WORLD ARMIES

Second Edition

WORLD ARMIES
Second Edition

JOHN KEEGAN

GALE RESEARCH COMPANY · BOOK TOWER · DETROIT, MICHIGAN 48226

© John Keegan, 1979, 1983

First edition published 1979

This edition is published in the United States, its possessions
and Canada by the GALE RESEARCH COMPANY, Book Tower, Detroit, MI 48226.

Library of Congress Cataloging in Publication Data

Main entry under title:

World armies.

    1. Armed Forces.   I. Keegan, John, 1934-
UA15.W68 1983   355   83-8964
ISBN 0-8103-1515-7

Printed in Great Britain

THE CONTRIBUTORS

Simon Baynham, Department of Political and Social Studies, Royal Military Academy, Sandhurst

James Brown, Government Department, Southern Methodist University

Stewart Drummond, Extramural Department, University of Southampton

Gwynne Dyer, formerly of the Department of War Studies, Royal Military Academy, Sandhurst

Adrian English, FRIBA

Mrs Catherine Eyre

Colonel K. C. Eyre, Canadian Armed Forces

Major F. A. Godfrey (Retired), Department of War Studies, Royal Military Academy, Sandhurst

T. A. Heathcote, Curator, Royal Military Academy, Sandhurst Museum

Richard Holmes, Department of War Studies, Royal Military Academy, Sandhurst

David Isby, MA

John Keegan, Department of War Studies, Royal Military Academy, Sandhurst

Nigel de Lee, Department of War Studies, Royal Military Academy, Sandhurst

L. L. Mathews, formerly Colonial Service

Matthew Midlane, Department of Political and Social Studies, Royal Military Academy, Sandhurst

John Pimlott, Department of War Studies, Royal Military Academy, Sandhurst

Colonel John Skinner, late Royal Army Ordnance Corps

Richard Snailham, Department of Political and Social Studies, Royal Military Academy, Sandhurst

CONTENTS

FOREWORD

by

Morris Janowitz, Professor of Sociology, University of Chicago,
and Chairman, Inter-University Seminar on Armed Forces
and Society

Armies are universal institutions. There are no nation States playing a role in world politics in which the political leaders have deliberately taken the decision not to maintain an army. The military, and especially the ground forces, reflect the supremacy and the resulting dilemmas of nationalism in the modern historical period. In fact, to speak of a nation State means to designate the scope and corporate form of its army.

It is self-evident that the continued development of armies is not simply the result of industrial and economic development or of the mere accumulation of past aspirations, accomplishments and failures of the armed forces. Among the plethora of new nations which came into being with the decline of Western imperialism after World War II, there was not a single case of a ruling group which did not explicitly — and very often energetically — organise an army. The push to create these armies has in many cases led to the downfall of these ruling groups or political leaders.

In the contemporary period, the universality of armies is dramatised by the common and uniform terminology for describing the military enterprise; the term 'the military balance', for example, has come to have a world-wide currency. It is a language which strives for precision but which is not without its 'reification' of military reality. The idea of the 'military balance' rests on the accumulation of statistical measures and indicators which are designed to be summed into an estimate of politico — military potentials. These measures encompass the men (and the women) under arms classified into the variety of categories which reflect their military status. It includes the number and types of weapons; and wherever possible this information is translated into monetary units. These sums emerge as an essential aspect of the self-conceptions of the military profession in a technological age. These data become basic elements in the imagery and rhetoric with which political leaders think about the world community. The military balance protrudes continuously into the mass media and into popular discourse about war, peace and the hope for conflict resolution.

But armies are historical, social and political institutions. Statistical indicators remain partial, and subject to distortion; they must be supplemented by a concern with organisational forms. Armies are institutions which have some common characteristics because they are organised to make use of military technology and to apply a logic of making war and deterring war. But each army has its own special characteristics which flow from its operational history, its cultural setting and its political attachments. John Keegan's *World Armies* is a world-wide survey of armies as human bureaucracies; the emphasis is on the special and particular features of each army. The idea of a world-wide survey in the institutional *genre* is truly attractive. The book represents an immense amount of work by the editor and his collaborators and the result enriches our understanding of the armies of the world, giving succinct presentations without loss of essential detail. The end result is a series of institutional portraits which give a clearer but more complex meaning to the military balance and which offer a fuller understanding of the political meaning of armies as they actually exist and continue to evolve.

Chicago, 1979   M.J.

EDITOR'S PREFACE

The origins of this book are easily explained. In 1972 Dr John Paxton asked me to assist him with the army entries in the long-established *Statesman's Year-Book* which he edits for The Macmillan Press. I readily agreed. But, while I found those for the older and larger countries fairly easy to complete, information about the armies of the newer and smaller countries proved hard to uncover. I tried a variety of sources and, as disappointment grew at the paucity of the material they yielded, came to feel that I was failing to find a book which obviously existed but must be hiding itself from me — a comprehensive guide to the armies of the world. Once the idea of such a book was fully formed in my mind, a little reflection told me that no such thing was published in English. Enquiry revealed that there was nothing similar in French, German, or any language that I could read. And I was ultimately convinced that no such thing was published anywhere.

It was a short step for John Paxton to suggest to The Macmillan Press that I should undertake the preparation of such a work and to their agreeing to it. Our reasons coincided: that armies, far from losing their importance as the rise of air power and the development of nuclear weapons had seemed earlier in the century to suggest they would, were now among the most significant institutions in many countries in the world, even if that significance was to be measured in political rather than strictly military terms. In mainland Latin America, a majority of the States were under direct military rule, as was also the case over wide areas of Africa and Asia. In many other countries the army, if not ruling directly, was the unchallenged arbiter of who should rule, on what terms and for how long. And in others still, a guarantee of the army's support was the first assurance sought by any government in time of crisis. Nor were such countries always necessarily among the young nations. It may be remembered that President de Gaulle, on his hasty return from Romania to face the *événements* of May, 1968, made the headquarters of the First French Army his first port of call. Finally, in the communist world, army and party typically formed a single and indissoluble apparatus of power, through which mutual suspicion and interest were more or less smoothly worked out, at the expense of all other groups in society.

This worldwise rise of armies to political and social prominence should surprise no realistic observer of the contemporary scene. For, in the words of Professor S. E. Finer, 'at first sight the political advantages of the army *vis-à-vis* other and civilian groupings are overwhelming. It possesses vastly superior organisation. And it possesses *arms*. The wonder, therefore, is not why it rebels against its civilian masters, but why it ever obeys them.' That question, of which Professor Finer is a leading analyst, has come to be treated as one of the greatest importance by modern political scientists who have, under the title of 'civil—military relations', accorded independent status to the enquiry as a major subdivision of their discipline. Professor Finer's particular contribution to it has been to investigate the motives and circumstances disposing armies to intervene in politics and to suggest a theoretical framework of 'levels' of intervention — progressively 'influence', 'pressure', 'displacement' and 'supplantment'. Displacement and supplantment characterise military politics in the countries of what Professor Finer calls 'lower political culture'. In developed political cultures it is

the minor levels of intervention — pressure and the perfectly legitimate exercise of influence — to which armies resort. And what political scientists must seek to explain there is why armies in general confine themselves to such comparatively restrained uses of their power. Those who have sought to do so are chiefly Americans, and notably Professors Samuel Huntington and Morris Janowitz (the latter has generously contributed a Foreword to this book). To the former we owe the idea of the rise of 'professionalism' in modern armies, a concept he employs to demonstrate how the leaders of armies in the Western world have been progressively integrated into the educated middle class and persuaded to adopt its outlook, manners and responsibilities. To Professor Janowitz we owe the first detailed sociological profile of a 'professionalised' military group, as well as an interesting theory of how such a military sub-culture may be expected to evolve in the future.

The work of these scholars — and of their European *confrères*, notably Demeter in Germany and Girardet in France — has transformed over the last 30 years our whole understanding of military societies. But it is nevertheless possible still to feel that a great deal remains to be done for the study of armies. Their work, largely undertaken in universities, has necessarily been done at some distance from the military institutions on which it concentrates. It has tended as a result to represent armies as monolithic in structure and likely to reveal an internal texture as uniform as their outward appearance. Those who work near or within armies are rapidly made aware, however, of how deceptive this apparent uniformity is, and of the extent to which an army may reproduce within itself the social and cultural divisions, regional patriotisms, sub-group ('regimental') loyalties, personal followings and similar fragmentations which compartmentalise large and powerful organisations everywhere. An intimate knowledge of one army, moreover, quickly provides clues to the discovery of internal divisions peculiar to others and thereby to a pattern of differences between armies in general. These differences are an inconvenience to political scientists, for whom 'army', like 'civil service', 'judiciary' or 'police', is a useful piece of political shorthand which may be made to stand as a term of fixed value in many of their commoner equations. It is, for example, generally taken to mean 'the sole bearer of arms within the State'. In many countries, however, the army is only one of two or more armed bodies under State control, and less important for internal political purposes than the armed police or workers' militia. It is generally taken to mean 'the automatic guarantor of the State's authority'; but in many countries the army is disqualified or exempts itself from involvement in the internal affairs of the State. It is generally taken to mean 'the embodiment of the popular will to defend the national territory'; but in a number of countries anti-militarist feeling is so strong that the army's military role is scarcely more than symbolic. The catalogue of ways in which any particular army may be shown to diverge from the hazily defined and loosely used concept of 'the army' might be continued for some time.

The principal aim of this book therefore is to provide a portrait of each army in its domestic context, historical, social and political as well as military. Each main entry is arranged in a standard form, containing nine headings: History and Introduction; Strength and Budget; Command and Constitutional Status; Role, Commitment, Deployment and Recent Operations; Organisation (Arms of Service and Operational); Recruitment, Training and Reserves; Equipment and Arms Industry; Rank, Dress and Distinctions; and Current Developments. The hope is that through this scheme of treatment a picture of each army will emerge revealing not only its military capability – how and where recruited, how armed and by whom, where stationed, to what alliances committed, in what operations most recently engaged and how successfully – but also its relationship to the government and administration of the State to which it belongs; its kinship with the population; its affinities with, or antipathies to, significant groups within society; its role in the national historical experience and its own particular cultural and social character.

Because the editorial emphasis lies on the domestic rather than the international status of each army, entries may sometimes seem longer than the military worth of a particular army might be thought to justify. Thus an army like the Argentinian (which has fought no war for a hundred years) receives as much space as the British, which is not only larger but has been almost continuously in action, abroad or in the empire, for over a century. The latter, however, plays no appreciable political role in national affairs, while the activities of the former have been of paramount importance. In many cases, however, both the length and quality of entries has been affected by the paucity of trustworthy information available to the contributors. Reliable information was most easily obtained in the case of the armies of the democracies,

and then in those of the communist States, which are closely studied by Western observers even if they publish little about themselves. It was least easily acquired in the case of the small, new States where the armies, though often of little military worth, are crucial institutions and therefore both anxious and able to censor news about their shortcomings. The editor and contributors are keenly aware of the consequent gaps and obscurities, they are confident that a new edition will generate the flow of information necessary to equalise the quality of all entries in subsequent years.

They have nevertheless received a great deal of assistance from many quarters, for which they acknowledge their gratitude. The editor would in particular like to thank the International Institute for Strategic Studies, and its Deputy Director, Colonel Jonathan Alford, for permission to draw freely on its *Military Balance* wherever appropriate. Those familiar with that indispensable publication will recognise whenever material has been taken from it; it provides in particular most of the information in the Strength and Budget section of the entries. His thanks go also to the contributors, with whom it has been a consistent pleasure to work; despite the length of time taken in compilation, a happy spirit of co-operation has prevailed between all. He would finally also like to thank his wife, whose natural interests are not in military things but who has given constant encouragement and advice, all of which was deeply valued.

Camberley, 1983   J.K.

INTRODUCTION

by

Professor Michael Howard, CBE, MC, FBA,
Chichele Professor of the History of War,
University of Oxford

A book on the world's armies published before 1914 would have been strikingly different from this one. In the first place, instead of listing well over 140 countries, it would have comprised perhaps a couple of dozen: the States of Europe (including the new, militant nations of the Balkans); the USA; Turkey; Japan; and perhaps Latin America. Secondly, much of its interest would still have attached to the splendour of the uniforms it depicted; soldiers were still reluctant to believe that their capacity to survive, let alone fight, in war depended on their being as indistinguishable as possible from the mud and dust of the battlefield. Thirdly, the weapons depicted would have been comparatively simple. Cavalry was armed with lance, sabre, and carbine, infantry with rifle and bayonet, artillery with standard field or heavy pieces. In the supporting arms, indeed, twentieth-century technology was beginning to make its mark. Bicycle and field-telegraph detachments would have been listed, and observation-balloon units were beginning to experiment with primitive aircraft. But all this was marginal. Finally, with the possible exception of Latin America, there would have been no question about the function of these armies. It was to fight one another, in a great war that was universally expected and would be likely to involve them all.

If it did nothing else, the present volume would show how completely the world has been transformed by World Wars I and II. The old European armies, where they survive at all, are swamped by those of the States which have arisen on the ruins of their empires, and are dwarfed by those of the two superpowers (though the giant military potential of the Russian Empire was there even in 1914 for those who had eyes to see). Brilliant uniform has ceased to be a feature of any serious army. All dress as simply and inconspicuously as possible, and the *machismo* which once found expression in military elegance now attaches to the weapons with which the forces are armed, and a ruggedness emphasised by the very casualness of dress. The weapons of even the smallest of armies, though often easy enough to operate, are of a complexity of construction such as only the most advanced technological societies can produce. An interesting exercise would be to go through the entries in this book and see from what a small number of suppliers all this military hardware actually derives.

Finally, and perhaps most interestingly of all, is the question of the role of these armies; why they exist at all, and what enemy they expect to fight. In some cases, such as the Israeli army, the answer is only too obvious. For others — say that of New Zealand — a certain political sophistication is needed to discern a role at all. For some — Iran/Iraq, India/Pakistan — there are significant regional rivalries. For those of the USSR, the USA and their European allies, there is the great central confrontation. For China there is the looming presence of the Soviet Union, for Vietnam the looming presence of China, for Thailand, perhaps, the looming presence of Vietnam.

But the great majority of the armies here listed do not owe their existence to any particular military threat. In European nations like Britain and France they are historic institutions as old as the community itself, which have adapted themselves from generation to generation to new needs, as they have adapted themselves to new weapons. As for new States — the 77 listed in these pages which have been established since 1945 — their sovereign status demands, in the eyes of their own peoples, that they should display a readiness to defend their independence by the establishment of their own military institutions, even of the most minuscule and representational kind. And once established, these institutions acquire a self-image and a perception of the world around them which makes their growth virtually inexorable. Considerations of international prestige are almost inseparable from those of functional need. Expectations of threat become self-fulfilling prophecies. Hence the armourers thrive.

One final observation. Pre-1914 European armies, with the exception of the French, were *royal* forces. Their mystique was based on loyalty to a monarch, as that of the British army still is. But today many, perhaps most, armies derive their mystique from a movement of national liberation or a war of independence, which has usually involved social revolution as well. It was a tradition established even before 1914 in Latin American armies. But the armies of the USSR (in 1918—21), of Yugoslavia (in 1941—5) and of Israel (from 1936—49), literally created themselves, as they created a new social and political order, by fighting. They are thus in a special sense the symbols of their States and of the revolutions which brought them into being.

Most armies of Third World States, even (perhaps especially) those which did not have to struggle for independence, see themselves in the same way. In such armies the tradition of revolution, of the freedom fighter, blends uneasily with that of the military professional dedicated to the maintenance of State power against both external and, if necessary, internal threats to its security. In France, the USSR and Israel the transition from revolutionary to professional force is complete. In the newer States, especially those professing varying degrees of revolutionary socialism, the armed forces are still in a state of uneasy and unstable equilibrium. But if history is any guide, sooner or later they will all eventually settle into a professional mould, hierarchical, disciplined, deeply concerned with the technology of their profession and seeking escape from the political complexities of the society which surrounds them in an elaborate sub-culture of their own. But when these complexities become unendurable, the armies move out of their barracks and try to remake society in their own image. In a large number of the cases listed here they already have; and once they have done so it is not easy to get them back into their barracks again.

This is therefore not just a book for military enthusiasts. It is a valuable guide for anyone who seeks to understand the complex and disturbed societies that between them make up the contemporary world.

All Souls College, Oxford, 1979   M.E.H.

A NOTE ON ABBREVIATIONS, UNITS AND FORMATIONS

A NOTE ON ABBREVIATIONS

It was the intention to exclude all abbreviations from the text, since it is meant to be as useful to the non-specialist as to the specialist. A few abbreviations have nevertheless crept in, while others have in practice come to look preferable to the cumbersome phrases for which they stand (cf. APC and Armoured Personnel Carrier). These are the most frequent occurrences:

AAM	air-to-air missile
AFV	armoured fighting vehicle
APC	armoured personnel carrier
ATGW	anti-tank guided weapon
COIN	counter-insurgency (aircraft)
CPB	coastal patrol boat
FB	fighter—bomber
FGA	fighter—ground attack
FPB	fast patrol boat
FPBG	fast patrol boat with guided missiles
LST	landing ship, tank
LCT	landing craft, tank
MICV	mechanised infantry combat vehicle
MTB	motor torpedo boat
RCL	recoilless (rifle)
RL	rocket launcher
SAM	surface-to-air missile
SP	self propelled (gun or howitzer)
SPG	self propelled gun
SSM	surface-to-surface missile
TOW	tube-launched, optically-sighted, wire-guided anti-tank missile

A NOTE ON UNITS AND FORMATIONS

Military specialists distinguish between a military *unit*, in which only one arm of service (e.g. infantry, artillery) is represented, and a *formation*, in which two or more are represented. Almost without exception, formations are larger than units, from a mixture of which they are composed.

Units

Section (or Squad): 6—10 men; about three sections to a:—
Platoon: 30—40 men; about three platoons to a:—
Company: 150—250 men; about three companies to a battalion (see below)
(Battery: the equivalent of an infantry company in the artillery)
(Squadron: the equivalent of an infantry company in the cavalry or armoured branch)
Battalion: 750—1000 men
Regiment: (*a*) a unit of several battalions; (*b*) a battalion of artillery, cavalry or armour

Formations

Brigade: three or more battalions, with attached support and service units; about 5000 men; if armoured, about 100 tanks
Division: two or more brigades, with its own artillery, support and service units; 10,000—17,000 men; if armoured, 150—300 tanks
Corps: two or more divisions
Army: two or more corps
Army Group: two or more armies (known as a *Front* in the Soviet army)

Sections are commanded by corporals or sergeants; platoons by sergeants or lieutenants; companies (batteries, squadrons) by captains or majors; battalions by lieutenant-colonels; brigades by brigadiers or colonels; divisions by major-generals; and corps by lieutenant-generals.

MAJOR ITEMS OF
MILITARY EQUIPMENT

Note: The items of equipment chosen for illustration are generally those which have been produced in the largest number; most have been sold or supplied widely beyond the country of origin, but some items have been illustrated as examples of the products of newly established or re-established arms industries.

Fig 1. Chieftain Mark 5 main battle tank. Britain. Crew, 4; armament, 120mm gun; weight, 55,000 kg; in service with Iran, Jordan, Kuwait, Oman, United Kingdom. (*Royal Ordnance Factory*)

Fig 2. Scorpion light tank (CVR(T)). Britain. Crew, 4; armament, 76mm gun; weight, 8,000 kg; in service with Belgium, Brunei, Honduras, Iran, Ireland, Malayasia, New Zealand, Nigeria, Oman, Philippines, Tanzania, Thailand, UAE and United Kingdom, (*Alvis Limited*)

Fig 3. Leopard 2 main battle tank. West Germany. Crew, 4; armament, 120mm gun; weight, 55,150 kg; in service with Federal Republic of Germany, Netherlands; Mark 1 also in service with Australia, Belgium, Canada, Denmark, Greece, Italy, Norway, and Turkey. (*Krauss Maffei*)

Fig 4. Merkava main battle tank. Israel. Crew, 4 (may also carry 8 infantrymen); armament, 105mm gun; weight 56,000 kg.

Fig 5. M60A1 main battle tank. USA. Crew, 4; armament, 105mm gun; weight, 49,000 kg; in service with Austria, Egypt, Iran, Italy, Jordan, Morocco, South Korea, Saudi Arabia, Singapore, Somalia, Spain, Sudan, Tunisia, USA and North Yemen. (*Austrian Army*)

Fig 6. M1 Abrams main battle tank. USA. Crew, 4; armament, 105mm gun; weight, 54,432 kg (*US Army*)

Fig 7. T-54 main battle tank. USSR. Crew, 4; armament, 100mm gun; weight, 36,000 kg; in service with nearly fifty countries in Eastern Europe, Africa, the Middle East and Asia. (*Israeli Ministry of Defence*)

Fig 8. T-62 main battle tank. USSR. Crew, 4; Armament, 115mm gun; weight, 40,000 kg; in service with over twenty countries in Eastern Europe, Africa, the Middle East and Asia. (*TASS*)

Fig 9. T-72 main battle tank. USSR. Crew 3; armament, 125mm gun; weight, 38,000 kg; in service with Algeria, Bulgaria, Cuba, Czechoslovakia, East Germany, Hungary, India, Iraq, Libya, Poland, Romania, Syria and USSR. (*US Army*)

Fig 10. AMX-13 light tank. France. Crew, 3; armament, 90mm gun; weight, 15,000 kg; in service with Algeria, Argentina, Chile, Dominican Republic, Djibouti, Ecuador, El Salvador, France, India, Indonesia, Ivory Coast, Lebanon, Morocco, Netherlands, Nepal, Peru, Saudi Arabia, Singapore, Tunisia, Venezuela. (*Dutch Army*)

Fig 11. AMX-30 main battle tank. France. Crew, 4; armament, 105mm gun; weight, 36,000 kg; in service with Chile, France, Greece, Iraq, Lebanon, Qatar, Saudi Arabia, Spain (made under licence) and Venezuela. (*GIAT*)

Fig 12. Type 61 main battle tank. Japan. Crew, 4; armament, 90mm gun; weight, 33,500 kg; only in service in Japan. (*Kensuke Etabe*)

Fig 13. Marder mechanised infantry combat vehicle. West Germany. Crew, 4 + 6 infantrymen; armament, 20mm cannon, 2 machine guns; weight, 28,000 kg; in service in West Germany. (*West German Army*)

Fig 14. **M-113 armoured personnel carrier.** USA. Crew, 2 + 11 infantrymen; weight, 11,000 kg; in service with about fifty countries in Western Europe, Africa, Asia, the Middle East, Latin America and Australasia. The version shown is a M901 Improved TOW vehicle, TOW is seen in flight (*Emerson*)

Fig 15. **M2 Bradley infantry fighting vehicle.** USA. Crew, 3 + 6 infantrymen; armament 25mm cannon, twin TOW missile launcher, 1 machine gun; weight 22,000 kg. (*FMC Corporation*)

Fig 16. BMP-1 mechanised infantry combat vehicle. USSR. Crew. 3 + 8 infantrymen; armament, 73mm gun, *Sagger* missile launcher, 1 machine gun; weight 13,500 kg; in service with Afghanistan, Algeria, Cuba, Czechoslovakia, Egypt, Ethiopia, East Germany, Hungary, Iran, India, Iraq, North Korea, Libya, Poland, Syria and USSR. (*TASS*)

Fig 17. AMX-10P mechanised infantry combat vehicle. France. Crew, 3 + 8 infantrymen; armament, 20mm cannon, 1 machine gun; weight, 14,200 kg; in service with France, Greece, Indonesia, Mexico, Morocco, Qatar, Saudi Arabia and UAE. (*GIAT*)

Fig 18. VAB (Véhicule de l'Avant Blindé) armoured personnel carrier. France. Crew, 2 + 10 infantrymen; armament, 1 heavy machine gun; weight, 14,200 kg; in service with France, Ivory Coast, Lebanon, Mauritius, Morocco, Qatar, UAE and other countries. (*RVI*)

Fig 19. Type 73 armoured personnel carrier. Japan. Crew, 3 + 9 infantrymen; armament, 1 heavy, 1 light machine gun; weight, 13,300 kg. (*Kensuke Ebate*)

Fig 20. EE-11 Urutu armoured personnel carrier. Brazil, Crew, 2 + 12 infantrymen; armament, 1 heavy machine gun; weight, 13,000 kg; in service with Bolivia, Brazil, Chile, Colombia, Iraq, Libya and other countries. (*ENGESA*)

Fig 21. AML-90 armoured car. France. Crew, 3; armament, 90mm gun; weight, 5,500 kg; in service with over thirty countries in Africa, Western Europe, Latin America, the Middle East and Asia, produced under licence in South Africa as the *Eland*. (*Panhard*)

Fig 22. M109A2 155mm self-propelled howitzer. USA. Crew, 6; weight, 24,000 kg; in service with nearly thirty countries in Western Europe, Asia and the Middle East. (*British Ministry of Defence*)

Fig 23. M110 203mm self-propelled howitzer. USA. Crew, 5; weight 26,500 kg; in service with Belgium, West Germany, Greece, Iran, Israel, Italy, Japan, Jordan, South Korea, Netherlands, Pakistan, Syria, Turkey, United Kingdom, USA and Vietnam. (*British Ministry of Defence*)

Fig 24. M-1973 152mm self-propelled howitzer. USSR. Crew, 6; weight 28,000 kg; in service with East Germany, Iraq, Libya, and other countries. (*US Army*)

Fig 25. AMX Mark F3 155mm self-propelled howitzer. France Crew, 2; weight, 17,400 kg; in service with Argentina, Chile, Ecuador, France, Kuwait, Morocco, Sudan, UAE and Venezuela. (*Creusot Loire*)

Fig 26. Gepard self-propelled anti-aircraft gun. West Germany. Crew, 3; armament, twin 35mm radar-controlled automatic cannon; weight, 44,800 kg; in service with Belgium, West Germany and the Netherlands. (*Dutch Army*)

Fig 27. ZSU-23-4 self-propelled anti-aircraft gun. USSR. Crew, 4; armament, quadruple 23mm radar-controlled automatic cannon; weight, 19,000 kg; in service with thirty countries in Eastern Europe, Africa, Asia and the Middle East. (*US Army*)

Fig 28. Rapier tracked anti-aircraft missile. Great Britain. Range, classified; in service with Abu Dhabi, Australia, Brunei, Iran, Oman, Qatar, Singapore, Switzerland and the USA. (*British Aerospace*)

Fig 29. Chaparral tracked anti-aircraft missile. USA. Range, classified; in service with Israel, Morocco, Taiwan, Tunisia and the USA. (*Israeli Ministry of Defence*)

Fig 30. Roland tracked anti-aircraft missile. International (France—Germany—USA). Range, classified; in service with Afghanistan, Brazil, France, West Germany and USA. (*MBB*)

Fig 31. FIM-92A Stinger man-portable anti-aircraft missile. USA. range, classified; weight, 15.8 kg; in service with USA and Britain. (*General Dynamics*)

Fig 32. SA-6 (Gainful) surface-to-air missile. USSR. Range (altitude), 4–18 km; in service with Egypt, Libya, Syria, USSR and Vietnam. (*TASS*)

Fig 33. SA-7 (Grail) man-portable anti-aircraft missile. USSR. Range (altitude) up to 9 km; in service widely in Eastern Europe and in Cuba, China, Egypt, Morocco, Syria, Vietnam, South Yemen and Yugoslavia. (*US Army*)

Fig 34. SA-8 (Gecko) surface-to-air missile. USSR. Range (altitude) 8—16 km. (*US Army*)

Fig 35. Milan anti-tank missile. International (France—Germany). Weight (with launcher) 28.5 kg; in service with over twenty countries in Western Europe, the Middle East and Asia. (*MBB*)

Fig 36. RPG-7 anti-tank rocket launcher. USSR. Weight, 9.25 kg; range, 300m; in service with all Warsaw Pact countries and widely in Africa, the Middle East and Asia.

Fig 37. Pershing 2 surface-to-surface missile. USA. Range, 650 km; conventional or nuclear (10–20) kt) warhead. (*Martin Marietta*)

Fig 38. Pluton surface-to-surface missile. France. Range 120 km; nuclear (15–25 kt) warhead. (*ECPA*)

Fig 39. FROG-7 surface-to-surface missile. USSR. Range, 60 km; conventional or nuclear (low-yield) warhead; in service with the Warsaw Pact countries and in Egypt, Iraq, Libya, North Korea, Syria and USSR. (*Franz Kosar*)

MAP SECTION

US Army Abroad

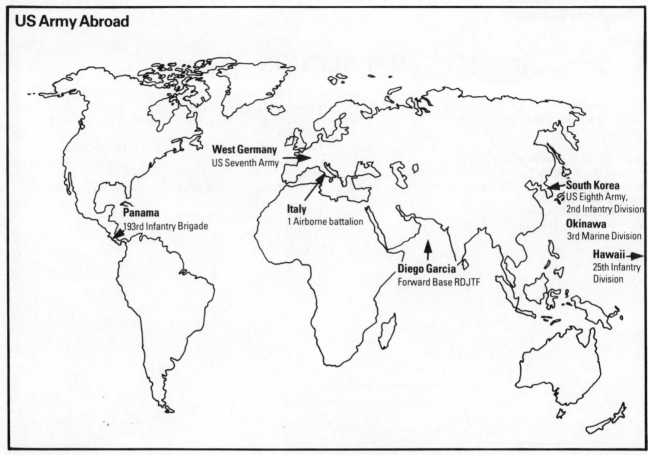

West Germany
US Seventh Army

South Korea
US Eighth Army,
2nd Infantry Division

Okinawa
3rd Marine Division

Italy
1 Airborne battalion

Panama
193rd Infantry Brigade

Hawaii
25th Infantry
Division

Diego Garcia
Forward Base RDJTF

Major US Army Units and Headquarters

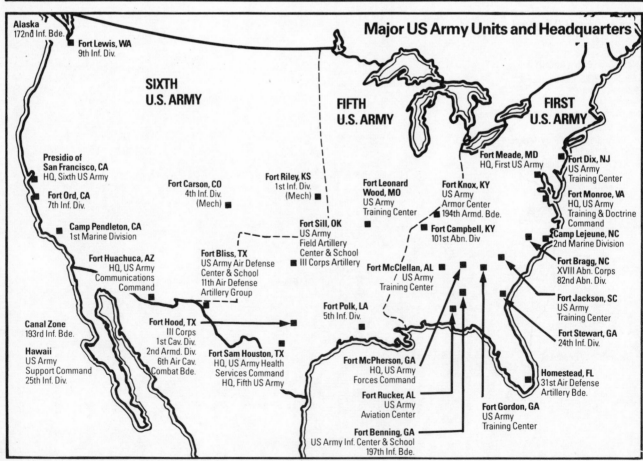

Alaska
172nd Inf. Bde.

Fort Lewis, WA
9th Inf. Div.

SIXTH U.S. ARMY

FIFTH U.S. ARMY

FIRST U.S. ARMY

Fort Meade, MD
HQ, First US Army

Fort Dix, NJ
US Army
Training Center

Presidio of San Francisco, CA
HQ, Sixth US Army

Fort Carson, CO
4th Inf. Div.
(Mech)

Fort Riley, KS
1st Inf. Div.
(Mech)

Fort Leonard Wood, MO
US Army
Training Center

Fort Knox, KY
US Army
Armor Center
194th Armd. Bde.

Fort Monroe, VA
HQ, US Army
Training & Doctrine
Command

Fort Ord, CA
7th Inf. Div.

Camp Lejeune, NC
2nd Marine Division

Camp Pendleton, CA
1st Marine Division

Fort Sill, OK
US Army
Field Artillery
Center & School
III Corps Artillery

Fort Campbell, KY
101st Abn. Div.

Fort Bragg, NC
XVIII Abn. Corps
82nd Abn. Div.

Fort Huachuca, AZ
HQ, US Army
Communications
Command

Fort Bliss, TX
US Army Air Defense
Center & School
11th Air Defense
Artillery Group

Fort McClellan, AL
US Army
Training Center

Fort Jackson, SC
US Army
Training Center

Canal Zone
193rd Inf. Bde.

Fort Polk, LA
5th Inf. Div.

Fort Stewart, GA
24th Inf. Div.

Fort Hood, TX
III Corps
1st Cav. Div.
2nd Armd. Div.
6th Air Cav.
Combat Bde.

Hawaii
US Army
Support Command
25th Inf. Div.

Fort Sam Houston, TX
HQ, US Army Health
Services Command
HQ, Fifth US Army

Fort McPherson, GA
HQ, US Army
Forces Command

Homestead, FL
31st Air Defense
Artillery Bde.

Fort Rucker, AL
US Army
Aviation Center

Fort Gordon, GA
US Army
Training Center

Fort Benning, GA
US Army Inf. Center & School
197th Inf. Bde.

British Army Abroad

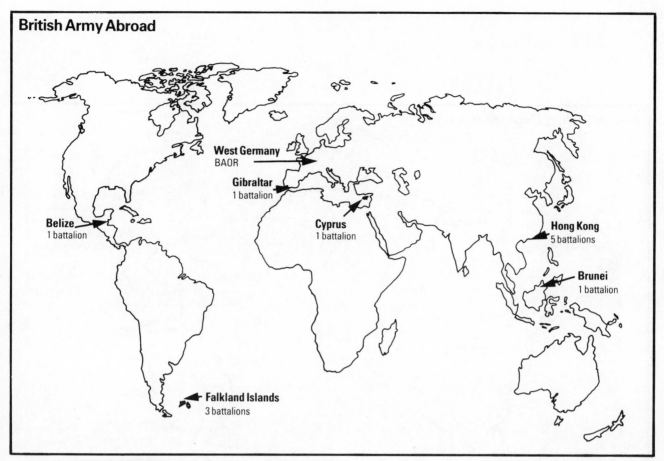

West Germany
BAOR

Gibraltar
1 battalion

Belize
1 battalion

Cyprus
1 battalion

Hong Kong
5 battalions

Brunei
1 battalion

Falkland Islands
3 battalions

French Army Abroad

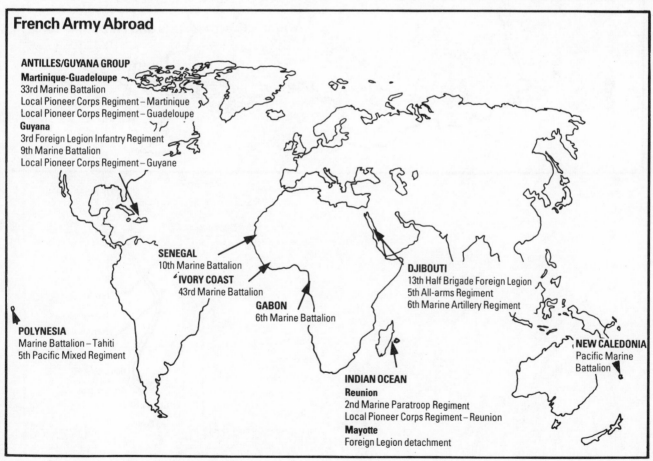

ANTILLES/GUYANA GROUP
Martinique-Guadeloupe
33rd Marine Battalion
Local Pioneer Corps Regiment – Martinique
Local Pioneer Corps Regiment – Guadeloupe
Guyana
3rd Foreign Legion Infantry Regiment
9th Marine Battalion
Local Pioneer Corps Regiment – Guyane

SENEGAL
10th Marine Battalion

IVORY COAST
43rd Marine Battalion

GABON
6th Marine Battalion

DJIBOUTI
13th Half Brigade Foreign Legion
5th All-arms Regiment
6th Marine Artillery Regiment

POLYNESIA
Marine Battalion – Tahiti
5th Pacific Mixed Regiment

INDIAN OCEAN
Reunion
2nd Marine Paratroop Regiment
Local Pioneer Corps Regiment – Reunion
Mayotte
Foreign Legion detachment

NEW CALEDONIA
Pacific Marine
Battalion

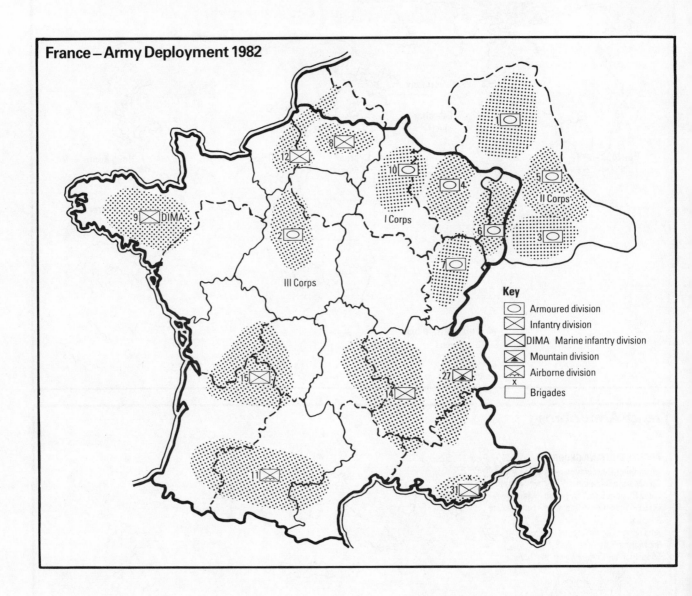

France – Army Deployment 1982

Key
- ⬭ Armoured division
- ⊠ Infantry division
- DIMA ⊠ Marine infantry division
- ⊠ Mountain division
- ⊠ Airborne division
- ▫ Brigades

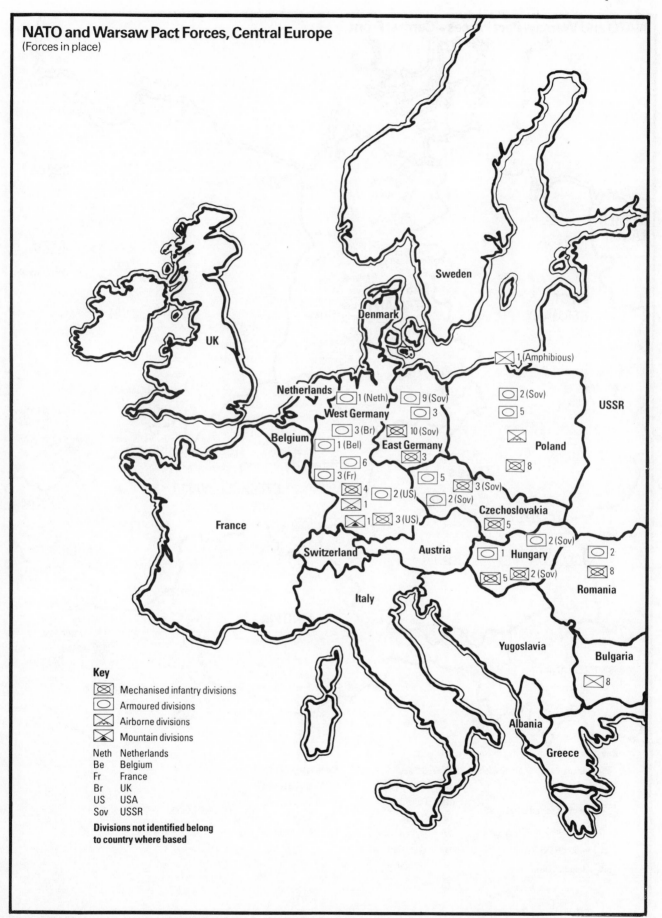

NATO and Warsaw Pact Forces, Central Europe
(Forces in place)

Key

- Mechanised infantry divisions
- Armoured divisions
- Airborne divisions
- Mountain divisions

Neth	Netherlands
Be	Belgium
Fr	France
Br	UK
US	USA
Sov	USSR

Divisions not identified belong to country where based

NATO and Warsaw Pact Forces – Central Front

Key

- Mechanised infantry division
- Armoured division
- Mechanised infantry brigade
- Armoured brigade
- Airborne division
- Mountain Division

Be	Belgian	Neth	Netherlands
Br	British	NVA	East German
Can	Canadian	P	Polish
Cz	Czech	Sov	Soviet
Fr	French	US	American
Ge	West German	H	Hungarian

Soviet Military Districts

(with designations of divisions)
1. Leningrad (HQ Petrozavdonsk). 2. Baltic (Riga). 3. Belorussian (Minsk). 4. Moscow (Moscow). 5. Carpathian (Lvov).
6. Odessa (Odessa). 7. Kiev (Kiev). 8. Caucasus (Rostov). 9. Transcaucasus (Tbilisi). 10. Volga (Kuibyshev). 11. Urals
(Sverdlovsk). 12. Turkestan (Tashkent). 13. Central Asia (Alma Ata). 14. Siberia (Novosibirsk). 15. Transbaikal (Chita).
16. Far Eastern (Khabarovsk).

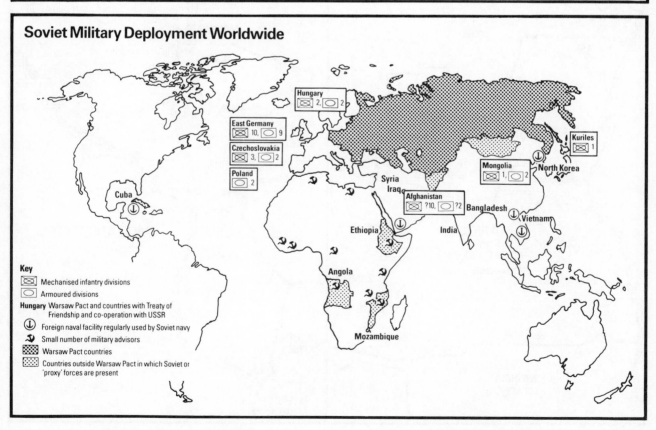

Soviet Military Deployment Worldwide

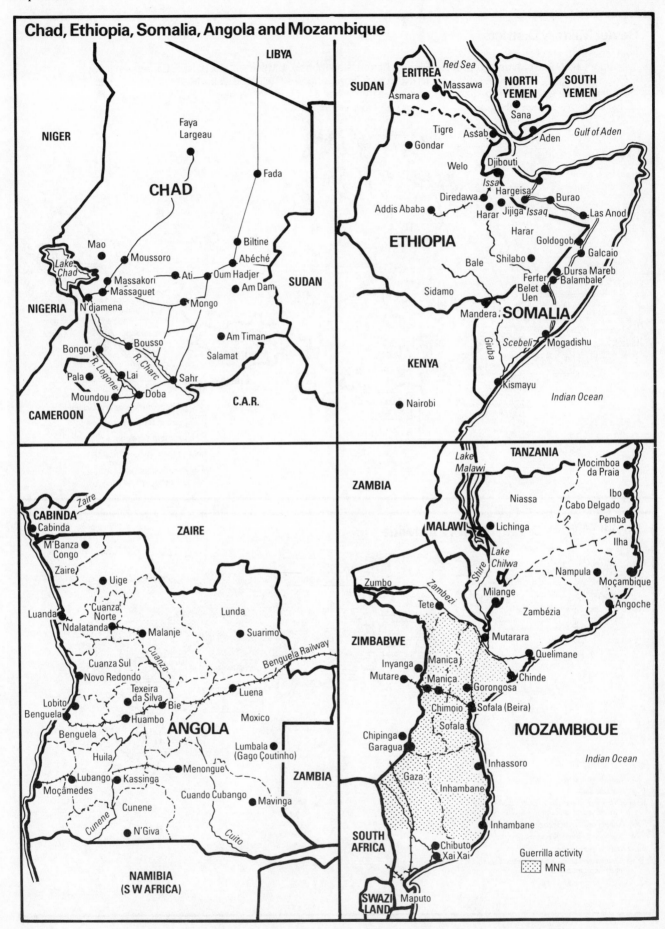

Chad, Ethiopia, Somalia, Angola and Mozambique

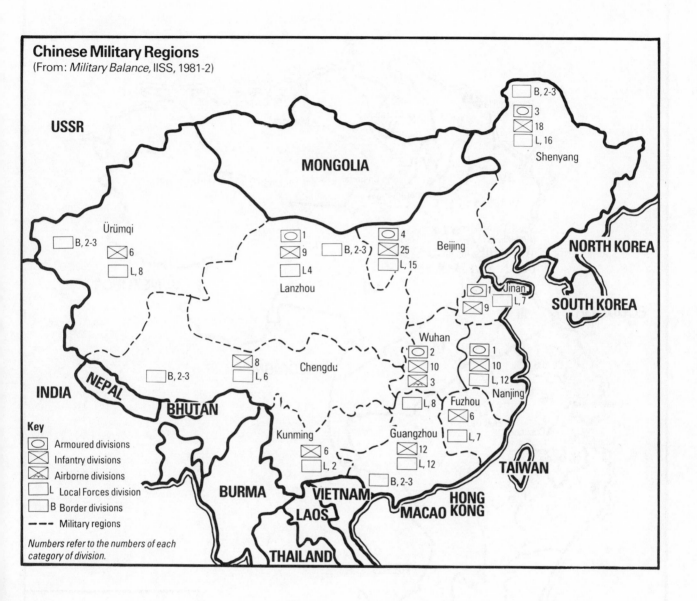

Chinese Military Regions
(From: *Military Balance*, IISS, 1981-2)

USSR

MONGOLIA

B, 2-3
○ 3
⊠ 18
L, 16
Shenyang

Ürümqi
B, 2-3
⊠ 6
L, 8

○ 1
⊠ 9
L 4
Lanzhou

○ 4
B, 2-3   ⊠ 25
L, 15
Beijing

NORTH KOREA

○ 1   Jinan
⊠ 9   L, 7

SOUTH KOREA

Wuhan
○ 2
⊠ 10
⊠ 3
L, 8

○ 1
⊠ 10
L, 12
Nanjing

Fuzhou
⊠ 6
L, 7

INDIA **NEPAL**

BHUTAN

⊠ 8
B, 2-3   L, 6
Chengdu

Key
○ Armoured divisions
⊠ Infantry divisions
⊠ Airborne divisions
L Local Forces division
B Border divisions
--- Military regions

Numbers refer to the numbers of each category of division.

BURMA

Kunming
⊠ 6
L, 2

Guangzhou
⊠ 12
L, 12

B, 2-3

VIETNAM
LAOS

MACAO **HONG KONG**

TAIWAN

THAILAND

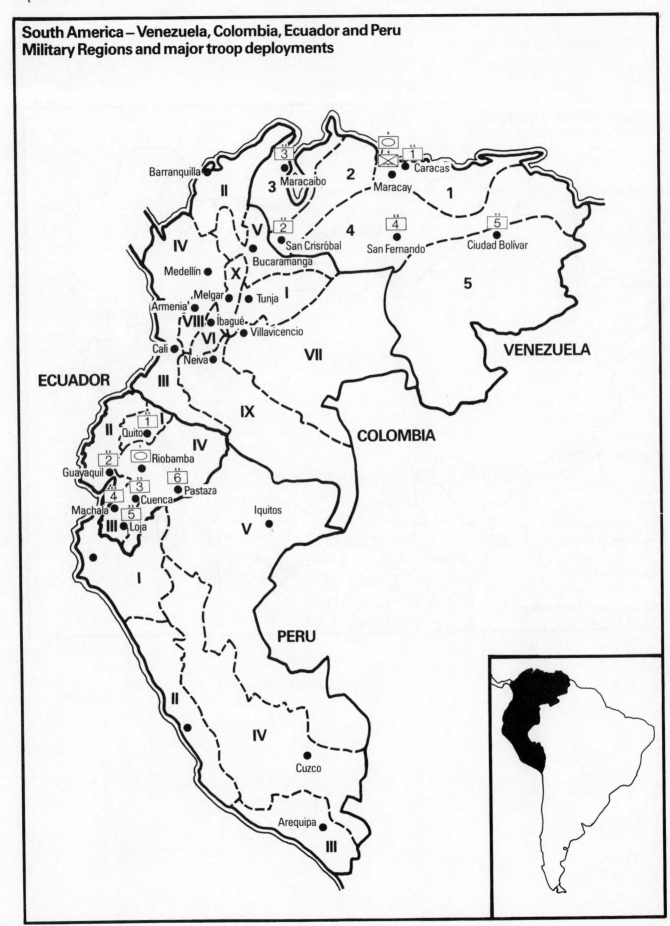

**South America – Venezuela, Colombia, Ecuador and Peru
Military Regions and major troop deployments**

Barranquilla

II

3 Maracaibo

2

Caracas

Maracay

1

III

San Crisróbal

V

4

San Fernando

4

Ciudad Bolívar

5

IV

Medellín

X

Bucaramanga

Melgar

Armenia

VIII Ibagué

Tunja

I

VI

Villavicencio

Cali

VII

Neiva

VENEZUELA

ECUADOR

III

IX

COLOMBIA

II Quito

1

IV

2 Riobamba

Guayaquil

3

6

Pastaza

4 Cuenca

Iquitos

Machala

III 5 Loja

V

I

PERU

II

IV

Cuzco

Arequipa

III

South America – Paraguay, Uruguay, Bolivia, Chile and Argentina
Military Regions and major troop deployment

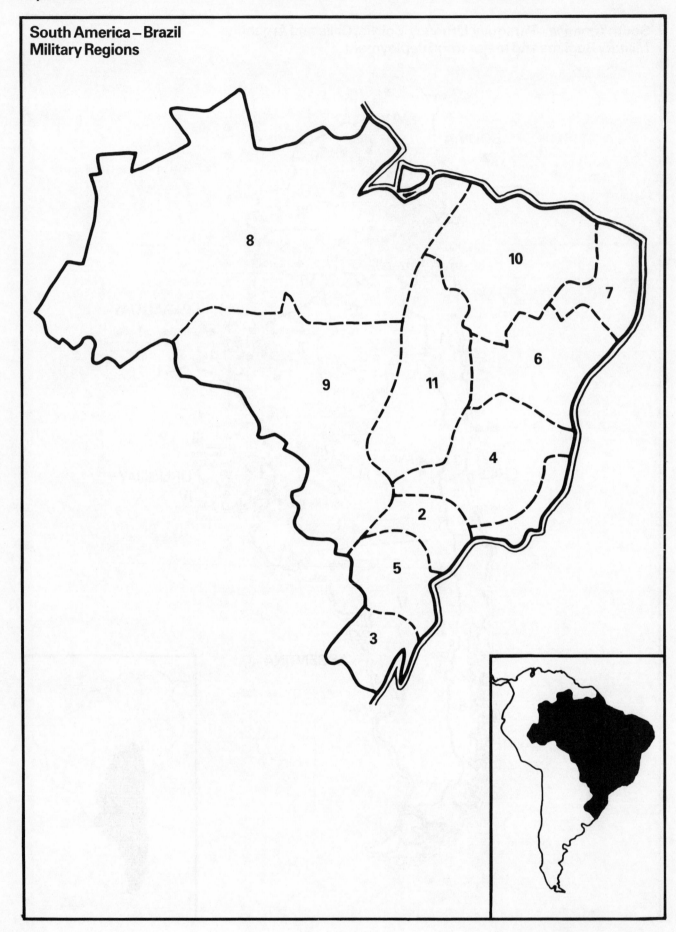

**South America – Brazil
Military Regions**

Central America – Military Regions and major troop deployment

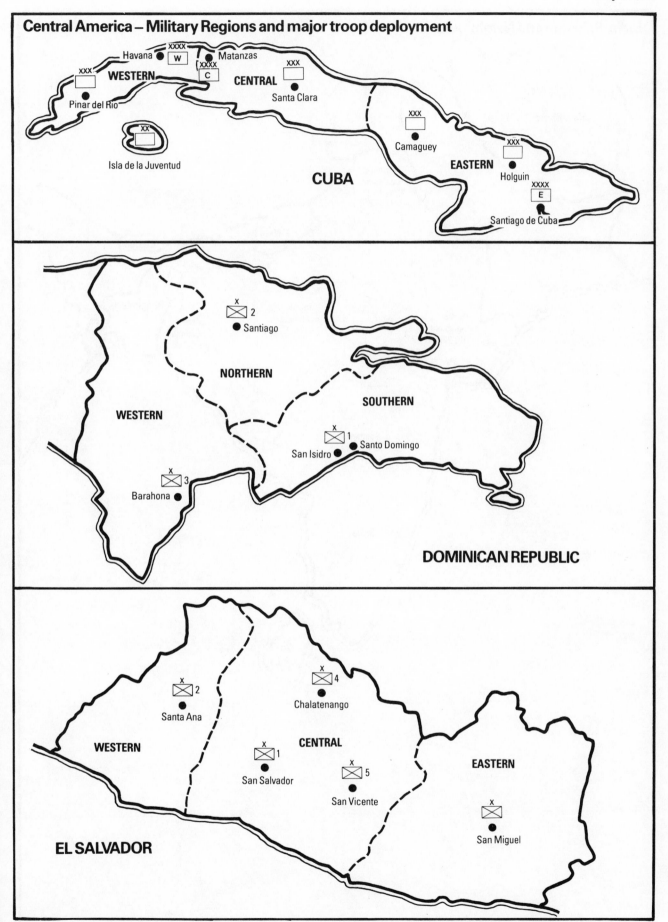

CUBA

WESTERN
CENTRAL
EASTERN

Havana
Pinar del Rio
Isla de la Juventud
Matanzas
Santa Clara
Camaguey
Holguin
Santiago de Cuba

DOMINICAN REPUBLIC

WESTERN
NORTHERN
SOUTHERN

Santiago
Santo Domingo
San Isidro
Barahona

EL SALVADOR

WESTERN
CENTRAL
EASTERN

Santa Ana
Chalatenango
San Salvador
San Vicente
San Miguel

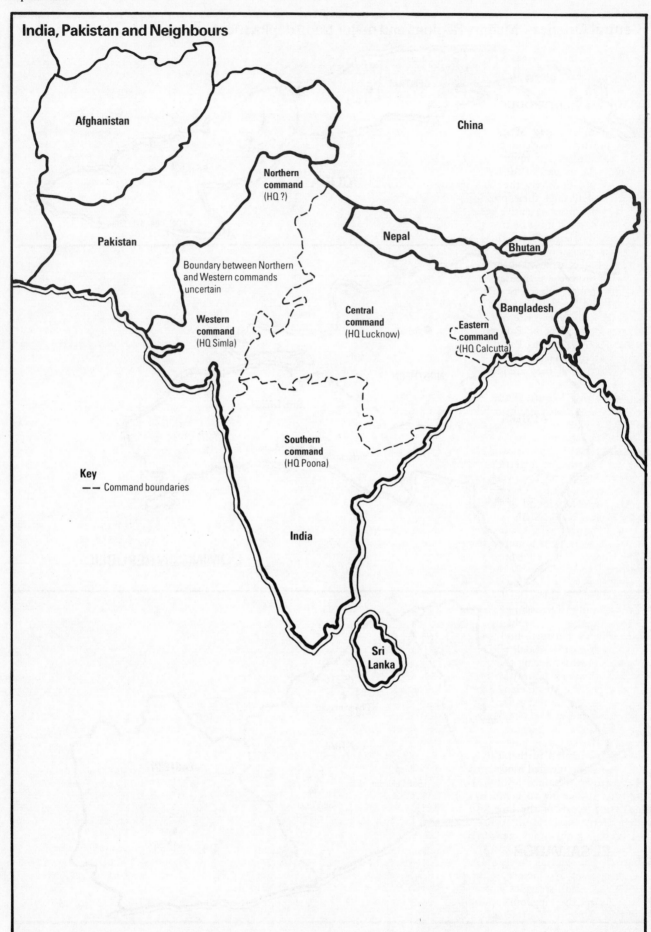

India, Pakistan and Neighbours

Afghanistan

China

Pakistan

Northern
command
(HQ ?)

Nepal

Bhutan

Boundary between Northern
and Western commands
uncertain

Western
command
(HQ Simla)

Central
command
(HQ Lucknow)

Eastern
command
(HQ Calcutta)

Bangladesh

Southern
command
(HQ Poona)

Key
–– Command boundaries

India

Sri
Lanka

AFGHANISTAN

HISTORY AND INTRODUCTION

Afghanistan, like two of its three neighbours – the Soviet Union and Iran – is a country where the dominant national group constitutes not much more than half the population, and lives in only part of the total area. Unlike the Persians or the Russians, however, the Pushtoons have only relatively recently established their political independence and their rule over the more extensive areas they now control. A large part of the reason must be that their superb military qualities were usually defeated by their equal devotion to a tribal form of organisation in which feud, faction and an ingrained distrust of all centralised authority were paramount.

The Pushtoons are the nation, split into a myriad of great and little tribes, sub-tribes and clans, who speak the Pushto language and live south and east of the Hindu Kush (broadly speaking, the south-eastern half of Afghanistan, and the north-western parts of Pakistan). They are also known in English as Afghans, as Pakhtuns (Pushtoon as pronounced in the eastern dialects), and as Pathans (an Indian corruption of the word), but they are identically the same people under all these names.

The historic origins of the Pushtoon people are obscure, but for a long time they have been the dominant population in the area. They have provided many soldiers and some noted commanders to the imperial armies that have swept repeatedly through their land, which was always a major corridor of trade, of migration and especially of invasion (of northern India), but for a very long time they failed to assert themselves as a nation.

After one last round of Persian conquest by the military phenomenon Nadir Shah, who overran Afghanistan on his way to conquer Delhi, the history of Afghanistan as such begins with Nadir Shah's murder by his own officers in 1747. Independence for the Pushtoons became possible, for he had smashed Moghul power, but no powerful Persian State survived him, and the waves of nomad conquerors were no longer rolling periodically from the central Asian reservoir (thanks mainly to Russian expansion).

The kingdom of Afghanistan was actually founded by Nadir Shah's personal body-guard, who happened to be recruited from the Abdali tribe of Pushtoons, from the area around Kandahar. Seeing the opportunity (and having fallen out with the Persian army commanders anyway) they raced home, called the Abdali clans together, had their commander, the 23-year-old Ahmed Khan, chosen as King, and set about conquering the rest of Afghanistan and its neighbourhood. Ahmed Shah, as he became, proved to be good at it, rapidly seizing all of what is now Afghanistan, and then devoting himself to conquest further afield, especially in rich northern India, which he invaded nine times before his death in 1772.

The crown remained in the same tribe (renamed the Durrani) for the next two centuries, but that tribe comprised less than a tenth of the Pushtoon population. The fiercely independent instincts of other Pushtoon tribes and the fractured, mountainous geography of the country made necessary an extremely loose, semi-feudal system of administration. The central power's weakness was exacerbated by the absence of a principle of primogeniture, leading to repeated succession struggles within the dynasty. After Ahmed Shah's death, the kingdom rapidly declined in power and in cohesion.

The capital was moved from Kandahar to Kabul by his successor, but upon the latter's death in 1793 there set in almost half a century in which monarchs were frequently assassinated or deposed, amidst recurrent civil war. During this time of troubles all territories beyond Afghanistan proper was lost to the rising Sikh power to the east: not only the Punjab and Kashmir, but also all the territories between the Indus river and the hills. This latter loss was of permanent importance, for these territories – today the North-West Frontier Province and the northern parts of Baluchistan province in Pakistan – contain almost half of the total Pushtoon population. Shortly afterwards, in the Second Sikh War of 1848, all these lost territories would pass into the hands of the British Indian Empire, and thence a century later to the successor State of Pakistan. It is a grievance which still dominates Afghanistan's foreign relations.

The advent of British power in north-western India was also disastrous for Afghanistan in a more direct and immediate sense. Just at the time when a single ruler, Dost Muhammad, had at last succeeded in having himself crowned as ruler of a united Afghanistan again, in 1837, British Russophobia led to the first of three British invasions of Afghanistan. Then, as later, Britain's fears that the gradual Russian expansion in central Asia could lead to a Tsarist ataack on India via Afghanistan were so exaggerated and ill-founded as to verge on the paranoid. The 1838 invasion, for example, was occasioned by the appearance of one Lithuanian-born Russian junior officer in Kabul. But such anxieties were to govern British policy towards Afghanistan for a century, and eventually to reduce the State to something near a dependency (though not a colony).

The 1838 British invasion succeeded easily, there being nothing worthy of the name 'army' surviving in Afghanistan, and for 2 years the country appeared to be settling down as another princely State requiring only token British forces to maintain order. In 1841, however, the whole country rose in revolt against brutal maladministration by foreigners, and catastrophe engulfed the British army attempting a winter retreat from Kabul. Subsequent British retaliation was spectacular, including exemplary massacres and the burning of Kabul, but the decision was taken to abandon the country. The puppet king was killed by his subjects, and Dost Muhammad resumed the throne.

He had more or less reunited the country by his death in 1863, and had instituted the policy of refusing entry to almost all foreigners, and banning foreign travel for almost all Afghans, which was to retard significant change in Afghanistan until well into the twentieth century. This self-imposed isolation undoubtedly aided in the difficult task of preserving the country's independence, caught as it was between the upper and nether millstones of Russian and British imperialism, but it also contributed to the fact that Afghanistan is today among the five poorest nations in the world (according to United Nations statistics), with over 95% illiteracy, not a single kilometre of railroad, and only half of those born surviving to adulthood.

Afghanistan's present population is officially estimated at about 18,000,000. It is not a homogeneous population: only about 11,000,000 are Pushtoons (though there are at least 6,000,000 more across the border in Pakistan). The majority of the remainder are Tajiks, speaking a dialect of Persian called Dari, most of whom live amongst the Pushtoons and under their hegemony, often as tenants. The Hazaras, a unique people of Mongolian descent about a million strong who are settled in the central massif west of Kabul, also speak Dari, while most of the million-plus central Asian Turks settled between the Hindu Kush and the Soviet border speak Uzbek. The majority of the nomads, numbering perhaps 2,000,000, are Pushtoons, Turcomans and a few Arab tribes. The total urban population is less than 1,500,000, and social patterns still remain fairly static.

This distribution of population is unchanged from the last century, and accounts for the difficilties faced by Sher Ali Khan, Dost Muhammad's successor, when he first sought to create a regular Afghan army on the European model in the 1870s. It proved impossible to draft or recruit soldiers from amongst the belligerent Pushtoon tribes (who were more concerned to retain the ability to defy the central authority), and those conscripts whom he was able to collect were drawn almost exclusively from among the non-tribal and socially inferior Hazaras and Tajiks. Though they were dressed and (sketchily) equipped on European lines, they were utterly without officers capable of training or commanding them.

In 1875 the Russian border in central Asia arrived at Afghanistan, which shortly led to renewed British demands for concessions from Kabul, amounting to the loss of Afghan independence, in order to guarantee that the Russians would be kept firmly out. Sher Ali's refusal was followed by the second British invasion of Afghanistan, in 1878, and his new-model army proved only 'a uniformed mob, whose sole cohesive force lay in the tendency of its members to flee at the same moment'. As before, the conquest was easy, but the occupation one of mounting expense in lives and money, and by 1881 Britain had withdrawn again.

The man who then emerged as King, Abdur Rahman, known deservedly as 'the assassin' by his countrymen, was probably Afghanistan's most hated ruler, but by the time he died 20 years later he had single-handedly dragged Afghanistan forward into the twentieth century. His principal tools in establishing and strengthening central authority were bribery, murder, torture and above all the regular army, which he at once began to rebuild and expand.

Abdur Rahman brought in a kind of conscription to replace the previous forced levy: the new system, known as *hasht nafri* (eight men) required each village to send one out of every eight men between twenty and forty in turn for a 2 year period of duty, and to pay the costs of his uniform and keep. It was less effectively enforced against the Pushtoon tribes, so the bulk of the army remained Tajiks and Hazaras, low in morale and not very efficient, but there was now regular pay and modern firearms (though ammunition was generally so scarce as to preclude target practice). The officer corps — almost entirely Pushtoon, as with all other branches of the State administrative structure — were considerably improved by the suppression of nepotism. With the aid of liberal British finanical aid, an arsenal was constructed in Kabul to reduce dependence on foreign sources for small arms and other ordnance, supervised training courses were introduced, troops were organised into regiments, brigades and divisions, containing battalions of artillery, and a formal (and harsh) code of discipline was imposed. It was this army, under the command of Abdur Rahman's general, Ghulam Haidar Charkhi, which cemented the unity of modern Afghanistan in more than a dozen major campaigns against rebels which the ruler frankly referred to as 'civil wars'.

It was also during Abdur Rahman's reign that Afghanistan's important borders were defined. In 1893 the Durand Line, fixing Afghanistan's eastern border, was accepted by Kabul under the veiled threat of yet another British invasion, although it cut off all the Yusufzai tribe and divided the powerful Waziris, Mohmands and Afridis, as well as many smaller ones. Abdur Rahman also had to agree to deal with other nations only through British mediation, but in return received an annual British subsidy. Two years later, in 1895, the 700 mile Russo—Afghan border was surveyed and agreed. (The short Chinese frontier was not finally delimited until 1965, and there is still no formal agreement — though no dispute either — with Iran.)

The transition from Abdur Rahman to his son Habibullah in 1901 was unimpeded by violence, in defiance of Afghan tradition. The new ruler pursued a careful policy of slow modernisation, always aware and cautious of the existence of powerful conservative (mostly Islamic) resistance. A few roads and factories were built, Afghanistan's first public school along European lines founded, the first newspaper was published, and Habibullah managed to keep Afghanistan out of World War I despite strenuous German and Turkish attempts to bring it in. But when he was assassinated in 1919, his successor embarked on a far more daring and dangerous policy of rapid change.

King Amanullah, who came to the throne in 1919, at once declared Afghanistan fully independent from Britain in both foreign and internal affairs, which promptly led to the Third Afghan War. It amounted to hardly more than border clashes, however, and in the peace Britain recognised Afghanistan's independence, Kabul then proceeded to open diplomatic relations with Britain and the Soviet Union, and subsequently with other States as well.

Amanullah's first act on gaining power had been to double the army's pay, to guarantee their loyalty against contenders for the succession. Under this reign it got Turkish instructors, and a small air force was founded in 1924, with 11 Russian pilots to fly its aircraft. By the 1920s the army's organisation and administration were regularised on European lines, and in 1932 a military academy was opened. But it remained such an ineffective armed force that the only way of quelling any significant tribal revolt (amongst people who were, after all, characterised by their British opponents on the North-West Frontier as the best guerrilla fighters in the world) was to seek the support of other tribes against the rebels. When this didn't work, Amanullah fell.

The concerted opposition to Amanullah was mainly made possible by his radical policies for domestic change, including such items as the abolition of the veil and the official discouragement of polygamy. Religious and tribal leaders, their natural conservatism reinforced by a century of well-justified xenophobia, finally ganged up to unseat him, and his regular army, though loyal, proved insufficient. Indeed, in 1929 a large portion of it was wiped out north of Kabul by a mere bandit chieftain, who proceeded to replace Amanullah as Shah. He was in his turn displaced by Nadir Shah, a candidate from the traditional ruling family, who had the added attraction of being literate, in 1929. Nadir Shah was of a military background, and a former War Minister, and immediately embarked on a new effort to reorganise and revitalise the army, but in his turn he was assassinated in 1933.

His nineteen-year-old son Muhammad Zahir Shah succeeded him without difficulty, however, and proceeded to rule Afghanistan for the next 40 years until 1973. The first twenty of those were relatively placid, with Zahir Shah leaving most power in the hands of three trusted uncles, who ensured that the rate of change in the country should not again become so rapid as to arouse once more the opposition which had overthrown Amanullah. Afghanistan stayed out of World War II without any serious problems, and arrived in the early 1950s little altered from a generation before. The principal foreign military influences on the Afghan armed forces during this period, and indeed until the present, were those of the Soviet Union and Turkey, both of which have maintained military training missions in Afghanistan and accepted Afghan officers in their military educational establishments for most of the past 50 years.

In 1953, when a new prime minister with different ideas came into office, the armed forces of Afghanistan were still scarcely capable of suppressing a large tribal revolt. Infantry rifles dated from the previous century, and ammunition was so scarce and old that few soldiers had fired their weapons. Some of the tribes were significantly better armed. The artillery was antiquated, and the total strength of the air force was 12 aircraft which dated from World War I. There were no mechanised forces of any kind.

The new prime minister, who dominated Afghan history, with intervals, for the next quarter-century, was to change all that. He was Sardar (Prince) Muhammad Daud Khan, a member of the royal clan and doubly related to the King as cousin and brother-in-law. Educated at the Afghan Military School, he had risen in the army, showing great drive in putting down the last major tribal revolt in 1947, and just prior to 1953 he had been Minister of Defence. His first concern as Prime Minister was the modernisation of the army, and the decisions he then took have shaped not only Afghanistan's armed forces but also much of its diplomacy ever since.

Daud turned to the Russians for help in modernising his army. His reasons for doing so were complex, but most revealing of the priorities held by subsequent Afghan governments.

One urgent reason for modernising the army and strengthening the administration was the chronic problem of tribal revolt. It scarcely mattered whom the aid came from in this context, and indeed Afghanistan had long been asking the USA for assistance, quite without result. The other main reason for improving the armed forces, however, was 'Pushtoonistan', and in this case the source of the military aid was a rather sensitive subject.

The incorporation of almost half the Pushtoon population first into the Sikh State, and then into British India, had been accepted under protest by an Afghan government powerless to prevent it, but the incorporation of those territories into the new State of Pakistan in 1947 was totally unacceptable to Kabul. In 1947 the Afghan government denounced the Durand Line, which had defined Afghanistan's eastern border since 1893. It demanded that the Pushtoon-populated areas of Pakistan (extending as far as the line of the Indus, including Chitral, Swat and Peshawar, and continuing south through North-West Frontier Province as far as the Pushtoon area of northern Baluchistan) should be recognised as the State of 'Pushtoonistan' or 'Pakhtunistan'. At times Kabul has called for independence for this area, at times merely for autonomy, but its insistence on the principle has never varied. Afghanistan was, indeed, the only country to vote against Pakistan's admission to the United Nations.

All Afghans feel strongly about Pushtoonistan, but Daud, whose great-great-grandfather was the last Afghan governor in Peshawar, undoubtedly felt more strongly than most. Pakistan has been the only neighbouring State whom Afghans seriously consider a potential military opponent since 1947, and if the army were to be built up partly for that contingency — as was certainly the case — then there were certain definite disadvantages in linking oneself to American military aid. Principal among these was the fact that the United States was then engaged in constructing alliances to contain what it saw as Russian expansionism in the area, and was far more concerned to include Pakistan than Afghanistan.

One must also not overlook the simple fact that the only practical route for American military aid to reach land-locked Afghanistan in the 1950s was via Pakistan. Aid from the Russians, by contrast, would be subject neither to blockade nor to divided loyalties on the part of the donor.

In the eyes of almost all educated Afghans, moreover, there were few objections to accepting Soviet military aid. None of them for a moment believed in the possibility of a Soviet invasion. Subversion seemed implausible, given Afghan xenophobia, a pervasive police system, and the virtually total absence of anything resembling an industrial proletariat. The one previously existing barrier, the tendency to panic so prevalent in British Viceroys in India, had vanished with the viceroys.

Negotiations with the USA for military aid and some form of defence agreement continued during the first 2 years of Daud's Prime Ministership, and the break-down ostensibly came because of American refusal to extend a security guarantee to Afghanistan, but other factors were in fact more influential. In 1954 Pakistan signed a Mutual Defence Assistance Agreement with the USA, provided the latter with military bases, and joined SEATO; in the following year, both Pakistan and Iran joined the Baghdad Pact (now CEN-TO). When Mr. Khrushchev visited Kabul in 1956, offering a $100,000,000 Soviet loan, it took little persuasive power for the Prime Minister to get the assent of the *Loya Jirga* (traditional tribal council) to accepting Soviet military aid as well.

It was a decision that stuck. For a while trade and foreign aid were almost monopolised by the Soviet Union (between 1957 and 1972 60% of Afghanistan's foreign aid — $900,000,000 — came from the Soviet Union, and even now it takes more than half Afghanistan's trade), but in military aid the Soviet monopoly was virtually total, and survives to this day. The vastly expanded military forces are armed exclusively with Soviet equipment, the only foreign military advisers in the country for the past two decades have been Russians, and an entire generation of Afghan officers has matured under the predominant influence of Soviet military doctrine (often learned at military education establishments in the USSR).

There has never been any overt Soviet meddling in Afghan domestic politics, and in terms both of professional competence and of modern equipment the Afghan armed forces have benefited immensely from Soviet assistance. Most Afghans see Pakistan's difficulties with its American alliance since 1965 (a 10 year American arms embargo, for example) as confirmation of their wisdom in choosing otherwise. Not all Daud's innovations as Prime Minister survived him, but the Soviet military link has never been seriously questioned.

Daud's policies were adventurous both at home and abroad. He introduced 5 year economic plans, abolished the veil for women, and in 1961 began sending students to the Soviet Union. He pushed so hard on the Pushtoonistan issue that by 1961 there were Pakistan—Afghanistan border clashes and a rupture of diplomatic relations. While these policies alienated or frightened some Afghans, his apparent lack of interest in any sort of democratisation of the regime annoyed others of the *élite* equally. In 1963 he was forced to resign by Palace intrigues, and spent the following decade out of politics.

The new Prime Minister, Dr. Muhammad Yusuf, was the first from outside the royal family, and in 1964 he introduced a democratic constitution designed by young Kabul intellectuals. The parliament thus created never functioned properly, however, as the monarch timidly refused to permit political parties, and on the whole the governments of Dr. Yusuf and his successors were ineffective in producing any major change in the country's political or economic circumstances. This state of affairs continued for a decade, until abruptly ended by Afghanistan's first modern military coup in July, 1973.

The armed forces' loyalty to the King was normally assured by his direct control over personnel matters (all appointments of captain rank and above in both army and air force required his personal approval). Inevitably, a high proportion of senior promotions went to men drawn from families linked with the King by the ties of the Muhammadzai clan. The main motive force for the 1973 coup, beyond disillusionment with the pace of development under Zahir Shah's latter governments, seems to have been frustration amongst younger officers at the lack of promotion for those outside the kinship net.

The conspiracy was led by some 20 young army and air force officers, many of them trained in the Soviet Union and of more or less clearly defined leftist views, who constituted themselves into the 'Central Committee of the Revolution'. Muhammad Daud seems to have been brought into the plot only late in the planning, to serve as a figurehead. His key role in organising the modernisation of the armed forces made him a popular figure within the services, while his reforming but non-ideological zeal made him an encouraging and reassuring figure for civilian onlookers. The coup went off smoothly, aided no doubt by the fact that one of the leaders, Major Faiz Masoud, commanded the elite force guarding the King. A full list of Central Committee members was never published.

A republic was promptly declared, with Muhammad Daud (no longer using his princely title) as President. The radical young officers gradually discovered after 1973, however, that Daud had no intention of remaining a mere figurehead, and slowly lost ground before him. In early 1977 he proclaimed a new republican constitution, and an end to the purely military government. In April, 1978 the displaced and often demoted young radical officers of 1973 struck back, in a coup which killed Daud and much of the armed forces' high command amidst 2 days of severe fighting in Kabul. Subsequent political developments are described below.

STRENGTH AND BUDGET

The strength of the Afghan armed forces in 1982 was 46,000, a heavy decline from the figure quoted in the 1979 edition of *World Armies* (110,000). The army numbered 40,000 men, the bulk of them being conscripts, and the air force 6,000. There is a paramilitary force of 30,000 gendarmerie, under the control of the Ministry of Internal Affairs. A National Guard (presumably intended to reflect the political colour of the new regime and to defend its interests) was founded in May, 1978, is not identifiable.

Afghanistan's estimated defence expenditure for 1981 was $97,000,000; GNP was $3,230,000,000. All figures are untrustworthy

COMMAND AND CONSTITUTIONAL STATUS

The Communist government appears to consist of three tiers: in ascending order of authority, they are the Cabinet, the Revolutionary Council and the Central Committee of the People's Democratic Party. All members of all three bodies belong to the PDP, and the majority are civilians. This undoubtedly understates the degree of military influence in the government, however, as it was military officers who were secretly members of the PDP who made the coup while the civilian leadership was in jail, and as the only source of sup-

port for the new government's policies, given the virtual absence of mass organisations of any sort in Afghanistan, is the armed forces.

Command
President Babrak Karmal, who was brought from Russian by the Soviet invaders in December 1979, is titular commander-in-chief of the army (though reports claim he is at loggerheads with the Russians over the limitations even of his civil powers). The PDP, over which he presides, is riven into two factions – Flag (*Parcham*) and People (*Khala*) – and finds difficulty in agreeing national policy, even within such limits as Russia allows. The Defence Minister, General Rafi of the Flag faction, was sent to Russia in January 1982 to quell disagreements over his hard-line policy, and replaced by the Vice-President Abdul Qadir.

Operationally, the Afghan army may be presumed to be under the control of the Soviet commander in Afghanistan (in February 1982 the Soviet First Deputy Minister for Defence, Marshal Sokholov).

ROLE, COMMITMENT, DEPLOYMENT AND RECENT OPERATIONS

Since the Soviet invasion in December 1979 of Afghanistan, now occupied by ten Soviet motor rifle divisions and two airborne divisions, the task of the surviving elements of the Afghan army is to assist the occupying forces in suppressing revolt. This revolt, against the communist policies of the politicians who succeeded Daud, notably President Amin, was already in progress when the Soviets intervened, presumably with the intention of protecting their political nominees and allegedly at their invitation, but invasion has intensified and spread resistance. The Afghan army is wholly committed to anti-guerrilla operations, apparently largely to provide the screen behind which Soviet forces carry out the main fighting.

About 80% of the area of Afghanistan is said to be in rebel hands, and they are also said to move freely in such cities as Kabul by night. Four million refugees have nonetheless fled the country for Pakistan, and the fifteen main rebel groups (six active) are unable to agree on common policies or strategy, since divided along traditional tribal lines. Most of the fighting takes place in the mountains north and east of Kabul, the capital, which lies close to Pakistan. In 1981–2, however, fighting also spread to the western districts of Herat and the Southern district of Kandahar.

At a PDP conference held in Kabul in March, 1982, the interior minister claimed that the Afghan army had participated during 1980 in 1700 military actions, '800 without Soviet assistance', killing 10,000 counter-revolutionaries.

ORGANISATION

Arms of Service
The Afghan army is organised into three armoured divisions (of brigade strength) and 11 infantry divisions, all very under-strength (about 2500 men). There are two full-strength mountain infantry brigades, an artillery brigade of three regiments, two commando regiments and a parachute battalion.

The air force contains an air-defence division, incorporating Afghanistan's heavier anti-aircraft equipment. It is organised into a SAM brigade consisting of three battalions each controlling 40 SA-2 missiles, an AA brigade of two battalions equipped with 37mm, 85mm and 100mm AA guns, and a radar brigade of three battalions.

All functions are under-strength, demoralised and subject to constant desertion.

Operational

The Afghan army is organised into three army corps. Their headquarters, at Kabul, Gardez and Kandahar, are all within 50 Miles or so of the eastern border, facing the main passes leading down into Pakistan. There are also four separate divisions, stationed in areas of the country beyond the territorial boundaries of the three corps organisations, which report directly to the Ministry of Defence in Kabul. Only very light forces are deployed west and north of the Hindu Kush.

The principal air force fighter base is at Bagram, and the main bomber base is at Shir Dand (Sabzawar). Other air force installations are at Gardez, Ghazni, Herat, Jalalabad, Kandahar, Kunduz, Mazar-i-Sharif and Sherpur. Military airfields would probably not function very well without Soviet technical assistance, but they are all under Afghan control.

RECRUITMENT, TRAINING AND RESERVES

[Quoted from the first edition of *World Armies*.]

The Afghan army's regular officer corps is voluntarily recruited, and receives its training at the Afghan Military Academy. (Most regular officers are also graduates of the Military High School in Kabul, which takes boys from the age of ten.)

There is also a technical school and a school for each principal arm, and many officers subsequently train abroad. Most non-commissioned officers are also long-service regulars, and receive their training at an NCO's school, and sometimes also at technical schools within Afghanistan. Air force flying training is done at Mazar-i-Sharif, and the Air Academy at Sherpur has about 400 cadets. The majority of air force personnel are regulars.

A very high proportion of regular officers come from the royal clan and from other families closely associated with it. This recruitment pattern was effectively continued by Muhammad Daud after the creation of the republic in 1973, as a result of which there is an extremely wide social gap between officers and men. Despite the very rapid growth of ideological loyalties alongside the traditional kinship loyalties within the officer corps, and the far-reaching purges after the April, 1978 revolution, this situation still largely prevails.

The bulk of the army is provided by conscripts, who are called up between the ages of twenty-two and twenty-eight for 2 years' service in accordance with the Conscription Act of 1954. Youths in higher educational establishments do their service as conscript officers, and must serve only 1 year, most of which is spent at the Reserve Officers' School. All able-bodied men are liable for military service, but it is in fact selective service: the overall call-up figure for the year is decided by the army in consultation with the government, and apportioned between the provinces, but the actual selection of individuals who must serve is done by local arrangements within each province. A proportion of conscripts are drafted into the Labour Corps (employed mainly on public works).

Conscription theoretically applies to all Afghan males of military age, but certain tribes are in practice exempted in return for agreement to provide tribal levies in times of emergency. Others, such as the Kirghiz group in the Wakhan corridor extending to the Chinese frontier between the Soviet Union and Pakistan, assume responsibility for border patrols in their area in return for exemption. Wherever practical, conscripts are assigned to units widely separated from their own areas, to encourage the growth of national consciousness and to avoid a conflict of loyalties if the army becomes involved in internal security operations.

The organised reserves total 162,000 men, and are administered by General Reserve Headquarters in Kabul. Conscripts are placed on the reserve list upon discharge, and are liable for 2 month periods of refresher training any time during the next 22 years. There is a mobilisation organisation, and an officer reserve also exists. The several hundred thousand tribesmen living near the Pakistan frontier who would be available as irregular auxiliaries in an emergency have a loose reserve organisation to direct them, and in certain circumstances could prove a formidable problem (as Pakistan proved when it sent the tribes into Kashmir in 1948). Their potential effectiveness is enhanced by the fact that they are mostly fellow-tribesmen, and often close kinsmen, of the Afridi, Waziri, Mohmand, Bajauri and Mahsud tribes of Pushtoons on the Pakistan side of the border.

During the 1960s almost all higher technical and military instruction for the armed forces was provided by the Soviet Union, which as late as 1973 had over 1000 advisers with the Afghan army. Thousands of Afghan officers received training in the Soviet Union, while only a handful were sent elsewhere (USA, France and Turkey). After the 1973 coup, however, there were signs of major changes in this pattern.

Although there was no intention to reduce Afghanistan's dependence on the Soviet Union as its exclusive arms supplier, the number of Soviet advisers with the army was cut to no more than 200. Afghan officers continued to receive some of their training on Soviet equipment outside the country, but increasingly this was done in India (also almost exclusively Soviet-equipped in recent years), where the likelihood of Marxist influences making large inroads into the officer corps is less great. This reorientation had its roots in concern for the political trend within the Afghan officer corps; now that the 1978 coup has demonstrated the accuracy of that concern, it is to be expected that the direct Soviet role in training Afghan officers and technicians will once again increase. The number of Soviet military advisers in Afghanistan is now reported to be in the low thousands, and they are attached to many tactical units. Afghan officers are again attending Soviet military schools in considerable numbers.

It is impossible to make any firm statements about the current recruitment or training of the Afghan army, which is under Soviet control and has the greatest difficulty conscripting recruits and retaining those it inducts. Desertion is endemic; sometimes whole sub-units desert to the guerillas.

The IISS *Military Balance* refers to several forces recruited through political parties: *Sarandoli* (Defenders of the Revolution), organised in provincial regiments; regional 'Revolution Defence Groups'; Pioneers; Afghan Communist Party Guards; Khalki; Youth Militia; and the Pashtun Tribal Milita. However, most tribal forces are in action against the government and the Soviet army of occupation.

In January 1982 the government resorted to kidnapping men and youths stopped at road blocks to provide recruits, but widespread protests brought this method of conscription to a stop.

EQUIPMENT AND ARMS INDUSTRY

The Afghan army is wholly Soviet equipped and in the words of the IISS Military Balance it is not possible to differentiate between Soviet and Afghan holdings of identical equipment.

RANK, DRESS AND DISTINCTIONS

The rank and grade structure generally resembles the British pattern, with the additional ranks of third-lieutenant and senior captain. Rank insignia for regimental-grade officers consists of gold bars and gold-coloured stars (sunbursts) worn on green epaulettes: third-lieutenants wear one bar, second-lieutenants one bar and one star, first-lieutenants one bar and two stars, junior captains two bars and one star and senior captains two bars and two stars.

Field-grade officers wear gold-coloured crossed swords and gold stars on maroon epaulettes: majors wear crossed swords and one star, lieutenant-colonels crossed swords and two stars and colonels crossed swords and three stars. All field-grade officers also have maroon and gold cap cords and maroon collar tabs embossed with a gold stalk of corn.

General officers' rank is indicated by gold-coloured national crest emblems and stars worn on crimson epaulettes: brigadier-generals wear the crest and one star, major-generals the crest and two stars, lieutenant-generals the crest and three stars and generals the crest and four stars. The rank of field-marshal exists, but is rarely used. All general officers have gold cap cords and crimson collar tabs embossed with two gold stalks of corn.

More than a dozen military decorations and awards existed under the former regime, most of them including money, grants of land, or both, but it is not yet clear whether they will be maintained or altered by the new government.

CURRENT DEVELOPMENTS

President Muhammad Daud's regime was overthrown on April 27th, 1978 by a bloody coup led by officers belonging to the Afghan Communist Party. In the 2 days of fighting in the capital a large number of people were killed (the more plausible estimates range from 400 to 5000 dead). There was particularly heavy fighting around Central Corps headquarters and the Justice Ministry, where air force SU-7s made rocket attacks to aid the rebels, and in the vicinity of the 7th and 8th Divisions which were based near Kabul. President Daud's 1500 man guard held out in the former Royal Palace for 16 hours, until it was reduced to rubble by the fire of some 50 tanks and air force MiGs. Daud was captured and executed in the palace courtyard, after being compelled to watch the machine-gunning of some 30 members of his family including women and children.

The coup was carried out by relatively young officers, many of whom had been involved in more junior roles in the 1973 revolution and had subsequently been pushed aside or even demoted by Daud. Most units involved were from the air force or the armoured forces, the two branches where Soviet training influence has been greatest: the most prominent leaders were Colonel (later Brigadier-General) Dagarwal Abdul Khadir of the air force and Colonel Muhammad Aslam of the armoured corps. All the military leaders, however, subsequently proved to have been secretly members of the Communist Party.

The People's Democratic Party (it eschews the word 'Communist', in deference to the Muslim beliefs of the Afghan population) does not appear to have been a major influence on the young leftist officers who engineered the 1973 coup that brought Daud to power. Indeed, it split in the course of a controversy over supporting Daud's regime, the larger Khalq ('People') faction under Ahmad Tarakki's leadership refusing co-operation while the Parcham ('Flag') faction followed Moscow's orders and accepted places in Daud's government. Neither faction is known to have had any part in the numerous attempted coups and uprisings with which Daud had to contend in his first years in power: an attempted coup in September, 1973 from the centre of the political spectrum, involving a former prime minister and eight senior officers, conspiracies in December, 1973 and June, 1974 involving conservative mullahs and some junior officers

of strong Islamic convictions (in the latter case nearly 100 officers, apparently belonging to the Muslim Brotherhood); and an abortive uprising by the fundamentalist Jamaat Islami Afghanistan Party in 1975.

As Daud gradually consolidated his hold on power and subdued the Islamic right (and disappointed rivals of the political centre) however, he began to remove from positions of power the young radical officers whose support had previously been indispendable. The key act was probably his purge of Soviet-trained air force officers suspected of communist sympathies in April, 1974 (Brigadier-General Abdul Khadir, first Minister of Defence in the 1978 revolution, was demoted in that purge). The shadowy Central Committee of leftist officers who had invited Daud to lead their revolution met for the last time, it is believed, in late 1974. It now seems clear that it was at this time that considerable numbers of disappointed leftist officers formally joined the Khalq Party (secretly, of course).

During 1977 Daud removed the representatives of the dissident Parcham faction from his government, and the two branches of the Communist Party then reunited under the leadership of Mr. Tarakki. The immediate cause of the coup was the murder of the leader of the Parcham faction, Mir Akbar Khyber, allegedly by government agents. His funeral on April 17th, 1978 was attended by serious demonstrations, and the government began large-scale arrests of communist leaders: Mr. Tarakki and his civilian colleagues were jailed on April 24th. Perhaps anticipating similar arrests within the armed forces, military adherents of the Khalq Party launched the successful coup of April 27th, released Mr. Tarakki and appointed him President.

The regime took drastic measures to secure its hold on power against domestic opposition. Of some 60 to 80 army and air force generals in April, only about a dozen remained in their old commands in May; the rest had been killed in the fighting, were in jail, or had gone into hiding, while their jobs were being done by young majors and captains. The new police chief was an air force major (the air force contains more Khalq Party adherents, and is generally more leftist and pro-Soviet, than the army), and a National Guard was being formed to serve as a party militia. Extensive political purges were initiated in the armed and civil services, concentrating especially on members of the Muhammadzai clan, and there were reports of mass arrests in the clan's own territories. All provincial governors were dismissed and replaced by Military personnel (the Khalq Party having virtually no civilian members outside Kabul and Kandahar).

Tribal resistance to the new government began almost at once, notably in the Jalalabad region near the Pakistan border which is the seat of the Muhammadzais, and a National Rescue Front grouping the various tribal-cum-Islamic strands of opposition to the new regime was created in exile in Pakistan. In an attempt to defuse this problem, representatives of the main tribes were brought into the Revolutionary Council. There was also trouble in the army, with one division near Kabul reportedly being disarmed by troops loyal to the regime in June, 1978 after it had shown signs of revolt. Eighty officers were subsequently dismissed. A more serious falling out between the civilian leadership of the regime and their military supporters occurred in August, 1978 when Brigadier-General Khadir, who had been made Defence Minister, was arrested, together with the Army Chief of Staff on charges of 'anti-revolutionary plotting and treason'. This was followed shortly be a renewed split between the Parcham and Khalq factions and the expulsion of many members of the former from their government posts. Meanwhile guerrilla resistance to the new regime increased in late 1978 with the coalition of two Islamic parties, now known as the Movement of

Islamic Revolution, but remained concentrated in the eastern provinces near the Pakistani border.

The scale of the rebellion, however, and the threat it offered to the stability of the PDP regime prompted Soviet intervention in December 1979, the replacement of President Amin (who had taken power from Tarakki only in September) with Babrak Karmal, and the initiation of intensive and extensive anti-guerilla operations by the Soviet and the Afghan armies. The latter has dwindled away through desertion and by the disaffection of potential recruits. The latter has grown constantly in strength, from an initial commitment of 50,000 to its present strength of 12 divisions (said to be Category II and III divisions from neighbouring Military Districts of the USSR) plus two airborne divisions.

The campaign does not progress well either for the Soviet or Afghan armies. Excellent defensive terrain allows the guerillas to sustain resistance, despite their enemies' ample use of armour, air power (including many gunship helicopters) and, it has been alleged, chemical agents [US statements of November and December 1981].

The most favourable factor for the Soviet/Afghan forces is that the guerillas (*mujaheddin*) remain divided, largely along tribal lines. Seven main groups have been identified: the *Hizb-i-Islami* factions, two *Jamiat Islami*, two *Hartkat-i-Inqilabi* and the Afghan National Liberation Front. They are reported to have agreed on a union in March, 1982 at Peshawar, but from a people with a 'passion for discord', truly unified action seemed unlikely to result.

Gwynne Dyer
John Keegan

ALBANIA

HISTORY AND INTRODUCTION

The Albanian Party of Labour was founded in 1941, and played a leading role in the struggle against the Italian and German occupation forces. The Party's leader, Enver Hoxha, commanded the Liberation Army, and in October, 1941 he became head of the provincial government. Albania was declared a People's Republic in January, 1946 after elections in which Hoxha's party won an overwhelming majority.

Albania initially came within the Yugoslav sphere of influence, and there were even plans for the incorporation of Albania into the Yugoslav federation. The Tito—Stalin dispute led, however, to the severance of relations between Albania and Yugoslavia, and from 1949 to 1961 Albania was a Soviet satellite. Albania broke with Russia in 1961, and withdrew from the Warsaw Pact in 1968. Since 1961 she has followed the Chinese lead on ideological matters, and currently receives economic and military assistance from China.

STRENGTH AND BUDGET

Strength
Population: 2,730,000
Total armed forces: 43,100 (23,000 conscripts)
Army: 30,000
Navy: 3100; three submarines, 71 small craft
Air Force: 10,000, 100 combat aircraft
Internal Security Force and Frontier Guard: 13,000 (controlled by the Ministry of the Interior)

Budget
GNP (1978 estimate): $1,850,000,000
Defence expenditure (1981 estimate): $188,000,000

COMMAND AND CONSTITUTIONAL STATUS

Command
Hoxha holds the rank of army general, and until July, 1953 was *de facto* Commander-in-Chief of the Armed Forces. In 1953 the Minister of National Defence, a serving officer, took over the functions of Commander-in-Chief.

Constitutional Status
The People's Assembly is the supreme legislative organ. It is elected, for a 4 year term, by all citizens over the age of eighteen. The People's Assembly elects the Presidium, which, under the leadership of the President of the Presidium, carries out the functions of Head of State. The Council of Ministers is appointed by the Assembly. Hoxha is First Secretary of the Party of Labour, and Colonel-General Balluku is a member of the Party's Politburo and Minister of National Defence.

ROLE, COMMITMENT, DEPLOYMENT AND RECENT OPERATIONS

Role and Commitment
The Albanian armed forces have the dual roles of defending Albanian sovereignty and safeguarding the regime. All are stationed within the borders of Albania.

Deployment
The army forms one tank brigade and nine infantry brigades, all below strength, together with eight coast artillery battalions. The country is divided into two military districts, one in the north and the other in the south; it is impossible to assess the division of troops between military districts.

Recent Operations
The Albanian armed forces have participated in no military operations since World War II.

ORGANISATION

The Albanian army was, at least until 1961, organised along Soviet lines, but it is likely that it now follows Chinese organisational patterns. The tank brigade appears to consist of three tank battalions and a motor rifle battalion.

RECRUITMENT, TRAINING AND RESERVES

Recruitment and Training
Conscripts make up over half the army's total strength. Conscription is for 2 years in the army, and for 3 years in the air force, navy and paramilitary forces. Lack of sophisticated equipment means that most training time is relatively low-level.

Reserves
There are approximatley 100,000 regular reservists. In addition, the Society for Aid to the Army and for Defence (SHNUM) gives part-time paramilitary and civil-defence training to civilians. Pre-conscription military training was made obligatory in 1953.

EQUIPMENT AND ARMS INDUSTRY

Until Albania's break with the Soviet Union, almost all Albanian military equipment was of Soviet origin. A great deal of this remains in use, but it is being complemented with, and in some cases replaced by, Chinese equipment.

Small Arms: of Soviet origin, including PPSh, AK-47, RPD and RPK; and the M-10, M-49 and M-38 heavy machine-guns. Some World War II German weapons — MP-40, Mauser 98K, MG-34 and MG-42 — would be used by reservists. Chinese copies of Soviet small arms have been imported
Mortars: 82mm M-37, 120mm M-43 and 160mm M-43
Anti-tank: 14.5mm PTRD M-41 Soviet anti-tank rifle. 45mm M-37, 57mm M-43, 57mm M-55, 76.2mm M-42 and 85mm M-45 towed anti-tank guns
Anti-aircraft: 37mm M-38/39, 57mm M-50 and 85mm M-44 Soviet AA guns
Artillery: Soviet 152mm M-43 and M-37, 122mm M-38, 85mm M-45 and 76mm M-42 towed guns
Armour:
    Tanks: T34/85 (70). Soviet T-54 and its Chinese copy, T-59 (15). T-62 Chinese light tanks (possibly as many as 40).
    APC: about 20, including BA-64, BTR-40 and BTR-152
    SP gun: Soviet 76.2mm Su-76 anti-tank
Missiles: SA-2 Guideline

8

RANK, DRESS AND DISTINCTIONS

Rank and Dress
The Albanian army formerly wore Soviet-style uniforms and badges of rank. These now appear to have been replaced by Chinese-style tunics without badges of rank.

Distinctions
Numerous orders and decorations have been awarded to members of the armed forces. Some of these had Soviet equivalents, but it is not known how they have been affected by the break with the Soviet Union.

CURRENT DEVELOPMENTS

It is difficult to assess the military consequences of Albania's current close relations with China. If fighting efficiency was damaged by the Russo—Albanian rupture, it has now probably recovered. The Albanian army remains, nevertheless, a relatively primitive and unsophisticated force consisting primarily of infantry. Small-unit actions are stressed in training, and it is likely that these, carried out in mountainous areas, could hamper the advance of an invader.

Richard Holmes

ALGERIA

HISTORY AND INTRODUCTION

The Democratic People's Republic of Algeria was created by a prolonged military uprising against French rule in 1954–62, tying down half a million French troops at its height and costing up to a million Algerian lives. The armed forces, which have been the power base of Algeria's rulers since independence, claim this struggle as their accomplishment and (by inference) as their right to rule, but this is a considerable simplification of the actual history of the Algerian war.

Most of the senior members of the present officer corps, having gained their initial military experience as officers or NCOs in the French armed forces, joined the *Armée de Liberation Nationale* (ALN) which was created shortly after the Algerian rising of 1954 and was under the political control of the *Front de Liberation Nationale* (FLN), which set up an Algerian government in exile in Cairo in September, 1958. The ALN grew to number about 150,000 lightly armed men by independence in 1962. The great bulk of its forces were not involved in the fighting, however, being stationed along the frontiers of the neighbouring independent Arab States of Tunisia and Morocco, while the actual fighting was done by a fluctuating number of irregular 'internal' members of the ALN organised in six regional commands. Individuals were frequently transferred between the 'internal' and 'external' forces, but there was constant rivalry between the two leadership groups, the 'external' forces under their commander Colonel Houari Boumedienne claiming political leadership of the entire ALN.

Although French forces succeeded in re-establishing a large measure of control over Algeria during a brutal counter-insurgency campaign in the late 1950s, the political tolerance of the French public for the continuing high cost of the war in money and in conscripts' lives was steadily worn away. President De Gaulle originally came to power in France promising no surrender in Algeria but there was little French popular protest when he signed the treaty of Evian in 1962 providing for a referendum to determine whether or not Algeria was to remain a part of France. Algeria became independent later in 1962, and 1,000,000 French settlers — about one tenth of the population — left the country.

The simmering disagreements between the 'internal' and the 'external' wings of the ALN came to a head after independence was achieved. The FLN political leadership (previously based in Cairo) which had signed the Evian treaty, led by Ahmed Ben Bella, and the external wing of the ALN under Boumedienne vied for the allegiance of the commanders of the six regions into which the internal army was organised. When some proved reluctant to hand over the victory they felt they had been instrumental in winning to the external group which had spent the war outside Algeria's borders, recourse was had to the superior force of the semi-regular troops of the external army. In the autumn of 1962 Boumedienne sent 900 of his troops into Algiers, which was held by his adversaries, and the threat of full-scale civil war arose. In the end, however, a ceasefire agreement was signed which effectively acknowledged the primacy of the Ben Bella–Boumedienne faction.

Boumedienne was put in charge of the Defence Ministry and was appointed Commander-in-Chief of the Armed Forces by Ben Bella's government; one of his close associates was made Minister of the Interior. Boumedienne then embarked on a massive purge of the armed forces, in which he retained most of the officers who had previously served in the external wing of the ALN and dismissed or exiled a very large proportion of those associated with the internal wing. Only some 10,000 of the 50,000–60,000 men who had fought in the internal forces were taken into the *Armée Nationale Populaire* (ANP), as it was renamed in 1962, while the remainder (most of them Berbers) were demobilised.

During the first years of independence, personal rivalry and differences over policy led to a growing estrangement between the Commander-in-Chief of the Armed Forces and the Head of State; when Ben Bella tried to reduce the power of the military faction and to restore civilian control, he was ousted in a military coup led by Colonel Boumedienne in June, 1965. Boumedienne became President, and the army became the sole effective source of political power in the country, while the civilian political organisation of the FLN, though preserved, went into a steep decline. Ben Bella was placed under close house arrest, from which he only emerged fifteen years later.

Following the defeat of the attempted coup led by Col Tahar Zbini in 1967, the General Staff of the ALN was suppressed, and Boumedienne ruled both party and army essentially through his own personal network of followers for the remaining decades of his rule. The character of the regime was defined by his own equally devout commitments to Socialism and to conservative Islam, and the relative influence of the army in the system declined markedly.

Upon Boumediennes's death in December 1978, however, there was a marked resurgence of military influence; it was essentially the army which determined the choice of Col Benjedid Chadhi as his successor over civilian competitors like Abdelaziz Boutifhka, Foreign Minister for fifteen years, and Mohammed Yahyawi, the effective head of the FLN who had been close to Boumedienne. By 1980 Chadhi's power was sufficiently secure that he felt able to release Ben Bella from his long imprisonment, and to reward the armed forces for their support by re-establishing the General Staff. In 1981 he removed both Boutefhka and Yahyawi from the Control Committee of the FLN (together with other powerful civilian rivals he had inherited from the Boumedienne era), and even pardoned Col Zbini (who had been condemned to death in abstentia in 1969). In domestic policy he eased up considerably on the austere Socialism and puritanical Islam which his predecessor had rigidly imposed on the country, and abroad he took a considerably less militant line in supporting anybody and everybody's 'liberation movement', but he did not find it possible to abandon Algeria's long and draining commitment to support the Polisario guerillas of Moi in the Saharan war.

The armed forces were maintained at roughly the same strength (60,000–70,000) from independence until the late 1970s, but since then they have more than doubled, largely due to the possibility of a war with Morocco growing out of Algeria's support for the Polisario guerillas. National service has provided an additional conscript element since 1969, but most conscripts, after initial military training, are employed on non-military duties. The senior officers today are still for the most part Boumedienne's close associates from the days of the 'external' ALN, and real political power is now more than ever concentrated within a small circle of military officers despite the creation of a civilian and representative element in the government since 1976.

Algeria's domestic policies have been resolutely socialist throughout the period of independence, and its foreign policy has made it one of the leaders of the radical bloc in the Arab League, the Organisation for African Unity, and the Third World as a whole. During the 1960s and early 1970s it provided refuge, vocal support and sometimes actual aid to a wide assortment of guerrilla and revolutionary organisations and individuals, although in recent years it has shown more selectivity. It could be generally observed, however, that the Boumedienne regime's verbal radicalism was tempered by a considerable degree of caution in practice. In the early years this was probably due primarily to Algeria's military weakness (it was humiliatingly defeated by Morocco in a brief border war in 1963) but in the more recent period Algeria's caution probably owes more to the exigencies of its economic strategy. With a population of 20,000,000 growing at a rate of 3.4% a year (i.e. 35,000,000 by the year 2000) and only very limited arable land in the Mediterranean coastal belt, Algeria has committed itself to a crash programme of industrialisation to provide jobs and prosperity for the next generation. It must also bear a very high educational expenditure (30% of the budget) to train the workforce for that industrialised future. It is a monumental task — 70% of the population is still on the land, and agricultural techniques are still traditional in much of the country — but substantial progress has been achieved; illiteracy, which was about 80% at independence, is planned to be entirely eradicated in the younger generation by 1980. But Algeria is now irrevocably committed to its policy of rapid industrialisation (there has been a classic flight from the land, and the urban population now numbers hundreds of thousands of youthful job-seekers) and this strategy depends critically on oil and gas exports to pay for the investments required.

The oil price-rise after 1973 has been of great help (the first development plan in 1970–73 included investments of $8,000,000,000; the second plan, 1974–7, projected an investment of $27,600,000,000, two fifths of it in heavy industry), but Algeria's main problem is that most of its exportable hydrocarbons are in the form of gas not oil. Its oil production has still not recovered from the 1973 peak of 51,000,000 tons, and oil reserves may run out altogether in the mid-1980s; on the other hand it has almost unlimited gas reserves.

The political repercussions of this arise from the fact that the developing infrastructure of gas-processing plants will cost $28,000,000,000 in the years 1978–85, over half of which must be borrowed abroad, and the equally sensitive fact that the principal market for Algerian gas is the USA (which could go elsewhere for its gas). While it would be an exaggeration to say that these considerations have drastically altered the foreign policy of the Algerian government in recent years, it is nonetheless true that they would exercise a considerable restraining effect on any courses of action which might involve the direct commitment of Algerian armed forces in support of that policy. It should also be observed, however, that the prospect of continuously rising domestic prosperity (albeit from a very low level) would suggest that there is unlikely to be any early challenge to the armed forces' effective monopoly of political power in Algeria.

STRENGTH AND BUDGET

The Algerian armed forces total 168,000 men out of a population of 20 million. Of this total, the army has 150,000 men, the navy 6,000, and the air force 12,000. All three forces have approximately doubled in strength in the past five years. There are also 14,000 paramilitary Gendarmes (up from 10,000 in 1977) equipped with heavy weapons, and a Coastguard which operates a number of fast attack craft. There is a national service force of 6 month conscripts which in under the Ministry of Defence but is primarily employed on civic action projects. There are about 100,000 army reserves.

The military budget in 1982 was $856.8 m, approximately twice the 1978 figure but still a relatively modest share of the GNP of $36.8 m. The cause of the sharp rise in military spending is almost entirely the possibility of confrontation with Morocco over Algeria's support for the guerrillas who are attacking Moroccan and allied Mauritanian forces in the former Spanish Sahara which these two neighbouring States partitioned and annexed in late 1975.

COMMAND AND CONSTITUTIONAL STATUS

Colonel Houari Boumedienne, President, Head of State and Prime Minister since 1965, was Defence Minister and Commander-in-Chief of the Armed Forces from independence in 1962 until his death in December, 1978. He was then succeeded by Colonel Benjadid Chadli, who holds all the same offices with the exception of the prime minister. Chadli is assisted as Minister of Defence by two deputy ministers, Colonel Abdallah Benhouchet, who also holds the post of Inspector-General of the armed forces, and Colonel Kasdi-Merbah, formerly head of the military security branch. Day-to-day command of the army is the responsibility of the Secretary-General of the Ministry of National Defence, Col. Mustapha Belloucif.

The General Staff, created in 1964, suppressed in 1967 and recreated in 1980, has responsibility for the organisational, mobilization, budget and employment planning of the four armed services (including the National Gendarmerie). The formal organisation for the general control of armed forces operations is the Higher Council of Defence, consisting of the President and Minister of National Defence (both Chadli), the Ministers of the Interior and Foreign Affairs, and the Chairman of the Committee of National Defence in the National Assembly and two other members designated by the President; but in practice the President deals directly with the commanders of the armed forces and of the five military regions.

The armed forces have FLN party cells at all levels, and an elaborate organisation of political commissions reporting to the Political Commissariat at the Ministry of National Defence. This organisation is subordinate to the Political Bureau of the FLN.

In the last few years a considerable constitutional superstructure has been created for the regime. A 60,000 word document entitled *The National Charter*, which is 'the source of ideological legal and political reference for the institutions of the party and State at all levels' was widely debated and substantially amended — indeed, criticism got a bit out of hand — before being approved by a national referendum in June, 1976. This was followed by a referendum (without prior public discussion) in November, 1976 on a constitution granting all executive powers to the President, and effectively rendering the new Popular National Assembly a rubber stamp. In accordance with the constitution, President Boumedienne was elected to a renewable 6 year term of office in December, 1976 (he was the only candidate and received 99.95% of the valid votes), and parliamentary elections for the new 261 member assembly followed (only the FLN ran candidates) in

February, 1977. There is no evidence that any of this altered the actual focus of political power and control over the armed forces in Algeria, which remains in the presidency.

ROLE, COMMITMENT, DEPLOYMENT AND RECENT OPERATIONS

The principal roles of the Algerian armed forces remain the governing of the country and the protection of the regime. They have never faced a truly serious challenge in either capacity. The only likely source from which such a threat might arise at present is the Berber minority, many of whose members harbour separatist sentiments that have been stimulated further by the unrelenting official campaigns to 'Arabise' Algeria. However, the gendarmerie proved adequate to deal with the only recent outbreak of Berber resentment against the government, the Tizi-Ouzo riots of April, 1979, continually requiring aid for regular troops, and in general the probability of Berber disaffection can be regarded as chronic but not critical. If their aid were ever needed, the regular armed forces would certainly be willing and able to deal with the problem.

External defence has been a secondary role for the armed forces for most of Algeria's independent history, but it has been increasing in importance since the outbreak of the Polisario war. They do have a secondary role of external defence, however, and this has been increasing in importance since the commencement of the confrontation with Morocco over ex-Spanish Sahara in 1975. The military budget has risen sharply, and there has been a considerable concentration of forces near the Moroccan frontier, especially in the south near Tindouf, where the military airfield's runway has recently been lengthened and strengthened, and MiG-21s brought in.

The conflict with Morocco dates from the beginnings of Algerian independence, and springs not only from the diametrically opposed political characters of the regimes but also from serious border disputes. The latter are particularly sensitive in the south, where the historical accident of administrative boundaries within the French colonial empire has given Algeria the lion's share of the Sahara, including extensive areas that were more usually under Moroccan control or influence. This dispute led to a sharp border war (fought mainly in the south round Tindouf) in October, 1963 in which the new Algerian army, trained only in guerrilla tactics, was soundly beaten. Subsequent attempts to settle the borders by negotiation never achieved ratification, and during the early 1970s Algeria was accused by Rabat of being implicated in several attempts on King Hassan's life.

The current tension was caused by the secret agreement of 1974 between Morocco and Mauritania for the partition of the Spanish colonial territory of Western Sahara which lay between them. The local population of less than 100,000, whose guerrilla organisation, Polisario, was already getting arms and bases from the Algerians in its struggle against the Spanish, was strongly opposed to its partition. When Spain concurred with the Moroccan – Mauritanian partition plan for the colony in November, 1975 the deal was denounced by both Polisario and Algeria. Guerrilla operations from Algerian bases around Tindouf began against Moroccan and Mauritanian occupation troops, and in March, 1976 Algiers formally recognised the government-in-exile of the Saharan Arab Democratic Republic. Both Morocco and Mauritania thereupon severed diplomatic relations with Algeria.

The guerrilla war since 1976 has been fought mainly in the territory of the former Spanish colony and in Mauritania itself, although Polisario also raids into southern Morocco. It has succeeded in tying down up to a third of the Moroccan army, and has brought Mauritania to the brink of economic collapse, with constant raids on the communications links joining its few mines to the sea. Despite the ten-fold expansion of the Mauritanian army within 5 years, it became necessary in late 1977 for Morocco to send a number of troops to the aid of its ally. In mid-1978 Moroccan troops in Mauritania were officially stated to number 9000 (and unofficially estimated at 15,000), and Rabat itself was feeling the strain of the war.

Morocco has made it clear throughout the crisis that it regards Algeria as almost solely responsible for the activities, and even the existence, of Polisario, and has repeatedly raised the possibility that it might cross the Algerian border in the course of 'hot pursuit'. Algerian troops have therefore been redeployed into the threatened areas, and the tenuous lines of communication between thickly populated coastal Algeria and the flashpoints of the south-west border region near Tindouf have been systematically improved. The Algerian armed forces have also acquired new arms in large quantities, particularly from the Soviet Union.

In a war between Morocco and Algeria which was largely confined to the south, it is unlikely that either side would gain a decisive advantage given the present levels of forces and the state of the communications in the area. Should one side or the other begin to make substantial advances, however, it is very possible that the other might expand the conflict to the narrow densely settled coastal plain along the Mediterranean. The deployment of the full strength of the two countries' armed forces in the area might have the most serious consequences.

The Algerian armed forces have had no operational experience since the brief 1963 war. A battalion of infantry and a squadron of MiG-21s were sent to Egypt during the 1967 war, but the troops saw no action and eventually returned home (six MiGs were reportedly lost). Algerians proved themselves ferocious and capable fighters during the war of independence in 1954–62, when less than 50,000 of them succeeded in tying down half a million French troops, but that was a different kind of war and offers little guidance as to the organisational and operational capabilities of the present Algerian armed forces.

The army is extensively employed in civic action projects (especially the engineers and the conscript elements). Algeria has no external defence commitments, although it does maintain a close political relationship (that could conceivably have some military implications) with Libya.

The headquarters of all four armed forces are in the Ministry of National Defence in Algiers. Army bases are widely distributed throughout the country, with garrisons in all major cities and towns.

The principal navy base is at Mers-el-Kebir. Other naval bases are at Algiers, Annaba (Bône), Oran, Arzew, Batna, Philippeville and La Senia.

The main air force base is at Dar-el-Beida, near Algiers. Other major bases are at Boufarak, Paul-Cazelles, Marine, Oukar, Biskra, Algiers, Oran and Sidi-bel-Abbes. There are 30 additional medium air fields and about 20 minor ones in the country.

ORGANISATION

Arms of Service
The army contains the usual infantry, armoured, engineer, and artillery arms, and the full array of services. The navy, air force and gendarmerie are separate forces.

Operational
The army is organised into two armoured brigades, four

mechanised brigades, six motorised infantry brigades, one airborne special forces brigade, three independent tank battalions, two paratroop battalions, and some independent infantry battalions. There are five independent artillery battalions, eleven air defence battalions, four engineer battalions, and twelve independent companies of desert troops which garrison the Sahara region.

Since March, 1964 the original seven territorial military commands (*wilayas*) have been reduced in number to five larger ones, with headquarters as follows: Region I, Blida; Region II, Oran; Region III, Béchar (Colomb-Béchar); Region IV, Ouargla; and Region V, Constantine. Each region is commanded by a colonel who is directly subordinate to the Minister of National Defence rather than to the General Staff. The bulk of the army's forces are concentrated in Region II .

The air force consists of seven fighter-ground attack squadrons, four interceptor squadrons, one reconnaisance squadron, one light bomber squadron, one counter insurgency squadron and one transport squadron. There are also one helicopter squadron, an OCU and one SAM regiment.

RECRUITMENT, TRAINING AND RESERVES

Recruitment has never been a problem for the ANP, which is invariably oversubscribed with volunteers. The core of the army consists of regular troops, but compulsory conscription of male Algerians for a period of 6 months at the age of nineteen was instituted in 1968, primarily for nation-building and morale purposes. The conscripts spend much of their time on civic action projects. Preliminary military training in secondary schools and universities was instituted in November, 1967.

In the early phase of its conversion from a guerrilla force to a regular armed force in the early 1960s, the Algerian army was heavily dependent on foreign training assistance, and sent most of its officers abroad for military instruction. In line with its political orientation, Algeria took most of this aid from the Soviet Union or from the then-radical Egyptian government, although the French continued to make a large contribution to the training of the air force and gendarmerie.

Thousands of Algerian officers were trained in the Soviet Union in the 1960s, but most officer instruction is now done at home. The military college at Blida gives a 3 year course for army officers, and the air force academy at Tafraouine near Oran, founded in 1967, offers a course of similar length for air force officers. Flying training, previously carried out in France, has been established at Bou-Sfer (near Mers-el-Kebir) since 1970, but operational training is still done with Soviet assistance. Technical training for NCOs is provided at a school in Blida. There are now fewer than 1000 Soviet experts and only a couple of hundred French military personnel in Algeria lending training assistance.

Reserves are estimated to number up to 100,000, but no details are available on their organisation or state of readiness.

EQUIPMENT AND ARMS INDUSTRY

Algeria inherited a good deal of French arms and equipment in 1962, but almost all its subsequent arms purchases have been from the Soviet Union, with the result that 90% of its weapons are now Russian-made.

The Algerian army's main armoured strength consists of 400 T54/55, 200 T-62 and 30 T-72 tanks, supplemented by 50 AMX-13 light tanks and 50 AML-60 and 100 BRDM-2 armoured cars. The APCs consists of 500 BMP-1 MICV and

830 BTR-40, BTR-50, BTR-60, BTR-152 and Egyptian-made Walid. The artillery arm is particularly strong, consisting of over 600 guns and howitzers including 100 85mm guns, 350 SU-100 SP guns, and large numbers of 122mm and 152mm guns and howitzers. It also possesses 150 multiple rocket launchers of 122mm, 140mm and 240mm, and 180 120mm and 160mm mortars.

Anti-tank weapons include 230 guns of 25mm, 76mm and 85mm, and 20 Stagger and 180 Milan ATGW. Anti-aircraft equipment consists of 440 37mm, 57mm, 85mm, 100mm, 130mm towed AA guns and 100 25U-23-4 and 25U-57-2 SP AA guns, and an assortment of SA-6, SA-7 and SA-9 SAM. It is not clear whether the 14 FROG-4 SSM the army once had are still operational.

The nucleus of the air force has five MiG-15s delivered in 1962 by the Soviet Union. It now has 306 combat aircraft, most of which are Soviet built. Two of the seven FGA squadrons operate 60 MiG-17, two have 20 SU-7, three have about 40 MiG-23, and about 12 new SU-20s and eight old MiG-19s are not on squadron strength. Three of the four interceptor squadrons fly 95 MiG-21 MF/F, and the other has 18 newly delivered MiG-25 Foxbat A. The reconnaisance squadron operates a further four MiG-25R Foxbat B, and the light bomber squadron has 12 I1-28 (another 16 I1-28 are in storage). The main air-to-air weapon is Atoll AAM.

There is a COIN squadron operating 26 armed Magister aircraft, and a test squadron with eight AN-12, six C-130 It, three Caravelle, two Mystère-Falcon and one I1-18. The OCU has four MiG-15, and the six helicopter squadrons have 28 Mi-6, four Mi-6, 12 Mi-8, 37 armed Mi-24, five Puma, four Alouette, and six Hughes 269A. There is a marine reconnaisance squadron flying seven F-27, but it operates under navy control. The training command has MiG-15-17-21 UTI, SU-7U, MiG-23U, MiG-25U and T-34C aircraft, and various base flights operate six Beech King Air, two Super King Air T-200T (which are used for marine reconnaisance) and three Queen Air. The air force has a SAM regiment distributed amongst various air bases, with twenty SA-2 launchers (80 missiles and some SA-3 and SA-6 launchers).

The navy's main strength lies in missile-armed fast patrol boats; it has three Osa-I, eight Osa-II and six Komar FPBGs (four more on order) armed with Styx SSMs. It also has two Koni-class frigates with SA-N-4 SAM and two Nanuchka-class corvettes (more on order) with SA-N-4 SAM and SS-N-2 bis SSM. Other warships include 10 P-6 torpedo boats, six SO-1 subchasers, two fleet minesweepers of the Soviet T-43 class, one LST of the Polnocny class (two more on order).

The gendarmerie is also equipped with combat weapons, including about 50 cannon-armed AML armoured cars.

The coastguard operates two P-6 torpedo boats and 15 small Baglietto attack craft.

There is no Algerian arms industry of any consequence, but the armed forces do by now have a considerable capability for maintenance and repair.

Algeria is exclusively dependent on the Soviet Union for arms, but so long as the present regime and its policies persist this is unlikely to cause any embarrassment.

RANK, DRESS AND DISTINCTIONS

One of the most striking characteristics of the Algerian army is that it has one of the least inflated rank structures in the world. The rank of general exists, but nobody has actually been promoted to it since independence; the highest rank actually held is that of colonel, which is borne only by the Minister of National Defence, the commanders of the five military regions and some General Staff officers. There are, altogether, only about 50 field-grade officers at the top of an extremely broad rank pyramid numbering about 150 captains and 2000 lieutenants. Great reliance is placed on the large category of warrant officers.

ANP ranks, their English equivalents and the insignia of rank are given in the following table.

Liwa (General) — Not known, as none exists
Sagh el Tani (Colonel — Crescent device and two stars (not known)
   (Lieutenant-colonel) — Crescent device and one star
Sagh el Aouel (Major) — Crescent device
Dhabet el Tani (Captain) — Three stars
Dhabet (Lieutenant) — Two stars
Moulazem el Tani (Second-lieutenant) — One star
Moulazem el Aouel (Cadet) — One star of contrasting colour to the buttons
(not known)
   (Chief Warrant Officer) — Golden 'V' over three bars
Moulazem (Warrant Officer — Golden 'V' over two bars
Arif el Tani (Sergeant First Class) — Golden 'V' over one bar
Arif el Aouel (Sergeant) — Golden 'V'
Djoundi el Aouel (Corporal) — Two diagonal red stripes
(not known)
   (Private First Class) — (not known)
Djoundi (Private) — None

In practice, the ranks equivalent to lieutenant-colonel, chief warrant officer and private first class are not filled. The uniforms adopted by the Algerian army, navy and air force in 1964 bear a close resemblance in style and pattern to those of the United States armed forces.

Pay for armed forces personnel compares favourably with that of men with similar qualifications in civilian life. There is provision for health care, and disablement and retirement benefits, although details are not available. The army finances much of the expenses out of the profits of its own co-operative establishments making clothes, shoes and furniture. The army is, indeed, the biggest single employer in Algeria, providing work for over 30,000 civilians as well as employing 7000—8000 of its own members in running these co-operatives.

CURRENT DEVELOPMENTS

There is no reason to doubt the stability of the present regime in Algeria or of the military hierarchy on which it fundamentally depends of the ANP's relatively small cadre of senior officers have similar backgrounds — service in the French army as officers or NCOs, followed by years in the 'external wing' of the ALN — and have been closely associated for two decades. Political opposition movements are not permitted to function, and both the army and the State apparatus are pervaded by an efficient security network.

Algeria's status as a radical both within the Arab League (where it is a mainstay of the 'Rejection Front') and the Organisation of African Unity (where it is one of the core members of the developing coalition of 'progressive' States) is unlikely to change, but neither is its reputation for caution in action. The one issue which might lead it into a military clash, or even all-out war with Morocco, is the question of the former Spanish colony of Sahara, where it has granted support and bases to the Polisario guerrillas fighting against the Moroccan and Mauritanian annexation of that territory, and has given recognition and a home to the Saharan government-in-exile. Algerian anger at Spain's complicity in the partition agreement has also caused it to give facilities to the MPAIAC, the secessionist movement seeking independence for the Canary Islands, and this has led to a marked cooling of relations with Spain, but no open conflict is likely on this account.

In the case of the Sahara, Algeria's initial enthusiasm for the Polisario cause was considerably dampened by the Moroccan military successes of 1976—7, when Polisario's strategy of striking at the much weaker partner in the partition deal, Mauritania, was thwarted by the despatch of up to 15,000 Moroccan troops (official sources admit to 9000) and French fighter—bombers to Mauritania's aid. In early 1978 the Algerian press had ceased to dwell on the Saharan conflict, the representatives of the Saharan Arab Democratic Republic were considerably less visible in Algiers and there was talk of a negotiated settlement or simply a gradual fading away of the war. In July, 1978 however the Mauritanian government was overthrown by an army coup whose leading figures were suspected of wishing to escape from Moroccan influence, withdraw from Mauritania's share of the Sahara and end the war which had crippled Mauritania's economy. While Polisario at once responded by declaring a unilateral ceasefire to apply to Mauritania only, this development paradoxically put new heart into the Algerians to continue the confrontation with Morocco, in view of the possibility that Morocco's ally would seek to withdraw from the conflict or even to change sides.

This has also considerably increased the risk of a direct Moroccan—Algerian clash, since it is doubtful whether the large number of Moroccan troops in Mauritania would permit such a change, while some Mauritanians might actively seek Algerian aid to evict the Moroccans. If such a conflict occurred, the better Moroccan lines of communication in the far south would give Rabat a considerable advantage, although this is to some extent offset by superior Algerian air strength.

Gwynne Dyer

ANGOLA

HISTORY AND INTRODUCTION

Angola attained independence from Portugal in 1975 amid civil war conditions. The Zaïre-based FNLA, a non-Marxist resistance movement formed largely from the Bakongo people, stood in alliance with UNITA, an eastern Angolan insurgency movement supported by Zambia; both were in conflict with MPLA, a Marxist resistance movement, and the first to appear in Angola. The MPLA drew its support from a number of the *mestiço* community, the urban African population of Luanda (and some white working-class elements as well), and some sections of the Ovimbundu people. The Chinese supported the FNLA, a factor which appears to have influenced the decision of the USSR to intervene jointly with Cuba in favour of the MPLA. South Africa also supported UNITA, but its military intervention appears to have followed the USSR's decision to participate, contrary to much widely held popular belief. The 14,000 Cuban troops, together with considerable quantities of Soviet equipment, enabled the MPLA to gain a victory early in 1976. After the victory, the Cubans started to reduce their numbers; various crises in Angola have, however, led to their reinforcement to a little over the 1976 total. These crises have been the cause of unpopularity of the MPLA regime in certain rural areas, a specific coup attempt in May, 1977, considerable resumed UNITA activity in the east of Angola, and above all the continuing South African military occupation of Cunene province and its use as a sally port for hot-pursuit operations against the Namibian insurgency movement SWAPO (South West African Peoples Organisation), even further into Angola.

The Angolan regime has faced a number of internal political difficulties. In 1977 a mounting internal power struggle erupted into a plot to oust the President, Agostino Neto. The plot was the work of the Minister of the Interior, Nito Alves, and a senior army political officer, J. van Dunem; it was supported by a number of officers. The quick suppression of the plot and its failure to spark off general uprisings in the streets should be seen as a measure of the fear inspired by the regime rather than any indication of popularity or even acquiescence. The major consequence for the army was an increased representation in the MPLA Congress Central Committee and its important Political Committee; for the rest of the country the result of the coup attempt was a reassertion of party ideology and control, and a wave of arrests.

In 1979 President Neto died, and was succeeded by President J. E. dos Santos. The latter appears to be slightly less hard-line and more pragmatic in ideological terms, but is nevertheless constrained by the hard-liners within the MPLA Central Committee and the regime's dependence on Cuba and the Soviet Union in face of the combined challenge of UNITA and the South Africans. The regime has however struck a balance with Zaïre in the north; Zaïre's support for FNLA had control, perhaps annexation, of the oil-producing Cabinda enclave as an ulterior motive. The defeat of FNLA was check rather than check-mate to President Mobutu of Zaïre in this respect; Zaïre's unreal aspirations were only finally destroyed by the events of 1977 and 1978. In these two years incursions were launched into the Shaba province of Zaïre across the border from Angola, clearly with Angolan acquiescence, and it is alleged, some measure of Angolan – acquiescence, and it is alleged, some measure of Angolan –

and Cuban – support. Zaïre was obliged to seek outside military help on both occasions; the lesson was learnt and in late 1978 an agreement was reached by which both Angola and Zaïre undertook not to interfere in each other's internal affairs. This agreement appears to be holding; it relieves Angola of one external military threat, though FNLA and the small Cabinda separatist movement FLEC remain irritants. These are, however, small scale compared with the operations discussed below that have to be mounted in face of UNITA and the South Africans.

STRENGTH AND BUDGET

Population: 7,000,000
Armed Forces: Army, 35,000; Air Force, 1,500; Gendarmerie, 10,000; Workers' Militia ('Organisation of Popular Defence'), 500,000.
GNP: }
Defence Expenditure: } No figures available.

COMMAND AND CONSTITUTIONAL STATUS

President dos Santos is the titular commander of FAPLA, the Angolan People's Liberation Army. The Defence Minister, General H. ('Iko') Carreira is attending a long course at a Soviet Senior Command College; in his absence command of the FAPLA is in the hands of P. M. Tonha ('Pedale'). D. Da Silva, as Vice Minister for defence controls the militia.

Carreira's absence may indicate disfavour. He is a *mestiço* and as such open to criticism by UNITA and others. He appears to have been dropped from the MPLA Politburo.

The Cuban troops are seen in the official rhetoric as guardians of the revolution, an exercise in brotherly proletarian internationalisation to secure socialism, not primarily as troops of an allied power stationed in the territory to secure its inviolability. They total between 15–19,000, together with some 10,000 teachers, aid officials, etc, in addition. They country is divided into six military regions, north, east, central and west, south, Luanda and Cabinda.

ROLE, COMMITMENT, DEPLOYMENT AND RECENT OPERATIONS

FAPLA's present role is to try and contain UNITA and the South Africans. UNITA makes political capital from the hard-line ideology of Luanda, from the presence of the Cubans and the influence (though no longer the domination) of the *mestiços* in the MPLA; it draws ethnic support, virtually solid, from the peoples of the south-east, majority support from the central plateau Ovimbundu and some support from other ethnic groups; it draws military and financial support from South Africa, Morocco and possibly also France.

At present UNITA controls the provinces of Cuando Cubango and Moxico in the south-east, including a number of the towns. It operates freely on the central plateau and on occasions strikes into the north. Recent operations have taken place in Malanje province (where it may find support from followers of the former Minister of the Interior, Nito

15

Alves). It has stopped all but very occasional trains, these under heavy guard, on the Benguela railway line; even these very occasional trains are liable to protracted delay arising from sabotage which may occur almost anywhere along the length of the line.

The South Africans hold an area to the north of the existing formal Namibia-Angola border, and in practice roam freely around most of Huila and Cunene provinces and into the central south, occasionally conducting forays further north. Their forces inside Angola are estimated to total 5,500, organised into two motorised brigades, with further reinforcements in Namibia. South African operations are supported by air reconnaissance and air strikes. Troop-carrying helicopters are also used for raids, one such being mounted against a SWAPO base in South West Angola in March 1982, Pretoria claiming that over 200 SWAPO insurgents were killed. A number of other South African incursions and operations took place at the same time in the south-western Mossamedes area. Earlier, in a daring and spectacular seaborne commando-style operation, South African special forces blew up Angola's only oil refinery in a suburb of Luanda itself. Other air strikes have been directed at civilian industrial targets as well as FAPLA units.

The two forces co-ordinate activities on occasions, the South Africans taking a town and handing it over to UNITA, sometimes for temporary sometimes for permanent occupation.

Initially in the mid-1970s Cuban units were used to try and contain the South Africans; they performed poorly and were brushed aside by the South Africans with little difficulty. FAPLA, on its formation, was then deployed, sometimes mixed with Cubans in company-sized armoured personnel carrier detachments, supported by helicopters whose pilots and crews were East Germans; the operation of these detachments were controlled by Soviet officers.

The position now appears to be one in which the Cubans have been withdrawn to hold towns, factories and major installations, leaving FAPLA, under Soviet guidance and with the help of Soviet and East German specialists, fighting in the field.

In operations in August and September, 1982 FAPLA claimed that its 2nd Motorised Infantry Brigade administered a check to a South African column advancing on Lubango, the capital of Huila province, but further east a combined South African-UNITA force was operating apparently unrestrained north of Cassinga. FAPLA still remains an inadequate force for the challenge; while it is said to be improving somewhat, it is unlikely ever to be able to take on the South Africans on its own. At the time of writing, October 1982, operations have slackened, both sides awaiting the outcome of diplomatic negotiations. The August and September incursions, therefore, may have been mounted by Pretoria to make a specific political point.

ORGANISATION

The FAPLA is organised into two motorised infantry brigades (each composed of one tank and two infantry battalions), seventeen further infantry regiments and four anti-aircraft artillery brigades. The gendarmerie is formed into eleven battalions, a total to be increased to fifteen.

RECRUITMENT, TRAINING AND RESERVES

FAPLA is recruited by means of a compulsory two-years service system applied of areas and communities over which the government has authority and whose soldiers, it is hoped, will prove reliable. A number of officers are coastal *mestiços*.

Numbers of Cubans and Russians are employed in training and administration. A major problem facing the regime as a whole and the army in particular is the acute shortage of skilled labour and men with any form of technical training, so many in these categories (Portuguese *mestiços*, blacks and others) having departed in 1974–5. A twenty-year treaty of friendship with the USSR was signed in 1976. The details of this treaty were not published, but it is believed that they provided for massive aid in return for permanent Soviet maritime reconnaissance and naval installations. The probability is that in approximate terms there are some 700 Soviet advisers and technical experts, with some 250 East Germans. Their roles have been discussed above. It only needs to be added they very rarely appear on the actual field of battle, political capital being too easily made by their capture.

EQUIPMENT AND ARMS INDUSTRY

A number of conflicting reports exist on the quantities of Soviet equipment supplied to Angola; the confusion is compounded by the impossibility of distinguishing equipment belonging to the Cuban units from that belonging to FAPLA.

Some 100, possibly 150 or more T34 tanks, approximately 120 to 150 T54/55s and possibly a small number of T62s have been reported, with in addition 50–60 PT 76 tracked and 200 BRDM 1–2 wheeled armoured reconnaissance machines. Over 150 Soviet BTR 60 and BTR 152 armoured personnel carriers, 200 Soviet artillery pieces of various calibres, 76mm, 85mm, 100mm, 122mm, 130mm and 152mm together with fifty BM-21 artillery rocket launchers and a number of 120mm mortars may be in service. A few elderly ex-Wehrmacht 105mm guns taken from the Portuguese may also still be in service. Infantry unit weapons include 82mm mortars, RPG 7 grenade launchers, Sagger anti-tank guided weapons and SAM 7 anti-aircraft missiles. Other anti-aircraft weaponry includes Soviet 14.5mm, 23mm, and 37mm towed guns, the tracked self-propelled ZSU 23-4 and ZSU 57-2 machines, and SAM 3 (*Goa*) and SAM-6 (*Gainful*) anti-aircraft missiles, these latter equipments in small numbers only.

The Air Force includes two fighter ground attack squadrons of forty MiG-21, 25 MiG-17 and two Aeritalia G91 aircraft; one Fokker F27 maritime reconnaissance aircraft; two transport squadrons of some forty-five assorted medium and small transport aircraft of Soviet, US and Western European manufacture; two helicopter squadrons with between them thirty-five MI-8 and thirteen Alouette helicopters, and a small number of training aircraft. Swiss PC-7 Pilatus turbo-prop training aircraft are on order.

RANK, DRESS AND DISTINCTIONS

Little information is available. Units on parade wear a jungle type combat kit.

CURRENT DEVELOPMENTS

Angola must be viewed primarily as an overspill from the South African/Namibian situation. No one event could ensure a healthy non-committed independent national and military life for Angola more than a peaceful solution to the Namibian question; this, unfortunately, is improbable and Angola seems likely to need military assistance from someone to survive. If the French of the Portuguese agree to shoulder the defence of southern Angola against South African incursions Luanda might ask the Cubans to depart, though whether they would actually do so, or even whether the Soviet Union would accept the arrival of Western European troops at all, is doubtful. The present unsatisfactory situation may therefore last, but not necessarily so, as the Soviet Union could well weary of the cost of maintaining the Cuban presence, settle for a Cuban withdrawal and some acceptance of UNITA in the government in return for a guaranteed permanent South African withdrawal, particularly if no other Western troops were to arrive and the USSR could retain her maritime reconnaissance facility; this latter would be regarded as almost essential by Moscow. Some easement of the Namibian struggle would, however, seem a pre-requisite for such developments, and here South Africa is better placed to 'sweat it out', than the USSR, though for economic and domestic political reasons Pretoria, too, would like a Cuban withdrawal.

At the time of writing, October 1982, high-level international negotiations were reported to be taking place in Paris and Washington.

Internally, the Luanda regime remains inefficient and lacking in cohesion, a number of different views being held by members of the MPLA Politburo and Central Committee the differences being sometimes ideological (hard-line versus pragmatist), sometimes ethnic (*mestiço* versus pure black) and sometimes personal. The cost of defence, although no firm figures are available it is understood to amount to more than half the budget, compounds the country's plight. This latter is worsened by the disastrous falls in agricultural production since independence.

ADDENDUM

The last months of 1982 have seen a worsening of Angola's military situation. UNITA insurgents, operating in company sized detachments mounted a virtual siege of the central Angolan city of Muambo, imposing an economic stranglehold. Other UNITA groups mounted attacks, increasing both in frequency and effectiveness on several stretches of the Benguela railway line. Other UNITA attacks have been reported at Kandende, on the Luanda—Malange road, and at Calulo, 140 miles south of Luanda.

At the same time South African incursions in southern Angola became more daring, two major bridges carrying the important Jamba-Cassinga iron-ore railway being badly damaged near Namibe (formerly Mossamedes). The South African commandos made their attack from small boats launched from a warship.

Angola has signed a new military co-operation treaty with East Germany, details of which have not been released.

Lloyd Mathews

ARGENTINA

HISTORY AND INTRODUCTION

The Argentinian army, after the Brazilian the largest in South America, is a national and to some degree an international institution of the greatest significance. In its modern form it is of comparatively recent origin. But its predecessors were instrumental in expelling the Spanish colonial government from the country, in helping to liberate neighbouring Chile and Peru, in establishing Uruguay as an independent State and in preserving the power of the central government during long years of provincial turbulence. In modern times the army has played a cardinal political role in national affairs. From its ranks issued the most important and influential politician of twentieth century Latin American history, Juan Perón, whose ideas and achievements made their effects felt far beyond the continent. His fall from power, which the army itself brought about, has consigned the nation to endemic political crisis, and obliged the army to arbitrate at frequent intervals between those loyal to the political tradition he established and those who seek to control or reverse its revolutionary implications. As a result the army has acquired, perhaps unwillingly, a reputation as the most political in modern Latin America. At the same time it most nearly approaches European standards of military efficiency, professional autonomy and universality of conscriptive obligation. Its performance in the brief South Atlantic War of April/June 1982 was, however, disappointing, revealing serious shortcomings in the areas of leadership, morale and training and must occasion a critical re-appraisal of its military potential and of its continuing ability to serve as the final arbiter of the country's political life.

The first Argentinian military force was raised by the citizens of Buenos Aires to repel an invasion force sent by the British in 1806 after Spain had made alliance with Napoleon. Their two victories, known today as the *Reconquista* and the *Defensa*, are celebrated as national events because, though serving the immediate interests of Madrid, they demonstrated to the Buenos Aireans the power they possessed to determine their own affairs and led directly to the overthrow of the Spanish administration in 1810. The Spaniards retained forces in the north and west of the Vice-Royalty of the Río de la Plata, however, against which Buenos Aires had to send troops, but they failed to win for the future State those parts of the territory now known as Bolivia, Paraguay and Uruguay, the inhabitants of the latter region securing independence for themselves both from the Argentinians and the Portuguese in Brazil. It was not until the arrival of San Martín in 1814 that effective measures were taken to tackle the remaining centres of Spanish power. San Martín's Army of the Andes, largely Argentinian in composition, crossed the mountains in January, 1817 and 4 years later completed the liberation of the continent.

The Argentinians' part in this historic achievement would help eventually to establish them as the dominant nation of the south. But they could not begin to play that role, nor to function as an effective political society, until they had achieved their own unity. Argentina was, as to some extent it still remains, two lands in the 1820s, a vast hinterland (*campo*) over which the seaward-looking citizens (*portenos*) of Buenos Aires exercised only very tenuous authority. It was indeed not even formally a centralised State, but a loose federation

of provinces for dominance in which the *unitarios* of the 'port' and the *federales* of the 'camp' were to struggle for the next 40 years. It was not until the defeat of the provincial armies in 1861 that Argentina became a united republic. And even thereafter the provinces could find the men to wage civil war as late as 1880. But by then the national army, which in an embryo form had already fought wars against the Brazilians in the 1820s and against Paraguay in 1865–70, was too strong to be overcome from within. Within a generation its loyalty was to become the most prized political possession in the State.

The rise of the army as a modern institution may be taken to date from the creation of the Military Academy (*Colegio Militar de la Nación*) in 1869. Like most Latin American armies of the period, it had hitherto been officered by political appointees and soldiers of fortune. By 1896, however, when the Academy produced 122 second-lieutenants, entry to the officer corps was closed to non-professionals and within a decade almost all of its members, who numbered about 1700 in the period 1900–30, were Academy trained. This professionalisation of the officer corps was very much the achievement of General Roca, president between 1880 and 1886 and again from 1898 to 1904. A former minister of war and victor of the 'War of the Desert' (1879–83) against the Indians of the south, he also, during his second presidency, saw through the law which would transform the enlisted ranks of the army from an erratically recruited collection of regiments to a nationally conscripted force. This Ricchieri Law, so called after Roca's minister of war, obliged all twenty-year-olds to register for military service, selection to be made by a lottery. The term fixed was 1 year in the army, 2 years in the navy. The proportion enrolled from each annual contingent averaged about a third before 1914, but was still higher than that imposed in most Latin American countries and was reasonably socially representative, since grounds allowed for exemption were restricted.

Modernisation did not stop there. Like Chile during the same period, Argentina turned to Germany for help in the higher training and organisation of its army. A staff college (*Escuela Superior de Guerra*) was opened in 1900. Its director and four of its 10 professors were German officers. At the same time, Argentinian officers began to be sent to Germany to study in military schools or serve in German regiments, and Uriburu (later president), one of the most outstanding of this group, was, as Inspector General from 1923, to employ a German general (Faupel) as his personal adviser. German advisers were to remain with the army until 1940, making it both in outward appearance and in doctrine almost as Prussian an institution as the Chilean.

Unlike the Chilean however, the Argentinian army was from the outset of its development as a modern, professional institution, to be drawn into national politics, at first partially and sporadically but later wholeheartedly and continuously. Its modernisation coincided with very large-scale immigration from Europe, particularly from Italy and Spain, which was to raise the population from under 2,000,000 in 1870 to 4,000,000 in 1895 and to nearly 8,000,000 in 1914. This influx put the traditional ruling class under very heavy pressure, which manifested itself in the rise of a mass radical movement. A revolt against the Buenos Aires government in 1890 attracted military support in the provinces but was put down, as was another in 1905, which also commanded military support. The leader of the radicals, Yrigoyen, who was eventually elected to the presidency on an extended franchise in 1916, frankly solicited military support among the young modernising officers and rewarded those who had assisted him when he eventually achieved power, a foretaste of the fruits of political influence which the officers were not to forget. Those outside Yrigoyen's circle formed in 1921 an Argentinian version of those 'lodges' so prevalent in Latin American military circles, the Logia de San Martin, used the strength it gave them to impose their own choice as minister of war on Yrigoyen's successor and, when Yrigoyen was re-elected in 1928, to work for his downfall. It was in fact brought about in 1930 by an opponent of the San Martin Lodge, Uriburu, but the San Martin faction eventually succeeded in capturing the presidency for their candidate, Justo, at the elections of 1932.

Justo represented the anti-radical tendencies present both in the army and in civilian politics and ruled so selfishly that the period of his presidency and that of his successors has been called the Infamous Decade (1932–43). Effective opposition to his rule took the form not of a left-wing movement, however, but of a corporatist nationalism called 'integral nationalism', which borrowed many of its ideas from Mussolini's Italy and had important support among a group of army officers eventually known as the GOU (*Grupo de Oficiales Unidos*). Their leading light was Colonel Juan Perón, who had recently served as military attaché in Italy, and had taken a part in the coup of 1930. Deeply committed to corporatist ideals, conscious of the 'new' Argentinians' rejection of their immigrant fathers' socialism, fanatically nationalist, he used the position brought him by his part in the coup of June, 1943 which overthrew the conservative regime, to establish himself as a demagogic leader of the working class. That position was head of the department of labour and social security, which he quickly turned into the key ministry of the government. Through his influence over a succession of military presidents, he secured funds to create an advanced social-security system, financed out of the enormous revenues which Argentina's agriculture was earning in the international war economy, and so to ingratiate himself with the more powerful unions, to which he granted extensive legal bargaining powers. Meanwhile the military government attracted intense internal and external dislike for its open siding with the Axis. When the disgruntled officers of the Campo de Mayo garrison (the principal military station outside Buenos Aires and the usual breeding ground of coups) attempted to vent their frustration by demanding and achieving Perón's dismissal on October 9th, 1945 he appealed directly to his working-class followers (the *descamisados*) and 8 days later was triumphantly welcomed back by them from the custody in which he had been placed. In February, 1946 he was elected president by an overwhelming majority.

There followed 10 years of *Peronismo*, rule by President Perón in the spirit of what he called *Justicialismo*. The doctrine was not, as he claimed, an original one: its slogans were 'political sovereignty, economic independence, social justice'. But, in a country dominated economically by foreign investors and circumscribed diplomatically by the United States, and where many of the workers of town and country remained desperately poor among abundant natural riches, it had appeal, and all the more because Perón strove to give it substance. His continuing support of the trade unions and largesse to the social-security system coincided in the late 1940s, however, with worsening terms of trade, and so resulted in serious inflation and a halt to industrialisation. The latter programme had woken wide support in the army, which was committed to a policy of self-sufficiency in military equipment. Disappointment at this stagnation, alienation from the increasingly civilian entourage of the president and outrage at the nomination of Perón's wife, the magnetic Evita, as vice-president led in September, 1951 to a military and naval rebellion. Easily suppressed though it was by loyal troops, Perón used his authority, reinforced by his re-election in November, to purge both the navy and the army.

Economic conditions in his second term heightened his difficulties, however, forcing him to make concessions to the industrial and commercial classes and to sustain the momentum largely by a public quarrel with the Catholic Church. He was aware that this quarrel fed the hostility of many officers, who were ideologically (if not always spiritually) Catholic in outlook, and he attempted to reinsure himself against military rebellion by fostering the creation of militant union militias, though only after an abortive naval uprising in June, 1955. But the threat of a breach of its monopoly of arms was exactly that calculated to unite an army still deeply divided between pro- and anti-Peronistas, and on September 16th, exactly 3 months after the naval revolt, a major military and naval rebellion, against which even the remaining loyal units around Buenos Aires would not stand, brought Perón down. He resigned his functions to a military *junta* and retired first to Paraguay, later to Nicaragua and then to Spain.

This so-called 'liberating revolution' had been the work of armed factions rather than of the armed forces as a whole, notably the Córdoba garrison and the navy's marine infantry, a force ironically created by Perón to imitate the US Marine Corps. And after two months' of united support for the new military president, Lonardi, the factions reappeared. The navy and a strong group of anti-*Peronistas* in the army, later to be known as the Reds (*colorados*) overturned Lonardi and installed in his place an anti-*Peronista* general, Arumburu, whose policy for the extirpation of Peronist influence in the country was to restore elective constitutional government. He dealt harshly with a Peronist military uprising in June, for the first time in Argentinian history sending numbers of officers to the firing-squad. As a result, there was no opposition to his calling of elections in 1958, which returned a radical, Frondizi, to the presidency. Frondizi aimed to reintegrate the *Peronistas* into political life, and at the same time to cure Argentina's economic difficulties by a policy of encouraging foreign investment and the exporting industries. The results were to swing popular support to the intransigent *Peronistas*, whose gains at the provincial elections of 1962 were so great that the army dropped Frondizi and replaced him with an interim president until new elections could be held. These, in July, 1963 returned another radical, Illia. He inherited Frondizi's economic problems and persisted in his policies, particularly that of attempting to win back the *Peronistas* to constitutionalism, but without success. In June, 1966 the army, in which the faction known as the Blues (*azules*) (who shared Frondizi's and Illia's belief in the necessity of winning the *Peronistas* back to constitutionalism) were now dominant, lost faith in Illia's prospects, overturned him, and put the leader of the Blue faction, General Onganía, in power. His economic policies, even more deflationary in their effects than his predecessors had been, provoked a major popular uprising centred on Córdoba (the *Córdobazo*) in May, 1969 and the reverberations of the revolt led to the removal of his minister of economics, Vasena, and to the outbreak of terrorist outrages staged by left-wing groups, among which the left-wing Peronist *Montoneros* and the communist ERP (Popular Revolutionary Army) were to become the most prominent.

Uncertain about the economic future, the army vacillated for some months and then in June, 1970 replaced Onganía with General Levingston but found him an unsatisfactory substitute. In March, 1971 he was removed and General Lanusse installed in his place, with a stated commitment to introduce constitutional elections. By then, however, Perón, who had once before attempted to re-enter the country, had become an active force in national politics. His nominee, Campora, was returned at the presidential elections of May, 1973 and in the next month Perón came home. Campora at once stood down and Perón was elected in his place, with his second wife, Isabel, as vice-president. He proved to have no easy solutions either to the country's economic problems or to the growing menace of terrorism, which was mounted by groups which had now moved far to the left of the position he was prepared to support. Moreover, his health was failing. On his death in July, 1974 he was replaced as president by his wife, who took advice from Perón's former secretary, Lopez Rega. The army was prepared to lend her its support but not to tolerate the growing tide of violence, which was directed both against army installations and individual army officers. In December, 1975 an air force rising was put down but in March, 1976 the army, exasperated by economic chaos and the virtual breakdown of law and order, deposed President Isabel Perón and transferred executive and legislative power to a *junta*, with General Videla, the army Commander-in-Chief, as President.

General Videla was in turn replaced by General Roberto Viola from March until December 1981 when he was in turn superseded as Head of Government by General Leopoldo Galtieri, one of the prime movers in the coup which had deposed Isabel Perón.

Faced with growing internal unrest and imminent economic collapse, General Galtieri embarked on a brief but catastrophic war against Great Britain with the invasion of the Falkland Islands in April 1982 and was himself displaced by General Bignone following the Argentine defeat.

STRENGTH AND BUDGET

Population: 28,000,000
Army: 130,000
Navy: 36,000: 15 major warships and 16 building
Air Force; 20,000; 240 combat aircraft
GNP (1981): $124,600,000,000
Defence Expenditure (1981): $10,080,000,000

Information on defence spending is scarce and has become scarcer since the Army's return to power. As a proportion of the national budget, it has fluctuated about 12 per cent for some time. Following Argentina's defeat in the South Atlantic War, in which large quantities of military equipment were lost, defence spending may be expected to rise fairly dramatically despite the country's extremely poor economic condition.

COMMAND AND CONSTITUTIONAL STATUS

Argentina is a presidential republic, the President being elected by direct popular vote, and having powers to introduce his own legislation into the elected Senate and Congress. The provinces elect their own governors and legislators, but the President possesses powers to intervene in provincial affairs, either by the appointment of presidential *interventores*, or by the imposition of a state of siege (under Article 2 of the Constitution) which may be applied to the whole or part of the country. The President is Commander-in-Chief of the Armed Forces, but exercises control of them through the War, Air and Navy Ministers, who are serving officers.

The last legally installed President was Isabel Martinez de Perón, widow of General Perón, from whom she took over power on his death. Following widespread internal violence, severe economic difficulties, and her suspension of Congress to prevent her impeachment, the army removed her from office on March 24th, 1976 and declared that power had passed to a *junta* composed of the heads of the three services.

The *junta* announced that it would remain in power for 3 years. Meanwhile it dissolved Congress, the provincial legislatures and city councils, dismissed the provincial governors and interventors, suspended the activities of all political parties, trade unions and employers' and professional associations, decreed the continuation of the state of siege imposed in November, 1974 (and extended indefinitely in March, 1975), prohibited public meetings and the dissemination of 'alarmist' news and warned workers that they would be punished for absenteeism. On March 25th, the *junta* further announced that it would be the supreme organ of the State, would be responsible for choosing the President, Judges of the Supreme Law and the Attorney General. The head of state was to be a minister of the armed services (General Videla, Chief of Staff of the Army, was sworn in as President on March 29th), who would appoint the government and the provincial administrations. The formation of a new cabinet was announced on March 28th, in which all the portfolios but two (finance and education) were held by officers. Another announcement appointed a Legislative Advisory Commission, composed of three officers from each of the three services, to advise the *junta* on its legislative programme, and at the same time military representatives were placed in control of the General Confederation of Labour and the General Economic (employers') Confederation. On March 31st, 13 trade unions were put under military suspension and five extreme left-wing parties outlawed. On June 2nd, a law was passed establishing penalties for engaging in political or trade union activities, and abolishing in all 48 political parties and youth movements. In September, 1976 trade union legislation was introduced which imposed penalties for incitement to strike and for the imposition of lock-outs by employers, while in May the *junta* had outlined economic plans which were designed to produce a clean break with Peronist policies. Restrictions were to be lifted on the investment of foreign capital, some State-owned enterprises to be denationalised, some State monopolies to be broken, and the bureaucracy to be reduced sharply in size.

The *junta* has thus taken steps to impose its authority not only over the political but also the economic and social life of the country. Speaking in April, 1976 President Videla outlined its plan for the nation's future. It was to follow three stages: first, the assumption of power 'to avoid national disintegration'; second, the economic and political reorganisation of the country; and third, the strengthening of institutions with the object of achieving 'a democratic representative and federative government'. In December he explained that this meant avoiding 'a return to the pendulum movement according to which strong military governments give way to weak civilian governments'. On April 1st, 1977 he announced that the military government would continue for the foreseeable future, and that only when a fundamental reconstruction of the social and political system had been achieved could the *junta* 'install a democratic regime which expresses the joint aspirations of the armed forces and the civilian section'.

The Argentinian army has, therefore, like the Peruvian army, and perhaps in imitation of it, boldly embarked on an autonomous, long-term reform of its country's institutions — with the difference that it sees its task as requiring the dismantling of several State enterprises, rather than their creation, and the encouragement rather than restriction of investment from overseas. While one appears 'right-wing' in its ideology and the other 'left-wing', this is perhaps a reflection of the different economic and social conditions prevailing in each country. The end result desired in both by their armies would appear to be a healthy mixed economy guided by a healthy democratic regime.

ROLE, COMMITMENT, DEPLOYMENT AND RECENT OPERATIONS

Role

Apart from Brazil, Argentina is the only country in Latin America whose army regards itself as a credible defender of the national territory against external attack. The source of such attack is undefined. Though there are frontier disputes with Chile in the Andes and southern Patagonia, neither country could deploy a significant offensive from across the mountain chain. Towards Paraguay, Argentina has a protective rather than defensive attitude. Bolivia is a threat to none of her neighbours, and Uruguay, though feared in the 1960s as a source of ideological infection, is a military midget compared to Argentina. Brazil remains Argentina's only political enemy in the sub-continent. But though they are certainly rivals for its leadership, Argentina never more explicitly so than under Perón, war between the two would be geographically difficult and politically almost unthinkable. The only external use of Argentinian armed forces of any likelihood would therefore be in an amphibious operation against the Falkland Islands (Islas Malvinas), British possession of which is disputed. Such an operation was mounted during the first week in April 1982, the small British garrisons of the Falklands and South Georgia being rapidly overwhelmed. Massive British retaliation resulted in the recapture of South Georgia, after only nominal Argentine resistance, on April 25th and British landings in the Falklands on May 21st culminated in the surrender of all Argentine forces on June 14th. The Army's poor performance in the brief Anglo-Argentine war has seriously undermined its credibility in conventional military operations.

The army's main operational role is therefore internal and it has indeed been called upon to perform that role frequently and at times intensively since 1972 (see Recent Operations). Since 1900 the army has also attempted, as has no other in Latin America, to act as a 'school of the nation', through the conscription of a large proportion of the annual contingent. In recent years the army has also undertaken development engineering work in the Andes, the south and Patagonia. For the army's major and at times decisive political role, see Command and Constitutional Status.

Commitment

Argentina is a signatory of the two major Latin American defence pacts: the Act of Chapultepec (March/April, 1945) and the Rio Defence Treaty (September, 1947). By the first, Argentina, Bolivia, Brazil, Chile, Colombia, Costa Rica, Cuba, the Dominican Republic, Ecuador, Guatemala, Haiti, Honduras, Mexico, Nicaragua, Panama, Paraguay, Peru, Uruguay, Venezuela and the United States (its moving spirit) declared that any attack upon a member party would be construed as an attack upon all, and provided for the collective use of armed force to prevent or repel such aggression. By the second, the same parties (less Ecuador and Nicaragua) agreed to settle disputes between themselves by peaceful means and made further provisions for collective self-defence against external attack in any situation (Cuba withdrew from the

Rio Defence Treaty in March, 1960). The Charter of the Organisation of American States (to which the signatories of the Rio Treaty belong, with Barbados, El Salvador, Jamaica and Trinidad and Tobago) embodied the provisions of the Rio Treaty. Argentina, like most other Latin American countries has a bilateral military agreement with the United States which provides her with access to advice, training and equipment from the United States.

Relations with Brazil have greatly improved in recent years, arrangements for military co-operation falling just short of a formal mutual defence treaty. The respective spheres of influence of the two countries appear to have been amicably agreed and Brazil rendered some low-profile military assistance to Argentina during the Anglo-Argentine War. Both navies carry out regular joint manoeuvres and the two countries have concluded an agreement for mutual assistance in the field of nuclear research. Relations between both countries and the Republic of South Africa have also been strengthened and prior to the South Atlantic war it seemed as if co-operation between Argentina, Brazil and South Africa might have developed into a formal South Atlantic Treaty, with Paraguay and Uruguay as junior partners and possibly also involving Nigeria with the active, if largely covert, encouragement of the United States. The unequivocal support given by the United States to Great Britain during the Anglo-Argentine War antagonised all Latin American countries except Chile and would appear to have effectively sabotaged all movement towards the development of such a treaty.

Deployment

The national territory is divided into five Military Regions, as follows:

Region I (HQ Buenos Aires) covers the Federal Capital and most of the provinces of Buenos Aires and La Pampa.

Region II (HQ Rosario) covers the provinces of Entre Rios Corrientes, Misiones, Santa Fé, Formosa and the Chaco Territory.

Region III (HQ Córdoba) covers the Provinces of Córdoba, Mendoza, La Rioja, San Juan, San Luís and southern Catamarca.

Region IV (HQ Tucuman) covers the provinces of Salta, Jujuy, Tucumán, Santiago del Estero and northern Catamarca.

Region V (HQ Bahia Blanca) covers southern Buenos Aires and La Pampa and the provinces of Neuquén, Rio Negro, Chubut, Santa Cruz and the territories of Tierra del Fuego and the Argentine Antarctic in addition to the Malvinas (Falkland Islands).

Under the army re-organisation of 1964, the 1st, 2nd and 5th Military Regions were each garrisoned by an Army Corps of identical numerical designation whilst the 3rd and 4th Military Regions both came under the jurisdiction of the 3rd Army Corps, with its HQ at Córdoba. The expansion of the Army as a result of the tension with Chile over the Beagle Channel dispute (see Current Developments) involved the resurrection of a 4th Army Corps, responsible for the defence of the 4th Military Region.

Prior to 1964 the Army had comprised 5 Army Corps (including 1 Armoured, 7 Infantry and 2 Mountain Divisions) plus a Cavalry Corps of 3 Divisions. The 1964 re-organisation suppressed the 4th Army Corps and the Cavalry Corps and replaced the Division with the Brigade as the major tactical formation.

The 1st Army Corps (HQ Palermo Barracks, Buenos Aires) comprises the 1st Armoured Cavalry Brigade (HQ Tandil, Buenos Aires), the 10th Motorised Infantry Brigade (HQ Buenos Aires) and the Buenos Aires Detachment.

The 2nd Army Corps (HQ Rosario) consists of the 2nd Armoured Cavalry Brigade (HQ Paraná, Entre Rios), the 3rd Mechanised Infantry Brigade (HQ Curuzú-Cuatiá, Corrientes) and the 7th Jungle Brigade (HQ Corrientes).

The 3rd Army Corps (HQ Córdoba) consists of the 4th Airborne Brigade (HQ Córdoba) and the 8th Mountain Infantry Brigade (HQ Mendoza). This Corps also includes an independent Paratroop Training Regiment which is outside the brigade structure.

The 4th Army Corps (HQ Tucumán) consists of the 5th Mountain Infantry Brigade (HQ Tucumán) and the new 12th Motorised Infantry Brigade still forming with its HQ at Santiago del Estero. One of the three regiments of the 2nd Armoured Cavalry Brigade, based in the 2nd Corps area, is on semi-permanent detachment to this corps which also contains one of the three remaining horsed Cavalry Regiments.

The 5th Army Corps (HQ Bahia Blanca) comprises the 6th Mountain Infantry Brigade (HQ Esquel, Chubut), the 9th Motorised Infantry Brigade (HQ Comodoro Rivadavia) and the new 11th Motorised Infantry Brigade with its HQ at Bahia Blanca. This Corps includes two of the three remaining horsed Cavalry Regiments which are outside the brigade structure and subordinate to Corps HQ.

Recent Operations

Until the brief Anglo-Argentine War of 1982, Argentina had not been at war since 1870, the end of the war with Paraguay (1865−79); its declaration of hostilities against the Axis in March, 1945 being a diplomatic move. In the 1970s the army has however been frequently engaged in internal security duties and in anti-guerrilla operations, chiefly against ideological opponents of the government.

The most important groups, which came into being during the period of military government (1966−72) which preceded the return of the Peronista party, and then Perón, to power, are: the *Ejercito Revolucionario del Pueblo* (ERP − People's Revolutionary Army), a Trotskyite guerrilla movement formed in July, 1970 as the armed wing of the *Partido Revolucionario de los Trabajadores* (Workers' Revolutionary Party) and hostile both to the Argentinian Communist Party and the Peronistas, as well as to all parties to their right (it split it into three groups in 1973 and having formerly acted as an urban guerrilla organisation, announced the formation of rural units); the *Montoneros*, a Peronista guerrilla group which joined in October, 1973 with another, the *Fuerzas Armadas Revolucionarias* (FAR − Revolutionary Armed Forces) and became a challenge to orthodox Peronism (a political front, the Authentic Peronist Party, was set up in March, 1975); the *Alianza Anticomunista Argentina* (AAA) which emerged after Perón's death in July, 1974 to take revenge on the left-wing groups by reciprocal murder; and the *Fuerzas Armadas de Liberación* (FAL − Armed Forces of Liberation), a Maoist group of which little has been recently heard.

The left-wing groups have favoured urban terrorism, and their chosen methods of attack on organised society have been the selective murder of army officers, policemen and government officials and the kidnapping of the owners or representatives of large businesses. Very large sums of money (at least $14,000,000 in the case of an Esso executive kidnapped in March, 1974) have been extorted by the left-wing guerrilla groups in exchange for the release of their victims, who have been murdered if not ransomed. In 1974 the ERP embarked on a more military phase. In January 70 guerrillas attacked the barracks of the Azul garrison, killed the commanding officer and his wife and kidnapped a colonel. In Au-
gust 90 guerrillas attacked barracks at Catamarca but were repulsed; 19 were killed and 15 captured. In January, 1975 the ERP succeeded in shooting down a plane carrying many members of the Army General Staff, and in October, after two smaller but similar incidents, guerrillas hijacked a plane from Buenos Aires to Formosa, attacked the barracks and seized the airport. In August a frigate under construction had been dynamited and sunk in the Río Santiago naval shipyard. In 1975 the ERP set up a rural front in Tucumán province and the army deployed its 5th Brigade on large-scale operations. In February, 1976 it announced that it had discovered 30 ERP camps, ambushed a convoy of 32 ERP vehicles, and killed 174 terrorists for the loss of 20 soldiers.

There is no doubt that the ERP/Montoneros's open offensive against individual army officers and military installations was an important factor in predisposing the generals to intervene against President Isabel Perón's government in 1976. Since its coming to power, the level of terrorism in the countryside has somewhat diminished. The level of political violence in the towns, however, remains high. The Montoneros, who now seem more active than the ERP, began to concentrate on attacks on police stations in 1976. In June they killed the general commanding the police with a bomb planted at his house (two senior police chiefs have also been assassinated, in 1974 and 1975). In July the Montoneros blew up Police Headquarters in Buenos Aires, killing 18 people; in September a police bus in Rosario, killing ten; and in November the La Plata police headquarters, besides attacking a Buenos Aires police station in the same month. But the Montoneros also continued attacks on army leaders and installations: in October they exploded a bomb at a Buenos Aires officers' club, injuring fifty, and in February, 1977 another alongside a plane in which President Videla was taking off from a Buenos Aires airport. They had made two earlier bomb attempts on his life, in March and October, 1976.

The army killed, wounded and captured numerous ERP and Montonero terrorists during the same period. In December, 1975 during another ambitious attack on the Monte Chingollo arsenal outside Buenos Aires, 160 ERP members were killed (out of an estimated 500 taking part). In counter-operations of its own, five Montonero leaders were killed by the army in September, 1976 while it consistently claimed unspecified success against both ERP and Montoneros. Some of the casualties suffered by the terrorist organisations were the work of counter-terrorists, particularly the AAA, which in 1976 perpetrated murders of priests suspected of left-wing sympathies. In March, 1977 Amnesty International accused the military regime of condoning such counter-terrorism and of cruel and unlawful suppression of terrorism by its own security forces, accusations which the military government strenuously denied.

The army appears to have brought an end to rural guerrilla activity, but urban terrorism is likely to continue, though at a reduced level, for the foreseeable future.

The brief war with Great Britain, provoked by the invasions of the Falklands and South Georgia, was an almost unmitigated disaster for the Argentine Army, the performance of which, with some honourable exceptions, fell far below the minimum level of competence expected of the armed forces of a sophisticated modern state. Its failure to give even a reasonable account of itself in this, its first external war for over a century, must have repercussions in the willingness of the civilian population to tolerate its almost continuous interference in domestic politics. Comparable political repercussions to those experienced in Bolivia after that country's defeat by Paraguay in the Chaco War of 1932−35 may be expected.

ORGANISATION

Arms of Service

These consist of Infantry, Airborne, Mountain and Jungle troops, Cavalry (both armoured and horsed), Artillery, Aviation troops, Engineers (combat, construction and specialised e.g. amphibious), communications troops and services. Infantry and Cavalry are organised into regiments of which there are currently 32 of the former (of which four are Airborne, nine Mountain and 3 Jungle) and ten of the latter (one Presidential Escort, eight Armoured and three Horsed), all of which are numbered and some of which are also named. The 1st Infantry Regiment is called the *Patricios* after a militia unit composed largely of Irish immigrants which was prominent in repelling the British invasions of 1806–07 and wears traditional early nineteenth-century uniforms when performing ceremonial functions. This unit, together with the Presidential Escort, the *Regimiento de Granaderos a Caballo* 'General San Martín' forms a unit known as the *Destacamento Buenos Aires*, which is based at the federal capital and used largely for ceremonial purposes. The *Granaderos a Caballo* also wear historical uniforms, in this case reminiscent of the Prussian hussars of the Napoleonic Wars. The Cavalry also includes mechanised reconnaissance troops which are organised in Squadrons to provide the reconnaissance elements of armoured and mechanised field formations and Detachments in the case of others. The Artillery is organised primarily into Groups whilst the Engineers and other Arms and Services are organised in Battalions, Groups and independent Companies.

Operational

The basic operational formation is the Brigade of which there are now twelve: two armoured, one mechanised, four motorised, one airborne, three mountain and one jungle. Each consists essentially of three regiments of the basic arm, a company sized reconnaissance unit, a group of artillery, an air defence battery, an engineer company, a signals company and a logistic battalion. The numbering of Infantry and Cavalry Regiments is traditional but the support units of each brigade derive their numbers from those of the brigades which run in the simple numerical sequence from 1 to 12.

Each Army Corps has a variable number of combat and logistic support units numbered in the sequence commencing with 101 in the case of the 1st Army Corps and 121, 131, 141 and 151 respectively in the case of the other four Corps. These invariably include an anti-aircraft battalion, an engineer construction battalion and a logistic support battalion. The 1st Army Corps adds a regimental sized armoured reconnaissance unit and as has already been noted, 4th and 5th Corps each includes one or two horsed Cavalry Regiments whilst 3rd Corps has an independent Paratroop Regiment.

Further units numbered in the sequence commencing with 601 are to be found at Army level. These include the 601st Special Forces Group; a regimental-sized anti-aircraft unit; the 601st Combat Aviation Battalion, which operates the aircraft of the Army Aviation Command and an amphibious engineers battalion operating a number of small transport vessels and landing craft on the river system adjoining the Brazilian frontier.

The Marine Corps, which unlike the Army performed well in the Anglo-Argentine War, is approximately 10,000 strong and is organised into two Fleet Marine Forces, each with the strength of a weak amphibious infantry brigade and two independent battalions, one for river and one for Antarctic operations. There are also six independent security companies used for the immediate defence of naval shore installations. The 2nd Fleet Marine Force includes an amphibious recon-naissance group, a field artillery battalion, a heavy mortar company, an anti-tank company and an engineer company. The 1st Fleet Marine Force has no combat support units. Other independent units include two groups of commandos numbered in the 601 sequence used by the Army, an amphibious vehicles battalion operating approximately three dozen tracked landing vehicles, a full air defence regiment and a signals battalion.

Paramilitary

There are three major paramilitary forces: the *Gendermería Nacional*, the *Prefectura Naval Argentina* and the *Policía Federal*.

The 12,000 man *Gendermería Nacional*, which is primarily a frontier guard force, comes under army command and functions from three regional headquarters at Córdoba, Rosario and Bahia Blanca. Its main organic unit is the *Agrupación*, a level of command between that of a battalion and a regiment, each of which is in turn subdivided into squadrons, groups and sections. The Gendermeria is equipped with armoured cars, APCs and aircraft in addition to infantry, personal and support weapons.

The 9,000 man *Prefectura Naval* is a coastguard force under naval command concerned primarily with the prevention of smuggling, fishery protection, life-saving, the maintenance of navigational aids and the regulation of the national ports. In emergencies it can equip small landing forces and shore units with light infantry weapons and it operates a number of rotary and fixed-wing aircraft in addition to about 30 patrol vessels and craft.

The 22,000 man *Policía Federal* is primarily concerned with conventional police and internal security functions in the Federal Capital for which it has available a number of light armoured vehicles and aircraft in addition to light infantry weapons. It is also available to reinforce provincial police forces in cases of emergency.

RECRUITMENT, TRAINING AND RESERVES

Recruitment and Training

Although six out of the fourteen major Latin American countries have passed universal conscription laws, in practice only Cuba, Argentina and perhaps Brazil insist on their application; elsewhere service tends, in fact if not in law, to be selective. Argentina's law, the Ricchieri law as it is called after the Minister of War who sponsored it, was passed in 1901. As amended in 1905, it provided for 1 year of service in the army (or two in the navy, the choice to be decided by lottery). Naval service was subsequently reduced to 14 months, but the army and air force term is still 1 year. During the 1920s the law furnished an annual contingent of 20,000–25,000. The present size of the army contingent is about 63,000, with 15,000 regular NCOs and 5000 regular officers. During the tension with Chile over the Beagle Channel dispute (*see* Current Developments) the total effectives of the Army were increased from approximately 85,000 to 130,000 by the simple expedient of retaining the annual conscript contingent of about 65,000 for an extended period of service with the colours, the numbers of officers and NCOs normally about 5,000 and 15,000 respectively being augmented by reserve mobilisation.

Recruits all receive their basic training in the units to which they are assigned, further specialist training being received at the *Escuelas de Aplicación* of the various arms and services of which the Infantry, Cavalry and Artillery schools, as well as most of the supporting arms and services schools, are located at Campo de Mayo outside Buenos Aires, the Airborne Forces School being located at Córdoba whilst the Mountain and Jungle Warfare schools are located at Mendoza and Corrientes respectively. Regular NCOs are trained at the *Escuela de Suboficiales Sargento Cabral* at Campo de Mayo.

Regular officers are recruited from high-school graduates by competitive examination in academic subjects. The cadet training centre is the *Colegio Militar*, located at El Palomar, between Campo de Mayo and Buenos Aires (founded 1870). Since 1946 education there has been free. The number of cadets is about 750 and the course lasts 4 years. Staff College training is provided at the *Escuela Superior de Guerra*, Buenos Aires, founded in 1900 by a German military mission. German influence on the Argentine officer corps has been very strong. A German military mission remained in Argentina until 1940, and hundreds of Argentinian officers went to Germany for training during those 40 years. There is a higher war college at Buenos Aires, the *Centro de Altos Estudios*, which opened in 1943. The arms and services schools each have demonstration units of approximately regimental size. The *Colegio Militar* and the NCO School each have composite demonstration units, also of about the size of a regiment.

Since World War II, German influence on the Argentinian army has naturally waned, to be replaced by American. Many Argentinian officers now attend the American staff and war colleges, as well as the School of the Americas in the Canal Zone, where anti-guerrilla warfare techniques are taught.

A French military mission has also been active since the early 1970s, principally in connection with the manufacture and operation of French designed equipment under the 'Plan Europa' (*see* Equipment and Arms Industry).

Reserves

The military obligation lasts from the conscript's twentieth to forty-fifth year. The first ten are spent in the active army, one on duty, nine in the reserve; the next ten are spent in the National Guard, the last five in the Territorial Guard. The two Guards are paper forces, however, and the reserve is rarely, if ever, called out. In theory the reserve holds 600,000 men, the National Guard 200,000 and the Territorial Guard 50,000.

EQUIPMENT AND ARMS INDUSTRY

Argentina was the first Latin American country to embark on the manufacture of its own weapons for its army, the first to aim at self-sufficiency and, is today, the first to be within sight of achieving that aim (though still some way off).

San Martín organised the local manufacture of small arms for his army before he set off to liberate Chile and Peru in 1817. His factories remained in existence during the nineteenth century and are said to have turned out copies of light Krupp field-guns in the 1880s. Certainly German engineers helped in 1911 to set up a factory producing Mauser rifles, and other foreign experts later established plants to manufacture Browning pistols, Madsen and Colt light machine-guns, Stokes Brandt mortars and Bofors light field guns. Plans were formulated by the army as early as 1923 to systematise this manufacture, but it was not until October, 1941 that the appropriate State supervisory authority was set up. It was called the *Dirección General de Fabricaciones Militares* (DGFM) and took charge of the *Fabrica Militar de Aviones* at Córdoba and naval shipyard at Río Santiago. It later founded or took over the small-arms ammunition factory at Puerto Borghi, Santa Fé province, the Domingo Matheu small-arms factory at Rosario, Santa Fé province, the artillery ammunition plant at Río Tercero, Córdoba province and the

powder and explosives works at Villa Maria, Córdoba province. A military research establishment (CITEFA – *Instituto de Investigaciones Científicas y Técnicas de las Fuerzas Armadas*) was subsequently set up to assist the work of the DGFM, which since 1952 also put out work to private industry. As a result, military transport and armoured vehicles have been produced, wholly or in part, in Argentina. An early production of a tank, the 35 ton Nahuel DL-43 of 1943, was unsuccessful but the French AMX-13 has apparently been built (probably from imported parts) by Argentinian subsidiaries of Fiat and Kaiser.

An early production of a medium tank, entirely designed and developed in Argentina, the 35 ton DL-43 Nahuel of 1943, was entirely successful and in some respects superior to contemporary vehicles such as the US 'Sherman' but was unable to compete economically with the vast numbers of war surplus vehicles available at bargain prices after the end of World War II and production terminated after only ten examples had been built. Following the refusal of the United States to supply up-to-date material of the types required by Argentina, in the early 1970s, the so-called 'Plan Europa' was adopted whereby the focus shifted from the US to France, Germany and Italy as the main overseas sources of equipment supply. As a result of this, AMX-13 light tanks and AMX-UCI APCs were first acquired from France and later assembled under licence in Argentina as were numerous examples of the Italian Oto Melara Model 56 105mm pack howitzer and the Swiss Mowas Roland wheeled APC. A new tank (*Tanque Argentino Mediano – TAM*) and APC (*Vehículo Combate Infantería – VCI*), both designed by Thyssen-Henschel and based on the Marder combat vehicle, are now to be constructed in Argentina. The gun (an Argentinian development of the French 105mm) and the turret (which will be imported from Germany) are to be assembled at Río Tercero, and the whole vehicle completed at Buenos Aires. About 200 TAMs and 300 VCIs are to be built altogether, the proportion of Argentinian-made parts to each has not been revealed. It is claimed, however, that the 30 ton, 4-man tank is superior to the Leopard I and that Thyssen hope to export a development to other countries. More recently, a 155mm towed howitzer of local design has been successfully developed and placed in production. Argentina has a flourishing and well-developed aerospace and ship-building industry and it has been reckoned that the country could produce nuclear weapons, without outside assistance, within three years.

Pistol: Browning 9mm (Fábrica Militar de Armas Portatiles, Domingo Matheu, Rosario)
Sub-machine-gun: PA-3-DM 9mm (Fábrica Militar)
Rifle: FAL 7.62mm (Belgium; Fábrica Militar)
Machine-gun: FN 7.62mm (Belgium; Fábrica Militar) Browning H2 12.7mm
Mortars: FM 81mm; FM 120mm
Anti-armour weapons: 75mm, 90mm and 105mm RCLs (US and FM); SS-11 and SS-12 ATGW (French); Cobra 2000 ATGW (German); Mathogo ATGW (Argentine)
Air-defence weapons: 30mm HS 831 (Swiss); 40mm Bofors L/60 and L/70 (Swedish and US); Blowpipe SAM; Roland SAM; Tigercat SAM
Artillery: 105mm Model 56 (Italian; FM); 105mm M101 (US); 155mm M2 (US); 155mm (FM); 155mm F-3 SP (French)
Armour: M-113 APC (US; 200 in service); Mowas Roland APC (Swiss; 120 in service); AMX-VCI APC (French; 180 in service; TAM UCI APC (German-Argentine; 200 in service); Sherman Firefly medium tank (US-British; 120 in service); AMX-13 light tank (French; 120 in service); M-41 light tank (US; 50 in service); TAM medium tank

(German-Argentine; 150 in service); Kurassier tank destroyer (Austrian; 170 in service).

Aircraft: 60 fixed-wing aircraft and 60 helicopters. The Air Force has about 70 transport aircraft and 50 helicopters.

The Marines use the same personal and infantry support weapons as the Army. They also have 105mm howitzers and 88mm and 30mm anti-aircraft guns. A number of Panhard AML-90 armoured cars were lost in the Falklands and a number of EBR-90s are on order. Mowas Roland APCs are also operated and there were 20 LUTP-7 and 16 LARC-5 tracked landing vehicles in service prior to the South Atlantic War. The Marines also use Bantam ATGWs and Tigercat SAMs.

RANK, DRESS AND DISTINCTIONS

Officer rank is indicated on shoulder straps and epaulettes as follows:

Teniente General — Three gold suns + laurel wreath
General de División — Two gold suns + laurel wreath
General de Brigada — One gold sun + laurel wreath
Coronel — Three gold suns
Teniente Coronel — Two gold suns
Mayor — One gold sun
Capitán — Three silver suns
Teniente — Two silver suns
Segundo Teniente — One silver + one gold sun
Subteniente — One silver sun
NCOs wear a combination of broad and narrow chevrons.

There are a wide variety of dress, service and fatigue uniforms adapted for service in the wide range of climates found throughout the Republic. The basic colour is olive green. Officers service dress features dark green tunic and cap and beige trousers with brown footwear and leather equipment. Mountain troops wear German-type *Bergemütze* caps and have a white snow camouflage uniform. Jungle troops wear slouch hats and either dark green or dazzle camouflage uniforms. Airborne troops wear maroon berets and marine commandos dark green. The US M-42 steel helmet appears to have superseded both the German and Swiss types previously worn by some units. Many units, especially Cavalry Regiments, wear historic uniforms for ceremonial occasions.

There are two major national decorations: the Order of the Liberator San Martín and the Order of May. Other awards include the Order of Military Merit and the Medal for Antarctic Service.

CURRENT DEVELOPMENTS

The armed forces *junta* which took power in March, 1976 instituted severely authoritarian reforms. It announced that its aims were 'to enforce Christian moral values, eradicate subversion, extremism and corruption, revitalise the country's constitutional bodies and create a fair social and legal order'. This appeared to require, at the outset, the dissolution of congress, the provincial legislatures and city councils, trades unions, employers' associations, professional associations and political parties, and the dismissal of provincial governors and federal 'interventors' (the emissaries of the central government to whom in Argentinian law it may entrust delegated powers in the provinces, universities and trade unions). It further announced that it would remain in power for 3 years. Its economic policy, hastily designed to deal with a situation of collapsing exports and inflation of 600% per annum, included measures to encourage foreign investment, reduce

the size of the bureaucracy by one-sixth immediately, lower the artificially high exchange rate and put some State-owned enterprises onto the market. The other pressing requirement was to reduce the level of public violence, which had caused the deaths of 300 people in the first quarter of 1977. Many of these deaths were the work of the right-wing *Alianza Argentina Anticomunista* (AAA), which it was believed employed the services of off-duty policemen, but others were the responsibility of the left-wing groups, particularly the Montoneros and ERP. During 1975 they had directed their attacks mainly at army personnel and installations, but in the year after the military coup they turned their attention to the police. They were nevertheless also able to make three separate attempts on the life of the president, in March and October, 1976 and in February, 1977 when they exploded a bomb beside his aircraft as it was taking off.

During 1977 the level of violence was much reduced, as leaders and personnel of both groups were killed or arrested. Speaking to the nation in March, 1977 however, General Videla set no date for the elections he had promised on taking power. Legislative as well as executive functions remain with the *junta*, which has also taken effective control of organised labour. There are no signs, therefore, of any immediate return to civilian rule in Argentina, nor of dissension in the military government sufficient to hasten such a return.

During the late 1970s increasing tension with Chile over the disputed ownership of three small islands in the Beagle Channel, at the southern tip of the continent, led to a minor army re-organisation, an increase in the numbers of serving personnel, the creation of a number of new units and significant arms purchases abroad. An arbitral award in favour of Chile, by the Pope, as mediator, exacerbated rather than improved matters and there remains a real danger of hostilities between the two countries.

The military Government, led by General Leopoldo Galtieri, sought to detract popular attention from a rapidly deteriorating internal situation by the military adventure of the invasion of the Falkland Islands and South Georgia in April 1982. Although Argentina's subsequent ignominious defeat may to some extent be rationalised by the fact that it was suffered at the hands of a major NATO power, backed by one of the two super powers, the Army did not perform well or even creditably. This defeat has already had considerable political repercussions in Argentina and seems likely to have an even more far reaching political effect in the medium to long term.

Although the credibility of the Army has suffered considerably and enormous quantities of military equipment were lost in the brief but disastrous campaign, some of the losses have already been made good and despite near bankruptcy the military government is scouring the world's markets for war material. The fact that the defeat in the Falklands was suffered at the hands of a nuclear power seems certain to accelerate Argentina's own nuclear weapons programme. Likewise, efforts to achieve self-sufficiency in defence production, virtually abandoned since the end of the first Peronista era, seem most likely to be renewed.

Argentina may seek to redeem her military honour by a successful war against Chile but a second and better prepared attempt to annex the Falklands, failing some at present highly unlikely diplomatic solution of this problem, seems inevitable in the medium term. This could well prove a danger not merely to hemispheric but even to world peace.

John Keegan
Adrian English

25

AUSTRALIA

HISTORY AND INTRODUCTION

The Australian army is widely regarded as one of the most efficient, for its size, in the world today. It is a major strategic factor in the politics of south-east Asia and the Pacific, and the repository of a respectable, even awesome, military tradition. Yet it has a history, as an effective force, of less than 70 years, and has achieved its reputation largely in the face of strong domestic anti-militarist feeling.

Until 1870 Australia, then consisting of seven unfederated States, was defended by a garrison of British troops, the forbears of whom had been raised as early as 1789, sailing to New South Wales with the first convict ships in the same year. In 1870, however, following a British government decision to make the white colonies provide for their own defence, the garrison was withdrawn. The only military forces left to the States by this move were the locally-raised volunteers of New South Wales, Victoria and South Australia, brought into being after an earlier, partial withdrawal at the time of the Crimean War. Taking these units as a basis, the State governments went on, between 1871 and 1900, to form a three-tiered military system which was distinctly Australian. It consisted, in each State, of (a) a Permanent Force, mainly of administrative troops, but with some batteries of garrison artillery; (b) a Militia, a part-time, but paid, body of engineers, field artillery, cavalry and infantry; and (c) a Volunteer Force of part-time, unpaid infantry. It was from the Militia and Volunteers that New South Wales sent a contingent to the British army fighting in the Sudan in 1885, and all States contributed to the sizeable Australian contingents for the South African War of 1899—1902. It was in this latter conflict that the Australians first demonstrated their formidable military talents, particularly as mounted infantry against the Boer Commandos.

In 1901, when the Australian States were federated into a single Dominion, the various Permanent Forces were amalgamated, although the Militia and Volunteers remained under local control. However, the low military value of the part-timers, even for home defence, was undisguiseable, and in 1911, after a visit by Lord Kitchener, they were finally brought under Federal control and reorganised. Officers and NCOs were transferred from the Militia to a new Citizen Force, the two part-time forces were disbanded and all medically fit male Australians in the age-range 12—25 years were made liable for army training. Junior cadets (aged 12—14 years) and senior cadets (14—18 years) were required to perform 90—96 hours' drill each year, while the older men (18—25 years) had to do 16 days' training, eight continuously, in units of the new Citizen Force, which, although controlled centrally, was recruited and organised by the individual States. The universality and home-defence orientation of these arrangements suggests, in retrospect, that Australian military institutions were set to develop basically along Swiss lines, but this was not to be. In 1914 Australia, in common with other colonies, responded eagerly to Britain's call to arms and, in the ensuing upheaval, the Citizen Force structure was overthrown. Its members, although making up a nominal 92 battalions, were young (average age 19—21 years) and too little trained to be instantly embodied as an expeditionary force, while their terms of service did not include active duties overseas. Volunteers for an Australian Imperial Force (AIF)

were therefore requested as individuals, and out of the rush, swollen by many Citizen Force and old Militia men, the 1st Australian Infantry Division and 1st Australian Light Horse Brigade were formed in 4 weeks. These formations, merely a vanguard to many more, were sent to Egypt, from where the 1st Australian Division, joined up the later-raised 2nd and the New Zealand Division to form ANZAC (Australian and New Zealand Army Corps), was to make a heroic but militarily fruitless journey to Gallipoli in 1915.

The Citizen Force remained in existence throughout the war, with many of its members transferring from it to the Imperial Force as partially trained recruits. Australia's great military reputation was won, however, by the AIF which, although basically an *ad hoc* organisation, had put into the field by the end of the war in 1918 no less than five full infantry divisions and two divisions of light horse. The light horse remained in Egypt and Palestine during the Gallipoli campaign, and operated with spectacular success against the Turks throughout the conflict. The infantry, on the other hand, was transferred to France after 1915, and by the last year of the war the Australian Corps had come to form, with the Canadians, the spearhead of the British Expeditionary Force and its counterpart to the shock divisions with which Ludendorff opened his final, almost successful 1918 offensives. The Corps Commander, Monash, a mining engineer in civilian life, had revealed himself to be perhaps the most talented general on the British side, and the Australian soldier, although thought undisciplined and casual by his British allies, had acquired something of a reputation as a military superman.

The AIF disappeared at the end of the war, but its organisation and divisional titles, which now meant so much, were preserved in the Home Defence Force, which was itself reformed. Conscription remained, but the junior cadets were disbanded and compulsory training in the Citizen Force (confusingly re-named the Militia) was limited to periods in two successive years. In 1929, due to the economic depression, conscription was abandoned and numbers in the Militia dropped to 30,000. The result was that, when war broke out in 1939 — a war to which Australia was to respond as eagerly as in 1914 — the divisions of the Militia were at 40% strength only. Conscription was accordingly reintroduced, but the Militia's liability for service was still restricted to mainland Australia. To provide a force for intervention further afield, the government had once more to call for volunteers, this time to form the 2nd Australian Imperial Force.

World War II, unlike World War I, was, however, to bring an enemy — the Japanese — into Australian-controlled territory (in Papua—New Guinea) and to threaten the Dominion itself with invasion. These factors were to have two effects: they required the Australian government, firstly, to extend the Militia's liability for service to include the Australian-controlled territories beyond the mainland, and, secondly, to exercise a far stricter control over the employment of the 2nd AIF than it had done over the 1st. The 1st AIF had acted, in effect, as a powerful reinforcement to the *British* army; the 2nd AIF, although it served Britain magnificently in the Western Desert before, and even for some time after Japanese intervention — notably in the first defence of Tobruk and at Alamein — had to be employed from 1943 onwards in the Pacific as an *Australian* defence force. Popular demand for Australian control of its own armed forces could not, in addition, be ignored after heavy losses in the division isolated on Crete in May, 1941, and particularly after the pointless disembarkation, under British orders, of the 8th Division at Singapore 9 months later, straight into Japanese hands.

At the end of the war Australia did not, as in 1918, move at once to disband the AIF. A brigade group had to be found to represent Australia among the Allied forces of occupation in Japan, and from this brigade grew the sizeable regular army which exists today. The process of growth was by no means straightforward, however, incorporating a series of changes to the Australian military structure which began as early as 1947. In that year it was decided to revert to a voluntary system of enlistment for the Militia, hoping thereby to create another Citizen Force (now renamed the Citizen Military Forces, or CMF) of some 50,000 men who could act as a back-up and home-defence alternative to a Regular Army of 20,000. Unfortunately the Australian temperament is perhaps unsuited to peacetime volunterring, and after the beginning of the Korean War in 1950 has shown how small the CMF had become and how little an alternative it was to the Regular Army committed elsewhere, a National Service Training Scheme had to be introduced. Between 1951 and the scheme's suspension in 1959 approximately 30,000 trainees were enlisted each year for 98 days' full-time service followed by 2 years' part-time duty in the CMF; an arrangement which rapidly increased the size of the home-defence forces to some 85,000 men. While this was taking place, of course, the Regular Army was actively involved in the defence of Australian interests on the mainland of Asia, chiefly in Korea (1950–3) and Malaya (1948–60).

The next major change occurred in 1959–60, when the army as a whole, both Regular and CMF, was reorganised into what was called the 'pentropic' system, the basic unit of which was a 'battle group' of an enlarged infantry battalion with supporting arms. A pentropic division – two of which were formed, the 1st consisting of Regular and CMF units together, the 3rd solely of CMF volunteers – consisted of five such battle groups and a 'combat support group'. This organisation remained in effect until 1964, when a new form of selective conscription necessitated further change. Every male Australian, upon reaching the age of 18, took part in a ballot and, if chosen, was called up for 2 years in the Regular Army. Those who escaped continued to do military training, however, it being their task to man the CMF, now expanded into two separate divisions, the 2nd and 3rd, leaving the 1st as before, a combination of Regular and CMF units.

This reorganisation of 1964 constituted the beginning of a 'one-army' concept in Australia, a trend considerably reinforced when at the same time the charter of the CMF was amended to give them a follow-up role to regular troops in time of war, dispensing with their previous home-defence-only commitment. Although the CMF was not involved in the Vietnam conflict – Australian efforts in that theatre being left to the regular forces with their experience of counter-insurgency gained in Malaya and Borneo (1963–6) – and despite the end of National Service in December, 1972 which rapidly reduced overall military strength, this basic balance between full- and part-time soldiers still remains. In many ways it is perhaps the ideal so far as the Australian people are concerned, for with their anti-militarist tradition on the one hand and their history of eager response in emergencies on the other, a dependence upon one or the other of the two systems alone would involve many disadvantages. As it is, with a small but highly professional regular force gaining valuable experience and a fully trained CMF ready to act as reinforcements, the army as a whole seems well prepared to perform its task of defending Australian interests, wherever they may be deemed to lie.

STRENGTH AND BUDGET

Population: 15,065,000
Military service: voluntary
Army: 32,850 regulars; 31,738 (CMF)
Navy: 17,626; 18 major vessels, 29 smaller
Air force: 22,707; 81 combat aircraft
Defence expenditure (1980–1): $US 4,229,000,000

COMMAND AND CONSTITUTIONAL STATUS

Command
Following closely upon the British pattern of army administration and command structures, in 1964 a Ministry of Defence, co-ordinating army, navy and air force policy, was established, nominally under the control of the Governor-General of Australia as representative of H.M. Queen Elizabeth II, but actually the responsibility of a Minister of Defence, a civilian politician appointed by the political party in power. Under him, as the chief decision-making body, there is a Defence Council, the membership of which is:

The Minister of Defence	(Chairman)
The Chief of Defence Staff }	(Deputy Chairman)
The Secretary of Defence }	
The Chief of Naval Staff	
The Chief of General Staff	
The Chief of Air Staff	

The Secretaries of Foreign Affairs and of the Treasury, as interested parties in military decisions, are also vote members, and the Council may appoint other members at its discretion. The Council as a whole is responsible for all command and administration functions, while assisting the Minister in the formulation of defence policy.

Constitutional Status
Following the British pattern again, the Australian Commander-in-Chief, to whom all service personnel owe direct allegiance, is H.M. Queen Elizabeth II, although for purposes of convenience the Governor-General, as the monarch's representative in Australia, is invested with the power to raise and maintain the armed forces. In practice this has little effect, for unless government decisions are directly alien to Commonwealth interests, The Governor-General's military powers are purely nominal. One advantage of the system, however, is that the armed forces owe their allegiance not to the government in power but to a higher authority, so cutting down the possibility of military forces being used for purely political ends.

ROLE, COMMITMENT, DEPLOYMENT AND RECENT OPERATIONS

Role and Commitment
The basic role of the Australian army, in common with its counterparts in other countries, is the protection of the homeland itself from external and internal aggression. The latter threat has never appeared to be very great, and, with an adequate civilian police force, the army is unlikely to be called upon in this role. The threat of external aggression, however, is felt strongly, particularly after the experiences of 1941–5 with Japan and the growth of communist influence in Asia since the end of World War II. As a result, Australia now has a tradition of defence co-ordination with like-minded countries in her area and since 1945 has become a member of several multilateral defence arrangements. These

range from ANZUS Pact of 1951, whereby Australia, New Zealand and the United States agreed to support each other in the Pacific, through the SEATO Treaty of 1954 which covered collective defence in Asia, to the Five Power Defence Arrangements of 1971 for the protection of Malaysia against communist aggression. This latter agreement led to the formation of a combined ANZUK force of Australian, New Zealand and British troops, and although this has now lapsed, it does not seem incorrect to suppose that, in the event of trouble in Malaysia, Australian commitment will be renewed.

In 1981 the military aspect of the Five Power Defence Agreement bore fruit in the training exercise held in Queensland when all five nations including a rifle company from the UK participated in a ten day exercise. These annual exercises are to be hosted alternatively by the Australians and the New Zealand armies.

At the moment, however, the idea of defending Australia by having regular forces constantly in Asia has become less attractive, and the majority of the armed services remain in the home territories.

Deployment

With the exception of two Mirage squadrons of the Royal Australian Air Force, which remain in Malaysia/Singapore as part of the air-defence system laid down by the Five Power Defence Arrangements of 1971, all Australian forces are now concentrated in Australia itself. Representative forces of both the Regular Army and the CMF are stationed in each of the seven States, with some units in Papua—New Guinea.

Recent Operations

Since 1945 Australian forces have been involved solely in the Asian theatre, beginning with the Korean conflict of 1950—3. The bulk of their experience, however, has been in counter-insurgency and, with the British, New Zealand and Rhodesian armies, they may be regarded as amongst the most successful in this field. Starting with the Malayan emergency of the 1950s and including the Borneo confrontation of 1963—6, this experience perhaps culminated in Vietnam in the late 1960s, where the techniques employed by the Australian units (particularly the Special Air Service Regiment) surprised the Americans with their subtlety and success.

In 1980 the Australians provided a contingent of over 200 soldiers to the Peace Keeping Force in Zimbabwe during the transitional period between the ending of UDI and the formation of the state of Zimbabwe. The pattern of post-World War II operations for the army has been to soldier outside the Australian continent in concert with allies. In all cases this has meant that the logistic support for the army has been provided from other sources thereby leaving the Australian system of logistical support largely untried in battle.

In common with many other Western-style armies, the Australians have no recent experience of large-scale or armoured warfare.

ORGANISATION

The army is at present organised on the functional command system with three commands namely Field Force, Training and Logistics command. All HQs of these commands are situated on the East coast line including Melbourne. There are three Divisions, one regular and two CMF. The regular division has three brigade groups each with its own special role. One operates on light scales, one operates on conventional scales and the third is registered to train for armoured warfare. A parachute capability is also being developed.

Composition of the Regular Army

This is as follows:

1 infantry division HQ and 3 task force HQs
1 tank regiment   Royal Australian
2 cavalry/APC regiments }   Armoured Corps
6 infantry battalions (1st—6th Battalions, Royal Australian Regiment)
1 Special Air Service Regiment
4 artillery regiments (1 medium, 2 field and 1 light anti-aircraft)
1 aviation regiment
3 field engineer regiments
1 army survey regiment
2 signals regiments
1 logistic support force
Women's Royal Australian Army Corps

RECRUITMENT, TRAINING AND RESERVES

Recruitment

Regular Army

Since December, 1972 all military service in Australia is voluntary, and for those who choose to enter the Regular Army, the initial engagement is for 6 years, with re-engagement at the end of that period for either a further 6 or 3 years, up to the age of 55 years, when retirement is compulsory. Both men and women may enlist at any age between 17 and 43 years, although restrictions apply at both ends of the range: those under 18 years have to produce their parents' written consent; those over 35 may be expected to bring into the army some specialist skill. Australian subjects with 'a satisfactory civil record' and a good general education are obviously given preference, but both British and 'alien' subjects with resident status may enlist. Terms of service specify that soldiers may be sent 'anywhere within or beyond the limits of the Commonwealth of Australia', although it is laid down that no-one under the age of 18 years will leave the mainland, nor anyone under 19 years be sent on active service. Officer volunteers, on the other hand, must be between the ages of 19 and 25 years unless recruited from the ranks, and are expected to remain on permanent service up to the age of 55 years, although commissions may be resigned anytime after 3 years' service.

The CMF

For those volunteering for part-time service in the CMF the terms are very similar to those of the Regular Army. Both men and women have to be 17 years' old, although the rules governing older people do vary. Men up to 35 years of age may volunteer for Field Force duty (as the direct back-up to the Regular Army) and up to 45 years if 'other than Field Force'; women may join so long as they are under 30 years with no previous military experience, but if they are ex-regulars this may rise to 38 years. In all cases the initial engagement may be for 2, 3 or 6 years, with re-engagements for 2 year periods thereafter, up to the age of 48 years for men, 50 years for women. CMF officers tend to rise through the ranks, although ex-regular officers may have their commissions transferred.

Training

Regular Army

Officers chosen for the Regular Army are trained initially at one of two establishments. The older — the Royal Military College, Duntroon, founded in 1911 — involves a course lasting 4 years, during which the officer cadet is expected to follow both military and academic courses; indeed, the college is directly affiliated to the University of New South Wales, and all successful cadets receive a degree in arts, applied science or engineering when they are commissioned. At the Officer Cadet School, Portsea (Victoria), set up in 1951, however, the course is far shorter (11 months only), and does not include a great amount of academic work. Regardless of which establishment he attends, each newly commissioned officer is then sent to the specialist school of the arm-of-service he chooses. These schools, ranging from the Armoured Centre at Puckapunyal (Victoria) to the School of Army Aviation at Oakey (Queensland), also cater for the training of NCOs and private soldiers who attend arm-of-service courses after promotion or basic military training in their particular units.

The Government has decided to merge the initial academic training for all officers in the Australian Defence Force Academy to be located in Canberra. Once their initial training has been completed, special to arm training will follow, at the respective army, navy and air force establishments. This scheme is not without its service opponents and the recent change of Government may well delay these plans.

The CMF

All the CMF volunteers receive their basic training within the units they join, attending specialist courses at the appropriate schools on the same basis as the regulars.

EQUIPMENT AND ARMS INDUSTRY

The Australian defence industrial base is small. In the past almost total reliance has had to be placed on foreign firms to provide the weapons and equipment involving high technology. In the period 1980–82 the Government made it clear that greater efforts were to be made to boost home industry. A decision has been made to build under licence the UK Light 105 gun. In addition project Whaler is an ambitious endeavour to design and, if possible, build a family of armoured vehicles to replace the ageing M-113 fleet. The desire to increase the 'Australian Industrial Participation' in all foreign contracts involving defence procurement is clear evidence of this policy.

Arms and Equipment

Pistol: 9mm Browning L9A1 (Canada and Belgium)
Rifle: 7.62mm L1A1 (Australia); 5.56mm M-16 (USA) and 7.62mm Omark M-44 sniper (Australia)
Sub-machine-gun: 9mm SMG F1 (Australia) and 0.5in Browning heavy barrel M-2 (heavy; USA)
Machine-gun: 7.62mm M-60 (sustained fire; USA) and 7.62mm L4A4 (light; Britain)
Mortars: 81mm mortar F-1 (USA and Britain)
Anti-tank weapons: L-6 Wombat 120mm RCL (Australia) and Entac ATGW
Anti-aircraft weapons: 40mm AA guns, Redeye SAM (USA) and Rapier SAM (Britain)
Artillery: 5.5in gun (Britain; 34 in service), 105mm pack howitzer (Britain; 227 in service) and M-40 106 mm
Armour: M-113 APC (USA; 790 in service) and Leopard tank (Germany: 103 in service)
Aircraft: Bell 47 helicopter (USA; 29 in service) and Bell 206 B-1 helicoper (USA; 47 in service); Pilatus Porter

light aircraft (Switzerland; 16 in service) and Nomad light aircraft (11 in service)

Also 65 assorted watercraft in service, chiefly with the engineer and survey regiments.

RANK, DRESS AND DISTINCTIONS

Rank

General — Crossed sword and baton, one crown, one star
Lieutenant-general — Crossed sword and baton, one crown
Major-general — Crossed sword and baton, one star
Brigadier — One crown above three stars
Colonel — One crown above two stars (shoulder)
Lieutenant-colonel — One crown above one star (shoulder)
Major — One crown (shoulder)
Captain — Three stars (shoulder)
Lieutenant — Two stars (shoulder)
Second-lieutenant — One star (shoulder)
Warrant Officer I — Australian arms (sleeve)
Warrant Officer II — Crown (sleeve)
Staff sergeant — Crown above three chevrons (sleeve)
Sergeant — Three chevrons (sleeve)
Corporal — Two chevrons (sleeve)
Lance-corporal — One chevron (sleeve)
Private —

Dress

In common with the British and other Commonwealth armies, most patterns of dress take khaki as their basic colour. The only distinctive items of dress in the Australian army are the bush hat with the left side bent up, and an American-style steel helmet. Combat dress is uncamouflaged (except for certain styles of jungle warfare) and leggings are worn with most types of working dress. Officers' mess-dress follows the British pattern, and exists in both winter and summer styles.

Distinctions

Each unit or corps within the Australian army wears a distinctive cap badge, with matching collar devices and, in working dress, some form of shoulder title.

CURRENT DEVELOPMENTS

The main thrust of Australian military thinking is likely to concentrate on producing an effective command structure and with it a correct mix of conventional forces in order to operate effectively within the Australian continent. The paramount importance of sound logistical resupply operating in a hostile natural environment is one of considerable complexity since over 90 per cent of the army is located in the south-east and the obvious area of possible operations is in the North and West. Present strategical thinking is to develop a small core force which can be capable of rapid expansion as the threat demands. This core force will use the CMF for expansion and hence the need to try and improve the retention rate within the CMF to maintain the standard of training.

No-one can deny the professionalism of the Australian army, particularly in the role which it is most likely to be called upon to carry out — counter-insurgency. Therein lies its strength.

John Pimlott

AUSTRIA

HISTORY AND INTRODUCTION

The army of Austria, like the State which it serves, was within living memory one of the largest and most powerful in Europe. In the seventeenth century it had stood in the forefront of the defence of Europe from Ottoman invasion. In the eighteenth it offered the principal military counterweight to France in the struggle for continental supremacy. In the wars of the French Revolution and Empire it was the most constant element in the coalitions formed to overcome the Republic and to defeat Napoleon, and as late as 1915 it could conduct simultaneous operations against half the Russian and the whole of the Italian armies on two widely separated fronts. Moreover, it had produced during those centuries some of the most illustrious generals of history: Starhemberg, defender of Vienna against the Turks in 1682; Eugene of Savoy; the Archduke Charles; Schwarzenberg, the victor of Leipzig; Radetzky.

Its role within the Habsburg empire had been as important as its victories over the empire's foreign enemies. Grillparzer's poetic salutation to Radetzky, *'In deinem Lager ist Oesterreich'* ('In your camp is Austria') defies easy translation. But its importance is clear enough. In an empire of 10 nationalities and five religions, without common political institutions and lacking even a unified crown – the Archduchy of Austria and the Hungarian monarchy, though vested in the same person, were separate sovereignties – the army served as the only visible bond between the emperor's disparate subjects and the only organ through which they could jointly offer him their loyalty. As a means of attracting their loyalty it was remarkably successful. It is fashionable now to use instances of disaffection in the Slav regiments during World War I as evidence of the empire's impending dissolution. More remarkable is their infrequency. The army may not have fought very well between 1914 and 1918, but it held together almost to the end. It did not, like the Tsar's, 'vote for peace with its feet', nor, like the French or the Italian, suffer a mid-war collapse of morale. This devotion to duty is principally a testimony to its success, alone among the institutions of the empire, in solving the 'nationalities problem'. It did so by frankly recognising it, through the organisation of regiments on a linguistic basis, and at the same time discounting nationality in its promotion policy. The army's 'centre of gravity', like the empire's, was inevitably German; but anyone who took the trouble to make himself normally fluent in the language could rise within it as far as his ability could take him; the Croats in particular were certainly over-represented in the officer class, at the top of which were also found Poles, Italians, Slovenes and Romanians. The army also made liberal provision for cultural differences and traditions of its constituent contingents, so that at one end of the empire were found Muslim regiments of Bosnians, run in a spirit not dissimilar from those of the British Indian Army, at the other the Tiroler Kaiserjäger, whose independent mountaineer riflemen were allowed to organise themselves along lines more resembling the militia of neighbouring Switzerland than of the army of a bureaucratic monarchy.

Paradoxically, the collapse of the monarchy and the reduction of Austria to its German-speaking heartland did not diminish the political importance of the army. 'Remnant Austria', small as it was in size and population (6,500,000), was racked by internal problems and threatened by the territorial ambitions of the successor States. Its frontiers were eventually guaranteed by the intervention of the great powers, but they could not cure the dislike existing between the right-wing country people of the mountainous western half of the State and the left-wing town dwellers of Vienna and the eastern industrial areas. Both were armed, but so fearful was the new republic's first socialist government of right-wing reaction that it created its own socialist army, the *Volkswehr* (People's Army), to guarantee its hold on power. In the event, civil war was averted, and the *Volkswehr* transformed into an acceptable and reasonably apolitical State army, the *Bundeswehr*. However the population was not disarmed – in the Tirol there was a tradition as old as Switzerland's of the private possession of arms – and during the 1920s the loose associations of home guardsmen, which had briefly had their counterparts throughout central Europe in the immediate aftermath of the political collapse of 1918, coalesced into private armies under party control: the Social Democrats' *Schutzbund* and the Christian Socials' *Heimwehr*. In 1930 the latter entered parliament on its own account and in 1932, Dollfus, the new Christian Social Chancellor (a famous ex-Tiroler Kaiserjäger) was obliged to offer it cabinet seats as a means of maintaining his majority. Its leaders pressed him hard to take action against the *Schutzbund*, as did Mussolini, to whom he had turned for foreign support as an alternative to the all too pressing attentions of Hitler. Arms searches and arrests of Social Democrats provoked disaffection and eventually, in February, 1934, a general strike, and that in turn, civil war. Though the *Schutzbund* remained on the defensive, Dollfus took the decision to commit the army which, reluctantly and illadvisedly, brought in heavy weapons and shelled the working-class districts of Vienna – in particular the great municipal apartment blocks, the Karl-Marx-Hof and the Goethe-Hof, into submission.

Within four years, Austria, with its army, had disappeared inside Greater-Germany. But the civil war had left a mark on Austrian politics which persists to this day: it had cast the Social Democrats in the role of heroic defenders of democracy, truly anti-Fascist without being communist; and it had tainted the army with a reputation for partisan politics and heavy-handed repression, not dissimilar from that which the execrated Haynau had won for it by his pacification of Hungary in 1848.

As a 'victim of Nazi aggression', Austria was permitted to form its own government as soon as the war was over, a government of all the parties, Social Democrat, Communist and People's (the new Christian Socialists), through which each of the two occupying blocs, Soviet and Western, nevertheless hoped to establish an independent Austria favourable to its own cause. The Russians were frustrated in their hopes, as a result of the failure of the Austrian Communist Party to win seats at the polls, to secure key ministries or to gain control of the trade unions, and in 1955 agreed, after prolonged negotiation, to sign a State Treaty which re-established Austrian sovereignty, ended the occupation and transferred full power to the ruling Social Democrat–People's Party coalition, all within the context of Austria's 'perpetual neutrality'.

The intention of all parties to the treaty, domestic and

foreign, was to make of Austria another Switzerland, with which it shared a frontier and, in the western *Länder*, a cultural tradition. Militarily, however, the Austrian tradition was different from the Swiss and the years of occupation had left it with an embryo military structure quite unlike its neighbour's citizen militia. In their zones, the British, Americans and French had raised from the existing gendarmerie a mobile regiment of three *Alarm* battalions, as an internal security force, which played an important part in the suppression of the Communist campaign of industrial disorder in 1950. It was already foreseen as the nucleus of a State army and from 1952 its ranks were deliberately swelled to provide future leaders for the conscript force it was planned that Austria should raise on independence. The main function of that force should be the prevention of a communist bid for power in the wake of a Soviet withdrawal of its occupation troops. Evacuation led to no such bid, but the new State persisted nevertheless in the creation of what, for one so small, was quite a sizeable army, initially by the transfer of about half the gendarmerie – the 'B' or *Bereitschaftgendarmerie* (6500 men) – into the *Bundeswehr*, then through the mechanism of the draft.

Evidence accumulated during the first 10 years of independence that the planned military framework was too ambitious for Austria's population and economy: by 1960 it had grown to include 48 battalions, organised into nine brigades, one for each of the Federal *Länder*. But lingering anxieties for the security of the border, raised by the Hungarian uprising of 1956, and a bipartisan defence policy in the coalition government, deferred a serious reconsideration. The victory of the Social Democrats in 1970 brought the debate out into the open, and in particular the party's buried mistrust of a conventional standing army. Like most of the orthodox Socialist parties of Western Europe, it had always held, on ideological grounds, that a militia was preferable to a regular army, and it could find powerful arguments for moving to a militia system in Austria's contemporary situation: there was the convincing Swiss analogy; there was detente; there was the mounting cost of equipment, much of which had to be bought abroad; and there was the growing dislike among the military age-groups of prolonged conscript service.

Its original intention was to introduce a militia system based on 6 months' service. The army leadership was appalled. In part this was no doubt due to a certain rigidity of outlook, which was naturally formed by memories of, and in many cases personal links with, the *Kaiserheer* and its great imperial past (it is not insignificant that the Vienna Museum of Military History is without question the most magnificent in Europe). Armies are slower to change their characters than almost any other sort of institution, and an assumption of international status similar to Switzerland's could not be expected automatically to entail an inhabitation of Swiss military forms and attitudes, which themselves had taken 700 years to develop. In addition, the leadership was also genuinely alarmed by the dangers which adoption of a purely militia system would bring. Austria, unlike Switzerland, had frontiers with Warsaw Pact as well as NATO powers, offered both sides important strategic routes for the movement of their forces and had, as recently as 1968, had to man its own frontiers as a result of the 'Czech spring' and the Soviet measures taken against it.

The *Wehrgesetznovelle* of July, 1971 by which the parliament (*Nationalrat*) eventually instituted reform, represented therefore a compromise. Conscription was reduced from 9 months to 6 months and many of the units were scheduled for transformation from standing to militia (*Landwehr*) status, but provision was made for conscripts to volunteer

for an additional two months and so to provide the manpower, with the regular soldiers, for the maintenance of a number of Alert units (*Bereitschaftstruppe*), in the strength of about 15,000. At the same time a unified army headquarters, which had hitherto not been allowed to exist, was created and the territorial organisation of units, hitherto strictly federal in character, redrawn on more functional lines.

Organisationally, the Austrian army is still in a state of flux, and resistance to the new scheme, from both within and without the army, seems by no means dead, but the probability is that it is now set on a course of gradual assimilation to the Swiss form, which may well turn out to be, as the Social Democrats claim, what is militarily best for a small, neutral, democratic and federal State on the alpine slopes of central Europe.

STRENGTH AND BUDGET

Population: 7,504,800
Army: 13,000 regulars; 32,000 conscripts; 930,000 reservists of whom 60,000 are effective; 11,250 paramilitary (gendarmerie)
Air force: 2200 regulars; 2000 conscripts; 700 reservists; the air force forms part of the army (*Bundesheer*); 32 combat aircraft
GNP (1981 estimate): $65,500,000,000
Defence expenditure (1981): $767,700,000

COMMAND AND CONSTITUTIONAL STATUS

Austria is a Federal State, but defence is administered by the Federal Government. The President is Supreme Commander of the *Bundesheer*, but the government delegates operational control (*Verfugungsrecht*) to the Minister of Defence, who personally exercises executive command (*Befehlsgewalt*). Until July 1st, 1973 he dealt directly with the commanders of the three *Gruppen* into which Austria was divided for purposes of military command and administration. Since then, however, there has existed an army headquarters (*Armeekommando*) within the Ministry of Defence, the head of which is the Army Commander, appointed by the Ministry of Defence, to whom he is responsible for the training, operational readiness and command of the army. The Corps and Air Force Commanders are his immediate subordinates.

Like other neutral European States, Austria has a plan and organisation for 'total defence' (*umfassenden Landesverteidigung*), comprehending military, civil, economic and psychological (*geistige*) defence, which is co-ordinated in the Federal Chancellor's department.

ROLE, COMMITMENT, DEPLOYMENT AND RECENT OPERATIONS

Role
Austria, by declaration of its parliament, is a 'perpetually neutral' State (October 26th, 1955). Her neutrality is not guaranteed by any of the four former occupying powers and is not enshrined in the State Treaty (May 15th, 1955) by which she regained her independence and sovereignty, but, by her government's reckoning, has been explicitly or implicitly recognised by 61 countries. Austria therefore belongs to no alliance system but, unlike Switzerland, is a member of the United Nations.

The principal role of the *Bundesheer*, therefore, is to

Austria

defend Austrian neutrality which, it is recognised by ministerial resolution of May 11th, 1965, may be threatened in one or more of three ways: through an international crisis, such as that in Czechoslovakia in 1968 (*Krisenfall*); through a war between neighbouring States, when Austria might have to deny rights of passage to the combatants (*Neutralitätsfall*); through a direct attack on her territory (*Verteidigungsfall*). In the third, but not the other two cases, general mobilisation would be proclaimed, the fight would be opened as near the frontiers as possible and the aim would be to prevent at least the alpine area from falling to the aggressor.

Austria has, since 1960 (the Congo operation), also contributed contingents to United Nations peacekeeping forces. Because of her neutrality, this required a special law to be passed by the parliament; it provides for expeditions to be organised between the army and suitable volunteers from its ranks on a contractual basis.

Commitment
Austrian army and air units are committed wholly to defence of the national neutrality, on national soil, except for the volunteer battalions on United Nations duty.

Deployment
Until 1972, Austria was divided into three Group (*Gruppen*) zones: western, north-eastern and south-eastern, whose boundaries followed those of the appropriate States (*Länder*), each of which contained a reserve (*Landwehr*) brigade as well as regular formations; the latter were formed into 10 brigades, of which three were for training only. Under the reorganisation of 1972/3, the *Landwehr* brigades remain, but the regular formations are being reduced to six, organised into two divisions, each subordinate to a corps (*Korps*) headquarters, which replaces the group organisation. As the reorganisation is still in progress, clarity requires that both organisations should be given, and they are as follows.

Old Organisation
Gruppe I (HQ Vienna; Lower Austria and Burgenland): 1st Infantry Brigade; 3rd and 9th Armoured Brigades; 2nd (Training) Brigade; Vienna, Lower Austria and Burgenland *Landwehr* Brigades.
Gruppe II (HQ Graz; Styria and Carinthia): 5th and 7th Infantry Brigades; 10th (Training) Brigade; Styria and Carinthia *Landwehr* Brigades.
Gruppe III (Upper Austria, Salzburg, Tirol and Vorarlberg): 4th Armoured Brigade; 6th Infantry Brigade; 8th (Training) Brigade; Upper Austria, Tirol and Salzburg *Landwehr* Brigades.

New Organisation
I Korps (HQ Graz): Styria, Burgenland, Lower Austria and Vienna *Landwehr* Brigades.
II Korps (HQ Salzburg): Tirol, Carinthia, Upper Austria, Salzburg and Vorarlberg *Landwehr* Brigades. Between them these brigades are formed of 28 *Stammregimente*, which are training units. The organisation of the six regular brigades into divisions is still in progress, at present only 1st Panzergrenadier Divisions, of these is in existence.

Recent Operations
The Austrian army reckons its concentrations on the eastern frontier (*Grenzsicherungen*) during the Hungarian and Czech crises of 1956 and 1968 as operational experience; it also undertook disaster relief in the mountains during the great floods of 1965. Apart from the activities of its volunteer battalions with the United Nations Emergency Forces, it has seen no other active service. There are at present one infantry battalion in Cyprus and one in Syria.

ORGANISATION

Arms of Service
These are: *Panzertruppen* (armour), which includes armoured reconnaissance (*Panzeraufklärung*), *Infanterie* (*Panzergrenadier* – armoured infantry; *Jäger* – infantry; *Hochgebirgstruppen* – alpine infantry), *Artillerie*, *Fliegerabwehrartillerie* (air defence), *Pioniere* (engineers), *Telegraphentruppen* (signals), *Sanitätstruppen* (medical), *Militärseelsorgedienst* (chaplains), and *Versorgungstruppen*, which includes *Nachschub-Transport* (transport), *Intendanz* (supply) and *Instandsetzung* (repair and maintenance); the air force is collectively known as *Fliegertruppen* and forms an integral part of the army.

Operational
The Austrian operational organisation is based on the mechanised brigade, which consists of a headquarters (*Stab*) battalion, two artillery regiments and six combat battalions, of which three are tank (*Panzer*) and three mechanised infantry (*Panzergrenadier*). The infantry battalions have four companies, the tank and mechanised battalions three companies and the artillery regiments three batteries; in practice, each, since 1968, has been weaker than establishment by one company or battery. There are also signals, engineer, anti-tank and air-defence battalions (one of each).

There also exist a number of independent armoured, engineer, signal and service units.

The *Landwehr* (territorial reserve) is organised on the basis of frontier-defence (*Grenzschutz*) or local-defence (*Sicherungs*) companies, which are subordinate to regiments or independent battalions.

The regular brigades are formed from volunteers and conscripts on extended service; the *Mobile Landwehr* is formed from ordinary conscripts, led by regular officers and NCOs, and acts as a training organisation, but on mobilisation will in theory yield eight infantry brigades; the *Territoriale Landwehr* will be a reserve organisation of ex-conscripts, who will be liable for 60 days training spread over 13 years, and will form local defence units on mobilisation.

The air force, which forms part of the army and is largely regular, is organised into a flying (*Flieger*) and an air-defence (*Luftabwehr*) brigade. The former consists of a fighter–bomber wing (*Geschwader*) of three squadrons (*Staffeln*), a helicopter regiment of six squadrons (*Fliegerregiment 1*), and a training regiment (*Fliegerregiment 2*); the latter of three anti-aircraft gun battalions. There are air force bases at Langenlebarn, Linz, Zeltweg, Wiener Neustadt, Aigen im Ennstal and Graz-Thalerhof.

RECRUITMENT, TRAINING AND RESERVES

Recruitment
The original Armed Forces Law of 1955 made conscription universal and set the term of service at 9 months, but without provision for refresher training (a few days of reserve training were later instituted). Voluntary enlistment for longer periods, either in the officer or other ranks, was permitted. The new law of July 15th, 1971 reduced the period of conscription to 6 months, with liability for 60 days' refresher training in the *Landwehr* spread over 13 years. By volunteering to serve 8 months, conscripts can avoid refresher training (they thereby provide numbers for the regular formations); provision for voluntary regular enlistment remains.

Training
Training has hitherto taken place in the third training battalion of the regular brigades or in one of the three training

regiments (ex-brigades, Nos. 2 (Vienna), 8 (Salzburg) and 10 (Graz)). Henceforth it will take place in the appropriate provincial brigade of the *Mobile Landwehr*, to which conscripts will presumably continue to be drafted four times a year.

Regular officer training takes place at the *Maria Theresia Militär-Akademie* (founded 1752) at Wiener-Neustadt; the course lasts two years. The staff college (*Landesverteidigungsakademie*) is at Vienna; the course lasts 3 years.

Reserve officers have hitherto been trained in the *Einjährig-Freiwilligen-Kompanien* of the three training regiments, by volunteering to serve a full year of conscript duty. The new law perpetuates this system. But it is freely admitted that the system is imperfect, and that an adequate supply of reserve officers and NCOs may not be forthcoming.

Reserves

The Austrian system has consistently produced larger numbers of trained specialists than the reserve organisation can usefully employ, but insufficient infantrymen – the result of maintaining a standing force of all arms but a *Landwehr* of lightly equipped home-guard companies. Refresher training has, in consequence, been unpopular. The new system, which will train most conscripts as infantrymen, will rectify the imbalance, but it will leave the regular (*Bereitschaft*) brigades without a mobilisable reserve, and exaggerate the infantry character of the *Landwehr*, which will have an effective strength of about 120,000. Refresher training will be done in six periods of 10 days, either in the conscript's original *Mobile Landwehr* unit, which has a cadre of regular officers and NCOs, or in a company of the *Territoriale Landwehr*, which has none.

EQUIPMENT AND ARMS INDUSTRY

In imperial days, the Austrian arms industry, based on the Skoda works in what is now Czechoslovakia, was one of the most important in Europe; the state was self-sufficient in arms and exported heavy artillery and small arms. Of this industry, the Steyr combine (now Steyr–Daimler–Puch) remains, and, with VOEST, Linz, produces small arms and light armoured vehicles – though most of the production is of foreign models made under licence. The majority of Austrian heavy equipment is imported.

Pistol: Walther P38 9mm
Sub-machine-gun: MP-69 9mm (Steyr design and manufacture)
Rifle: StG-58 (Steyr version of 7.62mm FN)
Machine-gun: MG-42 7.62mm (Germany)
Heavy-machine-gun: M-2 0.5in (US)
Mortar: L-16A1 81mm (Great Britain; 300 in service), M-2 107mm (US; 100 in service) and M-30 120mm (USSR, Austrian built; 88 in service)
Anti-armour weapons: 74mm Miniman rocket-launcher (Sweden) and 66mm LAW rocket-launcher (US); 84mm Carl Gustav recoilless weapon (Sweden) and M-40 recoilless rifle (US; equips the anti-tank company of the infantry brigade and the anti-tank platoon of the infantry battalion); 85mm M-52 gun (Czechoslovakia; 240 in service; equips the *Landwehr* anti-tanks units)
Anti-aircraft weapons: M-58 20mm Oerlikon gun and M-65 35mm Oerlikon gun (Switzerland; equip the anti-aircraft batteries of the infantry brigades/battalions); M-42 40mm SP gun (US; equips the anti-aircraft batteries of the *Panzergrenadier* brigades); 55/57 40mm Bofors gun (Sweden; 59 in service equipping the anti-aircraft units of the *Landwehr*)

Artillery: M-42 105mm howitzer and M-1 155mm howitzer and some other artillery in the *Landwehr*; M-109 SP howitzer (US; 38 in service equipping the artillery of the *Panzergrenadier* brigade)
Armour: *Kürassier* tank-destroyer (153 in service; a marriage of the French AMX-13 turret with 105mm gun and the Austrian Saurer APC chassis; equips the anti-tank battalions); Saurer 4K4F APC (Steyr–Puch–Daimler, Saurer-Werke, Vienna; 470 in service; 60km/h; crew 10; equips the *Panzergrenadier* battalions); M-60 tanks (US; 170 in service equipping the *Panzer* battalions).
Aircraft: Saab 1050E fighter–bomber (Sweden; 38 in service equipping the fighter–bomber squadrons); Alouette II/III helicopters (France; 25 in service); Augusta-Bell 204 and 206 helicopters (US; 36 in service)

RANK, DRESS AND DISTINCTIONS

Austria preserves her traditional titles of rank, several of which have counterparts in no other army (though the delightful imperial oddity, *Feldmarschalleutnant* (major-general), has disappeared).

*General** (Major-General) – Three stars in a wreath
*Brigadier** (Brigadier) – One star in a wreath
Oberst (Colonel) – Three stars on gold patch
Oberstleutnant (Lieutenant-Colonel) – Two stars on gold patch
Major (Major) – One star on gold patch
Hauptmann† (Captain) – Three stars
Oberleutnant (Lieutenant) – Two stars
Leutnant (2nd Lieutenant) – One star

Fähnrich (Officer-Cadet) – One star over broad and narrow stripe
Vizeleutnant – One star over broad stripe
Offiziersstellvertreter – Three stars over two narrow stripes
Oberstabswachtmeister – Two stars over two narrow stripes
Stabswachtmeister – One star over two narrow stripes
Oberwachtmeister – Two stars over one narrow stripe
Wachtmeister – One star over one narrow stripe
Zugsführer – Three stars
Korporal – Two stars
Gefreiter – One star

Notes:
* the Austrians consider that these ranks equate with higher ones in foreign armies, that *General* (*der Infanterie*, etc.) is a full general, *Brigadier* a major-general and the senior *Oberst* a brigadier;
† *Rittmeister* in the armoured formations; the multiplicity of NCO ranks makes them difficult to equate with British or American: *Vizeleutnant* is a senior warrant officer, *Zugsführer* or *Wachtmeister* a sergeant, *Gefreiter* a lance-corporal. Badges of rank are worn on a collar-patch.

Austrian officers wear a grey service dress similar to the West German *Bundeswehr*'s. The combat dress is mottled camouflage suiting, worn with the NATO helmet or a ski cap.

CURRENT DEVELOPMENTS

The Austrian army is still in a state of flux. The failure to fully implement the reorganisation announced in 1973 has two root causes: (1) a shortage of funds – Austria spends less than 1% of GNP on defence and is reluctant to spend more because the necessary expenditure, for extra and more modern equipment, would have to be spent abroad; (2) an originally over-ambitious defence structure. Hindsight suggests that it would have been more sensible to have settled at the outset for a militia of the Swiss type, basing it perhaps on the traditions of the old *Tiroler Kaiserjäger*, which would have helped to commend militia service to the population (it is significant that the French *Chasseurs Alpins* and West German *Gebirgsjäger*, comparable organisations, are oversubscribed among the conscripts). The decision to organise instead a conventional, balanced all-arms force was understandable, in view of the imperial military tradition and of the apparent threat of invasion from across the eastern border, but it has resulted in an under-equipped and skeleton army and in the overproduction of specialists for whom no useful reserve employment can be found. The new army, consisting of a small regular combat force, a larger conscript militia and a reserve force of home guard companies is probably, as the high command argues, 'more in conformity with national requirements'. The main requirement is not to assure the defence of the country's frontiers, for given Austria's location, shape and size, the frontiers are indefensible against a superior aggressor; rather it is to organise the Austrian national will to defend her neutrality, even if in a hopeless battle, so that an aggressor will choose to avoid, rather than violate, her territory. But it will take some years before transition to the new organisation is complete.

John Keegan

BAHRAIN

HISTORY AND INTRODUCTION

See the entry under United Arab Emirates for the history of all the Trucial States of the Gulf until 1971.

Since Bahrain gained independence in 1971, it has led a fairly untroubled existence. The one external security threat, a long-standing Iranian claim to the island which had been revived when Britain announced its departure from the Gulf, was quietly dropped by Iran after a referendum in 1970 over-whelmingly rejected union with Iran.

The ruling family, the al-Khalifas, have controlled Bahrain, with one brief interruption, since 1783, and the ramifications of kinship connections create a direct loyalty in most other leading families of the State. In a gesture towards establishing representative institutions for his increasingly sophisticated population, the Ruler held elections in December, 1972 for a constituent assembly, and a national assembly convened the next year in accordance with the provisions of the new Constitution. It was dissolved in August, 1975 however and various 'leftists' were arrested. There was very little popular reaction, and many of the so-called 'leftists' would not merit that description in most other parts of the world.

Strength and Budget
Total armed forces are 2300, all of them army. The defence budget in 1981 was $135,000,000, a small proportion of the GNP of $2,210,000,000. The population of Bahrain is 400,000.

Command and Constitutional Status
The Commander-in-Chief is the Ruler, Shaikh Isa bin Sulman al-Khalifa, KCMG. The Minister of Defence is Shaikh Hamad bin Isa al-Khalifa.

Role, Commitment, Deployment and Recent Operations
The role of the army is solely internal security, in which it is assisted (or, at need, balanced) by the police force. It has no foreign commitments, no deployment abroad and no combat record.

The principal internal security threat to Bahrain is the large resident Iranian community, amounting to over half the total population, which is commercially prominent but almost totally excluded from the political/military power structure. The Ruler might find it difficult to retain control of some quarters of the capital city in the event of disturbances without Saudi help (which would undoubtedly be forth-coming). The real anxiety of the government, whether realistic or not, is that trouble with the Iranian community might cause or provide a pretext for an intervention by Iran.

Bahrain's only territorial dispute is with Qatar, which dis-putes Bahrain's right to the island of Huwar off the Qatari coast. The island is important because it affects the demarca-tion of territorial waters between the two States, and hence of possible sea-bed oil reserves.

Bahrain generally enjoys Saudi Arabian support in this dispute, and also depends on Saudi forces as a final reserve in case of trouble with the Iranian community. For this reason Bahrain has permitted Saudi Arabia to establish a major airbase at an old RAF airstrip south of the Awali—Zalaq road. The base, which is expected to become operational during 1978, has barracks, housing for Saudi air force officers and aircraft hangars, and will initially accommodate about 25 aircraft. It is Saudi Arabia's first military establishment beyond its own borders, and is integrated into the Saudi air-defence system.

At the time of the British withdrawal from the Gulf in the late 1960s, Bahrain offered the use of the base there to the United States navy instead. Limited American use of the base did follow, but following the 1973 Yom Kippur war the government asked the USA to vacate it. The agreement providing the United States Seventh Fleet with permanent port facilities for $4,000,000 per year was terminated (by common consent) in June, 1977, but the United States Department of Defense continues to run a naval school in Bahrain, and United States navy ships continue to make use of the port facilities on an *ad hoc* basis about as frequently as before.

Organisation

Arms of Service
The army consists of an infantry battalion, an armoured car squadron, an artillery battery and an air wing. There is also a coastguard.

Operational
Unknown.

RECRUITMENT, TRAINING AND RESERVES

There are some foreign officers on contract. The Iranian population is not significantly represented in the armed forces. There are no reserves.

EQUIPMENT AND ARMS INDUSTRY

The army has eight Saladin armoured cars, eight Ferret scout cars, 110 M-113 armoured personnel carriers and 20 AML 90 armoured cars. Its fire support consists of eight 105mm light guns, Mobat 120mm RCLs and six 81mm mortars.

Rank, Dress and Distinctions
Rank structure and uniforms are similar to those in the other Gulf Shaikhdoms.

CURRENT DEVELOPMENTS

See comments under same section of the entry on United Arab Emirates, which are also largely applicable to Bahrain.

Gwynne Dyer

BANGLADESH*

HISTORY AND INTRODUCTION

Bangladesh was born amidst vast carnage that exterminated a substantial proportion of the country's scanty educated *élite*. It is the large country of the world which stands closest to the Malthusian abyss, and a large body of opinion suspects that it may stand even closer to a political catastrophe of unparalleled scope. After less than 3 years of independence its civilian political institutions collapsed in ignominy and bloodshed, and only the army, itself a highly unstable organisation, now remains to defend the existing order.

At independence in 1971 Bangladesh was about the poorest country in the world. Literacy was less than 20%, one-quarter of all children died before the age of five, and over half of all families consumed less than the minimum acceptable daily intake of calories. The situation has since got worse, with food consumption continuing to decline, cloth consumption amounting to about one simple loin-cloth per person per year, and per capita income at the al-most meaningless level of $75.

The country is still only beginning the process of urbanisation, although the proportion of landless labourers in the countryside has risen to about 40%, and average farm size is 2 acres. Almost the entire country is a flat, fertile plain, much of it waterlogged for a large part of the year, but the population of 83,000,000 already creates a quite extraordinary pressure on the sole large economic resource: agriculture. The population is expected to double by the end of the century.

There are a few other areas of the world in almost as desperate an economic situation — some lie just across the Indian border, in West Bengal and Bihar provinces — but none so extensive, nor any which encompass an entire country. The creation of Bangladesh, a deprived agricultural area virtually bereft of any alternative resources, owes nothing to economic logic and everything to politics — in particular to communal politics based on religious divisions.

The emergence of a separate Muslim community within Bengal dates from the waves of conversion in the thirteenth and subsequent centuries, and by the period of British rule about two-thirds of the population in the eastern divisions of Bengal had long been Muslim, but they had never sought or achieved a political expression of their identity. As British rule approached its end, however, Bengali Muslims began to link up with those elsewhere in India, as the best strategy for opposing Hindu domination, although the Muslim League only replaced a local and quite separate party as the principal Muslim political party in Bengal in the early 1940s. From 1943, there was a Muslim League ministry in the province, and a rapid conversion of Muslims in Bengal (albeit even later than elsewhere) to the idea of Pakistan. (For details of the partition struggle, and the division of the old Indian Army between India and Pakistan, see the entries for those countries.)

In 1947 East Bengal became one of the five provinces of the new State of Pakistan, though it was more numerous than all the rest put together. From the beginning, however, there were immense differences between the two wings of the country. The traditions, customs, language and even the

appearance of Bengalis were greatly different from those of West Pakistanis, and the two wings were not complementary in their economies. West Pakistan ended up almost entirely Muslim after the mutual massacres in the partitioned Punjab in 1947; East Bengal, where such communal slaughter did not occur, retained a 13% Hindu minority.

Tensions and misunderstandings were inevitable in such a relationship, especially when the two halves of the country were separated by a thousand miles of fundamentally hostile India. They were, however, greatly exacerbated by the fact that virtually the entire leadership cadre of the new State was located in the West, and operated, consciously or otherwise, with Western perspectives.

All the cities which were successively the capitals of united Pakistan (Karachi, Lahore and Islamabad) were located in the West, and the far superior educational levels of the Punjabis in particular guaranteed Western dominance in the federal civil service. Indeed, by 1948 an influx of Punjabi officials and merchants was already making its presence felt and resented in the East. Similarly, the army which Pakistan inherited from the Indian Empire was comprised almost exclusively of Punjabis and Pathans from the West wing, due to the recruitment patterns of its predecessor. Although the East Bengal Regiment (infantry) was subsequently raised in the Eastern wing, and limited numbers of Bengalis also joined other arms and services, the army remained overwhelmingly West Pakistani in its personnel and orientations down to the end of united Pakistan in 1971. Its Western perspectives were accentuated by the fact that the 1947 and 1965 wars with India over Kashmir were fought exclusively on the West Pakstani border, and little attention was given to the defence of the Eastern wing. From 1958, when the army seized power in Pakistan, this meant that all political decisions in the country were also being taken by West Pakistanis.

Even before that, the political domination of West Pakistan had begun to rouse powerful resentments in Bengal. As early as March, 1948 Muhammad Ali Jinnah, Pakistan's first leader, declared Urdu to be the country's official language (though widely spoken by the educated Muslims of northern India, it was spoken by less than 1% of East Pakistan's population). The making of a constitution for Pakistan was delayed for most of a decade, contributing greatly to the discrediting of parliamentary democracy in the country, because of the determination of West Pakistanis that East Pakistan, though containing the majority of the population, should not be able to translate that directly into political power through the electoral system.

In 1958, the army seized power under General Ayub Khan, and East Pakistanis lost almost all political voice in federal affairs. Shortly afterwards Ayub dismissed his first choice as military governor in the East, General Azam Khan, who had enjoyed a certain local popularity, and from then almost to the end East Bengalis enjoyed very little voice in their own provincial affairs either. Amongst younger educated Bengalis resentment grew steadily against their effective exclusion from participation in federal politics, at what they saw as a gross imbalance between East and West in recruiting for the army and civil service, and against non-Bengali domination in commerce even in the East. There was massive vote-rigging in the East in 1965 when Ayub Khan had him-

*See also Appendix 2.

self re-elected President, and in the war with India later that year East Pakistan was practically denuded of troops and left to rely on the Chinese deterrent for protection.

From almost the start of the protests in the East against the privileged position of the Urdu language, the leader of the dissidents was Sheikh Mujibur Rahman, a man of extremely modest administrative talents but possessed of a brilliant flair for mass politics. He was imprisoned by the central government when direct rule was imposed in the East in 1954, on the grounds that he was a secessionist, though at that time and for long after his actual programme was merely one of limiting federal power strictly to defence and foreign affairs, with the retention by each wing of its own economic resources.

Mujib was subsequently released from prison and founded the Awami (People's) League to further his cause, but is growing popularity caused Ayub Khan to imprison him again in 1966. Anti-federal and outright secessionist sentiment in East Pakistan, though forced underground by Ayub's dictatorial rule, continued to gain strength, and burst into the open shortly after he was forced to resign in February, 1969. (Indeed, riots in the East played a large role in unseating him, though the various grievances of West Pakistanis probably played a more effective role.) General Yahya Khan succeeded him as interim President, with a commitment to return the country to democratic rule, and in the elections of December, 1970 Sheikh Mujib's Awami League won an overwhelming victory in the East, taking 160 of its 162 seats in the federal parliament.

The new constitution provided for representation by population, so Mujib's victory gave him an overall majority in the National Assembly, and with it the right to become Prime Minister and implement his sweeping programme of reform leading to a far looser federal system. West Pakistanis reacted with horror, and Mr. Zulfikar Ali Bhutto, whose Pakistan People's Party had enjoyed almost as complete a victory in the Western wing, refused to participate in the new parliament unless Mujib drastically modified his proposals. Mujib refused, and General Yahya Khan, with Bhutto's encouragement, thereupon refused to summon the parliament until he gave way. At the beginning of March, 1971 negotiations broke down, and on the 10th the Awami League forced the issue by staging a *de facto* seizure of power in East Pakistan after a general strike by the police and civil service. General Yahya's government responded by sending three more Pakistan army divisions by sea to reinforce the single division permanently stationed in the East, a large part of whose personnel were Bengalis.

An officer of that division, Ziaur Rahman, was the first to rise in open revolt and proclaim the independence of Bangladesh at Chittagong on March 15th, 1971. Mujib was arrested at once and taken to West Pakistan, and the majority of Bengali officers and men in the Pakistan army, some 28,000 men, were disarmed and similarly interned in the Western wing. General Niazi, the Pakistani commander in the East, rapidly regained control of all major centres, but with only some 80,000 troops (more could not be sent, because Islamabad had to retain them for the defence of the West in case the crisis led to war with India) he was unable to suppress completely the guerrilla resistance that sprang up all over the country.

The campaign of repression quickly developed into an army-led pogrom which seemed to be aimed at eliminating virtually the entire educated Bengali *élite*. Niazi also recruited some 20,000 irregulars, the so-called 'Razakars', from the loyal, non-Bengali-speaking Bihari community which had emigrated from eastern parts of India in 1947, and this force was responsible for some of the most hideous

massacres, particularly directed at the 9,000,000-strong Hindu minority. In the civil war which raged in East Pakistan between March and December, 1971 somewhere between 300,000 and 1,500,000 people were slaughtered, almost all of them Bengali-speakers and a very large proportion of them Hindus. By November about 10,000,000 refugees, including almost half the Hindus and amounting to one-seventh of the entire population, had fled across the border into India, where they continued to die amidst appalling conditions in the refugee camps that were hastily set up there.

The revolt's only hope for success from the first had been Indian intervention, but New Delhi prepared the ground carefully before acting. It encouraged the formation of guerrilla groups from amongst the refugees, the largest of them being the Mukhti Bahini, loyal to Mujib, and by the summer was arming them and sending them back across the frontier to harry the Pakistan army on a large scale, but the first tentative border crossings by the Indian army did not occur until late October. Indian forces were gradually built up on East Pakistan's frontiers, and finally, on December 4th, India struck with about eight divisions accompanied by some 50,000 Mukhti Bahini.

The fighting in the East lasted only 13 days, at the end of which all Pakistani forces there laid down their arms. There was also extensive fighting on the West Pakistan border, but Islamabad, faced with the impending transfer westward of the Indian forces that had been used in Bengal, accepted a ceasefire a day later. The People's Republic of Bangladesh was formally proclaimed (as a secular, not an Islamic, State), and rapidly received international recognition. (For further details on the 1971 war and the Mukhti Bahini's role, *see* Role, Commitment, Deployment and Recent Operations.)

Sheikh Mujib was released by Pakistan in January, 1972 and returned as a national hero and 'Father of the Nation' to become Bangladesh's first Prime Minister. He inherited an immensely difficult situation, with the economy devastated, a large part of the Bengali administrative class exterminated (about 60% of the police force had been killed, for example), and the country flooded with weapons held by guerrilla groups that were often reluctant to disband. Despite his popularity he also had a hidden handicap that was to grow more visible with the passage of time: he was 'India's man', in a deeply Muslim country which had used New Delhi's support to gain its independence, but did not on the whole harbour tender sentiments towards its giant neighbour. When all charitable allowances have been made, however, Mujib did everything imaginable to make the situation even worse.

It proved quite impossible to establish order in the country under Mujib. The Mukhti Bahini itself was integrated into the army, demobilised, or transformed into a territorial force trained by the regular army, but in several areas of Bangladesh wartime guerrilla leaders refused to relinquish their weapons and reigned as local warlords. A notable example was the force led by Kader 'Tiger' Siddiqi, a former student and a supporter of Mujib, who controlled the entire Tergail district with his troops until 1975. There was sporadic terrorism from right-wing Islamic and pro-Pakistan groups, from the pro-Chinese wing of the National Awami Party, and from Maoists allied to the Naxalites of West Bengal.

Most important of all, as it turned out, was the defection of the radical wing of the Awami League in 1972 and its reconstitution as the Jatyo Sanajtantrik Dal (JSD), which translates into English, rather unfortunately, as the National Socialist Party. It espoused an extreme version of social revolution, seeking the creation of a proletarian government based on 'the unity of the revolutionary soldiers, peasants, workers and students' which, in the view of many of its adherents, must be preceded by the wholesale massacre of the privileged educated classes. The JSD is rabidly anti-Indian, expects New Delhi to intervene against its revolution when it occurs, and believes that the best defence would be a 'people's army' based on local resistance. Even before it was forced underground in 1974, it had begun to pursue the strategy of creating its own clandestine People's Revolutionary Army (PRA) actually within the enlisted ranks of the regular Bangladesh army. The PRA was under the secret leadership of Colonel Abu Taher, a one-legged hero of the independence war who had been dismissed from the army in 1972 for his 'people's army' approach and his criticisms of Mujib.

Quite apart from the spreading subversion within its ranks, the full extent of which did not become evident until late 1975, the Bangladesh army suffered grieviously from dissension within its officer corps. The root cause was the fact that the bulk of Bangladesh's potential regular army, the former Pakistan army regulars of Bengali origin, spent the first 2 years of independence imprisoned in former West Pakistan. In the meantime Bangladesh's army was created out of those former regulars who had evaded capture, plus a larger proportion of Mukhti Bahini fighters. The choice of who was to be incorporated into the army, and in what rank, was heavily influenced by the question of loyalty to Mujib and the Awami League (whence, probably, the PRA gained its initial secret adherents in the army after it split from the Awami League in 1972). When the 28,000 Bengali regular officers and soldiers returned from captivity in Pakistan in early 1974, they were generally forced to take posts and ranks beneath those who had previously been junior to them. Three full battalions of the East Bengal Regiment, one of the best in the Pakistan army, returned intact, but were deliberately split up and dispersed throughout the army. This 'freedom fighters' versus 'repatriates' conflict bedevils Bangladesh to this day.

In part it was merely defensive tactics on the part of those who were already enjoying the fruits of office, but there was unquestionably also a certain Indian influence at work. Both Mujib and his Indian patrons suspected that these returnees might be more sympathetic to Pakistan and Islam, and rather less enthusiastic about Bangladesh's status as an Indo–Soviet client, than they were themselves. Exactly the same form of discrimination was applied against Bengali civil servants who had served in the West before 1971, and who were now left out in the cold by Mujib, although their exclusion effectively deprived the country of half its scanty surviving supply of experienced administrators. Not only did this policy create a severe problem of factionalism within the army officer corps; in the way of such things, it operated as a self-fulfilling prophecy, guaranteeing that those falling under suspicion would nourish a bitter resentment against Mujib and his Indian protectors.

They were by no means alone in Bangladesh in displaying a rapid growth of anti-Indian feeling, for as Mujib's initial popularity in the country melted away in consequence of his corruption, autocratic methods and economic failure, he turned increasingly to India and its Soviet near-ally for support. The final Indian army withdrawal from Bangladesh began in March, 1972 and Mujib was confirmed as Prime Minister by a sweeping majority exactly a year later, but he never quite let go of the Indo–Soviet lifeline. He damned himself forever in the eyes of many Bengali nationalists by signing the Indo–Bangladesh Friendship Treaty of 1972, which allowed the Dacca government to call on Indian aid in the event of internal disturbances.

Indian army officers were employed as training advisers to his brutal party militia, the Rakkhi Bahini, at its main camp at Savar outside Dacca. The Soviet Union, the first major power to recognise Bangladesh after the war, sent advisers and aid, including some weapons; it also sent some 20 vessels under a Soviet Rear-Admiral to clear Chittagong port. (They managed to spin it out until they were expelled after the August, 1975 revolt, thus setting the record for the world's longest minesweeping operation.) Nationalist Bengalis began to see their country as less than fully independent, and much of army opinion, the extreme revolutionary left, the middle classes and the fundamentalist Islamic right, began to unite in opposition to Mujib and the Indo–Soviet link. Other factors contributing to this perception included the government's agreement to let India construct the Farakka barrage across the Ganges river just above Bangladesh's border (because of its potentionally serious effects on agriculture in the country's western regions, Pakistan had never allowed this pre-1971), the failure of India to return most of the weapons of the four Pakistani divisions that were captured in the East in 1971, and the large role of Mujib's close political associates in the rackets smuggling rice and jute into India, which brought the economy to the brink of total collapse.

As opposition mounted, Mujib defensively tied himself even closer to India and the Soviet Union. In October, 1973 the Awami League formed an alliance with the pro-Soviet wing of the National Awami Party and with the pro-Moscow Communist Party in a joint programme to 'suppress terrorism', and the role of the Rakkhi Bahini was expanded. Following floods and widespread famine the Government declared a state of emergency in December, 1974 and suspended all constitutional rights. At the end of January, 1975 the Awami League-dominated parliament adopted a new constitution replacing the parliamentary with the presidential form of government: Mujib became President, with absolute powers, and created a one-party State by expanding his own organisations to embrace his pro-Soviet allies in the Bangladesh Peasants' and Workers' Awami League and banning all other parties.

By now the price of rice had increased 400% since 1971, corruption continued to flourish, and popular antipathy to the government and anti-Indian feeling were rising rapidly. Moreover, Mujib had good reason to suspect that he had lost the support of the army, infiltrated at the bottom by the PRA and increasingly pervaded by anti-Mujib sentiments within the officer corps as the 'returnees' struggled to displace his own privileged appointees and supporters. In the spring of 1975 he took his final and fatal decision: to expand his own Rakkhi Bahini into a force which could overawe the army.

In July of 1975 this paramilitary party army numbered 25,000 men (against 55,000 in the regular armed forces), but it had already been enjoying priority in the acquisition of new arms for some time. By Mujib's decisions at that time, however, the armed forces were to be held to their existing strength, while the Rakkhi Bahini would be expanded to 130,000 men, with a brigade positioned in each of Bangladesh's 19 districts, and would receive almost all new equipment purchases for the foreseeable future. In view of the embarrassment caused by the Indian army's training mission it was decided that in future Rakkhi Bahini officers would receive their training in India, and in July a special Indian air force aircraft flew the first 100 cadets off to undergo a year-long course at Dehra Dun, India's military academy. But by simultaneously challenging the army's role and underlining his own status as an Indian puppet, Mujib had signed his death warrant.

On August 15th, 1975 a colonel and six majors from the regular army surrounded the Presidential compound in Dacca with about 200 soldiers and proceeded to massacre Mujib, his entire family (except two daughters then abroad in West Germany) and all his household staff. Elsewhere in Dacca several others of his relatives were murdered. Perhaps by prior arrangement, the rebel officers proclaimed Mujib's Commerce Minister, Khondakar Mushtaq Ahmed, as the new President, and took up residence in the Presidential palace with him in order to retain direct control of the government. The army high command evidently had no previous knowledge of the coup, but in order to preserve discipline it at once declared its loyalty to the new President. (Most senior officers were relieved to be rid of Mujib, and approved of the majors' anti-Indian, anti-Soviet attitudes, though they did force one of the leaders, Major Dalim, to retract his initial declaration of an Islamic Republic in Bangladesh.)

The new regime's first measures won it the favour of most of the army, the extreme left, and the Islamic right alike. Senior Awami League politicians who had been too closely associated with Mujib were imprisoned and the hated Rakkhi Bahini was disbanded (though elements of it secretly survive). President Ahmed promised to rescind the ban on other political parties in exactly 1 year's time, and to hold elections at the end of February, 1977. For the moment, he also managed to contain the tensions in the army between the returnees and the civil war veterans, though the young majors rapidly set about promoting their own friends and supporters, and Mujib's appointees clearly had reason to fear for their positions in the future. In any case, there was little the army high command or anyone else could do at the time, for the rebel officers were from the army's only two armoured regiments, and their tanks were all over the capital.

In foreign affairs, Bangladesh carried out a rapid and almost total reversal of alliances, to the general approval of the great majority of the population. Pakistan, which had formally recognised Bangladesh in 1974 but had kept its distance from what it saw as an Indian satellite, opened diplomatic relations with Dacca in October, and soon all sorts of closer links, especially in trade, were being discussed. China, who had hitherto withheld recognition for the same reason, instantly recognised the new government in August, 1975 and exchanged ambassadors with Bangladesh in October. Relations were also established for the first time with a number of conservative and oil-rich Arab countries, especially Saudi Arabia, through the mediation of Pakistan's Prime Minister Bhutto.

The Indians and Russians withdrew to the security of their embassies and awaited events, while a thick frost settled on relations between Dacca and its former patrons. But the situation was inherently unstable, with the army riven by factions, numbers of formerly pro-Indian officers fearing for their careers, and even perhaps their lives, the political scene littered with secret and often well-armed revolutionary groups, and a handful of inexperienced and rather isolated junior officers in charge. The inevitable counter-coup came on November 3rd, 1975. As expected, it was led by the late Mujib's pro-Indian former protégés within the officer corps.

According to some reports, the coup was triggered by the murder of Mujib's surviving cabinet colleagues in Dacca jail on the order of the ruling group of majors, which led former Mujib supporters in the army to act while they still could. The extent to which India was informed of the plot in advance, if at all, is not known, though there were unconfirmed reports at the time that five Indian divisions were mobilised on Bangladesh's frontiers to go to its aid if necessary. The coup was led by the Deputy Chief of the Army General Staff, Brigadier Khalid Musharaf, an officer of known pro-Indian sentiments who had commanded the Mukhti Bahini units in the Comilla sector during the independence war. He surrounded President Ahmed's residence with troops and forced his resignation; the young majors were sent into exile to Bangkok (whence they moved to Libya), and the Army Chief of Staff, General Zia Rahman, a war hero renowned for his vehement anti-Indian opinions, was placed under arrest. Musharaf appointed himself Army Chief of Staff in Zia's place, had the Chief Justice of the Supreme Court, Abusadat Muhammad Sayem, sworn in as President on November 6th, and proclaimed the rehabilitation of the late Mujib as Father of the Nation.

Given the almost universally anti-Indian opinions of all significant political groups in Bangladesh, and the fear that Musharaf would invoke the Indo–Bangladesh Friendship Treaty and call in the Indian army to secure his position, the counter-coup was bound to meet with widespread popular resistance. Given also the fact that the advantage in numbers within the army already lay by 1975 with those who had left the Pakistan army peacefully, rather than with the war veterans, it was almost certainly foredoomed. But the manner in which it was undone came as a great shock: the coup was destroyed by a mutiny of the army's rank and file which represented perhaps the most significant challenge to the subcontinent's established social order since the Sepoy Mutiny of 1857, and came within a hair's breadth of success in its goal of total revolution.

The PRA, the military wing of the JSD, has since claimed the support of 70% of the enlisted men in Bangladesh's army: the events of November 7th–11th, 1975 demonstrated that this claim, if somewhat exaggerated, contains a considerable element of truth. As soon as Musharaf's coup occurred, the JSD leadership set its PRA cadres within the army into motion, distributing leaflets in the military cantonments on November 5th and 6th urging the private soldiers to attack their officers and overthrow the intriguers who had seized power. The mutiny it unleashed was to be aimed not just at removing the pro-Indian Khalid Musharaf, but at creating a general uprising against 'the bourgeois upper echelons of the officer corps and the bourgeoisie itself'.

The mutinies that broke out in army garrisons throughout the country on November 7th were only partly under JSD–PRA control, with many other soldiers just reacting to Islamic nationalism and anti-Indian fears. The Dacca Brigade's enlisted men were, however, largely under the control of Colonel Abu Taher, the head of the PRA, who emerged from hiding to lead their mutiny. Between 40 and 60 officers were massacred in Dacca alone (2–3% of the entire officer corps), and General Khalid Musharaf and his aides were killed by a PRA group while fleeing towards the airport. Colonel Abu Taher released General Zia Rahman, reinstated him as Army Chief of Staff, and presented him with the PRA's 'Twelve Demands' for wholesale revolutionary change within the army.

The first Demand, addressed to Zia himself, read: 'Our revolution is not for changing leadership only. This revolution is only for the interest of the poorer class. We have accepted you as our leader in this revolution. For that reason, you are to express very clearly that you are the leader of the poorer class. And for that, you are to change the structure of the armed forces.' Amongst the changes demanded to achieve the transformation from the 'army of the rich' to the 'army of the poor' were the abolition of all officer–man distinctions, and the creation of a rankless army on what the JSD imagines to be the Chinese pattern.

General Zia temporised, and was aided by the fact that most units outside Dacca were content to stop with overthrowing Khalid Musharaf. As Colonel Abu Taher himself admitted, given the short time available, the PRA had been unable to take control of the mutiny in most units. By November 9th Zia felt confident enough to ban a JSD rally in Dacca, and Taher went underground again. Two days later Zia made a nationwide speech condemning those who had tried to use his name 'for certain purposes', and making clear that his break with the JSD was complete. He succeeded, by the skin of his teeth, in re-establishing a semblance of central control over the army, but the educated and privileged minority which corporately runs Bangladesh had had a horrifying glimpse of the 'pit that lies only inches beneath the seemingly solid ground under their feet'.

Since November, 1975 there has been no surviving real possibility of a pro-Indian reversal in Bangladesh's internal politics, but the process of re-establishing discipline within the army, the only remaining pillar of authority in the country, has been delicate, difficult and even now is by no means certain of success. In the aftermath of the November events Abusadat Muhammad Sayem was left as President, with real power lying in the hands of the three service chiefs as Deputy Chief Martial Law Administrators: Zia for the army, Commodore Musharaf Hussain Khan for the navy, and Air Vice-Marshal M. G. Tawab for the air force. Zia from the first was *primus inter pares*, but his colleagues were equally anti-Indian: A. V. M. Tawab once described himself as being 'obsessed' with Indian interference in Bangladesh politics.

The most urgent priority was that of re-establishing the chain of command within the officer corps, and reasserting officers' authority over the private soldiers who had tasted power in November, 1975. The first few months were studded with recurrent abortive coups from within the faction-ridden officer corps, which included such bizarre events as a group of junior officers locking themselves inside their tanks and charging across the Dacca cantonment in an attempt to overthrow Zia. In the crisis of December 23rd, however, the army commander succeeded in forcing the withdrawal of the tanks which had ringed Dacca since Mujib's death to their depot at Bogra, 100 miles and several river crossings away.

General Zia Rahman's showdown with his rebellious junior officers came in April, 1976 when four of the majors who had led the original coup against Mujib suddenly returned from their Libyan exile and joined their comrades at the armoured depot at Bogra. With the support of Air Vice-Marshal Tawab, they demanded a share of political power and the transformation of Bangladesh into an Islamic republic. The officers of the two armoured regiments, the Bengal Lancers and the 1st Bengal Cavalry, mutinied when ordered to surrender the returned exiles, but General Zia succeeded in re-establishing control over the units in early May.

Air Vice-Marshal Tawab was dismissed, and the Bengal Lancers, the more deeply implicated unit, was disbanded and about half its 500 members brought up on disciplinary charges. General Zia was able to force the rebel officers to return to exile, but in July felt it necessary to give all but two of the 13 exiles diplomatic posts abroad in recognition of the continuing strength of their supporters within the army.

STRENGTH AND BUDGET

The Bangladesh army numbers 70,000 men, and also has under its command a paramilitary border security force of 30,000 men known as the Bangladesh Rifles. The navy has approximately 4000 men, and the air force 3000. The total armed forces strength of 71,000 represents a 270% increase since 1974, which mainly reflects the incorporation of ex-Pakistan army returnees since that time. The population of Bangladesh is 93,000,000, GNP about $10,400,000,000 (1980).

The estimated defence expenditure for 1980 was $153,000,000, a startling 200% increase over the 1975–6 defence budget, but it may well be that Bangladesh deliberately understated earlier expenditure. There are those who suspect that Bangladesh finds it more tactful to understate its defence expenses in view of its extremely high dependence on foreign aid and the possible adverse impression that the inflation of arms expenditure would create amongst the donors.

COMMAND AND CONSTITUTIONAL STATUS

The three services are commanded by their respective chiefs of staff, who are nominally co-equal, but in fact the Army Chief of Staff invariably and inevitably predominates because of his service's preponderant size. Under the martial law which has prevailed since 1975, the three chiefs of staff were theoretically all equal deputies to the President, who was Chief Martial Law Administrator. In November, 1976 however, the President transferred that office to the Army Chief of Staff, leaving himself only the ceremonial functions of civilian head of state, and effectively placing the other service chiefs in a subordinate position. This was largely cosmetic, as in fact the army commander had been ruling the country ever since late 1975. The true political situation was recognised in the presidential elections of June, 1978 in which General Zia Rahman received 80% of the poll.

ROLE, COMMITMENT, DEPLOYMENT AND RECENT OPERATIONS

Role
The Bangladesh army's principal roles, as discussed elsewhere, are internal security and, increasingly, the direct administration of the country's political life. In so far as it has an external role, both geography and political developments since 1975 designate India as Bangladesh's only possible enemy. Despite the tense relationship that prevailed between Dacca and New Delhi until recently, and the recurrent border clashes between the Bangladesh Rifles and Indian-backed guerrillas, however, the Bangladesh army has no serious pretentions to being able to defend the country against an Indian attack. This fact is reflected not only in its size, but in the scale and nature of its equipment, which is primarily only suitable for internal security operations.

This fact imposes a certain discretion on the Dacca government in its dealings with New Delhi, whatever the degree of hostility towards India that may prevail in Dacca. There are, nevertheless, certain real disincentives to an Indian invasion beyond those of political morality and international public relations. One is the Chinese military deterrent against such an Indian adventure, made available to Bangladesh because Peking views the subcontinent almost exclusively from the standpoint of wishing to confine Russian influence there. The other is the certainty of large-scale guerrilla resistance even after an Indian victory.

India has been seen by China as a Soviet near-ally since 1965 (although this may now be changing), and for that reason Chinese recognition of Bangladesh was withheld so long as Indian influence predominated in the country. Chinese sources have since revealed, however, that there were small-scale armed clashes on the Sino—Indian border both east and west of Nepal during August, 1975 at the time of the coup against Mujib which overthrew Indian influence in Bangladesh — 'second-class Ussuri River incidents', in the words of one Chinese official. It may not be going too far to suppose that these were staged by the Chinese to warn the Indians against seeking to intervene militarily in Bangladesh. It is certainly the case that the Chinese subsequently heavily reinforced their military strength along the Sikkim—Bhutan border area, where Indian territory between Bangladesh and Tibet narrows at one point to a mere 60-odd miles. (It is by no means certain, however, that the Chinese would be prepared actually to commit their forces to war against India even in aid of Bangladesh, as the logistical situation would hardly be in their favour.)

The second major disincentive to an Indian invasion is the fact that, although the Indian army could unquestionably walk over the Bangladesh regular forces, and under certain circumstances might be able to do so without facing intervention even from China, it would then face an unending guerrilla war in a hostile and densely populated countryside. Indeed, it is this logic, as much as political or ideological considerations, which impels the JSD to argue for the abolition of the regular army and its replacement by a mass 'people's army' organised for guerrilla resistance. The deterrent effect on India of the fact that successful invasion would merely be the opening of a protracted and probably unwinnable guerrilla war is not to be underestimated, especially since the political orientations and purpose of the guerrilla leadership most likely to emerge could easily prove to be a communicable disease, capable of infecting similar impoverished areas of eastern India.

None of this should be taken to suggest that India has actively contemplated military intervention in Bangladesh at any time since 1975, though its disappointment at Mujib's overthrow and the reorientation of Bangladesh's foreign policy was acute. These are, however, the basic calculations made in Bangladesh whenever the question of defending the country against its giant neighbour is considered.

Commitment and Deployment
The Bangladesh armed forces have no military commitments beyond their own frontiers. No Bangladesh troops are deployed outside the country.

Recent Operations
The bulk of the regular officers and men of Bengali origin in the Pakistan army were disarmed and interned at the very beginning of the revolt in East Pakistan in March, 1971 and sat out the war in West Pakistan. Those who remained free fought together with the guerrilla forces, principally the Mukhti Bahini, which were formed with New Delhi's aid on Indian territory during the remainder of that year. Some 50,000 Mukhti Bahini accompanied the Indian army when it crossed East Pakistan's borders in around 20 columns on December 4th, 1971 but they mostly played an auxiliary role as guides, interpreters and rear-area security forces in the rapid Indian advance that followed.

Indian army forces in the east were about 160,000 strong, giving them a two-to-one advantage over the Pakistan army defenders, who suffered the additional handicap of having to fight while surrounded by a hostile population. The Indians also enjoyed complete air superiority from the first day, and were much more mobile thanks to a more lavish scale of transport. As a result, the campaign was not so much one of direct military confrontations, in which the Mukhti Bahini might have got more involved, but rather a series

of rapid Indian flanking manoeuvres which enveloped the static Pakistan army garrisons. Indian troops gained the two principal rivers, the main defensive line chosen by General Niazi, the Pakistani commander, before Niazi's own troops could fall back on them, and were closing in on Dacca by the middle of the second week of fighting. Pakistan army morale, already shaky because of universal popular hostility, the certainty that no further help could be sent from the West, and the inevitability of eventual defeat, abruptly collapsed under these blows, and General Niazi surrendered his whole force of 85,000 men on December 16th, 1971.

The Mukhti Bahini was a great diplomatic asset to the Indians during the brief occupation period, helping moderate the inevitable frictions by acting as a buffer between foreign, mostly Hindu, troops and a prostrate and starving Muslim countryside. Some of its members had already been transformed into the core of the new Bangladesh army by the time the Indian withdrawal was completed in early 1972.

The Bangladesh army as such has never fought a war, but since December, 1975 it has been involved extensively in internal and border security operations (though its paramilitary adjunct, the Bangladesh Rifles, has borne the brunt of the latter). Its opponents, according to the Bangladesh government, have been pro-Mujib elements and non-Bengali tribal groups, in both cases armed and supported by India.

The first border incidents occurred in the months following Mujib's overthrow in August, 1975 mainly in the west and the south-east, but really serious trouble began on January 19th, 1976 with a series of co-ordinated assaults by guerrillas on dozens of Bangladesh Rifles and police posts lasting a week. These and subsequent assaults received supporting fire from the Indian Border Security Forces, whose Director-General was seriously wounded in one such exchange of fire in April, 1976. Dacca reported in January, 1977 that the IBSF had opened fire on Bangladesh border posts on 1316 occasions in the preceding year. General Zia Rahman has stated that several hundred guerrillas have been captured along the frontier with India, and have admitted that they were trained by Indian troops, in some cases as far away as Calcutta. In all there are some 30—50 guerrilla bases around the Bangladesh border, stated the General, with the Indian training camps run by the IBSF mainly concentrated in the northern area opposite Mymensingh.

Mymensingh province is also the location of the main internal guerrilla base area, run by Kader Siddiqi, a former student leader and 1971 guerrilla leader who has proclaimed his loyalty to the memory of Shaikh Mujib. He claims 30,000 followers, but the Dacca government estimates that his following of 'miscreants' is around 3000—3500. They are drawn mainly from the local Garo tribe, non-Bengali and mostly Christian, who straddle the Bangladesh—Assam border (there are about 40,000 within Bangladesh) and whom the guerrillas have promised an autonomous Garoland within Bangladesh. A similar insurgency exists at the other end of the country in the Chittagong Hill Tract, based mainly on the Buddhist Chakma tribe, of Burmese origin. Dacca has accused India of supplying arms and aid to both. During 1978 this resistance developed into full-scale guerrilla war, and a counter-insurgency campaign was launched.

Both the border incursions and the internal insurgencies seem well under control, and have not placed the Bangladesh army under any major strain. Though they have a certain nuisance value, it is difficult to envisage them actually threatening the present political order in Bangladesh, or even affecting in a significant way any future changes which it might undergo. The change of government in New Delhi in early 1977 has evidently brought an end to Indian support for domestic insurgents, although this flight of refugees from the Chittagong Hill Tracts into Indian territory (Tripura) continues to engage the concern of the Indian Government.

ORGANISATION

Arms of Service

The Bangladesh army is institutionally a fourth-generation descendant of the British army, by way of the armies of the Indian Empire and of Pakistan (with the modern Indian army as presiding midwife at the birth). The principal arms — infantry, armour, artillery and engineers — duplicate the British pattern, as do also the various services. A modified version of the British pattern of regimental organisation prevails within the arms, but the regimental lineages do not in general extend back beyond 1971.

The navy and air force (officially, the Air Wing of the Defence Forces) were both founded in 1972, and also conform largely to the inherited form of organisation. The paramilitary border defence force, the Bangladesh Rifles, is organised along the same lines as the regular infantry.

Operational

The army is organised into twelve infantry brigades (27 infantry battalions), two armoured regiments, ten artillery regiments, and six engineer battalions. There are five infantry divisional headquarters organisations in existence. Army headquarters are in Dacca, and the main tank depot is at Bogra; infantry units are distributed throughout the country.

The very small navy has its headquarters in Dacca, with its principal naval base in Chittagong. There is also a smaller base at Khulna.

The air force consists of one fighter squadron, one transport squadron, one helicopter squadron, and a training organisation disposing of a handful of aircraft. There are a number of airfields and landing strips designated as air force bases — Barisal, Chiringa, Chittagong, Cox's Bazaar, Dohazari, Hathazari, Ishurdi, Jessore, Kurmitola, Lalmonirhat, Saidpur and Tazgaon — but most of the air force's strength is in fact at Dacca, where the headquarters are also located.

RECRUITMENT, TRAINING AND RESERVES

Recruitment is by voluntary enlistment. Army recruiters can afford to be highly selective since the armed forces incorporate less than 0.1% of the population, and offer one of the most secure and well-rewarded occupations in the country.

Military training takes place almost entirely within Bangladesh since 1975 (previously there was some co-operation with the Indian army), and conforms to the usual pattern. There has recently been a strong emphasis on discipline and such morale-building incidentals as drill, smart new uniforms, and distinctive regimental marks, in an attempt to counteract the corrosive effects of the 1975 mutiny and subsequent effervescences on the army's cohesion and obedience.

There is no organised reserve system, except for the 36,000 strong Armed Police Reserve. The government has eschewed the creation of a popular militia, presumably because of its resemblance to the JSD–PRA concept of a 'people's army', and its vulnerability to penetration by that sort of subversive group.

EQUIPMENT AND ARMS INDUSTRY

The army has 30 Soviet T-54 medium tanks, 6 M-24 Chaffer light tanks (US; obsolete) and 30 105mm and five 25 pounder gun/howitzers. It also possesses some 81mm and 50 120mm mortars and a number of 106mm RCLs. Spares are short, some of the equipment is unserviceable, and even ammunition was so scarce in early 1976 that infantry officers were ordered to restrict target practice severely.

The Bangladesh navy has three frigates, both bought second-hand from Britain. It also has four large gunboats, four patrol craft, five armed river patrol craft, and one support vessel.

The air force has 20 F-6 ground attack aircraft and 6 MiG-21 fighters. The transport squadron operates a few AN-24 and AN-26 aircraft, while the helicopter squadron has four Alouette III, two Wessex, six Mi-8 and six Bell 212 helicopters. There are eight trainers. Spares are short and some aircraft cannot fly.

For armed forces the size of Bangladesh's, this must be one of the lowest scales of equipment in the world. It reflects not only the extreme poverty of the country, but also its brief but chequered political history. Bangladesh inherited little equipment from the Pakistan army units which surrendered on its soil in 1971 (though it did manage to salvage a few ex-Pakistan Sabre 6s, now non-operational, with which to found its air force.) In late 1972–4 the armed forces did receive modest deliveries of Soviet arms, which still comprise the bulk of their holdings, but a large share of military expenditure in those years was devoted to building up their now defunct paramilitary rival, the Rakkhi Bahini. Since the coup of August, 1975 Indian or Soviet arms have of course become unavailable, and an acute problem has arisen over the supply of spares for the armed forces' existing Soviet equipment.

The Bangladesh government, however, sees an urgent requirement for increasing and modernising its weapons, partly because it is presently unable to present even a minimal military deterrent to India, but even more because of the need to rebuild the armed forces' morale and self-respect. Since November, 1975 therefore, it has been in contact with China, Pakistan, Britain, West Germany, Libya and several other Muslim States in its search for arms. In mid-1976 a military mission was sent to the United States with an extremely optimistic shopping list that included 40–50 F-5 fighter–bombers, surface-to-air missiles, anti-aircraft guns, artillery, small arms, communications equipment and radars. Thus far, however, Bangladesh has only succeeded in acquiring two frigates, from Britain.

Bangladesh faces an unusual and delicate problem in seeking to buy arms abroad (apart from the fact that most arms suppliers are loth to annoy far larger India, which has vocally disapproved of Dacca's arms-buying ambitions, pointing out that there is no-one Bangladesh could use them against except India). Dacca's special problem stems from the fact that an extraordinarily large part of its income comes from foreign loans and grants, which are given mainly because of its great poverty. If large amounts of government expenditure were diverted to arms purchases, it would have a powerful negative effect on the willingness of foreign donors to supply more aid (especially since sales of grain sent as aid generate a very large share — figures of between 50 and 90% are quoted — of government revenue). It is hard to see how this difficulty can be circumvented by Bangladesh's government, so the prospects for the desired dramatic improvement in armed forces equipment seem less than bright.

There is no arms industry in Bangladesh.

RANK, DRESS AND DISTINCTIONS

Ranks and uniforms in the Bangladesh armed forces follow

the basic British patterns adopted by the Indian and Pakistani forces. No information is available on distinctions for gallantry.

CURRENT DEVELOPMENTS

No-one given the task of designing a country would put it where Bangladesh is (typhoons, tidal waves, one-third of the country regularly flooded each year). Neither would they people it so liberally, nor endow its people with such a volatile and anarchic temperament. Despite the temporary, dramatic improvements in Bangladesh's position that can be wrought by a series of good monsoons unaccompanied by the usual natural disasters – a 12% growth rate was recorded in 1975–6 – the country does largely merit its image as the international basketcase, the Malthusian nightmare on the brink of coming true.

What is less widely recognised is that such a disaster cannot approach, much less occur, without the most drastic political consequences. It is true that the chronic malnutrition from which two-thirds of the population suffers in normal times, not to mention the more severe effects of actual famine, tends to produce not revolt but rather passive acceptance of suffering. Nevertheless, there must inevitably be large numbers whose acute deprivation does not utterly incapacitate them, and who remain capable of the most violent reactions against those who do not share their lot. It is the prevailing, and probably accurate, perception of the narrow *élite* of educated and privileged Bangladeshis – there are perhaps 150,000 potential taxpayers in a nation of 80,000,000 – that the country faces the possibility of cataclysmic social revolution.

This perception, rather than India, defines the army's principal role: defence of the social order. The judgement was reinforced by the experience of November, 1975 which revealed that the enlisted ranks of the army had been penetrated to an astonishing degree by the JSD, perhaps the likeliest agent of such an upheaval (though there are other candidates). Since then there has been a thorough-going round-up of JSD cadres in the cities, and a determined effort to evict PRA adherents from the army, but it is by no means certain that the organisation has been decisively crippled.

In domestic affairs, General Zia has taken a liberal economic line, and the efficiency and honesty of the civil service has been dramatically improved. Bengali ex-members of the Pakistan Civil Service have been given jobs again, and the government takes great care to satisfy, as far as possible, the often competing demands of the army, civil service and police for enhanced career opportunities. Public security in the towns and countryside has been greatly improved.

In foreign relations, the government has followed a firmly anti-Indian line, maintaining close links with Pakistan (the re-establishment of former economic links – on a more equitable basis – has been strongly encouraged by both governments) and with China. Bangladesh has also turned to the West diplomatically, and has sought to make substantial arms purchases from Western countries (with the primary purpose of restoring the morale of the badly equipped armed forces).

Bangladesh's relations with India after the overthrow of Mujib and the failure of the counter-coup were bound to be bad, but from the end of 1975 they were made far worse by an apparent deliberate Indian policy of arming and supporting anti-Dacca guerrillas along and within the frontiers. The guerrillas were mainly drawn from those pro-Mujib refugees who fled the country in August, 1975 but India did not actually permit them to begin operations until after the failure of the November counter-coup. For some time

afterwards border clashes were continual, occasioning several dozen casualties a month in Bangladesh, and Dacca claimed that the Indian Border Security Forces frequently provided the guerrillas' attacks with covering fire from across the border. It also accused India of providing aid to two guerrilla forces within the country, one led by Mujib's former supporter 'Tiger' Siddiqi in the northern region around Mymensingh, and the other in the Chittagong Hill Tract near the Burmese border: Bangladesh reported the seizure of some 6000 weapons that had come across the border from India during 1976. India denied all these accusations, of course, and as late as January, 1977 Bangladesh–Indian talks on the problem ended in deadlock. (For further details on the border clashes and internal security operations, *see* Role, Commitment, Deployment and Recent Operations.)

Other irritants to Bangladesh–Indian relations have included the wounding of the Indian High Commissioner in Dacca by six JSD gunmen in November, 1975 and the rabidly anti-Indian tone of the controlled Bangladesh press, but the most important recent issue is unquestionably that of the Farakka dam. India extracted Bangladesh's consent to this $200,000,000 project during Mujib's rule, and it was completed 4 months after his death. It is located 11 miles above the point where the Ganges river enters Bangladesh, and its purpose is to divert much of the river's water westwards into its former main channel, the Hooghly river, from which the flow shifted in the seventeenth century, in order to deal with the severe problems of silting in Calcutta harbour 150 miles to the south. During the first dry season of its operation during 1976, however, this diversion had devastating effects on irrigation projects, industry and river navigation in the western districts of Bangladesh that depend mainly on the Ganges water, and Dacca accused India of 'an act of aggression against the economic sovereignty of Bangladesh'. Salt water moved far up the mouth of the Ganges, cutting the fish catch which is Bangladesh's main source of protein, the rice crop was badly affected, and electrical power production was crippled throughout the south-west of the country. Negotiations with India on this issue began in September, 1976 but made no early progress. Bangladesh subsequently went to the United Nations on this question, which General Zia termed 'a matter of survival'. An interim 5 year agreement on the sharing of the Ganges water was reached by India and Bangladesh in 1977.

India's strained relations with Bangladesh are understandable, in view of the fact that all major political groups within the country – the pro-Western military and educated civilian *élite*, the Islamic extreme right, the pro-Chinese communists, and the JSD – vie with each other in expressing their hostility towards India. Nevertheless India would be remarkably ill-advised in assisting any movement which seeks to displace the present government of Bangladesh, since one of the possible consequences would be precisely the social explosion the Bangladesh *élite* fears. The neighbouring regions of India are amongst the most poverty-stricken in that country, containing a population of some 200,000,000, 40% of whom, as in Bangladesh, are landless peasants, and revolution can be infectious even across frontiers. It is possible, of course, that with the change of government in New Delhi as a result of the March, 1977 elections, Indian policy towards Bangladesh will also change, and that India will gracefully resign itself to the loss of its influence in that nation.

Despite the apparent gradual improvement in the army's cohesion and discipline and in the state of public security over the course of 1976, General Zia finally baulked at the decision to return the country to democratic rule. The ban on political parties was duly lifted in August, 1976 in fulfilment of the promise made a year before, and elections were announced for February of the following year. No sooner had the parties reorganised themselves and begun their campaigns, however, than all the familiar signs of instability and inveterate factionalism in Bengali politics began to reappear, in mid-November, there, General Zia announced the indefinite postponement of the elections.

Faced with a strong reaction from the civilian political parties, Zia had the President transfer the office of Chief Martial Law Administrator to himself on November 29th, and promptly arrested most leading politicians including former President Khondaker Mushtaq Ahmed for 'prejudicial activities against the State'. They were subsequently awarded lengthy jail sentences. Zia himself became President in the elections of June, 1978.

The officer corps, however, continues to be riven by factions and is probably still coup-prone. Up to 75 junior officers were secretly tried and sentenced to imprisonment in 1976–7, and the continuing strength of the JSD in the enlisted ranks was shown by the events of September–October, 1977. On September 30th an army unit at Bogra mutinied, killing at least two officers; 2 days later, while the government's attention was distracted by negotiations with Japanese Red Army terrorists holding a hijacked jet at Dacca airport, there was a spontaneous uprising by airmen against their officers. The mutineers shot 11 officers, including six of Bangladesh's few fighter pilots, and the fighting spread to the airport and the main Dacca army cantonment's officer quarters before the mutineers were slaughtered by a loyal infantry unit. As many as 230 people, mostly military personnel, were killed in the fighting.

A number of senior air force officers were compulsorily retired in the following weeks, the army headquarters staff were reshuffled and the air force and navy commanders were relieved of their positions as Deputy Chief Martial Law Administrators. In late October, 1977 the government announced that 37 members of the army and air force had been executed for their parts in the affair, but unofficial reports suggest that up to 800 servicemen were convicted by secret military tribunals in the following 6 months, of whom 600, mostly from the air force, were executed by firing squad or hanging in Dacca. The most desperate turn taken in this faction fight was the murder at Chittagong on May 30th, 1981, of General Zia by fellow soldiers, allegedly led by Major-General Manzur, a divisional commander. The coup collapsed on June 1st, and Manzur was shot 'while attempting to escape'.

Manzur was closely identified with the 'freedom fighter' element in the army, those who had fought in the war of independence of 1971, whom Zia's 'repatriate' group (see Introduction) had largely removed from positions of influence in the army and government. The 'freedom fighters' were also associated with radical and even pro-Chinese elements in the country's political life. Twelve officers associated with Manzur were executed for mutiny, after trial by court-martial in Chittagong in September, 1981. All remining 'freedom fighters' were relieved of government posts.

Adbus Sattar, the Vice-President, was elected President in November, 1981, but almost at once ran into conflict with the army, whose leader, Lt-General H. M. Ershad, demanded its admission into the processes of government to relieve its 'frustration' and so 'stop further coups'. On March 24th, 1982, he unleashed a coup of his own — fortunately bloodless — and appointed himself 'Chief Martial Law Administrator'. A 'repatriate', he announced a 'holy war' against corruption and dedicated himself to transforming the economic state of the country by austerity, land reform and the encouragement of private investment. He exempted President Sattar from threat of arrest, declaring him to be an 'honourable man', but characterised him as 'unable to run the party' (the Bangladesh National Party) or give leadership to the Nation'. The general foresaw the possibility of holding new elections for a return to civilian rule in 'about two years'.

Gwynne Dyer
John Keegan

BELGIUM

HISTORY AND INTRODUCTION

In 1815 the 'powers' sought to create a 'buffer' State between France and Germany by combining the former Spanish Netherlands with the Dutch Netherlands. This uneasy political arrangement only lasted until 1831, when Belgium became an independent State. The powers intended to guarantee the new kingdom's perpetual neutrality and this suited the Belgians; after all, their country had been used as a battlefield by warring powers for several centuries.

Initially, it was hoped in Brussels that a neutralist policy would avoid the need for armed forces, but it was soon realised that something more than the *Garde Civique* was required to secure the newly founded nation. Soon after Leopold of Crowned Saxe-Coburg was the first King of the Belgians, he had the task, as Commander-in-Chief, of raising an army. It was formed on a selective basis: 'that is, young men had to register for service, but only about a quarter of each year's intake were called up; and those who found it inconvenient to serve were allowed to put forward substitutes'*.

Belgium occupied an area of Europe of outstanding strategic importance and longstanding vulnerability; its strategic significance stemmed from its position astride a main route between France and Germany, rather than from its size. It was, and still is, a small and densely populated country, measuring little more than 150 miles across from north to south and east to west. The Belgians, as a nation, were divided among themselves territorially, linguistically, and to a certain extent, culturally†. The 50 mile coastline was Belgium's only natural frontier, but the hilly third of the country in the south-east and the elaborate extensive drainage systems covering the remaining flat land provided considerable obstacles to ground movement. However, obstacles which were not to prove impenetrable.

Thus it was natural for Belgium to seek neutrality and remain aloof from the quarrels of her larger, more powerful neighbours. But at the same time she needed to extract guarantees of security from certain of the powers, i.e. Britain and France, and convince the nation that an army was needed. These three factors remained in conflict throughout the first one hundred years of Belgium's existence and it was their interaction which left the kingdom militarily unprepared to deal with invasion, twice in quick succession.

The Belgian army was needed, when international crises arose, for deployment along the nation's frontiers in fortresses and static defences facing three ways: east towards Germany, south towards France and even north towards the Netherlands. The problem was to maintain it at its authorised strength. In 1868 a recruiting law gave greater legal force to the annual drafting of conscripts, but the army remained understrength. In 1870, at the outbreak of the Franco–Prussian War, the Belgian army mobilised and a year later demobilised; an exercise that exposed serious military and administrative shortcomings. Yet, by the turn of the century, the modest target of a 20,000 strong army had still not been reached; but in 1909, the 'drawing of lots' was dropped as a basis of selection.

Troubles there may have been over maintaining the peacetime strength of the army, but early and significant advances were made in officer training. In 1834 the *École Royale Militaire* was founded in Brussels to train young officers, and close by the *École d'Application* was set up to complete the training of those officers destined for the technical arms and staff employment of that early period. In 1868, the Belgian *École de Guerre* began staff training and, with the other two schools, remains in Brussels to this day. All armies provide similar basic and staff training for their officers but a notable feature of the Belgian army's system, since very soon after its birth, has been the purposeful specialised training of officers for a career in what may be generally described as 'Military Administration'. Since those early days, suitably qualified officers, gaining experience all the time at various levels and in various appointments within the army, have managed service finances and dealt with personnel policies like 'conditions of service'. In contrast, in most other comparable armies the policy for such matters is in the hands of civil servants who seldom have any real service experience‡.

There could be no doubting the tremendous task that faced the Belgian government immediately prior to World War I. It needed a larger army, its 33,000 men providing only six small divisions, an under-equipped cavalry division and fortress troops. Signs grew clearer and more ominous that neutralist policies would fail and that the country would once more become the battlefield of the powers: this time Britain and France against Germany. But the war came too fast and caught the Belgian army in the midst of a major reorganisation. It played very little part in the first part of the war for King Albert decided that it should have no hand in the disastrous early campaigns until there was a chance of military success. The time was used to overhaul the army and train its soldiers. This paid off for, in 1915, it acquitted itself well when, from positions in the northern part of the line, it drove back the Germans as they launched their final offensive in Flanders.

After the war, in 1919, Belgium concluded a defence agreement with France and entered into a similar understanding with Britain. Belgian forces joined those of France occupying the Ruhr in 1923 until the task formally ceased with the signing of the Treaty of Locarno 2 years later. In 1923, the army comprised 12 divisions manned almost entirely by conscripts serving 13 months with the 'colours'; in 1924 eight active divisions remained with the other four placed in reserve; then, in 1926, only two active and two reserve divisions were retained. This quite drastic reduction reflected the need to save the expense of maintaining a standing army in peace-time of a size comparatively larger than before the 'war to end all wars'. This recaptured mood

---

* Foot, M.R.D., *Men in Uniform*, Weidenfeld and Nicolson, London, 87 (1961).

† Rather more than half of today's population of nearly 10 million live in the larger, generally more rural, northern part of the country, Flanders, and speak Flemish as their main language. The remainder live in the Walloon provinces in the south and are predominantly French speaking, as are the majority of *Bruxellois*.

‡ This notable feature of the Belgian army has led not only to smaller and generally more efficient headquarters staff, but also to a noticeable lack of administrative complications and 'burdens' even today. Both aspects are envied by those of other armies who are aware of their existence and value but do not enjoy their benefits.

stressed former tendencies towards neutralism, and emphasised the reliance placed upon the guarantees Britain, France, Germany and Italy made for the security of Belgium. Furthermore, the British and French undertook to intervene militarily should German forces cross to the west bank of the Rhine at any time in the future. During the inter-war years the Belgian army's main preoccupation was with strengthening fixed fortifications on pre-1914 lines and with modernising equipment.

Hitler's regime presaged peril and gloom, and general conscription had to be reintroduced. An army of 500,000 was approved in 1935 but, unfortunately, opposition in parliament hampered serious and effective rearmament at that time. Lack of funds particularly set back the modernisation of cavalry and artillery units. However, when Hitler reoccupied the Rhineland in the following year, parliamentary sanction was given for a 13 month conscription period, also for funds needed to strengthen fortifications and for equipment and mechanisation. Six active and 12 reserve infantry divisions were raised, together with two cavalry divisions and a corps of *Chasseurs Ardennais*. In that same year, 1936, it was also decided to follow a policy of neutrality more strongly.

The well-known and tragic sequence of events which led to the outbreak of World War II requires no elaboration here. As with other armies concerned with combating Nazi military adventurism, mobilisation was 'on and off'. When the order was eventually given the Belgian army encountered difficulties which were hastily tackled. Precautionary measures like anti-aircraft defence deployment and fixed fortress reinforcement were undertaken; all frontiers again were to be made secure. When Britain and France declared war on Nazi Germany on September 1st, 1939, the King formally announced Belgium's neutrality. Yet, even after Hitler had reaffirmed that there would be no invasion, he issued his infamous Instruction No. 6 on October 9th, which contained orders for the invasion of the Low Countries and also France.

When the period of 'phoney' war seemed to be drawing to a close, final mobilisation measures were taken in January, 1940. The Belgian army's strength was by this time 600,000. For once the problem was not an understrength military force; it was widespread paralysis of industry and public services caused by so many men being drafted for service. The bulk of the army took up defensive positions facing eastwards, behind a line which stretched from Antwerp in the north, along the Albert Canal to Liège, and southwards to Arlon in the Ardennes. From the Belgian standpoint, it was understandable for the government to impose as long a delay as possible before permitting British and French to enter the country. There was still hope that Hitler would keep his undertaking to recognise Belgian neutrality. Plans did exist for the deployment of British and French forces on Belgian soil, but they were secret, at least. Approval was given in early April when all the indications left no doubt as to Hitler's intention to invade. On May 15th when the Dutch army capitulated, there was chaos and panic in Limburg, the southernmost province of the Netherlands. There had been contact five days earlier between Belgian and German forces in the area of Maastricht, but now the whole area directly to the east of the central part of the Belgian defensive line lay open to a German advance. The line of the Meuse could not be held and, with the build-up of some 30 German divisions, reinforced by typical Stuka air attacks, the defences began to crumble. After valiant efforts to keep the line intact, further withdrawals and considerable losses forced the Belgian army to surrender during the night of May 27th/28th, 1940. Set against the might of the German invaders the weak home defence forces were no match. The war in Belgium lasted only 18 days. Belgian soldiers had fought as gallantly as any others but their army was simply not organised, equipped or

prepared for such an onslaught, and this was not confined to the Belgian army. The larger allies were made to suffer from being caught unawares too.

So the population were left to live with and resist hostile occupation forces; the Germans deported many thousands of Belgians during the long wait for liberation. It was a tribute to their national spirit, and must have been a boost for the nation's morale, that so soon after occupation Belgian servicemen and potential servicemen began arriving in Britain to take up arms. From the end of May, 1940 men, women and children used direct and indirect routes, some travelling via Portugal and others by way of the Belgian Congo, in order to reach Britain. A hospital and refugee centre was set up in Tenby, in south-west Wales, and this area became the temporary home for many Belgians during the war. With commendable speed and resource the 1st Battalion of Fusiliers was formed there by the end of October, 1940 and the 2nd Battalion of Fusiliers was formed there by July, 1941; by then some 1600 men had been equipped and trained. In January 1942 a group of Belgian forces concentrated in the Clacton area of Essex and it was there and then that the *1er Brigade d'Infanterie* was formed. The famous 'Liberation Brigade', as it became known, comprised three motorised units armed with heavy infantry weapons and integral means for reconnaissance. It also consisted of one armoured car squadron, one artillery battery of twelve field guns, one engineer company, a support unit and a liaison detachment. The force, like others of the nation stationed outside the homeland, proudly prepared for the day when it would help liberate the Kingdom of the Belgians.

The 'Liberation Brigade' played a successful part in the Normandy landings of August, 1944 as a component of the British 21st Army Group. By September 3rd Belgian units had reached Tournai and when the 11th British Armoured Division entered Brussels the next day, Belgian soldiers were in the van. The capital was again free. Six days later, Maastricht in Dutch Limburg was in allied hands and Belgium had been liberated, but for a determined 'pocket' of Germans on the coast near Antwerp.

Returning to May 8th, 1942, this was the date when a Belgian independent parachute company was formed in Britain. The original complement of 144 soldiers was swelled to 210 by January, 1943 and the company became part of and trained with the British 6th Airborne Division. A year later it was transferred to the British Special Air Service (SAS) Brigade for specialised training in clandestine operations. In July, 1944 liberation was stealthily heralded when Belgian parachutists dropped in small parties into various areas of their home country.

Commandos in the Belgian forces were, and still remain, a part of the army and, from 1940, an independent unit trained in Britain. In that year it fought in Norway and, in 1942, raided Madagascar, Bruneval, St. Nazaire and Dieppe. It became part of the celebrated international No. 10 Commando. Belgian commandos also fought in the Far East, Sicily, Italy, Greece, Normandy, Waalcheren and in Germany.

Colonial troops had served in the Belgian Congo since 1877 and the *Force Publique* was 18,000 strong in 1914; between the world wars it grew in size and its training became more effective. From 1940, operations were directed by the Belgian government-in-exile and co-ordinated with British land force deployment and employment in Africa. The force grew to 40,000 troops formed into three brigades, a river unit and support. It took part in the Abyssinian campaign of 1941, and then helped establish an overland route from Lagos through Fort Lamy and part of Sudan to Cairo. In February and March, 1943 a Belgian colonial motorised brigade of 2000 troops undertook the difficult journey by land from the Congo via Juba and Khartoum to Egypt, while a further 6000 troops were shipped to the Suez Canal. This Belgian expeditionary force fought in the Middle East. To add to the story of overseas commitments, a Belgian medical unit, the 10th Casualty Clearing Station, supported operations in Burma and later in Indonesia.

After the liberation of Belgium more volunteers were recruited, and six infantry and six fusilier battalions were formed and trained, as were six pioneer (auxiliary engineer) battalions. By the close of 1944 some 16,000 men were under arms and during the next two years the total rose to 24,000 formed into three divisions. Two of these divisions with supporting units remain as part of 1st Belgian Corps, integrated within NATO's Northern Army Group.

When the Russian menace arose in central Europe, so soon after World War II, to compound the lingering threat of possible German *revanchisme*, Belgium, like her neighbour Holland, preferred to join and support defensive pacts rather than return to introspective policies of neutralism. The Belgian government joined those of neighbouring countries as early as March, 1948 to formulate terms for a mutual assistance and security agreement. The Brussels treaty was signed by Belgium, Britain, France, Luxembourg and the Netherlands later that month. By September a Western Union Defence Organisation had been established with Field Marshal Montgomery as Chairman of the Commanders-in-Chief Committee, the French General de Lattre de Tassigny as Commander-in-Chief Land Forces, and with its headquarters at Fontainebleau in France. A year later Belgium was a signatory of the North Atlantic Treaty, and to NATO, like the European organisation it superseded, she contributed forces; this contribution confirmed the sharp reversal of former Belgian policies and tendencies. Ever since that time her defence policies have reflected an interdependent approach to her own and western Europe's security and the political acceptance of retaining only a small, though not insignificant, navy and air force while directing her major military effort towards maintaining her army. *La Force Terrestre* consists of an army corps assigned to NATO (*la Force d'Intervention*), landforces designated for home defence (*les Forces de l'Interieur*) and a tactical reserve of a parachute commando (a *corps d'élite*).

Throughout its short history the Belgian army had remained a conscripted force, raised on a selective basis, with a small regular cadre of officers and NCOs. The post-war requirement to make a permanent peacetime contribution to the alliance made a change necessary. A mixed service system, part volunteer and part conscript, was introduced with a gradual strengthening of the regular element over the years. In the past the army had been caught unprepared for action and tied down too much to static fortress-like defence. Ever since the incorporation of the largest part of the Belgian land forces within an allied command, it has been accepted policy to maintain an up-to-date, strong, combat-ready and mobile contribution.

The long-term intention, as expressed in the late 1950s, was 'to assemble forces composed one-third long-service regulars (people who intended to give the best part of their lives to armed service), one-third short-term conscripts called militiamen (*miliciens*) and one-third short-service regulars known as 'NATO technicians (*techniciens* — OTAN)*. Because the 'technician' scheme started well and swelled the ranks of the regular cadre, the government was able to reduce con-

scription in 1959 from 15 to 12 months. By the late 1960s the army's strength was almost half regular.

Other changes were introduced during the 1950s. British-pattern organisations and procedures were gradually replaced. A Service Corps, an Ordnance Corps and a Corps of Electrical and Mechanical Engineers, existed as a legacy of wartime service and training in Britain. Quartermaster, Transportation and Ordnance Corps were introduced in the 1950s on similar lines as in the American army, and later the supply, transportation and maintenance (repair) functions were combined within a single Logistic Corps. The common NATO staff organisation was introduced into all Belgian army field headquarters.

The way the Belgians and Dutch structured their fighting formations ran parallel and reflected the process which both armies went through, in the 1950s in particular, of following American organisational patterns as well as purchasing more American combat equipment. They adopted the 'pentomic' organisation for their infantry divisions whereby each was composed of five 'battle groups'. Conventional brigades were eliminated and each new battle group, an enlarged infantry battalion with tank and artillery support, was to be capable of independent operations. When the Americans decided that this structure was unsuitable for Central Region operations, and changed in the early 1960s to divisions of three brigades, the Belgians and the Dutch had to consider an alternative structure for their field armies. About this time, NATO tried to introduce a 'standard' division of three brigades as the most appropriate main fighting formation for the central front and endeavoured to get nations involved to accept and introduce it. Only Belgium fully complied, but when the army discovered that it was alone in adopting the LAND-CENT division* in all detail, it saw no reason to resist introducing its own modifications to structure and composition as they became necessary. During the 1960s, the division contained brigade groups and divisional troops and the view prevailed in the Belgian army, and elsewhere, that strong and moderately self-contained brigades were best to cope with the fluid operations envisaged. But as the variety and complexity of weapons, vehicles and equipment grew, so did the demand for men to man them and by the late 1960s personnel costs were beginning to inflate as well. In an effort to conserve manpower the Belgians, like the Dutch, replaced divisional headquarters by a command post from which the divisional commander and a small tactical staff were to conduct the battle involving two or more brigades. Combat support and logistic support units were withdrawn from divisions to be retained at corps level for allocation forward as necessary. The division, therefore, became a 'framework' and the brigade group with organic combat and logistic support remained the basic fighting formation. This is the situation today; structurally the Belgian field army is similar to the Dutch but the composition of formations and organisation of units differ.

Since the alliance was formed Belgian officers and soldiers have served alongside colleagues of other nationalities in NATO headquarters and a small number of multinationally manned units. The 1st Belgian Corps, *La Force d'Intervention*, co-operates and trains at formation and unit levels with other NATO nations who contribute contingents to the Northern Army Group. Until recently most of the Belgian corps has been stationed in the Federal Republic of Germany, but currently nearly half of its active units are being withdrawn to be barracked in Belgium. This is to save costs and

---

* Foot, M.R.D., *op. cit.*, pp. 88, 90. The Dutch introduced a very similar 'technician' scheme in order to produce 'key' specialists like tank crew, mechanics, electricians, etc. who require long training and particular expertise.

* HQ LANDCENT was at that time the superior land force headquarters for the Central Region; it was part of the Allied Forces Central Europe (AFCENT) at Fontainebleau.

Belgium

for political and social reasons. Many Belgians do not understand why, after 30 years of peace, almost the whole of the fighting part of their army should be located in Germany. Because practically all of their active formations are assigned to NATO, most regular officers and soldiers have spent the majority of their service in Germany where they may have married local girls, where their families have lived for many years, and where their children have been educated. Tours of duty in Germany are popular with the army and their families and the Belgian Corps is as proud to be part of Northern Army Group as the allied NATO command is proud to have them. The operational disadvantages and problems of keeping such a large part of the corps in Belgium, so far from its battle areas, will be examined later.

It would be difficult for Belgians to overlook NATO. Its headquarters is on the outskirts of Brussels, and SHAPE is only some 30km away near Mons. National defence policy strongly emphasises continuing support for NATO and the Euro group, and the Prime Minister, Mr Tindemans**, leads a strong body of opinion within and outside his country which favours closer European union, including common defence policies and joint equipment procurement. Like the Dutch, Belgians regard 'rationalisation' and 'specialisation' of tasks among NATO forces as a means of helping smaller nations, like their own, to continue to make worthwhile military contributions. Already, through internal rationalisation, a unified Medical Service supports the three Belgian armed services; clearly those who run the country's defence will seek and support further measures on a multinational scale. In 1975, Belgium spent less on defence per head of the population than Germany and the Netherlands, but approximately the same as Britain†.

STRENGTH AND BUDGET

Population: 9,904,000
Army: 68,700 (26,900 conscripts)
Navy: 4300; four major vessels, 38 smaller
Air force: 20,500, 164 combat aircraft
GNP (1981 estimate): $100,840,000,000
Defence expenditure (1982): $2,878,000,000.

COMMAND AND CONSTITUTIONAL STATUS

Command
The King is Commander-in-Chief. The government controls the Belgian armed forces through a Minister of Defence and a small Defence Ministry which incorporates a General or Joint Staff and a Central Administrative Staff both headed by lieutenant-generals. From a separate location, also in Brussels, the Army Headquarters headed by the Chief of Army Staff (also a lieutenant-general) controls subordinate formations (see Figure 1).

Constitutional Status
In principle, universal service has always been a feature of Belgian life. Every male Belgian citizen must carry out military service according to the law and the obligation

lasts for 15 years unless mobilisation prolongs the period of liability indefinitely. In practice, the law provides for numerous exemptions and deferments for men considered indispensable, or who are excused or barred for various reasons*.

ROLE, COMMITMENT, DEPLOYMENT AND RECENT OPERATIONS

Role and Commitment
Since the end of her colonial responsibilities in 1960 Belgium's standing forces have been totally geared to continental defence roles and commitments. The army has three main tasks: to provide an army corps of two divisions and supporting troops for the Northern Army Group; to defend the homeland; and to furnish logistic and all other forms of support for NATO contingents and home defence forces from the army base in Belgium (see Figure 1). In addition, the army's tactical reserve of a composite parachute-commando regiment, manned by volunteers, is capable of intervention on the central front or the flanks of NATO. A battalion of this regiment is assigned to the Allied Command Europe Mobile Force (AMF). But Belgium's role in support of the alliance is not limited to providing tactical formations and units complete with their organic support; she offers to other member nations vital logistic facilities such as ports like Antwerp, depots, staging areas and lines of communication eastwards into the operational areas of NATO's Central Region. Belgium may no longer provide the potential battlefield in any future conflict of conventional forces in Europe, but much of the country will certainly become a congested and vulnerable logistic base in the event of an emergency arising.

Deployment
Until recently only one of the four active brigades in the 1st Belgian Corps was located in Belgium in peacetime; now this has been increased to two brigades, a divisional headquarters and some supporting units so that approximately half the corps has been moved back from Germany. The consequent lengthening of deployment times from peacetime locations to operational areas causes a reduction of combat readiness and particular problems if a surprise emergency arises. The plans for the 1st Belgian Corps to be wholly manned by regular officers, NCOs and soldiers will promote combat readiness because of the higher standard of training and military proficiency generated among longer serving personnel. Formations and units take part in exercises which acquaint all ranks with their operational areas and tasks, and deployment on exercise reduces the time taken to reach these areas during an emergency, for forces in being. Reserve formations and units still have to be mobilised as well as deployed, and their availability could depend to a crucial extent on timely political decisions†.

Recent Operations
Except for military operations in the Belgian Congo (including the intervention in Stanleyville in 1964) and Rwanda—Burundi (which finished in 1961), the Belgian army has had no active service experience since World War II. Currently training teams are employed in the Congo, Rwanda and Burundi.

** The Tindemans Report on the Future of the European Community.
† The comparison is made between NATO countries contributing forces to Northern Army Group, remembering that Germany in particular makes substantial contributions to Central Army Group and NATO's Baltic Approaches Command. The figures for 1975 (dollar per head of population) were: Germany 260; the Netherlands 215; Belgium 185; and Britain 184.

* 'Tout citoyen belge doit accomplir le service militaire': Conscription of Law, September 2nd, 1957, Chapter II, Article 2, paragraph 1 quoted in Foot, M.R.D., op. cit., pp. 88 and 89, which also gives details of the law, its application and exempted/defined categories.
† This is the case for all nations contributing contingents to a NATO formation.

48

In a lightning operation over the period May 19th—22nd, 1978, 1750 Para-commandos landed in Shaba province of Zaïre to protect the survivors of anti-European massacres.

ORGANISATION

Arms of Service
The army comprises:
1. Cavalry (*Chasseurs à Cheval, Guides et Lanciers* manning tank and reconnaissance battalions).
2. Infantry (*Grenadiers, Carabiniers, Chasseurs, Ardennais, Linie* and the *Parachute-commando Régiment*).
3. Artillery and Engineers (*Artillerie et Genie*).
4. Aviation.
5. Logistic, Signals and Medical Corps (*Troupes de Logis, Transmissions et Santé*).
6. Military Police.
7. General Staff and Military Administrators (*see* Table 2).

Operational
The recently completed reorganisation of Army headquarters, which is still under trial, is based on a version of the American 'Planning, Programming and Budgeting System', and is staffed throughout at officer level by the military. Land forces stationed in Germany are collectively identified by the title *Force Belge en Allemagne* (FBA); units stationed at home in Belgium are subordinated to Headquarters, Home Defence Forces. The home 'Operations and Training Organisation' comprises: subordinate military headquarters commanding home defence units which co-ordinate measures with paramilitary (gendarmerie) and civilian authorities on a provincial basis; these consist of 11 motorised infantry regiments and four motorised infantry battalions the large parachute-commando regiment held in tactical reserve; and various training establishments. The functions of the 'Mobilisation' and 'Logistics' organisations are self-explanatory and provide army base support for Intervention and Home Defence Forces (*see* Figure 1).

The FBA includes the Belgian Corps and a small national logistic support command staff (of about 13 officers in peacetime). The corps structure has been described in outline earlier: strong and moderately self-sufficient brigades, only small tactical command posts at divisional level, and support retained at corps for allocation forward as required (*see* Table 1). Three mechanised brigades and an armoured brigade are 'active', one further mechanised brigade and a motorised brigade are 'reserve' formations. Some combat support units are 'reserve' and a larger proportion of logistic units fall into this category. The corps is completely mechanised: all infantry is APC-mounted and artillery self-propelled.

RECRUITMENT, TRAINING AND RESERVES

Recruitment
Plans are currently being implemented to produce an all-regular Intervention Force by 1978 when it is anticipated that the volunteer element of the army will have grown from the present 55% to a projected 75%. Since the announcement of the new plans, recruitment has been most encouraging but there are misgivings in some circles that this is largely attributable to a higher than normal amount of civilian unemployment. The plan also involves manning home defence units, apart from small regular cadres, with non-regulars. By 1978, the intention is to reduce national service to 6 months; at present, conscripts serve for 9 months in units in Germany and 11 months if serving in Belgium.

Thus, conscription will be retained with the 'active' period reduced to what will virtually become a training course. Roughly the same number of young men will be called up for national service as now; probably one in four eligible males will be enlisted.

There is a feeling among Belgians that a predominantly conscript army integrates more easily with the populace, because a conscript is merely a citizen doing his national service. Some mistrust the idea of building an army with such a high proportion of regulars. Such an army could grow apart from the nation, could be used as an extension of political power, and could be used against 'strikes'. On the other hand, those who wish to see military proficiency continuing to improve welcome the manning of three-quarters of the army, and especially the Belgian Corps, with soldiers serving on a volunteer basis. To achieve this aim will require consistently good recruiting and there are doubts that the present strength of the Corps will be maintained because of future manpower shortages. The present success with recruiting may be sustained by the recent moving back of more corps units to Belgium from Germany because it is easier to recruit when units are based at home. The current situation is encouraging for Belgium and for NATO, and has even temporarily retarded the planned intake of women into the regular forces.

Training
Individual basic training of soldiers takes 2—3 months, depending on arm and function, followed by continuation training in units or on courses at schools. The higher proportion of regulars, and this is growing in the Belgian army, the lower the initial training overheads and, naturally, the higher the standards achieved during their longer term of service. Potential regular officers undergo two alternative categories of training: an 'all weapons' course of 4 years or a 'polytechnic' course for 5 years. Later in their careers, when they attend the École de Guerre*, there are again two possibilities: the Staff Course or the Administration and Finance Course. Those wishing to become officers must first pass an examination in their second language (Flemish or French as the case may be) before commissioning; then officers must pass another similar examination in order to qualify for promotion to major. The schism over language means that candidates for promotion to higher rank must fit into a 50—50 allocation scheme to ensure linguistic balance. The army order of battle contains Flemish- and French-speaking brigades and units, and at divisional level and upwards all orders are published in both languages. Documents for general circulation like training pamphlets and teaching précis are also produced in both languages.

Reserves
There are specified training requirements for reservist officers, NCOs and private soldiers, and the government may recall any number of men to the 'colours' if an emergency arises. Former conscripts attend training camps regularly for the first five years after national service, some filling appointments in the two 'reserve' brigades (*see* Table 1). From 1978 when conscription is reduced to six months, it is probable that only one in 16 will be recalled for periodical training in units of these two brigades.

---

* Selection is as stiff as in other comparable armies. Those wishing to qualify must first pass examinations in both English and German; this is additional to their bi-lingual requirements in Flemish and French.

Figure 1   MINISTRY OF DEFENCE AND TOP LEVELS OF ARMY COMMAND

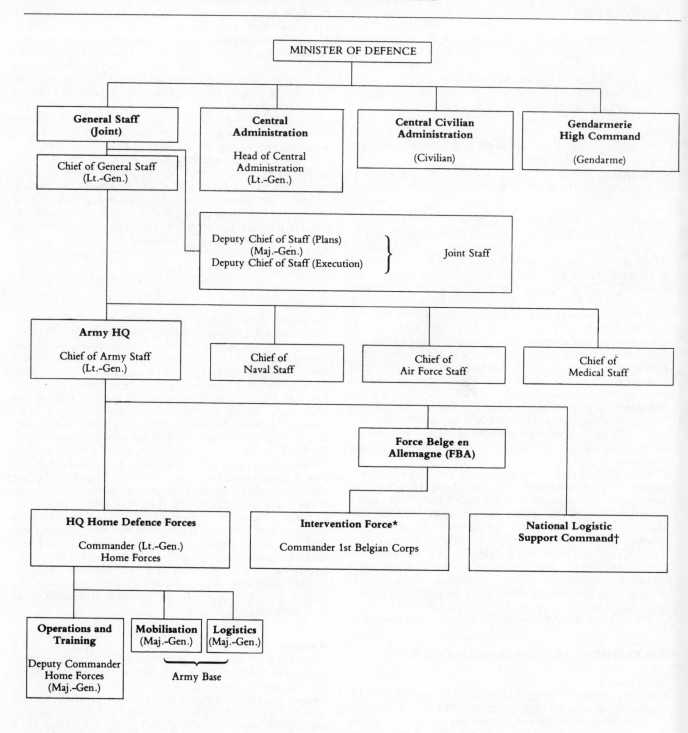

*Some units are already stationed in Belgium and therefore not technically FBA.
†Very small *État Major Terrestre FBA* based in Cologne with Corps HQ.

Table 1   THE 1ST BELGIAN CORPS

HEADQUARTERS

Commander (Lt.-Gen.)
Chief of Staff (Col.)

Corps Combat Troops	Active Division HQ	Active Division HQ	Reserve Division HQ	Corps Logistic Troops	Corps Signals and Provost
Three Reconnaissance Battalions	Three Mechanised Brigades		One Mechanised Brigade	Logistic Regiments*	Signal Battalions and Companies
Artillery Group (Maj.-Gen.) with Battalions and Heavy Batteries	One Brigade		One Motorised Brigade	Transport Regiments*	Military Police Companies
				Medical Regiments*	
Engineer Battalions					
Aviation Squadrons					

Mechanised Brigade	Armoured Brigade	Reserve Brigades
2 x Mechanised Infantry Buses	As for Mechanised Brigade but for one additional Tank Bn.	Differences from 'active' versions:
1 x Tank Bn. (40 Leopards)		1. Mechanised Bde. has a Recce. sqn. in place of one Infantry Bn.
1 x Artillery Bn. (18 SP guns)		
1 x Anti-Tank Bn. (12 Jägdpanzerkanone, 12 Milan)†		2. Motorised Bde. only has one Infantry Bn. and one Tank Sqn.
1 x Engineer Co.		
1 x Supply Co.		
1 x Maintenance Co.		3. Both have organic support.
1 x Postal Detachment		

* Regiments commanded by colonels consist of a number of battalions. The logistic regiments undertake supply, including integral transport and maintenance (repair).

† Being introduced. The Jägdpanzerkanone is a 'tank destroyer', a high-velocity gun mounted on a tank chassis, but not in a turret.

EQUIPMENT AND ARMS INDUSTRY

Since World War II the Belgian armaments industry has become prominent mainly through its success and skill in producing small arms. *Fabrique Nationale* (FN) is a familiar trade name in the many armies equipped with the Belgian self-loading rifle (SLR). Today the country's industry manufactures or assembles, or both, equipment developed elsewhere, e.g., the German Leopard tank and the British Combat Vehicle Reconnaissance Tracked (CVRT) made under licence for the army.

Equipment in service includes: 334 Leopard main battle tank (MBT) 133 Scorpian light tanks; AMX 13 (French) and M-75 (American) Spartan APCs; Lance, 8in self-propelled howitzer (M-110); 155mm self-propelled howitzer (M-109); 105mm self-propelled howitzer (M-108); 20mm light anti-aircraft gun; Hawk surface-to-air missile; 4.2in, 81mm and 60mm mortars; Milan anti-tank guided missile (APC and jeep mounted); 7mm Vigneron M-2 machine pistol; 9mm Browning pistol; 7.62mm FN general purpose machine-gun (GPMG) and light machine-gun (LMG); 7.62mm FN SLR.

Scimitar and Jagdjianzer anti-armour vehicles and Grejiand air defence vehicles have recently been introduced.

RANK, DRESS AND DISTINCTIONS

A similarity with British army uniform remains: ceremonial dress for officers is blue 'patrols' with regimental accoutrements; service dress, battle dress, berets and 1937-pattern webbing are worn; officers continue to use 'British warm' overcoats. Service dress is made from a khaki heavy- or light (summer)-weight material and the useful battle-dress keeps its long-service style. Arm or regimental badges are

On collar patches	Gold stars	Gold bars below stars	Silver star
Lieutenant-general	3	2	—
Major-general	2	2	—
Colonel	3	1	—
Lieutenant-colonel	2	1	—
Major	1	1	—
Captain-commandant	3	1 (above stars)	—
Captain	3	—	—
Lieutenant	2	—	—
Second Lieutenant	1	—	—
Adjutant	—	—	1

On lower sleeve	
Adjutant-chief (RSM)	One silver star above a palm bar
First sergeant-major	Three silver bars (space) two silver bars
First sergeant	Two silver bars (space) two silver bars
Sergeant	One silver bar (space) two silver bars
Corporal-chef	One silver bar, one red bar, one silver bar
Corporal	Two silver bars

Table 2   ARMS OF SERVICE

	Collar Patch	Shoulder(*) or collar(†) Badge
General officers	Black with crimson edge	Gold-winged thunderbolt†
Cavalry		
Chasseurs à Cheval	Orange	Hunting horn and crossed sabres*
Guides	Crimson with green edge	Crown over crossed sabres*
Lanciers	White with or without black edge	Crossed lances*
Infantry		
Grenadiers	Red	Grenade*,†
Carabiniers	Dark green with yellow edge	Hunting horn*,†
Chasseurs Ardennais	Dark green with red edge	Boar's head†, Crown*
Linie (of the Line)	Red with black edge	Crown*
Parachute-commando	Crimson	Winged sword* (1st and 3rd Battalions)
Regiment	Black with white edge	Dagger* (2nd Battalion)
Artillery		
Artillerie	Dark blue with red edge	Crossed cannon barrels behind vertical rocket (Horse Artillery has superimposed horseshoe)
Engineers		
Génie	Black with red edge	Roman helmet†
Aviation		
Aviation	Light (horizon) blue	
Supply Transportation and Maintenance (Repair)		
Troupes de Logis	Light blue	Crowned cog-wheel, bearing wing and two lightning flashes*
Signals		
Troupes de Transmissions	Black with white edge	Flaming torch and lightning flashes*
Medical Service		
Troupes de Santé	Maroon	Snake coiled round staff*
Military Police	Scarlet	

* Shoulder badge.
† Collar badge.

worn on khaki peak caps. Generals wear crimson hat bands and 'winged thunderbolts' above their rank badges in gold embroidery on collar patches. All ranks wear collar patches, the colour of which denotes arm or regiment, and some have regimental badges as well (*see* Table 2). Combat dress, in denim material, is drab green in colour.

Brigadier's rank does not exist in the Belgian army*, but an extra rank is inserted between captain and major, that of captain-commandant. In a battalion a commandant (abbreviated rank title) normally commands a company, squadron or battery. Officers and adjutants (senior warrant officers) wear embroidered badges of rank on coloured collar patches, and NCO's rank insignia are sewn onto the lower sleeve (*see* Table 2).

* Colonels command brigades and a colonel acts as Chief of Staff, 1st Belgian Corps.

CURRENT DEVELOPMENTS

The strength of the Belgian army has been reducing and now totals about 69,000 men, including some 27,000 conscripts. Significant progress has been made with regular recruiting with the aim of making the 1st Belgian Corps a totally volunteer force. It is planned to man all home defence and army base units with non-regulars, except for small cadres. A similar proportion of 'active' and 'reserve' units to that which exists at present will be maintained in the 1st Belgian Corps, but more units are now housed in Belgium than before. The army retains its high standards of military discipline and proficiency and has not had the same problems with conscripts experienced in the Dutch army. Officers and soldiers may join any union although there are independent army trade unions; in Belgium, unions are not automatically left-wing or socialist-affiliated as in the Netherlands and some other countries.

Defence expenditure stands at 2% of the gross national product* and it is hoped to increase spending by 3% each year at constant prices. The 'conversion' costs to create an army three-quarters regular is supplementary to this annual increase. Equipment and other capital investment take up 25% of the military budget, personnel costs now exceed 50% and operating costs have dropped below 25%. Belgium strongly supports NATO and Eurogroup, and particularly efforts to standardise equipment and to economise on development, production and procurement costs. The economic downturn in Belgium, more severe than in most European countries is hampering defence procurement and the maintenance of current defence establishments.

John Skinner
John Keegan

BELIZE

Belize is the only country of the English-speaking Caribbean in which armed forces are primarily for external defence rather than internal security. Although the Belize Defence Force was only officially created at the beginning of 1978, and the bulk of the responsibility for defending the country still rests on the British troops stationed there, it seems likely that Belize's armed forces will eventually grow to a relatively larger size than those of other members of the Caribbean Community (CARICOM), which it joined in 1974.

The reason for this also accounts for the fact that Belize (formerly British Honduras, renamed in 1973) has still not achieved full formal independence from Britain: its entire territory is claimed by neighbouring Guatemala. Belize has had full internal self-government since 1964, and has long been as desirous of independence as Britain is eager to grant it. The problem is that Belizeans are convinced that only the small British defence forces stationed there (and the prospect of their rapid reinforcement in an emergency) deter the Guatemalan army from marching in. Belize will not accept full independence without a continuing defence guarantee, and Britain is not willing to extend such a guarantee after independence.

Belize was first settled by British wood-cutters in 1638, and has been in continuous British possession ever since. Britain's presence there was never formally recognised by Spain, however, and when the Central American States became independent in 1821, Guatemala inherited and pursued the Spanish claim to Belize. Finally, in 1859, the present frontier was agreed by a convention between Britain and Guatemala, in return for which Britain undertook to construct a road from Guatemala's land-locked Petén region through Belize to the Caribbean coast. This road was never built, however, and in 1940 Guatemala repudiated the convention and revived its claim. There is also a dormant Mexican claim to the northern part of the country, which Mexico has stated it would waive if Belize became independent, but would revive if Guatemala attempted to annex the British colony.

Since 1945 all Guatemalan constitutions have insisted that the entire territory of Belize is part of Guatemala, and all its inhabitants Guatemalan citizens. There have been regularly repeated Guatemalan threats to invade the country, necessitating the permanent stationing of a British garrison there. The claim has now been made into a major element in Guatemalan nationalism, and is frequently used by a harrassed government to distract attention from difficulties at home, or by the extreme right wing to bring pressure against a government it feels is becoming too conciliatory.

There is also an apparently genuine fear in Guatemalan military circles that an independent Belize could become a base for leftist guerrilla operations against the existing regime. Indeed, the Guatemalan army insisted that arms and supplies were coming in via Belize during the rural guerrilla campaigns of the 1960s, although all outside observers were convinced that the guerrilla supply lines ran through the wild and unpopulated areas along the northern border with Mexico. This fear has not been lessened by Cuba's vocal support for Belizean independence, including the unsolicited offer of military aid in the country's defence.

These various factors within Guatemala have led to repeated outbursts of sabre-rattling accompanied by threatening military concentrations along the Belizean frontier. Combined with the steady growth in size and combat effectiveness of the Guatemalan armed forces, they have caused a considerable rise in the size of the British garrison in Belize over the past decade. The pattern has been one of urgent reinforcement in a crisis, followed by subsequent reduction — in 1972 the aircraft carrier *Ark Royal* and several thousand British troops were dispatched to the area; in 1975 an extra battalion of troops and a squadron of Harriers were flown in on short notice; and in July, 1977 the same reinforcements were sent again — but the permanent British garrison in non-crisis periods has risen from around 750 men in 1970 to over 1500 in mid-1978.

The Belizean population these troops are defending numbers only 145,000, in a largely empty territory of about 8000 square miles. It is an extraordinarily mixed population. Although the principal groups are of Caribbean/African and Spanish/Indian descent, in about equal numbers, it includes Asians and white Spanish-speakers, mestizo and Indian refugees from various uprisings in Mexico in the north, blacks with Irish names, pure Mayan Indians and Chinese (including the descendants of an entire Chinese village that emigrated *en masse* during the Boxer Rebellion), and such curiosities as the Black Caribs (Carib Indians deported from the Windward Islands mingled with Africans) and 3000 Mennonites who moved down from Mexico in 1958. The Prime Minister is part Welsh, part Mayan Indian.

Approximately two-thirds of the population are English speaking, one-third primarily Spanish speaking (although an 'open-door' immigration policy, creating a steady inflow from the overcrowded islands of the West Indies, is tending to reinforce the English-speaking element). Virtually all identify themselves as Belizeans, and have no wish to be connected to Guatemala in any way. The independence movement which emerged in 1949, under the title of the People's United Party, has dominated Belizean politics ever since, and its leader, George Price, has been Prime Minister since full internal self-government was granted in 1964. The small opposition party opposes independence, but principally out of fear of Guatemala.

The Belizean government, while unwilling to accept independence without a reliable external defence guarantee, has conducted a long and increasingly successful campaign to muster international support on behalf of its right to self-determination. It has succeeded in persuading not only the Commonwealth conferences but also the General Assembly of the United Nations to adopt resolutions supporting its independence by overwhelming majorities each year since 1975. The English-speaking nations of the Caribbean naturally support it unanimously. More importantly, perhaps, it has recently succeeded in attracting support for its rejection of Guatemalan claims from Latin American nations, including most of those which are nearby: Mexico, Colombia, Venezuela, Panamá and Cost Rica. (Guatemala broke off diplomatic relations with Panamá in 1977 over this decision.) Honduras is also favourably disposed to Belizean independence, and the only remaining opponents within Central America are Guatemala's fellow right-wing governments in El Salvador (which has promised Guatemala military aid in case of war over Belize) and Nicaragua.

It was as part of this drive to assure diplomatic and military support for its independence that Belize created its own armed forces, by a law which went into effect on January 1st, 1978. (The actual constitution of the force began early in the previous year.) The nucleus of the Belize Defence Force is the former Special Force of the Belize Police, which was transferred whole to the new organisation, while the bulk of the early recruits were drawn from the Belize Volunteer Guard, a home guard force which had previously acted as a police reserve.

By the end of 1980 a military force of about infantry battalion strength, including special signals, transport and ordnance elements had been trained. Recruitment is voluntary, and the terms of service are not known. The former Belize Volunteer Guard now serves as a reserve organisation for the Defence Force. Ranks, uniforms, equipment and organisation follow British models, and most training is provided by regular British units stationed in Belize.

British forces stationed in the country include a minimum of one infantry battalion (rotated at regular intervals), an armoured reconnaissance troop, an artillery battery, a troop of sappers, an Army Air Corps detachment and a squadron of the RAF Regiment for airfield defence. There is always at least one Royal Navy frigate on call with Marines embarked, and in times of high tension the defence forces have been reinforced within 2–3 days by an additional infantry battalion, another frigate and a squadron of Harrier VTOL fighter–bombers.

Although some potential for infiltration exists in the Maya Mountains along the southern part of the Belize—Guatemala border, the principal route of any possible invasion would be along the single road connecting the two countries and leading eastward to the new inland capital, Belmopan, and to Belize City on the coast, the principal town. There are Guatemalan commando bases at Melchor de Mencos near this border-crossing point, and a substantial proportion of the British troops in Belize is stationed at Holdfast Camp near San Ignacio on the other side of the frontier. An attack along this line could be greatly slowed, however, by blowing the single suspension bridge which crosses the Belize River near San Ignacio. Another exposed area is near Punta Gorda in the extreme south (where offshore oil exploration is underway), as the bulk of the Guatemalan navy is now stationed at the country's sole Caribbean port — Puerto Barrios, only 30 miles away.

The only key strategic point, however, and the one on which the British and Belizean defence effort is concentrated above all, is Belize airport, where the 2100yd runway is the only one in the country able to take jet transport aircraft and so to guarantee a rapid flow of reinforcements. Airport Camp is also the headquarters of British forces in Belize, and following Guatemala's recent acquisition of 12 Arava transport aircraft from Israel there was concern that a rapid airborne assault could seize the airport and effectively isolate the country from reinforcements. It is now heavily defended by Bofors guns and Tiger Cat surface-to-air missiles, however, so this does not seem a serious danger.

Britain has engaged in continual negotiations with Guatemala over the past few years in an attempt to find some solution that would permit it to grant Belize independence without the need to give it an open-ended defence guarantee, and in late 1977 to early 1978 London actually discussed the cession of a substantial proportion of Belize's territory to Guatemala in return for a recognised and secure independence for the remainder. This approach had strong United States support, and reportedly included the further inducement of British and United States finance for a $100,000,000 oil refinery in Guatemala. The negotiations began by discussing the transfer of 2000 square miles of southern Belize to Guatemala (one quarter of the country's area, and the region which contains the suspected oil reserves and mineral deposits that are Belize's main hope of future prosperity). It is not clear whether Britain ever had the Belize government's approval for this idea; it is known that the offer was dropped first to 1500 square miles, and then to 1000, in an attempt to secure Belize's agreement, before Prime Minister Price made the entire affair public and stated that his country was determined to insist on its full territorial integrity.

Nevertheless, this demonstration of British eagerness to be rid of its embarrasing commitment in Belize and to make territorial concessions (as the sovereign power) to hasten the day of its withdrawal (although, it was stated, such concessions would require the consent of the Belize government and people) has understandably alarmed the Belize government while hardening Guatemalan determination to press their claim. It has led Belize to hold active consultations with the governments of Guyana, Trinidad and Jamaica on the possibility of a joint military guarantee of Belizean independence by the CARICOM countries, though their tiny armed forces would make such a guarantee ineffective unless the troops of larger Caribbean powers like Venzuela or Mexico were also on call. Pending the creation of some such arrangement, Belize will probably have to continue to rely on the British garrison and its own growing Defence Force, while foregoing the luxury of formal independence. Britain's reaction to the Argentinian seizure of the Falklands in April 1982, and the continuing presence of British forces in Belize (one infantry battalion, one armoured reconnaissance troop, an artillery battery, one light air defence troop, one engineer squadron, one helicopter flight, one Rapier detachment, four Harrier and four Puma aircraft, and a frigate), certainly assures the extreme unlikelihood of Guatemala attempting military action.

Gwynne Dyer
John Keegan

BENIN*

HISTORY AND INTRODUCTION

This country is one of the poorest in Africa. Its intractable and apparently insoluble economic difficulties have been the main cause of its internal instability since the attainment of independence from France in 1960. The country has presented a depressing picture of confusion, coups, strikes, plots and abortive coups, scandals and ethnic rivalries. A major contributory cause of this sequence has also been the existence of a large and ambitious *élite* clan, political and military, which has exploited regional and other differences.

In 1960 Prime Minister Maga (President from 1961) was in power; his government lasted until riots and strikes in October, 1963 when the army, under Colonel Soglo, took power. The army made way for a government headed by two of Maga's rivals: Apithy (President) and Ahomadegbe (Prime Minister) in 1964. In 1965 the army, again under Soglo, returned to power in circumstances of disorder; initially it attempted to rule through a civilian, Congacou, but later in the year Soglo took over himself. At the end of 1967 Soglo was removed by a group of younger officers who, along ethnic and political lines, were themselves sharply divided. These attempted to rule through a Military Revolutionary Committee; finding this impossible they handed authority to the Army Commander, Colonel Alley. Alley disliked military involvement in government and returned power to a civilian regime in 1968, again amidst conditions of confusion and recrimination.

This regime found itself heavily dependent on Colonel Kouandete, Alley's principal rival in the army, which led Alley to attempt a coup; this failed and Alley was arrested. Kouandete then assumed power in 1969 and permitted both the return to the country, and to political life, of Maga, Apithy and Ahomadegbe, in a triumvirate. This in turn led to increasing unrest, disunity, disobedience and abortive coups in the army, and to yet one more successful coup, by a northern officer, Major Kerekou, in 1972. Kerekou's government has lasted longer, and has proved slightly less inefficient, than any post-independence government in Porto Novo. Its policy has been one of political disengagement from France together with increasing Marxist rhetoric, without too sharp an alienation from indispensable French economic and military aid. In January, 1975 there was an abortive coup involving one unit that attempted to overthrow Kerekou, the most serious of three such plots in the period 1972 to 1975; this was followed shortly afterwards by a political scandal in which it was alleged that the Defence Minister was caught in bed with the President's wife.

Periodic strikes and demonstrations, suppressed with some severity, suggested that Kerekou's government was not solving Benin's problems any more than its numerous predecessors. In January, 1977 a most extraordinary event took place: a group of airborne soldiers, some of pale complexion, attacked the Presidential Palace in a seemingly very casual style. The attack was unsuccessful. Benin rhetoric alleged that Togo, Gabon and Morocco organised the raid, with French financial and logistic help. Other explanations that have been offered suggest either that the shooting arose from a feud between the army and the gendarmerie, or, somewhat less likely, that

the affair was arranged by Kerekou himself to rally support and dispose of opponents. Of all these explanations, a measure of Moroccan complicity seems the least improbable, Morocco being aggrieved at Benin's support for Polisario claims in the former Spanish Sahara.

The present scene appears to be one of resumed factional strife, corruption and perhaps a nascent underground resistance movement. Below Kerekou, the most powerful figures are Azonhiko, a Fon who controls the gendarmerie, and Colonel Ohouens of the Army who like Kerekou, comes from the north.

STRENGTH AND BUDGET

Population: 3,500,000 (approximate)
Armed forces: Army of 3000, an air force of 100, and a gendarmerie of 1100.
GNP: $1,000,000 (estimate)
Defence expenditure: Not known.

COMMAND AND CONSTITUTIONAL STATUS

Colonel M. Kerekou is President of Benin, President of the Military Revolutionary Council and Minister for Defence; under him the 'Director-General' of the Ministry for Defence is Lieut-Colonel P. Koffi. The Army Chief of Staff is Colonel B. Ohouens.

ROLE, COMMITMENT, DEPLOYMENT AND RECENT OPERATIONS

Benin's *Forces Armees Populaires*, are under the Kerekou regime, supposed to be committed to the government's revolutionary and development policies. In defence terms, relations with Togo are very strained. Benin's dissidents having moved there. The border is guarded. Relations with Nigeria appear to be satisfactory.

ORGANISATION

Benin's army is composed of two infantry battalions, a company described as para-commando, a reconnaissance squadron and an artillery battery. One report also suggests an engineer sub-unit.

The para-commando company is normally stationed at Ouidah, and one each of the infantry battalions is in the north and south of the country, respectively.

Army headquarters is at Parakou, the air force headquarters and base is at Porto Novo.

A grandiose reorganisation scheme was proclaimed late in 1976 in which all State services were to fall into three groups. The first is to comprise the army, police, customs, fire, border guards, gendarmerie and forest service; the second is to be a public security force; and the third a people's militia. North Korean assistance has been reported both in the late 1960s and at present. Reports of sizeable Cuban and Soviet advisory staffs need to be treated with caution, though small missions from both countries may well be present.

* For general notes on African armies, see Appendix 1.

RECRUITMENT, TRAINING AND RESERVES

The army is raised by a somewhat random system of 18 months' national service. There is intense ethnic rivalry among the officers. The majority of soldiers come from the north.

Ideological training is said to form an important part of the soldiers' basic training syllabus.

EQUIPMENT AND ARMS INDUSTRY

Benin has no arms industry. Its army's original equipment all came from France, with the exception of seven M-8 U5 armoured-cars. More recently Soviet equipment has arrived. This includes AK47 rifles, RPG7 grenade launchers, eight BRDM-1 reconnaissance vehicles and ten PT76 light tanks. The original French equipment included 81 and 60mm mortars, and a few 105mm howitzers. Recently West Germany presented Benin with 20 scout cars and six UNIMOG personnel/load carriers. The air unit comprises 100 men. The machines are seven light transport aircraft, Russian, French, Dutch and American, two small army co-operation machines, and two helicopters.

RANK DRESS AND DISTINCTIONS

Those generally follow the French pattern except that officers wear peaked caps and not the *képi*.

CURRENT DEVELOPMENTS

The Benin army lacks credibility. It has never succeeded in retaining popular support for its interventions in political life. Just as the triumvirate, or eternal triangle, of Maga, Apithy and Ahomadegbe represented the regional interests of the north, the south and the Fon, respectively, so in the army have the personalities of Kerekou, Kouandete, Alley and Soglo.

There have also been sharp, at times bitter, divisions between the older and more experienced officers who had risen from the ranks of France's colonial army, and the newer generation of young men trained at St-Cyr-Coëtquidan and elsewhere. Soglo and Alley represented the older generation, and Kouandete and Kerekou the younger generation. Under Kerekou the latter group appear to have gained almost complete ascendancy.

The Soviet Union has of course gained considerable influence under Kerekou, contacts with Libya have also been developed. However both France and Benin have taken care to avoid a complete cessation of military contacts and France may, despite ideological differences, return at least in part to her former influence.

Lloyd Mathews

BHUTAN

The Kingdom of Bhutan, a country similar to Switzerland in size and topography, situated on the Indian–Chinese border, has existed in a state of uneasy dependency on India ever since the British East India Company concluded a treaty with the ruling family in 1774. By a subsequent treaty of 1910 the kingdom agreed to let Britain handle its foreign affairs, and this responsibility was assumed by New Delhi on Indian independence in 1947. According to the most recent treaty, renegotiated in 1949, Bhutan 'agrees to be guided by the advice of India' in its foreign policy.

Bhutanese officials frequently claim that this advice is not necessarily binding, but New Delhi insists that it is, and in practice Bhutan accepts this fact. Thus, for example, Bhutan does not dare to resume trade with Tibet, which was banned in 1960 when Sino–Indian hostility was fast becoming serious, nor to have diplomatic contact with its Chinese neighbour. India's influence, based on its overwhelming military dominance in the area and its physical control over all access to Bhutan for trade or travel, is reinforced by the fact that its economic aid to the kingdom finances almost all of the country's development plan.

Indeed, New Delhi is so conscious of the need to preserve its exclusive influence in this strategically hypersensitive area – at Bhutan's western end only 10 miles separate China from the 50 mile-wide corridor connecting the main part of India to all its north-eastern provinces – that it has shown itself extremely jealous of the United Nations, its principal rival in the provisions of aid to Bhutan. Bhutan is one of the world's highest per capita recipients of UN aid (around $10 per capita), but UN experts travelling to Bhutan are habitually subjected to administrative harrassment while passing through India.

The Indian solicitousness for Bhutan's welfare is particularly pronounced in matters of defence. In addition to providing a resident military mission in the capital, Thimpu, and furnishing most of the aid and training for Bhutan's small army, India maintains an undisclosed number of its own troops in the country. Reports that as much as a division of Indian troops is based in the country are certainly exaggerated, but it is beyond question that regular Indian army units help the Bhutanese to patrol their northern border with China, and that contingency plans exist for their rapid reinforcement in a crisis. It is generally believed that the imposition of a prohibitive entry fee for foreign tourists in 1975, which strangled the infant tourist industry, was made at India's insistence, to avoid the embarrassment of foreign visitors freely roaming about Bhutan and observing the scale of the Indian military presence. Those foreign tourists who do enter Bhutan may travel only in groups accompanied by guide/interpreters, and are restricted to the central areas.

With its external defence task effectively taken over by the Indian army, the role of the Bhutanese army is mainly internal security. In this regard, there is little by way of sophisticated political dissent, as Bhutan is one of the least-developed countries in the world: annual per capita income is under $60, over 95% of the population are illiterate peasant farmers living in isolated valleys, and there are only four settlements with populations of over 10,000. In a population of 1,200,000, there are only 18,300 students attending school.

Political parties are illegal, and King Jigme Singye Wangchuk rules virtually as an absolute monarch, appointing his own Council of Ministers to run the government. There is a National Assembly of 150 members (100 indirectly elected village elders, 10 monastic representatives and 40 government appointees) which has the power to enact legislation, accept or reject the appointment of royal ministers, and even every 3 years to hold a vote of confidence on which the King's continued reign is contingent, but in practice it presents no obstacle to royal rule.

The principal potential source of instability which might call for the army to exercise its internal security role is the composition of the population. Approximately 60% are Bhotias, the dominant, Tibetan-related group which speaks the national language, Dzongkha, but about 25%, living mainly in the western districts, are Gurungs, a Nepalese group. The remaining 15% are made up of an Assamese minority in the south-east and various small indigenous or migrant tribes. There is also a small but relatively well-educated community of about 5000 Tibetan refugees, politically loyal to the exiled Dalai Lama: in 1974 a group of them were arrested when the government discovered a plot to assassinate the newly crowned King, who was then 18 years old.

The principal instrument for containing the often severe inter-communal rivalries is the army, a force of about 4000 men which is directly under royal control. Military service is obligatory for all males, with liability extending from the age of 18 years to fifty, but in practice there are invariably sufficient volunteers to fill the ranks. There is in addition a militia numbering about 15,000 which serves as a local security force and reserve.

The army is trained by Indian officers, and all of its weapons – light infantry weapons only – are derived from India. Uniforms, ranks and organisational structure are also modelled on the Indian army. Annual defence expenditure is unknown, but cannot be large as the total government expenditure in 1978 was only 65,100,000 ngultrums (the ngultrum has the same value as the Indian rupee). There is almost certainly an Indian subsidy to the Bhutanese military budget as well, however.

Gwynne Dyer

BOLIVIA

HISTORY AND INTRODUCTION

Bolivia has an extremely violent history, the result both of frequent internal revolution and of bloody foreign war. A very high proportion of her rulers have been military men and, in modern times, the army has directly exercised power for long periods; at the same time, Bolivia is one of the few countries in Latin America in which the army has been defeated and humbled in the course of political conflict. It has a better reason than most Latin American armies, therefore, to appreciate the importance of armed force in internal politics.

Bolivia, originally Upper Peru, seceded from that newly independent State in 1825, but chose to call itself after the liberator who had secured the independence of both countries. An Andean State with a very large majority of depressed and illiterate Indian peasants in its population, the country and its politics were to be dominated by the white creole class throughout the nineteenth century and for much of the twentieth. The first president, Sucre, Bolívar's principal aide, was succeeded by the ambitious Santa Cruz (1829–39), who succeeded in dragooning Peru back into a confederation with his domain. The confederation was dissolved as a result of the battle of Yungay (*see* Chile). He was succeeded in turn by a succession of caudillos, almost all of whom ruled by brute force through *ad hoc* armies. The defeat of Daza's army in the War of the Pacific (*see* Chile and Peru) inflicted on the country a disastrous loss of territory and its access to the sea, recovery of which is still a major issue in Bolivian politics and diplomacy, and so discredited caudillism as a system that the country was thereafter able to enjoy several decades of reasonably constitutional government, in which the army played an intermediary role between liberal and conservative factions.

The emergence of the army as a properly organised force does not, however, antedate 1891, when a Bolivian graduate of the French *École de Guerre* was brought home to open the military academy (*Colegio Militar*), which found a home first in Sucre, then in Oruro and eventually (1899) in La Paz. Shortly afterwards, in step with developments in neighbouring countries, foreign missions were invited into the country to help with the reorganisation and retraining, first a French mission in 1905, which created a rudimentary general staff, and then, more fashionably, a German mission which arrived in 1911. Its head, Major Kundt, was appointed head of the general staff, and a subordinate director of the *Colegio Militar*. The mission went home in 1914 but Kundt returned in 1921, was named Minister of Defence in 1925, so pleased was the government by his skill in arranging military parades, but fell from favour in 1931 for meddling in politics.

The army's involvement in politics, dormant since the previous century, was reawoken by its defeat at the hands of Paraguay (*see* that entry) in the Chaco War of 1932–8. Young officers, led by Colonel Toro, impatient with the ineptitude the civilian government had shown in the management of the war, and outraged at the heavy losses (60,000 dead, mostly Indians) the army had suffered in consequence, overthrew it in 1936 and installed a colonels' regime which proclaimed a collectivist policy modelled on current European Fascist programmes. It invited an Italian military mission into the country in 1938 to establish a staff college and to reform the general staff discredited by the Chaco War, and also founded an arms school to improve the training of all officers.

The suicide of Colonel-President Busch in 1939 allowed the oligarchy to reassert its power and rule through a succession of older generals, but in 1943 the members of a military 'lodge', the *Razón de Patria*, founded while they were held prisoner by the Paraguayans, made common cause with the radical political party, the National Revolutionary Movement (MNR), took power and reintroduced the national socialist policies (the emphasis was socialist rather than nationalist) with which Toro and Busch had experimented. Their motives for doing so are easily explained. Bolivia is a poor country of enormous natural wealth, 'a beggar sitting on a golden throne', as the local proverb has it. Most of the wealth takes the form of deposits of minerals, mainly tin, and of oil, the exploitation of which, and profit from which were, to an extent even greater than was once true of Peru, in foreign hands. The young officers, led by Major/President Villaroel, and the MNR, led by Paz Estenssoro, made it their ambition to retain the bulk of these profits inside the country. In reaction the mining companies used their wealth to foment disturbances against the government, in one of which Villaroel was lynched.

The traditional ruling class regained power, purged the army and exiled the political undesirables. MNR nevertheless won the presidential elections of 1951 and, when prevented from assuming power by a right-wing military *junta*, organised an armed political militia, chiefly of miners, and overthrew it in April, 1952. The passage of events which ensued is almost unprecedented in the modern history of any State: the army was not technically disbanded, but it was largely ignored, and its place taken by the three militias of the miners, factory workers and peasants. Some purging of the officer corps took place (though early reports that 80% were dismissed have been proved untrue, the real figure being nearer 25%), and about two-thirds of the conscripts sent home. The remaining personnel did what they could to maintain barracks and equipment, while the militiamen performed most of the army's traditional duties, to the extent of refusing officers access to armouries and arsenals. The *Colegio Militar* received a class of 'MNR cadets' who were graduated after 10 months' training and told at their commissioning parade by the party leader, Paz Estenssoro, that the 'new army' was an instrument of production and a builder of schools and roads, as well as the defender of the nation.

Meanwhile the MNR hurried through a number of fundamental reforms, none of which, given the grossly unequal character of Bolivian society and its economic dependency on outside interests, was premature: the extension of the franchise to all adults, the breaking up of the great absentee-landlord estates, and the nationalisation of the three major tin-mining companies. Over the latter the government overreached itself. By 1961, after a collapse of the world tin market, the nationalised mines had become a major economic embarrassment to the government, which was obliged to turn to the army, now somewhat restored in strength and standing, to overawe the miners' militia so that a sensible reduction of their inflated labour force could be effected.

This reversal of MNR's policies was seen as a betrayal by

many of its supporters and Paz was able to secure re-election in 1960 only by engaging the army as his ally. In order to contain what had become endemic violence in Cochabamba and Santa Cruz departments, the two were declared virtually autonomous military zones in 1960, under military *interventores*. One of these, General Barrientos, made it his price to Paz, who unprecedentedly sought re-election in 1964, that he should take him as his vice-presidential candidate. There were good political grounds for doing so, in that the general belonged to the pro-MNR faction inside the army, and had a strong following among the peasants of the eastern departments where he had been *interventor*. No sooner elected, however, than he ousted Paz, alleging that the president's policies were divisive and unpatriotic, and took power himself, with the support and endorsement of the armed forces commander, Ovando, himself an MNR general, political radical and economic nationalist. The two men nevertheless dealt firmly with the continuing disturbances in the mines, eagerly courted American support for the economy and used the skills learnt by the hundreds of officers they sent to the United States School of the Americas to put down ruthlessly Ché Guevara's attempt in 1967 to foment trouble among the peasants of the east. Barrientos was killed in a helicopter crash in 1969, and was briefly succeeded by his vice-president, but after 4 months Ovando took power and restated a full programme of left-wing aims, including the nationalisation of the Gulf Oil Company. An internal army coup, led by the rightist General Miranda, removed him from the presidency after a year but did not succeed in capturing power, which passed to another left-wing general, Torres. He promised 'a popular, nationalist government resting on four pillars – the peasant farmers, the workers, the students and the armed forces', showed open hostility to the United States, extended contacts with Russia and eastern Europe and appeared to be building a constituency among the army's NCOs. It may have been this last development which prompted the right within the army, led by the able young commander of the *Colegio Militar*, to move against him, which it did decisively after some misfired attempts in August, 1971.

General Banzer was toppled by a military coup in July 1978 and replaced by General Juan Pereda Asbún, who in his turn was replaced by General David Padilla, in November of the same year. Elections in July 1978 were inconclusive and Dr Walter Guevara was chosen as an agreed interim President. General Padilla yielded up the presidency to Dr Guevara who was immediately overthrown by a coup led by Colonel Natusch Busch. Colonel Natusch however failed to secure the support of the rest of the Armed Forces and Congress named Señora Lidia Gueiler as the first woman President of Bolivia on November 20th, 1979. Señora Gueiler was overthrown by a coup led by General Luis García Meza on July 18th, 1980. In October 1982, Dr Hernán Siles Suazo, who had previously been President for a brief period in 1960 again assumed the presidency as leader of a left-wing coalition, his cabinet including two communists.

STRENGTH AND BUDGET

Population: (estimated 1981) 5,600,000
Army: 20,000
Navy: (river and lake) 2,600 including Marines; 37 small craft
Air Force: 4,000; 38 combat aircraft
Paramilitary: 5,000
GNP: (1981) $7,400,000,000
Defence Expenditure: (1981) $177,700,000

A very high proportion of the national budget (about 24%) was devoted to defence before the 1952 coup. It then declined to about 7% and rose slowly during the 1960s to about 13%. Bolivia has benefited particularly generously from United States military assistance and Agency for International Development payments, the latter used chiefly for rural development work sponsored by the army engineers.

COMMAND AND CONSTITUTIONAL STATUS

The President is Commander-in-Chief. Since 1964 the post has usually been held by a soldier. He exercises direct command over the army, air force, police and navy (formerly the River and Lake Froce, established 1963). The commanders of the four services direct their own staffs. The former post of Commander-in-Chief of the Armed Forces, always held by an army officer, was abolished in July, 1970 as a result of an internal army faction-fight, and replaced by the Superior Council of National Defence, on which senior officers of all services sit. It is an advisory body to the presidency. The Ministry of National Defence, traditionally held by a soldier before the 1964 coup, but not always since, is administrative in function; it does not exercise command. Staffs are organised on the American system.

Though Bolivia enjoyed a period of stable, civilian government between 1880 and 1930, its political history is so full of revolution, dictatorship and constitutional upsets, that it is difficult to point to norms in the arrangements of civil – military relations in the country.

ROLE, COMMITMENT, DEPLOYMENT AND RECENT OPERATIONS

Role

Though the army has fought in two of South America's major wars, and is now in effective control of the government, a close American military observer* ascribes it a comparatively modest institutional role: 'It is not an operational force, and, despite sporadic employment of a few units against guerrilla groups and organised violence in the mining areas, it has never developed an operational "mystique". Emphasis has been, rather, on supporting an army presence throughout the national territory, maintaining frontier garrisons and protecting the central government apparatus'. The repossession of access to the sea is a national ambition.

Commitment

Bolivia is a signatory of the two main Latin American defence treaties, Chapultepec and Rio, and has a bi-lateral military assistance agreement with the USA, but is not committed to any other external military responsibility.

Deployment

The country is divided into six Military Regions, as follows:

Región Militar 1 (HQ La Paz) covers most of La Paz Department.
Región Militar 2 (HQ Sucre) covers department of Cochabamba and most of Chuquisaca.
Región Militar 3 (HQ Tarija) covers departments of Tarija, eastern Chuquisaca and Santa Cruz.
Región Militar 4 (HQ Potosí) covers departments of Oruro and Potosí.
Región Militar 5 (HQ Trinidad) covers most of Santa Cruz and Beni Departments.

---

* Corbett, Charles C., *The Latin American Military as a Socio-Political Force*, University of Miami Press (1972).

Región Militar 6 (HQ Cobija) covers department of Pando and parts of La Paz and Beni.

Originally each Region was garrisoned by a nominal Division. The number of Divisions was however increased first to eight and more recently, to ten. The present tactical organisation, adopted in the late 1970s seeks to superimpose a Corps structure on these Divisions. There will ultimately be four Army Corps as follows:

Army Corps I (HQ Oruro), which is already partially formed, will combine the 1st Division (HQ Viacha) with the 2nd Division (HQ Challapata) and the 10th Division, still in process of formation with its HQ at Tupiza.
Army Corps II (HQ Santa Cruz), which is also partially formed, will combine the 3rd Division (HQ Villamontes) with the 4th Division (HQ Camiri) and the 5th Division (HQ Roboré).
Army Corps III, still in process of formation, will combine the 7th Division (HQ Cochabamba) with the 8th Division (HQ Santa Cruz).
Army Corps IV, also incomplete, will combine the 6th Division at (HQ Riberalta) with the new 9th Division (HQ Trinidad).

The composition of the Divisions is not standard, the strongest being the 1st, 2nd, 3rd and 7th whilst some consist of only one regiment.

Deployment

The country is divided into nine military regions, which correspond with the administrative departments, and are further sub-divided into circumscriptions and districts, the latter chiefly for recruiting purposes. The army is organised into 10 'divisions', based one in each of the regions, but with an additional 'division' at Viacha in La Paz Department. There are headquarters at Viacha, Oruro, Villa Montes, Sucre, Camiri, Roboré, Santa Cruz, Riberalta, Trinidad, Cochabamba, Cobija, Potosí and Tarija. The main bases are at Miraflores barracks, La Paz and at Cochabamba (Seventh Division) which houses the staff college, the arms school, the NCO's school and the special troops school, with its parachute battalion. Troop strength in each of the garrisons rarely exceeds a thousand. The six engineer battalions operate in the interior on development projects. The two ranger battalions are also in the interior. The infantry battalions are scattered between the headquarters, one in each. The cavalry, motorised and artillery regiments are at the main bases.

Recent Operations

With covert American assistance, the Bolivian army successfully concluded in 1967 what has become the most celebrated (or notorious) anti-guerrilla operation in recent Latin American history: the extinction of Ché Guevara's band on the headwaters of the Rio Grande, where he was seeking to foment people's war among an uncomprehending peasantry. There has been no serious attempt since.

ORGANISATION

The Army is divided into Combat Arms: Infantry, Cavalry, Armoured Troops, Artillery, Engineers and Signals and Logistic Support Services which include Intendance, Transport, War Material and Medical. Infantry, Cavalry and Artillery are organised in regiments whilst Armoured Troops and Engineers are organised in battalions. The remaining Arms and Services are largely organised at company level. There are 17 Infantry Regiments (including 2 Motorised, 3 Andean and

2 Ranger), 6 Cavalry and 3 Artillery Regiments; 1 Paratroop, 2 Armoured and 5 Engineer Battalions. With the exception of the Paratroop Battalion, which is attached to the Centro de Instrucción de Tropas Especiales at Cochabamba, all Regiments have both names and numbers.

The Bolivian State Police (Corps of Police and *Carabineros* of Bolivia) is modelled on the *Carabineros de Chile*. It is a centrally controlled, militarised force, which may be treated as a reserve of the army in time of war. A 'brigade' is stationed in each of the departments, divided into urban and rural sections. There are additional detachments in troubled areas, such as San Ignacio de Velasco and Tupiza, and two separate regiments in the capital. The strength of the corps in 1970 was 5000, of which half was stationed in La Paz. It was reorganised and trained on American lines by an American training mission in 1976.

RECRUITMENT, TRAINING AND RESERVES

Recruitment and Training

Since 1904 recruitment has been by conscription of the male population at the age of eighteen. In practice, only a proportion of the annual contingent is enlisted, apparently on a haphazard basis of selection. Almost all the conscripts are Indians. NCOs are time-expired conscripts.

Officers are recruited exclusively from the military academy (*Colegio Militar*, founded 1891) at La Paz, entry to which is highly competitive; there are about 800 to 1000 applicants for 100 to 150 places each year, of whom about 75 to 85 eventually graduate. Recruitment is exclusively from the white or *mestizo* middle class. Subsequent training is given at the arms school (*Escuela de Aplicación de Armas*) and, for the chosen, at the staff college (*Escuela de Estado Mayor*, founded 1938), both at Cochabamba. There is a war college (*Escuela de Altos Estudios Militares*, founded 1960) for senior servicemen and civilians at La Paz. Officers go every year to schools in Argentina, Brazil, Peru and the United States, postings which are much coveted. There is a military engineering school at La Paz, to which the army's engineer officers may go for a professional qualification. NCOs are trained at the *Sargento Paredes Escuela de Clases*, Cochabamba. Conscripts are trained in the units.

At Cochabamba there is also the *Centro de Instrucción de Tropas Especiales* which has an attached Paratroop Battalion. The *Centro de Instrucción de Operaciones en la Selva*, at Riberalta, trains troops in jungle warfare. There is a Special Forces school, with US instructors, at Santa Cruz.

An Italian military mission founded the staff college; Argentinian and American military missions have influenced officer training since 1956.

Reserves

Apart from the police and the pool of discharged conscripts, there appear to be no reserves. The workers' militias might be called on in the case of war.

EQUIPMENT AND ARMS INDUSTRY

Although hand grenades were manufactured during the Chaco War, Bolivia currently appears to have no arms industry and must import all military equipment, including small arms ammunition. The United States was the main source of supply until the mid 1970s although quantities of second-hand equipment, including artillery pieces, were acquired as gifts from Argentina, from which country quantities of small arms ammunition were also purchased. During the past ten years, Bolivia has also purchased quantities of weapons and equipment from Switzerland, France, Germany, Spain, Israel and more recently Brazil, Taiwan and Austria.

Rifles: SG 510 7.62mm (Switzerland); G3 7.62mm (Germany); Galil 7.62mm (Israel)

Sub-machine-guns: M-3A1 (US); Uzi (Israel) Machine-guns: M-2 12.7mm (U.S.) M-1917 7.62mm (US); M-1919 7.62mm (US)

Anti-armour: 106mm RCL (US)

Mortars: Brandt 60mm (French); Brandt 81 mm (French); 4.2"(US)

Artillery: M101 105mm howitzer (US); M116 75mm howitzer (US); Bofors 40mm L/40 (Swedish via Argentina)

Armour: Kürassier tank destroyer (Austria; 30 in service); EE-9 Cascavel armoured car (Brazil; 16 in service); U-150 Commando armoured car (US; 10 in service); EE-11 Urutu APC (Brazil; 24 in service); Mowag Roland APC (Switzerland; 20 in service); M113 APC (US; 18 in service)

Aircraft: The Army operates 4 light aircraft; the Air Force has about 36 transport aircraft and about 30 helicopters.

RANK, DRESS AND DISTINCTIONS

Both officers and NCOs are distinguished by rank insignia on shoulder straps or epaulettes as follows:

General — Three large gold stars
General de División — Two large gold stars
General de Brigada — One large gold star
Coronel — Three small gold stars with central stripe in branch colour on shoulder strap
Teniente Coronel — Two small gold stars with central stripe in branch colour on shoulder strap
Mayor — One small gold star with central stripe in branch colour on shoulder strap
Capitán — Three small silver stars on plain shoulder strap
Teniente — Two small silver stars on plain shoulder strap
Sub Teniente — One small silver star on plain shoulder strap
Suboficial Primero — Three chevrons in branch colour, point uppermost
Suboficial Segundo — Two chevrons in branch colour, point uppermost
Suboficial Tercero — One chevron in branch colour, point uppermost
Sargento Primero — Three horizontal bars in branch colour
Sargento Segundo — Two horizontal bars in branch colour
Cabo — One horizontal bar in branch colour

Officers have a grey service uniform of decidedly Germanic cut. Other ranks wear grey-green service uniforms on the Altiplano; khaki-beige in the tropical lowlands. The US M-42 steel helmet appears to have largely replaced the German helmet formerly worn. Dress uniforms are extremely Germanic, including spiked helmets. The 1st *Colorados* Infantry Regiment, which performs ceremonial duties at La Paz, has a French 'Second Empire' style uniform, with red jackets and kepis and white trousers. The 4th *Insavi* Cavalry Regiment, which also performs ceremonial duties at La Paz, also has a red uniform with a bearskin headgear.

The principal Bolivian decoration is the 'Cóndor of the Andes'. There are also an Order of Military Merit, a Service Cross, the Iron Star and the Chaco War Medal.

CURRENT DEVELOPMENTS

Colonel Banzer's presidency was one of the most unsettled periods of modern Bolivian history, not only for the country but also for the army and the rest of the armed forces. There were, besides the announcements of forestalled coups, four major military rebellions, one by the right-wing faction and three by the left-wing faction within the armed forces. In December, 1972 supporters of Torres and Barrientos staged a mutiny at the El Alto air base, near La Paz, as a result of which Banzer dismissed the Chief of Staff. In May, 1973 Colonel Selich, a former Minister of the interior to Banzer and commander of the ranger battalion which had played the key role in his coup, was arrested re-entering the country from exile and died in the hands of the police. Señor Arce, the current Minister of the Interior and first civilian to be appointed to Banzer's cabinet, disclosed that Selich's death was murder, which led to a protest by the commander of the key Cochabamba garrison, and another by the *Falange Socialista Boliviana*, the MNR's main party of opposition which commanded a considerable following in the armed forces, and to the resignation of Señor Arce. Claiming the threat of a coup, Banzer replaced all the leaders of the armed forces and assumed direct supreme command himself. In January, 1974 while he was visiting the south of the country there was a revolt by the *Tarapaca* armoured regiment in La Paz, where its officers seized the presidential palace. They were expelled without bloodshed, but a month later Banzer, who claimed that the officers were *barrientistas* (i.e. supporters of his left-wing predecessor), dismissed his civilian—military cabinet and replaced it with an all-officer one. In November of the same year, a left-wing military rising had to be put down with troops brought from La Paz. And in January, 1976 alleging the discovery of a 'vast communist plot', the President replaced all the service commanders-in-chief.

All this had taken place against the background of continuing civil strife. In January, 1974 peasants and workers of the Cochabamba region closed the roads into the city, which had to be opened by military action at the cost, the Catholic hierarchy alleged, of a hundred civilian lives. A 'state of siege' was proclaimed, which was extended in April for another 3 months, the underlying cause of the disturbance, namely high inflation and static wages, not having been cured. In November, 1974 as a result of the military rebellion in Santa Cruz, the President postponed indefinitely the elections which he had first promised for mid-1974, then postponed until 1975 because of his decision to concentrate national attention on the recovery of 'access to the sea' (*see* Chile). There were further strikes and disturbances in January, 1975 despite the existence of the 'state of siege' proclaimed in November. It was lifted in February, but had to be reimposed again in January, 1976 following the murder in Argentina of ex-President Torres, his widow alleged at the hands of the Bolivian military attaché in that country. Troops were sent to occupy the mining regions and remained there even after the 'state of siege' was lifted in July.

In November, 1977 the internal state of the country had stabilised for President Banzer to announce the advancement of elections from 1980, the date he had set in November 1974, to 1978. He also laid down a timetable for return to civilian rule: first, a stage of 'institutionalisation', when the parties and trade unions, placed 'in recess' in November, 1974 would be allowed to operate again, and then in 1980 a stage of 'constitutionalisation' when an elected government would reintroduce constitutional forms, of a new sort. But he warned that certain exiled left-wing leaders would not be allowed to return, nor to benefit from amnesty. He also insisted that his decision to bring forward elections was a decision of the armed forces, not influenced by external events, which implied a warning to dissidents within the country. The fall of Banzer ushered in another period of extreme political instability.

Chronic internal instability remains a major problem. Foreign policy is largely concentrated on regaining access to the sea, lost in the Pacific War. In pursuit of this, Bolivia is informally allied with Peru which also aspires to regain its lost southern provinces despite having abdicated all claim to them by the Treaty of Tacna Arica of 1929. Revenues from the illicit trade in cocaine have given a boost to the depressed economy and made increased funds available to permit a modest expansion and re-equipment of the Armed Forces which until recently lacked any true capability for conventional military operations. Whilst the immediate fear of hostilities between Peru and Chile has faded somewhat, Bolivia would certainly offer military assistance to any country at war with Chile. Bolivian support for Argentina during the South Atlantic War, which took the form of an offer to make the entire transport force of the Bolivian Air Force available to Argentina, must be seen more in the context of Argentino-Chilean rivalry and the Beagle Channel dispute than that of Latin American solidarity. The possibility of Bolivia engaging in any unilateral military action against any of its neighbours is extremely remote.

John Keegan
Adrian English

BOTSWANA

HISTORY AND INTRODUCTION

The Republic of Botswana attained independence in 1966, having previously been the British territory of Bechuanaland. An exceedingly poor country, Botswana hoped to avoid the necessity of raising an army, but overspill from the conflict in Rhodesia, in the form of the arrival of insurgents and of 'hot pursuit' operations, led to the raising of a small army in 1977. The majority of the first soliders were drawn from the Police Mobile Unit, whose deputy commissioner became the first commander of the Botswana Defence Force. At first the inspiration and equipment of the Botswana Defence Force were both British, more recently the Soviet Union has gained influence.

STRENGTH AND BUDGET

Strength
Population: 900,000 (estimated)
Total Armed Forces: 3,000
Army: 2,850
Air wing: 150
Barrack Police: 1,250

Budget
GNP: $600m (approximate)
Defence Expenditure: $29.3m (1980)

COMMAND AND CONSTITUTIONAL STATUS

The President of the Republic, Quett Masire, is commander-in-chief of the armed forces, the army commander is Major General Mompati Merafe who has as his deputy, Brigadier I. Khama, son of the country's first President, Sir Seretse Khama.

ROLE, COMMITMENT, DEPLOYMENT AND RECENT OPERATIONS

The Botswana Defence Force's role is counter-penetration and counter-insurgency. It is concerned with incursions by South African forces, especially from the Caprivi Strip area where a number of incidents have occurred. Counter-insurgency is seen mainly as a problem of insurgency occasioned by refugees turned insurgent rather than of local discontented.

ORGANISATION

The Botswana Defence Force is organised into a battalion group from which sub-units are sent out for particular missions. A second battalion group is envisaged.

RECRUITMENT, TRAINING AND RESERVES

Recruitment is voluntary, there appears to be no shortage of quantity, but constraints include physical fitness, and in respect of future NCOs and officers, the limited supply of educated manpower.

A small Botswana Defence Force Reserve exists. Some personnel, including officers have been trained in Britain.

Training concentrates on expertise in long range savannah and desert operations.

Indian Army personnel have arrived to supervise training with the new Soviet equipment.

Discipline is said to be good.

EQUIPMENT

Original equipment was almost entirely British, SLR, 81mm mortar, 84mm Carl Gustav RCL, and a number of Land Rovers. Then some captured insurgent Russian or Russian-patterned weaponry became available. Recent reliable reports note the arrival of a number of Soviet AK47 rifles and one hundred SAM 7 missiles, further reports claim 30 Soviet BTR 60 a.p.c.s have been delivered. The USA has also shown interest, 20 Commando Cadillac Gage light armoured car reconnaissance vehicles suitable for operations in bush terrain having also arrived. Motor-cycles are also used for the movement of small sub-units.

The air wing has been expanded to include five Britten Norman *Defender* light army co-operation aircraft, three *Skyvan* STOL transports, two Cessna 152 and six *Bulldog* light training machines.

RANK, DRESS AND DISTINCTIONS

These generally follow the British pattern.

CURRENT DEVELOPMENTS

The last two years have seen a marked increase in Soviet interest in Botswana, where a large Soviet Embassy has opened. This interest is of course only part of the Soviet Union's posture against South Africa. However, this posture and the known radical views of Brigadier Khama may well lead to situations in which sharper skirmishes with South African forces than those hitherto may take place.

ADDENDUM

The possibility of Botswana's amalgamating with the South African 'homeland' state of Bophututswana is being considered. An important military consideration would be the possibility of greater security for Botswana against South African 'hot pursuit' operations.

Lloyd Mathews

BRAZIL

HISTORY AND INTRODUCTION

Even when Brazil's armed forces have seemed to conform to the pattern of political behaviour familiar amongst the Spanish-speaking countries of Latin America, the resemblance has been more apparent than real. The only case of overt and prolonged military takeover of the governing function in Brazil has been the period since 1964, and neither in its motives nor in its goals is this period of military rule fully comparable to those which are typical of military coups in Spanish-American countries.

While there has been a certain convergence of political behaviour amongst all Latin American armed forces due to the influence of USA-derived counter-insurgency doctrine in the past two decades, the fundamental distinctions which characterise the Brazilian armed forces remain dominant. The difference of greater historical weight is the fact that Brazil did not experience savage and lengthy war which would have made the armed forces the pre-eminent institution of the State (as was true almost everywhere else in Latin America) in order to achieve its independence. Latterly, the fact that this country, unlike any of its Latin American fellows, can and does nourish the ambition to become a great power on a world scale in the twenty-first century has also profoundly affected the behaviour of Brazil's armed forces.

During the period of Portuguese rule, which lasted for over half of Brazil's history as an area of European settlement, the imperial government preferred to depend on officers and men recruited mainly in the home country to fight the colonial wars which were waged against Spain in La Plata and against Dutch incursions in the north-east. Portuguese imperial administraton exercised a far looser control than the Spanish, however, and from an early time landholders were made responsible for defending themselves against Indian attacks, slave risings and even foreign incursions. Thus, nearly every plantation in Brazil had its private army, numbering in the hundreds or even thousands, under the purely nominal control of the Portuguese administration. Following the period 1580—1640 when Portugal fell under Spanish rule, and the Dutch took advantage of Spanish neglect to seize Recife and establish control over the entire northern coast of Brazil, it was primarily native volunteer forces of this type, organised as the *Terco de Ordenanças* (Regimental Command), which expelled the Dutch from Brazil in 1654 and founded an independent Brazilian military tradition.

The Napoleonic Wars prepared the way for Brazilian independence. When Portugal itself was occupied by French forces in 1808, Brazil became the residence of the royal family and the governing centre of the shrinking but still impressive Portuguese empire. The possibility of a revolution like that which burst on Spain's American empire in 1810 was met by the decision to raise Brazil to dominion status within the empire in 1815, and by the policy of reserving the highest posts of command in the army and navy for men from the Iberian peninsula.

The hostility of creole officers to this policy, and the resentment of the native economic oligarchy at heavy taxation which went to support the perpetuation of an empire run largely for Portugal's benefit, constituted the possible sources of a Brazilian revolution on the Spanish-American model, but Braganza family politics soon foreclosed this avenue of development. King John VI and the imperial government belatedly returned to Lisbon in 1821, but in the following year his son Pedro, who had remained behind in Brazil, declared in São Paulo for 'independence or death'. He was crowned Emperor of Brazil in December, 1822 and thus Brazilian independence was achieved almost without bloodshed, the Portuguese troops in the country either swearing allegiance to Pedro, or offering only token resistance before accepting repatriation.

This peaceful transition to independence was largely the handiwork of the distinguished scholar and statesman Jose Bonifacio de Andrade e Silva, an intelligent and subtle conservative who was one of Pedro's first and closest advisors. Andrade e Silva's purpose was precisely to avoid the chronic violence, the importation of radical political ideas derived from Rousseau and the French revolution, and the military domination of civilian affairs which was already becoming evident as Spanish-speaking America's inheritance from the long wars of independence, and he was almost entirely successful. The Brazilian armed forces were deprived of the opportunity to make themselves the heroes of the independence struggle, and the economy and society were left untouched and unaltered by the ravages of war.

The Brazilian armed forces declined even further in public esteem compared to those of their neighbours during the reign of Pedro I, due to his continued preference for retaining Portuguese-born officers in the higher ranks and his war against Argentina, begun in 1828, which led to the creation of the buffer state of Uruguay. Even before Brazil finally lost the war, its unpopularity was causing young men to flee their homes in order to avoid military service, and it had become necessary to bring in numbers of German and Irish mercenaries. In 1831 Pedro I was forced to abdicate in favour of his five-year-old son and to return to Portugal, but again it was civilians who were at the head of the Brazilian political forces compelling this change.

During the succeeding 15 years Brazil was wracked by major separatist of federalist revolts in almost every region, fought largely by armies raised by levies on the plantations, but also involving desertions of regular units to the revolutionary side on some occasions. The centralised authority of the government survived, however, and the rebellions soon died out after Pedro II's assumption of full powers in 1840 (at the age of fourteen) ended the interregnum. The Brazilian armed forces, though always consulted and taken into account by the emperor's advisors, remained a subsidiary element in the empire's government at least until the 1870s.

The war against Argentina in 1852, resulting in the downfall of the Argentine dictator Juan Manuel de Rosas, had little effect on the size or status of the Brazilian armed forces, but the long and hard-fought War of the Triple Alliance (Brazil, Uruguay and Argentina against Paraguay) in 1864—70 had a profound influence on the future attitudes and actions of the Brazilian armed forces. At the beginning of the war the Brazilian army totalled only 17,000; by the end it had over 100,000 men in the field, and had suffered between one-third and one-half of that number in casualties. While its strength was quickly reduced again after the war, the army's new sense of its own importance, sharpened by the manifest ingratitude of the civilian authorities, worked a permanent change in the army's view of its proper relationship with the State.

The years after 1870 saw the onset of a steep decline in the stability of the empire's political structure in any case, due to Church—State quarrels, the growing pressure to emancipate Brazil's slaves, and the progressive decline in the Emperor's health, but it was the changes taking place in the army which were of the greatest importance. Indeed, it could be argued that the years 1870—89, culminating in the almost bloodless military overthrow of the empire, were the period when the Brazilian army's distinctive character and pattern of behaviour emerged and became settled.

The army officer corps of the 1870s and 1880s had already become a self-conscious institution, jealous of its prerogatives and resentful of the way in which the armed forces were being starved of funds by the governments of the day. The officers were largely of lower-middle-class origin, the army being one of the very few avenues of rapid social advancement available in imperial Brazil, and they had little sympathy for the slave-owning aristocracy of the north-east or for the imperial system of which it was a principal buttress. Commanding an army in which the enlisted men were almost exclusively Negro ex-slaves, army officers were familiar with the abolitionist arguments and generally supported them. The then-fashionable positivist theories of Auguste Comte, with their stress upon progress and social authority, became virtually gospel in the military academy by the mid-1880s, predisposing a whole generation of officers to republicanism and activism.

On a less-exalted level, officers were encouraged to enter politics by competing civilian parties, and from 1883 the increasingly sensitive officer corps as a whole became embroiled in an interconnected tangle of bitter disputes with the government — the so-called 'military question' — over quite petty points of personal privilege. The final straw may have been the government decision in 1889 to organise a National and Civic Guard which would equal the army in strength by the end of the year, but the collapse of the empire was already a foregone conclusion (slavery was abolished early that year). On November 15th, 1889 Marshal Manoel Deodoro da Fonseca, the acknowledged leader of the officer corps, announced the overthrow of the government and declared a republic. There would never again be a government in Brazil that did not rely upon at least tacit military support.

It is important to observe, however, that a tradition of direct military rule did not become established. Marshal Deodoro made himself President and instituted a frankly military regime that was continued by his immediate successor, Marshal Floriano Peixoto, but widespread disorders in outlying areas and sharp rivalry between the monarchically inclined navy (predominantly white and of aristocratic origins) and the republican, ethnically mixed army prevented the emergence of a settled military regime. This was not desired by Brazil's military leaders in any case. Marshal Deodoro helped to draft an explicitly civilian constitution for the republic, and in 1894 Marshal Peixoto passed the presidency into civilian hands, where it remained until 1964 (although a general was elected to the presidency in 1910—14).

In most respects, indeed, the Brazilian republic in its first three decades was little different from the empire it replaced; it remained a plantation economy dominated by the same political class that had monopolised leadership under the empire, strongly regional and with only rudimentary public opinion. The most noteworthy changes were the great enhancement in the social status of military officers (accompanied by a marked improvement in their economic conditions), and a continued high level of military influence from behind the scenes on the course of civilian politics. One might perhaps also attribute the heightened interest in material progress in post-imperial Brazil to the armed forces, which thanks to a well-developed military education system then possessed a very high proportion of Brazil's technically and scientifically oriented personnel.

By the 1920's, however, Brazil was beginning to evolve the rudiments of a modern economic and social structure. The shift of the economic centre of gravity from the north-east to the industrialising south-central region was almost complete, and there was for the first time an urban working class (albeit a small one) in Brazil's growing cities. The continuing influence of the positivist tradition on the army's junior officers though not on their seniors) was clearly demonstrated in the quixotic revolt of the Copacabana garrison in 1922, and the far more serious Tenente (Lieutenant) uprising in São Paulo in 1924. While these revolts by officers of lower-middle class origins can best be explained as a generalised protest against the corruption and stagnation of the existing regime, given specific direction by their technical military training and their professional orientation towards disciplined organisation, the programme of the Tenentes prefigured much that was typical of the Vargas regime in 1930—45 and of the military governments since 1964.

The Tenente revolutionaries of 1924 demanded minimum wages for labourers and regulation of work for women and children, while strongly opposing the anarcho-syndicalist trends that were then prevalent in Brazil's largely immigrant industrial workforce. While not opposed to private capital, they favoured State ownership of natural resources, and took a far more nationalistic attitude towards international trade than was then prevalent in Brazil or anywhere else in Latin America. They favoured the development of Brazil's vast interior frontier and the expansion of government's role in order to protect the common man. They saw government as a benevolently authoritarian institution, and the armed forces as redeemer of the nation. It is scarcely surprising that many of them ended up as collaborators in Vargas's proto-fascist 'New State', while others (notably Luiz Carlos Prestes) subsequently became leaders of the Brazilian Communist Party. Nor is it surprising that the senior officers who created the post-1964 military regime were themselves junior officers during the ferment in the army in the 1920s.

The 1924 revolt was quickly suppressed by loyal military forces, and even the 5,000 mile march of the *Coluna Invicta* (invincible column) through the Brazilian backlands led by Luiz Carlos Prestes was over by 1927. But it was the same sort of officers in the army (including some of the original Tenentes, newly returned from exile) who provided the leadership for the armed revolt which brought Getulio Vargas to the presidency in 1930 after his Liberal Alliance had been cheated at the polls. Although many of the Tenentes soon defected when Vargas showed himself willing to compromise with senior officers and the established political forces (and some took part in the abortive revolt of 1932), others continued to support him even after he inaugurated his corporatist 'Estado Novo' in 1937. So did their senior officers, who were equally attracted by his lavish spending on the armed forces and by his authoritarian emphasis on order and industrial development.

The initially undifferentiated reformism of the junior ranks in the armed forces had already split into communist and anti-communist strands by 1935, however, when almost the entire firepower of the abortive communist *putsch* of that year was provided by dissident army officers and NCOs. The post-1964 purges have now eliminated this communist strand of opinion from the regular armed forces, but it can be argued that all of Brazil's native political movements aimed at imposing radical reform from above had their origins in the armed forces of the 1920s and 1930s.

The initial military support for Vargas's authoritarian State began to wane rapidly, however, once he began to seek to replace his declining middle-class support by building a new political base amongst the working class. Brazil's participation in World War II (it was the only Latin American State to send armed forces to Europe) contributed to the army's soaring prestige, and thoroughly permeated the army with the anti-fascist sentiments that animated the alliance within which it fought. As a result, the army forced the resignation of Vargas, the dismantling of the corporate State, and the holding of democratic elections in 1945.

The democratic 'interlude' of 1954–64 (as it now appears) found the armed forces continuously involved in politics, while always refusing the last step of direct intervention. The problem which confronted the army in this period was one which is familiar to armies in most rapidly industrialising States that attempt to maintain a democratic system: the military priorities of rapid economic development and national discipline repeatedly clash with the tendency of democratic politicians in such States to seek support amongst urban workers by promising immediate and rapid improvement in living standards. Thus the armed forces had to permit a protégé of Vargas's to assume the presidency in 1945, unless they were prepared to invalidate the elections entirely. In 1950 they had to allow Vargas himself to return to power, though only on the understanding that he would not renew his attempt to build support on the left. When his Minister of Labour, Joao Goulart, did attempt such a manoeuvre in 1954, senior military officers forced his dismissal, and later in the year demanded Vargas's own withdrawal. Instead, Vargas committed suicide.

The last 10 years of the democratic regime in Brazil were marked by repeated civil–military clashes, including brief military interventions in 1955 and 1961 in which the soldiers withdrew again after obtaining their immediate political objectives. Military candidates for the presidency were soundly defeated in the elections of 1950, 1955 and 1960, and those defeats were accepted by the armed forces, but the successful civilian candidates in each case were compelled to rule within the constraints imposed upon them by military opinion. The principal issue was invariably the concern of the armed forces that politicians should not make demagogic appeals to the growing urban working-class electorate (numbering about 5,000,000 by 1950).

The main restraint on full military takeover before 1964 was the existence of a dominant faction within the army which, with powerful civilian political allies, persisted in believing that the existing democratic political structure could be manipulated to contain this danger. Harder-line officers within the army, and the generally more conservative navy and air force, were effectively deterred from pushing for comprehensive intervention in politics by the fear of splitting the armed forces. The crises of the period were generally resolved by compromises like that of 1961, when the leftward-leaning Vice President Joao Goulart was permitted to succeed to the office of president after his predecessor had resigned in frustration, but only on condition that his powers be restricted by a change to a parliamentary rather than a presidential form of government. Throughout this period, moreover, there were steadily mounting numbers of officers serving on detached duty in key positions in civilian government departments and national agencies concerned with industrial development (the figure of 1100 has been suggested for 1961), which gave the armed forces further confidence that their views would be heeded.

This civil–military *modus vivendi* broke down permanently in 1964 for a number of reasons. President Goulart's drive to recover full powers, his political co-operation with the Communist Party, and his tacit encouragement of a militantly nationalist left-wing movement in order to increase his freedom of manoeuvre all alarmed the armed forces, while the dire economic situation – runaway inflation and rising popular unrest – seemed to them to demand decisive action which his government was politically incapable of taking. The most important motives for the military takeover, however, were the heightened attention paid to internal security questions by the armed forces in this post-Castro period, when armies all over Latin America were frantically preparing themselves to deal with communist insurgencies (real or not), and the specific suspicion that President Goulart was trying to build up a following among non-commissioned officers that would counterbalance the officers' corporate political influence. On March 25th, 1964 Goulart indicated that some 3000 sailors and marines who had rebelled against their officers, calling for basic social reforms, would receive an amnesty; on March 31st–April 2nd the armed forces, with support from several State governors and most of the country's powerful economic groups, deposed Goulart.

Although few officers could have envisaged at the time that the armed forces would still be ruling Brazil a decade and a half later, the intervention was from the first a new departure in Brazilian history. Contrary to civilian expectations, the soldiers did not retire in favour of some new civilian politician. They arrested over 7000 persons on charges of subversion and corruption within the first week (including a great many politicians), issued decrees empowering the high command to suspend constitutional guarantees, cancel the mandates of elected officials at all levels, and deprive individuals of the right to vote or hold office for 10 years, and on April 11th, 1964 they compelled a decimated Congress to elect Marshal Humberto Castelo Branco to serve out Goulart's unexpired term. By the end of 1964 President Castelo Branco had removed some 9000 military officers and over 100 elected politicians from office as part of the 'moral rehabilitation of Brazil', while 378 of the country's most influential political and intellectual leaders had been deprived of their political rights.

The perceived threat of total social breakdown and Castroite insurgency which played a large part in motivating the military coup of 1964 was a mirage, but in broader terms Brazil's military leaders had accurately analysed the country's political problems. They were remarkably sophisticated men by Latin American military standards: almost all belonged to the circle of commanders who had fought in Italy during World War II, and had participated in the founding of the Superior War College in 1949. In this school senior officers of the three services and selected civilians had been engaged in continuous study of Brazil's political, economic and military situation and had evolved a common set of priorities in which (alongside an increasingly explicit anti-communism) first place was given to a strong nationalist drive to make Brazil a genuine great power – by the turn of the century, in the usual formulation. The USA-promoted counter-insurgency doctrines which were such a powerful influence on all Latin American armies in the early 1960s lent a sharper edge to their anxieties about Brazilian domestic developments, but the basic thrust of policy is more clearly illustrated in the growing penetration of armed forces officers into executive positions in the nationalised industries throughout the period after 1950.

The corporate view of the Superior War College on Brazil's political malaise quite accurately saw the basic problem to be the inability of the established order (including the armed forces themselves) to come to terms with the political power gained by the radical, labour-based popular movement created by Vargas. (The analogy with Perón in Argentina is close). Moreover, in the view of many senior officers and their civilian associates (especially in the economics faculties of the universities), it would not be possible to achieve the rate of economic growth necessary to achieve Brazil's great-power ambitions if the political structure were forced to accede to the demands of this movement for immediate and large rises in the living standards of the mass of Brazilians. Therefore, if the existing political structure could not contain these demands, one must be created that could.

It was by such a logical progression that Brazilian senior officers arrived, half-unawares, at the necessity of creating a permanent military government. It was not a conclusion accepted all at once, nor indeed has it ever been accepted in precisely those terms. Each step towards it was taken with as strict an observance of the constitutional forms as the military leadership felt the situation allowed – not a great deal, in some cases. Throughout this period there has been visible behind the manoeuvring of hard- and soft-line factions within the armed forces a persistent hankering to evolve some sort of restructured political system (such as the attempt to create a two-party system by *fiat*) that would safeguard the military position and the great goal of world-power status while permitting some popular safety valve in the form of a more or less representative government. Thus, for example, while the rulers of Brazil since 1964 have all been army-dominated generals, there have been regular elections – held under varying degrees of coercion – in an attempt to gain popular validation of their position.

The presidential elections scheduled for 1965 were postponed, but President Castelo Branco proceeded with the elections for governors in half of the 22 States. When more than half the winners proved to be from amongst the opposition candidates, however, the military government moved quickly to entrench itself. In the same month Castelo Branco issued Institutional Act No. 2, in which he asserted his right to suspend Congress and rule by decree, and decreed that in future the president would be elected indirectly by the Congress. He also dissolved all existing political parties and ordered the creation of an official government party, ARENA, and a tame opposition party, the MDB. In October, 1966 Congress obediently elected his successor, Marshal Artur da Costa e Silva, the man chosen by the armed forces, to the presidency, and in 1967 a new constitution was enacted by Congress that further increased the power of the presidency at its own expense.

His legal position thus assured, President da Costa e Silva proceeded to a partial 'civilianisation' of the government – half his 22 Cabinet members were civilians – and to a 'humanising' of the harsh austerity measures that had been imposed by his predecessor in a largely successful attempt to bring down the catastrophic rate of inflation. This trend was soon halted, however, by the emergence at last of the Marxist insurgency that the armed forces had been anticipating for so long.

The first Castroite rural guerrilla band, which was rounded up in Minas Gerais in 1967, included many non-commissioned officers who had been dismissed from the army in 1964, while the two best-known leaders of the urban guerrillas who had largely supplanted them by 1969, Carlos Marighela and Carlos Lamarca, were former army captains; but the main strength of the movement lay in radical middle-class university students for whom all other avenues of political expression had been closed by 1968. The urban guerrillas' bank robberies, raids on military installations and kidnappings (during 1969-70 they kidnapped the ambassadors of the USA, West Germany and Switzerland) were designed to harass and embarrass the government, and did not add up to a strategy offering any discernible prospect of success, but the military government's reaction was extreme.

In December, 1968 Congress was recessed indefinitely and a further wave of arrests was carried out; in September, 1969 just after President Costa e Silva succumbed to a stroke, the country was declared to be in a state of 'internal revolutionary war'. General Emilio Garastazu Medici, former Head of the National Intelligence Service, was selected by the Armed Forces High Command to serve as president for the next 5 years, and a campaign of unrestricted official terror – including regular use of torture, kidnappings and death squads – was unleashed against the leftist guerrillas and those suspected of being associated with them. It accomplished its aim so effectively that the guerrillas were a moribund force by 1971, and in February, 1973 the four main guerrilla organisations jointly recognised that their campaign had failed (while not retracting their ideological commitment to armed insurrection in the long term). Shortly after General Ernesto Geisel succeeded to the presidency in 1974, a series of transfers and arrests within the army brought an end to the worst excesses of the governmental campaign of counter-terror.

With the guerrilla crisis past, Geisel resumed the armed forces' attempt to institutionalise the regime, allowing relatively free elections to Congress in 1974 (in which the opposition MDB won the senatorial race in 16 of the 22 States) and lifting censorship on most of the press in the following year. The intractable difficulties involved in trying to reconcile a measure of democracy with the armed forces' wishes for Brazil were underlined once more in 1977, however, when the MDB defeated government-sponsored judicial reforms in Congress. Geisel responded by closing Congress, and re-writing the electoral rules so that senators and State governors will no longer be elected directly, but rather chosen by government-controlled electoral colleges.

While the army's direct tenure of power has lengthened far beyond its original expectations due to its inability to create a stable civilian political structure that will function to its own satisfaction, its central ambition of achieving rapid economic growth has nevertheless been largely fulfilled. Following a short period of stringent austerity while the economic chaos of 1964 was being brought under control, Brazil regularly achieved 10% economic growth rates in the late 1960s and early 1970s. Being heavily dependent on imported oil, it was exceptionally hard hit by the 1973–4 oil crisis and subsequent price increases, but within a couple of years had recovered to a quite respectable 6% growth rate. If this pattern can be maintained, the goal of becoming a fully industrialised power of the first rank within a single generation remains within reach.

The price of this rapid growth is paid by the mass of the working population, especially in the crowded cities, whose real income has fallen considerably since the coup of 1964. It is the classic formula for rapid industrialisation under any political dispensation – squeezing the resources for investment out of the mass of the population – but it underlines the political dilemma of Brazil's military rulers. While the senior officers of the armed forces are loosely aligned into harder- and softer-line factions, over the issues of authoritarian rule versus the maintenance of the constitutional facade, of straightforward repression of dissent versus relative tolerance, of lenient policies on foreign trade and investment versus economic nationalism and etatism, they are alike hemmed in by the realisation that they cannot pursue their economic/political goal of making Brazil a great power quickly and at the same time enjoy the sort of popular support that would make genuinely representative institutions possible. When forced to choose between these alternatives, as they regularly are, they invariably prefer the former.

General João Baptista de Oliveira Figueiredo succeeded General Geisel to the Presidency on March 15th, 1979. Although General Figueiredo appears to have liberalised the military regime to a considerable extent, including an amnesty for political prisoners in August 1979 and the licencing of new political parties in October of the same year, there seems to be no immediate prospect of a return to civilian rule. Considerable labour unrest, particularly in 1980, has not arrested the liberalisation process but helps to ensure that the military government feels that the country is not ready for a return to democracy.

STRENGTH AND BUDGET

Population: 125,000,000
Army: 183,000 (including 132,000 conscripts)
Navy: 47,000 (including 15,000 Marines and 3,000 Naval Aviation); 27 major vessels
Air Force: 42,000; 230 combat aircraft
Paramilitary: 185,000
GNP: (1980) $240,980,000,000
Defence Expenditure: (1980) $2,020,000,000

Under the Brazilian constitution, 1 year's military service is compulsory for all males, but in fact conscription is highly selective as over 1,000,000 Brazilian males reach military age each year, far exceeding the armed forces' requirements. The total strength of the armed forces is a modest 0.25% of Brazil's population of 115,000,000.

There is no organised reserve system, but the immediate reserve of trained men is estimated to be about 1,115,000. Paramilitary forces under armed forces command include the military police (sometimes known as the State Militia) numbering around 185,000 men, which serves as an auxiliary reserve force for the army.

Although defence spending has increased in absolute terms, it has in fact shown a decrease in real value since 1965.

COMMAND AND CONSTITUTIONAL STATUS

Under Section VI, Articles 90–93 of the Constitution of 1969, the navy, army and air force are permanent institutions under the authority of the President of the Republic. Their size, composition and budget are to be voted annually by Congress upon the recommendation of the President. If Congress is not in session, these matters are to be handled by decree law.

In his capacity as Supreme Commander of the Armed Forces, the President is constitutionally allowed to declare war after it has been authorised by Congress, and without such authorisation in case of foreign aggression occurring between legislative sessions. He is also authorised to declare partial or total mobilisation and to proclaim the existence of a state of siege and rule by decree. The president is indirectly elected to a term of 5 years by an electoral college consisting of all members of the National Congress, three delegates from each State legislature, and one extra delegate for each half-million voters. Since all these electors are themselves chosen by one or another form of electoral college, it is quite simple for the military government to arrange the election of a new president once the armed

forces have decided who it should be. The president is not immediately eligible for re-election.

In his military capacity the president is assisted by government organs including the National Security Council, the President's Military Household, the Armed Forces General Staff and the Ministries of the Army, Navy and Air Force. (There is no overall Ministry of Defence in Brazil, as navy and air force anxieties about army domination have always made its creation impossible despite the army's most strenuous efforts to create such a body.)

According to Article 87 of the Constitution the National Security Council (NSC) is the highest-ranking body to advise the President in the formulation and execution of national security policy; it also bears general responsibility for strategic defence planning. The NSC is made up of the President, Vice-President, all 16 Cabinet Ministers (about half of whom are usually military officers), the Chief of the Armed Forces General Staff, the Chiefs of Staff of the Navy, Army and Air Force, the Chief of the President's Military Household, and the generals and admirals commanding major commands. It is, in other words, so large in membership as to be of only ceremonial significance, but an abbreviated version of it is believed to function as an actual executive body.

The Ministers of the Army, Navy and Air Force are invariably military personnel appointed by the President for an indefinite tenure of office, and are responsible for the supervision and control of their respective forces. They report directly to the President except in matters of concern to other services, in which case they co-ordinate them through the Chief of the Armed Forces General Staff.

The Armed Forces General Staff is a joint all-service organisation without command functions, charged with the development of war plans and organisation and with inter-service administrative co-ordination. The President's Military Household, besides having responsibility for the security of the presidential palace, acts as the President's chief instrument of liaison with the armed forces ministries and other departments of government.

The actual (as opposed to constitutional) source of the President's authority, the real body which chooses presidents, and the final arbiter of major policy decisions in Brazil, is the so-called 'College of Generals', an informal organisation of about 120 army and air force generals, 60 admirals and 60 brigadiers. Within this body the army is much the most influential body of opinion, and the views of the 10 generals on the Army High Command (*see* Organisation: Arms of Service) are of particular moment. It is within the 'College of Generals', hidden from public view, that real politics in Brazil takes place; its relative importance in the Brazilian scheme of things may be deduced from the fact that only one of Brazil's four recent military presidents (Geisel) has succeeded in obtaining its approval for his own candidate as successor.

ROLE, COMMITMENT, DEPLOYMENT AND RECENT OPERATIONS

In fact, and even in constitutional law, a principal role of the armed forces since the foundation of the republic in 1889 has been to exercise the 'moderating power' previously provided by the emperor over the politics of the country, and to guarantee its unity. Some clause to this effect has been incorporated in every Brazilian constitution since 1891, and has been seen by the army as giving it the right and the duty of arbitration when political crises occurred. In the earlier years of the republic this function was largely exercised in defence of national unity and federal authority, as the armed forces were the main organisation of truly national scope in a country riven by regional rivalries. Increasingly in recent decades, as regional particularism receded, the army's 'moderating power' has been applied to the arbitration of political conflicts on the federal level, and since 1964 has been expanded to encompass the suppression of civilian politics and direct military rule. In terms both of Brazil's history and of the army's own preoccupations, this has long been its primary role.

National military defence has taken second place because of Brazil's relatively safe geopolitical situation: the country has actively fought in only one war in this century, and that only by way of an expeditionary force fighting in Europe. It does have genuine military concerns, however, both within the South American continent and in the wider field of the East—West confrontation.

Brazil occupies 3/7ths of South America and has approximately half the continent's population. It has more neighbours than any other sovereign State except the USSR: only Chile and Ecuador among South American countries do not share a common border with it. As the sole Portuguese-speaking nation in an otherwise Spanish-speaking continent, it is very much the odd nation out, and as a relative giant with great ambitions it often excites suspicion and anxiety amongst its smaller neighbours.

This anxiety is particularly acute because most of Brazil's borders with her neighbours run through sparsely populated Amazonia, a hinterland into which the Andean nations have scarcely pushed the borders of settlement and development, but where on the other side of the frontier Brazilian settlers are pushing forward in greater numbers each year. Seven thousand miles of new roads have been cut through the Amazonian forests of Brazil in the past decade, running to the borders of Venezuela, Peru, Bolivia, Guyana, and almost to Surinam, and where the roads go the settlers quickly follow. In a few places (notably in the empty eastern plains of Bolivia) they are already spilling across these unmarked frontiers, and wherever they go they trade only with Brazil.

Although almost all of Brazil's frontiers with her neighbours were formally settled by a series of agreements concluded in 1910 (and in only one case, over territory disputed with Bolivia, did Brazilian troops become directly involved), nevertheless there exists a continuing nervousness amongst those Andean nations whose own Amazonian territories are almost totally undeveloped. This anxiety played a large part in causing the lengthy delays in the negotiation of a 'multilateral co-operation pact' for the co-ordinated development of Amazonian water resources and the protection of the local ecology which was proposed by Brazil to its western and northern neighbours (it was finally agreed in mid-1978). The fact that the Brazilian armed forces are very heavily engaged in providing transportation and other essential services in these frontier regions is seen as a matter of sheer practicality in Brazil, but is a further cause of suspicion of Brazil's expansionary designs amongst its neighbours — so much so, in Peru's case, that it has deliberately refrained from building its section of the Transamazonia road, planned to link the Atlantic and Pacific coasts of the continent, and now completed within Brazil.

In addition to this general suspicion, there exists an acute and long-standing rivalry between Brazil and Argentina, founded in the wars of the Plata region in colonial times and during the nineteenth century, and nourished by the ambition of each nation to be the leading power in South America. Each country's armed forces have traditionally set their requirements for sophisticated weapons largely in terms of maintaining the military balance with the other, and even the question of the acquisition of nuclear weapons (which has

been seriously discussed in both Argentina and Brazil — *see* Equipment and Arms Industry) has been examined almost exclusively in terms of the rival's possible intentions in the same direction.

There are no Argentine—Brazilian border disputes, and indeed the common frontier between the two countries is very short, but there is great rivalry between the two for predominant influence in the buffer States of Paraguay and Uruguay. Latterly Brazil has been notably successful in making major inroads in this historically Argentine sphere of influence, and conflicting Paraguayan—Brazilian and Paraguayan—Argentine projects for the construction of enormous hydroelectric dams on the Parana river are now causing great friction between Brasilia and Buenos Aires.

An exacerbating factor in this rivalry has been Brazil's close identification with, and extensive aid to, the ruling military *junta* in Chile, a country with which Argentina has an active territorial dispute. Peru and Bolivia also both have major boundary disputes with Chile, and both fear Brazilian 'expansionism', so that there is even talk from time to time of a Peruvian—Bolivian—Argentine axis emerging to confront a Brazilian—Chilean axis. This does not seem likely in practice, however.

To cope with these not very imminent potential threats in its locality, Brazil simply pursues its traditional defensive strategy. This is made relatively easy because jungles, mountains and swamps, accessible only by a few large rivers and (on the Brazilian side) a few new roads, cover almost all of Brazil's frontiers with its neighbours. Only the southern borders, with Uruguay, Argentina and Paraguay, are relatively easy country for military operations, and close enough to Brazil's urban-industrialised heartland, so it is not surprising that the Third Army Corps in the south is the biggest in Brazil. The largest concentration of air force strength is in the same region.

Brazil's defensive strategy was made necessary by the difficulty in concentrating military power quickly in any particular region of the country to repel invasion. This required that the army be carefully deployed within the country to cover a number of critical points (a distribution which also facilitated the army's anti-separatist and 'moderating' role). Since it was only where rivers crossed the Brazilian frontier that a serious invasion could take place, strategic defence requirements were met by the creation of a special command known as the Frontier Elements Group which, through units stationed at ports of river entry, controlled all movements in and out of the country via water transportation. The bulk of the army was based near the important coastal cities and industrial areas and adjacent to the southern borders with Uruguay and Argentina, with about 15% based in the 'hump' of the north-east in deference to anxieties about a threat to that strategically important region which controls the 'narrows' of the south Atlantic in a possible global confrontation.

In actual fact, the possibility of Brazil's becoming involved in international conflict within South America during the middle decades of the twentieth century was assessed as virtually nil even by Brazilian military planners themselves: while these deployments were (and still are) largely maintained, military attention was focussed at higher and lower levels, on World War II/cold war externally and on internal security at home. Now, however, the internal security threat seems decisively defeated and the Pax Americana extended by Washington over Latin America is becoming frayed at the edges: Brazilian like other South American generals again see serious wars within the continent as a contingency that must be planned for. Thus the strategic priorities of the Brazilian General Staff may now be stated to be the maintenance of a defensive shield around the Rio—São Paulo—Brasilia triangle, the ability to operate at sea throughout the south Atlantic, and a capability to operate on land and in the air throughout the River Plate basin.

A recent addition to this list is an ability to operate in the Surinam—French Guiana region in the period following withdrawal of the colonial power — a requirement justified by Brazil by reference to the possibility of a power vacuum in these underpopulated and underdeveloped neighbours which might attract Cuban or Soviet intervention, but seen with considerable suspicion in Venezuela as part of a Brazilian drive to gain access to the Caribbean.

In support of these strategic priorities the Brazilian armed forces have undergone an extensive modernisation programme in the past decade: the air force has acquired Mirage and F-5 supersonic fighters and the navy is receiving a considerable number of new warships to boost its anti-submarine and general warfare capabilities. Specific programmes which illustrate the growing regional emphasis of Brazilian strategic thinking include the acquisition of Roland surface-to-air missiles and Cobra ATGWs, the formation and equipment by the navy of a support brigade of marines complete with landing craft, and the formation in 1977 of a second parachute brigade of 7000 men which is theoretically capable of operating anywhere in South America within 12 hours.

Brazil's external commitments include membership in the United Nations, the Organization of American States, and its military counterpart, the Inter-American Defense Board. In practice its military activities abroad (with the exception of some army units with the United Nations Emergency Force at Suez and some air force elements with the UN force in the Congo in the 1960s) have been almost exclusively in association with the USA. This link extends back to the time of World War II, when Brazil joined the Allied war effort after German submarines had begun attacking Brazilian commercial vessels.

It had done the same thing for the same reason part of the way through World War I, and it was considered preferable in Washington that it restrict itself to the same kind of logistical contributions that it had made in the earlier conflict: collaboration of the Brazilian navy with Allied forces in the anti-submarine battle in the south Atlantic, the delivery of strategic minerals and other raw materials to Allied industry, and the granting of air and naval bases to the USA in north-eastern Brazil permitting United States forces to transit through Natal *en route* to Europe and Africa. Brazil provided all these services (and the Brazilian constitution still contains a duplicate of the clause that was then inserted permitting the president to authorise the basing or transit of foreign forces on Brazilian territory), but it also insisted on doing more.

In an early display of that determination to emerge from the regional into the world scene which has marked Brazil's armed forces in recent decades, they insisted on sending an expeditionary force to Europe. Washington, which had mixed feelings about the modernisation of Latin American armed forces, attempted to block Brazil's plans, and did succeed in limiting its contribution to one infantry division and one fighter group — about 25,000 men. They entered combat in mid-1944 in Italy as part of the United States Fifth Army, were in almost continuous action for over 200 days, and proved themselves able to meet the standards of European warfare. The Brazilian Expeditionary Force was not just the first and only military unit in history to leave South America to engage in combat in Europe; it also thereby made the Brazilian armed forces the only ones on the continent (except for a small Colombian contingent that

fought in Korea) with any direct experience of modern warfare. It would not be excessive to say that the army's experience in Italy did more than anything else to mould both the international and the professional orientations of subsequent Brazilian senior officers down to the present.

Since 1945 the Brazilian armed forces have participated in frequent air and naval exercises with the USA and neighbouring countries in the south Atlantic, and in 1965 sent one of the first contingents to the Inter-American Peace Forces which intervened in the civil war in the Dominican Republic (the IAPF commander was a Brazilian officer). A close military association was developed with the USA, which sent a joint service mission to Brazil in 1948 to help establish the Superior War College that has since been the greatest single influence on senior officers' thinking. A full-scale American military mission was set up in Brazil in 1963, and between 1950 and 1970 United States grant aid to the Brazilian armed forces was $217,700,000 plus a further $27,600,000 worth of excess stocks.

Since the arrival in office of President Geisel in 1974, however, the once close links between Brasilia and Washington have been considerably loosened. In part this is a natural reaction to the fact that neither Brazil nor the USA is still in the militantly anti-communist frame of mind that helped to cement the alliance so closely during the Cold War. In part it derives from the exigencies of Brazil's ambitious economic growth plans, which absolutely require it to trade with anyone, regardless of ideology, and have made considerably sharper Brazilian resentments against the USA's trade policies. In the largest part, however, the estrangement of Washington and Brasilia is attributable to the growing divergence of interests and priorities as Brazil pursues its aim of becoming the local South American superpower, and an independent great power on the global stage.

The first clear signs of a new pragmatism in Brazilian foreign policy came in 1974, when General Geisel established diplomatic relations with Peking. In 1975 Brazil recognised the Marxist MPLA government in Angola several months before its final victory in the civil war there, and in the same year it voted for the UN resolution condemning Zionism as racism. These can all be seen as gestures intended to assist Brazil's export offensive in new markets, notably Africa and the Middle East, though they show a new willingness to ignore the USA's objections. The 1975 agreement between Brazil and West Germany on nuclear co-operation, however, was an unmistakable gesture of total independence, for it involved — as Washington was well aware — the eventual creation in Brazil of an independent capacity to build nuclear weapons.

While the increasingly severe but unsuccessful pressure exerted by Washington on both Brasilia and Bonn to cancel this agreement was probably the main factor in alienating Brazil from the USA in the past few years, the final straw was the United States Senate requirement that its own State Department provide reports on human rights violations in each of the 80 countries that were receiving American military aid. When such a report on Brazil was duly furnished to the United States Congress in March, 1977 the Brazilian government formally renounced any further American military aid even before Congress had a chance to consider it. The sum involved was not large — some $50,000,000 — and can easily enough be made up by Brazil, but the gesture was of prime importance in establishing that the old semi-paternal attitude of Washington towards Brazil was no longer acceptable. The two countries remain allies, but they now have a more distant and distinctly more turbulent relationship than at any time since 1945.

ORGANISATION

Arms of Service

Each of the three armed services operates as a separate agency within its own sphere of competence, but with common subordination to the authority of the president and the decisions of the National Security Council. The logistical procurement and distribution systems are also separate, and interservice rivalries and jealousies are considerable.

The minister for each armed force is appointed by the president and is invariably a major-general or vice-admiral; he exercises actual command over his service, and his office serves as general headquarters. The Minister of the Army is assisted in carrying out his duties by a secretariat, *ad hoc* commissions as necessary, and the Army General Staff sections. He also heads the High Command of the Army, a sort of army cabinet of political as well as military significance: it is made up of the Minister, the Chief of Staff, Ministry of the Army department heads, and the commanding generals of the four field armies (i.e. about 10 men). Meetings of the High Command generally occur monthly.

The Ministry of the Army is organised into five principal branches, grouping the Chief of Staff, High Command and Supreme Council of Comptrollership under the Elements of General Control; the Ordnance, Training and Research, Services, Personnel, and Engineering and Communications Departments under the Elements of Sectoral Control; the I, II, III and IV Armies, the Amazon Military Command and the Planalto Military Command under the Ground Forces; the Minister's Staff, the Secretary-General's Department, the Legal Advisor, the Public Relations Centre, the Intelligence Centre, and the Directorate of Finance and Accounting under the Administrative Directorates; and 28 other directorates under the Special Elements.

The Army follows the usual Latin American practice of distinguishing between Combat Arms and Supporting Services, the former consisting of Infantry, Cavalry, Armoured Troops, Artillery, Engineers and Signals and the latter embracing Supply and Transport, War Material and Medical services and Military Police. The Infantry, Cavalry and Armour are organised in regiments, there being also independent battalions of Infantry and Armour and independent squadrons of Cavalry, most of which is now mechanised. The basic unit of Artillery is the Group whilst the remaining arms and services are organised into battalions, groups and independent companies.

The present tactical and territorial organisation dates from 1967 when the existing Armoured Division, 4 Mechanised Divisions, 7 Infantry Divisions and Airborne Detachment were re-organised into eight combined arms 'Army Divisions', which were in turn grouped in pairs into four Armies, one for each of the four existing Military Zones, which were then in their turn subdivided into Military Regions, each garrisoned by a Division. Two new military Commands were also created, those of Amazonia and Planalto, the former being divided into two Military Regions, each garrisoned by a mixed brigade and the latter containing only one Military Region garrisoned by a single brigade and a number of independent units. The Army Divisions each consist of from three to six brigades which may be armoured, mechanised, armoured or mechanised cavalry, infantry (either armoured, mechanised or motorised) or airborne. There are thus over 30 brigades of various types including a single armoured and two airborne brigades. The Amazon Command includes five jungle warfare battalions.

The Marines are organised primarily into an Amphibious Division, the strength of which approximates rather to that of a brigade with three infantry battalions, an Artillery group and an Engineer battalion. There is also a Special Operations battalion and there are 10 Security Groups of variable size entrusted with the defence of naval shore establishments.

The air force, made an independent service in 1943, is commanded by the Air Force Minister, assisted by an Air Cabinet for administrative and strategic planning functions and by the Air Chief of Staff and Air General Staff for operational control and direction. As in the navy, but unlike the army, the chain of command descends from the Minister through the Chief of Staff to the commanders of the major tactical units. The Air Cabinet consists of a chief (who is an air force general officer), a secretariat, and five sections responsible for study and information, public relations, administration, legal affairs, and congressional liaison.

The air force's combat elements are organised on a squadron basis, consisting of one interceptor, two fighter—ground attack, eight counter-insurgency, one ASW, one maritime reconnaissance, four search-and-rescue, 12 transport and three liaison squadrons. It also provides over 100 observation planes for army use and possesses large numbers of helicopters and trainers.

Operational

Since 1953, and in accordance with a law passed in that year, the operational organisation of each of the Brazilian armed forces has been territorially based, the army being divided into four principal zones, the air force six and the navy seven.

The principal army organisations corresponding to these zones are the four numbered armies, with headquarters at Rio de Janeiro (1st Army), São Paulo (IInd Army), Pôrto Alegro (IIIrd Army) and Recife (IVth Army). These zones are further divided into military regions whose boundaries are those of the State borders (though they may contain more than one State). The lightly populated north and north-west of the country do not fall under any of the numbered armies, but are controlled separately by the Amazon Military Command. Other special commands are the Brasília Military Command and the Frontier Elements Group (*see* Role, Commitment, Deployment and Recent Operations) which operates under IIIrd Army control.

There are 11 military regions (*Region Militar*), each consisting of one or several States and belonging to the following military commands:

Ist Army:	1st RM: Espiritu Santo, Guanabara, Rio de Janeiro
	4th RM: Minas Gerais
IInd Army:	2nd RM: São Paulo
	9th RM: Mato Grosso
IIIrd Army:	3rd RM: Rio Grande do Sul
	5th RM: Paraná and Santa Catarina
IVth Army:	6th RM: Bahía and Sergipe
	7th RM: Rio Grande do Norte, Paraíba, Pernambuco and Alagoas
Amazon Military Command:	8th RM: Acre, Amapa, Amazonas, Pará, Rondonia and Roraima
	10th RH: Ceará, Maranhão and Piauí
Brasilia Military Command:	11th RM: Brasília Federal District and Goias

The IIIrd Army is the strongest in troops by a considerable

margin; 1st and 3rd RMs have almost always been the military regions with the largest concentration of ground forces.

The Brazilian navy divides the country into six operational districts, each of which has a commandant exercising full command over the ships, forces, installations and personnel assigned to his territory. The headquarters of the Naval Districts are: First, Rio de Janeiro; Second, Salvador; Third, Recife; Fourth, Belém; Fifth, Florianópolis; and Sixth, São Paulo. The relatively new Seventh Naval District is in fact the Brasília Naval Command.

The main naval bases are the large complex in the Rio de Janeiro—Guanabara Bay area, and other large bases at Belém, Natal, Recife and Salvador. The navy also maintains a river base at Ladario near Corumba on the Paraguay River in southern Mato Grosso State, whose forces come under the operational control of the Frontier Elements Group.

The Fleet Air Arm, formed in 1965 after a lengthy inter-service struggle with the air force, has its headquarters at São Pedro da Aldeia Naval Air Station. It only controls helicopters devoted to maritime warfare purposes, however; under the compromise imposed by Marshal Castelo Branco, the air force continues to operate all fixed-wing SAR, MR and ASW aircraft, including the squadron of S-2E Tracker ASW aircraft embarked aboard the navy's only aircraft carrier.

The Brazilian air force contains both regional and functional commands, each of which in varying degrees are superimposed on the basic squadron structure. The six Regional Air Commands (COMARs), with headquarters in parentheses, control the following areas:

1° COMAR (Belém) — Acre, Amapá, Amazonas, Pará, Rondônia and Roraima and the northern part of Mato Grosso

2° COMAR (Recife) — Alagoas, Bahía, Ceará, most of Maranhão, Pernambuco, Piauí, Rio Grande do Norte and the mid-Atlantic island territory of Fernando de Noronha

3° COMAR (Rio de Janeiro) — Rio de Janeiro and the larger part of Minas Gerais

4° COMAR (São Paulo) — São Paulo and the central and southern parts of Mato Grosso

5° COMAR (Pôrto Alegre) — Paraná, Rio Grande do Sul and Santa Catarina

6° COMAR (Brasília) — Brasília Federal District, Goías, western Minas Gerais and a small part of Maranhão

While these COMARs provide the local support facilities for the air force's combat squadrons, however, they do not exercise full operational control over them. The three specialised commands which do so are the *Comando de Defesa Aerea* (Air Defence Command), the *Comando Aerotático* (Tactical Air Command) and the *Comando Costeiro* (Coastal Command).

The sole squadron under the control of the Air Defence Command is the *1ª Ala de Defesa Aerea* (ALADA), based at Anápolis AFB some 80 miles south-west of Brasília. It is envisaged that the command should eventually possess a substantial interceptor force supported by SAM batteries in an integrated air-defence system, but at the moment the 1st ALADA is only of squadron strength, consisting of 15 Mirage IIIEBR and four two-seat Mirage IIIDBR interceptors (known as the F-103E and D, respectively, in the Brazilian air force). There is, however, a growing system of computerised air-traffic control and air-defence radars known as SISDACTA, installed under contract by the French Thomson-CSF Company, which in its present phase (DACTA II) covers all of south-eastern Brazil up to the cities of

Brasília and Belo Horzonte. This network is under Air Defence Command control.

By far the largest combat command is Tactical Air Command, which controls the fighter—ground attack and counter-insurgency/reconnaissance squadrons. The most powerful of these are the *1°* and *2° Esquadrão*s of *I Grupo de Aviação de Caça* (*GAvÇa*), based at Santa Cruz AFB near Rio de Janeiro and flying F-5E Tiger II supersonic fighter—ground attack aircraft. The other three fighter squadrons, the *1°* and *2° Esquadrão*s of *IV GAvÇa* at Fortaleza AFB in Ceará State and the *1° Esquadrão*s of *XIV GAvÇa* at Canoas AFB near Pôrto Alegre, are equipped with Brazilian-made AT-26 Xavantes.

The counter-insurgency component of the Tactical Air Command consists of five *Esquadrãos Mistos de Reconhecimento e Ataque* (Reconnaissance and Attack Squadrons): *1° EMRA* at Belém and *2° EMRA* at Recife, both flying the older T-25 Universal Is, and *3° EMRA* at Galeão AFB near Rio de Janeiro, *4° EMRA* at Cumbica AFB near São Paulo and *5° EMRA* at Canoas AFB near Pôrto Alegre, all flying AT-26 Xavantes.

The *Comando Aerotático* also controls the three *Esquadrãos de Ligação e Observação* (Liaison and Observation Squadrons), which operate a mix of light aircraft and helicopters with counter-insurgency capabilities. The *1° ELO* at Campo dos Afonços near Rio de Janeiro operates the Neiva L-42 Regente, Bell 206A Jetrangers and Cessna 0-1E Bird Dogs; the *2° ELO* at San Pedro de Aldea flies Neiva T-25 Universal Is; and the *3° ELO* at Pôrto Alegre has Bell UH-IH Iroquois, O-1E Bird Dogs and L-42 Regentes.

Coastal Command controls only two squadrons: the *2° Esquadrão* of the *Grupo de Aviação Embarcada* (there is no 1st squadron), shore-based at Santa Cruz AFB near Rio de Janeiro, which flies the S-2E Trackers that operate from the navy's aircraft carrier; and the *1° Esquadrão*s of the *VII Grupo de Aviação* based at Salvador, which operates EMB-111Ms in a maritime reconnaissance role. There are plans, however, to expand the Coastal Command to at least four squadrons of EMB-111Ms (a maritime patrol derivative of the Bandeirante light transport) and one long-range maritime reconnaissance squadron flying an aircraft equivalent to the P-3E Orion by the early 1980s.

The other functional commands of the Brazilian air force are: the *Comando de Transportos Aéreos* (Air Transport Command), which exercises overall control over all air-transport elements (although these come under the direct command of the COMARs in which they are based); the Comando Geral de Apoio, responsible for repair, maintenance and storage depots; the Comando Geral do Ar, which supervises all ground staff, FAB troops, etc.; and the Comando Geral de Pessoal, responsible for personnel and general administrative matters.

The principal air bases of the Brazilian air force, other than those already mentioned, are at Balterra, Cachijo, Guarantinqueta, Jacareacanga, Manaus, Natal and Santarém. These mainly house air-transport squadrons. In addition, however, there are approximately another 150 airfields and bases from which the Brazilian air force operates on a regular basis.

In the event of mobilisation, the principal reserve force available is the Military Police (also known as the State Militia). These forces are organised on a military basis, hold military titles, bear military weapons including automatic rifles and rocket launchers, and are commanded by an active-duty army officer. According to Decree Law No. 667 of July 2nd, 1969 they are under the operational control of the Ministry of the Army, with command channels extending from the Army General Staff through the numbered armies and special commands to the individual military regions embracing one or more States and territories.

RECRUITMENT, TRAINING AND RESERVES

According to the compulsory military service law of 1908, embodied in all successive constitutions, military service is obligatory for all Brazilian males between the ages of twenty-one and forty-five. They must report for examination at the age of eighteen, and serve 1 year on active service at the age of twenty-one. They then pass to the reserve of the army 'first line', in which they spend 8 years, followed by 14 years in the army 'second line'. There is a theoretical obligation for men in the reserve of the 'first line' to spend 2—4 weeks' training each year, and in order to qualify for public office a man must prove he is a reservist, has discharged his military obligation, or has been officially exempted.

The great majority of Brazilians, however, fall into the last category. Well over a million Brazilian males reach the age of twenty-one each year, and the armed forces' present requirement for conscripts is only 113,000. Even in the army, which takes all but 3000 of these conscripts, the proportion of regulars is almost 40% and has been steadily rising over time, while the number of conscripts accepted annually has been falling in absolute terms even as the armed forces expand. Thus, conscription is highly selective.

Conscript soldiers bear no distinguishing outward insignia, but within the armed forces they are regarded as transients, not quite equal to the long-service volunteers. Many are from deprived rural backgrounds, and are bereft of skills and often illiterate when they join the army. In addition to basic military skills, they are taught to read and write, when necessary, and often acquire simple industrially useful skills which will aid them on their return to civilian life.

The training of conscripts is primarily the responsibility of the commanders of the military regions containing the units to which they are assigned. In general, conscripts serve near their own municipality, and it is not unknown for them to be allowed to return to their homes for the evening or even for lunch in the latter stages of their training. The year of active duty is mostly devoted to training, in a series of instructional stages passing from school of the soldier to basic unit training, specialised weapons training and manoeuvres, which lasts 9 months. During the last 3 months the conscripts function as regular members of their units, but it is quite common for them to be discharged a month or two early. Most conscripts are from the poorer classes of society, and may indeed find the good, regular meals, decent accommodation and medical attention offered by the army superior to anything they have known in civilian life, so military service is not unpopular. Conscripts returning to civil life are guaranteed the right to return to their former employment.

As may be gathered from this account, conscription provides virtually none of the army's combat strength, and is primarily a means of training a large infantry reserve. Brazil's real armed forces are the approximately 160,000 regulars, all of them volunteers, and for them there exists an extensive and highly developed system of training establishments — by far the oldest and most sophisticated in Latin America.

Enlisted ranks in the regular army, after basic training, will attend courses at various points in their career at their relevant branch school, and at the Sergeant-at-Arms School if they rise to the higher non-commissioned ranks. Naval enlisted personnel begin training at one of the Seamen's Apprenticeship schools that operate at Fortaleza, Natal,

Recife, Salvador, Vitória and Florianópolis, or if educationally qualified for petty officer rank will attend courses at the Admiral Tamandaré Instruction Centre in Natal or the Admiral Wandenkolk Instruction Centre in Rio de Janeiro between the ages of sixteen and nineteen. Air force personnel who rise to non-commissioned rank attend a variety of specialised courses at the Specialists' School at Guaratinguetá in the State of São Paulo.

The educational system for army officers is one of the most comprehensive in the world. For over 90% of officers now serving it began with an army-supported military high school which they entered at the age of twelve (though as recently as World War II only 40% of army officers entered by this route). If they achieved an acceptable academic record on graduation, they then entered the Military Academy of Agulhas Negras (Black Needles), named after the black towers which dominate its entrance. This school is a lineal descendant of the Fortification School founded in Rio de Janeiro in 1699, later known as the Royal Military Academy, and undergoing several further changes of name and location before settling into its present name and location in Rio in 1951. Cadets attend the Academy for 4 years, taking the same subjects for the first two, then choosing their branch of the army and receiving special training in that branch during the final two, before graduating and receiving their commission. Medical officers receive their commissions by direct entry after graduation from civilian institutions, however, and need not attend the Military Academy.

Having commenced service with their units, junior officers must attend a course at the Officers' Improvement School during the new few years, and may also receive further specialised training at one of the branch schools: Engineers, Anti-aircraft, Coast Artillery, Communications, Material, Health, Veterinary Science and Physical Education. The major hurdle in any line officer's career, however, is gaining entrance to the 3 year General Staff College (*Escola de Comando e Estado Maior do Exército* — ECEME).

Admission to the ECEME is by competitive written examination, and the pass rate is generally less than one-quarter of the applicants. Not only is the ECEME the key institution in creating an *élite* identity in the Brazilian army's senior officer corps, but graduation from it is a formal prerequisite for promotion to the rank of general, for appointment to the teaching staff of any military school, or for service on the general staff of any senior command. It is a demanding and extremely wide-ranging course.

The summit of the military educational system (and the only level on which officers of all three services, plus civilians, attend the same institution) is the Superior War College (*Escola Superior de Guerra* — ESG), the so-called 'Sorbonne' of Brazil, founded in 1949. This institution, located in historic Fort São João in Rio de Janeiro, functions essentially as a postgraduate school for exceptionally promising general and field-grade officers of all three Brazilian services, under the direct control of the Armed Forces General Staff. Approximately half of its students are civilians prominent in industry, commerce, the professions, the civil service and politics, and its focus is on security policy at the highest level. It has been the principal source of the Brazilian officer corps' corporate view of its roles and responsibilities in the past two decades, and could be argued to be the most important political institution in Brazil. (See the note at the end of this section for further details on the curriculum and political significance of the ESG.)

Naval officers are educated at the Naval Academy on Villegaignan Island in Guanabara Bay, which is a descendant of the Royal Midshipman's Academy founded in 1808. The course consists of 4 years' academic work at the Academy and 1 year on a cruise ship, at the end of which the mid-shipmen receive their commissions. Officers subsequently attend courses at one of the series of specialist schools maintained for the various branches, and successful candidates will eventually proceed to a 9 month course at the Naval War College (equivalent to the Army Staff College). Classes are generally composed of about 60 officers, of whom two-thirds are line officers and the remainder from the Engineer, Supply, Medical and Marine Corps. Other officer schools are the Naval Research Institute, which co-ordinates and develops scientific and technological research of relevance to the navy, and the Aero-Naval Instruction and Training Centre, founded in 1955, which trains both naval and air force personnel for carrier-borne air operations.

There are two separate officers' educational systems in the air force, one for flying officers and the other for specialists. Flying personnel begin by attending the Air Cadets' Preparatory School at Barbacena in the State of Minas Gerais, where an average of 600 students receive training which leads to automatic entry into the Air Force Academy, the main institution providing flying officers to the Brazilian air force.

Non-flying specialist officers attend the Aeronautics School at Campo dos Afonços in Guanabara. They then proceed either to the Specialist Officers and Guards School at the Bacacheri Air Base in Curítba, Paraná, where they are instructed in aircraft maintenance, armament, communications, photography, meteorology or supply, according to their speciality (and where air force infantrymen are trained in air-base guard and defence duties), or to the Aeronautical Technological Institute at São José dos Campos, São Paulo, where prospective aeronautical and electrical engineers undergo a 5 year course conducted on a high technical and scientific level.

At a later stage in their careers, air force officers will attend the Officers' Advanced Training School at São Paulo Air Force Base prior to achieving field-grade rank for instruction in command, leadership and administrative duties. If successful in competitive entrance examinations, flying, administrative and medical officers may subsequently attend the Command and Staff School in Guanabara. As in most air forces, general's rank is usually reserved for flying personnel. Air force generals like navy admirals, will probably spend a year at the Superior War College.

In general it may be said that conscripts come from the working classes (most others being easily able to obtain the necessary exemption) and that most non-commissioned officers come from the middle classes, though a substantial proportion have working-class backgrounds. Before 1930 commissions were limited almost entirely to those of high birth, but increasing educational opportunities and the greater military emphasis on academic qualifications then led to progressively larger contingents of men of middle- and even working-class origins joining the officer corps. By the middle 1960s the army's officer corps was predominantly composed of men drawn from rural middle and lower-middle income groups, with a majority of them still coming (as was traditional) from outlying, less prosperous States or from the dynamic State of Rio Grande do Sul in the far south. Three of Brazil's four military presidents between 1964 and 1978 were from Rio Grande do Sul.

The consequences of this shift in terms of officers' social perspectives were less strking than might be imagined, how-ever, for Brazilian officers are automatically accorded high social status regardless of previous origins. Any effects of this shift in the base of recruitment have been further at-tenuated by the growing trend towards the creation of a military caste in Brazil: whereas only 21% of cadets ad-mitted to the Military Academy in 1941–3 came from military families, the proportion had climbed to 35% by 1962–6, and may now be even higher. It should also be observed that the navy is much more class- and race-conscious than the other Brazilian services; as late as 1962 the Naval Academy had graduated only a dozen mulattos and no negroes (in a country where these two groups comprise, respectively, about a quarter and a tenth of the population).

Conditions of service at all rank levels in the armed forces are favourable by comparison with the standards prevailing for civilians of similar experience and education. There is adequate food, accommodation and medical care even for conscripts. Base pay for regulars is not particularly high, but there are periodic salary increases for blocks of years of completed service, quarters, family and ration allowances, hazardous duty and hardship pay, and periodic cost-of-living increases which bring the total sum received by officers and NCOs to a level at least equal to that of their civilian counterparts. There has been no recourse to inflation of the rank structure in order to reward officers more lavishly – in 1964, the latest year for which a figure is available, fewer than 15% of Brazilian officers held colonel's or general's rank. Retirement pensions are relatively generous, and senior officers may also look forward to a smooth transition into well-paying jobs in government-owned industry or the private sector (in which they may well have accumulated considerable experience even when on active duty).

In view of the effort and expense devoted to training conscripts who immediately pass into the first-line reserve, it is surprising how little formal structure there is to the Brazilian reserve organisation. Potential officers are grouped into three classes: class one, those retired officers who are still capable of immediate command or staff duty when recalled; class two, those military officers who have retired early, officers on active duty with the State police forces, graduates of the officers' reserve training schools and sergeants in the reserve who have had at least 5 years' active duty service; class three, other civilians of good educational background. Similarly, there are three classes of potential enlisted personnel: class one, all men who have served on active duty, either as conscripts or reserves; class two, enlisted members of State police organisations, graduates of the reserve sergeants' school and all those who have completed military training courses in an authorised civic organisation; class three, all others under forty-five (the great majority) who received indefinite deferments of military service because they were in excess of requirements.

There is, however, no formal system of reserve military units, and only rarely are former conscripts required to do annual refresher courses. It seems probable that only a hand-ful of recently retired officers, and the preceding two or three years' groups of conscripts, would be of any immediate use to the armed forces in the event of mobilisation. There is not, in any case, equipment available for more.

The more valuable and more readily available reserve for the army, at least in so far as internal security duties are concerned, is unquestionably the military police, also known as the State Militias. These forces, armed, organised and trained along military lines, are under the operational control of the Ministry of the Army, and number about 200,000–250,000 men. The police districts correspond to the military regions, and these forces offer the additional advantage that, much more than the army, their own numbers are greatest in the largest centres of population: in São Paulo they are 67,000 strong, in Minas Gerais 30,000, in Guanabara 24,000 and in Rio Grande do Sul 19,000. They are not equipped for full-scale war, but could readily relieve the army of all in-ternal security responsibilities and free regular troops.

Brazil

Note on the Superior War College

From the beginning of Brazilian independence, army officers have been more closely involved in the industrial and technological life of the country than in any other Latin American republic, since until 1874 the Military Academy was the nation's only source of both civil and military engineers. Even up to the 1920s the Academy was still training the majority of the country's engineers. The modern Brazilian officer corps' deep involvement in every facet of the country's political, economic and industrial activities, however, is a direct result of the doctrines formulated at the Superior War College (ESG).

There was probably a predisposition to political activism amongst its founders in 1949 in any case, since virtually all of them shared two key experiences: participation in the 1930 revolution, with its strong echoes of the social reformism of the Tenente rebellions of the 1920s; and experience of the Italian campaign in 1944–5, which whetted their desire to turn Brazil into a great power able to play an active role in global politics. At least as significant in moulding the ESG's perspectives, however, was the extremely large part in setting it up and guiding its early course that was played by the United States military advisory mission that arrived in Brazil in 1948 and remained until 1960.

By the mid-1950s, it seems clear, the influence of United States military doctrines and preoccupations had totally supplanted the previous French influence established by General Gamelin's mission between the two world wars. By that time, also, United States military missions in Latin America were turning increasingly to exporting new United States doctrines on the military's role in counter-insurgency, civic action and nation building, evolved in response to the revolutionary warfare techniques that were enjoying such success in China, Vietnam, Algeria and (ultimately) Cuba. Latin American armies were encouraged to study the social and political conditions which facilitated the growth of revolutionary protest, and to develop doctrines and techniques to prevent or crush such movements. Inevitably, they were drawn into consideration of how to alter those conditions – and the more professional the army, the more coherent and far-reaching would be its analysis of the existing internal situation.

In the highly professional Brazilian army, already committed to turning Brazil into a great power and tempted to help it along the path by direct intervention, these doctrines fell on fertile ground. The RSG began to develop a corporate view which directly linked national security (primarily from internal subversion) with national development, and accordingly to direct its attention to all the aspects of civilian policy-making which could affect such issues. During the 1950s, therefore, growing numbers of prominent civilians were invited to take part in the ESG's courses, and as early as 1959 the school's chief ideologue, Colonel Golbery do Couto e Silva, was arguing that the principal threat to Brazil's national security (the armed forces' responsibility) was not external aggression but 'limited warfare, localised conflict and above all indirect communist aggression, which capitalises on local discontents, the frustrations of misery and hunger, and just nationalist anxieties'. Thus the armed forces' main responsibility was to formulate a national security policy which would bring irresponsible politicians under control, foster rapid national development and impose a strong centralised discipline to avert revolutionary outbreaks.

The shift in Brazilian military perspectives and purposes can be measured in a number of ways. The curriculum of the ESG became ever broader, with the seven academic divisions devoted to: (1) political affairs; (2) psychological/social affairs; (3) economic affairs; (4) military affairs; (5) logistical and mobilisation affairs; (6) intelligence and counter-intelligence; and (7) doctrine and co-ordination. The proportion of civilians at the ESG, collaborating with the officers in studies of such varied topics as inflation, banking reform, agrarian problems, voting systems, transportation and education, as well as the more customary subjects like conventional and guerrilla warfare, swelled steadily, and created the nexus of contacts between like-minded soldiers and civilians which made possible the 1964 coup. By 1966, the ESG had graduated 599 military officers, but also 224 leading figures in private industry and commerce, 200 from government ministries, 97 from other government agencies, 39 Congressmen, 23 Federal or State Judges, and 107 other civilian professionals such as professors, economists, writers, doctors and priests. During the same period, even larger numbers of serving Brazilian officers were going into government ministries and national agencies devoted to industrial development on detached duty.

As late as 1960, it may be argued, this new national security perspective of the ESG, which automatically impelled its graduates towards taking charge of Brazil's chaotic economic, political and social life, was not shared by the army as a whole. By that time, however, the changed emphasis had already had its effect on the General Staff College (ECEME), which was and remains the principal vehicle for disseminating doctrine through the officer corps as a whole. In 1956 the ECEME curriculum contained no formal allocation of hours to the study of counter-insurgency warfare, internal security and communism; 10 years later, it devoted 222 hours to internal security, 129 hours to irregular warfare, and only 24 hours to the old professional preoccupation of conventional land warfare. Similarly, commencing in 1961 the *Boletim de Informações*, a newsletter distributed by the General Staff to key troop commanders, began systematically to disseminate the new ESG doctrines to all units.

With the passage of more than another decade, and the apparently decisive defeat of the guerrilla threat in the intervening period, the emphasis in the ECEME and ESG curricula is swinging back towards the more conventional military subjects, though there is no reduction in the stress placed on what other equivalent institutions would regard as the civilian subjects of economics, sociology and planning. The ESG remains the central institution providing theoretical direction to the Brazilian armed forces' drive to raise their nation to great-power status, and the meeting ground where the links between the soldiers and the civilian 'technocrats', who have jointly run Brazil for the past decade and a half, are forged.

The ideology and role of the ESG were summed up in 1976 by the then Chief of Staff of the Armed Forces, General Antonio Jorge Correa, at the ceremony marking the opening of its new academic year. 'Nothing', he said, 'will stop Brazil becoming a great power . . . . It has to be remembered that ideal solutions, solutions that mark the destiny of great nations, appear as a result of difficulties.' The ESG was developing from 'a laboratory of ideas aimed at perfecting and strengthening national security' into an actual producer of solutions. The institute was producing an *élite* of military and civilians capable of running the country, and had already graduated some 3000 members of this *élite*.

EQUIPMENT AND ARMS INDUSTRY

Rifles: IMBEL 7.62mm M-964 (Brazil); G3 7.62mm (Brazil – German licence); FN FAL 7.62mm (Brazil – Belgian licence)
Sub-machine-guns: M-972 9mm (Italy)

Machine-guns: M-1917A1 7.62mm (U.S.); M-1 27mm (U.S.)

Mortars: 60mm IMBEL (Brazil); 81mm IMBEL (Brazil); 81mm (U.S.); 120mm IMBEL (Brazil); 4.2″ (U.S.)

Anti-armour: 106mm RCL (Brazil); Cobra ATGW (Brazil – German licence); 108mm rocket launcher (Brazil); 114mm rocket launcher (Brazil)

Artillery: 105mm howitzer (Brazil); M-101A1 105mm howitzer (U.S.); M-114A1 155mm howitzer (U.S.)

Air defence weapons: 40mm L/70 (Sweden) 40mm L/60 (Sweden/U.S.); Roland SAM (France); Hawk SAM (U.S.)

Armour: M-4 Sherman medium tank (U.S.; 60 in service); M-41A3 light tank (U.S.) with Brazilian modifications; 250 in service); X1A light tank (U.S. M-3 light rebuilt in Brazil; 90 in service); M-3A1 light tank (U.S.; 50 in service); EE-9 Cascavel armoured car (Brazil; 120 in service); EE-11 Urutu APC (Brazil; 150 in service); M-113 APC (U.S.; 500 in service); M-59 APC (U.S.; 150 in service)

Aircraft: Air Force has about 180 transport and 60 light aircraft and about 40 helicopters

These are impressive armed forces in any case by Latin American standards, but the most noteworthy thing about the Brazilian forces' equipment is that at least 40% of their needs – unofficially estimated at $350,000,000 upwards a year – are now manufactured at home. Since the cancellation of the 25 year-old military assistance agreement with the USA in March, 1977 the Brazilians have placed even greater emphasis on producing their own weapons (with the help of licencing agreements, etc. where need be), and may soon be meeting above 75% of their requirements without suffering any severe penalty in terms of performance. Indeed, Brazil is now unquestionably the largest and most technically advanced arms producer in the third world, and in the past few years has even begun to appear in force in the military export market.

Brazil began modestly enough in the early 1960s by commencing production of a rifle under licence from the FNB Company of Belgium, the Italian Beretta pistol and a USA-patented heavy machine-gun, and by 1968 was meeting the army's requirements for cross-country vehicles from domestic production. In that year the army began a development plan for the construction of Brazilian-designed and produced armoured vehicles, floating bridges, rockets and rocket launchers, field radios and anti-tank missiles, while the navy launched a 10 year modernisation plan, now completed, which envisaged the development of naval shipbuilding capabilities in the Rio de Janeiro area to the point where they were able to produce modern destroyers at home. At the same time, the nascent Brazilian aircraft industry was offered strong government incentives to rapid growth. In 1970 the principal Brazilian aircraft company, Embraer, produced its first two aircraft, and in the following year the first prototype of the Brazilian-designed Cascavel armoured car was completed by the Engesa company.

Now all the items envisaged in the army's 1968 programme, and a great many other weapons, are being built in Brazil. Embraer's aircraft production in 1977 was just short of 700 planes, and the Brazilian air force's inventory of aircraft is over half home-produced. Engesa now produces a complete range of wheeled armoured vehicles, including amphibious APCs, and in 1977 secured export orders for more than 400 at a price of about $400,000 each. The last two of a batch of six Vosper Thoneycroft-designed destroyers equipped with variable-depth sonar, ASW helicopters, surface-to-surface and surface-to-air missiles, were completed recently in Brazilian shipyards.

Many of the more sophisticated components must still be produced from foreign designs under licence, of course: Brazil is building Cobra anti-tank missiles and light automatic cannon in collaboration with West German groups, and heavy weapons in co-operation with Oto Melara of Italy. The Xavante ground-attack aircraft is a version of the MB-326 produced under licence from the Italian company of Aermacchi, the British Ferranti company has created a joint company with the Brazilian armed forces for the local manufacture of the Argus 700 (an advanced mini-computer used to control weapons systems) and negotiations with Aerospatiale of France for licence production of helicopters in Brazil have been reported. In many cases, it is still necessary to import entire sub-assemblies (including jet engines, some radars and sonars), but the rate of advance of the Brazilian armaments industry over the past decade has been little short of astonishing. A Brazilian-designed tank and a military-*cum*-civilian medium transport aircraft are now being contemplated.

A substantial portion of the arms industry is directly controlled by the armed forces. The navy runs its own shipyards and repair facilities, and the main naval shipyard in Guanabara Bay not only builds naval vessels but also accepts contracts for commercial vessels when capacity permits. The army maintains eight munitions factories – four in Rio de Janeiro and the rest in Minas Gerais, São Paulo and Paraná – and four arsenals, and is effectively self-sufficient in small arms and in all categories of ammunition, explosives and chemicals. The activities of these facilities, and the standards of civilian factories producing items for military use, are supervised by Imbel, a State-owned company established by presidential decree in 1975, and run by the Army Ministry. Imbel is also the main government instrument in seeking out (mostly Western European) arms producers interested in setting up joint ventures in Brazil, and in negotiating arms sales abroad.

The two giants of the Brazilian arms industry are Embraer and Engesa, both of which are located (together with many of Brazil's other private arms manufacturers) in the industrial city of São Jose dos Campos between São Paulo and Rio de Janeiro. In addition to building the Xavante and six other designs under licence, Embraer produces the very successful Bandeirante twin-turboprop transport and several other models of its own design for both military and civilian markets, and even produces assemblies for use in United States-produced combat aircraft like the F-5 Tiger II; it is the only non-United States company amongst the world's 10 biggest manufacturers in the 'general aviation' class. Engesa now has in series production: the EE-9 Cascavel, an armoured car of world-wide competitiveness which can be fitted with either a 20mm automatic cannon or a 90mm gun and carries 14 infantrymen; the EE-11 Urutu (a fully amphibious APC of sophisticated but rugged design); and the EE-17 Sucuri, armed with a 105mm gun firing fin-stabilised projectiles.

Nearby is the company of Avibras, specialising in the manufacture of solid-fuel artillery rockets for the Brazilian army – the 108-R, with a 7.5km range and 16.8kg launch weight, is already in service with the Brazilian army together with the associated X2 16 tube launcher designed for towing from any army vehicle including jeeps. Nearing series production are the X20 rocket (35kg warhead and 35km range) and a 3 round trailer/launcher, together with the X40 spin-stabilised battlefield support rocket (150kg warhead, 68km range) and a single-round trailer launcher, both of which have been extensively test-fired at the army's Marambaia Test Centre in Rio de Janeiro. There are proposals for even larger tactical rockets (the X300, for example, with a 1500kg warhead deliverable at ranges of about 350km), and a longer-range missile test site has been chosen in the north-eastern part of the country. Avibras is also reliably reported to be working on its own designs for air-to-air and surface-to-air missiles.

A large part of the strategy guiding the development of Brazil's arms industry is directed towards the creation of a military export sector catering primarily for the third world which will support the costs of domestic design and production. Early results have been good, since Brazil is able to offer technically satisfactory and robust weapons that are designed to withstand the harsh environmental conditions and indifferent maintenance which prevail in many third-world countries. Moreover, production costs are substantially lower than in high-wage industrial countries, and the Brazilian armed forces' willingness to drop back in the delivery queue in order to allow arms producers to secure export orders permits Brazilian firms to offer usually prompt delivery to foreign buyers.

The principal exporters so far have been Embraer and Engesa. Since the Embraer made its first military export sale of five Bandeirantes to Uruguay in 1975, it has sold six Bandeirantes and 11 EMB-111s (the maritime reconnaissance variant) to Chile; 10 Bandeirantes, 10 Xavante fighters and eight Uirapuru trainers to Paraguay; 12 Uirapurus and 18 Xavante fighters to Bolivia; and recently broke into the African market by selling six Xavantes to Togo and six Bandeirantes to Sudan. Engesa's armoured cars have proven extremely successful: after selling 30 Cascavels to Chile and 20 to Qatar in 1976, it secured an order for 400 Cascavels and Urutus from Libya in mid-1977. Imbel is also reported to have had discussions with delegations from Iraq, Turkey and Abu Dhabi regarding large purchases of Engesa-built armoured vehicles. Even the Brazilian navy finally entered the export market in July, 1977 accepting an order from the Chilean navy for 10 Brazilian-designed and built fast patrol boats.

It is likely that this export drive will continue and expand, providing a firmer base for Brazil's defence industry and thus bringing the goal of near self-sufficiency in arms closer within reach. It is plausible to suggest that within a decade nothing (with the possible exception of supersonic combat aircraft) will be outside the capabilities of the Brazilian defence industry.

Note on Nuclear Weapons Potential

The huge commercial deal between Brazil and West Germany in June, 1975 for the purchase of a complete 'nuclear fuel cycle' (uranium enrichment plant, eight 1100 MW reactors and fuel reprocessing plant) has led to acute anxieties in Argentina and amongst those concerned to prevent nuclear proliferation elsewhere that Brazil has embarked on a course leading to the production of nuclear weapons. It was the first agreement ever for the wholesale transfer of an entire nuclear technology from one nation to another. In view of the extreme antagonism it aroused outside the two countries involved — the USA's attempts to persuade West Germany and Brazil to cancel the deal severely strained Washington's relations with both countries, and the Dutch government almost fell over its participation in the associated agreement by the URENCO consortium (Britain, the Netherlands and West Germany) to supply enriched uranium to Brazil until its own enrichment facilities are completed — it will probably be the last such deal. But the German nuclear industry faces a commercial collapse at home, and this huge export deal could well mean the difference between survival and bankruptcy, so the Bonn government has steadfastly supported its nuclear exporters despite all pressures.

While all aspects of the Brazilian—German nuclear programme have been made subject to the strictest International Atomic Energy Agency supervision by a 1976 agreement, the concern about possible Brazilian nuclear weapons continues unabated. Brazil has possible motives in its historical rivalry with Argentina, whose nuclear programme is much further advanced (the first Argentine power reactor went on stream in 1974, and the industry there is based largely on local technology and expertise). Both these countries, moreover, have refused to sign the Nuclear Non-Proliferation Treaty on the grounds that it is discriminatory. Brazil's sheer desire to possess all the appurtenances and prestige of a great power is seen as an additional motive. It is alleged with some truth that once the entire nuclear cycle, from mining uranium (of which Brazil has an ample supply) through enriching it, using it in nuclear power reactors, and finally reprocessing it to extract the potentially weapons-grade plutonium, is contained within the country, then deception of IAEA inspectors, or outright rejection of them and denunciation of IAEA controls, is a much greater possibility.

Thus international (not to mention Argentinian) concern has focused primarily on the enrichment and reprocessing plants, which do indeed indicate a determination to achieve nuclear self-sufficiency for whatever purposes. The parallel argument that Brazil has no economic need for so much nuclear power so soon, especially when it will prove to be more expensive than the hydroelectric power of which the country still has large untapped reserves, is however, less convincing. Even if the official forecasts that Brazilian energy requirements in the year 2000 will be between 180,000MW and 200,000MW (on the assumption that national energy consumption will continue to double every 7 years) should prove to be on the high side, the total exploitable hydroelectirc potential of the country is probably only about 120,000MW — and a very large share of that is in the Amazon basin, at the other end of the country from the industrial areas where most of the demand is concentrated. Since Brazil is by far the poorest of the large continental countries in fossil fuel resources, it is calculated that nuclear energy will have to provide a rapidly growing share of electrical power after 1990 — the president of Nuclebras has suggested that it will need 75,000MW of installed nuclear power by the turn of the century, which is greater than the present nuclear power generating capacity of the USA.

The West German deal does fit in with these expectations — the first two 1300MW reactors, sited alongside Brazil's one existing 625MW Westinghouse-built reactor on Itaorna Beach at Angra dos Reis in Rio de Janeiro State, will probably not be ready until 1985 and 1987, while the remaining six reactors plus the enrichment and reprocessing plants will more likely come into service at the end of the 1980s and the beginning of the 1990s. Part of the agreement provides that the Brazilian share in the manufacture of reactor components should rise from 30% for the first two to about 85% for the final one, thus paving the way for a new generation of Brazilian-produced reactors in the 1990s.

A nuclear power programme of these dimensions does provide sound commercial and foreign exchange reasons for building one's own enrichment and reprocessing plants, although they are also the key to a possible nuclear weapons programme. It is very likely that Brazil's military leaders had in mind both independence from foreign sources of supply which might make them critically vulnerable to external pressures, and also a potential ability to build nuclear weapons, when they insisted that these ancillary facilities be included in any deal — and it was an absolute condition of any purchase, being indeed the main reason that Brasília chose West German suppliers over Americans who were legally unable to supply such plant. The remark made by the commanding general of the Brazilian First Army at the time the agreement was made in 1975, to the effect that it 'constitutes a decisive step that reinforces the country's sovereignty', predicting that Brazil 'would be transformed into a great power', undoubtedly does reflect the attitude of the Brazilian military leadership as a whole.

There is probably not, however, any intention on the part of Brazil to proceed to the production of nuclear weapons as soon as it becomes technically feasible in the late 1980s (and very probably of paying an extremely high price for thus violating the agreement to submit to IAEA inspection). Indeed, to evince any immediate interest in nuclear weapons would serve merely as a stimulus to the Argentine nuclear programme, which is currently years ahead of Brazilian capabilities. In so far as the agreement with West Germany on nuclear technology has a direct military significance for the present generation of Brazilian leaders, it is more that of discouraging the Argentinians from embarking on the development of nuclear weapons by demonstrating that Brazil can compete, and of achieving eventual nuclear technological parity with Argentina in order to afford themselves the option of making nuclear weapons rapidly in an emergency.

RANK, DRESS AND DISTINCTIONS

Ranks in the Brazilian armed forces are the same as those in the services of the USA, except that five-star air force and army general officers bear the title of marshal of the air force or army. Generally, however, these ranks are left vacant.

Insignia for army and air force general officers are from one to five silver stars worn on shoulder boards, ascending from one for brigadier-general to five for marshal. Field-grade army officers wear a combination of stars with sunbursts and plain five-pointed stars, worn without shoulder boards — colonels have three stars with sunbursts, lieutenant-colonels two with sunbursts and one plain and majors one with sunburst and two plain. Company-grade army officers wear plain stars — three for captain, two for first-lieutenant and one for second-lieutenant. Field- and company-grade air force officers wear the same arrangements of stars, but in place of sunbursts the stars are supported by varying numbers of gold metal bands. Naval officers' rank insignia is gold bands worn on the sleeve or on shoulder boards, the numbers of stripes being the same as in the United States Navy but the top band having a small loop as in the British Royal Navy.

All three services have a variety of uniforms including full dress, dress, service, and manoeuvre or fatigue uniforms. The army service uniform is dark green, the navy's is dark blue, and the air force's a lighter blue.

The principal decoration for bravery in the line of duty is the Combat Cross (*Cruz de Combate*), established in 1944 and awarded in two classes — gold and silver. The first class is awarded to individuals only, and the second may be awarded to members of a group or military unit. The Blood Cross of the Armed Forces, established in 1945, is awarded to military personnel for wounds received in military action. The Campaign Medal, created in 1944, was granted to military personnel for distinguished service in Europe in 1944–5.

There are also a number of medals awarded for noncombat achievements, of which the highest is the National Order of Merit Medal, established in 1946 for both military personnel and civilians of distinguished merit. There are five classes in this order (Grand Cross, Grand Officer, Commander, Officer and Knight), of which the highest is awarded to marshals, generals, their naval equivalents, and military officers who have completed 30 years of service. The Military Medal, established in 1901, is granted to officers of all services on the completion of each 10 year bracket of continuous

service: bronze for 10 years; silver for twenty; gold for thirty; and a platinum clasp for forty. The War Services Medal, created in 1943, has a series of stars on the ribbon denoting the three classes: three stars, combat duty; two stars, patrol duty; and one star, base duty.

All three services have special achievement medals to be awarded to officers and men of their own branches for distinguished service and for excellence in service schools and academies. There are also a number of other medals which may be awarded to Brazilian service personnel, as well as to civilians, for distinguished service to the country in various fields.

CURRENT DEVELOPMENTS

The only major political division of opinion in the Brazilian officer corps of today, after two decades of ESG indoctrination and the post-1964 purges that removed some 20% of the officer corps for excessively democratic or leftist views, is between those who prefer to continue running Brazil publicly and those who would prefer to retire behind a tactical smokescreen of civilianisation and partial redemocratisation. Virtually all, however, are in agreement that their goal to make Brazil a great power, and that that goal requires the armed forces to exercise at least a close supervision over the affairs of State.

So long as internal pressures do not become acute, it is likely that the officer corps will not choose to withdraw fully from its public politically directing role, though a further relaxation of the internal political controls may well occur. Active terrorism and organised subversive groups have been effectively removed from the scene, and there are no signs pointing to their early revival. The past decade and a half, moreover, have seen the steady expansion of personal links and common interests amongst Brazilian senior officers, the civilian technocrats who administer the government on their behalf, and the rapidly growing industrial and commercial sectors of the economy. While prediction is risky, Brazil seems one of the less likely candidates for radical political change in the near future.

As regards purely military affairs, the slow but steady increase in the size and modernity of the Brazilian armed forces will probably continue, together with the rise of an independent Brazilian arms-producing and exporting industry. Despite chronic tensions with Argentina and the shadowy emerging outline of a Brazilian—Chilean axis opposed to an Argentinian—Peruvian one, the probability of open military conflict in South America remains low (though it has increased appreciably in the past decade). The persistent inter-service rivalry in the Brazilian armed forces will probably continue to block the creation of a unified Ministry of Defence, but the army's numerical preponderance allows it to exercise effective leadership and avoid damaging splits. The safest short-term prediction in the military field, as in the political field, therefore, is more of the same. Relations with Argentina have dramatically improved during the past three years to a point just short of a formal treaty of mutual defence. Military co-operation is especially marked between the respective Navies and an accord for mutual assistance in the field of nuclear research was reached in 1981. Relations with South Africa are also good and positive moves in the direction of the development of a South Atlantic Treaty organisation, with the active if low-key encouragement of the United States and embracing Argentina, Brazil, Uruguay, Paraguay, South Africa and possibly Nigeria, were under way when the Anglo-Argentine War upset the delicate strategic balance in the area.

Gwynne Dyer
Adrian English

BRUNEI

Brunei, a sultanate on the northern coast of Borneo consisting of two nearby enclaves totalling 2226 square miles, is the only Asian equivalent to the oil-rich mini-States of the southern Persian Gulf. Its 170,000 people benefit from oil revenues that in 1977 amounted to almost $900,000,000, and to defend this tempting wealth it maintains relatively large armed forces: 2750 troops of its own, plus a battalion of Gurkha troops on loan from Britain.

Internally the State functions as an absolute monarchy, ruled by the young Sultan Sir Hassanal Bolkiah Waddaulah, but Britain remains responsible for its defence and external relations. It has now been agreed with Britain, which had been exerting heavy pressure on the Sultan to break this link for a number of years, that it will become a fully independent State responsible for its own defence in December, 1983.

The Muslim sultanate of Brunei at one time ruled the greater part of the Borneo coast and even extended into the southern Philippines, but by the time Britain formally extended its protection over the State in 1888 successive concessions to the rajahs of Sarawak had reduced it to its present diminutive dimensions. It remained a backward and impoverished country until the discovery of the first oilfied in 1920, after which it rapidly rose in prosperity to become the richest State in Asia in terms of per capita national income.

Brunei failed to join the Federation of Malaysia when it was formed in 1963 because of the former sultan's insistence on retaining control of the oil revenues and his desire to be next in line for election to Malaysia's rotating Kingship (demands which Kuala Lumpur refused to grant). As a result, both segments of the State are entirely surrounded on the landward side by the Malaysian State of Sarawak. The political turbulence caused by the question of joining Malaysia was largely responsible for the State's one political upheaval, an abortive revolt by the now outlawed Parti Rakyat Brunei (Brunei People's Party) in 1962 which was suppressed with help from British troops.

Subsequent relations with Malaysia were cool but correct until 1973, when a group of political detainees belonging to the Brunei People's Party escaped from prison and were given political refuge in Malaysia. Following a period of acute political tension, relations with Malaysia were restored to a more normal tenor in 1977, but it is known that the Malaysian Foreign Ministry has been conducting delicate secret negotiations with Brunei in an attempt to persuade it to join the Malaysian Federation when British protection is finally withdrawn. Kuala Lumpur is anxious that an independent Brunei might be vulnerable to 'outside forces', especially in view of the autocratic system of government and the past history of attempted revolt, but there has been no indication that Brunei's ruler is partial to such a solution.

Indeed it is entirely clear that the Sultan's preference would have been for the indefinite continuation of the present arrangement whereby Britain takes responsibility for his defence and foreign relations. (The amended treaty governing this relationship was concluded in 1971). Britain, however, has been eager to terminate this relationship for at least a decade, since it no longer maintains any other military outposts east of Suez except for Hong Kong, and since it is continually being upbraided by the United Nations decolonisation committee for holding Brunei as a colony.

Following talks in London in 1978, it was announced that the Sultanate would receive its full independence in 1983. It was also agreed that the British army's contribution to Brunei's defence, the battalion of Gurkhas stationed at the main oil town of Serai (whose costs are borne entirely by the Sultanante), would not be withdrawn until September, 1983. The Sultan is believed to be in direct negotiation with the government of Nepal to retain their services after that date, presumably under the command of contract officers.

Internally, the major preoccupation of the government is security, with approximately half the budget being devoted to the armed forces, the Royal Brunei Police, and the Department of Security and Intelligence. Expenditure on the armed forces in 1981 was $US195,000,000.

The armed forces are known as the Royal Brunei Malay Regiment: all naval and air elements form part of the army. Ground forces consist of two infantry battalions (the second of which was only formed in 1975, and reached full strength in 1978), and one armoured reconnaissance squadron, a light air defence battery and a small engineer unit. There are plans to form a third battalion, but the fact that recruitment is voluntary and the acute manpower shortage in the state — is is estimated that the available military manpower pool is only about 4000 — mean that this is unlikely to be complete until well into the 1980s.

Army training, equipment, uniforms and rank structure all conform closely to British models, and most of the senior command positions are filled by some 60 expatriate British officers. The commanding officer of the RBMR is Colonel Norman Roberts. There is a substantial effort underway to train suitable Malay officers to replace the expatriates, and in 1977 there were almost 100 recruits undergoing training in Britain, but it is estimated that no indigenous personnel will be senior or experienced enough to take command of the regiment until 1984.

The naval and air elements of the RBMR comprise about 350 men, and ambitious expansion plans are being delayed by the shortage of trained pilots and naval officers. The naval element is based at Muara, the State's only commerical port; it is envisaged that the air wing will eventually be based at the international airport near Bandar Seri Begawan, the capital.

The major weapons of the ground forces include 16 Scorpion light tanks, 24 Sankey APCs and 16 81mm mortars. The navy has recently taken delivery of three missile-firing fast patrol boats, and also maintains three gunboats, 24 assault craft, three river patrol boats and two landing craft. The air wing has one HS-748 transport, two Cherokee training aircraft, and two Bell 206, 6 BO-105, and 11 Bell 212 helicopters. Brunei is also planning to buy a Rapier air-defence system from Britain for an estimated price of about $60,000.000.

Paramilitary forces available to the government consists of the 1750-strong Royal Brunei Police. There is no organised reserve system. Pay, allowances and retirement benefits are generous, and conditions of service are good.

The transition to full independence and the projected withdrawal of the Gurkha battalion in 1983 are viewed with some trepidation by the government, but all visible indications are that the internal security situation is not threatening. The banned Parti Rakyat Brunei which led the 1962 revolt, and is still seen as the major threat, split in 1975, and Malaysia has recently been showing much less sympathy to refugees of that party. The RBMR, the police and the 235 man Department of Security and Intelligence present convincing obstacles to any attempt to overthrow the exising government which is based on purely internal support, but so long as the government fails to incorporate any representative element whatever, the possibility of internal trouble cannot be entirely discounted.

Gwynne Dyer
John Keegan

BULGARIA

HISTORY AND INTRODUCTION

The Bulgarian army is, in a sense, older than the Bulgarian state. The army can trace its origins back to the 'Bulgarian Legion' which fought with the Serbs against the Turks in 1862, although it was not until 1878 that Bulgaria gained autonomy. The history of Bulgaria has been marked by conflict. The Bulgarians defeated their traditional enemies, the Serbs, in 1885—6, and in 1912 joined the Balkan League's victorious campaign against Turkey. Bulgaria was defeated by Serbia the following year, but in 1915 she joined the central powers, occupied much Serbian territory, and managed to contain an Allied expeditionary force based on Solonika. Bulgaria was, however, eventually compelled to surrender, and the Treaty of Neuilly (1919) forced her to cede some of her territory to Yugoslavia and Greece.

In 1914 Bulgaria became an ally of the Axis powers, declaring war on the western Allies but not on the Soviet Union. The Germans used Bulgaria as a staging area for their invasion of Greece, but Bulgarian forces were not actually involved in the fighting. The Bulgarian army remained unengaged until September, 1944 when Soviet troops reached the borders of Bulgaria. The government rapidly capitulated, and Bulgarian forces thereafter fought against the Germans, under Soviet control.

The Fatherland Front, a communist-dominated coalition, had been formed in 1942, and it assumed power following the Soviet invasion. It won an overwhelming majority in the elections of October, 1946 and the Moscow-trained Bulgarian communist Georgi Dimitrov became Prime Minister as well as First Secretary of the Party. The constitutional monarchy had been ended following a referendum in September, 1946, although it was not until after the signing of a formal peace treaty in February, 1947 that Bulgaria officially became a communist State.

The Bulgarian army was thoroughly sovietised in the period 1944—51. Personnel of unreliable political views were purged, Bulgarian-born Soviet officers were moved into key appointments and 'deputy commanders' were introduced to act as political commissars. By 1951 the army had been thoroughly re-equipped with Soviet arms and equipment, and appeared to be a staunch and potentially effective Soviet ally. Although the Bulgarian army has now been outstripped in both size and combat potential by other Warsaw Pact armies, it remains a solid, if unsophisticated, force.

STRENGTH AND BUDGET

Population: 8,950,000
Army: 105,000 (70,000 conscripts)
Navy: 9,000 (6,000 conscripts), two submarines, 74 small
    craft, and combatants, 12 combat aircraft
Air Force: 34,000 (18,000 conscripts) 260 combat aircraft
Border Guards: 15,000
Security Police: 7,500
People's Territorial Militia: 150,000
Defence Expenditure (1981): $1.346 billion

COMMAND AND CONSTITUTIONAL STATUS

Command
The Bulgarian Army command is organised along standard Warsaw Pact lines, with a Minister of Defence being both the highest-ranking uniformed officer and a political functionary and member of the Central Committee, directly responsible to the head of state. The Minister of Defence has responsible to him the military district commanders, service chiefs, and a number of Deputy Ministers of Defence, including the Chief of Staff and heads of the political Administration, Rear Services, Training, and Administration.

Constitutional Status
Bulgaria is a People's Republic, governed according to the Constitution of May, 1971. The National Assembly, elected every 5 years by all citizens over the age of eighteen, elects the State Council, the supreme organ of state power. The State Council's chairman, Todor Zhikov, is also First Secretary of the Communist party. The Council of Ministers, appointed by the National Assembly, is the supreme executive and administrative body. The National Assembly appoints and dismisses the commander-in-chief, and the State Council gives general guidance for the country's defence and security; it also appoints and dismisses senior commanders. The constitution states that military service is compulsory for all male citizens.

ROLE, COMMITMENT, DEPLOYMENT AND RECENT OPERATIONS

Role and Commitment
The army has the roles of national defence and the maintenance of the regime. Bulgaria is a member of the Warsaw Pact, and her forces would come under Warsaw Pact command in the event of major war.

Deployment
All Bulgarian forces are normally stationed within Bulgaria, although units as well as individuals go to the Soviet Union for training.

Recent Operations
One Bulgarian motorised rifle regiment participated in the invasion of Czechoslovakia in 1968.

ORGANISATION

Arms of Service
These are similar to those of the Soviet army.

Operational
All units follow basic Soviet patterns, but are smaller. The tank brigades would probably operate in support of the

motorised rifle divisions. In the 1970s, some motorised rifle units were using trucks in place of APCs. Each military district headquarters appears to function as a field army upon mobilisation.

Deployment
1st Army/Military District HQ; Sofia
1st Guards Training Motorised Rifle Division: Sofia
28th Motorised Rifle Division; Blagoevgrad
9th Tank Brigade; Knayzhevo
? SCUD Missile Brigade; Samokov
2nd Army/Military District HQ; Plovdiv
17th Motorised Rifle Division; Khaskovo
2nd Motorised Rifle Division; Stara Zagora
19th Training Rifle Division; Pazardzhik
5th Tank Brigade; Kazanluk
11th Tank Brigade; Karlovo
? SCUD Missile Brigade; Karlovo
3rd Army/Military District HQ; Sliven
3rd Motorised Rifle Division; Burgas
7th Motorised Rifle Division; Yambol
18th Training Rifle Division; Shumen
13th Tank Brigade; Sliven
24th Tank Brigade; Aytos
? SCUD Missile Brigade; Yambol
? Airborne Regiment; Burgas

The training divisions are believed to be at cadre strength.

Non-divisional units include:
Four artillery regiments, four anti-aircraft artillery regiments, one mountain battalion, two reconnaissance battalions, special commando companies, two Naval Coast artillery regiments with 20 batteries, two independent *Samlet* Naval Coast Defence Missile battalions, three Naval Guard companies, 30 Air and Air Defence Force SAM sites.

RECRUITMENT, TRAINING AND RESERVES

Recruitment and Training
All officers and the great majority of NCOs are professional. Conscription is for 2 years in the army and air force, and for 3 years in the navy. There is less emphasis on technical training than in the Soviet army, but training in general seems vigorous and effective. Bulgaria participates in Warsaw Pact Exercises.

Reserves
200–225,000 army reserves are in various categories of the reserve. Reserve training is not emphasised and is inadequate by Western standards.

The People's Militia, under the Ministry of Internal Affairs, is 150,000 strong. Armed with old-model infantry weapons, its units are organised on a territorial basis throughout the country.

The Frontier troops, 15,000 strong, are part of the Army and responsible for border security and rear area protection in time of war. They are deployed along the borders – including that with Romania – and armed with infantry weapons and armoured vehicles.

The *Trudovak* are the Army Construction Troops. Similar to the Soviet model, they are used on construction projects throughout the country. The personnel are serving conscripts.

The Ministry of the Interior MVR Security forces, 24,000 strong, are charged with maintenance of the regime against internal threats.

EQUIPMENT AND ARMS INDUSTRY

Equipment
Small arms: 9mm PM pistol, standard equipment is AKM/AKMS 7.62mm assault rifle, PK/PKM 7.62mm general purpose machine gun. Lower readiness and reserve units use PpSh SMG, SKS carbine, RPK, RPD, RP-46, all in 7.62mm
Mortars: 82mm M-1942, 350 120mm M-1938 and M-1943, 160mm M-1943 and M-1953
Anti-tank: RPG-7 grenade launcher, 90 57mm ZIS-2, 150 73mm SPG-9, 82mm B-10 RR, *Sagger, Snapper* STGMs.
Anti-aircraft: 23mm ZU-23, 37mm M-1938, 57mm S-60, 100mm KS-19, ZSU-23-4,
Artillery: Soviet-built 76mm, 85mm, 100mm, 122mm (400 reported), 130mm, 152mm (100 reported) guns and howitzers. BM-21 multiple rocket launchers (100 reported)
Armour: Tanks: 150–300 T-34/85, 1,500–1,800 T-54/55s, 0–100 T-62s, 60 T-72s.
Reconnaissance Vehicles: PT-76 (250 reported), BRDMs (250 reported)
Infantry Combat Vehicles: BMP-1
APCs: 1,500–2,000 BTR-152, BTR-50, BTR-60, OT-62, MT-LB.
SP Guns: Su-100 100mm
Aircraft: MiG-17 (148), MiG-21 (80), MiG-23 (24), An-24, Tu-134, An-2 transports, Mi-2, Mi-4 Mi-24, Ka-25 helicopters.
Naval: 2 submarines, 5 escorts, 4 OSA Class PPB with Styx SSM, 6 PT boats, 11 patrol craft, 28 minesweepers, 27 landing craft, 1 replenishment ship, Mi-2, Mi-4, Mi-14 helicopters.
Missiles: 36 FROG-7, 30 SCUD-A and -B, SA-2, SA-3 (about 180 total), SA-4, SA-6, SA-7, SAMs.

Arms Industry
Bulgaria produces small arms and ammunition.

RANK, DRESS AND DISTINCTIONS

Rank
Badges of rank are worn on the shoulder-board, and are almost identical to those of the Soviet army. The Bulgarian army has, however, fewer ranks than its Soviet counterpart: the various ranks of marshal do not exist, and there are no ensigns. The Bulgarian *starschina* wears a broad braid 'T' on his epaulette, a badge now replaced by a broad braid stripe in the Soviet army.

Dress
Officers and soldiers in walking-out dress wear an olive-brown open-necked tunic and olive-brown trousers, black shoes and an olive-brown peaked cap with a red band. Shoulder-boards and collar-patches are in arm of service colours, and metal arm-of-service insignia are worn on the collar-patch. Working dress consists of an olive-brown tunic with a high collar, olive-brown trousers gathered by cloth anklets over black boots. Soldiers wear an olive-brown sidecap with a red star on the front and a national emblem on the left; officers wear a peaked cap. A long-skirted blouse is worn in summer. Combat dress is similar, and is worn with Soviet-style steel helmets and Soviet equipment. Tank suits and NBC protective clothing are also of Soviet pattern. Greatcoats and fur caps are worn in winter. The Dimitrov Mausoleum Guard composed of specially selected conscripts, wears an elaborate

Bulgaria

ceremonial uniform based on a white hussar-style dolman in summer and a red dolman in winter.

Distinctions

Numerous orders and decorations are awarded by the Bulgarian People's Republic. The highest order is the Order of Georgi Dimitrov, awarded to Bulgarian soldiers and civilians as well as to foreigners.

CURRENT DEVELOPMENTS

Despite being the most loyal to the Soviet Union of any of the Warsaw Pact allies, Bulgaria is still a low priority recipient of modern equipment. The appearance of some new weapons such as the T-72 tank and Mi-24 helicopter, coupled with recent (1982) Warsaw Pact exercises which include seaborne reinforcement of Bulgaria from the Soviet Union, may point to some changes.

Richard Holmes
David Isby

BURMA*

HISTORY AND INTRODUCTION

Burma was the first country of the British Commonwealth of Nations to leave the association on gaining independence, which it did in 1948, declaring itself at the same time a republic. The political leaders who won independence had first made their names and established their power as members of a nationalist military organisation, and Burma is today still led by one of those original 'thirty comrades'. Despite their success in winning independence from the British, however, their movement did not subsequently succeed in making itself acceptable to the heterogeneous population of the country as a whole, much of which is, and has been for many years, in open revolt against the central government. As a result, the army is continuously engaged in counter-insurgency operations in many of the 'minority' areas, and is indeed unable to penetrate some of the more remote frontier regions. The army is, however, more than a mere agent of political coercion. At the highest level, its leadership is indentical with that of the ruling Burma Socialist Programme Party and is committed to its one-party system of government and its policies of social and economic development and external non-alignment.

The modern Burmese army, unlike the Indian and Pakistani, is only tenuously descended from that of the colonial era. Until 1937, Burma, which Britain had annexed in successive stages between 1824 and 1886, was a dependency of the Indian Empire, garrisoned by a regiment of the Indian Army which, though called the 20th Burma Rifles, did not enlist Burmese proper.† Some Burmese were recruited into the Burmese Military Police, a paramilitary force, but they were outnumbered by Indians and Gurkhas and by representatives of the Burman minorities — Karens, Kachins and Chins — who also supplied the bulk of the Burma Rifles. At the approach of World War II, the Burma Rifles was expanded from four to 14 battalions, but the proportion of Burmese enlisted did not increase.

Most of these hastily-raised and undertained battalions melted away during the British retreat from Burma in the face of the Japanese invasion in 1942. Only one, the 2nd Bruma Rifles, kept together, and into it were drafted the survivors of the rest, most of them Karens of the Irrawaddy delta, about 1000 in number. The battalion fought throughout the rest of the Burma campaign and played a particularly useful reconnaissance role during the two Chindit operations behind Japanese lines.

In terms of numbers, and of future political and military significance, however, the most important group of Burmese soldiers served on the other side from the British during most of the war years. This was the Burma National Army, raised by Burmese patriots, under Japanese patronage, with the aim of bringing their country to independence. Its leaders, as self-styled *Thakins* (masters), had cut their political teeth in prewar university and parliamentary nationalist agitation,

through which they attracted the attention of a Japanese agent who arranged, in early 1941, for 30 of them to visit Japan for military training. Their leader, Aung San, had already been there on a preliminary visit and on their joint return he became head of a clandestine Burma Independence Army. It actually took part, at the side of the Japanese, in the expulsion of the British from the country in 1942, but its military value was low and was quite offset by the unrest its subsequent oppression of the minorities within the country caused. In July, 1942 it was disbanded by Japanese order. The Japanese had nevertheless decided to vest the government of the country in the nationalist movement, and in August conferred power on a group which included Aung San. He was allowed to re-raise a military force, which was called first the Burma Defence Army and then the Burma National Army, and employed to maintain internal security — a necessary duty in view of the disaffection of the minorities, which the British successfully fostered. It grew eventually to a size of nine battalions, and even took a minor part in operations against the British; but worsening relations with the Japanese, who mistreated its personnel and frustrated Aung San's efforts to build it into an independent national force, prompted him to make contact with the British and arrange for it to change sides at a convenient moment. This it did on their approach towards Rangoon in March, 1945.

The BNA and its leaders thus ended the war on the winning side, under the new title of Patriotic Burmese Forces (PBF). It quickly moved into an even more advantageous position within the country. While the British garrison was progressively withdrawn for demobilisation, former BNA troops were recruited in sizable numbers into the new Burmese Regular Army, and into the reorganised Military Police. The principle of enlistment which Aung San forced the British to concede was by 'class', so that while battalions of Karen, Kachin and Chin Rifles were separately established, in recognition of their wartime service, five new wholly Burmese battalions (1st and 3rd—6th) of the Burma Rifles were also created, as well as several wholly Burmese battalions of the Military Police. The majority of the Burmese recruits into both were former members of supporters of the BNA, and the surplus were directed by Aung San into a private army of his political party, the Anti-Fascist People's Freedom League, known as the People's Volunteer Organisation. It soon had branches in every district and town and, with an AFPFL network within the public services, provided the movement virtually with a parallel authority within the State.

Open conflict between the government and the AFPFL over the timing and conditions of independence — the principle of which the British conceded — had been certain since the reinstitution of the colonial regime. It was precipitated spontaneously by a police strike, over a mundane but pressing issue of pay, in September, 1946 which the AFPFL, seeing their opportunity, turned into a general strike. Lacking the means to maintain order, and with the PVO drilling in the streets, the British governor invited Aung San to head a new Executive Council, formed largely of AFPFL members. Aung San accepted and almost immediately demanded the grant of full independence under the threat of rebellion. In January, 1947 he was promised that it would come into effect within 1 year.

The British acted apparently in the belief that the min-

---

* See also Appendix 2.
† 'Burmese' is commonly used to signify the Burmese-speaking majority, 'Burman' the whole indigenous population, which includes several large minorities of mainly hill-dwelling people — Shans, Kachins, Karens, Chins, Mons, Arakanese — as well as many small tribal groups.

orities, about 30% of the population, would accept the legitimacy of a unitary State, and that Aung San was undisputed leader of the nationalist movement. Neither belief, as the British were well aware, was sound. The Burmese communists, who had been purged from the AFPFL, were in open rebellion, and were themselves split into a Red Flag (Trotskyite) and White Flag (Stalinist) group, while still inside the movement were many rivals for Aung San's position, notably U Saw, a pre-war prime minister. In the population at large, the minorities remained deeply suspicious of Burmese intentions, and were adamant for local autonomy and the entrenchment of the right of secession.

By a remarkable effort of personal diplomacy, Aung San managed to reconcile all the hill-people, except the Karens, to his independence scheme, which would have allowed them a measure of autonomy, and, with that success behind him, went on to sweep the polls at the election for the Constituent Assembly in April, 1947. Three months later, however, at one of the first constituent cabinets, henchmen of U Saw broke into the meeting and machine-gunned to death most of those present, including Aung San. They, including U Saw, were executed soon after. But the death of *Bogyoke* ('the great general' as he continues to be known in Burma) robbed the country of its chance of a smooth transition to independence. His successor, U Nu, though a senior Thakin, lacked his popularity and authority and was faced from the outset by rebellion. At first it was offered mainly by the Red Flag communists and by the Muslim *Mujahids* of the north Arakan, but within 6 months they had been joined by White Flag communists, much of the PVO, some ex-BNA battalions of the regular army and the Union Military Police, some of the 1st Kachin Rifles and, among the other minorities, the Karen National Defence Organisation and the Mon National Defence Organisation. By March, 1949 15 months after independence, full-scale war was raging over the greater part of the country and, with the exception of Rangoon, all the important towns were in rebel hands.

Fortunately the rebels were quite disunited and, indeed, in most cases mutually antagonistic. Even more fortunately, and very creditably, most of the Karen, Chin and Kachin battalions remained loyal, even though called on to fight their own people, and despite the example of the bulk of the Burmese battalions that defected to the communists in July—August, 1948. Through their efforts (and despite the mutiny in February, 1949 of the hitherto loyal Karen battalions) the government held on and by November, 1949 had wrested the initiative from its enemies. About that time their number was swelled by the appearance of a refugee army of Nationalist Chinese inside the eastern Shan States but these 'KMTs' (*Kuomintang*) constituted a problem which could be temporarily shelved and dealt with separately. Against the insurgents proper, the Burmese army pressed forward to recover half the territory of the State, and most of the important towns, by the end of 1950. It grew greatly in strength, from 9 to 41 battalions, between 1952 and 1953, and by the end of 1954 had virtually destroyed the Karen National Defence Organisation and the *Mujahids*, and had greatly reduced the numbers of the White and Red Flag communists and their allies the PVO mutineers. It was also able to deal severely, in 1953—4, with the KMTs, even though they had recruited numbers of Shans and had apparently been reinforced directly from Taiwan.

The very military success of the government in the regions produced, however, grave political problems at the centre. The absence of a parliamentary opposition, which is what the rebels would have provided had they not taken to the jungle, encouraged faction fighting in the AFPFL, which by 1958 had gone as far as the creation of new private armies, financed by the proceeds of corruption which was rife in the party's ranks. 'The situation was closely approaching the sad spectacle of 1948—9', warned the Commander-in-Chief, General Ne Win, in a speech to parliament, and the only solution to it, in the judgement of wide sections of opinion, was to confer power temporarily on the army. The view was shared by U Nu who on October 26th, 1958 requested Ne Win to take office, with powers to restore order sufficiently for new and free elections to be held.

During the following 15 months the army set itself three tasks: to re-establish peace and the rule of law; to implant democracy; and to establish a socialist economy. To that end young officers were introduced into most public agencies, the police strengthened, the counter-insurgency prosecuted more vigorously, squatters resettled, and public corruption severely punished. While it does not seem that much progress was made with any but its first task, the army nevertheless proceeded to sponsor the promised election, a year later than originally scheduled, in February, 1960. The electorate returned U Nu's branch (now non-socialist) of the AFPFL by a large majority and the army returned to barracks, or rather to the full-time prosecution of the war in the provinces.

U Nu's rejection of socialism, though it had won him temporary popularity by making his wing of the AFPFL seem a new — and therefore perhaps uncorrupt — party, failed, however, to win stability for his government. To gain new supporters, he had given promises, particularly to the Buddhists, which he proved unable to keep. He had also offered the minorities, particularly the Shans, increased autonomy and, when he seemed about to allow them to secede (as the Constitution strictly allowed them to do), the army once more intervened, this time on its own initiative. On March 2nd, 1962, the Rangoon garrison, under the orders of Ne Win, occupied the government buildings and installed a military cabinet in power.

The precipitating cause of the coup was probably the desire to preserve national unity, of which the army, like that of so many other countries, regarded itself as the fundamental guardian. But there were other reasons for the army's decision to seize power. One was a widespread contempt for the politicians and their parties — similar to that which had prompted Ayub Khan to stage his coup in Pakistan in 1958. But, paradoxically, the failure of these socialist parties to make good their programmes had generated a popular desire for more, not less, socialism and, because of its roots in the pre-war nationalist struggle, the army's leadership also saw itself as guardians of the purity of 'Burmese socialism'. As a result, the regime of which Ne Win became the head more closely resembled that of Nasser's Egypt than those military regimes which came to power elsewhere in Asia in the same years.

It differed from the Nasserite model, however, in constituting itself as a political *corps d'élite* rather than as the spearhead of a mass movement. The military leadership constituted itself a Revolutionary Council on taking power, dissolved parliament, and disbanded the political parties (March 28th, 1964), having meanwhile created its own Burma Socialist Programme Party. Entry to that party was made, however, deliberately difficult and its membership, even today, does not seem to extend far beyond the upper ranks of the army and the administration* (which in many cases are co-terminous). Admission requires the assent of the Revolutionary Council and members are obliged 'to accept

---

* In 1973 President Ne Win declared his intention of transforming the BSPP into a mass movement, the People's Party. That did not happen. Ne Win was replaced as head of state by U San Yu, a former Vice-Chief of the Army Staff.

out of conviction *The Burmese Way to Socialism'*, a fairly orthodox statement of Marxist belief which the Council published in April, 1962 as its party creed. In some sense, therefore, the BSPP may be seen as a Leninist revolutionary cadre rather than as a ruling political party.

Yet the party does rule and in the years between 1962 and 1972 did so in a very direct manner. The revision of the Constitution, undertaken by a mixed military—civilian committee between 1971 and 1973, has replaced direct rule with a more representative form, but the personnel has not changed and effective power rests where it did before, among the leadership of the armed forces. The political and economic consequences for Burma of so many years of Marxist—military government have not been happy. The economy, which has been progressively nationalised, is stagnant and the fundamental political problems, which require a federal solution, have not been tackled at root. As a military body, however, the rank and file of the army remain efficient and well-motivated and their purely military achievements against the rebels in recent years have been considerable. Rebellion is now almost exclusively confined to the border areas and the number of active dissidents has been reduced to an easily manageable figure (perhaps 15,000). Having preserved the unity of the country, and largely restored law and order, the next task of the army will be progressively to shed its power and inaugurate an era of permanent civilian administration.

STRENGTH AND BUDGET

Population: 32,445,000 (of which 30% are non-Burmese minorities)
Army: 163,000
Navy: 7000 (one frigate, 4 corvettes, 88 small craft.
Air force: 9000 (16 combat aircraft)
Paramilitary: 38,000 paramilitary police; 35,000 militia
GNP (1981 estimate) $4,800,000,000
Defence expenditure (1981) $189,000,000

COMMAND AND CONSTITUTIONAL STATUS

The 1974 Constitution, which restored a measure of representative government after 12 years of government by decree, transferred power from the Revolutionary Council — set up by the coup of 1962 — to a one party (Burma Socialist Programme Party) civilian government. The membership of the new Council of Ministers is close to that of the former Revolutionary Council, whose military members — the large majority — had dropped their ranks in 1972. Real political power, as well as control of the armed froces, remains in the hands of the President, ex-General Ne Win, and his close supporters, most of them ex-officers. He is empowered, by virtue of emergency provisions embodied in the new Constitution of December, 1973 (the product of a national referendum) to employ the army in virtually any situation and any guise he chooses. Its officers are deeply involved in politics and in many cases are elected members of the government. Party influence permeates throughout the army, though the creation of a 'commissar' system has been avoided; instead, commanding officers act as both military and party chiefs within their own units, and are promoted on the basis of professional competence and party loyalty in equal measure.

The supreme governing and policy-making body is the Council of State, which is chosen by the People's Assembly (first elections to which took place in January, 1974). The Chairman, is also *ex officio* President of Burma. The Council's defence powers, which require endorsement by the People's Assembly, include the declaration of martial law, states of emergency and mobilisation.

The supreme executive body is the Council of Ministers, which implements the orders of the Council of State and resolutions of the People's Assembly. Specifically, it is charged with the management of national defence, maintenance of law and order and the budget. Ministers and their deputies may be serving officers; officers elected to the Council of State, however, must retire from the service.

The head of the defence organisation is the Minister of Defence, who also acts as Chief of Staff of the defence forces. The Defence Ministry is a joint integrated headquarters, exercising complete political, operational, financial and administrative control over the forces and the defence industries. There are Vice-Chiefs of Staff for each of the three services but, although the navy and air force have responsibility for their own operations and training, their influence within the defence organisation is slight. The army dominates by virtue of its much greater size.

ROLE, DEPLOYMENT, COMMITMENT AND RECENT OPERATIONS

Role

Because of Burma's unaligned foreign policy, external defence is not a major preoccupation of the Burmese army. India and Thailand are benevolent neighbours, Laos has internal problems and China, though having cause for disagreement on a number of issues, some now settled, some still outstanding, in practice chooses to maintain good relations.

The maintenance of internal security is thus the army's principal task, but it is not discharged in a purely military way. During the Revolutionary Council period, 1962—74, the administrative machinery of Burma proper at division, district, sub-division, township and village levels was organised in Security and Administration Committees, the chairmen of which, except at village level, were serving officers, who were also either commanders of units operating within the area or in close liaison with them. The administration in the States (Karen, Kayah, Kachin and Shan, and the special division of the Chins) was differently organised, for historical reasons, but was also strongly military. Since the reintroduction of a nominally civilian government in 1974 these arrangements have been modified, but the administration remains, nevertheless, under close military supervision. The commanders of the nine regional commands, in particular, wield great power.

Deployment

Units are deployed under nine regional commands, the boundaries of which correspond exactly or approximately with those of the seven divisions of the States. Each command has at its disposal one to three Tactical Operation Commands (TOCs), equivalent to a brigade, containing three to four infantry battalions. They are deployed as shown in Table 1. In addition, the Ministry of Defence disposes of three divisions, numbered 77, 88 and 99, each fielding three TOCs and comprising 10 infantry battalions, which are allotted as necessary to the regional commands. All are at present deployed in the eastern hills. There are reports that three new divisions have been organised.

Commitment

Burma has no military treaty with any other State and does not allow foreign troops to enter her territory (though Chinese troops may have tacitly been allowed to operate against the KMTs in 1961—2). Aid and advice have been received intermittently from the British, Yugoslavs, Russians

Table 1

Regional command	Division or State	Number of TOCs
North-west	Special Division of the Chins, Magwe (northern), Mandalay (northern), Sagaing (southern)	Two
Western	Arakan, Magwe (southern)	One
Central	Mandalay (southern), Pegu (northern)	One
South-west	Irrawaddy	Two
Rangoon	Pegu (southern)	—
Northern	Sagaing (northern), Kachin	Two
North-east	Shan (northern), North-east Special District*	Two
Eastern	Shan (southern), Kayah	Three
South-east	Karen, Tenasserim	Three

* East of the Salween river; the army does not operate in this area.

and Chinese, but the policy of the army is to rely on its own training resources and to procure arms from abroad, if that is necessary, by cash purchase.

Recent Operations

'Recent operations' merge imperceptibly with 'past operations' in Burma, for the rebellions with which the army is continuously occupied have been running uninterruptedly since independence and have their origins in the ethnic and political character of the country. The dissident groups are fewer today than in 1948, but those which survive were active then, if under a different name or names, and are still devoted to aims declared at that time. They fall into three categories: (1) the communists, whose quarrel with the government is ideological (though historically also personal) and who now operate in the Shan States on the Chinese border. Formerly split into White Flag (Stalinist) and Red Flag (Trotskyist) wings, the latter were effectively destroyed by the capture of their leader. Thakin Soe, in 1970. The White Flags, who had long operated in Arakan, Pegu and the Irrawaddy delta, concentrated their activity in the Shan States in 1968, following the assassination of their leader, and in order to enjoy readier access to the aid which the Chinese surreptitiously give them. They number between 3000 and 6000 and have an alliance of convenience with the Shan and Kachin rebels. (2) The dissidents among the minorities, mainly Shans, Mons, Karens, Kachins, Chins and Arakanese. Each group desires autonomy for its own region, but they are disunited (although short-lived alliances have been formed: the most recent is the National Democratic United Front, to which the communists have made overtures). The most important groups are: the Karen National Unity Party, the New Mon State Party, the Karen National Defence Organisation, the Chin National Organisation, the Arakan Liberation Party, the Kachin Independence Army (about 4000 fighters) and the Shan State Army (about 4000 fighters). A group of dissident Burmese exiles, founded by U Nu in 1969 and based originally in Thailand, called the Parliamentary Democracy Party, is also sporadically active. (3) The Kuomintang (KMT), whose presence on Burmese soil owes nothing to internal causes. They are a remnant of Chiang Kai-shek's army which made its way into eastern Burma after the Communist victory in 1949, and are now principally engaged in the opium trade, though they commit the occasional 'political' act and remain in contact with the Taiwan government.

The army can claim a considerable degree of success against the rebels in recent years, particularly over the communists in Pegu in 1968–72, but this must be measured against a marked upsurge of rebel activity in the mid-1960s, brought about by Ne Win's policy of centralism. The rebels remain strong and popular enough in their own areas to stage quite spectacular attacks on government forces. The most serious in recent years have been the seizure of the town of Mong Mah in Shan State near the Chinese border by 4000 communists in November, 1973 who were dislodged only by a fierce counter-attack supported by aircraft, and the seizure of the town of Myawaddy in March, 1974 by 2000 Karens. They kept 150 government troops surrounded for 5 days until they were released by a force of 2000 soldiers supported by aircraft. Government interference with the opium trade, on which all dissident groups depend for income, also frequently leads to fighting, as with the quite unpolitical Lah tribesmen of the Thai borderland in January, 1973. Student disorders and industrial strikes, caused by economic grievances, also required the intervention of the army in several large towns in 1974.

ORGANISATION

Arms of Service

The army contains as well as ordnance, service, medical and military police corps units, small signal and engineer units, three field artillery regiments, one anti-aircraft regiment, and two armoured regiments (one tank and one armoured car) both with obsolete (and in the case of the tanks, antiquated) equipment. It is, however, overwhelmingly an infantry force, which has retained something of a 'regimental' system deriving originally from the British. The regiments are: Burma Regiment, 89 battalions; Burma Rifles, six battalions; Kachin Rifles, five battalions; Chin Rifles, four battalions; Shan Rifles, one battalion; Kayah Rifles, one battalion; and Light Infantry Regiment, nine battalions. Official policy is to reduce the regiments recruited on an ethnic basis, and to man all units with a mixture of people. Thus the government has consistently refused Arakanese requests for the formation of an Arakan regiment. However, many battalions are still recruited from a single people only, and this is true of battalions of the all-Union Burma Regiment, some of which, for example, are exclusively composed of domiciled Gurkhas (numbers of whom are settled in the Kachin and Shan States).

Operational

A battalion is organised into four rifle companies of three platoons, plus a support company with mortar, machine-gun and recoilless rifle platoons, and an administrative company. The establishment is 27 officers and 723 other ranks but the normal strength is about 500. Three or four battalions form a Tactical Operations Command; three TOCs form a division. Artillery and armoured units are deployed only as required.

RECRUITMENT, TRAINING AND RESERVES

Military service is voluntary. Pay is not now higher than in comparable civil employment, but the perquisites offered by the army — free rations, clothing, accommodation and medical care — raise the military standard of living higher than the civilian. There is therefore little difficulty in recruiting either officers or men. The recruitment policy is to man all units on a mixed-race basis, but numbers are still recruited from a single minority.

Officer training is conducted at the Defence Services Academy, Maymyo, near Mandalay, founded in 1955. It is a tri-service school, at which the cadets complete a four-year degree course and are indoctrinated for membership of the Burma Socialist Programme Party. An Officer Training School commissions university graduates after a four-month course and selected serving soldiers after 18 months. The superior training of officers is conducted at the Command and General Staff College, an eight-month course, and the National Defence College, Rangoon.

Soldiers are trained in their unit depots: non-commissioned officers are trained at the Non-Commissioned Officers School; the various corps — Artillery, Armour, Signals — maintain schools of technical training.

There are virtually no reserves for the army. The Territorials (sitwundans) founded at independence and numbering originally about 14 battalions have gradually been absorbed into the regular army. The other forces — kins (village home guards) and the Special Police Reserve — are local part-time organisations.

EQUIPMENT AND ARMS INDUSTRY

Equipment is largely of British and American pattern and is mostly obsolete, but some is gradually being replaced by locally manufactured light arms and small quantities of heavy weapons from abroad. Burmese government policy is to purchase foreign equipment, rather than seek gifts, in accordance with its foreign policy of non-alignment. The local arms industry is of recent foundation and limited scope and output, but the country is believed to be self-sufficient in small arms ammunition.

Apart from old patterns of small arms, the most important types of weapons are believed to be as follows:

Rifle: 7.62mm G-3 (German; Burmese made)
Light machine-gun: 7.62mm G-4 (German; Burmese made)
Grenade launcher: 40mm M-79 (USA)
   light: types unknown
   heavy: 120mm Soltam (Israel)
Anti-armour weapons: Six and 17 pounder anti-tank guns (obsolete British; 50 in service)
Air-defence weapons: 40mm and 3.7in guns (obsolete British; about 10 in service)
Artillery: 76mm mountain gun (Yugoslavia; 120 in service); 105mm howitzer (USA; 80 in service); 25 Comet tanks (British; obsolete)
Armour: Humber armoured car (obsolete British; 40 in service); Ferret scout car (obsolete British; 45 in service)
Aircraft: the air force operates 16 old ground-attack fighters, 17 transports and 43 helicopters

RANK, DRESS AND DISTINCTIONS

In its early years the Burmese army wore British-style tropical uniform, unit insignia and badges of rank. It may still do so; but there is some evidence that it has reverted to the badges of rank and rank titles of the old Japanese Imperial Army, under whose aegis the Burma National Army was formed during the war. The leaders of the army received their training at the hands of the Japanese, and it is said that strong traces of Japanese influence remain, evident in a marked formality, sharp distinction between ranks and deference towards superiors.

CURRENT DEVELOPMENTS

The military tradition is strong in Burma. The British chose to believe that the Burmese did not make good soldiers, but the basis of the State which they overthrew in the nineteenth century was in fact military, and the resistance it offered them in their three Burmese wars was considerable. An unfortunate consequence of British military policy towards the Burmese was, however, that they did not include a modern, apolitical army in the administrative apparatus they bequeathed to the Burmese at independence. Political opposition to colonial rule had taken, perhaps in reaction to the British dismissal of the Burmese soldierly qualities, a specifically military form, and it was perhaps inevitable, therefore, that post-independence governments should have failed to achieve a satisfactory separation of military and civil power in the State and the subordination of the one to the other.

The tradition of dacoity — semi-criminal, semi-political banditry — was also strong, and was fostered by wartime conditions. The hill peoples in particular were armed and encouraged to war against the Japanese, and thereby learnt habits of disaffection not easily unlearnt in peacetime. It was perhaps also inevitable, therefore, that opposition to the independent government should take violent forms with both its ideological and ethnic opponents. What could not be foreseen was that the army, after winning a remarkable victory in a civil war it seemed destined to lose, and after then withdrawing from the centre of the stage for 10 years, should have re-emerged to subject the country to probably the most comprehensively military regime of all of those that have sprung up in the world since 1945. For the Burmese army did not seek merely to supplant the politicians, but also the country's civil servants and many of its native as well as foreign businessmen. Through the nationalisation of the greater part of the country's industry and trade (since partly reversed), the army achieved perhaps a greater degree of control of the conditions of national life than that attempted by soldiers anywhere. On top of its political and economic programme, it also propagated its own political philosophy — *The Burmese Way to Socialism* — which, though an unexciting mélange of Marxism and Buddhist ethical tenets, stands as an almost unique attempt by a military regime to implant a distinctive, intellectually coherent ideology on its subjects.

The wonder is that, amidst its political preoccupations, it has found time and energy to prosecute the war which originally gave it the pretext for political intervention, and to such effect. During the last 6 years it has made real headway against the internal dissidents — minorities and communists alike — and has also achieved the self-confidence and political maturity to begin the painful and difficult process of divesting itself of power and rebuilding a civilian administration. Through its veil of secrecy, a remarkable, and in many ways admirable, process of political and military achievement is perceptible.

John Keegan

BURUNDI

HISTORY AND INTRODUCTION

This small African State was a colony of Germany until 1918, and of Belgium until 1962. Its major problem, however, originated in the 16th century when a pastoral Para-Nilotic ethnic group, the Tutsi, imposed themselves as a dominant people upon an agricultural Bantu peasantry, the Hutu. Extremely complex social relationships — divisions among the Tutsi and to a lesser extent the Hutu also — differentiate the clash of the two major groups in Burundi from the not dissimilar but more simplistic clash in Rwanda; the consequences however were those of violence and bloodshed on an even greater scale both before and after the departure of the Belgians. A tradition of political murder began in 1957, but the even more serious pattern of selective killings of leading Hutu personalities and educated men by the dominant Tutsi factions of the time began in 1965, and was repeated in 1969 and 1971, on the latter two occasions many leaders of losing Tutsi factions perishing at the same time. A gendarmerie officer, Micombero, took power in 1966 ending the monarchy. A full-scale revolt of the Hutu took place in 1972 in which thousands (probably between 80,000 and 100,000) lost their lives either in the revolt or the subsequent repression, both sides aiming at a 'final solution' with almost Hitlerian literalism. Torture, disembowelling and crucifixions were reported. In 1976 the Head of State, Colonel Micombero, was overthrown by a group of officers headed by Lieutenant-Colonel Bagaza, who pledged themselves to 'clean up' Burundi's affairs.

In this aim he has made progress, the country has become more stable and the national political party, UPRONA (Unity for National Progress) has been revived. Communal tensions have been reduced from frenetic passion to smouldering distrust.

STRENGTH AND BUDGET

Population: 4,250,000 (approximately)
Strength: a national army of 6500 including the former gendarmerie now brought into one force.
GNP: $600,000,000 (estimate).
Defence expenditure: $35,000,000 (approximate).

COMMAND AND CONSTITUTIONAL STATUS

The head of State Lieutenant-Colonel J. B. Bagaza. The Supreme Revolutionary Council established in 1976 has been abolished and replaced by a Central Committee and a Policy Committee of the ruling party. The Head of Security is Colonel S. Nzohabonayo, and the Army Chief of Staff is Colonel A. Niyungeko.

ROLE, COMMITMENT, DEPLOYMENT AND RECENT OPERATIONS

The Burundi army and gendarmerie both played leading parts in the 1972 repression.

Burundi's borders represent a threat — chiefly from the continuing likelihood of the Hutu group attempting to cross, from safety, in the hope of overthrowing the regime, but also on occasions of border dispute such as that with Zaïre in 1981, when both countries moved troops to the border. There were no clashes.

ORGANISATION

This appears to comprise two infantry battalions and a 'parachute' battalion all at Bujumbura, one other 'commando' battalion, an armoured-car unit, the former gendarmerie detachments and logistic sub-units.

RECRUITMENT, TRAINING AND RESERVES

The army is very largely Tutsi.

Belgian officers and advisers, who had become linked with one of the Tutsi factions, were returned home in 1968. Chinese assistance was used briefly in the mid-1960s.

French military assistance, including personnel (probably on contract) appears to have played an unattractive role in the 1972 repression. A military training and an aid agreement was signed with France in 1969. Units of the Zaïre army also maintained order in the capital, Bujumbura, while the Burundi army suppressed the revolution in the rural areas.

An armed forces training school exists.

Recent policy appears to aim at identifying the army with development work, agriculture, school and road building etc., on occasions.

EQUIPMENT AND ARMS INDUSTRY

Small arms have arrived from a variety of sources; vehicles (including those of UNICEF) were commandeered for use in the 1972 repression. Twelve AML-90 Lynx and fifteen AML-60 armoured cars have been delivered over the last three years, together with some troop carrying lorries. Older equipment (perhaps no longer serviceable) includes fifteen US 75mm howitzers and a few Soviet 82mm mortars and 14.5mm AA guns. One report notes Shorland armoured cars on order, together with *Blindicide* 83mm anti tank missiles.

The air unit possesses three helicopters (Alouette) and three Dakota transports. On order are three Italian Marchetti SF 260 COIN aircraft.

RANK, DRESS AND DISTINCTION

Such information as is available suggests a modification of Belgian styles and insignia.

CURRENT DEVELOPMENTS

The Burundi army has hitherto existed to perpetuate rule of the country by an ethnic minority. Whether it can become a more truly national institution, which the Hutu 85% majority of the population might perceive as legitimate, is open to doubt. It is perhaps the country's major political question.

Lloyd Mathews

CAMEROUN*

HISTORY AND INTRODUCTION

Cameroun, a former French possession, became independent in 1960; it was formed from the bulk of the former German colony of Kamerun which had passed into French administration. To it was added in 1961 one of the two parts of Kamerun that had been administered by Britain (the other opted for union with Nigeria). The State is a Federation, but the vastly larger Francophone area predominates. In addition to the division caused by its colonial past, Cameroun also has ethnic divisions, and a religious one in that the northern part of the territory has a considerable Muslim population.

The country gradually became a one-party State; since 1960 the Head of State has been President A. Ahidjo. This continuity has, however, not been without opposition. In the last years of the colonial period a revolt broke out among the Bamileke people which continued for a period after independence and was only put down by French troops. Further trouble among the Bamileke reappeared in the late 1960s, Chinese support for the insurgents being alleged. French troops again played a part in the suppression, to all intents and purposes complete by 1970. The Cameroun authorities exacted severe punishments on those alleged to be leaders. By a new co-operation agreement with France signed in 1974, the French garrisons at Douala and Koutaba were withdrawn.

Cameroun has experienced severe economic difficulties over the last few years. Popular discontent is stifled by the authoritarian nature of the regime, but there is growing evidence of resentment.

STRENGTH AND BUDGET

Population: 8,750,000 (approximate).
Armed Forces: 7300 — an army of 6600; navy and air force of 300—350 each; paramilitary forces totalling some 6000 and comprising a *Sureté Nationale*, a gendarmerie, a *Brigade Mixte Mobile* and a security service known as the *Direction de Documentation*.
GNP: $5,250,000,000 (estimate).
Defence expenditure: $63,000,000.

COMMAND AND CONSTITUTIONAL STATUS

The President of the Republic, A. Ahidjo, is the supreme authority. The Minister for Defence is M. Abdoulaye, General P. Semengue is Inspector-General of the Armed Forces, and Colonel T. Malongue is Commander of Ground Forces.

ROLE, COMMITMENT, DEPLOYMENT AND RECENT OPERATIONS

The Army's roles are that of internal security and defence against threats from neighbours. Cameroun adjoins six countries. The war in Chad has given Cameroun a refugee problem and anxieties over Libyan aspirations. Suspicion of Congo's intentions and her support for Cameroun dissidents occurs from time to time. Although with the fall of Macias

* For general notes on African armies, see Appendix 1.

Nguema relations with Equatorial Guinea have improved units have periodically to be seen to be vigilant on the border. Cameroun was never at ease with the Bokassa regime in the Central African Republic, though here too difficulties have eased. Recent years, however, have seen several sharp border disputes with Nigeria, on two occasions conflict resulting. The second of these in 1981 resulted in Nigerian occupation of a disputed border area, after a naval engagement and a Nigerian air strike. The problem remains delicate as Cameroun wishes to establish a liquefied natural gas plant very close to another border area still in dispute. In respect of internal security, Cameroun forces were of course employed during the Bamileke troubles and in the containment of university unrest at Yaoundé in 1973.

ORGANISATION

Cameroun's army consists of four infantry battalions based at Yaounde, Kutuba, Douala and Baffoussam, an armoured reconnaissance battalion, a parachute battalion, an artillery and an anti-aircraft artillery battery together with small engineer, signals and transport units. The country is divided into ten military districts each headed by a colonel or a lieutenant-colonel. These are moved around frequently to avoid any gaining too great a local influence.

The gendarmerie is organised into six units.

RECRUITMENT, TRAINING AND RESERVES

The recruitment of the army was voluntary until 1975 when a system of obligatory military training for all fit men to prepare them for service in the police, army or gendarmerie, was announced.

French training facilities have been used since independence; a small French training staff still remains, and reports suggest a few French-born officers, probably contract personnel, present in Cameroun uniform.

EQUIPMENT AND ARMS INDUSTRY

Cameroun possesses a miniscule arms manufacturing capacity, the German firm of F. Werner operating a small-arms plant at Garona.

The immediate post-independence equipment of the Army included French infantry weapons, including 81mm and 60mm mortars, US M-8 armoured-cars and M-3 half-tracks, some British Ferret scout cars and French 75mm guns. Re-equipment has included Belgian M-101 105mm howitzers, Milan anti-tank missiles, 26 US Commando Gage Light armoured cars/armoured personnel carriers, twelve armed with a 90mm gun, eight with a 20mm, three for troop transportation, two adapted for recovery work and one for command, and important provisions for Cameroun's anti-aircraft unit, 201 anti-aircraft battery. This latter has received or is receiving Swedish 40mm Bofors guns and Swiss 35mm Oerlikon guns to replace the older Chinese 37mm and 14.5mm equipments, together with the *Superfledermaus* radar control system and British Snipe targets for training. 201 Battery is normally located at Edea. Infantry weapons include 60mm

Cameroun

and 81mm mortars. Some older 57mm anti tank guns and 89mm rocket launchers may still be in service.

The air force possesses six Alphajet fighters and four Magister COIN machines, two large C-130 Hercules transports, eleven smaller transport aircraft of different types, a liaison aircraft, two maritime reconnaissance aircraft, and a helicopter fleet of one Puma, one Lama, three Alouettes, one Ml-4 and four Gazelles.

The main airfield is at Garoua.

The gendarmerie, together with the reconnaissance unit, possess a first order of 27 Commando vehicles; these were petrol-engined but may be re-engined for diesel.

The purchase of Italian FIROS artillery rocket launchers is being considered.

RANK, DRESS AND DISTINCTIONS

These follow the French pattern; the *képi* is however replaced by a peaked cap in the army.

CURRENT DEVELOPMENTS

The Cameroun army is a small force that has hitherto met its country's modest needs. There is no doubt however that it can only operate a 'hedgehog' defence policy against any serious challenge from Nigeria – i.e. to hold out long enough to gather inter-African or international support. Re-equipment appears to be designed to achieve this limited aim, – and also to please restive officers.

ADDENDUM

In a surprise move in October 1982 – and after first forewarning Paris – President Ahidjo resigned. His successor, President P. Biya is a southern Christian; his appointment will serve to redress a political balance that had tended to favour the north, particularly in the last Ahidjo years. Few other major changes are likely.

Lloyd Mathews

CANADA

HISTORY AND INTRODUCTION

With the passing of the British North America Act in 1867, Canada became a self-governing Dominion within the British Empire. While the Canada of today is a huge nation that sprawls over 3,200,000 square miles, the original Federation encompassed only a comparatively small area centred on the St. Lawrence river valley. The geographic expansion of the country on an east–west axis occupied the remainder of the nineteenth century. Development of the Arctic did not even begin until after World War I, and even today the high north remains largely a frontier land.

Carving a nation out of a wilderness was a major endeavour. Fortunately, the task was not complicated by the need for elaborate and costly defence measures. Many factors contributed to his favourable situation. First and foremost, there was the security of isolation. The vast expanses of the Atlantic and Pacific were effective barriers to aggession while, to the north, the polar wastes were even more formidable obstacles. The ubiquitous Royal Navy added another layer of safety. Then there was the United States.

In the late nineteenth century, the United States was yet to emerge as a world power, but the tremendous potential of that country was evident. During the American Civil War (1860–1865) relations between the Union and Britain had deteriorated steadily but the trend had stopped short of war. In Canada, apprehension over possible American designs on the north had been one of the factors leading to confederation. In 1871, however, the Treaty of Washington between the United States and Britain removed sources of friction arising out of the events of the civil war. As long as amicable relations with the United States was a cornerstone of imperial foreign policy, Canada's southern frontier was secure. Given these conditions, there was no imperative to develop the defence establishment. Strategic security, an economic depression in the years following confederation and the pressing needs of nation-building, all contributed to the initial impoverishment of the Canadian 'army'.

Canada inherited the beginnings of a military establishment from Britain, and, until very recently, the British connection was the most important military fact in the Dominion. In the early years of nationhood, military enthusiasm ran high. The 'threat' from the United States had not been resolved: Fenians, attempting to embarrass Great Britain into resolving the Irish home-rule problem, periodically launched small raids from American States into Canada. In 1870 there was a minor rebellion in the Red River Colony to the west which warranted the raising of a small expeditionary force composed of British regulars and Canadian militiamen to put it down. British regular units stationed in Canada also provided training facilities and instructors. In 1871, however, the British units were withdrawn and Canada was left to fend for herself.

Canada's 'army' was known as the Militia, and had three components. The Reserve Militia was supposedly composed of all the able-bodied men in the country between the ages of 16 and 60, but there was no organisation, no equipment and no mobilisation plan. The force could not even be dignified with the term 'paper army', since there were not even nominal rolls of those eligible to serve. All that can be said of the Reserve Militia is that it represented some vague potential.

The Non-permanent Active Militia, on the other hand, had somewhat more substance. It was the major element of the Canadian defence establishment. Even so, it was a modest organisation, composed of part-time volunteers who served only 14 days a year. Organisation, doctrine, equipment and customs closely followed the British model. In its early years the force consisted solely of cavalry, artillery and infantry units, but in the decade preceeding the outbreak of World War I a start was made in creating the necessary support arms, services and staffs required by a balanced field force. From 1867 to 1914, the strength of the Active Militia grew in fits and starts from 25,000 to a pre-war peak of about 50,000 all ranks.

The third component of the Militia was the Permanent Force, the Canadian equivalent of a standing army. The force was originally raised in the early 1870s to maintain the various military works left by the departing British. Its role quickly evolved into that of a training cadre for the Active Militia. In this respect, its early successes were limited as it proved difficult for this miniscule army to find time even to train itself. In August, 1914, it numbered less than 2000.

With this tiny, ill-trained ill-equipped force, Canada went to war. Yet the Militia was well off compared to the rest of the defence establishment. There was no air force nor did the Militia own any aircraft. The newly created Royal Canadian Navy was foundering on the shoals of political disagreement. The question as to whether Canada should simply contribute to the upkeep of the Royal Navy, or attempt to raise her own maritime forces had not been satisfactorily resolved before the war. The RCN consisted of two cruisers, one on each coast.

The Dominion's war effort focused upon the army. A divisional-size expeditionary force was raised in a matter of weeks and dispatched to Britain. Canada balked most strongly when the War Office made known its intention to break up the force into reinforcement drafts for British units. Despite initial problems in obtaining qualified senior commanders and staff officers, it was never accepted — in Canada — that Canadian forces would fight other than together. For the initial years of conflict, Britain provided the senior officers. By war's end, however, what had grown to a corps of four divisions was commanded and staffed almost exclusively by Canadians — most of them pre-war Militia officers.

Six hundred thousand Canadians, out of a total population of 12,000,000, served during World War I; 60,000 died. By 1917, the replacement requirements of the Expeditionary Force forced a reluctant government to resort to conscription.

Their reluctance was well founded. There was a fundamental difference in perception of the war, and Canada's proper role in it, between English- and French-speaking sections of the country. In general, English-speaking Canadians were much more attuned to the Imperial connection than were their Francophone countrymen. This, the fact that the command structure operated exclusively in English, and an incredibly inept recruiting programme, resulted in a distinct lack of enthusiasm for the war in the province of Quebec. Conscription virtually divided the country into two mutually hostile camps.

Having fought the war to end all wars, Canada quickly returned to the pre-war pattern in military affairs. To the Active Militia and Permanent Force were added a nascent navy and air force, but in no sense was the defence establishment regarded as being a key facet of the national effort. The great depression brought a slashed defence budget. When the inevitability of another conflict with Germany became apparent in the late 1930s, the Canadian rearmament programme was inevitably a matter of too little, too late. Britain, Canada's traditional source of equipment, was fully engaged in her own rearmament programme, and precious little was available for Canada. In 1939, fewer men underwent the 14 days of annual training than had on the eve of war in 1914.

The World War II pattern of Canadian military effort was essentially similar to that of World War I. In a spasm response, a million men and women were recruited into the forces over the 6 years of war. The focus of the Canadian war effort was the Atlantic and Europe, with the majority of personnel serving in the army. Mindful of the conscription crisis of World War I, the government adopted a policy of 'conscription if necessary, but not necessarily conscription'. While many men were conscripted for service in Canada, only a few thousand of them were eventually drafted overseas.

With the beginning of the cold war, Canada gave up her traditional reliance upon the Militia and opted for collective security and forces-in-being. Co-operation with the United States for the defence of North America, which had begun in the early months of World War II, was continued and expanded in the air and on the ground. Canadian membership in NATO brought an initial commitment of an air division of four wings and a 6000-man brigade group to Europe.

Canada has been a strong supporter of UN military operations. A brigade group served in Korea, and elements of the Canadian forces have participated in every one of the numerous peace-keeping and truce-observation bodies that the UN has formed over the last two decades.

Post-war strength of the forces peaked in the early 1960s when the Canadian defence establishment numbered some 120,000 regulars, of whom 50,000 were army (50,000 air force, 20,000 navy). In the same period, the Militia declined in size and importance when compared to its traditional status.

The most significant event in Canadian post-war military development was the integration and unification of the forces in the mid and late 1960s. In the place of individual services Canada opted for a single Armed Force. The project held the prospect of increased flexibility, lower manpower requirements, and a greater portion of the defence budget being available for capital expenditure. Functional commands were created: Mobile Command became the post-integration equivalent of the Canadian army. A series of reorganisations, restructurings and changes of priorities have followed unification. Overall force levels have dropped steadily to where they now stand at about 65% of their former post-war high. The impact of inflation, rising absolute costs of military hardware, and increasing operating costs have cut severely into that portion of the defence budget available for capital expenditure. At the end of 1975, Mobile Command was stretched to its apparent limit in terms of manageable tasks, personnel and equipment. A defence structure review is currently underway.

STRENGTH AND BUDGET

Population: 24,200,000
Canadian Armed Forces: 82,000 regulars, 21,000 reserves.
Land Element (army) Mobile Command: 17,034 regulars, 15,500 reserves.
Canadian Mechanised Battle Group in Europe (NATO): 3200 regulars
Navy: 20 major vessels, 12 smaller
Air force: 15,300, 208 combat aircraft

GNP (1981): $282,870,000,000
Defence expenditure (1982–3): $5,710,000,000

COMMAND AND CONSTITUTIONAL STATUS

Command
Her Majesty, Queen Elizabeth II, Queen of Canada is Head of State. The Governor-General, her representative and as such is the titular Commander-in-Chief of the Canadian Armed Forces. The Federal cabinet is responsible for all matters of defence policy. A bipartisan Standing Committee on External Affairs and National Defence of the House of Commons assists the cabinet in its deliberations. The Chief of the Defence Staff (CDS) is the senior military advisor to the government and is responsible for the conduct of all operations of the Canadian Armed Forces. Within the unified force structure there are no chiefs of individual services, although the commanders of the three environmental commands correspond roughly to such positions.

The Department of National Defence is headed by the Ministry of National Defence. The Deputy Minister and the Chief of Defence Staff are directly responsible to him. The five functional commands are under the direct command of the CDS, who is assisted in exercising direction and control by the staffs of National Defence Headquarters.

Constitutional Status
In 1982, Her Majesty the Queen proclaimed the new Constitution which replaced British North America Act. In assigning Federal and Provincial responsibilities, defence is given to the Federal government. The Militia Act, Naval Service Act and Air Force Act were all eliminated in 1950 by a single National Defence Act (NDA), although the three traditional services remained distinct entities. In 1968, the NDA was amended by the Canadian Forces Reorganisation Act which eliminated the individual services, replacing them with a unified Canadian Armed Forces.

The National Defence Act is the source of authority for the Minister of National Defence and the CDS. The Deputy Minister of National Defence, the senior civil servant in the Department, draws his authority from a variety of acts; his prime responsibility is the financial administration of the Department.

ROLE, COMMITMENTS, DEPLOYMENT AND RECENT OPERATIONS

Role
The role of the Canadian Armed Forces flows from the stated national aims that:

a. Canada will continue secure as an independent political entity.
b. Canada and all Canadians will enjoy enlarging prosperity.
c. All Canadians will see in the life they have and the contribution they make to humanity something worthwhile preserving in identity and purpose.

Defence priorities are:

a. Surveillance of Canadian territory and coastlines, i.e. the protection of Canadian sovereignty.
b. Defence of North America in co-operation with US forces.
c. Fulfilment of such NATO commitments as may be agreed upon.
d. Performance of such international peacekeeping roles as Canada may, from time to time, assume.

Commitment

'Army' commitments of the Canadian Armed Forces include those fulfilled by elements of Mobile Command in Canada and the land component of Canadian Forces Europe. Canadian-based units are all multi-tasked.

Force commitments may be divided into four categories:

a. *Defence of North America*. A major land invasion of the continent is inconceivable at this time. To deal with any small-scale incursion or raid, Canada maintains three air-portable brigade groups, and two squadrons of CF5 aircraft in the ground attack/reconnaissance role. The United States Army has a similar sized force in the same role. On operations involving protection of Canadian sovereignty, the Canadian Forces would act alone.

b. *Internal Security*. The Chief of Defence Staff has a legal obligation to respond to requests for aid of the civil power and aid of civil authority. Such requests for military assistance must be raised by the provincial Attorneys-General. While any Canadian-based unit in the forces is liable for internal security duties, such calls are normally placed on Mobile Command units because of their particular skills and capabilities.

c. *NATO*. Army components of Canada's NATO commitment include a small mechanised brigade group deployed in the CENTAG area of Germany and a Canadian-based air mobile battalion as part of the Allied Commander Europe's Mobile Force (Land) North (AMF(L) North). Under certain conditions the AMF(L) commitment could be built up to brigade group strength by deploying the Canadian Air-Sea Transportable (CAST) Brigade Group.

d. *United Nations*. An air mobile force of battalion group size from Mobile Command is maintained on UN standby in Canada. The Canadian Airborne Regiment currently has this responsibility.

Deployment

Mobile Command (HQ; St Hubert, Quebec)

The current deployment of Mobile Command is not based upon any tactical or strategic command, although the nationwide location of units reflects the requirement to respond to requests for aid to the civil power. The deployment has been largely determined by historical association, financial restraints, and political/economic considerations. The Command is responsible for Canadian Forces Bases at Calgary, Alberta; Gagetown, New Brunswick; London, Ontario; Montreal, Quebec; Petawawa, Ontario; Shilo, Manitoba; Suffield, Alberta; and Valcartier, Quebec, Mobile Command exercises command and control over the following major formations.

1 Brigade

Artillery: 3rd Regiment, Royal Canadian Horse Artillery (Shilo, Manitoba).
Armour: Lord Strathcona's Horse (Royal Canadian) (Calgary, Alberta).
Infantry: 1st Ballation, Princess Patricia's Canadian Light Infantry (Calgary); 2nd Battalion, Princes Patricia's Canadian Light Infantry (Winnipeg, Manitoba); 3rd Battalion, Princess Patricia's Canadian Light Infantry (Esquimalt, British Columbia).
Special Service Force: (all units located at CFB Petawawa, Ontario, except 1 RCR)
Artillery: 2nd Regiment, Royal Canadian Horse Artillery.
Armour: 8th Canadian Hussars (Princess Louise's).

Infantry: 1st Battalion, The Royal Canadian Regiment (London Ontario); Canadian Airborne Regiment.
The Canadian Airborne Regiment: (all units located at CFB Edmonton).
1er Commando Aeroporte (Francophone unit); 2nd Airborne Commando, 3rd Airborne Commando.
5e Groupe de Brigade (all units located at CFB Valcartier, Quebec, except 2R22eR, a Francophone formation).
Artillery: 5e Regiment d'Artillerie Legere du Canada.
Armour: 12e Regiment Blinde du Canada.
Infantry: (2nd Battalion, The Royal Canadian Regiment); 2e Battalion, Royal 22e Regiment (La Citadelle, Quebec City); 3e Battalion, Royal 22e Regiment.
Combat Training Centre: (all units located at CFB Gagetown, New Brunswick).
Combat Training Centre (Armour, Artillery, Infantry Schools; C Sqn Royal Canadian Dragoons and 22 Field Squadron Engineers).
1st Canadian Signal Regiment (CFB Kingston, Ontario).
Militia Areas: HQ Pacific Militia Area (Vancouver, British Columbia); HQ Prairie Militia Area (Winnipeg, Manitoba); HQ Central Militia Area (Toronto, Ontario); Quartier General Secteur de L'Est (Montreal, Quebec (Francophone area); HQ Atlantic Militia Area (Halifax, Nova Scotia).

Canadian Forces Europe (HQ: Lahr, West Germany).
All land components are located in Lahr, West Germany, with the exception of 3 Canadian Mechanised Commando.

4 Canadian Mechanised Brigade Group

Artillery: 1st Regiment, Royal Canadian Horse Artillery.
Armour: The Royal Canadian Dragoons.
Infantry: 1er Battalion, Royal 22e Regiment, 3 Canadian Machanised Commando (Baden-Soellingen).

Note: both the NATO brigade and all Mobile Command formations include a full range of engineer, communications, service support, medical, and air-control units.

Engineer -- 4 Combat Engineer Regiment.

United Nations

Current commitments include a 426-man force based on an infantry battalion in Nicosia District, Cyprus, as part of UNFICYP. UN tours are of 6 months' duration. Rotation in UNFICYP is carried out on a unit basis, in UNEF II on a man-for-man basis.

In addition, Canada provides observers to several other UN operations.

Recent Operations

Combat

Major operations in the twentieth century include a four-division corps fighting on the western front in World War I, and a field army of five divisions in north-west Europe during World War II. Canada's last combat operation saw the deployment of an infantry brigade group to Korea.

Peacekeeping

Included among these operations are Egypt 1956–67 (UNEF), the Congo, Kashmir, Cyprus and UNEF II 1973–). In addition, Canada participated in two peacekeeping (or war watching!) operations in Indo-China. Canadian Land Forces have a very high level of expertise and experience in UN-type operations.

Aid of the Civil Power

In the autumn of 1970, a series of incidents involving radical

Quebec 'separatists' caused the Federal government to declare a state of 'apprehended insurrection' and invoke the War Measures Act giving the police wider powers than normal. The majority of Mobile Command units were deployed into the Ottawa-Montreal area in aid of the civil power, where they remained until the crises ended later in the same year.

ORGANISATION

National Defence Headquarters (NDHQ) exercises command and control over the five functional commands of the Canadian forces, these being Maritime Command (navy), Mobile Command (army), Air Command (air force), Canadian Forces Europe and Communications Command. The latter two are separate and distinct from the environmental commands. The Canadian Forces Training System and miscellaneous minor establishments independent of any command are controlled directly by NDHQ.

Mobile Command consists of two brigade groups, each composed of: one light artillery regiment, one light armoured regiment, one combat engineer regiment, two or three infantry battalions, and supporting units; The Special Service Force (SSF), a light brigade is similar to the other two however the infantry position is the Canadian AMF(L) Battalion and an airborne Regiment of three large companies. Artillery and engineer elements in the SSF have an airborne capability. A Combat Training Centre, which supplies specialised training to all levels; an airborne regiment composed of two small battalions (commandos) and support arms and services; a signal regiment; and an airborne centre. A mechanised brigade group forms the land element in Canadian Forces Europe.

Note: Of the 27 officer classifications and 65 military trades, only a small portion – the combat arms and the combat support specialties – can be identified as uniquely land or 'army' oriented. Members of support services (i.e. logisticians, communicators, etc) and professional specialties (i.e. doctors, dentists, lawyers, etc) cannot be identified by environment. Men and women in these specialties can and do move from environment to environment. It would not be in the least extraordinary, for example, for a medical assistant to do one tour at sea aboard a destroyer escort, and find himself attached to a mechanised infantry battalion for the next.

RECRUITMENT, TRAINING, RESERVES AND CADETS

Recruitment
There is no conscription in Canada, and service in both the regular forces and the reserve is completely voluntary. Recruiting of both men and women is designed to fill overall requirements, while assignment to specific branches or trades is based upon a combination of vacancies available, individual interest and ability. The basic period of enrolment is 4 years.

The composition of the Canadian Armed Forces is designed to reflect national aspirations. Current recruiting aims at balancing the forces on a 73%-Anglophone-27%-Francophone level. Bilingualism is encouraged through an extensive system of language courses and other more subtle incentives. A study group is presently examining the need to identify and designate several thousand establishment positions as requiring a bilingual incumbent. Similarly, women are eligible to serve in all but the combat trades.

Training
Other-rank recruits are trained at common forces-wide recruit training schools. There are two of these facilities, one catering to the needs of Anglophone candidates, the other for Francophones. Basic and advanced trades training is carried out at branch schools where, again, instruction is offered in both official languages. There is also a full range of NCO academies where formal instruction in command and technical skills is provided.

Officer recruits enter the forces through several programmes, the most important of which is the Regular Officer Training Plan (ROTP). Selected candidates attend one of the three Canadian military colleges or a civilian university. Basic training is carried out in the summer during the break in the academic year. Commissioning usually follows attainment of a baccalaureat degree.

The Staff Training Programme includes a Forces Staff School for junior officers, a Land Forces Command and Staff College (senior captains), a Forces Staff College (majors) and a National Defence College (lieutenant-colonels and colonels). Selected officers pursue advanced academic degrees on an 'as required' basis.

Reserves
The Militia is the land component of the Canadian Forces Reserve. All arms, support arms and services are represented in the Reserve, although the largest organised field force is the battalion. Militia units are liked to a high degree to regular formations of Mobile Command.

There is no compulsion on the individual militiamen to attend annual training concentrations, although career progression is naturally highly dependent upon such participation. Current Canadian law makes no provision to ensure the job security of militiamen undergoing annual training. This anomaly has been identified and legislation is apparently under consideration to correct it.

Cadets
The cadet movement in Canada is moderately strong. As part of the Department of National Defence's contribution to national development, the cadet movement aims at developing leadership skills, good citizenship and self-confidence in young Canadians. The production of recruits for the regular forces is not a primary objective of the cadet programme, although a significant proportion of recruits have had some cadet experience.

The traditional service affiliations have been retained by cadets. Army cadets number 26,000 out of a total 62,000 in the entire cadet organisation. 404 of the 972 cadet corps are army. Participation in cadets is voluntary and is open to both boys and girls.

EQUIPMENT AND ARMS INDUSTRY

Equipment

Small Arms
   Pistol: 9mm Browning (Belgium; made in Canada)
   Sub-machine-gun: 9mm Stirling (UK; made in Canada)
   Rifle/automatic rifle: 7.62mm NATO FN C1/C2 (Belgium; made in Canada)
   General purpose machine-gun: 7.62mm NATO Browning 1919 (USA)
   Light anti-tank weapon: 66m LAW (USA)
   Medium anti-tank weapon: 84mm Carl Gustaf recoilless gun (Sweden)
Support Weapons
   Mortar: 81mm L5 (UK)
   Heavy machine-gun: 0.50in Browning HB M2 (USA)
   Heavy anti-tank weapon: 106mm M40 A1 recoilless rifle (USA), (SS11 B1 ATGM (France)) TOW (USA)

Anti-aircraft weapons: Blowpipe LLAD SAM (UK), 40mm Bofors (Sweden) fixed mount point defence of Canadian NATO air bases
Artillery: 105mm L5 pack howitzer (Italy)—equips Airborne and AMF(L) batteries; 195mm C1 (M1A1 USA) towed howitzer; 155m M109 (USA) SP howitzer

Armour
APC: M113 (USA), Grizzly
Recce: M113 1/2 Lynx (USA), Cougar
Tank: Leopard I (German) (114 in service)

Aircraft
Light observation helicopter: CH-136
Utility helicopter: Bell CUH-IN (USA)
Medium helicopter: Boeing CH47-C Chinook (USA)
Light tactical fighter: Northrop CF5 (USA) (Being replaced by McDonald Douglas F18)

Note: tactical air resources belong to Air Command but are under the operational control of appropriate land formations.

Arms Industry
Minor items of clothing and equipment are mostly manufactured in Canada from Canadian designs. In the 1950s Canada attempted to design and build major items of equipment such as an APC and a supersonic interceptor. The failure of these projects to reach a production stage despite considerable sums of money being spent on research and development was a bitter experience for the country. Today, with the exception of warships, most major equipment is of foreign design. Much of this is manufactured in Canada under licence and modified to meet specific Canadian needs. Such a method is naturally preferred to buying 'off the shelf', but the latter approach was necessary for armour, artillery and helicopters.

In 1974, Canada exported a total of $280,500,000 in military equipment. About two-thirds of military exports are consistently purchased by the United States, and most of the remainder by NATO allies. Over the past 10 years, however, Canadian firms have sold military equipment to a total of 73 countries. A government agency, Canadian Commercial Corporation, has been formed to act as a go-between in such sales; all privately arranged sales require an export permit from the Department of External Affairs. Exports consist mainly of aircraft, aero-engines and parts, electronics, and radio equipment.

Not included in the above statistics are the nuclear reactors which have been sold abroad with the stipulation that these be used for peaceful purposes only. India's Candu reactor was used to produce her first nuclear device.

RANK, DRESS AND DISTINCTIONS

General — Four maple leaves
Lieutenant-General — Three maple leaves
Major-General — Two maple leaves
Brigadier-General — One maple leaf
Colonel — Four wide stripes
Lieutenant-Colonel — Three wide stripes
Major — Two wide stripes bracketing a narrow stripe
Captain — Two wide stripes
Lieutenant — One narrow stripe above one wide stripe
Second-Lieutenant — One wide stripe
Officer Cadet — One narrow stripe

Chief Warrant Officer — Coat of Arms of Canada
Master Warrant Officer — Crown and laurel wreath

Warrant Officer — Crown
Sergeant — Three chevrons
Master-Corporal — Maple leaf over two chevrons
Corporal — Two chevrons
Trained Private — One chevron

Gold-coloured rank badges are worn by general officers on shoulder straps, by all other officers and warrant officers on the lower arm, and by NCOs on the upper arm.

Dress and Distinctions
Canadian parade and walking-out dress is a rifle-green tunic and trousers, and peaked forage cap or beret. Work dress is also rifle green, usually worn open at the throat. Combat clothing is Canadian-designed olive drab uniform with a US-pattern steel helmet. Troops of the Special Service Force wear a camouflaged jump smock. Branch or regimental badges are worn on the collar and on the cap.

CURRENT DEVELOPMENTS

The 'army' and, for that matter, the entire Canadian Armed Forces, currently is stretched to the absolute limit of capability. Economies have been created by manpower reductions and 'multi-tasking' all Canada-based units. In the same vein, equipment procurement programmes have been held in abeyance.

While Mobile Command elements have maintained their capability to respond to the full range of their current missions, serious difficulties could be expected to arise if the Command were ever called upon to fulfil several missions at the same time. The planned use of Militia elements in times of crisis helps to alleviate this problem to some extent.

A large number of equipment types are currently reaching the end of useful life. Several major purchases have been made to maintain capability levels and tasks. Chief among these was replacement of the Centurion main battle tank deployed in Europe by the Leopard. New artillery and tactical air-defence weapons are urgently required. The land element was not alone in its need for new equipment. Air Command recently replaced the long-range patrol aircraft to meet both anti-submarine warfare commitments and the needs of sovereignty protection. A new generation of fighter aircraft and FIB will also be provided in the near future. Present force development plans aim at eventually providing 20% of the defence budget for such capital procurement.

Unification has been a modest success, although changed perceptions of the international situation, new defence priorities and spiralling inflation have negated many of the project's promised advantages. The trauma of the change has passed and the system has proved to be workable. There is no significant call for 'de-unification' either within the Department of National Defence or without.

The current first defence priority — the protection of sovereignty — has not been easily assimilated by Mobile Command. The focus of concern to date has been upon the northern territories, but in the absence of a clearly defined challenge to national sovereignty, operations had been oriented towards the provision of a symbolic presence and the development of an improved operating capability in that often hostile environment.

Peacekeeping has been, on the whole, an unhappy venture. The short-term stability provided by the interposition of a UN force has not, in general, led to the hoped for long-term peace. Still, peacekeeping operations are taken very seriously by Mobile Command and UN training is a standard feature of the annual training cycle, UN operations provide a high level of individual satisfaction, in as much as participation is commonly perceived as a significant contribution to world order and tranquility.

In many ways, Canada's contemporary strategic situation today is analagous to that which existed in the early years. The umbrella of the American deterrent covers the country, and sheer distance and isolation still removes the nation from the arena of intermediate- and low-level conflict that disrupts other areas of the globe. Defence policy and force capability are not a major national issue. The main focus of national concern is the state of the domestic economy. Should this situation change over the next few years (and it is difficult to envisage the nature of such a change) the greatest strength of the Canadian forces will probably be found to lie in the professionalism of its individual members.

K. C. Eyre
Catherine Eyre
John Keegan

CAPE VERDE

Cape Verde, a former island group possession of Portugal, attained independence from Portugal in 1975. The same political party, Party for the Independence of Guinea and Cape Verde (PAIGC), conducted the struggle in both territories, a struggle amounting in its final stages to a military conventional war in the mainland territory, but one amounting to sporadic acts of sabotage only in the islands. The independence struggle over, however, the paths of the two territories began to diverge. For a brief while lip-service was paid to the concept of an eventual union but such a development now seems out of the question.

The small size of the territory precludes any significant force. The Government, headed by President A. Pereira with as his Defence Minister Colonel H. Chantre has a small 'Popular Militia' at its disposal, together with, for a time after independence, a small East German training cadre. The government also owns two Antonov AN 26 aircraft. This force, the precise size of which is reported to be a battalion of 6-700, appears to be maintained for internal security purposes only. It possesses eight BRDM-2 armoured reconnaissance vehicles and a few 3.5 inch rocket launchers. Rifles and light machine guns will almost certainly also be Soviet basic issues, supplied by East Germany.

As with other lusophone States, a cautious rapprochement with the former colonial power is in progress and reports of some very small-scale Portuguese military training assistance and provision of equipment have been received.

Lloyd Mathews

CENTRAL AFRICAN REPUBLIC

HISTORY AND INTRODUCTION

The Central African Republic attained independence from France in 1960; in the colonial period this territory had been named after its two main rivers, Oubangui-Chari. It remained under a civilian government until December 31st, 1965 when a military coup took place, the army being headed by its commander, (the then) Lieutenant-Colonel J. B. Bokassa. The reasons for the coup appear to have been allegations of corruption and nepotism, too close an involvement with China, and a budgetary crisis. Colonel Bokassa first promoted himself to Marshal, and then, in 1976, proclaimed himself Emperor.

A coronation ceremony, as costly as it was bizarre, followed. His rule became increasingly despotic, in the last year descending to mindless killings in which the Emperor appeared personally to be involved. Attempts were made to overthrow Bokassa in 1969, 1973, 1974 and 1976 all without success. Bokassa's days, however, became numbered when his excesses and brutalities proved too much for the French, whose support he had hitherto enjoyed. A brief reprieve was secured by the presence of units of the Zaïre army early in 1979. These troops suppressed student unrest, the Empire's own troops not being considered sufficiently reliable. Later in the year however a French airborne force ejected Bokassa in 'Operation Barracuda' and restored the former President Dacko. At the same time the permanent French garrison, withdrawn in 1971, was re-established. Dacko however proved unable to rebuild the shattered economy or maintain political stability, and in September 1981 almost certainly with covert French support, the Army Chief of Staff, General Kolingba, seized power at the head of a Military Committee for National Recovery. Kolingba's rule has so far proved the best the territory has enjoyed since independence and a March 1982 attempt was foiled. Much mystery surrounds this event, reflecting it would appear divisions among the French as much as divisions at Bangui. Radical French political activists gave the plotters some support which has led the Kolingba regime to a cautious view of French aims; on the other hand French officials played a decisive part in ending the coup attempt.

Some friction exists between the peoples of the north and the south in the Central African Republic. The present regime is strongly southern, the fallen Emperor and his associates were largely northern Baka.

France retains a strong uranium mining interest in the Central African Republic however, and is likely to support any government which preserves it; Kolingba here meets French needs very satisfactorily. The size of the immediate post-coup French military presence has been reduced; at present some 750 troops are posted to Bouar and a little under 400 to Bangui.

STRENGTH AND BUDGET

Population: 2,300,000 (approximate).
Armed forces: Army 1,860, Air Force 300, Gendarmerie not known, perhaps 1,000.

* For general notes on African armies, see Appendix 1.

GDP: $500m (estimate)
Defence expenditure: $12m (approximate)

COMMAND AND CONSTITUTIONAL STATUS

The President, Major General A. Kolingba is also Minister for Defence and Army Chief of Staff. The Committee for National Recovery is composed of some thirty senior officers.

ROLE, COMMITMENT, DEPLOYMENT AND RECENT OPERATIONS

The Central African Republic's army role is one of internal security. France is likely to take care of any external threat, at any rate for the time being.

ORGANISATION

The Central African Republic's army consists of one infantry battalion, supported by engineer transport and signals subunits. Although detachments are posted elsewhere, most of the battalion is located at Bouar. Since the fall of Bokassa the sizes of the various forces have all been slightly reduced.

RECRUITMENT, TRAINING AND RESERVES

A selective national service operates, two years' service being required. A military training centre for basic, cadre and officer training exists at Bouar.

EQUIPMENT AND ARMS INDUSTRY

Until recently all equipment for the army was French, but Soviet and Israeli rifles and sub-machine carbines were noted in 1977. The infantry battalion's armoury includes 81mm mortars and a few RPG-7 and 106mm anti-tank weapons. One report also suggests twenty-two Soviet BRDM-2 vehicles. Ten old British Ferret scout cars are also on the paper strength, if not actually still in service. The air force is equipped with two SOCATA Rallye, one Douglas DC4 and three Douglas C47 aircraft for transport, seven Broussard MH-521 liaison aircraft and, in respect of helicopters, four Sikorski H34 and one Alouette. The state of repair is not known.

RANK, DRESS AND DISTINCTIONS

These follow the French pattern, except that peaked caps have replaced the *képi*.

CURRENT DEVELOPMENTS

This army has been put to strange purposes; one of these the 1972 public beating-up of prisoners in Bangui ('one soldier per prisoner' in the words of Bokassa) attracting world criticism. Imperial ceremonial then became the major priority. After the fall of Bokassa the French made considerable efforts to discipline and train the army, not without success.

The Central African Republic however remains a pawn in the French African game. If the French feel that the Republic is vital, either in terms of resources or as a general base for intervention elsewhere in Africa they will ensure stability and the country's integrity. If France is indifferent the Central African Republic's future may be bleak.

ADDENDUM

As an expression of his displeasure with France, and perhaps also to blackmail Paris into greater financial aid, the Kolingba government accepted Libyan military aid in the autumn of 1982. This aid, it is reported, takes the forty-four T-62 tanks, eight BRDM armoured vehicles, heavy mortars and lorries together with a sixty-strong Libyan training mission. These are lodged at a camp at Damara, some distance from the French garrison, and the Libyan personnel are not allowed into Bangui.

Lloyd Mathews

CHAD*

HISTORY AND INTRODUCTION

The former French colony of Chad attained independence in 1960. It is a very large, mostly semi-desert country, but with a southern and western section of greater population and better vegetation. This geographical division is approximately matched by a major ethnic one; in the semi-desert areas Moslem peoples, mostly nomad, feel kinship with the north of Africa. In the south and west are negro peoples, Christian and animist. The lack of homogeneity in Chad, one of the most divided of Africa's new nations, is the root cause of the violence and bitter conflict which has plagued the country since 1968.

From independence to a military coup in 1975 Chad was ruled by President François (later Ngarta) Tombalbaye; his government was largely one of Sara and Majingaye peoples from the south and west. Tombalbaye's government proved less and less able to meet the demands of the situation, made worse by administrative incompetence and, in the early 1970s, by drought. Plots to overthrow him were alleged in 1963, 1967, 1971, 1972 and 1973. In 1975 he was overthrown and killed in a coup to which the French may well have been complicit. His successor, General Malloum, assumed power at the head of a Council of Military Officers.

Malloum, however, proved no more capable than Tombalbaye in containing the major threat to Chad's stability, the revolt of the Moslem north, which had begun in 1968. Tombalbaye, because of Chad's immediate response to the call of de Gaulle in 1940, was able to draw on considerable French support. The French garrison was deployed, and later further troops were brought from France. Zaïre sent a small air liaison unit, US help also arrived and Israel trained a 200 strong Chad parachute unit. The northern insurgents, styling themselves FROLINAT (Freedom and Liberation for Chad), were, however, able to draw on an increasing measure of Libyan support with the result that by as early as 1972 some 50 French and over 500 Chad soldiers had already been killed, among the former being the son of the French commanding general, Cortadellas. Fighting occurred chiefly in the north, the Tibesti-Borkou-Ennedi areas.

With the departure and death of de Gaulle, and France's increasing appetite for energy resources, French policy began to be modified in the early 1970s, in order to maintain profitable economic relationships with Libya. French military involvement was reduced, and French troops withdrawn from most of the combat zones in 1971 and 1972, leading to bitter reproaches from Tombalbaye and later, after France dealt directly with the insurgents following the abduction of the wife of a French development official, Mme Claustre, also provoking further bitter reproaches from Malloum, the latter asking for French withdrawal. He almost certainly did not mean this to be taken literally, and while some French units were withdrawn it seems others remained, sometimes in Chad uniforms, and a new agreement in 1976 provided for a returned French presence of several hundred 'advisers'. These in theory were not to be committed in battle, in practive evidence suggests that on occasions they were, notably in delaying the fall of Ounianga-Kebir in Borkou, to FROLINAT in 1977. They also served to buttress Malloum's position, conspiracies to overthrow him being discovered in both 1976 and 1977.

To about this time, the mid-1970s, the FROLINAT versus government struggle had appeared to be a straight north versus south contest, the north also serving Libyan interests. At this time Libyan regular forces had entered and occupied the extreme north-west area of Chad, Aouzou (believed to contain mineral wealth), and insurgents controlled most of the centre and the rest of the north, with the Malloum government attempting to hold a line stretching approximately across the middle of the country. The apparently clear-cut divide however how began to become several-sided. One group had in fact broken away from FROLINAT earlier in the decade in favour of a negotiated solution; whether regional interests or growing insurgent concern over long-term Libyan aims, or a mixture of both, was the main cause of this and the divisions within FROLINAT to follow, remains unclear.

In March 1978 Colonel Qadaffi of Libya accepted, amid much publicity, a cease-fire on the basis of Chad promises of political reform, but only a minority of the groups amongst the insurgents were willing to respond. Later in the year the largest township in the north and the final outpost of Chad government authority, Faya-Largeau, fell to the insurgents who also took a number of military prisoners. The continuation of insurgent activity stung the French into a much more resolute resistance, over 1,500 soldiers being despatched to Chad to support the Malloum regime. These, together with Chad's own forces (of course mainly southern recruited) inflicted a number of sharp reverses on to the insurgents, notably one near Ati in which the Chad army surrounded FROLINAT detachments while French aircraft delivered lethal strikes. The insurgent advance on the capital N'Djamena (formerly Fort Lamy) was stopped. But French casualties began to arouse embarrassing criticism in France, which once again sought to effect some mediation.

As a result of this in July a new agreement was signed between Hissen Habre, leader of one of the factions composing FROLINAT, and General Malloum. By this agreement, Malloum remained Head of State, with Habre as Prime Minister. Two new government bodies, a Committee of National Union and a Committee of Defence and Security were established with members equal in number from both the Malloum and Habre camps, and it was also agreed that the followers of Habre and other FROLINAT members so disposed should be incorporated into the Chad Army. While at one level this agreement appeared a triumph of moderation, at another level it illuminated the fact that Habre had lost influence and power within FROLINAT to Goukouni Oueddei, the leader of the largest and most militant faction.

Habre's appeal to FROLINAT, then, reflected his weakness at the time; he had only partial success. Oueddei's majority following resenting the continued presence of the French, on which Malloum insisted. Fighting between the various FROLINAT factions then began; some but not all of these again turned to Libya.

The French general in command at the time of the formation of the Malloum-Habre dyarchy, General Bredeche, viewed the new regime with both doubt and disfavour and wanted France to act offensively and crush FROLINAT. He was replaced by General Forest, who with an increased force of some 2,000, a squadron of Jaguar air-to-ground strike aircraft and a surveillance system made a military effort limited only to defending the survival of the lawful government in N'Djamena. This policy was at first not entirely without success (probably due more to divided counsels in Tripoli than anything else), but was to fall apart for two reasons, a measure of Libyan reassertion and the incompatibility of Malloum and Habre, the former increasingly under the influence of hard-line southern officers led by Lieut-Colonel Kamougue, who hated Habre. The dyarchy fell apart; with some Sudanese support at international and local levels and a considerable supply of French weaponry at battlefield level, Habre's forces entered N'Djamena in February 1979 — with French forces, reinforced in case of a successful thrust by Oueddei, standing by doing nothing despite the very heavy bloodshed. At this point, then, the situation was one in which the different FROLINAT groupings, most but not all in varying measure acknowledging Oueddei (the son of an important northern chieftain) as their head controlling the north, Habre with his *Forces Armées du Nord* (FAN) controlling the centre, and the remainder of the Old Chad Army under Malloum and Kamougue controlling the south. FROLINAT's internal divisions, however, began again to become acute, besides Oueddei's followers, there were others, the Chad Liberation Movement (MPLT) led by Abubakar Abdurahman, M. Abba's Peoples Liberation Army and a 'Vulcan Force' led by A. Acyl.

Habre's triumph aroused the south, massacres of non-Moslems following. A number of Sahel African countries attempted to mediate between him and Oueddei, these attempts led to another 'government of national unity', (GUNT) in which Oueddei and Habre reached an agreement by which the new leader of the MPLT, Lol Shawa (Abdurahman having been assassinated) became head of state, Habre and Oueddei both agreeing to be Ministers. The French undertook to withdraw and an all-African force to secure order was agreed upon, a reflection of the interest of a new party, Nigeria, which wished to see a French departure.

The Lol Shawa regine, however, was unacceptable to Libya as it contained no representatives of Abba's Peoples Liberation Army of Acyl's Vulcan Force, both Libyan protegés; it was also unacceptable to the south, as the Malloum-Kamougue dimension was also unrepresented. Libya proceeded firstly to arm its own protegés and in an exercise of ultracynical *real politik*, to arm the Christian southern forces as well and then launch a full invasion of the north of Chad. The French were therefore asked to stay on by Lol Shawa, but France's eyes had begun to turn temporarily away from Habre and towards Oueddei as the man most likely to end the political conflicts, now once again overspilling into full scale military operations following the Libyan attack. This, although by a force of over 2,500 Libyan Regular troops, was in fact halted by the temporary union of the Oueddei and Habre factions. But the French judged Lol Shawa to be ineffective and they also wished to see Kamougue included in the Chad regime. So with French support, Oueddei succeeded the ineffective Lol Shawa as President, with Kamougue as Vice President and Habre as a Minister. However, Oueddei once in supreme power and in the belief that if he promised to keep the Libyans out the French would cease from giving any further support to his arch-enemy, proceeded to dismiss Habre who returned to the battlefield.

Oueddei's regime therefore solved nothing. By mid-1980 Chad's miseries and chaos had worsened, some dozen armed factions competing for power, national or local. At this point the most important still appeared to be the former Oueddei mainstream FROLINAT, the military force of which was known as the FAP (*Forces Armées Populaires*); with Oueddei in power they were the nearest equivalent to a legal Chad army. Their main opponents, in an opposition weakened by irreconcilability were Habre's FAN operating in the east of Chad, and Kamougue's *Forces Armées Tchadiennes* (FAT), the quondam largely southern, regulars. Habre's forces were supported by one or two of the smaller factions, Oueddei's by some five pro-Libyan factions, of which Acyl's was the most important. The departure of Habre had, however, the effect of crystallising Libyan interest upon Oueddei, especially on the pro-Tripoli factions operating in his interest, and Libyan forces amounting in total to some four brigades and including artillery rocket launchers, parachute troops and mechanised units moved into Chad.

Despite this Libyan support for his main opponent, Habre's campaign, beginning seriously in May and June 1980, gathered much initial strength and success, not only against the Oueddei forces, but also against those of Kamougue as well; one major reason for this being Habre's charges that Oueddei, and also Kamougue, were both the agents of the Libyans. Habre then appeared temporarily to lose momentum. OAU and other international support for Oueddei was one major cause of this apparent decline; a second cause was a closer measure of co-ordination between Oueddei, his linked factions, and Kamougue whose fortunes were on the decline and who needed to secure himself in a linkage with what appeared to be at the time the likely winner, Oueddei. In a return for support Oueddei made Kamougue Vice President. Habre was also experiencing friction between his own FAN and one of his main supporting factions, the MPLT.

More significant though, in the light of the events to unfold in 1982, were renewed jealousies, turning to violent fighting between Oueddei's FAP and his militantly pro-Libyan supporting faction headed by Acyl. The clashes led to the involvement of Libyan troops in support of the Acyl followers, to the acute embarrassment of Oueddei and to the great advantage of Habre. Early in 1982 Habre's attacks once more began to meet with success, in February the FAN secured a spectacular victory over the FAP. Faced with reverses, both the Oueddei grouping of factions and the FAT started to disintegrate, Acyl leaving Oueddei in May and the FAT experiencing internal fighting created by units dissatisfied with Kamougue's leadership, the dissatisfied units receiving a measure of support from Habre. The Libyans had been recalled, and the OAU peace-keeping force despatched to Chad supposedly to secure Oueddei was not directed to intervene in his interest against Habre's advancing FAN. This absence of intervention reflected the growing distrust of Libya among the contributing countries, especially Nigeria. Another country profoundly distrustful of Libya, Egypt, provided military supplies for Habre's FAN, in Sudanese aircraft.

On June 19th, Habre's FAN entered the battered, burnt-out wreck of N'Djamena. Oueddei and Acyl fled into exile, the latter dying in a flying accident a littler later. Kamougue also departed into exile; the divisions in his FAT reflected not only dissatisfaction with his leadership but also rivalries between the Mbai Sara, Majingaye and Ngambaye peoples. Habre has been, and will continue to be able to draw leaders and some support from elements that had deserted Kamouge's cause. Overall Habre's former opponents are now scattered and in the greatest disorder, while Habre himself heads a military organisation of some 4,000 equipped with some French, some Egyptian and some captured or abandoned Libyan material. In his task of rebuilding a shattered economy and restoring a normal political ilife, Habre can count on measures of French, Egyptian and Sudanese support, and also Nigerian if southerners are seen to be reconciled; the list of ministers announced by Habre in late October 1982 includes a number of southern names.

It will be seen from these paragraphs that few of the

normal section headings under which information is set out in this volume can apply to Chad at the present moment. The country has been an arena in which various factions have fought, often very bloodly for power over the last fourteen years. The old Chad regular army became one, and not the most important, of these factions; as it declined so it increasingly lost effectiveness, credibility and legitimacy. No plans for the shape and size of Chad's future forces have yet been announced by President Habre or his Defence Minister, Rotouang Yoma. No illusions are, however, harboured by Habre as to where the main danger to his regime lies. In very recent statements he has noted the continuing Libyan occupation of the north-western Aouzou area and has claimed that Libyan Forces are preparing military bases elsewhere in the north of Chad with a view to continuing their interference in the country's internal affairs.

ADDENDUM

The Former Chad President, Oueddei, has formed a rival government at Bardai, in the north with Libyan support. Fighting has once again broken out in the north, the centre and the east; Oueddei has linked together most of the factions and individuals that have in the past been opposed to Habre, and Libyan military aid has been reported.

Habre is trying to unite his FAN with those units and individuals of the old Chad Army that can be trusted, and also to form a combat group to be based at Faya-Largeau. An Army commander for the new army, Major I. Debbi, has been appointed.

Lloyd Matthews

CHILE

HISTORY AND INTRODUCTION

The history of the Chilean army differs from that of most other Latin American armies in two important respects: its victories in campaigns fought since independence have been the means of adding greatly to the national territory; and, for the greater part of its existence, it has remained obedient to the control of elected civilian governments. All the more surprising, therefore, has been its assumption, with the other armed forces, of governmental powers since 1973.

The Chilean army traces its origins to the opening battles against Spain in 1810–14. A remote frontier province of the Spanish empire, isolated by the Andes to the east, desert in the north and unsubdued Indians (the Araucanians) in the south, Chile easily expelled the colonial administration in 1810 but its tiny volunteer army, led by Bernardo O'Higgins, was easily overcome by a Spanish army of reconquest at Rancagua in October, 1914. O'Higgins took its remnants to join San Martín at Mendoza in Argentina, with him recrossed the Andes and at Chacabuco in February, 1817 and Maipú in April, 1818 fought the battles which established Chilean independence for good. A hastily created Chilean navy, commanded by the cashiered British admiral Cochrane, then played the decisive role in expelling Spain's last army in the Americas from Peru. By then O'Higgins had been overthrown as national leader by another hero of the independence campaign, Freire, who became the central figure in a struggle for power between the regions and the capital, Santiago, which lasted from 1823 until 1830. It was ended by the defeat of Freire at Yircay in April, 1830 which established in power a centralising faction of great land-owners, led by Prieto and Portales. They made it their first concern to rid the country of military factions and to unify the army, and then to promulgate an effective constitution, so successfully in the latter respect that it remained in force until 1925.

They were also successful in their military policies. The military academy (*Escuela Militar*) was founded in 1832, and from it the army increasingly drew a steady supply of professionally trained officers, thus avoiding the troubles suffered by so many other Latin American countries at the hands of self-made or politically appointed officers. As a counterweight to the army a provincial militia, the *Guardia Civil*, officered by the wealthy classes, was also created in 1832, but proved superfluous. The purged army displayed from the start an admirable loyalty to the government and, within 6 years of Prieto and Portales coming to power, refreshed its reputation as the source and guardian of national independence by its conduct in the war of 1836–9 against the Confederation of Bolivia and Peru. The murder of Portales by a Chilean renegade made the war a popular issue and the eventual victory of the army, under General Bulnes, at Yungay in January, 1839 was hailed as a 'Second Independence'.

Bulnes and his successors ruled Chile without serious internal dissent for the next 50 years. The role of the army during this era of the 'Autocratic', and later the 'Liberal' Republics, was strictly external. The short-lived and long-range war against Spain, in 1866, in alliance with Ecuador, Peru and Bolivia, involved only the navy. But in 1843 the army embarked on the penetration of the far south, where the Araucanian Indians remained unsubdued, British and French ships were reconnoitring the coast, and the frontier with Argentina was undelineated. Under the protection of the army, settlers began to occupy land around Valdivia, many of them Germans who were in years to come to make an important contribution to Chilean life. The pacification culminated in the Araucanian rebellion of 1859–61 and was only completed in 1883, when the Indians of the south and the Santiago government signed a treaty establishing the integrity of the tribal lands, by then much reduced in extent. Meanwhile the army had fought a regular and even more important war against the country's northern neighbours, Peru and Bolivia, over possession of the newly discovered mineral wealth of the desert provinces of Antofagasta, Tarapacá, Tacna and Arica. Unregarded until the 1860s, the provinces were then assigned by Bolivian–Chilean agreement to administration by the former, while Chile was granted favourable terms to exploit the nitrate deposits. In 1878 a new ruler of Bolivia abrogated the agreement, with Peruvian endorsement, and in 1879 Chile put the issue to the test of war. The ensuing War of the Pacific, the most important internal war fought in South America, began badly for Chile, who was defeated at sea, but her acquisition of a modern ironclad quickly gave her back naval primacy. On land her army defeated the Bolivians at Tacna in 1880 and the Peruvians at Miraflores and Chorillos later in the year. Lima was occupied in January, 1881. The Peruvians insisted on maintaining resistance in the mountains for another 2 years, but were brought to make peace in 1883. That treaty, and another signed with Bolivia in the following year, consigned all the disputed territory to the victors, deprived Bolivia of her access to the sea, and left Chile the dominant power on the Pacific coast.

Her military superiority was shortly to be reinforced by the activity of a remarkable foreign military adviser, the Prussian Emil Koerner, who arrived at the invitation of the Minister of War in 1886 to reform the *Escuela Militar*. Koerner quite quickly established his ascendancy over the whole Chilean military establishment and when in 1891 a disputed presidential election divided the army he became head of the rebel general staff. Their victories at Concón and Placilla were effectively his achievement. This short and unbloody civil war established Congress, dominated by the land-owning, commercial and mining interests, as the leading power in the State, replacing the hitherto paramount presidency. It also gave the army a reminder of the power it possessed to determine the course of national politics, in which it had not seriously intervened for 60 years. But its immediate effect was to accelerate the Prussianisation of the officer corps. In November, 1891 Koerner became Chief of the General Staff, a post he retained until 1910, and he used his office not only to introduce German military training methods, instructors, uniforms and organisation, but also to foster that spirit of military self-importance which was such a baleful influence on the politics of his homeland.

The Prussianised Chilean army became a model for others in Latin America. Its officers were sought after as instructors by the armies of Ecuador, Venezuela, Colombia and El Salvador, while the obvious superiority of their professional knowledge led Argentina and Bolivia to go directly to Germany for military tutorship. But the congressional government which the army had established served its sponsors badly. The services were neglected throughout the first two decades of the century, which also saw the collapse of the nitrate industry as the result of the development of a synthetic substitute by European firms, upon which Chilean prosperity depended. By 1920 both the army and the electorate were disaffected from the oligarchy which controlled the congressional system, and 12 years of unhappy and complex politics, dominated by military intervention, were to result. Alessandri, a political leader from the nitrate fields, was elected President in 1920 but failed to pass his progressive legislation through the oligarchic congress. Its obstruction prompted a group of young officers, broadly sympathetic to his policies and hostile to the selfishness of the entrenched property-owners, to engineer a coup which brought him by roundabout means back to power in 1925. With the assistance of the leading soldier—politician, Colonel Ibáñez, he promulgated a new constitution, which legalised trade unions and introduced a social security system, but, on the termination of his presidency, power passed to Ibáñez himself who became President by the resignation of his own puppet in 1927. By purging the army and borrowing abroad, Ibáñez sustained himself in power until the effects of the great depression were experienced in Chile in 1931. Ten different administrations held office in 1931–2, the last a so-called Socialist Republic led by an air commodore of Anglo-Saxon descent, Marmaduke Grove. Its farcical demise consolidated a growing resolution in the armed forces to disentangle itself from politics, with which they had nothing more to do for 40 years. The re-emergence of Ibáñez, who became President in 1952, was of personal, not institutional, significance.

Its apoliticality survived the appearance of a Popular Front government in 1938, the reappearance of Ibáñez and a strongly reformist Christian Democrat government in 1964. The election of President Allende at the head of a Marxist-inclined Popular Unity government in 1970 reawoke, however, the armed forces' political concerns. Despite the attested sympathy of many officers for the Chilean underprivileged, and their lack of patience with the vested interest of the landowning and industrial oligarchy, their strong nationalism would have no truck with the threat of foreign intervention — Soviet or Cuban — which the Allende regime presented, while their instincts for order were affronted by the continuous industrial strife which Allende's expropriatory policies generated. Chile's besetting inflationary difficulty became uncontrollable in 1973, middle-class anti-government strikes became continuous and on September 11th the armed forces unleashed a coup. President Allende was killed (or committed suicide) in the presidential palace and a *junta*, headed by the Army Commander, General Pinochet, took power in his place. Congress was suspended and the *junta* announced its intention to govern by decree. This combined action by the army, navy, air force and police, who had not hitherto always found it easy to agree either on service or on political issues, was in itself evidence of the degree to which Allende had united opposition to his government. And it was further evidence of the hesitation which the forces had had to overcome before moving against him that his two last cabinets had included representatives of all the services, who had joined it in an attempt to help his government ride out the storm by making a common front to prevailing economic and social difficulties. In so doing, the armed forces were acting very much in the spirit of their traditions. It is the policies of the military government since the coup, in particular its declaration of intent to retain the reins of power, which mark a new departure.

STRENGTH AND BUDGET

Population: 11,300,000
Army: 53,000
Navy: 29,000 (including 5,000 Marines); 19 major vessels
Air Force: 15,000; 90 combat aircraft
Paramilitary: 27,000 Carabineros (National Police)
GNP: (1980) $28,000,000,000
Defence Expenditure: (1980) $1,436,000,000

In the period 1953–66, Chile benefited particularly generously from United States military aid, receiving in military grants and surplus stocks assistance second only to that given to Brazil and, in *per capita* terms, more than any other Latin American country. Most of the money and equipment went, however, to the navy and air force. Internal spending was also less generous to the army; its share of the defence budget declined in the 1960s while that of the other two services rose. Under the Allende government, the share of the budget devoted to the armed forces rose slightly, and the army benefited thereby. Subsequently the level of inflation (about 600% at its worst) makes computations about the level of military spending difficult.

COMMAND AND CONSTITUTIONAL STATUS

Article 71 of the 1925 Constitution, still technically in force, allots to the President the responsibility of preserving internal law and order and assuring the national defence. He is Commander-in-Chief of the Armed Forces, and may command directly with the approval of the Senate. As Commander-in-Chief he is advised in military affairs by the Supreme Council of National Security, which consists of the Ministers of National Defence, Foreign Relations, Finance, Development, Economics and Reconstruction; by the Commanders of the Army, Navy and Air Force; and by the Chief of the National Defence Staff. In time of peace, control of the armed forces is vested in the Minister of War, who is advised by the National Defence General Staff. He deals directly with the commanders of the services. The office of the Commander-in-Chief of the Army consists of his deputy, chief of staff, and three staff sections, organised on the German pattern: (1) operations; (2) intelligence; and (3) personnel and logistics; there is also a training section. The Inspector-General of the Army is separately subordinate to the Commander-in-Chief.

Since 1973 command of the armed forces has been exercised by the ex-Commander-in-Chief of the Army, General Pinochet, first as Head of the *junta*, then as Supreme Head of State and, since December, 1974 as President (by his own decree). Congress has been abolished, and the *junta* acts as the legislature. An 18 man Council of State, to act as consultative body, was created in January, 1976 but the armed forces, meaning largely in practice the army and *Carabineros*, exercise power directly and without civilian supervision or check. The 'state of siege' declared on September 11th, 1973 is still in force and though President Pinochet promulgated on the third anniversary of the coup a constitutional guarantee of the rights of citizens, he accompanied it with an extension of the states of emergency which the government might declare, including a 'state of latent emergency'. The remaining non-Marxist political parties were dissolved in March, 1976 and it is the armed forces' declared intention to retain power for the foreseeable future, until prosperity has been restored and the danger of a Marxist return extinguished.

The 'state of siege' ended in March 1978 and a new Constitution was approved by 67.5% of the voters in a national referendum in September 1980. This provides for a return to democratic government after a minimum period of eight years during which General Pinochet will remain in office as President.

ROLE, COMMITMENT, DEPLOYMENT AND RECENT OPERATIONS

The 1925 Constitution declares the tasks of the armed forces to be the defence of the national territory and the preservation of internal law and order, under the authority of the President. Since 1973, and very much against the traditional pattern of Chilean politics, the armed forces have ruled directly.

The army is not commited to any external role, and is bound only by the normal South American military treaties (Chapultepec Mutual Defence Pact of 1945 and the Rio Defence Pact of Non-Aggression of 1947). Like most other Latin American countries, Chile is also the signatory of a Military Assistance Pact with the United States (April, 1952) by which she promises to render access to raw materials and support in defence of the hemisphere in return for American military protection. Chile has benefited particularly generously from American equipment and military aid deliveries.

The country is nevertheless in dispute with Bolivia and Argentina, and potentially with Peru, over borders, and its troop deployments reflect these disputes. The country is divided for military purposes into six divisions (also known as Internal Security Complexes) thus (from north to south): 6, HQ Iquique; 1, HQ Antofagasta; 2, HQ Santiago; 3, HQ Concepción; 4, HQ Valdivia; and 5, HQ Punta Arenas. Divisions 6 (bordering Peru and Bolivia) and 5 (where Chile is in dispute with Argentina) are disproportionately well-garrisoned. So too is Division 2, containing both Santiago, Valparaiso and the main military training centres.

ORGANISATION

Arms of Service

The Chilean Army, the influence of which is widespread amongst so many other Latin American armies, distinguishes between combatant Arms and logistic Services. The former comprise Infantry, Special Forces, Cavalry, Armour, Artillery, Engineers and Signals; the latter Intendence, War Material, Transport, Medical, Veterinary and Military Police. The Infantry, Cavalry, Armoured Forces and Engineers are organised in regiments which are both numbered and named. The Artillery is organised in groups whilst the Signals and logistic Services are organised in battalions and groups. The Special Forces form a single battalion.

There are 24 regiments of Infantry of which 18 are motorised and 6 mountain troops. The number of battalions per regiment varies from two to four. Mountain Infantry regiments include a reconnaissance section and a group of mountain artillery and thus resemble brigades in their composition. There are 6 horsed and 2 mechanised Cavalry Regiments, the latter equipped with tanks and other tracked vehicles. The 2 Armoured Regiments are classed as Infantry and consist of 2 battalions apiece. Artillery is now organised in groups of which there are 9 in all. There is one Engineer Regiment, at Army level and 6 divisional Engineer Battalions.

Operational

Operationally the Army is divided into six Divisions, each of which consists, in theory, of 3 Infantry Regiments, 1 Andean Regiment, a Cavalry Brigade of 2 Regiments, an Artillery Group, an Engineer Battalion and supporting services. Recent tensions with both Argentina and Peru have occasioned some

redeployments so that the composition of the Divisions is no longer standard. Some now include as many as five Infantry Regiments, only two appear to have a full Cavalry Brigade and two (2nd and 6th) each include an Armoured Regiment. The strongest formations are the 1st, 2nd, 5th and 6th Divisions, the 3rd and 4th being apparently below establishment.

The 5,000 strong Marine Corps is organised in four 'Detachments' corresponding to the four Naval Zones into which the country is divided. Each of these consists of a variable combination of Infantry, Field, Coastal and Anti-aircraft artillery.

Anti-aircraft defence, apart from the close defence of army and naval units, is the responsibility of the Air Force which deploys 5 anti-aircraft groups, one subordinate to each of its five Wings.

The national police force, the 27,000 strong *Carabineros de Chile*, is organised into six zones corresponding to the army's six divisional areas and each of which is in turn subdivided into *prefecturas, suprefecturas, comisarías, subcomisarías, tenecias, retenes* and *puestos avanzados*. The Carabineros includes a marine and an air section.

RECRUITMENT, TRAINING AND RESERVES

By the Obligatory Service Law of 1900, which was modelled on current German legislation, all Chilean males become eligible for service at the age of nineteen. The term of service is 1 year, though in practice conscripts are released after 9 months. By recent decision, 10% of those conscripted must be illiterates, military service being seen as one of the most effective means of combating illiteracy, which is still over 10% in the country at large. The annual contingent numbers about 30,000, of whom about two-thirds are selected, by lottery. Training is conducted in the units to which conscripts are assigned. Three-fifths of the army is composed of volunteers, who may be trained at the army schools.

Officers are recruited from high-school graduates, and receive 5 years' training (three academic, two military) at the *Escuela Militar*, Santiago (founded 1832). Superior training is given at the Staff College (*Academia de Guerra*), Santiago; there is also a tri-service/civilian war college, *Academia de Defensa Nacional*, at Santiago, attendance at which is necessary for promotion to senior ranks. Military engineer specialists are trained at the *Academia Politécnica Militar*, Santiago. There are several arms schools: Infantry (San Bernardo, near Santiago), Cavalry (Quillota), Artillery (Linares), Armour (Autofagasta), Engineer (Tejas Verdes), Signals (Santiago), Mountain (Rio Blanco), Parachute (Colina Air Base, Santiago) and Special Forces (Peldehue); the Sergeants' and Soldiers' Specialists' Schools are at Santiago.

Chile's military academies have a high reputation in South America and students come to them annually from El Salvador, Ecuador, Honduras, Dominican Republic, Paraguay and Venezuela. Chilean officers also regularly attend the United States School of the Americas, Panama Canal Zone, and the Inter-American Defense College, Washington, for reasons of diplomacy rather than necessity.

The Obligatory Service Law consigns ex-conscripts to 12 years' service in the active reserve and thirteen in the second reserve, to the age of forty-five. The effective size of the army reserve is said to be 160,000. Estimates vary, however, and there is no evidence that reserve formations are effective or that reservists receive useful refresher training.

EQUIPMENT AND ARMS INDUSTRY

Although a highly industrialised state, by South American

standards, with one sixth of the work force employed in manufacturing, Chile did not, until recently, have an arms industry although several small naval vessels have in the past been built in local yards and the construction of light aircraft has also taken place sporadically. The almost universal boycott of the military regime, enforced after the overthrow of the Allende Government in 1973 threw the Chileans back upon their own resources and local industrial potential was accordingly expanded. Although most weapons and military equipment are still imported, certain western countries, notably Great Britain and the United States, having recently adopted a more rational attitude towards the Chilean Military Government, Chile now manufactures its own explosives and small-arms ammunition and is commencing the production of armoured vehicles (by agreement with the Swiss Mowas corporation), anti-aircraft weapons of local development, aircraft (in collaboration with the Spanish aerospace industry) and naval vessels up to the size of landing ships, small patrol craft and naval auxiliaries.

Rifle: SIG 510 7.62mm (Switzerland); 63 7.62mm (Germany)
Sub-machine-gun: Madsen 9mm (Denmark); MAC M-10 0.45″ (US)
Machine-guns: MG-42 7.62mm (Germany); M2 12.7mm (US)
Mortars: 120mm (France); 81mm M-29 (US); 81mm M-1 (US); 60mm M-19 (US)
Anti-armour weapons: 106mm M-40A1 RCL (US); Milan ATGW
Air defence weapons: 20mm (Switzerland); 40mm L/60 (Sweden/US)
Artillery: 105mm M-101 (US); 105mm Mod. 56 (Italy); 155mm F.3 SPH (France)
Armour: AMX-30 (France; 21 in service); AMX-13 (France; 47 in service); M-4 medium tank (US; 74 in service); M-41 light tank (US; 60 in service) M3 light tank (US; survivors of 40 used for training); EE-9 Cascavel armoured car (Brazil; 30 in service); EE-11 Urutu APC (Brazil; 30 in service); M-113 APC (US; 100 in service)
Aircraft: The Army has about 40 light fixed-wing aircraft and over 30 helicopters. The Air Force has about 30 transport aircraft and 20 helicopters.

RANK, DRESS AND DISTINCTIONS

General de División — Three stars on shoulder boards
General de Brigada — Two stars on shoulder boards
Brigadier — One star on shoulder board
Coronel — Three stars on shoulder plaits
Teniente Coronel — Two stars on shoulder plaits
Mayor — One star on shoulder plaits
Capitán — Three stars on shoulder straps
Teniente 1 — Two stars on shoulder straps
Teniente 2 — One star on shoulder straps

Suboficial Mayor — Three gold stripes
Suboficial — Two gold stripes, star
Sargento 1 — Two gold stripes
Sargento 2 — One gold stripe
Cabo 1 — Two red stripes
Cabo 2 — One red stripe
Soldado 1 — One star, one bar
Soldado 2 — One star

At the turn of the century, the Chilean army was dressed in Prussian-style complete. Ceremonial uniforms are still Prussian. The army goosesteps on ceremonial occasions.

Service uniforms are grey and of decidedly Germanic cut. The US M-42 steel helmet appears to have largely replaced the German 'coal-scuttle' model formerly worn. Arms and Services are distinguished by coloured cloth collar patches as follows: infantry — red; cavalry — sky blue; armoured forces — yellow; artillery — black; engineers — blue; signals — white. Special Forces wear a black beret. Full dress uniforms reveal strong German influence although combat dress is of US pattern.

There are ten awards — three decorations and seven medals. The decorations are the *Estrella Militar de las Fuerzas Armadas*, awarded to officers for long service, the decoration *Al Valor* awarded to officers and other ranks for heroism and the decoration *Presidente de la República* which is automatically given to generals and admirals on promotion. The medals include *Diosa Minerva* for staff officers, the *Cruz de Malta* for officers who graduate first in their respective classes in the Academies of the Armed Forces, the *Orden al Mérito*, the *Condecoración Nacional, Medalla de Tropa*, awarded to enlisted personnel for long service and the *Al Deber* for conspicuous devotion to duty.

CURRENT DEVELOPMENTS

Despite unmistakable evidence of disaffection from the Popular Unity Government over a wide spectrum of society, the military coup of 1973 attracted obloquy from progressive and left-wing opinion throughout the world. More general disquiet was voiced at the news which followed in the wake of the coup of the harshness of measures taken against Allende's supporters. By the military government's own account in October, 1975 it still held over 4000 detainees either awaiting trial or without charge and, a year before, had held 10,000. It was also disquieting that in March, 1976 the 'state of siege' instituted at the moment of the coup was again extended, and all remaining political parties, including those of the centre like the Christian Democrats, who had pledged their support to the government, were disbanded, as those of the Popular Unity Alliance had already been. In January, 1976 the Chief of Staff of the Armed Forces, General Stark, was obliged to resign, apparently in consequence of protests he had voiced the previous month, with 10 other generals, at the harsh effects of the government's deflationary policies on the poorest classes. General Pinochet, who had become President by decree in December, 1974 appeared unmoved by this opposition from within the ranks of the armed forces. On the third anniversary of the coup, he announced his programme of 'Authoritarian Democracy', by which legislative power would be vested in the *junta*, executive power with the President, and only the judiciary remain independent. The aim of the regime would be to create conditions of political and economic stability such that the 'sectarianism' and 'chaos' of the Allende years could not recur.

A certain liberalisation of the military regime has been noted over the past three years. This has been accompanied by considerable economic development and a halt in the rate of inflation.

This period has also been characterised by increasing tension with neighbouring countries, notably Argentina and Peru. The Beagle Channel dispute with Argentina brought both countries to the brink of war and occasioned an expansion and partial re-organisation of the Chilean Armed Forces. Motivated by the threat of hostilities with Argentina, Chile alone amongst the countries of Latin America failed to support Argentina in the South Atlantic War with Great Britain. Following the defeat of the latter, there is again a real danger that the Argentine Armed Forces may seek to retrieve their honour in a military adventure aimed against Chile. Although the boycott of the Pinochet regime enforced by most western countries following the overthrow of Allende is now largely a dead letter, it has left the Chilean Armed Forces at something of a material disadvantage vis-à-vis both Argentina and Peru, although the danger of hostilities against the latter has diminished considerably with the restoration of civilian government.

John Keegan
Adrian English

PEOPLE'S REPUBLIC OF CHINA

HISTORY AND INTRODUCTION

The formation of the Chinese People's Liberation Army was announced by Mao Tse-tung in July 1946, by which time regular communist armed forces had been in existence for some 19 years.

After the collapse of the Manchu dynasty in October, 1911 northern and central China steadily became ungovernable, despite attempts at military dictatorship and then imperial restoration by the warlord Yuan Shih-k'ai. In southern China, based on Canton, two radical movements emerged. The first was the Kuomintang (KMT), a movement initially committed to the principles of liberal democracy and social reform led by Dr Sun Yat-sen until his death in 1925, thereafter dominated by the Generalissimo Chiang Kai-shek. The communist party of China (CPC) was founded in 1921. In 1923, following advice from the Comintern and the Soviet regime in Moscow, it formed a United Front with the KMT. The communist intention was to assist the KMT in its plans to overthrow the warlords who had reduced much of China to chaos, and unite the country under a strong central government. At the same time the CPC would infiltrate all the organs of the KMT, and ultimately transform it into a vehicle for a Marxist revolution in China. In view of these intentions, the CPC did not create a revolutionary army of their own, but set about gaining influence and control within the KMT forces. Dr Sun Yat-sen adopted Bolshevik forms of organisation (but not Bolshevik political objectives), and many communists became political officers attached to KMT units. They also took great interest in the process of political indoctrination carried out at the Whampoa Military Academy, the training school for KMT officers.

In 1926 the KMT army embarked upon the 'northern expedition', a strategic offensive to put down the squabbling cliques of warlords that culminated in the capture of Peking in 1928. The 4th Corps of the KMT army, called the 'Ironsides', consisted of some 30,000 Cantonese, and had been heavily infiltrated by the CPC. As the 4th Corps moved northwards, its communist members organised the peasants, setting up Peasant Associations, and encouraging them to attack or intimidate landlords into redistributing their lands, or reducing rents. By the spring of 1927 there were 50,000 Ironsides of whom some 30% were committed to the communist cause.

In the spring and summer an ideological split emerged in the KMT, between a right-wing faction led by Chiang Kai-shek based on Shanghai and a left-wing faction based on Hankow. The CPC supported the Hankow faction. Chiang triumphed, the Hankow faction submitted and abandoned their communist supporters. The right wing purged the KMT of its known CPC members. The response of the CPC Central Committee was to order a series of urban uprisings.

On August 1st, 1927 there was a communist rising in Nanch'ang. The communist forces consisted of the 'Ironsides', a proportion of the garrison of the city (which consisted of KMT officers cadets, led by their commander, Chu Teh, formerly an officer in the army of the Warlord of Yunnan), and a ragged force of peasants, KMT deserters, and strikers from the Hanyang coal mines, led by Mao Tse-tung. Chu Teh proclaimed the foundation of the Red Army, and Mao named his followers the '1st Workers' and Peasants' Red Army'. These events marked the emergence of the first distinct communist armed forces in China.

The Nanch'ang rising had little success, and indeed from 1927 until 1937 the Red forces in China had little respite from a constant round of defeat and retreat. They could do nothing in the face of superior enemy forces but survive, prepare for the future, and lay the foundations for an enduring romantic legend.

As KMT reinforcements moved on Nanch'ang the Red troops, having failed to gain the expected degree of support from the urban proletariat of the city, retreated. Attempts to inspire or support urban uprisings in Canton, Shanghai and other cities failed, and by late in 1927 the forces of Chu and Mao, much depleted by enemy action, disease, starvation and desertion, took refuge in Chingkangshan, a mountainous wilderness, where they merged their troops with those of indigenous bandits. From Chingkangshan they set out to politicise the local peasantry, and set up a soviet.

In June, 1928 the Comintern and the 6th National Congress of the CPC approved the formation of the Red Army. By this time there were at least eight soviets, most of them ephemeral, in existence in China, and all had forces of a sort. The most substantial were at Chingkangshan, where Mao and Chu commanded some 10,000 men and women, of whom approximately 2500 were armed.

Early in 1929 Mao and Chu were forced to evacuate Chingkangshan by an effective KMT blockade that starved them out. On the move, southwards, they relied upon peasants to supply their food, fill up the ranks with recruits, and give intelligence as to the activities of hostile forces. Such support was secured by the usual political activity, the most popular form of action being attacks upon the landlords and their militia, the Min Tuan, in order to obtain arms and rice. The retreat from Chingkangshan ended in south Kiangsi, after the pursuing forces had run out of steam. The Reds settled down to construct a soviet.

In the meanwhile, the senior CPC members with the Red Forces had discussed military policy in conference at Kut'ien. Here it was agreed that the Red Army must at all times accept the absolute authority of the CPC, and the principle of political control was established. But, there were disagreements over strategy and tactics; Mao denounced Red Army commanders, many of whom had been trained in warlord armies under Japanese or German influence, as 'bourgeois militarists', and called upon them to abandon conventional military operations for guerrilla activities in order to ensure survival.

In 1930, there were further disputes over strategy. The Central Committee of the CPC ordered new attacks on cities in order to spark off an urban revolt against the KMT. Mao believed such attacks would fail, would be costly, and would induce no useful response from the urban populations. He favoured continued guerrilla and political activities designed to gain support from the peasants and so gain control of the countryside. Despite his arguments, formal assaults were made on a number of cities held by the KMT. Some were temporarily successful, but once the KMT responded cities capture by the Reds were quickly lost. The workers failed to rise in support. The attacks did little but provoke a vigorous counter-attack by the KMT.

Between the autumn of 1930 and the autumn of 1934 the

KMT launched five 'encirclement campaigns' against the Reds. These campaigns were intended to annihilate the CPC. The Reds fought all but the last in conventional manner with their permanent forces, and relied upon sympathetic peasants behind the KMT lines to supplement their regular operations with guerrilla attacks. The Red forces had some success, and some good luck too. On occasions they could 'lure deep' an enemy formation; by pinprick attacks from many directions anger the enemy commander so that his troops could be drawn, over-extended, isolated, exhausted by long marches, then ambushed, or encircled and assaulted. In this way the Red forces obtained weapons, ammunition and equipment. In 1932 the Reds launched an effective pre-emptive spoiling attack upon the surrounding KMT forces. In 1931, they were saved by the repercussions of the Mukden Incident, that distracted the attention of the enemy commanders. Red political activity continued to be effective, even amongst enemy forces. In 1931 a brigade from the army of the 'Christian Warlord' Feng Yu-Hsiang defected to the Reds, and in 1932 the KMT 28th Route Army of some 20,000 men did the same. By summer 1933 the Reds had sufficient trained men to allow a reorganisation of forces in which they created 'divisions', each of some 6000 men, organised on a triangular basis.

In October, 1933 KMT forces launched the 5th encirclement campaign against the Kiangsi soviet. By September, 1934 they had reduced its area by half. Red Forces found it increasingly difficult to evade strong KMT columns, and when Red units fought KMT units at equal odds, they were always defeated. Also, the soviet could no longer feed its inhabitants. Mao and Chu decided that they must break out and go to find a more inaccessible and more secure rural base area elsewhere. Accordingly, they broke out, not without loss, and having left a stay-behind party in south Kiangsi to carry on political and guerrilla work, moved south-west. Red forces in the Hsiang-o-hsi soviet in west Hunan and west Hupei, and in the Oyuwan soviet in the Ta-pieh-shan mountains, were ordered to join them. In this way the Red Army commenced the 'long march', which was performed by three separate columns. All of them suffered great privations on their journeys, which were 6000–8000 miles in length, and great loss due to severe climatic conditions, rough terrain, shortages of food, and action by hostile KMT, warlord and tribal forces. The column from south Kiangsi was almost pinned on the Yangtze, and then on the Tatu, by pursuing enemy troops.

The Red forces eventually concentrated in north Shensi in autumn, 1936 where they set about the creation of a defensive base area. Some 35,000 regular Red troops were formed into seven 'divisions' and deployed to defend the base should it be attacked. Guerrilla forces were sent out beyond the base area to enlarge it by political activity.

Meanwhile, Chiang Kai-shek laboriously deployed KMT and allied warlord units so as to encircle the north Shensi soviet, and prepare to reduce it. However, the Reds managed to persuade many of his senior commanders that the KMT should form a united front with Red forces in order to repel the Japanese, who by December, 1936 were reinforcing their troops on the outskirts of Peking. In December, 1936 Chiang arrived at Sian to supervise the extermination of the north Shensi soviet. He was kidnapped by senior officers led by Chang Hsueh-liang, warlord of Manchuria, and forced to accept a united front.

So, in 1937 the Red forces in north Shensi formed the KMT 8th Route Army, an army of three divisions. In September, 1937 the 115th division commanded by Lin Piao ambushed a Japanese mechanised column at Ping Sing pass, and as a result furnished the Red Army with 50 field guns,

their first substantial body of ordnance. Apart from this exploit, which was used to the utmost by CPC propaganda, the Reds did little fighting against the Japanese until 1940. Until then the 8th Route Army stood ready to defend the base area, guerrillas concentrated their attention upon landlords and KMT irregular forces, and CPC work teams encouraged the peasants to arm and organise themselves into local self-defence corps. In April, 1938 the activities of the 8th Route Army were supplemented by those of the KMT New 4th Route Army, a communist force of divisional size located on the southern bank of the Yangtze.

In summer, 1940 the Reds launched the '100 Regiments Campaign', which was their only large-scale offensive against the Japanese invaders. Approximately half a million Red soldiers took part. Activity was concentrated in northern China. Red troops assisted by peasants mobilised by local CPC members and political officers of the Red Army first wrecked roads, railways and bridges, then attacked isolated Japanese posts. The second phase was more difficult and had less success than the first. The Japanese responded in the period between summer, 1941 and summer, 1942 by the 'Three All' campaign, based on the principles of 'kill all, destroy all, burn all'. The Japanese did not attempt to pursue Red forces and bring them to battle, instead they controlled, reduced and punished the rural population upon whom the Red troops relied for intelligence and logistic support. Their campaign was a great blow to the Reds, and from 1942 until the Japanese surrender of 1945, they reverted to low-level guerrilla and political activities directed against the KMT, Min Tuan and collaborationist 'puppet troops'. Meanwhile, in spring, 1941 the KMT, losing patience with the failure of the Red forces to make suicidal attacks upon the Japanese, and with their continued political action in the countryside, broke up the United Front by attacking the New 4th Route Army.

By summer, 1945 the Red forces had grown in size, and large areas of countryside were sympathetic to the CPC, especially in northern and central China. In August, 1945 the Japanese surrendered, and the Reds instantly went into action. The 8th Route Army increased by calling up half-trained peasants from 400,000 to 800,000 men in a few weeks; the New 4th Route Army increased from 80,000 to 110,000. The Red forces were reorganised for the civil war. Eventually the regular elements fought in five field armies, each one of which acted within a distinct and usually independent theatre of operations. In the initial phase of the civil war the Reds created a new army, the 4th Field Army, which was sent north under the command of Lin Piao to seize Manchuria, the main industrial base area of China. The Second and Third Field Armies moved into central and northern China to obstruct the advance of KMT forces coming from the south-west. They tore up roads and railways to deprive the KMT of the advantages of having motor transport and locomotives. The Reds armed themselves and new recruits at the expense of the defeated Japanese. All over central and northern China columns of disconsolate Japanese soldiers, stripped to their loincloths by destitute Red soldiers, trailed north-eastwards. In Manchuria, with some assistance from the Soviet occupation forces, the 4th Field Army acquired medium artillery and tanks. These unfamiliar weapons had at first to be operated by Japanese prisoners; they were later worked by deserters from the KMT armies.

Meanwhile the KMT forces fought their way northwards, with American help, and soon appeared to be in possession of the whole of China. But, although the KMT garrisoned great cities and towns, and patrolled major lines of communication, it could not catch and annihilate the Red forces, or control the countryside. The communists surrounded, isolated and starved towns, and when relief columns were sent they ambushed them or stopped them by blocking the roads. They also swiftly surrounded and wiped out KMT units whenever they were able to concentrate decisively superior forces. By summer, 1947 the KMT forces, affected by internal political dissension, were weary and demoralised, made fatalistic and defeatist by CPC propaganda, and the PLA went over to the offensive. Slowly, one by one, the cities in Manchuria were taken, by blockade, bombardment and massed infantry assault. Each communist victory brought in floods of recruits, many of them deserters or prematurely demobilised soldiers from the KMT army. By October, 1948 the five field armies were all well established and were all making successful attacks upon the KMT. In November, 1948 at the battle of Suchow, elements of several field armies co-ordinated operations to defeat the best of the KMT modernised divisions, and deal a deathblow to the military arm of Chiang Kai-shek's regime. In January, 1949 the Peking–Tientsin pocket fell, and in April, 1949 Red forces crossed the Yangtze almost unopposed. Chiang Kai-shek and the best of his remaining forces fled to Taiwan as the PLA mopped up in the South and south-west. On October 1st, 1949 the Chinese People's Republic was proclaimed.

At that point the PLA was transformed; it was not longer purely the military arm of the revolutionary movement – it took on the new role of an instrument of state obliged to defend national interests. The first commitment was to complete the destruction of the enemy, and this entailed pursuit and annihilation of the KMT forces on Taiwan. However, amphibious assaults on Quemoy and Matsu made by units of the 3rd Field Army, were repulsed with great loss. Attempts to reach Taiwan itself were swiftly ruled out by American naval measures.

Another commitment was to reestablish Chinese control over certain peripheral areas, and in particular, over Tibet. Action was taken in summer, 1950. Five divisions of the 2nd Field Army and two of the 1st Field Army moved into Tibet and quickly induced the Dalai Lama to submit to the authority of Peking.

Meanwhile, an apparent threat to the security and integrity of metropolitan China arose as a result of the progress of the UN forces in Korea. As a result of this perceived threat the PLA crossed the frontiers of China for the first time, encountered fully equipped modern forces with catastrophic casualties as a consequence, and in an effort to modernise itself came for a number of years under strong Soviet influence.

In autumn, 1950 some 300,000 Chinese Peoples' Volunteers (CPV), drawn mainly from the 4th Field Army, secretly crossed the Yalu and prepared to counterattack the advancing UN forces. The attack had initial success, but at great cost, and was stopped by UN firepower in spring, 1951. The Chinese commanders discovered that in Korea they lacked the room for manoeuvre and support from the rural population that had guaranteed survival and success in China. They leaned heavily on the Soviet Union for weapons, equipment, training, organisation and doctrine. By 1953, when the Korean War ground to a halt, the CPV resembled a Soviet force on much reduced scales of equipment. There were some 21 Corps, each consisting of three infantry divisions, most having some integral field artillery, in Korea. In addition the CPV deployed nine artillery divisions, two tank divisions, and some 1800 modern aircraft. The last of the CPV left Korea in 1958.

Soviet influence persisted, with the PLA adopting many of the characteristics of a conventional army, until the Sino–Soviet relationship began to decay in the late 1950s. As Mao and his immediate followers prepared for the 'great leap forward', they decided to purge the PLA in order to make it

once more an instrument of radical political change. An assault was made upon Soviet military ideas and forms of organisation in 1959. The need for modernisation and a formal rank structure was questioned and under the auspices of the 'officers to the ranks' scheme all officers were sent to serve as private soldiers for 30 days a year. Those who protested against such changes, including Peng Teh-huai, the Minister of Defence, were dismissed and purged. Lin Piao was made Minister of Defence with instructions to reawaken the revolutionary radical spirit in the PLA. Gradually the Soviet concepts instilled since 1951 were discredited and eradicated. Despite the internal turmoil, the PLA remained an effective military force, and proved the point by suppressing a revolt in Tibet in 1959, and soundly beating the Indian Army in a series of border clashes in 1962.

By 1964 Mao was satisfied that the PLA was once more fit to school the nation in revolutionary politics. He sent PLA propaganda teams into cities and villages to promote a 'learn from the PLA' movement, and to encourage the people as a whole to purge and revitalise the CPC. As the 'great proletarian cultural revolution' was launched in the mid-1960s, Red Guards were sent to help propaganda teams from the General Political Department of the PLA. Other units of the PLA were drawn into the political mäelstrom, first the militia and local forces, which were closely connected with the local CPC leaders under attack by the radicals, then, as violent chaos ensued in parts of the country, main units of the ground forces. In autumn, 1966 revolutionary committees were set up to discharge the functions of local administration, the normal machinery having been discredited or destroyed during the purges. By summer, 1967 the PLA was in control of these revolutionary committees, and rapidly gained a predominance on CPC and State committees at all levels. At the behest of senior commanders the Red Guards were put down, the the Cultural Revolution brought to a close. In restoring order the PLA had gained power.

It is probable than an important motive for the intervention of the PLA was that the disruption caused by the purges and resistance to the purges imperilled the efficiency of the armed forces at a time when China seemed to be under dire threat from the Americans to the south, and the Russians to the north.

The PLA continued to consolidate its political position. In 1969 Lin Piao was named as Mao's political heir. In the same year the PLA engaged in a number of serious border clashes with Soviet forces, particularly along the frontier of Sinkiang and along the Ussuri river. In the latter area the PLA scored a notable propaganda victory in a clash at Chen Pao island.

In 1971 the political position of the PLA was seriously undermined by the death, in mysterious circumstances, of Lin Piao. He was killed whilst fleeing by air towards the northern frontier of Manchuria. He had subsequently been accused by official Chinese sources of planning a *coup d'état* and the assassination of Mao. After 1971 the PLA gradually lost ground. CPC cadres replaced PLA commanders on vital committees. In 1973 most commanders of military regions were moved, thereby cutting them off from carefully nurtured local power bases. The military budget reached a peak in 1970, and then declined. In spring, 1976 Teng Hsiao-p'ing, who had been made PLA Chief of Staff in October, 1975 was removed from all his offices. The Minister of Defence, Yeh Chien-ying, came under political pressure and propaganda attack by radical elements once more attempting to push the PLA leftwards. However, in 1976 the PLA began a political resurgence. After the death of Mao in September the radical 'gang of four', led by Chiang Ching, attempted to seize power. The army gave firm support to Hua Kuo-feng who had been appointed Mao's deputy in May. In October Hua was confirmed as true legitimate successor of Mao. The 'gang of four' were subjected to increasingly intense criticism, arrested and expelled from the party, and then vanished to an unknown fate. The PLA suppressed disorders instigated in Shanghai and rural areas in the south by radical sympathisers.

In spring, 1977 Teng Hsiao-ping was gradually rehabilitated, and in July he was restored to office, including the position of Chief of Staff of the PLA. Under his direction the PLA is preparing to modernise, and to acquire weapons and armaments plant from foreign sources, including the EEC, to improve fire power and mobility.

STRENGTH AND BUDGET

The PLA ground forces maintain approximately 3,150,000 men in their regular units, of whom some 1,000,000 or so are deployed in independent divisions and regiments. The rest are organised in the corps of the main forces and supporting arms.

The main forces consist of some 12 armoured divisions, each with about 10,000 men. There are 119 infantry divisions, each with a strength of some 14,000. There are 37 artillery divisions (17 field, 4 anti-tank, 6 anti-aircraft) fifty engineer regiments and 14 railway divisions provide transport and other forms of support.

The local forces are organised into 97 divisions and some 130 regiments (including Border Guards).

The ground forces are reckoned to have some 10,500 tanks, 4000 APCs and 11,800 artillery tubes.

The trained elements of the militia have strength of some 12,000,000, but of these only some 4,300,000 are armed. An urban Militia consisting of trade union members has a strength of about six million.

The Public Security Forces deployed as frontier guards are armed as light infantry and number some 300,000.

There are no reliable figures available as to the Chinese GNP or the Chinese military budget. Western estimates of GNP vary between $280 and $570 billion; defence expenditure of $11,870,000,000 was disclosed (for the first time) in 1981 (20% of government expenditure).

COMMAND AND CONSTITUTIONAL STATUS

Command

The PLA is both the military instrument of the Chinese People's Republic, and as such the defender of Chinese national interests as defined by the State; and the armed force of the CPC, and so the violent servant of a revolutionary political movement. The structure of command at all levels reflects the dichotomy in the character of the PLA. It is based upon two principles. The first of these can be summarised as the slogan 'politics in command', and was established at the Kut'ien Conference in 1929. It was reaffirmed in Aritcle 15 of the Constitution of the CPR adopted on January 17th, 1975, part of which reads, 'The Chairman of the Central Committee of the Communist Party of China commands the country's armed forces'. The second principle derives from the first, and is that of 'dual command' — in effect, of joint control of military activities at all levels by political and military officials. Machinery for the exercise of dual command was created in 1930; a revolutionary military committee was set up to collaborate with commanders in strategic planning, and political commissars with powers to countersign all orders were sent to field units.

The system of dual command persists. Organs of the CPC are parallel to organs of State. The National Defence Council, the highest State institution concerned with defence, is watched and supervised by the Military Affairs Committee, a subcommittee of the Central Committee of the CPC which came into existence in 1949. These two bodies supervise the work of the Ministry of Defence. The Ministry is served by several departments; the Ground Forces General Staff, the General Rear Services Department (GRSD), the General Political Department (GPD), the Navy Department and the Air Force Department. The General Staff is organised along conventional lines, and is divided into subdepartments dealing with operations, intelligence, etc. Every department and subdepartment has a CPC committee within it. The General Staff exercises command over the military regions (MRs), military region HQs exercise immediate control over main force corps in their regions and supervise the work of subordinate military districts (MDs). Military districts control local forces, independent units of the regular forces, and paramilitary forces such as the Militia. HQs at military region, military district and corps level maintain close liaison with local CPC committees.

The General Rear Services Department supervises all work concerned with the supply and transport of the PLA. It directly administers or indirectly controls the production and distribution of centrally produced warlike stores, controls all large-scale movements of troops, and all major engineering and construction works. It supervises the activities of the Production and Construction Corps, and of the General Militia when engaged on production or construction tasks.

The General Political Department directs the work of the commissars with PLA units and also keeps watch on the political reliability of other departments.

During the 'great leap forward' the PLA extended its authority over Public Security Forces border guards, who were formerly under the command of the Ministry of Public Security. In the period of the cultural revolution the PLA took over the command of the People's Armed Police and the militia from local CPC organisations. These forces are now controlled by military district HQs.

The Urban Militia, a force originally raised by local CPC committees in 1968 as the Workers Provost Corps, is now under the control of trade union committees.

The actual application of the principles of 'politics in command' and 'dual command' at lower levels has varied with circumstances. Until 1949 the authority of commissars was enhanced by their operational value to commanders. By their political work commissars secured vital supplies, labour service, intelligence and fresh recruits from the peasantry. They also inspired loyalty, enthusiasm and self discipline amongst the soldiers of the Red forces. Discipline in Red Army units depended to a great extent upon political indoctrination, and was self-enforced at unit level. Every unit had a soldiers' council organised and led by CPC cells. These councils discussed the conduct of training and operations, and the behaviour of individuals at all levels, before and after action. When in action, soldiers were expected to render absolute obedience to the orders of a commander. Soldiers who were disobedient or hesitant in action were hauled before their unit Soldiers' Council at the earliest possible moment, and were often sent for execution. The task of the commander was thereby simplified; his work was simply to plan and execute operations or training schemes; administration and discipline were dealt with by the commissar and the soldiers themselves.

The power and status of commissars was greatly reduced as a result of PLA involvement in the Korean War. As the CPV adopted conventional operations, organisation and equipment under Russian advice, commanders became less inclined to allow commissars their previous right to examine, discuss and countersign operational orders. Commissars were no longer a vital link with the rural population, as the North Korean peasants failed to respond to their propaganda, and anyway, supply, discipline and administration were regularised with Soviet help. The system of dual command and politics in command was no longer in operation at unit level; commissars were regarded by their commanders not as equals, but as political assistants whose main role was to look after the morale and welfare of the troops. This attitude persisted after the major commitment to Korea ended. PLA commanders neglected political work in order to achieve a greater degree of technical military competence. CPC members within the PLA declined in numbers and lapsed into quiescence. By 1959 Mao was afraid that the PLA might lose its revolutionary character and become a bureaucratic instrument of the state rather than remain a militant arm of a revolutionary CPC. He acted to restore the importance of commissars and of the CPC within the PLA. Lin Piao became Minister of Defence, and worked to reinvigorate the communist movement within the PLA. By 1964 there was a CPC cell in 80% of the platoons of the PLA, and Mao considered that it could be used to guarantee a safe and successful purge of the civil CPC. Commissars were very active during the Cultural Revolution, but do not seem to have gained much power at the expense of commanders within the PLA itself. For a while their influence was greatly reduced after the PLA took political power and the General Political Department was thoroughly purged. It would appear that commissars are still unable to exert their claimed equal authority with commanders of an equal level when dealing with operational matters. But, they do wield great influence. They normally act as secretary to the unit CPC Committee which a commander will always consult before taking an important decision. They also perform certain important administrative functions; they carry out the political indoctrination of the troops; advise on promotions and postings; control resettlement; see to the morale and personal welfare of the soldiers; conduct security screenings; run military courts and boards; organise entertainments and unit newspapers; are responsible for psychological warfare in the event of war; and handle the business of civil—military relations.

Constitutional Status
The constitutional status of the PLA has been a matter of political contention. Since 1949 the PLA has always been available as a 'temporary reserve government' should the normal machinery of civil administration break down. In the case of the cultural revolution the PLA took over control, not only of the machinery of the state, but also that of the CPC.

Between 1949 and 1952 the PLA ruled China by martial law. But, in 1952 it handed over day to day business to civil authority. The principle of ultimate CPC authority was maintained until 1967; in 1959 the Minister of Defence, Peng Teh-huai was dismissed after a disagreement with Mao; in 1965 the Chief of Staff, Lo Jui-ch'ing was dismissed in similar circumstances.

However, the PLA always had great influence and political power, based upon the five field army connections, each of which had close links with a particular geographical area, and great influence over CPC leaders within it. It has been suggested that China is in informal terms a loose federation based upon these field army connections whose centres of power are: 1st Field Army, north-west China; 2nd Field Army, south-west China; 3rd Field Army, central and eastern China; 4th Field Army, Manchuria and Canton; 5th Field Army, north China, including Peking.

During the 'great leap forward' Mao showed a deep desire to purge the PLA of Soviet influences and ideas, make it an integral part of the Chinese masses, and draw it into Chinese political life. This desire was resisted by the regular forces of the PLA. But, during the cultural revolution the PLA regulars were drawn into political struggles in spite of their desire to abstain.

Having radicalised the PLA, and in particular the GPD, by 1964, Mao sent the commissars into the country to reform the CPC. By 1966 it was clear that the commissars had failed. Mao decided that a 'great proletarian cultural revolution' was required to reawake the Chinese revolution. He sent the Red Guards, some 50,000,000 students, to reinforce the commissars. The Red Guards were initially organised by the commissars, and were supplied and transported by the General Rear Services Department (GRSD). As the Red Guards began their assault on local CPC committees, local forces under MD commanders were drawn in on the side of local CPC branches. Main-force units were on the whole loyal to the central government, and some were politically radical, but they were concered to maintain readiness against the Soviet and American external threats, and anxious not to be involved in domestic politics. In January, 1967 local forces were ordered by Peking to support the Red Guards, but apparently refused to do so. In response, the Red Guards criticised the PLA as a whole, which alienated some main-force units. In April, 1967 the Red Guards attacked and destroyed local CPC branches and local government committees. Local forces of the PLA moved in an attempt to protect the local CPC and officials, and there were armed clashes with Red Guards. In the summer of 1967 the PLA main-force commanders decided that they could not longer tolerate the violent chaos that existed in many areas. In July, the senior commanders of the Wuhan military region captured and held three senior members of the Cultural Revolution Group from Peking, as a protest. In August, 1967 the PLA commanders induced the central authorities in Peking to order an end to the Cultural Revolution, and instruct the Red Guards to return home. PLA regular forces moved in to enforce these orders. PLA commanders took control of revolutionary committees and took over the administration of local government; a move which virtually made China a federal state in formal terms. PLA commanders also took control of national bodies, and gained power in the Central Committee of the CPC and the Politburo. The followers of Lin Paio's 4th Field Army were in a particularly strong position. In 1969 Lin was named as Mao's successor. The CPC was a military dictatorship at all levels; the PLA ruled the CPC.

However, the radicals led by Mao, were absolutely opposed to 'military polycentrism' and set out to destroy it. By 1971 Lin's position was so weakened that he is said to have planned a *coup d'etat* and the assassination of Mao. Whilst fleeing northwards with some of his senior cronies he was killed. The power of the PLA was swiftly reduced. In 1973 eight of the eleven MR commanders were moved away from their original MR and Field Army areas; their vital local political connections were broken and 'military polycentrism' was ended.

After the death of Mao, a majority of the Military Region commanders supported Hua Kuo-feng and Teng Hsia-ping against the 'Gang of Four', thereby consolidating their political influence and military prospects. The CPC re-established civil control at local and national levels. The constitutional position of the PLA was defined in the Constitution of 1975 as follows:

'The Chinese People's Liberation Army and the people's militia are the workers' and peasants' own armed forces led by the communist party of China . . .'

The principle put forward at Kut'ien has been readopted.

ROLE, COMMITMENT, DEPLOYMENT AND RECENT OPERATIONS

Role

Article 15 of the 1975 Constitution of the CPR stated:

'The Chinese People's Liberation Army is at all times a fighting force, and simultaneously a working force and a production force.

The task of the armed forces of the People's Republic of China is to safeguard the achievements of the socialist revolution and socialist construction, to defend the sovereignty, territorial integrity and security of the State, and to guard against subversion and aggression by imperialism, social imperialism and their lackeys.'

This passage makes clear the fact that the PLA is not a purely military force; it is extensively used for economic purposes and plays a great part in production and construction work; it is also used for political work, such as the soldiers' education and indoctrination of the masses.

The extent to which the PLA should divert its energies from the military role in order to take part in the economic and political life of the country has been a matter of dispute. Career commanders have in the past protested that the involvement of the PLA in non-military work is inimical to military efficiency and readiness and so renders China vulnerable to external attack. The radical political elements in China, supported by Mao, have argued that the PLA must be fully integrated with the life of the masses in order to counter internal threats that are far more dangerous than external enemies. They also claim that invaders should be defeated by a 'people's war', and that success in such a war depends more upon the maintenance of popular support, and so on political work, than it does on the existence of highly equipped and trained regular forces.

Actual policy as to the role of the PLA is a compromise between these two points of view. The PLA main forces spend most of their time training and preparing to fight any invader on a conventional basis, and are being slowly modernised in their equipment. The local forces, regular and irregular, spend a great deal more time on economic and political work.

The primary role of the main forces, which are organised into corps and Armies under MR HQs, is to defend the territory of the CPR against invasion. Until the late 1960s the CPR believed that the main threat was of invasion by KMT forces from Taiwan, supplemented by American naval and air attacks. Since the late 1960s the CPR has regarded the Soviet Union and its Asian allies such as India as the main threat to Chinese security. The CPR now fears encirclement by the Soviet Union, and believes that the Russians may attempt to stir up rebellion by national minorities in peripheral areas of China, especially Sinkiang and Inner Mongolia. There is also considered to be a possibility of a Soviet conventional invasion against Peking from the Mongolian SSR, Chinese nuclear activities in Sinkiang, and the main Chinese industrial base area in Manchuria.

Maoists believe that the best way to defeat an invader is to resort to the strategy of 'people's war'. If such a strategy were employed, as invading forces advanced into China, PLA regular forces would withdraw to wage a protracted war. The enemy would occasionally be briefly attacked in order to draw him, so that his forces could be 'lured deep' into difficult terrain. The regular forces would defend rural base areas by blocking action, whilst guerrillas harassed enemy lines of communication. Eventually the enemy would be induced to disperse his units in a vain attempt to force elusive

PLA forces to stand and fight. Then the PLA regular forces would use superior mobility on foot and superior intelligence to concentrate greatly superior forces in the vicinity of selected enemy units, isolate, encircle and annihilate them. Tactics would be simple and consist mainly of massed close assaults by infantry at night with artillery support. Military Regions would have considerable autonomy under such a strategy. In effect, the defence of China would be operationally decentralised. Logistics would also be decentralised; the PLA would rely on the friendly rural population to supply their needs.

But, it is unlikely that the main forces would resort to a purely people's war strategy. Career commanders would prefer to use modernised regular forces to conduct a firm conventional linear defence of the frontiers of the CPR. Ideally, they would employ a 'forward defence'; make a surprise pre-emptive advance beyond the threatened frontiers in order to spoil enemy preparations for attack, then go over to the defensive and set up a strong line. Such a strategy would require careful co-ordination of MRs by the General Staff. Probably, in the event of an invasion, the main forces would fight a series of conventional delaying actions whilst other elements of the PLA conducted a people's war behind enemy lines.

The main forces might also have an offensive role, although this is unlikely due to the military superiority of the primary enemies of the CPR. However, it is not impossible that the CPR would one day employ the PLA to 'restore the ancient frontiers of China', by seizing areas of territory in dispute along the frontiers or invading Taiwan. The PLA can also be used to punish small neighbours who defy China or damage Chinese interests, as in the case of Vietnam in 1979. The threat of offensive action against Soviet allies and satellites in Asia could be of value to Chinese diplomacy. There is no real disagreement as to how the PLA main forces would wage an offensive campaign. The first state would be to analyse the character of the enemy forces, and select the weakest elements for attack. Next, the PLA commanders would analyse the seat of the war and identify the key terrain, this being an area of critical importance to the enemy, usually on their potential line of retreat. This key terrain would then be seized and held by the primary force whilst secondary forces delayed or stopped enemy reinforcements; or, secondary forces would take or threaten the key terrain whilst primary forces lay in wait to ambush and wipe out enemy reinforcements. The object of offensive action would always be the complete destruction of enemy military units, not the gaining of ground. So tactical principles favour the concentration of greatly superior firepower on the battlefield as a precondition of any attack, and the employment of manoeuvres to ensure the double envelopment or encirclement of the enemy to prevent his escape. Strong enemy forces would be reduced to weakness by long marches, isolation and blockade before being attacked. The destruction of a weak enemy force would be reckoned a greater success than the reduction, containment or enforced retreat of one far greater. The most favoured form of battle would seem to be the strategic ambush.

The roles of local forces are less purely military.

The independent divisions and regiments of the PLA are controlled by MD HQs. In peacetime they are deployed to maintain internal security, which is of particular importance in peripheral regions of the CPR. They are also extensively used to carry out production and construction work. In wartime they would lead the irregular forces in guerrilla actions against the rear areas of enemy forces. They would operate within their MDs.

The Public Security Forces in peacetime have an internal security role, and also patrol the coasts of frontiers of the

CPR. In wartime they would be consolidated and used as independent units.

The Peoples' Armed Police carry on normal police business.

The Production and Construction Corps are employed primarily in economic work, especially in opening up new lands to agriculture and industry in the sparsely inhabited border regions of China. However, they have also been employed in the construction of field fortifications in frontier areas; and as they are partially armed and work in politically sensitive areas, they also have an internal security and border role.

The Militia consists of two main elements. The Common Militia is unarmed and its primary role is as a supplier of labour for production and construction. In the event of war it would provide main force and independent units and guerrillas with logistic support, coolies, recruits, food, intelligence and transport units. The Armed and Basic Militia would in wartime form guerrilla forces for local self defence and raids in enemy rear areas. They would also supply drafts to the regular forces. In peacetime the Armed Militia polices the countryside, patrols frontiers and coasts, and does a great deal of political work.

The PLA is an almost exclusively defensive force, but it serves a movement which subscribes to an aggressive revolutionary ideology. The PLA is incapable of attempting to spread revolution by conquest, but it does assist movements waging wars of national liberation by providing advisers, advice, training facilities and limited amounts of basic equipment. It is also prepared to send production and construction troops abroad to perform major engineering tasks; for example, the PLA built the Tanzam railway in Tanzania and until recently was building a highway in northern Laos.

Commitment

The most important commitment of the PLA is to protect the CPR and CPC from rebellion or invasion. It is also committed by the constitution to protect the 'just rights and interests of overseas Chinese', but it is difficult to see how this commitment could be effectively discharged. The PLA is also committed to complete the revolution in China by bringing Taiwan under the authority of the CPR. It is further committed, in theory, to restore the rightful frontiers of China, to recover lands annexed in the past by neighbours, mainly Russia.

The CPR has few formal commitments that bind it to take military action beyond the frontiers of China. There is an informal commitment to assist in the protection of the countries of Indo-China. During the Vietnamese war the PLA sent engineer and anti-aircraft units to assist the defence of North Vietnam.

The CPR has firmer commitments in regard to North Korea and Pakistan.

The Alliance signed with USSR in 1950 directed against Japan and any ally of Japan expired on April 10, 1980. There are non-aggression pacts with Afghanistan, Burma and Kampuchea.

The PLA is committed to the maintenance of strong forces along the frontier with Vietnam, and still has some advisers attached to anti-Vietnamese guerrillas in northern Laos.

Deployment

The Militia and other local forces are dispersed throughout the whole area of inhabited China to carry out their internal security duties.

The deployment of the main forces has been fairly static since 1949. This is partly because the PLA lacks mobility, because PLA units depend upon the local population for supplies, and because units developed strong local political connections which they are reluctant to break. However, in the late 1960s some formations were moved to reinforce the borders with the Soviet Union and the Mongolian SSR. It is estimated that there are now some 1,000,000 regular soldiers concentrated in the vulnerable frontier areas of Manchuria, Inner Mongolia, Sinkiang and Szechwan. These troops are supported by three production and construction corps, in all about 40 divisions, active in Heilungkiang, Inner Mongolia and Lanchow. In addition, there is a concentration of mechanised forces in the Foochow MR, opposite Taiwan. There are also usually some armoured units deployed near Peking for political reasons. A strategic reserve of mobile forces is usually located between the Yangtze and Yellow rivers.

Estimated strengths of main force units in MRs are given in Organisation Section.

Recent Operations

The PLA was engaged in no large scale operations between the armistice of 1953 in Korea and the Vietnam war of 1979.

The main operations of the PLA have been designed to crush rebellions in sensitive border areas. In 1959 a large scale rebellion in Tibet was crushed, although Tibetan guerrillas are still active in remote parts of the autonomous region. In the 1960s, there were uprisings by national minorities in Sinkiang and Inner Mongolia, and the PLA put these down. The PLA has also assisted in the establishment of Chinese settlers in these areas in an attempt to stabilise and secure them.

The PLA has been involved in numerous frontier clashes along the disputed borders of China. In 1962 PLA units successfully seized the Aksai Chin and certain strategic passes formerly administered by the Indian North-East Frontier Agency. Since the emergence of the Sino—Soviet dispute into public view, the PLA has been engaged in thousands of frontier incidents of varying scale with Soviet forces. The most spectacular of these occurred at Chen Pao island in 1969.

In the spring of 1979, the PLA was involved in a short war against Vietnam. The Main Force troops who took part performed creditably, but various deficiencies in equipment were clearly revealed during the fighting. The lessons of 1979 may induce the CPR to give a higher priority to the modernisation of the PLA.

The PLA had no experience of large-scale conventional operations between 1953, when the Korean War ended, and spring, 1979. The Sino-Vietnamese war of 1979 lasted from February 18th to March 6th, but its repercussions persist in the form of incessant and violent incidents along the common frontier.

The conduct of operations in Vietnam revealed the strength and weakness of the PLA. Briefly, it was strong in the human factors, such as morale, ingenuity and numbers, but weak in material. It was short of modern weapons and had very little motor transport.

The Chinese campaign took the form of a strong but limited and carefully controlled incursion to punish and frighten the government of Vietnam. Chinese troops advanced into North Vietnam along five axes, to swamp and deceive the enemy command, and to take advantage of the number of soldiers available. It has been estimated that some 33 divisions were committed to the offensive. Having taken a number of border towns in the first phase of the offensive, the PLA paused, then advanced deeper into Vietnam, to the edge of the Red River delta. At this stage, it clearly threatened the security of Hanoi and Haiphong, and the Vietnamese hastily reinforced in the area. But the advance was not resumed.

After some days, the PLA withdrew into China, retiring in good order.

Throughout the punitive expedition, the use of force was carefully orchestrated as part of a complex of psychological, political and diplomatic measures. The action of the troops emphasised or helped to conceal political measures and developments. Conversely, diplomatic and political statements were issued to support the military operations; for example, both during the advance and just before the withdrawal, the Vietnamese were deceived as to the immediate intentions of the PLA.

The Chinese soldiers generally performed well, but did suffer from their lack of modern equipment. Because transport was primitive, the infantry could not advance for more than two or three days without pausing to let resupply of food and ammunition catch up with them. Casualties were severe, due to a lack of powerful support weapons, and to the primitiveness of medical services. Despite these deficiencies, there was no obvious loss of cohesion or discipline. The PLA high command appears to have been satisfied with the army's performance.

ORGANISATION

The PLA contains two types of forces: main forces and local forces. Main forces are controlled by MR HQs, local forces by MD HQs. In the event of an invasion, MRs would probably act as autonomous theatre commands, with limited co-ordination from the General Staff. All but two of the MRs contain several MDs, as given below. MD boundaries usually coincide with province boundaries.

In the 1950s the main forces were organised on Soviet lines, and in the 1960s they tried and rejected the American 'Pentomic' form of organisation. Now they are organised on a conventional triangular pattern.

An army of which there are about 42, consists of three infantry divisions and may have an armoured division attached. An infantry division consists of three infantry regiments, a field artillery regiment, air-defence battalion, reconnaissance battalion, and engineer and administration contingents. Approximately two thirds of the infantry divisions have a tank regiment attached; such a regiment would consist of a tank battalion, a battalion of self-propelled artillery, and a reconnaissance unit of armoured cars or motor cycles. An infantry regiment consists of three rifle battalions, a heavy weapons battalion equipped with mortars and anti-tank guns, and a heavy-machine-gun battery.

An armoured division consists of two tank regiments, an infantry regiment, an air-defence battalion and a reconnaissance company of armoured cars or light tanks.

Local Forces of the PLA are regular forces under the command of MD HQs. There are some 97, some independent divisions, and 130 independent regiments. They are organised on the same triangular pattern as the main force units, but are much more lightly equipped. Some, but not all, have integral light artillery and anti-tank support; none has tanks. Public security forces are organised as independent units for war purposes.

The Militia are under the control of local MDs and CPC committees. They can be divided into three types. The Common Militia consists of the entire population of military age not enrolled in other forces. It is unarmed, and serves as a source of labour, potential recruits and means of political control. The Basic Militia of about 20 million receives a few days of basic military training a year, but is not armed. In the event of war it would provide recruits and logistic units, and form village self-defence corps for local guerrilla operations. The Armed Militia of 5,000,000—7,000,000 are politically reliable, given basic training, and paid for their service. They are armed with basic small arms on a permanent basis. They are organised in companies of 130 — an HQ plus three platoons of 40 each. A platoon consists of an HQ and three sections. Patrols are normally carried out by platoon-sized units. Some of these troops are trained as air-defence units.

There are some 14 divisions of engineer, railway and transport troops under the control of the GRSD. In wartime they would probably come under the command of MR HQs as support troops. They would also no doubt greatly increase their size by conscripting coolie, wheelbarrow and other support units from the Common Militia.

The GRSD also exercises supervision over the troops of the Production and Construction Corps, who are organised in divisions and corps on a military pattern.

RECRUITMENT, TRAINING AND RESERVES

Recruitment
The PLA recruits by conscription. Article 26 of the 1975 Constitution states:

> 'It is the lofty duty of every citizen to defend the motherland and resist aggression. It is the honourable obligation of citizens to perform military service according to law.'

Conscription was originally established in principle by the 1949 constitution, but due to the Korean War was not put into effect until 1954. Until that year the Militia was the main source of recruits.

All men and women become liable for military service at the age of 18, but conscription for the regular forces is selective. About 10% of the 9 million potential recruits that come of age each year are trained for 2—4 years' service with main force or independent units. A small proportion of these may opt for long service and become instructors or junior

MR	MDs	Divisions
Lanchow	Kansu, Ninghsia, Shensi, Tsinghai:	1 armoured, 9 infantry, 4 local, 2—3 border
Sinkiang	Sinkiang:	0 amoured, 6 infantry, 8 local, 2—3 border
Chengtu	Szechwan, Tibet:	0 armoured, 8 infantry, 6 local, 2—3 border
Kunming	Kweichow, Yunnan:	0 armoured, 6 infantry, 2 local
Wuhan	Honan, Hupeh:	2 armoured, 10 infantry, 3 airborne (Air Force), 8 local
Foochow	Fukien, Kiangsi:	0 armoured, 6 infantry, 7 local
Nanking	Anhwei, Chekiang, Kiangsu:	1 armoured, 10 infantry, 12 local
Canton	Hunan, Kwangsi, Kwangtung:	0 armoured, 12 infantry, 12 local, 2—3 border
Shenyang	Heilungkiang, Kirin, Liaoning:	3 armoured, 18 infantry, 16 local, 2—3 border
Peking	Hopeh, Inner Mongolia, Shansi:	4 armoured, 25 infantry, 15 local
Tsinan	Shantung:	1 armoured, 9 infantry, 7 local

commanders. Those selected for the regular force must be politically reliable and of a high degree of physical fitness. Those not selected for the regular forces are automatically enrolled in the Militia.

Training

The training of regular soldiers places great emphasis on political and psychological aspects of soldiering. A great deal of time is spent indoctrinating soldiers and convincing them that political motivation and high morale can enable them to overcome enemies with superior firepower.

Military training as such concentrates upon basic skills. Recruits do a great deal of weapon training with rifles, machine-guns, mortars, grenades and mines. A drawback is that due to shortages of ammunition, live firing exercises are rare. Physical fitness and personal mobility are also stressed; even regular soldiers do a lot of physical labour, especially at harvest time, and PLA units conduct long route marches of about 30 miles twice a week. Tactical training concentrates upon fieldcraft and small scale operations; in particular, ambushes, patrols, infiltration and close assault at night.

Large scale exercises are rare. The largest manoeuvres conducted so far have been at divisional level. The PLA uses map exercises and war games to train senior commanders.

Reserves

The whole population of military age constitutes a potential reserve. The Armed and Basic Militia units are a more immediate source of trained and half-trained drafts for the regular forces. Until 1958 the regular forces sent those who had completed their military service into a special reserve; these men and women now join the Militia where they often serve as instructors and junior leaders.

EQUIPMENT AND ARMS INDUSTRY

Equipment

By Western and Soviet standards the PLA is seriously underequipped. The regular forces (main forces and independent units) are adequately supplied with rifles, sub-machine-guns, machine-guns (light and heavy), bazookas, light anti-tank guns and small field guns. Most of these weapons were suplied by the Soviet Union before 1962, or are later Chinese copies or adaptations of Soviet designs. Tanks, APCs and motor transport vehicles are in short supply. Most armoured vehicles are obsolete Soviet models or Chinese copies of obsolete Soviet models. However, the PLA is now receiving a limited number of Chinese models; a battle tank; a light reconnaissance tank; and a lightly armoured, highly mobile APC. The lack of motor transport is a serious defect in the PLA; it means that to a large extent strategic movements must be made by rail, and tactical movements on foot. It also means that time must be spent creating stockpiles before any large-scale manoeuvre can be undertaken because resupply is extremely limited. There is a serious shortage of

Local Force units have infantry small arms, but lack heavy weapons. They have some heavy machine guns and mortars, and perhaps a few light anti-tank weapons. Very few have any field artillery.

Some elements of the Production and Construction Corps are armed with small arms and mortars.

Public Security Forces are armed with infantry small arms only.

The Militia are only partially armed. Of the Armed Militia, some two thirds carry obsolete rifles and light machine-guns, the rest make do with grenades or improvised weapons. In the event of war the Militia would be expected to produce

simple weapons such as mines from their own resources, and also arm and resupply themselves by capture from the enemy.

Arms Industry

The CPR is equipping its main forces with modern weapons, but the process is slow. The industrial base capable of producing sophisticated weapons has hardly expanded since the withdrawal of Soviet aid in 1962, and many Maoists question the need for mechanisation, citing the Maoist principle of 'men over weapons'. However, the CPR has recently begun production of Chinese-designed tanks, APCs and aircraft in accordance with the policy of strategic self-sufficiency. Armaments factories are controlled by the GRSD and the MR HQs, and are concentrated in established industrial areas; in particular in the Nanking, Peking and Shenyang MRs.

MRs are expected to be self-sufficient in food, clothing and other basic stores. In the event of war the PLA would depend upon the peasants and the enemy for such commodities.

RANK, DRESS AND DISTINCTIONS

There are no ranks as such in the PLA. Personnel are classified as commanders, commissars or fighters. Commanders hold appointments rather than ranks. Between 1953 and 1958 the PLA started to adopt a Soviet type of rank structure, and created an officer corps on the Soviet model in 1955. In 1958 this development was attacked by the central authorities, and the privileges of officers were steadily eroded. In 1965 all ranks and badges of distinction were abolished.

Commanders are selected for political reliability first and military ability second. They are trained in techniques of leadership and basic tactics in military academies on 18-month courses, then do 6 months' service in the ranks before taking up their first command. They are expected to lead in battle and training by personal example. Commanders at all levels are required to submit to criticism from subordinates, but in action would expect orders to be obeyed without question.

The uniform of the PLA consists of a green suit of quilted jacket and trousers and peaked cap. Regular soldiers wear red collar patches. The badge is a five-pointed red star.

Militia forces often wear civilian clothes and identify themselves as members of the PLA by wearing armbands.

CURRENT DEVELOPMENTS

The PLA is not an army in the Western sense of the word in that it has important economic and political functions as well as military ones. It is a conglomeration of bodies, only some of which are primarily military in their character.

The main forces of the PLA resemble the army of a second-rate European military power of the 1930s. They are short of every military commodity except manpower. They are predominantly infantry, organised on a modern basis, but not so equipped. Their policy of self-sufficiency, with consequent dependence on local sources of supply, allied to their lack of motor transport, renders them strategically immobile. Strategic immobility has resulted in the formation of strong local attachments that make them politically powerful. The soldiers in these units are tough, fit, highly mobile on foot, and well trained in basic infantry skills, except for accurate shooting. No doubt they would be formidable in nocturnal close assault, ambush and other minor operations. A serious weakness of these forces is the fact that their commanders have had no experience of large scale operations since 1953, and hardly any of large scale exercises. They would probably be effective in defence of their own well-known MRs against an invader. It is unlikely that they could mount a successful strategic offensive against a sophisticated enemy beyond the frontiers of the CPR. The PLA may create an effective modern striking force with sufficient firepower and mobility to carry out such an offensive in the future, but current progress towards such a development is slow. For the immediate future the main forces, backed up by the independent units and the paramilitary forces, are likely to guarantee the CPR against a conventional invasion, and perhaps allow it to threaten small neighbours. They will not enable the CPR to project strong military influence beyond its own immediate periphery.

In regard to the internal role of the PLA it would seem that the CPC has re-established itself in command of the CPR. But the PLA is very powerful, especially in the provinces, and in the event of a failure of order could no doubt take control of the country as it did during the cultural revolution and the power struggles after the death of Mao.

Nigel De Lee

COLOMBIA

HISTORY AND INTRODUCTION

The Colombian army stands apart from others in Latin America, in that it combines very considerable operational experience, second only (and that recently) to that of the Cuban, with a professional aloofness from political affairs which, though not always maintained, is unquestionably sincere. The single period of military government to which it has subjected the country (1953—7) was brought about by internal disorders of a scale and intensity which elsewhere might have been taken by the armed forces to justify their more or less permanent assumption of power.

The modern Colombian army dates from the period known in domestic administrative history as the *Reforma Militar*, 1909—11, when a Chilean military mission, which had been invited into the country to pass on its German-taught skills, did away with the haphazard system of temporary enlistment of officers and soldiers, established recruitment and training on a professional basis and founded the staff college for the higher training of officers. The army thus reformed was one with a history very similar to that of its neighbours in Ecuador and Venezuela, the survivor of nearly a century of internal revolutions and civil wars, in which its role as a national institution had been frequently challenged by provincial and personal armies following the fortunes of party, region or caudillo in the quest for dominance. It had begun as the liberating army of Bolívar, which he had led across the Andes from Venezuela to surprise the Spanish garrison of Bogotá in 1819 and win the decisive battle of Boyacá. His subsequent victories in Venezuela laid the basis for his creation of the Republic of Gran Colombia, uniting the present territories of Venezuela, Ecuador and Colombia. But he proved unable to hold the territories together in peacetime and the union was dissolved in 1830.

The forces which drove apart the territories of Gran Colombia are known for convenience as 'centralism' and 'federalism', but they were not quelled by the dissolution. As in so many other Latin American countries during the nineteenth century, Colombian politics after the dissolution took on the character of a struggle between parties representing exactly those same principles, but with the particular difference that centralism became closely identified with the church. Colombia and Ecuador compete for the title of the most Catholic country in Latin America, and though the competition is artificial Colombia is unquestionably a country in which the church arouses passionate loyalties and their antithesis. The liberals, who were generally federalists, were driven into fierce anti-clerical positions, in which they usually found themselves at odds with the national army — though so uncertain was the power of the central government that the national army could be at times outnumbered and defeated by provincial armies led by local leaders. Thus, when the army imposed its own government on the country in 1854, four former Presidents, of both liberal and conservative complexion, led personal armies to the capital and ousted it. The leader of a personal army was in power from 1863 to 1867, when the official army overthrew him by a barracks revolt (one of the familiar *cuartelazos* of Latin American politics). Moreover, against the background of struggle for control of the centre, the countryside was the scene of almost endemic warfare between neighbouring valleys, towns and villages. The strong conservative Presidency of Núñez, 1880—94, imposed some order but on his death full-scale civil war, the notorious 'Thousand Days', broke out and at its end in 1902 had caused 100,000 casualties. The disruption in national life which the war brought about allowed the United States to arrange the secession of Panama without serious local hindrance, though the deed was to rankle for many years afterwards. But it also imposed the peace of exhaustion on the country, and a temporary renunciation of resort to force by both liberals and conservatives. An important outcome of the armistice was the reorganisation of the army, known as the *Reforma Militar*, one object of which was to turn it into the sort of professional and career institution which would end its involvement in party politics and equip it to deal impartially with factional attacks on the central power of the Republic.

The reform was successful, in that the army was not thereafter drawn into national politics for nearly 50 years. It became what the reformers wanted it to be, a career force, recruited from conscripts chosen by an equitable lottery, and officered by serious-minded young men from the provincial middle class. The ruling *élite*, whether liberal or conservative, forebore from making attempts to enlist its support in their party struggles. The deep-seated divisions in the country, scarcely alleviated by efforts to industrialise and to redistribute the untilled land of the latifundia by the liberal President Lopez (1934—8), nevertheless persisted. It was to be expected, therefore, that when a magnetic political leader arose, as he did in the person of Gaítan, a liberal who promised genuine economic and political reform, he should command an enormous following. His murder in the streets of Bogotá in 1948 led to catastrophic rioting (the *bogotazo*, which left 5000 dead) and accelerated a civil war in the countryside which had been simmering since 1946.

This extraordinary and terrible conflict, simply known in Colombia as *La Violencia*, was eventually to bring about the deaths of 200,000 people. It was 'not primarily a class struggle or even a spontaneous *jacquerie* . . . Though the liberals and communists (who called a conference of guerrilla leaders in 1952) attempted to give it political orientation and coherence, the violence remained largely unco-ordinated, purposeless and localised . . . The causes of *La Violencia* were complex and no doubt stemmed in part from the dormant regional rivalries and political feuds between local conservative and liberal bosses in the nineteenth century, which the polarisation of political attitudes in the 1940s had revived. Following the murder of Gaítan and the *bogotazo*, each side became convinced that the other was bent on its destruction.' Curiously, the violence remained confined to the countryside and, despite the peculiarly horrible form it took (reminiscent of nothing as much as the worst excesses of the Mau Mau in Kenya), remained unknown not only to the outside world but also to the populations of the big cities. The army, which had to attempt to contain it, was nevertheless well aware of what was going on and in June, 1953, impatient with the failure of the traditional politicians to deal with a crisis that threatened to destroy the country, the commander of the army, Rojas Pinilla, deposed the President and took power himself. The army's intervention was generally welcomed by the leaders of both the conservative and liberal parties.

His 4 years of power did succeed in reducing the level of

120

rural violence, partly by the application of new counter-insurgency techniques taught by the American-established Ranger School (*Escuela de Lanceros*). In 1957, however, he attempted to prolong his presidency and was overthrown by an alliance of conservative and liberals, with support from the army. The parties thereupon swore a 16 year truce and established a National Front to assure settled coalition government under which fundamental reforms of the country's problems could be tackled.

A 'ten-year plan' was agreed, which won the approval of the American-backed Alliance for Progress and attracted a considerable flow of foreign investment into the country, and an Agrarian Reform Institute was set up with the aim of buying out the latifundia, increasing the holdings of the poorest peasants and reducing the country's dependence on coffee as a source of foreign income. These measures achieved some success in damping popular discontent, but the tradition of armed independence had, by the 1960s, become institutionalised in the countryside. A number of 'peasant republics' had come into existence in the valleys of the Andes south of Bogotá and on the headwaters of the Amazon. In the 1950s they had come under the influence of left-wing parties and in the early 1960s were judged to be a threat to the security of the State. In 1962 the army therefore embarked on what was to be a major counter-insurgency operation. Its outcome is described under Current Developments.

Despite the responsibility laid on the army for preserving the security of the State, and the weakening of the pact sworn by liberals and conservatives in 1957 (which allowed, for example, Rojas Pinilla to campaign as a nominal independent conservative in the 1970 elections), it has shown no signs of re-entering the political arena. Whether, with so many examples of military intervention confronting it from neighbouring States (whose problems Colombia very largely shares), it can maintain its impartiality, it is impossible to predict. Current information does not suggest the existence of a strong *peruanista* faction in the Colombian officer corps.

STRENGTH AND BUDGET

Population: 27,520,000
Army: 57,000
Navy: 7,200 (including 2,500 marines); 10 major vessels
Air Force: 3,800; 40 combat aircraft
Paramilitary: 50,000 National Police
GNP: (1980) $32,740,000
Defence Expenditure: (1980) $301,100,000

The Colombian army has tripled in size since the late 1940s as a result of the need to suppress internal disorder in the country. The largest increase took place in the early 1950s, when *La Violencia* was at its height, and the size of the army has now decreased slightly from the 50,000 it reached in the mid-1960s.

Information about the military budget is difficult to obtain. The military share of the budget is believed to be about 16%, four-fifths of which is spent on personnel costs. Equipment purchases have for many years been a small factor.

COMMAND AND CONSTITUTIONAL STATUS

Article 120 of the 1968 Constitution empowers the President 'to control the public force, confer military ranks, preserve public order throughout the territory and re-establish it if it is disturbed, direct operations of war as Commander-in-Chief and provide for the external security of the Republic'.

As Commander-in-Chief the President is advised by the Supreme Council of National Defence (composed of the Ministers of Government (Interior), Foreign Affairs and Finance) and the High Military Council (composed of the Commanding General of the Armed Forces, the Chief of Staff of the Armed Forces, the Commanders of the Army, Navy and Air Force, the Commander of the Military Institutes Brigade, the Director of the Staff College and the Directory of the Military Industry Division). The Minister of National Defence, who is a serving officer, has administrative rather than command functions. The President exercises command through the Commanding General of the Armed Forces, whose own staff is the Armed Forces General Staff (*Estado General Mayor de Fuerzas Armadas*) under its Chief of Staff. This and the staffs of the three services are organised on the American model. The national police and various inter-service organisations (Directorate-General of Services and Military Industries Division) are also on the same chain of command as the commanders of the three armed services.

Although Colombia was under direct military rule between 1953 and 1957, and army officers have at other times been intimately involved in internal politics as individuals or groups, the Colombain army has generally during the present century preserved a professional aloofness from government. Its domestic reputation is as a professional and impartial organ of the State.

ROLE, COMMITMENT, DEPLOYMENT AND RECENT OPERATIONS

Because of the very deep-seated and violent party antipathies in Colombia, which have subjected the country to the longest and bloodiest internal disorders in Latin America, the army has a particularly important role not only as a force for the imposition of social discipline but also as an independent and impartial national institution which, all in all, it has very creditably discharged. It is also a successful protector of the national territory; the border dispute with Peru for possession of the Amazonian outpost of Leticia in 1932 ended in Colombia's favour. Colombia is a particularly devoted supporter of the United Nations, sent troops to the Emergency Force in Eygpt in 1956 and maintained an infantry battalion (thrice replaced) in Korea during the Korean war. The country is a signatory of the Chapultepec and Rio Pacts and has a military assistance agreement with the United States.

1st military Region (HQ Boyacá) covers National Capital and most of Boyacá department.
2nd Military Region (HQ Barranguilla) covers departments of Guajira, Magdalena, Bolívar, César and parts of Córdoba.
3rd Military Region (HQ Cali) covers departments of Valle del Cauca, Cauca, Nariño, Putumayo and part of Choco.
4th Military Region (HQ Medellín) covers Antioquia, most of Choco and parts of Córdoba.
5th Military Region (HQ Bucaramanga) covers departments of Arauca and Norte de Santander.
6th Military Region (HQ Ibagué) covers Tolima department.
7th Military Region (HQ Villavicencio) covers departments of Meta, Vichada, Vaupés and part of Boyacá.
8th Military Region (HQ Armenia) covers departments of Quindio and Rigaralda.
9th Military Region (HQ Neiva) covers Huila and Caqueta departments.
10th Military Region (HQ Melgar) covers parts of Cundinamarca and Tolima.

There is also a considerable concentration of troops, particularly instructional units, around Bogotá, the capital. The army has waged a serious internal security campaign against political militias and resistance groups since 1948, with intense periods of activity in 1953–6 and 1962–6. At least three guerrilla organisatons continue to operate inside the country, but do not seriously disturb internal order.

ORGANISATION

The Army is organised into the following branches: Infantry, Cavalry, Mechanised Troops, Artillery, Engineers, Signals, Intendence, War Material, Transport, Medical, Veterinary and Military Police. Infantry, Artillery and Engineers are organised into battalions; the Cavalry and Mechanised Troops are organised in groups. Supporting services, organised at company level, are further organised into combined Service battalions in the brigades. All units are named and numbered. There are 26 Infantry Battalions, a combined arms Presidential Guard Battalion, a Paratroop Battalion, a Ranger Battalion, one Mechanised and 6 Cavalry Groups (most of which are also mechanised), 6 Artillery Battalions, an Anti-aircraft Artillery Battalion and 6 Engineer Battalions. In addition the Infantry, Cavalry, Artillery and Engineer Schools each has a demonstration battalion or Group at full strength. The Brigades consist nominally of 3 Infantry Battalions, 1 Cavalry Group, 1 Artillery Battalion, 1 Engineer Battalion and 1 Service Battalion but only The 1st to 6th Brigades are at full strength, the remaining four having only 2 Infantry Battalions apiece and lacking combat support units. The Infantry Battalions are numbered sequentially throughout the Brigades, the combat and logistic support units deriving their numbers from those of the parent brigades. The Ranger and Paratroop Battalions are army level units and are stationed at Bogotá and Villavincencio, respectively. There is also an independent Mechanised Group at Bogotá. The Anti-aircraft Battalion is stationed at Barranca Bermeja.

The police are a national force (*Policía Nacional de Colombia*), which have been under the control of the Minister of Defence since 1960, and were organised into a single body in 1961. Some of those in the rural areas, who have received special training, are known as *Carabineros*. The force in 1976 numbered about 35,000.

RECRUITMENT, TRAINING AND RESERVES

Since 1886 universal conscription has been the law of the land. It was not enforced until this century and has never been applied to the whole annual contingent of males of military age. Decree 3338 of 1961 reiterated the provision that all Colombian men between eighteen and fifty were liable for military service, but the system in force is nevertheless selective. Of the 160,000 Colombian males who become eighteen each year, a large number (students in higher education, principal breadwinners and clerics) are immediately exempted. The names of the others are then entered in a lottery, held at municipal level. Sufficient names are drawn, together with those of two substitutes for each, to provide a recruit contingent of about 20,000. Service is for 2 years. Recruits are trained in branch schools rather than units, which accords a higher operational value to Colombian units than prevails in most Latin American conscript armies.

Officers are recruited by competitive examination among high school students and trained at the cadet school, Bogotá. Continuation training is provided at the arms schools and staff training, for selected candidates, at the war college (*Escuela Superior de Guerra*) which was founded in 1909 by a Chilean military mission. The collection of schools and training units, most of which are around Bogotá, form the Military Institutes Brigade. An important new foundation (1955) is the *Escuela de Lanceros* (Ranger School), established with American help to train the Colombian army in counterinsurgency and jungle warfare. Several thousand Colombians have also been trained at the United States School of the Americas in the Canal Zone. With the assistance of the United States military assistance group in the country, the army also began in 1962 an extensive civil-aid programme in the countryside. Part of the programme was designed to end illiteracy among army recruits (illiterates form about a quarter of the intake, which corresponds with the proportion in the population at large).

Time-expired conscripts remain on the reserve, which is divided into three classes, to the age of forty-five. Its size is calculated at between 250,000 and 300,000, but its military value is probably very low.

EQUIPMENT AND ARMS INDUSTRY

Colombia manufactures small-arms ammunition, but imports all its arms and equipment. Most of it is American and the rest French. The army's equipment is largely obsolete or obsolescent.

By the early 1980s most tracked AFVs were out of service and some Cavalry units were de-mechanised and re-horsed as an interim measure pending the acquisition of new equipment. In 1981, it was announced that 200 wheeled AFVs were being purchased from Brazil. Subsequently, it was also announced that new field artillery equipment was being acquired although no details of the quantities involved or their origins were revealed. It is also reported that a new main battle tank of unspecified type and origin is to be acquired.

Rifles: G3 7.62mm (Germany); SAFN 49 7.62mm (France)
Sub-machine-guns: Madsen M-46, M-50 and M-53 7.62mm (Denmark)
Machine-guns: M-2 12.7mm (US); M-1917 7.62mm (US); M-1919 7.62mm (US); Browning Automatic Rifle 7.62mm (US)
Mortars: 60mm (US); 81mm (US); 105mm (US)
Anti-armour weapons: 75mm RCL (US); 105mm RCL (US)
Artillery: M-101 105mm (US); M-116 75mm (US)
Air defence weapons: 40mm L/60 (Sweden and US)
Armour: M-4A3 medium tank (US); M3A1 light tanks (US); M-8 armoured car (US); M-20 armoured utility vehicle (US); M-3A2 half-track APC (US); EE-3 Jararaca scout car (Brazil); EE-9 Cascavel armoured car (Brazil); EE-11 Urutu APC (Brazil)
Aircraft: The Air Force operates about 40 transport aircraft and 30 helicopters.

RANK, DRESS AND DISTINCTIONS

General de División — Two gold suns
General de Brigada — One gold sun
Coronel — Three gold stars and bar
Teniente Coronel — Two gold stars and bar
Mayor — One gold star and bar
Capitán — Three gold stars
Teniente — Two gold stars
Subteniente — One gold star

Service and combat uniforms are American in style. Dress

uniforms are Germanic in style and the Presidential Guard has a distinctly Prussian uniform, complete with spiked helmet. There are a number of orders and decorations, including the Military Orders of San Mateo, San Carlos and Boyacá.

CURRENT DEVELOPMENTS

During *La Violencia* a number of so-called 'self-defensive zones', later to be called 'peasant republics', came into existence in central Colombia, the largest of them, Marquetalia, in the south of the State of Tolima. Rojas Pinilla's declaration of an amnesty at the start of his presidency did much to quell these elsewhere but in this remote area the Colombian communist party worked to transform the 'peasant republics' into foci of insurrectionary activity. Their armed bands caused little trouble outside the immediate areas they occupied but, as autonomous and potentially subversive centres, they were judged a threat by the National Front government which ousted Rojas Pinilla and in 1962 operations were opened to reduce them. The task was entrusted to the army's 6th Brigade, which eventually was joined by two others, and in March, 1965 the Marquetalia area was cleared of guerrillas and brought under direct government control. The survivors of the bands which escaped from the district went to form a new, mobile guerrilla force, under orthdox communist leadership, known as the *Fuerzas Armadas Revolucionarias Colombianas* (FARC), which was to remain mildly active in central Colombia. At the same time another left-wing guerrilla force, the *Ejército de Liberación Nacional* (ELN), founded by an admirer of Castro, Fabio Vásquez, began to operate in north-eastern Colombia, in the department of Santander. It at first made little impact until it was joined by the most notable left-wing leader of the period, the charismatic ex-priest Camilo Torres, who was killed in its ranks in the course of an operation by the 8th Brigade, specially formed to deal with the ELN, in February, 1966. Early in January, 1968 a third left-wing guerrilla movement, claiming Maoist allegiance, opened a campaign in the northern department of Bolívar. All remain active, but at such a low level of activity that none constitutes a serious threat either to internal security or to the stability of the government. Nevertheless, there is widespread political alienation in the country and profound economic and social distress. Though the army is capable of dealing with the current level of violence, which is far lower than that which it had to tackle in the 1950s or even in its campaign against the peasant republics in the 1960s, military power does not offer the solution to Colombia's problems.

John Keegan
Adrian English

COMORO ISLANDS

The Comoro Islands, consisting of four main islands and a number of smaller ones with a total area of 2236 km^2 and a population of about 300,000 occupy a potentially important strategic position at the northern end of the Moçambique Channel (between the Malagasy Republic and the east African coast) through which passes 90% of the Arab and Iranian oil destined for Europe. The islands are virtually without visible means of support, and the average annual per capita income about $50 makes them a leading contender for the title of poorest country in the world. There is however, a large armed force, devoted entirely to internal security duties, which has been variously reported at strengths of up to 11,000 men.

The four main islands of Grande Comore, Anjouan, Mayotte and Mohéli are ethnically very mixed, having been subjected to successive waves of settlement from the Malagasy Republic, Indonesia, Arab countries, Africa and Iran, with further variety being added subsequently by Portuguese and French colonisers and their imported Indian and Chinese plantation workers. On all of the islands the dominant language is a kind of Malagasy patois with degrees of Arabic and Swahili influence that vary from one island to another.

Culturally all of the islands except Mayotte have been most strongly influenced by Arab culture and have adopted the Muslim faith. The traditional ruling *élite* was an amalgamation of the original Arab conquerors (no longer racially distinct) and the Shirazis, of Iranian origin, who arrived via Zanzibar in the seventeenth century. Although an Arab–Shirazi sultanate also ruled on Mayotte, that island has retained a strongly Indian and Malagasy character, and the inhabitants became for the most part adherents of the Roman Catholic church over the course of the last three centuries.

This deep division between Mayotte (population about 40,000) and the other islands was the principal stumbling block in the way of a smooth progression to independence from France, since the inhabitants of Mayotte, with bitter memories of Arab–Shirazi rule, had no intention of being submerged in an Islamic Comoran State run from Moroni on Grande Comore. It is also clear, however, that France was extremely reluctant to surrender Mayotte, the only island whose deepwater harbour potential makes it a possible strategic base.

Paris therefore consented to the demand by the inhabitants of Mayotte that the referendum on independence in 1974 be held separately on each island. The three Muslim islands voted almost unanimously for independence, but the population of Mayotte voted 65% against independence. In an attempt to forestall the expected separation of Mayotte from the other islands, the Comoran Chamber of Deputies voted for an immediate unilateral declaration of independence on July 6th, 1975 and elected Ahmad Abdallah, the President of the Executive Council since 1972, as President of the new State. This declaration of independence, however, had no practical effect on Mayotte, which remained under the conrol of France.

Less than a month later, on August 3rd, 1975 President Ahmad Abdallah was ousted by a coup mounted by the principal opposition parties, making use of mercenary forces provided by Colonel Bob Denard, a well-known French Basque soldier-of-fortune who had been providing mercenary services in a large number of African countries ever since the Congo troubles of the early 1960s. The Comoran leader of this coup was Ali Soilih, who was formally appointed President by the Revolutionary Council on January 2nd, 1976. At the same time France extended formal recognition to the Comoro Islands, but when President Soilih attempted to mount an unarmed landing on Mayotte and followed that by nationalising all French assets on the islands, Paris replied by withdrawing all its personnel including its indispensable teachers and doctors.

At this point the Comoros faced economic disaster, with only 675 tons of rice remaining to take the islanders through 6 months to the next harvest. International emergency aid succeeded in staving off a famine, but the chaotic and brutal rule of President Soilih during the next 34 months reduced the islands to a truly terrible state. Proclaiming a 'cultural revolution', he dismissed the entire civil service of 3500, replacing them mainly with semi-literate high-school students, and ordered the burning of every file in the government records. The voting age was lowered to fourteen, and even telephones and typewriters were systematically smashed in the regime's revolutionary zeal.

Traditional Comoro customs such as elaborate marriage ceremonies were banned, and a complete break with the past was proclaimed. A formal political system of 'direct democracy' on the Libyan model was proclaimed, but actual enforcement of the dictator's decrees was placed in the hands of a 'people's army' or presidential militia comprised mainly of tough young men between the ages of sixteen and twenty. The stated purpose of the army was 'revolutionary construction', plus a vague future commitment to 'the reconquest of Mayotte', but its main activities were extortion and terrorism on behalf of the regime. Entire villages suspected of disloyalty were frequently razed and their inhabitants tortured and murdered. Large numbers of refugees fled to Mayotte.

Further troubles heaped on the Comoros included anti-Comoran riots in the Malagasy Republic which forced the mass repatriation of the 60,000 Comoran immigrants in the Majunga region to already severely overpopulated Grande Comore and Anjouan, and an abortive rising on the latter island in June, 1976 which was savagely suppressed. A certain tenuous contact was maintained with Tanzania, whose interest in keeping Indian Ocean islands out of the hands of the great powers caused it to lend President Soilih a few Tanzanian military advisers, but a Comoran application to join the Arab League in 1977 was met with little enthusiasm. The regime's other main external contacts were with Libya and China (which maintained the only foreign diplomatic mission in the country), and despite considerable foreign aid from Arab sources the economy had almost totally disintegrated by early 1978. Almost all the foreign development aid that was received was diverted to buying military equipment and paying foreign advisers (i.e. mercenaries). Food production had declined drastically, disease was rife and infant mortality was soaring.

At this point reappeared Colonel Bob Denard, this time in league with former president Ahmad Abdallah whom he had overthrown on Ali Soilih's behalf less than 3 years before. On the night of May 13th, 1978 Denard led 50 mercenaries, armed only with sawn-off shotguns and hand grenades, ashore from a French-registered trawler anchored off Moroni, and seized control of the government. Resistance was minimal — only three presidential guards were killed, and one mercenary was wounded in the arm — and in 2 hours Ali Soilih was a prisoner. After taking part in a re-enactment of the invasion for the benefit of a French television team which fortuitously arrived in the islands, Ali Soilih was shot and killed 'while trying to escape 2 days later.

The new government was announced as a 'political—military directorate' consisting of two Co-Presidents, Ahmad Abdallah and his colleague Muhammad Ahmad, and Colonel Denard as Defence Minister, Commander-in-Chief of the Armed Forces and Chief of Police. Denard assumed Comoran citizenship, embraced Islam, and took the new name of Said Mustapha Mohadjou in order better to fit his new role of 'participating in national reconstruction and forming a viable army and police force of quality'. This did not suffice to calm the indignation of other African nations, most of which are understandably terrified by the idea of white mercenary involvement in African domestic politics, and there was talk of a boycott of the Comoros by the Organisation of African Unity. Accordingly, Colonel Denard agreed to resign his posts and leave the country on September 27th, 1978.

A few days later a referendum on a new constitution was held which yielded a 99.31% affirmative vote, and Co-President Muhammed Ahmad resigned in order to clear the way for Ahmad Abdallah to assume the presidency. The new constitution is of the federal type, leaving the way clear for the accession of Mayotte at some future date, but this does not seem likely any time soon. A referendum held on February 8th, 1976 resulted in a 99.4% vote for retaining that island's links with France, and in a further referendum on May 11th of that year Mayotte voted against remaining an Overseas Territory (TOM) of France, preferring the closer connection involved in becoming an Overseas Department (DOM). Paris promised to implement the electorate's wishes, although the United Nations recognises the government in Moroni as sole representative of the whole island group.

The future composition of the Comoros army is unclear, but it is certain that the regime will continue to need such a force for internal security purposes. It is very probable that much of its strength will continue to consist of the youthful members of the former 'people's army', if only because they are too dangerous to be left wandering around outside it, and that numbers of Denard's mercenaries will be retained in some more tactful capacity in an effort to train and discipline the force. The future of the strategic island of Mayotte seems for the moment to be securely tied to France, and the island is gradually developing into a major French base in the southern Indian Ocean, with several thousand French military personnel in residence or in transit at most times.

Gwynne Dyer

CONGO*

HISTORY AND INTRODUCTION

The former French colony of Middle Congo attained independence in 1960, styling itself Congo; it is often referred to as Congo—Brazzaville. Its history since independence has been turbulent and confusing, the mixture of ethnic, political and armed forces' rivalries being peculiarly complex. At independence the government was headed by the Abbé Youlou — pro-French and right wing, from the centre of the country. His government fell in 1963; strikes and riots led to his downfall. Although French troops were flown in to protect lives and property, the French did not seek to perpetuate the Abbé's regime. He was succeeded by President Massemba-Debat — moderate left, also from the centre of the country — at the head of a government which included non-political soldiers and a number of left-wing socialists. This government moved rapidly leftwards, the more moderate ministers being replaced and an armed youth movement created; an attempt by the army to overthrow the government and destroy the youth movement in 1966 was suppressed by 200 Cuban troops of another body — a newly formed people's militia. In 1968—9 the country entered a period of turmoil: Massemba-Debat first dissolved the legislature, next a military coup under Captains Ngouabi and Raoul took place, then for a brief period Massemba-Debat and the army attempted to govern jointly though a larger National Revolutionary Council. This failed and Massemba-Debat resigned while the army attacked and destroyed the People's Militia and armed youth movement supporters in a 2 day engagement. Finally within the army, Captain Ngouabi emerged as the dominant figure, his popularity being based on support from northern Mbochi Kouyou soldiers, the majority group in the army.

Ngouabi remained Head of State until 1977; a Kouyou, representing northern interests, he met with increasing opposition from the south and centre expressed both in conservative and extreme-left political views. Lieutenant A. Diawara, who led an insurrectionary movement from 1972 until his death in 1973, was a Lari from the geographical centre of the territory, but of extreme-left ideology. Other plots and abortive coups were also reported in this period.

Events came to a head in March, 1977 when Ngouabi made a rough attempt to broaden the basis of his government and liberalise the regime. In a confused and violent reaction by several groups of officers, Ngouabi was killed: the blame was laid upon the luckless Massemba-Debat who was subsequently executed. The new regime was headed by another junior officer, J. Yhombi-Opongo. Emerging as an increasingly important figure was Yhombi's deputy, Denis Sassou Ngouesso, who favoured closer links with the USSR; Sassou held the Defence portfolio. In February 1979 Yhombi was removed from office; resentment against his opulent lifestyle and doubts over his mental stability were the main causes. Sassou became Head of State but despite his ideological preferences almost immediately sought French aid, with considerable success, as all the USSR would offer was insufficient and, in the event, often not delivered. Sassou's regime has therefore continued the strange mixture of official Marxist-Leninist rhetoric and growing links with American capital

and French aid which characterised its two predecessors. The most powerful figures in Sassou's government are northerners and Marxist hard-liners, but there are important counter-balancing moderate and southern groupings. The politics of the Congo are essentially those of three themes: north versus centre and south, free enterprise versus Marxism, and rival factions within the army and the police. None of the grouping runs parallel, and the police gendarmerie is additionally divided into at least two rival security departments and a border guard, and it is said that different sections of the army staff do, in practice, control different units of the army. A national assembly exists, but is of little significance and is in any case limited to members of the one permitted party, the Congolese Labour Party.

A noteworthy feature of the Congo is that half of its population lives in towns: one-fifth of the country's population lives in Brazzaville; this and certain other historical events of the colonial period have served to produce more acute tensions amidst changing societies than elsewhere. Other causes of instability include a high birth rate and a high primary literary rate.

STRENGTH AND BUDGET

Population: 1,500,000 (approximate).
Armed Forces: 8700, including the army of 8000 with an air force of 500, a navy of 200, a police gendarmerie of approximately 1500 and a new people's militia said to be of some 2000.
GNP: $900,000,000 (estimate).
Defence Expenditure: $80,000,000 (approximate).

COMMAND AND CONSTITUTIONAL STATUS

President Colonel D. Sassou-Ngouesso remains Commander-in-Chief. The Minister for Defence is Colonel N'Gollo. The army is styled the People's National Army; its chief of staff is Colonel E. Elenga.

ROLE, COMMITMENT, DEPLOYMENT AND RECENT OPERATIONS

The Congo has been so preoccupied with its own affairs that its army has had little time for preparations to meet external threats. Relations with Zaïre pass through phases of friendship and hostility — Zaïre was alleged to have supported Diawara's 1972 rising — and the Congo River Bank and land border is occasionally guarded, particularly in the Brazzaville area. Recently the confused situation on the Cabinda border led to some reinforcement of units in the area.

In 1971, following an unsuccessful coup attempt in which many police gendarmerie officers were involved, it was announced that the gendarmerie was to be dissolved and its duties given to the army. How this has been effected in practice, and the position of the new people's militia is in these changed circumstances not known. One distinct possibility is that the people's militia is simply a polite name for the small permanent Cuban presence, with the cosmetic addition of a few Congolese, the whole forming a small *Waffen SS.*

---

* For general notes on African armies, see Appendix 1.

ORGANISATION

The formal army is composed of an armoured unit, an infantry battalion, a 'parachute commando' battalion and an engineer and an artillery unit; how far former police gendarmerie units have been linked to the army structure is not known.

RECRUITMENT, TRAINING AND RESERVES

Traditionally the army has been largely recruited voluntarily from northern peoples, notably the Mbochi Kouyou; the Ngouabi government generally preserved this arrangement. Nevertheless the members of the gendarmerie drafted into the army in 1971 constitute a different ethnic following — and conflicting loyalties. In the early 1960s many of the officers were southerners, chiefly Bakongo. These have now mostly been replaced by northerners.

At independence France agreed to supply cadres and training staff, but these became associated with the Youlou government and no further staff were sent after his fall. (The two army mutinies that occurred in the Youlou period appear to have been anti-French).

A Soviet military mission at least 100 strong, and an East German mission only slightly smaller assist with military training. There are also in the Congo permanently based, a Cuban military unit of approximately 600 supposedly concerned with the national youth movement, while a further 3,000 Cuban troops use rest camp facilities near Pointe-Noire on rotation from Angola.

EQUIPMENT AND ARMS INDUSTRY

The armoured unit possesses fifteen Chinese type 59 and fourteen type 62 tanks, together with some 35 Soviet T54/T55 vehicles. The army also possesses twelve PT76 light reconnaissance tanks and 25 BRDM 1 or BRDM 2 armoured vehicles. The 'Parachute-Commando' battalion and the infantry battalion have between them 20 BTR-50 tracked armoured personnel carriers, and 24 BTR-60 and 44 BTR-152 wheeled carriers. The Soviet equipment originated from Cuba and China rather than the USSR. The artillery possesses ten 100mm and eight 122mm Soviet pieces, and six French 75mm guns. There are also unknown — but small — numbers of 82 and 120mm mortars, 57mm, 76mm and 100mm anti-tank guns, 57mm rocket launchers and 37mm anti aircraft guns. One report claims a recent delivery of new Soviet weapons including BM 21-artillery rocket launchers.

The air force operates one MIG-15 and twenty MIG-17 fighter aircraft, all obsolete. For transport purposes one Fokker F28, five Antonov 24, five Ilyushin 14 and three C47 provide an ill-assorted mixture. There are in addition approximately six light liaison aircraft and four French Alouette and one Puma helicopters.

RANK, DRESS AND DISTINCTIONS

These follow French patterns; the *képi* is however replaced by a peaked cap.

CURRENT DEVELOPMENTS

The army is a doubtfully loyal armed political support group for the regime in power. Its combat value in action with an enemy army would be virtually nil and the serviceability of its apparently impressive force of armoured fighting vehicles is unlikely to extend much beyond independence day parades.

Lloyd Mathews

COSTA RICA

Costa Rica has always been unique in Central America. It was a small, relatively prosperous white nation of small-property-owning farmers in a region of extremely backward, deeply divided countries with very large Indian and mestizo populations which were dominated by tiny *élites* of rich land-owners. It has been consistently ruled by civilian, democratic governments, while all its neighbours have spent the greater part of their histories under military rule. In 1948 it added a further distinction: it abolished its army entirely, converted the main barracks in San José into a museum of fine arts, and devoted its military budget to education.

Costa Rica has shared both the international environment of its neighbours and their economic problems. It formed part of the Captaincy-General of Guatemala in the Spanish colonial period, was briefly incorporated into the Mexican empire of Maximiliano de Iturbide in 1821–3, and was part of the Confederation of Central America until it broke up in 1838. It fought a serious border war with Nicaragua in the dying days of the Confederation in 1836, and its army played a large part in the war of 1853–7 which defeated the troops of the North American filibuster William Walker in Nicaragua. In 1921 a border dispute with Panama led to armed clashes (the boundary was settled by treaty in 1944).

Throughout the colonial period and the nineteenth century Costa Ricans mostly lived by subsistence agriculture, just like their Central American neighbours. In the twentieth century the country's income has derived largely from the export of tropical agricultural products, coffee, bananas and cotton, just like the rest of Central America. The 2,000,000 Costa Ricans do not have richer lands, or more land per person, than elsewhere in the isthmus.

Yet Costa Rica's per captia GNP is approximately twice that of Guatemala, Honduras and El Salvador. Education is free and compulsory, and the literacy rate is the highest in Latin America. The sole episode of military dictatorship in the country's history occurred in 1870–72, and no soldier has been elected to the presidency since 1917.

The main reason for these striking differences is that the entire country was settled by immigrants from Galicia and other parts of northern Spain. There were never many Indians in the territory, and so the *latifundia* system never became established in what is now Costa Rica; the immigrants settled down to become a homogeneous society of peasant farmers. After independence, therefore, the alliance between the army and the large landowners so familiar elsewhere in Latin America never developed, and the army had little incentive to intervene in politics. Similarly, when the development of an export-oriented cash economy and influences from the outside world began to move Costa Rican politics leftwards in the first half of this century, there was no army–landowner alliance to thwart it as there was elsewhere.

By the 1940s, consequently, both major Costa Rican political parties had adopted greater or lesser amounts of social-democratic doctrine, and the ruling National Republican Party of President Teodoro Picado Michalski was actually in a close relationship with the Popular Vanguard Party, the 'popular front' version of the small but vigorous Costa Rican Communist Party. When Picado lost the 1948 Presidential election to Otilio Ulate of the rival National Liberation Party, however, the NRP-controlled Congress attempted to nullify the election result. This led to an outbreak of civil war which lasted 2 months, and ended with the decision to abolish the regular armed forces.

The leader of the NRP, José Figueres, organised a rebel army to enforce the results of the election; the regular army continued to obey the incumbent government, and President Picado also permitted the communist leaders to organise some 2000 armed and disciplined followers to aid it. After several bloody clashes the popular forces led by Figueres defeated both the regular army and the communist militia, and Ulate was duly installed as president. Immediately after the rebel victory the regular army was disbanded, and a constitutional amendment of 1949 forbade the establishment or maintenance of a national army in future. A temporary military force may only be organised for urgent reasons of national defence.

Since then Costa Rica has relied for its defence and internal security primarily on the Civil Guard, a relatively small but well-trained volunteer force having both police and para-military duties. It numbers about 3000 men, all long-service volunteers, and functions as a police force in the national capital, San José, and the six provincial capitals. (A separate force called the Town and Village Police, numbering some 2500 men and trained to less exacting standards, maintains public order in other parts of the national territory).

The Civil Guard, approximately half of which is stationed in San José, is organised essentially along military lines, with military rank titles and terminology, and equipment designed primarily for tactical military, rather than civil police, operatons. It includes some special units, such as the *élite* Presidential Guard, the Traffic Force, the Detective Force, and a small Air and Sea Force with four coastal patrol boats and a few Cessna light aircraft, but the bulk of its strength is organised in companies ranging from 80 to 350 men. Companies are rotated periodically between mountain and coastal provinces. The Third Company, a large unit base in the capital through which personnel are rotated for training from throughout the nation, functions as a ready reserve and has charge of the arms and ammunition of the entire Civil Guard.

The President of the Republic is commander-in-chief of all public forces; the Civil Guard is under the jurisdiction of the Minister of Public Security, with a civilian Director-General of Public Forces in charge of day-to-day operations. However, the Minister of Government provides the budgetary allocation for supplies and equipment (the 1966 budget was $2,300,000), and the Minister of the Presidency has control over the National Police School. The senior officer of the Guard, with the title of Director, holds the rank of colonel.

The Civil Guard is one of the best-trained forces in Latin America. The National Police School, founded in 1963, provides both recruit trair.ing and higher-level courses, and almost 10% of the Guard's personnel have received specialised training outside the country (principally in the United States army schools in the Canal Zone, or in the USA). Ranks, uniforms and rank insignia are virtually identical with those of the United States army. Most of the Civil Guard's armament and equipment has been furnished through United States military assistance programmes, administered by a United States army Mission accredited to the country. United States military assistance amounted to $1,800,000 in the years 1950–70, plus an additional $113,000 in excess military stocks.

It will be clear from the foregoing that Costa Rica's claim to have abolished its armed forces is an amiable deception, or at least an exaggeration. What it has done, with notable success, is to restrict its armed forces to the minimum level actually necessary to maintain public order in a fairly stable country, and to demilitarise them.

The Civil Guard, despite its small size, has shown itself entirely capable of handling problems along the border like those of 1949 and 1955, when Costa Rican exiles launched small invasions from Nicaraguan territory. To contend with a hypothetical military confrontation of larger magnitude — the only conceivable one being a clash over the border dispute with Nicaragua — the Guard could deploy almost all its regular forces on the frontier (there is a volunteer reserve of several thousand who meet weekly for drill and instruction, and could take over many internal security duties in any emergency). Should the highly trained units of the Civil Guard prove unable to deal with such forces of the Nicaraguan army as could be detached from guarding the government in Managua (which seems improbable), it has behind it an entire nation of peasant farmers who are familiar with firearms.

In times past Coata Rica's standard response to border provocations has been to call in observers from the Organisation of American States to stabilise the situation: this worked in 1949 and 1955, when the Nicaraguan government was training Costa Rican exiles to invade the country. It prefers to have recourse to the OAS (to whose peace-keeping force it contributed a Civil Guard contingent during the 1965 Dominican civil war) rather than to the UN, or to the moribund Central American international institutions. Though Costa Rica belongs to the Organization of Central American States and the Central American Common Market, it does not belong to the Central American Defence Council (CONDECA), which it regards as being a league for the defence of right-wing military rule dominated by Guatemala, El Salvador and Honduras.

Relations with Nicaragua have indeed varied between cool and hostile. In addition to the intense ideological antipathy the Somoza military dynasty of Nicaragua feels towards its democratic, 'leftist' neighbour to the south, there exists a serious border dispute between the two countries over the San Juan river region on the Pacific Coast: in 1969 Nicaraguan maps were published showing the boundary 18 miles within Costa Rican territory. The Nicaraguan regime tends to stoke up this dispute as a diversionary tactic at times of internal difficulties, and in late 1977 a Nicaraguan aircraft strafed a launch on the San Juan river which had the Costa Rican Minister of Public Security on board. The dispute is not likely, however, to escalate into a full-scale military conflict.

There have, however, been signs that the Sandinista guerrillas, who launched a full-scale rebellion in Nicaragua in late 1978, have made use of Costa Rican bases for some of their forays. Diplomatic relations between the two countries were severed in late November and since then there have been outbreaks of border fighting between Sandinista guerrillas and Nicaraguan Guardsmen.

Costa Rica's original solution to the problem of military intervention in politics has been an outstanding success. The Civil Guard has shown itself to be an entirely professional, obedient and apolitical force. Civilian governments and democratic elections have succeeded one another without undue turbulence since 1948.

The various governments led by Figueres's National Liberation Party pursued moderately social-democratic policies, established friendly relations with socialist States, and in 1975 restored the Communist and other extreme left-wing parties to legality, all without encountering the extreme right-wing violence customary in other Central American States. There was an alleged plot with Guatemalan support to overthrow the President in 1976, and there are the usual sporadic bombing campaigns by right- and left-wing extremists which are now familiar in most of the world's countries, but the constitution remains safe and the Civil Guard obedient. In February, 1978 the leader of the opposition Unity Coalition, Rodrigo Carazo, was elected to the Presidency in an election which was exemplary for its peacefulness and honesty.

Gwynne Dyer

CUBA

HISTORY AND INTRODUCTION

Cuba is governed by the leaders of a guerrilla movement which overthrew the former regime in 1959 and who have preserved from those heroic days the ethos and aims as well as the appearance of revolutionary soldiers. The great majority of those at the head of every sector of public life in Cuba hold military rank, affect a military style, represent their aims and methods in military language and encourage the militarisation of the enterprises over which they preside. At the outset, the military model to which they conformed was that of the guerrilla band. As the 'revolution' has 'matured', the political style of the regime — which adopted an open and orthodox Soviet-communist alignment in 1961 — has approximated more closely to one based on a conventional regular army of the communist pattern. The Cuban Communist Party is, nevertheless, a far more 'military' organisation than any of its counterparts within the rest of the Soviet orbit. The army which the regime has created, and which has become in the last 3 years an important instrument of Soviet power in Africa, has developed from its revolutionary origins into a wholly orthodox version of the Soviet-style regular army, organised for the internal and external defence of the State, the indoctrination and training of the nation's youth and for operations overseas in the furtherance of the aims of the Soviet bloc.

The army which Fidel Castro and his July 26th Movement defeated in 1959 had been brought into being by the American provisional government of Cuba, after the United States had expelled the Spanish colonial government in 1908. Based on the *Guardia Rural*, a militarised police force, the Cuban army did not aspire to, or indeed reach, a much higher level of organisation in its first 20 years of existence. It did not attract the sons of the established classes, but tended to be officered by promoted sergeants, and accordingly was held in low esteem. Under the dictatorship of Machado, however, the army began to be used as an arm of the administration, which much increased its importance, and also the resentment of those *oficinistas* (would-be officers) who had been denied promotion. Machado's isolation from popular support prompted a group of *oficinista* sergeants in 1933 to lead a coup against him. Its success led to the dismissal of the entire officer corps and its replacement by sergeants favoured by the *golpistas*, foremost among whom was the future dictator, Fulgencio Batista. At first as Chief-of-Staff and then (1940) as President, Batista ruled Cuba until 1944, when his populist tendencies prompted him to hold elections under conditions which allowed the electorate a free choice. It fell upon the democrat Grau San Martín, whom he had installed after the 1933 coup, and who passed the succession to an ally in 1948. On the eve of the presidential elections of 1952, Batista returned from his place of exile in Florida, organised old friends in the upper ranks of the army and seized power before it could be legitimately transferred. Cuba's large and well-educated middle-class were outraged by the coup, which Batista consolidated by brutal repression of protest, and a number of groups began organising armed rebellion against him. One of these, led by Fidel Castro, then a law student, attacked the Moncada barracks on July 26th, 1953 but was repulsed, and many of its members were murdered in the aftermath. Castro was tried, but released on amnesty in 1955,

and at once organised a new resistance group, entered the country in December, 1956 and set up a guerrilla base in the mountains of Oriente province, the Sierra Maestra. Batista deployed the army against them, the high point of his campaign being an encircling attack in June, 1958 at San Domingo. It failed and thereafter Castro, who by then had numerous supporters in the towns, went over to the offensive. There was little fighting. Batista's army became demoralised by its inability to find and hit the guerrillas and by its evident unpopularity. Its morale collapsed and on January 1st, 1959, as Castro's emboldened forces (which never numbered more than 2000) entered the main cities, Batista fled abroad.

Castro's guerrilla army, one of whose principal leaders was the later-to-be-legendary Ché Guevara, was quickly swelled by covert supporters and bandwaggon-jumpers into a large popular militia. And at first a large armed force was needed, to repel the anti-Castroists who attempted to invade the country (including the group who landed with American support at the Bay of Pigs in April, 1961) and who remained at large in the interior. But this so-called 'anti-bandit campaign', which allegedly destroyed 179 bands of infiltrators or insurrectionaries (particularly in the Escambray mountains, Las Villas province), was largely over by 1963, in which year Castro announced, despite an earlier rejection of the step, his decision to introduce conscript service and so form a conventional army. He had many reasons for doing so, but one may have been a waning faith in the invincibility of the guerrilla approach, following the failure of expeditions to Haiti, the Dominican Republic, Nicaragua, Guatemala and Panama. Thereafter the chief proponent of the export of revolution through guerrilla warfare was to be Ché Guevara, who was to be killed in 1967 in an unsuccessful attempt to transplant it to Bolivia. But the most important reasons for the introduction of conscription were the need to discipline and indoctrinate the youth of the country in Marxist principles, which had become the official creed of the regime in 1961, and to provide a large mass of cheap labour to increase and diversify agricultural output. During the middle and late 1960s the army played a major role in agriculture; farm machinery was in fact concentrated in 1967 in the Ché Guevara Brigade, run by officers seconded from mechanised units.

America's forthright reaction to Russia's attempt to establish missile bases on the territory of its new ally in 1962 had inhibited the development of the Cuban armed forces as a strategic force. In early 1972, however, a large Soviet training mission entered the country, bringing with it much modern equipment to supplement that already supplied. The size of the army, which had fallen to under 100,000 from the peak of 300,000 it had reached during the 'anti-bandit campaign' in 1963, began to rise. The reason for this expansion was revealed in early 1975 when Cuban forces, transported by Russian ships and planes, began to appear in Angola at the side of the MPLA guerrillas. That movement, after Portugal's announcement of her intention to withdraw from the colony, had agreed to share power with the two other independence movements. But, on the FNLA's alignment with Peking, Russia apparently decided to see that the MPLA won, and deployed the Cubans as a proxy instrument of her strategy. The intervention was a remarkable success and the

Cuban expeditionary force, to the extreme disquiet of the Western powers, and against their vain protests, has subsequently appeared in Somalia, Ethiopia, Moçambique and in smaller numbers in half a dozen other African countries. Foiled initially in his own continent, Castro and his army are busily propagating the revolution across the Atlantic.

STRENGTH AND BUDGET

Population: 9,900,000
Army: 180,000
Navy: 10,000; 4 major vessels, 90 smaller craft
Air force: 16,000; 190 combat aircraft; 24 air-defence missile battalions
Paramilitary: 15,000 State security troops; 3000 Frontier Guards; 100,000 Labour Army; 500,000 Territorial Militia
GNP (1980 estimate): $18,400,000,000
Defence expenditure (1980 estimate): $1,126,000,000

Under the Batista regime the proportion of the budget devoted to defence varied between 15 and 25%. More recent figures are difficult to come by. It has been estimated that the proportion in 1965 was 8.4%. It is certainly now very much higher but is covered to a large extent by subsidy from the Soviet Union. Castro is reported to have announced in 1970 that Russia had supplied military equipment to Cuba to the value of $1,500,000,000.

COMMAND AND CONSTITUTIONAL STATUS

Article 129 of the Fundamental Law (Constitution) appoints the President as Supreme Commander, but the position is nominal. Fidel Castro, as Prime Minister and First Secretary of the Cuban Communist Party is Commander-in-Chief. The Minister of the Revolutionary Armed Forces (his brother, Raúl Castro) stands at the head of the chain of command, which runs to the general staff of the armed forces, headed by a vice-minister/chief of staff, assisted by a vice-minister for supply. The chain then separates into three: one branch runs to the chief of operations and the operational units; another to the chiefs of armour, artillery, *Defensa Civil*, and the political sections (commissars); and the third to the paramilitary forces (Frontier Guard, etc.) The Council of Ministers is empowered to fix the size of the armed forces and decide on their organisation. In practice, power resides with the Central Committee of the Cuban Communist Party, which is two-thirds military in composition (in that its members wear uniform and hold military rank), and more particularly with the Politburo of the Central Committee, of which three-quarters hold military rank. Castro, as Commander-in-Chief, is believed to deal directly with the commanders of operational formations, and the Minister of the Armed Forces to play a chiefly administrative role.

As in all communist armies, the commissar system is an important element in the control and indoctrination of the units. Under the head of the Political Section, communist party cells work in each formation and unit down to company level. The head of the cell has authority equal to that of the formation or unit commander, except in purely military matters. His mission is 'to assure military loyalty and efficiency and help leaders in the strict fulfilment of their assigned duties, to give instruction in Marxist principles to the unit's members, to prevent deviation from the socialist line and guard against defeatism'.

Cuban units operating in Africa seem to have generally been under the operational control of Soviet commanders.

ROLE, COMMITMENT, DEPLOYMENT AND RECENT OPERATIONS

Role

Cuba under Castro is a highly militarised society. Military service is obligatory and genuinely universal, and its object is not only to provide a large standing army and an even larger reserve, which it does, nor even to furnish a plentiful supply of cheap agricultural labour, which it also does, but to politicise, and above all discipline, Cuban youth. Military influence pervades the highest political levels. Almost all Cubans of importance hold military rank and wear military uniform. The language and ethos of the ruling party, the Communist Party of Cuba, are very military and hark back to the heroic guerrilla days of the leaders in the Sierrra Maestra. Attempts to distinguish, therefore, an army role distinct from that of the apparatus of the State are more difficult than in other countries, even other communist countries. Nevertheless, it is possible to point to: the defence of the national territory; civic aid and rural development; the maintenance, with the paramilitary organisations, of internal security; the clandestine training of foreign military and guerrilla personnel; and the execution of military missions abroad, particularly in Africa, under the aegis of the Soviet Union. That role began with the deployment of Cuban units to Angola in 1975.

Commitment

Cuba is still legally a signatory of the Chapultepec and Rio Defence Pacts and a member of the Organisation of American States, but has been excluded from its workings by a decision of OAS foreign ministers since 1962. Although Cuba has a close military association with the Soviet Union, and has received a great deal of financial and military aid from her, the two countries have no military agreement which has been made public.

Deployment

Information on the Cuban Revolutionary Army is scarce but there are known to be three major geographical Commands, as follows:

Western (HQ Havana) covering the capital and the provinces of Havana and Pinar del Rio.
Central (HQ Matanzas) covering the provinces of Matanzas, Villa Clara, Cienfuegos and Sancti Spiritus.
Eastern (HQ Santiago de Cuba) covering provinces of Santiago de Cuba, Guantánamo, Granma, Holsüín, Las Tunas, Camagüey and Ciego de Avila.

Each Command is garrisoned by an Army, subdivided into a variable number of Army Corps, each of three Infantry Divisions. Each Army also contains a single Armoured Division and a Mechanised Division. The Eastern and Central Armies each consists of only one Army Corps with headquarters at Pinar del Rio and Las Villas respectively. The Eastern Army contains two Army Corps, the respective headquarters of which are at Camagüey and Holgüín. The Western and Central Armies thus each appear to have a total of 5 divisions, whilst the Eastern Army seems to consist of 8 divisions.

The Isle of Youth (formerly Isle of Pines) has the status of a separate military region and is garrisoned by an Infantry Division, which brings the total number of this type of formation to 13. There are also 8 independent Infantry Regiments, with a static defence role and at least as many independent battalions with a similar function. Of the independent Regiments, the origins of which date back to pre-revolutionary times, three are believed to be located at or in

Cuba

the vicinity of Havana and one each at Santiago, Camagüey, Santa Clara, Matanzas and Pinar del Rio. Independent battalions are thought to be located at Cienfuegos, Sancti Spiritus, Ciego de Avila, Tunas, Holgüín, Bayamo and Guantánamo. There is also a General Staff Security Battalion, attached to Army headquarters at Havana. Army forces deployed in Cuba are completed by an Airborne Assault and Landing Brigade and an Artillery Division which controls all non-divisional artillery units. The Navy includes an Amphibious Assault Battalion and a number of security units for the defence of its shore installations. The Navy also mans some coast defence batteries equipped with SSC-2A SSMs. The Air Force mans 30 batteries of SA-2 and SA-3 SAMs.

Apart from the Armed Forces proper, there are several types of well-equipped paramilitary troops. These include the Ministry of the Interior Special Troops, which include two para-commando battalions and the Border Troops, also under the jurisdiction of the Ministry of the Interior, and which include a coast guard element with approximately 20 small vessels. The Department of State Security, the Cuban equivalent of the Soviet KGB, also under the control of the Ministry of the Interior, has about 10,000 Paramilitary troops.

The Cuban Expeditionary Forces in Angola and Ethiopia, each respectively have the status of an Army as jointly have the Foreign Military Assistance Forces deployed in smaller numbers in other countries. Total Cuban personnel deployed outside the country, by no means all of whom are military, are believed to number as follows:

Afghanistan: 100 military advisers.
Algeria: 170 military and civilian advisers.
Angola: 5,000 military and 3,000 civilian advisers.
Congo: 750 military and 200 civilian personnel.
Ethiopia: 6,000 almost entirely military personnel.
Grenada: 300 military and civilian advisers.
Guinea-Bissau: 100 military and 50 civilian personnel.
Iraq: 2,200 mainly military personnel.
Libya: 3,000 military and civilian advisers.
Malagasy: 50 military advisers.
Mozambique: 750 military and 150 civilian personnel.
Nicaragua: 200 military and 3,000 civilian personnel.
Sao Tomé: 75 civilian medical personnel.
South Yemen: 800 military personnel.
Tanzania: 100 civilian personnel.
Zambia: 25 military advisers.

Recent Operations
Following the falling-out between the three nationalist guerrilla movements which acceded to power after Portugal's decision to withdraw from Angola, Cuban units appeared in that country (early 1975), transported there in Soviet ships and aeroplanes. They joined forces with the Moscow-aligned MPLA, and fought three campaigns during the course of 1975: the first in the north against the FNLA guerrillas, whom they succeeded in driving into Zaïre (the guerrillas have since returned in some numbers); the second in the south, where South African forces had entered the country, but withdrew before making serious contact with the Cubans; the third in the east, against the UNITA guerrillas, whom they did not succeed altogether in subduing. Although the campaign was regarded as finished by early 1976, and a large number of Cubans were withdrawn, revived activity by UNITA, and to a lesser extent by the FNLA, has brought Cuban reinforcements back into the country, so that the number deployed there is reckoned to equal that present at the height of the campaign – about 15,000. Some are reported to have been involved in the unsuccessful invasion of Shaba province (Katanga) of Zaïre in March, 1977 by the

'ex-Katangese gendarmerie'. Cuban casualties in Angola are reported by their guerrilla enemies to be high but probably do not exceed a few hundred dead.

Cuban troops were next reported present in Somalia, but, following Russia's decision to back the Ethiopians in the Somali—Ethiopian border war, were transferred to Ethiopia, where they were deployed in late 1977. They took a major part in the Ethiopian counter-offensive which regained the Ogaden province from the Somalis in February—March, 1978. They were again reported to have suffered heavy casualties but these were probably exaggerated. Cuba gave active support to the Sandinista revolution in Nicaragua, mainly by the provision of arms and equipment. Since the success of the revolution in that country, a low level of Cuban military assistance seems to have continued including, the provision of advisers and instructors in the handling of small quantities of heavy military equipment apparently recently transferred but principally in the form of technical assistance in the rebuilding of the country's civilian infrastructure. Cuba has also supported the left-wing guerrillas in El Salvador, mainly morally but also with the supply of very limited quantities of military equipment. As can be seen from the above list, Cuban military and civilian advisers are widely active in Third World countries with a left-of-centre political orientation.

ORGANISATION

Information on the domestic and operational organisation of the Cuban Revolutionary Army is scanty. The Infantry, Cavalry, Armoured Forces and Artillery are organised into both regiments and independent battalions; Engineers, Signals, Medical and Logistic services in battalions and companies. Although Soviet military doctrines are supreme, the organisation of the Army does not follow Soviet models as closely as might be expected, resembling rather that of the Chinese People's Liberation Army or the Vietnamese People's Army. Based on the known composition of the tactical formations, there would appear to be at least 59 Infantry Regiments, 8 or more independent infantry battalions, 2 paratroop battalions; 12 Mechanised Cavalry and Armoured Regiments plus 11 independent armoured and 13 motorised reconnaissance battalions; 24 Artillery Regiments, 24 Air Defence Regiments and 11 Engineer Battalions. The overall strength is considerably less than that indicated by this relative proliferation of units, the establishments of the units being considerably less than in normal practice. A Cuban Infantry Regiment, at full peace establishment, numbers only 1,010 all ranks and a battalion 349. Armoured regiments consist of only 720 all ranks and tank battalions muster a mere 110. There are also three levels of combat readiness ranging from units at full establishment to those containing only a cadre of regular personnel. The home service Army consists of 3 Armoured Divisions, of which only one, stationed at Havana, is believed to be at full strength, 3 Mechanised Divisions, which may be almost fully manned and 13 Infantry Divisions, the majority, if not all of which are only cadres requiring reserve mobilisation to bring them up to operational strength. The full peace-time establishments of the three types of Cuban division are 6,200, 8,200 and 5,900 respectively.

There are a number of paramilitary organisations. They are: the Frontier Guard Corps, which are the armed customs guards; the Frontier Guards, about 3000 strong, whose principal role is to guard the perimeter of the American naval base at Guantánamo; the *Lucha Contra Bandidos*, a corps of rural vigilantes originally formed to trace incursions by anti-Castroists, but now engaged on rural development work (if still indeed a recognisable entity); the Young Labour Army (EJT), in which conscript youths unsuitable for military service do agricultural labour and rural development work, and which has absorbed all previously existing worker youth organisations; and the militia, known until 1969 as the *Milicia de la Defensa*, but then renamed the *Defensa Civil*. The militia, at the outset a mass organisation to which the party and the leadership accorded great importance, has been progressively downgraded in status. It was originally divided into combat companies, composed of men and women under thirty, and guard companies, composed of men and women between thirty and fifty. Its role was to 'guard the interests of the people by protecting the manufacturing and commercial installations of the country, and standing ready to defend the nation's cities in the event of hostilities while the regular forces are away at the front'. It was urban in composition and numbered at its height about 250,000. Originally its members held arms, with which they practised on ranges which were set up in all cities, and also practised guerrilla tactics. Arms were subsequently withdrawn and held in central locations. Its rural equivalent was the Workers' Militia, the peasant members of which were initially encouraged to work 20 days in the month in the fields and to spend the other ten in military training. Its importance has now also apparently been reduced.

Air defence is the responsibility of the Air-Defence Forces of the air force, which man 24 missile battalions equipped with Russian SA-2 and SA-3 missiles.

RECRUITMENT, TRAINING AND RESERVES

Castro's original declaration on seizing power, at the head of a force of guerrilla volunteers, was that 'we will not establish military service because it is not right to force a man to put on a uniform and a helmet, to give him a rifle and force him to march'. Four years later, however, he announced that conscription, together with compulsory secondary education, would be introduced, to prevent the emergence of the 'parasitical element, the potential *lumpen* of tomorrow'. His brother Raúl, the Minister of Defence, when introducing the compulsory military service law on November 12th, 1963 denied that it had been designed 'to do away with wasters' but nevertheless announced that the low starting age of seventeen had been chosen to include as many school-leavers as possible, who would be divided into two classes, those who would actually be allowed to bear arms and those who would do agricultural work, 'the wasters, *lumpen* and counter-revolutionaries'. In practice, all conscripts, who served for 3 years, spent part of their time in the fields or at civic-aid projects. This is still believed to be the case with units stationed in Cuba, whose members spend between a quarter and a third of their service (*Servicio Militar Obligado*) on non-military work. Recruits are inducted in April—May each year and given their basic training in a recruit-training centre, of which there is one in each of the field army areas (east, centre, west). They receive advanced training in their units. Technicians are trained at the Military Technical Institute, Manano, Havana.

Officers may be chosen in one of three ways: by direct appointment; by volunteering; or by selection from the ranks of the conscripts, this last being effectually the main route. There are a number of officer-training institutions: the Military Academy, for infantry officers; the Camilo Cienfuegos Artillery School, for artillery officers; and the Antonio Macco Interservice Cadet School for armoured, mechanised, signals, engineer and other officers. Higher military studies

are also conducted in these schools, apparently by Soviet personnel. Cadets must be between sixteen and twenty-one and most belong to the *Unión de Jóvenes Comunistas.*

In the late 1960s the government set up a number of military preparatory schools, called Camilo Cienfuegos Schools, and there is now one in each of the six provinces. Pupils (called *Camilitos*) are aged ten to sixteen and receive a normal education along with their military training. They are apparently intended to supply the officer-training institutions. The total number of pupils in the early 1970s was about 16,000.

Time-expired conscripts go to form the reserve, which now numbers about 90,000. Conscripts who so volunteer may engage as regular soldiers for a 5 year term and as many as half are said to do so, though only a small proportion are accepted.

The militia, which used to form a parallel army, available for duty in emergency, has been progressively downgraded in importance. In April, 1973 all militiamen were given the honorary rank of *subteniente* in the Revolutionary Armed Forces but ordered to cease wearing their militia uniforms and accorded the right to wear military uniforms only when called upon to perform military duty.

EQUIPMENT AND ARMS INDUSTRY

Before Castro's seizure of power, the Cuban army was equipped with American equipment, much of it obsolete (the infantry generally carried the 1903 Springfield). It has subsequently been re-equipped with Soviet weapons, though some American equipment may not yet have passed out of service. The country does not yet manufacture any equipment, though it may now produce some small-arms ammunition.

Rifles: AKMS 7.62mm (USSR); AKM 7.62mm (USSR); AK-47 7.62mm (USSR); M-52 7.62mm (Czechoslovakia)
Sub-machine-gun: M-23 9mm (Czechoslovakia)
Machine-guns: PK 7.62mm (USSR); RPK 7.62mm (USSR); DPM 7.62mm (USSR); RP-46 7.62mm (USSR); RPD 7.62mm (USSR); DShKM 12.7mm (USSR)
Anti-armour weapons: ZIS-2 57mm A/T gun (USSR); ZIS-3 76.2mm A/T gun (USSR); D-44 85mm A/T gun (USSR); D-48 85mm A/T gun (USSR); Sagger ATGW (USSR); Snapper ATGW (USSR)
Mortars: M-1937 82mm (USSR); M-1938 120mm (USSR); M-1943 160mm (USSR)
Artillery: M-30 122mm (USSR); A-19 122mm (USSR); D-74 122mm (USSR); M-46 130mm (USSR); D-1 152mm (USSR); ML-20 152mm (USSR); D-20 152mm (USSR); SU-100 100mm SPG (USSR); Frog-5 rocket launcher (USSR); SSC-2A SSMs (USSR)
Air-defence weapons: ZPU-1 14.5mm (USSR); ZPU-2 14.5mm (USSR); ZPU-4 14.5mm (USSR); TR-152AZPU SP twin 14.5mm (USSR); ZU-23 23mm (USSR); M-53/59 SP twin 30mm (Czechoslovakia); M-1939 37mm (USSR); S-60 57mm (USSR); ZSU-57-2 SP twin 57mm (USSR); KS-12 85mm (USSR); KS-12A 85mm (USSR); KS-19 100mm (USSR); SA-2 SAM (USSR); SA-3 SAM (USSR); SA-7 SAM (USSR)
Armour: T-62 MBT (USSR); T-54/55 medium tank (USSR); T-34 medium tank (USSR); PT-76 light tank (USSR); BROM-1 scout car (USSR); BROM-2 scout car (USSR); BTR-40 (USSR); BTR-60 APC (USSR); BTR-152 APC (USSR)
Aircraft: The Air Force operates about 50 transports and over 100 helicopters.

RANK, DRESS AND DISTINCTIONS

Until 1973, the highest rank held by any Cuban officer (including Fidel Castro as Commander-in-Chief was that of *Comandante*, which means both 'major' and 'commander'. Below that were two ranks of captain and three of lieutenant. In 1973 Castro introduced a new rank system which conformed more closely to the traditional. He explained his innovation thus: that the armed forces had been distinguished by their modesty in uniform and rank but that the revolution had become more mature and the armed forces with it. They also needed to match the practices of the Russian and other allied armies. His new system, common in Latin America, divided officers into three groups: generals, chiefs and officers (called by him 'superior', 'first' and 'subaltern'). The ranks are:

> *Comandante de Ejéricito*
> *Comandante de Cuerpo*
> *Comandante de División*
> *Comandante de Brigada*
> *Coronel*
> *Teniente Coronel*
> *Mayor*
> *Capitán*
> *Teniente Primero*
> *Teniente*
> *Subteniente*

Under the old system, the highest ranks wore gold stars, while those corresponding to colonel and below wore gold chevrons.

Cuban army dress still follows, despite the Russian alliance, the United States army-surplus styles worn by Castro and his followers in the Sierra Maestra. A more sober uniform for senior officers has been seen, and Castro now dresses on ceremonial occasions in the style of senior officers of Warsaw Pact armies.

CURRENT DEVELOPMENTS

The Cuban army is now operationally the most experienced in Latin America and, though limited for manpower, the most powerful. It is unable, in the face of United States control of American waters, to operate either in the Caribbean or on the mainland, where the governments with the exception of those of Guyana and Nicaragua and to a lesser extent, Mexico are uniformly hostile to the Castro regime and all now sufficiently in control of their own populations and territories to deny it a base, however remote, from which to propagate rebellion, as Ché Guevara tried to do in Bolivia in 1967. While it remains Castro's declared policy to transplant the 'Cuban revolution' to the rest of Latin America, it seems likely therefore that the Cuban army will continue to be engaged only in those areas where the Soviet government is able to sponsor its operations. At present this means Africa, though Cuba also has close links with anti-Western governments and organisations in the Middle East and south-east Asia. The United States and its allies have not as yet found any means of translating their hostility to the Cuban army's intervention into effective opposition.

Cuba joined with the majority of other Latin American countries in supporting Argentina in the South Atlantic War, offering 'unlimited military assistance', which was not availed of by the Argentine junta. It remains to be seen to what extent, if any, this gesture of Latin American solidarity may have increased the Castro regime's acceptability to the predominantly right-wing governments of the area and whether Cuba can exploit the undoubted opprobrium earned in Latin America by the US by its support for Britain, an extra-hemispheric and former imperial power, against one of its own Latin American allies.

John Keegan
Adrian English

CYPRUS

HISTORY AND INTRODUCTION

The turbulent recent history of Cyprus, which has turned it into something approaching an armed camp, has been dominated by Greek—Turkish rivalries at two levels. One field of conflict has been between the Greek—Cypriot majority (about 80% of the island's 650,000 people) and the Turkish-Cypriot minority over mainly local issues, but in recent decades this has been consistently overshadowed by the conflicting interests of the two mother-countries.

For Greeks, Cyprus is the last unrecovered portion of the Greek irredenta (apart from formerly Greek areas of present-day Turkey, which are forever lost through a change in the population itself from Hellenic to Turkish). The in-gathering of the irredenta has been the main focus and purpose of Greek nationalism in the modern era, and so Cyprus remains a powerful emotional factor in Greek politics.

The Greek Cypriots have never been ruled from Athens and have traditionally entertained mixed feelings about throwing in their lot with their mainland relatives, whom they see as relatively backward economically and politically, and prone to recurrent military dictatorships. Nevertheless the emotional attraction of Greek unity is strong, and so the Greeks of Cyprus have found their politics dominated by violent disagreements about the desirability and practicability of *enosis* (union with Greece).

The question of practicability arises because of adamant Turkish opposition to the union of Greece and Cyprus. The opposition proceeds in part from sympathetic support for the Turkish-Cypriot minority, which would lose all effective political voice if submerged in a sea of 10,000,000 Greeks and sees its own future in such a case as one of gradual disappearance through emigration, but there is also a strategic motive in Ankara. A cursory glance at Greek—Turkish relations over the past century and a half convinces most Turks that the possibility of yet another war with Athens must be numbered among the strategic contingencies they face, however good Greek—Turkish relations may be at a given moment.

In such a possible conflict at some future time, possession of the island of Cyprus, only 40 miles from the Turkish south coast, would give the Greek air force, and to a lesser extent the navy, large strategic advantages. From Cyprus bases Greek aircraft could attack targets in virtually all parts of Turkey, and would require Turkish air defences to deal with a threat from a quite different direction. However hypothetical such calculations may seem, they play a substantial role in Turkish military thinking, and greatly fortify the opposition of Ankara to *enosis* which derives from purely political and emotional grounds.

Cyprus has been Hellenised since the middle of the first millenium BC, when Greek colonies were founded in the island and rapidly eroded the former Phoenician influences. In 1579, however, the expanding Ottoman Empire conquered Cyprus, which it was to hold for the next three centuries. Ottoman rule was by no means totally unpopular — the conquerors ended the feudal status of the peasantry, restored the independence of the Greek Orthodox Church, and allowed a considerable degree of self-government to the subject Christian community through the *millet* system. Conforming to their usual pattern, the Ottomans made little or no attempt to proselytise the Christian majority on behalf of Islam.

They did settle about 30,000 demobilised Turkish soldiers in Cyprus, however, in order to provide a loyal resident garrison cheaply. These Turkish Muslims (plus a certain number of later immigrants) were the origin of the severe communal problem which has plagued Cyprus for the past century, for they proved almost wholly resistant to the pressures towards assimilation that usually operate against such minorities.

Cyprus passed peacefully under the control of the British Empire in 1878, in order to provide Britain with an eastern Mediterranean base from which it could assist in the defence of the Ottoman Empire against Russia. Sovereignty was not transferred to Britain until 1914, however, when Britain and Turkey found themselves on opposite sides in World War I, and London actually offered the island to Greece in the following year in an unsuccessful attempt to induce Athens to join the Entente Powers. The offer did not remain open, however, and from 1925 Cyprus was administered as a Crown Colony.

Over the succeeding three decades the movement for *enosis* grew steadily amongst the Greek-Cypriot majority. At the same time the strategic importance of Cyprus to Britain gradually increased as its other Mediterranean base areas one by one gained independence. A British poposal in 1954 to create a restricted form of constitutional government in Cyprus leading to self-government within the Commonwealth was accepted by the Turkish community, but rejected by the *enosists*. The latent conflict burst into the open in the following year, when a guerrilla movement known as the National Organisation of Cypriot Fighters (*Ethniki Organosis Kyprion Agoniston* – EOKA) began active operations to evict Britain from Cyprus and achieve union with Greece.

EOKA's terrorist campaign, assisted by clandestine aid from Greece, was led by General George Grivas and tacitly supported by Archbishop Makarios, the religious leader of the Greek-Orthodox majority on the island. The latter was exiled to the Seychelles in March, 1956 but the campaign steadily gained ground through the later 1950s, tying down about 10,000 British soldiers. The Turkish community readily collaborated with the British authorities against EOKA, and the first serious outbreaks of Greek—Turkish strife occurred in 1958.

In 1959, however, the EOKA leadership split, with Makarios accepting the 'Macmillan Plan' for independence without *enosis*. According to the London Agreement of 1960 neither partition of the island nor union with another State would be permitted, and its independence would be guaranteed by Britain, Greece and Turkey. Makarios returned to Cyprus and was elected the new Republic's first President, while Grivas fled to Greece. Cyprus became independent in August, 1960. There remained deeply aggrieved minorities, however, amongst the unreconciled *enosists* and amongst Turkish Cypriots who would have preferred partition.

Under the 1960 Constitution, Cyprus had a Greek President and a Turkish Vice-President, with both the Cabinet and the House of Representatives split 70%—30% between the Greek and Turkish communities. The Turkish Vice-President had a veto over certain subjects, and separate majorities in both communal groups in the House were required to pass financial legislation. There were to be separate Turkish municipal governments in the main towns, and separate communal Chambers to deal with religion, education and cultural matters.

The public services were constitutionally obliged to employ 70% Greeks and 30% Turks, and the 2000-man army was split 60%—40%. Greece received the right to station 950 troops on the island, and Turkey 650, to safeguard the rights of their respective communities. Britain retained sovereign rights over large base areas, and all three States were granted the right to intervene, together or separately, to uphold this settlement.

Such cumbersome arrangements were seen to be necessary to prevent civil strife, but even with much good will on either side they might have proved impossible to work. As it was, there was no good will, and disputes over the Turkish municipalities, Turkish-Cypriot vetoes on Makarios's attempts to integrate fully the army and public services, and other issues led to total deadlock in only 3 years. In November, 1963 Makarios formally proposed constitutional reforms which would sweep away most of the Turkish community's entrenched safeguards, and all co-operation ended.

Underground groups in both communities were already preparing for conflict, and full-scale civil war broke out in December, 1963. The Turkish community, scattered throughout the island, was shut up by dozens of separate sieges round their villages or the Turkish quarters of various towns, and some massacres occurred when local defences collapsed. Atrocities grew common on both sides, the number of irregulars under arms rose rapidly, and aid flowed in to the combatants from Greece and Turkey. Tension grew to dangerous levels between the two mother countries.

The arrival of UN forces (UNFICYP) in March, 1964 ended the worst of the fighting, but the bi-communal republic was effectively at an end. For the next 11 years the Turkish community lived under a form of modified siege, and the institutions of government in Cyprus passed entirely into Greek hands. By mid-1965, moreover, Makarios's desired constitutional changes had all been passed into law, transforming the State into a unitary, majority-dominated Republic with single municipalities, no Turkish veto, and no separate communal electoral rolls.

The bi-communal army provided by the 1960 Constitution was also ended for practical purposes, although it was only officially disbanded in 1968, and in June, 1964 the (now totally Greek) House of Representatives established a National Guard in which all male Cypriots between eighteen and fifty-nine — all Greeks, in practice — were liable to 6 months' service. The term of service was extended to 1 year at the end of 1964, and is now 2 years. A Greek-Cypriot navy was also created in 1964, with the primary purpose of preventing the landing of arms to the beleaguered Turkish community, and grew to include six 'torpedo boats', two larger patrol craft (a third was sunk by the Turkish air force in 1964) and ten smaller craft. The vessels were mostly provided by the Soviet Union.

The main purpose of this measure was to bring the various irregular Greek forces under government control, but it failed in that aim. In late June, 1964 Grivas returned to the island from Greece and took effective command both of the new National Guard and of 'volunteer' Greek forces. He took his orders from the Ministry of National Defence in Athens, and a proposal by Makarios to transfer control to the Cyprus Ministry of Defence in 1966 was sharply rejected by both Grivas and the Greek government.

The politics of Greek Cyprus for the next decade were dominated by the struggle between Makarios, who had reluctantly concluded that *enosis* was impossible at least for the moment as it would cause a Turkish invasion, and those in Cyprus and in Greece who persisted in the struggle to achieve union. Makarios had been driven to this conclusion by the events of June, 1964 when Turkey had indeed come very close to mounting an invasion to rescue the Turkish Cypriots. Only a direct warning to Ankara from the USA's President Johnson had prevented it.

A possible solution arose in 1967, after a coup in Athens brought the Greek army to power, when Turkey offered to accept *enosis* in return for military bases in the island and 10% of the territory, but it was rejected by the Colonel's regime in Athens. By the end of 1967 Turkey and Greece were again on the brink of war, after a massacre of Turkish villagers in November by the Greek Cypriot National Guard.

American intervention once again secured Turkish demobilisation, but Athens was compelled to withdraw Grivas from the island. Both the Greek and Turkish army contingents stationed in the island were reduced once more to the numbers permitted by the 1960 Constitution. At the end of 1967, however, the Turkish Cypriots announced a 'Transitional Administration' to run their affairs until the 1960 Constitution was restored, with a legislature drawn from the Turkish members of the old House, and despite Greek-Cypriot denunciations of its illegality it operated thenceforward as the *de facto* government of the besieged and scattered Turks.

There were sporadic inter-communal talks over the next 5 years, and the blockade of the Turkish Cypriots was eased somewhat except in the Turkish quarter of Nicosia. No progress was made on the central issues, however, and the blockaded Turks had little share in the rapidly rising prosperity of the island under the impact of mass tourism. Indeed, under this severe economic pressure the Turkish-Cypriot community was rapidly shrinking through emigration — between 1963 and 1974 almost one-sixth of the community left the island.

Makarios was re-elected President in 1970 by the Greeks, and Rauf Denktash was elected as Vice-President in the same year by the Turkish community. Increasingly, however, the Greek-Cypriot community was split into two armed camps, with the Athens government scarcely concealing its support of the *enosists*. Pro-*enosis* terrorism against the Makarios government was resumed in 1969 by the newly formed National Front, which attempted to assassinate the Archbishop in the following year.

Late in 1971 Grivas again returned to the island, with the secret support of the Greek government, and rapidly transformed the National Front into a more effective organisation called EOKA-B. The Greek-Cypriot National Guard, still under the effective control of Greek army officers, was a tool of uncertain loyalty to Makarios, who was therefore forced in early 1972 to dismiss his anti-Athens ministers and admit some moderate *enosists* to his government.

Makarios did not cease to resist the folly of *enosis*, however. He secured arms from Czechoslovakia, and created his own paramilitary counter-balance to the Athens-dominated National Guard in the form of a Special Police Reserve. During 1973 he succeeded in dismissing numerous police and National Guard officers who were suspected of being active EOKA supporters, and the EOKA terror campaign was flagging by the time Grivas died of a heart attack in January, 1974.

Meanwhile, however, a new military *junta* had come to power in Athens, more enthusiastically pro-*enosis* and less cautious than its predecessor. Suspecting that it might take direct action against him, Makarios carried out a further purge of EOKA supporters in the police, civil service and National Guard in June, 1974. He then wrote to the Greek government on July 2nd, 1974 accusing it of giving arms and subsidies to EOKA and of using the Greek army officers attached to the National Guard as a centre of subversion. He demanded their withdrawal, and published the letter.

The Greek *junta*, with a ruthlessness nearly as great as its ignorance, replied by ordering his overthrow. On July 15th, 1974 the National Guard, led by Greek army officers, launched a coup in Nicosia, defeated the Special Police Reserve, and attacked the Presidential Palace. Makarios barely escaped with his life, fleeing to a British base and thence to Britain, while the National Guard installed as President the former EOKA gunman Nicos Sampson, who was known to have personally directed massacres of Turkish Cypriots.

Sampson declared Cyprus a 'Hellenic Republic', and his followers talked of achieving *enosis* by the end of the year. They turned at once to hunting down and murdering Makarios supporters, of whom up to 2000 were killed in the following week, but serious massacres of isolated Turkish communities did not begin until the Turkish invasion 5 days later.

It has been argued that the Greek colonels launched their coup against Makarios in the hope of restoring their own rapidly deteriorating position in Greece, and that they actually failed to realise that Turkey would react militarily to the threat of *enosis*. It is also possible, having regard to the level of intelligence they displayed in other actions, that they simply neglected to think matters through. The result, in either case, was to call down the ultimate disaster in Cyprus.

The Turkish government instantly announced its intention of intervening in response to this flagrant violation of the 1960 agreement, and Prime Minister Bülent Ecevit flew to London to seek British support as co-guarantor of Cyprus independence. When the British government refused to act, the Turkish invasion went ahead on July 20th. (For details of military operations in Cyprus in 1974, *see* Role, Commitment, Deployment and Recent Operations.)

The Turkish landings near Kyrenia on the northern coast rapidly overcame the resistance of the Greek-Cypriot National Guard and the small Greek army forces on the island, though they were powerless to prevent massacres of Turkish Cypriots elsewhere. Greece itself mobilised, but the shambles that ensued in an army which had neglected its military duties for the past 7 years, and the obvious impossibility of intervening in the fighting in Cyprus, quickly persuaded even the Greek army's own generals to withdraw their support from the bewildered and panic-stricken *junta* in Athens. Turkey declared a ceasefire on Cyprus on July 22nd, when the Turkish army held a narrow bridgehead extending inland from the northern coast to the outskirts of Nicosia, and on the following day both the Sampson regime and the Greek military government resigned. United Nations forces did not become involved in the fighting.

Negotiations soon afterwards began in Geneva between the Turkish government and the new civilian government of Greece headed by Constantine Karamanlis. They broke down, however, when the Greek government rejected Ankara's proposal to create a federal republic in Cyprus organised on a cantonal basis. The Turkish map would have given the Turkish Cypriots control over various areas amounting to just over 30% of the island.

When the proposal was refused, Ankara decided to seek a more radical solution by military force — to carve out a single, continuous area in which all the Turkish Cypriots might live in safety, though still within the context of an independent and federal State. The Turkish military advance was renewed on August 14th, 1974 and Greek-Cypriot military resistance promptly collapsed. The Turkish army's advance halted when it had reached a line running approximately Morphou—" Nicosia—Famagusta, encompassing about 36% of the territory of Cyprus.

There has been no further military activity in Cyprus since August, 1974 and the ceasefire line has not moved. The great majority of former Greek-Cypriot residents of the Turkish-occupied territory fled in 1974, and all but a few hundred of the others have since been induced to leave. Virtually all Turkish Cypriots originally living south of that line (half the Turkish-Cypriot population) had managed to get themselves to the north by the end of 1975, many of them via the British base area in which they had taken refuge in 1974. The situation can be viewed as one in which almost half of the island's population (around 200,000 Greeks and 90,000 Turks) have become temporary refugees, or more realistically as an enforced and permanent exchange of populations to create two ethnically homogeneous areas.

The Turkish government's position remains that of seeking an independent and federal republic on Cyprus, though obviously no longer on the basis of the 1960 Constitution. It rejects the possibility of partition and 'double enosis'. In pursuit of its objectives Ankara permitted the declaration of the 'Turkish Federated State of Cyprus' in 1975 — rather like the sound of one hand clapping, since there is no Cyprus federation — but it will not allow the Turkish Cypriots to declare their full independence.

The Greek-Cypriot government, again under Archbishop Makarios, and supported by Athens, refused to accept this *fait accompli*. In 1976 it was prepared to consider some federal solution provided the boundaries of the Turkish zone were radically moved back to allow the majority of Greek-Cypriot refugees to return to their homes. These homes have long since been occupied by Turkish-Cypriot refugees from the south, however (as has happened, in reverse, to the homes the latter abandoned). With each passing year the scope for alterations in the *de facto* boundary becomes less.

The death of Archbishop Makarios in 1977 changed little, for his successor, Spyros Kyprianou (confirmed as president in the 1978 elections) has consistently pursued the same policy. The re-election of Rauf Denktash as President of the TFCS in 1981 ensured that the Turkish-Cypriot side too would continue willing at least to discuss the possibility of a federal solution that could put the shattered island together again. However, the progress of the inter-communal negotiations, held under UN auspices, has been virtually imperceptible.

Cyprus remains pre-eminently a place of arms, with two separate armies — Turkish, Greek, British, Turkish Cypriot and Greek Cypriot — quartered on its soil, plus the UN contingent drawn from eight outside nations. In an island whose population is less than 750,000, there are almost 60,000 soldiers under arms. The major fighting, however, is probably over. At the cost of a catastrophe, the Cyprus problem has been 'solved', though only with the passage of time are the various participants in the tragedy likely to reconcile themselves to the solution.

STRENGTH AND BUDGET

The Cyprus National Guard, which is predominantly Greek-Cypriot in composition (including all the conscripts), but includes some 450 Greek Army officers and NCOs on secondment, has a regular strength of 10,000 men. This is a very considerable reduction from the approximately 40,000 men (including some 10,000 Greek Army regulars) who made up the strength of the National Guard in the late 1960s. Reserves number 30,000 of whom 8500 are immediately available for service, and the remainder are second line. Paramilitary forces include 3000 armed police. The defence budget of the (Greek) Cyprus government in 1981 was $27.2 million, which amounted to less then 2 per cent of the GNP.

The Turkish-Cypriot security force, exclusively Turkish in membership, has a regular strength of 4,500 men. This is also a major decline from the average of 10–15,000 troops who were serving in the Turkish Defence Organisation of the late 1960s. Reserves are 15,500, of which 5,500 are immediately available and the remainder second line.

TCSF defence expenditure in 1982 was $4.98 million, but this was almost certainly supplemented by hidden subsidies from Ankara.

There are, in addition to these indigenous armed forces, four other military organisations present in Cyprus. The Turkish armed forces in early 1977 had approximately 24,000 troops in the island (down from the 1974 peak of almost 40,000), whose expenses are met by the Turkish military budget. Greece maintains 1300 troops (including 350 commandos) in the island in addition to personnel attached to the Cyprus National Guard. Their cost is covered by the Greek defence budget.

The payment due to Cyprus for the use of the bases, however, has now become a matter of dispute. Under the 1960 treaty Britain agreed to give Cyprus a once-and-for-all payment of £12 million over 5 years, and to review further and every 5 years 'taking all factors into account', including the financial requirements of the government of the Republic. Cyprus now argues that this clause obliges Britain to make further payments so long as she retains the bases, and that on this basis, at current prices, Britain now owes Cyprus arrears of approximately £250 million. Britain's position is that Britain's aid to Cyprus has no connection with the bases, which are British sovereign territory and were never part of the Republic; that any moral obligation is discharged by Britain's contribution to the UN peacekeeping force; and that Cyprus (or at any rate the territory ruled by the Greek-Cypriot majority) is a resounding economic success which is not in need of further financial aid. This dispute will provide innocent amusement for many, and lucrative employment for a few for many years to come.

The British armed forces maintain about 4000 army and air force personnel (and another 4000 dependents) in the Sovereign Base Areas of Dhekelia and Akrotiri, whose costs are covered by the British defence budget.

United Nations Forces in Cyprus (UNFICYP) have a strength of 2778 men (down from almost 7000 in the mid-1960s), whose costs are paid by voluntary contributions from 59 UN member nations (none of which belongs to the Soviet bloc). The cost of UNFICYP since 1964 has been over $250,000,000.

COMMAND AND CONSTITUTIONAL STATUS

The Cyprus National Guard is ultimately reponsible to the President of the Republic of Cyprus, an office held by Mr. Spyros Kyprianou since Archbishop Makarios's death in August, 1977. Direct political control and responsibility is exercised by the Minister of the Interior and Defence, currently Mr. Christodoulos Veniamin. There remains a small number of mainland Greek army officers serving with the Cyprus National Guard on detached duty, but it is less subject to control from Athens than at any previous time in its history.

The 'Turkish-Cypriot Security Force' was created by the National Assembly of the Turkish Federated State of Cyprus in a law of November 24th, 1976 to serve as the regular army of that State, itself only proclaimed in February, 1975. It is the old 'Turkish Fighters' militia of the Turkish-Cypriot community in a new guise, and like its predecessor is principally officered by members of the Turkish army on secondment who have years of experience in Cyprus. The new army is commanded by a brigadier-general of the Turkish regular army, but for constitutional purposes he is responsible directly to the President of the T.F.S.C., Mr. Rauf Denktash, whom he advises on all matters of security. There is a Minister of Defence, but the army commander is in control of both administration and operational functions. He also controls the police and the radio station.

British forces in Cyprus are controlled by the Ministry of Defence in London. UNFICYP's commander in Cyprus is responsible to the Secretary-General of the United Nations.

Turkish regular forces in Cyprus are administratively part of the 2nd Army Corps (HQ Konya), but their commander-in-chief is directly responsible to the Ministry of National Defence in Ankara, and is not the command of the President of the T.F.S.C. He is also martial law commander in the Turkish-occupied part of the island.

Greek regular troops on the island are presumably controlled by the Ministry of Defence in Athens, in consultation with the Cyprus governments.

ROLE, COMMITMENT, DEPLOYMENT AND RECENT OPERATIONS

Role, Commitment and Deployment

The Cyprus National Guard, deployed throughout the Greek-Cypriot controlled south of the island, has the primary role of defending that territory, but is manifestly incapable of doing so against the Turkish forces now in Cyprus, should they be ordered to advance further. Its more significant role, therefore, is to maintain the authority of the elected government in the face of the still numerous irregular armed groups illegally maintained by political organisations, notably those of the EDEK party and of the banned EOKA-B.

The Turkish-Cypriot Security Force is deployed throughout the north of the island, and serves as an auxiliary to the Turkish regular army in the defence of the territory and in the various civic action programmes undertaken by the latter. It has little real autonomy.

The British forces are in Cyprus by bilateral agreement, not as members of NATO, but it is nevertheless in the latter capacity that their presence is of strategic signficance. Before the 1975 British Defence White Paper there were two squadrons of Vulcan nuclear bombers protected by Lightning fighters based on Cyprus, but the RAF no longer maintains combat aircraft in the island. Its facilities — a large military airfield, an electronic surveillance station at Dhekelia, the huge RAF radar station in the Troodos mountains — nevertheless remain valuable to NATO in the eastern Mediterranean, and may indeed have grown in value since the post-1974 American difficulties with base rights in Greece and Turkey.

On calculations of purely national interest, Britain might well abandon its extensive Cyprus base areas — which cover 3% of the island's territory — but it maintains its presence in the interests of NATO. A further consideration is the probability of a further Turkish military advance if the airbase were to become available to the Greek air force, or if Greek-Cypriot forces were enabled by a British withdrawal to occupy the Sovereign Base Area of Dhekelia, which runs right up to the suburbs of Turkish-occupied Famagusta. The

4000 British servicemen in Cyprus are roughly evenly divided between the army base at Dhekelia and the air force installations at Akrotiri.

UN peacekeeping forces in Cyprus are headquartered in the Greek part of Nicosia, but are deployed throughout the island. Their initial function was to safeguard the fragile ceasefire established in the days when Greeks and Turks lived in closely intermingled communities in all of Cyprus, and has thus been much eased by the far clearer single dividing line established since 1974. Their duties are solely those of surveillance and mediation, and they are authorised to use their weapons only for self-defence.

Turkish army forces in Cyprus are deployed throughout the northern part of the island. Their task is to maintain the security of the Turkish-Cypriot community and to maintain the borders established in 1974 until and unless they should be modified by negotiations. They serve the additional unstated purpose of providing a most persuasive deterrent against any attempt by frustrated Greek Cypriots to engage in any form of guerrilla attacks against the Turkish areas, since they have the undoubted ability to seize the remaining three-fifths of the island in a very short time.

Recent Operations

During the 1974 crisis the Cyprus National Guard was employed first against the Special Police Reserve and other forces seeking to defend President Makarios's government, and less than a week later against the Turkish seaborne and airborne forces that intervened in the island. Despite the political turmoil in which the National Guard were inevitably caught up, it fought well in the battles against greatly superior Turkish forces. Much of its scanty armour and artillery was lost at the beginning in the morning of July 20th, in a futile attempt to defend the beaches west of Kyrenia against overwhelming Turkish naval and air forces, but it succeeded in keeping the strategic St. Hilarion Pass leading south towards Nicosia closed for the better part of 2 days against Turkish paratroops.

It did manage, just barely, to deny Nicosia airport to the Turks until the first ceasefire intervened on July 22nd (thus necessitating the construction since 1974 of new civil airports at Ercan and Larnaca to serve the two halves of the divided island). During the succeeding month it performed creditably enough around the fringes of the gradually expanding Turkish army lodgement, although shaken by yet another political upheaval in the Greek-Cypriot community when the result of the coup was reversed by the resignation of the Sampson government. Its resistance collapsed rapidly and completely, however, in the face of the second Turkish offensive of mid-August, which was launched by a force by then enlarged to 40,000 men and 200 tanks.

The other Cypriot armed force, the 'Turkish Fighters', as it was then called, played an entirely subsidiary role in the main operations in the north of the island in 1974, owing to the presence of Turkish regular forces. It did, however, succeed in defending most of the besieged Turkish-Cypriot communities out of reach of the Turkish army's protection in the south — most notably in the case of the Turkish quarter of Famagusta, which was under siege without water for over 3 weeks until relieved by the Turkish army.

For the Turkish army's role in the operations, see the entry on Turkey. Neither the British nor the UN forces in Cyprus took any part in the 1974 fighting.

ORGANISATION

The Cyprus National Guard is organised into 20 under-strength infantry battalions (to be filled out upon mobilisa-tion), plus one armoured battalion, two reconnaisance/mechanised infantry battalions, 7 artillery battalions, eight support units, and a light air wing. The Turkish-Cypriot Security Force consists of seven infantry battalions.

The British force in Cyprus consists of two infantry battalions and a reconnaissance force, plus RAF personnel.

UNFICYP is made up of infantry and military police contingents from seven countries: Australia, Austria, Britain, Canada, Denmark, Ireland and Sweden. The largest contributors are Britain (823 troops) and Canada (474 troops) whose contingents are regular force battalion units. The Scandinavian contingents consist mainly of military reservists recruited directly from civilian life.

The Turkish army in Cyprus consists of a corps of two infantry divisions, organised on the standard Turkish pattern, Greek regular forces consist of an infantry battalion, a commando unit, and administrative personnel.

RECRUITMENT, TRAINING AND RESERVES

The Cyprus National Guard is made up primarily of conscripts who join at the age of eighteen and do 26 months' service, after which they join the reserve. They are trained by a small cadre of regular officers and NCOs, assisted by some Greek army regular officers on secondment. On mobilisation, the force can rapidly expand to about 40,000 men.

The Turkish-Cypriot Security Force consists of conscripts called up at eighteen, who serve for 24 months (22 months for NCOs). They are trained by Turkish army regular officers on detached duty. On mobilisation, the forces' strength would rise to 20,000 men.

EQUIPMENT AND ARMS INDUSTRY

Both Greek-Cypriot and Turkish-Cypriot forces are armed mainly with light infantry weapons of the patterns used in the respective mother countries. Prior to 1974 the Greek-Cypriot forces possessed some dozens of antiquated armoured vehicles, but most of those were lost on the beaches at the time of the invasion. The Cyprus National Guard is now reported to have 10 T-34 tanks, 17 BTR-50 APCs, 20 EE-9 Cascavel and 20 Marmon-Harrington armoured cars, plus approximately one hundred 100mm, 105mm, and 25-pounder guns and 75mm howitzers and a number of 40mm and 3.7 in AA guns. Twenty further EE-9 Cascavels are on order from Brazil. The force also possesses one 30-ft patrol craft and about 12 light spotter aircraft, but Turkish reports that it has been given 32 old F-84 fighter bombers and a number of *Chapparal* SAMs by Greece have not been confirmed. The Turkish-Cypriot Security Force possesses some T-34 tanks, but is almost entirely dependent on Turkish regular forces for heavy weapons and air support. There are currently estimated to be about 150 Turkish tanks (M-46 and M-48) on the island supported by M-113 APCs and 212 105mm, 155mm and 203mm guns and howitzers and 40mm AA guns. Greek reports that the Turks have introduced Milan anti-tank missiles and a battery of Hawk SAMs onto the island have not been confirmed.

RANK, DRESS AND DISTINCTIONS

Both Turkish-Cypriot and Greek-Cypriot forces closely follow the models of the armies of the respective mother countries. The former, indeed, wear Turkish army uniforms, the only distinguishing feature being the cap-badge (a wolf's head instead of the Turkish army's crescent and star).

CURRENT DEVELOPMENTS

The Turkish government has repeatedly stated its goal in Cyprus to be the reconstitution of the Republic as a federal State incorporating two autonomous communal entities, each possessing very wide powers of self-government in its own zone. It has resisted pressure from the right wing in Turkey for annexation, and from the Turkish-Cypriot government for a declaration of full independence for the northern part of the island, and maintains that its forces will be withdrawn from the island once a federal solution has been negotiated.

By 1975 Archbishop Makarios had accepted this sort of settlement in principle, but the main stumbling block — apart from the abyss of mistrust separating the two sides — was the size of the Turkish component in such a federal Cyprus. The present Turkish-occupied area, at 36% of the island's surface, is approximately twice the proportion of Turkish Cypriots in the total population, although it corresponds somewhat more closely to the actual proportion of land registered to Turkish-Cypriot owners before the upheaval of 1974. Negotiations between the two Cypriot sides actually began during the first half of 1977, but soon broke down on this question of how much land the Turkish Cypriots should hand back. There has been no public discussion on what kind of army a federal Cyprus should have, although it seems certain that the Turkish Cypriots would insist on maintaining their separate force.

The stalled inter-communal negotiations were resumed in September 1980, after the appointment on August 1 of Dr Hugo Gobbi as the UN Secretary General's special representative in Cyprus. Towards the end of 1981, having made virtually no progress, he boldly presented a document seeking to blend the positions of the two sides — the so-called 'Waldheim Evaluation' — which has become the (unacknowledged) basis for all subsequent discussions. The Greek-Cypriot and Turkish-Cypriot sides remain fundamentally opposed on such basic questions as the nature of the reconstructed Cypriot state, the powers to be given to the central government and the extent to which the Turkish-Cypriot minority should be given equal rights with the Greek-Cypriot majority, but a number of lesser issues have been agreed.

The negotiations continue to be heavily influenced by political developments in the two mother countries. The advent of a military regime in Turkey in 1980 may actually have made the Turkish negotiation position more flexible (for Turkish civilian governments are greatly constrained by their chronic concern about the military reactions to any concessions they make), but the election of a Socialist government led by prime minister Andreas Papandreou in Greece in October, 1981, has undoubtedly complicated matters considerably.

Much of Papandreou's political appeal at home derives from his unremitting hostility to all things Turkish. Soon after he assumed office he sought to persuade the Greek-Cypriot government that the intercommunal talks were a total waste of time and should be abandoned. Greece and Cyprus would be better employed, he argued, in launching an all-out diplomatic 'crusade' to force the Turkish army to withdraw unconditionally from Cyprus.

However, in April 1982 Cyprus's President Kyprianou, in order to ensure his own re-election in 1983, concluded an electoral pact with AKEL, the powerful, pro-Moscow Communist party of Cyprus, which pledged him to purse the intercommunal talks as 'the most suitable procedure for a solution of the Cyprus question'. As a consequence, the governments in Athens and Nicosia have become estranged to a degree not seen since early 1974 — and it is difficult to imagine the Turkish government agreeing to any Cyprus settlement which is rejected by Athens.

Greek—Turkish disputes in the Aeagean Sea, the resolution of the Cyprus problem, and the relations of Ankara and Athens with Washington (particularly over questions of American bases and arms supplies) have become so intertwined diplomatically that any formal ratification of the new facts created in Cyprus in 1974, accompanied by territorial adjustments, seems unlikely in the near future. The realities are plain to almost everyone, however (although Greek Cypriots find them very unpalatable) and it is therefore improbable that there would be any return to open hostilities in Cyprus.

Gwynne Dyer

CZECHOSLOVAKIA

HISTORY AND INTRODUCTION

Unlike Hungary and Poland, Czechoslovakia was not even a 'historical nation' when, in the autumn of 1918, she emerged from the dissolution of the Hapsburg Empire. Her territory included Bohemia, Moravia, Slovakia and part of Silesia, and contained not only Czechs and Slovaks but also Germans, Magyars and Ruthenians. Nevertheless, the new republic possessed excellent natural resources and thriving industry, and made steady progress under the sound leadership of Thomas Masaryk. It was, ironically, external pressure which aggravated the problem of national minorities and led to the republic's collapse. German *Anschluss* with Austria in March, 1938 was followed by agitation amongst the German minority of the Sudetenland (northern Bohemia) who demanded unification with the *Reich*. Czechoslovakia was abandoned by her allies at Munich in September, 1938; Germany annexed the Sudetenland in October, and Slovakia gained autonomy. The remnants of Bohemia and Moravia did not survive for long: in March, 1939 Hitler proclaimed them a German protectorate and his troops occupied them without resistance.

Elements of the Czechoslovakian army escaped abroad after the German invasion, and during World War II Czech forces were sponsored by both the western allies and the Soviet Union. In April, 1945 with the collapse of Germany imminent, Churchill and Truman agreed in principle upon the desirability of liberating at least part of Bohemia. In the event, however, the Americans decided to halt on the line Karlový Vary–Plzeň–České Budějovice, and it was Soviet tanks which swept into Prague in the first week in May. On April 4th a provisional Government of National Unity had been formed in Moscow under the pre-war President, Dr. Eduard Beneš, who had spent the war heading the London-based government in exile. The government was set up after a week's haggling between Beneš, aided by his Foreign Minister, Jan Masaryk, and the Moscow-based communists led by Klement Gottwald. Although the government contained only seven communists, they were an influential minority. It was also significant that the Ministry of War was entrusted to the 'non-political' figure of General Lukvík Svoboda, commander of the Czech corps which had been organised under Soviet auspices.

United States forces withdrew from western Bohemia in the winter of 1945, and with them went the last external source of support for anti-communist Czech politicians. The Czech Communist Party (KSČ) grew in strength, and obtained 38% of the popular vote in the first post-war elections, held in May, 1946. Not only was the KSČ the largest single party, it also possessed a narrow parliamentary majority, thanks to its alliance with the social democrats. Beneš therefore appointed Gottwald Premier, and the latter's 26 man cabinet included nine communists and three social democrats. This cabinet voted, rather surprisingly in view of its membership, to join the Marshall Plan, but Gottwald and Masaryk were summoned to Moscow where an enraged Stalin complained that this was an unfriendly act. The cabinet promptly reversed its decision, bringing Czechoslovakia firmly within the Soviet economic sphere.

Predictions that the communist share of the popular vote would be greatly reduced in the 1948 elections encouraged the communists to increase their propaganda and prepare for direct action. On February 13th, 1948 a crisis broke when the non-communist members of Gottwald's cabinet tendered their resignation. A Soviet minister, V. A. Zorin, warned Masaryk that 'reactionary elements' were at work within Czechoslovakia, and noted that the Soviet Union looked forward to Gottwald's eventual success. The veiled threat of Soviet intervention was not all Beneš had to contend with. The communist-dominated People's Militias were issued with arms and ordered to prepare for a struggle against 'reactionaries', and Svoboda warned that 'the army goes with the nation', and confined all senior anti-communist officers to their quarters. Beneš had no choice but to approve Gottwald's new cabinet, which contained a majority of communists. Masaryk remained Foreign Minister, but died in suspicious circumstances 2 weeks later and was replaced by the communist Vladimir Clementis.

The *putsch* of February, 1948 was followed by a rapid increase in Party membership, the removal of the Party's opponents from positions of power, and the introduction of a new constitution. The communists swept home with a massive majority in the May elections, and Beneš resigned rather than approve the new constitution; he died on September 3rd. Gottwald became President in mid-July, and Antonín Zápotocký took over as Premier. Gottwald himself died in April, 1953 but not before he had carried out a massive purge of the Party, the armed forces, the civil service and the church. Numerous communists of long standing perished; Svoboda himself was arrested in late 1951 and imprisoned for 'treason'. Despite the occasional glimmer of liberalism, Czechoslovakia steadily followed the Moscow line under the Presidencies of Zápotocký and his successor Antonín Novotný. There was, however, some relaxation after Josef Lenárt became Premier in 1963.

In the 1950s, the Czech Army was thoroughly 'Sovietised'. While never as extensive as the Soviet control of the Polish Army, a 1,000-strong military mission had 'advisors' down to regimental level. Organisation, doctrine, training and even uniforms conformed to the Soviet model. The Czech arms industry geared up for large-scale production, often with Soviet-designed weapons. Between 1950 and 1953, for example, Czech weapons production increased over 900%. In 1951, the strength of the Czech Army doubled and the border and security troops quadrupled. Operationally, the Czechs were to provide one operational group of armies, which was to be subordinated to Soviet command. This shifted, around 1960, to providing ten divisions as the first echelon of a southwestern front, with a wartime mission of driving along the axis Pilsen-Karlsruhe.

Novotný came under increasing pressure from students, intellectuals and Slovak nationalists, and in January, 1968 lost the first round of a struggle for power. The posts of President and First Party Secretary were separated, and, although Novotný retained the former office for the time being, the latter post went to the Slovak communist Alexander Dubček. It was in an atmosphere of growing pressure for changes in policies and leaders that Novotný at last resigned as President, on March 22nd. The rehabilitated General Ludvík Svoboda was elected in his place; it was a significant coincidence that *svoboda* means 'freedom' in Czech.

The fall of Novotný was preceded by a group of highly-placed conservative generals who either contemplated or, apparently, actually attempted to use military force to support Novotný, organising troop exercises in the direction of Prague during the Party Plenum session that resulted in Novotný's fall. Action from the central government, especially the Main Political Administration of the Army prevented the troops being used and the plotters were arrested, fired, or 'committed suicide'.

Dubček's action programme – an attempt to pursue a Czechoslovak way to socialism and to reject Soviet insistence on continued class struggle – was approved by the party's Central Committee in early April. Many of the victims of Gottwald's purges were rehabilitated, and there was a general air of hope and enthusiasm. This euphoria did not last long. Soviet pressure on Dubček increased, and the Soviet press hinted at 'counter-revolution' and 'reaction' in Prague.

There is evidence that reformist elements in the Czech Army wished to move away from their being simply an element in overall Soviet strategy and wished to re-establish a national Czech defence strategy. In mid-May a military mission under the Soviet Minister of Defence, Marshal Grechko, visited Czechoslovakia, giving rise to rumours of imminent Soviet military intervention. In late July the Soviet Politburo and the Czechoslovak Presidium met at the little village of Čierna-nad-Tisou on the border between Czechoslovakia, Hungary and the Soviet Union. The meeting resulted in the signing of the empty Bratislava Declaration on August 3rd, and did nothing to avert the Soviet invasion, launched late on Tuesday, August 20th. Some Czech reformist military leaders may have considered the possibility of such an invasion, and submitted plans to the Politburo for resistance, which were not accepted.

Dubček and his colleagues decided, no doubt wisely, not to meet the invasion with armed resistance. There was, however, a good deal of passive resistance on the part of the civilian population, which suffered a number of casualties. Dubček was arrested, along with several other liberal politicians, and, although he was released shortly afterwards, the erosion of his power had begun. Most of the liberal measures of the 'Prague spring' were rescinded during the autumn, an amendment to the constitution made Czechoslovakia a federated State, and, in April, 1969 Dr. Gustáv Husák, Head of the Slovak Communist Party, was elected First Party Secretary in place of Dubček, who was subsequently sent to Turkey as ambassador. Dubček's complete disgrace was not long delayed; in late June, 1970 he was dismissed from his diplomatic post and expelled from the Party. There was no massive purge on the scale of 1951–2, but few of Dubček's supporters were allowed to retain any positions of power or influence. Oldřich Černik, Premier during the 'Prague spring' but an advocate of compromise following the Soviet invasion, was replaced as Premier by Lubomir Strougal, a former close adherent of Novotný.

A series of bilateral agreements sealed the work of the Warsaw Pact armies. The Moscow Agreement of 26 August, 1968 abandoned the Czech reforms. A status of forces agreement for the stationing of Soviet troops was concluded on 16 October. A 20-year treaty of friendship, cooperation and mutual assistance was signed in May 1970.

An immediate purge of the highest-ranking backers of the Dubček regime took place in the Armed Forces. General Prchilik, leader of the military wing of the reform movement and head of the Main Political Administration, was the first to lose his job. Anti-Soviet demonstrations and the less-purged Party's outlook on the Soviet 'liberators' resulted, in the spring of 1969, in a threat to use force by the Army's new commanders, hand-picked in Moscow. They were aided by Soviet officers performing much of the day-to-day work of the Czech Army. Many of these Soviets have remained, although not as numerous as they were in the 1950s.

The purges were extensive. 11,000 officers and 30,000 NCOs were removed from the Army. In 1968, fully 57.8% of all officers under 30 resigned. To replace them, crash courses were set up for those of proven political loyalty. The shortages in command personnel have never been made up, and the Czech Army still suffers from its loss of officers to purges and resignations. Even worse, the post-1968 political appointees are now reaching command rank, and are proving to be bungling even by Warsaw Pact standards. Purges continued until 1975. Other steps to maintain party control were the re-establishment of a Department for Military Affairs in the Central Committee and the transfer of Military Counterintelligence and the Border Troops to Ministry of the Interior Command.

There have been relatively few changes in Czechoslovakia since the re-establishment of Moscow-dominated communism in 1968–9. Husák and Strougal are First Secretary and Premier, respectively, and the aged Svoboda still inhabits Prague's Hradčany Castle. In 1973 Czechoslovakia made some efforts to normalise her foreign relations, and in December a treaty was concluded with the Federal Republic of Germany. It is unlikely that there will be another 'Prague spring' in the foreseeable future; the Soviet Union's determination to maintain an authoritarian communist regime in Czechoslovakia remains unaltered, and the five Soviet divisions currently stationed in Czechoslovakia lend weight to this determination.

STRENGTH AND BUDGET

Population: 15,450,000
Army: 142,500
Air force: 54,000; 482 combat aircraft
Paramilitary: 11,000 Border Troops; 2500 Civil Defence
    Troops
People's militia: 120,000
GNP (1981 estimate): $73.1–121 billion
Defence expenditure: (1981) $3.796 billion

COMMAND AND CONSTITUTIONAL STATUS

Command

The President of the Republic is the nominal Commander-in-Chief, but the actual command of the Army follows a standard Warsaw-Pact style Ministry of Defence. This Ministry is responsible to the Head of State through the Council of Defence, established by the Law of 31 January, 1969. The Council's seven to nine members include the Minister of Defence and are all drawn from the highest ranks of Czech leadership. There are also separate Defence Councils in the governments of the Czech and Slovak Republics.

The Minister of Defence, as in all Warsaw Pact nations except Romania, assumes the nation's highest military rank while holding his position. He has responsible to him various Deputy Ministers of Defence, the service chiefs, the Chief of Staff, and the two Military District Commanders. Also following standard Warsaw Pact pattern, the Main Political Directorate of the Ministry of National Defence is responsible for political training and indoctrination throughout the Army, and has its representatives down to company level. The Directorate itself is directly responsible to the Central Committee of the Czechoslovakian Communist Party.

The Main Political Administration is part of the Ministry of Defence, although responsible directly to the Central Committee of the Party.

Constitutional Status

The Constitution of July, 1960 made Czechoslovakia a Socialist Republic, and an amendment of October, 1968 introduced the current federal system. The federation consists of two nations of equal rights, the Czechs and Slovaks, forming two republics, each with its own government. The Federal Assembly, elected for 5 years, is the supreme organ of State power. It has two components: the House of the People, with members proportionate to the population of the republics, containing the 138 Czechs and 62 Slovaks; and the House of Nations, with 75 members from each republic. The Federal Assembly elects the President for a 5 year term, and the President appoints the government, the supreme executive body. Each republic has its own government and elective National Council, and is responsible for all matters except foreign relations, overseas trade, communications and defence, which are specifically reserved for the federal government.

ROLE, COMMITMENT, DEPLOYMENT AND RECENT OPERATIONS

Role and Commitment

The Czechoslovakian Army is subordinated to Warsaw Pact command, and would be employed, apparently in Army or divisional size units, under Soviet operational-level command. It would be committed to Southern Germany in the event of hostilities. Its territorial defence mission is very much secondary to its Warsaw Pact offensive mission.

Deployment

Ministry of Defence; Prague
Western Military District; Tábor
1st Army HQ; Pribram
1st Tank Division; Slany
4th Tank Division; Havlickuv Brod
2nd Motorised Rifle Division; Susice
3rd Motorised Rifle Division; Kromeritz
15th Motorised Rifle Division; Cĕské Budejovice
19th Motorised Rifle Division; Pizeň
20th Motorised Rifle Division; Karlovy Vary
9th Tank Division; Tábor
311th SCUD Missile Brigade; Stara Boleslav
321st SCUD Missile Brigade; Rokycany
331st SCUD Missile Brigade; Hranice
Eastern Military District; Trenčin
13th Tank Division; Topolcany
14th Tank Division; Presŏv
22nd Airborne Regiment; Pronitz bei Olmutz
?   Commando Battalion; ?

Non-divisional units include six engineer brigades, two artillery brigades, one anti-aircraft artillery brigade, two anti-tank regiments. The Air and Air Defence Forces have three divisions with six SAM regiments and 40 SA-2 and SA-3 sites with 240 launchers.

Reportedly, one tank division is at readiness Category I, two each in Categories II and III. Three motorised rifle divisions are Category I, one each Category II and Category III.

Recent Operations

The Czechoslovakian army has been involved in no recent military operations; in 1968 it did not offer armed resistance to the Soviet invasion. It participates, however, in the normal run of Warsaw Pact military exercises.

ORGANISATION

Arms of Service

The Czechoslovakian army is divided into Arms (*Zbranĕ*), Auxiliary Arms (*Pomocné Zbranĕ*) and Services (*Sluẑby*), as follows:

Arms: motor rifle, armour, artillery, engineers
Auxiliary Arms: signals, chemical troops, transport troops
Service: medical, quartermaster, ordnance, administration, justice, topographic.

Operational

Units are organised on basically Soviet lines but with some differences. For example, motorised rifle companies normally have seven APCs instead of 10 or 11 as in the Soviet Army. Other adaptations are made to reflect the use of Czech-designed equipment in some roles.

RECRUITMENT, TRAINING AND RESERVES

Recruitment

This is by means of conscription. Military service is for 2 years in the army, 27 months in the border troops and internal security forces, and 3 years in the air force. Sixty-six per cent of the armed forces are conscripts.

Training

This is similar to that of the Soviet ground forces. The army is subject to the same sort of political supervision that exists in other Warsaw Pact States, and political training takes up a significant proportion of training time.

Reserves

Reserve obligation continues when Czechoslovakians leave military service. Under the Law of 18 April 1961, service is in the first-line reserves to age 40, then in the second line to age 60. Reservist training is limited. The People's Militia is unique amongst the Warsaw Pact nations in that it is basically, as in 1948, the Party's private army. All members are party members and the First Secretary himself is the Commander-in-Chief. This force grew in importance after 1968. 140,000 strong, it now has AFVs, heavy weapons, and air defence weapons. Larger, brigade-equivalent headquarters have apparently been formed. Its main function remains internal security.

The Frontier Guard (PS) is under the Ministry of the Interior and is responsible for border security. The Interior Guard (VS), also under the Ministry of the Interior, is responsible for internal security. The highest echelon units are battalion-equivalents.

EQUIPMENT AND ARMS INDUSTRY

Czechoslovakia is the most industrialised Soviet satellite. She has a thriving arms industry, and her armed forces use numerous Czech-designed and Czech-produced items of equipment.

Equipment

Small arms: M-50 machine pistol, 7.62mm short, and M-24/26 machine pistol, 7.62mm short; M-52/57 automatic rifle, similar to Soviet SKS (Simonov), for the 7.62mm M-43 round; M-58 assault rifle, 7.62mm M-43, very similar to Soviet AK-47; M-1952/7 7.62mm M-43 belt-fed light machine-gun (M-58 is standard rifle)
Mortars: Soviet 120mm and 82mm
Anti-tank: P-27 Pancĕrovka rocket projector, similar to

Czechoslovakia

Soviet RPG-7; RPG-18; T-21 Tarašnice 82mm and M-59A 82mm recoilless guns; M-52 85mm gun, similar to Soviet M-45, and M-55 100mm gun, similar to Soviet M-55; the Soviet M-43 and M-55 are both in use
Anti-aircraft: DShK-Vierling quadruple 12.7mm machine-gun (this is the Soviet DShK gun on a Czech-designed mounting); M-53 30mm twin cannon; M-53/59 30mm twin cannon on Praga V3S armoured vehicle; 57mm cannon, similar to Soviet M-50; ZSU-23—4; (500 57mm reported)
Artillery: Mainly Soviet-designed: 150 100mm, 300—600 122mm, 25 130mm, 122mm SP, 152mm SP, 200 RM-70 122mm MRL, 120 130mm MRL
Armour: Tanks: 3,400-3,600 main battle tanks, mainly T-54/55s, but up to 1,000 T-72s may be in the force structure
Infantry Combat Vehicles: 950 BMP-1
APCS: 2,800 OT-62/64
Scout Cars: 1,250 OT-65 and BRDMs
Missiles: Sagger and *Spigot* ATGMs, 40 FROG-7, 27 SCUD-B, 250 SA-2 and SA-3, SA-4, SA-6, SA-9, SA-7.

Arms Industry

The Škoda factory at Plzěn had an international reputation for the manufacture of high-quality arms long before the birth of Czechoslovakia as an independent State and the battle-tried British Bren light machine-gun was modelled upon a weapon designed in Brno. The thriving Czechoslovakian arms industry currently produces a wide range of military equipment, and is easily the most important non-Soviet arms industry within the Warsaw Pact. Some Czech-produced equipment is, naturally, of Soviet design, or is closely based upon a Soviet prototype, but many such items – like the Czech version of the BM-21 – are substantial improvements upon the Soviet originals. Other equipment is of Czech design – the Tatra and Praga range of vehicles are particularly worthy of note. Czechoslovakia has had considerable success in the export of military equipment: the SKOT, for example, is currently in service in Poland, Hungary, Egypt, India, Morocco, the Sudan, Syria and Uganda. Many exported T-55 Tanks are Czech made, for example Iraq. The workmanship on Czech weapons is normally superior to soviet-built examples.

RANK, DRESS AND DISTINCTIONS

Rank

All badges of rank are worn on the epaulette.

Officers
Armádni general – Gold edged epaulette, four stars above crossed maces and wreath
Generálplukovnik – Gold-edged epaulette, three stars above crossed maces and wreath
Generálporučik – Gold-edged epaulette, two stars above crossed maces and wreath
Generálmajor – Gold-edged epaulette, one star above crossed maces and wreath
Plukovnik – Gold-edged epaulette, three stars with crossed maces above
Podplukovnik – Gold-edged epaulette, two stars with crossed maces above
Major – Gold-edged epaulette, one star with crossed maces above
Kapitán – Four stars with crossed maces above
Nadporučik – Three stars with crossed maces above
Poručik – Two stars with crossed maces above
Podporučik – One star with crossed maces above

Officers' stars and buttons are gold. Stars are arranged as follows: generals – stars one above another; plukovnik, nad-poručik – stars in inverted 'V'; kapitán – stars in inverted 'Y'; podplukovnik and poručik – stars side-by-side.

Warrant Officers
Nadpraporčik – Silver-edged epaulette, three silver stars, one above another
Praporčik – Silver-edged epaulette, two silver stars, one above another
Podpraporčik – Silver-edged epaulette, one silver star

Regular NCOs
Nadrotmistr – Three silver stars, one above another
Rotmistr – Two silver stars, one above another
Rotný – One silver star

Conscript NCOs and men
Četař – Three round white studs, side by side
Desátnik – Two round white studs, side by side
Svobodnik – One round white stud
Vojin – Plain epaulette

Dress

There are five basic forms of dress with certain variations. Ceremonial parade dress (which is relatively uncommon), parade dress and walking-out dress are based upon an olive-brown tunic with open collar and four pockets, worn with a light khaki shirt, black tie and olive-brown trousers. Embellishments depend upon the order of dress: black- and yellow-braided belts are worn in ceremonial dress; leather belts, with Sam Brownes for officers, are worn in parade dress; while in walking-out dress no belts are worn. Black boots and gaiters are worn in ceremonial parade and parade dress, and shoes are worn in walking-out dress. Officers, warrant officers and regular NCOs wear an olive-brown peaked cap in all the above orders of dress, but conscripts wear an olive-brown sidecap in walking-out dress.

For everyday wear in summer, officers and soliders have a greyish shirt-blouse of *blouson* cut; this garment has an open neck and two breast pockets, is buttoned at wrist and waist and is worn outside the olive-brown trousers. A green combat suit with brown camouflage dashes, with camouflaged field cap or steel helmet and black boots and gaiters, is worn in field dress. The Czechoslovakian army employs the usual specialist clothing. NBC suits and tank-suits are of the Soviet pattern, and parachute units have a special mottled combat suit and brown leather protective helmet. Tank crews and paratroopers wear berets in certain orders of dress; those of the former are black, and those of the latter red. Olive-brown double-breasted calf-length greatcoats are worn, with most orders of dress, in the winter. Arm of service badges are, in the main, self-explanatory. The cap-badge consists of a lion rampant on a pentagonal shield, and a national red, white and blue roundel is worn on the left upper arm in most orders of dress.

Distinctions

Numerous decorations, among them the Military Order of the White Lion for Victory and the General Milan Restslav Stefanik 'Sobol' award, were in use before 1955. In the latter year several new decorations were instituted, most of them with precise Soviet equivalents. The Order of Clement Gottwald is the Czech equivalent of the Order of Lenin. The Order of the Red Banner, Order of the Red Star, Medal for Merit in the Defence of the Homeland and Medal for Service to the Homeland are awarded for outstanding achievement, meritorious service and long service.

CURRENT DEVELOPMENTS

The shadow of 1968 still hangs over the Czech military. While it would appear that the widespread Soviet control has achieved as much reliability as can be expected, nationalist and anti-Soviet sentiment endures. The Czech officer corps has been highly politicised. The Czech Army is an integral part of the Warsaw Pact's offensive strategy in the Central Sector.

Richard Holmes
David Isby

DENMARK

HISTORY AND INTRODUCTION

Like its neighbour Sweden, with which for several centuries it disputed the mastery of the Baltic sea and coasts, Denmark is the inheritor of a great military tradition, but also the protagonist, in more recent times, of a strong and idealistic creed of neutrality and pacifism. Belief in this creed, at the peak of its strength before World War II, was seriously undermined by German behaviour to Denmark during 1940—45 and, in the post-war years, Denmark has adopted a more partisan foreign policy and a more robust defence posture than at any time since the mid-nineteenth century. Pacifist and neutralist tendencies remain strong nonetheless, and are reflected in the reductions Denmark has recently made in the size of her armed forces, in the numbers conscripted for military service and in the length of the conscripts' terms.

The pacifist strain in Danish politics may be due in part to the fact that the army, unlike the Swedish, lacks really deep roots as a popular institution. In the eighteenth century the powerful land-owning nobility obliged the monarchy to introduce a measure, known as the *Stavnsbaand*, which bound the peasantry to their estates – a return to feudalism – obliged them to perform free labour and used the threat of conscription into the army against those who proved refractory. The system was abolished in 1788 but the army retained its status as an oppressive instrument of State power. The campaign to retain the 'Duchies' – the partly German provinces of Schleswig-Holstein – in 1848—50 aroused popular enthusiasm, which was further fuelled by the remarkable Danish victories of Fredericia, July 6th, 1849, and Isted, July 25th, 1850, over the army of the German Confederation. In addition the liberal Constitution of 1849 included Article 81, which made military service a universal obligation. However, the decisive success of the Prussian and Austrian armies in the Second Schleswig-Holstein War of 1863—4, the heavy casualties suffered in the concluding battle of Dippul, the economic crisis which resulted from the cost of the war, and the loss of population and territory, all contributed to put an end to Denmark's aspirations to independent military power.

For a country which had, at various times in the past held the crowns of England; headed a Union of all the Scandinavian countries (and retained Norway until 1814); ruled the islands of the north Atlantic (Greenland and the Faroes remain Danish); owned territory on the southern Baltic coast as far east as Estonia; founded trading stations in West Africa and the East and West Indies; maintained a navy of European importance; and, between 1429 and 1857, exacted dues from all shipping passing in and out of the Baltic, the defeat of 1864 therefore marked a revolution in national affairs. The Danes accepted its logic, nevertheless, with remarkable realism, the only domestic military disputes ensuing up to the outbreak of World War II being over exactly how small an armed force they should maintain. Until 1901, defence expenditure was concentrated on fortifying Copenhagen against a future German attack. Thereafter the impossibility of resisting a German invasion was recognised, and Denmark adopted a policy of seeking to convince Germany that she 'could be trusted to defend herself against aggressors harbouring hostile intentions against Germany'. As a result, she agreed to mine the Great Belt at the outbreak of World

War I. After the war, the coalition of Social Democrats and the pacifist Radical Liberals which held power for most of the inter-war period and became one of the governments most strongly committed to the League of Nations' ideals, adopted a completely neutralist policy and reduced the Danish army almost to a token force.

The advantage which Germany took of Denmark on April 9th, 1940 when the country was invaded without warning, and the ordeal of occupation, which took the form of German military government after 1943, produced a strong reaction against neutralism in post-war Denmark. Some attempt was first made to find future security in a pan-Scandinavian defence union but eventually the country decided to accede, with certain limitations (*see under* Command and Constitutional Status) to NATO. All three services were considerably enlarged from the pre-war size and expensively re-equipped, with American aid.

An interesting and significant post-war development was the creation of the Home Guard (*Hjemme Vaernet*). A voluntary organisation, now 70,000 strong, it was founded upon, and largely by, the Danish resistance movement in 1945 and achieved statutory recognition in 1949. Initially it represented a certain popular contempt for, and suspicion of, the regular army, which had not opposed the German invasion (chiefly because it had been given no orders to do so). In addition it had remained in existence under German occupation until 1943 and had provided formed contingents to the 'foreign volunteer units' of the *Wehrmacht* and the *Waffen SS* for the campaign in Russia. In a sense therefore, the Home Guard represents an 'alternative' military principle in Danish life, and stands as a keeper of the nation's military conscience. Though the enthusiasts who brought it into being are now being taken from it by age, it continues to maintain its strength, all the more remarkable when compulsory military service in the standing army grows apparently more unpopular with young Danes.

STRENGTH AND BUDGET

Population: 5,125,000
Army: 18,000 plus 59,000 reserves
Navy: 5800 (10 frigates, 5 submarines, 56 smaller vessels)
Air force: 7400; 112 combat aircraft
Home Guard: 57,000 (voluntary)
GNP (1981): $57,580,000,000
Defence expenditure (1982): $1,102,000,000

Denmark publishes a combined defence budget, in which the army element is difficult to isolate. As a result of the 1973 agreement between the major parties, defence expenditure is to be calculated in April, 1972 prices over the fiscal years 1973—7 inclusive and to rise somewhat. During the same period, as a result of the move towards substituting regulars for conscripts in the Standing Force and the consequent saving in training costs, it is expected that the sums available for procurement will somewhat increase. The army has several major items of equipment (*see under* Equipment and Arms Industry) which it intends to add to its inventory during the term of this defence budgetary period.

COMMAND AND CONSTITUTIONAL STATUS

Constitutionally, the Sovereign is Head of the Armed Services. In practice, command resides with the Ministry of Defence and the services.

Denmark has a unified defence ministry and a single defence command. The Chief of Defence, Head of the Defence Command, is a serving officer, whose Deputy is the Chief of the Defence Staff; together with the Chiefs of the Army, Navy and Air Force and the Commander, Danish Operational Forces, they form the Defence Council. Operational control of the army, as one element of the forces, rests with the Chief of Defence; but at a time of tension he may transfer command to the Commander Danish Operational Forces; as explained in the next section, the Commander Danish Operational Forces is also the NATO Baltic Approaches Commander (COMBALTAP) who, when appropriate, transfers Danish forces to NATO control, which he then exercises as a NATO commander; his Principal Land Subordinate Commander (COMLANDJUT) is alternately a Danish and then a German officer.

The Head of the Army is not an operational commander, though he is operational adviser to the Defence Commander in the Defence Council; his principal service role is as inspector of his own service and commander of the army's schools and training function. He is not head of the army element of the Home Guard, which is directly subordinate to the Ministry of Defence through its own Home Guard Command; at the head of that command are a Civilian Commissioner and a Military Commander, who is also Inspector of the Army Home Guard.

Parliament (*Folketing*) exercises very close supervision over Danish defence, and all recent defence legislation has come about as a result of political bargaining between the main parties. During debates on defence matters, Parliament calls the heads of the various services to give evidence before it, and to submit papers directly to it.

Denmark has a written constitution, Article 81 of which lays down the duty of 'every man capable of bearing arms . . . with his own body to contribute towards the defence of his native land'. The successive Defence Acts (the most important are those of 1950, 1960, 1969 and 1973) also have constitutional force, as do the General Operational Instructions issued as a Royal Decree of March 6th, 1952 and amended on April 26th, 1961. This remarkably forthright document, framed in the light of the events of April 9th, 1940, lays on all Danish servicemen the duty of resisting violation of the national territory without waiting for receipt of orders, disobeying orders to cease fighting unless their legal validity is established beyond doubt, and disregarding orders issued by superiors who have fallen into enemy hands.

The right of conscientious objection is recognised and about 15% of eligible Danes invoke the right annually. A code of military law exists and military courts have jurisdiction over servicemen.

ROLE, COMMITMENT, DEPLOYMENT AND RECENT OPERATIONS

Role
The peacetime role of the Danish army has been officially defined as 'participation in the surveillance of Danish territory, repelling of violations of Danish land territory, preparation for the execution of war tasks, through its peacetime existence to contribute towards forcing a potential aggressor to take such preparatory measures so that his intentions will be revealed in due time and, at an alert, to guard and secure such installations which are of importance to the overall national defence'; the wartime role is defined as countering a surprise attack and gaining time for mobilisation, maintaining the fight to allow Allied forces time to arrive and then continuing the fight jointly with Allied forces.

Commitments
Denmark is a member of NATO. Her ground forces are subordinate to the Commander Danish Operational Forces who is also always NATO Commander Allied Forces Baltic Approaches (COMBALTAP). He is subordinate, as a Danish national commander, to the Chief of Defence and so to the Danish government; as a NATO commander he is subordinate to CINCNORTH but the superior of the NATO Commander Allied Land Forces Schleswig-Holstein and Jutland (COMLANDJUT), alternately a Danish and then a German officer who commands both Danish and German ground forces (the latter the 6th Panzer Grenadier Division). The Danish land forces are therefore under the control of a NATO commander and are earmarked for NATO commitment, but will be transferred to NATO command only at the decision of the Danish government. The Local Defence Forces, the Home Guard and any part of the Field Army in Western Land Command, which is excluded from the agreement with NATO, would remain at all times under Danish national command.

The Danish United Nations Battalion, which is financed by the Ministry of Foreign Affairs, forms part of the joint Scandinvian force made permanently available to the United Nations and is either abroad on emergency duty (at present it is in Cyprus) or on call.

Although a full military member of NATO, Denmark does not permit the stationing of foreign troops on Danish soil (except in Greenland) and, until 1963, did not allow foreign NATO troops to exercise on her territory. She still does not allow foreign NATO troops to set foot on Bornholm, out of deference to the Soviet view that that island was evacuated by Russian troops in 1946 on such an understanding. She does not allow the stationing of nuclear weapons on her territory.

Deployment
Operationally, the Danish land area is divided into a Western Land Command, Eastern Land Command and the Bornholm Region. Eastern Command contains two of the Standing Force brigades, Western Command the other three. Bornholm contains an independent force consisting of an infantry battalion and some armour and artillery. For territorial defence, Denmark is divided into seven regions, three in Jutland, one in Funen, two on Zealand and one on Bornholm, under which are subordinated the 500 Home Guard companies and the 21 Local Defence Forces battalions.

Recent Operations
The Danish army has not been to war since 1864. It sent medical units, under United Nations auspices, to the Korean War, 1950–3.

ORGANISATION

The army is organised into supply troops, signals, engineers, artillery, army aviation, infantry and armoured troops (excavalry). The latter include the old regiments of infantry and cavalry, some of which trace their origin to the seventeenth century – the Jutland Dragoons (1670), the Guards Hussars (1762), the Zealand (1614) and Funen (1614) Life Regiments, the Schleswig Regiment of Foot (1778), the Kings and the

Denmark

Royal Footguards — and which form the link between the standing and the reserve army. The 1st battalions of these regiments belong to the standing force and are manned by regulars, the 2nd—4th battalions are training units or belong to the Local Defence Forces. The other corps serving the army are tri-service: the Judge Advocate Corps, the Medical Corps, the Defence Construction Service, the Quartermaster Corps and the Defence Intelligence Service.

Operational Divisions

The army is divided operationally into the Field Army, which is earmarked to operate with NATO, and the Local Defence Forces. The Field Army consists of three elements: the Standing Force and the Augmentation Force (together known as the Covering Force), and the Field Army Reserve, consisting of the Covering Force Reserve and other reserve (mainly support) units. The Covering Force consists essentially of five small armoured infantry brigades, three on Jutland and two on Zealand, each of which contains an armoured infantry battalion (two armoured infantry companies and one tank company); a tank battalion (two tank companies and one armoured infantry company); an artillery battalion (two SP howitzer batteries and one air-defence battery); and an armoured reconnaissance squadron. In addition there also exists an infantry battalion on Bornholm and the Royal Lifeguard Battalion at Copenhagen. The Augmentation Force consists of company-sized units sufficient to add a company to each of the Standing Force battalions; the Covering Force Reserve would add one armoured infantry battalion and one motorised infantry battalion to each of the brigades.

The Local Defence Forces, based on the seven military regions, consist of seven headquarters companies, 21 infantry battalions, two tank battalions, seven artillery battalions, seven engineer companies and some tank-destroyer squadrons; the infantry battalions are not equipped for mobile operations and are formed of reservists, who do only a few days annual refresher training, and who would probably come into existence only on mobilisation. The Home Guard, a voluntary organisation 57,300 strong, forms about 500 local defence companies; the personnel keep their weapons and equipment at home. The numerical strength of the various categories are: Field Army Standing Force, 8500; Field Army Augmentation Force, 6000; Field Army Reserve, 43,000; Local Defence Forces, 16,000; Home Guard, 57,300. To these should be added a Training Force of about 5750 (engaged in training conscripts and reservists), 7250 in headquarters, depots and schools, and a United Nations Battalion of 350 (in Cyprus).

RECRUITMENT, TRAINING AND RESERVES

Conscription remains (in strict constitutional theory) the principle on which all the Danish armed forces have been recruited since 1849. As a result of the defence agreement concluded between the four major parties in 1973, however, the attempt has recently been made to increase the proportion of regulars serving in the forces, with the object of manning the Standing Force wholly, and the Augmentation Force partly, with regulars, retaining conscripts only in the training units to provide reservists for the Field Army Reserve. The term of service for the conscripts was reduced to 9 months in 1973; regulars must enlist for 54, 63 or 72 months.

Training is at present carried out in the training battalions of the regiments (the active battalions of which form the units of the Standing Force) and, for specialists, in the various schools. In future, training is to be concentrated in the schools; all artillery personnel, for example, will be trained at

the Army Fire Support School at Varde, West Jutland, and all infantry personnel at the Army Combat School at Oxboel, West Jutland. Conscript NCOs and officers are also trained at these schools, senior NCOs and officers having to serve for 18 months instead of nine. Regular officers are trained at the Defence College, Copenhagen, a tri-service institution which is also the staff college.

The Home Guard recruits are trained in Home Guard centres near their own homes, either in their spare time or in periods of 4 days for which compensation for loss of wages may be paid. In the first year recruits train for 100 hours per year, in the second and third year for 50 hours per year, thereafter for 24 hours per year.

The reserves are formed, for the most part, of complete units of ex-conscripts who started their service together. After completing their 9 months' training, they proceed *en bloc* to the reserve, either by way of the Augmentation Force, with which units remain for 18 months, or directly to the Field Army Reserve or the Local Defence Force, with which the unit remains for 5 years. The reserve liability then effectively ceases; except for the shorter duration of the reserve liability, this system of *en bloc* transfer of trained conscript units to the reserve is similar to the Swedish. Reserves number about 70,000 (Augmentation Force 4500, Field Army Reserve 41,000 and Local Defence Forces 24,000).

EQUIPMENT AND ARMS INDUSTRY

Denmark formerly possessed an important source of small-arms manufacture in the firm of Madsen, a pioneer manufacturer of automatic weapons, but the firm has now given up armament work. The country's armed forces have, since the war, been re-equipped with foreign military equipment, largely at American expense, though that aid ceased in 1967. The additional burden that has been thrown on the Danish budget is one of the principal reasons underlying the political campaign for the reduction in the size and capabilities of the armed forces. Re-equipment is nevertheless proceeding: major items to be procured in 1975—7 include Leopard tanks to replace the ageing Centurions; a replacement for the army and Home Guard rifle; and other items such as APCs, vehicles, radios, artillery VT-fused ammunition, tank ammunition, fixed-wing aircraft, land mines, electronic equipment and radios.

Equipment

Pistol: 9mm Browning FN
SMG: 9mm M-49 Hovea (Swedish Husqvana)
Rifle: 7.62mm GM 50 (the American M-1 Garand, converted by Beretta) and 7.62mm GM 66 (German G-3, replacing the above)
Machine-gun: 7.62mm MG 62 (German MG42/59, Rheinmetal)
Mortars: 60mm M-51 Fa (USA), 81mm M-57 Fa (made by Danish Vabenarsenalat) and 120mm M-50 Fa (Hotchkiss-Brandt) Vabenarsenalat
Anti-armour weapons: 84mm Carl Gustav RCL (Swedish); 106mm M-56 RCL(USA) and TOW guided missile (USA)
Anti-defence weapons: Redeye SAM (USA) and 40mm L/70 Bofors gun (USA; equips the air-defence batteries of the armoured infantry brigades; 36 in service)
Artillery: M-109 SP howitzer (USA; equips the artillery battalions of the armoured infantry brigades; 72 in service) and M-55 203mm howitzer (USA; 12 in service); 155mm guns (24 in service); 105mm howitzers (96 in service)
Armour: M-113 APC (USA; equips the infantry companies of the armoured infantry brigades; 650 in service);

Centurion tank (Britain; partly equips the tank companies of the armoured infantry brigades; 88 in service); Leopard 1 tank (Germany; 120 in service, replacing the Centurions); M-41 light tank (USA; equips the armoured reconnaissance companies of the armoured infantry brigades; 48 in service)
Aircraft: 500A Hughes helicopters (12 in service); Saab T-17 light aircraft (12 in service)

There is a variety of older equipment in use by the Reserve, the Local Defence Forces and the Home Guard, including towed 155mm howitzers and guns and 105mm howitzers (270 pieces in all).

RANK, DRESS AND DISTINCTIONS

Rank

General (General) — Three large gold stars
Generallöjtnant (Lieutenant-General) — Two large gold stars
Generalmajor (Major-General) — One large gold star
Oberst (Colonel) — Three smaller gold stars
Oberstlöjtnant (Lieutenant-Colonel) — Two smaller gold stars
Kaptajn (Major) — One smaller gold star
Kaptajnlöjtnant (Captain) — Three small gold stars
Premierlöjtnant — Two small gold stars
Löjtnant — One* small gold star
Sekondlöjtnant — One small gold star

Overfenrik — Four chevrons, point up, three arcs under
Fenrik — Four chevrons, point up, two arcs under
Oversrgent — Four chevrons, point up, one arc under
Sergent — Three† chevrons, point up
Korporal — Two† chevrons, point up
Overkonstabel I — Three bars
Overkonstabel II — Two bars
Konstabel — One bar

Note: officers' badges are worn on the shoulder strap, other ranks' on the upper sleeve; * also with a gold triangle; † also worn with an arc if the wearer is a regular.

Dress

For everyday wear a khaki uniform of British 'battledress' style, with beret or side-hat; the combat dress is green, worn with the NATO steel helmet; a walking-out dress of dark-green jacket and dark-grey trousers has recently been issued. The Royal Lifeguard wear on ceremonial occasions an early nineteenth century uniform of bearskin cap, scarlet tunic, white crossbelts and sky-blue trousers.

CURRENT DEVELOPMENTS

Defence policy is traditionally a matter for hard bargaining between the parties, of which there are more than in most Western democracies and of which several have long-established pacifist beliefs. It is against this background that Denmark's recent reduction in the size of the armed forces should be seen; and if the defence policy of the mushroom Poujadist Progressive Party (which won 28 seats in the *Folketing* in December, 1973 and advocated disbanding the armed forces and installing an automatic telephone system which would say 'We surrender' in Russian) appears eccentric, it should be remembered that the respected Social Democrats had suggested in the 1930s reducing the Danish army to a 'watch' of 800 men.

In domestic terms, therefore, the current downward trend of military investment and of the liability to conscription is understandable. Its sense is reinforced by the fact that Denmark lacks geographical defences: it is almost completely flat, and Jutland, the peninsula, has no important water obstacles. The hostility of males of military age (only one-third of whom are required for military duty) to conscription, and the high rate of registrations of conscientious objection (15%) may also be seen as an exaggeration of a phenomenon almost world-wide in the 1970s. And there remains among all Danes a fear of German intentions towards their country and suspicion of the long-term consequences of close military association with Germany in NATO.

Nevertheless, even if it is argued that the defence establishment erected by the 1960 Defence Agreement was too large for the Danish population and economy to support, and if it is accepted that the 1973 Defence Agreement between the parties (including for the first time the anti-military Radical Liberals) allows for a larger establishment than proposed by the long dominant Social Democrats in 1970 (which would have reduced the conscript's term to 5—6 months and the size of the Standing Force to 7000), the new defence establishment is a matter of legitimate concern, which has been forcibly expressed to the NATO Defence Planning Committee. Its views, as they affected the new organisation of the Danish army (reduced since 1970 from 20 to 14 first-line battalions), was that the shortening of the conscription term (from 14 to 9 months since 1969) would 'diminish the effectiveness of units manned mainly by conscripts and reserve personnel' (i.e. the Augmentation Force), and that it would entail the devotion of a larger proportion of the defence budget to personnel at the expense of 'much needed re-equipment'. It did not mention, though it might have done so, that the new Danish 'brigades' are possibly the smallest formations in any European army to be accorded that designation (they are in effect only battle groups). It did, however, touch upon the most serious consequence of the diminution of Danish first-line ground defence: the protection of the Baltic outlets. The Danish army could never have been expected to contribute largely to NATO's order of battle on the Central Front, but the Soviet bloc possesses a sizeable amphibious force in the Baltic, including a Polish amphibious division, an East German special forces group and a Russian naval infantry division, which might be expected to have the islands and peninsula of Denmark, which block egress to the North Sea, as its principal objective.

John Keegan

DJIBOUTI

HISTORY AND INTRODUCTION

Djibouti is a small, independent state that exists today as a consequence of the desire of France, during the 'scramble for Africa' period, to have a port that controlled an entrance to the Red Sea in rivalry to that of Britain in Aden. It has a mixed population of some 40% Afars (kinsmen of the Danakil communities living in the Ethiopian province of Eritrea) and some 55% Issas, one of the main Somali clans. The balance is composed of Arabs and other immigrant communities. The final ingredient in the predicament of Djibouti is that the port lies at the end of the only railway into the Ethiopian highlands, linking Addis Ababa to the sea. During the last years of colonial rule, at a time when Djibouti was desired by the Ethiopians because of the rail link, and by Somalia as part of Somalia's irrenditist ambitions, the French renamed the territory as the 'French Coast of the Afars and Issas'; they also tried by a variety of measures to weaken the Somali majority. They did this not simply to prolong a colonial rule ended elsewhere in francophone black Africa in 1960, but also because were the territory to pass to either Somalia or Ethiopia, there was every likelihood of a violent reaction by the other.

By the mid-1970s however, pressures for change emerged. The Afars became restless under the stigma of being one of Africa's last colonies, the more perceptive of them also came to see they could never rule the territory on their own. Some too were attracted by the revolutionary rhetoric of Ethiopia. France shrewdly perceived that Somali Issa leaders, once in office, were unlikely to pass the territory on a plate to Mogadishu as a remote province. French harassment of the Issa ceased, and a reconciliation begun, which led to flag independence in 1977 under a government in which political leaders of both communities figured. The new government immediately signed a treaty with France, giving Paris the right to maintain a strong garrison. The post-independence government — under President Gouled Hassan, an Issa, and with since December 1977 an Afar Prime Minister — has still a major problem of creating a national unity. The problem's dimensions can be seen by occasional restlessness and violence, the worst outbreak being in late 1977 when bombs were thrown, and the 1981 decision to make Djibouti a one-party state. But there are, nevertheless, signs that a new sense of statehood may be emerging even if one of its major components is a common appreciation of the tight rope the territory has to walk.

A factor to Djibouti's advantage is the number of friends she has abroad besides France. The USA has provided generous aid (mostly military credits); other aid donors include China, Taiwan, South Korea, Pakistan, Saudi Arabia, Iraq, Oman, Algeria and Libya.

STRENGTH AND BUDGET

Population: 310,000.
Armed Forces: Army, 2,600; Air Force, 80; Navy 20, Gendarmerie 2,100.
GNP: $275,000,000 (estimate).

COMMAND AND CONSTITUTIONAL STATUS

The President of Djibouti, President Gouled Hassan Aptidion, is commander-in-chief of Djibouti's armed forces. The Minister for Defence is Mr Habib Mohamed Loita and the Armed Forces Chief of Staff is Colonel Fathi Ahmed.

ROLE, COMMITMENT, DEPLOYMENT AND RECENT OPERATIONS

Djibouti's armed forces exist firstly to secure the state against a military incursion from either Ethiopia or Somalia, the former perhaps backed by the USSR, and secondly to assist in the preservation of law and order within the territory. In the former role, Djibouti's small armed forces would be supported by the French garrison; the combined forces would be adequate (and have so far proved to be so) to secure for Djibouti a 'Hong Kong' defence posture — the territory could not be taken over without several days of fighting during which Djibouti's friends would be able to mobilise considerable diplomatic support and perhaps even military reinforcement.

The French units, under a 1977 military protocol, may only be deployed in the event of foreign aggression, and then only at the request of the Djibouti government. They are expressly forbidden from operating in support of the Djibouti government in the event of internal unrest.

ORGANISATION

Djibouti's forces are all, technically, part of the Army, and they are built around an infantry regiment, an armoured squadron, a 'border commando battalion', a parachute company and a logistics support unit.

(The French Forces include the 13th *Demi Brigade* of the Foreign Legion, the 5th *Regiment Inter Armes d'Outre Mer* (composed of an infantry company, two squadrons of AMX-13 tanks, a towed 155mm and 105mm gun battery and an anti-aircraft battery of 40mm and 30mm guns), the Vexin Air Force Squadron of Mirage IIIs and (usually) a French naval unit).

RECRUITMENT, TRAINING AND RESERVES

France has hitherto enjoyed a virtual monopoly training position and joint exercises take place regularly. Recent reports, however, suggest that the USA is assuming responsibility for training and equipping a military engineering unit. The armed forces appear to have no recruitment problems though reports suggest the personnel is disproportionately Afar.

No reserves are known to exist.

Pakistan, Libya and Algeria have made small contributions to the equipment of the gendarmerie in the provision of barbed wire (Pakistan), BRDM-2 and BTR-40 vehicles and radio equipment (Libya), and training facilities (Algeria).

EQUIPMENT AND ARMS INDUSTRY

No local arms industry exists. The Army's equipment is a mixture of French and Soviet, the latter mostly supplied by Libya. In terms of armour it includes twelve BRDM-2, eight AML-90 Panhard and two AML-60 Panhard armoured vehicles, twelve BTR-60 armoured personnel carriers, and French 81mm and 120mm mortars, and 89mm and 106mm anti-tank weapons. One report also notes the arrival of a small number of 105mm pack howitzers.

The Air Force consists of four small transport aircraft, a light liaison machine and one Alouette II helicopter.

RANK, DRESS AND DISTINCTIONS

These generally follow the French pattern, except the *képi* is not worn, being replaced by a peaked cap.

CURRENT DEVELOPMENTS

The 'new dimension' to Djibouti's situation is, of course, that of US interest in Djibouti as a possible staging post for the Rapid Deployment Force. A number of US Navy ships have visited the port in recent months.

Other factors affecting the situation are the world recession and the general tension in the Horn of Africa which have reduced Djibouti's value as a port (Ethiopia trades through Assab whenever she can) and a growing anti-French restiveness among the younger generation of Somalis. In the event of a return to prosperity, and congestion at Assab with a consequent increased Ethiopian use of Djibouti, a future Djibouti government might be tempted to cut the link with France.

For the moment, however, with Ethiopia still unstable, the present regime is likely to look on France as its main protector for several years ahead. France, with its continuing naval interest in the Indian Ocean, is equally likely to continue providing its garrison.

Lloyd Mathews

DOMINICAN REPUBLIC

HISTORY AND INTRODUCTION

From the first days of its independence from Spain in 1821 the history of the Dominican Republic has been dominated by military events and military men, but it did not actually acquire a regular army in the contemporary sense until about a century later. Since then, it has usually been the new United States-founded regular army which has determined the course of Dominican affairs.

The island of Hispaniola, Spain's first base in the New World, rapidly lost its importance after the end of the sixteenth century, and a century later the western third of it was ceded by Spain to France. This has had a profound effect on shaping the Dominican Republic's environment and priorities, for shortly after the outbreak of the French Revolution the black slaves of Haiti revolted and seized control of that country.

With the support of French revolutionary troops Toussaint l'Ouverture's ex-slave army conquered the Spanish-ruled two-thirds of the island in 1801 and ruled it until the Dominican population revolted in 1808. They routed a French military force at the battle of Palo Hincado and completed the liberation of the Spanish-speaking part of the island with a successful siege of Santo Domingo.

The return to Spanish rule was short-lived, however, and the Dominican Republic's first experience of independence in 1821 even briefer, for in the following year it was overrun and subjugated once again by Haitian armies. The brutal 22 year occupation which followed is vividly remembered in the Dominican Republic even today as the 'Period of Africanisation', and left a lasting fear and suspicion of Haiti which has ever since been the principal public justification for a strong Dominican army.

Through the remainder of the nineteenth century the justification was not without substance, for although the Dominican Republic was refounded after a successful revolt in 1844 its Haitian ex-rulers made repeated attempts to reconquer it during the succeeding decades. Although the Dominican Republic itself has a far larger black element in its population than any other Spanish-speaking republic — 60% are mulatto and 12% black — the traditional hostility to Haiti has strong racial undertones. One of the military strongmen who ruled the republic during the 1860s, Pedro de Santana, even persuaded Spain to re-annex it as a means of gaining protection from the Haitian threat, but after a 2 year revolt Spanish rule was overthrown by the Dominicans in 1865.

Throughout the nineteenth and early twentieth centuries the Dominican Republic was a society dominated by a mostly white land-owning *élite* which monopolised both government and army senior ranks. The mass of the population lived in wretched poverty and ignorance in subsistence agriculture, or as landless labourers on the sugar-cane estates. Political power was extremely decentralised: there was nominally a national army and a central administration, but in fact most power usually lay in the hands of local *caudillos* who made themselves provincial governors and recruited military units under their own control.

There periodically arose more powerful *caudillos* who succeeded in hanging onto the presidency by establishing effective control over the provincial governors and their militias — notably General Ulises Heureaux, whose truly bestial tyranny lasted from 1882 to 1899. The more general pattern, however, was that of rapid changes of president brought about through often bloody civil wars, as one or another of the provincial governors expanded the forces under his control by the most brutal and arbitrary means of recruitment and made his bid for the top position. In the period 1844—1916 the Dominican Republic had 43 presidents, almost all 'generals' who had successfully promoted themselves from the ranks of the provincial *caudillos* — and 39 military uprisings.

At the end of each round of fighting the ignorant, impressed militia troops would be released or desert (if they had not already succeeded in doing so), and many would take their weapons with them and turn to banditry, while the national army would shrink to some scores of officers drawing regular salaries and little else. At the time of the American occupation in 1916, for example, the military budget provided for an army of 900 men, but most of the ranks were filled by 'phantom troops' whose salaries were pocketed by the officers. The forces that could be rapidly raised by any of the 10 provincial governors seeking to seize central power would so greatly outnumber this tiny force that the only defence available to the government was to authorise other loyal governors to expand their own military forces, and embark on yet another civil war.

This dreary succession of meaningless wars fought largely by unwilling and amateur armies was brought to an end by the United States occupation of the Dominican Republic in 1916. It was the natural conclusions of a process of growing United States intervention that had begun with the establishment of a customs receivership in 1905. As in the other United States military interventions which were taking place around the Caribbean at the same period (Haiti, Nicaragua, Cuba and Panamá), it proceeded from a desire to establish order in the interests of United States creditors and an overwhelming conviction of the exportability of American political institutions.

As in all the other cases, a key element in the USA's strategy for establishing order was the disbanding of the turbulent old armies and their replacement by efficient, non-political 'constabulary' forces. The result of this experiment, in the Dominican Republic as everywhere else, was to create new armies which were far more efficient in seizing and holding political power themselves. The noteworthy difference, in the Dominican case, was that the creation of this army transformed the social structure of the power-holding group.

The existing civilian and military *élite* of the republic were virtually interchangeable, both being derived from the same small class of wealthy land-owners. In contrast to the other United States interventions, however, the United States was unable to find collaborators from this group in sufficient numbers, with the result that in the case of the Dominican Republic the intervention was direct and total. On November 29th, 1916 the Dominican Republic was declared under the military administration of the USA, a force of United States Marines was put ashore, and the entire structure of government and army was taken over. For the next 8 years the Dominican Republic was ruled by a United States Military Governor advised and aided by a cabinet of United States Marine officers. One of their first measures was to deprive the semi-independent provincial governors of their military power and effectively to hand over their authority to American officers. By 1917 the army and navy had been abolished, United States Marine troops were acting as police in the cities and maintaining order (sometimes with extremely unfortunate results) in the countryside, and the creation of a new 'Dominican Constabulary Guard' was taken in hand.

However, this new centralised military force, trained and at the beginning commanded by United States Marines – almost all NCOs who were given temporary officer rank for the purpose – failed completely in its attempt to recruit Dominicans of education and some respectability to serve as officers. The old *élite* boycotted the new armed force being created by the occupiers, whose ranks were accordingly filled from the illiterate lower strata of Dominican society, while its officers were mostly adventurers of doubtful antecedents. The military efficiency of the Guard nevertheless progressed rapidly – the Haina Military Academy was founded 30 miles north of the capital in 1921, and alongside it a training centre for enlisted men – but the long-term result was the destruction of the political power of the Dominican Republic's traditional *élite*.

The outstanding representative of this process was Rafael Leónidas Trujillo Molina, a man of lower-middle-class origin and possibly the possessor of a criminal record (all records were subsequently destroyed in a providential fire) who joined the Guard as a second-lieutenant in 1919, and by early 1924 was a major and Commander of the North, holding one of the two senior field commands in the Dominican Republic's first centralised, modern army.

In 1924, satisfied that the conditions for public order had been established, the USA supervised the election of a civilian president and then withdrew the Marines, in confidence that the new constabulary force – now called the 'Dominican National Police' – would safeguard its achievement. In the succeeding 4 years Trujillo was promoted to lieutenant-colonel and Chief of Staff of the force, which was renamed the 'National Army' in 1928. By 1930 he was the most powerful man in the country, at the head of a powerful military force which had practically no ties or debts to the traditional power structure, and after a brief outburst of violence he was elected to the presidency unopposed.

Within a decade Trujillo had promoted himself to Generalissimo and renamed the capital city after himself. During his 31 years of rule he expanded the army to 15 times the size it had been at the time of the United States occupation, playing skilfully on Dominican fears of Haitian invasion, and he and his family and cronies ended up owning almost half the country's land and fixed assets.

Trujillo maintained his authority by a lavish use of the tools of terror that had traditionally been used by Dominican *caudillos*, but equally importantly by a lavish distribution of favours to the army's officers. He also created a counterbalancing force by building a relatively large air force, and deliberately encouraged the growth of rival cliques within the officer corps of both services. His was a new kind of dictatorship, perhaps the most absolute ever seen in Latin America: he promoted the growth of a personality cult of something approaching North Korean proportions, and personally ran or dominated every aspect of social, economic, intellectual and even religious life within his small empire.

By the time he was assassinated in 1961, he had ruled for twice as long as any previous Dominican dictator, a feat that can probably be attributed to the fact that he was the first of his kind to have a centralised and disciplined army at his command. But the sheer longevity and flamboyance of Trujillo tends to mask a more fundamental transformation that took place in the Dominican Republic during this period.

Up to 1916 the dominant group in Dominican society was a civilian/military land-holding upper class which used non-professional armed forces to settle its own quarrels over power. By the time Trujillo was killed a new and greatly privileged military caste, originally recruited from a quite different section of the population, was using a professional army to rule the Dominican Republic in its own interests. The old *élite* were virtually out of the running, and the only rivals to the military interest were the new social groups (business men, professionals and urban labour) which had grown up thanks to the very considerable economic growth the Republic enjoyed in the 1940s and 1950s.

By and large this privileged position of the Dominican officer corps has been preserved since Trujillo's death. It has long ago ceased to draw its members from its original ill-educated sources low down on the social scale, of course, for it is now one of the most attractive careers in the country; some of the better-educated entrants of more recent decades have even espoused reformist or socialist ideas.

The presence of such ideas – indeed, of any coherent political ideas – in the officer corps was not immediately evident upon Trujillo's death. His assassins were rival officers within the regime, most of whom were quickly hunted down, and for some months in late 1961 his son and heir retained control of the armed forces and governed through the puppet president Joaquín Balaguer. This successor regime rapidly collapsed under intense United States and internal pressure, however, and in 1962 the Dominican Republic had its first free elections in 38 years. Juan Bosch, a reformer of the democratic left who had American support, won the presidency, and his Dominican Revolutionary Party (PRD) swept both houses of Congress. But his reforms, and in particular his toleration of legal communist parties at a time when Cuba was spreading panic through the Caribbean, soon frightened sectors of the armed forces as well as the business *élite* and the church. Seven months after the election they combined to overthrow and deport the constitutional government. In its place they put a Triumvirate of civil politicians eventually led by Donald J. Reid Cabral, who was 'advised' by the high command of the armed forces.

The armed forces themselves were badly split by factional struggles, however. During 1963–5 different groups of junior- and middle-rank officers began to intrigue in favour of the ousted President Bosch or ex-President Balaguer (who had undergone a transformation in his post-1962 exile into the leader of the democratic centre-right). These rival groups, as well as idealists who simply wanted the armed forces out of politics and the holding of elections, and some simply ambitious or adventurous young officers, were engaged in almost continuous plotting during the last year of the Triumvirate, often in opposition to each other, but all under the same ambiguous banner of 'constitutionalism': the need to wipe out the effects of the 1962 coup. When economic crisis and an ill-advised drive against corruption in the armed forces lost Reid his last supporters in the business and military higher echelons during 1964, his overthrow became inevitable.

What started as a simple colonels' coup grew into a full-scale civil war accompanied by massive United States military intervention because of the differing goals and inevitable isolation of the various groups of military plotters, and the preconceptions and misinformation of the influential United States embassy. The coup that overthrew Reid in late April, 1965 was actually launched by a pro-Bosch group of officers amongst whom Police Colonel Francisco Caamaño Deñó eventually emerged as leader; most of the more senior army officers and the navy and air force high commands, however, distrusted Bosch and favoured the establishment of a military *junta*. Within a day the coup leaders controlled the Presidential Palace and central Santo Domingo, while air force planes and navy warships were strafing and bombarding the Palace and armoured units under the command of Colonel Elías Wessín y Wessín were attempting to fight their way into the city.

Disposing of relatively small regular forces, the Constitutionalists and leaders armed the urban populace and accepted support from various extreme leftist and communist groups. Wessín's tank forces succeeded at first in penetrating some distance into the city, amidst battles causing hundreds of casualties, most of them civilian. Within 4 days, however, the advance of Wessín's forces had been stopped, the morale of his troops collapsed, and the Dominican armed forces began to disintegrate.

The United States embassy, which had long since ceased to favour Bosch's return and supported the *'junta* solution' from the start, was growing increasingly panicky about the prominence of leftist groups in the Constitutionalist forces and entertaining visions of a 'second Cuba'. At this point, it recommended full United States military intervention. On April 30th the USA began to land a force of 23,000 Marine and army troops outside Santo Domingo. They were later given a scanty diplomatic covering by the dispatch of contingents numbering about 2000 troops from some Latin American countries, and the elevation of the whole into an Inter-American Peacekeeping Force under the auspices of the Organization of American States.

This intervention effectively smothered the fighting, and a ceasefire was signed on May 6th. Subsequent negotiations succeeded in re-unifying the armed forces under a single command, the main leaders of both factions including Wessín and Caamaño being sent abroad. The rest of the officers who had fought on the Constitutionalist side, it was agreed, would be reintegrated into the army. In September, 1965 a Provisional Government was established under a neutral civilian figure, Hector García Godoy, which ruled by decree until elections were held in June, 1966. Both Bosch and Balaguer returned from exile to contest the elections, which were won by the latter, and the OAS intervention force was then withdrawn.

Balaguer also won the 1970 and 1974 elections (unopposed), and proved to be a moderate and conciliatory president. He even tactfully attempted to reduce the influence of the armed forces and their share of the national wealth, by adroitly exploiting the intense and almost Byzantine rivalries amongst the various cliques of officers. The prevailing opinion within the officer corps as a whole, however, has been far to the right since 1965: the promise to re-integrate the rebel Constitutionalist officers into the army was generally ignored, and those few who gained re-admission were isolated at a single military base where they remained. The armed forces were the most substantial obstacle to even the modest programme of reform that Balaguer has attempted to carry out in recent years.

Since 1961, with brief exceptions, the armed forces have not directly ruled the nation, but they continue to be a comparatively large force enjoying unusually generous pay and fringe benefits. The most significant indicator of the officer corps' actual position in the country and the economy is the fact that, contrary to the usual Latin American pattern, it is not private land-owners but the armed forces who have been the principal hindrance to land reform. Senior officers' perquisites included the right to concessions from the State Sugar Corporation to grow sugar on the vast Stage lands (the former possessions of the Trujillo family), the area of the concession corresponding to seniority. Few of them ever saw the land, but at harvest-time the State Corporation 'bought' the sugar from them. Understandably, the armed forces did not show much enthusiasm for redistributing these lands to landless peasants.

STRENGTH AND BUDGET

Population: 5,900,000
Army: 14,000
Navy: 4,500 (including marines); 3 major vessels
Air Force: 3,500
Paramilitary: 10,000 National Police
GNP: (1981) $7,100,000,000
Defence Expenditure: (1981) $117,800,000

COMMAND AND CONSTITUTIONAL STATUS

The 1966 Constitution describes the forces as obedient and non-political, with the purposes of defending the independence and integrity of the republic, maintaining public order, and upholding the Constitution and the laws. The President of the Republic, elected for a 4 year term, is Supreme Chief of the Armed Forces and Police Forces, but must not have engaged in any active military or police service for at least a year prior to his election.

The President appoints the Secretary of State for the Armed Forces, who in turn appoints three Deputy Secretaries of State for the Army, Navy and Air Force with the President's approval. The Secretary of State, usually an army major-general, and his three deputies are all military personnel, and within the chain of command. These officers are primarily responsible for policy-making and supervision; operational control of the forces is in the hands of the three Chiefs of Staff — an army major-general, an air force brigadier-general and a navy commodore — while day-to-day administration is done by their respective General Staffs.

The National Police, a paramilitary force, are under the control of the Secretary of State for Interior and the Police, a Presidential appointee. The Director-General is an army officer, but is subordinate to the Secretary of State.

ROLE, COMMITMENT, DEPLOYMENT AND RECENT OPERATIONS

The Dominican army's principal roles are national defence and the maintenance of internal security, including defence against guerrilla landings or attacks. Despite the overwhelming superiority of the Dominican armed forces, which outnumber the Haitian forces almost three to one and are far better equipped, the lengthy and brutal Haitian occupation of the country is still remembered and resented, and defence against Haiti is seen as a real priority. Even in recent decades there have been recurrent war scares, usually because of each government's habit of intriguing against the other or due to the continuing pressure of illegal immigration from overcrowded and far poorer Haiti into the Dominican Republic.

The last actual clashes were in 1937, when Trujillo's forces massacred at least 10,000 seasonally immigrant Haitian cane-cutters and the two countries went to the brink of full-scale war. Trujillo habitually intrigued for the overthrow of Haitian governments which were not subservient to him, and repeated the practice in the first years after Dr Duvalier established his comparably totalitarian regime in the neighbouring republic, but external pressures against both dictators soon forced them to sign a secret mutual assistance pact in 1958.

Duvalier was deeply alarmed by the subsequent assasination of Trujillo in 1961 and the rise to power of the democratic leftist Juan Bosch, and commenced to plot Bosch's overthrow. Bosch brought charges before the OAS and moved troops to the border in 1963, whereupon Haiti severed diplomatic relations. The crisis escalated to the point where Bosch was threatening to recognise a Haitian government-in-exile and Venezuela offered him military assistance. The Triumvirate which deposed Bosch was unable to restore diplomatic relations with Haiti, and in 1964 the Dominican army was mobilised. Since the end of the civil war and the accession of Joaquín Balaguer to the Presidency in 1966, however, relations between the two countries have improved considerably, and in 1972 after the elder Duvalier's death, his son even entered into an agreement with the Dominican Republic to expand trade between them.

Nevertheless, historical anxieties and the ever-present danger of a confrontation over the Dominican Republic's attempts to control illegal Haitian immigration mean that the 193 mile border with Haiti and the narrow valley's leading eastwards from it are still primary security concerns for the Dominican armed forces. The border, closed for much of the two countries' independent history, has been open again in recent years, though only where the main road between the two capitals crosses it, but even this link has been allowed to fall into an almost impassable state of disrepair. In any conceivable military confrontation between the Dominican Republic and Haiti the Dominican regular forces would enjoy an overwhelming superiority, but Santo Domingo is fully conscious of the old Haitian tradition of raising huge amateur armies at short notice, and of the fact that the Haitian side of the border is far more densely populated than the Dominican.

The Dominican Republic's other international relations have predominantly been with the USA, although in Trujillo's last years he was engaged in several feuds with other Latin American presidents (his attempt to arrange the assassination of Venezuelan President Romulo Betancourt in 1960, which resulted in the wounding of the latter, brought on the OAS economic and political sanctions which hastened his own overthrow in 1961). Subsequent Dominican governments have been little involved in hemispheric politics, and the country at present has no defence commitments beyond its border. It belongs to the OAS and the UN.

In its other main role, that of maintaining internal security, the Dominican army acts in close co-operation with the National Police, a paramilitary force of 10,000 men whose Director-General is an army general. Suppression of urban riots and rural disorders of a political nature is generally left to the police, with the army held in reserve.

Guerrilla movements have not presented major problems despite the proximity of Cuba, and the Dominican armed forces are now extremely well trained and equipped to deal with any such outbreaks. (They include a battalion whose training has been along the same lines as the United States' 'Green Berets'.) Two small guerrilla landings on the coast in the first years of Castro's regime in Cuba were easily wiped out, and a prolonged campaign of right-wing terror and assassination in 1966–71, perpetrated by an unofficial group known as 'La Banda' within the National Police, killed or drove into exile most of the prominent left-wing political activists in the country.

The ultra-right- and left-wing leaders of the 1965 civil war both subsequently tried and failed to overthrow President Balaguer's government, and are no longer a threat. General Wessín was caught in the midst of a conspiracy in 1971, and was shown on television while a premature recording of his voice announcing the fall of the government was played, before being handed over to the armed forces commanders, who sent him into exile in Spain. The left-wing leader, Colonel Caamaño Deñó, who had disappeared from

his post as military attaché in London in 1966, made a quixotic attempt to overthrow Balaguer by landing on the south coast in February, 1973 with a handful of supporters, but they were hunted down and killed in 10 days. Another landing by Dominican emigrés in June, 1975 was equally unsuccessful. At the moment, especially in view of the fact that Cuba has ceased to support Latin American guerrilla adventures in recent years, the likelihood of a major outbreak of guerrilla warfare in the Dominican Republic seems small.

All branches of the armed forces participate in civic action programmes, principally in rural areas. The army has a special responsibility for forest conservation and re-forestation, and the Directorate-General of Forestry has been removed from the jurisdiction of the Secetary of State for Agriculture and placed under the Secretary of State for the Armed Forces.

The country is divided into three defence zones as follows:

Southern Defence Zone (HQ Santo Domingo) covers area between San Cristóbal and the Mona Passage approximating to the provinces of Peravia, San Cristóbal, El Seibo, San Pedro de Marcorís, La Romana, La Altagracia and the national district of Santo Domingo.

Northern Defence Zone (HQ Santiago) covers area extending from Puerto Plata to the Samana peninsula and approximating to the provinces of Puerto Plata, Santiago, La Vega, Espaillat, Salcedo, Duarte, Sánchez Ramírez, Maria Trinidad Sánchez, and Samaná.

Western Defence Zone (HQ Barahona) covers area adjoining Haitian frontier and extending from Valverde in the north to Azúa in the south to cover the provinces of Azúa, Dajabón, Montecristi, Santiago Rodríguez, La Estrelleta, San Juan, Bahoruco, Independencia, Pedernales and Barahona.

Each zone is garrisoned by an infantry brigade and a variable complement of units outside the brigade structure. Basically, the Southern Zone is garrisoned by the 1st Infantry Brigade, the Northern Zone by the 2nd Infantry Brigade and the Western Zone by the 3rd Infantry Brigade. The Southern Zone contains about 50% of the entire effectives of the Army.

The operations section of the National Police, which bears primary responsibility for the preservation of public order, is divided into four regional commands, with headquarters at Santo Domingo, San Pedro de Macorís, Santiago de los Caballeros and Barahona.

The only recent major military operation undertaken by the Dominican armed forces was the civil war of 1965, which was not a fair test of their operational capabilities since they were fighting themselves.

ORGANISATION

Arms of Service

The Dominican Army consists of Infantry, Armour, Artillery, Engineers, Communications, Supply, War Material, Transport, Medical and Military Police units. The basic unit is the battalion, into which all combat arms are organised. There are 10 Infantry battalions, a Presidential Guard Battalion, a Mounted Rifle Battalion, an Armoured Battalion, three Artillery Battalions, one Engineer Battalion, one Transport and one Ordnance Battalions. Each Brigade consists bascially of three Infantry Battalions. The 1st Brigade adds reconnaissance, supply, transport and medical companies. The Mounted Rifle and Engineer battalions also come under the jurisdiction of this Brigade although not forming an organic part of it. There is a Support Command which administers the Presidential Guard Battalion and the sole War Material (Ordnance) battalion and includes Supply and Military Police companies. Artillery is organized as a separate command with a regimental structure and two battalions. The Armed Forces Training Centre, at San Isidro, controls the sole Armoured Battalion, the *Batallón Blindado '27 de Febrero'*, an Infantry Battalion and an Artillery Battalion. Under the Trujillo regime these formed a separate Brigade (4th) enjoying semi-autonomous status under the Ministry of Defense and thus forming, in effect, a fourth armed force. Its location at the principal base of the Dominican Air Force gave rise to the erroneous belief that the Air Force was equipped with tanks.

The General Staffs for all three armed forces are divided into the same five sections: personnel, intelligence, operations, logistics and public relations. Each service also has an administrative judge advocate section.

The National Police is run by a Director-General who is an army general officer. He has three Assistant Director-Generals, heading the three main sections of the National Police: administration and support, police operations and special operations (the secret police).

Operational
The basic operational unit is the Brigade, one of which is assigned to each Defense Zone. Only the 1st Brigade has organic tactical and logistic support units. Artillery is not organic to the Brigades, batteries being detached from the two battalions of the Artillery Command and deployed with the Brigades as operational requirements dictate. Although the 4th Brigade was officially abolished in the early 1970s, its constituent units still approximate to the effectives of a US Army Armoured Command of the World War II period.

The Navy includes some units of marine commandos, including under-water demolition units and there is a group of para-commandos incorporated in the Air Force's Base Defense Command. The Air Force appears to control all air-defense units.

The air force is divided into two operational squadrons, one of fighter-bombers, the other a COIN/training unit. There is also a transport squadron, a helicopter squadron and a training wing. Air force headquarters is at San Isidro; other air bases are at Santo Domingo, Puerta Plata, Santiago, La Romana, Saibo, Barahona, La Vega, Monte Cristi and Azua.

The navy is divided for administrative purposes into three zones: Santo Domingo (where naval headquarters are also located). Puerto Plata in the north and Barahona in the south. The main naval bases are at Las Calderas and San Pedro de Macorís. Besides its maritime forces, the navy also maintains a commando battalion.

RECRUITMENT, TRAINING AND RESERVES

The 1966 Constitution authorises conscription for males between eighteen and fifty-four, but in fact all vacancies in the Dominican forces are easily filled by voluntary enlistment. Military service tends to be a long-term career and even enlisted men often stay on until retirement age.

Army enlisted men receive basic training at a centre near San Isidro air force base, navy personnel at Las Calderas, 50 miles west of the capital, and air force recruits at San Isidor air force base. Subsequent training is conducted within army and air force units and aboard naval vessels; at Bani in Peravia province is the Vocational School of the Armed Forces and National Police, where members of all branches who are about to return to civilian life receive training in various semi-skilled trades.

Officer candidates must possess a high school diploma and pass strict physical examinations. Each of the three services maintains a military academy which graduates about 50 students a year after a 4 year course. Air force cadets attend the army academy at Haina for the first 2 years before going on to the air force school for special training; the naval academy runs its own full 4 year course.

Infantry officers of captain and lieutenant rank attend a 6 month basic course before being appointed to company commands. The army also conducts a 10 month command and staff course for officers between captain and lieutenant-colonel rank to prepare them for battalion command. More advanced officer training for all three services is done at United States military education facilities in the Panama Canal Zone and in the USA itself, under the terms of the Military Assistance Agreement of 1962.

Following the 1965 civil war a National Police Academy was established with assistance from the USA. National Police students also attend advanced courses in the Panama Canal Zone and at the International Police Academy in Washington, D.C.

Pay and conditions of service are more generous than those prevailing in comparable occupations in civilian life, and service personnel benefit from medical services and special shopping facilities. All members of the armed forces who have served honourably are entitled to pensions of 75% of their highest pay after 30 years of service (twenty for some special categories like flying personnel). Compulsory retirement age is fifty for enlisted personnel, rising to sixty for colonels and lieutenant-colonels, and seventy for general officers.

There is a law which requires all those not enlisted in the regular forces to do 2 months/year of service in the reserves, but it is not widely applied. The size and state of preparedness of the reserve organisation is not known.

EQUIPMENT AND ARMS INDUSTRY

The Dominican Republic has a small defence industry and in the past has produced automatic weapons of local design and development and small naval vessels. Current production is limited to small arms ammunition, uniforms and personal equipment and all major weapons and equipment must be imported.

Rifles: FN FAL 7.62mm (Belgium); CETME 7.62mm (Spain); G3 7.62mm (Germany)
Sub-machine-guns: Thompson 0.45" (US); Beretta 9mm (Italy); San Cristobal Mk 3 0.30" (Dominican)
Machine-guns: BAR 0.30" (US); M-1919 0.30" (US) M-2 0.50" (US); FN MAG 7.62mm (Belgium); M-60A1 7.62mm (US)
Mortars: 81mm (US)
Artillery: M-101 105mm (US); 105mm m/40 (Sweden)
Air-defence weapons: 40mm L/60 (Sweden)
Armour: M-3 light tank (US); L-600 light tank (Sweden); AMX-13 light tank (France); M-3A1 scount car (US); Landsverk Lynx armoured car (Sweden); U-150 armoured car (US)
Aircraft: The Air Force has about 15 transport aircraft and 15 helicopters.

RANK, DRESS AND DISTINCTIONS

Dominican officer ranks are the same as those in the United States armed forces, although there are not normally any officers above major-general/rear-admiral rank. The rank structure is very inflated, with 41 generals and admirals for only 18,500 men. Army and air force company-grade officers wear one, two or three silver laurel leaves on shoulder-boards; field-grade officers wear a metallic replica of the national coat of arms surmounted by one, two or three silver laurel leaves; brigadier and major-generals wear the coat of arms with one or two silver stars. Enlisted personnel wear a series of olive-green chevrons on the upper sleeve.

The uniforms of the Dominican armed forces closely resemble those of the corresponding services in the USA. The normal service uniform is khaki; dress uniforms, blue in winter, white in summer.

The highest Dominican awards are the Order of Merit Duarte, Sánchez and Mella; the Order of Christopher Columbus; and the Captain General Santana Military Order. These are followed by the orders of army, navy, air force and police merit. The highest two awards are also granted to civilians and foreigners for distinguished service to the Dominican Republic; the remaining five are reserved for military personnel.

CURRENT DEVELOPMENTS

In the May, 1978 elections President Balaguer, having ruled for 12 years, was defeated by the candidate of the PRD, Antonio Guzman. There was almost a military coup during the counting of the ballots, when National Police units (which are under the authority of the armed forces) intervened at the central electoral headquarters in Santo Domingo, ejected the election officials and stopped the count. It was evident that this move did not have the united support of the armed forces high command, however, despite their anxiety about a victory for the party on whose behalf the rebels had acted during the 1965 civil war.

After a day of confusion, Balaguer asserted his authority over the armed forces, who withdrew the units from the electoral headquarters and allowed Guzman's victory to be verified. While there was undoubtedly strong pressure from the USA and the Organization of American States (which had an electoral observer team present) to prevent the setting aside of the election results, the credit for the obedience shown by the armed forces must ultimately go to Balaguer, who had pursued the goal of gradually reducing the armed forces to their constitutionally ordained subordination to the civil power through the whole period of his Presidency. He proved himself a master at playing off the competing factions in the armed forces against each other in order to accomplish this aim.

Until about 1970 Balaguer was not in full control of the armed forces and the National Police, elements of which were involved in a secret terrorist campaign that murdered hundreds of PRD and other left-wing leading figures. In July, 1971 however, the influential right-wing leader in the civil war, General Wessín, was caught red-handed while attempting to mount a coup, and was sent into exile with the concurrence of the armed forces chiefs. In October, 1971 Balaguer replaced General Enrique Pérez y Pérez as Commander of the National Police by his own long-standing associate, General Neit Nivar Seijas, with instructions to end the violence. By the end of the year La Banda had been disbanded, and the official terror campaign had died away.

The popularity Nivar Seijas gained in this operation, and the sheer fact that he had done it, aroused much resentment amongst the leading ultra-right-wing officers of the armed forces. They succeeded in having him kicked upstairs as Secretary to the Presidency in 1972, while General Pérez y Pérez was made Army Commander. Political terrorism began to rise again in the country, and in 1973 Juan Bosch resigned as leader of the PRD, leaving the left hopelessly divided and leaderless.

After Balaguer won his third term of office in 1974, however, he felt strong enough to challenge the dominant ultra-right groups in the armed forces hierarchy by re-appointing Major-General Nivar Seijas as National Police Commander. As soon as he did this in May, 1975 the Army Chief of Staff, General Pérez, resigned together with his associates the Secretary of State for the Armed Forces, and the Air Force and Navy Chiefs of Staff. Balaguer simply accepted their resignations, briefly took over the armed forces department himself, and then appointed new men. As a consolation prize, however, General Pérez was subsequently appointed as Secretary of State for the Interior and the National Police.

The most dangerous phase of the process, that of gradually reducing the armed forces' share of government expenditure, was already safely past in 1978. The failure of the half-hearted military intervention in the 1978 elections would seem to confirm the new subordinate status of the armed forces, at least so long as an adroit manipulator of the deep factional divisions in the officer corps occupies the presidential office.

There is no serious revolutionary organisation in the Dominican Republic at the moment — the communists are split into four small, squabbling fragments — but the present conditions could well be conducive to the rise of one. The Republic, which enjoyed an extremely high economic growth rate in 1970—75 (over 10% a year) due to the boom in sugar prices, has been hit harder than any other country in the world by their collapse in 1976: sugar contributes one-fifth of GNP, and two-thirds of export revenues. Average per capita income is close to $1000 a year, a respectable figure for Latin America, but it is grossly maldistributed: even in the boom years unemployment and under-employment were estimated at 40% of the adult population, and over half the population are undernourished.

The government has great difficulties in doing much about this. Haitian cane-cutters have been banned (which could cause trouble), and the redistribution of State lands has been accelerated, but there would be strong resistance from land-owners and army officers to a more radical land reform programme designed to relieve rural poverty. Most of the Dominican population is still rural, two-thirds of it living in the fertile plains of the north-east around Santiago, but the capital of Santo Domingo across the mountains on the south coast has tripled in size since 1960, and now numbers over 1,000,000 people. Vast slums now ring it to the north, and even less is being done about the misery of their inhabitants.

While such conditions may be breeding grounds for radical popular movements, however, there is some prospect that the new government may be able to tackle social problems in a more decisive manner. At the same time, the PRD of 1978 is a moderate centre-left party, long shorn of the radical elements that were present in it in the mid-1960s. The current President, Antonio Guzman, is of a background — businessman and cattle-rancher — which is unlikely to alarm the more extreme right-wing elements in the armed forces sufficiently to unite them in a coup against him. His first step was to dismiss Balaguer's closest military associates, Secretary of State for the Armed Forces Lieutenant-General Juan René Beauchamp and the commander of the Santo Domingo garrison, General Neit Nivar Seijas. Provided he shows the same skill as Balaguer in the management of military factional rivalries, the present status of the Dominican armed forces is likely to continue.

Gwynne Dyer
Adrian English

157

ECUADOR

HISTORY AND INTRODUCTION

Ecuador is at present under a military government, which took power in 1972. That turn of events cannot be said, however, to mark an unnatural interruption in the course of Ecuadorian politics which, to a degree unusual even in Latin America, are an arena of abrupt and unconstitutional changes of regime. Between 1925 and 1962 there were 29 changes of president, only two of whom held office for their full term. Most of these changes, moreover, were brought about by political rather than military means and, though military intervention in politics is not unusual, the turbulence of Ecuadorian political life does not stem from military caprice. It depends rather upon intense personal rivalries for the support of a very narrowly drawn electorate. The current military regime promises to broaden the electoral base and, in its economic policy, has also given evidence of a radical and nationalist inclination. There is a precedent for its behaviour in the declarations of the officers who made the coup of 1925, which was avowedly left wing in intentions. The current regime is certainly not left wing, and has made its hostility to the left-wing parties clear, but seems determined to break the power of the old oligarchy and to win for Ecuador a fair share of the revenue from her natural resources, hitherto exploited by foreign-based companies.

Ecuador, originally a part of Gran Colombia, became independent of that successor State in 1830 and for 15 years was ruled by a lieutenant of Bolívar, General Flores. On the overthrow of his personal rule there followed 15 years of turbulent rule by anti-clerical liberal politicians, until in 1860, with the military assistance of Flores, a remarkable conservative and Catholic politician, García Moreno, inherited the presidency. During his 15 years of power, Ecuador was transformed into a theocracy, in which the church was elevated to the highest place of honour, the country dedicated to the Sacred Heart of Jesus and the army's regiments given such names as Soldiers of the Infant Jesus, Volunteers of the Cross and Guardians of the Virgin. But the army was also reorganised and put on a modern footing, as were the other institutions of the State. Moreno, though a fanatic, was a highly efficient one to whom Ecuador owes its emergence as a modern State. His fall ushered in 20 years of chaos and civil war, and then an era of liberal presidencies (1897–1916), which unmade his theocratic structures. Politics remained, however, the concern of the urban and propertied minority, and the majority of illiterate and landless Indians had no say in its workings. The first genuine liberalisation of the system was brought about by a military coup in 1925, the work of a military 'lodge', the *Liga Militar*, formed by officers from the inland sierra, who sponsored a left-wing government. Their success blunted their left-wing impulses, however, and they quickly became servants of the traditional oligarchy, which continued to monopolise power through a 'waltz of the presidents' until 1944. The army then again intervened to place in the presidential palace the politician who has dominated Ecuadorian politics almost ever since, José Velasco Ibarra. Political life since his arrival may be said to have taken the form of a dialectic between him and the leaders of the armed forces, in which they and he alternately champion opposed political positions. Standing for no fixed position except opposition to the traditional ruling class, his policies

have 'smacked at different times of conservatism, liberalism, *justicialismo* (Peronism) and moderate reformism'. But the army, too (and the air force, which has a 'progressive' reputation), has espoused a variety of positions during the same period. Thus it turned Velasco out in 1947 when his demagoguery took one of its rightist turns, and installed a *junta* in 1963–6 which promised an expropriatory land reform, but removed Velasco in 1972 largely for fear of his threat to sponsor candidates from the left-wing alliance *Concentración de Fuerzas Populares* in the forthcoming elections, his breach with the United States over fishing rights and his meetings with Castro and Allende of Chile.

The military regime, which held power until 1979, was sternly right-wing, but also showed itself ready to quarrel with the United States, particularly over oil exploitation and fishing rights and to prepare with apparent sincerity for the extension of the franchise and of the representative character of congress. Elections were duly held in 1979 and a new Constitution came into force on August 10th, 1979, on which date Jaime Roldos Aguilera was sworn in as democratically elected civilian President.

The erratic and at times unconfident political behaviour of the Ecuadorian army may stem in part from its compromised role as defender of the national territory. In 1904 the country was obliged under pressure to surrender a large slice of Amazonian territory in the Oriente to Brazil, and in 1941 the army fought and lost a war with Peru in the same area. The country was obliged to concede Peru's annexation of more Amazonian territory by the Protocol of Rio in the following year. There have again been border clashes in the area in the last 2 years.

A serious frontier incident occurred in January 1981 and fighting lasted for several weeks before a cease fire was agreed early in February.

STRENGTH AND BUDGET

Population: 8,350,000
Army: 30,000
Navy: 4000 (including 1000 marines); 10 major vessels, 15 smaller
Air force: 4000; 48 combat aircraft
Paramilitary: 5000 National Police
GNP (1980 estimate): $10,840,000,000
Defence expenditure (1980): $194,000,000

The Constitution of 1946 lays down that defence, with education, shall receive preferential consideration in the apportioning of the budget, and the Ecuadorian armed forces are traditionally accustomed to receive a remarkably large share – about 25% in the 1940s and 1950s. As late as 1968 they received 19.5%, the bulk of which went to the army. The army has also benefited generously from American military assistance.

COMMAND AND CONSTITUTIONAL STATUS

The Constitution of 1946, in force before the military seizure of power in 1972 (when it was replaced by the Constitution of 1945), invested command in the President, who was advised by a National Security Council and the Joint Chiefs of Staff of the Armed Forces. The forces were under the administrative control of the Minister of Defence, to whom the commanders of the three services answered through the Chief of Staff of the Armed Forces. The Constitution defined the armed forces as 'non-deliberative', meaning that they were not to take any share in State policy-making, though a member of the armed forces sat *ex officio* as their representative in the senate. Congress was to fix annually the size of the armed forces, and to approve all promotions to the rank of colonel and above by secret ballot. Defence expenditure was, with education, to receive preferential treatment in apportioning the budget.

The military regime which took power in 1972, though nominally bound by the provisions of the Constitution of 1945 (the fifteenth to be introduced since 1830), has in practice been ruled by a *junta* of the heads of the armed services, following the deposition of the military Head of State, President Lara, in January, 1976. All political activity has suspended, but three committees, charged respectively with revising the 1945 Constitution, drafting a new one to replace it and drawing up a new electoral and party law, sat. The first two sat reported, and recommend an extension of the franchise to illiterates, a single chamber congress and the sponsoring of all presidential candidates by an established political party. The committee producing a new electoral law did not report; the drawing up of new electoral registers, begun in 1976, suffered delay; and the elections promised for January 1978 were, in April, 1977, postponed. The government therefore continued to rule by decree, through a cabinet which was largely military in composition. Since the return to civilian government in 1979, the previous command structure and constitutional status of the armed forces has been restored.

ROLE, COMMITMENT, DEPLOYMENT AND RECENT OPERATIONS

Article 153 of the 1946 Constitution (revoked by the military regime in 1972 and replaced by the 1945 Constitution) prescribes that 'for the defence of the Republic and the maintenance of constitutional order there shall be a military armed force in accordance with law'. This role has been reaffirmed since the return to civilian government.

The national territory is divided into four military zones as follows:

1st Military Zone (HQ Quito) covers provinces of Pichincha, Imbabura and Tulcán
2nd Military Zone (HQ Guayaquil) covers provinces of Guayas, los Rios, Esmeraldas and Manabí.
3rd Military Zone (HQ Cuenca) covers provinces of Azuay, Loja, El Oro and Cañar.
4th Military Zone (HQ Pastaza) covers the eastern provinces.

The Army is divided into six Divisions, each of one or two brigades and deployed as follows:

Division 1 (HQ Quito) garrisons the 1st Military Zone and includes an infantry and a jungle brigade (3rd Infantry and 9th Jungle, both with HQ at Quito).
Division 2 (HQ Guayaquil) garrisons the 2nd Military Zone and appears to consist of only one brigade (1st with HQ at Guayaquil).
Division 3 (HQ Cuenca), Division 4 (HQ Machala) and Division 5 (HQ Loja) together garrison the 3rd Military Zone which consequently contains the highest concentration of troops.

Division 6 (HQ Pastaza) is the Ecuadorian Army's Jungle Division and garrisons the 4th Military Zone.

There are six Infantry, two Mechanised, one Special Forces and three Jungle Brigades. Of these only the 1st Infantry (HQ Guayaquil), 3rd Infantry (HQ Quito), 5th Infantry (HQ Cuenca), 7th Infantry (HQ Loja and 9th Jungle Brigades have been positively identified and located. The 1st Special Forces Brigade has its HQ at Quito but divides its two constituent Groups between Quito and San Camilo. Infantry and Jungle brigades appear to be numbered in the same numerical sequence although the Special Forces Brigade duplicates the number of the Infantry brigade at Guayaquil. It would seem reasonable to assume that the two Mechanised brigades may be numbered 1 and 2. One of these is believed to have its HQ at Riobamba. A new numbering system, adopted in the early 1980s, appears to prefix the traditional numerical designation of the infantry brigades with that of the parent Division. Thus the 3rd and 9th Brigades (both apparently part of the 1st Division) are now known as the 13th and 19th respectively.

Ecuador has no external military commitments; the country is a signatory of the Chapultepec and Rio Pacts; it has a military assistance agreement with the United States. The national territory is divided into six military zones, with headquarters at Quito (capital), Guayaquil, Cuenca, Machala and Loja; the sixth zone comprises the Oriente region on the Amazon headwaters. The two motorised battalions of the army are stationed at Quito and Guayaquil. The nine infantry battalions and 10 independent companies are stationed in the 19 provinces, according to population. There is a small unit on the Galápagos. There is a Presidential Guard squadron at Quito and a horsed cavalry squadron in the headquarters town of the other military regions. The parachute and air-defence battalions are stationed at Quito; the parachute battalion has an alternative base at Salinas, on the coast. The three armoured squadrons are probably stationed at the capital, together with the three artillery 'groups' (? batteries) and the two engineer battalions (though they may be in the interior).

Border clashes between Ecuadorian and Peruvian troops were reported between June, 1976 and January, 1977 on the disputed frontier in the Oriente, but are said to have been ceased by agreement. Peru and Ecuador fought a war over the border in 1941 and Ecuador was brought to accept a frontier adjustment in Peru's favour by the Treaty of Rio in 1942. Much more serious clashes, which threatened to develop into full-scale hostilities, occurred in January–February 1981.

ORGANISATION

The Army is organised into the following branches: Infantry, Special Forces, Cavalry, Mechanised Troops, Artillery, Engineers, Signals, Intendence, War Material, Transport, Medical and Veterinary. Infantry, Mechanised Troops and Engineers are organised in battalions, whilst Special Forces, Cavalry and Artillery are organised in groups. There are also independent motorised reconnaissance squadrons attached to the 1st, 2nd and 3rd Brigades. Brigades consist basically of two battalion-sized units, some having in addition a Cavalry Group (horsed or mechanised), an Artillery Group and an Engineer Battalion. There are in all 23 Infantry and Mechanised Battalions, two Groups of Special Forces, a Presidential Escort Squadron, three horsed and five mechanised Cavalry Groups, three Motorised Reconnaissance Squadrons, three Groups of Artillery, one Air Defence Battalion and two Engineer Battalions. Recent purchases of artillery and air defence equipment indicate that the number of units of this army may be expected to increase in the near future.

There are three battalions of Marines, one of which garrisons the Galápagos Islands (Archipielago de Colón). Another performs garrison duties in support of naval shore establishments on the Pacific coast with detachments on the river system of the Oriente. The third battalion is an amphibious assault unit. The air force has one para-commando squadron.

The National Police is a centralised force with a 'corps' in each province. Those in Quito and Guayaquil are about 700 strong. The country is divided into four police districts, controlled by the Ministry of Government

RECRUITMENT, TRAINING AND RESERVES

Recruitment and Training

Universal conscription is decreed by law, but recruitment is in practice selective. Few Indians are conscripted. The size of the annual available contingent is about 45,000 of which one-fifth is inducted. The choice is made by selective service boards in each provincial capital. Only-sons, students and principal breadwinners are exempted. Recruits are enlisted at twenty for 2 years' service. They are trained in the units, which are more than training organisations.

Officers are recruited by competitive examination from high-school students and trained in the *Colegio Militar* at Quito; the course lasts 5 years, and is a mixture of military and academic instruction; about 60 army and air force cadets graduate annually. There is an arms school (*Escuela de Perfeccionamiento*) at Quito, which trains officers in the specialisms of their own arms, and runs courses for other ranks of the cavalry, artillery, infantry, engineers and signals. Staff training is conducted at the *Colegio de Guerra*, Quito; the course lasts 2 years. In 1972 the military government founded a tri-service school, modelled on the Peruvian CAEM, called the Institute for Higher National Studies. The main influence on Ecuadorian military education has been Chilean. A Chilean military mission, bringing newly learnt German methods, came to the country in 1900. It continued to be responsible for most of their training at the Staff College until 1962. The Staff College itself was founded in 1922 by an Italian military mission, which also set up the Arms School at Quito.

Two specialist schools of importance are the parachute school at Salinas, on the coast, and the jungle-warfare training school (special forces school) in the Oriente region. Another is the School for Industrial Apprenticeships (*Centro Militar de Apprendizaje Industrial*), Latacunga, Cotopaxi province, founded in 1962, which trains conscripts who volunteer for an additional year's service in automotive engineering and electronics.

Reserves

Time-expired conscripts form a reserve, the size of which is undisclosed, but is probably about 50,000. In May, 1972 some reservists were called up to take part in manoeuvres held in the San Antonio training area.

EQUIPMENT AND ARMS INDUSTRY

Ecuador has no arms industry, and does not appear to manufacture even small-arms ammunition. Most of the army's equipment is American, some of it obsolete, though in recent years some items have been purchased from France. For its size, it is among the better-equipped Latin American armies.

Rifles: FN FAL 7.62mm (Belgium)
Sub-machine-gun: Uzi 9mm (Israel)
Machine-guns: FN MAG 7.62mm (Belgium); M-1919 7.62mm (US)
Mortars: 81mm (US)
Anti-armour weapons: 90mm and 106mm RCLs (US)
Artillery: M-101 105mm (US); Model 56 105mm (Italy); Mk F3 155mm SPH (France)
Air-defence weapons: 40mm L/60 (US); 40mm L/70 (Sweden); Vulcan M-167 20mm (US); M-163 20mm (US); Chapparal SAM (US); Blowpipe SAM (Britain)
Armcur: AMX-13 light tank (France; 81 in service); M-3 light tank (US ; 30 in service); AML 245 H60/90 armoured car (France; 27 in service); AMX-VCI APC (France; 20 in service); M-113 APC (US; 20 in service)
Aircraft: The Army operates about 20 fixed-wing aircraft and 6 helicopters. The Air Force has about 30 transport aircraft and 20 helicopters

RANK, DRESS AND DISTINCTIONS

General de Ejército — Two gold stars, national crest
General de División — One gold star, national crest
Coronel — Three gold stars
Teniente Coronel — Two gold stars
Mayor — One gold star
Capitán — Three silver stars
Teniente — Two silver stars
Subteniente — One silver star

The service dress of the army is grey. Combat dress is American in colour and style. Officers wear a full dress of purple tunic and black trousers. There is a War Cross, instituted after the war of 1941 with Peru.

CURRENT DEVELOPMENTS

The military government which took power on February 15th, 1972, headed by General Lara, the army commander, issued a 13-point 'Philosophy and Plan of Action of the Armed Forces' which declared the regime to be 'nationalist, military and revolutionary', and to have as its aims 'social justice, redemption of the humble, and transformation of the country's basic structures in order to benefit the country's less-favoured social strata'. The main ways in which this programme could be brought about are through land reform in the sierra, where most of the Indians work on the property of large estate-owners, and by taking a larger share in the revenues of the foreign-owned extractive industries. The government did not (unlike the *junta* of 1962–6) make any move towards land reform, but it encroached sharply on the interests of the foreign oil companies. In June, 1974 it took a 25% interest in the holdings of the Gulf–Texaco consortium, and in January, 1977 nationalised the Gulf holdings in the country. It also gave strong evidence of its wish to establish civilian democratic government in the country on a new and more stable basis. After February, 1977 three committees sat to draft a new constitution and prepare new electoral and party laws. Elections were promised in 1977 for 1978 and were being postponed only, by the government's account, because of delays in preparing new electoral rolls.

On the other hand, there is also evidence that it was less committed to change than its words promised. In October, 1974 the Minister of National Resources, Captain Ampudia, was removed from office because of his 'strongly nationalistic oil policy'. In January, 1976 President Lara was overthrown in an internal coup after announcing plans for a speedy return to civilian rule, and in the following June, Colonel Levoyer, the Minister of the Interior, was removed from office by the new *junta* after announcing a return to civilian rule by January, 1978. The *junta* also dealt harshly with internal disorder. In July, 1977 the heads of two of the major trade union organisations were imprisoned for leading strikes and in October a strike of sugar-cane workers was put down with over a hundred deaths.

There have been two military uprisings since the coup of 1972, one against Lara in September, 1975 which was put down with little bloodshed, and another, apparently opportunist, at the time of Lara's deposition in January, 1976. Lara was also obliged to replace the commanders of the navy and the air force in February, 1972 when they resigned in protest at the 'predominating influence' of the army over the new military government. It is therefore difficult to define the character and inclination of the military government. The *junta* was probably, as its political and trade union opponents accused, right wing and fearful of change, but it cannot be said that that attitude characterises the outlook of the officer corps as a whole. The reality seems to be that the armed forces are as fragmented politically as is the Ecuadorian 'political nation', and as much the plaything of *personalismo* as the electorate and the congress in the days of former civilian governments.

The Armed Forces did permit free elections in 1979 resulting in the election of a civilian President. Increasing labour unrest, culminating in wide-spread strikes towards the end of 1981 and 1982, have severely threatened the stability of the new civilian government and may prompt the military to intervene in politics once again. The major external problem is the continuing frontier tension with Peru, both countries deploying a major portion of their respective armed forces in the frontier region, with the likelihood of further incidents and a real possibility of their escalation into full-scale warfare.

John Keegan
Adrian English

EGYPT

HISTORY AND INTRODUCTION

Despite an ancient tradition of almost two millenia as a great military power under the Pharaohs, Egypt virtually lost its military significance before the beginning of the Christian era. Successively conquered and ruled by Persians, Greeks, Romans, Arabs, Turks, French and British, the Egyptian population ceased to be regarded, or to regard itself, as a militarily competent people. There was a brief renaissance of Egyptian military power in the early nineteenth century under the rule of Muhammad Ali, an Albanian adventurer nominally in the Ottoman service, and Egyptian armies fought well in the Greek War of Independence and the Syrian wars of that period, but this premature effort to create a modern Egyptian army lapsed after the deaths of Muhammad Ali and his son Ibrahim in mid-century.

When British power first began to establish itself in Egypt later in the century, it was opposed by an uprising led by Lieutenant-Colonel Ahmad Arabi in 1882. British troops put down the revolt, and the army created by Muhammad Ali was disbanded. In its place, a new colonial-style Egyptian army was created by the British, commanded and largely staffed by British officers. The Egyptian officers serving under them were almost invariably chosen from wealthy families of high social standing, while the enlisted men serving in the army were members of the poorest classes who were unable to pay the exemption fee by which military service could be avoided. This army fought indifferently in the Sudan and other nearby countries for the British, but regular British regiments were maintained in the country for the defence of the vital Suez Canal installations.

Egypt never formally lost its independence during the period of British rule, and in 1918 the Egyptain government took advantage of the stresses placed upon Britain by World War I to demand successfully that the command and staff posts within the army be handed over to Egyptian officers. There remained a British inspector-general in a supervisory position, but his post was abolished by the Anglo—Egyptian treaty of 1936, which also provided for the withdrawal of some British garrison troops. Up to this time the Egyptian army still remained a body incapable of acting as a national mobilising force because of the ultra-conservative views of its wealthy officer corps and the immense social gulf between officers and men, but another development of the same year was to alter this situation fundamentally. It was in 1936 that the rules for admission to the Egyptian Military Academy were changed to allow the sons of middle-class families to enter.

The graduates of the Military Academy classes of 1938, 1939 and 1940 were a different breed: nationalists, anti-monarchists, and, from the start, revolutionaries. During the campaigns in the Libyan desert in 1940—43 many of them were involved in intrigues with the Axis forces across the frontier aimed at expelling the British from Egypt, and many ended up in jail as a result. They all fought in the unsuccessful war against newborn Israel from May 1948 to February 1949, and it was their anger at the corruption and ineptness of the monarchy, which they held responsible for that defeat, which caused them to form the secret Free Officers' Movement in 1949.

In July, 1952 they seized power, forcing King Farouk to abdicate; Egypt became a republic in the following June, with General Muhammad Neguib as President and Prime Minister. He was of an older and more conservative generation, however, and it was Colonel Gamal Abdul Nasser, the Deputy Prime Minister, who became acting Head of State when the younger Free Officers ousted Neguib in November, 1954. A new constitution was introduced in 1956, and Nasser was elected President.

It would be a great exaggeration to state that Egypt has been ruled from 1952 to the present by the 1938, 1939 and 1940 graduating classes of the Egyptian Military Academy. Nasser belonged to this group, however, as did his successor Anwar Sadat, and what even today remains a high proportion of the most senior Egyptian officers. They were colleagues in nationalist conspiracy from 1940 onwards, and in government from 1952; despite many later splits and intrigues, they remain a goup with a distinctive identity. It was from their early ideals that 'Nasserist' rule took its character: barely disguised permanent military rule (but with the army in the background), activist, anti-imperialist, anti-Israel, and devoted to a nebulous and authoritarian concept of socialism and social change. Despite the official pan-Arabism which was enthusiastically purveyed so long as Nasser lived, the majority of this leadership generation were deeply nationalistic men in a more narrow Egyptian context, and saw pan-Arabism principally as a vehicle for restoring Egypt to great-power status. There have been great changes of emphasis in Egyptian domestic and foreign policy since Nasser's death, particularly as regards socialism, 'anti-imperialism' and policy towards Israel, but many of the characteristic priorities and attitudes of the earlier period remain. There also remains a segment of the officer corps, of unknown size, which secretly preserves the 'Nasserist' ideology in its original form.

Nasser nationalised the Suez Canal in July, 1956 largely in an effort to obtain revenue to finance the building of the Aswan dam. His seizure of the Canal was opposed by the British and French governments, and in the late October and early November of 1956 British and French forces attacked targets in the Nile Delta while the Israelis advanced through the Mitla pass into Sinai. Although international pressure brought about a rapid ceasefire and allied withdrawal, the episode served to push Egypt further into the arms of the communist bloc, from which she had already begun receiving large quantities of arms in the previous year.

In February, 1958 Egypt and Syria formed the United Arab Republic, but Syria withdrew from the union following a change of regime in September, 1961. Egypt continued to strengthen her ties with the Soviet Union: Khrushchev visited Egypt in May, 1964; he was followed by Kosygin in August, 1965 and May, 1966. Nasser, meanwhile, stepped up his propaganda against not only Israel but also the 'imperialists' and their allies in the Arab world. Between 1962 and 1967 he gave substantial military assistance to the republican forces in the civil war in the Yemen: at one time about one-third of the Egyptian army was deployed there. The fighting in the Yemen was, however, overshadowed by the Six-Day War of June, 1967 in which Egypt and her allies suffered a severe defeat at the hands of the Israelis. Egyptian forces were driven across the Suez Canal, and their losses in manpower and equipment were very heavy. Israeli forces remained in occupation of the entire Sinai peninsula.

Russia immediately came to Egypt's aid with plentiful

162

arms supplies; the losses of the war were made good, and a sophisticated air-defence system was installed along the Suez Canal. There were 2500 Soviet advisers in Egypt by the end of October, 1967 and this figure rose to 15,000 by mid-1970. Numerous clashes between Egyptian and Israeli ground and air forces occurred during this period, and a small number of Soviet pilots were shot down. A ceasefire came into effect on August 1st, 1970, under the terms of which both sides agreed upon a military standstill for 32 miles on each side of the Canal. This agreement was not fully honoured by Egypt, and SA-2 and SA-3 missiles were subsequently deployed in sites near the canal.

There was considerable unrest within the army following the 1967 defeat, but a planned military coup was nipped in the bud. Nasser died in September, 1970 and was succeeded as President by Colonel Anwar Sadat, who initially continued his predecessor's policy of friendship towards Russia. Relations between the Soviet Union and the Arab world deteriorated steadily, however, and in July, 1972 Sadat ordered most of his Russian advisers to leave. He also attempted to strengthen the ties between Egypt and her allies: a federation of Libya, Syria and the Arab Republic of Egypt came into force in February, 1972 but had little real effect. In 1972–3 a gradual union of Egypt and Libya was agreed upon, but once again the measure had few practical consequences.

Sadat's unsatisfactory relations with the Soviet Union convinced him that Russia did not seek another war in the Middle East; American support for Israel seemed, moreover, likely to continue. He therefore planned a limited military offensive which would provoke an international crisis, as a result of which the superpowers might compel Israel to make concessions. The planning for Operation *Badr* began in October, 1972 when General Ahmed Ismail was appointed Minister of War, with General Saadeddin al-Shazli as his Chief of Staff. Ismail was appointed Commander-in-Chief of the federated forces of Egypt and Syria in January, 1973 and expanded his existing plan to permit operations on two fronts. Detailed planning went on, in the utmost secrecy, from February, 1973 and was assisted by close co-operation between Ismail and his Syrian opposite number, Major-General Mustafa Tlas.

Intensive training was accompanied by an elaborate deception plan: the latter was so effective that the Americans knew of the imminent offensive only hours before it commenced. The Egyptian attack was launched on October 6th, when the Israelis were celebrating Yom Kippur, the Day of Atonement. The Suez Canal was crossed in strength and the Israeli Bar-Lev defence line invested, while on the Syrian front five divisions advanced into the Golan. It took some time for the superpowers to react, but on October 10th Russia began a massive airlift of arms to Egypt and Syria, and the USA commenced a similar airlift to Israel 4 days later. The Israeli counter-offensive, which met with considerable success on the Syrian front and made more limited gains on the Egyptian front, helped convince Kosygin of the necessity of a ceasefire, but it was not until October 22nd that he was able to persuade Sadat to agree to a compromise formula. This agreement did not bring about an immediate cessation of hostilities, and it was only after President Nixon had brought American forces to nuclear alert that Russia agreed to the establishment of a UN force to supervise the ceasefire.

The armistice was bitterly attacked by Libya's Colonel Gadaffi, and was unpopular with many Egyptian and Syrian officers. The 1973 war was nevertheless a partial victory for the Egyptian army, which emerged with greatly enhanced morale and self-confidence. The Egyptians were justly proud of their crossing of the Suez Canal, carried out in the face of serious natural and artificial obstacles in the presence of a strongly entrenched enemy. As a result of Dr Kissinger's initiatives, a disengagement on the Suez front was agreed upon in 1975, and the Egyptians later regained the entire Sinai peninsula.

Further progress towards a peace settlement with Israel proved impossible on the terms Egypt was insisting upon at that time. It was clearly possible for Egypt to arrive at a separate peace with Israel in which the Sinai peninsula would be returned to Egyptian sovereignty, v.ith demilitarisation, observer forces and other safeguards in the area to guarantee against any surprise attacks in future, but the demands Cairo felt compelled to raise on behalf of other Arabs — notably the return of the Golan Heights to Syria, the creation of a self-governing homeland for the Palestinians in the West Bank and the Gaza Strip, and the restoration of East Jerusalem to Arab rule — were unacceptable to any conceivable Israeli government. On the other hand, Egypt was deterred from accepting a separate peace by the certain knowledge that to do so would mean isolation in the Arab world.

President Sadat's negotiating strategy after 1973 was to rely on the USA to bring sufficient pressure on Israel to extract the necessary concessions for a general Arab–Israeli peace settlement. This reorientation of Egyptian policy greatly annoyed Moscow, which retaliated by embargoing almost all arms deliveries to Egypt, and then by refusing even to supply the necessary spare parts for Egypt's almost wholly Soviet-equipped armed forces. Sadat responded by ordering all Soviet military advisers out of Egypt in 1974, and subsequently withdrawing the Soviet Mediterranean squadron's port facilities at Alexandria as well. The Soviet–Egyptian Friendship Treaty was abrogated in 1976. However, this did nothing to solve his basic problem, which was that without adequate spares the Egyptian armed forces were becoming steadily less capable of combat — nor could his growing purchases of Western Military equipment even begin to fill the gap. Thus Egypt was even less able to use the threat of military action as a bargaining lever against Israel, while the declining effectiveness of the armed forces was causing a dangerous unrest in the officer corps.

The domestic political situation was also deteriorating steadily in the period 1975–7, as the Egyptain civil population waited with increasing impatience for the peace and prosperity which they had been promised would follow the 1973 war. Amongst the general population there was little sympathy for the Palestinians, on whose behalf it was reckoned Egypt had sacrificed enough already, and no understanding of the wider Arab political situation which deterred President Sadat from making peace with Israel in return for the recovery solely of occupied Egyptian territories.

The immense drain of Egyptain resources into military expenditure for the confrontation with Israel (amounting in many years to one-third of the entire GNP) over a period of three decades were widely seen as the main reason why Egypt, from being the most prosperous and developed Arab country in 1948, has now become one of the poorest. The appalling poverty and congestion of Egyptian cities have made them political powderkegs, where urban mobs easily exploited by the leftist or Islamic rightist opponents of the regime can appear on the streets at a moment's notice. It is clear, moreover, that this situation cannot be defused unless much government expenditure can be redirected from defence and unless foreign investment flows in in very large volumes — and neither of those things could occur until a peace treaty was concluded with Israel. Thus the savage food riots in Cairo in January, 1977 when for a time the army lost control of the streets, were probably the main impetus that impelled President Sadat to change his negotiating strategy.

In November, 1977 Sadat astonished the world by paying a visit to the Israeli Knesset in Jerusalem. Over the succeeding year of negotiations it became clear that he was actually pursuing a separate peace with Israel, while bargaining as best he could for those other Arab interests on which Israeli diplomacy was far less likely to be yielding. In the peace treaty which was signed between Israel and Egypt in early 1979 this impression was confirmed.

The treaty provided for the return of all occupied Egyptian territory in the Sinai peninsula over a period of 3 years, in return for full diplomatic relations and free movement between the two countries. Military security for both parties is provided by a wide demilitarised zone on the Egyptian side of the frontier and further zones of limited armament in the rest of the Sinai peninsula and in a narrow zone on the Israeli side of the border, with UN forces patrolling the Egyptian–Israeli border and the western shore of the Gulf of Aqaba, acting as a buffer between Gaza and Sinai, and assuring freedom of passage through the Strait of Tiran.

Provisions for the settlement of the Palestinian problem are much less precise, involving the election of a representative government in the West Bank and Gaza Strip which will, however, remain occupied by Israeli security forces for a 5 year interim period. It is stated that the final status of the area and its boundaries will then be determined in negotiations between Egypt, Jordan, the Palestinian elected authorities (not the Palestine Liberation Organisation) and Israel, but all parties will have a veto on any decisions taken. On the subject of occupied Syrian territories there is not a word.

It is not surprising that Syria, the PLO and a number of radical Arab States stated their unequivocal opposition to this settlement and declared Sadat a traitor to the Arab cause, but such opposition had little significant effect on Egyptian internal affairs. At the time of writing even the conservative Arab States were keeping their distance from the Egyptian–Israeli settlement, but of these only Saudi Arabia, as a major contributor to the Egyptian budget, is of any great consequence to Cairo. It is scarcely conceivable that Saudi Arabia would adopt any course of action which might encourage the overthrow of Sadat and the re-emergence of a politically radical regime in Egypt – nor, indeed, that it would willingly do anything which might create a heightened danger of an Arab–Israeli war. Consequently, the main factors which will determine the success or failure of Sadat's historic gamble on peace are the reactions of the Egyptian armed forces and the civil population.

So long as peace brings some perceptible improvements in living standards, civilian opinion in Egypt is unlikely to turn decisively against the regime. The armed forces are a more difficult proposition, since they are losing not only their major reason for existence over the past 30 years, namely the confrontation with Israel, but also the swollen military budgets that were thre result of that confrontation. Substantial numerical reductions in the forces and a reorientation towards different tasks calling for different types of equipment seem inevitable over the medium term, and could provide many officers with strong personal and professional reasons for opposing the regime and its policies. On the other hand, if the changes are carried out with sufficient slowness and sensitivity, and if adequate sums of money and alternative employments are available to ease the transition, there is no reason that the task cannot be accomplished without outbreaks of resistance – especially as the armed forces are thoroughly penetrated at every level by the intelligence services of the regime.

For further comments on the Eyptian government's strategy for achieving a comprehensive restructuring of the armed forces and a transition from a war to a peace footing without encountering violent opposition, and on its prospects of success, see under the headings Role, Commitment and Deployment, and Current Developments.

STRENGTH AND BUDGET

The Egyptian armed forces have total strength of 452,000 men, of whom 255,000 are conscripts. They comprise a modest 1% of the population of 42,600,000. The combined strength of the army and the Air-Defence Command (the latter consisting of army troops, but organisationally a separate service) is 405,000 men, with reserves numbering approximately 300,000. The navy has 20,000 men, plus 15,000 reserves. The air force has 27,500 men, all regulars, and about 20,000 reserves.

There are, in addition, paramilitary forces numbering about 139,000 men, made up of the National Guard (60,000), the Frontier Corps (12,000), Defence and Security Forces (60,000) and Coast Guard (7000). The Coast Guard and Frontier Corps are organisationally part of the army.

The Egyptian defence budget in 1981–82 was $2,100,000,000, a figure representing about one-tenth of the GNP of $20,600,000,000. This would appear to be a substantial decline from the 1975–6 defence budget of $4,370,000,000, but that may be misleading, since in recent years Egyptian military expenditure has been subsidised to an undisclosed but very considerable extent by Saudi Arabia and the smaller Gulf States. It is probable, indeed, that most if not all of Egyptian arms purchases from Western countries requiring payment in hard currencies have been paid for by Saudi Arabia. This makes the surprisingly low figure for military expenditure unreliable as an index of military effort, but very significant nevertheless as an indicator of the decreasing defence burden on the Egyptian economy.

This is a most significant decline from the 1975–76 defence budget of $4,370,000,000, and may represent an even sharper decline in actual Egyptian spending on arms since, prior to the signature of the peace treaty with Israel, Egypt was receiving undisclosed but very considerable subsidies for arms purchased from Saudi Arabia and the smaller Gulf States. In view of the fact that the armed forces have continued to grow in strength numerically – they have increased by 58,000 since 1978 – spending on Egyptian arms and forces per capita has at least halved since 1975.

COMMAND AND CONSTITUTIONAL STATUS

The Egyptian constitution proclaims that 'sovereignty is of the people along'. The People's Assembly, whose 360 members are elected for a 5 year term, is the supreme legislative body. The President, elected for a 6 year term, is the supreme executive authority, and appoints the Council of Ministers, which comprises the Prime Minister, Deputy Prime Ministers and other Ministers. The mission of the armed forces, according to the same constitution, is 'the protection of the socialist gains of the popular struggle, the safeguarding of the country and the security and integrity of its territory'.

The President is Supreme Commander of the Armed Forces, and has an enormous amount of control over them. He appoints the Ministers of Defence and War Production (both serving officers) and the Commander-in-Chief directly, and is empowered by the constitution to appoint all other military officials as well. He presides over the National Defence Council, the senior policy-making body of the government in matters affecting military affairs. He may declare a state of emergency, make treaties and, after obtaining the approval of the People's Assembly, declare war. (In practice, as both 1967 and 1973 showed, this approval may be retroactive.) By the provisions of decrees issued by the President himself, he is the final authority of review of courts martial and must approve all officer promotions. He may also take away seniority, reduce an officer in rank, or reduce him to enlisted status. Moreover, he may delegate these powers to whomever he chooses.

The National Defence Council, a consultative and advisory body without executive powers, assists the President in the formulation of defence policy. Its membership consists of the Prime Minister, the Ministers of Defence, War Production, Foreign Affairs, Interior, Economy and Foreign Trade, the Commander-in-Chief, the Director of the Intelligence Service, the Chiefs of the Army, Navy and Air Force, the Assistant Minister for Air Defence, and other selected officials.

The Minister of Defence has control over the armed forces budget and over economic, industrial and policy matters affecting the military. He is also responsible for the reserves and for veterans' affairs. The Commander-in-Chief controls all four components of the armed forces and is responsible for their organisation, training, armament and administration. In practice these two offices have usually been held by a single officer: the incumbent appointed in October, 1978 was Lieutenant-General Kamal Hassan Ali, the former Chief of Army Intelligence.

Immediately subordinate to the Defence Minister and Commander-in-Chief is the Deputy Commander-in-Chief, who also functions as Chief of Staff and Commander of the Army. According to the formal organisational structure the Commanders of the Navy and Air Force are responsible to this officer in his capacity as Chief of Staff, but these lines of command have not always been strictly observed. In his other capacity, as Commander of the Army, this officer is in charge of the three field armies and the various other army commands such as training, material and intelligence. In most of Egypt's recent wars, it has been the Chief of Staff who has exercised direct control over the conduct of military operations. From October 3rd, 1978 the officer holding this post was Major-General Ahmed Badawi, a front-line brigade commander in 1973 and subsequently Commander of the Third Army.

After the catastrophic loss of most of the Egyptian air force on the ground in the 1967 war, all the Egyptian air-defence troops were placed into a separate Air-Defence Command on the Soviet model. The officer in command of these forces bears the title of Assistant Minister for Air Defence, but despite his cabinet rank he is presumably answerable to the Chief of Staff for operational matters. The nine air force squadrons of air-defence interceptors are operationally subordinate to Air-Defence Command, not to the Commander of the Air Force.

The Defence ministry, army headquarters and Air-Defence Command headquarters are all in the Cairo area.

The headquarters of the Commander of the Navy are at Ras al-Tin, just west of Alexandria. He is assisted by a Deputy Commander who serves as Chief of Staff, and a staff consisting of five departments responsible for personnel, training, operations, logistics and technical services. Control of operational forces is exercised by a selected senior officer designated Commander of the Fleet.

Air force headquarters are at Heliopolis Air Force Base near Cairo. The Commander of the Air Force has a deputy who serves as his Chief of Staff, and a general staff composed of the chiefs of administration, operations, training, logistics, engineering and supply.

Of the paramilitary forces, the Frontier Force and the Coast Guard come under the control of the army, and the National Guard under the Ministry of Defence. The Defence and Security Forces responsible for the guarding of important public installations and for instruction and supervision of the civil-defence organisation, also come under the control of the Ministry of Defence, but they work with representatives of the Ministry of the Interior in their civil-defence role since that ministry is formally responsible for this task.

ROLE, COMMITMENT AND DEPLOYMENT

The roles of the Egyptian armed forces in the period 1950–70 were four: the elimination of Israel as a political entity and, after 1967, the reconquest of occupied Egyptian territory as a preliminary to that goal; defence against any attempt by 'imperialist powers' to reassert foreign domination over the region; intervention in intra-Arab hostilities in the service of the pan-Arab and 'progressive' causes; and the suppression of any internal uprisings, riots, etc. Defence against external (i.e. European) aggression rapidly lost its urgent priority after the Anglo–French attack of 1956, however, as it became clear that the old imperial powers had lost their will or ability to intervene directly in the Middle East, and so Egyptian deployments from about 1960 were organised to meet the other three tasks.

Prior to 1967 the country was divided for military purposes into four administrative area commands: the Sinai peninsula, the Suez Canal, the Nile Delta, and the long, narrow ribbon of the Nile Valley extending southwards to Sudan, each with major army units under command. The vast desert areas to the east and west of the Nile Valley, comprising some 90% of Egypt's area, were not included in any of the commands. They were the sole responsiblity of the Frontier Corps, consisting of a few thousand tough, disciplined troops, mostly mounted on horses and camels, who manned widely separated garrisons and carried out reconnaissance patrols in the border regions.

Since 1967, the army has been continuously in a field command organisation, consisting of I Corps, centred on Cairo with outlying units in the Delta and up the Nile, serving primarily as a reserve and support formation; II Corps, holding the Suez front from the Mediterranean to a point just south of Ismailia; and III Corps, guarding the front from there to the Red Sea. In these circumstances, the old administrative area commands have ceased to function, but the practical effects of the new organisation was the same: the bulk of army troops were facing Israel, while adequate forces were held in the populated regions (and especially around Cairo) for internal security duties. As before, the desert areas remained the responsibility of the Frontier Corps. When it was necessary to supply an intervention force for use in intra-Arab conflicts, as when a large Egyptian expeditionary force was dispatched to fight on the republican side in the North Yemen civil war in 1962–7, the forces were drawn equally from all commands, and operated in the field as an independent command.

This pattern of deployment and the priorities underlying it persisted down to 1973, and indeed are still formally in effect today. Moreover, Egypt's defence commitments beyond the direct confrontation with Israel also formally remain in force; its membership in the League of Arab States, which includes the Arab Defence Council and the Unified Arab Command among its subsidiary bodies; its separate defence agreements with Jordan, Iraq and Libya; and its membership with Syria and Libya in the Federation of Arab Republics, which envisages a federal defence council and a unified military command (and briefly in 1973 actually did have a joint Egyptian–Syrian command). But the Arab League has never actually had Egyptian forces placed at its disposal (and has formally suspended Egypt from membership), while Syria and Libya all openly advocate the overthrow of the Egyptian government for its peace agreement with Israel. Even the mutual defence agreement with Jordan must be considered in abeyance.

In other words, Egypt's overwhelming concentration of land forces on the Sinai front facing Israel, and its residual military obligations to various inter-Arab alliances and organisations whose principal purpose was to co-ordinate the battle against Israel, have all become obsolete. While a need to maintain military forces near the Israeli border will doubtless persist indefinitely, it no longer calls for such a great weight of forces: the commitment to eradicate Israel is gone, and the occupied territories have been recovered. The military role in internal security is unchanged, but is adequately met by the normal distribution of support forces in the populated areas of the country. As for the intervention role, it has changed in purpose under the present leadership from that of backing 'progressive' and revolutionary forces in the Arab world under Nasser to that of preserving moderate and conservative regimes, but it has actually expanded in scope to include not just the Arab world but much of Africa.

Within the shell of the old force structure, one is beginning to see the emerging outlines of a new pattern of armed forces organisation and deployment conforming to the new military priorities, which are essentially two-fold: a defensive capability on the Israeli border, and a highly mobile intervention force capable of operating not only (or even primarily) in Arab countries, but also in the northern and central parts of the African continent.

For the first task, it is necessary to maintain and refurbish at least a significant proportion of what may be called the 'old' army: the armour-heavy, Soviet-equipped force which was built up over the past 30 years to fight Israel. Since the bulk of army officers have made their career in this force and will continue to do so, it cannot be neglected for political reasons; in any case, a credible defence force against Israel will still be required even after full peace is established. The necessary degree of modernisation of this force is being carried out with Western aid, but there is no question that it is being allowed to run down considerably from the peak strength achieved in 1973. (For details, see Equipment and Arms Industry.)

Parallel to this 'old' army, an intervention force is being created which will allow Egypt to effect events in countries to the east, south and west of her. In Arab terms the key-stone of this policy is the mutual defence treaty signed between Egypt and Sudan in July, 1976 (after the most recent Libyan attempt to overthrow the Sudanese government) and the financial support and political backing of Saudi Arabia. Other nations with which Egypt more or less closely co-ordinates policy in this area are the USA, France and Morocco. The shared perception of all these countries is that the major threat to regional stability in the Arab world, and especially in Africa, is the collaboration of the Soviet Union with local radical regimes like Libya, Angola and Ethiopia in attempts to overthrow moderate and conservative regimes. For various reasons of their own both Saudi Arabia and the USA find it unsuitable to provide intervention forces to cope with such threats themselves, but are prepared to support a volunteer like Egypt with money and arms supplies.

Thus one finds that a very substantial proportion of Egyptian arms purchases from Western countries since 1975 (mostly paid for by Saudi Arabia) have been of weapons far more suited to the low-intensity combat environment likely to be encountered by intervention forces in Africa than to the sophisticated and deadly battlefields of another Arab—Israeli war: C-130 Hercules transport aircraft and F-5E fighter—bombers from America, Alpha Jet strike/trainer aircraft from France, and Commando helicopters and SRN-6 hovercraft from Britain. In seeking permission to buy the F-5Es from the USA, President Sadat was quite explicit that they were intended to create a defence (and intervention) capability in Egypt's African border regions where the Soviet/Cuban presence was a growing threat, i.e. in the Ethiopia—Sudan—Uganda—Chad—Libya area.

Indeed, minor instances of such Egyptian military interventions have already occurred. During 1977—8 Egyptian pilots and other military aid specialists were sent to Zaïre, alongside French and Moroccan forces, to aid that country in repelling an invasion by rebels based in Angola. Egyptian military advisers (and according to some reports, Egyptian military supplies) went to assist the Chad government in resisting the attacks of Libyan-backed rebels. Egyptian transport aircraft illegally overflew Kenya in the process of delivering military aid to Somalia during the final phases of the Ogaden war, and Egyptian commandos were involved in a disastrously bungled operation in Cyprus to rescue the hostages in an airliner hijacked by Palestinian terrorists. The most notable instance of this sort of operation was the brief Egyptian—Libyan border war in July, 1977 (see Recent Operations).

Hitherto there has been no evidence that the command structure of the armed forces has been substantially changed to take account of these new priorities and missions, but the Libyan clash has occasioned a significant redeployment of Egyptian forces. It is now understood that about 15% of the armed forces' combat strength — about 35,000 men, 200 tanks and 80—100 combat aircraft — are positioned along and behind the Mersa Matruh—Sollum front in the Western Desert facing Libya. They probably come under the control of I Army Corps in Cairo, but it is possible that they may constitute a separate command.

If current trends continue, it may be anticipated that progressively larger proportions of the Egyptian defence effort will be directed away from the Israeli border, with the emphasis in the newer forces being placed on long-range maritime and air-transport capabilities in support of operations in Africa at some distance from Egyptian bases. However, the breach with Saudi Arabia after Egypt's conclusion of a separate peace with Israel halted the flow of subsidies and hence has slowed the acquisition of weapons and equipment suited to this new role.

RECENT OPERATIONS

The recent operations of the Egyptian army are of very great political and military significance. Not only have they affected the balance of power in the Middle East and relations between the superpowers, but they have also provided practical examples of the potentialities of modern weapons and tactics.

The Egyptian army suffered total defeat in the Six-Day War of 1967, largely as a result of the pre-emptive Israeli air strike which destroyed much of the Egyptian air force on the ground and thereby deprived the army of air cover. Egyptian forces in Sinai, some seven divisions in all, were deployed in what General André Beaufre called 'a curious Soviet style' in a number of strong defensive positions. The Egyptian front was penetrated by three major thrusts: several positions were taken by direct assault, and retreating units were severely mauled by the Israeli air force. Israeli victory was, though, by no means cost-free. Some formations fought doggedly: a brigade defending Rafa lost about a thousand men before it was overrun. A number of Israeli senior officers commented that the Egyptian army's greatest weakness was its officer corps — Egyptian soldiers, when well led, were capable of giving a good account of themselves.

The 1973 campaign provided the Egyptian army with considerable compensation for the humiliations of 1967. The strategic considerations were, admittedly, somewhat different: the war had limited political aims, and the military planning of Egyptian operations was consequently linked to an attainable political objective. Ismail correctly assessed the strengths of weaknesses of the Israelis: he noted their air superiority, technical skill and American support, against which he weighed their long lines of communication, manpower difficulties, vulnerable economy and dangerous over-confidence.

The crossing of the Suez Canal and the breaching of the Israeli Bar-Lev line were the most serious practical problems facing the Egyptians. The Canal was a significant obstacle in itself, and the Israelis had strengthened it by increasing the height and width of the sand bank on its eastern edge. Opening gaps in this bank with explosives or bulldozers would be time-consuming, but it was impossible to cross it with vehicles until adequate breaches had been made. An Egyptian engineer officer discovered that high-pressure water hoses could successfully open a gap in such an obstacle, and steps were accordingly taken to breach the bank by this means. While the breaching was in progress, infantry armed with anti-tank and anti-aircraft missiles were to scale the slope to prevent Israeli armour or aircraft from interfering with the engineers. The strength of the air defence on the Egyptian side of the Canal was, in any case, likely to make Israeli air operations in the vicinity of the Canal both difficult and costly. Once the Canal and sand bank had been crossed and the Bar-Lev line pierced, Egyptian armoured formations, with integral air defence, would be able to press on into Sinai.

Intensive training for the crossing was carried out on an Egyptian-held loop of the Canal and on stretches of the Nile. Ismail took particular care to eliminate 'trench fever' which had infected the Egyptian army as a result of its long emphasis on defence. He also endeavoured to revitalise the officer corps, paying particular attention to the leadership ability of junior officers. Ismail's training programme met with considerable success. His deception plan was similarly fruitful. Defensive positions were constructed on the west bank of the Canal, to give the Israelis the impression that the Egyptians proposed to remain on the defensive. Bridging equipment was camouflaged in large hides near the Canal, and a feint road-building project was commenced in the marshy ground at the northern end of the Canal.

The Egyptian assault began on the early afternoon of October 6th. The defenders of the Bar-Lev line were taken by surprise, and missile-armed Egyptian infantry held off Israeli armour and aircraft while Egyptian tanks crossed the Canal. Two armoured and two infantry divisions formed the first wave of the attack, and by October 13th the Egyptians had pushed about 1000 tanks into Sinai, taken most of the Bar-Lev forts and all but destroyed an Israeli armoured brigade which had attempted to counter-attack. Up to this point Egyptian forces enjoyed the military advantages of following a well-prepared, highly detailed operational plan, and of standing on the tactical defensive against an enemy who was not adequately trained for attacks against their sophisticated range of anti-aircraft missiles and automatic guns. In retrospect it appears that the impact of Egypt's

anti-tank missiles was less significant for the outcome of the battle than was believed at the time (except in the very first stage of the war, when no other anti-tank defences were available to the Egyptians east of the Canal), but the Israeli armour suffered grievously from being unable to count on its usual air support when operating under the umbrella of anti-aircraft defences extending well forward from the Egyptian lines.

By the mid-point of the war, however, anxiety about the shallowness of Egyptian positions in the east bank of the Canal, a certain degree of over-confidence in the Egyptian command, and the urgent need to draw off the main weight of Israeli strength from hard-pressed Syria conspired to make the Egyptians change their tactics. Abandoning the tactical defensive, Egyptian armour went out in strength beyond the cover of their own anti-air and anti-tank defences, seeking a decisive battle. They found it, and within the space of 12 hours they lost it. On October 14th, the Israelis got the best of a massive armoured battle in the area of the Mitla and Gidi passes, and on the night of October 15th/16th they managed to force a crossing of the Canal just north of the Great Bitter Lake. By October 17th a firm bridgehead was established on the west bank, and Israeli armour pushed southwards to encircle the Egyptian Third Army. The ceasefire came barely in time to save the Third Army from collapse, but left the Israelis in possession of a belt of Egyptian territory running from Ismailia to the Gulf of Suez. The Egyptians nevertheless remained in strength on the east bank of the Canal, and subsequent negotiations were to enable them to take possession of the territory between the Canal and the western ends of the crucial Sinai passes.

The Israeli General Arik Sharon admitted that the Egyptian army had performed infinitely better than in previous campaigns. 'I have been fighting for 25 years,' he remarked, 'and all the rest were just battles. This was a real war.' General Ismail maintained that the Egyptians had changed the world's opinion of them, and to some extent he was right. In strictly military terms the Egyptians and their Syrian allies had lost more territory than they had gained, but this loss was to a great extent remedied by subsequent disengagement agreements. The war had certainly fulfilled most of its political objectives: the Middle East was brought forcefully to the attention of the superpowers, who exerted pressure to bring about a cessation of hostilities and a more lasting peace. America's attitude was doubtless heavily influenced by Arab use of the potent oil weapon: on November 20th the hitherto conservative Saudi Arabia announced the suspension of its oil exports to the USA.

The Egyptian army's performance had been impressive but by no means flawless. The crossing of the Suez Canal and the breaching of the Bar-Lev line were carried out with almost textbook precision. Subsequent operations were less creditable. The Egyptian high command reacted slowly to a fluid situation: Egyptian response to the Israeli crossing of the Canal was painfully slow. The war nevertheless did much to efface the shame of 1967. The Egyptian high command had shown that it could plan and execute complex operations, junior leadership had clearly improved and the army's morale had, in the main, been remarkably high.

The main Egyptian military operation since 1973 was the brief, limited attack on Libya in July, 1977. This was undertaken in response to an extensive Libyan-sponsored campaign of sabotage and subversion in Egypt, aimed at displacing President Sadat. The Egyptian attack, similarly, was intended to provide the occasion for all Libyan opposition elements to unite and overthrow Colonel Qadaffi.

The attack was well-prepared in advance, and was launched on July 21st with no warning. Egyptian armour crossed the frontier, while air force raids hit the major Libyan air base at Al Adem near Tobruk without encountering opposition. Little damage was done to the base, however, and subsequent raids were opposed by Libyan SAM defences. The army reported that it had put the Libyan 9th Armoured Battalion out of action, with 50% of its equipment destroyed, but this was not confirmed. The fighting on the ground never moved far from the frontiers, and after 4 days a ceasefire was accepted by both sides. The Egyptian political aim was not achieved, as the fighting served only to rally the Libyan population to the support of Colonel Qadaffi, but the military performance, at least of these picked troops, was satisfactory in most respects.

ORGANISATION

Branch of Service

The army is primarily an infantry force; the other combat branches are armour, artillery, engineers, airborne and commando. The services consist of supply and transport, military works and survey, signals, chemical, medical and the other usual specialties. The army contains the Frontier Corps, which patrols the desert borders, and the Coast Guard, which has a coast-defence combat mission in wartime and in peacetime concentrates on anti-smuggling operations.

Naval officers and ratings are divided into the usual specialties more or less along the lines followed by the British Royal Navy. There are not naval aviators, nor is there any marine corps, but there is an element of naval infantry whose principal purpose is commando raids.

Air force flying personnel are classed as pilots, navigators and observers; there are the usual variety of branches for non-flying specialists. The Air-Defence Command is a separate service.

Operational

The Egyptian army's tactical organisation revolves around the division and brigade structure. There are three armoured divisions, four mechanised infantry divisions, three infantry divisions, plus two Republican Guard Brigades.

The armoured divisions contain two armoured and one mechanised brigade each, the mechanised divisions one armoured and two mechanised brigades. Infantry divisions have one mechanised and two infantry brigades. There are a further two independent armour brigades of nine independent infantry brigades, plus two airmobile brigades, a parachute brigade and 7 commando groups which form the core of the intervention force. The army has 12 artillery brigades, 2 heavy mortar brigades, two SSM regiments and six ATGW brigades.

An armoured brigade contains three tank battalions, and an AA company with guns and missiles together with motorised infantry, armoured reconnaissance, engineer, signals and headquarters companies. A mechanised brigade has three mechanised infantry battalions, supported by a tank battalion and mortar, AA, anti-tank, pioneer, armoured reconnaissance, signals and headquarters companies. An artillery brigade normally contains a battalion of M-63 122mm D-30 howitzers, a battalion of 122mm D-74 guns, three battalions of M-38 122mm howitzers, a battalion of 160mm and 240mm heavy mortars, an anti-tank battalion with SU-100s, a light anti-tank company with Sagger ATGWs mounted on GAZ 69 jeeps, and anti-aircraft, signals, engineer, mechanised infantry and headquarters companies. Artillery battalions usually contain four batteries of guns/howitzers.

The field army comprises three corps. I Corps, base mainly in the lower Nile valley and the Delta with forces extending westwards towards Libya, is the main repository of training and support formations and also the home of most of the commando, airmobile and paratroop units which are the army's main contribution to Egypt's new capability for intervention abroad. The security of the government in Cairo is ultimately guaranteed by the outsized Republican Guard brigades, which are not in the corps organisation. II and III Corps, hold the northern and southern parts of the Suez front, facing Israel, respectively.

The greater part of the operational structure and doctrine of the Egyptian army is still derived from the Soviet Union, but there has been a slow, steady shift towards Western operating procedures as increasing amounts of Western-built equipment enter the Egyptian inventory.

The navy's principal operating base is at Ras al-Tin (Alexandria), with other Mediterranean bases at Port Said and Mersa Matruh but a portion has been kept in the Red Sea permanently since 1967 with bases at Port Tewfiq, Hurghada and Safaqa. The fleet is organised into four major commands: destroyer, submarine, mine warfare and torpedo boats. There is no marine corps but a naval infantry force is maintained.

The air force has an administrative superstructure of air regiments (one bomber regiment, three interceptor regiments and five FGA regiments) but the basic tactical unit is the squadron. There are also twelve helicopter squadrons, two reconnaisance squadrons, one MR squadron and five transport squadrons. The interceptor squadrons come under the operational control of Air-Defence Command.

RECRUITMENT, TRAINING AND RESERVES

The National Military Service Law of 1956 imposed an obligation to perform 3 years of military service on all Egyptian males not specifically exempted by law. Males are required to register for national service at the age of sixteen, but none is inducted before twenty or over thirty-five. Service may be performed in other quasi-military public services — work battalions, police, fire departments or the prison administration — and thirteen specific categories of people receive automatic exemption: the physically unfit, only sons, sole supporters of a family, etc. There are also discretionary exemptions for government employees and essential industry workers, and deferments for university students up to the time they leave school or to the age of twenty-eight, but on the whole the system has worked fairly and eliminated most of the old abuses.

The armed forces only require an annual intake of about 100,000 recruits to maintain their present level, however, while the number of fit men reaching military age each year is several times greater than that. Accordingly, the system is actually one of selective service. The country is divided into draft zones, and conscripts are selected annually by zonal councils composed of senior military officers, civil officials of the governorate and a team of medical officers. Local mayors and village chiefs participate in examining the prospective recruits. After exemptions and deferments have been ruled on, conscripts are chosen by lot from the available pool of eligible men, and the names forwarded to the Draft Administration in Cairo.

Military service is not unattractive to many Egyptians, as it offers better living conditions and prospects for advancement than are available to a large proportion of the community in civilian life. Thus NCOs in all services are almost always regulars, chosen from amongst qualified volunteers from the ranks, and the services can afford to be highly selective in whom they accept. Indeed, even in the enlisted ranks most air force personnel are volunteer regulars. In the navy, volunteers and conscripts are about equal in numbers below NCO level. Only in the army are a large majority of the lower ranks conscripts.

Basic training for new troops follows the usual indoctrination pattern, but the Egyptian forces have to pay special attention to raising the educational level of some conscripts to the point where they can cope with modern weapons and techniques. For many years it was necessary to give simple literacy training to large numbers of new recruits; this is no longer a major problem, but other basic education courses still have to be given to many conscripts. The training is done at the 'Liberation Schools' run by the army, some of which can grant secondary school certificates qualifying graduates for university entrance.

After basic training and any necessary remedial instruction, army recruits usually attend the branch school of their assigned arm or service, located at one of several training centres throughout the country, for a period of from 3 to 6 months. They then participate in the annual cycle of army training, commencing with individual weapons training at the beginning of the year and working up to army-wide exercises in the autumn.

At the end of the period of obligatory military service, selected volunteers attend a command school and are accepted as regular NCOs. There is a wide variety of opportunities for specialised technical training for NCOs both at local units and at branch schools. Many NCOs have received advanced training abroad at Soviet-bloc branch, staff or technical schools, or latterly at their Western equivalents. The army runs an advanced career school for senior NCOs at Almazah in Cairo.

Navy enlisted men go from basic training to 6 months of shipboard duty, followed by 6 months of advanced training that qualifies them for a specialist school. Successful candidates then attend specialist courses in quartermaster, communications, armament, supply or seamanship. Individual ship commanders are responsible for training their own crews, but there are further technical courses and an advanced career school for NCOs at the navy's training centre at Ras al-Tin.

Air force enlisted training is mainly devoted to developing ground-crew skills, and after basic training almost all airmen are sent to the technical schools — aviation mechanics, radio, radar, ordnance and aerial photography — which are located at Heliopolis Air Force Base near Cairo. At the highest level, there is an interservice school conducted at Ministry of Defence level for exceptionally well qualified NCOs which includes on-the-job training in senior-staff operations.

Egypt is usually fortunate amongst Arab nations in having this large, competent and experienced cadre of NCOs. On average they have had more than 10 years' service and experience of at least one war; thanks to the comprehensive technical and professional education system they are also likely to be proficient in their specialty. In many ways, they constitute the backbone of the Egyptian armed forces.

Regular officers are trained in the three service academies and in the tri-service Armed Forces Technical College. Admission requirements vary somewhat, but generally provide that candidates have general secondary certificates or high school diplomas with good average grades, be under twenty-one (the air force takes college graduates up to twenty-four), be of good character and never have been married. They must also pass competitive examinations and physical-fitness tests. Certain preferences are given to sons of serving and retired officers and to sons and brothers of those killed in war.

The Military Academy, sometimes called the War College, is in Cairo. It provides a 3 year course which includes comprehensive infantry and leadership training as well as a rigorous academic programme. Graduates are commissioned as second-lieutenants and go on to specialised courses conducted by their own branch schools before joining their units.

Both navy midshipmen and air force cadets also spend the first year of their training at the Military Academy, as do prospective students of the Armed Forces Technical College. Navy midshipmen then proceed to the Naval Academy at Ras al-Tin for 3 years, of which the first two are largely devoted to academic work and the third is spend mostly at sea. Air force cadets go from their year at the Military Academy to 3 years at the Air Force Academy at Bilbeis, 25 miles north-east of Cairo, where they pursue a curriculum divided into three 1 year terms of theoretical, technical and scientific training and interspersed with 250 hours of flying instruction. Upon completion of flying training and after passing the academic examinations, graduates are appointed pilot lieutenants and granted a bachelor of aviation degree. Those who fail to qualify as pilots may be given ground administrative assignments or may revert to the army. The Navigators' School and the Observers' School are also part of the Academy at Bilbeis, and much of their curricula is common with that of the other cadets.

The Armed Forces Technical College in Cairo was founded to produce competent technical officers for all the services: applicants must have a particularly good academic record in science, and must pass examinations in algebra, trigonometry, analytical geometry and mechnical engineering. They must also complete a 1 month selection camp, and 1 year at the Military Academy. Their 3 years of training are divided into intermediate, higher and scientific research stages, after which they graduate as first-lieutenants. Since 1969 civilians have also been allowed to attend the College; on the other hand naval technical officers now spend only 1 year there, followed by two further years at the Naval Technical College which was opened at Ras al-Tin in 1969.

Enlisted men who can qualify are eligible for entry into any of the academies.

There is an extensive system of technical, branch and staff schools providing for the further education of Egyptian military officers. Probably the most important is the Army Staff College, founded in 1939, offering instruction to officers of major/lieutenant-colonel rank. The syllabus includes tactics, logistics, organisation, planning and administration up to divisional level. Much attention is given to the specific circumstances of the Middle East.

The highest level of the military educational system is the Nasser Institute, founded in 1964, which gives senior officers time and opportunity to consider the problems of war on a broader scale. Strategy, tactics, and the political, economic and social aspects of national mobilisation are part of the curriculum. Large numbers of officers of both middle and senior rank also attend staff colleges and other advanced schools abroad: in the first years after independence these were mostly in Britain, France and the USA; after 1955 they shifted to Soviet-bloc countries, and since 1973 they have been mainly in the West once again.

While this may make for a confusion of doctrines, it certainly does tend to broaden officers' perspectives. There is little question today than an Egyptian officer at divisional- or corps-command level is the professional equal of his Russian, American, German or Israeli equivalent. He will have had the benefit of his own good military educational system; experience at a Soviet or a Western senior staff college (or, in some cases, both); and the inestimable advantage, shared only by his Israeli opposite number, of having commanded forces in full-scale modern warfare at every stage of his career, as a junior officer in 1956, a field-grade officer in 1967 and a brigadier in 1973.

Egyptian reserves officially number 300,000 men for the

army 20,000 for the air force and 15,000 for the navy. When enlisted men finish their 3 year duty they are placed in the reserves for 9 years, during which the government can recall them for an additional 3 years. It is possible for college students to fulfil their military obligations by taking military training in term and spending parts of their vacations in military labour battalions; indeed some form of military training is obligatory for all male and unmarried female college students, and passing military examinations is a prerequisite for graduation. Those who wish may seek commissions by attending the Reserve Officers' Academy at Faid, about 30 miles north-west of Suez.

Reserves are used extensively in the various military training programmes in schools and civil-defence organisations, but it is not clear how useful they are for combat purposes. Some, certainly, are members of clearly defined units that train together and can reasonably be counted as part of the army's fighting strength on mobilisation; these would be a few tens of thousands. The remainder include a large number who have sufficiently fresh military experience (in the previous 3–4 years) to be useful as individual reinforcements or replacements to existing units, and many men of this category have been mobilised in past crises.

EQUIPMENT AND ARMS INDUSTRY

The main armoured strength of the army consists of 1,250 T-54/55, 600 T-62 and 250 M-60 (i.e. M-60A3) medium tanks (with a further 189 M-60A3s on order), plus 30 PT-76 light tanks. These are supplemented by 300 BRDM-1/-2 scout cars and 200 BMP-1 M1CV. The mechanised infantry are borne in a total of 2,500 OT-62, BTR-40/-50/-60/-152 and Walid APC and 300 M-113A2 APC, (750 more M-113A2 APC on order).

The artillery arm consists of 1,300 85mm, 100mm, 122mm, 130mm, 152mm and 180mm towed guns and howitzers, plus about 200 SU-100 and ISU-152 SP guns, plus 360 120mm M-43, 160mm M-53 and 240mm M-63 mortars and 300 122mm, 140mm and 240mm multiple rocket launchers. 100 M-106A2 and M-125A2 mortar carriers are on order. There are 12 FRGG-7 and 12 Scud B ##M.

The anti-tank armoury consists of 900 57mm and 100mm ATK guns, 900 82mm B-10 and 107mm B-11 recoilless rifles, and approximately 1,000 Sagger, Snapper, Swatter, Milan, Beeswing, Swingfire and TOW ATGW, 52 M-901 AFV mounting TOW, 200 TOW launchers plus 4,000 missiles (including 2,500 improved TOW), and 2000 Swingfire ATGW are on order.

The army's integral air-defence weapons (under Air Defence Command administrative control) comprise 350 ZSU-23-4 and ZSU-57-2 SP AA guns, SA-7 and SA-9 SAM, and 16 Crotale SAM (four more on order).

The Air Defence Command is equipped with 360 SA-2 SAMs on 80 sites and 200 SA-3 SAMs on 65 sites, plus six Improved Hawk and 16 Crotale mobile Sam. A further six batteries of improved Hawk are on order. Air Defence Command also has 2,500 37mm, 40mm, 57mm, 85mm and 100mm AA guns. Associated radars are Far Song, Low Blow and Straight Flus (missile/gun) and Squint Eye and Long Track (EW).

The air force has a total of 429 combat aircraft, down from 612 in 1978, and many of the remaining Soviet-supplied aircraft are grounded for lack of spares.

The premier air defence weapon is the three regiments of interceptors which operate under the control of the Air Defence Command, though they belong administratively in the air force. They consist of seven squadrons equipped with 142 MiG-21 MF/U and two with 2C F-16A.

The remaining combat strength, which fights under air force operational control, consists of one bomber squadron with 14 TU-16 (some carrying AS-5 ASM), two reconnaissance squadrons, six Mirage 5SDR, 12 MiG 21R and 20 Su-7, four helicopter squadrons with 60 Gazelle (24 equipped with HOT and ATGW), and five fighter-ground attack regiments: two with 35 F-4E and 48 Chinese-built F-6 (MiG-19), two with 50 MiG-17 and 40 SU-7BM, and one with 46 Mirage 5. There are 60 F-16 on order (some of which are intended to replace the F-4E, now being sold to Turkey which the Egyptian air force has had difficulty in maintaining), together with 20 Mirage 2000, 16 Mirage 5 E2 and 20 Gazelle.

The Egyptian air force also has one marine reconnaissance squadron with five IL-28; a transport brigade of five squadrons with 18 C-130 H Hercules (six more on order), 18 Il-14, 10 An-12, 20 DHC-5D, four Falcon 20, one Boeing 707 and one Boeing 737; eight utility helicopter squadrons with 20 Mi-4 55 Mi-8, 28 Commando and 15 CH-47C (four AS-61 on order); and two EC-130H electronic intelligence gathering aircraft. Air force trainers consist of 30 MiG-15UTI, 80 L-29, 60 Gomhouria, 36 Yak-18, four Chinese FT-6, five Mirage 5SDD and four F-16B. (45 Alpha-Jet are on order, of which 15 are also configured for ground attack.)

Standard air-to-air weapons are AA-2 Atoll, R-530, Sparrow and Sidewinder AAM; air-to-surface missiles in service are AS-1, AS-5 Maverick and HOT. In addition the aircraft currently in general service, the Egyptian air force has approximately 50 MiG-21, 17 MiG-23 BN/U, 72 MiG-17, 47 Su-7, 40 Su-2Q, 43 F-6, three An-24 and 12 Mi-6 in storage.

The Egyptian navy has four ex-Soviet 'W' class submarine and eight 'R' class (six ex-Soviet, two ex-Chinese), five destroyers (from Skory-class, one ex-British Z-class), and three ex-British frigates (one Hunt class, one Black Swan class, and one River-class now used as a submarine support ship). The main striking force is the 19 missile-firing fast attack craft (eight Osa-I with Styx SSM and SA-7 SAM, four Fomar, five P-6 and two Vosper-built Ramadan-class with Otomat SSM). One more P-6 and four more Ramadan are on order. There are also 16 fast torpedo boats (ten P-6, four P-4, two Shershen), 14 fast patrol boats (four Shershen with BM-21 MRL and SA-7 SAM, ten P-6), twelve large patrol boats of SO-1 class (some with SA-7 or BM-21). Other vessels include ten ocean minesweepers (six T-43 and four Yurka-class), four inshore m/s (two T-301, two K-8 class), three Polnocny-class LCT, 14 LCU (ten Vydra, four SMB1-class), and three SRN-6 hovercraft (14 more on order). The navy has an ASW helicopter squadron with six Sea King Mk 47, and a coastal defence unit (using army troops, but under naval control) which disposes of 130mm guns and 30 Otomat and Samlet SSM launchers.

The striking point to emerge from these figures is that Egypt has made little effort to replace the approximately 800 tanks that were lost in the 1973 war, let alone to match the subsequent further expansion of the Israeli forces. The Egyptian armoured force of today consists largely of what was still surviving on the last day of that war, less subsequent attrition. The same is true for most other categories of armoured vehicle and all types of artillery. The extent of Egyptian loss of interest in maintaining an offensive capability against Israel may be measured by the fact that Egypt now has substantially fewer main battle tanks than Syria or Iraq.

Little new has been bought for the army since 1973, except anti-tank guided weapons: Swingfire and TOW to extend the anti-tank cover over a wider area than the old first-generation Soviet ATGWs in Egyptian hands could do, and Milan and Beeswing for the nearer distances. But this is scarcely surprising in that Egypt no longer expects to have to attack Israel — for a defensive war her arms are probably sufficient, and tanks are not the sort of delicate machinery that instantly fail if the flow of spare parts slows. Thus the stringent Soviet arms embargo against Egypt has not had marked effects on the army's efficiency and readiness, nor has it been seen as expedient or necessary to buy the army new weapons. It is here an advantage, of course, that tanks and other bulky steel weapons do not deteriorate if left in a desert climate.

One can see at the most nothing more than a policy of replacing old with new in the navy's weapons-buying pattern since 1973. Air-Defence Command's purchase of Crotale and improved HAWK SAMs is understandable in view of the fact that its SA-2 and SA-3 missiles, the heart of its system on the Canal, are now approaching an age at which their reliability will fade (none has been supplied since 1973, and their 'shelf life' is estimated at 5 years).

By far the greatest problems caused by the Soviet refusal to supply spare parts for weapons Moscow had previously sold to Egypt have been experienced by the air force, whose numbers of operational aircraft and average monthly flying hours declined drastically over the period 1973–8, though flying hours have recovered considerably as western aircraft have been delivered.

For the rest the Egyptians have been reduced to reconditioning old aircraft wherever they could, and trying to create their own domestic arms industry as a long-term solution to the problem of arms embargoes. In early 1977 the Soviet Union finally returned 50 of 175 MiG-21 engines that had been sent there for overhaul, but apart from that most of the work has been done by China and Britain.

The Chinese began supplying Egypt with desperately needed spare parts for its 90 old MiG-17s in July, 1976 reportedly in exchange for a MiG-23 which they used as a model (fitted with licence-built British Spey engines) for their own new F-8 fighter soon to be produced in Sian. Chinese assistance may have extended to the supply of new engines for MiG-17s, and a military protocol was signed by the two countries in late 1976, but most of the reconditioning work is in fact being done by British firms.

The most urgent item on the list was undoubtedly the 200-plus MiG-21s that provide the backbone of the Egyptian air force. The Hawker Siddeley side of British Aerospace and Rolls Royce were deeply involved in servicing the engines of some 80 MiG-21s in early 1978, and the aircraft have been successfully tested with a Smiths Industries head-up weapons delivery system. Vosper Thorneycroft agreed in 1977 to overhaul and update the navy's Russian-built missile boats. Other British firms have been involved in the overhaul of the army's ageing T-54/55 tanks.

Arab Organisation for Industrialisation

The only long-term answer to Arab arms dependence on fickle outside suppliers has long been recognised to be the establishment of a domestic arms industry — or perhaps two, to supply the conservative and the 'radical' countries, respectively. In the aftermath of the 1973 war a number of Arab conservative States found themselves in a position to fund such a development, thanks to greatly increased oil revenues. Not having the large skilled labour forces themselves that would make such a transfer of technological skills from the industrial countries possible, they found in Egypt a similarly pro-Western, conservative State which could supply the workforce for such an Arab arms industry.

Thus was created in May, 1975 the Arab Military Industrial Organisation (subsequently renamed the Arab Organisation for Industrialisation — AOI), with a founding capital of $1,040,000,000 contributed by Saudi Arabia, Qatar, the United Arab Emirates and Egypt. The Chairman was Ashraf Marwan, President Sadat's son-in-law. Kuwait, which was asked to join and to contribute $400,000,000 to the organisation's capital, consistently refused to do so because of doubts about the enterprise's commercial viability. This was perhaps not surprising, in view of the AOI's serious under-capitalisation, but various Western arms manufacturers were nevertheless prepared to enter into co-production and technology transfer agreements with the organisation because of the privileged access to the large Arab market which it offered. It was intended that any arms produced by AOI plants should be sold to most or all of the participating States, not just to that in which a particular factory is located.

However, the AOI agreed with several American concerns in February, 1978 to establish a joint company for the manufacture of military electronic equipment in Saudi Arabia and has studies underway to build arms factories in Qatar and the United Arab Emirates as part of a strategy to disperse its facilities 'to avoid their being targets of attack in times of crisis', it was always recognised that the bulk of its plants must be in Egypt, the only member with any existing industrial expertise and capacity. The idea was to build on the small existing Egyptian arms industry, the only one in the Arab world, by injecting large amounts of Western capital and technology.

The Egyptian arms industry began to be developed even before the 1952 revolution, and got a significant impulse when a centralised Ministry of War Production was created after the 1956 war. It moved from production of small arms like the 7.62mm Rashid assault rifle and the 9mm Port Said sub-machine-gun (a copy of the Swedish Carl Gustav M-45 built under licence) to limited production of the now obsolescent Walid APC (powered by a German Deutz engine and externally resembling a four-wheeled version of the BTR-152) and of an SP gun (essentially a marriage of an M-63 122mm gun with a T-34 tank chassis). All kinds of ammunition and minor military equipment are produced, and the four existing munitions factories, now under AOI auspices, have recently been producing spare parts for tanks and mobile bridge-laying equipment. They are also carrying out such modifications to existing equipment as the fitting of anti-tank missiles to T-62 tanks and Gazelle helicopters and the mounting of SA-7 anti-aircraft missiles on American Motors jeeps (now being produced in Egypt).

Egypt's pre-1973 essays in the production of more sophisticated weapons, however, were uniformly unsuccessful. In 1949 Egypt began turning out light training aircraft under licence from various European countries (of which the air force's Gomhouria trainers are the sole surviving examples), but a large expenditure of money and effort in the 1950s in an attempt to design and produce an Egyptian jet fighter with the aid of German experts failed to result in a useful product, and the project was eventually shelved. A parallel attempt to produce surface-to-surface missiles, also with the aid of a German team, was begun and halted again three times in 1948–60; it was announced in 1966 that three types of missiles had been produced, but they never achieved sufficient reliability to become operational with the armed forces. Research in nuclear fusion began in 1955, and a Soviet-built research reactor was installed at Inchass, a Cairo suburb, in 1961, but weapons research was never seriously pursued.

It was against this background of repeated failure to develop a sophisticated arms industry based on local resources that the basic AOI strategy of involving Western manufacturers in the upgrading of the Egyptian armaments industry was formulated. Its concrete results so far, apart from the agreement to produce 12,000 American Motors Corporation jeeps per year, have been an $80,000,000 contract with British Aerospace in December, 1977 to set up a production line in the outskirts of Cairo to produce the Swingfire long-range anti-tank guided weapon, and a further set of contracts worth $665,000,000 in early 1978 to build Lynx 10 seat military helicopters in Egypt. The Swingfire is being built by a joint company called Arab British Dynamics, with six AOI representatives on the board and a British managing director. Two similar companies, the Arab British Helicopter Company and the Arab British Engine Company, have been created in partnership with Westland Aircraft and Rolls Royce to build the Lynx helicopters and their Gem jet engines at the Helwan aircraft factory 18 miles outside Cairo. The first 20 helicopters are to be imported whole from Britain, the next thirty assembled locally from imported parts, and subsequent models to have increasingly large proportions of locally manufactured components – an eventual production rate of four per month is envisaged, with probable market of some 250 Lynxes eventually forecast in the various Arab armies.

The choice of a fixed-wing combat aircraft to be produced by AOI has been the subject of excessive speculation and repeated premature announcements, but at the time of writing it appears to have settled on the Franco–German Alpha Jet, a technically undemanding trainer/strike aircraft on which the Egyptian aircraft industry can build up its expertise. After almost 3 years of negotiation the AOI signed a contract with the French Marcel Dassault Aircraft Company in October, 1978 for the purchase of 14 Alpha Jets to be followed by the assembly of 150 more (again with increasing Egyptian input) at the Helwan aircraft manufacturing complex. This deal is reportedly linked with others to be concluded with SNECMA (the French aero-engine company), and with Matra (the missile manufacturing group) and the Thomson-CSF electronics groups to assemble Crotale surface-to-air missiles and to produce surveillance radars and communications equipment for AOI. The arrangement with Dassault also calls for the establishment of an assembly line in Egypt for the very advanced Mirage 2000 fighter as soon as it enters production in France, but since that is not scheduled to occur in France until 1982 it allows considerable time for Egyptian skills and manufacturing capabilities to be developed.

An element of doubt about the future states of the AOI has been introduced by the signature of the Egyptian–Israeli peace treaty, and was further exacerbated by President Sadat's dismissal of its chairman. Ashraf Marwan, in October, 1978, but it is unlikely that these events will lead to the collapse of the organisation. So long as the present regime survives, Egypt will continue to be seen as a safe home for their armaments industry by the conservative Arab States which are providing most of the money and much of the market, and the attractions of that market provide a sufficient incentive to Western arms manufacturers to enter into arrangements with AOI.

RANK, DRESS AND DISTINCTIONS

The titles of rank are the same in all four services, and equate to the same levels of base pay and privileges. Like the uniforms, unit insignia and much else, they derive from British models, and are shown with their corresponding British army ranks. Officers wear their insignia on epaulettes; other ranks on sleeves.

Mushir (Field Marshal) – Eagle, wreath, crossed swords

Fariq Awwal (General) – Eagle, two stars, crossed scimitars

Fariq (Lieutenant-general) – Eagle, one star, crossed scimitars

Liwa (Major-general) – Eagle, crossed scimitars

'Amid (Brigadier) – Eagle and three stars

'Aqid (Colonel) – Eagle and two stars

Muqaddim (Lieutenant-colonel) – Eagle and one star

Ra'id (Major) – Eagle

Naqib (Captain) – Three stars

Mulazim Awwal (Lieutenant) – Two stars

Mulazim (Second-lieutenant) – One star

Musa'id (Warrant Officer) – Epaulettes without insignia, triangle on right sleeve

Raqib Awwal (Sergeant-major) – Four stripes on right sleeve

Raqib (Sergeant) – Three stripes

'Arif (Corporal) – Two stripes

Jundi (Private) – One stripe

Officers and men of the various branches of the army (engineers, infantry, armour, etc.) and of the navy (seamen, communications, weapons, etc.) wear distinctive insignia on their sleeves. Men serving in specialist units such as the paratroops or commandos wear various badges denoting their expertise and experience. Air force personnel do not wear branch insignia, but flying personnel wear badges on the left breast – the national ensign with a wing on either side for pilots, one one side only for navigators and observers.

Pay and allowances for both officers and enlisted men are good by comparison with what individuals of comparable skills could expect to receive in the civilian economy, and there is specialist pay and hazardous-duty pay in addition for dangerous assignments such as flying, submarine duty and commando service. Rapid inflation has narrowed the gap between military and civilian pay in real terms in recent years, and there may even have been a slight fall in more junior officers' real income, but there remain the considerable advantages for all servicemen of relatively generous leave, decent medical care and educational opportunities, plus the cash benefits of pensions, longevity pay, family allowances and care for servicemen's families which are generally unavailable or very limited in civil life. Officers' social status remains high, and ordinary servicemen are highly regarded by the public as patriots doing a difficult job.

Officers and NCOs have separate accommodations, and married quarters exist in most garrison posts for regular troops. Unmarried enlisted men and conscripts live in barracks. Food is ample and good, often superior to that consumed by the average civilian. Discipline is strict, even harsh, but is recognised to be administered fairly. The class-ridden officer–man relations of the old Egyptian army have been largely eradicated.

Egyptian uniforms generally follow the British pattern in all services, though naturally with the emphasis on lightweight clothing. The army's service and dress uniforms are closely similar to British army models, but both functional clothing (for tank crews and other specialists) and combat dress are now based mainly on Soviet patterns. The navy wears white uniforms most of the time, but does have dark blue uniforms for winter use. The air force usually wears khaki uniforms with light-blue garrison or service caps; officers generally wear a 'bush jacket' with the sleeves rolled up.

The system of awards and distinctions was radically revised at the time of the Revolution, eliminating all distinctions with a royal connotation, and was codified in its present form in 1966. All major distinctions carry with them a monthly cash bonus ranging from £E10 to £E2.50 which is payable throughout the individual's service career and is subsequently added to his (or his family's) pension.

The highest decoration is the Star of Honour; it is awarded to officers for 'exceptional service, sacrifice and extreme prowess in the face of the enemy'. In addition to the cash bonus, it carries with it the guarantee of free education at all levels for the holder's brothers and children.

The other major decorations in order of precedence are the Military Star and the Military Medal of the Republic (gold and silver classes), which are awarded, respectively, to officers and men for courage on the battlefield; and the Medal of Courage and the Military Medal of Duty (each in gold, silver and bronze classes), which are granted to officers and men for 'distinguished acts of bravery' and for 'loyalty, devotion to duty and good conduct', respectively. There is another group of awards that are awarded for outstanding service or for participation in particular events or campaigns.

CURRENT DEVELOPMENTS

The effective disappearance of any Egyptian offensive capability against Israel, and indeed the probability that even Egypt's ability to defend itself against an Israeli attack has gravely deteriorated, is the quite inevitable consequence of the political strategy initiated by Sadat and continued by Mubarak. It was clear from the beginning that the Soviet Union, Egypt's sole source of arms from 1955 to 1973, would not continue to supply weapons once Sadat embarked on his 'American strategy' for reaching a peace settlement with Israel (though the completeness and devastating effect of the Soviet embargo on spare parts may not have been anticipated).

It was equally clear that Western arms suppliers could not quickly fill the gap, both because Egypt's financial resources and the ability of its armed forces to change over quickly to Western armaments would not permit it, and because the USA in particular would be reluctant to supply Cairo with large quantities of advanced weapons so long as any possibility of an Egyptian–Israeli military conflict lingered on.

In effect, therefore, the decline of Egyptian military capabilities against Israel was foreseen and discounted in advance, as being of little political significance in a situation where peace with Israel was the goal of Egyptian policy. It is now evident that Sadat reckoned not to have to deal with serious domestic popular opposition to peace with Israel, and that he was prepared if necessary to disregard the reactions of the rest of the Arab world, assuming that the 'radicals' would fulminate ineffectually while his conservative allies and financial supporters would eventually accept his policy lest worse befall (i.e. the re-emergence of a radical regime in Egypt). What could not be so easily discounted was the possible reaction of the armed forces, either on the political ground that their sacred mission was being betrayed, or on the professional ground that their organisation was being allowed to deteriorate.

It is possible that one reason for Sadat's gradual reorientation of the armed forces towards an interventionist role in the service of Western and 'moderate' interests in Africa (in addition to the obvious purposes of keeping radical and pro-Soviet regimes away from Egypt's borders, winning American support, and gratifying Saudi Arabia) was to provide the Egyptian officer corps with a new and professionally attractive role. The need for some such compensation was amply demonstrated by the mid-1978 defection of General Shazli, probably the officer who still commanded the highest respect in the Egyptian armed forces despite his previous well-publicised disagreements with Sadat's policies and his post of semi-exile as Ambassador to Lisbon.

The state of dissatisfaction prevailing in the Egyptian officer corps, which had already moved Sadat to promote the Air Force Commander Husni Mubarak to the Vice-Presidency in 1975 in an attempt to placate the armed forces, was certainly intensified after Sadat's November, 1977 visit to Jerusalem, when it became clear that he was determined to conclude a separate peace with Israel if efforts at a more comprehensive settlement failed. It is understood that about 130 officers were retired or transferred immediately after Sadat went to Israel, and armed forces senior officers' public statements in succeeding months did not always contain the usual fulsome and unstinting praise of the President.

The internal politics of the Egyptian armed forces are more than usually inaccessible to outside observers, but there has clearly been concern in the Egyptian government since late 1977 over the possibility of a coup. The political upheavals in Egypt during the brief experiment with 'democratisation' in spring 1977 to spring 1978, the fact that two of Sadat's own appointees resigned the Foreign Ministry within a year (unable to keep up with the rapid development of his peace offensive), and above all the alarming popular dissatisfaction with the state of the economy revealed by the January, 1977 food riots, all served to underline the critical degree to which Sadat's rule depended on the continued support of the armed forces.

When the long expected coup against President Sadat occurred, however, it was of an entirely unanticipated nature. On October 6, 1981 the President was taking the salute at a military parade in Cairo held annually to celebrate the initiation of the successful attack across the Suez Canal against Israel in 1973. During the parade a truck towing a heavy artillery piece stopped in front of the saluting base, apparently because of mechanical failure, but, when the President rose to see what was happening, the crew left the vehicle, charged the saluting base with automatic weapons firing and killed him with seven others, wounding twenty-nine more (including the Vice-President and former commander of the air force, Husni Mubarak). The assassins, who were all arrested, proved to be members of an Islamic fundamentalist sect, Al Jihad (the Holy War), which was loosely connected with a better-known group, Takfir wal-Hijira. Their aim, apparently, was to replace Sadat with an Islamic fundamentalist, Professor Omar Ahmed Rahman of Asyut University, and establish an Iranian-style regime. In the aftermath of the assassination, seven hundred fundamentalists were arrested and thirty officers and 104 soldiers purged from the army. The arrests provoked severe rioting in several cities, including Asyut, and over fifty rioters were killed in battles with the police. Vice-President Mubarak was nevertheless able to establish his authority without real difficulty and swiftly affirmed his purpose of continuing to rule Egypt by the policies which Sadat had instituted, including the foreign policy of friendship with the United States and accord with Israel. So far (March 1982) the armed forces appear to accept the perpetuation.

Gwynne Dyer
John Keegan

EQUATORIAL GUINEA

HISTORY AND INTRODUCTION

Equatorial Guinea is the nation which was formed by the union of Spain's two former sub-Saharan African possessions into one independent State in 1968; the two possessions were Rio Muni, on the West African coast and the island of Fernando Poo certain small groups of islands also form part of the State. At independence a small Spanish *Guardia Civil* garrison remained, for external defence and internal security. In the February—April, 1969 political crisis, during which anti-white riots occurred, a new independence force, the *Guardia National*, was instituted and the Spanish unit withdrawn. The Head of State, President Macias Nguema, presided over one of Africa's most bloodily tyrannical regimes until his overthrow in 1979 following an invasion, launched from Fernando Poo and led by a kinsman, Obiang Nguema, who, on the revolt's success, became President. The invasion was a murky event, a number of foreign countries offering a little help and a number more claiming to have done so after the revolt succeeded. Morocco supplied a Presidential Guard that is only now being withdrawn. The new regime, although authoritarian, is not notably despotic in its methods; it has also closed down the Cuban staging facility for military personnel bound for Angola. What appears to have been a coup attempt in April 1981 was foiled by the President's Moroccan guard. A small number of opposition groups operate, ineffectively, from exile.

STRENGTH AND BUDGET

Population: 260,000 approximately.
Armed Forces: Army, 1400; Air Force, 50; Gendarmerie, 2000.
GNP:
Defence Expenditure: } no figures available.

COMMAND AND CONSTITUTIONAL STATUS

The Republic's President, President Obiang Nguema Mbasogo holds the post of Minister for Defence and Chief of the Armed Forces. The senior ranking officer is Lieut-Colonel F. M. Onana, Inspector of the *Forces Armées de Guinée Equatoriale*. Power lies with an HMC, or Supreme Military Council.

ROLE, COMMITMENT, DEPLOYMENT AND RECENT OPERATIONS

The role of both *Guardia* is essentially one of internal security, or armed political support for the President. Equatorial Guinea had a dispute with Gabon over certain off-shore islands; this was settled by the mediation of Congo and Zaïre in 1972.

ORGANISATION

The *Guardia National* (Army) is composed of one infantry type unit of four companies, together with a supporting logistical company. The *Guardia Civil* (gendarmerie) consists of two large company detachments, one each for the mainland and Fernando Poo.

RECRUITMENT, TRAINING AND RESERVES

The forces have a high percentage of mainland Fang soldiers both in the ranks and in the hierarchy.

The present president is a Fang, as was his predecessor. Discrimination against soldiers of ethnic groups other than Fang, in particular the Bubi, was very marked in Macias Nguema's day but seems now to have been diminished; some HMC members are Bubi. The Fang have never been popular in the islands.

Immediately after independence a small cadre of Spaniards trained the Army, these soon departed and Cuban assistance was used, officers being sent to Cuba and also, according to some reports a small Cuban training team operating in Equatorial Guinea itself. The new regime has made fresh arrangements. A small Moroccan cadre is operating in Guinea, two sub-units of the Army are to be trained in Spain, and Spanish officers and NCOs are to be posted to them.

EQUIPMENT AND ARMS INDUSTRY

The force was equipped with Spanish small arms at independence. Soviet armoured vehicles, ten BRDM-2s and ten BTR-152s then arrived together with RPG-7 grenade launchers and light mortars. Unconfirmed reports note deliveries by North Korea of small numbers of Chinese infantry 35mm rocket launchers.

RANK, DRESS AND DISTINCTIONS

These generally follow the Spanish system. One distinctive feature of this small force is its custom of conducting its ceremonial parades entirely by bugle call, no words of command being given.

CURRENT DEVELOPMENTS

The *Guardia National* exists primarily to support the regime. Spanish assurances of protection of the inviolability of the nation appear to have been given, though whether Spain would wish to embroil herself with Nigeria should the latter decide to annex Fernando Poo is doubtful. At present Nigeria does not seem interested in Fernando Poo, though annexation was considered earlier at a time of much persecution of Nigerian labourers on the island. Spain believes Equatorial Guinea may possess off-shore oil resources.

ADDENDUM

Recent reports state that the two *Guardia* forces have now been merged, and that the regime is becoming more despotic in its methods, in particular in its treatment of communities other than the Fang.

Lloyd Mathews

ETHIOPIA

HISTORY AND INTRODUCTION

Ethiopians not only have an ancient military tradition but also a country which geographically is ideally suited to its exercise. An island of Christianity in an almost encircling sea of Islam, the mountain fastnesses of the Amhara peoples have over the centuries suffered attacks from Arab, Somali, British, Egyptian, Dervish and, more recently, Italian armies.

The cult of the hero is deep-rooted in Amhara society. The warrior who killed another man was traditionally venerated and it was never difficult for Negus, Ras or a lesser chieftain to raise a private army. These flourished until the mid-1940s and it was only slowly that the Emperors Tewodros II (1855—68), Yohannes IV (1872—89) and Menelik II (1889—1913), who by conquest greatly extended the Amhara and Shoan kingdoms to the east, south and west introduced the concept of a national army. Menelik, in whose time massive arms imports began, had to stem the first serious wave of Italian aggression, and Adowa (1896) was the first big defeat of a colonial army by an African.

Haile Selassie became Regent in 1916 and Emperor in 1930, and was the real creator of the Ethiopian armed forces who were, ironically, to topple him in 1974. He formed the Imperial Bodyguard in 1917 and sent some young men to St. Cyr in the 1920s. Belgian, Russian, Swedish and Swiss officers helped institute training programmes and a school for officers was established at Holeta in 1934 — but too late to have much impact on Mussolini's invasion of October, 1935. Barefoot Ethiopian units, armed with spears and antique rifles, were routed, and although a patriotic resistance continued, the modern organisation of the army had to wait until Haile Selassie's return from exile with the Allied forces who overran the Italian East African Empire in 1941.

For 10 years the British Military Mission trained and equipped 10 infantry battalions, a regiment of artillery and one of armoured cars. In 1951, in line with the Truman Doctrine, the United States took over. In exchange for the use of Kagnew communications base in Eritrea, United States military aid began to pour in. The 1953 Mutual Defence Agreement set up the Military Assistance Advisory Group (MAAG) and United States equipment and weaponry became standard. Between the early 1950s and 1977 the United States was the primary supplier of military hardware and training.

Other nations played their part, however: Swedes helped set up an air force in 1947 and Norwegians a navy in 1955. The Israelis have trained paratroops, and Britain, France and India have also provided a modest amount of aid and training assistance. The Haile Selassie I Military Academy was launched on Sandhurst lines at Harar in 1958 and staffed by Indian army officers up to 1971. Until the early 1970s a succession of Ethiopian officer cadets came to RMA Sandhurst, and majors and the occasional lieutenant-colonel and naval lieutenant-commander to the Staff College, Camberley.

Ethiopian units fought for the United Nations with some distinction in Korea (1951—4) and with rather less in the Congo (1960—4). These units came from the Imperial Bodyguard, an over-privileged and somewhat pampered force which comprised 6000 of a 26,000-strong army, and was in 1960 radically purged as a result of the unsuccessful December coup in which it was deeply implicated.

The educated military *élite*, many of them trained abroad, others conversant with Western standards through their professional or social contacts, always showed some impatience to modernise their country, and despite the Emperor's policy of cementing their loyalty by regular grants of *gashas of land, some ambivalence* in their attitude towards him. Between 1960 and 1974 there were a number of plots and rumours of plots against the regime involving senior army officers, but all of them were defused (and the leaders usually executed) at an early stage. However, it was the discontent of predominantly Holeta-trained junior officers and NCOs with their low rates of pay, the internal injustices within the army, and a despair at the seemingly interminable war against secessionist guerrillas in Eritrea which led to the creeping coup of 1974.

Ethiopia's army revolt began as a minor insurrection by a group of young army officers in Borana. Widespread mutinies led to governmental changes and the imprisonment and execution of notables. The Armed Forces Co-ordinating Committee (AFCC) was formed in April and seized control of the country in June. In September Haile Selassie was deposed, the AFCC became the Provisional Military Administrative Council, or *Derg*, and proceeded to rule the country with General Aman Andom, an Eritrean, as Head of State. In November General Aman, with 59 other top ministers and generals, was assassinated, and Brigadier-General Teferi Bante, Chairman of the *Derg*, took his place. He in his turn was assassinated in the February, 1977, pre-dawn coup, power devolving to the man who had since early 1974 dominated army, *Derg* and country — Lieutenant-Colonel Mengistu Haile Mariam. Ultimate control continues to be exercised by Mengistu. Nevertheless there is evidence to suggest that there is some opposition in the *Derg* to the new personality cult now surrounding him.

The *Derg* originally consisted of about 120 junior officers and NCOs, but intra-junta disputes (based on ideological considerations and personal antagonisms) and assassinations of *Derg* members by anti-government urban guerrillas — mainly members of EDRP, the strongly anti-militarist left-wing opposition group — have reduced it in number to about 40, of whom 15 comprise its inner circle. Of the original inner group of 15 only three — including Mengistu — are still alive. According to reports emanating from diplomatic and government sources between 1978 and 1983, the ruling military junta also now includes a number of Soviet and Cuban advisers. A small but significant tilt towards Moscow and its allies in already pro-Soviet Ethiopia took place at the end of 1979 following the visit in November of Erich Honecker, the East German state and party leader. A twenty-year treaty of friendship between the GDR and Ethiopia was signed. The two leaders laid the foundation stone of a Karl Marx monument in Addis Ababa. East German personnel are also believed to be involved in the creation of a new political party structure, COPWE, (See Command and Constitutional Status).

During the first five years following the 1974 revolution, pro- and anti-government factions settled differences with 'revolutionary violence' on the streets of the capital. By 1978, a reign of terror — with nightly murders and torturing of so-called 'counter-revolutionaries' by undisciplined urban defence militia men and soldiers — was the order of the day. Today the streets of the capital are again calm. Urban admin-

175

istration in Ethiopia has been handed over to groups of residents known as *kebeles*, each of which has its own court and volunteer police-squad. In this way, the regime has consolidated its grip on urban areas.

STRENGTH AND BUDGET

Population: (1982) 30,500,000.
Army: 244,500 (This includes the People's Militia, consisting in 1982 of some 150,000, which has now been incorporated in the army). The size of the army has quadrupled in four years, rising from 6 Divisions to 20.
Mobile emergency police force: 9000.
GNP: $4,090,000,000 (1980 estimate).
Defence budget: (1980) $362,800,000 (estimate). This was 46% of the whole budget in 1981.

COMMAND AND CONSTITUTIONAL STATUS

The army is controlled by the Marxist Provisional Military Administrative Council or *Derg*, whose leading figure in April 1983 was the Head of State and Army Commander, Lieutenant-Colonel Mengistu Haile Mariam.

The *Derg* had in late 1976 been taking steps to begin a civilianisation of the government in response to pressure from the Marxist Ethiopian People's Revolutionary Party (EPRP), the army, students and the former Confederation of Ethiopian Labour Unions (CELU). To this end it set up the People's Provisional Political Office – later renamed the Provisional Office for Mass Organisational Affairs – under Dr Hailu Fida (by October, 1977, Hailu, previously principal policy adviser to Mengistu, had fallen out of favour and is believed to have been jailed and executed). But the shoot-out of February 3rd, 1977, in which the previous Head of State, Brigadier-General Teferi Bante, and six other leading members of the *Derg* were killed, hindered these moves. For the next four years, there was no sign of an increase in civilian influence at the expense of the military. Indeed, Lieutenant-Colonel Mengistu, who survived the affray, gained a reputation as a hard-line militarist as did his close rival, the *Derg*'s First Vice-Chairman, Lieutenant-Colonel Atnafu Abate, until his execution in a bloody purge in November, 1977. The *Derg* moved against independent trade unions and leftist political groups (including *Was*, the labour league, in 1978, and *Meison* and *Echaat*, two opposition parties, both of which were proscribed in 1977) and arrested their leaders.

ROLE, COMMITMENT, DEPLOYMENT AND RECENT OPERATIONS

Since the early 1960s internal and external threats to two regions have done much to determine the role of the Ethiopian army.

The most intractable problem has been in the former Italian colony of Eritrea, where predominantly Muslim movements (but backed by Christian Eritreans) have sought to reverse its absorption by Haile Selassie into the Empire as the 14th province in November, 1962. A long-drawn-out campaign by the Eritrean Liberation Front (ELF) – founded in 1958 to demand autonomy for Eritrea – and the Ethiopian People's Liberation Front (EPLF) – the main guerrilla movement and strongly Marxist-Leninist – aided by various Arab States, has sapped the army's strength and morale. There have been mutinies and defections and the 2nd Division had at least five commanders between 1976–1979.

Even in the Emperor's day it looked as if it was a struggle that could not be won militarily and his replacement in 1974 by General Aman Andom, himself an Eritrean, held out hopes of an end to the fighting and the concession of some measure of self-government to the province. General Aman Andom's murder, however, showed that the *Derg*, and in particular its strongman, the then Major Mengistu, was determined on a military solution.

Various expedients have been tried since the ELF launched a major new attack against 2nd Division army positions in and around Asmara early in 1975: the *Derg*, in April and May, 1976, offered 'regional autonomy' for Eritrea, but at the same time pursued contradictory policies – a new, 6th Division (the Nebalbal or 'Flame' Division) was raised and part of it sent north, and the ill-fated mustering of a peasant army (People's Militia) of 35,000 ended in disaster when it, too, marched north only to be scattered by guerrilla forces in Tigre. The attempt to defeat Eritrean secessionists with a huge peasant army of 150,000 in the summer of 1977 had little apparent effect until heavy armour and large numbers of regulars were brought in under the command of General Ivanovitch Petrov, who masterminded the Ogaden victory, in mid-1978.

Until about February, 1977 much of the guerrilla activity in the province was near the border with Sudan to the west of Gondar, but in July the Ethiopian forces suffered a major defeat when the city of Keren, on an important road junction 50 miles north-west of Asmara, was seized by Eritrean rebels after a four-day artillery bombardment. In August the strategically important town of Mandafara was also in the hands of guerrilla forces. This only left Massawa, Agordat, Barentu, Asmara, Assab and a few small garrisons in government hands although the first three of these were under siege at this stage.

By September, 1977, Agordat had fallen to the rebels after one of the bloodiest battles of the war, Barentu had been almost starved into submission and all the other government-held towns – including the provincial capital of Asmara and Massawa – were encircled and could only be supplied from the air. In October guerrillas severed Asmara's last remaining lifeline to the sea at Massawa, and in mid-December Massawa itself was captured.

In the face of these reverses there was a determined stepping up of anti-insurgent operations by the Ethiopian army in towns which it held in Eritrea, but this achieved little except to send fresh waves of refugees fleeing into neighbouring Sudan, adding to the 150,000 Eritrean refugees already there. However, the guerrillas suffered severe setbacks in mid-1978, when Ethiopian forces cut off in Asmara smashed their way out following a major troop and tank offensive to relieve the city. By September government forces had raised the sieges of Asmara and Massawa and captured more than 30 towns. In November the rebels suffered their last grave defeat when Keren was recaptured.

In the past, independent reports have suggested that in spite of heavy Eritrean losses (some 30,000 are estimated to have lost their lives and about 900,000 have been displaced) the nature of the terrain has minimised the possibility of an outright victory by government forces. But although the rebel armies held almost all the province after three years' intensification of the war of secession, the use of Cuban and Soviet forces has now transformed the situation. Although earlier Eritrean reports that Soviet, Cuban and South Yemeni pilots have flown MIG-23s in action against rebel forces remain unconfirmed, it is clear that Soviet, East German and Cuban advisers are playing a key role and that troops from Cuba, South Yemen (and probably East Germany) have taken part in ground operations against the rebels. Even the most conservative intelligence reports suggest that there are at least 1500 Soviet military personnel and 15,000 Cubans in Ethiopia

— and these have been used by the *Derg* with increasing effect since 1978—79.

Between February and May, 1982, a big offensive, Operation Red Star, was launched in the north. Eight divisions were deployed there and Lieutenant-Colonel Mengistu personally directed operations from Asmara. Although some inroads were made on Eritrean positions, the offensive failed. Whilst the rebels lost 4,000 killed and wounded the Ethiopians lost some 30,000. The town of Nacfa, the scene of an Ethiopian army defeat in January, 1980, was again not taken.

Possibly the most significant factor in this government reverse was the turn of events in Tigre, the Christian, Tigrinya-speaking province which lies to the south of Eritrea across the Mareb River. The hostility of many Tigreans to the *Derg* probably stems from the popularity of their former governor, Ras Mangashia Seyoum, a loyal supporter of Haile Selassie who was forced to flee in the 1974 revolution. Since then, however, the Marxist Tigrean People's Liberation Front (TPLF) has filled the vacuum and since 1979 gone from strength to strength. Aided by the Eritrean People's Liberation Front (EPLF), whose current leader, Issyas Aferworki, is a Christian from a part of Eritrea close to Tigre, the TPLF have repeatedly threatened the vital north-south highway from Addis Ababa to Asmara. Ethiopian army convoys, heavily armed, take three weeks to reach Asmara from Dessie instead of the normal 36 hours. The TPLF have also extended their operations south and east into Wollo and even Shoa. 4,000 of their guerrillas are fighting alongside the 10,000-strong EPLF forces inside Eritrea. All this has made the task of the Ethiopian army in Eritrea doubly difficult. Detachments in Makalle and Axum are now normally reinforced from the air and the severely mountainous countryside on either side of the road is barely controlled at all. Four Tigrean towns were reported captured by the TPLF in July 1982.

There are signs in early 1983 that Eritrean rebels and Ethiopian government are alike taking a slightly less intransigent stance, prompted, respectively, by Saudi Arabia and Sudan. But Mengistu, despite Russian coolness, still seems set on a military solution to this 25-year-old problem and, with some recent help from the Israelis, is preparing yet another offensive.

Prospects for its success seem slender. Army morale is low, despite an effective doubling of salaries in late 1981, and defections still occur. Disaffection continues in many other regions — the Ethiopian Democratic Union (EDU) is occasionally active in Wollega and ties down a number of battalions, whilst further east the Galla-based Oromo Liberation Front has had a new lease of life: Brigadier-General Gebre, lately of the Ethiopian Army, now directs it.

But still a most damaging distraction comes from further south. The second major area of tension has been in the south-eastern desert lands of the Ogaden, claimed by Somalia. The Somali Republic has long pursued an irredentist policy towards the Ogaden province of Ethiopia by claiming that the area is populated by 500,000 Somali tribesmen. This territorial claim has been pursued by illegal but covertly supported Somali guerrilla action on both sides of the border which has led to several clashes between the Ethiopian and Somali regular forces. Just as the 2nd Division ('The Army of the North') has been tied down for many years in and around Asmara, so the 3rd Division ('The Army of the East') has long been based in Harar and deployed southwards in the Haud and Ogaden whenever President Siad Barre has made expansionist references to a 'Greater Somalia'.

In 1964 sporadic guerrilla action in the area flared up into a two-day war but both sides were forced to stop fighting when they ran into logistical problems. At a conference in March the two countries agreed to the establishment of a demilitarised border zone, but minor skirmishes continued for another twelve years, and in 1976 the West Somali Liberation Front (WSLF) swung into motion and briefly captured the town of Imi. By mid-1977 the guerrilla incursions were being heavily supported by Somali troops and weapons, and by November the WSLF was in control of virtually the entire province with the exception of the cities of Harar and Dire-dawa. At the end of 1977 Somalia and Ethiopia were engaged in open military confrontation but the tide of battle began to turn in Ethiopia's favour when the army, heavily backed by Soviet and Cuban 'advisers', units of the 'peasant army' and vast supplies of Soviet military hardware, mounted a massive counter-offensive from the provincial capital of Harar at the beginning of 1978. On March 9th Somalia accepted defeat in the Ogaden by announcing withdrawal of its troops from Ethiopian territory, but guerrilla activities in the province continue.

At its height 40,000 regular Ethiopian troops and 80,000 People's Militiamen were involved in the Ogaden against 80,000 regular and irregular Somalis, plus an unknown number of WSLF insurgents. The Ethiopian successes were the result of improved supplies and a consequent rise in army morale, the launching of a Militia which was better trained than the shambles of the previous year and the inpouring of Russian 'advice' and weaponry — scores of T-54 tanks, 600 armoured vehicles 400 artillery pieces, including BM-21 multiple rocket launchers (Stalin Organs).

Throughout 1979 Somalia continued to support guerrillas operating in the Ogaden. The WSLF, however, always claimed that it functioned independently. Its operations were mainly against convoys linking the Ogaden centres occupied by Cuban forces (said to number 11,000 in 1981) and Ethiopian units. In retaliation Ethiopia harboured within her frontiers the Somali Salvation Front, a movement opposed to President Siad Barre, which in December, 1979, killed 37 Somali troops at Dolo. In attempts to secure their approaches to the Ogaden, the Ethiopian army continued to harass elements of the Oromo Liberation Front in Bale and Sidamo provinces and drove many thousands of Galla and Borana refugees into Somalia.

In the summer of 1980 a seven-week battle for the Ogaden settlement of Warder, 90 miles north west of the Somali border, ended in defeat for the pro-Somali forces. But fears that the Ethiopians with Soviet support might invade Somalia during 1980 and unseat the increasingly pro-American President Barre proved unfounded. Nevertheless, Ethiopia now clearly held the initiative in the region.

In July, 1982, the Ethiopian army did invade Somalia. 3000 men, supported by tanks, crossed the frontier but were checked after 18 miles at Balamballe and Geldogob. There they have remained, on the wrong side of this ill-defined frontier, and are now quietly entrenched. There is sporadic artillery fire. Patrols go out and generally return. Two armies, two miles apart, observe one another warily. It is, however, clear that the 20,000 Ethiopians, with the 5,000-strong Somali Salvation Democratic Front (an amalgam of dissident Somali groups brought together in October 1981) could at any time, with their superior air cover and armoured strength, push on into Somalia and topple President Barre.

Another eye is always kept cocked in the direction of Djibouti, formerly the French Territory of the Afars and the Issas, which received its independence on June 27th, 1977. If Ethiopia ever loses control of the ports of Massawa and Assab to an autonomous Eritrea, the rail link from Addis Ababa to Djibouti — which is the main outlet and point of entry for Ethiopia's trade — will assume even greater importance.

The Afars are an Ethiopian people while the Issas are a Somali clan. The constitution of Somalia includes claims to

Djibouti but Addis Ababa is determined not to allow it to fall into Somali hands. Both countries are concerned about each other's intentions and rightly suspect each other of wanting to annex the tiny enclave. Somalia has provided aid for a small guerrilla group, the Front for the Liberation of the Somali Coast (FLCS) which was founded in 1960, while Ethiopia has given support to the Afar ex-premier of Djibouti, Ali Aref. But Ethiopia also faces a revolt among its own Afar population and is worried lest the Ethiopian Afars, led by Ali Mireh, should break away and form a new entity with Djibouti. Addis Ababa's railway link with Djibouti port was closed for much of 1977 as a result of the repeated destruction of rail bridges by guerrillas of the WSLF. Because of its dependence on Djibouti, Ethiopia would almost certainly regard any attempts by Mogadishu to annex the territory as a *casus belli*, but a deterrent to such a scenario exists in the shape of 4500 troops retained by the French in their former colony.

Relations between Addis Ababa and Khartoum have also been strained. Sudan shelters about 250,000 Ethiopian refugees — some of them officers and men from the 'Army of the North'. President Nimiery has complained that the Ethiopian Marxists have tried to foment trouble in his country as a smokescreen to their own difficulties. If provoked further he could well step up aid to the Eritrean and Tigrean liberation movements (he already allows these groups to use Sudanese territory as a base camp) and to the right-wing Ethiopian Democratic Union (EDU), based in Khartoum. Formed by exiled senior army officers and officials of the Emperor, the EDU operates in the Gojjam, Begemdir and Wollega provinces of north-western Ethiopia. Little has been heard of this group since the fall of its strongholds at Humera and Metema to *Derg* forces in mid-1977. Groups of freedom fighters, or *tagays*, armed with captured weapons, still exist.

Over the past 20 years the army has been called in to dampen internal unrest in Gojjam (where civil disturbances broke out in 1967–8), in Bale and Sidamo provinces (where the Oromo Liberation Front is active), and more recently in Addis Ababa itself where it searches houses, maintains the curfew and protects the members of the *Derg*.

All in all there are six identifiable rebel movements within Ethiopia demanding autonomy or independence, and a number of other minor armed groups fighting for the overthrow of the regime or a change in its ideological orientation — all of which require the attentions of the army. To complete Ethiopia's all-round discomfiture she shares long frontiers with two hostile neighbours, whilst not much further away parts of the Arab world are opposed either to her Marxism or her putative anti-Muslim stance in Eritrea. Any of these powers could, at the most, intervene (as Somalia has already shown), or at least, continue to support rebel movements within Ethiopia.

ORGANISATION

Twenty notionally 8000-man divisions (14 infantry, three motorised infantry, two mountain, one light). Eight of these divisions are currently in the north — the 2nd, 14th, 15th, 21st and parts of the 6th and 7th in Eritrea; the 16th, 18th and parts of the 6th and 7th in Tigre. Others including the 8th at Shimbo, are in the Ogaden. There are also four parachute/commando brigades, 20 tank battalions, 30 artillery battalions, 15 air defence battalions and 2 engineer battalions. The 3500-strong airforce remain based at Debra Zeit near the capital, and the 2500-man navy in Massawa and Assah.

RECRUITMENT, TRAINING AND RESERVES

Service in the army has generally been voluntary and has always been popular since, as in many other African States, it is an avenue to social and economic advancement. The ancient martial tradition ensures that much local prestige attaches to a soldier's uniform. It has not therefore been difficult to build up one of the largest armies in Africa and the second largest (after Nigeria) in Black Africa.

Most of the officers in Haile Selassie's day were recruited from the landowning class. Many others moved into it when a grateful Emperor rewarded their loyalty by settling land on them (the *Derg*'s sweeping land reforms have now dispossessed them and caused much bitterness, especially in the Asmara-based 2nd Division). Some three-quarters of the parents of the intake at the former Haile Selassie I Military Academy, founded at Harar in 1958, owned land. In educational terms the post-war officer corps have formed a significant section of the social *élite*, representing an eighth of all Ethiopians who had been educated beyond the secondary level.

Officially the recruitment of officers and men has taken no account of their geographical or ethnic origin within the country. Nevertheless Amharas have preponderated in the officer corps (constituting about half of all officers) although they account for less than a quarter of the country's population. Tigreans, constituting a tenth of the population, account for a fifth of officers although their proportion was almost a quarter in 1970. The remaining 30% of officers have been drawn mainly from the Eritrea and Oromo (Galla) regions. Enlisted men have been recruited almost equally from the Amhara and Galla areas (35% each) and only 30% from elsewhere. Thus, as in many other African armies, there is a marked difference in the ethnic and regional base of the officer corps and the ranks.

In the late 1950s and early 1960s the best 12th-grade boys from the secondary schools were drafted into the army for life and most of them were happy to end up at Harar. These became regular officers, whereas the officer school at Holeta gave short-service commissions only. NCOs went there to gain commissions, too. Many of the current differences within the army stem from a developing Harar — Holeta animosity. The more traditionalist product of Harar shared little common ground with the upstart, potential revolutionaries of Holeta, who always regarded themselves as poor cousins and who are exemplified by the present Head of State, the ambitious, unattractive Lieutenant-Colonel Mengistu.

Reserves are probably entirely committed.

Recently there have been reports of inter-tribal antagonisms within the army, particularly between the Anharas and members of the Oromo ethnic group. This source of cleavage was illustrated in the clash between Mengistu, from the Walamo tribe (part of the larger Oromo ethnic group) and the ill-fated Lieutenant-Colonel Atnafu Abate, a member of the Amhara tribe. A few months before his bloody execution in November, 1977 — perhaps anticipating what was to happen — Atnafu Abate moved his headquarters into the compound of the 4th Division (which had a simple majority of Amharas), and seldom moved from there. Reliable reports indicate that since November, 1977 Lieutenant-Colonel Mengistu has been guarded by several hundred loyal Walamo soldiers, showing both the extent of ethnic tensions in the army and the Ethiopian strongman's fear of a coup.

By 1960 an air-force school was established at Debra Zeit (adjoining the air force base), and a naval cadet school at Massawa. These schools were expanded to become academies in 1968.

EQUIPMENT AND ARMS INDUSTRY

Until mid-1977 the army's equipment was almost wholly American. Between 1952 and 1976 the USA provided Ethiopia with $275,000,000 in military assistance. This level of aid was larger than that of all her other donor governments together and four times that given by the USA to 13 other tropical African States.

Before the war with Somalia began in June, 1977 Ethiopia had 35 M-60 medium tanks, 70 M-41 light tanks, 90 M-113 APCs and 55 French AML-60 armoured cars, though the ELF has claimed to have knocked out many of these. Howitzers and mortars were at that time all of American pattern. The standard infantry combat rifle remains the M-1 carbine. Israel — fearful that Arab control of the Red Sea would threaten her vital oil lifeline — has continued to supply weapons to Ethiopia including air-to-air missiles, cluster bombs and probably napalm.

After 1975 U.S. military aid became somewhat attenuated: in March of that year only $7,000,000 was forthcoming in response to the *Derg's* request for $25,000,000 to stave off the secessionist threat in Eritrea. This marked the beginning of America's re-evaluation of its military aid programme to Ethiopia, but despite increasing internal anarchy and mounting left-wing extremism some aid continued for another 18 months. In April, 1976 eight F-5 fighter bombers were supplied. A year later in April, 1977 the *junta* expelled its American military advisers.

The Soviet Union quickly filled the military aid vacuum and in August, 1977 it began delivery of the equivalent of some $385,000,000 in arms. Since mid-1977 deliveries from the USSR are believed to have included: 400 T-54/55 and a few T-62 tanks; 60 older T-34s; 200 other assorted armoured vehicles; more than 300 guns of various calibres from 100mm to 152mm; as well as mortars, anti-aircraft guns and several batteries of BM-21 rocket launchers. SAM-3 and SAM-7 missiles and Sagger anti-tank guided weapons have also been supplied, together with large quantities of small-arms ammunition, spare parts and communications equipment. Thirty American M-47 tanks have also been received from Yugoslavia. The air force, which had 35 combat aircraft in early 1977, has been supplemented by approximately 60 MiG-21s and a few of the older MiG-17s.

The USA continued to shore up a hostile Marxist State for almost 3 years after the 1974 coup because it was felt (quite rightly in view of subsequent developments) that if she did not the Soviet Union would fill the gap. Ethiopia continued to ask for American aid because if it dried up she feared there would be a dangerous hiatus during which she would have an acute short-term rearmament and retraining problem. As it was the Ethiopian army experienced considerable difficulties in the handling and operation of its newly acquired Soviet equipment during the last few months of 1977 and the first quarter of 1978 when the massive airlift of Soviet arms to Ethiopia took place. However the dislocations were not as severe as expected and the military has largely adjusted to the switch in the source of arms.

The peasant militia units inherited American MI-4s and MI-6s from the army, who now have Czech and Russian weapons, including AK-47s.

RANK, DRESS AND DISTINCTIONS

Ranks are after the British style, dress is American. Officers of the *Derg* are now seen in No. 3 dress of tan khaki long-sleeved shirts and trousers, cherry-coloured chokers, black webbing belts (like the British 1937 pattern) and green U.S. army overseas caps (sidehats). A black aiguillette is worn on the left shoulder by senior officers, and badges of rank appear on the open-necked shirt collar.

CURRENT DEVELOPMENTS

The outlook for the Ethiopian army today is still grave though the situation appeared even more dire in the face of apparent imminent defeat at the hands of the Somalis in the Ogaden during the latter months of 1977. At one time it seemed as though the whole country might fragment into a series of petty states, but this has not in fact occurred. The army's control over the remoter regions is tenuous, especially in the north and east. Lieutenant-Colonel Mengistu has admitted that there is rebellion in eight of the 14 provinces. After the failure of Operation Red Star in Eritrea and Tigre early in 1982 the more successful incursions into Somalia offer him the classic chance to divert public attention away from the northern humiliations.

The size of the army increased by almost 50% between 1976 and 1978 and has since multiplied fourfold. But after all the purges and defections since the 1974 coup the quality of the training and leadership of any new units must be doubted. The 6th (Flame) Division seems to be, partly at least, a sort of Praetorian Guard to protect the *Derg* and the Head of State from assassination attempts, of which there have already been many.

The morale of officers and men is low and their loyalty to the *Derg*, which in the late 1970s seemed to have degenerated into a kind of Marxist Mafia with the occasional Valentine's Day massacres, must be at least questionable. There have been rumours of conspiracies against the ruling military *junta* from elements of the 4th Division, as well as numerous demonstrations of disaffection and mutiny from front line army units serving in Eritrea and the Ogaden. There has been particular anxiety about the loyalty of the Harar-based 3rd Division (in October, 1977 some of its units mutinied and retreated in disorder from the fighting at Jijiga) and there have been persistent reports of regulars being forced into battle only through the persuasion of militia units. This mood of disenchantment with the regime has been largely responsible for Ethiopia's poor performance on its two main battlefronts and explains why Mengistu has had to lean so heavily on his Soviet and Cuban 'advisers' for support in both the administration of the country and trying to eradicate the guerrilla insurgency in Eritrea and elsewhere.

There have been important political developments. The events leading to the overthrow of the Emperor in 1974 had radicalised large sections of the Ethiopian population; it was not possible simply to crush the increasingly nationalistic and fragmentary nature of opposition movements. First hints of a change in direction came in 1981 when the *Derg* began the process of widening its political base. The vehicle was COPWE, the Political Commission to Establish a Worker's Party, given legal status in December that year. Ethiopia's nascent political party is tasked with taking control of all political cadres in the country, including those from the military party, *Seded*. Despite extensive Soviet military assistance to the regime, Lieutenant-Colonel Mengistu seems reluctant to permit the domination of COPWE by pro-Moscow groups. And interestingly, in a speech during the second congress of COPWE in January 1983, Mengistu revealed that Ethiopia is to open its doors to foreign investors, including those from the West, for the first time since the revolution.

Equipment, weapons and ammunition which were running short due to the cutback and eventual suspension of American military aid are now being provided by the USSR, but the *Derg* will find it increasingly difficult to disentangle itself from the wider political ambitions of its new communist allies. The future of Ethiopia and its army remains bleak: unfortunately the country is too strategically important to be left to determine its own future. Ethiopia is seen to affect the entire balance of power in the Horn of Africa and to weigh heavily in the world political conflict between East and West. For a long time to come the fortunes of the army, and its relationship with the civilian population as a whole, will be inextricably tied up with the activities of rebel guerrillas, the designs of Ethiopia's neighbours and the interests of the wider international community.

Simon Baynham
Richard Snailham

FIJI

Fiji is the largest country by far amongst the South Pacific island States, with an area of 7055 square miles and a population of about 645,000 people living on 106 inhabited islands, of which the two largest islands, Viti Levu and Vanua Levu, account for over six-sevenths of the national territory. The army was established under the Fiji Military Ordinance, 1949, and passed under national control when Fiji achieved independence within the British Commonwealth on October 10th, 1970.

The Fiji islands were first settled by Melanesian colonists, and already contained a long-established population, divided into many warring tribes, when they were first sighted by Europeans in 1643. European visitors became numerous in the nineteenth century, when sandalwood from Fiji became a valuable export commodity, and the usual consequences ensued. The principal gifts of European sailors to the islands were rum, muskets and syphilis, and in the latter part of the nineteenth century the islands were ravaged by disease and constant, bloody tribal wars. They were taken into the British Empire in 1874, and were gradually reduced to order.

The British attempt to develop sugar-cane cultivation in the islands, however, was directly responsible for the principal political problem which faces Fiji today — and one in which the army and police are potentially significant. Native Fijians proved unwilling to engage in the brutal physical labour involved in growing sugar, so around the turn of the century the British began to introduce Indian labourers into the islands. Over the next four decades approximately 60,000 Indian immigrants arrived, and their descendents today account for 51% of the population. Native Fijians of Melanesian origin are only 42%, the remainder of the population being small European, Eurasian and Chinese minorities.

Almost all Fiji's exportable commodities except gold are agricultural — primarily sugar, copra and ginger — and the vast majority of farmers are of Indian origin. Indians also have a dominant position in commerce and the professions. This causes a certain resentment amongst the Fijians who have become a minority in their own country, but it scarcely compares with the resentment felt by the Indian community against its legal disabilities. These revolve mainly around the ownership of land, which has a great spiritual significance for Fijians (even if they are not inclined to farm it).

To safeguard Fijian hereditary land, the constitution prevents non-Fijians from acquiring it. This means in practice that 90% of agricultural land is owned by Fijian nobles or communally by Fijian villagers, but that most of it is actually worked by Indian tenant farmers who are forbidden by law from acquiring leases of more than 30 years. This is the most important instance — though far from the only one — of what Indians see as systematic discrimination against them on behalf of the less-competitive native Fijians. (Another recently revealed case which caused a considerable outcry was the relevation that Fijians were being deliberately favoured over Indians in admission to the University of the South Pacific.) After four or even five generations in Fiji, Indians feel themselves still to be treated as second-class citizens.

The tension engendered by this rose sharply as a consequence of the two elections of 1977. For the previous 10 years, since before independence, Fiji had been governed by the Alliance Party of Prime Minister Ratu Sir Kamisese Mara, a nominally multiracial party which supports the present laws granting indigenous Fijians various special advantages. It naturally received most of the votes of these Fijians, but also garnered some support from Indians and minority races who felt that this was the safest course. Since the electoral system provides for a number of communal seats for which voters are segregated into separate racial electoral rolls, and the indigenous Fijian population has a disproportionate share of these seats, the Alliance Party invariably succeeded in gaining a majority in Parliament.

In the April, 1977 elections, however, a new, explicitly racialist party known as the Fijian National Party emerged, which campaigned on the slogan 'Fiji for the Fijians' and advocated the deportation of the Indians in the population. This party succeeded in splitting the Fijian vote, and in driving enough Indians back into the arms of their own communal party, the National Federation Party (which seeks to end the ban on the sale of land to non-Fijians), that it caused the defeat of the Alliance Party.

Divisions within the victorious National Federation Party permitted Prime Minister Ratu Mara to retain office and call new elections. These were held in September, 1977 with Sakeasi Butadokra, the leader of the breakaway Fijian National Party, in jail for prejudicing the public peace. The elections resulted in a landslide victory for the Alliance Party, to which many of the defecting Fijian voters had returned, alarmed that their defection had almost brought the Indian communal party to power. The Alliance Party again forms the government, and all is superficially as it was before, but there is now a greatly heightened tension and concern about inter-communal relations in Fiji.

The Royal Fijian Military Forces (RFMF) are overwhelmingly Fijian in membership both in the regular force and the reserves, although there is no barrier to the entry of Indian or minority citizens to either the enlisted ranks or the officer corps. The first line of defence in internal security matters, the Fijian Police Force, is also predominantly Fijian, but it does have about 30% Indian personnel.

The Fijian army, 1924 strong, consists of one regular infantry battalion, one Conservation Corps battalion, one Territorial (reserve) battalion, one engineer squadron and one artillery troop. Major weapons are 4 25-pounder guns and 10 81mm mortars. There is also a naval squadron, consisting principally of three converted minesweepers which are employed as fisheries protection vessels to enforce Fiji's newly declared 200 mile maritime economic zone. All form part of the RFMF.

The regular force of the army is recruited entirely by volunteer enlistment for long engagements. Enlisted men are trained primarily in New Zealand; officer training is done in Britain at the Royal Military Academy Sandhurst, or at the Australian Military College. These arrangements allow not only for basic and initial training in a military environment of greater sophistication than Fiji, but also extend to the provision to the RFMF of higher technical and professional training for its officers and men.

The Conservation Corps is primarily a means of relieving unemployment and upgrading rural skills, although it does provide military training as well. Those who serve in it, for periods of 6 months to 1 year, work at such tasks as road-building or the maintenance of public buildings, while receiving instruction in useful skills such as carpentry or machinery operation. Most members of the Conservation Corps and discharged regulars pass directly into the Territorials, a reserve force which is organisationally a single battalion, but which has many more members than normal for such a unit. Reservists may be called up for training, or permitted to volunteer for periods of continuous service: of the 500 man Fijian unit now serving wth the UNIFIL peacekeeping force in Lebanon only 200 are regulars, the remaining 300 being Territorials who have taken the opportunity and volunteered. Fijians also serve in Lebanon with UNIFIL.

Ranks and badges of rank within the RFMF are similar to those in Britain. The usual uniform is green-khaki shirts and shorts or long trousers.

The Fiji Police Force, with a strength of 1488 men, bears primary responsibility for internal security. It is a centralised force organised on the British model, with its own training school at Nasese (near Suva, the capital). In normal circumstances Fijian police do not carry arms on duty. Fijian members of the force wear blue shirts, white *sulus*, red cummerbunds and sandals; Indian members wear blue caps, shirts, trousers, and black shoes.

There have been few overt racial incidents in Fiji despite the recent rise in political tension. The composition of the armed forces and police, although not consciously designed for this purpose, contributes considerably to this relatively stable situation by ensuring that the racial minority has a majority within the security forces.

Gwynne Dyer
John Keegan

FINLAND

HISTORY AND INTRODUCTION

Finland's army occupies a very special place in national history and society, having been the instrument of the State's creation in 1918 — in admittedly controversial circumstances — and the embodiment of the popular will in the epic 'winter war' against the Soviet Union in 1939–40.

The Finns, a people of mysterious origin, neither Slav nor Teutonic, speaking a language apparently akin to Magyar, were conquered and christianised by their Swedish neighbours in the twelfth century. Conquest did not lead to subjection: when Sweden's moment of empire came in the seventeenth century, Finland provided her army with homogeneous regiments of infantry and cavalry, whose exploits at Breitenfeld and Lützen still arouse pride, and with individual recruits sufficient to make Gustavus Adolphus's army one-third Finnish. Out of the leaders of these fighting Finns was to grow a Swedish-speaking native nobility whose oppressiveness was remarkable even among the warrior societies of the Baltic regions. They were also remarkably successful in fending off the series of invasions which, as Swedish power declined, Russia launched across the Finnish border. But at the beginning of the nineteenth century this nobility, deciding its interests would be better protected by Russian than Swedish suzerainty, offered their country to the Tzar and, despite bitter military resistance to his armies by the Finnish rank-and-file (1808–9), managed to deliver it to him. The bargain they drove was, nevertheless, broadly advantageous to Finland as a whole, for the Grand Duchy, while retaining its legislative and fiscal autonomy, was henceforth assured of Russian military protection, without corresponding military liability, since the Finns were specifically exempted from conscription. For much of the nineteenth century indeed, while the country prospered and national self-awareness grew, Finland supported no military force at all, except a battalion of regular guardsmen for whom the Tzar paid; though, at the same time, the Swedish-speaking nobility, for whose sons a cadet school had been founded at Hamina (Frederickshamn) in 1821, furnished the Tzar, as did the rest of his Baltic aristocracy, with a sizeable proportion of his officers.

Finland's enjoyment of the best of both worlds, political and military, was to attract at the end of the century the hostility of the ascendant 'Russifiers' in the Tzar's government, who saw in the privileged military status of the Grand Duchy's citizens the making of an issue which could be used towards an overall reduction of its resented autonomy. Since 1878, when Alexander II had given back to Finland a national militia — one plank in his policy of offsetting a passing desire for reunification with Sweden by fostering local patriotism — all young Finns had been liable to short-term conscription within Finland, under Finnish officers. In 1898 the Russifiers tried to assimilate this liability to the Imperial norm: 4 years' service in Russian regiments anywhere in the empire. Recognising the thin end of a wedge, the Finnish Diet protested and was stripped by edict of its powers. Passive resistance within Finland prevented the imposition of the Imperial conscription law — though not the dissolution of the Militia, the cadet school and, in 1905, the Guards Battalion — long enough for the policy of the Russifiers to be defeated by the 1905 Revolution; and a well-timed general strike, organised by the large, new, tough-minded Social Democratic Party and policed by its own Red Guard (whose bourgeois student counterpart was called the White Guard), then procured the restoration of the Diet with an enlarged authority and on an extended franchise. But the military consequences for Russia, reinforced by a second attempt at Russification from 1909, was that few Finns were willing to fight for the Tzar when war came in 1914. On the contrary: Finland's principal contribution of manpower was made to the other side, the numbers of young Finns (many of them ex-White Guards) who 'patriotically' emigrated to Germany at the outbreak allowing the Kaiser to authorise, in May, 1915, the formation of the 27th 'Prussian' *Jäger* Battalion which was wholly Finnish in composition. It was briefly engaged on the eastern front but, its members seeing themselves as soldiers of an 'army in exile' whose foremost duty was to preserve it intact against the day of national opportunity, secured its permanent withdrawal to barracks in December, 1916. When that day dawned in the aftermath of the February Revolution, these *Jägers* were to play a decisive role, for the presiding power in Finland, the Social Democrats, then proved unable to organise the smooth transition from the status of Russian autonomous province to that, desired by all classes and parties, of a truly independent State. By losing control of their own Red Guards, whose insolent behaviour throughout the summer of 1917 alarmed both peasants and middle classes, they gave the covert White Guard organisation (which had kept itself in existence throughout the years since 1905 under the guise of athletic clubs and volunteer fire brigades) the pretext it needed to seek arms from abroad. By losing the critical election of October, 1917 it surrendered power to a collection of right-wing parties which the working class, rightly or wrongly, associated with the White Guard and social repression: thus also giving Bolshevik Russia a pretext for renewed intervention in Finnish affairs. For though the Bolsheviks were the first government to recognise Finnish independence, proclaimed by the new Diet in December, 1917, they were not really prepared to see a politically hostile and potentially pro-German regime established so close to home. When, therefore, in January, 1918 the Red Guards seized Helsinki and proclaimed a Socialist Workers' Republic, Lenin at once made available to them arms, personnel and advice.

The Red Guards did not take the need for Russian help seriously, for they had thought their *coup d'état* would secure them in power. What it provoked nevertheless, was a civil war in which, despite considerable Russian assistance, they were soundly beaten. What beat them was the arrival of the *Jägers*, a better force than any they could muster, the White Guards, and the remarkable military leadership of Mannerheim — eventually reinforced by plentiful German assistance. But Mannerheim's role was crucial. The most illustrious of the Tzar's many Finnish Officers, like most of them a sibling of the Swedish-speaking nobility, he had escaped from the Bolsheviks just in time to be offered command of the White forces, which he at once directed against the northern capital of the Reds, Tampere. Despite inferiority of numbers, he succeeded in capturing it on April 5th, after a siege of several weeks, and then, leading his still half-organised force southwards, sandwiched the remainder of the Red Army between it and the advancing

Finland

Germans, the Baltic Division of von der Goltz, which had landed at Hanko on April 3rd. By the middle of May, Helsinki was in Mannerheim's hands and the civil war over. Mannerheim's part was still not played out, however, for it was he who persuaded his fellow Whites that they must not, as many wished, make their new state a puppet of Germany and insisted on the preservation of a strong army as a guarantee against that outcome. On the collapse of Germany, and the fall of the pro-German party, he briefly became Head of State.

The wounds of the civil war were slow to heal in Finland: over 24,000 Finns had died, 10,000 of them Reds who had succumbed to starvation or atrocity at White hands, and a smaller number of Whites who were the victims of Red atrocity. Finland was also not to make her peace with Russia until October, 1920 when most of Carelia, Finland's easternmost province, was ceded to the Soviets (but the Arctic port of Petsamo allotted to Finland). In the era of reconstruction which followed, military priorities naturally receded in importance, but conscription was re-established on the 1878 pattern and a typical small-nation conscript army slowly created. In 1932, legislation prescribed that all able-bodied Finns should spend their twenty-second year under arms and thereafter serve in the reserve until the age of forty. The regular component was limited to officers, NCOs and instructors, and the permanent institutions to a cadet school (1919), Reserve Officer School (1919) and War College (1924). An unusual feature of Finland's military structure was provided, however, by the *Suojeluskunta* (Civic Guard), which bears comparison with the contemporary Austrian *Heimwehr*. It was 100,000 strong and separate from the reserve (though most of its numbers were reservists), voluntary in character, yet recognised by the State. It was nothing more nor less than the White Guard, which remained in being as a standing check on the militant Social Democratic organisations; considerable hostility existed between the two. Trade unions, for example, refused to accept Civic Guards as members. The Guard also had a numerous Women's branch, called *Lotta Svärd*, after a Finnish literary heroine.

All these service-people were to be needed — and dissensions were forgotten — when, in November, 1939 Russia declared war on Finland by ultimatum. The Russians undoubtedly expected to get what they wanted — part of Carelia and the Hanko peninsula — without opposition. To their great embarrassment, the tiny Finnish army of nine divisions, about 135,000 strong, inflicted on them a whole series of defeats and it was only after 3 months of fighting on a static line that the Red Army was eventually able to break through. The Finns' highly individualistic *motti* tactics (small ski-unit infiltration of the forests) had again frustrated Russia's policy towards Finland; Finnish national pride, which had fuelled the success of their army, was no whit diminished by the annexations upon which Russia insisted. As soon, however, as Hitler declared war on Russia, the Finns took their opportunity to win back from the Soviets the ground they had been forced to surrender, and, to demonstrate their independence of the Germans, they thereafter maintained only a token offensive against the Russians, with whom, their sense of history told them, they must one day come to an accommodation.

The accommodation, arrived at by the armistice of September, 1944, itself brought about by a shattering Soviet counter-offensive, gave back to Russia both the disputed territories of 1939 and the Arctic part of Petsamo. It also imposed upward limits, codified by the Paris Peace Treaty of February 10th, 1947 and on the size of the Finnish armed forces, which was henceforward to contain only 34,400 soldiers including frontier guards and anti-aircraft gunners, 4500 sailors with no more than 10,000 tons of shipping, and 3000 airmen with no more than 60 aircraft, none of them bombers. But that Finland still possesses not only an independent armed force, but also the bulk of her national territory and her undiminished sovereignty, is in part testimony to the respect in which Russia holds the military ability of her people and her army. It is usual for foreigners to think of the Finns as pioneers of social welfare and political democracy; their fundamentally martial spirit and history, one of the most remarkable in Europe, should also be remembered.

STRENGTH AND BUDGET

Population: 4,810,000
Army: 31,400 (24,000 conscripts); 3600 frontier guards
Reserves: 690,000
GNP (1981): $712,000,000,000
Military expenditure (1981): $666,000,000.

The strength of the navy is 2500 (two corvettes, 54 smaller craft) and of the air force 3000 (43 combat aircraft).

COMMAND AND CONSTITUTIONAL STATUS

Command of the Finnish Armed Forces is vested in the President of the Republic (who is himself indirectly elected by an electoral college). He is also responsible for Finland's foreign policy. He may in time of war delegate his military authority. Parliamentary control of the forces and their budget is exercised through the Minister of Defence, who is the administrative authority; his executive agency is the Ministry of Defence. Military command is in the hands of the Commander-in-Chief of the Defence Forces, a serving officer seconded from General Headquarters, the supreme command of the army. The army has its own Chief of General Headquarters and Chief of Staff. (The navy and air force have their own Chiefs and Staffs, subordinate to the Commander-in-Chief of the Defence Forces.) Finland may therefore be said to have a unified defence command structure in which, as is historically understandable, the army is paramount.

Three international treaties impose certain limitations and obligations on the role of the Finnish Armed Forces:
1. The Agreement of Friendship, Co-Operation and Mutual Assistance with Soviet Russia, signed 1948, obliges Finland to use all her forces against aggression directed at the Soviet Union through Finnish territory.
2. The Paris Peace Treaty between Finland, Soviet Russia, Great Britain and other States, signed 1947, limits the size of the armed forces to 41,900 and prescribes the existence of paramilitary forces (such as the Civic Guard and *Lotta, q.v.*).
3. The Agreement with Sweden over the Swedish-speaking Aäland islands, signed 1929 and 1940, demilitarises those islands and exempts their inhabitants from military service but obliges Finland to provide for their defence.

ROLE, COMMITMENT, DEPLOYMENT AND RECENT OPERATIONS

Role
Because of Finland's neutrality, reinforced by that of her neighbour Sweden, and her special relationship with Russia, the role of her army is strictly limited. A bill currently under

preparation for parliament defines these limitations: it recognises that the standing army cannot do more than offer a resistance at the frontiers if aggression is threatened, being specifically forbidden, by international treaty, from operating outside its own frontiers. But the very large reserves, which include almost the whole male population between twenty-two and sixty, are looked to as a means of defending the nation, its legal system and the circumstances of its people. If Finland, therefore, were threatened with large-scale invasions, the standing army would deploy and control the nation's strength in an effort to resist it, as it did in 1940. It is the existence of these reserves, together with Finland's formidable military record, which lends credibility to her reserve forces.

A subsidiary role of the army is to promote the peoples' willingness to defend their country and their physical fitness. This highly traditionalist view of the army as a 'School of the Nation' is very much in the spirit of the national character. An additional role which the Finns, together with other Scandinavians, have taken up since 1945, is that of providing international peace-keeping forces to the United Nations.

Commitment
Some Finnish servicemen and units belong to the 'Nordic Stand-by Forces in United Nations' Service' set up by Sweden, Finland, Denmark and Norway in 1964 to provide the UN with a readily available source of peace-keepers. About 400 Finns are on UN duty in the Middle East.

The remainder of Finland's army is committed in the normal way to the national defence.

Deployment
Finland is divided into seven military areas. Each area contains a brigade, and some also additional units: Armoured Brigade (HQ Parola), Nylands Brigade (HQ Dragsvik; the language of the brigade is Swedish), Pohjan Brigade (HQ Oulu), Kainuun Brigade (HQ Kajaani), Porin Brigade (HQ Säkylä), Karjalan Brigade (HQ Kouvola) and Savon Brigade (HQ Mikkeli). There is also a guard battalion at Helsinki, and light infantry battalions in Hame, Pojois-Karjala, Kymi, Nyland and Lappi (Lappland).

These control the operational forces, which also train the conscripts. Military Training Institutes, to which most of the remaining personnel are allotted, are subordinate directly to General Headquarters.

Recent Operations
Apart from duties with the UN already mentioned, Finland has not taken part in any operations since World War II.

ORGANISATION

Arms of Service
The army is divided into infantry, field artillery, coast artillery, anti-aircraft artillery, engineers, signals and logistic troops (which include medical services). The armoured units belong to the infantry; coastal artillery works in direct liaison with the navy. The Frontier Guards, a paramilitary force, are normally under the control of the Interior Ministry, and anti-aircraft artillery works in direct liaison with the air force.

Operational Organisation
Operational organisation and territorial location of the army is combined in Finland. The country is organised into seven military areas, each of which contains a brigade (one of which is an armoured brigade). The establishment of each

of these brigades is: two infantry battalions; one artillery battalion of one field and one air-defence battery; one engineer company; one signal company; and one training battalion (third infantry battalion on mobilisation).

The five largest military areas each has a military hospital and a military transport company.

There are in addition seven independent infantry battalions which, like the Lappland *Jäger* Battalion, are assigned either to regions of particularly difficult terrain or to liaison with the coastal artillery. A number of independent regiments and battalions of field, coastal and air defence artillery exist.

Frontier Guards
The Frontier Guards, numbering 3700, are a paramilitary constabulary which acts in peace-time as a border-security force and coastguard; it is trained in guerrilla tactics for war. Conscripts may perform their military service in major Frontier Guard units, of which there are seven: four land units in the four northern, western and eastern military areas, and three coastguard units in the three southern coastal military areas. Officers and NCOs are recruited and trained in the same way as for the army, but receive special-to-arm instruction at the Frontier Guard schools. Conscript training is designed to provide reserves for guerrilla forces which the Frontier Guards would activate in wartime.

Within the areas in which they operate – the thinly populated borders and the Baltic archipelago – the Frontier Guards exercise police powers and work closely with the civil police.

RECRUITMENT, TRAINING AND RESERVES

Recruitment
All Finns, if fit, are liable for military service and enter training at the age of twenty or twenty-one. The length of service is 240 days, after which conscripts pass to the reserve, in which they remain to the age of fifty. As reservists they are liable for 40 days' refresher training in 7–10 day periods (if NCOs or technicians, for 75 days). Those selected for technical training, as reserve NCOs, or as reserve officers, serve 330 days; reserve officers are liable, after conscript duty, for 100 days' refresher training and remain in the reserves until sixty.

Regular officers and NCOs (there are virtually no regular private soldiers) enter as conscripts and then transfer either to the Officer Corps (Lieutenant to General) or to the partially coterminous NCO Corps (Staff-Sergeant to senior Lieutenant).

Training
NCOs are trained at the NCO Institute in three successive 6 month courses, the last of which promotes successful candidates to lieutenant's rank. Would-be regular officers, having completed the Reserve Officer School course, go to the Military Academy for 2½ years; candidates must possess the Finnish School matriculation certificate. During the last year, cadets attend their arms school. After 4 years' service as a lieutenant, an officer does an 8–10 month captain's course in his arm school, and sits the captain's promotion examination.

Successful candidates may then sit the examination for the tri-service War College course, which leads to general staff posts via another competitive examination. The course is of 2 years for general staff and 3 years for technical officers. It also provides courses for civil servants who occupy defence-related posts.

Officers not successful in the War College examination are

usually later trained at a senior officer's course which qualifies them for promotion to lieutenant-colonel.

Conscripts, of whom an annual total of 40,000 are inducted three times a year (February, June and October) are trained for 8–10 weeks, generally in the units in which they will serve. Besides the acquisition of special-to-arm skills, there is a high emphasis on developing their will to defend the country, their physical fitness and their ability to move and survive in the country's difficult terrain and extreme climate. All infantry recruits are trained in orienteering (individual cross-country running off a map and against the clock).

Each arm of the service has at least one school or institute:

Infantry: Combat School, Parachute School
Artillery: Artillery School (ranges at Rovaniemi, northern Finland), Coastal Artillery School, Anti-Aircraft School
Engineers: Engineer School
Signals: Signal School
Logistics: Logistic Training Centre, Ordnance School, Veterinary School

Reserves

About 38,000 reservists are put through refresher courses each year, either in complete reserve units or at the permanent schools.

EQUIPMENT AND ARMS INDUSTRY

Small arms: M-62 7.62mm assault rifles and LMG (Russia)
Mortars: 81 mm mortar (Britain) and 120mm mortar (Russia)
Anti-tank missiles: SS11 (France) wire-guided missiles; 55mm and 95mm recoilless projectile launchers (Russia)
Artillery: 122mm and 130mm field guns (Russia); 122mm and 152mm howitzers (Russia)
Anti-aircraft: ZSU-57mm and ZU-23mm (both twin-barrelled; Russia), SA-3, SA-7 missiles (Russia)
Artillery: 35mm Oerlikon (Denmark); 40mm Bofors (Sweden)
APC: BTR 50 P (Russia), BMP (Russia)
Tanks: T-54, T-55 medium tanks and PT-76 reconnaissance tanks (Russia).

Finland manufactures little military equipment of her own. The most important manufacturers are Kemira (ammunition), SISU (Suomeni Auto-Teollisuus, which produces the A-45 four-wheel-drive truck, the KB-45 cross-country vehicle, the Terra cross-country tractor, the Terri motor sledge) and Tampella (mortars).

RANK, DRESS AND DISTINCTIONS

Commissioned ranks are lieutenant, senior lieutenant, captain, major, lieutenant-colonel, colonel, major-general, lieutenant-general and general. (Mannerheim held the unique rank of Marshal.)

Regular non-commissioned ranks are staff-sergeant, sergeant-major, lieutenant and senior lieutenant.

Conscript ranks are private, corporal and sergeant.

The Finnish army wears an extremely simple grey-green uniform with collar and tie; badges of rank are worn on the collar. Major-, lieutenant- and full generals wear respectively one, two or three Finnish lions. A mottled camouflage suit is worn in the field, with knee-boots, and white smocks and trousers in winter.

CURRENT DEVELOPMENTS

Finland's army ought, given the diplomatic situation of the country, to be either the puppet of a foreign power, or a decorative irrelevance. In practice, it is an independent force of high fighting value, which continues to enjoy wide popular support. Its strengths are in its well-proved ability to use the country's terrain and climate to advantage; every Finn skis from childhood, so that its winter-warfare capability is probably unmatched by any army in the world, while the skill and training of its engineers in barrage construction makes the approach to the Finnish heartland through the lakeland of the south-east an even more militarily questionable procedure than it looks on the map.

It is ironic that a neutral State like Finland, almost alone among the democracies of Europe, should continue to believe in the army as the 'School of the Nation' and see it as 'the Nation in Arms'. But that it continues to do. Although there has recently been agitation to loosen the hold of the President (who enjoys wide powers in Finland) and of General Headquarters on the army, and increase parliamentary control, the army remains an 'above party' institution of great popularity, which is reinforced by its distinguished role as a United Nations peace-keeping force.

John Keegan

FRANCE

HISTORY AND INTRODUCTION

The French army disputes with the British the title of the oldest of Europe's (and of the world's) national armies. It is notable as a social or political institution for other important reasons: for the principle of universal conscription on which it was early established and for the equation made by its Revolutionary leaders between the performance of military service and enjoyment of the rights of citizenship — two principles very much alive in the modern world; for its function as a vehicle of revolutionary change between 1789 and 1815; for its adoption of the role of 'school of the nation' in the late nineteenth century; and for its frequent intervention in French domestic politics at moments of crisis (e.g. de Gaulle's recall to power in 1958 and the Algerian *Putsch*). It is also important for its almost single-handed creation of the French colonial empire and — on the purely military side — for the primacy it exercised among European armies for almost 200 years (1650–1850). It pioneered the modern sciences of gunnery, siege-craft, military engineering and fortification and made fundamental innovations in principles of staffwork and organisation.

1400–1600

The origins of the French army, like those of most other European armies, are traced to the decline of the feudal military system, in the middle of the fifteenth century. The mercenary bands which had come into being, first to supplement, then to replace knight-service, proved an unstable factor in a kingdom plagued by foreign aggression and internal strife. Successive kings attempted to bring them permanently onto their payroll, while seeking a cheaper but equally efficient substitute from among their own subjects. Hence the existence, at the beginning of the sixteenth century, of *'compagnies d'ordonnance'* of native noblemen, the ancestors of today's *Arme blindée/cavalerie*; of a royal artillery; and of numerous *bandes* of mercenaries from which today's infantry descends.

1600–1800

The success achieved by the French kings in amalgamating these disparate elements into a single disciplined force may be recalled by reading the long roll of its seventeenth and eighteenth century campaigns against Austria, Britain, Holland, the German States and Spain. But despite the reputation it had come to enjoy by 1789 as the leading European army, it was then, as much as any other French institution, ripe for reform. The nobility monopolised commissioned rank and the officer's career was emphatically not one open to talents. When the Paris mob rose, the Royal Army offered little resistance and while the majority of officers fled abroad, it transferred its loyalty to the Revolution. Many of the new leaders emerged from its ranks; others, like Napoleon, captain in the *declassé* Artillery, were former royal officers who saw their chance with the new order. Threatened almost at once by foreign invasion, the army, filled out with raw conscripts, saved the Revolution at Valmy in 1793. Reorganised by a War Minister of genius, Carnot, it was by 1796 pushing the Revolution beyond the frontiers of France. By 1800, when Captain Napoleon had vaulted to the First Consulship direct from the battlefield, it was poised to dominate Europe.

1800–1918

Militarily, the Napoleonic years were the most brilliant in the history of the French — and perhaps of any other army. And victory at the front was matched at the rear by the establishment of the first modern war economy and society. Wherever Napoleon moved, moreover, existing regiments and droves of conscripts — Italian, Spanish, German — were drafted into the *Grande Armée*. By 1815, France had become an almost wholly militarised society, while the elements of the Napoleonic military and administrative system had been disseminated throughout western Europe. The legacy was as important, in its way, as that of the Revolution's ideology.

Ultimately, Napoleon's exactions exhausted France, and the defeats of 1814–15 were an inevitable outcome of his misuse of country and army. As the restored Bourbons rightly suspected, however, the army's loyalty remained with Napoleon even after his downfall, and in order to break that tie, Louis XVIII disbanded all the regiments and reformed them as *Légions Départementales* of infantry and cavalry. He retained both the *Garde Nationale*, the armed revolutionary citizenry which, by 1815, had become a comfortably bourgeois force (and so a counterweight either to the army or the mob), and the principle of conscription, administered on a selective basis which spared the middle class. The latter system survived until 1870, when its disastrous effects were revealed in the Franco–Prussian War.

Louis's retention of the *Garde Nationale* also proved ill-judged, for in 1830 it was material in finally dethroning the Bourbons. Disregarded by Napoleon III, who lavished money on his successful (but small) regular army, it again sprang into prominence after the regulars' defeat in 1870: its men formed the garrison of Paris and the provincial armies whose unskilful bravery robbed the Prussians of complete victory. The Third Republic's government, anxious 'to recreate on French soil an exact copy of the army which had defeated Napoleon III's', yet unwilling 'to put a gun on the shoulder of every socialist', which it reckoned the introduction of Prussia's conscriptive system would achieve, was slow to find the answer to republican military needs. But when eventually rebuilt, the army proved in many ways the most brave, successful and politically subordinate of any France had known. However 'anti-republican' the Dreyfus affair implied it to be, it devoted itself between 1870 and 1914 almost wholly to '*la revanche*' and preparation for it. And as the 'school of the nation', of which 1,700,000 citizens were to die between 1914 and 1918, it was remarkably successful in communicating to its conscripts the spirit of obedience and self-sacrifice so characteristic of its pre-1914 outlook.

1918–1968

The sufferings of World War I, which fell disproportionately on to the French army, broke its morale in 1917 and it was only slowly brought back to play a part in final victory. Appalled by the price of victory France affirmed her determination that it should never be paid again — and so authoritatively that in 1940 the reservists took their leaders at their word. The German occupation which resulted put all French officers in a exquisite dilemma, which only a few solved by rallying to de Gaulle's army in exile. Upon those who did, and returned victorious in 1944, fell the duty of rebuilding the army — as it had been rebuilt in 1870.

The results this time were different. For de Gaulle's army had been built on the colonial garrisons outside Vichy's control. It was strongly 'imperial' in spirit and, when called upon to fight two colonial wars in quick succession — first in Indo-China, 1946–54, then in Algeria, 1954–62, it took the government at perhaps better than its word. Most of the empire had been won by nineteenth century soldiers acting almost independently of Paris. The army now resolved to retain it, independent of the wishes of Paris, and, when Paris wavered in 1958, effectively dissolved the Fourth Republic and recalled de Gaulle.

He repaid his debt to the army in false coin, granting independence to Algeria despite the defeat the guerrillas had suffered at the army's hands. But the 'imperial' element in the army allowed him to do so by overplaying its bluff, which was called by the conscripts. They were unwilling to prolong the parachutists' war for no end they valued. However, when young men of the same age-group rioted to demand de Gaulle's removal during May, 1968, the army, to which he turned at once for support (the explanation of his 'disappearance' from Paris on May 19th), gave it him. In doing so, it remained loyal to the majority of its traditions. More often than not, the French army supports constitutional authority.

STRENGTH AND BUDGET

Strength

Population: 53,750,000
Army: 330,000
Gendarmerie: 76,000
Total defence forces: 502,000 (navy 68,500; air force 103,600)
Conscripts in defence forces: 273,000 (of whom 66% are in the army)
Reserves
   Army: 400,000 (of whom 75% allotted to D.O.T. — see later)
   Gendarmerie: 80,000

Budget

GNP (1976 estimate): $353,200,000,000
Defence expenditure (1977): $11,720,000,000
Third (1971–5) procurement budget: Fr. 82, 400,000,000
Army allocation: Fr. 17,140,000,000 (20.8%)

COMMAND

Political

1. The Commander in Chief of the three Armées – de Terre (army), de Mer (navy), de l'Air (Air Force) – is the President of the Republic. The main defence decisions are taken by him, though he consults the Conseil Supérieur de la Défense Nationale (a consultative body) and confers with the Comité de Défense (a committee of ministers). It was believed that M. Pompidou, to a far greater extent than General de Gaulle, devolved defence decisions onto the Prime Minister, whose organ of defence decision is the Comité Restreint de Défense (a defence sub-committee, personal to him). President Giscard is believed to pursue the same approach.
2. The Ministre des Armées controls the day-to-day administration of defence. He is assisted by a Secrétaire-général, whose staff also serves the President and administers all other important defence committees. It is half military and half civilian in composition. He is also assisted by a Ministerial Armaments Delegation (see Equipment and Arms Industry). The French parliament debates and votes the defence budget.

Military

1. The Chief of Defence Staff (État-major des Armées) heads the fully unified defence system which France has possessed since 1961. He is also Vice-Chairman of a Chiefs of Staff Committee, and directly oversees the operations of the three services, since their units are organised on functional lines into four main forces:
   (a) Forces Inter-Armées d'Intervention (tri-service).
   (b) Forces Nucléaire Stratégique (air and missile units)
   (c) Forces de Manoeuvre (army and air)
   (d) Forces de Défense Opérationelle du Territoire (D.O.T., mainly army).
2. The Service Chiefs of Staff are responsible for appropriate non-operational matters. The Army Chief (État-major de l'Armée de Terre) commands:
   (a) Six military regions in France.
   (b) The First French Army (Including army units in the French Forces in Germany).
   (c) Army units in four joint overseas commands:
      (i)   French Polynesia (HQ Tahiti).
      (ii) South Indian Ocean (HQ Réunion).
      (iii) West Indies (Antilles-Guyane) (HQ Fort de France, Martinique).
      (iv) Pacific (HQ Noumea, New Caledonia).

Also under command are the French troops in West Africa at Djibouti.

ROLE, COMMITMENT, DEPLOYMENT AND RECENT OPERATIONS

Role

Between 1948 and 1964 the promulgation of a series of government decrees established a 'total' concept of defence, in obedience to which distinctions between 'peace' and 'war' which formerly had important legal implications were abolished, and military and civilian structures of the State unified. In practice, the roles of the army remain the traditional ones of national defence, assistance to allies and protection of overseas interests. Internal security, because of the large paramilitary police force, is of secondary importance.

Commitment

France, though not a military partner, remains a member of NATO. She has had, since 1964, a bilateral treaty with the German government which permits her to maintain three of her divisions on German soil, and in practice their operational tasks and staffs are closely integrated with NATO's. She also has bilateral defence agreements with 11 of her former territories: Cameroun, Benin, Ivory Coast, Niger, Mauritania, Senegal, Togo, Central African Republic, Congo, Gabon and Djibouti.

Deployment

Force de Manoeuvre

The army component consists principally of the First French Army (the retitled Armée du Rhin et Danube which Marshal de Lattre led in the Liberation Campaign of 1944–5), three of whose divisions are stationed in Germany, while the remaining four are in France. Its I and II Corps (Table 1) contain tactical nuclear missile regiments, which are under the direct control of the President. The III Corps (Versailles) consists of one armoured division.

Forces d'Intervention

The army component (Forces Terrestres d'Intervention) consists principally of (a) the 11th (Parachute) Division, located

Table 1 I, II and III Corps

Armoured Division (H.Q.)

I CORPS (H.Q. NANCY)
4th (Nancy)
7th (Besancon)
6th (Strasbourg)
10th (Chalons)

II CORPS (H.Q. BADEN—OOS)
1st (Trier)
3rd (Freiburg)
5th (Landau)

III CORPS (VERSAILLES)
2nd (Versailles)

at Tarbes, Hautes-Pyrénées with two airborne brigades (20th and 25th); the 9th (Amphibious) Division, located at St-Malo, and the 31st Brigade (Overseas Intervention), stationed at Aubagne, near Marseilles. It consists of the 21st R.I.Ma and 22nd R.E.I. and is specifically equipped and intended for rapid reaction in the Mediterranean. The French navy's marines, *Groupement Commando de Fusiliers-Marins*, stationed at Brest, also act as part of the intervention force.

Army Units in Overseas Commands
These comprise, in the Ivory Coast, 43rd BIMa; in Senegal, 10th B.I.Ma.; in Gabon, 6th B.I.Ma.; in Martinique, 33rd R.I.Ma. in Réunion, 2nd R.P.I.Ma.; in Tahiti, 5th Regiment Mixte Pacifique (Foreign Legion) or B.I.Ma. Tahiti; in New Caledonia, R.I.Ma. Pacifique; in Mayotte, a Foreign Legion company; in Djibouti, 13th D.B.L.E., 6th R.A.Ma, 5th R.I.A.O.M.

Forces de Défense Opérationelle du Territoire (D.O.T.)
The army element is known as the *Forces du Territoire* and its organisation has, since the 1950s, been closely integrated with the civil administrative structure. This step was prompted initially by the wave of 'insurrectionary' strikes of 1947—8, which revealed that in times of widespread disorder the central government, which has always exercised very direct control over the provinces, needed an intermediate organisational tier between it and the *départements* if it were to act effectively. Hence the grouping of the 95 *départements* into six 'super-prefectures' known as *Zones de Défense*. The *Régions Militaires*, whose number has been reduced to six, have been made to correspond geographically and their commanding generals are the military colleagues of the 'super-prefects'.

In times of emergency, they would form joint staffs, and pool their forces. These consist, on the civil side, of the urban police, the riot police (*Compagnies Républicaines de Sécurité*; C.R.S.) and the two intelligence services of the Ministry of the Interior, the *Renseignements Généraux* (R.G.) (political intelligence), and the *Surveillance du Territoire* (S.T.) counter-espionage. On the military side the available forces comprise the *Gendarmerie Nationale* (rural police and internal security companies, normally under civil control), of the 21 'commando' regiments and four armoured-car regiments of the army's *Forces du Territoire*, and, if mobilisation was declared, of 95 reserve regiments (*Régiments Divisionnaires*), one to be raised in each *département*.

The army maintains a small military liaison team in each *département*, working with the perfect, and a larger staff, under a *Général Divisionnaire*, in each of the 21 *Circumscriptions d'Action Régionale*. These civil circumscriptions, which are subdivisions of the six *régions*, correspond geographically to the 21 *Divisions Militaires*. Before mobilisation can be declared, three preliminary states of emergency must be declared: *troubles* (civilian authority operations); *mise en garde* (the military assume authority); and *état de siège*. It is, however, difficult to envisage this elaborate machinery being called into action in contemporary circumstances, and this lack of credibility is reflected in the unpopularity of service in the D.O.T. among regular soldiers.

Recent Operations
Although the French have fought two large colonial wars since 1945 (indo-China 1946—54 and Algeria 1954—62) and suffered in that period proportionately higher casualties, particularly in officers, than any army except the American, Chinese and Vietnamese, it has had very little operational experience in the last 10 years. Its most notable involvement has been in the anti-guerrilla campaign in the Republic of Chad, where the 6th Mixed Regiment and the 2nd Foreign Legion Parachute Regiment have been engaged side by side with the small and undertrained local army against anti-government rebels since 1968. The campaign attracted unfavourable political attention in France in 1971, however, despite the very small casualties suffered (49 up to September, 1972), and the Legionaires have subsequently been withdrawn, President Tombalbaye announcing that his troops (7000 strong) would henceforth assume responsibility for internal security. A parachute company was also stationed in the then Central African Republic from 1967 to September, 1969 at the request of the then President Bokassa.

The French army, so active in internal politics through the period 1958—62 (i.e. through its acquiescence in the disturbances of May, 1958 in Algeria, Corsica and metropolitan France, which brought de Gaulle to power; through the complicity of certain units in the abortive anti-Gaullist revolt in Algiers of January, 1960, known as 'the week of the barricades'; and through the 'generals' *putsch*' of April 22nd, 1961) has subsequently taken no overt part in the political life of the nation. It was not called out of barracks during the *événements* (the anti-de Gaulle riots of May, 1968) which

Administrative Structure of the D.O.T.

(a)	Civil administrative areas	(b)	Military administrative areas	(c)	Civil authorities
(d)	Military authorities	(e)	Local gendarmerie units		

(a)	Zone de défense (6)	Circonscription d'action (21)	Département (95)	
(b)	Région militaire (6)	Division militaire (21)	—	
(c)	Préfet de défense (6)	Préfet de circonscription (21)	Préfet (95)	
(d)	Général commandant (6)	Général divisionnaire (21)	Military liaison team (95)	
(e)	Commandement de région (6)	Légion (21)	Groupement (95)	

France

were suppressed by the civil police and the gendarmerie. A French parachute battalion, 2 R.E.P., intervened at Kolwezi, Zaïre, on May 19th, 1978 to rescue survivors of the anti-European massacres (see also Belgium), and a battalion of Infanterie de Marine, 3 R.P.I.M., arrived in Lebanon in March, 1978 to form part of the UN peacekeeping force. The parachutists were quickly withdrawn, but the peacekeeping unit remains.

ORGANISATION

Arms of Service
The modern French army is really an amalgamation of three historically separate forces: the home army (Armée du Métropole); the Army of Africa, which formed part of the metropolitan army but was stationed and largely recruited in north and west Africa; and the Colonial Army (Troupes Coloniales), which at different times was under the command of the Ministries of the Navy and the Colonies. The Army of Africa (which included the Foreign Legion), was the creation originally of the Orleanist Monarchy of 1830–48, which initiated the penetration of the continent; the Colonial Army descends from the colonial garrisons of the old pre-revolutionary Ministry of the Navy, and its surviving regiments are once again known as Troupes de Marine (not to be confused with the Fusiliers-Marins, the modern French navy's marines). The metropolitan army's infantry and cavalry also claim descent from the pre-revolutionary regiments, but very few can trace an unbroken lineage. There is, finally, a fourth component of the army: the Gendarmerie Nationale, which polices the countryside, provides internal security units and is effectively commanded by the Ministry of the Interior. Its origins are also pre-revolutionary.

Infantry
These diverse historical origins help to explain the existence of four different sorts of units within the infantry: Infanterie Métropolitaine (36 regiments); 12 battalions or groupements of Chasseurs (six alpine, six mechanised); six regiments of the Foreign Legion; and 19 regiments of Infanterie de Marine, some still locally recruited (e.g. in the Pacific and the West Indies). Two of the metropolitan, five of the marine and one of the legion infantry regiments are parachutists. Tours of duty in the parachute regiments have been restricted in length since the 1960s, because of the dissident reputation the parachutists won in Algeria; officers may now serve only for about 3 years up to the rank of captain, and about 4 years altogether thereafter. All regiments are now organised as single battalions, but those which are mechanised contain both armoured-infantry and tanks, while some of the Marine troops are mixed units (Régiments Inter-Armes d'Outre-Mer: RIAOM) which serve overseas. Regimental abbreviations, almost always used, are:

R.I. – Régiment d'Infanterie
R.I.Méca – Régiment d'Infanterie Mécanisée
R.I.M. – Régiment d'Infanterie Motorisée
R.I.Ma. – Régiment d'Infanterie de Marine

B.I.Ma. – Bataillon d'Infanterie de Marine
G.C – Groupement de Chasseurs
B.C.A. – Bataillon de Chasseurs Alpins
R.E.I. – Régiment Étranger d'Infanterie
D.B.L.E. – Demi-brigade de la Légion Étrangère
R.P. – Régiment Parachutiste (e.g. R.E.P. = Régiment Étranger Parachutiste)

Cavalry
The Cavalry consists of 30 regiments, which preserve the ancient titles of Dragons (R.D.), Cuirassiers (R.C.), Hussards (R.H.) and Chasseurs à Cheval (R.C. à Ch.). The 1er Spahis (ex-north African cavalry), the Régiment Étranger de Cavalerie (R.E.C.), and the 501ème Régiment de Chars de Combat (the original tank regiment) have also been kept in being for historical reasons. In theory, Cuirassiers man heavy tanks, Dragons light tanks, Hussards heavy armoured cars and Chasseurs light armoured cars, but these distinctions are not strictly observed. Some Dragon regiments are now mechanised infantry in the Force de Manœuvre, and three marine regiments (R.I.C.M., R.M.T. and 21ème R.I.Ma.) are armoured.

Other Arms
The Artillery contains both metropolitan and Marine (R.A.Ma.) regiments. However, the Génie (Engineers), Transmissions (Signals), Train (Transport) and Aviation Légère de l'Armée de Terre – A.L.A.T. (Army Air Corps) are organised on straightforward functional lines. So too is the Service du Matériel, which supplies and maintains stores and equipment, the Service de l'Intendance (food and pay – assisted by the Trésor), and the Service des Essences (fuel supply).

Minor Services
Aumônerie (chaplains); Service Vétérinaire (veterinary); Justice Militaire (legal services); Pionniers (military labour); Poste Militaire (mail); and Prévôte (military police provided by gendarmerie); Personnel Féminin de l'Armée de Terre (P.F.A.T.) (women's service).

Operational Organisation
The French army underwent a major operational re-organisation between 1976–81, which has increased the number of corps from two to three and, the number of divisions from seven to fifteen. The new divisions, in which the brigade structure has been abolished (except in the parachute division), are smaller than before (about 7000 men), the corps have more units, and the 'Army' and 'General Reserve' units have been increased in number. Observers comment that the new organisation is designed to fit the army particularly for operations on the nuclear battlefield. But four of the new divisions are infantry formations (8th, 12th, 14th, 15th), whose function appears chiefly to be 'Operational Defence of the Territory'. In time of mobilisation, they would be joined by fourteen reserve divisions, ten to be formed from divisions of the active army, four from the units of the major training schools.

Titles of Sub-units Within Arms

Infantry:	régiment,	(bataillon),	compagnie,	section,	groupe
Cavalry:	régiment,	–	escadron,	peloton,	–
Artillery:	régiment,	groupe,	batterie,	–	–
Engineers:	régiment,	bataillon,	compagnie,	section,	escouade
Transport:	–	groupe,	compagnie,	peloton,	–

Army and General Reserve Troops consist of: one signals regiment, one electronic warfare regiment, one long range reconnaissance regiment, two aviation regiments, eight engineer regiments (three amphibious), one nuclear missile (Pluton) regiment, one air defence (Hawk) regiment, eight artillery regiments, ten transport regiments.

The *Corps* (I, II, III) consists of: two nuclear missile (Pluton) regiments, four air defence regiments (Roland and Hawk), two artillery regiments, a motorised infantry regiment, two armoured reconnaissance regiments (with AMX 10 RC), two aviation regiments (72 helicopters each) and a fleet of 30 light helicopters, two engineer regiments, a NBC battalion, a traffic control regiment, three signal regiments, a locating regiment, and a logistic brigade (10,000 men, 2800 vehicles, with supply, transport, medical and repair functions).

The *armoured division* (1st, 2nd, 3rd, 4th, 5th, 6th, 7th and 10th) consists of two tank regiments (each 53 AMX 30 and an armoured infantry squadron), two mechanised battalions (each 20 AMX 30 and 42 AMX 10 armoured personnel carriers), an artillery regiment (24 155mm GCT self-propelled howitzers), an engineer regiment, an anti-tank company and a headquarters and logistic regiment (*régiment de commandement et soutien*).

The *infantry division* (8th, 12th, 14th, 15th) consists of an armoured reconnaissance regiment (AMX 10 RC and VAB), three infantry battalions (VAB), an artillery regiment (24 155mm howitzers), an engineer company and a headquarters and logistic regiment. The *amphibious* division (9th DIMa) is similarly organised. The *alpine* division (27th DIA) has six infantry (*Chasseurs alpins*) battalions and lighter equipment. The *parachute* (11th) division has kept the brigade structure: its two brigades consist of three parachute battalions and a headquarters and logistic battalion; divisional troops consist of an administrative and logistic battalion, a reconnaissance regiment, an artillery regiment (120mm mortars) and an engineer regiment.

Reserve Organisation. The re-organisation of the active army, which was aimed at abolishing the distinction between the 'forces of manoeuvre' and the 'territorial defence forces', is paralleled by a new reserve structure, which produces fourteen reserve infantry divisions. Four of these, based in the 3rd, 4th and 5th Military Regions, are to be formed around the local training schools (artillery, infantry, engineer, armour, NCO and parachute); the other ten are to be formed from the local active divisions, and are numbered accordingly: 102nd/104th, 107th, 108th, 109th, 110th, 112th, 114th, 115th, 127th. There a number of non-divisional reserve units in excess.

Gendarmerie Nationale
This national police force, though controlled day-to-day by the Ministry of the Interior, belongs to the army. It has a dual organisation: (a) the *Gendarmerie Mobile*, organised into *Groupements*, *Escadrons* (of which there are 130) and *Pelotons* and equipped *inter alia* with armoured cars and helicopters, provides internal security units (and traffic police); (b) the *Gendarmerie Départementale* is the rural police force, but also an important intelligence-gathering agency. It maintains a *Brigade* (5—40 men) in each of France's 3000 cantons, a *Compagnie* headquarters at the next administrative level, the *Arrondissement*, and a *Groupement* headquarters in the main town of the *Département*. *Mobile* and *départementale* units are controlled at the next level by a *Légion* under a *Commandement de Région*, whose chief would come under command of the 'super-prefect' in times of emergency, but normally takes orders from Paris. The *Garde Républicaine* are the best known Gendarmerie unit, and protect the President's residence, besides providing ceremonial guards on occasions of state.

The Gendarmerie formed in 1973—4 an anti-terrorist unit, *Groupe d'Intervention de la Gendarmerie Nationale* (GIGN) now based near Paris. It consists of 56 men organised into four teams and had mounted 200 operations up to October 1981, securing the release of 483 people held hostage.

RECRUITMENT AND TRAINING

Officers

Cadet Training
Regular officers (*officers de carrière*) are recruited, (a) by competitive examinations (*concours*) among school leavers who have completed a 2 year course of preparatory studies, and (b) by commissioning NCOs.

Most officer training is carried out at Coëtquidan (Morbihan) in Brittany, to which the *École Spéciale Militaire de St-Cyr* was moved in 1946. Also located there is the *École Militaire Inter-Armes*, where selected NCOs are trained. Training at the E.S.M. is for 3 years (2 until 1981); at the E.M.I.A. for 1 year. Each school produces about 250 officers a year; E.S.M. graduates enjoy a 10% higher rate of pay up to the rank of Commandant, and thereafter rather better promotion prospects. On commissioning into their different arms of service, *sous-lieutenants* go for a 1 year course to the appropriate *école d'application* (special-to-arm-school):

Infanterie: Montpellier
Arme blindée/Cavalerie: Saumur
Artillerie: Draguignan
Génie: Angers
Transmissions: Montargis
Train: Tours
Matériel: Bourges
Gendarmerie: Melun

On promotion to captain (age about thirty), officers return to their *école d'application* for 6 months.

Higher Military Education
Junior staff officers are trained, after selection, at the *École d'État-major*; more important is to succeed in the competitive examination (84% fail) for entry to the *École Supérieure de Guerre* (located with the former in the *École Militaire* building in Paris). Entry takes place at major rank, age 38—42 years, and is an essential precondition for command of a major fighting unit. The highest level of military education is provided at the *Centre des Hautes Études Militaires* (same building) where about 20 officers of colonel rank train for the most senior defence posts; co-located is the *Institut des Hautes Études de Défense Nationale*, for senior civil servants. The two higher institutes work in harness.

Other Officers
Four other sorts of officer are found in the French army: technical officers, selected by *concours* from among NCOs; old NCOs, near to retirement, commissioned direct as *sous-lieutenants*; suitable civilian candidates awarded short-service commissions, and suitable conscripts (particularly those who have completed a voluntary period of *préparation militaire* as schoolboys) commissioned as *sous-lieutenants de réserve*.

Technical Officer Training
Regular officers may proceed at captain rank to the *Enseignement Militaire Supérieur Scientifique et Technique* for training in weapons technology, electronics, etc. and usually thereafter remain in those fields.

France

Medical Officers
They receive both their medical and military training at the military medical school in Lyon.

École Polytechnique
This famous school, once the source of all French artillery and engineer officers and still run as a military establishment, no longer supplies more than the odd individual to the army. Its cadets (*Les X*) surrender their commissions on graduating and enter civilian State service or private firms.

Military Schools
The army runs six military boarding schools (*Collèges Militaires*) with favourable terms for sons of living and dead soldiers. The most famous is the Prytanée de la Flèche; the others are set in the restored buildings of the original St-Cyr, and at Aix-en-Provence, Le Mans, Autumn and Tampon (Ile de Réunion in the Indian Ocean). Subsequent military service is optional but common.

Current Situation in Officer Recruitment and Training
The French officer retains his traditionally high social standing, though it is somewhat affected by the widening gap between military and other professional salaries. The St-Cyr quota is filled each year without a lowering of standards, though the number competing declines. Recruiting is also localised, many more *Cyrards* coming from the east and extreme west than from the north and centre. The most notable trend since the war has been for St-Cyr to become self-recruiting; in 1954–8 an average of 44% of *Cyrards* were themselves the sons of soldiers and the proportion continues slowly to increase.

The French officer corps seems to have recovered from the strains it underwent during the years of the Fourth Republic and of de Gaulle. It has been much reduced in size, many officers having been induced to retire prematurely by handsome gratuities, and promotion, though still slow by British and American standards, has quickened. A deliberate attempt has been made, by the political and military leadership alike, to banish memories of empire and to lead the army back to the traditions of 'silence' and of 'defence of the homeland' characteristic of its spirit between 1870 and 1914. The French army remains, nevertheless, essentially right-wing and catholic in temperament, and is still characterised by internal cliques and political patronage to a degree which British and American soldiers would find surprising. No survey of French domestic or foreign affairs should leave the mood of the officer corps out of account.

NCOs and Soldiers

Conscription and Regular Soldiers
All Frenchmen on reaching the age of 18 years become liable for military service and about 75% of each annual contingent is inducted. There are deferments for students (*see* Current Developments). The term of service has been reduced from 16 months to 1 year. It is also possible to enlist as a regular soldier on a 5 year engagement. All NCOs in the Foreign Legion and many of the *Troupes de Marine* are regulars; so too are the NCOs above the rank of corporal.

Conscript training, which is carried out in the regiments, lasts 6 months: 4 months basic, one in camp, one at a commando centre. One result of this system is that regiments devote half their annual working life to training. The *Troupes de Marine*, Foreign Legion and some other branches have their own training regiments.

NCOs
Suitable candidates are sent after enlistment, to training either at the *École de Sous-officiers d'Active* (ESOA) at the appropriate arms school (*Écoles d'Application*) or to the *École Nationale de Sous-Officiers d'Active* (ENSOA) at St-Maixent (founded 1963). The standard of training is high, but except in the technical corps they receive less responsibility than in the British or American armies.

EQUIPMENT AND ARMS INDUSTRY

Control
France has had one of the leading armaments industries of Europe since the seventeenth century. As well as ship-building, it now includes explosives, weapons, aircraft and aerospace industries. Research, development and production are under the sole direct control of a senior civil servant, the Ministerial Delegate for Armament (DMA), an immediate subordinate of the Minister of Defence. His delegation has various technical directorates: those supplying equipment to the army are the technical directorates for ground armament (DTAT — *Direction Technique des Armements Terrestres*), missiles (DTEn — *engins*) and powders and explosives (DP — *poudres*); the army also deals with those for aeronautical equipment (DCTA — *Constructions Aéronautiques*) and for research and testing (DRME — *Recherches et Moyens d'Essai*). DRME does not conduct research itself, but collates military requirements and oversees their development in private or public centres.

Production
The French armaments industry is mainly financed and controlled by the State, and much of it is fully nationalised. Some weapons factories have been State-owned since the eighteenth century.

Weapons Factories
1. *Armoured Vehicle Manufacturers:* Société de Construction Mécaniques Panhard et Levassor: 18 Ave. d'Ivry, Paris — armoured cars and personnel carriers. Direction Techniques des Armements Terrestres (DTAT): HQ Caserne Sully, 92-St Cloud — tanks, APCs, self-propelled artillery; many works throughout France, main centres at St-Étienne and Châtelerault.
2. *Gun Manufacturers:* DTAT.
3. *Infantry Weapons:* DTAT.
4. *Helicopters and Aircraft:* Aérospatiale (amalgamation, 1970, of Nord Aviation and Sud Aviation); HQ: 12 Ave. Bosquet, Paris; works throughout France at St Aubin-de-Médoc, Bourges, Cannes, Châteauroux, Châtillon, Courbevoie, La Courneuve, Les Mureaux, Marignane, Meaulte, Nantes, Puteaux, St Nazaire, Suresnes and Toulouse.
5. *Radar and Electronic Equipment:* Thomson C.S.F., rue des Mathurins, 92-Bagneux. Electronique Marcel Dassault, 55 Quai Carnot, 92-St Cloud.
6. *Missiles and Projectiles:* Luchaire S.A., 180 Boulevard Haussmann. Constructions Navales et Industrielles de la Méditerranée (C.N.I.M.), 50 Champs Élysées, Paris — RAP 14 missile. Direction Technique des Engins (DTEn) (*see* DMA earlier).
Direction des Poudres (*see* DMA above) — explosives, shells and small-arms ammunition. Aérospatiale (*see* above) — helicopters; SS-11, ENTAC and HOT anti-tank missiles.

In the last five years, these factories have provided the army with an extensive range of new and high-quality equipment, particularly for the armoured, artillery and missile units. Some equipment has been jointly produced with German manufacturers.

Equipment Suppliers

The major items of equipment supplied to the French army are:

Light Aircraft: Broussard: liaison six to eight seats/casualty evacuation (two stretchers). Nord 3400: observation, two seats (Aérospatiale)

Light Helicopters: Alouette II and Alouette III; under replacement by SA341 Gazelle (Aérospatiale) which carries 4 HOT anti-tank missiles.

Heavy Helicopters: SA-330 (*hélicoptère de manœuvre*); designed to carry a section of 12 infantrymen in all-weather conditions (Aérospatiale/Westland)

Medium Tanks: AMX-30: 32.5 tons, 105mm gun, cross-country speed 21—25 mph, crew of four, equips the tank regiments in the mechanised brigades; AMX 32: 40 tons, 105mm rifled or 120mm smooth-bore is replacing

Light Tanks: AMX-13: 14.5 tons, 90mm gun (and sometimes four SS-11 anti-tank missiles), cross-country speed 25 mph, crew of three; equips the tank companies in the mechanised regiments and the light tank regiment in the motorised brigade

Armoured Cars: AMX 10 RC (105mm gun) is replacing the EBR (*Engin Blindé de Reconnaissance*): 13 tons, 90mm gun, maximum speed 60mph, crew of four; equips the reconnaissance regiments of the corps and divisions. AML (*auto-mitrailleuse légère*): 5 tons, 90mm gun or 60mm mortar, maximum speed 60 mph, crew of three; equips the armoured regiment in the alpine division.

Armoured Personnel Carriers: The AMX 10P (20mm gun, carrying a section of nine men) is replacing the AMX 13 in the mechanised battalions of the armoured division. The VAB (wheeled) equips the infantry battalions of the in infantry divisions and corps infantry regiment.

Artillery: 105mm SP howitzer on AMX 13 chassis (range 14200m); equips the infantry divisional artillery regiment, but is being replaced by 155mm TR towed howitzer. The 155mm SP howitzer on AMX 13 chassis equips the armoured divisional artillery regiment but is being replaced by the 155mm AVFI gun (on AMX 30 chassis). The 30mm anti-aircraft twin gun on AMX 13 chassis is being replaced by similar on AMX 30 chassis, supplemented by Roland missile on AMX 30 chassis.

Missiles: Besides Roland, which equips the corps air defence regiment, and Hawk, the French army employs the STRIM 89mm rocket, HOT and Milan anti-armour missiles. The corps and army tactical missile regiments are equipped with the all-French Pluton, on AMX 30 chassis, which has a 15—20KT warhead and maximum range of 120km. Pluton is under presidential control.

Engineer Equipment: There is an excellent range of bridges and ferries based on the low-pressure-tyred Gillois vehicle

Ground Surveillance. (a) *Radars:* Rasura and *Olifan* man-portable short-range radars. (b) *Radios:* PP11, PP12, man-portable company and platoon sets, 5—15 miles range

Support Weapons and Small Arms: There are five sorts of mortar — three of 120mm which equip the support company in infantry regiments and two of 80mm which are in the rifle companies. The *machine-gun* serves as both a light and medium weapon. It is the same calibre as the *rifle*. The *sub-machine-gun* is issued to over half the men in the infantry company, and the riflemen are only trained to hit targets at 200m (except for three *tireurs d'élite* who are equipped with sniper's rifles).

DRESS, DISTINCTIONS, RANK, COLOURS AND DECORATIONS

Dress

'Horizon blue', which was adopted in place of the famous red trousers and blue *capote* in 1915, gave way in the 1930s to khaki, which has been worn ever since; the present style is reminiscent of British service dress; officers wear a slightly paler colour than men. Both wear buff cotton summer uniform. The cylindrical peaked képi, in a distinctive 'Arm' colour, is still worn by officers, NCOs and certain entire units (e.g. the Legion) on formal occasions; otherwise they, with the rest of the army, wear a blue beret (red for parachutists). The *Chasseurs* wear a huge version (*la marmite*) and a dark-blue uniform. Officers have a simple evening uniform whose colour recalls 'horizon blue'. Of the magnificent full dress of the nineteenth century, the *Garde Républicaine* preserve the cuirassier and infantry versions; St-Cyr still wears its red trousers and white and red plumes (*le casoar*) and the white gloves its young men donned for battle in August, 1914; the *Polytechnique* keeps its frock coats and cocked hats and the 1st *Spahis* their red and white Moorish cloaks.

Distinctions

Soldiers indicate their regiment and arm of service in a variety of ways. Most units wear a metal pendant badge on the right

Arm		Colour	Cap Badge
Infantry		Dark blue	Flaming grenade
Foreign Legion		Grass-green and red	Legion's grenade
Chasseurs {	mécanisés		
	alpins	Yellow	Huntsman's horn
Cavalry {	Dragons	White	
	Cuirassiers	Red	
	Hussards	Light blue	Mounted knight
	Chasseurs à Cheval	Green	
Artillery		Red	Crossed cannon
Engineers		Black velvet	Breastplate and helmet
Transmissions		Black velvet	Breastplate and helmet with a 'T'
Train		Light green	—
Matériel		Light blue	—
Médical		Dark red	Rod of Aesculapius

breast pocket; designs recall the regimental history where appropriate. The beret badge, and the colour of the shoulder-straps and of a sleeve lozenge, indicate arm of service.

Parachutists wear a winged dagger in the beret; *Troupes de Marine* an anchor on their shoulder-straps. There are a number of other minor distinctions.

Rank

Rank is indicated by sleeve *chevrons* (point upmost) for NCOs, shoulder stripes (*galons*) for officers and stars for generals:

Maréchal (Field-Marshal)* — Seven gold stars
Général d'Armée (General) — Five gold stars
Général de Corps d'Armée (Lieutenant-General) — Four gold stars
Général de Division (Major-General) — Three gold stars
Général de Brigade (Brigadier) — Two gold stars
Colonel (Colonel) — Five gold stripes
Lieutenant-Colonel (Lieutenant-Colonel) — Three gold, two silver stripes
Commandant (Major)† — Four gold stripes
Capitaine (Captain) — Three gold stripes
Lieutenant (Lieutenant) — Two gold stripes
Sous-Lieutenant (2nd Lieutenant) — One gold stripe
Aspirant (Officer-Cadet) (reserve rank) — One gold stripe broken by red

Adjutant-Chef (Warrant Officer Class I) — Two thin gold stripes
Adjutant (Warrant Officer Class II) — Two thin silver stripes
Sergent-Major (Staff-Sergeant)‡ — Four gold chevrons
Sergent-Chef (Colour-Sergeant)‡ — Three gold chevrons
Sergent (Sergeant)‡ — One gold chevron
Caporal-Chef (Lance-Sergeant)§ — One gold, two red chevrons
Caporal (Corporal)§ — Two red chevrons
Soldat de 1ère Classe (Lance-Corporal) — One red chevron
Soldat de 2me Classe (Private) —

Notes: * Marshal of France is not a rank but a '*Dignité d'État*' (high State honour). It can be conferred only on a general who has led an army to victory against the enemy. Allowed to lapse after 1870, it was not conferred again until 1918; after 1945 it was conferred on Generals Leclerc, Juin and de Lattre de Tassigny. There are no living Marshals.
† Commandants known as *Chef de Bataillon* in the infantry, *Chef d'Escadrons* in the cavalry and *Chef d'Escadron* in the artillery.
‡ Substitute *Maréchal des Logis* for *Sergeant* in cavalry and artillery.
§ Substitute *Brigadier* for *Caporal* in cavalry and artillery.

Colours

Each French unit '*formant corps*' (having a permanent and constitutional existence) possesses a tricolour standard or colour, appropriately inscribed. It is carried on ceremonial parades and may be 'decorated', in token of the unit's performance in battle, with the *Légion d'Honneur, Médaille Militaire*, etc.

Decorations

French awards for bravery or for meritorious service are: the *Légion d'Honneur* (five classes), the *Médaille Militaire* (for bravery or victorious generalship only); *Croix de guerre; Croix de la Valeur Militaire* (Algeria). All are awarded both to officers and men.

CURRENT DEVELOPMENTS

The French army, which at the end of World War II had lost almost everything of an army's substance — modern equipment, trained soldiers, reserves, reputation — has remade itself and its name during the intervening years in the most impressive fashion. The convulsions brought on by the Algerian war may now be seen as temporary — though the army did so much to create the French empire, its centre of gravity has always been in the *métropole*, to which its heart has now returned. To a notable degree however, the post-war army has been 'Gaullist' in spirit. Its nucleus was the Free French Forces which rallied to the General after 1940 and returned with him to France in 1944; despite their subsequent disagreements, it was the army which recalled him to power in 1958.

The army is on a noticeably easier footing with the nation than is the case, say, in Germany. Despite the high proportion of the annual class actually conscripted (about 300,000 out of 400,000 for the three services), a recent poll revealed that more than 50% of young Frenchmen accept the principle of National Service and there are few conscientious objectors (objection is very difficult to establish, however: it was only legitimised by law in 1968 and successful objectors have to serve 2 years instead of 1 year, as non-combatants). The *lycée* riots of March and April, 1973 against the new conscription law (which lowered the term of service 1 year) were a middle-class protest against a restriction of deferments (*le sursis*) for university students — originally demanded after *les événements* of 1968, by representatives of the middle-class students, to reduce the 'unfair' burden which fell on working-class youth. The working classes and the army are equally insistent that, given 1 years' service, all conscripts must take their turn between 18 and 21 years of age. The army declares it impossible to run units full of 25 year-old married men with university degrees. The working classes know that many graduates, in consequence, escape military service altogether.

The concentration of defence expenditure on the creation of the strategic forces (nuclear ballistic missiles, bombers and submarines) has deprived the army of much of the equipment it would have liked to receive during the last 5 years. Its field forces (the *forces de manœuvre* and *d'intervention*) are nevertheless among the very best equipped and trained in Europe, and the current thinking about its deployment has, since the tacit abandonment of the Gaullist '*tous azimuths*' strategy in the late 1960s, brought its operational plans back into line with those of the Western alliance.

REORGANISATION

Important organisational changes, still not wholly completed, were introduced in 1977. The aim of the changes is to abolish the difference of function between the *Forces de Manœuvre, D.O.T.* and *Forces d'Intervention* and to increase the number of operational formations.

The number of Military Regions has been reduced to six. The number of divisions has been increased to fifteen, of which eight are armoured, four infantry, one parachute, one alpine and one amphibious. The alpine and parachute divisions are the existing 27th and 11th, the latter unchanged in strength. All the other divisions are smaller: the armoured divisions consist of two tank battalions of four tank squadrons each and two infantry battalions each of two tank squadrons and two infantry companies in APCs. The infantry divisions consist of an armoured car squadron and three infantry companies in wheeled APCs. The alpine division consists of six alpine battalions. Except in the parachute division, the brigade is abolished.

Three divisions (1st, 3rd and 5th, all armoured) are stationed in Germany, instead of two as before. Of the others, 4th, 6th, 7th and 10th Armoured are stationed in the Sixth Military Region (eastern France); 2nd and 8th Armoured and 12th Infantry in the First and Second Military Regions (central and northern France); 14th Infantry and 27th Alpine in the Fifth Military Region (south-eastern France); 11th Parachute and 15th Infantry in the Fourth Military Region (south-western France); and the 9th *Division d'Infanterie de Marine* in the Third Military Region (north-western France).

The headquarters of the Military Regions are: First, Paris; Second, Lille; Third, Rennes; Fourth, Bordeaux; Fifth, Lyon; Sixth, Metz. The four new divisions which will form the new *I Corps* (4th, 6th, 7th and 10th, which were formed in 1977–8) have their headquarters at Nancy, Strasbourg, Besançon and Chalons, respectively. The 9th, 14th and 15th, have their headquarters at St-Malo, Lyon and Limoges. The Alpine Division has its headquarters at Grenoble.

The most recent formation is the 31st Brigade, based near Marseilles, dedicated to amphibious/airborne intervention in the Mediterranean region.

Since the last edition of *World Armies*, the army has undergone an extensive re-equipment, which continues. Although its organisation better suits it to operations on a projected nuclear rather than conventional battlefield, the last five years have seen it raised to a new level of efficiency and aptitude.

John Keegan

GABON*

HISTORY AND INTRODUCTION

Gabon, along with most of France's colonies in Africa, attained independence in 1960, but because of its small size and considerable mineral wealth has maintained very close links with France, in whose hands the exploitation of Gabon's uranium, oil and manganese very largely lie. It was because of these interests that French forces intervened in Gabon's internal affairs in 1964; the President, Leon Mba, had been arrested by a group of 150 soldiers led by three subalterns and a gendarmerie leiutenant. The small French garrison of 150 'community troops' was invited by the Vice-President to rescue President Mba and restore his government, which, with the aid of some reinforcements from Dakar, they quickly achieved. Since that time there have been no further military challenges to President Mba or to his successor, President Bongo. Nevertheless, the latter has sought to reduce France's monopoly position in Gabon's defence and defence supply arrangements without alienating France, a policy pursued with some success.

The Bongo government is however becoming increasingly authoritarian and its security service has acquired a very unpleasant reputation for arbitrary arrests of critics of the regime.

STRENGTH AND BUDGET

Population: 700,000 (approximate) of which the largest ethnic group is the Fang who total 200,000 (approximately)

Armed Forces: 2,000 (1,500 Army, 200 Navy, 300 Air Force), plus a para-military security force of 1,000 a gendarmerie of 1,700 and a presidential guard of 500.

GNP: $3,700,000,000

Defence Expenditure: Not known

COMMAND AND CONSTITUTIONAL STATUS

The President of the Republic, Omar Bongo, is Commander-in-Chief. The Minister for Defence is J. M. Epigat. The Chief of Staff is General H. G. Pounah, and the Gendarmerie commander is General A. Nzong.

ROLE, COMMITMENT, DEPLOYMENT AND RECENT OPERATIONS

No special role or commitment is perceived for the Gabon army other than general internal and external security; the para-commando company of the Gabon army was however despatched to the Shaba Province of Zaire from June to November 1978 as part of the pan-African force.

* For general notes on African armies, see Appendix 1.

ORGANISATION

The Gabon army comprises one large all-arms battalion, eight independent infantry companies together with an engineer company, a 'paracommando' company and a reconnaissance company. The army's headquarters, the logistic, reconnaissance and paracommando companies are all in Libreville; the other company detachments are at Mouila, Oyem, France-ville, Tchibanga, Makokou, Pana and Cocobeach. A small women's unit exists, but may be one of part-time reservists only.

The Presidential Guard is better equipped, possessing light field and anti-aircraft artillery – all French 75mm, 40mm and 20mm weapons. It is stationed in Libreville. Certain aircraft of the air force are included in the Guard.

The gendarmerie is commanded from Libreville and is divided into brigades. The Northern Brigade has companies at Libreville, Makokou and Oyem; the Southern Brigade has companies at Port Gentil, Lambaréné, Mouila and Tchibanga; and the Eastern Brigade has a company at Moanda with detachments at Franceville and Koula Moutou.

RECRUITMENT, TRAINING AND RESERVES

The ethnic composition of the army has been estimated at 40% Fang, 40% Bapounou and 20% Omyene and others. Training assistance is provided by France and a close relationship exists between the French garrison and the Gabon Army; both for example parade on occasions such as July 14th or Armistice Day. Gabon personnel also train in the USA, Morocco, Senegal, the Ivory Coast and West Germany.

The gendarmerie's training school is located at Owendo.

EQUIPMENT AND ARMS INDUSTRY

The Army has sixteen Brazilian Cascavel and fifteen Panhard AML armoured cars, both equipped with 90mm guns, six US Commando and twelve French Berliet VXB-170 armoured troop carriers, French 81mm mortars and 106mm rocket launchers. Some elderly British Ferret armoured vehicles may also be still in service. Anti-aircraft weapons include ten 37mm and two 40mm guns. Some of these artillery and mortar equipments are, according to one report, maintained by the Presidential Guard. The para-commando company is equipped with Chinese AK-47 rifles. Reports not yet confirmed suggest that fifteen HE-60 armoured troop carriers, nine AML-60 armoured cars and an unspecified number of 105mm howitzers may be on order. A late report does, however, confirm an order of five Cadillac Gage light armoured cars for the Presidential Guard.

The Air Force possesses a strike capacity with its seven Mirage-5 fighter bombers. An interesting recent addition is four Brazilian EMBRAER EMB-11 patrol aircraft which can be used for maritime reconnaissance, ECM operations or even as air to ground rocket launchers. Also in service are one Hercules two 'stretched' Super-Hercules, three Douglas C-47 and three Nord Noratlas transport aircraft, seven smaller communication and liaison machines, four Puma and three Alouette helicopters.

RANK, DRESS AND DISTINCTIONS

Uniforms and the rank structure follow the French model, including the *képi*. Two national orders exist, the Order of the Equatorial Stav and the National Order.

CURRENT DEVELOPMENTS

Until the Portuguese revolution Gabon's small size and belief that France would secure her frontiers kept her armed forces small in scale. The events in Angola and the continuing apparent leftward move of Congo-Brazzaville appear to have been the main factors leading to the sizeable increases in military and air expenditure of recent years.

Lloyd Mathews

GAMBIA

In the colonial era 'The Gambia Company' of the Royal West African Frontier existed in peacetime, and Gambian contingents participated with other British West African troops in the German East African campaign of World War I and the Italian East African and Burma campaigns of World War II.

When Gambia became independent, in 1965 the government of the time decided the new state would not need an army and the company was disbanded. A company-sized detachment of the Gambia Police, styled the Field Force, was raised by voluntary recruitment in its stead, and was expanded over the years to a total of some 350—400. Some of its officers, and on occasions detachments of the Force, trained in Britain, and its equipment extended to eight Ferret scout cars, four US M-20 armoured utility vehicles and 3.5 rocket launchers. But the external defence of Gambia was from independence, seen to be based upon a defence treaty, duly negotiated and signed, with Senegal.

Gambia enjoyed remarkable political stability until June 1981 when some 130 members of the Police Field Force mutinied, attempting to seize power and instal a radical regime as a protest against the conservatism and *immobilisme* of Gambia's politics. Senegalese troops were called upon by Gambia's President, Sir Daudi Jawara; these, assisted it is said by British specialist personnel flown out and tasked to rescue Jawara's family restored order and suppressed the mutiny, though not without difficulty and bloodshed. The event, however, brought into immediacy the question of the long-term future of Gambia as a viable independent state (the present population total is an estimated 60,000) a question partly resolved by the decision to form a confederal union with Senegal. An agreement has been negotiated, details and procedures are at the time of writing being finalised. They appear to provide for a loose association, both states retaining separate sovereignty and the President of Senegal and the President of Gambia being President and Vice President respectively of the Confederation which is to have a confederal assembly selected by the legislatures of the two component areas, these legislatures to survive. An economic and monetary union is also envisaged. In respect of the armed forces, the President of the Confederation is to assume the direction of the armed forces and be responsible for overall confederal defence and security, but the President of Gambia remaining Commander-in-Chief of local Gambian forces.

In the meantime Gambia's defence lies in Senegal's hands, the Field Force having been disbanded; a new gendarmerie is to be raised in due course.

Lloyd Mathews

GERMAN DEMOCRATIC REPUBLIC

HISTORY AND INTRODUCTION

Although any German armed force is necessarily the inheritor of a long and immensely powerful military tradition, and in this the *Nationale Volksarmee* is no exception, its immediate origins are recent. Exactly how recent is a matter of dispute, depending on the significance allotted to successive measures of militarisation of the police force instituted in the Soviet zone between 1945 and 1952. By the latter date, however, the existence of an embryo national army on East German soil was, though forcefully denied by the Soviet government, undisguisable. It took the form of the *Kasernierte Volkspolizei* (Barracked People's Police), equipped with ex-*Wehrmacht* weapons, recruited in many cases from returned prisoners-of-war and numbering about 80,000 men organised into six divisions. Its recruitment was by voluntary enlistment and, though many of the very large number of deserters from it who made their way to the West revealed that they had volunteered in Russia in order to secure their release from prisoners-of-war camps, the force did attract, particularly at officer level, numbers of veteran communists, young party enthusiasts, or genuine converts from the traditional military class who were inspired by the challenge of creating a 'people's army' for a German communist State.

The motives of the Soviet government, on the one hand, and of the communist leadership of the Soviet zone, on the other, in permitting and fostering such a creation, are difficult to analyse. The Russians had, and still have, a genuine and understandable fear of German armed force; the German Communist Party (or Socialist Unity Party (S.E.D.) as the Communist and Social Democrat Parties were known after their shotgun union in 1945) equally had good reason to fear a reborn German army, the ruthlessness of military reaction against the 'popular' movements of 1848 and 1918 being a major theme of its own folklore.

The explanation of Soviet policy would seem to lie at several levels: a desire to reduce its own military budget by allowing East Germany to provide partly for its own defence against the 'aggressive NATO alliance'; a recognition that, for the authenticity of the sovereignty of an East German Communist State (whose creation was announced in October, 1949) to be accepted abroad, it should possess its own armed forces; a preference for domestic disturbances (should they arise) to be put down by German, rather than Russian, troops; a determination to match step-by-step all West German measures of remilitarisation, even if that should mean at times anticipating them. Russia has always represented each new departure in her East German policy as a response to an allegedly similar development in the Federal Republic; she has also been careful not to violate the strict letter of the Nuremberg Judgements — the East German army, for example, possessing in theory no General Staff, since that body was declared criminal by the International Military Tribunal.

The attitude of the S.E.D. (*Sozialistische Einheitsparte Deutschland*) was probably more straightforward. Being at the outset neither chosen nor loved by the population of which the Soviets had made it, within carefully restricted limits, the master, it was anxious to provide itself with a native armed force which would deter demonstrations of dissent and safeguard the regime from violence should it

break out. Its leaders, most of whom had spent long periods in Russia, believed that they knew how the party could bind the infant army to its will without danger of subsequently losing control of it.

The evolution of the Barracked Police into the People's Army (including air and sea branches) had several significant landmarks. The original Alert Units (*Bereitseinheiten* — a word, like many others in the East German military vocabulary, with Nazi echoes) were at first under regional (*Bezirk*) control, but in October, 1948 were centralised under the Ministry of the Interior. The First Minister was Willi Stoph, with Wilhelm Zaisser ('General Gomez' of the Spanish Civil War) as his Commander of Barracked Police, and Heinz Hoffman, also an ex-International Brigadier and a graduate of the Moscow Frunze Academy, as Deputy Commander (Zaisser, subsequently First Minister of State Security, 1950, was purged for 'defeatism' after the East German rising of June, 1953). In 1952, following a Soviet appeal for all-German elections and a promise of 'her own armed force' to a re-united and neutralised Germany — an appeal apparently intended to halt West German rearmament — there was a noticeable relaxing of Soviet and S.E.D. attempts to camouflage the existence of the Barracked Police. It was given Soviet-style military uniforms and two additional armed bodies — the Factory Combat Groups (*Kampfgruppen*) and the Sport and Technology Association (*Gesellschaft für Sport und Technik*) — came into being. Despite this strengthening of the military resources of the DDR, it was to suffer in the following year its most humiliating setback: a countrywide rising, most violent in East Berlin, against its policies and legitimacy. Over 300,000 people took part in strikes and demonstrations and, to add to the alarm of the S.E.D., they were joined by a significant number of its own soldiers, who did not as a body appear disposed to put down the disturbances.

The 1953 rising set back the evolution of the East German armed forces. Training and organisational development was curtailed and the Soviets took back the Air Force's MiG-15 jet fighters. The lasting distrust it created, combined with the Russian's distrust of Germans, helped to create the especially thorough Soviet controls that the East German armed forces of today operate under.

Among subsequent recuperative measures instituted by the party, which included an expansion of the combat groups, was a thorough purge of the army: about 12,000 men, out of 80,000 serving, were dismissed. There has subsequently been no evidence of serious disaffection. This may in part be attributed to the ending of the army's ambiguous status in 1956, when on January 18th, 12 days after West Germany's induction of her first conscripts, the act creating the National People's Army and the Ministry of National Defence was carried by the *Volkskammer* (Parliament). Traditional uniforms were reintroduced at the same time, Soviet advisers were henceforth progressively withdrawn from units, and on January 28th the Political Consultative Committee of the Warsaw Pact admitted the N.V.A. to its United Armed Forces.

Since 1965, the N.V.A. has belonged to the Pact's First Strategic Echelon — those forces which would immediately take the field in the event of conflict with NATO forces. This promotion of the army to the first rank of Soviet-bloc troops is chiefly due to the increase in quality and reliability of its soldiers brought about by the introduction of universal conscription in 1962 (Act of Parliament, January 24th), a measure made possible by the building of the Berlin Wall in the previous August (the constant exodus of men of military age to the West via West Berlin was one of the factors which drove the S.E.D. to this extreme measure). But the N.V.A.'s skill in handling modern Soviet equipment, with which Russia has been increasingly generous, has contributed also to its gain in prestige and efficiency. Because of its small size – both absolute and proportionate to the population – it is the smallest of the Pact armies – the N.V.A. can never play a major role in Soviet strategy. Nor, given what we know of Soviet policy towards East Germany, is it likely that Russia would wish that it should. Nevertheless, it has become within the last 10 years an army of adequate quality, well-equipped and, at officer level at least, wholly loyal to the regime which it serves. This loyalty is in any case assured by the remarkably complex system of control and supervision which the party has embedded in the army's structure and which is described in another section. It is an index of its reliability that the East German government apparently insisted, and the Soviet government certainly agreed, that part of it should be used in the invasion of Czechoslovakia in 1968.

Technically, the *Nationale Volksarmee* is a tri-service organisation, the army (*Landstreitkräfte*) being only one element in it with the sea and air branches. Of these, however, the army proper is by far the most important. Unlike the old German army, however, whose insistence on being the 'sole bearer of arms within the State' underlay its conflict with Hitler, it is not the only armed force upon which the regime can call. The other militarised offshoots of the People's Police (*Deutsche Volkspolizei*), namely the Frontier Troops (*Grenztruppen*), the Alert Units (*Bereitseinheiten*) and the Guard Regiment of the Ministry of State Security (*Wach Regiment der M.S.G.*), together with the combat groups, provide the party with an ultimate counter-balance against the army's power, a feature of political organisation common to all States of the Soviet bloc.

In its own series of 'checks and balances', East Germany has spawned a remarkable number of paramilitary organisations.

The Border Troops, about 50,000 strong, are under the Defence Ministry, but with their own chain of command, service schools, and separate authorities. They are not, for example, under the peacetime operational command of the Military Districts where they are located. Until 1974, they were part of the Army.

The Frontier Troops (H.Q. Plauen, near Karl Marx Stadt (Chemnitz) are directly controlled by the Minister. The paramilitary forces, including the combat groups, are under the orders of the Regional Commands (*Bezirk-Kommandos*) of the People's Police, answering to the Police Praesidium in Berlin–Basdorf.

In addition to the Alert Units, the People's Police fields the Transport Police (of eight districts, armed with infantry weapons and RPG-7s), the *Schutzpolizei*, the Traffic Police, the Passport and Registrations Police, and the Criminal Police. Only the last of these is equivalent to a Western police force. It is also considered the least important.

In addition to commanding its own armed force in the 'Felix Dzerzhinsky' Guard regiment of six battalions intended for internal security duties, the Ministry for State Security also controls the Main Adminstration for Reconnaissance (HfA), the main East German espionage arm.

The Combat Groups (*Kampfgruppen*) started as an unarmed party militia, but have now become a 500,000 man territorial army, about half of which could be deployed.

They are subject, through the 14 *Bezirke* regional headquarters to the Ministry of the Interior. Its primary function is internal security. It would also be used for rear area security, service support, and in secondary sectors in any future conflict.

The Society for Sport and Technology (GST) is modelled on the Soviet DOSAAF. It is responsible for pre-conscription training of youth and also for reservist training. It has 450,000 members and is responsible to the Ministry of National Defence.

Civil Defence forces, under the Ministry of National Defence, have a cadre of about 3,000, but will coordinate the activities of a wide range of military, paramilitary, party, and civilian functions in time of war.

The Navy controls most of the assets of the former Coastal Border brigade. As well as controlling Border Troops and Water Police elements, the Navy has committed five beach patrol battalions, two 'divisions' of two companies each afloat, one boat group, 34 vessels including 18 Kondor-I class coastal minesweepers, *Samlet* coastal surface-to-surface missiles, and reportedly 152mm coastal guns.

STRENGTH AND BUDGET

Population: 16,750,000
Army: 113,000 active (including 67,000 conscripts), 250,000 reserves
Air Force: 38,000 (including 15,000 conscripts), 30,000 reserves, 374 combat aircraft
Navy: 15,000 (including 10,000 conscripts), 25,000 reserves. 200 ships, mainly small craft
Border Troops: 50,000
Ministry for State Security Guard Regiment: 6,000
Police Alert Units: 15,000
Transport Police: 8,500
Kampfgruppen: 500,000
GNP (1981): $96.8–142.13 billion
Defence Expenditure (1982): $7.39 billion

COMMAND AND CONSTITUTIONAL STATUS

Command of the 'people's army' is complicated, it being subordinated not only to the authority of the State but also to the Central Committee of the Socialist Unity Party, and its Politburo to the United Command of the Warsaw Pact and, for operational purposes, to the Commander of the Group of Soviet Forces in Germany (possibly also of neighbouring Soviet Groups).

Constitutionally, the army is immediately subordinate to the Minister of National Defence who, according to the act creating it, organises and leads the N.V.A. in accordance with the laws, decrees and decisions of the People's Chamber. Its tasks are 'decided by the Council of Ministers'. As in most communist countries, however, it is in the party's rather than the State's organs that real power resides, ministers also holding senior posts in the Central Committee and possibly in the Politburo, where policy is ultimately decided. In East Germany, the key agency of the military system appears to be the Commission for National Security, a dependancy of the Politburo, of which Erich Honecker is Chief. He is also Secretary of the State's superior military policy-making body, the National Defence Council (of which Stoph is Chairman), but the routine work of his Politburo Commission is carried out by the Security Department of the Central Committee of the Party (of which Stoph is again Chairman and Honecker First Secretary).

Party control over the military is even more thorough than in other Warsaw Pact armies. The Main Political Administration of the Armed Forces, headed by General Heinz Kessler, former Chief of Armed Forces Main Staff. The Main Political Administration has a unique dual status as a division of both the Ministry of National Defence (with General Kessler as a Deputy Minister of Defence) and a Department of the Central Committee of the Socialist Unity Party. The Soviet-style political officers, present down to company level, are responsible to the Main Political Administration. Parallel with this are Party organisations at all levels of command (virtually all officers are party members) and organisations of the Free German Youth (FDJ), the Party's youth organisation. Reportedly, 80% of the troops are members. These organisations are responsible to the Central Committee through the Main Political Administration.

The State Security Service (SSD), responsible to the Ministry of the Interior, acts as a check on the Political Administration with a network of agents and informers throughout the military, similar to the use of the KGB in Soviet units.

The units and the personnel of the N.V.A. are supervised, therefore, with a strictness and thoroughness unknown and probably intolerable to Western soldiers. Control, moreover, is not merely passive; because political education (4 hours weekly for soldiers; 8 hours monthly for officers) is compulsory, the party exercises through that medium a positive check on the political motivation and enthusiasm of all service personnel. An even more positive check is provided through the surveillance of the Ministry of State Security; it maintains a liaison officer in every formation and unit down to battalion level besides, it is authoritatively reported, running a network of clandestine informers throughout the services at every level. They report to one of the main branches of the Ministry of National Defence (the Administration 2000) which is in effect an office of the Ministry of State Security, reporting to its own minister, and through him back to the Politburo. It is also believed to be in liaison with the Russian K.G.B.

The formal staff structure of the N.V.A. is unlike that of a Western army. Because the Nuremberg Tribunal declared the German General Staff a criminal organisation, it has none in the orthodox sense. The field force is commanded directly by the Minister of National Defence (together with the navy and air force combat units) as are the Administrations (British 'Directorates') of the various arms – artillery, armour and engineers – and certain specialised departments like the (excellent) military publishers, the military prosecutor and the Sports and Technology Association. The Main Staff, which approaches most nearly the status of a Western General Staff, is one of five principal sub-divisions of the Ministry of National Defence (excluding the air force and navy sub-divisions) which are headed by Deputy Ministers. Two of these are supply and procurement branches, one is the training branch, another the Chief Political Administration already mentioned; the last is the Main Staff, whose duties are operational planning, intelligence, control of signals and the co-ordination of communications with the Warsaw Pact networks, finance, recruitment and records. It thus approximates to the 'A' and 'Q' branches of a British General Staff, or the G-1, 2 and 4 of an American General Staff, without its G (British) and G-2 (American) elements. The oddity of the arrangement is explained by the Soviet's resolve to keep operational control of the N.V.A. above that of all the satellite armies in its own hands.

Operationally, the N.V.A., it is believed, would be commanded thus: the three divisions of Military District V would come under the orders of the Commander of the Soviet

Group of Forces in Germany, which has its H.Q. at the old German Army Headquarters at Wunsdorf—Zossen; the three divisions of Military District III would come under the orders of the Soviet Commander of the Northern Group, headquarters at Liegnitz, Poland.

The East German armed forces are much more subject to external command than any other Warsaw Pact nation. They are the only armed force wholly subordinated to Warsaw Pact command in peacetime. The bi-lateral Status of Forces Agreement with the Soviet Union allows the Soviets substantial control. Soviet troops positions and movements are outside East German control, unlike in Poland and Hungary. Further, the Supreme Commander of Group Soviet Forces Germany can declare a State of Emergency in East Germany in response to external and internal conditions and then eliminate any threat – the only limitation that he consult with the East German government. This gives the Soviet Army basic veto powers in East German affairs.

The Joint Warsaw Pact command gives the Soviets a great deal of influence over East German day-to-day matters. There are 80 Soviet staff officers reportedly in the East German Defence Ministry and Soviet generals are included in high-level planning discussions. Soviet officers are attached down to division level in peacetime, regimental level in time of war, and provide an alternative chain of command.

The closeness of the Soviet control of the East German Army extends even to the soldier's oath: on joining the colours, he swears to stand by the USSR and world socialism.

ROLE, COMMITMENT, DEPLOYMENT AND RECENT OPERATIONS

Role

The N.V.A.'s original role, in the words of an expert, was 'outwardly to be a symbol of the sovereignty of the German Democratic Republic and ... a countermeasure to the *Bundeswehr*. Inside East Germany it was to be accepted by the population as a continuation of traditions and to serve as a reliable support for the regime'. Since 1965 (at the latest) the N.V.A. has belonged to the First Strategic Echelon of the Warsaw Pact, that group of forces earmarked for immediate operations in the event of military conflict with NATO in central Europe. Its field force is sufficient to form two Soviet-style armies (equivalent to NATO corps), a grouping to which the Pact allows independent operational status, but it is more likely that it would operate as two groups of three divisions within a Soviet front (equivalent to a NATO army group) under direct Soviet command. The Frontier Troops of the N.V.A. would provide its covering force in wartime, in peace their role is that of preventing free passage across the DDR's borders in any direction. The role of the other paramilitary and security forces includes the deterrence and suppression of internal disorder, the provision of counterweights to the army and the militarisation of the population for political ends.

Commitment

The N.V.A. is an independent force only in theory. In actuality, it is the most totally integrated force within overall Warsaw Pact planning – the price of being in the 'front line', as declared in 1965. N.V.A. units, which will probably be committed in army or, at very least, divisional sized forces under Soviet operational command in wartime, leave the territorial defence mission to the paramilitary forces.

Deployment

The six divisions of the field force are stationed in two military districts: III (Leipzig) and V (Neubrandenburg). The remaining operational units come directly under the Ministry of Defence's headquarters at Strausberg, east of Berlin. This deployment produces a heavy concentration of military strength in the northern and southern districts and around Berlin, but little in the central area. The Magdeburg district contains no N.V.A. unit, though across it runs the direct route to Berlin from the West.

The Frontier Troops are responsible to the Minister of Defence through Frontier Troops Command at Paetz bei Koenigswursterhausen, under which are the Frontier Command North at Stendal, Frontier Command Centre at Berlin-Karlhorst, and Frontier Command South at Erfurt. Both the Centre and North commands have naval and coastal units which, together with the Navy and the Ministry of the Interior Water Police are under the Navy's operational Coastal Brigade.

Each of the three Frontier commands has six Frontier regiments and two training regiments. There are also two independent regiments to cover the Polish and Czech frontiers. An independent border crossing-point regiment handles traffic to and from Berlin.

The 21 Alert Units (*Berettseinheiten*) of the People's Police are deployed one to each of the 14 Districts (*Bezirke*), with one extra in Magdeburg, Halle, Leipzig and Potsdam, and these are under the control of the Police Praesidium in Berlin—Basdorf.

The Hundreds and Battalions (General and Heavy) of the paramilitary 'Combat Groups of the Working Class' *Kampfgruppen der Arbeiterklasse*) are centred on the populated areas which provide their membership; likewise the Basic Organisations of the Sport and Technology Associations and the Order Groups of the Free German Youth (F.D.J.).

Military Districts (*Armies*)   Each contains two motor rifle divisions and one armoured division (all on the Soviet establishment), together with army troops: one SCUD surface-to-surface missile brigade; one artillery regiment, one air-defence regiment, one signals regiment, one artillery-locating regiment, one engineer battalion, one anti-tank battalion, one transport battalion, one nuclear—chemical warfare company and one (non-operational) NCO training regiment. The units of Northern Army (H.Q. Neubrandenberg) are stationed as follows: 1st and 8th Motor Rifle Divisions, Potsdam and Schwerin; 9th Armoured Division, Eggesin; SCUD missile brigade, Demen; artillery and artillery-locating regiments, anti-tank battalion and NCO training regiment, Torgelow; air-defence regiment, Prenzlav; signals regiment, Neubrandenberg; engineer and transport battalions, and nuclear-chemical company, Pasewalk. One motorised rifle regiment in this area is trained in amphibious operations. The units of the Southern Army (H.Q. Leipzig) are stationed as follows: 4th and 11th Motor Rifle Divisions, Erfurt and Halle; 7th Armoured Division, Dresden; SCUD missile brigade, Hermsdorf; artillery, artillery-locating, air-defence and signals regiments, Leipzig; anti-tank battalion, Wolfen; transport battalion, Cottbus; engineer battalion, Gera; nuclear—chemical company, Grossenheim; NCO training regiments, Eilenberg. Most non-divisional units are numbered as either the 3rd or 5th, depending on which District they are stationed in.

The Ministry of Defence troops (H.Q. Strausberg) are stationed as follows: guard regiment, Eggersdorf; signals regiment, Niederlehme; railway construction regiment, Doberling; engineer regiment, Storkow; transport regiment, Strausberg; rocket brigade, Bruck; bridging and electronic-warfare regiments, Dessay; 40th and 5th 'Willi Sanger' air-borne battalion, Prora on the island of Rugen in the Baltic (these battalions are trained for unconventional warfare operations); one battalion-sized special warfare force, southern East Germany (two companies of which are equipped with M48 tanks and M113 APCs in *Bundeswehr* markings).

Recent Operations

Two divisions of the N.V.A. took part in the Soviet invasion of Czechoslovakia in 1968, under close Soviet control. They were not deployed in the populated areas and appear to have returned home after 5 days. N.V.A. divisions have taken part in major Warsaw Pact exercises.

Since the mid-1970s, East Germany has deployed substantial military and political missions abroad, considerably more than any other Warsaw Pact state. According to US Department of Defence figures, the following East German military and civilian advisors were deployed in 1981: Angola, 450; Congo, 15; Ethiopia, 550; Guinea, 125; Moxambique, 100; Tanzania, 15; Algeria, 250; Iraq, 160; North Yemen, 5; South Yemen, 325; Syria, 210; Afghanistan, 'substantial numbers' (probably several hundred). East Germans in Afghanistan are in charge of rebuilding the Kabul Regime's police and intelligence forces. The East German military advisors in Angola have been conducting extensive training of Angolan military units. There have been frequent, but unconfirmed, allegations that these East German advisors also help train SWAPO guerrilla forces for operations in Namibia.

ORGANISATION

Arms of Service

Being a new creation, the N.V.A. has a corporate organisation uncomplicated by traditional or sentimental factors. The main branches are: infantry (*Infanterie*); armour (*Panzer*); artillery and rocket troops (*Artillerie und Rakententruppen*): engineers and technical troops (*Pionere und Technische Truppen*); signals (*Nachrichten*). These are known as the 'operational' troops. The 'rear-service' (*ruckwartige Dienst*) are procurement, supply and transport troops. The medical and administrative services are also separate, as is the political service (officers only).

Operational

The East German Army is the only non-Soviet Warsaw Pact Army whose tactical unit organization — divisions and below — follow more or less exactly the Soviet model, without national adaptations.

Normally, Frontier regiments consist of three 408-man, four company battalions. Those around Berlin have a different organisation. They are armed with a full range of infantry and light anti-tank weapons and are motorised, primarily in wheeled armoured and unarmoured vehicles.

The Alert Units of the People's Police are organised as battalions with three motorised and one APC company, a heavy weapons company and a headquarters company. The four battalions line of the Guard Regiment of the Ministry of State Security are similar. This regiment also has a heavy weapons battalion and a training battalion.

The Combat Groups form either general or heavy battalions (the latter are also know as Battalions of the Regional Reserve). Each is organised into three to four hundred, of three platoons of three sections. The heavy battalions, of which about 130 exist, are motorised and have some mortars and anti-tank weapons.

The Sport and Technology Association is divided into regional unions (based on the 14 *Bezirke*, then into district unions (based on the *Kreise*), then into basic organisations, centred on factories, agricultural enterprises and schools.

RECRUITMENT, TRAINING AND RESERVES

Recruitment

Until 1962 the army was voluntarily recruited, in the early

days largely from ex-officers and soldiers of the *Wehrmacht* who, having been identified as sympathetic to the S.E.D. through their having joined the Free Germany Committee or the anti-Fascist schools in prison camp, were released directly from captivity into the People's Police. About 40–50% of N.V.A. soldiers are still volunteers but, by act of the *Volks-kammer* of January 24th, 1962, universal conscription applies in East Germany and conscripts are enrolled in all three services (including the Frontier Troops). The term of service is 18 months; would-be regulars enlist either for 'short' (3 year) or 'career' (12 year) service, but must first complete their 'basic' 18 months. But despite the notional 'universality of conscription', the full contingent is not recruited each year, and about 45% of the N.V.A. are regulars. The right of conscientious objection is partially recognised: those who refuse to bear arms because of 'religious or similar views' are conscripted into construction units (*Baueinheiten*).

Officers, originally ex-members of the *Wehrmacht* or veteran communists with military experience, are today recruited directly from secondary schools (in which case they are exempt from 'basic' service) or else are chosen from suitable conscripts or serving volunteers. School entrants must show university-entrance qualifications. Officers enlist for 10 years, the age limits for service in each rank being: captain, thirty-five; major, forty; lieutenant-colonel, forty-five; colonel, fifty; major-general, sixty-five. The N.V.A. takes pride in its claim that it now has an officer corps largely 'proletarian' in origin.

Officers were originally commissioned solely for political loyalty and often lacked professionalism – in 1956 only 11% of the officers had graduated from high school and only 2.6% had any college education. The 1960s saw increasing requirements, with the Ernst Thaelmann Academy founded in 1963 and a series of technical officer academies established in 1971. By 1974, 22% of the officers were college graduates and another 66% had the equivalent of a vocational degree. Today, all officers must pass examinations in a military-technical speciality, administration and political education, and an equivalent civilian profession.

Training

Conscripts are called up (and released) twice a year, at the beginning of December and June. Their first 4 weeks are spent in a 'recruit unit', where they learn drill and discipline; at the end of it the recruits are received into their operational units with considerable ceremony. At a parade of the whole regiment, where the band plays, each swears on the colour a long and solemn oath binding him to preserve the Soviet alliance and the cause of Socialism, and to give unconditional obedience to his superiors, under pain of 'harsh punishment ... and the contempt of the working people'. He then receives his personal weapon from a member of the local Combat Group, an act intended to symbolize the bond between the proletariat and the People's Army, and listens to an address by a local party official. A full member of his regiment, he next proceeds to 'individual' and then 'section' training in weapon handling and minor tactics; in the subsequent training periods of each of his 'military half-years' he acquires skill on a second weapon and in using a wireless set. When sufficiently trained, he takes part in the 'unit' and 'formation' training his regiment undergoes, at the appropriate stage of the 'half-year'. The emphasis of the training, as in all Soviet-bloc armies, is on offensive and night-fighting operations. Conscripts spend much time out of doors and, like all citizens of the DDR, are expected to attain very high standards of physical fitness. About a quarter of all training time is devoted to political indoctrination under the unit's political officer.

Frontier troops, selected for their political reliability, spend their first 6 months in special training units, where they are further screened by State Security, and receive 'border training' and intensive political indoctrination.

NCOs selected during their first 'half-year' of training, are sent either to the NCO training regiment of their military district (III – Eilenburg; V – Torgelow) or, since room does not allow for all, to the NCO training company of their unit. The emphasis of training seems to lie rather on the technical than the man-management side, the object being to produce a man who can look after equipment, rather than lead men.

Since 1963 officers have been trained at the Ernst Thalmann Officer School at Lobau, near Dresden. The course lasts 4 years and is run on Soviet lines, with a high emphasis on military theory and much political indoctrination; the military training is designed to fit graduates for command of a platoon. Final examinations are deemed equivalent in standard to those of higher civilian schools and qualify graduates for careers in civil administration should they leave the army.

East Germany conducts more professional military education in the Soviet Union than other Warsaw Pact nations, over 120 officers a year training at Soviet institutions, helping to maintain N.V.A. integration within Soviet concepts to an extent never achieved with any other Warsaw Pact Army.

Frontier troops officers are trained separately at the Rosa Luxemburg School at Plauen, the course lasting 3 years.

Scientific and technical officers are sent to study at the civilian engineering college at Berlin–Lichtenberg, while its civilian graduates are eligible for direct commissions.

Medical officers are commissioned directly from the Department of Military Medicine at Greifswald University, near Rostock.

Higher military training of officers of colonel and equivalent rank of all three services is at the Friedrich Engels Military Academy at Dresden (founded January 5th, 1959 and named after 'the co-founder of Marxism and first military theoretician of the working class'). The course lasts 2 years, is modelled on that of the Moscow Frunze Academy attended by several of the N.V.A.'s most senior officers, and is conducted at regimental/divisional level, its diploma being deemed equivalent to a university degree. (It is believed those officers promoted to general rank go for 2–3 years' training in Russia.)

The training of political officers, concentrated at a school at Treptow until its closure in 1961, is now conducted at special courses. The original brand of political officer, like his Soviet counterpart, caused much offence to commanders by reason of his military inexperience; political officers are now recruited solely from the active army.

For a short time the N.V.A. ran a cadet school, modelled on the Soviet military boarding schools, but it was closed in 1956 'to reduce the danger of the separation of the officer corps from other functionaries'.

Reserve

The military obligation extends from the age of eighteen to fifty for soldiers and to sixty for officers. The reserve is divided into two groups, the first of men up to thirty-five, on which the combat units would draw, the senior of older men who would staff rear services. Reservists are liable for reserve training of twenty-one months, spread over several years. The 'surplus' – those men not conscripted at eighteen because numbers exceeded requirements – are also liable for training as reservists on the same terms as ex-conscripts. Party functionaries, skilled workers and students, who are largely exempted from conscription, are particularly required to perform this sort of reserve training; party functionaries are then granted military rank commensurate with their political status. The strength of the effective reserve is calculated at 200,000 but might be as high as 350,000. East German reserve training is considered extensive and efficient by Warsaw Pact standards — much more so, in fact, than any other Pact member, including the Soviet Union.

EQUIPMENT AND ARMS INDUSTRY

The DDR has no arms industry to speak of — a deliberate measure of Soviet control — and produces only small arms (copies of Soviet models), signal and optical equipment (The best-made in the Warsaw Pact and used in many Soviet systems), transport vehicles and components. The equipment authority of the N.V.A. is the Department of Special Requirements of the State Planning Commission, headed by a major-general. It works in co-operation with the Research Council, the State Secretariat of Research and Technology and the Council of the National Economy.

Equipment of Soviet design manufactured in East Germany includes the army's 9mm Makarov pistol, the AK-47 assault rifle, the 7.62mm light and medium machine-guns, the 82mm and 120mm mortars, and the RPG-7 and SPG-9 light anti-tank missiles. There is a light mortar, the S-53 of East German design and manufacture. Otherwise, all material is imported from Russia or the Warsaw Pact states.

During the 1970s, the N.V.A.'s equipment was upgraded. It is now clear that it has the highest priority for new weapons among the Warsaw Pact states. T-72 main battle tanks (possibly Polish and Czech built) are replacing T-54/55s. Such new systems as self-propelled 122mm and 152mm self-propelled howitzers, SA-9 SAMs, and similar equipment are in service. The weapons used by the N.V.A. are not significantly different from those used by GSFG.

1,500 T-54/55 and T-72 MBTs, 1600 more in storage.
AFVs: 500 BRDM scout cars, 700 BMP IFVs, 1,000 BTR-152, -50, and -60 and MT-LB APCs.
Artillery: 122mm towed and SP, 130mm, 152mm towed and SP, BM-21 and RM-70 122mm MRLs. 24 FROG-7, 18 SCUD-B SSMs, 120mm mortars, 100mm AT guns.
AT weapons: full Soviet range, from RPG-7s up. Includes 85mm AT guns, 100mm AT guns, 73mm SPG-9, *Sagger* and Spigot ATGMs.
Infantry Weapons: full Soviet line, including RPG-18 and other late model equipment.
Air Defence: ZSU-23-4, 57mm S-60, SA-4, SA-6, SA-7, SA-9. Air Defence forces also have SA-2 and SA-3.

RANK, DRESS AND DISTINCTIONS

Ranks and Their Badges

Officers
Armeegeneral — Four stars on woven gold and silver shoulder straps
Oberstgeneral — Three stars on woven gold and silver shoulder straps
Generalleutnant — Two stars on woven gold and silver shoulder straps
Generalmajor — One star on woven gold and silver shoulder straps
Oberst — Three stars on woven silver shoulder straps
Oberstleutnant — Two stars on woven silver shoulder straps
Major — One star on woven silver shoulder straps
Hauptmann — Four stars on flat silver shoulder straps
Oberleutnant — Three stars on flat silver shoulder straps

Leutnant — Two stars on flat silver shoulder straps
Unterleutnant — One star on flat silver shoulder straps

Soldiers
Stabsfeldwebel — Three stars on grey shoulder straps edged with silver
Oberfeldwebel — Two stars on grey shoulder straps edged with silver
Feldwebel — One star on grey shoulder straps edged with silver
Unteroffizier — Silver edged shoulder strap
Stabsgefreiter — Two stripes on shoulder strap
Gefreiter — One stripe on shoulder strap
Soldat — —

Dress

Successive changes in the style of the N.V.A.'s dress provide one of the clearest examples of how deep and subtle is the significance — symbolic and ideological — of a national military uniform. The Barracked Police originally wore police blue. In 1952, however, on the party's unveiling of the military status, they adopted uniforms of Soviet colour and cut. These proved unpopular both with their wearers and, more importantly, with the East German population, and in 1956 therefore, on the official declaration of the N.V.A.'s existence, a uniform almost indistinguishable from the *Wehrmacht*'s field-grey (itself descended from the combat dress of World War I and preserved by Seeckt during the years of the Hundred Thousand Man Army as a promise of renaissance), was introduced. The colour chosen, stone-grey (*steingrau*), was slightly different and the helmet adopted was an experimental model of 1944 rather than the notorious coalscuttle, but in almost every other respect, including such details as badges of rank, it echoed exactly the garb of the past — the past of the Hitler years as much as of the Second Reich. This required political justification and in his speech proclaiming the existence of the new army Stoph was at pains to offer it. 'There are important progressive traditions in the military history of our people, which found their expression in the uniform,' he argued. 'German imperialism and fascism . . . degraded (it) as a symbol of military and national honour . . . . In the National People's Army, the German uniform will have a true patriotic meaning as an expression of resolute readiness for the defence of our democratic achievements. In these uniforms, but with red armbands, the armed workers in 1918 chased out the Kaiser; the Hamburg workers, miners from the Ruhr, workers and peasants from Saxony and Thuringia fought against the Nationalist *Freikorps* and the reactionary *Reichswehr*. In these uniforms in World War II many officers and soldiers came forward in the National Committee 'Free Germany' against the Hitler Fascist Army.' However disingenuously this speech reads, it does seem that the S.E.D.'s decision to revert to the traditional uniform has been a successful one in endearing the N.V.A. to the people. However, recent changes in style, notably the abandonment of the old-fashioned high collar in favour of open lapels with a shirt and tie beneath, suggest that the leadership has decided that its use of the Seeckt–*Wehrmacht* style was too blatant an attempt to establish a false continuity.

Among other traditional uniform details worn are the facing colours (*Waffenfarbe*) of the different arms: Armour, pink; Artillery, red; Engineers, black; Infantry, white; Technical troops, black; Signals, lemon; Medical Corps, dark blue; Rear Services, dark green; Frontier Troops, light green; Air Defence, light blue.

Parachutists wear a light-blue beret. The Guard Regiment wears a traditional-style ribbon above the left cuff, reading

N.V.A. WACHREGIMENT (the State Security Guard Regiment wears a similar one, reading *WACHREGT. F. DZIER-ZYNSKI*, the name of the founder of the Russian secret police). Bandsmen wear traditional silver 'swallow's nest' epaulettes, and officers carry *Wehrmacht*-pattern sabres on ceremonial parades and wear the old black and silver girdle. They wear a Nazi-style ceremonial dagger on formal occasions. The regimental colour of each regiment of the N.V.A. is a black—red—yellow tricolour, gold fringed, mounted on a traditional spear-headed staff, bearing the insignia of the State on a roundel encircled with the words 'For the defence of Workers' and Peasants' Power'.

Distinctions

The DDR awards many State decorations. Of the military, the most important are: the Scharnhorst Order, the Battle Order of Merit (three classes), the Medal of Comradeship in Arms (three classes), the Merit Medal (three classes) and the Medal for Faithful Service (three classes — 15, 10 and 5 years). Soviet medals won fighting *against* Germany in World War II may be, and are, worn by a (decreasing) number of senior officers; medals won in the *Wehrmacht* may not be worn (as they may be in the *Bundeswehr*).

CURRENT DEVELOPMENTS

Perhaps the most interesting thing about the N.V.A. is that it should exist at all. The Russians, for the best of reasons, have a powerful fear of Germans in arms, and feel an apparently genuine anxiety over the existence of the *Bundeswehr*. Indeed they have always pretended that the N.V.A. came into existence only after, and because of, the *Bundeswehr*'s creation, and though examination reveals this pretence for what it is, it is difficult to produce explanations which are convincing to Western minds of Russia's foster fatherhood of the N.V.A. Economy is a more obvious one, and the desire to discipline East German youth another — though it is partially invalidated by the delay in the introduction of conscription. Perhaps the real reasons are less tangible: the view that East Germany required an army as proof to the world of her sovereign status; the ideological requirement for a State founded on the basis of 'struggle' to possess the means to fight (it is significant that all the satellite States possess armies as well as police forces); a suspicion that German militarism was so deep-rooted as to make any German regime which lacked its own army fundamentally 'illegitimate' in the eyes of its subjects.

Whatever their reasons, the Russians have nevertheless taken steps to see that the N.V.A. remains, proportionate to population, the smallest of the Warsaw pact armies (1 soldier:170 citizens as against 1:150 in Poland; 1:100 in Czechoslovakia; and 1:70 in Bulgaria); in absolute terms it is the second smallest of all, only 10,000 stronger than that of Hungary, which has only 10,000,000 instead of 17,000,000 people. They have also provided domestic counterweights to it, in the form of large security forces under the control of the Ministries of the Interior and State Security, numbering 70,000, and of the Combat Groups. Although much political emphasis is laid on the popular ownership of the Peoples' Army and its warm relationship with the proletariat,

the existence of these independent forces, standard as they are to communist regimes, testifies to the S.E.D.'s and the Russians' fundamental lack of trust in the subservience of *any* German army.

The East German military and paramilitary forces have a value different from those existing in other Warsaw Pact states is that they exist independent of national traditions and missions to a greater extent than any other nation in the Pact. There has been more of a conscious effort to try and link the military and paramilitary services with the Party and the State as one. Thus for every 10,000 GDR citizens (in 1978—79 figures) 433 are members of military or paramilitary organisations (not including reserves). The comparative figure is 185 for the Soviet Union, 210 for Czechoslovakia and 115 in Poland.

Virtually all males aged 18—26 pass through East German military or paramilitary ranks, making them a powerful force for socialisation and indoctrination.

East German law recognises conscientious objection, the only Warsaw Pact country to do so. Conscientious objectors serve in construction battalions which are normally unarmed, but they are not exempted from service.

It appears, nevertheless, that the N.V.A.'s real concern is with professional efficiency and not with any political role it might choose to play in the future. Militarily, it is an efficient, well-trained and well-equipped army. Its NCOs are said to lack the status necessary to their rank, a problem common to modern conscript armies, but the motivation and quality of the officers appears quite satisfactory and the morale of the soldiers adequate. As a body, the army is over-supervised, the influence of the S.E.D. being too intrusive at every level for comfort, while the senior ranks are filled with men whose political dependability probably exceeds their military talent; but this apart the N.V.A. must be reckoned a useful component of the Soviet-bloc forces.

The N.V.A. lacks many of the tensions that can be seen in other Warsaw Pact armies, between nationalism and commitment to following the Soviet Union, and between territorial defence and participating in the overall offensive thrust of Warsaw Pact strategy. The N.V.A., with nationalism not a basically anti-Russian force as it is in the rest of the pact (except for Bulgaria), can wholeheartedly support its role as a fully-fledged member of the Pact's 'front line'. This ties in well with the Army's key mission of socialisation and indoctrination, which it shares with the paramilitary organisations.

When asked whether the N.V.A. was any good a *Bundeswehr* officer replied 'Yes, it is a very good army. It is a German Army'. US Army officers attached to Group Soviet Forces Germany as liaison comment on the superior discipline and efficiency of the N.V.A. compared to their Soviet comrades-in-arms, which reflects in things such as better N.V.A. convoy driving to leaving their bivouac areas in better condition. Whether this would translate into superior combat effectiveness, especially in action against the *Bundeswehr*, is hard to say. It remains that the N.V.A. has a seriousness, a purpose, and an aura of overall efficiency and competence that exceeds anything else seen in the Soviet Union's allies.

Richard Holmes
David Isby

GERMAN FEDERAL REPUBLIC

HISTORY AND INTRODUCTION

The role of the army in the history of Germany has been more important than that of almost any other major State's. For united Germany – the Second Reich of 1871, of which the West and East German States are the successors – was the product of a military alliance transformed into a political federation through the victories of confederated armies. Their head, the Prussian King and German Emperor, owed his rise to primacy over his princely rivals almost wholly to the pre-eminence of his soldiers.

Professionally, moreover, Germany's army has played a leading role among the world's military institutions comparable to that taken by her universities in European and American academic life: it has offered a model of excellence which has had a world-wide influence. Not only was the Prussian *Kriegsakademie* (founded on the same day in 1810 as its neighbour, the University of Berlin) to become the prototype of all modern staff colleges; the General Staff which it supplied with graduates developed the division of duty and methods of work which all other staffs were to follow. The conscriptive system it administered, based upon the short-service enlistment in local units of all fit males, was also to set a pattern adopted by most States which either sought, or were compelled to compete in, the major military league (and which had important effects on their political and social evolution). While, in war, the German army time and again demonstrated an enviable capacity to hit upon a spectacular tactical or strategic solution of whatever problems with which unfamiliar technology or political adversity confronted it – in 1940 *blitzkrieg*, in 1870 the strategic use of railways, in 1810 the Krümper system of clandestine re-armament, in 1740 the battle-winning 'oblique order'. In every century since the eighteenth it has been the nursery of military prodigies – Frederick the Great, Gneisenau, Schlieffen, Guderian, Manstein, Rommel – and the throne-room of military titans – Blücher, Moltke, Frederick Charles, Hindenburg, Ludendorff – while at the beginning of the nineteenth century it produced, from the same intellectual climate which nurtured Hegel and Marx, the only universal philosopher of war, General Karl von Clausewitz.

Clausewitz, the Krümper system and the Kriegsakademie were each in their different ways distinctively Prussian, as in origin was much else that has come down into Germany's twentieth-century military system. But the Prussian army was only one among several which went to make up the army of unified Germany. Germany ununified possessed numbers; indeed the eighteenth century Germany of *Kleinstaaterei* could show almost as many armies as it could States, and while most were very small – perhaps only a single regiment maintained for show and hired out to a richer prince in order to defray the expense it cost its royal commander – some were sizeable: the Bavarian and Saxon were large enough to take the field independently. The history of these armies is often fascinating, most of all those which fought for the British in America and Spain or, as many did, for Napoleon in Russia; that of the Bavarian, which retained its independence even after 1871 and whose lively ghost could confront the Weimar Republic with the threat of military secession as late as 1923, is one of real significance in modern German affairs. But for the most part their history has been lost to

view, submerged within the much larger story of the Prussian army, into which after 1871 they were physically incorporated (unless they had already been disbanded in penalty for choosing the wrong side in the Austro–Prussian War, like the Hanoverian which, as Wellington's King's German Legion, had written its own epic in Spain and at Waterloo and, going out in a blaze of glory, almost defeated the Prussian force sent to overawe it in 1866 at the battle of Langensalza). Thus the armies of Brunswick, Oldenburg and the Hansa towns survived after 1870 only as individual regiments on the Prussian list, that of Mecklenburg as a brigade, that of Hesse as a division and those of Saxony and Württemberg, the largest, as corps, their kings, by treaties of capitulation (an ancient word surviving from the days of mercenary warfare and signifying an agreement to hire troops) accepting the Prussian Crown's authority over their men in everything but honorific and cermonial detail.

The story of the German Army has been taken by modern historians to mean, therefore, that of the Prussian; and not without reason, for if looked at in terms of the law of natural selection it was the Prussian which proved itself, among the other species of army active in Germany, most successful at adapting to its environment. Its evolution, however, has been Lamarckian rather than Darwinian in character, a process of conscious self-improvement directed towards a concrete end: that of military and political primacy first within the Prussian heartland, next within Germany, then central Europe, ultimately over the continent itself. This is not to argue that Frederick William I looked forward to, or would even have approved of, the foreign policy of William II, still less of Hitler. His often quoted admonition to his son, the future Frederick the Great, 'You must not think about imaginary things; fix your mind on real ones. Have money and a good army,' were the words of a cautious husbandman of his fledgling State's resources, not of a would-be world conqueror. Even so, it was a matter of central satisfaction to him that he had made the difficult transition of status from '*rio mercenaire*' to one who could wage war '*nach eigener Conniventz*' – at his own convenience. And while the habit of waging war *nach eigener Conniventz* was certainly not uniquely Prussian, it was one in which the Hohenzollerns persisted longer than most, calculated their chances more finely and achieved the most spectacular run of success.

The Prussian army's evolution had effects in Prussia itself as well as on its neighbours. Through it the very nature of the State, and eventually that of Germany, was to be determined, while the process also exerted important influences on the development of German society as a whole. How this came to be is complex to explain, but if a single cause is looked for it will be found in the transformation of Prussian nobility into an exclusive officer class, whose view of what place in society it should hold and what form that society should take, were equally inflexible. Originally a coterie of minor landowners, firmly planted in the soil of their small estates and looking to horizons not more distant than their own boundaries, they were successfully wooed from private and feudal concerns to public and military concerns by the efforts of a succession of rulers – the Great Elector, Frederick William I, Frederick the Great. This royal persistence was understandable, for if Prussia was to become an efficient centralised State the Crown needed both to break the selfish parochialism of the landowners and to provide itself with a loyal native bureaucracy, civil and military. To enlist the Junkers into royal service was, therefore, to catch two birds from the same bush; but in doing so, the crown was unwillingly creating an alternative centre of power within the State, and of a dangerously monopolistic character, for the Junkers quickly came to look on the apprenticing of their sons to the army not as a duty they owed the Crown but as one it owed them, and them alone.

As long as Prussia remained a simple monarchical State, as it did throughout the years (1740—86) when Frederick the Great was teaching its army the secret of invincibility, the special relationship between the officers and the Crown was a relatively harmless feature of its structure. The evil effects of the Junkers' monopoly was not to be grasped until military defeat (by Napoleon in 1806) had shaken the foundations on which the monarcho-military State had been based. That those who attempted to rebuild it on different foundations were themselves soldiers, e.g. Scharnhorst, Gneisenau and Boyen, disguised for a while the military caste's opposition to change. That it did not then or later resist some of the reformers' policies — those, for example, which made conscription genuinely universal or cast the army in the role of 'School of the Nation', further camouflaged its inflexibility. But its opposition to the recruitment of officers by competition, which would have substituted brains for birth as the selective principle, and to the creation of a popular militia (Landwehr) which would have been officered by the despised (and feared) bourgeoisie, revealed both its true attitude and the isolation of the reformers within their own class. The reactionaries' eventually successful counter-attack further revealed how superficial were the changes which the reformers did bring about; the Landwehr was reduced from a citizen force to the regular army's reserve and the lessons which the army (as the nation's schoolmaster) taught its conscripts was that of unbending obedience to the Crown.

However, the officer corps's victory did not end there. During the 'critical battles' for the future of Prussia (those of 1819, 1848, 1866 and 1918) it was the opponents of constitutional reform, liberation and democracy who were the most effective fighters, and they were usually either soldiers or their close allies. The liberals recognised whence their opponents drew their power: 'It is significant that the Prussian liberals in 1848 and in the years 1862—6 sought, first and foremost, to win control of the army, realising that control of the State would follow if this could be acquired. This challenge the leaders of the army met with highly effective political tactics. In 1848 they defeated the demand that the army should be bound by an oath to the new constitution (whose promulgation they had, however, failed to block), a dangerous exemption confirmed in all constitutional arrangements until 1919. In the so-called Konfliktzeit of the 1860s they effectively defied the right of parliament to influence (military) matters and fruther demonstrated that the army was responsible to the Crown alone. Finally, after the unification of 1871, when (parliament) sought to win . . . the right to question the War Minister, the army leaders adroitly deprived that official of most of his functions and relegated authority in all matters of command, organisation and personnel to utterly irresponsible army agencies. (Thus) until 1918 they were able successfully to block the introduction into Germany of . . . the minimal requirements of representative government, namely ministerial responsibility and effective parliamentary control over State administration and policy. Indeed even when the monarchy collapsed in 1918 and Germany acquired a republican constitution, the forces of resistance carried on their fight and were willing in the end, in order to destroy the democratic system, to place the fate of their country in the hands of Adolf Hitler.'

Not everyone would follow Professor Gordon Craig, magisterial though his authority on the subject is, to that final conclusion. The story of the German army up to 1914 is indeed one of its rooted opposition to change, exemplified by its preservation of the right of officers to be tried by their peers instead of by civil magistrates (hence the virtual abolition of courts-martial in today's Bundeswehr) and its (successful) efforts to transform middle-class officers, when at last they had to be admitted in numbers, into Junker facsimiles. But the attitudes of the army after 1918 were, it can be argued, quite as much, if not more, influenced by the experience it and Germany had undergone during World War I than by anything which had passed before, for that experience had been unprecedented and traumatic. Two million Germans had been killed, wide swathes of territory surrendered and the Kaiser dethroned. The vast wartime army had demobilised itself without its officers' permission, civil war had broken out in half a dozen German cities and provinces and the organs of government, such as survived, had been left for a time without the means to exert their authority or indeed even to protect themselves against common rioters, let alone dedicated revolutionaries. It was with these consequences that the German officer corps had to deal in 1918; to argue retrospectively from the accommodation to which it came with Hitler in 1933—4 that its aim throughout the Weimar years was to solve the problems of defeat by confiding them to a new strong man, does justice neither to its intelligence or the facts.

The army was indeed changed by the war just as was Germany itself. Obliged to recognise that the old monarchical State was doomed, less because of its obnoxiousness to the Germans than to the victorious Allies, it was the General Staff itself which presented the ultimatum to the Kaiser, in the hope that his departure would spare the country dismemberment and disarmament, and, when that proved unavailing, decided to take upon itself the duty of preserving national unity. Leaderless in a leaderless State, the army made itself in effect the new sovereign, holding itself 'above party' and pledged to intervene in the affairs of the Republic only if government should fail to preserve public order or compromise German sovereignty. This is not to say that Seeckt, creator of the 100,000 man army allowed to Germany by the Versailles treaty, liked the Republic, any more than did Field-Marshal Hindenburg, its president from 1925—34, while the feelings of their juniors was yet more tepid. All nevertheless served it dutifully enough to convince Hitler that he could seize its machinery only through the parliamentary process, and it was only after he had done so that the Reichswehr transferred their loyalties to him. That loyalty moreover, remained qualified, his demagogy being distasteful to their fundamentally conservative instincts, and his adventurism in foreign policy alarming to the prudence they had learnt since 1914. If Hitler captured the army — and the evidence usually adduced is that of its passivity during the excesses of the 'blood purge' and its meek acceptance of his presidency in August, 1934 — he did so less by persuading its leaders that they and he shared common interests than by using against them the same mixture of threats, bribes and false alarms with which he had won German votes between 1930—33. Most potent of these threats was that to legalise the party militia, Röhm's SA, as an 'alternative army', most potent of his bribes were the largesse of promotions he conferred through the initiative of large-scale rearmament in 1935; most potent of the false alarms were the calumnies his henchmen laid against the army's leaders, Blomberg and Fritsch, in 1938. The mixture produced the effects Hitler had hoped for. The Röhm and the Blomberg—Fritsch affairs sapped the army's self-confidence, and rearmament's benefactions to individuals blunted its collective conscience. He took command and led it to war.

Whether, had his leadership continued to yield cheap victories after 1941, its conscience would have stirred again, is an unanswerable question. That stir it did in 1943–4, when a handful of regular officers of the pre-Hitler army glimpsed the loom of catastrophe, is well-known, as is the means they selected to avert it: the assassination of Hitler in his own headquarters. Their abortive tyrannicide was unsuccessful in both the short- and long-term. Immediately, it deprived the army of what was left of its independence, and paradoxically, by confirming the Allies' conception of it as 'a State within a State', it strengthened their resolve to deprive a reconstituted Germany of an army for good. East and West stood united in 1945 over that issue as over no other.

The reappearance of a (West) German army only 11 years after the 'permanent' demobilisation of the *Wehrmacht* is, in a sense, therefore, one of the most surprising events of the post-war world; in another, given the outbreak of the Cold War and the creation of a clandestine army in Soviet-occupied Germany, it is not surprising at all. By 1950 the British, Americans and French had convinced themselves, from a calculation of relative strengths, Russian intentions and the level of economic sacrifice their populations were prepared to make in the case of collective security, that they could not maintain a credible land defence of the East—West border (manned at the time by only five divisions against 175 Russian in central Europe and European Russia) without German assistance. But the creation of a new *Wehrmacht* (*Bundeswehr* was the term eventually chosen) raised issues beyond the simply strategic. Not only was there the abrogation of inter-Allied agreements and the aggravation of Soviet mistrust to be considered. German rearmament raised in France (and not in France alone) anxieties almost as fierce as fears of Russian intentions, and in German liberals and socialists the spectre of a reborn 'State within a State', with all the threats to the safety of democracy that entailed, and of a remilitarised (by which they understood 'rebrutalised') society. Many Germans, moreover, though not specifically hostile to rearmament, disliked the prospect, because it conflicted with their passionate desire to lead quiet private lives after three decades of turbulence, an attitude summarised as '*ohne mich*' ('count me out'). The *Bundeswehr*, it was clear, would have to be a very different army from any that Germany had known before. It would have to be commanded by a supranational authority; it would have to be wholly subordinated to the civil power; and it would have to make itself acceptable to a generally apathetic but, in parts, actively antipathetic population.

The difficulty of finding ways to meet the first two of these aims (the third is not yet wholly achieved) meant that the raising of the *Bundeswehr*, from conception to institution, was to take 6 years. The external difficulties took longest to overcome. The first solution, proposed by France and endorsed by Winston Churchill in August, 1950 was for a European army, under a European Defence Minister, into which German units could be drafted without it being necessary to raise a German army at all. In negotiation the European army became a Defence Community (EDC) and the European Minister a board of nine commissioners, supervising divisions, instead of the battalions originally proposed as the largest homogeneous units. But so smoothly did agreement grow, that the Allies meantime unilaterally abolished their control commissions, ended the state of war and recognised West Germany as a sovereign State. These diplo-

matic measures were contained in a Treaty of Bonn, signed in May, 1952, with the military agreements in a Treaty of Paris, signed the following day, the force of the former being conditional upon the ratification of the latter by all parties. In France its debate in the Assembly was delayed until August, 1954 and, for a variety of reasons, it then found insufficient support. This created an awkward situation. Although the Treaty of Bonn had been signed conditionally, the non-communist world had for 2 years treated the Federal Republic as if it were fully sovereign, and there was now 'little except good faith to prevent the Germans rearming' particularly as their government knew that America had wished that they should, ever since it had been decided that their help was needed. As Britain had greatly contributed to the delay in framing the terms of the E.D.C., and thus postponed French ratification of the Treaty of Paris, it was up to her to retrieve the situation, which she did by proposing the formation of a Western European Union (W.E.U.), to include Germany and Italy. The establishment of this body, largely consultative though it has to be, generated the diplomatic goodwill necessary for the admission of Germany to NATO, and provided the Federal Republic with the occasion to limit voluntarily the military contribution it would make to the alliance to levels acceptable to France and the lesser powers. As specified in the Paris Agreement of October, 1954, these limitations included the renunciation of the right to manufacture biological, chemical and nuclear weapons, or to alter her boundaries or seek re-unification of Germany by force. The size of the German army was fixed at twelve divisions, of the air force at 1000 combat planes, all of which would be assigned to NATO and commanded by SACEUR.

Meanwhile, the Federal government had gone some way to settle the internal political difficulties attendant on rearmament. An 'Office of the Commissioner of the Federal Chancellor for Questions Connected with the Increasing of Allied Troops' (called the Blank Office after its first and only incumbent) had been set up in October, 1950. It had two main tasks: the formulation of an 'idea of the Bundeswehr' and the preparation of the legislation which would transform idea into reality. Foremost among the ex-officers to advise Blank was Graf Baudissin, with whom is associated the development of the '*Staatsbürger in Uniform*' (Citizen in Uniform) concept on which the *Bundeswehr* was to be built. He summarised its sense in these words, 'The inner structure of the armed forces in a free society must be such that young soldiers can complete their military training without fundamental break with their civilian environment.' An end then, to separate military courts and to 'sergeants' rule' (bullying and beating, characteristic of the Prussian army). The Basic Law (the constitutional Foundation of the Republic enacted in 1949) was to govern the army, its soldiers were to be guaranteed their constitutional rights and they and their officers were to be taught a view of the soldiers' and leaders' role through a scheme of '*Innere Führung*' (moral leadership). And to see that Parliament's and Society's will in these matters was enforced, there were to be a Parliamentary Defence Committee with permanent powers of enquiry, and a Defence Commissioner (*Wehrbeauftrager*) (based on a Swedish example): to him all members of the forces were to have the right of direct, confidential appeal in matters of basic constitutional rights.

This protection of the citizen's rights was vital if the *Bundeswehr* was to commend itself to the population of the Republic, for it had been early recognised (though not by Colonel von Bonin, first Chief of Planning, who advocated a small all-volunteer force) that it would have to be conscriptive. The government also hoped, by assuring parliamentary control and the soldier's constitutional rights, to made the establishment of the *Bundeswehr* bi-partisan in policy. In that it failed. The SPD (Socialist party) assented to several of the defence bills of 1954–7, in particular the one which set up a Screening Commission to exclude undesirable officers (and which rejected several members of the Blank Office) at the office of the Defence Commissioner, but it opposed almost all the others. Nevertheless the necessary acts were passed (*see* Command and Constitutional Status). In July, 1955 the first volunteers were recruited and in January, 1956 the first units established. In July half of the Federal Border Guard, created by the Adenauer government in 1950 to emphasise to the Allies Germany's defencelessness, was integrated, and in April, 1957 the first 10,000 conscripts were inducted. By 1960, the *Bundeswehr* numbered 256,000, of which 158,000 belonged to the army, organised into seven divisions. Progress towards its full strength of 12 divisions, reached in 1965, proceeded smoothly. Considerable expenditure in armaments have subsequently made them the best equipped of all on NATO's Central Front. Militarily, the German army is again a formidable force. The electorate appear to accept that the danger of its becoming 'a State within a State' are effectively checked by the severe constitutional restraints in which it operates. The army itself carries no aspiration to any such status.

STRENGTH AND BUDGET

Strength

Population: 61,665,000 (including West Berlin)
Army: 35,000 (conscripts 180,000)
Navy: 36,400; 172 vessels (mainly small craft)
Air force: 106,000; 548 combat aircraft
Paramilitary forces: 20,000 Federal Border Police and 15,000 *Länder* Alert Police
Reserves: army, 615,000; navy 27,000; air force 85,000
Territorial Army: 441,000

Budget

Defence expenditure for 1982 was about DM44,000,000,000. The cost of the army is not shown separately. Nevertheless, some published information throws light on it: in 1973 the operating cost of an armoured brigade (equipment procurement cost DM250,000,000) was DM82,300,000 of which DM59,000,000 was personnel costs; the operating cost of an armoured infantry brigade (equipment procurement cost DM260,000,000) was DM82,800,000 of which DM57,200,000 was personnel costs; the operating cost of an infantry brigade (equipment procurement cost DM165,000,000 was DM76,100,000 of which DM56,300,000 was personnel costs. At the same time it was calculated that the annual personnel cost of an officer, and NCO and a conscript private was DM36,300, DM23,570 and DM11,660 respectively.

COMMAND AND CONSTITUTIONAL STATUS

Command

Control of the armed forces is divided between the parliament and the executive. Parliament (*Bundestag*) is responsible for defence legislation, the military budget and, when necessary, the declaration of a state of war (*Verteidigungsfall*). Two investigatory agencies work to it: the Defence Committee, composed of members of parliament, which has the powers of a parliamentary committee of enquiry, and the Defence Commissioner, whose role is to assist parliament in exercising its supervisory powers and to protect the constitutional rights of citizens while they serve in the armed forces. The

executive's powers are divided. The Federal President is, unusually, not titular commander-in-chief; his powers are limited to the appointment and dismissal of civil and military officers, the regulation of the system of ranks and design of uniforms; and the proclamation of a state of war. The Federal Security Council, a Cabinet committee to which the *Bundeswehr* Chief of Staff belongs, co-ordinates the direction of defence affairs. The Federal Minister of Defence is Commander-in-Chief of the *Bundeswehr* in peacetime, and responsible for its management. He is assisted by a junior minister (Parliamentary Secretary) and two State Secretaries, one for administration, the other for armaments. To him work directly the five senior Chiefs of Staff: *Bundeswehr*, Army, Navy, Air Force and Medical Service. Each of their staffs is organised into seven sections: I Personnel and Training, II Intelligence, III Operations, IV Organisation, V Logistics, VI Planning and VII Communications, Electronics and Weapon Development. For historical reasons (the condemnation of the General Staffs of the Wehrmacht and the Army as criminal organisations by the Nuremburg International Military Tribunal) the Chiefs of Staff are entitled *Inspekteure* (e.g. *Inspekteur des Heeres* – Chief of Staff of the Army) and their staff as *Führungsstab* (e.g. *Führungsstab des Heeres*).

Operational command of the army is exercised, moreover, not by an organ of the German government or *Bundeswehr* but by NATO officers. The chain of command runs from SACEUR (an American Officer) to Commander, AFCENT and through him to the Commanders CENTAG and NORTHAG. The former commands, with other NATO forces, II and III (German Corps and the latter I (German) Corps. Command of the 6th *Panzergrenadier Division* in Schleswig-Holstein is exercised by Commander AFNORTH under SACEUR. Thus the highest national level of operational command in the German army is at Corps headquarters. Command of the Territorial Army is in the hands of the minister, however, together with that of the General Army Office and of *Bundeswehr* installations.

Constitutional Status

The Basic Law (*Grundgesetz*) on which the Federal Republic was founded said almost nothing about the status of its army, not unnaturally since none existed at the time (1949) nor was envisaged for the future. It did not, however, prohibit the raising of an army (as it did the waging of aggressive war) so that when, in 1956, the Federal Government proceeded to create one it found no serious legal impediment to its so doing. Given the strict protection of the rights of the individual enshrined in the Basic Law, however, and the hostility of the Socialist opposition party to, as well as international suspicion of, the rearmament policy, the government did find it necessary to pass a whole range of new laws and constitutional amendments defining the army's place in the Federal State and of the citizen's rights while in uniform. Of these the most interesting are: the Servicemen's Act, which stipulates, that 'he is to be instructed in the rights of the people of all nations according to international law' as well as in his own constitutional rights and responsibilities; the Military Penal Act, which lays down that the soldier remains under the jurisdiction of the civil courts; and the Military Appeals Act, which allows the soldier to lodge complaints and appeals to the civil courts. Thus the exemption of the soldier from the civil jurisdiction, the cause of multiple inequities in Imperial Germany, is forbidden. The enforcement of the new constitutional order is guaranteed, moreover, by the activity of the Parliamentary Defence Commissioner, the first of whom, Count Baudissin, firmly established the concept of the 'citizen in uniform' as the basis for relations between army and State (*see also* the first and the next sections).

ROLE, COMMITMENT, DEPLOYMENT AND RECENT OPERATIONS

Role

This has been much debated (*see* History and Introduction, and Command and Constitutional Status) and is more closely circumscribed by domestic law and international agreement than most other armies'. Like theirs, the German army's role is both external and internal: the protection of the national territory; and the maintenance of 'the existence (and) free democratic basic order of the Federation' (Article 91 of the Basic Law). By the Paris Agreements of October 23rd, 1954, by which the British, American and French terminated their occupation of West Germany, recognised it as a sovereign State, invited it to join NATO, and agreed to the creation of a German military force, the Federal government undertook to limit the size of that force to the maxima negotiated in the European Defence Community Treaty of May, 1952 (i.e. 12 divisions), to abstain from the manufacture of atomic, biological and chemical weapons, and to refrain from seeking to bring about the reunification of Germany or to alter the boundaries of the Federal Republic by forceful means. Command of the forces whose raising was authorised by the Paris Agreements was to be vested in the Supreme Allied Commander Europe (SACEUR). These provisions defined the international status of the *Bundeswehr*, and they remain effective. Meanwhile the Federal government had to revise its own constitution to provide legally for the existence of the new national army. The Basic Law was virtually silent on the matter, containing only a guarantee of the right to refuse military service (Article 4), and a prohibition of the waging of aggressive war and reservation of the right to manufacture weapons (Article 26). Article 91 did permit the Federal government, however, to intervene in the affairs of the *Länder* for self-defensive purposes and amendments to that and others (notably 87, which allowed 'Federal frontier protection authorities' to be raised) provided the constitutional basis for the *Bundestag* to vote the amendments necessary to the creation of an army. But constitutionally the army may, in peacetime, operate only 'to protect civilian installations and to regulate traffic' and where the performance of its defensive mission requires (Article 17) or, in cases of emergency, when the police and *Bundesgrenzschutz* have both failed to suppress disorder and those causing it 'are organised and armed with military weapons'. In both cases a State of Defence (*Verteidigungsfall*) must previously have been proclaimed by the *Bundestag* by a two-thirds majority of those voting, which must represent a simply majority of elected members (Article 115). Thus German law limits the role of the army to that of (*a*) obeying the orders of a supranational commander (SACEUR) except when (*b*) parliament authorises its employment on the national territory for purposes strictly defined in nature and limited in time. The legal purity of this doctrine has been somewhat muddied by the creation of the Territorial Army (*see* Organisation) which is not assigned to NATO; but it too may only be employed operationally after a State of Defence has been proclaimed.

The operational doctrine (*Kriegsbild und Auftrag*) of the army conforms to that of NATO which since its birth has been explicitly based on 'forward defence' — the defeat of a Warsaw Pact attack as near the eastern border as possible, by the use of conventional forces in the first instances and by nuclear weapons only as a last resort. The German army is naturally less happy with the doctrine of 'flexible response' as a means of operating the 'forward strategy' which wa instituted in 1967, since it suggests a willingness by NATO t surrender larger areas of German territory than most German would care to lose, as a means of postponing the momen when nuclear weapons would be employed — more of whic would then explode on German soil. The German arm therefore trains particularly seriously for the compensator NATO plan to commit major conventional forces at or nea the border and to wage an offensive defence.

Commitment

The field forces of the army are all assigned to NATO. Th units of the Territorial Army act either as training or suppor units for the field army or as home defence units, which ma be employed only when a 'state of defence' has been pro claimed. Germany is a member of NATO, of Western Euro pean Union and has bilateral agreements with the Unite States and with France (under which the French divisions ar stationed in Baden—Württemberg).

Deployment

Because the territory of West Germany is, in effect if not i law, permanently organised for war, appropriate details ar included under Organisation.

Recent Operations

The German army has taken part in no operations since it re-formation.

ORGANISATION

Arms of Service

The German army, having been rebuilt from scratch in 1956 has, as might be expected, a highly functional domesti structure. No attempt has been made to perpetuate o revive links with the regiments or corps of the past, as Seeck tried to do after 1921; though individual infantry an cavalry/armoured units stationed in appropriate district nevertheless unofficially adopt the identities of vanishe Imperial regiments, the adoption of these fictional ancestrie is heavily disfavoured by the Defence ministry.

The arms of service are:
1. Infantry (*Infanterie*) which includes armoured infan try (*Panzergrenadiere*), mountain infantry (*Gebirgs jäger*), parachute infantry (*Fallschirmjäger*) and anti tank troops (*Panzerjäger*).
2. Armour (*Panzertruppe*) which includes tank units (*Panzer*) and reconnaissance (*Panzeraufklärung*).
3. Artillery (*Artillerie*) which does *not* include the large tactical guided missile (Pershing) — units which are manned by the air force.
4. Anti-aircraft Artillery (*Flugabwehrartillerie*) which does *not* include large surface-to-air missiles (Hawk and Nike—Hercules) — units which are manned by the air force.
5. Engineers (*Pioniertruppe*).
6. Signals (*Fernmeldetruppe*).
7. Army Aviation (*Heeresflieger*).
8. Technical Services (*Technischetruppe*), which embrace transport, supply, storage maintenance and repair units.
9. Medical Service (*Sanitätsdienst*), a tri-service body.
10. Nuclear—Biological—Chemical Defence Corps (*ABC-Abwehrtruppe*).
11. Military Police (*Feldjäger*).
12. Band Service (*Militarmusik*).
13. Intelligence Corps (*Frontnachrichtentruppe*).

14. Psychological Warfare Corps (*Psychologische Kampf-führungtruppe*).

Operational

The army is divided into a Field Army (*Feldheer*) and a Territorial Army (*Territorialheer*). The Field Army consists of the major fighting units, which are earmarked for assignment to NATO in case of war. The Territorial Army would remain under national control even in time of war and consists of all the other army units, including the headquarters (*Heeresamt*) and all army schools, colleges and academies.

The Field Army is organised into three corps (I, HQ Münster; II, HQ Ulm; and III, HQ Koblenz) and an independent division (*6 Panzergranadierdivision*) based at Neumünster in Schleswig–Holstein which works with the Danish army (*q.v.*). The corps control three to four divisions each; the divisions control three brigades each. There are 12 divisions in all (six armoured, four armoured infantry, one mountain and one airborne – the latter's brigades distributed between the corps) and 36 brigades (17 armoured, 15 armoured infantry, one mountain and three airborne). The divisional headquarters are:

I Corps: 1 *Panzerdivision*, Hannover
           3 *Panzerdivision*, Buxtehude
           7 *Panzerdivision*, Unna
          11 *Panzerdivision*, Oldenburg
II Corps: 4 *Panzergrenadierdivision*, Regensburg
          10 *Panzerdivision*, Sigmaringen
           8 *Gebirgsdivision*, Garmisch–Partenkirchen
           9 *Luftlandedivision*, Bruchsal
III Corps: 2 *Panzergrendierdivision*, Kassel
           5 *Panzerdivision*, Diez/Lahn
          12 *Panzerdivision*, Wurzburg

The three brigades of the airborne division (27, 25, 26) are allocated to I, II and III Corps respectively.

Each corps has a sizeable complement of combat and support units. The most important *combat* units under direct corps command are: the corps infantry battalions; the corps artillery brigade, with one Lance Rocket Battalion (six launchers); two heavy artillery battalions (18 175mm SP howitzers); one corps anti-aircraft regiment (80 guns and Roland); one corps engineer brigade with up to eight battalions of various types (heavy, bridging, etc.); one signals brigade with two signals and one electronic warfare battalion; one corps of aviation command (126 light and medium helicopters for anti-tank observation and troop transport).

Each division (except the airborne) also directly controls a number of combat and support units. The most important of these combat units are: one divisional armoured reconnaissance battalion (19 APCs, 34 tanks); one divisional artillery regiment, with one gun battalion (six 203mm SP howitzers,) and one rocket battalion (18 FH, 16 110mm multiple rocket launchers); one divisional anti-aircraft battalion (36 Gepard); one divisional engineer battalion; one signals battalion; one divisional aviation squadron (10 light helicopters).

The brigade, of which a division controls three, may be one of four types: (*a*) armoured, (*b*) armoured infantry, (*c*) mountain infantry and (*d*) airborne. The airborne division contains only airborne brigades; the armoured divisions contain one armoured infantry and two armoured brigades; the armoured infantry division contains one armoured and two armoured infantry brigades; the mountain division contains one mountain, one armoured infantry and one armoured brigade.

The amoured brigade contains two tank battalions (110 tanks), one armoured infantry battalion (46 APCs) and one artillery battalion (18 155mm SP howitzers); the armoured infantry brigade contains two armoured infantry battalions (92 APCs), one armoured battalion (54 tanks) and one artillery battalion (18 155mm SP howitzers); in the mountain brigade the infantry are all carried in wheeled vehicles and the artillery battalion is equipped with 105mm pack howitzers; the airborne brigade contains three parachute battalions and light supporting units (airborne engineer company, anti-tank company, etc.). Armoured and armoured infantry brigades now all contain the cadre for a fourth battalion of mixed tank and APC companies, to be brought up to full strength on mobilisation.

The Territorial Army, whose main task is to defend the rear areas in event of war, is organised, as part of the Organisation for Territorial Defence (*Territoriale Verteidigung*), on a geographical basis, the boundaries of its sub-divisions coinciding with those of administrative areas with which it is in liaison. There are three Territorial Commands (*Territorial Kommando*): *Nord* – HQ Mönchengladbach, *Sud* – HQ Heidelberg, and *Schleswig – Holstein* – HQ Kiel. At the next level downward, *Schleswig–Holstein* oversees Military District (*Wehrbereich*) I – HQ Kiel; *Nord* oversees Military Districts II (the Länder of Niedersachsen and Bremen – HQ Hannover) and III (Nordrhein–Westfalen – HQ Düsseldorf); *Sud* oversees Military Districts IV (Hessen, Rheinland–Pfalz, Saarland – HQ Mainz), V (Württemberg–Baden – HQ Stuttgart) and VI (Bavaria – HQ Munich). The Military Districts are sub-divided into Defence Regions (*Verteidigungsbereichs*) of which there are 27, coterminous with one or more administrative districts (*Regierungsbezirke*) of the Länder, which are further sub-divided into 80 Defence Sub-regions (*Verteidigungskreise*), coterminous with one or more city or rural districts (*Stadt-Landkreise*). They liaise with NATO army groups, corps divisions and brigades respectively.

The Territorial Army's *combat* units are of three sorts: (*a*) Home Defence Groups (*Heimatschutzkommandos*), of which twelve are in existence, two each in Military Districts I–VI; (*b*) 15 Home Defence Regiments in the Defence Regions; and (*c*) 150 Home Defence Companies in the Defence Sub-regions and 300 Security Platoons. The Home Defence Groups are effectively amoured infantry brigades; in peace each contains about 2800 men, of whom all but 15% are conscripts undergoing training. The infantry regiments of the Defence Regions have a permanent cadre but are manned by reservists, who do 14 days' annual training. The Security Companies of the Defence Sub-regions are entirely reservist in composition and based in the areas where there reservists live. The equipment of all these combat units is held at local centres manned by serving soldiers. The Territorial Army also contains numbers of engineer battalions, whose task is to create defensive obstacles and demolitions, as well as signal and supply units for the support both of the Territorial and the Field Armies. The corps depots of the Field Army are filled by units of the Territorial Army from depots administered by the Army National Command.

Besides these combat and support units, the Territorial Army nominally controls all other units, commands, agencies and schools of the army which are neither part of the Field Army or the Army Staff. In practice, the majority are administered directly by the General Army Office (*Heeresamt*) at Cologne (*see* Command and Constitutional Status), the principal subordinate headquarters of the Army Staff. It has dual responsibilities: as a subordinate headquarters of the Army Staff it is responsible for the organisation, training and logistical support of the Field and Territorial Armies, and the provision and maintenance of equipment; as Command Headquarters for Army Installations, it supervises the Army Officer School (Hannover), the 22 arms and service schools and the Army Material Command which holds and handles stocks for supply to units.

Paramilitary Forces

The Minister of the Interior controls the Federal Border Guard (*Bundesgrenzschutz* – BGS), established in 1950 under Article 87 of the Basic Law as a counter force to the East German *Grenztruppen*. It numbered 10,000 (since 1953 20,000) and is organised into four commands, which control several *Gruppen*, each of two to three battalions. The force is a fully motorised militarised police, equipped with light armoured vehicles (e.g. the BGS Sonderwagen, built by the Swiss firm MOWAG), mortars, anti-armour weapons, 20mm cannon and infantry small arms. Its role is limited to a strip 30km deep along the Federal border, unless its use is invoked under Article 91 of the Basic Law, which allows the Federal government, in the face of a threat to 'the existence or free democratic order' of the *Bund* or one of its constituent *Land*, to centralise police forces under its control. About half of the BGS was transferred to the *Bundeswehr* in 1956 to constitute its original units. An anti-terrorist unit (GSG9) now forms part of the BGS and has achieved a high reputation. It overwhelmed a group of hijackers of a Lufthansa airliner at Mogadishu in 1977 in spectacular style.

Each *Land* also controls a number of Police Alert Units (*Bereitschaftpolizei*). The Federal government requested the Western Powers in August, 1950 in view of the disturbed internal situation in Germany to permit the formation of a militarised Federal Police. The request was refused, but permission given for each *Land* to raise a barracked police (equivalent to the *Kasernierte Volkspolizei* already in existence in East Germany) to a strength of 30,000, which would in emergency quell disturbances. The *Bereitschaftpolizei* are organised in battalions of the same type as those of the BGS, and all German police recruits serve 2 years in one as a preliminary to normal duty. Under Article 91, these battalions may be placed under Federal control or that of another *Land* which has need of them.

RECRUITMENT, TRAINING AND RESERVES

Recruitment

There are three forms of service: conscript, army-service regular and career regular.

The first members of the *Bundeswehr* were all regulars (Volunteer's Law of July 16th, 1955), many of them ex-members of the *Wehrmacht*, selected by a Personnel Advisory Committee appointed by the *Bundestag* with the concurrence of all parties (except the tiny *Deutsche Partei*). It admitted 6000 applicants, having rejected about 600 ex-soldiers. On July 6th, 1956 the *Bundestag*, however, had also passed the Conscriptive Law, which provided for the compulsory recruitment of annual contingents, initially for a period of 12 months. The period was extended to 18 months in January, 1963 and reduced to 15 months on January 1st, 1973. Until April, 1965 the minimum recruiting age was twenty, then eighteen, but in practice nineteen is normal. Deferment for those undergoing professional training is permitted as is the performance of shortened military service for certain categories of recruits. The legal right of conscientious objection is strictly preserved; initially, indeed, the legal difficulty was to make military service constitutional, for although the Basic Law establishing the *Bundesrepublik* did not prescribe remilitarisation, it so tightly enshrined a whole range of personal freedoms that the imposition of military discipline on citizen-conscripts, indeed even on volunteers, would have seriously infringed the law. Some 30 constitutional amendments had in consequence to be passed, many of them not without lengthy parliamentary tussles. Objections must be confined on conscientious grounds to all use of force as between States, but need not be religiously based. The objector is interviewed by a board of four, one appointed by the Minister of Defence, three by the *Land* in which he lives. If successful, he must perform useful social service for the full term of his service. The numbers applying were low during the first 12 years of conscription, about 3400 a year; 70% were university students or high-school graduates, and 80% applied successfully. In 1968, apparently as a result of the outbreak of student and youth dissent in many Western countries, the number jumped to 12,000 and reached 33,792 in 1972. Of the 1973 contingent born in 1953, 6.7% (27,589) about half of whom were high-school graduates, had filed objections by September 30th, a number 2.5% up on the equivalent period for 1972, and of these 2278 were already serving. There are now sufficient 'alternative service spaces' for successful applicants.

If the *Bundeswehr* were dependent wholly on conscripted youth for its recruits, and needed all that were available, the situation would be serious. However, even after objectors have fallen out, it has an annual class of over 300,000 from whom to choose and takes only about two-thirds, a practice which gives rise to a familiar complaint about the inequity of conscription. Its selectivity is determined by its need to fill many technical and command posts with regulars who form about 55% of the army's strength. This is 5% fewer than the army would prefer, but is adequate, though again the length of engagement for which regulars volunteer is shorter than the army would wish. Regulars may enlist for any term between 21 months and 15 years and, if promoted sergeant, may between the ages of twenty-five and twenty-eight apply for a career appointment guaranteeing employment to fifty-two, and thereafter a pension. There are about five times as many applicants as places for these career posts.

Training

Soldiers

The shortening of basic military service from 18 to 15 months (soon to be restored to the former length) has necessitated a simplification of the conscript's training. He is no longer given a preliminary training as an infantryman but, during his 3 months' basic training, begins at once to learn his individual skill – that of tank gunner, radar operator, etc. – though with some instruction in drill and self-defence. This is carried out in one of 15 Basic Training Units which form part of the Home Defence Groups of the Territorial Army. His remaining 12 months are spent in his operational unit, where he receives unit training, the syllabus for which is divided into four 3 month periods, which can be taught in any sequence (since any sub-unit will contain soldiers in their 2nd, 3rd, 4th or 5th 3 months of service). Thus unit training is a cycle which can be entered at any quarter of the year and left 12 months later. The system naturally throws a considerable strain on the energy and intelligence of the junior officers and NCOs who must make it work, but it appears to be efficient.

NCOs

Future NCOs, selected if possible after 5–8 months' service, are trained first in their parent units, then at a 3 month Basic NCO course in the school of the Arm to which they belong. Of these the most important are: Infantry and Armour – Combat Schools (Hammelburg), II and III (Münster); Artillery) – Idar–Oberstein; Anti-aircraft – Rendsburg; Engineer – Munich; Signals – Feldafing; Military Police – Sonthofen; Army Air Corps – Buckerburg; Technical Corps – I (Aachen) and II (Bremen). There are besides some specialist schools: Paratroop (Altenstadt); Mountain and Winter Warfare (Mittenweld); Missiles (Eschweiller); NBC (Sonthofen); Engineer Construction Academy (Munich) and Machine Engineering School (Darmstadt). After three satisfactory years of service in the *Unteroffizier* rank, suitable candidates go forward to the Advanced NCO courses held at Sonthofen or Aachen (Army NCO Schools I and II). Each is then trained there for 6−33 months depending on the length of his engagement, both in his speciality and for eventual civilian employment in a related occupation, and is tested for suitability for promotion to career NCO or specialist officer.

The *Bundeswehr's* new training and education policy, announced on January 18th, 1973, is to integrate its courses with those of the Federal education system so that specialist military training will automatically fit servicemen for civilian employment on discharge, a policy dictated by national economic requirements and the need to make military service more attractive. A corollary is that selection for training depends very much on the recruit's pre-service education − NCO training, for example, being the prerogative of men who have completed an apprenticeship or middle school. However, the *Bundeswehr* runs 31 vocational schools which provide both a 'second educational route' to advancement, for poorly educated recruits enlisting for 8 years or more, as well as 3 year courses in civilian skills open to all long-service and career NCOs on discharge.

Officers

Their system of training has been radically revised. Hitherto, all (reserve, short-service, long-service and career) have proceeded from basic military training of the sort undergone by conscripts to a short period of regimental service and then to Officer Candidate School at the school of their Arm, where after six months they took the officer examination. After that, short-service, long-service and career officers attended courses at one of the three Army Officer Schools (*Heeresoffizierschule*) at Hamburg, Hannover or Munich, and took a course whose length depended on that of their engagement. This system persists for short and long-service officers (under 12 years' engagement). However, Career officers, and long-service officers engaged for 12−15 years, now proceed from Officer Candidate School to one of the two new *Bundeswehr* universities established on October 1st, 1973 by (*a*) the transformation of the Officer School at Hamburg and (*b*) by the fusion of the Air Force Technical Academy with the Army Officer School and one of the army's three technical colleges, all at Munich. Training at these universities lasts 4 years and leads to the grant of a degree, the subjects for which are strongly scientific in character. After 8 years of commissioned service, officers are obliged to proceed to 'Grade C' education, meaning a long or short course at the Armed Forces Staff College (*Führungsakademie der Bundeswehr*) at Hamburg. Only about 85−90% are chosen for the short staff course, qualifying them for S1, 2, 3 or 4 posts (subordinate staff appointments). The remaining 10−15% do 2 years' training preceded by 4 months' language training, and emerge qualified for the G (major staff) appointments. The system is reminiscent of the distinction maintained at the old *Kriegsakademie* between the training of 'troop' staff officers and future members of the Great General Staff. A 'Grade D' level of training is planned for lieutenant-colonels and above, but not yet instituted, though the *Führungsakademie* already runs a National Defence Course for senior officers.

The army (or the *Bundeswehr*) maintains a number of other schools attended by army officers, of which the best known is that at Koblenz for *Innere Führung* (an untranslat-

able term − perhaps 'moral leadership'). Its foundation was insisted upon by idealists among the planning group which set up the *Bundeswehr*, and was intended to teach officers a civic approach to their profession − to replace that 'caste' attitude held typical of the old Prussian officer corps. Originally much derided, it now seems tolerated by, though not very influential within, the *Bundeswehr*. The technical colleges at Darmstadt (*Akademie für Maschinenwesen*) conducts diploma courses (equivalent to those run by the civilian *Technische Hochschulen*) for officers proceeding to technical staff appointments. There are also the *Bundeswehr* Logistic School (Hamburg); Administration and Technical Academy (Mannheim; also trains civil servants); Language School (Euskirchen); Psychological Warfare School (Euskirchen); Intelligence School (Bad Ems); and Physical Training School (Sonthofen). The *Bundeswehr* Medical Academy (Munich) does not train doctors, who are recruited from civilian universities (at which suitably qualified volunteers may also be financed): it provides military medical training to the already qualified, and is therefore not an equivalent of the French military medical school at Lyons.

The *Bundeswehr* universities and vocation schools attract professional interest in Germany as the only educational institutions run under central government control; the Basic Law reserved supervision of education to the *Länder* which results in considerable discrepancies of syllabus and standards from *Land* to *Land*.

Reserves

These total 1,800,000 in all of which 540,000 are available for mobilisation. As a result of the reduction of military service from 18 to 15 months, conscripts are liable for instant recall in the first three months after discharge. Officers and NCOs are liable for recall up to the age of sixty, ex-regulars of all ranks up to sixty-five. Reservists are held in the strength of two types of units: those of the Territorial Army (*see* Organisation) and the replacement pool of the Field Army.

EQUIPMENT AND ARMS INDUSTRY

Germany entered both World Wars I and II with one of the largest, most comprehensive and versatile arms industries in the world, though on the second occasion rebuilt at great speed on the much diminished base to which it had been reduced by Allied fiat after the Versailles treaty. After 1945, the German armaments industry, heavily damaged by the Allied strategic bombing campaign, was even more drastically reduced than in 1918. The factories in the Soviet zone of occupation were stripped of their machine-tools, which were sent to Russia; those in the Western zones of occupation were, when rebuilt, re-tooled for civilian production. Between 1945 and 1956 no military equipment of any sort was produced in the Federal Republic, nor very much in the first years of rearmament. By the early 1960s, however, a great deal of public and private investment in heavy industry, usually in those firms with a history of armaments manufacture − Henschel, Messerschmitt and Blohm − had allowed West Germany to begin production of major items of equipment. It is today almost self-sufficient, though its policy is not, as it was before 1939, to design as well as produce all equipment: most of its military aircraft are foreign designs produced under licence and it shares design and development of other items with foreign governments, notably in the field of anti-tank weapons and armoured vehicles.

The major arms producers are Krauss−Maffei AG of Munich (Leopard tank); Thyssen Rheinstahl Henschel of

German Federal Republic

Kassel (Jagdpanzer tank-destroyer, Marder APC, and other armoured vehicles); Hanomag (military vehicles); Messerschmitt–Bölkow–Blöhm of Munich (anti-tank missiles); Carl Walther of Ulm, Heckler and Koch of Oberndorf, Rheinmettal of Dusseldorf (small arms); Diehl Mettalwerk of Nürnberg (anti-armour weapons).

Equipment

Small Arms
Pistol: 9mm PI Walther
Sub-machine-gun:: 9mm Uzi (Israel)
(Assault) rifle: 7.62mm G3 (Heckler and Koch; German version of the Spanish CETME)
Machine-gun: 7.62mm MG3 Rheinmettal (the World War II MG-42)

20mm HS 820 Cannon
   Hispano–Suiza (Swiss) } Mounted on the Marder APC
20mm Rh 202 Cannon
   Rheinmettal

Mortars: 120mm MRS-120-2 Soltan (Israel; equips the support company of the infantry battalion) 120mm Tampella (Israel; equips the support company of the airborne battalion)
Anti-armour weapons: PZF 44mm one-man rocket launcher (Diehl; the infantry platoon anti-tank weapon) Milan guided missile (Messerschmitt–Bölkow; the company anti-tank weapon); TOW guided missile (America; equips the anti-tank company of the brigade); HOT guided missile (French; equips the anti-tank company of the brigade)
Anti-aircraft weapons: Roland surface-to-air missile equips the corps anti-aircraft battalions); 35mm twin self-propelled Gepard (German–Swiss; equips the divisional anti-aircraft battalion)
Artillery: 105mm pack-howitzer (Italy; equips the artillery battalion of the mountain brigade); 155mm FH 70 howitzer; equips divisional artillery battalion; 155mm M-109 SP howitzer (America; equips the brigade artillery battalions (*not* the mountain or airborne brigades); 175mm M-107 SP gun (America; equips two battalions of the corps artillery); 203mm M-110 SP howitzer (America; equips one battery of the divisional artillery; can fire a nuclear shell (held in American custody)); 110mm rocket-launcher, 110SF (36 tubes to each launcher; equips one battalion of the divisional artillery); 'Lance' surface-to-surface missile (America; equips one battalion of the corps artillery)
Armour: APC Marder (Rheinstahl–Hensche; equips the *Panzergrenadier* battalion); APC M-113 (America; equips some *Panzergrenadier* battalions); Armoured car: Spahpanzer 2 Luchs (Rheinstahl–Henschel; replacing the Hotchkiss; 8-wheeled, 20mm cannon, 100k.p.h.); Tank-destroyer: Jaguar carrier (20 HOT guided missiles; equips the tank-destroyer companies of brigades); Tank: Leopard 1 and 2 (Krauss–Maffei; 105mm gun (British), crew 4; range 600km, weight 40tonnes; engine, Daimler 830h.p.; equips most panzer battalions); Tank: M-48 (America; equips some panzer battalions; under replacement by Leopard 2)
Aircraft: Alouette II light helicopter (France; equips the divisional aviation squadron and the observation/liaison squadron of the corps aviation command); Bell UH-DI light transport helicopter (America; equips the light transport regiment of the corps aviation command); Sikorsky CH-53 DG medium transport helicopter (America; equips the medium transport regiment of the corps aviation command); BO105 (German; equips the anti-tank helicopter regiment of the corps aviation command).

RANK, DRESS AND DISTINCTIONS

Rank

General — Four stars and oak wreath
Generalleutnant — Three stars and oak wreath
Generalmajor — Two stars and oak wreath
Brigadegeneral — One star and oak wreath
Oberst — Three stars and oak wreath
Oberstleutnant — Two stars and oak wreath
Major — One star and oak wreath
Hauptmann — Three stars (no wreath)
Oberleutnant — Two stars (no wreath)
Leutnant — One star (no wreath)

Oberstabsfeldwebel — Bronze edging, looped chevron, two chevrons
Stabsfeldwebel — Bronze edging, looped chevron, one chevron
Hauptfeldwebel — Bronze edging, looped chevron
Oberfeldwebel — Bronze edging, two chevrons
Feldwebel — Bronze edging, one chevron
Stabsunteroffizier — Bronze edging
Unteroffizier — Bronze edging (part)
Hauptgefreiter — Three half-chevrons
Obergefreiter — Two half-chevrons
Gefreiter — One half-chevron
Grenadier (etc.) — —

All badges of rank are worn (since 1973) on the shoulder strap. Generals' badges of rank are in gold, the rest in silver. Generals preserve the gold-embroidered scarlet patches, derived from the 26th *Altlarisch* Regiment of Frederick the Great and worn by the generals of the Kaisers' army and the *Wehrmacht*. The many gradations of NCO rank are also a historical relic, and are very difficult to relate to those of other armies.

Dress

The *Bundeswehr* has also preserved its traditional facing colours (*Waffenfarbe*) of the arms of service, worn as piping on trousers, hats, shoulder straps and collar badges: General Staff maroon; Armour pink; Armoured Reconnaissance yellow; Artillery brick red; Anti-aircraft Artillery coral red; Engineers black; Signals lemon yellow; Infantry grass green; Technical Troops blue; Army Aviation light grey; Nuclear/Chemical Troops crimson; Military Police orange; Military Bands white; Medical Corps dark blue.

As in East Germany (q.v.), the question of what the new army should wear proved a distinctly problematical matter at the time of rearmament in 1956. In the *Bundesrepublik*, it was one on which the public spoke its mind and that of her former enemies was consulted. A return to *Wehrmacht* styles was dismissed and a distinctly civilian design adopted, with short boots in place of the famous 'dice boxes' and an American helmet in place of the 'coal scuttle'. The moderation proved overdone, for the new style did not find favour with those who had to wear it, and it has subsequently undergone a subtle re-militarisation. It remains, however, fairly simple and civilian, and a not particularly traditional dress: light-grey jacket, dark-grey trousers and a peaked cap for walking-out; 'moss-grey' combat suit. Tank crew wear black berets, parachutists maroon, *Jäger* green, *Panzergrenadiere* brown; the mountain troops wear the ski-cap with its edelweiss badge. All ranks wear the black–red–yellow national cockade on their hats.

Distinctions

All *Bundeswehr* regiments carry a colour (*Truppenfahne*), black–red–gold, with the black eagle in the centre, carried on a traditional spear-pointed staff. Recruits are sworn into the regiment holding an edge of the colour. Some medals have been created for the *Bundeswehr* but restrictions on its role have prevented the earning of many: an exception is the 1962 Hamburg flood-catastrophe medal.

CURRENT DEVELOPMENTS

Since the publication of the last edition of *World Armies* in 1979, the army of the Federal German Republic has completed a major reorganisation, which makes it a more formidable force than ever. The direction of change, to what is called Structure No 4, is towards strengthening the brigades and divisions, in part by transferring units and equipment to them from the corps, in part by the replacement of old equipment with new. Apart from the mountain and parachute divisions, which remain on a separate organisation, all divisions now consist exclusively of armoured and armoured infantry brigades; the two *Jäger* divisions (2nd and 4th), formerly infantry, have been transformed into armoured infantry divisions, while 1st, 7th and 11th divisions are now fully armoured. Even in the mountain division, only one brigade remains specialist infantry; the other two are amoured and armoured infantry respectively. The brigades of the parachute division, which are allotted one to each of the three corps, are trained and equipped for the role of rapid intervention against amoured incursions. Some old equipment (American M-48 tanks and M-113 armoured personnel carriers) is still in service; but it is rapidly being replaced by Leopard 2 and Marder.

A further change furnishes each brigade with the cadre for a fourth battalion, of tanks and infantry mixed, to be formed on mobilisation, and each division with the cadre for a fourth brigade (of infantry). On mobilisation, the strength of the field army would therefore rise from 36 to 57 brigades.

The Territorial Army, which is under national command, has also grown impressively in strength. Six of the Home Defence Brigades Type A have been formed; they consist of two motorised infantry battalions, two tank battalions (equipped with the M-48s shed from the Field Army, and an artillery battalion; six Type B brigades are under organisation, and will consist of two infantry, one tank and one artillery battalions. In addition, fifteen Home Defence Regiments, each of three infantry battalions, are now in existence, together with 150 Home Defence Companies and 300 Security Platoons.

The growing strength of the Warsaw Pact armies appears now to bulk larger with German public opinion than the residual anti-military feeling which was noticeable ten years ago, and also counterbalances youthful opposition to the obligations of national service. The German army, already the largest in NATO's Central Region, must therefore certainly be counted the most formidable.

John Keegan

GHANA*

HISTORY AND INTRODUCTION

Ghana attained independence from Britain in 1957, the first African colony of any European power to do so. As the Gold Coast, Ghana had been ruled by Britain in a manner generally both efficient and progressive. From the days of Governor Sir Gordon Guggisberg in the 1920s, effort had been spent on the education of an African elite, a policy that equipped Ghana well in terms of professional men at independence but was nevertheless to carry within it, unforeseen, an elitism that in turn was to engender radicalism. The radicalism has made appeal at times of economic difficulty. These times have increased in number and in gravity when Ghana's rulers pursue narrow socialistic policies, invest in prestige projects of doubtful value and create economic institutions that work only to give jobs to political clients. Failure to expand and diversify constructively has meant that Ghana's traditional exports, expecially cocoa, serve less and less to meet her import needs and preferences. These latter may often reflect the personal preferences of the elite, so worsening the problems and the resentments.

President Nkrumah, Ghana's ruler until his overthrow in a military and police coup in 1966 became increasingly frustrated at the slow pace of development after independence. This frustration led Nkrumah increasingly to a slatternly form of political radicalism. This radicalism perturbed the elite, who were in any case and with very good reason shocked by Nkrumah's despotic pretensions, the decay of politics, corruption and economic mismanagement. The first coup installed a 'National Liberation Council' of conservative army and police officers which gave Ghana a military government remarkable for its tolerance, absence of political prisoners and attempts to eradicate nepotism and corruption; unfortunately its development record was disappointing and Ghana's overall economic situation deteriorated. After a commendably free election in 1969, Ghana returned to civilian rule. The new premier, K. Busia, however, made a number of political and economic misjudgements that led to his overthrow in 1972 by a second military coup. The second military government, unlike the first of Generals Ankrah and Afrifa which saw itself as a caretaker regime aiming to return to parliamentary democracy, held that a period of military rule was necessary in order to initiate reform of many of the country's institutions. The regime's leader, Colonel I. Acheampong, envisaged 'union government', in practice a no-party state, to include a legislature elected but with no political links, as an eventual aim. Acheampong, after a not unpromising start, soon however found the innovatory role of economic and political saviour of the nation too much for the army and himself; he and some of his associates fell to corruption and his methods became increasingly arbitrary. The methods included open harassment of the elite. In July 1978 Acheampong was removed from office by General F. Akuffo, who tried to follow in the path of the first military regime's caretaker style, by arranging elections to be held in 1979.

At this point the radical sector of Ghana's life, the urban unemployed, under-employed and blue collar workers,

produced a new champion, Flight-Lieutenant Jerry Rawlings, an air force officer of part-British, part-Ghanaian parentage, of mercurial temperament and a record of indiscipline. Rawlings seized power in June 1979 at the head of an Armed Forces Revolutionary Council composed of junior ranks, in some cases private soldiers; the seizure was accomplished only with bloodshed, the Army Commander, General Odartey-Wellington, being killed in the fighting. Further bloodshed followed when Generals Afrifa, Acheampong and three other senior officers were all executed, supposedly for corruption, without any form of trial and, in the case of Afrifa, simply for reasons of political revenge; the corruption charge against the others had rather more validity. Harassment, amounting at times almost to a pogrom, of the professional classes and the elite, (including attacks upon and beating-up of a large number of the Army's best officers by soldiers and NCOs) followed, a military PIT (pre-trial investigation team) becoming notorious.

Under some external pressure Rawlings agreed to allow the election planned by General Akuffo to take place; he and his followers in turn exercised internal pressures that ensured the return of a government, headed by President Limann pledged to a resumption of many of Nkrumah's radical policies. Limann, however, became almost paralysed by the sharply worsening economic predicament of Ghana – which needed drastic and politically unpopular measures – on the one hand, and the presence in the wings of Rawlings – now to an increasing extent the prisoner of forces he had unleashed – on the other.

In January, 1982 Rawlings, totally dissatisfied with Limann and urged on by extreme radical followers, removed the President from office, installing himself as head of a Provisional National Defence Council the membership of which includes the Chief of the Defence Staff, a dissenting Catholic priest, a warrant officer and a sergeant, and a trade union leader and a student leader. 'Peoples Defence Committees' now watch and harass any entrepreneurial activity, critics of the regime disappear, many of the country's ablest officials and professional men have fled abroad.

Ghana's armed forces were once among the best in Africa. They took pride in their descent from the Gold Coast Regiment of the former Royal West African Frontier Force. This regiment served in the Togo and German East Africa campaigns of World War I (being very highly rated by General Smuts) and in the Italian East Africa and Burma campaigns of World War II. A Ghanaian brigade, still including at the time a number of British officers, served with success in the UN Congo Expeditionary Force in 1960–62. It was, however, from the Congo period that the Ghana army became disenchanted with President Nkrumah, a disaffection that came to a head in 1964–5 when, in addition to major national abuses of power, he raised a rival military *Waffen-SS* style formation and starved the army of funds. Proposed defence expenditure reductions were also an important contributory cause of the 1972 coup.

It must be assumed that the upheavals of the last three years have destroyed the discipline and efficiency of the armed forces and a long period of reconstruction is going to be necessary. There is evidence of detachments from units fighting against each other, general abnegation of responsibility by officers, particular harassment of Ewe personnel

---

* For general notes on African armies, see Appendix 1.

from the eastern part of the country and clashes and shoot-outs with sections of the civil community in a number of places. The 'Peoples Defence Commitees' exist in military units.

STRENGTH AND BUDGET

Population: 12,750,000
Armed Forces: Army 12,500; Air Force 1400; Border Guard Force 5000
GNP: ⎫ not known
Defence Expenditure: ⎭

COMMAND AND CONSTITUTIONAL STATUS

The army, now the 'People's Army' is under command of Flight-Lieutenant J. Rawlings as Head of State. Mr Riley-Poku is Minister for Defence and Brigadier J. Nunoo-Mensah is Chief of the Defence Staff.

ROLE, COMMITMENT, DEPLOYMENT AND RECENT OPERATIONS

The large size of the Ghana army is legacy of the grandiose ambitions that President Nkrumah entertained for his country, a size which successor governments have been unwilling or unable to reduce substantially. The army does, however, have certain specific commitments, notably that in relation to Togo. The Ewe ethnic group lives on both sides of the border, the majority on the Togo side, and any Ghana government is periodically faced with a secessionist movement; the issues are complex, being further complicated by the fact that the present border is not that of the old German Togoland colony, but further east (i.e. to Ghana's advantage). A need for a strong force to overawe Togo is perceived, and Togo complicity in conspiracies to overthrow the government are periodically alleged. At present Togo is much criticised for providing refuge to members of the elite.

Other recent commitments include border patrolling (to prevent the outward smuggling of cocoa, for which a better price can be found in neighbouring Francophone States) and the despatch of one battalion to the United Nations Command in Sinai and later one to the Lebanon. UNIFIL, the United Nations Lebanon Force was in fact under the command of a Ghanaian officer, Major-General E. Erskine.

ORGANISATION

The army is composed of two brigades of three infantry battalions each, supported by an armoured car reconnaissance battalion, a field engineer battalion, a mortar battalion, an airborne battalion and a signals battalion. A seventh battalion was disbanded, though the parachute battalion, disbanded by the 1969–72 civilian government, is being reformed. It will lack any real capacity for dropping.

The brigade headquarters are at Accra (1st Brigade) and Kumasi (2nd Brigade). Battalions are generally posted to Accra, Tema and Takoradi (1st Brigade) and Kumasi, Sunyani and Tamale (2nd Brigade).

Army headquarters is at Burma Camp, Accra. The Border Guard force is organised into three battalions and is has hitherto mainly deployed in the Eastern Region; lately however units have been deployed in the west to stop smuggling cocoa out to the Ivory Coast.

The air bases are at Tamale and Takoradi.

RECRUITMENT, TRAINING AND RESERVES

Recruitment is voluntary. The army still contains a large number of soldiers from the poorer ethnic groups of northern Ghana and also a few from francophone States further north attracted by the conditions of service. Recruits are trained at the combined services basic training centre at Kumasi. There is a military cadet academy (with a 2 year course), a school of infantry and a junior officers course, at Teshie, near Accra.

With British assistance a small staff college opened recently at Teshie and subsequently moved to a large prestige building from the Nkrumah era in Accra. Field training is perceived to fall under two main headings: forest training and savannah training; units are expected to be proficient in both.

For a period of three years after independence, the Ghana army relied heavily on British assistance and British officers in command appointments, a reliance largely caused by Nkrumah's doubling of the army's size. In 1961 however, almost all of the British officers were repatriated and British assistance was replaced by Canadian instructors, on a much reduced scale; but officers are still sent to Britain for staff training and also a few cadets to Sandhurst. One or two cadets were sent to Pakistan; Israel and the Soviet Union both promised military help, but apart from the provision of Israeli mortars and some very out-of-date Soviet equipment, the assistance appears to have been negligible. After the fall of Nkrumah there was an increased use of British facilities in the N.L.C. period including battalion exchange visits in 1968 and 1969. Since 1970, foreign exchange has proved the largest obstacle to further overseas training, though the arrangements whereby a small number of officers, cadets and specialists train in Britain, has so far continued.

Foreign exchange shortages have had two other specifically military consequences. All units are required to grow a proportion of their own food in unit farms, and much of the army's transport is earmarked as a 'task force' to help the civil administration.

EQUIPMENT AND ARMS INDUSTRY

The Reconnaissance Regiment is equipped with Mowag Piranha armoured-cars of which Ghana possesses 100, a very small number of older Saladin and Ferret vehicles may still be serviceable. The mortar battalion is equipped with twenty Tampella 100mm mortars, and the infantry battalions carry 81mm mortars, and 84mm Carl Gustav rocket launchers.

The Air Force possesses a light air-to-ground strike squadron of twelve Aeromacchi MB-326 machines, two transport squadrons that between them operate eight Britten-Norman Islanders and six Short Skyvans, a light transport/communication squadron of five F-27 and F-28 aircraft, a training squadron of ten Bulldog machines, together with two Alouette and two Bell 212 helicopters.

The shortage of foreign exchange has seriously affected the supply of spare parts and fuel for field training.

RANK, DRESS AND DISTINCTIONS

The Ghana army uniforms still closely follow British patterns in rank structure, dress and uniform embellishments. The different battalions have distinctive belts or lanyards, rank insignia differ from those of Britain only in the replacement of the crown by a national emblem. Gold braid on caps again follows the British model. Distinctive, however, is the scarlet ceremonial parade tunic, worn above dark-blue trousers with a red stripe.

CURRENT DEVELOPMENTS

Ghana's once proud and efficient little army is now no more. The future, like the future of the country, will depend on the measure of success obtained by Rawlings and the PNDC in restoring some form of discipline and social cohesion, and in pursuing constructive economic policies. Rawlings appears now to recognise the need for both, and is known personally to have berated units with the worst breakdown in discipline. Whether he will be able to carry some of his more extreme associates with him is debatable. The alternative would most likely prove to be further social disintegration and violence.

In military terms, Ghana will remain enfeebled for at least a number of years, but it is unlikely that any of her neighbours other than Togo would see any gain by taking advantage of it; Togo's own internal problems and the need for any government in Lomé not to alienate Paris are perhaps the most optimistic features of the Ghanaian military scene.

ADDENDUM

In November 1982 a fresh upheaval in Ghana occurred, the details and implications of which are still unclear. It seems that the sergeant member of the PNDC, along with other NCOs, attempted to overthrow the Rawlings government, though the attempt was a failure. Shooting and casualties occurred. The sergeant and the NCOs were arrested. Although the sergeant was known to hold militant leftist views, government rhetoric lays blame on right-wingers and on Britain, probably for political convenience. Brigadier Nunoo-Mensah resigned before the coup attempt. The senior ranking officer now is the Army Commander, Brigadier A. Quainoo.

Lloyd Mathews

GREECE

HISTORY AND INTRODUCTION

In the course of this century Greece has fought in five wars, endured two foreign occupations, and suffered a catastrophic civil war, which might be thought enough to keep its army fully occupied. That is not the case, however: since 1900 Greece has also experienced 10 major military *coups d'état*, several bouts of fighting between army factions, and a host of minor military upheavals.

This dismal pattern is not fundamentally due to the army's lack of discipline (though that has often enough suffered from the consequences of political involvement). The basic clash between the military and the civilian ethos in Greece, indeed, arises from the fact that the army is the only effective corporate institution of wide membership in the entire Greek nation, with a vision of an orderly, 'Western' Greece that is utterly at odds with the fiercely fractious individualism that is the Greek reality in politics, business and private life. Some officers are seduced by the universal civilian systems of patronage and so drawn into the political arena, while others are driven by disgust verging on despair to try their hand at uprooting such systems by firm military rule.

The Greek army of today, even after the shattering experience of the collapse of the most recent period of military rule in 1974, still has clearly identifiable patterns of behaviour and belief that can be traced to its past experiences over a century and a half of turbulent Greek history. The only period which has not left a residue, surprisingly, is the Greek War of Independence itself, ending in the establishment of an independent Greek national State in the Balkans for the first time in history. The semi-regular soldiers and semi-brigand armed bands that fought in that struggle were almost all disbanded immediately afterwards, and the bulk of the Greek army during the first decade after 1833 was in fact comprised of 3500 Bavarian soldiers who arrived in that year with the new King Otto. Only a handful of Greeks were retained in military service, and employed as the Athens garrison.

The first act of self-assertion of a genuinely Greek army was the mutiny of that garrison in 1843, which succeeded in extracting a constitution of sorts from King Otto and also insisted upon the Hellenisation of the army. The tradition of German training and methods in the army, however, was not broken by this upheaval, or even by the overthrow and expulsion of Otto 20 years later. The new dynasty, though Danish by origin, maintained the German orientation of its predecessor in military matters. The army's close personal links with the monarchy, and that of the monarchy with the German court, actually grew more influential with the passage of time: at the outbreak of World War I the new King Constantine (who had personally commanded the army in the successful Balkan Wars in 1912–13 as Crown Prince) was married to the Kaiser's sister, and convinced that a German victory was inevitable. This was one of the strands that was to prepare the way for the catastrophe that is Greek history from 1915–50.

The second strand was the growth in Greece after about 1850 of *Megali Idea* (the Great Idea) as the focus and goal of all nationalist sentiment. It was nothing less than a project to reverse several centuries of history in Asia Minor, and re-establish Byzantium. Way-stations along this road were to include the rounding out of Greece's frontiers in Europe to embrace all those areas containing Greek majorities or even large Greek minorities (a process more or less completed by the Balkan Wars), and the ingathering of the various islands like Crete and Cyprus which had majority Greek populations. The ultimate goal, however, was nothing less than the recapture and re-Hellenisation of Constantinople (Istanbul) and of at least the western parts of Anatolia, where a considerable Greek minority had continued to live and even to flourish during over five centuries of Ottoman Turkish rule. From the mid-nineteenth century onwards devotion to *Megali Idea* became the litmus test of nationalist virtue, and the dominating theme in Greek foreign policy, leading to ever more adventurous and even reckless foreign policies.

The third strand in preparing the disaster was the politicisation of the Greek army. Greek governmental chaos in the late nineteenth century (an average of one government every 9 months between 1864 and 1908) was appalling, but it owed little to the army. The Greek army had never been neutral in politics, of course – no Greek individual or institution is permitted that luxury – but it had not been a particularly coup-prone army. The key event in establishing the very different twentieth century pattern of army behaviour was the coup of 1909, which was directed (like so many since) at a government which had failed to measure up to the demands of *Megali Idea*, by giving in to international pressure not to declare a union with Crete. (The Cretan situation was very similar to that in Cyprus 50 years later.) Not only did the army revolt set a new precedent for military intervention, but it also actually brought to power Eleftherios Venizelos, the Cretan politician who was to dominate the next 20 years of Greek history.

These three strands came together in 1915, when King Constantine and the bulk of the army's senior officers, pro-German or at least convinced of German military superiority, insisted on remaining neutral. For Venizelos and the passionate adherents of the Great Idea, however, the war was Greece's golden opportunity: by fighting on the side of the *Entente* powers Greece could demand and get the lion's share of Anatolian Turkey in the post-war share-out of territory. The quarrel between Prime Minister Venizelos and the King, abetted by the representatives in Athens of the warring powers, rapidly led to the division of the army and the country between a republican regime based in the north at Salonika and committed to the allied cause, and a royal government and army based in Athens and determined on neutralism. The French occupation of Athens in 1916 (and of the whole country by mid-1917) ended the visible divisions, but the bitter monarchist–republican split was to dominate Greek politics for the next 30 years. Traces of it can be discerned even today.

In the short run it led to the participation of the Greek army (thoroughly purged of 1500 monarchist officers) in the final offensives of 1918 in the Balkans, and to a share in the occupation of long-desired Constantinople. Venizelos eagerly agreed to provide Greek troops for occupation duties in Anatolia as well, and by 1920 the Great Idea seemed to be on the brink of success. At that moment the young King, in whose favour the pro-German Constantine had abdicated the throne in 1916, suddenly died, and Constantine himself returned, to be approved overwhelmingly in a national referendum. Venizelos went into exile, Constantine re-instated all the purged monarchist officers and ejected Veni-zelos' republican supporters instead, and the army was sent marching off into the heart of Anatolia in search of decisive victory over the Turkish nationalist forces of Mustafa Kemal (Ataturk).

The military disaster that overtook that army in 1922 was in a sense inevitable, for there was never any realistic possib-ility that Greece could establish control over Western Anatolia in face of the hostility of a large and determined Turkish majority. But the successive purges, and the blind factional stubbornness that had infected all areas of Greek politics including the army, was certainly a contributing factor to the scale of the disaster, whose shock is still reverberating in Greece today. In the space of a few weeks, the entire Greek population, some 1,250,000 people, were swept out of Anatolia ahead of the victorious Turkish army, and 3000 years of continuous Greek settlement on the eastern shores of the Aegean came to an abrupt and permanent end. The Greek army was utterly shattered, and a number of refugees from Anatolia equal to one quarter of the native population was suddenly dumped on an impoverished Greece unable to feed and shelter even its own population.

The Venizelos/republican faction had begun the adventure, the monarchist faction had taken it over on the way to catas-trophe, and each could and would blame the other in the harshest terms for decades into the future. In the immedi-ate aftermath of the Anatolian disaster Constantine went into exile again, the republican officers seized control of the army once more, and the monarchist commander-in-chief and five former cabinet members were executed. It was a measure of the unutterable bitterness of the mutual recrim-inations, hatreds and fears that now came to dominate Greece, as the unhealed divisions distorted both political and military life, and another precedent for the future.

The army had in some senses been the arbiter of power ever since 1843, but it was in the chaotic years 1922—36 that the tradition of military intervention in the modern style took root. In those years there were 19 changes of government, seven military coups and an almost constant flow of abortive plots. Moreover, every royalist or republican coup or counter-coup by the army — or the navy — and every change of civil government became the occasion, more than ever before, for yet another purge of politically suspect members of the officer corps, in the search for a wholly illusory security. Not only did military intervention in politics became established, but political meddling with the army became the accepted *quid pro quo*. Hundreds and even thousands of officers were purged as governments flickered past, now military, now civilian, this one monarchist, that one republican. Executions were not unknown.

This anarchic period was ended by a coup by royalist officers in 1935 that managed to hold on to power. The monarchy was restored, the ageing Venizelos was sentenced to death *in absentia* (and two of his colleagues in the flesh), and within a year General John Metaxas had emerged as military dictator under the King. His rule was widely char-acterised as fascist (in the strict, rather than merely the pejorative sense of the word) by those who confused it with the populist right-wing regimes then typical of central Europe, but it was in fact in a purely Greek tradition of mili-tary rule which had already established itself in the 1920s, and was not without crude similarities to the pattern of administration that then prevailed also in the neighbouring Turkey of Ataturk. In the Greek case, however, it proved both more extreme and longer lived.

The puritanical values of Greek military governments, and the stumbling means by which they have sought to impose them on an unwilling Greek population, have been remark-ably similar throughout this century, from General Pangalos in 1926 through General Metaxas in 1936—40 to Colonel Papadopoulos in 1967—73. All were devoted to an ideal of 'Hellenic—Christian civilisation' in which the Greeks were not the squabbling, venal mortals of reality but the noble ab-stract beings of an impossible mythological past, and all were determined to transform their countrymen from the former to the latter state by the sharp smack of barracks discipline. It gave rise to a frustration entirely understandable inside the army, where the dominant virtues were order, duty and patriotism, and to an ambition utterly hopeless in reality.

Pangalos, like all his successors, began by censoring the press, exiling his opponents, and demanding efficiency from the civil service, but soon he could think of little better to do than to forbid women to wear skirts more than 14 inches above the ground. Metaxas followed much the same course, with the added attractions of social welfare measures (directed most notably towards the rural population), public works and the construction of a massive security police apparatus. Thirty years later the colonels around Papadopoulos were pursuing precisely the same path yet again (complete with compulsory haircuts for hirsute tourists at the Greek border), and hectoring and cajoling the population to be worthy of their Greek heritage in a tone of voice almost identical to Metaxas's (one observer, indeed, has referred to their per-formance as 'a gigantic act of historical ventriloquism').

The one element in the army's ideology which was new in Metaxas' time, though it has been prominent ever since, was a rigid and fanatical anti-communism. It began when the tiny Greek Communist Party, based mainly amongst the destitute Anatolian refugees, briefly achieved a position of balance of power in the mid-1930s, but it had to wait for the 1940s to reach its full flowering. Meanwhile, Greece was invaded by Italy in 1940. Initial Greek resistance to the incompetent Italian attack was successful, and Metaxas died before the German invasion of the subsequent spring destroyed Greek resistance. There then ensued 4 years of occupation, follow-ed by 3 years of civil war. During the decade of the 1940s over 10% of the Greek population died due to the fighing or to starvation, and an already poor country was laid waste.

As in many other occupied countries of Europe, the com-munists of Greece, with their highly secretive administrative structure, proved to be the most effective group in the organisation of a resistance movement. By early 1943 their own force, ELAS (National Popular Liberation Army) was by far the largest of the Greek guerrilla organisations. By no means all their fighters were communists — many were simply republicans disgusted by the futile quarrels of the exiled monarchist government — but the leadership was firmly in communist hands. This leadership showed its hand prematurely in the summer of 1943, however, in the so-called 'first round', when under the mistaken impression that the forthcoming Allied landings would be not in Italy but in Greece, the communists launched surprise attacks aimed at destroying all the other Greek resistance movements. By the end of the year only one survived, in a distant corner of the country, while the communists controlled virtually all the rest of Greece except for the German-occupied main towns and communications routes.

This premature revelation of their purposes was ultimately fatal for the Greek communists, however, as it caused a gradual drift of republicans into alliance with the exiled monarchist government, and alerted the British in the Medi-terranean to the true situation in Greece. The communists succeeded in fomenting a major anti-monarchist mutiny in the Greek army in exile in Egypt in the summer of 1944, just before the Germans evacuated the country and the legal

220

government returned, but British military forces were sent to Athens to support the government in lieu of its own troops. When they arrived they found ELAS forces in control in fully nine-tenths of Greece, and the showdown came in December, 1944 when the communist forces refused the British commander's demand that they observe an agreement to disband all guerrilla units and reform within a Greek national army. In the so-called 'second round', communist forces took four-fifths of Athens, including the harbour and one of the two airports, and fought their way to within 300 yards of the British Embassy which was serving as allied headquarters, but British reinforcements were urgently sent over from Italy and succeeded in re-establishing control. By January, 1945 the second round was over, and ELAS agreed to surrender its arms (probably on Stalin's orders, pursuant to his 'percentage agreement' with Churchill).

However, there then began a white terror, directed not only at known communists, but at anyone who had been associated with ELAS in the fight against the Germans. The vengeance campaign was headed by monarchists and some former collaborators, but received strong support from the security forces (which has been purged of all left-wing elements after the 1944 mutiny). In less than a year 3000 people were officially condemned to death, at least another 500 murdered, and there were 20,000 in prison with a further 50,000 facing prosecution. It was in these circumstances that ELAS took up arms again for the 'third round', by far the worst, in 1946. There ensured 3 years of full-scale civil war, now centred in northern Greece where the communists were receiving aid from Albania, Yugoslavia and Bulgaria, which cost 150,000 casualties and made a million people refugees. The remnants of the economy were utterly ruined, and political reconstruction did not even get underway; between 1945 and 1952 there were over 20 Greek governments, with an average life of 150 days. The army was gradually rebuilt during the fighting with British and then American aid, and in the formative experience of the civil war tempered the obsessive anti-communism that has characterised it ever since.

At just this time, however, there occurred two remarkable changes of fortune which transformed Greek prospects, and led to a 15 year period of stable democratic politics and rising prosperity unprecedented in modern Greek history. The first was General (later Field-Marshal) Alexander Papagos, a military hero from both the Italian and the civil wars, who refrained from seizing power by the usual *coup d'état*. Instead he exploited his popularity to win power by elections (modelling himself consciously on de Gaulle) in 1952, and succeeded in passing on a stabilised political system to his successor, Constantine Karamanlis, in 1955. He was greatly aided in this by the second stroke of luck: the change from bankrupt Britain to wealthy America as the constitutional government's principal outside supporter upon the proclamation of the Truman Doctrine in 1947.

The consequence was an immense flow of American aid and investment that fuelled Greece's startlingly rapid economic recovery and expansion through the 1950s and early 1960s. By making hitherto undreamt of sums available to the government, for allocation by the usual patronage channels, it may also have been the main factor in enabling Karamanlis to rule as Prime Minister for eight unbroken years, twice as long as anyone else in modern Greek history. For the army, particularly after Greece's accession to the NATO treaty in 1952, it meant a flood of modern American weapons and a new role (at least in theory) as a member of a large alliance. Although its political perceptions and priorities were little changed by the close relationship with the United States, it did end up using almost exclusively American military assumptions, procedures and weapons.

Politically, the army remained an enclave of anti-communism and strongly authoritarian ideas, best typified perhaps by the ultra-right-wing secret organisation IDEA (Sacred Union of Greek Officers) which was founded in the early 1950s. This orientation, though not out of harmony with the general political atmosphere at the end of the Civil War, led to increasing hostility and suspicion between the army and civilian politics as the latter drifted leftward over the succeeding years.

The primary cause of that leftward drift was unquestionably the Cyprus problem, which first emerged in 1950, but grew far more acute after the EOKA guerrillas began operations there in 1955. The failure of NATO to take a firm position in favour of the Greek case, due to the fact that Turkey was also a NATO member, occasioned a steadily rising agitation against NATO links in Greece, and the resultant growth of the far-left EDA (United Democratic Front) to the position of second-largest party. Karamanlis's staunchly conservative government resisted these pressures (an agreement on storing American nuclear weapons in Greece was finally signed in 1959) and in 1960 the crisis seemed to have ended with a settlement that the government could defend. The respite proved only temporary, however; the newly founded Centre Union Party of George Papandreou, the grand old man of republican Greek politics and a one-time *protégé* of Venizelos, quickly joined the EDA in condemning the 1960 compromise creating a bi-national Cypriot republic as an unprincipled betrayal of the sacred Greek national cause for a mess of American pottage. *Megali Idea* re-emerged to dominate Greek politics, with consequences almost as grave as before.

Papandreou's party scraped a narrow victory in the 1963 elections. When it then resigned in December, 1963 to seek a larger majority (which it eventually got), President—Archbishop Makarios of Cyprus exploited the political paralysis in Athens and in Ankara (where there was also a caretaker cabinet) to abrogate the rights guaranteed to Turkish—Cypriots under the 1960 Constitution. The large-scale fighting in Cyprus that followed, accompanied by an acute Greek—Turkish crisis which came close to war, spelled the end of political stability in Greece. Greek impotence to impose Athens's preferred solution in Cyprus was reflected in a mounting verbal hostility of the government against NATO, and Papandreou's reckless rhetoric encouraged the renewed polarisation of Greek politics. The right was greatly alarmed by the rapid advancement of Papandreou's son Andreas, who came to symbolise the re-emergent left, and by the growth of Soviet influence in Cyprus. In the time-honoured Greek way, everybody began to scent foreign intrigue and domestic plots, a perception given some substance by the uncovering of the so-called Aspida (Shield) group of young left-wing Greek officers in Cyprus, who were reputed to be planning a republican coup. Only some 28 officers were implicated, but Andreas Papandreou was accused of being involved with them.

The final blow to Greek political stability was the elder Papandreou's attempt to reconstruct the Greek officer corps by purging its right-wing senior officers, many of whom owed their advancement to Metaxas, and all of whom were immured in a 30 year-old right-wing tradition of royalism and extreme anti-communism. When Papandreou's own Defence Minister refused to accept a new list of army transfers and promotions in July, 1965 the King refused to allow the Prime Minister himself to assume the Defence post on the grounds that his son was under suspicion with regard to the Aspida affair. Papandreou resigned, and the King hastily appointed a new, conservative government. The last 18 months until the inevitable army coup was a scene of chaotic disorder as the left-wing parties furiously attacked the King, the government and the army amidst violent street demonstrations, and right-wing groups retaliated with the implicit approval of the security forces.

The coup of April 21st, 1967 that inflicted a 'mercy killing' on Greek democracy (the phrase is Constantine Karamanlis's) came from the army, as expected, but not from its leadership. A virtually unknown group of colonels seized power in an almost bloodless operation and proceeded in time honoured fashion to 'cleanse' the nation of the excesses produced by unfettered democracy. The leader, Colonel George Papadopoulos, was Head of the Greek Intelligence Service, giving substance to the instant Greek conclusion that the coup had been sponsored by the American CIA, but there was neither evidence nor logical reason to support such a provenance. The number of officers directly involved in the coup numbered no more than 300 in the 9000-strong officer corps, but they unquestionably represented a much broader body of sentiment in the army.

All the familiar measures were taken: martial law, censorship, the banning of strikes and public demonstrations, the arrest of 7000 people in a few days (though all but about 1000 had been released by 1969), a purge of the civil service and the professions, loyalty tests for university students, etc. The Communist Parties remained illegal, of course, and all left-wing political activists became the object of severe repressive measures. There was also the customary authoritarian imposition of the rural and *petit-bourgeois* moral values that prevailed in the officer corps: a ban on long hair, mini-skirts, music in public places after midnight, and such deplorably 'Eastern' Greek customs as smashing crockery in cafes.

The 'Hellenic—Christian' version of the Greek nation, with strong emphasis on the unity of Orthodox Church and State, on the artificial *Katharevousa* version of the language which was invented in the last century as a bridge between modern demotic Greek and the 'pure' language of classical times, and on the Apollonian rather than the Dionysian version of Greek culture, was relentlessly imposed on the resistant Greek reality. In the economic sphere also the *junta*, made up almost entirely of former village boys raised in grinding rural poverty, pursued the usual course of Greek military regimes: strict financial discipline, and stabilisation of the currency (after severe inflation in the last years of civilian government), together with a determined drive for economic growth which met with some success.

The military regime of 1967—74 was not precisely fascist, though it indulged in much brutality and some torture of prisoners. It shared certain features with classical fascism — a populist tone, ultra-nationalism, moral conservatism and anti-establishment radicalism — but it created neither a totalitarian party nor effective mass organisations. It was certainly not royalist: the colonels regarded the most senior, royalist officers as being just as much tainted by corruption as the old political establishment, and purged them from the army at once. When the King made his feeble attempt at a counter-coup in December, 1967 they sent him packing into exile and appointed one of their number as 'Regent'. Their initial base in the army (patronage soon extended it) was the so-called 'captain's parliament' of some 150 junior officers whose ideas were not far from Nasserist, although that too lost its impetus once the fruits of power began to be enjoyed by the new rulers.

The long-term political programme of the colonels' *junta*, such as it was, envisaged a gradual transition to some form of 'guided democracy' under army supervision, after the passage of an indeterminate number of years. The leading regime figures resigned their army commissions in early 1968, and

proceeded to erect a civilianised façade for the regime. The process went so far as the creation of a republic, approved by referendum in July, 1973, but the only real source of the regime's power remained the army. As the leading figures of the *junta* came ever more closely to resemble the stereotypically corrupted civilian politicians they had replaced, so their support in the army melted away. Following the brutal suppression of rioting at the Athens Polytechnic in November, 1973 (34 dead, and almost a thousand injured), the discredited Papadopoulos government was overturned in a bloodless coup led by General Phaedon Ghizikis. This short-lived second *junta* was, if anything, even less competent than its predecessor, especially in foreign affairs.

Greece had already become seriously isolated under the first military regime: its membership of the Council of Europe was suspended and its progress towards Common Market membership halted, while its relations with Turkey became increasingly strained by the Cyprus problem. Under Ghizikis, and due directly to his attempts to undermine the government of Archbishop Makarios, this problem rapidly turned into a full-blown crisis. With a dazzling combination of ruthlessness and ignorance, the Greek military government conspired at the violent overthrow and attempted assassination of Makarios by the Greek-Cypriot National Guard under the leadership of Greek army officers in July, 1974. Athens apparently expected that the Turks, under American pressure, would accept this *fait accompli*, and made no serious preparations for any alternative outcome.

The consequence, of course, was the Turkish invasion of Cyprus, and the sudden eruption of a Turkish—Greek confrontation for which the regime was utterly unprepared. Greece was quite incapable of bringing military pressure to bear in the vicinity of Cyprus, which is 600 miles from Greece and only 60 miles from Turkey. The panic-stricken mobilisation of the Greek armed forces to face the contingency of war with Turkey in the Aegean sea and along the Thracian border revealed that 7 years of soldiers in government had rotted the military efficiency of the armed forces. With the dazed government evidently preparing to sleep-walk into an already lost war, army units in the north refused to accept its orders, and the *junta* collapsed less than 96 hours after the Turkish invasion of Cyprus. In a matter of days a provisional civilian government had been re-established under the leadership of former Prime Minister Constantine Karamanlis, who returned from 11 years of self-imposed exile in France.

War with Turkey was averted, although the military tension between the two countries has remained high ever since. In elections held later in 1974 in an atmosphere of continuing crisis, Mr Karamanlis's conservative New Democracy Party won 54.4% of the vote and secured over two-thirds of the seats in the national parliament. Andreas Papandreou's Pan-Hellenic Socialist Movement (PASOK) won only 14% of the votes, and the two newly legalised Communist Parties a mere 9½%.

The issue of the monarchy was swiftly closed by a referendum confirming the republic, and in January, 1975 a new Constitution (modelled closely on the pre-coup Constitution of 1952) was adopted. The leading *junta* members and the more notorious torturers were tired and imprisoned, and the army purged of the more prominent adherents of the previous regime. Civilian democracy was re-established with remarkable speed and unanimity, and the books were ostensibly closed on the past.

The legacy of the *junta* years and the 1974 humiliation still dominates Greek foreign relations, however. Since that date the country has been engaged in a crash rearmament programme to counter the perceived Turkish threat, involving extremely heavy expenditure of foreign exchange. Greek bitterness at the unwillingness of their NATO allies to take their side against Turkey in the 1974 crisis led to the immediate withdrawal of the Greek armed forces from the alliance's military command, though Greece remained a member of the political organisation. Resentment at American dealings with the *junta* during the years of military rule has been fortified by a widely shared Greek conviction that the 1974 disaster was somehow the result of a devious American plot, with the consequence that anti-American public opinion has forced the government to restrict American base rights in the country drastically. Even the Greek application to become a full member of the European Economic Communities, which was formally submitted in the course of 1977, attracted the hostility of the left in Greek politics.

The elections of November, 1977, moreover, showed that the conservatism of the Greek electorate in 1974, in the midst of an acute crisis, was more apparent than real. Mr Karamanlis's party was re-elected with a severely reduced popular vote of less than 42% (although it still won enough parliamentary seats to govern alone), while the combined communist vote rose to 12% and PASOK's support soared to 25.3%. These latter parties advocated Greek withdrawal from NATO, the closing of American bases, and a policy of non-alignment. And in the subsequent elections, in October, 1981, PASOK actually won power, under the leadership of Andreas Papandreou (son of the earlier prime minister), with 48% of the popular vote and an absolute majority of 172 seats in the 300-member parliament.

In the interval between these two elections, however, Prime Minister Karamanlis, who clearly foresaw this possibility did much to ensure that immediate and radical change would not intervene, and to reassure the army about the prospect of a socialist government. In May, 1980, having resigned the prime ministership in favour of his lieutenant, George Rallis, he was elected to the presidency. Since the president has the power to dissolve parliament and call new elections, this provided the army with a guarantee that there would be a reliable conservative backstop to any rash acts committed by a socialist government up to 1985, which is past the date of the next parliamentary elections.

By the time the conservative government left office in late 1981, moreover, it had presented its successor with a fait accompli on the question of entering into direct negotiations with Turkey and the issue at dispute between the two countries (the Turkish and Greek Foreign Ministers met in Ankara in June, 1980), on the reintegration of Greece into NATO's military command structure (the Rogers Agreement of October, 1980), and on entry into the EEC (Greece became the tenth member on 1 January, 1981). The only outstanding alliance issue was that of the US bases in Greece, on which Greek-US talks broke down in June 1981.

Even during the election campaign Mr Papandreou began to moderate his previously extreme positions on most of these issues: EEC membership would be renegotiated in pursuit of special terms for Greece, and then put to a referendum; American bases would have to go in the end, but would need to be phased out over a period of time; NATO membership was basically undesirable, but must be seen in the light of Greece's need for arms and support in order to defend herself against the real enemy, Turkey. On the last issue, Papandreou was adamant; his view, which unquestionably derives from personal conviction as well as political expediency, is that Turkey is a menacing and aggressive neighbour with whom no negotiations are likely to prove fruitful, and that the Greek armed forces must be prepared for war with Turkey. This not only accords with Greek popular opinion, but is extremely reassuring to the armed forces: socialist rulers are

less frightening if they are rabid ultra-nationalists who wish to shower the soldiers with weapons. Mr Papandreou assumed office in late 1981 with no difficulty whatever, retaining the Defence Ministry for himself both as a precaution and as a gesture of respect towards the armed forces. The Greek army is firmly back in the barracks, and seems likely to remain there at least for some time. The significance of the 'weekend purge' of February 26–7, 1983, when twenty Greek generals were relieved of command following reports of alleged preparations for a coup under cover of large-scale exercises in northern Greece, has not been explained. Rumours of such an abortive coup were subsequently and emphatically denied by the government.

STRENGTH AND BUDGET

The total regular strength of the Greek armed forces is 206,500, up from 161,000 in 1975 as a result of the confrontation with Turkey. Of these, 152,000 are conscripts serving for a period of 22 months (24 months in the air force, 26 months in the navy). 2.2% of the total Greek population is under arms, a ratio surpassed in the entire world only by Israel, Syria, Jordan, Taiwan and North Korea.

Army strength is 163,000 (125,000 conscripts), with about 270,000 reservists. The navy numbers 19,500 (12,000 conscripts) with an additional 24,000 reservists. The air force has 24,000 personnel (15,000 conscripts) and about 30,000 reservists. The principal paramilitary forces are 25,000 Gendarmerie and 100,000 National Guard.

The defence budget in 1978 was $2,273,000,000. This was 20.3% of government spending, down from a peak of 25.5% in 1975, but it still represents 5.7% of GNP (highest proportions in NATO except for the USA).

COMMAND AND CONSTITUTIONAL STATUS

The Commander-in-Chief of the Greek Armed Forces is the President, elected by Parliament for a 5 year term. The office is currently occupied by Mr Constantine Karamanlis. He has the authority to declare war and to conclude peace treaties; in exceptional circumstances he may preside over the Cabinet, or suspend Parliament for a period not exceeding 30 days. He may also call together the Council of the Republic, a body made up of all former democratic Presidents and Prime Ministers, plus the current President, Prime Minister and Leader of the Opposition, which may authorise the President to dissolve Parliament.

The three services are integrated under the Ministry of National Defence. The responsible Ministr is the prime minister, Andreas Papandreou. Until recently the Defence Minister's immediate subordinate was the Armed Forces Commander, under whom were separate Commanders of the Army, Navy, Air Force and Gendarmerie. In August, 1977 however, this structure, introduced by the colonels, was replaced by the pre-1968 command structure in order to reduce the danger of military takeover. The most senior serving officer is now the Chief of the National Defence General Staff, a post in which officers of the three services alternate. The Chiefs of the Army, Navy and Air Force General Staffs are separately and directly responsible to the Ministry of National Defence for matters pertaining to their own services, and the entire structure of semi-autonomous high commands has been abolished.

ROLE, COMMITMENT, DEPLOYMENT AND RECENT OPERATIONS

Role

The Greek armed forces have two primary roles in defence of the country: the long-standing tasks of defending the north of the country against Soviet attack, and assisting in the maintenance of Western control over the eastern Mediterranean in wartime, which are the responsibilities allotted to Greece as a NATO member; and the more recent and now higher priority role of establishing at least an equilibrium of power with Turkey.

Defence against the Soviet threat means essentially defence of the border with Bulgaria. There is no perceived military threat from non-aligned Yugoslavia, with whom relations have been cordial since shortly after Marshal Tito ceased aiding Greek communist forces in the Civil War of 1946—9. Diplomatic relations with Albania were only established in 1971, and there is little warmth in them due to the acute ideological differences and a lingering border dispute (there is a Greek minority in southern Albania), but as in the Yugoslavian case there is not anxiety in Athens about a possible military confrontation. Neither Yugoslavia nor Albania, of course, is a member of the Warsaw Pact, and both States are if anything more concerned about the threat of Soviet invasion than Greece itself.

The Bulgarian threat, on the other hand, is taken seriously. There are no Soviet troops stationed permanently in Bulgaria in peace time, but the Bulgarian armed forces of 148,000 men possess almost twice as many tanks as Greece. The geography of north-eastern Greece, moreover, makes it very difficult to defend: a strip of land several hundred miles long between Bulgaria and the Aegean Sea, averaging only 30—50 miles wide. Although it is likely that in any general European war the bulk of Bulgarian forces would be directed eastwards towards the strategically vital objectives of Istanbul and the Straits, few Greeks doubt that a substantial proportion would be reserved for an attack into western Thrace. Although the region has been thoroughly Hellenised since it fell to Greece in the second Balkan War of 1913, Bulgaria's resentment at having been robbed of its spoils from the First Balkan War of 1912, and thus of its long-sought sea-coast on the Aegean, has been a constant if sometimes muted theme of Bulgarian nationalism ever since.

The other role of the Greek armed forces, defence against Turkey, has been growing in significance ever since the first Cyprus crisis, but it was after 1974 that it took over as the first priority. It is the perception not only of the possibility of war with Turkey over Cyprus but of a longer-term Turkish expansionism aimed at Greek islands and perhaps even mainland territories (however dubious in fact) that has caused such a dramatic rise in Greek defence budgets and armed forces manpower since 1974. Obviously, this has helped to downgrade the NATO link, since NATO obviously cannot be of assistance in the event of a war between two of its own members.

The likeliest trigger of a war with Turkey, and its focal point, in the Greek view, would be the waters around the Greek islands which fringe the west and south-west coasts of Anatolia. These have given rise to a dispute, independent of the Cyprus question although exacerbated by it, over the proper demarcation line on the seabed of the Aegean. Athens insists that the distribution of Greek islands across the entire sea gives it rights to over 90% of the seabed, while Ankara claims that the respective continental mainlands should be the point of reference for the drawing of a median line, Greek islands to the east of that line generating seabed rights only under their individual territorial waters. (Such a solution would give Turkey 35—40% of the Aegean seabed.) The discovery of modest quantities of offshore oil in the northern part of the Aegean, together with unofficial claims raised by Turkish extremists to the offshore Greek islands, have lent even greater sharpness to the dispute.

As a result, Greece has remilitarised its islands off the Turkish mainland in defiance of the Lausanne treaty, pointing to the creation of a 4th Turkish Army on the Aegean coast as justification, and has spent large sums on the fortification of the larger ones. Considerable Greek army forces have also been repositioned closer to the Turkish land border in Thrace. In recognition of the fact that any war with Turkey would be fought mainly in the Aegean, where naval and air forces would be decisive, the thrust of the massive Greek rearmament programme since 1974 has been directed towards ensuring that at least the navy and air force are comparable in numbers and quality to their Turkish equivalents, even if Greece cannot hope to match an opponent with four times the population in the numerical strength of its ground forces.

It would be easy to exaggerate the effect of this reorientation of defence priorities on the actual disposition of forces, however. The number of troops absorbed by the defence of the Aegean islands is relatively small, and the bulk of the Greek army has to be in roughly the same north-eastern area whether its potential opponent is Bulgaria or Turkey. Similarly, the Greek navy and air force are primarily intended for Aegean operations whether the crisis should be one with the Warsaw Pact or with its own NATO neighbour.

Commitment

Greece's main military commitments are its membership of NATO, and its bilateral arrangements with the USA providing American base facilities in the country. Both of these arrangements, however, have been subjected to severe strain since 1974, and the terms have been changed considerably.

Greece withdrew its forces from NATO command to peacetime on August 14th, 1974 and placed them all under exclusively national command. Since then it has refused to allow the ships or aircraft of its nearest NATO ally, Turkey, to operate in its part of the Aegean, and it has withdrawn its contingent from the staff of NATO South-Eastern Headquarters in Izmir. Athens also withdrew in 1974 from the NATO Defence Planning Committee in Brussels, and for 3 years refused to take part in NATO exercises involving Turkish units. Greece's reintegration into NATO's military command structure, which became an urgent priority for the conservative government of Athens as the 1981 election approached (with the probability of a socialist victory), was formally agreed with General Bernard Rogers, SACEUR, in October, 1983. It was based on a partition of NATO's former command in south-eastern Europe, which had embraced both Greece and Turkey. In June, 1978, the former headquarters at Izmir had been handed over to Turkey, since in practice it had only controlled Turkish land forces and the Turkish First Tactical Air Force; it was now agreed that Greek land and air forces committed to NATO would be controlled from a separate headquarters at Larissa in central Greece. Both these headquarters would report to NATO Southern Headquarters in Naples, but Turkish forces would not use Greek territory or communication channels, nor be provided with any information from the Greek radar systems forming part of the NADGE (NATO Air Defence Ground Environment) system. Both Turkey and Greece agreed to defer settlement of their major outstanding dispute relating to the new command structure, that of military air command zones in the Aegean, until after Greece's re-entry into NATO, since that was most urgent.

However, despite ratification of Greece's re-entry by the Greek parliament in October 1980, the regional NATO command centre at Larissa, the link which would actually tie the Greek armed forces into NATO operations, has not yet been established. The dispute over mid-air traffic control in the Aegean (which had been allocated solely to Greece by NATO before 1974, but had devolved largely on Turkey during Greece's absence) was not easily settled, since it became entangled with other territorial issues with Greece and Turkey, like seabed rights. Greece insists on retaining its previous control of Aegean aerospace right up to the Turkish coast and, since Prime Minister Papandreou assumed power, has linked satisfaction of Turkey's demand with any further moves towards applying the Rogers agreement.

The special Greek defence relationship with the USA has also been greatly affected by the events of 1974. Unlike Turkey, Greece has not been subjected to an American arms embargo, but American bases have become as sensitive an issue as they are now in Turkey. After 18 months of negotiations a tentative agreement was reached at the end of 1976, which provided for the closure of three of the seven American bases in the country. The remaining four (the Sixth Fleet's air—naval support base at Suda Bay, Crete; the air force communications station at Iraklion, Crete; the Naval Commander centre at Nea Makri near Athens; and the USAF logistical support base at Hellenikon airport near Athens) would shift from American to Greek command, with up to 50% Greek personnel. The 4000 American servicemen in Greece would lose their extraterritorial rights, and the USA would cease to have the right to conduct 'combat operations' or to store nuclear weapons in any of these 'facilities', as the bases have been renamed. This new defence co-operation agreement was initialled in Athens on July 28th, 1977, and is fairly satisfactory to both sides so far as the bases themselves are concerned. However, it has been put into effect because successive Greek governments have tried to attach other political and financial conditions to implementation, specifically, that the US (or NATO) guarantee Greece's eastern frontier against Turkish attack, and that US military sales and aid to Greece and Turkey should be kept at the traditional 7-to-10 ratio to preserve a balance of power in the area. These are the two demands, unacceptable to Washington, which led to the breakdown of negotiations in June, 1981. Despite the militant anti-Americanism of the new socialist government, and its firm commitment to shut the bases it has continued to negotiate with the United States on exactly the same terms, with just as little success. In the meantime, the bases remain available to the US on the 1976 terms.

Deployment

Two of the four Greek army corps are located on the northern frontiers with Bulgaria and Turkey. The third and fourth, which cover the rest of the country, also provide the troops for the recently remilitarised islands along the Anatolian west coast. Total numbers deployed in these islands are not known, but there have been reports of over 10,000 in Rhodes alone. There are 1300 Greek troops including 350 commandos in Cyprus in addition to 450 officers and NCOs who are serving on secondment as cadres on the Greek-Cypriot North Command.

The major navy bases are at Piraeus, Salonika, Valos, Mitilini, Suda Bay, Salamis and Rhodes.

All 40 of Greece's LTV A7 Corsair IIs are based at Suda Bay in Crete.

The general southward and eastward shift of the Greek defence forces naturally reflects the concern in Athens about a possible war with Turkey. In such a war, it is reckoned by both sides, major advances by either party would be unlikely along the Thracian border, nor would air strikes against bases and cities accomplish anything decisive. The focal point of such a war would unquestionably be the Aegean islands, especially the large ones only a few miles off the Turkish coast (but hundreds of miles from mainland Greece) which might be seized as hostages for a favourable peace. Fighting in such an area would be decided by air and naval engagements, and in view of the considerable range disadvantage Greek forces would suffer the trend towards forward basing of Greek forces is unsurprising.

Recent Operations

The Greek armed forces have not fought since 1949, with the exception of a contingent sent to the Korean war and the small number of Greek troops who were in Cyprus in 1963–74.

ORGANISATION

Arms of Service

The Greek army is primarily an infantry force, consisting of 11 infantry divisions, one armoured division and three independent armoured brigades, one mechanised division, one para-commando division and 13 field artillery battalions (another is forming). There is also a marine infantry brigade, 3 AA artillery Battalions, three SSM battalions (with 12 Honest John missiles each), 2 SAM battalions (with improved Hawk), and 14 army aviation companies and one independent flight.

The tank division has six tank battalions of 55 tanks each, four motorised infantry battalions (750 men and 60 APCs) and reconnaissance battalions, three SP artillery battalions (18 105mm SPs) and one mixed artillery battalion (10 SP howitzers of 155mm and 203mm), plus a combat engineer battalion, communications battalion, army air corps company and logistical support sub-unit. Total strength is 13,000 men and 360 tanks. The independent armoured brigade consists of two tank battalions, one motorised infantry battalion, one SP artillery battalion and other arms and services in proportion; total 3600 men and 119 tanks. The para-commando division consists of one parachute and one marine brigade, plus one commando and one marine battalion.

Greek infantry divisions closely resemble the motorised infantry formations of other NATO countries. There is a headquarters company plus three infantry regiments of three battalions each, and anti-tank APC and Army Air Corps companies. The strength of a Greek infantry division can range up to 14,300 men, with 62 tanks, 80 APCs, 1800 vehicles, six airplanes, four helicopters, 76 howitzers of 203.2mm, 155mm and 105mm, 114 mortars, 50 106mm RCLs and up to 450 AT weapons. They are all trained for combat in both nuclear and non-nuclear conditions. Greek military concepts, doctrine and combat training are almost wholly American in origin.

Reserves

The army reserves are organised into three territorial and 17 Sub-Commands controlling 12 independent infantry brigades and about 100 Home Guard battalions (most of which man coastal defences).

The Greek air force is divided into Tactical, Training and Material Commands. Tactical Air Force has seven combat wings containing eleven FGA squadrons, five interceptor squadrons and one FGA/reconnaissance squadron; one independent wing of three squadrons; and one MR squadron, nine base flights and three helicopter squadrons. Training Command operates five squadrons.

Operational

The armed forces are divided into three military regions, two of which are located in northern (Thessalonika) and north-eastern Greece. The third army, headquarters Athens, controls forces in the rest of Greece and the islands.

RECRUITMENT, TRAINING AND RESERVES

Less than a quarter of the Army's strength — some 37,000 men — are long-service regulars, almost all of them officers, NCOs and specialist trades. The remainder of the army is made up of conscripts doing their compulsory 22 months' military service. Military liability continues for the 21st to the 50th year, with trained conscripts passing into the First Reserve for 19 years, and 10 years in the Second Reserve.

Recruit contingents are called up every 3 months. Since the rapid post-1974 expansion of the army the number of young men entering the appropriate age group each year has not been adequate to meet requirements, due to a birth rate that has been static for some time. Accordingly the Greek government introduced a bill in 1977 to open armed forces careers up for women (hitherto they had been restricted to the nursing corps), and to make women between the ages of twenty and thirty-two liable to compulsory military service for a period of 14 months. Married women, mothers of illegitimate children, nuns and orphans would be automatically exempted, but it was hoped that up to 12,000 women could be brought in each year, to serve in non-combatant positions and release men for combat duties. Present female strength in the armed forces is only 834 women.

EQUIPMENT AND ARMS INDUSTRY

The Greek army's armoured force consists of 100 M-26, 300 M-47, 818 M-48 and 285 AMX-30 medium tanks, 170 M-24 light tanks and 180 M-8 and 130 M-20 armoured cars. A further 55 AMX-30 tanks are on order from France, and 106 Leopard I tanks from West Germany. APCs include 820 M-113, 240 AMX-10P MICV, 160 Leonidas, 460 M-59, 460 M-3 half-tracks, and 120 M-2.

The artillery component consists of 600 25-pounder and 36 M-107 and 175mm guns, and 108 75mm and M-56 105mm pack howitzers (12 more on order); 180 M-101 105mm, 270 M-114A1 155mm and 72 M-115 203mm towed howitzers; and 126 M-52A1 105mm, 54 M-44 and 60 M-109A2 155mm, and 20 M-110 203mm SP howitzers. (48 more M-109A2 155mm SP howitzers on order.) Other weapons 36 Honest John SSM and 200 M-20 75mm and 700 106mm plus some M-18 57mm and M-67 90mm recoilless rifles. (350 more 96mm RLC on order).

Anti-tank weapons include 64 M-18 and 32 Kuerassier SP ATK guns (48 more Kuerassier on order), and SS01, Milan, 400 Cobra and 1431 TOW ATGW (56 more TOW launchers on order). Air defence weapons consist of RH-202 twin 20mm and 40mm AA guns, Redeye SAM, two battalions of improved Hawk with 108 missiles, and 37 Chaparral SAM with 600 missiles.

The army's reserve formations possess a variety of older equipment including light tanks, M-20 armoured cars, M-2 and M-3 APCs, 75mm pack howitzers, 25-pounder guns, 105mm guns and howitzers, 57mm, 75mm and 106mm RCL, and 40mm AA guns.

The main strength of the Green navy is ten submarines, 16 destroyers (5 with ASROC), six frigates (one with Harpoon SSM and Sea Sparrow SAM), 25 fast attack craft (eight with Exocet, six with Penguin SSM), nine coastal patrol craft, 2 coastal minelayers and 13 coastal minesweepers, plus 84 landing craft. Two further frigates and 50 assault landing craft are on order, plus additional Harpoon SSM and Aspide SAM. The navy maintains two ASW helicopter squadrons, one equipped with 13 AB-212 and the other with 5 Alouette III.

The Greek Air Force has 11 FGA squadrons, three equipped with 54 A-7H and 6 TA-7H Corsair IIs, two with 36 F-4 and RF-4, two with 40 F/TF-104 G, two with 42 F-5A/B and RF-5, and two in reserve with 54 F-84F. There are five interceptor squadrons, one with 18 F-4E, one with 21 F-5A1B, two with 36 Mirage F-1CG and one with 24 F-104S. The FGA/reconnaissance squadron operates 20 F/RF48-F and 8RF-4E, and the MR squadron flies 8 HU-16B Albatross. The Air Force has one SAM wing, consisting of one battalion with 36 Nike Hercules and one with 36 Nike Ajax. Reflecting the bewildering variety of combat aircraft which it operates, it has in service Sparrow, Sidewinder, Super Sidewinder, Falcon and R-550 Magic AAM (plus 280 AIM-7M Sparrow and 300 Super Sidewinder on order) and Maverick and Bull pip ASM (200 additional Maverick on order). It is also purchasing 40 Skyguard Air Defence systems, supplemented by extra twin 35mm AA guns.

There are three independent squadrons operating 12 C-1BOH Hercules, six YS-11, 21 Noratlas, eight C-47, seven CL-215 and one Gulfstream aircraft. The three helicopter squadrons have six AB-205A, two AB-206A, ten Bell 47G, eight UH-19D, two AB-212 and eight CH-47C. Training Command's five squadrons have 36 T-2E, 20 T-41A, and 24 T-37B/C aircraft, some of which are armed. There are nine base flights, disposing of 48 T-33 and six C-47 aircraft and eight AB-205A helicopters.

Greece's domestic arms-building capability is at present not very great, but a parliamentary bill introduced in early 1977 provided assistance to State-owned and private factories manufacturing armaments in order to attract advanced foreign technology. The government explained that international political events had created new problems potentially affecting the regular supply of weapons, and it was announced that the government in collaboration with the heads of the three services had produced a draft plan for producing in Greece a large part of the necessary equipment and arms. The first result of this was the call for tenders for a new main battle tank to be built in Greece. Tenders were received in July, 1977 from France (offering improved AMX-30s and AMX-13s), Germany (Leopard I and Marder), Italy (Lion I, an improved Leopard I built under licence) and Britain (which offered either the Chieftain or the Vickers Mk. 14) but in September, 1979 plans for setting up a tank factory in Greece were postponed indefinitely due to financial stringency and the greater emphasis being given to new weapons and the air force and navy. A number of La Combattante II class guided missile fast patrol boats have now been built under licence in Greece by Hellenic Shipyards. It is likely that Greece's next major purchase of military aircraft — it is in the market for 100 to 130 new generation warplanes by 1983, an order likely to be worth $5 billion — will include some element of local co-production. Indeed George Petsos, a senior air official of the Ministry of Defence, has now been given specific responsibility for seeking co-production agreements in Greek owned purchases in order to develop the Greek armaments industry and for diversifying the foreign sources of supply as far as possible in order to reduce Greek dependence on the United States.

RANK, DRESS AND DISTINCTIONS

Ranks follow the British system and uniforms have always been closely similar to the British in colour and design. Recently, however, a uniform more American in style has been introduced.

A distinctive visual element in the Greek army are the Royal Guard, or *Evzones*. They wear traditional mountaineer dress, including the tasselled cap, embroidered waistcoat and pleated white *fustanella* skirt.

CURRENT DEVELOPMENTS

The likelihood of war with Turkey is not high, and has certainly declined considerably since 1974. It is, nevertheless, a matter of almost obsessive concern in Greece.

It can be said with some assurance that Greece would have lost such a war in 1974. The subsequent Greek arms build-up and the effects of the American arms embargo against Turkey (later lifted in May, 1978), have altered the balance to an appreciable extent, however, and there has also been a recovery in the morale of the Greek armed forces. While it remains virtually impossible for Greece to *win* a war with Turkey, since geography offers it few opportunities to strike at Turkish vital interests, it is now also improbable that Greece could *lose* such a war decisively in the limited amount of time that would likely be available before a ceasefire was imposed.

In fact, such a war has always been far less probable than it is generally seen in Greece (both at governmental and at street level), since Turkey does not actually harbour secret ambitions for territorial expansion against Greece. At least, that is what the Turks say, and what almost all other non-Greek observers believe. The disputes between Turkey and Greece are about specific issues, and nothing more; primarily, Cyprus and the waters and seabed demarcation in the Aegean.

The Cyprus problem is now effectively 'solved', at great cost (though the solution is not yet ratified by anybody). The Papandreou government's outrage at the situation is voiced loudly and often, but even the Greek-Cypriot government in Nicosia refuses to join Athens in a futile crusade to force the Turks out, choosing instead to continue with the UN-supervised inter-communal talks. Further fighting in Cyprus is improbable, and the island is therefore unlikely to become the trigger in a Greek-Turkish war.

The Aegean seabed dispute is considered more dangerous, and is further exacerbated by continual Greek protests about Turkey's 'violation' of Greek airspace. (Greece claims territorial waters to 6 miles around all its Aegean islands, but by a decree of 1931 claims a ten-mile air space; the further four-mile extension is not recognised by Turkey and is source of continual friction, especially during Turkish military exercises.) The Athens government frequently threatens to extend its Aegean territorial waters (and air space) to 12 miles in order to solve the problem — but that would be the one action that actually would carry a strong likelihood of leading to war.

At a stroke, a 12-mile territorial limit around the multitudinous Greek Islands would reduce the contested area of Aegean seabed from about 100,000 square km to 45,000 — the rest being added to the 60,000 sq. km. already under Greek sovereignty, with 6-mile territorial waters. It would also extend Greek sovereignty to 75% of Aegean air space, and render access to much of the Turkish west Coast by sea or air impossible except by passage through Greek territory. Other powers, like the Soviet Union and the USA, would be greatly annoyed by such an action by Greece; Turkey had made it plain that such a unilateral move could lead to war. Despite the Papandreou government's aversion to any direct diplomatic negotiations with Turkey, Ankara's position is sufficiently clear to Athens, and it is unlikely to hazard such a move.

The government in Athens sees any threat to Greece from the Warsaw Pact as distinctly secondary in importance, if plausible at all, though this belief has not been translated into changes in troop dispositions, for example, in view of Greece's NATO connexions. However, Prime Minister Papandreou has actively pursued his proposal for a Balkan nuclear-free zone as a means of lessening tensions in the region. While Bulgaria responded warmly and Romania (which originally raised the idea in the 1950s) also sound interested, Yugoslavia was cool to the idea, and Turkey and Albania totally negative. At the moment, the plan appears to be utterly stalled.

Greece's relations with its own officers have been much smoother than anticipated under Papandreou's leadership: there is no longer even public talk of a referendum on membership of the Common Market; the US bases are still in Greece and showing no signs of imminent departure; and Greece is still formally integrated into NATO's military command despite the missing headquarters at Larissa. The likelihood that the Papandreou goverment would ever actually close the US bases or pull out of NATO is rendered diminishingly small by the government's obsession with the Turkish menace: such actions, after all, would cut Greece off from NATO weapons, supplies and aid, and force the Western alliance to align itself more closely with Turkey. As for EEC membership, the government no longer ever mentions a referendum in the issue.

The probability of renewed military intervention in politics in Greece is low at the moment partly because there is no particular incentive for intervention — actual government foreign and domestic policies do not threaten values held dear by the officer corps, whatever the rhetoric in which they are couched, and partly because the soldiers have the Turkish threat to keep them busy. Moreover, for the military point of view, the government is 'sound' (i.e. ultra-nationalist and defence-minded) on this all-important question. Nor have the PASOK government's measures to heal the historic wounds caused by the 'civil' war — recognition of the patriotic role of those who fought in the Communist Resistance Movement during the 2nd world War, and free repatriation of and restoration of Greek citizenship to the Communist political refugees, estimated to number (with families) anything from 30,000 to 100,000 people today, who have been living in exile in Eastern Europe and the Soviet Union since the end of the civil war — caused a serious breach of the armed forces.

If there does begin to be armed forces unrest against the government, it will arise more probably from the kind of government meddling with the navy's internal arrangements at the behest of PASOK ranks, which encroaches on the army's denuded autonomy. In November 1982, for example, the government announced the abolition of security screening students entering Greek military academies (a device previously used to ensure no left-wingers joined the officer corps), which led to an outcry about the consequent probable infiltration of Communists into the armed forces. PASOK is also committed to the 'democratisation' of the military services, and although actual changes to the end of 1982 were limited to such things as abolishing shaven heads for recruits and permitting conscripts to wear own clothes off duty, the changed atmosphere has led to such phenomena as the growth of clandestine 'servicemen's committees' seeking such further changes as political and union rights for servicemen, the reduction of conscripted service to 12 months, improved living conditions in barracks, and an end to the isolation of enlisted men from society. There is alleged to have been a secret nationwide assembly of the servicemen's committees in August 1982, but it is difficult to gauge their real strength, and they certainly do not enjoy government support.

The fundamental anti-communism of the Greek armed forces remains a serious factor in the Greek political equation, but the real relationship of Greek officers to their national political culture cannot be defined so narrowly: the clash of approved values and modes of behaviour is almost total. To the extent that army officers possess a professional orientation, they are attracted to order, co-operative effort, discipline, efficiency, hierarchy and an austere patriotism towards an idealised State. The Greek in the street (and in the government), on the other hand, thrives on conflict in every area of his private and public life, has minimal tolerance for formal rules or even for political stability, and at the same time is enmeshed in an ever-ramifying patronage network which provides the real framework on which the nation's affairs are conducted.

These conflicting perspectives combine with more specific factors to produce a profound alienation of the army from the élitist circles that dominate Greek democratic politics. A majority of army officers are recruited from the lower middle class (the sons of traders, shopkeepers, junior civil servants, etc.) and some from the relatively prosperous elements of the peasantry. A very high proportion are from the provinces. They tend to react towards the prosperity of the established political, professional and commercial *élite* with a mixture of envy and contempt. They respond variously and at different times by seeking advancement through affiliation with the civilian patronage systems that extend into the army, by seeking self-protection through joining together in the kind of secret and semi-secret societies which repeatedly emerge in the army, or by seeking to cleanse the civilian society by military rule.

The army's efficiency (at least relative to other Greek institutions) and freedom from the blatant patronage and exchange of favours which dominates all other sectors of Greek life, were achieved quite early, as indispensable conditions of its military effectiveness. It makes army officers despise the near-anarchy and shifting patronage constellations which usually pass for civilian control in Greece. (The politicians in return despise the soldiers as *stenokephalos* — narrow-headed or stupid.) The army is not so much right wing, as permanently tempted to impose that austere social discipline which is so utterly lacking in real Greek culture. Since none of this has changed since 1974, there is no reason to believe that the cycle of intervention and withdrawal has been finally and decisively broken.

James Brown
Gwynne Dyer

GUATEMALA

HISTORY AND INTRODUCTION

Guatemala is the historical 'great power' of Central America, considerably bigger and more populous than any of its neighbours to the south. During the colonial era it was the centre of an isthmus-wide political jurisdiction, however loosely enforced, and its neighbours are still chronically suspicious of Guatemalan aspirations to reunification of the area. In fact, however, Guatemala's attention during the twentieth century has been focused almost entirely on its internal affairs and on relations with the USA, the two processes whose interactions define modern Guatemalan history. In this situation, the armed forces have virtually lost interest in external affairs and have become ever more deeply involved in internal security matters, so that they now constitute a corporate (if sometimed disguised) permanent government.

The great dividing line in Guatemalan history is 1944. Before that time it conformed entirely to the Central American pattern. Afterwards, it embarked on a course of radical political and social change which was largely sponsored by elements within the army's officer corps, and which was a precursor in various ways of the Cuban Revolution of Fidel Castro and of the reformist *peruanista* tendencies that emerged in various other Latin American armies in the course of the 1960s. While in Guatemala this pioneering phase of military radicalism was stifled within a decade, the after-effects of it are largely responsible for the fact that the country has been in a chronic state of low-level civil war since the middle 1960s, with a casualty toll of about 20,000 dead.

The early period of Guatemalan history was similar to that of other parts of Spanish America. Central America was conquered by Pedro de Alvarado and 300 Spanish soldiers, the decisive battle being won against Tecún Umán, chieftain of the Maya-Quiche Indians of Guatemala, in 1524. What is now Guatemala became the capital and most populous part of the Captaincy-General of Guatemala, extending from Chiapas and Tabasco provinces of modern Mexico down to the present Panamanian border, but lacking the mineral wealth of Mexico or the Andes it remained a backward and neglected area even by the standards of Spanish America. The intermarriage of Spanish settlers with the Indians of the Guatemala highlands gradually produced a mestizo population of European custom and culture, known as *ladinos*, who lived alongside an Indian population still speaking its own languages and pursuing its own customs.

This situation persists to the present day, although *ladino* has lost most of its racial connotations and is applied to anyone who speaks Spanish as his mother tongue and adopts European behaviour. Between 40 and 50% of Guatemalans may still be classified as Indians, speaking Spanish poorly or not at all and living largely traditional lives in Indian villages where land is held communally. Indians and *ladinos* live alongside each other throughout the central highlands (which contained 90% of the population until this century, and still are the home of the majority), but there is little social contact between the two groups. The densely settled provinces in the western half of the highlands all have large Indian majorities, while the provinces east of Guatemala City are predominantly *ladino*.

Guatemala achieved its independence in 1821 without effort of its own, as a consequence of the successful Mexican revolt against Spanish rule, but it then had to drive out a Mexican army of occupation in 1823. Within a few years it became part of the Central American Confederation, held together by the army of the Honduran General Francisco Morazán. The majority of the Guatemalan *élite* in this period were of conservative, and hence anti-federalist, political orientation, however, and the shaky confederation was destroyed in 1838 by a ragtag army of Guatemalans led by the illiterate *ladino* general Rafael Carrera, who ruled Guatemala with arbitrary ruthlessness until his death in 1865.

In so far as the chaotic politics of the isthmus at this time rose beyond the level of mere personal advantage, it ranged liberal, anticlerical, federalist elements in each national *élite* against conservative, church-oriented, separatist factions. Carrera fell into the latter group, and in the wars of mutual intervention on behalf of liberal or conservative factions in neighbouring countries which wracked Central America in mid-century he three times led Guatemalan armies against coalitions between El Salvador and Honduras: in 1839, 1850 and 1863. Each time he captured San Salvador, but withdrew after bringing friendly local factions to power.

Guatemalan armies up to this time, however, were totally amateur and *ad hoc* organisations. The foundation of a professional military tradition (in the service of a revived drive for Central American unification) was the work of Carrera's great liberal successor, General Justo Rufino Barrios, who seized power in 1870. He was a gifted ruler who has become the Guatemalan national hero; in 14 years of drastic reform he destroyed the Church's privileges, introduced commercial agriculture in the form of coffee estates and banana plantations, built roads and initiated a rail system.

Within a year of taking power, in 1871, he founded a regular national army, which proved its worth in yet another victorious war against El Salvador in 1876. In 1874 he created a national military academy, La Escuela Politécnica, in Guatemala City, which began to produce officers with proper professional qualifications. In the end, having failed to achieve regional reunification by diplomatic means, he proclaimed himself supreme commander of the 'Army of Central America' in 1885 to achieve his aims by force, only to be killed in the very first battle on the Salvadorean frontier. But although his forces collapsed upon his death, and Guatemala was ruled by a succession of other essentially civilian liberal politicians until 1898, Barrios had laid the groundwork for political domination of the country by real generals whose basic careers were in the army: between 1871 and the present, 18 out of 23 Guatemalan presidents have been military men.

The Escuela Politécnica survived, and produced a steady flow of 'school' officers who gradually raised the professional standards in an army largely commanded by 'line' officers who had received the traditional direct commissions from civilian life. By the turn of the century there was at least a portion of the officer corps for which the army was a career, and a French military mission was employed in improving the standard of training. In 1906 Guatemala fought its last international war, again against El Salvador; both sides were persuaded by Mexico and the USA to accept arbitration, and apart from some minor border clashes in 1935 there have been no serious conflicts between the two countries since then.

During most of the early part of the twentieth century Guatemala was ruled by two military dictators in the classical Latin American mould: men who exercised a highly arbitrary and personalistic rule that used the armed forces merely as one instrument of oppression amongst others. From 1898 to 1920 the country suffered under the brutal and primitive dictatorship of Manuel Estrada Cabrera. After a chaotic interim period in the 1920s the government was seized in 1931 by General Jorge Ubico, with decisive assistance from the USA. His rule, while equally arbitrary, was distinguished by an unusual degree of fiscal integrity and a quite unprecedented degree of centralisation: it was in the period 1931–44 that almost all local centres of power were subjugated to the government in Guatemala City. It has been observed that Guatemala during his reign resembled a 'model jail'.

Two of the consequences of Ubico's relatively efficient and honest rule, however, were largely responsible for the dramatic break with previous Guatemalan history that occurred in 1944. As a result of his public works projects — especially a vast expansion of transportation and communications facilities — his emphasis on economic development, and his expansion of the government bureaucracy, Ubico assisted in the great expansion of the middle class, especially in the capital where commerce, industry, the professions and government offices were all heavily concentrated. A self-conscious and comparatively large group of people emerged who were still totally excluded from power and ignored by the traditional ruling alliance of generals and great land-owners.

Ubico's second important, though unwitting, contribution to the 1944 revolution was drastically to reform the military academy. At his request a United States army officer was appointed to command it in 1935, with instructions to 'make the Escuela Politécnica as near like West Point as was possible under conditions here'. Entrance requirements were greatly stiffened and competitive examinations replaced influence as the means of gaining a place; discipline was upgraded, the curriculum modernised, a merit system introduced and the academy considerably expanded. By the mid-1940s these reforms had produced a well-trained, professional junior officer corps, including a number of individuals of middle-class origin. Unsurprisingly, they found themselves dissatisfied with service in an army in which almost all the senior officers were their professional inferiors, promotion was solely by personal favour of the dictator, and there were 80 generals for 15,000 men.

The first revolution of 1944, in May–July, was the work of the new middle classes. The pro-democratic propaganda with which the Allies flooded Latin America during World War II, although directed at arousing hostility against the Fascist powers in Europe and Japan, had made old-style dictatorships like Ubico's seem obsolescent and inappropriate. Under the influence of a general strike which had succeeded in overthrowing the similar dictator Hernández Martínez in neighbouring El Salvador in April, 1944, university students in Guatemala City demanded certain changes within their own faculties. These were conceded, to everyone's surprise, and with the smell of victory in their nostrils the students rapidly escalated their demands. They were joined by professional and other middle-class groups in the capital in peaceful demonstrations culminating in a general strike — and Ubico went quietly.

He left behind him, however, a *junta* of three generals, from whom his handpicked Congress chose General Frederico Ponce to serve as provisional President pending the organisation of free nationwide elections. The exultant students and their middle-class allies proceeded to create a multitude of political parties, and by August an intellectual, Juan José Arévalo, who had been abroad teaching at an Argentine university, had won the support of many of these parties with his vague doctrine of 'spiritual socialism'.

It was, however, the senior officers of the army acting through Ponce, together with their allies in the Congress and amongst the great land-owning families, who were really still in charge of Guatemala. They were playing an unusually subtle game, allowing free expression and a certain political effervescence in the belief that in due course it would blow itself out and eventually allow them to bring a candidate of their own preference to the Presidency through the familiar fixed elections. Arévalo's soaring popularity alarmed them, however, and by September Ponce's government was increasingly reverting to the old tactics of repression and assassination of opponents. It looked as though the Guatemalan revolution, like its model in El Salvador, was running into the sand.

What made Guatemala different was its large, disgruntled and professional junior officer corps. The old army was sufficiently aware of the danger to keep most academy graduates away from the capital — only six academy graduates of recent years held appointments in Guatemala City, and those included the provisional President's sons — but even those few were enough. On October 20th, 1944 the presidential guard was led in rebellion by two young officers, Major Francisco Javier Arana, commanding the army's one tank battalion, and Captain Jacobo Arbenz. Arms were distributed to students, and after a brief battle the outgunned loyal troops in the capital surrendered. All 80 generals were sent into exile and the rank was abolished. Arana and Arbenz formed a new *junta*, together with one civilian, which supervised the elections of December, 1944 that duly brought Arévalo to the Presidency. Both coup leaders were promoted to colonel, the highest remaining army rank; Arana became Chief of the Armed Forces, and Arbenz became Minister of National Defence.

The young officers who led the coup of October, 1944 had no clearly formulated programme. Arbenz was a 'school' officer, and very popular with even more junior officers from his time as a lecturer at the academy, but Arana was a 'line' officer belonging intellectually to an older generation. The motives that moved them and their military supporters in 1944 were an amalgam of the idealistic — revulsion against Ubico's bloody though efficient rule, and an attraction towards the glowing future of liberty and prosperity promised by the intoxicated student revolutionaries after Ubico's fall — and the severely practical. Amongst the latter must be mentioned the very bad pay (newly commissioned lieutenants earned $24 a month), the blockage in promotions caused by the huge top-hamper of generals and colonels, and the prospects of rapid advancement that invariably accompany a successful coup.

Arana and Arbenz duly achieved such promotion, and many of their own close associates also benefited from promotion or government jobs. It should be noted, however, that throughout the 1944–54 period the officer corps as a corporate entity was not directly involved in the governing of the country, nor was a majority of its members active in politics. Officers benefited generally from higher salaries, opportunities to study abroad, and promotions into the vacancies created by the purge of the senior ranks. They were generally favourably disposed to the regime's nationalist goals, however opposed many of the more conservative officers may have been to its social policies.

The presidency of Dr Arévalo, which began in early 1945 with such high hopes and with the support of a variety of revolutionary parties, proved unable to produce the miracles of reform that were looked for. Partly this can be attributed to Arévalo himself: he proved to be an agile survivor in the face of the dozen plots and attempted coups which were directed against him in 1945–9 and a master of political expediency, but his mystical variety of 'spiritual socialism' lacked a clear programme. Unions, free to organise and to strike at last, proliferated and spread, as did peasant organisations in the countryside, and a social security law and a labour code were enacted by Congress, but few really fundamental measures of reform were even attempted. The influence of powerful conservative groups was still great, and they found a protector, figurehead and prospective presidential candidate for 1951 in the semi-autonomous Chief of the Armed Forces, Colonel Arana. With the army still potentially the arbiter of politics, radical parties similarly offered to support the Minister of Defence, Colonel Arbenz.

Arana, who had operated as a brake on all government reform policies by his scarcely concealed willingness to contemplate a coup, was assassinated in 1949 by individuals associated with Arbenz. Some conservative officers in the army revolted in reaction to this event, but the bulk of the army remained obedient to the government and the revolt was crushed. Afterwards most remaining officers of an openly conservative disposition were purged, and Arbenz emerged as the undisputed power behind the throne. In the 1951 elections he succeeded Arévalo to the presidency.

Arbenz was much more determined and competent both as a social reformer and as a political organiser: he adopted really effective land reform as his basic goal, and actually began to carry it through. He nationalised the extensive holdings of the United Fruit Company virtually without compensation, thus appealing to the anti-American sentiments of almost every Guatemalan. But he made two great errors (although neither may have been avoidable): he allied himself too closely with the Guatemalan Communist Party, and he then continued to trust that the army would support him in all circumstances.

The Guatemalan Communist Party was small — in 1944 it had only a few hundred members, and even in 1954 it had only 4000 — and it had no illusions about being able to seize power through Arbenz in the foreseeable future. But it was remarkably well organised, and had complete control of the national trade union organisation and a dominant voice in the national peasant organisation by 1952, when it was finally legalised. Even in the coalition of 'revolutionary' parties which supported Arbenz's government it was much smaller than the two major parties, but it did hold the balance of power between them. Its members were relatively free from the scandal and corruption that were rotting the other parties after almost a decade in power, and Arbenz came to rely upon it quite heavily in certain areas: the application of the land reform measures, for example, was entrusted largely to the communists.

However necessary communist support may have been to Arbenz's policies at home, it inevitably spelled trouble with the USA, which was then at the height of its Cold War panic about communist infiltration in Latin America. Actions such as the nationalisation of American property in Guatemala and denunciation of United States policy in Latin America by diplomatic representatives of Guatemala were merely additional goals to American intervention; the mere fact of a legal Communist Party being represented in the Guatemalan government was sufficient in itself. During 1953 the United States Central Intelligence Agency began organising and arming exiled Guatemalan opposition elements

under the command of Colonel Carlos Castillo Armas, a right-wing supporter of the assassinated Colonel Arana who had fled the country after leading an unsuccessful revolt in 1950.

As these preparations advanced President Arbenz was forced increasingly to rely upon communist support, which caused mounting concern in the army. Contrary to some assertions, the Communist Party never systematically attempted to gain a party of adherents in the army (although individual officers were members or sympathisers); it did, however, begin to infiltrate the police heavily, and made preparations for the arming of a peasants' and workers' militia in case the army should refuse to fight the expected invasion. During late 1953 and early 1954, as Arbenz was forced into a corner by the tide of events, the secret police began mass arrests of opposition figures, accompanied by brutal tortures and some murders, while various communist luminaries from other Latin American countries (including 'Che' Guevara of later fame) arrived to give him aid and advice.

Castillo's 'Army of Liberation', numbering only a few hundred men, crossed the frontier from Honduras on June 18th, 1954, but was contained by loyal government forces after advancing only 20 miles. The popular uprising against Arbenz which he had hoped for failed to materialise, and he made no further advance until the issue had been decided in Guatemala City. The deciding factor there was not the army's hostility to Arbenz, much less its support for Castillo or the USA, but rather its anxiety about the intentions of the communists towards itself.

In a classic example of the self-fulfilling prophecy, the Communist Party's concern to guard against army disloyalty by creating an armed workers' and peasants' militia had created acute suspicions within the army that the communists were aiming to supplant the armed forces entirely, or even (in the more lurid versions) to massacre the officer corps. This professional jealousy had been raised to fever pitch by a shipment of arms which had arrived in Guatemala by ship from Poland the month before. Arbenz had only turned to a communist country for arms after being refused them everywhere else, and it was never clear whether they were intended for the militia, the army or even revolutionary forces in some neighbouring country, but the army suspected the worst and intercepted the shipment on the docks. Therefore when, on June 25th, Arbenz instructed his loyal Chief of the Armed Forces to furnish arms to paramilitary workers' groups and the revolutionary parties, the army refused to comply. On June 27th representatives of the officer corps met with Arbenz and demanded his resignation. He meekly complied.

All resistance at once collapsed, although Castillo's Army of Liberation did not at once proceed to the capital. Arbenz had lost much popular support through the damage done to living standards by his extreme economic nationalism, and the entire structure of government-supported mass organisations ceased to function almost at once, while the communists and most other members of the government took refuge in foreign embassies. It is important to note, however, that the army finally withdrew its support from Arbenz not because of his economic and social policies or even because of his communist support, but mainly over the essentially professional issue of preserving its monopoly of the national defence role.

This was borne out by all that followed. The army command strongly resisted the elevation of Colonel Castillo Armas to the Presidency, which was only achieved after a week's delay and under intense American pressure. The entire cadet corps of the Politécnica assaulted and beat up a small contingent of the 'Army of Liberation' shortly after it arrived in Guatemala City: some were sent home and others abroad on scholarships, and the Politécnica was closed for 2 years, but no overt disciplinary action could be taken against the cadets by Castillo because most of the officer corps saw the action as little short of heroic. There was great resentment in the regular army at the enforced integration of 'Army of Liberation' members into its ranks. In the eyes of most of the officer corps the entire episode was seen primarily as a humiliating demonstration of the United States' ability to manipulate Guatemalan affairs, and it was only by dint of the most stringent disciplinary measures, large-scale purges of officers and extremely alert intelligence services that the Castillo regime was able to survive.

Following a series of executions Castillo established himself in power, and had himself confirmed as president in an uncontested election in October, 1954. Unions and peasant organisations were effectively banned, left-wing politicians were hunted down and eliminated by the secret Committee of National Defence, and much of the land expropriated under the agrarian reform was returned to the large land-owners. Both for the enforcement of the retrograde land reform, and as a counterweight against the army, he relied heavily on the National Liberation Movement (MLN), an extreme right-wing private army composed mainly of smaller landowners from the country's eastern region. There was considerable economic aid from the USA, but basic social problems were neglected.

Castillo was assassinated by a reputedly communist palace guard in July, 1957 and a successor in the same mould who won a rigged election had to step aside after popular protests enjoying the army's support. The man who was chosen in the relatively honest re-run of the election in January, 1958 was General Miguel Ydígoras Fuentes, a former senior official under the ruthless dictator Ubico in the early 1940s.

Ydígoras was an extreme conservative, which probably attracted as many in the officer corps as it alienated others, but the decisive factor in winning him the army's support was that he was, at the outset, anti-American and ultra-nationalist. This relationship changed, however, after the emergence of Fidel Castro's regime in Cuba as an overtly communist government, for Ydígoras's extreme anti-communism led him to volunteer Guatemala to the USA as a training base for the Cuban exiles whom the CIA was training and equipping to overthrow Castro. This large Cuban force arrived at Retalhuleu on the Pacific coast of Guatemala in mid-1960 to train for the Bay of Pigs invasion that took place in the following year.

Even to the anti-communists who then, as always, predominated in the Guatemalan officer corps, this admission of United States-backed foreign forces to Guatemala was an extreme affront to national honour. Within months, on November 13th, 1960 a group of officers and men led by Colonel Rafael Sessan Pereira seized a barracks outside Guatemala City while another group succeeded in taking over the military base at Zacapa in eastern Guatemala and the Atlantic-coast port of Puerto Barrios. It took Ydígoras's government 4 days to quell the revolt, and he had to call on assistance from five United States naval vessels and from bomber aircraft piloted by Cuban exiles from the training base at Retalhuleu.

This incident marked the real start of Guatemala's chronic problem of guerrilla insurgency, for several of the young officers implicated in this abortive coup, after brief periods of exile in neighbouring countries, returned to provide the first generation of leadership for the leftist guerrilla movements that have operated ever since. (For a more thorough treatment of the genesis and course of the guerrilla war in Guatemala, see Recent Operations.) For Ydígoras, the use of these foreign forces was a step which irrevocably condemned him in the eyes of most officers. He survived an attempted revolt by a faction of the Guatemalan air force in November, 1962 but was forced out by his own Minister of War, Colonel Enrique Peralta Azurdia, in March, 1963.

Peralta was himself an extreme conservative; indeed, one of the announced reasons for the coup was the fact that Ydígoras had allowed the former leftist president Juan Arévalo back into the country to run in the presidential election that was scheduled for December, 1963. (Ironically, the possibility that Arévalo might win the election was instrumental in providing United States support for the coup.) Peralta ruled Guatemala under state of siege until 1966, and it was under his regime that the subsequent and still subsisting real political system of the country was evolved and established.

By the early 1960s the army's corporate professional identity was fully established, and the period of direct military rule under Peralta convinced it that it was at least as fit to govern the country as its civilian rivals. Thanks in part to the politicising effect of the United States-supplied counter-insurgency training which so many Guatemalan officers received from the late 1950s on, the officer corps had a clear view of itself as the most coherent and selfless instrument for national development available to the country. Although it still had to deal with other powerful interest groups in the country, it was no longer their client; its resources and above all its unity and sense of purpose were comparatively so much greater that the relationship was reversed.

Thus it became the duty and responsibility of the army to take over the government of the country on a permanent basis — though constitutional forms would be observed, and even figurehead civilian presidents were permissible. Guatemalan politics since 1963 have effectively moved inside the armed forces: the 4000 strong private army of the MLN in the east which more openly espouses the cause of the extreme right, civilian forces (including the right-wing death squads), and even the left-wing guerrilla movements, can be seen essentially as instruments of factions within the officer corps.

Inside that exclusive group there remain a variety of ideological views, ranging from far-right to near-left. Indeed, even the élite on the far-left of Guatemalan politics may be considered part of the officer corps, except that those officers have taken off their uniforms and are leading guerrillas in the field. The entire spectrum of officer opinion is united by extreme nationalism, strong anti-Americanism (although the right wing has often had to suppress this sentiment in order to get aid in its struggle against the left) and an intense corporate bond. This bond is so strong that it has been reported that the guerrilla leader Yon Sosa came in from the bush on one occasion to attend an evening party given by members of his class (promoción) from the military academy, despite their official status as enemies.

It is simply not known how the shifting balance of advantage amongst the different ideological views within the Guatemalan officer corps is determined, although latterly it has seemed to be left largely to the decision of more or less free national elections amongst presidential candidates approved by the army. Thus the vehemently anti-American and ultra-right-wing government of Colonel Peralta was succeeded in 1966 by the elected government of Julio César Méndez Montengro, a distinguished civilian law professor identified with the reformist cause. He had to agree, however, that the Defence Minister would be chosen by the army and would be responsible only to the army and not to him.

Within 4 months of his taking office the guerrilla threat, which had been growing through the early 1960s, became so acute that he had to declare a state of siege and hand most powers over to the army. The army also had to swallow its prejudice and permit United States troops (Green Berets and Ranger Special Forces) to assist the Guatemalan army in its intensive rural counter-insurgency operations. After 1968 the focus of guerrilla activities moved to the urban areas, but the intensity of the battle remained so high that army opinion shifted decisively in favour of a military president, the celebrated 'guerrilla-killer' Colonel Araña Osorio, in the 1970 elections.

Since 1972 the guerrilla and terrorist war in Guatemala has decreased markedly in intensity, and the concomitant slackening of the political tensions within the army was sufficiently great that the voters in the 1974 presidential elections were offered a choice of three generals: one conservative, one moderate and one liberal. The reputedly most conservative candidate, General Kjell Laugerud García, won, though not only narrowly (and subsequently proved to be less right-wing than had been thought). This pattern of presenting the voters with a choice of officers may be becoming established, for it was repeated in 1978, when the presidential candidates were Colonel Enrique Peralta Azurdia (extreme right, Head of State 1963–6), General Romeo Lucas García (centre-right) and General Ricardo Peralta Méndez (centre-left). The victor, in a count which was as always disputed by the losers, was General Lucas García.

Lucas García was ousted by a coup in March 1982 and replaced by a three-man junta led by General Efraím Rios Montt. General Rios Montt initially acted to improve the human rights situation by disarming the death squads which had previously operated from an annexe to the Presidential Palace, disguised as an Evangelical mission, which action, combined with an avowed anti-communist posture, prompted a renewal of US military assistance. More recently, an apparently planned programme of genocide against the Indians of the department of El Quiché in northern Guatemala has raised questions concerning the international acceptability of the Rios Montt regime.

STRENGTH AND BUDGET

Population: 7,260,000
Army: 17,000
Navy: 1,000 (included in Army); 30 minor vessels
Air Force: 600 (included in Army); 10 combat aircraft
Paramilitary: National Police: 9,500; Treasury Police (Border Guard): 2,100
GNP: (1981) $7,900,000,000
Defence Expenditure: (1981) $90,700,000

COMMAND AND CONSTITUTIONAL STATUS

The President of the Republic is identified in the 1966 Constitution as the commanding general of the army, which for constitutional purposes embraces all the armed services. He is elected to a 4 year term, and is ineligible for re-election. He appoints his own Cabinet without consultation with the legislature. The constitution contains a bill of rights guaranteeing the usual freedoms, but the frequently invoked Law of Public Order permits him to abrogate the rights and rule by decree by proclaiming any of four states of emergency ranging in severity from a 'state of prevention' to a total state of siege and war. Formal declaration of war, the conclusion of peace treaties, and the national budget (including defence) must receive Congressional assent, but in Guatemalan conditions this does not constitute an impediment to the President's power.

The President issues military instructions through the Minister of National Defence, who is invariably an army officer. The President is explicitly empowered to: decree mobilisation and demobilisation; grant promotions to all ranks of officers; confer military decorations and honours; and grant special pensions. There is a strictly consultative body, the Superior Council of National Defence, made up of the Minister of Defence and senior commanders, which advises the President on both military and political affairs and acts as the Superior Tribunal of the Armed Forces (the senior court of military justice). On operational military matters the President deals directly with the Minister of Defence and his Chief of Staff.

The constitution provides, however, that the army is to be governed principally by its own constitutive law and by military laws and regulations as approved by the Minister of National Defence, and in practice even soldier-presidents do not have total control over the army, which functions as a self-regulating body. The Minister of National Defence enjoys considerable autonomy: it is he who appoints the six military zone commanders and also the Commander of Reserves in each of the 22 departments of the country. The Commanders of Reserves are the military counterparts of the civil Governors appointed by the President, and in times of national emergency the Governors must yield their civil authority to these military officers.

The Army Chief of Staff exercises operational control over all the armed forces except the Palace and Presidential Guard, which receives its orders directly from the President. The Chief of Staff supervises the General Staff, which coordinates the policy, logistical and administrative functions of all three services. He controls the Territorial Commands which contain most of the operational units, and also the Special Commands and the Chiefs of Arms and Services.

The country is divided into six military zones, each including one or more of the 22 departments. Each military zone is commanded by a brigadier or colonel of one of the combat arms. These major territorial commands control the reserve structure in their areas, consisting of a Commander of Reserves in each department with basically administrative duties of controlling the reserve elements and the conscription organisation, but also with responsibility for some minor regular force units. The so-called Special Commands, which do not come under the authority of the zone commanders, are the Air Force, Navy, Military Forces Command, Military Bases Command, and Military Education Centres.

The Director General of the National Police is usually a senior army officer on loan from the Department of Defence, as are numerous other supervisory officers in the force, and the force has a military-style organisation. The police command structure is composed of a small staff in charge of operational divisions in the central headquarters and the five regional zones outside the capital, thus coinciding with the army's territorial command structure. The Director General of the National Police reports directly to the Minister of Government on all operational and administrative matters, while the Chief of the Border Patrol reports to the Minister of the Treasury, but in periods of national emergency both are subordinate to the army high command, and local regional army commanders assume command of police elements within their areas. Both forces have played a large role in the counter-insurgency operations of the past 15 years.

ROLE, COMMITMENT, DEPLOYMENT AND RECENT OPERATIONS

The 1966 Constitution states that the military establishment 'is designed to maintain the independence, sovereignty, and the honour of the nation, the integrity of its territory, and peace within the republic'. In practice the army has had little concern for the defence of the country's territorial boundaries in recent decades, and has been preoccupied almost entirely with the maintenance of internal security. Since 1962 it has been engaged in continuous military operations against an active and powerful guerrilla movement operating both in the countryside and within the cities. Starting at about the same date, it has assumed the additional role of being the effective government of the country, and has had to acquire new skills and devote much attention to the new tasks which this role entails.

Guatemala has no serious outstanding border disputes with its neighbours to the south, Honduras and El Salvador, although the latter retains a lingering suspicion about Guatemalan pretensions to leadership in Central America. The border with its huge neighbour to the north, Mexico, is well defined, and sparsely populated on both sides along most of its length; it has never been a cause of dispute. A dispute with Mexico over fishing rights in coastal waters in 1959 actually led to shots being exchanged and a temporary break in diplomatic relations, but the breach has long since been repaired. In terms of external enemies, there is no one in sight for the Guatemalan army to defend the country against.

There is, however, an extremely serious border dispute with the former British colony of Belize to the east, since Guatemala formally claims that entire territory. Belize's population of 175,000 is predominantly of Carribean origin and English-speaking, and the territory has been under British control for over three centuries, but Britain's presence there was never formally recognised by Spain. After Guatemala achieved its independence a treaty was concluded with Britain in 1859 in which the present frontier was agreed, on condition that Britain construct a road across Belize linking Guatemala with the Atlantic. This condition was never fulfilled, however, and since 1945 all Guatemalan constitutions have stated that Belize is part of the national territory, and that all Belizeans are Guatemalan citizens.

Partly because of its potential as a diversionary tactic in times of political crisis within Guatemala, the claim to Belize has now become a major element in Guatemalan nationalism. There have been repeated sabre-rattling incidents in which Guatemala has threatened to invade Belize, and a pattern has developed in which the normal British garrison of about 1500 troops in Belize has to be urgently reinforced on a temporary basis every 2 or 3 years – as in 1972, 1975 and 1977 – in response to bellicose statements in Guatemala City. This threat tends to be the particular prerogative of the extreme right, and there have been occasions in which the private army of the National Liberation Movement has offered to invade Belize from its stronghold in the neighbouring eastern provinces of Guatemala if the regular army were not up to the job.

In addition to its membership in the United Nations and the Organisation of American States, Guatemala has had senior officer representation since 1945 on the Inter-American Defence Board, the military planning organisation affiliated to the OAS. It is a member of the Organisation of Central American States, established in 1962, and Guatemala City is the headquarters for the permanent joint military staff of the Council for Central American Defence (CONDECA), the military branch of this organisation founded in 1963 with the participation of all the nations of the isthmus except Panamá and Cost Rica. Both CONDECA and its parent organisation OCAS liaise with their hemispheric counterparts, the Inter-American Defence Board and the OAS, but they are independent organisations. During the mid-1960s CONDECA conducted a series of joint exercises under United States aegis, concentrating on counter-guerrilla operations, but this form of co-operation has since lapsed. Indeed, with the emergence of a more radical form of military government in Honduras, CONDECA has now effectively become an alliance between the right-wing States of Guatemala and El Salvador.

This alliance does have a certain military potential, but it is in the area of intervention by one government's armed forces against an internal threat to an allied government, and would probably not be conducted under the auspices of CONDECA. There have allegedly been minor instances of this sort of mutual military aid in the past, as when Guatamalan air force planes were reportedly used to bomb rebels advancing to the capital of El Salvador in 1972, and there was speculation that similar assistance in larger quantities might be provided by Guatemala and El Salvador to the beleaguered Nicaraguan government during the 1978 civil war if the military situation required it.

This did not materialise and the beleaguered Salvadorean regime has sufficient domestic problems to rule out any offers of military assistance to Guatemala in the foreseeable future. There are no Guatermalan troops deployed beyond the national borders at the moment, and there remains an extreme aversion to the possibility of foreign troops, however friendly, being based on Guatemalan soil.

Recent Operations

The Guatemalan army's principal concern for the past two decades has not been the country's neighbours but its internal security situation. Since 1962 it has been involved in continuous large-scale counter-insurgency operations, with a death toll (mostly civilians and guerrillas) that undoubtedly exceeds 20,000 by now, and could be a good deal more. The rural violence actually began in the east of the country in the 1950s, when peasant resistance to the repossession by landowners of lands which had been expropriated under Arbenz's government was crushed by private right-wing armies, notably the MLN, but the start of true guerrilla warfare dates from shortly after the November 13th, 1960 military revolt against the government of President Ydígoras Fuentes. It was a typically nationalist revolt, triggered by army resentment at the presence of a Cuban exile military training camp under United States control on Guatemalan soil, although it would be true to say that most of the officers involved in it were basically more sympathetic to Arbenz than to his ultraconservative successors.

One group of rebels seized Fort Matamoros near Guatemala City, killing some loyal officers and escaping with troops and armaments; the other seized the military base of Zacapa and the major port of Puerto Barrios in the east of the country, and held them for 4 days before being dislodged by government troops supported by Cuban exiles flying bombing missions and by the United States navy. The defeated rebels escaped into Mexico, Honduras and El Salvador, but within 4 months some were back in the country seeking to found rural guerrilla movments. The most prominent were Lieutenants Marco Antonio Yon Sosa (of Chinese extraction) and Luís Augusto Turcios Lima, both of whom had already received training in counter-insurgency tactics from the United States army.

At first these young officers had no Marxist connections at all, and the guerrilla movements they set up in Zacapa and the Sierra de las Minas in the east of the country were intended to serve as the nucleus for a general uprising and the immediate overthrow of Ydígoras. There was indeed a rapid rise in bloody popular disturbances during the following 2 months, but then Ydígoras effectively gave in to the army and filled all his Cabinet posts with regular officers (a year before he was formally overthrown). The guerrilla leaders were thus forced to consider a longer-term strategy, and to seek civilian political allies. In late 1962 both Yon Sosa's MR-13 and Turcios Lima's separate but allied group agreed to an alliance with the underground Guatemalan Communist Party under the name *Fuerzas Armadas Rebeldes* FAR – Insurgent Armed Forces).

It should be stressed, however, that the Communist Party never had any control over the guerrilla groups, nor was it ever committed solely to the military seizure of power. Like most Latin American communist parties of that time it was wedded to the Soviet doctrine that a 'bourgeois revolution' must come before a socialist one, and that its place would be as a legal party in a leftist coalition, giving history an occasional push in the right direction. For the communists, the guerrillas were mainly a means of bringing pressure on the existing system in order to achieve that intermediate stage. Neither guerrilla leader was ever really a communist, although Turcios Lima finished up in an ideological position very near Castro's at the end of his political self-education. Yon Sosa, in contrast, conducted a lengthy flirtation with the Trotskyites of the Fourth International in 1964–6, and effectively held his MR-13 organisation separate from the FAR. But neither political association proved satisfactory to the young officers leading the guerrilla movements, whose pragmatically evolved revolutionary ideology did not fit into either the Trotskyist or the communist doctrinal strait-jackets, and whose essentially nationalist orientation put them more in the tradition of Arbenz and of the Nicaraguan guerrilla leader Augusto Sandino (*see* Nicaragua, History and Introduction) than in that of Marx, Lenin and Mao. In 1967 MR-13 was reabsorbed within the FAR, with Yon Sosa, totally disillusioned with the Trotskyists, in overall command. Early in 1968 the FAR as a whole, irritated beyond endurance at the Guatemalan Communist Party's adherence to the Moscow line of de-emphasising guerrilla struggle in Latin America, denounced its alliance with the communists in the bitterest of terms.

By this time the guerrillas had grown to represent a major threat to the survival of the Guatemalan regime, but as a result they were also coming under far greater pressure than before. The years 1963–4 had been occupied in the gradual construction of guerrilla base areas (*focos*), primarily in the three easternmost provinces of Izabal, Zacapa and Chiqui-mula, and in 'armed propaganda' amongst the generally receptive peasant population, but by 1965–6 the guerrillas were expanding into new rural areas and had begun to carry out operations in the capital. In November, 1966 shortly after the inauguration of the elected civilian president Julio Méndez Montenegro, he was compelled to declare a state of siege, effectively hand control over to the army, and to call in United States Green Berets and Ranger Special Forces to assist in an all-out counter-insurgency campaign. Unfortunately for the guerrillas of the FAR (at that time still at odds with the smaller MR-13), their leader Turcios Lima had been killed in a car accident in Guatemala City the month before, and his successor César Montes was a civilian who lacked the former's extensive contacts within the army.

Colonel Carlos Araña Osorio, an extremely ruthless commander, was placed in charge of Zacapa province and given half the Guatemalan army plus United States Special Forces units. He also created and armed unofficial vigilante groups who were given *carte blanche* to use the most extreme methods in eradicating 'communist sympathisers' and extracting intelligence from the local peasantry. (These groups gradually coalesced into two main anti-communist organisations, the *Mano Blanco* ('White Hand') and the *Consejo Anti-Communista de Guatemala* (CODEG) which survive to the present day and are the authors of most of the extreme right-wing terrorism and death-squad activities). Araña then proceeded to fight a remarkably successful counter-insurgency campaign in the east in 1966–8, forcing the guerrillas onto the defensive, cutting into their strength severely and keeping them continuously on the run. The estimated cost of his search-and-destroy methods in 2 years was 4000 deaths, of whom the great majority were innocent peasants; 28 United States soldiers were also killed.

By 1968 the guerrillas had been forced to move most of their operations into the cities: in January, 1968 they succeeded in killing the United States military and naval attachés, and in August the American ambassador was killed while resisting a kidnap attempt. The right-wing death squads replied with indiscriminate murder of anyone known or suspected to be sympathetic to the left: it was known that numbers of army officers were involved in their activities, but the extent to which the army high command secretly enouraged their activities is unknown. During 1969 and 1970 this war of mutual assassination turned into the chronic problem, costing over a thousand lives a year, which has plagued Guatemala ever since (in 1970) the FAR even kidnapped and murdered the West German ambassador), and which has effectively stulified any responsible political initiative from either left or right.

During 1969 and 1970 the FAR, having effectively lost its old bases in the eastern provinces, began trying to move into the countryside once more, this time in the Pacific coastal province of Escuintla, the predominantly Indian areas in the western highlands around Quetzalenango, and along the Mexican border. It was there that Yon Sosa was killed in 1970 in a clash with Mexican troops, leaving César Montes in command of the FAR. In the same year Colonel Araño Osorio, famed as the 'guerrilla killer', was elected to the presidency. He set about applying the tactics he had employed in Zacapa to the elimination of the rural guerrilla movement nationwide (this time without United States troops in support), and by the end of 1973 he had substantially succeeded.

However, like the war of assassination by the right against the left, the rural guerrilla struggle has now become ingrown. In 1975 there was a resurgence of guerrilla activities in three of the previously affected areas: Zacapa–Chiquimula, west of Guatemala City, and along the Mexican border. The FAR was now known as the Guerrilla Army of the Poor (EGP), but it was essentially the same organisation, back in such strength that it was necessary for the Guatemalan army to conduct joint operations with the Honduran army in the Zacapa and Chiquimula foothills during 1975. Rural operations continued at a lower level in 1976 and 1977.

In early 1979 the EGP was estimated at 300 combatants, still commanded by César Montes, and organised in four different commands. The one urban command was in Guatemala City, and of the three rural commands the strongest was in the mountainous Indian areas north-west of the capital. A second had been re-established in Escuintla on the tropical Pacific coast, and the weakest was in Zacapa. The EGP unit in the capital was co-operating closely with the communists, although tensions between the guerrillas and the communists still remain. There is absolutely no sign that the guerrillas can overthrow the army-dominated government, or that the army can permanently eradicate the guerrillas; the country seems doomed to a low-level war of assassination, guerrilla attacks and counter-insurgency operations for the foreseeable future. Between June and November, 1978 a total of 770 bodies bearing the marks of torture were found in various parts of Guatemala; in January, 1979 a Christian Democratic politician, Alberto Fuentes Mohr, was murdered in the capital, probably by a death squad of the extreme right.

The Rios Montt regime has acted resolutely against left-wing guerrillas, showing little discrimination towards neutral non-combatants in an apparent campaign of extermination in areas previously controlled by subversive elements.

ORGANISATION

Arms of Service
The military establishment as a whole is divided into the active duty components (*Fuerza Permanente*) and a large reserve. The combat arms of the regular force are the infantry, cavalry, artillery, engineers, air force and navy. (The latter two, though enjoying a considerable organisational independence, are ultimately considered to be part of a single armed force, which by sheer strength of numbers is really the army.) There are the usual service corps such as ordnance, military police, medical, and so on. Each branch is headed by a Chief of Arm or Service who is directly subordinate to the Chief of Staff.

The Infantry is organised into battalions of which there are 15 plus a Paratroop/Special Forces battalion and a regimental-sized Special Forces group. The Cavalry is organised into one Armoured Battalion and 4 mechanised reconnaissance squadrons. There are four groups of field artillery and one anti-aircraft battery. There is a single battalion of Engineers.

Operational
The six Military Zones form the infra-structure of the Army's reserve organisation and not all contain permanent garrisons of regular troops. The principal tactical formation is the Brigade, of which there are four. Two of these, the 'Mariscal Zavala' and 'Guardia de Honor' brigades have their headquarters at Guatemala City. A third brigade is deployed along the Pacific coast with its headquarters at San José whilst the remaining brigade is currently deployed along the frontier with Belize, with its headquarters at Puerto Barrios. The Presidential Guard (not to be confused with the 'Guardia de Honor' brigade) effectively forms a fifth brigade whilst the *Agrupación Táctica de Seguridad del Ejército*, is a sub-brigade-sized formation with a counter-insurgency function, also based at Guatemala City where approximately 60% of the total effectives of the Army are normally located. The Brigades, all of which are named but which do not appear to have numerical designations, each consists of three infantry battalions, a reconnaissance squadron and an artillery group, with an operational headquarters and a logistic support company. Four marine rifle companies come under the operational control of the Navy although the latter theoretically forms part of the same unified Armed Force as the Army and Air Force.

RECRUITMENT, TRAINING AND RESERVES

By law all male citizens between the ages of eighteen and fifty have an obligation to perform military service, but most are permitted to discharge this by service in the reserves between the ages of eighteen and thirty. Only about 5% of the estimated 60,000 men who register for military service each year on reaching eighteen are actually inducted into the regular forces; of these the great majority are Indians, and only a few *ladinos*. The term of service in the infantry and some other branches with low technical requirements is 1 year; in most of the others, 2 years.

Draft intakes are received four times a year. After the preliminary selection and medical examination have been carried out by the Commander of Reserves in each department, recruits are lined up by height and selected by representatives of the various arms. The Palace Guard gets the first choice, followed by the artillery, cavalry, infantry, engineers, air force and the various services, in that order. Basic training, including weaponry, physical education and instruction in elementary Spanish for the substantial proportion of recruits who do not speak it, is done in the special recruit centres, and usually lasts 16 weeks. Since 1945 the army has maintained a Literacy Department, and puts great emphasis on teaching all its recruits to read and write Spanish, but this instruction does not commence until they reach their units. Those who are already literate and have some education will be selected for assignments demanding higher technical skills; the actual instruction is usually provided by on-the-job training within the units.

Until the 1960s the Guatemalan army had always deliberately limited the numbers and responsibilities of senior NCOs for fear that they might become an institution which could challenge the position of the officer corps: most volunteers were allowed only one re-enlistment and few advanced beyond corporal's rank. The greater technical and operational demands on the army in the past two decades have caused this situation to change, however, and now three-quarters of army personnel are long-service volunteers. *Ladinos* in particular are encouraged to volunteer at the end of their obligatory service, and pay for volunteers has been made competitive with the civilian economy. The Guatemalan army now has about the usual proportion of enlisted personnel serving in the various sergeant ranks, and regulations provide for a career of up to 20 years. Non-commissioned officers' academies have been opened within the country, and numbers of NCOs also attend the United States Army School of the Americas in Panamá for technical training.

Officer recruitments is primarily through the *Escuela Politécnica*, to which cadets who have been successful in competitive examinations administered in each department of Guatemala are admitted at the age of fourteen or fifteen. They are now mostly drawn from middle-class families, and the proportion of cadets drawn from military families is lower than average for Latin American armies.

Graduates of the 4 year course at the Military Academy are granted a diploma in Science and Letters, commissioned as second-lieutenants in the infantry, and immediately posted to operational units. After 2 years' infantry service they may apply to transfer to other arms or services, including the air force and navy. Most air force pilots are trained to fly in the USA, with a few going to Venezuela or Mexico; the majority of naval officers receive their specialist training in Guatemala, but some have attended the Venezuelan or Argentine naval academies. Some officers, with diplomas good enough to qualify for university entrance, take degrees in such fields as medicine and law. Graduates of the Guatemalan or foreign military academies are known as *de escuela* (from the school); the few who are promoted from the ranks are known as *de linea* (from the line).

Post-academy training of army officers is provided by the School of Applied Tactics (*Escuela de Aplicación*), founded in 1941, which offers a variety of combat arms courses for all officer grades. Approximately 80% of company-grade officers re qualified parachutists, and a large majority of officers also attend professional courses abroad. In the past most of these have gone to United States army schools in the USA or the Panama Canal Zone, but others have gone to France, Italy, Spain, West Germany, Mexico and Argentina.

One of the striking features of the Guatemalan army is the extraordinarily strong corporate identity of the officer corps, which is reinforced by the institutions of the *promoción* and *centenarió*. The members of each year's graduating class at the Military Academy (*promoción*) recognise a special loyalty to each other throughout their careers, exchanging mutual favours and making allowances for shortcomings in a way that would not normally occur between members of different *promociōns*. The *centenario* relationship is a similar, even stronger bond between two individuals, generally 2 or 3 years apart in seniority, who share the same last two digits in the consecutive numbers which are assigned to all cadets entering the Academy — say, 543 and 643. The elder of the two is particularly responsible for the younger's welfare throughout his service career. These special loyalties will frequently take priority over factional and political divisions within the officer corps.

One factor that tends to vitiate the strong corporate bond of the officer corps, however, is the inadequate pay which is received by all ranks: it is expected that an officer will seek additional income beyond the base pay for his grade. The two principal ways of achieving this are to acquire one of the limited number of military appointments which carries with it a *sobresueldo* — an additional stipend — or to engage in private enterprise, which is perfectly permissible except that officers may not own liquor factories or run night clubs. Most officers in fact choose to invest in land, or if possible to obtain land by official grant in the lightly populated colonisation areas, supplementing their incomes with the rent obtained. Both these solutions, however, are highly conducive to power-seeking and influence-peddling within the army, and may be as important as political ideology in shaping its internal factions.

In addition to its normal training activities, the army when not engaged in active combat operations devotes considerable time and effort to civic-action projects. These include the provision of school lunches and the construction of schools, road construction (a major activity of engineer units), the regular dispatch of medical teams to villages in remote areas, and work connected with opening up for settlement the practically uninhabited northern province of El Petén, which occupies over one-fourth of the national area.

By law reservists — that is, everyone eligible for military service at eighteen who is not inducted into the regular army — must train every weekend in the first year, one weekend per month in the second year, every 3 months in the third year, and every 6 months in the fourth. Regular army units in the area are responsible for providing the training programme, and the reserve structure in each department is supervised by the local Commander of Reserves. Two federally subsidised schools give military instruction to high-school graduates and grant them reserve commissions as second-lieutenants. These provisions are not invariably observed, however, and the amount of training received by reservists seems inadequate to make them very useful militarily. The mobilisation system, such as it is, is not tested in practice.

EQUIPMENT AND ARMS INDUSTRY

Guatemala has no indigenous defence industry and all military equipment must be imported. Since the end of World War II, the United States has been the principal source of supply, although the purchase of large quantities of principally Czech arms, from the Soviet bloc, by the Arbenz Guzmán regime, in 1954, provided the principal rationalisation for its overthrow by a CIA engineered invasion. Following the refusal of the Carter administration in the United States to supply the type and quantity of Material required, Guatemala turned increasingly to alternative sources of supply, mainly Israel.

Rifles: Gallil 7.62mm (Israel)
Sub-machine-gun: Uzi 9mm (Israel)
Machine-guns: M1919 0.30″ (US)
Mortars: M-1 81mm (US); M-2 60mm (US); M-2 4.2″ (US)
Artillery: M-101 105mm (US); M-118 75mm (US); M-12 L16 75mm (Germany via Czechoslovakia)
Air-defense-weapons: 40mm L/60 (Sweden/US); 20mm (Switzerland)
Armour: M4 medium tank (US); 10 in service); M-3 light tank (US); 10 in service); AMX-13 (France via Austria; 8 in service); M-8 armoured car (US; 8 in service), M-3A1 scout car (US; 15 in service); M-113 APC (US); 15 in service); RBY-1 scout car (Israel; 10 in service); V-150 armoured car (US; 7 in service)
Aircraft: The Air Force has about 20 transports and 30 helicopters.

RANK, DRESS AND DISTINCTIONS

Ranks and insignia of rank have been standardised within all the members of CONDECA, including Guatemala, and are similar to those of the United States army. All ranks above colonel were abolished in the Guatemalan army in 1944, but the rank of brigadier-general was reinstated in 1968 and is now the highest rank held by serving officers.

Guatemalan troops wear khaki shirts and trousers and peaked caps for both work and dress uniforms; field uniforms are of American pattern. In addition to garrison uniforms similar to those of the enlisted ranks, Guatemalan officers wear an olive-green woollen gabardine uniform of roll collar jacket and trousers. Dress uniforms for officers and dark blue, with a gold belt and narrow gold stripes down the trouser legs. Officers' rank insignia are worn on shoulder-boards, or on shirt collars when no jacket is worn.

Camouflage coveralls are increasingly used as a field uniform. A fibreglass ballistic helmet of Israeli manufacture appears to be replacing the US M42 steel helmet previously worn.

The highest military decoration in Guatemala, presented only by the President, is the Order of the Quetzal in the grade of the Grand Cross (*La Ordén del Quetzal en la grado do Gran Cruz*). Other decorations, in order of precedence, are: the Cross of Military Merit, grades I, II and III; the Cross of Distinguished Services; and the Medal of Achievement in the Services.

CURRENT DEVELOPMENTS

With the doubtful benefit of hindsight it has become commonplace to impute to the military revolutionaries of 1944 (and likewise to their successors of the 1960s) motives, ideologies and programmes which they did not then possess. Thus the Arbenz of 1954, with his close alliance with the Communist Party and his hemispheric status as a sort of proto-Castro, is confused with the young Captain Arbenz of 1944. Similarly the Trotskyite guerrilla leader Yon Sosa and his pro-Peking ally Turcios Lima of the Fuerzas Armadas Rebeldes in, say,

1965, are confused with the two naïve young army lieutenants who took part in the abortive nationalist coup of November 13th, 1960. This misconception has then been extrapolated to reach the unwarranted conclusion that the junior 'school'-trained officer corps of the Guatemalan army was a secret hotbed of Marxist revolutionaries. Nothing could be further from the truth. Arbenz was no more than an ambitious young nationalist with reformist sympathies in 1944. The only places where Yon Sosa and Turcios Lima could have been systematically exposed to Marxist ideology prior to their part in the 1960 revolt (when they were respectively twenty-two and nineteen) was in the anti-communist indoctrination courses given at the Guatemalan military academy which they had entered at the age of fifteen, or in the United States army counter-insurgency courses which they subsequently attended at Fort Gulick in the Canal Zone and Fort Benning, Georgia. The Guatamalan army was indeed changing its character and its role rapidly in this period, but it was not corporately becoming a radical force. Rather, it was acquiring a consciously professional officer corps, increasingly confident of its own political abilities and increasingly nationalist in ideology. One of the first big changes in the army after 1944 was that 'line' officers who were still young enough were encouraged to attend the academy to acquire a professional training. It is true that the post-1940 'school' officers, being on average better educated and frequently of middle-class origins (not to mention being younger) did tend to have a more reformist and interventionist attitude to politics, but that does not mean they shared a common ideology.

What they did share, apart from ambition to better their own and the army's status, was a desire to build a more modern, more powerful Guatemala, less vulnerable to external (American) intervention. For many this did lead to the conclusion that the stranglehold of the old social structure must be broken, and that drastic reforms were required to set free the energies of the nation. Even if for some this in turn led to a leftist political orientation, it was more often social reform in the service of national power and independence than the other way around. By the later 1960s, the most common view in the officer corps (now almost all 'school'-trained) was that the army was the most effective force for modernisation and the most trustworthy guarantor of political stability in the country, and that it was fully competent to rule Guatemala. The old alliances between the army and other powerful groups in society became much less equal, and the army arrogated to itself the corporate role of (sometimes disguised) leading political force in the country. This is quite different from the old individualistic model of military dictatorship, and has developed into a system with considerable stability.

This sort of development is scarcely unknown in other Latin American armies in recent years — Peru and Brazil spring to mind, on the left and the right, respectively — s the obvious questions arise: why did Guatemala experienc the entirely untypical events of 1944—54, and why did i continue to produce young officers capable of changing rapidly into Marxist guerrilla leaders right through th 1960s?

The answer is probably a matter of dates. The Guatemalan revolution of 1944 was not predestined to follow the cours it traced up to the disaster of 1954, but it could only tak that path at all because it was the first such revolution in Latin America. In subsequent cases where similar potentialitie existed, local conservative forces or the USA were alerte and could move decisively to stop things in time. Once th model of an even temporarily successful left-wing nationalis government had been demonstrated in Guatemala, however it could not be forgotten in less than a generation, and s the goals and methods that were espoused under Arben. in the early 1950s are still widely disseminated, in a mucl more vivid fashion than in countries where they remain pure speculation, waiting to be adopted by dissatisfied youn; officers in search of a cause or a lever.

The number of such young officers within the army i now much smaller than it used to be, however, for 15 year of guerrilla war against Marxists has shifted the spectrun of political opinion inside the army a considerable distance back towards the right. The officer corps remains an ultra nationalist (and therefore essentially anti-American) bod) of men, but a large number of officers have renewed o strengthened the traditional close connection with the economically dominant and politically right-wing faction of Guatemalan civilian society. Factionalism inside the army continues to be restrained by the very powerful instinc for corporate solidarity amongst the officer corps, and i further contained within bounds by the realisation that only a united army can continue to exercise effective rule ove the country as it does at present.

There is little prospect that the army will voluntarily withdraw from this role, since it conceives of itself as a efficient instrument for national development (and enjoy many privileges as a result of its prominence). Neither i the army likely to split irremediably on factional lines. A for the continuing guerrilla challenge, it is unlikely to achieve major success in the foreseeable future, as the Guatemalar army is now probably the most effective fighting force in Central America with high professional expertise in counter insurgency operations. The Salvadorean Army, after almos four years of sustained high-level counter-insurgency opera tions, must now be regarded as a serious challenger for thi position.

Gwynne Dye
Adrian Englis

238

GUINEA BISSAU

HISTORY AND INTRODUCTION

This former Portuguese colony declared itself independent in 1973, the proclamation being issued from an area from which Portuguese forces had been ejected in the final phase of a protracted insurgency campaign at times more resembling a limited conventional war. The Portuguese government conceded independence (at a small ceremony in Lisbon at which no Guinea's were present) in 1974. In the independence struggle the lead was taken by the PAIGC, a Marxist party of rigid ideology, and led by Amilcar Cabral, an important figure in the theory of Marxist guerrilla movements and Third World development writing. The party was common to both Guinea–Bissau and Cape Verde, aiming at a post-independence union. In 1973 Cabral was assassinated (probably by a Portuguese 'special operation'); he was succeeded by his brother Luis. L. Cabral became president of the mainland territory at independence, but was ousted in November 1980 in a coup led by J. B. Vieira ('Nino' as he is less formally named) a famous insurgent leader in the liberation struggle. Nino has favoured re-opening contacts with the West and has refused Soviet requests for a maritime reconnaissance facility. A return to constitutional government with elections (one party but probably a choice of candidate) has been promised, but extreme Marxist hard-line opposition to these developments still exists, and may have been the motive behind two abortive 1981–2 coup attempts, one involving the tank unit posted in Bissau. A number of officers were *limogés*.

STRENGTH AND BUDGET

Population: 800,000
Armed Forces: Army 6000, Air Force 50; para-military militia 5000
GNP: $200,000,000 (estimate)
Defence Expenditure: No figure available

COMMAND AND CONSTITUTIONAL STATUS

The President, J. B. Vieira, is Commander-in-Chief of the country's forces. After the abortive coup attempt all armed forces were placed under the direction of the President's office, I. Camara being Vice-Minister for the Armed Forces.

ROLE, COMMITMENT, DEPLOYMENT AND RECENT OPERATIONS

In the struggle against the Portuguese from 1963 to 1974 the PAIGC (the one permitted party) created the People's Revolutionary Armed Forces (FARP) on Maoist lines with an elite hard core plus locally based irregular guerrillas and with a militia as an auxiliary.

In the actual fighting, the FARP divided the territory into sectors within which one 'bi-group' operated. A bi-group was some 30 men in strength with a commander and a political commissar, and was equipped from a variety of weapons including Soviet AK-47s and RPDs (and their Chinese equivalents), Goryunov M-49 machine-guns, PPsh-41 and 43 carbines, Degtyrew 1938/46 12.7mm machine-guns, the Chinese 75mm type 52 recoilless gun, and Soviet RPG-2 and sometimes RPG-7 weapons; a few units also held Soviet mortars and latterly SAM-7 surface-to-air man-pack missiles. A few special units sited in Guinea or Senegal were equipped with Soviet 122mm field guns, but these appear to have been only loaned (from Nigeria) and may now have been returned. Decisive to the outcome of the campaign was the use of SAM-7, which destroyed the Portuguese capacity to airlift troops to areas in which PAIGC units were operating.

One report notes that a small Guinea-Bissau contingent served with the MPLA and Cuban forces in Angola in 1975–76 and in São Tomé for a period from 1978. Guinea-Bissau's forces, military and para-military, rounded up a group described as 'counter-revolutionaries' in November, 1978; this group, it was alleged, was composed of mercenaries and former Portuguese colonial soldiers, and was said to have crossed into Guinea-Bissau secretly from Senegal.

ORGANISATION

The FARP consists of four infantry battalions, probably under strength, a tank battalion (in practice little more than a squadron), and an engineer company.

RECRUITMENT, TRAINING AND RESERVES

In the campaign against the Portuguese the Balanta and Nalu ethnic groups supported the PAIGC, while the Fula frequently supported the Portuguese. This is likely to have left its mark on the ethnic composition of the FARP.

EQUIPMENT AND ARMS INDUSTRY

The tank squadron possesses 10–12 T-34 tanks. One unconfirmed report notes also a battalion's worth of T-54 tanks, but this seems unlikely. Thirty Soviet armoured personnel carriers are in service, mostly BTR-40s or BTR-152s but including a few BTR-60s. Another unconfirmed report adds small numbers of BRDM-2 and PT-76 vehicles, again the probability does not seem great. From the guerrilla campaign remain small numbers of 85mm and 122mm guns, 120mm mortars, 89mm rocket launchers, and 75mm recoilless launchers, and 23mm and 57mm anti-aircraft guns together with SAM-7 equipments. The air unit possesses two Dornier Do-27, two YAK-40 light transports and a Cessna 337 light aircraft, together with two Alouette and one MI-8 helicopters. The 105mm guns were originally *Wehrmacht* and then Portuguese. One report notes fifty light armoured carriers, for loads or personnel, on order from the French Citroën firm

RANK, DRESS AND DISTINCTIONS

A simple form of combat jungle uniform is all that has been reported in respect of dress. Until 1974 there was only one officer rank, Commandant. The structure now provides for Commandant, Senior Commandant and Brigade Commandant.

CURRENT DEVELOPMENTS

Although ideologically far apart from Senegal, Guinea-Bissau prefers at present to cultivate that country's friendship rather than that of Marxist Guinea (Conakry). One reason for this is fear of Sekon Toure's designs for an eventual annexation and his immediate claims upon the two Piolan islands. Another is that Bissau wishes to effect a reconciliation with its Fula community; these carry some weight in Dakar. A defence treaty with Senegal is reported to have been signed.

It is accepted that the original plan of a union with Cape Verde is for the time being dead.

Lloyd Mathews

GUINEA CONAKRY*

HISTORY AND INTRODUCTION

Guinea, a French colony in the colonial era, rejected French Community membership terms in 1958, opting for a complete independence even at the cost of all links with France. The cost proved to be very considerable, and was made worse by a poor level of economic performance under a regime of austere xenophobic Marxist socialism. The government of Guinea, since 1958, has been in the hands of President Sekou Toure. Various plots to overthrow him have been reported and others have been alleged. These have often been followed by purges and trials, sometimes followed by executions, the most recent occurring in 1969, 1971, 1973, 1976 and 1980 (the latter attempt on Toure's life being described officially as a *crime crapuleuse*). In some plots the complicity of Senegal and the Ivory Coast was alleged.

A Soviet maritime reconnaissance squadron was based on Conakry until 1979, when Sekou Toure's increasing suspicions of Soviet interventions in Africa led to its closure. Sekou Toure has, however, maintained cordial relations with other European Communist countries and, in a skilful balancing act, significantly improved relations with France.

STRENGTH AND BUDGET

Population: 5,750,000 (approximate)
Armed Forces: 9000 (army), 600 (navy) and 800 (air force) with a para-military militia force of approximately 9000
GNP: $1,200,000,000 (estimate)
Defence Expenditure: no figure available

COMMAND AND CONSTITUTIONAL STATUS

President Sekou Toure, as Head of State, is Commander-in-Chief. The Minister of Defence is General Lansana Diana.

ROLE, COMMITMENT, DEPLOYMENT AND RECENT OPERATIONS

A Guinea battalion (described as commanded by a lieutenant and including six political commissars) was sent to the UN Congo Force in 1960. It was equipped with mortars and heavy machine-guns, and its discipline appeared poor: its general unsuitability prevented it being put to any real test and it was soon withdrawn.

Since then Guinean instructors and personnel have assisted the anti-Portuguese P.A.I.G.C. insurgents in Guinea–Bissau, and have occasionally appeared in a harassing role on the borders of Senegal, Ivory Coast and Liberia, all at one time or another being the subject of accusations of sponsoring counter-revolutionary conspiracies. In 1971 Guinean troops were sent to Sierra Leone at the request of President S. Stevens while his own army was reorganised. These all returned to Guinea within 2 years. A similar service was provided briefly to Master-Sergeant Doe after his coup in Liberia.

The Guinea army signally failed to contain the Portuguese-sponsored raiding incursion into Conakry from the sea in 1970, the aim of which was to destroy P.A.I.G.C. headquarters.

The army has also been given commitments in the field of development, road-making, farm projects and minor construction work.

ORGANISATION

The army is composed of five infantry battalions, a tank battalion, an artillery battalion, a commando battalion, a special forces unit and an engineer unit. It appears that the militia was reduced in size and reorganised into battalions in 1971–2. Some form of militia reserve may still exist, though this may be indistinguishable from local branches of P.D.G. party activists.

RECRUITMENT, TRAINING AND RESERVE

A system of national civic service, or which military service may be an option, is in force.

Training assistance has been obtained from West Germany and the USSR. The German assistance was reduced in the late 1960s and withdrawn entirely in 1970. Soviet assistance has now probably been withdrawn, but one report suggests it may have been replaced by East Germany.

EQUIPMENT AND ARMS INDUSTRY

Guinea's equipment is Soviet-patterned, but obtained from China and Czechoslovakia as well as the USSR. The tank battalion is equipped with fifteen T-34 and thirty T-54/55 tanks. Other armoured vehicles include ten (one report suggests twenty) PT-76 reconnaissance light tanks, twenty-five BRDM-1 or 2 armoured patrol vehicles, a number, between forty and sixty-five, armoured troop carriers, either BTR-40, BTR-60 or BTR-152 and unspecified numbers of Soviet 76mm, 85mm and French 105mm and Soviet 122mm guns, 57mm anti-tank guns and 37mm, 57mm and 100mm anti aircraft guns. Infantry weapons of course also follow Warsaw Pact patterns and include RPG-2 and RPG-7. One report suggests that the army possesses SAM-7 light surface to air missiles; this is very likely as they were supplied to the PAIGC.

The Air Force possesses three M₁G-21 and ten MiG-17 fighter machines, with two MiG-15 machines, now used for training also available if necessary, as a strike force. For transport, eight Ilyushin-14s, two Ilyushin-18s, four Antonov-24s and two Antonov-12s are in service, with three smaller liaison aircraft and ten training machines. There are three helicopters, a Bell 47, a Puma, and a Gazelle.

RANK, DRESS AND DISTINCTIONS

The rank structure appears to remain French in its nomenclature and connotations; however, actual appointments do not seem always to be related to rank. Uniforms are of Soviet style, including ankle boots and side caps.

* For general notes on African armies, see Appendix 1.

Guinea-Conakry

CURRENT DEVELOPMENTS

Reliable information is extremely hard to obtain, and other reports often conflict. It is probably correct to assert, however, that for a variety of economic and logistic reasons, little could be undertaken without considerable Soviet or other Warsaw Pact support. Such support seems now much less likely and Guinea appears more anxious to reach 'live and let live' understanding arrangements with her neighbours. These in turn, and in recognition of the relaxed nature of the regime in the 1980s, the freeing of many political detainees and the ending of strident propaganda attacks on non-Marxist regimes governments, are in turn becoming better disposed towards Conakry. Sekon Toure is on his way to respectability, though the continuance in detention of a number of detainees remains a stumbling block in the way of full general, or in particular full French, acceptability.

Lloyd Mathews

GUYANA

Although one of the mainland South American republics, Guyana is unique among them in being English-speaking, and having remained a dependent State of Great Britain, until 1966.

Venezuela lays claim to about two-thirds of Guyanan territory but the dispute was laid in abeyance for 12 years by the 1970 Protocol of Trinidad. There is also a border dispute with Surinam, which led to an armed clash on the border in 1969, but it has been quelled by an agreement to demilitarise the area. There was a minor internal disturbance in 1969, the so-called Rupununi rebellion, fomented by white ranchers among the Amerindians in the interior, but it was put down without difficulty. Guyana received international notoriety with the Church of God and Jones sect massacre in 1978. Guyana's real troubles are more deep-seated. The population divides almost exactly into Negro and Indian (Hindu) halves, who follow different leadership and are unable to co-operate either politically or socially. The negro People's National Congress, led by Forbes Burnham, has been in power since 1968. He is Defence Minister as well as Prime Minister and the Defence Force is under his personal control. it is increasingly negro in composition. In the event of serious racial distrubances, its impartiality would therefore be in Although it contains a number of Indians, recruited when the force was under British control, it is increasingly negro in composition. In the event of serious racial disturbances, its impartiality would therefore be in doubt. Hitherto, however, it has not been called upon to play a major internal security role.

STRENGTH AND BUDGET

Population: 870,000
Army: 5,000
Navy: (part of Army); 10 small craft
Air Force: (part of Army); no combat aircraft
Paramilitary: 5,000
GNP (1980): $559,000,000
Defence Expenditure (1981): $24,200,000

COMMAND AND CONSTITUTIONAL STATUS

The Guayana Defence Force is under the direct command of the President.

ROLE, COMMITMENT, DEPLOYMENT AND RECENT OPERATIONS

The ostensible function of the Guyana Defence Force is the defence of the country against external aggession. Its size and limited equipment militate against its potential effectiveness in this role and it has become increasingly a partisan internal security force. In accordance with this development, the bulk of its effectives are deployed in the vicinity of the capital.

ORGANISATION

The Guyana Defence Force combines the country's land, sea and air forces under a single unified command. Until recently the land forces consisted of two composite battalions, each consisting of headquarters, three rifle companies and a support company. In the case of the 1st Battalion, the support company was a heavy weapons unit and operated all the heavy equipment of the Guyana Defence Force. In the case of the 2nd Battalion, the support company was an engineer unit. In 1980, a third battalion and an artillery battery, equipped with heavy mortars, were raised and the composition of the three infantry battalions was standardised. It is not known whether any separate mechanised or engineer units have been formed.

RECRUITMENT, TRAINING AND RESERVES

Recruitment is on a voluntary and increasingly racialist basis with preference to negro recruits. Before independence, the Guyana Defence Force was trained by British personnel. It seems possible that some covert Cuban training assistance may have been recently received. The trained reserve consists of three companies.

EQUIPMENT AND ARMS INDUSTRY

Guyana produces no defence material.

Rifle: G3 7.62mm (Germany)
Machine-guns: L7A2 7.62mm (Britain); Bren 7.62mm (Britain)
Mortars: 81mm (Britain); 82mm (Soviet Union); 120mm (Soviet Union)
Air-defence weapons: SA-7 SAM (Soviet Union)
Armour: Shorland scout car (Britain)
Aircraft: There are about 10 light transport aircraft and 6 helicopters

RANK, DRESS AND DISTINCTIONS

Uniforms are of British tropical type. Rank insignia follow British practice.

CURRENT DEVELOPMENTS

The most notable recent developments are the increasingly Marxist orientation of the Forbes Burnham government, which was re-elected in 1980 and the increasing political predominance of the negro element of the population.

A worsening economic situation and racial and demographic pressures have a potential for internal disruption. Although Venezuela strongly supported the Argentine invasion of the Falkland Islands, the possibility of military action to support Venezuelan claims to more than half of the country's total area seems unlikely.

John Keegan
Adrian English

HAITI

HISTORY AND INTRODUCTION

There have been two basic kinds of army alternating or co-existing in Haitian history since the heroic period of the wars of independence in the late eighteenth and early nineteenth centuries: relatively small regular forces with a modicum of training and discipline, and larger, ill-disciplined groups of armed men whose sole military capabilities were against either the domestic population or the government. Both kinds have generally acted ruthlessly in pursuit of their own interests, but the level of bloodshed and random terror attendant on this process has been lower when disciplined forces predominated in the military establishment. At the moment Haiti's armed forces are in slow transition from the gangs of hoodlums that were dominant in the 1960s back towards a somewhat more professional armed force.

Haiti, the western third of the Caribbean island of Hispaniola, has had three complete changes of dominant population in the past 500 years: from the Indians to the Spaniards shortly after Columbus's voyage of discovery in 1492; from the Spaniards to the French in 1697, and from French to Africans in 1791–1804. It was during the last period and the few succeeding decades that the basic conditions of modern Haiti's existence were established.

When the French Revolution broke out in 1789 Haiti was France's richest colony, with a population of 35,000 whites, 35,000 mulattos and about half a million black slaves. The majority of the slaves spoke only African languages and a form of pidgin French (which have subsequently blended to create the 'creole' which is spoken by 90% of the population) and practised traditional religions in a form called *vodun* (voodoo). The mulattos, however, were French in language and culture and Catholic in religion. They were active in commerce, and owned one-third of the black slaves.

The great slave revolt which broke out in 1791 and ended by exterminating all the whites in Haiti was led by self-taught black generals — Toussaint L'Ouverture, Jean-Jacques Dessalines and Henri Christophe — who have become Haiti's national military heroes. The French revolutionary government decreed emancipation, and in alliance with French troops the black Haitian forces overran the Spanish part of the island (now the Dominican Republic) in 1798. In 1800, however, there occurred the first of many black–mulatto clashes, the War of the Castes, won by Toussaint's black forces.

He was shortly afterwards treacherously seized and deported to France, where he died in jail, but the French campaign to reconquer the country and reimpose slavery ordered by Napoleon was defeated by Dessalines with British help. In the course of the fighting the remaining whites were wiped out, and Dessalines emerged in 1804 as the Emperor of an independent black-ruled Haiti. He was assassinated in 1806 and mulattoes regained control of the south and west of the country under President Alexandre Pétion, but the black General Henri Christophe ruled in the north as King Henry until his suicide in 1820. Thereupon the mulatto leader Jean-Pierre Boyer reunited the country, and in 1822 conquered the new Dominican Republic which was just emerging from Spanish rule in the rest of the island.

The main themes of Haitian politics were firmly established by then: permanent competition for power between the French-acculturated mulatto minority and black demagogues appealing to the rural peasnat masses, who were already lapsing into a primitive subsistence agriculture; and intense national and racial hostility between the Haitians and their Dominican neighbours, who refer to the Haitian occupation as the 'Period of Ethiopianisation'.

By 1843 the third major characteristic of Haitian politics had appeared; the army, an unpopular career amongst the commercially oriented mulattos, had become predominantly black, and overthrew mulatto rule. Control of the Dominican Republic was lost in the following year (though the Emperor Faustin made repeated attempts to reconquer it in the 1850s). Haiti for the next 70 years was ruled by a succession of brutal, often illiterate, negro generals who succeeded for a time (often after much fighting) in gaining control of the army and thus the Presidential Palace.

For most of this period the army averaged about 6000 men, a strength which seems to have been determined largely by the impossibility of looting enough money from the extremely limited public funds to keep the loyalty of a larger number. For practical purposes the sole activity of government was the distribution of legally collected and illegally extorted money amongst its supporters, while the countryside was effectively ungoverned. The army was a totally unprofessional body consisting of the shifting retinues of military adventurers whose goal was political power, with the consequence that it spent a great deal of time fighting itself.

Towards the end of this period the political/military situation became so chaotic — there were six presidents in 1911–15, none of whom lasted a year and all of whom died violently — that the USA intervened. It had already established a customs receivership in 1905, and it was then at the height of its Caribbean interventionist phase, sending in the marines to take control, create reliable 'constabulary-style' forces, and establish orderly government. The USA's occupation of Haiti lasted from 1915 to 1934 and encountered no resistance from the army as such, although there was almost continuous guerrilla warfare in some rural areas against the American marines.

The main changes effected by the USA were the restoration of mulatto rule — the USA governed through a series of mulatto puppet presidents — and the creation of the first modern Haitian army. The old force was entirely disbanded, and marine instructors set about creating a small professional military force (3000 in 1934) which would be efficient, obedient and outside of politics. Inevitably, however, it was a predominantly negro force, so the basic Haitian equation was not changed.

The restored mulatto supremacy under President Sténio Vincent survived the withdrawal of the United States marines in 1934 due to its effective alliance with this new army and the threat of renewed United States intervention (the USA's control over Haitian customs was not relinquished until 1941). The momentum of the USA's reforms was sufficient to ensure the election of another educated mulatto. Elie Lescot, to the Presidency in 1941, but in 1946 the black army, supported by the racially resentful mass of the population, ended this second period of mulatto domination. With the 500-man Palace Guard in the lead, the army took advantage of a general strike to oust Lescot and bring about the election of an anti-mulatto black President, Dumarsais Estimé.

When the latter attempted to ensure his continuation in office by a constitutional amendment in 1950, the army intervened again and brought Colonel Paul Magloire, the leader of the 1946 *junta*, to the Presidency himself. The army's traditional role as the supreme political force in Haiti was restored, although this comparatively well-trained and efficient force exercised its control as a unified and irresistible force issuing decrees, rather than through the bloody factional military uprisings which were typical of Haiti's old army. The army did not neglect its own interests, of course (20% of the national budget was reserved to it, and it had grown to 5000 men by 1956), but it was a far better educated force — all the officers were literate, and many were graduates of the military academy which had been founded in 1941. It had progressed some distance beyond its previous, purely predatory role in Haitian politics, and under Estimé and even under the markedly more conservative Magloire some social and economic advances were made.

This phase was ended, however, when Magloire sought to extend his term of office illegally in 1956. The army overthrew him, but had no agreed candidate to replace him. After some months of chaos, when various candidates from among the 'men of 1946' competed for army support, a black American-educated doctor called François Duvalier succeeded in gaining the support of a majority of the key army officers and so got himself elected President. This was a fatal mistake for the professional army, for Duvalier promptly proceeded to destroy it as a potential rival for power.

Adroitly playing off one military faction against another Duvalier successively removed most high-ranking officers from the active list, while constantly reshuffling unit commanders to guard against a coup. Not only former supporters of his rivals were removed, but also his own supporters of 1957. The Army Chief of Staff was deprived of the prerogative of selecting the commanders of key posts and also of operational control over the two *élite* units stationed in the capital (the Presidential Guard and the Dessalines Battalion), both of which were assumed by the President himself. As an additional precaution, the bulk of the army's ordnance was moved to storage areas in the basement of the presidential palace and its surrounding grounds. By 1960 or 1961, the army's officer corps had been thoroughly purged, the empty places being filled by Duvalier henchmen, while its combat capabilities had been completely destroyed.

Duvalier chose instead to rely on irregular security forces for internal repression, as a counterbalance to the untrustworthy regular army, and to a considerable degree even as the first line of external defence. It was a deliberate reversion to the type of armed forces that had been predominant in the pre-American intervention era.

The principal force created for this purpose was the National Security Volunteers, whose members (averaging 14,000 during the 1960s) received the equivalent of army basic training, but were paid no salaries. They served in normal times as Duvalier's local paramilitary organisation in the outlying districts, drawing money as needed from local community budgets, but could be mobilised when required either to repel attempted guerrilla landings or to overawe the army.

For enforcement in the capital and for the more active repression of dissent Duvalier relied on the *Tontons Macoutes* (named after the scrounging 'Uncle Strawbag' of Haitian folk legend who kidnaps small children and puts them in sacks).

Members of this force of between 1500 and 5000 men, wearing civilian clothes but carrying side-arms, were omnipresent in all government organisations and also in the more important private enterprises, operating as Duvalier's personal intelligence network, control agency, extortion ring and private executioners. Recruited largely from the criminal underworld, they were immune from interference by other government agencies (including the army), and were responsible for most of the atrocities which were Duvalier's main instrument of rule.

With the National Security Volunteers as his army, the *Tontons Macoutes* as his secret police, and the emasculated regular armed forces pushed far into the background, 'Papa Doc' Duvalier was able to rule undisturbed until his death in 1971 (he had made himself President-for-Life in 1964). Five times during his reign there were landings by armed Haitian exiles, including former army officers, seeking to start a popular rising against him, but in each case they were quickly killed or captured by his security forces. The lack of response in the countryside to these various invasions was partly due to the efficiency of his security forces and the traditional political apathy of the illiterate, undernourished peasantry. There is no doubt, however, that Dr Duvalier also exerted a powerful hold on their loyalties through his anti-*élite*, and anti-mulatto demagoguery and his astute exploitation of the voodoo priests to spread the belief that he was a great magician.

The stability of his regime was demonstrated by the contemptuous ease with which he withstood intense United States pressure to stand down at the end of his elected term. He cancelled the USA's aid programmes himself, and waited calmly for American fear of the spread of Cuban influence (only 50 miles separate the two islands) to bring Washington back to supporting him — as it duly did in 1964. The best proof of the regime's strength, however, was the fact that the position of President-for-Life was inherited smoothly by his nineteen-year-old son Jean-Claude Duvalier on his death from natural causes in 1971.

The rule of 'Baby Doc' Duvalier has seen modest and sporadic gestures towards liberalisation punctuated by sharp reversals. The fundamental conflict is between the 'old guard' of the regime, led by 'Papa Doc's' widow Maman Simone ('The Guardian of the Sacred Torch of the Revolution') and Henri Siclait (Head of the State Agency which provides most of the Duvalier family's illicit income, estimated at $17,000,000 a year), and the younger and better-educated 'technocrats' whom the new President-for-Life has gathered around him. Immediately after the old dictator's death in 1971 a number of the worst *Tonton Macoute* warlords were dismissed. A new Secretary of State for Interior and National Defence, Paul Blanchet, together with two other young ministers, pursued a nationalist line (largely unsuccessfully) against foreign enterprises which had been attracted by Haiti's cheap labour, and even attempted to enforce the labour laws on minimum pay and working conditions.

It was largely as a part of this competition between the young and the old guard that the new government began to improve the status of the army, while downgrading that of the irregular forces in which the old power-holders were entrenched. Since 1971 the National Security Volunteers have been halved in number, and placed under the operational control of the army. The *Tonton Macoutes* still exist but are considerably less visible, and their worst excesses have been curbed. The army has been given better training, and new *élite* counter-insurgency units (the 'Leopards') have been trained to do what was once primarily a militia job.

The Haitian army's effective political power is still negligible, but its status has been raised considerably relative to the regime's paramilitary forces. It remains an obedient tool in the hands of the President-for-Life, but it is an extremely effective tool for internal control: it contains within itself not only the country's police forces, but also its main telecommunications network. Most of it still has little or no capability for conventional combat, but certain units have been restored to an operational status, and morale and discipline have certainly improved.

Military service remains a respected career, and both officers and men are strongly conscious of Haiti's considerable heritage of military achievement in the early nineteenth century. It is possible to envisage circumstances in which the army would regain its former prominence, and no longer play a subordinate role in Haitian affairs.

STRENGTH AND BUDGET

The strength of the Haitian armed forces is 7500 men, of which the army accounts for over 7000. There is a small aviation corps of about 200 men and a coastguard of about 300 men. Numbers on strength have not changed significantly since the late 1950s, and indeed are quite close to those prevailing a century ago. They amount to only 0.1% of Haiti's population of over 6,000,000.

The principal paramilitary force is the National Security Volunteers, a militia organisation which has been drastically reduced in numbers since the death of the elder Duvalier in 1971. It now numbers an estimated 5000–7000 men, the majority of whom are pursuing their private occupations most of the time. There are also the *Tontons Macoutes*, the not very secret police of the regime, who do not have any formal military organisation. Their numbers have apparently been reduced since 1971, but were not known reliably either then or now: estimates range from 1500 to 8000.

The 1976 defence budget was $10,800,000, amounting to exactly 25% of total government expenditure of $43,200,000. This was almost exactly the same share of the total budget it received in 1965, and was just under 1% of the GNP of $1,100,000,000. As much again, however, was probably spent legally on the paramilitary forces. Estimated GNP in 1980 was $1,555,000,000 and defence expenditure $15,300,000.

COMMAND AND CONSTITUTIONAL STATUS

The President-for-Life, Jean-Claude Duvalier, is the Commander-in-Chief of the Haitian Armed Forces, and appoints all officers. He also has personal control over the two *élite* units in the capital: the Presidential Guard of some 700 men, housed on the ground floor and basement of the Presidential Palace, and the Dessalines Battalion, quartered in the Caserne Dessalines on the grounds behind the palace. Most of the army's main items of ordnance are also kept beneath the palace or in the grounds; there are still machine-gun bunkers along the low walls of the palace, but the anti-aircraft guns have now been removed from the lawn.

The Secretary of State for Interior and National Defence is formally in the chain of command. The senior military officer is the Chief of the General Staff, who also serves as Commander of the Armed Forces; he is usually a major-general. In what was believed to be a pre-emptive move to forestall a coup or at least a mutiny in the armed forces, the President abruptly dismissed the Chief of Staff and his deputy in 1978. The armed forces have a unified system, with the small air force and coastguard under the same commander; police forces are part of the army. Since 1971 the National Security Volunteers have also been under the control of the General Staff, but the secret police (*Tontons Macoutes*) are not.

ROLE, COMMITMENT, DEPLOYMENT AND RECENT OPERATIONS

The principal role of the Haitian army for the past century has been internal security, an orientation which is clearly reflected in its organisation and deployment. Only three units, numbering no more than 2000 men at most, are capable of conventional military operations; of those, two (the Presidential Guard and the Dessalines Battalion) are employed in guarding the President-for-Life, while the third (the 'Leopards') is primarily a counter-insurgency unit. The remainder of the army consists of the Port-au-Prince Police Force and constabulary forces distributed amongst the six military departments in rural areas.

Haiti belongs to the UN and the Organization of American States, but has no external defence commitments. The principal external defence concern throughout Haiti's history has been the Dominican Republic with which it shares the island. Since 1960 there has also been a potential threat from Cuba, but Haiti relies on the presence of United States naval forces (based at Guantánamo Bay in Cuba and elsewhere in the region) to prevent anything larger than small boatloads of armed Haitian exiles from reaching its shores from Cuba.

The Dominican–Haitian antipathy goes back almost to the creation of the two States – Haiti conquered its neighbour in 1822 and ruled it brutally for the next 22 years – and has been strengthened by subsequent events. There is a constant source of friction in the large number of impoverished Haitians who enter the Dominican Republic illegally to seek work as cane-cutters (at five times the wages they could command at home). The last major crisis was in 1937 when the Dominican army, under the dictator Rafael Leónidas Trujillo Molina, massacred at least 12,000 Haitian seasonal agricultural workers.

The border between the two countries has been closed for a large part of their history, but in the twentieth century the relationship has been dominated not so much by the fear of invasion as by the fact that each has habitually attempted to influence internal political struggles in the other by encouraging plots and/or providing a base for political exiles from its neighbour. Thus in 1949–51 each country accused the other of aggression through sponsoring plots against the existing government in the neighbouring State (an OAS investigating committee found both charges accurate). Trujillo, who had attempted to overthrow any Haitian government which was not dependent upon him since 1930, tried again in the first year of Duvalier's rule, but external pressures against both dictators soon forced them to sign a secret mutual assistance pact in 1958.

After Trujillo's assassination and the election of the leftist candidate Juan Bosch to the Dominican Presidency in 1962 relations again became extremely bad, with constant charges and counter-charges of political intervention. After the American-assisted right-wing victory in the 1965 Dominican civil war and the election of President Joaquín Balaguer in Santo Domingo the following year the crisis atmosphere evaporated, though tensions have continued.

An actual invasion of one country by the other is not very likely in the late twentieth century, however. Certainly the grossly inferior strength of the Haitian armed forces (which are outnumbered 3:1 by the Dominicans) and the pattern of military deployment in both countries suggest that it is not a prospect taken very seriously in either capital.

Political intrigues against the neighbouring government have also stopped since Balaguer's election in 1966, and in 1972 the two countries signed an agreement for the expansion of trade and the improvement of communications between them.

The only recent operations of the Haitian army has been against handfuls of armed exiles seeking to create a guerrilla movement against the regime, and they have been uniformly successful in liquidating all such incursions rapidly. There are well over a quarter of a million Haitians in exile, but they do not represent a mortal danger to the regime in themselves: most are settled abroad and are not deeply involved in Haitian affairs any more, while the relatively few active opponents of the government operating from exile are decisively hampered in trying to found an anti-Duvalier guerrilla movement by the gulf that separates them — mostly middle class by Haitian standards, and with a large mulatto contingent — from the world of the Haitian peasant.

ORGANISATION

Arms of Service

The army is made up of 35 companies of infantry (21 of which operate in dispersed units as District Police in areas outside the capital); six companies of the Port-au-Prince Police Force; the Fire Brigade in the capital; and the Prison Guard Company running the National Penitentiary and Fort Dimanche (for political prisoners) in the capital and five other prisons. There are small units which are trained to handle the few old artillery pieces and light tanks, and there are specialised transportation, medical, engineering and communications units. The communications section is of special importance, since it maintains radio-telephone and telephone links with the headquarters of the six military departments, which in turn have at least telephone links with the military districts, subdistricts and rural sections. In many rural areas the army has the only telephone, and is thus the only direct link with all branches of the government in the local and national capitals.

The aviation corps is a single composite squadron which mans both military aircraft and the civilian airline. Both it and the coastguard come under the control of the armed forces general staff in Dessalines Barracks in the capital, which contains four sections: personnel, intelligence, operations and logistics.

Operational

The army is organised into nine Military Departments. Three are in the capital: the Presidential Guard (four companies totalling about 750 men, quartered in the Presidential Palace); Dessalines Barracks (which includes the Dessalines Battalion and headquarters troops); and the Port-au-Prince Police Force of some 600 men. The rest of the country is divided into six Military Departments: North-West, North, Artibonite, West, Centre and South — amongst which are distributed 21 companies operating as a police force in the provincial towns and rural areas. Each of these commands is divided into military districts and sub-districts, below which are the rural posts, each headed by an enlisted man. The militia force (the National Security Volunteers) is under the operational control of Defence Headquarters, and is organised on lines roughly parallel to those of the regional Military Departments.

The only army units which possess any mobility or capability for tactical military operations are the Presidential Guard, the Dessalines Battalion and the Leopards (three companies of commando troops who have been trained in counter-insurgency operations by a Miami-based private company).

The main aviation corps base is at Port-au-Prince airfield; there are ten other cities with airfields able to accommodate medium-sized transport aircraft. The coastguard has several bases around the coasts.

RECRUITMENT, TRAINING AND RESERVES

Recruitment is entirely voluntary, and there are always many more applicants than vacancies. Military service is a lifetime career offering considerable prestige, with material rewards well above those prevailing in most comparable civilian occupations. For commissioned officers there is also the prospect of rapid social and political advancement, although for the past 20 years the very top positions have been closed to them. Conditions of service are good compared to civilian life, including medical care and pensions equal to half the monthly pay on retirement after 25 years of service. Mandatory retirement age is sixty for officers and fifty for enlisted men.

Officer training is provided at the military academy at Frères, founded in 1941, which offers a 3 year course for about 60 cadets. There is also a training school for non-commissioned officers, the *Camp d'Application*.

There are no army reserves, but the National Security Volunteers, still approximately equal in numbers to the regular army, have all received basic military training.

EQUIPMENT AND ARMS INDUSTRY

Almost all equipment is of United States origins and is largely obsolete.

Rifle: M1 0.39″ (US)
Sub-machine-guns: Thompson M1928 0.45″ (US); Uzi 9mm (Israel)
Machine-guns: M1919 0.3″ (US); M2 0.5″ (US)
Anti-armour weapons: M3A1 37mm anti-tank gun (US); M1 57mm anti-tank gun (US); M18 57mm RCL
Mortars: M1 81mm (US); M19 60mm (US)
Artillery: M101 105mm (US); M116 75mm (US)
Air-defence weapons: 40mm L/60 (Sweden/US)
Armour: M3 light tank (US; 9 in service); V-150 scout car (US; 6 in service); M113 APC (US; 6 in service)
Aircraft: Air Force has about 10 transport aircraft and a similar number of helicopters.

RANK, DRESS AND DISTINCTIONS

Haitian titles of military rank correspond to those of the United States army. Army and air force officer insignia are worn on shoulder boards, and consist of one, two or three chevrons for company-grade officers, one, two or three small gold stars for field-grade officers, and one, two or three larger silver stars for general officers. Coastguard insignia on dress uniforms are the usual naval gold bands worn on the sleeve.

All three services have khaki fatigue and garrison uniforms of conventional design except the Port-au-Prince Police, who wear similar uniforms in light blue. *Elite* army units have dress and parade uniforms of dark blue, and officers of all three services have full dress white uniforms. Army officers also sometimes wear green blouses with beige slacks, or with riding breeches and boots.

The *Tonton Macoutes* wear blue jeans or black suits with sunglasses. They do not wear badges of rank.

The principal decorations for valour in combat or in police action, reserved for military personnel, are the Military Medal and the Distinguished Service Medal. There are also long-service medals awarded at various intervals to both officers and men.

CURRENT DEVELOPMENTS

President-for-Life Jean-Claude Duvalier was only born in 1951, so no early change in the regime by constitutional means is at all likely. He has now survived half as long as his father in the Presidency, so he has clearly established his own network of supporters and no longer depends solely on the elder Duvalier's adherents. Indeed, in the first years of his rule he made considerable efforts to dislodge some of the latter group from key positions, with some success.

The limits of his power were demonstrated in April, 1976 however, when he was forced to accept a reshuffle of government posts engineered by the old guard. His own choice in the key post of Secretary of State for the Interior and National Defence, Paul Blanchet, was replaced by Pierre Bamby, former private secretary to 'Papa Doc' and a particularly bloodstained functionary who had personally organised several massacres of opposition elements. Duvalier managed to dismiss Bamby in May, 1977 justifying it as a pre-emption of expected American criticism on human rights, and replaced him with one of his own closest aides, former Justice Minister Aurélien Jeanty, but it is evident that there is a somewhat precarious balance of forces between the younger and older generations amongst the ruling family and their associates.

Whichever faction eventually triumphs, it is virtually certain that power will remain within the circle of the present ruling civilian and military élite. The Haitian opposition in exile is split into a great many ineffectual and squabbling groups, and there is no organised underground resistance at home (virtually the entire leadership of the Haitian Communist Party was machine-gunned to death by the *Tontons Macoutes* while meeting in a house in Port-au-Prince in 1969). There are very occasionally hit-and-run raids by exile groups — in 1976 a 'commando group' of exile youths landed from North America and killed a dozen *Tonton Macoutes* before escaping across the Dominican border — but they do not represent a serious threat to the regime. In the parliamentary elections of February, 1979 which the President had meant to use to displace some of the more powerful adherents of his mother and the 'Old Guard', the latter emerged triumphant. Mrs Duvalier has also secured the removal of her son's chief adviser, Mines and Energy Minister Henri Bayard. Unusual signs of instability were evident after the election, when there were 10 days of riots in provincial cities and several hundred arrests.

Precisely what role the army might play in the intra-regime competition in the future cannot be predicted, but the focus of the recent power struggle on control of the National Defence Department confirms the impression that the army is now a far larger factor in Haitian politics than it was five or ten years ago. There is no direct evidence that it has yet begun to behave again as an independent actor, but it seems likely that the same generational split exists in the officer corps as in the civilian apparatus of the regime. With its paramilitary rivals substantially reduced in size and influence, it would not be surprising if the army eventually resumed its leading role in Haitian affairs.

None of this is likely to alter the increasingly grim basic fact about Haiti: its terrible and growing poverty. It has long been the poorest and least developed country of the Western Hemisphere: 75—80% of the population are illiterate, and 90% live by primitive subsistence agriculture and receive a cash income averaging less than $1.00 a week. Most Haitians lead an existence which is close to that in West Africa before colonisation.

All this has been true ever since Haitian independence 175 years ago: what has changed is the population. Haiti is an extremely small country — about 10,000 square miles, of which less than a third is arable land. The population is already over 5,000,000 and growing fast, with the result that the effective population density in the settled rural areas is already over 1500 per square mile. Even advanced agricultural techniques will not easily support such a population. The primitive agricultural techniques in use are rapidly destroying the fertility of the land, while the hills have long been denuded of trees in order to provide firewood and room for coffee planting, leading to a rapid erosion.

Quite simply, the country is rapidly turning into a desert, while the population pressure on the land continues to mount. Already famine is chronic in parts of the north-west, and malnutrition is the norm in most of Haiti. From 5,000,000 people and 3000 square miles of arable land now, the country may reach the turn of the century with 10,000,000 people and virtually no cultivable land. Such a trend virtually guarantees growing political turmoil and suggests that any future government will be critically dependent on the armed forces for its survival.

Gwynne Dyer

HONDURAS

HISTORY AND INTRODUCTION

The Honduran army, despite an apparently lengthy history, is in fact an exceedingly new military institution. For practical purposes it is much the youngest army in Central America, and its rapid growth and politically adventurous character are causing grave concern amongst all three of Honduras's neighbours.

Since their humiliating defeat in the 1969 war with El Salvador, the Honduran armed forces have tripled in size. Moreover, during the past 5 years the Honduran army has displayed an increasing inclination towards that brand of military socialism which is associated with the 'Peruvian' or 'Portuguese' models, a potentially infectious development which is even more disturbing to the rulers of neighbouring Central American States.

It may seem surprising that such anxieties might be entertained about a country which has frequently been described as the 'definitive banana republic', and 'the most retarded of the Central American States' – especially since those epithets were entirely true as recently as 15 years ago. In a curious way, however, such facts help to explain the current pattern of developments in Honduras.

While it is perfectly true that virtually all of Honduras's foreign exchange is derived from bananas, for example, the intensive development of that industry by large foreign companies along the northern coast (where there is also a substantial black West Indian minority of more advanced political ideas) was instrumental in the creation of the first real Honduran labour movement. This example spread to other urban workers in the inland capital of Tegucigalpa, and subsequently to peasant organisations as well, during the 1950s and 1960s, and has fundamentally changed the balance of Honduran politics. Even that influence does not begin to compare with the emergence of a cohesive and potentially radical professional military establishment, however. Its radicalism is largely a function of its newness, which in turn derives from the extreme backwardness and lack of central institutions in Honduran social structure until very recently.

At first glance Honduran history from the end of Spanish rule in 1821 seems simply an exaggerated version of the typical Central American pattern: there were 134 coups in the next 134 years, with a rather higher frequency in the nineteenth than the twentieth century. Foreign armies were more often involved in these violent changes of government than was common elsewhere in the isthmus, but this was presumably only a reflection of Honduras's extreme weakness and disorganisation. All of the governments that ruled Honduras were corrupt and conservative, and most of the presidents bore the title of 'general'. But the image this creates of a Honduran military institution with an inveterate disposition to seize power and govern in its own interests is wholly illusory: in fact the first truly *military* coup in the conventional sense only occurred in Honduras in 1957, for the simple reason that there was not any recognisable military institution in the country until about 1950.

There were, to be sure, any number of organisations calling themselves 'armies', but they were purely transitory phenomena. There never developed in Honduras the sort of stable military institution with strong corporate identity and interests that evolved in Guatemala and El Salvador in the nineteenth century. Honduran 'armies' were purely instrumental in politics, as the armed expression of the power of some 'political party' (which in reality was itself simply the personal following of some powerful individual).

This was the natural consequence of the character of Honduran society. Honduras was, and to a large extent still is, a land of small isolated peasant communities. It is a racially homogeneous society (over 90% are mestizo, and the white minority which traditionally dominated politics in its neighbours is an exiguous 1% in Honduras). It also lacks the usual sharply defined class structure (although approximately 600 families owned almost a third of the land, there was not the tight oligarchy of rich land-owners which monopolised national politics elsewhere).

In such a decentralised society, political power was acquired by creating a local guerrilla band, making alliances with similar aspiring politicians, and overthrowing the government. The 'army' that had defended the last bunch of rascals was dispersed, and one's own guerrilla commanders became the officers of the new national 'army'. The newly confirmed generals then returned to civilian life, usually as provincial governors, while the decentralised military structure would be staffed by lower-level leaders of the guerrilla band.

For practical purposes there would be no enlisted men in the 'army' in peacetime, merely militia lists of men in each district who would be theoretically available when it became necessary to fight off the attacks of the next upward-mobile guerrilla band. If the challengers won, then once again the national 'army' would be disbanded and their own forces substituted. Power changed hands by fighting, as a rule, but politics was civilian; while there was always a Honduran 'army' (if not two or three), the personnel would change completely from time to time, and there was no professional military institution.

This pattern persisted well into the twentieth century. One unusually far-sighted President, Miguel Dávila, tried to secure his position by founding a Military Academy and an Artillery School between 1903 and 1906 (importing a Chilean colonel and a French sergeant to direct them), but all their graduates were dismissed from the army after the next revolution in 1911, and both schools were frequently closed until the 1920s. The real beginnings of the Honduran military profession had to wait until a period of political stability was achieved under the iron rule of President Tiburcio Carías Andino in 1933–49.

Carias himself achieved power by the traditional route. He was apprenticed to his family's band of guerrillas at the age of sixteen, commanded a detachment fighting for the Nicaraguan *caudillo* José Santos Zelaya in 1907, and eventually had himself made a general of the Honduran army after he had become the most powerful political figure in the country. His decision to create a corps of trained professional officers was manifestly directed towards improving the counter-insurgency abilities of the Honduran armed forces.

As early as 1924 he had been impressed by the counter-insurgency potential of aerial bombardment (a small Honduran Air Corps had been created in 1922), and his first step was to found a Military Aviation School in 1934 with United States aid. By 1942 Honduras had 22 aircraft manned by United States-trained pilots, which proved very useful in maintaining his rule. (This was the origin of the markedly higher status which the Honduran air force still enjoys in the armed forces, by comparison with other Central American States.)

The process of creeping professionalisation, with United States aid, continued with the creation of a Basic Arms School to train both officers and men in 1946, and the founding of the Francisco Morazán Military Academy to train officer cadets in 1952. Large numbers of officers also attended year-long courses at the United States Army School of the Americas in the Canal Zone. Parallel to these military educational developments was a United States Military Assistance Programme to create more mobile formations equipped for conventional combat and counter-insurgency operations in the army, which had hitherto been a wholly regional and militia-based organisation: the First Infantry Battalion was formed in 1947 along United States Army lines, and four further infantry, engineer and artillery battalions followed.

Educational standards were progressively raised at the Military Academy – in 1956 a programme of civilian education leading to a full secondary school-level qualification in arts and sciences was introduced alongside the military subjects – and a military officer's career for the first time became an attractive alternative for ambitious young Hondurans. In the same period entrance standards were steadily raised, which had the effect – given the shortcomings of the Honduran rural school system – of shifting the officer recruitment base from the traditional rural sources to the urban lower-middle class (by 1961 almost half the cadets came from towns of over 10,000, compared with 14% of the general population). This factor undoubtedly explains much of the greater political radicalism of the generation of officers reaching senior rank in the middle 1970s (discussed later), but already by 1957 the army had become sufficiently professionalised to carry out the first autonomously military coup, independent of civilian politicians, in Honduran history.

It was a hesitant intervention, occurring only after 2 years of political chaos and widespread violence. Carías's handpicked successor had controlled the presidency from 1949 to 1955, but when the strong-man decided to return to power himself in the election of that year his National Party, rotted by decades of power, split in two, allowing the Liberal Party candidate Ramón Villeda Morales to win a clear majority. He was denied his victory by some adroit political chicanery, however, and in 1956 a National Party leader was installed in the presidency instead. Shortly afterwards a group of young officers overthrew him and held new elections for a constituent assembly, which duly installed Villeda Morales as President in late 1957.

The intervention was not motivated by party considerations, though many of the young officers may have been in sympathy with Villeda's liberal ideas. It was an act of institutional self-defence, intended to preserve the newly professional army from the injuries that the turbulent old political system, now apparently returning, had traditionally inflicted on the army's cohesion and status. This was most evident in the 1957 Constitution, which contained an unusual provision that the President's orders to the military were to be obeyed only if given through the Chief of the Armed Forces. It also granted the army the explicit right to disobey executive commands which were viewed as violating the Constitution, gave the Armed Forces Commander the right to appeal Presidential orders to Congress, and stripped the civilian government of all meaningful control over military promotions and assignments (see Command and Constitutional Status).

The Villeda Morales government's pro-labour measures and its generally liberal outlook certainly created some hostility amongst more conservative soldiers, but the reason

for its overthrow by the coup of 1963 was once again the defence of the new military institution's autonomy. This was threatened by two specific measures: the creation of a paramilitary Civil Guard of 2500 men directly under the President's command in 1959, in a deliberate attempt to counterbalance the influence of the armed forces, and the campaign promise of the Liberal candidate in the forthcoming 1963 elections to remove the offending clauses on military autonomy from the constitution. When it became clear that this candidate, Modesto Rodas Alvarado, would probably win the election, the armed forces under the leadership of air force Colonel Osvaldo López Arellano overthrew the government and cancelled the elections.

This time the armed forces stayed in power; the new Constitution of 1965 repeated the clauses about military autonomy, and Colonel López became President. The rival Civil Guard was abolished, and replaced by the Special Security Corps (CES), which is staffed almost entirely by ex-army men. Although López observed the constitutional ban against a president succeeding himself, and permitted a civilian candidate of the conservative National Party to be elected in 1971, he retained his position as Chief of the Armed Forces 'in the interest of national unity'. The civilian interlude lasted little more than a year; in December, 1972 the figurehead president was eased out of power in a bloodless coup and López announced that he would serve out the remainder of his 6 year term. López was deposed by a military coup in April 1975 and replaced by General Juan Melgar Castro, who was in turn deposed by the Armed Forces in August 1978. A three man military junta, led by General Policarpo Paz García, ruled the country until April 1980 when a promise to restore constitutional government was fulfilled by the holding of free elections. General Paz was elected Provisional President until elections for a constitutional President could be held.

Up to about 1970 the new military domination of Honduran political life can be seen mainly as the defensive action of a recent and still vulnerable profession. The political style was typical of the wave of military interventions that swept Latin America in the early 1960s in reaction to the Castroite guerrilla threat (though there has never been any communist guerrilla activity in Honduras). López's first government was conservative, oppressive, blindly hostile to organised labour (which he characterised as 'an agent of international communism'), and extremely compliant to foreign investment interests.

Two developments have now transformed the perspectives of the Honduran armed forces, however. One was their defeat in the 1969 'Football War' with El Salvador (see Role, Commitment, Deployment and Recent Operations), which has led to a very rapid expansion of the armed forces and a greater emphasis on conventional warfare capabilities. The other was the rise to senior rank of academy-trained officers of urban lower-middle-class background, which has radically altered the armed forces' political stance. The pressures in this direction was already evident during the first years of López's second term, when he changed to nationalist and reformist policies, and since his removal in 1975 the influence of the powerful peruanista faction in the officer corps has been ever more evident. (See Current Developments.)

Honduras is also unique in that a former military dictator, who gained power by violent means, earned sufficient respect in government to be democratically elected as President by a left-of-centre constitutional assembly.

STRENGTH AND BUDGET

Population: 4,000,000
Army: 11,500

Navy: 300; 7 minor vessels
Air Force: 1,200; 30 combat aircraft
Paramilitary: 3,000 man Civil Guard
GNP: (1981) $2,270,000,000
Defence Expenditure: (1981) $41,300,000

COMMAND AND CONSTITUTIONAL STATUS

The President of the Republic is Commander-in-Chief of the Armed Forces, with the right to declare war and make peace, to send Honduran troops abroad and allow foreign troops to enter the country, and to name officers up to the rank of captain on the recommendation of the Chief of the Armed Forces. Officers of higher rank are appointed by Congress on the joint recommendation of these two persons. The President's authority is severely limited, however, by special constitutional provisions which give the Chief of the Armed Forces the right to disobey Presidential orders which are believed to violate the constitution, and obliges the President to relay all his orders through the Chief of the Armed Forces. In practice, moreover, the Chief of the Armed Forces has full control over all officers' appointments.

There is a Secretary of Defence with cabinet rank, heading the Department of Defence, but he is outside the chain of command and the Department deals only with administrative matters.

More important is the Superior Council of National Defence, an advisory body comprised of the President, the Secretary of Defence, the Chief of the Armed Forces, the Chief of Staff of the Armed Forces, and all the top military commanders. Its principal constitutional function is to select candidates for Chief of the Armed Forces for a 6 year term if the job falls vacant, and to remove incumbents when necessary. This has the effect of removing such questions from the control of the President, since all but two of its members (originally eight, but now reportedly twenty-two) are military officers.

The Chief of the Armed Forces exercises direct operational control over all subordinate commands, and is in charge of all military assignments including those of unit and zone commanders (except for the Presidential General Staff and Presidential Guard).

These provisions were originally designed to ensure armed forces' independence from civilian presidential control; they now function as a means by which the collective leadership of the armed forces can exercise control over a military president. The expanded Superior Council of National Defence has become the principal arena in which armed forces' policy is debated and decided, and the means of guaranteeing that the officer occupying the presidency does not grow over-mighty.

To this end, it is essential that the President should not also occupy the office of Chief of the Armed Forces, and it is noteworthy that the first step in removing López Arellano was to deprive him of the latter position in 1974. It is through this body, rather than through the President, that the *peruanista* faction of the officer corps exerts its influence.

ROLE, COMMITMENT, DEPLOYMENT AND RECENT OPERATIONS

Up to 1969 the primary role of the Honduran armed forces was considered to be internal security, but the war with El Salvador in that year has since led to much greater emphasis on external defence. Long-standing border disputes with other neighbours were formally settled with Guatemala in 1933 and with Nicaragua in 1961, but the ideological

hostility of both these countries' governments has also caused some anxiety in Tegucigalpa.

The internal security task has been largely delegated to the paramilitary CES, now expanded to about 3000 men, which maintains a large force in the capital and small but relatively competent detachments in all provincial towns and cities. Since the disbanding of the Civil Guard in 1963 the armed forces have had total control of the internal security apparatus — most CES officers and men are drawn directly from the armed forces — but there is a deliberate policy of keeping the armed forces proper out of the often distasteful business of dealing with rural unrest, and so preserving a favourable public image of the army. The armed forces are not likely to be drawn into large-scale security operations in the future unless CES units prove inadequate to deal with the task. On the other hand, the army and the air force both run large and highly visible civic action programmes, concentrating on short-term projects in education, health, agriculture and highway construction.

There are army troops deployed throughout the country in six military zone commands, but the bulk of the combat units are concentrated in the 'special army corps', which are headquartered near the two major cities of Tegucigalpa and San Pedro Sula, with substantial detachments along the El Salvador border. There is also a larger than usual concentration of military forces in Gracias a Dios province, at the Atlantic end of the Nicaraguan border, which includes the territory whose ownership was disputed by Nicaragua prior to 1960.

Honduras belongs to the United Nations, the Organization of American States, the Central American Common Market and the Organization of Central American States. It has only once sent troops abroad — a 250-man contingent was dispatched to the Dominican Republic in 1965 as part of the OAS peace-keeping force — and there are no foreign bases on its territory. Honduras's relations with the OCAS and its military sub-organisation, the Central American Defense Council, have been rather cool in recent years, due to the domination of the latter body by the right-wing governments of its neighbours. The CACM has never fully recovered from the 1969 war between El Salvador and Honduras, which was followed by border closure and trade restrictions between these two centrally placed members for a number of years.

The principal recent operation of the Honduran armed forces was the 1969 war, which was triggered by riots against a Honduran football team visiting San Salvador for the World Cup play-offs, and counter-riots against Salvadorean immigrants in Honduras. The real cause, however, was the presence in Honduras of about 300,000 immigrants, many of them illegal, from the overcrowded countryside of El Salvador (where populaton density is almost ten times as high). There was great Honduran resentment against these immigrants from what is, after all, a somewhat richer country, who made up fully one-eighth of the resident population in 1969, and the government was not above using them as scapegoats. Additional causes for concern were the specific border disputes between the two countries, and much wider expansionist ideas which circulated freely in El Salvador.

The serious fighting in the war lasted only a week, though there were up to 2000 people killed in the fighting and anti-Salvadorean riots in Honduras, and over 100,000 Salvadorean immigrants became refugees. The war on the ground was characterised by steady Salvadorean advances of up to 20 miles against the small and ill-equipped Honduran army along the Pan-American Highway leading east towards Tegucigalpa, and northwards near the Guatemalan frontier towards the Caribbean coast city of San Pedro Sula. Both sides employed air strikes extensively against military and civilian targets, but the most effective attack was the Honduran raid on El Salvador's main oil refinery at Acajutla. The fighting was ended with the introduction of OAS observers, and Salvadorean forces evacuated all occupied Honduran territory within a month. (For further details, see El Salvador: Recent Operations.)

Border clashes continued until 1971, when a 2km demilitarised zone was created along the frontier. There were renewed border clashes in July, 1976 when Honduras accused El Salvador of launching an invasion, and tensions continue to run high. The principal result of the war in Honduras has been a resolve to expand the combat elements of the armed forces rapidly and to undertake a major military re-equipment programme, in order to avoid in the future any possibility of a military humiliation similar to 1969.

Mediation attempts, under the patronage of the President of Peru, finally bore fruit, after prolonged negotiations, in November 1980 and a peace treaty was signed by both Honduras and El Salvador. The current internal problems of the latter country render a further outbreak of hostilities highly unlikely in the forseeable future.

ORGANISATION

Arms of service

The Army consists of Infantry, Artillery, Engineers, Signals, Supply and Medical Services. There are no units designated as Cavalry or Mechanised and all armoured vehicles in service are operated by infantry units. The basic organic unit is the battalion of which there are 11 of Infantry, two of Artillery and one of Engineers. Two of the Infantry battalions (1st and 5th) form the Presidential Guard, based at Tegucigalpa. The only major tactical formation is the *Agrupación Táctica del Ejército* which combines the 2nd, 8th and 9th Infantry Battalions and appears to operate most of the available armoured vehicles. Another partially mechanised unit is the 6th *Centauros* Infantry Battalion. Little is published about the deployment of the units of the Honduran Army but the *Agrupación Táctica* would appear to be located in the vicinity of the frontier with El Salvador, although this deployment may be expected to change as the major external threat is now perceived to be the left-wing revolutionary government of Nicaragua.

Operational

The Presidential Guard is under the personal command of the President. All other army units, and also the six military zone commanders, are under the direct command of the Chief of the Armed Forces, who is assisted by a general staff operating at armed forces headquarters in the capital. The air force is an autonomous organisation, but is also controlled directly by the Chief of the Armed Forces. The *Agrupación Táctica* appears to be the major operational element, the independent infantry battalions performing a relatively static defence role in the six military zones. The Presidential Guard and the Artillery and Engineer battalions would seem to form a sort of strategic reserve.

RECRUITMENT, TRAINING AND RESERVES

The constitution makes military service compulsory for all male citizens, but during peacetime the armed forces are composed mainly of volunteers, the benefits available to soldiers being more than sufficient to fill the ranks. Citizens are potentially liable for up to 18 months' compulsory service between the ages of eighteen and thirty-two, but the average length of time conscripts actually spend on active service is 8 months, with subsequent reserve training. For many enlisted men military service is their first contact with the modern world and their only experience of formal education. The armed forces therefore provide literacy programmes, and often some trades or agricultural training to servicemen shortly before they return to civilian life.

Until 1957 Honduran officers were almost all promoted from the ranks, but since then the main source of officers has been direct-entry primary-school graduates to the Francisco Morazán Military School in the capital. There are stiff competitive entry examinations, with the ratio of applicants to places as high as 15:1, and the Academy provides a comprehensive 5 year course of military and academic studies. Graduating cadets receive the rank of sublieutenant (2nd Lt.), and most receive scholarships for an additional year of military study abroad, usually at the United States Army School of the Americas in the Panama Canal Zone. Air force pilots, cadets and technicians receive fairly extensive training at the Military Aviation School at Toncontín. Advanced training is provided by the First Infantry Battalion in Tegucigalpa and by comparable artillery and engineer model formations. Officers' staff and advanced technical training is mostly done abroad, primarily in the Canal Zone and the USA, but to a limited extent in Europe as well. The excuse of the disastrous 1969 war was used by the more professional junior officers to purge many of the older and less competent officers, and to introduce a compulsory retirement age.

The reserve system is theoretically all-embracing, and many civilians with virtually no training were mobilised in 1969. The unsatisfactory results of that experience have led to the creation of a more organised reserve system, but the number of trained men actually available for mobilisation is unknown.

EQUIPMENT AND ARMS INDUSTRY

Honduras has no local defence industry and all equipment must be imported, the United States being the major equipment supplier. US military aid to Honduras has been stepped up since the victory of the Sandinista revolution in Nicaragua.

Rifles: FN FAL 7.62mm (Belgium); M16A1 5.56mm (US); M1 0.30″ (US)
Sub-machine-guns: Uzi 9mm (Israel); Thompson 0.45″ (US)
Anti-armour weapons: M18 57mm RCL (US)
Mortars: 81mm (France); 120mm (France)
Artillery: M101 105mm (US); M116 75mm (US)
Armour: M3 light tank (US); Staghound armoured car (US); Scorpion light tank (Britain)
Aircraft: The Air Force operates about 12 transports and a similar number of helicopters

RANK, DRESS AND DISTINCTIONS

Rank structure generally follows that of the United States army, with the exception that sublieutenant is substituted for second-lieutenant, and brigade and division generals for the equivalent American ranks of brigadier-general and major-general. There are no higher ranks in the Honduran armed forces. Officers' rank insignia are one, two or three gold bars for company-grade officers, one, two or three gold stars for field grades, and four or five silver stars for general officers, in order of increasing seniority. Air force personnel are distinguished only by corps insignia, and by wings worn on the jacket or shirt pocket where appropriate.

The basic service uniform is olive-green fatigues with cloth or garrison caps; with the substitution of a helmet, a canvas belt and khaki leggings, this becomes the field uniform, worn on exercises, guard duty and parades. The service dress uniform is khaki in summer, and olive green in winter. Officers' dress uniforms are navy-blue trousers with a gold stripe, white shirt, black tie, a white or navy-blue jacket according to the season, epaulettes, and a navy-blue hat with black peak and gold chinstrap.

The highest military award is the Decoration for Merit, which comes in several classes. Other distinctions include the Heroic Valour Decoration, the Distinguished Service Cross and Medal, the Flying Cross, the Soldier's Medal for outstanding enlisted performance, and the Conduct Medal.

CURRENT DEVELOPMENTS

The influence of a group of young army officers who favour radical social reforms was already evident early in President López Arellano's second term, when he reversed his previous policies by introducing limited measures of land reform, providing government support for the formation of trade unions, terminating concessions to foreign mining companies and nationalising the foreign-owned lumber industries. Once the Peruvian-influenced faction had established a dominant position in the Superior Council of the Armed Forces, however, it forced López to relinquish his position as Chief of the Armed Forces in March, 1974 to Colonel Juan Melgar Castro, a compromise candidate acceptable to both radicals and the more moderate reformers.

López's position was further undermined by his apparent inability to cope with the task of national reconstruction following the disastrous Hurricane Fifi in late 1974, and allegations that he had accepted bribes from United Brands, a large American-owned company that dominated the vitally important production and export of bananas. López was removed by the army in March, 1975 and his place as President assumed by Colonel Melgar Castro (who was simultaneously obliged to relinquish his office of Chief of the Armed Forces, however).

The allegations of corruption which finally caused the Superior Council of National Defence to unseat López Arellano in 1975 also accounted for President Melgar Castro in 1978. He was accused of involvement, along with other high-ranking officials, in a $30,000,000-a-year operation smuggling cocaine from Colombia to the USA, and on August 7th, 1978 was removed from power in a bloodless coup. The three members of the *junta* which replaced him were General Policarpo Juan Paz García, Chief of the Armed Forces and Commanding General of the Army, Lieutenant-Colonel Domingo Alvarez, Chief of the Air Force, and Lieutenant-Colonel Amilcar Zelaya Rodriguez, Chief of the Public Security Forces. The Liberals won 35 out of 71 seats in the National Constituent Assembly in the 1980 elections and Roberto Suazo Córdoba, a Liberal, was elected President of the Assembly which subsequently ratified General Paz García as Provisional President. A new Constitution is being drafted.

Honduras is the second least developed country in the Western Hemisphere, with appalling poverty, an extremely low literacy rate, widespread malnutrition, and only a minute industrialised sector of the economy – not precisely the place where military radicals would be expected to emerge, or to succeed in their efforts at root-and-branch reform. That such a process has actually begun is mainly due to the very newness of the military profession in Honduras, which lacks the conservative traditions and institutional alliances of the older Latin American armed forces. At the same time, the lack of powerful competing organisations has allowed the army to establish rapidly an unusually high degree of control over national life, and (together with the 1969 war) has allowed it to embark on a programme of military expansion and re-equipment whose only Latin American counterpart – allowing for differences of scale – is in Peru.

Gwynne Dyer
Adrian English

HUNGARY

HISTORY AND INTRODUCTION

Although Hungary emerged as a fully independent State only at the end of World War I, she had a long and colourful national tradition which looked back as far as the coronation of St. Stephen on Christmas Day, 1000. Centuries of Hapsburg dominance were unable to suppress Hungarian nationalism, and the establishment, in 1867, of the Dual Monarchy gave Hungary a large measure of autonomy within the Hapsburg Empire. Certain matters, notably defence and foreign affairs, were the responsibility of common, rather than national, ministries, but even in these fields Hungary made significant contributions to the Empire as a whole. Hungarian influence helped prevent Austrian interference in German affairs, while in the sphere of defence Hungary provided the Imperial and Royal armies with large numbers of troops, among them the light cavalry for which Hungary was rightly famed. It is interesting to note that, just as Polish military dress served as the basis for lancer uniforms in other European armies, so the costume of Hungarian light horsemen became institutionalised as hussar uniform.

Hungary suffered severely as a result of her involvement in World War I. She was dismembered as the Hapsburg Empire collapsed: Slovakia was occupied by the Czechoslovakians, and Transylvania by the Romanians. A Republic was declared in November, 1918 under the presidency of Count Mihály Károlyi, who resigned in March, 1919 when it became clear that the Allies intended to strip Hungary of her national minorities. Power passed into the hands of the Communist Béla Kun who, confident in Russian support, formed a Red Army and tried to recover the lost territories by force. The expected Russian help was not forthcoming, and Béla Kun fled to Austria on August 4th, 1919; the Romanians took Budapest 2 days later.

Romanian occupation of Hungary's capital was short-lived. The Allies were, though, not prepared to conclude an agreement with the conservative regime which succeeded that of Béla Kun, and it was not until November that an acceptable provisional government was formed. The Treaty of Trianon deprived Hungary of most of her non-Magyar elements, which were given to Czechoslovakia, Romania, Yugoslavia and Austria: well over two-thirds of historic Hungary was lost. The new parliament, elected in January, 1920 annulled all measures enacted by the previous post-war regimes: the monarchy was restored, and on March 1st Admiral Miklós Horthy was elected Regent and entrusted with the powers normally exercised by the Crown. The former Emperor Karl made two attempts, in March and October, 1921 to claim the throne, but was thwarted by the Allies as well as by anti-legitimists within Hungary.

The Hungarian economy, aided by a substantial loan from the League of Nations, made an excellent recovery. The decade commencing in 1921 saw the dominance of Count István Bethlen, under whom Hungary became an authoritarian, but not totalitarian, State. Many of the country's serious social and economic problems remained unsolved, and Bethlen's fall, itself a consequence of the financial crisis, was followed by a period of unrest from which intense right-wing anti-semitic radicalism emerged. Gyula Gömbös, who became Prime Minister in October, 1932 pursued a policy of *rapprochement* with Germany, motivated by a desire to recover Hungary's historic frontiers with German assistance as well as by certain ideological sympathies with Nazism. Gömbös died in October, 1936 and his successors brought Hungary more closely within the sphere of German and Italian influence. Count Pál Telecki took over as Prime Minister in early 1939. He was initially fortunate: Hungary re-acquired Ruthenia in March, 1939 and was not compelled by Germany to join her when war broke out. Telecki's luck could not last: in the spring of 1941 German troops passed through Hungary on their way to attack Yugoslavia, and Telecki, fearing that this would drag Hungary into the war, committed suicide.

Hungary sent a small force to assist the Germans in their invasion of Russia, but soon came under pressure to increase this military involvement. Horthy, convinced that the Allies would ultimately win the war, appointed the liberal Miklós Kállay Prime Minister in March, 1942 but 2 years later Hitler forced Horthy to appoint an overtly collaborationist government. Thousands of Hungarian Jews were deported, and Hungarian forces on the Eastern Front, badly mauled at Voronezh in January, 1943, were reinforced with hastily trained drafts. In October, 1944 Horthy concluded an armistice with the Russians, but was seized and deposed by the Germans as soon as he announced the news. Soviet liberation of Hungary was completed in April, 1945. A provisional government, formed at Debrecen in December, 1944, took over the running of the country, having signed an armistice by which all territorial gains since 1938 were renounced. The peace treaty of February, 1947 restored the 1920 frontiers, with a minor variation, in Czechoslovakia's favour, in the north; it also placed certain limits upon the size of the Hungarian armed forces.

Although the provisional government contained only two communists, increasing pressure from the parties of the left led to the formation in June, 1948 of the powerful Communist 'Workers' Party', which gained an overwhelming majority in the May, 1949 elections. Hungary was proclaimed a People's Republic, and real power was concentrated in the hands of the Party's First Secretary, Mátyás Rákosi. In 1949 there was a struggle for power within the Party, the victory of whose Soviet-inspired faction was accompanied by a purge within the army, civil service, judiciary and church. Rákosi remained dominant until July, 1953 when Imre Nagy became Prime Minister in his place. Rákosi, however, remained Party Secretary, and in the spring of 1955 he secured the dismissal of Nagy, whose reforms had been bitterly opposed by Hungarian Stalinists. Rákosi himself survived only a year, and was forced to resign in July, 1956. He was succeeded by his political associate Ernö Gerö, whose policy of repression led to the revolt of October 23rd, 1956. The Hungarian army proved unwilling to resist the demonstrators, and Soviet troops were forced to leave Budapest. Nagy was swept into power at the head of a coalition government: numerous reforms were promised, and hundreds of political prisoners were freed. Hungary's new-found freedom was short-lived. Soviet reinforcements began to enter the country in late October, and on the night of November 3rd/4th the military leaders of the revolt were seized as they negotiated with the Russians. At dawn on November 4th, Soviet forces swept into action, and the revolt was snuffed out within a matter of days.

The Soviet offensive was accompanied by the establishment, behind Russian lines, of a new government headed by János Kádár, and it was this body which assumed power in Budapest following the collapse of the revolt. Kádár was Prime Minister from late 1956 until 1958, and again from 1961 until 1965. He remained Party Secretary throughout, and continues to hold this office today. Despite its origins, the Kádár regime has proved more stable and less austere than those of Rákosi or Gerö, and numerous economic reforms have been instituted, notably in 1968.

The events of 1956 were certainly a watershed for the Hungarian Army. The officer corps was replaced over a ten-year period by younger men with acceptable 'proletariat' backgrounds. Political controls have been tightened. The Soviets maintain a considerable military mission and occupy key logistics and command, control, and communication sites within Hungary, preventing any independent action by the Hungarians. The Soviet Southern Group of Forces remain as very much an army of occupation. Although Hungary has permitted internal reforms and flexibility, especially in economics, the party's monopoly of power has not been challenged and it continues to follow the Soviet line in foreign affairs.

STRENGTH AND BUDGET

Population: 10,750,000
Army: 85,000 (plus 130,000 reserves)
Air and Air Defence Force: 21,000 (plus 13,000 reserves)
    152 combat aircraft
Border Guards: 15,000
Security Troops: 15,000
Worker's Militia: 60,000
GNP: $37.7—52.8 billion (1981 estimate)
Defence Expenditure: $1.318 billion (1981 estimate)

COMMAND AND CONSTITUTIONAL STATUS

While officers are appointed and dismissed in the name of the Presidential Council, actual day-to-day decision-making is the responsibility of the Minister of Defence, who is both a member of the Party's Central Committee and the highest-ranking officer in the armed services. Under him he has the chiefs of the Army, Air, and Air Defence Force, the head of the Main Political Administration, the Chief of Staff, and a number of Inspectorates, all headed by Deputy Ministers of Defence.

Command
The Minister of Defence is responsible, through the Council of Ministers, to the Prime Minister. He has under him a number of Directorates, each headed by a Deputy Minister of Defence. These are believed to include the Directorates for Training, Rear Services, Administration, and the Political Directorate. The Chief of the General Staff is also a Deputy Minister for Defence. Hungary is the only Warsaw Pact state not to have followed the Soviet model in forming Military Districts.

Constitutional Status
Hungary is a People's Republic, governed according to the Constitution of August, 1949 as amended in April, 1972. Parliament, elected every 4 years, is the highest organ of State power. It elects the Presidential Council, composed of the President, two vice-presidents and seventeen other members. The Presidential Council exercises power when Parliament is not in session. It also recommends the election or removal by Parliament of the Council of Ministers, the highest organ

of State administration. The Prime Minister heads the Council of Ministers. The Prime Minister is also a member of the Central Committee of the Hungarian Socialist Workers' Party, whose First Secretary is János Kádár. The Party exercises a high degree of control over all social, political and economic activity: this control is, in the case of the armed forces, exercised through a political directorate within the Ministry of Defence. All individuals have a constitutional liability for military service: the Constitution states that 'military service and the defence of their country are the duties of all citizens'.

ROLE, COMMITMENT, DEPLOYMENT, AND RECENT OPERATIONS

Role and Commitment
The Hungarian armed forces are subordinated to overall Warsaw Pact command and direction. In wartime, Hungarian operational units would be part of a Soviet *Front*. Hungarian forces could be used to move into Austria. It is known that in the 1950s Soviet planning for a Warsaw Pact invasion of Yugoslavia included a large role for the Hungarian Army.

Deployment
5th Army HQ; Szekesfehervar
III Corps HQ; Cegled
5th Tank Division; Tata
17th Motorised Rifle Division; Zalaegerszig
9th Motorised Rifle Division; Kaposvar
27th Motorised Rifle Division; Kiskunfelegyhaza
12th Motorised Rifle Division; Gyongyos
8th (4th?) Motorised Rifle Division; Nyiregyhaza
? Airborne Battalion;
? SCUD Missile Brigade; Tapoica

One motorised rifle division is believed to be at cadre strength. There may be an additional hostilities-only cadre motorised rifle division. Four divisions are considered 'high readiness', two 'lower readiness', but all are, on paper, supposed to be available for operations seven days after mobilisation.

Non-divisional units include: one artillery brigade, one anti-aircraft artillery regiment, one SAM regiment, one airborne battalion, at least one commando battalion, and the Danube Flotilla with 700 men and 15 craft.

Recent Operations
Elements of two Hungarian divisions participated in the invasion of Czechoslovakia in 1968. They operated under very rigid Soviet control, and it has been suggested that their performance was not impressive. Hungarian troops take part in the normal run of Warsaw Pact exercises.

ORGANISATION

Arms of Service
These are similar to those of the Soviet ground forces.

Operational
Units and formations are basically organised on the Soviet pattern, although they are smaller and follow earlier Soviet equipment levels.

RECRUITMENT, TRAINING AND RESERVES

Recruitment and Training
About 60% of Hungarian servicemen are 2 year conscripts; the remainder are extended service and regular NCOs, and

regular officers. There is compulsory pre-conscription military training, the length of which was increased by legislation in early 1976. Training has much in common with that of the Soviet ground forces, and includes substantial amounts of political education.

Reserves

About 130–148,000 Army reservists are available to be recalled, although reserve training is limited by Western standards.

The Worker's Militia, 60,000 strong, is under the Ministry of the Interior. A part-time force, it is armed with older infantry weapons and has units throughout the country.

The Frontier Guard of 15,000 men is under the Ministry of the Interior, although it would probably come under Army operational command in wartime. It is divided into a number of district commands, each containing several battalions. It controls all frontier traffic and protects the borders.

The Internal Security Troops, 15,000 strong, are under the Ministry of the Interior. Their mission is the suppression of internal dissent or rebellion, although in wartime they could be used for rear area protection.

EQUIPMENT AND ARMS INDUSTRY

Equipment

The overwhelming majority of Hungarian military equipment is of Soviet design, although some items are produced, with modifications, within Hungary.

Small arms: M-48 SMG 7.62mm short, copied from the obsolete Soviet M-41 PPSH; 7.62mm assault rifle (similar to AK-47, but has hollow plastic butt and pistol grip); other small arms are of Soviet design
Anti-tank: RPG-7 rocket launchers, 150 73mm SPG-9, B-11 107mm RR, 150 85mm and 100mm AT guns
Artillery: 250–360 122mm howitzers, 40–150 122mm SP howitzers, 100 152mm guns/hows, 50–150 BM-21 MRLs.
Anti-Aircraft: 57mm towed, ZSU-23-4, ZSU-57-2
Armour: Tanks: about 1200 T-54/55s, 100 T-72s
Reconnaissance vehicles: 100 PT-76 light tanks, and about 600 BTR-40 BPs. FUG M-1963s and FUG M-1966s; the latter two vehicles are also used by the Polish and Czechoslovakian armies, where they are known as OT-65s and OT-66s; they are designed and produced in Hungary; FUG M-1963 is turretless, while FUG M-1966 mounts a turret containing a 23mm cannon and a 7.62mm MG
APCs: BTR-40s, BTR-60s, BTR-50 PKs and BTR-152s, MT-LB, 1,400 total BMP-1s Micr.
Aircraft: 152 combat aircraft. 120 MiG-21 in six squadrons, 20 MiG-23 in one squadron, 12 Mi-24 in one squadron; about 36 AN-2, AN-24, AN-26, Il-14, Tu-134 transports, 48 helicopters, Mi-4, Mi-8, Ka-26
Missiles: 24 FROG, 12 SCUD, Sagger ATGM, 150 SA-2 and SA-3, 80 SA-6, SA-7, 50 SA-9.

Arms Industry

Hungary produces its own Soviet-designed small arms, ammunition, and the indigenous FUG scout cars and Csepel trucks, both of which display a great deal of components commonality with other Warsaw Pact vehicles.

RANK, DRESS AND DISTINCTIONS

Rank

Officers (worn on the epaulette)
  Hadseregtábornok — Four silver stars on gold braid epaulette

  Vezérezredes — Three silver stars on gold braid epaulette
  Altábornagy — Two silver stars on gold braid epaulette
  Vezérörnagy — One silver star on gold braid epaulette
  Ezredes — Three silver stars on partially braided epaulette
  Alezredes — Two silver stars on partially braided epaulette
  Örnagy — One silver star on partially braided epaulette
  Százados — Three gold stars on epaulette
  Főhadnagy — Two gold stars on epaulette
  Hadnagy — One gold star on epaulette
  Alhadnagy — One silver star on epaulette with vertical strip of gold braid

Note: all officers' epaulettes are edged with twisted gold braid

Regular NCOs (worn on the epaulette)
  Főtörzsőrmester — Three silver stars above horizontal braid band
  Törzsőrmester — Two silver stars above horizontal braid band
  Őrmester — One silver star above horizontal braid band

Note: all regular NCOs have an edging of twisted silver braid to their epaulettes.

Long-service NCOs (worn on the epaulette)
  Főtörzsőrmester — As for regular NCOs, but without braid edging to epaulette
  Törzsőrmester — As for regular NCOs, but without braid edging to epaulette
  Őrmester — As for regular NCOs but without braid edging to epaulette
  Szakaszvezető — Three small stars in inverted 'V'
  Tizedes — Two small stars, side-by-side

Conscripts (worn on collar) — with arm of service insignia
  Szakaszvezető — Three small silver stars in inverted 'V'
  Tizedes — Two small silver stars, one above the other
  Őrvezető — One silver star
  Honvéd — No badge of rank

Dress

Parade dress consists of a light-brown single-breasted tunic and trousers of the same colour, worn with a Soviet pattern steel helmet. Walking-out dress is similar, but a light-brown peaked cap replaces the helmet, and shoes, rather than boots and anklets, are worn. A short khaki blouse replaces the tunic for walking-out in summer. Officers may be seen in a special gala walking-out dress with white-peaked cap and white tunic. Khaki denim blouse and trousers, with a soft khaki peaked cap, are worn in barrack dress. Two types of dress may be countered in the field: one closely resembles barrack dress, and the other consists of a mottled green and brown jacket and trousers. Boots and webbing anklets are black; equipment, NBC protective clothing and tank suits are of the Soviet pattern.

Arm-of-service badges are worn on the collar in parade and walking-out dress. These insignia are in yellow metal and are, in the main, self explanatory. Arm-of-service colours are worn, in the same order of dress, on collar patches and cap piping; they also form the background colour of officers' epaulettes. Most arms and services wear green patches and piping. Armoured troops wear black, while generals, field artillery and air-defence artillery wear red. All ranks wear a shield bearing the letters MN in silver on the upper left arm of all except barrack and combat dress.

Distinctions

Most of the decorations currently awarded were instituted in

March, 1953. The senior order is the Order of Merit of the People's Republic of Hungary, conferred on both soldiers and civilians. The senior title is Hero of Socialist Labour.

CURRENT DEVELOPMENTS

While the Soviet Union is disliked by most of the Hungarian people, the officers of the Army are all hand-picked for loyalty, and the way the Soviets have integrated Hungarian forces into overall Warsaw Pact planning, as in Czechoslovakia in 1968, seems to point that Hungary would fight with their allies if the order came from Moscow. In a general war, they could be used to move through Austria. Soviet planning for a war with Yugoslavia in the 1950s is known to have envisaged a considerable role for the Hungarian Army. The Hungarian Army appears to be a credible part of the Warsaw Pact force structure.

Richard Holmes
David Isby

INDIA*

HISTORY AND INTRODUCTION

The Army of the Indian Republic traces its descent in un-broken line from the armies raised and maintained by the British in India, at first through the agency of the East India Company, and then under the British King — Emperor and his Government of India.

Although in the ancient Hindu empires there were standing armies, and regular troops organised into corporate bodies, the conventional method of raising troops in India, when the European merchant adventurers arrived in the sixteenth century, was the *jagirdari* system. This, like the feudal system in Europe, was a system of military tenure, except that in India the assignee, or *jagirdar*, held not the land, but the right to collect the tax produced by the land allotted to him. With the proceeds of this wealth he was required to maintain a stated number of armed troopers and horses, and to pay thier wages for a specified limited time if they were called up for government service. This system was used by the early Muslim conquerors, the Sultans of mediaeval Delhi and south India, by their neighbouring Hindu kingdoms, and by the Mughal empire and its successor States. As was the case with the European feudal system, as long as the central Govern-ment was powerful enough to enforce its authority over its powerful fief-holders, the *jagirdari* system was economic and simple to operate, but when the central power declined, these vassals tended to become independent rulers setting up their own dynasties, and to use their military contingents as their own personal forces.

The type of army produced by this system was very like the feudal arrays of mediaeval Europe. The main fighting arm was the cavalry, yeoman landholders with their sons and retainers, and their own (or their proprietors') horses and weapons, armed with sword, lance, shield and dagger, and possibly a matchlock for artistic effect. Each trooper was the business end of a weapons system, consisting of grooms, grass-cutters, tent-pitchers, armourers and so on, forming a vast dismounted element. The central govern-ment provided a nucleus of full-time professional troops, including the artillery park, and a few disciplined infantry-men employed as bodyguards and household troops.

As the Mughal empire declined in the early eighteenth century, its various provinces turned into independent successor States, each contending with the other for control of land and sources of wealth. India once more became prey to invasion by armies from Afghanistan. In the north-western plains, the militant Sikhs of the Punjab began to carve out their own kingdoms. In central India the renascent Hindu power of the Maratha confederacy established new dynasties, and the Rajput kingdoms also threw off the yoke of Muslim domination. The European trading companies with settlements in India imported Europe's wars into the already war-torn sub-continent, and by diplomacy, gold, bluff and sheer military power, established themselves as minor Indian powers on their own account.

Against the old fashioned hordes of individual Indian horsemen, the disciplined fire-power and parade-ground manoeuvres of well-trained European infantry and field

* See also Appendix 2.

artillery were bound to be victorious. Only the lack of manpower held them back, until the French, followed by the British, discovered that Indian soldiers, dressed, trained and equipped in the European way, were a passable sub-stitute for the home-grown product, and were cheaper and easier to raise.

The battle of Palasi (Plassey) in 1757, where 900 British soldiers and 2000 Indian sepoys overthrew a combined Indian host of 50,000 in a morning, and where the greater part of that host never came into action at all because the British had bought off its commanders, showed equally the moral and military bankruptcy of the existing Indian system. Britain's naval supremacy, and the involvement of her European rivals in wars at home, left her the only real European power in India after 1763. By 1822 the British had become not merely a major power in India, but the paramount power. In 1858 they abolished the titular rem-nants of the Mughal dynasty, and the British Crown replaced the East India Company as the agency of British rule, a process formally completed in 1877 when Parliament sanc-tioned the Queen of England, adding the style 'Empress of India' to her titles.

By the middle of the nineteenth century the superior military organisation and technology of the British had given them direct control over the most fertile and populous areas of the sub-continent. The only areas to avoid direct annexa-tion were those composed of jungle, desert or mountain, which were both unprofitable to govern and unsuitable for European tactics. While the ferocity of Indian soldiers, the ability of their commanders and the weight of their numbers often made the British pay dearly for their victories, and at times even scored local success, the only native armies to meet the British in the plains on level terms were the Marathas and the Punjab kingdom of Lahore, both of which, and especially the latter, maintained standing armies in imitation of the British system, with good field artillery, and trained by European military advisers.

From the earliest times, the British forces in India were divided into three separate and independent armies: those of Bengal, Madras and Bombay, the three 'presidencies' from which the British had extended their rule over provinces of India. Bengal was directly ruled by the Governor-General of India, and the Bengal Army was directly under the Com-mander-in-Chief, India. The other two presidencies and their armies had their own Governors and Commanders-in-Chief who were only indirectly controlled by the Government of India, in Bengal. Each army was made up mainly of Indian units under European officers, but also included a few units in which all ranks were recruited from the United Kingdom for permanent Indian service. These were all employees of the East India Company, but each army also included a small contingent of units from the regular British army, stationed in India and periodically relieved by other units from the UK or elsewhere in the British empire. During their tour of duty in India, the pay and other running costs of British army units were provided from the revenues of the Government of India, not by the British tax-payer. The reason for this was that these soldiers were defending India, and if they were not required there they could be disbanded and the British taxpayer spared the cost of maintaining them.

The great watershed in the political and military history

258

of British India was the great Mutiny of 1857–8. The contributing causes of the Mutiny were varied. It was, as evidenced by the degree of support given to it by many Indian princes and ordinary people, in part a protest against the seemingly endless, and often unjustified, annexation of Indian States by the British. It was also a protest against the way in which the British, as they took over territory, interfered with ancient, if inhumane, religious customs, and brought in modern inventions and modern practices, undermining the rigid system of caste division on which Hindu society rested. Another reason was the vicious system of giving extra pay for duty at frontier stations or for civilian employment, which encouraged officers to transfer away from their own regiments, and resulted in regiments in rear areas, where the Mutiny broke out, having few officers actually in post.

The peculiar frightfulness of this Mutiny, which was virtually confined to the Bengal Army and the north Indian plains, was that it took place in a settled area. Not only did the mutineers, supported by local mobs, murder European officers and civilians, but also their wives, and most horrible of all in the eyes of the British soldiers (far away from their own families), their little children as well. The Mutiny was fought, and quelled, with all the ferocity associated with servile wars, the innocent suffering with the guilty, and never again was there so trusting a relationship between Briton and Indian as had previously been enjoyed.

The native element of the Indian Army was reduced in size from 226,000 to 150,000. The European element was raised from 40,000 to 75,000, all from the 225,000 strong British Regular Army, into which the East India Company's European troops were incorporated. Indian artillery was reduced to a handful of mountain batteries, officered by the Royal Artillery, and Indian sappers and miners were placed under the Royal Engineers. The East India Company was abolished, and its Indian troops, with their British officers, became servants of the Crown controlled by the newly established India Office, whose Secretary of State sat in the Cabinet in London. The India Office was in fact an amalgam of the East India Company's home establishment, and the Board of Control for India was a government agency through which the Company's political affairs had been effectively regulated by Parliament since 1784. The Indian Army, including its British contingent, was controlled by the Secretary of State for India, not the Secretary of State for War, and the Commander-in-Chief, India, was responsible to the Governor-General of India and the India Office, not to the Commander-in-Chief of the British army. Two out of the three Commanders-in-Chief of the local Indian armies (Bengal, Madras and Bombay) were provided by the British army, and when a post was given to a general of an Indian army, his successor had to be from the British. Troops from the Indian establishment could be used for overseas campaigns unconnected with Indian defence needs, but in such cases they were paid for from British, rather than Indian, revenues.

With only 150,000 men to recruit from a population of 400,000,000 people, in a country where military service was generally regarded as an honourable and desirable profession, the British could afford to be very selective. During the late nineteenth and early twentieth centuries, they increasingly restricted recruiting to certain classes and communities, predominantly from the Punjab and northern frontier areas. One reason for this was the historical fact that the mutinous Bengal Army had been defeated with the aid of new troops raised from the recently conquered province of the Punjab. The men from this part of India are generally taller and sturdier in physique than men from the central and southern areas. The Punjab is also the home of the Sikhs or 'disciples', originally a peaceful religious group, whose members were driven by Mughal persecution to adopt warlike practices, and who had many old scores to settle with the last Emperor in Delhi, where the mutineers set up their capital. From their record in the Mutiny, the Punjabis were deemed to be more trustworthy and better soldiers than the men of the U.P. (Uttar Pradesh – the north India plain) who had formed a majority of the old Bengal Army. When that army was reformed, the Punjab units filled up the vacant places in its list, and the number of 'Hindustani' units was gradually reduced. A similar process occurred in the two smaller armies. The poor performance of some Bombay units during the Second Afghan War, and some Madras units during the Third Burma War, resulted in a sweeping condemnation of the material from which these armies were recruited. Critics included officers of the larger Bengal Army, smarting from the airs adopted by officers and men of the two armies which had not mutinied. It was argued that in India there were many communities. Some were naturally warlike, brave and manly. Others were timid, weak and effete, either from the effects of generations of conquest and oppression or from the enervating effects of a tropical climate, or because years of peace under the British had made them unaccustomed, and therefore unfit, to bear arms. Most 'martial' classes, as defined by this theory, came from the Punjab and the northern borders, where there was a long history of fighting and other disturbances, whereas the 'non-martial' classes included almost by definition the majority of the population of western and southern India, the areas allotted to the Bombay and Madras Armies, respectively.

What the advocates of this theory failed to remember was the adage that there are no bad troops, only bad officers. As long as the Bombay and Madras armies were restricted to their own districts, the chance of active service, and in particular frontier service, was minimal. This state of affairs, while reflecting great credit on the political management of the country, was unpopular with the British officers of those armies, for although the soldiers did not wish to serve far away from their home in peace-time, the officers had little chance of distinction unless they did so. Accordingly, the best officers tried to join the Bengal Army, and the worst were content to stay in the peaceful south. Under such officers, several units proved unfit for combat when the chance came, and their failure was made the pretext for the gradual restriction of recruitment to an ever-narrowing number of communities. The so-called martial classes, on analysis, proved to be essentially agricultural peasant proprietors, among the educationally most backward and (perhaps on that account) politically the most inert, in the whole of the Indian empire.

The reform of the Indian Army in 1902 under Lord Kitchener attempted to remedy the situation by bringing all units into a common sequence, and abolishing the terms Bengal, Madras and Bombay. (The separate armies and commanders-in-chief had been abolished in 1895.) Every unit became liable for peace-time service anywhere in India, including the north-west frontier, where skirmishes with the Pathan tribes were always liable to occur. This was used, however, as a pretext to reduce still further the number of 'down-country' regiments, and replace them by men of the desired 'martial classes'.

Kitchener's reforms produced an army intended primarily for the defence of India's north-west frontier against aggression by local tribal, or European (i.e. Russian), forces. Internal security (the actual occupation and holding down of India) was given secondary consideration in view of the apparent stability of the British position, although units were to be given equal practice in both roles. The field army consisted of nine infantry divisions and eight cavalry brigades. The divisions were each to have an Indian cavalry regiment, a field brigade and a mountain brigade of artillery, three infantry brigades of one British and two or three Indian battalions, a pioneer battalion, sappers and miners, and medical units. As had been the case since 1857, the Indian troops carried firearms of a pattern discarded by the British on re-arming with better weapons.

It was this army, designed and trained virtually as a colonial auxiliary of the powerful British forces, that was flung into the holocaust of World War I. Two army corps were in action against the Germans in France and Flanders by November, 1914, and by their sacrifice helped the small band of British Regular and part-time Territorial soldiers hold the line until Kitchener's New British Armies could be trained and sent to the front. Another Indian Expeditionary Force went to Mesopotamia, to fight a bloody campaign against the Turks. Others fought in Palestine, East Africa and Salonika. By 1918, more than half a million Indian soldiers were under arms. Although officers and men endured the test and stood the strain, the system which supported them did not. The low number of British officers in each unit (eight to a battalion instead of twenty-four in the case of the British army) meant that a small number of officer casualties had a serious effect on the fighting capacity of units — especially as they could not easily be replaced in the esteem, or even the comprehension, of their solders. The careful balance of classes and communities between the troops and companies of a unit, created over a period of years, could be wiped out in an hour by the mass destruction wrought by modern weapons. Indian officers and NCOs from one community could not easily be posted to command men of another, even within the same regiment. A system built to withstand the casualties, suffered by tens and twenties, in a frontier war, collapsed when asked to deal with casualties, suffered by the hundred. The favoured martial classes were unable, sometimes unwilling, to meet all the demands made on them by recruiting parties. High prices on the farm, high wages in the factories, both proved strong counter-attractions to young men whose first priority was to feed their own family rather than fight for a distant King-Emperor in a cause they dimly understood. The valour, determination and good conduct of those who did join up, and who fought in distant lands for the British, even though their own homes, families and liberties were not threatened, and who endured the risk of wounds, disease and death in every unpleasant and extreme form, must always be a shining example of what the ordinary Indian soldier (the sepoy or *sipahi*) can achieve.

A number of reforms were introduced in the post-war period. Units were renumbered and regrouped, the cavalry reduced in number and the infantry formed into large regiments each with a number of battalions able to send reinforcements to one another. The ancient *silladari* system, whereby the trooper (or *sawar*), in return for a higher rate of pay, supplied a cash deposit and paid monthly dues to his commanding officer for the supply and upkeep of horse and clothing, was at last abolished. However, the army still looked towards the north-west frontier, now fearing the red dawn of Soviet Russia, and ignored the north-east, where the rising sun of Japan was to be the real enemy. Although in the stress of war many classes had been regarded as at least temporarily martial, the small peacetime army once again denied their young men the chance of service, and restricted entry to the traditional groups. What could not be changed was the forward pace of political development. Despite official attempts to portray the leaders of the nationalist movement as agitators and ringleaders, whom the British and Indian soldiers were defending against assault by real and savage enemies, political discontent grew steadily. Troops were increasingly used to quell civil disturbances, to the detriment of their training for war. By 1939 the one-third of the British regular army normally stationed in India was little more than a garrison force, unable to be withdrawn for service elsewhere for fear of weakening the British hold over the country.

A further reform was conceded only reluctantly, under pressure from Indian public opinion. This was the 'Indianisation' of the officer corps. Before World War I, the commissioned officers of Indian units were all expatriate Britons, educated as cadets at the Royal Military College, Sandhurst with their British army contemporaries. Indian officers did not hold commissions, and were promoted only after long service in the ranks. They acted as sub-unit leaders and as advisers and assistants to their British squadron, company or battery commanders.

From the early years of the twentieth century, Indian nationalists began to ask why, when Indians were able to enter the highest ranks of the judiciary, the civil service and other branches of government employment, they were excluded from service as commissioned officers in their own army. The victories of the Japanese forces in the Russo—Japanese war had shown that Asian officers could successfully employ the techniques of modern war, and there was no reason why Indian officers should not be as good as the Japanese.

The British argued that the young men of the martial classes lacked the necessary Western education, and that the sons of the middle-class urban intelligentsia, who were educated, were non-martial. The martial classes replied that they had shed their blood in the British cause, and had been promised commissions during the Great War, and that it would be unwise for the British to alienate those on whose support the British position rested. The urban *élite* pointed out that war experience had shown that men of all classes could be brave, and that an independent India would be one nation, not a collection of communities. The British dragged their feet, partly on grounds of the ultimate security of their rule, partly because the Indian Army officers had traditionally been drawn from the less affluent end of the British middle class. Every one of the limited number of vacancies given to a young Indian meant one less for a young Briton, at a time of world recession and large-scale unemployment. A further difficulty was the imagined reluctance of British officers to serve under men of a different race and colour. Nonetheless a small but steadily increasing number of Indian cadets of 'martial' and 'non-martial' background, were commissioned, until the outbreak of World War II swept away such scruples, and large numbers of Indians were granted war-time commissions.

A further subject of controversy between the British and Indian politicians was the type of armament issued to Indian soldiers. Nationalist spokesmen asked why, if the British really meant to see India a self-governing dominion, Indian soldiers had to be worse armed than their British comrades. The answer was, again, military security, but as this was at variance with declared policy, the British had to yield. The first batteries of Indian field artillery were formed in 1936, and anti-aircraft batteries were raised shortly afterwards. By 1945 the Indian artillery consisted of more than 80 regiments of all natures. In the case of the cavalry arm, a combination of 'horse' tradition, demands for internal security and the cost of new vehicles, resulted in the Indian cavalryman being even slower than his British counterparts to convert to a mechanised role. During the 1930s, Afghanistan and Iran, who were still regarded as the most likely enemy, each had more tanks than the Indian Army. When the first Indian cavalry was motorised, it was given unarmoured lorries to drive it to the battle, and trained to dismount and fight on foot. The collapse of many Indian units before the Japanese onslaught in Malaya and Burma was due in part to a feeling of having been let down by their British rulers, in the inferior nature of their equipment. Of the 60,000 Indian officers and men taken prisoner, one third joined the Indian National Army, a force raised by the Japanese to fight for an independent India and spearhead the march on Delhi. In the event this force achieved little, but it was a serious warning to the British that Indian soldiers shared the aspirations of their fellow citizens, and their blind support could not be taken for granted.

During World War II the Indian Army rose to a strength of 2,500,000 men of all classes. It saw service in north Africa, Eritrea, the Middle East, Europe, Burma, Malaya, and elsewhere in south-east Asia. It operated the most complex mechanical and electrical equipment, and the most modern weapons, tanks and artillery. The collapse of the 'martial class' theory was hastened by this expansion, for it was the urban, educated soldier who proved most useful in a modern army, and the backward farm boys who had to struggle to achieve the desired standard. As in World War I, although the traditional martial classes fought well and bravely, men from other backgrounds proved their valour too.

In 1947 the Indian empire and its local forces divided into the two Dominions of India and Pakistan, each with its own army. Of the 500,000 men then under the arms about one-third went to Pakistan, two-thirds to India. Wherever possible unit identities were preserved, often by posting Muslim and Hindu or Sikh soldiers between units to ensure a religious homogeneity. Pakistan made it clear that no non-Muslims were acceptable in the army of a State whose whole existence was based on a desire to defend the Islamic way of life; but India, a secular State, accepted Muslim soldiers from her own territory with open arms.

After independence the Indian army emerged as a long-service all-volunteer regular army of about 280,000 men. This was by no means an inevitable or natural development, for many argued in favour of a short-service conscript army, to build national unity, on the Japanese model. Others advocated a militia system such as the Chinese Communist People's Liberation Army. Some felt that the survivors of the Indian National Army, who had fought for independence, should have a place in the new army. There were even suggestions that the army, which had after all been a tool of the imperialist oppressors, should purge its guilty past by massive civil-aid projects alongside the workers and peasants, digging ditches, reaping the harvest and building roads (Gandhi even advocated cleaning sewers).

The forces of military conservation withstood these attacks, and many senior officers encouraged the continuity of pre-independence institutions (such as the officers' mess system) in order to maintain high standards of efficiency and *esprit de corps*. British Indian military traditions were maintained not because they were British, but because they were the Army's, and the Indian Army continued to commemorate victories won over Indian enemies as well as those won over Afghans, Turks or Germans. Political respectability was won as early as 1948, when the army went into action in defence of the new India. A short action in Hyderabad ensured the incorporation of that State into the Indian Union. In Kashmir, Pathan tribesmen, carried in Pakistani army lorries, under Pakistani army officers, and finally with regular Pakistani army support, waged a major old-style frontier campaign against Indian troops hurriedly brought up from the plains. In 1961 a 'walk-over' in Goa against the unresisting Portuguese nevertheless revealed serious logistic weaknesses – the result of 14 years' continuous neglect of the army by

politicians committed to non-violence and neutralism.

In 1962 Sino–Indian border disputes in the Himalayas led to serious fighting in which the Indian army suffered a major defeat, with 3000 of its soldiers killed or missing, and 4000 taken prisoner. Indian troops found themselves with their Lee Enfield bolt-action rifles against AK-47 assault rifles, their pack howitzers outranged by heavy mortars, their thin cotton uniforms against Chinese quilted clothing. And, whereas the Chinese were acclimatised, Indian soldiers went down in droves from the effect of altitude sickness and frost-bite. While the men fought bravely when they had the chance, poor generalship and bad staff work made their sacrifice of no avail. There was slackness at lower levels too – signallers opening on the same frequency every day so that they could be easily jammed, axes and digging tools forgotten, anti-tank weapons left behind. Above all the logistic problems of fighting a campaign in the Himalayas with inadequate communications had been gravely underestimated.

The Indian army arose from this defeat like a phoenix from the ashes. The politicians abandoned non-alignment and bought weapons from whoever would sell. Public opinion supported the expenditure of scarce resources on military hardware. Ten new mountain divisions were formed (the British, for all their fighting on the hills of the north-west frontier, had never formed Indian mountain troops other than their pack batteries). Regular army strength was doubled to 750,000 men, incompetent generals were removed, and the army, under new leaders, adopted a new spirit of urgency and realism.

In September, 1965 India and Pakistan waged a conventional war against each other in the plains of the north west. Fighting lasted about 21 days, both sides being trained and equipped in Western style. The major engagement, the tank battle of Sialkot, lasting over 2 weeks, was the largest tank battle at that time since the end of World War II. Pakistani Patton tanks, though technically better than India's Centurion's, proved too complicated for their crews to maintain. The battle was a drawn one, each side losing about 300 tanks, 4000–5000 men, and 50 combat aircraft. Indian infantry proved less effective than the Pakistanis' at patrolling and infiltration, and the Royal Pakistan Artillery and Royal Pakistan Air Force scored notable successes against Indian field and light air-defence batteries. One of the most important lessons was that India could not rely on British resupply in such emergencies. The British government, in the interests of 'neutrality', cut off the supply of spares and ammunition for the British-built equipment it had sold to India. Severing links forged over many years, the Indian army turned away from dependence on the British, and made up its deficiencies with Soviet-designed material, much of it from Czechoslovakia.

In 1971 India intervened in the struggle for independence then being waged in East Pakistan. Within 12 days the Indian army smashed its way across the plains and rivers of east Bengal to Dacca. The Pakistani garrison, some four and a half divisions well provisioned and supplied, were completely overwhelmed by the three Indian corps (each of two or three divisions, mostly mountain troops) opposed to them. Many Pakistani units fought fiercely, but it was clear that with the whole country opposed to them they could do no more than fight a delaying campaign hoping for foreign intervention or successes in the west. The speed, ferocity, and flexibility of the Indian attack, including a parachute brigade drop, brought about a more rapid and spectacular victory than either side anticipated.

On the western front both sides fought a tank war, as in 1965. Infantry held defensive positions along rivers and minefields while the armoured troops manoeuvred between them. Indian Special Forces harassed the Pakistani rear areas more successfully than in 1965, and the Pakistani air force, not trusting its mainly Bengali ground crews, ceded air supremacy to the Indians. When Dacca fell, Pakistan had taken no bargaining counters in the west, and the whole campaign must be counted a victory for Indian arms.

STRENGTH AND BUDGET

Population: 688,600,000
Army: 944,000
Navy: 47,000; 40 major vessels, including one aircraft carrier, one cruiser, two missile destroyers, 21 frigates and eight submarines; 48 smaller vessels
Air force: 113,000; 635 combat aircraft
Paramilitary forces: 260,000
GNP (1981) $157,800,000,000
Defence expenditure (1981–2): $5,260,000,000.

COMMAND AND CONSTITUTIONAL STATUS

Supreme command is vested in the President of the Republic of India. Political control is exercised by the Minister of Defence, but policy is determined by the Political Affairs Committee of the Cabinet, of which that minister is a member. It is chaired by the Prime Minister. Internal Defence Ministry policy is determined by the Defence Minister's Committee, which consists of, besides him, the Minister of Defence Production, the three Service Chiefs, the Defence Secretary, the Financial Adviser (Defence) and the Scientific Adviser. A parallel committee is the Defence Minister's Production and Supply Committee on which additional civil servants sit. The ministry is a tri-service organisation, and its activities are co-ordinated by the Secretary, a civil servant, and his secretariat. It provides the secretariat for the Defence Minister's Committee, and the Production and Supply Committee and the Chiefs of Staff Committee. It also oversees the main interservice organisations, the Production and Inspection Organisation, Research and Development Organisation, Directorate-General of Medical Services, National Cadet Corps, Historical Section, Joint Cipher Bureau and the interservice colleges and academy.

A special branch of the Ministry of Finance, namely the Ministry of Finance (Defence), under the Financial Advisers, controls military expenditure and advises the Minister of Defence on financial aspects of defence policy. Its head is a subordinate of the Minister of Finance.

Ministers are Members of Parliament (which has its own parliamentary consultative committee on defence) and they are required to answer to parliament on defence policy, particularly during the regular defence debates.

There is a history of disagreement between the Chiefs of Staff (particularly the Army Chief of Staff) and the Minister of Defence, originally occasioned by the low standing of the Defence Minister in the hierarchy of the ruling Congress Party, which was traditionally anti-militarist in outlook, and the lack of experience of its nominees to the post. A subsequent over-compensation when the able and strong-minded Krishna Menon was appointed in 1957, led to personal and policy disagreements with the equally strong-minded General Thimmaya, who was retired in 1961, and to his replacement by a General Kaul, whom the army felt to be a Menon protégé. The *débâcle* of the China–India War of 1962 led to Menon's demotion and eventually to Kaul's retirement. More recently the Congress Party and the army appear to have developed a

warmer mutual regard and a smoother system for the management of defence.

Although the three Chiefs of Staff are co-equal, the Army Chief of Staff (formerly the Commander-in-Chief) was historically superior and continues to enjoy effective primacy within his own Army Headquarters in the Ministry of Defence; he is assisted by four Staffs, which bear the traditional British titles of: the General Staff (of which he is directly Head), the Adjutant-General's Branch, the Quartermaster-General's Branch and the Master-General of the Ordnance's Branch. They are responsible, respectively, for operations, personnel, supply and procurement. Each supervises a number of Directorates, the Heads of which are administrative superiors of their own arm of service or of a particular military function. Thus the Director of Military Operations and the Director of the armoured corps, infantry and other fighting arms both answer to the Chief of the Army Staff (as Chief of the General Staff), the Director of Supplies and Transport answers to the Quartermaster-General and the Director of Ordnance Services answers to the Master-General. The State Commands, and the field formations, are under direct command of the Army Chief of Staff.

ROLE, COMMITMENT, DEPLOYMENT AND RECENT OPERATIONS

Role
Under the British, the Indian army was trained to fight wars, particularly minor imperial wars, rather than to maintain internal security, for which the police, or, their efforts failing, British or Gurkha units, were principally employed; only in emergencies were Indian units used to quell political riots or communal disturbances, it being considered, understandably, that such duty put the army's national, caste or religious loyalties under too great a strain. The coming of independence and the movements of population concomitant on partition having largely removed the old causes of political and communal unrest, the army has not often, despite its inheritance of the internal security role of tribal pacification which the British exercised right to the end, though now in Assam rather than the north-west frontier. It has also been an instrument of national unification, the Princely States (particularly Hyderabad) and the foreign enclave of Goa having been incorporated into India by the (peaceful) action of the Indian army. The army has been one of the United Nations most valuable sources of troops for its peace-keeping work and it is a duty to which it attaches great importance. It has not, however, undertaken to any extent a 'nation building' role, for reasons which its peculiar and limited recruitment explain (*see* The Bangladesh War, 1971). Nor does it devote any particular effort to civil assistance work — road building or civil engineering — except in areas of military importance. In many respects, indeed, the army remains what the British left it: a highly trained and dedicated military instrument, concerned principally with the defence of the borders of India.

Commitment
India is an unaligned State. No foreign troops are stationed on its territory and, since the withdrawal of the army from Bangladesh in 1972, none of its own is stationed abroad (except for individuals in the UN Emergency Force, as already mentioned).

Deployment
India is divided into five Commands: Southern (HQ Poona), Western (HQ Simla), Central (HQ Lucknow), Eastern (HQ

Calcutta) and northern (HQ undisclosed). Southern Command covers the area of the States of Rajasthan, Gujarat, Maharashtra, Mysore, Andhra Pradesh, Kerala and Tamil Nadu. Central Command covers Madhya Pradesh, Uttar Pradesh, Bihar and Orissa. Eastern Command covers West Bengal, Assam, Tripura, Manipur, Nagaland and Arunachal Pradesh (North-East Frontier Agency). Western Command covers Jammu and Kashmir (Indian sector), Haryana, Punjab and Himachal Pradesh. Northern Command has been created by dividing Western Command; its exact area is undisclosed. All border on foreign territory: Southern on Pakistan; Western (and Northern) on Pakistan and China; Central on China and Nepal; and Eastern on Bhutan, China, Burma and Bangladesh (which it almost surrounds). The frontier with Nepal, Sikkim, Bhutan and Bangladesh is militarily inactive, but there are major concentrations of forces on the Pakistan and Chinese borders, as well as a large internal security force in Assam, Nagaland and Mizoram. The exact allocation of forces between commands is not published, but it is believed that Western Command contains three corps (I, XII and XV) each of six divisions, including 1st Armoured Division and seventeen other divisions, some of which are mountain divisions; that Central Command contains II and XXXIII Corps with four Divisions (4th, 9th 20th and 23rd); Eastern Command contains some mountain divisions and the 8th and 57th Divisions on internal security duty, with the Assam Rifles in Nagaland; the remainder of the fighting formations, including the 6th Armoured Division, are in Southern Command, whose forces constitute a central reserve.

Recent Operations

Since independence in 1947 the Indian army has become one of the most experienced and combat-tested armies in action. Before this its units had been engaged in three major fronts — Burma, north Africa and Italy — against the Japanese, Germans and Italians, respectively for most of World War II. Unhappily much of the Indian army's warfare since 1947 has been of a semi-fraternal character, against the Pakistani army — its 'other half', many of whose senior officers are former brothers-in-arms of their Indian counterparts.

The Indian army's major campaigns are as follows.

Kashmir 1947—8

A princely State whose population was ruled by a Hindu Maharaja, it attempted to remain independent of both Pakistan and India on partition. A Muslim uprising obliged the Maharaja to call for Indian aid, in return for which he acceded to the Indian Union on October 22nd, 1947. But the success of the Indians in driving the insurgents and their Pakistani *Azad* (Free) *Kashmir* allies out of positions which penetrated Pakistan's Punjab frontier prompted the Pakistan army to intervene and led to a direct India—Pakistan conflict during 1948. The fighting, however, was on a small scale and of sporadic nature and was eventually brought to an end by United Nations negotiations in December, 1948. The ceasefire left India in possession of the Vale of Kashmir and the Pakistanis in possession of the mountains.

Nagaland 1956—present

The Nagas, a tribal people living astride the mountainous border of Burma, were reluctant to accept the transfer from British to Indian rule, even though the Indians maintained the policy of minimal interference in their affairs. Demands for independence from India were voiced, and rejected, and in 1956 open insurrection broke out. The original number of Naga 'effectives' was 1500—2500, but many more joined the rebellion, obliging the Indians to increase the strength of the

local paramilitary Assam Rifles (now 18 battalions strong and largely Gurkha in recruitment) and to commit regular troops. In 1966 a sympathetic rebellion erupted among the Mizo hill people of Mizoram. The temperature of the fighting, which continues, has fluctuated but at any one time engaged the presence of 20—30 battalions of troops. Their problems are compounded by the access 'hostiles' have to sanctuary on the far side of the Burmese frontier, in an area not under the control of the Burmese government.

Himalayan Conflict with China, 1962

The Sino—Indian border east, and west of Tibet followed a line which the Chinese regard as having been arbitrarily imposed on them by the British during the era of Chinese weakness in the nineteenth and early twentieth centuries. It had been declared Chinese communist policy before their seizure of power to recover the 'lost' territories and to occupy ('liberate') such former feudal dependencies as Tibet. Tibet was occupied by China in 1950 and thenceforward the communists inherited a policy of aggressive control of the *de facto* frontier, which led to sporadic conflict with the troops with which the Indian government in their turn began to reinforce the Himalayan regions. The two main areas of confrontation were east and west of Tibet, the North—East Frontier Agency, Himachal Pradesh and Ladakh, respectively, and on October 20th, 1962 the Chinese opened large-scale attacks in both sectors. The Indian forward positions were very quickly overrun, a penetration of 30 miles made into Ladakh and in the N.E.F.A. the whole Indian 4th Division were effectively disabled with the loss of its 7th Brigade. India appealed for help to Britain and America, who hastily ferried equipment, but on November 20th the Chinese announced a unilateral ceasefire and their intention to withdraw 20km north of the MacMahon Line (the disputed line of demarcation) in Ladakh, and of the 'line of actual control of November 7th, 1959' in the N.E.F.A. The withdrawal was completed by January 15th, 1963.

The debacle, which led to the removal of the Defence Minister, Krishna Menon, and the Chief of Staff, General Kaul, provoked national outrage, and led to an immediate and large-scale expansion of defence investment and of army numbers, and to a reorganisation of the army for mountain warfare. The development of the Indian Army as a modern fighting force dates from this episode.

Indo—Pakistani (Undeclared) War, 1965

India's humiliation in the 1962 war led to a worsening of her relations with Pakistan, whch was thereby emboldened to harden its own attitude to the policing of its disputed frontiers with India in Kashmir and the Rann of Kutch (south of Karachi). There was an increase in the number of troops on the ceasefire line and in April—May, 1965 a series of clashes between regular troops in the Rann of Kutch which led in September to the outbreak of a 22 day 'undeclared war' along the western frontier. It was precipitated by the incursion on August 5th of 3000 Muslim freedom fighters into Indian Kashmir, which prompted the Indian government to send regular troops to destroy their 'staging posts' in Pakistani Kashmir. In response President Ayub Khan launched a tank attack in the Chamba sector on September 1st, and 3 weeks of fighting followed. It was again brought to an end by United Nations intervention, reinforced by the imposition of an Anglo—American embargo on arms shipments to either side. The military result was a territorial stalemate, minor gains or losses on each side of the ceasefire line cancelling each other out, but the fighting saw the largest-scale tank battle since the end of World War II — from which the Indians emerged winners in numbers of tanks destroyed — and it also testified to a considerable level of military efficiency on both sides, and, it was said, to a marked improvement in the quality of the Indian army since 1962.

Mizo Uprising, 1966

A minor insurrection among the Mizo hill people of southern Assam required the intervention of the army and added to its internal security responsibilities in the area. Unrest continues.

The Bangladesh War, 1971

The Indo—Pakistani conflict was brought on by a declaration of independence by the 'eastern wing' of Pakistan. Its Bengali population had long found themselves the poor relations of their Punjabi compatriots in the 'western wing' and the triumph of the secessionist Awami League in the 1970 elections provided the opportunity to break the links between them. West Pakistan, fearing economic hardship and international demotion should secession succeed, reinforced the units of the Pakistan army in the country and embarked on suppression. Between March and December, over 1,000,000 Bengalese fled from East Pakistan ('Bangladesh', as its Awami league leaders had proclaimed it) and had to be succoured by the Indians in refugee camps near the border. Some of them, with Bengali elements of the East Bengal Rifles, instituted their own campaign against the West Pakistanis and their Bihari allies in Bangladesh, and the fighting between these 'Mukti Bahini' and the Pakistan army soon took on the form of a guerrilla war. After much diplomatic activity by both India and Pakistan, the former seeking international recognition for Bangladesh, the latter foreign support for its campaign of repression, India invaded Bangladesh on December 4th. At the same time fighting broke out on the West Pakistan frontier. In the east, where India deployed eight divisions against Pakistan's four, and could also count on the assistance of 50,000 Mukti Bahini, the campaign was short and completely successful. Within 13 days the whole of Bangladesh had been overrun by concentric advance from 20 starting points and all western troops made prisoners (about 85,000 in all). In the west the war opened on the evening of December 3rd with a Pakistani air strike on Indian airfields, modelled on the pre-emptive strikes with which Israel had assured its success against the Arabs in 1967. India had, however, taken precautions against just such an attack and its effects were small. Pakistan's ground attack which followed was equally unsuccessful: although Pakistani forces fought on unequal terms elsewhere, equality prevailed in the west (12 divisions to 13) but they were unable to cut Indian communications into the Vale of Kashmir, regarded by both sides as the key sector, and were actually obliged to yield ground in Sind. At the ceasefire, declared unilaterally by India on December 16th, and accepted by Pakistan the following day, India held 2750 square miles of Pakistani territory. In human and material casualties Pakistan was also the loser, having lost 8000 men killed to India's 3000, 220 tanks destroyed to 83, and 83 aircraft destroyed to 54; at sea 22 ships (including 2 submarines) to India's 1. In the words of the Institute of Strategic Studies Survey for 1971, 'The outcome was a triumph for the reorganisation of the Indian army after the 1962 Chinese invasion (which) had hardly got under way by the time of the 1965 war . . . It resulted in a complete transformation of the military equation in the sub-continent'.

United Nations Peace-Keeping Duty

India has taken a major part in UN operations since 1948. She has maintained observers on the Egypt—Israel border, in Lebanon and in Yemen, sent a contingent to West Irian in 1962—3, a large force to the Congo (Zaïre) 1960—4 and a field ambulance to Korea, 1950—3. Senior Indian officers have also served as individuals in UN peace-keeping forces.

ORGANISATION

Arms of Service

The domestic organisation of the army, virtually unchanged from the British—Indian, is strongly 'regimental' in character. Most of the infantry and cavalry regiments trace an unbroken ancestry into the mid-nineteenth century and some into the eighteenth (via a web of amalgamations which only experts understand). The infantry regiments are 'family' units, not operational units, their several battalions (six to fifteen in number) rarely serving together in the same formation. The cavalry regiments are equally 'family' bodies but are of a single battalion-sized unit only. Both are generally raised on a 'community' basis (i.e. from the same territorial/linguistic/caste group), a practice again inherited from the British, and officers and men serve throughout their regimental career in the same regiment (though officers not necessarily in the same battalion). In the corps, 'community' recruiting is not the rule; but the engineers preserve the old 'Presidency' division into Madras, Bengal and Bombay groups and recruit accordingly, and the artillery tends to recruit still from the 'martial races' (communities) favoured by the British.

The infantry regiments inherited from the British in order of place in the line are: Punjab Regiment (formerly 2nd Punjab Regiment; senior battalion raised 1751); Grenadiers (1779); Mahratta Light Infantry (1768); Rajputana Rifles (1775); Rajput Regiment (1798); Jat Regiment (1803); Sikh Regiment (1846); Dogra Regiment (1887); Garwhal Rifles (1891). During World War II the following were raised: the Madras Regiment; the Kumaon Regiment; the Assam Regiment; the Bihar Regiment; the Mahar (Machine-Gun) Regiment; the Sikh Light Infantry; the Parachute Regiment. Since independence the Brigade of Guards and the Jammu and Kashmir Rifles have been raised. A Naga Regiment was raised in the late 1960s and also the Ladakh Scouts (see Paramilitary Forces).

The Indians divided with the British the 10 regiments of Gurkha (now spelt Gorkha) Rifles, retaining the 1st, 3rd, 4th, 5th (Frontier Force), 8th and 9th. They subsequently raised the 11th, to accommodate the surplus of Gurkhas who did not wish to transfer to the British army.

The cavalry regiments in order of precedence are: President's Bodyguard (formerly the Viceroy's Bodyguard: raised 1775); 1st Skinners Horse (1803); 2nd Lancers (1809); 3rd Cavalry (1841); 4th Horse (1857); 7th Light Cavalry (1788); 8th Light Cavalry (1787); 9th Deccan Horse (1854); 14th Scinde Horse (1839); 16th Light Cavalry (1776); 17th Poona Horse (1817); 18th Cavalry (1842); 21st Central India Horse (1858). Raised since independence are: 61st, 62nd and 63rd Cavalry. These regiments together form the Armoured Corps. The Training Regiment, Armoured Corps Centre, Ferozepore, it the 15th Lancers.

There are in addition to these combatant regiments a number of paramilitary forces under the control of the central government, the Ministry of External Affairs, or of the States, which descend from the frontier constabulary, the Frontier Scouts and the armed elements of the Indian Police of British days. The most important are the Assam Rifles (not to be confused with the Assam Regiment) which is under the control of the Ministry of External Affairs and is responsible for internal security in Assam, and the Border Security Force.

The corps of the Indian army are: Regiment of Artillery; Corps of Engineers (Madras, Bengal and Bombay Groups); Corps of Signals; Army Service Corps; Army Ordnance Corps;

Corps of Electrical and Mechanical Engineers, Remount, Veterinary and Farm Corps; Corps of Military Police; Army Educational Corps. The Medical Corps forms part of the tri-service Armed Forces Medical Service.

Operational

The organisation of units and formations is on British lines, through corps, divisions, brigades and battalions/regiments. There are two armoured divisions (being re-organised into brigades), eighteen infantry divisions, eleven mountain divisions, five independent armoured brigades, seven independent infantry brigades, one parachute brigade and seventeen independent artillery brigades, including about 20 air-defence regiments. Corps, divisions and independent brigades identified in the 1971 war were: I, II, IV, XI, XV, XXXIII Corps; 1 and 6 Armoured Divisions; 2, 4 (Mountain), 5, 6 (Mountain), 7, 8, 9, 10, 14, 15, 17, 19, 20, 23, 26, 27 and 57 Infantry Divisions; 1 and 2 Independent Armoured Brigades; 191 Independent Infantry Brigades; 50 Parachute Brigade.

Paramilitary Forces

The British—Indian Empire maintained large paramilitary forces, consisting of three main elements: armed units of the Indian Police, which were organised on a provincial basis; the Frontier Constabulary, which maintained law and order on the 'administered' side of the troublesome northern (particularly north-west) frontier; and the Frontier Corps or Scouts, which, under the control of the Indian Political Service of the Home Affairs Department, exercised influence on the 'unadministered' side of the frontier. The Scouts were wholly Muslim in composition and all the Frontier Corps — Northern Scouts, Gilgit Scouts, Chitral Scouts, Khyber Rifles, Kurram Militia, Tochi Scouts, South Wazierstan Scouts, Zhob Militia, Pishin Scouts, Makran Levies and Chagai Levies — went to Pakistan on partition.

The (independent) Government of India preserved the police structure and its remaining elements intact. Each State has its complement of armed police (e.g. the Rajasthan Armed Constabulary which played a part in the opening stage of the war with Pakistan in 1965). The government has created its own equivalent to the armed constabularies in the Central Reserve Police Force, now 60 battalions strong, distributed between 17 Group Centres (it has also assumed the functions of the old railway police) as well as a Central Industrial Security Force, which polices 'public sector undertakings'. In 1965, following the border war with Pakistan, the government created a Border Security Force: its composition is unclear — it obviously fulfils the role of the old Frontier Constabulary and it may have absorbed the Armed Constabularies of the States on the borders; it numbers 100,000. A separate force, the Assam Rifles, now 21 battalions strong and largely recruited from Gurkhas, comes directly under the Ministry of Home Affairs. The Ladakh Scouts, raised in the 1960s and fulfilling the function of the old Frontier Corps which went to Pakistan, is an army unit operating in the high Himalayas.

RECRUITMENT, TRAINING AND RESERVES

Recruitment

Recruitment to the Indian army is an extremely complex, and nowadays politically sensitive, matter. It can be understood only in historical terms, in particular in terms of the nature of the Indian mutiny of 1857. That uprising of the Bengal army against the British was put down largely through the loyalty to the British of the Bombay (and to a lesser extent of the Madras) army and of the various irregular

forces, foremost among which was the Punjab Irregular (later Frontier) Force. The Bengal army was chiefly recruited from high-caste Hindus of Oudh, whereas the other forces were not. In consequence, and in the aftermath, the British resolved to diversify recruiting and to favour those tribes, castes and sects which had sided with them. These so-called 'martial races' were chiefly people of the north-west and north — Punjabi Muslims, Sikhs and Gurkhas. The reorganised Indian army came therefore to consist of regiments which were composed either of a single 'race' of proved loyalty and fighting worth (e.g. Gurkhas, recruited from outside British India) or of a mixture (organised into separate companies in squadrons within the regiment) of other 'martial races'. In time, the issue of loyalty receded but the value-judgement of 'martial worth' gained strength. The British came to consider the peoples of south, central and eastern India to be of little military value (inexplicably since it was with soldiers of these regions that they had conquered the sub-continent) and recruited preponderately from the Punjab, Rajputana, United Provinces, Baluchistan and other north-western and northern areas, and chose only those of high-caste (if Hindu) or of established military reputation (if Muslim). Thus, of the technically casteless Sikhs, the British preferred Jat Sikhs, whose ancestors were high-caste Hindus, to Mazbi Sikhs, whose ancestors were low-caste.

Independent India is avowedly a secular State, which does not favour one caste at the expense of another (unless to attempt to improve the lot of its low-caste and untouchable citizens through 'scheduled caste' legislation). Nevertheless, by 1947 so ingrained had the belief in the desirability of recruiting the 'martial races' become in the army itself — most of whose Indian officers (KCOs) were themselves of the 'martial races' — that it has proved impossible significantly to alter the system. In January, 1949 orders were officially issued to abolish recruitment by classes (the British euphemism for 'martial races') in all arms of service. This is explained in an Indian government publication* which goes on to say, 'For administrative reasons arising out of previous commitments and locations of troops, it was not possible to implement this decision immediately in the case of the infantry and the armoured corps' (i.e. the bulk of the pre-partition army and that providing its combat edge). 'Regiments composed of particular classes, through several decades, developed a certain kind of cohesion and while steps are taken to broad-base their composition, it is essential to ensure that the sentimental attachment arising out of such composition is not suddenly disturbed.' In practice, it has not even been gradually disturbed. The Indian army preserves intact the composition of the historic 'class' and 'class company' regiments; an example of the first sort is the Sikh Regiment, while the Punjab Regiment is an example of the second. However, in the regiments raised during World War II and since, the army with the warm encouragement of the government instituted an eclectic recruitment policy. The Madras Regiment, for example, enlists Indians of every religion and language of southern India, and the Mahar Regiment, which originally recruited only Mahars, recruits many 'scheduled castes' (i.e. untouchables). It seems probable that other technically 'mixed' regiments, like the Brigade of Guards and the Parachute Regiment, are effectively selective, but in the reverse direction, favouring the 'martial races' once more.

It would be unfair to suggest that the army is not attempting to unfreeze the 'community' character of its fighting regiments (as it has certainly unfrozen that of the

* Veukakeshwaran, A. L., *Defence Organisation in India*, Government of India, New Delhi (1969).

services, which are manned from a wide range of 'communities'). Since 1963 there have been deliberate efforts to introduce new 'community' representations into single or restricted 'community' regiments, but it seems that the pattern of recruiting at present is as follows:

'Pure'

Mahratta Light Infantry: high-caste Maharashtra Hindus
Jat Regiment: middle-caste Hindus of Rajastan and Uttar Pradesh
Sikh Regiment: high-caste Sikhs
Dogra Regiment: Dogras (high-caste northern Hindus)
Garwhal Rifles: Garwhalis (Himalayan foothills)
Kumaon Regiment: Kumaonis (Himalayan foothills)
Assam Regiment: Assamese*
Gorkha Rifles: Gurkhas of Nepal

Mixed Company

Punjab Regiment: Sikhs and Punjabi Hindus, high-caste Maharashtra Hindus and Muslims
Rajputana Rifles: Jat, Hindu and Muslim companies
Rajput Regiment: some battalions purely Rajput (high-caste Rajasthan Hindus), others Bengali
Jammu and Kashmir Regiments: Kashmiri Sikhs, Dogras and Muslims

Totally Mixed

Brigade of Guards: in fact consists of separate battalions of Rajputs, Punjabis and other 'martial' communities
Parachute Regiment: separate battalions of 'martial' communities
Madras Regiment: south Indians, completely mixed
Bihar Regiment: eastern low-caste Hindus and Christians
Mahar Regiment: 'scheduled caste' northern Hindus

The armoured corps is generally recruited from the 'martial races' (particularly Jats, Sikhs, Dogras, Rajputs and Maharashtras), and to a lesser extent this also applies to the artillery. The Madras, Bengal and Bombay Groups of the Corps of Engineers (under the British, respectively, the Madras, Bengal and Bombay Sappers and Miners) recruit within their own regions and fairly widely through the communities. The services are all of mixed recruitment.

The recruitment of officers is officially not influenced by 'community' considerations. In fact, the Indian King's Commissioned Officers of the British—Indian army were 'martial' almost to a man, and the proportion remained high for many years thereafter; in 1954—5 about one-third of the army cadets at the National Defence Academy were Punjabis and 15% came from Delhi and its region, while West Bengal and Andhra Pradesh ('non-martial' regions) supplied less than 1%. Since 1962, when the great expansion of the army began, recruitment has broadened, aided by a fall in officers' living standards and a rise in the frequency and duration of postings to the Himalayan frontiers; in consequence many traditionally military families have chosen to send their sons into better-paid and less-onerous careers. It seems probable, however, that within the infantry, cavalry and artillery the officers still come predominantly from the martial communities. Community does not, however, determine with which regiment an officer will serve, nor does language — the 'command' language of the army is Hindi (though English is much spoken).

There is some difficulty in recruiting officers, standards of selection remaining high. By contrast there is none in recruiting soldiers, about 10 applicants presenting themselves

* The Assam Rifles is almost completely composed of Gurkhas.

for each vacancy. The prestige of the 'jawan' remains very high in rural India, and his economic status enviable. Nevertheless, there is considerable recruiting outside India: it is estimated that the army, the Assam Rifles and the Border Security Forces contain about 90,000 Gurkhas.

Training

Infantry recruits are trained in the training battalions of their regiment, others in training units of their corps. Advanced training for officers, JCOs and NCOs of the various arms and services is provided at the Armoured Corps Centre, School of Artillery, College of Military Engineering, School of Signals and Army Signals School, Infantry School, Army Service Corps School, Army Ordnance School, Electrical and Mechanical School, Intelligence Training School, School of Physical Training. Army Educational Centre and School, Army Air Transport School, School of Mechanical Transport and the Corps of Military Police Centre and School. Mountain region training is provided at the School of Mountain Warfare, Darjeeling.

There are a number of tri-service schools for specialist and higher studies, e.g. Land/Air Warfare School, School of Foreign Languages and the Armed Forces Medical College.

Officer training is at three levels: pre-cadet, cadet and staff. In order to improve officer recruitment, the Indian government, developing an idea originating with the British, has created a number (in 1962 eleven) of 'Sainik' schools which provide a British public-school education for would-be applicants to the National Defence Academy. The Army Cadet College at Nowgong provides similar preparation to suitable serving soldiers. The National Defence Academy (age of entry 15—17 years, length of course 3 years) is situated at Khadakvasla, near Poona, and educates cadets of the three services. Army cadets then proceed to the Indian Military Academy, Dehra Dun (age of entry eighteen; length of course 1 year). The I.M.A. is also open to 'Direct Entry Cadets' from high school or university and to technical graduates. Special-to-arm training is given to freshly commissioned officers in the centre or school of his arm. Staff training for captains and majors who pass the competitive examination is given at the Defence Services Staff College, Wellington, south India (course 1 year) and senior staff training at the National Defence College, Delhi, a tri-service institution (course 1 year; civil servants also attend). Indian officers regularly attend overseas staff colleges.

Reserves

Under British rule, India had three reserve forces: the Regular Reserve of the Indian army, composed of time-expired soldiers; the Auxiliary Force (India) — the A.F.I., a volunteer force of Europeans and Anglo-Indians, most of the latter railwaymen as the titles of their units revealed (e.g. The Great Indian Peninsular Railway Regiment); and a small Territorial Force (raised 1920), for India volunteers.

The military value of both the Auxiliary and Territorial Forces was small and they disappeared at independence, understandably so in the case of the A.F.I., since its principal role was as a buttress of British power. In 1951, however, the Indian government decided to re-raise a Territorial army, but it proved difficult to recruit and in 1956 an amending act was passed to draft certain categories of government servant into its ranks. Meanwhile, in May, 1955 the government decided to set up a National Volunteer Force (Lok Sahayak Sena) to give basic military training to 500,000 men, who would not be liable for military service. The idea seems to have been to create a peoples' militia on the Chinese pattern: the force was not to be under control of the army.

In 1965, however, the *Lok Sena* was disbanded, on the creation of a Home Guard, 1,000,000 strong, in the villages, and at the same time the Territorial Army was reorganised and strengthened. It is claimed that 100 units of the T.A. were embodied in 1971.

India now has two reserve forces, the regular army reserve of 200,000 trained soldiers, and a Territorial Army of 40,000. Additionally, there exists a National Cadet Corps, training in which is compulsory for male students in all government colleges.

EQUIPMENT AND ARMS INDUSTRY

Arms industries have been long established in India. The Moghul, Mahratta and Sikh States had their own, the Sikhs in particular producing artillery pieces of the first quality. The East India Company was also quick to establish arms and ammunition factories, a gun foundry being established at Dinajpur in 1768. After the Mutiny of 1857, however, the government instituted a policy of restricting the quantity and nature of arms issued to Indian units: the Indian infantry and cavalry received weapons of an older generation than those carried by the British, and Indian artillery units (except for a few light mountain batteries) were disbanded altogether. The production of weapons in India consequently declined and it was not until the winning of World War II, when the impossibility of equipping the greatly expanded Indian army from British factories became evident, that belated efforts were made to increase the military productivity of the sub-continent.

The Indian army at independence in 1947 was therefore ill-equipped and lacked the means to re-equip itself fully from existing factories. It was to persist in that state for over a decade, as a result of the policies of eschewing foreign military aid (part of the diplomacy of non-alignment) and of concentrating investment in civil projects. These policies, admirable as they were in developing country, were overturned by China's attack on India in 1962. Strategic necessity and popular outcry compelled the government both to accept foreign (largely Russian and British) military assistance, both in the form of goods and cash, and to increase its own investment in military plant.

There are now over 20 defence plants in operation: Jabalpur (vehicle plant), Chandigargh, Shahjahanpur, Kanpur, Bhandara, Varangaon, Nasik, Kirkee, Bombay, Ishapore, Calcutta, Koraput, Secunderbad, Hyderabad, Bangalore (aircraft and electronics), Avadi (tank plant), Vishakhapatnam, Tiruchirapalli, Khamaria, Ambajahari, Aruvankadu, Ambarnath and Muradnagar. India produces most of its own small arms, artillery, ammunition, assembles its own military transport vehicles, builds its own tank, and manufactures high-performance combat aircraft, soon to its own design. It is not yet militarily self-sufficient, but may well become so within the next decade. The cost has been grave; about 20% of government expenditure goes on defence.

Pistol: 9mm Browning HP (Belgium)
Sub-machine-gun: 9mm Sterling (Britain; Indian manufacture)
Rifle: 7.62mm Ishapore (Indian version of Belgian type)
Machine-gun: 7.62mm LAA4 (British Bren; Indian manufacture) and 7.62mm MAG 58 (Belgian FN)
Mortars: 81mm MI6A1 (Britain; Indian manufacture) and 4.2in Brandt (France; Indian manufacture)
Anti-armour weapons: 57mm RCL (USA; infantry platoon anti-armour weapon); 106mm RCL (USA; equips the support company of the infantry battalion); SS-11 ATGW (France; equips the support company of the infantry battalion); ENTAC ATGW (France; equips the support company of the infantry battalion); 100mm anti-tank gun (USSR; equips the support company of the infantry battalion); Harjron missile
Air-defence weapons: 40mm L60/70 gun (Britain; equips the light-air-defence batteries); 3.7in gun (Britain; equips the heavy-air-defence batteries); Tigercat SAM (Britain; equips the missile-defence batteries; 40 in service) ZSU-23/4 guns (USSR); SA-6, SA-9 missiles (USSR)
Artillery: 75mm pack howitzer (USA; obsolescent); 75mm howitzer 75/24 (India; equipping mountain batteries); 76mm mountain howitzer (Yugoslavia; equipping mountain batteries); 25-pounder gun — howitzer (Britain; Indian manufacture; divisional artillery under replacement by Indian gun); 100mm gun (USSR; divisional artillery); 105mm (USA; under replacement); 105mm pack howitzer (Italian–British; divisional artillery); 105mm Abbot SP gun (Britain; equips the artillery of the armoured brigades); 130mm gun (USSR; divisional medium artillery); 5.5in (Britain; under replacement); 152mm gun (USSR; divisional medium artillery); S-23 180mm (USSR)
Armour: APCs: BTR 50/152 (USSR), OT-62 and OT-64 (2A) (Czechoslovakia) (about 700 in service; equip the infantry of the armoured brigades); Light tank: AMX-13 (France; equips some of the armoured regiments; 140 in service); Medium tank: T-54/55 (USSR; equips some of the armoured regiments; 950 in service); T-72 (USSR, 100 in service) and Vijayanta (India; equips most of the armoured regiments; 1100 in service)
Aircraft: The Indian Air Force operates 220 helicopters, including 60 Soviet transport and some Alouette (French) machines, the latter with anti-armour missiles. It also operates 10 fixed wing transport squadrons.

RANK, DRESS AND DISTINCTIONS

Rank

India has preserved the unusual rank structure inherited from the British, who divided the officers of their units into three groups in ascending order: NCOs; native officers (later Viceroy's Commissioned Officers — VCOs); and British officers (later when Indians were admitted to the group, King's Commissioned Officers — KCOs). The intermediate rank of VCO originated from the earliest days of the British–Indian Army, when British officers were few in number and native gentlemen of military experience were naturally employed to fill officers' posts. The system was then retained for reasons of economy and efficiency, and survives into independence through the force of tradition. VCOs are now known as Junior Commissioned Officers (JCOs); they are always promoted from within the ranks of the regiment, in which they fill the majority of junior command appointments (Platoon Commander, etc.). The senior JCO (Subedar-major) acts as principal assistant to the commanding officer.

Officers
*Field Marshal — Asoka lions badge, crossed batons in wreath
General — Asoka lions badge, three stars, crossed swords
Lieutenant-general — Asoka lions badge, two stars, crossed swords
Major-general — Asoka lions badge, one star, crossed swords
Brigadier — Asoka lions badge, three stars
Colonel — Asoka lions badge, two stars

* The rank was created for General Manekshaw, the victor of the 1971 war and the then Chief of the Army Staff.

India

Lieutenant-colonel — Asoka lions badge, one star
Major — Asoka lions badge
Captain — Three stars
Lieutenant — Two stars
Second-lieutenant — One star

JCOs
Subedar-major — Asoka lions badge on cloth backing
Subedar — Two stars on cloth backing
Naib subedar — One star on cloth backing

NCOs
Havildar — Three chevrons
Naik — Two chevrons
Lance-naik — One chevron
Sepoy — —

In the cavalry, the title of subedar is replaced by *risaldar*, havildar by *dafadar* and sepoy by *sowar* (rifleman in rifle regiments). Private soldiers are collectively known as 'jawans'.

Dress

Dress is strongly 'regimental', each regiment jealously preserving its particular distinctions (colour and shape of turban, etc.) which have been inherited from the British—Indian Army, and remain, with the removal of imperial symbols, identical. The every-day order of dress is khaki drill, cut to traditional British Indian Army patterns. The President's Bodyguard retains the scarlet ceremonial uniforms worn in Viceregal days.

Distinctions

Servicemen who won British or British Indian awards before independence retain them, but India has instituted its own system of decorations: the Param Vir Chakra, equivalent to the Victoria Cross, for outstanding bravery in the face of the enemy; the Maha Vir Chakra and the Vir Chakra for acts of lesser bravery; and the Asoka Chakra, class 1, 2 and 3, for bravery other than in the face of the enemy. They are awarded with regard to rank.

Indian infantry regiments (rifles excepted) carry two Colours on parade, the President's and the Regimental; cavalry regiments carry a standard or guidon.

CURRENT DEVELOPMENTS

The Indian army, for over a hundred years before 1947 the most important implement of military power in south and south-east Asia, has staged a remarkable recovery from the decline it underwent in the first two decades of independence. Its triumph in the 1971 Bangladesh war has shown it to be markedly superior to the Pakistani army (with which it never-theless retains a curious step-brotherhood through the common parentage); its ability to police and, if necessary defend the Himalayan frontier with China since its expansion re-equipment, reorganisation and retraining after 1962 appears distinctly credible.

Its life is, however, not problem-free. The cost of maintaining an army of 900,000 throws an increasing strain on the Indian economy and budget, particularly in view of its need to match, largely from domestic resources, the equipment of neighbouring armies which are either militarily self-sufficient, like China, or the beneficiaries of generous foreign aid, like Pakistan. It has a particular problem in recruiting sufficient officers of the right quality, difficult to understand in view of the graduate and middle-class unemployment prevailing in the country, but nonetheless real for that. It has a more general recruiting difficulty, in that the government, and it itself, are committed to the principles of secularity and equality of opportunity for all communities of the Indian population. 'We are all Ksatriya (members of the martial caste) now', said Defence Minister Chavau in 1965, but its component units have particular recruiting traditions, which they are unwilling to modify. The solution of that particular problem must wait, however upon a general transformation of Indian society. In the shorter term, it is threatened by the danger of its induction into the political life of the country. The Imperial Indian Army was notably 'apolitical' — given of course, that its British officers were instruments of British imperial rule. That army nonetheless successfully transmitted to the army of independence, chiefly through the careful selection and training of Indian officers at Sandhurst and the Indian Military Academy, the belief that the political and military careers are absolutely separate. As a result, and almost alone among the armies of ex-colonial States, the Indian army has remained wholly uninvolved in domestic politics, but that has also been due to the central government's success in ruling largely by consent. In consequence such internal disorders as have occurred have not exceeded the ability of the strong and disciplined armed police forces to repress them. The assumption of emergency powers by Mrs Gandhi's government in 1975 threatened to set in train events which might have brought the Indian army's admirable apoliticality to an end. As it happened, the 'emergency' was ended by an electoral reverse and, in the subsequent settling of accounts the army was again untouched by criticism of its role during that controversial period. Her return to power and the endemic communal problems of the country contrive to leave the army beyond politics.

John Keegan

[History and Introduction: T. A. Heathcote]

INDONESIA

HISTORY AND INTRODUCTION

The Republic of Indonesia was proclaimed somewhat hesitatingly by Mr Sukarno and Dr Hatta on August 17th, 1945. Within a few weeks it was involved in a struggle for existence which lasted for some 4 years, and during those weeks the various elements which were eventually to make up the Indonesian army exploded into action all over Java and Sumatra. These fighting units frquently were very different in their origins and subscribed to very different political ideologies. They were in many cases ill-disciplined and for some time many sections were not really under the control of the army commanders. For these reasons they added elements of tumult and additional conflict to the already turbulent and complex pattern of the Indonesian revolution; but there was more than this to be noted about the armed forces in the revolution. Sometimes sections backed particular political parties and so entered into the disputes over leadership and political strategy, while at others the army or major parts of it played an independent role at odds with the civilian government. There was, as a result of this, no unity of outlook in the army, no sense of any subordination to civilian powers, but rather a tradition of being involved in politics, and above all a sense that the army was at least equal to political parties in its contribution to the direction and ultimate success of the revolution. The struggle for independence produced an attitude of mind as a consequence of which the army came to believe that it had as much right (or perhaps a greater right) to help in shaping society as any other group or institution; but it also produced an army that was far from agreed about how society should be shaped.

During the colonial period the Royal Dutch East India Army (KNIL) had controlled the archipelago. In 1940 it was just under 40,000 strong, but was mostly officered by Europeans and Eurasians. A very large section of the rank and file and NCOs were recruited among the Chrisitan population of Menado and Amboina. This continued to be the case when the war with Japan ended, and the KNIL was rebuilt and used in the fighting against the nationalists in Java and Sumatra.

In 1950, shortly after independence, the KNIL was disbanded, 26,000 out of the total strength of 65,000 being incorporated into the Indonesian army, the remainder being either demobilised or becoming members of the Netherlands army. Those who joined the Indonesian army were not given positions of prominence, even where their training might have suggested it. Thus, the Indonesian army has no institutional links with the KNIL, but there were some individuals who had been officers in the KNIL in 1940 and who joined the revolution, and they did have a disproportionate influence. One such was General Nasution who had been to the Bandung Military Academy, but more commonly Indonesian army officers had been NCOs in the KNIL and later received training as officers by the Japanese. President Suharto comes into this category.

The purpose of the Japanese in giving Indonesians military training was to create local defence forces for their own purposes, not to provide local peoples with an instrument to further their national ambitions. Nevertheless, a large number received some sort of training. Those who were officers were imbued with the Japanese 'fighting spirit', and in addition many of them were indoctrinated with a fanatical hatred of things Western. The result was that when the war ended, while there was nothing that could strictly be termed an army, there was a mass of fighting potential. It was led by young men, often very young, fanatically brave and reckless, and determined to use it to prevent the re-establishment of colonial rule, but with very little sense of discipline and little understanding of military organisation or strategy. It has been estimated that in the early years of the independence struggle, perhaps 500,000 men were in some way or other linked with a fighting unit.

The most important of the organisations set up by the Japanese was the PETA (Fatherland Defence Force). Eventually it numbered 37,000, organised in 69 battalions (in Java and Bali), and was officered by Indonesians up to the level of battalion commander. Some 3000 officers were trained altogether, amongst them being President Suharto who rose to be a company commander, and a former Commander-in-Chief, General Jani, who was murdered in the abortive Gestapu coup of 1965, and was a platoon commander. In addition there was the Hei-ho, a sort of Home Guard numbering just over 26,000, but entirely Japanese officered, and various paramilitary organisations from which derived the guerrilla forces known as 'Lascars'. The latter were often uncontrollable, and gave more than their fair share of trouble to all concerned, friend or foe. Much more important, qualitatively, were the officers trained in guerrilla tactics at three special centres set up by the Japanese, and who, according to Pauker, were the hard core of the resistance to the Allies when they returned in 1945.

Battalion commanders were drawn overwhelmingly from the traditional *élites* – the minor aristocracy and Islamic leaders – rather than from the Western educated. Officers of more junior rank were very young and frequently students, and they tended to be particularly influenced by the values of their Japanese teachers. One effect of this was to make much of the army unsympathetic to political leaders like Sjahrir and Hatta who were striving for a settlement, and were thought to be too willing to accept the point of view of the Dutch. Twice, a part of the army went as far as rebelling against the Republic's political leaders, and on the first occasion there was widespread sympathy with the rebels. In July, 1946 the 3rd Division of General Sudarsono kidnapped Sjahrir (who was Prime Minister at the time) in an attempt, in alliance with Tan Malakka's Fighting Front (PP), to wrench the Republic on to a more radical course. Sjahrir had been involved in a political struggle with the PP for some months. He was well aware of the sympathy of important sections of the army to PP, and built up the Siliwangi Division which was controlled by men who were Dutch trained. Together with the Mobile Police Brigade, they were responsible directly to him and it was units from these forces that rescued him. A real danger of civil war within the army existed, until Sukarno persuaded the Commander-in-Chief, General Sudirman, to come off the fence and leave Tan Malakka without significant army support. Two years later, army units were again involved in an attempted left-wing coup, when the 4th Division supported the proclamation of a communist government at Madiun, in September, 1948. Once more the Siliwangi Division was instrumental in restoring the situation. On this occasion, Sudirman was firmly loyal to the government, but even so it was estimated that 35% of the army supported the People's Democratic Front (FDR). One reason for the rising, or at least its timing, was a plan of the Prime Minister, Dr Hatta, to rationalise the army, reducing it from its large and rather unwieldy form to one appreciably smaller, and most importantly, more disciplined, centrally organised and controlled. This would have undermined the influence of the communists and other radicals, although the main intention of the government was to deal with the military weaknesses which had been only too apparent at the time of the 1st Dutch Police Action of July, 1947. The reduction would have involved a rapid reduction of the army from 360,000 to 160,000, but it was far from complete when the 2nd Dutch Police Action led to the overrunning of the Republic's remaining territory in Java, and the capture of most leading Republicans.

Political authority was transferred to Republican leaders in Sumatra who were still at liberty, but in the months after the 2nd Police Action it was the army in Java which kept the spirit of Indonesian nationalism alive through a guerrilla campaign which made life difficult for the Dutch. It is perhaps an exaggeration to say that this compelled the Dutch to negotiate, but one can understand the army's pride in its achievements, and also its feeling that the politicians came to terms too readily when accepting the Roem—van Royen Agreement. Many of them would have preferred to have fought longer, and gained more favourable conditions in the financial area, and a more satisfactory settlement over New Guinea. They may have been wrong in this, but their belief that it was true has shaped their relations with the civilian leadership to a very significant degree.

So far the analysis has been confined to what happened in Java, and this is reasonable for it was the area within which the drama was to a very large extent played out. Nevertheless Sumatra was also very much involved. It had been controlled by the Japanese 7th Army whose headquarters were at Singapore, and this meant that although a policy similar to that of the 6th Army in Java and Bali was followed, and analogous organisations set up to train Sumatrans in self-defence, the revolution in Sumatra was somewhat apart and followed a course which had its own, and rather different, logic. The links with Java were somewhat tenuous, and in the case of military units there was, as a consequence, a quite independent development. Essentially there were two armies. In contrast, in east Indonesia (Kalimantan, Sulawesi and the eastern islands) the Japanese navy had been in control and followed a more conservative policy, not training local groups. Here the Allies regained control with relative ease and handed power back to the Dutch in an orderly way, and therefore these islands did not contribute any units to the Indonesian army (except, of course, for those members of the KNIL who were absorbed in 1950). It is therefore clear that when independence came at the end of 1949, the Indonesian army was no more than the sum of its parts, and these parts differed in many ways from each other according to whether they were guerrilla or 'regular' units, whether they originated (and remained based) in Sumatra or Java (and indeed which part of Java), whether their officers were predominantly Dutch trained or Japanese trained, and where their political loyalties lay. One should note finally that throughout the struggle for independence, operations had tended to be at battalion level, a tendency encouraged by the need to conduct guerrilla operations after the 1st and, even more, the 2nd Dutch Police Actions. Thus the army had a somewhat nebulous existence at higher levels; above battalion or brigade level, it had hardly operated as an army, its senior officers had not handled large units and had a limited appreciation of strategy. Independence would require a for-

midable measure of consolidation and unification to be carried through.

STRENGTH AND BUDGET

Population: 156,000,000
Army: 200,000
Navy: 40,000 (including 12,000 marines)
Air force: 29,000; 45 combat aircraft (about 170 others held in store)
Paramilitary: 12,000 armed police (Police Mobile Brigade); 70,000 militia
GNP: (1980): $67,660,000,000
Defence expenditure (1981 estimate): $ 2,690,000,000

The armed forces in 1966 numbered about 500,000 and the military budget represented almost 5% of the GNP. Since then the number has been reduced to 320,000 (1971—3) and then further to 247,000 (1977). The army's size has declined rather less, and in 1977 was 180,000, almost three-quarters of the armed forces. The defence budget was at first cut back even more severely and in 1970—1 was only 2.25% of GNP. During the period of retrenchment, the reason for which was the priority given to economic development, the naval and air forces suffered worst, with the result that much of their more sophisticated equipment became unservicable and no replacements occurred. These two services were permitted in the mid-1970s to order ships for coastal defence, and aircraft for surveillance and reconnassance, transport, ground attack and counter-insurgency work. This new equipment was either absolutely central for the defence of a vast archipelago, or intended for use in close collaboration with the army and thus enhancing its efficiency. It should be noted, however, that in 1977—8 the air force was allowed to order 12F-5E, four F-5F and eight Hawk aircraft at a total cost of $130,000,000, marking a sharp break with previous policy, and probably indicating a need to raise the morale of the service. The same applies to a less degree to the navy.

COMMAND AND CONSTITUTIONAL STATUS

The unity of the armed forces has been a fundamental concern of *Orba* (the military government period). Once the services had been purged of those considered disloyal or worse, a number of organisational changes took place aimed at reinforcing unity. In 1967 separate service ministries disappeared and in 1969 separate Commanders-in-Chief also went. At the top is the Ministry of Defence and Security, at first headed by President Suharto, and then from 1973—8 by General Panggabean who also held the position of Commander-in-Chief of the Armed Forces. He was replaced in March 1978 by General Yusuf. In place of the separate Commanders are largely managerial Chiefs of Staff for each service.

It is perhaps appropriate at this stage to note the current terminology used for the armed forces and its component services. The armed forces are known collectively as ABRI (Angleatan Bersenjata Republik Indonesia), and consists of four services. These are:

The army, ADRI (Angkatan Darat Republik Indonesia),
The navy, ALRI (Angkatan Laut Republik Indonesia),
The air force, AURI (Angkatan Udara Republik Indonesia),
The police, POLRI (Kepolisian Negara Republik Indonesia)

The first three, the fighting services, are known as the TNI (Tentara Nasional Indonesia). This jargon, and much similar to it, is used almost to the exclusion of more normal language in Indonesian military studies.

ROLE, COMMITMENT, DEPLOYMENT AND RECENT OPERATIONS

Role, Commitment and Deployment

It was a fundamental belief of *Orba* that economics is supreme and this it probably still holds. It governed its diplomacy to a considerable extent, in that the pressing need for aid and private investment in the late 1960s and early 1970s inevitably entailed a peaceful and essentially pro-Western policy. It also led to self-denial over re-equipment on the part of the armed forces, though, as we shall see, this has ceased to be so to a quite significant extent in the last 2 or 3 years. This emphasis on the pursuit of economic success came from a belief that it is the most important factor in avoiding conflict in society, the basic aim of *Orba*. Experience has resulted in some doubts as to whether it is as simple as this, and this is a question we shall have to return to in the final section. The virtual elimination of political party activity has the same motivation. A prosperous, depoliticised society is a united one, the argument runs, and in turn a united society helps ensure the unity of the armed forces. As we shall see a number of organisational changes have been introduced to the same end. Here, of course, the argument comes full circle for a united army is the ultimate guarantee of all the policies leading to national unity.

In practice the army has displayed few, if any, differences about ultimate goals, but there have been disputes about means. In the years after Gestapu, when policy lines were more fluid, a distinctly different line was advocated by General Dharsono of the Siliwangi Division — which may be termed a more openly anti-Sukarno line and a more Western approach. Dharsono fell out of favour, and power and influence became concentrated particularly in the hands of Diponegoro officers. This division has its base in central Java and its officers were more compromising, more indirect in their approach to their ends, more traditional and less Western in their attitudes. Suharto shared this approach, as indeed did Sukarno. It is one of the factors which gave a unity of outlook to the *Orba* and armed forces leadership during the crucial early years.

The Siliwangi–Diponegoro split, although it still exists in some senses, is far less significant than it was in the 1960s There is an obvious difference of attitude between the Javanese divisions, and it is almost inconceivable for a Diponegoro general to be appointed to command the Siliwangi, but it is no longer valid to refer to them as having totally different cultural attitudes. There are certainly differences in society between Westernisers and traditional Javanese, and representatives of both will be found in the army, but it is not institutionalised any longer. It would be more important to point to the antipathy of ABRI to those who wish to bring Islam into politics and government.

The Indonesian army has had a fairly active life in the operational sense; it has however been even more constantly engaged in politics. The intensity of its involvement in political matters during the independence struggle made it unlikely that it would readily accept a subordinate role in which it was the mere instrument of the government. This was true even when a smooth working arrangement with the cabinet existed in the earliest days, for as Herbert Feith argues, army leaders emphasised that ' . . . the army was and would remain a political body . . . composed of nationalists who had joined the force from political conviction, not to earn a living, and could not therefore be stripped of political

influence . . . Withdrawing their subordinates from politics at regional and local levels implied a *quid pro quo*. That *quid pro quo* was a great amount of influence for themselves as army leaders in all such affairs as affected the army's interests and tasks.'

During the early 1950s they came to feel not only that they did not have the influence that they expected, but that they were being prevented from carrying out their tasks effectively by the way in which parliament and the political parties operated. They were not free to deal with Darul Islam in the way they would have preferred because of the influence of some Islamic politicians. Policies agreed on for re-equipping the army were not carried through, and although at the beginning some measure of modernisation and reorganisation was achieved, further steps were frustrated. Not only was this so, but political parties sucked the army into their own conflicts, which had the effect of both deepening political divisions inside the army and even worse dragging its affairs through the mire.

In 1952 Parliament, with Sukarno playing a Macchiavellian role in the wings, frustrated policies aimed at reorganising the army throught the elimination of those who were unable to meet the standards demanded in a modern army. This threatened those who continued to hold to the more inspirational approach of the 'fighting spirit', among whom were many friends and allies of the President. A number of army leaders including the Chief of Staff, Nasution, had already been thinking of an anti-Parliamentary coup, and now in a confused episode in October, 1952, they attempted what is probably best construed as an attempt to press Sukarno to bring about constitutional change. It was frustrated by the President and used by him to replace Nasution by a member of the opposition PETA group, Bambeng Sugeng.

He could not hold his position, and a further crisis in 1955 brought Nasution back, as Major-General, to the position of Chief of Staff. His return was to have a decisive impact on constitutional development and in shaping civil–military relations. Although he was not undisputed master of the army for a year or so, his views, certainly from 1957, can be said broadly to be those of the army. They may be summarised as follows. He had a profound antipathy to political parties for the way in which they encouraged disputes and opened up differences, and through their activities in parliament and elsewhere caused indecision, inefficiency and, worst of all, subversion of the unity of the nation and the army. Parliamentary government encouraged the political parties in these undesirable activities, and it was therefore preferable to have a Presidential system of government with an executive to some extent insulated from both parties and the assembly (which should be at most consultative).

Elections held in 1955 made the system of parliamentary government even more difficult to operate than before, and as the deadlock continued both army and President determined that there should be a fundamental change in the constitutional arrangements. Before this was achieved the nation went through a serious crisis with its climax in the civil war of 1958, and in this the army was divided even more than the nation. The divisions in Sumatra and the other islands had never been integrated with those of Java or controlled very effectively from the centre. In 1956–7 a number of regional grievances surfaced, particularly concerned with restrictions on trade, and army units in the outer islands took the lead in organising smuggling on a large scale. It is not going too far to talk of *de facto* economic autonomy. A year later in 1958 this regional discontent joined with political opposition to the constitutional plans of the President and discontent about his economic policies, and resulted in the PRRI rebellion.

271

Nasution had during 1957 devoted a lot of energy to conciliation of regional commanders, but once rebellion was proclaimed he seems to have had no doubt about the need to crush it. He acted swiftly and decisively, and in restoring unity so rapidly brought the army back to the position of power and influence it had had in 1949. His standing was also greatly enhanced, and as a result much was done to remedy the unsatisfactory situation which had developed in the early and middle 1950s. The army's own command structure was changed so as to weaken the position of commanders in the regions, and for the first time a really unified army existed. It was inevitably dominated by the Javanese divisions, particularly the Siliwangi and the Diponegoro (based on Central Java), and ideas emanating from Java consequently guided its progress and development.

In addition to this the army ensured that when Sukarno's conception of guided democracy was given constitutional form, the position they required for themselves was institutionalised. The new system provided for the army (and other national institutions) to play a direct role in political life as a functional group, allocated seats to it in the People's Consultative Assembly (theoretically the most powerful organ of government), and allowed it to be represented in the Cabinet. In its role as a functioning group it had a duty to be politically active in securing the aims of the national ideology and the national purpose. At the same time, of course, the army was still considered as an instrument of government for the maintenance of security, and in this way we have the emergence of the concept of the army's Dual Function.

The army was already involved in the economy, having taken over control of the Dutch enterprises following the expulsion of the Dutch in 1957 in order to forestall the communist trade unions. With its new view of an extended role in society, the army sought further economic influence to remedy the rather poor performance of previous years. But by far the most important enlargement of its area of involvement in society came from the formulation of the new defence policy, Territorial Defence, and its corollary Territorial Management. These ideas, based on the experience of 1945—9 and influenced by foreign doctrines of 'total' national defence by the whole population, were put forward as the only logical defence policy for a poor under-industrialised country which at the same time insisted on following an independent, non-aligned foreign policy.

The defence scenario envisaged falls into three phases. In the first phase the enemy was if possible to be prevented from making a landing, but given the weakness of the navy and air force this was likely to fail. The second phase would be dominated by the army which, using tactics involving the maximum flexibility and mobility, would inflict constant damage on the enemy while avoiding any action likely to involve its own destruction. During this phase preparations would be made for a counter-offensive in the final phase to drive the enemy out. The success of this policy, particularly in Phase II, would depend upon there being total national resistance. This meant that the army would need the full co-operation of the civilian population who would need to be prepared to advance. The army was only too well aware that, in the various insurgencies of the 1950s, it had not been very successful, and had not been able to rely upon civilian assistance even where it should have been possible to gain it. This led to a wide ranging analysis of its relations with the population as a whole, and to the conclusion that it was an essential part of its tasks to assist in land reform and agricultural improvement, the development of co-operatives or of local industry, and the construction of roads, schools, mosques or whatever was needed by the villagers. These ideas were first used in the successful campaign of the Siliwangi Division against the Darul Islam which led to its final defeat in 1962.

On the grounds that it was a prerequisite of national defence, these policies were made the basis for a national programme of Civic Action. No one was naïve enough to ignore the fact that in undertaking a Civic Action programme, the army was engaging in a socio—political campaign which in an area like Central Java competed with the activities of the Indonesian Communist Party (PKI). To take in one stage further. Civil Action might be of value in national defence, it was even more likely to be important in the case of conflict between the army and the PKI. Not surprisingly the PKI was intensely hostile to the whole concept, but at the beginning the army was able to impose considerable restrictions on what the PKI could say and do. The fact that it managed to survive, and from about 1962 to re-emerge as a serious political force, was due to President Sukarno's need to break out of the straight-jacket of consensus imposed on him by the army. To gain freedom of action he did everything he could to build up the parties and particularly the PKI, and then to act as a pivot around which the parties and army moved. This balance of forces he termed NASAKOM — involving national religious and communist blocks each of which represented a significant section of the nation, and therefore could not be ignored. NASAKOM represented a consensus totally alien to that which the army had created in 1958—9 and one which it greatly disliked. It had never forgiven the PKI for the stab in the back in 1948 at Madiun, quite apart from its rejection of its social and political philosophy.

The change in the army's fortunes paradoxically came about through the two military campaigns of the 1960s, the West Irian conflict and Malaysian Confrontation. The former greatly strengthened the President's position, for he was closely associated from the beginning with the demand for a transfer of sovereignty, and his diplomacy brought it about. The PKI as the most vocal of anti-imperialists also benefitted. In the case of the services, the Navy and Air Force gained most from the West Irian affair in that they were considerably expanded and received much modern equipment. Their political weight increased, and they were encouraged to use it in an independent way by Sukarno. This division in the services was made more worrying to the army by the fact that radical influences grew in all services, particularly in the air force. Confrontation had more far reaching effects, for the PKI was very much in the forefront, demanding more and more effective action, accusing the army of being lukewarm, and using the whole episode to demand changes of policy and changes in society which would strengthen its position and open up new possibilities. As in 1957 the army took over foreign enterprises to pre-empt the communist trade unions and so again extended its economic influence, but the PKI mounted a violent campaign for land reform, and a noisy and sustained one for the creation of a Fifth Force to consist of armed peasants and workers. This would take over the task of Confronting Malaysia from the other four services. It was a demand which the army equally strenuously resisted, but it indicated the extent to which the PKI was on the rampage.

In contrast the army was on the defensive, uncertain of its path and itself divided. Those who had seen the extent to which the West Irian affair had changed the political scene must have been concerned about another glorious war of liberation. If Britain chose to stand her ground the prospects were somewhat uninviting, and indeed promised little but trouble; while victory, if West Irian were a guide, seemed likely to advance the fortunes of the army's rivals rather than its own. But many were far from cautious, looking forward much more to the expected glory, and unattracted by the alternative of Civic Action. Equally, it was difficult to withstand Sukarno's vivid flow of oratory denouncing the Malaysian concept as an OLDEFO (Old Established Forces, a Sukarno acronym for Western imperialists and their lackeys) plot to frustrate the democratic wishes of the North Kalimantan people. The split in the army was symbolised by the promotion of General Yani as army Chief of Staff in place of Nasution who was given the somewhat empty post of Chief of Staff of the Armed Forces in June, 1962. Nasution was steadily reduced in stature over the next 2 years, and increasingly Sukarno was apparently able to impose his will.

Nevertheless the overt moves of the PKI to increase its power met with solid army resistance, and it was probably this which led to the Gestapu plot with its elimination of several of the key figures of the army. Gestapu showed the extent of the PKI's penetration of the services. Not only was the Chief of the Air Force deeply involved and the Halim air base the scene of the mutilation of the generals, but the army itself was seen to have been affected. Considerable sections of the Diponegoro Division had been subverted, and it has been stated that 430 officers had eventually to be purged.

More fundamentally, the events immediately following, involving the massacre of hundreds of thousands of communists and their supporters, showed how deep and bitter the divisions in Indonesian society had become. Sukarno did his best to protect them against the wrath of the army and the knives of Muslim youths and others, but failed and in failing brought about the collapse of the political structure on which his dominance had been based. For a while those who still sympathised with him or held him in some awe prevented his removal from office. But after March 11th, 1966 when General Suharto, the victor of Gestapu, was granted wide ranging executive powers, the office did not mean much. It meant nothing at all a year later when Suharto was sworn in as Acting President. In this way began Orba (Orde Baru — a new order), the third period of constitutional history since 1949, and one this time entirely shaped by the army.

Constitutionally there were not fundamental changes. The establishment of a Presidential Constitution in 1958 had, as we have seen, been brought about with Nasution's approval, and the institutions of Guided Democracy had provided a place for the armed forces. That place was now to be much larger, and those forces in society which had perverted Guided Democracy were in contrast to have no place. But the legal relationships between institutions were unaltered. The People's Consultative Assembly (MPR) which lays down policy lines and elects the President was to consist of 920 members, 460 being Members of Parliament and a further 112 being selected in proportion to party strength, 131 coming from provincial assemblies, 10 representing less successful parties, while 207 were nominated by the President from the armed forces and other functional groups. In Parliament, of the 460 members, 100 were nominees of the President again from the armed forces and functional groups, and 360 elected. Elections held in 1977 resulted in the government sponsored group (Sekber Golkar — Joint Secretariat of Functional Groups) winning 231 seats. Thus in Parliament the government could rely on the support of 331 representatives of functional groups, and in the MPR it could rely on an even higher percentage. The other parties represented in Parliament and MPR are the Partai Pesatuan Pembangunan (PPP) which is the most significant of them and represents Islam, and the Partai Demokrasi Indonesia which combines Christians and those of a secular disposition. One writer has contrasted the NASAKOM structure of Sukarno with the NASAGOLAB as he terms it, i.e. National plus Religious plus Golkar plus Armed Forces. The last two are obviously overwhelmingly preponderant, and reflect the almost total dominance of government by the armed forces and those groups which identify with the armed forces. The way in which the electoral laws were designed to suit the armed forces, and the election campaigns of 1971 and 1977 were managed by them in favour of their chosen instrument, Golkar, equally reflected the power of the army and its determination that that power should be sustained.

However, in Orba the armed forces have penetrated into society in many other ways than simply the constitutional and political, indeed there is no significant aspect of the nation's life with which they are not concerned. Territorial Defence and Territorial Management have been enormously expanded into what the former Minister of Defence, General Panggabean, named 'Total People's Defence and Security'. The logic of this concept is that defence and security involve the whole people as well as the armed forces, and that the effectiveness of the people (and the armed forces) depends upon the economy, the educational system, the social structure, the moral and cultural vitality of the nation, and so on. Ultimately it is difficult to make any fundamental distinction between the two functions of the armed forces, that of serving defence and security, and that of acting as a social force. Indeed critics of this development have said that Dual Functionalism (Dwi Fungsi), as it is known, has no meaning whatsoever in the current context, and there is only one function, that is, there is total control of society by ABRI.

At the highest level, military personnel are found in charge of economic enterprises, the most obvious example being that of Pertamina which was built up by General Ibnu Sutowo, running local government — provincial governors are members of the armed forces — and in control of public utilities. ABRI recognises this as being a vital part of its activities. Officers who undertake these tasks have to resign from the active list, and they then come under the classification of Kekaryaan (Civilian Duties). There is a Kekaryaan section at HANKAM (Department of Defence and Security) with a Chief of Staff overseen by a Kekaryaan Committee of some considerable power, which is concerned with the placing of ABRI personnel in the economy and public life. Not only is this so, but the highest mililitary academic institution, the National Defence College (LEMHANNAS), has recently become rather more like a National College of Administration than its name would imply, and is training senior officers of the rank of brigadier and above for their civilian tasks, rather than being centred on defence studies. It is now virtually a requisite for appointment to top administrative positions to have passed through it.

At one time the rationale for Dwi Fungsi, especially in the economic sphere, was that the armed forces were the Samurai of Indonesia, but in the last few years this view has been looked at rather sceptically. One reason has been the evident failures, above all the heroic misjudgements of Ibnu Sutowo in the management of the national oil conglomerate Pertamina, which piled up such enormous debts that it required the Bank of Indonesia to use all its resources to rescue the company, and indeed the State. It is argued that there is no obvious evidence that members of ABRI are abler in managerial terms, although it is accepted that ABRI is the most significant modernising force in the country. Dwi Fungsi brings with it the dangers of abuse of power and of corruption, and critics say that the negative sides of Kekaryaan are at least as prominent as its more positive ones.

When one turns to look at the Civic Mission in its more traditional form as envisaged by Nasution, army units are seen to be involved at various levels. In rural areas they build roads, schools and mosques, and help in small irrigation projects. Sometimes, and this is particularly the case in the outer islands, they are involved in more ambitious schemes. In Central Sulawesi there is an enormous project for bringing 17,000 ha of land into cultivation, though, one should hasten to add, this is not being managed even primarily by the army. One army battalion has a specific amount of land allocated to it, which it is bringing into rice cultivation. Further north, in Menado, numbers of Bailey bridges have been erected to improve communications.

Two features of the Civic Mission must be stressed. One is the way the army is integrated at every level into local society. The Provincial Liaison Committee at the Daerah (Province) level is headed by the KODAM commander (see later, p. 321), and at each level downwards the same is true. Every village in the country has its village NCO who works closely with the local police and the village head, and puts up proposals to the KODIM (see later, p.321) for implementation. The other is the extent to which the army prepares its officers for these activities and organises itself for them. As will be seen, much time is spent at Staff College in analysing the social situation, and training officers for carrying out the civic mission (see later, p. 322). In addition the army staff organisation besides having four branches which deal with such standard military matters as operations, intelligence, personnel and logistics has a fifth branch known as *territorial*. On the one hand this devotes itself to the specific defence aspects of territorial defence, but it is also concerned with the Civic Mission as such. This pattern of organisation is found at all levels from the KOWILHAN (see p. 321) to the smallest administrative unit. It need hardly be added that such a system, besides preparing for territorial defence, provides an internal intelligence network covering every island and every village.

Recent Operations

The Indonesian army was involved in fighting almost before it was born. It was often necessary in August and September, 1945 to fight the Japanese for arms, although the severity of the fighting varied considerably. Admiral Mountbatten had ordered the Japanese not to surrender to unauthorised persons, an order often disobeyed or impossible to carry out. He also ordered them to hold certain key towns where prisoners of war and internees (APWI) were concentrated, and severe fighting occurred at Bandung and Semarang. When British forces landed, they moved to protect the APWI where possible and a number of actions took place, notably a series of running battles on the road from Djakarta to Bandung and in the Semarang—Mageland area of central Java. At Surabaya a major battle occurred in which the Indonesians fought fanatically against the 5th Indian Division, incurring 5000 casualties of whom probably 2000 were killed. This battle is considered by some to have been decisive in dissuading the British from making an attempt to conquer Java, although in fact all the evidence points to their never having had such intentions. Apart from this, it was the first major battle and the most bloody encounter of the war for independence, and in consequence November 10th is celebrated in Indonesia as Heroes' Day. The whole campaign pinned down three British (Indian Army) divisions from October, 1945 until May, 1946 when they began to withdraw, which is a tribute to the tenacity of the Indonesians. It could also be argued, however, that it left them less able to withstand the Dutch Police Action of July, 1947 which resulted in the rather rapid seizure of the economically significant areas of Sumatra and most of Java apart from the central area. Resistance could only take the form of guerrilla action, and this was a constant problem for the Dutch. Preparations had been made to continue this in central Java, and when the Dutch did over-

run this area in December, 1948 they did not find their occupation a very comfortable one. Nevertheless, it was not crucial, international pressure being far more important in persuading the Dutch to grant independence eventually.

The army was involved in a number of small operations in 1950, when the Republic destroyed the federal structure. In the process it, like Indonesia itself, established a new unity. The most important operation was that undertaken against the South Moluccan rebellion, which was extinguished easily enough apart from a prolonged guerrilla struggle on Ceram island. In addition the Darul Islam rebellion west Java also was a thorn in its flesh. The army which still contained so many guerrillas was not at all successful in dealing with its problems of guerrilla war. In 1958, it was divided among itself, with much of the army in Sumatra and Sulawesi joining with pro-Western politicians and experts in the PRRI—Permesta rebellion. General Nasution dealt with these swiftly and efficiently, even though they involved air- and sea-borne landings. At the same time it must be added that the rebels showed little appetite for battle and even less tactical skill in preparing to defend airfields or beaches. They had hoped not for a war but for a political deal. But, as in the previous cases the Permesta guerrillas in Sulawesi held out for several years after the main forces had been destroyed. Not until the Siliwangi had adopted a more socio—political approach, later as we shall see developed into the doctrine of Territorial Management, was it to find a solution to guerrilla war. By 1962 the Darul Islam had at last been eliminated as a result of what across the Straits of Malacca was called a 'hearts and minds' campaign.

By 1960 the Dutch were once more the real enemy and the scene of activities was west New Guinea. The army had little chance to show its ability, however, since the Dutch had sufficient control of sea and air to prevent all but scattered landings. In any case Sukarno relied more on isolating the Dutch diplomatically, and force was threatened and used only so far as it was necessary to jog the USA into a 'mediating' position. It may have been that he had similar intentions when mounting the Confrontation of Malaysia, but it did not work out that way. Britain and Malaysia were not forced into a diplomatic corner. Militarily the Indonesian army was pulled into a campaign it did not want and was not technically equipped to deal with. 1963 and early 1964 showed that the Borneo dissidents trained in Indonesia were ineffective politically and militarily. The weakness of the Indonesian air and naval services prevented any but the most trivial action against the Malaysian peninsula. And so in the latter part of 1964 and throughout 1965, the Indonesian army engaged the British and Malaysian armies in a furtive war along the long frontier between Kalimantan and Sarawak/Sabah. The Indonesians fought competently and bravely, but could not match the experience, particularly of the Gurkha battalions, nor did they have the helicopters or logistic back-up which enabled so few British units to cover such a large territory. By the time Sukarno was fatally weakened by the Gestapu affair, the TNI recognised that it had been neutralised and was anxious to end the affair.

Since then there have been actions in 1965—8 to deal with the supporters of Gestapu, with PKI guerrilla activities in north-west Kalimantan and central Java, and the rather more important involvement in Timor. Indonesian units, reputedly volunteers, were landed in Portuguese Timor on December 7th, 1975 after pro-Indonesian parties had called on them for help against the left-wing Fretilin forces which controlled much of the half-island. The Indonesian forces were not well organised and suffered considerable casualties. Ten years of concentration on internal security and the civic mission at the expense of training and preparation for such operations are considered by many to have been an important reason. They did not find it difficult to control the bulk of the half island, but remnants of Fretilin formed guerrilla forces which 2½ years later were still in existence. The army had evidently forgotten the lessons of the early 1960s and lost the abilities they showed during Confrontation, and it has taken 2 years to re-learn them. Both there, and in West Irian to a smaller extent, heavy handed sweeps, burning of villages and similar actions were commonly used, and as usual were counter-productive. A high percentage of combat forces have now had a spell of duty in Timor and combat training has also been increased in the various commands. This is one of the reasons why there is confident talk of the imminent end of the Timor guerrilla war, though West Irian remains a problem, and a more intractable one to which there is no military solution possible, only a political one.

ORGANISATION

A considerable number of army personnel, estimated at about a third of its total strength, are believed to be involved in civil and administrative duties at any given time. Combat forces consist of 13 infantry brigades (39 infantry battalions) and two air-borne brigades (six battalions), together with an armoured cavalry brigade. In addition to this there are four independent battalions of para-commandos, a field artillery regiment, an air defence regiment, four para/commando (Special Forces) groups, four engineer construction battalions, eight field engineer battalions and 37 independent infantry, artillery and engineer battalions. Of these, six brigades are under KOSTRAD: three infantry brigades, the armoured cavalry brigade and the two air-borne ones. These are capable of being deployed as two divisions, and while at present they are all stationed in Java, there is talk of some deployment in the outer islands.

The armed forces are organised according to a territorial system. There are four regional commands (originally six) known as KOWILHAN, covering Sumatra and north-west Kalimantan the case of KOWILHAN I; Java, Madura and Nusa Tenggara (Lesser Sunda Islands) in that of KOWILHAN II; Sulawesi and the remainder of Kalimantan in that of KOWILHAN III; and the Moluccas and west Irian in that of KOWILHAN IV. Army generals command the first three, the fourth being under an Admiral, but each is a combined head-quarters. Beneath, there are separate organisations for each service. In the case of the army there are 17 KODAMs (Daerah Military Commands). These are two-brigade strong in the three Java KODAMs and in Jakarta Command and are then headed by major-generals. Elsewhere they are of brigade strength or the equivalent. Beneath them are KOREMs (in Java), KODIMs at district, i.e. *Kabupaten* level and KORAMILs at the sub-district (*ketjamatan*) level. These territorial commands, besides being concerned with simple defence matters, are also involved in quasi-political affairs, being responsible for intelligence, internal security and liaison with elected bodies and officials in carrying out the mission of the armed forces. It should be noted that these KODAMs (and in the case of the navy and air force the eight KODAERALs and five KODAVs, respectively) are the highest level at which individual services function separately. Apart from the ordinary Combat Commands there is also KOSTRAD, the Strategic Reserve Command. It was from his position as Head of KOSTRAD that General Suharto was able to organise resistance to the Gestapu plot, and it can be seen as a strike force directly under central command.

The Daerah Military Commands (KODAM) are:

I   Iskandarmuda (Aceh)
II   Bukit Barisan (north Sumatra)
III 17 Agustua (west Sumatra)
IV   Sriwijaya (south Sumatra)
V   Jaya (Jakarta)
VI   Siliwangi (west Java)
VII Diponegoro (central Java)
VIII Brawijaya (east Java)
IX   Mulawarman (east Kalimantan)
X   Lambung Mangkurat (south Kalimantan)
XI   Tambun Bungai (central Kalimantan)
XII Tanjungpura (west Kalimantan)
XIII Merdeka (north and central Sulawesi)
XIV Hasanuddin (south and south-east Sulawesi)
XV   Pattimura (Maluku)
XVI Udayana (Lesser Sundas)
XVII Centrawasih (west Irian)

KOSTRAD, under the direct control of the ministry, has 16–19,000 men, organised into one armoured and three infantry brigades, with an artillery regiment and an air combat command of two airborne brigades. KOPNESANDHA, the Special Forces Command, has 4500 men in four para/commando groups.

The Fourth Service: The Police

The police are the second largest service in terms of numbers and include a Mobile Brigade. They do not have a territorial organisation as the other services, and are not represented at the KOWILHAN joint service headquarters. The highest level of command is the KOMDAK, of which there are seventeen, coinciding with the KODAM. The police in these are responsible to the Governor of the Daerah, and through him to the Home Minister, and less significantly to the elected Daerah assembly. They wear medium-brown uniforms with similar insignia to those of the army.

The Marines: The infantry is organised into two regiments of three battalions each with a close support regiment, three amphibious assault, one artillery and one air defence battalions. Bases are at Jakarta and Surabaya.

RECRUITMENT, TRAINING AND RESERVES

The Indonesian army is essentially a volunteer army. Conscription exists in theory and occasionally specialists such as doctors, engineers and lawyers are conscripted for limited periods. Recruits undergo a basic training of 3–4 months at the regimental centre of the KODAM, followed by a further period of perhaps 4 months of specialist corps training at the appropriate national corps centre. They are then posted to the KODAM for battalion service, and after 1–2 years they rise to the rank of corporal or sergeant, the criterion for promotion being essentially length of service or skill, not leadership qualities. NCOs attend courses and have to pass promotion subjects, and each KODAM has a regimental centre for training, although this is primarily infantry training. The centres are generally well run.

Officers have to pass through the various academies. Entry is highly competitive, and is open to those who at the age of 18 years have had 12 years of schooling and have the appropriate leaving certificate. The demand for places is so great that it is possible to cream off the most able in society – 100,000 apply each year. There are four academies, of which the most important is the Magelang Academy. It is at one and the same time the Army Academy and the general Academy, and all ABRI cadets spend their first year at the general Academy, only then going on to the specialist (Army, Navy or Air Force) Academies where they study for a further 3 years. They come together again at the end of the course when they graduate as second-lieutenants or the other service equivalents.

Officers serve 2–3 years before promotion as lieutenant, a further 3 years before becoming captains, and then 4 years before achieving the rank of major. Only after achieving that rank is promotion by ability and personal character. Before looking at the Staff College system, it is worth noting that there are two other ways to gain commissions. There is the Officer Candidate School at Bandung which provides a path for NCOs to become officers. This is an extremely tough course, mentally and physically, and lasts 9 months. Candidates have to have reached the rank of sergeant, and so they graduate at about the age of 23 or 24 years. It is an avenue of promotion particularly for administrators and technicians. There is, secondly, professional entry direct from the universities to provide doctors and engineers as required.

Staff College organisation was reshaped in 1974, prior to which there were four Staff Colleges (SESKO). They were brought together under the title of SESKOABRI (Armed Forces Command and Staff Colleges). In practice, however, the services still run their own colleges, to which officers go with the rank of major, but it is necessary to emphasise the Joint Wing Staff College (SESKOGUB). This has a particular significance in that it takes rather more senior officers, at the level of lieutenant-colonel, and it is fairly clear that it is preparing the middle to senior rank officers who have already passed through their own special colleges for their role in civil affairs. No foreign students have so far been admitted to SESKOGUB. Even in the case of SESKO army course (SESKOADRI), a considerable amount of time is taken up in studying the social background and it is necessary to emphasise the war both military training, and training for the civic mission and for Kekaryaan, are built in to officer training, and increasingly so at the senior levels. In 1974 the Army Staff College was busily preparing its officers for the elections to be held in 1977 and providing them with ideological viewpoints, e.g. a bias against Islam in politics. As noted before it is by no means easy, nor would the Indonesians consider it desirable, to make any fundamental distinction between military training and training for the role in society. It can bring its problems, and some have argued that it has meant that officers are less well prepared to carry out their professional military tasks, a view which many observers of the Timor operation would whole-heartedly endorse.

EQUIPMENT AND ARMS INDUSTRY

Indonesia has a local small-arms industry and manufactures 7.62mm and 9mm ammunition. The army's heavy equipment is imported. Most is British, French or Russian, but since the breach with the Soviet Union the Russian equipment is short of spares. It is known that much equipment is out of service but, as there is little current operational need for equipment heavier than small arms, this is not a serious military impediment.

Rifle: 7.62mm BM-59 (Italy; made at Bandung arsenal)
Sub-machine-gun: 9mm PM Model VIII (Indonesia; made at Bandung arsenal)
Machine-gun: 0.30in Madsen (Denmark; made at Bandung arsenal) and 7.62mm DPM and SMG (USSR)
Mortar: 120mm M-43 (USSR; 200 in service)
Anti-armour weapons: 90 and 106mm M-40 recoilless rifle (USA) (France)
Air-defence weapons: 40mm L60/70 Bofors (Sweden; Britain; 90 in service) and 57mm M-50 gun (USSR; 200 in service)

Artillery: 76mm M-48B-1 pack howitzer (Yugoslavia; 180 in service), 105mm M-101 howitzer (USA; 18 in service) and 122mm M-55 gun/howitzer (USSR)
Armour: Ferret scout car (Britain; 60 in service); Saladin armoured car (Britain; 75 in service); 60 Saracen, 200 AMX-VC1, 60 Commando APC BTR 40 and BTR 152 (USSR: 130 in service); M-5 Stuart light tank (USA; obsolete), PT-76 light tank (USSR; 75 in service) and AMX-13 light tank (France; 93 in service)
Aircraft: Two Alouette III, 6 Bell 205, 16 BO-105 helicopters; three light aircraft. The air force operates 18 C-130s and 12 C-47s, as well as about 55 other transports and observation aircraft

Two further comments must be made about the heavy equipment. While all the armour can be used to control student unrest and for similar internal purposes, the only really serviceable armoured vehicles are the AMX-13s which are being rebuilt and of which about fifty were ready in mid-1978, and the V-150 wheeled armoured cars mounting either 90mm cannon or twin 30mm machine-guns, which have recently been purchased. The artillery branch suffers desperately from lack of ammunition which prevents proper training of gunners, while poor maintenance in all fields is recognised as a serious problem. The bottleneck here is lack of trained technicians, something of which ADRI is only too conscious.

RANK, DRESS AND DISTINCTIONS

Ranks and Insignia
Working and combat uniforms are of an olive drab colour. The insignia worn by the various ranks are as follows:

General — Four stars
Lieutenant-general — Three stars
Major-general — Two stars
Brigadier-general — One star
Colonel — Three emblems which are a stylised version of a nut
Lieutenant-colonel — Two such emblems
Major — One such emblem
Captain — Three bars
Lieutenant — Two bars
Second-lieutenant — One bar
Candidate officer (equivalent to cadet) — One bar in outline
First assistant lieutenant (Equivalent to WO1) — Two zig-zag bars
Second assistant lieutenant (equivalent to WO2) — One zig-zag bar

The above insignia are in yellow metal, In the case of ceremonial and service dress they are worn on epaulettes on both shoulders. On combat uniforms generals wear them on both collar tips, all other commissioned officers and assistant lieutenants wearing them on the right collar tip only.

Sergeant-major — Four yellow chevrons
Chief sergeant — Three yellow chevrons
Sergeant class I — Two yellow chevrons
Sergeant class II — One yellow chevron
Corporal class I — Two red chevrons
Corporal class II — One red chevron
Private class I — Two red bars
Private class II — One red bar

These badges of rank are worn on both arms in all dress, and are of cloth.

CURRENT DEVELOPMENTS

It has been suggested earlier that economic success has not automatically meant the avoidance of conflict, indeed some aspects of the way in which economic growth has been achieved have increased conflict. Members of ABRI, notably those who are involved in economic activities, have been accused of corruption, as indeed have those in a position to place lucrative contracts. Their links with businessmen, particularly Chinese businessmen and with other foreign interests, have been particularly commented on. The Chinese are considered to have made an absolute killing out of *Orba*, and there is also widespread hostility to foreign capital, particularly Japanese and American. Part of the revival of the Sukarno cult comes from those who agree with his former demand to stand on one's own two feet.

There is also a sense in which the army does not really seem confident that economic success does produce unity, and when any criticism occurs, far from taking a relaxed attitude and waiting for economic growth to take care of the problem, it overreacts to it. This could be seen most clearly in January, 1974 when the visit of Prime Minister Tanaka of Japan led to the Malari riots, and, more recently, at the beginning of 1978 when the students demanded that someone other than Suharto should stand for President. Their demonstrations were met by a very heavy-handed response, most notably at the University of Yogyakarta. It is interesting to note that General Dharsono, the former Siliwangi commander, who became the first Secretary General of ASEAN, lost that position when he came out in favour of the students, accepting their argument that economic disparities had grown under *Orba* and that there was need for action. Dharsono's dismissal was an example of over-reaction, but it is significant that he and those who shared his views to some extent, such as Nasution, were brushed aside without difficulty.

Generally ABRI has managed to handle its crises reasonably well. General Sumitro, who at the time of the Malari riots was Head of KOPKAMTIB(Command for the Restoration of Peace and Order) and whose policy of allowing more open discussion and the expression of differences was considered to have encouraged the violence, was retired with no serious repercussions. And when the affairs of Pertamina led to the need for a stupendous rescue operation to deal with the debts run up by Ibnu Sutowo, Sutowo was removed from his office and replaced with the minimum of disturbance. It has, of course, to be admitted that it did nothing to boost the image of ABRI as the source of infallible and dynamic tycoons. It would be too much to expect 15 years to pass without some differences between leading figures, or the occasional hiccup (even if Pertamina was more of a violent spasm), but it is not apparent that these differences have led to any fundamental divisions within ABRI.

It is frequently asked whether there is a serious division between the old guard, the generation of 1945, and the new Magelang generation, that is to say those who are the products of the academies and do not have the nationalist and political background of their elders — and, if so, what is the difference. The Magelang generation could be expected to be more professional, and there have been rumours of discontent about the handling of Timor amongst them. This generation includes all those up to the rank of colonel and some above, and they must in any case begin to take over the senior positions to a considerable degree in the next few years. It does seem unlikely that the new men will readily abandon the power held by their elders, but the prospect of change gives scope for the most interesting speculation, particularly since it will come as President Suharto draws to the end of his third term.

Stuart Drummond

IRAN

HISTORY AND INTRODUCTION

The history of modern Iran since 1921 has been utterly dominated by two powerful and autocratic Shahs, each of whom climbed to a position of total control mainly by means of an intimate alliance with the Iranian army. With the exception of the period 1941–53, during the troubled early years of the last Shah's reign, the relationship between Shah and army was the key to Iranian politics.

The prestige of the old Persian army, and eventually the larger part of Iran's independence, were destroyed in the course of the nineteenth century by the arrival of Russian and British influence in the area. Russian military power appeared on the Caucasian frontier when the Tsar accepted the Georgian crown in 1800, and in the first major military clash in 1827 the Persian army, though it fought well, was utterly defeated by Russian forces. The treaty of Turkoman-chai in 1828 fixed the present Russian–Iranian border, but without the counterweight of British pressure there is little doubt that Russian imperial forces (which also arrived on Iran's north-eastern borders later in the century) would have made further substantial incursions into Persian territory. As it was, the middle and later parts of the nineteenth century in Iran saw a continuous Anglo–Russian struggle for influence which preserved the country's territorial integrity, but virtually extinguished its independence. Central authority steadily diminished, the Persian crown became hopelessly indebted to foreign (mostly Russian) creditors, and the old Persian army ceased to be a serious military force.

The ancestor of the modern Iranian army was the Cossack Brigade, founded by Nasir-ed-Din Shah after he had been impressed by the Cossack guard of honour provided him on his way through the Russian Caucasus during his second European trip in 1878. It was not only trained but also commanded by Russian officers, and was the first military force in Iran to be organised and equipped on European models. By the early twentieth century the old army was in headlong decline, and the Cossack Brigade, plus a gendarmerie trained and commanded by Swedish officers, were the only efficient forces of order available to the Iranian crown. They were far too small, however, to make any impact on the problems of external pressure and internal fragmentation that beset the Persian government.

The first nationalist reaction of a recognisably modern type to Iran's plight was the Constitutional Movement of 1906. Though its motives were mixed and its strategy confused, it was principally an attempt by the tiny handful of educated Iranians to rescue their country from its humiliations by reforming its domestic institutions to make them able to resist foreign pressures more successfully. They drew support from the less articulate anger of the Persian masses against foreign arrogance and domestic decay, but their own programme was typical of such a time and place, putting its faith in the direct transplant of the liberal democratic political institutions of contemporary Europe as a means of restoring Iran's power and prosperity. The Court, traditionalist and despotic, but also bankrupt and militarily helpless, gave in to their demands, and granted a constitution and an elected national assembly (*Majlis*) in October, 1906.

Whatever hope of national regeneration such a programme ever offered, however, was immediately dashed by the Anglo–Russian Entente of 1907. As part of the alliance-making process leading up to World War I, Britain and Russia composed their differences along their imperial borderlands in Asia and thereby ended the rivalry which had been Iran's sole guarantee of independence in the previous 75 years. The two empires agreed to divide Iran into spheres of influence, and northern Iran, including the capital, Tehran, fell into the Russian sphere.

The Russian imperial government rightly regarded the Constitutional Movement as a nationalist threat to its dominant position in its agreed zone of Iran, and immediately began to incite and assist the new Shah in attempts to suppress the *Majlis*. By June, 1908, using the Russian-officered Cossack Brigade as his weapon, he had succeeded, but further turmoil ensued. In July, 1909 Bakhtiyari tribesmen and other revolutionary forces marched on Tehran in defence of the Constitution, defeated the Cossack Brigade outside the city and deposed him (he took refuge in the Russian Embassy), after which the *Majlis* did enjoy nominal control over his 11-year-old son Ahmad Shah. But the revolutionaries soon fell into disagreement, and in 1911 Russian troops were introduced into Iran to overthrow their influence. The northern part of the country remained in virtual Russian military occupation up to 1917.

Iran remained neutral in World War I, though it was inevitably sympathetic to the Central Powers who were fighting its British and Russian tormentors. The government remained a helpless onlooker as Turks and Russians fought repeatedly on its soil, a German equivalent to T. E. Lawrence called Wassmuss raised the Qashqai tribes in revolt against British forces in the province of Fars, and both Britain and Russia raised large forces on its territory. In 1916 the Russians expanded the Cossack Brigade to divisional strength and re-equipped it to fight the Turks, while Britain raised the South Persian Rifles, a mixed British–Indian–Persian force, to control the south of the country.

In early 1917, however, came a stroke of great good fortune for Iran: the revolution in Petrograd. Over the summer of 1917 the Russian armies in Iran melted away, and with them the semi-colonial status to which the country had been reduced. The Bolsheviks subsequently renounced all the privileges the Tsarist regime had gained in Iran in the Irano–Soviet treaty of 1921 (though Article 6 did give them the right to send troops into the country if it should ever become a base for anti-Soviet activities, and subsequently provided the legal pretext for the 1941 invasion). The only obstacle to Iranian independence still remaining was the British position in the country.

The British government, now free at last from Russian rivalry, concluded a comprehensive agreement with Ahmad Shah in 1919 to consolidate its influence in Iran. There were to be British advisers in the economic and military fields, Britain would monopolise the sale of arms to a new Persian army which it would also help in organising, and there were the usual provisions for a foreign loan. The agreement was kept secret for some time, in knowledge of the storm of nationalist protest which it would unleash. As a first step the Russian officers of the Cossack Brigade were all dismissed in October, 1920 and Persian members of the force (some of whom had been allowed to serve in junior officer ranks) promoted to take their places.

This proved to be the undoing of British plans for Iran, for it led directly to a military coup by the Cossack Brigade less than 5 months later. The storm of protest awakened by the revelation of the British agreement led to several plots by Iranian nationalists against the government, and one of them, headed by a politician called Zia ed-Din Tabatabai, succeeded in gaining the support of the new Persian commander of the Cossack Brigade, Reza Khan. In February, 1921 Reza marched his troops to Tehran and seized power; Tabatabai became Prime Minister, and Reza Minister of War and Commander-in-Chief of all Iranian forces. The agreement with Britain was formally denounced at once.

It is clear that there was an element of military self-interest in this on the part of the newly promoted Persian officers of the Brigade, who understandably disliked the prospect of British officers taking the places of the recently departed Russians. But it is equally clear that Reza Khan, at least, was moved not only by personal ambition but by a powerful sentiment of nationalist resentment against foreign domination.

Reza was then 42 years old, and had spent all his adult life up to that time in the Cossack Brigade. He was a man of modest origins and no formal education, but endowed with immense will and skilled in intrigue. Within a few months he had forced the civilian Tabatabai to flee abroad. By August of 1921 he had more than tripled the military budget (which thus grew to exceed civilian expenditure four-fold). He then embarked on a programme to expand the army (based on the Cossack Brigade) in order to restore central control in outlying parts of Iran, a task which was largely accomplished by 1924.

Reza Khan did not choose to become Prime Minister until 1923, and there was further hesitation (he considered the possibility of a republic) before he forced the abdication of the reigning monarch and had himself declared Shah in 1925, taking the family name Pahlavi for his new dynasty. He ruled Iran for the next 16 years as a total autocrat, brooking no opposition and delegating virtually no authority.

Reza Shah saw himself as a nationalist moderniser in exactly the same tradition as his neighbour Ataturk (the only visit he ever made abroad was to Turkey in 1934), but he was a far less sophisticated man, and Iran was then a much more backward place. The army always came first in his scheme of things, not only because his dominant goal was the creation of an armed force strong enough to maintain internal control and deter foreign aggression, but also because his position was directly dependent on the loyalty of his senior military commanders. He introduced universal conscription and spent heavily to equip the ever-growing army with modern weapons, and even in his projects to improve communications, the educational system, etc. the army's needs got first priority. He changed the titles of military rank from the Turkish of the Zajar dynasty to Iranian (said to be drawn from the Old Persian of the Sassanid period) and emphasised the great military tradition of Iran's distant past. Throughout his reign, the army held the dominant position in all Iranian communities, the civilian authorities in practice being subordinate to the local military commanders.

Under Reza Shah Iran was more unified and tranquil than it had been for over a century, and a certain amount of material progress was achieved, but he grew ever more tyrannical and jealous of opposition. Several hundred political murders may be laid to his account, as he systematically eliminated all possible rivals in political life, and he amassed a vast personal fortune. When the army he had so painstakingly created collapsed after only a couple of days' resistance to the Anglo—Soviet invasion in 1941, his credit with it collapsed. He abdicated, and died in exile in South Africa in 1944.

Iran stayed neutral when war broke out in Europe in 1939,

but considerations of trade, anti-Russian sentiment and the Shah's strong anti-Communism inclined the government to be pro-German. When the Soviet Union entered the war in 1941, Iran became the only available year-round route by which supplies could be sent to it from abroad. By that time too, Britain, contemplating the expansion of German influence into the Arab Middle East, had become concerned for the safety of its vital oil-fields in Iran. When Reza Shah failed to comply with the terms of an Anglo—Soviet ultimatum, British and Russian troops invaded on August 26th, 1941. Reza's 22-year-old son Muhammad Reza Pahlavi came to the throne with a shattered army, a country wholly under foreign occupation, and a doubtful future.

The young Shah had no real political experience, having spent 5 years in school in Switzerland and then several years in the Iranian Military Academy, from which he had only recently graduated. He at once freed political prisoners and gave his father's wealth to the nation, in order to strengthen his own precarious position, but for the next 12 years his power remained severely circumscribed by the Constitution (which his father had been able to ignore).

During the wartime occupation successive civilian governments came and went rapidly, unable to contend with the uncontrollable inflation and growing loss of central control. A 1942 Anglo—Russian—Iranian treaty purportedly legitimised the occupation and provided for all foreign troops to be withdrawn within 6 months after the war's end, but the Soviet occupiers exploited their position to foster the growth of a Communist party — Tudeh — and of separatist movements in the areas near the Soviet border. Throughout 1946 they supported 'independent' governments in the Azerbaijani and Kurdish regions of north-western Iran.

Both Shah and army gained considerably in popular prestige from the re-entry of Iranian troops into Azerbaijan in 1946 (though the success had much to do with strong American pressure on the Soviet Union), but mass civilian parties continued to dominate the political scene. A strong Communist movement and an even stronger ultra-nationalist movement alternately competed for power by the most demagogic means, and collaborated against the dominating position of the hated Anglo—Iranian Oil Company which controlled the oilfields. The crisis came when Dr. Muhammad Musaddiq, a radical nationalist, became Prime Minister in April, 1951. Within days he nationalised the oilfields, beginning a two-year crisis with Britain that led to a worldwide boycott against Iranian oil and a rupture of diplomatic relations with London in October, 1952. Musaddiq also became Minister of War in July, 1952 and at once began purging the army of officers he believed loyal to the Shah. Within two months, 25 generals had been dismissed, the Guards Division in Tehran was split into independent units, and plans were made to strip the Shah of his powers as Commander-in-Chief. Both the Shah and his army commanders concluded that the entire existing order was threatened, and so did the United States, which had now replaced Britain as the dominant Western power in Iran.

On August 13th, 1953 the Shah dismissed Musaddiq and named General Fazlullah Zahedi as Prime Minister in his place. At first the stroke miscarried: the Imperial Guard officer who delivered the firman of dismissal to Musaddiq was arrested by forces loyal to the Prime Minister, General Zahedi went into hiding (reputedly in the United States Embassy), and the Shah discreetly fled abroad, his throne apparently lost. But on August 19th General Zahedi led a military coup that overthrew Musaddiq, and became Prime Minister. The Shah returned, and Musaddiq, having been duly court-martialled, went to jail.

It took the founder of the Pahlavi dynasty only 4 years to

climb to absolute power with the help of the army; it took his son 20 years, but from August, 1953 the path was smooth. The regime each year quite rightly celebrates the 'momentous' date of August 19th as marking the true beginning of the Shah's rule.

The corresponding enhancement in the army's position was instantaneous (though a massive purge of Tudeh and other pro-Communist members of the army began only a month after the coup, leading to the execution of scores and the imprisonment of hundreds of officers and men). The defence budget, which had been $43,000,000 and falling in Musaddiq's last year in power, rose steadily to $144,000,000 in 1965. The army was re-equipped and expanded, offering ample scope for promotion, with the help of substantial amounts of American aid, and an American training mission was attached to it. Political life was also purged by the end of 1954, to the accompaniment of thousands of arrests, and the Majlis subsided into its subsequent state of ceremonial powerlessness.

The latter 1950s were characterised by two trends: Iran's increasing involvement in Western defence arrangements, and the gradual consolidation of the Shah's control over the army. A new oil agreement was reached with Britain and America in 1954, and the following year Iran joined the Baghdad Pact (now CENTO). In March, 1959 a bilateral defence pact was concluded between the United States and Iran, by which the former promised to use appropriate means, including armed force, in the event of aggression against Iran.

Immediately after the 1953 coup there is little doubt that the Shah was directly dependent on the goodwill of his senior army officers, but he at once began to work to extend his control over them, using in particular his control over all senior appointments. By April, 1955 Zahedi resigned as Prime Minister, and the Shah began to take a more active role in the administration. There were attempts by the army to resist this trend – in 1958 General Vali-i Zanani was arrested when a plot was uncovered – but by the early 1960s the Shah's control was virtually complete.

Iranian army officers enjoy very extensive privileges, the armed forces continue to expand, affording rapid promotion, and collectively the officer corps is still the foundation and guarantee of the regime's power. But many senior posts are occupied by officers closely connected with the Royal Family by marriage and/or business interests, and the officer corps as a whole is under close supervision by several competing and highly efficient internal security organisations – SAVAK is merely the best known – which are also engaged in watching each other.

Operating from this base of power, the Shah embarked on a successful campaign to break the power of all the powerful conservative institutions in the land in the early 1960s, in order to clear the way for the rapid modernisation and industrialisation of Iran which was as much his own goal as his father's. The key strategy was the White Revolution inaugurated in 1962. Its centrepiece was a partial land reform, though it also included such things as a literacy corps of volunteer school-leavers sent out to instruct in the villages (even now illiteracy is 55%). The general tenor of the enterprise was a sort of monarchical populism, whose propaganda saturated every area of Iranian public life.

By the middle of the 1960s the Shah's power was virtually untrammelled, and he was able to embark on ambitious foreign policy and headlong State-directed industrialisation programmes. In March, 1975 the political façade of the regime was adjusted, when the controlled two-party system was abruptly abandoned in favour of a one-party State in which the new Rastakhiz (National Resurgence) Party monopolised political activity. The denial of political freedom, and popular opposition

to the Shah's modernisation programme, created an alliance of middle and lower class majorities to his rule. It was that which brought about his fall in January 1979.

STRENGTH AND BUDGET

The strength of the Iranian armed forces is 235,000, of which 150,000 are army. A large proportion of the army's strength is conscripts, but almost all officers and non-commissioned officers are regulars. The population of Iran is 39,100,000.

The navy has 10,000 men, and the air force 35,000, of whom a smaller proportion are conscripts. They were first organised as branches of the army in 1924 and 1927, respectively, but were elevated into separate services equal in status to the army in 1955. The paramilitary Gendarmerie of 5000 men, almost all volunteers, is organised on a regimental basis. It is equipped with light aircraft, helicopters and 40 patrol boats. There are also numbers of Islamic militias.

The revised Iranian military budget for 1981 was $4,400,000,000.

In recent years before the Shah's fall between 50 and 80% of Iranian military expenditure had been devoted to foreign exchange purchases: since 1972 Iran bought approximately $18,200,000,000 of arms from the USA alone. Western inflation, a 15 month freeze on oil prices, and falling oil consumption in the industrial countries brought about the reappearance of a deficit in the Iranian balance of payments in 1976, which accounts for the fall in the 1977–8 defence budget. (It was originally planned to be $10,550,000,000.) By the end of 1976 Iran was actually pressuring foreign contractors on defence projects and potential suppliers of sophisticated military equipment to accept barter payments in crude oil, with only partial success. The principal effect of the fall in expenditure has been to delay the construction of Iran's extremely large naval and air base at Chah Bahar on the Indian Ocean.

COMMAND AND CONSTITUTIONAL STATUS

Since the deposition of the Shah in January 1979 Iran has been an Islamic Republic (referendum of March). Command of the armed forces rests with the President (elected 1981), exercised through the Prime Minister, Minister of Defence and Commander of the Armed Forces. However, ultimate power depends from the *Velayat Faqhih* (Religious Leader), Ayatollah Khomeini, who exercises it in a fashion not restrained by constitutional provisions.

ROLE, COMMITMENT, DEPLOYMENT AND RECENT OPERATIONS

The Iranian army has three principal roles in external policy, corresponding to the three main threats to Iran's security. In approximate order of importance, these latter are: the 1100 mile border with the Soviet Union; the lengthy frontier with the radical Iraqi regime; and the stability of the small Arab shaikhdoms on the southern side of the Persian Gulf, which potentially dominate the vulnerable sea route along which almost all Iran's trade, including oil exports, must travel.

The corresponding military tasks are: to maintain at least a minimum deterrent force against a Soviet attack; to establish and maintain military superiority over Iraq; and to maintain a quick-reaction intervention force for use in the Gulf. In accord with these priorities, the three main Iranian army headquarters are located at: Tehran, controlling forces on the Soviet border; Kermanshah, controlling those on the Iraqi border; and Shiraz facing the Gulf.

Lesser or at least less-urgent duties falling on the armed forces include counter-insurgency operations against the dormant Baluchi separatist movement in the barren south-east, the creation of a degree of Iranian air and maritime superiority in the western Indian Ocean and the maintenance of an overall military balance with the rapidly expanding forces of Saudi Arabia. There are no perceived security threats along the Pakistan or Turkish frontiers.

The April, 1978 coup which brought a leftist, pro-Moscow government to power in Afghanistan has reportedly occasioned a limited increase in the forces deployed in Iran's sparsely populated north-east along the Afghan border. Tehran's anxieties, however, centre much more on the possible destabilisation and disintegration of Pakistan due to Afghan intrigues, and on the presence of about a million Afghan immigrant workers in Iran, than on the unlikely contingency of a direct military confrontation with Afghanistan.

Though the Soviet threat to Iranian security is potentially far more serious than any other, relations with Moscow have been consistently good since the Shah first visited the Russian capital in 1965. The volume of Russo—Iranian trade is quite large, and Tehran has even bought a considerable quantity of arms from the Soviet Union. But the Russians have invaded Iran three times in this century, and if the Penkovsky papers are to be believed they had contingency plans to try it again as late as the Cuban missile crisis of 1962.

As a consequence, Iran views the present deployment of considerable Iranian armed forces facing the Soviet frontier not as an impenetrable defence — which it certainly is not — but as a trip wire ('a lock in the door', he calls it) which would hold up a Russian invasion long enough for the West to demonstrate its determination to defend Iran and its oil.

The great bulk of the Soviet armed forces are presently deployed facing NATO in Europe and China in the Far East, and it is a reasonable assumption that they will become increasingly stretched as Chinese military capabilities improve. The question then arises: could the Soviet Union possibly withdraw forces on the scale required for many months from either or both of these major fronts, in order to invade or merely blackmail Iran? It is arguable that a credible conventional deterrent against Soviet invasion is potentially available to Iran in the next decade.

The second (and generally more evident) Iranian defence priority is Iraq. The two countries nearly went to war over the Shatt-al-Arab dispute in 1969, and again over Iranian support for Kurdish rebels in the north of Iraq in 1974—5. The most sensitive issue between the two countries for many years was the Shatt-al-Arab, the waterway by which the combined Tigris and Euphrates rivers reach the Persian Gulf. The Shatt is the avenue by which all Iran's oil reaches the sea, but by a treaty imposed by the British in Iraq earlier in the century the international border ran not down the middle, but along the Iranian shore. This gave Iraq a potential stranglehold on Iran's trade lifeline.

In 1969 Iran re-opened the question of the border in the Shatt, and for the next 6 years relations between the two countries were extremely tense. Occasional border clashes and mutual expulsions of minority populations were followed in 1974 by large-scale Iranian logistical support for the Kurdish separatists fighting in the north of Iraq. Not only did Tehran allow the Kurdish insurgents free movement across the border areas in their control; it also reportedly supplied them with artillery and anti-aircraft weapons. It was a potentially risky strategy, for Iran has a much more numerous Kurdish minority on its own side of the border, but it worked.

By late 1974 the larger part of the Iraqi army was tied down by the relentless Kurdish war in the northern provinces, and the overstretched Baghdad regime came to terms. In early 1975 it agreed to redraw the international boundary down the centre of the Shatt-al-Arab. In return Iran dropped all support for the Kurdish revolt and closed the border, whereupon Kurdish resistance in Iraq promptly collapsed. It was a major victory for Iran, and was due at least in large part to the fact that Iraq did not dare escalate the conflict into an open clash with Iran's growing armed forces. Saddam Hussein, who came to power in Iraq four years later resolved to take the risk, thus initiating the current Iraq—Iran war. [See Iraq.]

ORGANISATION

Arms of Service

Since the collapse of the Shah's organisation, firm statements about the Iranian forces are difficult to make. Large numbers of regular servicemen were killed or deserted after 1979, and extant formations shrank in size. However, it seems that the army consists of four armoured divisions, four infantry divisions and one airborne division. Air defence is provided by a SAM battalion equipped with Hawk missiles and there is a separate Army Aviation Command. All 'divisions' are more probably brigades.

The principal arms are infantry, armour and artillery, but there are also separate specialities for engineers, aviation, paratroops, alpine troops and anti-aircraft troops. Supply services are controlled by Logistics Support Command, one of the largest organisations in the army, which is also responsible for carrying out almost all of the construction work and base maintenance required by the army. One of the most important new elements in the army is the Revolutionary Guard Corps (*Pasdaran*), whose Islamic Zealots have fought with great bravery against the Israelis.

Operational

There are three field armies: The First Army, with headquarters in Kermanshah; the Second Army, headquarters Tehran; and the Third Army, headquarters Shiraz. Aviation Command has its headquarters at Isfahan.

Iranian Navy headquarters are at Khorramshahr, the major naval base. Other bases are at Bandar Pahlavi (on the Caspian Sea, where only patrol boats are maintained), Bushire, Kharg Island and Bandar Abbas, while a large new base for Indian Ocean operations is being built at Chah Bahar near the Pakistani border. The navy also controls a squadron of six maritime reconnaissance aircraft, an anti-submarine warfare squadron of six helicopters, a transport squadron of 10 aircraft and 48 helicopters, and three marine battalions.

The Iranian Air Force is organised into 22 fighter—ground-attack squadrons, one reconnaissance squadron, five medium transport squadrons, five light and two tanker squadrons. It seems that only about 90 combat aircraft are serviceable. Air force headquarters are in Tehran, and other major air bases are at Ahwaz, Dezful, Doshan-Tapeh, Galeh-Marghi, Hamadan, Isfahan (the principal training centre), Mashhad, Mehrabad, Shiraz, Tabriz and Zahidan.

RECRUITMENT, TRAINING AND RESERVES

[The Islamic revolution has quite upset the organisation of the Iranian armed forces. This section is largely based on the entry of 1979, amended as information permits.]

Basic military manpower is provided by universal conscription at the age of twenty-one, for a period of 2 years. Graduates of secondary schools and universities serve for shorter periods, having already received military training in these educational establishments, and are usually granted commissions: first-lieutenant for those with doctorates, second-lieutenant for those with bachelor's degrees and third-lieutenant for high-school graduates. Exemptions are generally available for those who are the sole support of their families, and for students until they have completed their educations. Former employers are obliged by law to offer discharged conscripts a job at least equal to that that they last held before entering military service.

Recruits receive 13 weeks' basic training at one of six induction centres, and are then assigned to organisations for unit and advanced training. All conscripts are required to learn to read and write before being discharged, adequate instruction being provided, and many learn a trade as part of their service duties or through special instruction in the last 3 months of their service. The manpower available considerably exceeds military requirements, and large numbers of suitably qualified men are instead directed into the various community assistance organisations – the Literacy Corps, Development and Agricultural Extension Corps, Health Corps and Equity Corps (legal aid) – or into the gendarmerie, to serve the equivalent of their military obligation.

The bulk of the officers and NCOs are regulars. Regular officers are commissioned after a 3 year course at the Military College, which is open to secondary-school graduates possessing character references from a general officer or a member of parliament, and who pass a competitive entrance examination. They are subsequently trained in combat tactics at the training centres run by the different branches of the army, which also provide officers and NCOs with advanced courses in their specialties.

Higher military education is provided by the Army Staff College and the War Academy. The National Defence University, founded in 1968, amalgamated the high command, joint staff and senior management schools. Iran's armed forces are largely self-sufficient in military education.

Iranian army reserves are officially stated to be 400,000 men. The Military Service Law of 1969 requires men to serve in the reserve for a total of 40 years, but not beyond the age of sixty. The service is broken into five periods: 2 years of active service; 6 years in the active reserve; and three further periods of 8 years, 9 years, and whatever years remain to the age of sixty. During the active reserve period they are required to train for 30 days a year, although this provision is not always enforced. Reserve officers generally go through the college military training systems, and then receive 6 months of intensive training at one of the major branch centres – infantry, armour or artillery – at the beginning of their active service.

The principal paramilitary force is officially the Iranian Gendarmerie, numbering 7000 men with light aircraft, helicopters and 40 patrol boats. The structure is military, and the officers come from the army; the great majority of the enlisted ranks also began their service in the army. The gendarmerie is responsible for security in rural areas and towns of under 5000 people, and provides the country's border guard. In peacetime it is under the control of the Ministry of the Interior, although it co-operates closely with the army in controlling internal disturbances. In wartime it would come under army direction; some specialised groups are capable of combat duty, but its primary mission would be rear-area security.

There is now a large number of paramilitary Islamic militias of which the Revolutionary Guard, 40,000 strong is the most important.

EQUIPMENT AND ARMS INDUSTRY

Since the outbreak of war in 1980, the Iranian military inventory has been heavily depleted by combat losses. Its armoured strength now consists of 420 Chieftain, 300 M-47/48, 200 M-60A1 and 190 T54-62 medium tanks and 100 Scorpion light tanks. The infantry is partly mechanised, using about 1580 M-113 and BTR-40/50/60/152 APCs. Artillery strength comprises about 1000 guns and howitzers, including: 105mm and 155mm; various numbers of 75mm, 130mm and 175mm SPs; and 203mm SPs of American and Soviet manufacture. Lighter fire-support weapons include M-21 RLs and 106mm RCLs.

Anti-tank missiles are a mixture of ENTACs, SS-11s, Dragon and TOWs. There are 1800 anti-aircraft weapons, mainly Russian built, including 23mm, 35mm, 40mm, 57mm (80SP), 85mm and ZSU-2.3-4 and ZSU-57-2SP guns, and Hawk, Improved Hawk and SA-7 surface-to-air missiles.

Army Aviation Command disposes of 65 light aircraft and 470 helicopters. The types are: F-27, Shrike Commander, Cessna 185, O-2A and Cessna 310 aircraft; and AH-1J, Bell 214A, Huskie, AB-205A and CH-47C helicopters. Iran has been living from hand-to-mouth during the Iraq war, buying replacement equipment and spares where it may on the open market.

RANK, DRESS AND DISTINCTIONS

The Iranian armed forces continue to bear the conventional military ranks and wear the uniforms common before the Islamic revolution. All other information is unreliable.

CURRENT DEVELOPMENTS

After a humiliating and costly setback at the beginning of the Gulf War (September 22nd, 1980), the Iranian armed forces have made a remarkable recovery. Despite heavy losses of equipment and experienced personnel (by purge and desertion as well as battle), the army succeeded in expelling the Iraqis from Iranian territory and is now carrying the offensive onto their soil. Its loyalty to the Islamic regime appears solid. Its fighting quality has been enhanced by the adhesion of large numbers of Revolutionary Guards, dedicated defenders of the Ayatollah's regime.

Shortages of equipment must, however, now limit the army's capacity to sustain the offensive.

Gwynne Dyer
John Keegan

IRAQ

HISTORY AND INTRODUCTION

Iraq is renowned throughout the Arab world for the extraordinary turbulence and extreme violence of its domestic politics, which have been largely dominated by army factions for the past four decades (and overwhelmingly since 1958). Between 1956 and 1973 there was scarcely a year in which there was not a coup or an attempted coup. Between 1961 and 1975 there were only a couple of years in which substantial proportions of the army – up to 80%, in some years – were not committed to high-intensity regular military operations against Kurdish and other revolts. Since the establishment of the Ba'ath regime in 1968 there has been greater political stability, and since 1975 the Kurdish insurgency has been quiescent, but both these achievements are maintained only by a ruthless and utterly uncompromising military–political dictatorship.

Iraq is unquestionably one of the world's most difficult countries to govern, and it is idle to suppose that it could be successfully ruled at this point by any other method. Few other countries are so seriously divided in language and religion, with no natural majority. Few have such a powerful system of local, clan and family loyalties still flourishing beneath the formal political and administrative structures. Hardly any have so deeply entrenched a tradition of violent intrigue in politics at every level: no powerful man in Iraq moves about without a small platoon of bodyguards. Even the strident pan-Arabism of post-1958 regimes (and especially of the post-1968 Ba'athist regime, which is so purist that it finds it hard to co-operate even with other radical nationalist regimes devoted to Arab unity) serves only to conceal the fact that Iraq is the least 'Arab' country in the Arab world.

The explanation for all these phenomena lies in that series of misfortunes and catastrophes which is Iraq's history. At the beginning of recorded history it was one of the two wealthiest and most densely populated countries on Earth – at the beginning of the second millennium BC the population was about 1,000,000, and by the seventh century BC, under the Assyrian Empire, it probably touched 2,000,000. But even then it was subject to two recurring catastrophes which caused sudden great drops in population: periodic rises in the water table due to over-irrigation which would ruin most of the arable land of lower Mesopotamia through excessive salinity, and waves of conquest sweeping across the unprotected flatlands which form the Iraqi heartland.

Much of the population was Arabised after the Arab conquest in the seventh century AD, and as the centre of the Abassid caliphate the country enjoyed a golden age of civilised prosperity in the ninth century, rising to a record population of 2,500,000. But once again the water table rose, destroying the country's agriculture, and the ruin was completed by a century of appallingly destructive invasions in the thirteenth and fourteenth centuries by the Mongols under Hulagu Khan, followed by the hordes of Timur the Lame. By 1300 the population had dropped to 1,000,000, and five centuries later it was even slightly below that.

The experience of these five centuries, undoubtedly the darkest period in Iraq's long history, was the main influence that shaped the fundamental character of Iraqi political behaviour: extreme loyalty to one's own particular small group, usually linked by blood ties, and total hostility and distrust towards all beyond that group. It was the only means of survival in a country which became an impoverished borderland repeatedly devastated by invading armies and bereft of any significant or lasting civil administration.

Between the death of Timur in 1405 and 1831, Iraq was successively conquered by two Turcoman confederations, the Kara Koyunlu (Black Sheep) and the Ak Koyunlu (White Sheep), by the Safavid dynasty of Iran, by the Ottoman Turks, by the Persians again, and finally by the Ottomans again in 1638 after two unsuccessful invasions. The Ottomans soon lost all practical control outside Baghdad to various local potentates, however, and the attempts of two determined Ottoman governors in the first half of the eighteenth century to extend their authority over the whole country were thwarted by yet another devastating series of Persian invasions in 1729–43. They were repelled, but the country then fell under the rule of a slave (Mamluk) army, its soldiers mostly recruited from Georgia and converted to Islam as youths, which misgoverned Baghdad and Basra provinces until 1831, amidst continuous internal strife, yet another Persian invasion, and raids of growing intensity by the recently created Wahhabi State of central Arabia. Throughout this period, moreover, there were continual revolts by the great Arab tribal confederacies of Iraq and the Kurdish tribes of the north against whatever degree of local government authority did exist, and an unending series of raids out of the great Arabian desert to the south by nomadic tribes.

In 1831 the Ottoman authorities succeeded in exterminating the Mamluk army, and thereafter created a degree of central government and introduced certain imports from the modern world to Iraq – a telegraph and postal service, steamboats on the rivers, conscription for the army – but in almost all respects the Iraq of 1900 was hardly different from that of 1500. Development after 1900 was more rapid, but with coming of World War I the country was conquered by the British Indian Army – Baghdad fell in 1917. Under the British military administration which ruled until 1920, its borders were defined as those of the Ottoman provinces of Basra, Baghdad and Mosul (although possession of the latter, mainly Kurdish, province was disputed by Turkey until 1926).

The independent country that was thus created under a British mandate from the League of Nations was culturally, economically and socially the most backward part of the Arab world at that time, except for the Arabian peninsula. Literacy and urbanisation were both well below 5%, extreme poverty was virtually universal, and traditions of civil government or civic co-operation were non-existent. Only in the previous decade had a nascent concept of Arab national identity begun to spread amongst the small educated class, especially amongst the Arabs of Baghdad province who belong to the orthodox Sunni sect which predominates throughout the rest of the Arab world. Even this, however, was scarcely to be found at all amongst the Arabs of Basra province in the south along the Euphrates river, where the majority of the population belonged to the Shiite sect of Islam and had close connections with Iran, where that sect predominates. The northern third of the country, Mosul province, was not Arab at all, but Kurdish, and had been included within its border by the British because of its promising oil deposits.

The basic problem of rule within the arbitrarily defined

State of Iraq created in 1920, therefore, can be defined in terms of the population: about 25% are Sunni Arabs, 35% are Shiite Arabs and 20% are Sunni Kurds. (The remainder include Turks, Christian Assyrians and other smaller minorities.) Of all these groups, only the Sunni Arabs of Baghdad feel an instinctive attachment to the pan-Arab ideal. Under the Ottomans, themselves defenders of Sunni orthodoxy, Shiite Arabs were excluded from all participation in official activities, and the deep cleavage between the two Arab communities of Iraq continues today. The Kurds of Iraq form part of one of the largest submerged nations in the world, some 7,000,000–8,000,000 people split up between Iran, Iraq, Turkey and Syria. Only 2,000,000 Kurds live in Iraq, but they form a far higher proportion of the population than in any of the neighbouring States. Therefore, although they have fared far better in Iraq than elsewhere in terms of recognition of their language, right to local autonomy, etc. it is also in Iraq that their demands and their power have been greatest.

The solution to the problem of who rules Iraq, for which the Ottomans prepared the way and which was adopted by the British and continues undiminished in the republic, is that the Sunni Arabs run everything. For the Turks, it was a question of religious doctrine; for the British, one of convenience; for all of Iraq's post-independence regimes, the central issue of politics. It will be obvious that if no external imperial power is present to enforce this order of things, Sunni Arab rule can only be maintained by an authoritarian domestic government backed by strong military forces, and such has invariably been the case.

In recent decades this domination of the State by Sunni Arabs is explained (usually quite ingenuously) not to be discrimination against other sections of the population, but rather a preference for those who are dedicated to the cause of pan-Arab unity. It can just as well be argued, however, that the extraordinary and fanatical dedication of the Sunni Arabs of Iraq to the pan-Arab cause, far exceeding that of governments in more homogeneous Arab countries, is a justification of their privileged status and a means of perpetuating it. In more practical terms, there has been from the very inception of the Iraqi State a love/hate relationship with Syria, the one Arab country with which union would have practical significance: on the one hand, the declared goal of Syrian–Iraqi unification would create a State in which a majority of the population were reliable Arab patriots; on the other hand, the Sunni Arabs of Iraq would be a minority within that majority.

The British acceptance of Sunni Arab dominance in the mandate period in Iraq was not entirely deliberate. Partly because they owed the Hashemite ruling family of the Hejaz in what is now south-western Saudi Arabia a debt of gratitude for its military assistance against the Turks in World War I, and partly because they were anxious about the stirrings of Arab nationalism amongst the Sunni Arabs of Baghdad, the British imported the Hashemite Amir Faisal ibn Husain in 1921 to rule as King of Iraq. With him, however, came the Arab officers of the Ottoman Army who had defected to help Faisal lead the Hejazi tribal forces in the Arab Revolt during World War I.

Only Sunni Muslims were granted commissions in the Ottoman Army prior to the Young Turk Revolution of 1908. Moreover, a very large majority of the Arab officers in the Ottoman Army were recruited from Iraq, principally because there were more attractive civilian careers open to educated Arabs in more developed Syria which simply did not exist at that time in Iraq. Therefore, a large majority of the Arab officers who were infected by the rampant nationalism of their Turkish fellow officers in the Committee of Union and Progress after the 1908 Revolution, who responded by founding rival nationalist secret societies in the Ottoman Army (notably al-'Ahd – the Covenant) after 1910, and who then defected to provide the professional core of the Hejazi army in the Arab Revolt, were in fact Sunni Muslims from around Baghdad.

These were the men who came to Iraq with King Faisal, who formed the officer corps of the new Iraqi army, and who effectively dominated both the army and increasingly civilian politics was well for the next generation: the most influential of them even at the time of the Arab Revolt in 1916–18, Nuri as-Said, was the central figure in Iraqi politics from the 1930s onwards, and was Prime Minister as late as 1958.

Until the decision to place King Faisal on the newly created throne of Iraq, Britain had controlled the country with its own occupation forces and with the so-called Iraqi Levies, a paramilitary force recruited primarily from the non-Arab minorities like the Kurds and Assyrians. The new Iraqi army that was founded in July, 1921, however, was drawn principally from the Arab population, and it was the ex-Ottoman Army, ex-Hejaz Army Iraqi officers who became its officer corps. General Nuri as-Said was the first Chief of Staff. By 1925 the army numbered 7500 men, and by 1936 had reached 23,000. A military academy was founded in Baghdad in 1924, followed by a staff college in 1928. Numbers of officers were also sent to Britain or India for advanced military training, and Britain provided instructors, advisers, arms and equipment in Iraq.

By 1936 the Iraqi army and the newly created air force were bodies of a reputable professional standard, although of course the great bulk of their operational tasks were in the internal security category against the continual tribal revolts. The officer corps, although as riven by personal cliques and factions as was the rest of Iraqi political life, was composed predominantly of Sunni Arabs, with some Kurds, drawing its recruits from the local political and economic *élites*.

In 1932 the British mandate over Iraq was terminated and the country gained full formal independence, but its actual dependent relationship with Britain scarcely changed: a 25 year treaty of alliance signed with Britain in 1930 provided for full consultation in foreign affairs, permitted the free passage of British troops through the country, and granted Britain two major airbases at Habbaniyah and Shu'aiba. Iraq was, however, one of the few Arab countries which were not fully under the control of European empires, and there was a steady growth in opinion in the officer corps from the simple anti-Ottomanism of the early years towards a broader anti-imperialist version of Arab nationalism. Discontent with the 'foreign' monarchy and with British indirect rule grew steadily.

This was only indirectly manifested in the military coup of 1936, the first such event in the Arab world. The short-lived regime of General Baqr Sidqi and his reformist followers was principally concerned to broaden the narrow circle of individuals with access to political power beyond the small group around the monarch, and had few specifically nationalist aims: indeed, Baqr Sidqi himself was a Kurd. His regime was unsuccessful and he was assassinated in 1937, but the government remained in military hands.

There was a growing number of Arab nationalist officers and, like those in Syria and Egypt at the same time, their opposition to Anglo–French imperial rule in the Middle East made them extremely susceptible to the advances of Nazi Germany. A group of Sunni Arab officers later known as the Golden Square, together with associated civilian supporters, elaborated a programme of Arab nationalism and anti-British imperialism which borrowed heavily from fascist political style and had strong support from local German representatives. Iraq duly severed its diplomatic relations with Germany when war broke out in 1939, but in 1941 the government was overthrown by the army leadership.

The new government, under the nominal leadership of General Rashid 'Ali al-Gaylani and with real control exercised by the Golden Square, announced its non-belligerent intentions and refused British troops the right of passage. British troops then attacked Iraq, while the Iraqi army besieged the RAF base at Habbaniyah near Baghdad. After only 29 days of fighting resistance collapsed, and a pro-British government returned to office. During the remainder of the war Iraq was occupied by the British. After a thorough purge of nationalist officers and wholesale reorganisation the Iraqi army was reduced virtually to an auxiliary unit of the British army, under the strict surveillance of British officers co-operating with officers loyal to the monarchy.

British occupation troops were withdrawn after 1945, and for the next 13 years Iraqi politics appeared to revert to the pre-war model, with growing oil revenues to help lubricate the creaking machinery of the monarchy and reward its privileged supports. 12,000 Iraqi troops were sent to fight in the first campaign against Israel in 1948; and Iraqi forces were again sent to the brother Hashemite kingdom of Jordan during the 1956 Suez War (though on that occasion they saw no action), but none of this disturbed the regime's close and indispensable links with Britain and the West. Indeed, in 1955 Iraq joined with Britain, Turkey, Iran and Pakistan to form an anti-communist, anti-Soviet alliance known as the Baghdad Pact (later CENTO, after Iraq's withdrawal). But inside the army dissatisfaction at the regime's corruption and its slavish dependence on Western support was growing, and new, more radical political views were spreading into the army.

The most important of these was the Ba'ath (Renaissance) Party, which had been founded in 1943 in Syria by Michel Aflaq, a French-educated Christian Syrian intellectual. It was a movement with tremendous potential appeal to Iraqi Arabs as well, being socialist, anti-imperialist and dedicated to the creation of a single Arab State from Basra to the Atlantic — with the initial goal of creating a 'Greater Syria' including Iraq, Palestine and Jordan. The foundation of the Iraqi branch of the party took place in 1949, immediately after the Arab defeat in the war in Palestine, apparently at the inspiration mainly of Palestinian refugees and Iraqi students who had been educated in Syria. It grew rapidly in secrecy, adopting the cellular organisation familiar in Communist Parties working underground, and in 1954 it was erected into a full 'regional' (i.e. Iraqi) branch of the 'national' (i.e. pan-Arab) Ba'athist movement.

The closing years of the Iraqi monarchy were characterised by extreme repression — massacres of jailed political activists, the suppression of all political parties, and from the time of the Suez crisis in October, 1956 continuous martial law — but the regime was unable to prevent the spread of new ideas amongst the Sunni Arab population and especially the army officer corps. The Ba'ath Party had strong competitors in the Iraqi Communist Party and the Nasserist group which hoped to emulate the achievements of the Egyptian Free Officers' Movement of 1952, but all were prepared to co-operate at least for the limited purpose of overthrowing the monarchy and breaking Iraq's unequal alliance with the West.

The receptivity of army officers to these groups was greatly enhanced by the fact that the Military College in Baghdad had been thrown open to a much wider range of applicants after the Baqr Sidqi coup of 1936. The newer breed of officer, drawn increasingly from lower-middle-class and small-town

Sunni Arab society rather than from the privileged upper classes of Baghdad, was reaching the key major—colonel rank bracket in the early 1950s, and responded readily to all these revolutionary ideologies. Nasserists, Ba'athists and communists in the army all co-operated in the unsuccessful attempted coup of 1956, and were again associated to a greater or lesser extent with the successful coup of July 14th, 1958 in which King Faisal II, the Crown Prince and Prime Minister Nuri as-Said were all killed. Iraq was declared a republic, left the Baghdad Pact, and turned to the Soviet Union as its principal arms supplier. Large numbers of executions took place, and the communists rapidly organised a paramilitary force known as the People's Resistance Force which was particularly strong in the Kurdish areas.

The two principal architects of the coup were Brigadier (later General) 'Abd al-Karim Kassem and Colonel (later Field-Marshal) 'Abd as-Salam Muhammad Aref, commanding the two armoured brigades near Damascus. Kassem was an ultra-nationalist of leftist inclination, but without formal links with any of the conspiratorial political parties, while Aref was loosely associated with the Ba'ath. In the power struggle that followed Kassem won, and by November, Aref, having failed to overthrow Kassem in an attempted coup staged in Mosul with Nasserist and Ba'athist support, was on trial on charges of treason. Within a year, despite several outbreaks of armed resistance, all Nasserist, Ba'athist and communist officers had been excluded from the government, and the communist militia had been forcibly disbanded. In October, 1959 Kassem was the target of an assassination attempt in central Baghdad led by Saddam Hussein Tikriti of the Ba'athist Party (then a 22 year-old student and Ba'athist gunman, now the strongman of Iraq). Kassem escaped with a wounded shoulder, while the severely wounded would-be assassin escaped to Syria, followed by those Ba'ath leaders who escaped arrest.

Kassem's period of violent and xenophobic rule initiated all the themes which have since dominated Iraq's political and military history: hostility to almost all neighbouring States, domination of Iraqi politics by soldiers, an extreme position in favour of pan-Arab union combined with bad relations with almost all existing Arab governments, the imposition from above of an authoritarian version of 'Arab socialism', and close links with the Soviet Union. It also saw the first of the series of sweeping purges, summary executions and outright bloodbaths which, repeated numerous times as coups brought different governments to power, have by now winnowed down the army officer corps to a relatively homogeneous remainder that is Arab, Sunni and either members of, or at least passively loyal to, the Ba'ath Party.

Kassem's regime made enemies outside Iraq, by claiming Kuwait at that country's independence in 1961, thus angering the conservative Arab States, and by disputing Nasser's claim to leadership of the radical Arab group. It made even more enemies inside Iraq by ruthlessly repressing Ba'athists, Nasserists and Kurds. The refusal of the regime to grant Kurdish demands for autonomy was the biggest single factor that weakened its hold on power, for as a result the Kurds rose in revolt in March, 1961 under Mustafa Barzani. Control was lost over much of the north within months, and by 1962 the Iraqi army was heavily engaged in a war that was to last, with interruptions, for 14 years. For the course of the Kurdish revolt, see Recent Operations. An alliance of officers loyal to Colonel Aref, co-leader of the 1958 revolt, and of Ba'athist officers succeeded in carrying out a coup in February, 1963: Kassem himself was captured and shot, and Colonel Aref became President with the Ba'athist officer Ahmad Hassan al-Bakr as Prime Minister. Pro-Kassem, pro-Nasser and communist officers and civil servants and those of

Kurdish origin were thoroughly purged, and numbers were executed after mass trials. The Ba'athist militia, the National Guard, also massacred several thousand communists without trial.

Shortly afterwards a Ba'athist regime also seized power in Syria, and a federal union between Iraq, Egypt and Syria was tentatively agreed in April, 1963. This led to a split in the Iraqi Ba'ath Party between extremist pan-Arab elements and the more moderate faction which feared the consequences of precipitate union. When the moderate faction gained control of the Iraqi Regional (national) Command of the party in November, 1963 the extremist faction made an unsuccessful attempt at a *coup d'état* in the course of which air force elements attacked the Presidential Palace and the Ministry of Defence. President Aref assumed full powers, and crushed the Ba'athist paramilitary National Guard in street fighting; some moderate Ba'athists remained in his government, but the party had again lost its hold on power. One important consequence of this episode was to confirm the dominant role of the military wing within the Ba'athist Party, as it was clear that the party's loss of power had been largely due to the extent to which the civilian wing had alienated the professional officer class as a whole with its attempt to create a paramilitary rival in the National Guard.

Muhammad Aref's regime survived an attempted coup by Nasserist officers in early 1966, and 2 months after his death in a helicopter crash in April of that year his brother and successor in the presidency, Major-General Abd al-Rahman Aref, had to crush another attempted coup mounted by the same elements in the army. The Six-Day War of 1967 found the army in a transitional period; most of its equipment was by now of Soviet origin, but training doctrines were still British and the number of Soviet advisers was kept to a bare minimum. Iraqi troops were dispatched to assist on the Jordanian front, but were badly mauled by the Israeli air force before they could even get into action.

The regime of the second Aref brother staggered on into 1968, though generally reckoned both corrupt and inefficient, until it was overthrown by the sudden and bloodless coup of April 17th, 1968. This time it was a coup of solely Ba'athist inspiration: Aref went into exile, and the Ba'athist general who had briefly been Prime Minister in 1963, Ahmad Hassan al-Bakr, became President. The army was purged once again, and members of former governments were given long jail sentences or died in mysterious circumstances. Westerners were expelled in large numbers, the remaining Western interests in the country including the oil companies' holdings were nationalised and the full apparatus of an authoritarian police State was rapidly put in place. Public executions were commonplace, including the hanging of 11 Iraqi citizens, of whom nine were Jews, from lamp-posts in Baghdad's main square as 'spies for the United States, Israel, imperialism and Zionism'. Amongst those who made televised confessions of having been agents of the CIA and Israel after secret trials were a former president, two former prime ministers, a former Army Chief of Staff, the military leader of the Kurds and a son of the spiritual leader of the Iraqi Shiites: by early 1970 there had been over 100 public executions.

These extreme measures worked, for they gradually put an end to the cycle of coups: President al-Bakr and the Ba'ath Party are still in power. The army has been made an exclusively Ba'ath preserve, and there has even been some progress in reviving the influence of the civilian wing of the Ba'ath Party. This has been particularly evident in the rise to power of al-Bakr's protégé, Saddam Hussein, who first came to prominence when he attempted to machine-gun Kassem in 1959 and is now Vice-President of the Revolutionary Command Council (RCC) (although he found it tactful to take an honorary degree from the Military Academy and to assume the military rank of general in 1976).

While the professional jealousy of army officers for rival claimants to power and also genuine political and ideological differences do play a real part in Iraqi politics, however, it is evident that, under the Ba'ath as much as under the Aref brothers or Kassem, the real foundation and structure of power in Iraq are still the alliances formed between officers and civilians who are linked by ties of blood or locality. This phenomenon, typical throughout Iraq's modern history, finds its major expression at present in the so-called 'Tikriti gang' which dominates the Ba'athist regime.

Tikrit is a small town of some 30,000 people, located about 100 miles north of Baghdad, which was the birthplace of President al-Bakr. It was also the home of Air Marshal Hardan al-Tikriti, first Vice-President of the RCC, and of his successor Saddam Hussein, who is now the effective ruler of Iraq. Many other prominent figures of the regime are also Tikritis, including General Adnan Khairallah Talfah (a brother-in-law of Saddam Hussein), who in October, 1977 took over the post of Defence Minister which had been held since 1973 by the now-ailing President al-Bakr.

This is not to say that the bitter civil—military rivalry within the Ba'athist hierarchy has been ended, nor that the Tikriti faction does not have its own internal quarrels. In 1970 Hardan al-Tikriti attempted a coup to halt the rising influence of Saddam Hussein. (He failed, and was murdered in Kuwait the following year, while forty other officers and civilians were executed by the regime.) In July, 1971 there was another attempted coup by army and air force officers. In 1973 the civilian security chief, Nazim Kazzar, attempted to destroy the dominant military influence within the RCC in another abortive coup (Defence Minister Hamad Shihab was killed, and another prominent military member, Saadoun Ghaidan, was wounded). But in general the Tikritis stick together, and have such a strong representation in the upper echelons of the armed forces that there have been no further coup attempts since 1973.

While Iraq under the Ba'ath continues to be a near-totalitarian State, the killing or torture of opponents of the regime is now conducted in secret, and a significant degree of *détente* has been achieved with rival internal forces. The two most striking achievements of Vice-President Saddam Hussein have been the creation of a National Progressive Front enlisting the support of the Iraqi Communist Party for the regime in 1973 (although it is still allowed to operate only within the narrow bounds permitted by the Ba'ath Party), and the pacification of the Kurdish north in 1975 after 15 years of intermittent war, an achievement made possible by a diplomatic agreement with Iran. The development of the internal economy has been extremely rapid in recent years, due mainly to Iraq's rising oil production (which will exceed that of Iran within the next few years) and the greatly heightened oil prices since 1973.

There has also been a significant easing in the virulently hostile policies which Iraq pursued towards most of its neighbours and the world beyond in the early years of the Ba'ath regime. The long-standing dispute with Kuwait was reduced in negotiations in 1977 to a mere disagreement over the terms of lease of Kuwaiti territory which had been forcibly seized by Iraq in an earlier period, and the border between the two countries was reopened. The bitterly hostile relations with Iran caused by territorial disputes and Iranian aid to Iraq's Kurdish insurgents, which more than once had threatened to erupt into full-scale war, became cool but correct after the remarkably statesmanlike gesture of Saddam Hussein in 1975 when he abandoned Iraq's territorial claims in return for Iranian abandonment of the Kurdish revolt.

Even the most venomous quarrel in the entire Arab world – that between the Iraqi and the Syrian governments and Ba'ath Parties – was at least temporarily composed in 1978. The quarrel, which led to a complete split in 1966 and the creation by both the Iraqi and Syrian 'regional' Ba'ath Parties of rival 'national' (pan-Arab) Ba'ath commands, was nominally about esoteric ideological differences, but actually owed a great deal more to personal and factional rivalries and the fear within each party that it would be manipulated or dominated by the other. A significant material point of difference arose after the accession to power of the current Syrian Ba'athist leader, Hafez al-Asad, in 1970, when the Syrian regime officially accepted the possibility of a negotiated peace settlement with a sovereign and still-surviving Israel – something no Iraqi Ba'athist leader has ever reconciled himself to. The need for a united Arab radical front in face of Egypt's peace negotiations with Israel finally overcame even the bitter Syrian–Iraqi hostility, however, and in October, 1978 the borders between the two countries were reopened, the military forces which both sides had kept stationed there were withdrawn, and the two nations formed a military co-operative committee to draft a defence agreement to serve as the basis for full military union between them. There have been many such agreements in the past between these and other Arab States, none of which has lasted, but just the fact that the Baghdad regime would have anything to do with the Syrian Ba'athists is in itself a most significant sign of Iraq's growing pragmatism in foreign affairs.

This pragmatism has its finest hour in Iraq's relationship with the Soviet Union, its main arms supplier since 1958. The Ba'athist regime signed a 15 year 'Friendship and Co-operation Treaty' with the Soviet Union in 1972 from which it reaps significant economic, military and diplomatic benefits, but it has not been allowed to compromise the regime's independence in any way. Iraq has been careful to diversify its sources of arms supply (principally to France) and maintains extensive economic and trading links with most Western countries. Although Baghdad shares with Moscow a generalised hostility to the 'imperialist West', its specific foreign policies are as often as not opposed to those of the Soviet Union: over the Kuwaiti and Iranian confrontations in the past, over the legitimacy of Israel and the desirability of a negotiated Middle East peace, and most recently and sharply over the Soviet presence and policies in the Horn of Africa. No Soviet objections were permitted to stand in the way of Iraq's proposed re-establishment of diplomatic relations with the USA (broken since 1967) in 1977, although those negotiations eventually failed for other reasons. The regime ruthlessly executes local communists who attempt to step beyond the narrow political sphere allotted to them.

The present Iraqi regime resembles all those since 1958 in being essentially a government of Sunni Arabs over Iraq's other minorities, in being xenophobic and fanatically pan-Arab, while avoiding actual commitments to political union with other Arab States, and in being ultimately dependent upon its supporters in the army. It differs in having created a mass civilian party (the Iraqi Ba'ath Party, estimated to have 5000 members in 1968, now has 50,000–60,000 regular members, around half a million 'friends and supporters', and another million 'adherents', by its own reckoning), in having enough money to keep its supporters and other Iraqis at least passively contented, and in having established an efficient semi-totalitarian system. The key to its survival is still the army, however, and here too it has apparently been remarkably effective in removing all non-Ba'ath officers from sensitive positions. While severe civil–military tensions remain, they are mainly within the Ba'ath Party, which dominates both spheres. As a result of all this, the regime certainly has a far more secure hold on power than any of its predecessors, and can probably continue to pursue its totally independent course in foreign policy.

STRENGTH AND BUDGET

The strength of the Iraqi armed forces in 1982 was 342,250 men, of whom 300,000 were in the army, 38,000 in the air force (of whom 10,000 are Air-Defence personnel) and 4000 in the navy. Army reserves are about 75,000 and the main paramilitary force is the Ba'ath Party militia (the People's Army) consisting of approximately 7000 men trained and equipped on the military model. There are also 4800 'security troops' under the control of the Ministry of the Interior.

There has been a steady increase in the size of the armed forces from 23,000 in 1936, to 50,000 in 1958, to 82,000 in 1966, followed by a leap of more than 150% to today's figure. This has been made possible in part by the extremely rapid growth rate (over 3% per annum) of Iraq's population, which now numbers 13,600,000, but is mainly due to the four-fold rise in government oil revenues after 1973.

Iraq's defence expenditure in 1980 was 491,500,000 dinars ($2,900,000,000 from a GNP of $38,980,000,000.)

COMMAND AND CONSTITUTIONAL STATUS

The President of Iraq, Saddam Hussein (assumed power July 16th, 1979), is also President of the Revolutionary Command Council (the supreme executive and legislative body), the Prime Minister of the Council of Ministers (cabinet), the Secretary-General of the Regional (Iraqi) Ba'ath Command (the Party's executive body) and Commander-in-Chief of the Armed Forces.

In the Provincial Constitution of 1968 the Revolutionary Command Council is identified as the highest authority in the country, with full executive powers and also with legislative powers pending the election of a National Assembly (an event which has yet to occur). The precise channels by which the body's decisions are transmitted to the armed forces have not been publicly identified, but in practice it may be assumed that control is exercised by President Saddam Hussein.

The other vital element in maintaining the stability of the regime is direct control over the Baghdad garrison and the general reserve. Direct command of the Baghdad garrison (the Republican Guards mechanised brigade, one infantry division and one independent armoured brigade) is exercised by the President.

The general reserve, consisting of one armoured and one mechanised division, one special forces brigade and one independent infantry brigade, is like the Baghdad garrison commanded by officers who are considered the most loyal to the regime. In past years it was based to Tikrit, 100 miles north of Baghdad, which is the power base of the ruling faction within the Ba'ath Party. (In 1969 Iraq's 14 provinces were increased to 16 departments, and Tikrit became a separate administrative division.) Apart from the Baghdad garrison and the general reserve from Tikrit, all other army formations as kept well away from the capital, and in times of tension may even be routed around it when moving from one part of the country to another.

Under the Minister of Defence, who is believed to be formally in the chain of command, operational control is the duty of the Chief of the General Staff, also based at the Ministry of Defence in Baghdad. This officer is also invariably the Chief of Staff of the Army. The Commander of the

Air Force, which is a separate service, is nonetheless subordinated to the army in the person of the Chief of the General Staff; air force headquarters are in Baghdad. The small navy is an integral component of the army, and the Commander of the Navy comes under the control of the Chief of Staff of the Army (although the distinction is a purely technical one, he being the same person as the Chief of the General Staff). Navy headquarters are at Basra.

ROLE, COMMITMENT, DEPLOYMENT AND RECENT OPERATIONS

Role and Commitment

The Iraqi army organises and deploys itself in support of three principal roles: defence of its own position within the regime; defence of the regime as a whole against enemies, primarily the other national minorities; and defence or attack against external enemies.

The first role, that of safeguarding the ruling faction within the Ba'ath Party from its rivals and of defending the large influence of the armed forces within the Party, is achieved by political manoeuvre backed by specialised troops – the Baghdad garrison and, to a considerable extent, the general reserve at Tikrit – which are mainly devoted to this role. They are equipped more or less in the standard way, but it is, for example, scarcely conceivable that the troops of the Baghdad garrison would ever be sent away from the capital in support of some other commitment. The forces against which these troops might be called upon to fight are primarily the People's Army maintained by the civilian wing of the Ba'ath Party (whose strength in the capital is not significantly inferior to that of the army's Baghdad garrison except in armour), or rebel army or air force units.

Deployment

The second main role, that of controlling Iraq's non-Sunni Arab communities, is what usually occupies the greater part of the army. In the case of the Shiite Arabs of the south this has not called for more than riot-control duties which are performed by combat units that do not have specialised riot-control equipment. In the case of the Kurds, however, the maintenance of control has involved the army and air force in protracted conventional military campaigns as well as an unending counter-insurgency task. (For details of the Kurdish campaigns, see Recent Operations.)

On average, therefore, about half the army has been stationed in the north for the past 20 years. This is not as great a disadvantage for the third role (external defence) as it might seem, however, for the main external threats to the country in this period have been seen as coming from Syria and Iran. In both cases the principal avenue of attack would be into the north of Iraq, which also contains the vital oil fields which are the most important point to defend, so the centre of gravity of the army and air force is in the right place for defence against external attack anyway. Drawing also on the general reserve stationed at Tikrit, about half way between Baghdad and Mosul, the principal city of the north, the Iraqi army has repeatedly shown itself able to concentrate approximately half its total strength against either Iran or Syria within a very short time, without exposing the oilfields to danger or relinquishing control of the Kurdish areas.

The normal deployment of the army around the country, at times when there is no particular border defence or counter-insurgency task demanding priority, is a good indication of the relative importance assigned by the Baghdad regime to various threats. In early 1977 it was as follows: at Mosul, covering the Turkish and Syrian borders and protecting the approach to the Kirkuk oilfields in the event of further hostilities with the Kurds in the north, one armoured and one mechanised division and one independent infantry brigade; at Kirkuk, controlling the southern part of Kurdistan and covering the northern part of the Iranian border, one armoured and two infantry divisions; at Tikrit, serving as general reserve and equidistant from Baghdad and the central part of the Iranian border, one armoured and one mechanised division, one special forces brigade and one independent infantry brigade; at Baghdad, one Republican Guard mechanised brigade, one infantry division and one independent armoured brigade; and in the south around Basra, covering the Kuwaiti border and the southern part of the Iranian frontier, one armoured and one infantry division.

Since the settlement of all outstanding issues with Iran in 1975 (for the confrontation with Iran, see Recent Operations), the defence of that frontier has not been given a very high priority. In the event that it should again become important, one would again expect to see Iraq in an essentially defensive posture. This is due not only to the greater size and superior equipment of Iranian forces that could be deployed along the frontier, but also to the arguments of terrain. While Iran's vital oil terminals and general ports of Khorramshahr and Abadan in the south are right on the river that forms the border, the extremely narrow neck of Iraqi territory leading down from Basra to the Gulf, averaging about 30 miles wide, would make it very difficult for Iraq to mount an offensive into Iranian territory there, while an Iranian river-crossing could quite possibly cut Iraq off from the sea. In the north, by contrast, the mountains begin at the Iranian frontier and offer no strategically significant targets to an Iraqi attack anyway, while going the other way both Baghdad and Iraq's main oil area around Kirkuk are only 80 miles from the border across fairly good tank country.

Access to the Gulf is a major Iraqi defence concern, since most of the country's imports and exports (including, since the 1975 opening of a pipe-line southwards from the oilfields, over one-third of its oil exports) must pass through the Gulf. Iraq has built up a small navy of missile-armed fast patrol boats to defend access to its 30 miles of coastline at the head of the Gulf and to its main ports a short distance up the Shatt al-Arab, but basically the problem is insoluble since Iran controls the exit from the Gulf to the Indian Ocean from bases well out of range of Iraqi forces. The government's natural anxiety at being the only radical regime in an area otherwise populated by conservative, pro-Western States had made it the main obstacle to the conclusion of a Gulf security pact, a goal avidly sought by some of its neighbours. It was Iraq's dissent which prevented the realisation of such a pact at the meeting of littoral States held in Oman in 1976, since it felt unable to agree to a rule excluding outside naval forces from the Gulf. The other States would feel perfectly secure in their own numbers and naval strength if the United States navy were excluded from the Gulf, but for Iraq the only equaliser is the ability of the Soviet navy to cruise in these waters.

Iraq's nervousness about its access to the Gulf also lies at the root of its continuing dispute with Kuwait, which has stimulated the latter into an arms build-up aimed at matching Iraqi forces deployed in the vicinity. The claim to all of Kuwait raised by the Kassem regime in 1961 has long since been dropped, but in order to protect the approaches to its sole naval base of Umm-Qasr, the only regular Soviet naval port of call in the Gulf, Iraq has long occupied the Kuwaiti islands of Warba and Bubiyan. There have also been Iraqi incursions into Kuwaiti territory at Samita on the mainland side of the channel leading to Umm-Qasr, notably in 1973, and further border clashes occurred in 1976. Following a visit by the Kuwaiti Defence Minister to Baghdad in July,

1977 the border between the two countries was reopened for the first time in 5 years. Iraq has proposed a solution whereby it would lease the islands for military purposes, together with a coastal strip of the opposite mainland which is still under Kuwaiti control, while permitting the Kuwaiti civil administration to return to the islands, but at the end of 1978 there had been no agreement on the precise terms of this solution.

The desert half of Iraq extending south and west to the Saudi Arabian, Jordanian and Syrian borders contains little population and almost nothing of economic importance except oil pipe-lines, and the same is largely true on the other side of those borders. Iraq has some minor border disputes with Saudi Arabia, and bitter ideological quarrels with both the Saudis and Jordan, but large-scale hostilities on the Saudi Arabian or Jordanian borders are both logistically and strategically implausible. The 12 year vendetta between the rival Ba'athist regimes in Damascus and Baghdad (given at least a temporary burial in October, 1978) repeatedly led to the protagonists concentrating a couple of divisions each on their common frontier, but the considerable distances between the Syrian—Iraqi frontier and strategically significant objectives in either country make it unlikely that anything more serious than large skirmishes would ever occur. There have never been military tensions along Iraq's border in the north with Turkey, although extensive counter-insurgency operations against the Kurds have been carried out on the Iraqi side.

What remains to be considered is that Iraqi armed forces' capabilities against Israel. Iraqi contingents have fought in three of the four Arab—Israeli wars (in 1967 they arrived too late for the fighting, although about 20,000 Iraqi troops remained in Jordan and Syria until January, 1971). In any future war where they were trying to reach the front after the outbreak of hostilities they would again suffer heavy Israeli air attack while their columns and convoys were crossing Syria, as they did in 1967 and 1973, and they would again be thrown into combat piecemeal, with probably disastrous results. Moreover, the range of some of the new aircraft recently acquired by Israel brings Iraq's oil fields within reasonable attack range, and it is known that the Iraqi air force has recently mounted 24 hour combat patrols above the oil installations at times of high tension in Arab—Israeli relations.

This did not prevent Israel from destroying the Iraqi nuclear plant near Baghdad in June 1981, by an F-16 raid.

Since the outbreak of the Iraq—Iran war on September 22nd, 1980, fighting has required the deployment of almost the whole Iraqi army to the Shatt-el-Arab front, south of Basra (though some forces were deployed on the border further north, and a few remained in Kurdistan for security reasons).

Recent Operations

The Iraqi army's only recent experience of high-intensity conventional combat was in 1973, when an armoured formation arrived on the Golan front 10 days after the war began. It was caught by Israeli aircraft and artillery while still deploying, and lost about 100 tanks in a couple of hours.

In counter-insurgency operations, on the other hand, only the Sudanese army in the Arab world can begin to approach the Iraqi army's experience. It easily destroyed a brief guerrilla campaign in the southern marshes of the country led by a breakaway faction of the Iraqi Communist Party in 1969—71, but its main field of operations from 1961 to 1975 was in Iraqi Kurdistan.

The Kurds, divided between four nations since the partition of the Ottoman Empire in 1918, constitute a larger proportion of the total population in Iraq (about 20%) than in any other country, and sporadically revolted even during the period of British rule. Immediately after World War II, when the Soviet Union was maintaining a 'Kurdish Republic' in Russian-occupied north-western Iran, Moscow provided military aid to a more serious Kurdish rebellion in Iraq led by the feudal chieftain General Mullah Mustafa Barzani. When American pressure forced the Russians to withdraw from Iran the aid dried up and Barzani was obliged to go into exile in the Soviet Union, but he returned in 1958 on the overthrow of the monarchy. He established himself as the titular head of the Kurdish Democratic Party (KDP), a theoretically socialist grouping dedicated only to Kurdish autonomy within Iraq, but in reality he always overshadowed it as a powerful military leader drawing his strength from traditional tribal loyalties.

Following unsuccessful negotiations with the Kassem government for Kurdish autonomy. Barzani declared an independent Kurdish State in March, 1961 and in the course of the next year drove Iraqi government forces out of all the Kurish areas along the Turkish and Iranian frontiers. The war then settled into a pattern that lasted throughout the 1960s: a spring and summer offensive by government forces, with the ground won in that offensive then being regained by the Kurds in the autumn and winter. Barzani had tacit Soviet support, though little direct military aid, and the Iraqi army proved unable to cope with the combination of almost universal Kurdish support for the revolt and the exceedingly difficult mountainous terrain. The war was punctuated by a negotiated ceasefire in 1964 and in 1966, based on major concessions by Baghdad on Kurdish national rights, and a section of the Kurdish population led by Jalal Talabani even rallied to the Iraqi side on the second occasion, but a final settlement and a complete end to the fighting were never achieved.

Following the Ba'athist coup of 1968 the fighting was resumed in full intensity, and by 1969 the Kurdish rebel army (about 15,000 strong) was even shelling the vital oil installations at Kirkuk on the disputed border between Kurdistan and Iraq proper. In 1970 the Ba'ath regime produced a 15 point peace plan which granted most Kurdish demands: Kurdish representation in the government, equal status for the Kurdish language in the north, government acceptance and support for Barzani's troops as an official Iraqi frontier force, the appointment of Kurdish officials in Kurdish majority areas, and constitutional recognition that Iraq was a bi-national State inhabited by Arabs and Kurds. Fighting stopped almost immediately, but over the following years it became evident that the Baghdad government had no intention of fulfilling most of its promises. A number of attempts were made to assassinate Barzani and his closest aides, and the autonomy statute promulgated by Baghdad after the agreed delay in April, 1974 failed to satisfy Kurdish expectations in a number of respects: notably, in denying Kurds representation on the Revolutionary Command Council, and in excluding from the Kurdish autonomous area the districts around Kirkuk containing the main oilfields, where the Kurds claimed to be in the majority.

Barzani and his militia, the Pesh Merga, resumed fighting immediately and by the latter part of 1974 the war was being fought at a hitherto unprecedented intensity. Most of the Iraqi army was deployed in Kurdistan, suffering heavy casualties, while the air force was employed in making saturation bombing attacks on Kurdish villages in rebel-held areas. It became a war of semi-conventional character, with brigade-sized engagements occurring at frequent intervals. The Kurds were amply supplied with heavy weapons, including artillery and anti-aircraft guns, and the Iraqi army was unable to subdue the resistance. Most of the districts along the border were completely under KDP administration.

The great difference in 1974 was that the Kurds had the active support of Iran and the tacit support of the USA, and large quantities of weapons and supplies were flowing into them across the Iranian border. Following a lengthy series of border incidents, Iran had denounced the 1937 treaty defining its border with Iraq, and demanded revisions along the Shatt al-Arab, the river which gives access both to Iraq's only ports and to Iran's main oil termini. The 1937 agreement imposed by the British had placed the frontier on the Iranian bank, making the river exclusively Iraqi territory, and Iran demanded that the frontier be recognised as running down the centre of the river. Tehran's military support for the Kurdish insurgency was entirely a means of extorting Iraqi agreement to this claim (Iran, after all, cannot afford to play with Kurdish autonomy, having more Kurds within its borders than Iraq), but Barzani made the fatal error of making himself wholly dependent on Iran's support.

Iran's strategy worked: in March, 1975 at the OPEC meeting in Algiers, Iraq agreed to settle the border dispute on Iran's terms, and to cease supporting revolutionary groups in Iran. In return, Tehran agreed to end 'infiltrations of a subversive character', that is, to end all support for the Kurdish revolt. Kurdish resistance promptly collapsed, and by May, 1975 200,000 Kurds had fled across the border to Iranian refugee camps. Barzani retired to the USA, almost totally discredited, and Iraqi government forces occupied all of Kurdistan.

Baghdad formally maintained the Kurdish autonomy statute and proclaimed an amnesty for Pesh Merga soldiers. Some 50,000 of the returning refugees, however, were forcibly resettled in southern Iraq, and the entire Kurdish area remains saturated with Iraqi army units. Extensive fortifications have been built around Kirkuk and Mosul. Kurdish sources claim that Baghdad is following a policy of Arabisation in these vital areas of mixed population, by bringing in large numbers of Arab settlers from the south, and that a 25 mile strip of land along the Turkish and Persian borders is being systematically emptied of its Kurdish population. On the other hand, about 40,000 Kurds were allowed to return to Kurdistan from the south in April, 1977.

Following the shock defeat in 1973, the KDP splintered into a number of warring factions, but by 1977 guerrilla attacks were again becoming frequent in Iraq's Kurdish areas. The bulk of the fighting, however, was between two rival Kurdish groups: the KDP—Provisional Leadership, which claims to have inherited Barzani's mantle, and the Patriotic Union of Kurdistan (PUK). The latter was an alliance between Jalal Talabani's original group of that name (he had long since broken his links with Baghdad), the Association of Marxist—Leninists of Kurdistan, and Ali Askari's Socialist Movement of Kurdistan. The KDP—PL, having renounced any dependence on outside sources of aid like Iran and the USA, and having reverted to a strategy of protracted guerrilla warfare, officially adopted a socialist programme for the first time in 1976. The PUK, based in Damascus, received strong support from Syria, Iraq's inveterate enemy, in attempting to revive the revolt.

In a major clash in July, 1978 near the Iranian border the KDP—PL claimed to have captured 400 PUK fighters, including Ali Askari, 'Supreme Military Commander', and all its other leaders operating inside the country except Talabani himself. The PUK's ability to challenge the long-established KDP for control of the 'second revolution', as it is known, has been further sapped by the reconciliation between Syria and Iraq which, if it lasts, will cut the PUK off from its supplies and arms. The potential for a renewed large-scale Kurdish revolt

is still in existence, but it is unlikely that it will actually flare into major warfare again in the near future.

The outbreak of the Iraq—Iran war on September 22nd, 1980, involved the army in by far the most intense fighting it has experienced since independence (and some of the heaviest fighting anywhere in the world since 1945).

Attacking on a 300-mile front, on the pretext of a continuing dispute over the Shatt-el-Arab frontier, but probably in the hope of toppling the Islamic regime in Iran, Saddam Hussein's forces had considerable early success. They penetrated as far as the oil town of Abadan and seized territory extensively in the 'Arab' province of Khuzistan. After a year of stalemates, however, they were counter-attacked at the end of 1981. In March the Iranians secured a considerably success near Deshful, and in May recaptured Khorramshahr. In June, conceding the failure of his offensive, Saddam Hussein withdrew his troops from Iranian territory since when they have been defending their own against increasingly heavy attacks from the Iranians. In the context of equipment losses suffered by both sides and the nature of the terrain, the war seems likely to become one of pure attrition, as long as it lasts.

ORGANISATION

Arms of Service
The army is divided into combat arms — infantry, armour, artillery and engineers — and services essentially along British lines. There are also *elite* units such as the Republican Guards brigade and the Special Forces brigade. The air force is organisationally separate, although under the effective operational control of the Army Chief of Staff through his other appointment as Chief of the General Staff. It is divided into flying and non-flying personnel, and the latter group is further divided into various technical specialities, along the same lines as the British Royal Air Force. The small navy is an integral part of the army.

Operational
The army is organised into six armoured, three mechanised and four mountain infantry divisions, plus three special forces brigades and one Republican Guards brigade. Divisional organisation is triangular: armoured divisions have two armoured and one mechanised brigade, mechanised divisions have one armoured and two mechanised brigades, and infantry divisions have one mechanised and two motorised brigades, in each case with supporting artillery, anti-aircraft and in some cases SSM units. Each brigade contains three regiments. A standard infantry division averages about 12,000 men; armoured divisions have considerably smaller numbers of personnel. Divisions are moved about internally according to changing priorities in internal security and border defence.

The air force has a squadron organisation, and consists of one bomber squadron, one light bomber squadron, 11 fighter—ground attack squadrons and five interceptor squadrons. There are also two large transport squadrons and 11 helicopter squadrons, plus a large number of training aircraft. The 10,000 strong Air-Defence component of the air force operates the fixed and mobile SAM units, but not the army's lavish array of anti-aircraft guns and SAM-7s. The principal operational air bases are at Baghdad, at Kirkuk and Mosul in the north, and near Basra in the south.

The navy has the normal organisation of ship and shore commands, all centred at Basra, the site of naval headquarters, and nearby at Umm-Qasr, the main naval port.

RECRUITMENT, TRAINING AND RESERVES

Conscription for 2 years of military service, liability extending for all males from the age of eighteen to forty, has been extablished in Iraq since 1934; it has been extended for 'the duration' since the outbreak of war. It was only after 1958, however, that the National Defence Law abolished the provision whereby conscripts could purchase exemption from military service, and until quite recently there had been only limited success in applying the law in Kurdish-populated areas. State employees in essential jobs and certain categories of students and religious leaders are entitled to deferment or exemption, but by and large the law is fairly and strictly applied: this largely explains the steady numerical growth of the Iraqi army, which is simply accepting each year the larger number of conscripts produced by the rapidly expanding population.

Induction of recruits normally occurs at the age of eighteen, and after his 2 years of active service the conscript is automatically placed in a reserve status for an additional 18 years. The army also encourages voluntary enlistments for successive 2 year periods, commencing either directly from civilian life or at the completion of conscript service, and enlisted personnel are eligible for pension after 15 years of service or upon reaching the age of forty-five. A substantial proportion of the enlisted strength of the Iraqi army, including almost all NCOs, is made up of these career personnel. Almost all air force and navy personnel are volunteers.

Following basic recruit training, conscripts receive on-the-job training with their assigned units. Most conscripts are of rural background and limited education, but are familiar with firearms; they adapt readily to military service.

For regular personnel, the army maintains service schools for the combat arms, as well as for the technical and administrative services, mostly in the Baghdad area; they provide courses for both officers and NCOs. About 150 Soviet advisers are in the country to assist in training Iraqi troops in the use of the more advanced Soviet weapons in use, and numbers of NCOs as well as officers have been sent abroad for training. After 20 years of primary reliance on the Soviet Union as arms supplier, Iraqi army tactical doctrines have shifted considerably from the former British model towards the Soviet pattern, although this transformation has been both retarded and to some extent redirected by the fact that most of the army's actual combat experience in this period has been in counter-insurgency operations.

Most army officers are graduates of the Military College, founded in 1924, which is located in the south-western section of Baghdad at Rustamiyeh. Candidates must be secondary-school graduates between 16 and 21 years of age, and must succeed in competitive entrance examinations. In practice the large majority of the 250—300 cadets enrolled each year are Sunni Arabs, and in recent years there has been a concerted attempt to ensure that most are members of the Ba'ath Party associated with the dominant factions within that party. Cadets are divided into two groups, combatant (combat arms) and administrative (the various technical services); they study common subjects during the first 2 years of the course, but specialise according to their branch in the final year. Upon graduation they receive commissions as second-lieutenants in the regular army.

There is also a Reserve College, founded in 1952, which provides separate 1 year courses for conscripts holding secondary school qualifications or academic degrees; the latter course also provides military training for professional specialists such as doctors and legal personnel who join the regular army. About 2000 reserve officers are graduated each year, of whom only a small percentage subsequently serve on active duty for short periods. Those with professional degrees or qualifications receive commissions as second lieutenants, the remainder as warrant officers.

Air force flying personnel are trained at the Air Force Flying College at Shu'aiba Air Base near Basra, founded in 1950. It also conducts courses for the training of technical specialists. Beginning in 1976 some 30 Iraqi pilots a year were also being trained to fly by the RAF Training Command in Britain, but the recent coolness in Anglo—Iraqi relations may lead to the ending of this agreement.

Company-grade officers receive further training in tactical and technical subjects in the various branch training establishments maintained by the army, and also abroad. Army and air force officers selected for higher command and staff responsibilities attend a 2 year course at the Staff College in Rustamiyeh, founded in 1928, whose curriculum is basically modelled on that of the British Army Staff College at Camberley. Selected Iraqi officers also attend Staff Colleges in the Soviet Union and Britain.

The army's reserves are stated to number about 250,000 men, with graduates of the Reserve College providing an officer reserve as well, but there is not unit organisation for the reserves, nor are they called up for training at regular intervals. Those who have completed active service as conscripts within the preceding 5 years, however, provide an ample reservoir of soldiers with reasonably fresh experience to serve as reinforcements or replacements for existing regular units in an emergency. There are not figures available for air force reserves, but they would not be very numerous.

EQUIPMENT AND ARMS INDUSTRY

The main armoured strength of the Iraqi army is its 2300 T-54/-55/-62/-72 medium tanks, with the latter predominating. It also has 100 PT-76 light tanks. Large numbers of tank transporters are in use and further T-62s are on order from the Soviet Union.

Amongst the total of 3000 other armoured fighting vehicles the great majority are Soviet BMP and BTR-50P and Czech OT-62B APCs. Wheeled APCs include the old BTR-152 and the newer BTR-60P; light reconnaissance duties are performed by BTR-40P amphibious vehicles, some in a special anti-tank version mounting a six-launcher AT-3 Sagger system. There are small numbers of French-built Panhard AMLs, and other foreign designs — Cascavel and MOWAG etc.

The artillery arm has 19 FROG-7 surface-to-surface missiles (80km range) and 9 Scud B SSMs (300km range). Further Scud Bs are one order. Self-propelled artillery includes 90 SU-100 and 40 ISU-122 SP guns. The remaining 800 artillery pieces, all of Soviet make, towed: 75mm and 85mm guns; M-37 and M-38 122mm howitzers; modern M-63 122mm gun/howitzers; M-54/46 130mm guns; and M-37, M-43 and M-55 152mm howitzers. The standard mortars are Soviet M-37 81mm, M-38 and M-43 120mm, and some 160mm. Rocket launchers are of the BM-21 122mm type, carried on URAL-375D trucks.

The main burden of anti-tank defence is now borne by Soviet AT-3 Sagger and French SS-11 HOT and Milan ATGWs, but there remain limited numbers of Soviet M-44 100mm and M-45 85mm ATK guns. B-10 82mm and B-11 107mm recoilless rifles are also in use, and RPG-7 anti-tank rockets are issued to the infantry in large numbers.

The army has a total of approximately 1200 Soviet-made AA guns. There are some of the old-calibre M-44 85mm and M-49 100mm AA guns, but the great majority are modern small-calibre automatic weapons: S-60 57mm cannons in both the single towed and twin self-propelled (ZSU-57-2) versions, M-38/39 37mm cannons in single and twin towed versions, 23mm cannon in the twin towed (ZU-23) and quadruple self-propelled (ZSU-23-4) version, and Vladimirov KPV 14.5 heavy machine-guns in twin and quadruple mounts carried on a wide variety of vehicles. The SA-7 Strela man-portable surface-to-air missile is used in large numbers by the infantry. Larger SAMs, including the mobile SA-6s, are operated by the air force.

The standard infantry weapon is the Kalashnikov AKM in both the Soviet version and the East German MPiKM version; soft-skinned transport vehicles are about half Soviet, half East German.

The air force has about 330 combat aircraft, of which the majority are Soviet built, with some French and British types. Bomber strength is 12 TU-22 medium bombers and 10 Il-28 light bombers. The five interceptor squadrons are equipped with 115 MiG-21s. Of the 12 FGA squadrons, four fly 80 MiG-23Bs, three have 60 SU-7Bs, three have 30SU-20s and two have 20 Hunter FB59/FR10s. The one COIN squadron flies 12 Jet Provost T52s. 72F-1C Mirage fighters and four Mirage F-1B trainers are on order from France, with deliveries scheduled to begin in 1979.

Transport aircraft include 10 An-2s, eight An-12s, eight An-24s, two An-26s, two Tu-124s, 13 Il-14s and two Herons. A number of Il-76 transports are on order from the Soviet Union.

The helicopter squadrons fly 35 Mi-4, 14 Mi-6, 80 Mi-8, 47 Alouette III, eight Super Frelon, 40 Gazelle and three Puma helicopters. There are reports that at least some of these helicopters have been equipped as gunships for use in counter-insurgency operations. Air force training aircraft include MiG-15/-21/-23Us, SU-7Us, Hunter T69s, 10 Yak-11s, 12L-29s and eight L-39s.

The standard air-to-air weapon is the AA-2 Atoll AAM and the air-to-surface missile is the AS-11/12 ASM. However, R.550 Magic AAMs and Exocet ASMs are on order from France.

The naval component's principal fighting strength is its six Osa-I and eight Osa-II fast patrol boats armed with Styx surface-to-surface missiles. It also has 10 P-6 torpedo boats, three SO-1-class submarine chasers, two large Poluchat-class patrol craft, six smaller coastal patrol boats, five mine-sweepers (two T-43-class, three inshore) and three Polnocny-class LCTs. All naval equipment is Soviet built.

Army and air force workshops have a considerable main-tenance and repair capability, and serviceability rates are quite good by Middle Eastern standards, but apart from this there is no arms industry in the country. The need to import all weapons, spares and even most varieties of ammunition creates a certain vulnerability, which is exacerbated by the fact that over 95% of Iraqi weapons since 1958 have been provided by a single supplier – the Soviet Union. In any conflict on its eastern frontiers, moreover, Iraq would prob-ably be unable to make use of its vulnerable and easily block-aded ports on the Shatt al-Arab, and would be completely dependent on aerial resupply.

In an attempt to diversify its source of arms, therefore, Iraq has increasingly turned to Western suppliers in recent years, and especially to France, with which it has a partic-ularly close commercial relationship (Iraq is France's largest Middle Eastern oil supplier after Saudi Arabia, and there are an estimated $4,000,000,000 worth of French industrial projects underway in the country). The agreement to purchase 72 Mirage fighters, additional helicopters, and French air-to-air and air-to-surface missiles was concluded during French Prime Minister Raymond Barre's visit to Baghdad in 1977. Baghdad has also engaged in discussions with West Germany

about the purchase of a modern radar network for the air force, and with Brazil concerning the acquisition of training aircraft. Much the greater part of Iraqi defence purchasing, however, will probably continue to be from the Soviet Union.

Iraqi is a signatory of the Nuclear Non-Proliferation Treaty, but much concern has been expressed in some quarters recently about the kind of fuel that is to be supplied by France for the 70 MW Osiris-type research reactor (Osirak) which is being constructed at Taiwatha in northern Iraq under the terms of the Franco–Iraqi nuclear accord of November, 1975. France is committed to supply 70kg of 93% enriched uranium by the time the reactor is completed in 1980, and other Western countries have made strong representations to France about his since it would provide Iraq with sufficient quantities of easily extractable weapons-grade uranium to make at least one nuclear bomb. France is now testing an alternative uranium fuel known as 'caramel' for the Osiris-class reactors which is enriched to only 7 or 8% and is thus unsuitable for weapons, but there is consid-erable doubt as to whether this will be available in commer-cial quantities by 1980.

RANK, DRESS AND DISTINCTIONS

Ranks in the Iraqi army generally follow the old Ottoman nomenclature, adapted to the British army's rank structure. Insignia of rank are worn on shoulder straps by army and air force officers (air force officers add flight wings at the outer edge of the strap). Naval officers wear gold stripes indentical to those of the British Royal Navy. Non-commissioned officers' ranks are shown by black stripes worn on the upper sleeves, with branches of service shown by distinctive em-blems, coloured cap piping and collar patches.

Mushir (Field Marshal) – Crossed sabres within olive wreath, Arab eagle towards centre
Muhib (General) – Crossed sabres, two stars, Arab eagle
Fariq (Lieutenant-general) – Crossed sabres, one star, Arab eagle
Liwa' (Major-general) – Crossed sabres, Arab eagle
Zaim (Brigadier) – Three stars forming triangle, Arab eagle
'Aqid (Colonel) – Two stars in line, Arab eagle
Muqaddam (Lieutenant-colonel) – One star, Arab eagle
Rais Awal (Major) – Arab eagle
Rais (Captain) – Three stars
Mulazim Awal (Lieutenant) – Two stars
Mulazim Thani (Second-lieutenant) – One star

Naib Dabit (Warrant Officer) – Arab eagle on upper sleeve
Rais Urafa Widha (Regimental Sergeant-major) – Arab eagle on lower sleeve
Rais Urafa Widha (Company Sergeant-major) – Four slant-ing stripes on upper sleeve
Rais Urafa (Company Quartermaster Sergeant) – Three slanting stripes, surmounted by Arab eagle
'Arif (Sergeant) – Three slanting stripes
Naib Arif (Corporal) – Two slanting stripes
Jundi Awal (Lance-corporal) – One slanting stripe
Jundi (Private) – –

Promotion of enlisted men is based on recommendations by superior officers, written proficiency examinations and time in grade. Minimum time in grade before promotion is: for privates, 1 year; for lance-corporals, 1½ years; for corporals, 2 years; for sergeants, 2½ years; for sergeant-majors, 4 years;

and for warrant officers, 3 years for each consecutive advancement through the eight classes within the rank. Before 1966 all officer ranks had a minimum time in grade of 4 years, but a law of that year permits the President of the Republic to grant up to 3 years' credit to any officer for distinguished service.

Pay and allowances in the armed forces compare favourably with salaries and wages for civilians of similar qualifications. Discipline is very strict, and distinctions between the various ranks are wide. Officers have powers to confine other officers of more junior rank after summary trial, for varying periods depending on the difference in rank, and may even order flogging of enlisted men (three lashes maximum by a captain, seven by a colonel).

Iraqi army officers' uniforms are similar to those of the British army: field uniform of beret or helmet, battledress jacket and trousers, web belt and short leggings; service dress of single-breasted jacket with patch pockets, khaki shirt and tie, and trousers without cuffs; and dress and mess dress uniforms. Except in the field British-style garrison caps are worn, with coloured piping to denote the branch of service, except for the armoured corps, who wear black berets. Winter field and garrison uniforms are olive-drab wool; summer equivalents are in light-tan gabardine or cotton twill. Specialised combat clothing is now mainly of Soviet design.

The highest Iraqi distinction is the Decoration of the Republic, which is granted to soldiers, civilians and distinguished foreigners for services to the nation. The Rafidain Military Medal, in three classes, is awarded to both soldiers and civilians, and is exceptionally presented to foreigners. The Bravery Medal and the General Service Medal are awarded to both soldiers and civilians for outstanding courage and for distinguished service during active military operations or in time of war. There are also campaign medals for the 1941 revolt, the Palestine War, the 1958 Revolution, the 1963 Revolutions and the war against the Kurds (the Medal of the Suppression of the Rebellion in the North), awarded to those who were in military service at the time or participated in the various revolutions.

CURRENT DEVELOPMENTS

Stability has three dimensons in Iraq: the intra-regime factional balance, and especially the civil—military balance; inter-communal relations between the various Iraqi minorities; and Iraq's relationship with the rest of the Arab world. As always, there are serious potential threats in all three areas, but nevertheless the present regime looks more solid and lasting than any in Iraq's modern history.

After the decades of coup and counter-coup which eliminated so many other major groups and parties in the Iraqi *élite*, and a decade of vigilant and ruthless suppression of dissents by the Ba'ath Party, there are no longer any discernible political challengers to the Party's control of Iraq's military and political *élite*. The only other political force permitted to operate within the Arab community, the Communist Party, is closely circumscribed in its activities: it belongs to the National Progressive Front, but has only two members in the Cabinet and none on the high policy-making arm of the government, the Revolutionary Command Council (RCC).

No party except the Ba'ath is permitted to organise political activity within the armed forces (a condition the communists agreed to in 1971), and any rival attempt to do so is instantly detected and crushed: 21 communists were hanged in May, 1978 for attempting to form secret groups within the army. Potential opposition figures are even tracked down abroad. One of two Iraqis awaiting trail in England in late 1978 for the assassination of General Abdul Razzak al-Nayef (briefly Prime Minister as head of the non-Ba'athist military officers who collaborated in the seizure of power in 1968, but then expelled from the country and the government by Ba'athist officers) was Fahad Shaker, the younger brother of Saadoun Shaker, head of Iraqi intelligence and a senior member of the RCC.

The exceptional secretiveness of the regime renders it opaque so far as the details of factional manoeuvres are concerned, but it is clear that the civil—military struggle is heating up as the departure of President al-Bakr approaches. For most of the past decade the stronghold of the generally more moderate military wing of the party has been the Revolutionary Command Council, while the Ba'ath Regional (Iraqi) Command has been dominated by the radical civilian factions within the party. Five officers formed the first RCC in 1968: some civilians were subsequently introduced, but after successive purges the RCC had again been reduced by mid-1977 to President al-Bakr and one other original member, plus Saddam Hussein and two other new members both of whom had served the President in a military capacity. In September, 1977, however, all 15 full members of the Ba'ath Regional Command plus two candidate members (almost all civilian) were added to the RCC, giving it a decidedly civilian flavour.

This should not necessarily be taken as a decisive shift of power, although the military wing is clearly on the defensive and feels particularly threatened by Saddam Hussein's policy in recent years of introducing *en masse* a new generation of young Ba'athists, loyal to himself, into the officer corps, where they are gradually rising in rank. The execution of 21 communists in 1978 on charges of infiltrating the army (some of whom had been convicted as long ago as 1975) may well have been a warning to the radical civilian wing of the party not to seek an alliance with the Communist Party against the military wing. The outcome of a civilian—military showdown is entirely unpredictable now, given the civilian wing's allies in the junior ranks of the officer corps and its control over the 75,000 strong and well armed party militia, the People's Army.

The second dimension of stability, that of the relations between the various minority communities of Iraq, is easier to assess. The Sunni Arabs are securely in charge, there is no discernible separate political organisation for the Shiite community at all, and one faction of the Kurdish Democratic Party is included within the National Progressive Front. It is unlikely that the pro-government part of the KDP accurately represents the feelings of more than a significant minority of Kurds, but after the total defeat of 1975 and the subsequent drastic measures taken by Baghdad, a renewal of the Kurdish revolt on a similar scale is improbable in the near future. Most of the renewed fighting in the north (spilling over into Turkey's Kurdish areas as well) in 1977—8 appears to have been between rival Kurdish factions, and even if the KDP did establish its dominance by mid-1978, as has been reported, a really serious renewal of the Kurdish war would not be possible without major outside support. There have been suspicions in Baghdad of Turkish, Iranian and even Soviet support for the Kurds during the past year, but there is no evidence that this is the case.

The case of the Shiite Arabs of the south is similar: without external support no really serious trouble is to be expected. The potential is there is terms of dissatisfaction and resentment amongst the Shiite population: there were major riots in the Shiite holy cities of Najaf and Karbala in February, 1977 which were promptly and bloodily suppressed by the army. Baghdad's main anxiety, however, was that an ultra-nationalist regime of strongly religious character would supplant the Shah in neighbouring Iran. The Shah's departure into exile in January, 1979 means that this is still a possibility. If there is encouragement and support for Iraqi Shiites from the new government in Shiite Iran, then the present Baghdad regime could face a problem fully as serious as the recently ended Kurdish revolt — especially since there would be a strong likelihood that it would have to face both problems at once.

In the third principal dimension of survival — its international relations — the Iraqi regime currently enjoys an unusually favourable situation. For the first time since the 1958 revolution Iraq has no major dispute potentially involving a military confrontation with any of its neighbours. The last such dispute, with Syria, was ended in October, 1978 by a spectacular reconciliation aimed at creating a joint 'Eastern Front' against Israel to make up for the loss of Egyptian military support. Moreover, it now has formally correct relations with every single Arab regime except Egypt, and has at least for the moment ceased to support the campaign of assassination against moderate elements within the Palestine Liberation Organisation that was waged by radical Iraqi-based Palestinian groups through most of 1978.

The present inter-Arab cordiality will last only so long as no Arab regime breaks ranks and approves Egypt's peace policy, however, and Iraq's reconciliations with Syria and Iran must both be reckoned fragile. Renewed hostility towards Syria is perhaps the likelier of the two, but would not expose the regime to serious danger. The probability of major battles on the Iraqi—Syrian frontier has always been small, despite the repeated alarms of the past decade, since neither side would willingly commit large forces to combat there: Syria's principal defence concerns are at the other end of the country, on the Israeli frontier and in Lebanon, while Iraq's are along the Iranian border and in Kurdistan. A new confrontation between Iraq and the newly formed Iranian regime would be a more serious military threat, but would be likely to take the form of internal security operations against revolts receiving Iranian encouragement rather than of large-scale combat operations on the Iranian border.

The Iraqi army's ability to contain such internal revolts, if not to suppress them entirely, is not in doubt. It now has a homogeneous and professionally well-qualified officer corps with very extensive experience of counter-insurgency operations. It is hard to imagine that even the most severe factional rivalries within the Ba'ath Party would be permitted so to disrupt the armed forces as to jeopardise the exising structure of power in the country.

Failure in the war with Iran may, however, change that. While the army is fully extended in defending the Shatt-el-Arab frontier against the Iranians, the present leadership is probably safe. A prolonged pause in the fighting, allowing time for reflection on recent mistakes, may alter the army's outlook.

Gwynne Dyer

IRISH REPUBLIC

HISTORY AND INTRODUCTION

The Irish Defence Forces, which consist largely of the army, with an integral air corps and naval service, see their origins in the Irish Volunteers, founded in Dublin in November, 1913 by Professor Eoin MacNeill of the Gaelic League. The foundation was open and indeed perfectly legal, under the current United Kingdom legislation governing volunteer forces, which had been enacted to regularise the spontaneous creation of the Volunteer Rifle Corps of 1859. It was also under that legislation that the Ulster Volunteer Force (U.V.F.) had been founded in the northern counties the previous year. But, just as the U.V.F. had been founded to offer physical resistance, if necessary, to the imposition of the Irish Home Rule Bill ('Ulster Will Fight and Ulster Will Be Right'), by no means a purpose which the volunteer legislation had been designed to countenance, the foundation of the Irish Volunteers had a local political purpose: to counterweigh the U.V.F. and threaten the Westminster parliament with armed resistance if the Home Rule Bill were not enacted. It was only to the first of these intentions that MacNeill, the mildest of intellectuals, was dedicated; but the second was the real intention of his fellow committee members, whose loyalties lay towards the underground and revolutionary Irish Republican Brotherhood (I.R.B.).

Though hidden from the British, the I.R.B. connection became apparent to the leader of the constitutional Irish National Party, John Redmond, M.P., who managed to secure a controlling position within the Irish Volunteers and, on the outbreak of war in 1914, to lead the vast majority of its members (170,000 out of 180,000) into support for the British war effort. His belief was that a demonstration of loyalty would guarantee the grant of Home Rule (enacted but postponed at hostilities) after the war. The I.R.B. and the other extreme nationalist groups, including the tiny socialist Irish Citizen Army, took the contrary and time-hallowed view that 'England's difficulty was Ireland's opportunity' and prepared for rebellion. Their plans were discovered and countermanded by MacNeill, at the moment they were to strike in Easter week, 1916, but the Military Council of the I.R.B., meeting in Liberty Hall, Dublin, headquarters of the Irish Citizen Army, on Easter Sunday, April 23rd, decided nevertheless to proceed and the following day seized key points in the city with the handful of Irish Volunteers who answered their call, and the Irish Citizen Army. In all their force numbered 1200 and after a week's fighting their resistance was overcome.

The rising had not been popular in Ireland, but the execution of the leaders by the British turned opinion in their favour. Demand for full independence became widespread and in the 'khaki' election of December, 1918 for the United Kingdom parliament the majority of the candidates elected for Irish constituencies were nominees of Sinn Fein, the nationalist umbrella organisation. They refused to go to Westminster and met in Dublin, where they proclaimed themselves to be Dáil Éireann (the Irish parliament) and the legitimate government of Ireland. The Irish Volunteers, who came after August, 1918 to be known as the Irish Republican Army, were regarded as its armed force.

However, though the I.R.A.'s Chief of Staff, Richard Mulcahy, and Director of Intelligence, Michael Collins, were members of the Dáil, and Collins indeed its Minister of Finance, the I.R.A. was not under its direct control, either formally or, worse, practically. Éamon de Valéra, the Prime Minister, defined the relationship in April, 1919 thus: 'the Minister for Defence (Cathal Brugha) is of course in close association with the voluntary military forces which are the foundation of the national army'; but it was not such a close association that it could prevent individual I.R.A. groups taking independent action against the British army or the Royal Irish Constabulary. It was, in fact, an unauthorised killing of two constables at Soloheadbeag, County Tipperary, on January 21st, 1919, the day of the Dáil's first meeting, which precipitated the outbreak of open war between the nationalist movement and the British government and army.

The war lasted until July, 1921 and caused the deaths of about 600 soldiers and policemen, and 750 Irish people, mostly I.R.A. men. The I.R.A.'s armed strength never exceeded 3000, the British army's deployed strength being about 50,000, besides the R.I.C. and its emergency-raised forces, the 'Black and Tans' and the Auxiliaries. Michael Collins later admitted to the British that at the end his forces were almost beaten, but the war ended with a truce and negotiations for a treaty. Its terms were for sovereignty of an Irish Free State of 26 of the 32 Irish counties, within the British Commonwealth, something less than the all-Ireland republic of which the Dáil claimed to be the government. Many of its members, including de Valéra, declared their unwillingness to settle for less and, after a general election in June, 1922 had returned a pro-treaty majority, left the Dáil. The I.R.A. split along pro- and anti-treaty lines, occupied key points in various cities and in late June opened hostilities against each other. The pro-treaty faction, armed by the British and with the machinery of government behind it, quickly got the upper hand, but the campaign then resolved itself into guerrilla war and was not ended until July, 1923, and then principally by the implementation of a ruthless policy of reprisals: 77 anti-treaty prisoners were executed without trial by the Free State government.

Its army, founded on the pro-treaty faction of the I.R.A. but swelled by volunteers, had by then reached a strength of over 50,000, from which figure it was gradually run down in the first three years of peace, though not without difficulty; in March, 1924 a mutiny broke out among discontented officers, disgruntled both by the turn of political events inside the country and the terms of demobilisation, though more strongly by the latter, and it had to be settled by a mixture of force and bribes. Strength gradually fell from 15,000 to 11,000 in the mid-1920s but in 1930 had fallen to about 5000, near which it remained until the outbreak of World War II.

That the government felt obliged to retain a conventional army in being, while it also maintained a large and efficient national police force, was protected by the Royal Navy (which enjoyed the use of certain Irish ports until 1938), and consistently pursued a non-aligned foreign policy, cannot wholly be explained by reference to the argument that an army is one of the outward marks of sovereignty cherished by newly established states. The nationalist movement had always rested its case for nationhood upon a more abstract foundation, that of distinctive Irish culture, language and morality, and had carried this case forward into independence (under which the propagation of the Irish language in the public services – including the army – and its compulsory instruction in schools became one of the minor irritants of everyday life). The Free State's maintenance of its army in being is really explained by the underground survival of the anti-treaty guerrillas, who continued to call themselves the Irish Republican Army, who denied the legality of the Irish Free State, mounted violent attacks on its officials and claimed in some sense to represent legitimate power in Ireland. The I.R.A. called itself, in Irish, *Oglaigh na hEireann*, the title of the Irish Volunteers, which was also that borne by what it called the 'Free State Army'. That army was not needed to repress the I.R.A., for which the police (*Garda Siochana*) was a match, and indeed the government was at some pains to exclude it from anti-I.R.A. operations, for fear that by involving it some semblance might be given of a civil war still in progress. Thus the army principally existed to deny the claim of the I.R.A. itself to be the Irish army and to represent the pure spirit of nationalism – a claim which it maintained all the more strongly after de Valéra led the political Republicans into parliamentary life in 1927 (under the confusing party title of *Fianna Fáil*, Soldiers of Destiny, a monogram of which formed part of the Irish Volunteers' (and therefore also the Irish Free State Army's) badge. The election of *Fianna Fáil* to power in 1933 damned it for good in the eyes of the I.R.A., which in December, 1938, by a tortuous process of legal argument, declared itself to have inherited the sovereign power of the second *Dáil* and its 'Army Council', therefore to be the legitimate government of the Republic of Ireland.

Its activities had constantly invoked the State's use of emergency powers against it, particularly in the mid-1920s and early 1930s, but after the assumption of its claim to represent sovereign and legitimate power in the land, the organisation was swiftly declared unlawful (August, 1939). It was then conducting a campaign of terrorist explosions in Britain and, on the outbreak of war, when the Irish Free State (since 1937 *Eire* or Ireland) declared its neutrality, most of its more active members in Ireland were arrested and interned. It seemed thereafter destined to fade into obscurity. During the war, meanwhile, the Irish Defence Forces rose to almost the strength they had had during the civil war, while at least 50,000 citizens served in the British forces. An important element of the forces were the Volunteers, a force formed by the *Fianna Fáil* government in 1934 to provide a deliberate counter-attraction to the I.R.A. among young men of military inclinations in the countryside; the I.R.A itself admitted that it very greatly diminished their recruiting.

After the war, the army was reduced again to a strength of about 11,000, with the pre-war Volunteers and the wartime Local Defence Force consolidated as a volunteer reserve known as the *Forsa Cosanta Aitiuil*, 37,000 strong. The army had proved itself by now an efficient and trustworthy force, generally acceptable to the population at large. If it had faults, they were those of the country itself: poverty, provincialism and lack of opportunity. Because Irish citizens, even after the State's departure from the Commonwealth in 1948 (when it became 'The Republic of Ireland'), continued to be treated for almost all purposes as British citizens when resident in Britain, to which they had unrestricted right of entry, and because pay, conditions of service and opportunities for foreign travel were all better in the British army, it was the British army rather than the Irish army which most Irish would-be soldiers thought of joining first (or sometimes second – about 7000 men deserted from the Irish forces to join the British during World War II).

During the 1960s two developments impinged to vary the routine of Irish army life. The first was United Nations duty, first in the Congo, where two specially formed battalions served between 1960 and 1964, and later in Cyprus and Egypt. The second, less happy, was the violent political upheaval in Northern Ireland. The Irish government has shown itself as anxious as always to deal with such political violence as the emergency has caused within the Republic itself through the police, but the army has nevertheless to some extent been drawn in. At the outbreak, in 1969, when many northern Catholics took refuge from Protestant violence in the Republic, the Irish government, in order to demonstrate its concern, opened army camps to the refugees and sent medical units to the border. The resurgence of the I.R.A., which moved swiftly to profit from the troubles, and the finding of evidence in 1970 that some officers of the intelligence branch had assisted in gun-running into the north, with the approval of some strongly nationalist members of the *Fianna Fáil* party then in power, aroused the government's old fears for the army's political purity. Two battalions were formed for duty on the border, in testimony of the government's determination to maintain law and order on their territory (whether threatened by the I.R.A. or by intruding northern Protestant terrorists), but they were instructed to act only 'in aid of the civil power', which meant under the direction of the police. It seems that fears of provoking even the appearance of a renewal of civil war, which the spectacle of Irish soldiers firing on Irishmen might give, remain as strong as ever.

Despite recent enlargements of its role, and much improved pay and conditions of service, made possible by the successful management of the Irish economy over the last two decades, the lot of the Irish army is not therefore altogether a happy one. The Irish are an extremely military people. Their ancient literature, resurrected by nationalism and a powerful ingredient of their political myths, is one of warrior sagas. For several centuries, from the 16th onwards, they provided European armies with a constant supply of soldiers, many of whom made glittering military reputations. At times they have furnished almost half the strength of the British army (and they formed almost the whole of the strength of the East India Company's European Regiments). This mercenary service was largely forced upon them, for want of economic and social opportunity at home, but it has left its marks. One of these is the existence of competing military traditions: that of the British army itself, and that of the 'wild geese' of the emigration, as well as that of the post-independence Irish army, to which must also be added the sinister but thrilling tradition of the underground I.R.A. It is difficult therefore for the Irish army to present itself as a central national institution, and it is praiseworthy that it should have sustained its difficult role over 50 years as successfully as it has.

STRENGTH AND BUDGET

Population: 3,440,000
Army: 15,157; reserves, 720; volunteer reserve (*Forsa Cosanta Aitiuil*), 21,045
Navy: 1097; eight small warships
Air force: 1155; 14 combat aircraft
GNP (1981): $17,490,000,000
Defence expenditure (1981): $278,090,000

For the greater part of the State's existence, the defence budget has been very small, both absolutely and as a proportion of government expenditure. In 1965 it stood at only £10,000,000, and represented a little over 1% of GNP, about the lowest figure for national defence expenditure in the developed world. Almost all the money went on personnel and maintenance costs. Under the pressure of the Northern Ireland situation, the government has considerably increased defence expenditure, both to acquire badly needed new equipment and to add to the numbers in the armed forces. Nevertheless, expenditure remains below 2% of GNP and the bulk continues to be spent on man-power costs rather than procurement. This is understandable, for the armed forces' need for expensive equipment is limited by their essentially internal security role.

COMMAND AND CONSTITUTIONAL STATUS

The legal basis of the Irish army's foundation lay in Article 46 of the Irish Free State's Constitution, which conferred on the *Oireachtas* (the *Dáil*, lower house, and Senate) the exclusive right to raise and maintain an armed force, which was given statutory force by the Act to make Temporary Provisions in Relation to the Defence of *Saorstát Éireann* (Irish Free State), passed on August 3rd, 1923; the army was actually established (though of course it was already in existence) by Proclamation of the Executive Council (cabinet) on October 1st, 1924. The Defence Forces (Temporary Provisions) Act of 1924, annually re-enacted, remained the basis of military legislation until 1954, when the Defence Act was passed; amended in 1960, to allow the despatch of contingents outside the national territory for United Nations duty, and supplemented by Regulations issued under it, it continues to govern the command, organisation, military law and discipline of the armed forces.

The President (*an tUachtaran Éireann*) is also Supreme Commander; under his direction, military command is exercised by the government through the Minister for Defence. He is assisted and advised by the Council of Defence which consists of two civil members (the Parliamentary Secretary to the Minister and the Secretary of the Department of Defence) and three military members (the Chief of Staff, the Adjutant-General and the Quartermaster-General). These last two officers are Heads of the Personnel and Material Branches of the Military Staff, respectively. The Chief of Staff (*an tAire Cosanta*), assisted by Directors of Intelligence, Operations, Training, and Planning and Research, is the executive commander; he also (not the Adjutant-General) is responsible for officers' appointments and promotions. The Directors of the corps form the Technical and Supply Staff on the Military Staff; Artillery, Cavalry and Signals work to the Chief of Staff; Medical and Military Police work to the Adjutant-General; and Engineers, Ordnance and Supply and Transport work to the Quartermaster-General. The Commanders of the Air Corps and the Naval Service act directly under the Chief of Staff.

The discipline of the army is governed by its own code of military law, administered by the Judge-Advocate-General. During periods of political violence, the government has also used military officers as judges in a military tribunal to try cases of terrorism, when intimidation of witnesses, juries and civil justices made the normal legal processes inoperable. It sat in 1931, 1934 and during World War II, and had powers to intern and to impose capital punishment, during the latter period without right of appeal against its verdicts.

ROLE, COMMITMENT, DEPLOYMENT AND RECENT OPERATIONS

Role
The official handbook of the Irish Defence Forces describes the army as 'defensive in title and in primary mission'; and it is indeed difficult to visualise circumstances in which it would need (or be able) to perform any but a defensive role. Another, though unmentioned, task, however, is to protect the government against armed attack from within the State, as well as to act, as is normal, as its ultimate guarantor. The army (still 'The Free State Army' to extreme Republicans) had its origins in insurrection and civil war, some of the losing party to which still do not regard it as over, and the army exists in some sense therefore chiefly to prevent a recurrence. During the current troubles in Northern Ireland it has, besides mounting border patrols, also taken part in the suppression of terrorist incidents within the Republic, provided explosives experts to defuse terrorist bombs, and prison perimeter guards to prevent the violent liberation of Republican convicts.

Commitment
Ireland's neutrality precludes the commitment of her army to any alliance. In 1960, however, the current Defence Act was amended to allow contingents to be sent outside the national territory in order to take part in United Nations emergency operations 'of a police character'; contingents and observers have subsequently been so sent.

Irish officers regularly attend the American, West German and British staff colleges.

Deployment
From 1924 to 1976 there existed three Commands: Eastern (HQ Dublin) corresponding roughly to the province of Leinster; Western (HQ Athlone) corresponding to Connaught; and Southern (HQ Cork) corresponding to Munster (the boundaries did not in fact exactly follow either the boundaries of the provinces or their constituent counties). The Curragh Camp, formerly the British army's centre in Ireland, had the status of a separate Command, and contained most of the army's schools and central services. Since 1977, the country has been divided into four territorial Commands, as follows:

Southern Command (HQ Cork) covers counties Cork, Kerry, Limerick and Tipperary, the southern portion of Clare and the western portions of Waterford and Offaly.
Eastern Command (HQ Dublin) covers counties Dublin, Meath, Louth, Monaghan, Carlow, east Cavan and the northern portions of Kildare and Wicklow.
Western Command (HQ Athlone) covers counties Donegal, Sligo, Mayo, Galway, Roscommon, Leitrim, Longford and Westmeath, together with the western portion of Cavan and north Clare.
Curragh Command (HQ Curragh Camp, Co. Kildare) covers most of counties Kildare and Wicklow and all of Wexford, Laois, Carlow and Kilkenny and the eastern portions of Waterford and Offaly.

Each Command is garrisoned by a regular brigade and a variable complement of FCA (Volunteer Territorial Reserve) units. The headquarters of the brigades coincide with those of the Commands in which they are located. Eastern Command has also an 'Infantry Force', a formation combining two regular reinforced infantry battalions under a small operational headquarters but without logistic support units. Western Command has a reinforced infantry battalion, outside the brigade structure. Curragh Command contains most of the training establishments and includes the sole tank squadron and the headquarters of the Air Defence Regiment, in addition to the recently formed Ranger unit. In 1982 there was also a reinforced infantry battalion serving with the United Nations Emergency Force in Lebanon. The deployment of the major tactical formations and units is as follows:

Irish Republic

Southern Command:
1st Brigade (HQ Cork)
FCA Group, Southern Command (HQ Cork) comprising:
  6 Infantry Battalions
  1 Motorised Reconnaissance Squadron
  2 Field Artillery Regiments
  2 Air Defence Batteries
  1 Field Engineer Company

Eastern Command:
2nd Brigade (HQ Dublin)
Eastern Command Infantry Force (HQ Gormanston, Co. Meath)
FCA Group Eastern Command (HQ Dublin) comprising:
  4 Infantry Battalions
  1 Motorised Reconnaissance Squadron
  1 Field Artillery Regiment
  1 Air Defence Battery
  1 Field Engineer Company

Western Command:
4th Brigade (HQ Athlone)
28th Infantry Battalion (Reinforced) (HQ Finner Camp, Bundoran)
FCA Group Western Command (HQ Athlone) comprising:
  6 Infantry Battalions
  1 Motorised Reconnaissance Squadron
  2 Field Artillery Regiments
  1 Field Engineer Company

Curragh Command:
6th Brigade (HQ Curragh Camp, Co. Kildare)
Army Ranger Unit (Curragh Camp)
1st Tank Squadron (Curragh Camp)
1st Air Defence Regiment (HQ Curragh Camp)
FCA Group Curragh Command (HQ Curragh Camp) comprising:
  2 Infantry Battalions
  1 Field Artillery Regiment

UNIFIL
52nd Infantry Battalion (reinforced) (HQ Tibnin, Lebanon)

It will be noted that there are no 3rd or 5th Brigades. These were predominantly FCA manned formatons under the ill-starred 'integrated' organisation adopted in 1959, under which tactical formations and even units, in the case of the Artillery, consisted of a mix of regular and FCA personnel in the approximate ratio of 1:2 in favour of the latter. Both Brigades vanished under the new organisation adopted in 1978.

Recent Operations
The Army mobilised and expanded to a strength of two Divisions and two independent Brigades during the World War II period.

Since 1960, units of the Irish Army have been on almost continuous service with various United Nations Emergency Forces. Eight Battalions (32nd to 39th, inclusive), two infantry groups (1st and 2nd), two armoured car squadrons (2nd and 3rd) and a Brigade headquarters (9th) served in the ex-Belgian Congo between 1960 and 1964. Three Battalions (40th to 42nd, inclusive) and twenty infantry groups (3rd to 13th and 18th to 26th, both inclusive) served in Cyprus between 1964 and 1974 when increased activity by subversive organisations prompted Ireland's withdrawal from the Cyprus operation. By the end of 1982, ten Battalions (43rd to 52nd, inclusive), each reinforced with an armoured car

troop, an APC company and a section of heavy mortars, either had served or were serving with the United Nations Forces in Lebanon.

The outbreak of sectarian violence in Northern Ireland, which for a time threatened to spill over into the Republic, prompted the formation of four infantry groups (14th to 17th, inclusive) to patrol the border between the two parts of the island in 1969. These were subsequently consolidated into two new Battalions (27th and 28th) in 1973 and joined by a third (29th) two years later. The Irish Army, with which the I.R.A. has avoided any direct confrontation, has been involved in a heavy internal security commitment from the early 1970s to date.

ORGANISATION

Arms of Service
These are, in order of precedence: Infantry (in Gaelic, *Cor Coisithe*), Artillery (*Cor Airtleire*), Cavalry (*Cor Marcra*), Engineers (*Cor Inealltoiri*), Signals (*Cor Comharthafochta*), Ordnance (*Cor Ordanais*), Supply and Transport (*Cor Solathair Agus Iompair*), Medical Corps (*Cor Liachta*), Military Police (*Cor Poilini Airm*) and Air Corps (*Aer Cor*); the Naval Service and the Observer Corps also form part of the unified Defence Forces.

The volunteer territorial reserve force is known as the *Forsa Cosanta Aitiuil* (Local Defence Force), usually shortened to FCA. The largest permanent unit is the battalion, which is found only in the Infantry and which has three companies for home service or four or more for UN duty. FCA infantry battalions may have as few as three or as many as six companies. The Artillery is organised in Regiments which may have from two to four batteries. Units of the other arms are organised only at company level. There are 11 regular and 18 FCA Infantry Battalions, one regular Tank and one Armoured Car Squadrons, three regular and three FCA Motor Reconnaissance Squadrons, three regular and six FCA Field Artillery Regiments, one mixed regular and FCA Air Defence Regiment and three regular and three FCA Field Engineer Companies. Infantry Battalions are numbered in sequence from 1st to 6th, 12th and from 27th to 30th in the case of regular units and 7th to 11th, 13th to 24th and 31st in that of FCA units. There are no 25th or 26th Battalions and UN Service units are numbered sequentially onward from 32. Tactical and logistic support units take their numbers from those of their parent Brigades except in the case of the 6th Brigade, the Cavalry unit of which is the 1st Armoured Car Squadron and which has only one field battery (3rd) which is outside the regimental structure. FCA Motor Reconnaissance Squadrons are numbered 3rd, 5th and 11th, FCA Artillery Regiments being the 3rd, 5th and 6th to 9th inclusive. The FCA combat engineer units are the 3rd, 5th and 11th Field Companies.

Operational
The largest tactical formation is the Brigade, although two Divisions existed during the World War II 'Emergency' period. There are now four Brigades, each of which, in theory consists of three battalions, a mechanised cavalry reconnaissance unit, an artillery regiment and a company each of engineers, signals, supply and transport, medical corps and military police. In practice, the Brigades have only two battalions each, although presumably it is intended to raise four additional infantry battalions at some unspecified future date. The Brigades are particularly weak in armour and it may be surmised that long-term plans call for the addition of an armoured unit to each Brigade. The normal

home service battalions have only two rifle companies (one of which may be APC mounted) and a support company, those employed on Border security having a non-organic armoured car troop on semi-permanent attachment. The units raised on an ad hoc basis for UN service are significantly stronger, usually consisting of three companies with organic combat support sections. The battalions deployed with the United Nations forces in Lebanon are the strongest infantry units ever fielded by the Irish Army, each including an armoured car troop of four H-90 vehicles, a 13 vehicle APC company and a section of four 120mm heavy mortars.

The present tactical organisation of the Army, which appears to owe something to French doctrine, deploys the regular units as a manoeuvre force and the FCA as a territorial defence force, the role envisaged for the later force at its inception. As such, it appears to make the best possible use of the limited resources available in direct contradistinction to the unrealistic 'integrated' organisation which it replaced.

RECRUITMENT, TRAINING AND RESERVES

Recruitment of all ranks of both the Regular Army and Volunteer Reserve is by voluntary enlistment; conscription has never been imposed during the State's history (and Ireland was exempted from the conscription laws imposed in Britain during World War I, as indeed Northern Ireland was during and after World War II). Soldiers may enlist between the ages of seventeen and thirty-two (thirty-eight if they have previous service) for an initial term of 3 years, extendable to 3, 4, 6 or 9 years. Thereafter, re-engagement is permitted to allow service of 21 years, extendable by 2 year re-engagements to 31 years. The army is characterised by long service; in 1974 one man in three had 12 years' service and one in six had 20 years'; half those reaching the rank of company sergeant or company quartermaster sergeant had between 13 and 21 years' service.

Recruits undergo a basic training course of 16 weeks at the General Training Depot at the Curragh Camp, Kildare, where 13 of the army's 17 schools are concentrated. He completes his training with his unit. Specialist training in the school of his corps is carried on at the Curragh, as is the training of potential NCOs. Those so trained are promoted to corporal within their units, and then to higher ranks, as vacancies arise. The only schools not in the Curragh area are those of Ordnance, Music, Catering and Equitation, all of which are at Dublin.

Officers are recruited by competition from young men aged seventeen to twenty who must hold the school leaving certificate. They are trained for 2 years in the Cadet School of the Military College at the Curragh and, since 1969, complete their education at University College, Galway, from which they graduate with a degree. The officer's further training in the school of his corps takes place in his first year of service and then in his fifth, on promotion to captain. All officers in their fifteenth year attend the 9 month Command and Staff Course at the Military College. Promotion from the rank of captain is by selection; there is a compulsory retiring age of fifty-four for captains up to sixty-three for major-generals. Long service is the rule and promotion is slow.

Reserves consist of the Reserve of Officers and the Reserve of Men, First Line — ex-regulars who have an annual training commitment of 14–21 days' service, but which, because of the long regular service common in the army, totals only 700; and the Volunteer Reserve, Forsa Cosanta Aitiuil, about 16,000 strong. It provides (besides artillery batteries, signal and engineer companies and the like) 17 infantry battalions distributed by platoons and companies throughout the Re-

public as follows: the 24th Battalion, for example, in Donegal has companies in Letterkenny, South Donegal, Inishowen and North Donegal; the 20th Battalion, in Dublin, has an Irish-speaking company, Complacht na bbFian, and a student company, named after Patrick Pearse (a Gaelic scholar and one of the heroes of the 1916 Rebellion).

EQUIPMENT AND ARMS INDUSTRY

Although armoured fighting vehicles of original conception have been developed in the country and are produced abroad, under licence and a number of small naval vessels have been constructed for the Naval Service at the Hiberno-Dutch Verolme Shipyard, at Rushbrooke, Co. Cork, Ireland cannot be said to have a defence industry in the accepted sense of the word and almost all items of equipment, including even small arms ammunition, must be imported. Traditionally, Britain has been the main source of supply although the Swedish and French armaments industries have benefited from repeated orders by the Irish government.

Pistol: FN 9mm (Belgium)
Rifles: MK 33A2 5.56mm (Germany); FN FAL 7.62mm (Belgium); Lee-Enfield No. 4 0.303" (Britain)
Sub-machine-guns: MK 53 5.56mm (Germany); Carl Gustav KPist 45 9mm (Sweden)
Machine-guns: FN MAG 7.62mm (Belgium); Bren 0.303" (Britain); Vickers 0.303" (Britain)
Anti-armour weapons: Carl Gustav 84mm RL (Sweden); PV-1110 90mm RCL (Sweden); MILAN ATGW (France)
Mortars: Thomson-Brandt 60mm (France); Thomson-Brandt 81mm (France); Thomson-Brandt 120mm (France)
Artillery: Light Gun 105mm (Britain); 25 pounder Mk II (Britain)
Air-defence weapons: Mk 1 40mm L/60 (Sweden); 40mm L/70 (Sweden); RBS-70 SAM (Sweden)
Armour: Scorpion light tank (Britain); 12 in service); AML 245 H-90 armoured car (France; 28 in service); AML 245 H-60 armoured car (France; 32 in service); Landsverk 180 armoured car (Sweden; 6 in service); Leyland armoured car (Britain/Ireland; 3 in service); AML VTT M3 APC (France; 60 in service); Timoney APC (Ireland; 10 in service); Unimos armoured scout car (Germany/Sweden; 15 in service)
Aircraft: The Air Corps operates 11 helicopters.

RANK, DRESS AND DISTINCTIONS

General — Crossed swords inside a wreath, three pips
Lieutenant-general — Crossed swords inside a wreath, two pips
Major-general — Crossed swords inside a wreath, one pip
Colonel — Crossed swords, two pips
Lieutenant-colonel — Crossed swords, one pip
Commandant — Crossed swords
Captain — Three pips
Lieutenant — Two pips
Second-lieutenant — One pip

Sergeant-major — Two bars
Battalion quartermaster sergeant — One bar
Company Sergeant — Three wavy chevrons, army badge over
Company quartermaster-sergeant — Three wavy chevrons, specialist badge over
Sergeant — Three wavy chevrons
Corporal — Two wavy chevrons
Acting corporal — One wavy chevron

Partially trained and fully trained privates wear two and three stars on the sleeve, respectively; rank badges of officers and the two senior NCO ranks are worn on the shoulder strap, and of the other NCOs on the upper sleeve. Officers' badges are in metal, other ranks in red cloth; generals wear red gorget patches.

The Irish army's uniform has always closely resembled the British, as did that of the few Irish Volunteers who fitted themselves out in uniform style. A few deliberate distinctions have from time to time been adopted – at first, officers wore a pistol in a low-slung holster, and during the 1930s the whole army wore the German coal-scuttle helmet – but today the uniform is scarcely distinguishable from the British army's, except for its greenish shade. Service dress, pullover order and combat kit are the main orders of dress. Officers wear a peaked cap and Sam Browne belt with service dress. Other ranks wear a black beret, and the Cavalry Corps a loose beret with trailing ribbons, wrongly called a 'glengarry'.

CURRENT DEVELOPMENTS

Since joining the EEC in 1973, successive Irish Premiers and Foreign Ministers have reiterated that the Republic is prepared to participate in community defence whilst paradoxically continuing to stress the immutability of the traditional policy of neutrality. Irish neutrality is in fact an illusion and something of a pious fraud indulged in under the implicit security of the NATO umbrella. Ireland has benefited to a significant degree from EEC subsidies towards its endorsement of the community Exclusive Economic Zone and the recent spectacular expansion of the Naval Service, for many years the cinderella of the Defence Forces, would almost certainly not have taken place in the absence of Community financial assistance. Whilst Ireland would probably, if pressed, participate in an EEC-based military alliance, NATO continues to be regarded with an almost pathological suspicion, surprising in a country which, although theoretically non-aligned, is solidly pro-western. This aversion to NATO membership, cleverly nourished by a small but influential left-wing lobby, has its basis in a mistaken belief that participation in the North Atlantic Alliance would in some way endorse and perpetuate the partition of the country. A certain softening of entrenched traditional objections to participation in European defence received a severe set-back in the context of the Anglo-Argentine War. Whilst the Irish official position was scrupulously correct, condemning the illegality of Argentina's invasion of the Falkland Islands and their dependencies and supporting EEC economic sanctions against Argentina but withdrawing any appearance of supporting military action by a foreign country – in this case Britain – as is required under the Irish constitution, popular opinion was overwhelmingly pro-Argentine. This arose, not so much from the widespread low-level anglophobia, rooted in history, as in a conviction that the British Government, which had effectively provoked the Argentine invasion, was cynically avoiding a diplomatic solution and provoking a military one for domestic political reasons. This, in turn, re-awakened popular isolationism and has done irreparable harm to any possibility of an Irish Government being able to carry the referendum necessary for the constitutional amendment which would be required if the Republic were to join an EEC-based defensive alliance. Any possibility of Ireland abandoning its pseudo-neutrality in the foreseeable future therefore appears extremely remote.

John Keegan
Adrian English

ISRAEL

HISTORY AND INTRODUCTION

'The army of Israel was established by decree on May 26th, 1948, 12 days after the Declaration of Independence. This was a formality. The creation of the army had preceded and made possible the birth of the new State, whose allotted territory was invaded by the regular forces of five Arab States on the first day of its independence' (E. Luttwak and D. Horowitz, *The Israeli Army*, Allen Lane, 1974). Tendentious though Arab (and particularly Palestinian Arab) readers would find this statement, it fairly summarises in Israeli eyes the role which their armed force, *Zahal*, played in the formation of their State and the reason why it remains, in many respects, the most important of their national institutions. For the creation of a Jewish State in *Eretz Israel* ('the land of Israel'), even if short-lived, would in itself have been a realisation of the Zionist dream. But *Zahal* has done more than bring that about. In three subsequent wars it has consistently defeated the armies of its Arab neighbours and in the second of them more than doubled the area of territory under Israeli control. It has helped to turn several hundred thousand immigrants into Hebrew-speaking citizens. Its victories have immensely enhanced Israeli national and Jewish ethnic self-esteem, and it has done all of this — or so Israelis would claim — wihout compromising the egalitarian, internationalist, even pacifist, ideal on which Zionism was founded.

The pacific inclinations of the original Zionist settlers, who came to Palestine in the 1880s, are generally admitted. Many indeed had come to escape military service in Russia, where conscripted Jews were treated with particular indignity and harshness, and wanted only to live out quiet lives in the Old City or on the agricultural settlements supported by philanthropists like the Rothschilds and Montefiores. However, the second *aliyah* (wave of immigration), which began to reach Palestine in 1904, was composed of Jews with more positive and potentially more disruptive aims. It was not simply that they imbibed the ideas of Herzl's *Judenstaat* (1897), from which Zionism derived its modern political objective: 'a publicly recognised, legally secured home in Palestine for the Jewish people'. They were mainly socialists from eastern Europe, which housed the largest Jewish population in the world, but one sunk in ignorance and poverty, and they also believed that the salvation of their race lay in the creation of a genuine Jewish working class, of which they were resolved to make themselves the first members. Initially committed to the principle of day-wage labouring, since they shunned the idea of property owning and thought manual labour a good in itself, they were shortly persuaded that the reality was politically self-defeating. The hardships it entailed threatened to kill the strongest of them and drove the weaker back into the diaspora. They turned, therefore, to a new idea, that of the *kvutza*, the communal settlement, which might be co-operative (the *moshav*) or fully collective (the *kibbutz*) but which in either form seemed to offer the means to realise in full their Socialist–Zionist ideals: 'conquest of labour', as the idea of salvation through work was called; 'conquest of the land' (it was an important Zionist belief that the decay of Ottoman Palestine into desert and swamp was the consequence of the Jews' expulsion and could be reversed only by Jewish immigration); and a centre of attraction for that immigration itself.

The third *aliyah* which, encouraged by the British government's war-time promise of support in the establishment of a national home (the Balfour Declaration), began to arrive in Palestine in 1919, was committed in advance to the *kvutza* idea. But its numbers, eventually about 40,000, and the apparent favour they enjoyed from the new British administration governing under mandate from the League of Nations, brought to a head the trouble promised by the programme of the second *aliyah* yet hitherto ignored or denied by all but a handful of Zionists: conflict of interest and with the indigenous Arabs. They, resentful of the newcomers' competition for employment and fearful that land sold to Jews was lost to Arabs for good, initiated attacks on isolated communities of the *yishuv* (as the Jewish population called themselves) which resulted in several deaths. Police action put the violence down and a local slump calmed passions by halting and even reversing the tide of immigration. But violence flared up again briefly in 1929, perhaps at the instigation of the Arab leadership, and in 1936, after 90,000 fugitives from Nazi anti-semitism had entered the country in 2 years, it erupted in a full-scale Arab revolt, which was not to be extinguished for 3 years.

The Zionist response to Arab hostility expressed itself in three voices. The 'official' view, propagated by the World Zionist Organisation and the Jewish Agency (the semi-official government of the *yishuv*) was that it would be short-lived, for Jewish immigration could only increase the prosperity of all Palestinians and therefore foster harmony between them. The 'practical' Zionist view was that it was regrettable but must be borne, since Jews were accepted nowhere in the world and could best find a *modus vivendi* by asserting their identity and their rights, and merely heightened hostility to themselves by seeking to placate and accommodate. The 'revisionist' Zionists, a right-wing minority, went much further: they argued that the plight of the Jews internationally was much greater than that of the Arabs locally, that the Arabs had therefore no right to resist immigration, and that the Jews must overcome any resistance they offered by swamping them with numbers.

These views determined what military response the *yishuv* made to the Arab revolt. The Jewish Agency jointly organised with the British an official Jewish Settlement Police for the purely static defence of the more threatened *kvutzot*. The Labour-Zionists raised through *Haganah*, their part-time militia which had existed intermittently since 1920, a rather more aggressive force, *Fosh* (Field Companies), which was available for service away from home. The revisionists, disdaining *Haganah*'s doctrine of *havlagah* (self-restraint), formed an illegal national military organisation (*Irgun Zvai Leumi* — I.Z.L.) which carried out reprisals and practised terror on its own account. None of these forces, however, not even the Special Night Squads of the Settlement Police trained by the gentile Zionist Orde Wingate, a serving British officer, contributed much to the defeat of the revolt, which was effectively curtailed by the granting of political concessions to the Arabs.

The principal concession, a virtual halting of Jewish immigration, might have transformed the Arab revolt into a Jewish one, had not the outbreak of World War II compelled the Jews to co-operate in working for a British victory. A persistence in the policy of restricted immigration after the war was over, did in fact bring such a revolt on and prompted the British, after 2 years' unsuccessful effort to repress it, to announce their intention of surrendering the mandate and withdrawing their garrison. The United Nations, inheritors of the League's responsiblities, voted to partition the country, though lacking any means to enforce the decision, and in December, 1947 in anticipation of the independence which was to take effect on the following May 15th, open war broke out between the Jewish and Arab inhabitants.

Historians of *Zahal* now make much of its military ancestry: of *Hashomer*, the romantically bandoliered protectors of the villages of the second *aliyah*; of the Zion Mule Corps which served on Gallipoli and the Jewish Legion (38th—40th Battalions, Royal Fusiliers) enlisted for service under Allenby in Palestine in its conquest from the Turks; of *Fosh* and the Night Squads, and of the *Palmach* (*Plugo Machaz* — Striking Companies), the offensive organisation formed by *Haganah*ir during World War II and tolerated by the British while Palestine lay under threat of capture by Rommel. But the truth is that militarily none amounted to very much: the Mule Corps and the Jewish Legion were products of 'political' Zionism's effort to win the Balfour declaration; *Fosh* and the *Palmach* were products of the need experienced by any static militia (in this case *Haganah*), to have available mobile reinforcements against local emergencies (the Active Service Units of the Ulster Volunteers of 1914 might seem a parallel). Jewish Palestine was, in 1945, a virtually unarmed, soldierless and militarily quite inexperienced community, materially and morally unequipped to fight for statehood. The return of those who had fought under British colours in World War II, either as individuals or as members of the Jewish Brigade which Britain had reluctantly and tardily raised from the *yishuv* for service in Italy, brought home some 30,000 trained men. But the future State lacked the arms to equip them, and *Haganah* the experience to form them into a national army. Two years later, at the end of the guerrilla war against the British, *Haganah* disposed of only 13,000 small arms, while its organisation was still based on the home guards of the settlements.

The 'phoney war' of November, 1947 to May, 1948 was both the making and the salvation of *Haganah/Zahal*, since the British army's disengagement allowed the Jews freedom to train, arm and fight a 'Battle of the Roads' to maintain communication between their settlements, while its presence protected them from attack by the armies of the neighbouring Arab States. In February, 1948 *Haganah* proclaimed general mobilisation and by May could show on paper nine organised 'brigades', each 2000—4000 strong, reasonably mobile and named after the areas of settlement from which they operated. Six belonged to *Hish* (*Hel Sadeh* — 'Field Corps'), the regular element of *Haganah*, and three to the *Palmach*, still a semi-autonomous *corps d'élite* dominated by the left-wing *kibutzim* of the United group. The *Hish* brigades were: Golani (southern Galilee), Carmeli (Haifa), Alexandroni (Hadera), Kiryati (Tel Aviv), Givati (Tel Aviv) and Etzioni (Jerusalem). Those of *Palmach* were Yiftah (northern Galillee), Harel (Ramla) and Hanegev (the Negev).

Etzioni, attacked by the full weight of the Kingdom of Transjordan's Arab Legion, was overwhelmed in the first few days of the open war which broke out on, or slightly before, May 15th. The others were able to hold their own and to begin to implement the strategy which the *Haganah* had laid down in April — to secure the borders allotted by the United Nations to the Jewish State 'and those of the blocs of Jewish settlements and such Jewish population as were outside those borders'. The assault on the borders was mounted in the north by the armies of Syria, the Lebanon and Iraq, assisted by a Palestinian Arab Liberation Army; in

the south by that of Egypt; as well as in the east by the Arab Legion. But despite their strength, it was only on the east front with the Arab Legion, best-trained of the regular Arab armies and operating in a solidly Arab area, that the Jewish line was broken. The first of a series of truces, negotiated by the United Nations, brought the Jews a breathing space in June, by which they profited better than their enemies to import arms and raise men, and subsequent truces helped them consistently to improve their position. By the beginning of 1949, they had succeeded (though at the cost of 6000 dead, a grievous loss to a population of 650,000) in securing, and in many places improving on, the territorial allotment proposed by the United Nations; and they had broken the neighbouring Arab States' will to continue the fight. Armistices were signed with all of them between February and July, by which Israel's military victory — though neither her sovereignty nor her right to her conquests — was conceded by her enemies.

The War of Independence had done more than preserve the infant State. It has also transformed the disparate elements of its proto-army into a unified force capable of guaranteeing its future. These elements represented a variety of party affiliations, historical traditions and cultural elements in the life of the *yishuv*, e.g. *Haganah* (the populist Labour-Zionism of *Mapai*, the majority Socialist party), the *Palmach* (the more elitist and Soviet-inclined socialism of the minority *Mapam* party) and the United Kibbutz movement (I.Z.L. — the ruthless nationalism of 'revisionist' Zionism). But the pressure of war itself did not prove sufficient to reconcile their conflicting outlooks. It took the determination of the Prime Minister and Minister of Defence, Ben Gurion, to do so. At the outset of the war he had authorised the use of force to end I.Z.L.'s efforts to secure its own supply of arms, and had then broken up its independent formations. In addition, towards the end he had even insisted on the dissolution of the separate command structure of the *Palmach*, though that force had proved the most efficient in *Zahal* and had won almost single-handed Israel's greatest victory, the conquest of the Negev from Egypt. He rightly took the view, however that Israel could afford only one army and one military tradition, and that both must be 'above party'.

During his long post-war Premiership, with which he combined the Ministry of Defence, he administered a policy of appointments and promotions within the army designed to institutionalise the 'one army' idea (literally one army, for he kept the air and sea elements subordinate to the single General Staff). *Haganah* and the Jewish Brigade officers were preferred for command, I.Z.L. was frozen out altogether and *Palmach* veterans were initially restricted to non-operational posts, unless, like the rising star, Moshe Dayan, they belonged to his own *Mapai* party. Yet he was sensitive enough to the *Palmach*'s achievements to respect the tradition for which it particularly stood, that of the pioneering youth movement. While denying that the *Palmach* had a monopoly of it, and successfully seeking to imbue *Zahal*'s system of training with its spirit, in 1951 he authorised the formation of a special 'Fighting Pioneer Youth' Corps (*Nahal*) which was, in effect, a recreation of the *Palmach*, which had always combined military service with kibbutz work, under State auspices. A pioneer himself of the second *aliyah*, the creation was in any case a work of the heart.

The first serious test of the unified *Zahal* came in 1956 when, in concert with British and French forces, it was launched in an offensive against the Egyptian garrison of Sinai. Its Chief of Staff, Dayan, had been dissatsified with its performance in border defence in the early 1950s, and had done much to improve its training, junior leadership and command. Peres, Director-General of the Ministry of

Defence, had added to its inventory of weapons, which now included modern tanks and aircraft, and fresh waves of immigration had increased its numbers, so that it could field nine full-strength brigades in Sinai alone. But it remained an army chiefly of mobilised reserves. The pace and completeness of its victory, therefore, created a world-wide sensation, not diminished by its surrender, at Great Power insistence, of its conquests in Sinai, and the Israeli system, in which office-workers became infantrymen overnight and privates addressed generals by their first names, was held up as a model to older, more militarily and socially conventional armies. Those of other recently established States, in Africa and south-east Asia, seeing in *Zahal* a source of expertise hitherto thought available only from their former colonial overlords, competed to invite Israeli training teams to share their secrets of success with them. Some cautious military commentators pointed out that the Israelis had in Sinai outnumbered the Egyptians, who had also been under threat of attack by the French and British in their rear, but were generally ignored.

That it was right to ignore them was generally conceded in the aftermath of *Zahal*'s next war in 1967, when it defeated single-handed and in the same tempo the armies of all its neighbours (except Lebanon, which stood aside from the conflict). At the end of the Six-Day War (June 6th—11th) *Zahal* was proclaimed, almost as loudly by hard-headed experts as by exultant Zionists, the most perfect fighting instrument, size for size, in the world, and the superior of many larger. Indeed, its achievement is destined to stand, whatever the future brings, as one of the most remarkable of any army in the history of war. Even given that it hinged upon the success of a pre-emptive aerial attack on the bases of the Egyptian, Syrian and Jordanian air forces, which left their ground forces to do battle naked in some of the most open terrain in the world, the speed with which the Israeli armoured columns broke through fixed defences of great strength and depth and the impetus they developed in exploiting these breakthroughs spoke of military skills of the very highest order. The victory could not, moreover, be ascribed to superiority in arms, for the Arab armies deployed Soviet equipment as modern as that supplied by Western States to Israel; nor could it be ascribed to a ruthless disregard for casualties, for Israel suffered only 600 dead, a tenth of the loss of the War of Independence from a population which had grown to nearly 3,000,000.

Yet a price was to be paid for the war, if not immediately. It had to be paid in a greatly increased military budget (26% of GNP, or $483 per capita in 1970, the highest in the world), in a lengthened term of military service (36 months for the conscripts), in an extension of the reserve duty (from one to two or even three months per year), and, after the euphoria of victory had passed, in the anxieties of a constantly sharpened vigilance. For the defeats of 1967 had inflicted a humiliation on Israel's Arab neighbours which succeeded, as the sense of grievance it replaced had not, in generating among them a relentless desire for revenge and an urge to find the opportunity to inflict it. The opportunity, as the Israeli generals came to recognise, lay in their greatly extended lines of communication. Valuable though the possession of Sinai (the principal prize of 1967) was in deepening Israel's defensive cordon, it necessarily put some of the best of the army's standing brigades 150 miles beyond the political frontier and consigned them, as the defence of a water obstacle like the Suez Canal must, to a purely static role. This new development, for all the apparent security it brought, greatly complicated Israeli strategy, which had hitherto always been based on the manipulation to her advantage of short 'interior lines', which made possible, among other things, the delaying of

general mobilisation until the reality of a threat had been firmly identified, and allowed a deployment of force in the wrong direction to be rectified in short order.

Egypt's waging of what Israelis came to call the War of Attrition (1969—71) on the Suez Canal — a prolonged artillery duel — postponed perception of the changed situation, since it kept the Israelis at a high state of readiness, and at a time when the Egyptians had not recovered sufficiently from the defeat of 1967 to undertake a canal crossing. The negotiated lull which followed, however, brought Israel face to face with her new uncertainties. Her excellent intelligence services issued warnings to the government that it had detected signs of an impending attack in January, May and September, 1973, and on the second of these occasions partial mobilisation was ordered. Public criticism of what was reckoned an unnecessary expense deterred the government from issuing similar orders on the third occasion, and then again in October. Thus it was not until after the Egyptians and Syrians had begun their combined offensive on October 6th, the Day of Atonement (*Yom Kippur*), that the reserve brigades were called to their concentration centres and that those destined for the defence of Sinai began the long desert transit westwards. The outcome of the subsequent operations, tactically as brilliant and daring as anything *Zahal* had achieved, are described under Role, Commitment, Deployment and Recent Operations.

The political and military implications of the 1973 war, and of their meaning for *Zahal*, are discussed under Current Developments. But it may well be that 1973 marked a turning point in the development of Israel's army and of its relationship with the people and the State. Hitherto it had remained faithful with remarkable consistency to its animating spirit, which was very much that of the third *aliyah*, a spirit of youth, egalitarianism and buoyant optimism, which it in its turn derived from the ethos of the *Wandervogel* and other central European youth movements of pre-World War I Europe. Indeed, in a sense, *Zahal* was the greatest of Israel's youth movements, which, while the State matured into caution and the population grew urban and bourgeois, miraculously preserved the enthusiasm of the founding pioneers. It was that youthful enthusiasm which invested Israel's campaigns with their jamboree character, and their success which allowed Israelis to believe that enthusiasm, in war as well as in peace, overrode calculation as a means towards the object of one's desire. Israel faces in the future, however, choices to which the simplicities of the pioneers do not offer answers, and it is inevitable that *Zahal* will be changed by the choices that are made. It may return to the cautious, defensive spirit of the inter-war *Haganah*, dominated as it was by the moderate socialism of the second *aliyah*. Or it may turn towards the single-minded nationalism of the revisionists and the I.Z.L., whose influence has been so firmly extirpated from its leadership. But in any case, Israel has now been brought to recognise that war is too serious to be left to boy generals.

STRENGTH AND BUDGET

Population: 4,000,000 (excluding the occupied territories)
Army: 25,000 regulars; 110,000 conscripts (including women); 315,000 reservists
Air force: 21,000 regulars; 7000 conscripts; 7000 reservists; 634 combat aircraft
Navy: 5700 regulars; 3300 conscripts; 1000 reservists; three submarines; 70 small warships; 300 naval commandos
GNP (1981): $ 21,100,000,000
Defence expenditure (1981): $6,060,000,000

Israel has spent an unusually high proportion of government expenditure and of GNP on defence from the earliest days of the State. In the 1950s the proportion of GNP spent varied between 6% and 8%, while expenditure rose from $87,000,000 in 1950 to $209,000,000 in 1960. From the mid-1960s the proportion of GNP spent on defence rose into double figures (1966, 12.4%) and in 1971 reached 26% ($1,600,000,000). The latter figure was inflated by arms purchases from America costing $800,000,000 but public resistance to the level of taxation it entailed reduced expenditure in 1973 to 20% of GNP (32% of government expenditure). More recent details are not available, since the defence budget is a State secret. It is not debated on the floor of the *Knesset* (parliament), and the opposition parties are not officially informed of its provisions.

Israel has received a considerable amount of foreign aid towards defence purchases, either as a remittal of the cost (by West Germany in the 1960s), or as grants or low-cost loans (by America since 1967). In general, however, Israel has paid for what it has bought abroad, financing the transactions chiefly from the contributions of the international United Jewish Appeal which, with American governmental grants, has brought in $600,000,000 annually since the Six-Day War of 1967.

COMMAND AND CONSTITUTIONAL STATUS

Command

The three elements of command in *Zahal* are the Minister of Defence, the Chief of Staff and the Director-General of the Ministry*. Because, however, the Ministry was created only after *Zahal* had fought and won a crucial war, it is a relatively weak institution *vis-à-vis* the Staff (which, like it, is also tri-service in its purvue). Its most important functions seem to be in the financing and direction of the State-controlled defence industries. Such other duties as it carries out are those which the Staff have wished upon it.

The Staff has a dual organisation: operational and administrative. Administratively, the Chief of Staff controls, through one of the four appropriate branches [General Staff (i.e. Operations, or in its Hebrew acronym *Agam*), Manpower (*Akka*), Quartermaster (*Aga*) and Intelligence (*Amman*)], the Inspectorates of the various arms of service (*see* Organisation) and the various routine functions of recruiting, training and administration; administratively the air force and navy are also responsible to him but, because they are small in size and largely regular in composition, they in practice administer themselves. Operationally, the Chief of Staff works through a parallel chain of command to the three areas (Northern, Central and Southern), which in turn command divisions (*Ugdah*) and brigades, as well as to the air force and navy. In peacetime the Area Commands oversee all units stationed within their territory and the local defence units (*Haganah Merchavit*) of older reservists; in war, the Area Commands become operational headquarters. Because Southern Area faces the strongest foreign army (the Egyptian) and has the largest number of troops permanently at its disposal (including the 'school' units of the Armour Command located at Beersheba), its commander holds the rank of *Aluf* (*see* Rank, Dress and Distinctions), the other Area Commanders that of *Tat Aluf*.

Constitutional Status

The Israel Defence Forces (*Zahal*) were constituted by Order No. 4 of the State of Israel of May 26th, 1948, which had

* In Hebrew *Misrad Habitachon*, literally the Minister of Security.

four clauses. The first gave *Zahal* its name, the second laid down the procedure for general mobilisation*, the fourth forbade the maintenance of any other armed force on the territory of the State, and the third defined the form of the oath of loyalty to be sworn by each recruit: 'I swear and undertake' (those with religious objections to taking oaths may affirm), 'on my word of honour, to remain faithful to the State of Israel, to its laws and its legally constituted authorities, to accept without reservation the discipline of the Israel Defence Forces, to obey all orders and instructions given by its authorised commanders, and to dedicate all my strength and even to sacrifice my life in the defence of the homeland and the freedom of Israel'.

The order did not, however, name a commander-in-chief and the President of the State has never, as might have been expected, acceded to that role. Instead, the cabinet is invested with ultimate command authority on a collective basis, rather as is the Federal Council in Switzerland. In practice – though it may and does form *ad hoc* defence committees from its own members – it delegates its power to the Minister of Defence, 'who serves as the army's sole political master and is responsible to the cabinet and the *Knesset* (parliament) for all military matters. Parliamentary supervision, however, is weak, for though the *Knesset* maintains a standing committee on foreign policy and security, on which all parties are proportionally represented, its powers are limited to enquiry and report.

The meagre constitutional provisions for command of the armed forces might suggest that it is a matter of secondary importance in Israeli politics. The contrary is of course the case. For the greater part of the State's existence, the Prime Minister has combined the Ministry of Defence with his own office (1948–54 and 1955–63, David Ben Gurion, and 1963–7, Levi Eshkol). When he has not done so, the post has either been held by a politician of the first rank (e.g. Moshe Dayan, 1967–74) or else become a focus for fierce political conflict, as happened during Lavon's tenure in the short interruption of Ben Gurion's protracted Premiership from 1954–5. His attempts to extend the power of the Minister into technical military matters engaged the active hostility of the then Chief of Staff, Moshe Dayan, who held the view, which was also Ben Gurion's, that the Minister's role (though an extremely powerful one, for it included the right to proclaim mobilisation without prior reference even to the cabinet) was restricted, as far as it touched *Zahal*, to organisational questions and did not include operational matters. Lavon attempted to mobilise Labour Party (*Mapai*) and trade union (*Histadrut*) support for his line by proposing the creation of a national security council, which would have reduced the powers of Premier, Minister of Defence and Chief of Staff alike. But, despite the intrusion of *Mapai* and *Histadrut* into almost all public and private affairs in the country, they declined the chance to move into the executive control of defence, an act of self-denial which brought about Lavon's resignation.

A leading analyst of Israeli civil–military relations explains the self-denial thus: 'Such a body would have become political, and the traditional political party system established in *Histadrut*, in kibbutzim, in *Mapai*, in the Cabinet and in all of Israel's political and economic structures, would have turned *Zahal* back to the pre-independence era, when military structures were instruments for political influence. Under

* This Clause of the Order was amplified by the Defence Service Act of September 8th, 1949, which laid down the terms of recruitment and service.

that system, chief of staff would not be selected by merit but on a political basis .... This situation, duplicated on the lower levels of the army, would have dissolved the great achievements of *Zahal*'s unification, professionalisation and depoliticisation'†. But there was another even more important reason why the parties should agree that *Zahal* be kept insulated from that bane of Israeli politics, coalition bargaining. This was that committees breed indecision, while Israel's narrow depth of territory and dependence on reserve mobilisation make rapid decision essential to her survival. A coalition-based national security council, had it secured the right to interfere in the decision for mobilisaton, might have debated Israel into defeat. Joffre had warned the French Supreme War Council on August 1st, 1914 that by every 24 hours it delayed proclaiming general mobilisation, it surrendered 10km depth of the national territory, and the same principle, though to an even more urgent timetable, applied in Israel.

Until, 1973, Israel made provision against 'defeat through debate' by accepting the necessity for a direct, unsupervised relationship between the Minister of Defence and the Chief of Staff; it bore comparison with the right of personal access (*Immediatvortrag*) to the ruler won by the Chief of the Great General Staff in nineteenth-century Germany, which was justified by similar anxieties about the security of the frontiers. As a result of the report of Chief Justice Agranat's committee of enquiry into the circumstances of the outbreak of the *Yom Kippur* War of October, 1973 submitted to the cabinet on January 30th, 1975, it was decided, however, to set up just such a ministerial committee for defence as Lavon had wanted and failed to get 20 years before. It is to be composed of 10 members: the Prime Minister, the Ministers of Foreign Affairs, Defence and Justice, and one representative of each of the parties in the Labour coalition. It is to receive intelligence, to have control over the size, deployment, preparedness and equipment of the armed forces, and to have authority to decide on the conduct of military operations within the framework of government policy. Its proceedings will be secret but other Cabinet members will have the right to read its papers and to appeal against its decisions to the full Cabinet, though not to delay implementation of its decisions.

There is no means of judging whether the new system will be more or less likely to avert the danger of surprise attack. As with so much else in Israeli politics, the innovation is explained best perhaps in terms of personalities. The blame for the *Yom Kippur* War was believed to attach to the Defence Minister, Dayan, and to his tendency to trespass on the operational prerogatives of the Chief of Staff — exactly what he had objected to, when he himself was Chief of Staff, in Lavon's handling of the office. Because, however, the constitution does not define the Minister's responsibilities, he could not be blamed for delaying mobilisation nor for the army's subsequent bald-headed counter-offensive. But his responsibilities could be vested in a committee composed of his critics, if only until public opinion would allow a reversion to the former system — perhaps the original system by which the Premier combined his office with that of the Minister of Defence. It may be thought significant that the Prime Minister involved was one of Israel's foremost ex-soldiers, the Chief of Staff of the 1967 war, and that he took as his personal military adviser General Arik Sharon, the hero of the 1973 canal crossing.

† Perlmutter, A., *Military and Politics in Israel*, 91.

ROLE, COMMITMENT, DEPLOYMENT AND RECENT OPERATIONS

Role

'The primary function of *Zahal*', wrote Ben Gurion, the guiding spirit of its early days, in 1949, 'has been to safeguard the State. However, that is not its sole function. The army must also serve as an *educational and pioneering centre* for Israeli youth — for both those born here and newcomers. It is the duty of the army to educate a pioneer generation, healthy in body and spirit, courageous and loyal, which will unite the broken tribes and diasporas to prepare itself to fulfil the historical tasks of the State of Israel through self-realisation.' These words were no doubt partly a sop to the *Palmach* pioneer-soldiers and their supporters in the aftermath of its dissolution, and a palliative to the fears of the idealistic left that the creation of a standing army would irreversibly militarise the Israeli nation. The army, however, has, as he promised, acted throughout its existence as an important medium of education both in citizenship and in civilian skills, not the least useful of which in Israel is a knowledge of Hebrew. Yet necessarily its main service to a State born in war, thrice tested in subsequent wars and constantly harrassed across its frontiers, has been performed under arms. When Ben Gurion spoke of 'holy' or 'sacred' *Zahal*, as he was given to doing, it was its warrior, not its nation-building role, that he saluted.

Like other armed forces with a single-cut role — the Soviet army and the United States Marine Corps are examples — the Israeli army has developed a very strong operational doctrine with which to carry it out: that of the unrelenting offensive, led from the front. The roots of the doctrine are manifold; it undoubtedly owes a great deal to classical Prussian military theory, which made its way into Israeli thinking both through Marxism (of which Clausewitz is one of the minor deities) and through German literary culture. The example of the Germans themselves, and of their principal desert soldier, Rommel, is probably another, though unacknowledged, source; Manstein, the protagonist of 'fluid' operations, and Guderian, the exponent of 'forward control', would certainly have applauded Israel's style of making war. A teacher whom the army does acknowledge is Sir Basil Liddell Hart, whose ideas on the 'Indirect Approach' were also digested by those same Germans before World War II, while the British approach to officer training, which lays such high emphasis on example and self-sacrifice, is detectable also in Israeli leadership doctrine, where it was deliberately implanted by Wingate. But the most potent influence of all has undoubtedly been experience itself. Their weakness enforced a policy of boldness upon the Israelis from the outset, results justified in the War of Independence, and the campaigns of 1956 and 1967 gave it the force of principle. Arguments about how best the offensive should be applied have always flourished within the army, notably between the paratroopers, who favour fluidity and rapid changes of plan to profit from enemy mistakes, and the Armour Corps, which believes in the power of mechanical *blitzkrieg*, but, until the *Yom Kippur* War, the correctness of the offensive, or counter-offensive, had itself not been questioned. Since the reverses of the *Yom Kippur* War, however, the doctrine has undergone re-examination, not least because it depended, as did German *blitzkrieg* theory, upon an assumption of psychological — all too easily transmuted into a moral — superiority over the enemy. Israel's inability to keep her army mobilised for more than a few weeks without provoking the conomic collapse of the nation will compel her, in any future war, to seek a quick result, probably by offensive means. But the army now accepts that it cannot count on destroying Arab morale as it did in the past. What has been called by its critics the 'collapse theory' is now rejected.

Commitment
Israel, though a member of the United Nations, belongs to no alliance. Its existence is, however, implicitly guaranteed by the United States. The State has established military relationships with a number* of developing countries, e.g. Singapore, Burma, Uganda, Ethiopia and Ghana, through the work of *Zahal* training missions invited by their governments, chiefly between 1956 and 1970. Since the mobilisation of anti-Zionist feeling by the Arab governments in the Third World, most of these connections have lapsed.

Deployment
Identification of Israeli formations is made deliberately difficult by General Staff's refusal to reveal by what names or numbers they are known. In campaign accounts, brigades are referred to by letters or by their commander's forenames, but different authors are apparently issued by the General Staff with different lists of letters, e.g. A, M, X and Y brigades appear simultaneously on separate fronts in varous histories of the 1967 war. There is also little indication allowed of which brigades belong to the standing army and which to the reserves. Some exceptions are that the 1st (Golani) Brigade is known to be the training brigade of the conscript infantry, the 7th the 'School' Brigade of the Armour Corps, based at Beersheba, and the Jerusalem or Etzioni Brigade a multi-battalion reserve formation assigned to static duty around Jerusalem. The survival of these War of Independence titles and numbers suggests that the others are still kept in use and, as the pattern (if not the density) of Jewish settlement has not greatly changed over 25 years, that the present reserve formations may still come from the same areas and bear the same numbers. But that does not help to locate or identify the brigades of the standing army, of which it is generally agreed that there are eleven kept at full strength and six kept somewhere between full and half strength. Since the invasion of the Lebanon in June 1982, about one-third of the army has been fully mobilised and is in that country. The garrison on the Golan remains strong. The location of other units is subject to strict secrecy.

Recent Operations
Israel fought the fourth of her major wars between October 6th and 23rd, 1973, against Syria and Egypt, whose forces were joined by token contingents from Saudi Arabia, Kuwait, Algeria and Morocco, and by more sizeable elements of the Jordanian and Iraqi services. The war began in the north with a large-scale Syrian armoured offensive against the Israeli positions on the Golan Heights and Mount Hermon; and in Sinai by an Egyptian amphibious assault, in the strength of several divisions, on the Bar-Lev Line, constructed by the Israelis in 1968–9 to defend the captured east bank. The time chosen was the early afternoon of the Jewish Day of Atonement (*Yom Kippur*), the holiest festival of the religious year, which most Jews spend between home and synagogue; many conscripts are given leave for it.

There had been some indication that the attack was impending but, because a partial mobilisation on similar evidence in May had proved unnecessary and provoked criticism of the expense entailed, the Defence Minister, Moshe Dayan, and later the Cabinet, only decided on October

* Stated by Simon Peres to be 65.

5th to put the standing forces at advanced readiness. It was not until 7 a.m. on the morning of the attack itself that the evidence was judged — chiefly at the urging of the Chief of Staff, David Elazar — to justify a full call-out. This was arranged by the 'cellular' method: the transmission of a codeword to a select number, each of whom passed it in to 10 neighbours, and so on. Because units are formed on a neighbourhood basis in Israel, the cellular call-out achieves their mobilisation very quickly.

Not quickly enough on this occasion, however, to allow *Zahal* to oppose force with equal force on either front. In the north, the Israelis had permanently deployed two armoured brigades, including the 7th, the 'School' Brigade of the Armour Corps, both behind a deep anti-tank ditch which was backed by strong-points in 14 *telal*, the distinctive small volcanic hills of the area. Against these, the Syrians launched in the first wave three mechanised divisions, the 5th, 7th and 9th, with 600 tanks and 1400 other armoured vehicles; their task was to clear a way for the armoured reserve, 1st and 3rd Armoured Divisions and two independent armoured brigades, fielding another 1000 tanks. Such superiority would not have threatened the Israeli front's integrity had their air force been able to operate, as it had done with complete freedom and great success in 1967, in the ground-attack role. However, it was not: the Syrians had installed a dense screen of Russian SA-6 missiles and ZSU-23-4 anti-aircraft guns which, at the cost of 30 aircraft on the first day, *Zahal*'s pilots found they could not penetrate. Under its cover, the Syrians were able to engage the Israelis in tank-to-tank battles at odds of five to one. On the southern sector of the front, the standing brigade lost many of these battles, had its commander killed and was forced to give ground towards the Jordan, last line of defence of the Galilee plain. The 7th Brigade on the northern sector, handled by a commander who proved himself a brilliant practitioner of mobile defensive tactics, gave ground more slowly and inflicted heavy losses on the attackers, often by mounting local counter-attacks. On the extreme north, however, the Syrians seized the summit of Mount Hermon by helicopter assault.

By the evening of Sunday, October 7th, the Syrians had advanced south of the Kuneitra—Damascus road, 10 of the 17 miles which separated them from the Jordan. But they had suffered such heavy tank losses, partly because they had quit the cover of their anti-aircraft screen, that they had to spend the Monday reorganising, and renewed their attack only on Tuesday, October 9th. By then the Israelis had themselves committed their mobilised reserve brigades and, although they lost a little more ground south of Kuneitra, were able on Wednesday, October 10th, to counter-attack in force; by that evening they had returned to the 1967 ceasefire line. On October 11th they began to advance beyond it and by Saturday, October 13th had reached to within 35km of Damascus.

The first week of fighting on the Sinai front had seen no such upturn in Israeli fortunes. There the battle had opened on October 6th, at 1405 hours, with a 53 minute bombardment of the Bar-Lev Line by 1000 Egyptian guns, followed by a crossing of 10 brigades of infantry in assault boats. The company posts of the Line, garrisoned for the most part by reservists of the Etzioni Brigade fulfilling their annual recall liability, were weakly held and all but a few at once fell. The Egyptian infantrymen then moved forward about 6 miles into the desert, north and south of the Great Bitter Lake, and established an anti-tank guided-missile defence line. In their rear, sappers began breaching the high sand ramparts, erected by the Israelis, to allow egress for the tanks of the two follow-up armoured divisions which, that night, began to cross by bridge and ferry. Israeli aircraft which attempted to interfere ran into a missile and gun screen similar to that emplaced by the Syrians on the Golan.

Three Israeli standing armoured brigades were deployed in Sinai and the most forward, the 14th, suffered heavily in attempts to staunch the initial break-in. Gonen, the overall commander (one of the most successful brigadiers of 1967), kept his other two in their support positions until, on October 9th, sufficient of the mobilised brigades had made their way to him across Sinai (at a speed of 10 miles per hour — that of the tank transporters) to enable him to risk a counter-attack. When delivered, it proved a mistake; the 190th Brigade, unprotected by air cover, attempted an orthodox all-tank assault in close formation and was destroyed by salvos of Sagger missiles fired by the Egyptian infantrymen. Its commander was captured and later interrogated on Cairo television, a particular humiliation for *Zahal*, which in 1967 had had even fewer prisoners taken than it suffered fatal casualties. Thus deterred, the Israelis kept their gathering brigades beyond range of the Egyptian anti-tank and anti-air screens, waiting for the enemy to bring his own tanks, of which 1000 had now crossed to the east bank, forward of its protection. They did on Sunday, October 14th, and were repulsed, losing a quarter of their armour.

This success, coinciding with the relief of pressure on the Golan, and the concentration of four divisions (13 brigades) in Sinai, was taken by the Israelis as the opportunity they had awaited. The most aggressive of the divisional commanders, Arik Sharon, creator of the Israeli paratroopers, had proposed reducing the Egyptian bridgeheads by making a Canal counter-crossing into their rear and he was now given permission to take his two armoured brigades and two parachute brigades across. Choosing a point just north of the Great Bitter Lake, which divided the Egyptian bridgeheads, and a spot (at 'Chinese Farm') in the ramparts which the Israelis had built deliberately weak for that purpose, he breached a gap under cover of darkness — an element which he had taught the paratroopers to make their own — build a bridge and got onto the west bank by daylight of Tuesday, October 15th. For some time the Egyptians remained unaware of his presence, then underestimated in what strength he was across and, when eventually they concentrated force to expel him, found it insufficient. Despite heavy concentric attacks against the flanks of the corridor to Sharon's crossing-place (on the east bank), they were likewise unable to sever his communications, which the Israeli pilots also used as an air corridor through the missile screen to the west bank. With their support, Sharon drove columns southward, behind the Great Bitter Lake, to reach the southern course of the Canal proper on October 22nd and the towns of Suez on October 24th. By that bold stroke, he cut clear across the rear of the Egyptian Third Corps (wrongly called Third *Army* in communiqués) which, because of the interposition of the Great Bitter Lake and the Israeli trans-Canal corridor between it and Second Corps (Army), found itself completely marooned, without access to supplies, in the desert on the east bank.

On the following day a ceasefire, which had been called for in the United Nations Security Council on October 22nd, came into effect on both the Suez front and on the Golan front where, on October 21st, Israeli heliborne paratroopers had recaptured the summit of Mount Hermon. The war had cost the Israelis 2412 dead and 508 missing, and left 400 prisoners in enemy hands. It had also almost exhausted *Zahal*'s stock of munitions, calculated to feed a war of 30 days, and required the import from America during the conflict of weapons and supplies, including electronic counter-measure devices hitherto disdained, costing $2,200,000,000. It had also, despite Sharon's belated masterstroke, badly shaken the self-confidence of the Israeli people and of *Zahal*.

Their Arab neighbours had displayed military skills they were not believed to possess and the frontiers of 1967 had been shown to offer less than the total security their capture had been thought to have brought. Rapid mobilisation, though it had worked as well as before, had not saved the standing brigades from grievous loss in the opening battles, and air/armour *blitzkrieg* tactics, the orthodoxy of Israeli military philosophy, had for the first time failed. The consequences of these developments, as they affected *Zahal* and its leaders, are discussed under Curent Developments, together with the Litani river and 'Peace for Galilee' operations of 1978 and 1982.

ORGANISATION

Arms of Service

The domestic organisation of *Zahal* is highly centralised. All corps, including the air force (*Hel Avir* — Air Corps) and the navy (*Hel Yam* — Sea Corps), are regarded as belonging to a single service and, although the air force and navy do in practice enjoy considerable autonomy, all are subject to the authority of a single chief of staff, besides being administered by a single defence ministry.

There are 16 corps of the ground forces: the Armour (which includes armoured infantry); Artillery; Infantry and Parachute; Engineer; Signal; Ordnance; Supply and Transport; General Services; Women's (*Chem*); Medical; Military Police; Education; the Rabbinate; the Judge Advocate's Branch; Military Intelligence; and *Nahal*. The Supply and Transport Corps and the Ordnance Corps are administered by the Quartermaster Branch; the Education, Medical, Women's and Military Police Corps, the Rabbinate and the Judge Advocate's Branch are administered by the Manpower Branch, and the others by their own chiefs, who are technically Inspectors under the Chief of Staff. There are some exceptions: the Chief of Military Intelligence is the head of a branch of the General Staff, co-equal with Manpower and Quartermaster, the Chief of Armour is both inspector and the head of a command, thus having autonomy approaching that of the air force and navy commanders, and *Nahal* is also a separate command. This 'Pioneer Fighting Youth', for which its Hebrew acronym stands, is of political rather than military importance. Founded in 1951, it was intended to perpetuate the *Palmach*'s tradition of combining military work with agricultural work. Members of *Nahal*, a volunteer corps, go after training to help establish *kibbutzim* in frontier areas subject to enemy attack. It numbers about 5000 and garrisons about 30 settlements.

Operational

'We have never revealed', declared General Dayan in 1967, 'and I hope we never shall, what the size and numbers of the Israel Defence Forces are'. He and his successors have been remarkably successful not only in keeping these facts secret, but also the identity, location and organisation of its units.

The principal formation since the War of Independence has been the brigade, of which there are three types: armoured, (mechanised) infantry and parachute. During the 1956 War, however, experiments were made with a loose divisional formation, known as the *ugdah*, which appeared again in 1967 and, since 1973, has taken on the formal structure of a Western division, with three brigades (two armoured and one of mechanised infantry). Under the influence of Generals Elazar and Tal, who each successively commanded the Armour Corps and the General Staff (Operations) Branch, these formations became exceptionally 'tank heavy', with two tank battalions in the tank brigade and one in the infantry brigade.

A corps organisation (*gayessa*) was introduced in 1975.

Israel

The army was formerly believed to keep 11 brigades (five armoured, four infantry and two parachute) at full strength (i.e. as standing brigades) and six (one armoured, four mechanised and one parachute) at between full and half strength. Its fully mobilised strength (excluding lower-grade reserve brigades), is said to total 43 brigades. Careful identification of formations in the 1967 War sugggests, however, that only 23 came into contact with the enemy and it does not seem that more than 30 were deployed on the battlefronts in 1973. The difference between the identified and notionally total number – about 13 – is therefore, surprising.

The difference in organisation between armoured, parachute and infantry brigades is difficult to grasp. The armoured infantry belongs to the Armour Corps and, in 1967, some so-called 'armoured' brigades seem to have consisted chiefly of infantry belongs to the Armour Corps and, in 1967, some so-equally, have a tank battalion attached, as may infantry brigades, the only difference between them being that the parachutists are actually parachute trained.

The Israeli brigade organisation is triangular: three combat battalions, a reconnaissance unit, an artillery battalion, signals and engineers (though there are new regiments that it is 'square'). Battalions are also triangular, with three companies and, in the infantry, a support company. The artillery battalion has three batteries of four guns. A reasonably safe estimate of brigade organisation, therefore, is to say that armoured brigades are mainly composed of tank battalions, parachute brigades mainly of infantry battalions (probably mounted in half-tracks or APCs), and that infantry brigades, if of the standing army or first-line-reserve, are mainly composed of APC battalions with a tank battalion, while if of the second-line reserve they are probably carried in requisitioned civilian transport. All units are rather small by Western standards, with as few as 35 tanks in the tank battalion. The brigade reconnaissance unit is equipped with armoured cars, jeep-mounted anti-tank guns or now with captured Russian light armoured vehicles.

The great variety of equipment in Israeli hands further complicates analysis of the army's organisation. The standing brigades certainly have the newest of the bespoke equipment, while the oldest of the captured equipment goes to the lower-grade reserve formations. But in 1967, several of the reserve armoured brigades were as well-equipped as the standing ones. Equipment is not mixed in the battalions. Despite their standardisation of both bespoke and captured tanks, which all now have diesel engines and a 105mm gun, they outfit battalions with a single type. There have recently been reports of negotiations with at least one foreign country for the sale of some or all of the older captured Russian heavy armour.

Territorial Defence
The oldest classes of the reserve, those over fifty but perhaps also some men in their forties, are enrolled in the *Haganah Mercbavit*, the Home Defence Groups, which defend the villages and rural settlements. Over-age town dwellers are enrolled in Civil Defence. The units of *Nahal*, though formed of young people, remain at mobilisation in their *kibbutzim*, which it is their first task to defend.

Border Police
This is a paramilitary force of about 5000 which patrols the frontiers, particularly that with Jordan. Many of the Druze conscripts were formerly often posted into it.

RECRUITMENT, TRAINING AND RESERVES

Zahal is the best-known example of a civilian militia in the

world today. But exactly what sort of militia is it? In the aftermath of the War of Independence, when its leaders had to tackle the question of how best to secure their fragile State against the dangers of a new war, they examined the suitability of two military systems in particular: *Haganah's Hish*, a wholly part-time force, and the Swiss *Miliz* (*q.v.*), a large reserve army fed by a small annual conscript contingent. Yadin, the first Chief of Staff, actually visited Switzerland in 1949 to study the *Miliz*; and it is maintained that *Zahal's* organisation was based more closely upon it than on any other. Whatever the original inspiration, however, the resemblance between *Zahal* and the *Miliz* is now tenuous. In Switzerland, the initial term of service is very short (118 days), the first-line (*Aufzug*) combat units come into existence only for three weeks each year, while, for several winter months when even the training units are empty, Switzerland is virtually disarmed. Moreover, the ratio of cadres and conscripts under training to reserves is very low, about 6:100. In Israel the ratio is 36:100, the length of the initial term of service is 3 years and over half the combat units are kept permanently in being. In short, though *Zahal* is undoubtedly a militia, it approximates far more closely in organisation, if not in *esprit*, to the conscript armies of late nineteenth century Europe than to the National Guard of the burger republics of northern Europe. The reason is immediately apparent: France and Germany maintained large conscript armies between 1871 to 1914 because each feared the other's capacity (*a*) to achieve a surprise attack across the frontier with strong standing forces and (*b*) to follow it by a mass offensive with rapidly mobilised reserves. It is exactly those dangers which Israel faces and which produces in the Israeli military system so many features more reminiscent of those of the Third Republic or Second Reich (in which, for example, the ratio between standing army and reserves was 27:100) than of that of neutral Switzerland.

Recruitment
Conscription is universal, under the Defence Service Law of 1949. There is no voluntary enlistment and no special entrance for future officers. All fit Israelis are inducted at the age of eighteen, men for 3 years, women for two; this produces about 17,000 recruits a year. The small Druze and Circassian communities have, since 1955, also been liable, at their leaders' request, to conscription, but Arabs, Christian and Muslim alike, are exempt (they may volunteer, but none is known to), as are full-time theological (*Yeshiva*) students and the daughters of ultra-orthodox families; the latter concession was at one time the cause of serious political bickering in the country, but only 50% of eligible women are recruited in any case, the army being able to find suitable non-combatant employment for no more. Of the eligible men, 90% are recruited, a far higher proportion than in any other conscript army, explained both by Israel's exigent manpower requirements and by the importance placed on the army's 'melting pot' role in the education and assimilation of new immigrants. Older immigrants (men up to twenty-nine, women up to twenty-four) are subject to the same rules as those aged eighteen, those older still to shorter enlistments. Conscientious objection is not recognised by the law but, under discretionary powers granted to the Minister of Defence, ethical, though not political, objection is respected and exemptees are assigned to alternative civilian duty.

Training

Soldiers
Pre-service selection is rigorous, since the army's 'high-technology' style of warfare requires large numbers of

technically skilled entrants to the armoured, mechanised and artillery units. There is a particularly intensive course of selection for pilots. Selected recruits are distributed to training units, in which they serve 3 months, and then to the standing brigades and their support units. The aim is to get every able-bodied recruit into a combat formation; only the less fit and the specialist are found in support units. Suitable specialists are in short supply and the army runs a number of technical high schools, for those aged sixteen to eighteen, to provide technicians to the air force, navy, and signal, ordnance and engineer corps. It also provides in-service facilities for poorly educated recruits (usually north Africans or Yemenis) to get the elementary school certificate and it acts as a principal medium of Hebrew teaching in the immigrant community.

Officers and NCOs

After 3—5 months' service in a standing unit, suitable candidates are sent to NCO training school for 3 months. About 50% of recruits reach the rank of corporal. After further unit service, potential officers are selected from among them and are sent to the Officer Cadet School for 3 months, and then to a 3 month course at their corps school. The whole officer-producing process, from recruitment to commissioning, lasts 14—18 months (though it has tended to shorten since 1967 by an elimination of the NCO course for potential officers). At the end of conscript service, a final selection is made to choose regular officers. Because there is difficulty in finding enough suitable candidates (many of the suitable conscript officers preferring to return to civil life), the army runs a military cadet scheme, not dissimilar from the old German *Einjahrfreiwilliger* system. Boys from two of the country's foremost high schools, the Reali in Haifa and the Herzlia in Tel Aviv, spend their vacations at military duty and in return are granted the rank of corporal on enlistment. If commissioned, as most are, they are expected to serve an additional 2½ years beyond conscript service. Competition for cadetships is keen, six applicants appearing for each vacancy, though the education is not free*.

There is no promotion in the reserves from conscript NCO rank (except for promotion in the field). Some reserve officers, however, choose to attend courses, in their own time and at their own expense, which allow them to be promoted up to the rank of lieutenant-colonel. Promotion for regular officers is rapid: 4 years as a subaltern, and three in succeeding ranks, is the norm. Company commanders are therefore usually about twenty-five, battalion commanders thirty, brigade commanders thirty-five to forty, the Chief of Staff forty-five. Retirement is obligatory at fifty-five but most officers go out between forty and forty-five. It is official policy to encourage among them a 'two career' attitude and the interpenetration of military and civilian life in Israel makes it easy (too easy, some critics argue) for ex-officers to move into responsible and well-paid civilian jobs. Despite the rapidity of promotion, however, it is by no means automatic. Selection is rigorous, those passed over are compulsorily retired and failure in performance freezes a man in rank.

Officer training (except for the navy and air force, which is separate from the start) begins with a platoon commander's course, based on that of the *Palmach* and inculcating its spirit of 'follow me' (the motto of the Israeli officer corps and, in theory, the only order an officer may give under enemy fire). Thereafter training takes place within the officer's

own corps, with which he remains throughout his service (there are very strong corps rivalries in *Zahal*, particularly between armour and paratroops), though as much through rapid job-rotation as formal instruction. The army does hold, however, both a company commander's course (also open to reserve officers) and a staff course (a requirement for promotion to colonel rank) (*Poum — Pikud u Mate*, meaning Command and Staff), though there is no military academy or staff college as such. The army prefers to sharpen its officers' intellects by sending them on paid leave to civilian universities (25% have university degrees which facilitate the transition to a civilian career) or to widen them by a posting to foreign staff colleges. Most senior officers have followed both courses.

About a quarter also, though not necessarily the same quarter, are *kibbitzniks* or *Moshavniks*, though those groups form only about 8% of the Israeli population. This relationship between the communal settlements (in which the spirit of the State of Israel was born and nurtured) and the officer corps is well-known, and may be explained in a number of ways: firstly by the domination of all *élite* activity in Israel by *kibbutzniks*, secondly by the ethos of civic devotion and self-sacrifice inculcated in the *kibbutzim* (which have been accused of playing the same role in Israeli society as the public schools in British), and thirdly by the opportunity for advancement the army's promotion policy offered to young men whose ageing fathers virtually monopolised all the civilian posts of power and influence in the country. The first significant reduction of the abnormally high age of politicians in Israel has recently been brought about by the appearance in government of some of the country's abnormally young ex-generals.

Even if not *kibbuzniks*, most officers are *sabras* (native-born). Most conscripts, on the other hand, are immigrants, either Orientals or Slavs, this reflecting the low *sabra* birth rate and the continuingly high rate of immigration. Yet this 'ethnic' division does not (yet) seem to be a cause of resentment in the country. Even though the restricted career opportunities open to immigrants and the children of Orientals is threatening to become a cause of serious social and political tension in the country, *Zahal* is generally absolved of charges of discrimination and admired as the nation's one genuinely open institution.

Youth

All Jewish high-school youths must belong to *Gadna*, a paramilitary youth organisation administered by the Ministries of Defence and Education. Conscious of the genuine dangers in, and the damaging connotations attaching to, the State's sponsorship of such a movement, the government has charged it with a dual role: that of making the country's young 'defence minded', but of discouraging 'militarism' by turning their energies into social, agricultural and athletic activities. *Gadna*, however, is organised into battalions and provides courses in aviation, seamanship, signals and marksmanship 'for those interested'. A special branch of the General Staff exists to supervise it.

Reserves

The great majority of Israeli servicemen are reservists. Like the Swiss, they are encouraged to think of themselves as being on leave from their units, which are localised and can be activated in as little as 12 hours. There are two methods of recall: by proclamation, which brings out the whole army, or by the transmission of coded call-signs by radio, telephone, or word of mouth, which allows the mobilisation of selected units only. Reservists are divided into first and second line, the division apparently falling at the age of thirty-nine.

---

* It may be significant that these are the two oldest and most distinguished high schools in Israel. In 1914 the entire graduating class of the Herzlia was commissioned as officers into the Turkish army.

Men remain on the reserve until fifty-four, childless women to thirty-eight. The oldest reservists are assigned to the local defence groups of the static *Haganah Merchavit* or to Civil Defence, but the younger take to the field with the reserve brigades. Exactly which age-groups are assigned to fighting units of the mobile army and which to its services has varied with the strategic situation, and is kept a secret. Again, the parallel may be drawn with the secrecy surrounding reserve policy in France and Germany before 1914.

Reservists are also subject to annual training (the *milvim*), for a minimum of 1 day each month; those aged up to thirty-nine (childless women to thirty-four) must serve 31 days and officers and NCOs a further seven. Between 1967 and 1973 the annual liability rose to sixty or even more days a year, and many reserve units were deployed *en bloc* in the Bar-Lev Line for weeks at a time.

EQUIPMENT AND ARMS INDUSTRY

By the October War (of 1973) Israel was producing a wider range of artillery and infantry weapons, missiles and electronic equipment, aircraft, and battle tank and gun conversions, than any country in the world except Sweden and the Great Powers. The complex of Israeli research establishments and defence industries was engaged in a broad front effort that covered the full spectrum from nuclear physics to mechanical engineering. This achievement was the fruit of a decision, taken in 1967 and prompted on the one hand by Russian generosity with arms supplies to the defeated Arabs, on the other by the fear that America might not always be counted upon to deal likewise with Israel, that the country should, as far as possible, become self-sufficient in military equipment. The means to implement the decision lay to hand in the already existing State-owned defence industries, largely created by Simon Peres (in 1975 Minister of Defence) during his time as Director-General of the Ministry of Defence, 1959–65. The largest are Israel Aircraft Industries (I.A.I.), Tadiran (Israel Electronic Industries) and Ta'as (Israel Military Industries), which originated as the clandestine weapon-procurement branch of *Haganah*. A major collaborator in their work is the army's own Ordnance Corps which now has great experience in the re-arming and re-engineering of foreign military equipment, particularly tanks, both bespoke and captured.

Seen in perspective, the decision to aim for self-sufficiency was a logical extension of a trend in Israeli armament policy present at the founding of *Zahal*, and even before. Its first heavy weapon, the Davidka mortar, had had to be locally produced during the mandate in secret workshops, while so miscellaneous was such equipment as it was able to buy overseas during the War of Independence that its conversion to common standards was an urgent necessity requiring considerable industrial improvisation. From the early 1950s the State was able to buy new (instead of second-hand) equipment from abroad, the deals being financed out of its own booming exports, from the capital contributions of foreign Jews and from the West German government's reparations. It had, however, to buy when and where it could. Jet aircraft came from France and Britain, tanks from Britain and West Germany and, from the mid-1960s, armoured vehicles and aircraft from the United States. Moreover, these supplies were subject to interruption for diplomatic reasons at any time, were rationed by Great Power agreements to restrict levels of armaments in the area (notably the Tripartite Declaration by America, Britain and France of 1950) and continued to yield a very miscellaneous inventory of equipment, which the windfalls of victory in 1956 and 1967, welcome though they were, even further diversified.

Zahal's unwilling experimentation with this wide variety of equipment prompted it towards a companion decision to that for self-sufficiency: concentration on a strictly limited range of weapons. By 1967 the High Command had the clearest picture possible of the sort of weapons the wars it had to fight required, and specified that effort should not be wasted in producing a 'balanced' inventory. In aircraft, it decided to settle for an 'all-fighter' force, bought abroad but extensively modified, either by the manufacturer or in Israel, to perform interceptor and strike roles; in armour, to outfit the standing brigades with big-gun heavy-armour tanks (Centurions and Pattons), and to convert captured material to the same standard, but to keep older equipment (its by now antiquated Shermans) in service as long as it could safely be used by the reserve formations; in light military engineering, to produce a few types of weapon which would both satisfy its own requirements and capture export markets, a policy in which it has been successful: the Uzi sub-machine-gun and the Israeli–Finnish Tampella mortar are sold widely abroad, thus offsetting a little of its enormous arms bill.

The Israelis' armaments policy bears comparison with that of Switzerland, except that they are now moving to achieve self-sufficiency in types of equipment which neither Switzerland nor any other industrial country of their size attempts to manufacture. They have produced their own Mach 2 jet fighter (the Kfir) and a main battle tank, and certainly have in production an air-to-air missile (the Shafrir), a surface-to-surface missile (the Ze'ev (Wolf)), a Gabriel anti-shipping missile and the Reshef class of long-endurance missile boat. They are also widely believed to possess a nuclear weapon, or at least its disassembled parts, and a short-range (300 mile) ballistic missile, the Jericho, in which it might be fired.

Arms and Equipment

Rifle: 5.56mm Galil (Israeli manufacture based on Russian Kalashnikov); FN and G3 rifles not fully replaced in reserves

Sub-machine-gun: 9mm Uzi (Israeli design and manufacture)

Machine-gun: 7.62mm Browning (Belgium; Israeli manufacture)

Mortar: 60mm, 81mm, 120mm (light), 120mm (heavy) and 160 self-propelled (about 900 in service)

Anti-armour weapons: Cobra missile (West Germany), LAW (USA), TOW missile (USA), Cobra, Dragon (USA), Milan (France) missiles; 106mm recoilless rifle (USA); equips part of the brigade reconnaissance unit)

Anti-aircraft weapons: 20mm Vulcan/Chaparral gun (USA), 30mm Hispano–Suiza gun (Switzerland) and 40mm Bofors L-70 (Sweden/Britain) (about 900 in total in service); Redeye SA missile (USA); Hawk missile (USA; manned by the air force using 90 launchers)

Artillery: 155mm M-109 SP howitzer (USA), 155mm Soltam L-33 SP howitzer (French gun on Sherman chassis) and 155mm M-123 howitzer (USA) (about 600 in total in service); 175mm M-107 SP gun (USA; 60 in service); 203mm M-109 SP howitzer (USA; about 48 in service); 122mm M-76 gun (USSR), 122mm M-38 gun (USSR) and 130mm M-63 gun (USSR) (probably used in static role)

Armour: M-2 and M-3 half-track (ex-American, re-built); M-113 APC (USA); Walid (Israel) and BTR 40, 50, 60 and 152 (USSR) and BRDM (USSR) (about 4000 in total in service); Centurion main battle tank (Britain; 1100 in service); M-48/M-60 main battle tank (USA; 1660 in service); T-54/55 main battle tank (USSR; 250

in service); T-62 main battle tank (USSR; 150 in service); 200 Merkava main battle tanks (Israel); note that the total number of tanks is believed to be 3600

Aircraft: Phantom II F-4E fighter—ground attack (USA; 138 in service); Douglas A-4M fighter—ground attack (USA; 312 in service); Mirage III fighter—ground attack (France; 20 in service); 160 Kfir; 40 F-15; 14 F-16; about 125 large and small transport aircraft, and 150 large and small helicopters, are also in service, of French and American manufacture

RANK, DRESS AND DISTINCTIONS

Rank

Rav aluf†* (lieutenant-general) — Crossed sword and olive leaf
Aluf† (Major-general) — Crossed sword/two fig leaves
Tat aluf† (Brigadier) — Crossed sword/one fig leaf
Aluf mishne‡ (Colonel) — Three fig leaves
Sgan aluf (lieutenant-colonel) — Two fig leaves
Rav seren (Major) — One fig leaf
Seren (Captain) — Three bars
Segen (Lieutenant) — Two bars
Segen mishne (Second-lieutenant) — One bar

Rav samal rishon (Regimental sergeant-major) — Cuff badge
Rav samal (Sergeant-major) — Cuff badge
Samal rishon (Staff-sergeant) — Cuff badge
Samal (Sergeant) — Three horizontal white stripes
Rav turai (Corporal) — Two horizontal white stripes
Turai rishon (Lance-corporal) — One horizontal white stripe

Turai (Private) — —

Notes: * Held only by the Chief of Staff.
   † Introduced after the 1967 War to clear a promotion block — formerly the rank of aluf was regarded as equivalent to brigadier.
   ‡ Introduced after the War of Independence.

Officers badges are worn in bronze on the shoulder, NCOs badges in cloth on the upper sleeve. Rank titles are biblical in derivation and are common to army, navy and air force.

Dress

'Anyone', said Simon Peres, ex-Director-General of the Ministry of Defence, 'can see that we are by no means the best dressed army in the world; the principal outlay goes on armaments. Officers get issued with the same clothing as the men.' He might have added that, with conscription universal and its necessity as widely accepted, *Zahal* does not have to make its uniform seductive. It is not, moreover, strictly true that career officers are clothed exactly as the men. They possess a British-style service dress in olive drab, worn with a peaked cap. Their normal wear, however, is the issue cotton: drab for everyday, camouflage pattern for combat, worn with a khaki beret (maroon for parachutists, black for armour). An American-pattern steel helmet is issued.

Distinctions

Until 1967, no awards for bravery were given, it being official policy to expect bravery from all. But after 1967, 51 Chief of Staff's Mentions in Despatches were published and a bravery award in three classes is now being instituted. *Zahal* has issued campaign ribbons for each of its four major wars.

CURRENT DEVELOPMENTS

The life of the Israeli State and people is so bound up with that of *Zahal* that discussion of its present condition and its future can scarcely be disentangled from theirs. Economically, the cost of *Zahal*, which exceeded in 1974 the high it attained in 1972, is forcing the Israeli government to seek massive assistance abroad and the Israeli people to accept further sacrifices in their standard of living. In November, 1974 the Israeli pound was devalued from $0.238 to $0.167, largely because of expenditure on foreign arms, while taxes, already the heaviest in the world, were increased and subsidies on basic products reduced (the latter despite a campaign of demand by Oriental and east European immigrants for improved welfare payments). The 1974 defence budget is believed to have totalled $3,700,000,000, two and a half times the next largest previous appropriation, representing 38% of government expenditure and one-third of gross national product. Contributions from foreign Jews cannot meet the deficit this level of defence spending entails. It is not surprising, therefore, that Israel was reported in January, 1974 to have asked America for $2,200,000,000 in aid, of which $1,500,000,000 was for arms, and that Prime Minister Rabin, on his visit to Washington in September, 1974 is said to have been granted $4,500,000,000 spread over 1975/6/7. Much of it was needed to pay for the 50 Phantom fighters, 250 M-60 tanks and several sorts of missiles President Ford was also said to have promised him.

Israel's situation has also apparently worsened since 1973 at a strategic level, through her abandonment of the Suez Canal line (agreement signed with Egypt, January 18th, 1974), and more recently, of the Sinai passes. On the other hand, these concessions have brought her into a long-desired diplomatic dialogue with Egypt, whose severance of her ties with Russia further alleviates Israel's international situation, while America's stationing of observers in Sinai, between the Egyptian and Israeli front lines, is an important compensation for the security that possession of the passes provided. Militarily, the shortcomings revealed by the *Yom Kippur* War are said to have been made good: the mobilisation system has been streamlined (a partial mobilisation against Syria went off successfully on November 13th, 1974), transport capacity expanded (probably to shorten transit time across Sinai, which so delayed reinforcement of the Suez front in October, 1973), new fortifications built, and communications and electronic counter-measures (the latter an area of dangerous weakness as early losses in the air war of 1973 demonstrated) improved. *Zahal*'s commanders, after the restocking of 1973—4, believe that Israel has the means to wage a war of 1973's intensity for at least 21 days and to guarantee what have been laid down as current strategic priorities: to deny Arab armies the chance of gaining surprise, to avert the imposition of an air or sea blockade, to prevent the strategic bombing of the homeland and to achieve a quick victory if forced to fight a ground war — always given that avoidance of war, with its inevitable consequence of a renewed use by the Arabs of their oil embargo against Israel's foreign friends, now outweighs purely military considerations in the conduct of Israeli policy.

How fully *Zahal* itself has digested the changed circumstances with which the events of 1973 and their aftermath have faced Israel, is difficult to estimate. To an extent unparalleled in any other army, discussion of its strategic outlook, tactical doctrine and combat readiness turns on the personalities of its leaders. Much has been made of the displacement of 'armour' by 'parachute' generals since 1973, who are in turn seen to represent opposed philosophies of war making: the Armour Corps' rigid and bludgeoning, the parachutists' flexible and intuitive. It is true that the officers most severely censured in the Agranat report were from the Armour Corps, Elazar (the Chief of Staff) and Gonen (the Commander, until relieved, in Sinai), and likewise that Elazar's successor, Gur, and Sharon (the hero of the war), were parachutists. But Gur himself clearly displeased the Begin government by his 'hawkish' attitude to peace talks with Egypt, and was replaced in February, 1978 by General Raphael Eitan who, although a parachutist with a daredevil reputation, is on better personal terms with the political leadership. It has been announced that he is to oversee a reorganisation of *Zahal* which will give the army a separate command within the staff structure, as the navy and air force already have. It is expected that this will tend to reduce the direct involvement generals in the past have had in policy making, of which both Mr. Begin and his Defence Minister, Ezer Weizman, are known to be critical.

The Israeli army's operation of March 1978, to clear the south of Lebanon as far as the Litani river of Palestinian Liberation Organisation guerrillas, did not require a mobilisation of reservists. It was probably long contemplated, and contingency plans already laid. The supervision of the ceasefire line by United Nations contingents was only partial, but despite this Israeli forces were withdrawn from Lebanon by the middle of June, 1978.

In June 1982 they returned in a strength estimated at one-third of the army, occupied the South of the country (June 6—10) and laid siege to Beirut. The object of the operation, codenamed 'Peace for Galilee', was to expel the armed forces of the Palestine Liberation Organisation, which took refuge in West Beirut. A prolonged Israeli bombardment resulted in international intervention, most actively by the USA, and the consequent dispersion of the PLO (about 7000 armed men) to neighbouring Arab countries in small groups.

The Syrian army, badly hurt in tank battles in the South of the country and then in electronic warfare/strike duels in and over the Bekaa valley, was severely defeated in this operation. The Israeli army remains in place, now more dominant than ever before in the region.

John Keegan

ITALY

HISTORY AND INTRODUCTION

Italy produced the first modern armies: the bands of highly trained, full-time and (when in employment) well-paid mercenary soldiers with which the northern cities waged war against each other in the fourteenth and fifteenth centuries. But their epoch was short-lived, for, once Italy's stronger neighbours had learnt to raise professional armies of their own, the very disunity of the City States condemned them to invasion, defeat and dependence. It also condemned Italy to centuries of division and to clientage or foreign rule — under the Austrian Hapsburgs in the north and the Spanish Bourbons in the south — which left only the Papal States in the centre and Piedmont in the far north a conditional independence. Neither, by reason of their circumstances, maintained a large army or sought a warrior reputation.

Italy approached unification and statehood in the nineteenth century, therefore, without a strong military tradition or indeed the military means to rid the peninsula of its foreign overlords. Thus when the Kingdom of Sardinia—Piedmont (ruled by the House of Savoy, which had produced in Prince Eugene one of the greatest soldiers of modern times) raised the standard of national revival (*risorgimento*) against the Hapsburgs in 1848, its tiny army, though joined by volunteers from all over northern and central Italy, was easily beaten by superior Austrian power at Custozza and Novara. It was not until Napoleon III, for reasons of his own, brought his army to Piedmont's aid in 1859 that the Hapsburgs were forced to cede a portion of their Italian possessions; and not until 1866, when the newly proclaimed Kingdom of Italy joined in Prussia's attack on Austria (though without notable success), that the Venetian provinces were incorporated. By then the Bourbon Kingdom of the Two Sicilies had also fallen to Piedmont, thanks to the inspired guerrilla generalship of Garibaldi; and within 5 years the Papal States too were to be brought within its boundaries.

By that date the Italian army had won a certain military name. Its nucleus, the *Armata Sarda*, the royal army of the House of Savoy, had played an ostentatious part in the Crimean War on the Anglo—French side; it had produced in the La Marmora brothers a trio of generals known to the European public; and in the *Bersaglieri*, the romantically beplumed Piedmontese light infantry, it possessed a force which seemed to rival the French *Zouaves* in battlefield bravura. The army remained, nonetheless, an artificial and fragile creation. Established by royal decree on May 4th, 1861 as the *Esercito Italiano*, an amalgamation of the *Armata Sarda* with the forces of Modena, Tuscany, Parma and Bourbon Naples, and with the guerrilla bands of Garibaldi, it lacked a sense of unity and *esprit de corps*. The Piedmontese and Neapolitan armies had too recently been at war with each other to work easily in harness and the officers of both looked down on the adventurers of Garibaldi's Thousand who claimed equal status with them. The army, moreover, was unpopular with many of the new Kingdom's inhabitants, both because of the innovation of conscription and for its use in suppressing disorders caused by other administrative reforms which convulsed the south throughout 1861—5; and it was viewed by the devout, particularly after the forcible occupation of Rome in 1870 and the Pope's self-exile inside the Vatican, as an instrument of blasphemy. Over three-quarters of those

drafted for service in Basilicata, in the foot of Italy, in the 1860s took to the hills and even in 1910 one-fifth of southerners evaded military service.

By then, however, the army had gone some way to recommending itself to the population. In imitation of the German and French armies, it had taken to calling itself the 'School of the Nation', had indeed been called by a leading senator, Farini, in 1894, 'the only existing cement which holds the country together', and was indeed probably the only national (as opposed to provincial or municipal) institution with which a nineteenth-century Italian — the citizen of a still intensely regional country — came into contact. On the other hand, it had continued to incur odium for its role as an instrument of repression, particularly during the great outburst of agrarian unrest in 1898, and it had undergone two humiliating disasters on campaign in East Africa: Dogall in 1887 and Adowa in 1896; the latter was the worst defeat suffered by European troops at the hands of Africans during the conquest of the continent, a setback which interrupted for 40 years Italy's attempt to conquer Ethiopia and a blow to national self-esteem for which the conquest of Libya from Turkey in 1911—12 only partially compensated.

In the light of these circumstances, the performance of the Italian army in World War I, which it entered on the opening of hostilities with Austria in May, 1915 with the aim of conquering the last Italian-speaking provinces of the Hapsburg empire, was remarkable. Badly equipped and supplied, fielding only 25 divisions at the outset (a figure which quickly rose to 35 and to 65 by 1917), it at once undertook an offensive against the slopes of the Julian alps above the river Isonzo, and over the next 2 years, renewed the offensive no less than 10 times. The loss of life suffered and the conditions in which the troops were obliged to live and fight were appalling. By the autumn of 1917, nevertheless, the army was on the point of winning substantial gains from the Austrians, who accordingly sent urgently for help to the Germans. They organised a task-force of fresh, mountain-trained soldiers, skilfully selected a weak spot on the Italian front at Caporetto (Karfreit) and launched through it a brilliant alpine blitzkrieg which destroyed the Italian Second Army and forced the whole line back to the river Piave in the Lombard plain.

With French and British help the Italians, in the autumn of 1918, went over to the counter-offensive, in a battle they call Vittorio Veneto, and eventually recovered most of the ground lost the previous autumn. They were thus able at the peace to lay claim successfully to the '*Italia irridenta*' for which they had gone to war. But the war's sufferings — over 600,000 Italians had been killed — had not brought Italy internal peace. It had indeed brought on an open conflict between the socialists and Mussolini's new populist and nationalist party, the Fascists, which resulted in greater and greater illegality of behaviour between the two, which the sitting liberal government seemed unable to control, and culminated in Mussolini's March on Rome of October, 1922. There seems no doubt that many officers and ex-officers, whose careers had ended with the war, were in sympathy with Mussolini, but equally little doubt that the army as a whole opposed him and, with effective leadership, could and would have kept him from power. Mussolini was, however, effectively invited to usurp power by the King, to whom the army was unconditionally loyal, and it did not therefore resist his capture of the machinery of State.

It came, nonetheless, to regret it, for though his imperial policy allowed the army, in 1935—6, to avenge in Ethiopia the defeat of Adowa, he obliged it also to accept as a co-equal the socially uncouth Fascist militia; while in 1940 he committed it, unprepared and unequipped, to war at the side of Hitler against, first, the French and British, then the Greeks, then the Russians and eventually also the Americans. War with America, in which 6,000,000 Italians had made their homes, seemed to the majority of the nation almost as much a sacrilege as a folly; but the army had already suffered worse in the desert war against the British and in the campaign of Stalingrad against the Russians. It is now fashionable to decry the value of Italy's contribution to the Axis war effort; and it is true that much of the Italian army fought very badly and at times did not fight at all. On the other hand, those parts of it which had a modicum of modern equipment, fought well, while, as soon as Mussolini was overthrown and the successor regime accepted by the Allies as a co-belligerent, its remnants fought enthusiastically on the Allied side. These consisted of the *1° Raggruppamento Motorizzato*, formed in September, 1943 immediately after the armistice and attached to the United States Fifth Army, the *Corpo Italiano di Liberazione* and eventually six formations of divisional strength: *Cremona, Legnano, Friuli, Folgore, Mantova* and *Piceno* (on which the post-war army was eventually established). At the same time, the breach with Germany called into existence in northern Italy a partisan movement, which became a genuine expression of popular resistance and greatly impressed the Allied officers who were sent to advise it.

If the Italian army had fought badly in the war, it was largely because the war aroused little or no enthusiasm among Italians, who were moreover well aware that their army was unprepared for modern operations on a major scale. In coming to an assessment of the Italian army's worth, it is probably more instructive to reflect on its performance in World War I, in which its casualties were proportionately as heavy as those suffered by any other belligerent, its achievements by no means less and its one notorious failure, Caporetto, a crisis of morale scarcely different from that suffered by the French in May, 1917, by the British in March, 1918, and by the Germans at the end of the war.

There may, on the other hand, be something in the argument that the army, like so many of the other institutions of the modern Italian State, is essentially a northern creation foisted onto the centre and south by the process of political unification and never properly assimilated; it is significant that the units of high prestige, the *Bersaglieri* and *Alpini*, are northern in origin. Many Italians seem to accept this analysis. On the other hand, there is, as in France, strong left-wing hostility to the idea of reducing the army to a collection of high-prestige, all-regular units, which it is feared might be used against the left-wing parties in some future political crisis. It seems likely, therefore, that, as in France, the large conscript army will continue to exist precisely because of the doubts about its true military worth.

STRENGTH AND BUDGET

Population: 57,300,000
Army: 257,000 (190,000 conscripts); 550,000 reserves
Navy: 44,000 (including 750 marines); 27 major warships, 47 smaller craft
Air force: 70,000; 336 combat aircraft
Paramilitary forces: 90,000 Carabinieri; 72,000 Public Security Police

GNP (1976): $161,600,000,000
Defence expenditure (1977): $4,640,000,000

Two factors operate to restrict the military value of the sums, relatively and absolutely large, which Italy spends on defence: the first, a constant one, is the high level of personnel and operating expenditure; the second, a more recent one, is the rate of domestic inflation, which produced rises in equipment costs between 1973 and 1974 of the order of 40% Thus a Leopard tank, which in 1971 cost 180,000,000 lire, cost in 1975 300,000,000; over the same period, the cost of maintaining a conscript — and the Italian conscript receives nominal pay — rose from 960,000 lire to 1,600,000. The 1975 defence budget, though second only in size to the education budget, therefore yielded very little towards procurement and modernisation. Out of a budget of 2,451,000,000,000 lire, 1,433,000,000,000 was devoted to personnel costs, 46,000,000,000 to pensions, 255,000,000 to the maintenance of conscripts and 31,000,000,000 to running costs, leaving only 987,000,000,000 for procurement, research and modernisation, and this between the three services. The army needs to allocate a capital sum of 1,800,000,000,000— 2,000,000,000,000 lire to modernisation over the next 10 years, but receives at present only enough to complete its programme of modernisation in 25—30 years. And it is probable that the money should ideally be spent over a shorter period than 10 years, since large-scale re-equipment effectively ceased in the mid-1960s. As a result there are notable deficiencies in those equipment categories where technological change is rapid: anti-armour systems, air-defence systems and radio communications.

COMMAND AND CONSTITUTIONAL STATUS

The President of the Republic is titular Head of the Armed Forces, but control is exercised by the cabinet, the Defence Ministry and its administrative machine. Like most of the more important ministries, defence has a parallel council (but is appointed, not elected), which the government is bound to consult, and in this particular case it is a policy-forming, not consultative, body, the Supreme Defence Council (*Consiglio Suprema di Difesa*); its members are the President, the Prime Minister, the Foreign, Interior, Treasury, Industry and Defence Ministers and the Chief of the Defence General Staff. It must meet at least twice a year.

The Defence Ministry is a unified body whose minister works through two distinct chains of command. One is purely administrative and runs through the Defence Secretary General (a serving officer) to five Central Offices, responsible respectively for judicial and legislative affairs, budget and finance, organisation and methods, national mobilisation, and administrative inspections. The other is military; at its top is the Defence Secretary General and the Chiefs of Staff Committee, which consists of himself and the four chiefs of staff. Through the Defence Secretary General, it controls 19 General Directorates, which chiefly oversee personnel administration, procurement and supply of equipment and building, and works. It also advises the minister on operational planning, finance and organisation. The executive counterpart of the Chiefs of Staff Committee is the Armed Forces Supreme Board (the Defence Secretary General and the chief of staff of, and two general-rank officers of, each service) which meets either jointly or separately, depending on whether the agenda concerns one or more of the services.

The Defence Secretary General is therefore the central agent of the defence machine: upwards, he is directly responsible to the minister; to him are responsible the chiefs of staff. The Army Chief of Staff heads an Army General Staff divided into four Divisions — Personnel, Intelligence, Logistics and Operations; and six Inspectorates — Infantry and Cavalry, Artillery, Engineers, Signals, NBC Defence and Army Aviation. The Inspectorates' functions are advisory and administrative, the Divisions' executive.

The *Carabinieri*, which for day-to-day purposes comes under the control of the Minister of the Interior, is legally part of the army and its head, a serving lieutenant-general, is chosen from any branch of the army other than the *Carabinieri*. Those of its units integrated in army formations come under the orders of the formation commander.

The Chief of the Defence General Staff has his own staff within the Ministry of Defence which oversees joint defence policy and training; to him is also answerable the Chairman of the Technical and Scientific Defence Council, which carries out research and development for the Italian armed forces and allocates the research budget (on average $33,000,000 annually) between projects.

ROLE, COMMITMENT, DEPLOYMENT AND RECENT OPERATIONS

Role

As a result of the armistice of September, 1943 Italy became a co-belligerent of the Western Allies in the war against Germany (and Mussolini's rump State, the Italian Social Republic). It was not therefore disarmed at the end of the war but restrictions were laid on the size and equipment of its armed forces. In 1949 Italy became a founding member of NATO, and in 1951, at her insistence, the restrictions on the size of her armed forces were lifted by the Western Allies (against Russian protests) but that on her possessing nuclear weapons was left in force. Italy thus became a full military member of NATO, committed to building her land forces up to a strength of 12 divisions (a figure which has not been reached and has probably been tacitly abandoned). The exact purpose of an army of this size has never, however, been explicitly defined as a result of 'the fear successive governments have had of losing their precarious majorities by entering into open debate on defence policy. The Soviet Union and the Warsaw Pact are thus never mentioned by name as representing a threat in official government statements. Italy has never published a Defence White Paper and the Five-Year Plan of 1971 made no mention of defence whatsoever'. Nevertheless the Italian Foreign Ministry has stated that the main fole of the army, in collaboration with NATO, is 'the defence of the north-eastern frontier, air defence of the national territory' (in conjunction with the air force) and 'internal defence of the national territory. . . . In the general field of internal defence, the *Carabinieri* Corps, which is already responsible in peacetime — with the other armed corps of the State — for the general internal security of the nation, has a particularly important role.'

Commitment

The whole of the Italian Field Army (see Organisation) is committed to NATO; in the event of war, so too would be the Territorial Army and the military units of the *Carabinieri*. One *Alpini* battalion forms part of NATO's ACE Mobile Force. No Italian forces are stationed outside national territory but some American servicemen are stationed in Italy under NATO arrangements: the staff at AFSOUTH (Allied Forces Southern Europe) at Bagnoli, near Naples; the troops of SETAF (South European Task Force), which man two Sergeant battalions at Vicenza and Verona; the 8th Logistical

Command at Leghorn; and small air- and shore-based naval detachments.

Deployment

The bulk of the Italian Field Army is deployed on the frontier with Yugoslavia. Territorially, Italy is divided into six military regions (*Regione Militare*); North-West, North-East, Emilia—Tuscany, Central (including Sardinia), South and Sicily. These are further subdivided in 21 zones (*Zona Militare*) corresponding almost exactly with the 20 civil regions, and 65 military districts (*Distretto Militare*) which correspond with one or more of the 92 civil provinces. The regions are responsible for recruitment, internal security and mobilisation. Operationally, the army is divided into three corps (*Corpo d'Armata*) and five territorial commands (*Comando Territoriale*); the latter are situated in the four southern military regions and have few operational troops under their command (*See* Organisation) — the four Territorial infantry brigades and the *Granatiere di Sardegna* division at Rome (though the latter belongs to the Field Army and is assigned to NATO). The three corps are located in the two northern military regions: III Corps (HQ Milan) controls the *Centauro* armoured division (Novara/Civitavecchia), *Legnano* infantry division (Bergamo), *Cremona* infantry division (Turin) and *Taurinese* alpine brigade (Turin); IV Corps (HQ Bolzano) controls three alpine brigades — *Orobica* (Bolzano), *Tridentina* (Bressanone) and *Cadore* (Belluno); V Corps (HQ Vittorio Veneto) controls the *Ariete* armoured division (Pordenone), the independent armoured brigade *Pozzuolo del Friuli* (Gorizia), the *Julia* alpine brigade (Cividale), the missile brigade (Portogruaro), the *Lagunari* amphibious brigade (Venice), and the infantry divisions *Mantova* (Udine) and *Folgore* (Treviso); the *Folgore* parachute brigade, based at Pisa under *Comando Territoriale VII*, also belongs to the Field Army. There is a battlegroup of the Field Army, consisting of an infantry regiment and an artillery battalion, at Trieste.

The *Carabinieri*, like the army, has both an operational (mobile) and territorial organisation. Territorially, it is organised into three divisions (Milan, Rome and Naples), which control nine brigades (Turin, Milan, Padua, Bologna, Florence, Rome, Naples, Bari and Palermo) which in turn control 24 legions, subdivided into provincial groups. The mobile organisation consists of three infantry regiments of 11 battalions, a parachute battalion (which forms part of the *Folgore* brigade) and an armoured regiment, based at Rome.

Recent Operations

The Italian army has engaged in no operations (except for disaster relief) since World War II. The Public Security Police, and to a lesser extent the *Carabinieri*, have, however, been frequently involved in the suppression of internal disorder (as at Reggio Calabria in 1970) and terrorism, both of the right and left, and also in the control of banditry, which is still endemic in Sardinia and has not altogether died out in Sicily.

ORGANISATION

Arms of Service

There are eight: (1) armoured cavalry (*Cavalleria*), (2) artillery (*Artiglieria*) which is divided into field (*da Campagne*), medium (*Pesante Campale*), armoured (*Corazzata*) and horse (*a Cavallo*), (3) engineers (*Genio*), (4) signals (*Transmissioni*), (5) army air corps (*Aviazione Leggera del' Esercito*), (6) transport (*Automobilisti*), (7) logistics (*Commissariat*) which includes the medical and veterinary services, and supply, repair, administration and works, and (8) infantry (*Fanteria*) which is divided into infantry of the line (*de Linea*), grenadiers (*Granatieri di Sardegna*), mountain (*Alpini*), light (*Bersaglieri*), parachute (*Paracadutisti*), amphibious (*Lagunari*) and armoured (*Carristi*). The *Carristi* are really armoured troops, providing the tank crews of the armoured regiments; the *Bersaglieri* provide the armoured infantry of the armoured divisions and brigades; the *Granatieri di Sardegna* are permanently based at Rome (and are drawn from the tallest recruits); the *Lagunari* (*Reggimento Lagunari 'Serenissima'*) is based at Venice and equipped for amphibious operations in the lagoons and estuaries of the northern Adriatic; its three battalions are *Marghera*, *Isonzo* and *Piave*. The cavalry have preserved or revived the traditions of the old royal cavalry regiments (*Nizza, Piemonte, Savoia, Genova, Novara, Aosta, Montebello, Firenza, Saluzzo, Monferrato, Alessandria, Guide*) and provide the reconnaissance battalions of the corps and divisions (except for *Piemonte, Genova* and *Novara* which form the independent *Pozzo de Friuli* armoured brigade). A ninth arm of service is the *Carabinieri*, equivalent to the French *Gendarmerie Nationale*, but even more military in character; it provides not only the military police to the army but a whole armoured brigade. Unlike the army, the *Carabinieri* is an all-regular force.

Operational

The army is divided into the Field Army (*Esercito di Campagna*) and the Territorial Army (*Force per la Difesa Interna del Territorio*). The latter, through its five regional commands, exercises authority over recruiting, mobilisation and internal security/territorial defence. It disposes, however, of only four operational formations: the infantry brigades *Friuli* at Florence (*VII Comando Territoriale*), *Pinerolo* at Bari (*X Comando Territoriale*), *Trieste* at Bologna (*VI Comando Territoriale*) and *Aosta* at Palermo in Sicily (*XI Comando Territoriale*). These infantry brigades (*Brigata di Fanteria*) are organised into an infantry regiment of two battalions, a tank battalion (M-47) of two companies, a field artillery regiment of 18 105mm howitzers, a signals company and an engineer company, and an aviation flight; each of the infantry battalions has an APC company.

The Field Army, forming the Third Army (Designate) — *Comando Designato 3° Armata* — consists of the remaining operational units organised into three corps (III, IV and V) consisting of one armoured and three mechanised divisions, to independent mechanised and four independent motorised brigades, five alpine brigades, one airborne brigade, one amphibious group and one missile brigade. The organisation of the armoured division (*Divisione Corazzata*) *Ariete* is: one armoured reconnaissance battalion, one engineer battalion, one aviation flight, one artillery brigade (of three battalions of M-109s, one battalion of M-107s and one Hawk battalion), one signals battalion, and two armoured and one mechanised brigades; the armoured brigades each consist of a signals company, an engineer company, logistic troops, two tank battalions and a mechanised infantry battalion (*Bersaglieri*); the mechanised brigade consists of two *Bersaglieri* battalions, one tank battalion and the same support troops. The independent armoured brigade (*Brigata di Cavalleria*) *Pozzuolo del Friuli*, which provides the tactical reserve to V Corps, is similar in organisation to the divisional armoured brigades but its three battalions, each of three companies, are equipped with a mixture of Leopard tanks and APCs. The infantry divisions (*Divisione di Fanteria*) *Cremona*, *Legnano, Folgore, Mantova* and *Granatieri di Sardegna* consist of one reconnaissance battalion, one engineer battalion, one signal battalion, one artillery regiment (of two battalions

of 105mm howitzers, one battalion of 155mm howitzers and one light anti-aircraft battalion), one aviation flight, one mechanised regiment (of one tank battalion and one APC battalion with an anti-tank company) and two infantry regiments (each of three battalions and one company of 120mm mortars; one of the battalions in each regiment is to be motorised). The alpine brigades (*Brigata Alpina*) *Taurinese*, *Orobica, Tridentina, Cadore* and *Julia* consists of one signals company, one engineer company, one aviation flight, one parachute platoon, one mountain artillery regiment (of three battalions of 105mm howitzers and one battalion of 155mm howitzers) and a mountain infantry (*Alpini*) regiment (of three to four battalions, together with an APC company); all the troops of the brigades are mountain-trained and the supply columns contain mules. The parachute (*Paracadutisti*) brigade *Folgore* consists of one engineer company and one signal company, one aviation flight, one artillery battalion (of 18 105mm howitzers) and a parachute infantry regiment of two battalions (plus a *Carabinieri* battalion); all units are parachutable or air-portable. The amphibious brigade (*Lagunari*) consists of one signal company, one tank battalion and two or three APC battalions, together with its amphibious transport (which is not sufficient to carry all its vehicles). The missile brigade (*Brigata Missili*) deploys two Honest John missile battalions (now obsolescent and to be replaced by Lance and two M-55 203mm howitzer battalions), all capable of firing nuclear warheads (which are held by the American forces in Italy under dual-key arrangements); it also has an infantry battalion for local protection. The *Carabinieri* fields a number of operational military units, of which the most important are its three mechanised infantry regiments (containing in all 11 battalions), its parachute battalion (serving with the *Folgore* brigade) and its independent armoured regiment (equipped with tanks and APCs) based on Rome; it also provides a company of military police to each corps and division, and a platoon to each brigade.

The organisation of corps troops varies; in general each corps should dispose of one reconnaissance battalion, one tank battalion, one or two engineer battalions, several battalions of heavy artillery, one or more Hawk battalions, and signal and logistic troops, together with an aviation squadron of 10—18 helicopters.

The air force (*Aeronautica Militare Italiana* — AMI) shares the air-defence role with the army and deploys 12 air-defence groups with 96 Nike Hercules SAMs.

The navy has a small marine force: the *San Marco* regiment (1700 strong), and a commando and frogman group; two landing ships with 57 landing craft provide the sea lift for this force.

Paramilitary Forces

Besides the *Carabinieri* which legally forms part of the army, there exists also a barracked Public Security Police, under the control of the Ministry of the Interior, and 72,000 strong. The Ministry of Finance, one of the three Italian treasury ministries, controls another national police force, 5000 strong — the *Guardia di Finanza* (popularly the *Finanziere*), who combat smuggling. In cases of public disorder, it is the Public Security Police (commonly the *Celere*) who intervene; as a result, they are widely unpopular. The ordinary civil police are the *Vigili Urbani*, organised on a municipal basis.

RECRUITMENT, TRAINING AND RESERVES

Recruitment

The duty of military service is imposed on all fit, male Italians by the Constitution of 1947. The term of service has been, since 1973, 12 months in the army and air force, and 18 months in the navy from the age of twenty-one. Conscripts provide almost all the private soldiers in the army and a large number of the junior NCOs; they also, if suitably educated, may become reserve officers during their term of service. The right of conscientious objection is now recognised, but few Italians in practice choose to exercise it. Reservists remain on the reserves until forty-five and are recalled for occasional refresher training.

Training

The training of conscripts is carried out in three stages: first, at the *Centro Addestramento Reclute*, which are organised as 11 infantry regiments (*13, 28, 46, 48, 52, 60, 80, 84, 89, 152* and *2° Alpini*), and where the course lasts 3 months; it includes a course of *Addestramento d'Ardimento* modelled on American Ranger training. The remaining 4 months are spent in platoon training followed by company training. Specialists, after completing the first stage, proceed to the appropriate arms school.

Conscript NCOs are selected from the conscript contingent; those for the combatant arms are trained at NCO schools and then sent as corporals to their units, in which they may be promoted to the rank of reserve sergeant; those for the specialist arms are trained in the schools of their arm.

Conscript officers are selected from those with the high school certificate (*maturita*), undergo 5 months of training at the school of their arm and then proceed to their units with the rank of sergeant; if successful in that rank, they are promoted reserve lieutenant.

Regular Army officers (including those of the *Carabinieri*) are trained at the Military Academy in the Ducal Palace at Modena (in which were merged in 1948 the former Infantry and Cavalry Academy of Modena and the Engineer and Artillery Academy of Turin), where they spend 2 years, before proceeding for another 2 years to the application school of their arm: those of the infantry, cavalry, artillery, engineers and signals have been co-located since 1949 at Turin in the Palace of the Arsenal; the Transport Service School is Cecchignola, Rome; and the *Carabinieri* School is also at Rome.

Advanced training is given at the Staff College, Civitavecchia, where selected captains undergo a 2 year course; at the Joint General Staff School, Rome, for staff-trained officers of the three services; and at the Centre of Higher Military Studies, Rome, for senior officers and civil servants.

The army maintains a military preparatory school, the *Nunziatella* at Naples, founded by the Bourbons of Sicily in 1787, and now providing a boarding school education for would-be entrants to the Modena Academy.

The schools of the arms and branches are separate from the application schools, which are for officers, and provide specialist training for soldiers of all ranks; they include the infantry, alpine, parachute, mechanised and armoured, artillery, anti-aircraft artillery, engineers, signals, aviation, motorisation, medical veterinary, quartermaster, and administration schools. The army also maintains a number of technical institutes, particularly for the training of officers of the technical services, as well as foreign language, physical training and equitation schools.

The most important training area of the Italian army is Capo Teulada, Sardinia, where all armoured training is carried out.

EQUIPMENT AND ARMS INDUSTRY

Lacking domestic raw materials and any large public or private source of investment funds, Italy was slow to in-dustrialise. Under the stimulus of *Risorgimento*, however, a number of Italian families, encouraged by the Piedmont government, set up as large-scale manufacturers, and armaments formed from the outset one of their principal products. Notable among them were the Sicilian Orlando family, which took over the Ansaldo engineering enterprise and made weapons for Garibaldi and his Thousand, and the Breda family, pioneers of railway construction and steel-milling; and they were joined in the 1890s by the Agnelli family, the founders of Fiat and the first large-scale manufacturers of automobiles (and later, in 1915, of aircraft) in the country.

Italian industry was heavily protected by the State from the outset, however, used State subsidies to pay its dividends and suffered very gravely in the slump which followed World War I. It was largely rescued by Mussolini who, through the creation (1933) of a State industrial bank (*Instituto per la Ricostruzione Industriale* – IRI) provided the funds for many private endeavours to stay in business; this was far-sighted, for much Italian technology was original and of high quality.

IRI survived the collapse of Fascism and was taken over by the Republican government, which also inherited other wholly or partly State-owned enterprises and proceeded to apply the IRI principle (purchase of control without outright nationalisation) to other concerns. In order to rationalise its very extensive holdings, the government created in 1956 a new ministry (*Ministero delle Partecipazione Statali*). It now oversees most of the companies involved in armaments or defence-equipment production, with the notable exception of Fiat, which has retained its independence, and some foreign subsidiaries (in some of which it nevertheless has a stake).

Because of early and sustained State intervention, and because also of Mussolini's imperial and military ambitions, Italy has a large and comprehensive armaments industry. She produces military aircraft, naval ships, armoured vehicles and heavy as well as light ordnance, ammunition and propellants and a wide range of electronic and optical equipment. The most important firms producing weapons or equipment for the army are: Fiat (Turin), tanks and cross-country vehicles; OTO Melara (La Spezia), armoured vehicles, missile launchers and artillery pieces; Costruzione Aeronautiche Giovanni Augusta (a Bell associate), helicopters; SIAI Marchetti (Sesto Calende), helicopters and light aircraft; Whitehead Moto Fides (Leghorn), small arms; SNIA Viscosa (Colleferro), ammunition and propellants; SNIA Viscosa's subsidiary SIGME, surface-to-surface and anti-tank missiles; Breda (Brescia), anti-tank missiles and anti-aircraft guns; Contraves Italiana (Rome – an Oerlikon subsidiary), fire-control systems; SISTEL (Rome – a jointly owned subsidiary of Montecatini Edison, Contraves, Fiat, IRI's Finmeccanica and SNIA Viscosa), anti-aircraft missiles; Officine Galileo (Florence, Milan and La Spezia), fire-control systems and optics; OMI (Rome), optics and photogrammetric equipment; Montedel (Montecatini–Edison Elettronica) Elmer Division (Rome), radio equipment; and Beretta (Gardone-val Trompia), small arms.

Equipment

Pistol: 9mm Beretta M51
Sub-machine-gun: 9mm Beretta MAB 38/49
Rifle: 7.62mm BM 59
Machine-gun: MG 42/59 (Motofides, under licence from Rheinmetall – *see* Germany)
Mortars: 81mm (OTO Melara) and 120mm Hotchkiss-Brandt (OTO Melara – *see* France)

Anti-armour weapons: 3.5mm rocket launcher (USA); 106mm recoilless rifle M40 (USA); Cobra wire-guided missile (SIGME — *see* Germany); Mosquito wire-guided missile (Contraves — *see* Switzerland); and SS 11 wire-guided missile (Aerospatiale — *see* France)

Air-defence: Indigo missile (SISTEL), Hawk missile and Bofors 40/60 and 40/70 40mm guns

Artillery: 105/14 Model 56 pack howitzer (OTO Melara; equips the field artillery battalions of the infantry, alpine and parachute formations); M-109 155mm SP howitzer (USA; equips the artillery of the armoured formations); M-59 155mm gun (USA; equips the medium battalions of the infantry formations); M-107 175mm gun (USA; equips the gun battalions of the corps artillery); M-55 203mm howitzer (USA; equips the gun battalions of the corps artillery and missile brigade. (About 1500 artillery pieces of all calibres in service).

Missile: Lance (USA; equips the missile battalions of the missile brigade)

Armoured vehicles: M-113 APC (OTO Melara — *see* USA; equips the armoured infantry battalions of the army and *Carabinieri;* about 3600 in service). Equipping the army and *Carabinieri* tank battalions are the following: M-47 (OTO Melara — *see* USA; about 700 in service); M-60 (OTO Malera — *see* USA: about 200 in service); Leopard 2 (*see* Germany; 200 in service); and Leopard 3 (OTO Melara, Fiat and Lancia — *see* Germany; about 600 built or building)

Aircraft: equipping the brigade, divisional and corps light aviation are: A total of 150 Piper L18 and Cessna 01E Bird Dog light aircraft; 100 Agusta-Bell AB-47 helicopters; AB-206 A1 helicopters (coming into service); and a total of 130 AB-104 A1 helicopters and AB-205 A1 helicopters. Equipping the corps aviation squadrons are 26 Boeing-Vertol Chinook helicopters.

Much Italian equipment is obsolete or obsolescent, particularly in the anti-armour and air-defence fields, but there are modern models of many items of equipment under development or under consideration for purchase from abroad: the German—British—Italian FH 70 155mm howitzer; the *Sparviero* anti-tank missile (under development by Breda and Officine Galileo); the self-propelled SP 70 howitzer (also a German—British—Italian project based on the FH 70); the RS 80 multiple rocket launcher (German—British—Italian); the BR 51 GS multiple rocket launcher (Breda); the Spada low-level air-defence system (Selenia); the American TOW anti-tank missile (now coming into service); and the Folgore unguided anti-tank missile (Breda/SNIA), under development.

Italian equipment difficulties are certainly not the result of technical backwardness. Italy's success in marketing abroad the 105mm pack howitzer and in re-engineering the M-109 self-propelled howitzer demonstrate the forwardness of her ordnance industry. Her electronics industry is capable of producing a wide range of systems of the most advanced design and her aerospace and automotive industries of innovating or manufacturing under licence equipment of the first quality. Deficiencies in her arms industry have economic, and particularly budgetary, causes. If the Ministry of Defence succeeds in its stated aim of shifting the balance of defence expenditure away from personnel costs towards equipment procurement, there is no reason why the Italian army should not, in the 1980s, become one of the best-equipped in western Europe.

RANK, DRESS AND DISTINCTIONS

Rank

Generale di Corpo d'Armata designato d'Armata (general) — Four stars on silver-laced shoulder strap

Generale di Corpo d'Armata (lieutenant-general) — Three stars on silver-laced shoulder strap

Generale di Divisione (major-general) — Two stars on silver-laced shoulder strap

Generale di Brigata (brigadier) — One star on silver-laced shoulder strap

Colonello (colonel) — Three stars on yellow-edged shoulder strap

Tenente Colonello (lieutenant-colonel) — Two stars on yellow-edged shoulder strap

Maggiore (major) — one star on yellow-edged shoulder strap

Capitano (captain) — Three stars on shoulder strap

Tenente (lieutenant) — Two stars on shoulder strap

Sottotenente (second-lieutenant) — One star on shoulder strap

Aiutante di Battaglia — Three gold and two red stripes on shoulder strap

Maresciallo Maggiore — Three gold stripes on shoulder strap

Maresciallo Capo — Two gold stripes on shoulder strap

Maresciallo Ordinare — One gold stripe on shoulder strap

Sergente Maggiore — One thick chevron and two thin yellow chevrons

Sergente — One thick chevron and on thin yellow chevron

Caporal Maggiore — One thick chevron and two thin brown chevrons

Caporal — One thick chevron and one thin brown chevron

Soldato Scelto — One thick chevron

Soldato — —

Note: stars are silver, chevrons are worn on the upper arm.

Dress

The army has three main orders of dress, a khaki walking-out dress similar to the British (*Uniforme Ordinaria*), an every-day uniform almost identical to British battledress of World War II (*Uniforme di Servizio*) and a very boldly mottled camouflage combat dress (*Uniforme da Combattimento*). The steel helmet is of the same pattern as worn before and during World War II. A variety of other head-dress is worn: a black beret by armoured troops, a crimson beret by parachutists, a khaki beret by the *Granatieri;* the *Alpini* wear a felt hat decorated with an eagle's feather and the *Bersaglieri* wear their famous drooping bush of black cock's feathers on a leather hat (and on their steel helmets). All except the *Alpini* may also wear a khaki peaked cap.

Badges of different design and collar patches of different colours are also worn, distinguishing the corps, the different branches of the infantry and the regiments of cavalry. On parade, officers carry swords and wear a pale blue sash over the right shoulder.

The *Carabinieri* wear in everyday dress a white pouch-belt, and on ceremonial occasions a blue tailed coat and bicorn hat of early nineteenth-century design.

Italian units carry as the colour the national tricolour: green, white and red, on a pike, to which a pale blue 'cravat' bearing the unit's name and its honours is attached.

CURRENT DEVELOPMENTS

The Italian army is faced at present with several major problems. The first, and least important, concerns its political reliability. Since as far back as 1967, at the time of the so-called Lorenzo affair, the upper *echelons* of the army have been suspected by the Italian left wing of having plans laid for a *coup d'état*, to be unleashed in the event of the left acceding to power, or even simply to re-establish the neo-fascist party in power again. General De Lorenzo, subsequently Chief of the Army Staff, was in 1964 head of the *Carabinieri* and decided, without reference to the Minister of the Interior, and therefore improperly, to assemble files on persons to be arrested in the event of a political emergency. The total assembled reached 174,000 and, when word was leaked by the press in 1967, the general was dismissed as Chief of Staff and arraigned before a civil court. He was eventually exonerated and remained in public life, becoming first a monarchist and then a neo-fascist deputy, but scandal persisted even after his death in 1973. It was then revealed that a successor, General Miceli, had apparently had fore-knowledge of a coup planned by a leading neo-fascist, Prince Borghese, in 1970, which had been called off only at the last moment. Despite the dramatic nature of the allegations and counter-allegations, however, it is unrealistic to regard the Lorenzo—Miceli affair is evidence of the army's involvement in politics. It should be seen rather as a function of the fact that, for historical reasons, two Italian security forces — the *Carabinieri* and the secret service — are administratively branches of the armed forces. In a country with a highly polarised party system and a tradition of violence in politics, the Lorenzo—Miceli affair was almost predictable.

The second major problem concerns the size and efficiency of the army. It is now widely accepted in the country that the present size of the army, given the funds available to support it, militates against its efficiency, since far too much is spent on personnel and establishments and very little left — only about 15% — for procurement of new equipment. It has therefore been decided as a first step to reduce the number of men called up for national service, by about 45,000 (from 210,000) annually, to run existing formations at 70% strength and to reduce gradually the number of formations to meet the size of the national service contingents. The aim is to fall from 36 to 24 brigade-size formations, without any reduction in the number of the alpine and parachute brigades (which are admitted to be the best elements of the existing structure and the most popular with the conscripts). At the same time, some of the funds thus released are to be used to attract more regulars, of which there are shortages in both commissioned and non-commissioned ranks.

Since publication of the last edition of *World Armies*, the Italian army has undergone a major reorganisation designed to reduce it to a size at which funding could adequately support and maintain the remaining units. Brigades have been reduced from 36 to 24; those left are the missile, the air-borne and the five alpine brigades, nine brigades in three new mechanised divisions and three in the *Ariete* armoured division, two independent mechanised brigades and five motorised infantry brigades. The five alpine brigades are now all grouped in IV Corps, which is intended to play a normal as well as specialist role in the future. The training regiments have been abolished, and training is now carried out in battalions within the operational units. At the same time, much obsolete equipment has been replaced.

The *Carabinieri*, which is part of the army, has distinguished itself since 1981 by its success in repressing domestic terrorism, particularly of the Left (Red Brigades), but also of the Right. The condemning to life imprisonment of 25 leaders of the Red Brigades in February 1983 is regarded as marking a decisive victory in the struggle for domestic order.

John Keegan

IVORY COAST*

HISTORY AND INTRODUCTION

The Ivory Coast attained independence in 1960 and has maintained an uninterrupted record of stability and development since then; it has been argued though, that much of the post-independence development has been uneven and appears to benefit the Ivory Coast's former colonial master France as much as the Ivory Coast itself. Certainly very considerable French aid and investment have been placed in the Ivory Coast, whose President, F. Houphouet-Boigny, has been anxious to maintain and strengthen very close links with France. He is known to have a profound distrust both of Marxism and Islam, and a defence treaty with France is the cornerstone of his defence policy. Only very occasionally have suggestions appeared that political criticism of his policies exists. In 1963 over 100 people, including some ministers, were alleged to have been involved in a plot to overthrow the regime. None, however, was executed and many were released speedily as an act of clemency. In 1971 a middle-level military conspiracy was unearthed and seven officers of major, captain and lieutenant rank were sentenced to death. This plot however left an overall impression of a motivation of frustration and *ennui* rather than specific political aims.

Some recent student unrest has occurred. Political stability has been facilitated by the sustained economic performance; Ivory Coast, although affected by the world recession and also some mismanagement domestically, has suffered little in recent years and appears to have considerable prospects of oil revenue later in the decade. In ethnic terms, Houphouet-Boingy, a Baoule, presides over a Baoule hegemony structure that includes a number of key personnel in the armed services. This hegemony does not appear to arouse great resentment except among the Bete from the west of the country.

STRENGTH AND BUDGET

Population: 8,400,000 (approximate)
Armed forces: 3900, of which the navy comprises 400 and the air force 400 with in addition a barrack police gendarmerie.
GNP: no figure available
Defence Expenditure: not known

COMMAND AND CONSTITUTIONAL STATUS

Under the President of the Republic there is a civilian Minister for Defence, J. K. Banny; the Secretary of State for the Interior is a soldier. The Inspector-General of the Armed Force is Lieutenant-General I. Coulibaly, and the commander of the gendarmerie is Major General N. Daw Oumar.

* For general notes on African armies, see Appendix 1

ROLE, COMMITMENT, DEPLOYMENT AND RECENT OPERATIONS

In the early years of independence, defence was seen to be a continuing French responsibility, with the Ivory Coast's own small army to internal security. This view has now changed and some national defence role is seen: in practice this means attention being paid to the Ivory Coast's border with Guinea.

The French 4th *Régiment de Marine* remains stationed at Port Bouet, a force some 600 strong.

Ivory Coast is a member of ANAD, the treaty of mutual aid in the event of an attack signed by seven West African states.

Ivory Coast Army Medical personnel were included in the inter-African force sent to Kolwezi, Zaïre in 1978.

ORGANISATION

The Ivory Coast's army consists of a marine battalion, three infantry battalions, an armoured squadron, an artillery battery, an anti-aircraft artillery battery, an engineer battalion, a parachute company and a logistic unit. The gendarmerie is organised into four legions and the frontier guard into three detachments. The infantry battalions are stationed in Akouedo, Daloa and Bouake. The logistic unit is stationed in Abidjan and the artillery and air force Alpha-jets at Bouake.

RECRUITMENT, TRAINING AND RESERVES

The army is recruited by selective national service for six months. French training assistance has been present since independence, French officers still appearing in command and staff appointments. Use is made of French military schools and establishments; occasionally units are sent to France for training, and joint exercises with French troops are held annually. The Ivory Coast's French-directed training establishments provide basic military technical training for personnel from Gabon, Volta, Niger, Senegal and the Central African Republic. Personnel of the reconnaissance company are parachute-trained in France and in Togo.

EQUIPMENT AND ARMS INDUSTRY

All equipment is French. The armoured reconnaissance squadron operates five AMX-13 tanks and shares with other units six AML-90 and ten AML-60 armoured cars. Seven new ERC-90 armoured cars were delivered in 1981. Also in service are twenty-two M-3 armoured vehicles (of which six are equipped with twin 20mm guns), and a small number of other lightly armoured reconnaissance/troop carrying vehicles used by the gendarmerie. The army's artillery includes four 105mm howitzers and a small number of 120mm mortars. The infantry battalions possess French 81mm mortars. One report indicates that the anti-aircraft battery is equipped with ten towed 40mm guns. The air force possesses five Alpha jet light air to ground counter-insurgency aircraft (a sixth was lost in an accident), two C-130 Hercules, three C-47, three F-27 and two F-28 transport aircraft and twenty light liaison and training machines, together with three Puma, three Alouette and four Dauphin helicopters.

RANK, DRESS AND DISTINCTIONS

These follow French patterns, except that peaked caps have replaced the *képi*.

CURRENT DEVELOPMENTS

Until recently defence was not viewed seriously in Abidjan. The only possible enemy seemed to be Guinea, against whom some limited preparations were made. The presence of a French garrison was taken as token of a French protective role. At the turn of the decade however Libyan designs and instability elsewhere in Africa led to more attention being paid to the army, especially in respect of light armoured vehicles. This trend is likely to continue. The army is however expected to maintain a low political profile.

Lloyd Mathews

JAPAN

HISTORY AND INTRODUCTION

Article 9 of the Constitution of Japan, promulgated in November, 1946 runs:

'Aspiring sincerely to an international peace based on justice and order the Japanese people forever renounce war as a sovereign right of the nation and the threat of force as a means of settling international disputes.

In order to accomplish the aim of the preceding paragraph, land, sea and air forces, as well as other war potential, will never be maintained. The right of belligerency of the State will not be recognised.'

This article, based closely on a similar provision of the Kellog—Briand Pact of 1928, was included in the Constitution at the insistence of the American military government, which was largely responsible for its drafting, but with the apparently whole-hearted agreement of the Japanese government and people, in whom the experience of a long war of attrition culminating in nuclear attack, had extinguished not only aggressive intent, but also military spirit, altogether.

That this conversion was genuine is all the more remarkable in view of the strongly militaristic character of Japanese history and society. Since the twelfth century Japan had been governed by a military caste which maintained a rigorously feudal regime, interrupted occasionally by civil war between rival factions of *Samurai* — the feudal warriors — and though in the middle of the nineteenth century the political forms cherished by the *Samurai* had been overthrown, the caste itself had remained dominant within the modernised State, not only in its armed forces and government, but also within its burgeoning industrial and commercial life. Moreover, when the military monopoly of the *Samurai* was broken, as it was in the 1870s, by the introduction of conscription, the result was not a dilution of the military spirit of the Japanese but its transfusion, in full strength, to the population as a whole. The first serious engagement of the new European-style army was with the diehard, dispossessed *Samurai* of Satsuma province in 1877, and its victory prompted Yamagata, the government Commander-in-Chief, himself a *Samurai*, to observe that 'the Japanese, whether of the military class or not, originally sprang from the same blood, and when subjected to regular discipline, could scarcely fail to make soldiers worthy of the renowned bravery of their ancestors'. In the war with China (1894—5), and even more in that with Russia (1904—5), the Japanese peasant, who had been denied the 'knightly' right to bear arms until 30 years before, proved that he was a warrior of steadfast bravery, fierce aggressiveness and perfect subordination; more ominously for the Western empires, he also demonstrated that he was the master of modern tactics and of the most advanced weapons.

Despite the military evolution of the Japanese peasantry, however, the *Samurai*, or more particularly the Choshu clan, dominated the armed services until the early 1920s and dictated their ethos. That ethos expected of the State the provision of a special place for the armed forces within its structure — the reservation, for example, of the posts of Minister of War and Minister of the Navy for serving officers, who were each to be nominated by his own service; but it also required of the army and navy total and unquestioning subordination. The navy preserved that spirit to the end of World War II. But from the death in 1922 of Yamagata, the creator of the modern army and head of the Choshu clan, the army began to develop a different, more self-serving and menacing outlook. The composition of the officer corps had already begun to change, to include a growing number of men from the middle and small land-owning class and from the less important *Samurai* clans, or from none at all. They resented the clan favouritism which had determined promotion to that date, and were ready to manoeuvre for influence within the army in a way which would have outraged Yamagata. They were also much affected by feelings of solidarity with the peasantry, whom they knew as neighbours and tenants, and whose living standards suffered a disastrous decline from 1930 onwards. This was particularly true of the peasants of the north, the army's best recruiting ground (as it still is today). Ideas of a 'national socialist' flavour gained ground among those younger officers, even among those of General Staff headquarters; known colloquially as the 'Showa Restoration', this national socialist programme looked forward to the 'restoration' of the fortunes made by the new capitalist class to the Emperor, and of their power by the political parties. Wealth would then be controlled and authority exercised by a military dictatorship acting in his name. Abroad the frontiers of the State were to be extended into the territories of the defunct Chinese and moribund European empires.

These ideas had no prospect of acceptance either by the Emperor or any part of the Japanese establishment, and this fact led gradually to the growth of another and still more revolutionary idea within the ranks of the dissident officers — *gekokujo* — 'the overpowering of seniors by juniors'. As early as 1927 a secret society dedicated to plotting a *coup d'état* had come into existence within the army. The effects of world-wide depression, felt acutely in Japan, against which at its onset the more developed industrial powers brusquely closed their commercial frontiers, and the readiness of the civilian cabinet to co-operate nonetheless in disarmament agreements like the Washington Naval Treaty (judged disadvantageous and patronising by service opinion), strengthened the plotters' resolve. In September, 1931 the command of the Kwantung Army in Manchuria, acting on its own initiative and at the behest of a clique of fairly junior officers on its staff, ordered its units to seize the city of Mukden and subsequently to occupy the rest of the province.

The Kwantung Army was present in Manchuria by agreement with the Chinese government, and in order to defend the railway network against the disorders prevalent in warlord China. But what its leaders, prodded by extremist middle-rank officers, had in fact embarked upon was nothing less than the dismemberment of the Chinese State. In 1932 the Kwantung Army advanced into Inner Mongolia and obliged Chiang Kai-shek to create a wide demilitarised zone between Manchuria and Peking, while in the south, at Shanghai, it became embroiled in a full-scale battle for control of the city with his 19th Route Army, which lasted 6 weeks. Fighting was to break out again there in 1937 and also much more extensively in the north, apparently at the behest of a group of colonels in General Staff headquarters in Tokyo who felt that 'the time had come to settle accounts with Chiang'. The campaign developed into an advance up the Yangtse and culminated in the capture of his capital, Nanking. Shortly afterwards the Kwantung Army also became involved in border fighting with the Russians, which was to flare up again in the summer of 1939.

These external conflicts were complemented by a series of violent incidents at home, both between government and army and within the ranks of the army itself, all expressions of a growing and aggressive nationalism uncertain of the outlet it should take. The army itself was divided between two 'schools', the 'Control' and the 'Imperial Way', the former believing in a policy of expansion into China, the latter prepared to risk a renewal of the 1904 struggle with Russia for open mastery of east Asia. In 1936 adherents of the Imperial Way (*Kodo-ha*), in a 'now-or-never' spirit provoked by the court-martial of one of their own for the murder of General Nagata, unleashed a *coup de force* in Tokyo. Nagata, Chief of Officers' Postings and Promotions, was a leading member of the Control school (*Tosei-ha*) and had been bending his energies to the removal of Mazaki, the leading *Kodo-ha* general, at the moment of his murder. But it was less his success in that direction than his general determination to stamp on the *Kodo-ha* and the spirit of the 'Showa Restoration' which provoked its adherents to act. In the early morning of February 26th, units of the First Division, which had been warned for duty in Manchuria because of the *Kodo-ha* influence under which it had come in Tokyo, left their barracks, together with some individual sympathisers in the Imperial Guards Division, and went to the homes of leading members of the government. The prime minister escaped detection, but two former holders of the office were murdered, as was Mazaki's successor. The rebels, in a Japanese version of the *cuartelazo* so popular with the Spanish army in the nineteenth century (and to be practised again in Algeria in the 1960s), then occupied public buildings and barricaded off a sector of central Tokyo. After 4 days, in the expectation of a public trial at which they would publicise their case, the rebels, who numbered only 1500, gave themselves up. In the event they were secretly court-martialled and 13 of the ringleaders, none of whom had held higher rank than captain, were executed, together with the murderer of Nagata and the writer Kita Ikki, the ideologist behind the 'Showa Restoration'.

The incident led to a loss of respect by the population for the army, but not to a loss of its power. For, conscious of the slight, its leaders, now almost exclusively of the *Tosei-ha*, decided that they must repair the damage not by retreating from politics but by strengthening their grip on government. When a new cabinet was formed in the wake of the 'February Incident', its membership was largely dictated by the Minister of War, while its policies were laid down by the high command. They began to re-arm to a full war footing, signed the Anti-Comintern Pact with Hitler and Mussolini (the negotiations were actually carried out by the army, not the foreign office), and in 1937 removed an uncooperative prime minister and replaced him with a general. When his parade-ground manners united the diet against him the army accepted a civilian premier, but only because they recognised that in him, Prince Konoye, they had a supporter of their nationalist outlook. Konoye was not an aggressive imperialist, however, and attempted to moderate the army's resumed policy of expansion into China, but without success. In July, 1937 fighting broke out with Chiang's troops round Peking, and in August around Shanghai, where an American and a British naval ship were hit and Chiang's troops driven from Nanking, in which city atrocities were committed by the reservists called up for the campaign. Japan's international position was restored only by abject and public apology. The army's determination to press on into China, even at the expense of renewed conflict with Russia, remained nevertheless un-

shaken. There was a Russo—Japanese battle in Manchuria in the summer of 1938 and a more serious one, on the border of Mongolia, between May and September, 1939 out of which the Japanese came worst. But advances in central and southern China pressed deeper and deeper into Chiang's territory, cancelling out mistakes elsewhere.

The outbreak of World War II, and particularly the signing of the Russo—German non-aggression pact, regarded by the Japanese as a betrayal of the spirit of the Anti-Comintern Pact, brought a moderation of policies. But Hitler's spectacular victories of 1940 stilled the voice of caution. In September Japan signed a new Triparite Pact with Italy and Germany, and prevailed on Britain and Vichy France to assist in the prosecution of her war with China; Britain agreed to close the Burma Road bringing supplies to Chiang for 6 months, and France to allow Japanese soldiers into northern Indo-China to close the supply route from that direction. In July of the following year, Japan extracted the extra concession of bases in southern Indo-China, and when that move united American and British policy against her in the form of an economic embargo, began seriously to consider a Pacific war. Konoye, who had returned to the premiership after a cautionary resignation in 1939, opposed the prospect with all his strength, but felt himself unable to stand out against the combined contrary opinion of an Imperial Conference held in September. When he attempted to temporise nonetheless, on the grounds that the decision must await the outcome of talks with the Americans in Washington, he was replaced by his own war minister, General Tojo. He was an extreme exponent of the view that time was not on Japan's side and that she must make war at once if her whole position in the Pacific were not to be compromised for good. Against the better judgement of the navy, Japan was thenceforward steered inexorably towards war, which it began with the surprise attack on the American Pacific Fleet base at Pearl Harbour on December 7th, 1941.

The victories of December, 1941 and of the first 5 months of 1942 were as great as any country has won in any similar span of time, though rarely, perhaps never, over such a wide area. The most spectacular were the work of the navy and the naval air arm, and the land conquests of the Philippines and both the Dutch and British East Indies depended also upon the navy's transport of troops. But the army, if only lightly opposed by the outnumbered Dutch colonial army in the Indies, conducted a brillaint campaign against an equal enemy in Malaya, and one scarcely less noteworthy in Burma. The rapidity of its advance in both countries and the decisiveness of the battles it fought led its enemies to conclude that they had been opposed by a much superior force. This was, however, not the case. For the whole of the opening campaign, the Japanese committed a force of only 11 divisions, and the army which overran Malaya was actually outnumbered by the British defenders. The secret of the Japanese success lay in the high quality of the units engaged, and in the ruthlessness with which they operated. This was directed as much against themselves as the enemy: officers treated their soldiers 'with a severity that would have been thought barbaric even in the Prussian army'*, a practice which helps to explain, if not to excuse, their mistreatment of prisoners-of-war.

After the opening campaigns, the army made no more spectacular advances, in part because most of Japan's territorial ambitions had been satisfied, but more generally because it then came up against the growing force of its enemies' mobilising armies. It needed to keep the greater strength of its army in China, where Chiang carried on the

---

* Storry, Richard, *A History of Modern Japan*, Penguin, 1960.

fight against great odds in the interior and was obliged to wage a warfare of attrition or defence in the Pacific islands. Nevertheless, as late as 1944 it was able to find reserves sufficient to mount two major offensives: one against the American airheads in Chiang's territory, the other on the Indian border of Burma which had as its object nothing less than the invasion of Bengal. But its dominance in government, guaranteed by Tojo's occupancy of the premiership, could not be sustained once the steady roll of overseas defeats began to accumulate, as it did from June, 1944 onwards. The loss of Saipan, which gave the Americans a base from which they could bomb Tokyo, in June, 1944 and the failure of the Bengal offensive, led to the fall of Tojo's government. He was replaced by a retired general, Koiso, with a moderate as assistant prime minister. In April, 1945 the Koiso cabinet was replaced by one headed by Admiral Suzuki (who had nearly died of wounds suffered at the hands of the Tokyo mutineers in 1936). He came to power determined to secure some moderation of the allies' policy of unconditional surrender, but otherwise pessimistic of the outcome of the war. The destruction of the centres of Japan's 60 major cities by conventional bombing during the summer of 1945 persuaded almost everyone in government that peace must be made, and the dropping of the atomic bombs in August, that it must be made at once. But to the end the army took an inflexible line. The Minister of War, Anami, argued at the final Supreme Council meeting of the war that Japan should fight on, if only to get better terms, and eventually yielded only to the contrary view of the Emperor himself. He committed ritual suicide on the morning of the Emperor's broadcast announcing the surrender decision to the Japanese people. That same morning, August 15th, a group of officers in Tokyo attempted a final act of 'double patriotism', this time against the Emperor, whose 'real' as opposed to 'declared' will they claimed to represent. Having failed to persuade the commander of the First Guards Division to join them, they shot him dead, forged his signature to give them command of the division and used it to surround the palace which they searched in a vain attempt to find and destroy the recording of the Emperor's surrender broadcast before it could be transmitted.

They were overcome only by the bravery of the general commanding operational headquarters, who at the risk of his life visited the palace and talked the troops over to his side. It was an act which did something, but only a very little, to redeem the conduct of the army over the previous 15 years. 'Making all allowance for exceptions', as one of the most sympathetic of Western historians of Japan, Richard Storry, writes, 'the professional army abused its power by showing itself to be on the whole cruel, arrogant and stupid. Thoughtful, imaginative, politically gifted and sophisticated officers were over-shadowed, therefore, by narrow-minded bigots, prisoners of their own *neo-Samurai* mentality. These men . . . brought the good name of Japan into disrepute throughout Asia; and they very nearly destroyed for ever the monarchy and the State they were pledged to serve.'*

Storry's view is one which was widely, perhaps universally, adopted by the Japanese in the aftermath of the war, which was made manifest in the rise of a large-scale pacifist movement and which was given concrete form in Article 9 of the 1946 Constitution. The sincerity of the Japanese people's conversion to anti-militarism has been accepted by observers as widely opposed in ideological viewpoint as General MacArthur, who in 1947 said, 'Japan's spiritual revolution has been probably the greatest the world has ever known . . . I believe sincerely and absolutely that it is here to stay', and the Chinese Communist Foreign Minister Chi Peng-fei, who in 1973 said, 'Unless a country has self-defence power to

defend its own sovereignty, its independence cannot be protected. We are opposed to Japanese militarism, but we do not think Japan will permit the revival of militarism and, even if it were to be revived, it would be blocked by the Japanese people'. The principle of anti-militarism is entrenched in the policies of the socialist parties and guaranteed by their blocking minority in the Diet. The constitutionality of the Self-Defence Forces has been questioned from the moment of their creation, and their development (which is described under Command and Constitutional Status) has been opposed by sizable elements of the population at every step since 1954. The Self-Defence Forces are keenly aware both of the legal delicacy of their status and of the mere acquiescence in their existence which Japanese public opinion concedes. The transformation both of the structure of the Japanese state and the attitude of its people since 1945 therefore seems complete.

The influence of the Japanese Army has, nevertheless, continued to persist in a positive form elsewhere. Despite the narrow national self-interest which lay at the core of its anti-European policies preached and practised in east Asia before the war, its espousal of national independence movements and its direct involvement with their leaders has had an important effect on the character of post-war governments in at least three Far Eastern countries: Burma, Indonesia and South Korea. The high command of the armies of each of these countries contains men who were trained by the Japanese army. All three countries are ruled either by soldiers or by soldiers-turned-civilians, who emphasise their belief in an essentially military, anti-party approach to politics. And while none threatens to wage aggressive war, all have made the army the paramount institution in the State, and sought to win popular acceptance of that state of affairs persisting.

STRENGTH AND BUDGET

Population: 118,519,000
Army: 155,000; reserves 43,000
Navy: 45,000; 60 warships (including 14 submarines), 33 destroyers, 16 frigates, 67 smaller craft, 181 aircraft
Air force: 45,000; 314 combat aircraft
GNP (1981) $1,153,000,000,000
Defence expenditure (1981 estimate); $10,450,000,000

Japan has consistently maintained defence expenditure at a very low level, both absolutely and as a percentage of the budget and the gross national product. Expenditure as an absolute figure has increased over the period 1977–81 but only slightly; successive governments have come under increasingly heavy pressure from the American government to contribute a larger share to the costs of Pacific defence, but as yet without significant results.

COMMAND AND CONSTITUTIONAL STATUS

The origins of the Ground Self-Defence Force lie in the National Police Reserve, which General MacArthur, as Supreme Commander for the Allied Powers, authorised the prime minister to create in July, 1951. Its creation was sought by the Japanese government of the day as a means of securing internal law and order, which had been shaken by an abortive general strike in 1947 and by subsequent labour and political disturbances, and it was approved by the Americans apparently because of the denuding of the country of American occupation troops sent to Korea to fight the war there. Thereafter, however, the Americans consistently pushed the Japanese to transform the Police Reserve into a proper army, which could defend the country against external attack. The Japanese hope was that by guaranteeing internal stability themselves they could persuade America to take on permanent responsibility for the external defence of the country. The original Security Treaty of 1951 was therefore a provisional one, since the views of the two parties diverged widely over what the ultimate military status of Japan should be. In the following year the Japanese moved closer to the American point of view by renaming the Police Reserve the National Safety Force, merging it with the Maritime Safety Force and expanding its role to include external self-defence. On that basis a peace treaty and a full security treaty with the United States came into effect in the spring of 1952. In July, 1954 enabling legislation (the Defence Agency Establishment Law and the Self-Defence Forces Law) was put through the Diet which put the Self-Defence Forces on very much the footing which they occupy today.

That legislation vests command of the Self-Defence Forces in the Prime Minister. The Emperor has no connection with them; he has never reviewed Self-Defence Force units or visited their barracks and, in the view of a close observer, 'there is no way that the Self-Defence Forces can officially identify their military service with service to the Emperor'. The Prime Minister exercises command through the Defence Agency, a body which is not a ministry and is directly answerable to the Prime Minister's Office. The Director-General of the Defence Agency is the day-to-day commander of the forces, and he and his two principal assistants must be civilians (one is responsible for parliamentary relations, the other for internal administration). The Director-General, though a politician, is not a cabinet officer in his own right but an official of the Prime Minister's Office. The Ground, Air and Maritime Forces are not headed by commanders but by staffs, the chiefs of which form the Joint Staff Council, the highest uniformed authority in the Agency. In theory, however, its role is purely advisory to the Director-General, and recent expressions of dissatisfaction by senior officers at the constraints on the functions suggest that theory accords with practice.

Defence policy is determined by the National Defence Council, the members of which are the Prime Minister, Deputy Prime Minister, Foreign Minister, Minister of International Trade and Industry, Director-General of the Economic Planning Agency, Director-General of the Science and Technology Agency, the Chairman of the Public Safety Commission, a Counsellor for Intelligence and the Director-General of the Defence Agency. The Council, however, meets rarely and is said by a retired general to be 'an entity in name only'. Decisions in practice are taken by the Prime Minister with the Foreign Minister, Finance Minister, Minister of International Trade and Industry, and the Director-General of the Defence Agency. Parliament (the Diet) intervenes in defence affairs through a defence committee and by debate on defence expenditure and defence bills. Party lines on defence are, however, inflexibly drawn. Only the ruling Liberal Democratic Party is wholeheartedly committed to the maintenance of the Self-Defence Forces in their present form. The small Democratic Socialist Party is near it in policy, but the Komeito opposes the tie with America which makes the Self-Defence Forces viable, while the Socialists and Communists oppose their existence.

These two parties base their opposition in large part on the doubtful constitutionality of the Self-Defence Forces. This is a complex issue. Article 9 of the Constitution (see History and Introduction) indeed appears to forbid the creation of any military force, whether called a self-defence force or anything else. During discussion of the draft Constitution in 1946, however, the then prime minister made it

clear that it did not amount to the renunciation of the right of self-defence, only to the means of self-defence. When the National Police Reserve came into existence in 1950, the government argued that its creation was not a violation of Article 9 because the force was not capable of fighting a modern war, and used the same argument to justify the transformation of the reserve into the National Safety Force in 1952 and the Self-Defence Forces in 1954. After that date, as the forces grew in strength and acquired modern equipment, the government shifted its ground slightly, to claim that they did not constitute 'war potential' of the sort forbidden by the treaty, since they were defensive in purpose, and on that ground it has subsequently stood.

Opponents of the self-defence laws have constantly sought, however, to have the constitutionality of the government's policy tested in the courts, particularly the Supreme Court. The Self-Defence Forces have striven, largely successfully, to avoid such a testing, largely by taking care not to give their enemies issues on which to fight: for example, the forces are careful never to requisition land, but always to use land already in government possession. Nevertheless there have been four court reviews of the constitutional issue. In the first, in 1952, the leader of the Socialist Party, Suzuki, took the issue of constitutionality direct to the Supreme Court and asked for a ruling. The court declared itself incompetent, on the grounds that it was not a constitutional court but a final arbiter of cases, and that Suzuki's charge of unconstitutionality was not a case but an abstract issue. In 1959, in the Sunakawa case, it again declared itself incompetent, because the issue turned on a political decision, not a legal point. Demonstrators had protested at their expulsion from an American air base at Sunakawa, arguing that the Security Treaty of 1951, by which it was justified, was unconstitutional under Article 9. The court declared that the treaty was the outcome of a political decision and therefore not a matter for them to judge upon; but it further observed that Article 9 did not deny Japan the right to seek security by treaties with foreign powers, and that the stationing of foreign troops on her soil was accordingly legal. Again in 1962, when two brothers were charged with cutting a military telephone line at Eniwa and pleaded in defence the unconstitutionality of the defence law under which they were charged, the Sapporo District Court avoided a decision in the issue by declaring that the line was not a military one within the meaning of the law. In 1973, however, in the Naganuma case, the same district court, asked to judge the legality of the transfer of a plot of government forest to the Defence Agency, held the transfer illegal on the grounds that the Ministry of Agriculture could not make over land to an unconstitutional body, which it held the Defence Agency to be. The judge went further, by arguing that the Supreme Court's acceptance of 'political decision' as a reason for disqualifying itself from judgement was unsound, since by extension it would rob it of all powers of constitutional review.

The case has been appealed by the government to the higher courts, but the Supreme Court has yet to hand down a final judgement.

ROLE, COMMITMENT, DEPLOYMENT AND RECENT OPERATIONS

Role
The 'Basic National Defence Policy' adopted by the National Defence Council in 1957 laid down the following role for the Self-Defence Forces: to forestall direct and indirect aggression, overcome aggression in the case of its arising, and to defend the peace and independence of the country. To achieve this role, the SDF is dedicated to four policies: (a)

support of the activities of the United Nations; (*b*) promotion of the national welfare and enhancement of the spirit of patriotism, thereby laying a sound basis for national security; (*c*) the gradual development of an effective defensive power within the bounds of national capabilities to the extent necessary for self-defence; and (*d*) countering aggression by recourse to the security arrangements with America, pending effective functioning of the United Nations in preventing and repelling aggression. The Self-Defence Forces Law of 1954 also provides for the SDF to assist the civil police in the event of 'indirect aggression' or in other emergency; such help may be ordered by the prime minister (with the retrospective approval of the Diet) or given at the request of a prefectural governor (who must subsequently report his action to the prefectural assembly). Prefectural governors may also, under Article 83 of the Self-Defence Forces Law, request the assistance of the SDF in disaster relief. The SDF has been widely used in disaster relief, but never in a police role, to which there would certainly be wide and strong opposition from the public. There is no national emergency law in Japan.

Commitment

Japan has been a member of the United Nations since 1956 and has had a military alliance (Security Treaty) with the United States since 1951 (revised 1960 and now extended on a year-by-year basis). However, Japan furnishes no military assistance to the United Nations, since the Self-Defence Forces Law forbids troops to be sent out of the country, while the Security Treaty commits America to the defence of Japanese territory, but not vice versa. American air force units are still stationed in Japan, and its ports are used by the American navy, but an exchange of notes appended to the treaty prohibits America from changing without consultation the use of bases or the types of equipment stationed there, and from mounting combat operations from them.

Deployment

The islands of Japan are organised into five army areas: Northern Army (HQ Sapporo) in the island of Hokkaido (nearest the USSR); North-Eastern Army (HQ Sendei) in northern Honshu; Eastern Army (HQ Ichigaya, near Tokyo) in central Honshu and around the capital, Tokyo; Central Army (HQ Itami) in southern Honshu and the island of Shikoku (on which no major formation is based); and Western Army in Kyushu. Of the 13 divisions, four belong to Northern Army – 2nd (Asahigawa), 11th (Makomanai), 5th (Obihiro) and 7th (the armoured division; Chitose); two to North-Eastern Army – 9th (Aomori) and 6th (Jimmachi); two to Eastern Army – 12th (Soomagahara) and 1st (Nerima) (both these bases are near Tokyo); three to Central Army – 10th (Moriyama), 3rd (Itami) and 13th (Kaidichi); and two to Western Army – 4th (Fukuoka) and 8th (Kitakumamoto). The 1st Airborne Brigade (the only one) is located at Funabashi, near Tokyo. The largest concentration of troops is therefore opposite the Russian Far Eastern provinces, the Russian island of Sakhalin and the Kurile islands (to the three southernmost of which Japan lays claim); the Air Self-Defence Force is deployed exactly contrarily, with most of its bases west of Tokyo. Two composite brigades, location unknown, have recently been formed.

Recent Operations

The Ground Self-Defence Force has taken no part in military operations, of either an external or internal sort, since its formation. But, as a matter of policy, the Self-Defence Forces frequently lend help in disaster relief: between 1951 and 1969 they responded to 6600 calls, deploying a total of 3,000,000 personnel. They also share in government civil engineering projects and lend help to farmers: in 1966 58,000 members of the SDF spent some time on duty on the land.

ORGANISATION

Arms of Service

These are infantry, artillery, armour, engineers, ordnance, medical, army aviation, signals, quartermaster corps, transportation and service troops (which include military police, intelligence and other minor corps).

Operational

Organised originally on the American system, Japanese formations were in 1961 put onto a new and smaller establishment: six divisions and four brigades were turned into 13 divisions. These are of three types: A (or *Ko*), B (or *Otsu*) and C (or *Hei*); the latter is armoured (mechanised until 1980). The Type A divisions (2nd, 11th, 6th, 1st, 3rd, 13th and 4th) consist of four infantry regiments, one artillery regiment, one tank battalion, one anti-tank unit, one reconnaissance unit, one engineer battalion, one signal battalion, an ordnance unit, a quartermaster unit, a transport unit, a medical unit, and an aviation unit and service troops. The Type B divisions (5th, 9th, 12th, 10th and 8th) differ only in having three infantry regiments instead of four. The Type C division, 7th, is very similar to the Type B but has self-propelled artillery and a larger allotment of APCs, providing transport for the engineers and signallers as well as the infantry.

The units are small: the infantry 'regiment' is really a battalion of four rifle companies and a heavy mortar company. Thus the total strength of the Type A division is only 9000 and of the Type B and C only 7000; in NATO terms they are really brigades.

Divisions are directly subordinate to an army, each of which is allotted a number of combat units as army troops: all have an engineer brigade, and there are in addition one artillery and two air defence artillery brigades, as well as a signal brigade, a helicopter wing of 24 squadrons and a tank brigade, the latter stationed with the 7th Division in Chitose, Hokkaido.

Each of the three Air-Defence Forces of the Air Self-Defence Force deploys a Missile Group, equipped with Nike-J missiles; the army's own missile air defence consists of eight groups, each with 32 Hawk missiles.

Army aviation consists of 33 squadrons with 400 light aircraft and helicopters; the Air Self-Defence Force has a transport wing of 50 planes which could provide life for the airborne brigade.

RECRUITMENT, TRAINING AND RESERVES

Recruitment

Recruitment is by voluntary enlistment. It is organised in quarterly 'recruiting drives', carried out by selected members of the GSDF, who call themselves 'salesmen', and are based on the recruiting offices, one of which has been set up in each of the country's 47 prefectures. Recruiters categorise recruits as 'pure' (those who present themselves) and 'persuaded' (those whom the recruiters approach). In the late 1950s the proportions were about equal; now about 90% are 'persuaded'. Recruiters visit schools and universities, although they are banned by many, and draw up lists of eligible candidates from prefectural records. Candidates are then visited in their homes. The emphasis laid by recruiters in their 'sales talk' is on the personal advantage to the recruit in joining: on the technical training he will receive, which will improve his civilian employment prospects, and on the cash bonus — 100 days' pay after 2 years' service, 150 days' pay after 3 years' service. There is little difficulty in filling the vacancies in the Air and Maritime SDF, but more in finding the 20,000 recruits needed each year by the GSDF (only about 80% are found). Recruiting to the infantry is, as in all armies, the most difficult, and the northern and other rural prefectures (in which the SDF are least unpopular) are over-represented in the infantry, as well as in the army generally.

Recruits are free to leave the SDF at any time during their service, which is initially for 2 years. Recently about 20% have left in the first year, 8% during the second and 30% at the end of 2 years, leaving only 42% who re-enlist. There is a good deal of 'poaching' by industrial firms, chronically short of labour in the post-war boom, which the government attempts to minimise by threatening offenders who enjoy government defence contracts with non-renewal. The rapid turnover of personnel, particularly prevalent among the better educated and skilled recruits, makes the provision of junior NCOs difficult.

Officers are recruited either from school leavers or university graduates; a small number of pre-war officers, who were admitted to the army after a 'depurge' in 1955, remain, chiefly in the upper ranks, and some officers are promoted, via officer candidate school, from the non-commissioned ranks. There are 1200 officer vacancies each year, of which about 95% are filled.

Training

Recruits are trained first in the training brigades (1st with Eastern Army, 2nd with Central, 3rd with Western), then in their units. Specialist training is carried on at the branch schools: anti-aircraft at Chiba City; aviation at Obata, Mie Prefecture; engineer at Katsuta City; signal at Yokosuka City; ordnance at Ami, Ibaraki Prefecture; quartermaster at Matsudo City; transportation at Nerima-ku, Tokyo; service and intelligence, both at Kodaira City; medical at Setagaya-ku, Tokyo; chemical at Omiya City. Later training is carried on in units; the army's main training area, where formation manoeuvres are held, is at the foot of Mount Fuji.

Officers are trained at the tri-service Defence Academy, Yokosuka, near Tokyo (established 1952) for 4 years; the course is of degree level, and the annual army intake is about 300. About 100 officers are commissioned each year from the universities. Subsequent career and staff training is first in the branch school of his arm, and then, if selected, at the Staff College, Shinjuku-ku, Tokyo. Selected officers are later trained at the Joint Services Staff College, or at the National Defence College, both at Tokyo. The command and general staff course at the Staff College lasts 70 weeks.

A Youth Cadet Technical School, Yokosuka, offers technical training to students below military age in return for a promise of enlistment (a means of increasing the supply of scarce technicians, which many volunteer armies practice). Serving members of the GSDF may also be allotted places at civilian prefectural training centres (550 places yearly) which will fit them for future employment. Serving officers used also take up places in the graduate schools of the universities but have now been banned from doing so under student pressure.

Reserves

Ex-members of the GSDF do not incur a reserve liability (their number is now over 300,000) but a reserve (the Defence Officers Reserve Corps) exists, manned by volunteers, who perform a 5 day annual refresher course and receive generous reserve pay. The reserve may be embodied at the direction of the prime minister. Many of the reservists are not former members of the SDF, but civilians with an interest in military affairs. The GSDF reserve element numbers 39,000.

A number of ex-service associations exist: the SDF Friendship Association (*Jieitai Taiyukai*), a veterans' organisation, the Defence Association (*Boei Kyokai*) and the SDF Co-operation Association (*Jieitai Kyoryokukai*), which foster support for the SDF, and the SDF Parents' Association (*Jieitai Fukeikai*), which concerns itself with the welfare of servicemen.

A proposal by the Speaker of the House of Representatives in 1969 to form a volunteer 'local defence corps' 1,000,000 strong aroused predictable public outcry and was referred to the Liberal Democratic Party's security committee, which has not reported.

EQUIPMENT AND ARMS INDUSTRY

Despite the tepidity of popular attitudes to the Self-Defence Forces, the government has not sought to equip them from foreign sources, but has, through Japanese domestic industry, developed and produced an almost complete range of the most modern material, including ships and aircraft. The only categories not domestically produced are artillery, though it easily might be, and high-performance strike aircraft. But there is a growing demand from within the defence industry to make the American Phantom the last imported aircraft, which would be well within its capabilities: it already produces a supersonic trainer, the T-2. Japan is one of only eight countries to design, develop and produce its own tanks. It also designs and produces APCs, an anti-armour missile and a full range of small arms. It is self-sufficient in most types of munitions (though reserve stocks, officially computed at 2 months' worth, are believed to be much lower).

The government budgets for defence procurement over a 5 year period in what are known as Defence Build-up Plans. The Fourth (1972–6) is still in force. It had as its object for the Ground Self-Defence Force the procurement of 280 additional tanks (including 160 of the new Type 74), 170 additional APCs (including 136 of the new Type 73), 90 SP guns and 154 helicopters. Research on the new types is the responsibility of the Technical Research and Development Institute of the Defence Agency (established 1952), and procurement that of the Central Procurement Office. All equipment, however, is privately produced, the most important suppliers being, in order of importance, Mitsubishi Heavy Industries, Kawasaki Heavy Industries, Fuji Heavy Industries, Ishikawajima–Harima Heavy Industries, Nissan Motors, Mitsubishi Electric, Japan Electric, Tokyo Shibaura Electric, Hitachi Works and Shin Meiwa Industries.

An important element in the defence procurement and production system is the Defence Production Committee of *Keidanren* (Federation of Economic Organisations). Most large industrial enterprises are members of *Keidanren* and the DPC acts both as a negotiating body with the Defence Agency for firms producing defence equipment, and as a co-ordinating instrument between those firms. Its functions seem to be both the dissemination of defence information and the limitation of competition by agreement between interested enterprises. Despite its efforts, defence contracts appear to be generally unprofitable for Japanese industry.

Pistol: 0.45in Browning (USA)
Sub-machine-gun: 0.45in M-3 (USA) and 9mm SCK (Shin Chuo Kogyo, Tokyo)
Rifle: 7.62mm Type 64 (Howa Machinery Company)
Machine-gun: 7.62mm Type 62 (Nittoku Metal Industries)
Mortars: 60mm M-19 (USA), 81mm M-29 (USA) and 107mm M-30 (USA); 550 in service)

Japan

Anti-armour weapons: 57mm M-18 recoilless rifle (USA), 75mm M-20 recoilless rifle (USA), 106mm M-40 recoilless rifle (USA; some on Japanese Type 60 tracked carriers) and Type 64 and 79 guided missile; Kawasaki); TOW.

Air-defence weapons: 35mm L/90 twin gun (Switzerland), 40mm L/60 and 70 gun (Sweden—USA), 75mm M-51 gun (USA), Hawk missile (USA; 190 in service) and Nike-J (six Groups in Air Self-Defence Force; USA)

Artillery: M-2 105mm howitzer (USA; 360 in service; equips the field artillery battalions of the divisions); M-52 105mm SP howitzer (USA; 30 in service; equips the field artillery of the armoured division); M-1 155mm howitzer (USA; 220 in service; equips the medium artillery of the divisions); M-44 155mm SP howitzer (USA; 10 in service; equips the medium artillery of the armoured division). Equipping the independent artillery brigade/groups are the M-2 155mm gun (USA), M-115 203mm howitzer (USA) and Type 30 300mm free-flight rocket (Nissan) (some 155mm M-1 howitzers are probably also in these formations); Type 75 130mm multiple rocket launcher (30 in service). New Japanese 105mm and 155mm howitzers are also coming into service

Armour: Type 60 APC (eight men plus two crew; Mitsubishi and Komatsu; 430 in service; equips the battalions of the armoured division); (Type 73 APC (10 men plus two crew; Mitsubishi; 100 in service; equips the battalions of the armoured division); Type 61 medium tank (35 tons, 90mm gun, four man crew; Mitsubishi; 560 in service; equips the tank battalion in the divisions); Type 74 medium tank (38 tons, 155mm gun, four man crew; Mitsubishi; 150 in service; equips the tank battalion of the divisions)

Aircraft: 60 transport and communications aircraft in service, including the LM-1 (Fuji) and LR-1 (Mitsubishi); 270 helicopters, including 49 Vertol-107s and 83 UH-1Bs. All aircraft and helicopters are made in Japan, American models under licence by Kawasaki, Fuji or Mitsubishi.

RANK, DRESS AND DISTINCTIONS

Rank

General — Four large stars
Lieutenant-general — Three large stars
Major-general — Two large stars
Colonel — Three small stars, two bars
Lieutenant-colonel — Two small stars, two bars
Major — One small star, two bars
Captain — Three small stars, one bar
Lieutenant — Two small stars, one bar
Second-lieutenant — One small star, one bar

Non-commissioned officer 1 — Three Stripes, one star on shoulder strap
Non-commissioned officer 2 — Two stripes, one star on shoulder strap
Non-commissioned officer 3 — One stripe, one star on shoulder strap
Non-commissioned officer 4 — Three chevrons, one star
Non-commissioned officer 5 — Two chevrons, one star
Non-commissioned officer 6 — One chevron, one star

Officers' badges of rank are worn on the shoulder strap, NCOs' chevrons on the sleeve.

Dress

Both the service and the combat dress worn by the Ground Self-Defence Force are American in style. The American helmet is worn. Arms of service wear distinctive colours as piping : infantry, red; artillery, yellow; armour, orange; engineers, violet; ordnance, light green; medical, green; army aviation, light blue; signals, blue; quartermaster, brown; transportation, dark violet; others, dark blue. Members of the airborne brigade wear white piping. The cap badge insignia displays the dove of peace.

CURRENT DEVELOPMENTS

The Self-Defence Forces came into existence at the wish of the Americans, who were anxious to relieve themselves of the burden of Japanese defence in principle and all the more so when obliged to fight the Korean war. Reluctant though it was to agree, the Japanese government of the time acceded to American wishes because it believed in so doing that it could persuade the Americans to guarantee the external defence of the country. The Ground Self-Defence Force, though equipped with the full inventory of modern weapons, was designed to offer no more than the show of conventional defence, and to be objectively capable only of maintaining internal security — without the guarantee of which America could not be counted upon to maintain bases on Japanese soil.

The maintenance of internal law and order remains the principal role of the Ground Self-Defence Force, as the pattern of stationing of its units reveals. Although four are deployed in Hokkaido, the island nearest to Soviet territory from which the most likely external threat would be offered, the remaining nine are stationed close to Japan's major population centres. The quality and quantity of Japanese equipment, in particular its obsolescent artillery and small number of armoured vehicles, reinforces this view. However despite a persistent strain of violence in Japanese street politics, and the operations of a number of small left- and right-wing terrorist groups, law and order are generally respected by the Japanese, and no outbreak of violence has exceeded the powers of the police to contain it. The army has not therefore been called upon to intervene in civil affairs, and such intervention would be so deeply offensive to the Japanese electorate that no government would lightly contemplate ordering it.

Continuing American pressure on Japan to undertake a larger share of Pacific defence may oblige the Japanese government to reconsider its defence policies. There has already been some redeployment of force into the south of the islands, nearest Korea, and, if it is decided that a threat to Japan could develop from that direction, re-equipment of the Ground Self-Defence Force with modern weapons may become necessary (this newly deployed tri-service force is called the Tsushima Guard Post). The cost could certainly be afforded, since defence expenditures are low both absolutely and relatively. But the political price might be a high one to pay in a country whose public seems to have undergone lasting anti-militarist conversion.

John Keega

JORDAN

HISTORY AND INTRODUCTION

Jordan has been described as 'an army with a country attached to it'. Jordan has about 2.5% of its population in the armed forces, a proportion matched only by Syria in the Arab world, and amongst the bedouin tribes which comprise the regime's power base and define the country's character the ratio is three or four times higher. It has been estimated that one-quarter of the Jordanian economy depends directly or indirectly on the armed forces, a large part of whose expenditure derives from foreign aid.

It is in the political, psychological and historical fields, however, that the full truth of that statement may be observed. The country owes its sheer existence on the map to Britain's need to reward the bedouin Arab army led by the sons of the Sharif of Mecca which revolted against Ottoman rule in the Hejaz in 1916, and assisted Britain in defeating the Turks in Palestine and Syria at the end of World War I. Of the three independent Arab countries brought into existence in 1920 and ruled by various kings of this Hashemite dynasty, the Hejaz itself was conquered by Saudi Arabia in 1926, and the Hashemite king in Iraq was overthrown in 1958, but Transjordan, under its post-1948 name of Jordan, is still ruled by a Hashemite king.

Prior to 1948 the Kingdom of Transjordan, though containing a substantial sedentary population on the east bank of the Jordan River, was primarily a desert realm, the majority of whose population belonged to nomadic bedouin tribes closely linked with those of the northern Hejaz. (Indeed, some of the tribes had actually accompanied the Hashemite drive from the Hejaz.) In these circumstances, and with financial assistance from the British protecting power, it proved relatively easy for the new monarchy to establish itself and to create a system of tribal loyalties underpinning the regime similar to that which prevailed in the Hejaz. A miniature army was created in 1920–21, consisting at first of five officers, 75 mounted riflemen and 25 mounted machine-gunners for the purpose of maintaining internal order. By 1926 it had grown to 1600 men, and then gradually fell to a strength of 1200 in 1942. In Arabic it was known as the Arab Army (Al Jaysh al Arabi), perpetuating the title of the force led by the Hashemites against the Turks in World War I, but it was generally rendered in English as the Arab Legion.

The Arab Legion was officered, trained and paid for by Great Britain, but its troops were all Arabs drawn from the desert tribes. It grew into an effective, professional force, and performed well in World War II, fighting alongside British imperial forces in suppressing an Iraqi nationalist uprising in 1941 and in the invasion of Syria to evict Vichy forces the following year. At the end of the war it had risen to a strength of 8000 men, but shrank back to 6000 by 1948. When the British mandate over Transjordan was terminated in 1946 a large number of British officers remained behind on contract including the Legion's famous commander, Glubb Pasha, but measures were taken for the gradual replacement of these expatriates by Arab officers.

Although it had never been intended that the Arab Legion should fight an independent war and it lacked reserves of personnel, ammunition and supplies, it fought better than any other Arab force in the Arab–Israeli war that followed the British withdrawal from Palestine in May, 1948. Indeed, it won the only significant victories achieved by any Arab force, and succeeded in keeping almost half of the territory originally allotted to the Palestinian Arabs under the UN partition plan out of Israeli hands. This territory, now known as the West Bank and including the old city of Jerusalem, was subsequently incorporated into the kingdom, which changed its name to Jordan.

However, this annexation drastically altered the population balance of the kingdom by incorporating a majority of better-educated, more-prosperous, town-dwelling, politically aware Palestinian Arabs, who had no traditional allegiance to the monarchy, no tribal structure onto which loyalties could be grafted, and no particular reason to love the Jordanian king. Although the West Bank itself was seized by Israel in the 1967 war, the East Bank of the Jordan now also contains a large majority of Palestinians who have arrived there as waves of refugees from the Israeli conquests of 1948 and 1967.

The consequence has been that Jordan has been transformed from a country of about 500,000 with a clear bedouin majority in 1948 to a country of almost 3,000,000 people with a 2:1 Palestinian majority today. However great the repercussions of 1948 for Jordan in terms of creating an immense burden of expenditure for external defence against Israel, the most important result for the regime has been to turn the bedouin population on which it bases its power into a minority. In the broadest sense, this problem has been solved by basing the regime's power almost exclusively on the army, and recruiting the army almost exclusively from the loyal tribal population.

During the 1948 war the Arab Legion had been quickly expanded to 10,000 men. Faced with the requirements of maintaining internal order in the greatly expanded State and with the strong possibility of renewed war with Israel, the government continued this rapid expansion with British assistance and subsidies. The first armoured formation was created in 1952, and by 1956 the Legion numbered 25,000 men. On March 1st of that year the new king, Husain, dismissed the Legion's British Commander-in-Chief, General Glubb Pasha, and changed its name to the Jordan Arab Army; since then, it has been a wholly Arab force. At the same time the National Police was separated from it and placed under a Director of Public Security subordinate to the Minister of the Interior.

Insofar as a modern mechanised army requires large numbers of literate and semi-skilled soldiers, who were not to be found amongst the desert-dwelling nomads of central and eastern Jordan, the expansion and modernisation of the armed forces after 1948 created a demand for recruits of a kind who were only to be found in the urban, and most likely Palestinian, section of the population. Thus for the past three decades the armed forces have been torn between two conflicting requirements. Their political preference is for recruiting from the bedouin tribes who automatically gave their loyalty to the Hashemite lineage (which supposedly goes back to the Prophet Muhammad) and from their recently sedentarised descendants. Their professional need, on the other hand, is to recruit more highly skilled town-dwellers and Palestinians, despite the well-founded suspicion that many if not most of them are fundamentally hostile to the monarchy.

In the first phase of expansion the political danger of recruiting Palestinians was not fully appreciated, and indeed in 1956 the Chief of Staff, Ali Abu Nuwwar, was authorised to create a fourth infantry brigade composed mainly of urban Jordanians and Palestinians. When he attempted to carry out a coup with their support, however, the appropriate lesson was drawn. Further disturbances during 1958 led Husain to request the temporary despatch of a reinforced brigade of British troops and an RAF squadron.

After 1956 the army reverted to recruiting mainly tribesmen except for the technical services. A system of thorough political screening for all recruits was instituted, and it was accepted that the relatively small bedouin recruiting base precluded the option of a mass conscript army. Since then the emphasis has been on the creation of a fighting force combining the minimum possible numbers with the highest degree of combat efficiency. Even then the numbers required for Jordan's defence were comparatively large and so, in place of a high-turnover, politically unreliable conscript army Jordan chose to militarise a high proportion of the male bedouin population in a well-paid, all-volunteer regular army.

It has of course proved unavoidable that numbers of Palestinians be recruited to serve in the military specialities demanding a high level of education or specialist technical skills, and this has been done regularly, with reliance being placed on high pay, generous privileges and close political supervision to ensure their loyalty. When the Palestinian National Guard was dissolved by royal decree in 1965, due to the rising political activism of the Palestinian population, about 40% of its members were re-enlisted in the regular army after appropriate screening.

By 1967 the armed forces had grown to about 50,000 men, but Jordan was then enticed into the farcical Egyptian–Syrian–Jordanian joint command by falsified reports of Arab victories. In the brief war the small Jordanian air force was almost all destroyed on the ground, and the army was then driven out of the West Bank with heavy losses. Over half the economic resources of the kingdom were lost to Israel, and the impoverished remainder of the country was inundated by a new wave of refugees.

With the army virtually in ruins and the power of the Palestinian guerrilla organisations at its height, King Husain was forced to make a number of concessions to the Palestinians in 1969 and early 1970. These included the retirement, transfer or demotion of numbers of officers of tribal origin who were the King's own close supporters and who opposed the Palestinians' methods and aims. In the meantime, however, he was quickly reorganising and re-equipping his army with both Arab and American aid, and by September, 1970 he was able to challenge the power of the guerrilla organisations openly. The ensuing civil war saw bitter fighting between the Jordanian army and the Palestinian organisations both in the capital, Amman, and in the north of the country, as well as tank battles with Syrian armour sent south to intervene on the Palestinians' behalf, but the Army's loyalty held and the King won. All the Palestinian guerrillas were expelled from the country and their organisations banned. (Many ended up in Lebanon, thus initiating the sequence of events which triggered that country's civil war.)

Since the civil war the regime has been even more a target for Palestinian violence and incitements to revolt. In 1971 Prime Minister Wasfi al Tal was assassinated, and in November, 1972 the acting commander of a Jordanian armoured unit was discovered to have received a large sum of money from Palestinian guerrilla sources to organise a coup. Some 300 army and civilian personnel were arrested, and an air force pilot implicated in the plot attacked the royal palace with rocket fire and injured the King before dying in the ensuing crash. King Husain has by now survived at least eight assassination attempts. The obvious course of action was to reduce the number of Palestinians in the army still further, and this has now become easier to do since the younger, mostly settled generation of tribal Jordanians are far better educated and qualified than their fathers. It is estimated that the proportion of Palestinians in the armed forces is now well below 10%, of whom most are concentrated in the air force and the technical services. Plots against the King are still occasionally uncovered in the army (the latest allegedly in May, 1977 – see Current Developments), but there is no question that the great majority of armed forces personnel have a strong personal loyalty to the monarch.

Jordan stayed out of the 1973 Arab–Israeli war with the blessing of Egypt and Syria (since it had still not acquired a proper air-defence network and it would have been plainly suicidal to fight without one), but the army did send one armoured brigade to aid Syria on the Golan Heights when it appeared that the Israelis were about the break through in the south. In the 1974 Arab League summit meeting at Rabat which considered Arab post-war strategy, Jordan acquiesced in the declaration naming the Palestinian Liberation Organisation the 'sole legitimate representative of the Palestinian people', thus implicitly relinquishing its own claim to the West Bank, but this may prove not to have been an irrevocable decision (see Current Developments).

STRENGTH AND BUDGET

The armed forces of Jordan now number 72,800 men in a total estimated population of 3,158,000. The army is the dominant service, with 65,000 personnel, but the air force has tripled since 1971 to its current strength of 7500. The navy numbers only 300 men. There are 35,000 reserves, and paramilitary forces numbering about 11,000 made up of a 3500 man Mobile Police Force and 7500 man Civil Militia. Conscription has recently been introduced, but it is highly selective and is not expected to increase the size of the armed forces substantially.

The 1981 defence budget amounted to $424,000,000, out of an estimated GNP of $3,600,000,000, and was about a quarter of all government expenditure, but as usual a very large proportion of it was derived not from ordinary revenues but from foreign aid. United States military aid to Jordon in 1977–8 was almost $125,000,000, two-thirds of which was in the form of foreign military sales credits guaranteed by oil-rich Arab governments. In addition there were direct 'contributions to the war effort' of 52,000,000 dinars from Kuwait and 10,000,000 dinars from Saudi Arabia (although it is not certain that these contributions were incorporated into the ordinary military budget, more probably being devoted to payments on the Hawk missile system which is being bought for Jordan by the Gulf States at a price of over $500,000,000).

If these latter payments were counted in, the Jordanian defence budget would more closely resemble its 1967–73 pattern in that it would amount to about 45 to 50% of all government expenditure. It would also conform to the long-term pattern in which only half or less of the defence budget has been met from domestic resources. Broadly speaking, before 1957 the rest of Jordan's military expenditure was covered by grants and subsidies from Britain, and between 1957 and 1967 it was met by direct United States aid and by facilities and supplies furnished under the United States Military Assistance Program (MAP). Between 1967 and 1970 the Jordanian defence budget was subsidised by the oil-rich

Arab States to the extent of about $100,000,000 a year. After the civil war of 1970 this sum was halved as all Arab contributors except Saudi Arabia cut off their subsidies in disapproval, but the gap was entirely filled by renewed United States budgetary and MAP aid.

Since 1973 United States aid has continued at about the same level in constant dollars, while the Rabat conference in 1974 promised Jordan, as a 'confrontation State', an annual military subsidy of $150,000,000 a year from the oil-rich Arab States (though in practice it has usually been about half that figure). It will readily be seen that the Jordanian military budget, far from being a crushing burden on an impoverished economy, may even represent a net advantage to the economy in time of peace.

COMMAND AND CONSTITUTIONAL STATUS

The constitution states that 'the King is the Supreme Commander of the Army, Naval and Air Forces', the words 'supreme commander' having the same connotation as does 'commander-in-chief' when applied to the President of the United States of America. The King has the constitutional right to declare war, conclude peace and sign treaties, and to rule by decree under martial law or in a state of emergency (both of which are to be declared by decision of the Council of Ministers appointed by the King).

The army's role, as defined by the constitution, is 'restricted to the defence of the realm and its safety'. Its senior officer is the commander-in-chief in ordinary parlance, officially the commanding general of the Armed Forces General Command, based in Amman. He is in theory answerable to the Minister of Defence, but in practice that minister does not issue operational or policy directives unless they are ordered by the Prime Minister or the King. (Strong prime ministers, however, often combine their own office with that of Defence Minister.)

The Commander-in-Chief is also the Army Commander, and under martial law acts as military governor-general of the country. He is invariably a close personal acquaintance of the King, and is generally a scion of one of the leading bedouin clans. For practical purposes he has direct access to the King on all matters, and even in war acts in consultation with him rather than as an autonomous expert.

The main functions of the Ministry of Defence are administrative and logistical, and include the preparation of the military budget. It does not participate in the operational control of the armed forces.

The Commander-in-Chief's immediate subordinate at General Headquarters is the Chief of Staff, who heads a General Staff on the British model that directs the administration and operations of the army. The principal staff officers are the Director of Operations and the Director of Military Intelligence; special staff sections include the adjutant-general, quartermaster-general, surgeon-general, finance officer, signals officer and others. Since 1973 General Headquarters has also contained a new Directorate of General Intelligence whose director is responsible to the Commander-in-Chief; this directorate appears to be involved primarily with the collection of internal intelligence, especially within the armed forces, and seems not to have any direct relationship with the rest of the staff organisation.

The small navy is organisationally part of the army. The Royal Jordanian Air Force is semi-autonomous. Its commander, who is subordinate to the Commander-in-Chief and the Chief of Staff, carries out a degree of policy co-ordination with the Army General Staff, and receives some logistical support from the army, but he has his own staff for air force operations and administration. Air force headquarters are at Marka, near Amman.

This organisational framework greatly understates the King's influence on every aspect of armed forces operations and policy. He is himself a trained soldier, a graduate of the Royal Military Academy, Sandhurst, and a qualified pilot who personally test-flies all new air force aircraft. He devotes a large amount of his time to military affairs, personally approves all officer promotions and transfers, and cultivates a close personal connection with all ranks in the armed services. Jordan is essentially a praetorian State, in which the sole but sufficient condition for the survival of the monarchy is the personal loyalty of the armed forces to the Ruler, and so continuous close attention to this link has always been the King's first priority.

ROLE, COMMITMENT, DEPLOYMENT AND RECENT OPERATIONS

Role

Despite the fact that the Jordanian armed forces are equipped and trained primarily to fight a high-technology conventional war against formidable opponents, their internal security role is at least as important. Indeed, the operational engagements of Jordanian army units have more often occurred in this role than against outside enemies, primarily because of the unusually divided nature of its population. Apart from extreme cases like the September, 1970—July, 1971 civil war between the monarchy and the Palestinian guerrilla forces, which also took on some aspects of a conventional international war because of Syrian military intervention from the north, the army has frequently been employed in aid of the civil power in the cities where periodic outbursts by militant Palestinians have got beyond the limited capabilities of the civil police. Since 1971, however, there has been far less of this sort of thing, and so long as the army's loyalty to the King is not shaken — and it never has been — there is little likelihood that the internal security situation could get beyond its control in any case.

In its role of external defence, the army's main concern is of course Israel. (Syria was also a serious cause for worry in the 1960s, but has not been so since President Assad came to power there.) Notwithstanding the great improvement in the army's capabilities since 1967 and the recent acquisition of a comprehensive air-defence system, it must still be considered to have a strictly defensive posture: there is no reasonable prospect that it could mount offensive operations westwards across the Jordan into Israeli-held territory with more than transitory success. Even in defence, the army's forces are too few to offer an impenetrable resistance along the entire length of the Israeli—Jordanian border, especially in view of the shallowness of the populated and economically productive zone between the Jordan and the desert.

Commitment

Jordan is sufficiently strong to require the commitment of substantial Israeli forces to overcome it, however, and this does make it a considerable deterrent to an Israeli attack. In the opinion of most observers such an attack would be extremely unlikely in any case, as Israel has no wish to threaten the Hashemite throne. The one part of Jordan which is widely considered to be vulnerable is the north-east corner, which offers Israeli forces an opportunity to outflank Syria's dense defences on the Golan Heights by going round them to the south. Jordan itself recognises this, and keeps substantial forces in the field entrenched on the heights around Umm Qeis overlooking the Jordan River in this sector. This area was also one of the first to be brought under the coverage of Jordan's newly installed SAM system.

Jordan's international commitments, apart from membership in the United Nations and the Arab League, include a number of inter-Arab arrangements which formally involve defence co-ordination: the Defence Council and the Joint Command of the Arab League, a defence agreement with Egypt dating back to 1967, and membership in the loosely associated Eastern Front Command comprising Jordan, Syria, Iraq and the Palestine Liberation Army, which was set up in 1970. None of these institutions has any real military significance, however.

Jordanian defence links with Syria, however, are of some importance. Despite the sharp disparity of political systems, Syria's President Assad and Jordan's King Husain are personal friends who share what is effectively a single front with Israel, and they have accordingly created a Syrian–Jordanian consultative body to co-ordinate military policy. There are regular liaison visits between the Syrian and Jordanian Chiefs of Staff, and a number of Syrian army officers are attending military courses in Jordan and serving in the Jordanian Army Staff College. Consultations on a joint military defensive strategy take place regularly, and during 1976 consideration was given to creating an integrated air-defence operations centre. This would certainly make operational sense, since Amman and Damascus are little more than 100 miles apart, but the Jordanian decision to buy the American-made Improved Hawk SAM system, which is incompatible with Syria's Soviet-supplied air-defence radars and missiles, appears to have prevented the realisation of this scheme.

The other country with which Jordan attempts a degree of defence co-ordination is Saudi Arabia, although the latter is reluctant to conclude a military pact. It was reported in 1977, however, that Saudi Arabia had agreed to place all its northerly air bases at Jordan's disposal in the event of war with Israel. This is of considerable significance, as all of Jordan's own major air bases are only a few minutes' flying time from Israel, and its air force would stand a much better chance of escaping destruction on the ground if this sort of more-distant operating refuge were available. The most important facility the Saudis were alleged to have placed at Jordan's disposal is the air base at Tabuq (about 50 miles from the Jordanian–Saudi Arabian frontier), which is well protected by SAM defences.

Deployment

The smallness and proximity to the Israeli border of the settled parts of Jordan means that the army's main bases spread across the country provide a suitable initial deployment both for external defence and for internal security operations. The main base areas for the army are the complexes at Amman and az-Zarqa, with lesser installations in the north around Irbid–al-Mafraq and in the south at Ma'an, al-Aqaba and elsewhere. The two major all-weather airfields in use by the air force are at Marka near Amman (where the airstrip and some facilities will continue to be shared with Amman's civil international airport until the new Queen Alia International Airport opens at the end of 1979) and at al-Mafraq. Smaller airfields exist at Ma'an, al-Aqaba and elsewhere, and three new military airfields are being built in the interior of the country in order to provide the air force with a longer warning time of an Israeli air attack. The country's naval forces are all stationed at al-Aqaba, along the few miles of coastline Jordan possesses between Israel and Saudi Arabia on the Gulf of Aqaba.

The Jordanian Arab Army is so distinguished in Arab circles that it has furnished training missions to a number of countries in the Gulf, and currently has a training force operating with the Pakistani army. One Special Forces battalion served in Oman during the campaign in Dhofar province against the guerrilla forces of the Popular Front for the Liberation of Oman and the Arabian Gulf (PFLOAG), but was withdrawn before that war ended in 1975.

Recent Operations

The Jordanian armed forces have participated at full strength in two wars against Israel. In 1948 they proved to be the most effective of the Arab armies, securing the West Bank and East Jerusalem to the Hashemite throne. In the Six-Day War of 1967 they had little advance warning of hostilities, and were forced to fight without air cover after their air force had been destroyed on the ground in the first hours of the war. Their performance was therefore much less effective, and they were driven back across the Jordan with grievous losses. Even then, however, their resistance was distinguished by its tenacity in the face of superior numbers and overwhelming air attacks, and their forlorn defence of the Old City area of Jerusalem, where Israeli air power could not be brought to bear, cost Israel almost half its casualties in the entire war.

In the civil war of September, 1970 later known to the Palestinians as 'Black September', the Jordanian forces again demonstrated their combat efficiency and ruthlessness, especially in the heavy fighting encountered by the 40th Armoured Brigade in its offensives against PLO positions in the hilly country just south of the Syrian border and in its subsequent operations against intervening Syrian armoured forces. In the 1973 war it was again the 40th Armoured Brigade that was sent north by Jordan, this time to assist Syria's defence of the Golan Heights in the tenth day of the war. Driving north from Jasim towards Kuneitra with the intention of cutting into the narrow Israeli advance, it was left with unprotected flanks when the Syrians and Iraqis proved unable to give it the promised support, and lost 22 of its 80 Centurion tanks when it was outflanked by the Israelis outside al-Harra.

All of these operations, however, have confirmed the widely held opinion that the Jordanian army is a well-led and highly professional force which deserves a great deal of respect on the battlefield.

ORGANISATION

Arms of Service

The Jordanian army is organised into infantry, armour, artillery, engineers and service units. Armour is organised into numbered regiments as is mechanised infantry. Ordinary infantry is organised into battalions which both numbers and names, usually those of members of the Hashemite family or Islamic heroes.

Operational

The Jordanian army consists of five armoured and six mechanised brigades and two infantry brigades, a Royal Guard brigade, three special forces battalions with brigade super structure, two anti-aircraft brigades and 16 battalions of artillery.

In 1973, the latest period for which there is firm information, the Royal Jordanian Army was organised into a Western and an Eastern Command, under GHQ. Five divisions were formed in the war, but the normal formation is the brigade. Of these the following appear to have permanent existence: 40th and 60th Armoured (92nd and 99th also identified); the Royal Guards Brigade; and the Aliya, Hashimi, Hattin, Hussein, Imam Ali, Khalid, Qadisiya, Talal and Yarmuk infantry brigades.

Jordan

RECRUITMENT, TRAINING AND RESERVES

Recruitment is almost entirely by voluntary enlistment, with strong preference being given to recruits of bedouin tribal background from central and south Jordan south of Amman, rather than to urban Palestinians and Transjordanians from the area north of Amman (who are more oriented towards the town and village life of southern Syria and have on occasion made common cause with the Palestinians). Palestinians are rather more numerous in the air force and the technical services, but the infantry and armour are almost exclusively Transjordanian. Standards of recruitment developed in the old Arab Legion have been maintained, including political screening.

With a predominantly young and male population – in 1973 65% of the population was below the age of twenty-four, and of those 54% were male – there is no shortage of military manpower even given the policy of recruiting mainly among those of bedouin descent. A high unemployment rate, comparatively good pay scales in the armed forces, and a marked affinity for, and pride in, military service amongst those Jordanians of tribal background have assured that there would be a sufficient flow of volunteers forthcoming from this reservoir. The army also provides years' free training in vocational schools for selected boys aged thirteen who volunteer, with family consent, to serve at least one term of enlistment in the army upon completion of school.

The health and educational standards of recruits are good by regional standards: Jordan has an adult literacy rate of about 50%, and the army provides literacy training for those who need it. The recruits are typically tough and capable of endurance, and are easily moulded into excellent soldiers by the army's own training methods, which are again modelled on those of the British army.

The main personnel procurement problem has always been that of securing well-qualified technicians. It has become gradually less severe during the 1950s and 1960s, but the emergence of lucrative job opportunities elsewhere in the Middle East for technically qualified individuals in the 1970s, combined with the higher demand for technicians in a rapidly modernising military force, has brought the problem back in more acute form. It was primarily to solve this problem that Jordan put into effect a conscription law on January 1st, 1976, requiring every Jordanian male between the ages of nineteen and forty to serve in the armed forces for a period of 2 years, unless exempted by the authorities.

The application of this law has been highly selective in practice, most of the conscripts being the sort of technically qualified people (many of Palestinian origin) whom the army could not induce to volunteer. Those with a university degree are drafted into the officer corps, the remainder serving as privates or NCOs. The intake of conscripts is only planned to amount to 3500 per year, which means that the proportion of conscripts in the armed forces' stabilised total strength of 70,000 will not amount to more than 10%.

Junior officers for the army and air force are trained at the Jordanian Military Academy at al-Rusayfah, near az-Zarqa. They are drawn principally from urbanised families of tribal origin. The applicants must have a secondary school education and are carefully screened for loyalty. The course lasts for 2 years, and is modelled on that which used to exist at Britain's Royal Military Academy, Sandhurst prior to the recent drastic abbreviation of the Sandhurst curriculum. Upon graduation, cadets are commissioned as second-lieutenants in the army or air force. Very large numbers of Jordanian officers attend military schools and academies overseas after graduation for futher or specialist training: there are currently 300 in the USA, 40 in Britain and some attending the military academy in Taiwan. Direct commissioning from the ranks is not infrequent in the army, and the air force also grants direct commissions to technical specialists.

Air force pilots are trained to fly at the Royal Jordanian Air Academy at al-Mafraq, and some receive further training in the USA and Britain. These countries also make available technical training for non-flying officers and NCOs of the Jordanian air force. It is now proposed to convert the Royal Jordanian Air Academy into an Arab Air Academy, offering flying instruction to civil and military aviators on fixed-wing aircraft and helicopters from basic flight training to instructor-pilot level. Major-General William Maddox, former Commander of the United States Army Helicopter School, has been appointed Head of the Academy, which will move to Amman's present civil international airport when the new one opens in 1979. The Arab Air Academy is to be supported by an inter-Arab agreement, and is not intended to supersede training facilities already in existence elsewhere in the Arab world. The military part of the academy has been transferred to the Royal Jordanian Air Force, but will continue to share the same facilities.

More advanced levels of officer education are provided by the Jordanian Staff College, located at Naur south-west of Amman, where the course, of 1 year's duration, is closely modelled on that of the British Army Staff College at Camberley. Other Jordanian officers attend the course at Camberley, or its equivalent at the United States Army Command and General Staff College at Fort Leavenworth.

Pay and allowances in the Jordanian armed forces have historically been among the highest in the Middle East, especially for enlisted personnel, although they have of course been overtaken in many of the oil-rich States since 1973. Enlisted men receive cost-of-living and family allowances, and officers receive longevity pay and (for those above the rank of major) servant allowances. Other types of allowances are paid for special qualifications and dangerous duty, and there are good provisions for medical care and retirement benefits. Discipline is strict, even harsh, but generally fair. In most cases it would be true to say that Jordanian officers and soldiers enjoy a higher standard of living when not in the field that they could expect in civil life.

Jordan does not maintain an organised reserve structure. Discharged veterans who are still physically fit are subject to recall up to the age of forty, and would be mobilised through the main bases at Amman, az-Zarqa and al-Mafraq, but they would only be mobilised to expand the support services and provide combat replacements in the event of combat operations extending over a considerable period of time. For the short wars which are more typical of the area, the existing regular forces are already recruited up to the limit of budget capabilities to provide suitable equipment. The current total of reserves is about 30,000, but this figure may be expected to rise now that there is a steady flow of short-tern conscripts through the armed forces.

EQUIPMENT AND ARMS INDUSTRY

The Jordanian army's main armoured strength resides in its 350 M-47/-48 and M-60 United States-built medium tanks and its 189 older British-built Centurion medium tanks. These are supported by 140 Ferret scout cars, and 850 M-113 and 132 Saracen APCs. In addition to its 30 105mm and 146 155mm it has 49 203mm towed howitzers. It also disposes of large numbers of 81mm, 107mm and 120mm mortars; and 106mm and 120mm recoilless rifles. The standard personal weapon is the M-16.

333

For anti-tank defence, it relies upon TOW and Dragon ATGWs. A great deal of attention has been devoted to air defence in recent years. In addition to large numbers of the short-range man-portable Redeye SAMs and 200 M-42 40mm SP anti-aircraft guns, Jordan possesses an integrated system of Improved Hawk surface-to-air missile batteries supported by over 100 M-163 Vulcan 20mm AA guns, providing air-defence coverage for both military positions and Amman at a cost of $540,000,000 (paid for by Saudi Arabia). It also has numbers of Russian SA 2, 7 and 8 missiles.

As will be realised by reading this list, the Jordanian armed forces depend on the USA for approximately 90% of their weapons, with most of the remainder coming from Britain. The air force re-equipment programme is virtually complete, as is the creation of an integrated air-defence system. The substantial reinforcement of the army's tank strength and the mechanisation of two infantry divisions (plans to create a third mechanised division have been dropped) were substantially accomplished in the period 1973–8. Further large increases in the armed forces' size or weapons inventory are unlikely in the next few years.

At present there is no arms industry to speak of, although the capabilities of the army and air force maintenance workshops substantially exceed the Middle Eastern norm. There is, however, a plan to build a tank conversion facility in Jordan to up-gun and modernise the army's tanks and provide them with diesel engines. The projected factory is estimated to cost over $100,000,000 and would be the second-largest industry in Jordan. It would require an injection of funds by other Arab countries, but is well within Jordan's capability to operate and could prove valuable to other Arab armies as well.

RANK, DRESS AND DISTINCTIONS

The rank structures of the Jordanian army and air force are identical, and closely resemble that of the British army. Insignia of rank are worn on shoulder straps by officers; enlisted men wear chevrons, point downwards, on both upper sleeves. The basic colour of insignia and buttons in the army is gold; in the air force, silver.

Rank/British Equivalent/Insignia

  Al Malik (the King), (Supreme Commander) – Crossed sabres within a wreath, and one crown
  Mushir, (Field Marshal) – Crossed sabres within a wreath
  Fariq Awal, (General) – Crossed sabres, one star and one crown
  Fariq, (Lieutenant-general) – Crossed sabres and one crown
  'Amir Liwa', (Major-general) – Crossed sabres and one star
  Zaim, (Brigadier) – Crown and three stars
  'Aqid, (Colonel – Crown and two stars
  Muqaddam, (Lieutenant-colonel) – Crown and one star
  Raid, (Major) – Crown
  Rais, (Captain) – Three stars
  Mulazim Awal, (Lieutenant) – Two stars
  Mulazim Thami, (Second-lieutenant) – One star
  Murashah, (Cadet) White bar

  Waqil, (Warrant Officer) – Crown within wreath
  Naqib, (Sergeant-major) – Crown and three chevrons
  Naib, (Sergeant) – Three chevrons
  'Arif, (Corporal) – Two chevrons
  Jundi Awal, (Lance-corporal) – One chevron
  Jundi, (Private) –

All army personnel wear a gold-coloured metallic arc at the outer edge of their shoulder straps spelling out in Arabic

'The Arab Army'. Many units have authorised should patches or flashes, although these are not worn in comb. Air force flying personnel wear wings similar to those of t British Royal Air Force.

Army uniforms are brown wool; both field and garris uniforms are similar to those of the British army for bo officers and men. In summer, light-weight khaki uniforms desert tan are worn. Senior officers and staff college gradu tes wear red lapel patches and red hatbands.

Except in combat and field exercises, both officers a men frequently wear the red-and-white chequered Ar headcloth called the *kafiya* or *shmaag*, secured by a tw looped black cord called the *aigal*. In the field, infantry we brown berets, armour black, artillery blue and enginee maroon.

Air force uniforms are almost identical to those of t British Royal Air Force. The *kafiya* is almost never worn l air force personnel.

All decorations, honours and awards are conferred by t King. The highest award for valour by members of the arme forces and police, established in 1972, is the Hashemi Order of Grace (al-Nahda al-Hashemi al-Naamat). Oth awards, in descending order of precedence, are: the Order Military Gallantry (al-Nahda Agdam), the Order of the Re aissance (al-Nahda al-Ba'ath), and the Star of Jordan (a Kawkab al-Urdani). There are also service medals for Wor War II, 1948 and all subsequent campaigns and for 20 yea honourable service.

CURRENT DEVELOPMENTS

The demographic potential for an anti-Hashemite upheaval ever-present in Jordan, but in fact the country has been fa less turbulent since the PLO was expelled in the 1970–7 civil war ('Black September'). There has been little need t use the army in the internal security role, as had habitual been necessary during the 1960s. The army bulks so large i Jordanian affairs that it is impossible to conceive of radic political change in the country unless it is subverted fro within, or unless the country were to be subjected to massiv foreign intervention or serious defeat in war.

The likelihood of successful subversion in the army is ve low, in view of the great pains taken to guard against i Moreover, apart from some Palestinian factions, there is no no outside power that has any interest in encouraging th overthrow of the regime. It may be significant that the mo recent report of a planned military coup in Jordan, apparentl thwarted by the arrest of the plotters in late May, 1977, w allegedly uncovered thanks to information provided by th Soviet Union, which was approached by the plotters fo support. (Jordan has denied the entire episode.)

King Husain, the reigning expert in the art of survival i Arab politics, has consistently succeeded over the past fe years in finding a position which is acceptable or at lea tolerable to all the protagonists in the Arab–Israeli confro tation – 'rejectionist' States, conservative Arab States, bot super-powers and Israel. At the same time, while not openl questioning the decision of the 1974 Arab summit at Raba that Jordan should relinquish its claim to the West Bank, h has skilfully manoeuvred the country into a positon whe others might eventually turn to Jordan as the only possib solution to the Palestinian problem (perhaps in the form of Jordan–Palestine federal State now accepted by the Unite States).

Gwynne Dye
John Keega

KAMPUCHEA

Reliable information about the strength, composition, equipment and command of the army of Kampuchea, formerly the Khmer Liberation Army, is unavailable. In 1975, when it defeated the anti-communist forces led by Marshal Lon Nol, it was thought to number about 80,000–90,000, organised in four divisions and three independent regiments. It had been in existence since the late 1940s, when it fought a low-level guerrilla war against the French, but did not become significant until 1970, when it succeeded in wresting control of five northern provinces from the government. It was then supplied and assisted by the North Vietnamese. It then fell out with its former friends, and severe fighting took place on the border with the southern Vietnamese provinces. The reason for the attack on the Vietnamese border seems to have been an internal dispute between pro- and anti-Vietnamese factions in the government, in which the stronger anti-Vietnamese faction sought to compromise for good their opponents' relations with Vietnam by military action against that country.

In December 1978 the Vietnamese mounted a full-scale invasion, expelled the Khmer Rouge government, led by Pol Pot, and replaced it with one of their own creation, under Heng Samrin. The country was then officially styled the People's Republic of Kampuchea.

This Government has raised an army of its own, said to amount to 20,000 in strength, and to field four divisions (which must be under strength) and numbers of independent units of small size; the IISS *Military Balance* suggests fifty and also mentions the existence of various militias. All such information is speculative.

The army, with the 180,000 Vietnamese troops permanently based on Kampuchean territory, are engaged in a running war with opposition guerrillas whose bases are in or near the Thai border in the west. These forces consist of the Khmer Rouge, Pol Pot's guerrilla army, said to number 25,000 and still sporadically supplied with arms by China; the Khmer Serei, a non-communist alliance of ex-President Prince Sihanouk's Moulinaka, a smaller Sihanouk faction, and the KPNLF–Khmer People's National Liberation Front, which is said to field about 7000 fighters.

Inaccessible terrain, some local support and intermittent external supply allows the anti-Vietnamese forces to survive and sustain the fight. While Vietnamese troops are present in Kampuchea, however, it is quite impossible that their client regime can be overthrown.

John Keegan

KENYA*

HISTORY AND INTRODUCTION

Kenya attained independence in 1963 becoming a republic a year later. In colonial days the 3rd, 5th and 11th Battalions of the King's African Rifles had been recruited in Kenya, together with certain other smaller units. These and other war-time Kenya battalions of the King's African Rifles (KAR) served in the German East African campaign in World War I in the Italian East Africa, Madagascar and Burma campaigns of World War II, and since 1945 in counter-insurgency campaigning in Malaya (3rd Battalion only) and Kenya itself. These campaigns are recalled with pride, and are in no way seen as alien service.

Until the events of August 1982 the Armed Services had played no role in politics since independence. The involvement of the (then) Chief of the Defence Staff, Lieutenant-General J. M. Ndolo, in the so-called 'Kamba Plot' of 1971 is the sole exception to have appeared in public. Occasional rumours of individual officers' political ambitions and occasional unexpected retirements of certain officers suggest, however, that the army is not entirely free from the influence of events elsewhere in Africa.

The government, it is said, is anxious to identify the army with the overall social structure. Senior officers, for example, are encouraged to become landowners.

The Air Force Mutiny of August, 1982 appears to have made no appeal to the army most of whose units showed no reluctance to suppress the mutiny with bloodshed. While inter-service jealousies no doubt played a part here, ethnicity probably also did so, the large majority of air force personnel being Kikuyu and Luo while the army's soldiers were in the majority from Kenya's smaller ethnic groups. The one military unit that may have been involved was the newly-formed 'air cavalry' battalion. But equally those of its unfortunate members who undoubtedly were acting with the air force mutineers may have had no option.

The Air Force Mutiny has seriously weakened the political credibility of the government of President Daniel arap Moi (who succeeded President Kenyatta on the latter's death in 1978). It is now heavily dependent on the army for its survival; whether the army will make any political demands in return for its support is an open question. But the President and his ministers are now in no position to cross the army.

STRENGTH AND BUDGET

Population: 17,500,000 (approximate)
Armed Forces: Army, 13,000. There is also a barrack police force known as the General Service Unit, believed to be about 1800 strong. Before the Mutiny, the Air Force numbered 3000.
GNP: $6,400,000,000,000 (1980).
Defence Expenditure: $160,000,000 (1980).

COMMAND AND CONSTITUTIONAL STATUS

President Daniel arap Moi is Commander-in-Chief of the Armed Forces. There is at the time of writing no Minister

* For general notes on African armies, see Appendix 1.

for Defence, the previous incumbent, J. S. Gichuru, having died. Defence matters are dealt with by the Secretary of the Cabinet, J. Kiereini. The Chief of Staff of the Armed Forces is General J. Mulinge, and the Army Commander is Lieutenant General J. M. Sawe. After the mutiny, the Deputy Army Commander Lieut-General Mahmoud Mohammed, replaced the Air Force Commander, Major General P. Karinki, the latter being then arrested.

Army Headquarters are in Nairobi.

ROLE, COMMITMENT, DEPLOYMENT AND RECENT OPERATIONS

The Kenyan army is faced with one of Africa's most grave military problems in the defence of national frontiers. Somalia claims large areas of north-east Kenya and Amin's Uganda claimed a considerable area of western Kenya. In the first years of independence the Kenyan army was heavily committed in operations against Somali *Shifta*, or insurgent groups, supported by Somalia. The operations were conducted efficiently, as a result of which (and also as a result of government changes in Somalia) the insurgent attacks died down. Both problems remain latent and Somali reverses in Ethiopia may lead her to such compensation at Kenya's cost. Kenya has carefully preserved her good relations with Ethiopia despite the ideological differences so as to preserve a common front against Somali irredentism. But the ideological differences are total and while the USA backs Kenya the USSR backs Ethiopia adding a great power rivalry dimension to Kenya's ill-ease. Following the collapse of the East African Community relations with Tanzania are also frequently very cool.

A small Kenya Army detachment performed creditably with the Commonwealth Monitoring Force in Zimbabwe in 1980.

ORGANISATION

The Army is built around two infantry brigades one of three and one of two battalions, each brigade with an armoured unit. There is also an armoured reconnaissance battalion, two artillery units, two engineer units and a logistics unit in support. In formation in 1981 was a new 'air cavalry' battalion, a unit designed to be moved by assault helicopters to any conflict area. This new unit reflects Kenya's dilemma, of large areas and limited resources. If the aircraft and air personnel once more become available and reliable, other infantry units may be converted to the heliborne assault role.

RECRUITMENT, TRAINING AND RESERVES

In the colonial period the Kenya battalions of the KAR were largely recruited from the Kamba and Kalenjin (in particular Nandi) ethnic groups; with independence the army was based on something approaching a proportional system, though there is still a tendency for Kamba and Kalenjin to appear in a number of senior posts (in contrast to the barrack police, or General Service Units, as they are called, in which Kikuyu officers appear to be preponderant). Recruitment is by voluntary means. A few Kenyan-nationality Asians serve in the army. The Air Force was a very largely Kikuyu service.

Kenya gained — in relative east African terms — from being the last of the three territories to become independent. Both the late President Kenyatta's overall policy of national unity and reconciliation, and immediate military needs, led Kenya into a more close military relationship with Britain than either of its neighbours. A defence agreement was signed in 1964 by which Britain offered Kenya a substantial measure of British assistance and Britain was permitted to use training-area facilities in northern Kenya. At independence the first Kenyan officer to command a battalion was appointed, but Kenyatta retained the services of a British army general (on secondment), either as Army Commander or as Chief of the Defence Staff, until 1969. The very large British Army Training Team operated in Kenya until 1970, though these personnel had been withdrawn from unit or sub-unit command appointments earlier. Some British-born officers were also appointed on contract. A smaller British Army team reappeared in the mid-1970s and still remains. Although Israeli help was accepted in the mid-1960s and a few Kenyan army personnel are sent to countries other than Britain for training, these non-British arrangements form a minority. In the 1962–5 period a very large number of Kenyans passed through Sandhurst and Mons Officer Cadet School, smaller numbers continue to do so and also to attend courses at the Royal Military College of Science, the Staff College and the Royal College of Defence Studies. Kenya now trains the majority of its officer cadets at a special officer-training unit at Lanet, to which Malawi and Swaziland also send cadets.

The *Shifta* operations greatly improved the army's morale and efficiency.

Kenyatta saw benefits without constraints upon his military and foreign policy as a result of the British alliance — he was first of the East African leaders to seek British help in suppressing an army mutiny in January, 1964, and he firmly rejected the Soviet Union's offer of some elderly T-34 tanks as a gift and refused to accept into the Kenyan army a number of largely Luo cadets trained — under private political arrangements — in Bulgaria. Personnel trained in Israel were also not accepted unless they retrained in Kenya.

The administration, training and equipment of the army have since the mid-1970s been the subject of further reform, based on the need to develop from a small counter-insurgency force to a field army capable of withstanding air and armoured attacks. British advice was sought, but equipment purchased from a number of western countries as Britain was unwilling to offer the necessary long-term credits.

EQUIPMENT AND ARMS INDUSTRY

The Kenya Army's armoured units are equipped with Vickers Mark III tanks, the original orders of 60 were delivered but it is not certain how many of a third order for twelve more have in fact arrived. The armoured-cars include 40 AML-60 and AML-90 vehicles together with three elderly British Saracens, eight Shorlands and an unspecified number, perhaps a dozen, of Fox cars. One report suggests a further 20 AMLs, mainly AML-90s, are on order. There are also some 20 British Ferret cars, now probably almost worn-out. Armoured troops carrying facilities are provided by 50 UR-416 and twelve Panhard M-3 vehicles. The artillery consists of forty light and sixteen pack 105mm howitzers together with eight 120mm and twenty 81mm mortars. Anti-tank equipment includes eight Swingfire missile launchers, Milan systems, over fifty Carl Gustav rocket launchers and a small number of Landrover mounted WOMBAT recoil-less anti-tank guns. Rapier light battlefield surface to air missiles have been ordered and one report claims that some have been delivered; this however has not been confirmed.

At the time of writing (autumn 1982) Kenya has a number of aircraft but an enfeebled air force, a number of its personnel having been killed or involved in the Mutiny. Re-building the force will take several years, at least three and perhaps seven or more. The aircraft include ten Northrup F-5 E and two F-5F fighters with an air to ground strike capability, five BAC Strikemaster and twelve Hawk T52 counter-insurgency strike aircraft, fourteen Bulldog training machines, a transport fixed-wing fleet of five DHC-4 Caribon, six DHC-5 Buffalo and six Do-28D plus four light liaison machines. The helicopter force includes ten Puma and two Bell 47Gs, fifteen Hughes 500 MD Defender helicopters with TOW anti-tank guided weapons were ordered, some have been delivered and one crashed in August 1982. A further fifteen without TOW and two adapted for training are to arrive this year. Sidewinder missiles are also on order according to one report.

No aircraft were damaged or destroyed in the mutiny of August 1982.

RANK, DRESS AND DISTINCTIONS

The overall structure remains British patterned. The rank badges vary only with the replacement of the crown, and uniforms maintain the KAR style except that a special headdress has been introduced for ceremonial wear.

The air force kept military titles for its officer ranks.

CURRENT DEVELOPMENTS

Kenya's military future is very uncertain. Her strategic problem remains, and could become acute in the event of policy change in Somalia or Ethiopia. A large proportion of the Kenya Army is permanently on garrison duty in the north, a commitment which adds to its professionalism and also very probably to officer/soldier loyalties.

At the same time her increasingly overt political and military linkages with the West arouse internal domestic criticism, not always stifled. False interpretations have always been placed on the agreement by which British troops have been allowed a training facility in the northwest. Much more general criticism has been voiced of the new links with the USA which sees Kenya as an essential link in an American capacity to mount a rapid deployment force in the Middle East. American naval forces are frequent visitors to Mombasa. The USA on the other hand, has offered Kenya useful credit and aid facilities for its armed forces.

The third major factor in the uncertainty is Kenya's own domestic and social problems, in particular the high elitist structure of Kenya's society with its glaring contrasts of wealth and poverty, and the country's phenomenal birth-rate. It was not surprising that the junior leaders in the air force, mainly urban or peri-urban Kikuyu were in rapport with their Nairobi civilian counterparts; the object of the mutineers was evidently to introduce political radicalism.

Kenya's economy, too, has suffered in the general world recession conditions. The facts that Tanzania has suffered worse and that three of her neighbours, Uganda, Ethiopia and Somalia are all heavily pre-occupied with their own internal political and security problems are the best, if somewhat negative, grounds for any optimism.

Lloyd Mathews

NORTH KOREA

HISTORY AND INTRODUCTION

The Korean People's Army, at a strength of 430,000, ranks seventh in size in the world, immediately after the South Korean. Proportionate to the country's population of 16,000,000 its strength is unmatched, and only approached by that of Taiwan. No country in Europe, except the Soviet Union, has so many men under arms; by way of comparison, it is revealing to note that a State of nearly equal populousness, East Germany, also with a vital strategic frontier, maintains an army of only 105,000.

North Korea's highly militarised condition is the result of the failure to settle the problem of Korean unification after World War II (see the entry on South Korea), a failure first of agreement between the Western allies and the Russians, then of arms in the Korean War of 1950–53. But it is also, like the first of those failures and the war itself, the fruit of a particularly aggressive local ideology, compounded of Soviet-style communism, Korean nationalism and the 'cult of personality' of the North Korean leader, Marshal Kim Il Sung.

Kim Il Sung, born near Pyongyang the capital of North Korea, in 1912, was first heard of as the leader of a band of communist guerrillas operating, under Chinese Communist control, against the Japanese (who had annexed Korea in 1910) in Manchuria during the 1930s. After a year in a Japanese prison, he fled to the Soviet Far East in 1941, where he was trained in the Communist Party School at Khabarovsk. In September, 1945 he landed, wearing Russian uniform, at Wonsan with the Russian occupation force which, by agreement with the Western powers, was to garrison the country as far south as the 38th Parallel until its political future could be arranged. The method chosen was the holding of nation-wide elections under the aegis of the United Nations but, on the refusal of the Russians to allow the United Nations' commissioners to enter their occupation area, elections were held in the South only. The government formed by the elected assembly in May, 1948 was recognised in December as legitimate by the United Nations General Assembly, which called on the occupying powers to withdraw their forces as soon as practicable. Russia announced that she had done so on Christmas Day, by which time a government had also been set up in the North, under the Presidency of Kim Il Sung, who had taken office on September 10th.

Kim Il Sung's government claimed jurisdiction over the whole of Korea and was quick to embark on a programme of subversion inside the South, which soon developed into a campaign of cross-border raiding which the Southern government reciprocated. By the spring of 1950 the number of border incidents had reached several dozen a week, and both sides had deployed their armies in full strength along the 38th Parallel. That of North Korea's was much larger and stronger than the South's. Moreover, the latter was a recent creation, while Kim Il Sung's army was well-established. It consisted of two main elements, the Border Constabulary (Bo An Dae) and the People's Army (In Min Gun). The Border Constabulary, originally known as the Peace Preservation Corps, had been raised under Russian aegis from Korean communists who had fled to Soviet territory before September, 1945. In 1950 it numbered 50,000 and was organised in five brigades — 1st, 2nd, 3rd, 5th and 7th, equipped as light

infantry. The People's Army counted 10 divisions in June, 1950. Three (the 10th, 13th and 15th) were still forming and two (the 2nd and 3rd) were newly-raised. But the remaining five consisted of, or contained, veteran soldiers of Korean formations of the Chinese People's Liberation Army (CPLA). The 5th and 6th Divisions were the former Chinese 164th and 166th Divisions, the latter formed in 1942 from deserters from the Japanese Kwantung Army in Manchuria. The 7th Division had been made by transferring into it the Koreans from the Chinese 139th, 140th, 141st and 156th Divisions, while the 1st and 4th Divisions each contained one regiment of Korean veterans of the CPLA.

But while the manpower of the army owed most to the CPLA, its equipment was largely Russian. The most important items were the 120T-34 tanks of the 105th Armoured Brigade, but each of the divisions also had 12SU-76 SPGs as well as field and medium artillery. All formations were organised along Russian lines, and the character and tactical doctrine of the army were strongly Russian. Soviet officers had acted as training advisers to the army from the moment of its official formation in February, 1948 and were still present in large numbers in the summer of 1950.

To what extent Russia and China endorsed North Korea's decision to mount the invasion of the South which she launched on June 25th, 1950 remains a matter of argument. It seems unlikely that North Korea would have taken the decision independently. Her version of events is that the attack was launched in the opposite direction and that it was the South which was the aggressor. But that has not been generally accepted, either at the time or later. The United Nations Security Council, from which Russia had temporarily withdrawn, condemned North Korea as an aggressor on June 25th and voted to approve military action to restore peace in the area on June 27th.

While member nations, which meant principally the United States, deployed forces to South Korea to contain the invasion, the North Korean army made rapid progress southwards. It quickly destroyed most of the South Korean army and roughly handled the first American units, rapidly transported from Japan, which came to its support. By the beginning of August it had pinned the survivors of the opening campaign into a tiny bridgehead around the port of Pusan in the far south-east corner of the peninsula, from which the United Nations Forces looked unable to break out. A remarkable strategic gamble appeared to have paid off. On September 25th, however, the United Nations Commander, General MacArthur, delivered a long-prepared and finely calculated amphibious assault at Inchon, the port of Seoul, deep in the North Koreans' rear, and completely unhinged their front. Caught between the Inchon force and the Pusan garrison, who had simultaneously broken out of their perimeter, the North Koreans were, despite a precipitate retreat, almost destroyed as an army in the next fortnight. Out of some 130,000 soldiers who had entered the South, only about 30,000 made good their escape across the 38th Parallel, all in a broken state. Some formed bodies, cut off by the rapidity of the United Nations advance, remained in the mountains of the South where they gradually initiated guerrilla attacks against the rear of the United Nations army.

The intervention of the Chinese, as the United Nations advance neared their border with Korea, transformed the character of the war, which thenceforth became one of attrition along or close to the 38th Parallel, in which the bulk of the forces were provided by the Chinese 'Volunteer' Army, the Americans and the reconstituted South Korean army. The direction of the war passed from Kin Il Sung to the Chinese and the Russians, the latter supplying the munitions and equipment with which it was waged from the communist side. But, during the 3 years for which the campaign dragged on, the North Korean People's Army was gradually reconstituted, until by the signing of the ceasefire in July, 1953 it again numbered 10 divisions. Remarkably, in view of the humiliating collapse of September—October, 1950, Kim Il Sung remained as Head of State and nominal Commander-in-Chief of the People's Army. He seems in fact to have faced a challenge to his leadership from within the party in 1953, but forestalled it by instituting a purge. Three years later his authority was directly attacked at the party conference but he once again asserted his ascendancy, exiled his opponents and thenceforth sanctioned a 'cult of the personality' which has made him today a Korean Stalin.

Kim Il Sung's standing does not depend, however, simply upon his manipulation of the party's propaganda machine. He has also presided over a programme of economic development which achieved in the late 1950s a remarkable degree of success. North Korea has considerable natural resources, including coal and iron, and was left the infrastructure of a modern industrial base by the Japanese. Under Kim Il Sung's direction, and with plentiful aid from Russia, China and other communist countries, her mining, machine tool, chemical, textile and pharmaceutical industries were greatly expanded and hydroelectric capacity increased. In the 1960s however, economic growth slowed, due to the very heavy investment in military equipment — over 30% of government expenditure was allocated to the armed forces in 1968 — and to the interrruption of overseas aid. North Korea has oscillated in alignment between Moscow and Peking. Originally a Soviet protégé, the regime fell very much under Chinese influence during and after the Korean war, but continued to receive aid from both countries. When the Moscow—Peking split developed, Kim Il Sung sided generally with the Chinese, and between 1962 and 1964 there was an almost open break with Moscow, manifested by a withdrawal of Soviet and eastern bloc aid. Relations were normalised in 1965, when Premier Kosygin visited Pyongyang, and Soviet aid restored, but North Korea appears to remain more strongly committed to China than to Russia. Chinese aid, particularly in the form of oil which Korea lacks, outweighs Russian, and China's Asian policy is more in tune with Kim Il Sung's than Moscow's.

Both great communist powers must nevertheless feel some alarm over his long-term ambitions, which remain the reunification of the two Koreas, by force if necessary. They are obliged to provide him with the equipment which will match the massive armoury of South Korea, which is now partly supplied by its own industry, but neither can wish to see him use it aggressively. Russia needs to preserve the appearance of *détente* in the north-west Pacific as urgently as anywhere else, while China is anxious that the threat of involvement in another Asian war should not prompt America to disengage her forces, a valuable local counterweight, from the area. Without the material assistance and moral support of one or the other, Kim Il Sung cannot undertake military operations on any scale. Nevertheless, he maintains one of the most impressive military establishments in the world The North Korean army, recruited by universal long-term conscription, has once already proved itself a formidable fighting machine, is larger and far better equipped than in 1950, and appears wedded to the offensive tactical doctrine of the Soviet school in which it was brought up.

STRENGTH AND BUDGET

Population: 18,600,000
Army: 700,000
Navy: 33,000; 19 submarines, 4 frigates, 510 small craft
Air force: 51,000; 700 combat aircraft
Paramilitary forces: 38,000 security and border guards; militia of 760,000
GNP (1981): $18,800,000,000
Defence expenditure (1982): $1,700,000,000

COMMAND AND CONSTITUTIONAL STATUS

The constitutional status of the army is defined in Article 100 of the constitution, which was promulgated in September, 1948. The article is taken almost verbatim from the Soviet constitution and reads 'In order to defend the Democratic People's Republic of Korea, the Korean People's Army shall be organised. The mission of the Korean People's Army shall be to defend the independence of the fatherland and the people's freedom.' The army's relationship with the party is defined by an amendment of 1961 to the Rules of the Korean Workers' Party of 1956. The rules (66, 67 and 68) lay down that 'the Korean People's Army is the armed force of the Korean Workers' Party, that an Army Party Committee shall be organised and that it shall belong directly to the Central Committee of the Party'. It ordains the organisation of a General Political Bureau to organise and execute party activities inside the army and it enjoins the forging of links between party organisations within the army and with local party organisations and encourages its members and officers to seek office in such local organisations. In this it again follows Soviet example.

The Korean People's Army is a unified force, comprising army, navy and air force, which are commanded by a single chief of staff. As in the Soviet Union, and all other communist countries, however, command of the armed forces, though vested nominally in the apparatus of government, in fact resides in the party. In North Korea, the key organ of command is the Military Affairs Committee of the party, on which on June 26th, 1950 the Presidium of the Supreme People's Assembly conferred responsibility for prosecuting the war. It has remained the supreme arbiter of military affairs ever since. Its Chairman since 1950 has been Kim Il Sung, who is also President of the Republic, General Secretary of the Party and Supreme Commander of the Armed Forces, in which he holds the rank of marshal. Its other members, who usually number six, are always drawn from the most powerful men in the State, their standing being determined by their intimacy with the President and his family. No disclosures of its discussions or decisions are ever made. But it is known to control directly not only the armed forces but also the People's Militia and the provincial military committees of the party, each of which is run by a serving colonel acting as vice-chairman.

The Military Affairs Committee controls the formal governmental organ of command. This is the Ministry of National Defence, of which the minister is either a retired or serving officer; he has under him three vice-ministers, of whom one, a serving officer, also acts as Chief of the General Staff, commanding the three services. A second commands the General Bureau of Rear Services, and the third, who answers effectively directly to the party, is Chief of the General Politburo and Chairman of the Party Committee of the Korean People's Army, i.e. head of the political commissar structure. The Chief of the General Staff commands the operational services — Army, Mechanised Unit, Artillery Unit,

Air Force and Navy – and 14 staff bureaux, of which the most important are Operations, Reconnaissance (which oversees intelligence gathering in, and infiltration into, South Korea), Combat Training, Military Recruitment and Replacement (the personnel office). The importance of the Geology Bureau, another of the fourteen, may be greater than had been thought in view of the discovery of the border tunnels. The Director of Rear Services controls finance, building, munition production and the medical service. The Ordnance and Engineer Bureaux, however, are subordinate to the Chief of the General Staff.

He also shares authority with the Chief of the General Politburo over the Political Security and Court Martial Bureaux. The authority of the latter may be thought greater in those fields. The primacy of the party even in non-political affairs is in general very strongly stressed. As in all communist armies, the party oversees and interpenetrates the army at every level. There is a political vice commander (commissar) in each army, division, regiment, battalion and company, and there is a party committee in every army, division and regiment. In the battalion there is a 'primary party organisation' and in each company a cell, the nuclear party unit. It consists of the commander and vice-commander of each of the three platoons and of several private soldiers. About 20% of platoon members are believed to be party members; the proportion for higher ranks is of course much greater.

Party control over the Workers' and Peasants' Red Militia is even more complete, since its officers at provincial, *kun* (prefectural), and *ri* and *tong* (village and worksite) level are almost always the officials of the party organisation at the same local level.

ROLE, COMMITMENT, DEPLOYMENT AND RECENT OPERATIONS

The declared role of the army is the defence of the frontier with the South. Kim Il Sung openly hints, however, that it is ready to intervene in the South should 'revolution' occur there and, before the improvement of relations in 1972–4, the North Korean armed forces had conducted large-scale infiltration across the border and along the Southern coastline. The army also acts as an important medium of education of North Korean youth in the official ideology.

The flavour of the official role of the army, which corresponds closely with its actual one, is caught in this order of the day issued on the tenth anniversary (1969) of the founding of the Red Militia: 'Regarding it as the greatest honour and happiness to fight, devoting their youth and lives along the one road of the revolution, the one road of victory and glory indicated by the leader, they firmly resolve in their hearts to live up to the solicitude and trust of the Leader, their adoration of him being higher than the sky and deeper than the sea. They will show their love by thoroughly implementing the revolutionary line of our Party on stepping up economic construction and defence upbuilding in parallel, as put forth by the Leader; more solidly building up their combat capacity so that each can match one hundred foes; upholding the military line of the Party; defending the socialist Fatherland like an impregnable fortress; and making firm preparations to the full for bringing about earlier the great revolutionary event of the unification of the Fatherland.' The 'arming of the whole population' and the 'fortification of the entire country' are the two means consistently stressed towards the ultimate goal of reunification. The constitution of the People's Republic declares its capital to be Seoul.

North Korea, though it has security treaties with both Moscow and Peking that were reaffirmed in 1962 in the immediate aftermath of General Park's coup in South Korea, is not committed to assist in the defence of any foreign country. However, a number of North Korean pilots are believed to have flown in action over North Vietnam during the Indochina war during 1966–7. The regime also apparently has a general commitment to the encouragement and support of 'liberation movements' in many parts of the world. It has trained guerrilla fighters from many different countries and has been obliged at various times to withdraw its diplomats from Ghana, Burundi, the Central African Empire and Sri Lanka as a result of protests at its interference in their internal affairs.

The deployment of the North Korean army is cloaked in secrecy. It was reported in 1976 that its two armoured divisions had been moved up close behind the border with the South, which suggests that they had earlier been held back in reserve. The frontiers with Russia and China, particularly the latter, scarcely need defending, and it may be presumed therefore that the bulk of the 22 infantry divisions face the South Koreans across the border. However, the presence of South Korean marines on the Peklyong Do, the group of islands off the Haeju peninsula, and the agreement which allows free civil navigation of the mouth of the Han estuary, both of which lie north of the Demilitarised Zone, may prompt the North to keep sizeable concentrations of troops there.

The most recent operations of the army, which properly fall under the heading 'military engineering', are the construction of the tunnels under the Demilitarised Zone, the first of which was discovered in November, 1974. Eighteen are believed to have been built altogether, but only two have been counter-mined, the one originally found at Gorangpo, near Seoul, and another and much larger one east of Chorwon, the centre point of the North–South frontier. Five kilometres long and of six foot section, it would, when completed, have allowed thousands of troops an hour to enter the rear of the South Koreans' positions. The expense of counter-mining the tunnels is so high that the South Koreans (and the Americans, who have assisted them in their location) do not intend to proceed immediately against the others, but to monitor the surface over the suspected areas for signs of resumed activity.

Because of the effort and expense entailed, Western armies are not attuned to think of tunnelling as a useful military activity. Asian soldiers, however, are traditionally great diggers: the Japanese constructed enormously elaborate fortifications, which often included labyrinthine tunnels, throughout their island and mainland war zones during 1941–5. And what is called 'the waging of tunnel warfare' is actually a tenet of the Maoist doctrine of protracted warfare. Both the French and Americans in Indochina were chronically frustrated in their attempts to consolidate their possession of disputed regions by the existence of veritable mazes of tunnels, extending beneath hundreds of square miles of country, in which the Viet Minh and Viet Cong lived, maintained dumps and hospitals, and moved undetected from one tactical zone to another. The North Korean tunnels, though built on a more impressive scale than has been normal, may be seen as a completely conventional feature of the Asian communist approach to warfare.

The North Korean army has also engaged in active operations of a minor though menacing sort within the last 10 years. The most important formed part of its campaign of military infiltration of, and subversion within, the South in 1966–70. The South Koreans reported 566 infiltrations of the border in 1967 and in 1968 a 31-man unit described as belonging to the North Korean army's 124th Unit was found within 500 yards of the Blue House, the presidential palace in Seoul. Its members were killed in a gun battle and were later announced by the South Koreans to have been charged with the mission of assassinating President Park. There was a major North Korean coastal commando raid near Ulchin later in the same year. In 1970 the campaign tailed off, however, and infiltration stopped altogether between 1972 and 1974 while Kim Il Sung was pursuing negotiations for the peaceful reunification of the country. Relations have since sharply deteriorated once more and it is reported that North Korea's infiltration force now numbers 26,000. But the murder of two American officers in the Demilitarised Zone in August, 1976, horrifying though its manner, is probably best seen as an aberration of North Korean policy.

ORGANISATION

Arms of Service

These are those normal in a Soviet-style army: infantry, armoured troops, engineers, signals, ordnance and rear services. The latter include transportation and medical services as well as administration and construction.

Operational

The operational structure is unusual in that the armed forces form five branches under a single general staff. The air force and navy apart, the other three are the army, the mechanised arm and the artillery arm. It is perhaps simplest to think of the army being organised into three: the infantry divisions, the tank divisions and a strategic artillery force.

Infantry divisions, of which there are 35 are organised on old-style Soviet lines. They number about 9000 men each and comprise three infantry regiments of three battalions each, three artillery battalions of 18 tubes each (respectively 76.2mm field howitzers, 122mm medium guns and 120mm mortars), an anti-tank battalion of 18 57mm guns, an air-defence battalion with 24 37mm and four 14.5mm guns, an assault-gun battalion with 18 (?) 100mm SPGs, an engineer battalion, a signals battalion, a reconnaissance company and a chemical warfare company, with some small auxiliary units. The infantry regiments comprise, besides the infantry battalion, an air-defence battery with 14.5mm guns, a mortar company with six 120mm mortars, an artillery company with six 76.2mm howitzers, an engineer company, a signals company and a chemical warfare platoon, The infantry battalion, besides its three rifle companies, has a mortar company with six 82mm mortars, an anti-tank company with six 82mm recoilless rifles, and a heavy-machine-gun company.

The organisation of the two tank divisions three and five independent motorised divsion brigades probably follows that of the Soviet equivalents, and it is probable that all the 950APCs in the army are with these formations.

The 'artillery arm', best thought of as the artillery reserve of the army under direct control of the general staff, comprises three air-defence brigades, a missile regiment, two howitzer regiments, two mortar regiments and two 203mm gun battalions. But it may be that it has been expanded recently to accommodate the new Frog missiles (there are reports of two new missile regiments).

The infantry divisions of the army are grouped under nine corps headquarters, directly commanded by army headquarters under the general staff.

The Security Corps (*Choson Kyongbidae*) (Border Guards) is controlled by the Ministry of Public Security and is organised into regiments and companies. With other guards, these paramilitary forces number 38,000.

The Workers' and Peasants' Red Militia (*Nodong Chok-widae*), in which service is compulsory for all able-bodied males between the ages of eighteen and forty-five and all able-bodied females between the ages of eighteen and thirty-five, and which numbers about 760,000, is organised on a local basis. North Korea is divided into 10 provinces, subdivided into 175 prefectures (*kun*), themselves into villages (*ri*). The party organisation at *kun* level provides the regimental command, that at *ri* level the battalion command, while the personnel of the companies, platoons and sections is provided by the inhabitants or workers at hamlets and factories where they are organised. Battalions and regiments only take shape at times of major training. Weapons are provided by the provincial Public Security department, but are stored in factory or village premises. The object of the Red Militia, besides that of militarising the population, is to ensure the unyielding defence of each foot of the homeland. It must, however, also be prepared to wage guerrilla warfare if its positions are by-passed by an invader.

RECRUITMENT, TRAINING AND RESERVES

Until 1956 the army was recruited by voluntary enlistment. Conscription was then introduced, and is now universal for all able-bodied males from their twentieth year (the age of enlistment was raised from eighteen to twenty in 1965). The term of service is the longest in the world, 5 or 6 years being usual. The conditions of service are also abnormally harsh. Home leave, of which a short allowance was formerly granted to exemplary private soldiers, was abolished in 1969, while recreational time during the service day is closely supervised and free time almost non-existent. Pay is tiny. The only compensations for military service are abundant food and an honoured public status. To be deemed ineligible for service, on any but medical grounds, 'is to be saddled with a life-long social and political stigma'. 'Ineligibility' derives from a 'bad family background', usually meaning being the son of a capitalist or landowner under the former regime.

Recruits are trained in their units. As in all communist armies, a great deal of the training time is devoted to political education, apparently one quarter in the Korean army. Recruits, however, come to the army with some military knowledge, all having done at least 2 years in the Red Militia, which requires its members to perform at least 2 hours military training a week.

Officers, who may be on either regular or short-service enlistment, are selected from the Socialist Working Youth League, the young communist organisation, or from high schools or colleges, in all of which 200 hours of military training is carried on each year, and a reserve officer's examination held. (Students who fail their military courses are not allowed to proceed to the next year of military work.) There are three main officer training schools: the 1st Combined Officers Training School (which offers a 1 year course for short service officers), the 1st Combined Military Academy (which trains regular officers for 2—3 years) and the Army War College (which offers a 2—3 year staff course to captains, majors and lieutenant-colonels, and a 1 year course for more senior officers). Veterinary and medical officer cadets are trained at their own academies for 3 years and 5 years, respectively. The Tank and Joint Artillery Schools give specialist training to officers, cadets and NCOs of those branches. The quality of officer training in the People's Army is judged to be high.

RESERVES

Because the term of conscript service is so long in the People's Army, the size of the first line reserve must be consonantly smaller than for other armies of comparable size. If the annual contingent numbers 60,000 — perhaps a low estimate — the first-line reserve might be judged to number 268,000. It seems moreover unlikely that the State has sufficient equipment available to form large reserve units, and that the first line reserve is earmarked to provide replacements and mobilisation details. The true 'reserve' of the regular army is probably the Red Militia, which has the defensive task of protecting the homeland while the regular army performs the offensive mission on which its training lays such stress. But there are reports of 23 reserve divisions in skeleton (cadre) form.

EQUIPMENT AND ARMS INDUSTRY

North Korea counts among the most industrialised countries of East Asia: industrial income represented 65% of national income in 1969 and the officially reported production of coal and crude steel in 1970 was 27,000,000 and 2,000,000 tons, respectively. Over 40% of the work force was employed in industry, which now achieves machine-tool building. The bias of production is still, however, towards heavy industry and raw materials on the one hand, the traditional direction given it by the Japanese, and towards electronic and light-engineering goods on the other. Moreover, the public statistics bureau ceased to issue figures after 1969, when the current 7 year plan had begun to fall behind schedule, and it is now difficult to form a clear picture of the achievements of North Korean industry. Military investment is very high, but is believed to be devoted disproportionately to infrastructure — fortifications, roads and tunnels — rather than to the production of equipment, most of which still comes from China and Russia. It is probable that North Korea does not produce anything more complicated than small arms, some light weapons and light ammunition. It would be surprising if its defence industry was more developed than South Korea's, which is just approaching the production of medium artillery and the assembly of armoured vehicles.

Equipment
Equipment is very varied: much Russian, some Chinese, some captured American from the Korean war, some home produced, and of very mixed age. The Red Militia is equipped with obsolete or obsolescent models, intermixed with a little new material held by the better units. The army uses weapons of the generation before current Soviet models, except for its small arms.

Rifle: 7.62mm AK-47 (Russia; Korean made (?))
Machine-gun: 7.62mm PK/PKs (Russia; Korean made (?))
Mortar: 82mm M-37 (Russia; Korean made (?)), 120mm M-38 (Russia) and 160mm M-53 (Russia); these equip the mortar company of the infantry regiments and a battalion of the divisional artillery in the artillery reserve (9000 in service altogether)
Anti-armour weapons: RPG 2 and 7 rocket launchers (Russia; Korean made), 75mm M-20 recoilless rifle (USA; Chinese or Korean made), 82mm B-10 recoilless rifle (Russia; Korean made) and 57mm M-43 gun (Russia); these equip the divisional anti-tank battalion; Sagger missile
Air-defence weapons: 12.7mm machine-gun (Russia; Korean made); 14.5mm cannon (Russia); 37mm M-38 gun, 57mm M-50 gun, 57mm ZSU gun, 85mm M-44 gun and 100mm M-49 gun (all Russian; a total of about 5000 guns in service); SA-2 missile (Russia; a total of 250 in service with the air force) no SA-7 with army.
Artillery: 76.2mm howitzer and 122mm M-37 gun (both Russian; in the divisional artillery); 152mm M-37 howitzer

and 203mm M-55 gun (both Russian; in the artillery reserve); Frog 7 missile (at least 54 in service). There are about 4100 guns in service.
Armour: BTR 40 armoured car, BTR 60 APC, BTR 152 APC and M-67 APC (all Russian; a total of about 1000 in service, probably in the armoured divisions); SU 100 assault gun (Russia; equips the divisional assault gun battalion); PT-76 light tank (Russia; 100 in service) and T-62 light tank (China; 50 in service)*; T-34 medium tank (Russia; 300 in service), T-54/55 medium tanks (Russia) and T-59 medium tank (China) of which there are a total of 2200 in service
Aircraft: these are operated by the air force but, since that forms part of the People's Army, its units probably co-operate closely with the ground forces. It has about 40 Russian helicopters (Mi-4, Mi-8), 225 transports of several types, about 300 ground-attack fighters (MiG-15/17), 240 fighters (MiG-19 and MiG-21) and 80 light bombers.

RANK, DRESS AND DISTINCTIONS

The appearance and rank structure of the People's Army is closely modelled on the Soviet. There is a heavy emphasis on the deference due to senior rank, and there has never been, as in the Chinese People's Army, any attempt to democratise the army. The differential between the pay of junior soldiers and senior officers is very great; generals earn over two hundred and fifty times as much as privates.

Ranks

General — Four stars on shoulder strap
Colonel-general — Three stars on shoulder strap
Lieutenant-general — Two stars on shoulder strap
Major-general — One star on shoulder strap
Colonel — Three stars and two stripes on shoulder strap
Lieutenant-colonel — Two stars and two stripes on shoulder strap
Major — One star and two stripes on shoulder strap
Captain — Four stars and one stripe on shoulder strap
Senior lieutenant — Three stars and one stripe on shoulder strap
Lieutenant — Two stars and one stripe on shoulder strap
Junior lieutenant — One star and one stripe on shoulder strap

As in the Soviet army, there are a number of decorations, most of which carry material privileges. In descending order of importance, the principal ones are: the Gold Medal, with title of Labour Hero; the Order of the National Flag, 1st, 2nd and 3rd classes; and the Freedom and Independence Medal, 1st and 2nd classes. The latter is awarded to officers for bravery.

The uniform of the army is khaki, cut on Soviet lines and worn with a distinctive képi-style cap. Some units of the Red Militia wear army uniform, without insignia, as does the Public Security Force.

CURRENT DEVELOPMENTS

The People's Army is a vital institution of the North Korean State, since it is the only body which might challenge the authority of Kim Il Sung and his Korean Worker's Party and would be the principal instrument of his highly aggressive

---

* Not to be confused with the Russian T-62 medium tank.

foreign policy should he ever decide to move from the field of words and gestures to full-scale action.

The President is keenly aware of the theoretical danger which a military challenge offers to his personal rule. In 1968 he abruptly removed the three leading military men, charging them with failure to implement the party's basic military policy: fortifying the whole country, militarising the whole people and training each regular soldier to fill the rank next senior to his. It may be, however, that the root cause of the purge was a suspicion by Kim that the three threatened his personal position. More recently he has moved against O Chin-U, a comrade of his partisan days and lately Chief of Staff, apparently fearing that the general saw himself as his successor. Nevertheless, while Kim Il Sung retains his health and powers, a military intervention is extremely unlikely. The army is under the closest political scrutiny, while at the same time Kim Il Sung uses military men as some of his closest and most publicly honoured intimates.

In the immediate future, therefore, it is to the military, rather than the political, role of the army that observers should look. If military consumption has seriously distorted the development of the North Korean economy since the inception of the Seven Year Plan in 1961, it is because the army was charged almost immediately on its inception with a redoubling of preparations for 'reunification' with the South. Kim Il Sung is believed to regret the 'lost opportunity' of the student revolt of 1960 against the government of Syngman Rhee, and to have decided to let no new crisis in the South find him unready to take advantage of it. He also believes that America will at some time in the future withdraw her ground forces from the peninsula — as the Carter administration has given notice of its intention to do — and that their departure may provide him with the opportunity for military action which at present he does not dare risk. On the other hand, he must also be aware that the South, with twice the population of the North and an industrial base both larger and faster growing than his own, will soon be able to defend itself without American assistance. If he is to achieve his cherished and publicly proclaimed goal of reunification, he may be forced to provoke a conflict with the South in a narrow time gap between the departure of the Americans and the maturation of South Korea's military self-sufficiency. It is vitally important to his policy, therefore, that the combat edge of the army be constantly sharpened and its readiness for action instantaneous. He must be very aware, however, that his military suppliers (Russia and China) are neither of them keen on a new Korean war and stringently limit the amount and quality of the equipment they provide. His strategy may therefore be to accept reverses in a conventional campaign between the regular armies of North and South and to hope that through the 'militarisation of the whole population' and 'fortification of the whole country' he could emerge victorious from a protracted war, much of it fought on Northern rather than Southern territory. It is certainly significant that much of the regular army's efforts are devoted to tunnel building and that the interior of North Korea is mouseholed with tunnels over much of its area. Fighting defensively and to a strategy of protracted war, the People's Army and the Red Militia would make a formidable adversary.

Recent estimates by the International Institute for Strategic Studies suggest a very large expansion of the army in the last five years; an increase in the number of infantry divisions from 20 to 35, the formation of three motorised infantry divisions and the acquisition of about 1030 tanks. These figures may err on the generous side, but an increase of some considerable order has undoubtedly taken place. It makes the security of South Korea's frontier even more fragile than before.

John Keegan

SOUTH KOREA

HISTORY AND INTRODUCTION

The Republic of Korea, with a population of 34,000,000 and a land area of 34,000 square miles, maintains an army of 520,000, the sixth largest in the world after those of China, Russia, America, India and Vietnam. The government of the Republic has been in the hands of the army high command since a *coup d'état* in 1961. A third of the budget is devoted to defence and the population is constantly practised in civil defence measures. By these tests, South Korea must be counted one of the most militarised countries in the world. The reasons for this remarkable state of affairs derive from its experience in the Korean War of 1950—53 and the persisting state of ceasefire, rather than true peace, to which that conflict led.

Korea, annexed by Japan in 1910 after a thousand years of dependency from China, was occupied, through previous agreement between the Allies, by Russian and American forces in 1945. The Russians entered the north of the country, the Americans the south, and a demarcation line between their zones was fixed along the 38th Parallel. Both were committed to the reunification of the country under its own government but failed to agree on how that might be brought about and, having each established a regime friendly to themselves in their respective zones, withdrew their troops, the Russians in 1948, the Americans in 1949. Relations between the two successor regimes were extremely hostile from the outset and in June, 1950, after much cross-border raiding by both sides, the North Korean army invaded the south. The Americans, thanks to the temporary withdrawal of the Russians from the Security Council of the United Nations, were able to secure a condemnation of the act as one of aggression and to invoke the provisions of the United Nations Charter for military sanctions against it. American troops from Japan at once left for the front, and were quickly joined by others from the continental United States, while contingents from other United Nations countries hurried to join them, first a British brigade, and eventually units from the Australian, Belgian, Canadian, Colombian, Ethiopian, French, Greek, Luxembourg, Dutch, New Zealand, Philippines, Thai, Turkish and South African armed forces. Fifty-three nations altogether endorsed the United Nations' decision to take action.

But it was South Korea, not then a member of the United Nations, which provided the largest fighting force, larger than the American and eventually amounting to more than half the United Nations' ground combat command. In June, 1950 it fielded eight weak divisions. In the first months of fighting, when the North Koreans drove them and the Americans back into the tiny Pusan perimeter area in the south of the country, most were destroyed. When the Americans reversed the tide of war in September, by General MacArthur's brilliantly timed amphibious assault at Inchon, it was his divisions which led the great advance to the border with China. But when the Chinese, in early 1951, had pushed the United Nations' troops back to the 38th Parallel, where the fighting thereafter settled into stalemate, the South Koreans began to rebuild their army until at the ceasefire it numbered 16 divisions, manning three-quarters of the front. The Americans, moreover, conceded that it was in safe hands. The South Korean army had proved itself to be a very fierce fighting force indeed.

Its progress had been remarkable. In 1945, though the Koreans had acquired a reputation as tough, even brutal, soldiers in the Japanese army, and some Koreans had become officers in it, there existed no formed fighting force in the country. The Americans, in their zone, recognised the need for an armed force to police a disorderly countryside and created the Korean Constabulary. In 1948, shortly before they left the country, they transformed it into the Republic of Korean Army and on the eve of the outbreak of the war it numbered 94,000. But it had little artillery or armour while the North Koreans had 2000 guns and 240 Russian tanks. Though the South's population outnumbered the North's by 20 million to eight million, its army was therefore no match for the other and its initial defeat was wholly understandable. Parts of it having survived, however, American training and re-equipment and the mere experience of war quickly sufficed, through the medium of universal conscription, to turn it into a large and very capable army.

Its very size and efficiency were to yield predictable peacetime results. It was to become the most modern institution in the country and, while the North refused to negotiate a settled peace, its most important, swiftly dominating post-war society, 'By contrast, most other organisations in the nation were embryonic, parasitic or anaemic. In the name of the defence of freedom, South Korea had become an immense garrison.'

The freedom' for which the war had been fought was that of freedom from aggression rather than liberty of the subject, for President Rhee's pre-war regime had been distinctly autocratic in character. Its restoration in an even more autocratic form after the war, was not accepted, however, with the same previous passivity at home, and widespread student rioting at the suspect results of the National Assembly elections of 1960, which the army did nothing to suppress and the United States' representatives appeared to approve of, led to his downfall. A year later, after a period of ineffective civilian government, the army itself intervened. The coup of May 16th, 1961 was planned and led by a group of middle-ranking officers, identified as the 'eighth graduating class' of the Korean Military Academy (i.e. a group who had been cadets together in 1949), supported by some of the younger generals. Foremost among them was Chung Hee Park, then a major-general commanding the logistics base at Pusan. The coup came as a complete surprise to the rest of the army, including the First Army immediately north of the capital Seoul, and to the American commander of the United Nations Command and the United States' ambassador. The latter proposed to the incumbent President, General Yun, that the former be used to put down the coup, on the grounds that it would be followed by a second and a third, which would fatally weaken the political stability of the country. However, he refused, believing that an even worse outcome would be a division of the army into two warring camps. The coup was therefore allowed to succeed, its leaders taking over the government and constituting themselves a Supreme Council for National Reconstruction, in place of the cabinet. Of its 30 members, three were from the Marine Corps, one each from the air force and the navy, the rest all from the army.

About a third were of lieutenant-colonel or colonel rank.

The Council declared its object to be 'the reconstruction of the Republic of Korea as a genuine democratic republic' and at once began to purge political life of leading figures of the previous regime through a Political Activities Purification Law. It also announced that civilian rule would be restored by elections in May, 1963. As the date for elections approached, General Park, a peasant's son who had originally been commissioned into the Japanese army through the Imperial Military Academy at Tokyo, wavered in his promise 'to restore the government to honest and conscientious civilians and return to . . . proper military duties'. Having disqualified himself for the presidential election of 1963, he yielded to a soldier's demonstration (which lacked the appearance of spontaneity) and in March announced the prolongation of military rule for another 4 years. Appraised of American hostility to this change of plan, made concrete by refusal of a request for an extra $25,000,000 in aid, Park cancelled the prolongation but took his discharge from the army and, as a civilian, won the presidential election by a comfortable majority.

He has remained in power ever since, though elections are held regularly and an opposition party records large votes at the polls. Despite the appearance of democratic practice, the character of the regime is essentially authoritarian, with the army and the police providing its chief support; the Constitution of 1972 was suspended for several months as late as 1974. However, President Park from the outset made clear his belief that in the poorer Asian countries 'the people are more frightened of poverty and hunger than totalitarianism', and that the substance of democracy must wait upon the creation of a 'welfare state'. He has continued to affirm his intention of restoring civilian rule and he has also achieved extraordinary success in his economic programme. The GNP has increased by an average of 12% in every year of his Presidency, and a great deal of the growth has been consumed by the population, whose living standards have improved out of recognition in the period. Foreign economists predict that the country may reach a Japanese economic level within a generation. It is understandable therefore that the harsh censorship laws are sparingly invoked, and that the burden of defence costs and military service are borne uncomplainingly by the majority of the people (though not by many students and opposition politicians). While the population enjoys a rising standard of living, and as long as the North Koreans refuse to relax their aggressive posture, the military character of the government looks unlikely to change.

STRENGTH AND BUDGET

Population: 38,900,000
Army: 520,000
Navy: 25,000 (plus 24,000 marines); 18 warships, many smaller craft
Air force: 32,600; 444 combat aircraft
Reserves and paramilitary forces: 1,100,000 reserves; 2,400,000 also have a reserve liability; 3,400,000 militia (Homeland Reserve Defence Forces)
GNP (1981): $63,100,000,000
Defence expenditure (1981): $3,970,000,000

The Korean armed forces were built almost wholly with American aid payments, and maintained from the same source during, and for some years after, the war. As compensation for its withdrawal of one of its two divisions in 1971, the USA agreed to supply $1,500,000,000 in aid over the period 1971—5. But growth of the Korean economy had made the defence establishment increasingly self-supporting, and in 1976 the country embarked on a 5 year Armed Forces Improvement Plan, the aim of which is to make it able to repulse any attack from the North without outside help, except for American logistical support. The programme is expected to cost between $4,500,000,000 and $5,000,000,000, about two-thirds of which will be raised by a defence tax introduced in 1976.

COMMAND AND CONSTITUTIONAL STATUS

There have been three major constitutional revisions since the military coup of 1961, those of 1963 and 1972 notably increasing the executive power of the President and curtailing civil liberties. The President is Commander-in-Chief, and the armed forces are effectively only subject to his authority and jurisdiction. However, pursuant to the Taejon Agreement of 1950 between the then South Korean government and the United Nations Command, the operational control of the Korean armed forces is in the hands of the United Nations Commander, who is also always the Commander of the United States Forces in Korea. At the time of the 1961 coup, the United States commander complained that the movement of troops ordered by the conspirators was in breach of the Taejon agreement.

ROLE, COMMITMENT, DEPLOYMENT AND RECENT OPERATIONS

Role
In the late twentieth century, the military role of armies on the border between the communist and non-communist world has been diminished by the nuclear factor, while the political role of armies everywhere in the developing world has greatly increased. The political role of the army of South Korea, still a developing country, is self-evident but its military role remains, nevertheless, predominating. This is the consequence of the unsettled situation on the ceasefire line with North Korea, of the very large forces maintained by North Korea across it and of the evidence of the aggressive attitude maintained by the North Korean government. The army's role has therefore been defined officially as 'to ensure the success and realisation in peace of the Revitalising Reforms of the Nation (the programme of the 1961 coup leaders), to be the driving force for the advance of the Korean people and the restraining force against the outbreak of another war and disorder. . . . In order to restrain and cope with any kind of enemy surprise invasion, *and also to get final victory in any case* (italics supplied), immense combat strength should always be maintained in accordance with the "strength against strength" principle.' The army is thus maintained at a very high state of combat readiness, can manoeuvre in a strength of two corps (i.e. at the level of a major NATO or Warsaw Pact exercise) and is practised not only in conventional operations but also in mountain warfare and airborne, amphibious and snowfield operations 'applicable to the geographic and climatic characteristics of the Korean peninsula'.

The army also plays an important social role, both through training of the conscript classes, and in the organisation of the Homeland Reserve Forces, a militia largely based on the villages which benefit from the *Saemul* (New Village Movement). This is a programme of rural improvement through government investment and self-help, which touches to some degree every one of South Korea's 35,000 villages.

Commitment
South Korea is the beneficiary of the Mutual Defense Agree-

ment of 1953 with the USA, which binds the USA to provide the South Korean armed forces with equipment and training. It is also the beneficiary of a 16-nation (those which committed combat troops to the war) agreement of July, 1953 which pledges those nations again to unite and resist renewed aggression across the ceasefire line. The ceasefire line is supervised by the United Nations Command, of which the United States Commander in South Korea is also Commander, and by the United Nations Commission for the Unification and Rehabilitation of Korea, set up in 1950, though its duties are limited to observation and to reporting to the General Assembly. A number of the powers which fought under the United Nations Command (e.g. Britain) also maintain token forces which do duty at the ceasefire centre at Panmunjon in the Demilitarised Zone.

South Korea does not itself reciprocate these military commitments, since they are given to deter a specific threat, namely the violation of the country's territorial integrity. In token of its special relationship with the USA, however, it maintained two divisions (the Tiger and White Horse) and a marine brigade in South Vietnam during the American campaign there. In order to maximise the army's combat experience, about 300,000 Korean soldiers were rotated through those forces.

Deployment

The major combat formations of the army are deployed directly on the 151 mile ceasefire line. The western sector, where the line approaches to within 25 miles of Seoul, the capital and home of 7,000,000 inhabitants, is garrisoned by the Third Army of 10 divisions; the eastern sector is garrisoned by the First Army of eight divisions. The interior of the country, divided into four district commands, is garrisoned by the Second Army, whose units are chiefly training units. The islands and estuary of the Han river, west of Seoul, and the five islands collectively known as the Peklyong Do, close to the North Korean coast, are garrisoned by the Marine Corps, but also come under the United Nations Command.

Recent Operations

Since the war of 1950–53, and apart from the operations of the Tiger and White Horse Divisions in Vietnam, the South Korean army has not been engaged in operations. It has, however, had to cope with numerous North Korean transgressions of its borders, both by land and sea, notably in the period 1966–9. Since 1974 its engineers have also been engaged in detecting and destroying a series of major tunnels driving under the ceasefire line by the North Koreans, intended apparently as a means of moving an invading force of many thousands from North to South in a few hours.

ORGANISATION

Arms of Service

The internal organisation of the army is modelled on that of the United States army. Its main arms of service are infantry, artillery, armour, engineers, signal corps, ordnance corps and quartermaster corps. The marine corps is a separate entity under the administrative control of the navy.

Operational

The army is organised operationally into the First, Second and Third Armies. The Second is a training and administrative organisation, active in the interior of the country which is divided into four district commands. Major establishments which come under the Second Army are the Military Academy, the Army College, the Joint Services College, the War College, the recruit training centres, the service and technical schools,

the Combat Arms Command, the Logistic Command and the rear divisions. The Second Army is responsible for the security of the interior and the coast. The First and Third Armies provide the garrison of the ceasefire line and control the army's main fighting strength. Their 18 divisions are organised into five corps. The divisions are of the infantry type, apparently organised on traditional 'triangular' lines of three infantry regiments of three battalions, with three field- and one medium-artillery battalions. The armour is separately organised in two armoured brigades, in which most of the APCs are apparently deployed, and seven independent tank battalions. There are also two independent infantry brigades, five airborne brigades (although there is aircraft lift for less than one at a time), 30 independent artillery battalions, a missile battalion with Honest John missiles and two Nike Hercules air-defence battalions. The Marine Corps is organised in one division. A recent addition to the army's strength is the American TOW anti-tank missile, with which one battery in each division is now equipped.

RECRUITMENT, TRAINING AND RESERVES

Recruitment is by universal conscription. The term of service in the army and marines is 30 months.

Recruit training is carried out initially in the recruit training centres; specialist training is given at the arms schools, of which the Infantry, Artillery and Signals Schools are located at Kwangju in the south-west.

Regular officers are trained at the Korean Military Academy (run on West Point lines) and subsequently at the Staff College at Taegu in the south-east. Conscript and short-service officers are trained at the Third Military Academy.

Trained reserves now number 1,100,000 for the army and marines. The reserve mobilisation scheme is not made public, but it is presumed that on mobilisation some reservists would go to form new units in the Second Army and others would be used as reinforcements and replacements in the First and Third. In theory the reserves would treble the army's fighting strength, but only the younger reservists would be suitable for combat units, while equipment is lacking to fit out any sizeable number of reserve formations.

The Homeland Reserve Forces, 750,000 strong, are village home guards, who could not be used outside their localities, but would be useful to check guerrilla activity, which the North is expected to set in motion by the infiltration of small units by land, sea and air. Its guerrilla campaign behind the lines during the Korean war required a major diversion of United Nations effort to counter it.

EQUIPMENT AND ARMS INDUSTRY

The South Korean armed forces were built up with American equipment, and still exclusively use it. Rapid industrialisation in the last 10 years has allowed the country, however, to manufacture some items under licence and to assemble and refurbish others. Rifles and machine-guns are manufactured (Colt has recently opened a factory at Pusan), together with their ammunition, and some artillery, including the 155mm howitzer, though the latter is not yet in mass production. At the beginning of 1976 the government requested permission of the Americans to begin manufacturing the M-60 tank, but are still confined to refurbishing their M-47 and M-48 models, the guns of which they are anxious to change from the 90mm to the 105mm. Observers expect Korean industry soon to be capable of assembling aircraft and helicopters, though not perhaps the modern models which the air force needs to replace its ageing jet fighters. A first instalment of F-165 is now on order from the USA.

Rifle: 5.56mm M-16 (USA; Korean made)
Machine-gun: 7.62mm M-60 GPMG (USA; Korean made)
Mortar: 60mm M-2 (USA; Korean made), 81mm M-1 (USA; Korean made) and 4.2in M-30 (USA)
Anti-armour weapons: 57mm M-18 recoilless rifle (USA), 75mm M-20 recoilless rifle (USA), 106mm M-40 recoilless rifle (USA) and TOW guided missile (USA)
Air-defence weapons: 40mm L/60 and L/70 guns (Swedish Bofors; made in USA), Vulcan 20mm (USA; 66in Korea), Hawk missile (USA; 80in service) and Nike Hercules missile (USA; 100 in service)
Artillery: 105mm M-101 howitzer (USA), 155mm M-114 howitzer (USA; some Korean made), 155mm M-59 gun (USA), 175mm M-107 SP gun (USA), 203mm M-115 howitzer (USA) and Honest John missile (2000 artillery pieces in service)
Armour: M-113 APCs (USA; 500 in service), and M-47 and M-48 medium tanks (USA; 840 in service); some M-60 tanks are also in service
Aircraft: the army is dependent for air support on the air force, but the latter is effectively its air arm. It has 33 Phantom and 270 F-5 strike aircraft, but needs to replace its 50 Sabre interceptors with a more modern model. It also has 44 transports and 13 helicopters, with 80 more of the latter on order.

RANK, DRESS AND DISTINCTIONS

Ranks and badges of rank are indentical with those of the American army, and uniforms are very similar; the cadets of the Military Academy wear West Point-style grey and white on ceremonial occasions.

CURRENT DEVELOPMENTS

The decision of the Carter administration in February, 1977 to withdraw the Second Infantry Division from Korea was rescinded by the Reagan administration. In 1954 the strength of the American army in Korea was reduced to two divisions, forming with support units the Eighth Army. One of these divisions was subsequently withdrawn in 1971, to the loudly voiced alarm of the South Korean government. The withdrawal of the second would have left only one air-defence brigade in the country and one wing of the Fifth Air Force, based on Osan and Kunsan on the west coast. However, air, naval and marine forces in the Pacific can be deployed towards, or into, South Korea at short notice if necessary, as they were in August, 1976 when the killing of two American soldiers by North Koreans in the Demilitarised Zone of the ceasefire line brought a squadron of F-111 fighters from the continental United States, Phantoms and RF4s from Okinawa and B52 strategic bombers from Guam, within a week, as well as a naval surface squadron from the Seventh Fleet.

Air support is necessary to the South Koreans, since it is the one respect in which its forces are inferior to the North's. But even more important is the continuing presence of the United Nations Command, since its Commander is also the United States Forces Commander in the country. Because he exercises operational control over the South Korean armed forces, under the 1950 Taejon agreement, the United States automatically becomes involved in the defence of the country if the North invades. The phased withdrawal of all American ground troops from the country over a period of time, which the Carter administration had also adumbrated, would have left him without a convincing role, and perhaps led eventually to the dismantling of the United Command. It is a prospect which deeply perturbs the South Korean government.

Its capacity for self-defence is nevertheless impressive. The ceasefire line, which runs through the 2½ mile-wide Demilitarised Zone, is backed by a belt of fixed defences running back for 30 miles and manned by virtually the whole of the South Korean army. Its plan is to hold the line inflexibly, and destroy any North Korean invading force on it. In 1975 the American commander outlined a strategy for such a campaign, which would be concluded successfully in 9 days. In the first five, 1000 sorties a day would be flown by American strategic and tactical aircraft over the battle zone, to inflict crushing losses on the attackers, heightened by continuous artillery bombardment, and in the remaining 4 days South Korean infantry would restore the front. South Korean superiority in tanks and anti-tank weapons would ensure the failure of armoured penetrations.

American ground disengagement threatened this plan of some conviction. So too did the discovery, first made in November, 1974 of the existence of tunnels dug under the Demilitarised Zone from North to South, of dimensions which would allow the passage of thousands of troops an hour. About 18 tunnels are believed to exist. The South is exposed in another direction – that of the islands of the Peklyong Do group, which are closer to North Korean territory than to South Korea. They are heavily garrisoned and the South is determined to fight for them, if attacked, but would have difficulty in defending them.

In view of the diminished security of the South, and the continuing aggressive attitude of the North, Japan (South Korea's most important trading partner) has moved units of its army, traditionally concentrated in the north of their islands nearest Russia, to the south where they would be closer to South Korea. Japan is, however, unwilling at present to increase its defence spending to a level where it could act as an external guarantor of Korean territorial integrity. Moreover, its constitution forbids it to deploy its forces outside the national territory, while public opinion would find it difficult to support the provision of military assistance to a regime so openly authoritarian as the South Korean. South Korea remains, therefore, almost alone in the world, a country in which the army's ability to defend its frontiers against large-scale conventional attack is of prime importance in considering its future. No-one is more aware of this than the South Koreans themselves, who recognise that their new prosperity depends upon convincing foreign investors and traders of their ability to defend themselves.

The government and country has successfully surmounted the most dramatic and unsettling event in domestic affairs since 1950 – the assassination of President Park by the head of the Korean CIA, Kim Jae Kyu, on October 16th 1979. Kim's motives appeared to be those of pique at President Park's preference for the advice of others, as well as at accusations that the KCIA was not effectively repressing disorders which troubled the country in 1979; his intention appears to have been to invest the KCIA with political authority, leaving the army in charge only of defence affairs. Kim was, however, swiftly arrested by General Chung Seung Hwa, Chief of Staff, and tried for murder. Martial law was declared and General Chung appointed Martial Law Administrator on October 27th. The National Assembly decided meanwhile on a revision of the Constitution, aimed at a measure of liberalisation, and the National Conference for Unification announced the election to the presidency of the only candidate, Choi Kyu Ha, on December 6th. President Choi was a civilian and former diplomat, and a representative of a less authoritarian approach to government. But immediately after his election an attempt was made by General Chun, head of the Army Security

Command, to arrest General Chung on the grounds that he was party to Kim's assassination of President Park, and General Chung was subsequently imprisoned for complicity. General Chun's unathorised action went unpunished and President Choi was obliged to appoint generals to the key ministries of Justice, Interior and Defence at his insistence.

Internal disturbances continued, which the government accused political parties of fomenting. The arrest of a leader of the opposition New Democratic Party, Kim Dae Jung, provoked a major outburst in Kwangju, and led to an intensification of martial law repression. But continuing dissension caused the downfall of the civilian presidency in August and Choi's replacement with General Chun, who had added command of the KCIA to his appointments since his coup of the previous December.

President Chun was elected for a seven-year term in February 1981. The internal condition of the country — high economic achievement, authoritarian government and sporadic outbreaks of disorder — seems unchanged since the rule of President Park. The army remains the strongest and most important institution in the country.

John Keegan

KUWAIT

HISTORY AND INTRODUCTION

Kuwait began as one of a number of small fishing and trading settlements along the north coast of the Arabian peninsula, with a population related by clan and tribal links to those of Nejd in Saudi Arabia and the adjacent areas of desert Iraq. It eventually fell under Ottoman suzerainty, but retained its own autonomy under the government of the Sheikh, invariably selected from the leading Sabah clan. It passed painlessly under British protection in 1889, at a time when British influence was displacing Ottoman all along the southern shores of the upper Gulf. A treaty between Britain and Turkey in which the latter relinquished its claim to rule Kuwait from the neighbouring Basra Vilayet of Iraq was negotiated in 1913, but the outbreak of World War I prevented ratification and left the issue unresolved.

The subsequent discovery of oil in Kuwait made it the first of the small Gulf States to experience the benefits and problems of enormous wealth suddenly bestowed on a poor and backward community. The money allowed Kuwait to create the Middle East's first comprehensive welfare State by the 1950s, at a time when its neighbours were still just beginning their development, and the longer times it has had to reach its present level has allowed the country to avoid some of the more severe physical and psychological effects of ultra-rapid modernisation. It is today unquestionably the most mature and evenly developed of the Gulf States, and pre-eminent amongst them in commerce and finance.

Like all the small Arab States on the Gulf with the exception of oil-poor and relatively populous Oman, Kuwait has a majority of foreigners in its population: some 700,000 of the 1,160,000 residents are not citizens, and a substantial minority of these are not even Arabs. The proportion of non-citizens still shows a gradually rising trend, despite official concern about it, especially since a very large proportion of the foreign Arabs (perhaps half) are Palestinians. In fact, however, the ratio of citizens to foreigners is relatively high for the region, reflecting the longer period of prosperity which has produced an educated generation of native Kuwaitis. Moreover, the Egyptians and Palestinians who man much of the civil service and social services could not be dispensed with in any case, and have no history of meddling in local politics, which is purely a Kuwaiti matter. The estimated 130,000 Indians and Pakistanis in Kuwait, originally imported as temporary labour for specific projects for the most part, show every sign of becoming permanent as the sole source of semi-skilled labour for general construction and Kuwait's new industries, in which almost no Kuwaiti citizens are willing to work; these Asians have no political rights and dramatically lower living standards, and could become a serious source of unrest in the future.

Kuwait received its independence from Britain in 1961, and was immediately plunged into crisis when the regime in neighbouring Iraq resurrected the old Ottoman claim to Kuwait on its own behalf. The immediate crisis was overcome by emergency reinforcements of British troops, later replaced by an Arab League force, which dissuaded Baghdad from pursuing its claim by military means, but the long-term consequence was a rapid expansion of the small internal security-oriented army that had been trained by the British, into a comparatively large force equipped and trained for conventional battle. It is a process still underway today, and can be expected to continue for some time to come.

Internal security is not seen as a serious problem for the army, since the great majority of the country is empty desert, the population being concentrated in Kuwait City and a few much smaller towns. The ruling dynasty remains the supreme repository of political authority as well as the mainstay of the officer corps, especially in the more senior ranks. Many of the officers were trained at Sandhurst, and Britain continued to be the main provider of both training and military equipment until quite recently.

External security, on the other hand, is a serious problem because of border disputes, but even more because of Kuwait's highly exposed geographical situation. It is a very small and unpopulous country sandwiched between the three most powerful States of the region: Iraq, Saudi Arabia and Iran (which lies across the Gulf with only a few tens of miles of Iraqi coastline intervening). All three of these countries are heavily armed, and each is intensely suspicious, if not openly hostile, towards the other two. Moreover, the 'top' of the Gulf where Kuwait lies is where the most sensitive regions of each of its neighbours are located: Saudi Arabia's main oil-fields lying just south along the coast, Iraq's narrow outlet to the sea through the Shatt al-Arab and Iran's main oil-producing region. It lends a certain urgency to Kuwait's attempts to stay on at least moderately good terms with all three, and certainly explains why the country has always been the most enthusiastic supporter of that evergreen mirage — a Gulf mutual security pact.

Kuwait's specific border problems with Iraq are far more acute than with Saudi Arabia, although Baghdad abandoned its categorical claim to all of Kuwait in 1965. The longest standing dispute is over the Iraqi occupation of Bubiyan and Warba islands, traditionally Kuwaiti islands which lie across the exit from the Shatt al-Arab into the Gulf. This river, formed by the union of the Tigris and Euphrates in their lower courses, is Iraq's only means of maritime access to the Gulf and Indian Ocean, as nowhere along its 50km coastline is suitable for a port on the Gulf proper.

The Shatt al-Arab has growing strategic significance for Iraq since the pipelines taking oil exports westwards to the Mediterranean across Syria and Turkey are regarded as politically insecure (and indeed the Syrian line has been unusable since the beginning of the Lebanese civil war). The completion of a pipeline from the northern oilfields to the port of Fao on the Shatt in 1975 has therefore made this route as important for Iraq's oil exports as it already is for general imports, and the port of Umm Qasr opposite the island of Warba is the Iraqi navy's only base and the sole regular port of call in the Gulf for the Soviet navy. In these circumstances Iraq has made it absolutely clear that it will not evacuate Warba and Bubiyan islands, which could be used as bases from which to blockade the Shatt.

Kuwait closed its border with Iraq in 1972, and in the following year Iraqi forces occupied the Kuwaiti border post at Samita. Further forays into Kuwait's territory by Iraqi forces occurred in 1976, and relations between Kuwait and Baghdad were virtually non-existent. The contacts that began between the two governments in 1977 have led to a considerable easing of tensions (*see* Current Developments), but Iraq unquestionably remains Kuwait's primary defence concern.

Relations with its other large neighbour, Saudi Arabia, have not been without difficulties either, however. There was a lengthy dispute until 1966 over the demarcation of the neutral zone between the two countries, which contains rich oil reserves. Since the 1966 partition each country has administered its own share of the neutral zone as part of its own territory, while treating the on-shore oil production as an integral whole to be shared equally between the two. The question of the demarcation of territorial waters off the neutral zone was never decided, however, as Kuwait resists Saudi Arabia's claim that the rich off-shore oil reserves there should also be shared equally on the grounds that the territorial waters of the two countries were never in dispute.

From the middle of 1976 a Saudi–Kuwaiti joint commission met each month to discuss this dispute about the ownership of seabed oil reserves off the neutral zone, with Riyadh insisting that the 1966 agreement required equal sharing of them and Kuwait insisting that a resolution of the issue must await the long-delayed conclusion of the UN conference on the law of the sea. Kuwaiti–Saudi relations deteriorated sharply after differences over oil pricing policies at the December, 1976 OPEC conference, and in June, 1977 Saudi Arabian forces occupied the two offshore islands of Umm al-Maradem and Gharo in the disputed area.

While Kuwaiti–Iraqi relations have often been openly hostile, however, Kuwait's relationship with Saudi Arabia is never allowed to deteriorate to such a level. This is partly because Saudi Arabia is seen as the ultimate deterrent to any Iraqi move against Kuwait, and partly because the two ruling groups share common political perspectives both internally and internationally. Indeed, as Saudi Arabia's steady ascent to the position of local superpower in the Arabian peninsula has proceeded, so has its ability to influence events in the Gulf sheikhdoms; it is widely believed that Saudi disapproval for the faintly radical sentiments being expressed by some Kuwaiti parliamentarians was largely responsible for the Ruler's decision to dissolve the elected Kuwaiti National Assembly in August, 1976. This desire not to offend the Saudis is the main reason that Kuwait has not officially protested against the Saudi occupation of the offshore islands, and indeed formally denies that it has occurred.

In internal affairs, Kuwait's main concern is the political orientations of its large Palestinian resident population, and their influence on some Kuwaiti politicians. After 1976 it was evident that some Palestinians in senior civil service positions were being replaced by Egyptians, who were considered to be more reliable politically, but there have been no deportations. Kuwait contributes large sums of money to the Palestinian Liberation Organisation as part of its strategy for purchasing immunity from Palestinian radicalism on its own territory, and probably has the ability to foresee and control any outbreaks of Palestinian political activism on its own soil that might endanger its internal stability.

In external affairs, Kuwait is the most prominent and persistent volunteer for the post of mediator in almost all Gulf disputes, and is the most acceptable local choice for most of its quarrelsome neighbours. The great goal of Kuwait's foreign policy is the creation of a Gulf mutual security pact embracing all the littoral States, which it sees as a potential guarantee of the status quo, but its efforts have so far had little success.

In the meantime, its not inconsiderable armed forces (onefifth the size of Saudi Arabia's but with a greater combat capability than any other Arab Gulf State) will continue to expand. While they would not be able to defend Kuwait against all-out invasion by either Iraq or Iran (the two States

that figure most prominently in Kuwaiti defence contingency planning), they are large enough to ensure that no take-over could occur without a serious fight.

STRENGTH AND BUDGET

The Kuwaiti armed forces grew in strength from 600 in 1954 to 2500 in 1961, and to 7000 5 years later, and now stand at 12,400 officers and men. Conscription has now been introduced and further expansion is to be expected, but it should be borne in mind that the recruiting base is relatively narrow, consisting only of those 400,000 residents who are actually Kuwaiti citizens.

Defence spending in 1981 amounted to $1,300,000,000 of a GNP of $30,700,000,000. Following a major border clash with Iraq in 1973, however, a supplementary defence budget of $1,500,000,000 was introduced to pay for the rapid expansion of Kuwait's armed forces. A second special allocation of $2,800,000,000 was made when this was expended in early 1976, and a further supplementary defence budget of $1,500,000,000 was announced in March, 1977. Thus Kuwait's actual military budget since 1973, including capital expenditures, has not been the figure contained in the regular budget, fluctuating around the $200,000,000–$300,000,000 level, but more like $1,000,000,000 per year.

COMMAND AND CONSTITUTIONAL STATUS

The Ruler of Kuwait, Shaikh Jaber Ahmad Jaber al-Sabah, is the Commander-in-Chief of the Armed Forces, and the constitution (now suspended) gave him exclusive power to commission and discharge officers. The Minister of Defence and the Interior from 1968–78 was Shaikh Saad Abdullah Salem al-Sabah, from the other main branch of the al-Sabah family who presided over the expansion of the Kuwaiti armed forces from an internal security organisation to a fully-fledged external defence force; in February, 1978 he was formally designated Crown Prince and heir to the throne. The Chief of Staff is generally a member of the ruling Sabah clan.

The constitution that was partly suspended in 1976 is still officially in effect except for the provisions regarding the National Assembly. The constitution is now being revised by a working committee drawn mainly from the Council of Ministers, an appointed body, and there is speculation that the National Assembly could be revived in some form in the near future. The reality of power in Kuwait, however, especially as regards control over the armed forces, is that the Royal Family rules. Most senior command positions in the armed services are held by officers who are related to the family by blood or by marriage, and the highest positions are invariably held by men who are themselves powerful within the family. The internal security forces are commanded by an army officer.

ROLE, COMMITMENT, DEPLOYMENT AND RECENT OPERATIONS

The Kuwaiti armed forces are still to find a commitment in a possible agreement over Gulf security. Token armoured units served on the Suez front during the 1973 Arab–Israeli War, and there are recurrent alarms on the Iraqi frontier, where much of the ground forces are deployed. Although the official enemy is Israel, the actual focus of concern for Kuwaiti military planners is Iraq, which raised a claim to all of Kuwait at its independence in 1961, and still has serious border disputes with the country. Despite the recent easing of tensions this will continue to be the first defence priority.

The only other countries that are of direct security interest to Kuwait are its other neighbour, Saudi Arabia, and its near-neighbour, Iran. It is extremely improbable that military operations could ever occur between Kuwait and Saudi Arabia, however strained their relations may occasionally become, and the Saudis probably do not figure in contingency planning in the Kuwait General Staff except as possible allies against Iraq. Kuwait is also careful to maintain good relations with Iran, but there is undoubtedly a certain suspicion of Iran's intentions in all the Arab Gulf States.

While the Kuwait armed forces are certainly strong enough to defend their borders, territorial waters and air-space against limited incursions, even after the present expansion envisaged by the 7 year Defence Development Plan adopted in 1976 is completed, they will not be able to defend the country against an all-out Iranian or Iraqi onslaught. They would, however, be able to offer serious enough resistance to make it impossible for a surprise attack, launched without evident mobilisation and concentration of forces, to overrun the country in just one or two days, and thus could win the time for other forces to come to Kuwait's aid. That is probably their principal justification.

ORGANISATION

The 10,000 strong army is organised into two armoured brigades and three mechanised infantry brigades, while the 1900 man air force (not including expatriates) is operationally divided into one interceptor squadron, two fighter—bomber squadrons and three helicopter squadrons. One of the helicopter squadrons, equipped with Pumas, is devoted to troop transport, assault and logistical support; one of the two Gazelle squadrons is employed for observation, liaison and communications purposes, and the other is equipped with HOT missiles and dedicated to the anti-tank role. The small navy follows the usual pattern of naval organisation, and is all concentrated at a single base.

The internal detail of squadron, brigade and battalion structure, etc. conforms closely to the British model.

RECRUITMENT, TRAINING AND RESERVES

The officer corps is recruited mainly from among the ruling clan and related tribal groups, in order to ensure the loyalty of the forces to the regime. Many of the senior officers have been trained at Sandhurst, and no expense is spared in the training of any Kuwaiti officer, but some doubts must prevail as to whether the professional quality of the officer corps is uniformly as high as it might be if recruitment and promotion were more open to competition. However the same comment is true for almost every other State in the region.

Manpower for the rapidly expanding forces is being provided, since April, 1978 by the application of the new compulsory military service law. Under it all male Kuwaiti citizens are liable to perform 2 years military service between the ages of eighteen and thirty, thus yielding a potential conscript strength, additional to the existing regular component, of some 10,000 troops. Conscripts are normally inducted at the age of eighteen, although exemptions for various valid reasons and deferments for further education are generally available. The law has become necessary because it was proving impossible to attract sufficient Kuwaiti recruits for the planned expansion of the forces on a volunteer basis despite the very generous pay and conditions of service (Kuwaitis enjoy similar benefits in civil life), and because the government was unwilling to recruit volunteers from amongst the many alien residents.

Kuwait intends to create new military colleges and technical schools as part of its Defence Development Plan, but at the moment it remains heavily dependent upon foreign training assistance. Many Kuwaiti officers are sent abroad for training, particularly to Jordan, Pakistan, Britain and the USA, and a variety of foreign training missions are to be found in the country. The USA provides the training for the 1850 Kuwaiti troops who operate and support the Hawk missile systems and A-4 fighter—bombers Kuwait has bought from them, and 125 British officers are in the country to assist Kuwait in the operation of British-built aircraft and of its British-equipped armoured forces. France provides similar training for Kuwaiti military personnel operating Mirage interceptors.

Four Egyptian advisory teams are operating in Kuwait, training the army in infantry tactics, coastal defence and special forces techniques, and a number of Jordanian officers have been lent to Kuwait in various capacities. A Syrian military team is advising Kuwait on the introduction of conscription, while Pakistan is providing training aid in the development of Kuwait's nascent navy. About 20 Soviet military experts led by a general arrived in April, 1978 to oversee the training of Kuwaitis in the operation of the SA-6 and SA-7 SAM systems which are being acquired from the Soviet Union.

There is not at this time a formal reserve system in Kuwait, but it is anticipated that one will be introduced after the first batch of conscripts complete their military service in 1980.

EQUIPMENT AND ARMS INDUSTRY

The main armoured strength of the Kuwaiti army is 160 Chieftain, 70 Vickers and 10 Centurion medium tanks. Other armoured vehicles include 100 Saladin armoured cars, 80 Ferret scout cars and 97 M-113 and 130 Saracen APCs. The artillery, disposes of 10 25 pounder guns and 80 AMX 155mm SP howitzers; it also has some Frog missiles. It possesses a variety of anti-tank guided weapons, including, HOT, TOW and Vigilant.

Further equipment on order, includes an undisclosed number of Scorpion light tanks from Britain and $100,000,000 of SA-6 and SA-7 mobile SAM systems from the Soviet Union. There have been discussions with the USA on the purchase of an integrated command and control system for an estimated $85,000,000, and it is believed that Kuwait also plans to buy an undisclosed number of M-60 tanks and M-109 howitzers from the USA.

The air force is responsible for the operation of the 50 Improved Hawk missiles that provide the long-range SAM defences. They are grouped in four mobile batteries, but are based at fixed points on Kuwait's territory.

There is a very large programme of military construction underway in Kuwait, which includes a $100,000,000 military camp 20 miles from Kuwait City to be built by an Indian firm, a $29,000,000 naval base to be completed at the end of 1979 and a new air base being constructed by a consortium of Yugoslav firms.

Kuwait has no defence industry of its own, and has so far refused to join the Arab Organisation for Industrialisation (AOI) which is being funded by Saudi Arabia, Qatar and the United Arab Emirates to build advanced weapons in Egypt for the Arab countries. Kuwait's contribution to the AOI's founding capital has been set at $400,000,000, which was more than Kuwait was prepared to risk in an undertaking of whose management and commercial viability it was equally doubtful.

RANK, DRESS AND DISTINCTIONS

The army wears khaki. Ranks and badges of rank follow the British system.

CURRENT DEVELOPMENTS

The rapid modernisation and expansion of the Kuwaiti armed forces will doubtless continue for the next few years, as money is no constraint and conscription will supply the needed extra manpower. It would be reasonable to foresee a total strength of over 20,000 by the early 1980s, which should be more than enough to cope with any counter-insurgency problems – especially in terrain as inhospitable to insurgents as Kuwait's – and adequate to enable Kuwait to resist for 2 or 3 days against the improbable eventuality of a major military attack by one of its neighbours, in which time it could hope for aid from friends to arrive. The army by then will be a well-balanced, mobile force consisting largely of armoured and mechanised elements, including about 250 tanks. The air force, with perhaps 75 modern combat aircraft and comprehensive SAM coverage, likewise would be up to its task, and the navy should be nearing a match for Iraq's in the FPGBs which are most significant vessels in the narrow and shallow waters at the head of the Gulf.

In fact Kuwait's relations with Iraq, for long extremely tense, have recently undergone a considerable improvement. Following a visit to Baghdad by the Kuwait Defence Minister in July, 1977 the border between the two countries was reopened for the first time since 1972, and both sides withdrew their forces up to 10 miles from the frontier in what was described as a 'disengagement'. A joint ministerial committee was appointed to discuss the settlement of outstanding border disputes, principally the Iraqi occupation of Warba and Bubiyan islands and the area around the Samita border post seized by Iraq in 1973.

On the more serious of those issues, Iraq has indicated that it recognises Kuwaiti sovereignty over the islands, but that it is not prepared to withdraw its forces from them since they overlook the access from the head of the Gulf to its only naval base at Umm Qasr. Baghdad has instead proposed to return the civil administration and internal security responsibilities on the islands to Kuwait, and merely to lease them for military purposes together with a land corridor on the south side of the channel from Umm Qasr to the area lying opposite Warba Island. (This land, still under Kuwaiti control, overlooks an area where ships which are travelling up the channel bound for Umm Qasr must pass through Kuwaiti territorial waters.) Kuwait is not opposed to this solution in principle, although the two countries are still in disagreement on the freedom of action that Iraqi forces should be allowed on the islands. A substantial impediment to any final agreement, however, is Saudi opposition to a measure which would legally guarantee Iraqi access to the Gulf.

Nevertheless, Kuwait has supported Iraq in the Gulf War and while offering to mediate between Iraq and Iran, has allowed Iraqi troops to cross its territory. Early in the war, Kuwaiti oil installations at Umm al-Aish, near the Iraq border, were bombed by Iranian aircraft, but Kuwait did not respond by military means. Its position appears to be one of genuine neutrality (if not perhaps impartiality) in the conflict.

Gwynne Dyer
John Keegan

LAOS

Little reliable information is available about the Lao People's Liberation Army. It was originally known as the army of the Pathet Lao when it operated against the French in the early 1950s. After 1954, when the country's neutrality was established by international agreement at Geneva, the eastern half of the country passed effectively into Pathet Lao hands, and large numbers of North Vietnamese troops, who had first entered the country in 1952, began to be stationed there. Fighting between the Pathet Lao and the Royal Laotian Army was endemic and, despite further international efforts in 1973 to arrange a peaceful settlement, culminated in 1975 in the final defeat of the royal government's forces. The Lao People's Liberation Army, which is about 46,000 strong, and organised into about 70 infantry battalions, is distributed throughout the countryside, which is believed to be divided into five military regions. There is said to be recruitment by conscription, but it would be a new departure in Laos. About 45,000 soldiers of the Vietnamese People's Army, which formerly controlled the Pathet Lao army (as it still does) are permanently stationed on Laotian territory and the Laotian army is trained, organised and equipped on Vietnamese lines.

A variety of French, American, Russian and Chinese equipment is in Laotian hands, including 25 Russian PT-76 and 10 American M-24 light tanks, some Russian BTR-40 and American M-113 APCs, field and medium artillery pieces, light and medium mortars, and recoilless rifles. The air force has about 36 aircraft, mostly American T-28 trainers equipped for ground attack, about 30 transports and 50 helicopters. It is doubtful if the American aircraft are now all operational.

John Keegan

LEBANON

HISTORY AND INTRODUCTION

The Lebanon owes its existence as a State separated from its natural Syrian hinterland to the presence in the Mount Lebanon area north of Beirut of an Arabic-speaking but Christian population, the Maronite Catholics, who had retreated to this mountainous stronghold as a refuge from Muslim domination even before the time of the Crusades. Unlike the other Christian Arabs, who are predominantly Orthodox, the Maronites have always identified themselves with the West and have not regarded themselves primarily as Arabs. (Thus, for example, the Greek Orthodox Christians of Syria generally supported Islam against the West during the Crusades, while the Maronites sided with the Crusaders.)

During the nineteenth century, when the entire area was ruled by the Ottoman Empire, France succeeded in winning certain rights of autonomy for the Christians of Mount Lebanon, and a recognition of itself as their special protector. This relationship was consummated after World War I, when both Syria and the Lebanon became French mandated territories. Faced with strong resistance from nascent Arab nationalism elsewhere in its new possessions, Paris found it convenient to rely on the support of the Maronite Christians in the coastal districts, and created for them the separate State of Lebanon in which they were a majority of the population. Even in the 1920s, however, this 'Greater Lebanon', extending well beyond the traditional confines of Mount Lebanon, contained a large Muslim minority occupying lands which France preferred to attach to the Lebanon for strategic reasons.

Two of the three factors which led to the utter collapse of the Lebanese State in the mid-1970s were thus implicit in its creation: the fact that it was carved out of Syria (which has never agreed to open an embassy in Beirut since independence, on the grounds that both States are part of 'Greater Syria'); and the fact that it had been gerrymandered to incorporate a variety of Muslim and non-Maronite Christian groups into a Maronite-dominated State. Although higher Muslim birth rates soon turned the Maronites, and then the Christians as a whole, into a minority in the country, the well-organised Maronite militias ensured that the Lebanon continued to operate on the original basis of Christian predominance after it proclaimed independence in 1941.

Christian suspicions that they were becoming a minority had led them to prevent the holding of any national census after the early 1930s — there has not been one to this day — in order that they could maintain the fiction of a six-to-five Christian majority and a consequent dominant position in the government, where offices were allocated on a confessional basis proportional to population. The National Pact of 1943 (concluded before French forces finally left the country in 1946) enshrined a constitution which was in the nature of a contractual agreement between the various politico—religious communities of the Lebanon, allocating shares of governmental power between them. Under it, both the President of the Republic and the Commander-in-Chief of the Armed Forces were always to be Maronite, the Prime Minister was to be Sunni Muslim, and various lesser offices were guaranteed to the Druze, Shi'ite, Greek Orthodox and other communities.

The ultimate guarantee of Maronite pre-eminence in this system despite their declining share of population was their control of the Lebanese armed forces. These grew out of the *Troupes Spéciales du Levant* which the French mandatory authorities had organised as an internal security force in greater Syria in the 1920s. The founders of the Lebanese army were trained as officers in the *Troupes Spéciales*, and were transferred by the French to the independent Lebanese government in 1946.

The Lebanese army was always primarily intended for internal security duties, but as soon as possible the task of actually policing the country was handed over to the gendarmerie while the army assumed the role of ultimate guarantor of the integrity of the Lebanese political system. In the first decade after the French withdrawal it had little to do, as the system worked tolerably well. Nominally democratic, it was actually a highly fragmented system in which the notables (*za'im*) of the various confessional communities, holding power of an almost feudal character over their own groups, bargained with each other until a consensus on policy was achieved — or not, in which case the constellation of alliances would be reshuffled once more.

Already in 1948, however, the third factor which was eventually to destroy this system had emerged: the State of Israel. The creation of Israel on the Lebanon's southern border had two consequences for the latter. First, it contributed greatly to the awakening of a pan-Arab nationalism, tending in the 1950s and 1960s to follow a Nasserist line, politically radical and strongly anti-Western. This current of sentiment affected the Muslims of Lebanon at least as much as Arabs elsewhere, and increasingly alienated them from the pro-Western Maronite community which had welcomed the creation of Israel. The leftist character of this Nasserist ideology accentuated the split in the Lebanon, since it tended to be Christians who dominated the country's burgeoning commercial sector, while the most deprived segments of the population were mainly Muslim.

The second consequence of the creation of Israel was to land the Lebanon with a very large Palestinian refugee population — now numbering about 400,000, or over 10% of the total Lebanese population of around 3,000,000. The full significance of this was not to be seen until the Palestinians became a well-organised and well-armed radical political force in the late 1960s, but their mere presence, in 14 large refugee camps dispersed throughout the south and centre of the country, was a substantial influence in raising the Arab nationalist consciousness of the Lebanese Muslims.

The Palestinians did not play a major role, however, in the civil war of 1958, the first sign that the unique Lebanese political structure was breaking down. The war was caused by the spread of Nasserist ideas amongst sections of the Muslim populace who had been further roused by the Anglo—French—Israeli aggression against Egypt in 1956, and were seeking to end the Lebanon's policy of avoiding involvement in the Arab—Israeli confrontation. This, of course, required the overthrow of Maronite Christian dominance in the government, and the large Maronite militias (which had been in existence since the 1930s) soon became involved in large-scale clashes with the Muslim leftist forces. The army was not able to contain the fighting, and only the intervention of the USA, which landed a force of Marines in the Lebanon, prevented the disintegration of the State in 1958.

General Fuad Shehab, who was elected President under

the American aegis before the United States troops were withdrawn, succeeded in restoring stability to the Lebanese system for a decade, but made no progress in achieving reform and modernisation of the country's institutions before he was succeeded by President Charles Helou in 1964. The parliamentary façade of the Lebanese political system continued to operate under Shehab and Helou, but officers of the Military Intelligence, operating through a highly organised network of agents, were in effective control and determined the outcome of parliamentary elections. It was no more than a holding operation, however, on behalf of a Maronite concept of the Lebanon where the Maronites themselves were now no more than one-third of the population. After the election of President Franjieh in 1969 this network of agents was dismantled, but it could probably not have contained the pressures which were destabilising the Lebanon by them in any case.

The key development which initiated the slide of the Lebanon into catastrophic civil war — the sole cause of all the subsequent trouble, in the opinion of most Maronites, though that is much too simple an explanation — was the creation of militant Palestinian guerrilla organisations in the camps in the latter 1960s. Not only did the Palestinian guerrillas soon come to constitute a State within a State, but their guerrilla raids into Israel and terrorist activities elsewhere repeatedly brought down Israeli retaliatory raids on the Lebanon. The first of these was in December, 1968 when Israeli commandos destroyed 13 civilian airliners on the ground at Beirut airport in reprisal for an attack on an Israeli airliner in Athens by Palestinians who had allegedly been trained in Lebanon. It soon became customary for Israel to attack targets in the Lebanon in response to any Palestinian guerrilla activity, whether originating there or not, since it was far easier and safer than mounting raids into the well-armed Arab confrontation States: between mid-1968 and mid-1974 Israel mounted 44 major attacks into the Lebanon, killing approximately 880 Palestinian and Lebanese civilians as well as some guerrillas.

These raids had disastrous consequences for the authority of the Lebanese State, which was repeatedly shown to be incapable of defending its citizens, and for the tenuous cohesion of Lebanese society. The Lebanese army carried out military operations in April and October, 1969 seeking to remove guerrillas from the southern border areas, which led to armed clashes, but these clashes caused severe rioting by pro-Palestinian mobs in all the major cities, forcing the resignation of the Prime Minister. In November, 1969 the Lebanese Army Chief of Staff was compelled to conclude the famous Cairo agreement with Yasir Arafat of the Palestine Liberation Organisation, granting the guerrillas autonomy in the refugee camps and in the southern border regions.

Lebanon enjoyed a brief respite after September, 1970 when the Palestinian organisations were severely weakened by their defeat and expulsion from Jordan, but the main effect of 'Black September' in the longer run was to make the Lebanon an even more important base of Palestinian operations, as the only country where they were still free from government control. A particularly bold Israeli attack in April, 1973, when 35 Israeli commandos entered Beirut and assassinated three of the main PLO leaders and nine bystanders, moved the army to try once again to break the power of the Palestinians. In the following month the Lebanese army attacked the camps around Beirut, even employing fighter—bombers against them, but the fighting was a stand-off, and a further psychological defeat for the army and the State. Ominously, right-wing Christian militias were reported to have joined in the fighting for the first time.

What happened between 1968 and 1975 was that the limited basis of intercommunal co-operation which had made the old Lebanon workable was comprehensively destroyed. The younger and more radical sections of the Lebanese Muslim population, resentful of the domination of the State by a Maronite minority, sympathetic to the Palestinian and Arab cause, and aroused by the incessant Israeli attacks, drifted rapidly away from their traditional conservative leaders and into a proliferating variety of socialist and Nasserist parties which sought the wholesale reorganisation and reorientation of the Lebanese State. This basic trend was accentuated by a number of other factors: the fact that the divisions between rich and poor, and between Christian and Muslim, tended to coincide to a large extent; the tremendous growth of Beirut as the financial and commercial capital of the Middle East, which sucked huge numbers of unskilled Muslim poor from the countryside into the very centre of power; and most of all, perhaps, the new sense of pride and confidence in the wealth and power of the Arab world after the 1973 war and the oil boycott, which made Lebanese Muslims more unwilling than ever to accept Christian hegemony in their country.

Almost all of these new leftist, mostly Muslim groups (though numbers of Greek Orthodox Christians, resentful of Maronite dominance, also joined them) became loosely associated in the National Movement, an umbrella organisation founded in 1969 by Kamal Jumblat. Jumblat was the outstanding leftist leader in the Lebanon since the early 1950s (although his actual power derived not from his Progressive Socialist Party but from his position as feudal leader of the Druze minority). In the traditional Lebanese way, many of these leftist parties began to create their own militias in the early 1970s, although the great growth of the leftist militias occurred only after the civil war had begun.

The National Movement, whose programming included the abolition of the confessional system in Lebanese politics, the reorganisation of the army, and amendment of the citizenship and electoral laws — all intended to destroy the control of the Christian minority and to bring the Palestinians fully into Lebanese politics — was the organisation which provided the main institutional link with the Palestinian groups. The mainstream Palestine Liberation Organisation held itself more aloof from attempts to overthrow the existing Lebanese system than the more radical Rejectionist groups like the Popular Front for the Liberation of Palestine (PFLP), but all the Palestinians had learned from their bitter experience in Jordan that they needed the support of the mass of the local population. Clearly, changing the Lebanon in the way desired by the National Movement would make it a better base for all Palestinians, while for the extreme leftist factions it was natural to ally themselves directly with predominantly Muslim groups like the Nasserites, Jumblat's PSP, the communists and so on.

To the Maronites who had always dominated the Lebanon, the threat posed by this alliance was absolutely clear (although, since before 1975 the bulk of the armed forces on the Muslim —leftist—Palestinian side were Palestinian, the Maronites tended to concentrate mostly on the Palestinian 'foreigners' who were threatening to take over the country). They also tended to view the conflict in religious terms, whereas in fact being either Muslim or Greek Orthodox Lebanese or a Palestinian of any religion — and many Palestinians are Christian — simply meant that one was likely to see oneself as disadvantaged in the Lebanon, and belonging also to the greater Arab world. Only Maronite Christians had any real cause to be loyal to the kind of Lebanon that had been created for their benefit, and which held itself aloof from wider Arab concerns.

The Maronites began preparing to defend that Lebanon from the National Movement and the Palestinians in the early 1970s. The two main existing Maronite militias, Camille

Chamoun's National Liberal Party 'Tigers' and Pierre Gemayel's *Kata'ib* (Phalange), grew rapidly in membership, and even before he became President in 1970 Suleyman Franjieh founded a new militia of his own, the Zghorta Liberation Army. By 1974 major arms shipments were arriving at the port of Jounieh, in the heartland of Maronite territory north of Beirut, and the Maronite leaders were actively preparing for a showdown with the Palestinians.

In essence, therefore, what had happened in the Lebanon by 1975 was that a combination of the Palestinian presence, Israeli attacks, Arab nationalist ideas and rapid social change had destroyed the position of the traditional conservative leaders of the Muslim communities who had participated in and profited from the Lebanese system, and had created a new Muslim—leftist—Palestinian coalition which potentially had the numbers and the armed strength to overthrow it. The Maronites, still under their traditional leaders, saw it coming, and recognised that they would receive neither aid nor sympathy from anywhere else in the region, and only sympathy at most from Western powers who were more concerned to cultivate the good will of Arab oil producers. The Maronites therefore decided in desperation to strike first, in the hope of eliminating the Palestinians whom they blamed for all the changes that threatened to overwhelm them.

The opening shots of the civil war were in a massacre of a busload of 27 Palestinians in Beirut in April, 1975 by Phalange gunmen, and for the first month or so the fighting was restricted to clashes between Maronite militias and the more radical Palestinian groups. By the early summer, however, the crisis had developed into a full-scale civil war right across the country, with Muslim, leftist and Palestinian groups associated with the National Movement fighting the Maronite militias loosely grouped together as the Lebanese Front defending the status quo. Extremist Palestinian groups like the PFLP, the PFLP—General Command and Arab Liberation Front were heavily involved in the fighting throughout 1975, although the mainstream organisation *Al-Fatah* managed to stay clear of most of it until the end of the year, but from July, 1975 the main burden of the war on the anti-Maronite side was borne by the Lebanese leftists and Muslim militias, which expanded with great rapidity once the shooting started.

Given the high degree of segregation of the various Lebanese communities in the rural areas and even in the cities, the fighting soon took on a strongly territorial character, concentrating first of all on the elimination of enclaves belonging to the rival community and the 'cleansing' of mixed-community urban neighbourhoods, which involved some appalling massacres. Beirut was soon sharply divided between the Christian eastern districts and the Muslim western parts, and only the largely Shi'ite deep south and the central areas of the Maronite territory escaped heavy fighting. Once underway, the fighting rapidly did take on most of the characteristics of a religious war, with the result that the most horrible atrocities were frequently committed against unarmed civilians by both sides. The rapidly growing expenditure on ever heavier weapons by both sides was mainly met by radical Arab States so far as the Muslim—leftist coalition was concerned (Libya alone contributed $30,000,000—$40,000,000 during 1975), and on the Maronite side by a levy of 10 Lebanese pounds per family per month. Both sides supplemented these funds by robbing and looting banks and other commercial enterprises and by extortion. Maronite arms expenditure in 1975—6 was estimated at up to $600,000,000, spent mainly on the private arms market, but in the latter stages of the war militias were receiving large amounts of direct military aid from Egypt, and later from Israel, through Jounieh, the only port under their control. Muslim—leftist arms came principally from Iraq, Syria (at some stages of the war) and Libya.

There had been a considerable erosion of the dominant Maronite position in the army officer corps during the years 1958—75, but the high command remained a predominantly Christian organisation. The army's initial strategy was to hold itself aloof from the fighting, waiting for a decisive moment to commit its 17,000 men in defence of the status quo. The result, however, was that the bulk of the army simply melted away by desertion, its officers and men either retiring to their home districts or joining one of the rival militia organisations. Attempts to commit the armed forces at the climax of the war's first phase in January, 1976, when the Lebanese air force was used against Palestinian enclaves, simply led to the army's final fragmentation into four separate organisations (for details, see below.)

By the end of 1975, it had become clear to the Maronite leadership that they lacked the military strength to destroy the Muslim—Palestinian alliance and recreate the traditional Lebanese political system. They then modified their strategy and tried to set up a separate Christian State based on Mount Lebanon and the northern coast, with access to the port of Beirut and the Christian eastern parts of the city. This decision to seek partition, however, changed the character of the war, for the mainstream Palestinian guerrilla groups now committed their forces. This was partly because, as part of their strategy for consolidating their territory, the Maronites blockaded and attacked the Palestinian refugee camps in their prospective territory in January, 1976, but the PLO would have been compelled to intervene in the fighting directly in any case to prevent the creation of a Christian State in their rear which would inevitably be pro-Israeli.

More importantly, Syria, which had hitherto encouraged its traditional leftist clients while seeking to avoid damaging its new friendly links with France and the United States or provoking the Israelis, now intervened against the Christian forces. In January, 1976 it sent units of its Palestine Liberation Army (which is wholly loyal to Damascus, and equipped and organised to the same standards as the Syrian regular army) into Lebanon to forestall the Christian plan. Under this new and far greater pressure from the Palestinians and the Syrians, the Christians were soon clearly losing the war, and readily accepted a ceasefire at the end of January, 1976.

From this point on it was the Syrians who dominated the war in the Lebanon, and the key to their seemingly capricious changes of policy and alliance within the Lebanese tangle is to be sought in their fixed and long-standing purpose: to convert the Lebanon into an obedient satellite, as a way-station on the road to the recreation of 'Greater Syria' and as strategically vital territory which could protect the flank of Syrian defences on the Golan Heights while simultaneously opening the long-term possibility of creating a new front against Israel if necessary. They have always possessed the sheer military power to establish their control over the Lebanon by force, of course, but at all stages of the war they had to act with considerable caution because of the possibility of a violent Israeli military reaction.

At no time did Syria's aims coincide with those of even the moderate Palestinian groups (whose activities within Syria itself are very strictly controlled and confined), but during the first 8 months of the Lebanese civil war the Muslim—leftist—Palestinian coalition enjoyed Syrian support, including arms and financial aid. When it became clear in January, 1976 that this coalition was unlikely to be able to achieve fully its goal of creating an 'Arab' Lebanon, and that the most probable outcome would be the partition of the country and the emergence of a pro-Israeli Christian State flanking Syria's defences, Damascus felt compelled to escalate to direct intervention with its own Palestinian forces. Having stopped the Maronites short of partition and achieved a shaky ceasefire, Damascus then attempted to impose a moderate programme of reforms which would grant the Muslim population more representation and a greater share of power in the Lebanese government.

The Syrian intervention had decisively tipped the military scales against the Maronites, however. While the Christian militias were therefore disposed to agree to the Syrian proposals, the National Movement—Palestinian forces were not willing to abandon their advantage in return for this compromise settlement. Throughout January and February, 1976 the Lebanese leftists and the Palestinian forces incessantly broke the ceasefire to press forward, both in Beirut's hotel district and in the mountains, with the clear aim of crushing the beleaguered Maronite militias utterly.

This was utterly unacceptable to the Syrians on three counts: (1) their ability to convert the Lebanon into a satellite depended upon the country remaining divided between more or less evenly balanced factions; (2) a Lebanon run by a coalition of Nasserists and Palestinian guerrillas would be a most unwelcome neighbour for Syria; and (3) the prospect of such a Lebanon would almost certainly cause Israel to invade and occupy much of the country, which would be a strategic disaster for Syria even in the unlikely event that it did not cause a new Arab—Israeli war. Having failed to persuade the Lebanese Muslim and leftist forces and the Palestinians by argument to accept a compromise settlement, therefore, Syria turned to force.

In the spring of 1976 the Syrian-controlled Palestine Liberation Army regular units in the Lebanon and the Damascus-based *Saiqa* group of Palestinian guerrillas switched sides and began supporting the beleaguered Maronites. When this failed to turn the tide of the fighting, regular Syrian army units were committed on the Maronite side in the savage fighting of May and June. Syria did not even intervene to stop the terrible siege of the Tel al-Za'atar refugee camps, which culminated in a motorised assault by the Phalange and a ghastly massacre in August, 1976.

Nevertheless, the limited Syrian forces in Lebanon were still insufficient to break the resistance of the Palestinian—leftist militias, and over the summer of 1976 a political and military stalemate set in. In June the Arab League despatched an Arab Peace Force to Lebanon, comprising about 5000 troops from Libya, Sudan, Saudi Arabia and the Gulf States, but its efforts had little effect.

The stalemate was finally ended after Damascus got assurances that Israel would not react to a full-scale Syrian military occupation of Lebanon provided the Syrian army stopped at the line of the Litani River some 15 miles north of the Israeli border. In October, 1976, therefore, approximately 22,000 Syrian regulars with tanks and artillery broke the back of the Palestinian and Lebanese Muslim—leftist resistance. By the end of the month Syrian forces were all over the Lebanon except in the far south, and the Palestinians and the National Movement groups had accepted a ceasefire. A cloak of decency was dropped over the Syrian invasion by the Arab League, which at the Riyadh and Cairo summit conferences during October renamed the Syrian army in Lebanon the 'Arab Deterrent Force' (ADF), incorporating also token contingents from some other Arab countries which had been there in an ineffectual attempt to keep the peace since June.

The 19 months of war had virtually ruined the Lebanon. Between 40,000 and 60,000 people out of a population of 3,000,000 had been killed, and well over 100,000 injured — the great majority of them innocent civilians. An estimated 700,000 people had fled abroad, and many (including a high proportion of the country's most skilled people) have still not returned. $12,000,000,000 of property damage had been done, the centre of Beirut was a rubble-strewn wasteland,

and the trading and banking heart of the Lebanese economy had been destroyed. Moreover, the Maronites had effectively achieved a *de facto* partition of Lebanon: they had even commenced to build their own port and international airport in the area under their control. Above all, the country had lost its independence, probably irretrievably, to a thinly disguised Syrian occupation force.

Almost 3 years later, 35,000 troops of the Syrian army are still in the Lebanon, and are probably the only thing that prevents the civil war from re-igniting instantly. The Palestinian guerrilla groups have mostly returned to their camps, and the Lebanese leftist and Muslim militias have sent most of their men to their homes, still in possession of their weapons, to await further developments. Although Syrian patrols of the ADF do enter some of the areas held by the Maronite militias from time to time, the latter are still on a war footing and in full control of their areas. This is not surprising, as the Syrians have now 'switched sides' again and are attempting to destroy the Maronites' independent military position.

It was inevitable that the Syrian—Maronite alliance would end as soon as the Palestinians and their Lebanese allies were crushed, since Syria's purpose is to break the power of all the rival groups in the country and reconstruct a Lebanese government and army which will be subservient to Damascus. It has proved exceedingly difficult for Syria to accomplish this aim, however, because it is entirely contrary to Israel's interests.

So long as Syria was fighting the Palestinians, Israel felt no need to intervene. Since October, 1976, however, it has repeatedly demonstrated its determination not to allow the Syrian army to establish full control over the Maronite-held areas between east Beirut and Mount Lebanon, or over the buffer zone south of the Litani River in parts of which Israeli-assisted Christian militias have also been able to establish control since 1976.

The Syrian strategy in Lebanon since the war has been to create a pro-Syrian government and army and to construct a 'Broad National Front' embracing political forces drawn from both the polarised extremes of Lebanese politics. These institutions and groups would serve as a foundation on which to 'normalise' the Lebanon on a new basis involving a restructured constitution that more closely reflected the actual communal balance, and a close and subordinate relationship with Damascus. Militia groups would be disarmed, the Palestinians brought under State control and — presumably — Syrian troops would remain.

A start was made at building this new Lebanon just before the ceasefire, when a special day-long ceasefire was arranged in Beirut so that the Lebanese Chamber of Deputies, under overwhelming Syrian pressure, could install the pro-Syrian Elias Sarkis as the new Lebanese President and grant him power to rule by decree. This has since allowed Syria's actions in Lebanon to be covered by a double legitimacy, since they are carried out in the name of the ADF. which in turn is answerable to President Sarkis, who is Damascus's man. After the Syrian army had finally broken the Palestinian—leftist resistance and imposed a ceasefire in October, 1976 Sarkis appointed a close associate, Dr Selim Hoss, Prime Minister, and he in turn selected a cabinet of non-political 'technocrats'.

The next task was the recreation of the Lebanese army in a form which was politically obedient to Syria. This was particularly urgent as the Israeli refusal to let the Syrian army enter the south of Lebanon had meant that Palestinian—Christian fighting flared up there just when it had been damped down elsewhere in the country, and it was hoped that Lebanese army units might be able to stop it. In January, 1977 Lieutenant Ahmad al-Khatib, the leader of that part of the old Lebanese army which had broken away to fight on the Muslim—leftist side, was arrested and taken to Damascus. In March the strongly pro-Maronite Army Commander, Brigadier-General Hanna Said, was replaced by Brigadier-General Victor Khoury, an officer who, like Sarkis, had been a key figure in the Shehab regime, and who had fled to Syria in 1973 when the army was being purged of Shehabist elements. The head of the army's *Deuxième Bureau*, the Intelligence Section, was likewise replaced by a pro-Syrian officer, Major Juni Abdou, and in April, 1977 the nominal Lebanese commander of the ADF was replaced by another officer obedient to Damascus, Colonel Sami al-Khatib. But the creation of a pro-Syrian high command for the Lebanese army did not mean the re-creation of the army itself on a similar basis, which is a goal that still largely eludes Damascus.

From the Syrian point of view this has had particularly unfortunate consequences in the south, where Christian militias commanded by Maronite officers of the Lebanese army had succeeded in establishing a considerable measure of control with open support from Israel. When major Palestinian forces withdrawing from central Lebanon under Syrian military pressure re-entered the south in late 1976 they immediately came into conflict with these Christian forces, whom Israel was already providing with arms, supplies and fire support from across the border. Unable to send Syrian troops in, and lacking adequate numbers of Lebanese regular units, Damascus was reduced to supporting the Palestinian guerrillas fighting to end Christian—Israeli control over three major enclaves in the south even as it was still engaged in sporadic clashes with the Palestinian guerrillas around the camps further to the north. In two major bouts of fighting, in March—April and July, 1977, some 200,000 people, one-third of the south's population, became refugees. Each was ended by a ceasefire which left the positions basically unchanged, with Major Sa'ad Haddad's 'Lebanese Forces in the South' still controlling much of the border in league with the Israelis. The continuing fighting there threatened to restart the Palestinian—Christian war in the rest of Lebanon, and even to escalate into a Syrian—Israeli war.

The seriousness of these dangers was demonstrated in early 1978, when Syria permitted even larger numbers of Palestinian guerrillas — up to 3000 — to go south of the Litani River to increase the pressure on the Christian enclaves. Israel responded in March with a massive military invasion of the entire area, including saturation bombardments of suspected Palestinian positions by heavy artillery and aircraft. Lebanese civilian casualties were in the thousands, and a new wave of refugees descended on Lebanon's collapsing cities, but the Palestinians conducted an orderly fighting retreat and lost only a couple of hundred men.

If the guerrilla-killing aspect of the Israeli invasion miscarried, however, its purpose of removing Palestinians from the border areas was largely successful. Syrian army forces stayed well back from the line of the Litani River where they might have come into contact with the Israelis, and the latter did not withdraw until a new United Nations Peacekeeping Force (UNIFIL) of some 6000 men under the command of Ghanaian General Emmanuel Erskine had been hastily created to take their place in the buffer zone. Even so, Jerusalem supported the Christian militia in its refusal to permit UN troops to enter its own zone of control along the 60 mile frontier when the Israeli army finally handed over to the UN force and withdrew from Lebanon 3 months later. Israel also left the militia well supplied with tanks and other heavy weapons.

An attempt by President Sarkis and Syria to send 700 men of the Lebanese army into the south in mid-June, 1978 just after the Israeli withdrawal, was thwarted by the Christian militia, whose Israeli-supplied artillery halted them 25 miles short of their destination. This action was scarcely surprising,

as the 'Lebanese' troops in question were actually units of the breakaway 'Vanguards of Lebanon's Arab Army' which had fought for Syria in the civil war, now reincorporated into the Lebanese army. In early 1979 there was still no Lebanese government presence in the south, much of which was in effect controlled by Israel via the Christian militia forces. About 600 Palestinian guerrillas had infiltrated back into the area under UNIFIL control, and clashes between the UN troops and both the Palestinians and the Christian forces were common-place.

Syrian efforts to consolidate the control of the Sarkis government and 'normalise' the situation in the rest of Lebanon have had little more success. Clashes between Syrian troops and Palestinian forces have become much less frequent since 1977, although the Syrian army still keeps forces emplaced around most of the major Palestinian camps, but relations between the ADF and the Maronite militias have deteriorated into open hostilities. It has frequently been the militias who have initiated the clashes, but the basic problem is that the Maronites have no intention of falling in with Syria's plans for Lebanon's future.

The Syrian army could probably crush the militias and overrun eastern Beirut in an all-out offensive, but it would cost it more casualties than it is willing to accept. As it is, the Syrian army suffered about 1000 casualties in Lebanon during the 'peaceful' year of 1978. More importantly, Syria is restrained and the Maronites emboldened by the possibility that the Israeli armed forces would intervene to prevent conquest of the Maronite heartland — as Jerusalem has indeed hinted from time to time. In the circumstances, Syria has instead adopted a policy of attrition, aimed first of all at breaking the Maronite hold on east Beirut, by massive artillery bombardments which cause high Christian casualties (mostly civilian) and cost few Syrian lives.

In 3 days of concentrated and indiscriminate shelling of the Christian parts of Beirut by 300 artillery pieces and Katyusha rockets in July, 1978 the Syrian army killed about 400 people and laid waste residential areas that had largely survived the civil war fighting. The bombardment was only stopped after Israeli forces on the Golan Heights were placed on alert, Israeli fighters flew low over Beirut breaking the sound barrier, and President Sarkis threatened to resign. In the ensuing months, however, very large numbers of weapons, reportedly including artillery and some tanks, were sent to the Maronite forces by Israel, and renewed Maronite military provocations against the Syrians in Beirut in October, 1978 unleashed another week of intense bombardment of Christian east Beirut, causing at least 500 casualties. Syria made a determined effort to cut the bridges linking the Maronite-held parts of Beirut with the Christian hinterland to the north, but this clash too ended inconclusively in another ceasefire.

Thirty-one months after the end of the civil war, in other words, Syria had still not made significant progress towards any of its goals in Lebanon. The country has still effectively partitioned and the government had virtually no authority beyond that provided by the Syrian army. No progress had been made on the reconstruction of the constitution or of the economy, and very little on the rebuilding of the Lebanese army. The Maronites were totally hostile to Damascus, the Palestinians only conditionally reconciled to the Syrian presence, and Israeli influence probably exceeded that of Syria in almost half of Lebanon's territory.

On June 6 1982, Israel invaded the Southern Lebanon without warning, after mobilising approximately one third of its army. It swiftly brushed aside Syrian forces, destroying large quantities of equipment in heavy tank battles, and seized the line of the Beirut-Damascus road. The declared purpose f the invasion, called 'Peace for Galilee', has to achieve the expulsion of the Palestinian guerrillas from the country. When the PLO prolonged resistance from final positions its men had taken up in west Beirut, Israel subjected the city to bombardment. Eventually in September, following the intervention of the US government, the PLO fighters were evacuated to the neighbouring Arab countries which had agreed to receive them. Israel remained in occupation of Southern Lebanon, pending, by its own account, the withdrawal of Syrian troops from the country and the signing of a satisfactory peace treaty with the Lebanese government.

An international force of US, French, Italian and British troops occupied Beirut from the beginning of 1983 (after an earlier visit to oversee the Palestinian evacuation). Their presence was prompted by the massacres of Palestinians in the Sabra and Chatilla refugee camps in October 1982, said to be the work of Christian militias.

THE MILITIAS AND GUERRILLA FORCES IN LEBANON

[Current 1979 — present state obscure]
The following groups fought in the civil war. Their present strengths are not available, but in general it may be assumed that they could quickly return to the numbers they had during the war, which are given when known.

Maronite—Christian Forces

The Phalange
This was the largest force on the Maronite side, and probably counted 25,000 fighters at one time. It is associated with the *Kata'ib* Party headed by Pierre Gemayel, and is commanded by his sons Bashir and Amin. It drew its support mainly from the middle and lower classes of the Maronite community.

Bashir Gemayel also heads the unified military command of the Maronite militias, which constitute the military arm of the Lebanese Front headed by former President Camille Chamoun.

The Tigers
This is the militia of Camille Chamoun's National Liberal Party, and is led by his sons Dori and Dany. It rivalled the Phalange in size, and was more extremist politically. The National Liberal Party represents the conservative Christian establishment.

Zghorta Liberation Army (also known as the Giants Brigade)
The private militia of Suleyman Franjieh, who was President until September, 1976. It was much smaller than the two main Maronite militias, being recruited mainly from Franjieh's semi-feudal following in his family's home area, and was commanded by his son Tony. The latter was assassinated in mid-June, 1978.

The Maronite League
An extremist religious militia led by Shakir Abu Suleyman, a disciple of Father Sharbal Qasis. It numbered no more than a few thousand.

Guardians of the Cedar
Another extremist militia, first seen in July, 1975, and based in the Ashrafiye quarter of Beirut. Several thousand fighters.

Lebanese Forces in the South
This is a force of some 500 men, commanded by Major Sa'ad Haddad, whose core of regular soldiers has been filled out with Christian villagers living along the Israel border. It first came into prominence at the end of 1976, and is largely equipped with Israeli-supplied weapons. In close association with the Israeli army, it controls the southern frontier zone.

Since the Israeli invasion of June 1982, it has extended its reach; it was held responsible for the massacres in the Palestinian refugee camps in Beirut in October 1982.

Muslim—Leftist Forces

Progressive Socialist Party
Mainly significant for its leader Kamal Jumblat, the most prominent figure on the Lebanese left and leader of the National Movement coalition which grouped together the anti-Maronite forces during the civil war. The militia of the PSP itself was small, however, and mostly recruited from Jumblat's own Druze community. It fought primarily in the Mount Lebanon region. Jumblat was assassinated in March, 1977 and has been succeeded by his son Walid.

Popular Guard
The militia of the Lebanese Communist Party, drawn mainly from the underprivileged Shi'ite community. Numbers unknown, but probably 2000–3000.

Communist Labour Organisation
A radical leftist group headed by Muhsin Ibrahim. No formal militia organisation is acknowledged, but some of its members fought in formed bodies during the war.

Al-Mourabitou
The militia of the Independent Nasserites, led by Ibrahim Kuleilat. A strongly pro-Palestinian force which was the biggest leftist militia in Beirut during the war. Perhaps 15,000 men.

Firqat al-Nasr (The Victory Division)
A Nasserite group led by Najah Wakim and Kamal Shatila which fought the Phalange in the Beirut area, but did not resist the Syrians. The political party associated with it was the Nasserite Organisation — Union of the Toiling People's Forces. Strength under 5000.

Quwwat Nasir (The Forces of Nasser)
Militia belonging to the Nasserite Organisation — The Correctionist Movement, a breakaway group from the previously mentioned one, led by Isam Arab. Strength under 5000.

Popular Nasserite Organisation
Local militia in Sidon, led by Mustafa Sad. Strength under 1000.

Movement of October 24th
Local Sunni Muslim militia in Tripoli, strongly pro-Palestinian and leftist. Fought the Zghorta Liberation Army and later the Syrians. Strength 2500+.

The Ba'ath Party
Split into pro-Syrian and pro-Iraqi factions. The pro-Syrian group led by Isam Qansu stopped fighting after the Syrian intervention, but the pro-Iraqi faction's militia led by Abdulmajid al-Rafit continued to resist the Syrian forces. Neither group's militia was very large.

Syrian Socialist Nationalist Party
Leftist, also split into pro- and anti-Syrian factions. The former stopped fighting after the Syrian intervention. Neither faction exceeded 1000 fighters.

The Battalions of Lebanese Resistance (also known as *Hope*)
The military arm of the Movement of the Dispossessed, a

militant Shi'ite group led by Imam Musa al-Sadr (who was kidnapped in 1978 and has not since been seen). Took only a limited role in the fighting.

Palestinian Groups

These included *Fatah* (the biggest group, relatively moderate and not heavily involved in the fighting until 1976) and the PFLP, PFLP–General Command, PDFLP and ALF (all Rejection Front, in the thick of the fighting from the first). While all the above groups also fought the Syrian army in the summer and autumn of 1976, the *Saiqa* group changed sides. The PLA (Palestine Liberation Army) consists of regular military units run by the Syrians, which followed Damascus's lead throughout the war.

Total combat strength of the Palestinian guerrilla forces in the Lebanon was about 25,000.

Lebanese Army Factions

The Lebanese army, in addition to suffering a desertion rate far higher than 50%, broke into four separate forces during the course of the war.

The 'GHQ Army'

A small number of officers and men, mostly Christian, who remained obedient to the Army Commander, Brigadier-General Hanna Said. It took no part in the fighting.

Lebanese Arab Army

An organised body of Muslim enlisted men and junior officers which broke away in late 1975 under the leadership of Lieutenant Ahmad al-Khatib. From January, 1976 it fought on the Muslim–leftist side, and later against the Syrians. At its peak it numbered 3000–4000 men, but it withered away in the course of 1976 and was eventually reduced to a mere rump in the unoccupied far south.

Lebanon's Army

A Christian breakaway group commanded by Major Fuad Malik, which fought on the Maronite side and was closely associated with the National Liberals of Camille Chamoun.

The Vanguards of Lebanon's Arab Army

A small pro-Syrian force led by Lieutenant-Colonel Fahim al-Hajj, organised in May, 1976 to support the Syrian invasion of Lebanon.

STRENGTH AND BUDGET

The Lebanese Army is in the process of reforming after eight years of impotence. Its strength is said to be 22,000 men; the navy is 250 strong, the air force 1250 with 8 combat aircraft and 4 helicopters.

The defence budget for 1981 was $326,000,000 out of a GNP of $4,190,000,000.

There is a gendarmerie of 7500. Many armed militias continue to exist, which it is the government's ambition to disarm.

COMMAND AND CONSTITUTIONAL STATUS

Executive power is vested in the President, who must be a Maronite Christian. He is elected for a term of 6 years by the Chamber of Deputies, which is itself elected on a confessional basis, with 53 seats for Christians and 45 for Muslims. The present Chamber, which elected Elias Sarkis to the presidency under strong Syrian pressure in September, 1976, was itself elected in 1970, but the civil war caused a postponement of national elections.

The President appoints his own cabinet, including the Defence Minister (who is customarily Greek Orthodox) and the Commander-in-Chief of the Lebanese Armed Forces, the senior serving officer, who according to the National Pact of 1943 must be a member of the Maronite Christian sect. Under the new Army Law, replacing that of 1967, the Commander-in-Chief submits proposals for the appointment of army commanders to the Military Council, made up of senior military officers. If the appointees are not approved, the matter is referred to the Defence Council, comprising the President, the Prime Minister and the Ministers of Defence and Interior, whose decision is final.

The largest Arab armed force in the country is not the Lebanese army but the Arab Deterrent Force, over 90% of whose 37,000 troops are Syrian. The ADF is formally under the control of the Lebanese President, and its nominal commander is a Lebanese officer. In practice, however, the Syrian army in Lebanon receives its instructions from the General Staff in Damascus.

The various rightist, leftist and Palestinian militias in the country have no constitutional status. The 6000 United Nations troops of UNIFIL stationed in the south of Lebanon are responsible to the UN Secretary-General.

ROLE, COMMITMENT, DEPLOYMENT AND RECENT OPERATIONS

The role, commitment and recent operations of the various armed forces in Lebanon have been discussed in the section headed *History and Introduction*. The deployment of the Lebanese army is principally in and around Beirut and now in the South (since late 1982) the Beka'a valley in the northeast; it does not have any forces in the Maronite-held areas or in the area south of the Litani River. The Syrian army and other units of the ADF are concentrated in the Beka'a valley.

The Palestinian guerrilla forces have now largely been expelled. The Maronite militias remain in east Beirut, and on the coastline and in the mountains north of there to just south of Tripoli. The Muslim and leftist militias of the civil war are largely demobilised and in their home areas at the moment. The UN forces occupy the buffer zone between the Litani River and the Israeli border, with the exception of the strip close to the frontier which is controlled by the 'Lebanese Forces in the South', Haddad's Christian militia group enjoying Israeli support. Israeli forces, perhaps 30,000 strong, occupy the south of the country, to the Beirut-Damascus road. A British/US/French/Italian force is present in Beirut itself.

ORGANISATION

The army notionally consists of one armoured reconnaissance battalion, nine infantry battalions (all much under strength) and two artillery battalions; a mechanised brigade of one armoured and three infantry battalions also exists. Five infantry brigades are said to be forming.

The air force has one FGA squadron, one interceptor squadron (aircraft not in use) and one helicopter squadron.

RECRUITMENT, TRAINING AND RESERVES

Officer recruitment traditionally favoured Maronite Christians, and this preponderance is still reflected in the composition of the present officer corps. Enlisted men, on the other and, tended to be recruited from the poorer rural areas of the country, which are predominantly Muslim. Recruitment was voluntary, and training did not involve serious attention to modern conventional combat so far as the army was concerned. There was a military academy for officer training and an NCOs' school which provided some technical instruction; it is not known if they have been reopened.

Under the impact of the civil war, which drew an estimated 50,000 men into the various militias, the Lebanese Chamber of Deputies approved a law instituting compulsory military service in December, 1975. This law has not yet been put into effect widely, if indeed at all.

The only reserve available to the old Lebanese army was a few thousand former regular soldiers who had left the service at a young age, and a much larger number of people who had received a scanty military training in secondary school followed by a 1 month army summer camp after they had graduated from school. If conscription is put into practice, however, the future Lebanese army may develop a more useful reserve organisation.

EQUIPMENT AND ARMS INDUSTRY

The old Lebanese army was poorly equipped with antiquated weapons, which caused little concern as it was primarily an internal security force. Indeed, there were frequent debates between those wishing to stay clear of the Arab–Israeli conflict and those seeking a more active role in it as to whether it was even desirable to upgrade the armed forces' equipment, which were generally won by the former group. Thus, for example, in 1971 a deal to buy Crotale SAMs for the army was cancelled by the Lebanon with considerable financial loss to the country, and there were pressure groups within the government and even the armed forces wishing to sell off the high-performance Mirage fighters that had been bought for the air force just after the 1967 war.

The army's equipment is said to include 13 AMX-13 light 100 Saladin armoured cars, 127 M-113 armoured personnel carriers and 46 pieces of 122mm and 155mm artillery. Some Milan and TOW anti-armour missiles are held, and 25 U 2314 and Bofors anti-aircraft guns.

The navy has one large and three small patrol craft. The air force has one operational squadron of 8 Hunter F70 fighter-ground attack aircraft. The Helicopter squadron has 11 Alouette II/IIIs and 11 AB-212s. Training aircraft include six SA Bulldogs, and five Magisters. There are two transport aircraft: one Dove and one Turbo Commander 690A. There is an early warning/ground-control network, but much of it is not in use.

The paramilitary Internal Security Force has 30 Chaimite armoured cars. Its units are equipped with standard infantry personnel and support weapons.

RANK, DRESS AND DISTINCTIONS

The structure of the Lebanese armed forces parallels that of the French. Uniforms are similar to those worn by other eastern Arab armies.

CURRENT DEVELOPMENTS

In the aftermath of the Civil War, there was considerable talk in the Lebanon about plans to rebuild a well-equipped modern army which in the first stage would number 15,500 men and cost about $1,000,000,000 to equip properly, followed by a further expansion to some 40,000 men after the 1975 Conscription Law was put into effect, with still greater expenditure

to equip it properly. The expenditure involved, however, is entirely beyond the Lebanon's present means, and great difficulties are being experienced in reaching even the first-phase goal.

Indeed, the first line of difficulty in rebuilding the army has been political, since most of its troops were involved in the civil war on one side or the other, and the majority of its officers are Maronite Christians. Initially, the government sought to weed out those officers of the old army whom it did not want to keep by issuing a decree in February, 1977 ordering all army officers to submit their resignations within 3 months, the idea being that it would then accept or reject them according to its preferences. Although the deadline was extended to the end of 1977, however, only one-quarter of the officer corps complied, and a large proportion of those remaining were officers, whom the government did not want to re-employ.

The same problem applied with enlisted men, most of whom had become members of some Muslim–leftist or Maronite militia during the war. As a result, by late 1978 the government had succeeded in recruiting only two 'virgin' battalions, consisting of officers and men untainted by close links with one or another militia: these are stationed at Hadeth, a suburb of Beirut, and near the Presidential Palace at Ba'ada, and were until recently the only formations which could be counted on to obey orders.

The largest force, and the first to become available to the new army, was the Beka'a Command, consisting of some 3000 soldiers stationed in north and north-east Lebanon and commanded by the Commander-in-Chief's brother. In fact, however, the Beka'a Command was simply the 'Vanguards of Lebanon's Arab Army', the breakaway group which fought for the Syrians, under another name. Other units have been reshuffled in accordance with a secret army survey of the religious and communal affiliations of its troops so that entirely Christian units (most of whose troops will have fought in Christian militias) will be stationed in Christian areas, and all-Muslim areas.

What this means, in effect, is that few of the troops on the army's books would obey an order from the Defence Ministry without checking first either with the Israelis or with their local warlord. The sheer preponderance of Maronite officers likewise thwarted both Syria's desire to construct a reliably pro-Syrian high command, and the desire of Lebanese moderates to have a balanced and neutral high command.

The re-equipment of the army is also proceeding at a less than headlong pace. In mid-1977 the USA agreed to provide Lebanon with an immediate $25,000,000 credit for the purchase of 5000 M-16 rifles, 80 APCs and 105mm and 155mm guns, and promised a further $75,000,000 in credits over the following 2 years (which would be spent on heavier equipment). The USA also made an immediate donation of surplus armoured vehicles (Saracens and Saladins) which were transferred from Jordan to the Lebanon against replacement by the USA with newer vehicles, and undertook to provide training in the use of the American weapons to Lebanese officers and NCOs in the USA and through American advisers in Jordan and Saudi Arabia. The Lebanon has requested technical assistance from the USA in launching conscription for the armed forces during 1979.

In November, 1978 Lebanon's Defence Minister Fuad Boutros also sought French arms aid during a visit to Paris. The French government agreed to play a major role in reconstructing the Lebanese army, not only by supplying weapons but also by training cadets and officers in France. The arms purchases discussed were said to include AMX-30 medium tanks and AMX-13 light tanks, helicopters, anti-tank missiles, patrol boats and small arms. There was some discussion on a proposal for France to take over the maintenance of the Lebanon's unserviceable Mirage fighters and to reconstruct the radar system on Mount Hermon that was put out of action in the 1967 war. The package was reported to be worth about $300,000,000 of which the bulk was to be financed by Saudi Arabia.

The most hopeful prognosis for the Lebanese army — and for the Lebanon — is President Reagan's expressed aspiration that Lebanon should have 'only one army', a sentiment reinforced by his decision to station U.S. Marines in Beirut to sponsor the international force of French, Italian and British troops in the city, and to provide money for retraining and re-equipment. Israel's attitude to the rebuilding of the army remains obscure: a favourable one would depend upon the signing of an Israeli-Lebanese peace treaty on advantageous terms, which at present eludes the Israeli government.

Gwynne Dyer

LESOTHO

Lesotho is the former British territory of Basutoland, which attained independence in 1966. Its government, headed by Chief Leabua Jonathan is regarded by many as being too accommodating to South Africa, whose territory entirely surrounds Lesotho. The authoritarian style of Chief Jonathan's administration has also aroused resentment. Discontent has appeared recently in a militant form, the Lesotho Liberation Front, which operates (probably with tacit South African connivance) from the Qwaqwa and Bophuthatswana homelands; the South Africans in turn suspect that many of the refugee camps in Lesotho are in fact harbouring ANC militants. In September 1981 several spectacular bomb explosions occurred in Maseru, further violence followed in 1982. To counter this the Police Mobile Unit, the permenent barrack section of the police has been expanded into a military force under General J. Lekhanya. It has been trained by some former British Army personnel on contract and is equipped with British infantry weapons. Training includes counter-insurgency operations in Lesotho's mountainous terrain. Other equipment includes two Short Skyvan STOL aircraft.

Lesotho, like Botswana and Swaziland, is in danger of falling into the Lebanon predicament, involvement in a bitter racial conflict that is not of its making. South Africa may opt to see an unpopular regime maintaining itself in power with difficulty, as being preferable to a more broadly based popular government. The USSR is also interesting itself in Lesotho.

Lloyd Mathews

ADDENDUM

In December 1982 South African commandos raided the (South African) African National Congress's headquarters in Maseru, killing over 40 people without it appears, any loss to themselves. There is little that Lesotho will be able to do, on its own, to prevent further military raids of this type and the dangers of the Lebanon predicament appear to have increased.

LIBERIA

HISTORY AND INTRODUCTION

Liberia became independent in 1847. From 1822 a Militia had been in existence to protect the newly-arrived settlers from America. However no permanently established force existed until 1908, when the Liberia Frontier Force was created; its chief purpose was to pacify the interior and further to defend the interests of the coastal Americo-Liberian community in their control of the nation's economy. This force, when despatched to the interior, often lived off the area which it was pacifying, an additional communal punishment. It also recruited by frequently forcible methods. Its officers were drawn either from the coastal aristocracy or tribal elites, it started to receive United States military assistance in 1912, a US negro officer commanding the force until 1924. Assistance greatly increased during and after World War II. In 1962 after the independence of so many former colonies and also after a very poor performance by a battalion in the UN Congo Force, the role of the force was reviewed, and as The Liberian National Guard it emerged as a national army with a nascent professional spirit. After industrial troubles in 1966 the Liberian government decided to increase the Guard to its present size; at the same time the Militia which had continued a somewhat vague existence as a reserve was also overhauled. A major reason for the latter reform was the need for a check on the Guard; with its increasing professional ability appeared political ambitions among certain officers. The two forces then shared the former role of the Frontier Force, the preservation of the privileged position of the Americo-Liberians. This privileged position was expressed in political terms by the successive governments of the True Whig Party (TWP), in virtually undisputed power from 1870 to 1980. The TWP was in essence a grouping dominated, often corruptly and always expensively, by some 300 elite Americo-Liberian (i.e. black, but mainly coastal, and descendants of American negroes) families; what passed for political debate was rivalries amongst these families. President Tolbert (1971–1980) who followed President Tubman (1944–1971) made a limited attempt to broaden the basis of the regime by identification internationally with the rest of Africa and nationally with some of the neglected and underprivileged hinterland peoples, but signs of impending trouble were to be seen under both the last two TWP presidents; this dissatisfaction was, as far as the National Guard was concerned, evident in reports of a planned coup in 1963, arrests of senior officers in 1969 and 1970, the discovery of another coup conspiracy in 1973, and the rustification of the Defence Minister and a general in 1977. Recession and over-spending fuelled discontent which spilled over into bloody riots in Monrovia in April 1979, with further strikes later in the year.

In April 1980 the storm broke, with a coup led by a National Guard Master Sergeant, Samuel Doe, in which President Tolbert, members of his family and a small number of the Americo-Liberian elite were killed, others were beaten up or arrested; the more fortunate experienced only the looting of their property. A Peoples Redemption Council, composed initially of six sergeants, eight corporals and two privates, one from each of Liberia's fifteen provinces with one additional member (Doe) as Chairman, assumed power. At one level the event indicated the linkages that had been formed between the town workers and unemployed and the NCOs – from the same backgrounds; at another level the event marked a substantial transfer of formal power from the Americo-Liberians to the hinterland peoples, all fifteen members of the PRC being hinterlanders. Whether real power has been so fully transferred is much less clear, as after a period of victimisation and harassment of the Americo-Liberians Doe and the PRC found themselves faced both with an imperative economic need to regain United States aid and good will, and also an equally imperative need to use the Americo-Liberian officials, their expertise being irreplaceable. These needs led to the ending of some flirtations with regimes such as that of Cuba, the resumption of the American alliance including use of American military aid, and the release of Americo-Liberian detainees. Members of the expanded administration (a mixture of the better members of the civil service and of the TWP, former dissidents now returned and soldiers) favouring left-wing ideology or even non-alignment either resigned or were relegated to lesser roles. The situation remains confused. In ethnic terms there seems to be some advantage towards the Krahn people (of which Doe himself is a member) and the Kru; ex-TWP Krahns have often been preferred to more militant members of other communities. A return to civilian rule has been promised for 1985, but no firm constitutional arrangements have yet been finalised. Restlessness and indiscipline characterise the National Guard as a Field fighting force it is of little significance.

STRENGTH AND BUDGET

Population: 2,000,000
Armed Forces: Army 4900; Air Force 250; Militia 1750.
GNP } No figures available.
Defence Expenditure }

COMMAND AND CONSTITUTIONAL STATUS

Samuel Doe is the nation's overall Commander-in-Chief, and is now styled as such. Below him, growing in political significance, is General T. Quiwonkpah who has strongly pressed for return to Liberia's traditional American alliances.

ROLE, COMMITMENT, DEPLOYMENT AND RECENT OPERATIONS

Liberia perceives an external threat to her sovereignty from Guinea, particularly in the rich iron ore Mt. Nimba area, where occasional incursions by Guinean soldiers are rumoured. The main role of the armed forces, however, remains that of supporting the regime in power.

A formal defence treaty signed with the USA in 1959 provides for mutual support in the event of aggression, and the United States Military Mission was under President Tubman an integral part of the Department of National Defence.

ORGANISATION

The Guard comprises five infantry battalions and a Presidential Guards battalion, an artillery battalion, an engineer battalion and a logistic unit. Normal deployments provide for three National Guard and three Militia units in or near Monrovia, with the hinterland areas only thinly garrisoned.

RECRUITMENT, TRAINING AND RESERVES

Recruitment of soldiers is voluntary in peacetime, no ethnic group is favoured. Service in the Militia is in theory obligatory for all aged 16–45 a theory never applied, especially in the hinterland.

In the TWP era officers were mostly Americo-Liberians, or from hinterland elites co-operating with the political system. The coup saw a rash of promotions to subaltern and often field (i.e. major, lieutenant-colonel) rank of numbers of NCOs and on some occasions ordinary soldiers. General Quiwonkpah, not yet 30 years old, is a promoted NCO. Training standards, which had previously been notably poor, fell still further.

A US Army mission, of rather greater size and calibre than previous pre-coup teams, is now reported to be at work; one estimate notes the mission to be 200 strong. Joint exercises take place, and Liberian officers are sent to the USA for staff training.

A Liberian National Military Academy was founded in the 1960s. Some officers both prior to that time and since are products of an ROTC (Reserve Officers Training Corps) system at two Liberian university institutions.

Ostentation – and corruption – characterise a number of the senior military, especially those promoted rapidly after the coup.

The Militia convenes for training very infrequently (four times a year) and its combat value is virtually nil. It can, however, provide a mechanism for call-up of albeit virtually untrained, reservists. In the absence of any mobilisation plans, this could be useful.

EQUIPMENT AND ARMS INDUSTRY

All military equipment is American with the exception of a small number, some 20, of jeeps presented by China in July 1982; these will probably replace the World War II vintage M-3A1 scout cars, a dozen of which had survived to the time of the coup. The infantry is equipped with old M-1 rifles, some twenty 60mm and ten 81mm mortars, and a few 3.5 in rocket launchers. Other weapons include small numbers of 57mm and 106mm recoilless launchers, 75mm howitzers and eight 105mm pack-howitzers.

The air component is limited to two C-47 transports and fourteen light liaison aircraft, all varying models of Cessna machines.

The Militia is equipped with 1903 pattern US rifles, the bolts of which are not held in units but in central stores.

RANK, DRESS AND DISTINCTIONS

These generally follow US patterns, except that the rank of colonel is indicated by the Liberian crest.

As the Militia has to supply its own uniforms, its turn out is often individualistic, at times eccentric.

In addition to the civil honours system (The Liberian Order of African Redemption in three grades, The Order of the Star of Africa in five grades and The Most Venerable Order of Knighthood of the Pioneers of Liberia in five grades) the following military honours may be awarded, Distinguished Service Order, Distinguished Service Medal, Medal of Honour, Long Service Medal, Good Conduct Medal and Marksmanship Medal.

CURRENT DEVELOPMENTS

Since the coup Liberia has experienced a number of alleged dramatic political crises and counter-revolutionary conspiracies. One of these latter in May 1980 was said to have involved a former general and other pre-coup officers. Another conspiracy said to involve military personnel occurred in September 1980. In June 1981 thirteen junior ranks were reported to have been shot for involvement in a coup. In August 1981 several senior PRC members, including the Vice-President, Major General Thomas Weh Syen, together with three lieutenant colonels and a major were all executed. Other less dramatic political changes have involved political figures who had hoped the Doe regime would usher in a socialist revolution. Doe has survived the quarrelling and, having ended the initial excesses, he has also succeeded in gaining international recognition. He has, however, achieved little in effecting any real improvement in the country's desperate economic position.

It is difficult to avoid the conclusion that Commander-in-Chief Doe's coup has ended the domination of Liberian life by one faction, the old elite, simply to replace it by the domination of a new one – a few survivors from the TWP era, civilian opportunists and soldiers. The forces form one of the arenas in which internal jealousies among this new elite are contested.

Lloyd Mathews

LIBYA

HISTORY AND INTRODUCTION

Libya, with only 3,125,000 people and such unthreatening neighbours as Tunisia, Niger, Chad and Sudan, has the tenth largest force of medium tanks in the world. With the exception of Israel and Syria, all the other members of this select group with over 3000 tanks have at least ten times Libya's population. Libya is the limiting case in that class of oil-rich, population-poor States whose defence expenditure is neither constrained by circumstances nor directed against recognisable military threats.

The immense wealth derived from oil exports which allows Libya to cut such a bold figure on the international political and military stage is, however, of extremely recent origin. As recently as 15 years ago, it was one of the poorest and least-developed nations in the world. Almost all adult Libyans were born into a poverty-bound and deeply traditional society: the extreme and erratic courses of Libyan political and military policy since the money began to flood in are by no means solely attributable to the vagaries of a single leader. General Mu'ammar al-Qaddafi is in many ways representative of the responses of Libyan society as a whole to the abrupt transformation in its circumstances.

Libya's career as a political entity has been relatively brief. All its links with classical antiquity were broken by the Arab conquest of the seventh century AD, and even the Berber cultural substratum which still survives elsewhere in the Maghreb was totally submerged in Libya in the ninth and tenth centuries by large-scale immigration of Arabic-speaking nomadic tribes originally from the Najd in central Arabia. Of Cyrenaica in particular it may be said that no other part of the 'Arab world' except Arabia itself is more genuinely 'Arab' in ethnic terms. What little survived from the civilisation of classical, Abassid and Fatimid times was permanently destroyed by the catastrophic invasion of the Banu Hilal and Banu Suleim tribes in the eleventh century: agriculture was abandoned everywhere, and the country lapsed into a severely fragmented tribal society living in a semi-nomadic subsistence economy for over half a millennium.

Little improvement was brought by the Ottoman conquest of Libya in 1543, and the province was soon left to the administration of the local Pashas, Deys and the pirate captains whose captives provided most of the income of the small urban section. The three main inhabited regions of the country – Cyrenaica on the eastern coast, Tripolitania on the western coast and the extensive oasis complex of the Fezzan in the south – lived in almost complete isolation from each other, separated by hundreds of miles of desert, and even within each region tribal and family loyalties precluded any broader sense of identity. The very first glimmering of such an identity came only with the spread of the Sanusi religious brotherhood, founded in 1834 in Cyrenaica by Muhammad ibn 'Ali al-Sanusi, but it was not until this forgotten Ottoman province was exposed to foreign invasion in the early twentieth century that a broadly Libyan national consciousness began to take shape.

In 1911 Italy made an unprovoked attack on the Ottoman Empire with the purpose of seizing and colonising Libya; Italian troops were quickly landed and captured the few large coastal towns. The Turkish response, however, was to send arms and young army officers with experience of Balka guerrilla warfare (including Enver Pasha, later the Ottoma leader in World War I) to organise the Libyan population i guerrilla resistance. This they did, in close co-operation wit the leaders of the Sanusi order, and the Italians were succes fully confined to the coastal towns. Turkey, defeated in th Balkan Wars, was forced to cede Libya to Italy in late 191 and withdrew its officers, but the Sanusiya continued t resist fiercely. The Italians had still made little progress i the Sanusi stronghold of Cyrenaica, and had only a tenuou hold on the inland parts of Tripolitania, when in late 191 general war broke out in Europe, and Turkish arms and mil tary advisers once again began to reach Libya by submarin. The Italians were unable to deal with the Sanusi army, bu it was decisively defeated by the British when it attempte on Istanbul's orders to invade the Western Desert of Egyp in 1915. This led to a change of leadership in the Sanus which then passed to Sayyid Muhammad Idris, and a peac settlement was concluded which recognised him as the Am of the interior of Cyrenaica on condition that he end attack on the coastal towns and on Egypt.

The forced growth of Libyan national consciousnes under these conditions is seen in the fact that the Tripol tanians, who attempted to form a republic and expel the war weary Italians in 1918, recognised Muhammad Idris as Am of all Libya in 1921 in order to present a joint front in th negotiations for 'administrative independence' which wer held in Rome in that year. The negotiations failed, but eve under the vigorous military leadership of Mussolini's nev Libyan governor, Count Volpi, it took the Italians until 192 to pacify Tripolitania and disarm the population. The mai Sanusi bases in the oases of the south were occupied in th later 1920s, but it was not until 1931, after a barbed-wir fence had been built all along the Egyptian frontier and th tribes of Jebel Akhdar in central Cyrenaica had been pu into concentration camps, that resistance finally ended i Cyrenaica with the capture and hanging of Omar Mulhta the main Sanusi military leader.

The Italian rulers of Libya transformed the country during the brief tenure there, developing agriculture an building roads, towns and harbours, but it was all done fo the benefit of the relatively very large numbers of Italia peasant immigrants who were now encouraged to settl in the country. Libyans were discouraged from proceedin beyond a primary education, and very many of them los their lands to the immigrants. The extreme anti-Wester sentiment and the willingness to support virtually any movement anywhere in the world that portrays itself a 'anti-imperialist' which now characterise Libyan policy ow much to the fact that, unlike any other Arab State excep Algeria (which shares these policies), Libya was the victim of a deliberate programme of large-scale European colonisa tion.

There is also a largely unremarked historical reason fo Libya's uniquely uncompromising policy of pan-Arab nation ism and its extreme interpretation of the pan-Islamic ideal Qaddafi and his contemporaries were powerfully influence in their formative years by the propaganda on these topic preached by Cairo radio in Nasser's heyday – as they admi themselves – but they were in any case borne into a cultur which had been the first Arab society in the twentiet century to fight against European domination: their parents grew up while the resistance was still continuing.

In the circumstances prevailing in Libya in 1911–18, at a time when the Ottoman Empire was appealing strongly to the pan-Islamic ideal, there was an almost complete identity between local nationalism and pan-Islamic ideology in the Libyan resistance movement: no other twentieth-century Arab nationalist movement began within the framework of a Muslim religious order. As for the pan-Arab strand, at the formative stage of the Libyan resistance movement in 1914–15 it was advised by Ottoman officers of Arab origin who were already involved in secret pan-Arab revolutionary societies, like Nuri as-Said, later a military leader of the Arab revolt and Prime Minister of Iraq until 1958, and Aziz al-Masri, later the Egyptian senior officer who was the *éminence grise* behind the 1952 Free Officers' revolt. Due to the almost complete dearth of information about the currents of opinion within Libyan Arab society during the Italian and post-Italian colonial eras, the links between Libya's formative experience of nationalism and its present-day character cannot be traced, but it seems safe to say that modern Libya is acting within its own ideological tradition.

The modern Libyan armed forces have their origin in the Libyan Arab Forces (LAF) which were raised by the British authorities in Egypt at the beginning of World War II from amongst the Cyrenaican refugees who had taken asylum in Egypt after the collapse of the anti-Italian resistance a decade before. By 1940 the LAF, more popularly known as the Sanusi Army, numbered 600 officers and men. When two divisions of Cyrenaicans raised by the Italians fell almost intact into British hands in that year many of them elected to join the LAF, which thus expanded to a force of five battalions intended by the British for guerrilla operations in the Jebel Akhdar region. Because of the high mobility and considerable technical requirements of modern desert warfare, however, the LAF was in the end mostly used for ancillary duties such as guarding military installations and prisoners (although one battalion did take part in the fighting at Tobruk).

When the Italians were driven out of Libya the British saw no further need for this force, but the Sanusi Army was reluctant to disband and a majority of its members arranged to transfer to the local police force in Cyrenaica under the British military administration. During the years 1945–50 the country was administered by Britain with the greatest economy while its fate remained in doubt – at one point the Soviet Union was actively seeking the mandate for Libya from the United Nations – but eventually, in accordance with a United Nations resolution, Libya received its independence in December, 1951 as a monarchy under King Muhammad Idris, the Sanusi leader and hero of the earlier resistance movement. The veterans of the LAF then transferred from the police to form the nucleus of the Royal Libyan Army.

Libya was then an extremely poor country, with little to sell abroad except her strategic position, so in 1953 King Idris concluded a 20 year treaty granting Britain the right to maintain military bases in the country in return for substantial annual payments. In 1954 he concluded a similar 20 year treaty with the USA, and by the late 1950s Wheelus Air Force Base in Libya was the largest USAF base outside the USA. Oil was not discovered until 1959, and did not begin to be produced in significant quantities until 1962.

The King's main power base was in the strongly Sanusi areas of Cyrenaica, and as the years passed even that began to be undermined by the flood of Nasserist pan-Arab, anti-monarchical propaganda emanating from next-door Egypt. As the main Arab States involved in the confrontation with Israel became increasingly anti-Western and more closely tied with the Soviet Union in the period 1956–67, his close links with the Western powers and the presence of Western military bases on Libyan soil became an increasing embarrassment: there were serious student riots in 1964 and 1967.

In these circumstances the King grew increasingly to distrust his army, particularly as its original composition, consisting almost entirely of personnel of tribal extraction, began to be diluted by more skilled but politically less reliable city dwellers to cope with the greater technical requirements of a modern military organisation. Yet he was being encouraged by his Western allies to modernise his army (and his new navy and air force, founded in 1962 and 1963, respectively) in order to protect the oilfields, and incidentally to serve as a market for large imports of tanks and air-defence systems from Britain. His solution was to keep often ill-qualified Cyrenaican officers owing him personal loyalty in all important command positions, and to organise the force along regional and tribal lines, with the Cyrenaican bedouin forces being deployed in the politically more important areas including the two main cities of Tripoli and Benghazi. The army's strength was deliberately limited to 6500 men, and it was counterbalanced by a variety of armed police forces ranging from lightly armed territorial forces to the mobile National Security Force, equipped with helicopters and armoured cars, and the Cyrenaican Defence Force, a sort of praetorian guard recruited exclusively from tribes ruled by the Sanusi clan. The strength of these latter two forces in 1968 was 14,000 and their armament was not significantly inferior to that of the army: if the army bought tanks, the CDF was provided with anti-tank weapons, and vice-versa.

Even these elaborate measures failed to preserve the monarchy, which was overthrown in a bloodless coup on September 1st, 1969. As oil revenues had grown almost exponentially through the 1960s – by 1968 Libya was the second-largest Arab oil producer, with the great advantage, as a supplier to Europe, of being on the right side of the Suez Canal — the contrast between what might be done with those revenues for pan-Arab causes and for domestic living standards, and the conservative policies pursued by the King, had become painfully obvious to many Libyans. Qaddafi and the other young officers who seized power in 1969 have since revealed that they had been secretly discussing a Nasserist revolution for the previous 10 years, but by the time the revolution came virtually the entire Libyan population supported it. King Idris went into exile in Egypt, and the 'Revolutionary Command Council' (RCC) of 12 young officers declared the country a republic.

Most of the RCC officers in 1969 were from the lower strata of society – half were from tribal and peasant backgrounds – and their average age was twenty-eight. Qaddafi himself was twenty-seven, the son of a shepherd. They were the first generation to grow up with a truly national outlook, moulded in the army, and in origin were evenly distributed amongst the country's three main regions. Like most of their contemporaries in the army they were imbued with a pure Nasserist dedication to the pan-Arab cause, unsullied by any of the practical considerations and great-power ambitions which repeatedly distracted their Egyptian hero from his goal, and they had virtually unlimited funds at their disposal. At the same time they were almost all the products of a completely traditional and xenophobic society, and were determined to reassert that society's values. They at once embarked on a comprehensive restructuring of Libya's domestic society and its international relations.

The first priority was the unification of the armed forces,

which was accomplished by incorporating most of the National Security Force and the Cyrenaican Defence Force into the army, whose strength was thus tripled at a stroke to about 20,000 men. The entire leadership of generals and colonels was dismissed or retired (though usually on generous pensions), leaving the ranks of colonel and lieutenant-colonel held by some of the RCC members as the highest in the army. After an alleged coup attempt by the Ministers of Defence and the Interior in the first, largely civilian cabinet in December, 1969 at least one hundred other officers were retired, and members of the RCC took direct control of most branches of the government. The Sanusi tribes were disarmed, and the remaining police forces were placed under the Ministry of the Interior, which was headed by an RCC member. In 1971 a civilian militia known as the Popular Resistance Forces was created under the command of another RCC member, Major Khweildi al-Humaidi, and under the operational control of the Chief of Staff of the Libyan Armed Forces.

In domestic affairs the regime pursued a radical policy of Arab nationalism and Islamic fundamentalism. Alcoholic drinks and the use of languages other than Arabic were banned, all non-Muslim places of worship were closed, and such traditional Koranic punishments as the amputation of the hands of thieves were introduced. Most of the European and American experts employed in the country were rapidly replaced by Arabs from more advanced neighbouring countries, principally Egyptians and Tunisians, who soon came to account for one-sixth of the country's resident population as the regime's policy of creating a Libyan welfare State and a modern diversified industrial economy demanded ever larger numbers of foreigners with skills unavailable in the Libyan population itself. The law requiring Libyan ownership of all businesses in the country was strictly enforced for the first time, and the distribution facilities of the main oil companies operating in the country were nationalised — to be followed at a later date by their production facilities. In 1970 the property of all Italians and Jews remaining in the country was sequestrated and they were expelled from the country.

In its international relations with non-Arab countries, the new regime adopted a policy of strict non-alignment. The treaties permitting Britain and the USA to maintain military bases in the country was brought to an early end, and by mid-1970 all foreign forces had departed from Libya. Closer relations were maintained with France, which was seen as being less closely tied to either super-power and more favourably disposed to the Arab side in the confrontation with Israel, and most Libyan arms buying was transferred from Britain to France.

The armaments which the Libyan regime has been buying in ever-increasing amounts since 1970 are intended for the modernisation of the armed forces, which in turn are officially stated to be intended for the sole purpose of destroying the Israeli presence in the Middle East. Thus far greater stress was placed on creating first-class armoured and air forces than would otherwise be appropriate for a nation facing as few military threats on its own borders as Libya. In recent years these equipment acquisitions have clearly exceeded the ability of the Libyan armed forces to operate them even in terms of sheer manpower availability, and it must be assumed that a large proportion are destined for other Arab nations when they finally see the light and join Libya in one last victorious *jihad* against Israel.

Libya's priorities in foreign policy have always been principally within the Arab/Islamic world: first, and closely linked, come pan-Arab unification and the elimination of Isreal; second, at some distance, comes the support of other Islamic nations and minorities; third comes the support of other 'anti-imperialist' causes. Pan-Arab unification has always been seen in the context of republics: traditional Arab sheikhdoms and monarchies are viewed as obstacles to unification, and have been the constant target of Libyan-subsidised intrigues aimed at overthrowing them. Libya's attempts to further all of these aims have principally taken the form of the promise or the actual delivery of financial subsidies, and occasionally arms, paid out of its almost bottomless coffers. They have generally been characterised by a devastating naïvety on the part of Tripoli, and a cynical willingness to utter 'anti-imperialist', pan-Arab and/or pan-Islamic platitudes pleasing to Libyan ears on the part of the variegated beneficiaries.

The most striking demonstration of the regime's pan-Arabism was the enthusiasm with which it rushed headlong into agreements on unification with various other radical Arab regimes. In the very month he seized power, Qaddafi signed a loose confederal pact (the Tripoli Pact) with Egypt and the Sudan envisaging the eventual union of all three states, and in April, 1971 Egypt, Syria and Libya created the Federation of Arab Republics. Libya took an idealistic approach to these agreements, but for the other partners they were mere measures of expediency, intended only to secure Libyan financial aid and a certain propaganda appeal in the wider Arab world.

All the non-Libyan participants had strong but transient reasons for needing such a boost at the time: Nimeiri of Sudan had just seized power 6 months before the Tripoli Pact, and was facing powerful challenges both from the Ansar religious sect and from the Communist Party, while Nasser was still gravely shaken by his defeat in the 1967 war. Libya was indeed instrumental in saving the Sudanese regime during the 1971 communist coup in Khartoum, when it forced down a British civilian airliner bearing the coup leaders back to Sudan and handed them over to Nimeiri for execution, but thereafter Nimeiri, his power secure, lost interest in union. At the time of 1971 federation the new Egyptian leader, Anwar Sadat, was still facing a major internal challenge from the pro-Moscow Ali Sabri faction, and the Syrian leader Hafez al-Assad had just clambered to the top of the Ba'athist pile in Damascus, but as those two regimes grew in domestic strength over the following year they too lost interest in pursuing union with Libya.

To avoid the opprobrium of publicly spurning 'Arab unity' Sadat agreed in August, 1972 to total unification between Egypt and Libya by September, 1973 but despite such bizarre Libyan pressures as a 'popular march' on Cairo by 40,000 Libyans (which achieved no more than the destruction of an Egyptian border post), the appointed date passed without action. In the following month Egypt enraged the Libyan leadership by launching its 1973 war against Israel without previously informing Tripoli, and then burnt its bridges forever with the fundamentalists in Libya by revealing that it was a 'limited war' intended to lead a negotiated peace settlement with Israel. Qaddafi denounced it as an 'operetta war'; by the end of 1973 Egyptian—Libyan diplomatic relations had been ruptured, and Cairo had established a close relationship with a new source of financial assistance, Saudi Arabia.

There was one further essay towards Arab unity, when Qaddafi persuaded the ageing President Bourguiba to agree to the union of Libya and Tunisia after private talks in January, 1974 but this decision was immediately reversed when Tunisian Prime Minister Hadi Nouira, who had been abroad, returned to his country. Just as Qaddafi was left behind with his Nasserist goal of grand confrontation with Israel while almost all the Arab countries had moved into an era of gradual negotiation, so he was left isolated in his dreams of pan-Arab union, which had lost their dramatic appeal in the rest of the Arab world by the time he had come to power. His main response to those rebuffs, after 1973, was to seek to destroy those Arab regimes which had betrayed his ideals, and to accelerate greatly the expansion of the Libyan armed forces.

Qaddafi's regime had already acquired a reputation for its dangerous readiness to resort to violence and its unpredictability. Two attempts to overthrow and kill King Hassan of Morocco in 1971 and 1972 were subsidised by the Libyan intelligence service. Qaddafi had ordered an Egyptian submarine captain in 1973 (when the two countries were officially operating a joint command) to torpedo the British liner *Queen Elizabeth II* cruising towards Israel on charter to a group of Jewish tourists, in retaliation for the shooting down of a Libyan airliner that strayed over Israeli-occupied Sinai. (The submarine commander refused to obey the order.) But it was in 1974–5 that Tripoli set about systematically to overthrow the Arab regimes which had rejected its plans for union. The first target was Egypt, where Libyan agents began supporting various secret groups of Islamic extremists opposed to the existing regime in acts of sabotage and assassination. Several plots were directed against President Sadat's life, and the two countries had reached the point of large-scale border clashes by July, 1977 (*see* Recent Operations).

During 1975–6 the Libyan government supported two major attempts to overthrow and kill President Nimeiri of the Sudan: in the second of those attempts, in July, 1976 about 1000 Libyan-trained and equipped rebels succeeded in reaching Khartoum, and the city centre was heavily damaged in the fighting before they were suppressed. In the same year Libyan-trained agents were sent into Tunisia to kidnap or assassinate Prime Minister Nouira, who had thwarted the project for Libyan–Tunisian union. (They were captured, and confessed.)

Facing almost complete frustration in its programme for war against Israel and Arab union in the Mashreq (the Arab east), the Libyan regime turned its attention increasingly after 1974 towards its cherished project for a 'People's Maghreb', a union of the Arab west under radical regimes. It gave moral support (though not diplomatic recognition) to the 'Saharan Arab Democratic Republic' which was fighting to reverse the partition of the former Spanish Sahara between Morocco and Mauritania in 1975, and in December of that year committed its armed forces to a full military alliance with Algeria should the latter's provision of bases and support for the Saharan rebels draw it into war with Morocco.

Libya also recommended providing military aid to the Muslim tribal rebels of northern Chad (Frolinat) in 1975, after a coup in N'Djamena overthrew and killed the Chadian President, General Tambalbaye, with whom Libya had made a secret agreement in 1973 to cease supporting the rebels in return for Chadian silence on Libya's annexation of 37,000 square miles of Chad's northern territory (the 'Aouzou Strip'). The new Chadian regime of General Félix Malloum repudiated the agreement and protested publicly against the advance of the Libyan border up to 110 miles south, whereupon Libya began a process of escalating military involvement in support of Frolinat which now involves thousands of Libyan troops (*see* Recent Operations). Libya also annexed about 7500 square miles of territory along the Niger frontier in 1975, and backed a bloody coup attempt against Niger's President Kountché in Niamey in March, 1976 to forestall any protests. The coup failed, but President Kountché forebore to raise the question of his lost territory at an urgent meeting with the Libyan and Algerian leaders in the following month, and also agreed in principle to recognise

their protégé, the Saharan Arab Democratic Republic.

The orgy of conspiracy and intervention against Libya's neighbours after 1974 was paralleled by a sharp rise in Libya's indiscriminating aid to extremist and terrorist groups. In addition to its lavish financial assistance and provision of training, travel and communications facilities for the more violent and extremist sections of the Palestinian resistance movement, it was to be found supporting Dhofari rebels in Oman, Muslim secessionists in the Philippines and Thailand, the Irish Republican Army, secessionists in the Arab minority in Iran and Eritrean rebels in Ethiopia (until the revolution in Addis Ababa, and Soviet and Cuban arguments, persuaded it to change sides). African nationalist guerrillas and such regimes as President Amin's in Uganda and Emperor Bokassa's in the Central African Empire both benefited from Libyan largesse, and at the height of this phase in 1975–6 there is little doubt that non-Third World terrorist groups liek Germany's Red Army Faction and the Japanese Red Army were at least indirectly associated with some Libyan enterprises through the links which they had established with Palestinian extremist groups like Black June. Libyan aid to such groups is now considerably more discriminating, however, and support for acts of outright terrorism against innocent third parrties (aircraft hijackings and the like) has been withdrawn.

Thus one post-1973 Libyan response to the frustration of the regime's goals was all kinds of direct action against those forces which were seen as obstacles; the other has been a huge military build-up. Until about 1973 the expansion of the Libyan armed forces was aimed at the creation of modern, well-balanced forces of a size that Libya could reasonably expect to operate with its limited resources of skilled manpower, although even then there were severe shortages of pilots and skilled technicians. Most arms were bought from France, and although an agreement on oil co-operation had been concluded with Moscow in 1972 Libya's relationship with the Soviet Union was not close. It was not to be expected that France would co-operate in the scale of arms purchases that were now envisaged by Libya, however – nor indeed did France have the production capacity to fill such orders within a reasonable period of time – and in view of Libya's political isolation in the world the only potential supplier was the Soviet Union. Accordingly, Prime Minister Abdul Salam Jalloud visited Moscow in May, 1974 wth a lengthy shopping list of arms. The Soviet Union, aggrieved at its expulsion from Egypt and hungry for hard currency, agreed to supply the arms, and the first Soviet tanks were delivered in 1975. Since then Libyan armoured strength has virtually doubled every year, and annual cash payments for arms to the USSR have been estimated at well over $1,000,000,000 a year (occasioning a severe liquidity crisis even for wealthy Libya in 1977). Some Soviet advisers have been stationed in Libya and numbers of Libyan officers and men have been sent to the Soviet Union for training, but there is no indication that there is anything more than a cash deal; certainly there are no Soviet base facilities in Libya. (For further comments on the probable military purposes of this great expansion of the armed forces, *see* Role, Commitment, Deployment and Recent Operations.)

Throughout the decade since the 1969 revolution there have been almost continuous attempts to create some broader constitutional and popular base for the regime. The Arab Socialist Union (modelled after Nasser's political front in Egypt) was created in 1971 as the sole official party and an instrument of popular mobilisation. A 'cultural revolution' was launched in 1973 (directed, unlike its Chinese namesake, to the revival, not the destruction, of traditional cultural values) and 'popular committees' were formed in each geographical and functional unit of Libyan society to serve as the executive and legislative organs of government, with a General People's Congress (GPC) at the top which would eventually supplant the RCC. It did not do so, however, until 1977, when at its fourth congress the GPC officially changed the country's name to the Popular Socialist Libyan Arab Jamahiriya (an Arabic neologism coined from the words for 'republic' and 'masses' — 'peopledom' is the favoured translation). At that congress all power was officially vested in the people through People's Congresses, Popular Committees, Trade Unions, Vocational Syndicates and the General People's Congress. The RCC disappeared, and in its place the General Secretariat of the General People's Congress was established with Qaddafi as General Secretary.

It did not escape notice, however, that the membership of the General Secretariat was the same as that of the RCC; there has in fact been no progress whatever in moving from a personal to a more broadly based regime, and all power in Libya remains concentrated in the hands of Qaddafi and his dwindling band of military associates who carried out the 1969 revolution. That is not to imply that he is without popular support, however, and the regime's waning popularity was at least temporarily revived in the surge of patriotism which followed the brief war with Egypt in July, 1977. A more serious problem is the continuous decline of support within the army itself for Qaddafi's extremist foreign policies and his unfathomable objectives in acquiring so much unusable military equipment. Of the original 12 members of the RCC, only five are left, and there have been numerous arrests and some executions amongst other army officers. (For further details see Current Developments).

STRENGTH AND BUDGET

The manpower strength of the Libyan armed forces, which for years had hovered around the 25,000 mark, has been expanding rapidly since the effective introduction of conscription, and is now estimated to total 65,000. 55,000 of these serve in the army, 5000 in the air force and 5000 in the navy. The armed forces are now near the maximum figure that can be realistically sustained by a population the size of Libya's.

Libya had to rescind an earlier decree on conscription in 1967, when the withdrawal of workers from the civilian economy caused a severe labour shortage, but now as then this is a problem pertaining specifically to skilled labour, not to total manpower availability. From a native population of 3,125,000 Libyans, growing at a rate of 3.8% a year and weighted heavily in favour of the younger age groups, the country is able to provide the raw manpower for armed forces of this size especially since 40% of the adult labour force is now provided by foreigners, including the larger part of the skilled workforce. However, Libya still has difficulty in finding an adequate number of recruits with suitable backgrounds for mastering complex weapons systems.

The shortage of skilled personnel, rather than of sheer numbers, has been the main problem in the Libyan armed forces all along, and conscription will produce no quick answer to the acute shortage of trained manpower.

The Libyan defence budget in 1980 was $502,000,000 out of a GNP of $39,100,000,000, almost all derived from oil. This was just the housekeeping expenditure, however, and did not include most arms purchases from abroad. Estimates of expenditure on arms range up to $2,000,000,000 per annum since 1974, but exact figures are unavailable since the bulk of purchases were from the Soviet Union for undisclosed sums. Not all of this expenditure was for arms for Libya's own forces, however (substantial sums are believed to have been paid to Moscow for Soviet arms supplies to Syria), and the total may be exaggerated. If the lower estimate of about $1,000,000,000 per annum on arms purchases is closer to the truth, it would represent an unexceptional 20—25% of total annual Libyan expenditure on development, a proportion common amongst the wealthier Middle Eastern States. Even if the phasing of payments may cause occasional liquidity crises (as in 1977, when French arms deliveries were temporarily suspended due to Libya's falling into arrears on payment), the ability of the State to sustain this level of expenditure over the medium term is not in question. Much of Libya's arms debt to the Soviet Union is met partly by barter deals involving Libyan crude oil; a substantial proportion of the $400,000,000 due to Brazil for supplies of armoured cars is being paid in the same way.

Libyan subsidies to Arab groups and countries and to Muslim revolutionary groups worldwide come not from the military budget but from the separate Defence and Arab Co-operation Fund and the Jihad Fund. Subsidies to more sensitive groups, which would cause embarrassment if a Libyan link could be proved, come from secret funds; it has been reported that these are collected at least in part by a front known as the Africa Trading Company in Tripoli, which receives a 5% commission on some Libyan contracts with foreign suppliers, especially of military equipment.

COMMAND AND CONSTITUTIONAL STATUS

Major-General Mu'ammar al-Qaddafi is General-Secretary of the General Secretariat of the General People's Congress (a position organisationally corresponding to the Soviet post of Chairman of the Politburo, and for practical purposes equivalent to that of president and supreme executive) and Supreme Commander of the Armed Forces. The Head of the General Popular Committee (a position equivalent to Prime Minister), Mr Abdul Ali al-Obeidi, is not in the chain of command.

Defence remains the responsibility of the General Secretariat (the RCC under another name), although internal security has been transferred to the General People's Committee. The Chief of Staff of the Armed Forces, who also serves as Commander of the Army, is Lieutenant-Colonel Mustafa al-Kharrobi; both he and his predecessor until 1976, Lieutenant-Colonel Abu Bakar Yunis Jaber, were members of the RCC and are now members of the 5 man General Secretariat. The commanders of the navy and air force report directly to the Chief of Staff of the Armed Forces.

The transfer of internal security matters to the GPC is also less of a change than it seems, since the regular police remain under the command of an army officer, while the militia (the Popular Resistance Forces) has been commanded since its creation by Major Khweildi al-Humaidi, another member of the RCC and now of the General Secretariat. The Head of the Security and Military Intelligence Service, which serves both as internal secret police and as the executive arm for intrigues abroad, is his brother, Captain Abdul Majid al-Khweildi.

The chain of command below the level of the General Secretariat members is not known, but is largely irrelevant for an army of the size and character of the Libyan, where orders may pass directly from the General Secretariat to individual units. The various constitutional fictions which have been erected do not conceal the fact that all power over every aspect of armed forces administration, policy and operations remains collectively in the hands of the five surviving members of the RCC, now reconstituted as the General Secretariat: Major-General Qaddafi, the three officers named above, and Major Abdul Salam Jalloud.

ROLE, COMMITMENT, DEPLOYMENT AND RECENT OPERATIONS

The main announced role of the Libyan armed forces is war against Israel, and that is indeed the task for which they are configured. That is the reason for the acquisition of Tu-22 bombers with a 1400 mile range, and armoured forces grossly in excess of those required for Libya's own defence. Some token Libyan forces participated in the 1973 war in subsidiary capacities, but unless there should be a drastic change of regime and policy in Egypt there is now no way that Libyan ground forces can strike at Israel.

Libya's rapidly growing naval forces – General Qaddafi has predicted that Libya will have the 'third-largest navy in the Mediterranean' (presumably excluding the Soviet and American fleets) within a few years – and elements of its air force are capable of limited action against Israel in a Middle East war even without using Egyptian territory. The ranges, however, are too great to allow such action to have any major effect on the course of such a war, and the Israeli air force is able to reach the Libyan bases in Cyrenaica from which such operations would have to be launched.

The great build-up in Libyan armaments only began after this situation had already come into existence. Moreover, it is manifestly the case that the Libyan army, even expanded to the maximum size that conscription will permit, is not remotely capable of operating 3000 tanks unless it were to dispense entirely with the normal supporting arm – no other army operating that number of tanks has less than five times the manpower of the Libyan army. This has given rise to speculation about the Libyan reason for stockpiling such a large quantity of weapons.

Dismissing the suggestion that it is in fact a Soviet stockpile for Soviet use in an emergency, which is ruled out by the fact that the arms have been paid for in cash, that they are not maintained to Soviet standards and that the present Libyan regime is by no means a Soviet puppet, the most plausible explanation is that Libya proposes to be, in Qaddafi's words, 'the arsenal of Islam', waiting for the day when other Arab countries agree on the necessity of fighting Israel and have need of arms. At this point, Libya would enjoy a far larger voice in Arab counsels if she represented an immediate source of weapons in large quantities.

The only alternative explanation for the present arms policy is a total miscalculation of the capacity of the Libyan army to absorb weapons. In terms of sheer manpower the same comment cannot be applied to the weapons acquisitions of the navy and air force, but at present a substantial portion of Libya's combat aircraft are flown by foreign pilots on secondment.

The second principal role of the armed forces is internal security, but the officer corps also represents the main threat to the regime. There are no ethnic or religious minorities in Libya that might pose a threat to the regime, nor is it likely that popular disturbances like those in 1975 would be a serious danger so long as the army's loyalty to the regime is not shaken.

For practical purposes, it is neither Israel nor internal security that has been engaging the attention of the army's combat formations in the past few years, but rather quarrels along Libya's own frontiers. By far the most serious is with Egypt, which by 1977 had moved forces from Sinai into the Western Desert that were roughly equivalent in numbers to the entire Libyan army. Following 4 years of steadily worsening relations and numerous Libyan-supported attempts to subvert the Egyptian regime, Egypt launched a carefully prepared limited war – more by way of a larger raid, perhaps – against Libya in July, 1977, on the pretext of Libyan border violations.

The Libyans had ample advance notice of this: a Soviet note predicting and protesting against such an Egyptian attack was given to all Arab governments over 2 months beforehand. They appear nevertheless to have been taken by surprise by the timing of the assault, which was fixed by Cairo for July 21st in the belief that it was necessary to forestall Libyan action against the vulnerable Sudanese government. Egyptian armour drove across the border at Musaad, penetrating some 15 miles, and there were reports of Egyptian troops being landed by air at the oasis of al-Jaghbub some hundreds of miles south from the coast. At the same time Egyptian aircraft launched a large raid against the main Libyan interceptor base at El Adem; despite the lack of opposition this caused little damage, but another Egyptian raid 2 days later again caught the Libyans on the ground and had more success. A number of Libyan radar stations were also attacked and destroyed. On July 24th, both sides accepted a ceasefire mediated by Yassir Arafat of the Palestine Liberation Organisation.

The performance of the Libyan armed forces in this brief clash was unimpressive: the most reliable estimates are that Libya lost between 10 and 20 Mirages (mostly on the ground) and 30–40 tanks, against negligible Egyptian losses. Libya claimed that only its militia forces were engaged on the ground, but Egypt has stated that the Libyan 9th Armoured Battalion was put out of action with 50% of its equipment destroyed. Although the Egyptian operation was a military success, however, it had precisely the reverse effect to what Cairo had hoped for, which was a coalescing of the numerous dissatisfied sections of the Libyan population and army into a united front that would overthrow the regime. Instead the militia forces were mobilised, uniforms and weapons were distributed to the civilian population in prodigal quantities, and public opinion swung back behind the regime in an upsurge of patriotic emotion.

As a military problem, however, the Egyptian concentration of forces across the eastern frontier is now the major concern of Libya's military planners. The confrontation remains serious, with considerable potential for further clashes, and the larger part of the Libyan army is now stationed in the eastern part of the country.

Libya's other borders do not represent similar threats. Relations with Sudan are hostile and the border has been closed since 1975, but the small Sudanese armed forces pose no danger to Libya. Relations with Niger and Algeria are good, as they are with the island of Malta to the north. Relations with Tunisia have been strained for some time by a dispute over seabed demarcation in the Gulf of Gabès between the two countries, exacerbated by reports of a major oil find in the disputed area. This led to a small-scale naval confrontation between the two countries in 1977, but a larger clash is unlikely – Tunisia's armed forces are too greatly inferior to encourage anyone in authority in Tunis to seek a military solution, while Libya has adopted a posture of waiting for the aged and ailing President Bourguiba to be succeeded by what it hopes will be a politician more sympathetic to the idea of union with Libya.

Libya's remaining border, with Chad, is the other area in which the country's forces are concentrated; or rather, they are deployed across it, with a reported 4000 Libyan troops in the Aouzou strip area and even northern parts of undisputed Chadian territory, in support of the Frolinat guerrilla movement which is seeking to overthrow the government in N'Djamena. The rebellion of the northern Muslim tribes against the domination of Chad's government, commerce and army by black southerners began in 1966, but Libya first became actively involved in supporting Frolinat on a large scale after President Félix Malloum protested in 1975 against Libya's annexation of the Aouzou area, which had been condoned by his predecessor when it took place 2 years previously.

By supplying arms and aid on a large scale, Libya assured the ascendancy of its candidate, Goukkouni Wodei, leader of Frolinat's Second Army and son of the traditional spiritual leader of the Toubou tribal group that dominates the north, in the three-way factional struggle that had hamstrung Frolinat for some years. Even Goukkouni does not accept the Libyan annexation of Chadian territory, but the Tripoli government appears to be moved by a combination of Muslim solidarity and a conviction that Frolinat in power would raise less strenuous protests on the subject in world forums. Libya was also concerned by the military links between the Chadian government and France, for which reason it has also enjoyed Soviet support in its intervention.

Libya constructed an airstrip in the Aouzou region to ferry in supplies to the rebels, and a greatly expanded Frolinat Second Army, approximately 2500 strong, took the offensive in February, 1978 with Libyan troops allegedly in direct support. In mid-February the main garrison town of the north, Faya-Largeau, was overwhelmed by these forces, and 1500 prisoners were taken (30% of the entire Chadian army). The whole northern half of the country then rapidly fell to Frolinat forces. A report 800 Libyan regular troops supported by surface-to-air missiles were left to hold Faya-Largeau, which lies several hundred miles south of the area officially claimed by Libya.

A ceasefire in Chad was instigated by Libya in March, 1978 apparently in the hope that a coalition government including strong Frolinat representation could be installed in N'Djamena, but ceasefire violations provided France with an excuse to send 1200 troops and a squadron of Jaguar fighter—bombers to aid the Chadian government in April. Franco—Chadian counter-attacks then succeeded in pushing the Frolinat forces some distance back north from their most advanced positions. By July one of the disappointed rivals of Goukkouni for the leadership of Frolinat, Hissène Habre, had gone over to the government with his small army (approximately 500 men); in September he was appointed to the newly created post of Prime Minister by President Malloum in a gesture intended to conciliate Muslim northerners.

In late 1978 precarious ceasefires and sporadic negotiations continued to be interspersed with bouts of renewed fighting between Franco—Chadian and Frolinat forces along the front line running east—west across the country about 100 miles north of N'Djamena. Considerable numbers of French and Libyan troops remained in the country, but they had not clashed directly. Threre were no other Libyan troops deployed beyond the country's borders, 500 Libyan troops who had been sent to Lebanon as part of the Arab League peace-keeping force having been withdrawn in December, 1976. Reports that squadrons of Libyan aircraft have been sent to the aid of the Ethiopian and Ugandan governments for brief periods have never been confirmed.

ORGANISATION

Arms of Service
The division of arms and services follows the British pattern, the arms being infantry, armour, engineers and artillery.

There is an army aviation branch.

The air force also follows British RAF models in its basic division into flying and non-flying personnel, with numerous specialisations within the latter.

Operational
The Libyan army has 30 armoured battalions, 30 mechanised infantry battalions, one National Guard battalion, two special forces groups, and ten artillery, two anti-aircraft artillery and two SSM battalions. There is no divisional structure.

The air force is organised on a squadron basis. There are five fighter—ground attack squadrons and one FGA and one Operational Conversion Unit, three interceptor squadrons (plus an OCU), one COIN squadron, one reconnaissance squadron and one bomber squadron. There are also two transport, two training and four helicopter squadrons. The surface-to-air missile batteries are grouped into three SAM regiments.

It is not known whether squadrons are grouped together in a wing organisation, but there are several squadrons based at each of the air force's principal bases: Ukba bin Naf'i (formerly Wheelus AFB) near Tripoli, where there are MiGs and Tu-22s; Benghazi (shared with the civil airport), where there are more MiGs; Gamal-Abdul Nasser AFB (formerly El Adem) just south of Tobruk, where most of the Mirages are stationed; and Al Kufra, about 500 miles south of the coast near the Egyptian border. Most of these bases are shared with army units. In late 1977 there were reports that Libya was building a new base capable of accommodating 2000 men and at least 10 fighter aircraft in the Aouzou area recently annexed from Chad.

The navy is organised on the conventional ship, squadron and shore establishment basis. Naval headquarters and the principal naval base are at Tripoli; other naval bases are at Benghazi, Dernah, Tobruk, Bandiyah and Burayqah.

RECRUITMENT, TRAINING AND RESERVES

The Libyan constitution states that 'the defence of our homeland is the responsibility of every citizen. The whole people shall be trained militarily and armed by general military training.' This provision has been realised by the reintroduction of conscription and the enrolment of the fit adult population between 18 and 49 years of age (including many unmarried women) in the Popular Resistance Forces. Volunteers are enlisted in the regular forces for a period of 5 years; conscripts are drafted at the age of eighteen for 18 months' service in the armed forces, the great majority serving their terms in the army. In the event of war or other emergency, the law provides that males up to 32 years of age may be conscripted.

Following basic training, conscripts undergo further on-the-job training in their units. Numerous regular force personnel receive training abroad, principally in the Soviet Union, and there are substantial numbers of foreign military personnel in the country serving with training missions and providing technical skills as yet unavailable in the Libyan armed forces. The largest training mission is that of the Soviet Union, which has between 1000 and 2000 military and civilian personnel in Libya manning radar installations and missile sites, and helping to train tank crews and MiG pilots. There have been reports that Soviet aircrews are flying Tu-22 bombers of the Libyan air force pending the availability of Libyan aircrews capable of handling them, and this would certainly be the case with the MiG-25 Foxbats. Some non-Soviet Warsaw Pact military personnel also perform military training duties in Libya.

There are a number of French personnel in Libya maintaining the air force's Mirages, and the most promising Libyan pilots and ground crew are sent to France for further instruction. A large proportion of the Mirages are still flown by seconded Pakistani military pilots, and a Pakistani mission has primary responsibility for the training of the Libyan navy. The new Air Force Academy is largely staffed by Yugoslavs, and a 100 man Nationalist Chinese military group works with the Libyan army.

Libyan army officers are trained at the Military Academy in Benghazi, and work began on the construction of a maritime academy near Tripoli in 1978. The Air Foce Academy at Zawia near Misurata, opened in 1975, is now supported by an air force secondary college which was established at Ukba bin Naf'i AFB in 1978. The system is now being extended further downward, with the creation of a network of flying clubs across the country which are given jet training aircraft by the government and are intended to provide basic flight training for future pilots of all three armed forces. In time this comprehensive system should give Libya a generation of pilots fully qualified to operate the air force's combat aircraft without recourse to foreign assistance, but it will be the better part of a decade before the results begin to show themselves.

There is no information available on the size and structure of the Libyan reserves, although now that conscription has been applied it would seem natural that a reserve organisation should be introduced. The Popular Resistance Forces are a militia which undoubtedly has considerable significance as a political and morale factor, but the kind of training which these citizen forces receive, like the arms with which they are supplied (mainly personal weapons), suggests that they are not a major element in the military equation. Students are obliged to undergo militia training each year, and a militia cavalry division is being formed, but the military instruction provided to the rest of the force — that is, to ordinary citizens — is rudimentary.

Libya is presently training a pan-African Legion consisting of about 5000 non-citizens.

EQUIPMENT AND ARMS INDUSTRY

The main armoured strength of the Libyan army is 2,600 T-54/-55/-62 tanks, 200 OF-40 (Lion) and 300 T-72 (200 more on order). These are supplemented by 200 BRDM-2 and 300 EE-9 Cascavel armoured cars; Fiat 6616 armoured cars are on order from Italy. The Army's mechanised infantry battalions have 700 BMP MICV, 900 BTR-50/-60 and OT-62/-64, 200 EE-11 Urutu, 160 M-113A1 and some Fiat 6614 APCs. The artillery arm has been expanded greatly in the past few years, and now consists of 360 130mm guns, and about 600 M-101 105mm, 40 M-109 155mm SP, and considerable numbers of 122mm (including M-1974 SP) and 152mm (including M-1973 SP) howitzers. 200 Palmaira 155mm SP howitzers are on order. It also possesses about 600 multiple rocket launchers — BM-11 107mm, BM-21/ RM-70 122mm and M-51 130mm — and 200 M-106 recoilless rifles. It has 450 mortars of 81mm, 120mm, 160mm and 240mm. Longer-range bombardment capability relies on 48 FROG-7 and 70 Scud-B SSM and more Scud-B and C on order).

Anti-tank defence is provided by approximately 3,000 Sagger, Milan and Vigilant ATGW. Anti-aircraft weapons include 450 towed 23mm guns and ZSU-23-4 SP, 30mm guns including M-53/59 SP; 57mm guns, and SA-6/-7/-9 SAM.

The Navy's major warships are five Soviet supplied F-class submarines, one ex-British Vosper Mk 7 frigate with Otomat SSM and Albatross/Aspide SAM, and six corvettes; four Italian-built Wadi-Mragh-class 547 ton with Otomat SSM, one Vosper 440-ton, and one Nanuchka-II class. It is already strong in missile-aimed fast attack craft, having 12 Soviet Osa-II class with Styx SSM, three Vosper Thorney-croft-built Susa class with SS-12 SSM, two La Combattante II with Otomat SSM (eight more on order) and one Zwissen with SSM and SAM (13 more on order). The navy also has ten large patrol craft, two ex-Soviet Natya-class minesweepers, one landing ship dock (which serves as a logistic support and landing vessel, one Thorneycroft-built repair ship, two PS-700 LST, and three Polnocny-class and 2 C-107 LCTs. (Twelve more C-107s are on order.)

The Libyan Air Force has 555 combat aircraft, mainly of French and Soviet manufacture. There is one bomber squadron with 7 SV-22 Blinders and five FGA squadrons (plus an Operational Conversion Unit) operating 58 Mirage 5D/DD/DE, 100 SU-20/22 Fitter E/FJ, 32 MiG-23BM/U (140 more on order), five MiG-25U and 14 Mirage F-1AD (40 more on order). The three interceptor squadrons (plus OCU) have 32 Mirage F-1ED/BD, 143 MiG-23 Flogger E, 50 MiG-25 Foxbat A (50 more on order) and 72 MiG-21. There is one COIN squadron with 30 Yugoslav-built J-1 Jastreb, and one reconnaissance squadron with seven Mirage 5 DR and six MiG-25R.

The two transport squadrons have eight C-130 H Hercules, one Boeing 707, eight G-222 (twelve more on order), two Mystere-Falcon, four C-140 Jetstar, two CL-44, eight Il-76, two King Air and one Corvette 200. Ten Twin Otters are also on order. The four helicopter squadrons are ten Alouette III, nine AB-47, five AB-206 (armed), one AS-61A, two AB-212, eight Super Frelon (search and rescue), nineteen CH-47C, 20 Mi-2, two Mi-8, five Mi-14 and 25 Mi-24 (armed). Two A-109 and a number of Gazelle helicopters are on order. The two training squadrons have 61 Yugoslavian built Galeb and two Tu-22 Blinder D. Libya also has twelve Magister, 100 L-39z0, and 119 Siai Marchelle SF-260 WL (70 more on order). Some of the SF-260 may be the Warrior ground-attack or the Sea Warrior (armament and surveillance radar) versions, but the bulk are believed to be in use at the Air Force Academy at Zawia and in the government-sponsored flying clubs that provided *ab initio* flying training for prospective armed forces pilots.

The air force has three SAM regiments with a total of 60 Crotale launchers and approximately 300 SA-2/3/6 SAM. The standard air-to-air missiles are AA-2 Atoll and R-550 Magic (Super 530 AAM on order) and some helicopters carry Swatter ATGW.

There is very little by way of an arms industry in Libya. In July, 1978 Yugoslavia signed a contract to build a plant in Libya to manufacture ammunition and spare parts for the Soviet-made weapons of the Libyan army, but at present even workshop repair and maintenance facilities are both inadequate and manned to a considerable extent by foreign experts. A plan to set up an assembly plant in Libya to build the latter half of the large order for SF-260 trainers was abandoned in 1977.

A very large proportion of the Libyan armed forces' tanks and aircraft are in storage (approximately half of its tanks, and up to 450 of its combat aircraft). Proper storage facilities have now been constructed for most of this equipment, which suffered badly in the early stages of the build-up from being left out in the open for months with no protection or attention, but even now much of it is not maintained to Soviet standards, and deterioration may well be continuing at a slower rate.

General Qaddafi has repeatedly stated his intention of acquiring nuclear weapons, and secretly sent his closest associate, Major Jalloud, to China in an attempt to buy an atomic bomb only months after seizing power in 1969. It is believed in some quarters that a major reason for annexing the Aouzou strip from Chad was the suspected presence of rich uranium deposits in that area. For practical purposes, however, Libya has not the remotest possibility of developing its own nuclear weapons, even if the 10,000 kV research nuclear reactor contracted with the Soviet Union in June, 1975 and the 440 MW power reactor whose purchase from Moscow was agreed in late 1977, should both be delivered. It is not clear whether the 1976 French agreement to build a nuclear reactor in Libya is still valid.

RANK, DRESS AND DISTINCTIONS

Ranks in the Libyan armed forces follow the British pattern, with the standard Arabic terms being substituted for the three different forms in the British army, navy and air force. Since the 1969 coup, however, it has been the rule that the highest rank actually held by serving Libyan officers was lieutenant-colonel (Qaddafi's rank in 1969), and it is common for very influential Libyan officers to have the rank of major or even captain. Mu'ammar al-Qaddafi was promoted to the rank of general by the General People's Congress in 1977, but is still popularly known as 'Brother Colonel', and no other officers have been advanced to general's rank.

Pay for all ranks is generous even when compared to wages for comparable skills in Libya's buoyant civilian economy. Uniforms in the army and navy closely resemble those of the British; air force uniforms are modelled on those of the United States air force. The shoulder insignia for a colonel is a falcon crest with two stars; for a lieutenant-colonel, the same crest with one star. Majors wear only the falcon crest; captains, first-lieutenants and second-lieutenants wear three, two and one stars, respectively. No information is available on medals and distinctions in the Libyan armed forces.

CURRENT DEVELOPMENTS

In late 1978 Libya remained in a state of military alert on its Egyptian border, engaged in military operations within Chad and with considerable tension along its Tunisian and Sudanese borders. Its status of odd-man-out in the Arab world was no less pronounced than ever, although what was perceived as the urgent need to present a united Arab front against a possible Egyptian peace treaty with Israel had caused it to soft-pedal some of its outstanding quarrels with other Arab regimes: thus it overlooked its bitter opposition to Syrian policy in the Lebanon in order to join in a united Rejection Front condemning Egypt's intentions, and reduced its support for the Polisario guerrillas fighting against Morocco in the former Spanish Sahara in order not to drive King Hassan into open support for the Egyptian position. Apart from the role of the Libyan intelligence service in attempting to organise a coup to overthrow the Saudi Arabian government in July, 1977 (see later) and the continuing efforts to subvert President Sadat's regime in Egypt in the form of attempts to infiltrate the army and subsidies to extremist Islamic groups like the Muslim Brotherhood and the terrorist Society for Repentance and Retreat, no recent Libyan adventures in plotting the overthrow of other Arab regimes have come to light.

Domestically, the regime has lost much of its earlier popularity, but a combination of lavish public expenditure and efficient secret police supervision of potential civilian opponents effectively insulates it from potential challenges from that quarter. The peak of popular dissent represented

by the student riots of early 1975, when dozens of students were shot down by the army, has subsided markedly, although an estimated 700 political prisoners dating from all periods back to 1969 remain confined in Aziza barracks in Tripoli. Dispite repeated mass expulsions of Egyptian and Tunisian workers from Libya at moments of particular tension with those two neighbours, the predominantly Egyptian foreign community in Libya now numbers about 400,000, and is indispensable to the running of the administration, education and industry; it is not considered to pose a political threat to the regime.

The real cause for concern to the regime is undoubtedly the officer corps of the army itself. The waves of arrests after the banning of political parties in 1970 and the promulgation of the 'Cultural Revolution' in 1973 struck mostly at civilians on the Marxist and Islamic fundamentalist extremes of politics, but the three instances of military unrest in 1975 led to the arrest of at least 120 officers and about 130 of their civilian allies. The cause of all three — a joint declaration by 39 officers (who are still in jail) in March, 1975, a planned coup by the Chief of Military Transport and six colleagues of the Benghazi garrison in July, and a more serious coup attempt involving the commander of the Republican Guard and about half of the then-members of the RCC in August — was anxiety in the officer corps at the regime's almost total isolation in the Arab world and its rapidly growing military links with the Soviet Union. In the aftermath of the last coup attempt two leading RCC members, Planning Minister Major Omar Abdallah al-Meheishi and Foreign Minister Major Abdul Moneim al-Huni, defected to Egypt (where a Libyan assassination squad attempted to kill them in the following year) and two other RCC members were arrested.

No other plots against Qaddafi's almost total domination of the army and the country have since come so near success, but the regime's concern at the continuing grave unrest in the army was shown by its execution by firing squad of at least 22 officers accused of involvement in the 1975 plot in April, 1977. These death sentences, the first carried out in Libya since 1954, were soon followed by public hangings of other individuals accused of political crimes of violence, and reports continue to filter out of Libya of other executions of dissident army officers. An opposition movement of Libyan exiles in Europe known as Al-Tajammu al-Watani (National Grouping) began to smuggle anti-Qaddafi propaganda into Libya in 1976.

In January, 1978 the long-time head of Libya's Security and Military Intelligence Service, Captain Muhammad Idris al-Sharif, a close associate and childhood friend of Qaddafi who had planned the two coup attempts against Morocco's King Hassan, the two attempts to overthrow Sudan's President Nimeiri, countless attempts to kill Egypt's President Sadat and the plot to overthrow the Saudi regime in July, 1977, was arrested on charges of planning the overthrow of Qaddafi himself. According to the accusations against Captain Sharif he had been 'turned' by the Saudis, and in concert with Prince Turki, the chief of the Saudi Secret Service, had organised at least three attempts to assassinate General Qaddafi and his closest supporter, Major Jalloud, in the latter part of 1977. In the ensuing investigation the base commander at Uqba bin Naf'i airbase south of Tripoli, Captain Pilot Muhammad al-Said (Captain Sharif's brother-in-law) and about one hundred officers and men of the 7th Armoured Brigade stationed at that base were arrested, and further arrests were made at the military base in Benghazi.

It is not possible to state the degree of likelihood of a coup against the present Libyan regime, although the possibility clearly exists. The principal causes of dissatisfaction in the officer corps are still the Soviet connection and the apparent waste of money on arms which the armed forces cannot use and which rapidly deteriorate, instead of on a more balanced expansion of military capabilities. A growing additional source of unrest may well be the almost total blockage of promotion caused by the permanent alliance of still relatively young officers who came to prominence in the 1969 coup and who continue to occupy all command positions, together with their insistence on keeping their own former ranks of major/lieutenant-colonel and not permitting anyone else to advance even to field grade. On the other hand, the officer corps is still relatively small and relatively easy to keep under surveillance.

In external affairs, there is no sign that Libya proposes any serious change of policy. The military involvement in Chad continues, as does the military confrontation on the Egyptian border. Further armed attempts of Libyan inspiration to overthrow the Sudanese regime, however, seem to have been effectively deterred by the Sudanese—Egyptian alliance of 1975. The dispute with Tunisia over the demarcation of the oil-bearing seabed between the two countries continues to simmer, but is unlikely to flare into open violence. Further afield in the Arab world Libya remains effectively isolated, and unless there were to be radical changes in Egypt there is no way in which the Libyan armed forces could be used for what is proclaimed to be their primary purpose — war against Israel.

Gwynne Dyer

LUXEMBOURG

HISTORY AND INTRODUCTION

A founding member of NATO, Luxembourg revised its constitution in 1948 to abolish its 'perpetually neutral' status. Until 1967 its small army was conscripted; it is now a professional force.

COMMAND AND CONSTITUTIONAL STATUS

The Head of State, Grand Duke Jean, is Commander-in-Chief; executive control is exercised by the Minister of Public Forces, who in the present government also holds the portfolio of Public Health and Environment, and the Civil Service.

STRENGTH AND BUDGET

Population: 364,000
Army: 690; 500 gendarmerie
GNP (1981): $3,770.000,000
Defence expenditure (1982): $32,320,000

ROLE, COMMITMENT, DEPLOYMENT AND RECENT OPERATIONS

The Luxembourg infantry battalion is committed to NATO's ACE Mobile Force. It has not taken part in any recent operations.

ORGANISATION

The army is organised as a four-company battalion for airportable operations; there is also an independent company.

RECRUITMENT, TRAINING AND RESERVES

Recruitment is by voluntary enlistment for a minimum of 3 years. Conscription was abolished in 1967. Personnel were formerly trained by the Belgian army (but the son of the Grand Duke, himself a former Irish Guards officer, was recently commissioned from the Royal Military Academy, Sandhurst). On mobilisation, the country could begin to form a mobile brigade from reserves allotted to the Belgian army, but only after delay.

EQUIPMENT AND ARMS INDUSTRY

Although proportionally to population the most heavily industrialised country in Europe, Luxembourg has no arms industry. The battalion is equipped with NATO small arms and American infantry support weapons.

RANK, DRESS AND DISTINCTIONS

Ranks and rank insignia follow the British system, to brigadier. Dress is also British in appearance – service, battle and combat dress – worn with peaked cap or dark-blue beret. The badge is a crowned cypher 'J'.

CURRENT DEVELOPMENTS

The Luxembourg battalion, being all-regular, is a high-quality component of the ACE Mobile Force. But, though NATO has an air base and a logistic base in the Grand Duchy, the State's chief importance to the alliance is industrial.

John Keegan

MALAGASY REPUBLIC*

HISTORY AND INTRODUCTION

This vast island attained independence from France in 1960 as the Malagasy Republic. On account of a tradition of revolt against French rule it had not produced units of any size for the French Colonial Army, and its military establishment at independence and since has remained very small. Defence was seen, until 1972, to be primarily a French responsibility; France had posted to the Malagasy Republic a foreign legion and a marine regiment, together with air force and naval units. Malagasy political life remained stable under President Tsiranana until 1971 when a left-wing revolt broke out in the south-west area, causing a major political crisis. This worsened in 1972 when riots and student demonstrations on a large scale took place, as a result of which a Northern Merina aristocrat, General G. Ramunantsoa, the Minister of Defence, took effective power into his hands as Prime Minister with the left-wing gendarmerie Colonel R. Ratsimandrava, a non-aristocratic Merina, as Minister of the Interior. A few months later Tsiranana retired completely. The restlessness, however, continued with ethnic conflict occurring in December, 1972 when the coastal peoples attacked Tamatave as a gesture against the Merina domination of Malagasy life. The military government too, was divided, an abortive coup of dissident officers was suppressed in January, 1975, but with a fresh crisis occurring in the following month, when Ratsimandrava took over from Ramanantsoa, to be assassinated almost immediately, and in turn being replaced by the brief regime of General G. Andriamahazo. Ratsimandrava had been assassinated by police rebels, the remainder of a small unit especially raised for his own use by the former President Tsiranana; four days of fighting took place before the army finally suppressed this unit. In June, 1975 Andriamahazo was replaced by a left-wing naval officer, Commander D. Ratsiraka, as Head of State. Ratsiraka comes from the coast and has greatly reduced the plateau Merina hegemony. His policy is the introduction of 'Malagasy revolutionary socialism' based on local democracy. In practice this amounts to small scale populist capitalism, justified by much socialist rhetoric. Political conformity is expected, the regime often being severely authoritarian. Student riots occurred in 1978, 1980, 1981 and 1982, a very small number of people being killed on each occasion. Ratsiraka's hand was strengthened in late 1981 when the leading southern-based opposition movement sought membership of the ruling coalition of parties that forms the government, and again by a measure of electoral success in the 1982 elections. But evidence of discontent is plentiful, a coup conspiracy was 'unearthed' early in 1982 probably in an attempt to win support for the regime. Ratsiraka seems decreasingly able to manage the political scene — a complex one in which several parties of widely differing views bicker within the coalition and Ratsiraka's own party, the *Avant-Garde de la Revolution Malgache* is seen as epitomising the corruption affecting many aspects of Malgache life.

* For general notes on African armies, see Appendix 1.

STRENGTH AND BUDGET

Population: 9,000,000 (approximate).
Armed forces: Army 20,000, Air Force, 600 and a gendarmerie of 7—8000.
GDP: $2,900,000,000.
Defence Expenditure: Not known.

COMMAND AND CONSTITUTIONAL STATUS

President Ratsiraka is Head of State and as such commander of the armed forces.

ROLE, COMMITMENT, DEPLOYMENT AND RECENT OPERATIONS

The Ratsiraka government announced a specific role for the army in the development of a socialist Malagasy Republic. 'Forces of development' are to be established, drawn from six battalions based on provincial capitals, later a seventh was added and the name 'construction regiment' assumed. These heavily outnumber the combat units. For some reason, largely political hysteria, in September 1978 all Malagasy forces were mobilised in anticipation of a 'Mercenary raid'.

ORGANISATION

The army is organised on the basis of two all-arms units (battalions with integrated armour and artillery), an engineer battalion, a logistics battalion, a signals battalion and seven 'construction' regiments.

RECRUITMENT, TRAINING AND RESERVE

A system of national service (military or civic) for 18 months, is in operation: from this soldiers are selected. Both soldiers and officers have in the past been largely Merina.

French training assistance was provided until 1972. The Ramanantsoa government, compelled by pressure of public opinion, sought a new military agreement with France by which the French troops were withdrawn almost at once and the naval facilities shared only for an interim period. Regular French training staff survived for a little longer, but were all withdrawn by the end of the decade. Some of the local resident French community appear to have served for a while on contract. In the early 1980s various reports, none substantiated, have suggested small Cuban, North Korean or East European training staffs.

EQUIPMENT AND ARMS INDUSTRIES

The all-arms units are not well equipped. A small number of BRDM light armoured reconnaissance vehicles are believed to be in service, together with eight elderly US M-3 half track armoured personnel carriers, ten equally elderly British Ferret scout cars, a dozen 76mm guns and small but unspecified numbers of 81mm mortars, 106mm recoilless launchers and two PU-4 14.5mm anti-aircraft cannon. One report suggests small recent deliveries of Chinese type 69 and Soviet RPG-7 grenade launchers 105mm guns, believed to be US, are on order.

The Air Force operates a fighter squadron composed of four MIG-17 and eight MIG-21 aircraft, the latter supplied by North Korea. There is also a transport squadron of assorted machines, two YAK-40, one AN-12 Cub, three HS-748, four AN-26 Curl, five C-47 Skytrain and one C-53. There are also five light liaison aircraft and a helicopter force of one Bell 47, three Alouette and two MI-8 Hip machines.

RANK, DRESS AND DISTINCTIONS

Service uniform follows the French pattern. Ceremonial uniform is white with a coloured busby and plumes.

CURRENT DEVELOPMENTS

Malagasy does not see itself faced with any threat of invasion, little attention is therefore paid to forces designed to meet an external challenge.

The role of the 'construction' regiments may well extend to internal security, although they are ostensibly under the control of OMIPRA, the Office of Military Agricultural Production.

Lloyd Mathews

MALAWI*

HISTORY AND INTRODUCTION

On the dissolution in 1963 of the Federation of Rhodesia and Nyasaland, Nyasaland reverted to the status of a protectorate which it had held since 1891. In July, 1964 it became independent as Malawi, and in 1966 became a republic. Its armed forces consisted initially of the 1st (Nyasaland) Battalion of the King's African Rifles. This was slightly extended to form the Malawi army. In the colonial period battalions of the 1st K.A.R. fought in the World War I German East Africa Campaign where they suffered particularly severe casualties, and in Italian East Africa and Burma in World War II. A unit of the 1st K.A.R. also participated in the force sent to suppress John Chilembwe's rising against British rule in Nyasaland in 1915, one of the very few serious risings against British colonial rule in Africa. Shortly after independence the army had to assist the police force in foiling an attempted rising by the followers of H. Chipembere, a former Cabinet Minister with left-wing views, in the Fort Johnstone area in 1965, and in foiling a second attempted rising planned by another ex-Cabinet Minister, Y. Chisiza in 1967; this latter attempt took place on the Shire river, Chisiza's small party all being killed or captured. Since these events Malawi has remained very stable, though occasional ministerial re-shufflings are an indicator of tensions. President Banda's rule is very authoritarian; opposition within Malawi is covert but opposition organisations exist openly abroad, the most important being Lesoma, the Socialist League of Malawi, based in Maputo and Mafremo, the Malawi Freedom Movement, based in Dar es Salaam. The two are at loggerheads with each other, and additionally President Banda appears to have deprived Mafremo of its leader, an old political adversary, by granting him a pardon and permission to live out his days at home. Internally the government's mass organisations ensure discipline and security.

One further reason for Malawi's stability is that the government never made unreal development promises, but set itself certain practical and attainable aims, largely achieved. However, discontent and frustration do undoubtedly exist.

STRENGTH AND BUDGET

Population: 6,300,000.
Army: 4550; there is also a small barrack police unit of some 800, the army figure includes aviators.
GNP: $ 982,000,000.
Defence expenditure: $40.6,000,000.

COMMAND AND CONSTITUTIONAL STATUS

The Life President, Dr Hastings Banda, formerly held the title of Minister of Defence. Although he no longer does so, the title is held by no-one else and it is unlikely that he has ceased to exercise the function. Malawi is a one-party state, and the President is head of the party and government as well as of the state. The Army Commander is Major General M.M.

Khanga, who somewhat unexpectedly replaced the first Malawi general, Matewere, in 1980. Khanga comes from Dr Banda's home area in the centre of the country.

ROLE, COMMITMENT, DEPLOYMENT AND RECENT OPERATIONS

The army's role is frontier defence and internal security, but apart from minor technical frontier disputes (based on frontiers of the old Maravi African kingdom) with Mozambique, Zambia and Tanzania, Malawi has few alleged security problems, internal or external.

ORGANISATION

The army is organised into 1st, 2nd and 3rd Battalions, The Malawi Rifles (the battalions are small), a support battalion which includes a reconnaissance squadron of armoured cars and an artillery sub-unit, an infantry workshop, a military hospital and an ordnance depot. The permanent barrack installations are at Zomba, Lilongwe and Mzuzu.

RECRUITMENT, TRAINING AND RESERVES

Recruitment is by voluntary enlistment for 7 years, followed by 5 years with the reserve. British personnel formed a training team and European ex-Federation officers remained in post for some years after independence. An African battalion commander was only appointed in 1970 and Malawi's first African army commander only in 1972. Some Malawi officers are trained in Britain, the cadets on the Sandhurst short course and other officers at the Staff College and in specialist schools. Others are trained in Kenya. Malawi possesses its own small officer cadet school at Salima.

EQUIPMENT AND ARMS INDUSTRY

Malawi does not manufacture arms, equipment or munitions. Infantry weapons are the normal British range; some of the army's small arms were provided by South Africa in 1971 to contain Frelimo insurgents. The battalions possess 3.5 rocket launchers and 81mm mortars, the reconnaissance squadron possesses 12 Fox and an unknown small number, probably ten, BRDM-2 light armoured cars, and the artillery battery nine 105mm guns. Other equipment recently arrived includes Blowpipe light surface to air missiles. Some of the ten elderly Ferret armoured cars (also supplied by South Africa in the early 1970s) may still be serviceable.

The air unit possesses six Dornier Do-28 and six Do-27 transports, three Puma and one Alouette helicopters.

RANK, DRESS AND DISTINCTIONS

These follow the British system; the uniform is broadly that of the former King's African Rifles.

---

* For general notes on African armies, see Appendix 1.

Malawi

CURRENT DEVELOPMENTS

Malawi faces severe economic and geographic problems. A realignment of its foreign policy began in 1972, the formerly cordial relations with Portugal and South Africa becoming strained. This realignment was timely in view of the subsequent collapse of Portuguese power and the arrival of the new government in Mozambique, through which all rail traffic to Malawi must pass. But, overall, Malawi's general low-profile preference also serves to keep her from any border or overseas military commitments.

Lesoma, the main opposition group, claims adherents in the Army; two members of the air unit defected to Tanzania in 1981 and alleged that large numbers including the former Army Commander, were secret Lesoma adherents. The claim was certainly very exaggerated, and General Matewere, despite some reports that he was under arrest, appears to be enjoying an honourable retirement. Perhaps more seriously, Lesoma has announced the formation of a military wing. Lesoma is reported to be strongest in the north.

Lloyd Mathews

MALAYSIA

HISTORY AND INTRODUCTION

The Federation of Malaysia came into being in September, 1963. It was formed by enlarging the already existing Federation of Malaya to include the British Colonies of Singapore, Sarawak and Sabah (formerly British North Borneo). Singapore seceded from the Federation in 1965 and today Malaysia comprises 13 States. The two Borneo States of Sarawak and Sabah are collectively referred to as East Malaysia and the 11 States of Malaya as Peninsular Malaysia.

From the sixteenth century onwards until independence the Malaysian territories were inextricably bound up with the development of the European Far Eastern colonial empires. In 1824 the British influence was to become paramount in the territories making up the Federation and the Malaysian army properly speaking traces its origins back to the British period when in 1920 a proposal to form a Malay regiment was first put forward to the Council of the Federated Malay States. The idea was sponsored by the Sultan of Perak and the Yang di-Pertuan of Negri Sembilan and other lesser members of Malay ruling houses. It was only after considerable delay that on March 1st, 1933 an experimental company of Malay soldiers was formed and commenced training. Recruiting went ahead rapidly and by 1937 the unit had reached battalion strength. In that year it joined the 2nd Battalion of the Loyal Regiment and the 1st Battalion of the 17th Dogra Regiment to form the 1st Malayan Infantry Brigade. In July, 1941 the unit was officially named the 1st Battalion of the Malay Regiment. Recruiting continued and by December, 1941 the 2nd Battalion of the Malay Regiment was in existence and a regimental headquarters had been established on the west coast of the Malayan peninsula at Port Dickson in Negri Sembilan.

Both battalions of the Malay Regiment, though scarcely fully trained and totally without experience of active service, fought with the British army in the attempt to stem the advance of the Japanese forces down the Malayan peninsula to Singapore in December, 1941. They surrendered with British and Indian army units in Singapore on February 15th, 1942 but not before they had distinguished themselves in several minor clashes with Japanese troops invading the island.

The Regiment was reformed in 1946 when it was quickly brought back to its pre-war strength. With the outbreak of the Malayan Emergency in 1948 steps were taken to increase the strength of the Regiment to take on a bigger responsibility for anti-terrorist operations alongside the British battalions deployed throughout the peninsula. A third battalion was formed in February, 1949 and a fourth in November of the same year. In 1950 the first Malay officer cadets were sent to England for training at the Royal Military Academy, Sandhurst and by 1953 two more battalions had been formed making six in all.

As the name implies, the Malay Regiment was recruited solely from the Malay population of the Malayan peninsula. In 1953 it was decided to enlist into the army recruits from other sections of Malaya's multi-racial population in which the Chinese almost equalled the Malays in number and the Indians formed a not inconsiderable-minority. It was agreed that the Malay Regiment should continue to recruit only Malays but that two new multi-racial units should be formed – the Federation Regiment of Infantry and the Federation Armoured Car Regiment. By the end of 1954 both these units were committed to anti-terrorist operations and they quickly proved that racially integrated regiments were a feasible proposition.

In 1954 a further battalion of the Malay Regiment was formed and in the same year two Malay Staff Officers took up appointments at the Headquarters of the 1st Federal Division, having qualified at the British Army Staff College at Camberley. In 1954, also, the Federation Military College was established to train officer recruits. It was initially formed at the original Malay Regiment Headquarters at Pork Dickson but at an early stage it was transferred to a permanent location at Sungei Besi, closer to the Federal Capital of Kuala Lumpur.

In 1956, as a step towards Malayan independence, the Federal Armed Forces Council was created and in 1957, the year of independence, the Yang di-Pertuan Agong (the Paramount Ruler) of the Federation of Malaya became Supreme Commander of the Federation of Malaya Armed Forces.

Between 1957 and 1963 when the wider Federation was formed the army continued to expand. While considerable numbers of British army personnel remained seconded to fill crucial appointments, gradually more and more of these key jobs were taken over by Malayan officers and men.

In the early 1960s Malayan units saw service with United Nations forces in the Congo and at that time the Federation Regiment was amalgamated with the Federation Armoured Car Regiment to form the Malayan Reconnaissance Corps.

The foundation of the Federation of Malaysia in 1963 saw a further build up of military forces. The birth of the new State was confronted by the Indonesians who challenged the right of the Federation of Malaya to bring the territories of Sarawak and Sabah into a Malaysian Federation. President Sukarno felt that with the British departure from Borneo the whole island should fall naturally into the Indonesian sphere of influence.

Part of the plan to increase the size of the army to deal with 'confrontation' included the obviously necessary political move to recruit from the newly acquired East Malaysian States of Sabah and Sarawak.

Throughout the years of the Communist Emergency in Malaya the British army had employed Dayaks from Sarawak to assist British units as trackers and expert advisers in surviving and operating in jungle conditions. By 1955 these trackers, who had by then proved their great value, were organised into a small unit of company strength which adopted the title of the Sarawak Rangers. The name had first been used by the last white Rajah of Sarawak when for a brief period in the 1920s and 1930s he had raised a small military force largely to perform ceremonial duties and to act in support of the police in the suppression of minor internal disturbances.

On Malaysia Day the Sarawak Rangers were transferred to the new Malaysian army and renamed the 1st Battalion, the Malaysia Rangers. Recruiting, entirely in Sarawak, raised the unit to battalion strength and at the same time the 2nd Battalion, the Malaysia Rangers was recruited from Sabah. Since 1963 the number of battalions of the Malaysia Rangers has been increased to nine and the territorial and racial

Malaysia

connections of the original two battalions have withered away in the general process of expansion. In essence, the Malaysia Rangers have been used to further develop multi-racial recruiting from the whole of Malaysia. Commanding officers and most company commanders are found from the Malay Regiment which itself has in a sense remained élitist in that it is exclusive to the Malays.

STRENGTH AND BUDGET

Population: 146,661,000 (44% Malay, 36% Chinese, 10% Indian and Pakistani, 8% indigenous tribes (other than Malay) and 2% others)
Army: 80,000 regulars; reserves: approx. 26,000
Navy: 8100 regulars; 1000 reserves; two frigates, 46 smaller craft
Air force: 11000, 37 combat aircraft
GNP (1981): $24,810,000,000
Defence expenditure (1981): $2,050,000,000

COMMAND AND CONSTITUTIONAL STATUS

Command
The Supreme Head of State of Malaysia (the Yang di-Pertuan Agong) is elected for a period of 5 years by the Conference of Rulers of the Malay States of Peninsular Malaysia. He is a constitutional monarch and is, *ex officio*, Supreme Commander of the Malaysian Armed Forces. The three services operate independently but their activities are controlled and co-ordinated by the Armed Forces Council under the Chairmanship of the Minister of Defence. Since the Federation was formed in 1963 successive prime ministers have retained the office of Minister of Defence in their own hands.

The Ministry of Defence
The Armed Forces Council is responsible for command, discipline and administration of the armed forces. It is chaired by the Minister of Defence and includes the Chief of the Armed Forces Staff, the three service chiefs and two other senior military officers, the Secretary General of the Ministry of Defence, a representative of the State Rulers and an appointed member.

The Chief of the Armed Forces Staff's Committee, established by the authority of the Armed Forces Council, is responsible for joint planning and co-ordination of the armed forces. The committee is chaired by the Chief of the Armed Forces Staff, and its membership consists of the Chiefs of Staff of the Army, the Navy and the Air Force, the Chief of Personnel Staff, the Chief of Logistic Staff and the Chief of Staff of the Ministry of Defence.

There are nine staff divisions in the Ministry of Defence:

1. Joint Services Staff Division ⎫ These function on a
2. Personnel Division   ⎬ combined service basis
3. Logistics Division   ⎭
4. Army Division ⎫ These function for their own services and
5. Navy Division ⎬ as service command headquarters
6. Air Division   ⎭
7. Finance Division   ⎫ These are the civil
8. Secretarial Division ⎬ service divisions
9. General Administration Division ⎭

Constitutional Status
The Malaysian Constitution provides for the government of the Federation on Westminster lines. Parliament comprises the Yang di-Pertuan (Head of State), the Dewan Rakyat (House of Representatives) and the Dewan Negara (Senate).

While the army owes its allegiance to the Yang di-Pertuan Agong it is controlled by the government of the day formed from the majority party in the Dewan Rakyat.

There is one anomaly which perhaps deserves comment. According to the Constitution the Yang di-Pertuan is elected for a 5-year period by the Conference of Rulers of the Malay States of the former Federation of Malaya. This in effect means that the Governors of the States of Malacca, Penang, Sarawak and Sabah who are not the heads of hereditary houses, can never become the Yang di-Pertuan Agong. While this situation is not likely to create problems within Malacca or Penang, it is possible to envisage difficulties over divided loyalties for soldiers from Sarawak and Sabah if ever tensions were to build up between Peninsular Malaysia and East Malaysia.

ROLE, COMMITMENT, DEPLOYMENT AND RECENT OPERATIONS

Role and Commitment
The roles of the armed forces are to provide for the close defence of Malaysia against external attack, to secure the lines of communication between and within Malaysian territories and to support the police in ensuring that the authority of the lawful government of Malaysia can be effectively enforced.

While the armed forces are well equipped and trained to cope with the defence of the country against external attack they are hardly strong enough to provide a credible deterrent to a major power with aggressive intentions. Indeed, a former Prime Minister of Malaysia, Tunku Abdul Rahman, is on record as having said he would rather surrender than involve his whole country in widespread destruction.

Until the British withdrawal from Malaysia in 1971, the Anglo–Malayan Defence and Mutual Assistance Treaty of 1957 (extended in 1963 to cover the whole of Malaysia) offered some degree of security as was demonstrated during the period of Indonesian confrontation. After 1971, however, this security was considerably reduced despite the Five Powers Defence Agreement signed in 1971 between Malaysia, Singapore, Great Britain, Australia and New Zealand, which guaranteed consultations in the event of external attack.

The announcement of the British decision to withdraw forces from the Far East coincided with a renewed campaign by the Communist Party of Malaya's military arm, the Malayan National Liberation Army. Since 1968 the number of major incidents involving attacks both against members of the public and the security forces has steadily increased. The attacks have largely been mounted from jungle hideouts on the Thai–Malaya border and have spread further and further out into the peninsula. The resurgence of terrorist activity has led to more and more units of the armed forces being committted to internal security operations and also to moves by the government to increase the size of the armed forces.

Deployment
For some time now the army has been organised on a two divisional basis with the 1st Malaysian Infantry Division deployed in East Malaysia and the 2nd Malaysian Infantry Division in Peninsular Malaysia with its headquarters at Sungei Besi. As a result of an increased security and defence budget incorporated in the Third National Five Year Plan (1976–80) a third division is currently being formed. The two divisions were made up of eight brigades but with the creation of a third division a further three infantry brigades are to be formed. These plans are likely to result in an overall

increase in manpower from the 1976 level of 52,500 to somewhere in the region of 58,500 by 1980. While the redeployments resulting from the increased size of the army are not yet clear, it may reasonably be assumed that the new division will be available to support existing forces in both Peninsular and East Malaysia as the internal security situation demands.

Recent Operations
Units of the army have since 1968 been deployed on anti-terrorist operations on the Thai border where incursions by Communist groups have been and continue to be made. In the same way that terrorists use the remote Thai border areas as a sanctuary in the Peninsula, so do armed guerrillas use the even more inaccessible border between Sabah and Sarawak and Indonesia with the result that the armed forces are similarly deployed in that area.

There have been few spectacular successes for the army in these border operations. Just as during the Malayan Emergency from 1948—60 the terrorists retain the initiative and have the advantage of surprise. This allows them to strike at will in so many different places that it is almost impossible with the limited forces available to bring them to a decisive battle.

ORGANISATION

Arms of Service
There are 12 fighting arms and administrative corps in the army: infantry, reconnaissance, artillery, engineers, special service (commando), signals and intelligence; service corps (supplies and transport), ordnance corps, electrical and mechanical engineers, general service corps (medical, dental, pay and clerical) and provost.

The infantry comprises 26 battalions of the Royal Malay Regiment and 12 battalions of the Malaysia Rangers (multi-racial).

There are a number of training schools and establishments which include the Federation Royal Military College at Sungei Besi and the Recruit Training Centre at Port Dickson.

Operational Organisation
The present order of battle of the army is as follows: four divisional headquarters controlling twelve of 38 infantry battalions; three reconnaissance regiments; four artillery regiments; one mechanised regiment; one special service unit (to be increased to two); five signals regiments; and five engineer and administrative units. Paramilitary forces: a Police Field Force of 19,000, forming 21 battalions, of which two are recruited from aboriginals. The PFF undertakes anti-guerrilla patrols in the jungle.

RECRUITMENT, TRAINING AND RESERVES

The army is a volunteer force. The terms of service for both officers and men are very similar to those of the British army. Soldiers enlist for a period of full-time service followed by a stipulated number of years with the reserve. Currently the army reserve is estimated to be approximately 30,000. There is no requirement for training during reserve service unless a state of emergency is called. Within the Federation there is a territorial army, some units of which have, since 1968, seen extensive periods of mobilisation.

Recruitment
Any citizen of Malaysia of whatever race may present himself for recruitment into the army. The Royal Malay Regiment only accepts Malay recruits but all other arms and corps recruit on a multi-racial basis. Recruiting officers find no problem in obtaining volunteers and the general physical and mental ability of recruits is consequently high. Few Chinese youths, however, volunteer and the majority of those that do, opt for service in one or other of the technical arms.

Training
Officer training is carried out for the most part at the Federal Royal Military College although a few cadets from each intake are selected for training at overseas military schools and academies usually in countries of the British Commonwealth. Several are still sent each year for training at the Royal Military Academy, Sandhurst. More senior officers selected for staff training attend courses overseas often at the British Army Staff College at Camberley. Soldiers newly recruited receive their basic training at the Recruit Training Centre at Port Dickson followed by further training in the units to which they are posted. Specialist training is carried out at a variety of schools including the Catering School, Motor Transport School, Administrative School, E.M.E. School, Signal Schools Air Dispatch School and Intelligence School.

EQUIPMENT AND ARMS INDUSTRY

At the time Malaysia came into being in 1963 virtually all arms and equipment in use in the armed forces originated from British sources. Since then, as replacements and additions have become necessary, the army has looked further afield for its requirements. Today the major items comprise: 60 Ferret scout cars; 200 Commando APCs; 140 AMC/M-3 APCs; 10 5.5in medium guns; 92 105mm howitzers; and 35 40mm anti-aircraft guns.

There is currently no capacity for the manufacture of arms and equipment in Malaysia.

RANK, DRESS AND DISTINCTIONS

Rank

General — Crown and star over crossed kris and sheath
Lieutenant-general — Crown over crossed kris and sheath
Major-general — Star over crossed kris and sheath
Brigadier-general — Crown over three stars
Colonel — Crown over two stars
Lieutenant-colonel — Crown over one star
Major — Crown
Captain — Three stars
Lieutenant — Two stars
Second-lieutenant — One star

The badges of rank follow the British army pattern and are worn on the epaulette. The kris is a traditional Malay two-edged fighting dagger now carried on ceremonial occasions only by Malay royalty and dignitaries. The crown and star emblems are based on Malay Islamic designs.

Dress
For ceremonial parades the uniform basically comprises a white drill tunic and trousers. The Royal Malay Regiment in addition wear a brightly coloured Sarong from waist to knee over the white uniform. The head dress for the Royal Malay Regiment is a songkoh (traditional Malay headwear), while non-Malay troops wear either a peaked cap or beret.

Jungle-green bush jackets or shirts and slacks are worn for normal parade and barrack dress. Shorts with boots and puttees are an alternative within barracks and for drill parades.

On operations combat dress is worn. This consists of camouflaged bush jackets and slacks with a jungle hat (soft brimmed) and jungle boots. The latter are made of light canvas with rubber soles and lace up to below the knee.

Distinctions

A number of orders and medals are awarded for bravery and distinguished service both by the Federal Head of State (the Yang di-Pertuan Agong) on the advice of the Armed Forces Council and by the rulers of the various States within the Federation.

CURRENT DEVELOPMENTS

The Malaysian army is organised largely after the British model and the traditional British military values and ways of working appear to have been assimilated into almost every aspect of army life whether in the officers' mess, on the parade square or in the planning and conduct of operations by the staff. Most of the senior officers in the army received their military education either at Sandhurst or at Camberley and quite frequently at both.

The army is recruited on an entirely regular basis. While it is not easy to recruit from all races (the Chinese in particular are loath to come forward in any number), there is no shortage of suitable volunteers from among the Malays in Peninsular Malaysia or the indigenous tribes of East Malaysia.

The loyalty of the army to the government is currently beyond question but for it to remain so in the future depends on whether or not the government, which is dominated by Malays, can resolve the major political problems centering on the racial minorities within the country. It is not simply a question of whether the Malays can satisfy the political ambitions of the other races generally without weakening their own position. There are two distinct and separate problems: the first involves the Malaysian Chinese and the second the indigenous peoples of East Malaysia.

The Chinese element of the population causes problems in two directions. On the one hand there are those who look, perhaps, to Taiwan for their political ideals and who, since they tend to dominate the Malaysian economy, now want more say in the government. In contrast, there are those Chinese who look to Peking and seek (as they have done since 1948) to destroy the existing political system and set up one on the Peking Model.

The assimilation of the Borneo territories (Sarawak and Sabah) into the Federation has created a physically divided State (to be perhaps compared with Pakistan after 1947) in which one part, Peninsular Malaysia, is so dominant as to result in a distinct sense of imbalance between the two. The people of Sarawak and Sabah, where the Malays are very much in a minority, are inclined to be suspicious of the Kuala Lumpur government because of its domination by the Malays. Their feelings are exacerbated by the fact that their two States were, when they entered the Federation in 1963, and still are, far less well developed in terms of communications, hospitals, schools and other social amenities, than the States of Peninsular Malaysia.

If government succeeds in finding solutions to these problems the army will remain loyal to it. While all ranks, particularly the non-Malays, remain loyal the army will in all probability be effective in carrying out its internal security duties though the experience of the earlier Communist Emergency (1948—60) suggests that there could be difficulties in sustaining the morale of the army should it be subjected to a lengthy and exhausting commitment to arduous and frequently inconclusive anti-terrorist jungle operations.

F. A. Godfrey

REPUBLIC OF MALDIVES

The Maldive archipelago is a chain of 1196 coral islands with a total area of 115 square miles, located in the Indian Ocean about 400 miles south-west of India, and stretching almost 500 miles from north to south. The population of about 143,000 constitutes a distinctive nationality of Indo—Aryan stock speaking its own language, Divehi.

The Maldives have been settled by this population, making its living primarily by fishing and maritime trade, for about two millenia, and their relative geographical isolation and lack of important foreign resources have preserved them from any long-term colonial occupation. The Portuguese seized the islands in 1558 but were driven out in 1573, and a conquest by pirates from Malabar in 1752 lasted only 4 months. In 1887 the Maldives became a British protectorate, handing over responsibility for their defence and foreign affairs to the British governor in Ceylon, but the Sultans continued to exercise full internal control. Originally Buddhist, the islands have been 100% Sunni Muslim since 1153, when the ruler of the time was converted to Islam by a travelling Moroccan saint and ordered the entire population to follow suit.

The autocratic rule of the sultans was restricted by a constitution in 1932 following a court rebellion, and a short-lived republic was created in 1953 only to be reversed by a royal counter-coup within a year. From 1957 the islands were in fact ruled by the Prime Minister who became President when a referendum in 1968 approved the creation of the Second Republic. There is no official opposition nor any political parties, and there has been no Prime Minister since Ahmed Zaki fell foul of the President in 1975 and was banished to a distant island.

From 1957 to 1965 the Maldives were locked into a dispute with Britain over the terms, agreed in 1956 just before Ibrahim Nasir came to power, on which Gan Island in Addu Atoll at the extreme southern end of the archipelago was leased to the Royal Air Force as its main staging base to the Far East. During this period the 15,000 people of the three southernmost atolls seceded from the Maldives under the leadership of one Afif and declared an independent Republic of Suvadiva.

The dispute was finally resolved in July, 1965 when protectorate status was ended and the Maldives became fully independent and joined the United Nations. The secession was formally ended and Afif went into exile in the Seychelles. However, full control from Male, the capital, was not re-established until Britain prematurely terminated the lease and withdrew the RAF from Gan in March, 1976. Southern hostility to Male remains considerable, and has been exacerbated by the drastic fall in living standards occasioned by the closure of the base and the loss of over 800 jobs.

The primary role of the Maldivian National Guard, combining army and police functions, is internal security, and a considerable proportion of it has been deployed in these southernmost atolls since 1976. It is under the control of the Ministry of Public Safety. No details are available on the National Guard's size, training or equipment.

The Maldives' major strategic asset is the large air base at Gan. Immediately after the British left in March, 1976 thereby depriving the Maldives of an estimated $600,000 in foreign exchange per year (20% of total foreign income), the government began advertising in the international press that Gan was available for lease. It was withdrawn from the market after the Maldives joined the Non-Aligned Movement with Libyan sponsorship in August of that year, however, and in October, 1977 President Nasir rejected a $1,000,000 Soviet offer for the lease of the base.

In the growing international competition for Indian Ocean bases Gan has become one of the more attractive targets, and the Maldives was honoured by visits from the Iranian, United States, Indian and Sri Lankan navies in 1976—7. During the same period Libya, India and Pakistan opened the first foreign embassies in Male. However, President Nasir has stated that he does not wish to lease the island base to a superpower (nor, presumably, to a superpower's ally), and is seeking alternative ways of exploiting the facilities there. So long as his own power base remains secure and the National Guard loyal, it is unlikely that Gan will again be used as a military base. The Maldives became a member of the Commonwealth in July, 1982

Gwynne Dyer

MALI*

HISTORY AND INTRODUCTION

Mali attained independence from France in 1966; in the colonial period it was known as Soudan. For a few months a Federation of Mali, composed of the present Mali and Senegal, existed but this proved unworkable. During its brief period of life the Mali Federation sent a battalion formed of companies from both States to the UN Congo Force where it gained a great reputation.

From 1960 to 1968 Mali was ruled by President M. Keita; in 1968 he was overthrown by a military coup led by Lt. Moussa Traoré, who formed a Military Committee for National Liberation, mostly of officers of captain and subaltern ranks. More senior officers were retired, others who opposed the coup were arrested. The reasons for the coup appear to have been the radical socialism of Keita, economic stagnation, and the formation of a Chinese-trained and equipped People's Militia. Keita also enjoined the army to participate in radical political education and rural agricultural developments. In 1969 further arrests of dissident army officers said to be in a conspiracy followed, and in 1971 Traoré's principal aide and fellow conspirator of 1968, Diakite and one other senior officer, both of right-wing, Francophile views, were arrested for treason, and sentenced to long terms of imprisonment. More arrests followed in 1974.

In 1974 a new constitution promising a return to political rule in 5 years was promulgated, but arrangements for this have been very dilatory. In February, 1978 the Minister for Defence, Colonel Doukara, the Chiefs of Staff of the Army and Gendarmerie and other senior members of the military government were arrested; there have been other reports of restlessness both in the army and the nation as a whole.

The regime is not popular, being authoritarian in political style and inefficient in its handling of the economy. An attempted coup, led by a gendarmerie NCO was foiled in early 1981.

STRENGTH AND BUDGET

Population: 6,750,000 (approximate).
Armed Forces: 4600 Army, 300 Air Force, 5000 gendarmerie.
GNP: $700,000,000 (estimate).
Defence expenditure: $30,000,000 (approximate).

COMMAND AND CONSTITUTIONAL STATUS

The Head of State is Colonel Moussa Traoré. A military governor is head of the administration in each of the country's six regions.

ROLE, COMMITMENT, DEPLOYMENT AND RECENT OPERATIONS

The roles of the Mali army are defence against external threats and internal security. In 1974—5 Mali's border dispute with

Upper Volta reached a crisis and troops were sent to the disputed area. Clashes took place, but mediation by other west African States has succeeded in reducing the tension. The army performed well in Sahel drought relief work in 1974. More recently troops have been moved to the country's northern border. One major reason for this is the desire to prevent Polisario activity and recruiting; another reason may well have been the desire of the government to have personnel whose loyalty was in doubt some considerable distance away. Very recently a border dispute with Volta has necessitated further troop deployments

Mali is a member of ANAD, the treaty of mutual aid in the event of air attack signed by seven West African states.

ORGANISATION

The army comprises four infantry battalions, a tank company, a 'parachute battalion', an artillery unit, an anti-aircraft sub-unit and a small commando force.

RECRUITMENT, TRAINING AND RESERVES

A random system of 2 years' military or civic service exists.

Very early in her independent existence, Mali decided not to use French training aid or facilities, the French being asked to leave in 1961. The result was then a mixture of assistance from elsewhere superimposed upon pre-independence French training. In 1963 a number of officers were sent to the USA. By 1964 Keita had opted for Soviet help, and personnel were being sent to the USSR. Since the coup some limited training aid has been obtained from France. Air Force personnel are trained in the USSR.

An officers' school exists at Koti and an academy at Bamako.

Overall training standards are poor, and the results of this were to be seen in the confusion during some of the border commitments.

EQUIPMENT AND ARMS INDUSTRY

Mali has no arms industry. Most of its ageing military equipment is Soviet, dating from the Keita period. It includes some 20 T-34 and 25 T-54 tanks together with ten Chinese Type 62 light tanks, 20 BRDM-2 reconnaissance vehicles, 10 BTR-152 and 30 BTR-40 armoured personnel carriers. The artillery possesses 85mm and 100mm guns, 120mm mortars and 57mm anti-aircraft guns, the infantry is equipped with Soviet battalion weapons and 81mm mortars. The anti-aircraft battery is equipped with Soviet SAM-3 missiles. The air force machines include five MIG-17 fighters, two C47, three AN-2, two AN-24, two IL-14 and one Corvette 200 transport and communication aircraft; two MIG-15, six YAK-11 and six L-29 aircraft are used for training, and there are in addition two MI4 and one MI8 helicopters. One unconfirmed report notes a recent delivery of eight MIG-19 and fourteen MIG-21 aircraft and a small number of BTR-60 armoured personnel carriers from the USSR.

* For general notes on African armies, see Appendix 1.

RANK, DRESS AND DISTINCTIONS

These follow the French patterns, except that the *képi* is replaced by a peaked cap.

CURRENT DEVELOPMENTS

The Mali army is no longer the force which gave French Sudanese troops their redoubtable reputation. Ethnic rivalries and jealousies are strong and affect efficiency. The serviceability of much of the older Soviet equipment is doubtful. The poverty of Mali precludes any great expansion of her armed forces. On the other hand border anxieties occupy the attention of the army and provide some explanation of the longevity of the regime.

Recently, some debate upon a possible union with Guinea-Conakry has begun.

Lloyd Mathews

MALTA

As a group of three small islands commanding the relatively narrow passage between the eastern and western Mediterranean, most of Malta's history has been spent under one imperial rule or another, as maritime predominance in the Mediterranean passed from nation to nation. Over most of the past two centuries, therefore, it was under British rule, serving as a naval base and later also as an air base. During World War II it withstood the latest of a long series of sieges, and the entire island was collectively awarded the George Cross, Britain's highest civilian decoration for valour.

Even after Malta gained its independence in 1964 the mainstay of the economy remained the extensive British military facilities in the island, and a 10 year agreement was signed regulating the terms of the British military presence which also provided for Malta's defence. It was only with the election of a socialist government under Prime Minister Dom Mintoff in 1971 that the country began to pursue a non-aligned course in its international relations, and adopted the ultimate aim of ensuring its security and its income without the need for foreign military bases.

A new bases agreement was negotiated under which the rent paid by Britain (with contributions from other NATO powers) was greatly increased to £14,000,000 per annum. Only British forces were to use the bases, and they were to be used only for the purpose of defending the United Kingdom and NATO. Under no circumstances would they be used against any Arab country, and all British forces were to be withdrawn on termination of the new agreement in 1979. The last British troops left the island in March, 1979.

This leaves Malta with two rather large problems: to restructure the economy so as to make up for the lost income from the foreign military presence, and to find an alternative means of providing its military security. Some progress has been made on the first: the proportion of Malta's foreign exchange earnings derived from the British bases had fallen drastically to only 16% by 1975 (though their total contribution to the economy was still some $80,000,000 a year, a rather large sum for a country with only a third of a million people). On the question of security after the departure of the British forces, however, arrangements are still incomplete.

The Maltese army first took form in 1965, when the Government of Malta took over the three Maltese Territorial (reserve) Units hitherto maintained by the British army. In the following year these were reduced by amalgamation to two: The Light Air Defence Regiment RMA (T) and the 1st Battalion the King's Own Malta Regiment.

The regular Maltese units were transferred to Maltese government control in 1970: they consisted of the 1st Regiment Royal Malta Artillery, the RMA Band, and the Logistics unit. A Helicopter Flight was added in 1972, and with the raising in 1973 of three battalions of the Malta Pioneer Corps (*Dirghazn il-Maltin*), a paramilitary force recruited on a voluntary basis whose main purpose is to keep down the unemployment rate, the force had arrived at its present structure, and assumed its present title: The Armed Forces of Malta.

Armed Forces headquarters is at St Andrew's Barracks, and the Helicopter Flight is based at Luga Airport. Basic training is done in Malta, and specialised training, especially for the air section, has been provided by the armed forces of Libya, Italy, West Germany, Tunisia and North Korea. Maltese uniforms are patterned very closely on the British model. The Maltese defence budget in 1981 was $11.4m, just under one per cent of GNP.

Together with a 1,300-man police force, these formations seem more than ample to assure the internal security of the country.

Obviously, however, they have virtually no capability for external defence, although Malta remains a most desirable piece of strategic territory. Prime Minister Mintoff announced just before he was narrowly re-elected in 1976 that he intended to seek a guarantee of Malta's security through a treaty with all its immediate neighbours: France, Italy, Algeria, Tunisia and Libya. Not only would these powers guarantee the country's independence and neutrality, he suggested, but they might do so jointly through some yet-to-be-defined Mediterranean alliance. He even hinted that they might make use of Malta's extensive military facilities from time to time on a temporary basis, though there would be no permanent basing of foreign troops on the island in the future. They were to pay an annual sum of $56,000,000 in return for Malta's neutrality and occasional use of the bases.

The first state to respond directly to Mintoff's invitation was Italy, which in September, 1980, after consultation with its NATO allies, concluded an agreement whereby Malta would declare its neutrality and specifically guarantee that it would not adhere to any alliance, permit foreign military bases or soldiers on its soil, or extend ship-repair facilities to either US or Soviet warships in the Mediterranean. In return Italy made a lump-sum payment of approximately $20m in the form of soft loans and technical aid, and will provide an annual grant of about $5m. Italy agreed to consultations if Malta is attacked and guaranteed the island's independence. In December 1981 France and Algeria also agreed to support and guarantee Malta's neutrality.

Malta's relations remain cordial with all its other neighbours except Libya, with whom it has a dispute over the extent of their respective territorial waters.

An Italian oil exploration rig operating under Maltese government licence was compelled to cease operations by Libyan warships in 1980 and Malta retaliated by expelling some 50 Libyan military advisers from the island. Relations between the two neighbours remain cool, but not tense. Prime Minister Mintoff was re-elected in 1981, and his policy of 'passive neutralism' seems likely to be the basis of Maltese defence policy for the foreseeable future.

Gwynne Dyer

MAURITANIA

HISTORY AND INTRODUCTION

The Islamic Republic of Mauritania is one of the more artificial legacies of the colonial era. Like several other Sahel States its population is divided between a nomadic, Berber—Arab-related stock in the north of the country and a sedentary black African population in the extreme south, but uniquely amongst the Sahel States it is the northerners who have dominated the government.

When the country attained independence from France in 1960 Moors made up about 70% of the population, but by the 1980s the far higher birth rate amongst the African peasants along the right bank of the Senegal River in the far south had increased their share of the 1,500,000 population to about 50%.

The persistent droughts of the early 1970s had meanwhile virtually destroyed the traditional Moorish nomadic economy, wiping out 90% of their cattle and about half of their camel herds, thus forcing at least half of the Moorish population to adopt a sedentary and economically marginal existence on the fringes of the capital, Nouakchott (which has been growing since 1970 at 20% a year) and the other main towns. Nevertheless, the Moorish element of the population still dominates the government and the officer corps of the armed forces.

From the day of its independence Mauritania's existence has been threatened by the nature of its population. Morocco, to the north, did not drop its claim to all of Mauritania as a traditional Moroccan domain in the pre-colonial era until 1969, and the country was only admitted to the Arab League in 1973. Senegal, to the south, did not raise any equivalent claim to the southern areas of Mauritania which are inhabited by people who are racially, linguistically and culturally akin to the Senegalese, but there was nevertheless an implicit pull in that direction. As Mauritania's unity became ever more strained by the war it became involved in, in 1975, Senegal's President Léopold Senghor stated explicitly for the first time in January, 1978 that if the Mauritanian State should be destroyed as a result of the war over the Western Sahara, he would have to demand self-determination (i.e. union with Senegal) for Mauritania's black population in the far south.

Despite the inherent fissiparous tendencies of the country, Mauritania enjoyed a remarkably stable internal political situation — apart from the 1966—7 clashes between the then majority Moorish population and the negro southerners over the question of (Arabic) language instruction in the schools — until 1976. The government headed since 1960 by Moktar Ould Daddah effected a successful reconciliation over this question (while not losing its essentially Moorish character), and also succeeded in creating a significant export sector in the economy through the development of the Zouérate iron ore mines and the Akjoujt copper ore mines, although the country remained amongst the poorest in the world. Ould Daddah pursued a socialist policy in domestic affairs which won his single party, the Parti du Peuple Mauritanien, the tacit support of the clandestine Marxist Party, the Kadihines. In international affairs he followed a policy of prickly independence, terminating a defence treaty with France in 1972, and withdrawing from the French African currency bloc and creating a separate Mauritanian currency, the ougiya, in 1973. He subsequently nationalised the French mining interests. He maintained close links with Algeria in order to ward off the territorial pretensions of Morocco (which maintained its claim to a 'Greater Morocco', incorporating Mauritania as well as the Sahara, south-western Algeria and northern Mali, until 1969), and generally adhered to the positions of the radical bloc in inter-Arab affairs.

Mauritanian international policy underwent a radical reversal in October, 1974, however, when President Ould Daddah concluded a secret agreement with Morocco for the partition of the Spanish colony of (Western) Sahara which lay between the two countries. It was all the more extraordinary in that hitherto Mauritania had provided bases, support and much of the personnel for the guerrilla movement Frente Polisario which was fighting (not very effectively) for the independence of that Spanish colony. The abrupt switch of policy has been variously attributed to a mistaken belief that Algeria approved of the agreement, to a conviction that Morocco was determined to annex the territory anyway and that a Mauritanian-controlled buffer zone was therefore essential, and to sheer personal folly on the part of President Ould Daddah. The result, in any case, was to embroil Mauritania in a war which almost destroyed it.

Following the adroitly stage-managed Moroccan 'Green March' into the Spanish Sahara in 1975, Madrid hastily concluded a tripartite agreement with Morocco and Mauritania in November granting them the territory (and ignoring the United Nations' demand for a referendum on independence) in return for a continuing interest in the territory's rich phosphate mines at Bou Craa. This agreement, signed 6 days before Franco's death, was followed by the physical occupation of the territory by Morocco and Mauritania in early 1976. The southern area allocated to Mauritania was named Tiris el-Gharbia, and Nouakchott claimed that the support for the Mauritanian government expressed in the general elections which were held throughout the expanded national territory in August, 1976 obviated any need to hold a referendum in the former Spanish territory.

Well before that, however, it had become evident that the Marxist organisation Polisario was determined to resist the partition and annexation of the territory by Morocco and Mauritania, and that it enjoyed the whole-hearted support of Algeria in its struggle. Much of the scanty Saharan population (totalling less than 100,000) fled or was removed to refugee camps across the Algerian frontier around Tindouf, and arms and military bases were provided to Polisario in the same area. A government-in-exile of the 'Saharan Arab Democratic Republic', claiming sovereignty over the newly acquired Moroccan and Mauritanian territories, was set up in Algiers, and was recognised by Algeria and a number of other radical African States. By mid-1976, moreover, it was clear that Polisario's strategy was to strike primarily at the weaker of its two opponents, Mauritania, in the hope of destroying the alliance which had thwarted Saharan independence. (For details of the fighting in Mauritania, *see* Recent Operations.)

In the course of the succeeding 2 years the Mauritanian armed forces, a small constabulary force inherited from the era of French colonial rule, were expanded more than tenfold to cope with Polisario's assaults, and military expenditure rose to exceed 50% of the national budget, but no decisive result was obtained. Polisario columns continued to strike deep into Mauritania proper, as well as Tiris el-Gharbia, from their Algerian bases, and Mauritania's iron-ore exports were seriously curtailed by guerrilla raids on the railway between Zouérate and the sea. The formation of a joint defence pact with Morocco and arrangements for a joint military command (inevitably dominated by the Moroccans) in May, 1977, followed by the introduction of large numbers of Moroccan troops into the northern areas of the country, failed to end the raids, while rousing dormant Mauritanian suspicions about Morocco's annexationist desires. The provision of French air support and reconnaissance from bases in Senegal beginning in December, 1977 had a much more visible effect in restricting Polisario attacks, but it was nevertheless the case that both the Mauritanian armed forces and the populace at large were extremely demoralised by mid-1978.

Apart from the sheer strain and cost of the war effort, the ruling party's position was being undermined by the increasing alienation of its more radical erstwhile supporters, including the Kadihines and its own youth wing, as Moroccan and French influence grew increasingly pronounced in the country. (By the end of 1977 there were 300 French troops, and up to 10,000 Moroccan troops, in the country.) A considerable proportion of the Moorish population was in any case secretly sympathetic to the Polisario cause, and many actually had friends or relatives fighting with Polisario. Within the armed forces, the predominantly Moorish officer corps were equally affected by these influences, while the mainly negro enlisted ranks showed little enthusiasm for dying in a Moorish quarrel.

President Ould Daddah's anxiety about a coup was shown by his constant shuffling and reshuffling of senior officers' appointments, but by late 1977 he was no longer able to resist the military demand that he break with precedent and appoint an officer as Defence Minister. On July 10th, 1978 he was overthrown in a bloodless coup led by the Army Chief of Staff, Lieutenant-Colonel Mustapha Ould Muhammad Salek, who enjoyed general support within the army. A military *junta* of 18 officers, known as the Military Committee for National Recovery, took control and appointed a 16 man cabinet (including eight officers) to administer the affairs of the government. Two days later Polisario unilaterally declared a ceasefire (to apply to Mauritania only, not to Morocco), in the hope that the new Mauritanian regime would be willing to negotiate a peace settlement giving the guerrillas most of what they wanted.

The new Mauritanian regime is politically considerably to the right of Ould Daddah, and has strong links with the powerful former Emir of Mauritania, the major Hodh tribe in the east of the country, and other conservative forces. Despite its instant affirmation of adherence to Ould Daddah's close links with France and Morocco, it is clearly a nationalist regime that fears excessive Moroccan influence or even takeover. While quite prepared to relinquish the empty and valueless Tiris el-Gharbia in return for peace with Polisario, the *junta* is quite aware that the large numbers of Moroccan troops already on Mauritanian soil — certainly more than a match for the Mauritanian armed forces — do not permit it to seek a separate peace against Morocco's wishes. (For further comments, *see* **Current Developments.**)

STRENGTH AND BUDGET

The Mauritanian army in 1982 was estimated to number about 8,000, a sharp decline from the total that had been reached by the end of Mauritania's participation in the Sahara war in 1979. There are also about 2,500 paramilitary gendarmes and nomad units. The air force numbers about 150 men, and the navy 320.

The army expanded at an extremely rapid rate after 1975,

when its strength, stable since independence, was about 1500. The most rapid period of growth was in mid-1976 to mid-1977, when it grew from 3000 to about 12,000, after France had taken over almost the entire responsibility for training the new recruits. The armed forces amount to less than 1% of the national population; the enlisted ranks are mainly drawn from unemployed black Mauritanians living in the far south.

The defence budget for 1981 was $59,900,000, which is still a very large proportion of a GNP estimated at only $700m. It represents a considerable drop from 1978, however, when defence spending accounted for approximately a fifth of the entire GNP.

The hardships caused by this were even more acute because Polisario's strategy during the war was to undermine the Mauritanian economy.

By far the most vulnerable target was the iron ore mines at Zouerate, which earn about 80% of Mauritania's foreign exchange, and the 400 mile railway connecting them with the country's main port at Nouadhibou. Constant Polisario attacks cut output by 12.4% in 1977, and possibly by an even greater amount in 1978. The loss of revenue caused by this and the fall in world prices of iron ore, combined with the closure of the country's only copper ore mine at Akjoujt and the continuing severe effects of the prolonged Sahelian drought on the country's agriculture, resulted in a drastic reduction of government revenue at a time when military expenditure was making unprecedented demands upon it.

Without financial support amounting to a reported $400,000,000 in 1976—8 from the conservative Arab States, principally Saudi Arabia, the United Arab Emirates and Kuwait, the government would have gone bankrupt; even as it was, some civil servants were going unpaid for as much as 6 months, and it is beyond question that the severe economic hardships brought by the war played a large part in paving the way for the July, 1978 coup.

The new government has done all in its power to preserve the ceasefire, and has accelerated the trend back towards a liberal, private-enterprise economy that was already evident in the last year of Ould Daddah's rule, in an attempt to attract desperately needed foreign capital. Iron ore production is now being raised from the 8,400,000 tonne low of 1977 to 11,000,000 tonnes, and good progress has been made on securing the necessary $460,000,000 in foreign loans to open large new iron ore mines at El-Rhein in the Guelb area north of Zouérate. Both these improvements and the somewhat lower level of military demands on the tottering economy, however, are critically dependent on the maintenance of the ceasefire and an eventual peace settlement with Polisario.

COMMAND AND CONSTITUTIONAL STATUS

The constitution in effect since 1960 provided for a strong President elected by direct, universal suffrage for 5 years, who exercised control over the armed forces through a Minister of Defence (the incumbent of the latter post being always, until 1977, a civilian). The senior army officer was the Chief of Staff, who exercised executive command. The Inspector-General of the Armed Forces was chiefly responsible for matters of discipline and training. The country is divided into three military regions, with headquarters at Nouakchott (the south), Atar (the north) and Néma (the east). The navy and air force were subordinate to the army, but the Commander-in-Chief of the Gendarmerie was responsible to the Minister of the Interior.

Since the coup of July, 1978 however, the former President and most of his ministers have been in detention, and the constitution has been suspended. Colonel Ould Salek, while remaining Chief of Staff, also heads the 18 member Military

Committee for National Recovery, which in turn dominates the 16 member cabinet. Parliament has been dissolved and the precise relationship between the present organs of government has not been defined, but it is clear that the army makes all important decisions.

Since May 13th, 1977 the Mauritanian armed forces have been closely linked with those of Morocco by a defence agreement which provides for the stationing of Moroccan troops on Mauritanian soil and the co-ordination of military activities by means of a joint command organisation. The formal body known as the High Defence Committee meets once a month, but at least until Polisario's ceasefire in Mauritania in July, 1978 there were informal consultations between the military staffs of Mauritania and Morocco (and French liason officers co-ordinating French air force reconnaissance and strike sorties out of Senegal) on a daily basis. Despite the formal equality of representation, Mauritania is clearly the junior partner in this arrangement.

ROLE, COMMITMENT, DEPLOYMENT AND RECENT OPERATIONS

The role of the Mauritanian army, which was almost exclusively internal security until 1975, is now primarily defence against external threat, though all the fighting has been taking place within Mauritania. The fighting opened in December, 1975, when the Mauritanian army encountered Polisario resistance in the Noudhibou – Agüera region and inland at Fort Gouraud while occupying its share of the former Spanish Sahara. It acquitted itself well in these early encounters, and control was soon established over all centres of population in the territory. Soon afterwards, however, Polisario began to employ its since standard tactic of sending motorised raiding columns numbering up to 100 men or more long distances across the desert from their Algerian bases around Tindouf to carry out hit-and-run raids on targets within the former Spanish colony, and within Morocco and Mauritania proper. Given the vast distances and sparse population of Mauritania, discovering and dealing with these mobile raiding columns proved to be a task of considerably greater difficulty.

Early on in the war Polisario settled on Mauritania as its main target, on the grounds that it was much the weaker of its two enemies and that there existed a substantial sympathy for the organisation's aims amongst the members of the R'guibat, Izarguen and Touareg tribes of northern Mauritania – the same major tribes from which Polisario draws most of its Saharan recruits. For the same reason, the Mauritanian army has been unable to rely heavily on Moorish recruits for the war, and has depended mainly on black Africans from the Senegal River valley, who were both unenthusiastic about the war and unaccustomed to the desert conditions in which it was fought.

The extent of concealed opposition to Ould Daddah's Moroccan alliance was indicated by the daring Polisario raid which was mounted across hundreds of miles of open desert in June, 1976 against the Mauritanian capital, Nouakchott. The powerfully armed column was led in person by Polisario's Secretary-General, Ahmed el Wali, and the raid would probably not have been risked had not Polisario been counting on some form of rising in the capital co-ordinated with its attack. In the event, no such revolt occurred, however, and the bulk of the Polisario column, some 600 strong, was cut off and destroyed on its way back to Algeria, el Wali himself being amongst the dead. This was a major setback to Polisario, which confined itself to minor operations for the rest of the year while recruiting and training more troops, but by the

spring of 1977 it was ready to launch a full-scale offensive against Mauritania.

Polisario's raids, often cutting across the uninhabited north-western corner of Mali to strike into Mauritania from the east, were intended to isolate Morocco, either by forcing Nouakchott out of the war or by compelling Morocco to occupy its neighbour. They seen achieved notable success: on May 1st, 1977 Polisario forces took and held for several hours the mining centre of Zouérate, the best-defended site in the country, killing and capturing some French mining technicians and compelling the evacuation of most of the rest. (The Mauritanian garrison did not leave its barracks.) Within days, 600 Moroccan troops were flown in to defend Zouérate, and on May 13th a joint defence agreement was signed by Rabat and Nouakchott permitting the permanent stationing of Moroccan troops on Mauritanian territory. In June Polisario forces again stuck at Nouakchott, and Zouérate was hit twice more during 1977, while the railway from there to Nouadhibou was repeatedly cut and various smaller centres, including the military base at Tmeichatt, were the targets of other successful raids.

The Mauritanian army's casualties during 1977 probably totalled fewer than 500, but its inability to stop the Polisario raids, coupled with the resentment it felt at being largely supplanted by Moroccan troops and controlled by French advisers (the Moroccan expeditionary force in Mauritania had risen to about 10,000 troops by the end of 1977, while the number of French advisers had grown from 60 to over 300), contributed to a marked demoralisation of the Mauritanian armed forces. French also had 1200 troops in neighbouring Senegal ready for instant intervention if the military need arose, but the key step proved to be the stationing of a squadron of Jaguar fighter–bombers and a detachment of Breguet Atlantique reconnaissance aircraft in Senegal in December for operations over Mauritania.

During the first half of 1978, the combination of garrisons of tough Moroccan troops throughout northern Mauritania, good intelligence on Polisario movements provided by French reconnaissance aircraft, and on at least two occasions the annihilation of Polisario columns by Jaguar airstrikes, all served to reduce very considerably the guerrillas' freedom of movement in Mauritania. It did not, however, prevent the Mauritanian military coup of July 10th, 1978, since when Polisario has observed a ceasefire throughout the country in the hope that the new government will offer acceptable peace terms. The Moroccan garrisons remain in place, however, so Mauritania is far from a free agent in this regard.

The Mauritanian army's deployment during 1975–8 kept the airborne company and the paratroop commando company in the capital together with one of the three reconnaissance squadrons, the other two being stationed in the Néma and Atar military regions. The great majority of the motorised infantry squadrons which comprise the bulk of the army was deployed in the northern (Atar) military region, including Tiris el-Gharbia. Since the ceasefire a substantial number of the latter have been pulled back to Nouakchott, especially from Tiris el-Gharbia, for reasons which may not be entirely unconnected with the dispositions of Moroccan forces in Mauritania.

About 3000 Moroccan troops are in the extreme north of Mauritania, based in the towns of Ain ben Tili, Bir Moghrain and Dakhla along what has since 1976 been the Moroccan–Mauritanian border. There are two Moroccan battalions at Zouérate, the iron-ore mining centre in the north, and two more protecting the rail line to Nouadhibou and the port itself. A detachment of Moroccan F-5 fighter–bombers is also based at Noudhibou. The most significant Moroccan garrisons politically, however, may be the two battalions stationed at Atar and Akjoujt. The latter town has never been threatened by guerrillas, but is only 150 miles from the capital by a good road; the introduction of Moroccan troops there in January, 1978 caused demonstrations by the Mauritanian army. Almost all of Mauritania's main towns except Nouakchott itself now have Moroccan garrisons which are numerical comparable to their Mauritanian army garrisons, and are considerably superior to them in combat ability. combat ability.

Mauritania is a member of the United Nations, the Arab League and the Organisation of African States. There are no Mauritanian military commitments beyond the country's own borders, however.

ORGANISATION

The arms of service are modelled on those of the French army. The army is organised operationally into one infantry battalion, one artillery battalion, one Camel Corps unit, three armoured reconaissance squadrons, one AA battery, one engineer company and one parachute company.

RECRUITMENT, TRAINING AND RESERVES

The traditional recruiting pattern of the Mauritanian army was to draw its officers primarily from leading families in the Arab—Berber tribes of the desert north and centre, and to recruit its enlisted men from the black peasant population of the Rosso area near Senegal. In recent years the army began making a belated effort to balance its ranks more evenly between the country's major ethnic communities, but the demand for rapid expansion created by the war and the reluctance of many northern tribesmen to engage in what was essentially a Berber civil war caused a reversion towards the old pattern of recruitment. This had certain unfortunate effects, as the black recruits had no personal commitment to the war and little even to the country itself, as they regard themselves with some justice as second-class citizens of Mauritania. There is legal provision for 2 years' compulsory national service to be enforced nationwide, but in fact the army's needs are generally satisfied by the flow of volunteers from the Rosso area seeking refuge from unemployment.

From the time of independence France has provided training staff and assistance, and the majority of the present generation of Mauritanian senior officers were trained at French military academies. Since the war began in 1975 France has quintupled the number of its military advisers in the country and assumed the major part of the responsibility for training. A combined officers' and NCOs' school has been opened at Atar, with French instructors and a French-language curriculum.

There is no formal reserve organisation, but recent reports indicate that a new local home defence reserve has been created. The 2500 strong Gendarmerie, armed and equipped rather like the army, functions as an immediate reserve.

EQUIPMENT AND ARMS INDUSTRY

The army's equipment is predominantly French. Its reconnaissance squadrons use 15 EBR-75, 39 AML-60 and 14 AML-96 armoured cars. The infantry have 40 M-3 half-tracks and four M-3APCs. Infantry weapons are French, and light support weapons include 60mm and 81mm mortars and 57mm, 75mm and 106mm recoilless rifles. The army has no artillery or tanks, and is organised for mobile counter-insurgency warfare only. Air defence relies on 14.5mm, ZU-23-2 and 37mm AA guns and SA-7 SAM.

The small navy has eight patrol craft, one Patron-class, two Muny-class, three Barcelo class and two smaller vessels. The air force's combat element consists of five Defender and two Cessna 337 COIN aircraft. There are two Piper Cheyenne aircraft used for marine reconnaissance, and the transport flight has one DHC-5D, one Caravells, one Skyvan and one Islander.

There is no arms industry at all in Mauritania.

RANK, DRESS AND DISTINCTIONS

Ranks in the Mauritanian armed forces follow the French model, and both service and combat uniforms are patterned on their French equivalents. No information is available on medals and distinctions.

CURRENT DEVELOPMENTS

In early 1979 the ceasefire declared by Polisario (applying to Mauritania only) after the July, 1978 coup in Nouakchott was still holding, if precariously. Peace negotiations had been held with Polisario through a variety of intermediaries, including France, Libya (which furnished financial aid to Mauritania both before and after the coup despite its support for Polisario) and a committee of five 'wise men' (the Heads of State of Sudan, Tanzania, Guinea, Ivory Coast and Nigeria) set up by the Organisation of African Unity. No positive results have been achieved, however, probably due to the fact that the presence of 10,000 Moroccan troops in Mauritania, including some stationed at Akjoujt which could be seen as a force poised to intervene in Nouakchott if required, imposed a decisive limitation on the concessions Mauritania could make in order to gain a peace settlement.

It was clear throughout 1978 that Morocco itself was desirous of a peaceful solution to the Saharan war — indeed, there were abortive direct contacts between Morocco and Algeria — and despite Morocco's public protestations to the contrary Rabat would probably have accepted the plan proposed by France in late 1978. This proposed that Morocco should hold a referendum on the 1976 annexation in its part of the former Spanish Sahara, while Mauritania's share would be granted a special federal status (in which, though it was not explicitly stated, Polisario would be permitted to exercise power). This proposal was rejected by Polisario representatives in negotiations in Paris in September, 1978 however, and since then there have been several threats by Polisario to renew the war against Mauritania if a more satisfactory offer is not forthcoming. The death of President Houari Boumedienne, Polisario's strongest supporter in Algeria, in December, 1978 makes any assessment of Polisario's ability to wage such a renewed campaign problematical.

It is, however, clearly the case that it would be very difficult for the Mauritanian army to start fighting again. The Mauritanian garrison in the new Saharan territory of Tiris el-Gharbia has been substantially reduced, and the new attitude of the relatively few troops remaining there can best be described as 'very relaxed'. Both there, and in the northern part of Mauritania proper, it was Moroccan troops who bore the brunt of the fighting in late 1977 — early 1978, while on at least one occasion Mauritanian troops were involved in a demonstration against the Moroccan military presence. A renewal of the fighting, therefore, would probably lead quite rapidly to the establishment of de facto Moroccan control over much of northern Mauritania.

Gwynne Dyer
L. L. Mathews

MAURITIUS

HISTORY AND INTRODUCTION

Mauritius, a former British colony, attained independence in 1968. Its population is a remarkable ethnic mixture. The largest group, in a slight overall majority, are Hindu Indians, with Creoles (descendants of Europeans and Africans) and Indian sub-continent Muslims as the next groups in order of size. There are also very important but small Franco-Mauritian and Chinese minorities.

Until 1982 Mauritius had been ruled by a coalition of first-generation pro-Western nationalist conservative politicians under the leadership of Sir Seewosagur Ramgoolam. In June 1982 this regime received a shattering, total defeat in a general election at the hands of the *Mouvement Militant Mauricien* (MMM), a radical socialist grouping. Within this grouping the most influential leader is Paul Berenger, though the Premiership went to a Hindu, A. Jugnauth. The MMM's aims include a republican constitution, non-alignment and demilitarisation of the Indian Ocean, and in particular the return to Mauritius of the Chagos archipelago, including Diego Garcia.

Diego Garcia was detached from Mauritius, before the latter's independence, by Britain, which gave Mauritius a lump sum payment as compensation. The islanders were removed in distressing circumstances and Diego Garcia was then leased by Britain to the USA. The USA regards Diego Garcia as of prime importance in its Indian Ocean strategy. A bitter and embarrasing international wrangle can be anticipated, and anti-Western xenophobia over the issue is likely to be stirred up within Mauritius, particularly if the new regime's socialist policies fail to remedy the country's severe economic difficulties.

In the colonial period, a small part-time volunteer unit, the Royal Mauritius Regiment existed for home defence. It did not serve outside Mauritius in World War I; in World War II it was committed for lines of communication security work in the Madagascar campaign, at which point it mutinied. Inadequate training for the discomforts of an active service campaign was assessed as the cause.

STRENGTH AND BUDGET

Population: 950,000 (approximate)
Strength: The Police Special Mobile Force is a unit of approximately 800 serving within a police force the overall total of which is 3900

COMMAND AND CONSTITUTIONAL STATUS

At the time of writing, H. M. Queen Elixabeth II is Sovereign of Mauritius, with prerogative locally vested in the Governor-General, Sir Dayendranath Burrenchobay, with titular Commander-in-Chief authority but acting on the advice of the country's Prime Minister and Cabinet.

The MMM plans a republic with a non-executive President.

ROLE, COMMITMENT, DEPLOYMENT AND RECENT OPERATIONS

The task of the Special Mobile Force are seen as riot control and counter-insurgency operations, together with disaster relief and some civil aid work.

ORGANISATION

The Special Mobile Force is not an army in the formal sense, but a general service barrack police force trained on military lines in respect of internal security duties. For a number of years its two senior officers were a British Army lieutenant-colonel and a major.

RECRUITMENT, TRAINING AND RESERVES

Recruitment is by voluntary enlistment, for which there is no shortage of volunteers from all communities.

Some of the force's officers have been trained in military academies and schools, a few having passed through Sandhurst.

EQUIPMENT AND ARMS INDUSTRY

There is no arms industry. The force's small arms are all of British origin, its transport consists of Land-Rovers and light scout cars. The force possesses two helicopters — one being a gift from France, the other a gift from India.

RANK, DRESS AND DISTINCTIONS

These generally follow the British pattern.

CURRENT DEVELOPMENTS

Two general comments may be made: (a) The Special Mobile Force exists only for internal law and order. Whatever posture Mauritius may strike in Indian Ocean politics, an expansion of the force into an effective army of any account is out of the question; (b) Mauritius attracts the interest of the Indian Ocean naval powers for strategic reasons and a disturbed political life could in certain circumstances attract further attention, particularly from the Soviet Union.

Lloyd Mathews

MEXICO

HISTORY AND INTRODUCTION

The Mexican army differs both in its founding role and present status from almost all those of the major Spanish-American States. It did not, unlike the armies of Venezuela or Chile, win independence from the Spanish colonial government by force of arms — though its changing sides at a crucial moment was decisive in the struggle for independence. And it is not now, nor has it been for 50 years, a direct or even important influence on Mexican political life. On the other hand, its political role in the years between the gaining of independence in 1821 and the establishment of the modern Mexican governmental system in 1920—40 predominated over that of any other sector of Mexican society, making Mexican *caudillism* an exaggerated caricature of that distinctive feature of the nineteenth century Latin-American scene. scene.

Because the cause of Mexican independence succeeded by a reversal of loyalties rather than military victory, the modern Mexican army can claim a line of descent, however attenuated, from the royal army of the Viceroyalty of New Spain. But that army was not very ancient. Before the Seven Years' War (1756—63) Spain had maintained no effective army in the Viceroyalty (which then included the territory of the modern central American republics and much of the south-western United States). As a result of the difficulties experienced during that war in defending her overseas possessions, Spain decided to create an army for service in the Viceroyalty. It was to be composed of two classes of regiments: Spanish or 'peninsular' regiments, sent to America in rotation for a fixed period, and local or '*fijo*' regiments, raised in the Viceroyalty for permanent service there. It was also decided to retain and expand the units of urban and rural militia which hitherto had constituted Spain's only source of local military power, a very inadequate one at that. The result was that, after a number of false starts, the Army of New Spain numbered in 1800 about 30,000, organised into four regular regiments of infantry and two of dragoons, 10 militia regiments of infantry and nine of dragoons and cavalry, and numerous companies of coastal, frontier and town militia. The soldiers were recruited from the poor mestizo class and the officers from the white middle-class.

It was this army which moved into action against the rebels who, from 1810 onwards, rejected the rule of Napoleon's puppet government in Madrid and proclaimed their independence. They were too badly armed for the regular army, which was reinforced from Spain, to have much trouble beating them, but their cause was popular among the mestizo and Indian villagers, and became popular with the wealthier whites after the Liberal Revolution of 1820 in Spain. Independence was then made to look a way of preserving a conservative regime in Mexico and the conservative leaders cast about for a military man who might help them safely towards it. They found him in the person of a young captain, Agustin Iturbide, who secretly made contact with the principal guerrilla leader, Guerrero, agreed a programme for the country's political future with him and in 1821 presented the representative of the Spanish government with a *fait accompli*.

A minority of the Spanish regular soldiers in the country resisted, but the remainder did not and were eventually repatriated. Meanwhile, the viceroy had conceded defeat and signed a treaty recognising Mexican independence and, though the Spanish government disowned it, Mexico did effectively become a sovereign State from that date, first as an 'empire' under Iturbide (ruled 1821—2), then, when he was overthrown by his erstwhile henchman, Santa Anna, as a republic.

Santa Anna was to dominate political life from 1825 to 1855, through his control of the army, though not always as Head of State. A talented soldier, he defeated a Spanish attempt at reconquest in 1829, a French punitive expedition in 1838 and numbers of internal revolts, allegedly in the name of Centralism against Federalism, a familiar conflict in post-independence Latin America. But he failed to stop the secession of Texas, its accession to the United States, or the subsequent invasion of Mexico by American troops in 1846, designed to force Mexico to accept the new frontier. The costs of the war bankrupted the country, forced the government to appropriate church property and thus provoked new civil war in the country, which Santa Anna was recalled from exile to quell. Continuing internal disorder and foreign indebtedness prompted Napoleon III to intervene, ostensibly to recover European monies owing, actually to install his nominee, the Habsburg Maximilian, as emperor.

This extraordinary episode lasted from 1862 to 1867, when Juárez, one of Santa Anna's liberal opponents, led the patriotic armies to victory against their foreign emperor and re-established the republic. He ruled as president until 1872, but the coming man in the State had by then revealed himself to be the most successful of the anti-Maximilianist generals, Porfiro Díaz. It was he who had entered Mexico City as conqueror, and in 1876 he was elected president, largely through his military backing. He stood down in 1880 but was re-elected in 1884 and thenceforward ruled without interruption until 1910. Although the spirit of his government was supposed to be 'scientific', by which was meant modernising, he and his *Cientificos* in fact depended upon military power to maintain themselves in office. Diaz showed originality in the way he managed it. Recognising that the real danger to political stability lay in the ambitions of generals, not the discontents of their soldiers, he kept the generals docile by frequent transfers from one part of the country to another, sweetened by high salaries, honours and opportunities for graft. At the same time he shifted the responsibility for maintaining law and order from the army to a newly created armed police, the *rurales*, who were more directly under his thumb. He also, when opportunity offered, retired officers, thus reducing the very swollen size of the officer corps. By 1910, when he had held power for 30 years, the army consisted of 4000 officers, largely white and middle-class, 20,000 Indian soldiers, and 4000 *rurales*. The provincial armies, loyal to local *caudillos*, the bane of national life in the Santa Anna period, had disappeared.

By the end of the Diaz regime, which came in 1910, largely through popular resentment of its unfeelingness, summarily brought about a recreation of those armies. Revolutionary generals, like Zapata and Pancho Villa, claimed parity of status with career generals who had cannily changed sides at the right time, and the fighting between them and the regular army returned Mexico to the state of chaos it had known in the worst periods of the Santa Anna era. By 1920 there were 80,000 armed men abroad, few of them owning loyalty to the central government, commanded by generals who each claimed to embody political legitimacy. Taming this collection of disorderly bands was to be the main work of the anti-Porfirian government during the 1920s and early 1930s.

The period from 1920 to 1940 is known in modern Mexican history as the Revolution and, though there had been many before, it deserves that title for the real, irreversible changes which it worked in Mexican society. Foremost among these were the return of communal lands (*ejidos*) to their original village holders, the distribution of latifundia land to landless labourers, the energetic attempt to provide truly universal free education and, eventually, the expropriation of much foreign-owned extractive industry. None of this, least of all the land programme, could have been achieved without the subjection of the army to central government control. That this was eventually achieved was very much to the credit of a young Indian general of the anti-Porfirian revolution, Joaquin Amaro, who served as Secretary for War to President Calles in 1924–8. His methods resembed those which Díaz himself had used to tame the army 60 years before. He began by reforming the *Colegio Militar*, so that the new officer intakes should be properly educated, and he also opened a staff college (*Escuela Superior de Guerra*) and sent officers abroad to study. He improved the conditions of the soldiers, by raising their pay, modernising their barracks and generally working to attach their loyalty to the central government instead of the local commander. Finally, at the instigation of President Calles, he began a policy of frequent transfers of generals, denying them the chance to build a power-base in any one area. The predictable result was a generals' revolt in 1927. It attracted the support of only a quarter of the officers, most of whom were instantly dismissed.

The work of Amaro and Calles was carried on after 1934 by the latter's successor, General Cárdenas. He instituted promotion by merit and examination for officers up to the rank of colonel, and sent back to school those who failed. And in 1937 he institutionalised the political subservience to which he had reduced the officer corps by reorganising the Revolutionary Party on a basis of four 'sectors' — labour, peasant, popular and military. When accused by his critics of having brought the army into politics, he replied, 'It was already there. In fact, it has been dominating the situation and we did well to reduce its influence to one vote out of four'. Some senior generals, discerning the nature of the trap which this corporative arrangement had sprung on the army, raised a last banner of revolt, but it was easily put down. Against the danger of further trouble, the government permitted the raising of a workers' militia, which quickly came to outnumber the army two-to-one, but it proved not to be needed. Though a group of senior generals made a concerted effort to win the 1940 presidential elections for their man, the anti-army candidate, Camacho, himself a former general, easily won. He completed the work of Cárdenas by eliminating the short-lived military 'sector' from the official party (now renamed the Institutionalised Revolutionary Party), breaking up the military bloc in congress and retiring the remaining military trouble-makers.

The outbreak of World War II brought an additional boon to the party in that it gave the army, though it took no actual part in the fighting, the stimulus to concentrate on strictly professional matters: its training to defend the national territory, in concert with the United States, against foreign invasion. By the end of the war, the army had put its political past firmly behind it and was set fair on a course to become the least political in Latin America, a title which over the last 30 years it has unquestionably earned.

STRENGTH AND BUDGET

Population: 71,500,000
Army: 95,000
Navy: 24,000 (including naval aviation and marines); 44 major vessels
Air Force: 4,500; 50 combat aircraft
Paramilitary: 22,000 national police; 120,000 rural militia; 250,000 part-time 'conscripts' (see text)
GNP: (1981) $229,040,000,000
Defence expenditure: (1981) $1,403,000,000

The proportion of the national budget spent on defence is one of the lowest in Latin America. In 1973 it stood at 3.4% of which the army took the major share. Most of the spending goes on personnel and for fixed charges, since there has been very little investment in new equipment for many years.

Since the discovery of massive oil reserves, in the early 1970s, defence expenditure has increased dramatically, e.g. from $567,000,000 in 1979 to $884,000,000 in 1980 and $1,403,000,000 in 1981. It was also proposed to increase total armed forces manpower by 120,000. A manpower increase of 23,000 has occurred in the Army since 1978 whilst the Navy has increased its manpower by 6,500 although Air Force strength has actually fallen by 1,500 during the same period. It remains to be seen whether the country's current situation of near bankruptcy will halt or even reverse these trends.

COMMAND AND CONSTITUTIONAL STATUS

Mexico has a highly presidential system of government, with most executive power concentrated in the hands of the Head of State. He appoints not only ministers but also state governors and all military officers of the rank of colonel and above. He has the power to mobilise, with senatorial approval, and to suspend constitutional guarantee, under the same proviso. He is Commander-in-Chief of the Armed Forces, but day-to-day control is exercised by the Minister of Defence, to whom the army and air force commanders answer directly (the navy answers to the Minister of Marine).

Mexico, though by every test a democratic country is also effectively a one-party State. The party is the Institutional Revolutionary Party (PRI), which is organised on occupational lines. It has three 'sectors' — Popular, Farm and Labour, which by arrangement divide the constituencies between themselves before elections, i.e. in a constituency which has by agreement between the sectors been allotted to a Farm candidate, the other sectors will swing their vote behind him, in return for the Farm Sector's support in constituencies allotted to another. Until 1945 there was also a Military Sector, which resulted in the direct election to congress of servicemen (usually officers) on active duty. Although this arrangement has been dropped, officers continue to be elected to congress. Out of its 273 seats, between 20 and 30 were usually held by officers during the 1950s and 1960s.

Officers also often hold posts in the bureaucracy, either while on leave from the service or occasionally on active duty. The commanding general of a military zone, who is appointed by the President, is also his personal representative in the department (departments and military zones coincide) and is used by the population on occasions as a direct channel of communication with the Head of State when it is felt that the governor is not adequately representing the citizens' interests. He also acts as commander of the rural militia, which is both a counterweight to the regular army in the zone and a channel of intelligence to the central government.

ROLE, COMMITMENT, DEPLOYMENT AND RECENT OPERATIONS

Role

As a result of the measures successfully taken since the revolution of 1910 to depoliticise the army, it no longer plays any role in the choice or administration of government in Mexico. (It does, however, maintain order during elections.) Because of the cordial relations prevailing with the United States, that country's effective control of the Caribbean and eastern Pacific, and the weakness of Mexico's southern neighbours, the army has no external defensive role either. It is not deployed on the frontiers to any significant extent, but in the interior. This is a reflection of its principal mission, which is to deter, and if necessary suppress, rural and urban subversion, violence and disorder. It also carries out certain developmental duties, notably the reduction of illiteracy, not only among its soldiers, but also their families. Ceremonial figures largely in its activity; it is not unknown for a quarter of the strength of the armed forces to be assembled in Mexico City for a State occasion.

The army is responsible for the Sunday training of the 'conscripts'. But as the significance ascribed by the government to this activity is difficult to estimate, so too is its importance in the army's tasks.

Commitment

Mexico is a signatory of the two Latin American security treaties — the collective security treaty of Chapultepec and the non-aggression treaty of Rio. It also has a military assistance agreement with the United States. It has no military commitments to other nations.

Deployment

Mexico is divided for military purposes into 35 military zones. These correspond with the 31 States, except that three (Oaxaca, Veracruz and Guerrero) contain an additional military zone, and the Federal District is also a military zone. The State capital is in almost every case the military zone headquarters, in which resides the general commanding the zone. Most zones contain two infantry battalions, and some a cavalry regiment.

The Presidential Guard brigade, the two infantry brigades and the parachute brigade are stationed in the vicinity of the capital. The three marine infantry battalion headquarters are located in the capital, at Vera Cruz and at Mazatlán respectively, three of the security companies being subordinate to 1st Battalion headquarters at Mexico City, one each to the Gulf and Pacific Naval Command headquarters and one to each of the six Gulf and eight Pacific Naval Zones.

Recent Operations

Mexico's last foreign war was with the United States in 1846, unless the expulsion of the Emperor Maximilian in 1867 and the American puntive expedition of 1916 are included. In recent years, the army has been involved in a number of internal disturbances. Some of these partake of the character of traditional, localised 'social banditry', such as the insurrection by Lucio Cabanas in Guerrero State in 1967–74. He gave his group the name of the Party of the Poor. Other, more genuinely ideological groups which have attracted the attention of the army or police are the Communist League of September 23rd and the Revolutionary Action Movement (MAR). Many of the disturbances have been caused by univ-

ersity students, of which the worst was at Mexico City on the eve of the 1968 Olympic Games. There have been others at Morelia, Hermosillo and Tlaxcala in 1966, 1967 and 1973, respectively. The army has also been called in to quell local electoral disturbances, in Sonora in 1967, Tijuana in 1968. The army was also active in 1972 on the border with Guatemala, across which guerrillas had strayed from the neighbouring State. None of this activity has exceeded the scale of low-level police action.

ORGANISATION

The army is organised domestically into a number of branches: *Infantería*, *Caballería*, *Artillería*, *Zapadores* (Engineers, including *Ingenieros Constructores* and *Ingenieros Industriales*), *Servicio de Transmisiones* (Signals), *Intendencia* (Administration), Medical, Veterinary and Military Justice Services.

The cavalry, which is being slowly mechanised, principally with wheeled AFUs, is organised into 28 regiments. There are three artillery regiments and a number of independent battalions. The engineers and services are organised at regimental, battalion and company level.

Operationally, the largest formation is the brigade, of which there are four. Most of the army consists of isolated battalion-sized units, stationed in State capitals.

The Navy includes a marine force, organised into 19 companies, entrusted primarily with the defence and security of naval shore establishments and which are in turn subordinate to three battalion headquarters. The air force has a parachute battalion.

The police are organised on a Provincial (State) basis, but there is also a national police force of 22,000, the General Direction of Police and Traffic. It comes under the Ministry of Government.

In addition to the full-time organisations, there exists also a rural militia, originally raised by the governments from among the peasants to protect them from the 'White Terror' of the landlords at the time of the land distribution programme after the revolution of 1910. It was later used by the government in the 'war' with the church in 1926, and in 1929 received the name of the Rural Defence Corps. Its unit is the *peloton* of 11 men, which is under the immediate control of the governing body of the *ejido* (land-holding commune). The unit cannot be used outside the *ejido* to which it belongs without the permission of the Military Zone Commander, who then gives it orders. The militia is raised from volunteers aged between eighteen and fifty, is armed with obsolete weapons, but commands great respect within the *ejidos*. It is also greatly valued by the government as a source of intelligence from the countryside. In 1975 there were 80,000 mounted militiamen and 40,000 foot militiamen.

RECRUITMENT, TRAINING AND RESERVES

The recruitment and training of the Mexican army is highly individual. In theory, under the National Military Service Act of 1942, all males become liable for a year's service at the age of eighteen. In practice, this consists of some very simple marching and drill, without weapons or uniforms, in a park or the streets on Sunday mornings, supervised by a junior officer of the local garrison. The only end-product of the *conscriptos'* efforts is their acquisition of the *cartilla*, a document certifying completion of service, which must be produced when changing employment or address. Life without the *cartilla* is difficult for the Mexican male, and the control it offers the government over the male population seems to be the principal reason for maintaining the practice of Sunday morning training. However it also appears to be valued as a means of impressing the *conscriptos* with their status as citizens and children of the revolution.

The real army is regular, recruited from volunteers for 3 years. Re-enlistment is common. Most of the regulars are rural mestizos or Indians who have failed to find work, enjoy the army and re-enlist in the hope of promotion, which brings considerable benefits. Recruits are trained in their units, though there are a number of specialised schools for enlisted men, of which the most important is the *Escuela de Clases* (NCO School).

Officers are generally recruited from the urban middle or lower-middle class; a very large number are officers' sons. In this respect Mexico adheres to the modern trend for the profession to become self-recruiting. The military academy, founded in 1823, refounded in 1867, is the *Heroico Colegio Militar de Mexico*, at Chapultepec, Mexico City; 'heroic' refers to the spirited defence of the college against the American invaders in the war of 1846. Specialised training is given at the arms school (*Centro de Applicacíon y Perfeccionamiento*) and staff training at the *Escuela Superior de Guerra*. The course at the academy and the staff college lasts 4 years and 3 years, respectively. Observers judge that Mexican officer training is more specifically military than that common in most large Latin-American countries today. This may be deliberate government policy to inhibit the growth of political consciousness in the army.

The long-service army generates few reserves, although the ex-conscripts in theory form one.

EQUIPMENT AND ARMS INDUSTRY

Mexico has a small-scale arms industry, manufacturing a few infantry weapons; the *Fabrica Nacional de Municiones* manufactures arms ammunition. But most of its equipment, which is generally obsolescent or actually obsolete, was bought in the past from the United States. The army's equipment is sufficient for its role, but is much inferior to that in general use in Latin America. The plans for the expansion of the Armed Forces also include a re-equipment programme which may be curtailed as a result of the country's present economic difficulties.

Rifle: M1 0.30″ (US); H-33 5.56mm (Germany)
Sub-machine-gun: Thompson M-1921, M1 and M1A1 0.45″ (US); Mendoza 9mm (Mexico); H-53 5.56mm (Germany)
Machine-guns: M1917 0.30″ (US); M1919 0.3″ (US); M1917 0.3″ (US); BAR 0.30″ (US); Mendoza B-1933 7mm (Mexico); Madsen M-1934 7mm (Denmark; Mendoza RM-2 7.62mm (Mexico)
Anti-armour weapons: 37mm anti-tank gun (US)
Mortars: Stokes-Brandt 81mm (France); 4.2″ (US)
Artillery: M101 105mm (US); M116 75mm (US); M8 75mm SPH (US)
Anti-aircraft weapons: 12.7mm (France)
Armour: M4 medium tank (US; 25 in service) M3 light tank (US; 15 in service); M5 light tank (US); 10 in service); M8 armoured car (US); 50 in service); MAC-1 armoured car (US); 15 in service); Humber Mk. IV armoured car (Britain; 15 in service); Panhard ERC-90 armoured car (France; 40 on order) M3A1 scout car (US; 100 in service); HWK-11 APC (Germany; 15 in service); AMX-10P APC (France; on order)
Aircraft: The Air Force has about 90 transport aircraft and 30 helicopters.

Under the Armed Forces expansion programme, it was also intended to commence the production of tracked military vehicles of undisclosed type, with German technical assistance and of four separate types of wheeled military vehicles of indigenous design. This project may also be expected to be a victim of the prevailing economic situation.

RANK, DRESS AND DISTINCTIONS

General de Division — Three silver stars, eagle and wreath
General de Brigada — Two silver stars, eagle and wreath
General Brigadier — One silver star, eagle and wreath
Coronel — Three gold stars
Teniente Coronel — Two gold stars
Mayor — One gold star
Capitan Primiero — Three gold bars
Capitan Segundo — Two and a half gold bars
Teniente — Two gold bars
Subteniente — One gold bar
Sargento Primiero — Three horizontal stripes
Sargento Segundo — Two horizontal stripes
Cabo — One horizontal stripe
Soldado Primiero — One vertical stripe

Uniforms are tunic style, and vaguely Spanish in cut, for formal wear. Combat dress is American style; the American helmet is worn. Distinguishing colours are red for infantry, blue for cavalry, purple for artillery and black for engineers.

CURRENT DEVELOPMENTS

The internal state of Mexico is not entirely pacific. There were disturbances at the universities of Mexico City and Oaxaca in early 1977, and popular outbreaks in Juchitán in February, during which, it is alleged, 29 peasants were killed by the army. But to a surprising degree the country is free of serious threats to political stability and of organised sedition. The consistently unpolitical behaviour of the army over the last 40 years reflects this condition. Close observers nevertheless feel that the political consciousness of the army remains high, and that the involvement of individual officers in the processes of government is quite widespread. They also claim to detect a coming crisis of the 'institutionalised revolution', through its failure to adapt to changing times, unresponsiveness of its bureaucracy to popular needs, and overcentralisation of executive power in the presidency, which it will require force to overcome. All that can be said is that the signs of such a crisis are no clearer now than they have been for two or three decades, and that the army gives no evidence of an inclination to precipitate or forestall it.

President Lopez Portillo has adopted an independent line in foreign policy and has been highly critical of United States foreign policies, particularly in the Caribbean and Central America. The necessity of protecting the country's enormous oil reserves appears also to have prompted a re-assessment of Mexico's traditional defence policies as demonstrated in the plans for the expansion and re-equipment of the Armed Forces launched in the early 1980s. If brought to fruition, these would certainly result in an expanded role, both internal and external, for the Mexican Army.

John Keegan
Adrian English

MONGOLIA

HISTORY AND INTRODUCTION

Mongolia, in modern times a subject State of the Chinese Empire, secured its independence from Peking by unilateral action, and with Russian encouragement, in 1912. A small army was created with Russian assistance but it was unable to resist the Chinese when they returned to re-assert their suzerainty in 1919. However in 1921 a small revolutionary army, sponsored by a Soviet mission, defeated and expelled the Chinese garrison. The government established by the revolutionaries co-existed with the existing theocratic structure until the 1930s, when radical measures were taken to transform the country on the Soviet model. One of the most important measures was a purge of the high command of the army in 1937. Two years later the army took part in the Russian clash with Japanese troops at Kholhin Gol. It was also engaged during the short period of Russo—Japanese hostilities in 1945.

Russian troops have been stationed in Mongolia since 1932 (with a short intermission from 1956 to the early 1960s). The Mongolian People's Army is very much a product of Red Army training.

STRENGTH AND BUDGET

Population: 1,700,000
Army: 31,500
Air force: 3100; 12 combat aircraft
Paramilitary: 10,000 security police; border guards
Defence expenditure (1981 estimate): $239,600,000

COMMAND AND CONSTITUTIONAL STATUS

The High Command is organised on the Soviet model. The Minister of Defence, a member of the politburo, is a serving general and Commander-in-Chief of the Mongolian People's Army. A Political Directorate (commissar system) ensures Communist Party supervision of the army from within.

ROLE, COMMITMENT, DEPLOYMENT AND RECENT OPERATIONS

The vast size and small population of Mongolia make its defence by the People's Army quite impossible. Soviet power guarantees its borders, and considerable numbers of Soviet troops are stationed on its soil (perhaps four divisions, plus air defence, strategic missile and engineering units). Mongolia renewed its treaty of friendship and mutual defence with the Soviet Union in 1966, to last for 20 years.

The location of Mongolian People's Army units is not known but its engineering units (and perhaps others) have recently been engaged on construction work at the new industrial and coal-mining centre at Darkhan. Development work and literacy teaching are a major role of the army. It has taken no part in military operations since 1945.

ORGANISATION

The army is organised completely on Soviet lines. It comprises three brigades, possibly forming a division.

RECRUITMENT, TRAINING AND RESERVES

Recruitment is by conscription for 2 years at the age of eighteen. Conscription was introduced in the 1930s when it had the undesired effect of greatly increasing the number of Buddhist monks, since they were exempt. The dissolution of the monasteries after 1937 closed that line of escape from duty.

A Society for the Promotion of the Army, modelled on the Soviet DOSAAF and founded in 1961, has 100,000 members. Trained reserves are thought to number about 40,000.

EQUIPMENT AND ARMS INDUSTRY

Mongolia imports all its military equipment from the Soviet Union. Major items are: T-34 tanks; T-54/55 and T-62 tanks; BTR 60/152 APCs and BMP combat vehicles; SU-100 assault guns; 37mm and 57mm anti-aircraft guns; Snapper anti-armour missiles; and 76mm, 100mm, 130mm and 152mm guns and howitzers. The air force has 12 MiG-21 fighters, 30 transports, 10 helicopters and a battalion of SA-2 air-defence missile launchers.

RANK, DRESS AND DISTINCTIONS

These are entirely Soviet.

CURRENT DEVELOPMENTS

A buffer State between Russia and China, which still maintains its historic claim to suzerainty, Mongolia is necessarily committed to its Russian alliance. The tiny Mongolian People's Army is chiefly a symbol of national sovereignty.

John Keegan

MOROCCO

HISTORY AND INTRODUCTION

For much of the past thousand years Morocco has been the great power of north-western Africa, and its armies were often to be found in Spain, in the rest of the Maghreb, and far south into the Sahara. After almost a century of European domination, the country is beginning to re-emerge in this role, with a concomitantly great expansion in the size of its armed forces. The initial popular response to the policy has been almost universally favourable, but the need to provide greatly increased military expenditure out of an economy that is still relatively poor will almost certainly place considerable restraints on this role.

In the Arab world Morocco has always been isolated by its distance from the heartland of Arabic culture; even within the Maghreb it is effectively cut off from the east by the Atlas mountains. The original Berber inhabitants embraced Islam during the first wave of Arab conquest early in the eighth century, and took a large part in the succeeding conquest of most of Spain for Islam, but there was no extensive Arab settlement in this period. The great Idrisid, Almoravid and Almohad dynasties of medieval Morocco, whose rule extended at various times to central Spain, Libya and the Senegal River, were all based on Berber tribal support, and had their origin in religious movements of various kinds. The large-scale Arabisation of the Moroccan population did not commence until the eleventh and twelfth centuries, when bedouin tribes originally from Arabia, notably the Banu Hilal and Banu Suleim, began to penetrate into the Maghreb; the great bedouin invasions that thrust through the Atlas mountains and devastated the Moroccan lowlands only occurred in the declining years of the Merinid dynasty in the late thirteenth century. Even then, though the westward-facing lowlands along the central Moroccan coast became thoroughly Arabised, the mountains containing them to the north, east and south remain solidly Berber to this day. In 1982, Berber-speakers constituted at least 35% of the Moroccan population.

Political power, moreover, continued to be based on religion and on the support of Berber tribes. The present ruling dynasty, the Alawi Sharifs, arose in the late seventeenth century out of yet another wave of popular religious sentiment; it had its origin and tribal power base, like the Almoravids before it, in the Berbers of Saharan Morocco (the Tafilalet) in the far south. The loyalty of the army to the dynasty was ensured, as usual, by drawing most of its members from the Berbers of that region, and their special loyalty was repaid by giving their tribal leadership access to high office and virtually exclusive control of the hierarchy of the regular military establishment. The French and Spanish colonial authorities continued and reinforced this pattern of recruiting, as did the monarchy after the restoration of Moroccan independence in 1956. As recently as 1971 about 80% of the enlisted strength and over half of the officers in the Moroccan armed forces were Berber. Only in the rapid expansion of the armed forces since 1975 has there been any significant dilution of this policy.

Various coastal towns in Morocco had come under shorter or longer periods of European control from the time of the Spanish Reconquest and the rise of the European overseas empires onwards, by the actual encroachment of French and Spanish influence into the interior of the country only commenced after the French conquest of Algeria in 1830. The process was effectively completed when France and Spain divided Morocco into spheres of influence in 1904, although the formal French Protectorate of Morocco (with Spain deriving its authority over its share from France, not from the Sultan) was only proclaimed in 1912. In the earlier of these agreements, in 1904, the southern border of Morocco was fixed at $27° 40'$N, beyond which began Spain's Saharan territories: this division cut off all those southern desert regions sparsely inhabited by 'Moorish' tribes which had traditionally been regarded as Moroccan, though often not effectively controlled by the central government, and thus laid the ground for the various border disputes which have now brought war to the western Sahara.

It took the French colonial authorities only 2 years to establish firm control over lowland Morocco, but a further 20 years of hard fighting, punctuated by such formidable revolts as that led by Abd al-Krim in the Rif mountains in 1921—6, to pacify all the Berber-inhabited mountain and desert areas. They had scarcely finished this when they were confronted with a more modern form of nationalist resistance, the *Comité d'Action Marocaine*, drawing its support mainly from the towns. This organisation was dissolved in 1937, but nationalist agitation continued, leading to the creation of the Istiqlal (Independence) Party in 1943, whose aims enjoyed the full support of the powerless Sultan Muhammad V. However this movement did not find much favour amongst the conservative Berber tribesmen of Morocco, who were anti-foreign but even more opposed to Western-style modernisation, thus confirming the French and Spanish in their preference for maintaining the old royal system of recruiting troops from amongst the rural Berber population.

Morocco rallied to the cause of France in 1939, and to the Free French movement after the Anglo—American landings in 1942. Over 300,000 Moroccan troops fought with the French armed forces in North Africa, Italy and France, and large numbers subsequently served in the first Vietnam war. During the early 1950s, however, the nationalist agitation in Morocco became far more active, and in 1953 the figurehead Sultan refused to issue decrees on behalf of the actual French authorities. He was forced to go into exile after Berber tribesmen led by conservative local leaders began to converge on Morocco's main cities, and another member of the royal family was recognised as Sultan by the French. Outbreaks of anti-European violence spread, however, and following two attempts on his life the pretender to the throne renounced his claim in November, 1955 and Muhammad V returned to be acknowledged by the French as the legitimate Sultan.

Just prior to his return, a force known as the Army of National Liberation (*Armée de Libération Nationale* — ALN), formed around a core of Berber tribesmen who had fought in the French army in World War II and Vietnam, and loosely associated with the Istiqlal Party, began waging a large scale guerrilla campaign in the mountains against the occupying forces. Proclaiming that it was fighting for the liberation not only of Morocco but of all north Africa, it had succeeded by March, 1956 in wresting from the French control of the Rif and much of the Middle Atlas range. Faced as they were with a nationalist rising in Algeria that threatened their interests more closely, the French decided to cut their losses in Morocco.

A Franco—Moroccan declaration of March, 1956 decreed the Protectorate at an end and recognised Moroccan independence. An agreement with Spain ending the Spanish Protectorate followed in April, though the southern parts of the country were not evacuated by Madrid until 1958. In 1957, the Sultan assumed the title of King, and declared Prince Moulay Hassan heir to the throne.

Throughout the period of the Protectorate the armed forces in Morocco had consisted of French and Spanish forces, both of which accepted Moroccans in enlisted and commissioned grades along with French and Spanish nationals; at the time of independence there were about 50,000 Moroccans serving with these armies. The sole force under the control of the Sultan was the small Royal Guard, so after independence a military commission was appointed by the Sultan, including himself, the Crown Prince, ranking cabinet ministers, and French and Spanish army officers, to decide on the details of establishing national armed forces. Reda Guédira, a close associate of the Sultan, was named Minister of National Defence, and Crown Prince Hassan became Chief of the General Staff (the former has been one of the closest advisers of the latter since he became King in 1961).

In negotiations with the French and Spanish it was agreed that Moroccan units might transfer from their own forces to form the new Royal Moroccan Armed Forces (Forces Armées Royales — FAR), and that French and Spanish troops would remain in the country to safeguard order during the transitional period. During the first year attention was concentrated on creating an army: a small air force was founded at the end of 1956, and an even smaller navy in 1960, both of them being initially subordinate to the army. Fourteen thousand Moroccan personnel were transferred from the French army, and 10,000 from the Spanish armed forces; approximately 2000 French officers and NCOs remained on short-term contracts until crash training programmes at St-Cyr and Toledo Military Academies and the former colonial military academy at Dar al Bayda had produced a sufficient number of Moroccan officers. During 1956 Prince Hassan also negotiated the integration of the guerrilla ALN into the new army; about half of the 10,000 strong force joined the regular forces, bringing their total strength at the end of 1956 to about 30,000 men. All ALN personnel were sent on a 6 month training course, which for many included being taught how to read and write, and a limited number were granted commissions.

Another urgent task for the new government was the renegotiation of the Franco—American agreement of 1948 which had permitted the USA to create four large military bases in the country. These were the objects of vigorous protests by Moroccan nationalists and leftists, but despite talks between Hassan and American representatives in 1957, three of the bases were actually transferred to the USAF's Strategic Air Command and transformed into nuclear bomber bases in 1958. The issues was not resolved until late 1959, when the United States agreed to remove combat forces from Morocco; this was carried out in 1963 and the bases were formally transferred to Moroccan control, although small American military detachments remained at Kenitra and two nearby sites to man United States communications and monitoring facilities.

The principal external preoccupations of Morocco in this period, however, were the problems arising out of border disputes as the European colonial presence in north-western Africa gradually withdrew, leaving behind arbitrary boundaries that had been imposed on the area from outside. The more immediate problems had to do with the remaining Spanish enclaves in traditionally Moroccan territory: the Spanish-inhabited cities of Ceuta and Melilla on the Mediterranean coast, dating from the high tide of the Reconquest; the enclave of Ifni south of Agadir; and the huge desert areas of Saguia al Hamra and Rio de Oro lying to the south of Morocco's internationally recognised border.

In addition to these, however, Morocco also laid claim at independence to Mauritania, much of French Sudan (later Mali) and substantial areas of south-western Algeria, all of which were then still under French administration. Rabat's case rested on the traditional links of suzerainty and religious loyalty which the Muslim and largely Berber nomadic tribes of these areas had had with Morocco before the carving of colonial boundaries had begun. (It was never made entirely clear whether the claim extended to the extreme southern areas of Mali and Mauritania, where the population consists of sedentary black Africans.) Morocco further alleged, accurately enough, that Algeria, as a much earlier French possession and one which had been incorporated into France itself, had been consistently favoured by Paris in the drawing of the Saharan border between the two, so that Algeria's boundary had been pushed far west into areas whose inhabitants had traditionally looked to Morocco.

Morocco's newly forming regular army could not at first devote any attention to these concerns, since it was called on to suppress a widespread rebellion in the Rif in 1958—9. Prince Hassan took personal command of operations, and around 20,000 troops had be be committed to quell the rising. It would have been impolitic to pursue border claims against the French and Spanish empires with regular troops in any case in this period, when many officers and NCOs were still on loan from the armies of those two countries.

Moroccan irregular forces (the Armée de Libération de Grand Sahara) attacked Ifni and raided into Spanish Sahara and the northern fringes of Mauritania in late 1957 — early 1958, but hostilities ceased after the conclusion of a treaty in April, 1958 between Rabat and Madrid. Morocco did not recognise Spain's right to Ifni, Ceuta, Melilla or the Spanish Sahara, nor would it extend recognition to Mauritania when it became independent within the French Community in 1960 (thus long delaying Mauritania's acceptance into the Arab League), but it did not actively pursue these claims by military force during the 1960s.

Morocco's claims against Algeria, however, brought the two countries to war soon after the latter received its independence from France in 1962. The border south of Figuig had never been properly defined, and Moroccan forces entered the region south of Colomb—Béchar in Algeria in July, 1962. Fighting spread to the iron ore-rich Tindouf area in Algeria's extreme south-west in September, 1962 and by the latter part of 1963 Moroccan auxiliary forces had seized extensive areas for some 250 miles south-west of Colomb—Béchar. In October there was sharp fighting in this region. Morocco did somewhat better militarily, but a ceasefire on October 30th was followed by agreement on the creation of a demilitarised zone in February, 1964. Although the two regimes remained extremely hostile to each other on ideological grounds the border tension continued to abate, and in June, 1970 final agreement was reached on the delineation of the frontier, the disputed Gara—Djebilet area being assigned to Algeria but with provision for Morocco to have a share in a joint company to be established to exploit the rich iron-ore deposits in the area. This agreement, however, was never ratified.

The Moroccan government invariably enjoyed the unanimous support of all political parties and of the general populace in these border disputes, but in almost every other respect the monarchy's position deteriorated steadily almost from the moment of independence. The dominant conservative party, Istiqlal, was continuously frustrated in 1956–8 in its struggle to reduce the monarch's almost absolute powers, causing its more radical members to break away in 1959 under the leadership of Mehdi Ben Barka to create the National Union of Popular Forces (UNFP). This party at once became the object of severe repressive measures by the army and police, and in 1960 the King himself assumed the post of Prime Minister with the Crown Prince as his deputy. The latter assumed the title of King Hassan II and the post of Prime Minister on his father's death in February, 1961 and proceeded to push through a new constitution which theoretically established a constitutional monarchy with guaranteed personal and political freedoms. Istiqlal Party members were also removed from the cabinet in the succeeding year, however, and in the dubious 1963 elections a newly formed pro-monarchical party won the largest number of seats. Repressive action was then taken against both main opposition parties, and following an alleged coup attempt, almost the entire leadership of the UNFP was arrested. Many of them were held in solitary confinement, tortured and eventually sentenced to death, while Ben Barka himself, who had escaped to France, was kidnapped and murdered in 1965.

Faced with grave political unrest exacerbated by economic hardships in the cities, King Hassan created the paramilitary Mobile Intervention Companies with the *Sureté Nationale* (national police force), and these units together with elements of the regular army were used to suppress large-scale students' and workers' riots in Casablanca in March, 1965 that left over a hundred dead. The kindom continued through the latter half of the decade as a virtual police State, with the King depending for support primarily on his regular and paramilitary armed forces. Army officers also came to dominate the administration: by 1970 most of the 19 provincial governors were soldiers, as were also a large proportion of middle- and senior-level administrators in government departments. The state of emergency continued, with all political activity suppressed, until 1969, when a new constitution was followed by elections for a single-chamber legislature in 1970. The elections, however, were boycotted by all the opposition parties, and produced a meaningless chamber packed with 'King's men'.

Even the monarchy's main prop, the army, began to look extremely shaky in 1971, when a bloody coup attempt involving five of the thirteen serving generals almost succeeded. The precise motives of the coup have never been adequately explained: probably some combination of personal ambition, the temptation posed by a regime that seemed both weak and corrupt, and Libyan encouragement, would supply the answer. An additional motive that has been suggested is the concern of these right-wing generals at the relative political radicalism of some of the younger officers of urban background who were brought into the army in the 1960s to cope with the increasing technical demands of the more modern weapons that were being acquired.

The coup was headed by the Minister of the Royal Military Household, General Muhammad Medbouh, who led some 1400 military cadets in an attack on the King's palace at Skhirate in July, 1971 while he was celebrating his birthday in the company of government ministers, the foreign diplomatic corps and many other guests. At one point the rebels captured the King and his ministers, the Interior Ministry and the radio station, but loyal units overwhelmed them in less than 24 hours with the aid of many of the cadets, who had not initially been informed of the purpose of the operation. Four loyal generals a minister and an ambassador were killed and large numbers of guests wounded, and over

150 rebels were killed in the fighting, but the King escaped unhurt. Those of the five conspirator-generals who survived the fighting were summarily executed immediately afterwards, and over a thousand other army officers and men were sentenced to terms of from 1 year to life in prison.

The King's response to this upheaval, which left only four army generals alive, was to make General Muhammad Oufkir, long the regime's leading hatchetman (he had been found guilty *in absentia* of Ben Barka's murder by a French court), Minister of Defence and Chief of Staff, with almost complete control of the army and administration. He also launched an attack on corruption in the State services, and attempted to reach a reconciliation with the political opposition. Yet another constitution was declared in early 1972, but Istiqlal and the UNFP, briefly united in a National Front, boycotted the fraudulent referendum on it, and the planned elections were cancelled. In August, 1972 King Hassan narrowly survived a second coup attempt planned by General Oufkir himself: air force fighters tried to shoot down the plane in which he was travelling, and strafed the airport and the royal palace in Rabat. General Oufkir's death, together with that of the other leading conspirators, occurred immediately afterwards.

In later 1972 the Moroccan monarchy seemed to be nearing the end of the road: it had no support whatever from the country's organised political forces, and was so unable to trust the armed forces that most units were not allowed to have any ammunition under their own control. The senior officer corps were decimated and apparently almost totally disaffected, and civilian unrest was on the rise. There were serious student riots in January, 1973, and in March the capture of what were described as Libyan-supported rebels in the Atlas mountains led to widespread arrests of radicals in the major towns. Civil rights were even further curtailed, and 157 people, mainly UNFP militants, were tried by the Kenitra military tribunal on charges of terrorism and subversion: most received heavy sentences, and 15 were executed.

The regime's remarkably successful recovery from this desperate situation depended almost entirely on adroit appeals to Moroccan nationalism. One component, certainly, was an increased participation in pan-Arab affairs. This had already begun in 1967, when the Arab defeat in the Six Day War caused popular outbursts against the large and hitherto untroubled Jewish community in Morocco, leading to the emigration of about 90% of the Moroccan Jews (although, to its credit, the Moroccan government sought to protect the Jews and condemned the unofficial commercial boycott against them – the 25,000 who remain still have no legal restrictions against them, and there are indeed Jewish officers serving in the Moroccan air force). Morocco took a far more active role in Arab affairs thereafter, however, hosting Islamic and Arab League summit conferences in 1969, and recognising Mauritania and repairing its relations with Algeria in 1970. In February, 1973 at the very lowest point of the monarchy's popularity, King Hassan sent a Moroccan infantry brigade to the Syrian front. He was soon rewarded with a surge of popular support when it fought with distinction around Mount Hermon on the Golan Heights in the October, 1973 Yom Kippur War. (It was brought home in 1974.)

This success set the pattern for all that followed, but the focus then moved closer to home and to the emotional first priority of Moroccan patriotism: the creation of 'Greater Morocco'. Ifni had already been returned by Spain in 1969 without recourse to force. Moroccan attention now turned to the huge Spanish Sahara to the south, which had been the subject of a UN resolution in 1967 demanding that Spain should hold a referendum on self-determination for the territory in consultation with Morocco and Mauritania, both of which maintained claims against it. Algeria also had an interest in the territory, as offering the only practicable route to the sea from its own vast Saharan interior, and by 1971—2 all three neighbouring Arab States were supporting rival Saharan liberation movements. The Spanish project for a large-scale phosphate-mining enterprise in the territory was a further motive for Moroccan concern, as it threatened to cut into the market for Morocco's own phosphate exports, which are the country's principal source of foreign exchange.

The main impetus to Moroccan action, however, was nationalism (and the government's main hope was that the issue would create national unity). In July, 1974 the King held talks with the leaders of all the political parties as well as military and government officials to concert plans for a campaign to annex the Spanish Sahara, which Madrid was planning to erect into an independent State (with a population certainly much less than 100,000) which would remain closely linked to Spain. The immediate and unanimous reaction was enthusiasm and a quite remarkable degree of co-operation across the political spectrum: opposition leaders agreed to act as government envoys to foreign capitals, and made no serious protest when the King once more postponed promised elections until the crisis was past. In October, 1974 Morocco secured Mauritania's co-operation in a secret agreement for the partition of the territory, and in January, 1975 it increased the pressure on Spain by extending its campaign to include the enclaves of Ceuta and Melilla.

Algeria, as always Morocco's principal rival for influence in the Maghreb, responded by greatly increasing its aid to the Frente Polisario, the pro-Algiers, Marxist contender amongst the rival Saharan guerrilla movements, and there is some evidence of a secret agreement between Algeria and the moribund Spanish regime in October, 1975, as Franco lay dying, whereby Polisario would move in as the Spanish left to establish what would have amounted to an Algerian protectorate with privileges for Spanish investment. On October 15th, 1975 the United Nations' investigative mission reported that a majority of the Saharans favoured independence (which effectively rejected the Moroccan claim, based on historical rights). King Hassan's long-prepared riposte was to stage the so-called 'Green March' in which 350,000 unarmed Moroccans were trucked down to the desert frontier and marched across the border to take possession of the territory. The Spanish authorities allowed the marchers to advance some distance before halting them, and on November 14th the Madrid government signed an agreement by which it would withdraw from the territory in early 1976 without holding a referendum, and hand it over to a joint Moroccan—Mauritanian administration.

The Moroccan army marched in on December 11th, followed shortly by the tiny Mauritanian army, while the bulk of the population, some 30,000—70,000 people, fled, or were persuaded by Polisario to flee, to refugee camps near Tindouf just across the Algerian border. The Polisario guerrillas at once commenced a war of hit-and-run raids against the occupying forces from Algerian bases. As early as January, 1975 the Moroccan and Algerian armies clashed at Amgala inside the Saharan territory, but despite recurrent claims about a full Algerian—Moroccan war the struggle soon settled into a pattern of attritional warfare waged by the Algerian-supplied guerrillas against Moroccan and Mauritanian forces deployed mainly in fixed defensive positions. In March, 1976 a government-in-exile of the Saharan Arab Democratic Republic was set up on Algerian territory, recognised by Algeria (and subsequently by almost a dozen other radical Third World States), and a few days later Morocco broke off diplomatic relations with Algeria. The partition of the former

Spanish territory between the two occupying powers was completed in April, 1976, Morocco receiving the northern half containing the phosphate reserves and most of the population.

Taking advantage of the new spirit of national unity, the King then embarked on yet another attempt to reintroduce representative institutions. Municipal elections in November, 1976 were followed by national elections in June, 1977, the participation of all the opposition parties being ensured by making the party leaders Ministers without Portfolio in the pre-election period. The so-called Independents (the Royalist Party, in fact) secured the largest number of seats, but the main opposition parties are also represented in the cabinet apart from the third-ranking Socialist Union of Popular Forces (USFP), a breakaway group from the old UNFP and the only genuinely radical grouping with any significant following. The election also served as a substitute for any specific referendum on annexation in the newly acquired Saharan territories, now transformed into the three Moroccan provinces of El Aaiun, Smara and Boujdour.

The political benefits of the Saharan annexation for the monarchy have been huge, but its longer-term costs are also proving very considerable. To cope with the continuing guerrilla war, which extends into southern Morocco and almost all of Mauritania as well as the former Spanish territories, the Moroccan armed forces have increased by 50% in size since 1975. To meet the costs of the arms race with Algeria and to deal with the possibility of wider war, the defence budget has almost quadrupled since 1974. At a time when Moroccan finances are already severely strained by a sharp fall in the price of the country's main export, phosphates, the burden of these defence expenditures on the economy and on popular living standards may prove great enough to shatter the front of political unity that has been created.

The annexation of Spanish Sahara contravenes the basic rule of the Organisation of African Unity that colonial borders are inviolable, and as a result Morocco and Mauritania have become the focus of a bitter quarrel within that organisation which ranges them against the radical and many of the moderate members. The obligations of the developing alliance of conservative pro-Western States within the OAU, together with the need to keep the favour of Western arms suppliers, has caused Morocco to send large military expeditionary forces to the aid of the Zaïre government in 1977 and again in 1978. The pressures of the guerrilla war against fragile, impoverished Mauritania have necessitated the stationing of a 10,000 man Moroccan force in that country — which in turn inevitably reawakens Mauritanian fears of Moroccan expansionism, thus endangering the vital alliance with Mauritania. (For further comments on recent events, see Role, Commitment, Deployment and Recent Operations, and Current Developments. See also the entry for Mauritania.)

STRENGTH AND BUDGET

The total strength of the Moroccan armed forces in 1982 was 141,000 men, of whom 125,000 were in the army, 10,000 in the air force and 6000 (including 600 Marines) in the navy. This does not represent an inordinately large proportion of the population in arms for a country of Morocco's size, with 21,250,000 people, but it is a very sharp increase on the 1974 figure of approximately 50,000. The great bulk of the increased numbers is accounted for by the troops now deployed in Morocco's newly acquired Sahara territories, who number approximately 30,000 men. Paramilitary forces number 30,000, including 11,000 Sureté Nationale.

The growth in the defence budget has been even steeper, from $258,000,000 in 1975 to $1,110,000,000 in 1982. The greater part of the increased expenditure in the ordinary budget has been devoted to the acquisition of new weapons, as part of the urgent programme of military modernisation necessitated by the military confrontation with Algeria over the Sahara. The air force, which was particularly weak in comparison to its Algerian counterpart, has received the lion's share of the expenditure on new equipment: the order for 50 F-1 Mirages from France alone amounts to $650,000,000. Further large sums outside the military budget, amounting to $81,000,000 in 1978, have been devoted to civil development in the new Saharan provinces as part of a pacification programme.

The strains these expenditures have imposed on the Moroccan economy, already suffering from 4 years of bad harvests and a fall of about half in the world market price for phosphates, have been heavy. The growth rate fell from 8.5% in 1976 to only 1.3% in 1977, and foreign debt has quadrupled to $1,600,000,000 in the years 1974–7. This has necessitated a 30% cutback in the government's general expenditure on economic development, a wage freeze and an austerity programme causing a further sharp rise in the unemployment rate – unofficially 10% in the cities, but actually more like twice that. With a 3.4% annual growth rate in the population, this problem can only worsen, and there were signs in 1978 that popular enthusiasm for the expansion of Morocco was being gradually outweighed by distress at the economic hardships for which it is partly to blame.

COMMAND AND CONSTITUTIONAL STATUS

The armed forces (FAR) are under the direct command of the King, who is also the Chief of the General Staff. They continue to be part of the royal household, and are not technically an instrument of the government. The Ministry of Defence, which is under the government, is outside the chain of command, and concerns itself principally with logistics, supply, pensions, payrolls and related matters. Generally, however, the post of Minister of Defence is held by a general, and is combined with that of the Chief of Staff, an office currently held by General Ahmad Dlimi. In practice it is the Chief of Staff who controls all three armed forces, acting as the King's principal channel of command, and controlling individual units down to brigade and even battalion level.

Prior to 1971 the country was divided into six military zones, but these area commands were suppressed after the coup attempt in that year as providing too good a local power-base for aspiring coup-makers. There is little lateral co-ordination between military units, nor does the actual chain of command conform to the usual pyramidal structure, primarily in order to make the organisation of a coup more difficult. The Royal Air Force and Royal Navy are nominally separate services, but in practice their orders from the Chief of the General Staff (i.e. the King) also pass through the Army Chief of Staff.

The Royal Guard, a force of a few hundred men under the King's personal command, is technically part of the FAR. The Royal Gendarmerie, the principal rural police force, is an integral part of the army, and its commander and most of its officers are army officers. Its main unit structure is the company, each one being located in a different rural area· the companies are sub-divided into sections and brigades, and a special Mobile Group is maintained for rapid deployment in riot control and other emergencies.

The *Sureté Nationale* (national police) has primary responsibility for internal security and political intelligence, and shares with the FAR the duty of maintaining law and order in the major urban areas. The Director-General is usually an army officer, appointed directly by the King; the *Sureté* is not under the Ministry of the Interior and is, like the FAR, directly commanded by the King. Two-thirds of the 11,000 men are in the Urban or Judiciary Corps, performing ordinary police duties, but the Sixth Subdirectorate acts as the Kingdom's main secret police force, while the Mobile Intervention Companies (CMI), an active reserve police force of about 3000 officers and men, are employed both for riot control and to guard the King and senior officials.

The other main armed force in Morocco is the Auxiliary Forces, which are commanded by an inspector-general who is responsible to the Minister of the Interior. However he and most of his senior officers are serving on detached duty from the army, and are appointed directly by the King.

It is the King's general policy to avoid a clear demarcation of duties and authority amongst his various armed and para-military forces in order to retain a maximum degree of personal control. This includes the apparently intentional over-lapping of the territorial boundaries within which individual army units, *Sureté* detachments, Royal Gendarmerie elements and Auxiliary Forces companies operate, despite the operational difficulties and jurisdictional disputes which not infrequently result from such a state of affairs. In sum, the security forces are organised with an intricate and sophisticated system of internal checks and balances designed to reinforce the authority of the King and to counter any dangerous effects of the strong centralisation of control within each separate force.

ROLE, COMMITMENT, DEPLOYMENT AND RECENT OPERATIONS

The principal roles of the Moroccan army are internal security and external defence; the emphasis has shifted markedly from the former to the latter during the past 7 years, and almost one-half of the army is now deployed in a semi-combat role in the areas under attack by Polisario guerrillas.

Polisario's raids into the former Spanish Saharan territory, and also into Mauritania and the far south of pre-1976 Morocco, have required the stationing of some 30,000 FAR troops in the desert areas of Morocco's old and new territories, and a further 10,000 in allied Mauritania. In both cases the troops are deployed mainly in fixed positions defending the few targets worth attacking in these vast, empty territories, although they will occasionally sally forth when Polisario's small, highly mobile columns are located by reconnaissance aircraft. Claims issued by each side for casualties inflicted on the other are grossly inflated, but in some months Moroccan casualties may have amounted to as much as 100 men.

There is no military possibility that Polisario could physically dislodge Moroccan forces from their positions in the former Spanish Sahara, although they have consistently succeeded, since 1976, in preventing the operation of the extremely long and vulnerable conveyor belt which conveys phosphates from the Bou Craa mines, the territory's one significant economic resource, to the sea. (In the prevailing depressed state of the world phosphate market, this caused Morocco no distress, as it is well able to meet demand with production from other sources.) Polisario's strategy, as defined by the late Algerian President Boumedienne who was its principal supporter and supplier, was to wage an attritional battle which would cause a slow 'haemorrhaging' of Moroccan resources.

There are indications, however, that it is Polisario that

has been suffering most heavily from attrition of its scanty manpower resources, with diplomatic sources in Algiers suggesting an average loss rate of 60% on Polisario raids into Moroccan-held areas. Small numbers of Algerian troops have sometimes been killed or captured in clashes with Polisario columns near the Algerian border, and King Hassan has repeatedly asserted the right of hot pursuit and warned that he was prepared to contemplate full-scale war with Algeria, but in fact the Algerian armed forces have generally been careful to avoid offering direct provocation to Morocco in the area of operations.

Largely due to the relatively effective defence presented by Moroccan troops, Polisario began to concentrate on attacking the weaker partner in the Sahara partition agreement, Mauritania. A daring raid across hundreds of miles of desert to strike the Mauritanian capital of Nouakchott in June, 1976 ended in disaster when the returning column was caught by Moroccan and Mauritanian forces before reaching its Algerian bases, and Polisario's leader, Ahmed el Wali, was killed. Nevertheless, the strategy of striking at Mauritania's fragile economy and small, inexperienced army enjoyed considerable success, particularly by interrupting for long periods the movement of trains bearing the iron ore which is Mauritania's principal source of foreign exchange from the mines of Zouérate to the port of Nouadhibou. A direct attack on the mining compound at Zouérate in May, 1977 overwhelmed the inadequate Mauritanian defences, and though the Polisario column withdrew before reinforcements could arrive, they succeeded in causing the evacuation of most of the 400 French technicians needed to run the mines.

It was in response to this attack that Morocco and Mauritania signed a military assistance agreement on May 13th, 1977 setting up a High Defence Committee to co-ordinate defensive measures. Its principal practical effect was to permit the permanent stationing of Moroccan military garrisons at threatened points of Mauritania. This agreement has now led to the deployment of some 10,000 Moroccan troops in Mauritania (a number not far short of the total strength of Mauritania's own army), located not only in Zouérate, along the railway line to Nouadhibou, and at other centres in the north, but also at Akjoujt, a town linked to the capital by a fast road. As Mauritanian warweariness has increased, and particularly since the coup of July 10th, 1978 in Nouakchott brought a new Mauritanian government to power which was clearly interested in a peaceful compromise settlement to the dispute, these Moroccan troops have served as a form of guarantee against the defection of Rabat's smaller ally. Not unnaturally, they also revive amongst Mauritanians memories of earlier Moroccan claims against their entire country.

Even the presence of such a considerable number of Moroccan troops did not suffice to end Polisario raids into Mauritania. It was only after France sent several Atlantique long-range reconnaissance aircraft and a squadron of Jaguar fighter—bombers to Dakar in neighbouring Senegal in December, 1977, to assist in the defence of Mauritanian territory, that the defending forces began to gain the upper hand. Following the coup of July, 1978 Polisario declared a ceasefire against Mauritania, in the hope that a peace settlement relinquishing Mauritania's share of the Spanish Sahara could be negotiated with a new Nouakchott government, and shifted its military operations to Moroccan territory. Peace talks did indeed follow, although they were broken off in December, 1978 by Nouakchott, but throughout this period the Moroccan garrisons have remained in place throughout Mauritania. (*See also* Current Developments.)

The Saharan dispute has also created a need for Morocco to gain favour with potential Western arms suppliers and to prevent automatic application of the OAU rule on the inviolability of former colonial borders in Africa (which would result in condemnation of the Moroccan—Mauritanian partition agreement). The latter concern has caused Morocco to become *de facto* leader of a group of relatively pro-Western States within the OAU which are anxious about Soviet penetration into Africa, and to carry out military interventions in Africa in opposition to alleged Soviet initiatives. Thus in April, 1977 Morocco dispatched 1500 troops to Shaba province in Zaïre to repel an invasion by a rebel army returning from a long sojourn in Angola. The same troops were hurriedly reintroduced to Zaïre in early June, 1978 to deal with a renewed incursion from Angola; they were carried by American transport aircraft, and operated in conjunction with French and Belgian troops. Morocco has strongly supported French proposals for an inter-African intervention force to come to the aid of regimes which suffer attack from outside, and in November, 1978 King Hassan offered to organise and staff a pan-African army of 20,000 men to protect Angola's borders if Angola would send home the Cuban troops on its territory. These activities have won Morocco the strong support of France in particular, and have been successful in gaining the passive support of a group of African States in preventing the Saharan dispute from being officially considered and adjudicated upon by the OAU.

Apart from those 400 men in Equatorial Guinea, no Moroccan troops are currently deployed abroad. There are no foreign military bases on Moroccan territory, the last remaining United States communications facilities at Kenitra having been evacuated by American forces and handed over completely to the FAR in September, 1978.

ORGANISATION

Arms of Service
The internal organisation of the army into combat arms and services follows the French model; so does the branch structure of the navy. The air force, however, follows the American pattern. The Royal Gendarmerie and the Royal Guard constitute additional arms within the army.

Operational
The army consists of twelve mechanised infantry regiments, seven armoured groups, four amoured car squadrons, one paratroop brigade, one light security brigade, one Royal Guard battalion, five camel corps battalions, two desert cavalry battalions, nine artillery groups, one AA brigade, one paratroop brigade, one motorised battalion, three commando battalions, and four engineer battalions. The air force has no wing organisation; its squadrons consist of five fighter-bomber, one COIN, one transport and two helicopter squadrons, principal air bases include Kenitra, Sidi-Slimane, Ben-Guerir, Benslimane and Nouasser.

The main naval bases are at Casablanca, Safi, Agadir, Kenitra and Tangier.

RECRUITMENT, TRAINING AND RESERVES

Although the King decreed an 18 month period of service in the armed forces for all fit Moroccan males at the age of eighteen in 1967, it has always been possible to get almost all the recruits required on voluntary long-term enlistments. This is hardly surprising in view of the considerable unemployment in the Moroccan civilian economy. In addition, there exists a tradition of army service in some of the rural Berber areas from which the army has always drawn the bulk of its recruits. In 1971 it was estimated that only some 4000 conscripts were being inducted each year; the rapid expansion of the armed forces since 1975 may have increased the proportion of conscripts to some degree, but the majority of recruits are certainly still volunteers.

The principal source of officers for the FAR is the Royal Military Academy at Dar al Bayda near Meknés, where the course of instruction is modelled on that of St-Cyr. Some regular officers are also trained at approved foreign military academies, and individuals holding university degrees in certain subjects, such as engineering, or doctor's degrees in medicine, dentistry, veterinary science and chemistry, may receive direct commissions from civilian life on completion of a 6 month course at Dar al Bayda. There is also provision for NCOs with 12 years' service (of which 2 years must have been in one of the warrant officer grades) to receive commissions.

The officer corps still includes some dozens of senior officers who originally held commissions in the French or Spanish armies, and there is a small group of former NCOs, but the bulk of the middle- and junior-officer grades is now made up of post-independence graduates of Dar al Bayda. By and large this group tends to be of urban background, and to take a greater interest in politics.

Since 1971 pay rates for officers have been made comparable with those in the civil service (behind which they had previously lagged), and the pay of enlisted men and NCOs is comparable to, or better than, what they would receive in the civilian economy. There is the usual structure of allowances and special duty pay, and a pension programme exists for all military personnel. Maximum age-in-grade limits are forty-five for privates, fifty for warrant officers, and between fifty-one and sixty-one for officers of various ranks. The rate of re-enlistment is high, and soldiers tend to remain in the services until forced out by age.

The Moroccan army is a largely professional force whose training, done principally within the units, is adequate to the relatively undemanding technical level of its equipment. Its soldiers are mostly of a rural background, conditioned to hardship and harsh discipline, and have a reputation as fierce and tenacious fighters.

There is no organised reserve in the Moroccan army, but there exists a system for recalling ex-soldiers to active duty in an emergency.

EQUIPMENT AND ARMS INDUSTRY

The army is relatively short of armour for a force its size: it has 120 M-48 medium tanks (108 more on order) and 15 T-54s, plus 60 AMX-13 light tanks. It is considerably stronger in armoured cars, of which it possesses 1,000: AMX-10RC, EBR-75, AML-90 and M-8. A further 76 AMX-10RC and some AML-90 are on order. The mechanised infantry are borne in a wide variety of APCs: 364 M-113, 400 VAN (126 more on order), 40 M-3 half track, 50 OT-62/664, 15 UR-426, 80 Ratal, and Stage 4K-7FA.

The artillery arm has over 100 75mm, 76mm, 85mm, 100, SP and 105mm guns, and about 150 howitzers of 105mm, 130mm, 152mm and 155mm, including 36 M-109 155mm SP. The army's 1300 mortars are of 60mm, 81mm, 82mm and 120mm and it also has 36 BM-21 122mm multiple rocket launchers and STRIM-89 rocket launchers; recoilless rifles are 75mm and 106mm.

The army's anti-tank weaponry includes 20 M-56 90mm and 121 Kürassier 105mm SP ATK guns, and Dragon, Milan and TOW ATGW. Anti-aircraft defence relies on 100 26mm, 37mm, 57mm and 100mm AA guns and SA-7, chaparral and Crotale SAM; 40 M-163 Vulcan 20mm SP AA Systems are on order. Army aviation operates four Alouette II, three Gazelles and six A-169 helicopters.

It will be observed that in almost every category the army operates a mixture of French, Soviet and American equipment, which certainly complicates its logistical problems greatly. This is a consequence of its arms-purchasing history. Initially it was equipped with inherited French arms and was the recipient of considerable United States military aid, but at the height of the Algerian War Rabat, feeling that these supplies were inadequate and too slow in coming, turned to the Soviet Union for arms in 1960—61. The reversion to predominantly American and French arms in the 1970s has served to compound the problem further.

Under the threat of war with Algeria, the Moroccan air force has undergone a crash expansion programme since 1975 to make it capable of facing its much bigger Algerian counterpart.

It now has five fighter-ground attack squadrons, of which three operate 45 Mirage F-1 C/E, and two have 26 F-5A/B/E/F. Air-to-air weapons are R-550 Magic and Sidewinder AAMs. (381 Maverick ASM are on order). The COIN squadron has 22 Magister and four OV-10; the Transport squadron flies 11 C-130H (two more on order), three KC-130H, eight King Air, six Broussard, three DO-28D (seven more on order) and one Gulfstream.

The two helicopter squadrons have 33 AB-205A, five AB-206 (19 more on order), 13 AB-212, 27 Puma, four HH-43B and eleven CH-47C. There are also 24 Gazelle helicopters on order. Training units have eleven T-34C, eleven AS-201/18 Bravo, 28 SF-260M and 24 Alphajet.

The Moroccan navy is relatively small, its main offensive strength being five missile-firing fast attack craft: two French-built PR-72 type and three Cormoran class C Exocet SSM. (One further Cormoran class vessel and one Spanish Descubierta class missile armed frigate are on order). Its other vessels include three large and twelve coastal patrol craft (six P-32 coastal patrol craft on order) and one minesweeper. There is a naval infantry battalion of 600 men.

The Mobile Intervention Companys of the *Sureté Nationale* are equipped to a light military standard, and dispose of two Rallye aircraft and five Alouette II/III, three Zema, six Gazelle and six Puma helicopters.

There is no armaments industry in Morocco.

RANK, DRESS AND DISTINCTIONS

The rank structures of the Moroccan army and navy correspond to those of their French equivalents, except that there are only seven enlisted ranks. The rank structure of the air force, however, is modelled on that of the USAF.

Army and navy uniforms closely resemble the French, except for army officers' semidress and service uniforms, which are more like those worn in the United States army. The field uniform for all ranks is of olive-drab cotton, consisting of a jacket with web belt, straight trousers generally tucked into short canvas leggings, and a steel helmet or green beret. Service and semidress uniforms are also of olive-drab gabardine or wool; the former has a short battledress for all ranks, while officers' semidress uniform includes an open-necked shirt or a jacket, white shirt and black tie. In semidress uniform officers wear a service cap with visor, enlisted men the green beret. Traditional Moorish uniforms are retained for ceremonial wear.

Air force uniforms are of the same blue cloth worn by the USAF. Officers wear a blue service cap or beret, enlisted men a blue beret.

Army officers rank insignia is worn on shoulder boards of various colours denoting the various branches, red being the colour of the combat arms; air force officers' epaulettes are grey. Officer ranks in the army are indicated by various devices on the shoulder boards, but by sleeve stripes of gold braid in the air force. Warrant officers wear a silver star insignia on the shoulder loops of the coat or shirt, and enlisted men's ranks are shown by green diamond-shaped patches overlaid with a gold crown and various combinations of red and yellow chevrons, worn on the upper left sleeve of the winter uniform, and suspended from the left breast pocket of the shirt in the summer uniform. A gold crown is included in all insignia for all ranks.

CURRENT DEVELOPMENTS

On the available evidence, the Moroccan army has performed well in the low-level fighting in the Sahara region since 1975, though it has not been subjected to any severe tests there. There have been no recent instances of the sort of military indiscipline that threatened the throne in 1971—3, and popular support for the post-1975 Saharan policy and the consequent liberalisation of domestic political controls which it made possible have contributed to a very substantial relaxation in political tensions in Morocco. All Moroccan political parties, including even the communists, support Rabat's policy in the Sahara.

There is no possibility that Morocco could lose its new territories because of the efforts of the Polisario guerrillas, but the economic strains of preparing for a potential war with Algeria growing out of that dispute have been very great — particularly as they have come at a time when bad harvests and declining world phosphate prices put the Moroccan economy under considerable pressure. These strains will doubtless continue until Morocco's control over its new territories is internationally recognised, a goal towards which Rabat has been striving with mixed success.

Neither the USA nor the Soviet Union recognises Moroccan sovereignty over its share of the former Spanish Sahara. French support seems steadfast, but Spanish support has been wavering due to the greater economic importance of trade with Algeria, while the leader of the main Spanish opposition party, the socialists, has stated that he will repudiate the 1975 tripartite agreement between Spain, Morocco and Mauritania disposing of the territory if he should win power. (It was partly in response to that that Morocco reopened its claim to the Spanish enclaves of Ceuta and Melilla in October, 1978.) Morocco has hitherto succeeded in stalling a definitive OAU condemnation of its action in Sahara by threatening to withdraw from the organisation, but has no visible prospect of gaining approval from the OAU.

Rabat's problem was compounded by the coup of July, 1978 in Mauritania, where the new regime, despite its lip-service to the Moroccan alliance, was clearly desirous of concluding a peaceful settlement to the destructive war even at the expense of relinquishing its share of the former Spanish territory. Polisario, eager to split the allies, at once announced a ceasefire (applicable to Mauritania only) and talks took place in Mauritania in September and October. At the same time a *Comité des Sages* consisting of a mediating team from five African countries (Guinea, Ivory Coast, Nigeria, Tanzania and Sudan) was attempting to find a negotiated resolution to the conflict. Morocco's troops on Mauritanian soil are an effective guarantee against the latter's unilateral defection (and indeed Mauritanian discussions with Polisario broke down in December, 1978), but at the same time they provide an additional stimulus to Mauritanians anxious about Morocco's longer term ambitions to discover an exit from the conflict as quickly as possible.

Morocco's main concern must be to find some way of settling the Saharan quarrel peacefully without renouncing the gains that have restored the monarchy's popularity, and before a denunciation of the 1975 tripartite agreement by either Spain or Mauritania removes even the colour of legality that now attaches to its presence in those territories. Thus Morocco became involved during 1978 in direct secret negotiations with Algeria, seeking a settlement that would exchange guaranteed Algerian access to the Atlantic across the Sahara and some form of autonomous status within Morocco for the new Saharan provinces (presumably ratified by some form of referendum) for Algeria's recognition of Moroccan sovereignty in the area and the ending of Algiers' military support for Polisario. The death in December, 1978 of Algeria's President Boumedienne, Polisario's strongest supporter in Algiers, may have made this goal more attainable. However, it would also create a powerful temptation for Morocco to solve its problems by seeking a direct military confrontation with Algeria if the latter should be weakened by a lengthy succession struggle: in December, 1978 Algeria accused Morocco of using air force planes to drop arms to potential rebels amongst the discontented Berber tribes in the Kabyle east of Algiers.

If it should come to open war between Morocco and Algeria, Morocco's military situation is considerably more favourable than it was in 1975, and will continue its relative improvement as further arms deliveries take place. It is not to be anticipated, however, that it will match the Algerian forces in sheer numbers of tanks and combat aircraft, at least for the foreseeable future, and Rabat must also reckon with the possibility that Algiers might receive emergency shipments of arms from the Soviet Union in the event of war far more rapidly and in much larger quantities than Morocco could expect from France and the USA (if, indeed, it could expect anything at all from the United States in those circumstances — one of the curious aspects of the Maghreb's present alignments is that Algeria has a far more important commercial relationship with the United States than does Morocco).

Morocco's inferiority in military equipment *vis-à-vis* Algeria, however, is to a considerable extent compensated for by geographical and other considerations. In any fighting in the far south, Algeria's supply lines from the populated centres of the country would be considerably longer than Morocco's and for almost their whole length lie vulnerably exposed to attack from adjacent Moroccan border areas. Morocco's own lines of communication with the south, on the other hand, run along the coast, and are protected from Algerian interference by considerable mountain ranges.

In a full-scale war between the two, fighting would tend to shift northwards to the areas near the Mediterranean coast (where most of that part of the Moroccan army not committed in the far south, and a reported two-thirds of the Algerian army, are already concentrated). In this region, however, the terrain is eminently suitable for defence, and it is unlikely that any major advances would be possible by either side. In any case, it is improbable that either country would allow a clash over the Sahara to escalate to this extent.

Gwynne Dyer

406

MOZAMBIQUE

HISTORY AND INTRODUCTION

Mozambique attained independence in June 1975 after twelve years of mounting insurgency campaigning against Portuguese colonial rule; the campaign was almost entirely waged by Frelimo, now the ruling (and only) party. Frelimo is a revolutionary socialist party, and post-independence Mozambique is supposedly being reconstructed on its principles. The first seven years of independence have been eventful. Until 1981 Mozambique harboured, fed, trained and equipped insurgent groups operating against the Rhodesian regime. Both then and since there have been incidents on the South African border. In December 1975 some 400 troops mutinied in Maputo (formerly Lourenço Marques); the mutiny was however suppressed with small loss of life. Units of the Tanzanian Peoples Defence Force, probably two battalions, were reported to have arrived in Mozambique in May 1976, almost certainly to deal with another mutiny in the Cabo Delgado area. They were withdrawn by 1979 not, so far as is known, having been committed to any operational zone on the Rhodesian border. Until 1978 the Mozambique authorities resisted Soviet requests for permanent air and naval facilities although an East German radar watch system was installed. In March 1978 construction of more permanent Soviet air and naval installations was begun at Beira and Nacala. Protest against the severity of the Frelimo ideology and politics had begun even before independence, but in the late 1970s these developed into a considerable internal security problem to the regime with the emergency of the Mozambique National Resistance (MNR) as a specific military challenge. Until 1980 MNR enjoyed Rhodesian support, often including the provision of weapons and supplies, and on occasion helicopter lifts. After 1980 South African support and help enabled MNR to survive and develop. The MNR operates mainly in Manicaland, but also in Tete, Inhambana and Sofala provinces; the large Cabora Bassa dam may well also become a target. In November 1982 Beira's electricity was cut off, following sabotage, for several days. The MNR style is of bands of 100–200, their total is about 3000. Towns are rarely attacked, then only if remote, but roads, especially linked to mines, and railways especially railway bridges are preferred targets, often causing serious disruption. Their equipment includes small arms and wireless sets. MNR quite freely resorts to terror; when leading local Frelimo officials are captured they are mutilated. Some of the MNR were former Portuguese colonial soldiers.

Overall while many in government in Mozambique would welcome expanded contacts with the West, the need for Soviet military support in view of the present developments has had the effect of perpetuating close links with the USSR. At the time of writing, Mozambique's Minister of Defence was visiting London to consider purchase of weapon and surveillance systems.

STRENGTH AND BUDGET

Population: 11,500,000
Armed Forces: Army, 20,000; Air Force, 1000, together with a Border Guard of 6000 and a Peoples Militia of unknown size

GNP: ⎫
Defence Expenditure:⎭ no figures available

COMMAND AND CONSTITUTIONAL STATUS

The President of Mozambique, Samora Machel, is Commander in Chief of the country's armed forces and A. J. Chipande is Minister of Defence. Recently, to emphasise status and as part of the stiffening of the armed forces in face of the MNR threat, Machel conferred upon himself the rank of Field-Marshal and the rank of Lieutenant-General upon his Minister. Also given the rank of Lieutenant-General were A. Guebuza, the Deputy Minister and Chief Political Officer, and S. Marcos Mabote, the Chief of Staff.

ROLE, COMMITMENT, DEPLOYMENT AND RECENT OPERATIONS

Mozambique's forces (FPLM) have two roles, the maintenance of internal security in face of the MNR challenge, and the protection of the territory's frontiers, especially that with South Africa and also with Swaziland, aginst 'hot pursuit' operations.

These latter at the moment remain small-scale and are perhaps most conveniently noted first. They represent more a reminder of South Africa's military capacities than any attempt to destabilise the regime. The most spectacular South African operation to date was a very bold special forces raid on a suburb of Maputo, Matola, in January 1981; there is a considerable concentration of South African troops on the section of the border nearest to Maputo.

In the long insurgency campaign against the Portuguese, the Frelimo command's style was an unusual mixture of slow cautious ground tactics together with some original and daring strategic moves. In the latter stages of the campaign one of the hitherto most successful of the Portuguese African commanders, General Kaulza de Arriaga, was lured into committing and retaining the bulk of his forces into the north of the territory in Cabo Delgado and Niassa provinces. But at the same time the insurgents were preparing and eventually launching attacks much further south initially in Tete in 1971–2, and then in Manica and Sofala in 1973. This, together with the arrival on the scene of SAM-7 missiles which enabled Frelimo to shoot down the helicopters and aircraft bringing Portuguese forces to the scene of insurgent activity, proved decisive. At ground combat level, however, Frelimo's tactics were those of marching ants, a slow infantry marching speed reflecting a peasant liberation army philosophy.

For reasons both idcological and sentimental, Frelimo at first wished to keep this style of military organisation after independence, but has increasingly found that poachers have to be retrained and re-equipped, for all their poaching experience, if they are to be efficient game-keepers. Until 1979 Mozambique forces proved incapable of offering any effective opposition to Rhodesian airborne assault; poor command, poor training and also a lack of manpower were all major causes. By 1979, however, the results of Soviet retraining started to bear fruit and Rhodesian assaults began to meet effective opposition, especially from FPLM artillery fire. By the end of the Rhodesian conflict it had seemed, also, that MNR was being brought under control but 1981 and 1982 saw a return of MNR offensives. The Frelimo government responded by refurbishing the militia in areas under threat, the militia being issued with small arms, mostly rifles. In June and December 1981 major offensives were mounted by the FPLM against the MNR in Sofala and Manicaland; June 1982 saw a third major offensive, again in Manicaland, on this occasion involving, it is reported, 5000 troops, armour and artillery. The operation was supported by aircraft from the Zimbabwe Air Force and a battalion from the North Korean trained Fifth Brigade of the army. The offensive was far from being a crushing blow, only limited numbers of MNR being captured, and the movement embarking on attacks on railway lines and other installations elsewhere in Mozambique, notably in Sofaia and Inhambane provinces.

ORGANISATION

The FPLM standing forces are organised around a tank brigade, ten infantry brigades (each of three infantry battalions, two mechanised units, an artillery battalion, and anti aircraft defence unit and logistic detachments) a Presidential Guard unit and seven air defence units.

The Border Guard is organised into four brigades.

The new situation in Mozambique is reflected in the decision, taken in September 1981 to reintroduce a formal officer rank structure into the FPLM.

All officers have to be Frelimo members and political education forms an important part of all training programmes.

RECRUITMENT, TRAINING AND RESERVES

A system of two years' national service, of which the FPLM is one option, is in force, but it is unlikely to be comprehensive.

Men from the Makonde ethnic group formed a large part of Frelimo's military strength before independence; men from the Makua and Yao peoples figured conspicuously in Portuguese units. Although many of the Frelimo groups were demobilised and returned to their villages in 1974–5, and there also appears to have been some attempt to recruit former colonial African troops into the FPLM, the ethnic divisons of the insurgency period may well affect the composition of the new force, as also may the tendency of Mozambique's southern peoples to dominate the government hierarchy.

For some time East European training staffs have been at work in Mozambique, also until independence or shortly after, some Chinese instructors. The present situation appears to be one of some 500 training advisers, mostly Russian but including some East German, Romanians and Tanzanians as well. Cuban personnel have been noted in the past, very possibly only in transit; none are thought to be in Mozambique at present, though both a North Korean and surprisingly, a Portuguese team may be on their way. Personnel are of course also sent abroad, to the USSR in particular, for specialist training. A military academy, offering a three-year basic course for officers was recently opened in Nampula Province.

An important feature of FPLM training, a legacy of the liberation campaign, is the doctrine that the FPLM must ally itself with local populations by assisting with minor development tasks such as the construction of wells, light bridges, dams and villages.

EQUIPMENT AND ARMS INDUSTRY

The equipment of Mozambique's FPLM is a mixture of some quite modern Soviet equipment, much older Soviet equipment and some even older Portuguese pieces.

Over 200, perhaps as many as 350 Soviet T-34 and T-54 tanks are in service, together with a small number of PT-76 machines. There are also a number, between 35 and 100, BRDM-1 and 2 vehicles; some 200 BTR-40, 60 and 152 armoured personnel carriers; a number of artillery pieces, reported to be as high as 200 and including Soviet 76mm, 85mm, 100mm, 122mm and 130mm guns, together with some ex-Portuguese former *Wehrmacht* 105mm guns, an unknown number of BM-21 artillery rocket launchers; 60mm, 82mm and 120mm mortars, 75mm and 82mm recoilless launchers, Sagger anti-tank guided weapons, 20mm, ZU-23mm, 37mm, 57mm towed anti aircraft cannons and guns together with a small number of self-propelled ZSU-23-4 and SAM-3 units, together with SAM-7 equipments. Soviet amphibious K61 load carriers are also in service. A recent delivery of Soviet Sagger and Spigot anti-tank missiles has also been reported.

As noted already, in areas under MNR threat the Militia has been issued with rifles provided from a consignment provided by Portugal.

The air force includes 25 MiG-21 aircraft organised into two squadrons, a third squadron of older MiG-19 and MiG-17 aircraft has also been reported, a helicopter squadron of four armed Alouette and an unknown number of MI-8 machines, a transport squadron of one Tupoler TU-134 'Crusty', two Antonov AN-26 and two Noratlas Medium transports and some smaller communication aircraft, and a training squadron reported to include three MiG-15 and seven Czech Aero L-39 machines, the latter easily adaptable for a light counter-insurgency strike role.

RANK, DRESS AND DISTINCTIONS

Details of the rank insignia are not yet available. FPLM units wear shoulder-bands or brassards distinctive to each unit.

CURRENT DEVELOPMENTS

In the field of operations against the MNR, recent developments have already been noted. Mozambique seems destined for an uncertain, precarious, military future in the 1980s. Even if MNR is brought under control, a massive danger of becoming an overspill area for South Africa's problems, with Maputo as a form of Beirut, grows, unfortunately, ever more likely.

ADDENDUM

MNR activities intensified in the autumn of 1982, moving into the Beira area. The government claimed an important victory in which over 800 MNR insurgents were killed; the claim needs to be treated with reserve.

Zimbabwe's help was again requested, and at the time of writing it appears a Zimbabwe battalion is deployed guarding the oil-pipeline which pipes oil across Mozambique to Mutare (formerly Umtali) in Zimbabwe.

Lloyd Mathews

NEPAL

HISTORY AND INTRODUCTION

The Gurkhas of Nepal are the Swiss of south Asia, a mountain race famous for their bravery and military temperament who have fought as mercenaries in British and Indian service for 150 years; they are still eagerly recruited by both armies and also work as policemen and guards throughout the region. Yet, despite the existence of special military treaties with Britain and India — comparable to the military capitulations between Switzerland and France of former times — Nepal is and always has been a sovereign State, with its own army. It was indeed, through the prowess of that army that, alone among the smaller neighbours of British India, it retained its independence throughout the imperial era. For, although victorious in the Anglo—Nepalese war of 1814—16, the British found Gurkha resistance (admittedly much favoured by the mountainous terrain) so difficult to overcome that they did not push their victory to the point of annexation. Non-annexation remained their policy even though Anglo—Nepalese relations stayed troubled until the middle of the nineteenth century.

The Nepalese Kingdom of the war of 1814—16 was a recent creation, forged by the success of the Shah family of Gurkha, one of 46 small, neighbouring Himalayan States, in several decades of war with its neighbours which ended in 1769. It was the extension of this imperialism westwards into Garwhal and Kumaon, eastwards into Sikkim and southwards into the Terai, the border region between the Himalayas and the Indian plains, which brought Nepal into conflict with the British. The war brought an end to expansion, led to the expulsion of the Gurkhas from Sikkim and the annexation of part of the Terai and some of their hill conquests, but did not put a stop to quarrels among the leading families of Nepal itself. A succession of weak regencies resulted eventually in the extinction of royal power altogether in Nepal for over 100 years, when in 1846 Jung Bahadur Thapa became *vizir* (Prime Minister) and prevailed on the King to confer hereditary powers on his Rana family. Thenceforeward the royal family lived virtually prisoners within the palace while the Ranas, as a sort of Himalayan shogunate, exercised all functions of government on their behalf. It was during the early Rana years that relations between Nepal and British India were normalised and that Gurkhas, whose loyalty during the Indian Mutiny of 1857 contributed significantly to its suppression, became such a prized element in the Indian army. By World War I there were 20 battalions of Gurkha Rifles on its strength, and the actual numbers of Gurkhas who served during the war reached 200,000. In World War II 160,000 men served and, on the granting of independence to India in 1947, the new government of India and Britain jointly reached agreement with the government of Nepal to keep the regular battalions in existence, 12 going to India and eight to Britain. India and Britain were allowed to maintain the former imperial government's special recruiting rights within the country, and administer arrangements for the payment of pensions to discharged soldiers, which are an important element in the national and local economies of the Kingdom.

The Rana system did not survive the departure of the British from India. The monopolisation of all important posts in the civil service and the army by inner members of the family created, since the numbers of such posts did not increase proportionately with propagation, a body of disinherited but well-educated men who turned naturally for consolation to the Indian national movement south of the border. Organising themselves as the Nepali National Congress, they initiated an armed insurrection in the Terai in 1950. It received the tacit support of the Indian government which granted asylum to King Tribhuvan in its embassy in Nepal and then arranged for him to take residence on its soil when the Ranas deposed him. His declaration of sympathy with, and Indian support for, the insurrection ensured its success and in 1951 he returned to the throne and announced the institution of democratic government.

'Democratic' government as practised in Nepal has not taken a form recognised in the West, since political parties are not allowed to exist; the national assembly is indirectly elected and sits *in camera*, and the King generally appoints ministers, besides remaining constitutionally the executive head of government. King Mahendra (1955—72) was a consummate politician and, besides amending in 1960 the 1952 Constitution so as to increase the power of the executive, exercised all functions of royal authority by day-to-day manoeuvres. However, there is no suggestion that the King depends for his power on the support of the army or any other armed force. Obedience to the King derives from his divine status and to the religious respect which a deeply conservative people pay him. The army, loyal to the Ranas throughout their period of government, automatically transferred its loyalty to the King on his resumption of executive power in 1951, but obeys him for the same reasons as do the rest of his subjects. There is certainly no question of it conceiving itself to be a power behind the throne.

The Gurkhas in Foreign Service

Five battalions of Gurkhas (the 1/2nd and 2/2nd, 6th, 7th and 10th Gurkha Rifles) form part of the British army, the Gurkha Brigade in all numbering about 6000. Apart from one battalion serving on rotation in Britain and one in Brunei, financed by the Sultan, the remainder are stationed in Hong Kong. Their numbers have declined steeply in recent years and their future is uncertain. Eleven regiments of Gorkhas (the preferred spelling) serve in the Indian army (the 1st, 3rd—5th and 8th—11th), and each has several battalions. The exact number is not revealed. The Assam Rifles, a paramilitary force of many battalions, is largely formed from Gurkhas and others serve as individuals in non-Gurkha units of the Indian army. It is believed that there may be 100,000 Gurkhas altogether in Indian service. They also serve in the army and the armed police of Burma, where settlements of Gurkhas pensioned from the British-run Burma Rifles and Military Police grew up in the early twentieth century. The chief motive for enlistment among emigrant Gurkhas is to accumulate savings with which to add to family land holdings at home and to earn pensions. Landless Gurkhas are never enlisted in British regiments nor, it is believed, in Indian ones.

One battalion of Gurkhas, the 7th GR, served in 5 Brigade in the British Falklands campaigns, June 1982.

Nepal

STRENGTH AND BUDGET

Population: 14,600,000
Army: 25,000
GNP (1980 estimate): $1,990,000
Defence expenditure (1981 estimate): $22,200,000

COMMAND AND CONSTITUTIONAL STATUS

The Constitution of 1962, superseding that of 1952, declares the country to be a 'Constitutional Monarchical Hindu State'. The King, H. M. Mahárájádhirája Birendra Bikram Sháh Dev (King Birendra), is both titular and executive head of state, who chooses his council of ministers from an indirectly elected national *panchayat* (assembly); since 1979 this body is directly elected and advises the King on his choice of ministers. The last King, Mahendra, held the post of minister of defence for a long period after his resumption of direct rule in 1960. Moreover, the King is empowered, under Article 81 of the Constitution 'if (he) is of the opinion that a grave emergency exists whereby the security of the whole of Nepal or any part thereof is threatened by war, external aggression or internal disturbances, ... by proclamation (to) suspend any of the articles of the constitution indefinitely until such time as (he) is satisfied that grave emergency no longer exists'. In such circumstances the army would come directly under the control of the King. In practice it is always answerable to him, both because the government remains fundamentally monarchical in character and because the senior officers of the army are still drawn in the majority from court families.

ROLE, COMMITMENT, DEPLOYMENT AND RECENT OPERATIONS

Although several battalions of the army served the British outside Nepal under a special arrangement during World Wars I and II, three battalions fought on the Burma front in 1942–5 and 10 battalions did garrison duty in India during the partition crisis of 1947–8, the army's role is in practice an internal one. The special relationship with India, the Treaty of Peace and Friendship with China and the anxiety of both to preserve Nepal as a buffer zone effectively guarantee its frontiers – though Nepali dissidents based in India have been responsible for occasional disturbances in the south. For its part, Nepal, though not formally a neutralist State, has pursued a policy of non-alignment *vis-à-vis* the two countries since the Sino–Indian Himalayan war of 1962.

The army is deployed in four areas: the Royal Palace Brigade and No. 1 Brigade with service and support troops at Káthmándu, the capital, in central Nepal; No. 2 Brigade at Dharan and No. 3 Brigade at Biratnagar, both in eastern Nepal; and No. 4 Brigade at Nepalganj in western Nepal. Apart from a clash between a Nepalese and a Chinese patrol in the Kor La pass in 1960, for which China apologised, and sporadic action against Nepali Congress dissidents in the south, the army has not been involved in operations in recent years. Nepal's last war was that with the British in 1814–6.

A Nepalese battalion served in the United Nations Lebanon force (UNIFIL) in 1982.

ORGANISATION

The army is essentially a collection of units of battalion size or smaller. An artillery, an engineer and a signals regiment (all small), a parachute battalion and the Household Cavalry are at Káthmándu. Distributed between the five brigades are 12 battalions of infantry, most with long histories and distinctive names, such as: the Sri Nath (raised 1763), Purano Gorakh (1763), Sher (1807), Kali Bahadur (1831), Mahindra Dal (1845), Shamsher Dal (1845), the First Rifles, the Devi Dutt and the Gorakh Bahadur. The latter and the Kali Bahadur were formerly royal guards, stationed in the palace grounds, but in 1971 the late King Mahendra, in order to calm jealousies in the army, arranged for all battalions to do royal guard duty in rotation. Like those of the British and Indian armies, the battalions tend to recruit from particular areas; the Purano Gorakh, for example, recruits mainly Magars from western Nepal and the Kali Bahadur mainly Gurungs from the centre.

There is a small Army Air Support Transport Wing, under the command of the army headquarters. Headquarters is commanded by a chief of the army staff (a full general) with under him a chief of the general staff, adjutant general, quartermaster general and military secretary (all major-generals). The brigades are commanded by brigadier-generals; they consist of two (sometimes three) battalions, which are organised into three rifle and one support companies.

RECRUITMENT, TRAINING AND RESERVES

Nepal is a caste society and, though caste is much weaker than in India, its influence on army recruiting is strong. As in India, there are recognised 'martial races' – most upper caste and mainly agriculturalists. Unlike India, however, Nepal has a majority of martial races among the population, and its army is therefore fairly representative of the country's social character. Ranas, the traditional ruling class of the State, are, however, over-represented among the officers and particularly in the higher ranks, while soldiers are recruited from the land-owning peasantry. The landless classes are not enlisted. As already mentioned, individual regiments have their own recruiting areas, which confers a distinct local character on each of the battalions.

Soldiers are trained in their units. Officers are trained at the Indian Military Academy, and occasionally at Sandhurst. Some Indian officers serve as training advisers with the army in the Indian Military Liaison Group.

Service is entirely voluntary. The reserve structure is not known, but probably consists simply of the pool of time-expired regular soldiers.

EQUIPMENT AND ARMS INDUSTRY

Nepal has no arms industry. By Paragraph 2 of a letter exchanged with the copies of the Treaty of Peace and Friendship of 1950, between India and Nepal, 'any arms, ammunition or warlike material and equipment necessary for the security of Nepal that the Government of Nepal may import through the territory of India shall be so imported with the assistance and agreement of the Government of India. The Government of India will take steps for the smooth and expeditious transport of such arms and ammunition through India'. As all Nepal's importing routes lie through Indian territory, this agreement in effect obliges Nepal to purchase arms exclusively through India. In 1965 the country nevertheless purchased some weapons from Britain and America but, it is believed, by agreement between all four governments.

The army is equipped with British and Indian small arms, including the Ishapur 7.62mm self-loading rifle and the Bren gun converted to the same calibre. There is a little British heavy equipment: four 3.7in pack howitzers, four 4.2mm and 18 120mm mortars, and two 40mm anti-aircraft guns. The air transport wing has five small transports and five helicopters. Some French AMX-13 light tanks have recently been purchased.

RANK, DRESS AND DISTINCTIONS

The army wears khaki. The officers have a service dress of British style; the soldiers wear Indian-style khaki drill and pullovers, with the broad-brimmed Terai hat. Ranks follow the British system and are indicated for officers by a system of blazing-sun and crescent-moon symbols worn on the shoulder strap; generals also wear crossed swords and baton.

CURRENT DEVELOPMENTS

The army lives somewhat in the shadow of the two others which recruit Nepali mercenaries to serve in their ranks: the Indian and the British. It also lacks a distinctively military role, being confined to internal duties in a country which is generally very law-abiding and where disturbances, even transborder ones, fall well within the ability of the police to contain. In the circumstances, it might well be expected that the army would be deeply involved in political intrigue, there being no other outlet for the energies of its senior ranks, but this is not the case. The army, though 'political' in the sense of being deeply conservative and, in its upper ranks, socially exclusive, plays no part in Nepalese political life at all. It has a record of unswerving loyalty to constituted authority and the gradual change in the composition of its officer body since the end of Rana government shows no sign of altering the tradition.

John Keegan

NETHERLANDS

HISTORY AND INTRODUCTION

The founding of the 'Union of the Provinces' in 1477 and the declaration of the 'Republic of the United Provinces' a century later preceded the establishment of a kingdom which, with other changes of name and constitutional status, has become the Netherlands we know today. The long, narrow and flat country, with some land below sea-level, is wedged between Germany and the sea. The sea is held back by dykes; the land is crossed by innumerable canals and drainage systems constructed over the centuries, and now by a comprehensive network of modern roads and railways. These physical features, together with so many bridges, make an appreciation of the country's potentiality for the defender and for the attacker a challenging and interesting proposition.

During the kingdom's early years it was the Dutch navy that stole the limelight with several decisive victories at sea, and the marines, still part of the navy, also gained fame and repute. As the nation's eminence as a trading and colonial power grew, so did the navy's prominence. But while this was happening Dutch armies were fighting battles too, mainly against the Spanish and often in concert with the British. Yet the history of the Netherlands, though full of minor conflicts in earlier times, is not characterised by any underlying military aggressiveness. The Dutch have never been a martial race. The army has not been regarded as highly as the navy and, in peacetime, has not received the same recognition. Today, the Dutch army is the cause of disquiet in certain respects within the nation, and is viewed with some concern within NATO: it achieves another kind of prominence.

A Dutch army of some 28 infantry battalions, seven cavalry regiments and nine artillery batteries fought in the Waterloo campaigns. It was during the Napoleonic wars when the first efforts were made, nationally, to raise a new 'standing' army. This was to be a volunteer force to supplement the home guard, or *Landstorm*, which already existed. Recruiting problems caused this experiment to fail but here was the beginning of a new military structure that was to develop in concept, if not in actual armed strength, over the next century and a half; the beginning of a permanent cadre of regular officers and NCOs serving within a predominantly conscript militia, the *Landweer*.

At the Congress of Vienna in 1815, the Dutch and Spanish Netherlands were joined to form a 'buffer' State between France and Germany. The Kingdom of the United Netherlands broke apart only 15 years later when the Belgians revolted and the frontiers as we know them today were drawn at a conference of the Great Powers in London. The modern Dutch army can be said to date from 1830. Throughout the rest of the century efforts were made to create a volunteer army, but the manning requirements were never met. When mobilisation was called at the outbreak of the Franco—Prussian War in 1870 other military and administrative shortcomings were exposed. Dutch forces were not committed in this war, but clearly improvements were necessary. Liability for service with the colours was raised temporarily from 5 years to 7 years, but not all the intended reforms succeeded. At the turn of the century universal service was introduced in order to provide 23,000 men in the *Landweer*. In 1911, a *Landstorm* bill was passed in the States-General whereby all male adults, up to the age of forty, became liable for service in the home guard. This bill also gave the Crown the power to call out the *Landstorm* in a national emergency.

No real emergency arose, however, during World War I because the Netherlands' neutrality was respected. The government mobilised a home defence force comprising: a field army of four divisions and a cavalry brigade; a considerable number of infantry battalions and fortress artillery companies for static protection; and a sizable reserve. It was asserted at the time that the 458,000 troops embodied could have been doubled had further expansion been necessary. Following demobilisation at the end of World War I, there were repeated demands for drastic reductions in military expenditure. In fact, throughout the 1920s and 1930s the budget allocation to the land forces remained an acrimonious subject; during this period the army became run-down and ill-equipped, and particularly weak in artillery weapons. By that time, the Dutch army (or *Landmacht*) was organised on a militia basis. Some 20,000 men were called up for military training which varied in duration according to arm, but all were liable over a period of 6 years to undertake two spells of refresher training. In this way a reserve was established. The small regular cadre provided the commanders, staff officers, instructors and administrators. Between the wars, the *Landstorm* continued, on a volunteer basis, with a considerable commitment of training and home guard duties each year.

Events began to tell. In 1938, the government authorised a large increase in military funds mainly to cover the purchase of weapons and equipment needed quickly and in increasing quantity. That year, evidently, some 73,000 men were declared liable for military service, of whom only 43,000 were found to be available, and of these 19,500 were actually embodied. In 1939, an 'emergency' programme was drawn up even though great dependence was placed upon the country remaining neutral. In the event of war, elsewhere in Europe, some security forces would nevertheless be required. Hitler had affirmed, outwardly, that neutrality would be respected; it is known now that as early in the 'phoney' war as October 9th, soon after the British and French declared war on Nazi-Germany, the *Führer* had issued his Instruction No. 6 which contained orders for the invasion of the Netherlands as well as Belgium and France. So it came about.

On May 10th, 1940 German forces invaded the Kingdom. A home defence force of about 400,000 men (10 divisions mainly infantry, four horsed cavalry regiments and a few 'bicycle' units as well as artillery an supporting serv..:es) faced the enemy. After 5 days of fighting the position on land and in the air had become so hopeless that despite stout resistance the Dutch were forced to capitulate. The occupying power was not slow taking a variety of repressive measures. For example, regular army officers had to sign a parole undertaking not to engage in any anti-German activity. This was strengthened when, in 1942, former regular officers had to report periodically; in this way they were kept under surveillance and some were transported to prison camps. Nevertheless, a strong underground movement became established in the country during the war. The Dutch were active outside their country too.

During 1944, the *Prinses Irene* Brigade was training in Britain and later that year took part in the Normandy landings as part of the British 21st Army Group. The Brigade fought through Belgium and assisted with liberating their home country. It was disbanded in 1945 but the title *Prinses Irene* remains as the name of a guards regiment in the current regular army order of battle.

After the liberation of the southern provinces of the Netherlands, Dutchmen were recruited and trained for allied lines of communication duties. When the Germans surrendered in May, 1945 the Dutch government decided to raise an armed force of some 200,000 men to help with the occupation of Germany and the liberation of the Dutch East Indies which still remained in Japanese hands. Once again, military strengths did not match the plans and by December, 1946 the Dutch army amounted to about 117,000 excluding 47,000 serving in the Royal Netherlands Indies Army at the time. From the time the campaign in north-west Europe closed, attention was diverted to the Far East. Two divisions were raised, and were British equipped and trained, but as soon as they were ready to go, the war against Japan ended abruptly. However, three Dutch divisions arrived in the East Indies in 1946 to join two formed locally.

The Royal Netherlands Indies Army was a long-serving colonial force maintained by conscription and a large regular cadre. After the Japanese invasion many of its officers and soldiers were imprisoned. After the war and following liberation the State of Indonesia became independent and the Dutch forces were withdrawn. Many former members of the Indies army regular cadre therefore found themselves serving in Europe for the first time, and to this day there remains a strong East Indies element in the Dutch army. In 1974 the last colonial garrison force returned home when troops left Surinam. So, in 1975, the role of the Royal Netherlands Army (RNA) has become solely concerned with NATO and Europe, apart from a small component earmarked for United Nations duties.

To return to the troubled period in Europe of the late 1940s. The Netherlands joined her neighbours — Belgium, Britain, France and Luxembourg — in signing the Brussels Treaty of March, 1948. This mutual assistance pact was aimed at guaranteeing the collective security of the signatory nations. They felt threatened by the growing Russian military menace just as much as, if not more than, their fear of any German *revanchisme*. The creation of a Western Union Defence Organisation quickly followed, with its headquarters at Fontainebleau in France. Field-Marshal Montgomery became Chairman of the Commander-in-Chief Committee, and the French General de Lattre de Tassigny was appointed Commander-in-Chief Land Forces which included elements of the RNA. So began a movement away from Dutch neutrality and the process of integrating allied forces. NATO superseded the European organisation and Headquarters Allied Forces Central Europe (AFCENT) was set up at Fontainebleau; the endeavour to construct some form of collective defence as quickly as possible in the Central Region continued.

Also, in 1951, the Dutch government approved a 4 year armament programme and increased conscription from 12 to 18 months*. About that time a battalion joined the United Nations force in Korea. The main objective of the new programme was to produce five divisions for NATO of which one only would be activated at any time during peace. This one division was filled with conscripts and had a regular cadre. By 1954, the reserve of trained soldiers had grown to 220,000 (140,000 field army; 60,000 home defence; 18,000

anti-aircraft defence), and it claimed that all were mobilisable within 48 hours. During the 1950s the Dutch army changed over to certain NATO organisations and procedures like those operative now among their headquarters' staffs; it also began to switch from British to American equipment. Later the number of divisions in the field army order of battle were reduced to four and then, more recently, to three but with two activated divisions instead of just one. These two divisions comprise some reserve as well as active units. In the 1960s, the RNA adopted the brigade group as its basic field army fight formation and this remains so today, except that the detailed composition and readiness status of combat and support units within each brigade have changed. Initially, brigades were grouped within a modified Landcent divisional framework†. Later the division, as a formation, became only a means for tactically commanding a number of brigades. There is no combat support or logistic support resources at this level. The present structure will be described in more detail later.

In 1967, HQ AFCENT moved from Fontainebleau to Brunssum, in Dutch Limburg. RNA formations and units serve and train currently with their Belgian, British and German counterparts in Northern Army Group, and Dutch officers and NCOs serve on NATO's international staffs and in several multinationally manned support units.

The declared defence policy of the Dutch government, as described in its 1974 'Defence Note', is to support NATO strongly. A nation-wide opinion poll taken in 1974 indicated that over half of the nation supported NATO*. Stress is given to two particular points of universal interest in current defence policy: the 'specialisation' of military tasks within NATO and the role of tactical or battlefield nuclear weapons.

Apart from any 'rationalisation', like recent measures to amalgamate the certain functions of the medical services within the Dutch armed forces, defence policy emphasises that the armies of smaller countries may, in the future, have to relinquish an entire branch or capability, or even the whole of one armed service. In consequence the government has suggested that the Dutch navy takes over certain German commitments at sea in return for the *Bundeswehr* assuming Dutch land force commitments in Northern Army Group. This proposal is being studied. In parallel, the Belgian government has announced that it too will support 'rationalisation' and 'specialisation' along similar lines within NATO. The encouraging feature about these moves is that they are being conducted through Alliance channels.

Netherlands defence policy accepts the strategy of flexible response as the basis for military planning and the tactical conduct of operations, with the proviso that the role assigned to tactical or battlefield nuclear weapons should be relegated more to the background. The requirement to possess these weapons is accepted, but the need to raise the 'nuclear threshold' is stressed. This thoroughly sensible sentiment raises the vital issue of the conventional strength of the Dutch and other land force components assigned to, or

† HQ LANDCENT was the Land Forces headquarters for NATO's Central Region subordinate to HQ AFCENT. The 'LANDCENT division' was an attempt to produce a 'standard' division. The trouble was, and has been ever since, that NATO did not *insist* on its implementation. Hence, many national versions, and the situation as it exists today.

* For detailed results of the polls and other related information see C. C. Van den Heuvel's article 'Defence Motivation in the Netherlands', *NATO Review*, October (1975). The 'Defence Note' mentioned refers to the Government White Paper on Netherlands Defence Policy 1974—83, entitled *Our Very Existence at Stake*, The Hague, July 9th (1974).

* Article by Major Edgar O'Ballance, 'In Defence of Holland', *Army Quarterly* (1961).

earmarked for, the Central Region. Present Dutch defence policy does not seem to be aimed at any dramatic strengthening of the combat readiness or effectiveness of the conventional element.

STRENGTH AND BUDGET

Population: 14,178,000
Army: 67,000 (plus 145,000 reserves)
Navy: 17,000 (including 2900 marines); 20 major vessels, 50 smaller
Air force: 19,000; 172 combat aircraft
Paramilitary: 8700 gendarmerie; 4300 Home Guard
GNP (1981): $139,076,000,000
Defence expenditure (1982): $4,575,000,000

COMMAND AND CONSTITUTIONAL STATUS

Command
The Queen is Commander-in-Chief. The Government controls the Dutch army (*Koninklijke Landmacht*) through a Minister of Defence and a Defence Ministry. Also in The Hague, but in a separate location from the Ministry, the Army Headquarters exercises command over the subordinate formations and installations (*see* Figs. 1 and 2).

Constitutional Status
Apart from the normal enactments prolonging the existence of armed forces and approving their financing, the main constitutional feature concerns conscription which is perhaps natural within forces primarily based on a universal service system. Conscription is based on Section 194 of the Constitution which states that 'all Netherlanders who are able shall be bound to collaborate for the maintenance of the independence of the Kingdom and for the defence of its territory'. All male citizens of the Netherlands living in the country are registered for national service on February 1st of the year in which they reach the age of eighteen. About 10% of men registered are exempted before being called for medical examination for reasons such as service by brothers (i.e. if two brothers are serving or have already served) or because of training for Holy Orders. The Defence Minister announced that anyone liable for military service after July 1st, 1976 would not be called up if he had become a married man or a provider for a family before that date. The Netherlands Constitution offers the possibility of exceptions from military service on the grounds of serious objections of conscience.

ROLE, COMMITMENT, DEPLOYMENT AND RECENT OPERATIONS

Role and Commitment
The RNA has three main tasks: to provide an army corps of three divisions and supporting troops for Northern Army Group; to defend the Netherlands; and to furnish logistic and all other forms of support required by the Dutch contribution to NATO's Central Region and by the home defence force. Because some two thirds of the Dutch army consists of conscripts, their training is a heavy commitment; hence the separate training command and the many training establishments (Fig. 2). It may be the eventual intention to amalgamate the Army Training Command with the National Territorial Command.

Deployment
With the exception of one armoured brigade and a small number of other units stationed in Germany, the remainder of the 1st Netherlands Corps is located at home in peacetime. Therefore, most regular officers and NCOs spend the longest part of their service in barracks in the Netherlands, as do the conscripts. Exercises are conducted in the Federal Republic where troops become acquainted with their operational areas and tasks. In 1972, a commission of defence experts unanimously recommended that a second brigade and a second reconnaissance battalion should be stationed in the Federal Republic. They also pointed to the need for the earliest provisions of training areas in the Netherlands. Neither of these two improvements have so far been possible. The problems associated with the 'maldeployment' of NATO's land forces in the Central Region are well known and led the commission to state that, 'Permanent presence, preparedness and fast reaction capability should be the main features of our army' (Dutch White Paper, 1972). The time it would take the 1st Netherlands Corps to deploy to its operational areas means that an emergency arising, by surprise, would cause very great concern and difficulty.

Recent Operations
Dutch forces saw active service in the Dutch East Indies 1945–8 and Korea (1950–3) but since the early 1950s the RNA has received no experience of active service operations.

ORGANISATION

Arms of Service
The RNA comprises infantry (including a commando corps), cavalry, artillery, engineers, ordnance or technical service, signals, transportation, medical service, quartermasters and catering, military administration (including military finance, pay, education, etc.) and a legal service. The *Koninklijke Marechaussee* or Royal Military Constabulary, a predominantly volunteer force, not only has a joint service function but also exercises certain civil powers over public order and at national frontiers. Objections to military service relating specifically to conscience over the use of arms are recognised and men are posted to the Mobile Columns Corps which is a branch of the army dealing with such things as disaster relief, clearing of debris and medical assistance. The total length of service is the same as in the Arms.

The regiments and corps of the Royal Netherlands Army are as follows:

Infantry: *Garde Grenadiers, Garde Jagers, Garde Fuseliers, Prinses Irene, Regiment Chassé, Regiment Oranje Gelderland, Regiment Menno Van Coehoorn, Regiment Johan Willem Friso, Stoottroepen, Limburgse Jagers, Regiment Van Heutsz, Korps Commandotroepen*
Cavalry: *Huzaren Prins Alexander, Huzaren van Boreel, Huzaren Sytzema*
Artillery: *Veldartillerie*
Air Defence: *Luchtdoelartillerie*
Engineers: *Genie*
Technical Engineers: *Technische Dienst*
Signals: *Verbindings Dienst*
Transport: *Aan en Afvoer Troepen*
Medical: *Militair Geneeskundige Dienst*
Supply: *Intendance*
Military Administration: *Militaire Administratie*
Justice: *Militair Juridische Dienst*

There are also some small corps (technical staff, mobile columns corps (civil defence), bands, chaplains, women's

Figure 1 HIGHER DEFENCE ORGANISATION

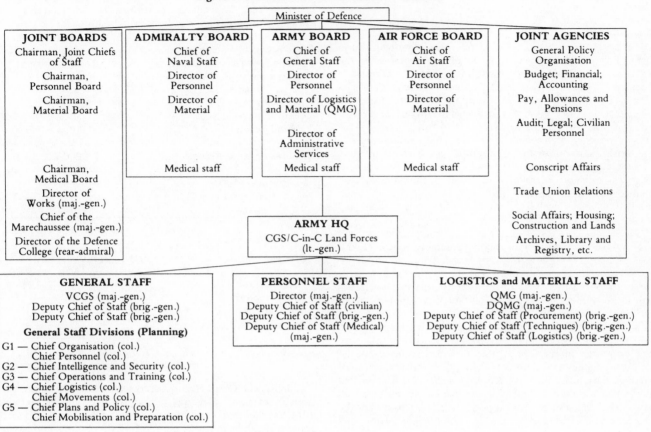

ARMY HQ
CGS/C-in-C Land Forces
(lt.-gen.)

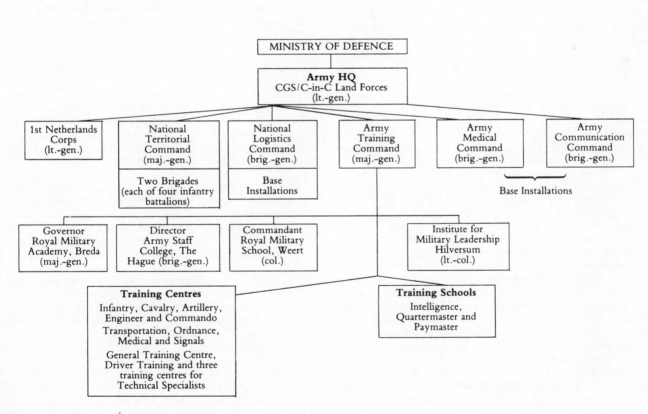

Figure 2

415

Netherlands

service (*Milva*) and military police supplied by the *Marechausee*).

Operational

The RNA is at present undergoing an extensive reorganisation and is being reduced in size; full details are contained in the Defence White Paper already mentioned. The 1st Netherlands Corps is organised in three parts: command and control elements, fighting elements and support elements. Like the Belgian army, the RNA has no divisional headquarters as such, but staffs are provided at divisional level to command tactically a number of brigades. The divisional commander has no combat-support or logistic-support resources of his own; these are either integral ('organic' is the military term) to brigades or allocated from corps level as the situation demands. Aviation, provost and signals support, although 'pooled' at corps level, have standard affiliations to divisional staffs.

At present only the two activated divisions are mechanised; the third, a reserve division, is being gradually converted and re-equipped to bring it to the same status. When the modernisation programme is complete, the 1st Netherlands Corps's three armoured brigades and six armoured infantry brigades will be fully mechanised with all infantry APC-borne and all artillery self-propelled, with the exception of a reserve infantry brigade. The armoured brigades will consist of two tank battalions, each equipped with 53 Leopard tanks, and one armoured infantry battalion of 67 APCs; the armoured infantry brigades will have one tank battalion and two armoured infantry battalions. Both types of brigade have a self-propelled artillery battalion and other organic combat support, as well as some signals and service support facilities. This makes the brigades, as the Dutch basic fighting formations, self-contained to an extent.

Only the two armoured brigades and four armoured infantry brigades belonging to the 1st and 4th Divisions are 'active'; the three in the 5th Division and the one additional infantry brigade are 'reserve' formations. Not all battalions in each brigade are 'active' or combat ready; some are 'RIM' and some 'mobilisable' which places them in 'reserve' status. The proportion of 'RIM' battalions is increasing under the current restructuring. 'RIM' units comprise conscripts who have left an 'active' battalion and are transferred as part of a complete company for a period of 18 months. 'RIM' units have a nucleus of regular officers and NCOs, whose permanent appointments in peacetime are in training centres and similar establishments, and have a proportion of former conscripts commissioned as officers or promoted to NCO rank. 'Mobilisable' units consist of a small regular element, and former conscript officers, NCOs and soldiers, who have either completed their 'RIM' tour, or who have been transferred direct from 'active' to 'reserve' service, where they complete the remainder of their military liability. 'Active' or combat-ready units, such as a tank or armoured infantry battalions, have a headquarters company, a training company and three 'manoeuvre' companies. Each manoeuvre company is filled with conscripts from the same national service intake and, apart from a small regular cadre, are replaced *en bloc*. This means that the standard of training is uneven within a battalion; also because conscripts automatically go on 'short leave' at the end of their service term, a complete company will be missing from the battalion at any one time. Hence, in peacetime an 'active' battalion is, at best, manned only up to two-thirds of its wartime establishment. The same type of structure and procedure applies to artillery, engineer, logistic and signals units. Under-implementation adds to the considerations of time and distance in any appreciation of combat readiness. Finally, 'active' units hold and use their own equipment, 'RIM' and 'mobilisable' units have their equipment stored in central locations. The procedures for drawing equipment are regularly practised.

Now that the reorganisation of the 1st Netherlands Corps is complete, strengths are:

Active (present in peacetime)	27,000
Active (in other peacetime appointments)	700
On 'short leave'	5,300
RIM } Reserve	17,600
Mobilisation }	31,200
Total wartime strength	81,900

or, expressed another way:

Combat units	Active	Reserve RIM	Reserve Mobilisable	Total
Tank battalions	5	5	$2\frac{1}{3}$	$12\frac{1}{3}$
Armoured infantry battalions	7	7	1	15
Infantry battalions	–	–	3	3
	12	12	$6\frac{1}{3}$	$30\frac{1}{3}$

Finally, the Corps Headquarters at Apeldoorn and the two 'active' Divisional Headquarters at Arnhem and Harderwijk in the Netherlands, are organised upon NATO standard staff system. In addition to the chiefs of staff — at corps a brigadier-general, and at division a colonel — there is the normal complement of staff officers organised into G-1, G-2, G-3 and G-4 branches backed by specialist staffs. A G-5 branch, at corps level only, deals with civil–military co-operation (CIMIC).

RECRUITMENT, TRAINING AND RESERVES

Recruitment

From February 1st, 1976 the term of national service was reduced from 16 to 14 months. The current universal service system involves a period of military training and employment (14 months) followed by 'short leave' (8 months), when the former conscript is liable to instant recall, maybe to a 'RIM' unit.

Every year about 45,000 young Dutchmen are called to the colours to national service; they represent about 40% of the total in their age group. Call-up is normally in the year in which the man reaches the age of twenty within the regulations of a selective system. About 30% of registered men summoned for medical examination are rejected as unfit for service.

The RNA runs a 'Technical Specialist' scheme involving a 4–6 year engagement and providing training in such key specialist functions as tank driving, mechanical maintenance, and so on. The target for recruitment is 5500 and, at present, the scheme is 60% successfully recruited.

Training

Initial basic training is conducted in central establishments (Fig. 2) and special to-arm training in units. Each 'manoeuvre' battalion (tank and armoured infantry) and many other supporting units have an organic training company. A conscript remains a private soldier throughout his service. If he

416

is recommended for employment as a reserve officer, he must start his national service earlier and then holds the rank of 'underofficer' during the period of his 'active' service. All officers and NCOs in the 'active' army are regulars and their standard of individual training is high.

Potential regular army officers spend 4 years at the Royal Military Academy, Breda. Later in their careers, officers may attend the Army Staff College course in The Hague. This lasts for 1 year and trains 10 students a year. All graduates are guaranteed a subsequent 'command' tour as lieutenant-colonels and the recent reduction of the Staff College's annual intake will enable the army to prolong the present over-short command tours (about 18 months) made necessary in order to fit in all those qualified. The Royal Military School at Weert provides centralised instruction for NCOs, and there is an Institute for Military Leadership at Hilversum.

Reserves

Under the provisions of the Conscription Act former conscripts remain on the reserve until their 35th birthday, although some officers continue until they are forty-five and some senior NCOs until they are forty. Reserve commitments vary, possibly incorporating an 'RIM' tour after the former conscript's 'short leave' has expired at the end of his period of national service. The majority of reservists will spend most of their period of reserve liability in 'mobilisable' units which are part of the field army or the home defence force (Fig. 2), or as individual reinforcements to convert other units from a peacetime to a wartime basis during a period of tension.

EQUIPMENT AND ARMS INDUSTRY

The Netherlands has never had a significant armaments industry, and even now, when electronics firms are producing more military equipment and DAF is manufacturing army vehicles, the percentage of national output devoted to defence represents a very small proportion compared to some other western European countries. The German Leopard tank is purchased complete, but a 'national' radio system is fitted in its turret.

Equipment currently in service includes:
Leopard (468 in service) and Centurion (343) main battle tanks AMX-13 light tanks (126 in service). M-113 (745), YP 408 (DAF) (742), AMX VCI (66) (tracked) TPR-765 (1051) APCs. Lance missile (6). 8in self-propelled howitzer (28) (M-110), 175mm self-propelled gun (12), 155mm self-propelled howitzer (M-109) (136), 155mm towed howitzer (USA) (140), 105mm self-propelled howitzer (AMX) (44) and 105mm towed howitzer (USA). L40/70 anti-aircraft gun and radar. 120mm mortar, 4.2in mortar and 81mm mortar. TOW and Dragon anti-tank guided missile and 106mm recoilless anti-tank rifle. 0.5in Browning machine-gun (APC mounted). 9mm sub-machine-gun (USA). 9mm Browning pistol (FN). 7.62mm self-loading rifle. General-purpose machine-gun. Light machine-gun (FN).

The re-equipment programme included the replacement of Honest John with Lance, but without a nuclear capability. The Netherlands is facing the same problems as her allied neighbours in providing sufficient financial resources to keep a credible military capability. In 1974, defence expenditure accounted for 3.8% of the GNP while the proportion of government expenditure going to defence has fallen over the last 20 years from one-fifth to one-eighth. Concurrently personnel costs have risen steeply during recent years as in all related forces, but none more so than in the Dutch case. The Dutch national serviceman is the best paid conscript in Europe and bonus payments for special terms of service engagement are commensurately high. All this means that proportionally less of the available defence budget remains for essential re-equipment and other operating costs. The recent governmental decision not to call up married men is said to stem from the desire to save some 25,000,000 guilders in subsidies paid to married national servicemen at present.

RANK, DRESS AND DISTINCTIONS

Ceremonial dress for officers in dark midnight blue. The jacket is high-collared with facings, badges and buttons; the trousers in the same shade have stripes in arm or regimental colours down their side. Service dress has a dark brown khaki jacket and fawn-grey trousers in heavy-weight material; officers and soldiers wear the same pattern uniform and convert it to shirt-sleeve order when appropriate. Officers also wear a light-weight summer uniform in a stone-coloured shade of material. Brown shoes are worn with all these forms of dress except ceremonial dress when black footwear is worn. Field service uniform comprises an American-style helmet, an olive combat suit, dark-green webbing and brown combat boots.

Rank badges are worn by officers, adjutants (senior warrant officers) and underofficers (national servicemen who will become reserve officers) on shoulder epaulettes, and by NCOs on the upper part of the right sleeve. Coloured arm or regimental patches behind badges are worn on the collar of service dress jackets.

CURRENT DEVELOPMENTS

The army's strength is given officially as 75,000 but at the time of writing has reduced to a figure nearer to 67,000, of which roughly 60% are conscripts. The army, like the navy and air force, is currently reorganising. It is the government's intention to create a 'new look' about the services by skimming military superstructures, creating a new training organisation, streamlining logistics and carrying out some inter-arm and inter-service integration. Simultaneously, the possible conversion to an all-regular army is being considered.

All of this is set against an unsettled background where basic principles of a military society have been challenged by large numbers of young Dutchmen. The concept of 'authority' is changing, there is growing pressure by conscripts to take part in the decision-making process, and armed forces are becoming compared with industrial undertakings. There is developing, mainly through Conscript Trade Unions, a process of questioning values and institutions and an increasing preparedness among representatives of younger generations to speak out more openly in favour of certain values and institutions in replacement of old, former ones. On the other hand, there is evidence of subversion by 'sleepers' which increases and fosters the signs of dissolution in the RNA.

In each west European country the same challenges to 'established' society exist; there is a feeling inside and outside the Netherlands that the 'movement' among their young has been allowed adversely to affect the army, in particular the three Dutch services, to an unreasonable extent. Unmilitary behaviour, ill-discipline and an almost deliberate show of military semi-competence are impressions engendered no doubt by a minority of conscripts, but they are impressions which have foundation in fact. How much this undermines military proficiency and combat readiness is outside the scope of this entry. A senior American general quite recently, and seriously, referred to the army as the 'Dutch Hair Force'; Mr Van der Heuvel optimistically reputed allegations of a disintegration of morale — on the contrary, he sees signs of the armed forces becoming more closely integrated with the people. In referring to external criticism of the long hair, untidy uniforms and undisciplined behaviour of Dutch soldiers, he has this to say: 'In certain circles in the Netherlands these articles are read with approval as they reflect their own views, but at the same time with a certain sense of shame because it hurts national pride. In other circles, however, such articles cause irritation, as they present — in their view — a very one-sided picture of the Dutch soldier. It is felt that even if long hair is regarded as symptom of a certain attitude, it goes much too far to use this as an essential element in criticism of the value of the Dutch armed forces. In this connection it is usually pointed out that he meets the requirements, and not infrequently achieves more than is expected from him'.

The two conscript trade unions are described in this article. The *Vereniging voor Dienst plichtige Militairen* (VVDM) is all-conscript and generally militant; it is the main trade union concerned with the armed services. The *Bond van Dienstplichtigen* (BVD) started as a protest group of socialist soldiers and former conscientious objectors and now lacks recognition and support. A third union, the *Algemene Vereniging van Nederlandse Militairen* (AVNM) is a moderate association mostly of conscripts, but some regulars, and is growing. Members of unions may demonstrate outside their barracks, but only inside if they have the permission of their commanding officers.

With so much emphasis also placed upon restructuring within the army itself, this is indeed a busy, eventful and challenging time for the competent regular cadre of officers and NCOs. In these matters, the RNA has traditionally looked towards the British army for guidance and a lead.

However, it seems that the restructuring plan adopted for the British corps in Northern Army Group has left Dutch officers perplexed and uncertain. Some feel that this will cause their army to swing even more towards the *Bundeswehr*.

No Netherlands government this century has felt much confidence in the feasibility of an autonomous defence policy. After World War II old neutralist aspirations were put away to be replaced by strong support for NATO and now hearty endorsement of any move to bring European union nearer to reality. It is not surprising, therefore, that defence policy should encourage developments along the lines of greater 'rationalisation' and 'specialisation' within NATO and a more pronounced degree of European interdependence in defence matters. Government spending on defence has never commended itself much to Dutch hearts and the current 'squeeze' is due in no small amount to generous pay scales, and even a '40-hour week' for servicemen from March 1st, 1976. Apparently there is now a campaign to pay soldiers the national minimum wage and this may help to share out defence funds available on a more equitable basis between personnel, equipment and operating costs. Financial forecasts up to 1980 put the defence share of national income at 3.7% which is the same as it is at the moment. There is pressure from left-wing politicians to reduce the proportion to 3%.

The uneasiness of the conscript force, tribulations of structural reorganisation and financial stringency make this a difficult time for the Dutch army. Its equipment, efficiency and, above all, the commitment of its conscripts have all improved greatly since the troubled 1970s, and it is now a truly effective element — if not as large as might be wished — in NATO's ground defence of Central Europe.

John Skinner
John Keegan

NEW ZEALAND

HISTORY AND INTRODUCTION

New Zealand enjoys a number of military advantages. The country is relatively isolated within the south Pacific, far from other powers; there are no land frontiers to protect; and since the Maori war of the 1860s internal harmony has been the norm. But these very advantages, if they are to be enjoyed, make the maintenance of armed forces essential. New Zealand has little heavy industry, so has to procure, through the channels of trade, many of its needs abroad, bringing the items in by sea. Sea lanes are vulnerable to attack, however, and armed forces are needed to protect them. In addition, if an enemy power did contemplate direct attack, the islands, with their 2000 miles of coast-line, would be difficult to defend, leaving the deterrent value of a capable armed force, working in conjunction with its counter-parts from other interested States, the only guarantee of long-term security. The maintenance of a small but professional regular army, backed by a fully trained reserve, is an integral part of this deterrence.

The islands of New Zealand became a British colony in 1840, and between then and a London decision of 1870 to make white colonies responsible for their own defence, regular troops of the British army constituted the bulk of the protecting force in the new settlements, achieving a maximum strength of over 10,000 during the Maori war. These regulars were supported, however, by locally raised troops, divided from an early date into two classifications which have always formed the basis of the New Zealand military structure. On the one hand there was a small Permanent Force, composed chiefly of artillery and engineers stationed in coastal regions, and on the other a group of part-time volunteer Militia units, based and recruited in local areas. When the British garrison was withdrawn in 1870, these forces were all that remained, but the strength of their organisation was shown 30 years later when a total of 10 contingents of mounted rifles (6500 officers and men), commanded from the Permanent Force but drawn from the Militia, were sent to assist Britain in the South African war. It was during this conflict that the resourcefulness and bravery of New Zealand soldiers first became manifest; characteristics associated with them ever since.

Nevertheless, with the growth of the colony and the forging of trade links, particularly with Britain and Australia, it soon became apparent that some form of military expansion and reorganisation was needed. Following the British pattern of the previous year, therefore, in 1909 the Militia was disbanded and a new force of part-time soldiers, known under the British title of Territorials, set up in local areas, subject to central control. In order to fill these new units, compulsory part-time military training for the entire male white population between the ages of eighteen and twenty-five was introduced, it being hoped thereby to preclude the need for a large regular army within the islands. At the same time the Permanent Force, although basically unchanged, began to take on the responsibility of staff duties, forming a skeleton command structure for the Territorials should they ever be mobilised.

The success of this scheme can best be seen in 1914, for New Zealand, responding to the British call-to-arms as eagerly as her Australian neighbour, was able to raise a complete infantry division, commanded from the Permanent Force and manned by the Territorials, in a very short time, with minimum recourse to civilian volunteers. This division (known as the New Zealand Expeditionary Force), in partnership with the 1st and 2nd Australian Divisions, formed what was known as ANZAC (Australian and New Zealand Army Corps), and as such was committed to the ill-fated Gallipoli campaign of 1915. Here it acquitted itself very well indeed, reinforcing the opinion of its troops first gained in South Africa a few years before. But casualties were heavy, and in 1916, by which time the remains of the Expeditionary Force had been moved to France, full-scale conscription for service overseas was regarded as the only way to maintain the necessary flow of reinforcements. This remained in force until the end of the war in 1918, by which time some 99,000 New Zealanders had been despatched abroad, with 16,700 losing their lives. From a colony containing little over a million people when the war broke out, this was no small sacrifice, especially in aid of a cause not directly affecting the south Pacific.

Once World War I was over, all ideas of full-scale conscription were abandoned, although the 1909 scheme did continue. Due to the economic recession, however, even that was dropped in 1930, causing the Territorials to revert in all but name to the old Militia system. Numbers dropped significantly, leading to a cut in the size of the Permanent Force, with the result that when war broke out again in 1939 the New Zealand government, although always strong in its advocacy of collective action to check agression, particularly in concert with Britain, could do little but promise military aid. It was not until the re-introduction of conscription in June, 1940 (by which time, it should be added, some 66,000 volunteers had already come forward) that a 2nd New Zealand Expeditionary Force, once again commanded from the Permanent Force and manned by the hastily augmented Territorials, could be formed for service overseas.

This Expeditionary Force, known also as the 2nd New Zealand Division, was sent initially to the Middle East to reinforce British efforts in that theatre, and saw hard service throughout the campaign. It suffered severe casualties in 1941 in Greece and Crete where the defence of the island was entrusted to its commander, Major-General Freyberg. After evacuation from Crete the division took part in the advance into Libya, and in June, 1942 played an important role, at Minkar Kuaim, in stemming the Axis advance into Egypt. It was one of the assaulting divisions at Alamein and was prominent in the pursuit of Axis forces until their surrender in Tunisia. In October, 1943 the division crossed to Italy where it saw further hard fighting, particularly around Monte Cassino. Meanwhile another division, numbered the 3rd, had been raised in New Zealand, and with the threat of Japanese expansion appearing nearer home, this force was committed solely to the war in the Pacific, fighting chiefly in the Solomon Islands. Altogether some 135,000 New Zealanders served overseas during World War II, and although the casualty figure of 10,000 killed did not match that of the previous war, the events of 1939—45 had a more profound effect upon military thinking.

The main reason for New Zealand's post-war reassessment of her armed forces was a realisation that they were needed, not merely as a reinforcement to the British army in times of crisis, but more importantly as protectors of the home islands themselves. The New Zealand authorities had not reacted to the Japanese threat in the same way as the Australians, who had withdrawn forces from the Middle East for service in the Pacific, but they were aware that the country was no longer as invulnerable as had been supposed. In addition, New Zealand, in co-operation with other powers, was expected not only to provide troops for occupation duties in the Far East immediately after the war, but also to contribute to the collective security of south-east Asia, a factor which led initially to the ANZUS Pact of 1951, followed by the SEATO Treaty of 1954 and Five Power Defence Arrangements of 1971 (see later). All of these commitments required the existence of armed forces on a relatively large scale, and although the basic military pattern of Permanent Force/ Territorials was not altered, a degree of reorganisation had to be introduced. Consequently in 1949 all male New Zealanders were made liable to a 14 week period of military training (altered to 10½ weeks in 1956) on becoming eighteen, to be followed by 60 days' service in the Territorials over the next 3 years. This persisted in essentials until 1968 when conscription by ballot was brought in, based on the law that all 'British subjects ordinarily resident in New Zealand' were liable for part-time service upon reaching 19 years of age. Those selected by this method – the average was reckoned to be about 2250 out of a possible 15,000 every year – were then called upon to do 12 weeks' training, followed by 3 years' Territorial service and 3 years in the Reserve. The scheme, and with it the whole idea of National Military Service, was abandoned in March, 1973 since which time the New Zealand army has been an all-volunteer force.

It will be noticed from the above description that at no time between 1948 and 1973 did conscription apply to the Permanent Force. That body (known more recently as the Regular Force) retained its voluntary status throughout, acing as a training and staff cadre, theoretically for use only when the Territorials were mobilised. In practice, however, it became usual, whenever the government's policy of collective security in the Asian theatre necessitated a commitment of troops, for volunteers to be called for from the Territorials. These men, under the command of officers and NCOs from the Regular Force would then form a special unit for service overseas: a traditional and well-tried New Zealand idea. Such units saw service in Korea (1950–53) with the United Nations force; in Malaya during the emergency (1948–60), and, between 1964 and 1971, in South Vietnam, where they joined an Australian task force in a mini-ANZAC. The system, distinctively New Zealand as it is, appeared to work well, and despite the change of government in 1973 which ended conscription and led to a policy more of home defence, its potential remains. Indeed, one infantry battalion continues to be deployed in Singapore as New Zealand's contribution to the Five Power Defence Arrangements, and there may be little doubt that it could be reinforced quickly, by the traditional method, should an emergency occur. In addition the Territorials, although now volunteers, are fully mobilised for the relatively long period of 12 weeks a year, giving them the training and experience to fill out and augment the Regular Force, preparatory to service in defence of the national interest.

STRENGTH AND BUDGET

Population: 3,160,000
Army: 5675 Regular Force; 5934 Territorials (mobilised for 12 weeks every year); 1412 Reserve Force
Navy: 2843; four frigates, four smaller craft
Air force: 4395; 32 combat aircraft
GNP (1981): $US 21,190,000,000
Defence expenditure (1981): $US 463,280,000

COMMAND AND CONSTITUTIONAL STATUS

Command

The Governor-General of New Zealand, as representative of H.M. Queen Elizabeth II, takes on the role of Commander-in-Chief and is empowered to raise and maintain all armed forces within the country. His duties have tended to be nominal, however, especially since 1964 when the command and administration of all three services (navy, army and air force) was placed under the central control of a Minister of Defence, appointed by the political party in power and charged with the formulation of an overall defence policy. He is aided in this task by a Secretary of Defence and Chief of Defence Staff as principal civilian and military advisers respectively, and operates within the context of a Defence Council, the membership of which is:

Minister of Defence (Chairman)
Chief of Defence Staff ⎫
Secretary of Defence ⎭ (Deputy Chairmen)

Chief of Naval Staff ⎫
Chief of General Staff ⎬ (Chiefs of Staff Committee)
Chief of Air Staff ⎭

The Secretaries of Foreign Affairs and the Treasury, as interested parties in defence decisions, are also vote members, and the Council may appoint other members at its discretion. It holds responsibility for both the command and administration of the armed forces, while assisting the Minister in formulating defence policy.

Below the Defence Council there exists a Defence Headquarters, comprising the Naval, Air and Army General Staffs and six functional branches (now in the process of being centralised) covering policy, personnel, support, administration, finance and management for each of the three services.

Constitutional Status

Following closely the patterns laid down in both Britain and Australia, all service personnel in New Zealand owe direct allegiance to H.M. Queen Elizabeth II as Commander-in-Chief, although for purposes of convenience the Governor-General, as already stated, is invested with the power to raise and maintain the armed forces. This is not designed to undermine the autonomy of the New Zealand government in defence matters and does not pre-suppose automatic support to Britain in time of crisis in Europe, for unless government decisions are obviously alien to Commonwealth interests, the Governor-General does not interfere. By owing allegiance not to the government in power but to a higher, permanent authority, however, the military forces are less likely to be used for purely political ends.

ROLE, COMMITMENT, DEPLOYMENT AND RECENT OPERATIONS

Role

The roles and missions of the New Zealand armed forces are officially stated in the *New Zealand Official Yearbook* as:

1. To maintain an ability to deploy, in the area immediately around New Zealand and in the south Pacific, forces to deal with situations affecting New Zealand's interests for which her allies would expect New Zealand to assume primary responsiblity.
2. To contribute to the protection of the air and sea communications vital to New Zealand.
3. To maintain an ability to contribute in time of war to the fullest extent possible towards the collective defence

of the friendly countries in the areas of primary strategic importance to New Zealand.

4. To contribute forces as appropriate to assist the United Nations, partners in defence arrangements and other friendly countries in keeping the peace and/or preventing escalation.

Commitment

The majority of New Zealand's defence commitments are centred upon the continent of Asia, and since the end of World War II she has become a member of several multinational defence arrangements. These range from the ANZUS Pact of 1951, whereby New Zealand, Australia and the United States agreed to support each other in the Pacific area, through the SEATO Treaty of 1954 (now being phased out) which covered collective defence in Asia, to the Five Power Defence Arrangements of 1971, designed to protect Malaysia in the event of further communist aggression. The last-mentioned agreement led to the formation of ANZUK, a combined force of New Zealand, Australian and British troops, and although both the Australians and British have allowed their commitments to lapse, New Zealand forces remain in Singapore under the title of NZ Force South East Asia. In 1980 a small contingent joined the multi-national Peace Keeping force in Zimbabwe.

Beyond the provisions of actual treaties, New Zealand also co-operates in defence matters with Indonesia, Papua New Guinea, Fiji and Tonga under the terms of a Mutual Assistance Programme, and feels very strongly her obligations under the United Nations Charter. Recently there have been nine New Zealand officers on UN duty in Kashmir and the Middle East.

Deployment

One battalion is stationed permanently in Singapore and the remaining units of the army are grouped into three Brigade groups, two stationed in North Island and the third in South Island. All Brigades consist of a mix of Regular and Territorial forces and form part of the Division which in peace time provides the core force. This concept enables the army to train and retain the expertise in a variety of conventional skills so that should the need arise there would be trained personel available to teach the Territorials. In addition there is a Ready Reaction Force permanently earmarked for rapid deployment.

Recent Operations

New Zealand military forces have been actively involved in campaigns on the continent of Asia three times since 1945. In 1950, at the start of the Korean war, a voluntarily recruited field regiment of artillery, with auxiliary units, was sent to join the United Nations force, remaining in action until the ceasefire in 1953. Between 1955 and 1960 New Zealand troops aided the British in countering communist insurgency in Malaya. Finally, between 1964 and 1971 New Zealand forces became involved in South Vietnam, reaching a maximum strength of 550 personnel, drawn chiefly from artillery and infantry units in 1967. These campaigns, particularly in Vietnam, provided useful training and experiences in counter-insurgency, a type of operation in which the New Zealanders, with their Australian allies, enjoyed considerable success. In addition to active service, however, the New Zealand army has gained a well-deserved reputation for aiding other countries in its area, particularly in the development of roads, harbours, reservoirs and pipe-lines as well as disaster relief. Army engineers have been stationed for development purposes in Thailand, the Gilbert and Ellice Islands and the Cook Islands, while all elements of the armed forces have contributed to disaster relief in Bangladesh, Fiji and Australia.

ORGANISATION

Arms of Service

Taking Regular and Territorial units together, the army comprises:

Royal Regiment of NZ Artillery, Royal NZ Armoured Corps (two squadrons), Corps of Royal NZ Engineers, Royal NZ Corps of Signals, Royal NZ Infantry Regiment (eight battalions), NZ Special Air Service, NZ Army Air Corps, Royal NZ Army Service Corps, Royal NZ Army Medical Corps, Royal NZ Army Ordnance Corps, Corps of Royal NZ Electrical and Mechanical Engineers, Royal NZ Dental Corps, Royal NZ Chaplains Department, NZ Army Pay Corps, NZ Army Legal Service, Royal NZ Provost Corps, Royal NZ Army Education Corps, Royal NZ Nursing Corps and NZ Women's Royal Army Corps.

Of these units, two infantry battalions and one artillery battery are all that are officially listed as Regular Force, but many of the corps and departments are permanently at cadre strength for administrative and preparation purposes.

Operational

In New Zealand the army is now organised into two commands, each directly responsible to Defence Headquarters for the performance of its functions:

1. *Home Command.* This provides the home support for the army in New Zealand; this Command is responsible for the function of the static organisation of the army, which it administers through seven geographical Army Area Commands, three major corps and the Army Training Group based at Waiouru.
2. *Field Force Command.* The army is structured to provide a Field Force of brigade size with associated support and logistic units for operational deployment in time of crisis, and Field Force Command, with its headquarters at Fort Cautley near Auckland, is responsible for those elements earmarked for this duty. The Field force is basically non-regular, but the infantry battalions and artillery battery which make up the Regular Force act as its core. In an emergency one brigade, with logistic support, could be mobilised almost immediately by adding Territorial units to the Regulars, and it is calculated that a second brigade, made up almost entirely of Territorials, would soon be ready as reinforcement.

Units and personnel in Singapore are under the command of NZ Force South East Asia.

RECRUITMENT, TRAINING AND RESERVES

Regular Force

Military service has always been voluntary in the Regular Force, and because of its relatively small size the authorities are able to indulge in fairly rigorous selection of recruits at both commissioned and enlisted levels. Military careers are popular with the Maori community, which provides about 25% of the enlisted strength and 40% of the infantry. Those who wish to become officers, presuming they do not rise through the ranks, have to pass aptitude and education tests before agreeing to serve an initial term of at least 8 years. They attend either the Royal Military College at Duntroon or the short course at Portsea. In addition some officers attend their own cadet course where their Territorial Officers are also trained. After graduation the officers return to New Zealand for specialist training in their units, although they may well be sent overseas again later in their careers, particularly when they rise to the level of staff duties.

Regular soldiers volunteer for a minimum period of 3 years (after which re-enlistment is favoured) and receive their training at corps schools or depots and in army units stationed within New Zealand or overseas. In certain cases specialised training may be received at overseas training establishments in England, Australia or the United States.

Regular servicemen, both officers and soldiers, are expected to enter the Reserve Force, presuming they do not join the Territorials, at the end of their enlistment period. To compensate for the lack of operational experience the army trains extensively with troops from Australia, USA and the UK. Annual exchange exercises are held at all levels and the opportunity to visit other countries and train with sophisticated weapons and equipment is an important aspect of this training.

Territorial Force

Since the end of Territorial conscription in March, 1973 recruits have been attracted to the force, with some success, by financial incentives. Males or females between the ages of 17 and 36 years may volunteer for Territorial service, enlisting for a minimum period of 3 years or until retirement age for rank achieved (normally fifty-five). After initial training within the units they join, these volunteers are expected to turn out full-time for 12 weeks a year (during which time their civilian jobs are protected by law) and to do a minimum of 20 days' training beyond. Officers for the Territorial Force are usually chosen from among the volunteers during the annual period of full-time training, although Regulars may transfer their commissions at the end of their period of service. Territorial specialist training is normally conducted within the units, but soldiers can be sent to the schools and depots of the Regular Force.

EQUIPMENT AND ARMS INDUSTRY

New Zealand is dependent on overseas suppliers for all major items of equipment and weapons. Close military links with Australia and joint military discussions are likely to lead to even closer co-operation over the standardisation of tactical doctrine and rationalisation of equipments. Joint exercises have highlighted the need for this consultation and the purchase of equipment in the future from traditional sources i.e. UK and USA may well depend on what and when the Australians decide to purchase.

Pistol: 9mm automatic L9 A1 (UK)
Rifle: 7.62mm L1A1 (Australia)
Machine-gun: 5.56mm M16A1 (USA; heavy), 7.62mm FN automatic L2A1 (USA; light), 7.62mm L4A4 Bren gun (UK; light) and 7.62mm L7A1 and L7A2 (UK; general purpose)
Mortars: 2in OML (UK) and 81mm OML L16A1 (UK)
Anti-tank weapons: 66mm M72 rocket (USA; light) and 106mm RCL M40A1 (USA; heavy; 23 in service)
Artillery: 5,5in field gun (UK; 10 in service) and 105mm howitzer (UK; 44 in service)
Armour: M-41 light tank (USA; 5 in service), and M-113 APC (USA; 72 in service)

RANK, DRESS AND DISTINCTIONS

Rank

General — Crossed sword and baton, one crown, one star
Lieutenant-general — Crossed sword and baton, one crown
Major-general — Crossed sword and baton, one star
Brigadier — One crown above three stars
Colonel — One crown above two stars
Lieutenant-colonel — One crown above one star
Major — One crown
Captain — Three stars
Lieutenant — Two stars
Second-lieutenant — One star

Warrant Officer I — Royal Arms
Warrant Officer II — Crown
Staff Sergeant — Crown above three chevrons
Sergeant — Three chevrons
Corporal — Two chevrons
Lance-corporal — One chevron
Private — —

Note: rank badges are worn by officers on shoulder straps, and on the upper arm by other ranks.

Dress

In common with the British and other Commonwealth armies, most patterns of dress take khaki as their basic colour. The only distinctive item of dress is an American-style steel helmet, the old bush hat, with its very high crown, appearing to have been phased out. Combat dress is uncamouflaged (except for certain styles of jungle warfare). Officers' mess-dress follows the British pattern and exists in both winter and summer styles.

Distinctions

Each unit or corps within the New Zealand army wears a distinctive cap badge, with matching collar devices and, in working-dress especially, some form of cloth or metal shoulder-title.

CURRENT DEVELOPMENTS

Because of its relatively small size and apparent isolation within the south Pacific, it would be tempting to dismiss the New Zealand army as an insignificant force. This would be something of a mistake. Successive New Zealand governments have formulated their defence policies well, realising the limitations of their country in both geographical and manpower terms, and have organised the armed forces accordingly. As a result, although the army, particularly in its Regular elements, is small, it is well-trained, widely experienced and capable of fairly rapid mobilisation in the event of emergency; characteristics shown on a number of occasions since 1945. Taking the priorities of New Zealand defence policy to be collective security in south-east Asia and the Pacific, the defence of the home islands and the protection of air and sea communications, those portions allotted to the army seem to be carried out well. When it is added that the same army contributes willingly to the United Nations and to the development of friendly countries in its area, it may be appreciated that it is a force of which New Zealand may be justly proud.

John Pimlott

NICARAGUA

HISTORY AND INTRODUCTION

Until the success of the Sandinista revolution in 1979, Nicaragua, together with Paraguay, was the last remaining stronghold of the tradition of the Latin American *Caudillo*, the strong military leader who ruled personally and absolutely through his control of the national armed forces. The Somoza family in fact constituted a dynasty of *Caudillos*, one or other of whom ruled the country for almost half a century, during which time the Nicaraguan National Guard, itself a unique force combining military, police and civil service functions, was always under the personal command of a family member.

The Somoza dynasty was itself a relic of the disastrously misguided policy of the United States in replacing the fragmented and badly organised military forces, in the countries of the Caribbean area subject to US intervention during the first 30 years of this century, with extremely efficient, well-trained and organised and theoretically apolitical military constabulary forces. In all five countries in which this policy was pursued, Nicaragua, Panama, Cuba, Haiti and the Dominican Republic, these forces became the stepping stones to political domination by their various commanders and in turn the instruments of their maintenance of power, a role which they were infinitely better qualified to play than were the forces which they replaced.

Nicaragua, which for practical purposes had no professional, national army during its first 100 years of independence and which suffered to an extraordinary degree, even by Central American standards, from the innumerable civil wars waged by the private armies of its main political factions, was especially ripe for such a development and whilst the Somoza dynasty was one of the most blood-thirsty and corrupt of all, it could be argued that the very efficiency of the form of military rule which it practised was an improvement on what had gone before.

It would be tedious and pointless to catalogue these upheavals, but the main outlines were simple. Nicaragua, like most of Central America, was in Spanish colonial times a country in which a large, illiterate, utterly impoverished mestizo population (now 69%) was dominated by an educated white minority of Spanish descent (now 19%), and in which all economic and political power was monopolised by a handful of extremely rich land-owning families. These families were divided into factions labelled 'liberal' and 'conservative' (more for convenience than because of any ideological distinctions), whose violent competition for power formed the substance of politics after independence from Spain in 1821.

In Nicaragua, however, these factions had a distinct territorial base in what were then the two main cities — the liberals in Leon, the conservatives in Granada — and warfare between them was chronic even before the Central American Republic collapsed and Nicaragua became fully independent in 1838. Both factions were inclined to summon military aid from abroad, which explains why Nicaragua was particularly prone to invasion. In 1845, for example, the conservatives sought aid from the armies of El Salvador and Honduras to topple a liberal government, and the invaders obligingly sacked the city of Leon. In the 1850s, the liberals invited in an army of adventurers commanded by the North American insurrectionist William Walker, who proceeded to have himself elected President before being ejected by the combined forces of the other central American States.

There were intervals of relative peace when one or other party established a lasting stranglehold on power — the conservatives in the 1870s and 1880s, the liberals under José Santos Zelaya in 1893—1909 — but there was never anything created that would fit the description of a national army; rather one party's militia was expanded and dignified with that title, while the other went underground. The armies were totally unprofessional, commanded by white officers prominent in the political factions and with the ranks filled by illiterate Indians pressed into service without distinction of age, fitness, or sometimes even of sex. Recruiting methods are summed up in a letter written by a young officer in the interior to his superior: 'Dear Colonel, I am sending you herewith forty volunteers who will fight for the cause so dear to us ... It will greatly help me, by the way, to secure others if you will make sure to return the ropes.'

Matters might have continued thus indefinitely, but the building of the Panama Canal and the growth of American investments in central American agriculture in the early years of this century created a new United States concern to end the turbulence in Nicaragua. In 1909 the USA precipitated the downfall of President Zelaya (who had been intriguing in the liberal tradition to bring about Central American union), and in 1912 it sent in the Marines to suppress a revolt against his conservative successor. Some of the Marines remained under the guise of a 'Legation Guard' until 1925, and as the most efficient armed force in the country they effectively assured the USA the right to choose Nicaragua's presidents, supervise the elections and secure its growing finanical, military and governmental interests in Nicaragua.

In 1925 the Marines were withdrawn, leaving behind a training mission that was to create a new, impartial National Guard that would supplant the traditional army and ensure democratic rule. Within months the government were overthrown by a coup, and the country reverted to all-out civil war, with the tiny new National Guard supporting one side and substantial Mexican aid being sent to the other. United States Marines were landed again in force in 1927, with the task of stopping the fighting and training a really powerful National Guard that would be led in its formative stages by Marine officers and NCOs.

This they duly did before they were withdrawn in 1933, and the Guard was indeed impartial (in the old sense, at least). The man selected as commander was Anastasio Somoza García, the American-educated son of a prosperous land-owning family; due to the relatively high wages offered and the difficulties of rapid expansion, numbers of criminals were among those enrolled in the ranks. All Nicaraguan political factions were disarmed, and the National Guard was soon committed to action alongside the Marines against the rebel general César Augusto Sandino, who had taken to guerrilla warfare in the north-western mountains against the American occupation. About 50 Marines and 50 Guardsmen were killed in combat against the guerrillas, but they were unable to eradicate them.

An officer training school was opened in 1930, and by dint of accelerated training programmes there were just enough Nicaraguan officers to command the Guard when the USA withdrew in 1933. This left the 2500-strong Guard as the main armed force in the country, and it was already totally loyal to its politically astute commander, Anastasio Somoza. The only possible rival was Sandino's 1000-odd guerrillas, who had had considerable success in their fighting against the Americans and had made their peace with the government as soon as the Americans were gone. Sandino was removed first, by assassination in 1934 and then the President (an uncle of Somoza, who had been installed as a figure-head but had developed ideas beyond his station) was ejected from office by the National Guard and forced into exile. In December 1936, Somoza had himself elected President, whilst retaining command of the National Guard.

The elder Somoza ruled unchallenged for 20 years, successfully riding out the Depression, World War II and border troubles with both Costa Rica and Honduras (see Role Commitment, Deployment and Recent Operations) thanks to his total control of the National Guard. He was assassinated in 1956, but the Presidency passed smoothly to his elder son Luís while the younger, Anastasio Jr, succeeded to the command of the National Guard.

There was a brief interregnum following Luís Somoza's death due to a heart attack in 1963, during which the Presidency was filled by René Guitiérrez, a close ally of the family. Following his death in 1966 and a violent election campaign, the younger son, Major-General Anastasio Somoza Debayle, succeeded to the Presidency in 1967, and continued to occupy it until his overthrow in 1979, except for a brief interlude in 1972–74 when a picked triumvirate was installed to alter the constitution so as to permit his re-election.

The Somoza dynasty accomplished a certain amount in developing Nicaragua economically, but its main achievement was to make the family stupefyingly rich. It is estimated to be worth up to $300,000,000, owning between 500,000 and 1,000,000 acres of land and controlling 44 of the country's most important companies. A considerable amount of this wealth and much public money was employed in lavishing favours on the National Guard which trebled its strength under the Somozas.

The system worked to ensure the loyalty of Guard officers to the regime, and of the men to their officers, apparently with complete success. Besides monetary rewards and social prestige, Guard Officers often secured important government posts after leaving the service. There had never been any indication of anti-regime opinion or serious factional division within the Guard, and it always showed itself ready and able to carry out whatever tasks of suppression of internal dissent it was required to perform. However, a growth in guerrilla activity and a significant cooling in the traditionally warm United States support for the Somoza regime created a new instability in the Nicaraguan internal situation.

The deterioration may have begun as long ago as December, 1972 when a disastrous earthquake destroyed the centre of Managua, killing 10,000 and rendering up to a quarter of a million people homeless. This emergency elicited large sums in international aid – at least $30,000,000 in the first 4 months – but reconstruction proved very slow. More than a year later the central area of Managua was still a virtual wasteland, and rumours were circulating that a very substantial proportion of the relief money had ended up in the pockets of the National Guard. The resurgence of guerrilla activity in 1974–6 contributed further to the unpopularity of the regime and the Guard, for it was met by martial law, strict censorship and widespread repressive measures that were not always aimed at the right targets.

The real crisis, however, began with General Somoza's heart attack in July, 1977 which removed him from circulation for several months. In October the FSLN guerrillas opened a new and much more serious offensive, concentrating

on bold armed attacks on Guard forces in Managua and the large provincial towns, which sometimes caused dozens of casualties. At the same time the guerrilla organisation broadened its programme from a narrow Marxist base to a 'national front' appeal, declaring itself 'pluri-classist' and 'pluri-ideological', and changed its strategy from a protracted guerrilla campaign to the goal of immediate 'popular insurrection'. It claimed (accurately) to have practising Catholics in its ranks, as well as members of the traditional Liberal and Conservative Parties. A group of prominent non-Marxist Nicaraguans from the business and professional community flew into exile in Costa Rica and issued a call for a new popular-front government which would include the FSLN.

Somoza's announcement in January, 1978 that he would not step down before his term expired in 1981 failed to quell the growing sense that his regime was tottering, and the murder of a prominent newspaper editor and opposition leader by pro-Somoza forces only intensified the wave of protests. Rioting in the main provincial towns by impoverished Indians, who appear to have been mobilised by the FSLN, was met by the National Guard with counter-violence that killed dozens of the rioters, and in February there was a 2 week national strike against the government in which employers and workers co-operated openly. In March Somoza's senior military aide, General Reynaldo Pérez Vega, was kidnapped and killed.

During the first seven months of 1978 over 300 persons were killed in the continual protests in the cities, and on August 11th Somoza attempted a reconciliation with moderate opposition opinion by relieving 30 of the 35 senior Guard officers of their duties on the grounds that they had used excessive force. Less than 2 weeks later on August 22nd, however, 25 guerrillas under the Command of the FSLN's senior field commander Eden Pastora ('Commander Zero') seized the National Palace in central Managua, killing eight National Guardsmen and taking almost 1000 hostages including Congressmen and close relatives of the President. They succeeded in bartering their hostages for $500,000, the release of 59 jailed guerrillas, and a flight to Panama.

The impression of weakness this created had two immediate effects. One was on the National Guard, where a number of senior officers were furious that Somoza had yielded to the guerrillas' demands and, fearful that Somoza might be planning to resign, immediately set about organising a coup to ensure that it should be they who replaced him. This plot was instantly discovered and crushed by Somoza, with the arrest on August 28th of 85 members of the Guard including 12 senior officers. The loyalty of the rest of the Guard remained unshaken.

The other effect of the guerrilla success at the National Palace, however, was to embolden civilian opponents of the regime. With only the loosest of co-ordination with the FSLN, if any, the Broad Opposition Front (Frente Amplio de Oposición – FAO), an alliance of middle-class and professional opponents of the regime, embarked on another nation-wide general strike, and citizens of the inland town of Matagalpa rose in open revolt. Both the strike and the revolts spread rapidly, and by the beginning of September, 1978 the nation was plunged into civil war. (For further details, see Role, Commitment, Deployment and Recent Operations.)

Following almost a year of bloody civil war, Somoza fled the country in July 1979, to be subsequently assassinated whilst in exile in Paraguay and was replaced by a junta of the Sandinista National Liberation Front, the provisional government representing an extraordinarily wide spectrum of political opinion varying from the moderate Right to the more-or-less-extreme Left. Following efforts to de-stabilise the revolutionary government, on the part of the United States, the left-wing elements of the Sandinista Government gained the ascendancy at the expense of its more moderate members and in 1980 it was announced that elections would be postponed until 1985.

STRENGTH AND BUDGET

By the end of the civil war, the strength of the National Guard had grown to over 10,000. Following the Sandinista victory, the National Guard was disbanded and replaced by popular militias pending the establishment of a new national army. Such a force was set up in mid-1980, although with a growing external threat from Somocista emigré forces, based principally in Honduras and armed and supported by the United States Government, the militias remain important.

    Population: 2,700,000
    Army: 15,000
    Navy: 200; 15 minor vessels
    Air force: 1,500; 20—25 combat aircraft
    Paramilitary: 5,000 Border Guard; 50,000 militia
    GNP (1981): $2,900,000,000
    Defence expenditure (1979): $100,000,000

COMMAND AND CONSTITUTIONAL STATUS

The constitution is currently suspended, pending the drafting of a new one. The Provisional Government of National Reconstruction consists of a five-man junta and 18 executive members of whom at least one is an avowed Marxist and two are Catholic priests. Although two of the original members resigned in protest at allegedly leftist trends, they were replaced by non-Marxists. Despite US propaganda claims to the contrary, it appears that the Provisional Government is attempting to steer a middle course between East and West and is mainly pre-occupied with the re-construction of the economy, wrecked by a succession of natural disasters, followed by the civil war.

The junta jointly exercises supreme command of the Revolutionary Armed Forces, through the Minister for Defence.

ROLE, COMMITMENT, DEPLOYMENT AND RECENT OPERATIONS

Role
The National Guard combined the functions of national defence with those of internal security and even performed several functions normally carried out by a national civil service, including the administration of the postal and telecommunications systems and of the national electric power network. These functions have now been separated and the role of the Sandinista Revolutionary Army is a conventional one.

Commitment
Nicaragua is a member of the United Nations and of the Organisation of American States and of the Central American Defence Council, which is subordinate to the latter. As a signatory to the Rio Treaty of Reciprocal Defence of 1947, the country is formally committed to hemispheric defence. US backing for Great Britain in the South Atlantic War against Argentina, a fellow signatory of the Rio Treaty, has rendered the effectiveness of this Treaty questionable. Paradoxically, the major perceived enemy of the present Nicaraguan administration is the United States.

Deployment
No details of the current deployment of the Nicaraguan Army are available. Following attacks across the Honduran frontier by US backed guerrillas, based in Honduras, there are known to be large concentrations of both regular Army and Militia forces in the frontier area.

Recent Operations
Since the victory of the Sandinista forces in the civil war, military operations have been confined to the defence of the country against the incursions of counter-revolutionary guerrillas, mainly in the vicinity of the Hondurian frontier and the defence of strategic points within the country.

ORGANISATION

The National Guard was organised primarily for internal security and as such its major tactical unit was a single reinforced battalion. There were also a Presidential Guard battalion, a mechanised company, a field battery, an anti-aircraft battery, an Engineer battalion and 16 local security companies, one in each of the country's 16 departments and of variable size.

It was announced in 1980 that the new Sandinista Revolutionary Army was to consist of 9 Infantry battalions, 1 armoured battalion, 2 field batteries, 1 air-defence battery and 1 engineer battalion, with a strength of approximately 15,000 all ranks.

RECRUITMENT, TRAINING AND RESERVES

The Nicaraguan constitution permits military service to be made obligatory for males at any time, but in practice the National Guard has always been able to fill its ranks by voluntary recruitment. Enlisted men usually volunteer for 3 year terms, and are drawn almost entirely from the lower classes, for whom the pay and living conditions are very attractive. They are paid wages well above those for jobs requiring comparable skills in the civilian economy, and receive free or subsidised housing and food, clothing, medical care and retirement benefits. They are trained at the National Guard Training School in Managua, which is commanded by President Somoza's son, Major Anastasio Somoza Portocarrera. Since the war in September, 1978 the Guard has also been recruiting numbers of American mercenaries.

The material benefits and prestige of an officer's career provides an ample supply of cadets for the national military academy. Numbers of officers attend the Chilean Military School, thus renewing a training relationship between the Nicaraguan and Chilean armies that commenced in the days before the United States military intervention and the creation of the National Guard. United States army and air force missions in Nicaragua provide further training, and many Nicaraguan officers attend the United States army courses in the Canal Zone and in the USA.

Serving members of the National Guard may not vote or hold any political office. There is a trained reserve of some 4000 men.

EQUIPMENT AND ARMS INDUSTRY

Traditionally the United States was the principal source of arms supply and military equipment, although the Somoza regime had occasional recourse to other countries as suppliers, as in the case of 26 F-51 Mustang fighter-bombers purchased in Sweden in 1954 and 45 Staghound armoured cars acquired in Israel in 1957. During and immediately prior to the civil war which overthrew Somoza, considerable quantities of equipment were also purchased from, *inter alia*, Israel, Spain and Taiwan. The Sandinista revolutionaries received limited quantities of light Soviet equipment from Cuba during the civil war and small quantities of largely obsolescent heavier equipment of Soviet origin appear to have been delivered, also from Cuba, during 1982. Contrary to the allegations of US propaganda, the Nicaraguans have not turned to the Soviet bloc as their exclusive suppliers of military hardware as evidenced by the 100,000,000 franc deal for the supply of French equipment, negotiated at the end of 1981.

Rifles: Galil 5.56mm (Israel); M16 5.56mm (US); AK-74 (USSR)

Sub-machine-guns: Uzi 9mm (Israel)

Machine-guns: BAR 0.30″ (US); M1917 0.30″ (US); M2 0.50″ (US)

Anti-armour weapons: M20 75mm RCL (US); RPA 68mm RL (France)

Mortars: 81mm (France); 120mm (France)

Artillery: M101 105mm (US); M-1941 105mm (USSR)

Air-defence weapons: 20mm (Switzerland); Z18-2 37mm (USSR); 40mm L/60 (Sweden)

Armour: M4 medium tank (US; 3 in service); T-54 medium tank USSR; 20 in service); Staghound armoured car (US via Israel); BTR-60 APC (USSR; 12 in service)

Aircraft: The Air Force operates about half-a-dozen transport aircraft and about a dozen helicopters; two Soviet-built Mi-8 helicopters are operated by civilian agencies and the French arms deal includes 2 Alouette IIIs.

RANK, DRESS AND DISTINCTIONS

The National Guard wore uniforms of US pattern and used the standard rank insignia agreed amongst the members of the Central American Defence Council. During the civil war, a fibre-glass helmet of Israeli manufacture, similar to that adopted by the Guatemalan Army, began to displace the US M42 steel helmet. No details of any changes in uniforms or rank insignia in the new Sandinista Revolutionary Army have been announced.

CURRENT DEVELOPMENTS

Since the triumph of the Sandinista Revolution, the governing junta has been engaged in attempting to rebuild the shattered economy and infrastructure of the country. In this they have been consistently and actively hindered by the United States although they have received considerable support from Cuba and from the Mexican and French governments. Whilst the new Nicaraguan administration has quite naturally accepted support and assistance from whatever countries which have been prepared to offer it, including very limited military assistance from Cuba, it seems determined to avoid excessively compromising involvement with either the Eastern or Western power blocs. As this neutralistic approach is interpreted as hostile by the US, which in turn is actively attempting to destabilise and bring down the new Nicaraguan regime, there is a real danger that the Nicaraguans may be driven closer to the Soviet camp. Uninspired United States foreign policy, which has already had the effect of increasing the influence of the more extreme left-wing members of the Sandinista Revolutionary Government, may thus bring about the very situation which it is at such pains to avoid, with tragic results for the Nicaraguan people.

Although the Argentine junta had offered the use of Argentine military personnel, to the United States, for the specific purpose of fighting Cuban and Nicaraguan influence in the Salvadorean civil war, shortly before the outbreak of the South Atlantic War, Nicaragua supported Argentina in its conflict with Britain and offered military assistance to the Argentine regime. This offer was not availed of and it remains to be seen whether this gesture of Latin American solidarity may broaden the acceptibility of the curent Nicaraguan administration amongst the predominantly right-wing regimes of the area, most of which regard the Sandinista Revolutionary government with extreme suspicion, if not outright hostility.

Gwynne Dyer
Adrian English

NIGER*

HISTORY AND INTRODUCTION

Niger, a former French colony, attained independence in 1960. At the time its government was headed by Hamani Diori, who, as President of the Republic, remained in power until 1974 when he was overthrown by a military coup. The main reasons for this were stresses created by the Sahel drought and dissatisfaction with the slow rate of national development, occasioned, according to some arguments, by exessive French profits from Niger's one economic asset, uranium, together with the general French dominance of the administration and the economy. Ethnic factors (the exclusion of Hausa–Fulani, Tuareg and Kanuri from effective power in the ruling party, largely Jerma and Sanghai dominated) may also have played a part. Further factors were corruption in the suite of the President, a project of Diori's to use the army for agricultural work and create a 'party militia' to reinforce his own position, and an unpopular defence pact with Libya. The death of President Pompidou in France gave the military conspirators a belief that France would not oppose the coup. Diori's long rule had earlier seen a military mutiny and insurrection in 1963 and an assassination attempt in 1965. The new government took the form of an eleven-member Supreme Military Council, presided over by Lieutenant-Colonel S. Kountche, which initially sought to reduce links with France.

An attempt by the Vice-President of the Council, Major Sani to replace Kountche by himself in July, 1975 was foiled, and Sani was imprisoned. A futher attempt to overthrow Kountche, headed by a Hausa army major and alleging Jerma domination of the army and government, took place early in 1976 and was equally unsuccessful. Libyan support for this attempted coup appears almost certain. As Niger's exploitation of uranium develops (now providing half of the state's revenue and over 70% of exports), so Libyan interest has increased. Fear of this Libyan interest has returned Niger to the French connection. Indeed to demonstrate France's interest in Niger 200 parachute soldiers were stationed temporarily at the mining town of Arlit.

STRENGTH AND BUDGET

Population: 5,500,000 (approximately)
Armed forces: army 2000; air force 100 plus a gendarmerie of about 1000, a ceremonial Republican Guard of 1100 and a Presidential Guard of 160
GNP: $2,000m (estimate)
Defence expenditure: $17.6m (1980)

COMMAND AND CONSTITUTIONAL STATUS

The Supreme Military Council headed by Colonel Kountche, as Head of State, is the supreme authority. Colonel Kountche is also Minister of Defence. The Chief of the Armed Forces is Major Ali Seibon.

* For general notes on African armies, see Appendix 1.

ROLE, COMMITMENT, DEPLOYMENT AND RECENT OPERATIONS

Internal security and defence against any external threat are the army's two roles; internal security has had implications affecting the army itself, as already noted. Niger had no border problems with its seven neighbours and the army has not to date been deployed to meet any perceived threat since independence, but suspicion of Libya has sharpened recently.

In 1974 army units distributed food and transported people from areas of extreme drought with noteworthy efficiency.

Niger is a member of ANAD, the treaty of mutual aid in the event of an attack signed by seven West African states.

ORGANISATION

The country is divided into three military districts, West (Niamey), North (Agadès) and East (Zinder).

The army is deployed into five company sized infantry detachments (at Niamey, Agadès, Zinder, N'Guigmi and Tahoua) and an armoured squadron, a parachute company and an engineer company, all (except the armoured squadron) at Niamey. A sixth company is to be raised for Dirbon, and a logistics company is also being formed.

The gendarmerie's headquarters is at Niamey with four regional groups for Niamey, Maradi, Zinder and Agadès. Further regional groups for Tahoua, Diffa and Dosso are proposed.

The Republican Guard operates 'pelotons nomades' based on Agadès, Tasker, Tchin–Tabaraden and Bilma.

The air force bases are at Zinder, Agadès and Tahoua.

RECRUITMENT, TRAINING AND RESERVES

Men are liable for call-up for 2 years; the system appears to be somewhat random.

French training assistance has been provided since 1960; in 1974 the French training personnel numbered 12 officers and 60 NCOs. These were all ordered out by the 1974 military government but recent reports indicate the return of a French training mission of approximately 60. West German assistance was provided for the engineer unit.

EQUIPMENT AND ARMS INDUSTRY

Niger's equipment is mainly French, and the infantry weaponry including 81mm mortars and 57mm and 85mm rocket launchers, are entirely so. The older vehicles in the Army's armoured unit, the 2nd Armoured Squadron stationed at Madewala, near Arlit, are ten M8 vehicles. Newer equipment includes eighteen Panhard AML-90 and eighteen AML HE-60/7; one report suggests a further ten AML-60/20/SERVAL vehicles are also in service. Transport of troops is undertaken by fourteen M3 Panhard carriers. Ten old US Army M-8 vehicles with 37mm cannon also remain in service.

The gendarmeries possess thirty radio-equipped BMW patrol vehicles delivered in 1982.

The air force includes two Lockheed C-130 Hercules, with it is reported a further two on order, one Douglas C-54, three Nord 2501 Noratlas and two Douglas C-47 transports, together ten assorted French and American light liaison aircraft. The government also possesses a Boeing 737 transport.

RANK, DRESS AND DISTINCTIONS

These follow the French pattern, except that the *képi* is not worn.

CURRENT DEVELOPMENTS

A very small military force which is unlikely to be committed to anything more than internal security, despite the very real fear of Libya, which it is hoped, with much justification that France will contain.

One of the infantry companies is reported to be noted for conversion to a second armoured sub-unit.

ADDENDUM

A second armoured squadron, to be located at Madawela, near Arlit, is in the process of formation. More AML-90 armoured cars are reported to be on order.

Lloyd Mathews

NIGERIA*

HISTORY AND INTRODUCTION

Nigeria's vast size and population (the latter being anything between 70m and 85m) give it an especial political and military significance in Africa; the size and population, however, represent aggregations of ethnic groups of sharply divided cultures and traditions. The preservation of unity will remain Nigeria's major problem for the foreseeable future, affecting every aspect of national life.

Britain's creation, the Federation of Nigeria, attained independence in 1960; the constitution of the Federation favoured the Muslim Northern Region. This northern domination, after a series of dramatic political events, came to an end with the first military coup of January, 1966. In this coup, young army officers (mostly Ibo from the Eastern Region) murdered the northern political leaders, one of whom had an especial religious significance in addition. Before long the peoples of the big northern cities started wreaking vengeance on their resident Ibo communities. The slaughter of the Ibos strengthened the already existing secession movement in the east, a movement based on resentment against the former northern political control, on the enterprise and energy of the Ibo people, on school leavers for whom no work could be found, and on a new economic self-confidence based on the oil industry. The result, in 1967, was the attempt by the Eastern Region to secede as Biafra, and the consequent civil war which lasted until 1970, from which the Federal government emerged as victorious. Nigerian unity was both preserved and strengthened by the generous conciliation and reconstruction programme of the Gowon government towards the Ibo, a programme for which oil profits could, fortunately, pay. Indeed there is some reason for thinking that the civil war, like that in the USA could have had an effect more unifying than divisive.

At the first military coup in January, 1966 the Army Commander of the time, Major-General J. Aguiyi-Ironsi, an Ibo, assumed power. He was, however, murdered by northern officers in July, 1966 principally for failing to discipline the young majors of January. The events of this month remain confused, but two disintegrative processes can be seen: pure ethnic hatred at the senior-officer and ordinary-soldier levels, and an anti-senior-officer radicalism at junior-commander levels. In the power vacuum, Colonel (later Major-General) Y. Gowon, a Middle Belt man proclaimed himself Head of a Supreme Military Council. This Council ruled Nigeria until July, 1975 when Gowon, whose amiable but indecisive personality made him an ineffective political leader — and one perceived by many as too pro-Western — was removed from office. The other military leaders judged the country not yet ready for a return to civilian rule, but also that a firmer hand was needed at the helm

A reformed Supreme Military Council headed by Brigadier (later Major-General) Murtala Muhammad (a Kano Hausa) assumed responsibility for the country. In an abortive coup in February, 1976 Murtala Muhammad was killed and his place as Head of Government and President of the Supreme Military Council was taken by Lieutenant-General O. Obasanjo, a Yoruba from the west. Among those alleged to have been involved in the abortive coup was the Commissioner for Defence, Major-General Bissalla; he and a number of other, mostly Middle Belt, officers of all levels were executed publicly, the shooting being prolonged. The strains (ethnic, political and ideological) and the personal relationships created by these events were testing both nationally and in the army; periodic reports of unrest or conspiracies in certain units persist. Obasanjo, put into office by senior officers primarily as a figurehead, developed a quietly effective style and personality of his own and was able to lead the country through a period of national constitutional debate in a Constituent Assembly, some quite creditably organised national and State elections in 1979, and in October of that year to a return to civilian rule. This well-managed withdrawal by the Army from power was a matter of great pride to Army and nation; this pride served, and to some extent still serves to curb political ambitions held by individual officers.

The new constitution is American-styled, with a strong executive president, a vice-president important as a political balancing figure, and ministers outside the legislature; its weak feature is that of elections every four years which in a country such as Nigeria means constant electoral fever. The winners in the 1979 election were the National Party of Nigeria (NPN) which emerged as the largest party, but without a complete majority in the legislature and with governments of other parties controlling a number of the nineteen States. The new President, Shehu Shagari, has made great efforts to try and build a national consensus, not without some success. He also, shortly after taking office, replaced the Army's two most senior — and highly political — officers with nominees of his own. However his government faces a number of difficulties, national cohesion and co-ordination within the complex federal constitutional system, external pre-occupations with Libya and Chad, some measure of corruption and most recently severe economic problems arising from Nigeria's inability to sell her oil. Elections are to be held in 1983.

The Nigerian army has its origin in the Nigeria Regiment, later The Queen's Own Nigeria Regiment, of the colonial Royal West Africa Frontier Force. Nigerian units participated with distinction in the Cameroun and German East Africa campaigns of World War I, in the Italian East Africa and Burma campaigns of World War II and also in the United Nations Congo Expeditionary Force. A battalion served briefly in Tanzania after the 1964 army mutiny there. For the bulk of the colonial period there were only two, sometimes three, battalions; in the 1950s expansion to a two-brigade army began but was not complete at independence, or even by 1966. The civil war saw a prodigious expansion of the army to three divisions of some 200,000 men at a time when many of the Army's most professional officers had been killed off. The Gowon government did not dare demobilise in any sizeable numbers, Murtala and Obasanjo carried out some reductions, but in the last Obasanjo years new military perceptions began to appear; these are discussed further below.

* For a general note on African armies, see Appendix 1.

429

STRENGTH AND BUDGET

Population: 77,000,000,000 (estimate)
Armed Forces: 138,000 (Army 125,000, Air Force 9000
    each, Navy, 4000).
GNP: $92,900,000,000
Defence Expenditure: $845,600,000

COMMAND AND CONSTITUTIONAL STATUS

The President, Shehu Shagari, is Commander-in-Chief. The Minister for Defence is Akanbi Oniyanga, the Chief of the Defence Staff is General S. Jalo, the Army Chief of Staff is General M. Wushishi, and the Air Force Chief of Staff Air Vice Marshal A. Bello.

ROLE, COMMITMENT, DEPLOYMENT AND RECENT OPERATIONS

A very brief survey of the Nigerian Civil War of 1967–70 is useful as it reveals instructive and very African features of value in assessing African armies and operations.

The war began with some spectacular Biafran successes, advancing into the Mid-West, even briefly occupying Benin City. Thereafter the Federals recovered the initiative and defeated the Biafrans at the battle of Ore, ejecting them from the Mid-West. The Federals a little later landed from the sea and took Port Harcourt, so capturing the whole coastline whose peoples were in any case opposed to an Ibo-led breakaway regime. These peoples were themselves not Ibo and preferred to be misgoverned from afar at Lagos than misgoverned too closely by the Ibo. Biafra was then cut off from the sea and the military campaign took the form of an investment of the Biafran-held area, the heartland of the Ibo people, by three divisions, the 1st in the North, the 2nd in the West and the 3rd (Marine Commando) in the South. The Federals faced a major logistic problem, the 1st Division, depending on neglected and often unpaved roads from the North, the 2nd Division had to cross the Niger and then supply itself over the river, and the 3rd Division had to be supplied by sea. The Biafrans could still score successes, one being the frustration of the Federal attempted to link the 1st and 3rd Divisions, so cutting Biafra in two. A contributory reason for this was that the 3rd Division commander, Adekunle, for his own reasons attempted to capture the Biafran capital, Umuahia, a project not part of the overall plan, and one which not only failed but obliged the Federal to abandon the important city of Owerri as well. The Biafran collapse in early 1970, however, was as much the result of the very African reason of protein deficiency than direct military action. Iboland's traditional supply of protein had been Middle Belt meat and imported stockfish. Both of these were cut off by the Federal advances and the Ibo, whose diet was always carbohydrate-heavy, suffered severely, especially after the loss of the northern food-growing areas. By the time of the Federal final offensive, their will to continue the struggle had been eroded.

The organisation of the Federal army in the civil war was a bizarre mixture of professional skill and chaos. It could hardly have been otherwise in view of the lack of trained officers and NCOs, the raw-recruit soldiers, the terrain and the climate. The Federal GHQ rarely in touch with events on the ground, moved at a very leisurely pace. The three divisional commanders were almost autonomous warlords, maintaining rival staffs at ports to commandeer newly-arrived equipment, and even maintaining rival purchasing missions abroad. Each division commandeered recruits, stores, etc, as it pleased. The bills were sent somewhat vaguely to GHQ.

The front-line fighting in its casualness and inefficiency wa equally strange to Western military minds — little or n fighting at night, no street fighting and few hand-to-hand encounters, military vehicles were embellished with fetishe of bones and feathers as well as camouflage nets. Attack were preceded by a bombardment — almost a code-signa for the defenders to withdraw, which they usually did, t appear elsewhere later. The attack would be launched and victory proclaimed. The hurriedly-recruited poorly-traine soldiers wasted prodigious quantities of ammunition. The Saracen and Ferret armoured cars spent more time in work shops than in action; the Federal's successes were gained b their small arms and mortars, and to some extent the artiller While excesses and atrocities undoubedly occurred, particu larly in the heat of battle, it is however more accurate to say they were exceptional; there was certainly no genocida policy and little of the mindless murdering that occurred i the Congo in 1960 and 1961. The Federal army on th march was described as 'the best defoliation agent every known', its columns were often supported by women camp followers of the traditional type. Beer fuelled the soldiers marijuana was also used. Towns occupied were instantly looted. Officers and NCOs were corrupt, selling stores an loot, and on occasions drawing the pay of soldiers killed ir action. Before an attack officers were liable to order me from their own home communities to safe duties in the rear Before an attack over which soldiers were apprehensive there were outbreaks of self-inflicted wounds in order to avoid th action. One very senior staff officer in a key position spent his time reading for a law degree. Commanders often had only the haziest idea of their forward line of own troops Divisions could include as many as eight 'brigades' and over thirty 'battalions', often scratch formations of 100–250 men commanded by a virtually untrained lieutenant.

The air force aircraft frequently lost their way. But despite the creaking and confusion, the Federal military system did work; there was an overall strategy, divisional commanders conformed to it for most of the time, discipline of a sort was generally maintained, sometimes by corporal punishment and the shooting of deserters. Soldiers were usually supplied with food and ammunition, signal communication systems worked more often than not, engineers constructed roads and bridges and infantry brigade and battalion officers often injected some tactical originality, for example feint attacks and ambushes, into their moves.

Since the end of the Civil War, one battalion of the Army has been on service with the United Nations Force in Lebanon, a brigade (the 33rd Infantry Brigade) was sent as part of 'Task Force Octopus', the inter-African Force sent to Chad. A Nigerian general, Ejiga, commanded the force which achieved nothing (through no fault of its own) during its stay from November 1981 to July 1982.

The Army has also had one domestic and two border commitments. In December 1980 extremist Muslim street violence broke out in Kano, in which several hundred people were killed; military units had to be called in to restore order. In March 1981 the best part of a division together with an air force squadron were despatched to Bornu, following fears of Libyan activities in Chad, two months later a border dispute with Cameroun over an area said to contain oil led to the despatch of again the best part of a division to the area concerned. Clashes occurred and the Nigerian Air Force is reported to have been committed in limited air-to-ground strike operations; one Nigerian aircraft was lost.

The present roles of the Nigerian Army are, naturally, firstly frontier defence; here the main threat is increasingly perceived by both non-Muslim and Muslim-Nigerians, as Libya. Cameroun is also seen as a military problem. Secondly a somewhat vague role, connected with Nigeria's aspirations for hegemony in Black Africa, is seen for the Army in the event of any Black African force being assembled to fight South Africa; this latter is also useful for justifying a defence budget. Thirdly a role in nation building is seen, the armed forces are to 'reflect the federal character of Nigeria' (i.e. as far as possible be recruited proportionately); some form of national service of which military service might be an option is under discussion.

There is every reason to think that the senior officers of the Nigerian armed services do not wish to see any form of renewed military intervention in politics. Some politicians have however spoken of a 'watchdog army' by which they appear to mean that military intervention might again be justified if politics became as corrupt and ethnically divisive as they were in the 1960–66 era. Some junior officers are known to be admirers of figures such as Master-Sergeant Doe of Liberia and Flight-Lieutenant Rawlings of Ghana – junior leaders who have seized power to initiate revolutionary changes. Occasional reports of unrest and suppressed coup conspiracies occur, notably one in Lagos in December 1980, one in Benin City in 1981 and one in Kaduna in April 1982. A handful of soldiers, according to these reports, were killed in the first two, but the third apparently saw several hundred deaths. These reports need to be treated with reserve for the time being.

ORGANISATION

Recent organisational changes reflect the changing perceptions. As a preparation for the return to civilian rule, three divisional areas were delineated from north to south for 1, 2 and 3 Infantry Divisions. This arrangement, deliberately crossing all ethnic, former Region and present State boundaries was devised to deny any divisional commander a geographical area with either ethnic or administrative homogeneity which might prove politically tempting. Each division possessed a mobile brigade whose units were to form a protective screen for the capital. A fourth formation, largely of logistic units was sited in the Lagos area.

These dispositions were already seen as dated by the return to civilian rule. The new order of battle is built around the 1st and 2nd Mechanised Divisions, the 3rd Armoured Division, and the 82nd (Airportable) Division. The first three are stretched across the country roughly on the former pattern. The 82nd Division (the number commemorates one of the World War II West African Divisions that distinguished itself in the Burma campaign) is stationed in South-East Nigeria for the Cameroun commitment. The Mechanised Divisions are being scaled down to three mechanised brigades each, the Armoured Division consists of four armoured and one mechanised brigade each, and the 82nd Division is composed of three brigades, one airborne, one airportable and one amphibious.

The division of the army into arms of service closely follows the British pattern; the arms are infantry, artillery, armour, engineers, signals, electrical and mechanical engineers, supply and transport, pay and ordnance. A chaplain's department exists of military priests, ministers and imams, and there is also an Army Medical Corps.

The Corps of infantry includes a Guards Brigade, but no battalions are linked to any particular town or region.

The air force is being organised into six groups and two supporting administrative units.

RECRUITMENT, TRAINING AND RESERVES

Recruitment (except in the period of the civil war) has hitherto been voluntary in Nigeria, indeed in the colonial period so popular in certain regions was military service that 'dash' (a bribe) would often be paid to ensure acceptance. The colonial-period pattern of the infantry and other teeth-arm units' soldiers being preponderantly Tiv, Idoma and other Middle Belt peoples with other significant contributions from Kanuri and Hausa, has continued; however a very high percentage of Yoruba in the engineers and other logistics units has recently been noted. The Shagari government has attempted to introduce a system of recruitment based on a quota for volunteers from each of the Federation's nineteen States; it is understood there are many loop-holes. Under the new constitution a compulsory national service with a military option is proposed.

The tumultuous events of the period since 1960 have left the Nigerian army with formidable problems. Until the late 1950s, merit was seen as the main criterion for a commission: the Northern Region objected to this and in 1961 a proportional system favouring the north was introduced. But this meant that by 1966 many of the middle-rank officers were either easterners or other able men from the southern half of the country irritated at the political control of the north – one cause of the dramas of January, 1966.

In purely career-structure terms, promotion was at first fast, due to Africanisation and expansion; for those who survived 1966 the promotion then became even faster. An *immobilisme* then ensued: the supporters and comrades-in-arms of General Gowon were rewarded but others felt frustrated. The July, 1975 coup removing Gowon also retired 17 colonels, 52 majors and 60 lieutenants. In the Obasanjo period it was noticeable that officers who had served in the 3rd Marine Commando division, which Obasanjo had commanded in the Civil War, enjoyed an advantage.

Distortions caused by events have also affected the NCOs' training; junior- and middle-level NCO's became neglected in the whirl of events and now the best warrant officers and sergeants, trained in the British period, became elderly. Their successors appear poorly trained.

For several years after independence the Nigerian army (and initially also its units) was commanded by a British officer; this system lasted despite the abrogation of the formal defence treaty, as a British general avoided the question of the region or origin of a successor. Cadets were sent to Britain for training both at Sandhurst and Mons O.C.S.; they were also sent to India, Ethiopia, Pakistan, Canada and Australia, while officers were sent to Britain, Canada and Pakistan for staff training. In the civil war the best that could be arranged was emergency courses of 3 to 4 months' duration; this is now the only training of vast numbers of Nigeria's officers. The education qualification was then (and it still remains) West African School Certificate. During and since the civil war use has been made of Soviet facilities, particularly for artillery and transport personnel, and of course, extensively in the air force. However, small numbers of cadets and staff officers were still sent to Britain (and occasionally elsewhere, for example, Ghana) for staff and higher-command training. A Nigerian Staff College opened at Jaji, near Kaduna, drawing on the help of British Loan Service Personnel. The first of two 6 month crash courses began in June, 1976 with 40 student officers including two brigadiers, 12 colonels and 26 lieutenant-colonels. A regular 1 year course system was introduced in 1977. A few students from other African armies may be accepted. A Nigerian Defence Academy, also at Kaduna, trains officer cadets on short-service (6 months) and regular (2½ years) courses. A number of Indian army instructors assist in the cadet training. There are several schools of infantry and other separate arms schools. The Nigerian navy owns two 350 ton modern landing craft; occasional small amphibious exercises take place, probably with an eye on an occupation of Fernando Po in the event of another Equatorial Guinea regime proving as unpleasant as that of the late Macías Nguema.

Readers will now have realised that many political, educational and ethnic factors will combine to determine promotion; it remains but to mention one more (already briefly noted) – corruption. The securing of attractive postings, or even passing promotion examinations, may all be governed by the local 'going-rate' as much as any other factor.

EQUIPMENT AND ARMS INDUSTRY

Nigeria is starting a small-arms manufacturing industry, the first country in Black Africa to do so. Until the civil war equipment for the army was purchased exclusively from Britain. With the outbreak of the civil war weapon sales to Nigeria became controversial in Britain, and the Nigerian army began the purchase of artillery pieces (76mm and 122 field guns) from the USSR to supplement their small numbers of British 25 pounder and 105mm guns. Britain's overall policy was the preservation of the Federation, seen as a British creation and as an area of the world containing a massive British investment. British policy for weapons sales was the supply of equipment viewed as 'traditional' (i.e. material sold before the conflict began) and at a total cost less than that supplied by the other major weapons supplier, the USSR, which supplied far fewer items of very costly equipment such as fighter aircraft. This arrangement enabled the Nigerians to purchase all they required of the material they needed most – infantry weapons and ammunition; further, since this material came from Britain it connoted British support for Federal policy and aims.

This background laid the foundations for an army whose equipment lacks homogeneity, subsequent weapon purchases have compounded this. Armoured units are built around Soviet T-55 tanks, of which Nigeria possesses at least 60 and possibly a further 40, and 50 British Scorpion light tanks. The Soviet tanks have NATO patterned signals equipment. Other armoured fighting vehicles include between 35 and 90 AML-60 or AML-90, and between 55 and 75 Fox, modern armoured-cars with survivors, now probably well under twenty, from an earlier order of Saladin vehicles; eighteen M3 VTT armoured troop carriers one or two of which may have been adapted for command or other purposes, fifty Austrian Steyr Daimler Puch armoured troop carriers of which again some may have been modified, and eight elderly Saracen armoured personnel carriers. Precise numbers of individual artillery weapons are also unclear; the weapons include 76mm, 105mm pack howitzers, 122mm (said to total 200) and 130mm guns, with 20mm and 40mm anti-aircraft guns together with 30 ZSU-23-4 tracked anti-aircraft units. Some 200 81mm mortars are said to be in service, the basic infantry weapon is the standard NATO Belgian FN FAL, but officers possess Swiss manufactured pistols. One recent report notes Soviet RPG-7 anti-tank grenade launchers said to have been purchased in the 1960s as still in service.

Other sophisticated ordnance includes RASIT and SHELTER battlefield radar surveillance equipment, and British SIMFIRE direct weapons effect simulators for training.

The Nigerian Air Force has also a formidable paper profile. A fighter/strike capacity is based upon three squadrons, one of twelve Alphajet and two of MiG-21 aircraft; each MiG squadron should consist of eighteen machines but one may have deficiencies supplemented by older MiG-17s. Two transport squadrons include between them six

Hercules C-130, five F-27, one F-28 and a Grumman Gulfstream II. For liaison search and rescue duties there is a helicopter squadron equipped with 20 West German BO-105 machines, and three squadrons that between them possess 37 Bulldog, 14 DO-28 and 3 Navajo light fixed-wing aircraft. For training there are the balance of the six MiG-17 aircraft not in the fighter squadrons, two trainer versions of the MiG-21, four trainer MiG-15 and 20 Czech Aero L29 Delfin machines. Many of these machines can be easily adapted for light air-to-ground strike work. The helicopter force, in addition to the BO-105s already noted includes thirteen Puma, ten Alouette IIs and three Whirlwinds. Some of these are retained in storage.

Extensive orders for a number of very expensive items were placed or under discussion in 1980 and 1981; it is not clear how many of these orders have been cancelled or delayed for financial reasons. Some undoubtedly have been deferred. These equipments include thirty-seven further Vickers Mark II battle tanks with laser sighting for their 105mm guns, plus a further five recovery vehicles, over 100 Brazilian EE9 Cascavel armoured-cars; folding float equipment for army engineers, twenty-five Italian tracked 155mm self-propelled guns, sixteen French mounted Roland mobile battlefield surface-to-air missile units. Blowpipe missiles, a large further order of AML-60 armoured cars, sixteen Hughes 300C training helicopters, four Aeritalia G-222 tactical troop transport aircraft, two maritime reconnaissance Fokker F-27s, three Lynx helicopters, four more Bulldog trainers, six Boeing CH47 Chinook helicopters and a number of Soviet Atoll air-to-air missiles. An even more ambitious project is the ordering from Austria of a complete factory for the assembly of Steyr Cuirassier light tank/tank destroyers.

RANK, DRESS AND DISTINCTIONS

The rank structure of the Nigerian army follows that of Britain, though successive rulers have tended to promote themselves further up the ladder. Murtala Muhammad becoming a general after the 1975 coup, and his successor, O. Obasanjo, being a lieutenant-general. Rank badges are patterned on those of the British army, the Nigerian eagle replacing the crown. Gold braid on the cap is also worn in accordance with British usage. The service and training uniform is also British patterned, though the ceremonial uniform, of a dark-green tunic with a patrol collar and very-light-coloured trousers, is a post-independence introduction. Staff officers wear red gorget patches of the British style. Some battalions wear distinctive plumes or hackles in their berets. Gloves are worn and swords are carried on ceremonial parades.

The Nigerian air force recently discarded military rank titles in favour of those in use in the British RAF.

Decorations include an Order of the Niger and an Order of the Federal Republic; both are awarded at different grades.

CURRENT DEVELOPMENTS

More perhaps than in any other African army, the transfer of the colonial army model has proved a very difficult experience. Reasons for conflict and jealousies abound in a vast land such as Nigeria with its diversity of peoples. There are additional frictions between soldiers of different cultures, languages and levels of education. Further frictions can arise from different foreign national training systems or hurried local courses through which officers have passed. Outside the barracks the officers may be seen as an expensive *élite* and even the soldiers as a 'labour aristocracy', a feeling in turn arousing resentment within the barrack gates. These frictions can affect all civil—military relationships at national, regional and local level particularly in a situation of economic scarcity; for all Nigeria's oil wealth, huge areas of the territory remain in abject poverty. The maintenance of an efficient, united, well-trained army is a formidable task.

Five factors impede the efficiency of the Nigerian Army. The first and most immediate is one of a very poor standard in technical maintenance. Preceding paragraphs have listed a formidable array of equipment; between a quarter and a third is all that is likely to be operational on any one occasion, a second third might be made ready within two or three weeks, the final third may well be unserviceable for many weeks or forever.

Corruption in the Army is also a serious problem (as it is in all Nigerian society); its effects cannot be quantified, but are damaging. The economic squeeze of 1982 may well have affected already inadequate supplies of spare parts, training expense, and efficiency generally. Finally there are two specific Nigerian psychology factors. One is arrogance, Nigerians see themselves as the giant of Africa, and overrate their own prowess and stability; this over-confidence could lead to major errors. The other, deep-rooted in all aspects of Nigerian life, is the lack of cohesion due to the weakness of the concept of national unity. At a local level this can mean men of one or several ethnic groups will not bother to do their best under an officer of another group. At a national level the weakness can mean that while many may be patriotic, even nationalistic, their aims and concepts may be totally different. Students of the period 1966—70 will endlessly come across instances in which a Nigerian officer, NCO or soldier said 'He was my closest friend in the army, now I see he was a traitor'. This comment would be made by a soldier of impeccably militant Nigerian patriotism in respect of another with similar views. Nigeria's army and indeed the Nigerian nation, will depend on some political consensus for an answer to the Austrian Emperor Franz Joseph's famous question: 'Patriot for whom? Is he patriot for me?'

Signs of an emergence of this consensus are not always encouraging. The forthcoming 1983 election may create tensions in which the Army has to hold the ring; its own internal cohesion could be severely tested in such circumstances.

ADDENDUM

The Nigerian Army had to be committed again to curb Muslim religous extremism in October 1982, the extremism, as in 1980 was caused by the followers of Mohammadu Marwa, leader of the fundamentalist Maitatsine sect. Marwa himself was killed in 1980 but his sect continued to gain support, its fundamentalism making an appeal among the poor. The Nigerian Army has ordered that soldiers found to be members or supporters of the sect will be discharged.

Further military purchase orders are, reliably, reported to include thirty Swedish Bofors FM-77B towed 155mm howitzers, fifty French twin 20mm gun equipped anti-aircraft armoured fighting vehicle, an unspecified number of American M2HB SACO heavy machine-guns, a further small order of Austrian Steyr Daimler Puch tracked armoured personnel carriers, a few of which are adapted to command or communication purposes and bringing to 70 the total number of these chassis, and a further fifty-five British Scorpion tanks, there to be fitted with a Belgian designed turret with a 90mm gun. The total Panhard AML fleet is now estimated to contain 124 AML-60s and twelve AML-90s.

The Defence Industries Corporation plant at Kaduna, developed and assisted by the West German Fritz Werner firm, the Italian Beretta firm and Belgium's FN, is now producing 7.62mm and 9mm ammunition, and Beretta light rifles and pistols. The manufacture of other weapons is being considered.

President Shagari, in a recent ministerial re-shuffle, assumed the post of Minister for Defence himself, probably with an eye to control of the armed forces during the 1983 Election Campaign.

Lloyd Mathews

NORWAY

HISTORY AND INTRODUCTION

The official date of formation of the Norwegian army is 1628, but it remained small — as did the population — and unimportant, a mere local appendage of the much stronger and farther-faring Danish army, until the transfer of national sovereignty from Denmark to the 'joint' kingdom of Sweden—Norway occurred in 1814. The Norwegians had resisted the forced union, compelling the Swedes to fight a token war for its consummation, and they made it a condition of their eventual acceptance that the Norwegian army should remain separate from the Swedish, and be officered exclusively by Norwegians and employed solely for the defence of Norway proper.

The separate identity of the army, and its role as effectual guarantor of national independence within the joint kingdom (of which the Swedish King was head, but the legislatures, bureaucracies and budgets distinct) ensured it a privileged place in Norwegian political life during the nineteenth century, and a consequential evolution along the lines current in major European armies during the same period. Initially established (by the *Storting* in 1816) on a basis of limited conscription (by lot among country dwellers only) for a long term (5 years) and with a sizeable regular element (the *hvervede*), it was placed in 1854 on a basis of universal conscription. The first-line was still to be recruited by lot, with purchase of substitutes permissible, but those escaping the draft were placed on the reserve (*landvern*, formed in 1837) and given a short military training. In 1885, the duration of the military obligation was further extended (though the training period was shortened, from 162 to 90 days). The male population was classed in 13 year groups, the first five of which were assigned to the line, the next four to the militia (*landvern*) and the last four to the territorial reserve (*landstorm*); at the same time, the regular *hvervede* was abolished. The parliamentary left would have preferred to make the army an even more popularly based institution, by transferring the burden of defence to the volunteer rifle clubs, whose emergence was a current pan-Scandinavian phenomenon, and which in 1884 had stiffened the *Storting*'s resolve in its battle with the King to abolish the royal power of veto. But the Norwegian establishment were suspicious of their political stance and rightly doubtful of their usefulness in a military crisis, of which the most probable was a confrontation with Sweden over the future of the union.

When that confrontation was brought on in 1904—5, the government made effective use of the power at its disposal, by ordering mobilisation, and the threat of war played its part in bringing Sweden to agree, eventually amicably, on the union's dissolution. Thereafter, the Norwegian army entered into a decline. The government perpetuated the policy of neutrality on which the joint Kingdom's diplomacy had been conducted since mid-century and which was entrenched by the powers' guarantee of Norwegian territorial integrity in 1907; protected thereby from aggression, and threatened no longer with political absorption by Sweden, the Norwegians progressively weakened their armed force. The trend was accelerated by the country's already strong and internationally recognised commitment to pacifist causes (for which reason Nobel had vested adjudication of his Peace Prize in

the *Storting* in 1901), and by the Norwegian left's dislike of the army as a symbol and, by its account, agent (actual or potential) of capitalist oppression. The left-wing youth movements had adopted the 'broken rifle' as their symbol in 1905 and made heroes of those who resisted conscription on ideological grounds (that trend was to reach its head in 1924—5, when 50 recruits refused training, and Tranmael, Secretary of the Labour Party, was imprisoned for sedition).

The first defence act after independence largely perpetuated the system of 1885, and actually extended the duration of military obligation (to the age of fifty-five) and of training (to 144 days). It also brought regiments into being and localised them in the six military districts into which the country was now divided. But after World War I, during which Norway joined Denmark and Sweden in declaring her neutrality, the country, under a left-wing government, adopted a defence policy of 'every reduction consistent with national safety'. In real terms this meant that in 1927 the intake of conscripts was cut by 30% and the cadre of officers and NCOs halved, and in 1935 the number of officers was again reduced to 470. Of serving soldiers, only a minute 'neutrality guard' was left on duty, though in theory 100,000 could be mobilised in an emergency.

The left's suspicions of the army (and the left was dominant in Norwegian politics throughout the inter-war years) had been heightened by its use by the short-lived Agrarian government of 1931—3 against strikers (e.g. in the 'battle of Melmed' in 1931) and by the activities of Vidkun Quisling, an ex-army officer, briefly Minister of Defence, 1931—3, the founder first of a voluntary militia (*Leidangen*) and then of a domestic Nazi party (*Nasjonal Samling*). As the events of April 9th, 1940 were to prove, however, the weakness to which the left had reduced the army was far more injurious to the nation than any imagined political reaction its regular officers might have essayed. Despite his military past, Quisling formed no following among the officers, 1700 of whom were deported to concentration camps during the German occupation. Also, it was regular army officers rather than the leaders of the left who did what could be done to oppose the unheralded German invasion. One of them, General Fleischer, earned the distinction, with the French General Béthouart, of inflicting on the Germans their first land defeat of the war, in the battle of Narvik.

Such was the state of Norwegian unpreparedness, however, that though half the army (50,000) managed to mobilise somehow and sustain the campaign for 2 months, it was unable to offer a co-ordinated resistance to the Germans and, despite British and French help (on the ground less effective than the action organised by the country-wise Norwegians themselves), was eventually forced to capitulate, take refuge in Sweden or escape to England. Out of the survivors the Norwegian government-in-exile raised a Norwegian brigade, based in Scotland, a unit of which, under a remarkable leader, Martin Linge, undertook daring and very effective commando raids against German installations in Norway, a campaign which culminated in the destruction of the Norske Hydro plant in 1943, the only source of heavy water for German nuclear weapons research. At the same time the Norwegians at home were organising their own partisan organisation, *Milorg* (an ironic allusion to the socialist minister Koht's words of 1936, 'every one is agreed that we cannot and will not have any strong military organisation'), which maintained the most active resistance consistent with the presence of 300,000 German troops in the country (one for every 10 Norwegians).

The occupation was brought to an end by the capitulation of Germany, rather than by liberation or national uprising. Nevertheless, its effects were decisive. Derry* wrote, 'National pride was deeply wounded by the ease with which their country was overrun. The short-term result was to blacken the reputation of the (left-wing) government of 1940 as inept blunderers, if not worse; the long-term result was to make the Norwegians defence-minded'. Every left-wing government since the war, and the complexion of government has remained generally left-wing, has given the full weight of its authority to building up and sustaining a respectable defence capacity; the only minister to have lost the confidence of the *Storting* during the same period was Hauge, the post-war Defence Minister, over his failure to establish smooth relations with the high command. Norway, after flirting briefly with the idea of helping to form a Scandinavian defence union, abandoned its habit of neutrality and joined NATO in 1949. The army, the navy and particularly the air force, were modernised with generous American help, but at a considerable cost to the Norwegian budget. In addition, out of the resistance movement grew an impressive parallel force to the army — the Home Guard, 80,000 strong, largely voluntary in composition and yet even today, when it must recruit chiefly from ex-conscripts who might be expected to have had their fill of military life, of an average age of under thirty. The Norwegians thus present an interesting example of a people whose attitudes to national military policy and personal military involvement have been transformed in a single generation.

STRENGTH AND BUDGET

Population: 4,100,000
Army: 24,400, of which 17,800 are conscripts; 122,000 reserves
Navy: 9400; 14 coastal submarines; five frigates; 60 smaller craft; 1600 coastal artillerymen manning 40 batteries
Air force: 8300; 114 combat aircraft
Home guard: 85,000, of whom 90% are in the army branch
GNP (1981): $49,370,000,000
Defence expenditure: $1,650,000,000

Norwegian defence expenditure, at 2% of GNP is comparatively low by NATO standards, but should be contrasted with the very small percentages spent in the decades between the wars. Post-war figures demonstrate an altogether higher degree of readiness on the part of Norwegians to spend for national military purposes. The defence budget has, nevertheless, declined since the 1960s when nearly 20% — admittedly offset by American aid — was spent in several years while re-equipment was proceeding. Recently most of the budget has been absorbed in personnel, logistic and administrative costs, leaving little for procurement. Replacement of equipment is hindered by Norway's lack of domestic defence industries and the consequent need to import. An adverse balance of payments, though compensated by invisible earnings, has yielded insufficient foreign currency to meet the ever growing costs of major defence items. The domestic oil boom may, however, henceforth make available the sums necessary to replace ageing equipment and fill gaps in the inventory.

* Derry, T. K., *A History of Modern Norway*, Oxford, 1973.

COMMAND AND CONSTITUTIONAL STATUS

The King is Commander-in-Chief of all three services, but executive control is vested in the elected government and exercised by the minister of defence; the defence committee of the *Storting* (parliament) has strong investigatory and advisory powers. The Norwegian command structure is an integrated tri-service organisation of which the head is the Chief of Defence, who is also the commander of the civilian defence services and whose deputy is the chief of the defence staff. The heads of the individual services (army, navy, air force and home guard) have the title of Inspector-General and their own staffs, but their role is restricted to recruitment, administration, organisation, tactics and doctrine. Operational command is in the hands of the Commanders North Norway (COMNOR) and South Norway (COMSONOR), who control integrated headquarters in which the individual service commanders have authority over their own forces. COMNOR is also the Commander of the Allied Task Force North Norway and, in certain circumstances, brings his national forces directly under the control of CINCNORTH, the NATO commander of the 'Northern Flank', always a British general whose headquarters are at Kolsaas outside Oslo.

ROLE, COMMITMENT, DEPLOYMENT AND RECENT OPERATIONS

Role

The several roles of the Norwegian army have been defined as: maintaining an efficient surveillance and warning system; guarding the sovereignty of Norwegian territory, by the deterrence, limitation or repulse of any violation; the rapid reinforcement of forces in exposed areas, and the maintenance of the necessary means; preparing and holding facilities for the reception of allied (i.e. NATO) reinforcements; providing contingents to the peace-keeping mission of the United Nations; in so far as possible, to render all assistance 'to society as a whole'. Norway, like Sweden and several other European States (e.g. Switzerland, Austria, Yugoslavia and West Germany), propagates a doctrine of 'total defence', which aims to create, in time of war: 'the largest possible military force with the highest possible quality; the best possible civilian support of the military; the best possible protection of civilian life and property; and the preservation, to the greatest extent possible, of national sovereignty'. With this in view, the operations of the army are to be integrated with those of the other services, the joint defence agencies, Civil Defence, the police, the health services and concerned economic and administrative organisations. In practice, the roles for which the army most frequently trains are the defence of Finnmark (the area bordering Russia in the far north), the reinforcement of the Finnmark force, the defence of southern Norway against airborne attack and the defence of the coast against seaborne invasion.

Commitment

Norway is a founder member of NATO and its Brigade North, the largest standing element of the army, is a NATO-earmarked force, which would come under command of CINC-NORTH in case of emergency. Most of the rest of the army is also earmarked, but would remain under direct national control. Like Sweden and Denmark, Norway also has earmarked, for United Nations emergency duty a number of military units, including an infantry battalion, and support and medical elements.

Certain restrictions have been unilaterally imposed on the stationing of foreign troops and weapons on Norwegian soil.

Norway

On February 1st, 1949, on the eve of its joining NATO, the government assured the Soviet Union that it would not permit the stationing of foreign troops on its territory 'as long as it was not attacked or threatened with attack, and in 1957 it also declared that it had no plans to set up stockpiles of nuclear weapons or to install launching sites for rockets. However, NATO forces, particularly the ACE Mobile Force, regularly exercise in Norway, and individual foreign servicemen in numbers gain experience of winter-warfare conditions there.

Deployment

Norway is divided into Northern and Southern Commands. The Southern (HQ Oslo), which contains most of the population, is also where the training organisations are based. The standing Brigade North (HQ Bardufoss, near Tromsö) is stationed in Northern Command (HQ Bodö). The mobilisation brigades and local defence forces are based on the centres of population, under four regional headquarters which are in process of establishment. The Home Guard (army) is organised into 18 districts, which correspond with the counties (*fylker*), divided into 90 sub-districts and about 500 local areas, the last roughly coterminous with the parishes (*kommuner*).

Recent Operations

Norway sent medical troops to Korea during the war of 1950—3; Norwegian battalions or observers have operated under the United Nations Emergency Force in Kashmir (1949—71), the Congo (1960—64), the Lebanon (1958), the Yemen (1963—4), in the Middle East on the Israeli border (1948—71) and subsequently in the Lebanon.

ORGANISATION

Arms of Service

The army is organised into infantry, cavalry, artillery, engineers, signals, transport, army aviation, logistics, repair and medical troops; the coast artillery forms part of the navy. Unlike the neighbouring Swedish and Danish armies, it has not maintained its historic regiments of infantry and cavalry, except for the Royal Footguards (*Hans Majestet Kongens Garde*); the reconnaissance units, however, preserve the title of 'dragoons'.

Operational

The standing Brigade North is organised into two infantry battalions, 1 tank company, one artillery battery and one air defence battery; the all-arms Group South consists of one infantry battalion, air companies as for the Brigade North; there are also some standing armoured squadrons and artillery regiments and the Royal Footguards Battalion in Oslo. The 11 mobilisation brigades (Regimental Combat Teams) are organised as the Brigade North, but are less mobile. The Home Guard (army) has as its basic operational unit the platoon, of which there are three to six in each local area, divided into sections of eight men and equipped for local defence only.

RECRUITMENT, TRAINING AND RESERVES

All fit male citizens are liable for military service from the age of twenty until forty-five; conscription has been imposed in Norway since before the union with Sweden in 1814 and has been universal since 1854. The term of service since 1973 has been 12 months. About 15,000 of the army's 18,000 soldiers are conscripts, who pass thence to the mobilisation

brigades of the reserves. Service in the Home Guard is voluntary; only about 400 of its members are regular servicemen.

Training lasts 3—8 months, the length depending on branch and specialisation, and takes place at the schools and training centres, which are located in southern Norway. The training centres provide basic training, which is completed after the conscript is transferred to his standing unit, and also contain officer- and NCO-candidate units; the schools are run by the respective corps, and train specialists as well as providing advanced courses for their own officers and NCOs. The Infantry and Signal Schools run frequent winter warfare courses for foreign students. Great emphasis is laid also on winter warfare in the training of all conscripts (whose general fitness on arrival is anyway higher than in most European armies); all must complete a 30 km cross-country ski test, and they are taught to survive blizzards without artificial shelter on the Arctic uplands.

Regular officers, who must be qualified for university entrance, have passed officer candidate school and served a year as NCOs, are trained at the Military Academy in Oslo, where the Staff College is also located.

Reserves number 130,000, the youngest of whom would form the 11 mobilisation brigades. The older are assigned to local defence units; far more important in local defence, however, is the Home Guard (*Heime Vernet*), which numbers 80,000, 90% of which belongs to the army branch (and 3% to anti-aircraft units). It is recruited partly by voluntary enlistment, partly by transfer of reservists from the mobilisation lists; a few conscripts are transferred directly. Its boast is that it can mobilse 10,000 men in 45 minutes, 40,000 in 2 hours, 60,000 in 3 hours and the whole in 4 hours. It is a completely voluntary body, whose members do 50 weekend hours, or six consecutive days, training each year. Home Guard officers and NCOs undergo an additional 14 days' training every 3 years at the two Home Guard Central Schools at Dombas and Torpo.

EQUIPMENT AND ARMS INDUSTRY

Most of the Norwegian army's equipment is imported; the Raufoss factory manufactures the 66mm M-72 LAW anti-armour weapon.

Pistol: P-38 Walther (West Germany)
Sub-machine-gun: MP40 (West Germany)
Rifle: G3 CETME (West Germany)
Machine-gun: MG42 (West Germany)
Mortars: 81mm M-29 (USA) and 107mm M-30 (USA)
Anti-armour weapons: 66mm LAW M-72, 84mm Carl Gustav (Sweden), 106mm M-40 RCL (USA), ENTAC ATGW (France) and TOW ATGW (USA)
Air-defence weapons: Rh-202 20mm cannon (West Germany); RBS-70 SAM; 40mm L/60 and L/70 guns (USA; in the army, air force and Home Guard air-defence units); and Nike Hercules missiles (in the four air force SAM batteries)
Artillery: 105mm and 155mm howitzer (250 in service) and 155mm M-109 SP howitzer (USA; 130 in service)
Armour: M-113 APC (USA); M-24 light tank (USA; up-gunned model of which there are 70 in service); M-48 tank (USA; 38 in service); and Leopard 1 tank (West Germany; 78 in service)
Aircraft: Piper L-18 (USA) and O-1E light aircraft (32 in service).

Note: the Home Guard is still equipped in part with older weapons.

RANK, DRESS AND DISTINCTIONS

Rank

General (general) — Three stars on gold lace
GenerallØytnant (lieutenant-general) — Two stars on gold lace
Generalmajor (major-general) — One star on gold lace
Oberst (colonel) — Three stars with silver lace edging
OberstlØytnant (lieutenant-colonel) — Two stars with silver lace edging
Major (major) — One star with silver lace edging
Kaptein (captain) — Three stars
LØytnant (lieutenant) — Two stars
Fenrik (second-lieutenant) — One star

Stabsersjant (sergeant-major) — Three chevrons, crown and bar over
Oversersjant (staff-sergeant) — Three chevrons, bar over
Sersjant (sergeant) — Three chevrons
Korporal (corporal) — Two chevrons
Vize korporal (lance-corporal) — One chevron

Stars are silver and are worn on the collar; chevrons are worn on the upper arm.

Dress and Distinctions

Officers wear a khaki British-style service dress. Every-day wear for all ranks is a khaki British-style battle dress, bearing a flash in the branch colour: cavalry, green and yellow; artillery, red and blue; engineers, blue and red; signals, blue and white; infantry, red; transport, blue and yellow; repair, red—blue—red; logistics, yellow; and medical, crimson. Combat dress is olive-green smock and trousers or, for winter, white ski overalls. Peaked cap, ski cap, beret or NATO helmet are worn as appropriate. The *Kongensgarde* preserves its magnificent early nineteenth century uniform with white crossbelts and bearskin cap. Veterans of the famous World War II raiding unit wear a shoulder title, *Kompani Linge*.

CURRENT DEVELOPMENTS

Norway is the only country in NATO, apart from Turkey, to share a frontier with Russia. Its neutralist past and its government's desire not to arouse Soviet antagonisms have combined to moderate its full military commitment to the alliance, by forswearing the basing of foreign troops or the stockpiling of nuclear weapons on its territory; and there is a small but consistent group of electors, about 5 to 7%, who are hostile to the country's membership of the alliance. It is from this same group that those are drawn who insist in seeing in the army's cadre of regular officers a potential source of threat to the country's democratic institutions. The army is confident enough of its standing with the population at large, however, to have allowed representative officers to appear in debate on radio and television with their accusers to rebut their charges, and it does not seem likely that they are widely believed. The Norwegians, indeed, though not a military people, are strongly committed both to a strong defence policy within the NATO ambit and to personal involvement in their own defence. Hardy and athletic, they make excellent individual soldiers, skilled particularly in winter warfare, accept conscription without complaint (the rate of conscientious objection is far lower than in neighbouring Denmark or Germany) and, by voluntary effort, have made the Norwegian Home Guard a popular militia of real military value. The asymmetric settlement of the country, which puts most of the population in the south while the military frontier is in the far north, indeed 250 miles north of the nearest railhead and connected with it by only a single road, makes the framing of a workable mobilisation plan difficult, and all the more so in view of the gross disparity between Norwegian and Soviet strength in the north (at least two divisions to one brigade). Norway counts upon the arrival of NATO help to hold the north if it were invaded, and hopes only to win enough time to allow such help (initially the ACE Mobile Force) to arrive. If the invasion were confined to the locality, and not part of a more general war, it might well prove that the Norwegian army, assisted by its excellent small navy and air force, might succeed in winning the time desired.

Seaborne or airborne landings anywhere in the populated areas would meet stiff resistance from the Home Guard. A danger with which Norway has not yet had to deal, but must, like Britain, prepare against, is terrorist sabotage or covert foreign attack on her off-shore oil installations. Primarily a naval task, it is judged nevertheless to require the commitment and training of soldiers. Norway may well find it necessary to raise a force of marines, something at present she does not possess.

John Keegan

OMAN

HISTORY AND INTRODUCTION

Since the late eighteenth century, Oman's close relationship with Great Britain relieved it of the need to provide its own defence against external attack. Its last reason to maintain armed forces capable of deployment beyond its borders disappeared when its east African possessions (including Zanzibar and Mombasa) were separated from it as a result of a disputed succession in 1856. For the next century, as the collapse of the country's maritime trade brought it ever deeper into poverty, the Sultan maintained only personal mercenary forces sufficient to secure his position at least in the coastal regions.

The Sultan's Armed Forces (SAF) have expanded nearly four-fold since Sultan Qabus overthrew his traditionalist father in a coup in July, 1970. Both the scale and the character of the expansion were almost entirely conditioned by the insurgency in the south-western province of Dhofar, and the wider possibilities of a development of that revolt northward into Oman proper, or a confrontation with the South Yemeni supporters of the revolt.

In 1970 the army was a wholly mercenary force of under 4000 men. Rather more than half the other ranks were Baluchis, recruited through the port of Gwadur in Pakistan, while the officers were almost entirely British, under contract or on secondment, with a few Pakistani officers at lower administrative levels. There were only 16 Omani officer, all lieutenants.

The old Sultan, whose faith in his subjects' loyalty was epitomised by this mercenary army, ran the province of Dhofar virtually as a private fief, with a separate, locally recruited defence force commanded by Pakistini officers. The province, whose 50,000–100,000 inhabitants speak south Arabian dialects related to Arabic and possess a distinctive local identity, has been permanently attached to the Sultanate of Oman since 1879, but it is separated from historical Oman by several hundred miles of virtually uninhabited desert and has strong separatist tendencies.

A local rebellion against the Sultan, beginning in 1963, gained much greater momentum after the departure of Britain from Aden in 1967 and the establishment of the Marxist-oriented Popular Democratic Republic of Yemen (PDRY) on the Dhofar frontier. With training and arms supplied by the People's Republic of China and Iraq, and a logistical base at Hauf just inside South Yemeni territory, the Popular Front for the Liberation of Oman (PFLO), as the Dhofar rebellion now calls itself, had established control by 1970 over almost all of Dhofar. Only about 10 miles around Salalah, the capital and main port, remained under the Sultan's control.

The old Sultan finally admitted the SAF to Dhofar in the late 1960s, but no noticeable improvement in the security situation followed. His steadfast refusal to grant any form of local autonomy to the Dhofaris, which was seen as the key problem, was a principal cause of his overthrow in 1970. Since then there has been an extremely rapid programme of expansion in the armed forces, largely paid out of newly available oil revenues, and a parallel programme of Omanisation to transform a mercenary force into a national army.

STRENGTH AND BUDGET

Oman's army has 15,000 officers and men in a total armed force numbering 18,000 (excluding expatriate personnel). The air force has 2000 personnel, and the navy currently has 1000. There are 1000 paramilitary gendarmerie, and an irregular tribal force in Dhofar – the *firqats* – now numbering about 3300. The population of Oman is 948,000.

The 1981 defence budget was ($1,690,000,000). Previous very heavy expenditure on defence, amounting to about three-fifths of Oman's annual oil revenue (which in turn accounts for 98% of total Oman government revenues), had forced Oman into deficit to the tune of $355,000,000 by 1975. It has had to borrow $124,000,000 on international markets since 1973, and reportedly received a special loan of $100,000,000 from Saudi Arabia in May, 1975.

COMMAND AND CONSTITUTIONAL STATUS

Lacking a constitution, Oman also lacks a formal constitutional status for its army. The Sultan, as ruler of an absolute monarchy, is Supreme Commander; his commanders-in-chief since his accession have been British officers on secondment, due to the absence of trained Omani officers of suitable rank and experience. The present Commander-in-Chief is Major-General Kenneth Perkins.

ROLE, COMMITMENT, DEPLOYMENT AND RECENT OPERATIONS

The primary role of the Oman army in the past 5 years has been the suppression of the Dhofar rebellion, though after 1973 offensive operations in Dhofar were increasingly dominated by the Iranian expeditionary force. The army's secondary role is the maintenance of internal security in Oman itself.

The latter mainly involves ensuring that there should be no resurgence of a separate centre of power in the mountainous inland areas, the former Imamate, whose fiercely independent and fanatical tribes were almost entirely free from control by Muscat betwen 1920 and 1955, and briefly again in 1957. Included in this role is the prevention of infiltration northward by PFLO cadres.

In support of these commitments the eighty infantry regiments (battalions) of the army are deployed into a Northern Command and the Dhofar Brigade. Omani battalions are rotated through the Dhofar operational area on a 9 month cycle. The tribal levies or *firqats* are returned to their own areas of Dhofar after training, and are not subject to rotation.

Oman's armed forces are not greatly inferior to those of the PDRY. The role of protecting power against larger threats from further away (and of a willing second in a possible clash with South Yemen) had largely passed from Britain to Iran by 1973; it has now presumably passed again to Saudi Arabia and Egypt.

Iran's intense interest in Oman's security arises from the fact that these two States control the Strait of Hormuz, through which all Persian Gulf traffic must pass. (Two of the three deep-water tanker channels actually pass through Oman's territorial waters.) It was the Iranian navy whose presence dominated in the waters round Oman, and the Shah guaranteed Oman's air-space.

In support of the latter commitment, Iran built a radar station in central Dhofar and stationed eight F-5 aircraft at the Thmarit airbase there until Oman took delivery from Britain of 12 Jaguar fighter—bombers equipped with the American-made Harpoon anti-shipping missiles (range 60 miles) in 1977. During the Shah's visit to Oman in December, 1977 the two rulers declared that they would henceforth be jointly responsible for the security of the Straits of Hormuz.

A complete Iranian brigade of 3500 men began operating in Dhofar in December, 1973 supported by their own artillery and heavy-lift helicopters. It was unquestionably the arrival of these troops, with their own self-contained logistics, that gave the Sultan's armed forces the numbers to go on the offensive.

Iranians subsequently comprised about half the actual combat troops in Dhofar. Though some progress had already been made in recovering control of the coastal plain from the rebels, it was only after the Iranians' arrival that sustained operations in the mountains which were the guerrillas' stronghold became possible year-round.

The operations were of an entirely conventional nature. First, control was regained of the road running inland from Salalah through the Qara mountains to Thamarit, and a barrier established along that line while guerrilla forces to the north-east of it were starved, hunted or bribed into submission. The operation was then duplicated on lines successively closer to the South Yemeni border across which all supplies flowed: the Hornbeam line (50 miles from South Yemen) in 1974, and the Damavand line (25 miles) in the autumn of 1975.

The first Iranian air attack on the South Yemeni supply centre of Hauf (which also houses the headquarters of the PFLO) was launched on October 17th, 1975, and a further military advance in late November brought Omani and Iranian forces right up to the South Yemen border. On December 11th, 1975 the Sultan declared that the war was won and the PFLO had been driven from Oman. British, Omani and Iranian casualties in the preceding two and a half years were about 500, the PFLO well over twice that figure. At the end of 1977, it was estimated that there were only about 40 guerrillas still active in Dhofar, and perhaps 200 more in camps across the South Yemen border. Approximately 1000 Iranian troops remained in Oman, apparently on a semi-permanent basis, but they were all withdrawn after the Iranian revolution of 1979 and replaced by 200 Egyptian troops.

Whilst South Yemen and the PFLO may remain the principal threat to Omani security, the recent focus of military attention has been within the Gulf. Oman has always considered that the smaller shaikhdoms to the west form part of Omani territory; although it did not actively pursue this claim when the United Arab Emirates was created in 1971, and accepted a UAE ambassador in Muscat, it has never returned the compliment. Recent events in the UAE, which emphasised the fragility of that State's unity, have probably played a part in the more determined line taken by Oman (although specific disputes have also played a part). There is no doubt that Oman would hope to gain at least the UAE territory separating the main body of the country from the strategically important Musandam peninsula commanding the southern side of the Straits of Hormuz in the event of the UAE's disintegration, if not Omani domination over the larger, oil-rich shaikhdoms lying further to the west.

Potentially the more serious Oman—UAE border dispute, since it directly involves Saudi Arabia as well, is over the Buraimi oasis. The long historical dispute between Abu Dhabi and Saudi Arabia over the ownership of the oasis, which lies on the UAE—Oman border, was settled between the two countries in 1975, but it was subsequently discovered that Shaikh Zayid of Abu Dhabi had also inadvertently signed away a considerable chunk of land which actually belonged to Oman. Intense pressure by Oman's Sultan Qabus, who has extensive influence in the shaikhdoms, obliged the UAE to convince Suadi Arabia in 1977 of the necessity of redrawing the maps defining the border in the 1975 treaty.

A more acute dispute arose in 1977 over the activities of Shaikh Saqr of Ras-al-Khaimah, the easternmost of the shaikhdoms, who has long been in the habit of nibbling at the borders of his neighbours both within the UAE and with Oman. The latter has long contended that Ras-al-Khaimah had illegally annexed certain border areas in Oman's detached territory of Ras Musandam, that it was prospecting for oil in Omani offshore zones and that it had expelled a number of Omanis from their homes. In November, 1977 an Omani naval vessel forced the suspension of drilling work at a Ras-al-Khaimah-licensed oil rig in the disputed offshore zone, and units of the Omani army, ostensibly on manoeuvres, lodged themselves 3 miles inside what Ras-al-Khaimah claims to be its territory. The incidents were resolved when Shaikh Zayid, the President of the UAE, strongly supported the Omani claims, but that cannot have helped the shaky cohesion of the seven 'united' emirates.

ORGANISATION

Arms of Service

The Oman army is organised largely on British models. The regular force consists of eight infantry battalions and one Royal Guard brigade. The battalions (1978) were: Muscat Regiment, Murlten Frontier Regiment, Desert Regiment, Jebel (i.e. Hill) Regiment, Frontier Force, Southern Regiment. The artillery is organised in three regiments one medium, two light, and there is a signals regiment, an armoured car regiment, a paratroop squadron and an engineer squadron. An air-defence regiment is now being formed, and a separate women's army corps is being set up (the first in the Arab world). The gendarmerie are a paramilitary force, nominally organised as a battalion, but of course never concentrated.

The *firqats* are bands of armed Dhofari tribesmen, the majority of whom are former rebels. They vary in strength from 50 to 150 men, all drawn from the same tribe. They receive modern rifles and are trained by a detachment of 60 Special Air Service troops (soon to be withdrawn) on loan from Britain, after which they are returned to their tribal areas as a form of regularly paid Home Guard.

The air force consists of one FGA/reconnaissance squadron, one FGA squadron, one COIN/training squadron, one tactical transport squadron, two transport squadrons and a helicopter squadron. There are two SAM squadrons for airfield defence duties.

Operational

There are two brigade headquarters organisations (besides the Royal Guard): one in the north and the other in Dhofar.

RECRUITMENT, TRAINING AND RESERVES

The programme of Omanisation of the SAF dominates all aspects of recruitment and training. At the moment there are still almost 450 British personnel serving with the SAF, including half the officer corps. In the ranks, progress has been rapid: mixed regiments have been separated into Omani and Baluchi units, and probably less than a third of the force is now mercenaries recruited from Pakistan. Pay and conditions of service have improved radically; a persion scheme, including widow's and disablement pensions, has been introduced, and regular accommodation including married quarters is now being provided.

Omanisation of the officer corps has inevitably been slower, in a country which had only three primary schools in 1970. At the end of 1975, however, there were 330 Omani officers, several dozen of whom had achieved the rank of major by accelerated promotion. The first Omani lieutenant-colonels were made during 1976, and by the end of 1977 all the infantry battalions (proviously commanded by British officers) were under Omanis. Most other units are to be fully Omanised in the following 4 years, and the commander-in-chief of the SAF should be Omani in 1981.

Recruit training, including general education, is done for all the services at the SAF training centre near Muscat. Basic officer training is also done there (all officer candidates must first serve at least a year in the ranks), while specialist training is done abroad — in Britain, Egypt, Jordan, Saudi Arabia and the Union of Arab Emirates. A services boys' school has been established, enrolling 200 pupils, from which many of the future officers and NCOs of the Omani forces will be drawn.

A technical school has been established for the air force, and the navy has begun to do its own training on a special-purpose training vessel. In view of the higher technological requirements of those services and the sophisticated equipment Oman has recently acquired, however, it seems probable that Oman (which had one fully qualified native-born pilot in early 1975) will remain dependent on foreign contract officers for some considerable time in the other two services.

Military service in Oman is voluntary, and there are no reserves.

EQUIPMENT AND ARMS INDUSTRY

Oman's military equipment is almost all of British manufacture. The army has 6 M-60 and 12 Chieftain tanks, 36 Saladin and some V-100 Commando armoured cars, and also Ferret scout cars. The artillery includes 24 25-pounders, 36 105mm and 12 130mm guns, 12 155mm SP howitzers and some 120mm mortars. Anti-tank defence is provided by American-made TOW missiles.

The air force's contribution to army operations is 12 Hunter ground-attack aircraft (transferred from Jordan), 7 Jaguars and 12 BAC-167 COIN aircraft. Tactical transport is provided by 20 AB-205, two AB-206A, and five AB-214 helicopters, and 15 Skyvan aircraft. Longer-range transport is the role of the air force's three BAC-111s, one VC-10, seven Britten-Norman Defenders and one Gulfstream. The SAM squadron has 28 Rapier SAMs and Blindfire radar.

The navy has three patrol vessels (the Royal Yacht and two ex-Dutch MCMs), one training ship, three fast patrol boats, four coastal patrol craft and three small landing craft. There are two minesweepers and a logistical support ship on order.

There is no local arms industry and only limited repair facilities.

RANK, DRESS AND DISTINCTIONS

Rank structure and badges of rank follow British practice. Uniforms are largely modelled on British patterns, with local headgear.

CURRENT DEVELOPMENTS

There may still be a few guerrillas in Dhofar, equipped with, amongst other things, SA-7 missiles that have succeeded in bringing down several SAF aircraft. The years during which it had a monopoly on indoctrination in the mountains guarantee the PFLO some residual passive support there for years to come. The *firqats*, though a useful force, are given to using their weapons against each other in tribal feuds, and as poachers turned gamekeepers might change sides again if it seemed advisable to do so.

Omani control of Dhofar will depend for a number of years, therefore, on either a large regular force in the province of an agreement with South Yemen. It is this latter which the Saudis, were recently trying to arrange, by offering substantial finanical aid to the impoverished Aden regime. At the end of 1977, however, this attempt had met with failure and lapsed at least temporarily, while South Yemen became actively involved alongside the Soviet Union and Cuba in sending military aid to the Ethiopian government in the war in the Horn.

The high defence expenditure of Oman will probably not drop drastically in the future even if the PFLO problem ends. Such levels of expenditure are quite commonplace in Oman's neighbourhood, where almost all the neighbours dispose of oil revenues far exceeding its own, and the need to keep up will make itself felt. This is especially the case since the possibility exists of conflict with UAE, or of intervention in that neighbour in support of Omani claims if it should actually disintetrate.

However, the Dhofar War was effectively brought to an end in April 1976, and the country may be regarded as wholly at peace. Relations with the VAE are friendly, and are now largely conducted through the recently established Gulf Co-operation Council.

Gwynne Dyer
John Keegan

PAKISTAN*

HISTORY AND INTRODUCTION

The Pakistan army is the Siamese twin of the Indian, from which it was surgically separated in the Partition of 1947. (For the history of the old Indian Army before 1947, see the entry on India.) Even now, it bears a closer resemblance to the Indian army than to any other (except perhaps the British, from which they both inherited many of their shared institutions and their predominating tone). This common inheritance has in some senses been enhanced by the fact that they have fought each other three times in their three decades of existence.

Other striking, if intangible, characteristics of both successors to the old Army of the Indian Empire, which set them apart from almost all others of the 'third world', are highly professional perspectives and the weight of tradition which mould their behaviour. They are not creations of recent vintage oriented primarily towards internal security — in the complexity of their internal structures and their attitudes towards the external world they more closely resemble the great historical armies of the industrial world — British, French, American or Russian. That is scarcely surprising, for they are the heirs of one of the premier military institutions of the last century and a half — the old Indian Army — which indeed began as just another instrument of colonial control, but in the twentieth century held its own in the biggest military leagues of the world — in Flanders against the Imperial Germany Army, in the western desert against Rommel, and in south-east Asia against the Japanese.

The domestic careers of the two armies have diverged radically since 1947 — while the Indian army has remained the loyal servant of the State, the Pakistan army has spent about half of the intervening period as its master. This was probably inevitable, given the comparative weakness and immaturity of the institutions of the new nation of Pakistan, its extreme vulnerability, and the relative shortage of competent civilian administrators and politicians. What is noteworthy, however is that the army, because of its apolitical traditions and its responsibility for external defence against very real threats, has usually managed to maintain its focus on its professional rather than its political roles. When it has intervened, it has done so corporately, at generals' level, for pragmatic reasons of efficiency and State security, and not from petty motives. The chain of discipline and command has never been broken, and the great bulk of the army has not become involved in the debilitating intrigues of the political arena.

In all its long life, nothing so became the old Army of the Indian Empire as the manner of its leavetaking. During all the turmoil of 1946—7, culminating in a horrible communal civil war, its discipline never broke. It is impossible to overestimate the importance of this fact, for by the middle of 1947 nothing else stood between the subcontinent and the sort of catastrophe, on a vastly larger scale, that engulfed the Congo in 1960. The human cost of Partition was atrociously high — over half a million dead, and about 14,000,000 refugees — but it could have been far worse but for the

* See also Appendix 2.

devotion to duty of almost all ranks, Hindu and Muslim alike, in the last months of the old Indian Army.

Not all echoes of the political strife rending the Indian Empire in its last years had been muffled by the Army's physical and political isolation from the civilian population, of course. The appallingly mishandled exemplary trial of three 'Indian National Army' officers (one Muslim, one Hindu and one Sikh) in late 1945 badly shook discipline in the armed forces (Almost 30% of the 70,000 Indian Army prisoners taken by the Japanese in the debacles in Singapore and Burma had eventually been persuaded to fight for the Japanese as the Indian National Army.) A chain reaction of mutinies in early 1946 swept almost every ship and establishment of the Royal Indian Navy. The remarkably rapid recovery of morale and discipline in the forces was at least partly due to the fact that both the Congress Party and the Muslim League, when they shortly afterwards realised that the British Labour Government really intended to leave India soon, drastically curtailed their agitation within the armed forces in order not to destroy an instrument they expected to inherit. Though discipline in the Army had undoubtedly become rather brittle, it held firm, and the Army was all the law and order there was in large northern areas of the subcontinent during the last desperate weeks of the British withdrawal.

A more fundamental reason for the unbroken discipline of the old Indian Army down to the end, however, was that the idea of Pakistan had grown with extreme rapidity, and had not had time to penetrate fully into the enclosed and distinctively different world of the Army by 1947. The word 'Pakistan' itself had only been coined in 1933, by a young Muslim Indian at Cambridge University, and the partition idea only began to gain wide support in the Muslim community in 1938, after the first provincial elections under the new Government of India Act aroused its dormant anxieties about Hindu domination. From then on the momentum of the partition idea grew with amazing speed — the 'Pakistan resolution was accepted by the Muslim League, then being rapidly transformed from a debating society to a mass movement by Muhammad Ali Jinnah, in 1940 — but as late as 1946 even most Hindu leaders of the nationalist Congress Party did not take it seriously.

Their incredulity was understandable, for carving a Muslim Pakistan out of the Indian Empire would result in an astonishingly clumsy and improbable political entity, of doubtful economic viabilty and sharing no unifying characteristic except religion. The British administrators of India were proud and protective of their handiwork, a subcontinent unified for the first time in its history, and therefore were equally loath to take the idea of partition seriously. In adopting this attitude, both the British and the Hindu leadership were showing a willful ignorance of the subcontinent's history and social realities.

In the Indian Empire of 1947, Hindus outnumbered Muslims three-to-one. There were Muslim majority areas in the north-west and north-east, but over most of northern India, and to a lesser extent in the south, Hindus and Muslims, lived in an intimate geographical intermingling, and had done so for centuries. Despite their physical proximity and their common ancestry (for most Indian Muslims were the descen-

dants of local converts at some past time), there had never
been any tendency towards intermarriage, or even a conver-
gency of customs. No two philosophies, no two sets of
traditions and assumptions about life could be more alien to
each other than the Hindu and the Muslim, and for most
Indians these considerations loomed larger than shared language, race and circumstances.

History, too, sharpened the antipathy of the two communities. For 1200 years, and in unbroken succession from
the twelfth to the eighteenth centuries, India's Hindus had
been the victims of wave after wave of Muslim conquest,
and the subjects of Muslim empires that had brutally subjugated and exploited the Hindu majority. Hindu prosperity
and status had grown greatly under the British Raj, however,
while the Muslim community's once-proud position had
fallen disastrously. For a long time after the Mutiny of 1857,
which was seen by the British as an attempt to restore the
(Muslim) Moghul Empire, Indian Muslims had been mis-
trusted and consequently discriminated against by the
British authorities, while their own reluctance to collaborate
with the new imperial power had allowed Hindus to gain a
predominating position in all the modern spheres of activity
—administration, industry, the professions — which grew up
under British rule. Even in the Army, Muslims were under-
represented in the officer corps, and especially in the more
technical branches.

A Muslim cultural renaissance got underway in India in
the late nineteenth century, with the foundation of the great
Muslim education institutions (though early on there occurred
the split between secularist modernisers and those who
stressed the traditional values of Islam which was to plague
independent Pakistan's early history). By the twentieth
century there was a small class of Muslim professionals and
intellectuals, and the Muslim League was founded in 1906.
But it was only when the Congress Party's campaign for
Indian independence began to show signs of making progress
in the 1930s that India's Muslims began to consider seriously
what their future would be in an independent India.

Many found it an extremely unattractive prospect. Congress was a secular party (as is the India it ruled after 1947 a
secular State) but its leadership and membership were overwhelmingly Hindu, and it was generally oblivious to the
special anxieties of the Muslim minority. Both within it and
outside it to the right, moreover, there was a body of Hindu
extremists who were actively anti-Muslim. Taking into
account the age-old antagonism between the two communities, and the prospect of the 'tyranny of the ballot-box'
that would be exercised by the Hindu majority after independence, a great many Indian Muslims came to see their
prosperity, their cultural survival, and even their mere
physical safety as lying only within an independent Muslim-
majority State. After 1940, under the single-minded leadership of Jinnah, this view was adopted by the Muslim League
and rapidly came to dominate the political perceptions of
Indian Muslims. Partition was, however, a solution to the
communal problem which was wholly and utterly unpalatable
to all India's Hindus, both because the probelm was not
theirs, and at a deeper level because of the immense significance of India's territory, and its rivers above all, in the
Hindu religion. To divide the country was not merely a
political device to be judged on its merits, it was a violation
of Mother India.

The latent conflict went critical in 1946, when the realis-
tion suddenly burst in upon Indian political leaders that the
British rulers, their credit and their will to rule quickly
ebbing away, were on the brink of departure. The Muslim
leadership's demands for partition before independence
became ever louder, and in its dissatisfaction with the Staf-

ford Cripps mission of March and with the intransigence of
the Congress Party it decreed August 16th, 1946 as Direct
Action Day. In teeming Calcutta the Muslim demonstrations
led to the worst communal riots for generations, with perhaps 5000 killed in 3 days, and the civil war was on. For the
next year communal mass killings flared in one locality
after another, in a crescendo of violence that culminated in
the horrors of August—November, 1947.

Throughout those 16 months the Indian Army was committed in aid to the civil power virtually to the last man,
while the politicians gradually came to terms with the
inevitability of partition. It was grossly overstretched, and
often unable to arrive in time when the sudden spasms of
communal fear and hatred led to massacres, especially in
rural areas, but its impartial and disciplined presence held the
ring long enough to give the political leaders time to work
out a deal. Indeed, the final shove which compelled the
Indian leaders to agree — the British announcement in
February, 1947 that the timetable for independence would
be drastically speeded up, with a final British withdrawal no
later than June, 1947 — was greatly influenced by the fact
that London feared the Army might not hold together much
past that date. Owing to demobilisation the number of British
officers in the Indian Army, war-swollen and already much
Indianised, was due to drop from 11,400 to only 4000 over
the 12 months from June, 1947.

By the end of April, 1946 Congress had come round to
recognising the inevitability of partition, as the only possibility for creating a strong central government in India. It did
demand and get the concession, however, that the Punjab
and Bengal, the two largest of the six provinces the Muslim
League demanded for Pakistan, must themselves be parti-
ioned (the undivided old Punjab was only 57% Muslim, and
Bengal also contained a huge Hindu minority). The Viceroy,
Lord Mountbatten, formally announced the decision on
partition on June 4th, to take effect 11 weeks later, and by
the end of the month government committees had been
established to apportion between the two successor States all
the institutions and resources of the Indian Empire — including the army.

The firm decision that the armed forces must split was
reached by the Partition Council on June 30th, and detailed
instructions were sent out to all units and formations. A
Joint Defence Council and the Armed Forces Reconstitution Committee were appointed to administer the division.
It was intended to have a single Supreme Commander until
the final sorting out of the Army on communal lines in
April, 1948, but at Jinnah's insistence each country was to
have some troops under its operational control on its own
territory from independence day, August 15th, 1947. Both
successor armies would have British officers as Commander-
in-Chief for a transitional period, and it was clear that Pakistan in particular would need to retain numbers of British
officers in its Army for a while, because of the severe shortage
of trained Muslim officers.

Some special difficulties lay in the way of creating a
Pakistan army out of the old united force at Partition. Pakistan was to receive an agreed portion of the military stores
held by the Army of the Raj, but the new Indian government
refused to deliver them after the outbreak of the Kashmir
conflict. Almost every ordnance factory lay on the wrong
side of the new frontier, as did most of the instructional
schools except the Quetta Staff College. Pakistan had to
create at once a new junior military academy at Kakul to
replace Dehra Dun, a new engineer centre at Risalpur, and all
the other schools and depots required by a modern army.

There had never been homogeneous Muslim units in the
old Army: the so-called 'class units' were entirely Hindu

(Mahrattas, Dogras, etc.) and went to India intact. Pakistan got only fragments of units, so it took far longer to reconstitute its army on an organised basis. Eventually it ended up with about a fourth of the personnel, but there was much confusion as individual officers, hitherto isolated from the communal disputes, hesitated between opting for India or Pakistan.

The problem was particularly acute because the main recruiting ground for the old Army had always been the north-west, and especially the Punjab (48% of the Army had come from that province in 1939, and even in the vastly expanded Army of 1947 well over a quarter did), so that many individuals found their homes and property on one side of the partition line in the Punjab, and their religious loyalties on the other. As a result of all this, there was still hardly a single completely formed unit of the Pakistan army in existence when the Kashmir troubles erupted in October, 1947. Several units in Pakistan still had Hindu or Sikh commanding officers, and there were Hindu officers holding appointments at Pakistan Army General Headquarters.

Another problem for Pakistan arising out of the old Indian Army recruiting patterns, though it did not become acute until after the military seizure of power a decade later, was that virtually all the officers and troops it inherited were Punjabis or Pathans (from North-West Frontier Province). There was hardly any representation of the Bengalis, a 'non-martial race' in the old parlance, though they constituted over half the populaton of the new country, and this extremely lopsided character of the army continued to plague Pakistan's politics down to the separation of East Pakistan in 1971.

With its small army, Pakistan on its foundation took over the bulk of the former defence tasks of the old Army — the Afhghan frontier and the tribes — besides what rapidly became a far more pressing matter, the 'internal frontiers' with far more powerful and increasingly hostile India. A degree of hostility was inevitable because of Hindu opposition to the whole idea of partition, not to mention the mutual slaughter of Muslims, Hindus and Sikhs that wracked the Punjab and neighbouring areas after independence day on August 15th, 1947, but the trigger for open and early military confrontation was the Princely State of Kashmir.

Most Princely States had been persuaded to opt for incorporation in the country more appropriate to their religion and location before independence day, but three held out. The two Muslim-ruled States of Junagadh and Hyderabad, which had largely Hindu populations and were physically surrounded by India, were forcibly brought into the Indian Union before the end of 1947 by short, sharp military operations, despite Pakistan's protests. Kashmir was in the opposite situation, with 77% of its 4,000,000 people Muslim and all its communications running westwards into West Pakistan, but ruled by a Hindu dynasty.

For a time the Hindu ruler played with the idea of full independence, but following an incursion of Muslim tribesmen from West Pakistan in October he hastily opted for India. The Delhi government at once responded by airlifting troops into Srinagar, the capital, which they narrowly saved from the invading Pathan irregulars. For the first months Pakistan was at a distinct disadvantage in the conflict that ensued, since it was unable to commit any regular units from its own army, still in the throes of reorganisation and fully occupied with escorting refugee columns in the Punjab, but over the succeeding 14 months there was a steady escalation in the fighting. The first Pakistani regular units were committed in March, 1948, and by the autumn of that year each side had forces committed amounting to several divisions. Just when full-scale war appeared inevitable, however, in December, 1948 the two sides suddenly agreed to an in-place ceasefire to be supervised by the United Nations which left the wealthier and more populous half of Kashmir in Indian hands. (For details of military operations in Kashmir and elsewhere, see Role, Commitment, Deployment and Recent Operations.)

Three decades later, despite two further rounds of fighting between India and Pakistan, the ceasefire line has not budged, and each country still claims all of Kashmir. UNMOGIP (United Nations Military Observer Group in India and Pakistan) still provides officers to supervise the ceasefire, and the two countries have never ceased to regard each other with intense suspicion. From its very foundation, therefore, the security preoccupation of the Pakistan army has been predetermined. Afghan invasion might be an occasional worry (it was in the early 1960s, and again to some extent since 1973), but Pakistan's main military problem has invariably been defined by the army as Indian military capabilities and intentions.

'The basic difficulty in Indo–Pakistani relations seems to be the very existence of Pakistan', one observer has remarked. If so, Pakistan's military problem was an enormous one, for at Partition India emerged as a State with four times Pakistan's population, ten times its industrial potential, and three times the armed forces. Almost as many Muslims remained in India as ended up in Pakistan, and practically all the processing plants for Pakistan's main cash crops (cotton in the west, jute in the east) ended up on the Indian side of the border. The two halves of Pakistan were separated by a thousand miles of northern India (and East Pakistan was virtually surrounded by Indian territory), while the sea voyage between the wings took 3000 miles and 10 days.

In this extraordinary State, a curious pattern of military perceptions emerged almost at once. East Pakistan, with 42,000,000 people, was far more vulnerable to Indian military action than West Pakistan, which then held 39,000,000. Indeed, it was probably indefensible militarily, but that makes it no less strange that there should have been no attempt to defend it. Until 1971, only one out of (eventually) 15 Pakistan divisions was based in the East. There was virtually no shooting there either in 1948 or in the 1965 war.

All military attention was focused on West Pakistan, where the great bulk of army personnel originated, and where the Kashmir confrontation was a physical fact. Lahore itself is only 15 miles from the Indian border, and the Kashmir ceasefire line follows the 150 mile Grand Trunk Road and railway between Lahore and Rawalpindi, the most important artery in Pakistan, at an average distance of around 50 miles. Given this acute geographical vulnerability and a bitter territorial dispute with a neighbour vastly more powerful than itself, it is scarcely surprising that Pakistan has always lavished unusually great attention on its armed forces. This was certainly reinforced by what might be called the ideological element in Pakistan.

The sole twentieth century parallel for Pakistan — a State created entirely by an idea — is Israel, which emerged only 10 months later. Both States got their opportunity because of the collapse of the long-established British empire, and both were founded against the violent opposition of the dominant population in the region. Both see their survival as threatened by the hostility of those more numerous neighbours, and a large proportion of the populations are refugees from places abroad where they suffered discrimination and violence. So in both States the prestige of the army is high, military affairs attract much attention (reinforced by the experience of recurrent war, in which both Israelis and Pakistanis see themselves always as innocent victims of aggression), and much is spent on the armed forces.

There is even a further parallel in domestic politics. The fundamental political tension in both States has been between those modernists, predominant in the civil service, the economy and the army, whose outlook is basically secular, and the traditionalists whose defence of old values and ways is immeasurably strengthened by the explicitly religious basis of the State. But two great differences stand out between Israel and Pakistan.

One was the lack in the Pakistan of 1947 of any unifying ideology or spirit more comprehensive than religion, for it possessed none of the cultural and even racial unity implied, and to some extent actually present, in the Zionist movement. Though West Pakistanis varied even among themselves, collectively they were as different in culture, temperament and appearance from the Bengalis of East Pakistan as Bavarians are from Portuguese. West Pakistan was six times the size of the East, but in the latter population densities were seven times higher. Geographically the Western Wing belonged to the Middle East, the East to south-east Asia: the West Pakistani villager got around by camel, the East Pakistani by boat. Shared religion was a bond, but Islam is a universalist religion, not the badge of a tightly defined chosen race, and so was a far less suitable definition for the boundaries of a State — especially one with a 1000 mile gap in the middle.

The second great distinction between Pakistan and Israel, which was in large part a consequence of the first, was that the army became increasingly involved in active politics, and was used to enforce the unity that was not instinctively felt. But its perspectives and its personnel were mostly Punjabi, and the consequences were ultimately fatal for the Pakistan of 1947.

Pakistan suffered a grave loss when its founder and only experienced leader, Muhammad Ali Jinnah, died only a year after independence. When his chief lieutenant, Liaquat Ali Khan, the Prime Minister, was assassinated in 1951, there remained no one of sufficient eminence to give the new and disparate country a clear lead. There followed the 'bad years' of 1952–8, when revolving door governments engaged in shady political deals amidst ramifying general corruption. Power lay in the hands of 'parties' that were mere personal followings ever splintering and reforming, and in the hands of influential civil servants. The Muslim League, always less cohesive organisationally than its Congress rival, disintegrated entirely in 1955, and the mere question of making a constitution deadlocked politics in the country for almost a decade. One of the two or three great issues, even then, was whether the federal assembly should be elected according to population (which would give East Pakistan the dominant voice) or whether the two wings should enjoy equal representation; until that issued was decided elections were out of the question.

By 1958 parliamentary democracy, so-called, was utterly discredited (though in fact the parliamentarians were merely the appointed representatives of provincial legislatures, long since dissolved, which had been elected before independence). As early as 1954 the army began to be drawn into politics, when the then Commander-in-Chief, General Ayub Khan, was opted into a Cabinet as Defence Minister after one of the 'civil service coups'. In 1958 the Prime Minister abruptly abrogated the new constitution (which had provided parity of representation between East and West), banned political parties, abolished the legislature, and proclaimed martial law. But he himself was tainted by the prevailing miasma of corruption and intrigue, and a few days later the martial law administrator, General Ayub, removed him and declared himself President.

The coup was efficient, bloodless and certainly popular.

The new cabinet consisted of President Ayub, three other generals and eight non-political civilians. There was a quick, thorough purge of the civil service, in which more junior army officers became directly involved in administering the State for a brief period, but by late 1959 they were almost all back in their contonments. One of Ayub's guiding principles was that the army should concentrate on its professional duties, and not get tangled up in politics any more than absolutely necessary. Martial law prevailed until 1962, when a new constitution was introduced proclaiming 'Basic Democracies', a form of indirect representation. Ayub was duly 'elected' President.

Pakistan's foreign policy was altered scarcely at all by the change of regime, for it had been largely determined by the confrontation with India from the beginning. For the first couple of years after 1947 the country followed a policy of formal non-alignment, seeking in vain to ensure its security through links with the Commonwealth and with other Muslim countries, but crises in 1950 and 1951 in which India concentrated forces on the Punjab border gave even greater urgency to finding an external source to provide the modern weapons Pakistan could not afford. Accordingly, in May, 1954 Pakistan concluded an agreement on military aid with the USA. Shortly afterwards, it joined the two pro-Western alliances in the region, the Baghdad Pact (later CENTO) and SEATO.

From the beginning the Pakistan—American alliance concealed a fundamental (and to some extent deliberate) misunderstanding. The United States was pursuing its policy of containment against what it perceived as a threat of Soviet expansionism, and sought to build up the Pakistani armed forces against that threat. To a lesser extent it sought military facilities on Pakistani territory (until 1968 it shared the use of Peshawar airbase, and until the 1960 incident in which Captain Gary Powers was shot down over Russian territory it flew secret U-2 reconnaissance missions over the Soviet Union from that base). Pakistan, on the other hand, was hardly at all concerned about the Soviet Union, with which it does not even share a common border, and wanted American military aid to assist in expanding and equipping its army to create a military balance within the subcontinent. Each party tactfully ignored the other's purposes. however, and under the 1954 agreement America promised to arm five and a half divisions with modern weapons, of which two would be armoured divisions. The build-up was remarkably prolonged, and the final completion date was eventually set for 1967. A further bilateral treaty with the United States followed in 1959.

The growth of Pakistan's armed forces over the later 1950s did establish a rough military balance in the subcontinent, although India, with its policy of non-alignment, was intensely suspicious of Pakistan's American link. The Indian military attack on the Portuguese colony of Goa in 1960 re-awakened Pakistani anxieties about New Delhi's tendencies towards military expansionism, and led it to begin cultivating relations as well with the People's Republic of China, then entering the bitterest phase of its frontier disputes with India. A further source of Pakistani anxiety about military security was deteriorating relations with Afghanistan (they were broken off completely in 1962) over the latter's claim to the Pathan-inhabited areas of Pakistan's North-West Frontier and Baluchistan provinces, but the most important cause for Islamabad's growing military worry was the 1962 Sino—Indian War.

During that conflict, which was seen at the time in the West as an unprovoked Chinese invasion, American and British military aid flooded into India. This was seen from Pakistan as misplaced sympathy, a poor repayment for its own open adherence to the Western alliance system, and a process which, if continued, would overthrow the military balance it had managed to establish between itself and India. Though Western military aid to India tapered off rapidly after 1962, its place was more than filled by a growing volume of Soviet military aid, as the Sino—Russian cold war came into the region, and the Indian armed forces began to undergo a rapid expansion and re-equipment. By 1965 an acute fear of impending Indian military superiority had gripped the Pakistani government and armed forces.

The trigger for the 1965 war was once again Kashmir. In December, 1964 the Indian government abolished the special status it had granted in 1950 to the zone of Kashmir under its occupation, and it became effectively just one more Indian State. The original Indian promise of a plebiscite amongst the predominantly Muslim population had never been honoured, and New Delhi's move was seen in Islamabad as an attempt to close the question of Kashmir once and for all as an international issue. Coupled with Pakistan's anxieties about India's growing armed forces (and at the same time its knowledge that a substantial proportion of them would be pinned down on the Himalayan frontier, and that the Chinese forces there would deter any Indian attack on East Pakistan), the Kashmir developments caused Islamabad to have recourse to military means to prevent the final incorporation of the State within India.

It is doubtful if Pakistan initially intended to wage full-scale regular warfare over the issue, but its introduction of guerrillas into the Indian-controlled sector of Kashmir in an attempt to stimulate a general revolt there in August, 1965 led to a rapid succession of counter-moves that transferred the focus of the fighting southwards to the Punjab border. There, in September, 1965 India and Pakistan fought a 22 day war involving the greater part of their regular armed forces and causing around 10,000 casualties. (For details, *see* Role, Commitment, Deployment and Recent Operations.) Neither side gained a decisive advantage, and on September 22nd, they both accepted a United Nations truce proposal. At Tashkent in the Soviet Union on January 10th, 1966 President Ayub Khan and Prime Minister Lal Bahadur Shastri of India signed an agreement for the exchange of prisoners and the mutual evacuation of territories seized during the fighting.

During the fighting Britain and America imposed an embargo on arms deliveries to both combatants, despite Pakistan's status as an ally of the latter. The British arms embargo was lifted in 1966, but the American ban on arms deliveries, except for spare parts, was maintained until 1975. This did not cause India any major difficulties, as its principal arms supplier was rapidly becoming the Soviet Union in any case, but for Pakistan it was a most serious matter. (Though in 1965, as again in 1971, it did receive some assistance in circumventing the United States embargo from the sympathetic Muslim States of Turkey, Iran and Indonesia). Much of the gap was filled by Chinese military aid, including tanks, combat aircraft, and enough equipment for about three divisions, on extremely favourable sale terms, but Pakistan was also forced to begin spending scarce foreign exchange on commercial arms purchases from France.

There was no immediate domestic reaction in Pakistan after the 1965 war, but when the military regime made the grave error of organising large-scale celebrations on its 10th anniversary in 1968 it released a wave of pent-up resentment at the autocracy, corruption and nepotism that had flourished increasingly in Ayub Khan's later years as President. Students and religious elements, followed by urban workers and even peasants (especially in the East) took part in a mounting wave of agitation and demonstrations. President Ayub Khan

made concession after concession, but could not quell the popular unrest or restore law and order. Within weeks he was compelled to resign by General Agha Muhammad Yahya Khan, his successor as Commander-in-Chief of the Army, who became President and reinstated martial law. His avowed (and apparently genuine) intention was to withdraw the army from politics and return the country to parliamentary, democratic rule. It was a decision that brought on the ultimate catastrophe for a united Pakistan.

Under Yahya Khan the 'Basic Democracies' were abandoned, and elections for a new Assembly were called. In deference to the intense resentment in East Pakistan at the way in which the West had dominated and exploited the more populous wing of the country, especially since the 1958 coup, it was decided that seats in the new Assembly should not be allocated on a basis of parity between the two wings, but in direct relation to the population of the country's main regions. (For further details on the growth of seccessionist sentiment in East Pakistan, and the army's role in that phenomenon, see the entry on Bangladesh.) This decision meant that East Pakistan would control 56% of the seats in the Assembly.

Pakistan's first ever federal general election was held in December, 1970. The Pakistan People's Party headed by Mr. Zulfiqar Ali Bhutto (who first came to prominence as Ayub Khan's Foreign Minister) swept the heavily populated areas of West Pakistan, but Shaikh Mujibur Rahman's Awami League won an even more total victory in the East.

The Awami League won 288 out of 300 seats for the Provincial Assembly; much more importantly, it won all but two of West Pakistan's 162 seats in the National Assembly (303 seats). Shaikh Majibur Rahman thereby gained the right to become Prime Minister and to enact his Six Point programme, embodying an extreme form of provincial autonomy and decentralisation and leaving only defence and foreign affairs to the federal government. Most Punjabis saw this programme as treasonable, and President Yahya Khan, with the encouragement of Mr. Bhutto, refused to convene the National Assembly until the Awami League modified its radical proposals for constitutional change.

In March negotiations broke down, and the Awami League then forced the issue by seizing effective power in the eastern wing following a general strike by the local police and civil service. On March 26th, 1971 the independence of Bangladesh was declared in Dacca, but the Indian support which was its only hope of success was not immediately forthcoming. Many of the Bengali troops in the single resident army division also supported the new State, but Islamabad had by then begun moving in three further divisions from the West, arrested Shaikh Mujib, and began a programme of vigorous repression. With the aid of the Razakars (a force of irregulars raised mostly from amongst the non-Bengali Muslim minority in East Pakistan) the army in the East embarked on systematic terror which seemed to be aimed at little short of the extermination of the Bengali political *élite* (and, incidentally, of the Hindu minority). By the time international war ended the army's efforts to maintain control of the East, in December of that year, an estimated 10,000,000 East Pakistanis — about a sixth of the population, including about half of the Hindu minority — had fled across the frontier to refugee camps in India.

The probability of Indian intervention in East Pakistan was great, both because of the eventually intolerable burden of refugees from the Pakistan army's operations in the East and because it presented Delhi with a once-in-a-lifetime chance to dismember its great rival in the subcontinent. Pakistan sought a Chinese guarantee (Mr. Bhutto went to Peking in November, when the crisis was reaching its peak), but China's attitude was more reserved than in 1962 or 1965. India, on the other hand, got wholehearted Russian support (a 20 year Indo—Soviet Treaty of Peace, Friendship and Co-operation was signed in August), and for months before December was arming, supporting and assisting large East Bengali guerrilla forces to operate across the border. The USA sought to prevent at least the dismemberment of West Pakistan, which it believed India to be considering at the time, and if possible to persuade the Pakistani government to grant autonomy and seek a peaceful settlement in the East. Washington believed it had got President Yahya's consent to this in November, and so informed New Delhi, but Indian forces struck in the East on December 4th.

The war lasted only 13 days in the East, concluding with a total debacle for the Pakistani forces and leaving 85,000 Pakistani troops as prisoners of war in Indian hands. Fighting in the West was also intense, with Pakistani forces at first on the offensive, but they gained little ground in the Punjab and Kashmir areas, and later suffered considerable territorial losses further south. With the surrender of Pakistan's forces in the East and the independence of Bangladesh, which at once got world recognition, large Indian forces became available for transfer to the Western front, and Pakistan concluded an armistice before the balance of forces there turned overwhelmingly against it. (For details on the 1971 war, see Role, Commitment, Deployment and Recent Operations.) Pakistan plummeted abruptly from a formidable rival to India and the fifth most populous State in the world, to a rump-State with only a tenth of India's population and approximately proportionate military and diplomatic leverage.

The speed with which Pakistan has reconciled itself to its losses and recovered its equilibrium is remarkable, however. Its economy quickly readjusted, and judgement against those responsible for Islamabad's blunders and the reconstruction of a semi-democratic political system were completed in little more than a year. Moreover, Pakistan has already rebuilt its military forces to a size larger than in 1971, though possessing less than half the previous population and a narrower economic base.

President Yahya Khan was dismissed from politics amidst universal execration, and Shaikh Mujibur Rahman was released from prison and allowed to go to Bangladesh one month after the war's end. Mr. Bhutto took over as Prime Minister, and the National Assembly met (less the members from the East) to agree a constitution setting up a federal, parliamentary system. Bhutto sought *rapprochement* with India, concluding the Simla Agreement for the withdrawal of both Pakistani and Indian troops from occupied areas along the common border in July, 1972. A further agreement in August, 1973 provided for a three-way repatriation of all prisoners of war held in India, Pakistan and Bangladesh, and in February, 1974 Pakistan formally recognised Bangladesh. In June, 1974 Mr. Bhutto paid his first state visit to Dacca.

Pakistan left the British Commonwealth in early 1972, in dissatisfaction with Britain's studiously neutral attitude during the 1971 war, and it also withdrew from SEATO within a short time of Mr. Bhutto's coming to power. However it has continued as an active member of CENTO and also maintains close bilateral relations with Saudi Arabia and the Gulf States, for whom it constitutes a major source of important military and civilian technical expertise.

Formal *détente* with India has continued: India and Pakistan again exchanged ambassadors in July, 1976 after a gap since 1971, and in September air and rail links between the two countries were restored for the first time since 1965. Since 1973, however, security preoccupations have re-emerged to plague Islamabad. On the one flank, the revolu-

tion in Afghanistan in that year brought back to power Muhammad Daud, the most ardent Afghan proponent of the Pakhtunistan State which would involve autonomy or independence for the Pathan areas of the North-West Frontier and Baluchistan, and Daud's overthrow in April, 1978 by a communist coup has further intensified Pakistani anxiety. Afghanistan is now a far more formidable military proposition than it was during the 1950s, and even short of direct conflict is in a position to lend aid and encouragement to the turbulent and anti-authoritarian tribes of the border regions. This has played at least some part in the persistent low-level insurgency Islamabad has had to contend with in Baluchistan since 1973, and in more sporadic upheavals in the North-West Frontier Province. As a result Mr. Bhutto banned Pakistan's main opposition party, the National Awami Party, in February, 1975. (Its strength was centred in those two provinces, where it formed the provincial governments until dismissed by Islamabad, and it was accused by the central government of autonomist and even secessionist tendencies.) The continuing troubles also led to the re-emergence of that quaint old British custom on the Frontier: local administration by fighter—bomber, with some recalcitrant tribes being disciplined by air raids on their villages (see Role, Commitment, Deployment and Recent Operations).

Pakistan discerns an even more serious threat in the Indian nuclear test of May, 1974 which it fears may portend the eventual development of Indian nuclear weapons despite New Delhi's vehement assurances to the contrary. It has given rise to a determination in Pakistan to obtain at least an option on nuclear weapons of its own, and the danger of nuclear proliferation thus created was a principal factor in the USA finally lifting its arms embargo on Pakistan in late 1975. Really large purchases of American arms, however, seem to be closely linked to a Pakistani commitment to forego this nuclear weapons option, so the situation remains unclear.

Between 1971 and 1977 the Pakistan army abstained from political involvement, both officers and civilians having learned some salutary lessons about its disadvantages in the period immediately preceding. Its personnel continue to be predominantly Punjabi (and to a lesser extent Pathan), but this now more closely reflects the character of the civilian population, as in post-1971 Pakistan Punjabis alone constitute over 60% of the population. The army's primary commitments continue to be to the maintenance of military forces of a size and efficiency adequate to deter any Indian pressures, and to the physical integrity of (former West) Pakistan.

Allegations of widespread vote-rigging in the March, 1977 national elections by the ruling Pakistan People's Party, however, led to the emergence of a coalition of all the opposition parties as the Pakistan National Alliance, and a prolonged period of violent rioting and civil disobedience campaigns in all of Pakistan's main cities. When Prime Minister Zulfiqar Ali Bhutto and the opposition alliance finally failed to agree on the terms for a new election in October, 1977 to resolve the crisis, the Pakistan armed forces intervened on July 5th under the leadership of the Army Chief, General Zia ul-Haq, to forestall open civil war. The armed forces' original intention was to supervise the October, 1977 elections and then return to its barracks, but Mr. Bhutto was subsequently placed on trial for murder and the elections postponed. In March, 1979 Pakistan was still under military rule.

STRENGTH AND BUDGET

The strength of Pakistan's armed forces is 478,600 men. Within this total, army strength is 450,000, including 29,000

Azad Kashmir troops. Navy strength is 11,000 men and air force strength is 17,600 men. The army's trained reserves are approximately half a million strong, while naval reserves number 5000 men and air force reserves 8000 men.

There are paramilitary forces totalling 109,100, consisting of 65,000 Frontier Corps, 15,000 Pakistan Rangers, 2000 Coastguard, 5100 Frontier Constabulary and 22,000 National Guard. The 25,000-strong Federal Security Forces, created by Mr. Bhutto in 1973, were disbanded by the martial law authorities in November, 1977 on the ground that they had been used by Bhutto as a personal instrument of repression and political intimidation (most of the members have been absorbed into the civil police force). In addition, there are four voluntary organisations which function as a form of home guard and second line defence (*see* Recruitment, Training and Reserves).

The defence budget for 1981 was $18,200,000,000. This represents approximately 7% of the GNP.

Pakistan's armed forces are actually larger numerically than they were in 1971, before the more populous half of the country was lost. Both in manpower and in defence expenditure Pakistan's military effort is about 40% of that of India, though the latter State has nine times Pakistan's population and GNP. The population of Pakistan is 88,950,000 (excluding Afghan refugees.)

COMMAND AND CONSTITUTIONAL STATUS

By the Federal Constitution adopted in April, 1973 the President is Head of State, but the advice of the Prime Minister, answerable together with his Cabinet to the Federal Legislature, is binding in all circumstances. The Prime Minister is automatically Defence Minister as well, and in time of war exercises Supreme Command over the armed forces.

The Higher Defence Organisation of Pakistan was reorganised in 1975, in the light of the experience of military catastrophe in 1971. It was brought into effect on March 1st, 1976 when General Muhammad Shariff assumed office as First Chairman, Joint Chiefs of Staff Committee (JCSC), a post which supersedes the old office of Commander-in-Chief. The general reorganisation rationalised a series of changes which had already seen the creation of a separate Defence Production Division within the Defence Department, the transfer of Naval Headquarters to the capital and preliminary arrangements to move Air Headquarters there as well, and the promotion of the Chief of Naval Staff and the Chief of Air Staff to the same rank as the Chief of Army Staff, to allow the three services equal say in defence planning. The structure is as follows.

As Minister of Defence, the Prime Minister is assisted by a Minister of State for Defence, who in addition to any duties particularly delegated to him, is responsible for military preparedness, defence planning, civil defence and the defence industries. The Defence Ministry's permanent head is the Secretary-General (Defence), who sits *ex officio* on the Defence Committee of the Cabinet and the Defence Council. The Defence Ministry is made up of the Defence Division, Defence Production Division, the Joint Chiefs of Staff Committee, and the three Service Headquarters (now all physically and administratively contained within the Ministry).

The supreme political authority in defence matters in Pakistan is the Defence Committee of the Cabinet (DCC), chaired by the Prime Minister, and including as permanent members of the Ministers of State for Defence and Foreign Affairs, the Ministers of Finance, the Interior, States and Frontier Regions, Kashmir Affairs, Information and Broadcasts, Communications, Commerce, Industries and Production. The Chairman of the JCSC, the three Chiefs of Staff, the Secretaries-General of Defence and Finance and the Secretaries of Defence, Foreign Affairs and Finance are also in attendance. The DCC's responsibility is to determine general strategic and defence policy and force goals, coordinate them with the actions of other Ministries, and to supervise the conduct of war. Executive supervision of military policy is carried out by a narrower body, the Defence Council, consisting of the Prime Minister, the Ministers of State for Defence and Foreign Affairs, the Minister of Finance, and the same soldiers and civil servants as attend the DCC. The Defence Council is also in direct charge of policy for the development of Pakistan's arms industry.

The highest military body is the JCSC, whose Chairman in wartime would also serve as Principal Staff Officer to the Prime Minister, and exercise such authority over the conduct of operations as was delegated to him by the latter. His term of office is normally 3 years, and he may be selected from any Service. Other members of the Committee are the three Service Chiefs of Staff, and the Secretary of the Defence Division. Beyond strategic and logistical matters, the JCSC is responsible for generating proposals on force size and structure, and advising the government on strategic communications, the siting and dispersion of major industries, and industrial mobilisation plans. The Secretariat of the JCSC is an inter-Service body organised into eight Directorates, of which the more important are (A) Operations/Plans, (B) Training, (E) Logistics and (G) Personnel.

The individual Service Chiefs of Staff continue to exercise command functions over their respective services through their Headquarters within the Ministry, and to have the right of direct access to the Prime Minister as Military Advisors.

It is difficult to assess how much of this formal structure has been functioning since the military coup of July 5th, 1977. General Muhammad Zia ul-Haq, the Army Chief of Staff, is Chief Martial Law Administrator; immediately after the coup he appointed a four-man military council led by himself to assist President Chaudhury in administering the country until the promised October elections. The other members were General M. Shariff, Chairman of the Joint Chiefs of Staff Committee; Admiral Muhammad Shariff, Navy Chief of Staff, and Air Marshal Zulfikar Ali Khan, Air Force Chief of Staff. After the indefinite postponement of those elections, this military council appointed an advisory council subordinate to itself, whose 16 members (generals, senior civil servants and a few retired politicians) act as departmental ministers. General Zia himself retained the posts of Chief Martial Law Administrator (presumably corresponding to that of Prime Minister in the above-described administrative structure), plus the portfolios of Defence, Defence Production, Information and Broadcasting, Atomic Energy and seven others. Other senior armed forces officers hold the portfolios of Interior, National Security, Industries and Production, Petroleum and Natural Resources, Kashmir Affairs, and States and Frontier Regions, so most of the committees listed above effectively consisted of the armed forces talking to themselves.

ROLE, COMMITMENT, DEPLOYMENT AND RECENT OPERATIONS

Role, Commitment and Deployment

The principal role of the Pakistan army continues to be the defence of Pakistan against India, a task considerably simplified militarily by the loss of the virtually indefensible eastern half of the country in 1971. Pakistan also recognises the possibility of a military threat from its opposite border with Afghanistan, however, and if it indulges in 'worst-case' contingency planning (as it almost certainly does) must allow for the improbable but daunting contingency of a co-ordinated attack and a two-front war. In such a case, it would have to place its hope for survival in a military intervention by China to draw off the weight of the Indian armed forces.

The army has also been used repeatedly in internal security operations, most notably in the savage war of repression it fought against Bengali nationalists in what was then East Pakistan between March and December of 1971. More recently, it has been employed in fighting guerrillas in Baluchistan, the empty south-western province of Pakistan, and in less continuous operations against insurgents in the North-West Frontier Province.

Pakistan is still formally linked to the USA by a military assistance agreement, and it remains a member of CENTO in alliance with Turkey, Britain and the USA. It has no specific commitments to lend aid beyond its own borders, however, and no Pakistani troops are deployed outside the country.

Recent Operations

1948

The Pakistan army fought its first war within 8 months of its creation, in the State of Kashmir which was disputed between India and Pakistan. Due to the chaotic conditions in the refugee-thronged Punjab and the rudimentary state of organisation of the new armed forces, however, the regular army did not participate in the first (and as it turned out, decisive) round of fighting in Kashmir.

The troubles in Kashmir, then still a Princely State, began in July, 1947 when the Ruler enlarged his army, which was almost exclusively Hindu and Sikh despite a predominantly Muslim population, and moved it towards the Punjab boundary. Muslim civilians there were ordered to surrender their privately held arms, and this was answered in Poonch province in September by a peasants' revolt which quickly overthrew the Ruler's control. That in turn contributed (together with the massacres in the neighbouring Punjab) to the outbreak of systematic anti-Muslim pogroms in Jammu, the southernmost part of the State and the only region with a Hindu majority. During the succeeding 11 weeks virtually the entire Muslim element of the population there, some half a million people, were killed or fled to the Western (Pakistani) Punjab.

With the connivance of at least some senior officials in the new Pakistani government, Pathan tribesmen from the frontier were transported to the borders of Kashmir, arriving there on October 19th. Their initial attack was badly mismanaged, many Muslims as well as Hindus being killed as they paused to loot on their way to the State's most important region, the Vale of Kashmir, but within a week they were approaching the outskirts of the capital, Srinagar. The Ruler fled, declaring his accession to the Indian Union as he did so, and airlifted Indian troops arrived in Srinagar on October 27th just in time to save the city. They then counter-attacked and drove the tribesmen back for a considerable distance.

Mr. Jinnah ordered the Pakistan army into Kashmir on October 27th, but his acting Commander-in-Chief, General Sir Douglas Gracey, refused to obey. After consulting with Field Marshal Auchinleck, officially Supreme Commander of both armies during the partition period, he pointed out that such a move, which would inevitably mean conflict with the Indian army (also then under a British Commander-in-Chief) would cause the instant withdrawal of all the British officers in the Pakistan army. Recognising that the Pakistan army could not do without British officers at that stage (and recognising also, perhaps, that it would probably lose in a confrontation with the Indian army, which was much larger, had numbers of all-Hindu units undisturbed by the uproar of partition, and enjoyed ample supplies of munitions, while Pakistan's share was being withheld by New Delhi), Mr. Jinnah withdrew his order. During the succeeding months he made do with supplying arms and other aid to the Pakistan fighters and the Azad ('free') Kashmir irregulars, who dated from the time of the Poonch revolt, and included large numbers of ex-soldiers. The fighting continued as a battle of attrition along a fairly stable front over the winter.

With the coming of spring and a major Indian build-up of forces in Kashmir, the first few Pakistan army units were sent into Kashmir in March, 1948. In response to a two-division Indian attack in May, which got within 18 miles of the Azad Kashmir capital of Muzaffarabad, much larger Pakistan regular forces were committed to battle (with the private approval of General Gracey). Reinforcements on both sides continued over the summer, and a further strong Indian offensive in October in Poonch province gained much ground, causing a large new wave of Muslim refugees. Pakistan's response was boldly to pull out most of its forces in the Punjab plains guarding Lahore, leaving its largest city only lightly guarded, and to move them into positions for a possible decisive counter-attack Indian communications in Poonch, the sole land link with Indian forces in the Vale of Kashmir. The attack never came, though, perhaps because of fear of an Indian counter-thrust against Lahore, and a ceasefire was suddenly agreed at the end of 1948. The positions held by the two armies in Kashmir have hardly changed at all since that time, and have gradually hardened into a *de facto* international frontier.

1965

The 1965 war was in large part a replay of the 1948 conflict with much greater forces, the military phase being initiated once again by Pakistani concern over the growing assimilation of Kashmir into India, an attempt to reverse the trend by the introduction of irregulars, and rapid escalation to the use of regular forces. After an initial border clash in April in the Rann of Kutch, a worthless area of salt desert well to the south of the Punjab, in which Pakistan came off best, the actual hostilities in Kashmir were initiated in August by the introduction of several thousand Islamabad-backed irregulars who, it was hoped, would trigger an anti-Indian rising amongst the overwhelmingly Muslim population of the Vale. The Indian army easily contained these incursions, however, and its counter-measures included several crossings of the ceasefire line and the seizure of strategic positions in Azad Kashmir.

Full-scale operations began on September 1st with a Pakistani attack by two brigades supported by tanks at Chhamb, at the extreme south-west of the ceasefire line, in an attempt to cut one of the two roads which were vital to the whole 150,000-man Indian garrison in Kashmir. It made significant progress, and the Indians expected it to be followed by a second thrust in Jammu to cut the only other road supporting their Kashmir positions. As Mr. Nehru had previously warned Pakistan, New Delhi's response was to launch an all-out attack on the Punjab border. It began on September 6th, with a three-pronged advance on Lahore, followed the next day by a second offensive against Sialkot, an important road and railway centre 50 miles to the north. By September 8th fighting had spread along a 1200 mile front, with an Indian advance underway as well in the uninhabited deserts of the Sind—Rajasthan border region 400 miles south of the Punjab.

At the outbreak of hostilities, it was estimated, there were eight (larger) Indian divisions on the West Pakistan border, plus three in Kashmir, against a total of seven divisions in

West Pakistan. There were another six Indian divisions stationed in the Himalayas and containing East Pakistan (where hardly any fighting occurred, probably due to the possibility of a Chinese reaction to an Indian attack there), and at least some of these forces were later brought west. In armoured forces the two sides were approximately equal, and India enjoyed air superiority at least in numbers. In the circumstances it is surprising that Pakistan should have felt any optimism, but it was misled by a certain conviction of the innate superiority of its own Muslim forces, and by a serious underestimation of the degree to which the Indian forces had already improved since their 1962 disaster at the hands of the Chinese. Far from being concerned at the possible outcome of a war with India, Field Marshal Ayub Khan, who personally directed Pakistan's military operations, had been known to boast that his tanks could reach New Delhi along the Grand Trunk Road (a distance of some 200 miles) in a matter of hours.

During the next 17 days the fighting was extremely heavy in the Punjab, but no decisive results were gained by either side. The Indian drive on Lahore got to within 5 miles of the city in places, but was effectively halted by the Pakistan action of blowing some 70 bridges across the BRB canal just east of the city. The main Pakistani counter-attack was made by their First Armoured Division south of Lahore, with the intention of swinging round behind the Indian forces and cutting the Grand Trunk Road east of Amritsar, but it was stopped by Indian forces just across the border. The second main Indian attack, which led to large and sustained tank battles over a period of a week, was made by the Indian First Armoured Division around Sialkot, and countered mainly by the Pakistan Sixth Armoured Division. At the ceasefire Indian forces were still fighting on the BRB canal east of Lahore, and the city of Sialkot was partly enveloped, but neither army was at the end of its strength. There were no major air raids on urban areas, and the Pakistanis generally got the best of the air battles with their superior aircraft.

At the end of the war India controlled about 720 square miles of Pakistani territory, most of it in the Punjab, while Pakistan held around 300 square miles of Indian territory of which most was empty Rajasthan desert. (The occupied territories were evacuated by the terms of the Tashkent agreement of January, 1966.) Indian casualties were estimated at 4000–6000, with up to 300 tanks and around 70 aircraft destroyed; Pakistani casualties numbered around 3000–5000, with about 250 tanks and 20 aircraft destroyed. Nevertheless, by the end of the fighting the Pakistan army was hurting badly; most of important terrain lost had been Pakistani, and ammunition was beginning to run low, while fresh Indian forces were arriving on the scene. At lower ranks both sides had fought bravely, though sometimes displaying a certain awkwardness in the use of advanced items of weaponry; it was generally agreed by outside observers that Indian commanders had displayed somewhat more imagination and flexibility in their tactics. One unarguable consequence of the war was to fix even more firmly the popular conviction in Pakistan that India's ultimate political purpose was the destruction of the country.

1971

The 1971 war was an unmitigated disaster for Pakistan, and a humiliating defeat for its army. It not only lost in areas where victory was not to be expected (i.e. East Pakistan), but it failed to do even as well as it should have done.

Once the declaration of Bangladesh independence was made in March, 1971 and the Pakistan army in the eastern wing of the country began its savage campaign of repression,

the fate of united Pakistan was effectively sealed. Even given the acute need for troops in the East to contain Bengali nationalism, Islamabad could not afford to weaken West Pakistan's defences in the general war with India which would, as President Yahya Khan announced in the autumn, be the certain consequence of Indian armed intervention in the Bengali province. That meant that General Niazi, the Pakistani commander in the East, had only four divisions plus about 20,000 irregulars, a total of some 93,000 men, and 23 aged jet fighters to defend 1400 miles of border and to contain the ever-swelling guerrilla forces operating within East Pakistan.

It is unquestionable, however, that his own tactics before the war increased the magnitude of his problem. From March onwards there was virtual civil war in the East, with Bengali villagers massacring the so-called 'Biharis' (non-Bengali-speaking Muslims who had come from India at Partition and were mostly loyal to a united Pakistan), and the Biharis in turn being organised into irregular units called Razakars by the Pakistan army to return this treatment with interest. The millions of refugees who fled to India constituted the raw material from which various guerrilla forces were created and armed by the Indian government, notably the Mukhti Bahini (People's Liberation Army), and sent back into East Pakistan to tie down Pakistan army forces. The most appalling slaughter took place during this phase of irregular fighting before the Indian invasion, with estimates of dead (mostly Bengali-speakers, and particularly Hindus) ranging from 300,000 to 1,500,000.

Pakistan's strategy, such as it was, took the form of a plan to launch a pre-emptive attack in the Punjab when the Indian invasion of East Pakistan seemed ready to proceed at last. There was plenty of notice of this, as Indian forces were gradually built up on East Pakistan's frontiers and border crossings by Indian regular troops became more frequent (the first occurred as early as October 27th). The final indication was given by the shift of four out of the ten Indian divisions on the Himalayan frontier to the East Pakistan border (the Himalayan passes were closed by snow at least until March, so no direct Chinese intervention would have been possible even if Peking had wished it).

Accordingly, Pakistan launched a co-ordinated series of air strikes on military airfields in north-west India at dusk on December 3rd, in emulation of Israeli tactics in 1967. After some delay, these were followed by a strong ground offensive in southern Kashmir and the northern Punjab. The Indians had also studied the 1967 war, however, and their aircraft were mostly well protected or dispersed. The following morning, December 4th, they invaded East Pakistan with about eight divisions – some 160,000 men – accompanied by perhaps 50,000 Mukhti Bahini.

All Pakistani air strength in the East was immobilised at once by an Indian raid that put the only jet runway out of commission, and the Indian advance, crossing the whole length of the frontier in more than 20 columns, advanced rapidly against weak opposition. General Niazi, recognising the impossibility of holding the frontier, had deployed his forces in defensive groups protecting the main towns and river crossings. The terrain was ideal for prolonged defence, but Indian forces avoided frontal assaults and moved round his positions in rapid flanking manoeuvres, assisted by an imaginative use of helicopters and paratroops. Position after position was abandoned by its Pakistani garrisons, but Indian forces reached the two main rivers – the fall-back Pakistani defensive line – before the bulk of the Pakistani defenders.

Cut off in a hostile countryside, with no possibility of reinforcements and no good news from the Western theatre of war, the Pakistan army's morale in the East began to crumble rapidly. Although the outcome of the campaign was a foregone conclusion after the first week, General Niazi's largely undamaged forces could have held on in Dacca and other strong defensive positions for weeks, perhaps months. But their will to fight had vanished, and General Niazi surrendered his whole force in Dacca on December 16th, only 13 days after the invasion and begun. Approximately 85,000 Pakistan army officers and troops became Indian prisoners of war.

The absence of any counterbalancing Pakistani successes in the West was in part a reflection of the way the military balance in the subcontinent had swung against Pakistan since the Indian army's reorganisation and expansion, begun after 1962, had been completed. While maintaining forces on the Chinese frontier and employing a 2:1 superiority against Pakistan's forces in the East, India was also able to provide a 3:2 superiority in troops in the West, and almost 2:1 in tanks (1270 for India against 700 for Pakistan). Indian air superiority was complete- in the East and almost 2:1 in the West, while at sea the Indian navy was hardly challenged at all.

As a result, Pakistan's initial armoured thrusts in southern Kashmir and the Punjab were halted almost at once, and a costly war of attrition ensued along the border. Further south in the Sind Desert the Indian army captured about 2750 square miles of territory, useful for post-war bargaining purposes, whereas the Pakistan army ended the war holding a mere 50 square miles of Indian territory. The much smaller Pakistan navy suffered severe losses (22 vessels) at the hands of the Indian navy, which lost only one ship, and the concentration of the Pakistan air force over the Punjab battlefields and in the air defence of Islamabad left large Pakistani cities like Karachi open to punishing air raids. The military situation was already becoming extremely serious for Pakistan in the West on December 16th when its forces in East Pakistan surrendered, raising the prospect that Indian forces could now be concentrated in the West. President Yahya Khan agreed on December 17th to the ceasefire which India had already announced, and was placed under house arrest the same day. Pakistani losses in the war, quite apart from the immense bag of prisoners taken by India in the East, were around twice those of the Indians.

An American carrier task force was deployed in the Bay of Bengal during the war in an attempt to moderate India's actions, but it was clear to all that this was entirely bluff, and that the USA would not contemplate the use of military force against India under any conceivable circumstances. Neither did China offer Pakistan anything more than commiserations. India, on the other hand, received the enthusiastic support of the Soviet Union, and demonstrated the transformation in its military strength that had been accomplished in the preceding 8 years by the programme of armed forces reorganisation and the creation of its own defence industries. The 1971 war did not create a radically new military balance in the subcontinent; it gave proof of one that had already come into existence.

Pakistan at once set about the lengthy process of rebuilding its military strength, but it also recognised that the disaster had been made more complete by a high degree of incompetence in the senior ranks of the army, caused in part by their pre-occupation with politics and consequent abandonment of their military duties. The 1976 White Paper on the Higher Organisation of Defence was scathing in its criticisms of the defence organisation prevailing in 1971: 'The defence policy had virtually become the responsibility of one man and his coterie . . . . The system of control and direction of the armed forces was a hodge-podge of colonial and totali-

tarian features . . . . The Defence Ministry itself was no more than a routine co-ordinating agency.'

There were, the White Paper revealed, no joint army—air or navy—air plans; there was not even a regular system of consultation between the services. All power had become concentrated in the General Headquarters (army), which was the base of operations of the Commander-in-Chief and Chief Martial Law Administrator, President Yahya Khan, and inter-service communications were so bad that the Chief of Naval Staff only heard of the outbreak of war through a radio news bulletin. The Army Chief of Staff had spent several days trying in vain to get in touch with the Commander-in-Chief before the initial Pakistani air strikes in the West, and stated later that he had 'not the faintest idea' what strategy his superior intended the army to follow them up with. 'The logical outcome of this state of affairs,' concluded the White Paper, 'was the whimsical, unplanned, partial and ill-fitting measures that were resorted to in the 1971 war and which resulted in the loss of half the country.'

It remains to be said only that martial law is the canker of armies, and that the Pakistan army by 1971 had been through three martial laws. There is little doubt that the glaring defects revealed in 1971 have since received close attention (the reorganisation of the higher command structure is detailed under Command and Constitutional Status). There is now once again martial law in Pakistan, however.

Internal Security Operations Post-1971
There were sporadic rebellions against the central government between 1958 and 1967 in the south-western province of Baluchistan, an extremely backward, mainly tribal area the size of Italy, but with only 2,500,000 people. The Baluchis are a distinct people, who also live across the border in south-eastern Iran and southern Afghanistan, and their leaders have always sought a wider autonomy within Pakistan from what they see as Punjabi control. Like the Pathans further north in North-West Frontier Province, their main political organisation since before Pakistan's independence has been a party now known as the National Awami Party (NAP).

The NAP, long banned, was legalised by Mr. Bhutto in early 1972, and formed the provincial government in both provinces following the elections later that year. The central government's suspicions about is eventual political purposes were soon reawakened, however, and the NAP was soon being accused by Bhutto of propagating the seditious notion that there were 'four or five nations' within Pakistan. The central authorities also concurred with Pakistan's neighbour, Iran, in seeing Baluchi nationalism as part of a complex conspiracy headed by India, the Soviet Union and Iraq to dismember Pakistan, merge the North-West Frontier Province with Afghanistan, and create an independent Baluchistan, thereby providing a pro-Soviet corridor to the Indian Ocean.

The pretext for moving against the NAP governments in the two provinces was provided by the 'discovery', on February 10th, 1973 of a huge cache of Soviet arms allegedly destined for Baluchistan in the Iraqi Embassy in Islamabad. There are strong grounds for believing that they were planted there with the complicity of the Pakistan authorities. Two days later President Bhutto dismissed the coalition government formed by the NAP in Baluchistan and removed the NAP governor of North-West Frontier Province (the coalition government there resigned in protest). Thereupon elements of the Bizenjo, Marri and Mengal tribes who had provided the backbone of political support for the NAP embarked on a guerrilla campaign in Baluchistan. The coup in Afghanistan later in the year, leading to the revival of the Afghan campaign in support of Pakhtunistan, caused further anxiety in Islamabad, and by the end of 1973 substantial

Pakistan army elements had been committed to the fighting in Baluchistan.

For the first year of the fighting, which began seriously in May of 1973, the army was largely on the defensive suffering serious losses in ambushes and unable to prevent frequent bomb explosions even in Quetta, the provincial capital. By early 1974, however, Pakistan army strength in Baluchistan had risen to about 50,000–60,000 troops, and reliable reports state that 25 Chinook helicopters provided by Tehran, complete with Iranian pilots, were also based in Quetta for use in the counter-insurgency operations. (Iran, with its own Baluchi minority across the border, took the revolt extremely seriously from the first.) In May, 1974 the government launched the first of the 'encirclement and suppression' operations, codenamed the Chamalang Campaign, and by the end of the year had succeeded in pushing the guerrillas out of the lowlands back into three mountainous areas, the tribal strongholds of the three major insurgent tribes.

The fighting then continued at a lower intensity, with up to 20,000 Baluchi guerrillas associated with the NAP or the more explicitly Marxist Baluch People's Liberation Front holding out in three mountainous areas east and south of Quetta: Marri-Bugti, Sarawan and Jhalawan. All main routes were guarded by blockhouses, towns were heavily garrisoned, and in the most affected areas much of the civilian population were resettled in so-called 'people's colonies' which, despite the army's denials, closely resemble the 'strategic villages' of classic counter-insurgency theory. Bhutto made no political moves towards reconciliation (the NAP was banned nationally in February, 1975 and its main civilian leaders arrested), and the federal forces were not successful in rooting out the hard core of the guerrilla units in the interior of their mountain strongholds.

In October, 1976 a Government White Paper stated that the Baluchistan rebellion had collapsed, with the surrender of 5500 rebel tribesmen, but this seems an excessively optimistic assessment. The casualty figures provided by the government — 385 killed in the preceding year, of whom 144 were members of the security forces — likewise seem improbably low. Reliable private Pakistani sources put Pakistan army dead and wounded since 1973 at between 3000 and 6000 men.

In the North-West Frontier Province disorders have been more sporadic and isolated, but nevertheless persistent. In September, 1976 there were reports that up to two divisions were used in Dir State in the tribal regions, in conjunction with the Pakistan air force, in a 10 day military operation which killed between 300 and 600 rebels and civilians. The following month tanks and aircraft were used to flatten the village of Wana, where tribesmen had been resisting army attempts to build a strategic road in the area.

Through these problems in the disaffected regions of the two western provinces were a steady drain on the army's resources and a thorn in the government's side, they were not in themselves a threat to the country's integrity. In Baluchistan, where the military difficulties were far greater, Mr. Bhutto's basic strategy was to hold the line militarily while cutting away at the roots of the tribal system (in April, 1976 he decreed the abolition of the Sardari — tribal chieftain — system) and to foster rapid development. Federal government investment in the province has increased greatly since the outbreak of fighting, and assistance from anxious Iran ($76,000,000 in 1975 alone for development projects in Baluchistan) is even larger than that from Islamabad.

Mr. Bhutto's overthrow by the army in July, 1977 has led to a substantial decrease in the intensity of fighting in Baluchistan. At the end of the year the military government amnestied all 50 leaders of the National Awami Party from Baluchistan and NWFP who were under trial on charges of sedition (although the ban on the NAP itself was maintained).

However, the left-wing coup in Afghanistan in April, 1978 was followed by some early signs that the new government in Kabul was inclined to renew Afghan support for the independence movements in the two border provinces. This has revived the nightmare of 1973–5 in Pakistan: the fear that a pro-Soviet Afghan regime might succeed in creating an independent Pakhtunistan and Baluchistan out of Pakistani and Iranian territory, with the purpose of establishing a corridor of Soviet-aligned States down to the Indian Ocean coast.

The Soviet invasion of Afghanistan in December 1979 and the civil war which broke out in its wake guarantee, however, that both the Afghan government and the Soviet Union will be too fully occupied inside Afghanistan's borders for some time to come to embark on adventures outside.

The military government's most serious security problem has been with the *Al Zulfiqar* guerillas who support the policies of Bhutto and are led by his son Mustaza. It has bases inside Afghanistan, and both the Pakistan police and army are active against its members and sympathisers. The problem is, however, entirely containable at present.

ORGANISATION

Arms of Service

The Pakistan army inherited from the British, and has largely preserved, a 'regimental' system of internal organisation. At Partition, those regiments with a majority of Muslim soldiers became Pakistani, while the corps were divided proportionately (30% of the old Indian Army was Muslim in 1947). In all, eight out of the 23 British–Indian infantry regiments (each being of several battalions) came to Pakistan, eight out of 21 cavalry regiments, and eight and a half out of 27 artillery regiments.

Unlike the Indians, however, who have preserved their regiments intact, the Pakistanis have somewhat amalgamated their infantry, which is now grouped into four multi-battalion regiments: the Punjab Regiment, the Frontier Force Regiment, the Baluch Regiment, and a new formation, the Azad Kashmir Regiment. The East Bengal Regiment (infantry) ceased to be part of the Pakistan army in 1971. The cavalry remain unchanged: 5th Horse (Probyn's), 6th Lancers (Watson's), 10th Cavalry (Guides), 11th Cavalry (Frontier Force), and 13th, 15th, 19th and 20th Lancers; four new regiments have been raised — 22nd, 23rd, 24th and 25th Cavalry. The other arms and the corps are: Pakistan Artillery, Engineers, Signals, Electrical and Mechanical Engineers, Ordnance, Military Police, Medical, Education, Clerks and Supply Services.

The air force is divided into Flying (operations), Administrative and Training Commands. Like the navy, its internal structure largely preserves the British pattern.

Operational

The army is organised into corps, divisions, brigades and battalions on British lines. There are two armoured divisions, 16 infantry divisions, four independent armoured brigades, five independent infantry brigades, seven artillery brigades, two air-defence brigades, six armoured reconnaissance regiments, one special service company, and five army aviation squadrons. A corps consists of two or more divisions commanded by a lieutenant-general, provided with a complete headquarters staff. Infantry divisions are made up of infantry, artillery, engineer, signals and supply units required for sustained independent action, and are organised into three brigades each consisting of three battalions. Divisional artillery and engineer units of battalion size are usually referred to as regiments Armoured divisions contain a varying number of tank battalions (also referred to as regiments), plus mechanised artillery and the usual support services.

Those units definitely identified as being in the West in 1917 were I, II and IV Corps; 1st and 6th Armoured Divisions, and 7th, 8th, 10th 11th 12th (Azad Kashmir), 15th, 17th, 19th, 23rd (Azad Kashmir) and 33rd Infantry. Divisions; and 8th Independent Armoured Brigade. The divisions lost in Bangladesh were the 9th, 14th, 16th and 36th; some, if not all, of these divisions have now been re-raised in the West.

Army headquarters has been moved from Rawalpindi to the Ministry of Defence in Islamabad. The present Chief of Army Staff is Lieutenant-General Zia ul-Haq.

The air force's former general headquarters at Peshawar, and naval headquarters in Karachi, have now also been transferred to the Ministry of Defence in Islamabad. The principal naval base and dockyard remains in Karachi. The air force is divided into two groups, with headquarters at Peshawar and Lahore; air force installations are at Chitral, Dergh Road (Lahore), Gilgit, Kohat, Malir, Mauripur, Miramshah, Peshawar, Risalpur, Samundri and Sargodha. There are three fighter squadrons, eight fighter–ground attack squadrons, one reconnaissance squadron, one light bomber squadron and one maritime reconnaissance squadron.

RECRUITMENT, TRAINING AND RESERVES

Recruitment in the armed forces is voluntary; enlistments are permitted from the age of seventeen and are usually for 7 year periods. The three services recruit separately, and have no difficulty in maintaining units at full strength, although the navy and air force sometimes have difficulty in getting recruits with the required special skills.

Officers must pass qualifying and physical examinations before appearing before the Inter-Service Selection Board for interview. A large proportion of successful candidates are graduates at the cadet colleges which were founded in the 1950s to raise the educational qualifications of applicants, or former members of the University Officers Training Corps, although these institutions carry neither the obligation nor the guarantee of admission to the Pakistan Military Academy.

The Academy, founded in 1948 at Kakul (near Rawalpindi) is the main source of regular officers, and provides a two and a half year course in military and academic subjects leading to a BA or BSc degree. The degrees are of a standard comparable to or higher than those awarded by Pakistani universities. The principal exception to this method of entry is in the procurement of officers for the Army Education Corps, charged with raising the educational standards of recruits entering the army: they are generally university graduates who attend a short military course at Kakul before being commissioned.

Newly commissioned Academy graduates are then given basic training in their arm or service at the appropriate corps school. These schools, which also provide subsequent specialist courses for officers and NCOs, include: the School of Infantry and Tactics and the School of Electrical and Mechanical Engineers at Quetta; the School of Artillery and the Armoured Corps School at Nowshera, the School of Signal Communications at Kohat and the School of Military Engineering at Risalpur (all in the vicinity of Peshawar); the Army Administration School at Murree, the Army Education School at Topa and the Army School of Music at Abbotabad (all around Rawalpindi); and the Army Aviation School

(which gives a 5 year course in flight training and artillery observation) and the Army Apprentice School both in Rawalpindi itself. The Apprentice School runs a 4 year course training technicians for the Signal Corps, Engineer Corps and the Corps of Electrical and Mechanical Engineers.

Higher military education is provided by the Command and Staff College at Quetta, originally established in 1905 for the British Indian Army. It offers a 10 month course in tactics, staff duties, administration and command up to division level, and attracts numbers of officers from other countries. Considerable numbers of senior Pakistan army officers also attend staff colleges abroad.

Pakistan navy officers attend the Military Academy for about 6 months, followed by about 18 months of academic instruction and naval training at the Naval Academy, which is located aboard the old light cruiser *Babur*. Further training is done on-the-job in the ships of the fleet. Naval ratings are trained in Karachi naval base at the Basic Training Establishment, known as *The Bahadur*, and subsequently at sea. The fleet periodically conducts joint exercises with other CENTO navies.

The Air Force College at Risalpur provides a 2 year course in academic and technical subjects and flying training, after which most students pass to the Fighter Leaders School for advanced flying and weapons training. The Air Force College of Aeronautical Engineering, affiliated to the University of Karachi, was opened in 1965 at Korangi Creek in Karachi to provide aeronautical engineers for the air force and the civil airlines, and grants a BSc degree in electrical and mechanical engineering; the associated apprentices' school gives technical training to air force NCOs. The highest level of instruction is provided at the Air Force Staff College at Dergh Road (near Karachi), which was opened in 1959 to give a 10 month course in higher command to selected senior officers. The air force has conducted joint exercises with fellow CENTO members Iran and Turkey.

Army recruits receive their basic training at the training centre maintained by the unit to which they are assigned, and with which they will generally remain throughout their service careers. Most regimental-sized garrisons have their own training centres, and basic training lasts from 4½ months to 12 months depending on the branch of service. Subsequent specialist training for NCOs is provided by the schools maintained by each arm and service. The army-wide annual training cycle starts with individual training from spring to autumn, commences unit training in October and frequently culminates in divisional or corps exercises in January.

The Army Education Corps operates schools in almost all company-sized units to improve the educational level of enlisted men and NCOs. The curriculum, which extends flexibly over a number of years, is designed to qualify participants for the Army Special Certificate of Education, approximately equivalent to graduation from secondary school. Specific educational qualifications are required for promotion in grade and for desirable duty assignments, and a large proportion of army enlisted men take part in the programme.

Army pay and welfare benefits compare favourably with those for similarly qualified people in civilian occupations, and much attention is paid to sport and recreation facilities. Retiring servicemen benefit from pre-release vocational training, pensions and welfare funds, a degree of preference in selection for some civil service posts, and land resettlement schemes. Morale is generally excellent, as is the relationship between soldiers and civilians, who hold them in high esteem.

The Pakistan armed forces possess a much more comprehensive and competent military training establishment than most Asian or Middle Eastern countries, and as a result their officers are in high demand in the small Arab States of the Gulf which are in the process of creating new armed forces. A large proportion of the combat aircraft of these countries, for example, is flown by ex-PAF pilots serving on loan or contract.

The regular army's reserves are extremely large at approximately 500,000 men, but there is not much by way of an organisation to deal with their mobilisation and deployment. Air force reserves are 8000 and navy reserves 5000. There are also 109,100 men in paramilitary regular forces in Pakistan, including some 65,000 hill tribesmen of the North-West Frontier Province are organised into the irregular Frontier Corps along the Afghanistan and Iran borders.

For those who have never done regular military service, or whose reserve liability has expired, there are four voluntary home defence corps. They have been reorganised since 1972, since their predecessors failed to give good service during the 1971 war, and together are supposed to constitute a second line of defence. They consist of a women's corps, a Mujahid (Crusaders) force, a Janbaz (Janissaries) force and a national cadet force.

In this scheme, which is based on the concept of a 'nation in arms', the women's corps is open to all fit persons of that gender, while the national cadet force is for male college and university students. The Mujahid force is open to men of eighteen to thirty who have no regular service experience, and provides them with a few month's initial training followed by periodic refresher courses of a month each. The Janbaz force is open to men from eighteen to fifty, and it is expected that ex-servicemen whose reserve liability has expired will form its backbone. These forces would be used primarily for civil defence and home guard duties in their own home districts in wartime.

EQUIPMENT AND ARMS INDUSTRY

Equipment

Pakistan's armed forces have one of the widest and most awkward mixtures of military equipment in the world, in terms of national origin. It is a logistical nightmare, involving major American, British, French, Russian and Chinese weapons, with Swedish thrown in for good measure. Pakistan's weapons, like geological strata, contain the history of its diplomatic triumphs and difficulties ever since its foundation.

From 1947 to 1954 Pakistan's military equipment was British, after which its equipment came from the USA until 1965. Between 1954 and 1970 Pakistan received $2,800,000,000 in American military aid, but after 1965 the United States' arms embargo restricted deliveries to spare parts. It then received Russian arms aid for a brief period, and Chinese military aid including Chen-6 fighters (an advanced Chinese version of the MiG-19), T-59 tanks and enough equipment for three infantry divisions. The Chinese aid still continues at a slower pace, and Pakistan also commenced buying arms from France (and, in one case, Sweden). Full-scale American arms sales to Pakistan (and India) also became possible in 1975, when the United States' embargo was finally lifted.

The Pakistan army's major equipment includes 250 American M-47/48 medium tanks, 35 Russian T-55s and 1000 Chinese T-59s. It also operates 50 M-24 light tanks, some M-4s and 15PT-76s. It has 550 M-113 APCs.

The army's artillery strength consists of about 1000 25-pounder, 75mm pack, 100mm, 105mm, 130mm and 155mm guns and howitzers, M-7 105mm SP guns, and 270 107mm and 120mm mortars. It possesses 57mm and M-36 90mm SP anti-tank guns; 75mm and 106mm RCL and Cobra ATGWs

(TOW ATGWs on order); and ZU-23, 30mm, 37mm, 40mm, 57mm and 3.7in AA guns. It also has nine batteries of Crotale SAMs.

The Army Aviation Wing has 40 O-1E and 45 Saab Supporter light aircraft, and 12 Mi-8, 35 Puma, 12 UH-1H, 23 Alouette III and 13 Bell 47G helicopters.

The navy has six fleet submarines and five SX-4-4 midget submarines. It operates one cruiser, nine destroyers, 21 patrol boats and smaller craft.

The air force has 219 combat aircraft.

Arms Industry

Pakistan's arms industry at the moment is largely restricted to repair and maintenance, and the manufacture of small arms, spare parts and ammunition for its wide variety of weapons types, this being carried out in two State arms factories, the larger of which is at Wah, near Rawalpindi. It has major projects underway to increase its capabilities, however, and envisages an eventual ability to manufacture submarines and missile boats, tanks, artillery and tank guns, military vehicles, missiles, radar and sophisticated electronic equipment. Seven new arms factories are already scheduled to be opened, and there is no doubt that Pakistan does have the skilled personnel gradually to achieve its ambitions. A major question is money, for large sums are clearly involved, but some assistance has already been made available by the wealthier Arab States. In November, 1976 for example, Saudi Arabia agreed to provide Pakistan with $1,100,000,000 to finance economic and military projects.

There is also the possibility of joint projects with Western manufacturers. In November, 1976 an agreement was concluded to manufacture about 60 Cessna T-41 basic trainers and 50 Hughes 500 helicopters a year in a factory near Campbellpur in Pakistan. Initially Pakistani input will be confined to the assembly of imported United States-built components, but there are plans to manufacture a gradually increasing number of parts locally. An already established aircraft industry, run by Pakistan Army Aviation at its main base at Dhamial (near Rawalpindi), manufactures Cessna O-1 observation and liaison aircraft (with 60% of components locally produced) and Alouette III helicopters at the rate of approximately one each per month. However, the most ambitious project, a proposal to assemble up to 70 Mirage F-1s a year in Pakistan for domestic use and sale to Middle Eastern countries, much discussed in 1974—5, has apparently run into difficulties because of Dassault's agreement with the Arab Organisation for Industrialisation in early 1977 to build Mirages in Egypt for sale throughout the Arab world. Instead, Pakistan opened a new aeronautical complex at Kamra, 40 miles north of Rawalpindi, in May, 1978 which will carry out all overhaul work on its existing Mirage III and V aircraft and end the need to send them to France for major maintenance work after July, 1979. This factory, which will eventually cost about $75,000,000, will also undertake the overhaul work on Pakistan's Chinese-built MiG-19s, and will build Swedish-designed Mashaak trainer aircraft under licence.

Whatever the longer-term successes of Pakistan's nascent arms industry may be, the government feels a short-term requirement to buy arms abroad. As a result of the ending of the United States' arms embargo in 1975, it has already ordered some smaller items such as TOW missiles, but the most urgent need is to replace its extremely aged F-86 ground-attack aircraft (and at a rather later date, its MiG-19s as well). In 1976, therefore, it sought permission to buy up to 110 A-7 Corsair II strike aircraft from the USA for $700,000,000. (These aircraft, like Pakistan's Mirages and MiG-19s, are capable of carrying small nuclear weapons, but they also have the range to reach almost anywhere in

India.) There is already some speculation that Pakistan may have to turn to Britain and/or France for about 100 Jaguars instead, for the American government is quite likely to forbid the sale unless it gets greater satisfaction from Pakistan on the key issue of nuclear weapons.

The Nuclear Option

The most controversial and important questions about Pakistan's arms industry revolve around what are still civilian industrial establishments, at least for the moment: can Pakistan's civil nuclear industry give it the capacity to build nuclear weapons, and will the government choose to do so? The question has been acute since India tested what it termed a 'peaceful nuclear device' at Pokaran (untactfully, within 90 miles of the Pakistan border) in May, 1974. The circumstantial evidence suggests that if Pakistan has not yet definitely decided to develop its own nuclear device (and it probably has not), then at least it is determined to obtain an option on such a decision at some later time which would be wholly invulnerable to outside pressure, and to shorten steadily the lead time required between decision and the production of a prototype nuclear weapon.

There are no signs that India is moving rapidly, or at all, from the nuclear device of 1974 to a nuclear weapons capability. Such a move would in any case have to wait until the early 1980s, when substantial quantities of unsafeguarded plutonium for a weapons programme become available with the entry into service of the first large Indian reactors built without foreign aid. Of course the Indian government has always denied any intention to proceed along such a course. But seen from Pakistan, such assurances offer little comfort, particularly since if India changed its mind then it could have nuclear weapons in significant numbers years ahead of Pakistan. Indian explanations about using nuclear explosions for civil engineering purposes ring even more falsely to Pakistanis than to others — though the real Indian motive in the 1974 test may well have been simply prestige, the civil engineering project most Pakistanis see as a likely task for Indian nuclear explosives is an abrupt and drastic programme of slum clearance in Pakistan's cities.

Even at a more realistic level, the possibility of Indian tactical nuclear weapons would pose an insuperable problem for Pakistan's defence forces: their only hope of survival in war would be to operate in extremely dispersed formations, while Indian forces could concentrate at will. Ever since the Indian nuclear test, therefore, Pakistan's civil and military leadership has been determined to acquire at the least a similar 'threshold' nuclear capability for their country, though after the first few months they found it preferable not to voice this determination publicly.

In 1975 it was estimated that Pakistan was 8 years away from a nuclear weapon if it embarked forthwith on a programme leading to that goal, but this was of course conditional upon Pakistan having access to certain key elements of nuclear technology from abroad. It already possessed one working reactor of 137 MW at Karachi, built with Canadian assistance during the 1960s. It has its own uranium ore, and could presumably fabricate the fuel itself if Canadian co-operation were withdrawn, though it currently lacks uranium enrichment facilities. The critical missing item was fuel processing plant which could extract from the spent nuclear fuel the plutonium with which to make relatively cheap (and relatively small) nuclear weapons. It now appears to have filled that gap, without which Pakistan's nuclear weapons capability would take far longer to achieve, although it was a near-run thing.

Claiming as justification a programme to build five or six large nuclear-power generating stations in the next 10 or 15 years, and 24 by the turn of the century, in order to make up for a lack of fossil fuel reserves and to meet future power requirements, Pakistan ordered a fuel reprocessing plant from France in March, 1976. In fact the first of these 600 MW reactors, at Chashma some 150 miles south of Rawalpindi, only began to be built in early 1977, and will not be completed until 1983. (It is to cost $527,000,000, including $222,000,000 in foreign exchange.) As the Canadian authorities observed, it was curious that Pakistan was buying the reprocessing plant before the reactors whose fuel they were to reprocess, especially since it is not economically sensible to run such a plant unless there are at least half a dozen large reactors to supply it. But Pakistan remained committed to the purchase.

The ending of the United States' arms embargo in 1975 was at least partly to give Washington bargaining leverage in Islamabad, so that conventional arms supplies from America might somehow be traded for Pakistani self-denial on nuclear matters. On December 17th, 1976 even France, the last major Western country in the business of exporting reprocessing plants, announced that it would sin no more. The French government stated that it would not cancel the sale of a reprocessing plant to Pakistan which had already been agreed, but indicated obliquely that it would be most grateful to be let off the hook. Islamabad, unsurprisingly, did not oblige.

So long as Pakistan adheres to this policy, American arms supplies on any large scale are unlikely — especially nuclear-capable strike aircraft. Within a week of Pakistan's refusal, Canada announced that it would end its nuclear co-operation with Pakistan, and end its supplies of enriched uranium and spare parts for the Karachi reactor it had helped build (the only large one Pakistan will have until 1983). In January, 1977 Mr. Aziz Ahmed, Minister of State for Defence and Foreign Affairs, replied that alternative sources were available to obtain fuel and spares for the plant, though there could be lengthy shutdowns if faults developed, and added that 'no third country has any right to demand that Pakistan abandon the reprocessing plant'.

It would therefore appear, barring a further change in French government policy, that Pakistan's nuclear option is assured. The French reprocessing plant will of course be provided under French controls which duplicate those of the 1969 International Atomic Energy Agency safeguards, and there is a Pakistani—Canadian agreement whereby the spent fuel from the Karachi reactor cannot be used without Ottawa's permission. But the latter agreement can be abrogated with 6 months' notice from either party, and the French-imposed safeguards on the reprocessing plant repudiated if and when it became necessary. Although the basis for a weapons programme thus created by the turn of the decade will be extremely austere even compared with Indian nuclear resources, it will provide Pakistan with what Islamabad regards as the indispensable option. That is, the ability to proceed rapidly across the 'threshold' to a nuclear explosion — say in 2 or 3 years — should the Indian nuclear programme show signs of turning to weapons development and production, without leaving a lengthy and acutely embarrassing interval when India would be nuclear-armed and Pakistan would not.

RANK, DRESS AND DISTINCTIONS

The rank structure and dress of all three armed services closely follow those of the old British Indian forces from which they are descended. The principal difference from the standard international rank system is the existence of a category of Junior Commissioned Officer (JCOs), promoted from enlisted rank after long and meritorious service. They fall between second-lieutenants and senior NCOs in the hierarchy, and although they rarely advance beyond JCO rank they frequently have responsibilities equivalent to those of junior officers in other armies because of their age and experience. The three grades of JCO, in descending order, are *subedar major*, *subedar* and *naib-subedar*; in armoured units the term *risaldar* is used instead of *subedar*.

There are two warrant officer grades, Class I and Class II, found only in the technical services. Other enlisted ranks are company *havildar major* (first sergeant), company quarter-master *havildar* (staff sergeant), *havildar* (sergeant), *naik* (corporal), *lance naik* (private first class/lance-corporal) and *sepoy* (private). In armoured units the term *dafadar* is substituted for *havildar*.

All military personnel are highly conscious of rank, and relations between officers of different ranks and between officers and NCOs are rather formal.

The highest Pakistani decoration for heroism in the presence of the enemy is the Nishan-i-Haidar: it is conferred regardless of rank, and carries a cash award of 10,000 rupees. The next highest award for valour in combat, given to officers only, is the Hilal-i-Juraat, bearing a cash award of 7000 rupees. The other awards for gallantry and distinguished service in battle are the Sitara-i-Juraat, awarded to officers the JCOs, and the Tamgha-i-Juraat, conferred on NCOs and privates; they carry cash awards of 5000 and 4000 rupees respectively. For valour or devotion to duty not in active operations against the enemy, officers and JCOs are awarded the Tamgha-i-Basalat Class I, NCOs and lower grades Class II; the cash awards are 4000 and 3000 rupees, respectively.

CURRENT DEVELOPMENTS

Pakistan is an economically viable State, verging on semi-industrialised status. Less than a quarter of its 75,000,000 people are literate, and around three-quarters are villagers, but it possesses a considerable industrial sector and a quite large work force of skilled and educated people. It is a poor country but relatively prosperous by south Asian standards.

It is also a very heavily armed country. Between a quarter and a third of regular budget expenditure goes on defence, and there are further hidden defence costs in the nuclear programme and the military industrial projects. The foreign exchange costs of arms-buying abroad are very heavy, and the consequent enormous trade gap is at present being covered mostly by heavy borrowings from Western and OPEC sources. Thanks to these efforts, however, Pakistan has been able since 1971 to recreate forces which, at least so far as the army is concerned, are not grievously inferior in strength to those that India is capable of deploying on its frontier (so long as a portion of India's forces remain committed to the Himalayan border).

Despite this, Pakistan remains acutely vulnerable to attack in the perceptions of its own rulers and soldiers. The possibility of India's developing nuclear weapons has caused a great deal of anxiety recently, and served to sharpen and reinforce the army's corporate image of India as an inveterate aggressor who will strike again when the time is ripe. And, given the fact that Pakistan is a Federal State made up of four provinces, each with a different linguistic and cultural group (Punjabis, Sindhis, Baluchis and Pathans), can the possibility of disorder leading to further fragmentation of the country, whether externally aided or not, cannot be entirely disregarded.

In fact, Pakistan is most unlikely to become involved voluntarily in a war with India in the medium-term future, or to get forced into one by the actions of its neighbours. On the one hand, it no longer believes, as it mistakenly did in 1965 and 1971, that it is capable of inflicting a decisive military defeat on the Indian army in the only theatre that counts, the Punjab. The balance of forces there is too evenly matched (with some slight advantage to the Indian side), and the long road and rail communications running parallel with the Indian border for almost 1000 miles from Karachi to the Punjab proved extremely vulnerable to Indian air action in 1971, as did Pakistan's sea communications to the Indian navy. Pakistan's expectations about the probable character of military operations have shifted significantly towards the strategically defensive since 1971 — only the improbable eventuality of a simultaneous large-scale Chinese attack on India could offer Pakistan any prospects for a big and lasting offensive success. On the other hand, any further disintegration in Pakistan is generally considered to be against New Delhi's interests, and a direct Indian attack would likely invoke tacit Chinese and American guarantees of Pakistan's territorial integrity.

Neither is further fragmentation of the country likely to occur from internal forces alone — while there is a genuine and quite powerful drive for autonomy in both of the western provinces, the population of Baluchistan is only some 2,500,000, and that of the North-West Frontier about 6,000,000. The rest of Pakistan's 78,000,000 people are Punjabis, Kashmiris and Sindhis, who feel their fate to be closely bound together, so the stresses are in no way analagous to those which tore the old Pakistan apart.

The principal instability in Pakistan at the moment lies in its internal politics. The military regime led by General Zia ul-Haq which took power in July, 1977 has had to prolong its intervention long past the brief period it originally intended, and now faces a problem of internal unrest.

Initially the coup was greeted with widespread relief, as the country's life and economy had been virtually paralysed by the 4-months of violent popular disturbances following the rigged national elections in March, and there was a genuine fear of civil war. The army felt obliged to intervene in its own defence, moreover, since there was growing restiveness in the junior- and middle-officer ranks at the unaccustomed public opprobrium the military forces were suffering as a result of their constant use in the streets in defence of Mr. Bhutto. But General Zia soon found he was no more able to reconcile the opposing political factions than any other mediator, and at the last moment he postponed indefinitely the re-run of the national elections which he had promised to hold in October, 1977.

There is reason to believe that one factor in the postponement was the fact that Mr. Bhutto's popular support, at its nadir in July, 1977, began to recover as soon as he was removed from office, while the opposition alliance began to disintegrate. This raised the prospect that Bhutto might win an honestly conducted election (as he surely would have, if by a smaller margin, even if the March elections had been free of abuses). That result would present the military regime with the unpleasant alternatives of setting aside the popular verdict by force, or accepting the return to office of a man with a score to pay against those officers who had overthrown and jailed him.

The reason given for postponing the election was the need to settle the charge of conspiracy to murder a political opponent which had been brought against Mr. Bhutto, a charge on which he was found guilty, and sentenced to death, in March, 1978. Whether or not the conviction was justified, this placed the regime in a new quandary: whether Bhutto was more dangerous to it dead or alive. His eventual execution in April, 1979 has not solved the problem.

Meanwhile, the probable duration of military rule continued to lengthen, despite all the army's well-founded concern about the deleterious effects of its prolonged presence in politics on military efficiency and discipline. In August, 1978, however, General Zia replaced his cabinet, which was mainly staffed with generals, with an all-civilian one, most of whose members were drawn from the coalition of conservative Islamic parties, the Pakistan National Alliance. A determined effort was launched to increase the role of Islam in public life and law – compulsory prayers for public servants, the prohibition of alcohol, the introduction of traditional Islamic punishments like amputation for various crimes – in an attempt to curry favour with rich, conservative Arab States and to appeal to the sole unifying force in Pakistan, its Muslim faith (just as Mr. Bhutto had done during the crisis preceding his overthrow). But the economy remained in dire straits, the bitter political divisions did not heal, and the prospect of finding a formula to provide Pakistan with a government enjoying public assent and support continued to recede.

General Zia, who became president in September 1978, seems resolved to continue his role with or without public support (of which, in practice, he enjoys a good deal), be-lieving that his policies of economic austerity and Islamic reformation are in the country's best interests.

His most pressing difficulties have been caused by the Soviet invasion of Afghanistan. At least three million refugees (one fifth of Afghanistan's population) is now in refuge on Pakistan territory, at a cost of £125 million a year, half of which Pakistan finds itself. The presence of strong Soviet forces just across its borders lends, moreover, a serious threat to Pakistan's security, anxious as the government always is for the stability of its western regions which lie between Afghan territory and the Indian Ocean.

However, the United States has done much to alleviate General Zia's anxieties by assurances of support and military and financial aid. The latter, granted on December 4th, 1981, was to consist of the delivery of 40 F-16 fighters and $3,200 million, over six years. An American offer to station troops on Pakistan soil was, however, rejected and, for its part, the Pakistani government re-affirmed its Islamic and non-aligned foreign policy. American aid is subject to Pakistan's observance of the Symington amendment, which interrupts aid should the beneficiary explode a nuclear weapon.

Gwynne Dyer
John Keegan

PANAMA

HISTORY AND INTRODUCTION

Panama differs from other Latin American States in that its independence dates not from the 1820s but from 1903, and that United States influence has not only dominated its experience, but was actually responsible for its creation. Indeed for the first three decades of its existence, Panama was effectively a United States protectorate, and the issue of the 10-mile-wide USA-controlled Canal Zone cutting right across the most populous part of the nation has latterly been a predominating factor in both domestic politics and foreign relations.

Although Panama is now generally considered to be part of Central America, it had no share in the formative experiences of the republics to the north during the nineteenth century, notably the failed experiment of Central American federation. Both in Spanish colonial times and throughout the nineteenth century it was governed from Bogotá, and from 1821 to 1903 was simply the northernmost province of Colombia. There was, indeed, little or no history of separatist sentiment in the province of Panama until a treaty was concluded between the USA and Colombia for the building of a canal across the isthmus of Panama just after the turn of the century.

That treaty, however, promised $10,000,000 in gold to Bogotá in return for the United States' concession to build and administer the canal, and when Colombia hesitated to ratify it the money potentially became available to any group of Panamanians who could successfully organise a secessionist movement and sign the treaty themselves. A Panamanian revolutionary clique duly organised a rebellion in 1903 with the aid of a French adventurer, Philippe Bunau-Varilla, who hastily signed a treaty in Washington that effectively granted the USA perpetual sovereign rights over the Canal Zone in return for the United States' recognition and $10,000,000.

This was considerably more than the Colombians had agreed to, and exceeded Bunau-Varilla's instructions, but it was necessary to get the treaty signed before a rival Colombian delegation arrived in Washington. The Frenchman was subsequently able to persuade the new Panamanian government to ratify it, but the treaty's terms and implications have dominated Panamanian life ever since.

The Panamanian army just after independence consisted of a handful of 'revolutionary' troops plus a battalion-strength unit of the Colombian army which had been bribed to desert. Within a year, however, the commander of this force was induced to attempt a *coup d'état* by a disgruntled faction of the civilian *élite*. The USA prevented the coup, and successfully pressed for the outright disbanding of the army. In its place a National Police Corps was created in 1904 to maintain internal security, but it rarely exceeded a strength of 1000 men during the next three decades. The republic relied upon United States troops stationed in the Canal Zone not only for external defence but often also for the maintenance of public order in emergencies as well.

This largely protected the government from the endemic Central American disease of military coups, though the police force soon became caught up in the intense rivalry between competing factions in the rich which oligarchy — the so-called 'first families', sometimes estimated to number around fifty — who totally dominated Panamanian politics. Following two such police interventions in politics in 1917 and 1918, both reversed by United States marines, an American citizen was appointed inspector-general and placed in charge of the entire force from 1919 to 1927. Marine Corps officers thoroughly reformed the Panamanian police, pursuing the elusive goal of turning it into a professional, apolitical force (just as their counterparts were doing in three other USA-occupied Caribbean countries at the same time), while United States military instructors provided it with modern weapons and methods.

In 1930, however, the USA adopted a policy of non-intervention in Panama. The following year, a revolution broke out against the traditional rule of the white aristocracy, and through the 1930s the national police were drawn increasingly into the role of arbiter between the ruling oligarchy and aspiring middle-class groups. By 1940 Panama had completed the transition from provincial backwater to a State abreast of the leading trends in Latin American politics (thanks largely to the Canal-derived economic growth which gave it the second-highest national income per capita in the region). That is to say, the traditional ruling group were on the defensive and seeking to co-opt allies in the new middle classes, while leftist and populist movements were gaining ground in the greatly expanded urban population — and sections of the 'army' (as the National Police Force was already coming to resemble) were becoming infected with their own versions of ultra-nationalist and reformist ideology that augured a much deeper and more continuous involvement in government.

Panama even produced a rough equivalent of Perón in Argentina or Vargas in Brazil, in the form of Arnulfo Arias, who seized power in a coup in 1940. He was an ultra-nationalist, populist demagogue, at that stage in his career inclined towards fascism, who eschewed the support of the prosperous white minority (12% of the population), and found his following amongst the mestizo majority (65%) and above all in black lower classes of the main cities (mainly descended from immigrants from the British West Indies who had been brought in to build the Canal). The police overthrew him in 1941, and for the rest of the decade Panama was ruled once more by conservative civilian presidents. The real power in Panama, however, was already the well-armed, highly disciplined National Police Corps, now grown to 2000 men, and from 1947 on its commander, Colonel José Antonio Remón, was the undisputed kingmaker in Panamanian politics.

Remón, like most of the force's officers, came from the non-propertied middle social group; moreover, he had been trained at a Mexican military academy, and was of a reformist bent. He actually brought Arnulfo Arias to the presidency in 1949—51, before assuming it himself in 1952. He introduced social-welfare measures and promoted agricultural and industrial development. For support he depended on the votes of the underprivileged, especially the blacks, and on the loyalty of the police force, which he cemented by showering it with material favours, increasing its size to 3000, and effectively granting it the status of an army in 1953 by converting it into the National Guard.

Remón was the commander principally responsible for the professionalisation and deliberate militarisation of the police force, both because of his own professional background (he was the first graduate of a military academy to enter the force) and because it was his principal power base in the country. Thus he established the Police Training School in 1946, completely restructured the force into a five-zone regional organisation, and eventually — with the fortuitous aid of the 'cold war' and United States military aid programmes — transformed it into a national military force.

The National Guard's domination of Panamanian politics was not ended by Remón's assassination in 1955, but the bulk of its officers were not radicals, and readily acquiesced in a reversion to rule by presidents drawn from the traditional civilian oligarchy. The steady progression of the Guard from police force to military organisation was not slowed, however: for the first time it began to attract Panamanian graduates of foreign military academics, and received standardised military equipment from the USA. Even more importantly, large numbers of officers and men received United States military training in the Canal Zone and the continental USA: 89 officers in 1953–62, and 265 in the next 7 years to 1969. The number who were attending police courses halved over the period, while the number attending military courses doubled.

It may be surmised that this training, directed at the officers of what was in fact a brand new military organisation with no native traditions, was instrumental in moulding the National Guard's subsequent political outlook. Especially after the Cuban revolution, these United States-run courses were directed primarily towards counter-insurgency; they stressed the inverse relationships between social justice and social violence, and emphasised the role of the military forces as an integral element in the process of development which might avert revolutionary upheaval.

The increasingly well-armed National Guard dealt easily with an invasion by some 80 Cuban guerrillas in April, 1959, and with several outbreaks of rural unrest in the early 1960s. It was indicative of its growing consciousness of a nationalist mission, however, that it stood aside during the rioting in January, 1964 against the USA's presence in the Canal Zone. This 4 day riot, leaving 18 Panamanians dead, was a turning point not only for Panama but also for the Guard itself, and the nationalist struggle against the USA's presence has played the key role in radicalising the politics of both ever since.

The Liberal (i.e. conservative) government of President Roberto F. Chiari negotiated three draft treaties with the USA in 1964–7 giving Panama a greater degree of control over the Canal. The inadequacy of the USA's concessions became the central issue of the 1968 elections, which were won by Arnulfo Arias, by now portraying himself as a radical leftist, who promptly denounced the treaties and demanded the USA's withdrawal. Significantly, the National Guard did not prevent his assumption of office on October 1st, 1968 and only deposed him 9 days later after he had attempted to reshuffle the Guard's high command to place his own supporters in charge.

The junta of three colonels which then took control appointed a fairly broadly based cabinet, but it was evident that the National Guard now contained officers straight out of the then-new peruanista mould. They were ultra-nationalists who, like the Peruvian junta, were determined on radical domestic reform, including genuine measures of land reform and the elimination of foreign (American) influence over the economy — with the additional, specifically Panamanian goal of the restoration of national sovereignty over the Canal Zone. They intended a revolution from above, for which purpose the army would remain in control for a lengthy period of time. In a coup within the coup, the colonels were replaced by reform-minded captains and majors before the end of 1968.

In Panama's case, however, the radical faction never gained full control. In March, 1969 its leader, Boris Martínez, a member of the newly created General Staff, was abruptly sent into exile. By the end of 1969 Colonel Omar Torrijos Herrera, having survived a coup attempt by other peruanista officers, had emerged as sole dictator.

Although there was a nominal return to civilian politics in 1972, when a National Assembly of Community Representatives was elected which drafted a new constitution and installed an indirectly elected civilian president, vice-president and legislative council, Torrijos, now a brigadier-general, remained Commander of the National Guard. He was also granted full executive powers for a 6 year period by a 'transitory provision' of the constitution, and named Chief of Government and Supreme Leader of the Panamanian Revolution. He relinquished the latter positions in October, 1978 when the National Assembly chose Aristides Royo as President. Free elections are promised for 1984, the end of Royo's 6 year term.

Under Torrijos both the government and the Guard itself became a great deal less corrupt than the previous norm. A marked feature of the past decade has been the concentration on land reform and on the integration of the rural half of Panamanian society, hitherto almost totally neglected by the urban-based oligarchy, into national life. The Guard is heavily involved in civic action programmes, and Torrijos had a distinctly populist style (spending most of his weekends in the villages).

Torrijos compensated for his gradualist and generally modest programme of domestic reform by adopting a rhetorically extreme position on the Canal issue ('We are prepared to follow the Ho Chi Minh route if necessary. That means terrorism, guerrilla operations and sabotage in a national-liberation war to regain our territory'), and a flamboyantly radical image (including a visit to Cuba). The National Guard, the vital base of his power, which had doubled in size in the decade before 1968, has since virtually doubled again.

From 1971, in an attempt to appeal to the strong peruanista faction in the Guard's officer corps, his government began to express admiration for the (then) socialist trends in the military governments of Peru and Bolivia. Despite the arrest or banishment of more than 70 dissident National Guard officers since Torrijos came to power, his power could still be challenged by either the peruanista or the right-wing factions in the officer corps. The ratification of the renegotiated Canal treaties by the United States Senate in April, 1977 however, had undoubtedly strengthened his position greatly.

On October 1st, 1979, a treaty was signed between Panama and the United States whereby the Panama Canal Zone would be handed over to Panama, in stages, between December 1979 and December 1999. Elections for the National Legislative Council were held in 1980, the Democratic Republican Revolutionary Party, effectively General Torrijos's main political support, gaining 60% of the available seats. Following the death of Torrijos, in an aircraft accident in 1981, no comparable strongman has emerged.

STRENGTH AND BUDGET

Population: 1,890,000.
Army: 11,000.
Navy: (included in Army); 15 small vessels.
Air Force: (included in Army); no combat aircraft.
Paramilitary: (included in Army).
GNP: (1978) $2,350,000,000.
Defence Expenditure: (1979) $30,100,000.

COMMAND AND CONSTITUTIONAL STATUS

According to the constitution, the President of the Republic is Commander-in-Chief of the National Guard, with the right freely to appoint and dismiss its senior officers and direct its operations. The chain of command passes through the Minister of Government and Justice to the Headquarters Command of the National Guard, which has as its principal officers the Commander, the Deputy Commander and the Secretary-General.

ROLE, COMMITMENT, DEPLOYMENT AND RECENT OPERATIONS

To a greater degree even than in most other Latin American armed forces, the Panamanian National Guard's principal role is seen by its leaders to be the maintenance of internal security against possible guerrilla operations and even more importantly against large-scale disturbances amongst the population. As part of its preventive strategy in this regard, National Guard troops spend much of their time on civic action projects, which are administered by a separate section of the General Staff.

There is no remaining problem with Colombia, which recognised Panama in 1914 and ratified a treaty defining its borders in 1921. The other land frontier, with Costa Rica, has occasionally been the scene of cross-border raids by Panamanian political exiles, but since Costa Rica does not maintain a conventional army there is no military threat to be countered. Panama's diplomatic relations with Guatemala were broken in May, 1977 after it stated its support for the independence of Belize, but it is not among those Caribbean nations which have talked of volunteering military contingents for the defence of an independent Belize.

For defence against threats from further away to the strategically important Panama Canal, Panama relies on the United States commitment to hemispheric defence, and specifically on the 10,000 United States troops based in the Canal Zone. These include an infantry brigade, a Special Forces group, two SAM battalions and an air force squadron, in addition to the personnel attached to the various States educational institutions for Latin American armed forces which are located in the Canal Zone, and the base personnel of the USAF bases at Albrook Field, Coca Sola, Howard and Río Alto, and the naval installations at Balboa and Colón.

Panama is a member of the United Nations and the Organization of American States, but has never contributed troops to any of their peace-keeping institutions – the Organisation of Central American States, its subordinate body the Central American Defence Council (CONDECA) and the Central American Common Market – though invited to do so, and has never participated in CONDECA joint manouevres.

The deployment of the National Guard is in accord with its primary mission of internal security. Well over half its strength is concentrated in the Panama City–Colón–Tocumén Airport area, which includes the capital, the main communications facilities, and the bulk of the nation's wealth and population. The remainder is distributed amongst the 10 zones into which the country is divided.

The Guard's only recent operations have been anti-riot duties in the capital, which it has performed efficiently.

ORGANISATION

The National Guard incorporates an air arm, with its headquarters and main base at Tocumén Airport, and a small naval service operating on both coasts, but it is administered as a single service from Headquarters Command at the central barracks in Panama City. Headquarters Command has directly controlled the five infantry companies since 1971, and runs the rest of the force through the Office of the Zone Commander and the General Staff. The former organisation directs the National Guard units in the country's 10 administrative divisions. The General Staff is divided into five sections: G-1, personnel; G-2, intelligence; G-3, operations (which also controls training activities, the Traffic Division, and air force and coastguard operations); G-4, logistics; and G-5 civic action.

There are, in addition, the following specialised units: the Presidential Guard (with quarters in the palace, and responsibility for the president's safety); the Bay Guard (attached to the Presidential Guard, and responsible for harbour security); the Cavalry Squadron (which is mounted only for ceremonial occasions and for crowd control); the Tocumén Airport Guard; the Public Order Company; and the National Department of Investigation (DENI, commonly called the secret police, and numbering about 300 agents).

The Guard's specifically military forces are rarely assembled together except in emergencies.

RECRUITMENT, TRAINING AND RESERVES

The Panamanian constitution permits the government to decree obligatory military service, but the Guard has always been able to achieve its desired numbers by voluntary recruitment. Recruiting is local, though centrally controlled as to numbers, and the requirement that recruits have 6 years of education is generally observed. There is no apparent discrimination on racial grounds either in the enlisted or commissioned ranks. For the great majority of its members the National Guard is a lifetime career, and 40 year-old privates are thus not uncommon.

Recruit training was haphazard until 1954, when the National Guard Orientation School was founded with the aid of a Venezuelan military mission. Recruits now receive there a 3 month course in military and police matters. An officers' school (the Police Academy) and one for NCOs were started in the early 1960s, but most of the existing senior officers have entered the commissioned ranks directly after graduating from foreign military academies. Almost all field-grade officers have attended the command and general staff courses at the United States Army School of the Americas at Fort Gulick in the Canal Zone, and many also go to the USA on courses. Large numbers of NCO's attend technical courses run by the United States Army in the Canal Zone.

Air force personnel are trained in Venezuela and Colombia, and at the Inter-American Air Force Academy in the Canal Zone.

The National Guard is an all-regular force, and there are no organised reserves.

EQUIPMENT AND ARMS INDUSTRY

The equipment of the ground forces of the National Guard is largely of United States origins although the recent years quantities of Belgian and Israeli material have been obtained. The major units of the coast guard elements and some transport aircraft are of British origins and three CASA Aviocar light transports are on order from Spain. No defence equipment is produced locally.

Rifles: M-1 0.30in (US); M-16 5.56mm (US); FN FAL 7.62mm (Belgium)
Sub-machine-guns: M-1928A1 0.45in (US); Uzi 9mm (Israel)

Machine-guns: M-1919A4 0.30in (US); FN MAG 7.62mm (Belgium)
Anti-armour weapons: M-20 3.5in RCL (US)
Mortars: M-2 60mm (US); Soltam 60mm (Israel)
Armour: V-150 armoured car (US; four in service); V-150 APC (US; 12 in service); V-300 APC (US; on order)
Aircraft: Approximately 30 light aircraft and transports and ten helicopters are operated by the air force elements of the National Guard.

RANK, DRESS AND DISTINCTIONS

Uniforms and ranks are similar to those of the USA, except for the Presidential Guard which has special uniforms for both daily duties and ceremonial occasions. Rank insignia conform to those adopted by the Central American Defence Council: company-grade officers wear one, two or three bars, field-grade officers one, two or three stars, and the Guard commander three laurel leaves on shoulder straps or shirt collar. Air force and coastguard officers wear the same insignia.

The highest award for merit given to National Guard members is the José Antonio Remón Cantera gold medal. There are six lesser awards for meritorious actions, and silver medals, bronze medals and bronze bars awarded for 20, 15, 10 and 5 years' service with the Guard.

CURRENT DEVELOPMENTS

Despite the death of General Torrijos, his policies continue to be broadly implemented. The Treaty with the United States, providing for the transfer of sovereignty over the Canal Zone to Panama, represents the realisation of the country's main foreign policy objective. As the date for the transfer approaches, the purely military elements of the National Guard may be expected to increase in importance. Considerable acquisitions of heavy equipment for its land, sea and air elements may also be expected.

Gwynne Dyer
Adrian English

PAPUA NEW GUINEA

HISTORY AND INTRODUCTION

Papua–New Guinea, the eastern half of the island of New Guinea lying to the north of Australia, was formed in 1919 by the merger of the protectorate of British New Guinea created in the south-eastern portion of the island in 1884 with the German colony established in the north-eastern part of the island (Schutzgebiet Kaiser-Wilhelms-Land und Bismarck-Archipel) in the same year. It then became the Mandated Territory of New Guinea, administered from Australia, and after being partly occupied by the Japanese and extensively fought over during World War II it became the United Nations Trust Territory of New Guinea in 1946. It became internally self-governing in 1973, and achieved independence as Papua–New Guinea on September 16th 1975.

Over 90% of Papua–New Guinea's population is engaged in subsistence agriculture, and lives still in small tribal communities which even 25 years ago were organised on the basis of a neolithic technology. As a consequence there is no nationwide cultural identity: the population, which is predominantly Melanesian and Papuan, with some Negrito, Micronesian and Polynesian enclaves, speaks over 700 different languages, and the number of ethnic blocs capable of independent political activity probably exceeds this number. The fragmentation is particularly acute in the mountainous interior – the Highlands – where population pressure on agricultural resources is also greatest. Pidgin English (Wantok) and two or three native languages serve as *linguae francae* for over half the population, with literacy amounting to about 15% in one or other of these languages. The threat or hint of secession is one of the principal currencies of political competition.

The Papua–New Guinea Defence Force has its origin in the Pacific Islands Regiment (PIR), of which the first battalion was raised in Port Moresby in 1940, with Australians filling all the officer and most of the NCO positions. Three further battalions were subsequently raised, and the regiment fought with distinction against the Japanese invaders in New Guinea for 3 years, split up for most of the time into small and scattered detachments performing reconnaissance duties for larger Australian and American units. It was disbanded in 1946, after the Japanese surrender.

With the onset of the Cold War, and after serious disturbances on Manus Island, the Australian government reformed the PIR. The first battalion was raised in Port Moresby, the administrative capital on the south coast, in 1951–2; a second battalion was raised with headquarters at Wewak on the northern coast in 1965. The same period, which saw Australia becoming deeply involved in the confrontation with Indonesia in Malaysia, also witnessed the development of major Australian army and air force bases in Papua–New Guinea and the partial refurbishment of the extensive World War II naval facilities on Manus Island.

The principal task of the Pacific Islands Regiment, however, was to provide continuous and wide-ranging patrols of about company strength throughout the mainland and the more important islands of Papua–New Guinea; it had no artillery or other heavy weapons, and the battalions hardly ever operated as a whole. The regiment did not become involved in the suppression of the large-scale civil disorders inspired by the Mataungan Association in the New Gazelle peninsula of New Britain Island in 1970 (although it was placed on alert), and devoted much of its time to 'civic action' enterprises. As late as 1971 it was still predominantly an Australian-officered force, with only 30 indigenous commissioned officers of whom just one had achieved the rank of major (he is now the Commandant of the Papua–New Guinea Defence Force). A Papua–New Guinea Division of the Royal Australian Navy was created at Manus in the Admiralty Islands in the 1960s, and gradually began to produce trained local personnel, but the foundation of an air arm did not occur until 1975, with the transfer of four C-47 transport aircraft from Australia.

Nevertheless, and despite an early record of disorders and disobedience, the PIR grew into what has been called the 'Super Tribe', an *elite* formation with superior pay and career opportunities whose level of efficiency considerably surpassed that of the other Western-style institutions being implanted in Papua–New Guinea, and whose members had subordinated their tribal loyalties to an organisational *esprit de corps* to a noteworthy extent. This characteristic has hitherto been of great assistance and comfort to the government, one of whose principal problems has been to cope with secessionist movements without conceding sovereignty, but also without using excessive military force. In this context, it is significant that some units have been trained in riot-control techniques.

Since the election of Mr Michael Somare as Chief Minister in 1972 on a platform of self-reliance and early independence, Papua–New Guinea's evolution into a viable political entity has been rapidly and remarkably smooth. In 1975, on the eve of independence, Papua–New Guinea was faced with a major secessionist threat in much of Papua, the more developed territory lying to the south of the central Owen Stanley range, which contains the capital, Port Moresby. Less significant in territorial extent, but perhaps even more important economically, was the secessionist movement in Bougainville Island, ethnically part of the Soloman Islands, which contains the copper mines that are Papua–New Guinea's chief source of foreign exchange. When Papua–New Guinea became independent, the Bougainville secessionists dismissed the provincial government and declared a separate Republic of the North Solomons.

A combination of patience, political adroitness and brisk military action succeeded in overcoming these difficulties in a short time, however. The handful of armed Papuan rebels were quickly run to ground, and the secessionist Papua Besena Party, though still commanding major support in the affected areas, is now peacefully participating in the national parliament. After waiting 6 months for the leaders of the Bougainville secession to fall into disputes among themselves, squads of Papua–New Guinea riot police were quickly brought in in April, 1976 and the secession collapsed. While considerable concessions on provincial autonomy were made (which are now being extended to other sensitive areas) the only advance over the terms on offer to Bougainville before the secession was the granting of permission to fly the Bougainville flag alongside the Papua–New Guinea flag. The main leader of the secession, Father John Momis, is now the Minister for Decentralisation in Port Moresby, and the Bougainville secessionist movement seems defunct at least for this political generation.

461

The post-independence defence relationship between Papua—New Guinea and the former colonial power, Australia, was not the subject of a formal treaty, which would have injured Papua—New Guinea's status as a non-aligned member of the Third World. Australia committed itself to assisting the development of the Papua—New Guinea Defence Forces, however, through a Defence Co-operation Agreement involving about $30,000,000 per annum in Australian aid, and in February, 1977 Prime Minister Somare of Papua—New Guinea and Prime Minister Malcolm Fraser of Australia issued a joint statement on the two countries' future relationship. It stressed the importance to both countries of continuing close co-operation in defence matters, and specifically provided for the attachment of Australian servicemen to the Papua—New Guinea Defence Force in non-combatant roles until they were no longer needed, the continued basing in Papua—New Guinea of formed units of the Australian armed forces to carry out engineering and air-transport functions still beyond the native forces' capacity, provisions for training of Papua—New Guinea Defence Force personnel both at home and in Australia, and various kinds of Australian assistance with transport, logistical and technical matters. In non-military areas, Australia has promised a minimum of $930,000,000 aid to Papua—New Guinea in the 5 years from July, 1976.

In the national elections held in Papua—New Guinea in June and July, 1977 both Mr Somare's Pangu Party and his coalition partner, the People's Progressive Party, emerged with increased representation. Later in the year the PPP suddenly withdrew from the coalition, but it was soon replaced by what had hitherto been the main opposition group, the United Party. This fluidity of political allegiances is not untypical of Papua—New Guinea, where politics is much more about regional interests than ideologies, but so far Mr Somare has shown himself an adroit manipulator of these regional pressure groups in the interest of national unity. His principal concern in foreign affairs at the moment — though it has serious potential domestic repercussions — is the troubled situation along the border with Indonesia's West Irian province that occupies the western half of the island of New Guinea. This is undoubtedly also the chief concern of the Papua—New Guinea Defence Forces. (*See* Role, Commitment, Deployment and Recent Operations.)

STRENGTH AND BUDGET

The strength of the Papua—New Guinea Defence Force in 1978 was 3775 men, of whom about 3400 were serving in the ground forces. This constituted just over 0.1% of Papua—New Guinea's population of 3,200,000 people, and seems to be a stable figure. The defence forces are complemented in the internal security role by the Papua—New Guinea Constabulary, a uniformed force of comparable size whose rural elements have roughly equivalent equipment and patrol duties. The Reserve Constabulary, a part-time volunteer force, is the principal reserve formation available to the government.

Defence expenditure in 1981 was $38,000,000 out of a GNP of $2,682,000,000. To this must be added, however, a substantial sum in Australian military aid under the Defence Co-operation Programme.

COMMAND AND CONSTITUTIONAL STATUS

Papua—New Guinea is a member of the Commonwealth, with executive power formally vested in H.M. Queen Elizabeth II. It is exercised on her behalf by the Governor-General, who is appointed by the Prime Minister and acts on the advice of the National Executive Council (the Cabinet) led by the Prime Minister. There is no office of Commander-in-Chief of the Defence Force, which is subject to the supervision and control of the National Executive Council through the Minister for Defence (Epel Tito). The Commander of the Papua—New Guinea Defence Force is Brigadier-General Gogo Mamae OBE, who is assisted by a small staff in his headquarters in Murray Barracks in Port Moresby.

The Papua—New Guinea Constabulary is controlled by the National Executive Council through the Minister for Police (currently Mr Patterson Lowa), and is commanded by a Commissioner of Police. Its administrative organisation and rank structure follow British colonial models; below the level of Constabulary Headquarters in Port Moresby, it operates through four territorial commands: First Division (Papua); Second Division (New Guinea highlands); Third Division (New Guinea coastal areas); and Fourth Division (New Guinea island territories).

ROLE, COMMITMENT, DEPLOYMENT AND RECENT OPERATIONS

The functions of the Defence Force are to defend Papua—New Guinea, and to aid the civil authorities in a civil disaster in the restoration of public order, or during a period of declared national emergency. In fact their primary potential role is as a last-resort guarantee of national unity, though they have not often been called on to act in this context. Their willingness to do so will be unquestioned so long as they retain their present character as a 'Super Tribe' which rises above the prevailing regional loyalties, and their ability to control secessionist movements is adequate to deal with the present scale of threats to national unity. Papua—New Guinea can probably also rely on direct Australian support in this context, if necessary, and at least on sympathetic understanding from its other big neighbour, Indonesia.

Papua—New Guinea belongs to the United Nations, the Commonwealth and the group of non-aligned nations, but maintains no foreign military alliances. Nevertheless it can rely upon Australian defence aid in meeting any military threat from outside the region, since its geographical location is of vital strategic importance to Australia itself. There is a continuing boundary dispute between Papua—New Guinea and Australia in the Torres Straits that separate them, arising from the action of Queensland in 1879 in extending the Australian border to encompass all the islands and waters to within a few hundred metres of the Papuan coastline, a disagreement made more serious by the high probability that the seabed in this area contains oil, but it is expected that a negotiated settlement adjusting the boundary in Papua—New Guinea's favour will eventually be reached.

The principal external threat which might engage the Papua—New Guinea Defence Force itself is the 600 mile border with the Indonesian-controlled western half of the island, West Irian. There are two negotiated agreements between Port Moresby and Jakarta delineating the border and the movement of people across it, but the Indonesian government is extremely sensitive on border security due to the persistent guerrilla movement in West Irian seeking secession from Indonesia. It is well aware that the cultural and ethnic links of West Irian are with Papua—New Guinea, not with distant Java, and that there is a reservoir of sympathy for the rebels in Papua—New Guinea. Some of the rebels talk of union with Papua—New Guinea, which disturbs Jakarta even more.

Originally part of the Dutch Empire in the East Indies, the western half of New Guinea was not granted its independence at the same time as Indonesia; it was handed over to Jakarta by the Dutch in 1962 after a lengthy but low-intensity Indonesian military campaign, mainly disguised as a 'liberation movement'. Indonesian annexation of 'West Irian' was theoretically approved by a referendum in 1969, but the domination of all levels of the administration by Indonesian outsiders and the flood of Indonesian immigrants (250,000 Javanese and Sumatrans have now settled amongst the 850,000 dark-skinned Melanesian natives) had already led to the emergence of a local guerrilla resistance movement 4 years earlier, in 1965. This movement, the Organisasi Papua Merdeka (OPM), carried out numerous raids through the later 1960s against Indonesian forces, concentrating its activities particularly in the area around the administrative capital of Jayapura, on the northern coast just west of the Papua–New Guinea border, where it enjoyed the greatest popular support. Numbers of refugees from Indonesian reprisals entered Papua–New Guinea along with the usual illegal immigrants seeking to benefit from its higher level of economic development, and the leaders of the OPM were from time to time in Port Moresby, where they got a sympathetic hearing in many circles.

After a period of relative inaction the OPM began operating again in the jungle mountains adjoining the Papua–New Guinea borders in 1975, and by 1977 its operations had caused the Indonesian government to carry out large-scale reprisal raids on villages suspected of harbouring rebels, including air attacks. A new wave of refugees began to cross the Papua–New Guinea border; the small units of the OPM, which may total no more than 200 full-time combatants, also began to use inaccessible parts of Papua–New Guinea just across the border as sanctuaries and, despite denials from both Jakarta and Port Moresby, it is clear that Indonesian troops repeatedly crossed the border in pursuit of them.

The Papua–New Guinea government is extremely anxious to avoid a clash with Indonesia, but the views of its own population prohibit it from active collaboration with Indonesian forces in suppressing the guerrillas using the cross-border area. An attempt to dissuade the West Irianese guerrillas from using Papua–New Guinea soil in their operations, involving an interview in Port Moresby between OPM leader General Seth Jafet Rumkoren and Papua–New Guinea Defence Force Commander Brigadier Diro (which led to intense speculation in the press about the Defence Force's loyalty to the civil government), failed to end the problem, nor did a further round of government discussions with Rumkoren and the rival OPM leader, Jacob Prai, in Port Moresby in April, 1978. Prime Minister Somare discussed the border problem with the Indonesian President, General Suharto, in a visit to Jakarta in May, 1977 and the Papua–New Guinea government subsequently sent 218 refugees back to West Irian, but the problem continued to worsen.

In May, 1978 the OPM abducted nine high Indonesian officials, including the Military Governor of the Jayapura district, the provincial intelligence chief, and the chairman of the provincial assembly. Indonesian forces repeatedly crossed the jungle border between Wutung and Bewani during the large-scale search and reprisal operations that followed, and at least one Papua–New Guinea village was bombed in error by Indonesian aircraft. Forced to react officially at last, the Papua–New Guinea Defence Force abruptly raised the force deployed in the northern border area to three companies – almost half the army's infantry strength – and transferred much of its air transport from Port Moresby to the area. This deployment was well advertised in advance, however, in order to give both the OPM guerrillas and any Indonesian patrols that were across the border time to get out of the way. At the end of 1978, the Papua–New Guinea Defence Force was still heavily concentrated along this border.

During the period 1979–82 the commitment remained one of border patrols, improving the training facilities and the quality of equipment. The major event of the period was the air move of a contingent of some 200 soldiers to Vanatu in 1980. This was in response to a request from the newly formed independent country for assistance in restoring law and order. This was the first overseas deployment on operations for the Papua–New Guinea Defence Force and gave a boost to the morale of the services and to the status of the country in the eyes of surrounding countries in the Southeast Pacific basin.

ORGANISATION

The Papua–New Guinea Defence Force consists of a ground element comprising two infantry battalions based at Port Moresby and Wewak, an engineer battalion, a signal squadron and some logistic units. Other main bases are at Lae and Manaus. Arms of service and internal organisation follow British/Australian patterns. The same is true of the air component, consisting of a single Air Transport Squadron based at Port Moresby, with other bases at Lae, Madang, Rabaul and Wewak, plus more than 400 usable airstrips throughout the country. The main landing strips within 20 miles of the border with West Irian in the north are Wutung, Bewani, Amanab and Green River. The naval component consists of a Patrol Craft Squadron based at Manus Island, and a Landing Craft Squadron based at Port Moresby.

RECRUITMENT, TRAINING AND RESERVES

All Papua–New Guinea Defence Force personnel are volunteers serving long engagements. Pay and promotion prospects are superior to those available in most civilian occupations, and competition for vacancies is keen. There is considerable Australian training assistance provided both at recruit level and within the operational army units, each of which has two medical officers and two training officers from the Australian armed forces attached to it. In 1978 the number of seconded Australian servicemen in Papua–New Guinea had fallen to 270, and it was expected that they would almost all be phased out by 1980. Papua–New Guinea Defence Force technical personnel, especially in the air component, continue to be sent to military and civil establishments in Australia for training, and it is anticipated that the requirement for direct Australian support for the air element will continue for a longer time. It is intended that a basic flying school should eventually be established in Papua–New Guinea, however.

Officers of all components are trained at the Papua–New Guinea Joint Services College at Lae, where the curriculum is a modified version of the Australian model and the bulk of instructors are furnished on loan by the Australian and New Zealand armed forces. For instruction in technical specialities and for higher military education, Papua–New Guinea Defence Force officers still go mainly to Australia.

The Papua–New Guinea Constabulary gives its recruits 6 months of training at the Central Police Training Centre at Bomana, and conducts year-long courses for officer candidates at the Police Training College on the same site. There is an additional on-the-job training period of 2 or 3 years for other ranks and officer candidates. Senior police officers attend courses abroad, in Australia, Britain and other Commonwealth countries.

EQUIPMENT AND ARMS INDUSTRY

The ground element of the Papua—New Guinea Defence Force is equipped with light infantry weapons, and transport and engineering equipment of Australian manufacture; it has no artillery or other heavy weapons. The naval element has five Australian-built Attack-class patrol craft and three LCHs. The air component flies three ex-RAAF C-47 transports and three GAF Nomad Mission Masters.

A plan to establish a national aircraft production capability by assembling Nomads in Papua—New Guinea was announced in late 1976, but there has been no significant progress towards achieving this goal. There is no arms industry in Papua—New Guinea at present.

RANK, DRESS AND DISTINCTIONS

The rank structure and uniforms of the Papua—New Guinea Defence Force follow Australian models.

CURRENT DEVELOPMENTS

After seven years of independence, the Papua—New Guinea Defence Force has continued to grow into a reliable, effective small force, drawn from all tribal areas and showing both maturity and self discipline. Australia continues to provide the major share of the defence budget although the cut-back required in 1981/82 has meant a drastic pruning of exercises schedules and the postponement of the purchase of new equipment. The major preoccupation of the army will continue to be the artificial frontier with West Irian. Cross-Border incursions by tribesmen of the same ethnic background seeking food, medicine or political haven still occur. The ability to respond quickly to such incursions is a major challenge to the Papua—New Guinea Defence Force. The development of a small ready-reaction force, with improved communications will do much to assist the defence forces in this task. Links with Canberra have been improved recently with the appointment of a Defence Adviser and this reflects the close ties which exist between Australia and the Papua—New Guinea Defence Force. Australia has a vested interest in ensuring that crossborder relations between PNG and West Irian remain favourable and the small but efficient Defence forces of PNG make a valuable contribution to this stability

Gwynne Dyer

PARAGUAY

HISTORY AND INTRODUCTION

Paraguay is a military dictatorship, now the longest lived in Latin America, the present ruler, General Alfredo Stroessner, having come to power in 1954. The army is the dominant institution in the country. Its officers, serving or retired, are strongly represented in the Council of Ministers and hold senior positions in the civil service and state enterprises. Although opposition parties exist, the ruling Colorado party consistently wins overwhelming majorities at elections, and the only effective voice of opposition in the country is raised by the church, with which the government is on bad terms. President Stroessner is now in his sixth term of office. A constitutional convention was elected to amend the constitution so as to allow him to serve a sixth, from 1978. Though there have been several attempts, real or merely reported, to overthrow him from within the armed forces, his position appears unassailable, and this despite the well-attested fact that the Paraguayans are perhaps the most bellicose people in the sub-continent.

Paraguay, completely land-locked, remote, poor and sparsely inhabited, has one of the most curious histories in South America. In the seventeenth and eighteenth centuries it was the main centre of the Jesuits' missionary efforts among the Indians, whom they organised in large, autonomous communes and protected against the depredations of the colonists. Their success and consequent unpopularity with the whites led to their expulsion in 1768, but they had ensured the survival of the indigenous population (*Guaranis*) almost intact, with the result that Paraguay has today a homogeneous population of largely Indian descent, and a living local language spoken by the majority of the inhabitants and supporting a lively national literature. Paraguay also became the first country to declare its independence of Spain, in 1811, largely by reaction against the efforts of the Argentinians to incorporate it in their own independence movement. The leader of the local movement was an extraordinary Spanish-educated lawyer, Francia, who defeated an Argentinian invasion and made himself dictator, which he remained until his death in 1840. His rule was completely arbitrary. He expelled all foreigners, allowed none in, and prevented Paraguayans from leaving the country. He severed trade links with the outside world, promoted self-sufficiency of a subsistence sort, persecuted the church and punished ferociously all disobedience to his whims and the least disrespect to his person. But his rule spared Paraguay the frightful civil and foreign wars which racked so much of South America in the independence era and left it a peaceful if not prosperous country. He was succeeded by the López presidents, father and son, whose policy was outward looking. But the father, Carlos, though he quarrelled with his neighbours, Argentina and Brazil, avoided war. The son, Francisco, overestimated his power. He built up between 1862 and 1864 an army of 50,000, the best in South America, and provocatively declared support for the anti-Brazilian party in Uruguay, over the control of which Brazil was in dispute with Argentina. The outcome of his intervention was to unite Brazil, Argentina and Uruguay against him in the War of the Triple Alliance, 1865–70. It was in this war that the Paraguayans first showed their ferocious and indomitable military prowess. Time after time they attacked at hopeless odds, to lose terribly but to continue the struggle elsewhere. It was ended only by the death in action of Francisco López himself. The country was bankrupted and devastated and had lost 300,000 of its 500,000 people. Among the survivors, women and children outnumbered men by none to one. The new generation was fathered by the Brazilian army of occupation which remained in the country until 1876.

The war, which transferred large tracts of territory to Brazil and Argentina, also broke that country's tradition of settled, if autocratic, government. Francisco López had not waged war without internal opposition and the parties which subsequently came into existence, the Colorados and Liberals, reflected those divisions. They were pushed to ridiculous, if familiar, extremes in the next 40 years, during which twenty-two presidents held office; there were no less than four in 1911. The army was the most frequent instrument of political change, and the chief source of political power. After 1912 there was a period of comparative stability, when the army sustained a succession of Liberals – Schaerer, Franco, the two Ayalas (the so-called 'literary presidents') – for their full terms, but the promise of peaceful progress was dashed by the onset of Paraguay's second great disaster, the Chaco War, in 1932. The Chaco, the northern extension of the pampas, had been claimed by Bolivia since 1811 but the claim had not been pressed. In the 1920s, however, Bolivia was alerted to the possibility of oil strikes in the Chaco. She had also long wanted a foothold in the River Paraguay, to restore her access to the sea lost in the war with Chile in 1883, and the failure of her claims to regain that coast in 1929 redoubled her interest in the river. There had been border clashes in 1927 and a serious shooting in 1928. In 1932 a full-scale war broke out. Bolivia brought her German-trained army out of the Andes into the low-lying Chaco where her brave soldiers died in thousands. So too, unfortunately, did Paraguay's for, though better acclimatised to the region, they were greatly outnumbered. Though they gained a victory and 20,000 square miles of territory, the male population was again reduced by tens of thousands. Bolivia, however, had been granted railway access to the river, which the population regarded as a humiliation. There followed as a result a succession of coups and counter-coups so frequently that the Paraguayans themselves described the period 1936–9 as *confusionismo*.

Confusionismo began with a seizure of power by a veteran of the war, Colonel Rafael Franco, in February, 1936. His policy was to inaugurate an Italian-style fascist regime, in which he was supported by many young officers in the army but, after provoking a series of revolts, he was removed by an army counter-coup in August, 1937. The *golpistas* replaced him with the president of the university, Paiva, who managed to hold peaceful elections in 1939. These returned the hero of the Chaco War, General Estigarribia, to power but his promising presidency was cut short by his death in an air crash the following year. In the meantime, however, he had replaced the comparatively liberal 1870 Consitution with a strongly presidential one and his successor, General Higineo Morínigo, the Minister of War, used it on his assumption of power to rule autocratically. He was elected to the presidency in 1943 in army-run elections, despite several armed uprisings against him. The disorder continued spasmodically, culminating in 1947 in a large-scale revolt by the Liberals and Febreristas (a left-wing party), who came to control wide areas of the country before they were defeated. In 1948 the army bought to power a Colorado candidate, González, but replaced him the following year with another Colorado, Chavez. He was eventually judged to be too influenced by Perón of Argentina and in 1954 was turned out by the Minister of War, General Alfredo Stroessner, a member of the small but powerful German immigrant community. The general has held power ever since, largely by his skill in manipulating the officer corps and rewarding chosen members with lucrative posts in government and State-controlled business enterprises. He has many opponents both inside the country, where the armed forces had his own Colorado party regularly produce dissidents, and outside, where a United Front for National Liberation occasionally stages cross-border raids from Argentina or Brazil. The best organised took place in 1960 and 1964. But he has crushed all opposition and has apparently no difficulty in retaining power, thanks to his absolute domination of the army. He has been careful to maintain cordial relations with the United States, from which he receives military and investment aid, and has cultivated friendship with authoritarian regimes abroad, notably those of South Africa and Taiwan, which also invest in Paraguay. Partly because of the difficult geographical approaches to the country, which lie across broad, easily patrolled rivers or inhospitable terrain, he has not been troubled by major guerrilla incursions. As long as he retains the loyalty of his officers, his government appears unshakable.

STRENGTH AND BUDGET

Population: 3,300,000
Army: 15,000
Navy: 2000 (including 500 marines); 15 small craft
Air force: 2000; 22 combat aircraft
GNP (1980: $5,330,000,000
Defence expenditure: (1980): $87,600,000

Over the last 15 years, Paraguay has consistently spent tetween 1.6 and 2.2% of its gross domestic product on defence, and about 20% of the national budget; of the latter figures, however, about a quarter is allotted to the upkeep of military farms and ranches, from which the armed forces are fed. The country has received appreciable quantities of United States military aid. The most recent deliveries were five Douglas DC-6s and 12 AT-6 Texan aircraft in 1975, all surplus to United States requirements.

COMMAND AND CONSTITUTIONAL STATUS

Under the 1967 Constitution, the President is Commander-in-Chief of the Armed Forces, and exercises dictatorial authority through his power to impose a 'state of siege' for prolonged periods over the whole area of the republic or designated parts of it. The western half of the country, the sparsely inhabited Chaco, is under permanent military government. The inhabited eastern half has been intermittently in a 'state of siege' since General Stroessner's assumption of power. He has the right to declare the 'state of siege' unilaterally, the only restraint on it being a requirement to inform Congress within 5 days of his reasons for declaring it and the areas of the country to which it extends.

The president directly controls the Armed Forces General Staff, to which the staffs of the army, navy, and air force are subordinate. The Ministry of National Defence, headed by a serving or retired officer, is outside the chain of command and concerns itself with budgetary, logistic and legal func-

tions. The President also, through the Ministry of the Interior, controls the National Police, the detachments of which are commanded by the government representative (*delegado*) in each department.

The president chairs all meetings of the officer promotion boards, which meet twice yearly on May 14th and December 31st, and personally approves or disapproves every promotion. He also makes all the more important military appointments, including those of serving or retired officers to governmental positions.

ROLE, COMMITMENT, DEPLOYMENT AND RECENT OPERATIONS

Role and Commitments

Now that Paraguay's frontier disputes with its neighbours have been settled (in the Triple Alliance and Great Chaco Wars), the army's role is chiefly an internal one. It provides, as it has done since 1870, the principal and perhaps only support of the ruling president, assists the police in the maintenance of internal law and order and, with the navy, exercises surveillance over the frontiers. In recent years it has also come to have an important developmental and civic role. Through its training of conscripts it reduces illiteracy in the population and teaches useful trades; and it performs direct civic aid, by the building of dams and bridges in the interior, the sinking of wells and provision of building materials for new settlements and village improvement. Its supervision of Indian affairs in the Chaco has given rise to hostile foreign comment; charges have been laid (by the British Anti-Slavery Society) of a deliberate policy of extermination of some tribes. The army has no external commitments. Argentina and Brazil maintain military missions in the country, and it also receives United States military aid.

Deployment

The country is divided into six Military Regions, as follows:
1st Military Region (HQ Aguncion) covers Central Department.
2nd Military Region (HQ Villarica) covers departments of Guairá, Caäzapá and Itapúa.
3rd Military Region (HQ San Juan Bautista de las Misiones) covers departments of Misiones and Neëmbucú.
4th Military Region (HQ Concepción) covers departments of Concepción, Amambay and San Pedro.
5th Military Region (HQ Puerto Presidente Stroessner) covers departments of Alto Paraná and Caäguazú.
6th Military Region (HQ Mariscal Estigarribia) covers the Chaco departments of Boquerón, Olimpo and Presidente Hayes.

Each Military Region is garrisoned by a nominal Infantry Division and a variable complement of other units. The 1st Military Region also contains the 1st Cavalry Division and most of the combat support units and training establishments. This Region also contains the headquarters of the Navy and Air Force, including the latter's Paratroop Regiment.

The bulk of the single Marine Regiment, together with some Naval Artillery units, is located on the Upper Paraguay river between the ports of Olimpo and Bahia Negra.

Recent Operations

Apart from the Civil War of 1947—48 and the sporadic coups, some of which, including that by means of which General Stroessner came to power in 1954, have involved considerable fighting, recent operations have been confined to the suppression of low level insurgency, principally during the 1960s.

ORGANISATION

The Army is divided into Combat Arms and Logistic Services. The Combat Arms are Infantry, Cavalry and Artillery, all of which are organised in regiments which are both numbered and named and Engineers, which are organised in battalions, which appear to be known by their numerical designations only. Signals and Transport each form single regiments, sub units of which are detached in support of the combat units. Intendence, War Material, Medical and Veterinary services are organised in support detachments of varying sizes.

Infantry regiments, of which there are six, have three battalions each, of which only one is active in peace time. The Presidential Escort Regiment is an elite combat unit, primarily of infantry but containing a small motorised element and military police unit. There is also the anomalously named *Regimiento Batallón 40*, stationed at Pilar, which is paradoxically an infantry unit organised on the lines of a cavalry regiment. In addition to the motorised infantry battalion attached to the 1st Cavalry Division, there is at least one more independent infantry battalion, stationed at Paraguarí and there are also two 'Frontier Battalions', stationed at Pilar and Puerto Presidente Stroessnner. Cavalry regiments have four squadrons each. There are two horsed and two mechanised Cavalry Regiments, the latter forming the 1st Cavalry Division, which is the Army's major tactical unit. This formation also includes a motorised infantry battalion and an artillery unit of indeterminate size known as the *Núcleo de Artillería de la Primera División de Caballería*. There is only one major artillery unit, the 1st 'General Bruguéz' Artillery Regiment, stationed at Paraguarí. There is an Engineer Command grouping together five engineer battalions which are deployed in the less-developed parts of the country and are largely employed on public works, such as road building.

A new tactical organisation, adopted in 1980, groups the existing Divisions under three Army Corps, as follows:
1st Army Corps (HQ Asunción) consists of the 1st Infantry Division (HQ Asunción), the 3rd Infantry Division (HQ San Juan Bautista) and the 1st Cavalry Division (HQ Nu-Guazú).
2nd Army Corps (HQ Villarica) combines the 2nd Infantry Division (HQ Villarica) with the 5th Infantry Division (HQ Puerto Presidente Stroessner) and the 1st Cavalry Detachment (HQ Encarnación).
3rd Army Corps (HQ Mariscal Estigarribia) comprises the 4th Infantry Division (HQ Concepción), the 6th Infantry Division (HQ Mariscal Estigarribia) and the *Pilcomayo* and *Cerrito* Detachments, with their HQs at Villa Hayes and Benjamín Aceval, respectively and a Cavalry Detachment based at Pedro Juan Caballero.

The establishment of each infantry division consists of a headquarters, three regiments and a logistic support battalion combining itendence, transport and medical units. Artillery is not organic to the divisions and is allocated to them on an ad-hoc basis. In peacetime each division normally contains only one skeletonised infantry regiment although the 1st and 3rd Divisions, forming part of the 1st Army Corps, each have two regiments.

Under the new tactical organisation, the single artillery regiment is grouped with the engineer battalions and signals units in a Combat Support Command.

The Presidential Escort Regiment is outside the divisional and corps organisation and comes under the direct command of the President of the Republic. It is not clear whether the frontier battalions are incorporated into the divisional structure.

The Navy includes one marine infantry regiment, the *Regimiento de Infantería de Marina 'Riachuelo'* and a nucleus of 'coastal' artillery manning fixed defences on the Upper Paraguay river.

The sole paratroop regiment, the *Regimiento de Paracaidistas 'Silvio Pettirossi'*, comes under Air Force command and is based at Luque near Asuncíon.

RECRUITMENT, TRAINING AND RESERVES

Recruitment of soldiers is by universal conscription, under Article 125 of the 1967 Constitution. The term of service is 18 months. Those exempted or living abroad must pay a military service tax, either to the Office of Internal Taxes or to a consulate. The annual contingent is about 20,000 strong, of which rather less than half is called for service, a proportion, nevertheless, much higher than in most South American countries; conscripts also serve in the police.

Soldiers are trained in the unit to which assigned. NCOs are chosen from promising conscripts and are trained at a variety of schools, including the Armaments School, the Engineer School and the Signal School, all located at Asuncíon. Officers, selected by competitive examination from high-school graduates, are trained at the *Colegio Militar*, Asuncíon (tri-service, 4 year course). Because of the civil as well as military career opportunities open to officers, admission to the military academy is eagerly sought for their sons by middle-class families. Many of the entrants are graduates of the *Liceo Militar*, a military boarding school at Asuncíon. Higher training is provided at the army and Air Force Command and General Staff College, and at the National War College (tri-service and civil service, founded 1968). Officers also attend the United States School of the Americas, and the Inter-American Defence College, Washington. The USA, with Brazil and Argentina, maintains a military mission in the country.

The army releases about 6000 trained conscripts each year but does not appear to maintain a reserve training programme or organisation.

EQUIPMENT AND ARMS INDUSTRY

In the past Paraguay has manufactured arms, including artillery pieces and during the Chaco War, a limited but efficient defence industry was built up under naval control, large quantities of hand grenades being manufactured together with personal equipment, aircraft bombs and even radio transmitters. No military equipment appears to be produced currently and even small arms ammunition seems to be imported. Equipment in use is extremely heterogeneous, including quantities of obsolete US material of World War II vintage, obtained both directly from its country of origin and third hand from Argentina and Brazil. Artillery pieces of British and Swedish origin have also been acquired, as gifts, from Brazil and Argentina.

Rifles: FN FAL 7.62mm (Belgium); M1 0.30″ (US)
Sub-machine-guns: Madsen Model 46 9mm (Denmark); Carl Gustav Kpist 45 9mm (Sweden); Uzi 9mm (Israel)
Machine-guns: M1917 7.62mm (US); M2 0.50″ (US); Madsen Model 1924 7.62mm (Denmark)
Anti-armour weapons: 75mm RCL (US)
Mortars: Stokes-Brandt 81mm (France); M2 4.2″ (US); M32 4.2″ (US)
Artillery: Bofors 75mm L/40 Model 1934 (Sweden via Argentina); Schneider 75mm 1927 (France); Schneider 105mm 1927 (France); Vickers 6″ (Britain via Brazil)
Armour: M4 medium tank (US); 10 in service); Sherman Firefly medium tank (US — British via Argentinia; 6 in

service); M3 light tank (US via Brazil; 12 in service);
Modified M8 armoured car (US via Brazil; 12 in service);
Modified M2 half-track APC (US via Brazil; 12 in service)
Aircraft: The Army operates 8 light aircraft and 3 heli-
copters. The Air Force has approximately 20 transport
aircraft and about a dozen helicopters.

RANK, DRESS AND DISTINCTIONS

The army wears a dark green service dress; the officers wear
white for ceremonial.

Mariscal (vacant since the Chaco War)
General — Four gold stars, wreath
General Mayor — Three gold stars, wreath
General de Brigada — Two gold stars, wreath
Coronel — Four gold stars
Teniente Coronel — Three gold stars
Mayor — Two gold stars
Capitan — Four small gold stars
1 Teniente — Three small gold stars
2 Teniente — Two small gold stars
Subteniente — One small gold star

The insignia of subaltern officers is worn on shoulder straps;
that of field and general officers on shoulder cords, officers
on combat or shirt sleeve order, when the equivalent US
insignia are worn on the collar.

CURRENT DEVELOPMENTS

The Paraguayan army is, with the national police, essentially
the chief prop of the incumbent regime, which is almost
wholly military in character. The Colorados, though in theory
the ruling party, are not an independent political force, but
the capitives of their nominee, General Stroessner. As long as
he retains the loyalty of his military subordinates, which he
has very skilfully done so far by a judicious allocation of
rewards and punishments, he appears irremovable. And while
he holds power, domestic political life will remain stultified.
External threats to the regime are negligible; the neighbouring regimes are also military in character and well disposed
towards the person of the president, while exiled dissidents
have little hope of launching successful attacks against the
regime across the country's difficult borders, or of establishing safe bases for guerrilla activity within the territory.

The army is not, however, simply an agent of repression.
It is deeply committed to civil action and development. An
important element in the training of conscripts is the teaching
of literacy and of useful tasks, particularly building work and
machine maintenance. And many units are devoted to development work in the interior. The army's five engineer battalions are committed to civil engineering projects, including
the building of roads and bridges, the digging of wells, building of water storage tanks, installation of pumping equipment
and the fabrication of bricks, tiles and other building materials for village schools and churches. The signal corps provides
radio and telephone communication to outlying settlements,
the military medical service furnishes medical care throughout the interior (as does the navy's medical service to communities along the rivers), while the army's veterinary service
is responsible for all veterinary care in the country. The air
force runs an internal air line, which provides subsidised
travel between isolated communities, and conducts the
national meteorological service.

The president's dual employment of his armed forces, in
repression and civil action, effectively nullifies internal
opposition to his regime, from all save one direction — that
of the church. The Paraguayan archdiocese of the Roman
Catholic church, once one of the most politically subservient
in South America, has become in recent years a frank and
open critic of authoritarian government and, because of its
national standing, a threat which Stroessner can neither
punish nor ignore. The archbiships of Asuncíon have thrice
excommunicated the Minister of the Interior for the mistreatment by his police of priests, and the present archbishop,
Rolon, has consistently condemned the regime for 'arbitrar-
iness, oppressiveness, monopoly of the media, favouritism,
corruption and severe mistreatment of prisoners'. The provincial clergy have identified themselves with the cause of the
landless peasants and have set up a number of co-operative
enterprises aimed at recovering land from absentee landlords.
Their work has involved them in direct clashes with the army
and police, particularly at Jejui, 190 miles north of Asuncíon,
in February, 1975. Hostility between the military regime and
the church may be expected to harden.

John Keegan
Adrian English

PERU

HISTORY AND INTRODUCTION

Peru is certainly not alone among Latin American republics in possessing an army which intervenes in politics, nor in that army regarding itself as the guardians of the nation's destiny and instrument of its economic and social development. But whereas most Latin American armies intervene in government only to bridge some political crisis, the Peruvian, which came to power by *coup d'état* in 1968, proclaimed its determination to remain in power until fundamental and irreversible changes in the nature of the Peruvian State and society have been achieved; and having apparently decided that these changes had been achieved, in July 1980, the Armed Forces handed back power to a democratically elected civilian government, ironically led by Fernando Belaúnde Terry, the man they had displaced from the presidency in 1968.

What is most surprising about the Peruvian army's recent and wholehearted involvement in politics is that it should come some 70 years after the definitive exclusion of the army from government had, in theory, been brought about. Until that moment its political role had been paramount from the foundation of the Republic in 1821, firstly because the Spanish combined power was stronger in Peru, the historic heartland of its South American empire, than elsewhere and the winning of independence demanded a constantly greater military effort, and secondly because the early years of the Republic's life were wracked by wars with neighbours (Colombia 1827, Chile 1838 and Bolivia 1841), incursions by exiled dissidents and internal struggles for power between armed parties. Stability was not imposed until the presidency of General Roman Castilla (1845–51), who took the important step of putting the army into a more regular basis. Like the other territories of Spanish South America, Peru had not been garrisoned by a properly constituted military force until the Bourbon administrative reforms of 1764. The force then constituted was made up of three elements: Spanish regiments serving temporarily abroad, Spanish regiments on permanent colonial service (*fijo* regiments) and colonial militias. The garrison proved far too small, however, to deal with the armies raised by Bolivar and Santa Cruz and new regiments were hastily raised after 1810, the men being mainly Indians and the officers creoles or mestizos. These regiments had defeated San Martin early in his campaign and had played a major part in the defeat of the Spaniards. Their leaders naturally expected to fulfil a similar role in the political life of the new Republic; they quickly squashed the grandees of the coastal cities, who regarded themselves as the legitimate inheritors of power, and thereafter used their military skills and resources to battle between themselves for control. As long as the army remained a collection of personal factions, such internal strife was inevitable. Castilla's efforts to regularise it were therefore crucial and, though only partially successful, pointed the way to the future.

Castilla allowed himself to become associated, however, with the liberal, anti-clerical interest among the coastal grandees and, through the conflict with the church and its supporters which ensued, to provoke a fresh round of internal strife which lasted until 1868. Internal differences were then overlaid by a sudden surge of economic development. Peru is immensely rich both in mineral resources and in deposits of guano (sea-bird manure), a by-product of its proximity to the richest fishing grounds in the world. It was guano and nitrates which generated the boom of the early 1870s, attracting capital from Europe and America for their exploitation, and for the creation of the railways to carry the materials to the coast. But the boom was mishandled by Colonel Balta (President, 1868–72) and at the presidential election of 1872 he was succeeded by Manuel Prado, the first civilian to hold the office and the leader of a new force in Peruvian politics, the Partido Civilista, a party drawing its support from the coastal grandees and dedicated to the establishment of constitutional government uninterrupted by military coups. One of Prado's first acts was to create a National Guard, recruited from the civilian population, to act as a counterweight to the army. The country's affairs continued, however, to be dominated by economic questions which led it in 1875 into a disastrous war with its neighbour Chile. It was not the first war she had fought. In 1859 there had been a border war with Ecuador, and in 1866 a local naval war with Spain, which was then attempting belatedly to reassert its influence in the Pacific; but neither had been serious. The War of the Pacific (1879–83) was to bankrupt and exhaust the country. The precipitating cause was a boundary dispute between Chile and Bolivia over a mineral-rich border province, in which Peru sided with Bolivia. Obliged to make good her guarantee of support, Peru at once lost her navy to a Chilean naval attack (Admiral Grau's death on the bridge of the monitor *Huascar* made him a Peruvian national hero), then lost her southern nitrate and guano regions on which she depended to finance the war to a land attack, and eventually the capital itself which the Chileans occupied in January, 1881. After 2 years of guerrilla warfare, the Peruvians were obliged to make a costly peace. In the aftermath, the country returned to military rule, but of so corrupt and inefficient a sort that in 1895 a civilian president was elected by an overwhelming majority. The era of military rule seemed to be over for good, and one of the first acts of the new civilian president Pierola was to import a French military mission and found a military college to teach the army European manners.

The ensuing 'golden age' of the oligarchy (1895–1919) was so called because it at last brought to the rich of the coastal cities and to the large estate owners ('the forty families') political power to control the social standing and wealth they had enjoyed since Spanish times. Unfortunately for their enjoyment of it, their inheritance also coincided with the rise of popular political power. Peruvian franchise was based on a literacy test in Spanish (and so remained until the last election of 1963). But the majority of the population, Quechua-speaking Indians of the Sierra and the Andean belts, were illiterate even in their own language, and therefore doubly disqualified. And until long after primary education was made compulsory in 1906, many of the Spanish-speaking mestizos of the Sierra and coast remained unable to pass the literacy test and so unable to vote. The literate lower and lower-middle class was, however, growing and the Partido Democratica, which had made common cause with the *civilistas* in the overthrow of the last military president, drew its strength largely from their votes. In 1912 it won its first election and one of its first acts was the reduction of the military budget. This was sufficient to provoke a Colonel Benavides to overthrow the President in 1914 and sponsor a *civilista* as his successor. And this development defined a trend which was to dominate Peruvian politics until World War II. The army had recognised that the lower class parties were hostile to its interests, that in combination with the upper class party they could assume civilian rule (chiefly by the use of the strike as a political weapon) and that the army's interests therefore lay in making common cause with the upper class party of which it became in effect the protector. Its tactics were to allow the upper class party to hold power, in return for concessions and favours, and they worked remarkably well for 30 years.

Government during those years was by no means strictly constitutional. Leguia, who became President in 1919, made himself effectively a dictator, until overthrown by a military coup in 1930. Cerro, leader of the coup, was assassinated and replaced by a soldier, Benavides, appointed by Congress. But the army remained generally in the background. Moreover, in 1939 the political process produced a president, Manuel Prado, who began to achieve success in what had become the major problem of Peruvian political life, the reconciliation of the working and lower-middle classes. Since the end of the 'golden days of the oligarchy' in 1919, those classes had found their political home in a remarkable home-grown party, the Alianza Popular Revolucionaria Americana (American Popular Revolutionary Alliance – APRA). Left-wing (but not orthodox Marxist), anti-American (since America was seen as the selfish exploiter of the country's resources) and pro-Indian, the party was founded in Mexico in 1924 by an outstanding Peruvian ideologist, Haya de la Torre, and was intended by him to become pan-Latin American in its influence, but took root only in his own country. Its early activities which included the fomentation of lower rank mutinies in the army and navy in 1932, made it hated and feared by the military but it gained such widespread support that by 1939, although outlawed, it was a force in Peruvian politics which could not be ignored. Prado, by playing its anti-fascist feelings, persuaded it to support his pro-Allied and therefore pro-American policies during World War II (which Peru entered in the last months) and eventually led it to participate in the 'negotiated' election of his successor in 1945. The new president, Bustamente, represented a new idea in Peruvian politics – Christian Democracy currently fashionable in Catholic Europe. But it lacked South American roots, failed to find a following and left its leader poised uncomfortably between the demands of the *Apristas* and the army. When he refused army demands to ban APRA a section of the army rose against him and, though the majority remained loyal, the generals decided he must go. He was replaced by Marshal Odría in October, 1948.

This return of the army to politics, legalised by Odría's winning of the presidential election of 1950, provoked a realignment of interests in Peru which has been compared to that between the Civilista and Democratica parties in 1895. The 'forty families' had come to accept that *aprismo* could not be dealt with by repression and that their own long-term interests required an accommodation with the left; APRA for its part had tired of underground politics and was anxious for legitimacy. They therefore jointly agreed in 1956 to support Manuel Prado, the wartime President, for a second term. He was elected, but only by a narrow margin, over the representative of a new party, Accion Popular. Its leader, Fernando Belaúnde, stood, as APRA had originally done, for the emancipation of the Indian peasantry, and at the 1962 elections again came close to winning with Haya de la Torre just ahead of him, and Marshal Odría (the *golpista* of 1948) a close third. The closeness of the elections threw it into the congress, which chose de la Torre, but the army were unwilling to accept their old *aprista* enemy and took

power, announcing that new elections would be held in 1963. These returned Belaúnde. He did not, however, command a majority in either house of congress, was forced to borrow abroad to finance his ambitious development programme, was confronted with extreme left-wing guerrilla risings in the interior and was prevented by his principles from offering the army the cabinet posts which would have guaranteed its support. Inflation eroded his popularity, while the army's involvement in the problems of the interior lent substance to the political theories its young leaders were imbibing at its new staff college, the Centre for Higher Military Studies (CAEM). On October 3rd, 1968 General Juan Velasco Alvarado, Chairman of the Joint Armed Forces Command, had Belaúnde put on an aeroplane for Buenos Aires, and announced the installation of a new military government.

This government demonstrated from the onset that it was unlike any military regime which the country had known before. Its justification for its seizure of power was the economic and administrative chaos into which Belaúnde's government had plunged the country, its pretext the unfavourable terms of the agreement he had recently signed with the American International Petroleum Company. But instead (as in 1962, or even in 1912) of declaring its intention of intervening only as a caretaker, it announced that its aims were revolutionary and its programme long term. Broadcasting on July 28th, General Alvarado stated that the revolution was not Marxist (a strange disclaimer for a Peruvian officer to make, and evidence of how greatly its internal temper had changed under the influence of the CAEM) but nationalist, and aimed at eliminating privilege and implementing the better distribution of wealth. He favoured the making of a new constitution, universal suffrage, nationalisation of selected national assets and the investment of foreign capital only on condition that the State shared in the profits. These were elements of the army's secret so-called 'Inca Programme' which was to be made public in 1974. Its preamble was then revealed to state that 'the armed forces, as executor and mainstay of the Peruvian revolution, will carry out the processes of change until they are irreversible'.

By 1974 the military government had shown how radical its programme in fact was. It had set the following as its specific aims: land reform and redistribution, particularly in the latifundia; expropriation of foreign oil and mining interests; the declaration and vigorous defence of a 200 mile fishing limit; administrative reform and an end to corruption; raising of lower-class living standards; the extension of educational opportunities to all; and, in general, the achievement of economic independence for the whole country. The principal object of its attentions were the foreign-owned exploitative corporations, in particular the Cerro de Pasco Corporation (which mined 50% of Peru's copper, lead and zinc), the International Petroleum Company (IPC, which had a virtual monopoly of oil production), the large haciendas (some over 200,000 hectares in area), the foreign-owned rail and telecommunications networks and the long-established coastal families whose wealth derived from arranging the export of the country's raw materials. In its first 6 years of power the military government expropriated the IPC's holdings (1969), established the 200 mile fishing limit and fired on American fishing vessels in its defence (1969), set up a State Corporation (Mineproperu) to control mineral exports (1971) and nationalised the telephone network, the largest railway company (1972), the Cerro de Pasco Corporation and all foreign fishmeal companies (1973), and the cotton industry (1974). As a token of its general distancing from the USA, it had also opened diplomatic relations with the USSR (1970), and China and Cuba (1971).

The explanation for this dramatic reversal of its hitherto

rigid defence of the traditional order cannot lie in the influence upon it of the CAEM, important though that institution undoubtedly was, nor in its exposure to the realities of life in the Sierra and Selva during the anti-guerrilla campaign of 1962–6, for all the impression that it left. It had certainly lost patience with the political parties of all complexions, and it was moved by a growing disgust for the foreign exploitation of the country's resources felt by most professional Peruvians. But these factors cannot be regarded as precipitating causes. What seems to have happened is that the army came to see itself as used by the rich, even when the rich appeared to be under its protection, decided that the policies of the rich were slowly but surely exciting a disastrous revolutionary condition and that the army alone possessed the cohesion, expertise and national standing necessary to avert the crisis. This decision to act 'in the national interest' is certainly not unique either in or outside Latin America. What made the Peruvian army's intervention unusual was that it did not seek to place itself at the head of an existing political movement nor to create its own, but 'in a country with the deepest political cleavages, both countrywide and along class lines . . . to set itself apart from, and from its point of view on top of, the domestic political struggle'. Its stance was that of platonic guardians, and its belief apparently was that by the disinterested implementation of the right policies it could make the Peruvian, willy-nilly, one people, free and prosperous in their own country. Whether its beliefs were justified will be tested by its return to power of a civilian government. Despite the universal Latin American scourge of inflation and an unemployment rate of 60%, Belaúnde's second administration has survived more than half its term, which is due to expire in 1985.

STRENGTH AND BUDGET

Population: 18,300,000
Army: 75,000
Navy: 21000 (including 3000 marines); 24 major vessels
Air force: 10,000; 138 combat aircraft
Paramilitary: 25,000 armed police
GNP (1981): $19,500,000,000
Defence expenditure (1981): $398,500,000

COMMAND AND CONSTITUTIONAL STATUS

The military leaders who overthrew the government of President Belaúnde in October, 1968 suspended Congress and promised a new constitution, proclaimed in 1979. Under Article 213 of the old, the armed forces were entrusted with 'the protection of the rights of the Republic, the enforcement of the constitution and the law and maintenance of public order' and it is under this provision that the junta presumably claimed legitimacy for its action. The Revolutionary Government of the Armed Forces rule by decree. It was headed by a general, as president. The cabinet was composed of military officers (though a civilian was admitted after the cabinet coup which overthrew President Alvarado in August, 1975). The Minister of War (Army) acted as prime minister and was a serving officer, as were the ministers of the navy and air force. In 1968 these ministers were also commanders-in-chief of their respective services. The posts were later separated but the Commander-in-Chief of the Army apparently had the succession to the premiership. The Head of the Office for Social Mobilisation, in effect the junta's own political movement, was a serving officer who sits as a minister in cabinet.

A major element in the system of military government was the group of corporations the government had set up to control the nationalised industries, of which the most important were Mineroperu (1971) which controls mining and mineral exploitation and exporting, and Pescaperu (1973) which controls fishmeal and fish oil production. The government also took full or partial control of the petroleum, cotton and cement industries, and of the Central Reserve Bank, telecommunications and railways, and instituted State investment in, and worker-management of, many other enterprises. Officers held key positions in all State institutions and the nationalised enterprises. In government itself a major role was played by the Corps of Officer Advisers to the Presidency, which was responsible for conceiving and directing the government's long-term policies.

Under the 1979 constitution, the chain of command runs directly from the President of the Republic to the commanders-in-chief of the Army, Navy and Air Force. Although, in the past, the commander-in-chief of the Army has also held the office of Minister of War, that office is purely an administrative one and is not in the direct chain of command. Traditionally the Ministers of War, Marine and Aviation have been serving officers. President Belaúnde, however, broke with this tradition, naming retired officers who had opposed the 1968 coup to these ministries.

The Joint Command is an advisory group, set up in 1957 and consisting of the chiefs of staff of the Army, Navy and Air Force, plus their assistants. Each of the armed forces appoints five or six officers of the rank of colonel (in the cases of the Army and Air Force) or captain (in the case of the Navy) to assist their respective chiefs of staff on the Joint Command, which is a planning group rather than an operational staff. The presidency of the Joint Command rotates annually amongst the three chiefs of staff.

Under the 1979 constitution, the Armed Forces are designated as the guarantors of 'The independence, sovereignty and territorial integrity of the Republic'. The President is designated as Supreme Commander of the Armed Forces with the authority to declare war or sign peace terms, following hostilities, although this authority may be used only 'with authorisation of the congress'. Promotions to the ranks of general and admiral must be confirmed by the senate and such promotions can be made only to fill existing vacancies thus effectively limiting the number of incumbents of these ranks at any given time.

Active duty military personnel renounce the right to vote and cannot hold public office until at least six months after retirement. Whether these elaborate precautions to exclude the Armed Forces from political activity will be effective in the long term, remains to be seen.

ROLE, COMMITMENT, DEPLOYMENT AND RECENT OPERATIONS

Role
In addition to their primary function of protecting the country from external aggression, the Armed Forces may, in specified emergencies, assume the responsibility for the maintenance of internal order, taking precedence over the police in this respect. The three Armed Forces perform many civic action duties in addition to their purely military functions and are particularly active in development projects in the under-developed eastern provinces and the Amazonian lowlands.

Commitment
Peru has no external military commitments; as a member of the United Nations it offered a contingent to the Emergency

Force set up to police the Middle East ceasefire line in 1956, but it was not among those chosen.

Deployment

Peru is divided into five military regions, with which the police (Guardia Civil) districts now correspond. These comprise the following provinces:

First (HQ Piura): Tumbés, Piura, Lambayeque, Cajamarca, Amazonas

Second (HQ Lima): La Libertad, Ancash, Lima, Huancavelica, Ica, Callao

Third (HQ Arequipa): Arequipa, Moquegua, Tacna

Fourth (HQ Cuzco): Puno, Cuzco, Apurimac, Junín, Pasco, Huánuco, San Martin, Ayacucho, Madre de Dios

Fifth (HQ Iquitos): Loreto

Information on the deployment of the units of the Peruvian Army is remarkably scarce. The major tactical formations are believed to be deployed as follows:

1st Military Region (HQ Piura):
1st Light Division (HQ Talara)
7th Light Division (HQ Tumbés)
8th Light Division (HQ Lambayaque)
1st Cavalry Division (HQ Sullana)
2nd Armoured Division (HQ Piura)

2nd Military Region (HQ Lima):
2nd Light Division (HQ Lima)
Airborne Division (HQ Callao)

3rd Military Region (HQ Arequipa):
3rd Light Division (HQ Moquegua)
6th Light Division (HQ Tacna)
1st Armoured Division (HQ Arequipa)

4th Military Region (HQ Cuzco):
4th Light Division (HQ Cuzco)

5th Military Region (HQ Iquitos):
5th Jungle Division (HQ Iquitos)

The heavy concentration of troops on the Ecuadorian frontier is notable.

Recent Operations

Apart from a minor frontier conflict with Ecuador in 1941, the Peruvian army has not been at war since its bitter struggle with Chile in the War of the Pacific (1879—83). Between 1962 and 1966, however, it waged a successful campaign against left-wing guerrilla risings in the interior of the country. The first of these, which took place in La Convencion valley in Madre de Dios province in 1962—3, was led by Hugo Blanco. A Trotskyist, he had formed his own movement, the Frente de Izquierda Revolucionaria (Left Revolutionary Front — FIR), with the object of leading the landless Quechua-speaking peasants to seize their holdings on the giant haciendas. The government did not at first oppose the activities of the FIR organisation syndicates and much land was effectively transferred to those who worked on it, but after Blanco had attacked a police post at Pucará in November, 1962 the military government, which had come to power in June, moved against him and his followers. He was captured and imprisoned in May, 1963 by which time the rebellion was extinct. But President Belaúnde, by then in power, formed the view that the dispossession of the peasants who had taken land was both unpolitic and unjust, and allowed most of those who had seized land to retain it. The army, whose eyes had been opened to the agrarian problem by its experience in the campaign, acquiesced in this judgement. It formed a harsher judgement however of the movements which rose in Ayacucho, Cuzco and Junín provinces in 1965—6. These were led by Cuban-inspired revolutionaries arther than aggressive reformers like Blanco, and were seen to pose a more distinctive and alien threat to the State, and were dealt with accordingly. The first of these was the Movimiento de Izquierda Revolucionaria (Movement of the Revolutionary Left — MIR) led by Luis de la Puente and other dissatisfied members of APRA. De la Puente, who had spent some time in Cuba, attempted to start a Castro-style guerrilla campaign in the foothills of the Andes in Cuzco province, but at once attracted strong military action and was defeated and killed in the period of September—October, 1965. A collaborator, Guillermo Lobaton, whose group was called Tupuc Amaru after an Inca hero (and from which the Uruguayan Tupamaros take their name) was defeated and killed in Junín in January, 1966 after a 6 month pursuit by the army. In the same month another group, belonging to the Ejercito de Liberacion Nacional (National Liberation Army — ELN), led by Hector Bejar and called Javier Heraud after the leader of an abortive rising who was killed in 1962 was decisively broken up. Despite the army's vigorous reaction, none of these groups was a serious military threat to the State; they failed to find a following among the peasants and were held at arms length by the orthodox (and most of the unorthodox) left-wing parties. Their revolt was intellectual in the extreme and utopian.

The army was briefly involved in the repression of a strike (for better pay) by Civil Guards in Lima in February, 1975. The majority of the Civil Guard remained unaffected.

A frontier incident during the last week in January, 1981, almost led to full scale hostilities against Ecuador. On January 22nd, an Ecuadorian Army patrol fired on a Peruvian helicopter flying in the sensitive border area, apparently without effect. Ecuadorian troops subsequently crossed the frontier and penetrated some 10km into territory recognised as Peruvian by the Protocol of Rio de Janeiro which ended the brief 1941 border war between the two countries. Ecuador had repudiated the Protocol and refused to ratify a peace treaty with Peru. Although both countries carried out a partial mobilisation of their respective Armed Forces and some skirmishing took place, intervention by the Organisation of American States prevented an escalation of the fighting. This area however remains a potential flash point.

ORGANISATION

Arms of Service

These are infantry, armoured troops, cavalry, artillery, engineers and services. The two cavalry regiments of the Presidential Guard are known as the Cuirassiers and the Hussars of Junín. The infantry, armoured troops and engineers are organised in numbered battalions, some of which are also named. The cavalry is organised in regiments and the artillery in groups.

Operational

The basic tactical formation of the Peruvian Army is the *División Ligera* (Light Division) which consists basically of four infantry battalions and an artillery group, to which may be added a cavalry regiment and/or an engineer battalion. There are eight such formations which resemble brigades rather than divisions in normal military usage. There are also two armoured divisions, a cavalry division and an airborne division, all of which also would appear to resemble brigades rather than divisions in their strength and organisation.

Although the Army has more than doubled its strength during the past 15 years, this would seem to have been accomplished by bringing existing units up to strength rather than by creating new units, the only major new formation to emerge during this period being a second armoured division. It would appear that there are approximately 35 infantry battalions (including two commando and one paratroop battalions), at least eight tank battalions, seven cavalry regiments, ten or more groups of artillery and at least six engineer battalions, plus a special engineer group operating in the Upper Amazon region.

The Navy includes a 3,000 strong Marine Corps, which is organised primarily as an amphibious brigade with defence and security detachments located at each of the major naval bases on the Pacific coast and the Upper Amazon.

There are two paramilitary police forces, the Republican Guard and the Civil Guard. Five police regions cover identical areas with those of the five Military Regions. The Civil Guard, formed in 1924 and trained by officers of the Spanish Guardia Civil, is the main national police force. It is organised into 59 *Comandancias* and includes a special anti-terrorist unit, the *Sinchi* battalion, based at Lima but available for service throughout the national territory. The Civil Guard is equipped with obsolescent light infantry weapons and has a number of armoured vehicles at its disposal. The Republican Guard patrols the country's land frontiers, guards public buildings and furnishes prison guards at penal institutions.

RECRUITMENT, TRAINING AND RESERVES

Recruitment and Training

The majority of the army (50,000) is composed of conscripts, who serve for 2 years. They are selected from a much larger annual contingent, by ballot among the white and mestizo population. Officers, most of whom come from middle-class mestizo families to whom an army career offers free education and a valued means of social elevation, are trained at the military academy at Chorrillos, near Lima (founded 1896) where the Staff College is also situated. By far the most significant element in the Peruvian military education system in recent years has been the Centro de Altos Estudios Militares (Centre for Higher Military Studies – CAEM). Founded in 1958, with a mainly civilian faculty, as a joint-services staff college it rapidly developed into a 'military school of public affairs'. Originally seven of the 10 months' instruction were devoted to social and economic affairs, and though the government later insisted on a reduction of the proportion, the threat of the school's instruction remained unchanged. It took as its basis Article 213 of the Constitution, which charges the army with the guardianship of national rights and sovereignty, analysed the prevailing social and political conditions to show how dominant were foreign and narrowly sectional interests, and outlined 'developmental' solutions to the country's besetting problems. It also implicitly preached the doctrine that the army, as the only truly disinterested national institution, was uniquely fitted to design and implement a development programme. Its influence in post-1968 government has been central – 13 of the first 19 cabinet ministers appointed after 1968 were CAEM graduates, and they almost entirely staffed the Council of Presidential Advisers.

The director of the school is appointed by the Joint Command of the Armed Services. It is divided into directorates – Academic, National Strategy, and Research and Development; the latter is a political and economic research department.

Reserves

These consist of the Reserve in which conscripts spend 10 years after active duty, and the National Guard, a second-line reserve, to whcih reservists then transfer. Both bodies appear, however, to be purely paper organisations.

EQUIPMENT AND ARMS INDUSTRY

Although Peru had a developing shipbuilding industry and in the past has assembled light aircraft, almost all military equipment must still be imported.

In the years following World War II, the United States was the principal supplier of arms and defence equipment. In the mid 1960s, French influence, always strong in Peruvian military circles, began to assert itself once more and quantities of equipment were acquired from Belgium and Switzerland in addition to France. During the early 1970s, with the growth of ties with Argentina, based on common enemity with Chile, some quantities of largely second and third hand material were also transferred to Peru by Argentina. The military regime, which held power from 1968–80, underlined its independence of the United States by engaging in massive purchases of Soviet equipment. Since the return of civilian government, Peru has returned to western countries as its major suppliers although the US no longer enjoys a monopoly. Peru's existing arsenal, which is impressive, must suffer from the extraordinarily heterogeneous origins of its equipment, the maintenance of which must pose a logistic nightmare.

Rifles: FN FAL 7.62mm (Belgium); G3 7.62mm (Germany); AK-47 7.62mm (USSR)
Sub-machine-guns: Uzi 9mm (Israel)
Machine-guns: FN MAG 7.62mm (Belgium)
Mortars: 81mm (France); 120mm (France)
Anti-armour weapons: 106mm RCLs (US); Cobra ATGW (Germany)
Artillery: M101 105mm (US); M-46 122mm (USSR); M-54 130mm (USSR); M114 155mm (US via Argentina); Mk. F.3 SPH (France)
Air-defence weapons: 40mm L/60 (Sweden/US); M-1938 76mm (USSR); ZSU-23-4 23mm SP (USSR); SA-2 SAM (USSR); SA-3 SAM (USSR)
Armour: M4 medium tank (US; 60 in service); AMX-13 light tank (France; 110 in service); T-54/55 medium tank (USSR; 350 in service); M48A2 medium tank (US; 50 on order); M113 APC (US some via Argentina; 200 in service + 150 on order); Mowas Roland APC (Switzerland; 112 in service); UR-416 APC (Germany; 106 in service); U-150 Commando APC (US some via Portugal); Fiat 6616 armoured car (Italy; 15 in service + 10 on order); SPz-12.3 armoured cars (Germany; 100 on order)

Aircraft: The Army operates about 50 helicopters and some half dozen light fixed-wing aircraft. The Air Force has approximately 80 transport aircraft and some 50 helicopters.

RANK, DRESS AND DISTINCTIONS

Service uniforms show heavy US and slight but perceptible German influence. Combat uniforms are similar to US and the US M42 steel helmet is standard. The Presidential Guard wears a French dragoon type uniform, complete with plumed brass helmet and all dress uniforms show a predominantly French influence as do officers rank insignia, worn on shoulder straps or cuffs as follows:

General de División – Three gold suns
General de Brigada – Two gold suns
Coronel – Six gold bars, grouped in threes

Teniente Coronel — Five gold bars, grouped in three and two
Mayor — Four gold bars, grouped in three and one
Capitán — Three gold bars
Teniente — Two gold bars
Subteniente — One gold bar

CURRENT DEVELOPMENTS

The most important recent development was the return to democratically elected civilian government. The Armed Forces appear to have loyally supported President Belaúnde, their erstwhile enemy, as President and seem to have accepted their role as defined under the 1979 constitution.

The frontier dispute with Ecuador remains the major source of international tension and although Peru still aspires to regain its lost southern provinces, the possibility of its resort to military means to bring this about seems to have diminished although the opportunity presented by any Argentino-Chilean conflict might prove hard to resist. Relations with Argentina are extremely cordial and Peru rendered positive support to Argentina during the South Atlantic War, transferring quantities of aircraft to Argentina to replace those lost in combat.

John Keegan
Adrian English

PHILIPPINES

HISTORY AND INTRODUCTION

The Philippine Islands, today an independent republic, were for most of the previous five centuries ruled by a foreign power: first Spain, then America, lastly if briefly by Japan. Spain conquered the islands, which number about 7000, at the end of the sixteenth century and ruled them until the end of the nineteenth. From the middle of that century, however, their rule was accepted with decreasing docility by the Filipinos. There was a serious mutiny among their native troops at Cavite in 1872, a major nationalist rising in 1896 and 1898 a further and successful nationalist rising which coincided with the outbreak of war between Spain and America. The Americans won a crushing naval victory over the Spanish fleet at Manila Bay but when their troops landed they found the Filipino insurgents in control of the mainland. The latter had declared their independence of Spain but they and the Americans soon fell out and, after a short but bitter war, the islands came under American rule. In 1935 the Americans raised the islands to the status of a Commonwealth under their protection, with its own army and an embryo navy and air force. But it continued to maintain on the islands its own garrison, which contained regiments of locally enlisted Philippine Scouts. It was these troops, with the Philippine army, which were attacked by the Japanese in December, 1941 and, after a heroic defence of the Manila area, on the Bataan peninsula and the island of Corregidor, were forced into surrender in February, 1942.

The Japanese, like the Spaniards and Americans, did not rule the islands without resistance. Foremost among the resistance groups which emerged during 1942 was the *Hukbo Ng Bayan Laban Sa Hapon*, or *Hukbalahaps*, or *Huks*, the People's Army against Japan. It was communist controlled, but supported by the Americans, and it had some success against the Japanese, though it more often attacked officials and policemen who had transferred their allegiance to them than the Japanese itself. At the end of the war, the Americans conferred independence on the islands but disowned the Huks and entrusted power to parties which had flourished under the Commonwealth. The new government's failure, however, to institute reform of the land tenure system, which kept the majority of the population in poverty on share-cropping tenancies, raised the fortunes of the Huks. Renamed in 1949 the *Hukbo Ng Mapagpalaya Sa Bayan* or People's Liberation Army, it had raised by 1950 a force of 15,000 armed men, enjoyed the support of half a million peasants in the rice-growing area of central Luzon, north and south of Manila, and stood poised to attack the city itself. The national armed police, the Philippine Constabulary, had lost the power to oppose it, and the Philippine army was not organised or equipped to engage it. Under the dynamic leadership of a new Secretary of Defence, Ramon Magsaysay, however, the army was transformed into an effective counter-insurgency force, while an enlightened land reform and resettlement programme was instituted at the same time to alleviate agricultural distress. By 1954 the back of the insurgency had been broken and by 1957, when Magsaysay had achieved the Presidency, the army was reorganised as an external defence force.

Filipinos, of whatever of the many ethnic groups inhabiting the islands, are renowned for their individual courage and warlike character. But they do not possess a long military tradition. The Spaniards raised few local regiments, and those chiefly from the Macabebe tribe of Pampanga province, a minority among the dominant Tagalogs of Luzon. The Americans, on their arrival, formed their first local units, Batson's Scouts, from the same tribe, and the Philippine Scouts, from which that force grew, remained an element of the United States army until 1941. The Army of the Commonwealth, established by a National Defence Act of December, 1935 was still in a formative stage when the Japanese attacked. It was a conscript force, inducting 40,000 recruits a year, and designed by its first commander, Douglas MacArthur, to deter a potential aggressor from landing on the islands. Its credibility depended, however, on the support of the United States Fleet and, when that was removed by the attack on Pearl Harbour, its defeat by the Japanese was predestined. Reformed after the war, it consisted until 1950 mainly of administrative, service and training elements, and had only two combat battalions. The Philippines Constabulary, established by the Americans in 1901, and organised on a provincial basis, bore the responsibility for maintaining law and order. From 1950 Magsaysay rapidly brought into being, with American aid, 26 battalion combat teams, equipped as light infantry. After their victory over the Huks, they were reorganised into conventional defence formations in 1957 and entered on the ground strength of the South-East Asia Collective Defence Treaty (SEATO). The Philippine Constabulary then resumed responsibility for internal security. But the outbreak of a separatist rebellion among the Muslim Moros of the southern Philippines, and the declaration of martial law in 1972, obliged the army to deploy its forces internally again, and greatly to increase their strength. Despite considerable success, the army and the Constabulary are still heavily committed in the southern islands of the republic.

STRENGTH AND BUDGET

Population: 50,350,000
Army: 70,000
Navy: 26,000 (including 7000 Marines); 8 frigates, 179 smaller craft
Air force: 16,800, 131 Combat aircraft
Paramilitary: 43,500 Philippine Constabulary; 65,000 Civilian Home Defence Forces
GNP (1981): $39,500,000,000
Defence expenditure (1981 estimate): $862,000,000

The expenses of suppressing the rebellion in the southern islands has raised the defence budget from $92,000,000 in 1972 to its present figure. An important offset is provided by the American government which granted $32,000,000 in aid in 1975 and $41,000,000 in 1977.

COMMAND AND CONSTITUTIONAL STATUS

The Philippines has a constitution modelled on that of the USA, which confers executive power on an elected President, who is Commander-in-Chief of the Armed Forces. In January, 1973 following the declaration of martial law in the previous

September, a constitutional amendment named the incumbent President, Ferdinand Marcos, President and Prime Minister without a fixed term of office (it had previously been 4 years). The Armed Forces of the Philippines, which include the army, navy, air force and Philippines Constabulary, are under the command of a single Chief of Staff and administered by a unified Department of National Defence. Its Head, a Departmental Secretary, is an assistant to the President.

ROLE, COMMITMENT, DEPLOYMENT AND RECENT OPERATIONS

Role
The official role of the army is to preserve the territorial integrity of the islands, of which there are over 7000. It has also played in recent years an important part in rural development, by the building of roads, wells and dams and by setting up schools and medical centres in the villages. Since 1972, however, it has been heavily engaged in the suppression of the Muslim separatist rebellion in the southern islands, and with political insurgency elsewhere.

Commitment
The Philippines are signatories of the 1954 SEATO treaty, but are not committed to deploy troops outside the islands. During the Korean war, however, it sent a representative force to the theatre of operations, maintaining an infantry battalion there (first the 10th Battalion Combat Team, then in succession the 20th, 14th and 2nd) between September, 1950 and May, 1955.

America is committed to the defence of the Philippines against external aggression, under the terms of a Mutual Defence Treaty of 1952, and to provide equipment and advice under a Military Assistance Pact. It enjoys in return, under an agreement first signed in 1947 and renewed in 1966, the use of two important base areas, and the Subic naval base of 40,000 acres on the west coast of Mindanao. Its lease runs until 1991, but President Marcos is anxious to retrieve Philippine sovereignty over the bases, which would allow him to join the ranks of the officially unaligned countries. The treaty is therefore under renegotiation.

Deployment
The bulk of the army is at present deployed in two recently established commands – CENCOM (Cotabato and Lanao provinces on Mindanao) and SOWESCOM (Zamboanga province on Mindanao and Sulo archipelago). It is reported that there are 25 battalions in each command, as well as sizeable Constabulary forces. The rebels are currently most active on Jolo island in the Sulus. The Constabulary is also engaged against a renascent Huk force, the Maoist New People's Army, on Luzon, where several thousand dissidents are active in Isabella province and smaller numbers in Camarines and Sorgoson. NPA activity has been reported from the island of Samar, and 10,000 troops have operated there since 1979.

Recent Operations
The war against the Muslim dissidents (Moros) of the south is of so intermittent and irregular a character as to defy easy description. The Moros, who are kin to their fellow Muslims in northern Borneo, were never properly subdued by the Spaniards and fought a serious campaign against them as late as 1840. They also sustained a guerrilla campaign against the Americans until 1913 at least. Their recent grievances appear to be the result of large-scale Christian immigration into Mindanao, ironically prompted by the government resettlement of former Huk supporters there in the late 1950s. In 1960 only 370,000 Christians lived in Cotabato province against 650,000 Muslims, but now there are 750,000. The 2,500,000 Moros were alarmed by the influx, but appear to have taken up the banner of separatism after the Philippines government itself laid claim to British North Borneo during the Anglo–Indonesian confrontation of the 1960s. Many now support the Moro National Liberation Front and its Bangsa Moro Army (Army of the Moro Nation). The BMA was reported by *Le Monde* in December, 1976 to have 72 battalions in the field, armed with M-16 and FLN rifles, 81mm mortars and rocket launchers. The government was reported by *The Far Eastern Economic Review* in April, 1976 to have deployed 50 battalions against them and to have raised 50,000 local members for the Civilian Home Defence Forces. The rebels are openly supported by Libya, which until 1976 transmitted supplies to them through Sabah, formerly British North Borneo, now a Federal State of Malaysia. The lull which fell over the war in 1976 is attributed to the failure in the Sabah elections of Mustafa bin Harun, its chief minister and a strong supporter of the Moros. Government and rebel versions of their activities are so much at variance that even casualty figures can only be guessed at, but a figure quoted by *The Times* (London) in September, 1976 is of 50,000 Muslim dead, 4000 government soldiers killed and 1,000,000 refugees.

In 1979 it was suggested that 35,000 government troops confronted 13,000 rebels and that 90,000 refugees had sought safety in Sabah. Subsequently, government development measures led to a lull in the fighting, also helped by the holding of elections for local assemblies. In February 1981 however, 119 government troops were murdered by Moslem rebels on the island of Pata, and fighting resumed in intensity.

ORGANISATION

The army, navy, air force and Constabulary form the Armed Forces of the Philippines under a single Chief of Staff. The army comprises infantry, armour, artillery, engineers, signals and logistics branches. Operationally it is organised into divisions and brigades, but the effective operational unit is the battalion. They are individually numbered, in a series from 1 to 50, and now apparently beyond.

The Constabulary has traditionally been organised into companies on a provincial basis, but larger units may have been formed for operations in the south. The Civilian Home Defence Forces are organised on a local basis.

RECRUITMENT, TRAINING AND RESERVES

Recruitment, until the outbreak of the war in the south, was by selective conscription. The very rapid expansion of the army from 16,000 in 1972 to over 50,000 in 1976, has been achieved by conscription on a much larger scale, but it has not yet become universal.

Recruits probably receive most of their training in these units. Officers are trained at the Philippines Military Academy at Baguio in northern Luzon. The class of 1974 was graduated 3 months early to provide officers for the war in the south.

EQUIPMENT AND ARMS INDUSTRY

In 1975 President Marcos announced his intention of making the Philippines self-sufficient in the production of small arms and ammunition, and in March, 1976 it was reported that the American Colt Industries had set up a factory in the country, with a credit of $8,000,000 from the United States Foreign

Military Sales fund, to manufacture M-16 rifles. All other equipment is imported from the USA. It consists of the normal range of American infantry weapons, including 75mm and 106mm recoilless rifles, 100 105mm howitzers, 40 4.2in mortars, M-41 tanks and 35 M-113 APCs. The BMA claim to have destroyed some of the latter with rocket launchers.

RANK, DRESS AND DISTINCTIONS

The army and the Constabulary are dressed in American style khaki, use American ranks and wear American pattern badges of rank. But under the Commonwealth (1934—41) the most senior rank was field-marshal, held by Douglas MacArthur.

CURRENT DEVELOPMENTS

Filipino society is traditionally abnormally violent. Both major parties (Liberal and Nationalists) are inured to their supporters being killed in dozens at elections, but everyday life is also marked by frequent murder and kidnapping, inspired by mercenary, political or personal motive. President Marcos used the first 3 years of martial law (1972—5) to act against entrenched lawlessness, and it was reputed in 1976 that he had in that period put down 200 'private armies' and 250 'crime syndicates' and recovered over 630,000 firearms from private hands. Experts regard the latter figure as in no way exaggerated.

The army and the Constabulary are not therefore undertaking a wholly unfamiliar task in their attempt to put down Moro rebellion in the south or Maoist insurgency on Mindanao. Being Filipino, they are accustomed to haphazard everyday violence. The rebellion in the south did, however, during 1974—5, assume proportions alarming even by Filipino standards, and the army appears at first not to have made an effective response to it. President Marcos expressed his own dissatisfaction by dismissing 40 generals of brigadier rank and above in November, 1975 and by earmarking the Commander of the Constabulary, Fidel Ramos, a West Point graduate, as next Chief of Staff. Since 1976, and assisted by the unseating of the Moros' chief foreign supporter in Sabah, the army has made considerably better progress in putting the rebellion down. It probably cannot be quelled for good without political concessions to the Moros and without direct development work in their regions to raise their standards of living. As a result of experience gained in the Huk campaign, the government is conscious of the importance of moderating military action with political inducement (Magsaysay called it the 'left hand, right hand method'), while the army is deeply experienced in rural development engineering. Its long-term prospects of success in the south appear favourable.

The Maoist NPA remains active in Luzon, and disorders in Samar island are said to be formented by the NPA. The government has also indicated the existence of a 'third force' of dissidents, the socialist National Liberation Army. The president himself was the target of conventional violence by old-time political opponents during and after the elections of June, 1981.

President Marcos is now, however, experiencing opposition from a different direction, that of the Catholic church, led by Cardinal Sin, once the government's staunchest supporter. The church complains of military excesses against the peasantry and suspected political opponent. In response to this weakening of his support, Marcos lifted martial law in January 1981 (imposed since 1972) and submitted himself to re-election in June. He was overwhelmingly returned. Changes made after the election were to replace the chief of staff with the head of the presidential security council, General Ver. General Ramos (see above) became Deputy Chief of Staff, while remaining head of the police and the Philippines Constabulary.

John Keegan

POLAND

HISTORY AND INTRODUCTION

If pre-*Risorgimento* Italy was little more than a geographical expression, it was in a more fortunate position than the Poland of 1914 which, divided between Prussia, Austria and Russia, lacked even geographical unity. The Polish Republic gradually coalesced, in the chaotic circumstances attending the collapse of tsarist Russia and the subsequent defeat of the Central Powers, between 1916 and 1919. In the latter year a constituent *Sejm* (Parliament) met, and the socialist Josef Pilsudski, the dominant figure in Polish history until his death in 1935, was confirmed in power.

The disordered state of eastern Europe made the creation of an effective army one of Pilsudski's first priorities, and the new Polish army, officered as it was by men who had gained valuable military experience in other armies, gave proof of its mettle when, in the summer of 1920, it hurled the Red Army back from the gates of Warsaw. This may have been the first major victory of the army of the Polish Republic, but it was by no means the first example of Polish military ability. For the previous century and a half, Poles, denied a national army of their own, had fought vigorously in the armies of other nations and had appeared, like the stormy petrels of revolution, in insurrections on both sides of the Atlantic.

The Constitution of 1922 was modelled on that of France, and its provision for a weak executive and strong legislature proved fatal in a nation beset by factionalism and lacking external security. Pilsudski, with the army's backing, staged a coup in 1926 and remained, for all practical purposes, dictator until his death. Poland was an excellent target for German aggrandisement following Hitler's annexation of the Sudetenland, for the free city of Danzig was a German-speaking enclave within Poland, and much of the population of western Poland was also of German origin. The German–Soviet pact of August 23rd, 1939 cleared the way for the German invasion of Poland, and the *Wehrmacht* struck only a week later. The Polish army had changed all too little since 1920; its excellent cavalry were no match for German armour, and the '18-day campaign' of September, 1939 witnessed its almost total destruction. On September 16th–17th the Russians moved into eastern Poland, most of which they formally annexed in November.

The occupation and division of Poland did not end Polish resistance. A government in exile, based first in France and later in Britain, controlled its own army in exile as well as a 'Home Army' of resistance fighters within Poland. The Russians, having initially interned Polish military personnel in their area of occupation, consented to the formation of a Polish army under General Władyslaw Anders, but this force, after repeated disagreements between its commanders and the Russians, was eventually allowed to depart, by way of Persia, for the West.

Relations between the Russians and the Polish government in exile deteriorated steadily, and in 1943 they broke down altogether. This breakdown was due partly to Polish suspicion of Soviet involvement in the Katyn massacre, and partly because of fears that the Russians had no intention of recognising Polish sovereignty east of the Curzon Line (which ran roughly Grodno–Brest–Lvov) once the Germans were expelled. In May, 1943 a Soviet-sponsored Polish division was formed under General Zygmunt Berling, and by the summer of 1944 the 'First Polish Army' was serving in Marshal Rokossovskii's First Bielorussian Front. The Russian-backed National Council of Poland, which included the Polish communists Bolesław Bierut and Władislaw Gomułka, formed a 'Lublin Committee' which took over the administration of Polish territory west of the Curzon Line as the Russian advance continued. In August, 1944 General Tadeusz Bor-Komorowski's Home Army rose in Warsaw, but, for reasons which remain disputed, the Russians failed to press forward to assist Komorowski, and the rising was suppressed.

A Government of National Unity was formed in June, 1945. It is significant that this body contained only two members of the British-backed government in exile. The Potsdam Conference of July–August, 1945 confirmed the Soviet view of Poland's boundaries, which were to run from the Oder and Neisse rivers in the west to the Curzon Line in the east. In the words of the German historian Hans Roos, 'The great powers had, therefore, moved the home of the Polish nation some 150 miles, on an average, to the west'. Large numbers of Germans were deported from the newly acquired territory on Poland's eastern borders, and the area was resettled by Poles. An obvious, if superficial, consequence of the changed status of the area was the large-scale change of place-names: Breslau became Wrocław, Liegnitz became Legnica, and so on.

In early 1947 elections were held, and the constituent *Sejm* produced a new constitution. A government was formed by Jozef Cyranciewicz, and it was no accident that its most influential members were also members of the Politburo of the Polish Workers Party (PPR). Nineteen-forty-seven witnessed the arrest of many of the PPR's opponents and the flight of both former members of the government in exile. In December, 1948 the communists consolidated their position when the PPR merged with the Polish Socialist Party (PPS) to form the Polish United Workers Party (PZPR).

The Polish army, formed around the nucleus of the Soviet-sponsored First Polish Army, numbered some 16 under-strength divisions in 1946. It was used largely for internal security duties and assisted with the deportation of Germans from eastern Poland. Also contributing to the new Army. were former members of the AL, the People's Army, the small Communist partisan force that resisted inside Poland.

In the 1945–49 period, Poland was in the grips of large-scale anti-Communist insurgency. Little reported in the West, this civil war was won by the Communists mainly by Soviet forces and troops of the Polish Communist Party's Internal Security Crops, the KBW. The Army, which had sent most of its wartime Soviet officers home, replacing them, in some cases, by pre-war officers or those who had fought with the British, only played a secondary role.

In 1948–49 the Party, on orders from Moscow, set to changing the Army with a vengeance. A large-scale purge of 'native' Polish communists and non-communists followed the re-Sovietisation of the Polish Army. Marshal Rokossovskii, the Soviet commander in Poland, became Polish Minister of War and Commander-in-Chief, and was soon given Polish citizenship and the rank of Marshal of Poland. All senior commands were given to Soviet officers many, but not all, like Rokossovskii, of Polish descent. The Polish Army was thus set up to be moulded into an extension of the Soviet Army, which is what occurred up until 1956.

In June 1956, Polish regular troops refused to fire on

rioting workers in Ponznan. Although a KBW brigade produced the required bloodbath, this set in motion events that resulted in the fall of the Polish Stalinists, the rise of Gomułka, and the 'de-Sovietisation' of the Polish military. In 1956, the Army largely remained in its barracks. Some Soviet-led Army units were prepared to move against Gomułka, but they were blocked by KBW, Navy and Air Force units, which took up defensive positions.

In following years the Army was reduced to about 200,000. Soviet troops in Poland were made subject to a status-of-forces agreement. While the Polish Army, Navy, and Air Force remained totally committed to the integrated Warsaw Pact command, the Poles evolved a separate 'branch' to cover a number of services the Defence of National Territory (OTK) forces. These include the Internal Defence Forces (WOW, the former KBW), the Territorial Defence Forces (OT), and the Air Defence Forces (WOPK), all under the Ministry of Defence, and the Frontier Defence Forces (WOPK), under the Interior Ministry in peacetime. These forces evolved in the 1965–70 era.

The modernisation of Polish forces started in 1956 and progressed through the 1960s, straining the Polish economy, resulting, after the fall of Gomułka, with the acceptance of a slower rate of growth for defence spending. Purges continued through the 1960s, the most notable being in 1967 when the Air Defence Force high command, any officers of Jewish background, and officers retaining ties with the old Soviet command were all removed.

Polish forces were used in the 1968 invasion of Czechoslovakia, their only external action since 1945, except for UN peacekeeping duties. It was obviously viewed, at the time and afterwards, with some distaste by the Army. There were criticisms of 'passivity' by Polish forces.

The fall of Gomułka in 1970 was preceded by the use of both internal security forces and regular troops to suppress rioting at Gdańsk. Mobile WOW brigades were conspicuous by their absence from the action. Gomułka's replacement, Edward Gierek, did not send in regular troops in the 1976 crisis. The August 1980 strike and the resultant crisis, which eventually led to the replacement of Gierek by Stanisław Kania and him, eventually, by former Defence Minister Jaruzelski, did not produce involvement of the Polish military until the imposition of martial law, after considerable Soviet pressure, in December 1981. Even at that time, the role of the Army was limited. The ZOMO and WOW carried most of the burden, although one armoured division was committed to internal security duties in the Gdynia-Gdańsk region.

STRENGTH AND BUDGET

Population: 35,900,000
Army: 207,000 with 500,000 reserves
Navy: 22,000 with 40,000 reserves, 4 submarines, one destroyer, about 100 smaller craft
Border Troops:
Territorial Defence Troops:
Citizen's Militia: 350,000
Internal Security:
GNP: (1981): $88.1–133.8 billion
Defence Expenditure 1981: $5.41 billion

COMMAND AND CONSTITUTIONAL STATUS

Command
The Polish High Command bears a strong resemblance to that of the Soviet Union and other Warsaw Pact States. The *Sejm* is 'the supreme organ of State authority'; it passes laws, and exercises control over the other organs of State authority and administration. It appoints, and may dismiss, the government and its ministers. The 15 man Council of State is elected by the *Sejm*, and its chairman is titular Head of State. The Council of State closely resembles the Supreme Soviet of the Soviet Union: it has wide powers, particularly when the *Sejm* is not in session. Executive power is exercised through the Council of Ministers. The real source of power is, however, the Politburo of the PZPR, and the Party's First Secretary, Edward Gierek, is undoubtedly the single most important figure in Polish politics.

The Minister of Defence is assisted by a number of Deputy Ministers, and his Ministry is composed of directorates and central directorates on the Soviet pattern. The Chief Political Directorate provides a link between the army and the Party. The Polish Ministry of Defence differs slightly from the standard Warsaw Pact model in that the only Deputy Ministers of Defence are the Chief of the General Staff, the Chief of the Main Political Directorate, the Chief Inspector of Training, and the Chief Inspector of Territorial Defence.

Constitutional Status
The Polish Constitution of July 22nd, 1952 is very similar to the current Soviet constitution. Article 6 declares that the Polish Armed Forces 'safeguard the sovereignty and independence of the Polish nation and its security and peace. Article 78 announces that military service is 'an honourable patriotic duty', and Article 84 affirms that serving soldiers have the right to vote. The imposition of long-term martial law and the emergence of a military man as the chief of state makes the military's role in Poland unique among the Warsaw Pact states.

ROLE, COMMITMENT, DEPLOYMENT AND RECENT OPERATIONS

Role and Commitment
The Polish Army is committed to its role in overall Warsaw Pact offensive strategy, but has evolved a separate, secondary force for the Territorial Defence Mission, the OTK forces.

Operationally, Polish Armies would probably be integrated, into Soviet Front-level commands, although there are reports that a Polish Front command was considered. Polish troops would also be involved in any trans-Baltic operations.

The realities of Polish politics, however, have meant that both of these roles have been superceded by the requirements of maintaining martial law, even though the Army itself has tried to keep its on-the-street commitment as little as possible. The Army's role as the prime supporter of the state has become its primary mission.

Deployment
Warsaw Military District HQ; Warsaw
1st Corps HQ, National Air Defence; Warsaw
1st Mechanised Division; Lebignovo
3rd Mechanised Division; Lublin
9th Mechanised Division; Rzeszow
6th Airborne Division; Cracow
1st Artillery Brigade; Wegorzowo
32nd SCUD Missile Brigade; Orzysz
Silesian Military District HQ; Wrocław
3rd Corps HQ, National Air Defence; Wrocław
5th Armoured Division; Gubin
10th Armoured Division; Opote
11th Armoured Division; Zagan
2nd Mechanised Division; Nysa

Poland

4th Mechanised Division; Krosno-Odryanskie
5th Artillery Brigade; Glogow
? SCUD Missile Brigade; Choszczano
? SCUD Missile Brigade; Biedrusko
? SCUD Missile Brigade; Bolesławiec
Pomeranian Military District HQ; Bydgoszcz
2nd Corps HQ, National Air Defence; Bydgoszcz
16th Armoured Division; Elblag
20th Armoured Division; Szczecinek
12th Mechanised Division; Szczecin
8th Mechanised Division; Koszalin
15th Mechanised Division; Olsztyn
7th Amphibious Assault Division; Gdańsk
6th Artillery Brigade; Toruń
Two Naval Infantry battalions; Gdynia
Three WOWO brigades; various locations
Six WOWO regiments; various locations
One OT brigade; ?
Eighteen OT regiments; various locations
Three Commando brigades; one per MD

Non-divisional units include 9 SAM regiments of the Air Defence Forces with 425 SA-2 and SA-3 at 50 sites; one artillery regiment, five anti-aircraft artillery regiments, three anti-tank regiments, one SA-4 SAM brigade.

The five tank divisions, the airborne division, and the amphibious assault division are all at Readiness Category I. Three motorised rifle divisions are Category I, two are Category II, and three, believed to be the three in the Warsaw Military District, are Category III.

Recent Operations

Aside from the UN detachments in Syria and Egypt, the only Polish military action outside its borders since 1945 was the involvement of two divisions (one of which was 6th Airborne), a number of non-divisional units, and tactical aircraft in the invasion of Czechoslovokia.

ORGANISATION

Arms of Service

Combat arms are: Mechanised, Rocket and Artillery, Armoured, Engineer, Signal, and Chemical. Technical Services are: Quartermaster, Ordnance, Medical, Veterinary, Automotive, Transportation, Radiotechnical, and Topography. Military Specialities are: Billeting and Construction, Justice, Administration, Military Police, and Political.

Operational

The operation organisation of the Polish Army fits into standard Soviet and Warsaw Pact models. Each military district could apparently become an Army-level headquarters. There is some evidence that, at least in the late 1960s, there was at least projected a Polish Front-level headquarters, which was to be formed from the Army Chief Inspectorate for Training Headquarters.

Polish tactical units follow basic Soviet patterns but include some significant differences. For example, mechanised companies have usually only seven APCs, as opposed to 10 or 11 in a Soviet motorised rifle company. In the early 1970s, Polish tank regiments did not have battalion headquarters subordinate to them, apparently commanding their companies directly. The Airborne and Amphibious Assault divisions are both small (the latter a brigade group by Western standards) and have unique organisations.

RECRUITMENT, TRAINING AND RESERVES

Recruitment

The forces were voluntarily recruited, mainly from former members of the Russian-sponsored Polish army, until the reintroduction of conscription in 1949. All males have a general liability for military service between the ages of eighteen and fifty; young men are normally called-up for 2 years' service in the army and air force, or 3 years in the navy and Territorial Defence Force. There are numerous grounds for exemption or deferment, and only about one-third of the male population of conscript age actually serves with the colours.

Training

Young Poles are, like their Soviet counterparts, liable for pre-conscription military training, and young men who escape regular service altogether are required to undergo part-time training. Individual training is very similar to that in the Soviet army, with a considerable proportion of training time being devoted to political instruction. Combined training with Soviet units commenced in 1955, and joint exercises have now become a standard feature of formation training. In September, 1973 for example, the Poles joined Soviet, East German and Czech troops in exercise *Quartet*, and the same nations participated in the larger exercise *October Storm* 2 years later. This pattern of joint exercises within the 'northern net' of Warsaw Pact forces has continued to the present day.

About 15% of the enlisted men and 80% of the officers belong to the Party or its youth organisations.

The officers and senior NCOs are largely professionals, although past political unrest have resulted in retention problems.

Anti-Soviet feeling is considerable among much of the Polish Army. The 6th Airborne Division is particularly noteworthy in its sentiments towards its allies.

Reserves

Reserves in the Polish Army, about 500,000 strong, would bring formations up to strength on mobilisation. As in many Warsaw Pact states, the degree of reservist refresher training is considerably less than in Western countries and the Polish press seems to emphasise the role of the reserves in the indoctrination and socialisation missions.

The Territorial Defence Troops (OT) are under the Ministry of Defence. They consist of independent regiments and battalions, with Territorial brigades commanding all the units in a province or region. In wartime, they would come under Army command and would be used for national defence. In peacetime, they also have a labour and construction mission.

The Internal Security Forces (WOW) are under the Ministry of the Interior, but are still responsible to the Chief Inspector for Territorial Defence of the Ministry of Defence. Organised in brigades, WOW troops are trained in standard infantry combat. In wartime, their mission is territorial defence. Currently, the WOW is the primary back-up to the martial law regime.

The Frontier Guard (WOP) is under the Ministry of Defence and responsible to the Chief Inspector for Territorial Defence. Organised in 1,500-2,300 man brigades, the WOP performs border security duties and has a wartime mission of territorial defence.

The Citizen's Militia (ORMO) is under the Ministry of the Interior and handles basic police duties. It has a part-time Voluntary Reserve (ROMO) and also handles secret police Security Service functions. The Motorised Unit's of the Citizen's Militia (ZOMO) are more heavily militarised and have carried the burden of internal policing since the declaration of martial law. They are trained in counter-insurgency operations and are armed with water-cannon trucks.

EQUIPMENT AND ARMS INDUSTRY

Most Polish equipment is of Soviet design, but there is domestic production of both Soviet and Czech-designed equipment.

Small Arms: standard Soviet types, produced in Poland, 7.62mm AKM and AKMS assault rifles, PKM/PK general purpose machine guns, RPK light machine gun
Anti-tank Weapons: RPG-7 rocket launcher RPG-18 disposable rocket launcher, 73mm SPG-9, 82mm, 107mm recoilless anti-tank guns. 450 85mm and 100mm towed guns. Sagger and Spigot ATGMS
Artillery: SP 122mm, SP 152mm, 122mm, 152mm, 130mm weapons. 122m BM-21, 130mm, 140mm and 240mm multiple rocket launcher. 82mm and 120mm mortars
Anti-Aircraft: 750 23mm, 37mm, 57mm, 85mm, 100mm towed. ZSU-23-4s
Armour: Tanks: 3,000 T-54/55, 100+ T-72, 130 PT-76 *APCS:* 5,500 BMP, OT-64, OT-62, MT-LB APCs *Reconnaissance:* 2,800 OT-65 and BRDM scout cars
Aircraft: 710 combat aircraft
Missiles: 51 FROG-3 and FROG-7, 36 SCUD, SA-2, SA-3, SA-4, SA-6, SA-7, SA-9

Arms Industry
Poland's arms industry is, among the satellite States within the Warsaw Pact, second only to that of Czechoslovakia. Several Soviet-designed items are produced under licence in Poland: these include the T-72, T-54/55, MiG-21, Yak-18 and Il-18. Other items are Polish-designed as well as Polish-built. The Star range of trucks is widely used, and the Poles produce the Polish–Czech OT-64 APC. The aircraft factories at Okęcie and Swidnik have produced the LiM-1 and LiM-5, Polish versions of the MiG-15 and MiG-17, and the Polish-designed TS-11 Iskra jet trainer. There is considerable collaboration in weapon design and production between Poland and Czechoslovakia.

RANK, DRESS AND DISTINCTIONS

Rank
Badges of rank are worn on the epaulete and, in most orders of dress, on the headgear.

Officers
Marshal of Poland — Crossed batons above twisted silver lace
General — Three silver stars above twisted silver lace
Major-general — Two silver stars above twisted silver lace
Brigadier — One silver star above twisted silver lace
Colonel — Three silver stars above two silver bars
Lieutenant-colonel — Two silver stars above two silver bars
Major — One silver star above two silver bars
Captain — Four silver stars
Lieutenant — Three silver stars
Second-lieutenant — Two silver stars

Soldiers
Warrant officer I — Two stars on braid-edged epaulette
Warrant officer II — One star on braid-edged epaulette
Senior sergeant — Two chevrons on braid-edged epaulette
Sergeant — One chevron on braid-edged epaulette
Junior sergeant — Three bars
Corporal — Two bars
Lance-corporal — One bar
Private — Plain epaulette

Dress
The turmoils of Polish history have not prevented the survival of numerous traditional features of Polish military uniform. The unmistakable silhouette of the *czapka*, an item of headgear which inspired the nineteenth-century lancer's cap, may still be seen above the more mundane field dress. The eagle cap-badge differs from that worn under the Grand Duchy of Warsaw only in having lost its crown, and the silver lace worn by generals has changed little since the same period.

Parade Dress. All ranks wear short khaki tunics with open collars, four patch pockets, and silver buttons. Collars and ties are khaki, as are the breeches or trousers which are worn tucked into high black boots. The flat forage-cap, with coloured band and black peak, bears badges of rank and the eagle cap-badge. When going on leave, Polish soldiers bend their round-topped forage caps under their arms, to, give it the square-topped appearance of a *czapka*. Officers wear Sam Browne-type belts, and carry sabres on certain occasions. Walking-out dress is similar, but shoes are worn instead of boots.

Everyday Dress. Khaki jacket and trousers tucked into boots, khaki side-cap. In summer the jacket may be replaced by a light-grey shirt.

Field Dress. Combat jacket and trousers, field-grey with black dashes for camouflage. Black equipment, boots and anklets. The square-topped *czapka* is replaced, when neccessary, by a steel helmet.

Tank and NBC suits are of Soviet design, but a distinctively Polish tank helmet is worn. Berets are popular: tank crews, when not wearing their helmets, wear black berets, airborne troops have red berets and marines blue berets. All berets bear, like the field-service *czapka*, the eagle badge. Carpathian-mountain units have their own characteristic uniform, which includes a broad-brimmed khaki hat with a plume and a long khaki cape clung over the left shoulder.

The Arm of Service to which an officer or soldier belongs may be seen from the insignia worn on his collar. All of these are, with the exception of the insignia of the Medical Corps, made of white metal, and most are self-explanatory. The badge of armoured units is a tank, artillery wear crossed cannon-barrels, construction united crossed pick and shovel, and so on. Arm of Service colours are worn on the cap-bands of forage caps. Most Arms of Service have red cap-bands, but among the exceptions are:
Armoured troops: Black with red piping
Internal Security Corps: Dark blue
Frontier Guard: Green
Military Police: White

Distinctions
Qualification and specialist badges, similar to those of the Soviet Armed Forces, are worn on the right breast. The Polish Democratic Republic has numerous orders and decorations, some of which are of traditional style and design and antedate communism in Poland. Among these are the prestigious orders of *Virtuti Militari* and *Polonia Restituta*. Decorations may like the Cross for Valour, be awarded for bravery in the field or, like the Armed Forces in the Service of the Fatherland Medal, reward long meritorious service.

Poland

CURRENT DEVELOPMENTS

No country is more geopolitically important to the Soviet Union than Poland. On the doorstep of the Soviet homeland as well as on the lines of communications to the potential fighting front in Germany, a strong and secure Polish Army is vital to the Soviets. Nationalism and ideology, however, have remained uneasy bedfellows despite a generation of indoctrination. While there seems no reason to doubt that the Polish Army would do its duty as part of the Warsaw Pact in any future conflict, the changing domestic situation must occupy the primary attention of all areas of the Polish government and party.

Richard Holmes
David Isby

PORTUGAL

HISTORY AND INTRODUCTION

On April 25th, 1974 a *coup d'état* by junior officers in the Portuguese army (and to a lesser degree the navy and air force), overthrew the authoritarian and corporatist government of Marcello Caetano, the political heir of Dr Antonio Salazar, who as effective ruler of Portugal for some 40 years was the most durable of modern dictators. The ensuing 18 months of political volatility, institutional instability and almost continuous military upheaval was characteristic more of the regimes of Latin America than those of Europe. Since late 1975 the armed forces have gradually returned to barracks and to the conventional role of defence against external threat. They have subordinated themselves to civilian constitutional government and at the time of writing it seems that the tendency towards military praetorianism has been stifled.

The origins of the Portuguese State are usually traced back to Alfonso I, who took the title of King of Portugal in 1139, whilst the institution of the *permanent* army in Portugal dates from 1640. Prior to this, the King's Army consisted of a cavalry, drawn from the nobility and their private forces, and an infantry of men of humbler origins. In each case their loyalty and responsibility to the king were based on the usual reciprocal obligations built into the feudal system. For some centuries the militia was the basis of Portuguese military organisation, it being completed in 1570.

The restoration of the Portuguese monarchy under John III after a period of Spanish domination (1580–1640) was the occasion for the creation of a permanent army to ensure national independence. All able-bodied men aged fifteen to sixty were eligible for conscription into new provincial defence forces. Although there were a number of methods of exemption from this duty, 4000 cavalrymen and 20,000 infantrymen were soon raised.

Cavalry were officially organised into regiments after 1707 and artillery, a form of which dates from as early as 1515, were more regularly organised from 1677 onwards. Artillery regiments, as such, first appeared in 1708. The Military Engineering Corps consisted of officers skilled in fortification and was later called the Royal Corps of Engineers. In 1812, during the Peninsula War, the initial permanent unit was formed, the Battalion of Artificer Engineers.

The first School of Fortifications and Military Architecture dates from the middle of the seventeenth century. After a number of name changes it became the Army School in 1837 and is now the Military Academy. In 1803 the *Colégio de Freitoria* was founded for the education of the sons of the officers of the Court Artillery Regiment. This became the Royal Military College in 1814 and now, as the Military College, prepares people for entry into the Military Academy. In the middle of the nineteenth century weaponry was rapidly improved and the forerunner of the present Practical Artillery School was set up at Vendas Novas to the east of Lisbon. In 1911 after the creation of the Republic (1910–26), the principle of compulsory military service was introduced, to be completed by all adult, fit males. In the same year the Central School for Officers (now the Institute for Higher Military Studies) was founded together with an organisation for the education of the sons of officers, NCOs and other ranks of the army and navy (now known as the Technical Military Institute for Army Trainees). In 1916 the first Military Aviation School was opened and in 1917 an Air Arm of the army was formed together with the introduction of naval aviation. An independent air force was finally created in 1925. The Royal Portuguese Navy can be dated from the reign of King Dinis, 1279–1325.

The army saw service in World War I after Germany had declared war on Portugal in March, 1916. Almost immediately an Expeditionary Corps began training and it sailed for France in January, 1917 under General Tamagrini de Abreus e Silva. Initially 25,000 strong, and later 40,000, it was divided into two divisions and suffered heavy losses in April, 1918 at the Battle of Lys.

Portugal officially remained neutral during the Spanish Civil War although Salazar was clearly more sympathetic to the Nationalists, whereas neutrality in World War II, although studiously expressed, was more pragmatic. In 1942, under severe pressure from Germany, Portugal agreed to sell the Nazis the scarce mineral wolfram whilst in the summer of 1943 the British government invoked its ancient alliance with Portugal to claim use of the Azores. Salazar complied with this request immediately.

Salazar formally took office as Prime Minister in 1932 but had been Finance Minister and *de facto* Premier since 1928. The government of which he became head had its origins in a military coup of 1926 which had brought to an end 16 years of perpetual economic and political crisis during which time the military had involved itself in politics on numerous occasions. General Carmona became President and Head of State in 1928, an office he held until 1951, whilst the Fascist or New State was inaugurated with the Corporativist Constitution of 1933. But whatever the egalitarian sounding rhetoric of that philosophy, Salazar's Portugal was dominated not by the institutions of corporativism but by the traditional power holders in Portuguese society: the church, the financial interest and the army. Of these three pressure groups the latter two were the more influential, especially considering the strong family links between the economic and military *élites*. Indeed numerous officers followed combined military and financial careers.

However, by the very nature of its control over armed force, it was the influence of the army that made Salazar's position secure, though its loyalty was never certain and his attitude to it was ambivalent. As we have seen, Salazar rose to power in the wake of an army coup, and at times, as an arch traditionalist, he could extol the virtues of the military. Thus he argued, 'The army has the secret of perpetual youth, and like the great and ancient family of noble descent it maintains and passes on its traditions so unimpaired and alive that it forms one in the same moral unity'.

How far Salazar was the creature of these forces is difficult to discern. In a recent book Neil Bruce has argued that Salazar was always, 'The front man of the right-wing generals, and the constitution he drew up . . . ensured that the ultimate arbiter in Portuguese politics would be the armed forces . . . it was the condition of the retention of his office as Prime Minister . . . from his appointment in 1928 he (Salazar) was only free to create policies, to innovate, to govern indeed, so long as he had the blessing of the army, the navy and later the air force'.

The constitutional position on which Bruce places so much

importance was Article 81 of the 1933 Constitution, which grants to the President the power of appointment and dismissal of the Prime Minister. Certainly it is true that all Portuguese Presidents until 1974 (and afterwards as it happens) were either Generals or Admirals and that in 1973, before the publication of his book *Portugal and the Future*, it was widely assumed that the successor to the ageing Admiral Tomás would be none other than General Antonio de Spinola. However, to read into all these arguments the conclusion that Portugal was, in effect, controlled by the military, is mistaken. Until Salazar's illness in 1968 the Presidency was merely a titular position, the winning candidate being the nominee of the National Union, an organisation created and totally dominated by Salazar. And, as Mario Soares points out, Salazar was a civilian and the military could never see him, unlike Franco in Spain, as themselves personified. Indeed Soares believes that at root Salazar despised soldiers.

Nor were civil—military relations in the Salazar years as harmonious as the outward stability of the regime would indicate. Military revolts and attempted coups were a common feature of the period, there being at least nine in Salazar's time and three in Caetano's. Of the military leaders in the post-1974 period, both Generals Gonzalves and Gomes are reported to have been implicated in earlier attempts to overthrow the government. Furthermore, a cursory glance at a list of oppositionists in the Salazar era would indicate how many were military men, the most notable being General Delgado and Captain Galvao. Portugal under Salazar was not a particularly harsh dictatorship, least of all when it dealt with opposition, military or otherwise, which emanated from the dominant groups in society. Thus although much has been written of the repressive nature of the PIDE (Secret Police, later renamed the DGS—Directorate General of Security), their viciousness was not on the whole vented on officers who had participated in failed coups. Confinement to barracks was a common punishment and more severe sentences such as exile were rare. Thus fear of draconian punishment would not be a major impediment in the planning of a coup.

Prior to 1958, the Portuguese officer corps had been a highly elitist, class ridden organisation, drawing its candidates from the economic aristocracy of the solid middle class. The army prohibited the recruitment of black officers and carefully scrutinised any prospective wife of an officer (she had to bring a dowry of £875 or have a university degree), and forced him to marry in church. This highly traditionalist and autocratic mode of officer selection was broken after 1958 when Salazar decided to remove all tuition fees from the Military Academy and for the first time provided the cadets with a salary. The effect of this was to draw into the officer corps and provide a career structure for men who had more tentative links with the regime than previous generations of officers.

During the 1960s the loyalty of the Portuguese armed forces which, as we have seen, was always tentative, was further shaken by two specific events: the expulsion from the Indian colony of Goa and the onset of the African wars. Both bit deep into the mystique of Portuguese colonial ideology and its concept of a Pan-Lusitanian community. The loss of Goa in December, 1961 affected the army in two ways. In simple military terms it was a humiliating defeat but of greater importance was its political impact. Salazar, who was then also Minister of Defence, hled the army commander publicly responsible, a slight and shame which the army never forgave him.

But in the long term the more profound influence was that engendered by the colonial wars in Africa which began with an uprising in Angola in March, 1961. In retrospect it is clear that the Portuguese administration had neither the resources nor the political will-power to sustain a prolonged guerrilla war although at the time the great emphasis placed on the ideological content of Portuguese policy obscured the harsher realities of economic decline coupled with growing military dissatisfaction.

The particular events which brought unrest to a head and precipitated the coup were to be narrowly based professional ones, involving in the main regular army officers, but equally important was the long-term socialising effect of the African wars which were to reawaken the political ideas generated by the modest social upheaval of the 1960s. Many young officers, and especially the conscripts, started questioning the legitimacy of the war. How widespread or thorough going this radicalisation was, seemed to vary from person to person, and in many it instilled little more than an opposition to a colonial war which by 1974 was unlikely to be won. But for some such as Captain Diniz Almeida its effect was dramatic. He argued: ' . . . in Angola and Moçambique we came across black men living very poorly and found it difficult to shoot a man who is fighting with all his senses. And there developed an important phrase, we said to one another, "If I were a black man I too would be a terrorist. We had no cause to fight them." '

Clearly, if attitudes such as these were at all wide spread, and many commentators argue that they were, then the morale and effectiveness of the army must have been crucially undermined.

However, as important as the politicisation of the army was the standing of the officer corps itself. Changes in the pattern of regular officer recruitment proved insufficient to provide enough officers to staff an army in Africa of over 150,000. Fewer and fewer of the traditional *élite* volunteered to join the army and evasion of conscription was enormous. Admissions to the Military Academy dropped dramatically; in 1961—2 there had been 257, in 1973—4 only 88. (At the time of the coup over 400 places were unfilled.) To combat this deficiency more and more university students were conscripted, many as officers and some of whom as noted political activists had been given the choice of the army or prison! Therefore by the early 1970s the preconditions for revolution had been satisfied. A major pillar of the regime had been infiltrated and its loyalty eroded. The regular officer corps were dispirited and disillusioned by a war which could not be won and many of the conscript officers felt little allegiance for a regime of which they had never been a part.

In July, 1973 the Defence Minister issued Degree Law 353/73 which allowed university-trained conscript officers to convert to regular commissions, avoid the 4 years' regular officer course and maintain the seniority they held as conscripts. The regular officers regarded this as yet another humiliation to their professional status; meetings were hurriedly called and protests sent to the government. Initially the meetings merely discussed professional grievances, but by December, 1973 when the government had refused to compromise, the discussions became overtly political, and one group, calling itself the Co-ordinating Committee of the Captains' Movement, accepted that no change would occur without the overthrow of Caetano's government.

A coup became all the more likely when the Deputy Chief of Staff, General Spinola, published his book *Portugal and the Future*, which although highly conservative in basic outlook contained an attack on traditional colonial policy. At the same time Caetano faced opposition from a number of well-known figures on the right of Portuguese politics (including it is said the President, Admiral Tomás and the former Commander-in-Chief in Moçambique, General Kaulza de Arriaga).

On March 14th, 1974, in a last despairing effort to gain support, Caetano ordered senior officers to attend a ceremony at the Presidential Palace to endorse the overseas policy. The Chief of Staff, Costa Gomes and his deputy, Spinola, refused to attend and on Tomás's insistence they were dismissed. Two days later there was an abortive coup by the Fifth Infantry at Caldas da Rainha and on April 25th, 1974 the Armed Forces Movement (MFA) overthrew the Caetano government.

STRENGTH AND BUDGET

Population: 9,971,000
Army: 41,000 (including 10,000 conscripts).
Navy: 13,400 (including 2,687 marines and 6,200 conscripts) 3 submarines, 17 frigates.
Air Force: 12,000 (including 3,500 conscripts and 2,500 paratroops) 87 combat aircraft.
GNP: (1981) $22,063,000,000
Defence expenditure: 1982 estimate $844,200,000
Paramilitary forces: 28,000 (approximately 14,600 National Republican Guard, 16,100 Public Security Police; 7,500 Fiscal Guard.)

Unlike any other NATO country, Portugal was continually involved in colonial wars in Africa from 1961 to 1974. Consequently although the Portuguese contribution to NATO has been slight, the size and expense of the Portuguese armed forces was disproportionately high when related to population and GNP. In 1974 the population was about 8,500,000, a decline of over 500,000 from the 1962 figure, caused by widespread emigration to avoid conscription and to enjoy a higher standard of living in the EEC.

At the watershed point of 1974 the total size of the Portuguese armed forces has been estimated at 282,000, a not wholly reliable figure and one which excludes black African troops in the colonies. The white army was between 170,000 and 180,000, which was about 12% of the men aged between eighteen and forty-five. This was made up of two tank regiments, eight cavalry regiments, 25 infantry regiments, one coastal artillery regiment, three AA artillery regiments, eight engineer battalions and eight signals battalions.

The air force (1974) was 16,000 strong, had 800 aircraft (152 combat) and contributed one maritime reconnaissance squadron to NATO. There was a parachute regiment of 4000 under air force command. The navy of 19,500 included 3300 marines. Reserves for all forces numbered nearly 500,000.

The Republican National Guard (GNR) were an *élite* paramilitary corps concerned with internal security. In 1974 these numbered 9700 and were not disbanded in the post-coup period, although the leadership was changed. The armed border patrol (*Guarda Fiscal*) had 5600 of all ranks, and the Police 13,700. In 1936 Salazar established the Portuguese Legion, a voluntary, armed, Home Guard which strongly supported the ideology of the regime. This was abolished in 1974 as was the 14,000 strong special riot police (PSP), the *Mocidade* (a quasi-fascist youth movement) and, of course, the Secret Police (DGS).

No fully accurate statistics are available as to how many Portuguese troops served in the African colonial wars. Prior to 1961, about 50–75% of the Colonial Army was African and the European troop level in each colony was never more than 3000 (and usually much less). In April, 1974 Portugal probably had 33,000 troops in Guinea (of which 17,000 were white), 70,000 in Angola (40,000 white) and 60,000–65,000 in Moçambique (20,000–25,000 white). A very high percentage of the European men were regular and conscript troops whereas the African figure includes a wide range of paramilitary militia and police groupings. One estimate was

that about 35% of the army units were black African. The Portuguese did compile official statistics of African troop levels and put them at 60% of the total, though this seems somewhat on the high side. It may well be that these were produced to substantiate the Portuguese ideology of non-racialism and the claim that all inhabitants of the overseas provinces (officially not colonies) were citizens of a wider and united Portuguese community. Indeed it is the case that in some instances the Portuguese conscripted Africans since the conscription law made no distinctions based on colour or birthplace.

Africans were deployed in a variety of units: local militia in defence of fortified villages known as *aldeamentos*; regular and usually racially integrated army units; and certain *élite* units (mainly African although commanded by Europeans). Of this latter group the most controversial were the *Flechas* (arrows) who operated in Moçambique as a long-range reconnaissance group and were reportedly controlled by the security police, the DGS. (It is reported that 1116 DGS personnel operated in Angola and 665 in Moçambique.) The *Flechas* and other *élite* African units were distinct in both their role and the higher degree of political indoctrination they received. In addition they were granted special privileges, the *Flechas*, for instance, being exempt from taxation. Over and above those formations cited above a number of white paramilitary, home-guard-type organisations operated in the colonies.

In 1973 it was estimated that total Portuguese casualties since 1961 were 13,000 dead and 65,000 wounded. If these figures are correct it suggests a very high rate in relation to population numbers involved. The period of army national service was 2 years, though at times soldiers had to serve for up to 4 years. (The air force period was 3 years, the navy 4 years.) In practice, many soldiers remained in uniform rather longer than necessary as attractive incentives were offered for further periods of colonial service. However, as early as 1967 it was admitted that of 80,000 men called up as many as 14,000 had evaded conscription. This manpower loss and the consequential emigration of the young from Portugal steadily increased until 1974.

The Post-1974 Period
Since 1974 conscription has been sharply reduced, as has the size of the Portuguese Armed Forces. The size and budget for the armed forces since 1970 is detailed below. It should be noted that Portugal has experienced very heavy inflation in the last decade, (1981 23.9%).

COMMAND AND CONSTITUTIONAL STATUS

The period since 1974 has been characterised by constant upheaval in military and political institutions, and by regular

Table 1 *Armed Forces Size. 1970–82*

1970	229,000
1971	244,000
1972	260,000
1973	276,000
1974	282,000
1975	204,000
1976	83,000
1977	79,000
1978	82,000
1979	81,000
1980	83,000
1981	71,000
1982	67,000

Table 2   *Armed Forces' Budget for the years 1970–1982*

Year	Amount (millions of escudos)	as a % of GDP
1970	12,538	7.0
1971	14,699	7.4
1972	16,046	6.9
1973	16,736	6.0
1974	25,108	7.4
1975	19,898	5.3
1976	18,845	4.0
1977	22,082	3.5
1978	27,354	3.5
1979	34,343	3.5
1980	42,159	3.4
1981	49,000	3.6
1982	49,870	

alternation of governing factions, parties and individuals. During this period there have been 15 governments, 10 Prime Ministers (2 military) and 3 Presidents (all military) together with an almost infinite range of competing political ideologies.

The initial programme of the Armed Forces Movement (MFA) was not particularly radical and in essence promised the creation of a western liberal democracy and the abolition of all the oppressive features of the former dictatorship. On external matters the programme committed Portugal to previously negotiated international treaties and to the speedy end to the colonial wars. In the manner of all military governments the MFA promised to return to barracks after democratic elections. General Spinola, the new President, symbolised the moderation of the programme.

However, Spinola's Presidency was to last a mere 5 months, a period in which he was unable to secure a firm base for his authority. He had wide popular appeal but in crucial sections of the community, particularly the industrial working class, he was viewed with suspicion for his association with the previous regime. Constitutionally, his position was uncertain for it rested on appointment by the '*Junta* of National Salvation', a body composed of seven senior officers, whom he himself had nominated. Theoretically the most important institution of the new polity was the Council of State, which had legislative authority and which consisted of the *junta*, seven members of the Co-ordinating Committee and seven 'public figures', also chosen by Spinola. But despite this superficial institutional dominance Spinola was never able to reconcile the competing interests and policies in post-coup Portugal. His first Prime Minister resigned in July, unable to obtain approval for a Presidential election (which would legitimise Spinola's position) and increase powers for himself as Premier. He was succeeded by Colonel (later General) Vasco Gonzalves, the choice of the MFA, not Spinola, and a man whom many thought was a card-carrying member of the Communist Party.

Whilst the MFA were undoubtedly politically inexperienced, they knew what they opposed, namely a return to fascism, and in Spinola they increasingly saw a man who might do just that. Thus each clash between them was seen by the MFA as an attack on the legitimacy of the revolution, and in each dispute they were further radicalised. Internal strife was exacerbated by industrial unrest and Spinola's opposition to colonial independence, which culminated in September, 1974 in Spinola's attempt to rally support by a march of his supporters, the 'silent majority'. In this he failed and under extreme pressure resigned, to be replaced by his

friend and far more politically astute colleague, General Costa Gomes.

The Spinola/MFA struggle was not the only significant feature of this period. Perhaps even more important was the increasing influence of the Portuguese Communist Party (PCP) on the MFA and the process of *saneamento* (purging or cleansing) which in the first weeks after the coup removed nearly 100 generals and admirals regarded as potential opponents of the new government.

The first few months after the coup also saw the formation of Copcon and the decision to turn the 5th Division of the General Staff into a propaganda unit. Copcon (Operational Command for the Continent) operated as an internal security force and played an ever increasing role in Portuguese politics until it was disbanded in November, 1975. It was headed by Major (later General, now Major) Otelo Carvalho, the architect of the coup and the chief proponent of the Cuban or Castroite solution for Portugal. The Fifth Division was dominated by the PCP and was later to gain control of much of the press, radio and television and to be foremost in the process of cultural dynamisation (the attempt to radicalise the traditionalist and highly conservative Portuguese peasantry).

In the wake of the attempted Spinola counter-coup of March, 1975 and as a reaction to it, the MFA moved increasingly to the left, agreed to a further period of *saneamento* and made major institutional changes. The *junta*, Council of State and MFA Co-ordinating Committee were dissolved and replaced by a Supreme Revolutionary Council (SRC) with full legislative powers.

The intention of the military to institutionalise further and implant their position was made clear by the pact the MFA forced the political parties to sign on April 11th, 1975, 2 weeks before the Constituent Assembly elections. The pact, in the form of a draft constitution, was a complete *volte-face* from the programme the MFA had issued a year earlier. Whereas the original intention had been for the military to return, after elections, 'to their specific mission of external defence', they were now to be given a political role which ensured their supreme authority for 5 years. Thus the power of the elected Constituent Assembly to draft its own constitution was severely limited.

Any lingering unity within the armed forces was rapidly eroded in the post-election months as Premier Gonzalves moved Portugal towards Eastern European style communism, whilst after some hesitation General Carvalho appeared to opt for a policy modelled on Cuba.

The rapid drift to the left was halted in mid-summer by a resurgence of the latent conservatism of the Portuguese north and resulted in the burning of numerous Communist Party offices. At the same time a group of MFA officers called for a reversion to a democratic and leftward-looking socialism, which was neither elitist and bureaucratic as the Eastern European model, nor bourgeois and capitalist as a liberal democracy.

In late August the Gonzalves government collapsed and the Fifth Division, the most vocal, influential and radical mouthpiece of the communist element in the MFA, was abolished. A new administration under Admiral Azevedo was formed but was unable to govern in the near anarchy of the mounting crisis. During this period military discipline reached its nadir with the formation of the left-wing soldiers' organisation, the SUV (United Soldiers Will Win). Their support for Carvalho's individualistic tactics and refusal to obey orders without prior 'democratic' discussion were to prove unacceptable to a number of more conservative officers.

In November 1975 a group of senior officers at last recognised that continued political involvement on the scale existing at the time was incompatible with the survival of the armed forces as a structured discipline and credible entity. Under the leadership of General Ramallio Eanes an alliance of moderate officers restored unity to the armed forces and ousted the leftist leaders.

Since 1975 the role of the armed forces in politics has been progressively reduced although their nominal position remained important, In February, 1976 a new pact was signed between the armed forces and the political parties under which the Council of the Revolution, a body of 19 officers retained the right to veto legislation. And under article 273 of the 1976 constitution the armed forces had a duty, 'to secure the continuation of the revolution and ensure the conditions under which Portuguese society may expect a peaceful and pluralistic transition to democracy and socialism.' In June 1976, General Eanes was elected President of Portugal, easily defeating leftist candidates. Although Eanes remained Commander-in-Chief of the Armed Forces and President of the Council of the Revolution, he used his influence to diminish military power and return soldiers to barracks. In August, 1976, he announced that membership of the Council of the Revolution was in future to be incompatible with holding a regional command. Effectively, officers had to decide whether they were soldiers or politicians.

Between 1976 and 1982 civilian governments came and went, and Portugal moved from one political and economic crisis to another. Eanes had a stormy relationship with politicians of both centre and left but, despite his austere manner, remained popular with the people. In December 1980 he was re-elected for a further five-year term as President. In February 1981 he renounced the post of Commander-in-Chief of the Armed Forces and in July, 1982 the Portuguese constitution was revised, the Council of the Revolution abolished and the radical elements of the 1976 constitution excised. A new Supreme Defence Council was set up but this body is to have no political authority.

ROLE, COMMITMENT, DEPLOYMENT AND RECENT OPERATIONS

In the period after April, 1974 the Portuguese forces shrank from a predominantly externally based force of 200,000 (all units) to a domestically based one of 67,000. It now exists to fulfil two basic roles: that of contributing, however modestly, to NATO; and in providing a counter-insurgency force for domestic use. Portugal has been a loyal member of NATO since its formation in 1949, this support being based on both ideological and military considerations. Salazar was a staunch anti-communist and naturally this found expression in an ardent support for NATO, but membership of the Alliance also afforded the intensely nationalistic Portuguese an opportunity to satisfy their yearnings to play a role in great-power politics. At the more instrumental level, NATO membership gave not only basic defence but also provided her with more sophisticated and expensive weaponry than would otherwise have been available.

Portugal's main contribution to Alliance security has been through the strategic importance of the Azores, already noted in the context of World War II and vital for the use of the air base at Lajes by the Americans to resupply Israel during the 1973 Middle East War. On April 8th, 1975 Prime Minister Vasco Gonzalves said that this facility would not be granted again but this decision was reversed by Eanes and in June 1979 an agreement was signed which allowed the United States to retain the base until 1983. In return the United States was to provide Portugal with $140m of aid. At present the agreement is again being renegotiated.

In the early years of the coup, Portuguese relations with NATO were uneasy. The Portuguese Socialist Party's policy was that of nonalignment, some elements in the Army were sympathetic to Cuba and the Portuguese Communist Party was avowedly Stalinist and pro-Moscow. Portugal was excluded from NATO intelligence reports and absented herself from the NATO Nuclear Planning Club. After 1977 Portugal gradually reestablished her links with NATO and in 1978 created a NATO Brigade. During 1980 the army again participated in NATO exercises and the same year Portugal rejoined the Nuclear Planning Group.

NATO has Atlantic naval command bases in both Lisbon (IBERLANT) and Madeira, and the Germans have an air force training base at Beja. Neither of these can be considered crucial to the Alliance.

ORGANISATION

In January, 1970 the Ministry of the Army was incorporated within the Ministry of Defence, which was given full responsibility for defence matters. The Chief of the General Staff was given command of operational troops which had previously rested with individual service chiefs. Also in 1970 the territorial organisation of the army was reformed into six military regions with headquarters in Coimbra, Oporto, Tomar, Euora, Lisbon and the Algarve. Metropolitan Portugal also included commands in Madeira and the Azores. Overseas Portuguese military regions were in Moçambique (divided into five Territorial Commands) and Angola (divided into three). Further territorial commands existed in Cape Verde, São Tomé and Principe, Portuguese Guinea, Macao and Timor.

In 1975 the Portuguese metropolitan regions were abolished and replaced by North, Central and South, each commanded by a senior MFA officer in the Supreme Revolutionary Council (now called the Council of the Revolution). Subsequently command of a region and a seat on the SRC became incompatible and in 1982 the Council of the Revolution was abolished. Today there are four military regions in Portugal (Coimbra, Oporto, Evora and Lisbon) and two island commands. (Canaries and Azores).

In 1975 all army regiments which had been known by number alone were renamed after their local recruitment catchment area. To some extent this formalised a pre-existing situation since traditionally units have recruited on a regional basis. During the crisis period of 1974—6 the political stance of particular regiments depended as much on this (i.e. regiments from the north tended to be conservative, as did that area) as on factors such as the political influence of individual officers. Today this political alignment has disappeared. The army consists of a mixed (infantry/armour), two armoured cavalry regiments, 12 infantry regiments, one independent infantry battalion, one commando regiment, 6 artillery regiments, a Special Forces Battalion and various engineer, signal and support regiments.

RECRUITMENT, TRAINING AND RESERVES

Recruitment is by conscription, the current term (reduced from the 4 years it reached at the height of the African wars) being 16 months. Recruits are trained in the Recruit School and then in the units. Conscripts may become corporals (*Cabo Miliciano*) and, by competition, sergeants, but NCOs are usually recruited from volunteers. Some of these come from the military preparatory school (*Pupilas do Exercito*). Corporals must attend the corporals' school (*Escola de Cabos*). Sergeants are trained in the school of their arm (*Escola*

Practica) and, for promotion, at the Central School for Sergeants.

Officers are trained at the Military Academy. They are recruited in a variety of ways: some are sergeants from the Central School, most are high-school graduates. Conscripts who have been selected for and have passed the conscript officer course may also become regular officers, and careers in the technical arms are open to *Pupilas do Exercito* with technical qualifications. Officers are trained subsequently in their arm's school, and staff officers, selected by competition, are trained at the Institute for Higher Military Studies. The Military Academy and the Institute are located in Lisbon.

Reserves number on paper about half a million, but as the Portuguese army is in the process of reduction its reserve strength and organisation are at present not of practical interest.

EQUIPMENT AND ARMS INDUSTRY

Portugal produces most of the light weaponry and ammunition she requires and has a thriving export business, particularly in ammunition. Other equipment she produces include: 9mm model 48 and 9mm model 63 sub-machine-guns (made by Fabrica Militar de Braco de Prata — FBP); 7.62mm G3 rifle on licence; grenades made by FBP; and 61mm and 81mm FBP mortars. In 1961 Germany arranged the transfer of 10,000 Israeli Uzi sub-machine-guns. Heavier equipment used is as follows.

Armour: 62, M-47; 23 M-48 tanks; 11 M-24 light tanks; 100 Panhard/AMC armoured cars, 32 Ferret Mk 4 Scout cars; 86 M-113 and 82 Chaimite armoured personnel carriers
Artillery: 68 5.5in; 54 M-101 AI 105mm towed; various coastal artillery
Air-Defence Weapons: 351 40mm AA guns
Anti-Armour Weapons: 90mm and 106mm recoilless rifles (82 and 127 in service) and 21 TOW ATGW

RANK, DRESS AND DISTINCTIONS

The service dress of the army is grey. A camouflaged combat dress is worn.

Marshal — Four gold stars
Chief of the General Staff — Four silver stars
General — Three silver stars
Brigadier — Two silver stars
Colonel — One wide and three narrow gold bars
Lieutenant-colonel — One wide and two narrow gold bars
Major — One wide and one narrow gold bar
Captain — Three narrow gold bars
Lieutenant — Two narrow gold bars
Sub-lieutenant — One narrow gold bar

It should be noted that the rank of general is not subdivided into full, lieutenant- and major-generals. Prior to 1974 this conglomeration of officers in one rank resulted in some confusion as to status and hierarchy.

The orders and decorations of Portugal in 1974 reflected the religious tradition and the emphasis on history in Portuguese nationhood. The decorations include the Ribbon of the Three Orders (worn by the President as Grand Master of all Portuguese military orders; first instituted in 1552); Military Order of the Tower and the Sword (the most important Portuguese decoration for valour in battle, and courage, service and command on campaign; 1495); Military Merit (a recent creation); Military Order Avis (oldest Portuguese military order; established in 1162); Military Order of Christ (awarded for distinguished service to Portugal and mankind; 1356); Military Order of St. James of the Sword (for artistic and academic merit, 1175); and the Order of Prince Henry the Navigator (for academic and other merit in regard to the sea; 1960). Other medals of valour and good service include the Military Valour Medal, the Exemplary Conduct Medal, the Distinguished Service Medal and the War Cross. In December, 1981 former Presidents Spinola and Costa Gomes were elevated to the rank of Marshal.

CURRENT DEVELOPMENTS

It now seems probable that after the turbulent years of 1974—6 the Portuguese army has relinquished any serious role in political life. Any judgement of this kind must, however, remain tentative since the development is both recent and in historical terms quite novel. Nor have Portuguese politics become sufficiently stable or the economy sufficiently healthy to presume that the army will remain constitutionally quiescent. Nevertheless there are strong signs that the military itself recognises the damage done to its credibility and effectiveness during the years of revolution and that it will not repeat the experience. The presence of the popular and strong, if rather dour, figure of General Eanes as President, is also likely to help current constitutionalism in government.

In the last three or four years the army has placed great emphasis on its re-establishment of a modest, but to Portugal, important role in NATO. This development is likely to continue, as is Portugal's request that aid be provided to equip its NATO brigade with modern weaponry.

The strategic position of Portugal remains important to the Alliance although the recent entry of Spain into NATO's formal structure somewhat diminishes this. It seems likely that the United States will again be granted base rights at Lajes in the Azores and may well develop this facility as a staging post for a Rapid Deployment Force.

During 1982 there were some signs that links might be recreated between the Portuguese military and the forces of her former colonies in Africa. A top level army mission visited Mozambique and a tentative agreement has been reached for Portugal to provide training and equipment for President Machel's forces.

Matthew Midlane

QATAR

HISTORY AND INTRODUCTION

See the entry under United Arab Emirates for the history of all the Trucial States of the Gulf until 1971 (p. 747).

A provisional constitution for Qatar was introduced in 1970, a year before independence. The first Cabinet, formed in accordance with it, contained the Ruler as Prime Minister and Minister for Oil, and Royal Family members in six of the other nine ministries. This was known as constitutional monarchy.

Sheikh Ahmad bin Ali al-Thani, the ruler for 15 years, was deposed in February, 1972 in a bloodless coup by his cousin Sheikh Khalifa bin Hamad al-Thani, who had gained the support of most of the Family. He now governs as Prime Minister, in a Council of Ministers nine of whose other 13 ministers also belong to the al-Thani family. There is also an Advisory Council of 20 appointed members, who will one day be elected instead.

STRENGTH AND BUDGET

The strength of the Qatar armed forces is 5000 excluding expatriate personnel. There are maritime and air components, but all are part of the army.

The defence budget for 1981 was announced to be around $893,000,000. Recent capital expenditure, has included over $100,000,000 for new barracks, a naval base and an air base, plus contributions to the Arab Organisation for Industrialisation (intended to finance the creation of an Arab arms industry based in Egypt). Qatar's population is 240,000 and its GNP in 1981 was estimated at $6,580,000,000.

COMMAND AND CONSTITUTIONAL STATUS

The Ruler, Sheikh Khalifa bin Hamad al-Thani, is Supreme Commander. His son, Major-General Sheikh Hamad bin Khalifa al-Thani, is Commander-in-Chief and Minister of Defence.

ROLE, COMMITMENT, DEPLOYMENT AND RECENT OPERATIONS

The only serious role of the Qatar army is internal security. The limited external defence capability which currently exists serves principally to avoid offering the invitation to external threat which would be presented by the complete absence of defences. The rather more ambitious air-defence capability which is envisaged by present arms-purchasing plans is not so much related to the direct defence of Qatar itself as to a co-ordinated inter-State programme to create a credible air defence for the Arab side of the Gulf. Qatar has no commitments nor forces deployed abroad, and has never fought a war.

The internal security problem arises mainly from the fact that only 50,000 of the 200,000 population are actually native Qataris. Almost half the residents are skilled or un-skilled workers on fixed-term contracts, who poses no

political problem, but there are permanently resident populations of about 20,000 Palestinians and between 30,000 and 50,000 Iranians.

There is a major territorial dispute with neighbouring Bahrain over the small island of Huwar, which lies only a few miles off Qatar's coast but is currently garrisoned by Bahrain. The principal significance of the dispute lies in the island's implications for the demarcation of territorial waters in which oil might be found. Saudi Arabia has offered to mediate, but has strained relations with Qatar and has recently built an air base in Bahrain.

ORGANISATION

The army is made up of one tank regiment, one Royal Guard infantry battalion and five infantry battalions. There are also maritime and air elements, with eight large gunboats and nine combat aircraft.

RECRUITMENT, TRAINING AND RESERVES

The Qatari personnel of the army are drawn largely from non-urban members of the leading tribes, and many officers belong to the Royal Family. The majority of the enlisted ranks are recruited from the bedouin tribes who move freely between Saudi Arabia and Qatar. There are numbers of expatriate personnel from Britain, other Arab countries and Pakistan. There are no reserves, but the tribes are armed.

EQUIPMENT AND ARMS INDUSTRY

The army has 24 AMX-30 medium tanks, 136 VAB personnel carriers (France), 30 AMX-10P MICVs, 25 Saracen APCs and 10 Ferret scout cars. The artillery has eight 25 pounder guns and six 155mm howitzers. There are some Tigereat air defence missiles and the infantry has 81mm mortars. There are improved Hawk surface-to-air missiles on order.

There is no arms industry.

RANK, DRESS AND DISTINCTIONS

Qatari military ranks follow the standard eastern Arab nomenclature. Uniforms are similar to those in the other Gulf sheikhdoms.

CURRENT DEVELOPMENTS

The most important question in Qatar for several years has been the dispute within the Royal Family over the succession to the present Ruler. The latter succeeded in having his eldest son, who is also Commander-in-Chief of the Armed Forces (see Command and Constitutional Status) named Crown Prince in 1977, but the rival claim of the ruler's younger brother, Sheikh Suhaim, has continued to unsettle

Qatari politics. In the course of the dispute Sheikh Suhaim has armed many of the more distant branches of the extensive Royal Family, and has sought Saudi Arabian support with some success. There is a precedent for a Saudi show of armed strength along the border to influence the internal politics of Qatar: it happened in 1972, when Saudi Arabia supported the inter-family coup, organised by Sheikh Suhaim, which brought the present Ruler to power.

See also the comments under Current Developments in the entry on the United Arab Emirates, which are largely applicable to Qatar.

Gwynne Dyer
John Keegan

ROMANIA

HISTORY AND INTRODUCTION

The Danubian Principalities which were to form Romania became autonomous within the Ottoman Empire in 1859, and the nation gained independence in 1878. Prince Karl of Hohenzollern-Sigmaringen became King, as Carol I, in 1866, and it was largely due to the predilections of the Royal Family that Romania did not enter World War I on the side of the Allies until the Summer of 1916. Romania's adherence to the Allied cause brought her the territories of Bessarabia and Transylvania.

Romania, as a member of the Little Entente, was subject to a good deal of French influence during the inter-war years, but the government was also under growing pressure from the right. In 1940 Romania was forced to yield considerable territory to Russia, Hungary and Bulgaria; Carol II abdicated in September, and the pro-German Marshal Ion Antonescu came to power. Romania entered the war in June 1941, and sent more troops to the Eastern Front than did all Germany's other allies combined. The Romanian army suffered heavy losses in the fighting in the east, particularly during the Stalingrad operation, and by the summer of 1944 it had been forced back to the eastern border of Romania. Soviet forces had already entered the country through the Iasi gap when, on August 23rd, King Michael and his adherents overthrew Antonescu and joined the Allies. This *volte face* came too late to avert Soviet occupation and, as in many other eastern European countries, the presence of Soviet troops proved a useful asset to local communists. The communists secured the most important government posts following the 1946 elections; Michael was forced to abdicate in December, 1947 and Romania was declared a People's Republic.

With two divisions formed by the Soviets from Romanian prisoners as its cadre, the Romanian Worker's Party set about forming a Communist army soon after it seized power in early 1945. In 1945—47, the army strength was reduced and officers and NCOs with connections with the previous regime were removed to be replaced by those loyal to Communism.

The revitalisation of the Army started in December 1947 with the appointment of Smil Bodnaras as Minister of the Armed Forces. Large numbers of Soviet weapons began to arrive. A large Soviet military mission was sent to Romania and Romanian officers and technicians were sent to the Soviet Union for training, and the Army was soon forced into the Soviet mould. Romania became a member of the Warsaw Pact when it was formed. Manpower policies dictated a reduction in size of the army from a peak of 15 divisions in the 1950s.

Nationalism began to guide Romanian policies increasingly in the early 1960s, and these tendencies became more pronounced after Nicolae Ceausescu became First Secretary in 1965. In 1964 and 1967, Romanian units participated in Warsaw Pact exercises in Bulgaria. Since then, only staffs or small units have been involved. Soviet influence was reduced with the withdrawal of the occupation forces in 1958 and the reduction of the military mission in 1960.

Romania has pursued a foreign policy that shows a degree of independence from the Soviet Union, although internally the Communist Party shows no flexibility towards sharing of power and continues repression of potential dissidents. In 1978, Ceasescu stressed that Romanian forces were national and not under the Supreme Military Command of the Warsaw Pact. This increased national defence emphasis was earlier seen in the withdrawal of the Soviet military mission in 1970—72, the formation of the Patriotic Guard for territorial defence against a Soviet-led invasion in 1968, and the re-orientation of Romanian forces against such an invasion. Romania has condemned the Soviet invasion of Czechoslovakia in 1968 and of Afghanistan in 1979.

STRENGTH AND BUDGET

Population: 22,400,000
Army: 140,000
Navy: 7,000; 124 small craft
Air force: 30,000; 328 combat aircraft
Border troops and internal security forces: 37,000
People's Militia: about 900,000
GNP (1981) $77.1—120 billion
Defence expenditure (1981) 1.4 billion

COMMAND AND CONSTITUTIONAL STATUS

Command
The President and Chief of State, Nicole Ceausescu, is the Supreme Commander of the Armed Forces under the constitutional amendment of March, 1974. He is also a member of the Defence Council, which follows the Soviet model, and the Council of Ministers. (The other members being the Ministers of the Armed Forces and Internal Affairs. (He is also the superior of the Minister of the Armed Forces.)

The Minister of the Armed Forces has direct responsibility for Romania's defence. Directly subordinate to him are the Directorates for Political Affairs, Rear Services, and Training, all headed by Deputy Ministers. The Chief of the General Staff is also responsible to the Minister and also holds the post of Deputy Minister. The chiefs of the four services — army, navy, air and air defence forces, and frontier troops, report directly to the Minister, as does the commanders of the Cluj and Bucharest Military Districts.

As in most Warsaw Pact countries, the Minister is a political appointee who also holds military rank, although in Romania this need not be the highest military rank.

Administered by the Ministry of the Armed Forces, but rather responsible to the Central Committee of the Romanian Communist Party, is the Higher Political Council, which is in charge of political education and indoctrination throughout the armed forces.

CONSTITUTIONAL STATUS

Supreme authority is vested in the unicameral Grand National Assembly, elected every 5 years. The State Council, the permanent executive body, is elected by the Grand National Assembly, as is the President. The Council of Ministers is the supreme administrative body. Both the Grand National Assembly and the State Council can appoint and recall the Supreme Commander of the Armed Forces. In addition, the State Council establishes military ranks and grants the ranks of marshal, general and admiral. Article 40 of the Constitution states that military service 'is a duty of honour for the citizens of the Socialist Republic of Romania.

ROLE, COMMITMENT, DEPLOYMENT AND RECENT OPERATIONS

Role, Commitment and Deployment
As a member of the Warsaw Pact, Romania is pledged to carry out the goals and objective of that alliance. However, in reality, territorial defence outside the Warsaw Pact framework is the actual primary mission of the Romanian Army. The Romanian Army is deployed against a Soviet thrust from the north, coupled with other forces positioned to meet a Hungarian attack into the areas of Romania that Hungary still claims. Other troops are in position to cover the Bulgarian border but Romania remains, today as in 1916, basically indefensible with its own resources. Soviet occupation troops withdrew in 1958 and the military mission was reduced in 1960.

Recent Operations
Romanian troops have not seen combat since 1945. They did not participate in the 1968 invasion of Czechsolovokia. As a matter of national policy they refuse to permit Warsaw Pact units to pass through on their way to manoeuvres. Although Romanian units have participated in selected Warsaw Pact exercises in the 1960s and 1970s, they are normally only represented by staff officers.

ORGANISATION

Arms of Service
The combat arms are Infantry, Armour, Artillery, Engineers, Signal, Chemical, and Cavalry. Under the Directorate of Rear Services are the Quartermaster, Medical, Veterinary, Administrative Technical, and rail and motor transportation branches. Other branches deal with Military Justice and Military Music.

Operational
The Romanian Army has two operational Armies, the Second and the Third, which correspond to the two peacetime Military Districts. Operational Deployments, in peacetime are:

Second Army HQ; Bucharest
4th (?) Tank Division; Bucharest
1st Motorised Rifle Division; Bucharest
2nd Motorised Rifle Division; Craiova
9th Motorised Rifle Division; Constanta
10th Motorised Rifle Division; Iasi
? Motorised Rifle Division; Braila
4th Mountain Brigade; Curtea de Arges
8th Artillery Brigade; Focsani
17th Artillery Brigade; Birlad
? SCUD Missle Brigade; Tecuci
Third Army HQ; Cluj
6 (57?) Tank Division; Tirgu Mures
11th Motorised Rifle Division; Oradea
18th Motorised Rifle Division; Timisoara
81st Motorised Rifle Division; Dej
2nd Mountain Brigade; Brasov
? SCUD Missile Brigade; Ineu
? Airborne Regiment; ?
? Naval Infantry Battalion; Giurgia

One MRD is believed to be at cadre strength. The tank divisions and four motorised rifle divisions are believed to be at Category I (approximately 80% strength). The other three MRDs are believed to be at lower strength.

The airborne regiment and the naval infantry battalion are both believed to be relatively small units.

Romanian non-divisional units are believed to also include two artillery, two anti-aircraft artillery, and four anti-tank regiments.

Unit organisation follows older Soviet patterns. Tank battalions, for example, have 21 tanks, where the Soviets have 31. Motorised Rifle companies often have less APCs than their Soviet equivalent. In the early-mid 1970s, it was known that the Romanians did not have enough APCs for all their motorised rifle units and were using trucks. The domestic production of APCs since then is believed to have made up most, if not all, of these shortfalls and units in the higher-readiness divisions may be at Soviet-type scales of equipment.

RECRUITMENT TRAINING AND RESERVES

Recruitment and Training
Service is 16 months conscription, followed by many years obligation in the reserve (to age 50) or the Patriotic Guard. There are professional NCOs, but, as in all Warsaw Pact armies, never enough. Training roughly follows the Soviet model. NCOs may volunteer for 4-year enlistments.

Reserves
About 450,000 regular army reservists will bring Romanian units up to combat strength in the event of mobilisation. They may also permit the mobilisation of one or two hostilities-only divisions.

The Patriotic Guard, 700,000 strong, was organised by the Law of 12 November, 1968, as a response to the Soviet invasion of Czechoslovakia and as an attempt to give Romania a Yugoslav-style territorial defence capability. While there are regular army cadres, the Patriotic Guard is normally under the Ministry of Internal Affairs, although it would probably come under Army operational command in the event of mobilisation. Patriotic Guard units are formed in factories, villages, and government bureaus. There is widespread liability for service, which includes women as well as men.

OTHER GROUND FORCES

The Frontier Troops
About 17,000 strong, the Frontier Troops are a separate service, co-equal with the Army. Its highest unit is the regiment. The Frontier Troops are responsible for border security and, in the event of mobilisation, their units would probably come under Army operational Command.

The Security Troops
About 20,000 strong and responsible to the Ministry of Internal Affairs, the basic tactical unit of the Security Troops is the battalion, with administrative brigades. Its primary mission is against internal enemies of the regime, but it will also secure the Army's rear areas in event of mobilisation.

Naval Coast Defence
About 1,500 strong in peacetime, plus a 500-man Naval Infantry battalion, this force has 100 coastal guns in 18 batteries. Two Naval Infantry regiments would reportedly be raised from reservists on mobilisation.

EQUIPMENT AND ARMS INDUSTRY

Small arms: of Soviet origins, although Mauserrifles remain for Militia training.

Mortars: Soviet-designed 82mm and 120mm (750-1000 in service) Anti-Tank RPG-7 rocket launcher, 73mm SPG-9, 82mm B-10 RR, 76mm, 85mm, 100mm guns.

Artillery: 76mm, 85mm, 600+ 122mm howitzers, 150 152mm weapons, BM-21 122mm MRLs, 150 130mm MRL, other heavy guns.

Armour: Tanks: 200 T-34/85, 1,600 T-54/55 and M-77 (Romanian rebuilt) tanks. some T-72s in service. *Scout Cars:* 600 BRDMs, BTR-40 APCs; 2,000 BTR-152, BTR-50, BTR-60, OT-810, TAB-72 (Romanian-produced BTR-60PB) *SP Guns:* 100 SU-100

Anti-Aircraft Artillery: 650 30mm, 37mm, 57mm, 100mm guns ZSU-23-4s

Aircraft: 70 MiG-17, 240 MiG-21, 18 I1-28, 30 transports, 95 helicopters

Missiles: 20 SAM sites with 108 SA-2, SA-6, SA-7 SAMs, Snapper and Sagger ATGMs, 30 FROG, 20 SCUD

Arms Industry

Romania produces Soviet-designed small arms, and armoured personnel carriers. It also rebuilds and improves tanks to the extent they are substantially new vehicles.

RANK, DRESS AND DISTINCTIONS

Rank

Officers' ranks and badges of rank are similar to those of the Soviet ground forces. Epaulettes are, however, smaller than their Soviet equivalents, and are piped with arms-of-service colours rather than with red.

Non-commissioned ranks are indicated by bars of gold braid worn on the epaulette.

Senior NCOs — bars are worn on epaulette of arm-of-service colour

Plutonier-adjutant — Three broad braid bars
Plutonier-maior — Two broad braid bars surmounted by one narrow braid bar
Plutonier — Two broad braid bars
Sergent-maior — One broad braid bar surmounted by one narrow braid bar

Junior NCOs and men — bars worn on plain epaulette

Sergent — One broad braid bar
Caporal — Two broad braid bars edged with arm-of-service piping
Soldat-fruntas — One broad braid bar edged with arm-of-service piping
Soldat — No badge of rank

Specialists — a number of specialist technician's ranks exist in the armour, artillery, signals, motor transport and technical troops. Badges of rank are worn on an epaulette of arm-of-service colour.

Maistru militar principal — Three gold chevrons surmounted by three short gold bars
Maistru militar clasa Ia — Two gold chevrons surmounted by three short gold bars
Maistru militar clasa IIa — Two gold chevrons surmounted by two short gold bars
Maistru militar clasa IIIa — Two gold chevrons surmounted by one short gold bar
Maistru militar clasa IVa — Two gold chevrons with no bars

Dress

Parade dress consists of a Romanian pattern steel helmet, light-brown tunic worn with khaki shirt and tie, together with light-brown trousers tucked into black boots. Officers wear Sam Browne belts. Walking-out dress is similar, but a large peaked cap with a band in the arm-of-service colour replaces the steel helmet, and black shoes replace boots. Both officers and men have a working uniform based on a single-breasted tunic with a fly front, high collar and four concealed pockets worn with brown trousers tucked into boots; officers generally wear peaked caps and soldiers sidecaps A camouflage combat dress is gradually replacing the old-style long-skirted blouse. Equipment, tank suits and NBC protective clothing are of the Soviet pattern. Mountain troops are distinguished by large grey berets.

Arm of service is indicated by a system of badges and colours worn in parade, walking-out and every-day dress. Badges are made of white or yellow metal; they are worn on the epaulette and are, in the main, self-explanatory. Arm of-service colours are worn on the collar patches, epaulettes and peaked cap. The most common colours are:

Red — infantry, administration, quartermaster, justice, music
Black — armour, artillery, engineers, signals, technical troops and motor transport
Dark Green — mountain troops
Light Green — frontier troops

Distinctions

These include two titles, 'Hero of the Romanian Socialist Republic' and 'Hero of Socialist Labour of the Romanian People's Republic' and a number of orders, the most senior of which are 'The Victory of Socialism', 'Star of the Romanian Socialist Republic' and 'Twenty-Third August'.

CURRENT DEVELOPMENTS

Romania has not moved fully away from the standard Soviet—Warsaw Pact force structure, but has accommodated it to a primary mission of territorial defence while maintaining, through staff participation in exercises and maintenance of support for joint activities, a secondary presence as part of the Warsaw Pact. Soviet wartime planning apparently does not envision a major role for the Romanian Army.

Richard Holmes
David Isby

RWANDA

HISTORY AND INTRODUCTION

Rwanda was one of East Africa's pre-colonial interlacustrine kingdoms in which in the sixteenth century a Para-Nilotic pastoral people, the Tutsi, established an ascendancy over a Bantu agricultural peasantry, the Hutu. With its similarly constituted neighbour Burundi, Rwanda passed into German hands in the 1890s, and then into Belgian hands in 1919. The Belgians followed the German policy of 'indirect rule' through the Tutsi *Mwami* (king) and the Tutsi hierarchy until the very end of the colonial period, when policy was abruptly changed to favour the very much more numerous Hutu. Bloodshed and the exile of thousands of Tutsi in late 1959 ensued. Further massacres of Tutsi followed in 1963 and 1965–6 following incursions by groups of armed Tutsi refugees. The country then appeared to settle down until 1973, when early in the year further massacres of Tutsi occurred. In July, 1973 the National Guard (army) seized power; the coup was said to reflect dissatisfaction with President Kayibanda's limited gesture of conciliation to the Tutsi which had retained a certain number of them in positions of importance. General Habyarimana, a northern Hutu opposed Kayibanda's southern Hutu moderation;

After nine years of authoritarian government in which Habyarimana progressively replaced military officers by civilians, the country returned to formal civilian rule in 1981, this taking the form of a one-party system, members of which are elected to a legislature. Habyarimana remained in office as Head of State. Habyarimana's regime once securely in power, commenced a new policy of ethnic reconciliation which has achieved some success, Habyarimana himself surviving a plot to overthrow him the central figure of which was a southern Hutu Army Major who at the time represented the extreme anti-Tutsi faction.

STRENGTH AND BUDGET

Population: 5,250,000 (approximate)
Army: 5,000 plus a further 150 air personnel who form part of the army, plus a barrack police of 1200
GDP: $959m (approximate)
Defence expenditure: $22.3m

COMMAND AND CONSTITUTIONAL STATUS

The President, Major-General J. Habyarimana, also holds the portfolio of Minister of Defence.

ROLE, COMMITMENT, DEPLOYMENT AND RECENT OPERATIONS

Since independence in 1962 the Rwanda army has been engaged in defending Hutu majority rule against Tutsi *inyenzi* (i.e. literally 'cockroaches') incursions; these have dwindled in significance and are now negligible.

ORGANISATION

The army is composed of a reconnaissance squadron, a small-sized 'commando' battalion together with eight infantry companies and an engineer sub-unit.

RECRUITMENT, TRAINING AND RESERVES

Recruitment is by voluntary service, but in practice is almost entirely limited to Hutu.

A small Belgian training cadre has been assisting with the training of the army, a French team trains the barracks police.

EQUIPMENT AND ARMS INDUSTRY

The army is equipped with twenty-seven AML-60 armoured cars, and very small numbers of 57mm guns and 81mm mortars. The air unit has three transport aircraft, a Boeing 707 and two C-47s, six liaison light aircraft, three training Magisters and two Alouette III helicopters. A small number of M-3 armoured personnel carriers and 83mm *Blindicide* rocket launchers are reported to have been ordered from France and Belgium.

RANK, DRESS AND DISTINCTIONS

These generally follow the Belgian pattern.

CURRENT DEVELOPMENTS

Rwanda's army was raised to assert the power of the Hutu ethnic majority; there now seems some hope that a wider national consensus may emerge.

Lloyd Mathews

EL SALVADOR

HISTORY AND INTRODUCTION

The Salvadorean army has much the longest tradition of professionalism in Central America. Its comparatively extensive reserve and Territorial Army organisation, in a compact and relatively cohesive nation, give it a highly visible role in all parts of the Republic, which has been further enhanced by its continuous control of the government since 1931. The generally high esteem which the army has enjoyed amongst the population has been reinforced by its successful combat performance in the 1969 war with neighbouring Honduras and by the subsequent continuing tension with that country. In the past few years, however, this image has been considerably tarnished by its repressive operations against growing revolutionary movements and those presumed to be sympathetic with their aims.

The first genuinely Salvadorean army was created in 1824, shortly after the Spanish withdrawal in 1821, when General Manuel Arce, first president of the Central American federation, drew together the large number of independent dragoon squadrons that had been combatting the incursions of the Mexican Emperor Iturbide under a centralised command. El Salvador has always been the most devout advocate of federation amongst the Central American States, and this force was extensively used in the numerous military campaigns needed to hold the federation together. When it finally disintegrated in 1838—9, the independent republic of El Salvador inherited most of the federation's forces as the nucleus of its own army.

The country spent the remainder of the nineteenth century almost incessantly at war either internally, or with its neighbours, or both at the same time, in a sort of mutual intervention process with Honduras, Guatemala and Nicaragua, as the rival political cliques of liberals and conservatives struggled for power in each country. (This tradition has not entirely died: the Guatemalan air force is believed to have made bombing raids in defence of the ruling military government in El Salvador during the attempted rebellion of 1972, and Guatemala and El Salvador are widely believed — especially by Honduras — to have a clandestine military alliance against the spread of radicalism in the isthmus under the cloak of the looser and broader Central American Defence Council.) Prior to the fall of the Somoza regime in Nicaragua, that country was believed to be the third party to such an alliance. The current domestic problems of both Guatemala and El Salvador render it highly unlikely that either would have any spare military capacity for operations outside its own frontiers.

In the circumstances of perpetual warfare which prevailed in the nineteenth century, geographically vulnerable El Salvador had strong incentives to raise the professional standards of its armed forces. It turned repeatedly to foreign military missions for assistance, including a French mission in the early 1860s that effected a drastic army reorganisation and assisted in the foundation in 1867 of Central America's first military academy (now the Military Polytechnical School), and a German military mission in the 1890s to train artillery units.

By far the most important influence in shaping the Salvadorean army until the 1950s, however, was the succession of Chilean military missions which directed military training and operations almost continuously between 1901 and 1957. A close rapport between the two national officer corps was created by the participation of a number of Chilean officers in the 1906 war against Guatemala (El Salvador's last campaign until 1969). The Chilean influence was enhanced by the creation of the War College (now the Command and General Staff College) in 1941, which was directed by Chilean officers until 1957. The result was the wholesale transfer of the largely Prussian-derived military ethics and procedures of the Chilean army (dating from General Emil Koerner's reform of the Chilean army in 1885) to the Salvadorean army.

Although the United States army has taken over the provision of foreign training assistance since 1957, leading to the adoption of United States procedures and doctrines by the Salvadorean army, and although there is now little institutional contact between the Chilean and Salvadorean military establishments, this heritage is still discernible in the remarkable *élan* of the Salvadorean officer corps. It is strongly conscious of the Salvadorean military tradition (a generally successful record in war, and a deserved reputation for efficiency) and is imbued with a powerful sense of its own professional and *élite* status. The rigid Salvadorean military code of honour, with its stress on selfless patriotism and a Spartan dedication to duty, continues to be a major if intangible factor distinguishing the army from its counterparts in neighbouring countries.

The presence of the Salvadorean armed forces in politics as an independent actor rather than a mere instrument is of relatively recent origin. Until the 1920s the officer corps were drawn almost exclusively from the same tiny white minority of Spanish-descended 'creoles' who dominated the nation's economy and politics. The yawning gap between this rich white minority, dominated by the 'fourteen families' — actually about thirty extensive clans — who own most of the land and control around 50% of the national income, and the impoverished peasant mass of the population, 90% of them landless and almost all of them mestizo, grew even wider as the country's overwhelmingly agricultural economy became devoted to growing coffee for export after the turn of the century, but it was some time before the political danger grew severe enough to necessitate direct military control.

The impetus to military intervention was provided by the catastrophic fall in coffee prices and hence in national income during the Great Depression, which led to widespread peasant revolts (characterised by the government as 'communist') in 1930 and 1931. In response to this emergency the Minister of War, General Maximiliano Hernández Martínez, staged a military coup in 1931, ruthlessly restored order in the countryside, and ruled the country until 1944. His emphasis on political stability and financial solvency gratified the civilian economic *élite*. At the same time his extensive programme of public works (including schools, roads and public services, although definitely not land reform) and his appealing personal eccentricities — he was a theosophist and a practising wizard, claiming the ability to read minds and producing magical formulae to improve the harvest or halt a smallpox epidemic — provided him with a genuine popular following.

By the time he was ousted in 1944, by a general strike in

the capital city, the basis for a more permanent and uniquely Salvadorean form of military rule had almost matured. The growing pressure of population on limited rural resources, the rise of urban labour and middle-class commercial and professional groups, the changing composition of the officer corps, and above all the influence of the 1944 leftist military revolution in neighbouring Guatemala very nearly led to a similarly radical transformation of the Salvadorean political scene, but after a sharp struggle within the army the generals reasserted control and brought one of their number to the presidency. It was not until 1948 that a coup by reform-minded colonels and majors seized power and inaugurated an era of 'controlled revolution' under military direction which has continued to today.

What has been remarkable about this regime is that it has sought to transform the national economy, raise the living standards of the masses, and thus avert violent social revolution by seeking the (often unwilling) co-operation of the land-owning élite. It has generally avoided the excesses of totally reactionary military regimes, on the one hand, and the dangerous experiments of the *peruanista* school on the other, thus making some modest progress while ensuring its own stability. While there are undoubtedly more radical officers in the Salvadorean army (they were involved in revolts in 1960 and 1972) as well as ultra-conservative ones, the dominant group of moderate reformers has managed to pass the presidency down from one hand-picked successor to another through three decades of rule. It has avoided both the violent changes of government and foreign intervention that have plagued Guatemala, and (at least until recently) the widespread peasant insurgencies and the urban guerrilla warfare of right and left that have characterised that unfortunate country.

Part of the explanation for this phenomenon undoubtedly lies in the strong sense of national mission which permeates the Salvadorean officer corps: it naturally prefers a policy which allows enough change to avert the risk of social upheaval, which would be damaging to the armed forces and could expose a weakened nation to various dangers of external intervention, while it eschews a radical programme for wholesale change for precisely the same reasons. (The Salvadorean military ethic stresses the army's ultimate responsibility for the well-being of the State, and raises no explicit barrier to full military control of the country.) Other factors which have made this policy possible include the relatively enlightened self-interest of the Salvadorean élite, which can usually be made to see the dangers that worry the army, and to acquiesce in the measures of social reform necessary to avert them (so long as extensive land-reform is not among them), and the homogeneous, close-knit quality of Salvadorean rural society — no Indian population to speak of, and dense agricultural settlement over the whole surface of the country — which enhances the sense of national unity and provides little scope for guerrilla activity.

By far the most significant factor in determining the middle-of-the-road reformism of the Salvadorean army since 1948, however, has been the unusual direction of the change in the recruitment base of the officer corps since the 1920s. While in most Latin American countries rising educational standards in military academy admission policies have shifted the source of officers overwhelmingly to the urban lower middle classes, who are typically hostile to the old land-owner monopoly of power but neglectful of the needs of the rural masses of the population, the change in El Salvador had a different character. There the officer corps has gradually come to be recruited predominantly from the mestizo majority living in the rural areas, while very few come from the capital. It is especially noteworthy that many young men have been sponsored for military careers by landowners who considered them reliable and promising, and that these ties are subsequently maintained both socially and, to some extent, politically.

Thus, for example, Major Oscar Osorio, one of the leaders of the military *junta* after the 1948 revolution and President from 1950 to 1956, began life as a peasant farm-worker, enlisted in the army, and rose through the ranks. Under his rule public housing projects were begun, urban labour was given the rights to organise and bargain collectively, an extensive programme of public works was inaugurated, and the army began to be involved in 'civic action' work — but no land reform measures were introduced, and peasant unions were not permitted. The army sponsored the creation of the Revolutionary Party of Democratic Unification (PRUD) to co-opt the support of the urban middle classes in particular, and in 1956 the Presidency was passed on to Osorio's Minister of the Interior, Lieutenant-Colonel José María Lemus.

A sharp decline in the prices of coffee and cotton brought economic hardship and widespread political unrest in the late 1950s, causing the government to impose extremely harsh repressive measures, and prompting a bloodless coup by left-wing officers and allied intellectuals led by Colonel Cesar Yánez Urías in 1960. It was in turn overthrown by more moderate army officers anxious about its 'Castroite' tendencies in January, 1961, and a new constitution was adopted in 1962. The officially sponsored PRUD was refounded as the Party of National Conciliation (PCN), and Lieutenant-Colonel Julio Adalberto Rivera, the *junta*'s leader, assumed the presidency. In the face of the increasing danger posed by the example of the Cuban revolution a number of civilians (technocrats) were admitted to the cabinet, which pursued an extensive programme of social legislation (including minimum wage laws, progressive income taxes, and credit for small farmers) and even made an extremely modest start on land redistribution. The pattern was continued by Colonel Fidel Sánchez Hernández, the PCN candidate, chosen by Rivera, who succeeded to the presidency in 1967.

The attention of the Salvadorean army, which had been focussed on internal dangers for a generation, was abruptly shifted to external defence by the brief war with Honduras in 1969 (*see* Role, Commitment, Deployment and Recent Operations). The aftermath of the war brought economic hardship, due to a large influx of refugees and to the continuing closure of the Honduras border, which severely crippled El Salvador's attempt to turn itself into the export-oriented industrial heartland of the Central American Common Market. These difficulties were greatly aggravated by the slump in coffee and cotton prices after 1968, and conspired to cause a serious deterioration in the security situation in El Salvador.

Sánchez Hernández's personal secretary, Colonel Arturo Armanda Molina, was duly elected President as his successor in February, 1972, but barely survived an attempted coup a month later by left-wing *peruanista* officers in favour of his left-wing opponent, José Napoleón Duarte. Over 100 people were killed in the fighting, and dissident military officers have since become involved in the left-wing guerrilla movements and right-wing death squads which have sprung up in El Salvador (*see* Current Developments).

The regime has been forced into an increasingly harsh policy of repression in recent years, and since 1975 the internal security situation has moved steadily closer to that state of chronic civil war which characterises neighbouring Guatemala. Colonel Molina's chosen successor, General Carlos Humberto Romero, was duly elected President in February, 1977, but at least 30 people were killed in post-election disturbances.

Romero was deposed by a *coup d'état* in October 1979 and replaced by a five-man junta with two military and three civilian members. In December 1980, José Napoleón Duarte, a Christian Democrat, was sworn in as President with Colonel Jaime Abdul Gutiérrez, who had led the coup against Romero, as Vice-President.

From the end of 1978 onwards, chronic low-level insurgency developed into something approaching a full-scale civil war, the number of (largely civilian) dead being estimated at between 35,000 and 40,000 by the middle of 1982. Fortunately, the agreement reached with Honduras, in November 1980, whereby the state of war between El Salvador and that country was finally terminated and a peace treaty between the two countries signed, permitted the Armed Forces to devote their undivided energies to internal security. However, despite massive financial and military assistance from the United States, the regime was able only to establish a fragile equilibrium between its forces and those of the left-wing guerrillas of the Farabundo Martí National Liberation Front which united all left-wing opposition to the government. Whilst the guerrillas have been unable to win a decisive military victory over the forces of the official government, which now appears to enjoy only limited minority support, the government forces have failed equally to suffocate guerrilla activity. Blatantly fraudulent elections, held in 1982, led to the defeat of Duarte and the strengthening of the extreme political Right, led by Roberto d'Aubisson, who as President of the constituent assembly is the real power behind figure-head President Alvaro Magaña.

STRENGTH AND BUDGET

Population: 4,800,000
Army: 15,000
Navy: 150; 8 minor vessels
Air force: 1,000; 24 combat aircraft
Paramilitary: 4,000 National Guard; 3,000 National Police; 2,000 Treasury Police
GNP: (1981) $3,330,000,000
Defence Expenditure: $116,200,000. This figure is highly misleading in the context of the massive military aid given to the Salvadorean government by the United States

COMMAND AND CONSTITUTIONAL STATUS

The President of the Republic is Commander-in-Chief of the Armed Forces, and appoints the Minister of National Defence and his under-secretaries. He is not constitutionally permitted to be an army officer on active duty, but in practice this has simply meant that all the presidents since 1944 have resigned their military commissions immediately before campaigning for the presidency. The Minister of National Defence is always an officer and is in the chain of command, with responsibility for executing the President's orders. The Deputy Minister of National Defence is charged with administrative duties, but has no command functions.

The Chief of the General Staff is the senior serving officer, and commands the forces in the field directly. He is himself the Chief of the Army, and has operational control over the Chiefs of the Navy and the Air Force. His headquarters also controls the reserves and the three internal security forces: the National Guard, the National Police and the Treasury Police (which are all usually commanded by army officers).

ROLE, COMMITMENT, DEPLOYMENT AND RECENT OPERATIONS

The principal military role of the Salvadorean army, unusually for Central America, has always been seen as external defence. This orientation has been encouraged by its distinguished record in local wars (a source of great pride to all Salvadoreans), by its higher level of professionalism imbibed through close training associations with the armies of much larger nations and not least by the sheer physical vulnerability of El Salvador, a nation only 200 miles long and a maximum of 62 miles wide. By the same token the densely populated Salvadorean countryside offers few of the conventional physical sanctuaries for internal guerrilla movements, and the security problem is even further reduced by the fact that rural districts are semi-militarised through the extensive reserve and Territorial Army organisations.

In these circumstances, the armed forces have been able to leave internal security to the various police forces under their control, with direct military intervention in civil disorders only invoked as a last resort. These forces are: the National Police, a conventional police force organised in its present form in 1945 to provide police protection in the larger cities and towns; the National Guard, formed in 1912 by Spanish officers who modelled it on the Spanish Civil Guard, whose 3000 men are responsible for rural constabulary duties; and the Treasury Police, a small force of 500 men organised in 1926 to carry out customs and anti-smuggling duties. All three are paramilitary in organisation, but only the National Guard has military significance: it wears army uniforms and carries standard infantry weapons, and is organised into 14 companies distributed geographically throughout the country in five infantry commands. It works in close co-ordination with the army in anti-guerrilla operations, but is not expected to take part in combat operations.

The regular armed forces concentrate on training for regular military operations, but much effort is also expended on civic action projects, which are administered by a separate organisation directly under the Minister. The army's Corps of Engineers is largely responsible for the country's relatively comprehensive and well-maintained road network, and other units operate over 500 literacy centres throughout the country and assist in public health projects. These tasks are facilitated by the army's pattern of deployment, which distributes units fairly evenly across the country in permanent association with particular districts, and provides some military presence in even the smallest communities to carry out reserve training. This deployment does not clash with the major defence concern since 1969, namely the possibility of another war with Honduras, since about three-quarters of El Salvador's land borders are with that country, and no point in the country is more than 100 miles from Honduras territory.

El Salvador is a member of the UN, the Organization of American States, and the various Central American institutions: the Organization of Central American States; its military organ, the Central American Defence Council (CONDECA); and the Central American Common Market. The CACM has been virtually paralysed since 1969 by the Honduras – El Salvador dispute, however, and the OCAS and CONDECA have decreasing relevance as neither Costa Rica nor Honduras subscribes to the right-wing military orientations of the dominant members. Effectively El Salvador now forms part of a bloc of relatively conservative military-ruled States, together with Guatemala there is extensive co-operation in anti-guerrilla operations, and there may be provisions for mutual intervention against attempts to overthrow the regimes. In July, 1977 El Salvador promised military assistance to Guatemala in the event of war over the Belize dispute.

The dominating factor in Salvadorean military thinking, however, is still the confrontation with Honduras. Although the incidents that sparked the 1969 war took place at World Cup soccer matches between the two countries, prompting the press to name it the 'football war', the real motives were much more serious, and have not since been removed. The basic problem is that El Salvador is the second most densely populated nation in the Western Hemisphere, with over 500 people per square mile and a population growing at 3.5% a year; land hunger is acute, and can only grow more so. Honduras, by contrast, is a larger country with much empty land and an average population density only one-tenth as great.

Illegal Salvadorean immigration into Honduras grew extremely rapidly during the 1960s. By 1969 the immigrants numbered some 300,000 (one-eighth of the Honduras population), and had become the target of intense hostility in the cities of Honduras. The Salvadorean government made no attempt to control this flow, and became vocally resentful when legislation was passed in Tegucigalpa excluding the immigrants from the benefits of the Honduras land reform programme. The intense nationalism on both sides was heightened by the expansionist ideas of many Salvadoreans: before the war maps were circulating in El Salvador showing the country more than doubled in size, with Honduras cut off from the Pacific coast and confined to the area north and east of Tegucigalpa. The rioting against Salvadorean immigrants in Honduras in 1969, touched off by the mistreatment of a Honduran football team in San Salvador, was only the spark that ignited a war that had been brewing for some time.

The El Salvador government called up the reserves and President Sánchez took to the field to direct operations, as Salvadorean refugees poured across the border. Salvadorean forces struck across the border on July 14th at three separate points, while the two countries' air forces each struck at military, communications and industrial targets in the other (both capitals' international airports were bombed, and El Salvador's main oil refinery at Acajutla on the coast was severely damaged). On the ground the Salvadorean army was successful from the first, driving some 25 miles east along the Pan-American Highway, and seizing the major Honduras town of Ocotepeque across the northern frontier (most of its inhabitants fled into Guatemala).

Honduras instantly accepted the OAS ceasefire call issued on July 14th, but El Salvador continued its advance at a slower pace and refused to consider withdrawal until Honduras gave guarantees of safety for the Salvadorean immigrant population. The fighting continued at a diminished intensity until July 29th, when the OAS formally branded El Salvador the aggressor and threatened to institute full economic sanctions against the country if its troops were not withdrawn from Honduras territory. The Salvadorean withdrawal began on July 30th under the supervision of OAS observers, and was completed by August 5th, 1969.

The war left 3000–4000 dead (including civilians), and saddled El Salvador with the burden of at least 100,000 refugees. It also resulted in the permanent closure of the border (despite numerous mediation attempts by other Latin American States,) which has caused grave damage to the Central American Common Market and the growing Salvadorean industrial sector which was founded on the assumption that that larger market would be available. Above all, it has stimulated a more than threefold expansion of the Honduras armed forces since 1970, adding greatly to El Salvador's external security problem.

Border clashes between the two countries continued until 1971, when a 1.8 mile (3km) demilitarised zone was agreed along the common frontier. In early 1976 El Salvador and Honduras agreed to place their boundary dispute in the hands of a mediator, but later in the year there were renewed border clashes, with Honduras accusing El Salvador of launching an invasion.

Since the first half of 1979, the Armed Forces have been increasingly involved in the internal security functions previously entrusted to the police. Counter-insurgency operations have escalated to the level of pitched battles with organised guerrilla forces during 1981–82. Although the guerrillas have invariably melted away once faced by significant numbers of regular troops, the Armed Forces have failed either to eliminate guerrilla activity or even to confine it to specific areas. The most daring guerrilla operation was the mortar attack on Ilopango air base, the headquarters of the Salvadorean Air Force, or January 27th, 1982, which resulted in the destruction of five fighter bombers, six helicopters and three transport aircraft and severe damage to another fighter-bomber, a light strike aircraft, two more transports and an additional helicopter, equivalent to almost 30% of the total effective aircraft strength available.

ORGANISATION

Arms of Service

The Army consists of Infantry, Cavalry, Artillery, Engineers, Signals and the usual logistic services. Infantry, Cavalry and Artillery are organised into regiments; Special Forces, Air Defence Troops and Engineers into battalions and groups. The logistic and medical services are organised at company level. There are six regular and twelve reserve Infantry Regiments of three battalions each, only the first battalions of the regular regiments being mobilised in peace-time. There is a single Paratroop Battalion and prior to the current civil war situation there were two Special Forces groups. Three additional battalions with a specific COIN orientation have been organised, trained and equipped with US assistance since the first half of 1981. The Cavalry is organised as a single composite mechanised regiment. The Artillery also forms a single regiment, of two battalions. There is also an anti-aircraft battalion and an engineer battalion.

Operational

The country is divided into three Defence Zones as follows:
Western Zone (HQ Santa Ana) covers the departments of Santa Ana, Sonsonate and Ahuachapán.
Central Zone (HQ San Salvador) covers San Salvador, La Libertad, La Paz, Chalatenango and San Vicente.
Eastern Zone (HQ San Miguel) covers San Miguel, Usulután, Cuscatlán and La Unión.

The boundaries of the Zones coincide with those of their component Departments.

Prior to the present civil war, each Zone was garrisoned by an Infantry Brigade of two regiments, the 1st Infantry Brigade and most the combat and logistic support elements being located in the Central Zone, the 2nd Brigade in the Western Zone and the 3rd Brigade in the Eastern Zone. Squadron elements of the single Cavalry Regiment and batteries of the two field artillery battalions being deployed in support of the brigades on an ad hoc basis in accordance with operational requirements. A fourth Brigade, manned partly by Nicaraguan mercenaries, supporters of the former Nicaraguan dictator Somoza and for the most part former members of the Nicaraguan National Guard and veterans of that country's civil war, was raised in the early months of 1981 and deployed in the vicinity of Chalatenango in the Central Zone. From mid 1981, a fifth Brigade, consisting of the US trained and equipped *Atlacatl, Atonal* and *Belloso anti-guerrilla* battalions, also existed and was in action in the region of San Vicente, also in the Central Zone. The Paratroop and Anti-aircraft battalions, although part of the Army, come under the operational command of the Air Force.

RECRUITMENT, TRAINING AND RESERVES

Although the constitution provides for universal military service, in practice the armed forces are a regular professional force maintained on a volunteer basis. Conditions for the serviceman compare favourably with those in civilian life, including relatively good pay, ample leave, decent food and quarters, strict but not harsh discipline, medical care and retirement benefits (50% of base pay after 20 years, 100% after 30), so there is no shortage of volunteers. Vacancies are filled as they occur, by lot amongst qualified applicants for regular status from the semi-annual class of conscripts. The escalation of the civil war has caused a larger proportion of the annual conscript class to be called to the colours, Army strength having increased two-and-a-half fold since 1979.

The remainder of the conscripts fulfil their constitutional obligation to perform 18 months' military service between the ages of eighteen and thirty by participating in weekly training sessions conducted by the regular army in or near their own home community. Training is usually limited to drill, weapons familiarisation and military discipline, but all military personnel released from active duty are also placed on this 'active reserve' list to constitute a nucleus of trained men. These fill the ranks of the second and third battalions of the regular Infantry Regiments and bring these and the other units of the regular Army up to full established strength on mobilisation. This reserve of 30,000 men has a battalion structure manning 12 reserve Infantry Regiments and an efficient mobilisation organisation; during the 1969 war the army was rapidly expanded in this way from five to eighteen infantry battalions.

At the age of thirty 'active reserve' members are reassigned to the Territorial Service, in which obligations theoretically continue until sixty. Its main function is to provide a framework of military authority throughout the rural areas of the country.

Regular officers of all three services are trained at the military academy, to which entry is by competitive examination for candidates with a minimum of 4 years' secondary schooling. The syllabus is divided between academic and military subjects, with the students' time devoted in about equal portions to classroom work and field exercises. Academic standards are good, and they graduate with a bachelor's degree after 4 years and receive commissions as sub-lieutenants in the army. The academy is located just west of the capital, and the student body averages 150; only 15–20 officers are graduated into the Salvadorean army each year, however, and there is a substantial contingent of students from other Central American countries.

In 1968 the government created a para-military peasant organisation, ORDEN, which is used both as an intelligence-gathering network and a counter-insurgency force in rural areas. Its strength in 1978 was estimated to be 80,000 men.

Salvadorean navy and air force officers get additional specialised training at the Navy School and the Aviation School. Like army officers they may also attend US armed forces courses in the Panama Canal Zone, but El Salvador is uniquely well endowed with military higher educational facilities in Central America. These include the Arms and Services School providing a 6 month course in advanced military subjects (stressing joint and combined operations) for field-grade officers, individual service schools providing advanced technical training in their various specialities, and the Command and General Staff College, which provides graduate studies in military science and a variety of academic subjects to students of lieutenant-colonel or colonel level.

Regular NCOs receive instruction at the Non-commissioned Officers' School, created in the 1890s and an independent institution since 1908, as well as at branch schools of the various arms and services. Numbers of senior NCOs are also sent abroad for advanced courses.

Recruit training includes literacy courses where necessary, and there is a considerable in-service programme to raise the academic standards and technical competence of enlisted men. Many garrisons open their literacy centres to the local population.

EQUIPMENT AND ARMS INDUSTRY

Although the most highly industrialised country of Central America, El Salvador has no domestic defence industry and imports all military equipment and weapons. From World War II until the 1969 war with Honduras, the United States was the primary supplier although in the aftermath of that war equipment was acquired from a variety of sources of which France and Israel were probably the most important. Massive US military aid has ensured that once more large quantities of US equipment have been received by the Salvadorean Armed Forces.

Rifles: M14 7.62mm (US); G3 5.56mm (Germany); M16 5.56mm (US)
Sub-machine-gun: Uzi 9mm (Israel)
Machine-guns: M1919 0.30″ (US); Madsen Model 1954 7.62mm (Denmark); M60 7.62mm (US)
Anti-armour weapons: 80mm rocket launcher (Israel); 57mm RCL (US)
Mortars: 81mm (France)
Artillery: M101 105mm (US)
Air-defence weapons: 40mm L/60 (Sweden)
Armour: AMX-13 light tank (France 12 in service); AML 245 H-90 armoured car (France; 18 in service); M113 APC (US via Israel; 10 in service); UR-416 APC (Germany; 20 in service)
Aircraft: The Air Force operates approximately 16 transport aircraft and 30 helicopters.

RANK, DRESS AND DISTINCTIONS

Army and air force officer ranks are identical, and follow the usual international system with the exceptions that second-lieutenants are known as sub-lieutenants, and that there is only one general officer grade, with the title simply of general. Rank insignia (in order of increasing seniority) are one, two or three bars; one, two or three gold stars; and a single laurel leaf, worn on shoulder straps. There are four NCO ranks: corporal, sub-sergeant, sergeant and technical sergeant, for which the insignia are two red chevrons, one gold chevron, two gold chevrons and two gold chevrons over the letter 'T', respectively.

Naval officers have the same ranks as the United States navy, with the exception that there is only one grade of flag rank, known simply as admiral. Naval NCOs and enlisted men, however, are known by their equivalent army grades.

The basic army garrison uniform is khaki shirt and dark-green trousers, with a garrison cap; the air force uniform is the same in a light-blue colour. With the addition of leggings, helmet and field equipment, the garrison dress becomes the combat uniform. Army and air force officers and technical sergeants also have service uniforms of coat and trousers in their respective uniform colours, and dark-blue dress uniforms for both services. The navy wears the traditional navy-blue uniform in winter, and whites in summer. There is also a khaki service uniform.

The highest Salvadorean decoration is the National Order of José Matías Delgado, established in 1916, which is presented in five grades (the highest being reserved for Heads of State). The award is limited to 25 living nationals, including military personnel. Other military decorations, all created in 1946, are the Laureate Medal of Military Merit, awarded for valour in combat, the Medal of Military Merit, granted for distinguished services, and the Military Cross, a decoration presented in various grades for 10—25 years of active service.

CURRENT DEVELOPMENTS

Although the army's main concern is still external defence, it has been drawn increasingly into internal security operations by the deteriorating political situation of recent years. The principal cause of the troubles is unquestionably the grave shortage of land in a thickly populated country with an overwhelmingly rural population, and the reluctance of successive military governments to confront the economic *élite* openly by undertaking large-scale redistribution of land. Rural insurgency has been on the rise since the beginning of the 1970s, and latterly the army has faced growing opposition from university students and urban intellectuals as well.

The most active of the armed revolutionary movements is the People's Revolutionary Army (ERP), an originally Casto-ite group which concentrates on assassinations and raids on rural police stations. It simultaneously seized eight local radio stations in the capital and provincial towns to broadcast its message for an hour in late 1975, and has latterly shown considerable effectiveness in stimulating peasant seizures of land on the great estates, relying on over-reaction by the security forces to win it more recruits. It is reported to have a national directorate of five members, and three regional committees for the western, central and eastern districts. A breakaway organisation, the Farabundo Martí Popular Forces of Liberation, has been more active in the cities, and there are also at least two other small splinter movements.

In 1978 there appeared a new guerrilla organisation, the Armed Force of National Resistance (FARN), whose relationship with the two older movements is not clear. It pursues a campaign of assassination of government supporters, and has recently taken to kidnapping foreign businessmen.

Since 1975 El Salvador has also seen the emergence of ultra-right-wing terrorist groups, first the Falange and latterly the White Fighting Union (UGB), which seems to have absorbed its predecessor. Its death squads are almost as hostile to the government's limited programme of land reform by compulsory purchase as to the extreme left-wing movements. During 1977 the guerrillas killed an ex-President and the Foreign Minister, while numbers of prominent leftist intellectuals were murdered by the death squads. The government also came into increasing conflict with the Roman Catholic Church (a majority of whose priests in El Salvador are foreign missionaries), and especially with the Jesuit order: in May, 1977 the Archdiocese of San Salvador reported that six priests had been killed and 25 others arrested, tortured or deported in the previous 6 months.

Since early in 1979, the Farabundo Martí organisation has succeeded in uniting all left-wing guerrilla groups in the Farabundo Martí National Liberation Front. The Government and Armed Forces have become increasingly identified with the political Right. The civil war, which has been waged with great ferocity on both sides, appeared to have reached a stage of near total stalemate at the end of 1982.

Gwynne Dyer
Adrian English

SAO TOME

This small ex-Portuguese colony, which attained independence in 1975, has a population of only some 80,000. Its normal security force is one of a 160 strong barrack police gendarmerie.

The territory had, for reasons which are far from clear, a garrison of about 1000 troops from Angola and a small contingent from Guinea-Bissau for a while from 1978. The reasons given by the São Tomé Head of State, President P. da Costa, were violations of territorial waters by unidentified foreign ships. The garrison is understood now to have been withdrawn. One report claimed that a Cuban unit had also been present. President da Costa denied this, but admitted that a very small Cuban training team was at work.

Two attempts appear to have been made to overthrow the regime. In 1977 a conspiracy, 'Cobra 77' was reported, two former ministers and a gendarmerie officer, all in exile, were named and sentenced *in absentia*. In 1979 President da Costa abolished the post of prime minister. The dismissed premier, Mr. Trouvonada, attempted later in the year to organise a coup to overthrow President da Costa, the coup attempt was a failure and Mr Trouvonada was arrested.

Although São Tomé's strategic significance must be minimal, the territory seems to command some measure of international interest.

Lloyd Mathews

SAUDI ARABIA

HISTORY AND INTRODUCTION

Between 1964 and 1976 Saudi Arabian spending on defence increased approximately one hundred fold to a total of $10,360,000,000, a figure comparable to the British or French defence budget. In the same period, the Royal Saudi Army no more than doubled, to a mere 40,000 men. The contrast not only highlights the enormous scale of Saudi Arabia's oil-derived wealth, but also its relatively recent advent. Even more importantly, so far as defence is concerned, it illustrates the point that wealth is not directly translatable into military power unless other resources are also present. The native Saudi Arabian population is only some 4,000,000–5,000,000 people, most of them only emerging from a medieval society in this generation, spread across almost a million square miles of territory. The population is in no way adequate to support pretensions to major military power, and Saudi Arabia does not have such pretentions.

Nevertheless the kingdom does have a strong military tradition, not only because of the warrior customs of the bedouins who made up much of its population until recently, but also because it was created by military conquest within living memory. It was created, moreover, by a unique and extremely effective military institution, known as the *Ikhwan*, which lives on even today as the National Guard, one of the kingdom's two parallel armies.

The fortunes of the al-Saud dynasty first rose in the eighteenth century when an ancestor of the present ruler concluded an alliance with Muhammad ibn Abd al-Wahhab, the founder of a militantly puritanical religious movement which sought to 'cleanse' the Islam then practised in the Nejd (the north-eastern part of Arabia) of various abuses which had become established there. The appeal of Wahnabism to the nomadic tribemen combined with the military leadership of the first Saud enabled him to establish his rule and the Wahhabite doctrine over the larger part of the peninsula. By the latter part of the nineteenth century, however, internecine strife and local rivalries had destroyed the grip of the Saud family, and it was left to young Abdul Aziz ibn Saud (born 1880) to reconquer the peninsula and unite it under one rule for the first time in many centuries.

The first step was taken in January, 1902, when the young Abdul Aziz and a small band of followers recaptured Riyadh, the former seat of the Saudi emirate, which had fallen to rival tribes of the great Shammar tribal confederacy of northern Arabia (extending also into Iraq and Syria) under the leadership of the Rashid family. By 1906, the Saudi forces had regained the central Nejd.

Recognising his need for a more reliable source of support than fickle tribal alliances, Abdul Aziz sent Wahhabi missionaries to encourage the tribes to settle in Ikhwan (religious brotherhood) communities to which he gave seed, farm tools, money, arms and ammunition, in return for the support of their warriors in his campaign to unite the peninsula. In each community mosques, schools and homes were built and religious teachers were provided.

The villages grew rapidly in number, and soon it was possible for Abdul Aziz to mobilise 25,000 men in 96 hours, although in most of his campaigns only 5000–10,000 were actually employed. The Ikhwan were first used in battle in 1913, to quell a revolt by the Mutayr tribe, force out Ottoman occupying troops and win the Saudi emirate access to the Persian Gulf, thus bringing under its control the Eastern Region where all the country's oil wealth now lies. During World War I, Abdul Aziz concluded a treaty with Britain in 1915 that gave him the money and arms to pursue his battle against the rival Rashid dynasty, which culminated in the Saudi capture of the Rashidi capital, Hail, in 1921. Abdul Aziz thus became Sultan of Nejd, recognised and endorsed by the British who were the dominant power in the Persian Gulf, and by 1922 the Ikhwan forces were in control of all the desert lands from the 'fertile crescent' in the north to the 'empty quarter' in the south-east.

Abdul Aziz's only remaining rival in the Arabic peninsula was the Hashemite Kingdom of the Hejaz, in the west along the Red Sea coast, which contained the holy cities of Mecca and Medina. When King Husain of the Hejaz laid claim to the Caliphate of Islam in 1924, the Ikhwan forces were sent against him by Abdul Aziz, and after 15 months the last besieged strongholds of the Hashemites surrendered in December, 1925. All of Arabia was united under Saudi rule, save the British protectorates along the Persian Gulf coast and the thickly populated Yemen in the south-west.

Abdul Aziz's next great task was to unite this kingdom, in which tribal loyalties were still strong and few outside the Nejd adhered to the Wahhabi doctrine, and to bring under control the unruly instrument of his victories, the Ikhwan. These warriors had always had a tendency to get out of hand, committing some brutal massacres like that at Taif in the Hejaz in 1924, and they were not willing to stop raiding simply because the kingdom had now expanded to its practical limits, its borders having reached British-protected territories to the north, east and south. Throughout the later 1920s undisciplined tribal Ikhwan forces raided into Kuwait, Iraq and Transjordan, all British mandates or protectorates, despite Abdul Aziz's orders to stop. Meanwhile, however, the monarch laboured to build up the small regular army he had founded as a counterweight to the Ikhwan in 1926, and in January, 1930, with air support from four newly acquired aircraft flown by British pilots, his regular army decisively defeated the Ikhwan in battle. The chronic internal warfare which had been Arabia's lot for centures then effectively ceased, except for a small border war between Saudi Arabia and Yemen in 1931–4.

The foundations of the future prosperity of the kingdom were laid in 1933, when the first oil fields were discovered in the Eastern Province and Saudi Arabia granted a huge concession to the Standard Oil Company of California. (It was considered a severe blow to Britain's hitherto monopoly position in the Gulf, but the King explained: 'The U.S. is far away from Arabia, and unlike any European power has no designs on it'.) Its political independence was thus safeguarded, but through the 1930s and 1940s Saudi Arabia remained a barren, backward, impoverished country in which no influences from the modern world were permitted to enter. What money came from the oil was hoarded, and virtually no development occurred except in the armed forces.

These, being the foundation of the dynasty's power, received close attention. After the Ikhwan had been smashed in 1930, they were permitted to reappear in the guise of the 'White Army' (renamed the National Guard in 1962) as a bedouin militia under much tighter royal control. They thus served as a counterbalance to the small and lightly equipped units of regular troops and the Royal Guard which were maintained throughout the 1930s at a modest strength, and were then taken in hand by Britain and the USA during World War II with the intention of forming a professional army in Saudi Arabia along the lines of the Jordanian Arab Legion. For this purpose, training missions were sent to the Kingdom to instruct the troops in the use of communications, light ordnance and military transport, and a small number of Saudis, almost all members of the royal family, were sent to Sandhurst for further training. After 1952, the USA took exclusive charge of military training with the explicit purpose of creating a modern regular army and a small air force, and numbers of Egyptian officers also collaborated with this training project until the growing political hostility between Nasser's radical government and Saudi Arabia's ultra-conservative regime forced their withdrawal. None of the targets that the USA had set for the growth of Saudi Arabian forces was met, however, principally because of manpower bottlenecks.

The problem was that the main pillar of the Saudi tribal confederation which ruled the country was the Nejdi tribes, but very few Nejdis had the background and education to make them promising material as officers or technicians in a modern army, let alone an air force. The solution which was eventually adopted was to permit generally better qualified men from the Hejaz, with its relatively sophisticated cities, to be recruited in large numbers to fill the gap. This trend has been accelerating, and Hejazis now form the backbone of the Saudi regular army and are an even larger proportion in the technologically more demanding air force. Senior command positions still remained almost exclusively in the hands of members of the large royal family, but it was rightly felt that Hejazis were less instinctively loyal to the Saudi dynasty and more open to the political influences sweeping the rest of the Arab world, so it was unsurprising that the National Guard based on the Nejdi tribal levies should have been expanded in parallel with the regular army as a precautionary measure. It was only in about 1965 that the regular army exceeded the National Guard in total strength. Even today the latter is under an entirely separate chain of command, and has exclusive responsibility for guarding the crucial oil fields in the Eastern Province, where there are no regular army troops whatever.

The reason for the more rapid expansion of the regular army in the 1960s was the civil war in North Yemen, where Egypt and Saudi Arabia ended up supporting different sides. Saudi Arabia had sent a token battalion to participate in the 1948 war in Palestine, but had remained generally aloof from the concerns and trends of the Wider Arab world. In the late 1950s and the 1960s, however, with monarchies being overthrown or attacked throughout the Arab world and the fortunes of the 'revolutionary' regimes in the ascendant, the kingdom found those concerns arriving at its own doorstep. Following the overthrow of the Imam of (North) Yemen in 1962, the Saudis armed and supported conservative tribal forces resisting the new republican military regime, and Egypt introduced a large expeditionary force into the country to support the republicans. Units of the National Guard and the regular army were posted all along the Yemeni border, although none became directly involved in the fighting, and the regular army began to be built up as quickly as possible.

After the Arab–Israeli war in June, 1967 the need for Egypt to keep its army closer to home made itself felt, and Egyptian troops were withdrawn from the Yemen leaving a shaky compromise settlement in that ravaged country, but the radical outside forces seeking to revolutionise the Saudi kingdom did not cease their incitements to revolt. In June and September, 1969 there were serious attempts to carry out a military coup against the dynasty, both originating in the air force where the influence of the outside world was inevitably at its greatest.

That the monarchy survived these pressures to emerge in the 1970s apparently stronger than ever – to the great surprise of so many who had predicted its fall throughout the 1960s – is probably due mainly to the fact that it had reformed itself in time. Abdul Aziz, who died in 1953, had kept his money in iron coffers, but his successor King Saud bin Abdul Aziz proved irresponsible, dissolute and profligate, and permitted many other royal princes to behave in a similar fashion. As before, there was little development of the kingdom, but there was now also scandalous contrast between the ruler's luxurious wealth and the subjects' poverty. What saved the dynasty was the fact that headship of the family (and thus the throne) is granted in Arabian custom not by primogeniture but by consensus of the family's leading members. King Abdul Aziz had left 42 living sons, so the family already numbered over a thousand, and many members were well aware that under Saud the kingdom was heading for disaster: in March, 1964 the family transferred the administration of the kingdom to King Saud's younger brother, Crown Prince Faisal, and in November of the same year Saud was deposed.

Under King Faisal bin Abdul Aziz, who ruled from 1964 until he was assassinated by a deranged nephew in March, 1975, the kingdom's somewhat compromised fortunes were restored. A firm grip was taken on the administration of the country, and systematic development of its human and natural resources began for the first time (although always with care not to introduce destabilising foreign influences). The carefree spending habits of individual princes were controlled, oil production was raised and the kingdom's share in the oil profits was increased, thus greatly increasing available revenue in the late 1960s. Much of this was devoted to the modernisation of the army, and some also to providing aid for those Arab countries directly involved in the confrontation with Israel, thus purchasing external goodwill that had previously been absent. A more active, although still very cautious foreign policy was adopted: closer links with Egypt, an attempt to persuade Bahrain and Qatar to join with the other seven lower Gulf emirates in the United Arab Emirates in 1971, and mediation between Jordan and the Palestine Liberation Organisation during the civil war in Jordan in the same year. An attempt by the new Marxist regime of South Yemen to assert a border claim against Saudia Arabia in 1969 was rebuffed by armed force, but the kingdom clearly recognised the limits of its military power: it made no attempt to intervene when Iran seized the Gulf islands of the Tumbs and Abu Musa in November, 1971.

The Saudi-led embargo imposed by the Arab oil-producing States against the USA and the Netherlands after the 1973 Arab–Israeli war, together with progressive cuts in oil production for other customers which at one point reached 30%, demonstrated to the entire world the potentially decisive effect of the 'oil weapon'. Saudi Arabia, as the second-largest producer and largest exporter of oil in the world, with reserves amounting to an estimated quarter of the world's remaining supply (and where new discoveries have exceeded production each year since 1933), was universally seen as the sole real owner of the oil weapon, and its diplomatic importance accordingly soared. So did its wealth: the first consequence of the embargo was the four-fold rise in oil prices, which suddenly conferred on Saudi Arabia an annual income of over $10,000 per capita (in a country with 85% illiteracy). The most striking feature of this wealth, moreover, was its extreme fluidity: even now Saudi Arabia's Gross National Product, around 95% of which is derived from oil revenues, is only about half the size of the Netherlands', but almost all of Saudi Arabia's money is available to be spent or given in aid abroad – indeed, very little of it can possibly be spent at home. Thus a country whose actual GNP is less than Switzerland's has a world economic importance as an importer of goods and services and a provider of foreign aid comparable to that of West Germany, Japan or the Soviet Union.

A very substantial proportion of post-1973 Saudi Arabian expenditure abroad has gone on military goods and services – in the 5 years 1973–8 Riyadh spent $15,000,000,000 on these in the USA alone – but it is frequently overlooked that despite the lavish expenditure the military ambitions of the country are quite modest. About 90% of the money spent abroad on military purposes has been devoted to contracts for construction work on support facilities and training assistance, and only about one-tenth on actual weaponry. When the current expansion and re-equipment programme is completed in the early 1980s Saudi Arabia's army will be roughly comparable in numbers and quality of equipment to that of Jordan today, and its navy and air force will be of similar size and sophistication to Algeria's. There is simply not the qualified manpower available for anything more ambitious, and so Saudi military policy aims only at a credible defensive capability on its own territory and a degree of military superiority in its own immediate neighbourhood, the Arabian peninsula.

For influence further abroad, Riyadh has relied principally on its own version of 'dollar diplomacy' – the provision of very large amounts of financial aid (almost certainly equalling its military expenditure in the post-1973 period) to the other States of the Arab world in order to create a stable political environment which is congenial to the survival of conservative monarchies like itself. In an Arab world which outside the Arabian peninsula is populated for the most part with ageing 'revolutionary' regimes that have outlasted their natural spans plus a few delicately poised monarchical survivors, this policy has had notable success. Massive Saudi subsidies have not only allowed President Sadat to retain control of desperately impoverished Egypt, but have been of great help in assuring the survival of Jordan's King Husain and Syria's President Asad. Other Saudi subsidies have helped King Hassan of Morocco in his confrontation with Algeria and Sudan's President Nimeiri in his struggle to avoid overthrow by radical neighbours in Libya and Ethiopia, while the North Yemen regime is virtually a Saudi pensioner.

Nearer home Saudi diplomacy has been rather more activist. The closure in 1975 and 1976 of the elected assemblies of Bahrain and Kuwait, the only two such representative bodies in the Gulf, is widely attributed to Saudi anxieties about the possible growth of radical influence through them and its transmission to Saudi Arabia itself. It is possible that there was Saudi encouragement for the coup that overthrew North Yemen's President Ibrahim al-Hamdi in 1977 just as he was going to enter serious talks on reunification with radical South Yemen. But even in the Arabian peninsula Riyadh has eschewed the use of its own armed forces: it tacitly accepted the presence of Iranian troops in Oman to fight the Marxist guerrillas in Dhofar in 1973–7, restricting itself to providing Oman with financial aid, and it made a determined if ultimately unsuccessful attempt to buy off the Marxist government of South Yemen in 1977 with promises of large sums of money for development aid in that extremely poor country. A similar financial inducement undoubtedly did have an effect in inducing the Somali regime to expel its Soviet military advisers in 1977.

On the key question which divides the Arab world, the Arab–Israeli dispute, as in most other intra-Arab disputes, Saudi diplomacy has sought to avoid total commitment to one side or the other, preferring to assume the role of a rich mediator who can ease the pains of compromise with large sums of money. Thus, for example, it played a key role in instituting the final and more or less effective ceasefire in the Lebanese civil war in October, 1976 by first putting the Syrian regime in serious financial straits by cutting its subsidies, and then providing ratification for the dominant Syrian position in Lebanon by approving the designation of the Syrian army there as an 'Arab Deterrent (peace-keeping) Force' in return for Syria's acceptance of Egypt's second disengagement agreement with Israel. Equally nervous of the ultimate intentions of then imperial Iran and of Ba'athist Iraq, its two militarily far more powerful neighbours to the north, Riyadh declined to participate in any Gulf security pact which excluded either, thus dooming the initiative to create such a pact which was launched by some of the smaller Gulf States in 1976.

Saudi Arabian foreign policy, aimed at maintaining a safe and stable environment in its own region, recognises three imperatives. First, the advance of communist influence (which it regards as synonymous with Soviet influence) in the area must be prevented. Secondly, there must not be another Arab–Israeli war. Thirdly, the West, which is Saudi Arabia's main market for oil and principal supplier of goods, must not undergo a severe economic decline. All three of these objectives, which are substantially interrelated in Saudi eyes, dictate a close 'special relationship' between Saudi Arabia and the USA.

Riyadh no longer regards any of the so-called radical regimes in its vicinity except South Yemen as a serious political threat, even despite the close relationship of Iraq and Syria with the Soviet Union as principal arms supplier, for it recognises that they have become fundamentally conservative in defence of their own positions. It is even happier, of course, when it can help to persuade former Soviet arms clients like Kuwait and Jordan from embarking on the purchase of Soviet arms. Saudi Arabia has become extremely alarmed by recent Soviet advances in the region – the communist coup in Afghanistan, the advent of Soviet, Cuban and East German troops in considerable numbers in Ethiopia and South Yemen, and above all the possibility that revolutionary Iran might slide into the hands of the pro-Moscow left. Thus it tried unsuccessfully to obtain Western arms aid for Somalia, and in early 1979 was still subsidising the Eritrean rebels who restrict Ethiopian access to the Red Sea coast and make the establishment of Soviet bases there improbable. It secured United States arms aid for the government of North Yemen in order to help contain the menace of South Yemen, and in late 1978 made a little-noticed security arrangement with Iraq against the possibility of an expansionary Iran.

In general, Riyadh regarded a revival of Islamic observance, with the full support of law, as a major prophylactic against the spread of communism, and had successfully encouraged many of its major aid recipients in the Middle East, from Pakistan to the Sudan, to take steps in that direction. (It recognised, however, that in at least two neighbouring States – Iraq and Syria – where the regimes were drawn from a religious minority, such pressures were not without their own dangers.) In only one instance, concerning perhaps the two most fragile Arab regimes of all – those of Egypt and the Sudan – did Saudi Arabia give direct support to a mutual security pact designed to ward off threats from radical forces (in Libya and Ethiopia, which both enjoy Soviet support), but even in that case Riyadh was unable to offer direct military support. Its funds are virtually limitless, but its military means are very modest.

Saudi Arabia is well aware that most of the regimes whose survival it is attempting to guarantee in the interests of stability are very weak and brittle — indeed, its own ability to wield such influence over them by mere promises of money is a measure of their isolation and desperation — and rightly fears that another Middle East war would bring tumbling down the whole rickety structure of regional security it has been trying to create. Not least, it would virtually compel Saudi Arabia itself to institute a new oil embargo, thus destroying the relationship with the USA which it regards as crucial to its survival, even if it did not mean Israeli attacks on the oil fields (as it well might). Saudi Arabia has therefore regarded an Arab–Israeli peace settlement as a high priority since 1973, and either openly or tacitly supported Egypt's President Sadat in his efforts to achieve it. (Soon after King Faisal's assassination in 1975, the new government stated that the existence of Israel could be accepted by it if all occupied Arab territories were returned and proper provision were made for the Palestinian people.)

Saudi Arabia is also well aware, however, that any separate Egyptian–Israeli peace settlement which effectively neglects the Palestinians will be fundamentally destructive of the whole edifice of mutual security it has been trying to construct, and since the inception of the Sadat initiative in November, 1977 which seemed to Riyadh to be aimed at just such a peace (however well disguised) it has climbed back up on the fence. With substantial numbers of immigrant Palestinians in its own population and far larger proportions in some of its small Gulf neighbours, Saudi Arabia has always been fully conscious of the need to maintain relatively good relations with the Palestine Liberation Organisation, and in November, 1978 it was a leading participant in the Arab summit meeting in Baghdad which sought to persuade, bribe or frighten Egypt back into the Arab fold.

But both in its anti-Soviet activities (Riyadh has not had diplomatic relations with Moscow since 1938) and in its efforts to assist the achievement of a lasting Middle East peace settlement, the Saudi government is fundamentally dependent on United States government support and assistance. To a far greater extent than between the Americans and any other non-industrial State, the relationship is one of recognised mutual dependency, for Saudi Arabia supplies a quarter of the USA's oil and has over $40,000,000,000 invested in the USA. Riyadh not only recognises this mutual dependency, but does all in its power to increase it. After all, it is only United States arms sales and political and economic support that can really contain the expansion of Soviet influence in the region, at least in Riyadh's view, and it was also felt that only American pressure could extract the concessions from Israel for a peace treaty which would be acceptable to all the directly involved Arab participants in the struggle.

Riyadh therefore welcomes the prospect that its ambitious military and civil development programme may require 100,000 Americans to be resident in Saudi Arabia by the early 1980s. It seeks to make itself indispensable to the West by keeping its oil production consistently at a far higher level of daily output than would be required by its own current finanical needs, and by campaigning in OPEC, often with considerable success, to hold the price of crude oil down so as not to damage the economies of its main customers, the industrialised States. In return for all these services, Saudi Arabia expects strong Western and especially American support, not only in its own efforts to create adequate defensive armed forces, but also in its broader objectives: the effective containment of Soviet influence in its region and the achievement of an Arab–Israeli peace which will be genuinely stabilising. Although it has suffered considerable disappointment in both these latter objectives in the past few years, it still seems bound to stick to this strategy as no obvious alternatives exist. This situation has undoubtedly created a dangerously large amount of psychological dependence on United States support in the Saudi *élite*, however, of just the type which paralysed the Iranian ruling group when United States support seemed to be weakening noticeably in the last months before the Shah's overthrow in early 1979. It was noteworthy that the Riyadh government requested and got a visit by a squadron of USAF F-15s in early 1979 as a token of continuing United States commitment to its security.

However well or ill the Saudi government manages its external security environment, it will be irrelevant if internal stability should become seriously disturbed, and yet it is inevitable that massive dislocations must be caused by the course of rapid economic transformation, paid for by vast amounts of money, that Saudi Arabia has chosen. For one thing, it has involved the importation of about 2,000,000 foreigners, amounting to about one-third of the population and ranging from Yemeni labourers to American financial consultants. Even if groups within this immigrant community do not grow to represent an internal security threat themselves, their presence in such numbers could well accelerate the erosion of the traditional values of Saudi society which provide the underpinning for the existing patriarchal political system.

Even before King Faisal was succeeded by the present ruler, King Khalid bin Abdul Aziz, in 1975, the basic decision had already been taken that the only possible response to the vast new wealth conferred by the oil price increase of 1973 was to adopt a policy of rapid economic development in every field. The risks of plunging an ill-prepared Saudi population into the bewildering complexities of a fully-fledged late-twentieth century industrialised welfare State, great though they were, were still seen to be less great than the probable consequences of denying them the fruits of the kingdom's wealth and leaving the country a weak and backward place exposed to every sort of economic exploitation and external threat. Accordingly, the 1975–80 development plan allotted $142,000,000,000 to the creation of infrastructure, industry and welfare services and the education and training of young Saudi Arabians to manage their wealthy new society. At the same time, every precaution has been taken to ensure that the population's moral values, social customs and political attitudes, grounded in the fundamentalist Wahhabite interpretation of Sunni Islam, should not be subverted by this new society. There is no doubt that this is a goal which has been adopted by the government for its own sake, but it cannot escape notice that success or failure in achieving it also closely affects the future of the existing system of rule.

The largest single share of this immense development expenditure, between a quarter and a third of the total, has been budgeted for the security forces (and since the Defence Ministry usually manages to spend its annual budget, whereas most other ministries habitually underspend by as much as 50%, the actual defence share may be greater than that). In view of the government's known concern about the effects of rapid modernisation, it is not surprising that such a large proportion of this expenditure has gone on the comforts rather than the weapons of the armed forces: military pay and allowances are extremely high, and the amounts devoted to living quarters, recreational facilities and supporting infrastructure are staggering, e.g. Assad Military City near Al-

Kharj, one of half a dozen 'military cities' being built around the country, will cost an estimated $15,000,000,000. Nor is it surprising that expenditure on the National Guard, although much less in absolute terms, has risen just as sharply as that on the regular army.

The degree of alarm felt about the possible consequences of extremely rapid change for the stability of Saudi Arabian society and the security of the regime is, indeed, the principal policy issue which divides the political leadership of Saudi Arabia — that is to say, the Saudi royal family, which by now numbers some 7000 members. There are few advocates of no change whatever, and no advocates of total and deliberate Westernisation, but there is a clearly discernible dividing line between supporters of the present pace of change and those who believe a more measured rate would be safer for the society and the dynasty. This difference of opinion has tended, for not particularly logical but excellent political reasons, to congeal along the same lines as the rivalries between various branches of the royal family. The armed forces are intimately concerned in it, for while the supporters of the present commitment to ultra-rapid development control the regular armed forces, those traditionalists who are opposed to this approach are naturally more influential amongst the tribes, and their leading representative controls the National Guard. This is not to suggest that the two rival armies are in any sense in confrontation with each other (although each was indeed originally intended to be a check on the other), but it does mean that military policy is to an extent influenced both by the broader policy dispute and by the factional manoeuvres of the rival branches of the Saudi family.

King Fahd, who succeeded King Khalid in June, 1982, is executive Head of State, and has long run the government. There are at least 2000 princes in the House of Saud, but the principal rivalry has traditionally been between two branches descended from different wives of the kingdom's founder, King Abdul Aziz bin Saud. Such rivalries are not merely intra-family, but also to a considerable extent inter-tribal rivalries, as King Abdul Aziz followed the usual custom of selecting his wives from the most powerful tribes in order to cement their loyalty to him. One branch, headed by the sons of a wife belonging to the powerful Jilwa family of the northeastern Shammar tribe, includes the late King Faisal, King Khalid and the Second Deputy Prime Minister and Head of the National Guard, Prince Abdullah bin Abdul Aziz.

The other important branch, descended from Abdul Aziz's favourite wife, Hassa bint Sudairi of the influential Sudairi tribe, includes seven full brothers who monopolise control of the kingdom's regular armed forces. The most senior of the 'Sudairi Seven' King Fahd himself, who is also Prime Minister. Others include: Prince Sultan, Minister of Defence and Aviation and Inspector-General of the Armed Forces; Prince Turki, Deputy Minister of Defence and Chief of Military Intelligence; Prince Nayif, Minister of the Interior (and thus in charge of the police, the Frontier Force and the Coast Guard); Prince Ahmad, Nayif's deputy; and Prince Salman, the governor of the capital, Riyadh. An effective ally of the Sudairis is Prince Saud al-Faisal, Foreign Minister and son of King Faisal who was assassinated in 1975, who is a leading advocate of the training and employment in government service of an *élite* group of (mostly non-royal) technocrats and administrators who will enable Saudi Arabia to make the transition from a tribal society to a modern State as smoothly as possible. His own ministry is the leading example of this policy.

By and large, the Jilwa branch of the family tends to be more closely identified with the conservative tribes and is considerably more anxious about the impact of the present rate of change in Saudi Arabia, while the Sudairi branch are

supporters of rapid socio—economic development and modernisation. King Fahd has filled the Council of Ministers (cabinet) not only with his brothers but with other princes and technocrats loyal to himself, while the concern of the Jilwa branch at this excessive Sudairi domination was the main reason that King Khalid appointed Prince Abdullah Second Deputy Prime Minister in addition to his post as Commander of the National Guard.

While the royal family invariably closes ranks against the rest of the world, and is far too conscious of the need to maintain solidarity easily to split in even the most intense circumstances of internal rivalry, it cannot be ignored that a considerable part of military policy is determined by the desire of the Sudairis and the Jilwas to enhance the relative importance of the armed forces under their control and consolidate their authority over them. They are both deeply entrenched in their respective positions — Prince Sultan has been Minister of Defence, and Prince Abdullah Head of the National Guard, since 1962 — and each strongly resists any attempt to expand the influence of the other.

It was widely believed that King Khalid wished to abdicate, in view of his ill-health, but this was not possible until the question of who should be Crown Prince upon Fahd's succession to the throne was decided. King Khalid and the Jilwa branch wished to counterbalance the Sudairi influence by selecting Prince Abdullah as the next Crown Prince, but the Sudairi predominance which succeeded in ensuring the selection of Prince Fahd as Crown Prince in 1975 effectively thwarted this compromise. In a series of meetings of senior princes in August, 1977 it was proposed that the King eventually go into retirement, retaining the royal title but leaving all real power in the hands of Crown Prince Fahd; when Crown Prince Fahd finally succeeded to the throne, Prince Abdullah would then become Crown Prince in his place. As his price for agreeing to this arrangement, however, Crown Prince Fahd stipulated that Prince Abdullah could only become his eventual successor if he at once relinquished his control of the National Guard in favour of a Sudairi, Prince Salman, who would proceed to integrate it into the regular army. Since this would place all the armed forces of the kingdom under the exclusive control of the Sudairis, and required Prince Abdullah to relinquish his power base now in return for a future promise, it proved unacceptable, and the question of King Khalid's retirement or abdication had to be postponed.

Since that time the Sudairis have worked to reduce the effectiveness of the National Guard or even integrate it into the armed forces proper, while advancing the claim of Prince Sultan, or perhaps Prince Turki, to be the next Crown Prince. In July, 1977 Prince Fahd is reported to have presented a plan to restrict the purchase of heavy armaments to the regular armed forces, simultaneously curtailing the complement of the National Guard and limiting its weaponry to light equipment so as to convert it into something much closer to a police force than its present status as an autonomous paramilitary organisation. There is no evidence that this plan was accepted, however, and indeed the National Guard has expanded significantly over the past several years.

On King Khalid's death in June 1983, he was succeeded by King Fahd, who immediately named Prince Abdullah Crown Prince and First Deputy Prime Minister. Prince Sultan became Second Deputy Prime Minister. Both retain their respective military posts.

STRENGTH AND BUDGET

The total strength of all Saudi Arabian regular forces is 52,500, of which the Royal Saudi Army accounts for 35,000. The air force has 15,000 personnel, and the navy's strength is 2200 men. All three services are chronically below authorised strength due to recruiting problems.

The National Guard has a strength of about 25,000 men. The paramilitary Frontier Force and Coast Guard number an additional 6500 men. Thus uniformed personnel may account for as much as 7% of native Saudi manpower. This represents a very considerable proportion of the population for a country whose manpower shortages have compelled it to import a foreign labour force of over 2,000,000 — so that there are more foreigners than natives in the employed adult male population — and it is unlikely that even conscription could radically increase the present military manpower figures.

Saudi defence expenditure in 1981 was $24,400,000,000; GNP was $118,990,000,000.

COMMAND AND CONSTITUTIONAL STATUS

Saudi Arabia is an absolute monarchy, with no parliament or political parties. The King is Commander-in-Chief of the Armed Forces. He appoints a Council of Ministers (cabinet), which he leads as Prime Minister; the Crown Prince is First Deputy Prime Minister. The Council of Ministers serves as the instrument of royal authority in both legislative and executive matters; about half the ministers are princes.

The Council of Ministers has been in existence since 1953, but its role is largely to formulate policy and recommend its execution, not to decide itself. Actual decision-making on matters of high policy is concentrated within the royal family. On day-to-day matters the King may consult only with Crown Prince Fahd (on government matters) or Prince Abdullah (on tribal matters). Other decisions might involve all forty or so members of the Council of Elder Princes. In all cases professional advice would be sought from ministers or advisers (Kamal Adham, for example, has advised both King Faisal and King Khalid on defence matters), but the ultimate decisions lie within these royal conclaves.

Defence policy is formally set by the High Defence Council (established in 1961), whose members are the King, the Ministers of Defence and Aviation, Finance and National Economy, Communications and Foreign Affairs, and the Chief of Staff. The Minister of Defence and Aviation, and Inspector-General of the Armed Forces since 1962, Prince Sultan bin Abdul Aziz, exercises supervision and control over the army, navy and air force as well as control of all civil aviation. There are two deputy ministers, one for military affairs and one for civil aviation; the former is Prince Turki, the brother of the minister, who also has charge of military intelligence.

Within the ministry, a Chief of Staff (invariably an army officer) is directly responsible to the minister for the supervision of the activities of the three forces. He also exercises direct command over the army, but the other services have their own commanders. The Commander of the Air Force is General Assad Zuhair. The Chief of Staff is assisted by four staff directors responsible for personnel (G-1), intelligence (G-2), operations and training (G-3) and logistics (G-4). Saudi military staff organisation exactly duplicates that of the United States armed forces. The country is divided into nine area commands, which serve as intermediate headquarters between the Ministry of Defence and Aviation and units in the field.

The National Guard is under the personal control of the King through a commander appointed by him: since 1962 the Commander of the National Guard has been Prince Abdullah bin Abdul Aziz. He also holds an appointment within the Ministry of Defence and Aviation as Controller of Militia Reserves; whether these would be added to the National Guard or the regular army upon mobilisation is not clear.

The Frontier Force, the Coast Guard and the internal security forces are controlled by the Ministry of the Interior.

Senior members of the royal family invariably hold the highest command positions in both the armed forces and the National Guard, and the armed forces as a corporate entity have little or no influence on the government or the regime. There are some 40 younger princes serving in various branches of the armed forces, who together with numerous members of families closely allied to the royal family serving in the officer corps, constitute an extremely effective informal network for intelligence-gathering and, if need be, control.

ROLE, COMMITMENT, DEPLOYMENT AND RECENT OPERATIONS

The armed forces have the mission of safeguarding the integrity of the national boundaries and seaward frontiers to protect the country from invasion. In times of internal disorder, they also have the responsibility for restoring the internal security of the kingdom. The National Guard has exclusive control of the oil-producing Eastern Province, and the general mission of supporting and assisting the forces responsible for maintaining internal security. It is also intended to assist the regular armed forces in repelling an invasion. However, its most important, if unstated, mission is to suppress military insurgencies. Special anti-insurgent units are maintained within both the National Guard and the regular army.

There are two possible sources of internal threat to the security of the regime: the armed forces themselves, and certain elements within the large immigrant community. The former are permeated at all levels with members and adherents of the royal family, and are lavishly rewarded. Moreover, a substantial part of the regular army as well as all of the National Guard is recruited from bedouin groups who owe tribal loyalty to the regime (though the continuing steep decline in the kingdom's genuinely tribal population, now down to half a million, is quickly eroding this reliable recruiting base). The two armies are sufficently closely matched to preclude any easy military takeover of power, and too separate in command and composition to make co-ordination between them easy. The air force is recognised by the regime as the most likely source of a coup attempt because its personnel are so much more exposed to external influences — and it is indeed where all three known coup plots have originated — but it is relatively easily immobilised by the withdrawal of indispensable technical support provided by Britain and the USA.

The question of the immigrant community is a complex one. The more rapidly Saudi Arabia develops its economy, and thus both its defence capability and the means with which to improve the education, skills and well-being of its own population, the more rapidly will this alien population also rise. It already exceeds 2,000,000, on most estimates, and hardly one in three employees in industry is a native Saudi. But the immigrant community is in fact a variety of separate communities doing different sorts of things: over a million Yemenis employed mainly in manual labour, together with Sudanese, Koreans and others; around 250,000 Egyptians mostly working as teachers, civil servants and technical specialists; some 150,000 Indians and Pakistanis working as artisans, technicians and in the liberal professions; up to 100,000 resident Europeans and Americans in a variety of commercial, managerial and training functions; plus Palestinians, Philippinos, Syrians, Chinese from Taiwan, Lebanese and many others. For Saudi Arabia, the potentially dangerous groups are seen as the Yemenis — because of their sheer numbers, and because South Yemen is a Marxist State — and to a much lesser extent the Palestinians. Other immigrant groups are seen as being too small, or politically too uninvolved in Arab affairs, to represent a serious threat to stability. Two recent indications of Saudi concern were a decree forbidding resident Yemenis from engaging in retail trade — as numbers had been doing for up to 20 years — and a new preference for construction contracts of the type concluded by South Korea and Taiwan, in which the labour force is imported by the contractor when work begins, and is taken away again when it finishes.

Riyadh views the Arabian peninsula as a single political arena, however, and it is clear that the smaller Gulf States are more seriously threatened by this problem of immigrants than is Saudi Arabia itself. Fully one-third of Kuwait's residents are Palestinians, and as little as 20% of the population of some of the shaikhdoms further east may still be native. Any political upheaval there could not help but affect Saudi interests. Thus the Saudi Interior Ministry maintains a very close liaison and co-ordinates security measures with the internal security forces of its Gulf neighbours, while the Foreign Ministry is keenly aware of the potentially disastrous effects of policies which were seen to betray Palestinian interests. In a regional conflict with any potential opponent except Israel, moreover, Saudi Arabia might have to reckon with the possibility of an internal 'Fifth Column', which would have to be dealt with primarily by the National Guard.

As regards direct military challenges as opposed to subversion, Saudi Arabia identifies four areas of potential conflict: the Red Sea — south-eastern Arabia region, where the Marxist, Soviet-aided and Cuban-aided regimes of Ethiopia and South Yemen are considered a potential strategic threat; the Persian Gulf, where Iranian intentions have always been viewed with suspicion; Iraq; and Israel.

The rapid growth of a Soviet and Cuban presence in Ethiopia and South Yemen in recent years has caused great concern in Riyadh. It was in response to this development that Saudi Arabia has come closest to making a defensive alliance, when it acted as sponsor and principal financial contributor to the Egyptian—Sudanese alliance of July, 1976. The possibility of a blockade of the southern entrance to the Red Sea, the Bab-el-Mandeb, has led to a concentration on increasing Saudi naval strength on this coast, and major land —air bases are being built in the previously neglected southwest of the country. Great attention is given to ensuring the continued friendship of North Yemen, by far the more populous of the two Yemens and the home of most of Saudi Arabia's Yemeni immigrants.

Until the mid-1978 coup which brought a more rigidly Marxist faction to power in Aden, Riyadh was also attempting to purchase the neutrality of South Yemen with offers of temptingly large amounts of aid. The rearmament of the North Yemeni armed forces with United States weapons is being paid for by Riyadh, and when border clashes broke out between the two Yemens in early 1979 Saudi Arabia placed its armed forces on alert and quickly obtained Washington's permission to use its United States-supplied weapons in defence of North Yemen if necessary. This is the area in which Saudi Arabia would be least reluctant to engage in military operations, both because of its extreme sensitivity and because, barring a massive influx of Soviet and Cuban military personnel, it could reasonably expect at least to hold its own against South Yemen's forces. Saudi aid also continues to flow to Eritrean guerrilla movements in order to prevent re-establishment of full control by Ethiopia over its Red Sea coastal regions.

The Gulf is another matter, both because any serious fighting there could damage the vital oil fields and because Saudi Arabia would be gravely overmatched. While in the latter days of the Shah's regime Riyadh had a decent working relationship with Iran on the question of maintaining Gulf security, there was always a considerable degree of Saudi unease and suspicion about the sheer size and eventual purposes of the Iranian armed forces. The Iranian revolution of early 1979 at least temporarily destroyed the effectiveness of those forces, but it could be quickly recreated by a regime in Tehran enjoying full authority. Moreover, it is not possible for Riyadh to foresee what the character and policies of such a regime might be, so the question of defence against Iran has certainly not disappeared from the Saudi strategic lexicon.

Apart from the potential internal security problem posed by the presence of large Iranian communities in some of the smaller Gulf shaikhdoms, the principal direct military threat from Iran would be an air threat. In addition to making what arrangements it can to defend its oil fields with its own air force, Saudi Arabia has therefore actively pursued the creation of what amounts to an integrated air-defence network on the southern side of the Gulf. Thus, for example, it contributed $50,000,000 to the cost of the Omani air-defence system in 1977, and encouraged tiny Qatar (population 200,000, of whom only 40,000 are Qataris) in its purchase of 30 Mirage F-1 fighters, which only make senses in the context of an integrated air defence of the southern Gulf. It was for the same purpose that Saudi Arabia began constructing its first military base abroad in 1978: an air base with a capacity for 25 aircraft on the site of the old British air strip south of the Awali—Zalaq road in Bahrain.

Beyond purely military measures, Saudi Arabia has since 1974 taken a consistently moderate stance in its own share of the numerous border disputes along the frontiers of the 10 emirates between Kuwait and Oman, and has assumed a mediating role in others, in order to minimise the opportunities for the intrusion of Iranian influence into the many territorial quarrels that bedevil the emirates. Riyadh can do little, however, about the geographical position of Iran which allows it to dominate the exit from the Persian Gulf, and it is at least partly as a measure of strategic precaution against the blockade of the Strait of Hormuz that a pipeline is now being constructed from the oil fields of the Eastern Province across to the Red Sea coast of the country. In view of the vulnerability to blockade of the Red Sea as well, negotiations have also taken place with Oman for the construction of a pipeline that would take Saudi oil directly across the 'empty quarter' and the mountains to the coast of Dhofar on the Arabian Sea.

While the ostensibly militant radicalism of the Ba'athist regime in Baghdad since 1968, combined with the very impressive Soviet-equipped armed forces at Baghdad's disposal, might suggest that Iraq was a principal strategic pre-occupation of Saudi Arabia's, it has almost never been so. Virtually the only possible cause of conflict between the two has been the lengthy territorial dispute between Iraq and Kuwait, in which Riyadh has a commitment to preserve the independence, and perhaps also the territorial integrity, of the latter. In view of Iraq's enormous military problems elsewhere, however, the Kuwait dispute has never attained the level of a fully-fledged crisis since 1961, and would be most unlikely to do so in the foreseeable future. In any case, the triumph of revolutionary Shiite nationalism in Iran poses a mortal threat to the survival of the Ba'athist regime, based as it is on a small clique within the Sunni Arab minority around Baghdad, in a country where over two-thirds of the population are Kurds or Shiite Arabs. In early 1979, indeed,

Iraq and Saudi Arabia came to a semi-clandestine arrangement for co-operation in security matters.

The fourth potential enemy of Saudi Arabia is Israel, although as always Riyadh may be depended upon to avoid a direct military role in any future Arab—Israeli war if possible. This is the merest common sense, since its compact ground and air forces would make very little difference to the balance between the huge military machines of Israel and the Arab 'confrontation States', while it would stand a very good chance of losing a high proportion of its scarce skilled-weapons operators. A few days' intensive combat in a war like that of 1973, for example, could cost Saudi Arabia half the trained fighter pilots whom it has managed to produce over the past 10 years. The disincentives to direct Saudi participation in such a war have grown far greater, moreover, since the Israeli air force has acquired aircraft with the range capabilities to make heavy strikes against the Eastern Province oil fields.

For Israel to take such an extreme step, of course, would imply that it was sufficiently desperate to ignore the wrath of its American ally which would thus lose its major source of imported oil for an indefinite period, so it may be argued that it is not a very likely eventuality, and therefore not such a serious disincentive to Saudi participation in war against Israel after all. On the other hand, the destruction of the Gulf oil fields would also deprive the Arab front-line States of the principal source of financial aid which would allow them to pay for a war and for the subsequent massive re-equipment programme that would be necessary, so there would not be any pressure from them on Saudi Arabia to take an active part in a war against Israel and thus put those vital assets at risk. The most that one would be likely to see by way of Saudi participation in a future Arab—Israeli war would be the dispatch of token Saudi ground forces to the reserve echelon, like the 4000 Saudi troops who were stationed on the Golan Heights and the 7000 who were based in Jordan from October, 1973 until the end of 1976.

The principal military threat to Saudi Arabia in the event of another Arab—Israeli war, therefore, would be that of Israeli air attack. Indeed, following the announcement in May, 1978 that the USA would sell Saudi Arabia 60 F-15 fighters for delivery beginning in late 1981, Israel warned that it might be necessary in another war to launch 'pre-emptive strikes' against Saudi military facilities. This was probably part of the Israeli campaign to abort the sale, however, as the F-15s being bought by Saudi Arabia are not at all the same aircraft as the F-15s that have been sold to Israel. They lack the multiple wing-racks for delivery of air-to-ground weapons, they have only three instead of five 'hard points' in order to limit the amount of payload, they have a simplified avionics system with reduced capabilities and they lack the 'fast pack' special fuel system which extends the aircraft's range. They are, in other words, F-15s in name only, and they have been chosen by Saudi Arabia to replace its ageing Lightning interceptors partly for prestige reasons, and partly because they require only one pilot and are actually simpler to fly and maintain than the very complex Lightnings. Only forty-five are fighters (the other fifteen are trainers), which is hardly an excessive number to provide interceptor capabilities over a million square miles of territory. Moreover, United States restrictions on the geographical deployment of the F-15s apparently do not permit them to be based at Tabuq in north-western Saudi Arabia, the only air base from which they could reach even Eilat within Israel (even despite the fact that there are currently Lightning interceptors at that base). In practice Saudi Arabia has not now, and will not have in the foreseeable future, a serious capability to attack Israel by air from its own bases.

Saudi Arabia's air force, therefore, is almost purely defensive. The F-15s, when they arrive, will be based at the same airfields (with the exception of Tabuq) that now operate Lightnings: Dhahran in the Eastern Province, Taif near Mecca and Khamis Mushayt near the North Yemen border. From these bases, in co-ordination with the country's extensive surface-to-air missile defences, they could offer a measure of protection to the Mecca—Medina—Jiddah region, the Riyadh area, and the oil fields around Dhahran. The country's principal strike aircraft, the relatively simple F-5s, are trained mainly for ground-attack missions in support of the army, and for the anti-shipping role (with Maverick missiles) in the Persian Gulf and the Red Sea. The small navy is wholly devoted to the task of holding open those nearby sea lanes of communication, and has no blue water capability.

The army is mainly based in four vast (and vastly expensive) 'military cities' which contain training, maintenance and logistical facilities, as well as housing and all the other facilities required by a large civilian dependent community. They are co-located with air bases in most cases, and are heavily defended by surface-to-air missiles. They are: Tabuq, in the north-west, where the army's existing armoured brigade and its French training mission are located; King Khalid Military City at Hafar al-Batin in the north-east, close to the Iraqi and Kuwaiti borders; Assad Military City at Al-Kharj, about 60 miles south-east of Riyadh, where the nascent national armaments industry is also situated, and Khamis Mushayt in the mountains of southern Asir, some 60 miles north of the North Yemen border. The National Guard, whose logistical system and training facilities are as separate as its command structure, is building two similar military cities at Al-Hasa, just north of Hofuf amongst the oil fields of the Eastern Province which are its prime military responsibility, and at Qassim, south of Buraidah in the centre of Nejd Province from which it draws most of its recruits.

There are up to 30,000 American, British and French military and civilian personnel in Saudi Arabia engaged in training, maintaining and supplying the Saudi armed forces, but no foreign military units are based in the country. In early 1979 the only Saudi units deployed beyond the country's borders were some air force personnel in Bahrain, and a battalion force of 1200 men who were sent to the Lebanon in mid-1976 as part of the Arab Deterrent Force seeking to keep the peace there. Saudi Arabia's only known military commitment to another Arab State was an agreement with Jordan in August, 1977 whereby Jordan could make use of air bases in northern Saudi Arabia (presumably Turayf, Gurayat and perhaps Tabuq) in the event of war with Israel, in order to give the Jordanian air force the strategic depth it lacks on its own territory, where all air bases are only a few minutes' flying time from Israel. It is not known whether the agreement would permit Jordanian aircraft to fly combat missions against Israel directly from these bases.

Apart from one battalion which took part in the Palestine war of 1948, sporadic clashes along the North Yemen border during the civil war in that country in the early 1960s, and skirmishes along the ill-defined South Yemen border in 1974—6, the Saudi armed forces have not been engaged in combat since well before World War II. A Saudi brigade was, however, attached, in 1973 to the Jordanian army which took part in the Arab—Israeli war.

ORGANISATION

Arms of Service
The arms and services of the Royal Saudi Army correspond

exactly to those of the United States army. The air force and navy branch structure is also identical to the American equivalents. The National Guard, however, has a less elaborately differentiated structure.

Operational

The Royal Saudi Army contains two armoured brigades (one fully equipped with French tanks and one in cadre equipped with American tanks), two mechanised brigades, two infantry brigades, two paratroop battalions and a special forces company together forming an airborne brigade, one Royal Guard regiment (recruited exclusively from tribal sources) and four artillery battalions. There are also 18 anti-aircraft artillery batteries and 18 surface-to-air missile batteries (the latter operate under air force control). The Royal Guard Regiment has three battalions.

The air force has three fighter—bomber squadrons with 65 F-5Es, one interceptor squadron with Lightnings, three operational conversion units with F-5B/Fs and F-15s, two transport squadrons and two helicopter squadrons. There are also training squadrons and a tanker flight. The major air bases are at Riyadh (HQ), Dhahran, Jiddah, Tabuq, Khamis Mushayt, Taif, Abhar, Medina and Yanbo.

The navy does not have a flotilla or squadron organisation. The principal naval bases are at Al Qatif/Jubail on the Persian Gulf and at Jiddah on the Red Sea. There are other navy bases at Ras Tanura, Dammam and Yanbo, coast guard bases at Ash Sharmah, Qisan and Haqi, and a logistics port under construction at Ras al-Mishab.

The National Guard is organised on tribal lines with tribal leaders in charge, and not all of it serves full time. It has a total of 20 battalions, of which four have been mechanised by the provision of V-150 Commando armoured cars and Vulcan anti-aircraft guns; there are also 24 irregular infantry battalions.

RECRUITMENT, TRAINING AND RESERVES

Service in the Saudi armed forces is voluntary, except in the National Guard where the system of customary tribal levies still persists to some extent. This further complicates the basic manpower problem of the armed forces — that of acquiring sufficient numbers of qualified recruits from a small population where modern education and ways of living are very recent developments. (In 1975, the literacy rate in Saudi Arabia was only 15%.) The lack of compulsion in recruitment means that the armed forces must compete for the small number of qualified potential recruits with a commercial sector where very large rewards may be had for lower qualifications and in conditions of considerably greater comfort.

The armed forces attempt to compete by offering excellent social and medical services, high quality accomodation, an education system superior to that provided by the Ministry of Education, and relatively high pay. To catch up with soaring wage rates in the private sector, military salaries were doubled for all ranks in March, 1977 even at a time when the government was trying to restrain pay rises in the public sector to combat inflation. Military pay rates are now higher than in any other part of the public services, but they still do not compare favourably with the money available in the private sector, and all the armed forces are chronically under strength. In February, 1978 the Deputy Minister of Defence and Aviation announced that a law for the introduction of conscription was being considered, but as it is not to be obligatory it is unlikely that it would greatly improve matters.

Recruitment for the regular armed forces is done on a nationwide basis, and units do not have any territorial links; the National Guard, on the other hand, recruits each of its units from a specific area. Enlistments are for 3 year terms. A career as a military officer is open to any Saudi citizen (including those who have been naturalised for a period of at least 5 years) who meets the physical and mental qualifications and is at least 18 years old. A large proportion of officer candidates are drawn from the basic military schools located in the larger cities, like the Military Preparatory School in Riyadh, which since the 1950s have offered a free education in elementary and intermediate subjects to young men who agree to enter the Royal Military College to become officers.

The Royal Military College in Riyadh is the principal source of junior officers for the army. It offers a 3 year course of instruction in academic and military subjects, and grants its graduates commissions as second-lieutenants. Newly appointed second-lieutenants serve on probation for 2 years before being confirmed in rank; if their performance has not been satisfactory they are then transferred to another unit for an additional 1 year probationary period, and if still unsatisfactory are released from the service. Graduates of technical schools may obtain direct commissions as second-lieutenants, and university graduates with science degrees are also granted additional seniority on entry, or even a higher rank, on a scale determined by comparing their years of study with the 3 years of study in the Royal Military College.

Air force pilots are trained at the King Faisal Air Academy at Riyadh airport. Candidates must have secondary school certificates; the 3 year course of military, academic and flying training produces second-lieutenants who are qualified to wings standard and are able to speak good English, in which language almost all subsequent training is conducted. The academy has also trained officers from Qatar, Sudan, Bahrain, North Yemen and Uganda; to relieve the pressure of numbers, some Saudi cadets are sent to the USA each year for flight training.

Naval officers are currently trained in the USA, but the construction of a new naval college has been budgeted for. National Guard officers are trained at the camp at Khasam al-An, about 15 miles from Riyadh, where a $133,000,000 construction project to build a military academy for the National Guard will be completed in late 1980.

Basic training for army and National Guard enlisted men is provided by Saudi NCOs and officers, but almost all subsequent specialised training comes within one of the numerous contract training schemes provided by foreign armed forces or private companies, with foreign personnel as supervisors or even as instructors. In the case of the navy, the youngest service, most training even for enlisted ranks is still conducted in the USA, particularly at San Diego, California. In late 1975 the air force concluded an agreement whereby 100 Saudi recruits would be sent to Lackland Air Force Base in San Antonio, Texas every 3 months for a course including 4 weeks of basic training, 59 weeks of English, and 1 year of mathematics and science instruction, followed by specialist training at a technical school.

Training in the Saudi armed forces is patterned on that in the United States armed forces, and is controlled by the training section of the G-3 (Operations and Training) Office in the General Staff. This office administers the military school system, which in addition to the army and air force academies includes army branch schools for infantry, armour (at Tabuq), artillery (Khamis Mushayt), communications, physical training, ordnance, engineering, military police, military administration, nursing and military music, and also the air force's Technical Studies Institute at Dhahran, which offers basic and advanced training to air force warrant officers in 43 aeronautical, electronics and air-control specialities. The training section of G-3 also liaises with the national military missions which supervise the large foreign training programmes that provide most of the senior staff for all these schools. The United States Military Training Mission numbers about 250 officers and NCOs of all three services who are responsible for supervising both direct training assistance by United States military personnel and the larger number of civilian personnel working on the extremely large contracts for providing training, construction and logistical support services to the armed forces – a total of perhaps 30,000 Americans. A French training mission performs a similar function for the several hundred French military personnel training the Saudi army's armoured brigade, and a senior British air force officer supervises the fulfilment of British training contracts.

The principal army contract with a private company is with the Bendix Corporation, for the provision of army logistical and maintenance services and the training of Saudi personnel to run them. There is also a contract with the Raytheon Corporation for the maintenance of the army's Hawk and Improved Hawk SAMs and the training of their crews. The air force depends much more heavily on such arrangements: a 4 year, $1,240,000,000 contract with the British Aircraft Corporation for servicing and maintaining the Saudi air force and operating the Air Academy and Technical Studies Institute, involving some 2000 British civilians and running until the end of 1980, is supplemented by a series of 'Peace Hawk' programmes run by the Northrop Corporation for the maintenance of F-5 fighters and the training of their air and ground crews, and contracts with Lockheed Georgia and Lockheed Aircraft Services to provide similar services for the air force's C-130 aircraft and for various major communications functions. There is also a Pakistan air force advisory mission. The navy is being built up almost from scratch under a package deal signed directly with the United States government in 1974, whose cost has grown to over $2,000,000,000. The Coast Guard is being trained by the Avco Corporation.

The most comprehensive foreign involvement in training is the $77,000,000 contract with the Vinnell Corporation of California to provide all the training on handling and maintenance of modern weapons and military vehicles necessary to convert four National Guard battalions of about 1000 men each into regular-style formations – three mechanised infantry battalions and one light artillery battalion – and to assist in the modernisation of the entire Guard. About 75 United States army officers are also involved in this programme, but the Vinnell Corporation's civilian trainers (mostly ex-United States Special Forces), numbering not far from a thousand, bear most of the responsibility. The training is being done at Khasam al-An. Small British, Pakistani and Jordanian military training missions also work with the National Guard.

Discipline in the Saudi regular forces is strict but not harsh. In the National Guard it varies widely between units, amongst which regular pay is the only common denominator. (The Guard is partly an institution for making payments to the tribes and getting money to the villages.) Some Guard units will put in only an occasional appearance, while others, like those being trained by Vinnell, are comparable to regular army units. The Commander of the National Guard, Prince Abdullah, can influence standards to a considerable extent, but much depends on the attitude towards training of the local tribal chief who leads each battalion.

Conditions of service in the regular forces are good, and pay is the highest of any armed forces in the Middle East.

Cash living allowances, housing allowances and clothing allowances are provided to officers and warrant officers, and officers also receive a servant allowance. Additional allowances are granted to officers in certain positions of command or who perform hazardous duties, and NCOs and privates may qualify for special allowances classified into 16 pay categories according to skills. Officers are entitled to 45 days of regular leave and 60 days of field leave per year, NCOs and privates to 1 month of each. Retirement provisions for officers and NCOs are generous, and they are eligible for retirement after 15 years of service.

The only reserve organisation, apart from the National Guard, is a militia force of 15,000.

EQUIPMENT AND ARMS INDUSTRY

The Saudi army enjoys the dubious luxury of possessing two main-battle-tank systems: 300 AMX-30s acquired from France and 150 American M-60s (150 more on order). It also has 150 Scorpion light tanks (100 more on order), and some AMX-13 and 60 M-41 light tanks. There are 200 AML-60/-90 and some Staghound and Greyhound armoured cars, and some Ferret and 100 Fox scout cars.

The army has 250 AMX-10P MICVs, with a further 60 on order. There are 600 M-113 and Panhard M-3 APCs; it is believed that the eventual requirement of the mechanised brigades is 1100. The artillery arm, largely French-equipped, has 105mm pack howitzers and 105mm and 155mm SP howitzers. There are also 60mm, 81mm and 4.2in mortars and 75mm recoilless rifles. Anti-tank guided weapons are TOW, SS-11 and Dragon. Anti-aircraft defence is provided by: M-163 Vulcan 20mm SP, M-42 40mm SP and AMX-30SA SP guns; Redeye and Shahine (Crotale SP) SAMs with the combat units; and 10 batteries of Hawk and six batteries of Improved Hawk surface-to-air missiles in fixed locations (total Hawk missiles: 580).

The National Guard has 240 150 V-150 Commando APCs and Vulcan AA guns. Some 105mm howitzers and TOW anti-tank missiles.

The mixture of American, French and British equipment in use by the Saudi armed forces must create some complex logistical problems, which can only be compounded by the fact that some entire weapons systems, like the air force's F-5s or the army's Hawk missiles, are separately maintained by different private corporations. It will also not escape notice that this scale of equipment, while not unimpressive, does not correspond to an average annual defence budget of around $25,000,000,000. Spending on infrastructure, most of it going to the United States Army Corps of Engineers (which has moved its European headquarters to Saudi Arabia because of the volume of business there), accounts for between 85% and 90% of Saudi defence spending in recent years. When the major contracts for the construction of the military cities, logistics ports and other major facilities are completed in the early 1980s, defence spending must drop drastically unless far more ambitious weapons purchases are undertaken. Since the present forces are already at the limit of their absorptive capacity for new weaponry, such a further programme of weapons buying would only be embarked upon if effective conscription were to be introduced to raise sharply the number of qualified recruits available to the armed forces.

The only arms industry in Saudi Arabia is the Al Kharj Arsenal, where United States small arms (M16s, M1s, and M60 0.30in and 0.50in calibre machine-guns) are produced under licence, together with light ammunition and rockets. The factory is government-owned, and staffed with United

States and West German advisers. More ambitious arms-production plans all fall under the aegis of the Arab Organisation for Industrialisation (AOI), in which Saudi Arabia is a partner with Egypt, Qatar and the United Arab Emirates (*see* Egypt for details). There have been proposals to locate much of the electronics production of the AOI at Al Kharj.

RANK, DRESS AND DISTINCTIONS

The rank system of the Saudi armed forces corresponds to that of the United States armed forces; standard eastern Arab rank nomenclature is used in all services.

Military distinctions are classified as decorations (which carry a monetary reward payable to the recipient for the rest of his life), achievement medals and medals. Decorations include the King Abdul Aziz ibn Saud Decoration, the King Saud Star and the National Military Decoration. Achievement medals include the Efficiency Medal, the Medal of Merit and the Appreciation Medal. Medals include the Long Service and Good Example Medal, the Exceptional Promotion Medal, the War Wounded Medal and the Palestine Medal.

CURRENT DEVELOPMENTS

Saudi Arabia now possesses compact but very well equipped armed forces of a good professional standard. However, the question of technical proficiency in the use of such sophisticated equipment, and even more in its maintenance, is a problem which takes considerably longer to overcome. The good military aptitudes of Saudi recruits is beyond question, but for at least another generaton there will remain a serious problem in the average level of education of the population, which is made far more severe by the intense competition for scarce trained manpower in the Saudi economy. The problem will be further intensified by the rapid decline of the tribal sector of Saudi society from which the forces have always drawn a relatively high proportion of their recruits, and yet the government is reluctant to introduce effective measures of conscription on both political and economic grounds: native Saudi manpower is equally short in the civilian economy, which is increasingly dominated by foreigners, and a wholesale shift of the base of recruitment towards towns and cities would tend to bring politically disturbing new elements into the armed forces.

In the circumstances, the armed forces are not likely to undergo further dramatic expansion. They are in any case adequate at their present size to offer a stout initial defence of Saudi territory against any likely regional threats. Against a more prolonged attack by a major regional power, or any challenge from an outside great power, the country must continue to rely on its friends and allies, as it lacks the manpower to create an entirely autonomous defence.

A further restriction on Saudi Arabia's military autonomy is its dependence on foreign, principally American, assistance for the maintenance and even the operation of its forces. This is most pronounced in the air force where, for example, it is estimated that the country will depend on American support to operate its F-15s well into the 1990s. Though few in numbers, Saudi pilots are entirely competent to operate the aircraft – many of them have now exceeded 1000 hours in Lightnings, and anyone who can fly a Lightning can certainly fly an F-15 – but despite the most intensive and expensive training programmes the ground support and logistical back-up are still largely dependent on foreign personnel. It may not be true that the Saudi armed forces would instantly cease to function if the USA disapproved of Saudi policy so strongly that it withdrew its personnel, but the air force would certainly lose most of its operational effectiveness after only a week of high-intensity operations, and even the army would be largely immobilised in a month or two.

It is highly unlikely, however, that the regime would ever get into a position so strongly opposed to that of the USA. Saudi Arabia's rulers are not 'pro-Western' in the conventional sense: they quite accurately regard the Western and Soviet blocs as two variants of an alien 'Western' culture, and see themselves as the guardians of Islamic culture and the Muslim community against the pernicious effects of that culture in either manifestation. Both on moral grounds and for practical considerations of political survival, they seek to restrict their dealings with the West to financial and military relationships and technology transfer; they do not want Western political and cultural influences to penetrate their own society, although they are fully aware of the difficulty of preventing this from happening. But both on the practical ground that Western allies are less hostile to the survival of the conservative traditional form of government in Arabia, and on the moral ground that communism in any of its guises is a far more serious threat to Islamic morality (it is, after all, explicitly atheist), the Saudi regime is inevitably allied with the West – which is also inevitably its main commercial partner.

This does not mean, however, that the country is in any way an American satellite. Its economic importance gives it considerable freedom of action, and it makes its own judgements about regional affairs. These are sometimes strongly opposed to American policy, as was the case in 1978 when Riyadh viewed Washington's attempt to achieve what amounted to a separate Egyptian–Israeli peace treaty with the utmost misgivings. In the aftermath of the fall of the Shah in Iran, the Saudi regime in early 1979 was also extremely concerned about the willingness of America to come to the aid of its allies in the Middle East – an anxiety that was amply demonstrated in Riyadh's strong reaction to the outbreak of fighting between North and South Yemen in early 1979. Saudi Arabia's armed forces were put on alert and all leave cancelled, and clearance was hastily obtained from Washington to use the country's American-supplied weapons in defence of North Yemen.

The actual scale of external threats to Saudi Arabia's security in early 1979 did not seem very serious, however, nor was it likely that internal security problems of major importance would arise either from the immigrant population or from the dispute over the succession in the royal family. The instinctive solidarity of the royal family and its clear awareness of the grave dangers of an open split seemed certain to contain the succession dispute within reasonable bounds. Despite rapid modernisation the regime retains the respect of almost all Saudi Arabian citizens for its success as the defender of Islamic values, the bringer of prosperity and the author of the great enhancement in Saudi Arabia's position in the world.

As to the possibility of a military coup against the regime, which is probably the most serious of an assortment of potential threats to the regime none of which is very serious, it seemed no greater than before. There was allegedly a plot for a military coup uncovered in May or June, 1977 involving 13 pilots at Tabuq air base, in which air attacks on government buildings and royal palaces in Jeddah and Riyadh would have been followed by the proclamation of an Arabian republic. Two of the implicated pilots reportedly escaped with their aircraft to Baghdad and the remainder were arrested, and for a time all aircraft were forbidden to carry munitions and restricted to enough fuel for only 30 minutes' flying time.

By Libya's own admission this was a plot inspired by the

Head of the Libyan Security and Military Intelligence Service, Captain Muhammed Idris al-Sharif. Libya further alleges that al-Sharif was subsequently 'turned' by the Saudis and at the direction of Prince Turki, Chief of Saudi Military Intelligence, organised at least three attempts to assassinate Libya's General Qaddafi before being arrested in early 1978. What proportion of this is true cannot be known; it is, in any case, not exceptional in the normal course of inter-Arab relations, and simply serves to emphasise that the air force's officers and warrant officers are the likeliest source of a military coup in Saudi Arabia.

The most violent event to have taken place recently in Saudi Arabia was of religious, not political inspiration. On November 20th, 1979, the first day of the Islamic fifteenth century, a group of 2—300 Muslim fundamentalists, claiming to act in the name of a new *Mahdi* (leader of a holy war), seized the Grand Mosque in Mecca, holiest place of Islam. On November 25th following the promulgation of an exemption from laws against the use of arms in the Mosque by an Islamic court, 2200 Saudi troops entered the mosque with armour and light artillery. Fighting continued until December 3rd, in its first stages allegedly directed by five French officers skilled in anti-terrorist tactics.

Of the 170 rebels taken alive, 63 were subsequently executed; 127 soldiers were killed and 451 injured in the fighting. A variety of agents later spoke of Iranian involvement, of anti-royalist statements made by the rebels, of disturbances in other parts of Saudi Arabia and of disaffection in the armed forces; but none was substantiated.

Gwynne Dyer
John Keegan

SENEGAL*

HISTORY AND INTRODUCTION

Senegal attained independence from France in 1960. For a few months Senegal formed part of the Federation of Mali uniting the two former French colonies of Soudan and Senegal. This union, however, proved unworkable, but during its brief period of life the Mali Federation sent a battalion formed of companies from both States to the United Nations Congo Force, where it gained a great reputation. From 1960 to 1981, Senegal was ruled by President L. Senghor. In general, Senghor's period of government was tranquil although economic development was disappointing; somewhat isolated attempts by rivals to overthrow Senghor occurred in 1962 and 1967, and 1968–9 saw major student and labour demonstrations. These events excepted, Senegal has enjoyed remarkable stability, and Senghor's retirement passed off without hitch. His successor, A. Diouf presides over a regime that permits several political parties and some lively political debate. The continuing decline of, and weaknesses in, Senegal's economic performance are now the greatest threat to stability.

The army specifically refused to intervene when a political leader who felt that he, rather than Diouf, should have been Senghor's successor and called for elections under army supervision.

STRENGTH AND BUDGET

Population: 5,500,000 (approximate)
Armed forces: 9560 of which 500 are air force and 700
  navy, plus a gendarmerie of 6000
GNP: $2,230,000,000
Defence expenditure: $60,000,000 (approximate)

COMMAND AND CONSTITUTIONAL STATUS

The President of the Republic, A. Diouf is the Head of State: The Minister for the Armed Forces is D. Sow and the Chief of Staff is General Idrissa Fall. The gendarmerie is commanded by Brigadier-General W. Faye.

ROLE, COMMITMENT, DEPLOYMENT AND RECENT OPERATIONS

Senegal is a member of ANAD, the treaty of mutual aid in the event of an attack signed by seven West African States.

Senegal has committed one battalion for service in the United Nations Force firstly in Egypt and then later in Lebanon; another was sent to Chad with the inter-African force, 1981–82. These commitments were generally supported by public opinion in Senegal. The inclusion of a Senegal contingent in the French-organised force sent to the Shaba province of Zaire in 1978, however attracted sharp domestic political criticism in Dakar.

Until the Polisario insurgency against Mauritania, to the north of Senegal, the Casamance area in the south was the territory's major military problem. Casamance adjoins both Guinea–Conakry, whose regime has always been hostile to

* For general notes on African armies, see Appendix 1.

Dakar, and Guinea–Bissau. Before the collapse of Portuguese rule insurgents operated against Portugal from the safety of the Casamance, sometimes attracting Portuguese hot pursuit across the border; after 1974 the problem continued for a while in a new form as former Portuguese African colonial soldiers, in flight from the new regime, occupied areas of the Casamance and proved an embarrassment to the authorities. With the opening of the Polisario's attacks on Mauritania, with whom Senegal is on friendly terms, anxiety centred upon the northern border until Mauritania withdrew from the conflict.

For more general defence, reliance has been placed on French garrisons. Until 1974 France maintained a garrison of some 2250, of which over 1000 were soldiers, the remainder being naval and air force personnel. In 1974 the French base at Dakar was transferred to Senegal, though France retained the right to use it. The French garrison was also reduced to its present level – a battalion of marines at Bel Air Camp, near Dakar.

In July 1981, following the mutiny of the Gambia Police Field Force, President Sir D. Jawara requested the help of Senegalese troops in suppressing the mutiny. These troops quickly arrived in Senegal and in a manner generally but not invariably efficient, restored order, either killing or capturing the mutineers. Some casualties were sustained.

In 1982 the Senegal government allowed British military aircraft to refuel at Dakar on their way to Ascension for the Falklands operation.

ORGANISATION

The Senegal army consists of five infantry battalions, an armoured-car reconnaissance squadron, an engineer battalion, two parachute sub-units, two marine sub-units, an artillery unit, a training battalion and three construction companies.

The country is divided into four military zones: West (Dakar), North (St Louis), South (Bignona) and East (Tambacounda).

One battalion is at Dakar and one at St Louis, and a third is in the south (present deployment not known). The marine, parachute, reconnaissance and artillery sub-units are normally posted to Dakar, with the engineer unit at Bargny. The officer cadet school is at Thies. The main air force base is at Ouakam, near Dakar.

RECRUITMENT, TRAINING AND RESERVES

A random system of national military service operates: the term of service for those selected was extended from 18 months to two years in 1974. No ethnic group appears to be in any position of advantage and little ethnic friction is evident.

France has provided the greatest measure of training and equipment assistance since 1960, a mission some 450 strong being at work in the early 1960s. This is now reduced to a level of some 20 officers and 20 NCOs. There has also been a limited amount of United States military assistance, a small United States army team serving in Senegal in the late 1960s. Occasionally Senegalese cadets are sent to Sandhurst.

Joint exercises with visiting French units and the French garrison are held at intervals.

Senegal legislation has recently been altered to allow for women to join the army, probably for communications or medical duties.

EQUIPMENT AND ARMS INDUSTRY

The armoured-car squadron possesses the largest share in the country's total force of thirty AML-60, twenty-four AML-90 and fourteen elderly US M-8 and M-20 armoured cars. The armed forces also possess a number of Panhard M-3 armoured troop carriers, the precise number is unclear, reports varying between twelve and forty, and twelve Berliet UXB 170 armoured troop carriers. The latter, with perhaps even some of the Panhards, may belong to the gendarmerie rather than the Army. The artillery possesses six US 105mm howitzers and a small number of 40mm anti-aircraft guns. One report also suggests a few very elderly US 75mm pack howitzers may also still remain. Also in service are an up-dated range of French infantry battalion weapons, eight 81mm mortars and a small number of Milan anti-tank guided weapons. The gendarmerie possesses some UNIMOG load personnel carriers.

The Air Force has no fighter or air to ground strike capacity, being limited to six C-47, one Caravelle and six F-27 transports, one Corvette liaison aircraft, and four Magister, two Broussard and one Cessna training aircraft. In an emergency the Magisters and the Cessna could be used for light bombing. The Air Force also possesses a small number of helicopters; one report notes one Gazelle and one Puma, another six Pumas.

Equally unclear is the order book, which may according to reports include Alouette helicopters and one or more Brazilian Embraer EMB-111 patrol aircraft, probably intended for maritime reconnaissance.

RANK, DRESS AND DISTINCTIONS

These follow the traditional French colonial pattern, except that the *képi* is not worn. A horsed gendarmerie Presidential Guard unit wears long red cloaks. The marines wear a white uniform with a cap similar to those of the French Navy.

CURRENT DEVELOPMENTS

A number of factors, including a sharply developing distrust of Libya and Guinea-Conakry (both of which supported critics of the regime), domestic unrest arising from economic conditions, the reduction of the French garrison and the presence of a second revolutionary government on Senegal's borders led Senegal to take a more serious view of defence than seemed necessary in the 1960s, hence the recent expansion of the army.

The 1981 confederal union with Gambia will in practice mean that Senegal's army will be the military force to defend both territories. Its competent intervention proved a political triumph for Diouf, on whom, at the time of writing, fortune is smiling. His own political skill enables him to manage the rival political parties and Muslim sects, the economic situation has slightly improved and perhaps most important of all for Senegal's stability, Diouf's political style is regarded as exemplary by President Mitterand, perhaps Senegal's surest shield in a hostile world.

Lloyd Mathews

SEYCHELLES

The Seychelles, a group of 87 islands in the north-western part of the Indian Ocean with a total area of 171 square miles and a population of about 166,000, were first colonised by the French in the middle of the eighteenth century. They subsequently passed under British rule in 1794, though the predominant language remains French. They attained independence as a republic in the British Commonwealth in June, 1976.

The government at independence was led by President James R. Mancham, the leader of the majority Seychelles Democratic Party, but it was a coalition incorporating also the principal left-wing party, the Seychelles People's United Party. The leader of the latter party, Albert René, was Vice-President. Government economic policy concentrated heavily on the development of the tourist industry, in which a large share of new investment came from Saudi Arabian private sources, and foreign policy was distinctly pro-Western. No attempt was made to create armed forces, internal security being left entirely in the hands of the civil police.

While President Mancham was abroad in June, 1977 however, a group of Vice-President René's supporters who are believed to have received training in Tanzania, carried out a sudden coup. Two policemen guarding the police arsenal were killed, control was thereby gained over the few rifles then available in the country, and the coup was complete. Albert René declared himself President, the constitution was suspended and parliament dissolved. Rule is now by presidential decree.

Since its inception President René's regime has shown extreme nervousness about the possibility of a counter-coup and has formed an army of men recruited from supporters of his party. It now numbers 1000, organised as an infantry battalion, an artillery troop and a support unit, equipped with six Russian BRD armoured carriers, three 122mm guns, mortars, and SA-7 missiles. In addition, about 150 Tanzanian troops have been brought in as 'advisers', their expenses being paid by the Seychelles government. In early 1979 the Seychelles navy took delivery of its first major vessel, an ex-French minesweeper of 400 tons which will be used as a patrol boat to control the newly declared 200 mile economic zone. A Britten—Norman Islander patrol aircraft has been acquired for the same purpose, together with three light aircraft and two Alouette III helicopters.

The government takes a politically polarised view of African politics, and in May, 1978 accused members of the Kenyan government of complicity in an alleged plot to mount an invasion of some 200 mercenaries by sea from Mombasa while President René was away on a visit to Peking. At the same time it was announced that large arms caches had been discovered on the main island, Mahé which were intended for use in the alleged counter-coup attempt, and 21 people were arrested in the capital. The Seychelles army's duties, in addition to the control of internal dissent, are now considered to include defence against an invasion by such a mercenary force as was supposed to have been gathered in Kenya.

Tanzanian support for René's coup in the Seychelles stems partly from ideological sympathy, but also owes much to Dar-es-Salaam's concern that there should be no superpower bases in the Indian Ocean. Although Mancham's government had never suggested that the good harbour at Victoria, the capital, might be made available for such a purpose, his general political stance and in particular his refusal to consider the islands part of Africa, had given rise to suspicions on this account in Tanzania and the Malagasy Republic.

President René has taken a lead in trying to end the growing naval competition in the Indian Ocean, calling a conference of Indian Ocean island States in Victoria in late April, 1978 to bring pressure on the USA to give up its naval/air base on Diego Garcia island and on the Soviet Union to withdraw its fleet from the region. The conference was attended by representatives of the governments of the Seychelles, Malagasy Republic, the Comoro Islands (since overthrown) and of the left-wing opposition parties in Mauritius and Réunion. It is doubtful if this attempt to create an Indian Ocean neutralist bloc under the patronage of the Malagasy Republic and Tanzania will enjoy significant success, but as long as President René's army and Tanzanian advisers are able to preserve his own power there are unlikely to be any foreign bases in the Seychelles.

Since the last edition of *World Armies* President René has twice more come under threat of deposition. In November 1979, he announced the discovery of a plot to overthrow him 'sponsored' from abroad and with the co-operation of mercenaries standing ready in Durban. The Tanzanian contingent of 250 was reinforced by 300 more soldiers, and many people arrested. (In October there had been demonstrations against René's plan to introduce 'national service' for youth). In November 1981 a group of South African-based mercenaries did invade the islands, apparently to overthrow the government, but their arms were detected when their airliner landed at the airport. Although they managed to return to South Africa in a hijacked aircraft, they were then arrested and tried by the South African government. Their leader, Colonel Mike Hoare, of Congo mercenary fame, and a number of others were subsequently sentenced to long terms of imprisonment. The South African and Kenyan governments denied complicity in the affair. Fighting at the airport at Victoria, capital of the islands, was claimed to have caused $2m damage.

Gwynne Dyer

SIERRA LEONE*

HISTORY AND INTRODUCTION

Sierra Leone attained independence from Britain in 1961 and until 1967 maintained political stability. In 1967 the governing party was defeated at the polls, but before the victorious former opposition party could assume power, the Army Commander, Brigadier Lansana, intervened. He was, however, overthrown by a group of officers headed by Brigadier Juxon-Smith; these formed a National Reformation Council. This Council survived only briefly, to be in turn overthrown by a 'sergeants' coup in 1968, which imprisoned almost all the officers and facilitated the return of the 1967 election winner, Siaka Stevens, as Prime Minister. Stevens then ruled by emergency legislation and banned the formation of any new political parties, although allowing the continuance of an existing opposition party. The return of Stevens marked the shift of power away from the coast to the hinterland peoples, in particular the Temne.

A further crisis arose in 1971 when members of the army attempted to assassinate Stevens – the attempt was mishandled (the major in command admitted subsequently to being inebriated) – but the Army Commander, Brigadier Bangura, resentful at growing Guinean influence, attempted to take over. This reaction was repudiated by the battalion commander, and he and other officers were arrested – Bangura and three others being subsequently executed. Stevens requested protection from Guinea, who supplied troops, and a republic with Stevens as Executive President was proclaimed. The Guinean troops then returned home shortly afterwards. A further crisis arose in 1977 when in atmosphere of repression and protest demonstrations, and despite much violent intimidation, the opposition party managed to secure some gains in an election. As a riposte Stevens declared a one-party state, Guinean troops again providing a temporary security force. Since then the regime has become markedly more authoritarian, inefficient and corrupt; its internal security force outnumber the Army. The events of 1982, noted below, suggest the present Sierra Leone state may be nearing the point of collapse.

Sierra Leone units participated in the World War I German East African Campaign and in the World War II Italian East Africa and Burma Campaigns.

STRENGTH AND BUDGET

Population: 3,500,000
Armed Forces: 3150 (this total includes naval and air force personnel and two internal security forces, the (uniformed) ISU (Internal Security Unit) of some 1000, and the non-uniformed special Security Department (SSD) also some 1000 or more, perhaps 2000
GNP: No figure available
Defence Expenditure: $21,000,000 (approximate)

COMMAND AND CONSTITUTIONAL STATUS

The President of the Republic, S. Stevens, as Head of State is Commander-in-Chief of the Armed Forces. The Internal Security Unit is, however, responsible to the senior Vice President, S. Koroma.

ROLE, COMMITMENT, DEPLOYMENT AND RECENT OPERATIONS

The Sierra Leone army has no overt political role, though it is tasked to assist with agricultural development. No external threat to the territory is perceived.

ORGANISATION

The army approximately 3000 strong, is based on a battalion group with mortar support, an armoured squadron, and a signals/engineer squadron. An air unit of 25 men and a seaward defence unit of 150 men form part of the army.

There is also a construction battalion, used apparently for agricultural purposes. The effective battalion group is posted to Freetown, the construction unit is stationed at Makeni.

RECRUITMENT, TRAINING AND RESERVES

Service is voluntary. A pattern existed in the early 1960s, but has now disappeared, by which the small numbers of officers were drawn mainly from the coastal creole community and soldiers recruited from the large hinterland ethnic groups. It is, however, reported that very recently a preference for recruiting ordinary soldiers from the most remote of the inland areas has developed. In 1961 only eight of the army's 37 officers were local, and the government at the time saw no necessity for any rapid localisation. Some of the NCOs involved in the 1968 coup – 'the Anti-Corruption Revolutionary Movement' – were commissioned by the Stevens government, and other junior officers released and reinstated. Some Israeli training assistance was accepted in the 1960s. In the late 1970s some personnel, including potential officers, were sent to Egypt, Tanzania and to Ghana for training, and a few also to Britain. Chinese and Cuban training teams, representing personal preferences of two leading political figures were also reported training in different camps near Freetown at the time, but these may have been at work with the ISU. The result, then, is a mixture of background and training.

A small number of women, including officers, serve in the force.

The ISU is reported to be recruited, in approximate terms, 25% Limba (Steven's own ethnic group) and 75% Temne (the ethnic group of the Vice President). Its training is reported to have been Cuban and Chinese.

The President is said to have recruited a small personal guard, for himself and other key political figures, from Palestinians.

Some recent advice suggests that the standard of training of the Army has been deliberately allowed to fall while the standard of training of the para-military forces has received especial attention.

Sierra Leone

EQUIPMENT AND ARMS INDUSTRY

Sierra Leone has, it is reported, a small armaments industry manufacturing light weaponry for the Palestine Liberation Organization. The Army possesses four Saladin armoured cars and ten Mowag Piranha armoured personnel carriers. Some survivors of ten Ferret armoured scout cars may still remain serviceable. One report notes a battery of ten 25 pdr guns. The infantry possesses 81mm and 60mm mortars of British and French origin, but is said to suffer from an acute shortage of all types of ammunition.

The air unit in late 1982 ordered two Aerospatiale Ecureuil helicopters. One report notes the unit already possesses two Hughes 500 light helicopters and one larger West German BO-105 machine. There are also three small transport aircraft.

RANK, DRESS AND DISTINCTIONS

These follow the British pattern.

CURRENT DEVELOPMENTS

The events of 1982, to the time of writing, make singularly depressing reading. In January two military coup conspiracies, one of major/captain level and one of more senior officers linked with certain political figures and possibly with elements in the ISU were discovered. A few killings and a number of arrests (including several officers) followed. In May an election was held in a climate of violence, scandals, intimidation and corruption. The Cabinet formed after the election makes some gesture to national reconciliation and unity, appearing somewhat to reduce Limba and Temne influence in favour of the Mende in particular. Resentment against the Afro-Lebanese community, some members (not the most reputable) of which are financing Stevens, continues to grow.

The country is near bankruptcy, Stevens is at least 79, probably more, the senior Vice President is a sick man, there is general public revulsion against the jobbery, corruption and authoritarianism of the regime. Some form of radical upheaval seems inevitable; the future, even the cohesion, of the Army in such circumstances can only be described as uncertain.

Lloyd Mathews

ADDENDUM

Recent reports suggest that the events of January 1982 may in fact have been only a propaganda move by the government to justify certain arrests and retirements that it wished to make. The declining political situation worsened still further in the last months of 1982.

SINGAPORE

HISTORY AND INTRODUCTION

Singapore, the great trading city of the Straits of Malacca founded by the British in 1819, owed its rise in almost equal measure to the military and financial investment in the island made by them during the next 100 years and to the simultaneous immigration of a large and industrious Chinese population. Chosen between World Wars I and II to be the main British naval base in the Far East, it nevertheless fell quickly to the Japanese in 1942 but, at the end of the war, it became again the centre of British power in south-east Asia. When Britain, having defeated a communist insurrection in neighbouring Malaya, decided to withdraw from the country, she therefore excluded the island from the independence arrangements made with the Malayans. But her reasons were not exclusively strategic. To have included the largely Chinese-settled Singapore in a unitary Malayan State would have been to outnumber the Malays in their own homeland, since the mainland also contained a large Chinese population. Consequently Singapore, when it became fully independent in 1963, did so as a separate entity. Its new Prime Minister, Lee Kuan Yew, impatient with the constriction this arrangement imposed, was a prime mover in a different solution, which came into force the following year: by it the Malayan Federation became the Malaysian Federation, to include not only Malaya and Singapore, but the largely Malay States in British Borneo, Sarawak and Sabah. But, though this new federation got the racial arithmetic right, it did not cure Malay suspicion of Chinese ambitions and, after only a year of association, Singapore was asked to leave the Federation in August, 1965.

Among the many other problems separation threw up, defence was crucial. As a member of the Federation, Singapore had been protected not only by local old-Commonwealth forces, but also by the Federation's large, experienced but chiefly Malay, armed forces. The protection of the latter had gone and the indefinite presence of old-Commonwealth forces was not guaranteed. Singapore had therefore to begin to plan her own defence. There was virtually no military tradition among the population. The Singapore Volunteer Rifle Corps, the oldest voluntary force in the empire, had become by 1939 the Straits Settlements Volunteer Force, but it was a part-time body, based partly on the mainland and recruited from Europeans and Indians; the Chinese settlers preserved their traditional distaste for militarism. The Force was destroyed in the defence of the island in 1942 and not properly reformed until 1948. But it remained a small, local and chiefly voluntary body. During Federation a Federation Regiment had been formed, in an attempt to recruit Chinese, but it remained Malay dominated. On separation, Singaporean Chinese members of the Federal armed forces returned to Singapore and it was upon these, and the Volunteers (renamed in 1954 the Singapore Military Forces) that the new State's armed forces were built. National service was made obligatory in 1967, much thought given to the form of armed forces the conscripts should man, Israeli advisers invited to train them, and heavy investment made in the purchase of foreign equipment. Firmly democratic though the Republic is, its government is effectively one-party and socialist, and it was not surprising therefore that the government's original idea was to produce forces as popular as possible in character

— a militia rather than a regular army. Its thinking cannot have been uninfluenced, moreover, by the Chinese military renaissance and the egalitarian spirit of the Chinese Peoples' Army which had brought it about. The status of officers was therefore minimised and many hopes stored in the development of a part-time citizen volunteer force (the People's Defence Force) to provide the numbers the defence of the island required, without putting the State in thrall to its own guardians. Little has been said explicitly, but the impression is that thinking has changed, perhaps as a result of Israeli advice. A 'people's army' requires space and time if its operations are to be successful, and Singapore has neither. The Singapore Armed Forces have therefore evolved on more conventional lines.

STRENGTH AND BUDGET

Population (1982): 2,400,000
Army: 35,000 (120,000 reserves)
Navy: 3000; 22 small craft
Air force: 4000; 93 combat aircraft
Police and paramilitary forces: 37,500
GNP (1981): $26,300,000,000
Defence expenditure (1981): $1,500,000,000

COMMAND AND CONSTITUTIONAL STATUS

Singapore is a parliamentary republic with cabinet government. The President, elected by parliament for a 4 year term, is titular Commander-in-Chief. Executive authority is vested in the Minister of Defence, a civilian member of parliament, who is answerable to it. Defence debates are held regularly. The Ministry of Defence oversees the unified armed forces and is divided into general staff, manpower, logistics and intelligence divisions. Until 1970 it was combined with the Ministry of the Interior, which is now responsible for the Vigilante Corps as well as the police.

ROLE, COMMITMENT, DEPLOYMENT AND RECENT OPERATIONS

The role of the Singapore Armed Forces is defence of the frontiers, maintenance of internal security and youth training. Two other roles have been hinted at: the concrete one of seizing and holding Singapore's water supplies on the Malaysian mainland in the event of a hostile regime coming to power in that country, and the intangible one of assuring actual and potential investors and traders, both native and foreign, on whom Singapore as a mercantile City-State depends for a living, that its resources cannot be seized by *coup de main*. As the Prime Minister told students at Nayang University in 1969, 'Without adequate security forces of our own to make a significant contribution to joint security arrangements, investment may slow down. If people believe that we are weak and defenceless, even our own wealthy citizens will move part of their capital abroad.'

At the time he spoke, Singapore was the beneficiary of a bilateral defence agreement between Malaysia and Britain which put Singapore under the protection of British armed forces and stationed units from each of them inside her territory. This agreement was subsequently replaced by the Five-Nation Defence Agreement of 1971 (Britain–Australia–New Zealand–Malaysia–Singapore) which extended weaker guarantees and reduced the size of the Old Commonwealth force deployed on Singaporean territory. Originally the ANZUK brigade, of one Australian, one New Zealand and one British battalion, even that has now been reduced to a shadow. In the aftermath of the disengagement from Vietnam, Australia withdrew her battalion, while Britain withdrew hers in March, 1976 in pursuance of the 'withdrawal from East of Suez' policy, determined for economic reasons. New Zealand maintains her infantry battalion and an air-transport squadron, and Australia two fighter squadrons, which are integrated in the Air-Defence System for Malaysia and Singapore set up by the 1971 agreement. The crucial clause of that agreement reads 'In the event of any form of armed attack externally organised or supported or the threat of such attack against Malaysia or Singapore, (the five) governments would immediately consult together for the purpose of deciding what measures would be taken jointly or separately in relation to such attack or threat'. Singapore thus still enjoys the benefits of an external defence commitment rather than participating actively in one, but some observers doubt the value of the five-power agreement as an effective guarantee, reading the clause to mean that the old-Commonwealth governments would require a joint appeal from Singapore and Malaysia before feeling free to act in their defence. Because of the nature of Singaporean–Malaysian relations, Malaysia might not join in the appeal if the external threat were directed against Singapore alone.

Singapore's armed forces are deployed exclusively within her own territory, the 55 islands of Singapore. The two senior Singaporean battalions, then forming part of the Malaysian Federal Armed Forces, served in Borneo during the confrontation with Indonesia, but independent Sinagpore's armed forces have not taken part in any operations.

ORGANISATION

Since 1968, the Singapore Armed Forces have been a unified service, divided into Territorial, Maritime and Air-Defence Commands, which correspond to the army, navy and air force. The latter are small, though Air-Defence Command has 93 combat aircraft, including 35 Hunter and 37 A-4 fighter–ground attack aircraft and 21 F-5 fighters.

Territorial Command oversees the regular forces, the reserves and the People's Defence Force, a volunteer part-time organisation. The regular forces consist of the Singapore Armoured Corps. Singapore Artillery, Singapore Engineers, Singapore Signals and the Singapore Infantry Regiment, of nine battalions. Operationally it is organised into the Armoured Brigade (of one tank, one reconnaissance and two APC battalions), the 1st Singapore Infantry Brigade (which commands the People's Defence Force) and the 2nd and 3rd Singapore Infantry Brigades (which command the regular units: (9 infantry battalions, six artillery battalions, six engineer battalions and one signal battalion). The People's Defence Force consists of six infantry 3 engineer and six artillery battalions. Two air-defence missile squadrons belong to the Air-Defence Command.

RECRUITMENT, TRAINING AND RESERVES

The army, which has been deliberately modelled upon the Israeli, and trained by Israeli officers, is designed to consist of an active element, led by a small regular cadre and manned by national servicemen, and a much larger reserve element. It

appears that originally the People's Defence Force was intended to take charge of the reserves, but the two are now apparently distinct.

National service, which as in Israel is designed to create a sense of common nationhood among disparate groups – here Chinese, Malays and Indians – was fully introduced in 1967 and is a universal obligation on all fit males aged eighteen. The term of service is comparatively long, from 24 to 36 months. National servicemen are trained in the School of Basic Military Training. Officers and NCOs are trained at the Singapore Armed Forces Training Institute, Jurong, which also contains a School of Advance Training for Officers, in effect a staff college. Regular officers are also trained abroad, at the Australian and British military academies and staff colleges. The People's Defence Force has its own training centre.

Army reservists now number 45,000 and there are 18 reserve battalions. National service can also be performed in the police and the Vigilante Corps, set up at the beginning of the confrontation with Indonesia, which is now a civil defence organisation. Their ex-national servicemen become their reservists.

EQUIPMENT AND ARMS INDUSTRY

There is a small arms ammunition factory at Jurong. Other military equipment is imported, from Britain, America, Israel, France and Sweden. The basic small arm is the American M-16 Armalite rifle, and its machine-gun derivatives.

The artillery is equipped with the American 155mm howitzer (30 in service), the American M-40 recoilless rifle (60 in service) and the Israeli 120mm mortar. The armoured corps has French AMX-13 light tanks (200 in service, bought from Israel), American M-113 APCs (500 in service) and V-200 Commando armoured cars, made by Cadillac Gage (450 in service).

The air-defence squadrons are equipped with the British Bloodhound and Rapier missiles.

RANK, DRESS AND DISTINCTIONS

There is a common uniform (dark green) for all branches of the armed forces, which use army ranks. These follow the British system and are indicated for officers by a combination of stars and the Singaporean lion crest.

CURRENT DEVELOPMENTS

For its size, the army element of the Singapore Armed Forces is one of the best forces in south-east Asia, well armed and well trained. Defence spending per capita ($US170 in 1975–6) is among the highest in Asia, and has contributed significantly both to the external imbalance of payments and internal inflation, which are besetting problems of the State. It is the government's judgement, however, that Singapore is a commercially credible entity only if it demonstrates its ability to defend itself, even though the exact nature of the military threat it might face is not spelled out. Against anything but a major attack by a foreign power, the Singapore army appears to offer a convincing defence. In local military terms, Singapore is a great power, having both the money to buy a comparatively large armoured force, and the skills to man and maintain the vehicles. It is significant that the navy has seven tank landing ships which give the armed forces the ability to deploy armour in the amphibious role in the Malay Archipelago.

John Keegan

SOLOMON ISLANDS

The Solomon Islands, which received their independence from Britain in July, 1978, are two parallel chains of mountainous islands (with some outlying coral atolls) extending south-east of Papua—New Guinea, with a population of about 215,000 people. The six major islands of Choiseul, New Georgia, Santa Isabel, Guadalcanal, Malaita and San Cristobal contain over three-quarters of the population, and one island alone, Malaita, has almost a third. The country's total area is about the same as Belgium's, but spread across an area of sea larger than western Europe.

The population of the main islands, some 90% of the whole, is Melanesian; that of the coral atolls is Polynesian. There are small Micronesian, Chinese and European minorities. English is the official language and Pidgin English the *lingua franca*, but some 40 different languages and dialects are in use. Until the middle nineteenth century there was chronic inter-island warfare, accompanied by headhunting, and in the latter part of the century the islands were extensively raided by 'blackbirders' seeking labour for the Queensland and Fiji sugar plantations.

The Solomon Islands came under British rule between 1893 and 1900 and the population was almost wholly converted to Christianity. Very little development took place until World War II, however, when the area was the scene of intensive fighting between United States and Japanese forces in 1942–3. The former capital, Tulagi, was destroyed, and both the international airport and the new capital and principal port, Honiara, on the island of Guadalcanal, owe their existence to the construction work of the United States forces.

Modest economic development began after the war, concentrated on fish, timber, copra and minerals. The islands are lightly populated with the exception of Malaita, and although most inhabitants live outside a cash economy there is little real deprivation. For almost 15 years after the war the island of Malaita was effectively beyond British administrative control, dominated by an anti-British movement known as 'Marching Rule' (a corruption of *Ma'asina* — brotherhood), a cargo cult which believed that if the British were expelled American ships bearing cigarettes, chocolate and much else would reappear over the horizon. Following the suppression of Marching Rule local councils were created, initiating a process which culminated in the establishment of internal self-government by a Council of Ministers answerable to an elected Legislative Assembly in January, 1976. The remaining British responsibility for foreign affairs, defence and internal security was transferred to Prime Minister Peter Kenilorea's government on independence in July, 1978.

The principal security force under British rule was the Solomon Islands Police Force, and for the moment at least this force of some 350 men continues to function as the sole instrument for defence and internal security. It operates in a gendarmerie role, and would be the only paramilitary force available to deal with attempted insurrection or secession.

The SIPF was always recruited from indigenous Solomon Islanders so far as was possible, but the scarcity of qualified men resulted in most of its officers being British, and many of its enlisted ranks being recruited from the Fiji Islands. These foreigners are now being replaced by Solomon Islanders as rapidly as possible. Training for all ranks is provided at the Police Training School in Honiara, but numbers of officer candidates have also been sent abroad to training establishments in Britain, Papua—New Guinea and Fiji. All officers are promoted from the ranks. Working uniforms are khaki shirt and shorts, blue beret and black sandals; ceremonial dress is a white tunic, blue *sulu* (short sarong) and black sandals. A red sash and superimposed black belt are worn with both uniforms.

The country is divided into four zones for political administration, to which the SIPF districts correspond: Western District (Choiseul Island and the Shortland and New Georgia groups, headquarters Gizo Island); Eastern District (Santa Cruz and San Cristobal, headquarters Kirakira on the latter island); Malaita District (Malaita, Sikaiana and Ontong Java Atoll, headquarters, Auki on Malaita); and Central District (Santa Isabel, Guadalcanal, Bellona, Rennell, and the Russell and Florida groups, headquarters Honiara).

The main security problem confronting the country is actual and potential secessionist movements. The strongest such movement is in the Western District, whose 45,000 inhabitants feel themselves both different (they are considerably darker than other Solomon Islanders), and culturally and ethnically superior. They also feel victimised, in that the Western District is by far the most commercially developed region of the country and contributes the greater part of government revenue, but receives a much smaller proportion of government expenditure. Both this secessionist movement and other less-widely supported ones draw added vigour from resentment at the domination of the central government by Malaitans. It may be doubted whether the SIPF at its present strength could contain a serious attempt by the Western District to break away, and there has been some talk of expanding it.

Gwynne Dyer

SOMALIA

HISTORY AND INTRODUCTION

The Somali Democratic Republic attained independence in 1960. Having been divided by Britain and Italy in the colonial period, the two former colonies were merged to form one territory. After a restless period of civilian political government, the army staged a coup in 1969, placing a Supreme Military Council headed by Major-General Muhammad Siyad Barre in power.

Somalia's national problems are unique in sub-Saharan Africa. Unlike the vast majority of black African States, Somalia is a nation – a country of one homogenous ethnic group with its own traditions, culture and language. But sections of the Somali nation lie outside the frontiers drawn by Britain, France, Italy and Ethiopia: the Somalis claim that north-east Kenya, Djibouti and the Haud and Ogaden areas of Ethiopia are also part of the Somali nation. While an overall Somali ethnic homogeneity, Islam, and a national resentment over Somali areas apparently lost contributes at one level to unity; at another level the Somali state is unfortunately an arena in which the rivalries of the major Somali clans compete, sometimes with violence. There are six major clans; of these the two Sab clans, Rahanwin and Digil are less important than the four Sameli, the Dir of the north-west, the Isaq of the north, the Darod of the main hinterland, and the Hawiye of the coast: the Darod amount to some 25% of the total population, and are at times prone to quarrel amongst themselves, two sub-clans the Marehan and the Mijerteyn in particular being opposed to each other. The Somali temperament, evolved in harsh climatic conditions where feuds over water and grazing can flash up very quickly, is one disposed to blood-feuds and vendettas. The July 1960 independence government, in broad terms, reflected a southern domination, of Hawiye and Darod, changes in political balances in the years before the 1969 coup had the effect of bringing more northerners, Dir and Isaq into the government but at the same time splitting the Darod. In terms of formal political life the changes led to so great an expansion of the ruling party that it declined to being simply a stage in which competing factions strove for ascendancy in an atmosphere of increasing sectarian particularism, nepotism and corruption, eventually culminating in the assassination of the President, Shirmake, shortly before the coup.

The head of the incoming military regime, General Siyad Barre, saw 'scientific socialism' imposed with great severity as the solution to the problems of Somalia's divisions. In clan terms the coup represented a Darod reassertion. Barre's ideological preference led him to friendship with Soviet Union, which initially welcomed the opportunity for influence in a strategically important area of the world. By a treaty of 1974 an era of close co-operation appeared to have begun, with considerable Soviet development and military assistance and in return, Somali permission for the establishment of Soviet air and maritime reconnaissance facilities. These were duly opened in several Somali towns, Berbera and Mogadishu (including the Uanle Uen airfield and radar surveillance at Agfoi), airfields at Hargeisa and Galcao, and marine installations at Birikao and certain off-shore islands. The Somali government nevertheless firmly denied the existence of these installations.

In 1977–78 Somalia, in pursuit of its historic claims and in the belief that Ethiopia had been enfeebled by revolution, sponsored an assault to regain the lost Haud and Ogaden territories; the possibility that the Soviets might decide Ethiopia was more important to Moscow than Somalia appears not to have occurred to them. The operations were entrusted to a 'West Somalia Liberation Front' (WSLF), which by its equipment and training appears to have been largely selected units and personnel of the Somali army under an alias. Another 'Abo Liberation Front' operated in south Ethiopia, and was also a largely Somali army force. The WSLF, clearly meeting with mass popular approval in the Ogden, took the town of Jijiga and advanced to the gates of Harar. Here it was held in check, Cuban reinforcements and Soviet-led Ethiopian units were brought to the area and in February–March, 1978 the Somalis were ejected, suffering severe losses in both manpower and equipment. The out-of-date Soviet equipment, poorly maintained and used in the hands of poorly-trained Somali soldiers or insurgents proved no match for the Cubans and the Soviet-trained Ethiopians with more up-to-date and better-serviced armour and artillery. The Somalis appear to have suffered particularly severely at the hands of the Ethiopian air force, although it must remain in doubt as to how many of this air force's pilots were actually Ethiopian. The shattered Somali forces withdrew in disorder back into Somalia harried from the air until they had re-crossed the border, and on a few occasions bombed within Somalia itself as a further admonishment. Clan vendettas among the senior Somali officers led to divided counsels and confusion.

The catastrophe, and the destruction of much of Somalia's military capacity, had initially a temporary unifying effect on the Somalis; anger also terminated the Soviet alliance. Somalia turned to the West, in particular to the USA, Egypt and Saudi Arabia (Somalia, somewhat surprisingly, is a member of the Arab League). American use of Somali facilities replaced that of the departing Soviets who had never been popular. For the Americans, Somalia is a useful link in the Rapid Deployment Force chain.

In internal political terms, the catastrophe soon began to undermine Barre's position. After the brief rallying to the cause factions began to appear attributing blame for the disaster on to Barre, whose position was additionally worsened by economic difficulties and growing popular resentment against the severely authoritarian nature of his rule. Barre's first response was an attempt to place a legal wig on the point of his sword by returning Somalia to 'civilian rule' in the form of a rubber stamp parliament the members of which are all drawn from the party formed in 1976 by Barre himself, the Somali Revolutionary Socialist Party, (SRSP). This limited form of civilian rule very far from defused the mounting internal political crisis, which began to assume a military form receiving support from Somali opponents of Barre resident in and supported by Ethiopia and South Yemen.

The first manifestation of this militant opposition was as early as April 1978, when a group of officers almost entirely drawn from the Darod Mijerteyn sub-clan were exposed by Barre, himself a Marehan Darod, as planning a coup, seventeen were executed. A 'Somali Salvation Front'

(SOSAF) opened in Addis Ababa, also largely Mijerteyn and including a number of officers. Other groups have opened in London and elsewhere since.

Barre, increasingly under pressure, suspended his newly-recreated legislature and reappointed a Supreme Revolutionary Council, almost entirely military officers, in 1980, at the same time declaring a state of emergency. Key appointments in the Council were given to Marehan close associates of Barre, notably the appointment of Barre's son-in-law General Ahmed Suleiman, to be in charge of the security apparatus. Early in 1982 fresh indications of discontent were evident, with mutinies and defections of officers to SOSAF in several northern-based military units: a number of officers and men were also executed for supposedly supporting other exiled opposition groups. Riots in Hargeisa, in which a number of people were killed, also aroused bitter recrimination. In yet another move to try and recapture some popular (and also United States) goodwill, Barre released one of the former prime ministers from the pre-coup era from prison and reappointed one of Somalia's most capable officers, Lieutenant-General Mohammed Ali Samantar, as Minister for Defence. Samantar had been one of Barre's closest collaborators in his earlier more successful years of rule, but had been *limogé*, probably for being too capable and well-respected for Barre's own comfort.

In 1981 the SOSAF amalgamated with another left-wing exile organisation to form the Somali Salvation Democratic Front (SSDF); the SSDF also benefited from a gift of weaponry from Libya. It remains a largely Mijerteyn-run organisation though other northerners are also included, and it was effectively reinforced in 1982 by the defection to it of an important Somali army general.

STRENGTH AND BUDGET

The population of Somalia is estimated to be about 4,000,000; it has recently been inflated by Somali refugees who, having supported the WSLF in the 1977—78 campaign, have felt it no longer safe to live in Ethiopia. A figure of between 4—4,500,000 is therefore the best available.

The Army — in theory — totals some 60,000, with an air force of 2000, a police force of 8000, a border guard force of 1500 and a People's Militia of anything up to 20,000.

No figures in respect of GNP or Defence Expenditure are available.

COMMAND AND CONSTITUTIONAL STATUS

Initially the military government ruled through a 19-member Supreme Military Council, of which Major General Muhammad Siyad Barre was President; he also held the appointment of Commander-in-Chief. With the return of 'civilian rule' and also after its suspension Barre retained his offices as head of state and commander-in-chief (together with that of Secretary General of the SRSP). In 1982, Lieutenant General Mohammed Ali Samantar became Minister for Defence in the emergency following the northern mutinies and riots.

ROLE, COMMITMENT DEPLOYMENT AND RECENT OPERATIONS

The disasters of 1977—78 and the emerging military challenge of the SSDF have already been outlined. At present two divisions of the Somali Army are deployed containing twin SSDF thrusts along Somalia's long western border. The 4th Division is operating in the thin 'waist' area of the Ogaden,

the President's Marehan home area, where the SSDF have occupied two towns, Balambale and Goldogob; the 5th Division operates further south in the Belet Uen area. The SSDF appear to have cut the main Mogadishu-Hargeisa road, a vital highway. The Somali divisions do not appear to have the capacity to eject the SSDF, the latter supported as they are by very powerful Ethiopian contingents. Indeed some reports state that the SSDF are limited by a reconnaissance role only and that the other 'units' are Ethiopian regulars, up to 15,000 in strength with artillery and armour. The SSDF may well pursue a joint campaign of attrition of the Somali Army at the front together with a guerilla campaign behind the front line in the hope of destablising Barre. The Somali commander, General Yusuf Ahmed Salhan, is handicapped by very limited anti-tank gun and missile capacity and virtually no anti-aircraft capacity to counter the strikes of Ethiopia's MiG 21 and MiG 23s. The SSDF claim that to mid-August, the Somali Army had lost 2500 dead with a further 4000 wounded and 300 captured, together with a further 1800 deserted. They also claim to have destroyed sixty armoured vehicles and two MiG-19 aircraft. These claims may not be greatly exaggerated.

ORGANISATION

The formal organisation of the Somalia army provides in theory for an army of three army corps of seven divisions, built up from three armoured brigades, twenty infantry brigades, a surface-to-air missile brigade, a commando brigade, and thirteen field and ten anti-aircraft artillery battalions. Even before the 1977—78 Ogaden campaign, the establishments were larger than the force that could actually be put into the field. The position now will have worsened.

The People's Militia or Gulwadayasha (Pioneers of Victory) is in a sense an internal security reserve; political loyalty and militancy are its bases and its duties include surveillance of, and reporting upon, political dissidents. To ensure security still further, a National Security Service also exists; Soviet KGB officers were reported to be attached to this organisation at one time. The force was mobilised early in 1977, but does not appear to have been committed. It includes women's units.

EQUIPMENT AND ARMS INDUSTRY

Reports on the quantities of Soviet military equipment delivered to Somalia are as varied as the reports on the serviceability of much of this equipment. Reports on the deliveries of replacement equipment after the 1977—78 catas-trophe are confusing. What follows is therefore largely an estimate.

The Somali Army probably has some 60 elderly T-34, forty T-54/55 and 40 Centurion tanks in service, together with 50 BRDM-2 and some 120 BTR-40 — 60 and a further 100 BTR-152 armoured personnel carriers. Post 1977—78 replacements have included unspecified numbers of V-150 Commando and (perhaps 200) Fiat 6614 vehicles.

The artillery includes about 180 assorted Soviet 76mm, 85mm, 100mm, 122mm and 152mm guns and BM-21 rocket launchers, together with 81mm and 120mm mortars, 106mm recoilless weapons and a small number of Milan, RPG-7 and type 69 anti-tank guided missile equipments. Anti-aircraft weaponry includes uncertain numbers of a range of Soviet anti-aircraft fire power, 14.5mm, 23mm, 37mm, 57mm, and 100mm guns, approximately a dozen tracked ZSU-23/4 guns, and some 30 SAM-2 Guideline and SAM-3 Goa surface to air missiles. Ammunition is critically short for the guns and many of the missiles may not be in operational order.

On paper, the air force can muster only one light bomber squadron of three Ilyushin 28 Beagle bombers; three fighter squadrons with between them seven MiG-21 and thirty Chinese built MiG-19 (F.6) aircraft; three air-to-ground strike squadrons of which two possess nine MiG-17s and one six Siai Marchetti SF-260 Warrior propeller-driven machines; a transport squadron of nine medium transports, some Soviet Antonov 24 or 26s, three C-47s and four Aeritalia G-222s; a helicopter squadron of four Mi-4 (Hound), two Mi-8 (Hip), one Agusta-Bell 204 and two Agusta-Bell 212 helicopters; and a training unit of six Piaggio 148 primary trainers and two MiG-15s. On order are said to be nine further SF 260 Warriors, a number of the more advanced jet Siai Marchetti 211 machines, two Piaggio P166 light transports and two further AB-212 helicopters.

The police force possesses two Dornier DO-28 liaison aircraft.

Probably only a small proportion of the aircraft are in anything approaching a combat effective state. Spare parts and trained personnel are often non-existent.

RECRUITMENT, TRAINING AND RESERVES

Members of the very large Darod clan were preponderant in the military hierarchy in 1969, but the rapid expansion of the Somali army appears to have reduced this. Recruitment until 1982 was voluntary; the majority comes from the Sameli group of clans, the Sab being disadvantaged. A small number of women serve in the Army. In 1982 compulsory recruitment of young men in the north and in the Mogadishu area was reported; this compulsory recruitment may have, however, had political rather than military causes – the removal from the streets of disaffected young men.

At independence Somalia possessed a very small, poorly trained and equipped army. The officers of this army had been trained in Britain, Egypt and Italy; a group of these, from the north, staged an abortive coup in 1961. After the military coup, however, the army was expanded and modernised with the help of Russian and Cuban military and political instructors. A very large number of Somali military personnel were sent to the USSR for training. It was never possible with certainty to distinguish, in terms of numbers, between those Soviet military, air and naval personnel posted to specific Soviet military bases in Somalia and those whose primary duties were the training of Somalis.

Training of recruits, originally a six months' programme, has been recently reduced to three months. Professional efficiency will therefore suffer. Chinese instructors have been trying to train aircrews, and are reported to have experienced very limited success only.

RANK, DRESS AND DISTINCTIONS

Normal uniform is of a light-grey colour; its style follows the Italian pattern.

CURRENT DEVELOPMENTS

These need to be considered at two levels. At the international level the USA, like the USSR, is more interested in Ethiopia than in Somalia. The USA's August 1982 supply of weaponry to Somalia (two airlifts including some armoured personnel carriers equipped with TOW anti-tank missiles, M-16 rifles, battlefield radar, signals and transport equipment) fell short of Somalia's hopes both in quantity and in nature – no anti-aircraft weaponry was included. This limitation probably reflects the USA's wishes to preclude any Somali adventurism and limit the country's capability to simply one of survival, and by this moderation secure a peaceful withdrawal of the Ethiopians from Somalia and the Cubans and Soviets from Ethiopia. Barre himself is not fully trusted in the USA, and his policies and actions cause frequent embarrassment.

Other Western and Arab nations have been similarly cautious and restrained for much the same reasons.

Ethiopia, using the SSDF, could topple Barre and may in fact proceed to do so in the hope of installing a pro-Soviet and pro-Ethiopian regime in Mogadishu — and also to distract attention from Ethiopia's own internal economic and insurgency problems. However, Ethiopia may also realise that a military thrust capable of toppling Barre might no longer be one that could be presented simply as SSDF to Africa and the rest of the world, and Ethiopia might incur odium for intervention.

At the front where Somali army units oppose the SSDF and their Ethiopian patrons, morale is said to be very low, with deficiencies in all essential items from ammunition to boots.

Opponents and critics of Barre alike may well believe an answer to the problem will arise from an internal upheaval in Somalia itself. This might take the form of a replacement of Barre by Samantar, of an uprising by army junior leaders, or by a political street revolution. Somalia's domestic story is a wretched one the increasing despotism of the Barre regime has already been outlined. To many it appears that all that Barre can offer to a country distracted by ever worsening economic problems and burdened with over a million starving refugees is a personality cult suggesting he is one in a line of Somali militant nationalists, a true descendant of Mohamed Abdille Hassan, the 'Mad Mullah' of the early years of this century.

It seems safe to predict only that Somalia's national ethos, the heady mixture of socialism, Islam, irredentist nationalism and inter-clan fighting will continue for the forseeable future. The events of 1977–78 are an excellent illustration of the drug-like effects of this mixture. Barre almost certainly was opposed to the venture, but found himself under such clan and irredentist pressure that to survive he found action inescapable. The country will probably never prosper until at least the latter two ingredients of its ethos, irredentism and clan rivalries, have in some way been cooled.

Lloyd Mathews

ADDENDUM

Intermittent fighting continues in the Ogaden. The Somali Army appears to have stopped a major thrust by the SSDF in September in the Goldogobs area, the Army claims to have inflicted over 200 casualties on the SSDF. A lull followed until late November when a further clash occurred, the SSDF claiming on this occasion to have killed 34 Somali soldiers for the loss of 10 of their own men.

SOUTH AFRICA

HISTORY AND INTRODUCTION

The roots of the contemporary South African military system can be traced back through both the British and Afrikaner (Dutch) traditions to the earliest days of European colonisation at the Cape of Good Hope. Although the Dutch East India Company provided a small number of troops to garrison the Cape, their function was seen as that of defence against external threat, and in particular, against possible attack by other European powers. However by 1657, five years after the initial settlement by Van Riebeck, it became necessary to raise a force for protection against attack from internal indigenous enemies. Thus began a specific South African contribution to military history.

In 1657 a militia was formed from the free, adult, male Burghers of the Cape for protection against marauding Hottentots and Bushmen. Service in the militia was compulsory and by 1762 included periods of annual training for both foot and mounted units, though organisation did not extend to equipment, for Burghers paraded in their best clothes and provided their own weapons.

Inevitably, organisation and structure were somewhat *ad hoc* in the early years, but one important transitory feature was the practice of Burghers electing their own officers. In the following decades as Burgher settlement moved tentatively inland, a new unit of defence was created — the Commando, a highly mobile force, ultimately to be used against a variety of diverse opponents including Hottentots, Bantu-speaking peoples, and not least, the British. Like the Burgher militia from which it evolved, the Commando system was based on the principle of compulsory service, though in addition often included the non-white servants of the Commandos. (A continuing theme in South African history has been the ever-changing attitude on the part of the Afrikaner to the use of non-white troops, especially in a combatant role.)

Throughout the following two centuries or more, until Union in 1910, South African military history is characterised by a complex mosaic of interaction and warfare between the various peoples of the region. On the one hand this is exemplified by the almost constant battles between black and white in the various frontier and 'Kaffir' wars, essentially being conflicts of territorial expansion and defence, whilst on the other, less frequent but often more bloody struggles within racial groups, culminating with the 2nd Boer War of 1899–1902. During this period the military traditions of the Boer or Afrikaners and the British became even more distinct, the Boers refining their fast-raiding commando tactics in the decades after the Great Trek (1834) in both the Orange Free State and the South African (Transvaal) Republic, whilst in the main the Cape and Natal retained the British system (and British troops) of voluntarism, the Drill Book and strict march discipline. In the final analysis neither tradition has proved individually sufficient and the legacies of both remain within the present South African Defence Force.

The formation of the Union of South Africa in 1910 inevitably foreshadowed the creation of specifically South African armed forces to replace the Imperial garrison of 30,000 although at the request of the new Prime Minister, General Botha, the latter were not finally withdrawn until the onset of World War I in 1914. After discussion with the British government, a Union Defence Force was established by the Defence Act of 1912. From the outset the permanent force was fairly small (2500 mounted police in five regiments and five batteries of artillery), but to be supplemented by a much larger reserve of some 25,000 formed into an active citizen force of embryonic regiments and men formed into rifle associations. This latter group satisfied the desires of those who hankered after the old Commando system, abolished by the British in 1902, as did the stipulation that military service was intended to be compulsory. (Provision at this time was also made for coastal defence, a small branch of the RNVR and a Flying Corps.)

In the period since Union the South African Defence Force (SADF) has been used operationally on a variety of occasions, at times amidst great controversy, particularly in terms of participation in World Wars I and II. In both instances strongly Republican elements within the Afrikaner community opposed entry in support of Britain, in 1914 resulting in a brief mutiny of senior generals. Non-white troops were used in both wars, combatant in World War I, non-combatant in World War II. Elsewhere the armed forces were used to quell a strike on the Witwatersrand in 1922 whilst later air force squadrons were involved in both the Berlin Airlift and the Korean War.

Since 1948 South African political life has been dominated by the National Party who have won every general election in that period. Committed in their early years to Republicanism (achieved in 1961) and to an ideology of apartheid or racial separation, these policies have been of signal importance in the development of the SADF and defence policy.

STRENGTH AND BUDGET

Strength

In the period from the Korean War until 1960 the South African Defence Force had very limited manpowers, a small budget, little or no serious role and was almost wholly dependent upon the United Kingdom. However in 1960, the year of the Sharpeville incident, the South African government came to recognise that the force of African Nationalism, both internally and on the wider African continent, might pose serious security problems. In recent years these fears have been fully realised. At the same time the government claimed that the strategic position of South Africa, its vast mineral reserves and its commitment to anti-communism, made it both a target for and a buffer against, Soviet expansionism in the region. Consequently the last 20 years has seen an enormous rise in the manpower, capability and budget of the SADF.

Total Population:
29,681,000 (including the 'Homelands').
Whites 4,400,000 (15%); Coloureds (Mixed Race): 3,600,000 (8.9%); Asians: 800,000 (2.7%); Black Africans: 21,800,000 (73.4%).

South Africa

Army:
70,000. Made up of approximately 10,000 white regulars (Permanent Force, PF), 5—7000 Black PF, 2000 white women and between 50—60,000 conscripts on two year tours. *See* Black Forces and National Service, below.

Reserves:
Citizen Force (CF): 130,000; Commandos: 100,000; plus rifle clubs, women's pistol clubs and a Cadet Force in over 600 schools. Virtually all reserves are white. *See* Citizen Force and Commandos below.

Police (1981)
White 18,370.
'Black' (including Coloured andAsian) 15,901.
Active Reserve 21,500 (of which over 18,000 are white).

In 1981 there was a shortfall of 24% on the Regular Police establishment. In the same year about 150 Blacks held commissioned rank and three had reached the level of Lt Colonel. In recent years Black Police have been armed.

Many police are trained in paramilitary techniques and some have been used specifically in that role, particularly in Rhodesia (as Volunteers) and in the Caprivi Strip, as well as in African townships. Legislation in 1980 gave authority for police to be deployed outside the Republic.

South African Navy

Permanent Force	3200
Marines	1900
National Service	1500
Reserves	2000

South African Air Force

Permanent Force	9000
National Service	1000
Reserves	25000

Budget
For selected, post-war years, the budget is as shown in the next column.

The 1977 budget was reduced in retrospect because France refused to confirm sales of warships to South Africa. The funds for this purchase were added to the 1978—9 estimates. Figures from 1975—6 to 1981—2 reflect total defence expenditure as indicated in South African Defence White Papers. It indicates, for instance, the sale of Defence Bonds to the general public.

The Defence Budget for recent years broke down in the following manner: (Quantities quoted are in millions of Rand)

Year	Amount (millions Rand)	As % of GNP	As % of of budget
1948	23		
1952—3	47		
1959—60	29		
1960—61	45		
1961—2	72		
1963—4	150		
1964—5	217		
1969—70	271	2.3	16.0
1972—3	335	2.1	11.8
1973—4	472	2.6	13.5
1974—5	692	3.2	16
1975—6	1043	4.1	15
1976—7	1408	4.9	17
1977—8	1940	5.1	19.0
1978—9	1976	4.2	16.3
1979—80	2189	4.5	16.6
1980—81	2074		
1981—2	2603		16.0
1982—3	3068		

COMMAND AND CONSTITUTIONAL STATUS

Constitutionally the Commander-in-Chief of the SADF is President of the Republic, though in practice the executive functions are the responsibility of the Prime Minister and the Minister of Defence. The State Security Council coordinates internal and external security matters. At the time of writing (January 1983) South Africa seems likely to introduce an executive Presidential system which may alter these relationships. The SADF is lead by a tri-service Chief of the SADF (presently General C. L. Viljoen). Although the formal position of the military remains as above, i.e. subordinate to the civil authority, their influence in government and policy making has risen appreciably in recent years. This is due in part to the rising threat to South African security and the growth of the SADF to meet this threat and at the personality level to the fact that the Prime Minister, P. W. Botha was Defence Minister from 1966 until 1980 and replaced himself in that role by the forceful Chief of SADF General Magnus Molan (who retired from the Army to enter Parliament).

	1978—79	1978—80	1980—81	1981—82
Command and Control	170.2	180.1	221.2	247.3
Landward Defence	1008.9	1134.9	1032.7	1293.6
Air Defence	90.5	74.2	42.3	62.4
Maritime Defence	111.5	127.5	111.7	128.4
General Training	71.4	80.1	68.5	100.26
Logistic Support	476.1	510.7	561.6	710.5
Personnel Support	43.8	78.8	32.0	52.9
General Support (Operating)	3.9	4.1	4.5	7.8
Total Costs				
Operating costs	1069.0	1152.8		
Fixed assets	907.3	1036.2		
Total expenditure	1976.3	2189.0	2074.5	2602.9

ROLE, COMMITMENT, DEPLOYMENT AND RECENT OPERATIONS

It has become commonplace to point out that in the last twenty or more years, South African foreign policy and defence policy have been moulded in the face of almost universal condemnation of the policy of apartheid, whilst at the same time South Africa has tried to convince the somewhat sceptical Western powers of her crucial strategic importance in any conflict with the Soviet Union.

In the years immediately after World War II the picture seemed less depressing for South African policy-makers. The Union had contributed significantly to the Allied War effort, and she was an important member of the Commonwealth. General Smuts had been instrumental in helping to create the United Nations, the Afro-Asian countries (later to be hostile to the very existence of the South African State) were not yet independent, and most crucially in terms of South Africa's perception of the world, her leaders were violently anti-communist. Consequently, South Africa had high hopes of playing a valued role in Western security arrangements. However, these aspirations were soon dashed. South Africa welcomed the creation of NATO (and also SEATO and ANZUS), but was disappointed that its treaty provisions did not cover the south Atlantic. The Union took part in defence conferences concerning the Middle East (MEDO Conference, June 1951) and in attempts to create some form of African defence community (Nairobi, 1951 and Dakar, 1954). All were abortive; the only positive arrangement which was negotiated was the 'Exchange of Letters on Defence Matters', of July 1955, the so-called Simonstown Agreement which was later subject to enormous controversy. The Simonstown Agreement was not even an alliance, containing little by way of specific reciprocal commitments, and concerned solely with the use of the Simonstown Base facilities and the limited sale by Britain to South Africa of naval equipment. The agreement was ended by a further exchange of letters in 1975.

During the 1960s, South Africa's isolated position was further excerbated by the growth of Afro-Asian power at the United Nations which resulted in December, 1963 in the Security Council calling on all member-states to ban arms sales to the Republic. Although never fully implemented by all countries, France being the most notable defaulter, the resolution did create enormous difficulties of supply, resulting in part in South Africa's decision to be a self-sufficient as possible in arms production.

Despite the diplomatic stagnation of the early 1960s South Africa's military build-up in that period enabled the Republic to contend that her defence role should be acknowledged as that of guardian of the south Atlantic against the 'menace' of communism. Whilst unable to form a South Atlantic Treaty Organisation (SATO), as she had hoped, the Republic's military and economic preponderance in the southern African region appeared to result in some success for the policy of accommodation towards African states to the north. (This policy, strands of which can be traced even to the era of Malan and Strydon in the early 1950s, has in recent years been called, synonymously, Dialogue, the Outward-Looking Movement and *Détente*.)

The role of the South African Defence Force must be seen in the context of the need to defend the Republic's internal policies against subversion, guerrilla warfare, or conventional warfare, and also in terms of the strategic considerations of Soviet penetration of the Indian Ocean. Whilst the military response to the two threats is essentially distinct, the South African army being concerned very little with the latter, the political implications are obviously interrelated, since the delicate question of apartheid inside South Africa, leading as

it does to the conventional and guerrilla threat, prevents the West utilising South Africa's geopolitical and strategic advantages to deter the perceived Soviet threat.

Until the middle 1970s, the landward defence of the Republic relied primarily on the existence of large buffer states to the north, either white-ruled, or, if black-governed, economically dependent on South Africa. Thus despite occasional internal unrest as a result of the policies of apartheid South Africa felt untroubled by military threat from neighbouring states. It was in this context that South African ministers regularly invoked the UN Charter requirement of non-interference in the internal affairs of other states as a means of deflecting criticism of her own domestic policies. However this period of relative tranquility came to an abrupt end with the coup in Lisbon in April 1974 and the consequential independence of Angola and Mozambique in 1975. At the same time South Africa found herself in a conumdrum over the escalating war in Rhodesia. On the one hand white South Africans felt a certain sympathy for Ian Smith's regime and the Republic gave aid to the Rhodesian government by means of sanctions and by provision of paramilitary police. However the war also destabilised the region and focused world attention on the conflict, both to the disadvantage of South Africa.

WAR IN SOUTHERN AFRICA, 1975–1983

South Africa and Angola 1975–6

It was as a consequence of these developments and as a response to the growth of SWAPO (South West African Peoples Organisation) activities that in June, 1975 the SADF took over responsibility for the security of the northern South West African/Namibian border from the South African Police.

Although the level of insurgency in the years before 1975 was comparatively low it was apparent that South Africa faced formidable security problems in Namibia, for as it is well known, even a small number of guerrillas can bottle up massively superior conventional forces. This is particularly true of northern Namibia where the border is over 1000 miles long, where SWAPO recruit most of their support (from the Ovambo) and where lines of communication and logistic support to South Africa itself stretch over inhospitable desert for nearly 1000 miles. These difficulties were magnified by the change of circumstances in the wake of the Lisbon coup when the Portuguese government announced that Angola would become independent in November, 1975. Clearly independence might imperil South Africa's economic interests in the Cunene River hydro-electric scheme in Southern Angola as well as providing a possible safe haven for SWAPO guerrillas but most important of all was the psychological impact on white South African attitudes of the prospect of a radical 'marxist' government in Luanda.

The military events of 1975–76 remain obscure and few accounts agree in detail.* Reports do agree that in mid-August 1975 South African Troops occupied the hydro-electric stations at Ruacana and Caluesque. On August 22nd a battalion strong South African force attacked Pereira d'Eca, 100 miles east of Cunene and in strategic terms unrelated to it. From about this time it seems that South Africa finally decided to support one nationalist movement UNITA (under the leadership of Jonas Savinbi) against the more dominant and radical MPLA (led by Agostinho Neto) and to install

---

* For the most informative account see *R. Hallet*, 'The South African Intervention in Angola 1975–6'. *African Affairs*, July 1978. See also I.D.A.F. *The Apartheid War Machine* (1980), P. Moorcraft, *Africa's Superpower* (1981).

UNITA and Savinbi in control in the capital Luanda by independence day, November 11th, 1975. A joint SADF/ UNITA force, code named Zulu occupied Pereira d'Eca on October 19th and then with armoured car and mortar reinforcement moved rapidly northwards and took Lobito and Benouela on November 7th. It was here that Zulu faced the formidable Soviet multiple rocket launchers, the 'Stalin Organ', which were to hold up the advance beyond the critical date of November 11th. A few days later Zulu continued its threat northward but was held and eventually repulsed by the MPLA, with Cuban regulars to the fore, at the Queve river.

Three other battle groups named Orange, Foxbat and X Ray, operated from mid-November in the central and east central regions of Angola. Each were combined SADF/UNITA forces. For the next two months something of a military stalemate ensued during which time intense diplomatic pressure on South Africa took its toll. The MPLA became widely recognised in Africa, South Africa was condemned by even the most conservative of African States and crucially United States and European support failed to materialise. By late January, 1976 all South African forces withdrew.

The precise role of the Cuban forces has been deliberately ignored in this brief review. South Africa regularly asserted that one major reason for her invasion was the presence of Cuban soldiers acting as proxy for the Soviet Union, but whilst it seems certain that some advisers were in Angola in early 1975, the bulk were airlifted in mid November, i.e. well after the South African intervention. However it also seems likely that heavy material support to the MPLA had already been committed by Cuba and was timed to arrive by sea for independence.

At the peak of her involvement there were probably about 2000 South African troops in Angola together with as many UNITA and mercenary troops and strong supporting armoured artillery. South Africa's reversal in Angola was primarily diplomatic rather than military and within the Republic the incursion is always described as a glorious victory over an enemy superior in number and sustained and led by the Cubans. Nevertheless the end result was the creation of a hostile government on Namibia's borders, a failure to deal a death blow to SWAPO bases, and some psychological damage to White South Africa with the death (of 33) and capture (of 4) of the soldiers.

Military Events 1976—82

Whilst the South African invasion of Angola in 1975—76 was the most significant military engagement in recent South African history it became the precursor for regular interventions into neighbouring states. To date the most important area of activity remains the Namibian/Angolan border where the political impasse in negotiations between South Africa and the UN has provided a favourable environment for the growth of SWAPO guerrilla activity. To counter this South Africa maintains as many as 30,000 soldiers in Namibia and in May, 1978 and March, 1979 launched large-scale airborne attacks on guerrilla bases in Angola. These attacks penetrated over 150 miles into Angola. SWAPO activity and attacks increased in 1980 but the movement exposed itself to very heavy casualities and in June, 1980 had its operational headquarters in Angola destroyed in another South African raid. As many as 200 SWAPO and 16 South African soldiers died in the raid. Over 1000 SWAPO members were killed in 1980.

In August, 1980 a separate SWA/Namibia Territorial Force was set up and in January, 1981 compulsory military service was introduced for all male Namibians, of whatever colour, aged 18—24. (Exemption was given to those living in the border area who were likely to support SWAPO.)

In August, 1981 South Africa launched Operation Protea into Angola; easily the largest incursion since 1976. A multi-pronged force attacked SWAPO bases, dashed 200 kilometres north to cut off the retreat of guerrilla forces and destroyed both a Soviet headquarters and an armoured column. In the latter attack two Soviet colonels were killed and a Soviet NCO captured. It is reported that hundreds of SWAPO and MPLA soldiers were killed and between 3—4000 tons of equipment captured, including at least 16 Soviet-built tanks.

Further raids took place in 1981 and 1982 although the overall scale of activity was somewhat lighter in 1982. South African sources claim that 1268 SWAPO guerrillas were killed in 1982 for the loss of 77 of their own men.

In the last two years South African politicians have regularly asserted their right to attack and destroy hostile forces wherever they are located. To this end preemptive strikes have been launched against bases in a number of neighbouring states in addition to Angola. In March 1978 legislation allowed the SADF to clear a 16 kilometre area around the Republic borders if security so required and in March 1981 control of part of South Africa's northern border was transferred from the police to the army.

In July 1977, the Deputy Commissioner for Police confirmed that a large police task force had been stationed along South Africa's borders with Botswana, Mozambique, Rhodesia and Swaziland to prevent infiltration of men who had left the country for military training. South African sources suggest that at least 4000 guerrillas are being trained abroad.

In January, 1981 South African forces entered Mozambique and attacked buildings used by members of the banned (in South Africa) African National Congress. A number of ANC members were killed. It is widely reported that South Africa is providing material aid for the anti-government movement, the Mozambique National Resistance (MNR) and that an MNR raid on a Mozambique oil depot in December, 1982 took place with the active participation of South African soldiers.

December, 1982 also witnessed a South African military attack on ANC bases near Maseru the capital of Lesotho, resulting in approximately 30 deaths. It is also reported that South African troops have been involved, if only on a small scale, in Swaziland and Zimbabwe.

ORGANISATION

Although consisting of the conventional services of army, navy and air force together with a separate South African Medical Service, the SADF is organised, particularly at its apex, on the basis of tri-service integration.

In recent years the organisation of landward defence has been restricted to meet the task of countering all forms of insurgency, whilst at the same time maintaining a credible conventional force. Since these two tasks are essentially distinct the army, and its reserve, has been subdivided into (a) a counter insurgency and counter terrorism force (COIN) and (b) a conventional force. Given the nature of counter insurgency in particular the likely length of operation and the need for specialised local knowledge the COIN force has been decentralised to nine territorial commands. Within this basic structure the army consists of a Permanent Force (with national servicemen under training), a Citizen Force (with reserves under training) and the specially tasked reserve force, the Commandos. Each command is staffed by Permanent Force members who provide the officers, NCOs and basic infrastructure and together with the conscripted National Servicemen are the ever present element of the SADF. Combining with these are reserve units of the Citizen Force and where appropriate the Commandos. Easily the most important of these Commandos is that of SWA/Namibia which was given separate status in 1980. Otherwise, the South African army is divided into 11 functional corps. There are: South African Artillery (Field Branch), Anti-Aircraft Artillery, Infantry, Armoured, Engineer, Signal, Technical Service, Administrative Service, Military Police, Intelligence and Women. In 1979 a separate Parachute Brigade was formed from existing units. Its role is that of a Quick Reaction Force.

Table 1 provides details in order of battle of the Divisional and Territorial structure of the South African Army. Recent changes to the Commandos and Army expansion may make elements of this out of date.

TABLE 1

Order of battle of the army

DIVISIONAL STRUCTURES

7th Division (Johannesburg)

71st Motorised Brigade (Cape Town):
    Cape Town Highlanders (Cape Town)
    Cape Town Rifles (Cape Town)
    Western Provinces Regiment (Stellenbosch)
72nd Motorised Brigade (Johannesburg):
    Johannesburg Regiment (Johannesburg)
    1st Battalion Transvaal Scottish (Johannesburg)
    2nd Battalion Transvaal (Johannesburg)
73rd Motorised Brigade (Vereening):
    Rand Light Infantry (Johannesburg)
    Regiment Louw Werpner (Ladybrand)
    Kimberley Regiment (Kimberley)
Divisional Troops:
    Light Horse Regiment (AC) (Johannesburg)
    Cape Town Field Artillery (Capetown)
    14th Field Artillery (Potchefstroom)
    7th LAA Regiment (−)

8th Division

81st Armoured Brigade (Pretoria):
    Pretoria Highlanders (Pretoria)
    Pretoria Regiment (Pretoria)
    Regiment Boland (Pretoria)
82nd Mechanised Brigade (Potchefstroom):
    Regiment de la Rey (Germiston)
    Regiment de Wet (Kroonstat)
    Witwatersrand Regiment (Germiston)
84th Motorised Brigade (Durban):
    1st Battalion Royal Durban Light Infantry (Durban)
    2nd Battalion Royal Durban Light Infantry (Durban)
    Prince Alfred's Guard (Port Elizabeth)
Divisional Troops:
    Umvoiti Mounted Rifles (Armoured Corps) (Greytown)
    Transvaal Staats Artillery (Greytown)
    Transvaal Horse Artillery (Greytown)

TERRITORIAL STRUCTURE

Western Province Command (Cape Town)
    Cape Garrison Artillery (Cape Town)
    101st Signals Squadron (Cape Town)
    Cape Corps Service Battalion (Eerste River)
    6th BOD (Cape Town)
    Command Workshops (Cape Town)
    2nd Military Hospital (Wynberg)
    3rd Field Ambulance (Wynberg)
    11th STD (Wynberg)
    Cape Flats Commando (Wynberg)
    Worcester Commando (Wynberg)
    Stellenbosch Commando (Wynberg)
    10th AA Regiment (Youngsfield)
    4th Electronic Workshops (Youngsfield)

Eastern Province Command (Port Elizabeth):
    6th South African Infantry (Grahamstown)
    84th Technical Service Corps (Grahamstown)
    11th Commando (Kimberley)
    East Cape Province Commando (Kimberley)
    Port Elizabeth Commando (Kimberley)
    Danei Theron Combat School (Kimberley)

Natal Command (Durban):
    5th South African Infantry (Ladysmith)
    15th Maintenance Unit (Durban)
    Tugela Commando (Durban)
    Umvioti Commando (Durban)

Orange Free State Command (Bloemfontein)
    2nd Field Engineering Regiment (Bethlehem)
    17th Field Squadron (Bethlehem)
    35th Engineering Supplementary Unit (Kroonstat)
    Tank Squadron 1st Special Service Brigade (Bloemfontein)
    1st South African Infantry (Bloemfontein)
    1st Parachute Battalion (Bloemfontein)
    3rd Military Battalion (Bloemfontein)
    Parachute Commando (Kroonstat)
    School of Engineering (Kroonstat)
    Transvaal Command (Voortrekkehoogte)
    2nd Signals Regiment (Voortrekkehoogte)
    5th B.O.D. (Pretoria)
    61st Brigade Workshop (Lyttleon)
    81 Brigade Workshop (Lyttleon)
    Pretoria Oos Commando (−)
    Horse and Dog Centre (Voortrekkehoogte)
    South African Military College (Voortrekkehoogte)
    Technical Service Centre (Voortrekkehoogte)
    Services School (Voortrekkehoogte)
    SAMS Training Centre (Voortrekkehoogte)
    School of Technical Training (Pretoria)
    Command Workshop (−)
    Frankfort Commando (−)

North Western Command (Pochesfstroom):
    3rd South African Infantry (−)
    Command Workshop (−)

Witwatersrand Command (Johannesburg)
    Johannesburg Noord Commando (Johannesburg)
    Southern Cape Command (Oudts−Hoorn)
    South West Africa (Windhoek)
    (see Namibia)

Permanent Force (PF)
The PF is the core of a largely conscript and reserve army. It contains roughly 20% of the Army (10,000 white regulars, 5−7000 black regulars) and has been rapidly expanded in recent years. It has an increasing number of 'black' soldiers (see below). In the late 1970s the army experienced a severe shortage of senior NCOs, junior officers, and good quality instructors.

National Service
Until the early 1960s, the Defence Force consisted of volunteers backed up by a part-time civilian reserve. In 1962 national service was introduced based on a ballot system, and

in 1967 this was replaced by compulsory military service for all fit, white, adult males. The period of national service has been progressively increased and from January, 1978 the 12 month requirements was extended to 24 months.

Citizen Force

Citizen Force units are fed by national servicemen but in recent years have been under strength. In the main the Citizen Force is organised in a conventional manner with infantry, artillery, etc. Some do belong to the Force for Counter Insurgency and Terrorism (see above). Since the South African army has few permanent operational units except those under training as national servicemen, the Citizen Force is the mainstay of the conventional forces. The Citizen Force is organised as a corps, comprising two divisions, each with a number of brigades. The corps headquarters is in Pretoria and divisional and brigade headquarters (where they exist) are staffed by Permanent Force personnel, and are found in the main population area. It is in the Citizen Force that regimental traditions are most strongly preserved.

In June 1982 the period a conscript had to serve in the CF after leaving the PF (National Service element) was increased from 8 to 12 years. Within this period he has a maximum commitment of 720 days. These are divided into 6, two year cycles, of 120 days each. In any *one* year a member of the CF may have to serve up to 90 days, of which 60 days may be in the operational area. The 1982 South African Defence White Paper said that in terms of a flow of units to the border the CF needed 10 units in existence for each one which could be on operational duty in Namibia or elsewhere.

After completing CF service an individual is transferred to the Active Citizen Force Reserve for 5 years where he can be placed on active duty on order of the Minister of Defence. Finally an individual is transferred to the Commandos (see below) where he serves until he is 60.

The CF is 46% of the whole SADF.

Commandos

The Commandos were reorganised in June 1982 as a result of a shortfall in manpower of some 37% and as a recognition that increased guerrilla activity inside South Africa posed new threats. The Chief of the SADF General Viljoen has described recent ANC tactics as those of 'area war' rather than 'border war' and argued that the Commandos ought to be restructured to meet this new challenge. Essentially Commandos will be locally-based militia who are tasked with the protection of their own locality. Whilst in the past the Commando system was voluntary and very much based on traditions derived from the Afrikaner past it will now become largely a conscript organisation. It will be manned by those who have completed their various National Service and CF commitments and each individual will be required to serve up to 12 days per year until they are 60. Some individuals may fulfil greater Commando commitments in lieu of other forms of service. There are three types of Commando:

(1) *Country Commando*

A unit to protect local areas especially designated keypoints. They will work closely with the police and will have an anti-terrorist role.

(2) *Urban Commando*

The task will be to assist the police with crowd control, cordons, road blocks and curfews.

(3) *Industrial Commando*

Organised to protect national installations of strategic import-

ance. Members of the Commando will be drawn from the specific industry to be protected.

There are 13 Commando air squadrons with private aircraft.

'Black Forces'

Given the nature of South African society the employment of 'black soldiers', particularly in a combat role, has always been controversial. Coloured and black African units which had served in a variety of roles in the two World Wars were disbanded after 1945.

In 1963 the South African Cape Coloured Corps (Cape Corps) was reformed and began combat training in 1978. Since 1978 it has been regularly used in Namibia. The Cape Corps has now expanded and includes a small element of National Servicemen and Commandos (both voluntary). Since 1975 a number of coloured soldiers have become officers. Plans to conscript coloured youths have recently been dropped as it was recognised that the loyalty of non-volunteers could not be guaranteed. There are probably now in excess of 4000 coloureds in the army. Coloureds and Indians also serve in the South African Navy.

Rather more of a difficulty was posed by the question of black African recruitment for this touches at the very fundamentals of white attitudes. Nevertheless after widespread debate the recruitment of black soldiers began in 1976 at Lenz in the Transvaal. After 1978 21 Battalion, as it was called, became a training organisation for recruits from other newly-formed ethnic units. It is not entirely clear from South African statements whether ethnic units recruit solely from individual tribal groups or from any black who lives in the catchment area. Presently there are battalions (not of full strength) of Zulu, Venda, Shangaan and Swazi. Some of these units have served in combat in Namibia. There are probably about 1500 Black African members of the PF and in recent years efforts have been made to move towards equal pay and status, regardless of rank.

Clearly there are political and military obstacles to a too rapid growth of black recruitment, since white public opinion moves slowly and the depth and extent of black loyalty to the regime must be in doubt. Chief Bothelezi, Prime Minister of Kwa Zulu, has refused to visit or recognise the Zulu unit.

Nevertheless senior officers of the SADF are keen to extend the system. They argue that black recruitment will both ease pressure on white conscripts and provide proof of their assertion that South Africa is involved in a war against communism and not an inter-racial conflict. As General Malan put it in 1977 'I want to emphasize that the door of this People's Army is open to people of all colours. In fact black and brown soldiers make up 20% of the total force in the operational area'.

Namibia

The Namibian Territorial Force has developed out of pre-existing units including a number of black units. Military service is compulsory for all population groups (males, aged 18–24) except those living in the border area. In addition to South African Regular and Citizen Force units the Force includes two Bushman 'battalions' and Ovambo and Kavango battalions together with a multi-ethnic battalion (no. 41 and highly controversial in consisting of 'mercenaries') a parachute battalion, and newer ethnic units.

Bantustans/Homelands

Since 1976 South Africa has granted 'independence' to Transkei (1976), Bophuthatswana (1977), Venda (1979) and Ciskei (1981). Although none of these 'states' is internationally recognised each has a small defence force, trained and largely led and financed by South Africa. The Transkeian army is led by Maj-Gen Reid-Daly former commander of the Rhodesian Selous Scouts. Each 'Homeland' army is of about battalion strength.

At present the Bantustans support South African policies although the fact that Transkei renounced her non-aggression pact with the Republic between 1978—80 indicates a possible future area and source of instability.

RECRUITMENT, TRAINING AND RESERVES

Recruitment

The majority of personnel in the SADF are conscripted national servicemen, but in recent years the small volunteer Permanent Force has consistently fallen short of establishment. This shortfall is considered acute and resulted in a major recruiting drive in the early 1980s, and the greater employment of women and non-whites. (By 1980 women made up 7% of the SADF.) Although training is in both Afrikaans and English, recruitment for the army has been much better from amongst Afrikaners, and indeed there seems to be some antipathy from the English-speaking community to voluntary military service. Within the conscript element, drug abuse and low morale pose considerable problems from a minority.

Training

All officers in the SADF train at the Military Academy at Saldanha Bay. The basic training system is divided into three phases and lasts two years, whilst about 30% of students complete an extra two years at the academy and graduate with a B.Mil degree. During the basic two years, army officer cadets will disperse to the various arms schools and units for up to 15 months. The most important of such establishments is the Infantry School at Oudshoorn, which caters for all soldiers and officers up to the rank of major. Officers may go later to the Army Staff College or the tri-service Defence College in Pretoria. For political reasons, few officers now train abroad, although it is reported that links exist with Israeli defence establishments. Certainly the SADF has been greatly influenced in both training and tactical developments by the experience of Israel, an experience which, as a similarly beleaguered and isolated State, South Africa finds particularly relevant.

Reserve

See under Strength and Budget, and Role, Commitment, Deployment and Recent Operations, for size, nature and deployment of reserve forces.

EQUIPMENT AND ARMS INDUSTRY

Arms Industry

In consequence of the over-increasing international furore over South Africa's domestic policies, and the United Nations' arms embargo first imposed in 1963, the Republic decided both to diversify her sources of supply whilst at the same time attempting to become as self-sufficient as possible through the development of a major arms industry. The United Nations arms embargo became mandatory in November 1977.

A Munitions Production Board was set up in December, 1964, later becoming the Armaments Board. This organisation has control over the manufacture, procurement, supply and defence research for the SADF. In January, 1969 the Armaments Development and Production Corporation of South Africa (ARMSCOR) was set up with a share of capital of R100,000,000 and in May, 1967 the Atlas Aircraft Corporation was formed which is now a subsidiary of ARMSCOR. ARMSCOR assets are now over R1,300,000,000, its annual budget over R1,500,000,000 and employs 29,000 people directly and a further 76,000 via subcontractors. These institutions manufacture equipment under licences granted some years ago by France and Italy but more importantly South Africa now produced a range of military equipment entirely designed locally. To a large extent South Africa is now self-sufficient in the arms she needs (with the exception of tanks). This includes all small arms, bombs, mortars, armoured cars and APCs. Training and combat aircraft are made under licence.

Recently the Republic has produced a 127mm Multiple Rocket Launcher (to counter the 'Stalin Organ'); a 155mm Artillery gun, the R-5; a six wheeled self propelled vehicle, the R-6, on which the R-5 is fitted; and a new 5.56, infantry assault weapon the R-4. ARMSCOR hopes to become a significant arms exporter in future years and believes the, 'tried and tested in battle' label will give impetus to their goal.

Equipment

The weapons and equipment used by the South African army (and other services in the SADF) include:*

1. About 250 Centurion/Olifant tanks; many very old but some acquired in the 1970s from Jordan and India. Perhaps 60 very old Comet and Sherman tanks, about 20 captured Soviet tanks (T-34 and PT-76), 90 M-41 light tanks.
2. 1500 Eland armoured cars, 230 Ferret Scout Cars, over 1000 Ratel and Saracen AFC, 500 light AFC.
3. 65 25-pds, 75 5.5in and 6.5—155mm, 50 Sexton 25 pds, 15 M7 105mm self propelled guns. 127mm multiple rocket launchers; various mortar and anti-tank guns; various anti-aircraft guns.
4. 120 ENTAC, Milan, 24 Cactus (Crotale), 54 Tiger surface-to-air missiles.

   * *Military Balance 1982—83* with amendments

South Africa has been quite ingenious at purchasing equipment via intermediaries or on the black market so as to avoid the UN arms embargo.

Nuclear Potential

A great deal of controversy has surrounded South Africa's nuclear capability fuelled by the Republic's refusal to sign the Nuclear Non-Proliferation Treaty. A recent UN document sums the issue up in this way: 'There is no doubt that South Africa has the technical capability and the necessary means of delivery. South Africa has vast uranium resources of her own . . an unsafeguarded enrichment facility capable of producing weapon-grade uranium.' An unexplained explosion in the Southern Ocean in 1979 led many to believe South Africa had tested a nuclear device. There is, however, no conclusive proof of this. The utility of a weapon, if South Africa had one, is difficult to judge. In strictly military terms it may be marginal since unlike Israel, with whom the situation is often compared, there is no need for deterrence against possible military defeat. Nevertheless South African leaders have threatened neighbouring states with armageddon (tantalysingly refusing to say if they actually have a weapon) and the possibility of its existence may enhance both South Africa's bargaining powers as well as her white citizen's morale.

RANK, DRESS AND DISTINCTIONS

The rank structure of the South African army broadly follows the British pattern. The term commandant replaces lieutenant-colonel and the army is usually commanded by a lieutenant-general.

In the Citizen Force, particular regimental names are derived from British titles, e.g. The Cape Town Highlanders, Durban Light Infantry, Transvaal Scottish.

New uniforms have recently been introduced which dispense with the heterogeneous dress based on regimental traditions. As well as being more functional, the uniforms move towards a common style for the whole of the Defence Force. In general, orders, decorations and medals are similar for all services in the SADF, though in some instances different ribbons may be worn.

The Cape of Good Hope Decoration (CGH), and the Honoris Crux Gold (HCG) are the highest awards for bravery, whilst the Order of the Star of South Africa (Class 1 SSA) is awarded to the most senior officers for especially meritorious service.

CURRENT DEVELOPMENTS

Ever increasingly in recent years South Africa has become a society at arms, a state which believes itself under siege. Since 1974 the Republic has lost the protective buffer states, or *cordon sanitaire*, on her borders and with them the military and psychological security they offered. Since 1977 the Republic has developed a 'total national strategy' aimed at combating the 'total onslaught on South Africa'. As one General put it in 1977 'We already exist in political, economic and ideological circumstances usually associated with a state of war'. The responses to this perceived threat have been many fold. The size and budget of the SADF has risen enormously as has the military commitment of white conscripts, the role of black soldiers has been greatly expanded and the influence of the military extended into the centre of government. The military voice is heard both more regularly and in more sophisticated terms for army leaders often point out that the defence of the Republic is 80% political and only 20% military. To this end greater emphasis is placed on attempts to win the 'hearts and minds' of the black population of South Africa.

In one sense however the 'militarisation of South Africa' is as much as response to a feeling on encirclement and a sense of betrayal by the West as it is to genuine military threat. Certainly there have been an increasing number of guerrilla attacks on installations within South Africa and a general increase in activities in Namibia. All these can easily be dealt with by the army. However it does seem probable that the next few years will see regular 'hot pursuit' raids by South Africa into neighbouring territories and a continuation and perhaps increase in sabotage within the Republic which however limited in the physical damage it can do to the state may have a severe psychological impact on the white electorate. At the time of writing negotiations over the future of Namibia seem likely to recommence. Many believe that South Africa's bargaining position has been enhanced since President Reagan took office since at present the United States is demanding a solution which links Namibian independence to the removal of Cuban troops from Angola. The future stability of a number of states in the region may well depend on the outcome of these negotiations.

Matthew Midlane

SPAIN

HISTORY AND INTRODUCTION

The Spanish army is a historical and national institution of the first importance. It is generally regarded as being the first national army in the modern sense and was certainly the first to exercise power on a continental scale. It was also the first imperial army of modern times, and a pioneering and modernising influence on the emergent national armies of sixteenth-century Europe. In the twilight and aftermath of Spain's imperial centuries it became something else: the principal instrument of change, for better or worse, in the political life of the country, a role it began to pursue immediately after the expulsion of Napoleon's armies from the country in 1814 and may not yet have laid down.

The achievement of the Spanish military establishment at the beginning of the sixteenth century was to create an army of permanent regiments (*Tercio*), the ownership of which was indisputably in the hands of the Crown and not of their commanding officers. The means for this creation were twofold: the existence of large numbers of experienced soldiers, veterans of the reconquest of southern Spain from the Moors, and the influx of bullion from the newly discovered Spanish empire in America, which provided the funds to purchase their loyalty and obedience. Certain technical military advances, notably the tactical co-ordination of new types of firearms worked out by Gonsalvo of Cordova, *el Gran Capitán*, lent the *Tercios*, at the same time, formidable battlefield efficiency. Wherever the Spanish army fought in the sixteenth century, in or beyond the extensive European dominions the Hapsburg heritage brought the Kingdom, the *Tercios* were generally invincible.

The *Tercios*, however, were never wholly, or even largely, Spanish in recruitment and, with the dissipation of Spanish wealth in the seventeenth century, their foreign recruits and their strength ebbed away. The eighteenth-century army became as backward as the Spanish State and economy, and was destroyed in the first months of fighting against Napoleon. Though a shadow army fought with Wellington throughout the Peninsular War, it was he and his soldiers, not the royal army, which eventually turned the invader out. But if the army had not fought, many Spaniards had, in the 'little war' (*Guerrilla*) whose prosecution turned the Spanish front into a running sore on the skin of the Napoleonic empire, and these guerrilla leaders insisted on being incorporated into the peacetime army at the restoration of 1814 without a compensating retirement of useless regulars. At the same time the surviving hierarchy of the army successfully determined, in the teeth of the hostility of the *cortes* (parliament), the return of absolute royal rule, while ruthlessly snubbing many of the new guerrilla officers whose military records were so much better than their own. Many of the guerrilla officers reacted by espousing the 'liberal' principles which were anathema to the military hierarchy, but were also held by numbers of younger officers from the middle class and veterans of captivity in France where they had been initiated into Freemasonry. Thus were implanted in the Spanish army the factors which were to make it a major force in Spanish political life for the next century and a half: swollen numbers of officers, which condemned most to discontented inactivity and all to miserable pay, even though their pay would usually consume the greater part of the Spanish military budget; and deep divisions in the officer corps over the struggle between liberalism and absolutism which would express themselves at best in disaffection, at worst in civil war. These divisions and imbalances in a major national institution were to be exacerbated by almost uninterrupted failure in a succession of imperial campaigns and by the outbreak of separatist insurrections within the Kingdom itself. Yet step by step with the pace of Spain's international decline, and all concrete evidence to the contrary, the army came to regard itself as uniquely embodying the 'Spanish' character and virtues, and deserving therefore of a degree of social respect and political consideration which the people and the State grew equally unwilling to concede it. Popular respect was all the more closely withheld because of the vile conditions in which the conscripts spent their military service and the ease with which the better off bought exemptions from its performance. Finally, and despite their unvictorious character, the colonial campaigns threw up a band of officers who, as volunteers for service abroad, conceived a hearty contempt for those who rotted at home and which was returned in distaste for their uncouth manners, learnt in the field, and resentment at their claims to more rapid advancement.

In 1881 a Liberal deputy calculated that there had already been 81 military revolts in nineteenth-century Spain, varying in gravity from the *cuartelazo*, when a rebellious unit would take possession of its barracks and await events, through the *pronunciamento*, a public declaration of military demands, sometimes accompanied by force, to the *coup d'état*. Yet the trend of military intervention, and the greater number of the revolts, were (conventional expectations to the contrary) liberal in character. After the restoration of absolute monarchy by the old military hierarchy in 1812, a series of minor military revolts against absolutism culminated in a successful demand for the re-institution of the constitution in 1820. When a French army restored absolute power to the king in 1823, it was the army rather than the parties which made the only serious efforts to retrieve constitutionalism in the military-inspired rebellions of 1830 and 1831. During the dynastic First Carlist War of 1833–40, though the army rallied round the legitimist party, it took the opportunity to secure a partial return to constitutionalism in 1834 and a full return in 1836. Between 1840–3 Spanish government was in the hands of a military regent, Espartero, who was also the most liberal ruler Spain had hitherto had, and, during the period of moderate reaction which conservative soldiers subsequently brought about, he was returned to power by military action in 1854–6. The rebellion of 1868, which ended Moderate rule and inaugurated the First Republic, was also led by soldiers.

But from the restoration of the Bourbons in 1874, the trend of military politics changed direction. Thereafter it was to be conservative, even reactionary, rather than liberal. The reasons for this were several. Perhaps first was the permeation of political consciousness into the Spanish peasantry and proletariat, where the liberal tendency took socialist and anarchist forms from which the officer corps recoiled. Parallel with these movements was the growth of separatist tendencies in the commercially successful north-east, Catalonia and the Basque country. Both movements were the cause of disorders which the army was frequently called to suppress and, from having itself been the principal agent of disorder in the first half of the century, the army began to look on itself as both symbol and instrument of internal peace and national unity, and deserving of national respect for that reason. At the same time, however, the army found itself drawn into a series of colonial wars, the most serious since those culminating in the loss of the South American colonies at the beginning of the century, and, paradoxically, insisted all the more stridently on its right to respect as its ineptitude in the field became more evident.

The Cuban and Philippine campaigns of 1895–8, culminating in the United States' intervention on the rebels' side, were disasters, deeply humiliating for Spain's name abroad and a cause of widespread suffering to the Spanish people, whose conscript sons died abroad in their thousands of disease and neglect. The fault was partly, but only partly, the government's, for its failure properly to equip and supply the army was chiefly due to the officer corps' resistance to any reduction in its size. Their salaries, in 1900, consumed 80,000,000 pesetas of a military budget of 138,000,000 pesetas; their numbers, which had rarely sunk below 20,000 during the previous century, stood at 24,705, while the men numbered only 80,000 and, at one point in the next few years, the ratio of officers to men actually approached one to one. At the same time French officers' salaries consumed only one-seventh of the military budget, with one officer to 23 men. Little wonder that victory was so elusive, or that the Moroccan war which began in 1908 should have protracted itself in mismanaged stalemate. Attempts by the government to revitalise the officer corps by promoting the few successful Moroccan campaigners – the *africanistas* – only provoked insubordination among the stay-at-homes, who formed so-called Defence *Juntas*, the chief object of which was to defend the professional *status quo*.

The *junteros* were only one of several intransigent groups – radicals, syndicalists, Basque and Catalan separatists – whose extreme and conflicting demands brought all Spanish governments of World War I and post-war years under acute pressure. The second decade of the century was indeed one prolonged political crisis in Spain, which any one of several component elements – general strike, agrarian revolt, terrorism of the left and right, separatist insurrection – might have brought to a head. But in the end it was military events and military reaction to them which did so. In 1921 a resurgence of the Moroccan war resulted in disaster at Annual: 8000 Spanish troops were massacred and the Spanish town of Melilla was saved only by the energies of two of the most prominent *africanistas*, General Sanjurjo and Major Francisco Franco of the Foreign Legion. The government abruptly veered in the direction of withdrawal – *abandonismo* – and a leading general, Primo de Rivera, unleashed against it a military conspiracy which in 1923 invested him with dictatorial powers.

The Primo dictatorship was not particularly repressive and, in concert with the French, it did bring the Moroccan war to a successful conclusion, the army's first military success for 50 years and the only one of any magnitude since O'Donnell's annexation of the Moroccan possessions in 1859–60. But it failed to reduce significantly the size of the officer corps, which still stood at 22,000 in 1930, without thereby mollifying any of the factions into which the army was still divided, and it failed to heal any of the wider divisions within Spanish society itself – those between rich and poor, monarchists and radicals, trades unionists and employers, landowners and peasants, the Catalans and Basques and the rest of Spain. In 1930 Primo became aware that he had lost the support of the army and effectively brought his own dictatorship to an end. The King, Alfonso XIII, installed another interim military dictatorship which proceeded to

hold municipal elections. When the towns voted overwhelmingly for republican candidates he and the generals withdrew, he into exile, they into barracks.

The new republican War Minister, Azana, had made a special study of military affairs, unusual in a socialist of the period. As early as 1919 he had written that 'the abolition of the existing military system is a matter of life and death', and he used the impetus generated by the republicans' electoral success to tackle the problem of the army head on. He reduced the number of divisions in the army from sixteen to eight and abolished its special legal jurisdiction, but above all, by the offer of generous retirement terms, achieved a massive reduction in the size of the officer corps. Within a month it declined in numbers from 22,000 to about half that figure. The army accepted the cuts unmurmuringly. But they were not, as Azana thought, to solve the Spanish military problem, for the surviving officers included some of the most energetic in the army, jealous of its honour and profoundly suspicious of the republican government's policies and abilities. In 1932 Sanjurjo, the saviour of Melilla, attempted a monarchist coup (the *sanjurjada*) and, though the right–centre interlude inaugurated by the elections of 1933 calmed military anxieties, particularly by the strong line taken over the socialist rising in Asturias in 1934, the return of the left republicans, as a Popular Front government, in February, 1936 inflamed them again. Public disorder had reached new heights, with organised terror visited by the ultras of left and right on each other, attacks on the police, fighting between the police and the landless peasants, massing of armed worker militias in the industrial towns and of right-wing militias in the Carlist north, and, most offensive to the army and to the lower-middle class from which the majority of its officers sprang, incendiary attacks on churches and convents. Army plotters, led by General Mola, mooted a coup in April, 1936 but failed to bring it to fruition. In July the army found greater resolution. Led by Mola on the mainland and Franco in Morocco, army units issued a *pronunciamento* against the Popular Front government and seized the centres of administration. In the Basque country, Catalonia and central and southern Spain their revolt failed or was not attempted, the army either being loyal to the government or judging local action against it injudicious. But most of northern Spain at once fell into their hands, as did a bridgehead in Cádiz province through which the Army of Africa was transhipped from Morocco. The revolt was immediately resisted, both by loyal units and by the republican militias, and within a week it was clear that the outcome was not to be a *coup d'état* but civil war.

The war was to last until March, 1939, polarise opinion in Europe, involve the direct intervention of Italian and German forces on the Nationalist side (as the rebels became known) and of Russians on the Republican, entail the deaths in battle or by atrocity of over 400,000 Spaniards, and bring Franco, proclaimed ruler of the Spanish State in 1938, a bitter victory. Its rights and wrongs, now embedded in the mythologies of right and left throughout the political world, defy judgement. But viewed as an episode in the Spanish army's long dialogue with the Spanish people and polity, it was clearly climactic. It was as a soldier in the *pronunciamento* tradition that Franco had instituted the revolt and, however political his manipulations of the parties which survived the war, it was as a military dictator that he ruled Spain until his death. Careful though he was to court the support of the church, and energetic in the renovation of the Spanish economy, it was upon the army and the forces of order – police and Civil Guard – that he based his power. All that the republic had taken away from the army he gave back to it – the Captaincies-General, the military governorships of the provinces, the autonomous legal jurisdiction. Curiously he gave back to it also its poverty and swollen numbers. In 1960 there were still 15,000 officers in an army of 150,000 conscripts, living on pay so low that 80% found it necessary to take a second, civilian job. It was as if this most reckless of *caudillos* shrank from the one act of modernisation which would irretrievably change the nature of the Spanish State.

Some efforts to reform the career of officers have been undertaken by the democratic government, but the profession remains largely unreconstructed.

STRENGTH AND BUDGET

Population: 37,900,000,000
Army: 225,000 (190,000 conscripts)
Navy: 54,000 (including 11,000 marines); 40 major vessels, 100 smaller
Air force: 41,000; 157 combat aircraft
Paramilitary forces: 65,000 civil guards; 40,000 armed police
GNP (1981): $191,700,000,000
Defence expenditure (1981): $3,650,000,000

After many years of financial starvation, the Spanish armed forces have benefited from increased spending in the last 20 years. This is in part the product of greater national prosperity, in part the fruit of direct payments made by America in return for the grant of air and naval base facilities. Between 1971 and 1976 America offered credits of $125,000,000, and $20,000,000 of direct aid for re-equipment; between 1953 and 1964 she had contributed $600,000,000. The greater portion of the equipment budget in recent years has, however, gone on the air force which, until the 1960s, was still equipped with propeller-driven aircraft of World War II. The army has begun to receive new equipment in the last decade, and lists shortage of armour, in comparison with other Western European armies of the same size, has begun to be made good.

COMMAND AND CONSTITUTIONAL STATUS

Spain, after 40 years of Franco's personal dictatorship, has recently completed its return to parliamentary democracy. A new Constitution came into effect in 1978, which defines the role and status of the army, the source of authority over it and the duties of Spaniards towards it. Constitutionally, the armed forces constitute a single army (by the Constitutive Law of 1878) which includes, besides the army proper, the navy and the air force, and the Forces of Public Order (of which the Civil Guard and the Armed Police are the most important elements). Their function is to 'guarantee the unity and independence of the country, the integrity of her territory, national security and the defence of the institutional system' (the 'institutional system' means the arrangements for the representation of the individual through, and only through, the family, the municipality and the State trade unions introduced by Franco during his tenure of office). Article IV of the Law of the National Movement lays down that 'the integrity of the country and its independence are the supreme exigencies of the national community. The Armed Forces of Spain, the guarantee of her security and the expression of the heroic virtues of her people, must possess the strength necessary for the better service of the country.' The Head of State (formerly Franco, now the King, Juan Carlos) 'exercises the supreme command of the army, navy and air force; (and) safeguards the maintenance of public order at home and the security of the State abroad', but, under him, the Home Office (*Gobernación*) exercises the supreme command of the security forces of the State, com-

posed of the General Police Corps, the Armed and Traffic Police, the Civil Guard Corps and all other units of security and vigilance . . . 'In case of need it may solicit, through the appropriate channels, the co-operation of military units.' Its authority is thus separate from that of the service ministries and staffs. Each service (army, navy and air force) has its own staff and own ministry. In addition there is a Supreme Staff on a tri-service basis. The ministers and chiefs of staff of the three services, the Chief of the Supreme Staff, the President of the Government (Prime Minister) and co-opted ministers and officials from the National Defence *Junta* which 'proposes to the government the general lines to be taken in respect of security and national defence'. The Army and Navy Ministers are usually serving officers.

Article 7 of *Los Fuero de los Españoles* lays down that 'Bearing arms in the service of their country is a mark of honour for the Spanish people. All Spaniards are obliged to render this service when called upon to do so by law.'

ROLE, COMMITMENT, DEPLOYMENT AND RECENT OPERATIONS

Role
The role of the Spanish army has already been defined, and differs legally not at all from that of most armies. Given Spain's history, however, the internal role of the Spanish army is of greater significance than in most European countries. Salvador de Madariaga, Spain's greatest modern historian, once described the army as 'utterly useless' but at the same time 'indispensable' because it provides the 'minimum of outward and mechanical order' without which the country cannot progress towards 'inner and spiritual order'. Militarily the army is now a great deal more efficient than when he wrote, but his view of it as a force essentially for stability rather than for action holds true. Its quality of creative inertia is recognised and valued by the State, which takes care to see that it is never directly involved in the suppression of disturbances, which are left to the police force. That they are militarised is beside the point. The army is the ultimate deterrent: unused, it threatens any force of disorder with extinction; used, it threatens the ultimate catastrophe of renewed civil war. The leadership of the army, moreover, appears extremely sensitive to its deterrent role and determined, whatever its retrospective judgement about the rights and wrongs of 1936, to stand above party in the future. And, though 'above party except against those of the extreme left' is probably a sensible qualification, so too is 'and of the extreme right'. The army consistently set its face against efforts by the *Falange* (Franco's official party of State, though devoid of power) to raise its own party militia; the proliferation of such bodies under the Republic and the former monarchy it remembers as being the precipitating cause of disorder in Spain's dark years.

The army has deliberately exercised another role during the 40 year peace: that of the 'school of the nation'. In an atmosphere of bitter division and recrimination following the civil war, it provided the one forum in which young Spaniards from every background and region — republican, nationalist and separatist — were forced to mingle. However successful or unsuccessful its efforts at indoctrination of the recruits — 2,000,000 passed through its ranks between 1940 and 1965 — in the official ideology, its mere imposition of propinquity on the sons of former enemies was a healing act.

Commitment
Spain became a member of NATO in 1982. By a bi-lateral agreement, first negotiated in 1953, the United States has also progressively extended guarantees of support for Spain

against an external military threat. Spain signed in 1970 a defence agreement with France, integrating their Mediterranean air-defence systems and arranging for the sale of arms from France to Spain. The nature of Spain's contribution to NATO is still being worked out.

Deployment

Spain is divided into nine military regions, each under a Captain-General: I (HQ Madrid) New Castile and Estremadura; II (HQ Seville) Andalucía less the provinces of Málaga, Granada and Almería; III (HQ Valencia) Valencia and Murcia; IV (HQ Barcelona) Catalonia; V (HQ Saragossa) Aragón; VI (HQ Burgos) Vascongadas (the Basque country), Navarre and Old Castile; VII (HQ Vallodolid) Asturias and León; VIII (HQ Corunna) Galicia; IX (HQ Granada) the provinces of Málaga, Granada and Almería, with Melilla on the Moroccan coast; Ceuta on the Moroccan coast belongs to Military Region II. Each of the regions is garrisoned by units of the Territorial Defence forces of the army: one Territorial Defence Brigade in each region, with one extra each for Madrid and Barcelona. There is also a reinforcement brigade in Granada. There is an alpine brigade in the Saragossa Region, and two mountain divisions (brigade strength only), in the Barcelona and Burgos Regions, stationed respectively at Lérida (4th) and Pamplona (5th). Ceuta and Melilla are garrisoned by two Foreign Legion regiments and four of *Regulares* (north African troops), the garrisons numbering 9000 and 10,000, respectively. There are 6000 troops in the Balearics (Majorca, Minorca and Ibiza) and 6000 in the Canaries. There is a coast artillery brigade in the Straits of Gibraltar and five other coast artillery regiments.

The units of the Intervention forces are distributed as follows: 1st Armoured Division *Brunete* and the parachute brigade in Madrid, 2nd Mechanised Infantry Division *Guzman el Bueno* in Seville and 3rd Motorised (to be Mechanised) Infantry Division *Maestrazgo* in Valencia. The air-portable brigade is the VIIIth Military Region and the armoured cavalry brigade is in Salamanca (1st Military Region).

A Royal Guards Brigade is stationed near the King's residence, the Zarzuela Palace, outside Madrid, and an army headquarters brigade in Madrid. Both are new formations.

Recent Operations

The Spanish army has been engaged in no operations since the end of the Civil War in 1939.

ORGANISATION

Arms of Service

There are five traditional arms of service: infantry (*Infantería*), cavalry (*Cabellería*), artillery (*Artillería*), engineers (*Ingenieros*) and services (*Intendencía*). Spanish regiments preserve their ancient numbers and some claim ancestry from the *Tercios* of 1535 but their lineage was broken at the civil war, after which the army was remade. This is not true of the Foreign Legion (*La Legión de Extranjeros*), founded in 1921, of which the three regiments (*Tercios*) are known as *Gran Capitán* (1st), *Duque de Alba* (2nd) and *Don Juan de Austria* (3rd). Also separate from the army are the *Regulares*, raised in 1911, the north African regiments of the Moroccan enclaves.

Operational

The army is divided into two halves: the Intervention Forces (*Fuerzas de Intervención Inmediata* — F.I.I.) organised for mobile operations anywhere in Spain or its overseas possessions, and the Territorial Defence forces (*Fuerzas de Defensa Operativa del Territorio* — F.D.O.T.) for the defence of the area in which they are stationed. Their separation is modelled on that of the French army.

The armoured, mechanised and motorised divisions (three in all) of the F.I.I. are organised in three brigades each, of which one is a cadre formation. Thus the armoured division has two armoured brigades, the mechanised division one mechanised and one motorised brigade, and the motorised division two motorised brigades; the latter is to become a mechanised division. The armoured cavalry brigade has three regiments, each of three companies of tanks and APCs. The parachute brigade has three parachute battalions and the air-portable brigade two infantry battalions and a third in cadre.

In the F.D.O.T., the three mountain brigades (one is counted as a high mountain or alpine brigade) consist each of three mountain infantry battalions, a mountain engineer battalion and a service battalion. The two mountain divisions to which the brigades belong also have each a motorised infantry battalion, an artillery regiment, a parachute company, an engineer battalion and an aviation battalion. The Territorial Defence brigades consist of three infantry battalions, an artillery battalion, a service battalion, a reconnaissance company, an engineer company and a signals company.

The Foreign Legion regiments (*Tercio* — also the name by which the Legion is often collectively known) consist each of two battalions (*Bandera*), the *Regulares* of several battalions (*Tabor*).

In addition to the formations of the F.I.I. and F.D.O.T. there exist a number of units of indeterminate status whose location is not certain. The most important are a heavy artillery brigade, formerly equipped with 203mm howitzers and Honest John missiles, and an air-defence battalion with Hawk and Nike Hercules missiles. The army aviation squadrons have 60 helicopters. The air force provides the army with the bulk of its ground-attack transport and liaison aircraft and helicopters. These belong to two air commands, the *Aviación Táctica* (Tactical Air Force) with stations at Madrid, Valencia and Vallodolid and the *Mando de Transporte* (Transport Command). The Spanish navy has a force of 8000 marines, organised in four regiments and two independent groups, and stationed chiefly in the islands.

One attack and one transport helicopter battalions have recently been formed.

Paramilitary Forces

Spain is a heavily policed country, with several forces under the control of the Home Office (*Gobernación*). Besides the General Police Corps of the larger municipalities there are two other national police forces of considerable importance. The first is the Armed Police (*Policia Armada*), about 40,000 strong, which act as riot police (on the lines of the pre-civil war Republican Assault Guards) and security guards in the big cities. The second is the best known and arguably most redoubtable armed force in Spain, the Civil Guard (*Guardia Civil*). About 65,000 strong (stronger if the Customs Guards (*Caribeneros*) are included), it is recruited from ex-servicemen and commanded by an army general. Its members, who are paid about 50% more than their equivalent ranks in the army, are always armed and patrol in pairs throughout the towns and countryside of Spain. The government uses Civil Guard units, unlike those of the army, without hesitation against riot, dissent and political crime. The force, the counterpart of the French *Gendarmerie* and Italian *Carabinieri*, is to an even greater extent than they an explicit symbol and instrument of government authority, recognised during the Franco years to be the regime's most important immediate guarantee.

RECRUITMENT, TRAINING AND RESERVES

Military service is a universal obligation in Spain, and about 100,000 young men are conscripted each year for 16 months. Regular service is also possible, and there are about 30,000 regular soldiers (besides officers). The Foreign Legion is completely regular and, apart from a few Portuguese, recruited almost entirely from Spaniards (unlike the French Foreign Legion, in which French citizens are debarred from serving).

Officers, of whom there are about 20,000, are recruited from suitable school leavers and trained at the *Academia General Militar* at Saragossa. About 70% are the sons of soliders, and of those the majority the sons of NCOs rather than officers. Staff training is carried on at the *Escuela Superior del Ejército* at Madrid.

The number of reserves is not made public but in theory is sufficient to transform each of the Territorial defence brigades into a division of three brigades and to man the cadre brigade in the two mountain divisions and the three mobile divisions. As late as the 1960s, however, there was no system of refresher training for the reservists, who on discharge were simply placed on the lists of discharged soldiers.

EQUIPMENT AND ARMS INDUSTRY

The Spanish arms industry is not highly developed and, except for small arms and ammunition, and some artillery and its ammunition, most weapons, munitions and military equipment are imported. The three most important armament firms are EN de Santa Barbara, Esperanza and Bonifacio Echiverria.

Rifle: 7.62mm CETME (EN de Santa Barbara; a very successful design which has been adopted by the German *Bundeswehr*)
Machine-gun: 7.62mm 42/58 (German; Spanish manufacture)
Mortar: 60mm, 81mm and 120mm (all Esperanza)
Anti-armour weapons: 106mm M-40 recoilless rifle (USA), Milan missile (France), Cobra missile (Italy), and Dragon and HOT missiles
Air-defence weapons: 40mm L/60 and L/70 guns (Swedish Oerlikon) and 90mm M-2 guns (USA); Hawk and Nike Hercules missiles and Improved Hawk (forming the missile group)
Artillery: 105mm pack howitzers (Italy; equipping the mountain artillery); a total of 1000 105mm M-1 howitzers (USA; equipping the artillery of the infantry brigades) and 155mm M-2 howitzers (USA; equipping the medium-artillery regiments); a total of 80 105mm M-37 SP guns (equipping the field regiments of the mobile brigades) plus 155mm M-44 SP guns and 175mm M-107 SP guns (equipping the medium regiments of the mobile brigades); 108mm, 216mm and 300mm multiple rocket launchers (Spain)
Armour: AML 60/90 armoured cars (France; 60 in service); M-113 APCs (USA; 500 in service, equipping the mechanised brigades); M-41 light tanks (USA; in the mechanised, armoured and armoured cavalry brigades; 180 in service); M-47 and M-48 medium tanks (USA; in the armoured cavalry and armoured brigades; 475 in service); AMX-30 medium tanks (France; in the armoured brigades; 520 in service)
Aircraft: army aviation has 130 helicopters of various types, including UH-1B/H, Alouettes and CH-47.

RANK, DRESS AND DISTINCTIONS

The Spanish army wears khaki in everyday dress. The officers' uniform is a British-style service dress, with which a sword and waist sash are worn on ceremonial occasions. Combat dress is also khaki, worn with a NATO helmet; the German coalscuttle helmet has been given up. Paratroopers wear a mottled combat dress. The Foreign Legion wears light green, with a tasselled side cap. Marines wear dark blue. The Civil Guard wear dark green, with the famous 'aeroplane' tricorn hat in patent leather.

Capitán General (general) – Four stars around crossed sword and staff
Teniente General (lieutenant-general) – Three stars around crossed sword and staff
General de División (major-general) – Two stars around crossed sword and staff
General de Brigada (brigadier) – One star around crossed sword and staff
Coronel (colonel) – Three eight-pointed stars on the cuff
Teniente Coronel (lieutenant-colonel) – Two eight-pointed stars on the cuff
Comandante (major) – One eight-pointed star on the cuff
Capitán (captain) – Three six-pointed stars on the cuff
Teniente (lieutenant) – Two six-pointed stars on the cuff
Alférez Alumno (second-lieutenant) – One six-pointed star on the cuff

Alférez – One six-pointed star on the cuff
Brigada – One thick gold stripe on the cuff
Sargento – Three thin gold stripes on the cuff
Cabo Primero – One thin gold stripe on the cuff
Cabo Segundo – Three diagonal red stripes on the cuff
Soldato Especialisto – One red chevron on the sleeve

The title, but not the rank, of Captain-General is held by the commanders of the nine Military Regions.

CURRENT DEVELOPMENTS

Fears widely expressed within and without Spain since the death of Franco, that the armed forces were the chief stumbling block to democratic progress, were substantiated by the seizure of the parliament building (*Cortes*) on February 23rd, 1981 by soldiers of the Civil Guard. They were led by Lt-Colonel Tejero, who had been imprisoned in 1978 for plotting to overthrow the government. The 1981 plot was better prepared and more widely-based, involving the movement of the *Brunete* armoured division to the capital to reinforce Tejero's Civil Guards once the members of parliament and ministers had been confined. A Captain-General, Milans del Bosch (Valencia) and the Vice-Chief of Staff, Armada Comyn, were the most senior supporters of the plot, but there were others, both in and outside the *Brunete* division. The coup was squashed by the initiative of King Juan Carlos, who used a private communication network to contact other leaders of the armed forces and assure their loyalty. Faced with evidence of the plot's collapse, and of the king's outraged reaction, which his televised broadcast to the nation during the night substantiated, Tejero surrendered the following morning. He, Milans del Bosch, Armada and numbers of lesser plotters were subsequently tried and convicted. Tejero and Milano del Bosch were sentenced to thirty years.

Subsequently there have been reports of a number of other plots and acts of dissension by officers of the armed forces. Some middle-rank officers were arrested in June 1981 for alleged plotting and in December an anti-government manifesto signed by 100 officers and men from Medina-based units was published. Several officers were subsequently relieved of command. On October 2nd, 1982, three colonels were arrested for plotting a new coup, timed to take place on the eve of the general election of October 27th. One of the conspirators had previously visited General Milans del Bosch in prison. The king has subsequently redoubled his efforts to remind the army of its duty of obedience to the constitution and himself, and rumours of plots have subsided. Unprecedently the Supreme Court, acting under new constitutional provisions, has revised the findings of the court-martial which tried the Tejero conspirators very much extending their sentences in many cases.

At the time of going to press (March 1983) the newly-elected Socialist Defence Minister, Narcis Sorra, has just announced plans to reduce the size of the Spanish army by 90,000 and national service from 15 to 12 months. The officer corps is to be cut by 25%. Promotion is no longer to be by seniority alone but largely by merit and, apparently, political moderation also. A unified Ministry of Defence is to be set up, pay improved and officers' education liberalised. The 1965 organisation of the army on territorial lines is to be replaced by the creation of 'mobile operational forces'. This presages true modernisation at last.

John Keegan

SRI LANKA*

HISTORY AND INTRODUCTION

Before becoming independent of Britain (by whom it had
been annexed in 1796) in 1948, Sri Lanka — Ceylon as it
then was — had no regular, locally recruited force. The
British army provided the garrison, never a large one, since
the country was tranquil and threatened by no external
force. The only indigenous military force was the volunteer,
part-time Ceylon Defence Force; the Ceylon Light Infantry was the most important unit, together with some
small volunteer units; many of the volunteers were locally
employed Europeans. The permanent cadre was British.

On independence, a regular Ceylonese infantry battalion,
the 1st Ceylon Infantry Regiment, was formed. In 1950 it
assumed the title of the 1st Battalion Ceylon Light Infantry
and the old C.L.I. became the 2nd (Volunteer) Battalion.
Subsequently two other regular regiments were formed, the
Sinha (Lion) Regiment and the Genuna Watch (each also has
a volunteer battalion). The army has been engaged in the
suppression of internal disorders in 1958 and 1971, but has
not operated from, and is not confronted by any threat
from, outside the island. It has also remained happily untouched by the racial, ideological and religious animosities
which divide Ceylonese society. A small, smart and efficient
force, it bears comparison, in its social and political status,
with its giant neighbour, the Indian army.

STRENGTH AND BUDGET

Population: 14,900,000
Army: 11,000
Navy: 2825; 27 small craft
Air force: 2600
GNP (1980): $4,070,000,000
Defence expenditure (1981 estimate): $29,420,000

COMMAND AND CONSTITUTIONAL STATUS

The President of the Republic (who is appointed by the
Prime Minister) is titular Commander-in-Chief of the Armed
Forces; the Minister of Defence (formerly the Prime Minister)
is politically responsible for the army, which is commanded
by a major-general. The army has, since independence,
played no independent role in the affairs of the country
(though 10 officers were convicted in 1962 for alleged complicity in an anti-government plot, and twelve more arrested,
again for alleged plotting, in 1966, but acquitted by the
Supreme Court).

ROLE, COMMITMENT, DEPLOYMENT AND RECENT
OPERATIONS

The army's principal role is to provide the ultimate support
to the police in the maintenance of law and order. The
country is neutralist and has no external commitments. The
deployment of the army outside the capital area is not

* See also Appendix 2.

known. It has not acted operationally since the internal
disorders which centred on Galle, in 1971.

ORGANISATION

Arms of Service
The army, divided into a regular and volunteer force, has,
like the Indian, a British-style regimental system. The three
regular infantry regiments (the 1st Battalion Sri Lanka Light
Infantry, the 1st Battalion The Sinha (Lion) Regiment and
the 1st Battalion The Genuna Watch) are independently
recruited organisations; officers generally serve in the same
battalion throughout their regimental career. The other
regular arms are: the Ceylon Armoured Corps (one armoured-
car reconnaissance regiment); the Ceylon Artillery (one field-
artillery regiment); the Ceylon Engineers (one field squadron);
the Ceylon Signals (one signal squadron) and the Ceylon
Army Service Corps, Ordnance Corps, Electrical and Mechanical Engineers, Medical Corps, Military Police and General
Service Corps. The volunteer force consists of: three infantry
battalions (the 2nd (Volunteer) Battalions of the Sri Lanka
Light Infantry, Sinha Regiment and Genuna Watch); an
engineer regiment (development and construction); a unit of
the Army Service Corps and the Army Medical Corps; four
pioneer battalions and one guard battalion of the Sri Lanka
Army Pioneer Corps; and two battalions of the Sri Lanka
National Guard. The air force also has an airfield construction
battalion and four squadrons of airfield guards (Sri Lanka Air
Force Regiment). Recent reports suggest the creation of two
main regular infantry battalions and another armoured
reconnaissance regiment — though numbers of soldiers have
not increased proportionately.

Operational
The regular battalions are now said to form five brigades with
two reserve battalions in each. There has been a steady
increase in the number of reserve battalions, prompted by
Tamil disturbances in the north.

RECRUITMENT, TRAINING AND RESERVES

Recruitment is by voluntary enlistment; in practice, the army
is almost completely Sinhalese Buddhist, other communal
groups not being accepted. Training of soldiers is carried out
at the Army Training Centre, Diyatalawa. Officers, formerly
trained at the British, Indian and Pakistani Academies, are
also now trained at Diyatalawa, but go for staff training to
Britain and India. There are specialist engineer, and electrical
and mechanical engineer service corps schools; other specialist
training is carried on in units. The volunteer force provides
the reserves.

EQUIPMENT AND ARMS INDUSTRY

The country has no arms industry. Its infantry weapons
are of British origin. The army has some Russian light
artillery (76mm and 85mm) and APCs (BTR 152; 10 in

service) and some obsolescent British armoured vehicles (18 Saladin armoured cars and 15 Ferret scout cars).

RANK, DRESS AND DISTINCTIONS

Ranks are British and most of the uniform and distinction badges of the former British-run Ceylon Defence Force, suitably adapted, have been retained. The Sri Lanka Light Infantry, for example, retains its Prince of Wales' feathers badge, with the plumes replaced by drooping sheaves of paddy.

CURRENT DEVELOPMENTS

Despite Sri Lanka's grave religious, ideological and ethnic troubles, now heightened by economic hardships, the army remains a loyal and cohesive force. This is due partly to the comparatively high standard of living it is able to offer its soldiers and to the high quality of the officers, trained in a tradition of apoliticism, which it is able to recruit. It also has to do with the policy, inaugurated after 1962, of recruiting only from the Sinhalese Buddhist community, which consistently monopolises the government.

Since 1980 there has been a resurgence in violence against the government by Tamils of the Jaffna region in the north of the island. The group claiming responsibility calls itself Liberation Tigers and seeks separate status for the 1,400,000 Tamils who are Sri Lanka citizens (the 1,000,000 Tamils of Indian or stateless citizenship remain passive). A state of emergency against terrorism was declared in August, 1981, but violence continues. Two soldiers, the first military victims, were killed in an ambush in Jaffna in October, 1981.

John Keegan

SUDAN

HISTORY AND INTRODUCTION

Sudan must be high on the list of the world's most difficult countries to govern, the difficulties are reflected in every aspect of its military situation. One of Africa's largest countries, an Arab Muslim north and an approximately 25% black African animist or Christian southern minority represents one main theme of internal dissent; there are however a number of others, notably internal divisions within the South, and a new oil discovery based assertiveness in the western provinces. An overall poverty (Sudan still figures on the UN's list of the world's ten least developed countries) creates a permanent climate of frustration and bitterness.

The country's configuration is a legacy of history, Egypt's wish to control the Upper Nile and an area of black Africa as a source of labour, and a later British colonial takeover of Egypt's claim. The Mahdist rising of 1881–5 should be seen in part as a northern Sudanese rejection of Egypt's claims, suspicion of Egypt still remains an important strand in Sudanese politics. Sudan was a British colony in practice, though an 'Anglo-Egyptian condominium' in strict theory, until independence in 1956. During this period military force consisted (apart from a permanent British garrison) of Sudanese units with British and Egyptian officers until 1924, when unrest and mutiny broke out; after the troubles were over a purely Sudanese Sudan Defence Force of Sudanese soldiers and British personnel with no Egyptians was created. The SDF performed well in the 1940–41 Italian East Africa campaign and it was hoped that it would form a prop of the post-independence state. Unfortunately even before independence, the Southern contingent had mutinied in 1955, murdering its northern officers.

The events in the Sudan since independence illustrate only too clearly the problems facing any government in El Khartum. At independence the ruling party represented a moderate local conservative nationalism of Mahdist tradition but it proved unable to cope with a growing insurgency in the South that soon developed into a full scale civil war, to last sixteen years, kill at least a third of a million people, devastate the South and destroy its economy. As the situation worsened the political order collapsed, the country initially passing to the first military government of General Abboud following a coup in 1958. Abboud was in most respects a military version of the conservative political style he ousted, and was to prove as unsuccessful, his regime collapsing in disorders and strikes in 1964. A period of instability followed, government formally in the hands of civilian political figures, but these heavily dependent on the army, greatly expanded as a result of the Southern conflict. The other features of this period, all reflecting Sudan's lack of real cohesion, were evident Israeli and pre-Revolution Ethiopian interest in exacerbating Sudan's Southern conflict, the remarkable growth of the Sudan Communist Party, and the emergence within the army of a new generaton of officers, Nasserist, anti-Western and radical. The politicians contained a number of coup attempts, but by the end of the decade the system was again bankrupt. In May 1969 Colonel (later successively General and Field Marshal) Jaafar al Nemery took power at the head of a grouping of radical officers. Nemery remains in power at the time of writing (February 1983) but the buffetings of Sudan's problems have changed its style from the heady radicalism of the May Revolution to a pragmatic, at times almost desperate, search for groupings, or factions within critical groupings, that can be turned to political support for a regime that must, inevitably with the passing of time, be increasingly under criticism.

Nemery's first two years were marked by radical and Communist internal politics and rhetoric, friendship with Libya and Egypt, and the crushing, in a very bloody operation in which several thousand were killed, of a Mahdist uprising of the Ansar sect in 1970. In 1971, however, Communist officers made an attempt to replace Nemery in a coup; unwisely from their point of view they spared his life and after a number of adventures he was able to regain power with the aid of loyal units and an Egyptian contingent. Retribution fell on the Communist and other radical officers, and Nemery began a developing move to the right in politics and to Western and Egyptian alliances in foreign affairs.

His authority at home, and stature abroad, was very greatly increased in the next year, 1972, by a successful ending to the civil war in the South. The Ethiopians were bought off by a promise that Sudan would no longer support Eritrean insurgency; with Ethiopia removed from the scene the Israeli connection was cut off. The South was given a large measure of autonomy under a Higher Executive Council, and the 1st Division, the Sudan Army's garrison in the South was restructured to provide for one half of its soldiers to be southerners (including many insurgents) and a Southern insurgency leader Joseph Lagu, was given command of the Division. There followed two years of Southern reconstruction and general national economic up-turn.

The year 1975 however saw renewed drama. Nemery had, and still has, to be cautious on pan-Arab issues if he has to keep the South in line. Opposition to this caution led to abortive coup attempts by the Mahdists with Libyan support in 1975 and in 1976. The first attempt was easily suppressed, the second, supported by columns of vehicles full of armed revolutionaries entering Sudan from Libya led to two days of street fighting in El Khartum, nearly 1000 people killed and great destruction of property. Nemery was exceedingly lucky to survive. Egyptian air and military support played a very important role in the coup's suppression.

The whole episode gave Nemery breathing space; the victory however did not solve any of Sudan's main problems, indeed these worsened when Marxist Ethiopia joined an embittered Libya to present Sudan with a new source of anxiety on its frontiers, so increasing Nemery's need for Egyptian and other Arab, especially Saudi, support, The latter became more difficult to obtain after Sadat's attempted *rapprochement* with Israel, which Nemery at first supported but later has attempted to distance himself: Egyptian support for the regime, never popular, has developed into a highly controversial issue.

In the late 1970s then – at a time when north-eastern Africa was becoming increasingly under either Soviet or US tutelage – a new external dimension of opposition to Nemery's policy of 'national reconciliation' included support by Ethiopia for Mahdist exiles, a move countered by Nemery firstly by a return to support for Ethiopia's running sore, the Eritreans, and later a second 'we will stop if you will stop' agreement with Addis Ababa in 1979. No such agreement with Libya was ever remotely possible, and the Libyan training camps for Sudan dissidents become a feature of the scene from this time. At home, Nemery set out bravely to seek a reconciliation with his domestic opponents using the political party of his own creation, the Sudan Socialist Union, as a 'broad church'. Some of the Mahdist Angars, including their leader agreed, others did not, nor did most of the followers of Nemery's other major domestic opponent, Sherif al Hindi's Unionist Democratic Party. By the end of the decade, however, strains within the 'national reconciliation' were evident at several levels. At the national level Sadiq had again departed to exile in protest against Camp David and the Egyptian connection, a coup conspiracy, probably based on Darfur, had been unearthed and a series of major military and political reshuffles and dismissals together with promises of further devolutionary arrangements for the north, east and west to balance those already existing in the South gave further evidence of criticism and restlessness. In the South there had been at least two military mutinies, and a more extreme grouping led by Lagu had replaced the more moderate grouping at the 1978 elections for the Southern Assembly; a statement that needs added to it the rider that the winning grouping both represented a protest against the domination of Southern political life by the Dinka ethnic group and an overall mounting suspicion of El Khartum's Egyptian and Saudi connections. Externally the endless civil war in Chad provided Sudan both with a cautionary tale and also a consequential increasing concern, that at times was having to be translated into military support (usually with Egypt) for the Habre facton lest the Libyan supported Ouddei faction prevailed and so gave El Khartum yet another frontier problem. Sadiq's break with Nemery however necessitated a curious — and very temporary — Nemery–Qaddafi *rapprochement* in 1979, the former anxious to contain Qaddafi support for the Mahdists, and Qaddafi persuading Nemery to qualify his support for Sadat's peace initiatives, a move rewarded also by much needed Saudi economic help and improved relations with other Arab lands. At street level, 1979 saw a wave of strikes and riots, and at least two attempts on Nemery's life.

The improved relations with the non-Egyptian Arab world set Nemery off to a good start for the 1980s in the North. Mismanagement by Lagu and astute political manoeuvrings by Nemery resulted in the removal of Lagu and a return to power of more moderate Southerners. However as the year progressed the usual problems all reappeared, in 1981 and 1982 to develop into an acute form. In the national legislature the running passed into the hands of Muslim Brotherhood, Mahdist and Unionist Democrats; within the Army another military coup conspiracy was discovered, followed by yet another in March 1981. In the mosques a new militancy was being voiced, in the western provinces of Darfur and Kordofan, provinces adjoining Libya, oil discoveries began to create new local political assertions, but despite the discoveries the overall state of the economy continued to worsen, accentuating dependence on Western help. The divide-and-rule possibilities arising from sharp new part political and part ethnic (i.e. Dinka versus non-Dinka led by the Zande) faction bickering in the South were of little comfort to the regime. The next year, 1981 saw border clashes with Libyan forces following some Libyan bombing raids, these all remained small-scale despite refuge (and Egyptian re-supply and re-armament) for the Habre forces in the Chad conflict on Sudanese soil. Darfur's trade lies mostly with Libya and the need to conciliate the area was seen by El Khartum as overriding. The year's difficulties also included bitter divisions within the one permitted party and the suspension of the national and all regional assemblies; in the South a provisional government headed by a Muslim general was installed

with talk of the division of the South in to further regions, increasingly demanded by Northern Muslim militants, but opposed in the South as the probable consequences become more clear. In the face of these centrifugal tendencies all that Nemery was able to do in 1982 was to undertake yet a further round of military and political reshuffles, conclude a 'Charter of Integration' with Egypt popular in the North but deeply suspect in the South — and to survive.

This lengthy and complex political introduction is necessary in order to illuminate how cancerous to any coherent military policy the regional and ethnic divisions are; the whole Sudan political order can be shaken by an issue such as the siting of an oil refinery or a ban on the traditional Christmas Day march of Christians through El Khartum. The tangle of Sudan's internal rivalries, compounded by backers outside, set against an ever fiercer competition for such economic recourses as may be available creates, despite the long tenure of office by Nemery, permanent crisis. The departure of Nemery would only create fresh dimensions of crisis and the long-term prospects for Sudan's survival in its present form must be assessed as doubtful.

STRENGTH AND BUDGET

Population: 19,300,000
Armed Forces: Total 58,000, including an army of 53,000, an air force of 3000 and a navy of 2000. Paramilitary forces include a Border Guard of 2500 and a Republican Guard of 500.
GNP:
Defence Expenditure: } No reliable figures available

COMMAND AND CONSTITUTIONAL STATUS

The President Jaafar al Nemery is Commander-in-Chief; he recently promoted himself to be a Field Marshal for additional authority and to avoid regulations relating to lengths of tours of duty for general officers.

It should be noted that the July 1976 treaty with Egypt, signed in the aftermath of the appalling fighting following the coup attempt of that year, provides for both governments to support each other in the event of an attack, this latter is not formally defined by includes domestic upheavals. How far in practice Egypt might intervene is, of course, another matter.

The country is divided into six major commands, El Khartum; Central (Al Ubayyid); Eastern (Qadarif); Western (Al Fashir); Northern (Shendi); Southern (Juba).

A senior officers Congress of General officers meets to advise the President and other ministers, a sign of the power of the military. A number of senior military officers are seconded to civil administrative departments. A Joint Defence Council and Joint Chiefs of Staffs organisation with Egypt also exists; standardisation of equipment and training has been adopted as a general aim.

ROLE, COMMITMENT, DEPLOYMENT AND RECENT OPERATIONS

At independence the army existed for light internal security duties and shortly afterwards had to be greatly expanded for operations against the Southern insurgents, the *Anya Nya*. After the ending of the Southern conflict, the Army found itself increasingly involved in border commitments, these necessitating its development from a gendarmerie to a field army.

The country has frontiers with seven other nations, of these the long borders with Libya, Chad and Ethiopia all require military surveillance, as on occasions do those with Uganda and Zaïre. Only those with Egypt, Kenya and the Central African Republic require little military watch.

Sudan contributed a brigade of troops to the defence of the Suez canal after the 1967 conflict, these were brought back in Egyptian aircraft at the time of the 1976 coup. Another 1000 strong force was sent to join Arab forces in Lebanon, but this was withdrawn at the end of the 1970s. In December 1982 a contingent, size not specified but unlikely to be large, was sent to support Iraq in the Gulf War.

The present perceived threats are firstly and above all from Libya. Sudan realises that it cannot hope to match the scale of the Libyan forces, and believes they may best be destroyed from the air while on the advance across the long desert distances. Generally similar thinking governs the next assessed threat, Ethiopia. In the event of an Ethiopian attack Sudan feels it can rely on Saudi help, particularly in the Red Sea; Saudi naval units freely use Sudanese ports. The third perceived danger is infiltration, by small columns of enemy soldiers in disguise; the Egyptian alliance and the garrisons of the major towns, it is hoped, would deny success to infiltrators. The last role, and likely to be once again the 'growth industry' is internal security especially in the South but also possibly in the West. Very recent reports suggest that small-scale counter-insurgency operations have already had to be commenced in the South.

One final factor must be taken into account in any description of the deployment of Sudan's Army, perceptions of loyalty. Units distrusted for one reason or another are likely to be posted away from seats of power.

ORGANISATION

The Sudan Army is built around two armoured, seven infantry and one parachute brigades, supported by three artillery regiments, three gun and one missile anti-aircraft artillery regiments and an engineer regiment.

The organisation of arms of the Army follow the British pattern.

RECRUITMENT, TRAINING AND RESERVES

In the main colonial era, the army was recruited in the North, mainly from the Beja ethnic group. In the last colonial years a deliberate attempt to recruit Southerners was begun for units in Equatoria, these are already noted mutinied in 1955. After the end of the civil war, the First Division was reconstituted to provide for ethnic units, of Northerners and Southerners in about equal proportion; since 1972 Southerners have gained a majority. The Division's officers are largely Southern. Elsewhere in the Army units are either entirely Northerners, or the few Southerners serving do so under northern officers.

In theory a system of two years' conscription exists. In practice numbers so produced exceed the numbers required and service can be seen as voluntary. No reserve system exists.

Officer training takes place at El Khartum and at Arms Schools; these are at Jubaytt (infantry) Atbara (artillery) Shajara (armour) and in El Khartum for the various logistic services. A Staff College at El Khartum also exists.

Until 1970 British training assistance was used, to be replaced by the Soviets from the May Revolution to 1972 (for the bulk of assistance) and 1977 (for the final ending of the Soviet role). British assistance returned, on a very small scale, in 1973 and continues. Egyptian help, on a much larger scale, has been in use since 1970. Personnel are sent abroad for training to Egypt, the USA, Pakistan and Britain. A few went to the Soviet Union in the early 1970s.

EQUIPMENT AND ARMS INDUSTRY

Sudan possesses no arms industry. The variety of her equipment reflects the changes in political directions over the years, and who has been willing to provide funds or credits.

The armoured units possess some 70 T-54, 50 T-55 and 17 T-34 Soviet tanks, 50 M-60 A1 and 50 M-41 American tanks, and 27 Chinese type 62 tanks. Armoured personnel carriers and reconnaissance vehicles are an equally confusing mix of 40 Saladin and 50 Ferret British armoured cars, a dozen or so BTR-40 and a small number of BRDM-1 and 2 Soviet vehicles, sixty Czech OT-64s, some Chinese K-63s, approximately 40 British Saracen armoured personnel carriers and 40 V-150 Commandos, with small and unknown numbers of M-113 and Egyptian Walid vehicles. The artillery includes 55 British 25 pdr guns, 40 Soviet 100mm guns, 20 M-101 US 105mm howitzers, 18 Soviet 122mm howitzers and 11 155mm US howitzers. A limited number of 120mm mortars are in service, together with 30 85mm anti-tank guns. Anti-aircraft weaponry includes 80 37mm and 80 40mm guns, a small number of larger anti-aircraft guns together with 24 M-163 Vulcan 20mm self-propelled anti-aircraft equipments; missile systems include 20 SAM-2 Guidelines, a number of SA-7 Grails and HAWK missiles.

Further orders for M-113 armoured personnel carriers, 155mm howitzers M-163 self-propelled anti-aircraft equipments and HAWK missiles have been placed.

The air force comprises two fighter/air-to-ground attack squadrons. One of these is a mixture of four F-5s, and 8 MiG-21s, the other a mixture of the Chinese version of the MiG-17 and the Chinese MiG-19. A transport squadron is centred upon six C-130 Hercules, four DHC-5Ds, eight Turbo-Porters and seven EMB-110 P-2s with one or two other miscellaneous machines. A helicopter squadron of 15 M1-8, two Puma and ten BO-105 exists, but the Soviet machines are reported to be in poor repair. Some of the training aircraft could be put to counter-insurgency uses if necessary. These training machines include five BAC-145s, two Jet Provosts, three of the training version of the MiG-15 and two of the training version of the MiG-21s, together with two each of the training versions of the Chinese edition of the MiG-17 and -19s.

On order are further F-5E and Hercules aircraft.

RANK, DRESS AND DISTINCTIONS

The rank structure of the Sudan Army still follows that of the British Army, an eagle replacing the British crown on officer's insignia and a star replacing the British crown on non-commissioned officer's badges.

CURRENT DEVELOPMENTS

At the time of writing (late February 1983) rumours of a planned Libyan attack on Sudan led to a US naval deployment in the Mediterranean, the USA being keenly sensitive to a threat to any link in what might have to be a Rapid Deployment Force chain.

The event, whether the rumours were correct or false, is symptomatic of the whole Sudan dilemma, which appears likely to be compounded by the Libyan decision to support a Northern-based Queddei provisional regime in Chad in an attempt to eject the Habre government, well disposed to El Khartum. Also, Sudan, perhaps rashly but understandably in view of Libya's consistent support for Nemery's opponents, permits an anti-Qaddafi radio to broadcast to Libya from El Khartum.

The future remains very uncertain and unpredictable. A key factor will be the steadiness, or otherwise, of the Army; a number of its senior officers are, it is rumoured, very critical of Nemery and drawn to the Muslim Brotherhood or Sadiq's Mahdist movement.

Lloyd Mathews

SURINAM

The Republic of Surinam, a former Dutch colony on the north-eastern coast of South America which received its independence in 1975, has a population of about 448,000 people. Although inter-racial relations are relatively harmonious, given that Surinam has probably the most variegated population mixture in the world, anxiety that the end of Dutch rule would result in the kind of racial hostility and domination by a single group that prevails in neighbouring Guyana was at the root of most emigrants' choice.

Surinam, first colonised by the British in the early seventeenth century, passed under Dutch rule in 1667, and spent the next two centuries as a typical West Indian sugar-planting economy, with a minority of whites and a large African slave population. When slavery was finally abolished in Dutch possessions in 1863, the black population fled the land, as they had previously done throughout the West Indies. As in Guyana, the solution adopted was to bring in indentured labour from India, but also in Surinam's case from the Indonesian island of Java.

By the first half of the twentieth century the population consisted of about 31% Creoles (black and mixed race), 37% Hindustanis (from India, but so called to distinguish them from the indigenous Indians, and including Muslims as well as Hindus), 15% Javanese, 10% Bush Negro (the descendants of escaped slaves, living in the interior and retaining much of their African culture), 2.5% native Indians, 2% Chinese, 1% Europeans, 1% Lebanese, and a scattering of others. Most groups had retained their own language and customs: the Creoles spoke Dutch, most of the people originating from the Indian sub-continent spoke Hindi, the Indonesians spoke Javanese, and Chinese, English, French and Spanish were also in use. Most people spoke the purely local patois, Sranan Tongo, also known as taki-taki. The population was 45% Christian, 28% Hindu and 20% Muslim.

The Creoles are overwhelmingly urban, and most work in the swollen public services (which provide 28% of all employment in Surinam) or in the bauxite industry which earns 90% of the country's foreign exchange. The once predominantly rural Hindustanis and Javanese have left their farms in huge numbers to flock to the cities, where they dominate all aspects of commercial activity (together with the small Lebanese and Chinese minorities). Most of the country's area (about the size of England) is rich in unexploited timber and minerals, but even the majority of the arable land is unused, while half the population lives in greater Paramaribo, the capital. Surinam is relatively prosperous by South American standards, with a per capita annual income of well over $1000.

Surinam was granted full internal self-government in 1954, becoming an equal partner with the Netherlands Antilles and Holland itself in the Kingdom of the Netherlands. There was little pressure for independence from the governments of the 1950s and 1960s, the last of which, in 1969–73, was a Hindustani-dominated coalition which nevertheless incorporated numbers of Creoles (including the Prime Minister). This government fell after a wave of strikes and violence in 1973, and in the ensuing election the political parties separated on communal lines more sharply than ever before. The election was won by Mr Henck Arron's National Party of Surinam, an exclusively Creole party of socialist orientation, and the ensuing government was a coalition between this group, two smaller Creole parties of more radical leftist tone, and the Javanese community's party. In the much tenser racial atmosphere which now prevailed, Prime Minister Arron was unable to find any leading figure of the Hindustani community who would join his government.

The new government at once demanded independence, to the considerable relief of The Hague, and arrangements were rapidly finalised for the termination of Dutch rule in November, 1975. Dutch promises of post-independence aid were unusually generous, amounting to $1,500,000,000 over the following decade, but it was also agreed that the Dutch armed forces would be withdrawn, handing over the responsibility for defence and internal security to the newly formed Surinam Armed Forces. Since, giving the overwhelming predominance of Creoles in all branches of the State service, the new armed forces were bound to be a largely Creole institution, the Hindustani community in particular were gravely concerned that the post-independence course of events would duplicate that in Guyana, with a black minority government manipulating the political system to keep itself in power indefinitely with the support of a black army and police force. There was also concern amongst the large Hindustani merchant community at the socialist government's policies on nationalisation.

As a result of these misgivings, the main Hindustani political parties withheld their assent to the new constitution and resisted independence until only 5 days before the event, when they finally accepted the inevitable. In response to repeated demands from the other racial groups that the new armed forces should be recruited on the basis of racial quotas, the Creole-dominated government bluntly refused, stating that Surinamese were Surinamese. Consequently, the new army did indeed turn out to be a predominantly Creole force.

It was the fear of future racial clashes which was the prime motive force behind the extraordinary wave of emigration in 1974–5. It would appear, moreover, that the prospect of a largely black army and the Guyanese analogy led to a relatively high proportion of Hindustanis joining the emigrants: no statistics are available, but the clear victory of Prime Minister Arron's coalition in the October, 1977 elections, compared to its previous narrow margin, would seem to suggest that there has been an appreciable shift in the racial balance of the remaining Surinamese population.

STRENGTH AND BUDGET

Population: 448,000
Army: 1,000
Navy: (included in Army); 10 small vessels
Air Force (in process of formation as part of Army); 4 light aircraft on order
GNP (1978): $455,556,000

COMMAND AND CONSTITUTIONAL STATUS

The Commander-in-Chief is the President. Executive power rests with the Prime Minister, who is also Minister of Defence.

ROLE, COMMITMENT, DEPLOYMENT AND RECENT OPERATIONS

In addition to their internal security duties, the Surinam Armed Forces have a potential external defence role, in that Surinam has border disputes with two of its three neighbours. The southern border with Brazil has not become an issue, but disputes over which tributaries are the true sources of the rivers which define the international borders exist with both Guyana and French Guiana, Surinam's neighbours to the west and east. In each case, a substantial area of sparsely inhabited territory at the inland end of the common border is disputed, amounting to some 6000 square miles on the Guyanese frontier and somewhat less than half that on the French Guiana side. Since the land disputed with Guyana lies in the bauxite belt, and the territory claimed by French Guiana is believed to contain gold, both are of some economic significance, and development of these resources is being delayed by the uncertainty about ownership. With Guyana, the dispute has come near to armed clashes in the past.

Surinam belongs to the United Nations and the Organization of American States, but is non-aligned in foreign policy. The border dispute with Guyana has prevented it from joining the Caribbean Community. It has an agreement with the Netherlands providing training facilities for its armed forces, but there is no defence treaty.

ORGANISATION

The Surinam Armed Forces that were created in 1975 now number over 1000 men. They comprise a single unified force, of which all but a tiny proportion are land forces.

RECRUITMENT, TRAINING AND RESERVES

Recruitment is by voluntary enlistment, and initial training is done within the country. Officer candidates, however, attend the Dutch military college, and in 1979 there were about 30 warrant officers receiving instruction in the Netherlands in various technical specialities.

EQUIPMENT AND ARMS INDUSTRY

Surinam produces no defence material.

Rifle: FN FAL 7.62mm (Belgium)
Sub-machine-gun: M3A1 0.45″ (US)
Machine-gun: FN MAG 7.62mm (Belgium)
Armour: DAF YP-408 APC (Netherlands)
Aircraft: four light aircraft on order

RANK, DRESS AND DISTINCTIONS

Uniforms and rank insignia follow Netherlands practice.

CURRENT DEVELOPMENTS

The most significant recent development was the coup d'etat of August 1980 which established a right of centre government

Gwynne Dyer
Adrian English

SWAZILAND

HISTORY AND INTRODUCTION

Swaziland remained a British Territory after the formation of the Union of South Africa in 1910 and continued, albeit somewhat neglected, as such until independence in 1968. Immediately prior to independence unrest had necessitated the presence of a battalion of British troops. At independence the country assumed the form of a monarchy, in theory constitutional, but perhaps more correctly described as an enlightened despotism. The parliamentary constitution was suspended by the king, Sobhuza II in 1973. A new constitution, providing for a legislature composed of members first selected by local meetings then approved by the king and then elected to form an electoral college which would make the final selection of legislators for both legislatures, was introduced in 1978. In September 1982 King Sobhuza II died, his successor has not yet been selected and the head of State is the Queen Regent (or *Indlovuhazi*, or Great She-Elephant), with a government headed by the Prime Minister, Prince Mabandla Dlamini. In practice the (royal) Dlamini clan dominate Swaziland's life. Whether the political structure will long survive the death of the 82 year old monarch is not clear; much of the loyalty he inspired was personal to him and his family and lineage have a reputation for corruption. The rural areas are generally conservative; the measure of political stability will depend on whether the government can win support in the towns. Overt political opposition groups operate with some difficulty. An underground opposition movement, the Swaziland Liberation Movement, exists, its size and support cannot at present be assessed.

STRENGTH AND BUDGET

Population: 550,000
Armed Forces: An army of 1000—1200; there is also a para-military police unit
GNP: Not available
Defence Expenditure: Not available.

COMMAND AND CONSTITUTIONAL STATUS

The Prime Minister is Commander-in-Chief of the Umbutfo Swaziland Defence Force, the name of the Army.

ROLE, COMMITMENT, DEPLOYMENT AND RECENT OPERATIONS

The Swaziland Army is a new organisation, for the first years of independence Swaziland had hoped to avoid this commitment and expense. The army exists to serve three specific roles; to maintain internal security, specifically against any insurgency mounted by SWALIMO (The Swaziland Liberation Movement) and to guard Swaziland's frontiers against their use by Mozambique-based African National Congress insurgency striking westward towards the Rand across Swaziland, and perhaps to join forces with SWALIMO *en route*. A third role is now emerging; the Swaziland claim to the Ingwaruma (Tongaland) area of northern Natal which would give Swazi-

land access to the sea. At present this area is included within the Kwazulu ethnic 'homeland', but Pretoria is considering giving it to Swaziland, a large percentage of its population being Swazi. The Kwazulu homeland government led by Chief Buthelezi, the most effective black political leader in South Africa (and as such one Pretoria would like to see weakened) has pledged opposition at any and every stage if the transfer is effected.

ORGANISATION

The Army is very small, at present composed of four independent units each of 150—250 men, a fifth is planned. The whole may then be grouped together in a battalion/regimental structure. The independent units operate as border guards.

RECRUITMENT, TRAINING AND RESERVES

Recruitment is by voluntary selection. There is no ethnic problem, Swaziland being homogenous. A number of women were initially recruited for clerical and other administrative duties; this has, apparently, not proved a success. Officers are trained in Britain and Kenya. Senior officers are often former policemen.

Much of Swaziland's army is still in an early, improvised stage. Transport, for example, has to take its place in the queue at the mechanical transport workshops of the Works Department.

The army experienced serious disciplinary problems, soldiers committing armed robbery and other acts of violence, in the late 1970s. Discipline appears now to have improved.

EQUIPMENT AND ARMS INDUSTRIES

The basic equipment is NATO infantry weaponry, of either British or South African origin. Covert South African help, in the form of weapon and perhaps credit, supply can be assumed.

RANK, DRESS AND DISTINCTIONS

These are modelled on those of the British Army.

CURRENT DEVELOPMENTS

Swaziland stands in increasing danger of being caught up, as Lebanon, in the overspill of a situation not of its own making. Insurgent activity into South Africa from Mozambique is almost certain to increase, an accession of territory in the Ingwavuma area could be a doubly-poisoned chalice forming an area of the country not ethnically homogenous and therefore not of general loyalty, and also an area not respected by Mozambique-based insurgents anxious to strike south. No military power that Swaziland is likely to be able to deploy will be sufficient to preserve territorial integrity.

Lloyd Mathews

SWEDEN

HISTORY AND INTRODUCTION

The Swedish military system, like the Swiss, rests upon the militia principle, within a framework of so-called 'total defence'. Its rationale is to present an aggressor with the prospect of having to confront a whole nation in arms, equipped with modern, domestically produced arms, trained to operate in extremes of climate and protected from indiscriminate attack on the population and essential services by a network of deep shelters and strong fortifications. To an extent even greater than the Swiss, the Swedes are determined to show that they are prepared to make extensive economic and social sacrifices to defend their neutrality.

Swedish neutrality is effectively over a century old, while the kingdom has not been involved in war (then against France) since 1814. Her adoption of neutrality, however, follows, like Switzerland's, on a long period of intense military activity, devoted, as Switzerland's was not, to territorial aggrandisement and imperial purpose. This 'imperial' episode in Swedish history began in the sixteenth century when the collapse of the power of the Teutonic Knights, long established on the southern shore of the Baltic, provoked the littoral States into a struggle for dominance in the region. Denmark, with which Sweden had recently been unified, Russia, recovering from a long decline, and Poland, still a strong State, were all anxious to seize the leading position. But it was Sweden, under a new and remarkable dynasty, the Vasas, which was, over the next 200 years, ultimately to do so. The aim of the original Vasa, Gustaf I (1523–60), was chiefly to unify his kingdom and consolidate its boundaries, in which he was remarkably successful. His descendant, Gustaf II Adolph (Gustavus Adolphus) (1611–32), made use of the national army he inherited from him to establish Sweden as the greatest power in northern Europe. Intervening on the side of the Protestant German princes in the Thirty Years' War, he won a succession of brilliant victories and, before his death in battle at Lützen, added considerably to Swedish territory. At the end of the century another fighting king, Charles XII (1697–1718), of even more bellicose character, reaped the whirlwind of Sweden's expansionist policy. Attacked simultaneously by Denmark, Saxony, Poland and Russia, he nevertheless succeeded in forcing the first three to make peace and then carried the war into Russia, eventually as far as the Black Sea. Ultimately defeated at Poltava in 1712, he succeeded in regaining his homeland and in staving off the consequences for another 6 years, but after his death in battle against the Danes, his successor was obliged to make peace and surrender almost all the territory gained during the preceding century.

Despite the collapse of the Swedish empire, the kingdom's achievements were remarkable, and all the more so since they were gained with a conscripted native army, not one of foreigners or mercenaries like those fielded by most of her enemies. Sweden enjoyed, and enjoys still, certain important strategic advantages, notably the deep forests and indented coastline which make her frontiers difficult and dangerous to violate, but her population was small — proportionate to surface area, very small indeed — her economy primitive and her financial resources exiguous. The Vasas

had succeeded nevertheless in raising what is generally regarded as the first national army in Europe (1544) and sustaining it in fighting efficiency for 200 years. Even after the death of Charles XII it remained a formidable force; and the system on which it was raised and maintained, moreover, allowed its gradual transformation into a modern citizen militia without the provocation of any of those civil–military disputes which have marred the constitutional development of other warrior States.

This system, established by Carl XI at the end of the seventeenth century, and made possible as a result of his expropriation (reduktion) of the over-powerful nobles, was known as the indelningsverket or allotment system. On of the land exacted from the nobles were settled the conscript soldiers of the provincial regiments on plots appropriate to their ranks, from the produce of which they were supported. Frequent mustering ensured that they did not allow their agricultural interests to erode their military efficiency. So deeply rooted did the provincial regiments become in Swedish social life that most have survived to this day, thus being the only military units to rival in unbroken descent the regiments of the British army.

In time, however, agriculture sapped the fighting spirit of the army, which did badly in Sweden's later wars, so much so that in 1808 they were unable to resist Russian attempts to impose on them her policy of friendship with Napoleon and were forced to surrender Finland, Swedish since the fourteenth century, almost without a struggle. Despite a temporary recovery under Bernadotte (an ex-Napoleonic marshal whom the Swedes persuaded to accept the succession in 1811, as a result of which the crowns of Sweden and Norway were united in 1814), the decline of the army continued.

Sweden continued nevertheless to behave as if her military power were intact, sending troops to help Denmark protect Schleswig–Holstein in 1848, negotiating in 1855 with Britain and France a treaty guaranteeing her against the consequences of her currently anti-Russian foreign policy, and allowing Swedish troops to serve as volunteers with the Danes during their unsuccessful war with Austria and Prussia in 1864. However, the lightning victories of the Prussians in 1866 and 1870 ultimately convinced Sweden — and Britain as well — that some far-reaching reform of their military system was necessary. That conviction had already brought forth from the middle class, as it had also done in Britain, a voluntary militia, the Sharpshooters, founded in 1860 and soon 40,000 strong, but lacking, like the British rifle volunteers of 1859 (q.v.), military effectiveness. What was really needed, it was seen, was an army based on general conscription and supported out of central funds and, after two decades of dispute with the farmers (still numerically predominant and still directly responsible for the bulk of military costs), such an army was created. In 1885 military service for the peasant soldiers was increased to 42 days annually and 30% of the land tax remitted by the government; in 1895, as a result of Russian threats to Finland and growing tension with Norway (which was to recover its full independence in 1905) general conscription was introduced with an 8 month term of service; and in 1901 the indelningsverket was finally abolished.

It was on a system of general short-term conscription that Sweden has organised her armed forces ever since, though the period of service has fluctuated considerably. In 1924 it was reduced to 4 months, in 1936 raised — in view of Sweden's patent unpreparedness at a time of growing international tension — to 6 months, and during World War II set at 360–450 days, near which it remains today. The introduction of general conscription was associated with the adoption of a formally neutral foreign policy. Though popular feeling was notably pro-German during World War I and anti-Russian during the Russo–Finnish War of 1939–40 (in which Swedish volunteers joined on the Finnish side), official Swedish policy from 1914 onwards was neutralist and has become increasingly strongly so. It is also idealistic, Scandinavia having been in the 1920s and 1930s perhaps more strongly committed to the League of Nations idea and to the vision of general disarmament than any other region in the world, a commitment which almost disarmed Denmark and Norway and brought Swedish preparedness to a low ebb. It is also strongly 'Scandinavian' in character: both immediately before and after World War II Sweden was deeply interested in the co-ordination of defence measures with her neighbours, a policy which almost led in 1948 to the formation of a Nordic Defence Union.

In the last resort, however, Sweden remains intensely independent in spirit. 'Even England suffered occupation in the eleventh century; Sweden has never known it . . . In her enjoyment of such an advantage, she is probably unique among the nations of the Old World, and such things do affect, in ways often difficult to define, a people's character'. It is not difficult to define the way it has affected the Swedish people's attitude to defence. Inheritors of a pioneering, colonising, warrior tradition, descendants of soldiers who won victories across the whole of northern Europe for 200 years, practitioners of a technology (military as well as civil) as advanced as any in the developed world, devotees of a cult of physical hardiness which their high standard of living seems to heighten rather than sap, the Swedes have a genuine determination to protect their own sovereignty and a belief in their power to do so. Their army, moreover, is a popular institution, and politically a beneficent one: 'The constitutional development of every country seems to be related — sometimes closely related — to its military system; and the fact that a great part of the Swedish population took an active part in the armed forces of the country interposed a real obstacle in the way of the establishment of any absolute form of government . . . the nature of the Swedish army, and (not least) the way it was paid, protected Sweden from the perilous choice between military efficiency and civil liberty.'* That judgement relates to the seventeenth and eighteenth century. What the Swedes have achieved in the twentieth is a very high level of military efficiency and its reconciliation with civil and personal liberties as extensive as any in the world.

STRENGTH AND BUDGET

Population: 8,323,000
Army: 9000 regulars; 9000 reservists on duty; 36,000 conscripts in initial training; 80,000 conscripts on refresher training
Navy: 22,000; 12 submarines, 21 destroyers, 150 smaller craft
Air force: 14,000; 421 combat aircraft
GNP (1982 estimate): $110,900,000,000
Defence expenditure, 1982–3: $3,220,000,000
Reserves: total mobilisable strength is given as 700,000; the size of the contingent on reserve refresher training in army units in any one year is about 80,000 and would

represent one-third to one-quarter of the army's effective reserves, which therefore probably number 350,000; in addition, the voluntary home guard of pre-conscripts and ex-reservists numbers 100,000

The defence budget is voted by parliament but, under a recently introduced system, itemised votes — for catering, ammunition, etc. — have been discontinued and the army has been allocated funds for the creation of different sorts of brigades, as it judges fit. Defence spending is fairly high — in 1969 about 15% of the budget, of which figure the army received less than a third — and, at constant prices, has doubled in the last 15 years (from 4,107,000,000 kronor in 1959 to 9,752,000,000 kronor in 1975).

COMMAND AND CONSTITUTIONAL STATUS

Swedish defence is organised and controlled within a system of Total Defence, comprehending Military, Economic, Civil and Psychological Defence (cf. the Swiss and Austrian defence organisation). The King and parliament jointly exercise supreme command: the King in name only (since 1973 he has been a Head-of-State without powers), parliament directly through the powers of the ministers responsible and indirectly through its Permanent Defence Committee. In peace, the Minister of Defence is responsible for the co-ordination and control of Total Defence; in war, his powers would pass to the Prime Minister. However, even in peace the Prime Minister acts as Chairman of the National Defence Council (which is the meeting point of the military defence structure) under its Supreme Command, and the rest of the Total Defence Structure, under the so-called Central Command. The Council consists of, besides the Prime Minister, the Supreme Commander, the heads of the most important civilian Total Defence authorities and one of the Civil Commissioners of the six Military Command Areas (militärområde) into which Sweden is divided, together with such ministers as the Prime Minister may summon. Its policy is executed by the Total Defence Staff Committee on the civil side and by the Supreme Command on the military side; the Supreme Commander is at present Chairman of the Total Defence Staff Committee.

Within the Military Command Areas, the borders of which follow the boundaries of groups of counties (län), defence authority is vested in the six Commanding Generals and six civil Commissioners, of whom the former are directly subordinate to the Supreme Commander. Subordinate to the Commanding Generals are the Military District Commanders; their areas of responsibility correspond geographically with the counties, and the County Administrations exercise defence responsibilities on the civil side, under the Commissioners.

A number of semi-autonomous bodies form part of the Swedish defence structure, notably the Material Administration of the Armed Forces — the Military Procurement Agency, the Fortifications Administration, the National Defence Research Institute and the Medical Board of the Armed Forces. There are also a large number of voluntary organisations devoted to defence activity.

ROLE, COMMITMENT, DEPLOYMENT AND RECENT OPERATIONS

Role
Sweden has taken part in no war since 1815 and has been effectively a 'permanently neutral' State since 1855, when,

*Roberts, Michael, Essays in Swedish History, London, 9, 1967.

Sweden

to avoid involvement in the Baltic episode of the Crimean War, she negotiated a guarantee of integrity from Britain and France. Her neutrality does not exclude her from belonging to pacts or alliances, since both before and after World War II Sweden showed interest in joining a Nordic Defence Union, which would have protected the neutrality of Denmark and Norway (with whom she had made a joint declaration of neutrality in 1912, renewed in August, 1914) along with her own. She is also a member of the United Nations and one of the most frequent contributors to the organisation's Emergency Force (in which over a third of Sweden's regular officers have served), but it does preclude her joining a great power bloc. A semi-official definition of her international position is 'non-alignment in peace leading to neutrality in war'. The role of the Swedish army is to preserve that neutrality. Subsidiary roles are the training of the nation's youth for national service and the fostering of the national will to resist.

Commitment

The army is therefore wholly committed to the territorial defence of the kingdom, except for such volunteers as are on United Nations duty. Since 1964, the four Nordic countries have maintained a permanent contribution to the Emergency Force. Sweden's units are at present a battalion in Cyprus and a detatchment in Lebanon.

Deployment

Sweden is divided into 26 Defence Districts, grouped into six Regional Commands. The Defence Districts coincide geographically in almost every case with the countries (*län*) and each contains a number of regiments (*regementen*) and corps (*kår*), totalling 49 in all. These are training units and are the descendants of the old provincial regiments and corps.

The Upper Norrland Command (HQ Boden) comprises the counties (*län*) of Västerbotten and Norrbotten; the Lower Norrland Command (HQ Östersund) comprises Västernorrland, Jämtland and Gävleborg (north); the Bergslagen Command (HQ Karlstad) comprises Örebro, Värmland and Kopparberg; the Eastern Command (HQ Strängnäs) comprises Östergottland, Södermannland, Stockholm, Uppsala, Västmannland and Gävleborg (south), together with the independent Island of Gotland command; the Western Command (HQ Skövde) comprises Halland, Göteborg and Bohus, Älveborg and Skaraborg; the Southern Command (HQ Kristianstad) comprises Malmöhus, Kristianstad, Blekinge, Kronoberg, Jönköping and Kalmar.

The mobilisable strength is reckoned to be 30 brigades, raised territorially in about equal proportion to the number of training regiments; the exact number and distribution is not revealed. Mobilisation stores are held in about 2000 dumps, distributed throughout the inhabited areas. In addition, there exist about 100 mobile (bicycle) battalions of older reservists (territorial defence) and 500 static defence companies. The voluntary Home Guard (*Hemvärnet*) is a separate force. The 'Coast Jäger', belonging to the naval coastal artillery, are a marine commando force operating in the islands.

The Swedish air force, though separate from the army, is organised for air defence into regions which roughly correspond with the Area Commands, but the fighter—bombers, which co-operate with the army, belong to the First Air Command, which is directly subordinate to the Supreme Commander.

Recent Operations

The Swedish army was last involved in war in 1814, against Napoleon. Swedish contingents are a permanent element of the United Nations Emergency Force, however, as already discussed, and Swedish military missions have trained troops in the Congo Free State (1883–1914), in Persia (1911–15) and in Ethiopia (1934–6 and 1945–64). During World War II about 9000 Swedish officers and men volunteered, on an individual basis, to fight for Finland against Russia, in the Swedish Volunteer Corps, the Hangö Battalion and the Svir Company.

ORGANISATION

Arms of Service

There are seven arms and services: infantry, armour (including armoured cavalry), artillery, air defence, engineers, signals and maintenance troops. The directorates of these are subordinate to the Army Chief of Staff, and with Section I (Organisation and Equipment), Section II (Tactics and Training) and the Camp Commandants' Office, they form the principal branches of the Army Staff (the Home Guard Staff, Central Conscript Bureau and the Army Administration are separate organisations directly subordinate to the Army Commander-in-Chief). More important to the conscript, and to Swedish military tradition and ethos, are the *regementen* and *kår*, many of which can trace their descent from the seventeenth century. They are locally based, train the conscripts from the surrounding district and provide the mobilisation structure for the operational brigades (see below). The infantry regiments (with their headquarters) are: *1 Svea livgarde* (Upplands Bro); *2 Värmlands Regemente* (Karlstad); *3 Livregementetgrenadjärer* (Örebro); *4 Livgrenadjärregementet* (Linköping); *5 Jämtlands Fältjägar* (Östersund); *11 Kronoberg* (Växjö); *12 Norra Småland* (Eskjö); *13 Dalregementet* (Falun); *14 Hälsinge* (Gavle); *15 Älvsborg* (Borås); *16 Halland* (Halmstad); *17 Bohuslän* (Uddevalla); *19 Norbotten* (Boden); *30 Västerbotten* (Umeå); *21 Västernorrland* (Sollefteå); *22 Lapplands Jäger* (Kiruna). The armoured regiments are: *1 Göta Livgarde* (Enköping); *2 Skånska Dragonregementet* (Hässleholm); *4 Skaraborg*

Command

	Infantry	Cavalry	Armour	Artillery	Anti-aircraft	Engineers	Signals	Service
Upper Norrland	2	1	1	1	1	1	1	—
Lower Norrland	2	—	—	1	1	—	—	1
Bergslagen	3	—	—	1	—	—	—	—
East	3	1*	3	2	2	1	1	1
West	3	1	1	—	1	—	1	1
South	2	—	3	2	1	1	—	1

*The Royal Lifeguards; the remaining cavalry are armoured reconnaissance.

(Skövde); *5 Norbottens Pansarbataljon* (Boden); *6 Norra Skånska* (Kristianstad); *7 Södra Skånska* (Ystad and Revinghed); *10 Södermansland* (Strängnäs); and *18 Gotland* (Visby). Regiment 5 (P5) forms with Infantry Regiment *19* (119) a combined unit. The (armoured) cavalry regiments are: *K1 Livgardets Dragoner* (Stockholm), The Royal Bodyguard; *K2 Livregementets Husarer* (Skövde); and *K4 Norrlands Dragoner* (Umeå). The other regiments or *kår*, which are not basic training units, are artillery, air defence, engineer or maintenance; also organised into regiments, though belonging strictly to the navy, is the coast artillery. The artillery comprises: *A1 Svea Artilleriregemente* (Linköping); *A3 Wendes* (Kristianstad); *A4 Norrland* (Östersund); *A6 Småland* (Jönköping); *A7 Gotland* (Visby); *A8 Boden* (Boden); and *19 Bergslagen* (Kristinehamm). The air-defence regiments are: *Lv2 Gotlands Luftvärnsbataljon* (Visby); *Lv3 Roslagens Luftvärnsregemente* (Norrtälje); *Lv4 Skånska* (Malmö); *Lv5 Sundvall* (Sundvall); *Lv6 Göta* (Göteborg); and *Lv7 Luleå* (Luleå). The engineer regiments are: *Ing. 1 Svea Ingenjörregemente* (Södertälje); *Ing. 2 Göta* (Eksjö); and *Ing. 3 Boden* (Boden). The signal regiments are: *S1 Upplands Regemente*; *S2 Göta Signalregemente* (Karlsborg); and *S3 Norrlands Signalbataljon* (Boden). The maintenance (*träng*) regiments are: *T1 Svea Trängregemente* (Linköping); *T2 Göta* (Karlsborg); *T3 Norrland* (Solleften); and *T4 Shånska* (Hässleholm). The coast artillery regiments are: *KA1 Vaxholms Kustartileriregemente* (Vaxholm); *KA2 Karlskrona* (Karlskrona); *KA3 Gotland* (Fårösund); *KA4 Älvsborg* (Göteborg); and *KA5 Härnösand* (Härnösand). An army aviation battalion and eleven artillery aviation platoons have recently been formed.

Operational

The basic formation to be found on mobilisation would be the brigade, of which there are three types: armoured (*pansar*), infantry and Norrland (the northern half of Sweden is so-called). It is planned to raise five, nineteen and four, respectively, of these types. The organisation of the armoured brigade is an armoured reconnaissance company; an HQ company; two anti-tank companies (84mm Carl Gustav recoilless gun, Bantam missile and 90mm recoilless gun); an artillery battalion (one battery of four 155mm howitzers, two batteries of six 105mm 4140 howitzers); an air-defence company (Red Eye and 20mm cannon); an engineer battalion; a maintenance battalion; and three armoured battalions (each of two tank companies and two APC companies, an artillery company (105mm) and a maintenance company); total strength about 5000 men. The infantry brigade has the same reconnaissance, engineer, HQ, air-defence and maintenance units, but also one anti-tank company; one assault-gun company; one artillery battalion with three batteries of six 105mm howitzers; and three rifle battalions (each of an HQ company, one mortar company equipped with 120mm and 81mm mortars, one maintenance company and four rifle companies). The HQ company and the rifle companies each have a 90mm recoilless anti-tank gun platoon, and each rifle section has two 84mm Carl Gustav anti-tank weapons. The organisation of a Norrland brigade is very similar, except that its means of transport are different. Both infantry and Norrland brigades are trained to move infantrymen by towing: in the infantry brigade behind a tractor and power take-off trailer, and in the Norrland brigade behind a Laplander tracked all-weather vehicle. In snow, the troops are towed on skis, in ordinary conditions on bicycles. This system had been adopted because Sweden lacks the oil fuel resources to sustain a fully motorised army in action for any length of time (though the cost of fully motorising the army would probably also be prohibitive). The Laplander

vehicles are military, the tractors are to be brought by the local farmers to the mobilisation centres when required; an infantry battalion needs 94 tractors for full mobility. The number of anti-tank weapons in the brigades is to be noted: every other infantryman has an anti-tank weapon. There are also large allotments of anti-tank mines to the brigades.

On mobilisation, the brigades would operate under divisional headquarters. The organisation of divisional troops is one air-defence battalion of two batteries of six 40mm guns and one battery of six 57mm guns; one artillery regiment with one gun battalion of nine 155mm guns and two howitzer battalions with 12 150mm howitzers; and one transport battalion of three companies each with 55 tractors.

The older reservists would form about 100 bicycle battalions, armed with older heavy weapons and small arms, and 400–500 static defence companies.

The voluntary home guard (*Hemvärnet*), 100,000 strong, keeps its weapons at home and forms sections, platoons and companies.

RECRUITMENT, TRAINING AND RESERVES

The personnel of the army is divided into four types: regular, conscript, civil–military and civilian. The civilians are employed on clerical, administrative and stores work; the civilian–military are technicians, doctors and dentists. The conscript personnel consist of privates, junior NCOs and junior officers while the regular cadre consists of officers and senior NCOs. The Swedish regular rank structure is an unusual one, consisting of 'regimental' officers who correspond to the regular officers of other armies; 'company' officers, whose role corresponds to that of warrant officers; and 'platoon' officers, who are equivalent to senior NCOs. Some 'regimental' officers are recruited from the 'company' officer corps and about one-third of the 'platoon' officer corps eventually become 'company' officers'. This system has been adopted to improve recruiting of NCOs, which, in Sweden's high-wage egalitarian society; has been very poor in recent years.

Recruitment

This is by universal conscription of all male citizens at the age of eighteen. The annual contingent is about 40,000. Conscientious objection is allowed, but objectors (except those belonging to certain recognised religious groups) must perform alternative civilian service of 540 days within the Total Defence context; those refusing are imprisoned. The number of authentic conscientious objections registered has risen recently (750–1000 annually), but not at the same rate as in Germany or Holland.

Training

Conscripts are called to their local military district regiment (infantry or armour), examined and then allotted to the appropriate training unit, which may be the military district regiment itself or a specialist unit. The shortest term of service, for drivers, etc. is 255 days (Category G). Most conscripts serve 300 days (Category F) as riflemen. Tank commanders (Category E) and those selected for corporal serve 345 days. Conscript NCOs and conscript officers serve 450 and 540 days, respectively. Conscripts are called up, according to the length of service they will perform, at roughly monthly intervals, those with the longest to do starting first. In this way a future field unit is formed, proceeds to unit training, and is then placed, at the end of its conscripts' term, on a reserve footing.

Conscript corporals ('group commanders'), selected at the outset, undergo special leadership training before joining the ordinary conscripts in the training units. So too do conscript senior NCOs ('platoon commanders'), though they start their training even earlier than the corporals. Successful 'platoon commanders' may volunteer for conscript officer training, which lasts 6 months at a cadet school.

Regular 'platoon' officers undergo a year's training on top of their conscript term. From their ranks are selected the 'company' officers who follow a year's course at their school in Uppsala. 'Regimental' officers proceed via the conscript officer training route. After that term of service, they enter the Military Academy at Karlsborg for a year's course.

Staff training is conducted at the Royal Swedish Staff College, Stockholm, on a tri-service basis. There has also existed since 1951 a National Defence College, serving the Total Defence organisation, at which military and civil-service personnel study with representatives from civilian organisations and private industry.

Reserves

The liability for military service endures to the age of forty-seven, reservists being technically 'on leave' until then. Refresher training takes place after an interval of 2 years from conscript service and then at intervals of 4 years, making five periods of 18 days in all. The first two to three periods are spent in the reservist's field unit — deactivated when he and his comrades completed their conscript term — which is mobilised for the occasion at its mobilisation centre. Reserve refresher training is thus also a practice mobilisation. The last two or three periods are spent in the reservist's local territorial unit.

Corporals and Category E reservists serve an additional 7 days on each refresher course, senior ranks an additional 14 days. Moreover, they all undergo, in the interval between the four-yearly refresher courses, a special period of training: 32 days for officers, 11 days for the rest.

For all reservists, there are also five separate mobilisation practices of 1–2 days. On mobilisation, nine out of ten command appointments are filled by reservists.

EQUIPMENT AND ARMS INDUSTRY

Sweden has one of the oldest established and now most comprehensive arms industries in the world. Its vast mineral resources (particularly of high-grade iron ore and copper), its enormous forests which provided charcoal for smelting, and its plentiful water power, allowed the country in the seventeenth century to become, through the application of royal and foreign capital and immigrant technical skill, a leading exporter of cannon: in 1641 her exports of guns were equal in number to the total of shipborne cannon in the French navy and in 1694 her cannon were reaching Britain, Holland and Portugal as well as Russia and many of the German States. It was not until the second half of the nineteenth century, however, with the coming of the railway and the refinement of the national banking system, that the Swedish engineering industry began to diversify: between 1870 and 1900 the number of engineering workers increased six-fold and the number of engineering works five-fold. A high level of universal education equipped the workforce for advanced industrial enterprise and the country's artificial isolation from world markets in two world wars encouraged self-sufficiency. As a result, Sweden, with a population of less than 9,000,000, has an industrial base of a size and complexity unmatched by many much large developed countries. It includes shipbuilding, aircraft and motor-vehicle industries, all of which are involved in military, as well as civilian, production. The most important defence-orientated firms are the Volvo Corporation, whose subsidiary Svenska Flygmotor produces jet engines and Bolinder Munktell tracked vehicles; Saab—Scania (factories at Linköping, Jönköping and Södertälje) which produces aircraft, missiles and vehicles; Bofors, at Karlskrona, which produces artillery, armoured vehicles, missiles, ammunition and explosives; Förenade Fabriksverken (FFV). at Eskilstuna, which produces small-arms, anti-tank weapons, ammunition and missiles; Hagglunds, at Örnsköldsvik and Mellansel, which produces armoured vehicles; Norma at Åmotfors, which produces small-arms ammunition; and a number of electronic firms — L. M. Ericsson of Stockholm, Philips of Stockholm, Svenska Radio (with factories at Bromma and Kumla), and Standard Radio and Telefon (an ITT subsidiary), all of which produce radar, laser, infra-red and air-defence control systems, fuses and radio communication systems.

About 10% of Swedish military equipment is purchased abroad, since it is a principle, laid down in 1973, that the most favourable bid, whether foreign or domestic, must be accepted when contracts are put to tender (rare exceptions are made for protective reasons). The rest is Swedish made (but includes 15% foreign components). There is an elaborate but effective system for arriving at contracts. Fundamental research on defence equipment requirements is carried out by the National Defence Research Institute (F.O.A.), which is directly responsible to the government but acts on the advice of the services and the procurement agency, the Material Administration of the Armed Forces (F.M.V.). Great importance is attached to writing the specification for new equipment, since finance does not usually allow the manufacture of alternative prototypes, as well as to giving it a 'Swedish profile' — suitability for use by a militia army in an extreme climate and for manufacture within the domestic economy. Development is largely carried out by Swedish industry, at a cost of about $140,000,000 (7% of the defence budget). Annual purchases by the Material Administration of finished equipment amount to $500,000,000 (25% of the defence budget and 6% of the Swedish engineering industry's sales).

The research and procurement process has been remarkably successful in producing equipment universally recognised to be of the first quality, particularly of artillery, anti-aircraft artillery, anti-tank weapons, aircraft and armour, much of which is widely exported. National neutrality imposes restrictions on the export of material to nations actually in conflict, but has not prevented Swedish industry acquiring a virtual Western-world monopoly, for example, of the manufacture, either directly or by granting of licences, of 40mm and 57mm anti-aircraft guns. Some Swedish designs, on the other hand, have proved too advanced or too distinctively 'Swedish' to attract foreign sales, notably the remarkable 'S' turretless tank, now re-equipping the armoured brigades.

Sub-machine-gun: 9mm M-45 Carl Gustav (FFV)
Rifle: 7.62mm Automatkarbin 4 (Swedish-made Spanish CETME)
Machine-gun: M-58 7.62mm (Swedish-made Belgian FN)
Mortars: 81mm M/29 (Swedish-made French Stokes—Brandt) and 120mm M/41 (Swedish-made Finnish Tampella)
Anti-armour weapons: Pansarskott M/68 Miniman (FFV one-shot throw-away missile); 84mm Granatgevär M/48c Carl Gustav recoilless weapon (FFV); 90mm Pansarvärn-spjäs 1110 Huggpipan recoilless gun (Bofors; equips the

brigade anti-tank companies); Robot 53 Bantam wire-guided missile (Bofors); TOW missile (on order) (U.S.)

Anti-aircraft weapons: 20mm M/40 Ivakan (Bofors) automatic cannon (equips the brigade air-defence companies); 40mm L/70 M/48 Ivakan (Bofors) gun (equips the divisional air-defence battalion); 57mm M/54 Ivakan (Bofors) gun (equips the divisional air-defence battalion); Rb 69 Red Eye shoulder-fired missile (*see* USA; equips the brigade air-defence companies); Rb 67 Hawk missile (*see* USA; in separate Hawk unit(s)); Rb 68 Bloodhound 2 (*see* Britain; in air force air-defence battalions)

Artillery: 105mm 4140 howitzer (Bofors; equips the brigade artillery – replacement of the older M/39 and M/40 by the 4140 is in progress); 155mm F howitzer (Swedish-made French M-1950; in the divisional and armoured brigade artillery); 155m 77 semi-SP howitzer (Bofors; replacing the 155mm F); 155m BK 1A (L/50) self-loading SP gun (Bofors; in the divisional artillery; this is a highly advanced weapon, with a traversing turret, 14 round magazine and 25km range); Assault gun: IKV 103 105mm (obsolescent; in the brigade assault gun and anti-tank companies) FH-77 155mm howitzer (Anglo-German; on order)

Armour: Tank-destroyer: IKV 91 90mm gun (Bofors; replacing the IKV 103); APC: PBV (Pansarbandvagn) 302 (FFV; two crew plus 10 men; in the armoured battalions of the armoured brigades); Tank: STRV (Stridsvagn) 101, 102 (British Centurion; in the armoured battalions) and STRV 103B (Bofors; replacing the Centurion; this is the 'S' tank, a turretless vehicle which trains its 105mm gun by moving the whole vehicle with an elaborate hydraulic system; it has aroused great interest among tank experts)

Aircraft: 66 Bulldogs, 5 Augusta-Bell 204Bs and 4 Jet Ranger helicopters

RANK, DRESS AND DISTINCTIONS

Rank

General (general) – Crossed batons, four stars

General-löjtnant (lieutenant-general) – Crossed batons, three stars, one oak leaf

General-major (major-general) – Crossed batons, two stars, two oak leaves

Överste av 1 graden (brigadier) – Crown, four stars

Överste (colonel) – Crown, three stars

Överste-löjtnant (lieutenant-colonel) – Crown, two stars

Major (major) – Crown, one star

Kapten (captain) – Three stars

Löjtnant (lieutenant) – Two stars

Fänrik (second-lieutenant) – One star

Förvaltare | (warrant officer, approx.) – Three buttons
Fanjunkar | – Two buttons
Sergeant (staff-sergeant, approx.) – One button

Rustmästare (sergeant, approx.) – One thick bar, three thin bars

Överfurir (sergeant, approx.) – Four thin bars

Furir (corporal, approx.) – Three thin bars

Korpral | (lance-corporal, approx.) – Two thin bars
Vice-korpral | – One thin bar

Badges of rank are worn on the shoulder strap. Generals also wear three embroidered golden oak leaves on the collar. In combat and barrack dress, the rank badges are also worn on one side of the collar, the arm of service badge on the other. The regimental number is worn on the shoulder strap by colonels and below. Officer cadets wear one, two or three gold chevrons on the shoulder strap.

Dress

Formal dress is dark-grey tunic and trousers and peaked cap, with gold buttons and badges. Everyday wear is dark-green battledress. Combat dress is field grey. The steel helmet has cloth ear flaps and peak for winter wear. White snow clothes are worn in winter in the north. The Royal Guards wear nineteenth-century ceremonial uniforms.

Regimental and *kår* badges are as follows: armour, crossed swords; artillery, crossed cannon barrels; engineers, crossed axes, sword and wheel; infantry, crossed rifles.

CURRENT DEVELOPMENTS

The organisation of the Swedish army remains the most impressive example of the militia principle in action to be found outside Israel. The morale of the serving soldiers, the commitment of the youth of military age and the support of the general population are high. Sweden's defence problem is not therefore, as it is in some other Western European countries, a human one. It is economic. The country has been marvellously successful at designing and developing military equipment of the first class for much of this century. But it is now widely felt that the costs of the next generation of equipment, particularly of aircraft but also of ground fighting vehicles and ordnance, which already alarm the defence ministries of the large military powers, may be too great for Sweden to bear. The effects of the recession of the 1970s have been felt particularly severely there but, even if that were not so, it would seem probable that the country, if it is to provide its servicemen with equipment of the standard to which they are accustomed, will have to purchase from abroad. Although foreign equipment has been purchased before, the quantities have been kept small, with a view to avoiding any compromise of the principle of neutrality. If Sweden is now obliged to buy in large quantities, she may find herself committed willy-nilly to an alliance with her supplier. The issue is of even greater importance for Swedish diplomacy than for Swedish defence.

John Keegan

SWITZERLAND

HISTORY AND INTRODUCTION

It is widely known that modern Switzerland possesses no standing army as such, relying on the part-time service of its whole adult population as its principal means of national defence. However, there is a great deal more to the military character of the Swiss than that. *'Point d'Argent, point de Suisse'* ('no money, no Swiss') — Racine's aphorism, though overquoted and often misapplied, conveys two of the most important facts: that they were in their time well-known mercenaries, and that their services were distinctly worth buying. So well worth buying that as late as 1791, two centuries after Switzerland had ceased to act as an independent military power, the Bourbons maintained 11 Swiss regiments on the roll of the French army, besides the Swiss Guards (who were to be massacred the following year in defence of the Tuileries). In addition, Louis XVIII, at his restoration, actually renegotiated the agreement with the Swiss confederation under which these troops were recruited, thus providing his house with three Swiss regiments until its final fall in 1830. That demise severed a connection of 400 years, during which the Swiss had served not only the French (though they were always their principal employers) but most of the armies of western and central Europe including the Swedes, the Dutch and, in the seventeenth century, the English. However, though the official connection was broken, Switzerland continued to provide France, via the Foreign Legion, with a steady stream of excellent soldiers (even after enlistment was declared illegal in 1927 by the Federal government), besides furnishing the Pope, as it still does with the law's approval, with his personal guard (established by Pope Julius II in 1505).

The great military reputation of the Swiss was won, however, not in the service of foreign States but in defence of their own land and liberties, at a very early date and by tactical methods which marked a reversal of a centuries-old trend in European military development. In the thirteenth century, the Swiss, partly through the decay of imperial power (for they were technically vassals of the Holy Roman Empire, the *Reich*), and partly through the natural inaccessibility of their homeland, achieved an effective independence of their overlords. Threatened with submission to feudal status by the ascendant Habsburgs, Archdukes of Austria and soon to be Emperors, the foresters of the three cantons of Schwyz, Uri and Unterwalden met at the Rütli meadow on August 1st, 1291 to swear an 'eternal' treaty of mutual defence. Thereafter these mountaineers successfully maintained their resistance to Habsburg encroachments, and in the battle of Morgarten on November 15th, 1315 they achieved the massacre of a Habsburg army which was foolish enough to penetrate one of the narrow valleys which they were so adept at defending. This was an event of startling importance for two reasons: its was a victory of peasants over their feudal betters and of infantry over cavalry. Socially the former was the more shocking, but technically the latter had wider ramifications, for cavalry had consistently beaten infantry since the eleventh century. In practice, the victory threatened a socio-military revolution, for the social structure of the lands surrounding the forest and mountain cantons was built on the ascendancy of the mounted knight; to demonstrate his military fallibilty was to threaten the settled order of things. The demonstration would have been, nonetheless, of purely local importance had the free cantons remained three in number, but during the fourteenth century they gained adherents: Lucerne in 1332, Zurich in 1351 (the town's adherence was important for the wealth and sophistication they bought to the confederation), Glarus and Zug in 1352, and in 1353 Berne which had 14 years before won a distinctively 'Swiss' victory over the Burgundian nobility at Laupen. These accretions, together with purchases and conquests of, or unilateral alliance with, neighbouring communities not yet admitted to the Confederation, gradually transformed it from an assemblage of would-be free men into an independent power with foreign interests of its own to pursue. Their pursuit involved it, during the fifteenth and early sixteenth centuries, in direct conflict (or alliance) with the great powers: the Habsburgs as always, France, Burgundy, the northern Italian cities and the Papacy.

In almost every battlefield encounter of these years the Swiss were successful, and the nature of one of their rare defeats, the 'mad' battle of St. Jacob-en-Birs, against the Dauphin Louis in 1444, demonstrated why: though outnumbered fifteen to one, the Swiss forded a river in the face of their enemies, attacked and broke into their formation and fought in its centre throughout the day until they were surrounded by 2000 enemy dead, and were themselves killed to a man. The Dauphin returned to France, persuaded that the Swiss were unbeatable; and so they believed themselves to be, in the dense, pike-studded phalanx in which they chose to fight. Besides being overwhelmingly self-confident, they were 'hardy, used to privations and painstakingly drilled . . .' and singled out from other races by 'their preference for killing rather than taking prisoners, their refusal to sacrifice order for plunder, their ruthless punishment of waverers', and their unconcern for the fate of their own wounded. Nor did their strength lie solely in their Kamikaze tactics. The Confederation possessed a remarkable military organisation which 'rested on compulsory military service from the age of sixteen to nearly sixty, on the training of the young men, and on pike-drill; periodical inspections ensured the use and upkeep of weapons . . . by an elaborate system of signals and intelligence, the army when required, could be rapidly mobilised; in the latter half of the fifteenth century the Diet could call up between 50,000 and 60,000 men' (an enormous number for the times; *see later* for comparison with the modern Swiss system).

By the beginning of the sixteenth century, the military importance of Switzerland in European affairs underwent an abrupt eclipse. Its causes have been variously ascribed: to a sudden loss of self-confidence engendered by the defeat of a Swiss army in the battle of Mariginano in 1515, to the signing of the treaty of 'perpetual peace' with France in 1516, to a recognition of the lowering effect of mercenary service on the interests of the Confederation as a whole, to an abrupt outdating of Swiss tactics by the appearance on the battlefield of effective firearms, to which their dense columns of pikemen were extremely vulnerable. None of these explanations is sufficient, for the Swiss continued after 1515 to fight abroad, both as mercenaries and, for a while, in their own cause, and adapted successfully to gunpowder warfare. The real reason is probably simpler, besides being inherent in the federal character of their union: it was that, under the impact of the Reformation (of which two of the most important leaders, Zwingli and Calvin, were Swiss-born), the minimum basis of co-operation between the cantons necessary to the pursuit of a common policy, disappeared. The Swiss had frequently disagreed among themselves – the Battle of St. Jacob had been fought in consequence of a civil war – and the coming of religious disunity (the central cantons around Lucerne remained staunchly Catholic) institutionalised the internal divisions.

In the wider European context, however, religious warfare provided the Swiss for the next 150 years with the most rewarding opportunity for mercenary services that they had yet been offered. Like all mountain peoples, they could win even at the best of times only a frugal living from their native valleys, and emigration was to them a necessary mechanism of economic survival, on a seasonal if not a longer time-scale. Their physical toughness and warlike reputation made their surplus population, like that of such other mountain peoples as the Scottish Highlanders, the Albanians and the Nepalese, readily saleable to foreign military paymasters; but the central situation of their homeland gave them, unlike the Scots and the Nepalese, ready access to several competing markets and hence a much higher return on their physical and moral capital than these other mountaineers enjoyed. France was always their principal employer, and found it in her interest to guard Swiss unity and formal neutrality throughout the wars of the sixteenth and seventeenth centuries, but they also fought, on a strictly contractual basis, for most other European States as well, including their ancient enemies the Hapsburgs. They even fought on opposite sides, a rare eventuality which agreement between the cantons was supposed to avert: at Malplaquet there were Swiss regiments in Villar's and Marlborough's armies.

However, by then – the beginning of the eighteenth century – the dampening of religious animosities in Europe had deprived the Swiss of the more lucrative opportunities for mercenary service, but in compensation had also relaxed the sectarian stresses which had threatened the fragile unity of the Confederation for 200 years. The Swiss continued to provide foreigners with soldiers – though on the formal, bureaucratic footing which the new regular armies of the dynasties required, rather than on the old heady, freebooting basis – but the Confederation itself was gradually undergoing a transformation into the sober, industrious, productive country which the world knows today. In the process, which much increased the power of property owners at the expense of peasants and artisans, it seems to have lost much of its legendary military power, for in the face of French revolutionary armies, invited into their homeland by native sympathisers in 1798, the Swiss militia crumbled. In the long run, however, the collapse of the patrician regime in the cantons may be thought to have been a good thing, for although the Helvetian Republic created by the French Directory was quite foreign in character to Swiss institutions, being highly centralised, the patrician regime it replaced was itself far removed in spirit from the peasant democracy of the forest cantons, while French interference led directly to the remarkably apt constitution imposed by Napoleon (through the Mediation Act of 1803) and to the eventual recognition of Swiss neutrality by Napoleon's victorious enemies in 1815.

The nub of the Napoleonic constitution was the resurrection of the cantons as 'living autonomous units' and the transfer of national defence, but not of military taxation, into federal hands. 'By providing for a cantonally apportioned federal tax, Napoleon thus solved the problem of the financing of the contingents which had for centuries baffled Swiss statesmanship and thereby paralysed Swiss national defence.'

Not that the Swiss benefited from this solution while his power persisted, his imposts on their manpower – which provided the splendid contingents who fought so bravely to assure the crossings of the Beresina in the retreat from Moscow – leaving the homeland so weakly defended that the allies made of that weakness a justification for their infringement of their neutrality in 1813. The powers declared that they 'could not admit a neutrality which existed in name. They would recognise it when the State was free and independent.' It was a warning which the Swiss took to heart and have guarded ever since, and explains the very great size of the army, relative to the population, which they have always subsequently maintained.

The acts of 1803 and 1815 did not solve all Switzerland's problems. The 1803 constitution was drastically revised in 1815 by the patricians of Berne, Zurich and Lucerne, very much to their advantage, while the Confederation's neighbours frequently intervened in its affairs, which were, at mid-century, much agitated by religious antagonisms between the Catholic and Protestant cantons. These antagonisms led, in 1846, to a minor civil war (the *Sonderbund* war), provoked by the Catholics' determination to set up a military organisation of their own separate from the Confederation's. The Diet thereupon elected a General Dufour (the first of only four to have been appointed: Dufour in 1846 and 1856; Herzog 1870; Nille 1914; Guissan 1939) whose brisk and relatively bloodless campaign collapsed the *Sonderbund*'s forces and led to a reconciliation of the cantons and an important democratisation of the constitution.

Switzerland's military history, internal and external, has been subsequently uneventful. The army was mobilised in 1856, successfully to outface a threat of Prussian intervention, in 1870 because of the French–Prussian operations on her borders, and in 1914 and 1939 as a precaution against the Powers violating her neutrality. It is in the mediation of disputes and in the alleviation of suffering caused by war that Switzerland has, during the last century and a quarter, made her mark on the world's battlefields, where her inverted national colours – a red cross on a white field – have come to symbolise impartial relief of distress and to recall the work of the greatest of her modern citizens, Henri Dunant, author of *Un Souvenir de Solférino* and founder of the International Red Cross. The Swiss army remains, nonetheless, a national institution of the greatest importance, symbolising the unity of the cantons and the determination of the Confederacy in the last resort to guarantee its own independence. Socially, it stands for the principle of equality in Swiss life, its officer corps in no sense forming an officer class; practically, it provides the means for the Swiss electorate to render direct and continuing service to the State and to exercise, therefore, their powers as citizens as of right. In its international military aspect, the Swiss army serves as the most telling example of a citizen militia, besides being a force to be reckoned with by major modern armies.

STRENGTH AND BUDGET

Population: 6,370,000

Army: 3500 regulars; 34,000 active conscripts; reserves (mostly army) 580,000 of whom 400,000 do refresher training each year)

Air force: 9000 active; 334 combat aircraft (serviced by civilians)

GNP (1982 estimate): $100,030,000,000

Defence expenditure (1981): $1,780,000,000

COMMAND AND CONSTITUTIONAL STATUS

Command

The Swiss system knows neither a personal supreme commander nor, except in time of war or general mobilisation, a commander-in-chief. The rank of general, except when a commander-in-chief is elected by parliament, remains in abeyance. Supreme command is vested in the 7 man Federal Council (*Bundesrat*). Its functions are exercised by the Councillor for Military Affairs, through the Federal Military Department, which has, under a General Secretariat, three main divisions or *Gruppen*: General Staff (*Generalstabsdienst*), Training (*Ausbildung*) and Armaments (*Rustungsdienst*). The commanders of the four army corps also form part of the Department. The last four officers and the Chiefs of the General Staff and of Training hold the rank of *Oberstkorpskommandant* (Colonel-Corps Commander, equivalent to lieutenant-general). The Heads of the Secretariat and of Armaments are civilians. The Commander of the Air Force, organically part of the army, is on a par with the corps commanders.

These officials and officers form the Federal Military Defence Council (*Kommission für Militarische Landesverteidigung*) which lays down higher military policy. In another guise this council acts as the Minister's Command Staff (*Leitungsstab*).

Constitutional Status

Military service is so intertwined with civil life in Switzerland that the strict 'constitutional status' of the army means perhaps less to the average Swiss than its everyday reality. The army's status is nevertheless very precisely defined by the Federal Constitution of 1874, the second article of which lays down that 'the purpose for which the Confederation is formed is to secure the independence of the fatherland against foreign nations, and to maintain peace and good order within'; article 11 forbids Swiss citizens to enlist as foreign mercenaries; article 13 forbids the Confederation to maintain a standing (i.e. regular) army; article 18 enjoins universal conscription and the soldier's duty to retain his weapons at home; articles 19 and 20 lay down the respective military responsibilities of the Confederation and cantons; article 21 prescribes that units shall be composed of men from the same canton. Articles 85 and 102 regulate military taxation. The distinctive features of the Swiss military system are thus fully and very prominently enshrined in Switzerland's basic law; indeed, as we have seen, Swiss nationhood is arguably military before it is political, cultural or economic.

ROLE, COMMITMENT, DEPLOYMENT AND RECENT OPERATIONS

Role and Commitment

The role of the army is to preserve the permanent neutrality of Switzerland and is wholly self-defensive. The country belongs to no alliance system, is not even a member of the U.N.O. (though it did belong to the League of Nations) and is pledged not to attack any other country under any circumstances. The army's new plans do not envisage it operating outside Swiss territory, although its defensive doctrine is 'aggressive defence'; by that is apparently meant a programme of powerful counter-attacks against the flanks and rear of an invader supported by air interdiction of his lines of communication. Until 1961, when an important *Truppenordnung* (the acts of the Federal Assembly which regulate defence) revised the structures and tasks of the army, the doctrine was one of rigid defence of a series of river lines.

The new doctrine is one of fluid defence of the lowlands by the Field Army Corps, the frontier brigades acting as a covering force for the mobilisation of the border and field divisions, which would offer the main resistance, while the mechanised divisions manoeuvred for a counter-attack in which a very thorough demolition of communications would hamper enemy movement. About 6000 sites in the country are permanently prepared for demolition. The alpine heartland, defended by III *Gebirgsarmeekorps*, is regarded as a last-ditch national redoubt, its territorial, fortress and redoubt brigades being trained to defend its prepared strongpoints, with the mountain divisions providing an active defence. Sections of the army are earmarked to assist the civil population in the event of 'disaster', whether this be natural or manmade (e.g. as a result of military attack) and are used for firstaid, traffic direction, rescue and avalanche duty as part of their normal peace-time service. Since 1970, there has existed a Central Organisation for Co-ordinated Defence (*Zentralstelle für Gesamtverteidigung*) with joint civil—military organs at every level from the Federal to the commander, whch directs the emergency services of the State in any emergency. It has three main branches of activity: military defence, civil defence and 'spiritual defence', and in this last may be seen as carrying on the work of the formidable *Heer und Haus*, a voluntary organisation set up during World War II under the patronage of the then Commander-in-Chief, General Guisan, to invest the policy of neutrality with popular moral authority.

Deployment

The country is divided into four military or corps areas (*Korpsbereiche*): I, II and IV Field Army (*Feldarmee*) and III Mountain (*Gebirgsarmee*) Army Corps (always written 1, 2 and 4 FAK, and 3 GAK). The limits of the 3 GAK area coincide with those of the central ranges, and the southern sub-alpine cantons; those of FAK 1 with the north-western cantons around Berne; those of FAK 2 with the north-central cantons around Lucerne; and those of FAK 4 with the northeastern cantons around Zurich. The border areas of the country are the responsibility of Border Brigades (*Grenzbrigaden*) subordinate to one or other of the Corps.

Recent Operations

The army has taken no part in active warfare since the minor civil war of the *Sonderbund* in 1846. Its last major engagements were against the French in 1798–9, when the Confederation was defeated and occupied. However, Switzerland kept 650,000 men under arms throughout 1939–44.

ORGANISATION

Arms of Service

There are 10 Arms of Service: infantry; mechanised and motorised troops; artillery; anti-aircraft troops; engineer and fortress troops; signals; medical; veterinary; supply; and civil defence troops. The air force counts as a further 'arm of service'. The mechanised and motorised troops are the descendants of the old cavalry, each corps possessing a motorised regiment still called 'Dragonerregiment'. Engineer regiments are called 'Genieregimenter', signals regiments 'Ubermittlungsregimenter' and transport battalions 'Nachschubbataillone'. Infantry battalions are 'Fusilierbataillone'.

Operational

Of greater importance in the structure of the army are the principles of territorial recruitment and age classification. It is divided into three classes (*Heeresklassen*), the *Aufzug* or

Élite of men aged twenty to thirty-two, the *Landwehr* of men aged thirty-three to forty-two and the *Landsturm* of men aged forty-three to fifty (*see* next section). The Field Army (*Feldarmee*) is drawn from the *Aufzug* and the majority of its units are recruited partly for historical reasons, but largely for linguistic and practical reasons, on a territorial basis. The Constitution (Article 21) lays down that this shall be a universal rule, but in practice only the infantry and motorised/mechanised units are strictly cantonal in composition. The *Landwehr* provides men for the Border, Redoubt and Fortress Brigades attached to the corps (*see* later), while the *Landsturm* provides men for supply and transport duties in the Territorial brigades attached to the corps, and for guard, security and civil-defence duties in the Territorial regions and districts (*Kreise*), where they are organised into air-defence (*Luftschutz*) battalions and companies.

Organisation of the Field Army

Army Troops
Outside the four corps organisations, the Field Army disposes of a motorised infantry battalion (*Motordragonerbataillon*), two engineer regiments, two signals regiments and some supply and support units.

Composition of the Corps
The four corps each dispose of three divisions and several brigades. Divisions are either field (*Feld*), mechanised (*Mechanisierte*), or mountain (*Gebirgs*).

FAK 1: *Mechanisiertedivision 1, Felddivision 2 and 3*, and three *Grenzbrigaden*. The corps is chiefly French-speaking.
FAK 2: *Mech. div. 4, Felddiv. 5 and 8*, and three *Grenzbrig.*
FAK 4: *Mech. div. 2, Felddiv. 6 and 7*, and three *Grenzbrig.*
GAK 3: *Gebirgsdivisionen 9, 10 and 12*, three *Grenzbrig.* three fortress brigades (*Festungsbrigaden*) and three redoubt brigades (*Reduitbrigaden*). As *Corps Troops* each of the FAK disposes of the following units: one helicopter squadron (17 Alouette IIs or IIIs), one light-aircraft flight (eight PC-6s); one *Dragonerregiment* (mounted/motorised infantry – in process of reorganisation); one *Radfahrregiment* (cyclists); one *Genieregiment* (engineers) with one engineer battalion, one bridging battalion and one mining battalion; one *Ubermittlungsbataillon* (signals); one *Naachschubbataillon* (supply and transport); one *Krankentransportbataillon* (medical); and one *Verkehrsregelungsbataillon* (traffic control). The Mountain Corps has a mountain infantry regiment in place of the dragoon and cyclist regiments, and its engineer regiment has one engineer and one cable-car battalion. Six 'Territorial Zones', numbers 1, 2, 4, 9, 10 and 12, have replaced the former Territorial Brigades, and have local defence responsibilities.

Composition of the Divisions
Mechanised Division   Two armoured (*Panzer*), each with one anti-tank company and one mortar company, and two tank battalions (these each with two tank and two APC companies); one motorised infantry regiment of three APC battalions; two artillery regiments – one self-propelled (*Haubitz*) regiment of two battalions (*Abteilungen*), each *Abteilung* of three batteries of six guns (M-109, 155mm) and one towed (*Artillerie*) regiment of two *Abteilungen* (one *Abteilung* of three batteries of six 105mm pack howitzers and one *Abteilung* of three batteries of six 105mm guns; one air-defence *Abteilung* of three batteries (24 guns); one engineer (*Pionier*) APC battalion; one signals battalion (*Fernmeldeabteilung*); one medical (*Sanitat*) battalion, one transport (*Nachschub*) battalion, one maintenance (*Feldzeug*) battalion; one traffic-

control (*Verkehrregelungs*) company. Division organisation under change.

Field Division   One armoured battalion (three tank and one APC companies); three infantry regiments (these with three rifle (*Füsilier*) battalions and one support (*Infanterie*) battalion); two artillery regiments – one *Haubitz* regiment of two *Abteilungen*, each of three batteries of six howitzers (105mm pack howitzers) and one *Artillerie* regiment of two *Abteilungen* (one similar to the *Haubitz Abteilung*, and one of three batteries of six 105mm guns); air-defence, engineer, signals and support troops as in mechanised division. Divisional organisation under change .

Mountain Division   Similar to the Field Division but lacks the armoured battalion. The support troops are known collectively as the *Gebirgstrainkolonnen*. Divisional organisation under change.

Border Fortress and Redoubt Brigades   These each dispose of one to two infantry regiments (each of two to four *Füsilier* battalions), one engineer, one anti-tank, one air-defence and one signals company, one artillery *Abteilung* and some supply troops. Organisation under change.

Air and Air-defence Command   This belongs to the air force and disposes of numerous air-defence units in its *Fliegerabwehrbrigade Nr. 33*: six regiments each of three *Abteilungen*, each of three batteries of 20mm and 35mm guns; one regiment of two *Abteilungen*, each of two batteries of Bloodhound missiles. Its airfield brigade (*Flugplatzbrigade Nr. 32*) disposes of 12 static batteries of 20mm or 35mm guns. A further nine similar batteries provide dam defence. The air force also has a small parachute unit (*Fallschirmgrenadiere Kompanie Nr. 17*) and another is planned.

Fortress Guard   An important element of the army is the *Festungswachtcorps* (Fortress Guard), the only sizable permanent element of the army. It consists of 20 companies 50–250 men each) which maintain the arsenals, barracks and fortresses. It has an important equivalent in the *Uberwachungsgeschwader* of the air corps, four fighter squadrons which are, in effect, a standing air-defence force.

RECRUITMENT, TRAINING AND RESERVES

It is widely known that the Swiss have a highly distinctive recruitment and training system (often wrongly called unique, for the Swedish and Israeli are similar) but its precise workings remain more obscure, which is perhaps why its virtues are invoked in argument by militarists and antimilitarists alike. Its principal elements are (*a*) the absence of a standing army – there are only 3000 permanent personnel, (*b*) the universality of the military obligation – all fit Swiss males are inducted at twenty, (*c*) the long duration of service – all soldiers remain in the army until fifty, being technically 'on leave' when returned to civil life from training, (*d*) the short duration of training – 4 months at any one time, (*e*) the retention of weapons in private hands – each soldier keeps his personal weapon in his home and (*g*) the localisation of units – the unit to which the soldier generally belongs is based in, controlled by, and would normally defend, his own canton. 'Recruitment', 'Training' and 'Reserves' have therefore each a special connotation in Switzerland, since all fit adult males are soldiers by virtue of their citizenship (and, it might be said, citizens by virtue of being soldiers) and are theoretically under training throughout their prime manhood;

and, since they are granted 'leave' not 'discharge', belong always to the army, not to its reserves, which do not in theory exist. In practice, its separation into the *Auszug* (*Élite*), *Landwehr* and *Landsturm* (composed of men aged twenty to thirty-two, thirty-three to forty-two and forty-three to fifty, respectively) amounts to a reserve system.

Recruitment

In their nineteenth year, all Swiss males are examined for military service. About 10% are disqualified and 80% are passed for military service; another 10% are passed for 'auxiliary service' — in effect exemption for personal or career reasons. This produces an annual class of 30,000. It is inducted in two halves (February–May and July–November) in its members' twentieth year. There is no provision for conscientious objection in Switzerland. 'Military service, as we understand it, can only be service in a military unit. Thus, according to Swiss law, it cannot take the form of a *Civil* Service. There is only the possibility of assignment to noncombatant medical service. If a citizen refuses to do such service, he is prosecuted under the penal code, even if he appeals to religious motives, since the Swiss Constitution does not grant absolute religious liberty and freedom of conscience. In a conflict between religious liberty and compulsory military service, the latter has priority. The conscientious objectors are merely granted certain alleviations in serving sentence; nor are those sentenced suspended in their civil rights' (speech by H. R. Kurz, Federal Military Information Service, January, 1971). About 60–70 objectors, mainly members of religious sects, are sentenced each year.

Training

Those aged twenty are allotted to the various arms, e.g. infantry, artillery, etc. in groups called 'recruit schools' (*Rekrutenschulen*), of a size to allow manoeuvres in battalion strength at the end of the course. That lasts 118 days in all, the first seventy of which are spent in the barracks where the 'recruit school' is based; the next 42 days are spent in the field, twenty-one on section and platoon tactics, the following twenty-one on battalion exercise. The last week is spent back at barracks on inspection and demobilisation.

Throughout their recruit service, each pair of the three to six companies which form a recruit school is under the supervision of one of Switzerland's few regular officers (called 'instructing officers', *Instruktionsoffiziere*), but the company training is directed by other militiamen, NCOs or officers, whose 118 days' stint is itself part of their training obligation. The corporals who oversee the section training are militiamen of the previous years' recruit school who have been judged suitable for promotion and, in the 27 days prior to the recruit school they train, have themselves been given NCO training (*Unteroffiziersschule*) by 'instructing officers'. The lieutenants are former corporals who have been invited to do officer training (*Offiziersschule*) of 118 days. Higher ranks — militia captains, majors and colonels — are officers who, by invitation, have completed a statutory number of recruit schools as instructors and training courses as pupils. The system, in short, bears comparison with the monitorial system prevalent in British and French State Schools during the early days of compulsory universal education in the last century.

None of the NCO or officer training time exempts its recipients from the annual 3 weeks training (*Wiederholungskurse*) performed by the operational units to which they belong. Indeed before each annual training, they have to perform a short refresher course (*Kadervorkurse*). They then proceed, with the eight youngest classes of soldiers, to form and train as operational units for 3 weeks. The *Landwehr*

perform a similar unit training every 2 years, the *Landsturm* every 4 years.

The regular officers are given an orthodox military training and education of 1 year at the Military Academy in Zurich, to which they may later return for higher training. Regular NCOs of whom there are very few, receive only the militia training normal to their rank.

EQUIPMENT AND ARMS INDUSTRY

Like others of Europe's smaller highly industrialised States with a tradition of neutrality (e.g. Belgium, Sweden and Denmark), Switzerland has a long-established and versatile arms industry of high reputation. The country, though importing several sorts of heavy equipment, manufactures its own small arms, some of its own artillery and its own tank.

The equipment authority for the Swiss armed forces is the Armaments Group (*Gruppe für Rustungsdienst*) of the Federal military department; it has equal status to the General Staff and training groups. It has three branches (a) *Technical* which oversees research, (b) *Commercial* which deals with private national and overseas arms supplies and (c) *Military Workshops* which directs the six Federal arms factories. Armaments policy is decided by the General Staff, which then turns to the Armaments Group for research and procurement. The broad basis of Swiss armaments policy is that the country should be as little dependent as possible on foreign sources of supply (i.e. autarky), but that the national armaments industry should not attempt to produce material at uncompetitive cost. (A policy not always fulfilled: it is said that the P61 and P68 tanks cost 50% more than a comparable foreign model.) As there are parliamentary embargoes on the export of military equipment, this means that it concentrates on research and development of equipment items with which it has already had some success. Parliament also controls the introduction of new equipment by requiring that its production/procurement costs be voted separately from its research costs. Swiss policy also leans heavily on the principle of modification and modernisation, a good deal of its equipment being updated versions of old models. Nevertheless, the Armaments Group spends £120,000,000,000 annually on research, and has spent £1,500,000,000 since 1960 on new equipment (including fighter aircraft).

The five State factories are: Eidgenossische Konstruktionswerkstatte (manufactures the P61/68 tank), Thun; Eid. Munitionsfabrik, Aldorf; Eid. Waffenfabrik, Berne; and Eid. Pulverfabrik, Nimmis. The most important private arms manufacturers are: Schweigrische Industrie Gesellschaft, Neuhausen am Rheinfall (manufactures the standard rifle and machine-gun); Hispano–Suiza, Geneva and Oerlikon, Zurich (the latter now controls the former; both manufacture automatic cannon and anti-aircraft weapons); Contraves AG, Zurich (manufactures fire-control equipment).

ARMS AND EQUIPMENT

Pistol: 9mm P49 (SIG)
(Assault) rifle: 7.5mm Sturmgewehr 57 (SIG)
Medium-light-machine-gun: 7.5mm MG51 (MG42) (Eid. Waffenfabrik, Berne)
Mortars: 81mm MW33 (Eid. Munitionsfabrik, Thun), 81mm MW72 (Eid. Munitionsfabrik, Thun) and 120mm MW4 (Eid. Munitionsfabrik, Thun)
Anti-tank weapons: ROK Rohr 58, Bantam guided missile (Aktiebolager Bofors, Sweden); PAK 50 and 57 90mm gun (Swiss make equipping the support company of the fusilier battalions); PAK 106mm M40AI recoilless rifle

(USA make equipping anti-tank companies); and Dragon (US)

Anti-aircraft weapons: 20mm FLAMK 43 (Hispano–Oerlikon) and 20mm FLAMK 54 (Hispano–Oerlikon) equipping the air-defence *Abteilungen* of the divisions; two guns also in each artillery battery and 12 in the air-defence company of the infantry regiments; the 75 light batteries of army, air field and dam defence also contain these guns; 34 FLAMK 28 (Waffenfabrik, Berne) equipping partly the airfield and dam-defence batteries; FLAMK twin-35mm 63 (Swedish Oerlikon) equipping two batteries of the divisional air-defence *Abteilung* (12 guns) and partly equipping the regiment of *Fliegerabwehr Brigade Nr. 33* (army air defence); Bloodhound SAM (British Aircraft Corporation) equipping the rocket regiment of *Fliegerabwehr Brigade Nr. 32*

Artillery: 105mm H46 pack howitzer (Swedish Bofors; equipping the pack howitzer *Abteilungen* of the divisions); 105mm SK 35 gun (Swedish Bofors; equipping the gun *Abteilungen* of the divisions); and 155mm M-109U self-propelled howitzer (USA; equipping the self-propelled regiment of the mechanised divisions)

Armour: M-113 APC (USA) equipping the *Panzergrenadier* companies of the mechanised divisions (about 1050 in service); Centurion Mk III main battle tank with 20 pounder gun (Britain) equipping the armoured battalion of the field divisions (Swiss designation Pz55); Centurion Mk V and Mk VII main battle tanks with 105mm guns (Britain) equipping the armoured regiment of *Mech.div. 2* (Swiss designation Pz57; about 300 in service); Pz61 main battle tank (Eid. Konstruktionwerkstatte, Thun, Switzerland) with 105mm gun (British–Swiss make; 630bhp Daimler engine (German); 37 tonnes; 300km range; speed 50kph; armour not known; crew 4; equips the armoured regiment of *Mech.div 4*; about 150 in service); Pz68 main battle tank (details as for Pz61, except for weight (36 tonnes), speed (55kph) and range (350km) equipping the armoured regiment of *Mech.div. 1*; about 170 in service)

Aircraft: Alouette II and III light helicopters (France, Aerospatiale) and Dornier AB-47 light helicopter and Pilatus PC6 light aircraft (Swiss Pilatus Flugzeugwerke, Lucerne) equipping *Fliegergeschwader 25*

RANK, DRESS AND DISTINCTIONS

Rank

General (vacant) – Four stars
Oberstkorpskommandant (lieutenant-general) – Three stars
Oberstdivisionär (major-general) – Two stars
Oberstbrigadier (brigadier) – One star
Oberst – Three wide stripes
Oberstleutnant – Two wide stripes
Major – One wide stripe
Hauptmann – Three narrow stripes
Oberleutnant – Two narrow stripes
Leutnant – One narrow stripe

Adjutant–Unteroffizier – One chevron and Swiss cross over two chevrons
Feldwebel – Swiss cross over two chevrons
Fourier – Two chevrons, Swiss cross between
Wachtmeister – Swiss cross over one chevron
Korporal – One chevron
Gefreiter – One bar
Füsilier, etc. –

Note: rank badges in gold; worn by officers on shoulder straps, on upper arm by other ranks

Dress

Swiss parade and walking-out dress, which is of an almost Maoist modesty of design, is an open-necked blue-grey tunic with breeches or trousers. Officers wear a képi, soldiers a side-hat. The combat dress is startling: a very fiercely mottled camouflage jacket and trousers and a steel helmet of gigantic size and apparently mediaeval construction. Specialist badges are worn on the service dress, together with branch facing colours on collar and shoulder-straps, as follows: armour, lemon yellow; artillery, crimson; engineers, black; signals, light grey; infantry, dark green; medical, bright blue; air defence, dark blue; maintenance, violet; supply, green; territorials, orange; and fortress, red.

CURRENT DEVELOPMENTS

The Swiss have been almost completely successful in avoiding any of the dissension which has plagued the conscript armies of the Western democracies during the last 10 years. This must be attributed to the long tradition of genuinely universal military service in Switzerland, to the army's experience in the handling of large annual intakes of twenty-year-olds, to the well-established inadmissability of conscientious objection and the obligation to pay sizable military exemption taxes in the case of foreign residents, to the well-known 'clubbability' of the Swiss (among whose multifarious organisations ex-service clubs are numerous and popular) and, perhaps most important, to the very short duration of the initial training period (as opposed to the long duration of the military liability itself).

The latter factor has grave disadvantages, since for 18 weeks of the year, November to February, Switzerland is virtually demobilised, the Recruit Schools and the Repetition Courses being over and the 'instructing' officers and NCOs busy in their offices and workshops. It is true that these are the months of bad weather when movement even on the plateau is difficult. It is also true that 600,000 men can be mobilised at 48 hours' notice, but the intermittent military timetable to which the Swiss army runs and its conscripts are trained, raises serious questions about how effective it would be when mobilised. The quality of Swiss military equipment is certainly good and the tasks for which the soldiers are trained relatively simple, and likely to be performed in a familiar neighbourhood. But the fact remains that after two years' service the majority of the conscripts have had only 138 days' training. Even in those NATO armies which have reduced the duration of national service below 2 years, conscripts receive three times as much training in the same period.

On the other hand, it is difficult to see with what Switzerland might replace the militia. A standing army would be difficult to recruit in such a high-wage economy, and very much more expensive to support. It could never equal the size of the militia, and could not therefore by itself perform the multiplicity of tasks which Switzerland's defensive plan requires in an emergency. It would almost certainly offer a more convincing counter attack capability than does the militia but the opponents of the standing idea would certainly argue that, given Switzerland's small population and area, counter attack alone could not assure her survival if things had come to all-out war with one of her more powerful neighbours. In such occurrence, it would be a united effort by the whole population which would do most to halt an invasion of the homeland. As long as the principle and fact

559

of the militia remain part of the Swiss way of life – and both are deeply embedded in it – such a united effort would be forthcoming. If tampered with, the will to resist might be dangerously weakened. Questions about the measurable efficiency of the Swiss army may, therefore, seem irrelevant. In an important sense, the militia is Switzerland, and vice versa, and attempts to meddle with that relationship, say by increasing the size of the professional component and reducing the conscripts' tasks to that of local defence, could only do harm.

John Keegan

SYRIA

HISTORY AND INTRODUCTION

Since 1945 the Syrian army has been involved in three major wars and innumerable minor skirmishes with Israel, large-scale military interventions in Jordan and Lebanon, military confrontations with its other two neighbours, Turkey and Iraq, and a total of 21 coups against its own government. It has grown to a regular strength of 200,000 men (300,000 on mobilisation), and absorbs almost one fifth of the entire GNP. It disposes of the most modern weapons in such numbers that it surpasses the British and French armies in total weaponry, although those countries have seven times Syria's population and about fifty times its GNP.

This army, which dominates every aspect of Syrian political and economic life, had its origin in the *Troupes Spéciales du Levant* (originally called the Syrian Legion) which the French created in their newly acquired Middle Eastern possessions after World War I. This territory, comprising what is now Syria and Lebanon, was part of the old Otto-man province of Syria (which had also included Palestine), and had been under Turkish rule for centuries. In the decade preceding the war the very first intellectual stirrings of Arab nationalism had begun in the cities of Syria, and in 1920–22 King Faisal supported by officers of the 'Arab Army' from the Hejaz, which had helped drive the Turks out of Syria in 1918, attempted to rule an independent Syrian-Arab State from Damascus with support from local nationalist elements. In the end, however, the conflicts between a king from Arabia, ex-Ottoman officers mostly hailing from Iraq, and Syrian intellectuals, merchants and notables became too sharp to contain, and it required little military effort for the French to establish their control over the whole country.

The local forces France then created for internal security purposes, however, were built up with the potential threat of Syrian-Arab nationalism very much in mind, and so the pat-tern of recruitment avoided Sunni Muslim Arabs of urban background as much as possible. The Sunni Muslim Arabs of the cities and plains of central Syria make up about 65% of Syria's population, but there is also a 13% Christain min-ority, a small Kurdish minority (albeit Sunni) in the north-east, and a variety of heterodox Muslim or ethnic minorities – Circassian, Druze and Alawite – making up about 17% of the total population, in the mountainous western parts of the country. It was from these minorities, and particularly from the Alawites, that the French recruited most of their *Troupes Spéciales*, on the principle of divide and rule.

The so-called *Troupes Supplémentaires*, consisting of an Alawite battalion, and Druze, Circassian and Kurdish squad-rons, were mainly deployed in their own areas, but the min-orities also constituted a clear majority of the officers and other ranks of the *Troupes Spéciales*. There was, indeed, little inclination on the part of Sunni Arabs to join the force, not only because it was an instrument of alien rule, but because aversion to military service was deeply ingrained in the peasant population after centuries of Ottoman conscription methods. Educated Syrian Arabs, enjoying many more attractive alternatives for advancement in commerce, govern-ment and the professions than their Iraqi counterparts, had never shown the same inclination towards the profession of military officer. Thus in 1938 the *Troupes Spéciales*, num-bering some 10,000 men and 306 officers (of whom only 88 were French, mainly in the higher ranks), contained a majority of Syrians who were of rural background and minority origins. Those urban Sunnis who did become officers were of the lower-middle classes, not from the Syrian political and economic *élite*.

It was these troops who became the core of the new Syrian army after independence. Vichy French control in Syria was overthrown in 1941 by a British and Free French invasion after a futile resistance in which the *Troupes Spéciales* took part, and simultaneously a group of Syrian nationalists proclaimed an independent republic. After a period of military occupation French powers were effectively transferred to a Syrian government in January, 1944, and full independence was achieved in April, 1946. The former *Troupes Spéciales* became the Syrian army, serving the first government to rule an independent and united Syria since the fall of the Ummayad Empire in the eighth century. An air force was founded in 1948 and a navy in 1950.

The new Syrian State almost at once became embroiled in the 1948 Palestine war, in which its troops were severely handled by the victorious Israelis. In immediate reaction to this there were three coups in 1949 led by former officers of the *Troupes Spéciales*, of which the last, headed by Colonel Adib Shishakli, succeeded in retaining power until 1954. The successor government survived numerous further coup attempts and took the country into a federal union with Egypt as the United Arab Republic in 1958, but the extreme resentment of Syrian army officers at being forced to play a subordinate role to the more numerous and powerful Egyp-tians in the new joint army was the main motive force behind yet another coup in 1961 that took Syria out of the union. A further successful coup followed in March, 1962, and a third in March, 1963.

The seemingly endless succession of coups and attempted coups between 1949 and 1963 arose from two principal facts. First, the Arab–Israeli confrontation, arising at the very birth of Syrian independence, created an emphasis on defence which guaranteed that the army would be the most powerful force in the State. Syria was more deeply involved in the conflict than almost any other Arab State both because it was so vulnerable to Israeli attack (Damascus was only 40 miles from the Israeli border) and because the emotional identification with the Palestinians, who were historically indistinguishable from the Syrians, was greater than any-where else. The second reason for the coups was the fact that this overwhelmingly dominant army was internally divided into bitterly hostile factions, in which generational rivalry played a large part.

Colonel Shishakli, like most Syrian senior officers of the 1950s, was a graduate of the French Military Academy at St-Cyr. Like his colleagues, he had developed strong links with the conservative civilian *élite*, and the factions which they formed were allied to parallel factions in that *élite*. Below them in the military hierarchy, however, were younger officers of a more radical disposition, who had attended the military academy at Homs, had been exposed to the radical Arab nationalist ideology expounded by al-Husri, Minister of Education just after independence, and had been deeply influenced by the example and ideas of Egypt's President Nasser. They generally came from the same ethnic and social background as their predecessors in the *Troupes Spéciales* –

from the minority groups, especially Alawites, and from the peasantry and lower-middle classes – but the prevailing intellectual environment and the monopolisation of lucrative alliances with the civilian *élite* by their superiors both drove them in the same direction: anti-colonialism (and consequently anti-Western sentiments) and socialism. The continuous conflict between these two main rival groups of officers, greatly complicated by a proliferation of officer factions because of personal ambition or community allegiance, was the predominant factor in the acute political instability of Syria's government in the 1950s and early 1960s.

The first time that radical nationalist officers achieved power in 1954. No sooner had they done so than Syria began to come under great pressure to adhere to the Western-dominated Baghdad Pact which was then being constructed in the region as part of the West's Cold War strategy against the Soviet Union. These pressures soon extended to Turkish and Iraqi troop movements along the Syrian border, but the new regime was strongly opposed to the Baghdad Pact, which it saw as an instrument for renewed Western hegemony in the area and a distraction from the more important problem of Israel. It was at this point, in 1955, that the Soviet Union first offered diplomatic support to Syria, and also showed willingness to provide the country with the modern arms which the West had refused to sell it. The relationship which began with the delivery of Soviet and Czech arms and the arrival of Warsaw Pact military advisers in that year was more firmly cemented by Soviet promises of support for Syria during the Anglo–French–Israeli attack on Egypt in 1956, a renewed attempt by the Baghdad Pact to precipitate the fall of the Syrian regime through the creation of threatening troop concentrations along the Turkish border, and the Anglo–American military interventions in Jordan and Lebanon in 1958.

The position which the Soviet Union achieved in these years as the principal supplier of arms and training assistance to the Syrian forces has survived all the subsequent changes of regime and vicissitudes of policy. After the emergence of the radical neo-Ba'athist regime in 1966, Soviet military assistance became far more lavish, and it has been indispensable in making possible the expansion of the Syrian army from the 60,000 men and 400 tanks of 1965 to the 200,000 men and 2600 tanks of today. The remarkable stability of this relationship, in comparison to the history of Soviet relations with other Arab countries, derives largely from the fact that the Syrians have never allowed the Soviet Union to gain a disproportionate influence in the internal affairs of the country or army: they have never permitted the Russians military base facilities, nor have Soviet officers and NCOs ever been placed in positions of command over Syrian troops. Consequently, there has not been the kind of anti-Soviet backlash that occurred in Egypt. Despite the deliberate diversion of some Syrian arms purchases to alternative suppliers in the interest of diversification in recent years, and a considerably greater Soviet reluctance to supply arms except for cash payment, the Syrian–Soviet military relationship remains a basic and seemingly indispensable component of Syrian military policy.

The relatively greater stability of Syria's military governments since 1963, which at last permitted a rapid development of the country's economy, was due to the final, inevitable settlement of the generational feud within the officer corps in favour of the younger group in the March, 1963 coup. In contrast to earlier left-wing and radical-nationalist regimes, the group who seized power in 1963 had a political doctrine and a party framework which allowed them to survive. The doctrine was that of the Ba'ath (Renais-

sance) Party, which combined pan-Arab nationalism with a rather incoherent version of Marxist socialism.

The Ba'ath Party was founded in 1943 in Syria by Michel Aflaq, a French-educated Christain Syrian intellectual. It was a movement with tremendous potential appeal to young Syrian officers, being socialist, anti-imperialist and dedicated to the creation of a single Arab State from Morocco to Iraq – with the initial goal of creating a 'Greater Syria' including Iraq, Palestine and Jordan. It adopted early a cellular structure similar to that of underground communist parties, making it an ideal vehicle for political intrigue and the co-ordination of military coups. If once it attained power, moreover, the party's secretive organisation and totalitarian methods made it an ideal instrument with which a relatively small and isolated group of military officers might hope to control and mobilise the entire nation, while its pan-Arab aspect offered the prospect of greatly enhancing Syria's influence in the Arab world. By the early 1960s the Ba'ath Party had far outdistanced Nasserism or communism in its adherents amongst the radical younger officers who had been trained since 1945, and had also attracted large numbers of young Syrian civilian intellectuals.

The coup of March, 1963 was of a different kind from those that had gone before, therefore, and following an attempted counter-coup in July of that year the Ba'athist officers ruthlessly proceeded to eliminate all further centres of resistance within the army, and began the process of economic, political and sometimes physical liquidation of the traditional civilian *élite*. At the head of this government was the army commander, Major-General Amin al-Hafiz, but the majority of his cabinet members were younger Ba'athist officers.

The Ba'athist Party had spread to Iraq as early as 1949, and in 1954 the Iraqi organisation had been erected into a full 'regional' (i.e. Iraqi) branch of the 'national' (i.e. pan-Arab) Ba'athist movement. It chanced that early 1963 was also the first time that a Ba'athist-dominated coup seized power in Iraq, and accordingly one of the then frequent projects for Arab union was tentatively agreed between Syria, Iraq and Egypt in April, 1963. The project collapsed, however, when the Ba'athist regime in Baghdad was overthrown in November of the same year. Since then Syria's Ba'athists have shown little desire in practice to repeat the experiments of 1958–61 and 1963 in pan-Arab unification, despite their theoretical commitment to Arab unity. By the time a fellow Ba'athist regime had re-emerged in Iraq in 1966, indeed, the two main branches of the Ba'ath Party in Syria and Iraq had irrevocably split, nominally over ideological differences, but actually because each feared being dominated by the other. From 1966 to 1978, indeed, the two neighbouring Ba'athist regimes were the bitterest enemies in the entire Arab world. The real explanation for this is probably to be sought in the fact that Syria and Iraq are inevitably the major rivals in the contest for influence or control over the entire 'fertile crescent' which is an unchanging feature of inter-Arab politics.

After a result of disagreements within the Ba'athist Party, a new coup in February, 1966 brought the so-called neo-Ba'athist groups of Dr Nureddin al-Atasi to power, and gave increased influence to civilian elements within the Party. The succeeding 4 years saw the most extreme and brutal totalitarian regime imposed on Syria, with even the small property-owning and merchant classes being effectively destroyed or driven into exile. The army's officer corps became almost totally politicised, with military competence and attention to duty ceasing to figure at all in the selection of officers for promotion. This had much to do with the Syrian army's disastrous defeat in the June, 1967 war with Israel, as a result of which the Golan Heights came under Israeli occupation, and the front line moved appreciably closer to Damascus. (For further comments, *see* Role, Commitment, Deployment and Recent Operations.) Ironically, the military disaster led to a rallying of public support for the Atasi regime, and Syrian equipment losses were quickly made good by the Soviet Union. Soviet influence reached its apogee in Syria in 1968–70, with limited naval facilities being granted to the Soviet navy at the ports of Latakia and Tartus. The same period witnessed a steady rise in the relative influence of the more radical civilian wing of the Ba'ath Party, accompanied by ever greater repression of dissent at home and a growing recklessness abroad. The culmination of the latter was the Syrian decision to intervene in the Jordan civil war of 1970 on behalf of the Palestinian guerrillas, despite the manifest probability that this would result in an Israeli military response which could not be contained by the Syrian army.

Numbers of military officers were greatly opposed to this venture, and none more than the Defence Minister, Lieutenant-General Hafiz al-Asad, a senior Ba'athist who also served as commander of the air force (he was himself a former fighter pilot). The government overruled his protests and dispatched a Syrian armoured column into northern Jordan, but Asad as head of the air force withheld air support; as a consequence the Syrian force was badly mauled by Jordanian tanks and aircraft, and then forced to withdraw by a combination of Israeli threats and Soviet and American pressure. Those responsible for the fiasco were discredited in the eyes of the army, and in November, 1970 the more moderate military wing of the Ba'ath Party seized power under the leadership of Asad in the so-called 'correctionist movement'. Asad was elected President in 1971.

Behind the ideological quarrels and policy disputes which were the apparent substance of intra-Ba'ath politics in the 1960s, however, the reality was somewhat different. The policy disputes were real, as was the evident rivalry between the military and civilian wings of the party, but the actual formation of factions within the officer corps of the armed forces was based primarily on the existing pattern of recruitment from minority communities. Army officers, as in most Arab countries, had been the first major group to become collectively committed to pan-Arab unity, radical transformation of economic and social structures, and the planned expansion of the national economic base, even if, as in Syria, most of them did not belong to the urban Sunni educated *élite* which might be thought the most likely group to adopt these goals. But officers remained Druzes, Circassians, Alawites or Christians even when they had become Ba'ath members, and in the murderous struggle for power in a system without rules which was the reality of Syrian politics after 1949, and especially after 1963, the only trustworthy allies were those who were bound to one by ties of blood and community. Thus military factions were almost always based primarily on groups of a single community, and in view of their predominance in the army the most powerful factions were Alawite. Never was this more true than of the group led by General Asad which has ruled Syria since 1970, and which now utterly dominates the higher command positions in the armed forces and the intelligence services despite the Alawites' mere 11% share of the population.

President Asad's regime was initially extremely popular in Syria, however, because it ended the veritable reign of terror of the previous 4 years. It continued the drive to construct a strong socialist and centralised State controlled by an army-dominated administration, but there was a great easing of economic and political restrictions and a consequent surge of economic growth. The economic liberalisation produced a 159% growth in the GNP between 1970 and 1975, despite the destruction of an estimated $1,800,000,000 worth of industrial infrastructure by Israeli bombing attacks on economic targets during the 1973 war; and the unaccustomed personal style of Asad's leadership reconciled many Syrians to the apparently permanent rule of a totalitarian party dominated by soldiers belonging to non-Sunni minority groups. Asad also took the trouble to erect a certain pseudo-democratic façade to shield this reality: a new constitution was approved by plebiscite in 1973 creating an elected People's Council (legislative assembly), and the National Progessive Front was created by adding the communists, Nasserists and other socialist groups to the governing party (while carefully preserving the actual Ba'athist monopoly of power).

While likewise preserving the control of his own Alawite supporters over the senior command positions in the armed forces, Asad showed great energy in ensuring that the hordes of 'political' officers without adequate military abilities who had risen in the army in the late 1960s were replaced by competent professional officers. This, even more than the lavish provision of arms by the Soviet Union, was the reason for the markedly better performance of the Syrian army in the 1973 Middle Eastern War. (*See* Role, Commitment, Deployment and Recent Operations.)

Asad co-operated with some hesitancy in the post-war disengagement process mediated by United States Secretary of State Henry Kissinger in 1974–5. Syria accepted the possibility of peace with Israel if the occupied Arab territories were returned and an acceptable settlement could be obtained for the Palestinians (which retreat from militancy was the ostensible cause of an even more intense hostility on the part of Iraq, culminating in a crisis in 1975 that required the dispatch of substantial Syrian forces to the Iraqi frontier). But Asad was also aware of the fact that Israeli concessions to Egypt were far more likely than was the return of occupied Syrian territory, not to mention Israeli assent to the creation of a Palestinian State, and he was therefore wary of the possibility that Egypt might make a separate peace with Israel, leaving over-matched Syria to face the huge Israeli military machine virtually alone. From the time of Egypt's second Sinai Disengagement Agreement in 1975 this fear appeared to be becoming a reality, and Syria went into opposition to the 'peace process' as pursued by the USA and Egypt's President Sadat. This did not, however, prevent Damascus from maintaining quite cordial diplomatic relations with the USA and other Western countries (in marked contrast to the pre-1970 regimes), as it gave Syria much more room for manoeuvre than its previous sole reliance on close ties with the Soviet Union.

The growing isolation of Egypt in the Arab world after 1975 enabled Syria to embark with a greater chance of success on a policy which the effective withdrawal of Egypt from the Arab–Israeli confrontation had in any case made necessary: the creation of a regional power position, based on influence in Lebanon and Jordan and over the Palestine Liberation Organisation, which would enable it to bargain more effectively in peace and to depend on an 'Eastern Front' of greater military power in case of war. Thus in August, 1975 the existing informal military co-ordination with Jordan was formalised in the establishment of a Supreme Syrian–Jordanian Military Command to co-ordinate defence preparations and military operations. A proposal was also made to the Palestine Liberation Organisation for the unification of political and military commands, but it was rejected by the Palestinians, who rightly feared Syrian domination. (In Syria since 1970 all Palestinian organisations except those totally subservient to Damascus have been severely restricted in their activities.)

However, the factor which came to dominate Syrian foreign policy after 1975, and has latterly had severe domestic repercussions as well, was the attempt to make use of the Lebanese civil war in order to establish a dominant Syrian position in that country. (For details of the origins and course of the war, including Syrian involvement, see the entry on Lebanon.) Syria has always regarded Lebanon, which was only made into a separate State during the period of the French mandate, as being something less than a foreign country — it never exchanged embassies with Beirut for this reason — and it had traditionally supported the Muslim majority in Lebanon, with its greater consciousness of Arab nationality, against the dominant Maronite Christian minority. During 1975 Syria continued in this course, supplying arms, money and encouragement to the Muslim—leftist coalition which in alliance with Palestinian guerrilla forces was fighting to overthrow Maronite control and convert Lebanon into a 'confrontation State'. In early 1976 it even sent in regular units of the Palestine Liberation Army (which operate under the exclusive control of Damascus) to avert a partition of the country by the Maronite forces. The consequence of this intervention, however, was to tip the balance in the war so strongly in the Muslim—Palestinian favour that the possibility arose of a clear-cut victory and the emergence of a radical Lebanese State under the control of Palestinians and Muslim leftists. Not only would Syria have had little or no influence in such a State, but it would also have created a grave threat to the political stability of Syria itself and a strong probability of war with Israel. Accordingly, Syria switched sides, and from May, 1976 its regular forces were sent into Lebanon in growing numbers to fight alongside the Christians against the Palestinians and Muslim leftists.

Syria's goal was to weaken the latter groups sufficiently that they would be compelled to accept a compromise settlement which would re-create the old Lebanese State, with a fairer share of power for the non-Maronite majority but with effective Syrian hegemony over the entire country. The Palestinians in particular fiercely resisted this prospect, which would deprive them of the one real base of operations they had left near Israel. Had the Syrian military operation been a rapid success, it might have done little damage to Damascus, but it was not possible for Syria to smother resistance by introducing overwhelming force into Lebanon for fear of exciting Israeli suspicions and causing a possible Israeli counter-intervention. The Palestinians held off the limited Syrian forces in fierce fighting in June, 1976 therefore, and the conflict dragged on for months more.

The financial and political cost of this extended Syrian operation was bad enough on the international scene, where pro-Palestinian Iraq stopped trans-shipping oil via Syria, thereby depriving the country of badly needed $150,000,000 in transit revenues, and Palestinian and Iraqi-inspired terrorist attacks in Syria multiplied. The domestic consequences of the Syrian change of side were even worse, however, for the Syrian population was confronted every day for months with the prospect of Syrian soldiers in alliance with Maronite Christians killing Muslim Arabs and Palestinians. To make matters worse, the Syrian government and army which were doing this were controlled by an unpopular minority, the Alawites, who for many orthodox Sunni Muslims fall beyond the boundaries of Islam. Since 1976, therefore, there has been a marked erosion in the acceptability of the regime to the Sunni Arab majority of Syrians, and an apparently locally based terrorist campaign concentrating on the assassination of prominent Alawites. This unrest has been exacerbated by serious economic difficulties largely caused by the direct cost of the Lebanese intervention (some $4,000,000 a day) and its political repercussions on other Arab countries'

aid and trade relations with Syria. The flow of aid from the Arab oil States to Syria as a 'confrontation State' fell from $690,000,000 in 1975 to only $355,000,000 in 1976.

The Lebanese civil war was ended in October, 1976 after Syria had obtained assurances via the USA of Israel's willingness to abstain from intervening if Damascus introduced enough troops into Lebanon to crush Palestinian resistance. This was duly done, and the subsequent Arab summit conference at Riyadh effectively recognised Syrian hegemony in Lebanon, while preserving appearances, by renaming Syria's army in Lebanon the Arab Deterrent Force (with small additional contingents contributed by some other Arab States). But while Damascus thus succeeded in ending the war, it has had little success in re-establishing the conditions for peace, and its army in Lebanon is probably still the only barrier to a resumption of the war. The Muslims and Palestinians were largely brought under control by the end of 1976, but Syria has still to establish its dominance in the parts of the country controlled by the Christian militias. Despite frequent bloody clashes between the Syrian troops of the ADF and the Maronite militias, it is not possible for Syria simply to smother the Christians with overwhelming military force as it did the Palestinians, principally because Israel, which had no objection to Syrians killing Palestinians, might go to war to prevent the Syrians from overrunning the Christians of Lebanon. As a consequence, there were still approximately 35,000 Syrian troops tied down in Lebanon, with little to show for their efforts, two and a half years after the civil war had ended.

Syria's political isolation in the Arab world eased during 1977, and the visit to Jerusalem of President Sadat of Egypt in November, 1977 completed the rehabilitation of Syria by arousing the almost unanimous opposition of the Arab world to what was seen as a plan to consummate an Egyptian—Israeli separate peace. Following the Camp David summit meeting in September, 1978, which seemed to outline the terms of such a treaty, even the long-hostile Iraqi regime effected a reconciliation with Syria in October, agreeing to the creation of a unified military command as a step towards eventual union of the two countries. There must remain serious doubts, however, whether this alliance of the two Ba'athist regimes will ever become more than declaratory.

STRENGTH AND BUDGET

The strength of the Syrian armed forces in 1981 was 222,500 regulars and 102,500 reservists, out of a total population of 8,900,000. The army was far the strongest service, with 170,000 regular officers and men and 100,000 first-line reservists for whom a full regular scale of equipment issue was immediately available. The air force numbered 50,000, all of whom were regulars. The navy is the smallest service by far, with only 2500 regulars and 2500 reservists. The Syrian armed forces incorporate a fourth branch, Air-Defence Command, on the Soviet model, with a strength of 20,000 men, but its personnel are drawn from the army and air force and are included within those totals.

Also included within the army totals, but in practice operating under a separate command, are some 15,000 Special Forces troops, and between 5000 and 10,000 'Detachments for the Defence of the Regime', which serve as a Praetorian Guard. Paramilitary forces include a Gendarmerie of 8000 men, and a Desert Guard (*Hajjana*) of some 1800 men who are principally employed in controlling the bedouins of the eastern desert.

Syrian defence expenditure in 1982 was $2,390,000,000 out of a GNP of $47,000,000,000. In addition to this, unknown further amounts are being spent on national security as 'development expenditure'

COMMAND AND CONSTITUTIONAL STATUS

All executive power is vested in the President, who also holds the office of Commander-in-Chief. In the circumstances prevailing in Syria, where the President is a military officer and depends for his survival on continued control over the army, this is far from being a ceremonial position. All senior military appointments, promotions and transfers are made by the President or his immediate entourage, and similarly all movements of major military units within the country must be approved by him. In reality, indeed, it is not so much the case that the President is the Commander-in-Chief as the other way round: the officer in effective control of the armed forces becomes the President, and acts as the representative of the army in the formal apparatus of the State.

The President appoints his own cabinet, which is not subject to approval by the elected People's Council, and controls the armed forces through the Ministry of Defence. The officer who is Minister of Defence is also the Deputy Commander-in-Chief and is thus in the chain of command. The present incumbent is a very close associate of President Asad, Major-General Mustafa Tlas.

The Chief of Staff of the Armed Forces, General Hikmet Shihabi, is also the Army Chief of Staff. The other three armed forces – air force, air defence and the small navy – have their own commanders and staffs, subordinate to the Chief of Staff of the Armed Forces, or in the navy's case subordinate to the local army commander responsible for the coastal region. The Commander of the Air Force is Major-General Subhi Haddad, with Major-General Adnan Jabi as Assistant Commander and Major-General Ibrahim Hassan as Chief of Staff. The Commander of the Air-Defence Forces is Major-General Ali Salih.

There are at least five major internal security and intelligence services in Syria, some of which fall under the Interior Ministry, while others are answerable to the Chief of Military Intelligence, Major-General Ali Duba. The co-ordinating authority, the National Security Council, is headed by General Muhammad Kholi, who is thus in effect Head of the Secret Police.

Outside of the normal command structure of the army stand the 105,000 strong 'Special Forces' commanded by General Ali Haydar, and the division-strength 'Detachments for the Defence of the Regime', commanded by the President's brother, Lieutenant-Colonel Rifat Asad. Both these formidable formations are recruited almost exclusively from Alawite areas, and are equipped with heavy weapons and tanks. The Detachments for the Defence of the Regime are permanently kept in Damascus protecting the Presidential Palace; the 'Special Forces', equally fanatical in their loyalty to President Asad, have been doing most of Syria's actual fighting in Lebanon since 1976. These two forces would constitute the principal defence of the regime against the rest of the army, should a confrontation arise.

Most of the above-named officers are Alawites. More than half have reached their present eminence since mid-1978, following a wave of transfers and retirements in which most of the remaining senior officers who had been associated with President Asad in the preparation of the 1970 coup were removed from sensitive military positions and replaced by officers who owe their rapid promotions to the present regime. The others are officers who have been very close to President Asad for a long time, and are regarded as ultra-loyalists – like the President's brother Rifat, and Generals Tlas, Shihabi, Duba and Kholi.

Indeed, these five men and one or two others constitute the President's informal inner circle. Regardless of their relative positions in the formal hierarchy of army or regime, they are the men who, together with the President, make all important decisions in Syria and, through the networks of influence they control, ensure that the decisions are carried out. This inner group has not been entirely free from dissension: in 1972 General Muhammad Umran, who was said to have been plotting with Alawite army officers against the regime, was assassinated in Lebanon, and in March, 1978 one of the most senior members of this group, General Naji Jamil, was abruptly removed from his posts as Air Force Commander, Head of the National Security Council and Deputy Defence Minister, allegedly for playing his own political game while in charge of the Syrian military intervention in Lebanon. On the whole, however, the members of the inner circle recognise their mutual dependence, and operate very effectively to safeguard their joint power.

ROLE, COMMITMENT, DEPLOYMENT AND RECENT OPERATIONS

The Syrian army's military role has always been of paramount importance in view of the Arab–Israeli conflict which has been in existence almost from the date of its creation. Its parallel political role has sometimes had deleterious consequences for its primary mission, however: to some extent this was true in the 1948 war, which was ineptly directed by an officer corps in which advancement depended on political influence more than on professional ability, and it was entirely true of the disastrous 1967 war. On that occasion Syrian troops held out grimly in many parts of the Golan Heights under an overwhelming Israeli assault, often only to find themselves deserted by their own officers, who owed their positions to their loyalty to the Ba'ath Party rather than to their courage or competence. Since 1970, however, the army's political role has been severely restricted to the senior officer ranks, and company- and field-grade officers are expected to be able commanders as well as loyal Ba'athists.

Syria belongs to the Arab Defence Council, a subsidiary body of the Arab League created in 1959, and to the Unified Arab Command, set up in 1964. These organisations have never had any practical influence on events, however, and nor did the Federation of Arab Republics, created by Egypt, Syria and Libya in 1971, despite its alleged common defence policy, the existence of a Federal Defence Council, and the appointment in January, 1973 of an Egyptian Commander-in-Chief of all Federation forces. The defence agreements which have been of any significance have all been bilateral ones.

The alliances with which Syria fought the June, 1967 war were the bilateral defence agreements with Egypt of November, 1966 and with Jordan in May, 1967, which provided for the establishment of a Defence Council and Joint Command. Although co-ordination between the allies was extremely poor in that war the arrangement remained in existence, and was later joined by Iraq. Bilateral defence pacts were concluded in Syria and Iraq in May, 1968 and July, 1969, but the hostility between the two regimes prevented them from developing any real military significance. Indeed, the refusal of Syria to allow substantial Iraqi forces to be stationed on Syrian soil in peacetime, for fear that the Iraqi Ba'athists would conspire with sympathetic members of the Syrian Ba'athists to overthrow the Damascus regime, was the reason that Iraqi forces arrived very late on the Golan Front in 1973 and were largely destroyed before even deploying.

The existing Eastern Front Command, a loosely organised structure which had grown out of these bilateral treaties between Syria, Jordan, Iraq and the Palestine Liberation Army, was reorganised into separate Jordanian and Syrian commands in December, 1970. This foreshadowed the events of 1973, when Egypt and Syria in the course of preparing their October attack on Israel agreed that Jordan should be allowed to abstain from participation in the war due to its extreme vulnerability. The presence of Saudi Arabian and Moroccan units in Syria in 1973, although under the auspices of the Arab Defence Council, was also in fact the result of informal bilateral consultations.

The most important of Syria's external defence relationships in the period leading up to 1973, however, was not with an Arab country at all, but with the Soviet Union. Russian arms and training assistance had been the mainstay of Syrian armed forces since the mid-1950s, but after the neo-Ba'ath coup of 1966 and the 1967 war the number and modernity of weapons supplied to Syria rose dramatically. Between 1966 and 1973 the Syrian air force's combat aircraft increased by 250% to 210, and the army's tank force almost quadrupled to 1500. Soviet generosity grew noticeably greater after the expulsion of 20,000 Russian troops and advisers and the curtailment of Soviet air and naval facilities in Egypt in 1972, which left Syria as Moscow's only trusted ally amongst the Arab front-line States. Soviet arms shipments in the first half of 1973 exceeded those of the whole of 1972. The qualitative difference was also great: Syria began to receive the SA-6 missiles which enabled it to erect an air-defence screen over the Golan Heights during the war only in the preceding 12 months.

The Syrian army went to war in October, 1973 enjoying four great advantages over 1967: a vastly expanded and improved armoury of weapons, officers who could be relied on to know their job and stay with the troops, the benefit of years of work by a greatly expanded Soviet advisory corps, and the inestimable advantage of surprise. In consequence, it naturally achieved some striking initial gains. But only those who were astonished to learn that properly trained and led Syrian troops could fight bravely and well would say that the Syrian army's performance in 1973 was anything more than passable.

The Egyptians had analysed the specific problem of fighting the imaginatively led Israeli armoured units, assessed the impact of the new anti-air and anti-tank guided weapons, and drastically modified Soviet tactical doctrine to suit the circumstances (although, to be fair, the Egyptians had the enormous logistical obstacle of the Suez Canal to encourage them to consider the merits of a swift advance followed by a solid defence against which the Israelis might beat themselves in vain). The Syrians, by contrast, slavishly followed Soviet tactical doctrine without the resources and reserves to justify such an all-out offensive strategy, and indeed without any political need to pursue such a strategy.

The Syrians committed between 800 and 1200 tanks — the bulk of their armoured force — to the first attack, pursuing an inflexible plan in which insufficient allowance had been made for the inevitable dislocations inflicted on the best-laid plans by actual combat. At heavy cost they overwhelmed the light Israeli covering force on the Golan Heights, but in the course of the fighting the first wave naturally became scattered and lost its momentum. Within 36 hours of the initial attack the Syrian armoured columns had outrun their cumbersome logistical system — though the distances involved were not large — and there was no 'second wave' available to pass through them and continue the attack. Syria simply did not have enough tanks for the strategy it adopted. To make matters worse, command control over Syrian formations was rapidly lost once forces became engaged. As a result the furthest advanced Syrian forces, exhausted, short of fuel, and not infrequently lost, were struck by the Israeli counter-attack which had been absolutely inevitable as soon as mobilisation had been completed (and indeed could have been predicted almost to the hour) and were rolled back rapidly past their start line. By previous Syrian standards, it was an achievement of some merit; by the standards the Syrian army must aspire to if it ever hopes to have the capability to fight Israel on something approaching equal terms, it left a great deal to be desired.

The extremely high rate of Syrian equipment losses, especially in tanks, and the possibility that the Israeli counter-attack might not stop short of Damascus caused the Soviet Union to begin a massive sea and air lift of military equipment to Syria on October 10th. The Syrian army proved to be much more formidable and better organised in defence, however, although Moscow did feel it necessary to indicate to the USA on October 11th that Soviet airborne divisions had been alerted to go to the defence of Damascus, and the headquarters staff of one Soviet division was reportedly flown in. In the fighting around Sa'sa on the road to Damascus the Syrian defensive tactics, based on armour working in co-operation with fortified strong-points, proved particularly effective. Nevertheless, the effective ending of the heavy fighting on the Syrian front only half-way through the 2 week war was caused not by either of these obstacles to a continued Israeli attack, but rather by the transfer of major Israeli forces to the south for the counter-attack on the Sinai front. The Israeli air force, however, was ordered to wage total war against the Syrian economy, and in a series of extremely effective raids almost crippled the economy and communications infrastructure of the country.

The 1973 war was certainly not a military victory for the Syrians. Despite the advantage of surprise and superior numbers, they ended up losing 600km^2 of territory in addition to the area they had lost in 1967. Syrian military casualties included about 5000 dead, and 800 tanks — over half their force — were destroyed. In the political circumstances of 1973, however, almost any military outcome short of the Israeli occupation of Damascus would have meant a political victory for Syria, simply by demonstrating that they were still a military threat which could not be ignored either by Israel or by the Great Powers, and so it proved: under the disengagement agreement of May, 1974 the Israelis withdrew from the additional Syrian territory they had captured.

Nor were the heavy losses suffered by the Syrian forces a serious military problem. Between October 10th and 23rd, 3750 tons of Soviet military equipment was airlifted to Syria, while a greater amount arrived by sea. In a massive resupply operation in the few months after the war the Soviet Union made good almost all of Syria's massive equipment losses in the war, although training replacements for the dead gunners, tank crews and pilots would take some time. Syria nevertheless felt sufficiently recovered militarily to embark on a limited war of attrition in January, 1974 on the Golan Heights which culminated in heavy infantry fighting for the peak of Mount Hermon in April, 1974, and continued until the disengagement agreement in May. Subsequent Soviet arms deliveries have increased Syrian military strength to well above the 1973 level.

Since 1974, apart from the brief deployment of two divisions along the Iraqi border in August, 1975, all the army's operational experience has been in Lebanon. The first Syrian offensive launched against the Muslim–Palestinian forces in June, 1976 was considerably less than a success, due probably to a combination of overconfidence and inadequate numbers. The Syrian regular forces in Lebanon were considerably augmented over the summer and early autumn, however, and the final Syrian drive against the Palestinians in October, 1976 was a complete success. Although there must have been severe morale problems in asking Muslim Syrian soldiers to fight Palestinians and Muslim Lebanese, no serious breakdowns of discipline have been reported.

The morale problem was greatly eased when Syria changed sides again in the Lebanese conflict after the ceasefire of October, 1976. Almost all subsequent fighting by the Syrian army in Lebanon has been against the Maronite Christian militias. There are nevertheless considerable discipline problems involved in having a large part of the Syrian army engaged in what amounts to occupation duties in a much more sophisticated country like Lebanon, and the army has to maintain a 'decontamination' or 'de-Lebanisation' centre near Homs to process returning soldiers who may have acquired a taste for such un-Syrian habits as smoking marijuana. Moreover, the sporadic clashes with the Maronite militias have caused quite considerable casualties to the Syrian army – very roughly, a thousand a year in 1977 and 1978 – and it may be an indication of the morale effects of this on Syrian troops who have no clear idea why they are in Lebanon that tours of duty there are kept short. Most of the actual fighting in Beirut is now done by the *élite* 'Special Forces' units whose chief virtue is their absolute, almost tribal, loyalty to the regime.

In late 1978 there were seven brigades of the Syrian army – about 35,000 men – committed to the Lebanon, where they comprised the overwhelming majority of the ADF and assured Syria predominant influence in Lebanese affairs. These were the only Syrian troops deployed beyond the country's borders. In compliance with strong Israeli warnings, however, there were no Syrian units south of the Litani River, some 10–15 miles form the Israeli frontier, and the intervening space is held by UN forces and an Israeli-supported Christain militia. Moreover, the Syrian forces were distributed all over the Lebanon, and were in no position either to mount a rapid attack against Israel or to respond quickly to an Israeli attack into Lebanon. The presence of Syrian troops in Lebanon thus certainly does not indicate that a new front has become available to the Arabs for military operations against Israel.

At the same time, the absence of 35,000 Syrian troops from the existing Golan front certainly makes it even less likely that Syria would willingly contemplate war with Israel. With the effective departure of Egypt from the ranks of the 'confrontation States', all that now remains of Arab military strength immediately adjacent to Israel is the depleted Syrian army in the Golan and the competent but small Jordanian army to the south. The military balance has hardly ever been less favourable to the Arabs. (For further comments on the present Israeli–Syrian military balance, *see* Current Developments.)

Syria's only option after the defection of Egypt's armed forces from the ranks of the confrontation States was to strive to organise a really solid 'Eastern Front' which might at least serve to deter an Israeli attack, even if it were not capable of any co-ordinated offensive action carrying a reasonable promise of success. The most vital component of such an Eastern Front so far as Syria is concerned is, of course, Jordan, and since 1973 Jordanian–Syrian defence links have been very strong.

Despite the gulf between the official ideologies of the two countries, King Husain of Jordan is a personal friend of President Asad, who may well have prevented his overthrow by refusing to lend air support to the Syrian army's intervention in the Jordanian civil war of 1970, and both leaders recognise that they share what is in strategic terms a single front against Israel. The existing defence relationship between the two was strengthened in 1975 by the creation of a Supreme Syrian–Jordanian Military Command, and although at the time it was motivated more by threats from Iraq than from Israel, it does have contemporary relevance for the latter confrontation as well. It has no executive control over either country's forces in peacetime, but there are regular liaison visits between the Syrian and Jordanian Chiefs of Staff, and there is a joint consultative body which meets to co-ordinate military policy.

Although it is understood that Jordan would stay out of a war between Syria and Israel if possible, the Jordanian army maintains strong forces in the extreme north of the country to avoid offering Israel the temptation of an easy outflanking move around the southern end of Syria's Golan defences, and it is certainly not excluded that some Jordanian forces might be sent into Syria to help out in another war, as indeed they were in 1973. However, on the very important question of creating an integrated air-defence operations centre to co-ordinate the defence of the two countries' airspace – which would certainly make sense operationally, since Damascus and Amman are only a bit more than 100 miles apart – discussions which were held during 1976 ended after Jordan decided to acquire an American-made Improved Hawk SAM system which is incompatible with Syria's Soviet-supplied equipment.

The one Arab State whose full adhesion to the Eastern Front Command might make it a militarily credible deterrent to an Israeli attack is Iraq, and until 1978 relations between Syria and the Baghdad regime were so bad that no possibility of this seemed to exist. In October, 1978 however, Iraq staged a grand reconciliation with Syria, and the two States signed a charter for joint action in 'all political, military, economic, cultural and information fields'. A Joint Higher Political Bureau was established to supervise all aspects of bilateral relations, to meet every 3 months alternatively in the two countries' capitals, and including in its membership the most powerful figures in both regimes. The most important of the four sub-committees that were simultaneously created is the Committee on Military Co-operation, charged with formulating a 'joint defence agreement that will lay the basis for full military union between the two countries'. Iraq also offered to send troops to strengthen Syrian defences in the Golan Heights at once. In the next meeting in late January, 1979 Syria and Iraq signed a mutual defence pact and agreed to proceed via unification of the two branches of the Ba'ath Party to a complete union of the countries into one State with 'one name, one flag, one national anthem and one President who will be alternately Syrian and Iraqi'.

The likelihood that either the Damascus or the Baghdad regime would relinquish even a portion of its control to a joint authority is still very small, however, and it was noticeable that no statement about stationing Iraqi troops in Syria was forthcoming. Although a united Syrian–Iraqi State would indeed be a formidable military, economic and political power, possessing plentiful oil wealth, 415,000 troops, 750 aircraft and 4400 tanks, it is most unlikely to come into existence. The real motive for the reconciliation was fear of the gathering threats that face Iraq due to the Iranian revolution, and that beset Syria due to its own military inferiority to Israel, the endless military commitment in Lebanon, and the defection of Egypt. The Syrian–Iraqi reconciliation amounts to an attempt to remove the distractions of political terrorism in the capitals and military mobilisations along the common border, in order to be better able to face the dangers which threaten both Iraq and Syria at the other end of their countries, along the borders with Iran and Israel.

The deployment of the Syrian army, in consonance with the country's main military preoccupation, is mainly in the south-west, between Damascus and the Golan front, in the Beka'a valley of Lebanon and eastwards from the southern end of the front, in an attempt to protect against Israeli flanking moves. Only light covering forces are maintained along Syria's other frontiers. Most other Syrian troops are located at bases, depots and training camps which are mainly located in and near the larger cities, thus also serving in the function of garrisons. The exception is Damascus, where no formed military units are permitted to enter except Rifat Asad's 'Detachments for the Defence of the Regime'.

The political and internal security roles of the army have been discussed in the preceding sections. It may be added that extensive use is made of the technique of maintaining rival and overlapping intelligence services, some of which concentrate on the armed forces, others on the civilian population at large. What is most striking, however, is the extent to which the army presence permeates civil life and civilian economic activities.

One third of all the motor vehicles in Syria carry the army's green licence plates, and lands, buildings and services have been requisitioned on a very large scale. The armed forces have the ability in practice to disregard the directives of other ministries and to reallocate to themselves resources of material, foreign exchange and industrial capacity which were originally planned for other purposes. There is also a very substantial sector of Syrian industry which is controlled by the army, sometimes with little evident relation to the needs of national defence. Over 200,000 civilians work in army-run enterprises. Taking this together with the effects of conscription and pre-military training in schools, and the omni-present military intelligence services, there can be scarcely a family in Syria which does not have regular contact with the army in one way or another.

The Syrian Army was unwillingly drawn into new hostilities by Israel's invasion of Southern Lebanon on June 6th, 1982. It suffered heavy tank losses in its withdrawal to the line of the Beirut-Damascus road, and subsequently further equipment losses, including the loss of aircraft, in Israel's attacks on its positions in the Beka'a valley, which employed the most modern methods of electronic target acquisition and weapon guidance and homing.

ORGANISATION

Arms of Service
The Syrian army is divided into the conventional arms — infantry, armoured, artillery, engineers — and services. Air-Defence Command, although it combines army and air force personnel under army command, does not have its own separate branch structure.

Operational
The general staff organisation is patterned on that of the French army, with four chiefs of bureaux charged with responsibility for personnel and administration, intelligence, operations and training, and logistics. There is also a special staff composed of the directors of the various technical functions and services. The military chain of command extends from General Headquarters in Damascus to the component field commanders and chiefs of the combat arms. Air force headquarters is also in Damascus. The navy's headquarters is near Latakia; its commander is subordinate to the local army commander in the area, and a Director of Naval Operations exercises direct control over all units afloat.

The Syrian army is made up of four armoured divisions, each with two armoured and one mechanised brigades, and two mechanised divisions which each have one armoured and two mechanised brigades. There are a further two independent armoured brigades, and four independent mechanised brigades and three independent infantry brigades. The army also contains two artillery brigades, five commando regiments, one paratroop regiment, two surface-to-surface missile regiments, one with Scud missiles and one with FROG-7s, and 26 SAM batteries with SA-2/-3/-6s. The internal organisation of all army combat units now closely parallels the Soviet model.

The Air-Defence Command, under army control, is organised into 50 fixed SAM batteries equipped with SA-2/-3s, 25 mobile batteries with SA-6/-8s, anti-aircraft artillery batteries of a variety of calibres, plus interceptor aircraft and air-defence radars provided by the air force.

The air force's tactical organisation consists of: eleven fighter—ground attack squadrons (three with MiG-17s, three with Su-7s); three fighter squadrons with MiG-23s and MiG-27s; 12 interceptor squadrons with MiG-21 PF/MF (under the operational control of Air Defence Command); and transport, helicopter and training squadrons. A reconnaissance squadron of MiG-25s was reported to be operating in Syria in 1976–7, presumably flown by Soviet pilots, but this appears to have been withdrawn. Major Syrian air bases are at Damascus, Hamah, Dumayr, Palmyra, Sahles, Sahra, Aleppo, Blay, Sayqat, Rasafa, Khalkhalah and Masiriyah.

The navy does not appear to have any permanent operational subdivisions; all units at sea are directly controlled by the Director of Naval Operations. The major naval bases are at Latakia and Baniyas.

RECRUITMENT, TRAINING AND RESERVES

Candidates who wish to become regular officers must be between 18 and 23 years of age, and in possession of a satisfactory school matriculation certificate. Selections for the military academies are made from among those who pass the entrance examination and are physically fit.

Army officers undergo a 2 year course of instruction at the Military Academy at Homs, which was founded in 1933 by the French. It is primarily a school for training infantry officers; graduates selected for other arms or services go on to additional specialised training at other army schools, or are sent abroad for instruction at foreign schools and academies. Since 1963, almost all foreign training has been done in Soviet and Eastern European institutions. Upon completion of the 2 year course at the Academy, graduates are commissioned as second-lieutenants.

The Air Force Academy, founded in 1960, is at Nayrab air base near Aleppo. It provides officer candidates with a 2 year course of instruction in theoretical, technical and scientific subjects, and basic flight training. The Naval Academy, founded in 1962, is at Latakia, and also provides a 2 year course of theoretical and practical instruction.

Most of the manpower of the armed forces is provided, at least in the first instance, by conscription, which was introduced by the Service of the Flag Law in 1953. All Syrian males, with a few exceptions, are liable to perform 30 months of military service (subject to extension at the discretion of the army) commencing at age 19 years, and subsequently to serve in the active reserve for 18 years. Some individuals with special qualifications of use to the State have to serve only 18 months, and deferments are available for students going on to university. The conscript classes, designated by their year of birth, are called up in two annual increments in March and September. Some conscripts, mostly college graduates, are selected for training as reserve officers, while most of those with school-leaving certificates become reserve NCOs (though not with the same authority as professional NCOs) after basic training. The remainder of the conscripts serve as privates.

Military training for many Syrian conscripts begins long before induction, in the *futuwah* programme for secondary-school pupils. Begun in 1956 with regular army instructors, it is now run by full-time civilian instructors who are usually reserve NCOs or officers. All male secondary school and university students attend compulsory weekly sessions of military training, and in the case of secondary school pupils compulsory annual summer training camps as well. The school-leaving examination includes military sciences and practical military examinations upon which pass or failure are contingent.

Once in the army, conscripts undergo basic training and then go on to their units where they receive further on-the-job training, most of which is conducted by NCOs. The units of the army operate the usual annual cycle of field training exercises. Conscripts selected for reserve officer training attend a concentrated 9 months course at the Reserve Officers' School in Aleppo, and are then assigned to a unit, usually in the infantry, as an officer candidate. Those whose performance has been satisfactory are granted commissions as reserve second-lieutenants 1 month before the end of their required 2 year tour of duty.

Medical officers are given direct commissions after short periods of military training: 6 months at the Military Academy for those going into the regular service and 3 months at the Reserve Officers' Academy for those fulfilling their national service obligations.

The professional NCO corps is drawn from conscripts who choose to enlist for an initial 5 year period in the regular army on completion of their obligatory service. Full status as a professional rather than a conscript NCO is not granted, however, until the end of the first term of voluntary enlistment. Those volunteers who fail to make NCO may re-enlist up to a maximum total time of 15 years in the service; professional NCOs are retired at forty-five, or at their own request after 20 years of service. There is a wide variety of opportunities for NCOs to receive specialised technical instruction and advanced schooling, both within their own branches and at advanced career technical schools which all three services maintain for senior NCOs. Engineers and other highly trained and technical personnel are also recruited directly by the army as NCOs by the inducements of high salaries and other privileges; this applies particularly to those who work in the army's research centres and maintenance workshops.

The general standard of individual training of the Syrian army in the late 1970s was good, and it was by then largely independent of Soviet training assistance except for specific highly advanced technical subjects. The estimated number of Soviet advisers with the Syrian armed forces in 1978 was 1800, down from 3500 a few years earlier, and the majority of those were assisting in the training of the air force and Air-Defence Command (where the Russians insist on placing one adviser with each SAM unit). The professional NCOs continued to be the backbone of the system, but officer recruitment, though still drawing disproportionately heavily on the minorities, was based on professional competence or promise rather than on the purely political grounds of the 1960s.

In general, quarters, food and pay in the Syrian army compare favourably with what the average serviceman could expect to receive in the civilian economy. Officers and NCOs have separate accommodation, including family housing for married regulars on most posts. Medical care is of a high standard, leave is 30 days a year for regulars and 15 days a year for conscripts, and there are a wide variety of supplements to basic pay for dependents, duty in a combat zone, subsistence and specialist qualifications which in many cases double the basic rate. Officers receive an allowance for servants. Retirement pay is adequate to live on, with NCOs qualifying for retirement after 20 years and officers after 25 years.

The reserves are almost all army, there being only 2500 naval reservists. The widely used figure of 100,000 army reservists represents an estimate of how many reservists the army could actually equip and fit into its formations upon mobilisation; the actual total of former conscripts with a continuing reserve liability is many times that figure. In practice the army would only bring back those who had completed their service within the previous 3—5 years, with the possible exception of reserve officers, as older men would be unfamiliar with much of the army's equipment. The mobilisation organisation for the reserves is maintained at a high level of readiness, and although not so quick-moving as that of the Israelis, could produce most of those reservists who are actually required at 3 or 4 days' notice.

EQUIPMENT AND ARMS INDUSTRY

The Syrian army's armoured strength consists of 1000 T-62, 2200 T-54/-55 and 790 T-72 medium tanks. The army has unknown numbers of BRDM reconnaissance vehicles and BMP MICVs. The mechanised infantry is borne in 1600 BTR-40/-50/-60/-152 and OT-64 APCs. Artillery strength consists of some 800 122mm, 130mm, 152mm and 180mm guns/howitzers, 2600 SU-100 and some ISU-122/-152 SP guns. These are supplemented by 122mm, 140mm and 240mm multiple rocket launchers, and 82mm, 120mm and 160mm mortars. For long-range bombardment of targets within Israel the army has 30 FROG-7 and 36 Scud surface-to-surface missiles.

The formerly standard Snapper, Swatter and Sagger ATGWs have now been supplemented by a purchase of 1000 Milan missiles from France. These are supported by 57mm, 85mm and 100mm towed and ZSU-23-4 and ZSU-57-2 self-propelled anti-aircraft guns, and SA-7/-9 surface-to-air missiles. There are further SA-6/-8/-9 SAMs on order. The army has 40 Gazelle helicopters.

Area air defence, as opposed to mobile point-defence AA weapons with the combat units, is the responsibility of Air-Defence Command. This controls 150 batteries of SA-2/-3 and 125 batteries of SA-6 missiles, AA guns, 12 squadrons of interceptor aircraft and a comprehensive air-defence radar network which, since 1973, has been extended to cover all the country's industrial areas.

The great majority of Syrian weapons are derived from the Soviet Union, and must almost certainly continue to be so, both because of the logistical problems that would arise if major items of military equipment from other countries had to be fitted into the structure, and more importantly because the Soviet Union is the only country willing to provide Syria with arms in the quantities and of the level of sophistication the country requires. Moreover, no other arms supplier has the sheer reserve industrial capacity to provide Syria rapidly with replacements for weapons losses of the scale that were experienced in 1973. Thus, although Syria has deliberately diversified its arms-purchasing policy since 1973 by acquiring specific items of Western military equipment which were superior to their Soviet equivalents – Milan anti-tank guided weapons, and Gazelle and Super Frelon helicopters from France, HOT ATGWs from the USA, AB-212 helicopters from Italy, all-terrain trucks from Germany, and ordnance production equipment from Austria – there is no alternative to the Soviet Union for most of its equipment needs.

There have, of course, been difficulties with Soviet arms supplies as well, on both political and financial grounds. The Soviet Union has used its virtual monopoly position from time to time in an attempt to influence Syrian policy by slowing down the delivery of weapons and spares – in early 1974, for example, when it was trying to persuade Syria to attend the Geneva conference on Middle East peace, and in 1976 during the Syrian military operations against the Palestinians in Lebanon. It also insisted on cash payment for its weapons nowadays, which posed a considerable problem for Syria in 1976–7 when the flow of financial assistance for military purposes from the Arab oil States had temporarily slowed down.

RANK, DRESS AND DISTINCTIONS

The military rank and grade structure is the same for all services and conforms to normal practices. In general, lieutenants command platoons and captains are in charge of companies; squad leaders are usually sergeants with corporals as assistants.

Officers' rank is shown on shoulder boards, NCOs' rank by chevrons of silver thread worn point upward on the upper sleeve; the background colour of the shoulder board or chevron indicates the branch of service.

Fariq (Lieutenant-general) – Crossed swords and two eagles
Liwa (Major-general) – Crossed swords and one eagle
Zaim (Brigadier-general) – Eagle and three stars
Aqid (Colonel) – Eagle and two stars
Muqaddam (Lieutenant-colonel) – Eagle and one star
Rais Awwal (Major) – Eagle
Rais (Captain) – Three stars
Mulazim Awwal (First-lieutenant) – Two stars
Mulazim (Second-lieutenant) – One star

Wakil Awwal (Chief warrant officer) – Three chevrons over two stars
Wakil (Warrant officer) – Three chevrons over one star
Raqib Awwal (First Sergeant) – Three chevrons
Raqib (Sergeant) – Two chevrons
Arif (Corporal) – Two inverted chevrons (point down)
Jundi Awwal(Private first class) – One inverted chevron
Jundi (Private) –

Army combat clothing is of Soviet pattern. Officers' service uniform is wool coat and trousers of British design, with a visored cap; enlisted men wear battledress with a garrison cap. The red-and-white chequered Arab head-dress, the *kaffiyah*, is sometimes worn by soldiers guarding important national buildings. The dress uniform, worn by officers only, is of dark blue with a gold-decorated upstanding collar, black shoes and gold-trimmed belt. Air force personnel wear the same uniforms as the army, and naval uniforms are similar to those of the British or American navies.

Decorations carry considerable prestige, and are distributed sparingly. In order of precedence, the decorations for valour or outstanding performance in war service are: the Medal of Military Honour (four classes), the Medal of Merit

(five classes), the Loyalty Medal (five classes) and the War Medal (four classes). They may be awarded to either military or civilian personnel. Any participant in hostile action against Israel is awarded the Palestine Medal, and those who receive wounds in combat receive the War Wounded Medal.

CURRENT DEVELOPMENTS

Syria's military position *vis-a-vis* Israel has substantially deteriorated since 1973. The country's holdings of major weapons have grown by more than 50% since then, and have more or less kept pace with the rate of modernisation on the other side, but Israel's own stocks of weapons have also grown by at least 50%. Moreover, fully two divisions of Syria's forces are tied down in Lebanon, in positions from which they could not rapidly take an effective part in any fighting. What makes the great difference, however, is the effective departure of Egypt's large armed forces from the Arab–Israeli military balance, thus leaving Syria alone (or at the most, with what help Jordan could provide) to withstand the full weight of an Israeli onslaught. For the first time in the post-war history of the region, it is probable that Israel would enjoy numerical superiority over Arab forces engaged in a war, in addition to its still existing advantages of superior equipment and better-trained operators.

The Syrian regime is currently also concerned about its internal security. The trouble began at the time when the Syrian army attacked the Palestinian and Muslim-leftist forces in Lebanon in June, 1976. Within months, a series of bomb explosions and assassinations of prominent figures associated with the regime – most of them Alawites – had begun in Syria: the seizure of the Semiramis Hotel in September, 1976, the assassination of the military commander of the Hamah region and two other officials in October, an attempt on the life of the Foreign Minister in December, and the murder of the Rector of Damascus University, a relative and close adviser of President Asad, in February, 1977. The first attacks were carried out by Palestinian guerrillas, and there was doubtless Iraqi money supporting the campaign, but it appears that the actual perpetrators of most of these attacks have been dissident groups within Syria's own Sunni majority, most probably belonging to the Muslim Brotherhood. To many Syrian Sunnis, already resentful of the rule of the Alawite clique surrounding President Asad, the action in Lebanon looked to be simply an Alawite–Christian alliance against Muslims.

Nor did the subsequent Syrian reversal of alliances in Lebanon end the ferment which had been unleashed. It also had its repercussions within the army, where between 70 and 100 junior officers were reported to have been arrested in Lebanon at the end of 1976 after protesting against Syria's actions there and their own poor promotion prospects. The assassinations continued – Colonel Razzaq, Commander of the Missile Regiment, was killed in June, 1977 and six people died in a bomb explosion outside Air-Defence Headquarters in Damascus in July – and the elections for the People's Assembly on July 31st–August 1st averaged only a 17% turnout despite President Asad's attempt to co-opt the support of conservative and religious opponents of the regime by permitting numbers of 'independent' candidates to run.

A series of public hangings in Damascus failed to end the assassinations of prominent Alawites, of which there were about another dozen in 1977, including another relative and personal associate of the President. Criticism also began to be voiced within the army against the prominent role of the President's brother, Rifat, demanding the integration of his Special Forces into the army and the unification of the intelligence services. Unverified but apparently reliable reports stated that Rifat Asad and his wife were wounded in an attack by dissident army officers in February, 1978, and during the succeeding months about 20 other prominent Alawites were killed, including two other relatives of the President. The Head of the Security Services was removed in March, 1978 apparently for having been implicated in dealings with dissident officers, and round-ups of Sunni youths in the main cities further frayed the ragged confessional harmony of Syria. In an attempt to ward off trouble, some 400 transfers and retirements of senior armed forces officers were made between July and December, 1978, while the civilian apparatus of the Ba'ath Party was simultaneously purged of branch leaders throughout the country who were opposed to the 'Rifat Asad line'. But in August the Chief of Police Personnel, Colonel Khalil, was machine-gunned outside his home, and a large bomb was dismantled near the home of Rifat Asad.

It also seems probably that the machine-gun attack in June 1979 on the military academy at Homs, when 60 — mostly Alawite — cadets were killed was an expression of Sunni hostility to the Asad regime. Further Sunni attacks on Asad's rule took the form of an enormous car bomb explosion in Damascus in November 1981 and a full-scale uprising in the northern city of Hams in February 1982, which lasted for three weeks, and was put down at the cost — it has been suggested — of 30,000 dead. This figure is probably exaggerated, but there is no doubt that many Sunnis, whether or not members of the Muslim Brotherhood, showed themselves ready to fight to the death against Alawite rule.

Syria's security problem externally is currently an extreme one. Israel's annexation of the Golan Heights in December 1981, though unilateral, gives the Israelis *de facto* possession of the most commanding terrain in the southern approaches to Damascus. The Israeli occupation of Southern Lebanon, 1982—3, allows them to outflank Damascus from the West and thereafter the Syrian Army's positions in the Beka'a Valley. Syria's losses, on the ground and in the air, resisting the Israeli advances in June 1982, were considerable and may not have been made good, despite reports of large shipments of new Soviet equipment.

Gwynne Dyer
John Keegan

TAIWAN

HISTORY AND INTRODUCTION

Defeated on the mainland of China by the Communist Chinese People's Liberation Army in 1949, at the end of a 3 year civil war, Chiang Kai-shek transported the remnants of his army, with American assistance, to Taiwan (Formosa), where he re-established his government, claiming for it legitimacy. His claim was effectively accepted by the USA until 1974.

Under Chiang Kai-shek's direct administration, and with generous American assistance, Taiwan has become one of the most prosperous States in Asia, with a fast-growing economy and a large export trade. But its most remarkable feature remains its enormous army, 320,000 strong, quite disproportionate to its defence needs and, as long as America remains the regime's patron, with no role outside the island.

STRENGTH AND BUDGET

Population: 18,200,000
Army: 310,000
Navy: 38,000 (plus 39,000 marines); two submarines, 32 frigates and destroyers, 104 others (many landing vessels)
Air force: 77,000; 484 combat aircraft
Paramilitary: 25,000
GNP (1980 estimate): $38,000,000,000
Defence expenditure (1980): $3,200,000,000

COMMAND AND CONSTITUTIONAL STATUS

The President is Commander-in-Chief and Head of the Supreme National Defence Council, to which is subordinate the National Security Bureau, the National Defence Planning Bureau and the Military Science and Research Committee. It is composed of the President and Vice-President, Chief of the General Staff, and Ministers of Defence, Interior, Finance and Foreign Affairs. The General Staff is effectively a joint service organisation and its chief is also the President's executive for command and the Defence Minister's executive for administration.

ROLE, COMMITMENT, DEPLOYMENT AND RECENT OPERATIONS

The role of the army on Taiwan must remain a matter for speculation. Chiang Kai-shek steadfastly insisted until his death in 1975 that he intended to lead it in the reconquest of mainland China. Even if the Americans were to permit the attempt today — and they control the waters and airspace around the island — it would certainly be summarily defeated by the C.P.L.A. And the Americans in any case would certainly not permit such a venture. Nor have they shown any readiness to employ the services of the army elsewhere. Its diplomatic usefulness as an 'army in being' seems therefore negligible. The only justification for sustaining its present inflated size would seem to be as a guarantee of the island's security in the event of America quitting the western Pacific.

About 80,000 men of the army are stationed on the islands of Quemoy and Matsu, which are within artillery range of the mainland. The garrison and their mainland counterparts regularly exchange fire, and the bombardments have in the past been very heavy, particularly in the early 1950s. Otherwise the army has taken no part in operations since 1949. It may or may not remain in contact with the handful of Nationalist soldiers hidden in the jungle on the Sino—Burmese border since 1949.

ORGANISATION

The army is organised on American lines. There are 12 'heavy' infantry divisions, six light infantry divisions, six armoured brigades, four tank regiments, three airborne brigades, and five air-defence missile battalions. The marines are organised into three divisions.

RECRUITMENT, TRAINING AND RESERVES

The army has gradually replaced the veterans brought from the mainland in 1949 with locally conscripted youths. Service is for 2 years, beginning at eighteen.

There is an elaborate officer-training system. The academy is modelled on West Point, and the command and general staff college on Leavenworth. The National Defence College at Fenshan is regarded as the descendant of the famous Whampoa Military Academy which produced so many of China's leaders in the 1920s (both Chiang Kai-shek and Chou En-lai served on the staff there).

Trained reserves number 1,000,000, for whom personal arms and equipment are available. It is claimed that all reservists can be mobilised within 10 days.

EQUIPMENT AND ARMS INDUSTRY

Taiwan is now a major industrial power and produces two-thirds of its defence equipment in the island including surface-to-air and surface-to-surface missiles. It does not yet make heavy equipment, but F-5 fighters and helicopters are assembled locally. Small arms are American models, manufactured locally. Heavier equipment is as follows:

Anti-armour weapons: 106mm M-40 recoilless rifle (USA); 500 in service) and 76mm M-18 SPG (USA; 150 in service)
Air-defence weapons: 40mm L/60 Bofors (Sweden; USA); 40mm L/60 M-42 SPG (USA); Chaparral missile, Nike-Hercules missile and Hawk missile
Artillery: 75mm M-116 pack howitzer (USA; 350 in service); 105mm M-101 howitzer (USA; 550 in service); 105mm M-52 SPH (USA); 155mm M-114 howitzer and 155mm M-59 gun (USA); 203mm M-55 howitzer (USA)
Armour: M-113 APC (USA; 1100 in service); M-41 light tank (USA; 1800 in service); M-47/48 tank (USA; 310 in service)
Aircraft: 127 helicopters (UH-1H and Hughes 500). The air force operates 106 military transports

RANK, DRESS AND DISTINCTIONS

The army is entirely American in appearance.

CURRENT DEVELOPMENTS

The army, with which the political leadership remains closely linked, has transformed itself since the 1950s from an ageing and defeated rearguard into a youthful and well-equipped fighting force, supplied from a steady source of manpower and an expanding local industrial base. Its size and state of training make it one of the most formidable armies in Asia, though it is deficient in modern armour. Yet its role, as anything except testimony to the unrealisable ambitions of the successors of Chiang Kai-shek, remains mysterious. Its maintenance, despite American aid (now much diminished) and Taiwan's growing wealth, is a serious strain on the economy. Unless the government foresees a time when American ships and aircraft will no longer deny the Formosan Strait to a mainland Chinese invasion force, it can have no reason for maintaining its military force at this level.

John Keegan

TANZANIA*

HISTORY AND INTRODUCTION

Tanzania came into existence in 1964 following the union of the former mainland State of Tanganyika with Zanzibar. Tanganyika had been a British territory until 1961, and Zanzibar until 1963. Following a revolution of January, 1964 in which the Arab Sultanate was overthrown Zanzibar's new African rulers sought a loose union with the mainland. Although Tanganyikan soldiers fought on the German side in the World War I German East Africa Campaign and for the British in the East African and Burma Campaigns of World War II, the military traditions now commemorated are those of resistance to imperial rule, notably the Hehe resistance to the Germans in 1896–8 and the Maji-Maji Rising of 1905–6. After the army mutiny of January, 1964 the Tanzanian government decided that the British model was unsuitable for a socialist African State (being argued to be elitist) and the Tanzanian People's Defence Forces (TPDF) are organised on more revolutionary principles. The politicisation of the armed forces has in general been successful; occasional minor military conspiracies are reported; a more serious conspiracy arising from the proposed new party and constitutional changes was widely rumoured early in 1977, with another to follow in 1980. This latter led to some withdrawal of troops from Uganda. These were said to have been sent to Zanzibar, but it is not clear whether, on this occasion, Zanzibar was to blame or merely being used as a familiar cover story for an anxiety nearer Dar es Salaam. Tanzania has no significant mainland ethnic rivalries.

STRENGTH AND BUDGET

Population: 20,000,000 (approximately)
Army: 38,000 plus an air force of 1000, a barrack police force, the Police Field Force, of over 1000, and the loosely-organised Workers Militia of some 50,000
GNP (estimate): $5,000,000,000
Defence expenditure: $53,000,000

COMMAND AND CONSTITUTIONAL STATUS

The President of the United Republic of Tanzania, *Mwalimu* J. K. Nyerere, is the Commander-in-Chief of the TPDF. The portfolio for Defence is now held by A. Twalipo. In the lifetime of Zanzibar's revolutionary leader, A. Karume, the islands (Zanzibar and Pemba) maintained their own small forces under the overall shadowy control of Dar-es-Salaam, but in practice available for use only for local purposes. Exercises only occasionally took place together, mainland units were occasionally posted to Pemba, and the islands' soldiers infrequently trained or served on the mainland. Mainland forces were not posted to Zanzibar Island other than on brief ceremonial occasions. After the murder of Karume in 1972, his successor, Aboud Jumbe, has brought the islands much closer to the mainland. The distinctive island units are being merged into truly national ones, and personnel freely exchanged. The union nevertheless remains

consociational and may come under strain when the capital is moved from Dar es Salaam to Dodoma.

A basic requirement for acceptance into the TPDF is membership of the newly formed CCM political party, this party being an amalgamation of the two former TANU and ASP Parties (mainland and island, respectively). There is a Political Commissar for the TPDF: unit and sub-unit commanders are expected to be the heads of CCM committees of their commands. All officers are expected to undertake party work. Officers may also be required to serve in general national administrative postings.

ROLE, COMMITMENT, DEPLOYMENT AND RECENT OPERATIONS

The TPDF appears to have several roles – the obvious one of national defence and security being the most important. Tanzania has had frontier and border anxieties since 1964 – Zaïre and Rwanda supplying refugees, some of whom were turbulent, and a frontier dispute occurring with Malawi later in the decade. From 1965 onwards Tanzania experienced anxieties over her border with Mozambique, Portuguese forces periodically crossing or overflying in pursuit of Frelimo insurgents. In 1971 the Uganda border dispute began following President Nyerere's support for the armed followers of the deposed President of Uganda, M. Obote, who was attempting to recover his position. President Amin's first retaliations included a brief incursion into north-west Tanzania, an air attack on Mwanza and a claim for a border area; he was also known to have larger ambitions for territorial acquisition at Tanzania's expense. In 1976, units, said to be two battalions, were sent to Mozambique, whether to support the Mozambique authorities in internal security or to assist in the defence of Mozambique against the Rhodesians, was far from clear, but no reports of their having been in action against the Rhodesian army were received.

In late October 1978, probably arising out of terminal convulsions within the Amin regime, Ugandan forces in considerable strength crossed into Tanzania to seize the disputed border area (known as the Kagera Salient); the attack was mounted with great ferocity, looting and killing. Some 10,000 people were later reported as missing by the Tanzanian authorities. The Tanzanians were caught by surprise, they were not able to defend the area and were only in a position to launch a counter-attack to clear the Salient in mid-November. The Tanzanians were able to draw on much OAU support, to the extent that Amin was able to portray his ejection as a concession. There then followed an interval, during which both sides prepared for war, Amin receiving deliveries of Italian helicopters and Soviet PT-76 tanks to reinforce a small number already in his possession and his Czech OT-64 wheeled armoured personnel carriers, SAM-7 missiles and Mig 21 aircraft. Over 2,000 Libyan military reservists (some no longer in their youth) were sent by Colonel Gadaffi and some reports alleged field guns, anti-tank guns, small arms and ammunition were all also provided.

In March 1979, having decided at whatever cost to his precarious economy that the threat of Amin must be removed, President Nyerere ordered an attack on Uganda, and a force

---

* For general notes on African armies, see Appendix 1.

574

of a little under 10,000 Tanzanian troops together with 1000 armed Ugandan exiles took to the field. Their plan was a two-pronged attack following a long-range artillery bombardment. One prong advanced towards Kampala along the coast of Lake Victoria via Masaka, another moved inland to Mbarara, turned north-west to Fort Portal and then swung east towards Kampala.

The Tanzanians, wisely if cautiously, based their advance on the speed of marching soldiers, not attempting armoured dashes; this style certainly reduced the number of their casualties. The concept owed much to Tanzanian contacts with Frelimo in Mozambique. Only very occasionally did Amin's forces mount effective opposition. The reasons for this are varied: no pay and low morale, shortages of ammunition (the supply of which was also an acute problem for the Tanzanians as the USSR and China both refused to help, it was rumoured that Britain persuaded India to assist), and a number of sabotage strikes behind the Ugandan lines by opponents of Amin. Another more military reason was the preference of the Ugandans to fight in and around their wheeled armoured troop-carriers so confining them to areas with roads and making them liable to TPDF encircling movements and anti-tank weapon assault from infantry.

Of the few very spirited battles mention need only be made of two in the early stages of the campaign in southern Uganda, at Mutukula and Lukaya, and a competently mounted assault on Entebbe Airport led by the Tanzanian brigadier Mwita Marwa on April 7th: with Entebbe captured Kampala was invested and Amin's defensive positions, mainly Libyan, bombarded, an Amin counter-attack was repulsed, and a Libyan column severely shot up in an ambush. By mid-April Kampala was taken and Amin's remnants were in full flight through Jinja northwards. A number were pursued, and either killed or captured. So badly had Amin misled the Libyan leader that one large Libyan transport aircraft full of fresh soldiers attempted to land at Entebbe after the airfield's capture by the Tanzanians; the machine was destroyed and the soldiers killed.

The campaign saw small-scale air operations by both the TPDF and Amin's air force, the latter with Libyan or Palestinian pilots; on one occasion two Libyan Tupolev Blinder aircraft bombed Mwanza in Tanzania to little effect. Overall, however, it was a slow, competent if unambitious, footsoldiers' war.

A number, probably 400 or more, of the Libyans were killed, others were returned to Libya after the fighting ended.

To strengthen his claim that he had no wish to interfere in Uganda's post-Amin political arrangements, Nyerere had allowed the entry into Kampala to be made by detachments of the Ugandan exiles, TPDF units only entering the city afterwards. There they remained until June 1981. Numbers were increased to over 25,000 in 1979 though later they were reduced when some units were required in Tanzania (see above). The troops, together with a Tanzanian police detachment still remaining, represented Nyerere's policy aims in Uganda, the formation of a pro-Tanzanian regime preferably headed by the former Ugandan President, Obote. While in Uganda, support costs of the TPDF force were paid by Uganda.

The TPDF is also expected to play a part in 'nation-building'; duties in this connection can include rural development work, political instruction and at times repressive enforcement of the Ujamaa (community village) re-settlement schemes. More recently taskings have included control of crime in the cities and border operations to prevent smuggling of crops for export at better prices and the loan of troops to maintain order on Zambia's Copper belt. The TPDF trained insurgents from Portuguese Africa and Zimbabwe prior to independence; a TPDF mission is currently training the newly formed Seychelles force.

ORGANISATION

The ground forces of the TPDF have, following a rapid expansion in the last decade, now reached considerable size. Two division headquarters have been set up, below them are available for allocation eight infantry brigades each of three battalions; a tank battalion, two field, two anti-aircraft, two mortar and two anti-tank artillery battalions, a surface-to-air missile battalion and two signal units. There may also be an engineer unit.

RECRUITMENT, TRAINING AND RESERVES

The formal colonial basis of preference for Nyamwezi and Hehe soldiers has ended; there appear now to be no ethnic preferences except that members of immigrant races seem to be debarred.

In the military units approximately half of the soldiers are regulars and half are national servicemen. A compulsory period of general State service is required from all young men. Some 3500–4000 of these per year may opt to spend most of their service in the military units – after an initial three months on general work (construction or bush clearance) men who meet the party membership qualifications already noted and who can read and write Swahili (the national language) are accepted for 21 months in the ranks. A Standard XII education is required from officer candidates.

Some abuses of the system – in particular party membership being sought in order to opt for the slightly more comfortable military national service – have been alleged. However, TPDF officers appear to have adjusted to their new roles without marked resentment of the loss of apparent elite status; only a few instances of officer subversion have been reported, the most serious being in early 1977. No admission of this was made in Tanzania. One explanation for the apparent acceptance by the officers of a more lowly status than elsewhere in Africa is that the loss of elite perquisites is only apparent and rhetorical and not real, with their privileges more carefully concerned than elsewhere.

In the early independence period of 1961–4, British officers trained – and commanded – units. The British officers left after the 1964 mutiny and assistance was received from Canada, Nigeria (a battalion of whose army was posted to Dar es Salaam while the Tanzanian force was being reconstituted), Ethiopia and West Germany. The USSR, China and the GDR played an initial role in setting up Zanzibar's small force. In this period mainland cadets continued to be sent to Britain for training. In the late 1960s, however, Tanzania's growing friendship with China led to an increasing number of Chinese military advisers and the despatch of cadres to China for training. China gradually asserted a monopoly position and from 1969 onwards it would appear that no Tanzanians trained abroad anywhere else, for a decade. More recently Cuban advisers have been reported; this could well prove to be the case as the Chinese became disenchanted with Tanzania following the latter's support for the Soviet-Cuban-aided MPLA in Angola.

The Workers Militia is seen as a reserve of manpower for home defence and the preservation of socialist policies. In theory, police officers, prison officers, TANU Youth League members and all State servicemen receive weapon training, but this is unlikely to be the case universally in practice.

There is also the barrack police force and a harbour and coastal defence unit.

Recent reports suggest the Force is not without disciplinary problems; theft, extortions and on occasions killings by soldiers have all been criticised locally.

EQUIPMENT AND ARMS INDUSTRY

Reports of the full extent of the Tanzanian armoury are incomplete and at times at variance with each other. It is most unlikely that all units are complete with all the equipments that the unit equipment tables set out.

Equipments reported include thirty Chinese type 59, thirty type 62 and 36 British Scorpion tanks, unspecified numbers of BRDM-2 armoured reconnaissance vehicles and BTR-40, BTR-152, type 56 and K-63 armoured personnel carriers, a range of Soviet and Chinese variants of Soviet 76mm, 122mm and 130mm guns; 82mm and 120mm mortars; 50 BM-21 artillery rocket launchers, over 500 75mm rocket launchers, unspecified numbers of ZPU 14.5mm and ZU 23mm anti aircraft guns with over 100 37mm weapons. Missiles noted include small numbers of SAM-3 and SAM-6 anti-aircraft systems, together with rather larger numbers of SAM-7 equipments. Basic infantry weapons include the normal Soviet battalion weapons, AK-47 rifles and RPG-7 grenade launchers.

The TPDF and air strength comprises three fighter/ground attack squadrons composed of eleven MiG-21, fifteen MiG-19 and three MiG-17 machines. The transport squadron possesses one AN-2, three HS-48, four DHC Buffalo and one Fokker F-28 aircraft. Training fixed-wing machines include two MiG-15 and six Piper Cherokees, and there are six Cessna 310A variants for liaison duties. Helicopters include two Bell 47, five Agusta Bell 205s and six 206s, together with two Boeing CH-47 Chinooks.

RANK, DRESS AND DISTINCTIONS

The formal rank structure remains British, as do several aspects of uniform and dress.

CURRENT DEVELOPMENTS

Tanzania is a very poor country covering a large area of terrain; a major asset however is that mainland Tanzania is remarkably free from ethnic jealousies. The recent economic recession has affected the economy, but the fear of Uganda and the wish to make some assertion in the Indian Ocean and in Mozambique led to the expansion of the armed forces. There are still Tanzanian detachments in Seychelles and in the Comores, their role being, by their symbolic presence rather than their fighting capacity, to keep away the troops of other interested nations. They do, however, also represent President Nyerere's ambition to something approaching a hegemony role in East Africa.

Lloyd Mathews

THAILAND

HISTORY AND INTRODUCTION

The Royal Thai Armed Forces, of which the Royal Thai Army forms the strongest and politically most important part, have more or less continuously exercised power inside Thailand for 40 years. The coup of 1932, organised by a conspiracy of progressive civilians and conservative officers, was designed to end the absolute power of the monarchy, which both groups agreed was a disabling hindrance to Thailand's evolution into modernity. The civilians' programme of modernisation subsequently alarmed their more cautious military partners into excluding them from government which, with interludes from 1944–7 and 1973–6, the army, usually but not always supported by the other armed forces, has controlled ever since. At times the army has encountered fierce opposition from sectors of the population, but its rule has on the whole been accepted by the majority, who are prosperous by Asian standards, accustomed to unrepresentative government and fiercely proud of Thai sovereignty. During the 1950s the government became alarmed by the spread of left-wing subversion, but it was in fact confined to the overseas Chinese community. During the 1960s a more popular communist insurgency developed in the remote regions on the borders of China and Laos, and its suppression has subsequently become a major governmental and military preoccupation. But popular revolution in the cities or central regions is not a threat with which the government is confronted.

The Thais are a vigorous and warlike people, whose ruling house is descended from a successful general who expelled the Burmese from the country at the end of the eighteenth century. The Rama dynasty subsequently added southern Laos to its possessions and established suzerainty over Cambodia. These acquisitions brought it into conflict with the French at the end of the nineteenth century, which might have led to its annexation, had Siam (as it was then known) not already learnt to practice a skillful diplomacy between the various powers competing for advantage in its area. The Royal House had also taken the precaution of seeking help in modernisation, the need for which it early recognised, from several rather than a single European State. Young noblemen were sent abroad to train as officers, for example, at the British, French, German and Russian military academies, while Chulalongkorn, Siam's great modernising king (1868–1910) made a Belgian his principal adviser.

It is difficult, therefore, to characterise the influences which directed the Thai army's development into a modern force (though the navy was heavily influenced by the British). But by the 1930s the army had acquired a modern organisation, based on conscription, which had been introduced in 1917, and a strong corporate sense. It was this modernising and corporate sense which impelled it to join with a group of young civil servants, led by the socialist Pridi Panomyong, to present King Prachatipok with an ultimatum demanding constitutional rule, in June, 1932 – though they were also influenced by the previous king's favouring of an alternative army, called the Wild Tigers, and, with the civil servants, by reductions in the size of the army and civil service made necessary by an economic crisis. Once installed, the new government quickly split, the officers expelled the civilians and thereafter ruled themselves. Their rule until December,

1938 however, was faithful to the spirit of the new constitution. But in that month General Pibun (Phibul) Songkhram, a leader of the 1932 coup and the defender of Bangkok against an unsuccessful absolutist counter-coup in 1933, succeeded to the premiership and quickly made the national assembly a puppet organisation. When the Japanese appeared in Indo-China in 1940, he quickly came to an accommodation with them and took advantage of their arrival to repossess by force the Laotian provinces Thailand (as Siam was known after 1939 – 'Thai' means 'free') had been obliged to cede to France in 1893. Japan's insistence on his accepting their troops on Thai territory led to a minor crisis of conscience, but was swiftly resolved through the inability of the Western powers to aid Thailand's defence. The country therefore spent the war, until August, 1944 as Japan's passive ally.

The course of military events then prompted the ruling group to disentagle itself from Pibun, thus allowing Thailand to emerge in 1945 on the right side, and ruled by the socialist civil servant, Pridi, who had taken part in the coup of 1932. Neither Pibun nor the army had taken the transfer of power to his hands in good part, however, and in April, 1948 Pibun, who had organised a military coup the previous November, returned as prime minister. He was to hold power until 1957, and to bring Thailand firmly into the Western orbit by his accession in 1954 to the South-East Asia Treaty Organisation, whose headquarters were established in Bangkok. But he ruled as moderator between new strong men, particularly the Head of Police, General Pao, and the Commander of the Army, General Sarit, rather than in his own right. The navy was badly disaffected from this police–army regime and in February, 1949 the Royal Thai Marines and a number of naval officers actually launched a pro-Pridi counter-coup. Its failure led to Pridi's departure to join the Chinese communists and a major purge of the marines and navy. In June, 1951 the navy, conscious of its decreasing political influence, staged another unsuccessful anti-army coup, and actually made Pibun prisoner for some days, after which it lost all political importance. That of the police was growing however, to the point where it rivalled that of the army, and, in its pursuit of 'subversive elements', aroused widespread hostility among the Thai middle class. Pibun and Pao combined this domestic policy with, after 1955, a foreign policy which was friendly to China – whose government had assured Pibun that the 'autonomous Thai State' it had established in south China was not a bridgehead for aggression against his country. This ambivalent policy led to a serious reverse for his administration at the February, 1957 elections and in September his nominee at the head of the army, General Sarit Tanaret, ousted him and took power himself.

General (later Field-Marshal) Sarit ruled dictatorially until his death in 1963. The assembly and the constitution were abolished, trade unions and political parties dissolved and martial law imposed. In 1959 a constitutional assembly was convened – containing, as was now established practice, a majority of nominated military members – and among the provisions it advanced was a draconian endorsement of arbitrary measures in the event of an emergency. This interim constitution remained the basis on which the army governed during the remaining years of Sarit's rule and under that of his protege and successor, Field-Marshal Thanom Kittikachorn. The constitution, which provided for the election of a consultative but not executive assembly, was eventually promulgated in 1968 and led to elections in February, 1969. These returned the pro-government party, but did not indemnify the assembly, which was dissolved by an internal coup in November, 1971. Thanom ruled directly until December, 1972 when he introduced a new interim constitution and a new assembly of entirely appointed members.

Thailand's growing student population were by now extremely hostile to the military regime and to the façade of representative government which it maintained. The king, moreover, was reported to have been affronted by the internal coup by which Thanom had dissolved the last assembly. When, in October, 1973 demonstrations broke out at Bangkok universities, Thanom and his deputy, Field-Marshal Praphas, quickly found themselves isolated and fled into exile. A civilian government was appointed. But two subsequent coups, in October, 1976 and October, 1977 restored military government.

STRENGTH AND BUDGET

Population: 49,000,000
Army: 60,000
Navy: 28,000 (including 10,000 marines); six major vessels, 118 smaller craft
Air force: 43,000; 149 combat aircraft
Paramilitary: 15,000 Border Patrol Police; 40,000 Provincial Police; 33,000 Volunteer Defence Corps
GNP (1980): $31,100,000,000
Defence expenditure (1981): $1,310,000,000

Defence expenditure in 1975 was about 17.5% of the national budget. In a country so long dominated by the armed forces, it has naturally long been high (between 20% and 32%, 1932—9) and is currently inflated by the demands of the counter-insurgency campaign. A great deal of military cost has been offset since 1954, however, by American military aid ($481,000,000, 1961—9) and by direct American defence expenditure for base construction and operation (about $300,000,000 a year, 1967—9). As a proportion of gross national product, however, combined defence and internal security costs have consistently stood at between 4% and 5% in the 1970s, which is high for an unindustrialised country.

COMMAND AND CONSTITUTIONAL STATUS

The interim constitution promulgated after the coup of 1977 was the eleventh since 1932. It was formally adopted in December 1978. Since most of the others were also written by military governments, whose policies have been closely similar, the constitutions have not varied much in the provisions they have made for command of the armed forces. The King, a constitutional monarch, is Commander-in-Chief, but takes no official part in the executive process (though he wields great influence, which he is believed to have used at the time of the 1973 anti-Thanom coup). Under the military regime which held power until 1973, Field-Marshal Thanom was Prime Minister, Minister of Defence and Supreme Commander of the Armed Forces, and thus held the first three positions on the chain of command. The Minister of the Interior, Field-Marshal Praphas, was also Deputy Prime Minister and Commander-in-Chief of the Army. These 'multi-hattings' have been common under Thai military government. The chain of command from the Supreme Commander ran to the commanders of the three services, who each had their own staffs. In the army, the commander-in-chief was served by

four staffs (general, special, technical and training) but dealt directly with his army areas (of which there are four) and with the combat forces operating within them. Outside the main chain of command, the supreme commander was supported, through his own supreme commander's headquarters, by logistic, intelligence, training, budgetary and inter-service staffs. The office of the under-secretary for defence, also answering to the supreme commander, oversaw administrative and supply departments, including fuel and military factories. The civilian government installed after the 1973 coup did away with the office of supreme commander (it has now been restored), and replaced it with a joint chiefs of staff committee, but otherwise left the machinery of command intact. Whatever formal command changes it made were irrelevant. Thai government is deeply militarised — though that does not mean that it is insensitive to civilian interests or pressures. As an American observer, Fred Riggs, has explained, 'The successive *coups d'état* by which ruling circles are modified and replaced have become as much a formula for changing *élites* as the periodical electoral battles which take place in the United States, or the cabinet crises in France during the Third and Fourth Republics. The succession of constitutional charters in the Thai polity have, correspondingly, scarcely more systemic significance than a change of party in England, perhaps less. The effective constitutional structure, which is unwritten, appears to have taken shape as a relatively stable pattern'. That pattern is of one-party government, of which the military form the executive arm. The opposition Democratic Party does not represent an ideological opposition, but a source of criticism of the government's behaviour and shortcomings.

ROLE, COMMITMENT, DEPLOYMENT AND RECENT OPERATIONS

Role
The Thai army has played a major political role in the country since 1932, when a group of officers took part in the bloodless coup which transformed the monarchy from absolutism to constitutionalism. The armed forces played a controlling role in the first constitutional government and between 1939 and 1944 a military dictatorship held power. After a civilian interlude, the army again seized power, which they held without interruption until 1973 and since 1976 the armed forces have controlled the government again. Undeniably, therefore, a principal role of the Thai army, usually in concert with the navy and the air force, has been governmental. Because of the insurgency in the north and north-east, a large area of the country is under direct military administration. The army, with the police, also has a major counter-insurgency role and, during the American campaign in Indo-China, it maintained a division in Vietnam and sent large numbers of troops to fight the Pathet Lao in Laos (it is reported that at one time there were 20,000 Thai soldiers there). A Thai battalion served in the United Nations Force in Korea.

Commitments
Since the winding-up of the South-East Asia Treaty Organisation in 1977, Thailand has no external military commitment, but has a military assistance agreement with the United States.

Deployment
Thailand is divided into four military regions: First, Second, Third and Fourth (formerly the Fifth Military Circle). First Army, with headquarters at Bangkok, provides the King's Guard and oversees the central and northern areas. The

cavalry division has its headquarters (Saraburi) in the First Army area, though its units are widely dispersed. The Second Army has its headquarters at Korat and oversees the north-east. The Third Army has its headquarters at Phitsanulok and oversees the south-east. The Fifth Military Circle has its headquarters at Nakhon Si Thammarat and oversees the isthmus and Malay border. The infantry divisions and the cavalry division are deployed in the three Army areas; the Fourth appears to dispose only of independent regiments. Most formations are broken down into battalion-size groups, widely dispersed in the countryside, with the largest concentrations in the north-east. The special forces have their headquarters at Lopburi, north of Bangkok. The air force has four airfield defence battalions at the four main forward air bases: Korat, U-Tapao, Nakhon Phanom and Udon.

Recent Operations

The Thai army, through its involvement on the American side in the Vietnam war and its campaign against the Pathet Lao in Laos, has considerable operational experience. Since 1965, when the Communist Party of Thailand a deliberate campaign of terrorism, it has been conducting a counter-insurgency campaign on its own territory in the north-east and far south, and in the north and west since 1967. The population in the north-east contains a large number of Laotians, the north of hill peoples (Meo, Aka and Lisu), the west of Karens and the far south of Muslim Malays, in whose region shelter the intact remnants of the Chinese communist terrorist bands defeated in the Malayan emergency (1948—62). The insurgencies in the north, west and south, though active, do not threaten to develop into full-scale rebellions, for a variety of local reasons. That in the north-east, which is nearest to the powerful communist States, does pose a threat to the authority and even stability of the Thai government. The CTs ('communist terrorists', as the insurgents are known) were growing in numbers and the reach of their activities extending until 1979. While there are reckoned to be only 400 in the west, 2000 (mainly Chinese communist veterans of the Malayan insurgency) in the south and 2000 in the north, the number in the north-east is estimated at 10,000, and in February, 1977 the Crown Prince's car was fired on in Phetchabun province in central Thailand. Between October and December, 1976 170 clashes between government forces and the insurgents were reported, a considerable increase on any comparable period (though probably a response to the coup of October). There were also clashes with Cambodian troops on the border of Prachin Buri province in January, 1977 following a Cambodian raid into Thai territory and the killing of a number of villagers. The level of Communist insurgency continued to rise after 1977 until activity was reported in 50 of the country's 71 provinces. The Vietnamese invasion of Kampuchea in December 1978 imposed a heavy setback on the Communist Party of Thailand (CPT) from which it has not yet recovered. The occupation of Kampuchean territory interrupted the flow of supplies from China, the CPT's patron; and, at the same time, the outbreak of fighting between Pol Pot's forces and those sponsored by Vietnam led to CPT units in Laos and Kampuchea being pressured to choose sides. Because of the long-standing connection with China, most chose to support Pol Pot and were accordingly expelled into Thai territory. There many CPT members or supporters, including many of the middle class who had joined after the troubles of 1976—7, surrendered to the government forces.

Some shift of CPT activity to the northern territories then resulted; but the racial balance there limits the scope of the party's acceptability. However, there was also a marked increase in terrorist acts in the far south, where the CPT has also long had units. General Harn, commander of the responsible 2nd Region, reported considerable success against them in April 1982, the destruction of three guerrilla camps and the reduction of their strength to 3000. He forecast their total defeat, after which his troops would move to the extreme south, to stamp out resistance by Muslim Malay separatists and the remaining fragment of the Chinese Communist terrorists refugee bands from Malaysia. At the same time General Saiyuol, the supreme commander, estimated that CPT guerrilla strength throughout Thailand had fallen from 10,000 to 7,000 and other reports stated that their numbers in the north, where CPT HQ had been shifted from the north-east, were no more than 1300—1400.

Temporarily therefore, the Thai army has achieved a very considerable mastery over the guerrilla problem. It has always been peripheral and promises to remain so.

ORGANISATION

The domestic organisation of the Royal Thai Army is similar to that of the American: there are armoured cavalry, infantry, artillery, engineer, signal, transporation, quartermaster, military police and other smaller branches. Operationally, the army adheres to the American organisation of the 1950s: divisions, regimental combat teams and regiments and then battalions. The seven divisions have three to four regimental combat teams (RCTs), each of three (occasionally four) infantry battalions. Five divisions include a small tank battalion. The divisional artillery has nine batteries of six howitzers and some medium howitzers. The cavalry division is equipped with armoured cars, light tanks and APCs, and there are some APCs in the infantry divisions. An armoured division of one tank, one mechanised and one cavalry regiment has recently been formed. Armoured companies are also dispersed and many of the artillery units are broken down, often into two-gun sections. The total number of infantry battalions is about seventy.

The marines of the Royal Thai Navy form two infantry regiments and an artillery group. The infantry have some amphibious personnel carriers. The parachute and special forces units of the army have been expanded to four battalions, and are well provided with air lift. The army also operates five aviation companies and a number of independent flights, two flying helicopters and light aircraft.

The Thai National Police Department is a large force (60,000), with a strong paramilitary element. The country is divided into nine police regions, of which III—IX (headquarters Korat, Udon, Chiang Mai, Phitsanulok, Nakhon Pathom, Nakhon Si Thammarat, Pattani) have insurgency problems. Each region has about 4000 Provincial Police, some of whom are organised into 50 man Special Action Forces, trained to respond quickly to insurgent activity. All regions but Region I also have 1500—2000 Border Patrol Police, a force founded in 1954 to deal with insurgency on the borders; it is military in organisaton and equipment. The Police Air Division operates some helicopters and light aircraft. There is also a Marine Police, which patrols the Mekong and Thai territorial waters. Numbers are: Marine Police, 1700; Border Patrol Police, 15,000; Provincial Police, 42,000. A programme to provide each of Thailand's 7000 tambons (clusters of villages) with a detachment of 12—20 Provincial Policemen is making progress.

In the insurgent areas there also exists the Volunteer Defence Corps, founded in 1954 and numbering 33,000 and consisting of villagers armed to defend their homes. The operational unit is the joint security team or village protection unit, formed of 10 villagers led by two policemen. There effectiveness is limited by lack of mobility.

RECRUITMENT, TRAINING AND RESERVES

Under the Military Service Act of 1954 every able-bodied Thai between the ages of twenty-one and thirty is obliged to serve 2 years in the armed forces, which means in practice usually the army. Monks and teachers are exempt; so too are naturalised citizens and the sons of aliens, an exemption designed to exclude overseas Chinese from the armed forces. In practice, the government also exempts most of the minorities: the Muslim Malays of the south, Karens of the west, the montagnards (Meo, Yao, Lisu, Aka and Lowa) of the north and north-west, and the Khmers (Cambodians) of the north-east. The army is thus almost exclusively composed of Buddhist Thais. By no means all the annual contingent is drafted; those exempted among the Thais are transferred to the 2nd Category of the Reserve. Conscripts are inducted twice a year, to the battalion nearest their home, in which they are trained and then serve.

Officers, who come for the most part from the middle class, are trained at the Chulachom Klao Royal Military Academy, near the royal palace in Bangkok, founded by King Chulalongkorn in 1887. Some cadets go to Britain and America to train. There is an army staff college for selected officers and an army war college for more senior officers. The highest level of training is provided at the armed forces staff college, the courses being composed of 35 senior officers of the three services. The national defence college trains officers and civil servants. The Ministry of Defence also runs a preparatory school to feed the three service cadet academies, and there is a military technical training school to train technical specialists. Each of the three armies has its own counter-insurgency school: the First Army's is located at Hua Hin, the Second's at Nam Pung Dam and the Third's at Lamphun.

There is an elaborate reserve structure. Time-expired conscripts are enrolled in the 1st Category of the Reserve for 7 years. Service in the 2nd and 3rd Categories, which also include untrained men, is for 10 and 6 years, respectively. The reserves are apparently not called out for training, nor is there sufficient equipment in the country to arm them.

EQUIPMENT AND ARMS INDUSTRY

The Thai armed forces are equipped with American arms, bought or supplied under agreement from the United States, though some older British equipment is still held. There is a small, recently established arms industry, which manufactures small-arms ammunition, explosives and the Heckler and Koch 5.56mm rifle.

Rifle: 7.62mm M-1 (USA), 5.56mm M16 (USA) and 5.56mm Hk33 (West Germany, manufactured under licence in Thailand)
Machine-gun: 7.62mm M-60 (USA)
Mortar: 81mm M-29 (USA)
Anti-armour weapons: 57mm M-18 and 106mm M-40 recoilless rifles (USA)
Air-defence weapons: L60/70 Bofors (Sweden and USA); Hawk missile (USA; 40 in service)
Artillery: 75mm M-116 pack howitzer (USA); 105mm M-101 howitzer (USA; 300 in service) and 155mm M-114 howitzer (USA; 80 in service)
Armour: Scorpion armoured car (Britain); M-113 APC (USA; 300 in service); 120 Commando (US) personnel carriers; LVTP-7 armoured amphibious carrier (USA);

M-24 light tank (USA; obsolete) and M-41 light tank (USA; 1200 in service); 50 M-48 tanks (US)
Aircraft: 208 helicopters in service, including 120 UH-1 B/Ds; 90 light aircraft. The air force operates 44 military transports and 100 helicopters

RANK, DRESS AND DISTINCTIONS

Thai ranks follow the British system up to the rank of field-marshal. The unusual rank of 'special colonel' is equivalent to brigadier. Uniforms are American in colour and style.

CURRENT DEVELOPMENTS

An internal military coup of October 20th, 1977 overthrew the government set up by the Administrative Reform Council in October, 1976. It was entirely bloodless and merely removed the civilian prime minister, Thanin Kraivichien, installed by the soldiers a year earlier. His fault seemed to have been that his policy was too right wing for the armed forces. He preached a fiercely anti-communist foreign policy line, which the armed forces thought made it impossible to come to any working arrangements with their newly communist neighbours in Laos and Cambodia (Democratic Kampuchea), while announcing that he foresaw a return to civilian rule no sooner than 12 years in the future. A coup against his government in March, 1977 by a disgruntled general retired in 1976, failed for lack of official backing (and the officer was – unusually in Thailand – executed), but by October the armed forces appear to have decided that they could no longer work with Thanin Kraivichien. His government was reformed and its structure reorganised into three: a secretariat command, dealing with the bureaucracy, headed by the Under-Secretary of the Prime Minister's Office, a military command, in charge of counter-insurgency and security affairs, led by the Under-Secretary for Defence; and a civilian command, dealing with economic and foreign affairs. The overall governing body, closely similar in composition to the Administrative Reform Council, is called 'Revolutionary Council Command', and was composed of 23 officers.

Elections held under the constitution of 1978 returned a majority of civilian members of political parties to parliament in April 1979. But military members of the upper house, where they formed an appointed majority insisted on the appointment of a cabinet nominated by military ministers. The premiership was assumed by General Kriangsak, who had held the office in the previous unelected government, and in March 1980 he handed power to the Commander-in-chief of the army, General Prem, as a result of a political crisis caused by economic difficulties. General Prem's government was the target of a determined military coup, on April 1st, 1981, which was put down only by the personal intervention of the king. In accordance with Thai traditions, the conspirators were largely amnestied shortly afterwards. General Sau, the deputy commander of the army, who had led the coup, fled to Burma. Colonel Prachak, whose 2nd Infantry Regiment had played a key role, was merely dismissed from service. The motives of the forty leading officers described as 'Young Turks', are said to have been similar to those of Nasser's 'Free Officers' in Egypt in 1952. And at the time of going to press, it appears that the army has once again asserted its control over the government of Thailand.

John Keegan

TOGO*

HISTORY AND INTRODUCTION

Togo attained independence in 1960; it had been a German colony until 1919 when a small part was detached and made over to British administration (subsequently being incorporated into the Gold Coast), and the rest to a French mandate, later trusteeship. In 1963 Togo's President, S. Olympio, was murdered by a group of mutinous army NCOs. In 1967 Olympio's successor, Grunitzky, was overthrown by Eyadema (one of the NCOs of 1963) who assumed the Presidency and Defence portfolio. Eyadem's rule is authoritarian, at times despotic; a personality cult of adulation for 'Le Guide' is very evident. A curious and still murky event occurred in 1977 when a group of foreigners attempted to overthrow Eyadema, without success. An opposition movement, mostly of exiles, appears to be gaining strength.

STRENGTH AND BUDGET

Population: 2,500,000 (approximately)
Armed Forces: 2700 (of which100 are air force and 100 navy) plus a gendarmerie of 1400 and certain small presidential guard units.
GDP: $900,000,000 (estimate)
Defence expenditure: $30,000,000 (approximate).

COMMAND AND CONSTITUTIONAL STATUS

President Gnassingbe (formerly Étienne) Eyadema is Head of State and Minister of Defence; the Inspector-General of the Army Colonel K. Kongo is also powerful. The gendarmerie is commanded by Commander Assih, a close associate of Eyadema. The key military district, Lome, is also commanded personally by Eyadema.

ROLE, COMMITMENT, DEPLOYMENT AND RECENT OPERATIONS

Togo's army has little real role and no special deployment. Relations with Ghana pass through successive periods of unease. The majority of the Ewe people live in Togo, a minority in Ghana. When the Ewe are well-represented in Ghana's government, relations are good, but when the Ewe are at a disadvantage, relations are cool. Togo has never abandoned the aspiration of reunification of the Ewe people under the Togo flag and gives some covert support to the secessionist movement in eastern Ghana. Togo's army acts as a safeguard against any sudden Ghanaian military retaliation or strike.

Since the accession to power of Colonel Kerekou in Benin, occasional friction occurs on the border.

Togo is a member of ANAD, the treaty of mutual aid in the event of an attack signed by seven West African States. A detachment of 160 Togo Army personnel was included in the inter-African force sent to Zaire in 1978.

ORGANISATION

The army consists of six battalions, two of infantry, one of motorised infantry, two parachute and one 'commando'; all are small units of little more than two companies. There is also an artillery battery and an engineer sub-unit. Army headquarters is at Tokoin. The country is divided into three military districts, Lome, Lama Kara and Temedji.

RECRUTIMENT, TRAINING AND RESERVES

A random system of national service — for two years — exists. The majority of the soldiers come from the north of the country, in particular from the Kabré, while a majority of the officers were either Ewe or Mina from the south, until the events of 1963, when the balance began to change. The small technical and logistic units, however, are mainly southern.

French assistance for military training has been used since independence although air force pilots are being trained in Zaire. A feature of Togo military training has been the number of joint exercises held with visiting French units, the French providing aircraft for parachute drops and logistic support. French observers have commented favourably on the physical fitness of the Togolese.

The army's cadres are trained at the National Instruction Centre at Lama Kara, the parachute and commando units are trained at Temedji, where the parachute units are also posted.

The Presidential Guard, some 1000 strong is said to have been North Korean trained while a small personal household bodyguard unit is Israeli-trained and equipped.

EQUIPMENT AND ARMS INDUSTRY

Togo has no arms industry. The army's basic infantry equipment is all French. The motorised unit includes ten United States M-8 armoured-cars and five modern French M-3 armoured personnel carriers; more recent deliveries also include three AML-60 and seven AML-90 French armoured-cars and four US army 105mm guns. A number between thirty and sixty, of UR-416 West German armoured troop carriers have also entered service, largely for the motorised infantry and a recent report notes a Libyan gift of two elderly Soviet T-54 tanks. The Air Force includes six Embraer EMB—326 Brazilian COIN aircraft, together with 5 Fouga Magister training aircraft that can also be used for COIN purposes. There are also one Fokker Fellowship, one Boeing 727 and two de Havilland Canada Buffalo transport aircraft for transport duties, together with two light liaison aircraft and one Puma and one Lama helicopter. Five Dassault Dornier Alphajets are reported to be on order.

RANK, DRESS AND DISTINCTION

These generally follow the French colonial troops pattern, except that the *képi* is not worn.

---

* For general notes on African armies, see Appendix 1.

CURRENT DEVELOPMENTS

A very small force, the Togo army could not defend the country in the event of an effective Ghanaian incursion, but this now appears unlikely. A number of the army's best officers are being used for civil administration tasks, and army units are also committed to development tasks on occasions.

The group of ex-NCOs, mostly but not all northerners who are now the army's senior officers, and who are linked by complicity in the Olympio murder and Grunitzky overthrow, are of the same tradition and from the same area as the majority of the soldiers. This gives the army a cohesion, although at some expense to its claim to be a truly national institution.

The Mitterand government views the present Togo government with some distaste, and would undoubtedly be less inclined to support it than the former Giscard administration in the event of trouble.

Lloyd Mathews

TONGA

The Kingdom of Tonga consists of 169 islands (36 inhabited) in the south-west Pacific, about 400 miles east of Fiji. Approximately 75% of its total land area of 385 square miles is arable, and it is accordingly one of the most densely settled of the Pacific island States, with a population of 90,100. It is also, by virtue of its position and its history, by far the least affected by Westernisation and tourism of all the south Pacific island groups, and preserves both its culture and its traditional political system. Over 99% of the population are Polynesian, and the principal language is Tongan (although English is also spoken).

The islands were first settled no later than the tenth century, and have been a unified kingdom for a least 700 years. Very few Europeans called there until the nineteenth century, and the first Christian convert was only made in 1829. In the same period the Tongans, who had always been involved in the inter-island wars of the region, became infected with both the cannibalism and the savage civil wars that were then devastating Fiji, and for several decades Tonga itself was immersed in a series of civil wars. The new monarchy that emerged from this period, displacing the centuries-old Tu'i Ha'atakalaua dynasty, was founded by the warrior aristocrat Taufa'ahau, who was converted to Christianity in 1834. He had ended the civil wars by 1852, and by the time he died in 1893 all the Tongans had been converted to Christianity. The present monarch, King Taufa'ahau Tupou IV, who came to the throne in 1965, is only the fourth of his line to reign in Tonga in almost 150 years.

The founder of the dynasty put Tonga under British protection in 1889 to protect it from the predatory colonialism of the other imperial powers which were then scourging the south Pacific, and the present king led it back into full independence in 1970, but the entire period of British sovereignty had virtually no effect on the domestic political structure of Tonga. That structure, created by the first Taufa'ahau as the only way of ending the civil wars, is the purest example of feudalism in existence in the world today. The kingdom was divided into 33 hereditary fiefs, each holder of which was responsible for order, and for allocating all but 5% of the land (which he might rent) equally among the local population. The sale of land to foreigners was forbidden. Each Tongan male aged sixteen had the right to claim 8¼ acres from his local noble, and had the right to pass the usufruct on to his heirs.

In practice, however, the nobles have always retained far more of the land for their own use (the present estimate is as much as 27%) and arbitrarily extracted dues in kind from their tenants. With the rapid growth in Tonga's population in the twentieth century (now 3% a year) it became impossible to allocate land to each Tongan even if the nobles had wished to, and massive unemployment now causes great numbers of Tongans to seek work abroad, principally in the factories of New Zealand. Between 1974 and 1977 10,000 Tongans obtained entry visas to New Zealand to seek work. Much of the aristocracy's land remains untilled, and much other land is only cultivated very inefficiently. The flight from the land has resulted in the massive depopulation of the outlying lands: 62% of the population now lives on the main island of the southern group, Tongatapu, and one-quarter is concentrated in the capital, Nuku'alofa. Largely as a result of this, within a country where agriculture offers the possibility of prosperity, the annual per capita income is under $250.

This full-blown feudal system is ruled by an absolute monarch answerable, in effect, only to the nobility. The King is Head of State and Head of Government. He appoints and presides over a Privy Council of six Ministers plus the royal governors of the other two main island groups, Ha'apai and Vava'u. The Prime Minister, Prince Tu'ipelehake Fatefehi, is the King's brother. The Legislative Assembly consists of seven Ministers of the Crown, seven nobles elected by their peers, and seven commoners elected by all literate adults who pay taxes.

The Tongan armed forces consist of the Royal Guard and the Tongan Defence Force. Their duties are exclusively internal security, with the exception of the tiny maritime component, consisting of two patrol craft based at Nuku'alofa. For external defence, Tonga effectively relies upon Western naval forces in the Pacific, in the first instance those of New Zealand. The latter is extremely solicitous of Tonga's total independence: when a Soviet delegation arrived in the kingdom in 1976 and offered to construct a new international airport and to improve the port facilities for use by Soviet fishing fleets, the Foreign Ministry in Wellington urgently sought to dissuade Tonga from accepting the offer. So did the King's powerful friends on the right wing of Japanese politics, and in the end the Soviet offer was refused.

To carry out its internal security role, the Tongan Defence Force has an active strength of about 200 men who receive basic infantry and riot-control training. They are recruited by voluntary enlistment for a period of 18 months' to 2 years' active service; in view of the very high unemployment rate amongst school-leavers, there is no difficulty in attracting enough volunteers. The enlisted ranks are trained in Tonga, but regular officers and NCOs receive training abroad, principally in New Zealand. On completion of active service, Tongan soldiers are assigned to a reserve organisation which numbers upwards of 1000 men. There is also a Royal Guard of some 20 men.

The Tongan Defence Force is equipped with British-pattern infantry weapons. Its soldiers wear khaki uniforms similar to those of the Australian army, except for the headgear, and also have a ceremonial uniform of dark blue for the enlisted ranks and white for officers. The latest available figure for the defence budget is $Tongan 74,000 (about $100,000) in 1972–3.

There have been no known serious protests or attacks against the interests of the aristocracy in Tonga, but the large numbers of Tongans who have been exposed to a different way of thinking while working in Auckland make it likely that such developments may come. The King himself has warned his nobles of this publicly, urging them to cultivate their lands themselves or hand them over to those who will and prophesying 'an inevitable rise of disorders' if this is not done, but he is not in a strong enough position to compel the aristocracy to comply.

Gwynne Dyer

TUNISIA

HISTORY AND INTRODUCTION

The modern Tunisian army has its roots in the French colonial period, and is the first national army that the country has possessed for a number of centuries. Under Carthage, and later under Arabised Berber rulers like Tariq, who conquered most of Spain for Islam in the early eighth century, the area which is now Tunisia had been a powerful military factor in the Mediterranean, but following the great Arab nomad invasions of the eleventh century it declined steeply in prosperity and power. In the sixteenth century the country, by then almost entirely Arabised, was conquered by the Ottoman Turks, but the local Ottoman administrators soon established a considerable degree of autonomy. In 1705 an Ottoman general who had been appointed the Bey (local governor) of Tunis succeeded in making the office hereditary in his family, and founded the Husainid dynasty which lasted until 1957. The Beys acknowledged at first only a tenuous Ottoman suzerainty and later none at all.

During the nineteenth century the Beys of Tunis tended to look towards France for support at home and abroad, and fell increasingly into debt as they sought French loans to bolster their power and modernise the country. Under the pretext of a threat to their Algerian possessions, the French declared a protectorate over Tunisia in 1881, which rapidly developed into a colonial regime in which the Beys were only powerless figureheads. There was considerable European settlement, and Tunisians were extensively recruited into the French armed forces, while Bizerte was developed into a naval base dominating the narrows of the central Mediterranean. The only exclusively Tunisian armed force during this period was the 600 men whom the Bey of Tunis was permitted to keep as a personal bodyguard.

Nationalist agitation for independence began in a serious way in 1934, when a young lawyer called Habib Bourguiba broke away from an ineffective proto-nationalist grouping to found his own Neo-Destour (constitutionalist) Party. Its growth was interrupted by World War II, when Tunisia was extensively fought over, coming first under German and then Anglo—American occupation, but in the early post-war years it expanded rapidly into an impressive organisation embracing all currents of Tunisian nationalist opinion. French attempts to defuse the agitation by granting local autonomy measures under the Bey of Tunis proved inadequate, and anti-French guerrilla bands, mostly made up of Tunisian veterans of the French army, began operations in the Cape Bon peninsula in 1952. Although suppressed there, by an intensive counter-insurgency campaign by the French Foreign Legion, the *fellaghas*, as they were known, reappeared in mountainous areas south of Tunis and conducted a classical small-scale guerrilla campaign from early 1954 to 1956. It was not so much this campaign, however, as the need to concentrate on the far more serious insurgency that had begun in 1954 in Algeria (which was an integral part of France with over a million European settlers) that impelled Paris to seek a settlement with Bourguiba in 1955. Agreement on internal self-government was reached with Neo-Destour in that year, but pressure from the communists and from a radical pan-Arabist faction within his own party compelled Bourguiba to hold out for complete independence, which was achieved in February, 1956. Bourguiba returned to Tunis to ride through the city on a white stallion to the ecstatic adulation of the crowds, and has utterly dominated Tunisian politics ever since. The monarchy was abolished in 1957.

The Tunisian National Army which was founded in 1956 consisted of about 1300 officers and men released from the French army, and some 850 men from the Beylical guard. Tunisians had fought for France with distinction in both World Wars and in the first Indochina War, and as late as 1957 there were still some 4000 Tunisians serving with the French armed forces. Most were transferred to the new Tunisian army in the course of the next year, and by early 1958 it had achieved a strength of some 6000. The key positions in this new army, however, did not go to French army veterans but to reliable party and resistance-movement members.

Independence in 1956 did not end frictions with the French, as they continued to occupy the giant naval base at Bizerte and as most of the regular units of the Algerian Army of National Liberation were based just inside the Tunisian border until the war in that country ended in Algerian independence in 1962. There were continual clashes over the Bizerte base, the most serious occurring in 1961 when Tunisian regular forces and party organisations attacked the base, which the French were refusing to evacuate. It cost the Tunisians about 1000 casualties, but the French left shortly afterwards. The Tunisian army had achieved a sufficient level of administrative and logistical organisation by 1960 to be able to contribute a 3100 man force to the United Nations Peacekeeping Force in the former Belgian Congo. A navy was created in 1959, and an air force in 1960. By 1965 the strength of the army had risen to 17,000.

The armed forces remained relatively modest in size and importance, however — in the first decade of independence, military expenditure never amounted to more than 2% of GNP — partly because there were no serious external threats to Tunisian sovereignty, but at least as much because they were not required to perform the bulk of the internal security function, as they had been in so many other newly independent countries.

President Bourguiba's Destour Socialist Party (PSD), as it was renamed in 1964, rapidly evolved into an all-embracing single party, despite the fact that the constitution makes provision for a multi-party regime. Since the Communist Party was banned in 1963, there have been no other political parties in Tunisia, and in its earlier years the PSD filled the role of a national vehicle for political participation and social and economic development far better than most other single parties. The single instance in which elements of the army were implicated in political intrigue, an alleged assassination plot against President Bourguiba by pan-Arabist officers in 1962, may also have played a role in causing the political leadership to downgrade the importance of the armed forces.

The stability and popularity of the regime and the very creditable rate of economic growth achieved by Tunisia — it now has the fifth highest per capita income in the African continent, over $1200 a year — all contributed to this domestic tranquility. Until recently, the army was only three times called upon to intervene against domestic disorders: during the 1967 Arab—Israeli war, when it was called in to suppress serious rioting in Tunis (President Bourguiba made a suitably tardy offer to send a token force to support the

Arabs, which was not taken up); against disgruntled villagers at the height of the collectivisation campaign in 1969; and against strikers in textile mills in the coastal village of Ksar Hellal in 1977. On all other occasions, the civil police and gendarmerie proved sufficient. Even after the emergence of a serious territorial dispute with Libya over sea-bed demarcation in 1967, it was not considered in Tunis that there was any serious external threat to the country, so little attention was paid to keeping the army's equipment up to date, let alone expanding its size.

Since the later 1960s, however, Tunisia's political regime has become more autocratic and more erratic, with serious potential consequences for domestic stability. Many attribute this principally to the effect of advancing age on the personality of the undisputed leader, Habib Bourguiba: although born only in 1903, and thus not astonishingly old as world leaders in single-party systems go, he has suffered at least two heart attacks, viral hepatitis, several nervous breakdowns and has been afflicted for many years with arteriosclerosis. Whether the cause is medical or not, his behaviour in the past decade has been both impulsive and increasingly jealous of potential rivals.

In 1965–9, Bourguiba permitted a radical Minister for Planning and Development, Ahmad Ben Salah, to plunge the country into an ill-prepared experiment in unfettered collectivism; when the resentful rural population was nearing revolt in 1969, Bourguiba abruptly jailed Ben Salah for treason (he escaped abroad in 1972) and totally reversed Tunisia's attitude towards capitalist free enterprise and foreign investment. In succeeding years he succeeded in ousting all the other major independent figures from the PSD: Ahmed Mestiri in 1972, during a controversy over liberalising the party structure in which Mestiri actually won the support of most party members; Bahi Ladgham in 1973; and Muhammad Masmoudi in 1974. Masmoudi, a pan-Arabist who was then Foreign Minister, had persuaded Bourguiba to make an agreement with Libya for unification of the two countries, only to have the President renege at the last minute. In 1974 Bourguiba was also designated President-for-Life.

By the latter part of the 1970s, therefore, there were a number of former leading PSD figures, some in exile abroad, some in opposition at home, who could serve as alternative focuses of loyalty. Two of them, moreover, were closely associated with a radical pan-Arab socialist alternative, and maintained close links with Libya: Ben Salah and Masmoudi.

Despite Tunisia's still quite respectable economic growth rate, the gap between rich and poor was becoming steadily and embarrassingly wider, especially in the cities, and an alarming problem of youth unemployment had appeared. After fluctuating around the million mark for about 2000 years, Tunisia's population entered the rapid growth phase associated with modernisation during the later nineteenth century, and now stands at 6,500,000, of whom 56% are below the age of twenty. The fact that the government has consistently dedicated 30% of public expenditure to education, and that almost one-fifth of the population is attending some educational institution at any given time, in a sense only makes matters worse, since it is commonplace in the Third World that masses of educated unemployed youths are politically much more dangerous than uneducated ones.

To these difficulties should be added the fact that the party and the State bureaucracy – which are effectively one – have grown less representative and more corrupt than they were in the early years of independence, and that all the leading ministers and party leaders are now preoccupied with the preliminary moves in the impending struggle for the succession to Bourguiba. This jockeying for position has increasingly involved competition for the loyalty of the army, which is seen as playing a potentially decisive role in the post-Bourguiba period that cannot be long delayed.

STRENGTH AND BUDGET

The total strength of the Tunisian armed forces is 28,600, of which the army accounts for 24,000. The navy's strength is 26,000 and the air force's 2000. 12,000 of the army's strength and 500 in each of the other two services are conscripts. There are also 5000 paramilitary National Police, organised in three battalions, and 3500 National Guards. It became evident during 1978 that the PSD has also created an armed party militia, still officially unacknowledged; its strength is unknown, but it certainly numbers in the thousands. The military budget has risen steadily from about $14,000,000 in 1965 to $211,000,000 in 1981. It is still, however, less than 3% of the GNP of $8,600,000,000.

COMMAND AND CONSTITUTIONAL STATUS

The Commander-in-Chief of the Tunisian armed forces is the President of the Republic, who has the constitutional right to make military appointments. The Ministry of National Defence is responsible for operational control as well as administrative, personnel and logistical matters. The Minister is appointed by the President: the present incumbent is Salaheddin Baly.

The officer at the top of the military hierarchy is the Chief of the General Staff; beneath him are the Chiefs of Staff of the Army, Navy and Air Force. There is also an Inspector-General of the Armed Forces, who bears responsibility for discipline and efficiency.

The paramilitary forces, i.e. the National Police (gendarmerie) and the National Guard, are both controlled by the Ministry of the Interior. It is not clear who actually controls the PSD militia.

ROLE, COMMITMENT, DEPLOYMENT AND RECENT OPERATIONS

The mission of the Tunisian army is defined as the defence of the country's territorial integrity, the maintenance of internal security and participation in military civic action. It has never been called upon to carry out the first mission, and has only a limited capability to do so. It is very rarely employed in the internal security role, being held back as a reserve if the task should prove beyond the abilities of the paramilitary forces. It spends a great deal of time performing its civic action responsibilities, and indeed those are the primary occupation of the conscript elements of the army once their basic training is completed.

Tunisia's only neighbours are Algeria and Libya. The former is greatly superior militarily due to its much larger population and considerable oil income; the latter incomparably superior, at least in equipment, by virtue of its enormous oil revenues. Both neighbouring regimes are ideologically far to the left of the Tunisian regime, far more deeply committed to the pan-Arab cause, and closely associated with the Soviet Union as an arms supplier in contrast to Tunisia's Western military ties. Libya's Colonel Qaddafi has held a considerable grudge against the Tunisian government since it backed out of a precipitate plan for uniting the two countries in 1974.

Yet, despite the fact that the Tunisian army could hardly resist the full weight of either neighbour's armed forces for as much as a week, the Tunisian government has never felt enough concern about this situation to seek either defensive alliances with other powers or the achievement of a better military balance through large-scale expansion of its own forces. In this apparent neglect of Tunisia's defence there is of course a just appreciation of the limited nature of its own resources, but more importantly a belief, probably justified, that the probability of a serious military clash with either neighbour is extremely small. In recent years this belief has been further bolstered by the fact that Algeria's armed forces are pre-occupied with Morocco, and Libya's with Egypt, but beyond this there are two permanent considerations which make a military attack on Tunisia unlikely: first, that a certain sense of Arab solidarity makes a resort to war less probable than it otherwise might be, and second, that the three countries, Libya, Tunisia and Algeria, live so much in isolation from each other that in practical terms it is hard to imagine an issue arising between them which would be sufficiently vital to justify more than, at most, border clashes and military demonstrations of resolve.

Even the frontier dispute with Libya which has existed since 1967, despite the fact that it involves oil, is not such as to threaten really serious conflict between the two. The quarrel involves the demarcation of the sea-bed in the Gulf of Gabes between the two countries. Libya's grant of drilling rights in the disputed area to ENI, the Italian oil company, led to a confrontation in May, 1977 when a Tunisian frigate intervened to stop operations on an Italian drilling rig in the area, and there was some discreet sabre-rattling for a time. It may even be the case that the Tunisian military modernisation programme announced in that year, notably involving the acquisition of anti-tank and anti-air weapons and naval vessels, was undertaken partly in apprehension of border clashes or maritime skirmishes with Libya arising out of the dispute, but it is hardly likely that this quarrel could lead to full-scale war between the two countries.

The bulk of the army is equipped not for conventional war but for internal security duties, and except for the Sahara regiment is fairly evenly distributed amongst the more heavily populated regions of the country. The air force is likewise oriented towards internal security duties, the bulk of its aircraft being principally suited to counter-insurgency operations.

The primary day-to-day responsibility for internal security, however, lies with the paramilitary forces of National Police and National Guard. The former is primarily an urban police force with the usual police duties, but it also includes a special riot-control unit, three battalions strong, which was created after the 1967 riots. The National Guard fulfils all the roles previously carried out by the French Gendarmerie in non-urban areas, and is organised on a military basis. It is composed mainly of former army privates and junior NCOs who have completed their military training and are in the army reserves; in time of emergency, it is responsible for aiding the army in counter-insurgency tasks.

Tunisia belongs to the UN, the Arab League and the Organisation of African Unity, but it has no military commitments beyond its own border. Except briefly in 1967, there has never been any suggestion that Tunisian forces might take part in the Arab—Israeli confrontation — and even then the offer was probably not meant to be taken seriously. The Tunisian armed forces have had no combat experience since independence.

ORGANISATION

Arms of Service

The Tunisian forces are modelled on the French, and the arms and services within the army follow the French pattern.

Operational

The army is organised into two combined arms regiments (each with one armed and two mechanised infantry battalions), one Sahara regiment, one para-commando regiment, one armed recconaisance regiment, two field infantry regiments, two AA artillery regiments and two engineer regiments. No higher level of operational control exists.

The air force consists of one fighter/training squadron, one training squadron and one helicopter squadron. The principal air base is Sidi Ahmed near Bizerte. Others are at Tunis (El Aouina), Monastir, Gabes, Sfax and Djerba.

The navy's main base is the former French installation at Bizerte. There is also a naval base at Tunis and Sasq.

The National Police includes three battalions originated and equipped in military bases.

RECRUITMENT, TRAINING AND RESERVES

The core of the Tunisian army is about 6000 long-service regulars, including the great majority of the army's officers and NCOs, who are recruited by voluntary enlistment. The remainder is made up of conscripts who serve for only 1 year, and acquire only basic military skills. Since the much smaller air force and navy are predominantly regular, they together contain over one-third of the regular strength of the armed forces.

All physically able male citizens reaching the age of twenty are required by law to serve for 1 year in the armed forces. There are generous exemptions available for those with dependents and certain other categories, and deferments are available for students. It is also possible for students, teachers, civil servants and certain groups of technicians to perform their national service in several shorter periods, rather than in a single 1 year stretch. Since the early 1960s, the number of 20 year-olds becoming available for military service each year has exceeded the armed forces' requirements by an ever growing margin, so that the system is now in fact selective service, with those who will actually have to serve selected by lot. Fewer than half of those who are eligible are actually conscripted. In 1978 Tunisia also commenced the conscription of young women, but in what numbers and in what roles is unknown.

Lycée and first-year university students receive a certain amount of pre-induction training at nearby army installations 1 day a week during the school year and in summer camps. Most of those who are conscripted will be trained as reserve officers or NCOs. The less-well-educated recruits who comprise the bulk of the annual intake receive not only training in basic military skills, but also instruction to bring them up to the equivalent of a sixth-grade education, including literacy training when required. The army also teaches recruits a number of trades, principally to do with construction, road building and machine operation, which it exploits in its own civic action programmes and then releases into the civilian economy.

Regular officer cadets have been trained since 1967 at the national military academy at Fondouk Djedad about 20 miles south of Tunis. The minimum qualification is a bachelor's degree, and admission is by competitive examination. After a 2 year course of instruction at the academy, most newly commissioned officers are sent abroad for further training, principally to France and the USA. The academy also provides more advanced combat arms training, but for instruction in many technical subjects it is still necessary for Tunisian regular officers and NCOs to attend courses abroad.

Conditions of service in the armed forces compare favourably with those prevailing in civilian life for most recruits from rural areas. Regular personnel receive pay and allowances competitive with what their skills would bring in the civilian economy, and there are pension programmes for all ranks.

Following active service, officers and enlisted men are required to become members of the reserve army for periods of 9 years in the first reserve and 15 years in the second reserve. Officers in the reserves are required to attend schools periodically to keep abreast of new techniques and mobilisation procedures, but the mobilisation organisation is hardly ever exercised.

EQUIPMENT AND ARMS INDUSTRY

Most Tunisian equipment is French or American, with small amounts of British, Austrian and Chinese. The army has 14 M-48 medium tanks (plus 54 M-60 A3 on order) and 55 AMX-13 and 20 M-41 light tanks, supplemented by 20 Saladin, 30 EBR-75 and ten AML armoured cars. The mechanised infantry travel in M-113A1, Steyr 4K-TFA and V-150 Commando APCs: total numbers do not exceed one hundred. The artillery is notably weak, comprising six 25-pounder guns, 40 105mm howitzers (10 SP) and ten 155mm howitzers, plus a number of 60mm, 81mm, 82mm and 107mm mortars. The acquisition of STRIM-89 rocket launchers in unstated quantities will not substantially change the situation.

A good deal of attention has been given to improving the army's anti-tank capabilities in recent years, however, and it now disposes of 400 TOW (800 more on order) in addition to its Milan and SS-11 ATGW' It also has 54 Kuerassier SPATK guns. Air defence, previously provided only by 45 37mm and 40mm AA guns, now depends mainly on 62 MIM-72 Chaparral SAM systems (including Vulcan guns). Army aviation consists of one Hughes 500 MD helicopter.

The navy has one frigate (ex-US Savage class), two Vosper fast attack craft, two ex-Chinese Shanghai-class FPBG, three P-48 patrol craft with SS-12 SSM, one Le Tougeux-class patrol boat, two minesweepers and ten coastal patrol boats. Three La Combattante-class fast attack craft with Exocet missiles, and two smaller attack craft, are on order.

The air force's COIN squadron has five MB-326K and three MB-326L. The fighter-ground attack squadron now forming will comprise twelve newly acquired F-5E7Fac. The training squadron has 17 SF-260, seven MB-326B, twelve T-6 and twelve Safir aircraft. The helicopter wing operates seven Alouette II, five Alouette III, four UH-1 It, one Puma, 18 AB-205, six Bell 205-Al and six AS-350B helicopters. The air force has one C-130 transport and four S208M liaison aircraft.

The three paramilitary battalions of the National Police have 110 Fiat 6614 APC.

RANK, DRESS AND DISTINCTIONS

The rank and grade structure of the Tunisian armed forces is similar to that of the French, except that the highest military rank authorised by law is major-general. Tunisian army uniforms resemble those of the eastern Arab armies, although certain French influences remain in matters such as collar patches. No information is available on medals and distinctions.

CURRENT DEVELOPMENTS

Despite President Bourguiba's age and infirmity he could well last for years, but all political decisions in Tunisia now, including decisions dealing with the affairs of the armed forces, have become entangled in the struggle for the succession. This is even true of the riots of January, 1978, the worst in the country's history, which cost over 100 lives and required army troops and tanks to be deployed in the streets of the major cities (although it was primarily the PSD party militiamen who did the killing).

The riots grew out of a general strike called by the head of the Tunisian trade union federation, Habib Achour, a major contender for power within the PSD, at least partly in order to assert his claim to the succession. The strike quickly degenerated into rioting and looting, carried out mainly by the hordes of jobless teenagers who throng all the cities, and for a time the authorities nearly lost control of the situation. Achour and 10 of the 13 man executive of the trade union federation were arrested, together with hundreds of other trade unionists. Both he and a senior colleague, Abderrazak Ghorbal, who had called for a 'worker's State', were sentenced to 10 years' hard labour for subversion in October, 1978, in a trial which fell far short of normal legal standards, but there remain many contenders for power both within and outside the regime.

The trend towards increasingly severe repression of dissent continued through 1979, and in January 1980, on the second anniversary of the riots, a force of sixty insurgents calling themselves the Tunisian Armed Resistance entered Tunisia from Algeria and attacked the mining town of Gafsa in the interior of the country. After enjoying some initial success due to the absence of most of the town's usual garrison in the neighbouring town of Nefta, some 60 km distant, where President Boumedienne was on holiday, the guerrillas were all killed or captured by the end of the month. The death toll in the fighting was 41. Thirteen of the surviving rioters were subsequently executed and the rest jailed.

Although the insurgents were all Tunisian nationals and Muslim activists, the inspiration and arms for the raid came from Libya, and indeed most had been recruited from the large community of Tunisian workers in the country. (Though they passed through Algiers on the way to Gafsa, the Algerian government were not involved.) During the five days of fighting the French navy, at Tunis's request, deployed a force of warships in the Gulf of Gabes between Tunisia and Libya in case there were plans to send further groups into Tunisia by sea, and in retaliation the Libyan government arranged for a mob to attack and sack the French embassy in Tripoli. The most disturbing aspect of the raid for the Bourguiba regime was that the raiders had met with some popular support in the first days of their presence in Gafsa.

In April 1980, however, Bourguiba's heir-designate, the long-serving Prime Minister Nedi Nouira, was forced to retire due to illness. His successor, Prime Minister Mohamed Mzala, at once reversed Nouira's policy and began a programme of liberalisation, commencing first with a restoration of the autonomy of the trade union federation UGTT and the freeing of all the union leaders who had been jailed in 1978 (though not all of them were allowed to resume their union offices). Against a background of successful strikes, Mzali then announced in April 1981 that other political parties would be recognised provided they observed the constitution, abjured violence, and had no foreign ties. The Tunisian Communist Party resumed a legal existence after 18 years, and two new parties emerged embodying the two major breakaway trends from the PSD: the Movement of Social Democrats, led by former Defence and Interior Minister Ahmed Mestui, who had been expelled from the PSD in 1971 for his 'liberal' tendencies, and the Movement of Popular Unity, a hard-line socialist party embodying the ideas of the exiled Ahmed Ben Salah.

The one political group who did not benefit from this indulgence was the Islamic fundamentalists, whose popular support among the deprived young has grown greatly in recent years. Following attacks by fanatics on foreign tourists, the government arrested over 100 leaders of the Islamic Tendency Movement in August 1981, and sentenced 84 of them to long jail terms on vague charges. Once they were out of the way, however, Mzali proceeded to hold elections for the Chamber of Deputies in November (President-for-Life Bourguiba's position was not at stake) in which, for the first time in a quarter century, the PSD faced open opposition. Much of the goodwill he had gleaned with his liberalisation was lost, however, when the PSD, fearful that things were going too far, rigged the actual elections so that it won an incredible 95% of the vote and all 136 seats in the Chamber of Deputies. Despite the legalisation of opposing parties, therefore, the real struggle for the succession to Bourguiba is still largely confined within the hierarchy of the PSD.

All this manoeuvring takes place against a background of deepening social unrest in Tunisia. Amongst the young in particular there is a growing current of extreme leftist sentiment, and also a strong Islamic fundamentalist movement even in this most Westernised of Arab countries. If the battle for the succession ends up in the streets, however, it is probably the army that will decide the issue, and so all the rival factions have been seeking to win the support of key individuals in the officer corps.

The state of opinion within the officer corps cannot be precisely gauged, as they are not encouraged to make political statements beyond announcements of their loyalty to the regime. That sharp differences of opinion about Tunisia's future course exist in the army is certain: in August, 1976 22 members of the armed forces were arrested for plotting subversion and another five disappeared, after which the commanders of units in the south were replaced by loyal officers from the capital. It can be stated in general terms, however, that the right-wing group which has dominated the PSD's upper ranks for the past dozen years, has been seeking to gain the army's support both by a generous military spending programme and by specific promotion policies.

The latter process centres on the removal or retirement from senior command positions of 'first generation' officers who fought for independence with Bourguiba and 'second generation' officers, promoted after independence, who were infected by pan-Arab sentiments and were deeply disappointed by Tunisia's lack of involvement in the 1967 war against Israel. Their replacements are generally 'third generation' officers who have been trained in French or United States military academies or are known for their pro-Western sympathies. In this way it is hoped to ward off leftist, Islamic and/or Libyan challenges when Bourguiba finally goes. It is simply not possible, however, to judge what the true opinions of the mass of middle-ranking army officers really are, and this may prove to be the most critical factor in determining the outcome.

Gwynne Dyer

TURKEY

HISTORY AND INTRODUCTION

Turkey is the only State in the Middle East with an army whose traditions genuinely extend back beyond the turn of the century. It stands in direct descent from the Ottoman Army, and its outlook has been moulded and matured by five centuries of experience as the army of a great power. By the same token, the army's relationship with the Turkish State, and the immense fund of goodwill it enjoys in the mass of the Turkish population as a heritage of many generations of sacrifice and gallantry in (mostly lost) wars as the borders of the Ottoman Empire contracted, are fundamentally different from the circumstances prevailing in almost all its neighbours. Despite many alarums and upheavals, the Turks basically like their army and are comfortable with it. In return, though it sometimes puts its claims rather more strongly than civilian politicians would prefer, it knows its place — and that place is not in sole charge of the Republic.

In some senses, the Ottoman Empire was an army that made itself into a State, and the prime role of the early Sultans was almost invariably that of supreme military commander. The relative power of the army compared to other institutions was correspondingly always high within the Empire, and in time a succession of military interventions contributed substantially to its decline. This was a particularly marked phenomenon in the latter days of the Janissary army — a unique Turkish institution in which the army was comprised of Yenicheri ('new troops') who were conscripted from the non-Muslim subject populations in early youth, converted to Islam, and constituted into a professional, regular force. Eventually, and inevitably, this corps of men became a militarily useless body with entrenched privileges and reactionary views, leading the first of the reforming Sultans, Selim III, to attempt to replace them with a new army modelled on the Empire's successful European rivals.

His reforms were collectively known as the Nizam-i Jedid (New Order), but their focus, as in all subsequent efforts to modernise the Ottoman Empire from above in the nineteenth century, was on the military institutions which alone could save the empire from its encroaching enemies. Thus the new volunteer military force modelled on contemporary Western armies which was created in 1792, complete with military and naval schools where education on Western technical subjects was given by French officers, itself became known as the Nizam-i Jedid. The Janissaries, fearing for their privileges, revolted 13 years later, murdering many of the leading reformers and forcing the abolition of the new-style army and the Sultan's abdication in 1807, but the need for reform was too great to be postponed forever. The next great reforming Sultan, Mahmud II, effectively recreated the Nizam-i Jedid in 1826, and shortly afterwards annihilated the Janissary corps, once more in revolt, by massed cannon fire in the centre of Istanbul. This massacre is known to Turkish history as the 'Auspicious Incident'.

The regular army that then emerged is the lineal ancestor of the Turkish army of today. From that time onwards, too, the phenomenon became visible which was to dominate Turkish history for the next century, and influence it strongly down to the present: the leading role of army officers as reformers and Westernisers. For it was they, earlier and more comprehensively than any other Ottoman Turks, who were taught European languages and given Western education in the military schools which were now founded to train the officer corps of the regular army. It was also they who were best placed to see the disastrous gulf between the decaying traditional institutions of the Empire and the new forms of organisation that underlay European successes, they who bore the most direct responsibility for the series of catastrophic military defeats caused by this gulf, and they who were best placed to do something about it. Inevitably, they became first reformers, then revolutionaries.

Eventually, in 1908, it was army officers who carried out the Young Turk Revolution that inaugurated the last desperate race to rescue the Empire by turning it into a European-style State. Within a couple of years, they transformed the empire into a constitutional democracy with an elective parliament, remodelled practically every institution in sight along Western lines, and extended the right (and duty) of military service to the non-Turkish and non-Muslim populations of the empire. In practice, they also turned the State into a military dictatorship, run by an oligarchy of young Turkish nationalist officers (the average age of the leading rebel officers of 1908 was late twenties), and within 6 years they had plunged the empire into its last disastrous war. By 1918 they were totally discredited, and the empire was militarily prostrate, awaiting partition amongst the victorious *entente* powers.

There was, however, a 'second team' of 'Young Turk officers', dissidents who had been excluded from the ruling group quite early on, who had all along favoured a 'Turkish' rather than an 'Ottoman' solution. That is to say, they had argued (rightly) that it was far too late to try and save the moribund multi-national empire, and that all energies should be devoted to the aim of somehow extricating an independent Turkish national State from the impending wreck. The most prominent of these nationalist officers was Mustafa Kemal, later called Ataturk; like his colleagues, he served loyally in military commands throughout World War I, rising to the rank of General and Pasha, and his group was available as an alternative leadership when military catastrophe finally discredited its ruling rivals.

Mustafa Kemal Ataturk and his companions then proceeded to create a military resistance movement in central Anatolia, and fight off French, Italian, Greek and British forces — at first unaided, later with Soviet Russian aid — in a part-guerrilla, part-regular war that ended in triumph, and in the creation of the Turkish Republic in 1923. (It was for this first successful war of nationalist resistance against imperialism, by the way, that the Soviets coined the technical Marxist term 'war of national liberation', later to gain general currency.) The Russians saw it in ideological terms as a war of the 'national bourgeoisie', but the Turks are probably more accurate in describing it as 'the war of the reserve officers'. It was the army that rescued a Turkish national State from the ruins of the Empire, just as an earlier Turkish army had founded it, and the army's driving force was a Western-oriented officer corps — regulars educated in the military schools in the key positions, and reserve officers with semi-Western educations (a great many of them school-teachers) as the mass behind them.

In the subsequent 15 years until his death in 1938, Ataturk, with the army's backing, rammed through the radical reforms which turned Turkey into the mirror image (so far as laws and State institutions go) of a European, secular State. He did Turkey an equally great service in firmly suppressing any tendencies in the army towards the praetorianism that had wrecked the 1908 revolution, and by firmly insisting on the total separation of military and civil functions. (He set the example himself, by resigning his military rank upon becoming President of the Republic.) It was the army's role, clearly stated in the constitution, to safeguard Ataturk's reforms and prevent backsliding, but not to rule itself.

To a very great extent, Ataturk's definition of the army's role within the State prevails even today. Multi-party democracy was introduced in Turkey in 1950, and despite several interruptions has been the predominant pattern ever since. Indeed in the quarter-century 1950–75, in all the region between Italy and India, Turkey's record as a liberal, parliamentary democracy was only matched by Israel and (perhaps) Greece. Whether the same will hold true for the next quarter-century is difficult to say.

The Turkish army never ceased to play a political role, even after 1958. In 1960, it intervened against the government of the day on the grounds that it was corrupt, that it was pandering to traditionalist, obscurantist and anti-Ataturkist sections of the population, and that it planned to rig the forthcoming elections. True or not, the reputation the army still enjoyed as a modernising, progressive force was shown by the fact that the intervention had the support of most Turkish intellectuals, including even the students. It hanged the Prime Minister and two of his associates — now generally admitted to have been a disastrous error — but it dealt firmly with those of its own officers who showed a taste for clinging to political power, and it handed the government back to civilian politicians after only a year. Moreover, it gave the Second Turkish Republic a considerably more democratic constitution than its predecessor had had.

It is undeniably true, however, that a great many Turkish senior officers, operating in an efficient environment of thorough military professionalism, felt a deep distaste for the unseemly compromises and sloppy half-measures of democratic politics, and occasionally had the urge to knock the politicians' heads together. Such sentiments lay behind the 'mini-coup' of March, 1971 when the army, without actually seeking to overthrow the constitution, nevertheless demanded and got the resignation of the Prime Minister. Its patience had been sorely tried by the government's apparent policy of masterly inactivity in the face of the terrorist campaign then troubling Turkish cities (the Turkish People's Liberation Army, now largely defunct), and it got the sucessor government to impose a state of modified martial law in all the main urban areas. It then embarked on a draconian round-up of leftists of all varieties, without much regard for the niceties of constitutional rights.

However, most of these prisoners were released within a year of the army's handing back full control to the politicians in October, 1973. Not only did it allow the 1973 election to be held, but it acquiesced in the subsequent curious coalition government of social democrats and Islamic radicals. (Ten years previously, it would not even have allowed the latter party to run for office. When the armed forces attempted to exercise their traditional right of nominating the President in March, 1973 the politicians almost unanimously resisted, and got their way. By 1974, the last of the four 'interventionist' service chiefs who had forced their ultimatum on the Prime Minister in 1971 had been retired without any fuss.

In the latter 1970s, however, everything went wrong for Turkey. The effects of oil price rises and the general world recession on the Turkish economy were greatly exacerbated by domestic factors, most notably a series of governments who were at best ineffectual, at worst totally paralysed by disagreements amongst the coalition parties. Various ministries of the state, including the police and security forces, were effectively colonised by the adherents of the political parties (including a neo-fascist and an Islamic fundamentalist party) whose ministers in the coalition governments gained control of them. The level of corruption and favouritism in all state-run organisations and institutions rose to unprecedented levels, and popular respect for them, and for the political parties, suffered a steep decline. At the same time terrorism by right- and left-wing extremist groups returned, with far greater ferocity than at the beginning of the 1970s.

The sources of crisis in Turkey were not merely financial and administrative, however. Indeed, the crisis was in large part a natural consequence of the success of Ataturk and his successors in transforming Turkey from a static peasant society imbued with Islamic values into a secular, semi-industrialised state whose official values were democratic and 'European'. Turkey, by the end of the 1970s, was a country almost half of whose 49,000,000 people were urbanised, and living in a 'Western' physical and economic environment — but of course many of them were first generation immigrants from the countryside and not particularly successful at dealing with its environment and culture. The crisis of identity which resulted, combined with severe economic and political difficulties, came close to causing the collapse of the entire Ataturkist system.

Similar circumstances in neighbouring Iran, where the social transformation had been more abrupt, and where there were neither a strong democratic tradition nor an army with an ideology independent of the autocratic rulers, led to a fundamentalist Islamic revival and the rejection of all Western values in 1979. Turkey was spared that but, by 1979, it was effectively bankrupt, with the government unable to import even the basic necessities of life, power cuts of up to six hours a day, and insufficient fuel to heat homes through the harsh winter. It was also in a state of undeclared civil war, with right-wing terrorists (enjoying the clandestine support of two smaller parties in the governing coalition) and left-wing terrorists (including many from the oppressed Kurdish minority in the south-east who used Marxism to cloak their separatist ambitions) waging a war of assassination against each other and the general public that was killing an average of 30 people a day, despite the fact that 20 of the 67 provinces were under martial law.

It was in these desperate circumstances that the armed forces, under the command of General Kenan Evien, finally intervened on 12 September, 1980, to the relief of almost everybody. All political parties and institutions were suspended, and the army proceeded to suppress the terrorism with ruthless thoroughness. In the ensuing two years over 66,000 people were detained for suspected terrorist activities, of whom over 8,000 had received prison sentences by the end of 1982, with a further 18,000 in detention awaiting trial. Huge quantities of illegally held arms were seized, including 40,000 rifles and half a million hand guns. But by 1982 deaths from terrorism had been reduced to an average of three per week.

The regime of austerity imposed by the armed forces led to a rapid economic recovery; by the end of 1982 exports had doubled, inflation was more than halved, shortages of imported products had ended, and the GNP was growing at 4% after two years of stagnation. Given these results and the return of civil peace, it is unsurprising that the new constitution submitted for popular approval in November 1982 received a 91% 'yes' vote, although (or perhaps because) it was less liberal than its predecessor. By the same referendum, General Evien was elected president for a seven-year term, with constitutional powers comparable to those enjoyed by French presidents since De Gaulle. Party elections are scheduled for late 1983 or early 1984, at which time the armed forces will once again hand power over to civilian politicians.

STRENGTH AND BUDGET

The strength of the Turkish armed forces is 569,000 (1.1% of the population of 47,000,000), of which 470,000 are army. The army is the largest in the Middle East, and the second-largest (after the USA's) within NATO. Most of the army's strength (420,000) is conscript; almost all officers and non-commissioned officers are regulars.

The navy has 46,000 men (36,000 conscripts), and the air force 53,000 (33,000 conscripts). Army reserves number approximately 700,000. The principal paramilitary force is the Gendarmerie, which consists of 120,000 men and includes three mobile brigades.

The Turkish military budget for 1981 was $2,630,000,000, which is approximately 4.5% of GNP. The gendarmerie budget is separate. Having reached a peak in 1975 due to the Cyprus conflict and the Aegean confrontation, Turkish military expenditure has since declined in relative terms from 26.7% to 20.7% of government expenditure, and from 9% of GNP to only half that proportion.

COMMAND AND CONSTITUTIONAL STATUS

The President of the Republic is Commander-in-Chief of the Armed Forces according to the constitution. Since all but one of Turkey's presidents have been retired military officers, this role tends to be more than merely ceremonial. The President's power is exercised through the Prime Minister and the Minister of National Defence. The executive commander of the armed forces is the Chief of the General Staff.

At the moment, President Evien is also Chief of Staff, and will retain that post until party elections and the hand-over to a civil government occur in 1983 or 1984. Subsequently he will relinquish his formal role, but few Turkish presidents have failed to keep close informal links with the armed forces high command. Precisely what the formal constitutional relationship between government and armed forces will be is not now entirely clear, and what follows is descriptive of what prevailed before 1980. It is unlikely to be changed radically.

This last institution is the one in which change is most unlikely to occur, for the relationship of President and Prime Minister are significantly changed by the new constitution. The president now has the right to dissolve the 400-seat single-chamber parliament at times of protracted governmental crisis, and to declare states of emergency or martial law without resort to parliament. He continues to appoint prime ministers, who then must win a vote of confidence in parliament, but since he himself is no longer elected by parliament, but rather by a separate national vote, his power relative to the Prime Minister is now significantly greater, and in future the NSC may supplant the Supreme Military Council as the most important executive body in times of military crisis or war.

ROLE, COMMITMENT, DEPLOYMENT AND RECENT OPERATIONS

The Turkish army is organised for national defence, and except in times of martial law has no authority to perform internal security functions. (However, the gendarmerie, which does have such functions, is commanded by army officers and co-operates closely with local army units, although in time of peace it is under the control of the Ministry of the Interior.)

For several centuries, Turkey's main military preoccupation has been Russia, against which it fought (as the Ottoman Empire) about a dozen wars, in the course of which it lost the richer half of its imperial possessions. Hostility and fear towards Muscovy are deeply ingrained in the Turkish national consciousness (and a substantial minority of the Turkish population are descended from refugees from the territories lost to Russian armies over the generations).

Turkish—Soviet relations were quite good in the period 1923–41, as a heritage of their collaboration in the period of the Turkish War of Independence and the Western interventions in the Russian Civil War, and as a result Turkey was able to adopt a neutral foreign policy for the first time in its history. However, the old anxieties were instantly reawakened by the Russian arrival in the Balkans in 1945 and Stalin's demands for territorial concessions from Turkey, and Ankara accordingly flung itself into the arms of the USA when the Truman Doctrine was promulgated in 1947.

In its initial enthusiasm for the Western alliance (and, undoubtedly, to earn some political credit) Turkey sent a brigade to join the United Nations forces fighting in Korea in October, 1950. In all, some 20,000 Turkish troops fought in Korea, and 717 died there. It was the first time the Turkish army had fought since 1922, and it showed that the Turkish military reputation for ferocious bravery and unyielding resistance was still as well merited as it had always been.

In 1952 Turkey was admitted to full membership of NATO, and in 1955 it joined the Baghdad Pact (later CENTO), whose headquarters is in Ankara. Its main assigned role in both alliances, however, was simply to defend its own strategically vital territory, and above all the Bosphorus and Dardenelles Straits giving access from the Black Sea to the Mediterranean. This entirely corresponded to the Turks' own security priorities, and between 1947 and 1973 military assistance from the USA totalled almost $6,000,000,000 in value.

The Turkish enthusiasm for NATO began to cool somewhat after the emergence of the Cyprus problem in the 1950s, since it raised the possibility of conflict with Greece, their nearest NATO ally. The estrangement was gradual (and is still far from complete), but it was exacerbated by American attempts to steer a middle course between contending Greek and Turkish claims. It was also hastened by the gradual apparent diminution in the Soviet threat (the Soviet government repudiated Stalin's territorial claims on Turkey in the early 1960s) and by the deliberate Turkish government attempts, in emulation of its Western allies, to achieve a measure of detente with the Soviet Union.

As successive Cyprus crises heightened Greek—Turkish hostility, Turkish military priorities gradually came to include the possibility of war with Greece in the Aegean, or of military intervention in Cyprus. When the climactic crisis came in Cyprus in July, 1974 the Turkish armed forces were prepared and equipped to carry out a swift sea and airborne invasion.

The 1974 crisis was caused by the ill-advised action of the Athens government in sponsoring a coup against Archbishop Makarios, President of Cyprus, using as its instrument the 12,000 man Greek-Cypriot National Guard, a semi-regular force which was commanded by Greek army regular officers. Makarios escaped with his life, but the coup leader, Nikos Sampson, an ex-EOKA terrorist renowned for his anti-Turkish attitudes, was established as President within 24 hours of the attack on the Presidential Palace in Nicosia on July 15th. Cyprus was proclaimed a 'Hellenic Republic', and the military junta in Athens, displaying an incompetence that rivalled its brutality, evidently believed that the path had been cleared for *enosis* – union of Cyprus with Greece – within a year. Astonishingly, and despite clear prior warnings from Ankara, the Greek government was of the opinion that Turkey would not react vigorously.

The Turkish government, fearing for the safety of the Turkish-Cypriot minority and determined not to allow *enosis* (which would create a Greek military stronghold flanking its south coast), first sought British co-operation in a joint intervention in Cyprus. Both countries, as co-guarantors of the 1960 treaty establishing Cypriot independence, had the right to intervene in defence of the constitution, but Britain refused to exercise its right, or even to allow Turkey to land its forces through the British Sovereign Base Areas on the south coast. There were also reports that Washington was considering the recognition of the Sampson regime. The Turkish government therefore decided to ignore British and American pressure for a non-military solution to the crisis, which it feared could all too easily lead to the consolidation of the new situation, and chose to exercise its right of unilateral intervention by invading Cyprus.

Cyprus's geographical position, some 300 miles from Crete and 500 from the Greek mainland, but only 40 miles from Turkey, guaranteed Turkey air and naval superiority in the area. The Cyprus National Guard was relatively short of heavy weapons – it disposed of only 32 tanks, 50 armoured cars and some medium artillery – so that there was no question of its being able to prevent an invasion. The Turkish landings commenced after dawn on July 20th, across the beaches west of Kyrenia and by paratroop landings at the Turkish-Cypriot village of Gönyeli, on the Kyrenia–Nicosia road south of the St. Hilarion Pass.

The initial landings were successful, but there was tough Greek and Greek-Cypriot resistance, especially in the Pass. Turkish forces barely succeeded in driving a wedge through to the beleaguered Turkish-Cypriot quarter of the capital before the first ceasefire supervened on July 22nd, and they failed to seize Nicosia airport. Inter-service co-ordination was generally satisfactory, although Turkish aircraft sank one of their own naval vessels by mistake.

At the time of the July ceasefire the Turkish army controlled only a small enclave extending inland from the northern coast at Kyrenia, and about half the Turkish-Cypriot population were still effectively hostages in Greek hands in the rest of the island. There were continual breaches of the ceasefire and a gradual expansion along the edges of the Turkish enclave during the next month. A conference convened in London on August 10th collapsed when the Greek side asked for more time to consider Turkish proposals for a permanent settlement in Cyprus on a cantonal, federal basis. Thereupon, having meanwhile built up its forces in the Cyprus bridgehead to about 40,000 men and 200 tanks, the Turkish army recommenced its advance in mid-August. Greek resistance collapsed rapidly under vastly superior air, armour and artillery bombardment, and by the time the second ceasefire was agreed on August 16th, the Turkish armed forces controlled the northern two-fifths of the island. They had also relieved the besieged Turkish-Cypriots in the city of Famagusta.

Over the next year, continuing population movements, some voluntary, some less so, more or less completed the physical separation of the Turkish- and Greek-Cypriot communities (although exacerbating even more the problem of Greek refugees, generally estimated to number almost 200,000). Since August, 1974 the Turkish government has insisted on a bizonal, not merely a cantonal, federal government for Cyprus, with the Turkish-Cypriot community remaining concentrated in a single contiguous area in the north. Recent negotiations between the two communities suggest that the Greek-Cypriot side has now reluctantly accepted this principle, though the final size of the Turkish-Cypriot area remains a subject for discussion. There is general consent, however, that some parts of Turkish-occupied northern Cyprus – 38% of the island's territory – will be handed back to accommodate some of the Greek refugees, and certain areas have been left deliberately empty by the Turkish authorities for this purpose. Turkish forces in Cyprus have gradually declined to a current size of about two divisions (25,000 men), and a permanent settlement would mean the removal of almost all of these as well.

During the 1974 crisis Turkey did not declare mobilisation (as Greece did), but elements of the First Army were concentrated on the Turco–Greek frontier in Thrace, while substantial air and naval forces were moved to the Aegean coast. Subsequently Turkey created a Fourth Army in the Aegean, outside the NATO command structure, but this was largely a symbolic gesture. For the most part, Fourth Army forces are those that were in the area before, simply transferred to a different chain of command. The same tendency was evinced in the government declaration in January, 1974 of an intention to create a bomber *force de frappe* within the air force which would operate outside the NATO command structure.

Only a small portion of the Turkish army has actually been shifted south since the confrontation with Greece over Cyprus, Aegean oil and other issues entered its severe phase in 1974, which may be taken to indicate one or both of two things: (*a*) the continuing preoccupation of the Turkish General Staff with the Soviet Union as the prime threat to security, if a less urgent one; and/or (*b*) the predominantly air and naval character that any war in the Aegean would assume. There is, of course, no serious possibility of a major Greek military incursion deep into Turkish territory.

Turkey's Greek problems since 1974 have shown themselves more in increased defence budgets, a greater stress on the development of a domestic arms industry (*see* Equipment and Arms Industry), and in difficulties with its allies. The US Congress placed an arms embargo on Turkey in December 1974, in an ill-advised attempt to force Turkish concessions on the Cyprus question, and Turkey responded by suspending the activities of US bases in Turkey, whose major importance is for electronic information gathering in the Southern Soviet Union and the Middle East. (The large NATO base in Izmir was not affected). The White House, which had never supported the embargo, did not succeed in having it wholly removed until 1978, by which time substantial damage had been done to the readiness of Turkish armed forces despite the efforts of its European NATO allies, notably West Germany, to fill the gap. Once the obstacle of the embargo was removed, a new Defence Cooperative Agreement regulating the status of the US bases was negotiated fairly rapidly, and signed in March 1980. This agreement, which places the bases under nominal Turkish command, is accompanied by annexes on the American military and economic aid and investment in Turkey's arms industry which may be expected over the subsequent five years, amounting to an average of $450 million a year.

The difficulties in the NATO command structure in the south-eastern Mediterranean which were occasioned by Greece's withdrawal from NATO's military command structure in 1974 were settled, so far as Turkey was concerned, in June 1978, when the former headquarters at Izmir was handed over to Turkey, since in practice it would only control Turkish land and naval forces and the Turkish First Tactical Air Force in wartime.

In an effort to ease the reintegration of Greece into NATO's military wing before the 1981 election, which was expected to bring an anti-NATO left-wing government to power in Athens, Turkey agreed in 1980 to postpone settlement of its dispute with Greece over NATO air command zones in the Aegean – the entire area had been under Greek control until 1974, but then devolved on Turkey – until after Greece's re-entry, and withdrew its veto in the NATO Council of Ministers, Greece formally rejoined the military command structure in October 1980, under an agreement which set up a separate NATO command for Greek forces with head-quarters at Larissa, both that headquarters and Izmir thenceforward to report separately to NATO's Southern Command in Naples. However, negotiations on this outstanding dispute with Greece, and with others over territorial waters and seabed demarcation in the Aegean, have been stalled since the PASOK government assumed power in Athens in October 1981. Prime Minister Papandreou, who pursues a vehemently anti-Turkish policy, has ended the high-level discussions with Ankara that were initiated under his predecessor, and the Greek headquarters at Larissa has not been activated.

Following the revolution in Iran, the former CENTO alliance which had linked that country with Turkey and Pakistan rapidly collapsed, and Turkey formally notified its withdrawal from it in March 1980. Ankara has observed a policy of strict neutrality in the war which began between its two eastern neighbours, Iran and Iraq, in September 1980, but it would be safe to say that it does have two particular interests in the outcome. Politically, it would certainly prefer that Iraq did not become another militant Islamic state on the Iranian model, since it faces a significant challenge of this sort in Turkey already. More importantly, however, it wants neither country to suffer so severe a defeat that fragmentation occurs, for that could lead to the creation of an independent Kurdish state along its present frontier with Iran or Iraq, and pose a grave problem for Turkey in containing the separatist ambitions of its own 8,000,000 Kurds in that region. Hitherto, however, the noticeable increase in the deployment of Turkish security forces in the south-east has been primarily in the form of Gendarmerie reinforcements for internal security duties.

ORGANISATION

Arms of Service
The Turkish army is still largely an infantry force based on peasant conscripts, albeit a very high-grade one, and this is reflected in the fact that it consists of 14 infantry divisions, and only two mechanised infantry divisions. There are, however, a further five independent armoured brigades and four mechanised infantry brigades, as well as eleven independent infantry brigades. There is also a parachute brigade and a commando brigade and eight armoured reconnaissance units, 36 artillery battalions, eight AA artillery battalions and a number of fortress defence regiments. The army also has four surface-to-surface missile battalions armed with Honest John missiles.

Operational
The Turkish General Staff, though it is invariably commanded by an army general and has a large majority of army officers, is in effect a joint staff. It is located in Ankara, and is organised into five major divisions for personnel, operations, planning, logistics and communications, designated J-1 to J-5, respectively. Staff officers in Ankara and in the field comprise a separate corps, all of whom are graduates of the 4 year course at the General Staff College in Istanbul. The headquarters of all three services are in Ankara, in constant close contact with the General Staff.

There are four Turkish army commands, each containing two or three corps. The First Army, headquarters Istanbul, controls forces in eastern Thrace on the Greek and Bulgarian borders. It is heavy in armour, and organised for mobile operations. The Second Army, headquarters Konya, is primarily responsible for the defence of the northern Anatolian coast east of the Straits, but also has logistical responsibility for the Turkish forces in Cyprus. The Third Army, whose headquarters has recently been moved from Erzerum to Erzincan, is responsible for the security of the Turkish–Soviet border area in eastern Anatolia. The newly created Fourth Army, headquarters Izmir, is responsible for the military security of the Aegean coastal region. The land forces also include a training command of five or six training divisions, three Communications Commands (West, Central and East), and several base commands.

The Turkish air force contains 31 squadrons, of which the majority are organised into two Tactical Air Forces. There are 15 fighter–ground attack squadrons, three interceptor squadrons, one reconnaissance squadron three training squadrons and six transport squadrons. It also possesses eight batteries of Nike–Ajax and Nike–Hercules surface-to-air missiles. A large part of the air force's strength, and all the SAM batteries, are concentrated in the region of Istanbul and the Straits. Major air bases are at Adana, Balikesir, Bandirma, Diyarbakir, Esluboğa, Eskişehir, Etimesgut (Ankara), Izmir, Merzifon, Sivas and Yesilköy (Istanbul); the First Tactical Air Force has its headquarters at Eskişehir in western Turkey, and the Third Tactical Air Force headquarters are at Diyarbekir in eastern Turkey. The air-defence and warning command, controlling an extensive radar network, is sometimes referred to as the Second Tactical Air Force.

The Turkish navy is composed of the North and South Sea Area Commands (Istanbul and Izmir) and several training commands. The sub-command in charge of operations in the Straits is also in Istanbul. Fleet Command, bearing primary responsibility for ship building, repair and supply, is at Gölçük, the naval base at the head of Izmit Bay in the Sea of Marmara. Other major naval bases are at Iskenderun, Samsun, Trabzon and Eregli.

The 110,000 man gendarmerie, armed with light infantry weapons is fully controlled by the army in wartime, and may also come under operational control of the army in whole or in part when states of emergency or martial law are declared. Even in peacetime it is commanded by a four-star army general, and the gendarmerie general staff is directed by an army major-general. Its personnel are derived from the army, and its uniforms, ranks, pay and equipment are the same. The gendarmerie organisation includes three mobile infantry brigades deployed in the Second and Third Army areas.

Under existing agreements, all of the Turkish navy, most of the air force, and 15 out of 17 army divisions are 'assigned' to NATO, although they remain – at least in time of peace – under the control of the Turkish military authorities. The NATO command structures in the region – Sixth Allied Tactical Air Force, and South-Eastern Command with responsibility for land forces – both have their headquarters at Izmir in western Turkey. Until recently both organisations were commanded by American generals, in order to avoid offence to the rival nationalisms of Greece and Turkey whose forces, together with some locally based American units, would be subordinated to these commands in wartime. This argument has ceased to be valid after Greece left the integrated command structure of the alliance after 1974, and since 1978 Sixth Allied Tactical Air Force and South-Eastern Command now comprised of Turkish forces has been commanded by Turkish generals with American deputies. The headquarters at Izmir, and a new allied headquarters at Larisa commanded by Greek officers, which would control Greek forces placed at the disposal of NATO, are both to be under the ultimate authority of Commander-in-Chief South in Naples. (Despite the formal agreement on Greek reintegration into NATO in 1980, however, the Larisa headquarters has not yet been activated.)

RECRUITMENT, TRAINING AND RESERVES

The regular officer corps of the Turkish army is trained at the Turkish Military Academy in Ankara, where cadets with a satisfactory standard of secondary education undergo a 3 year programme of military instruction and general education and receive commissions as second-lieutenants in the regular army upon graduation. About a thousand officers are graduated each year, and the historical tendency to over-produce junior officers, which has been aggravated by an inadequate rate of retirement at the top, has occasionally necessitated the wholesale retirement of officers in the middle ranks.

At appropriate stages in their careers, officers attend advanced courses in the schools run by their arm or service, and very large numbers have also been to courses in the USA and Western Europe. At the top of the army school system is the General Staff College in Istanbul, where selected officers who have passed the stiff entrance examinations pursue a 4 year programme of study and staff practice. Successful graduates become members of the *élite* General Staff Corps, and subsequently serve in the important command positions and on the General Staff.

Career NCOs are volunteers who enter on long-term enlistments after completing secondary school. They attend a course of about 2 years at the Non-Commissioned Officers' School in Ankara before being appointed corporals in the regular army.

The bulk of the armed forces' manpower (489,000 out of 569,000) is provided by conscripts doing 20 months of compulsory service. Fit males are generally called for service in their twentieth year, although induction may be deferred until completion of schooling or up to the age of thirty-two. There is no minimum educational or intelligence requirement. Those who are not secondary school graduates generally serve as privates; those who show ability may be appointed as acting NCOs in the lower grades, while university graduates almost invariably do their service as reserve officers.

Conscript recruits receive about 8 weeks of basic training (including literacy training if required) in the training divisions which are distributed around the country. (These are quite separate from the combat units of the field armies.) After basic training, recruits are assigned to a combat unit or, if qualified by education and aptitude, are sent to one of the army's branch schools for further training. The principal branch schools for the infantry are located in Istanbul and Çankiri; for engineers, at Kağithane near Istanbul; for artillery, at Polatli; for armour and for army aviation, at Ankara, and for commandos, at Eğridir. The technical services, such as ordnance, transportation and signal corps, maintain specialist schools in various parts of the country.

Reserve officers usually come to the army having already completed training programmes at the civilian universities. Required service is 20 months, but reserve officers may at the army's discretion contract for additional service of up to 26 years.

The navy has retained the former pattern of officer training, abandoned by the army in the 1950s: candidates generally attend the Naval Lyceum, a 3 year secondary school to which youths are admitted by competitive examination, before moving on to the Naval Academy where they undergo 4 years of naval and general education as midshipmen. They are then promoted to ensign, and serve a further probationary period of 2 years at sea before finally receiving full commissions in the regular navy. Both the Lyceum and the Academy are on Heybeli Island, in the Sea of Marmara off Istanbul, which also houses the headquarters of the navy's Training Command.

A similar system prevails in the training of NCOs; the Petty Officers' School in Istanbul accepts applicants at the age of twelve for 4 years of secondary and naval education, after which they are admitted as petty officer candidates and undergo a further 4 years of speciality training before being appointed as career petty officers of the lowest grade. Navy conscripts receive about 4 months' basic training, and serve the balance of their time in various duties ashore or afloat.

Air force regular officers are trained at the Air Force Academy in Eskişehir, where the Air Force Non-Commissioned Officers' School is also located. The latter school complex also provides specialist instruction in a variety of technical subjects, which is supplemented in some cases by instruction at civilian facilities or abroad. Pilot training is done at Çiğli, near Izmir. The air force relies on career airmen for operational and technical duties, generally restricting its proportionately small share of conscripts to administrative and guard duties.

Recently, a special once-only provision was made for those educated in universities abroad, or who had otherwise passed the usual age for military service due to educational reasons, to discharge their liability with a special abbreviated training period of only 4 months. This was seen by some as the entering wedge in tackling the problem of universal military service, which with the rapidly growing Turkish population (now 47,000,000, of whom some 42% are under fifteen) has been flooding the armed forces with more unskilled people than they can usefully employ, at some cost to the more important consideration of buying new equipment. Since universal military service is also seen as serving important educational and national purposes, however, especially in the case of the large Kurdish minority population of the south-east, there is still a considerable reluctance to change the system to one of selective or voluntary service.

Conscripts are placed on the reserve list at their local government office on completion of their 20 months' service. They are subject to recall until the age of forty-six if physically fit and not otherwise exempted, but there is no system of organised reserve units and no periodical refresher training is provided. It is estimated that the army could expect to be able to call up about 700,000 reservists who were reasonably fit, available, and with training recent enough to be useful, while the navy could call up about 70,000, and the air force 66,000.

Turkish armed forces' pay and allowances are adjusted periodically to keep them more or less equivalent to what is earned by persons of similar qualifications in civil life. The armed forces also run an extensive social-security system for their members called the Military Mutual Aid Association (OYAK). Regular officers and NCOs contribute about 10% of their salaries to the association fund, which is largely tax exempt. Participants may borrow from the fund for home purchases, and on retirement they receive back their investment plus accumulated interest and accrued dividend distribution. OYAK, whose director is a general officer on active service (the rest of the management is civilian) disposes of extremely large sums for investment, and has a considerable influence in the Turkish economy through its interests in the automobile industry, cement production, petrochemicals, textiles and other enterprises.

EQUIPMENT AND ARMY INDUSTRY

The Turkish army's armoured strength consists of 500 M-46, 3,000 M-48, 100 M-26, and 50 Leopard I tanks (20 more Leopards are on order). It also has M-8 armoured cars, and a variety of APCs including 2,000 M-113, 1,200 Commando, and some old M-2s and M-3s. The artillery armaments consist of 60 M-59 155mm towed and 36 M-107 175mm SP guns; 954 M-116 A1 75mm pack howitzers; 140 M-101A1 105mm, 288 M-114A1 155mm, and 116 M-115 203mm towed howitzers; 400 M-7/M-108 105mm, 210 M-46 155mm, and 48 M-110 203mm SP howitzers; and some 1,750, 60mm, 81mm, 4.2-in and 120mm mortars. The four SSM battalions have 54 Honest John missiles.

The army's anti-tank weapons consist of 1,200 57mm, 390 75mm and 800 106mm RCL, some M-18/M-36 76mm SP ATK guns, and Cobra, SS-11 and TOW ATGW. 2,500 Milan ATGW are on order. Anti-aircraft defences are made up of 300 twin 20mm, 900 40mm, some M-51 75mm and M-117/M-118 90mm AA guns. Army aviation has 118 aircraft (two DHC-2, 18 U-17, six Cessna 206, three Cessna 421, 15 Dornier DO-27, nine DO-28, 20 Baron, five T-42 and 40 Citabria 105S) and 204 helicopters (156 AN-204/-205, 20 Bell 47G and 48 UH-1H); 27 further UH-1H helicopters are on order.

The Turkish navy's major warships are 16 submarines (two in reserve and one more on order), 15 destroyers, two frigates (four more on order), 21 fast attack craft (two more on order), of which 13 are equipped with Harpoon or Penguin SSM, ten minelayers, 26 minesweepers and 75 landing craft. It also operates 53 coastal patrol craft and sixty other auxiliary ships (9 tankers), and anti-submarine air squadron possessing 18 S-2E tracker aircraft, two S-2A (in reserve) and three AB-204B and 16 AB-212 ASW helicopters. There is a marine infantry brigade of 5000 men organised in three infantry battalions and one artillery battalion (18 guns).

The Turkish air force has 402 combat aircraft, all but a few American designed. The 18 FGA squadrons consist of six with 84 F-5A/B, four with 66 F-100 C/D/F; four with 82 F-4E and eight RF-4E; and three with 62 F/TF-104G. Another 33 F-104 G and F-100 D/F are on order. The three interceptor squadrons fly 36 F-104S, and the one reconnaissance squadron has 16 RF-5As and F-5Bs. Airborne weapons include Sidewinder, Super Sidewinder, Sparrow, Falcon and Shofire AAM and AS-12, Bullpup and Maverick ASM. There are eight SAM squadrons with 36 Nike-Hercules and 36 Nike-Ajax SAM. Ten search-and-rescue and four ECM UH-iH helicopters are on order.

The six transport squadrons consist of two with seven C-130E Hercules and 20 C-160D Transall; three with 30 C-47A, and one VIP squadron with three Viscount 794s, two Islander aircraft and 12 UH-1D/H and five UH-19D helicopters. Approx. 33 more Transall aircraft are on order. The three transport squadrons have 24 T-34A, 25 T-37B/C, 60 T-38A, and 20 T-41D aircraft. Operational Conversion Units operate 12 G-91T and 36 F-100 C/F, there is one independent VIP flight with two C-47A, and nine base flights have 40 7-33A and two C-47A aircraft and two UH-1H helicopters.

The Gendarmerie's three mobile brigades have Commando APCs, and its maritime units have a number of patrol craft.

On the whole, The Turkish air force is equipped to a relatively modern standard, but navy and army equipment tends to be rather dated. This became a source of acute anxiety during 1974—8 when Turkey suffered an American arms embargo (at first complete, latterly on Turkish arms transfers other than cash transactions up to a limit of S175,000,000 a year). The Turkish response has been two-fold: an attempt to vary its source of weapons, previously exclusively the USA, by turning to Western European arms producers, and in the longer run an ambitious attempt to create its own arms industry.

The main alternative source of supply for Turkey has become West Germany, from where Turkey has bought (or produces under licence) tanks, ships, submarines and aircraft. Although the Turkish strategy of creating a domestic arms industry is taken very seriously, the country's straitened financial circumstances in the past half-decade have seriously retarded the effort. However, Turkey has been building naval vessels up to the size of destroyer escorts since the middle 1960s, and is now producing West German-designed type 209 submarines and Zwisser missile-firing fast patrol boats. Measures to ensure Turkish self-sufficiency in small arms, artillery, soft-skinned military vehicles and ammunition are already well in hand.

Turkey is of course only one of a number of nations in the Middle East region that are seeking to lessen their dependence on foreign arms suppliers, influenced either by the experience or the fear of suffering arms embargoes at critical moments. Indeed, during 1975 Ankara concludes separate agreements with Libya, Iran and Pakistan to make joint investments in armaments industry (detailed plans to be formulated later). But such co-operation, whether within the framework of the RCD or not, is unlikely to extend far beyond joint marketing arrangements for various nationally produced weapons. Of these various national programmes for arms independence, moreover, only the Turkish one is to be taken very seriously for the coming decade.

However, in the entire Middle East only Turkey and Israel possess the necessary combination of political will, financial resources, industrial base, technical skills and large market — Turkey, like Israel, estimates its annual replacement requirement for combat aircraft at 40—50 a year — needed to create and support a fully-fledged domestic arms industry. While Turkey, like Israel, can never hope to be fully independent of outside sources for some of the most advanced weapons technologies, there is every reason to believe that it will eventually achieve a quite substantial degree of self-sufficiency in arms.

RANK, DRESS AND DISTINCTIONS

The Turkish armed forces have a rank structure identical to that of the USA, and the nomenclature is the same for all three services (except for naval ranks above that of captain).

> *Maresal* (navy: *Büyük Amiral*) — General of the Army (Admiral of the Fleet, General of the Air Force)
> *Orgeneral* (navy: *Oramiral*) — General
> *Korgeneral* (navy: *Koramiral*) — Lieutenant-general
> *Tümgeneral* (navy: *Tümamiral*) — Major-general
> *Tuğgeneral* (navy: *Tuğamiral*) — Brigadier-general
> *Albay* — Colonel
> *Yarbay* — Lieutenant-colonel
> *Binbaşi* — Major
> *Yuzbasi* — Captain
> *Üsteğmen* — First-lieutenant
> *Teğmen* — Second-lieutenant
> *Kidemli Başçavuş* — Sergeant Major (Chief Petty Officer)
> *Başçavus* — Master Sergeant
> *Üstçavuş* — Sergeant First Class
> *Çavuş* — Sergeant
> *Onbaşi* — Corporal
> *Er* — Private

There are only four grades of NCO in the navy, the rank of *Onbaşi* not being in use.

Turkish army officers' uniforms are generally similar in cut to those of the United States army, and are dark olive-brown in colour. Enlisted men wear a British-type battledress, with trousers tucked into short leggings when in the field. Navy uniforms for both officers and men conform to the usual international style and are navy blue in colour; air force uniforms follow army patterns for both officers and men, but are light blue in colour.

Officer ranks in the army and air force are indicated by combinations of five-pointed gold stars and other insignia worn on shoulder straps. In ascending order of rank, company-grade officers wear one to three stars, field-grade officers wear a gold wreath device enclosing the Turkish crescent-moon-and-star with one to three stars, and general officers wear the same device on a red background with superimposed white crossed sabres plus one to four stars. 'Five-star' generals wear no stars, but only the same device as other general officers on a solid gold shoulder strap outlined by the basic service colour, olive green or light blue.

Naval officer ranks are indicated by gold stripes on the sleeves, the topmost being of medium width with a standing loop. Ensigns wear one medium stripe, lieutenants one medium and one narrow, lieutenants two medium, lieutenant-commanders three medium, commanders three medium and one narrow, captains four medium, commodores one medium and one wide, rear-admirals two medium and one wide, vice-admirals two medium and one narrow above one wide, admirals three medium above one wide and admirals of the fleet four medium above one wide.

NCO rank indications for all three services are chevrons of the same design, worn on the right sleeve with the 'V' pointing down. Army chevrons are dark gold, navy are white and air force are light gold. The number of stripes rises with rank, from one to five. Conscripts who hold acting appointments in the lower NCO grades wear red chevrons to distinguish them from regular NCOs.

CURRENT DEVELOPMENTS

The military role of the Turkish army is rather blurred at the moment: the serious threat is the Soviet Union, against which all of Turkey's diplomatic and military arrangements of the past three decades have been directed, but the urgent threat is Greece. Priorities have, as a result, become rather confused.

As a fighting man the Turkish soldier's reputation ranks extremely high — amongst the four or five most respected in the world, perhaps — and it is well deserved. Given intelligent leadership and adequate support, he is superb. The support is there, in the sense that the extraordinarily powerful Turkish reflex of national unity in times of crisis is as strong as ever, and that national pride in the army and in Turkish military prowess is still immense. The leadership also is more than adequate: the Turkish regular officer corps has high professional competence and a justified reputation for intelligence. Although discipline is extremely strict in the army, there is no gulf in class: the officer corps is not drawn from the upper class, but recruited on merit mainly from much lower social backgrounds, including the peasantry.

The army has very limited ability to operate at any distance from its border, but in defence it might be able to perform its primary strategic mission: to resist a full-scale Soviet attack until help arrived from NATO. It would be hindered by its relative lack of mobility, compared to Warsaw Pact forces, but a larger problem would probably be that of just how much NATO help would be available.

This lies at the root of the perennial doubts expressed by Turkish officers at NATO's official doctrine of 'flexible response'. For if help from NATO would be slow in coming, or inadequate in numbers when it arrived (perhaps because of prior commitments elsewhere), then this policy would involve sacrificing at least temporarily not only the relatively empty uplands of eastern Anatolia, but also thickly populated Thrace and quite probably Istanbul and the Straits. The latter is unthinkable, so official Turkish government policy states that the defence line is on the border.

The contradiction is somewhat eased by the fact that the Turkish army would probably not face large Soviet forces in a general European war, since they would be committed largely to the Central Front, and in such a case would almost certainly be able to contain Bulgarian (and perhaps Romanian) forces with limited Russian stiffening. On the other hand a Soviet onslaught directed specifically against Turkey, which would be almost impossible to contain, would also find Ankara's NATO allies in a better position to send swift and effective aid.

These calculations about a possible Turkish–Soviet confrontation have been overshadowed since 1974 by the possibility of war with Greece. Such a conflict in the Aegean, however, would be primarily an air and naval war, almost certainly with Turkey on the strategic offensive. The army's role would be largely confined to holding the border in Thrace (a task well within its capabilities, though penetration westwards into Greek Macedonia would be extremely difficult for reasons of geography and terrain) and to providing landing forces to attack and take hostage one or more of the Greek islands fringing the Aegean coast of Turkey. Neither country is in a position to strike at the heartlands of the other. In any case a Greek–Turkish war, never likely once the July, 1974 crisis was past is now — despite the arms race — a diminishing possibility. The Turkish and Greek Prime Ministers met at Montreux in March, 1978 to discuss the resolution of mutual problems, and negotiations between the two countries continue.

The Greek arms build-up and the United States arms embargo against Turkey led in the later 1970s to an official reformation of defence priorities. Shortly after Prime Minister Bülent Ecevit took office in January, 1978 he announced a 'new national security concept' for Turkey which effectively de-emphasised the NATO link and the Soviet threat, while stressing self-reliance, joint arms production agreements with Western Europe, and the primacy of the Greek threat. Turkey's decreased concern about the Soviet Union was underlined by a visit to Ankara by the Soviet Chief of Staff in April, 1978 (he publicly suggested that the two countries might 'benefit from the possibilities offered by a military relationship', but Turkish sources denied any intention to buy Soviet arms), and by Prime Minister Ecevit's visit to Moscow in June, during which the two countries signed an accord pledging friendly relations and binding them not to allow their territory to be used as a base for attack against each other.

However, the Soviet invasion of Afghanistan in 1979 put an end to the development of closer relations with the Soviet Union, and since the military coup of September 1981, the Turkish government has strongly re-emphasised its NATO and European links. Instead, the government has announced that it intends to apply for full membership in the EEC in the relatively near future (a prospect which causes considerable alarm in Brussels). At the same time, the advent of Prime Minister Papandreou in Athens has led to a significant worsening in Greek–Turkish relations, since he has avoided all direct negotiations with Ankara on the disputes between them, and indulges in considerable sabre-rattling over alleged Turkish infringements of Greek airspace in the Aegean. (These occur almost constantly, since Greece claims a ten-mile aerial zone around all its Aegean islands, while Turkey only recognises six miles.)

The only development which could conceivably involve the two neighbours in open hostilities, however, would be a unilateral Greek proclamation of a twelve-mile limit (instead of the existing six) in the waters around its Aegean islands. If unchallenged, this would effectively foreclose the Turkish claim to an equitable sharing of rights on the Aegean seabed outside territorial waters (since only 45,000 sq km of the total 160,000 sq km would then remain outside undisputably Greek territorial waters), and would render access to much of Turkey's Aegean coast impossible without passing through Greek waters or airspace. Ankara has indicated that there would be a military response to any Greek attempt to impose an expanded territorial limit of this sort.

The present intervention by the Turkish armed forces in politics seems to be receding according to plan, as others have before it, but it is clear that the residue of military influence after democracy has been restored will be much greater than on previous occasions. At present this meets with the approval of the great majority of the population, which has no wish to return to the chaos that prevailed in the late 1970s, but it may be the source of serious civil-military conflicts in the future. There is also some doubt about whether the armed forces themselves will permanently remain committed to the Ataturkist doctrines that have restrained their political activities over the past half-century, since repeated involvement in political affairs is tending to erode the traditional political neutrality of the officer corps.

Gwynne Dyer

UGANDA

HISTORY AND INTRODUCTION*

Uganda, a former British colony, attained independence in October 1962. On the departure of the last British Governor-General, the country became a republic with the traditional monarch of the country's largest ethnic group, the Baganda of the Lake Victoria and south-east, as Head of State. This monarch, Kabaka Mtesa II of Buganda in his own territory, was only Head of State in his personal capacity and in this referred to as Sir Edward Mutesa. The Prime Minister, Milton Obote was a northerner, the conflict that arose between them was to mark the move of power from the Bantu south, where it had lain with the British support for Buganda in the colonial period, to the Nilote north, from where Obote came. The conflict took the form of an acute constitutional crisis in 1966, at the end of which the Uganda Army moved on to the Kabaka's palace and the Kabaka was forced to flee, to exile and death from despair in Britain. Obote then ended the country's federal arrangements and proclaimed himself President of a unitary state.

Obote's triumph however was short-lived. His hope of creating a new national mobilisation by means of radical politics proved vain; the reasons are debatable but among them certainly were ethnic divisions and in particular Baganda resentments and general political ineptitude. More seriously, the 1966 events had made Obote dependent on the Army whose commander Idi Amin, came from the far Paranilote north-west and had already by 1966 begun to remove southern and some northern officers, on occasions by violence. A sign at the foot of the staircase leading from the ground floor of the Ministry of Defence 'No Politicians Beyond This Point' indicated where real power lay in this period. Amin's own community, the Kakwa, contained a number of Muslims. Amin himself being one.

In 1971 a sudden flare-up occurred, largely through misunderstandings, in the hitherto amicable Obote-Amin relationship. Amin mounted a coup ejecting Obote, abroad at the time. The coup marked a new shift in the locus of power, to the north-west, some but not all of whose leading figures styled themselves, as 'Nubi' (Nubian). Amin proclaimed that 'anyone could become a Nubi' by embracing Islam, and a number of career-seekers duly did so. Thus the Kakwa and the real Nubi, together with the Nubi converts, came increasingly to provide the military leaders (and therefore the real holders of power) as Uganda's nightmare decade developed. The Amin era has, correctly, become a byword for repression, violence, bloodshed and horror including the expulsion of the Asians, harassment and the killings of southerners, and before long northerners also. Less well-publicised was the deliberate extermination of Uganda's secondary, professional and university-educated manpower, wherever possible.

Finally, in 1978, Amin over-reached himself by mounting a second series of military operations against Tanzania. The reasons for this appear to have been unrest and conspiracies within Amin's army, terminal convulsions of a regime by then revolting even many who had previously supported it. The Tanzanians at first withdrew, then regained their lost territory, and then deciding Amin was a disgrace to the con-

tinent, moved in March 1979 to eject him. This was accomplished with relative ease, the Tanzanian forces being accompanied by a large number of Uganda exiles, reflecting most shades of political opinion opposed to Amin, but poorly co-ordinated and with the only grouping bearing arms being political adherents of Obote.

The benign President Lule was at first installed to head the new regime in Kampala, but it quickly became clear that the Tanzanian government had its own decided ideas as to who should rule Uganda, ideas based on a mixture of the desirability of restoring a legitimate authority and of socialist ideological sympathy. Their favourite was naturally therefore Obote. Lule was preremptorily ejected in November 1979; a second interim figure, Binaisa, followed a little later in May 1980. An election was held in late 1980 under arrangements made by the 'military commission' of the 'Uganda National Liberation Front', Obote emerging as the winner. The general opinion of observers of the election was that while there were few overt pressures applied on the electorate to vote for Obote, there were a number of very weighty covert ones. Throughout this period Tanzanian troops secured the capital and the south, at its greatest extent the Tanzanian garrison numbering some 25,000 troops together with several hundred police, Uganda paying huge sums ($142,000,000 in 1979) in support costs. Tanzanian numbers were reduced in 1980, and the troops (but not the police) withdrawn in 1981.

Predictably, Obote has again failed to create a new national unity, although he has modified some of his late 1960s radicalism. The south, in particular the Baganda — while not necessarily seeking a return of local traditional rulers — is never likely to forgive the man who so abruptly ended cherished traditions. No end to the continuing unrest in Uganda can therefore be foreseen.

In colonial days Uganda had contributed the 4th Battalion (and other wartime replications) to the King's African Rifles, with an excellent record of service in the German East Africa campaign in World War I, Somalia, Ethiopia and Burma in World War II, and in operations against Mau Mau in Kenya in the 1950s. A feature of the battalion however from the earliest years to World War II (as a legacy of the Nubian soldiers of Emin Pasha, Gordon's governor of Southern Sudan) was that the senior African ranks were north-westerners. Even though in World War II ascendancy passed to northerners the north-western tradition survived, the basis of the career of Idi Amin. At independence in 1962, the 4th KAR became Uganda's army, a second battalion being formed a little later and with a brigade-sized force of three battalions as an aim. After the events of 1966 Amin's leverage on the Obote government led to the purchase of Czech OT-64 personnel carriers and other expensive items; after the coup the Uganda army embarked on a rapid expansion, which was neither well-balanced nor resting on foundations of manpower capable of using or maintaining much of the prestigious new equipment — particularly in view of the progressive liquidation or flight of those of the army's trained personnel who crossed Amin. The total of this gimcrack force at its greatest extent was a little under 20,000. This, Amin's army was destroyed by the Tanzanians. Former soldiers of it, still in possession of their weapons and ammunition are still living as outlaw gangs, some loosely linked to two resistance movements, the 'Hippo Strike Force' and

* For general notes on African armies, see Appendix 1.

598

the rather more effective Northern Regiment, whose leaders include former senior officers of Amin in various northern and north-western area of Uganda, terrorising the inhabitants. Other partisan forces at work include the National Resistance Army, followers of Y. Museveni, a political figure who fell out with Obote, and the Uganda Freedom Movement. Both of these operate in several areas of the country the former mainly rural, the latter urban. The UFM's motivation appears revolutionary and ideological rather than ethnic, and they form the main components of an anti-Obote opposition front organisation, the Uganda Popular Front. But at the time of writing it is doubtful if they could mount action sufficient to overthrow Obote; although they have light weapons and mortars they lack ammunition. They do, however, kill a few soldiers and policemen each month. In addition to these guerilla groups (who may or may not wear uniform) there are numbers of ex-soldiers engaged in plain armed robbery, sometimes in uniform.

The Obote government is now trying to form a new army, the Uganda National Liberation Army. With the general lawlessness, killings and bomb explosions prevalent in many areas of the country, the paucity of trained cadres and the dubious legitimacy of the regime in the eyes of much of the public progress is very slow. Many reports indicate UNLA soldiers also participate in armed robberies and violence.

The Uganda government alleges Libyan support for the insurgents.

STRENGTH AND BUDGET

Population: 13,250,000
Armed Forces: Present strength is about 10,000 with in addition certain ethnic 'militia' units, purely political forces in total some 8–9000.
GNP: Not available
Defence Expenditure: Not available

COMMAND AND CONSTITUTIONAL STATUS

President M. Obote is Commander-in-Chief of the Uganda armed forces. The Minister for Defence is P. Muwanga, the Army Commander General T. Okello, and the Chief of Staff is Brigadier D. Oyite Ojok. The key figure is probably Ojok, a Lango as is the President.

ROLE, COMMITMENT, DEPLOYMENT AND RECENT OPERATIONS

Since independence, Uganda's army has had an eventful career. In January, 1964 the 1st Battalion of the Uganda Rifles mutinied, Amin, at that time a major, playing a very ambiguous role and emerging as the battalion's new commanding officer. In 1966 on Obote's orders, Amin directed an assault on the Kabaka's palace held by a tiny weakly armed force loyal to the Kabaka; this assault is now viewed by the Uganda army as a glorious achievement. After Amin took power the Uganda army not very efficiently repelled incursions by military groups wishing to restore President Obote, several in the north in 1971 and a more serious one in the south in 1972; this latter led to inconclusive sparring with Tanzanian forces. It also led to the brief appearance of Libyan units in Uganda, ostensibly to assist in defence against Tanzania, but more probably (since they never moved near the Tanzanian border) to withstand a rumoured British military operation to evacuate the Ugandan Asians. Its first real exhibition of incompetence however

was the army's complete failure to prevent or contain the Israeli assault on Entebbe in July 1976.

Amin entertained great ambitions for his country — the annexation of part of Western Kenya together with a part of north-western Tanzania and eventually an access to the Indian Ocean by the acquisition of the port of Tanga. These ambitions ensured that he had no local friends to support his regime other than Libya.

The disastrous conflict with Tanzania opened with an attempt in October 1978 by Amin to seize the disputed north-western border area, the Kagera Salient. The attack was mounted with great ferocity looting and killing. Some 10,000 people were apparently killed. The Tanzanians were caught by surprise, they were not able to defend the area and were only in a position to launch a counter-attack to clear the salient in mid-November. They were able to draw on much OAU support, to the extent that Amin was able to portray his ejection as a concession. There then followed an interval, during which both sides prepared for war, Amin receiving deliveries of Italian helicopters, Soviet PT-76 tanks to reinforce a small number already in his possession and his Czech OT-64 wheeled armoured personnel carriers, SAM-7 missiles and MiG-21 aircraft. Libyan military reservists (some no longer in their youth) were sent by Colonel Gadaffi and some reports alleged field guns, anti-tank guns, small arms and ammunition were all also provided.

In March 1979, having decided at whatever cost to his precarious economy that the threat of Amin must be removed, Nyerere ordered an attack on Uganda. A force of a little under 10,000 Tanzanian troops together with 1000 armed Ugandan exiles embarked upon a two-pronged attack, following a long range artillery bombardment. One prong advanced towards Kampala along the coast of Lake Victoria via Masaka, another moved inland to Mbarara, turned north-west to Fort Portal and then swung east towards Kampala.

The Tanzanians, wisely if cautiously, based their advance on the speed of marching soldiers, not attempting armoured dashes; this style certainly reduced the number of their casualties. Only very occasionally did Amin's forces mount effective opposition. The reasons for this are varied: no pay and low morale, shortages of ammunition and a number of sabotage strikes behind the Ugandan lines of opponents of Amin. Another more military reason was the rash preference of the Ugandans to fight in and around their wheeled armoured troop-carriers, confining them to areas with roads and making them liable to encircling movements and anti-tank weapon assault from Tanzanian infantry.

Of the few very spirited battles mention need only be made of two in the early stages of the campaign in southern Uganda, at Mutukula and Lukaya, and a competently-mounted Tanzanian assault on Entebbe Airport on April 7th. With Entebbe captured Kampala was invested and Amin's defensive positions, mainly Libyan, bombarded, an Amin counter attack was repulsed, and a Libyan column severely shot up in an ambush. By mid-April Kampala was taken and Amin's remnants were in full flight through Jinja northwards. A number were pursued, and either killed or captured. So badly had Amin misled the Libyan leader that one large Libyan transport aircraft full of fresh soldiers attempted to land at Entebbe after the airfield's capture by the Tanzanians, the machine was destroyed and the soldiers killed. As many as 400 Libyans may have been killed in the campaign.

The conflict saw small scale air operations by both the TPDF and Amin's air force, the latter with Libyan or Palestinian pilots; on one occasion two Libyan Tupolev Blinder aircraft bombed Mwanga in Tanzania to little effect. Overall, however, it was a slow, competent if unambitious foot-soldiers war, lost by the Ugandans despite the fact that they were on their own home ground – a measure of their own collapsed morale, over expansion and poor leadership.

ORGANISATION

It is intended that the UNLA will eventually be composed of three brigades, each of three battalions.

RECRUITMENT, TRAINING AND RESERVES

In the early post-independence period, training aid was provided by the British. This ended in 1964, following the Army mutiny. Israeli assistance was then sought, dubious financial arrangements forming a significant part of the package. After the coup, Amin initially turned to Britain, then with the worsening of relations, Cuban, Soviet, Libyan and Palestinian exile training staff all flitted across the increasingly murky stage. A few personnel were trained in the Sudan and other Muslim countries.

The new army was raised under Tanzanian auspices, Tanzanian training staff being used for the first 5000 men. With the departure of the Tanzanians, a North Korean team briefly appeared, and then disappeared. In 1982 a Commonwealth training team of thirty-nine was assembled under British direction, an interesting politico-military development. The majority of the members of the team are British and Australian, but others include representatives from Canada, Sierra Leone, Tanzania, Kenya, Jamaica and Guyana. A five-weeks' course for officers at the old 4th KAR's centre at Jinja is regarded as the team's most important commitment. A new North Korean team is also training UNLA units, supposedly in internal security.

Recruitment of the new Uganda Army is returning to the traditional northern majority, especially Teso, an arrangement of course suited to Obote. Surprisingly in view of their past record in the 4th KAR Acholi recruitment is less extensive; allegations that the Acholi are opposed to Obote and Acholi soldiers have been involved in many of the armed robberies have been made. The Acholi militia is, too, being scaled down while those of Lango and Teso are built up. Although General Okello is an Acholi, other senior appointments are increasingly filled by Teso and Lango. The majority of the armed Ugandans that entered the country with the Tanzanians were, as a result of exile politics, as it happened mainly westerners. After the liberation many of these were discharged.

One unit of UNLA, on duty in West Nile, mutinied in July, 1981 on account of non-delivery of food and pay.

Overall discipline and standards of training are both very poor; deserters provide recruits to the insurgent groups.

EQUIPMENT AND ARMS INDUSTRY

No details are available of the few items of equipment that was either not destroyed by the Tanzanians or not taken by them as booty after the war. Before the conflict Uganda possessed small numbers of T-54 tanks, BTR-152, BTR-40 and OT-64 and Saracen armoured personnel carriers, BRDM and PT-76 reconnaissance vehicles, 76mm and 122mm field guns, 40mm and 23mm anti aircraft guns together with SAM-7 missiles, 82mm and 100mm mortars, GSP assault pontoon ferries and K-61 amphibious load carriers. Some Sagger anti-tank missiles were also provided by Libya or the USSR, but it is not clear whether these were vehicle mounted or man-pack. The Air Force possessed some 30 MiG-15, -17 and -21 aircraft (the pilots mostly being Libyan or Palestinian) some transports and some helicopters.

It must be assumed that at the most only isolated pieces survive from this armoury, and such surviving items may be unserviceable with little prospect of technical staff becoming available to service them.

Some reports indicate that the Tanzanians have provided Uganda with small numbers of type 69 and RPG-7 grenade launchers.

Uganda has no arms industry. She has a further serious military handicap, a desperate fuel problem of both expense and transport, the latter being the necessity to cross Kenya.

RANK DRESS AND DISTINCTIONS

Rank and dress still generally follow the British pattern.

CURRENT DEVELOPMENTS

It is difficult to see any early end to lawlessness in Uganda; it is certainly most unlikely to end while any regime headed by President Obote remains in power. The army is likely to be used increasingly to impose and buttress President's regime, with the likelihood of further unfortunate consequences from this semi-political role.

It will be a long time before the majority of Uganda's population will again respect soldiers, either as individuals or as a legitimate force designed to protect the nation's security against a foreign threat.

Lloyd Mathews

UNITED ARAB EMIRATES (UAE)

HISTORY AND INTRODUCTION

For reasons of space, this introductory survey will deal with all seven Gulf Emirates which used to be known as the Trucial States. Developments since 1971 and the contemporary military situation in Qatar and Bahrain, who did not adhere to the United Arab Emirates, will be treated separately.

For most of its history the southern Persian Gulf coast between Kuwait and Oman has been a sparsely inhabited region making its living primarily from the sea (fishing, pearl culture and piracy). Periodically it came under the political control of neighbouring empires: Bahrain was sporadically under the rule of the Safavid empire of Iran between 1602 and 1782, and later most of the coast came under tenuous Ottoman sovereignty. Most of the time, however, actual political power lay in the hands of the small tribal confederacies based primarily on kinship ties which had established themselves along the coast. In the area later to become the Trucial States, there were only two real towns – Bahrain and Dubai, both making their money mainly from smuggling (now known as trade).

British imperial power was extended westwards from India into the Persian Gulf in the early nineteenth century principally to suppress piracy in the region. The first treaties with the eastern sheikhdoms were concluded in 1820, and were followed by others granting Britain further influence over the States until a final one in 1892. Similar British treaties with Bahrain were concluded in 1861, 1880 and 1892, and Qatar was finally brought into the system when Ottoman sovereignty was repudiated in 1916. All the treaties were virtually identical in effect: the sheikhly States granted Britain exclusive responsibility for their defence and foreign relations, gave up their right to have direct dealings with foreign States, and received British advisers at their courts. They got British subsidies in return, and collaborated in the suppression of piracy. There was little interference with domestic political arrangements, and the rulers all retained their personal bodyguards and autocratic privileges.

In the early twentieth century the Gulf States were still extremely poor, totally dominated by conservative Islam in their political and social life, and almost 100% Arab. But then oil began to be discovered: in 1932 in Bahrain, in 1949 in Qatar, and in Abu Dhabi in 1959. The avalanche of sudden wealth has already transformed these societies utterly – per capita income in Abu Dhabi, at $22,000 a year, is the highest in the world – and the changes are far from finished.

In Bahrain, the edifice of a welfare State is almost 40 years old, and change is no longer at such a headlong pace. Indeed, Bahrain's oil output is far less than those of the other major producers in the area, and its oil is expected to run out within another 20 years, so the State's strategy for future prosperity is focused on turning Bahrain into the commercial centre of the Gulf, and creating industries which will outlast the oil. Elsewhere the wealth is newer and greater, and the growth more frantic, although already there are numbers of industrial projects (mainly hydrocarbon-based) planned or under construction.

In all seven States, however certain common patterns have emerged. The autocratic rule of the sheikhs has not been seriously challenged, though the ruling families have occasionally substituted a less traditionalist sheikh for an older

incumbent. The local Arab populations, swimming in wealth but still socially conservative, have shown little inclination to protest the utter absence of genuinely representative institutions anywhere in the region. But the Arab citizen population, in almost every case, has become a minority – sometimes a small one – in its own country, as the foreign experts and workers needed to work the oil industry and administer the welfare state have flooded in.

At the turn of this decade Bahrain's population was 207,000; it has grown to 345,000 in the meantime (1979), and remains 70% indigenous. But Qatar's population has almost doubled to 205,000 people in the same period, and only 30,000 are native Qataris. The seven States making up the United Arab Emirates had 150,000 people in 1972; there are now 750,000, with the growth concentrated in Abu Dhabi and Dubai. Europeans run the oil installations and supervise the endless construction projects; Palestinians, Egyptians and Lebanese administer the country and run the education system; and masses of Baluchis, Pakistanis, Indians and other Asians do the labour. As little as 20% of the United Arab Emirates' population are now citizens; between two-thirds and three-quarters are from the Indian subcontinent. In Abu Dhabi, according to the local joke, it is hard to find anybody in the street who speaks Arabic.

A majority of resident foreigners, on top of all the stresses of rapid change, has led to a certain apparent political fragility in all of these States. Taking into account also the dominating presence of Iran in the Gulf, and the South Yemeni and Iraqi attempts at stimulating revolution in the area which had already begun in the late 1960s, it is scarcely surprising that the sheikhdoms greeted the British announcement of impending withdrawal from the Gulf in January, 1968 with less than undiluted enthusiasm.

As the Gulf sheikhdoms grew in importance due to their oil wealth in the 1950s, the British military presence in the area was gradually reinforced. By the end of the 1960s it amounted to some 9000 men, with their headquarters in Bahrain. After Britain's withdrawal from Aden in 1966, it commenced to construct a new base in Sharjah, which also became the base of the Trucial Oman Scouts, and internal security force officered and paid for by Britain. All this was due to disappear when Britain's withdrawal was completed in 1971, however, and the sheikhdoms would have independence thrust upon them.

This may have been a prerequisite for the continuation of the conservative sheikhly regimes, for the South-Yemeni-backed Popular Front for the Liberation of the Occupied Arab Gulf (PFLOAG), as it was then known, would otherwise have had the far easier target of British imperialism to attack. The rapidity of the British withdrawal came as a rude shock, however, and concentrated minds in the region wonderfully. All nine sheikhdoms formed a loose federation in July, 1968 with authority vested in a council of the nine rulers, and each State began building up military forces to the extent of its ability.

The federation thus formed enjoyed rather more success than most of the others encouraged by London during Britain's imperial twilight, although it was not total. In 1971 six of the sheikhdoms formed the United Arab Emirates, with their seat of government at Abu Dhabi, Dubai, Sharjah, Ajman, Umm al Qaiwain and Al-Fujairah. At that time the only one possessing substantial oil wealth was Abu Dhabi, although Dubai has subsequently begun producing oil on a large scale.

A seventh, eastward-lying sheikhdom, Ras al-Khaimak, held itself aloof for a time in the hope of discovering its own oil, and also because it hoped to extort military support from somewhere in its dispute with Iran over the Tunb Islands strategically situated near the Strait of Hormuz. The other sheikhdoms could offer nothing but moral support, however, while Britain was not prepared to intervene and Saudi Arabia then lacked the military strength to do so. Iran duly invaded and seized the disputed islands at the end of November, 1971 as soon as the British treaty of guarantee lapsed, and Ras al-Khaimah joined the United Arab Emirates in the following year.

The two westernmost states, Bahrain and Qatar, found it impossible to devise a satisfactory formula whereby they might remain in the federation. Each had had oil wealth for far longer, each had a population far larger at that time than any of the other seven, and especially in Bahrain's case there had been a much greater degree of development in education and the social services thanks to a full generation of oil-fuelled prosperity. Qatar and Bahrain went their separate ways, each receiving their independence from Britain at the same time as the United Arab Emirates in 1971. All three States joined the United Nations and the Arab League.

(Further developments in Bahrain and Qatar are discussed in the entries for those countries.)

The history of the United Arab Emirates since 1971 has been dominated by two processes: learning cope with the special indigestion of the very rich; and trying to create a real federal government over the heads of seven absolute rulers. The lead in the latter enterprise has been taken throughout by Sheikh Zaid of Abu Dhabi, but every step has had to be achieved by persuasion. Of course, Sheikh Zaid can be very persuasive indeed, for his State has the lion's share of the oil wealth – 1,600,000 barrels/day in 1976 – and is the only member with a large surplus of foreign exchange. Dubai is the commercial capital, as it contains the Union's only long-established town, and produces oil at the rate of 350,000 barrels/day; Sharjah has 50,000 barrels/day; Ras al-Khaimah began producing some oil at the end of 1977; and the other three members, despite a good deal of searching, have yet to find any. So subsidies from Abu Dhabi to the federal budget and thence to the poorer sheikhdoms have been the order of the day, and provide the motive power for Sheikh Zaid's programme for strengthening federal control.

Abu Dhabi has contributed the great bulk of the federal budget ever since 1971 (over 75% in 1975), and has consistently attempted to integrate the administration and the economy. Despite its preponderant wealth, however, each State continues to develop its own parallel facilities – five of the seven members have opened their own international airports in the past few years, Sharjah's and Dubai's being only 5 miles part – and federal institutions still resemble more an alliance than a federation. The National Assembly, which passes on, but does not initiate, legislation, consists of 40 members appointed individually by the ruling sheikhs, and supreme authority lies in the High Council of the Federation, where each of the seven rulers has a veto.

In December, 1973 Abu Dhabi disbanded its own government, some of its members becoming federal ministers, and subsequently Sheikh Zaid pledged 50% of his immense revenues to the federation. He has had some successes: in May, 1975 the High Council agreed on further centralisation measures, including the handing over of police and internal security forces to the federal Ministry of the Interior, and in

November Sharjah and al-Fujairah handed over their tiny National Guards to the federal government and abolished their flags. At the end of 1976 Abu Dhabi's ruler was chosen by his peers for a second 5 year term as federal President, and it was agreed that all other emirates should also contribute from their revenues to the federal budget according to a negotiated formula.

But the larger States did not follow suit in handing over their defence forces to the Union Defence Forces, and retained the right to maintain their separate armed forces. An agreement in May, 1976 to unify the federation's military forces was executed at the end of the year, but bore little fruit in terms of genuine integration. (*See* Command and Constitutional Status, and Role, Commitments, Deployment and Recent Operations.) The individual rulers continued to act as Heads of State, accepting official invitations from abroad without informing the Foreign Ministry, and issuing formal joint communiques with foreign leaders.

Sheikh Zaid evinced a certain reluctance to accept a second term as President in 1976 – perhaps as a pressure tactic – and immediately received a message by special envoy from the Shah of Iran, while the United Arab Emirates' Foreign Minister had to be sent off on an urgent mission to the Saudi capital. In the event, the Sheikh allowed himself to be persuaded, but the incident amply demonstrated the tender solicitude both his large neighbours display for the health and further integration of the federation.

Such an attitude on their part is the merest common sense, but it is only lately that they have been showing it. When the United Arab Emirates came into existence in 1971 it was on extremely bad terms with Iran, which had just annexed territories previously under the control of two of its members, and the federation's leaders suspected Tehran of having expansionist ambitions. Relations with Saudi Arabia were non-existent because of a dispute over the Liwa oases on the Abu Dhabi–Saudi border. But in late 1974 the territorial dispute was settled and Riyadh officially recognised the United Arab Emirates. In 1975 Sheikh Zaid paid a State visit to the Saudi capital, and at the end of the year he visited Tehran with whom relations have also improved greatly.

Iran's reconciliation with Iraq in the spring of 1975 is seen in the Gulf as having ended the ambitions of the latter to spread revolution in the area, at least for the moment. The end of the Dhofar war is widely assumed to mean an end also to South Yemen's active support for subversion in the United Arab Emirates.

A meeting of all eight Gulf States in Oman in November, 1976, with the aim of creating a regional agreement on security and co-operation, foundered, principally because of Iraqi opposition. Nevertheless, the territorial survival and political orientation of the State appear rather more assured than they did at its foundation. The principal threat is now probably the intense rivalries between the three largest sheikhdoms, Abu Dhabi, Dubai and Ras al-Khaimah, and particularly between the former two.

Dubai–Abu Dhabi rivalry was endemic even before 1971, and the ruler of Dubai has since attempted to match Abu Dhabi's great wealth derived from oil by pursuing a head-long and sometimes reckless expansion of industry, commerce and banking (two UAE banks were forced to close their doors in 1977). This policy has led to Dubai refusing to recognise federal authority in banking and other matters, to make no contributions whatever to the federal budget, and to guard jealously the effective independence of its own armed forces.

Sheikh Saqr bin Muhammad al-Qasimi, ruler of Ras al-Khaimah, was a late and reluctant adherent to the federation, and in recent years has been pursuing his own private territorial dispute with neighbouring Oman, much to the discomfiture of the federal authorities. The latter find little merit in Ras al-Khaimah's defence of its encroachments into Omani land and offshore zones, and are deeply concerned by the possibility of a clash with Oman; on the other hand, they can scarcely refuse to stand by one of the partners in the federation. The purpose of Sheikh Saqr's manoeuvres is privately seen by some other members of the UAE as an attempt to create his own base of power in case the UAE should disintegrate, possibly with a view to establishing a local Qawasim State uniting Ras al-Khaimah and Sharjah (the ruling families in both States are Qasimi). His decision to invite Soviet military technicians to the emirate is taken as another evidence of his disaffection.

Although these disputes are extremely serious, and very little real progress has been made in unifying such key federal institutions as the budget, the banking system and the armed forces, there are powerful countervailing factors which help to hold the UAE together. The most obvious of these is Abu Dhabi's enormous wealth, which underwrites virtually the whole of the federal budget and is almost the sole support of the small members with little or no oil of their own. The rulers of all the emirates have a clear and probably overriding interest in hanging together lest they hang separately. Finally, neither Saudi Arabia, which wields enormous influence in the UAE or Oman, would welcome the turmoil and uncertainty which would attend the break-up of the federation. In all probability, the seven sheikhs are stuck with one another permanently.

STRENGTH AND BUDGET

The strength of all the United Arab Emirates' armed forces at the end of 1982 was estimated to be 48,500 men, of which land forces amount to approximately 46,500, Naval forces number 1000 men, and air forces about 1500. The military budget in 1980 was $1,200,000,000, still a small proportion of a GNP estimated at $29,680,000,000.

The situation is complicated by the fact that, despite an agreement to integrate the various sheikhly armed forces, there still existed four separate military organisations until very recently. Troops of all the sheikhdoms appeared in the same uniform for the first time in December, 1976 and the unified force's operational structure closely duplicates that of the old separate armies.

Of the four defence forces in the United Arab Emirates, Abu Dhabi's has always predominated in size and influence. Besides Abu Dhabi's own defence force, moreover, the old federal forces got most of their pay from the ruler of that State, which contributes about 98% of the federal budget. For purposes of comparison, the strengths of the old separate forces on the eve of unification in 1976 were as follows: The Union Defence Forces (formed out of the former Trucial Oman Scouts) numbered 3000, but the largest were the Abu Dhabi Defence Forces, with 15,000 men. Dubai and Ras al-Khaimah maintained their own small defence forces of 2000 and 900 men, respectively.

COMMAND AND CONSTITUTIONAL STATUS

Under the terms agreed in the October, 1976 meeting of the High Council of the Union for the unification of all armed forces in the United Arab Emirates, the President (Sheikh Zaid bin Sultan al-Nhayyan, Ruler of Abu Dhabi) exercised direct control of the Union Security High Command, and acted at least temporarily as Commander-in-Chief. In his absence command was exercised by the Vice-President (Sheikh Rashid bin Said al-Maktum, Ruler of Dubai).

The Minister of Defence is Sheikh Muhammad bin Rashid al-Maktum, son of the Ruler of Dubai. The Minister appears to be responsible primarily for administrative, personnel and logistical matters. This responsibility he shares with the Deputy Commander, Sheikh Khalifa bin Zaid al-Nhayyan, son of the ruler of Abu Dhabi and current President. In December, 1976, as part of the process of integration, he decreed that arms purchases were to be made by the Ministry of Defence only: 'no emirates will be permitted in future to make their own contracts with arms suppliers'. The Minister of Defence does not appear to be in the chain of command, if so formal an arrangement exists.

Operational command of the integrated Union Defence Forces is exercised by the Chief of Staff, who is as before Major-General Awad Khalidi, a Jordanian. This officer also serves as military adviser to the President, and is responsible for carrying out the decisions of the Supreme Defence Council (another federal fixture of flexible make-up and ill-defined responsibilities).

There is rather less to the unification of the armed forces than meets the eye, for they are to be divided into three 'military regions', based on the three largest member States. Western Military Region in Abu Dhabi was initially placed under the command of Sheikh Sultan bin Zaid, son of the ruler of Abu Dhabi. Central Military Region in Dubai is commanded by Sheikh Ahmad bin Rashid, son of Dubai's ruler and hitherto Commander of the Dubai Defence Forces. Northern Military Region in Ras al-Khaimah is under the command of Sheikh Sultan bin Saqr, who happens to be the son of Sheikh Saqr al-Qasimi, ruler of Ras al-Khaimah.

The largely fictional nature of the unified command structure was demonstrated by an acute crisis in February, 1978 when the President, Sheikh Zaid of Abu Dhabi, named his 18 year old son Colonel Sultan bin Zaid (until then Commander of Western Military Region, i.e. Abu Dhabi's own forces) to the post of Commander-in-Chief and promoted him to Brigadier. As President, Sheikh Zaid had previously occupied the post himself as a purely nominal office; he apparently failed to consult with Sheikh Rashid of Dubai or with his son, the Defence Minister, before making the appointment.

The immediate response in Dubai was that officers in the local force announced that they were no longer taking orders from the federal authorities and that Dubai's troops had been put on 1 hour emergency alert. Subsequent declarations from both sides endeavoured to conceal the existence of any rift, but likewise it is to be doubted that the appointment achieved any substantial advance towards genuine integration. The refusal of Dubai forces to accept orders from the federal command structure was little more than an untactful revelation of an existing situation: for practical purposes all three of the chief contingents in the federal armed forces — those of Abu Dhabi (15,000 men), Dubai (3000 men) and Ras al-Khaimah (1000 men) retain full operational independence.

ROLE, COMMITMENT, DEPLOYMENT AND RECENT OPERATIONS

The principal potential role of all armed forces in the United Arab Emirates is probably internal security, though they have had no exercise in that role. There is also a certain prestige value in armed forces in such a heavily armed region (especially in the case of the forces hitherto maintained by the individual member States). The United Arab Emirates can afford them, and already its forces are considerably bigger than those of Oman or Kuwait.

United Arab Emirates

In terms of defence against external threats, the United Arab Emirates' foreign officials blandly refuse to identify any in the region, but there are two that probably occupy most military attention in the emirates. One is the possibility of Iranian attack — even though that would seem utterly remote so long as the present political regime survives. The other, even less plausible, would be a hypothetical American attempt to seize the Gulf oilfields in some ultimate crisis brought about by a prolonged and total oil embargo. Yet the United Arab Emirates (more precisely, Abu Dhabi) is engaged in building a small but high-quality air-defence system incorporating Mirage aircraft, Crotale and Rapier surface-to-air missiles, and an expensive network of low-level radar cover. Whether against Iranians, Americans or perhaps Iraqis, such a small defence system could not survive for very long, but it might win enough hours for someone else to come to the United Arab Emirates' aid, or at least (on the American hypothesis) to destroy the oilfields. And of course if things started going badly wrong in the Gulf, nearby States much closer to the United Arab Emirates' own size could conceivably turn into hostile regimes almost overnight.

The United Arab Emirates has no military commitments beyond its own borders. Its defence forces have never fought anybody. Some 700 United Arab Emirates' troops were sent to join the Arab League peacekeeping force in the Lebanon, at the end of the civil war in that country in late 1976.

ORGANISATION

Arms of Service
The land forces consist of one Royal Guard 'brigade', five light armoured battalions with light tanks and armoured cars, nine infantry battalions, three-artillery battalions and three-air-defence battalions.

Operational
The Union Defence Forces are organised in three regional commands: western, central and northern, with headquarters in Abu Dhabi, Dubai and Ras al-Khaimah, respectively.

RECRUITMENT, TRAINING AND RESERVES

Military service understandably holds few attractions for the fortunate few who are citizens of the United Arab Emirates, so a large proportion of the armed forces are foreign mercenaries, recruited principally from other Arab States (particularly Oman and Jordan), Pakistan and Britain. There are numbers of Jordanian officers; ex-Pakistani air force pilots fly most of the combat aircraft; and some rulers still show a certain preference for British officers on contract instead of 'other Arabs' who are regarded as more likely to carry infectious political diseases.

A very large proportion of the United Arab Emirates' army's rank and file, and of junior officers up to the rank of lieutenant, are from its much more populous but less wealthy neighbour, Oman. This is encouraged by the Oman government, which also attempts to retain their loyalty by lavish promises of free land and houses when they finally return home. Unsurprisingly, this causes certain doubts in the United Arab Emirates and elsewhere about the ultimate allegiance of much of the military personnel, and there have recently been United Arab Emirates' efforts to recruit more heavily in North Yemen to offset the Omani predominance in the armed forces. Following the difficulties along the United Arab Emirates—Oman border in late 1977, the armed forces, already well paid, received a 50% pay rise in early 1978.

A great many recruits come to the United Arab Emirates Defence Forces already trained and most subsequent technical training is also done outside the Emirates. Methods of training and tactical doctrines are largely on the British pattern. There is no reserve system.

A report in November, 1976 that the Ministry of Defence was drafting a law which would impose conscription on the federations's citizens, had not been confirmed at the time of writing. It is in any case unlikely to alter the federal forces' basically foreign complexion, as the Arab citizen population of the emirates — only one-fifth of the whole — numbers well under 200,000. Only full mobilisation of every fit adult male citizen would produce enough troops to man even the present armed forces; to maintain regular armed forces of that size with anything above a quarter of citizen troops is beyond the federation's demographic resources, even with conscription.

EQUIPMENT AND ARMS INDUSTRY

The ground forces have: 100 AMX-30 tanks and 60 Scorpion light tanks; some Saladin, six Shorland 90 AML-90 and some VBC-40 armoured cars; 60 Ferret scout cars; and 30 Saracen and 300 Panhard M-3 VAB and AMX-10. The artillery is provided with 50 105mm guns, and it also has 20 AMX 155mm SP howitzers. There are also 81mm mortars, and 120mm RCL and Vigilant ATGWs. Air defence is provided by Rapier and Crotale SAMs. There are 200 EE-9/11 armoured fighting vehicles on order from Brazil.

Maritime forces consist of 12 large patrol craft and 3 smaller boats.

The air arm of the Union Defence Forces consists of 24 Mirage Vs, ten Hunter ground-attack aircraft and ten MB-326 counter-insurgency aircraft. There are three C-130, and one G-222, four Islander, three DHC-4 and one Cessna 182 transports, and eight AB-205, six AB-206, three AB-212, 10 Alouette III and five Puma helicopters. Almost all the air forces of the federation previously belonged to Abu Dhabi. There are two G-222 and four DHC-5D transports, and 10 Mirage V fighters, on order.

There is no arms industry in the United Arab Emirates, but the State has contributed substantially to the consortium, also including Saudi Arabia. Qatar and Kuwait, which established the Arab Military Industrial Organisation in early 1975, with a founding capital of $1,040,000,000. The intention is to build advanced weapons for all the Arab countries in factories located in Egypt, using Gulf money, Egyptian skilled labour, and European designs and technical guidance. In late 1976 the first tentative deals with France for building Mirage aircraft in Egypt were announced, while the consortium was renamed the Arab Organisation for Industrialisation and reportedly had its capital increased to $4,000,000,000.

RANK, DRESS AND DISTINCTIONS

These follow the British style which prevailed in the Trucial States before independence.

CURRENT DEVELOPMENTS

There seems little chance that the United Arab Emirates' armed forces will be called on to fight anybody in the near future. Invasion from any quarter is improbable while the Iraq-Iran war lasts, and internal security is unquestionably the first priority.

In fact, the extraordinary population structure of the

State makes subversion a fairly unpromising enterprise. The large majority of residents who are foreigners from a wide variety of cultures and backgrounds are most unlikely to be susceptible to the sort of revolutionary blandishments that might appeal to citizen Arabs — a comment that applies equally to the armed forces. As for the indigenous population, they are extremely prosperous, and are closely bound to the ruling families in what are, after all, very small communities.

In any case, the main supporter of attempts to sow revolutionary seed in this fertile soil, the PDRY, is being gently dissuaded from such enterprises by Saudi Arabian subsidies.

The Aden-based Popular Front for the Liberation of the Occupied Arab Gulf, later renamed PFL Oman and the Arab Gulf, and still later in July, 1974 sub-divided into country-by-country organisations, of which that aimed at the United Arab Emirates was given the title National Front for the Liberation of the Arab Gulf (NFLAG), had never in any case got anywhere in the sheikhdoms. With the emergence of Saudi Arabia as a more active and flexible diplomatic actor under King Khalid, and the new Riyadh strategy towards South Yemen that emerged, this organisation may eventually be allowed simply to fade away by its sponsors in Aden.

If, despite all this, things should start to become unstable in the United Arab Emirates, its own defence forces are only the first of three lines of defence for the regime. Neither Iran nor Saudi Arabia would tolerate revolutionary change there, and both would intervene to prevent it — the order of precedence being fairly certainly Saudi Arabia first, with massive Iranian intervention only if the Saudis should somehow fail to restore the *status quo*.

There is a sort of domino theory about the stability of all the conservative States around the Gulf which is most strongly espoused by their own governments. With so much at stake, it is most improbable that a revolutionary movement could successfully establish itself in any of the small Gulf States without first capturing one of the larger neighbours who stand ready to crush any such outbreak.

The more immediate concern in 1978 was for the internal cohesion of the federation. Sheikhly rivalries continue un-abated, and the crisis over the command of the federal armed forces between Dubai and Abu Dhabi in February, 1978 (*see* Command and Constitutional Status) underlined the fact that no real military integration has yet been achieved. Ras al-Khaimah's independent course, which has brought it into serious territorial dispute with neighbouring Oman, nearly led to a military confrontation in November, 1977 when the latter's army and navy took active measures to curtail Ras al-Khaimah's activities in the disputed border and offshore regions. The United Arab Emirates' President's support of Oman's claims defused the confrontation, but further embittered relations between Abu Dhabi and Ras al-Khaimah; it is difficult to see how he could have done otherwise, in view of Iranian support for Oman and the predominance of Omani mercenaries in the ranks of the United Arab Emirates' armed forces, but it augured ill for the attempts that are underway to achieve greater integration.

A further unsettling factor was Iranian–Saudi Arabian rivalry for influence within the United Arab Emirates. Abu Dhabi and the small emirates have strong ties with Riyadh, whereas Iranian influence has always been powerful in Dubai. The latter was the only real town in the region before oil was discovered, a trading town of cosmopolitan make-up and outlook whose large merchant class was predominantly Iranian, and 'Arabism' has never been very important there. The conflicting influences were clearly seen at work during the crisis over the appointment of the Emir of Abu Dhabi's son to the post of Commander-in-Chief of the Armed Forces: the Saudi Arabian Defence Minister sent a message of congratulations to the new appointee, while the United Arab Emirates' own Defence Minister, the son of the Emir of Dubai, immediately went to Tehran for consultations and consolation. The unseating of the Shah, the rise of Islamicism in Iran and the outbreak of the Iran-Iraq war have, however, brought Iranian influence in the Emirates to a stop. Governmental suspicion of Iranian ambitions in the Gulf remains, but its anxieties are held in check while Iraq continues to engage Iran's military energies.

Gwynne Dyer
John Keegan

UNITED KINGDOM

HISTORY AND INTRODUCTION

The Regular Army has always occupied a rather anomalous position in British society. Since the formation of a permanent force over 300 years ago it has owed allegiance to the monarch while being effectively controlled by politicians who traditionally regard its existence as unconstitutional and a potential threat to civil liberties. It has always been reduced in size alarmingly during periods of peace — a process which continues today — yet has proved flexible enough to absorb and train large numbers of recruits, whether volunteers or conscripts, during times of national emergency. It has contained within its ranks all the latent conflict of the British class-structure, drawing its officers from the landed gentry and its soldiers from the lower orders, for much of its history, yet has never interfered in the politics of the State nor shown the slightest sign of class hostility. It has a tradition of conservatism in its tactical thinking, invariably fighting the first battle of a war on lessons drawn from the preceding conflict, but has not lost a major war since 1783. Finally, it has been despised in the folk-memory of the country, but now enjoys an enviable reputation as one of the most professional and capable armies in the world.

Some of the reasons behind this picture of confusion date back to the emergence of the army in the late seventeeth century. Up to that time it was widely felt that England had no need for a standing force, being adequately protected against external attack by the navy and internal trouble by locally raised, part-time militia units. Any move towards the establishment of permanent forces, it was argued, could only be for the purposes of political or religious repression, as indeed had been the case during the Civil War and its aftermath in the 1640s and 1650s. Thus, when the raising of standing regiments became a necessity with the beginnings of empire in the 1660s, the units were treated with considerable wariness and accepted by Parliament only on condition that they should never be stationed in England. Unfortunately James II (1685–8) ignored this stipulation, openly building up his army for use in the suppression of his religious and political opponents. Parliament took fright and, after engineering the King's deposition, made sure that his successors, although remaining as titular head of the army with some effective power, should enjoy no independent control of military forces. By the Declaration of Rights (1689) two important constitutional checks were imposed upon the monarch when Parliament took over responsibility for the cost and discipline of the army. Thereafter, if the force should ever be regarded as too large for public safety or politically dangerous, the House of Commons could refuse to vote money for its upkeep, which would lead to an immediate reduction, or to renew the annual Mutiny Act, which would oblige the King to disband an army thus freed from the strictures of discipline. As a further safeguard, the gradual introduction of purchased officer commissions ensured that men who invested their fortunes in the army were unlikely to upset the *status quo* by moving against either Parliament or the monarch for fear of losing their money.

This pattern of close political control of military affairs has continued to the present day, for although the purchase system disappeared in the 1870s, it is still the responsibility of Parliament to pay for the army, through the annual Defence Estimates, and to renew its terms of discipline, through the Army Act. Many commentators agree that it is this, above all else, that has successfully prevented military interference in the politics of Britain over the last 300 years. It should be added, however, that the same political control has often led to a dramatic fall in military efficiency, particularly during periods of peace, as Parliament has used its financial powers to reduce the size and cost of a basically distrusted force, augmenting it hurriedly in time of crisis.

The effects of this constant process of reduction and expansion may be seen throughout the army's history. They were at their worst between 1689 and 1870, as the army took on the roles which have shaped its development. During this period Britain was involved in major wars with European neighbours for about 80 years, and while they were going on the politicians did not starve the army of funds, enabling it to perform some remarkable feats of military skill. Under the Duke of Marlborough, particularly between 1704 and 1709, British soldiers placed themselves firmly on the map by defeating the most professional armies of the day, and their main battle-honours — Blenheim, Ramillies, Oudenarde and Malplaquet — still feature proudly on many regimental colours. One hundred years later the Duke of Wellington proved himself a natural successor to Marlborough, leading his troops to a new string of victories in the Iberian Peninsula between 1808 and 1814. His career, and with it the reputation of the British regular forces, reached its height with the defeat of Napoleon at Waterloo in 1815; a victory which was to be exploited by the politicians until the early campaigns of the Crimean War (1854–6) called their bluff by showing how inefficient the army had become. Meanwhile, during the eighteenth century an empire was gained — in America, Canada, the West Indies, the Mediterranean and parts of India — almost entirely through the exploits of British regiments, and although the colonies in America were lost beween 1775 and 1783, enough remained elsewhere to lay the foundations of Britain's maritime trade. These foundations were built upon during the Revolutionary and Napoleonic Wars (1793–1815), particularly in the West Indies and southern Africa, while the early decades of the nineteenth century saw a large-scale expansion of British interests in India, again in the wake of military action. Finally, in both the eighteenth and early nineteenth centuries, it was regular regiments which protected the homeland itself from invasion, even bringing the enemy to decisive battle within the country in 1746.

But as each war or national crisis ended, so did the flow of money, and for well over half the period in question the army had put up with cuts of alarming proportions, often being reduced to a third of its strength as soon as hostilities ceased. This had a number of detrimental effects. Within the army itself it led to a dangerous lack of interest in military affairs, particularly among the officers. Although competent and dedicated men undoubtedly existed, there were many who abused their positions. Commissions were purchased, often at inflated prices, purely as investments; officers absented themselves from duty or exchanged commissions with others less fortunate, simply to escape an unattractive posting; there was little attempt at tactical innovation or anything more than basic drill within the regiments. In short, the army stagnated during periods of peace, despite the reforming zeal of people such as the Duke of York who, as Commander-in-Chief between 1795 and 1827, tried desperately to stop absenteeism and purchase-abuse, even introducing a form of officer training when in 1802 the Royal Military College was opened under his auspices at Sandhurst. When such reforms were destroyed in the apathy of peace, the army quickly gained a reputation within society which lasted, in essentials, until the early years of the present century. The officer-class was widely regarded as amateurish, treating military service as an imposition while enjoying the social rewards of army life; the rank and file, obliged to join the service for terms limited only by death or old age, were despised as the very dregs of society. Little wonder that to enlist as a soldier was seen as the last resort before starvation and that the army during these periods of peace reached its nadir in both size and efficiency. Unfortunately this was the picture of military life which became etched in the folk-memory of Britain; a picture which was to remain at least until World War I, if not beyond.

Responsibility for improving this situation lay ultimately with the politicians, who had to be forced to recognise that the army was not merely a weapon to be ignored until a war broke out. Fortunately such a process took place between 1870 and 1914, beginning with a realisation that the army, heavily committed to the protection of a widespread empire, did not have the manpower resources or organisation to take part in a European war. The muddles and confusions of the Crimea showed how difficult it was to get an effective force into the field, while the growth of Prussian militarism, chiefly in the 1860s, implied that even if British soldiers appeared on the continent, they were going to be outclassed. The immediate reaction to the problem was to concentrate forces in Britain by withdrawing all those in white colonies, leaving the settlers to look after their own defence, but it soon became clear that this could only be a short-term solution. Consequently, between 1870 and 1881 a series of reforms were introduced by Edward Cardwell, Gladstone's Secretary of State for War, which altered the army and its organisation to a remarkable extent. The purchase system was abolished, short-term enlistments for private soldiers were introduced (consisting of 12-year engagements, six to be spent with the colours and six with the Reserve), and all infantry regiments were affiliated to local areas and reserve formations in Britain for the purposes of recruitment, the area name becoming part of the regimental title. In addition, each infantry unit was re-organised to consist of two battalions, one of which was to be abroad, policing the Empire, while the other was at home, fostering local connections and ready to fight in Europe if the need arose. The scheme as a whole was a considerable success. Men who before had not joined the army because of its unattractive terms of service, now came forward, usually to join the unit affiliated to their area of Britain; a capable Reserve force, allied closely to existing Regular formations, was formed from the old militia units and the more recent Rifle Volunteers, raised in the late 1850s; and, perhaps most important of all, a regimental system grew up in which officers no longer put their own convenience above their military careers and intense feelings of loyalty to a particular unit and its recruiting area were engendered. This, more than anything else, was to sustain the bulk of the army through the traumatic experiences of the twentieth century.

The reforms could not end there, however, for regardless of Cardwell's success in counteracting many of the old abuses, the army was still not prepared for modern war. The chief weakness lay in the field of command and administra-

tion, where the traditional political mistrust of militarism had long prevented the development of a General Staff, charged with advising the government on the preparedness and capabilities of the army in any given situation. This deficiency became obvious during the early disasters of the South African War (1899–1902) and reforms were quickly introduced. As early as 1902 a Committee of Imperial Defence was set up to co-ordinate military and naval policy-making at Cabinet level, and two years later Lord Esher, Chairman of a special War Office (Reconstruction) Committee, re-organised the whole administrative structure, centralising executive processes under the Secretary of State for War and introducing a General Staff. The scheme took until 1908 to finalise, by which time Lord Haldane as Secretary of State had come forward with more new ideas. Taking the Cardwell reforms as a base, he went one stage further by creating from the units stationed in Britain a coherent fighting force of two army corps (six infantry divisions) with a supporting cavalry division, ready to move into Europe as soon as a war developed. This British Expeditionary Force (BEF) was composed entirely of Regular formations, but as a back-up to them Haldane reorganised the Militia and Volunteer units into a new Reserve force — known as the Territorials — consisting of 14 self-supporting divisions. The modernisation of the army was complete.

This was just as well, for in August, 1914 Britain entered a conflict which was to stretch her military resources to the limit. At first, all appeared to go according to plan. The BEF was committed to Europe within a fortnight of the declaration of war, while Territorial units moved onto a war-footing, with some relieving Regular formations in the colonies. But Haldane's reforms had catered for campaigns of short duration only, and when the BEF was virtually wiped out at the battles of Mons and 1st Ypres in 1914, being replaced initially by the other Regular regiments and then, as casualties continued to mount, by the Territorials in 1915, a manpower shortage arose. To a certain extent this had been foreseen by Lord Kitchener who, when appointed Secretary for War at the outbreak of hostilities, had made an appeal for civilian volunteers which rapidly produced over 1,000,000 men, but they were untrained and, at prevailing rates of loss, could not be regarded as sufficient. The government had little choice except conscription — a method of recruitment without precedent in the history of Britain's standing army — and in January, 1916 the process began with a selective call-up of unmarried men between the ages of 18 and 30. At the time it was hoped that the decisive campaign of the war would take place on the Somme in the summer of 1916, so relatively few of the conscripts were trained, but when the Somme offensive resulted in the wholesale destruction of Kitchener's volunteers for little territorial or military gain (the casualty list for July 1st, 1916 alone being over 60,000, of whom 20,000 were killed) there was nothing else left. As the war dragged on into 1917 and 1918, casualty figures mounted and the net of conscription widened, eventually taking all fit males between 18 and 41, married as well as unmarried, until, when hostilities ceased, the army mustered nearly 6,000,000 men — its highest level ever. With such a force the enemy had eventually been beaten, not only in Europe but also in the Middle East, where Allenby conducted one of the few campaigns of brilliance to defeat the Turks, but the cost was exceptionally heavy, the final casualty figure standing at 745,000 killed. In such circumstances the British public, particularly in those towns and cities which had contributed so eagerly to the short-lived Kitchener battalions, was quite content to let the old pattern re-emerge and the politicians dismantle the military machine as soon as peace was restored.

The process of dismantlement was as complete as any that

had occurred before in the aftermath of war. Conscription — never popular with the people — was ended as early as December, 1918 causing the army to dwindle in size dramatically, regardless of the fact that its peace-time commitments had increased, initially with occupation duties in Germany and then with responsibility for the ex-German and Turkish colonies placed under League of Nations' mandate. In addition the government introduced a 'Ten-Year Rule' in 1919, specifying that defence-spending was not to be increased beyond prevailing levels as war in Europe was unlikely to reoccur in the next 10 years. This was all very well in 1919, but the rule was renewed, on the same ten-year reckoning, every year until the mid-1930s, causing a stagnation within the army which was reminiscent of the early-nineteenth century. By 1922 the force had been reduced to a mere 250,000 men; the Territorials had been re-organised and severely cut back; and the supply of new equipment had vitually ceased. This latter point was important, for during World War I Britain had led the world in the development of armoured warfare, and two men — Major-General J. F. C. Fuller and Captain B. H. Liddell Hart — had produced, or were to produce during the inter-war period, brilliantly viable theories on the use of armour which failed to make much impact upon the army, chiefly because the necessary equipment was not made available. The theories were taken up instead by the Germans, with devastating results.

For once, however, Britain was forced to recognise the parlous state of her defences before the peace-time period ended, when the Munich Crisis of 1938 jolted politicians into realising that another war with Germany was inevitable. Between then and the outbreak of hostilities a year later, the army was hurriedly prepared: the Territorial force was doubled in size; a degree of mechanisation was introduced, substituting tanks for the horses of the Regular Cavalry and their Yeomanry reserve; and, for the first time, a form of peace-time conscription was established, applicable to both unmarried men and women between the ages of 18 and 25. As a result, the army was large enough to take on the commitments of war in September, 1939 but, like so many times before, lacked the sustained training for immediate or easy victory. The string of initial defeats was long: in Norway and France in 1940 British soldiers had to retreat before the German onslaughts; in the north African desert, despite a brilliant campaign by O'Connor which routed the Italians in late 1940, the battles were long and hard for little appreciable gain, at least until 1942; in the Far East the Japanese attacks of late 1941/early 1942 swept all before them. It was not until the vast industrial and manpower resources of the United States had been committed to the British cause that the tide began to turn, and even then the road to final victory was hard. In north Africa it took Montgomery's victory at Alamein (October, 1942) and a seaborne invasion of Algeria (Operation *Torch* of November, 1942) to trap the German Afrika Korps between two advancing fronts. Elsewhere in the Mediterranean theatre, despite the surrender of Italy in 1943, it took until 1945 for the enemy to be decisively beaten, while in Europe the D-Day invasion (Operation *Overlord* of June, 1944) and the subsequent drive into the heart of Germany necessitated a commitment of men and material hitherto undreamed of. Finally, in the Far East, despite Slim's successful campaign in Burma in 1944/5, the Japanese did not surrender until atomic bombs had been dropped in August, 1945. The war had been total in almost every sense, and the British army, although ultimately victorious, had been incapable of defeating the enemy on its own in any theatre. The lesson was apparent: if the army was to be an effective influence in the post-war world it had to be allied to other, more powerful forces, preferably those of the United States, while maintaining its size and war-time efficiency. In 1945, there was to be no massive politically inspired reduction or return to the usual peace-time pattern.

The fact that the government accepted this new state of affairs was understandable from a purely practical point of view. In 1945 the army was being called upon not only to resume its pre-war colonial policing role, but also to establish large occupation forces in Europe and the Far East. In addition, with the Russian advance deep into Eastern Europe during the war, a new potential enemy had appeared, necessitating the maintenance of some form of instant fighting capability: a factor which led in 1949 to the establishment of the North Atlantic Treaty Organisation (NATO), with Britain, as a founder member, promising military contributions to a standing force in Western Europe. Such large commitments naturally required large numbers of men, and for this reason conscription had to remain, changing its name in 1948/9 to National Service, whereby all fit males aged 18 were obliged to do 2 years' Regular service, followed by 3 years in the Reserve. The troops were certainly needed, not only in Europe but also in the large numbers of colonies and mandated territories which had emerged from the war intent upon achieving independence from British rule. In many cases the eventual transfer of power was relatively easy, but elsewhere the local people could not wait for the political process to take its course, and the army had to be called upon to keep the peace. A series of campaigns — in Palestine (1945—8), Malaya (1948—60), Kenya (1952—60) and Cyprus (1955—9) — saw both volunteer and conscript soldiers learning techniques which were to help make the army one of the most adept in the world at counter-insurgency. At the same time, through its contribution to the United Nations' force in Korea (1950—3), the same army was continuing to gain experience of large-scale conventional war.

Nevertheless, the maintenance of such massive forces could not continue indefinitely. National Service was intensely unpopular among a people bred in the tradition of anti-militarism, the cost was enormous, and, as Britain withdrew from her Empire, the army's commitments diminished, while the country itself declined as a world power. The extent of this decline was shown in 1956, when despite a successful air and seaborne invasion of Egypt, designed to re-open the Suez Canal to international trade, Britain was forced to step down and withdraw her forces through economic pressure from the United States. In such circumstances a full-scale re-assessment of British defence policy was clearly called for, and this took place in 1957. Recognising the fact that as Britain no longer enjoyed a great deal of influence in world affairs, she no longer needed large armed forces, the politicians ordered a phasing-out of National Service and a drastic re-organisation of the army. The last conscript did not in fact complete his service until 1963, but by that time dramatic and far-reaching changes had taken place. Regiments were amalgamated (with some disappearing altogether) in order to cut down to the size of an all-volunteer force; the army was geared to a potential rather than a presence east of Suez; and Britain's commitment to NATO was afforded top priorty with the development of weapons and equipment for conventional war in Europe. In general terms this has remained as the shape of British defence policy ever since, and although counter-insurgency operations have continued to arise — in Borneo (1963—6), Radfan and Aden (1964—7) and, of course, Northern Ireland, where they still go on — the British Army of the Rhine (BAOR) maintains' priority. The army may be small, mustering only 172,500, but it is well-trained for its commitment to Europe and enjoys one of the best records in the world for successful counter-insurgency. It has certainly not fallen into the usual peace-time trap of complacency and stagnation since 1945, although how far its efficiency can be maintained in the face of constant economic pressure must be a subject of some speculation.

STRENGTH AND BUDGET

Population: 59,965,000
Army: 163,100 Regular Army, 139,000 Regular Reserves and 70,200 Territorial Army
Estimated GNP (1981): $449, 850,000,000
Defence expenditure (1982–3): $25,400,000,000

COMMAND AND CONSTITUTIONAL STATUS

Command
Supreme responsibility for national defence lies with the Prime Minister and the Cabinet, who are responsible for their actions to Parliament as a whole. The formulation of defence policy is the responsibility of the Secretary of State for Defence as political head of the Ministry of Defence (MOD), an administrative department set up in 1964 to co-ordinate control of all three armed services — navy, army and air force — as well as the procurement of defence equipment. The Secretary of State is assisted by a Minister of State and by three Under-Secretaries of State. They, together with the Chief of the Defence Staff, the three Chiefs of Staff, the Chief of Personnel and Logistics, the Chief Scientific Adviser, the Chief Executive of the Procurement Executive and the Permanent Under-Secretary of State for Defence, form the Defence Council, which deals with major defence policy under the chairmanship of the Secretary of State. The Chiefs of Staff Committee, comprising the Chief of the Defence Staff as chairman and the three Chiefs of Staff, is responsible for giving professional advice on strategy and operations. The day-to-day management of the army is the responsibility of the Army Board of the Defence Council.

Constitutional Status
Theoretically the monarch is still the head of the army, and it is to H.M. Queen Elizabeth II that all serving personnel swear allegiance. This is undoubtedly a contributing factor to the army's continuing non-interference in the politics of the State, but in practical terms its significance is slight. So far as Parliament is concerned, the army is still subject to the restraints imposed in 1689, and the annual Defence Estimates and Army Act repeatedly stress the civilian control of military affairs and reinforce the traditional idea that a standing force is maintained on sufferance only.

ROLE, COMMITMENT, DEPLOYMENT AND RECENT OPERATIONS

Role
The basic role of Britain's armed forces as a whole is to contribute to the defence of Europe, primarily against possible Soviet or Warsaw Pact aggression. This naturally entails contributions to the deterrent capabilities of NATO, with Britain playing an important part in the efforts of her European partners to assume, through closer co-operation, an increasing responsibility for Western defence. The army's first and most important role must therefore lie within Europe, defending the continent in co-operation with the NATO allies.

But other roles also arise. Chief amongst these is home defence, not merely against external attack, which is covered to a great extent by NATO, but more importantly, against internal trouble, of which the army's commitment to Northern Ireland is a prime example. In addition, six residual overseas responsibilities remain — Gibraltar, Hong Kong, the sovereign bases in Cyprus, Brunei, Belize (British Honduras) and the Falkland Islands — requiring the army to retain at least a capability in its traditional colonial policing role. Finally Britain's support for the United Nations occasionally necessitates military contributions to peacekeeping operations, chiefly in Cyprus.

Commitment
In line with role priorities, the army's main commitment is to NATO, with 55,000 troops comprising BAOR in northern Germany, and certain reserve formations earmarked for reinforcement duty, probably on the flanks (Norway or the Mediterranean), in the event of European war. Beyond NATO, Britain is a member of the Central Treaty Organisation (CENTO) and the South-East Asia Treaty Organisation (SEATO), as well as a participant, with Australia, New Zealand, Malaysia and Singapore, in the Five-Power Defence Arrangements of 1971, designed to protect Malaysia against further communist aggression. The last-mentioned agreement was the only one actually to involve a commitment of troops (with Australia and New Zealand a special ANZUK force was formed) but Britain's contribution has since lapsed. In fact, although Britain is still responsible for the defence and internal security of her remaining dependencies (leading to the maintenance of troops in Brunei, Hong Kong, Cyprus, Gibraltar and Belize), the vast majority of the army is now stationed in the United Kingdom (including Northern Ireland) and Germany.

Deployment
United Kingdom (United Kingdom Land Forces — UKLF):
1. United Kingdom Mobile Force (UKMF): (under command: one regular, two territorial brigades to reinforce Germany) two infantry brigades (mixed regular and territorial)
2. ACE Mobile Force (Land): one battalion group; one SAS regiment (less one squadron), and one Gurkha infantry battalion.
3. Home Defence: one brigade (mixed regular and territorial).
4. HQ Northern Ireland: three infantry brigade HQs; one armoured reconnaissance regiment and three squadrons; about six battalion-size units in an infantry role; one SAS, three engineer and two army aviation squadrons.

Germany
1. British Army of the Rhine (BAOR): one corps HQ, three divisional HQs, eight armoured brigades and one artillery division; total 55,000 men.
2. Berlin: one infantry brigade; total 3000 men.

Brunei: one Gurkha battalion.
Hong Kong: One brigade with one British and four Gurkha infantry battalions, one engineer squadron, and support units (garrison to be reduced to four battalions; total now 8000 men); Hong Kong Regiment (local volunteers).
Cyprus: One infantry battalion (less two companies), one armoured reconnaissance squadron with United Nations Force in Cyprus (UNFICYP), one infantry battalion, two infantry companies and one armoured reconnaissance squadron in garrison in Sovereign Base Areas.
Gibraltar: One infantry battalion.
Belize: One infantry battalion group.
Falklands: Two infantry battalions, air defence and support troops.
Military advisers and training teams at present in fifteen countries.

Royal Marines: This corps, part of the Royal Navy, maintains a brigade of Commandos (battalions) trained in an amphibious and Arctic warfare role.

Recent Operations

Since 1945, with the exceptions of Korea (1950–3) and Suez (1956), British army combat experience has been exclusively in the field of counter-insurgency. Beginning with Palestine in 1945 – a campaign which continued until 1948 – British soldiers have operated against insurgent organisations in Malaya (1948–60), Kenya (1952–60), Cyprus (1955–9), Radfan and Aden (1964–7) and Borneo (1963–6), and are currently involved in Northern Ireland (since 1969). In many ways the techniques adopted have differed little from those used in the colonial policing activities of the nineteenth and early twentieth centuries, but the close civil–military co-operation and excellent intelligence work which have characterised the army's conduct up to the present day have ensured a degree of success not enjoyed by other countries. Despite a recent resurgence of communist activity in Malaysia and a less-than-total destruction of insurgent organisations in Palestine, Cyprus and Aden when the various campaigns ended, the army has achieved enough to earn a description as one of the best counter-insurgency forces in the world. How far this has undermined its effectiveness in conventional warfare, however, is a subject of speculation, particularly now when units of BAOR spend a great deal of time training for, and serving in, Northern Ireland.

The most dramatic and, Korea apart, largest operation conducted by British armed forces since the Second World War took place in the South Atlantic between April 2nd and June 14th, 1982. The campaign opened when the Argentinians, who have never abandoned their claim to sovereignty over the Falklands (Islas Malvinas), tired of diplomatic negotiations to regulate their claim which were still in progress and landed a force at Port Stanley, the capital, in the early morning of April 2nd. It quickly overwhelmed the small party of Royal Marines in garrison there, expelled the British governor and took possession of the whole island group. Next day another Argentine force landed on the dependency of South Georgia where an even smaller Royal Marine detachment, after inflicting severe losses on the invaders, was also forced to surrender.

The British government at once announced that a Task Force would be despatched to the South Atlantic, the first elements of which sailed from West Country ports on April 5th. Ascension Island, midway point on the 8000 mile voyage, was to be activated as a replenishment base. The embarked troops of the Task Force consisted of 40, 42 and 45 Commando, Royal Marines (a Commando is a lightly equipped infantry battalion) and 2nd and 3rd Battalions, the Parachute Regiment, together forming 3 Commando Brigade. They were later to be joined by 5 Infantry Brigade, consisting of three battalions, the 2nd Scots Guards, 1st Welsh Guards and 7th Gurkha Rifles. Other combat units attached to the Task Force were 29 Commando Regiment, Royal Artillery and 59 Independent Commando Squadron, Royal Engineers (3 Brigade), one armoured troop of the Blues and Royals, T Battery, 12th Air Defence Regiment, RA (Rapiers) (attached 3 Brigade); two troops, 32 Guided Weapons Regiment, RA, 4th Field Regiment, RA, 36th Engineer Regiment, and 9th Parachute Squadron, RE and 656 Squadron, Army Air Corps; a marine helicopter squadron, a marine raiding squadron, sections of the Royal Marines Special Boats Squadron, elements of the Special Air Service and units of several other engineer regiments, together with support and service units from the corps of the army were also despatched.

The Argentine forces on the Falklands, drawn from the 3rd, 4th, 9th, 10th and 11th Brigades and the 3rd and 5th Marine Infantry Battalions, numbered about 12,000; the majority (8400) were based at Port Stanley, with detachments at Goose Green (1200) and on West Falkland. They included some armoured units (about 27 armoured vehicles) and five batteries of artillery, including three 155mm guns. The force was commanded by Brigadier General Menendez.

Operations opened with the recapture of South Georgia by 42 Commando and SAS units on April 25th, without fatal casualties on either side. On April 29th the Task Force arrived at the edge of the 200-mile 'exclusion zone' which the British cabinet had declared on April 12th and on May 1st SAS and SBS landings on the Falklands began. Next day the Argentine cruiser *General Belgrano*, which was approaching the exclusion zone, was sunk by the British nuclear submarine *Conqueror*; over 300 of the crew failed to survive.

The first British naval casualty was the destroyer *Sheffield*, sunk by an air-launched Exocet missile while on radar picket duty off the Falklands on May 4th. More naval losses were to follow when the Task Force entered the Falkland Sound between the two main islands of East and West Falkland on May 21st; between that date and May 25th the warships *Ardent*, *Antelope* and *Coventry* were lost to Argentine air strikes, together with the container ship *Atlantic Conveyor*, which was carrying essential heavy equipment for the troops as well as acting as an aircraft park for the vital Chinook helicopters. The initial landings on May 21st at San Carlos in Falkland Sound nevertheless succeeded. On May 28th the 2nd Parachute Regiment took the Goose Green position, in a bitter battle against superior numbers; its commanding officer, Colonel 'H' Jones, was killed at the head of his soldiers in an action which won him a posthumous Victoria Cross. Meanwhile the marine commandos had set out to march across East Falkland towards Port Stanley. The loss of the Chinook helicopters obliged the infantry to carry their necessities with them, such airlift as remained being required for the movement of artillery and engineer equipment.

On June 1st the troops of 5 Brigade, which had transhipped from the requisitioned liner *Queen Elizabeth 2* at South Georgia on May 28th landed at San Carlos. By June 2nd the 2nd Parachute Regiment, now attached to 5 Brigade, force marched to Bluff Cove ahead of the brigade's intended line of advance along the south side of the island. But, when the two Guards battalions followed in the logistic ships *Sir Galahad* and *Sir Tristram*, they were caught by Argentine aircraft at nearby Fitzroy. Fifty-one soldiers were killed by this airstrike, the Welsh Guards almost disabled as a fighting unit and the Scots Guards deprived of much of their equipment.

Despite this setback, Major-General Jeremy Moore, the Marine officer commanding the landing force, judged the situation ripe for a final assault. Port Stanley is protected from the interior by a range of hills and mountains which the brigades, supported by their artillery and the Harrier aircraft of the fleet and an RAF detachment, began to attack on June 11th. Three days of severe infantry fighting, conducted largely at night, led to a precipitate Argentine retreat. On June 14th General Menendez surrendered unconditionally to General Moore in Port Stanley. About 300 Argentinian soldiers were killed in the islands who, together with the drowned of the *Belgrano* and the downed pilots, comprise the 652 fatal casualties admitted by Buenos Aires. British losses from all three services totalled 255 dead and 777 wounded. Over 10,000 Argentine prisoners were repatriated via Uruguayan and Argentine ports during and immediately after hostilities. British aircraft losses were five Harriers to ground fire and four to accidents; 109 Argentine aircraft were destroyed, according to British claims.

The conduct of the campaign by the British services, including the Merchant Navy, won the unalloyed admiration of all impartial observers. It confirms that they represent, size for size, a supremely efficient instrument of force in the contemporary world.

ORGANISATION

Arms of Service
Taking Regular and TAVR units together, the army comprises:

1. Royal Armoured Corps: 11 Regular armoured regiments; eight regular and two Yeomanry (TAVR) armoured reconnaissance regiments
2. Royal Artillery: One Regular SSM regiments, three Regular SAM regiments, 17 other Regular regiments and five TAVR regiments.
3. Royal Engineers: 11 Regular regiments and seven TAVR regiments.
4. Royal Signals.
5. Infantry: Eight Guards battalions (Regular), 38 Regular infantry battalions and 38 RAVR infantry battalions.
6. Paratroops: Three Regular battalions and three TAVR battalions.
7. Gurkhas: Five Regular Infantry battalions with supporting services.
8. Special Air Service: One Regular regiment and two TAVR regiments.
9. Army Air Corps: Six Regular regiments.
10. Royal Army Chaplains Department.
11. Royal Corps of Transport.
12. Royal Army Medical Corps.
13. Royal Army Ordnance Corps.
14. Royal Electrical and Mechanical Engineers.
15. Royal Military Police.
16. Royal Army Pay Corps.
17. Royal Army Veterinary Corps.
18. Small Arms School Corps.
19. Royal Army Educational Corps.
20. Royal Army Dental Corps.
21. Royal Pioneer Corps.
22. Intelligence Corps.
23. Army Physical Training Corps.
24. Army Catering Corps.
25. Queen Alexandra's Royal Army Nursing Corps.
26. Women's Royal Army Corps.
27. Ulster Defence Regiment (TAVR): 11 battalions.

All the former Cavalry regiments are now represented within the Royal Armoured Corps, having been equipped with armour just before or during World War II. Horsed squadrons are maintained by the Household Cavalry (Life Guards, and Blues and Royals) for ceremonial duties, chiefly in London. Fifteen Cavalry regiments — the result of a series of amalgamations — still exist, retaining their old titles of Dragoon Guards, Hussars or Lancers, and they join four units of the Royal Tank Regiment to make up the Regular RAC formation. The old Yeomanry regiments — raised initially during the Revolutionary and Napoleonic Wars as a part-time cavalry reserve — are now represented by a mere two 'big' regiments — made up of squadrons drawn from different parts of the country — in the armoured role. Two other Yeomanry regiments do still exist, but are trained and equipped for infantry duties.

The 38 Regular Infantry battalions are all that remain of 110 such units which existed before the Cardwell reforms of the 1870s. These units — numbered 1–109 with the Rifle Brigade unnumbered — were reduced to 69 regiments by Cardwell, chiefly through a process of amalgamation, e.g. the 37th and 67th Foot became 1st and 2nd Battalions, The Hampshire Regiment. The advantages of this regimental system were two-fold: on the one hand it created a body to which both officers and men could feel intense loyalty; on the other, each individual regiment could act as a base upon which any number of battalions might be built up. At no time was the regiment as such a fighting unit, but during periods of crisis the number of battalions taking the name, and with it the loyalty and traditions of that regiment, could be immense. Thus, although in 1914 the Hampshire Regiment already mustered 1st and 2nd Regular battalions as well as 3rd (Special Reserve), 4th, 5th, 6th, 7th, 8th and 9th (Territorial) battalions, the Kitchener volunteers and later the conscripts of World War I could be orgnanised into further battalions, numbered 10th onwards. This system proved its worth during both World Wars and has been maintained, in essentials, ever since, creating a continuity of tradition which even the drastic amalgamations of the 1950s and 1960s — actions which helped reduce Cardwell's 69 regiments to the present-day 38 battalions — could not destroy. However, although certain TAVR infantry battalions still 'belong' to a parent Regular unit, the many changes which have affected the army since 1958 have resulted in some being organised as separate entities, with others tracing their history through the Yeomanry Cavalry!

The five Gurkha battalions are all that remain of the pre-1947 Indian Army. Recruited in Nepal with both their own and British officers in command, they constitute four Regiments of Infantry (one of which has two battalions) with separate Engineer, Signals and Transport services. The majority of the units are stationed in the Far East.

Operational
The chief operational command in the British army is 1st British Corps (BAOR) in northern Germany, which underwent change as a result of the 1974–5 Defence Review. Before the Review, this corps consisted of three divisions (numbered 1, 2 and 4) made up of five armoured bragades, one mechanised brigade, two artillery brigades (one conventional and one nuclear) and a separate brigade in West Berlin. By the reorganisation the command level of the brigade (and with it the rank of brigadier) disappeared and the British troops outside Berlin reallocated to a total of four armoured divisions, an artillery division and an infantry field force. The number of men stationed in Germany (55,000) did not change, but certain specialist functions hitherto enjoyed by all armoured and mechanical units (notably reconnaissance and anti-aircraft defence) were to be centralised in appropriate formations and parcelled out to individual divisions at need. This scheme was basically an economy measure, designed to help cut the army by 15,000 men through the dismantling of brigade staffs.

It was completely reversed in 1982, when the brigade was revived as a formation, and organisation returned to much the same state as before 1974. One brigade (5) is now earmarked as an overseas intervention force.

RECRUITMENT, TRAINING AND RESERVES

Recruitment
The army consists entirely of personnel serving on a voluntary basis. Those wishing to hold a commission, whether entering from civilian life or through the lower ranks, are chosen by a Regular Commissions Board (RCB) which assesses

their aptitude and educational qualifications over a three-day period. If successful, applicants may opt for short-, medium- or long-term engagements, receiving initial training at the Royal Military Academy (RMA) Sandhurst (see later). Engagements available to non-commissioned ranks range from 3 to 22 years, with a wide freedom of choice on the length and terms of service. In 1972 a new type of engagement was introduced for non-commissioned ranks, under which recruits are committed for a minimum period of productive service only (about 3 years) and, subject to that minimum, may leave at any time at 18 months' notice. Discharge may also be granted on compassionate grounds, by purchase, or on the grounds of conscience, for which there is an independent tribunal to assess cases.

Recruitment to the TAVR is usually on a local basis, with terms of service in the non-commissioned ranks similar to those for the Regular army. Officers for the TAVR are usually chosen from within the units, although Regulars are sometimes posted in for training and administrative purposes. It is also possible for a Regular officer to transfer his commission to the TAVR when his term of regular service ends.

Training

Since 1972 all initial officer training has been carried out at RMA Sandhurst. Successful applicants for Regular commissions, regardless of the length of their prospective engagements, enter the Academy at one of three dates during the year, receiving basic training in a Standard Military Course (SMC) which lasts approximately 6 months. All who survive this course are then commissioned as second-lieutenants, and those who have opted for a short-term engagement join their units. Those who wish to receive a permanent (long-term) commission, however, return to the RMA after two years' service for a further 6 months on a Regular Commission Course (RCC) consisting mainly of academic work in disciplines designed to lay a foundation of knowledge which can be built upon during their future careers. Upon completion of RCC the officers rejoin their units, but their academic training is not over. A few may go on to civilian universities, a number in the more technical arms are sent to the Royal Military College of Science at Shrivenham to do a degree course, and all are expected, through a Progressive Qualification Scheme (PQS) to pass written examinations, as well as practical aptitude tests, to rise from lieutenant to captain and captain to major. The results of these examinations, together with aptitude assessments, then determine whether the officer, upon attaining the rank of major, should attend the Staff College, Camberley, where an annual course, as the name implies, prepares students for staff duties and higher rank.

In addition, a proportion of officers are recruited directly from civilian universities upon graduation and others are sent to university as civilians on an army grant which obliges them to serve a minimum period (usually 5 years) after graduation. In both cases a six-month course at the RMA has to be attended before they join their units, and although their degrees can lead to exemption from some PQS examinations, these officers have to follow the same road as non-graduates to high rank. A short course at the RMA is held each year for TAVR officers, but their future rise through the commissioned ranks does not include attendance at Staff College.

Soldiers enlisting in the non-commissioned ranks receive basic military training at the central depot of their units, and may attend more specialist courses later in their careers. Most training, however, for both Regular and TAVR personnel, is done by the individual regiments on an internal basis. Some Regular soldiers, recruited at the age of 16, may join through the Army Apprentices College for technical arms, or the Junior Leaders Regiment for Royal Armoured Corps or Infantry. In either case these soldiers are regarded as future non-commissioned officers within their units.

Reserves

The army possesses two reserve forces. All officers and men, assuming they are still fit, are transferred to the Regular reserve upon completion of their Regular service, and are expected to be prepared to rejoin their units in an emergency. Their usefulness is obviously restricted to a certain time after the end of their Regular engagement, as they receive little additional training, but there are over 100,000 such men available, acting as a significant reserve potential. The Territorial Army (TA), on the other hand, is made up of soldiers who receive continuous training on a part-time basis, and although they muster 54,000 only, they are now capable not only of acting as a base upon which expansion could take place, but also as a direct reinforcement to the Regular army. One of the results of the 1974—5 Defence Review was, in fact, a complete assimilation of the TA into the Regular force — it had tended before to be rather an appendage — with all TA units being assigned to one of the three field forces in Britain, prepared to be sent as a direct reinforcement to BAOR or to remain in the home defence role. Those assigned to BAOR, now receive the same types of training and equipment as Regular units and have attained a very high standard of military skill, despite the restrictions inherent in their part-time nature.

EQUIPMENT AND ARMS INDUSTRY

Britain possesses a thriving arms industry, catering for both internal and export use. Responsibility for internal procurement (i.e. research, development and production) of defence equipment lies with the Procurement Executive within the Ministry of Defence, set up in 1971 to establish a closer liaison between the service users and the machinery for procurement, closer co-ordination with civilian industry in the formulation of programmes, and stronger and more accountable management.

The major part of research is undertaken by the Ministry of Defence's research and development establishments, but the Ministry also sponsors a substantial amount of research by industry and the universities. This requires a high initial investment — in 1975—6 the total cost of British equipment research and development was estimated at $554,000,000 — so attention has recently been concentrated upon more collaborative projects, particularly with NATO allies, which enable the cost of development and production to be shared. Examples of such collaboration range from the Tornado combat aircraft (developed by Britain, Italy and West Germany) to such Anglo-French projects as the Martel air-to-surface missile, and the Puma and Gazelle helicopters. Nevertheless, the importance of maintaining a sound national industrial base for defence procurement is recognised, and there is close consultation between government and industry both in the National Defence Industries Council and through other specialised machinery.

Following the development of defence equipment, either nationally or in co-operation with allies, production is usually undertaken by private industry on a contract basis or by the Royal Ordnance Factories. A Defence Sales organisation provides support, assistance and advice to British industry and the Royal Ordnance Factories in promoting the sales of defence equipment overseas. In 1980 the value of exports of British defence equipment was estimated to be about $5.37m.

ARMS AND EQUIPMENT

Note: all items are manufactured in Britain unless otherwise specified.

Pistol: 9mm L9A1 Browning automatic and 7.65mm Walther PP automatic (West Germany)
Rifle: 7.62mm L1A1 self-loading rifle and 7.62mm L42A1 converted No. 4 0.303in for sniping
Sub-machine-gun: 9mm L2A3 Stirling
Machine-gun: 7.62mm L7A1 GPMG, 7.62mm L8 tank MG coaxial, 7.62mm L20 helicopter MG, 7.62mm L37 tank MG cupola mounted, 0.300in L3A3 Browning M1919A4, 7.62mm L4A4 Bren and 0.5in L40A1 Browning spotting MG for infantry
Mortars: OML 2in and OML 81mm L16A1
Anti-tank weapons: rocket, 66mm Heat L1A1 (Norway); gun, 84mm infantry L14A1 Carl Gustav (Sweden); gun, 120mm RCL; cannon, 30mm Rarden L21E4; Swingfire ATGW; and Milan ATGW (Aerospatiale, France); some Swingfire mounted in Strike armoured vehicles in anti-tank squadrons.
Anti-aircraft weapons: 40mm L40/70 AA gun, Blowpipe SAM, Rapier SAM and Rapier/Blindfire SAM
Artillery: Abbot 105mm SP gun (100 in service) FH-120 155mm Howitzer (195 in service); M-109 155mm SP gun (USA; 101 in service), M-107 175mm (USA; 31 in service), M-110 203mm Cannon (USA; 16 in service) and 105mm pack howitzer/light gun (100 in service)
Surface-to-surface missiles: Honest John (being replaced by Lance; both USA)
Armour: Chieftain medium tank (900 in service), Scorpion FV-101 light tank (270 in service), Saladin armoured car (243 in service), Scimitar armoured car (290 in service), FV 438/FV 712 AFV (170 in service but Striker entering service), Ferret scout car (1429 in service), Fox scout car (200 in service), FV-432 APC (2338 in service) and Saracen APC (600 in service but Spartan entering service)
Aircraft: Beaver light aircraft (6 in service), Scout helicopter (110 in service), Alouette II helicopter (10 in service; French), Gazelle helicopters (155 in service; Anglo–French) and 90 Lynx helicopters.

RANK, DRESS AND DISTINCTIONS

Rank
Field Marshal – Crossed sword and baton in a wreath
General – Crossed sword and baton, one crown, one star
Lieutenant-General – Crossed sword and baton, one crown
Major-General – Crossed sword and baton, one star
Brigadier – One crown above three stars
Colonel – One crown above two stars
Lieutenant-Colonel – One crown above one star
Major – One crown
Captain – Three stars
Lieutenant – Two stars
Second-Lieutenant – One star

Warrant Officer I – Royal Arms
Warrant Officer II – Crown
Staff Sergeant – Crown above three chevrons
Sergeant – Three chevrons
Corporal – Two chevrons
Lance-Corporal – One chevron
Private –

Note: rank badges are worn by officers on each shoulder, by other ranks on each arm.

Dress
Most patterns of dress take khaki as their basic colour, with the beret (usually dark-blue) as the chief form of head-gear. Working dress for both officers and men now consists of pullover and trousers, the battle-dress having been phased out in 1972, and combat-dress is camouflaged. Full-dress, however, helps preserve peculiarities within individual regiments, ranging from the scarlet jackets and bear-skin busbies of the Foot Guards to the tartans of Scottish units. Officers' mess-dress takes this process even further, with scarlet jackets predominating for the infantry and blue for most of the corps.

Distinctions
Each unit in the British army wears its own cap or beret badge, with appropriate collar devices, and many wear some form of metal shoulder-title. Fusilier regiments, together with certain other units, wear distinctive feather hackles behind their cap badges, while all Scottish regiments wear bonnets and, in full-dress particularly, either the kilt or trews.

CURRENT DEVELOPMENTS

The British army persists with the re-equipment of its forces in Germany, where a new tank (the Challenger) is replacing the Chieftain, and new combat vehicles (the Spartan) the FV-432. Its recruiting difficulties have been completely eliminated by the current rise to high levels of male unemployment.

The most important event in the army's activities since the last publication of *World Armies* was the part it played in the re-capture of the Falkland Islands from the Argentinians, May 21st–June 14th, 1982. The high level of professional skill and physical fitness which the campaign revealed in the army has enhanced both its reputation and its own opinion of itself. Size for size, it is undoubtedly one of the most formidable fighting machines in the world.

John Pimlott
John Keegan

UNITED STATES OF AMERICA

HISTORY AND INTRODUCTION

The army of the USA belongs to that small and interesting group (the Chinese PLA being the next most notable member) whose existence antedates that of the States which they serve. Because of its founding role, the issue of who should command it, and how, attracted the closest attention of the fathers of the United States constitution. And this question of what control the civilian authority should exercise over the army, and of what influence the army should exert in domestic life, has remained a matter of importance – sometimes diminished, sometimes very prominent – ever since. Despite, rather than because of, this constant surveillance, the army's acceptance of its subordination to the civil power has, throughout its two centuries of life, remained absolute, its record unmarred even by so minor a blemish as the Curragh incident (*see* United Kingdom).

The significance of the army in American history does not, however, attach only to its part in securing the 13 colonies' independence from Britain, and preserving that of the Federal government thereafter. By its actions it has, at different times greatly extended the land frontiers of the Union, both by foreign conquest (as in the Mexican War of 1846) and by the defeat and pacification of the American Indian tribes in the period 1790–1890; opened to settlement great areas of the American interior; secured territory overseas (in the Caribbean and the Philippines (Spanish American War and Philippines Insurrection, 1898–1902); maintained, with the United States Marine Corps, a Pax Americana in the western hemisphere; won victories in two world wars which helped to establish America as the greatest power of the mid-twentieth century; and, most important of all, ensured, during the gravest crisis of American history (1861–5), the preservation of the Union itself. In a direction eccentric to the main trend of its activity, it has also during the twentieth century been the principal agent of America's policy of involvement in the affairs of mainland Asia, with results which, during the Vietnam War, awoke those powerful forces of antimilitarism which are constantly present in the American people's relationship with their professional soldiers.

So powerfully present was that antimilitarist feeling in the Founding Fathers that, after the departure of the British, they attempted, like the English at the restoration of Charles II, to dispense with an army altogether – and for much the same reason: unhappy experience of the exactions on property and freedom which standing armies impose. In 1784 Congress disbanded the Continental Army – the force of regulars it had voted to raise on June 14th, 1775 to supplement the disorderly colonial militias – except for 80 soldiers retained to guard stores at Pittsburgh and West Point. Relenting a little the following year, it authorised the creation of a single infantry regiment (today's Old 3rd, the senior American infantry regiment) and of two companies of artillery. And this tiny force was only gradually augmented, principally under the pressure of Indian resistance to settler expansion on the North-Western frontier, until the renewal of war with Britain in 1812.

At no time, however, did Congress attempt to disband the States' militias. Indeed it lacked after 1789 the power to do so, for although the new constitution reserved to Congress the right to raise (and therefore to disband) armies, the first amendment to it entrenched the rights of the people to bear arms and therefore to form militias. Thence stems the dichotomy in the American military system, strange to foreign thinking, between a federal regular army and the part-time voluntary forces of the States. Yet it had, in a sense, been present from the outset, for much of the fighting of the Revolutionary War had been done by militiamen, and the anti Federalists among the Founding Fathers had argued partly from self-interest, partly from political caution and partly from high-mindedness, that free States, united or not, both needed a militia and at the same time needed no more regular a form of military defence than a militia could supply.

As long as America's enemies remained on the far side of the Atlantic, this was a safe argument. And, except during the 1812 and the Mexican Wars, when the regular army was hastily expanded, it prevailed. Between 1790 and 1861 its peacetime strength never rose above 13,000 and sometimes sank as low as 5000. Professionally the most impressive element of the army during the years was not one of its fighting units, but rather the Military Academy at West Point, founded on the model of the Paris *École Polytéchnique* in 1803 and transformed by its great superintendent, Sylvanus Thayer, during his term of office (1817–33) into one of America's foremost centres of education. Its prominence and relatively large size (250 cadets) is explained by the function many of its graduates performed on leaving: rather than officer the army they were used by the government to plan and direct major public works, for which task the West Point engineering degree admirably qualified them (and to which few civilian universities, still orientated to the humanities, could offer an equivalent). It was their excellent engineering training which explains why so many West Pointers' names (like McClellan's) turn up on lists of directors of the early railway companies, why their intellectual standing, unlike their European comrades', has always been high among civilians, why the Corps of Engineers became, and remains, the principal agency for Federal public works in docks, harbours, irrigation and flood control, and why, when war between the States broke out in 1861, so tiny a body of professional officers (821 West Pointers were on active duty) yielded enough competent men to general armies numbering ultimately nearly 3,000,000.

'Competent' must be qualifed: though the four outstanding soldiers of the war – Grant, Lee, Jackson and Sherman (all West Pointers) – were commanders of world class, there was more bad generalship (much of it by West Pointers) in the Civil War than in any major conflict of modern history; and at the same time it would have required divine competence to make effective armies quickly out of the civilian hordes with which both North and South had to fight each other. The popular quality with which their improvisation necessarily invested the Civil War armies (and which revealed itself in the election of officers, a common impatience with the niceties of drill and turnout of which European armies made a fetish, and a general disregard for anything much but getting the job done and returning home) recalled the spirit of the Continental army; more important it laid down a pattern which was to repeat itself in the two world wars and which military commentators, foreign and native-born, were to hold distinctive of the American army itself and expressive of much that is fundamental in American society.

The Civil War inflicted on America higher proportional casualties than those suffered by any Western nation until 1914, and left behind, not unnaturally, a profound distaste for war which during the 1870s hardened again into a real antimilitarism. The prevailing mood then was one of what Samuel Huntington has called 'business pacifism', which compared business methods and achievement with the army's, to the latter's disadvantage. In sympathy to the nation's mood, Congress reduced the army's strength in 1877 to 27,000 and it remained at that level for 20 years, during which it became increasingly isolated from civil society both socially and physically: socially because the officers of the period were almost exclusively West Pointers and the soldiers new immigrants, and physically because its regiments lived far removed from the centres of population, fighting Indians on the western frontier. Yet, like the British army on frontier policing duty, an experience closely similar, it apparently suffered no harm from its isolation, which allowed its members to lead that life (brilliantly depicted in the paintings of Frederick Remington) of moderate danger in a fine climate by which soldiers appear most fulfilled. The only incidents to mar its agreeable *post-bellum* existence were the frequent calls made on the services for strike-breaking in the labour disputes brought on by rapid industrialisation (though the duty fell most heavily on the State militias which isolated enthusiasts kept alive during the 1870s and 1880s and were somewhat revitalised through the formation of the National Guard Association in 1879).

Yet for all their apparent indifference to the military necessity, Americans flocked to join the army when a war with Spain was manufactured in 1898. Within less than a year its strength had increased to 275,000 and while many of the recruits were National Guardsmen, the majority were first-time volunteers, of whom the best known was Theodore Roosevelt, whose rise to prominence dates from his command of the Roughriders (1st Volunteer Cavalry) in Cuba. Roosevelt's military motivation was Kiplingesque, and there is much to compare in the enthusiasm of the Americans for their war with Spain and of the British for theirs with the Boers. Moreover, though the Americans suffered no humiliations comparable to those of Magersfontein or Paardeburg, Cuba and the Philippines revealed shortcomings in their army which prompted the undertakings of reforms as far-reaching as those initiated in the British army after 1902. Perhaps, indeed, further-reaching, for the American army had even more ground to make up: it possessed before 1903 no general staff, no proper staff college, few 'special-to-arm' schools and no permanent organisations above regimental level, while its efficient command was hampered by a division of authority between the Secretary of War and the General-in-Chief (*see* Command and Constitutional Status).

A similar division in the British system has been healed by the abolition of the post of Commander-in-Chief in 1905. Elihu Root, appointed Secretary of War in 1899, and who was to establish himself as the greatest civil head the army has ever had, achieved the transformation of the Commanding General into a Chief of Staff in 1903 and at the same time persuaded Congress to provide him both with a General Staff and to feed it from new senior and junior staff colleges, the Command and General Staff College, Fort Leavenworth, and the Army War College, Washington. Root, who retired in 1904, had been much influenced in the policy-making by the writings of General Emory Upton (*The Military Policy of the United States*, published posthumously, 1904), whose dedicated professionalism, admiration for foreign

(particularly Prussian) practice, and contempt for the amateur, part-time and voluntary character of the national military institutions, branded him in the eyes of many as un-American. That he was not, for West Point, by its nature, had always produced a proportion of 'hard-nosed' military technocrats. But it was very American that the fight to direct the development of the 'New Army' (as Root's creation was called) should have been carried on between two generals who had each started life as military surgeons, an unthinkable origin for any senior European soldier. Frederick Ainsworth was a reactionary whose determination to preserve the powers of his own office of Adjutant-General meant resisting plans to centralise the scattered army posts, and who thereby won the strong support of interested Congressmen because it won additional Congressional support; it also meant resisting plans to supplant the National Guard with a more effective federal reserve for the regular army. Leonard Wood, whose plans these were, defeated Ainsworth in the end. But the American system was strong enough to leave him with only half of what he wanted: an experiment with centralised formations (the Maneuver Division of 1911) but not the federal reserve; the National Guard remained in 1914 (when he retired) the army's only reserve (though its organisation was somewhat improved as a result of the passing of the Dick Act in 1903).

As he had foreseen, though the President he served refused to contemplate the thought, the USA was about to confront the need to expand its armed forces even more suddenly and extensively than had been the case in April, 1861. Then Lincoln had thought 75,000 men enough to see the Civil War through. In 1917, on America's long, if under-standably delayed entry into World War I, Wilson was told by General Pershing, who had arrived in France in June, that he would need a million men at the front by the end of 1918; less than a year later he was to ask for 3,000,000 (or 66 divisions) by May, 1919 shortly revised to 80 divisions, and then again to 100 divisions. It is astonishing that in practice 43 divisions, out of 62 raised, actually reached France before the end of 1918, and that achievement would have been impossible but for the Mexican rebel 'Pancho' Villa's attacks on the Texan border in early 1916 which in turn prompted Congress to pass some anticipatory legislation. The National Defence Act of 1916 permitted an increase in the size of the regular army 175,000 but, familiar news to 'Uptonians' in the officer corps, it provided for strengthening the reserve by granting funds to the National Guard instead of a new federal force and, with a flash of anti-federalist caution, it laid limits on the number of extra officers who might serve on the General Staff in or near Washington. But the Selective Service Act, passed as soon as America declared war, provided the conscriptive powers necessary to achieve the expansion, much of it as divisions of a National Army, akin to the reserve Root and Upton had wanted, to be formed under federal control.

America's military contribution to the winning of World War I was not tangibly great. Pershing resisted Franco–British requests, first reasoned, then desperate, for piecemeal reinforcements, understandably wishing to withhold American troops from the front until a whole army of some 20 divisions could be assembled. When it was, the worst of the 1918 fighting was over, Germany having exhausted her strength just a little quicker than she had her enemies'. Pershing's American army was eventually allotted a secondary sector (the Meuse–Argonne) where its offensive, though conducted with a simple stand-up bravery not seen in France since the epic days of the Marne or the Somme, could not in any case have produced a decisive result. Nevertheless its intervention was the decisive factor in finishing the war for moral if not material reasons, its strength, vigour and apparently inexhaustible numbers, besides putting new heart into the British and French armies, revealing to the Germans how vain had become their generals' promise of victory.

Despite the extent of the army's achievement, and the apparent enjoyment with which most Americans had accepted conscripted service (to the introduction of which there was, thanks to the Civil War precedent, none of the political and moral hostility so strongly felt in Britain), it was allowed after 1918 to revert very quickly to its pre-war role and size (1921–36: 140,000). However, in the National Defence Act of 1920, Congress perpetuated the existence of a federal reserve (the Organised Reserve) separate from the Guard, in an 'Army of the United States' of which the regular army was to be the third component. The USA was divided into nine corps areas, each to contain one regular, two Guard and three reserve divisions (though for most of the period up to 1939 only three regular divisions had a peacetime existence). The Air Corps, raised during the war, was made a substantive element of the army, with its strength fixed (by the Air Corps Act of 1926) at 15,000.

This generally improved the organisation of the army but did little in practice to make it an efficient modern force, for while the Air Corps thrived on comparatively generous budgets, the ground elements had to make do during the penny-pinching inter-war years with the ageing equipment, much of it French, issued in 1918. Although Christie, the most inventive of contemporary tank designers, was an American, the army was allowed to purchase none of his models in bulk; indeed its Tank Corps was absorbed by the infantry in 1920. The soldiers moreover were given very little to do. The Marine Corps (raised in 1775) had by now finally fought off attempts to incorporate it into the army and established itself as America's Pacific and Caribbean police force. The fronters were quiet. The Philippines had organised its own army.

Public interest in the armed forces, such as there was, concentrated on the Air Corps which the mercurial General Billy Mitchell, preaching the same message as Trenchard in Britain, but in a more dramatic style, was determined to transform into a decisive element of American power. His efforts to have it separated from the army as an independent force, not eventually achieved until 1947, resulted in his court-martial in 1925. This sacrifice of his career was the most certain guarantee of the final success of his campaign that he could have arranged.

Otherwise the army spent the inter-war years at a humdrum round of garrison duty, occasionally relieved, in an unwelcome fashion, by internal security duty, as in the case of the dispersal of the Bonus Marchers (unemployed veterans demanding deferred gratuities) in Washington in 1932. During the worst of the recession the army also supervised the job-creation schemes organised by the federal government through the Civilian Conservation Corps. But the outbreak of war in Europe in 1939, even though Congress and the majority of the people were determined that America should take no part in it, brought a renewed spirit of activity and a massive increase of numbers. Fearful that Britain as well as France might fall to Germany, control of the Atlantic pass to Hitler and the security of the Western hemisphere be threatened, Congress in May, 1940 voted to increase the army to 375,000 (from 190,000). In August it authorised the President to embody the National Guard for federal service for 1 year and in September it voted for selective conscription (the Burke–Wadsworth Bill). By December, 1941 when Japan's attack on Pearl Harbour and Hitler's unilateral declaration of war on the USA ended the hesitation over involvement, the army had grown to a strength of 1,638,086, organised into 36 divisions. Because so much of America's

growing output of military material had been sent overseas to equip British (and later Soviet) forces, however, few of these new divisions possessed the means with which to fight, while almost none was under experienced leadership. The extraordinary pace and scale of the expansion bears comparison only with the creation of the previous American Expeditionary Force and of the Kitchener armies in 1914–15.

Unlike the AEF, the new American army would shortly have to fight as the major partner in the Western military alliance. Roosevelt and Marshall, the magisterial Chief of Staff who was to remain at the President's side throughout the war and do so much to guide the direction of allied strategy, were anxious to commit a major expeditionary force to battle in Europe in 1942. Dissuaded by the British from risking a cross-channel invasion of the continent, they dispatched the American II Corps to north Africa in November, 1942 as part of the Anglo–American First Army. Its three divisions were the vanguard of ninety-one which the army was to raise during the war (the Marine Corps was to field another six). In the ensuing Sicilian campaign, to which Roosevelt and Marshall reluctantly agreed, the size of the American contingent rose to four, in the invasion of Italy to five. By November there were seven American divisions in line, equal to the number of British and at the same time a major American invasion army was gathering in Britain for the much-postponed assault on north-west Europe. Eisenhower, Marshall's protégé and the commander of the original north African landing force, had been designated Supreme Commander of the Allied Liberation Army, in which the Americans would, after the initial landing, form the majority.

At the end of the battle of Normandy, which followed the audacious cross-channel invasion, Eisenhower assumed control, hitherto exercised by Montgomery, whose 11 British divisions were now outnumbered by 14 American. One British division actually had to be dissolved in order to provide reinforcements for those remaining, and thenceforward the American army was progressively to outdistance the British in size. At the end of the war in Europe, it counted twenty-three to eleven British, and was unquestionably the major partner in the victory.

In the Pacific theatre, where a British–Indian army engaged the Japanese in Burma throughout 1942–5, its strength had grown proportionately, though never, despite pressure from the United States Navy to the contrary, on a scale to inhibit operations in Europe. By the end of the war, there were 31 army divisions in the theatre, some transferred from Europe since the defeat of Hitler, but the majority of which had behind them 3 years of exhausting but triumphant amphibious island-hopping from New Guinea, Guadalcanal and the Philippines to Okinawa on the doorstep of the Japanese home islands.

Throughout the war, the air force, still technically as the Army Air Force a branch of the army, had maintained a major strategic bombing campaign against Germany, subsequently transferred to the Pacific theatre'. And the campaigns of the Army Ground Forces and the Army Air Forces had been supported by the work of the Army Service Forces – a three-fold division of an over-large organisation implemented in March, 1942. Over 8,000,000 Americans had worn khaki, and 2,000,000 had served in ground combat formations. They had shown remarkable and innovative military talent in airborne, armoured and amphibious operations, had pioneered a new 'joint' approach to the co-ordination of inter-service planning, staff work and command, and had produced, in MacArthur, one of the great strategists of the twentieth century, in Eisenhower the greatest inter-allied commander and in Patton one of the most dynamic battlefield leaders.

The immediate post-war years saw as radical a reduction of the strength of the army as it had suffered after 1918. The development of the atomic bomb persuaded the American people and its leaders that not only was there no excuse to delay the demobilisation of the wartime army almost in its entirety, but also that there would be little call in the future for traditional military forces to defend America's interests, since they could be consigned to the care of a small nuclear-equipped air force — after 1947 established as an independent entity. This optimistic forecast of America's military future was upset by the Korean War, which broke out on June 25th, 1950. The United Nations immediately invoked its security arrangements against the North Koreans, who had invaded South Korea, and the American occupation forces in Japan were mobilised to assist the South Korean army in repelling them. Its numbers proving inadequate, the American government was obliged to send forces from continental USA and to increase the size of the standing army. It had fallen to about 700,000, with only two divisions available for reinforcement of the occupation forces in Germany and Japan, and although Congress had in 1948 passed a selective service act to supplement with conscripts the supply of volunteers, it was to be operative for only 2 years. Confronted with the Korean crisis, Congress activated eight National Guard divisions and then introduced a Universal Military Training and Service Act (June, 1951) which, though applied selectively, did provide the army for the first time in its history with a permanent supply of peacetime conscripts. During the Korean War (not technically a war for America, but a peacekeeping operation) that provision was vital, since the scale of operations required the induction of 3,000,000 men and the maintenance of 20 divisions on a tactical footing.

In the aftermath of Korea, the USA was never again to allow the size of its army to fall to the dangerously low level it had reached in the late 1940s. Through its commitment to the North Atlantic Treaty Organisation, activated in 1949, it was bound to maintain the Seventh Army in Germany at a level of six divisions, but they had been allowed until 1950 to remain at skeleton strength. After 1955 they were properly reinforced, while in the USA a Continental Army Command (the predecessors of the present Forces Command) oversaw the gradual strengthening of American-based formations to realistic levels. Two Strategic Army Corps (III and XVIII Airborne) were earmarked for rapid deployment overseas in the event of emergency. Internally, the army reappraised its methods of training and standards of discipline in an effort to avoid future collapses of morale, displayed at the outset of the Korean involvement, which had deeply shocked old-school officers who had not themselves had to face Asian communist styles of warfare or treatment of prisoners of war.

President Johnson's decision to commit full American formations to ground warfare in Vietnam, which came in mid-1965, was initially seen by the reinvigorated and re-modelled peacetime army as a chance to display the new skills it had learned in the quietus since its last Asian involvement. Foremost among these were the techniques of irregular warfare pioneered by the Special Forces, which President Kennedy had greatly expanded as a means of extending American military power without committing full-scale military strength to foreign crisis centres. The Special Forces, who raised and led Vietnamese irregular units throughout the American involvement in the war, achieved much that was remarkable. But, after two and a half years of generally successful campaigning against the Viet Cong, the conventional formations of the army were badly shaken by the Viet Cong/North Vietnamese Tet offensive of 1968 (see Role and Recent Operations). Although

successful in suppressing it, they thereby lost control of much of the countryside, which they were never able to recover. The army was, moreover, from 1966 onwards afflicted by a very bitter domestic opposition both to the war itself and to its conduct, which heightened as the demands of the draft eventually extended to include almost the whole male population of draft age. In Vietnam, the disaffection of the conscripts became almost open once peace talks were opened with the North Vietnamese in 1969 and occasionally took the form of physical assault on superiors. It was exacerbated by drug abuse and by severe racial conflict outside the combat zones, most severely felt in units in the USA and Germany.

President Nixon's eventual disentanglement from the war was therefore warmly welcomed by the army's senior officers, as was the decision, enacted in mid-1974, to accept a 'zero draft' (without repealing the Military Service Act) and recruit the army by voluntary enlistment. It was believed that the voluntary system offered the army the best chance available to repair the damage done to its morale by the stresses of Vietnam and to transform it into a highly trained and motivated force, organised for the rapid reinforcement of the Seventh Army in Germany and for intervention overseas at points of crisis.

The last 10 years in the life of the American army have not been the happiest. It has come closer to losing a war than it has ever done before, and suffered acute internal disturbance in the process. It nevertheless remains a model of what the army of a great democratic State should be. For all the political anguish experienced in the USA over the war, no military leader improperly sought to influence either its conduct (as MacArthur was thought by some to have attempted during the Korean War) or the terms on which it was concluded. It has done its duty, dealt judiciously with breaches of its code of behaviour committed by its officers and soldiers during the war (and they were few) and accepted the judgement of the civilian authority constitutionally set over it throughout — as it has from the inauguration of the first President.

STRENGTH AND BUDGET

Population: 230,000,000
Army: 791,000 regulars 389,000 National Guard reserves; 225,000 army reserves
Marine Corps: 192,000 regulars; 37,000 reserves
Navy: 553,000; 204 major surface ships, 102 missile and attack submarines
Air force: 581,000; 3650 combat aircraft
GDP (1976); $2,924,800,000,000
Defence expenditure (1982–3): $215,000,000,000 (estimated)

COMMAND AND CONSTITUTIONAL STATUS

Command
The Commander-in-Chief of the three services is the President. Advised by the National Security Council, he directs policy and decision, through the Secretary of Defence and his Department (the Pentagon), with its many departments and agencies*. Of these the Joint Chiefs of Staff, chaired in turn by a soldier, sailor and airman (who is not the Chief of his own service staff and who has no vote, is the Secretary's executive, directly controlling the unified commands of the

* No ex-officer is eligible to serve as Secretary of Defence for the 10 years after he leaves the service: National Security Act, 1947.

American forces: Atlantic, Aerospace Defence, Pacific, Southern, Readiness, Strategic Air, Military Airlift and European. The staffs of the three services remain separate; they directly control those forces not assigned to Unified or Special Commands. For operational purposes, however, the controlling authority is the Joint Chiefs of Staff and the operational executive its J-3 division.

The Department of the Army, which is part of the Department of Defence, is headed by the Secretary of the Army, a presidential appointee, assisted by an under-secretary and five assistant secretaries, the latter responsible for (a) finance, (b) installations and logistics, (c) research and development, (d) manpower and reserves and (e) civil works. He exercises control of the army through the Chief of Staff, and he in turn through the Commanding Generals of the Field Commands. Of these there are now thirteen: Forces, Training and Doctrine, United States Army Europe, United States Army Japan, Eighth Army (Korea), Material, Communications, Health Services, Military Traffic Management, Criminal Investigation, Computer Systems, the Army Security Agency and the Washington Military District. (Reorganisation in 1973–4 did away with Continental, Combat Development, Air Defence, Intelligence, Pacific and Southern Commands.) Many of these are in turn subdivided, somewhat confusingly, into commands or armies (e.g. Forces Command controls First, Fifth and Sixth Armies in continental USA), nomenclature surviving from an older organisational scheme. The Reserve Army is commanded through nine Readiness Commands, subordinate to the First, Fifth and Sixth Armies, and overseen by a Chief of Army Reserve on the General Staff. The National Guard, because it is constitutionally a collection of State forces, is commanded by the Governors of the States, through their Adjutants-General, but the General Staff maintains a National Guard Bureau which standardises policy and training, and administers federal funds. Its chief, by jealously guarded statutory provision, has direct access to the Chief of Staff (and is a National Guard officer).

Constitutional Status

The framers of the constitution, who included in its preamble their intention to provide 'for the common defence' arranged that power over the army, as over other institutions of the Union, should be separately vested. Article 1, Section 8, allotted Congress the power 'to raise and support armies', 'to make rules for their government and regulation', 'to provide for organising, arming and disciplining militia, and for governing such part of them as may be employed in the service of the United States, and for 'calling forth the militia to execute the laws of the Union, suppress insurrection and repel invasions'. The appointment of officers in the militia was however reserved to the States, together with authority to train it 'according to the discipline prescribed by Congress'; while the second amendment to the constitution ('a well regulated militia being necessary to the Security of a free State, the right of the people to keep and bear arms shall not be infringed', 1789), established the right of the States to raise the militias to which the constitution referred. Finally, control of the army of the United States, and of the militia, while in federal service, was constitutionally vested in the President (Article II, Section 2); but, as a check on his executive military power, Article 1, Section 8, laid down that 'no appropriation to (the support of armies) shall be for a longer term than 2 years', and the appointment of officers is reserved to the Senate.

Many of the Founding Fathers had disapproved of giving constitutional endorsement to the existence of a federal army which they suspected would be a potential instrument of tyranny. Suspicion, though generally muted, has lingered ever since, expressing itself in mutual antipathy between the regular army and the militia (National Guard), in congressional struggles to restrict the army's autonomy and the size of its budget, and in successive readjustments of the relationship between the senior officer of the army on the one hand and the Secretary of War (later of the Army and then also of Defence) on the other. It was not until 1821 that the army was given an official head, and then only because during the war of 1812, 'civilian control of the military was interpreted by Congress to mean civilian command', with disastrous results. But the General in Chief (or Commanding General), whose post survived until 1903, was not a successful creation. Under a strong President (Polk in the Mexican War, Lincoln until his 'discovery' of Grant) he was merely a mouthpiece; under a weak President he tended to fight with the Secretary of War who, though his power was restricted in 1821 to the administrative side, often interfered in operations, the General's preserve. At the same time the General's own authority within the army was limited by the independence of his chiefs of bureaux (who had life tenure and reported directly to the Secretary) – so much so that General Schofield (1888–95) declared that 'under the government of the United States, an actual military commander of the army is not possible'.

The division of responsibilities, and the inefficiency and mutual hamstringing which resulted from it, had its parallels in the government of other nineteenth century armies, notably the British, and was eventually resolved at the same time and by the same methods: the institution (by Secretary Elihu Root in 1903) of a General Staff, whose chief surrendered nominal command for the status of principal professional adviser on the understanding that his domestic authority within the army should be virtually absolute. As a principle, it has been respected ever since, but its operation, particularly during World War II, when several service chiefs acquired immense politico–military influence by force of circumstance, has been erratic. The passing of the National Security Act of 1947, and the subsequent legislations and executive amendments to it, have, however, now shifted the balance of power decisively into civilian hands. The most important of these were the amended National Security Act of 1949, the Reorganisation Plan No. 6 and so-called Key West Agreement of 1953, and the Defence Reorganisation Act of 1958. The 1947 Act in itself was a half-measure, in that it subordinated the three services to a Secretary of Defence without giving him effective means of controlling them. As amended in 1949, they ceased to be 'executive departments' and by the Reorganisation Plan of 1953 the three Secretaries of the Army, Navy and Air Force were reduced in status to 'operating managers' under the Secretary of Defence, to whom were also subordinated all defence agencies, e.g. the Munitions and Research and Development Boards, which had an inter-service function. A few months later the Key West Agreement between the Chiefs of Staff of the three services further increased the authority of the Secretary of Defence, by prescribing as complete an integration of military functions as was possible, short of merging the three services. They were required furthermore to establish unified commands 'as necessary' – the tri-service organisations which were henceforward to be the most important agencies of American strategy. In 1958 the Defence Reorganisation Act re-aligned responsibilities within the defence structure so that the chain of command ran from the President to the Secretary of Defence to the Joint Chiefs to the unified commands; the naval and air staffs were taken out of the chain of command altogether (as the army had been by the Root reform of 1903) and the Joint Staff (whose head is appointed by the Secretary of Defence and which services the Joint Chiefs) was doubled in size (to 400 officers – now over 2000). Thus 'the Secretary, acting for the President has now been made solely responsible for defending the constitution... against all enemies, foreign and domestic. He was to maintain the security of the United States, its possessions, and areas of vital interest ... and safeguard internal security.' The Joint Chiefs meanwhile had their role reduced to one of advice, and their functions to the preparation of strategic plans and the 'provision of strategic direction'. But Congress, fearful of a movement towards the erection of a single service, removed provisions which would have allowed the Secretary of Defence to reassign functions between the services at will.

Civilian control is thus entrenched both in principle and practice; indeed Congress in the early 1960s expressed fear that the impact of military advice on decision making had become too limited (House Armed Forces Committee, Special Subcommittee on Defence Agencies, 87th Congress, 2nd Session, 1962, pp. 6631–4). Final judgement on the working of the defence bureaucracy in the direction of the Vietnam War may or may not bear out that fear.

Although the Secretary of the Army and the Army Staff now occupy a position several removes distant from the centre of strategic authority, they are not completely isolated from the processes of executive or legislative government. By an anomaly the Chief of Staff, through his membership of the Joint Chiefs Committee, may actually be more directly involved in decision-making than the Secretary of the Army, his nominal superior. Both, moreover, are in touch with Congress, through the investigative process run by the House and Senate Appropriations and Armed Forces Committees and their Defence Appropriations Sub-committees. The days of open combat between the services for a 'fair' share of appropriations, so notable a feature of Washington life in the 1940s and 1950s, are over. The army must still nevertheless justify its expenditure to Congress, besides being ready to answer any and every enquiry which Congress or its individual members submit: 'in an average year the Army might receive 60,000 letters, 75,000 telephone calls and 7500 personal visits from Congressmen'. To deal with all these matters the army maintains an Office of Legislative Liaison, with offices both in the Pentagon and the two Houses. It also prepares all legislation (which the army, like any other government agency, has the right to initiate). Such bills normally relate to the domestic affairs of the army and the pay, pensions and legal status of its members.

The National Guard, being the army of 'the Several States and territories', a 'single organisation with a double existence' – State and federal, and the beneficiary of both the 'army' and the 'militia' clauses of the constitution, has a special relationship with Congress. It comes under control of the President, as Commander-in-Chief, only after Congress has declared the existence of a national emergency. But its Washington lobby secured in 1933 the passage of an act which makes it a reserve of the regular army. Attempts to reorganise it against its will (as by McNamara in 1965) are usually fiercely and successfully resisted. The Army Reserve, though a federal body, also enjoys special Congressional protection, since its units, being static, tend to take on 'State' character.

Legally, the army (and the other services) possess wide disciplinary powers, set out in the Uniform Code of Military Justice, and may both try, sentence and punish offenders. The army maintains its own penal establishment, but long-sentence criminals are normally transferred to federal prisons to serve out their terms.

ROLE, COMMITMENT, DEPLOYMENT AND RECENT OPERATIONS

Role

Title 10, Section 3062 of the United States Code, lays down that 'it is the intent of Congress to provide an army that is capable ... with the other armed forces, of preserving the peace and security ... of the United States; ... supporting the national policies; implementing the national objectives; ... and overcoming any nations responsible for aggressive acts that imperil the peace and security of the United States'. In practice, it is traditionally upon the United States Marine Corps that the task of dealing with local threats to American interests overseas devolves (e.g. most recently in the Lebanon (1958) and in the initial stages of the intervention in the Dominican Republic (1965)). Moreover although Title 10, Section 3062 does not include the maintenance of internal security as a task of the army, it has frequently been so used, e.g. in 1860 to put down John Brown's rising at Harpers Ferry, in 1877 and 1894 to break railway strikes, in 1930 to disperse the Bonus Marchers in Washington and during the 1960s to suppress racial disorder. The army has also been used to capture runaway slaves before the Civil War, to run the Freedmen's Bureau after it and the 1300 camps of the Civilian Conservation Corps of the 1930s, to perform disaster relief, and to operate, through the Corps of Engineers, federal harbour, river and irrigation works throughout the USA. Constitutional or legal authority exists for all these activities. To a marked extent, however, the principal role of the American army is to fight wars, usually large wars, and in between to keep itself in readiness to do so.

Commitment

The USA maintains major army formations in Germany (including Berlin), South Korea, Italy, Japan (Okinawa) and the Panama Canal Zone, and embarked Marine Corps units in the Pacific and Mediterranean. It has bilateral treaties of military guarantee with Japan, Iran, Pakistan, South Korea, Spain and the Nationalist Republic of China (Taiwan), and with most of the members of the regional alliances to which it belongs: NATO, Organization of American States, ANZUS (Australia, New Zealand, Pakistan, the Philippines, Thailand and Great Britain). It also maintains military assistance advisory groups (MAAG) and other military missions in about 50 foreign countries (including all Latin American States except Cuba and Ecuador) and over 80 army attaché offices in foreign capitals.

Deployment

During 1973–4 the structure of the army, both in continental USA (CONUS) and outside (OCONUS), was much simplified, principally in order to reduce the number of servicemen employed on non-combat duty. Two major home commands (Air Defence and Army Intelligence) were eliminated, and also five overseas, of which Pacific, Alaska and Southern (Caribbean) were the most important. The two largest commands remaining in CONUS are Forces (FORSCOM) controlling all ground units, and Training and Doctrine (TRADOC) controlling all schools and training units. All others – Material, Communications, Health Services, Development, Military Traffic Management, Computer Systems and Criminal Investigation Commands, the Army Security Agency and the Military District of Washington – are Support, Procurement, Research or Administrative Agencies.

The territory of continental USA is divided into zones of three Armies – First, Fifth and Sixth, with headquarters at Fort Meade, Maryland; Fort Sam, Houston, Texas; and the Presidio of San Francisco, California – which administer all static army installations within their boundaries. It is further subdivided into nine Readiness Regions with headquarters in Fort Devens, Massachusetts; Fort Dix, New Jersey; Fort Meade, Maryland; Fort Gillem, Georgia; Fort Sheridan, Illinois; Fort Knox, Kentucky; Fort Sam, Houston, Texas; the Rocky Mountain Arsenal, Colorado; and the Presidio of San Francisco, California. The Readiness Regions are subordinate to the appropriate Army and are the medium of command of the local Army Reserve and National Guard units.

The field formations of the Active Army are subordinate, however, either to FORSCOM or to one of the armies overseas. FORSCOM directly controls two Corps (III and XVIII) and several independent brigades and regiments, besides the reinforcement divisions of the Seventh Army and those in strategic reserve. The divisions of the Active Army are thus commanded and deployed as follows:

Continental United States
XVIII Corps — Fort Bragg, North Carolina
82nd Airborne† — Fort Bragg, North Carolina
101st Air Assault† — Fort Campbell, Kentucky
III Corps — Fort Hood, Texas
1st Cavalry (Mechanised)† — Fort Hood, Texas
2nd Armoured* (less one brigade) — Fort Hood, Texas
1st Infantry (Mechanised) (less one brigade)* — Fort Riley, Kansas
9th Infantry† — Fort Lewis, Washington
4th Infantry (Mechanised)* (less one brigade) — Fort Carson, Colorado
5th Infantry (Mechanised) (two active and reserve brigades) — Fort Polk, Louisiana
24th Infantry (two active and reserve brigades) — Fort Stewart, Georgia
7th Infantry (two active and reserve brigades) — Fort Ord, California

Germany (Seventh Army, Heidelberg)
V Corps — Frankfurt
3rd Armoured — Hanau
8th Infantry (Mechanised) — Bad Kreuznach
VII Corps — Stuttgart
1st Armoured — Göppingen
3rd Infantry (Mechanised) — Würzburg
1st Brigade — Augsburg
1st Infantry (Mechanised) — Augsburg
plus one brigade each from 2nd Armoured and 4th Infantry (Mechanised)

Korea (Eighth Army and I Corps)
2nd Infantry (with 38th Air Defence Brigade)

Hawaii
25th Infantry

There are in addition six independent brigades: 6th Air Cavalry Combat Brigade at Fort Hood; 194th Armoured Brigade at Fort Knox; 197 Infantry at Fort Benning, Georgia; 172nd Infantry in Alaska; 193rd Infantry in Panama; and one in Berlin; there are also three large armoured regiments (2nd and 11th in Germany, 3rd at Fort Bliss, Texas) besides minor land units elsewhere, e.g. one airborne battalion in Italy and the headquarters of a Corps (*IX*) in Japan, and two Ranger Battalions at Fort Stewart, Georgia and Fort Lewis, Washington.

* Seventh Army reinforcements.
† Strategic Reserve.

The divisions of the Marine Corps are stationed thus:

Continental United States
1st Division (and 3rd Air Wing) — Camp Pendleton, California
2nd Division (and 2nd Air Wing) — Camp Lejeune, North Carolina

Pacific
3rd Division, less 1st Marine Brigade (and 1st Air Wing) — Okinawa
Part of the 1st Air Wing is stationed in Japan; the independent 1st Marine Brigade is in Hawaii.
The 7th Marine Amphibious Brigade forms part of the Rapid Deployment Joint Task Force.

The command structure of forces outside continental USA (OCONUS) now comprises only three major headquarters: United States Army Europe (USAREUR), United States Army Japan and Eighth Army in Korea, all controlled directly by the Department of the Army (in liaison with supranational authorities where appropriate: NATO in Europe and the United Nations Command in Korea).

Army Reserve
The Army Reserve is a voluntarily enlisted body of (1982) 225,000. It is administered through 19 Army Reserve Commads and is formed into 12 divisions (Training), two Maneuver Area Commands, four Military Police Commands, four Engineer Commands or Brigades, three Transportation Brigades, three Support Brigades, three Civil Affairs Brigades, nine Army Hospitals and three Infantry Brigades. The latter (157th Infantry Mechanised), HQ Horsham, Pennsylvania; 187th Infantry, HQ Boston, Massachusetts; and 205th Infantry, HQ Fort Snelling, Minnesota) are, with three independent infantry battalions, the Reserve's only true combat units. Some progress has been made however with a plan to associate Reserve units with those of the Active Army, to which in emergency they would act as formed reinforcements.

National Guard
The Army National Guard is a voluntarily enlisted body of (1982) 389,300. It is recruited and administered through the Adjutants-General of the 50 States and formed into eight Divisions: (*a*) 26th Infantry, Massachussetts; 28th Infantry, Pennsylvania; 38th Infantry, Indiana; 40th Infantry, California; 42nd Infantry, New York; 47th Infantry, Minnesota; 49th Armoured, Texas; and 50th Armoured, New Jersey, (*b*) 15 Separate Infantry Brigades: 29th Hawaii; 30th (Mechanised) Wisconsin; 33rd Illinois; 39th Arkansas; 41st Oregon; 45th Oklahoma; 48th (Mechanised) Georgia; 53rd Florida; 67th (Mechanised) Nebraska; 69th Kansas; 81st (Mechanised) Seattle; 92nd Puerto Rico; 218th (Mechanised) South Carolina; and 256th Louisiana, and (*c*) three separate Armoured Brigades: 30th Tennessee; 31st Alabama; and 155th Mississippi. It also provides 12 artillery, engineer, military police and support formations. Units of the Guard are commanded in peace by the Governor of the State in which they are located but, for training and operational purposes, the chain of command is from the Forces Command through its Readiness Regions. Under the new 'reserve components affiliation program' Guard units now perform training with the units of the Active Army to which they would act as formed reinforcements in emergency.

A Selected Reserve Force (SRF) of three divisions in size, formed from Guard and Reserve Units, is kept at an advanced state of readiness to mobilise in under 5 weeks.

Recent Operations

The United States army (or United States Marine Corps) has, since the end of World War II, thrice intervened in the affairs of foreign States and twice fought a major war. The interventions were in Lebanon in 1958, when three battalions of marines, and an army battle group, were landed at the request of the country's president to help avert the outbreak of civil war (the intervention was bloodless), again in 1982 and in the Dominican Republic in 1965 when marines and the 82nd Airborne Division occupied the capital between May and September, after a communist-inspired coup had overthrown the government. From 1962–75 the army and marines also maintained units in Thailand, which supported United States military advisers to the Royal Lao Army in Laos.

The two wars were in Korea (1950–53) and in Indo-China, 1965–72. The Korean War was long, large-scale (300,000 soldiers deployed) and costly, and falls outside the category of 'recent operations', but the army still lives with the aftermath of the Indo-China (Vietnam) War.

Its involvement in the region began, while France was still fighting its war there with the Vietminh, with the provision of money, equipment and training teams. After the defeat of the French, the United States army became responsible for training the new army of 150,000 of the Republic of (South) Vietnam and, from the onset of deliberate North Vietnamese subversion of the Southern government's authority in 1959, for the provision of numerous advisers to operate with ARVN (Army of the Republic of Vietnam) units in the field. By 1965 their numbers had grown to 27,000 but their efforts to stiffen the ARVN's resistance were unavailing, and in March of that year President Johnson decided to commit formed combat units in an attempt to avert an immediate seizure of power by the North Vietnamese/Viet Cong (NVA/VC). Their forces by then outnumbered those of the ARVN, which was losing a battalion each week in the fighting. Between 1965 and 1968 the United States army deployed 100 'maneuver battalions' (infantry, armour, airborne or ranger battalions) in the South and, having won at the outset some bloody full-scale battles for control of the highland frontier towns, embarked on a prolonged 'search and destroy' campaign in the countryside. Militarily, this demanded the creation of a new sort of unit – the helicopter-borne infantry battalion, with an immensely expensive support system to maintain it in action. Domestically it required a change from a programme of selective to near-universal conscription. The apparent success of the air-mobile units in the search and destroy campaign was very great. Politically, the progressive appetite of 'the draft' generated resistance from the young (and their parents) which took vociferous and sporadically violent forms and drew strength from the support of groups or individuals who, if not threatened personally by conscription, had moral or ideological objections to America's involvement in, or conduct of, the war. The anti-war movement had its hand greatly strengthened by the NVA/VC Tet offensive of February, 1968 during which 100 towns were attacked, Hué (the old imperial capital of Annam) occupied, and the American Embassy in central Saigon for a time besieged. The scale of this quite unexpected counter-offensive appeared to invalidate, fearful though its cost to the attackers was, the United States army's belief, and its commander General Westmoreland's firmly stated conviction, that it was winning the war. President Nixon, entering office in early 1969 and recognising the power of the anti-war movement at home and the improbability of American victory in the theatre of war itself, therefore instituted a policy of 'Vietnamisation'. It meant that the main burden of fighting was to be transferred to the ARVN, which was to be equipped for the task with arms and supplies on the scale hitherto enjoyed by the United States army. 'Vietnamisation' did not prevent the President's extension of the war in 1970 to Cambodia, whose neutralist leader had been brought publicly to protest at the growing (and well-known) use of his country's territory by the NVA/VC for their military purposes; but it did mean that by the end of 1972 the American army had ceased to operate combat units on Vietnamese soil.

A major element among many which brought the American government to decide on withdrawal from direct involvement in the war had been its effect upon the United States army and its soldiers, both regular and drafted, both in Vietnam and elsewhere. That effect, by and large, has been for the worse. At the height of the army's effort, 525,000 soldiers were deployed on the ground, representing 10 divisions (1st, 4th, 9th and 23rd American – now deactivated – and 25th Infantry; 1st Cavalry and 101st, both airmobile; and 1st and 3rd Marine) and five brigades. This deployment had reduced the strategic reserve in the continental United States to two divisions and brigades, and had deprived the Seventh Army in Germany of necessary resources. Morale in Vietnam after Tet was poor, expressing itself in widespread 'escape' from an unpopular war by drug-taking and in the occasional assassination of over-zealous junior leaders by their men. Many of the professionals, who had entered the campaign with enthusiasm and a determination to show the army 'combat ready', as it had not been at the outbreak of the Korean War in 1950, had become dispirited by the conscripts' discontent and by the seeming endlessness of the conflict. They were also depressed by reports of 'sympathetic' indiscipline in units at home and in Germany, and by the manifestation in the army of the racial tension and violence which disturbed domestic life during those years and which the black soldiers' recognition of their disproportionately high numbers in combat units exacerbated. The leadership of the army was also discouraged by the failure of its 'high technology' approach to counter-insurgency, on which high hopes had been based, to win tangible victories; they were also appalled by its cost in ammunition expenditure and equipment losses (up to 5000 helicopters a year) and by the suffering it inflicted on the civil population, friendly and not-so-friendly. President Nixon's decision in 1969 to 'Vietnamise' the war and progressively to return American units to the United States was therefore tacitly welcomed, as was that to institute a 'zero draft' (volunteer army) which flowed from it. Fears that sufficient volunteers to meet the army's prescribed all-regular strength (860,000) might not come forward have been proved exaggerated, at least in the context of a fairly severe economic recession; other fears that Vietnam had done irreparable damage to the army's morale, discipline and sense of duty appear groundless, the now all-regular force having apparently responded to its leaders' programme of regeneration in a satisfactory spirit. The quality of recruit, thanks to a surplus of applicants, has improved; meanwhile, whatever the other effects of Vietnam, it has meant that the great majority of the army's leaders have had combat experience.

ORGANISATION

Active Army

Arms of Service

These are known as 'branches' and are divided into 'arms' ('combat' and 'combat support' troops) and 'services' (providing either 'combat service support' or administrative services); three (Engineers, Military Police and Signals) are regarded as being both 'arms' and 'services', because of a multiple function.

The arms, in official order of precedence, are: Infantry, Corps of Engineers, Air Defence Artillery, Field Artillery Armour, Signals Corps, Military Police Corps and Military Intelligence Branch.

The services are likewise: Adjutant-General's Corps, Finance Corps, Quartermaster Corps, Army Medical Department (which comprises the Medical Corps, Army Nurse Corps, Dental Corps, Veterinary Corps, Medical Service Corps and Army Medical Specialist Corps), Chaplains, Judge Advocate General's Corps, Ordnance Corps, Chemical Corps, Women's Army Corps and Transportation Corps. Army aviation is organised, in deference to the air force, neither as an arm nor a service, but as an operational element of a fighting formation: its officers and men belong to other branches. The functions of most of the branches are explained by their titles; but the Adjutant-General's Corps deals with personnel affairs, the Chemical Corps with nuclear-biological-chemical warfare and the Quartermaster Corps is a supply organisation. Officers and men generally remain within the branch which they joined on entering the army. They spend little time with any one unit, however, as a result of the army's policy of diversifying their experience to the greatest extent possible. This turbulence can have an unfortunate effect on unit morale and efficiency and some attempt to offset it has been made with the introduction of the Combat Arms Regimental System (CARS). This, modelled on the regimental system of British army, confers on each combat unit the ancestry of one of the army's original regiments. It will also, from 1982 onwards, allow selected regiments (about 10% of the total) to enlist recruits on the promise they will serve with it for at least two tours of duty. The experiment is being watched with keen interest by the rest of the army.

Operational

The division is the key formation and since 1956 has been so organised that each of the three 'type' divisions – armoured, mechanised infantry and infantry – has a similar 'divisional base' (i.e. headquarters, support arms and services). They differ only in the number and type of allotted 'maneuver battalions', all of which have three 'maneuver' companies. The internal brigade organisation has been abolished, but each division contains three brigade headquarters which can control from two to five battalions as assigned by the divisional commander. Extra battalions, up to a total of 15, may be assigned by the corps commander. The artillery of the armoured and mechanised divisions can fire nuclear projectiles. The organisation of the airborne division is fairly similar to that of the 'type' divisions. That of the airmobile divisions is the subject of experiment (TRICAP, meaning 'triple capability').

The divisional base consists of: headquarters and HQ company; three brigade headquarters and HQ companies; one armoured cavalry (reconnaissance) squadron; one air-defence, one engineer and one signal battalion; one military police company; one aviation company (armoured and mechanised divisions) *or* one aviation battalion (infantry divisions), the divisional artillery – one Honest John battalion, three field artillery battalions (of 105mm howitzers in the infantry division, of 155mm SP howitzers in the armoured and mechanised divisions) and one 8in howitzer battalion (in the infantry division a mixed battalion of towed 8in and 155mm howitzers) – and a divisional support command (DISCOM) which contains one medical, one maintenance and one supply and transport battalion and administrative units. The air-defence battalion contains 24 20mm radar-controlled guns

and 24 Chaparral missile launchers. The aircraft strength is eighty-eight in the infantry divisions and sixty-one in the armoured and mechanised divisions, the difference being due to the large size of the infantry division's aviation unit, which has 37 helicopters instead of ten.

The 'maneuver' element of the division is:

Armoured division: six tank battalions and five mechanised infantry battalions
Mechanised infantry division: five tank battalions and six mechanised infantry battalions
Infantry Division: one tank battalion, one mechanised infantry battalion and eight infantry battalions (the tank battalion has 54 tanks)

The airborne division's organisation differs from that of the 'Type' divisions in that its nine battalions are all infantry, its artillery consists only of three 105mm howitzer battalions, and its signal, engineer, reconnaissance and other units are smaller in size and lighter in equipment.

The airmobile (Air Assault) division (which in Vietnam comprised helicopter-borne infantry battalions) is undergoing trials in triple capability role, for which it will probably be definitively organised with one helicopter and two conventional brigades.

Corps and Armies

The organisations of formations superior to the divisions has recently been changed (Echelon Above Divisions concept), to eliminate the numbered field army and its support command (FASCOM). Henceforward the corps is to be the main command and administrative formation intermediate between divisions and Theater Armies, e.g. United States Army Europe. The Theater Army will, however, retain its support command (TASCOM).

Corps troops will compromise: one corps headquarters and HQ company; the corps artillery (175mm gun, and Pershing and Sergeant missile battalions); one air-defence artillery; one engineer, one signal and one aviation brigade; one (or more) armoured cavalry (reconnaissance) regiment; one military intelligence, one psychological operations and one smoke generator battalion; one air cavalry squadron; one army security agency group; and the corps support commands (COSCOM) containing one medical and one civil affairs brigade, and transport, military police, administration, automatic data processing, movement control, material management, ammunition and support groups.

Theater Army troops comprise headquarters, artillery and air-defence artillery as assigned, and the support command (TASCOM) which contains personnel, medical, transportation, supply and maintenance, engineer and area support commands (respectively, in acronyms, PERSCOM, MEDCOM, TRANSCOM, SMCOM, ENCOM and ASCOM). The area in which these commands operate is known as the Communications Zone (COMMZ); the area forward of that, in which corps and divisions operate, is know as the Combat Zone.

Army Aviation

The United States air force jealously surveys army aviation to ensure that it does not encroach upon its functions or duplicate its equipment. In deference to American susceptibilities, army aviation is organised neither as an 'arm' nor a 'service'; it exists as a 'quasi-arm'. It is nevertheless a strong and important element of the army, with 18,000 fixed- and rotary-wing aircraft. All divisions have an aviation battalion, and each infantry division an aviation company. All divisional (armoured and mechanised) armoured cavalry (reconnaissance) squadrons have an 'air cavalry' (helicopter) troop.

Corps and armies contain additional light, medium and heavy helicopter units and fixed-wing units.

National Guard and Army Reserves

The organisation of units of these 'reserve components' is on paper exactly similar to those of the Active Army. In practice, the Army Reserve acts principally as a pool of reinforcements, though some progress is being made with 'affiliation programs' which will bring chosen units to a state of combat-readiness. It is intended that the National Guard should provide, in case of mobilisation and within 5 weeks, eight combat divisions, 18 separate combat brigades and some smaller units; but it is likely that effective mobilisation would take longer – neither Reserve furnishes formations larger than a division. A Selected Reserve Force (SRF), composed of elements of both reserves, is designed to provide immediate reinforcement of six divisions and three brigades on call.

The United States Marine Corps

Arms of Service

In theory, the USMC is a homogeneous corps. In practice, there is a strong division between the air and ground units, and within the ground units a fair degree of specialisation – artillery, amphibious transportation, military police, etc. The USMC does not, however, divide itself into 'arms' and 'services' as does the army.

Operational

The Corps consists of three active divisions (see Role, Commitment, Deployment and Recent Operations) and a reserve division. Each consists of three Marine regiments, each of three battalions of four rifle companies. Its support elements include: one artillery regiment; and one engineer, one reconnaissance, one anti-tank, one service, one medical and one headquarters battalion. Heavier support is assigned to so-called Force Troops, the equivalent of the army corps, but of variable composition. It is weaker in transport and supply facilities than an army division because much of its personnel, equipment and stores are seaborne; it is also weaker in artillery, because it can normally depend on the support of an affiliated Marine Air Wing (MAW) and of naval gunnery. A division provides the nucleus of the two Fleet Marine Forces: 2nd Division to the Atlantic Fleet (with a detachment to the Sixth Fleet in the Mediterranean) and 3rd Division to the Pacific Fleet. As needed, each Fleet Marine Force can provide a Marine Amphibious Unit (MAU – a battalion-sized landing team plus helicopter squadron) Brigade (MAO – regimental-sized landing team, plus helicopter group) or Force (MAF – a Marine division and Marine Air Wing).

An Air Wing has no fixed strength but usually contains eight fixed-wing tactical aircraft squadrons, three fixed-wing transport or observation squadrons and seven helicopter squadrons (heavy, medium, light and attack) in all about 400 aircraft. (Total in USMC Air Wings (1975): 1227 in active wings and 205 in reserve wings.)

Reserves

The Organised Marine Corps Reserve provides the manpower for the 4th Marine Division and 4th Marine Air Wing (Camp Pendleton, California). Reservists serve short terms to keep the division constantly in being. Members of the OMCR, like National Guardsmen, are ineligible for conscription and during the Vietnam war it quickly reached its authorised strength of 40,000. Between 1972–4 it fell to 32,000.

Paramilitary Forces

None exists at the Federal level, since the maintenance of law and order is the concern of the individual States. They rely on their National Guard units to contain disorders which overtax the power of the civil police. Against disorders which result from the refusal of a State government to operate federal law, the President may authorise the employment of Active Army troops (as did President Eisenhower at Little Rock, Arkansas in 1957); he may also lend Active Army units to a State Governor on request, as President Johnson did to the Governor of Michigan in 1967; disorder in both cases was the outcome of black–white conflict. Each State maintains a police force (usually State Troopers) with State-wide authority, outside the municipalities which possess their own police troops. Some of the larger municipalities have, since the outbreak of serious racial conflict in the early 1960s, formed 'Police Tactical Units' but neither these nor the State Troopers equate in size or resources or legal powers to the gendarmeries of European States.

RECRUITMENT, TRAINING AND RESERVES

Recruitment

Soldiers

Since June 30th 1974 the draft (the federal machinery of conscription) has been in 'zero operation', that is, the legal authority to conscript remains in force but the armed services have recruited by voluntary enlistment. The army's authorised strength is 785,000 and in the fiscal year 1973–4 182,000 volunteers were recruited.

In February 1980, however, President Carter announced the re-introduction of registration for selective service, and Congress voted the necessary funds in July. An amendment to include the registration of women was defeated in both houses. To maintain numbers at the required level 200,000 were required for 1974–5. To encourage enlistment a 'combat arms' bonus, a pay rise and the right to serve in a chosen unit were granted in 1973. Minimum enlistment is for 2 years. Re-engagement is permitted for additional periods as long as soldiers progress up the NCO or 'specialist' ladder. The 'specialist' ladder is equivalent to the NCOs', offering promotion from Specialist 4 (corporal) to Specialist 7 (sergeant first class) but without command responsibility. Under the 'cohort scheme', introduced in 1981, 10% of recruits are training in units in which they will serve together the first two years of their enlistment. The scheme is modelled on the British Regimental system.

Officers

Officers may be recuited either from the United States Military Academy, West Point (a small minority), or through the Reserve Officer Training Corps (ROTC) (the majority), or by promotion from the ranks (in very small numbers). Officers of specialist corps – Medical, Chaplains, Army Nurse Corps – are commissioned direct from civil life. ROTC officers are granted reserve commissions but may later apply to become regular officers; a few outstanding applicants are granted regular commissions from the onset. However, many serving officers remain 'Reserve Officers on Active Duty' throughout their career and retire as such on pension. Retirement on pension is possible for United States officers after 20 years. West Point officers must serve a minimum of 5 years from graduation. They are still selected, as they have been since 1843, by Congressmen (except for 14% of the academy's strength, selected by competitive examination among serving soldiers and deceased veterans' sons). Each

Congressman may nominate from his district one 'principal' and one 'alternative', or allow the academy to choose from six nominees. Most Congressmen submit applicants to examination on an approved syllabus before making their nomination. The system remains decentralised, nonetheless, and is an interesting example of the constitutional separation of powers.

Training

Soldiers

Soldiers receive 8 weeks of basic combat training at one of three training centres in the First, Fifth and Sixth Army areas, then proceed to individual training which may last from 5 to 44 weeks depending on specialisation (401 are taught by the army) at one of the Army Service Schools. He then joins his unit and enters its unit training cycle.

The Army Service Schools (which may also be attended by officers and NCOs) and are directed by the Training and Doctrine Command, are:

Adjutant General School, Fort Harrison, Ind.
Air Defence School, Fort Bliss, Tex.
Armour School, Fort Knox, Ky.
Artillery and Missile School, Fort Sill, Okla.
Aviation School, Fort Rucker, Ala.
Chaplain School, Fort Hamilton, N.Y.
Chemical School, Fort McClellan, Ala.
Civil Affairs School, Fort Gordon, Ga.
Combat Surveillance School, Fort Huachuca, Ariz.
Engineer School, Fort Belvoir, Va.
Finance School, Fort Harrison, Md.
Infantry School, Fort Benning, Ga.
Intelligence School, Fort Holabird, Md.
Judge Advocate General School, Charlottesville, Va.,
Management School, Fort Belvoir, Va.
Medical Field Services School, Fort Houston, Tex.
Military Police School, Fort Gordon, Ga.
Ordnance School, Aberdeen Proving Ground, Md.
Missile and Munitions School, Redstone Arsenal, Ala.
Primary Helicopters School, Fort Walters, Tex.
Quartermaster School, Fort Lee, Va.
Signal School, Fort Monmouth, N.J.
S.E. Signal School, Fort Gordon, Ga.
Special Warfare School, Fort Bragg, N.C.
Transportation School, Fort Eustis, Va.

The Northern Warfare Training Centre in Alaska teaches Arctic warfare and the School of the Americas, Panama Canal Zone, teaches jungle warfare, both to United States and Latin American soldiers; the medium of instruction is Spanish.

Officers

ROTC training is administered through four ROTC Regions under TRADOC and is offered in some 250 colleges and universities, including a number of civilian 'military academies' of which the oldest and best-known is the Virginia Military Institute (VMI) at which Stonewall Jackson taught and from which George C. Marshall graduated. Students joining ROTC receive part-time training, to fit in with their academic timetable spread over 4 years. They may be eligible for some pay and a contribution to their fees. On graduation, those commissioned into the Army Reserve proceed to branch training at the School (see above) of their branch.

The USMA course at West Point is of 4 years and is largely academic in character, its aim being to equip each cadet with a high-quality bachelor's degree in science, the arts or en-

gineering (the latter the traditional though now a minority subject). Military training is largely confined to the summer months, though military discipline prevails at all times. West Point graduates also proceed to branch training on graduation. All combat arm officers must complete Airborne and Ranger courses.

The branch training course lasts 9—16 weeks, and is followed by 3—8 years of regimental duty. Every regular officer must then complete his branch career course of 9 months, at the appropriate Army Service School. Thereafter officer training is on a selective basis, and selection is increasingly important for promotion. The Command and General Staff College, Fort Leavenworth, Kansas, offers a 1 year course to officers with 9—16 years' service, for which 60% of combat arms officers and 20% of services officers are selected; without its qualification, promotion beyond lieutenant-colonel is rare. The Armed Services Staff College, Norfolk, Virginia, is an inter-service school, offering a 5 month course, which 15% of regular officers attend as an alternative to the C and GSC (an officer may not attend both). The Army War College, Carlisle Barracks, Pennsylvania and the National War College and Industrial College of the Armed Forces, both at Fort McNair, Washington D.C., offer 1 year courses to officers with 15—23 years' service. About 15% of regular officers attend one of these Schools (the NWC and ICAF are inter-service); without that qualification, promotion to general rank is rare (of the 519 generals in the army in 1972, only two had not attended War College). The NWC and ICAF have recently been combined as the National Defense University.

The United States army, like the navy and air force, encourages and finances officers to gain higher degrees at civilian universities and it is now reckoned that possession of a master's degree is becoming a precondition for promotion to general. But the army also requires the specialist officers which its financing of in-service graduate education produces, while many officers seek such education with a view to finding a civilian career if promotion does not come their way. (In recent years, an increasing number of West Point graduates have used the esteem attaching to its bachelor's degree to leave the army at the earlier permissible point.)

The Marine Corps is and always has been an all-volunteer body. Its men receive basic training at Parris Island, South Carolina, and individual training at the Marine Corps Schools, Quantico, Virginia, which is also the training centre for officers recruited through ROTC or from the ranks. Regular officers are educated at the United States Naval Academy, Annapolis, Md.

Reserves

See Role, Commitment, Deployment and Recent Operations, and Organisation.

EQUIPMENT AND ARMS INDUSTRY

The United States is the largest arms exporter and has the largest arms industry in the non-communist world, but it is of comparatively recent origin: as late as 1917 the American army, on its arrival in Europe, had to be supplied with artillery by the French and tanks by the British (who had also provided many of the arms used by the North in the Civil War). It was not until President and Congress took the decision, early in World War II, to supply arms to Britain, first on a cash and carry basis, then on a lend-lease basis, that any sizeable fraction of the country's enormous industrial base was mobilised for war purposes. That it was mobilised with such speed and efficiency as to make America, by 1943, the

'Arsenal of Democracy', was due in part to a large portion of its capacity having lain idle since the slump of 1929–32 but in great measure to the adaptability of the labour force. Naturally, it was also an important contributory factor that much of American industrial capacity lay in automobile, aircraft, machinery, machine tools and chemical production, which required the minimum (though still very extensive) retooling to be turned to military purposes.

Had America reverted to custom, her industry would after 1945 have been demobilised and returned almost exclusively to civilian production. Much of it indeed was, and during 1947–9 the country underwent its worst severe post-war economic recession until 1973. Because, however, the scale of defence investment between 1941 and 1944 (in which period spending on war material increased from $2,100,000,000 to $57,700,000,000 at constant prices) industrial capacity had been created which would not quickly be converted to civilian use, and before reconversion was complete the outbreak of the Korean war had regenerated demand for its output. Continuing world tension and a rapidly changing arms technology have required ever since that large sections of American scientific, technological and industrial endeavour should be directed into defence research, development and production.

The United States army has itself become a major arms and munitions manufacturer operating (a) army ammunition plants at Radford, Virginia; Scranton, Pennsylvania; Milan and Holston, Tennessee; Marshall, Texas; Shreveport, Louisiana; Newport and Charlestown, Indiana; Burlington, Iowa; and Independence, Missouri; (b) army missile plants at Charlotte and Burlington, North Carolina; and Warren, Michigan; (c) the army ordnance plant at Joliet, Illinois; (d) the army tank–automotive plant at Cleveland, Ohio; (e) the army engine plant at Muskegon, Michigan; and (f) arsenals at Edgewood, Maryland; Frankford, Pennsylvania; Dover, New Jersey; Watertown and Watervliet, Massachusetts; Redstone, Alabama; Pine Bluff, Arkansas; Detroit, Michigan; Rock Island, Illinois; and Denver, Colorado. A very large number of private corporations manufacture equipment for the army, the most important are: Colt Industries, Hartford, Connecticut; Maremont Corporation, Saco, Maine (small arms); Bowen–McGlaughlin–York, York, Pennsylvania (artillery); Cadillac Gage Corporation, Detroit, Michigan; Pacific Car and Foundry Corporation, Renton, Washington; Chrysler Corporation, Detroit, Michigan; General Motors, Allison Division, Indianapolis, Indiana; Food Machinery and Chemical Corporation, San José, California (tracked and wheeled vehicles and tanks); Hughes Aircraft Company, Culver City, California; General Dynamics Corporation (Pomona Division), San Diego, California; Philco–Ford Corporation, Newport Beach, California; Sperry Rand Corporation, Salt Lake City, Utah; McDonnell–Douglas Corporation, Huntington Beach, California; Martin Marietta Corporation (Orlando Division), Orlando, Florida; LTV (Ling–Temco–Vought) Aerospace Corporation (Michigan Division), Warren, Michigan; Raytheon Company, Lexington, Massachusetts (anti-armour, surface-to-air, air-to-air, and surface-to-surface missiles); Boeing Company (Vertol Division), Seattle, Washington; Bell Aerospace Company, Buffalo, New York; and Sikorsky Aircraft, Stratford, Connecticut (army aircraft).

Equipment

Small Arms
  Pistol: 0.45 in Colt
  Rifle: M-16 5.56mm automatic (Colt)
  Sub-machine-gun: M-3 0.45 in
  Light machine-gun: M-14 A1 7.62mm (Colt)

Medium machine-gun: M-60 7.62mm (Maremont Corporation)
Grenade launcher: M-79 40mm
Grenade launcher (heavy): M-2 0.5 in (Browning)
Mortars: light: M-224 60mm; medium: M-29 81mm; heavy: M-30 4.2 in
Anti-armour weapons: light: M-72 66mm one-shot throw-away missile (General Dynamics); medium: M-47 Dragon missile (McDonnell–Douglas) (10,400 in service); heavy: M-151 TOW missile (Hughes Aircraft Co.; can be helicopter mounted) (6200); Hellfire
Anti-aircraft weapons: light: Redeye (one-man, shoulder-fired missile; General Dynamics); medium: M-139 20mm vehicle-mounted cannon (Hispano–Oerlikon; manufactured in United States army arsenals); M-163 Vulcan Air Defence System (M-61 20mm cannon on M-113 chassis; General Electric Co.; equips the air-defence battalion; 2600 in service); and Chaparral missile on M-548 truck (Philco–Ford; equips the air-defence battalion (600 in service); heavy: Hawk missile (Raytheon) (to be replaced by Patriot)
Artillery: light M-102 105mm howitzer (United States Army Arsenals; equips the artillery of the airborne and airmobile division); medium: M-114 155mm howitzer (United States Army Arsenals; equips the field artillery of the infantry division); M-109 155mm SP howitzer (Cadillac–Chrysler–Allison (General Motors); equips the field artillery of the armoured and mechanised division); heavy: M-110 8in SP howitzer (Bowen–McGlaughlin–York; equips the howitzer battalion of the infantry, armoured and mechanised division; can fire a nuclear shell) and M-107 175mm SP gun (Pacific Car and Foundry Co./FMC Corporation/Bowen–McGlaughlin–York; equips the gun battalion of the corps artillery)
Missile Artillery: Pershing guided missile (450 mile range, 1 KT warhead; Martin Marietta); Lance guided missile (70 mile range, 1 KT warhead; LTV Aero-Space Corp.)
Armour: APC: M-113 (Food Machinery and Chemical Corp.; equips the mechanised infantry battalion; exists in a variety of versions – M-114, M-577, etc.); Bradley Mechanised infantry combat vehicle coming into service. Light (reconnaissance) tank: M-551 General Sheridan (Allison (General Motors); now only in airborne units. Gun: 152mm Shillelagh smooth bore; engine 300 h.p.; range 350 miles; speed 45 m.p.h.; crew four); Medium tank: M-60 (Chrysler; equips the tank battalion. Gun: 105mm (some with Shillelagh, *see above*); engine 750 h.p.; range 310 miles; speed 30 m.p.h.; crew four). *Note:* some M-48 tanks are still in service. M-1 Abrams tank coming into service. About 12,000 tanks in service in all.
Aircraft: Observation helicopter: OH-6A Cayuse (Hughes Aircraft Co.; on issue to all divisional aviation units and to the divisional headquarters and artillery); Utility helicopter: UH-IC/D/G/H (various models), Iroquois (Huey) and Bell 204 (Bell Helicopter Co.; tactical armed transport eight soldiers); equips the divisional air cavalry troop, the divisional company, the combat aviation (battalion) and the combat aviation group of the air mobile division) Attack helicopter: AH-IG Huey Cobra (Bell 204) (Bell Helicopter Co.; two-seat gun-ship; employment as for Iroquois, which it complements); Medium transport helicopter: CH-47 Chinook (Boeing Vertol; the transport aircraft of the combat aviation group of the airmobile division)

The utility and attack helicopters are equipped with a variety of air-to-ground missiles, and machine-guns for anti-armour and anti-personnel missions.

Equipment in development: major items under development

United States of America

or coming into production are the Bradley mechanised infantry combat vehicle to replace the obsolescent M-113 APC; the Abrams M-1 main battle tank to replace the M-60; an advanced attack helicopter (AAH), for which Bell and Hughes have each submitted designs, and which will carry the Hellfire 'fire and forget' anti-armour missile; a utility and transport helicopter (UTTAS) to replace the AH-1 Huey; and a battlefield air-defence system, SMA-D. The heavy artillery is also to be re-equipped with a modern version of the M-110 8in self-propelled howitzer, replacing the old M-110 and the M-107 175mm gun; a new towed 105mm howitzer (XM-204) is also under development.

RANK, DRESS AND DISTINCTIONS

Commissioned Ranks

General of the Army — Five silver stars
General — Four silver stars
Lieutenant-general (*LTG*) — Three silver stars
Major-general (*MG*) — Two silver stars
Brigadier-general (*BG*) — One silver star
Colonel (*COL*) — Silver eagle
Lieutenant-colonel (*LTC*) — Silver leaf
Major — Gold leaf
Captain — Two silver bars
First-lieutenant — One silver bar
Second-lieutenant — One gold bar

Warrant Ranks

Warrant Officer W-4 — Three brown stripes on silver bar
Warrant Officer W-3 — Two brown stripes on silver bar
Warrant Officer W-2 — Three brown stripes on gold bar
Warrant Officer W-1 — Two brown stripes on gold bar

Enlisted Grades

Command Sergeant Major E-9 — Three chevrons, three rocker bars†, star and laurel between
Staff Sergeant Major E-9 — Three chevrons, three rocker bars, star between
First Sergeant E-8 — Three chevrons, three rocker bars, lozenge between
Master Sergeant E-8 — Three chevrons, three rocker bars
Platoon Sergeant (*Sergeant 1st Class*) *E-7* — Three chevrons two rocker bars
Staff Sergeant E-6 — Three chevrons, one rocker bar
Sergeant E-5 — Three chevrons
Corporal E-4 — Two chevrons
Private First Class E-3 — One chevron, one rocker bar
Private E-2 — One chevron
Recruit E-1 — —

Specialist Grades*

Specialist 7 — Three inverted rocker bars over eagle (*see* Specialist 4)
Specialist 6 — Two inverted rocker bars over eagle
Specialist 5 — One inverted rocker bar over eagle
Specialist 4 — Eagle on chevron-shaped patch

Commissioned ranks and warrant ranks wear badges of rank on the shoulder; enlisted grades on the upper sleeve.

* Specialists rank after the enlisted grade of the same number (Specialist 7 is equivalent to Platoon Sergeant E-7). Neither they nor the warrant officers (who mess with the commissioned officers) possess command authority.
† 'Rocker bars' are ellipses, ends upward, which join ends of upward-pointing chevrons.

Dress

Walking-out dress is a dark-green tunic and trousers, worn with pale-green shirt and black tie, and dark-green peaked cap; branch badges are worn on the lapel (the same in light khaki for summer). Officers may, and some ceremonial units do, wear a dark-blue version. Combat dress is dull-green tunic and trousers; the World War II (now NATO) helmet is still worn.

Distinctions

The army awards a variety of decorations, of which the highest for bravery is the (Congressional) Medal of Honour, instituted in July, 1861. Lesser awards for bravery are the Distinguished Service Cross and Medal, the Silver Star and the Bronze Star. The Purple Heart (instituted by George Washington in 1782 — re-instituted in 1933) is awarded for injury in combat, the Soldier's Medal for heroism not involving actual conflict. 'Commendation' medals may be awarded for lesser acts or achievements and especially distinguished units may be awarded Presidential Citations, a badge signifying this is worn by their members. These citations also decorate the colours, of which regiments carry two: a national colour (Stars and Stripes) and a regimental, in the appropriate branch colour (yellow for cavalry, blue for infantry, scarlet for artillery, etc.). The army has also awarded a large number of campaign medals.

CURRENT DEVELOPMENTS

The United States army has recovered well from the disabling experience it underwent in the Vietnam War. It has reorganised sensibly to produce a larger number of tactical formations than it could field before the war on a smaller manpower base, and is re-equipping them with a well-chosen range of new weapons. Its drug abuse, disciplinary and racial problems have been almost completely eliminated, its morale is high and the quality of volunteer it is able to recruit has been high during the economically depressed times in which the 'zero draft' has operated.

Its main difficulty is that its manpower requirements are, because of the short term for which most recruits enlist, very large and threaten indeed to exceed the numbers available. It has sought, as have the other services, to alleviate the problem by increasing the number of women enlisted, and their numbers multiplied four-fold in 4 years (from 13,000 to 51,000). Under equal opportunity legislation, it has also thrown open its career structure to women, excluding them only from combat assignments, which are forbidden to them by law. But that does not exclude them from non-combat duty in combat formations (above brigade level), to which many have been assigned. The willingness of male combat soldiers to accept routine orders from female superiors is thus becoming a subject for speculation in the ranks, since its reality cannot be long delayed.

Continuing difficulty in integrating women into formerly all-male units, however, and the unresolved issue of women's adaptability to combat conditions led to a pause in female recruiting at the end of 1981. As it now seems unlikely that the Equal Rights Amendment will be ratified by a sufficient number of states to become law, it is possible that the army will henceforth allow the proportion of enlisted women to diminish.

Operationally the most important development in the US Army since the last edition of *World Armies* has been the creation of the Rapid Deployment Joint Task Force (RDJTF), on March 1, 1980. On April 24th, 1981, the Defense Secretary announced that it will evolve into a unified command, with its own geographic responsibilities. The designated area will be South-West Asia, into which it will be RDJTF's mission to project US power as recognised in emergency. The force, commanded directly by the Joint Chiefs of Staff, has subordinate to it five fighter wings, and ancillary wings of surveillance, reconnaissance and transport squadrons; three naval carrier groups, a surface action group and squadrons of naval aircraft and logistic ships; a Marine amphibious brigade (7th); and three divisions (82nd, 101st, 24th Infantry) and one brigade (6th) of the army. The headquarters of RDJTF is at Tampa, Florida. Its forward operating base will be at Diego Garcia in the Indian Ocean; another island base is to be built off the coast of Oman. The aim of the RDJTF will be to position a battalion in the Persian Gulf area in 48 hours from warning, an airborne division in two weeks and a seaborne division in one month. Major exercises – 'Bright Star' in Egypt in 1980 and 'Bright Star 82' (1981) in Egypt, Sudan, Somalia and Oman – have already practised the necessary drills and deployments.

John Keegan

USSR

HISTORY AND INTRODUCTION

There is considerable truth in V. S. Soloviev's assertion that 'the history of Russia is the history of wars'. During the Middle Ages Russia was a loose collection of warring principalities, and in 1223 Mongol victory at the battle of the Kalka initiated a long period of Mongol rule. It was not until 1480 that Ivan III ceased paying tribute to the Mongols: he also styled himself 'ruler of all Russia', clearly stating the supremacy of his own principality, Moscow.

Ivan III conquered Novgorod in 1478, and Ivan IV brought yet more territory under Moscow's control: the khanates of Kazan and Astrakhan were overwhelmed in 1553 and 1556, respectively and substantial advances were made on the Volga, in the Crimea and in Siberia. The victories of the early tsars were won by armies of a markedly mediaeval character, consisting primarily of forces raised by great nobles, backed by small numbers of professional soldiers, the *streltsy*. An army of this sort had obvious disadvantages, and Peter the Great (1689–1725) set about providing Russia with an army more suitable for an expanding State. He disbanded the *streltsy*, after a bloody mutiny, and founded the Preobrazhensky and Semionovsky regiments, which may be regarded as the first units of the Russian regular army. A primitive form of conscription was introduced, and members of the nobility were obliged to serve as officers. Peter's army inflicted a decisive defeat upon Charles XII of Sweden at Poltava (1709), and the Peace of Nystadt (1721) made Russia a Baltic power. The capital was shifted from Moscow to the new city of St. Petersburg, and the bustling shipyards of the Neva gave Russia a fleet of Western-style warships.

The political trumoils which followed Peter's death did not prevent the continued improvement of the army. Its successes against the Turks brought Russia the lands between the Bug and the Dniester, and a short war with Persia saw the extension of Russian influence into Georgia and Transcaucasia. The most notable military leader of the period was General Alexander Suvorov, whose emphasis upon speed, decisiveness and the maintenance of morale was to make him an attractive figure even after the Revolution of 1917.

The accession of the unstable Paul I in 1796 brought with it the introduction of Prussian-style formalism. Although Paul reigned for only 5 years, the consequences of his military policies were to prove long-lasting. Paul was succeeded by his son Alexander I, whose initial liberalism was reflected as much in his dealings with the army as it was in his strivings for political reform. Alexander had, however, become suspicious and reactionary by the time of his death in 1825, and the army reverted to the parade-ground Prussianism of Paul I. Alexander's brother, Nicholas I, was a confirmed reactionary in all respects, and the army continued to be more concerned with the minutiae of dress and drill than with the need to improve tactics, training and recruitment. Nicholas's internal policy was based upon the three principles of autocracy, orthodoxy and nationalism. His foreign policy was heavily influenced by pan-Slavism, and his pressure upon Turkey led to the Crimean War of 1854–5. This conflict revealed the failings of the autocratic system and the weaknesses of the Russian army: it was a condemnation of a military system based upon long-service conscription and the extinction of individual initiative.

Alexander II was an'altogether more sympathetic character than his father Nicholas. Assisted by the capable Nicholai Miliutin he abolished serfdom in 1861 and subsequently introduced limited measures of local self-government. The army was reformed and universal conscription was introduced in 1874. The performance of Alexander's army was impressive. Russia's hold on the Caucasus was consolidated by the mid-1860s, and in central Asia Russian forces advanced to Tashkent, Samarkand and Khiva. Military victories over Turkey in the war of 1877–8, however, brought little material recompense, and the ensuring peace treaty damaged Russia's relations with Germany and Austria–Hungary.

Russian defeat in the Russo-Japanese war of 1904–5 discredited the regime and was followed by a wave of strikes and disturbances. The defeat was not an accurate index of the army's defects: it reflected rather the shortcomings of Russian strategy and the errors of senior commanders. These deficiencies had not been fully remedied when war broke out in 1914, and the disaster incurred by Russian forces at Tannenberg in East Prussia was the result of atrocious generalship and poor staff-work. Tannenberg did serious damage to the Russian army: losses in regular officers and NCOs, and in equipment, were very heavy, and confidence in the High Command was inevitably shaken. The army had better fortune in its struggle against the Austrians. The Brusilov offensive of 1916 inflicted irreparable damage upon the Austro–Hungarian army, but Russian casualties were, for the third year running, appallingly severe. Russia's economy and transport system proved unable to bear the strain of a long war, and serious food shortages contributed to war-weariness. The army's morale had, understandably, deteriorated, but it is significant that the first signs of collapse came not from the fighting units at the front but from replacement depots in Petrograd.

Revolution broke out in March, 1917. A liberal Provisional Government, dominated by middle-class intellectuals, was established following the tsar's abdication. In November this body was itself overthrown by Lenin and the Bolsheviks, who proclaimed a Federated Socialist Republic and in March, 1918 brought Russia out of the war with the treaty of Brest–Litovsk. The military logic behind the conclusion of peace was sound enough. The events of 1917 had inevitably worsened the already unsatisfactory state of the army. The Provisional Government had abolished military discipline and instituted soldiers' committees. Desertion was rife: over 2,000,000 men had left the colours by September, 1917. The Bolsheviks were faced with the urgent need to create an army both strong and reliable enough to defend them from their foreign enemies and internal opponents. They initially employed enthusiastic Communist Red Guards and sailors from the Baltic Fleet, but a decree of January 28th, 1918 brought the Red Army of Workers and Peasants into existence. Compulsory military service was reintroduced in April and conscription recommended in June. Many former imperial officers and NCOs were called up: some, like the future marshals Tukhachevski, Shaposhnikov and Egorov, rejoined the army voluntarily.

Essential though the employment of ex-officers was, it gave rise to problems of political reliability. The loyalty of these ex-officers, or 'military specialists', as they were known, was ensured by the attachment of a political commissar to every unit. The commissar system, which has survived, in a modified form, to the present day, was not without its disadvantages. All orders had to be signed by both commander and commissar, and it was not uncommon for there to be serious friction between the two individuals. The fighting against foreign interventionists and White forces dragged on until 1922. By this time the Red Army had developed considerably. It numbered over 5,000,000 men, organised conventionally in brigades and divisions. Discipline had to some extent been restored, but the system of dual command persisted and the concept of personal military rank was shunned. Two rival groups had crystallised within the army during the Civil War. One, the 'Red Cavalry' faction, included the future marshals Budenny, Voroshilov and Timoshenko: it enjoyed the influential support of Josef Stalin. The other faction was centred upon Leon Trotsky, Commissar for War and perhaps the single most important architect of victory in the fighting of 1918–22. Trotsky had opposed the Red Army's disastrous advance on Warsaw in the summer of 1920. He agreed with the military specialists that certain universal principles, as relevant to Soviet Russia as they were to the capitalist West, underlie military science. His rival, M. V. Frunze, claimed, on the other hand, that a Communist State should develop its own military ideology.

Trotsky was unseated in 1925 and replaced as War Commissar by Frunze. The latter died after only 5 months in office, but his reforms were of the greatest importance. The Red Army Staff was streamlined into the General Staff, and the country was divided into two armies, stationed in areas where fighting was still going on, and a number of military districts. The army, navy and air force were reorganised, and the power of the commissars was reduced. Tentative advances were also made towards the reintroduction of drill and smartness, but the egalitarian nature of military service was still stressed and commanders enjoyed no personal privileges.

K. E. Voroshilov became Commissar of the Army and Navy in December, 1925. Despite Frunze's reforms, the condition of the army left much to be desired: there was a serious shortage of modern equipment, and the position of the commander was far from satisfactory. Military collaboration between Germany and the Soviet Union had commenced in 1921, and by 1928 this co-operation was at an advanced stage. It ceased in 1933, but by this time the foundations of native Russian armaments industry had been laid. Western Siberia and the Urals were opened up to industry, and new industrial centres were established in European Russia. M. N. Tukhachevski, appointed Inspector of Armaments in 1931, was largely responsible for developing the tactical and strategic doctrine which, linked with the growing capacity of the Russian armaments industry, resulted in the mechanisation programme. Tukhachevski shared Frunze's belief that any attack upon the Soviet Union should be met with a massive counter-offensive, the aim of which should be rapid and decisive Soviet victory. He recognised the vast potential of armoured vehicles, and was well aware of the importance of inter-arm co-operation.

The first mechanised brigade was created in 1930, and several mechanised corps were set up 2 years later. In 1933 Tukhachevski's ideas were tried out in a series of major exercises in which mechanised units trained with parachutists, cavalry, infantry and artillery in a battle of breakthrough and encirclement. This period also witnessed the reorganisation of the central administration, whose existing bodies were replaced by the People's Commissariat of Defence, controlled by a Defence Commissar assisted by eleven deputies. The gradual increase in the proportion of commanders of proletarian origin made possible the improvement of their status. The commissars were reduced in improvement March,

1934 and personal ranks for some military commanders were reintroduced the following year. Five leading officers, including Voroshilov and Tukhachevski, were appointed to the new rank of Marshal of the Soviet Union. Steps were taken to improve officer education: a general staff academy was opened in 1936, and other military academies were improved and enlarged.

By 1936 the Red Army contained nearly 1,500,000 men, equipped with an impressive array of modern weapons. Its tactical doctrine was remarkably advanced, and many of its senior commanders were men of great ability. There were, however, numerous imperfections: officer and NCO training was still uneven, mechanisation was far from complete, and there was a substantial gap between tactical concepts and the real standard of training. Nor was the Red Army without a dangerous rival. The Peoples' Commissariat of Internal Affairs (NKVD) controlled not only the police, frontier guards and security troops, but also had its own well-equipped army of 150,000 men. There had been friction between the Red Army and the NKVD for some time, and the latter's activities in Spain during the Civil War served only to worsen army–NKVD relations. Purges within the Communist Party were by no means a new phenomenon, but that which commenced in the summer of 1936 was to have serious effects upon the army. The NKVD was more than ready to assist Stalin in his attempts to eliminate any possible political rivals, particularly when the latter were to be found within the army.

Several senior officers were arrested in May and June, 1937 and in the following month eight leading officers, including Tukhachevski himself, were arrested, tried for treason, and shot. During the next year up to 35,000 officers were executed, imprisoned or dismissed. They included three out of five Marshals of the Soviet Union, 13 out of 15 army commanders and all 11 Deputy Commissars of Defence. The purges had a cataclysmic effect upon morale: fear of denunciation dominated the lives of commanders and commissars at all levels. Officers of ability and experience were sacrificed, and the army was deprived of the men who had planned the mechanisation programme and correctly foreseen the pattern of future war. Yet even at the height of the purges the Red Army gave proof of its mettle. In the summer of 1938 Marshal V. K. Blukher, soon to fall victim to the NKVD, defeated the Japanese around Lake Khasan, south-West of Vladivostok, and a year later the Japanese were again vanquished, this time by G. K Zhukov, at Khalkin Gol on the Mongolian–Manchurian border.

The Ribbentrop–Molotov pact of August, 1939 paved the way for Russian occupation of eastern Poland the following month. The pact also placed the Baltic States within the Soviet sphere of influence, but although Latvia, Lithuania and Estonia gave Russia the required concessions, Finland proved obdurate. In late November the Red Army mounted an offensive against the Finns. The campaign initially went very badly for the Russians, and it was not until March, 1940 that Finland was at last forced to give up the unequal struggle.

The Russo–Finnish war revealed numerous shortcomings within the Red Army, and S. K. Timoshenko, who replaced Voroshilov as Defence Commissar, took steps to remedy these defects. The ranks of general and admiral were reintroduced in June, 1940 and in August the commissars, restored to eminence during the purges, were once more reduced in authority. A new code of military discipline came into force in October, and a personnel reshuffle took place within the Defence Commissariat and in the military districts. It was decided to form new mechanised corps, and Timoshenko himself kept a close watch upon the progress of training.

Timoshenko's reforms were only partially successful. They were impeded by equipment shortages, bickering amongst senior officers and a general air of false security. When the Germans lauched their invasion of Russia, early on the morning of June 22nd, 1941 they caught the Red Army in the midst of reorganisation and redeployment. Frontier defences were incomplete, and the Soviet forces stationed behind them were too weak to prevent the Germans from breaking through yet strong enough in armour and manpower for their destruction to have grave results. On June 23rd the *Stavka* (Supreme High Command) of the Armed Forces was set up, and Stalin took over from Timoshenko as its chairman early the next month. He also assumed the post of Commissar for Defence, and, in addition, presided over the State Defence Committee. Stalin was unable to check the German advance. Indeed, his insistence on holding ground at all costs often proved counter-productive, and the Red Army lost heavily in a series of battles of encirclement. German advanced units got to within a dozen miles of Moscow, but a counter-attack launched by Zhukov in early December thrust them back from the capital. Leningrad also held out, albeit at frightful cost to the civilian population.

In 1942 the Germans planned a major offensive with the oilfields around Baku as its prime strategic goal. The plan also called for the establishment of a defensive bulwark along part of the Volga, and the German 6th Army, charged with the task of seizing the industrial centre of Stalingrad and holding part of the Volga line, proved unable to capture the city and was itself enveloped by a Russian counter-offensive. The 6th Army held out until the end of January, 1943. Its collapse, the most serious reverse yet incurred by the *Wehrmacht*, gave a powerful boost to Soviet morale. The failure of German attempts to 'pinch out' the Kursk salient in the summer of 1943 was probably the turning-point in the war in the East: the battle saw the destruction of the last German armoured reserve. And, although Russian losses were also heavy, Soviet industry was by now producing 2000 armoured vehicles and 9000 aircraft each month, and the Kursk losses were soon rectified.

The initiative passed to the Red Army following its repulse of the Kursk offensive. Kharkov was recaptured on August 23rd, Smolensk fell in late September and Kiev in early November. The Russian summer offensive of 1944 brought about the destruction of the German Army Group Centre and the recapture of Minsk and Vilna. Before the year was out Russian troops had occupied Rumania, Finland and much of Hungary, and their advance continued in 1945. The final offensive began on April 16th. Russian soldiers entered the suburbs of Berlin on April 21st, and the city at last fell on May 2nd.

The war with Germany ended a fortnight later, but the Red Army's operations were by no means over. Russia declared war on Japan on August 8th, and on the next day three Soviet fronts (army groups) swept into Japanese-held Manchuria. The ensuing campaign was remarkable for the speed with which Russian armour advanced, the use of airborne troops to seize objectives ahead of the advancing divisions, and widespread reliance upon air supply. The offensive was dramatically successful: over 600,000 prisoners were taken, and the powerful Japanese Kwantung army simply ceased to exist. The lessons of the campaign were not lost on Soviet military theorists, and many of its ingredients were to become accepted as elements of standard military doctrine.

At the end of World War II the Red Army comprised some 500 divisions deployed from central Germany to Korea. It was, as Malcolm Mackintosh noted, 'the largest land army the world had ever seen'. Although reduced to about 175 divisions by the end of 1947 the Soviet army retained over 1,000,000 men in Eastern Europe. The reasons for this were

two-fold. Firstly, Russia was, at the time, unable to counter American nuclear power, and so planned to deter the USA by threatening a massive conventional invasion of Europe. Secondly, Soviet troops helped suppress anti-communist movements and thereby ensured the survival of local communist regimes.

In March, 1946 Stalin relinquished the post of Commissar for Defence. The Defence Commissariat was renamed the Ministry of Defence, and Marshal N. A. Bulganin, a political officer, became Minister. The titles 'Red Army' and 'Red Navy' disappeared, to be replaced by those of 'Soviet Army' and 'Soviet Navy'. There were some changes within the high command: Marshal A. M. Vasilevski took over the senior post of Chief of Staff of the Soviet Army and Navy, and Zhukov was confirmed as Commander-in-Chief of Ground Forces. Zhukov retained this post for only a few months: in July, 1946 he was sent to command the Odessa Military District. His fall from grace was a clear warning to all other senior officers, and it was not until Stalin's death in 1953 that the army escaped from the straitjacket imposed upon it by Stalin and the NKVD.

The high command established by the Collective Leadership, which took over following Stalin's death, bore a marked resemblance to that of 1946. Bulganin took over the Ministry of Defence, which had split into War and Navy Ministries from 1947 to 1953, with Vasilevski and Zhukov as his deputies. An abortive plot, centred upon the unattractive person of Lavrenti Beria, resulted in Beria's execution in December, 1953 and in the appointment of an army general to command the NKVD forces.

The death of Stalin, together with the explosion in August, 1953 of the first Soviet hydrogen bomb, gave new impetus to strategic debate. Theorists were not slow to point out that the old concept of linear frontier defence followed by a massive counter-attack was of limited value in the nuclear age. Premier G. M. Malenkov believed that the possession of nuclear weapons by both Russia and the USA would simply produce mutual deterrence: local conventional war was, he believed, infinitely more likely than full-scale global conflict. Malenkov's replacement by Bulganin in 1955 was accompanied by the elevation of Zhukov to the Ministry of Defence. The new leadership accepted the possibility of nuclear war, and took steps to improve air defence in order to blunt any strike by American bombers. The Air-Defence Command (PVO-Strany) became independent, being given the same status as the Ground Forces, air force and navy.

N. S. Khrushchev, who had served as a senior political officer on the Stalingrad front, assumed the key post of First Part Secretary in 1953 and retained it on Malenkov's fall 2 years later. He was to dominate Russian politics until his eventual replacement in October, 1964. The Khrushchev period witnessed the advancement of many senior officers of the so-called Stalingrad group, who had served with Khrushchev during the war. Marshal R. Ya. Malinovski became Commander-in-Chief of Ground Forces in 1956, and a number of Stalingrad officers obtained seats on the Party Central Committee at the Twentieth Party Congress. Zhukov was appointed a candidate member of the party's Presidium, an unprecedented honour for a professional soldier. He also initiated measures which were to have lasting importance. The corps was abolished as an intermediate command level between division and army. Plans were made to abolish mechanised divisions and armies and to replace rifle divisions with motor rifle divisions. There would eventually be two basic types of division — tank and motor rifle — and these would be grouped into tank and combined-arms armies.

It is scarcely surprising that there was friction between Zhukov and Khrushchev, particularly after the former, appointed a full member of the Presidium, felt entitled to expound upon non-military topics. He also came into conflict with the Political Directorate when he attempted to reduce the power of political officers and the time spent in political training. Zhukov was dismissed in October, 1957. He was replaced as Minister of Defence by Malinovski, and Marshal A. A. Grechko took over as Commander-in-Chief of Ground Forces.

Not all Zhukov's policies shared the fate of their author. The motorisation of rifle divisions began in 1958, tank armies began to replace the more cumbersome mechanised armies, and manpower was reduced towards a target figure of 140 divisions. Khrushchev's strategic doctrine, which emphasised the importance of nuclear rather than conventional weapons, led to the creation in 1960 of the Strategic Rocket Forces as the senior branch of the armed services. The Ground Forces ceased to be an independent command 4 years later, and were placed under the direct administration of the Ministry of Defence. They regained their former status in 1967, as part of a general trend towards the improvement of Russian conventional capabilities. The post-Khrushchev era also saw the reshaping of the officer corps. Many older officers died or were retired, and steps were taken to reorganise a command structure somewhat disorganised by the 'restructuring' carried out by Khrushchev.

The military service law of October 12th, 1967 which reduced the length of conscript service, lowered call-up age and revised retirement age-limits for all ranks, was a significant landmark in the Soviet army's development. It was probably inspired as much by internal motives — such as the army's need to compete for trained manpower with civilian industry — as by external threats posed by NATO or the USA. Although not all the law's provisions have proved totally successful, the measure has contributed to the excellent 'mixed' capability which has distinguished the Soviet armed forces in the post-Khrushchev period. The continuing development of the Strategic Rocket Forces has effectively closed the 'missile gap' of the 1960s. The Ground Forces retain an impressive ability to fight either a nuclear or a conventional war, and the substantial increase of Soviet naval strength has further broadened the Soviet Union's military capabilities.

STRENGTH AND BUDGET

Strength
Population: 269,650,000
Strategic Rocket Forces: 325,000
Ground Forces: 1,825,000
Air-Defence Forces (PVO-Strany): 630,000
Navy, including Naval Air Force, Naval Infantry, Coast Artillery and Rocket Troops: 450,000, 290 major warships, 273 submarines, about 837 smaller vessels
Air Force: 475,000; 4480 combat aircraft
Paramilitary: (a) KGB border guards, 300,000; (b) MVD security troops, 260,000; (c) civilian military training organisation (DOSAAF), 80,000,000 (claimed)

Defence Budget
There is some doubt as to what is included in the official defence budget. Such things as nuclear warheads, frontier guards and certain research and development programmes, are excluded. Even if allowance is made for these items, the total rouble cost of the budget does not reflect the real cost of defence expenditure to the national budget. It is also difficult to arrive at a dollar equivalent of this total rouble cost, for the official exchange rate does not accurately relate the purchasing power of rouble and dollar.

The 1981 budget, was 17,050,000,000 roubles but, making allowance for the artificial exchange rate, unreal price fixing and official exclusion of items which properly belong to the defence field, real expenditure was probably about S190 billion.

COMMAND AND CONSTITUTIONAL STATUS

Command
It is difficult and dangerous to draw precise conclusions about an organisation which, like the Soviet High Command, is both complex and secretive. Much remains unclear, and there is often a significant divergence between constitutional theory and military reality.

The Supreme Command
The Soviet Union is a federated State of 15 republics. Supreme authority is vested in the Supreme Soviet a large elective body which meets for only a few weeks each year. Article 108 of the Constitution declares that the Supreme Soviet is the 'highest body of State authority'. Since the Supreme Soviet is somewhat unwieldy in size and is rarely in session, its smaller Presidium, elected by members of the Supreme Soviet, carries out many of the latter's functions. The Presidium is specifically charged with the appointment and removal of commanders of the armed forces, the proclamation of war during the recess of the Supreme Soviet, the declaration of general or partial mobilisation and the imposition of martial law. The Council of Ministers is responsible to the Presidium and the Supreme Soviet, and also co-ordinates and directs the work of individual ministries.

In practical terms, however, real power is exercised by the Party's Secretariat and Politburo. There are some grounds for supposing that the Party's First Secretary is *de facto* Commander in Chief of the Armed Forces (and in May, 1976 First Secretary Brezhnev assumed the rank of Marshal of the Soviet Union). At the 22nd Party Congress in 1961 Marshal Malinovski referred to Khrushchev as 'Supreme Commander' of the Forces, and Marshal V. D. Sokolovski makes the same implication in his book *Military Strategy*. It is interesting to note that the then Minister of Defence, Marshal A. A. Grechko, was co-opted onto the Politburo in 1973 at the time of the SALT and MBFR discussions; this is not doubt an accurate pointer to the real source of top-level military decisions.

It is difficult to say with certainty what form the High Command would take in the event of war. It is, though, more than likely that a *Stavka* would be set up, transmitting its orders to the commanders of the various theatres of military operations.

The Ministry of Defence
The Minister of Defence has, since the creation of a unified ministry, always been a serving officer. The Minister is assisted by a Military Council, which normally includes the Commanders-in-Chief of the five Operational Branches, the Head of the Political Directorate, the Chief of the General Staff of the Armed Forces and the Head of the Chief Inspectorate.

The Chief of the General Staff of the Armed Forces is assisted by a number of Deputy Chiefs. The General Staff of the Armed Forces services six directorates, dealing with Operations, Intelligence, Topographical Service, Signals, Organisation and Mobilisation, and a Historical Section. It also provides the bulk of the staff officers employed in the Warsaw Pact Joint High Command. The Ministry includes, in addition, a number of other directorates with responsibilities for Personnel, Rear Services, Equipment and Military Justice. There is also a Chief Inspectorate and a Chief Political Directorate.

The Chief Political Directorate (GLAVPUR)
This body is at one and the same time a department of the Party's Central Committee and a directorate within the Ministry of Defence. It is headed by a Party official invested with military rank in order to take the appointment. His deputies are themselves, in the main, the senior political officers of the various Operational Branches. The Chief Political Directorate is responsible for the political reliability of the armed forces in both peace and war. Although direct responsibility for morale, discipline and political education lies with Commanders at all levels, they are aided by GLAVPUR personnel. All commanders, from those of the Operational Branches to to Community Commanders, have a Deputy Commander for Political Affairs (ZAMPOLIT) whose rank depands largely upon the level of command to which he is attached. The Political Administration of the Ground Forces is headed by a colonel-general, while a community would be likely to have a lieutenant as its ZAMPOLIT.

The Committee of State Security (KGB)
Russia has traditionally maintained a large and powerful secret police and security force, known from time to time as the Ochrana, Cheka, OGPU, NKVD and now as the KGB. The latter is the senior police organisation within the Soviet Union, and has its own well-equipped military forces which are quite independent of the Ministry of Defence. A special branch of the KGB deals with the security and political reliability of the army.

The Operational Branches
There are five main Operational Branches of the Soviet armed forces, each with its own commander-in-chief, deputy commanders (including, of course, a deputy commander for political affairs), and staff. The Strategic Rocket Forces are the senior branch. The details of their command structure are unknown, but it seems probable that there are at least two subordinate headquarters, one controlling MRBMs and IRBMs, and the other ICBMs. The Long-Range Air Force also comes under the command of the Strategic Rocket Forces, and it is likely that submarines armed with SLBMs are also subject to their operational control.

The Ground Forces are deployed in Groups of Forces in Eastern Europe and Military Districts within the Soviet Union. There are four Groups of Forces, of which the largest is the Group of Soviet Forces Germany (GSFG) with its headquarters at Zossen—Wunsdorf, near Berlin. The Northern Group of Forces is commanded from Legnica in Poland, the Central Group from Milovice, near Prague, and the Southern Group from Budapest. There are 16 Military Districts within the Soviet Union, each commanded by a Ground Forces officer with the title Commander of Troops. He is assisted by a Military Council, containing a Chief of Staff and a number of Deputy Commanders, and commands all forces within the Military District. This Military Council will also include the local Party Secretary.

The navy is commanded by Admiral of the Fleet of the Soviet Union S. G. Gorshkov, who has held the post since 1956. There are four major fleet commands – Northern, Baltic, Black Sea and Pacific – and a number of smaller flotillas. The navy controls its own Naval Air Force, which is largely land-based. It also possesses Coast Artillery and Rocket Troops, employed in the defence of ports and their approaches, and has a body of 12,000 Naval Infantry, carrying out the traditional tasks of marines, organised in regiments attached to fleets.

The Air-Defence Command (PVO-Strany) has four subordinate branches dealing with early warning systems, fighter aircraft, SAMs and ABMs. The Soviet Union is divided into a number of Air-Defence Districts, whose commanders are responsible for the co-ordination of the various means of air defence.

The air force in the most junior operational branch. It is in no sense an independent arm, for each of its branches is controlled by another operational branch.

The Warsaw Pact
The Pact was signed in Warsaw on May 14th, 1955 by the governments of the Soviet Union, Albania, Bulgaria, Czechoslovakia, East Germany, Hungary, Poland and Rumania. Albania, however, withdrew from the Pact in 1968. Article 4 of the Pact binds members to mutual defence in the case of armed aggression against any member, and Article 5 sets out the organisation of the Pact's Joint Command. The Pact has a Political Consultative Committee, a Joint Secretariat, a Permanent Commission and a Council of Foreign Ministers. Its highest military body is the Council of Defence Ministers, consisting of the Ministers of Defence of all the member States, assisted by a Military Council. The Joint High Command has its headquarters at Moscow and a forward headquarters at L'vov in the Ukraine, and is headed by a Soviet marshal with a Soviet general as his First Deputy Commander. The other Deputy Commanders are Ministers of Defence of member States. The Pact's Joint Staff is composed mainly of Soviet officers under the leadership of the Russian First Deputy Commander. The four Soviet groups of forces in Eastern Europe seem to be permanently assigned to the Pact, and forces stationed in the Baltic, Carpathian and Byelorussian Military Districts might well be allotted to the Pact in the event of war. In practical terms, though, the Pact is Soviet controlled. The forces of the member States would become operationally subordinate to the Soviet High Command in wartime, and even in peacetime the air defence of the Pact is controlled from Moscow by the Commander-in-Chief of the Soviet Air-Defence Command.

Constitutional Status
The Constitution of 1977, as amended to date, contains 174 articles in 9 chapters. It clearly asserts the obligation of all citizens to serve in the armed forces: Article 63 declares that 'military service is an honourable duty', and Article 62 states that 'defence of the Socialist Motherland is the sacred duty of every citizen'. This general obligation is, of course, more precisely defined in current military service legislation.

Individual Union Republics are permitted to enter into diplomatic relations with foreign powers. Issues of war and peace, and direction of the Armed Forces, are retained in the hands of the central government. The constitution lays down no limitations upon the use of military power or the employment of the armed forces. It does, though, guarantee the right of every citizen serving with the armed forces to vote and to seek elective office.

ROLE, COMMITMENT, DEPLOYMENT AND RECENT OPERATIONS

Role and Commitment
The role of the Soviet armed forces may broadly be termed as four-fold. Defence of the territory of the USSR is, naturally of prime importance. In this context Russian history has a considerable psychological impact: Russian has been invaded at least four times over the past 75 years, and the German invasion of 1941 has left an enduring scar. Secondly, the armed forces are intended to deter attack, particularly nuclear attack, but they are also designed to win any war

that might result if deterrence fails. The USSR has a clear commitment to maintain communist rule in certain of the countries of Eastern Europe: the invasions of Hungary and Czechoslovakia demonstrate how seriously this duty is taken. Finally, the armed forces are expected to support Russian political manoeuvres throughout the world. This support may take various forms, ranging from the supply of weapons to communist movements or nations, to the commitment of Soviet Ground or Air Forces to the defence of friendly States.

Soviet military doctrine is essentially concerned with what it terms 'nuclear rocket war', although it recognises the possibility that other types of conflict could arise. The balance between the nuclear and conventional elements of Soviet military thinking has shifted substantially within the past decade or so. Khrushchev emphasised 'minimum deterrence'; he hoped to deter the USA from launching an attack on the Soviet Union by threatening a Soviet counter-strike and, providing that this remained credible, he was content to accept a measure of United States nuclear superiority. Believing that deterrence made war between the superpowers unlikely, he was prepared to reduce Soviet conventional capabilities – hence his downgrading of Ground Forces. The Soviet Union has pursued a 'mixed' capability since the fall of Khrushchev. It has attained nuclear superiority over the USA: this has the dual effect of strengthening the deterrent value of its nuclear weapons while at the same time improving its ability actually to win a nuclear war should deterrence fail.

In February, 1963 over 18 months before the fall of Khrushchev, an article in *Red Star* announced that the Party had reached the conclusion that:

'the armed forces and the country as a whole must prepare for a war in which nuclear weapons will be widely used; which will represent a decisive, classic collision of two opposed world social systems, and which will be distinguished by unprecedented violence, dynamic force and high manoeuvrability of combat operations.'

Marshal Sokolovski took the argument a stage further, arguing that:

'Military strategy under the conditions of modern war becomes the strategy of deep nuclear rocket strikes in conjunction with the operations of all services of the armed forces in order to effect a simultaneous defeat and destruction of the economic potential and armed forces throughout enemy territory, thus accomplishing the war aims within a short time period.'

Sokolovski was at great pains to point out that, even in the nuclear age, military strategy was dependent upon politics: he noted, however, that statesmen could not violate or ignore the laws of military strategy with impunity.

Sokolovski, in common with other Soviet military authors, stresses the essentially defensive purposes of Soviet military power, but warns that the USA is pursuing a goal of world domination, and fears that war may eventually be unleashed by the aggressive activities of 'imperialistic madmen'. A massive Soviet counter-offensive would follow this aggression. Moreover, since the aggression itself would almost certainly involve the use of nuclear and chemical weapons, the Soviet response would itself employ such devices. This logic, curious though it may seem, is used to justify the great emphasis which the Soviet armed forces place upon offensive operations. There are, perhaps, more credible reasons for this preoccupation. The Soviet Union has vast tracts of thinly populated territory and long land borders and, as history so amply demonstrates, are vulnerable to invasion. Any form of linear frontier defence, even if militarily viable in the nuclear age, would be totally impossible because of the large amount of troops it would require. A mobile defensive war, fought within the boundaries of the Soviet Union, is clearly unacceptable: an offensive war, albeit fought in defence of Soviet interests, is therefore an eminently practical solution.

Soviet military doctrine stresses the primacy of offensive action. In his book *The Offensive*, Colonel A. A. Sidorenko emphasises that 'only the offensive leads to the attainment of victory over the enemy'. Defensive tactics are acceptable only on a temporary basis or in areas of secondary importance. Both Sidorenko and Sokolovskii emphasise that offensive operations are 'the main type of combat action for troops' and 'the basic means for solving the problems of armed conflict in land theatres'. There are three vital ingredients in the Soviet Offensive. The initial nuclear strike would have enemy nuclear delivery means, other targets in the deep rear and forward formations as its target. Airborne assaults would be used in conjunction with this strike to carry out acts of sabotage and destruction, to seize objectives of tactical significance, such as river crossings, or simply to 'leap-frog' ahead of the advancing troops. Tank and motor rifle formations would press forward along selected main axes of attack, exploiting breaches produced by the initial nuclear strike, and pushing on into the deep rear. Enemy reserves would, where possible, be attacked straight from the line of march, and the impetus of the attack would be sustained in order to prevent the successful occupation of defensive positions in depth.

Although Soviet theorists believe that nuclear weapons would almost inevitably be used in 'main sectors' in the event of a major war, they nevertheless point out the dangers of training exclusively for a short, fluid nuclear conflict. In the autumn of 1967 the Ground Forces, newly re-established as an independent operational branch, carried out the large-scale non-nuclear exercise DNEPR. This seems to have involved a brief attack by the 'enemy' force, rapidly followed by a massive counter-offensive, unrolling across an area roughly the size and shape of Western Europe. The exercise included the assault crossing of a major river obstacle, the Dnieper. This was conducted, in Sidorenko's words, 'simultaneously, in the entire zone of attack, across a front of tens of kilometres'. Helicopter assaults by motor rifle troops were used to seize vital ground on the enemy bank, and the whole attack was launched with the minimum of delay with assaulting formations crossing the river in the same formation in which they had advanced to the obstacle. The Russians continue to place great emphasis upon river crossing: it should be noted that the dramatically successful Egyptian crossing of the Suez Canal in October, 1973 was accomplished with the aid of large quantities of Soviet bridging and ferry equipment. Exercise DVINA, which took place in 1970, had both nuclear and conventional phases: it too involved the crossing of water obstacles.

In the event of major war the Soviet High Command would divide the world into a number of theatres of military operations, each under its own commander. A land theatre, say the Western European Theatre, would contain a number of Fronts, each equivalent to a Western Army Group, and probably named after the area in which they were to operate – First Western European Front, Second Western European Front, and so on. Each front would contain four or five tank and combined-arms armies, a tactical air army, and various supporting units.

The front's advance would be preceded by a large-scale strike, probably employing conventional, chemical and nuclear weapons. This would be planned by front headquarters, and would be likely to take about 4 hours to fire. Enemy nuclear delivery means would be the prime target, but headquarters, airfields and defensive positions would all be struck if located. Soviet nuclear weapons would mainly be fused to give a low air-burst, although ground bursts might be used against certain targets. The attack of the front's tank and combined-arms armies would be concentrated upon a number of 'axes of major effort', although the front commander would retain uncommitted formations and use them to reinforce any particular axis or exploit an enemy weakness. Secondary or holding attacks might be made in other sectors of the front's area with the aim of pinning the defender to his position and thereby enabling formations engaged on axes of major effort to encircle him or operate against his flanks and rear. The initial strike could also be exploited by airborne troops: during exercise DVINA an entire airborne division was dropped in a single wave.

A front might well advance with three of its five armies in the first line. Each of these armies would probably have an attack frontage of about 50km. An assaulting army's configuration would be much the same as that of a front: a five-division tank army could well lead with three divisions. The frontage over which these attacking divisions would operate would vary, but a division committed along an axis of major effort could assault on a frontage of as little as 5km. The army's remaining divisions could be used to reinforce or exploit, as occasion offered. A possible grouping for the three leading divisions of an army would be for two divisions, moving down an axis of major effort, to advance side-by-side with a combined frontage of up to 25km, while the other leading division would make a secondary attack, on a similar frontage, in another part of the army's sector. No effort would be made to maintain an unbroken front: the space between divisions would be covered only by reconnaissance units and flank security patrols.

Although Soviet military doctrine stresses the need for concentration of force, Russian theorists are not blind to the dangers of concentration on the nuclear battlefield. Considerable attention is therefore paid to the maintenance of depth in the assault. An attacking division could be concentrated along a narrow sector of front, but the distance from its leading reconnaissance elements to the last of its combatant units could be as much as 100km. Its advance would be made in two echelons, preceded by a strong reconnaissance detachment. The main weight of the division would be found in the first echelon: second-echelon units could be used to reinforce or replace the first echelon or to reduce centres of enemy resistance by-passed by the leading units.

In August, 1945 the Transbaikal Front advanced up to 800km in 10 days, and the 6th Guards Tank Army actually managed to average 100km/day. These impressive rates of advance were, admittedly, carried out over terrain which was well-suited to the use of armour, but they nonetheless showed that such swift operations were possible. It was not until the early years of this decade that the Soviet High Command recognised that similar rates of advance would be unattainable in future war in Western Europe. Nevertheless, basic Soviet tactical techniques, like the attack 'from the line of march' and the 'meeting engagement' are high-speed manoeuvres designed to ensure that the advance continues with the minimum loss of time. It is only if a Soviet formation were to be faced with an intact position held in strength that it would embark upon a set-piece attack with full preparatory fire. It seems likely that the Russians now plan to average about 50km/day for an operation lasting rather less than 2 weeks. This rate of advance would, of course, not be constant: the advance to contact and pursuit phases of the operation would obviously be swifter than the battle for the

main defensive zone, and the average rate of advance would itself decrease if nuclear weapons were not employed.

Possession of a well-ordered body of military doctrine which stresses the primacy of offensive action and deals in considerable detail with the conduct of the land battle has notable advantages for the Soviet armed forces. Planning, training and weapons procurement policies all reflect the prevailing doctrine, and the Ground Forces have developed an excellent capacity for waging the sort of war envisaged by Soviet theorists. Soviet equipment, although often less sophisticated than that used by Western powers, is usually simple and robust. The Ground Forces have a good river-crossing capability, and are well equipped for the delivery of, and defence against, chemical weapons. The aircraft of the tactical air armies would be likely to gain air superiority over their NATO opponents, thereby severely restricting NATO movement by day. Conversely, Soviet air-defence weapons are formidable in the extreme: major units and formations have large quantities of well-tried anti-aircraft weapons available. The impressive offensive capabilities of the Soviet Ground Forces have not been achieved without sacrifices, and it is not uncommon for Western observers to point out that Soviet tactical doctrine is unsubtle and to note the numerous restrictions imposed upon the initiative of junior and middle-rank commanders. These objections may indeed be justified, but they in no way invalidate the basic premise that wars are won by offensive action, and it is offensive action for which the Ground Forces are ideally suited.

If the operational role of the Ground Forces is reasonably clear cut, the same cannot be said of that of the navy. The current line of development of Soviet naval doctrine may be traced to the replacement of Admiral N. G. Kuznetsov by Admiral S. G. Gorshkov in 1955. Kuznetsov had clashed with Khrushchev over the composition of the navy: the former advocated the continued construction of cruisers, while the latter maintained that large naval units were of little value in the nuclear age. The fall of Kuznetsov was followed by the termination of the cruiser programme: naval research, development and construction were then concentrated upon submarines and guided-missile vessels. A substantial construction programme went on throughout the late 1960s and early 1970s: the Soviet navy now contains over 230 major surface combat vessels and 265 submarines. In terms of surface ships, submarines and naval aircraft Russia now has a superiority of something like 2:1 over her potential opponents in NATO.

Several roles are allotted to the Soviet navy. In a major war, nuclear submarines with SLBMs would be used to guarantee Russia's second strike capability, while Soviet antisubmarine units would endeavour to destroy enemy submarines whose SLBMs might be used against the Soviet Union. In a less clearly defined conflict Soviet naval power could be used against Western merchant ships: seaborne supplies to Western Europe could be seriously disrupted, if not entirely cut off, by Russian naval action. The Soviet navy also has numerous peacetime tasks. It carries out the traditional naval function of 'showing the flag', and is particularly useful for demonstrating to non-aligned countries the advances of Soviet technology. Visits to foreign ports can have more concrete purposes than mere propaganda: practical military aid is given to client States and satellites. Naval power can be used, in areas like the Mediterranean, to improve Soviet security and at the same time to diversify threats to the West.

Deployment

The Strategic Rocket Forces

Soviet ICBM complexes stretch in a broad band across the

Soviet Union, more or less parallel with the Trans-Siberian railway. MRBM and IRBM sites are located mainly near Russia's western borders, although some are positioned in frontier districts in the Far East and south-west.

The Ground Forces

These are deployed in the four groups of forces in Eastern Europe and the 16 military districts of the Soviet Union. There are three categories of Soviet division. Formation of Category 1 are at least 75% manned and 100% equipped, those of Category 2 are between 60 and 75% manned and fully equipped, although not necessarily with the latest equipment, while the divisions of Category 3 are up to 50% manned and are short of some equipment.

The Group of Soviet Forces Germany contains 19 Category 1 divisions, nine of them tank and ten motor rifle. They form five armies: 1st Guards Tank Army (HQ Dresden), 2nd Guards Tank Army, 8th and 20th Guards Armies (HQs Neustrelitz, Erfurt and Bernau) and 3rd Shock Army (HQ Magdeburg). The 16th Tactical Air Army is under the Group's command. The Northern Group (Poland) has only two tank divisions, the Central Group (Czechoslovakia) comprises two tank and three motor rifle divisions and the Southern Group (Hungary) has two tank and two motor rifle divisions. All these formations, like their counterparts in GSFG, are Category 1.

The bulk of forces within the Soviet Union are to be found in European Russia. Twenty-two tank divisions, 36 motor rifle divisions and five airborne divisions are stationed in the Moscow, Leningrad, Kiev, Odessa, Byelorussian, Baltic and Carpathian Military Districts. All the airborne divisions are Category 1, and the tank and motor rifle formations fall more or less evenly into all three categories. The North Caucasian and Transcaucasian Military Districts contain one Category 1 airborne division together with three tank and 19 motor rifle divisions half of them Category 2 and the remainder Category 3. The one tank division and five motor rifle divisions of the Volga and Urals Military Districts are all Category 3. The central Asian, Siberian, Transbaikal and Far Eastern Military Districts, together with the Mongolian People's Republic, contain one or two Category 1 airborne divisions, seven tank and 35 motor rifle divisions, divided between the three categories.

The Navy

The navy is deployed in four major fleets, of which the Northern Fleet, with an average strength of about 175 submarines and 60 surface combat units, is the largest. The Baltic Fleet normally consists of about 35 submarines and 55 major surface combat vessels, while the Pacific Fleet usually contains in the region of 105 submarines and 60 major surface combat ships. The Black Sea Fleet has an average strength of 25 submarines and 65 major surface combat units, a proportion of which are employed in the Mediterranean and Caspian flotillas. The navy also possesses 53 intelligence vessels, and these are often to be found in the North Sea, Atlantic or the Channel, engaged in electronic surveillance of NATO naval manoeuvres. The great majority of the 700 or so combat aircraft of the Naval Air Force are based in the Northern, Baltic and Black Sea Fleet areas, and the remainder are deployed in the Far East.

The Air-Defence Command

The missiles and fighters of the Air-Defence Command are intended primarily to defend the chief centres of population and industry and are mainly sited to guard against attack from the West. The GALOSH ABM system is deployed in four sites around Moscow.

The Air Force

The Air Force contains about 5300 combat aircraft, apart from the fighters and interceptors under the command of the Air-Defence Command. The majority of these belong to the Tactical Air Force, whose 4500 planes form 16 Tactical Air Armies, four of them — some 1500 aircraft — in Eastern Europe, and the remainder in 12 of the Soviet Union's Military Districts.

Overseas Commitments

Soviet military advisors are stationed in small numbers in Algeria, Iraq, Libya, Uganda, the People's Democratic Republic of South Yemen and the Yemen Arab Republic (North Yemen). About 1000 are currently to be found in Cuba and a significant but unestimated number in Angola, Mozambique and Ethiopia. The bulk of Soviet troops formerly stationed in Egypt were engaged in the air defence of the Suez Canal; they were organised on the lines of a Soviet air-defence district, and commanded by Colonel-General V. V. Okunev, Commander of the Moscow Air-Defence District, detached to Egypt in 1970. They were withdrawn in 1972.

Recent Operations

The Soviet Armed Forces have not been involved in any large-scale conventional operations since 1945. They have, however, been engaged in several clashes of varying intensity along the Sino—Soviet border, and have mounted three major internal security operations within the Warsaw Pact. The repression of the East Berlin rising of June, 1953 was the least important of these operations; the supression of the Hungarian revolt of November, 1956 was altogether more serious. General P. I. Batov moved eight divisions from his Carpathian Military District to assist the two Soviet divisions already in Hungary, and there was sporadic fighting which went on for about 3 days. The invasion of Czechoslovakia was by far the most significant of the three operations. It was planned while the Czechs and, indeed, most Western governments, were lulled into a false sense of security by the Bratislava Declaration of August 3rd. On August 7th Shtemenko took over as Chief of Staff of the Warsaw Pact forces and at once set about forming a command and signals network for a major operation. Certain Soviet specialists moved into Prague *incognito* on August 17th, and at 11p.m. on Tuesday, August 20th Warsaw Pact troops poured across 18 points on the Czech border. A large-scale airlift was mounted at Prague airport: the movement of air traffic was controlled from a 'civilian' Aeroflot plane which had landed earlier the same day. Perhaps 250,000 troops were involved in the early stages of the operation, rising to an estimated 600,000 by the end of August. Army General Pavlovski seems to have commanded the operation under the overall direction of Yakubovski. Elements of 24 Warsaw Pact divisions were initially employed: sixteen of these were Soviet, three Polish, two East German, two Hungarian and one Bulgarian. Czech military and security forces had been ordered not to resist the invaders, but there was some serious rioting, particularly in Prague, where a number of Soviet AFVs were destroyed.

Although the operation did reveal some minor flaws within the Soviet system — standards of map reading were far from perfect and the morale of some units suffered after contact with the hostile Czech population — it was an impressive demonstration of the Warsaw Pact's ability to plan and execute a rapid large-scale troop movement. The Prague airlift is perhaps the single most noteworthy military feature of the operation.

[For Afghanistan, see that entry.]

ORGANISATION

Arms of Service

The arms of service of the Ground Forces are as follows: tank; motor rifle; rocket troops and artillery; motor transport and military roads; chemical; engineer; pipelaying; signals and radio technical; military construction; railway and military communications; engineer technical; airborne; administration and intendance; medical; veterinary; and justice.

Operational

The Front

The Soviet front is roughly equivalent to a Western army group. Fronts do not exist in peacetime, but would be formed for operations from the Ground Forces divisions stationed in the groups of Soviet forces and the military districts. A number of fronts might be grouped together in a 'theatre of military operations'. There is not fixed organisation for a front, whose precise composition would depend upon its role. Under normal circumstances, though, a front would include two or three combined-arms armies, two tank armies and a tactical air army. Airborne forces, together with the requisite air transport, would be allocated to the front for a specific operation. The front would be amply provided with both combat and service support. It would be particularly strong in rocket and conventional artillery. The heaviest of its weapons would probably be the medium-range surface-to-surface nuclear missile Scaleboard, and it would certainly possess two brigades, each of nine launchers, of the shorter-range Scud missile, which has a conventional as well as a nuclear capability. The front's field artillery division would comprise about 160 guns and howitzers ranging in calibre from 122mm to 152mm. Two SA-2 regiments would provide the front with its heavy air defence: targets for the 18 launchers of each battalion would initially be detected by the front's early warning battalion. The prime role of the front's numerous engineers would be river crossing. Two engineer brigades and two independent regiments would man the PMP ferry-bridge, and two assault crossing battalions would provide lighter equipment. The front would probably contain two intelligence regiments: one, a reconnaissance intelligent unit, could be employed behind the enemy's lines, while the other, an intercept regiment, would be used to monitor enemy radio transmissions. At least two chemical-defence battalions would be attached to the front, and they might be joined by smoke-screen and other chemical units. Signals regiments, radio-relay battalions, independent ECM units and line-laying troops would complete a front's combat support. The largest element of service support within the front would be its transport brigade, consisting of a large but flexible number of road-transport and fuel-bowser battalions. The construction element within the front would consist of road and rail construction units, and would also include a fuel pipelaying brigade. An assortment of depots, maintenance units and minor services would, with two front hospitals and a number of independent medical units, complete the front's establishment

The Combined-Arms Army

A combined-arms army would contain three motor rifle divisions and a tank division, together with large amounts of combat support. Its artillery brigade would contain numerous guns, howitzers and multi-barrelled rocket launchers. These might be used at army level, or their control might be decentralised to those divisions which, in the army commander's opinion, required extra fire support. A nine-launcher Scud brigade would also be at the army commander's disposal. Air defence would be provided by one or two SA-2 regiments, each with 18 launchers, an SA-4 brigade and an early warning battalion. Large numbers of PMP ferry-bridges would be available in the two engineer regiments, who would be assisted by an assault-crossing battalion. Signals and ECM units, together with a reconnaissance company, helicopter squadron and chemical-defence battalion complete the army's combat support. Its service support would comprise a transport regiment, probably equipped with a high proportion of requisitioned civilian vehicles, and a number of medical, maintenance and static-depot units.

The Tank Army

The tank army's basic components are three or four tank divisions and one motor rifle division. It would also contain much the same combat and service support as the combined-arms army, although it would probably have no artillery brigade.

The Motor Rifle Division

The motor rifle division is descended from the old rifle division, but it is much more than merely a mechanised infantry division. Its formidable striking power is centred upon its three motor rifle regiments and its one tank regiment. Each motor rifle regiment contains three motor rifle battalions and a tank battalion. The motor rifle battalion has three motor rifle companies, each comprising three platoons of three sections. The battalion has its own anti-tank and mortar platoons, as well as a signals platoon and a small administrative echelon. The tank battalion of the motor rifle regiment is stronger than its equivalent within a tank regiment: it has three companies, each of three platoons, with four tanks per platoon. The motor-rifle regiment has its own artillery, which includes an ATGW battery with Sagger or Swatter missiles, an anti-aircraft battery of four ZSU 23-4 anti-aircraft tanks and four SA-9 SAMSs, and a battery of six 122mm howitzers. In all, the regiment contains 40 tanks and 112 APCs, together with a multitude of other armoured and soft-skinned vehicles. The division's tank regiment is an altogether smaller formation than the motor rifle regiment. It comprises three tank battalions, each of 31 tanks, together with combat and service support. Tank regiments have recently been given their own integral motor rifle troops, probably on the scale of at least one motor rifle company per tank regiment. They have no integral artillery apart from a battery of ZSU 23-4 anti-aircraft tanks. The motor rifle and tank regiments of the motor rifle division both possess reasonable river-crossing and chemical-decontamination facilities, but their repair and recovery resources are very limited.

The combat support of the motor rifle division is an impressive as the striking power of its regiments. The divisional artillery contains a Frog free-flight rocket battalion of four launchers, an artillery regiment of 54 122mm howitzers, a rocket-launcher battalion with 18 multi-barrelled rocket launchers, an anti-tank battalion of 18 100mm anti-tank guns, and anti-aircraft regiment of 24 57mm towed AA guns or a battalion of SA-6 or SA-8 anti-aircraft missiles; an artillery observation unit completes the divisional artillery's establishment. The division also possesses a strong reconnaissance battalion, an engineer battalion with good mine-clearing and river-crossing capabilities, a signals battalion and a chemical-defence company. It now seems likely that a tank reserve of up to 50 tanks is available at divisional level. The division's service support is, like that of the regiment, designed for lightness and mobility. Its repair and recovery facilities are limited, but it includes a 60 bed field hospital and a transport battalion.

The Tank Division

The tank division is a somewhat smaller formation than its motor rifle counterpart. It has three tank regiments, each containing 95 tanks, 93 of them in the regiment's three battalions and the remaining two in regimental headquarters. A motor rifle regiment, with 40 tanks of its own, is integral to the division, giving it a total strength of 335 tanks. The combat and service support of a tank division is very similar to that of a motor rifle division.

The Tactical Air Army

Although staffed almost entirely by air force personnel, tactical air armies are subordinate to the Ground Forces in both peace and war. The precise composition of a tactical air army is, like that of a front, subject to some variation. A typical army might consist of a headquarters controlling a number of air-defence fighter divisions, several fighter–ground attack divisions, and light bomber, transport and reconnaissance regiments. The army would have its own maintenance and ancillary services.

RECRUITMENT, TRAINING AND RESERVES

Recruitment

The majority of members of the armed forces are conscripts. The ratio of conscript to regular personnel varies between operational branches, but the Ground Forces, which contain the highest proportion of conscripts, it is about 65:35. The individual's general liability for military service is clearly stated in the Soviet constitution, and the Military Service Law of October 12th, 1967 which came into force on January 1st, 1968 provides the legal framework for conscription.

The 1967 law lowered the call-up period to 2 years in the Ground Forces and the air force, although it was fixed at 3 years for the navy and the KGB. There are two call-up periods each year, in May–June and November–December. Deferment from service may be granted on a wide variety of grounds, of which education is probably the most common. To gain deferment for this reason, however, the individual concerned must be pursuing a continuous course of full-time education. A man who obtains deferment up to the age of twenty-four is unlikely to be inducted for full-time service. About 1,250,000 conscripts, perhaps half the available total, are called up each year.

Most officers are recruited by way of the Military Schools (VU) and Special Military Schools (VVU). Applicants to these establishments must be between seventeen and twenty years of age; the majority of them come straight from civilian life, although serving conscripts may, with the permission of their commanding officers, seek admission. Examinations for VU and VVU take place in July, and are geared to the syllabus of secondary schools. Some young men, usually the sons of Communist Party officials or officers of the armed services, attend Suvorov and Nachimov schools (for the Ground Forces and navy, respectively) from the age of fifteen or sixteen, and then pass on to a VU or VVU. It is possible for a conscript to attain a commission, having first reached the rank of ensign (*praporschchik*). There is no foreign equivalent to the Soviet *praporschchik*, although he bears some resemblance to the French *adjutant* and the United States warrant officer. *Praporschchiki* and their naval equivalents were introduced in November, 1971 in an effort to replace the old category of 'extended servicemen' — re-enlisted conscripts. Extended servicemen or conscripts nearing the end of their service could apply for appointments as *praporschchiki*. Successful applicants enlisted for 5 years and can re-enlist, subject to efficiency, for 3 year and 5 year periods thereafter. The *praporschchik* scheme seems to have been designed to improve the senior NCO structure by creating a rank whose status and prospects make it attractive to the better elements among the conscripts. It has not been an unqualified success. The old extended service category still remains, for numerous extended servicemen were unable to qualify for appointment as *praporschchiki*. It is, though, likely that the scheme has improved incentives at the NCO level, and taken some of the more tedious and routine burdens from the backs of junior officers. A high proportion of *praporschchiki* seem likely to attain commissions, either in the regular forces or on the reserve. A third source of officers is the military departments of universities. University students carry out military training in these departments, and are appointed reserve officers, in which capacity they are liable for 2 years' duty with the regular forces.

Training

The 1967 law introduced compulsory preconscription military training. This is carried out at schools and other establishments, and is intended to consist of about 140 hours of training spread over a year to 18 months. The instructors are serving or retired officers, and the syllabus includes basic drill and tactics. By the end of 1974 about two thirds of conscripts had received a significant amount of preservice training. Schoolboys who fail to secure the certificate of military training at the end of preconscription training are denied a school-leaving certificate, which effectively denies them a worthwhile civilian career.

The conscript training cycle begins on December 1st, although the year is divided into two periods, each of 26 weeks, which commence with the arrival of the two annual conscript intakes. Induction procedure takes about 2 weeks, and is followed by 2 months' basic training, after which the conscript is posted to his unit. Potential NCOs are sent on a 6 month NCO course, from which they emerge as junior sergeants. Great emphasis is placed upon the standardisation of training, and the relatively short period of time available tends to produce an onerous and tightly structured daily training programme. Most conscripts will qualify in at least one trade, and may be taught another complementary skill; for example, a soldier whose first trade is a tank driver may also be trained as a tank gunner.

Officer training is naturally more thorough. The course at a VU lasts for 3 years, while that at a VVU may be either 4 or 5 years. Graduates of the latter establishments emerge with an appropriate technical qualification in addition to their junior lieutenant's commission. Despite the substantial academic content of officer training, officer cadets (*kursanty*) spend much of their time in the field, on training designed to reproduce, as accurately as possible, the stresses of modern war. This realistic battle simulation is also a feature of other aspects of Soviet training: the Soviet officer and soldier are likely to spend much longer training to operate in a chemical and nuclear environment than are their Western counterparts. The officer's education does not cease when he leaves his VU or VVU. In mid-career he will probably be sent on a command or technical specialisation course, lasting between 3 and 5 years, and officers destined for very high rank will be sent on the 2 year course at the General Staff Academy.

A significant proportion of training time is expended not on practical military instruction but upon political training. Officers and soldiers are all expected to receive certain regulation quantities of political training. A conscript will receive about 5 hours' training each week from his unit's ZAMPOLIT and his assistants, and officers must attend at least 50 hours of political instruction each year. In addition to formal classes, political training is also conducted in a number of other forms, since the ZAMPOLIT is closely involved in activities which might be considered sporting or recreational in a Western army. Officers are strongly encouraged to become Party or, if under the age of twenty-five, KOMSOMOL members. Party membership is by no means obligatory, but perhaps three-quarters of majors and officers of equivalent rank are Party members, and membership is almost a prerequisite for promotion to senior rank.

Reserves

The 1967 law gave rise to problems by reducing training time, but had the advantage of increasing the throughput of trained soldiers. About 1,250,000 conscripts pass onto the reserve each year, and they retain a reserve liability until they attain the age of fifty. Officers also go onto the reserve on retiring from the regular forces. It is difficult to estimate the current size of the reserve, but it could well be as high as 25,000,000 officers and men, of whom well over one-fifth have had regular service within the last 5 years. A paramilitary organisation, DOSAAF, gives part-time training in specialist skills such as shooting and parachuting.

EQUIPMENT AND ARMS INDUSTRY

Arms and Equipment

Small Arms: Pistol: Makarov 9mm (PM); Machine pistol: Stechkin 9mm (APS); Assault rifle: Kalashnikov 7.62mm (AKM); Light machine-gun: Kalashnikov 7.62mm (RPK); General purpose machine-gun: Kalashnikov 7.62mm long (PKS); Heavy machine-gun: Goryunov 7.6mm long (SGM) vehicle mounted; Degt-yarev-Shpagin 12.7mm (DShK) ground and air defence; and Vladimirov 14.5mm (KPV) ground and air defence

Mortars: 82mm M-1943 (parachute battalions), 120mm M-1943 (motor rifle battalions) and 160mm (used only in difficult terrain)

Anti-tank Weapons: Grenade launcher: RPG-7 (one per motor rifle section); Recoilless gun: B-10 82mm; Rocket launcher: SPG-9 76mm; Guns: SD-44 85mm, M-1955 100mm and T-12 100mm;

Anti-Aircraft Guns: 14.5mm ZPU-4 (four-barrelled towed), 23mm ZSU-23 (twin barrelled towed), 23mm ZSU-23-4 (four-barrelled AA tank), 57mm S-60 (single-barrelled towed) and 57mm ZSU-57-2 (twin-barrelled AA tank)

Artillery: Field guns and howitzers: 122mm howitzer D-30 (towed), 122mm field gun D-74 (towed), 130mm field gun M-46 (towed), 152mm howitzer D-1 (towed), 152mm howitzer D-20, 180mm heavy gun (towed, M-1973 152mm SP howitzer and M-1974 122mm SP gun Rocket launchers: 122mm BM-21 (truck-mounted; 40 tubes) and 140mm M-1965 (towed; 16 tubes)

Armour: Tanks: T55 main battle tank (100mm main armament, 36 tons in weight, crew of four), T62 main battle tank (115mm smoothbore main armament, 36.5 tons in weight, crew of four) and T10 obsolescent heavy tank (122mm main armament, 49 tons in weight, crew of four). A new main battle tank has entered service replacing the T55 and T62; it mounts a 125mm gun with an auto-loader and there are two versions: T64 and T12 with an improved chassis; Reconnaissance vehicles: PT-76 (amphibious light tank, 76mm gun, weight 14 tons, crew of three, now obsolescent), BRDM (several versions of this vehicle exist – one mounts a 14.5mm MG and another the Sagger missile; it can also be fitted with flag dispensers for NBC reconnaissance; weight 0–7 tons, crew 3–5) and BMP (reconnaissance variant); Assault guns: ASU-57 57mm gun (weight 3.4 tons) and ASU-85 85mm

gun (weight 15 tons); APCs: BMP tracked section APC (mounts 73mm smoothbore gun and is often fitted with Sagger), BTR-50P tracked section APC (mounts 14.5mm MG), BTR-50PK tracked section APC for the motor rifle troops of tank divisions, BTR-152 obsolescent wheeled section APC and BTR-60P obsolescent wheeled section APC (mounts 12.7mm MG). All the above APCs mount a 7.62mm MG in addition to any other armament

Aircraft: Several versions of many of the types listed below are currently in service. Names in *italics* are NATO recognition titles. Numbers in brackets are an estimate of quantities currently in service.

Tactical Air Force (4650): Yak-28 *Brewer* tactical attack bomber and Il-28 *Beagle* (175 in total); MiG-17 *Fresco* (220); Su-7 *Fitter*-A fighter–ground attack (500); MiG-23 *Flogger* variable-geometry aircraft, in interceptor (*Flogger*-A) and fighter–bomber (*Flogger*-B) versions (1100); MiG-21 *Fishbed* in fighter and interceptor versions (1450); Su-20 *Fitter*-B fighter–ground attack (an improved version of *Fitter*-A); Su-17 *Fitter*-C fighter–ground attack (300); Su-19 *Fencer* fighter–ground attack (120); An-12 *Cub* modified for ECM; and MiG-25 *Foxbat* (150); Air Transport Force (1300 fixed-wing aircraft and 2000 helicopters): Il-14 *Crate* obsolescent transport (a civil version remain in service with Aeroflot); An-8 *Camp* turboprop transport; An-24 *Coke* short- and medium-range turboprop transport; An-12 *Cub* General-purpose tactical transport; Il-18 *Coot* turboprop passenger/transport aircraft; An-22 *Cock* heavy transport (exceeded in size only by the Lockheed C5A Galaxy); Mi-1 *Hare* helicopter (now obsolescent); Mi-2 *Hoplite* general-purpose transport helicopter; Mi-4 *Hound* general-purpose helicopter (widely-used throughout the Warsaw Pact; Mi-6 *Hook* heavy transport helicopter (an armed version exists); Mi-8 *Hip* medium general-purpose helicopter; Mi-10 *Harke* transport helicopter designed to carry heavy loads slung beneath the fuselage; and Mi-24 *Hind* gunship and assault transport helicopter

Naval Vessels: MRBMs/IRBMs (690): SS-5 *Skean*; SS-4 *Sandal*, and SS-20 mobile IRBMs

Tactical nuclear weapons: Frog wheeled launcher (range 15–65km); *Scud*-B wheeled or tracked launcher (range 260km); and *Scaleboard* wheeled launcher (range 850km) ABMs: *Galosh* in four sites around Moscow (64); SAMs: SA-1 *Guild* (solid fuel, HE warhead; appears to be going out of service); SA-2 *Guideline* HE warhead (slant range about 25 miles); SA-3 *Goa* low level (slant range about 15 miles; mounted in pairs on tracked launcher; a naval version also exists); SA-4 *Ganef* medium range (mounted in pairs on tracked launcher); SA-5 *Gammon* long range, high level; and SA-6 *Gainful* medium range, low level (triple-mounted on tracked launcher); Coast defence: SS-N-3 *Shaddock*; Stand-off: *Kangaroo* for Tu-20 *Bear*; *Kipper* anti-shipping for Tu-16 *Badger*; and *Kitchen* for Tu-22 *Blinder*; Anti-tank: *Swatter* and *Sagger* HEAT warheads mounted on BRDMs (*Sagger* also exists in man-portable version)

Arms Industry

The Soviet Union has a large and well-developed arms industry. It is allotted a high priority by GOSPLAN, the State Planning Ministry, which produces overall industrial plans every 5 years or so. Standardisation of military equipment is relatively easily achieved, for both planning and production are totally subject to centralised control. Market forces, and the ambitions of individual armaments manufacturers, are thus of little consequence.

Although Soviet military equipment has become increasingly sophisticated over the past decade, there is a continuing emphasis upon producing items which are 'soldier-proof', being fairly simple to operate and maintain. There is also a tendency for designers to improve upon existing models rather than to develop new ones. Much Soviet equipment is widely used outside the Soviet Union, notably in the Warsaw Pact.

RANK, DRESS AND DISTINCTIONS

Rank

Officers
Officers show their rank on shoulder-boards which closely resemble those worn before the Revolution. There are three types of shoulder-board:
1. Gold braid for parade dress: plain braid for officers to the rank of colonel, decorated braid for generals.
2. Matt yellow for daily wear: generals have a decorated surface as in (1) above.
3. Khaki for wear in the field: generals have a matt-braid-like surface.

Marshal of the Soviet Union — Large five-pointed gold star with a national emblem above it
Chief Marshal of an Arm of Service — Large five-pointed gold star within a wreath, surmounted by the relevant arm-of-service badge
Marshal of an Arm of Service — Large five-pointed gold star surmounted by the relevant arm-or-service badge
Army General — Four medium silver stars
Colonel-General — Three medium silver stars
Lieutenant-General — Two medium silver stars
Major-General — One medium silver star
Colonel — Two red perpendicular lines, three silver stars in a pyramid
Lieutenant-Colonel — Two red perpendicular lines, two stars
Major — Two red perpendicular lines, one star
Captain — One red perpendicular line, four small silver stars, arranged in the form of an inverted 'Y'
Senior-Lieutenant — One red perpendicular line, three small silver stars in a pyramid
Lieutenant — One red perpendicular line, two small silver stars
Junior-Lieutenant — One red perpendicular line, one small silver star

Ensigns and Soldiers
Ensigns and soldiers also show their rank on shoulder-boards. There are only two types of shoulder-board for NCO ranks:
1. In arm-of-service colour for parade and everyday wear.
2. Khaki for wear in the field; badges of rank are red rather than yellow.

Ensign — Two small yellow stars
Officer cadet — Broad yellow edging to shoulder-board
Starshina — Broad yellow perpendicular line
Senior Sergeant — Broad yellow transverse stripe
Sergeant — Three thin yellow transverse stripes
Junior Sergeant — Two thin yellow transverse stripes
Efreitor — One thin yellow transverse stripe
Private — Plain shoulder-board

Dress
Soviet military uniforms underwent a major change in 1970–71. The new-style uniform is remarkably Western in appearance, although the typically Russian shoulder-boards have been retained. There are five basic forms of dress.

1. Parade Dress. Officers and ensigns wear a bottle-green tunic with a turned-down collar, bottle-green trousers tucked into high black boots, and a bottle-green forage-cap with red band. Soldiers wear a similar uniform in khaki. A ceremonial full dress, which includes a red plastron front to its tunic, is used by certain units on very special occasions.
2. Walking-out dress. This is similar to parade dress, but its embellishments, such as belts and aiguillettes, where worn, are less colourful.
3. Everyday dress. This is khaki for all ranks: the collars of officers' and ensigns' uniforms are turned down, and are worn with a collar and tie beneath, whereas soldiers have high collars. Soldiers normally wear their trousers tucked into their boots.
4. Working dress. This is worn by conscripts only, and consists of a khaki tunic with a high collar, and khaki trousers tucked into boots. It is worn with a khaki side-cap.
5. Field dress. All ranks wear high-collared khaki tunics and khaki trousers tucked into boots. Steel helmets are worn when appropriate. Officers and ensigns have plain khaki forage-caps, and soldiers often wear their working-dress side-caps in the field. Belts of the Sam Browne type are normally worn by officers and ensigns.

Grey greatcoats are worn, when necessary, with any of the above forms of dress: they are usually accompanied by grey fur hats. A number of special combat uniforms exist. The crews of AFVs wear black coveralls and ribbed helmet with integral headset. NBC protective suits are used by all troops in chemical and nuclear environments. Troops engaged on reconnaissance and special duties are issued with a mottled summer camouflage suit, and white winter camouflage is issued when appropriate. Airborne troops are something of a law unto themselves. They wear air force blue parade uniforms, and their khaki everyday uniforms have open collars, showing blue and white striped vests. They wear blue berets on some occasions, and have their own battle uniform of khaki coveralls and hood.

The operational branch and arm of service to which an officer, ensign, soldier or airman belongs is clearly shown on his uniform. Identification is made by means of arms of service colours and badges, shoulder boards, and collar and sleeve patches.

Arms-of-Service colours are as follows:

Motor rifle troops: Red
Rocket troops and artillery, armour, motor transport and military roads, railway and military communications, signals and radio technical, chemical, pipelaying, engineer, and all other technical troops: Black
Air force and airborne troops: Blue
Medical, military justice, administration and intendance: Magenta
KGB troops (but not border troops): Dark Blue
KGB border troops: Green
MVD troops: Russet

The shoulder-boards of soldiers and ensigns are in arm-of-service colour, except in field dress when they are khaki. Sergeants and below wear, in addition to their badges of rank, lettering on their shoulder-boards which indicate their operational branch. This lettering is in the same material as badges of rank, and is not worn on field shoulder-boards.

Examples of this lettering are

CA   Soviet Army
ГБ   KGB
BB   MVD

Collar patches are in the arm-of-service colour of the unit in which the wearer is serving. They are edged with gold in parade and walking-out uniforms, and bear the arm-of-service badge of the individual's parent arm.

Arm-of-service badges are small metal insignia worn on collar patches in parade, walking-out and everyday dress. In field dress all ranks carry their arm-of-service badge on the shoulder-board. Many of these badges are self-explanatory: the badge of armoured troops is a small tank, that of rocket troops and artillery is crossed cannon barrels, and so on.

Arms-of-service sleeve patches are large cloth badges with the arm-of-service badge woven in yellow on a background of the arm-of-service colour. They indicate the unit which the wearer is serving, rather than his parent arm, and are worn on the left upper arm in parade and walking-out dress. Airborne troops also wear them in everyday dress.

Distinctions

A wide variety of badges, medals and decorations are worn in the Soviet Armed Forces. Badges are awarded to soldiers for many reasons: passing training tests, physical proficiency, 'excellence' in specialist fields, and so on. Officers may also receive specialist qualification badges worn, like soldier's badges, on the right breast. The great majority of medals and decorations are worn on the left breast. Numerous campaign medals have been struck, and orders – like those of Suvorov and Kutuzov – were established following Russian victory at Stalingrad. The most coveted decoration is probably the gold star of a Hero of the Soviet Union.

CURRENT DEVELOPMENTS

The Soviet Armed Forces currently possess excellent capabilities for waging both nuclear and conventional war, although it must be remembered that Soviet military doctrine stresses the likelihood of any major conflict turning nuclear. Recent Russian naval developments are worthy of note, and the offensive potential of the Ground Forces – particularly the Groups of Forces in Eastern Europe – remains impressive. Centralised control of the Soviet economy contributes markedly to the efficiency of the arms industry, and Soviet military equipment, while retaining, in the main, its 'soldier-proof' characteristics, is tending to become increasingly-sophisticated.

If, however, the Soviet Armed Forces do not face all the problems encountered by their Western counterparts, they are by no means free from difficulties. Despite the reduction in the length of conscript service, and the energetic efforts of unit political officers, there is ample evidence that many young Russians regard their 2 years with the colours as anything but the happiest of their lives. The reduction in length of service has obviously lessened the time available for training, a diminution which, bearing in mind the further erosion of training time by political instruction, may well have damaging effects upon efficiency.

The Soviet Armed Forces share some of the recruitment and career-structure difficulties experienced by Western forces. Attempts to make the profession of arms an attractive career for suitable young men have not proved entirely successful: its seems likely that VU and VVU have recently been forced to lower their standards slightly The *praporshchik* scheme has not proved an unqualified triumph, and there are signs that the senior NCO situation is not entirely satisfactory. The effects that these shortcomings might have upon the overall efficiency of the armed forces are open to question. It is, though, unlikely that they seriously limit the ability of the Soviet Armed Forces to carry out their roles.

Richard Holmes

UPPER VOLTA

HISTORY AND INTRODUCTION

Upper Volta attained independence from France in 1960 and remained under civilian political rule until January, 1966. A military coup then took place which overthrew a regime by then unpopular; the coup was supported by the country's (relatively) powerful trade union movement. A military government headed by Colonel (later General) S. Lamizana was installed. Lamizana first attempted to return the country to civilian rule but this ended in violent disturbances. There followed a period of joint military and civilian rule, which in 1970 extended to elections for an assembly and a civilian prime minister. But friction, greatly exacerbated by the Sahel drought, occurred in the early 1970s; in 1974 the assembly was dissolved and the constitution suspended by a group of younger officers. These, it appears, then formed the effective power in the State, ruling through a National Council for Renewal, under which military officers had a considerable share in the governing of the country's 10 departments; a parallel system of 'defence zones' was also created. In 1976 Lamizana again announced an intention to return to civilian rule; this duly took place in 1977–78 and a number of political parties of widely differing policies emerged. More perhaps by the indifference (or cynicism) of the voters Lamizana was returned as President in Presidential elections; there was a very low percentage turn-out and Lamizana's main opponent secured a respectable total of the votes that were cast. Lamizana's renewed rule, although liberal was however not a success, major strikes hitting the country in 1980 and precipitating a new military coup led by Colonel Zaye Serbo. French connivance was rumoured. Serbo placed himself at the head of a *Comité-Militaire de Redressment pour le Progrés National*, put Lamizana and some of his closest official (but not his military) collaborators in detention; and promised radical reform. This promise has not been fulfilled, a failure that has brought Serbo into conflict with the trade union movement. So far Serbo has survived successfully, but it is reported that there are wide differences of opinion among the military, and loyalty to Serbo is far from universal.

STRENGTH AND BUDGET

Population: 7,000,000 (approximate)
Armed forces: 3775 Army, including a 75 strong army air unit, plus a gendarmerie of 900.
GNP: $850,000,000 (estimate)
Defence Expenditure: No figure available.

COMMAND AND CONSTITUTIONAL STATUS

Colonel I. Serbo as Head of State is Commander-in-Chief. The CMRPN has a rotating (and secret) membership. Originally composed mainly of young captains and majors, its membership from time to time now includes non-commissioned officers in order to try and ensure loyalty to the regime. The Chief of Staff of the Armed Forces is Major

General Y.G. Some. The Head of the Gendarmerie, a powerful figure, is Lieut-Colonel B. Neziem.

ROLE, COMMITMENT, DEPLOYMENT AND RECENT OPERATIONS

Upper Volta's army has two roles: internal security and the defence of the country's borders. A border dispute with Mali exists, Upper Volta holding an area of the Beli river near Agachev, important for grazing and also possibly for mineral wealth, to which Mali lays claim. The dispute became tense at the end of 1974 with border clashes; further clashes followed in June, 1975. The dispute still drags on, necessitating troop deployment on the border.

Upper Volta is a member of ANAD, the treaty of mutual aid in the event of an attack signed by seven West African states.

ORGANISATION

The army is composed of three infantry regiments, an artillery company, a reconnaissance squadron and a parachute company. One regiment with the reconnaissance company is posted to Ouagadougou; one other is at Bobo-Dioulasso. The three infantry regiments were formed out of five former under-strength battalions in 1980.

The gendarmerie's headquarters are at Ouagadougou, with four territorial companies stationed at Ouagadougou, Bobo-Dioulasso, Koudougou and Fada N'gourma; together with two mobile companies, one each at Ouagadougou and Bobo-Dioulasso.

RECRUITMENT, TRAINING AND RESERVES

The Mossi people are the largest (and best organised) ethnic group in the country, being just under one half of the total population. For this reason, and the very large number of Mossi traditionally in French colonial military service, they figure conspicuously in the Upper Volta army.

A basic training centre is located at Koudougou, and a military academy is being built at Kambouinsin.

Upper Volta has a technical military assistance and training treaty with France — but since independence there has been no French garrison. Some personnel train in Senegal, and Koudougou provides basic technical training for personnel from Senegal, Niger, Chad and Benin.

EQUIPMENT AND ARMS INDUSTRY

The Army possesses fifteen modern Panhard armoured-cars, eleven AML-60 and four AML-90, together with a number of older machines of doubtful serviceability, these include 30 Ferret scout cars and ten M-8 armoured cars. Thirteen M-3 VTT armoured troop carriers and four M-20 armoured utility vehicles have also been recently delivered. The artillery battery is equipped with a small number of 105mm howitzers, and the infantry regiments have 81 and 60mm mortars, together with 75mm rocket launchers.

---

* For general notes on African armies see Appendix 1.

Upper Volta

The small air unit is limited to transport and communication machines two C-47 Skytrain, two No 262 and two HS-748 transports, and five smaller liaison aircraft. Two Aérospatiale SA-361 helicopters are on order. These helicopters can be fitted to fire missiles, but it is not known whether the two on order are so equipped.

RANK, DRESS AND DISTINCTIONS

These follow the French pattern, though the *képi* is not worn.

CURRENT DEVELOPMENTS

Three main constraints upon any military developments stand out. Firstly, Upper Volta is one of the world's very poorest countries. Secondly the senior military personnel appear to be sharply divided; some reports suggest the commander of the Ouagadougou regiment, Colonel Kombascere, is in sympathy with radical politicians and trade union leaders. Thirdly Upper Volta has a tradition of urban radicalism. Linkages between urban poor and military junior leaders are not unlikely and will inevitably impair both military discipline and economic development. An added reason for anxiety is the confortable, often luxurious life-style of many senior officers, resentment over which was one of the major causes of the breakdown of discipline in neighbouring Ghana.

No news could be the best news from Upper Volta in the next few years.

ADDENDUM

On November 7th, 1982 the Zerbo government was overthrown, after some fighting, by a revolt organised by N.C.O.s and soldiers who formed a 'Provisional Council of Popular Salvation'. This council nominated an army medical officer, Major Jean-Baptiste Ouedraogo to be President and Minister for Defence. Major Ouedraogo is a Mossi, Volta's largest ethnic group.

Lloyd Mathews

URUGUAY

HISTORY AND INTRODUCTION

It was a concomitant of, and a precondition for, Uruguay's long-held reputation as the most stable and democratic State in Latin America that its army should be non-political. This was certainly the case until the early 1970s when, as a result of the internal revolutionary campaign conducted by the left-wing Movement of National Liberation (or *Tupamaros*, so named after the Indian resister of Spanish rule, Tupac Amaru), the army, in concert with the small navy and air force, progressively encroached on the autonomy of the government and eventually overthrew it in June, 1975. Uruguay thus joined the long list of Latin American republics under military rule, which the regime has given notice will not be lifted until 1981.

In striking contrast to the stability which Uruguay achieved in this century, its history in the nineteenth was disorderly to a degree unusual even in the region. Between 1828, when its independence was recognised by its neighbours Argentina and Brazil, each of which had laid claim to its territory, and 1890, there were nearly 40 revolutions, of which twelve were successful. Only three of the 23 governments which held power during the period were not challenged by revolt, and it was not until 1890 that the country got its first civilian president. All the rest had been soldiers, though, in the absence of a professional army, which did not emerge until the end of the century, 'soldiers' should really be understood to mean 'military adventurers'.

Demographically, economically and politically, Uruguay divides into two regions: that of the coast, centred on Montevideo, a great exporting and commercial centre; and the interior, which produces meat, hides and wool on great estates. Hostility between the two resulted in a 9 year siege of Montevideo from 1843 until 1852 (the Great War), with the city dwellers (*Colorados*, or Reds, from the colour they chose) backed by the Argentinians and the country party (*Blancos*, or Whites) backed by the Brazilians. Brazil took a large slice of the north as the price of her intervention and left a Blanco government nominally in power but, in 1863, joined with Argentina in supporting a Colorado invasion of the country from Paraguay, both countries hoping thereby to dismember the State further. The dictator of Paraguay, López, hoped however to make Uruguay his and his presumptions brought down upon him the combined wrath of the two larger annexationists. Uruguay joined them as an ally in the Paraguayan War which followed (1864—70), the result of which for her was to end Argentinian—Brazilian rivalry for her territory. The internal result was to bring the *Colorados* to power for the next 90 years and so gradually to suppress the endemic disorder in which the still sparsely populated country lived. The Paraguayan War had brought into being something like a national regular army (a national guard had been created with units in each town after the Great War, but had failed to flourish) and stable Colorado control of its hierarchy and promotions was an important factor contributing to the development of internal peace. The military academy was founded in 1885, after which adventurers were gradually excluded from its officer ranks.

But the most important factors making for stability towards and after the turn of the century were economic and political rather than military. Uruguay's rich agricultural interior and easy access to the seas made it a boom State, and attracted immigrants in hundreds of thousands from Europe, with moderate political traditions and no part in the feuds which had almost destroyed the country in mid-century. And in 1903 it elected as President one of the most remarkable men of modern Latin America, Jose Batlle, whose determination was to establish consensus politics, ending the *Colorado—Blanco* feud for good. His cure was to introduce collegiate government on the Swiss system, which gave the minority a share of seats with the majority on a Council of Government, designed to assist the president in his executive functions. Batlle was also during both his presidencies (1903—07 and 1911—15) to introduce legislation for universal and compulsory suffrage, mass education, State intervention in commerce and industry, social welfare payments and protection of trade union activity which was to win Uruguay during the 1920s and 1930s the reputation as the Sweden of South America.

The collapse of Uruguay's prosperity in the world slump of 1929—31 caused a return to dictatorship, of a mild sort, between 1931—8, and pure '*batllista*' government was not fully restored until 1951, when the presidency was actually abolished and the Council Government invested with the full executive power. But the army took no real part in government even during the years of the Terra dictatorship and acquiesced silently and decently in the '*batllista*' system. As late as 1960 Edward Lieuwen, the leading expert on Latin American militarism, could write:

> 'The country's extraordinary economic and social progress during the twentieth century has been paralleled by the assumption by the armed forces of a purely professional, purely military role.
>
> In Uruguay the armed forces at present are neither above the law nor beyond civilian control. The defense minister is uniformly a civilian. The career in arms is voluntary; there is no conscription. Personnel of the small professional army, navy and air force are isolated in military bases and other installations. The armed forces play only a minor, a disciplined and a completely subordinate role in the Uruguayan State'.

Within 12 years, the powers of government had passed almost completely to the armed forces. The reasons for this extraordinary and totally unexpected reversal in Uruguayan affairs result from the very success of the *batllista* achievement in producing the best-educated and most politically conscious electorate in Latin America, and thus that most sensitive to failures and short-comings in its elected government, and to the vulnerability of its economic system to movements of the world economy. Welfare Uruguay, with over half the work force on the government payroll, and with large welfare payments to make to any citizen thrown out of work, depended upon a ready and favourable market for its agricultural produce. An unfavourable balance of payments from the mid-1960s onwards resulted in raging inflation, the effects of which fell most heavily on the working class, and its social consequences brought to life the most dramatic and effective 'guerrilla' movement in Latin America, the Tupamaros. Recruited from the students educated in the free *batllista* university system, they robbed banks, kidnapped native and foreign notables (including the British ambassador) and infuriated the established class, to the point where in April, 1972 a 'state of internal war' was declared to exist. Thereafter the progression to full military rule (outlined under Command and Constitutional Status) became inexorable.

A new constitution, designed to pave the way for a return to democratic government, on lines acceptable to the military regime, was rejected by a referendum in December 1980.

STRENGTH AND BUDGET

Population: 3,000,000
Army: 22,000
Navy: 5000; four major vessels, seven smaller
Air force: 3000; 24 combat aircraft
GNP (1980): $9,770,000,000
Defence expenditure (1979 estimate): $211,600,000

The percentage of the budget spent on defence in 1973 was 10.2, the average throughout the 1960s being 8.1. The country has benefited very generously from American military assistance, the total received between 1950 and 1969 being about $40,000,000. The bulk of defence expenditure goes on the army, and is for running costs rather than equipment purchase.

COMMAND AND CONSTITUTIONAL STATUS

Since 1900 and until very recently, constitutional provisions in Uruguay have been designed to avert dictatorship and foster consensus. Between 1951 and 1967 the country was acutally run on the Swiss system. The presidency was abolished and executive power vested in a National Council of Government of nine members, six from the majority and three from the minority. The presidency was restored in 1967 as the result of a referendum and the revised constitution vested command of the armed forces in the President, who was also allotted power to regulate recruitment and the provision of personnel. The Congress was assigned powers to fix annually the size of the armed forces and to declare war. The Minister of National Defence had administrative control of the armed forces only, though they were subordinate to him on a day-to-day basis. Subordinate to each of the armed forces commanders was a chief of staff. There was no joint staff.

As a result of the internal crisis precipitated by the activities of the *Tupamaros*, the machinery prescribed by the 1967 Constitution has been very much altered. Although the country still has a civilian president, a former minister of health, he was installed by the armed forces as a result of a dispute between the service commanders and the former president, the last elected by popular vote, in June, 1975. By that date, power had already moved effectively to the armed forces, which had insisted on the dissolution of the Congress (Senate and Chamber of Deputies) in June, 1973 and its replacement by a 20 man Council of State. Even before that, it had effectively secured power to itself by requiring President Bordaberry, in February, 1973 to sanction the creation of a National Security Council (CONASED), composed of the commanders of the three services, and the Ministers of the Interior, Defence, Foreign Affairs and Economics, to function 'as an organ of military control over the administration'.

In June, 1975 the provisional president who replaced Bordaberry appointed a Council of the Nation, composed of 29 senior service officers and the existing Council of State, which 2 months later chose a president (the present one) for a 5 year term. In August, 1977 he announced a timetable for a return to democratic government: (1) the promulgation of a new constitution by 1980; (2) the election of a president, the candidate to be chosen by the two 'traditional' parties (*Colorados* and *Blancos*), with the approval of the armed forces, in November, 1981; (3) normal elections, of candidates from the traditional parties, in 1986.

Meanwhile the government rules by decree, constitutional measures and major laws being known as 'institutional acts'. The armed forces are in direct control of the central bank, State monopolies, posts and telegraphs, and fisheries. The press is banned or controlled. All left-wing parties have been dissolved and normal political and trade union activity is in abeyance. Divisions have been perceived within the armed forces over policy (between 'constitutionalists'; *'peruanistas'*, i.e. ultra-nationalists; and right-wingers, who take the military regime in Brazil as their model) but, through purges and dismissals, have been kept under control The temper of the military regime, though fiercely anti-left, is not reactionary. Generals have consistently expressed their disapproval of profiteering and corruption in the 'traditional' parties and, before taking power, openly voiced their unwillingness to act against the trade unions in an economic climate harshly unfavourable to the working-class. It is probable that the example of the military regime in Brazil, the country's neighbour, is that which most influences the army's policies.

ROLE, COMMITMENT, DEPLOYMENT AND RECENT OPERATIONS

The Constitution of 1967 enumerates 20 responsibilities of the Minister of Defence, of which the most important are defence against external aggression, and the preservation of national security and law and order. Uruguay is a signatory of the Rio and Chapultepec treaties, has sent troops to act as UN observers on the India—Pakistan border, has a constitutional provision permitting the entrance of foreign troops and the despatch of national troops abroad, with the approval of the general assembly, but has no current external commitments. There are four military regions. The army is at present deployed in Regions 1 and 2, around the major centres of population, particularly Montevideo, but maintains a presence in the interior and at the land frontier posts. Its engineer battalions are largely engaged on development work in the interior. Since the rise of the *Tupamaros* in the late 1960s, the army has been extensively committed to internal security duty, but operations have been of a police character. Uruguay sent military observers to the UN force supervising the Kashmir peace-line between 1949 and 1971.

The country is divided into four military regions as follows:

1st Military Region (HQ Salto), covering the departments of Artigas, Salto, Paysandú and Rio Negro.
2nd Military Region (HQ Mercedes), covering the departments of Soriano, Flores, Colonia and San José.
3rd Military Region (HQ Tacuarembó) covering the departments of Rivera, Tacuarembó, Durazno, Cerro Largo and Treinta y Tres.
4th Military Region (HQ Montevideo) covering the capital and the departments of Montevideo, Canelones, Florida, Lavalleja, Maldonado and Rocha.

Each Military Region is garrisoned by a nominal Division consisting of a three-battalion Infantry Brigade, a Cavalry Regiment, an Artillery Group, an anti-aircraft battery and an Engineer Battalion. Each Region also contains a variable proportion of non-divisional troops, thus the principal armoured formation, the 1st Tank Corps (actually a brigade of two mechanised cavalry regiments) is based at Tacuarembó, in the 3rd Military Region and the Army Parachute Infantry Corps (again a two-battalion brigade) has its HQ at Toledo in the 4th Military Region. There is a horsed Cavalry Brigade, of two regiments, based at Melo, in the 3rd Military Region and the 5th Engineer Battalion, an army level unit, is located in the 1st Military Region. There is also an anti-aircraft unit at Pando in the 4th Military Region. There are two units, with a largely ceremonial role, based at Montevideo, the 'Florida' Infantry Battalion and the *Blandengues de Artigas* Cavalry Regiment, both of which wear early nineteenth-century uniforms for cermonial duties.

Recent Operations

Recent operations of the Uruguayan Army have been confined to internal policing and civic action projects such as the public works carried out by its engineer battalions.

ORGANISATION

The Army consists of Infantry, Cavalry, Artillery, Engineers, Signals, Intendence, Transport, War Material, Medical and Veterinary services. The Infantry is organised into battalions, of which there are 15 (including one ceremonial and two of paratroops); the Cavalry in regiments, of which there are two mechanised and six horsed and one ceremonial; the Artillery in groups, of which there are five (4 field and 1 anti-aircraft) and the Engineers in battalions, of which there are also five. The four Divisions, each of which bears the number of the Military Region in which it is located, are administrative rather than operational formations, the highest effective tactical level of command being the Brigade, of which there are four Infantry, one Airborne, one Cavalry and one Mechanised. The Infantry Brigades have the same numbers as those of their parent Divisions, their constituent battalions being numbered sequentially. Likewise, the divisional artillery groups and engineer battalions derive their numerical designations from those of their parent Divisions as do the divisional cavalry regiments of the first three Divisions. The 4th and 5th (Mechanised) cavalry regiments however form the *Primer Cuerpo de Tanques* and hence the cavalry regiment of the 4th Division is the 6th rather than the 4th as might be expected. All units are numbered and some are named.

The Marine Infantry or, *Fusileros Navales*, are organised primarily as a single battalion, plus a number of security detachments.

The police number 17,000 and include at least two paramilitary units — the Republican Guard and the Metropolitan Guard, both stationed in Montevideo. The Montevideo branch of the National Police includes a Quick Action Unit specially formed to counter *Tupamaros* activity.

RECRUITMENT, TRAINING AND RESERVES

Unusually in Latin America, the army is recruited by voluntary enlistment. The soldiers contract for either 1 or 2 years' service, with the option of extending. There is no difficulty in attracting recruits. The men are trained in the units, specialists at the School of Arms and Services. Officers are also volunteers, chosen by competitive examination from high-school graduates. They are trained at the military academy (a 4 year course) and given branch training at the School of Arms and Services. There is an Army Command and Staff School for chosen staff candidates and a tri-service Military Institute of Superior Studies for senior officers.

The reserve is said to number 120,000, composed partly of time-expired soldiers, but largely of citizens who have undergone 'military preparatory training' at school. Its military value is probably low, but so to is the likelihood of a need for its use.

EQUIPMENT AND ARMS INDUSTRY

There is some light industry and a little heavy industry in the country, and small-arms ammunition is produced. The equipment of the army is imported, however, and is now almost all obsolescent or obsolete. Small arms are American. Heavier equipment is as follows:

Rifles: FN FAL 7.62mm (Belgium); M16 5.56mm (US)
Sub-machine-gun: M3A1 9mm (US); Uzi 9mm (Israel)
Machine-guns: BAR 0.30″ (US); Madsen Model 1937 7.62mm (Denmark); M2 0.50″ (US)
Anti-armour weapons: 106mm RCL (US); 57mm rocket projector (US)
Mortars: 81mm (US)
Artillery: M101 105mm (US)
Air-defence weapons: 40mm L/60 (Sweden/US)
Armour: M41 light tank (US) via Belgium; 22 in service); M24 light tank (US; 17 in service); M3A1 light tank (US; 18 in service); Scorpion light tank (British; 15 on order); FN-4-RM-63 armoured car (Belgium; 12 in service); M113 APC (US; 15 in service); M3A1 scout car (US; 10 in service)
Aircraft: The Air Force operates about 20 transport aircraft and about a dozen helicopters.

RANK, DRESS AND DISTINCTIONS

General de brigada — National emblem, two gold stars, oak leaves
Coronel — National emblem, one gold star
Teniente coronel — Crown, two sunbursts
Mayor — Crown, one sunburst
Capitán — Three sunbursts
Teniente — Two sunbursts
Teniente segundo — One and a half sunbursts
Subteniente — One sunburst

Uniform is American style. Distinguishing piping colours are worn: green for infantry; dark red for cavalry; black for engineers and signals; orange for ordnance; violet for medical and veterinary; brown for intendance and transportation; scarlet for artillery and general officers. There are no military medals or decorations.

CURRENT DEVELOPMENTS

As so many other Latin American armies which have usurped political power in the last 10 years have painfully discovered, the assumption of the responsibility of government has not abolished the necessity for political choice in Uruguay or exempted the army from its exigencies. Inflation, though somewhat reduced, continues at at high rate, despite a currency reform in 1976, and with it popular discontent and trade union protest. Twenty-two officers who had 'analysed' the current political situation in a document sent to the government in March, 1977 were dismissed from the army, and 30 more suspected of sympathising with them shortly afterwards. They may be presumed to belong to the ultra-nationalist *peruanista* wing who favour a more radical approach to the country's problems. In April a law was enacted providing for the retirement of officers 'whose activities compromise the purposes which should inspire their actions', a tautology enjoining an unattainable standard of loyalty. Now that the *Tupamaros* have been defeated as an effective force, the military government has the choice either of embarking on a full-blown Peruvian course, which the sophistication of the Uruguayan electorate probably makes both unfeasible and unthinkable, or of returning the country to civilian rule. That

it promised to do, under supervised conditions, by 1981. The rejection of the proposed new constitution, which was designed to prepare the way for a diluted form of democratic government, would appear to have delayed the hand over of power to a civilian administration.

John Keegan
Adrian English

VENEZUELA

HISTORY AND INTRODUCTION

Venezuela, cradle of Latin American independence, has 'a political history which can be told in the lives of its military dictators' and yet a political present in which the army plays a less intrusive role than perhaps anywhere else in mainland South America. Thanks to the very large oil revenues which the government enjoys, which give real hope for the economic transformation of the country, and the genuinely 'professional' outlook of the Venezuelan officer corps, the prospects for continuing civilian government appear promising.

Yet until 1958 Venezuela seemed bound to the wheel of an inflexible military dictatorship half a century old, and which seemed tolerable only be comparison with the era of civil war and personal caudillism which had preceded it. The country was born in war. Miranda, the Precursor as he is known in the annals of Latin American liberation, and Bolívar, the Liberator, were both Venezuelans, and Carabobo, the decisive battle for independence, was fought on Venezuelan soil. The country's secession from Bolívar's Gran Colombia, in which he temporarily united all the modern northern republics, was engineered by the commander of the Venezuelan army, General Paez, who became the country's first president and remained *de facto* ruler until 1848. His defeat at the hands of his nominee, General Monagas, in an abortive rebellion, merely ushered in a further period of personal rule, and one so arbitrary that it eventually brought about his violent overthrow in 1858. The parties who had combined against him, generally characterised as conservatives and liberals respectively, though all from the propertied classes, immediately fell out and the country embarked on a civil war (the Federalist War) which lasted for 5 years. The conservatives recalled General Paez in an attempt to win it but were ultimately defeated by Generals Falcon and Guzman Blanco. Falcon's presidency was challenged by a conservative revolt under the leadership of Monagas in 1868, and stable government was only restored by the counter-coup of Guzman Blanco in 1870.

Guzman Blanco ruled for 18 years, seen retrospectively as a golden age of peace, progress and culture. But the basis of his power was again military, and his regime was brought to an end by a provincial revolt. Four years of chaos (1888–92) were cured only by another dictatorial coup, led by the foremost general, Crespo and a disputed election at the term of his presidency led to a civil war (1897–9) which ushered in yet another military regime, that of General Cipriano Castro. An extortionate tyrant, Castro nevertheless gave Venezuela what it had hitherto lacked – a centralised army, with which his successor, General Juan Vicente Gómez, maintained himself in office from 1908 until 1935. López Contreras, the Minister of War and a serving general, quelled the disturbances which followed the death of the dictator by taking power himself, which he transferred to another, General Medina Angarita, at the end of his presidential term, while awarding himself the Ministry of War again and retaining effective authority.

He was preparing to resume the presidency at the 1945 election when, to the surprise of all but a handful of junior officers and left-wing politicians, the traditional establishment was swept off the board by a classic military conspiracy. The *junta* of professional officers, who had long chafed at being used to prop up regimes insensitive to the interests both of the army and the nation, initially sponsored a government of the leading left-wing party, *Acción Democrática*, under the presidency of the charismatic Rómulo Betancourt. Alarmed at its authentically reformist programme, however, the army took power itself in 1948 and held it for the next 10 years. The military leader, Pérez Jiménez, governed in a spirit of extravagant State investment and narrow repression, and came to grief at the hands of another left-wing-cum-military coup in 1958. Betancourt made a triumphant return to the presidency, overcame a series of internal left-wing rebellions and right-wing coups, and handed on power constitutionally to a candidate of his own party in 1964. The presidency passed to an opposition party (COPEI – Christian Socialist) candidate in 1968 and back to *Acción Democrática* in 1974.

Venezuela thus appears to have had only 20 years of non-military rule in its century and a half of independence. But the appearance is misleading, for 'military' is a word of more than usually imprecise meaning in the Venezuelan context. The 'army' with which the nineteenth-century *caudillos* sustained their power was in face a federation of local regiments, answerable to their provincial chiefs, into which the national army had dissolved after the secession from Gran Colombia. The provincial character of the 'army' reached its apogee during the Federalist War, when commissions were granted so freely that, even 10 years later, a census in the State of Carabobo revealed the existence, among a male population of 22,952, of 3450 commissioned officers, including 627 colonels and 449 generals. Paez had attempted to reform such absurdities by establishing a military academy, but the innovation has not been successful. The army which brought Castro to power in 1899 was a typically Venezuelan band of provincial partisans, motivated by hopes of political plunder.

Castro and his successor, Gómez, instituted between them, however, a fundamental transformation of Venezuela's military institutions which was to put their 'Andean' caudillism on a firmer basis than any of the former dictatorships had enjoyed and, at the same time, to promise an eventual end to caudillism itself. Their army, recruited chiefly in the Andean State of Táchira, was composed for the first time of literate townsmen, rather than uneducated peasants from the coast or the *llanos*, and therefore took readily to the reforms which their leaders introduced. These comprised the creation of a general staff and the organisation of a chain of command from it to the military commandants in each State, the establishment of a military academy and the importation of foreign training missions, initially from the Prussian-trained Chilean army, later from Belgium and France. Perhaps the most important of these initially was the general staff, which found ways of giving the local commandants no safe option but to accept its authority and put down local guerrilla bands which would not accept theirs. As a result the country had, by the end of Castro's presidency, a single army under effective presidential control.

In the longer run, however, it was the professionalisation of the army, through its own and the imported training institutions, which was to have the more important effect on Venezuelan political life. Castro and Gómez partially officered the army with men properly trained in the new military academy, but continued to commission political nominees

647

who were in general preferred for high command. And while Venezuela's traditional *élite* preserved their privileges, the junior officers remained badly paid and condemned to serve at menial tasks far from the capital. Those who went abroad for training, particularly in Peru, constrasted their lot particularly unfavourably with their fellow officers elsewhere. Military discontent first showed itself in the common cause made between the future leaders of *Acción Democrática* and some academy-trained officers in the abortive coup of April, 1928 against President Gómez. The intervention of the commander of the Caracas garrison, General López Contreras, spared many of the conspirators from the dictator's wrath but, though he was sympathetic to the rising spirit of professionalism within the army, his own management of national affairs, first as President (1936–41), then as *eminence grise* to General Medina (1941–5), deferred little to the young officers' aspirations. The prospect of his return to the presidency in 1946, and the continuation of the Andean hegemony over politics and the army which it entailed, therefore precipitated decisive military action. A secret society of young academy-trained officers, the *Unión Patriótica Militar*, acting in concert with Rómulo Betancourt's *Acción Democrática*, to which they had proposed revolution, instituted a rising on October 18th, 1945 and, after 5 days of internecine fighting which cost at least 500 casualties, took power.

The 1945 revolution marks a clear breach between what has been called the 'gendarmist State' and a regime of outright militarism. In the former, typified by the rule of Castro and Gómez, a military strongman 'uses a mercenary army to make himself national ruler, impose order, tames the army and uses it to maintain himself in power'. In the latter, the army rules directly and largely in its own interest. In Venezuela the transition was not clear cut. Medina, president between 1941 and 1945, had indeed attempted to demilitarise the existing government, and it was his success in doing so which in part created the revolutionary outlook of 1945. Demilitarisation continued during the first 3 years after 1945, when the army co-operated enthusiastically with the *Acción Democrática* government which it had brought to power. But the military mood which underlay both the army's overthrow of Medina and of its own chosen successor regime was consistent. Confronted by major regional and generational divides, on the one hand, and by the divisive policies of a too narrowly based political party on the other, the army acted both in 1945 and in 1948, when it took power back to itself, as a 'regulator', an agent of 'rectification', which alone among the institutions of the country and the State could act efficiently, uncorruptly and impartially.

The *coup d'état* of 1948 was to change the army's course, however. Delgado, leader of the three-man *junta* which overthrew the elected government, was mysteriously murdered in November, 1950 and his place taken by Pérez Jiménez, a colleague with none of his tact or standing with civilian society. Pérez Jiménez claimed to be alarmed by the policies of *Acción Democrática*, particularly its alleged plan to create an armed party militia, but it seems more likely that he feared their success would rob the army of its traditionally determinative role. His 10 years of power were certainly to be marked by an outright favouring of the army above every other sector of Venezuelan society. His arrangements with the foreign oil companies, far more preferential than those they had struck with the *Acción Democrática* regime, provided his treasury with plentiful funds, some of which he appropriated for his own use, some of which were invested in spectacular public works, but much of which was spent on the army itself. Salaries, long a subject of complaint with junior officers, had been raised in 1945 but were raised sharply again by Pérez Jiménez, to the highest level among Latin American armies, and supplemented by housing allowances and perquisites, which included the use of the Caracas Officers' Club, built by the dictator to be the most luxurious and costliest in the world. Favoured officers were promoted to the rank of general, in abeyance since 1945, were appointed again to political posts (from which officers had been removed by Medina) and allowed opportunities for graft. Officers suspected of disloyalty were, by contrast, ruthlessly persecuted by the National Security Police, which the dictator built up to a strength of 5000 and made the scourge of all opposition. The army itself, which remained only about 10,000 strong, was lavishly re-equipped, a development which gave great satisfaction to its career officers and NCOs, an increasing number of whom were also sent abroad for training.

The very lavishness of Pérez Jiménez's policies was to prove his ultimate undoing. Narrow though the army's view of its 'regulative' role was, it was based upon genuine idealism, to which the dictator's gross materialism was an affront. These feelings were particularly strong in the navy and air force, which were somewhat excluded from his largesse in any case. Despite the activities of the security police, the political parties had by 1957 organised a Patriotic *junta* whose object was the restoration of civilian rule, and similarly dedicated cells had begun to form in the armed forces. Two weeks after the dictator had held a rigged plebiscite to perpetuate his hold on power, on January 1st, 1958 army, navy and air force units rose, and planes bombed Caracas. Units loyal to Pérez Jiménez put the rising down, but it marked the end of his effective rule. On January 21st, the Patriotic *junta* called a general strike and, to avoid civil war, a group of his military supporters transferred their loyalty to the conspirators, who included, as in 1928 and 1945, the cadets of the Military School. Disorders continued until January 25th when the new *junta*, under Admiral Larrazábal, agreed to include two civilians in its ranks. It shortly afterwards promised free elections, to be held as quickly as possible.

The *junta* included and depended upon a high proportion of those officers of Andean origin, particularly from the province of Táchira, which had dominated both army and government since Castro's seizure of power in 1899. The demise of the *hegemonia andina* looked therefore by no means assured. But the experience of the army and the political parties under the 10 year dictatorship seemed to have taught both a new moderation and spirit of co-operation. The *junta* dealt severely with the leaders of the disorders, civilian and military, which swept the country between January and the presidential elections of December, 1958. The political parties, of which *Acción Democrática*, led by Rómulo Betancourt, re-emerged as the most powerful, campaigned in a moderate manner and agreed to pledge support to whichever candidate succeeded at the polls. Meanwhile the general staff was reorganised by the *junta*, and the most notorious of the *perezjimenista* officers exiled.

Rómulo Betancourt was returned as President, clearly if only narrowly ahead of Admiral Larrazábal, who at once marshalled the armed forces behind the legitimate Head of State. Their loyalty proved necessary to preserve the regime during its first 3 years of office, when it was frequently assailed by right- and left-wing coups, two of the latter being mounted by naval infantry units at Carúpano and Puerto Cabello in May and June, 1961. During 1962–3, left-wing violence of a more conventional sort was mounted by a splinter of *Acción Democrática*, the Movement of the Revolutionary Left (MIR), which with Communist Party support and help from Cuba organised a number of small bands in the countryside, particularly north-east and north-west, and waged low-level guerrilla operations. Their object appeared to be to provoke the army into a counter-coup, from which they hoped to profit, but the severity of Betnacourt's reaction, and the care he took to maintain his understanding with the military leadership, disappointed their hopes. An orderly election under an extended franchise resulted in the return of another *Acción Democrática* candidate in December, 1963 the extent of whose popular support completely deflated the guerrillas' claims to represent mass opinion.

Betancourt's policy of publicly flattering the army's wisdom and emphasising its predominant role, of privately sustaining warm personal relations with the military leaders, and of consistently fostering the material welfare of the armed forces has been pursued by his successors, with highly beneficial results. Venezuela has now enjoyed 20 years of civilian government and of almost unbroken internal peace, together with great prosperity, derived from the country's raw material revenues, and rapid developmental advance. The success of civilian government promises to prove self-sustaining and to preclude the occasion for a return to military rule.

STRENGTH AND BUDGET

Population: 17,000,000
Army: 27,000
Navy: 9000 (including 4000 marines); 11 major ships, 24 smaller; 12 aircraft
Air force: 5000; 87 combat aircraft
Paramilitary 20,000 National Guard
GNP (1980): $60,430,000,000
Defence expenditure (1980): $862,000,000

Venezuela has traditionally spent only a small portion of the national budget on defence. In the last year (1958) of the Pérez Jiménez regime, for example, it spent only 8.6%, compared to 29% in Brazil and 26% in Colombia. The reason for this moderation lies in the very large revenue which the government enjoys, largely derived from the sale of domestic oil, to the comparatively small size of the armed forces, and to their modest equipment. Unlike the States with 'great power' aspirations in South America, particularly Brazil and Argentina, Venezuela does not feel it necessary to buy or attempt to manufacture large surface ships, advanced combat aircraft or battle tanks.

COMMAND AND CONSTITUTIONAL STATUS

Venezuela, even among Latin American States, is notable for the number of constitutions which successive governments have granted. The present, promulgated in 1961 by Rómulo Betancourt's *Acción Democrática* congress, is the twenty-fourth. A highly idealistic document, it restores to congress and the States many of the powers which the Pérez Jiménez constitution of 1953 reserved to the presidency. Article 132 declares the National Armed Forces to be a non-political and obedient institution, organised by the State to ensure the national defence, the stability of democratic institutions, and respect for the constitution and the laws, the observance of which shall always be above any other obligation. The National Armed Forces shall be in the service of the Republic, and in no case in that of any person or political party. Article 190 declares that the President is Commander-in-Chief. He is advised by the Supreme Council of National Defence, which consists of the Cabinet, the Inspector-General of the Armed Forces, the Chief of the Joint Staff and the Commanders of the Army, Navy, Air Force and National Guard.

Executive control is vested in the Minister of Defence, who is advised by the Inspector-General of the Armed Forces but deals directly with the commanders of the services. In practice he works through the Chief of the Joint Staff, though that official is in theory outside the direct chain of command. Each of the services has its own staff, organised on the American pattern (as is the Joint Staff, which was established in 1958 as an anti-*perezjimenista* measure). The branches of the Army Staff normally double as branches of the Joint Staff.

ROLE, COMMITMENT, DEPLOYMENT AND RECENT OPERATIONS

The role of the army is well-defined by the Constitution. Historically, of course, it has acted either as the principal support of an autocratic ruler or as a government in its own right. Recently it has played an important part in protecting a democratic government from a violent overthrow. It also performs, though to a lesser extent than many Latin American armies, a civic action role. It has no external role of immediacy or importance, for though the country is in dispute over boundaries with Colombia and Guyana, the disputes remain diplomatic in spirit. Venezuela is a signatory of the mutual defence and non-aggression treaties of Chapultepec and Rio.

The country is divided into five military regions, as follows:

Región Militar 1 (HQ Caracas) covers federal capital and states of Carabobo, Aragua, Miranda, Sucre, Nueva Esparta and northern Anzoátegui.
Región Militar 2 (HQ San Cristóbal) covers states of Lara, Yaracuy, Táchira, Mérida and eastern Trujillo.
Región Militar 3 (HQ Maracaibo) covers states of Falcón, Zulia and western Trujillo.
Región Militar 4 (HQ San Fernando) covers states of Barinas, Portuguesa, Cojedes, Guárico, Apure, Monagas, southern Anzoátegui and the Delta Amacuro Territory.
Región Militar 5 (HQ Ciudad Bolívar) covers state of Bolívar and Amazonas Territory.

Each Military Region is garrisoned by a nominal infantry division and a variable complement of non-divisional units.

The army's main area of deployment has always been in and around Caracas, in which the Miraflores and San Carlos barracks have been traditional political storm centres, and at the large Maracay base to the west of the city. The Andean garrison, centred on San Cristóbal in Táchira State, has also always been strong. The old-established infantry battalions are distributed among the larger State capitals. The armoured units are based at Maracay. The new ranger battalions, raised during the 1970s, are based in the States which have experienced guerrilla activity, notably Sucre, Monagas, Anzoátegui, Falcón, Lara, Yaracuy, Portuguesa and Apure.

Operations against the guerrillas, organised by the MIR splinter of *Acción Democrática* the Communist Party of Venezuela, a small number of left-wing officers and other left-wing groups all actively supported by the Cuban regime, began in 1962 and were effectively concluded in 1965, although sporadic guerrilla activity continued for several years. The level of activity was always low, and easily contained by the army, National Guard and police.

ORGANISATION

The Army is divided into the usual Arms and Services, the former comprising Infantry, Cavalry, Armour, Artillery, engineers and Signals and the latter including Intendence,

Venezuela

War Material, Transport and Medical. There is also a small but expanding Army Aviation Service. The Infantry is organised in battalions of which there are a total of 28 (two Mechanised, eleven Line, thirteen Rifle and two Airborne). The Rifle Battalions (*Batallones de Cazadores*) are light infantry with a certain COIN orientation but cannot be accurately described as Rangers or Special Forces. There is a single Cavalry Regiment which is dispersed in squadron elements throughout the national territory. There are also three Armoured Battalions. The Artillery is organised in groups of which there are six Field and one Anti-aircraft. The Engineers are organised in five battalions. Although divisions exist, these appear to be administrative rather than operational formations and the effective tactical level of command is the battalion. The only major tactical formations are the *Agrupación Blindada No. 1*, a brigade-sized armoured unit which groups the 3 armoured battalions together with an artillery group at Maracay and the *Agrupación Aérotransportada Aragua*, a two battalion paratroop brigade, also based at Maracay. The Air Force includes a paratroop battalion, also based at Maracay and the Navy has three Marine Infantry Battalions, based at Puerto Cabello, Maiquetía and Carúpano.

The 20,000 man *Fuerzas Armadas de Co-operación*, generally referred to as the National Guard, is the fourth member of the Armed Forces and enjoys co-equal status with the Army, Navy and Air Force. Serving primarily as a federal police force, the National Guard also polices the country's land and sea frontiers, for which latter function it includes a coastguard element and a growing air detachment. There are three regional commands with headquarters at San Antonio de Táchira, Maracaibo and Caracas. The basic operational unit is the detachment which corresponds to an army battalion. There are eight of these under the direct command of general headquarters which serve as an intervention force in support of local detachments. The National Guard also provides guards for public buildings, penal institutions and major economic targets such as oil wells.

RECRUITMENT, TRAINING AND RESERVES

All Venezuelan males become liable for military service in their eighteenth year. The annual contingent numbers about 80,000, but only about a quarter are enlisted. There are generous exemptions for married men, teachers, high-school and university students, government employees, railway workers, clergy, only sons and brothers of servicemen. The requisite number is chosen from the remainder by lottery. The result is that the conscripts, who form the majority of the army, are from the rural and urban poor. They are mainly trained in the infantry battalions.

Officers and NCOs are all regulars. The NCOs are recruited from time-expired conscripts. The officers are selected by competitive examination from high-school students and trained at the *Escuela Militar* at Maracay; the course lasts for 4 years. Staff college training is given at the *Escuela Superior*, Chorrillos; there are branch schools for the infantry, artillery, armour, engineers, signals and transport at Maracay. The government also finances two military high schools, in Táchira and Caracas, to feed the *Escuela Militar* and to provide a supply of reserve officers.

Venezuela has a military assistance agreement with the United States, which has provided training missions in the past, and large numbers of Venezuelan officers and NCOs have undergone training at the United States School of the Americas; numbers of staff officers have attended the Inter-American Defense College, Washington. American influence on the organisation and doctrine of the army is strong.

There is no reserve organisation, but ex-conscripts are liable to recall in an emergency.

EQUIPMENT AND ARMS INDUSTRY

Venezuela has no domestic arms industry and most of its equipment has, since World War II, been imported from the United States. More recently the army has turned to Europe, and particularly France, with which the army has a historic connection, for equipment.

Rifle: FN FAL 7.62mm (Belgium)
Sub-machine-gun: Uzi 9mm (Israel/Belgium); Beretta 9mm (Italy)
Machine-gun: FN MAG 7.62mm (Belgium)
Anti-armour weapons: M40 106mm RCL (US); SS-11 ATGW (France)
Mortars: Thompson-Brandt 60mm (France); Thompson-Brandt 81mm (France); Thompson-Brandt 120mm (France)
Artillery: M101 105mm (US); Oto Melara Model 56 105mm (Italy); M3 155mm (US); Mk. F.3 155mm SPH (France)
Air-defence weapons: Bofors 40mm L/60 (Sweden)
Armour: AMX-30 medium tank (France; 142 in service); AMX-13 light tank (France; 40 in service); M18 76mm tank destroyer (US; 35 in service); Panhard AML 245 H-60/90 armoured car (France); AMX VCI APC (France; 40 in service)
Aircraft: The Army has about 10 light fixed-wing aircraft and 20 helicopters. The Air Force has about 30 transport aircraft and 50 helicopters.

RANK, DRESS AND DISTINCTIONS

Teniente General — Three gold sunbursts on shoulder cords
General de División — Two gold sunbursts on shoulder cords
General de Brigada — One gold sunburst on shoulder cords
Coronel — Three gold stars on shoulder cords
Teniente Coronel — Two gold stars on shoulder cords
Mayor — One gold star on shoulder cords
Capitán — Three small gold stars on shoulder straps
Teniente Primero — Two small gold stars on shoulder straps
Teniente — One small gold star on shoulder straps

The army wears a light khaki uniform in summer and dark-green in winter. Combat dress is American in style. There are many national decorations, including the Order of the Liberator, the Legion of National Defence and the Marshal Sucre Medal.

CURRENT DEVELOPMENTS

Venezuela's foremost national problem, until 1958, was undoubtedly the demilitarisation of its politics. After 20 years of civilian government it is possible to say that a very great deal of progress has been made towards solving it. Very serious problems nonetheless remain, even for a country of such abundant natural wealth. They include the redistribution of the land of the great estates, which *Acción Democrática* and COPEI have tackled energetically and intelligently, and the provision of employment for the hundreds of thousands of unemployed or semi-employed who inhabit the mushrooming slums of Caracas and the other large cities. The benevolence of the army is a necessary condition of progress towards their solution, since, despite its officer corps' genuine idealism and sense of national guardianship, the army's identification with the middle class and property ownership is a fact. In recent years all presidents, taking their cue from Rómulo Betancourt, have been at pains to flatter the army's self-esteem and pay tribute to the contribution it makes to national life. The civilian governments have also taken care to cushion both the officers' and the career NCOs' conditions of service. Their pay is the highest in the Latin American armies, they retire on full pay after 30 years' service, and officers have the right to employment in the civil service or State enterprises after leaving the army.

Paradoxically, the goverment must also take account of the existence, among a minority of officers, of radically left-wing sentiments. Divergent opinions of this sort are associated with the navy and the air force, which took a premier part in the overthrow of Pérez Jiménez, but the government cannot altogether, although it does in part, play at 'divide and rule' with the armed forces, since inter-service hostility is abhorrent to all of them, and politically dangerous into the bargain. Any Venezuelan government is therefore faced with the need for a particularly delicate manage-ment of its military establishment, whose loyalty is far more conditional than that upon which European governments can count. Expert observers include Venezuela in that group of countries in which 'it is likely that political power will continue to oscillate between the civilians and military men'. But the experiences of the last 20 years give grounds for optimism that power may have come to rest with the civilians, as long as they govern moderately and intelligently and the country remains prosperous.

Despite the traditionally slightly left of centre political orientation of the Acción Democrática dominated govern-ment, Venezuela has supported US policies in Central America. In the South Atlantic War, Venezuela backed up its verbal support of Argentina with offers of military assistance which were not availed of by that country. The Active support of Great Britain by the Reagan administration, which alienated most Latin American countries, may be expected to moderate Venezuelan support for United States foreign policy.

John Keegan
Adrian English

VIETNAM

HISTORY AND INTRODUCTION

The People's Army of Vietnam (*Quan Doi Nan Dan*), sometimes known as the Defence of the Homeland Army, is among the ten largest in the world, has had more, and more continuous, operational experience than any other since the end of World War II, can claim to have inflicted major setbacks on two Western armies during the period – the French and American – and is the instrument through which the independence of North Vietnam was secured between 1946 and 1954 and the territory of South Vietnam added to that of the People's (now the Socialist) Republic of Vietnam in 1975.

The army was created under the command of Vo Nguyen Giap at Cao Bang, on the Vietnamese–Chinese border, on December 22nd, 1944 as the Vietnam Propaganda and Liberation Army. It then consisted of 34 members and was somewhat expanded when in April, 1945 it merged with another nationalist force, Chu Van Tan's Army for National Salvation, composed of north-eastern tribesmen who had been recruited to the Viet Minh cause. The Viet Minh, a coalition of nationalist and Vietnamese communist bodies under communist leadership, personified by Nguyen Ai Quoc (Ho Chi Minh), had been formed at Chingsi in south China. One of its first acts was to send Giap into north Vietnam to organise a guerrilla force there. At that time Indochina, comprising the French-ruled Vietnamese territories of Tonking, Annam and Cochin-China and the French Protectorates of Laos and Cambodia, was still under French administration but also under the military occupation of the Japanese, who had come to an arrangement with the Vichy regime to use the territories as a staging area for their forthcoming campaign in south-east Asia. After the outbreak of war with America, American O.S.S. agents who reached Chiang Kai-shek's fastness in Chungking made contact with Giap and supplied him with weapons to use against the Japanese. Ho Chi Minh himself meanwhile became a member of an alternative coalition of Vietnamese nationalists, the Dong Minh Hoi, which had Chinese nationalist backing. Through it, Ho was able in October, 1945 to re-enter Vietnam and when the Japanese in March, 1945 dissolved the French administration, rightly supposing it to have accepted Gaullist leadership, Ho was able to extend his apparatus. When the Japanese themselves proclaimed a local capitulation in August, 1945 Ho prevailed on the Viceroy of Tonking, the Emperor Bo Dai's representative in the north, to lend his support to a National Liberation Committee, under Viet Minh control, which took over the administration of the territory. On August 23rd the Emperor abdicated in favour of the Viet Minh which on September 2nd proclaimed the Democratic Republic of Vietnam.

Neither the French nor the other Western allies were prepared to accept this arbitrary assumption of power, however, and two interim occupation forces were despatched to the country – a Nationalist Chinese to the north (Tonking) and a British to the south (Cochin-China and Annam). The Viet Minh was weak in the south and the British were easily able to establish their authority there and transfer it to a French army of reoccupation, under General Leclerc, when it arrived in October. In the north, where Ho's power was much better established, he looked to have a better chance of sustaining the pretensions to independence but was eventually obliged to treat with the French as a means of getting rid of the Chinese nationalists, whose intention was clearly to establish a puppet regime of their own. Negotiations with the French, who were willing to grant only limited independence, eventually broke down, however, and the Viet Minh, who made a desperate attempt to destroy the vanguard of the French reoccupation force by surprise, were driven out of Hanoi and the Red River Delta in December, 1946.

Thus began a war which was to last for 8 years. Ho and Giap retired with their skeleton army, about 10,000 strong, to the Viet Bac, the mountainous north-east, abutting onto China. They left behind them the infrastructure of a politico –guerrilla organisation in the villages and towns of the lowlands which grew steadily in importance despite the superiority of the French in conventional military strength. French efforts were concentrated during this first period of the war (1946–9) on asserting their presence in the countryside and on encircling Ho and Giap in the northern highlands. An essential element in the latter campaign was the holding of the Sino–Tonkingese frontier, marked by the *Route Coloniale 4* and the towns along it. The battle for *RC4* eventually became a full-scale campaign and yet did not stop the Chinese communists, after their arrival on the frontier in October, 1949 from passing advisers and large quantities of arms freely across it. With this accretion of strength Giap unleashed in September, 1950 a major offensive against the frontier towns on *RC4* and by the end of October had captured them all. It was a stunning defeat for the French.

In the following year, Giap made the mistake, however, of over-estimating his success. Believing that the war had reached what, in Maoist analysis of military operations, is called the stage of the 'general offensive', he brought his forces, now organised into five full divisions, down to the edge of the Red River Delta and made an all-out attempt to reach Hanoi. The French, under the inspired leadership of a newly arrived commander, the charismatic de Lattre de Tassigny, repulsed the attacks with great loss to the Viet Minh (at least 9000 killed). By mid-June, at the end of three major battles (Vinh-Yen, Mao-Khe, Ninh-Binh), Giap himself had suffered a defeat as serious as that he had inflicted the previous year and was obliged to withdraw his main force (*chu luc*) divisions into the Viet Bac. But he left behind him a greatly strengthened political and military structure, composed both of village guerrilas and regional semi-mobile regulars, in the countryside. As in 1947–9, the French largely ignored the countryside forces in new efforts, which occupied most of 1952–3, to bring the main force divisions to battle again and repeat the success they had won in the delta under de Lattre. By 'deep penetrations' along the northern rivers and by parachute descents into the Viet Bac, they strove to make the Viet Minh fight for fixed points of ground, where air power would tell. None of these operations had more than a temporary and local success, since Giap was well aware of their intentions and became adept at refusing battle, while profitably harrassing the flanks of the penetrations that the French made.

At the end of 1953 the French high command, desperate for a decisive battle and alarmed that the Viet Minh might repeat an earlier incursion into Laos, where a home-grown communist army, the Pathet Lao, was threatening the stability of the French-protected royal government, decided to construct an 'aero-terrestrial base' in the northern highlands across the route the Viet Minh must use if they wished to re-enter Laos. The spot chosen was Dien Bien Phu, on the Laotian border, 170 miles from Hanoi by air. The French counted on their air power, operating from the Dien Bien Phu airstrip in local support and from Hanoi on supply runs, to devastate the main force concentration they hoped Giap would assemble there. They were right in assuming that Giap would on this occasion accept battle but wrong in supposing that they could overcome. The Viet Minh managed to assemble, by man porterage over jungle tracks 300 miles long, a great weight of artillery and munitions in the hills overlooking the Dien Bien Phu airstrip. With this battering force, they opened a bombardment of the 'aero-terrestrial base' on March 13th, 1954 which immediately interrupted all landings and take-offs from the airstrip. The French succeeded in sustaining resistance there by parachute dropping of supplies and reinforcements, but were unable to provide effective local air cover to evacuate the wounded. After a heoroic resistance, the French garrison, numbering over 10,000, was obliged to surrender on May 8th. While the siege had distracted French attention, the Viet Minh had further extended their control over much of the lowland territory of Tonking and had asserted an important military presence in Annam. An international conference in session at Geneva, convened to decide the future of Vietnam (to which France had several times promised conditional independence) accepted the results of the fighting of 1954 as evidence that France no longer exercised effective jurisdiction and, with French acquiescence, drew up plans for the political future of Indo-China. Tonking became an independent State under Viet Minh (now openly communist) control, as the Democratic Republic of Vietnam. Annam and Cochin-China, where the Viet Minh had never been strong, also became independent, under a non-communist government, as the Republic of Viet-Vietnam. Laos and Cambodia ceased to be French Protectorates, but became subject to international supervision designed to avert their falling under the control either of the Viet Minh or anti-Viet Minh governments in Vietnam.

In the process of gaining independence there took place a major two-way shift of population between north and south. The largest movement was of Catholic Vietnamese from Tonking to the south, though numbers of declared Viet Minh also went from the south to the north; but the proportions were very unbalanced: about 900,000 from the north to the south, about 90,000 in the opposite direction. The imbalance was partly due to a decision by the Viet Minh to leave a number of their 'cadres' concealed in the south. The Geneva agreement had prescribed the holding of elections to bring about the unification of the two Vietnamese States, but there was clear lack of intention both in the north and south from the outset to accept reunification on anything except partisan terms.

The southern government, under the leadership of Ngo Dinh Diem, accepted American advice and aid from the beginning of its rule, particularly in the creation of an army. The French had created in 1948 a Vietnamese National Army (separate from the Vietnamese-recruited units of the French army) which eventually reached a strength of 100,000, and it was on that base that the South Vietnamese government built its Army of the Republic of Vietnam (ARVN). On American advice, it was organised into eight divisions, trained in conventional tactics to repel an invasion across the 17th Parallel (the provisional frontier and Demilitarised Zone separating the two Vietnams) which was regarded as the principal military threat the South had to face.

In fact, from 1957 onwards, it began to be confronted with the same pattern of rural insurgency, now organised by local communists who quickly came to be called Viet Cong, which the French had known. Between 1957 and 1960 several thousand government officials had been murdered in the villages and wide areas of the countryside ceased to be under effective government control. An attempt was made to establish, on the British model successfully carried out in Malaya, a chain of 'strategic hamlets', defended by village militias, which the Viet Cong could not penetrate, but it failed. In 1960 the southern insurgents proclaimed a National Liberation Front, with its National Liberation Army, and made clear that its programme was nothing less than the overthrow of the existing government and its replacement by one committed to Marxist forms.

In describing what happened thereafter, it is impossible to reconcile the versions of the two opposing sides. That of the NLF depicts a home-grown insurgency gradually overcoming, despite massive American assistance, the power of the southern government, to the point where the Americans were obliged to abandon it and it itself eventually collapsed. That of the South Vietnamese government and its American allies is completely contrary. While accepting the presence of a home-grown insurgency on the soil of the south, it insists that it survived only through the support of North Vietnamese units introduced by clandestine methods across the frontiers and supplied, down the 'Ho Chi Minh trail' through Laos and Cambodia, with munitions sent from North Vietnam but donated by Russia and China. It also insisted — and here the North Vietnamese version does not much differ — that the eventual collapse of the southern government was brought about by a full-scale invasion of the south by the north, after the Americans had withdrawn their troops and air support, in 1975.

The evidence for direct North Vietnamese involvement in the 'Viet Cong insurgency' is in fact incontrovertible. Photographs taken of supply columns on the 'Ho Chi Minh trail', captured stocks and documents and indeed captured personnel all point to the presence of People's Army units on southern territory and to wholehearted Hanoi support for the Viet Cong. It would indeed be difficult to disprove the south's case that the National Liberation Front and the Liberation Army were directly controlled from the north through southerners who had been original communist members of the Viet Minh. It would be almost equally difficult to show that the Viet Cong could have achieved their final victory without the presence of People's Army units on southern territory from early in their campaign.

That insurgency gathered pace from 1960, prompting the American government to reinforce heavily the numbers of military advisers it already had in South Vietnam. President Diem's government came under increasing internal and external criticism, as violence and his repressive response to its manifestations increased, and in November, 1963 he was overthrown and murdered by a political faction within the armed forces. The new government did no better at quelling the insurgency and in July, 1965 the United States government, using powers voted it by congress the previous August as a result of the Gulf of Tonking incident, decided to commit whole American units to the fighting. In heavy engagements during the autumn of 1965, these units were able to repel a full-scale North Vietnamese invasion of the south through the Southern Mountain Plateau and, during 1966–7, when American forces committed exceeded 250,000, and American air attacks on northern territory became continuous, the tide of war began to swing against the Viet Cong. The successful defence of Khe Sanh, besieged by three North Vietnamese divisions for 77 days in the spring of 1968, seemed an augury of eventual victory, which was cautiously predicted by the American commander, General Westmoreland. On January

21st, however, there was unleashed all over the south a mighty Viet Cong offensive, timed to coincide with the Vietnamese new year (Tet), which took both Americans and South Vietnamese completely by surprise and brought the war into almost every town of any size. Saigon itself was invaded by Viet Cong regulars and most of Hué, the ancient capital of the empire of Annam, taken over. At the end of a month's fighting, the Viet Cong and North Vietnamese People's Army had suffered 40,000 deaths, and failed in their objectives, but had attracted much of the fighting force of the six American divisions available for mobile operations (three others were tied to the Demilitarised Zone) and of the 150 South Vietnamese battalions out of the countryside, where they were never thereafter to re-establish control.

In April, Hanoi accepted an offer from President Johnson to negotiate for an end to the war. The talks, convened at Paris in May, were to last until January, 1973 while fighting continued in the countryside. Cambodia was invaded (May, 1970) and then Laos (February, 1971) by American and South Vietnamese troops in an effort to interrupt supplies and reinforcements from the north to the south, and the American air campaign against military targets in the north periodically halted and re-started to put negotiating pressure on Hanoi. But in July, 1969 the Americans had enunciated their determination to turn the conduct of the war over to the South Vietnamese (the Nixon Doctrine of 'arms not troops') and it was against that background that the diplomacy proceeded. The eventual agreement, which imposed a ceasefire and established an international control commision to supervise its observation, did little more than place that resolve on a public basis.

It did not end the fighting, though the re-equipped and revitalised ARVN which the Americans left behind after their withdrawal (completed January, 1973) showed itself far more effective at dealing with the Viet Cong after the Americans' departure than it had before their arrival. But the Viet Cong had by 1973 grown into an experienced and well-equipped force of 225,000, with the 15 divisions of the People's Army, much of it deployed in the south, to support it. By October, 1974 numbers of previously uncommitted North Vietnamese People's Army divisions had been brought down the Ho Chi Minh trail and emplaced on the border in the Southern Mountain Plateau. The ARVN, which had suffered heavily in its successful campaign to recapture the northern Quang Tri province and the highland region around An Loc in the summer of 1972, could not match either the weight of numbers or equipment that the enemy were able to deploy and, when the Viet Cong/People's Army offensive opened in March, 1975 it was swiftly forced to give ground. People's Army divisions first drove into the Southern Mountain Plateau, threatening to bisect the country, and then into Quang Tri in the north. Much of the South Vietnamese army, including the excellent marine division, was destroyed in the fighting for the northern town of Da Nang at the end of March, and by early April the People's Army controlled South Vietnam as far south as Nha Tranh, 200 miles from Saigon. During the next fortnight they maintained their pressure from west and north, driving the South Vietnamese army before them. On April 29th their forces surrounded Saigon and on the following day they received the unconditional surrender of the South Vietnamese government.

The appearance of the victorious army in the streets of Saigon, instantly renamed Ho Chi Minh City, removed all doubts about the identity of the conquerors. The units, including tank battalions equipped with Russian T-54s, were those of the Vietnamese People's Army. After a campaign lasting 20 years, it had achieved the unification of the country under communist rule.

STRENGTH AND BUDGET

Population: 56,000,000
Army: 1,000,000
Navy: 4000, 6 frigates, 84 smaller craft
Air force: 25,000, 470 combat aircraft (many in store)
Paramilitary: 70,000 armed security forces; a militia of 1,500,000

No trustworthy figures are available for military expenditure.

COMMAND AND CONSTITUTIONAL STATUS

Supreme command of the People's Army rests with the President, but control of its organisation, recruitment, budget, promotions and operations with the Politburo of the Central Committee of the Workers' Party. As a member of the Politburo, Minister of Defence, Commander-in-Chief, creator of the People's Army and architect of its victories (as well as it defeats, which should not be forgotten), General Vo Nguyen Giap must enjoy greater prestige than any politico—military commander at present in office anywhere in the world. Command, nevertheless, has always been exercised by committee, in which Giap has played the part of first among equals in the making of higher policy.

The High Command of the People's Army, of which the Minister of Defence and Commander-in-Chief is the Head, is organised into three main elements: the central political bureau (commissar system), which has cells as far down the military structure as the platoon; the supply staff, which procures and distributes military material and services; and the general staff. The latter is divided into bureaux for operations, intelligence, training, administration, armed (main) forces, popular forces (militia), personnel, communications and liaison.

ROLE, COMMITMENT, DEPLOYMENT AND RECENT OPERATIONS

Role
As in all communist States, the role of the army transcends purely military responsibilities. Soldiers form part of the National Assembly, its Standing Committee and of the Central Committee of the Workers' Party and its Politburo from which all power flows. The more or less continuous war which the party has fought since 1946 has naturally heightened the influence which military leaders exert. On the other hand, Ho Chi Minh, the creator of the communist State, was emphatically not a military man and as president, to which office the constitution in any case allots virtually unlimited power, he represented the political and ideological tradition in the communist system. He has been succeeded by a trusted friend, of the same background and outlook. Because of his advanced age, however, it seems unlikely that he is an effective president. This must enhance the power of other members of the politburo, in which military influence is strong.

Besides sharing in government, the army plays a major part in the indoctrination and leadership of the population through its control of the militia. Its resources have also become available, since the conquest of the south, for civic development and rural aid.

Commitment
Vietnam has a military assistance agreement with Russia, under which very large quantities of military equipment have been supplied. In July, 1977 she signed a series of agreements with Laos (where Vietnamese troops have operated for many

years). It is supposed that the agreements regularised the presence of Vietnamese units. In practical terms, Vietnam is committed to the defence of Laos.

Deployment

Vietnam is divided into a number of military regions. Two in the north are the North-Western, headquarters Son La, and the Fourth, headquarters Vinh. This would suggest that the government has preserved the four military zones delineated during the war against the French, the other two then being south and north of Hanoi. Since the conquest of South Vietnam, two military regions have been mentioned there — the Fifth and Seventh. The Viet Cong divided South Vietnam into three zones — the coastal plain, the highlands and the extreme south (Cochin-China). This evidence suggests that there are now seven military regions, with three to four divisions stationed in each.

About 45,000 Vietnamese troops are stationed in Laos, and have been there for many years, at least since 1961 in force, and in smaller numbers from French days. About 180,000 Vietnamese troops operate in Kampuchea.

Recent Operations

Vietnamese troops became engaged in fighting on the border with Kampuchea in mid-1977, following a worsening of relations between Hanoi and Pol Pot's Khmer Rouge regime. It was apparently provoked by the Khmer Rouge, for internal political reasons, but resulted in Vietnam 'straightening the frontier' in 1978 and then, in December, embarking on a full-scale invasion. The campaign swiftly brought the whole country into the hands of the Vietnamese, who subsequently set up in it a local party (KRP) friendly to themselves. The Khmer Rouge, however, and a small, right-wing guerrilla movement, the Khmer Serei, continue to operate in the west of the country, and their resistance requires the presence of 180,000 Vietnamese troops to contain it.

In January—February 1979 the Chinese, long Pol Pot's protectors, reacted to Vietnam's invasion of Kampuchea by a surprise attack on the northern border of Vietnam, in the Cao Bang and Lang Son regions, a campaigning ground well known to French soldiers in 1946—50. The object of the attack was probably punitive and admonitory; but it was fiercely resisted by the Vietnamese who, operating in excellent defensive terrain, inflicted heavy casualties on the Chinese and regained all the territory taken.

A dry-season offensive, the largest mounted since 1979, in early 1982 against the Khmer Rouge, and Serei, forces on the Thai border is reputed to have had little success.

ORGANISATION

Little is published about the domestic organisation of the Vietnamese People's Army, but it seems that it conforms to that common in communist armies — branches for infantry, artillery, engineers, signals, medical service, political directorate and rear services. The Air and Air-Defence Service forms part of the People's Army. Operationally it is organised into divisions and independent regiments. There are estimated to be 57 infantry divisions, armoured divisions, two marine divisions, six independent armoured brigades, seven engineer divisions, fifteen construction divisions, four engineer brigades. The division is composed of three infantry regiments each of three battalions, an artillery regiment, a tank battalion and support elements. The strength of a division is about 10,000 and of a regiment 2000—3000. Five of the divisions, Nos. 304, 308, 312, 316 and 320, were created about 1950 and have long and varied operational histories. The 304th Division, for example, was at both Dien Bien Phu in 1954

and Khe San in 1967. Other divisions identified are the 2nd, 3rd, 5th. 7th, 9th. 324th, 325th (sometimes numbered 325C), 335th, 338th, 341st and 610th. One of the best-known independent regiments is the 148th, which appears to have been more or less continuously in Laos since the 1950s. The VPA also includes an artillery command (which may be the 351st Heavy Division, also a 1950s creation), an engineer command (probably an offshoot of the 351st) 20 air-defence missile regiments, 40 air-defence gun regiments and 15 engineer regiments.

About ten of the Vietnamese People's Army divisions are formed from 'main force' units of the Liberation Army (Viet Cong), which have been absorbed since the unification of north and south in 1975.

It is not known how much, if anything, of the South Vietnamese Army (ARVN) has been absorbed into the People's Army, nor even whether its massive armoury has been taken into service. Some personnel, particularly from the paramilitary forces — the Regional Forces, Popular Forces, People's Self-Defence Force and Civilian Irregular Defence Groups — are known to have been enlisted on an individual basis.

North Vietnam had, before the conquest of the south, its own well-established paramilitary organisation: an armed police (Frontier, Coast and People's Armed Security Forces) totalling about 70,000; and an armed militia, numbering about 1,500,000.

RECRUITMENT, TRAINING AND RESERVES

The original People's Army was recruited through the peculiar structure of the army — the most active and best-motivated young men of the village guerrilla groups were chosen to go to the semi-mobile units of the provincial Regional Forces, and they in turn sent their best men to the Main Force (*chu luc*) (though it was possible also to join the last two directly). The party insisted that all its soldiers were volunteers, and that there was no conscription inside its liberated areas. Since the establishment of the communist State in 1953 conscription has been instituted, but it was supplemented during the Vietnam War by the 'Three Readies Drive' — a propaganda campaign which persuaded men to volunteer that they were 'ready to fight, ready to join the army, ready to go wherever needed', and which is said to have netted 1,500,000 signatories. The Vietnamese recruitment system seems therefore to be conscriptive, but to operate in a population whose men of military age have largely been persuaded also to declare themselves volunteers for military service. However, the communist party always met considerable resistance to efforts to recruit the non-Vietnamese minorities of the uplands and mountains. Some were won over by imaginative personal appeal (the 316th, 324th and 335th Divisions have a large minority element), but the majority expressed their ethnic hostility to the Vietnamese either by standing neutral or even by joining the French forces (during the Indochina war), or by enlisting to fight the Viet Cong and infiltrating North Vietnamese regulars in the south during the Vietnam War. It is not known to what extent the communist government has applied conscription to the minorities, or how willingly they have responded.

All Vietnamese of military age in the north receive some preliminary training in the village militias. They complete their training in units, probably in the training divisions. Officers, who are selected by the party apparatus, are trained in the officer training schools. Two, at Ha Giang and Bac Kan in the far north, had been established during the course of the war with the French. It is known that there are officer schools now at Thanh Hoa and Son Tay, south and just west of Hanoi, respectively.

The reserve is divided into two categories. The second category comprises men waiting for call-up. The first includes all those who have completed their compulsory military service (at least 2 years) and who are assigned to local reserve units, which have arms and equipment stored in convenient armouries and can be activated at short notice. They may number 500,000, perhaps more.

EQUIPMENT AND ARMS INDUSTRY

The Viet Minh began a village arms industry during their war against the French, but it produced only the most primitive sorts of weapons in very small quantities. Since independence in the north in 1954 they have expanded and re-equipped their arms industry, so that they can now manufacture small arms ammunition, some heavier ammunition (including shells for the American 105mm howitzer of which they captured numbers from the French) and some automatic weapons. The output was, however, quite insufficient to sustain the Viet Cong—North Vietnamese war effort in the south during the Vietnam War. Almost all the equipment used there, and to defend the north against American air attack, was supplied by China by Russia, over the Chinese border, through the port of Haiphong or through Cambodian ports. Spare parts and munitions for its now enormous arsenal of equipment must still come from its allies. It is not known what it will do with the equally large arsenal it inherited when the south was overrun, since munitions and spare parts for almost all those American weapons (the 105mm howitzer excepted) are of course unavailable.

Rifle: 7.62mm AK-47 (Russia; Chinese model also)
Machine-gun: 7.62mm RPK Kalashinkov (USSR) and 7.62mm PKS Kalashnikov (USSR). (Many older Russian and Chinese small arms also still in service)
Mortar: 82mm M-42 (USSR), 120mm M-43 (USSR) and 160mm M-43 (USSR) in the artillery battalion
Anti-armour weapons: RPG-7 rocket launcher (USSR); 57mm M-43 gun (USSR) and 85mm M-45 gun (USSR); 107mm B-11 recoilless rifle (USSR); 100mm M-45 gun (USSR); Sagger missile
Air-defence weapons: 14.5mm ZPU-2 and ZPU-4 guns (USSR); 23mm ZU-23 gun (USSR); 23mm ZSU-23-4 SPG (USSR); 37mm M-39 gun (USSR) and 57mm M-50 gun (USSR); 57mm ZSU-57-3 SPG (USSR); 85mm M-44 gun (USSR), 100mm M-49 gun (USSR) and 130mm M-55 gun (USSR); SA-2 (Guideline) missile (USSR), SA-3 (Goa) missile (USSR), SA-6 (Gainful) missile (USSR) and SA-7 (Grail) missile (USSR) and SA-9
Artillery: 105mm and M-101 howitzer (USA and 122mm M-38 howitzer (USSR); 130mm M-54 gun (USSR); 152mm M-55 gun/howitzer (USSR) also includes some American 155mm and 175mm artillery.

Armour: BTR 40/60, 152 APC (USSR); (1500 in service); 800 M-113 and Commando APC (US); PT-76 light tank (USSR) and Type 60 light tank (China) (450 in service); M-41 light tank (US; 150); T-34 tank (USSR) and T-54 and T-62 tank (USSR); T-59 (Chinese version of T-54), M-48 tanks (US); T-10 assault gun (USSR) and JSU-122 assault gun (USSR). There are about 1500 tanks in service with the army, of which 1500 are T-34/54/62 and 400 are M-48.

RANK, DRESS AND DISTINCTIONS

Unlike the Chinese People's Liberation Army, the Vietnamese People's Army uses conventional military rank titles, at least up to the rank of general. Like the CPLA, however, officers, at least in combat dress, bear no distinguishing mark. The uniform is a simple cotton tunic and trousers in khaki-green, with a red patch and a star on the collar. The most distinctive feature is the headdress, a tropical sun helmet made of pressed fibre and bearing a red star. It is from this that the regular soldiers (*bo doi*) get their nickname of 'hard hats'. A number of campaign medals have been issued, including one, much prized, for Dien Bien Phu.

CURRENT DEVELOPMENTS

The Vietnamese army is, after the Chinese, the second largest in Asia (and the third largest in the world) and immeasurably the most experienced. It appears able to sustain its intake of conscripts without detriment to the enormous objects of the state, and to maintain its very large inventory of equipment; though it is only the items of Soviet origin for which it can now easily acquire spare parts.

Bad relations with China, which resents its aspirations to great power status in South-east Asia, requires that a large proportion of its army remain in the northern border region. The resistance of the South to full social and economic integration in the Communist system also requires the maintenance of sizeable forces there. However, the main call on the VPA's strength is from Laos — where it keeps a garrison of 45,000 men — and Kampuchea, where 180,000 soldiers battle against the coalition of anti-Vietnamese Khmers (Khmer Rouge and Khmer Serei, a triple alliance of right-wing forces).

Military, Vietnam is unchallangeable in South-east Asia; even China would find it difficult to launch a large-scale war against Hanoi over the difficult and routeless terrain which divides the two countries. Politically, Vietnam's foreign policy objectives have now run up against the frontiers of acceptability, since Tahiland is the beneficiary of American military guarantees. Hanoi's fifty year battle for dominance in the Indo-Chinese region may therefore have reached its culmination.

John Keegan

WEST INDIES

JAMAICA

The origins of the Jamaica Regiment, the principal unit of the Jamaica Defence Force, ascend into the late eighteenth century. The West Indian islands were then, as they had been intermittently for 200 years, the scene of fighting between the European powers, and in 1795 a British officer raised a corps of islanders to help defend Martinique against the French. This, Malcolm's Corps of Rangers, was soon amalgamated with an existing body of men from Jamaica: the Corps of Dragoons, Pioneers and Artificers, which had originally been raised as the Carolina Corps in 1778, and used by the British to fight the rebels in the American War of Independence. Disbanded in Jamaica in 1783, its black soldiers were retained in government service as a semi-military labour force. The amalgamation of the two produced the unit which in 1798 was to be renamed the 1st West India Regiment and was to form the nucleus of the most important colonial force maintained by Britain outside India during the nineteenth century.

By 1799 there were 12 battalions of the West India Regiment in existence, a number which alarmed the white planter community considerably but was justified by the Westminster government on the ground that local regiments suffered a much lower mortality than white, which at times would be wiped out by disease. They proved their military worth by helping in the capture or retention of all the British colonies of the Caribbean during the wars of 1793–1815, and by accompanying Pakenham to New Orleans in the War of 1812. By 1819 the 12 battalions had been reduced to two – the 1st and 2nd West India Regiments. A third existed between 1840 and 1870 and a 4th and 5th briefly in the 1860s, but it was the two oldest which chiefly served the particular purpose for which the British government maintained the West India Regiment during the nineteenth century. This was the garrisoning of the Caribbean and British West Africa and, when necessary, colonial campaigning in West Africa. From 1812, soldiers of the W.I.R. were actually recruited in Sierra Leone, and from 1824, when the 2nd W.I.R. fought in the First Ashanti war in what is now Ghana, there was always one battalion on the west coast. In all the W.I.R. took part in 22 campaigns or expeditions before 1900 and fought in the Cameroons, east Africa and Palestine during World War I. Confusingly a British West Indies Regiment, eventually of 11 battalions, was raised from the militias and volunteer forces of the islands in 1915 and served in an auxiliary capacity during World War I. In World War II these local forces were re-embodied as the North Caribbean and South Caribbean Forces (1943), and an active service force, the Caribbean Regiment, was formed from it in 1944. But none saw action.

By then the old West India Regiment, always a corps of the regular British army, had ceased to exist. It had been disbanded in 1927, its band alone surviving as a ceremonial unit supported by the government of Jamaica. The various island volunteers and militias had remained in existence, however, and in 1959, as a result of the Federation of the Caribbean islands the year before, the West India Regiment was reconstituted, to be the nucleus of the Federal Army. On the dissolution of the Federation in 1962, following disagreement between the islands, the regiment was again dissolved,

its individual battalions becoming the property of the islands as they took independence. The 2nd Battalion went to Trinidad and Tobago, as the Trinidad and Tobago Regiment, the 1st and 3rd to Jamaica as the Jamaica Regiment. These units are now the main elements in the Defence Forces of these respective sovereign States.

The Jamaica Defence Force is divided into the Regular Force and the part-time National Reserve; both are tri-service in composition. The Regular Force consists of the 1st and 2nd (formed 1979) Battalions, Jamaica Regiment, infantry battalions of the British type; a Support and Service Battalion; the Force Coast Guard, with four fast patrol boats; and the Force Air Wing, with seven light aircraft and helicopters. The National Reserve consists of the 3rd Battalion Jamaica Regiment, an ordinary infantry battalion of part-time volunteers with a regular cadre, the five companies of which are scattered over the island; an Air Squadron; and a Coastguard Reserve. The Force is commanded by the Governor-General in name but in practice by the elected government. Officers are trained in Britain, India, Canada and Australia. The Force is equipped with British light weapons. It wears British style uniforms, badges of rank and insignia: its cap badge incorporates the wreath of Carolina laurel worn by the Carolina Corps and the Old West India Regiment. Its duties are to maintain internal security, which is threatened by the intense political rivalries and economic inequalities on the island. It was widely and successfully deployed to keep the peace during the 1975–6 General Election Campaign; there is no arms industry.

TRINIDAD AND TOBAGO

The Defence Force in its present form came into existence in 1962; for its previous history, see the entry on Jamaica (above). It consists principally of a single infantry battalion – the 1st Trinidad and Tobago Regiment with a support battalion. It is recruited by voluntary regular enlistment but has a part-time volunteer battalion. Officers are trained chiefly in Britain. It is equipped with British infantry weapons and wears British-style uniforms and badges of rank. Its role is to maintain internal law and order. There is a naval force which operates nine patrol craft and an airwing with two aircraft. The Governor-General is titular Commander-in-Chief but command is exercised by the elected government.

BARBADOS

The defence forces of this, the third most populous State of the former British West Indies, consists of a single volunteer part-time infantry battalion – the Barbados Regiment. It is only about 3000 strong. There are plans, not yet realised, to create a Barbados Defence Force, incorporating a larger Barbados Regiment and other units.

THE BAHAMAS, BERMUDA AND THE SMALLER WEST INDIAN STATES

The Bahamas has no defence force. Bermuda has a small infantry battalion – the Burmuda Regiment which is recruited by selective conscription and regular enlistment. The Associated States have small part-time volunteer defence forces: the Antigua Defence Force (75 all ranks), St. Kitts/Nevis Volunteer Defence Force (about 100 all ranks), Dominica Defence Force (about 100 all ranks), St. Lucia Defence Force (about 100 all ranks), the Grenada Volunteer Force (about 200 all ranks) and the Belize (formerly British Honduras) Defence Force (about 300, but in the process of ex-

pansion into a regular force). Britain retains responsibility for the external defence of these States. It does so also for Bermuda and the remaining dependent territories of the Caribbean. Britain maintains a garrison in Belize, to which Guatemala lays claim, and a naval force, with Royal Marines embarked, at Bermuda.

John Keegan

NORTH YEMEN

HISTORY AND INTRODUCTION

The governance of North Yemen is one of the closest approximations in the modern world to Thomas Hobbes' 'war of everyone against everyone'. The only two centres of power in the country are the army and the tribes, and the struggle for mastery both within and between the two forces is conducted virtually without rules and almost invariably by violence. Between October, 1977 and October, 1978 the country lost two presidents by assassination and experienced at least two other major coup attempts. Purges within the army, as the briefly successful contenders for power struggle to eliminate their enemies, have prevented it from attaining any serious measure of professional competence, and continuous intrigues, involving also the conservative, wealthy neighbour, Saudi Arabia, and the Marxist sister State, South Yemen, preclude any stabilisation of the situation. The fluidity of power in North Yemen is best exemplified by the rise to power of the late President Ahmad al-Ghashmi, assassinated in mid-1978, who made it all the way from corporal to lieutenant-colonel and Head of State by the age of thirtynine in a career marked by cynical intrigues an brutal murders.

The Yemen, north and south, is historically a single State which has always contained about half the population of the Arabian peninsula despite its small share (10%) of the region's territory, owing to the relative fertility of its soil and an adequate annual rainfall. Separated as it is by sea and vast tracts of sparsely inhabited desert from the rest of the world, it has also always been an extremely inward-looking, conservative and even xenophobic society. It was ruled by the Ottoman Turks until World War I, but the continuous uprisings against foreign rule made it the graveyard of the Turkish army (the folk-wisdom of Anatolia regarded a Turkish conscript posted to the Yemen as being as good as a dead man), and Ottoman rule was never firmly established in the mountains of the north which were the stronghold of the great tribal confederacies. These tribes belong to the Zaidi sect of the Shi'ite branch of Islam, and regarded the Sunni Turks as infidel interlopers. Amongst the population of the centre (including San'a', the capital), the coastal plain (the Tihama) and the south, however, there was markedly less resistance to Turkish rule, for this population is itself Sunni, of the Shafa'i school.

The Zaidi northern tribes traditionally elected in Imam with severely restricted temporal powers to serve as their leader, but from 1891 the Hamid al-Din family succeeded in making the Imamate hereditary in its own hands, and in expanding its political importance to something approaching the powers of a feudal monarchy. When the Turks left the Yemen in 1918 the Zaidi Imams set about the extension of their control over the entire country, and the political dominance they then established was such that even today it would be unthinkable for a Shafa'i Head of State to rule in San'a'. Even the Imams found it hard to control the great Zaidi tribes, dominated by the Hashed and Bakil confederacies centred in the north and north-east, but with adherents throughout the country. The Imam Yahya, who had ruled the country with an iron hand since 1918, was assassinated in 1948 in a palace coup supported by restive tribal factions opposed to his tight control, and his son Ahmad had to fight a major campaign against the rebel forces before re-establishing his control as Imam.

It was after this experience that the Imam Ahmad set out to build up a small army along modern lines which would enforce the power of the central government against the tribes. He purchased military equipment from the Soviet Union, and sent his new officers to be trained in Egypt and Iraq. The officers were deliberately chosen on non-tribal criteria, in order to ensure their loyalty to him. In a further measure to bolster central power, the Imam took his country into the United Arab Republic (Egypt, Syria and North Yemen) in 1958, but this federation was dissolved at the end of 1961 after the Syrians seceded. In the meantime, however, the officers of the new Yemeni regular army had been politicised by their contact with the Arab nationalism and radical socialist ideas of their Iraqi and Egyptian trainers, and had been made aware by their travels of the appallingly backward conditions which prevailed in the Yemen even by comparison with the central Arab world. When the Imam Ahmad died in 1962, a group of Nasserist, Ba'athist and socialist officers led by the commander of the Imam's personal guard, Colonel (later Marshal) Abdullah al-Sallal, seized power in San'a' in a military coup. With the support of the few like-minded civilians they founded a republican government which sought and received support from President Nasser of Egypt. The Imam, however, escaped, and enlisted the aid of the northern tribes and of Saudi Arabia. (The latter was then the target of Nasserist intrigues, and the Saudi regime was thus deeply concerned about the emergence of Nasserist influences on its southern borders.) The civil war that ensued in the Yemen was fought between the Republican Army of 10,000 men, soon totally overshadowed by an Egyptian expeditionary force that reached 70,000 troops at one stage, and the tribal confederacies of the north backed by Saudi money, arms and supplies. It took the form of a brutal and indecisive counter-insurgency struggle centred in the north, in which the Egyptians made lavish use of air power and even employed nerve gas against the tribal villages on a number of occasions. By 1967 over 200,000 Yemenis had died, but San'a's control still did not extend far beyond its northern approaches – and in that year Egypt suffered a crushing defeat at the hands of Israel in the Six-Day War. The Egyptian troops were now urgently needed at home, and Nasser was equally in need of Saudi financial aid to re-equip his shattered armed forces, so the Egyptian expeditionary force was withdrawn from the Yemen in accordance with a compromise settlement between Cairo and Riyadh. The republican government in San'a' remained and Saudi Arabia ceased to arm the tribes against it, but it was clearly understood by both sides that without Egyptian support the San'a' government would have to allow the tribes a very substantial share of power. In November, 1967 President Sallal was deposed while abroad, and a Republican Council was installed in San'a'. Sporadic fighting with the tribes continued until 1970, when Saudi Arabia assisted in a political reconciliation which accorded the tribes the share of power they felt to be their due: a new Consultative Council was created, with a substantial veto power over the government, whose head was Shaikh Abdullah al-Ahmar, leader of the Hashed confederacy, and most of whose members were his followers.

A further element had been added to Yemeni politics in November, 1967 when Britain withdrew from its Aden colony after a 4 year counter-insurgency campaign, leaving two rival guerrilla armies to dispute the future control of the new State of South Yemen (since 1970 called the People's Democratic Republic of Yemen). Of the two guerrilla armies, the more extreme Marxist organisation, the National Liberation Front, which had built up its support in the tribal areas by undermining the authority of the shaikhs, soon triumphed over the Front for the Liberation of Occupied South Yemen (FLOSY), which had been receiving support from San'a' and was mainly centred on the North Yemen immigrants who then made up much of the population of Aden City.

Following the NLF's victory, the FLOSY leadership, together with some 300,000 refugees from the North Yemeni community of Aden and from the displaced tribal leading families, fled into North Yemen, where they have ever since intrigued against the Aden regime, and on occasions mounted raids across the border. (The present North Yemeni Foreign Minister, Abdullah al-Asnaj, is the former leader of FLOSY.) During 1971–2 there was open border war between the two Yemens, with North Yemen receiving aid from Saudi Arabia and South Yemen getting military aid from the Soviet Union. At the end of the fighting, however, the Aden and San'a' regimes agreed to a total union of the two countries within 18 months. In view of the fact that one government was a tribally dominated conservative regime allied to Saudi Arabia and the other was the nearest thing to a communist regime in the Arab world, it is hardly astonishing that the union was not consummated. It is indicative of the strength of popular feeling in both parts that the Yemen is really one country divided only by an accident of colonial history, however, that the principle should have been espoused by two so dissimilar regimes.

By the early 1970s, therefore, all the harsh contrasts and bitter conflicts which divide the country and make it virtually ungovernable were already in existence. Of the 9,000,000 Yemenis, over 7,000,000 lived in the North, a state of extreme social conservatism and economic and political backwardness which was a protégé and pensioner of Saudi Arabia, with only the most tenuous tradition of centralised government continuously under challenge from powerful tribal forces. Just under 2,000,000 lived in the South, a State where tribal power counted for nothing, containing a considerably more sophisticated and urbanised population due to the period of British rule, but governed by one of the most politically extreme, savagely repressive and ruthlessly centralising regimes in the world, with close links to the Soviet bloc. Yet the sense of a single Yemeni nationhood persistently drives these two States to attempt union.

Within this basic division, other contradictions abound. The religious division between Shi'ite and Sunni is at least as important as any political conflict to most Yemenis and the religious border runs north of San'a', leaving the majority of North Yemen's population in the same camp as the south. Yet North Yemen is politically dominated by the Zaide Shi'ite tribes of the northern highlands. There is a standing temptation amongst the Shafa'i élite of San'a' and the south to collaborate with the South Yemen regime in order to overthrow Zaidi tribal domination – yet that élite in San'a' includes very large numbers of refugees who are implacably hostile to the Aden regime.

A further contradiction with incalculable consequences for both North Yemen and Saudi Arabia has arisen since the four-fold oil price increase of 1973 started the ultra-rapid development of the latter country, and led to the importation of about 1,000,000 North Yemeni labourers – one-third of the adult male population of North Yemen – to work on the vast construction projects that litter Saudi Arabia. Both North and South Yemen are almost totally undeveloped countries, but remittances from emigrant workers in Saudi Arabia now benefit North Yemen to the extent of over $1,000,000,000 a year, fuelling a severe inflation and an artificial boom in the economy. At the same time, the presence of so many North Yemeni workers in Saudi Arabia, rivalling in numbers the native working population, has made Riyadh desperately anxious that these immigrant workers should not come under radical influences through a change of regime at home in San'a'. As a result, Saudi aid covers North Yemen's budget deficits and pays the development of the armed forces.

All these contradictions have their echoes in the North Yemeni armed forces. A substantial Shafa'i element was introduced into the officer corps during the civil war, but since the end of the civil war the Zaidi predominance has been growing greater and the Shafa'is have been very much on the defensive. The political turbulence within the army makes rapid promotion as commonplace as sudden death, and by the mid-1970s officers with close tribal links, who had been excluded by both the Imam and the Sallal regime, were again rising into the higher ranks. The Saudis who provide much of the military budget have continually wavered between reinforcing the authority and cohesion of this army, and the alternative course of strengthening the northern tribes as the ultimate deterent to the appearance in San'a' of a radical regime allied with South Yemen. Generally they had done a bit of both: backing pro-Saudi military regimes in San'a' and even paying for the construction of roads in the north to facilitate counter-insurgency operations, but simultaneously cultivating the support of the northern tribes and spreading Saudi influence there (in the north and nort-east most vehicles are Saudi-registered and the principal currency is the Saudi riyal) in case the worst comes to the worst and the creation of a tribal buffer-State between south-eastern Saudi Arabia and a radical San'a' regime should become necessary.

From 1970 the principal institutional link between the Saudi and North Yemeni regimes was the Joint Yemeni–Saudi Co-ordinating Committee, chaired by the Saudi Defence and Aviation Minister, Prince Sultan bin Abdul Aziz, which channelled Saudi funds to various military and economic projects in North Yemen. Riyadh was generally content with the existing relationship between the two States, but it raised no strong objection to the coup by Lieutenant-Colonel Ibrahim al-Hamdi in June, 1974, nor to his manifest desire to strengthen the power of the central government over the tribes. It was clear to Riyadh even from its own experience that no stability or development would be possible so long as the tribes were in a position to thwart any changes, even if there was also a continuing Saudi interest in maintaining influence among the tribes as a sort of reserve position.

The 10 man Military Command Council created by Hamdi, himself a Zaidi, initially consisted of seven men, including three officers closely related to the leaders of the Hashed and Bakil confederacies. By 1975, however, Hamdi had expelled the three tribal representatives and reduced the MCC to four men: himself as President, Premier Abdul Aziz Abdul Ghani (a figure eminently acceptable to the Saudis), Chief of Staff Lieutenant-Colonel Ahmad al-Ghashmi (a Zaidi associated with the Hashed confederacy) and Paratroop Commander Major Abdullah Abdul Alem (a Shafa'i from the south). Riyadh was reassured, however, when Hamdi turned away from the Soviet Union as the country's main arms supplier after 1975, and with Saudi assistance arranged for the purchase of American arms. The naval facilities which were previously available to the Soviet navy at the North Yemen port of Hodeida were also withdrawn during the course of 1976. The Saudis therefore continued to support Hamdi when, having abolished the Consultative Council and purged the MCC, thus destroying the tribes' positions of influence in the central government, he became involved in an escalating confrontation with the great Zaidi tribes after 1975. The Hashed and Bakil confederacies responded to Hamdi's challenge first with a civil disobedience campaign, and then by ambushing army units in the north. By the spring of 1977 a small civil war had erupted again in the northern parts of the country, and the air force had been brought in to bomb the tribes.

There is little question but that by this time Saudi Arabia was becoming concerned by Hamdi's inability either to control the tribes or to compromise with them. At the same time Riyadh grew increasingly uneasy about the North Yemeni President's policy of seeking national reunification. At the end of 1976 he and Salim Rubayya Ali, the leader of the South Yemeni regime, issued a joint statement that 'rapid measures would be taken to unify the two parts of Yemen as a natural and necessary step . . . and as a strategic issue important to both countries'. In February, 1977 the two leaders met on the border and announced the creation of a Joint Council composed of themselves and their respective Ministers of Defence, Foreign Affairs, Economy, Trade and Planning to hasten the process of reunification. The South Yemeni leader paid one public and several clandestine visits to San'a' in the months that followed. At the same time the National Democratic Front, composed of six small leftist organisations and backed morally and financially by South Yemen, was encouraged to take a larger part in North Yemen's affairs. But in October, 1977 2 days before his scheduled first visit to Aden, President al-Hamdi was murdered in a *coup d'état*.

Hamdi's serious pursuit of the goal of Yemeni reunification undoubtedly caused some unease in Riyadh, although at the time Saudi Arabia was following its own policy of reconciliation with South Yemen in the hope of weaning it away from its links with the Soviet Union. Saudi Arabia and South Yemen had established diplomatic links in 1976, and throughout the following year there was much discussion about massive Saudi grants of aid to the impoverished country if it adopted a less stridently revolutionary foreign policy. At the end of 1976 Riyadh had succeeded in mediating a ceasefire on the South Yemen–Oman border, where Aden had previously been supporting Marxist guerrillas seeking the overthrow of the Oman government, and in retrospect it seems clear that the South Yemeni leader was not ill disposed to the Saudi proposals for a change of front. Indeed, that may have been part of the reason why he was murdered by domestic rivals in Mid-1978.

On the whole, therefore, the widely disseminated thesis that Hamdi's killers had Saudi support is not necessarily correct – even though his genuinely independent nationalist position, which has made him something of a hero for many educated Yemenis since his death, was arguably not in the Saudi interest. Despite all the trouble he was having with the tribes, moreover, the theory that the coup which killed him was made with the support of the tribes has no firm foundation. The likeliest explanation for Hamdi's murder was simply that his Chief of Staff and successor wanted to be president. Since violence is the only available route to power in North Yemen, that was the route he took.

The realities of the internal power structure in North Yemen offer innumerable opportunities for foreign conspirators to intervene in the course of domestic events, but they also make such intervention not a necessary element in violent local changes, as the structure itself guarantees that such violence will occur. The two main actors in politics are the tribes, who can field several hundred thousand more or less well-armed men at short notice, and the army, which has grown continuously in numbers from the 10,000 of civil war days to almost 40,000 now. But each major force is internally divided into many real or potential factions capable of acting separately: the tribal confederacies of the Hashed and Bakil are no friends to each other and have serious internal divisions, while the army's loosely organised brigades are often virtually the independent fiefs of their commanding officers, whose rise to that position is far more often due to their skill at intrigue than to their military ability. Thus, for example, Hamdi's purposes may have been idealistic and altogether praiseworthy from a Yemeni nationalist point of view, but his actual base of power consisted of precisely three brigades of troops, mostly stationed near the capital: the Amaliqah (Giants) Brigade in the Dhamar area, commanded by his brother Abdullah, the Paratroops Brigade, commanded by Major Abdullah Abdul Alem, a fellow member of the Military Command Council, and the Fourth Armoured Brigade commanded by Lieutenant-Colonel Ali Qannaf, Hamdi's brother-in-law. To overthrow the regime, it was only necessary to kill or isolate these men.

This was done, almost certainly at the instigation of Lieutenant-Colonel Ahmad al-Ghashmi, the Chief of Staff and another member of the 4 man MCC, in October, 1977. Both Hamdi brothers were murdered at a rest house maintained by one of them outside San'a' and two French women who were either at the house already or were brought there by the assassins were also killed and left there, in order to destroy Hamdi's considerable popularity amongst the puritanical Yemenis by disseminating the impression that he had been consorting with prostitutes. In a separate, simultaneous incident, Lieutenant-Colonel Qannaf, the Fourth Armoured Brigade Commander, was arrested elsewhere in San'a'. The Chief of Staff became President al-Ghashmi, and proceeded to purge all of Hamdi's supporters from the army. Saudi support continued under the new regime, and all suggestion of an imminent reunification of the two Yemens ceased, but there is no proof of prior Saudi knowledge of the coup.

It cannot be denied, however, that Ghashmi controlled a direct Saudi subsidy to military headquarters of $10,000,000 a month to finance officers' salaries and facilities while he was planning the coup, nor that he had a completely free hand in making military appointments. Moreover, he proved far more compliant to the Saudis than Hamdi had been in other matters of interest to Riyadh besides the suspension of the negotiations with Aden. The autonomous tribal area in the north were Saudi influence predominates, which had been dismantled by Hamdi, was reinstated by Ghashmi, and the National Democratic Front was fiercely suppressed. Saudi subsidies expanded rapidly, enabling Ghashmi to secure the army's loyalty by promptly doubling the pay for all ranks. Thanks mainly to Saudi largesse, North Yemen was able to sustain the astonishing import/export ratio of 100:1 in 1977–8.

Ghashmi nevertheless had considerable difficulty in establishing control over the country: in the first few months he survived several assassination attempts, and large-scale operations had to be conducted against the 'Giants' Brigade, the younger Hamdi brother's former regiment. A large number of armed forces personnel fled to the south, as did members of the National Democratic Front, and in the subsequent purges of the officer corps almost all Shafa's officers were removed from senior posts. The officer who conducted a suitably inconclusive inquiry into the motive for Hamdi's murder, Major Ali Shaybah, was made Chief of Staff in the following month, while the man widely believed to have been the actual killer, Lieutenant-Colonel Ali Abdullah Saleh, took over as Commander of the Fourth Armoured Brigade at the old airport just south of San'a'. This was the key brigade in the whole army because of its location.

The one remaining influential member of Hamdi's regime, the Commander of the Paratroops Brigade, Major Abdullah Abdul Alem, remained on the restructured Military Command Council for 6 months, apparently in the hope of securing a senior permanent position in the new regime, but when Ghashmi had himself 'elected' President by a specially convened Consultative Council in April, 1978, and dissolved the MCC without making any provision for Abdul Alem, the latter took himself off to his own Shafa'i home area of Hajjariya near the South Yemen border and raised the standard of revolt. He took several hundred men of his own Paratroops Brigade with him and was joined by others from the Giants Brigade, and succeeded in attracting some local support in the area around Adim where he dug himself in. It represented a major challenge to Zaidi dominance, in the heart of the Shafa'i area where that sect have attempted to establish an independent State of their own in the past, and San'a' mounted a considerable campaign involving armoured forces under the command of Colonel Ali Abdullah Saleh in order to dislodge Abdul Alem and drive him and his followers across the border. Subsequent rumours that in exile Major Abdul Alem sought to convince the South Yemen regime to support a major Shafa'i insurrection in the south seemed to be confirmed by the events of early 1979 (*see* Current Developments).

President Ahmad al-Ghashmi did not have long to enjoy his achievement of undisputed power, however; on June 24th, 1978 he was killed in his office together with a secret envoy from South Yemen's President Rubayya Ali, when the envoy's briefcase exploded upon being opened. Within 24 hours the South Yemeni President himself was stood against a wall and shot for his 'individualistic policies and actions' by forces loyal to the Secretary-General of South Yemen's monolithic National Front Party, Abdul Fattah Ismail, after a day of fierce fighting in Aden. A considerable number of South Yemeni refugees crossed the border into North Yemen, fleeing the fighting and the subsequent liquidation of the groups which had supported Rubayya Ali. San'a' promptly broke of relations with Aden, accusing the South Yemeni regime of organising President al-Ghashmi's assassination, and shortly thereafter Saudi Arabia achieved the unprecedented feat of persuading the Arab League to boycott the South Yemen regime. In San'a', the powerful Colonel Ali Abdullah Saleh asserted his right to the succession without challenge, and duly had himself 'elected' President shortly afterwards.

A bewildering variety of hypotheses has been offered for these bizarre events, but the explanation which seems most plausible, and is confirmed in all aspects except for one embarrassing detail by the South Yemeni regime, serves to illustrate how deeply entangled the political intrigues of the two Yemens have now become. It was known for some time before June, 1978 that the relations between President Rubayya Ali and party Secretary-General Ismail in Aden were at breaking point. This was commonly explained in terms of the former's 'moderate' Marxist views versus the latter's 'pro-Soviet and ultra-leftist' inclinations, but is quite adequately accounted for by the intense rivalry between two ambitious men schooled in the ruthless traditions of Yemeni politics and controlling separate power complexes within the totalitarian South Yemeni State. In early 1978 it was clear that Rubayya Ali was losing this struggle for power, as party leader Ismail was steadily expanding his control over the regular armed forces which were the President's main power base. The victors in the fighting of June 24th subsequently

alleged that Rubayya Ali had in desperation attempted to launch a coup against the rest of the leadership, and although in fact he may have been pre-empted by Ismail there is very little doubt that he was indeed planning to do so.

The South Yemenis further allege that President Rubayya Ali had secretly been in contact with President al-Ghashmi of North Yemen for months previous to June, 1978, which is partly confirmed by the visit of the secret envoy who brought the exploding briefcase to San'a' – and that the two presidents had been plotting to co-operate in the overthrow by Rubayya Ali of the National Front apparatus and the installation of a much more conservative regime in South Yemen, which would also be able to count on Saudi Arabian support.

The present Aden regime naturally will not reveal the rest of the story, but it seems probable that some of President Rubayya Ali's agents were actually double agents working for party Secretary-General Ismail, and that one of them succeeded in substituting the booby-trapped briefcase for the one containing the genuine documents that Rubayya Ali's envoy was bringing to Ghashmi. The explosion which killed Ghashmi was the signal for Ismail's supporters to strike against his fellow conspirator in Aden, Rubayya Ali, and to purge the South Yemen regime of any who were still tempted by the Saudi Arabian offers of lavish financial assistance in return for political moderation which had been extended over the previous few years.

The initial transfer of power in North Yemen from the assassinated President al-Ghashmi to President Ali Abdullah Saleh went smoothly, as the South Yemeni regime was pre-occupied with its own mini-civil war, but the totally Zaidi composition of the San'a' government and its scarcely concealed status as a Saudi Arabian satellite offered an irresistible target to Aden once its own house was in order. On October 15th, 1978 a military uprising took place in and around San'a', with clashes also occurring in Baida Province near the southern border. The revolt involved major military units including the First and Fifth Infantry Brigades and the Military Police, as well as civilian conspirators in the capital who were allegedly supplied with $2,000,000 and arms and explosives by Libya via South Yemen. The coup attempt had clearly involved infiltration of large parts of the armed forces by agents of the National Democratic Front exiles and/or Major Abdul Alem in South Yemen, and came very close to success; only the arrest of one key plotter, leading to a breakdown in communication between the rebel units at a crucial moment, the abstention of most of the armoured units and the loyalty of the air force saved the regime from overthrow. In the aftermath of the attempted coup at least 7000 persons were arrested, and there were numerous executions of officers and civilians implicated in the uprising. The rapid rotation of army commanders, provincial governors, ministers and officials which has been a feature of the Ghashmi and Saleh regimes (as an anti-coup measure) was subsequently accelerated further.

Having tried and failed with internal subversion, the South Yemen regime then turned to the sponsorship of an external invasion in its attempt to overthrow the pro-Saudi regime in San'a'. On February 20th, 1979 a force of National Democratic Front exiles attacked into North Yemen with strong support from the South Yemen armed forces, and in a short time fighting had spread along most of the border. At the time of writing military operations were still in progress.

STRENGTH AND BUDGET

The North Yemeni armed forces have grown about four-fold in the past 15 years, and now number 32,500 men, of whom

30,000 serve in the army. The air force has 1500 men and the navy 550. There is a paramilitary force of some 20,000 tribal levies that performs provincial security duties. Even including the latter, military forces amount to less than 1% of the population of 7,270,000, although military demands on the available manpower pool are considerably greater than that would imply, since about one-third of adult males are working abroad.

The present regime has the co-operation of the major tribes (President Saleh belongs to the Hashed confederacy), but their military potential remains most important. Even allowing for the substantial depletion of their manpower through massive temporary emigration to Saudi Arabia, the major tribes are probably still capable of fielding 200,000 armed men, and in their own northern highland territories represent a formidable military force.

Defence expenditure in 1980 was $331,000,000. The defence budget accounts for two-fifths of government expenditure, and is a notably high share of an estimated GNP of only S4,490,000,000. All North Yemen defence expenditure figures may be seriously misleading, however, as there are large Saudi Arabian subsidies to the North Yemen budget and there are also believed to be direct subventions paid to the armed forces general staff. Moreover, virtually the entire cost of recent North Yemeni arms purchases from the USA, amounting to almost $500,000,000, is being met by Riyadh.

COMMAND AND CONSTITUTIONAL STATUS

The President, chosen by a non-elected Consultative Council dominated by tribal representatives, is Commander-in-Chief of the Armed Forces. He appoints a cabinet headed by a Prime Minister, but there is no Minister of Defence. The armed forces stand directly under the President's authority, headed by the Chief of Staff. He exercises control over all three services. It is believed that the Head of the Central National Security Organisation (also referred to as the Director of Military Intelligence) stands outside this structure and reports directly to the President.

In practice, the army is the State, and whoever manages to secure control of it automatically becomes President and controls the civilian apparatus of the State as well, restricted only by the countervailing influence of the great tribal confederacies. (Since late 1977, the two forces have been effectively allied.) The unbridled competition for power within the officer corps is so intense, and the institutional structure so weak, that almost any ruthless and lucky officer can make it to the top — the current President, Ali Abdullah Saleh, was a lieutenant in 1974, and was only 31 years old when he became Head of State in mid-1978.

ROLE, COMMITMENT, DEPLOYMENT AND RECENT OPERATIONS

The role of the army is predominantly to maintain internal security, which generally means attempting to defend the centralising governments in San'a' against the power of the tribes. This was its role under the Imam, under Marshal Sallal during the civil war, and again under President Hamdi in 1974–7. As a natural consequence it enlisted substantial numbers of Shafa'i officers into senior positions, and tended to identify with 'progressive' political movements in the Arab world such as Nasserism, Ba'athism and Marxism. Despite the large increase in Zaidi and tribal influences after 1970, this remained true to some extent until Hamdi's assassination in 1977. Since then successive purges of the officer corps have converted it

into an overwhelmingly Zaidi force, no longer seeking actively to dominate the tribes, but acting almost as the agent of the northern tribes and of Saudi Arabia in the control of the Shafa'i areas, which are politically more inclined to the left and more enthusiastic about reunification with South Yemen even under its present regime. The fact that the tribes and the army are Shi'ite, whereas both Saudi Arabia and the Shafa'is are Sunni, does not seem to raise any obstacles to this political alliance.

In the course of carrying out this role, the army has increasingly become involved in a military confrontation with South Yemen, and a large part of its forces are now concentrated near the southern frontier. (A similar build-up of Saudi forces along the South Yemen frontier was evident in 1978.) It is still necessary to retain substantial forces in San'a' to ensure the security of the regime, however. The only North Yemeni forces deployed outside the country are 1500 troops serving with the Arab Deterrent Force in the Lebanon.

The great majority of the army's recent operations up to 1977 were counter-insurgency campaigns against the tribes in the north, although there were some clashes along the South Yemen border in 1971–2. At the time of writing the army was involved in another border war with South Yemen, and had recently been involved in fighting against itself. It has a considerable numerical superiority over the army of South Yemen, and is about equally well provided with similar sorts of weaponry. However, the severe internal divisions and successive purges which it has suffered in recent years give cause for doubt about its present effectiveness as a fighting force in sustained combat against a well-organised and similarly equipped army like that of its southern neighbour.

ORGANISATION

Arms of Service
The North Yemen army has the usual pattern of branch organisation into the various arms and services. Owing to the training role of the Soviet Union over a considerable number of years, many of its staff procedures and much of its unit organisation follow the Soviet model.

Operational
The army contains two infantry divisions consisting of one parachute brigade, nine infantry brigades (one reserve), one mechanised brigade and six plus two armoured brigades (one training), three artillery brigades and five anti-aircraft artillery battalions. Almost all of the 15 brigades are severely under-strength, some amounting to little more than big battalions, and a major objective of the 5 year modernisation programme initiated with Saudi support in 1976 is to reorganise the army into about half a dozen full-strength brigades.

The air force has one fighter squadron, one light bomber squadron, and transport, training and helicopter flights. The navy consists of some patrol craft and MTBs based at the main port, Hodeida.

RECRUITMENT, TRAINING AND RESERVES

The army is recruited on the basis of selective conscription, with military service beginning at the age of eighteen and lasting for 3 years. Almost all training beyond basic level is done abroad, mainly in Egypt and Saudi Arabia. There has been a Soviet military training mission in North Yemen for many years, and although all Soviet arms purchases ceased in 1976 there were still about 100 Soviet advisers with the army in early 1979. Indeed, during the border war at that time the North Yemeni Prime Minister publicly complained that since there were Soviet advisers with both sides, all movements of the North Yemeni army at once became known to South Yemen. He explained, however, that the North Yemeni army would continue to depend on the presence of Soviet instructors for some time, until the transition from Soviet to American weapons had been completed.

This transition, which began with the placing of the first North Yemeni arms orders in the USA in 1976, requires a different set of foreign advisers to be imported. It was envisaged that most of them − 75 or fewer − would be Saudi Arabian military personnel who were thoroughly familiar with United States weapons, with probably a small number of Americans as well. The great acceleration in United States arms deliveries occasioned by the border war in 1979 is likely to necessitate the presence of substantially greater numbers of Saudi or American military advisers, however, if the North Yemeni armed forces are to absorb these weapons in a reasonably short period of time.

Living conditions for North Yemeni conscripts are primitive, but not dissimilar to what they were accustomed to in civilian life. Pay was doubled for all ranks in late 1977 at the time Colonel Ahmad al-Ghashmi came to power, and is now roughly competitive with the amounts that can be earned by going to Saudi Arabia as an immigrant labourer. Since 1977 each soldier also received a daily ration of $12 worth of *qat*, the local narcotic shrub which is chewed habitually by most Yemenis.

There is a reserve of some kind in North Yemen, made up of ex-conscripts who have a residual reserve liability, but no information is available on its size, organisation or state of readiness. Tribal levies of 20,000 are said to exist.

EQUIPMENT AND ARMS INDUSTRY

The Saudi-sponsored transition by the North Yemen armed forces from Soviet to American arms supplies was initiated in March, 1976, when a United States military delegation visited San'a'. In the following month a $139,000,000 arms deal was signed with the USA covering the supply of howitzers, anti-aircraft guns, light weapons, ammunition and trucks, the cost being entirely covered by Saudi Arabia. Deliveries began in February, 1977 and were accelerated following the coup in South Yemen in June, 1978 which brought a more strongly pro-Soviet regime to power in Aden.

At the same time the United States administration also sought permission from Congress for the sale to North Yemen of $360,000,000 in additional weapons, including 12F-5 fighters, two C-130 transports, 50 M-60 tanks and 100M-113 APCs, to be delivered over the succeeding 3 years. These weapons were also to be paid for by Riyadh. The outbreak of fighting between North and South Yemen in February, 1979 caused the USA to employ an airlift to complete deliveries on the 1976 order, and the administration announced that it would commence deliveries on the subsequent order, including tanks and aircraft, without waiting the usual period in order to let Congress review the sale in view of the seriousness of the military situation.

Since 1976 the Soviet Union has allowed its military advisers to remain in North Yemen despite the marked pro-Western orientation of subsequent regimes in San'a', and has apparently not applied any restrictions on the delivery of spare parts for the largely Soviet-built equipment of the North Yemen forces. This policy may best be interpreted as a case of hanging on to established footholds and waiting for better times.

The main armoured strength of the North Yemen army consists of 150 T-34 50 T-54 64 M-60 tanks, supported by 50 Saladin armoured cars and some Ferret scout cars. There are 425 BTR-40/-152 and some Egyptian-made Walid and 90 American M-113 APCs. Artillery strength comprises 50 76mm and some 122mm guns, and 50 SU-100 SP guns, supported by 82mm and 120mm mortars, and 75mm recoilless rifles. Anti-tank defence depends mainly on 250 Vigilant TOW and Dragon ATGWs and anti-aircraft defence on 37mm 57mm and 85mm 2SU 23/4 and Vulcan AA guns. Additional United States artillery and anti-aircraft guns have been received, and 50 M-60 tanks and 100 M-113 APCs will be delivered during 1979.

The small navy has four large patrol craft (Poluchat-class) and four P-4-class MTBs, all based at Hodeida. The air force has 12 MiG-17 fighters and 14 Il-28 light bombers. The standard air-to-air weapon is AA-2 Atoll. Transports include three C-47s, two Short Skyvans and one Il-14; there are two AB-205 helicopters and one Mi-4. Trainers include four MiG-15UTIs, 18 Yak-11s and four F-5Bs which were transferred from Saudi Arabia in 1978 in order to speed the conversion of North Yemeni pilots to American aircraft. Twelve F-5E fighter—bombers and two C-130 transports are on order from the USA, and delivery was expected to take place in 1979. Some of the air force's existing aircraft are believed to be in storage owing to a shortage of pilots.

RANK, DRESS AND DISTINCTIONS

The rank structure of all the North Yemeni forces conforms to the usual international model, and employs standard eastern Arab nomenclature. No information is available on distinctions.

CURRENT DEVELOPMENTS

The situation of the North Yemen armed forces in early 1979 was difficult if not parlous. The officer corps had been heavily purged and deeply demoralised by the successive political upheavals of recent years, commanding officers were mostly young and had little military experience, and discipline was doubtful. The forces were also in the midst of an awkward transition from Soviet to American arms and particularly unready to fight a major conventional war against South Yemen, which seemed to be a significant possibility in early 1979. The military regime was heavily dependent on outside support from Saudi Arabia and the USA, and enjoyed little popular support in the southern and coastal parts of the country.

On February 20th, 1979 guerrillas of the exiled National Democratic Front in South Yemen in alliance with a group of former North Yemeni army officers led by Major Abdullah Abdul Alem calling itself the June Thirteenth Movement, and strongly supported by South Yemeni regular forces, attacked at a number of points along the lengthy and convoluted border between the two countries, which rises at some points to 10,000 feet. Within a week the South Yemen-backed forces were in control of three of the main North Yemeni towns along the border, Qataba, Bayda and Harib, and Saudi Arabia and the USA had both begun airlifts of arms and supplies to San'a'. There were also reports of disturbances in several military units in the interior of North Yemen.

In March 1979, however, the leaders of the two Yemens met and agreed on reunification and resumed discussions over the unification of their countries, first raised in 1972. Further progress was achieved in September 1981, when a joint statement was issued about the creation of common institutions, constituting a 'Yemen Council' and Joint Ministerial Committee.

Meanwhile the North Yemen's internal troubles persisted. The National Democratic Front. supported with funds and arms at various times by the Soviet Union, South Yemen and Libya (the latter said to supply $1m a month) maintained 8000 men on the South Yemen border. A ceasefire was intermittently in force but there was heavy fighting between it and government forces, said to amount to seven battalions, in August 1981.

At the same time the government was put under pressure by its external supporters. The Soviet Union, displeased by growing Saudi and American influence in the country, re-

quested the repayment of its loan of $360m worth of arms in September 1981, which was quite beyond the country's means. The Saudi government simultaneously reduced its regular payments in disapproval of internal political developments.

Until the two Yemens settle their differences, which they will find difficulty in doing while each remains tied to opposite patrons, armed opposition to the San'a' regime is likely to continue at a low level of intensity.

Gwynne Dyer
John Keegan

SOUTH YEMEN

HISTORY AND INTRODUCTION

South Yemen's origins as a coherent political entity extend back all of two decades. Though Britain had occupied the port of Aden for strategic reasons since 1839, and had created a network of treaties granting it advisory status with the various tribal shaikhs of the interior, only in the late 1930s and early 1940s did the British government even begin to extend the rudiments of a civil administration beyond the Aden colony. At the very time when British authorities began to think of a federation of shaikhdoms (in 1955), Arab nationalist sentiments were coming to dominate in the Aden colony.

The Anglo—French attack on Egypt in 1956 greatly accelerated the growth of the nationalist movement in Aden (where a majority of the workers were immigrants from North Yemen), and focused the hopes of many on President Nasser. The first strikes in Aden occurred in the same year, and soon Russian-made arms were finding their way to the tribes from North Yemen, which has always claimed the entire territory as its own.

In the late 1950s Aden was selected by Britain as a substitute for Suez as its major Middle Eastern base. In 1959 the South Arabian Federation was formed as part of a deliberate British policy of submerging the urban nationalism of the colony in the conservative mass of the rural population — a policy which culminated in the shotgun wedding of Colony and Federation in 1962. But 24 hours later the conservative Imam of (North) Yemen was overthrown, and a large Egyptian expeditionary force soon arrived in the Yemen to back the republicans in the civil war.

Violence began in South Yemen the following year under the aegis of the Front for the Liberation of Occupied South Yemen (FLOSY), with support from San'a' and Cairo. Soon, however, FLOSY gave birth to a splinter group, the National Liberation Front (NLF), comprised mainly of young Marxists who were disciples of the pan-Arab socialist movement headed by George Habbash. By 1964, when Britain promised to withdraw within 4 years, Britain was basically an onlooker at the civil war between FLOSY and the NLF.

The NLF adopted the strategy of winning over dissident tribesmen, turning them against their shaikhs, and gradually taking over the Protectorates, while FLOSY was largely confined to a North Yemeni immigrant following in the one large urban area, Aden. Egypt's withdrawal from North Yemen in the aftermath of its defeat in the 1967 Arab—Israeli war left FLOSY high and dry, and when Britain carried out an accelerated withdrawal from South Yemen the same year it handed over control to the NLF, as the strongest power on the ground. In a brief civil war immediately after the British departure, the NLF annihilated FLOSY's remaining strength.

The economy of the port of Aden has been in headlong decline since independence, due partly to the closure of the Suez Canal for most of that time. As a result of that and the campaign against FLOSY, the great majority of the estimated 100,000 North Yemenis have returned home, there to strengthen the opposition of the San'a' regime to the NLF. Despite an official commitment by both regimes to the eventual reunification of the Yemen, the ideological war between them continues unabated. South Yemen under the NLF became a unitary Marxist State — the shaikhs were executed or got out to live on Saudi stipends. Collectivisation, indoctrination and all the usual paraphernalia of the doctrinaire Marxist State were applied rigidly. The government is fanatically secretive and suspicious, and less detailed information is available about PDRY internal affairs than about almost any other State on Earth.

The National Front, the ruling party which grew out of the NLF, was torn by a bitter power struggle in 1967—9, culminating in the removal of President Qahtan al-Sha'abi by the radical leftists in June, 1969. A 3 man President Council was established under the chairmanship of Salim Rubayya Ali, who thus became President. His principal sources of power were his influence in the tribal hinterland and especially in the Hadhramaut, the eastern part of the country near Oman, and hence also in the regular army which was mainly recruited from these rural areas. His nearest rival in power was Abdul Fattah Ismail, whose main strength lay in his mastery of the party organisation. The third member was the Prime Minister and Defence Minister, Ali Nasir Muhammad. The country was renamed the People's Democratic Republic of Yemen (PDRY) in 1970, and the radical regime began the lengthy task of imposing absolute party control over both the armed forces and the administration.

The PDRY armed forces then consisted of the regular army, the General Security Units and the Popular Militia (an air force and navy were in the course of being created). The regular army had developed from the military forces that had existed in the territory at independence — the former Federal Regular Army (Aden Protectorate Levies), the Eastern Protectorate's Hadhrami Bedouin Legion and the Mukalla Regular Army — and had President Rubayya Ali as its Supreme Commander. The General Security Units, controlled by the Ministry of the Interior, normally performed only police and gendarmerie duties. The Popular Militia, however, came under the direct control of the NF, and was composed of workers, students and peasants who were regarded as being more 'revolutionary' in spirit than the regular forces or the General Security Units; it came under the effective control of party leader Abdul Fattah Ismail.

After 1969, the regular army and the General Security Units were thoroughly purged and reorganised. All British and royalist personnel had already been removed, but now officers belonging to the Awaliq tribes of the Fourth and Fifth Governorates, who were regarded as 'reactionary and traditional-minded', were purged, exiled or killed, and replaced mainly by officers from the Dathina area of the Third Governorate (which happened to be President Rubayya Ali's home territory). 'Revolutionary Military Commands' were introduced in the regular army in 1970, to subject soldiers and officers to intensive and continuous Marxist indoctrination, and Soviet military aid and advisers began to play a large role in the army. Like the civilian population, the army was forced into a posture of absolute and unquestioning obedience to the party; nevertheless, as became clear in retrospect even from the choice of those purged at this point, it also became an arena of conflict between the various factions within the regime.

South Yemen's external relations in the Arab world at this time were extremely turbulent. In addition to the North Yemenis who had fled after the defeat of FLOSY in 1967, at least 300,000 South Yemenis became refugees when the radical faction began mass round-ups of all potential opposition elements, accompanied by extreme brutality and a good deal of clandestine killing, after its victory in 1969. There had already been fighting against the Saudi Arabian army and air force in the Wadiah area of the common border in 1969, and the conservative Saudi regime, deeply concerned about the emergence of a radical Marxist State on its own borders, now organised many of the refugees into an 'Army of Deliverance' which unsuccessfully attempted to detach the Hadhramaut from South Yemen in an invasion in 1971. At the same time fighting flared on the North Yemen border, which harboured the refugee leadership of FLOSY and was closely aligned with Saudi Arabia; in October, 1972 this skirmishing erupted into open war, including air raids, for about 2 weeks.

In the ceasefire agreement mediated by the Arab League at the end of October, 1972 the two Yemens actually agreed to work for unification. This was indeed the fundamental desire of most Yemenis, who despite the division of the country in the colonial era have never ceased to see themselves as one nation. In view of the great ideological gulf between the regimes in Aden and San'a', however, nothing came of this agreement. Indeed, although fighting then subsided on Aden's North Yemeni and Saudi Arabian frontiers, it soon flared on the Omani border instead. There had been a local revolt against rule from Muscat in the neighbouring Omani Province of Dhofar since 1964, and soon after coming to power in 1967 the Aden regime had effectively taken control of it, transforming it into a Marxist revolutionary organisation known as the Popular Front for the Liberation of the Occupied Arab Gulf (PFLOAG). At first with Chinese assistance, and after 1972 with Soviet assistance, all channelled through the supply base of Hauf in the eastern PDRY, the PFLOAG guerrillas had succeeded by 1973 in overrunning virtually the whole of Dhofar Province except for the capital, Salalah. In December, 1973 however, a substantial number of Iranian troops were brought into Dhofar by agreement with the Sultan of Oman and proceeded to drive the guerrillas back towards the South Yemeni frontier. Oman claimed that 400–500 South Yemeni regulars were fighting with the Dhofari guerrillas as stiffening in the last phase of the war, but by the end of 1975 Iranian troops had reached the South Yemen border, and there had been instances of Iranian destroyers and aircraft attacking targets within South Yemen's easternmost region.

The end of the fighting in Dhofar, however, made it possible at last for Saudi Arabia, the local great power, to attempt a policy of *détente* with the radical South Yemeni regime, in which it had reason to believe that there were elements who would be willing to curb the regime's revolutionary adventures in return for massive Saudi subsidies to the desperately impoverished South Yemeni economy. In late 1975 Riyadh successfully arranged for the return of the body of an Iranian F-4 pilot shot down over South Yemeni territory, and capitalised on this contact to expand discussions to the point where an agreement to establish diplomatic relations was concluded in March, 1976. Although it was never stated publicly in so many words, the deal on offer by Riyadh was a very large amount of aid – some $400,000,000 was the most commonly discussed figure, which comes to almost 2 years' GNP for South Yemen – in return for Aden's ending support for revolutionary organisations beyond its own borders and breaking its close military and political ties with the Soviet Union. What the regime did internally would remain its own affair. While some members of the South Yemen ruling group, notably President Salim Rubayya Ali, seemed interested in at least some aspects of this package, others were totally opposed: party leader Abdul Fattah Ismail deliberately absented himself in Moscow to avoid being present for the March, 1976 reconciliation with Saudi Arabia.

An additional factor which attracted some South Yemeni leaders towards reconciliation with the Saudis was that the possibility of reunification of the two Yemens had by 1976 become more than a mere slogan. In June, 1974 the ultra-conservative, tribally dominated regime in North Yemen, which had refused to have anything to do with Aden, was overthrown by a young army officer, Lieutenant-Colonel Ibrahim al-Hamdi. While Hamdi continued to enjoy Saudi moral and financial support even after he came into serious conflict with the conservative tribes of the north in the course of his attempts to increase the powers of the central government, he was clearly a nationalist of much more 'progressive' ideas than any of his predecessors in San'a'. He even continued to enjoy Riyadh's support when he permitted the National Democratic Front, an organisation uniting six small North Yemeni leftist parties, to operate freely, and when he began to extend feelers to South Yemen on the subject of reunification in 1976 (counterbalancing this action by ending North Yemen's previous dependence on Soviet arms supplies).

Saudi Arabia's tacit support for Hamdi's proposals was due to the fact that they fitted into its own strategy for buying off South Yemen with a variety of inducements – and if it succeeded, a reunified Yemen in which the conservative north, over three times larger in population, would help further to contain an already tamed South Yemeni ruling party, would be highly desirable. In February, 1977 President Rubayya Ali of South Yemen and President al-Hamdi of North Yemen met on the border and announced the creation of a Joint Council composed of themselves and their respective Ministers of Defence, Foreign Affairs, Economy, Trade and Planning which would guide the process of reunification over a 4 year period. The South Yemeni leader paid one public and several clandestine visits to San'a' in the months that followed. A succession of South Yemeni ministers visited Saudi Arabia and the United Arab Emirates during 1977 discussing various kinds of financial and development aid which might be forthcoming, and in August President Rubayya Ali himself visited Saudi Arabia.

All this external diplomatic activity was closely connected with a major power struggle which was developing within the South Yemeni regime between the factions led by President Rubayya Ali and party leader Abdul Fattah Ismail. Issues of ideology and external policy were involved – Rubayya Ali advocated a gradual approach to social change and a *rapprochement* with Saudi Arabia, while Ismail was a rigidly orthodox Marxist who supported the radical policy of 'mass mobilisation' internally and opposed any weakening of the link with the Soviet Union – but these issues were interwoven with older quarrels arising from traditional tribal rivalries and personal disputes. Most of all the struggle was about sheer power – who would rule South Yemen – and the question of external relations with the Soviet Union or with Saudi Arabia became an issue which the rival factions used in their struggle, while the external powers who stood to win or lose by the outcome in turn used what influence they had to swing the balance in their favour. In terms of armed force, President Rubayya Ali as Commander-in-Chief, with Prime Minister and Defence Minister Ali Nasir Muhammad as at least a benevolent neutral, was able to rely on the support of the regular army to a considerable extent, while Abdul Fattah Ismail as party leader had almost exclusive control of the Cuban-trained and increasingly well-armed Popular Militia.

In October, 1975 Abdul Fattah Ismail succeeded in merging two smaller extreme leftist parties, the People's Vanguard (Ba'athist) and People's Democratic Union (Communist) Parties with the ruling National Front to create a new, broader single party, the Unified Political Organisation — National Front (UPONF), in which his own radical faction enjoyed stronger support. He was made Secretary-General of the UPONF, with President Salim Rubayya Ali as his deputy. This was interpreted as a victory for the hardliners, and the Soviet Union promised to continue supplying military and economic aid, but in a series of manoeuvres in December, 1975 to January, 1976 Rubayya Ali and his followers, depending heavily on their strong position in the Hadramaut, succeeded in reshuffling the UPONF's Central Committee and changing the composition of the government in their favour. This then left President Rubayya Ali free to pursue his policy of *détente* with Saudi Arabia and reunification with North Yemen through 1976 and early 1977.

During 1977, however, events abroad began to move rapidly to his disadvantage. The growing Soviet interest in supporting the beleaguered Ethiopian revolutionary regime in the Horn of Africa made South Yemen a far more important strategic base for Moscow, and the prospect that in a war between Ethiopia and Somalia the Soviet Union would be expelled from its existing Somali naval and air facilities further increased Aden's importance to Moscow. Promises of more generous Soviet military and economic aid began to be made to South Yemen, accompanied by requests for base facilities and tactful support for Abdul Fattah Ismail's faction of the leadership. Following the visit of Soviet Navy Commander-in-Chief Admiral Sergei Gorshkov to South Yemen in late 1976, Soviet First Deputy Defence Minister Sokolov visited Aden in February, 1977.

Cuba's Premier Fidel Castro arrived in March bearing a plan for a federation of 'revolutionary States' in the Red Sea area — Ethiopia, Somalia and South Yemen — which Rubayya Ali succeeded in rejecting, but he was compelled to rush his foreign minister to Riyadh to placate the nervous Saudis, and to give further reassurances to Saudi Foreign Minister Prince Saud al-Faisal, who paid a personal visit to Aden in April. Castro was followed in May, 1977 by a Soviet air force delegation led by General Shomatov (the prospect of having to airlift Soviet arms in large quantities to Ethiopia was already being considered), President Rubayya Ali persisted in his course, but Saudi Arabia's confidence in his ability to control the course of events in South Yemen was clearly declining as fast as its anxieties about Soviet intentions in the Red Sea and the Horn of Africa were rising: during a visit to Moscow in July, 1977 by Prime Minister and Defence Minister Ali Nasir Muhammad, Rubyya Ali had to hasten to Saudi Arabia to dispel the impression that Abdul Fattah Ismail's faction, with powerful support from the Soviet bloc, was gaining the upper hand. His parallel attempts to reassure North Yemen's President al-Hamdi that the unification project was still on course evidently succeeded, for Hamdi agreed to pay his first visit to Aden in October, 1977.

Hamdi, however, was murdered 2 days before his scheduled visit to Aden, and his successor (and the man who had arranged his assassination), Colonel Ahmad al-Ghashmi, was a strongly pro-Saudi officer which immediately suppressed the leftist National Democratic Front in North Yemen, and put an end to the talks with South Yemen on unification. There has been much speculation that Hamdi died because Saudi Arabia had concluded that President Rubayya Ali was unable to control the rise in influence of Secretary-General Abdul Fattah Ismail's faction in Aden, enjoying as it did such powerful support from the Soviet bloc, and that the reunification of Yemen therefore had to be stopped as it was likelier to result in the radicalisation of North Yemen than in the taming of South Yemen. Further confirmation of the apparent growth of Ismail's power in Aden had been provided by the fact that in September South Yemen had begun supplying

tanks and fighter aircraft (allegedly complete with crews) to a by then totally pro-Soviet Ethiopia — on the understanding that the South Yemeni equipment would be replaced by the Soviet Union — and by the visit of East German Defence Minister General Heinz Hoffman to Aden in October.

Whether or not the assassination of North Yemen's President al-Hamdi was a signal that Saudi Arabia had despaired of its efforts to achieve *détente* with South Yemen, it had an immediate impact in Aden which was very much to Rubayya Ali's disadvantage. Before October was out Prime Minister Ali Nasir Muhammad, who had hitherto also controlled the Defence Ministry and thus the regular army as a kind of counterbalance to Abdul Fattah Ismail's Popular Militia, was relieved of his post as Defence Minister. It went instead to Lieutenant-Colonel Ali Antar, a 'leftist' who was closely associated with Ismail's faction. Other cabinet changes in the same reshuffle also denoted a decline in Rubayya Ali's power.

During the succeeding months South Yemen became even more deeply committed to supporting Soviet strategy in the region. A full-scale Soviet air bridge was set up to fly in vast quantities of military equipment to Ethiopia, with all the aircraft staging through South Yemen, and units of South Yemeni combat troops were also sent to Ethiopia — notably in January, 1978 when a South Yemeni battalion committed to the Arab Deterrent Force in Lebanon was hastily withdrawn and sent directly to the defence of the Red Sea port of Massawa, which was under close siege by Eritrean guerrilla forces. By the end of 1977, moreover, border skirmishes between South Yemeni and Saudi Arabian troops had become common-place, with some more serious fighting at Wadiah in the western sector of the frontier. South Yemen's reward became clear in February, 1978 when Prime Minister Ali Nasir Muhammad, on a visit to Moscow, received far-reaching pledges of economic co-operation and a Soviet commitment to help double the size and strength of the South Yemeni armed forces. This prospect undoubtedly assisted the new, pro-Ismail Defence Minister, Colonel Ali Antar, in undermining President Rubayya Ali's previous influence in the regular armed forces. In April 150 senior army officers loyal to the President were arrested by the militia on Ismail's orders, and Ismail's key lieutenant, Minister of State Security Muhammad Said Yafai, attacked President Rubayya Ali publicly for having readmitted to the army some 300 soldiers who had formerly been discharged because of their hostility to the regime.

Following Defence Minister Antar's visit to Moscow in May, 1978 moreover, it was reported that a Soviet delegation led by Admiral Sergei Gorshkov arrived in Aden in early June under cover of secrecy to sign a 15 year agreement covering military and other aspects of co-operation. The agreement allegedly provided for Soviet assistance in the construction of a large new naval base in the Bay of Turbah which would offer the Soviet navy facilities for repair, storage, communications and monitoring; the construction of a new air base at Khormaksar near Aden with accommodation for 60 fighter aircraft (also offering facilities to the Soviet air force); a monitoring and communications station on Socotra Island; a large military installation at Mukalla on the road to Oman; and the delivery to the south Yemeni armed forces of some 30 MiG aircraft, five FPBs and a major radar network to cover the south of Saudi Arabia and parts of the Gulf.

By mid-1978, therefore, President Rubayya Ali had lost almost all influence over government policy to the rival faction led by Secretary-General Abdul Fattah Ismail, and his control over at least many of the units of the regular army. Given the arcane nature of South Yemeni politics, it is not possible to state with complete confidence the sequence of events which then led to the simultaneous assassination of the North Yemeni President, Rubayya Ali's execution and the outbreak of severe fighting between the army and the Popular Militia in South Yemen, but the version which is most plausible, and best substantiated by known events, is as follows.

Rubayya Ali, seeing no hope of restoring his crumbling position in South Yemen except with outside aid, apparently maintained secret contact with North Yemen's new leader, President Ahmad al-Ghashmi, despite the latter's known dependence on Saudi support and his suppression of the left in North Yemen. It is alleged that Rubayya Ali was planning a coup against the rest of the party leadership in Aden with the aid of units in the regular army that were still loyal to him, and that his contacts were to ensure instant North Yemeni and Saudi Arabian support for the coup in what was bound to be a delicately balanced situation in South Yemen. Some of Rubayya Ali's agents, however, were actually double agents working for Ismail, and one of them apparently succeded in substituting a booby-trapped briefcase for the one which the President's secret envoy was taking with him to North Yemen on June 24th, just as the coup was about to begin. When Rubayya Ali's unsuspecting envoy opened the briefcase in President al-Ghashmi's office in San'a', it exploded, killing both men.

It is not clear whether Rubayya Ali's coup ever actually got underway in Aden, or whether the heavy fighting in the city which broke out at the same time, accompanied by air strikes on the Presidential Palace, was due to units loyal to the President defending themselves against a pre-emptive attack by forces obedient to General-Secretary Abdul Fattah Ismail. Within a short time the President's forces in Aden City were defeated, however, and within a further 24 hours Rubayya Ali had been summarily tried, stood against a wall, and shot. Prime Minister Ali Nasir Muhammad was installed as President in his place, but the true undisputed ruler of South Yemen to emerge from the fighting was the hard-line General-Secretary of the UPONF, Abdul Fattah Ismail. He subsequently assumed the Presidency himself.

There was extensive fighting in various parts of the country as army officers and units loyal to President Rubayya Ali resisted Ismail's Popular Militia troops. Fighting was particularly heavy in the Third Governorate (Abyan), the President's home territory, where the local army commander led many soldiers up into the hills to conduct guerrilla warfare against the new regime, but there were also clashes in the First, Fourth and Six Governorates and throughout the eastern Hadhramaut. It was alleged (admittedly by refugees) that some of the Cuban troops in the country and two battalions of Ethiopians under Arabic-speaking officers, hastily sent by Addis Ababa in repayment for services rendered, were thrown in by the government to fill the gaps left by mass defections of regular army troops, and that several hundred Russian officers were placed in effective command of the South Yemeni army pending a thorough purge of all elements still loyal to the former President. It is certainly the case that there were large numbers of defections from the armed forces, including one entire unit (allegedly a brigade, but probably a battalion) that took refuge in North Yemen from the Beihan area. By November, 1978 however, almost all of the fighting had died down. The armed forces had been very extensively purged, with numerous executions, and even the mountainous areas along the borders with Oman and North Yemen were largely under government control. Consolidating his victory, Abdul Fattah Ismail transformed the UPONF coalition into a single 'Yemen Socialist Party' in October, 1978. The party's first congress afforded the Secretary-General and President Ali Nasir Muhammad an occasion to award themselves the

rank of brigadier, presumably to strengthen their authority over the army.

STRENGTH AND BUDGET

The strength of the PDRY's armed forces is 26,000 of which 22,000 are army. The 1000 man navy is subordinate to the army; the formal status of the 3000 man air force is unknown. In February, 1978 the Soviet Union pledged to double the size and strength of the armed forces over an unknown period of time. The population of the PDRY is 1,955,000.

Paramilitary forces, in the form of Public Security Force (1500 men) and the Popular Militia, at least notionally include every fit adult male in the population, but it is not known how closely this precept is adhered to in rural areas. Numbers of units in the Cuban-trained Popular Militia are now as well equipped as comparable infantry units in the regular army, as was demonstrated during the short civil war in June, 1978.

The military budget for 1980 was $123,700,000. This does not include expenditure on the Public Security Force, and it may not include the Popular Militia either. The estimated GNP is $996,500,000 which suggests that South Yemen, despite relatively large amounts of military aid from the Soviet Union, has one of the highest rates of military expenditure in the world.

COMMAND AND CONSTITUTIONAL STATUS

The executive organisation, effectively chosen by the single permitted party, is the Presidential Council. The President is Supreme Commander of the Armed Forces and exercises control through the Defence Minister, who is in the chain of command. Operational control is in the hands of the Chief of the General Staff; staff organisation is on the Soviet model, and Soviet military advisers are distributed throughout the army. Regional military commands coincide with the boundaries of the eight governorates into which the country is divided for administrative purposes.

The General Security Units are controlled by the Ministry of the Interior. The Popular Militia is directly controlled by the Secretary-General of the ruling party, and is at least as strong in numbers as the regular army. Following the fighting between the Popular Militia and units of the army loyal to the late President Rubayya Ali in June, 1978, numbers of army command positions, including senior staff jobs in Aden, were taken over by militia officers who were considered to be more reliable politically.

ROLE, COMMITMENT, DEPLOYMENT AND RECENT OPERATIONS

The role of the South Yemen regular army is the defence of the national territory against the country's three hostile neighbours. The role of the Popular Militia is the preservation of the regime against the army. The army's task is made rather difficult by the fact that North Yemen, Saudi Arabia and Oman all vehemently disapprove of the Aden regime, and together dispose of five times the armed forces, 10 times the population and 250 times the national income of South Yemen. The militia has recently demonstrated that it is entirely capable of performing its task.

In fact, the army's job of defending South Yemen is greatly eased by the fact that all the conservative countries of the Arabian peninsula have a strong aversion to creating a precedent for the overthrow of another country's regime by military invasion, or even of territorial changes imposed by force, and would be reluctant to embark on such a venture even to be rid of a regime they abhor as much as that in South Yemen. Moreover, the Aden regime can almost certainly rely on firm Soviet political and military support to prevent such an occurrence. The main problem the army has to deal with, therefore, is that of border clashes, although some of them have been of quite large scope in the past.

Recent operations have included border clashes with Saudi Arabia in 1969 and 1977, a small border war with North Yemen in October, 1972 involving air-strikes and small-scale military actions in a restricted area, and operations in support of the guerrillas of the Popular Front for the Liberation of Oman (as PFLOAG was renamed in 1974) fighting in Oman's Dhofar Province. The latter conflict involved Iranian and Omani air strikes into South Yemen's Hadhramaut Province and artillery duels across the border in 1975, but from 1976 onwards the Aden government refused to allow PFLO guerrillas to cross the border into Oman and shooting ceased.

As many as 2000 South Yemeni troops may have been involved in fighting in support of the Ethiopian government, principally in Eritrea, in 1977–8, but all were believed to have returned home before the end of 1978. The extensive fighting between the army and the Popular Militia in June, 1978 appears not to have done the former serious damage, as the army was committed on a large scale to the fighting that erupted along the North Yemen border in February, 1979 (see Current Developments). There is no real evidence as to the army's fighting ability in prolonged conventional combat against serious opposition, but it seems well enough trained and equipped to give a good account of itself.

Detailed information on deployment is unavailable. Both army and Popular Militia units are stationed throughout the eight governorates, and there are always substantial concentrations along the Oman and North Yemen borders. (The latter approaches to within 50 miles of Aden.) The lengthy border with Saudi Arabia runs through virtually uninhabited desert; exiles from South Yemen raid across it occasionally, but the South Yemen army maintains no military concentrations along it on a permanent basis except for a light screening force in the western sector. Major garrison towns include Aden, Mukalla and Hauf. There are not believed to be any South Yemeni troops deployed abroad.

The PDRY, like all Arab States, belongs to the Arab League and to its subsidiary military bodies, the Arab Defence Council and the Unified Arab Command and one Yemeni battalion was in Syria in 1982 as part of the Arab Deterrent force. The only significant military relationship maintained by the regime is with the Soviet Union and some of its allies, notably East Germany and Cuba, all of which supply military advisers to the country.

ORGANISATION

Arms of Service
The usual division of the army into combat arms (infantry, artillery, armour and engineers) and supporting services (signals, ordnance, transport, etc.) is observed. The branch structure of the Popular Militia, if any, is unknown.

Operational
The army is organised into 10 infantry brigades (each of three battalions), one armoured, one mechanised brigade, one artillery brigade, one (training) brigade, ten artillery battalions, a marine unit and one SAM brigade.

The air force has a conventional squadron organisation, consisting of one interceptor squadron (MiG-17s), one light bomber squadron, one transport squadron and one helicopter squadron. The main air base is at Khormaksar (Aden), which is also extensively used by the Soviet air force. Other air bases are at Al Dali, Mukayris, Lawdar, Bayshan al Qisab, Ansab, Ataq, Mukalla, Zamakah and Ir Fadhl Field.

The squadron or flotilla organisation of the navy, if any, is not known. The main naval bases are at Aden and Mukulla; a large new base for joint South Yemeni–Soviet use is being built in the Bay of Turbah.

RECRUITMENT, TRAINING AND RESERVES

Conscription for a period of 2 years was introduced in March, 1977 and the intention is to double the present size of the armed forces to about 40,000 men. It is not known if any conscripts are directed into the Popular Militia. There has been some discussion about sending young men to be trained in Cuba, as was done by the Ethiopians, but so far as is known all military training of conscripts is done at home. Further training in specialised subjects for senior NCOs and officers frequently has to be done abroad, however, mainly in the Soviet Union and East Germany.

Amongst the communist States which have sent training missions to South Yemen are the Soviet Union, East Germany, Cuba and North Korea. Considerably exaggerated figures are frequently quoted for the number of Soviet-bloc military advisers in the country, perhaps harking back to the quite high numbers of Soviet and Cuban military personnel who were based in the country briefly, or passed through it, in connection with the airlift of military aid to Ethiopia in 1977–78. The totals in early 1979, however, were between 400 and 800 Russians, about 300 Cubans and 300 East Germans and other Eastern Europeans, not all of whom were military personnel. The Soviet military advisers have primary responsibility for training assistance to the regular armed forces and the Cubans work mainly with the Popular Militia. The East Germans have specialised in the organisation and training of the police and internal security forces, including the much feared Revolutionary Security Organisation (the secret police), which is controlled by State Security Minister Muhammad Said Yafai, a close ally of President Abdul Fattah Ismail.

Apart from the Popular Militia, there was not known to be a reserve organisation in South Yemen, although with the introduction of conscription it would seem likely that one will eventually be created.

EQUIPMENT AND ARMS INDUSTRY

South Yemen operates mainly Soviet equipment, with some older British equipment from the pre-1970 period. The army's armour consists of 470 T-54/55 and T-66 tanks, supported by 10 Saladin armoured cars, 10 Ferret scout cars and 300 BTR-40/-152 APCs together with some BPM armoured vehicles. The artillery employs British 25 pounders and 105mm pack howitzers, and Soviet 85mm, 100mm and 130mm guns (360 in service) and 122mm and 130mm howitzers. Other weapons include BM14 and BM21 mobile rocket launchers, 81mm and 120mm mortars, and 122mm recoilless rifles. Anti-aircraft defence is provided by 37mm, 57mm, 85mm and ZSU-23-4 SP AA guns and SA-2 and 7 surface-to-air missiles. Anti-tank weapons probably include Sagger, Snapper or Swatter ATGWs. The standard personal weapon is the AK-47. In view of the June, 1978 agreement with the Soviet Union on the expansion of the armed forces, substantial further deliveries of Soviet weapons were received, and T-62 tanks were reported present in the South Yemeni units fighting on the North Yemen border in early 1979. Frog and SCUD surface-to-surface missiles (12) are in service.

The navy has the following: two SO-1-class and one Poluchat-class large patrol craft; two P-6 and four P-4-class MTBs; three Osa-I-class FPBGs with Styx surface-to-surface missiles; three ex-British Ham-class inshore minesweepers; two Polnocny-class and three ex-British medium LCTs; three Spear-class and one Interceptor-class patrol boats; and 15 ex-British small patrol craft.

The air force operates 12 MiG-21MF interceptors, 15 MiG-17 fighter—bombers and seven Il-28 light bombers. It has four Il-14 and three An-24 transports, and eight Mi-8 and some Mi-4 helicopters. There are three MiG-15 UTI trainers. The standard air-to-air weapon is AA-2 Atoll. It is believed that some aircraft are in storage owing to a shortage of pilots.

RANK, DRESS AND DISTINCTIONS

Regular armed forces ranks conform to international practice. No information is available on rank structure in the Popular Militia.

CURRENT DEVELOPMENTS

By the end of 1978 the regime appeared to be in full control of the army and the country, and its international alignment and military relationship with the Soviet Union seemed secure from further domestic challenge. By early 1979 it was confident enough to sponsor a major attack against North Yemen by exile forces from that country, with powerful support from South Yemeni regular forces.

There was considerable evidence that Aden had earlier had a hand in organising the major military revolt against the pro-Saudi, tribally dominated regime in San'a' in October, 1978. Following the suppression of that revolt further North Yemeni military and civilian refugees fled to South Yemen, where they joined earlier political refugees belonging to the leftist National Democratic Front (NDF) that had been banned

after the coup that overthrew President al-Hamdi in October, 1977, and military exiles who had taken part in an unsuccessful revolt led by Major Abdullah Abdul Alem in the southern part of North Yemen in April, 1978. (*See* the entry on North Yemen for further details.) The South Yemeni regime encouraged the NDF refugees to organise guerrilla forces in alliance with the June Thirteenth Movement formed by the exiled North Yemeni army officers, and on February 23rd, 1979 attacks were launched along most of the North Yemen frontier by South Yemeni regular units operating in concert with these guerrillas. Within a week a considerable area of North Yemeni territory along the frontier, including the three large towns of Qataba, Bayda and Harib were in rebel/South Yemeni hands, and the USA and Saudi Arabia had both begun airlifts of arms and supplies to San'a'. It did not seem likely that the South Yemeni attack was intended to penetrate far beyond the border areas, but rather to be aimed at sparking off an internal rebellion, or alternatively making it possible for the exiles to set up a rival provisional government in the territory seized for them by the South Yemeni forces.

Subsequently (*see* North Yemen) the two countries agreed to a ceasefire, and, in later talks, to move towards a unification of the two countries. But the difficulties obstructing such a solution of differences seem insurmountable.

Relations with Oman remain hostile. There was cross-border firing and patrol activity in March-June. Meanwhile, Soviet military aid to South Yemen increased. There were reports of the building of a Soviety command post at Jebel Hal, of a network of missile bases to protect Soviet, Cuban and Yemen military camps from attack from the south and of an amphibious training base at Ma'alla, near Aden, to train guerrillas from neighbouring states.

Gwynne Dyer
John Keegan

YUGOSLAVIA

HISTORY AND INTRODUCTION

The Kingdom of the Serbs, Croats and Slovenes was proclaimed on December 1st, 1918. It was made up of the independent Kingdoms of Serbia and Montenegro, the Austro—Hungarian provinces of Croatia—Slovonia, Dalmatia and Bosnia—Herzegovina, and small parts of Austria and Hungary. The new nation faced serious problems from the outset. Her borders were not confirmed until 1926, and the eventual settlement left numerous non-Yugoslav minorities — Magyars, Germans, Albanians and Romanians — within Yugoslavia. Of the population of about 12,000,000, just over half were Greek Orthodox, nearly 5,000,000 were Roman Catholic and over 1,000,000 were Moslem. The Royal Family, together with nearly half the population, was Serbian, and the Constitution of 1921 was merely a modified version of that of Serbia. The Constitution was sharply attacked by the Croatians, who demanded a federal union, and parliamentary debates grew so heated that Radić, the Croatian leader, was mortally wounded on the floor of the House in June, 1928.

In January the following year King Alexander decided that party passions were so inflamed that an extra-parliamentary solution should be sought: he therefore dispensed with parliament and Constitution, and set up a government under the nominal leadership of a general. All existing political parties were dissolved, and the formation of new ones required official authorisation. Alexander granted a new Constitution in September, 1931, but it was little more than a cloak for the continuation of royal dictatorship. On October 9th, 1934 Alexander was assassinated at Marseilles by an agent of the Croatian separatists. The young Paul II governed through a council of regency, dominated by his father's cousin, Prince Paul, who took some steps to liberalise the regime within the existing Constitution. Political parties were unofficially tolerated, and the Communist Party, banned in 1922, gained numerous adherents.

Josip Broz, subsequently known as Tito, a Croatian factory worker imprisoned in 1928 for illegal trade union activities, took over the leadership of the Communist Party in 1937. His energetic reorganisation of the party came at a time of deepening domestic and international crisis. The establishment of an autonomous Province of Croatia in August, 1939 failed to solve the problem of national minorities, and was followed by increasing Serbian, Slovenian and Moslem demands for self-government. The economy was dangerously dependent upon Germany, the disappearance of Czechoslovakia deprived Yugoslavia of her main source of arms, and the government's emergency economic measures contributed to the growing inflation. In March, 1941 after temporising as long as possible, the government at last bowed to German pressure and signed the anti-Comintern pact. The regency was thereupon overthrown by a coup in which army and air force officers played leading roles. King Paul was declared of age, and a new broadly representative government was formed.

The coup infuriated Hitler, who ordered that Yugoslavia should be smashed 'with merciless brutality'. On April 6th the Axis invasion commenced with a savage air attack on Belgrade. Organised resistance lasted only a few days: the government surrendered unconditionally on April 17th. Yugoslavia was then dismembered. Most of her components were placed under German or Italian rule, and an independent State of Croatia, run by the *Ustaši* as an Axis satellite, was established. The *Ustaši* embarked upon a policy of exterminating the Serbs within Croatia in a fashion which dismayed even the Germans and Italians, whose own behaviour in occupied territories was scarcely model.

Occupation was fiercely risisted. Armed bands were active in Serbia as early as May, 1941 and the German invasion of Russia brought the Yugoslav communists into the struggle. The conflict was bitter and confused, complicated by the existence of some pro-Axis factions as well as two major anti-Axis groups. General D. D. Mihailović's *ćetniks* were initially the largest and most prestigious group. They owed allegiance to King Peter's London-based government-in-exile, and enjoyed the support of the Western Allies. The communist partisans were led by Tito and supported by Russia; they eventually became recognised, even in the West, as the most effective of the resistance groups. The *ćetniks* and the partisans were often as hostile to one another as they were to the occupation forces, and the struggle was as much a civil war as a campaign against the invaders. The *ćetniks* had been almost totally destroyed by the spring of 1945, although it was not until March, 1946 that Mihailović himself was captured. He was executed, together with a number of other anti-communists, the following month.

The defeat of the Axis and the eradication of the *ćetniks* left Tito supreme. A communist-dominated provisional government was formed in March, 1945 and a constituent assembly met on November 29th. It immediately declared Yugoslavia a Federated People's Republic, and a federal constitution was approved in January, 1946. Yugoslavia was, in the early post-war years, a staunch ally of the Soviet Union: she was a founder member of Cominform, whose headquarters were set up in Belgrade. By late 1947, however, there was friction between Tito and Stalin over foreign policy, and in March, 1948 Stalin formally accused the Yugoslav Communist Party of revisionism and other anti-communist activities. The Yugoslav party denied the charges, but in June was expelled from Cominform and publicly castigated for ideological deviation.

Yugoslavia's break with the Soviet Union was followed by Soviet attempts to engineer Tito's overthrow by the party's central committee and by the army. The failure of these projects was followed by a purge of pro-Soviet members of the party, army and administration. Cominform stepped up its propaganda campaign in 1949, and the Soviet Union encouraged Yugoslavia's neighbours to press their territorial claims against her. Yugoslavia's economic severance from the Soviet bloc brought her economy to the verge of collapse, and forced her to look to the West for trade. In 1951 both France and America supplied Yugoslavia with arms, and the next few years saw increasing *rapprochement* between Yugoslavia and the West. There was a measure of relaxation within Yugoslavia: police powers were curbed in 1953—4, numerous collective farms were disbanded and steps were taken to decentralise elements of the administration. The Constitutional Law of January, 1953 introduced the office of President of the Republic, and played great emphasis upon the direct political participation of working people.

The death of Stalin, in March, 1953 removed a major obstacle to reconciliation between Yugoslavia and the Soviet

Union. A settlement was reached in 1955, and Tito himself visited Moscow the following year. The reconciliation proved short-lived: there were fundamental differences of opinion between Tito and Khrushchev, and by the summer of 1958 the Yugoslavs were once more accused of revisionism. The failure of the settlement with Russia encouraged Tito to increase his involvement with non-aligned States: he travelled extensively in Africa and Asia, and in September, 1961 sponsored a world conference of non-aligned States at Belgrade. Relations with Russia improved after 1961, but Yugoslav foreign policy remained firmly committed to non-alignment. Within Yugoslavia the trend towards the devolution of power and the increase of workers' control of industry went on: the Constitution of April, 1963 reaffirmed the rights of the working people, and set up a complex multicameral parliament.

The invasion of Czechoslovakia, in August, 1968 came as a shock to Yugoslavia, who feared that she might be treated in a similar manner. Tito and his Romanian counterpart immediately met and declared their determination to resist aggression, some military units moved to their war locations and a number of reservists were mobilised. The defence budget was increased in October, and in February, 1969 a territorial defence organisation, based on the concept of Total National Defence, was set up. Although the Soviet invasion never actually materialised – Yugoslav fears were undoubtedly somewhat exaggerated – the system of total defence remains an essential ingredient of Yugoslav defence policy.

Tito's undoubted success in maintaining Yugoslavia's independence should not be allowed to obscure the fact that the nation continues to face serious difficulties. There have been some rifts with the party: Vice-President Aleksander Ranković fell from power in an internal upheaval in the summer of 1966, and the veteran communist Milovan Djilas has been imprisoned on several occasions for his attacks on the regime. There have also been a number of strikes and some student unrest. The problem of nationalities, moreover, remains unsolved. Yugoslavia is, in the words of one authority, 'neither a homogeneous nation-state like Italy nor a fully multinational State like the Hapsburg Monarchy in the past or the USSR today'. Less than half the population belongs to the largest national group, the Serbs: there are four written and six spoken languages. Friction between the minorities persists, with economic, linguistic and cultural motivation, and some violence has been carried out by separatist movements. The move towards decentralisation and socialist direct democracy goes on, but there are fears that Tito's Yugoslavia will not survive its founder's death and that the federation will fragment under the pressure of nationalism. The effects of such fragmentation would not be purely domestic, but might all too easily provoke foreign intervention, with dangerous consequences for world peace. Recent events, such as the visit of General Lubcic to Russia in May, 1974 and General Kulikov's visit to Yugoslavia 6 months later, point to something of a *rapprochement* between Yugoslavia and the Soviet Union. Kulikov again visited Yugoslavia in April, 1976. If intended by the Russians as means towards exploiting inter-regional differences following the death of Marshal Tito, it was unsuccessful. Yugoslav federal unity survived his departure apparently without any trouble.

STRENGTH AND BUDGET

Population: 22,650,000
Army: 190,000 (140,000 conscripts)
Air force: 45,000; 400 combat aircraft

Navy: 15,500; nine submarines, one frigate, 125 smaller craft
Paramilitary: 1–3 million in a Territorial Defence Force; 20,000 frontier guards
GNP (1980): $69,867,000,000
Defence expenditure (1981): $2,870,000,000

COMMAND AND CONSTITUTIONAL STATUS

Command

The president is Commander-in-Chief of the Armed Forces. Day-to-day control is exercised by the Ministry of National Defence. There are seven military districts, based on Belgrade, Skopje, Split, Zagreb, Sarajevo and Ljubljana and another military in Serbia. The two major air commands are located at Zomun and Zagreb, and the navy, commanded from Split, has three regional commands based on Pula, Šibenik and Kotor/Trivat.

Constitutional Status

The Constitution of February, 1974 affirms that Yugoslavia is a Socialist Federal Republic, comprising the Socialist Republics of Serbia, Croatia, Macedonia, Montenegro, Slovenia and Bosnia–Herzegovina. The Socialist Republic of Serbia includes two autonomous regions: Voyvodina and Kosovo.

Collective presidency was established in 1971, and in 1974 the presidential body was reduced to nine members, one representative from each of the Republics and autonomous regions, and the President of the League of Communists of Yugoslavia. There is a bicameral Federal Assembly, whose members must be workers rather than professional politicians; it is assisted by an Executive Council of Ministers.

The constitution states, as a basic tenet, that Yugoslavia is devoted to 'peaceful coexistence and the principles of non-alignment'. It also declares that 'the armed forces of the Socialist Federal Republic of Yugoslavia are an integral entity, and consist of the Yugoslav People's Army as the joint armed force of all nations and nationalities and all working people and citizens, and the Territorial Defence Forces as the broadest form of organised armed resistance'.

ROLE, COMMITMENT, DEPLOYMENT AND RECENT OPERATIONS

Role and Commitment

In the words of Army General Ljubčić, 'Yugoslavia's armed forces are intended exclusively for the defence of the Socialist Federal Republic of Yugoslavia'. Yugoslavia subscribes to no military alliances, and all her forces are stationed within her borders. The concept of Total National Defence (TND) is paramount. Ljubčić suggests that 'TND points the way to the solution of the problem of how small- and medium-sized countries can successfully withstand aggression by a considerably stronger aggressor'. TND is designed to deter a potential aggressor and, if this deterrence fails, to ensure that 'every citizen, irrespective of sex, age, occupation and so on' resists the attack in one way or another. Ljubčić stresses that Yugoslavia's terrain favours small-unit defensive actions, and believes that the Vietnam war demonstrates that 'liberation forces' enjoying the support of the local population can defeat a sophisticated enemy.

Any attack on Yugoslavia would be met by 'comprehensive defence' beginning on the frontier and extending into the interior. The entire population would be involved in armed resistance, civil defence, armaments production or military engineering. There would be no front in the accepted sense:

units of the Territorial Defence Forces (TDF) would fight on in occupied areas, forcing the invader to pay careful attention to the security of his lines of communication. It is likely that the armoured formations of the Yugoslav People's Army (YPA) would fight delaying actions in the open country north and north-east of the Sava, Danube and Morava with the intention of inflicting casualties and giving the TDF time to arm and deploy.

Deployment
The YPA consists of eight infantry divisions, eight armoured brigades, 17 independent infantry brigades, one mountain brigade and a single airborne battalion. The armoured brigades seem to be grouped into divisional-sized formations around Sisak (Croatia), Kragujevac (Serbia) and Skopje (Macedonia). Armoured formations based on Sisak and Kragujevac are well placed to operate against an invader advancing through the good tank country of the Sava and Danube valleys.

Recent Operations
The YPA has been involved in no military operations since 1945. In 1971 a large-scale exercise, *Freedom 71*, was carried out: it involved both YPA and TDF. Although the Yugoslavs maintain that the exercise confirmed the practicability of their concept of TND, there have been suggestions, notably in the Austrian military press, that the exercise was not an unqualified success. Exercise *Kosovo 72* tested partisan operations, and exercise *Podgora 72* involved operations on the Adriatic Coast.

ORGANISATION

The concept of TND stresses the totality of national defence and the need for intimate co-operation between the YPA and TDF. There are, however, substantial organisational differences between the two forces.

Firstly the YPA has a full range of combatant arms and supporting services. Its formations come under the command of Military District HQs. Corps staffs would be formed only on mobilisation, but six army staffs, based on Military District HQs, exist in peacetime. The infantry divisions of the YPA comprise three or four infantry regiments, each containing three infantry battalions and a heavy weapons battalion, a tank battalion, an anti-tank battalion, an artillery regiment and various divisional troops. A tank division contains two tank brigades, a motorised infantry brigade, an artillery regiment and the usual divisional troops. Each tank brigade has three tank battalions, one or two motorised infantry battalions, an engineer company, artillery battery, quartermaster company and medical company. Army troops consist of one light and one heavy artillery regiment, a tank battalion or tank regiment, together with anti-aircraft, signals, engineer, medical and transport battalions.

Secondly the TDF is organised on the basis of existing socio—political communities: Socialist Republics, provinces, communes and factories. There are two major structures of TDF units. The *manoeuvrable* structure is made up of the larger TDF units under the control of republic, zone or province staffs; these units are intended to carry out mobile operations over a wide area. The *spatial* structure includes all other TDF units, which have the task of guarding key points, protecting the population, and so on.

RECRUITMENT, TRAINING AND RESERVES

Recruitment and Training
All Yugoslav citizens have some military liability: males may be called up for service in the YPA or TDF between the ages of sixteen and sixty-five. The YPA draws its recruits from all over Yugoslavia: conscripts serve in it for 15 months. Those conscripted into the navy or air force serve for 18 months. The YPA would be brought up to strength on mobilisation by the inclusion of reservists with recent regular service; others would serve in the TDF.

Schoolchildren receive compulsory military training, and the TDF carries out training on a part-time basis.

Reserves
There are about 500,000 army, navy and air force reservists with recent military service.

EQUIPMENT AND ARMS INDUSTRY

The Yugoslav armed forces use a very wide variety of arms and equipment. Although considerable efforts have been devoted to building up the domestic arms industry, the YPA still continues to employ numerous items of Soviet and American equipment. Units of the TDF are equipped mainly with older small arms and mortars.

Equipment
Small arms: 7.62mm M57 pistol (copy of Tokarev TT23), 9mm M65 pistol (based on Tokarev TT33), 7.62mm M49/57 SMG (copy of PPSh 41), 7.62mm M56 SMG (based on German MP 40), 7.62 M59/66 automatic rifle (copy of Soviet SKS), 7.62mm M64 assault rifle (now called M70, copy of Soviet AK-47), 7.62mm M65A and M65B (heavy barrel versions of M70, copied from Soviet Kalashnikov LMG), 7.62mm M53 SARAC LMG (copy of German MG42) and some bolt-action M-48 7.92mm carbines (based on the German Mauser 98K) which are still in service with the TDF

Mortars: (the Yugoslavs attach great importance to mortars, due, no doubt, to their usefulness in mountainous terrain); 50mm M-8 light mortar (similar to British 2in light mortar), 60mm M-57 (developed from United States 60mm M-2), 81mm M-31 (copy of United States 81mm M-1), 81mm M-68 (the Hotchkiss-Brandt MO-81-61L, built under licence in Yugoslavia), 120mm UBM-52 (the Hotchkiss-Brandt MO-120-AM50, built under licence in Yugoslavia). The Soviet M-38 and M-43 mortars are also used. M-60 rifle grenade

Anti-tank: M-57 anti-tank grenade launcher (similar to Czech P-27), M-18 57mm recoilless gun (United States design), M-20 75mm recoilless gun (United States design, mounted on a Zastava jeep), M-60 82mm recoilless gun (Yugoslav-designed and developed), M-65 105mm recoilless gun (replacing a similar United States weapon) The Soviet M-43 57mm and M-55 100mm anti-tank guns are also in use and Snapper and Sagger missiles

Anti-aircraft: most AA guns are of Soviet design, and include the ZSU-57-2 SP AA gun as well as a variety of towed weapons. The three-barrelled 20mm M-57 is manufactured in Yugoslavia under licence from Hispano—Suiza. Some World War II German 88mm FLAK-36 guns are still in use in emplacements on the Adriatic coast

Artillery: Towed guns include: 76mm M-48 B1 mountain howitzer (Yugoslav-produced; can be towed by vehicle or horses, or broken down for carriage on pack-mules), 105mm United States M-2 howitzer and its Yugoslav derivative the 105mm M-56 howitzer, 122mm Soviet M-38 130mm Soviet M-54, 152mm Soviet M-37 and 155mm United States M-2. German 105mm and 149mm howitzers are also in service; SP gun: 105mm United States

M7B2; Rocket launchers: 128mm M-66 32-barrelled rocket launcher mounted on trailer and 130mm M-51 Czech rocket launcher

Armour: Tanks: about a total of 1240 Soviet T-34/85s and T-54/-55s with 60 United Staes M-47 Pattons; Reconnaissance vehicles: Soviet PT-76 light tanks and BTR-40PB scout cars, and United States M-8 armoured cars; Assault guns and tank destroyers: Soviet ASU-57s and SU-100s, and United States 76.2mm M-18 Hellcat and 90mm M-36 Jackson tank destroyers; APCS: Soviet BTR-40s, -50Ps, -60Ps and -152s; United States M-3 half-tracks; Yugoslav-produced M-590 tracked APCs (carry 12 men and mount 12.7mm MGs); Yugoslav-produced M-980 MICVs (mounting 20mm cannon and two Sagger missiles)

Aircraft: Fighter—ground attack: United States F-84G Thunderjets (10), Yugoslav-produced Kraguj (15), Yugoslav-produced Galeb/Jastreb (95) and Yugoslav/Romanian Orao MRCAs; Fighter: a total of about 110 MiG-21Fs and United States F-86 Sabres; Reconnaissance: a total of 40 United States Lockheed RT-33As and Galeb/Jestrebs; Transports: a total of about 60 C-47 Dakotas, Il-14 Crates, Il-18 Coots, Li-2 Cabs and An-12 Cubs; Trainers: a total of about 90 Galebs, Lockheed T-33As plus a few MiG-21 UTI trainers; Helicopters: Westland S-55 Whirlwinds (15), Mi-4 Hounds (35) and Mi-8 Hips (25). 130 Gazelle SA-341s are on order. A small number of Alouette IIIs are probably still in service

Naval vessels: five submarines, one destroyer, three corvettes, 10 Osa-class patrol boats with Styx SSMs, 90 MTBs, patrol craft and minesweepers, and 30 landing craft

Missiles: Anti-tank: Snappers (mounted on Zastava jeeps and BTR-40Ps) and Saggers (mounted on BRT-40Ps); Anti-aircraft: eight SAM batteries with Soviet SAM-2s; SSM: Yugoslavia has no land-based SSM. The Soviet Styx SSM is used by her Osa patrol boats

Arms Industry

The Yugoslavs are well aware of the importance of building up the domestic arms industry, and a Federal Directorate is responsible for supervising the import and export of arms and, to a great extent, controls the domestic arms industry. Most home-produced items of Yugoslav military equipment are either copies of foreign equipment, or are foreign designs built under licence in Yugoslavia. The FAZ family of weapons (M64 and M65) are copies of Soviet weapons, and the Zastava jeep is a licenced copy of the Fiat AR-51. Lack of originality is, however, no great disadvantage, and the Yugoslav arms industry has made very considerable progress since 1970. The country is now producing its own infantry combat vehicle, the M-980.

RANK, DRESS AND DISTINCTIONS

Rank

General officers: gold-trimmed epaulette with crossed swords above laurel wreath at base
General armije — Four gold stars in inverted Y
General pukovnik — Three gold stars
General potpukovnik — Two gold stars
General maior — One gold star

Field Officers: gold-edged epaulette
Pukovnik — Three gold stars
Potpukovnik — Two gold stars
Maior — One gold star

Junior Officers: plain epaulette
Kapetan 1 klase — Four gold stars
Kapetan — Three gold stars
Poručnik — Two gold stars
Potporučnik — One gold star

NCOs and men: chevrons, worn point uppermost on the epaulette
Zastavnik — Broad gold chevron below thin gold chevron
Starji vodnik 1 klase — Four thin gold chevrons
Starji vodnik — Three thin gold chevrons
Vodnik 1 klase — Two thin gold chevrons
Vodnik — One thin gold chevron
Desetar — Two thin red chevrons
Razvodnik — One thin red chevron

Dress

Parade dress consists of open-necked grey tunic and trousers, black boots and grey webbing gaiters. Officers wear Sam Browne belts and other ranks black leather equipment of the German World War II pattern. Headgear is a grey steel helmet resembling the German 'coal-scuttle' helmet. Walking-out dress is similar, but boots are replaced by shoes; officers wear a grey peaked cap and other ranks a grey sidecap. An open-necked grey blouse with grey trousers, black shoes and headgear as for walking-out dress, is worn in summer. Grey denims are worn as barrack dress, and combat dress consists of grey jacket and trousers with black leather boots and equipment. NBC and tank suits are of the Soviet pattern. Mountain units may be seen wearing grey knee-breeches, long grey socks, black climbing boots and soft grey caps. Brass arm-of-service badges are worn on the collar in most orders of dress.

Distinctions

The Order of the Yugoslav Star and the Order of the Yugoslav Flag were founded by Tito in 1954 and 1947, respectively; both assumed their present form in 1961. Each order has several classes, and may be awarded to soldiers and civilians.

CURRENT DEVELOPMENTS

Impressive though the Yugoslav concept of TND appears, it is not without serious flaws. The system's prime aim is to deter aggression by threatening any potential invader with a long and costly struggle. If this deterrence fails, however, it is unlikely that Yugoslavia could fight unaided against a powerful aggressor for an indefinite period. The partisan tactics which proved successful during World War II might be less satisfactory in the face of an enemy equipped with modern weapons and large numbers of aircraft. It has also been suggested that the TDF's standard of training would seriously restrict its operations. Furthermore, although General Lubčić stresses that armaments production must be maintained in war-time, it is difficult to see how Yugoslav industry could be adequately protected from enemy air and missile attack.

Imperfect though the system of TND undoubtedly is, it is not without merit. Yugoslavia has managed to steer a middle course between East and West, and it continues, despite the strategic importance of its location, to avoid inclusion in either of the two great power blocs. TND is a powerful deterrent and, in the event of invasion, the Yugoslav armed forces would probably deny the aggressor victory until a third power or international organisation could intervene.

Richard Holmes

ZAÏRE

HISTORY AND INTRODUCTION

Until 1977 Zaïre saw itself as a country with especial qualifications for leadership in Africa: as the Congo, it was neither
French nor British, but Belgian. Zaïre further claimed links
with west Africa, through its small but important access to
the sea at the mouth of the Congo (Zaïre) River, and also
links with east Africa as Swahili is a *lingua franca* in much of
eastern Zaïre, and Swahili is an east-coast language.

Zaïre's attainment of independence in 1960, at the end of
an era of colonial rule distinguished by heavy paternalism
and lack of any real preparation for nationhood, was followed
by a period of the utmost confusion, violence and strife
necessitating the mounting of a large United Nations Expeditionary Force to bring some form of stability. Stability was
really only achieved in Zaïre with the return to power, in
1965 of General Mobutu, the Army Commander in a second
coup. For an initial period Zaïre's political and military prestige increased, but decline was to follow.

The Zaïre army has its origins in the *Force Publique* created
in 1888 in the sinister period of King Léopold II's personal
rule. For the most of the colonial period the *Force Publique*
was both defence force (with pacification commitments) and
gendarmerie. One of its distinctive features was a deliberate
Belgian policy of ethnic mixing and integration: this had
certain advantages but also could lead to amoral *déraciné*
behaviour as in 1960. In World War I units of the Force served
in the Cameroun and German East Africa campaigns, but it
was little used in World War II. In 1959 the Force was divided
into regular military units and gendarmerie, and at independence became the Congo National Army (ANC). These have
now become the FAZ (*Forces Armées Zaïroises*).

At independence the Force had no Congolese officers;
more important still the charisma of the authority to which
it owed its creation and loyalty had gone, and the ANC's
sub-*élite* status appeared insecure. Mutinies and collapse of
discipline resulted, with the consequent United Nations intervention. The ANC disintegrated into conflicting groups of
almost mindless gunmen, some linked to political factions
and supported and armed by revolutionary regimes elsewhere,
others solely concerned with plunder. As firstly Chief of Staff
and later Army Commander, Mobutu tried initially to create
a small nucleus of disciplined soldiers around him and then
recreate efficient units – he willingly accepted help both
from member units of the United Nations Force, and also a
small cadre of Belgian regulars. Finally he reabsorbed the
breakaway units who had been following the various Lum-
umba and Tshombe political factions. He continued to be
assisted by the Belgians, and then from 1962 onwards, also
by the USA on an increasingly large scale. But the ANC was
not strong enough to suppress the Simba rising, for which
European mercenaries had to be imported. It was against
these mercenaries and after his second coup, that Mobutu's
reformed ANC won its first real successes. The mercenaries,
who alleged that they had not been paid and refused to depart,
had allied themselves with mutinous soldiers from the Shaba
(Katanga) area, but the ANC, stiffened by United States
money and logistic support, forced them to withdraw via
Rwanda. One important defeat inflicted on the mercenaries
was the battle at Kamanyola in 1964. FAZ celebrates this
victory in a number of ways.

By the end of the 1960s the ANC seemed in some measure
to have returned to discipline and training. Young officers
trained abroad in Belgium, Britain or France had returned to
units, Kitona Base was beginning to appear a credible military
training centre and other service schools had opened. But
cases of indiscipline by soldiers – sale of weapons, robbery
with violence, and extortion, were still frequent and occur to
the present time with disturbing frequency.

Despite his military road to power, Mobutu's regime is not
essentially a military one: the President rarely appears in
uniform, and the style of the one-party regime, its quest for
'authenticity', and revolutionary songs and slogans, all indicate a search for a mass popular appeal; the President sees the
army as a people's revolutionary army – a crucible of revolutionary militancy and commitment. His regime has however,
always been very authoritarian, the President's office being
the centre of an exceedingly intricate pattern of relationships
which serve to keep the President informed on all events in
major State institutions. In 1974 rural development and
political education were laid down by the President as two
major military training priorities. In 1975 there was some
evidence of discontent among some senior army officers at
both the overall policy of the regime and the tasks it devolved
on to the army. Three former generals, a colonel and a major
were arrested, convicted and sentenced to death for conspiracy to overthrow the government in August–September,
1975. Further upheavals took place in 1977 and early 1978.
As a result of the army's feeble performance in the March,
1977 Shaba crisis (see below), Mobutu dismissed the Chief of
Staff and some 35 senior officers of general and colonel rank;
some of these appear to have, out of resentment, been involved in a conspiracy in February, 1978. This plot was discovered and further arrests of officers followed. Reports of a
rising in January, 1978 in the Kwilu area also circulated,
some noted the use of FAZ units in suppression of the revolt.
Other dismissals followed the Army and country's second
humiliation in Shaba in the summer of 1978. The situation
seems to have deteriorated further since 1979, with evident
student unrest (met by the drafting of rebellious freshmen
into the army) occasional strikes and an underground guerilla
resistance emerging in Kiru, Shaba and Haut-Zaïre. A number
of opposition groupings and movements have declared themselves, from the safety of European or other African capitals.
In Zaïre itself arrests and torture continue, giving the country
a notorious Human Rights record.

STRENGTH AND BUDGET

Population: 30,000,000 (approximate)
Army: 20,000 plus an air force of 2,500 and forty Gen-
    darmerie units totalling a further 20,000 or more.
GNP (estimate): $2,750,000,000 (estimate)
Defence expenditure: not known.

COMMAND AND CONSTITUTIONAL STATUS

President Mobutu Sese-Seko, an executive president, is the
Commander-in-Chief; General B. Nzongbi is commissioner
for defence and the Army Chief of Staff is General B. M.

676

Singa. Generals Nzongbi and Singa, the commanders of the ground forces, air force and gendarmerie, the chief of Intelligence and the military commander of Shaba Province are all men from Mobutu's home area, Equateur Province.

ROLE, COMMITMENT, DEPLOYMENT AND RECENT OPERATIONS

Zaïre's army has two main roles: defence against foreign aggression and internal security, a third commitment has been political propaganda and rural development.

Even prior to the dramatic events of 1977 and 1978 the army had been committed to internal security work, chiefly in the north-eastern area of the country and in the Lake Tanganyika area.

Small units of the Zaïre army were deployed in Angola in support of Holden Roberto's FNLA in 1975–6; their performance appears to have been poor. Relations with Congo–Brazzaville were also strained in this period (despite some rhetoric of reconciliation), and occasional border shootings occurred. With the victory of the MPLA Zaïre found herself with a serious military problem; her ambitions in the Cabinda area and her support for the FNLA made her the prime target for the victorious MPLA/Cuban forces, Zaïre's geographical configuration – long frontiers together with limited access to the sea rendering her particularly vulnerable. In March, 1977 with the clear connivance of the Angolan MPLA government a force of some 2000 (not the 5000 alleged by Zaïre) crossed the border into Zaïre's Shaba province, taking the town of Mutshatsha and advancing on the important mining town of Kolwezi. These insurgents were claimed to be Shaba inhabitants, seeking a liberation firstly of their province and secondly of Zaïre as a whole; they are more correctly to be seen as a Lunda ethnic movement following the 'tradition' of Tshombe's gendarmes. Cuban detachments were reported. The FAZ, however, withdrew precipitously, seeming to have no desire to stand and fight. The President appealed for help, and a Moroccan force arrived in French aircraft, with some French logistic support. As in Benin, the Moroccans had their own reason, the Polisario, for opposing any Marxist advance. This force of 1500 excellent soldiers quickly disposed of the insurgents. Zaïre rhetoric subsequently made great claims for the Zaïre units which had been rallied – these included a unit of pygmies equipped with bows and arrows – but the triumph such as it was, was a Moroccan one.

In May 1978 Zaïre suffered a second incursion, and a second military humiliation, when another Congolese National Liberation Front (FNLC) force under one 'General N. Mbumba' crossed into Shaba province from Angola and occupied Kolwezi, where in massacres they, probably with the assistance of out of control FAZ deserters, massacred some 200 Europeans and 500 Africans. At the urgent request of Mobutu French Foreign Legion parachute troops arrived with remarkable speed and efficiency, followed a little later by Belgian parachute troops and in a few days of 'flush out' operations ejected the insurgents from Zaïre with severe losses. Some of the insurgents fled out by way of Zambia. It seems the rebel force numbered some three thousand, though higher figures have been given. Some (with weapons concealed) had arrived in Kolwezi and Mutshatsha in plain clothes before the actual attack began, and these no doubt contributed to the rapid demoralisation of the Zaïre units in the area. The balance of reports suggest that at first the FAZ units, in their initial encounters with the insurgents, fought well, but very quickly lost heart; poor leadership may well have been the cause of this. The Kolwezi garrison commander, General Tshiveka, was later convicted of cowardice. Other analyses of the event attribute the FNLC's failure to inadequate sup-

port from the Angolan based Cubans and the poor leadership of 'General Mbumba'. The Zaïre government alleged the intervention was supported by the USSR, Cuba, Libya and Algeria, and Cubans were present in the FNLC units. No reliable evidence exists to support this, but it is not improbable.

After the ejection of the FNLC and the return of the French and Belgian troops, an inter-African force composed of units initially from Morocco and later from Senegal, Togo, Ivory Coast, Gabon, the Central African Empire and Egypt was assembled to secure the area, the respective units being flown in by United States military aircraft.

Zaïre and Angola, both wearied of the other's interventions, then signed a 'non-intervention in each other's affairs' agreement; at the time of writing this has been observed by both sides. There is a danger, however, that Western support for the UNITA movement in Angola might tempt Angola and Cuba once again to intervene in Zaïre as a means of retaliation for such support.

Zaïre, in an attempt to recover some military credibility sent a unit to the inter-African force despatched to Chad in November 1981. Like the rest of the force, it achieved nothing, and returned home in July 1982.

ORGANISATION

The present organisation of the Zaïre Army is unclear, one reason for this being politics. Formerly pride of place was given to the formation of a division, the Kamanyola Division. Doubts about the loyalty of some of its component units have, however, led to changes, the Division is now little more than a brigade and composed of units which, since they are not trusted, are short of supplies and pay. Favoured formations include the 21st Infantry Brigade in Shaba, trained by the Belgians, a commando unit in Equateur, also trained by the Belgians, the 3rd Commando Brigade at Kisangani trained by the Chinese who also train the Army's one armoured brigade and additional squadron, and the 31st Parachute Brigade trained by the French, who also train the logistics unit. The Belgians, it is reported, have begun to train some of the Kamanyola units.

RECRUITMENT, TRAINING AND RESERVES

Recruitment is voluntary. Until 1970 the Western part of Zaïre provided most of the recruits. After the 1978 events, recruitment in Bandundu and the two Kasai provinces was banned, and to all intents and purposes recruitment from Shaba has also ceased. The large majority of troops now come from Equateur Province.

Kitona Camp remains Zaïre's largest training centre, providing most of the army's basic training, together with training for specialist transport, signals and engineer units, and NCO and officer courses. Parachute training takes place at Ndjili and infantry training at Kotakoli.

Foreign training has been drawn from a number of sources. Some specialist personnel and cadets are trained in France, others in Britain. A small British team trained army engineers at Likasi. Belgium trains a number of military personnel of different ranks and arms. The USA does the same and has also maintained a military training mission. Italian personnel assist with air force training. Israeli instructors established the Ndjili parachute training facilities, but these all returned home in the 1960s. Moroccan training staff, in small numbers, arrived after the events in 1977. The present position is noted above; it only needs to be added that some units are in part actually officered by French officers.

The horrifying corruption in the government machine as a whole is mirrored in the Army where the already meagre pay is embezzled, and food, supplies and even vehicles sold off for private gain.

EQUIPMENT AND ARMS INDUSTRY

Zaïre has no arms industry and its equipment is drawn from many sources. The armoured units possess between 35 and 60 Chinese Type 62 light tanks and about 100 AML-60 and 40 AML-90 armoured cars; the type 62 tanks serve in Kamanyola units. Ten US M-60 tanks have also been reported. The numbers of armoured personnel carriers in service is also obscure, the main element is some 60 to 80 M-3 Panhard vehicles. An order for US M-113s was also placed for a number perhaps as high as 60; some appear to have been delivered. Some older Chinese K-63s, BTR-152s and US half track M-3s may also still be serviceable. The artillery include, small numbers of 75mm pack howitzers, 122mm and 130mm pieces, together with 82mm and 4.2 inch mortars. New French 120mm mortars are now under delivery. There are also 107mm rocket launchers and 57mm anti-tank guns, again in small numbers. Other weapons include limited issues of 57mm, 75mm and 106mm recoilless launchers and 37mm and 40mm anti-aircraft cannons. Signals equipment is French, and one report notes French 83mm rocket launchers to be on order.

The Air Force operates one fighter squadron of seven Mirage 5M and two counter insurgency squadrons, one of six Aeromacchi MB-326 and one of six North American AT-6 (Harvard) aircraft. The transport wing comprises a very mixed bag — six C-130 Hercules, two DC-6, two DHC Caribou, three Buffalo, eight C-47 Skytrain, and four C-54 machines. The liaison squadron of twenty Cessna 337 aircraft could with only slight modification have a limited counter insurgency value. Some thirty-five older light aircraft are still in service for training, there is a helicopter squadron of five Alouettes, five Pumas and one Super Frelon, and an order has been placed for four Fokker F-27 transports. Orders for French Aérospatiale Ecureuil helicopters and Siai-Marchetti S-211 light attack aircraft have also been reported.

RANK, DRESS AND DISTINCTIONS

These generally follow the Belgian pattern, except that a square or kerchief is worn around the neck in place of a collar and tie.

CURRENT DEVELOPMENT

President Mobutu survives for two reasons; firstly by subtlety and political blackmail he manages to secure not all the aid he needs, but just sufficient to survive, from the Western world (mainly a reluctant and bitterly critical IMF), and secondly because no one can foresee any alternative government that can be relied upon not to take, or not to allow to drift, this large and strategically important country full of Western investment into the Communist world. Zaïre is undoubtedly a prime Communist target, a fact often neglected by critics of CIA operations in Zaïre. Mobutu is also a skilled politician, the two Shaba humiliations have, paradoxically, been turned to some limited domestic political advantage, presenting Mobutu as the nation's saviour. His internal security arrangements and the French- and Belgian-trained army units serve also to buttress his otherwise shaky authority. Mobutu's regime is however one of the most repressive in the Africa of today, which coupled with its monumental administrative inefficiency and massive corruption from the Presidential entourage downwards must sooner or later lead to upheaval.

If the Army falls to internal divisions, either now or in an upheaval situation, Zaïre could return to the violence of the early 1960s. Mobutu has made little or no lasting contribution to the essential dilemma of this potentially quite prosperous African country, the alignment in some form of political consensus of the Kinshasa area, Shaba and the north-eastern Kisangani area. Only when a government emerges that can achieve this alignment will it have sufficient authority and legitimacy to produce a truly effective national army; expensive weapon purchases and regionally-recruited units trained with an eye to securing a highly unpopular regime are no substitute.

Lloyd Mathews

ZAMBIA*

HISTORY AND INTRODUCTION

Zambia's army's origins lie in the British colonial Northern Rhodesia Regiment (NRR) (Northern Rhodesia being the name of the territory as a British Protectorate); the NRR contributed battalions to operations in Italian East Africa and Burma in World War II, and one battalion to counter-insurgency operations in Malaya in the early 1950s. On the formation of the Federation of Rhodesia and Nyasaland in 1953, the NRR formed part of the Federal forces. At the dissolution of the Federation in 1963 the regiment reverted to Northern Rhodesia, forming the nucleus of Zambia's army at independence in 1964. At independence the army found itself committed in operations against the violent Lumpa religious sect; after Rhodesia's declaration of independence the military problems became very much more serious, and are noted later. The country has remained stable under the presidency of Kenneth Kaunda since independence, an achievement all the more remarkable in view of the strains occasioned by the Rhodesian war. Stresses have, however, been evident in a number of developments, political crises, the move to a one-party state and most recently the arrest of the Air Force commander, Major General C. Kabwe with allegations of a coup conspiracy. Another disturbing development is the great expansion of both the state security services, with the assistance of Soviet and GDR advisers, and the para-military forces.

STRENGTH AND BUDGET

Population: 6,200,000 (approximate).
Army: 13,000 plus an air force of 1800; a reserve of 1500 and para-military forces totalling approximately 1200.
GNP (estimate): $4 bn (approximate).
Defence expenditure: not known.

COMMAND AND CONSTITUTIONAL STATUS

The President of Zambia, Dr K. Kaunda, is the State's Commander-in-Chief; the Defence Minister is Mr W. Chakyula. The Army Commander is Lieut-General M. Masheke and the Air Force commander Major General Lungu. Although in 1972 the country became a one-party (UNIP) state and it was said that senior military officers might be liable to non-military responsibilities, little specific political instruction and linking of military units with the party organisation was reported for some time. More recently, however, army officers in uniform have attended UNIP rallies and conferences, and political instruction is being given in units.

ROLE, COMMITMENT, DEPLOYMENT AND RECENT OPERATIONS

Zambia's main military commitments since independence have been overspills from the conflicts in Angola, Namibia and Rhodesia, together with those arising from unrest in Zaïre; there is also a border dispute with Malawi which

surfaces from time to time. Until 1974 Portuguese 'hot-pursuit' incursions were frequent, together with a small number across from Rhodesia. In 1975 the Zambian Army intervened for the first time to suppress violent vendetta fighting between rival groups of Rhodesian insurgents, this intervention had to be repeated on a number of subsequent occasions. As the Rhodesian conflict worsened, together with the opening of guerilla activity in Namibia, Rhodesian 'hot pursuit' operations became more frequent. In one in 1978 a number of Zambian soldiers were killed. The Army also found itself committed to internal security work in the late 1970s, both on the Copperbelt and in pursuit of a local insurgent group, named after its leader Adamson Mushala who aspired to overthrow President Kaunda. In 1978 the Shaba insurgents, driven out of Zaïre by the French parachute troops, crossed into Zambia, a further call on the Zambian Army. Other Zaïre dissidents continue to cross — and misbehave on arrival — and a border dispute seems to be emerging. Zambia offers a small amount of overt and rather more covert support for SWAPO; this in turn has attracted South African 'hot pursuit' operations, the most serious of these being in early 1982 when a sizeable South African armoured force swept into Western Zambia. One factor perhaps for stability is an improvement in Zambia's relations with Angola; no support is now given to Angola's UNITA insurgents, and Zambia no longer has friction on this border.

One common feature, unfortunately, links the Zambian Army's reactions to their incursions, a feeble performance. A measure of this was the 'borrowing' of Tanzanian troops to maintain order on the Copperbelt in 1980.

The para-military forces are tasked for internal security, a commitment which evidently extends to being a counter balance to the Army. The majority of the para-military forces are deployed near Lusaka and Kabwe and around the Copperbelt.

ORGANISATION

The Zambian Army possesses an armoured regiment (i.e. a small armoured brigade that includes an armoured reconnaissance battalion), six infantry battalions, three artillery and two anti-aircraft batteries of the Zambian Artillery, the engineer squadron of the Zambia Corps of Engineers, two signals squadrons of the Zambia Corps of Signals, two logistics squadrons and two, perhaps now more, workshops.

An ambitious plan for an increase in the size of the army to twelve battalions was discarded in the late 1970s for economic reasons.

The para-military units are organised into a Police Mobile Unit (PMU) of 700 which forms a battalion of four companies, and a Police Para-military Unit (PPMU) of 500 which forms a battalion of three companies.

RECRUITMENT, TRAINING AND RESERVES

Recruitment of soldiers is by voluntary enlistment; no particular ethnic group appears to predominate, although there appears to be some feeling that the Bemba are under-represented. The Army includes over 1500 women.

---

* For general notes on African armies, see Appendix 1.

Zambia found itself very poorly prepared for an independent military existence as a consequence of its inclusion in the Rhodesian-dominated Federation of Rhodesia and Nyasaland until 1963. Cadets were first sent for training to Britain only in the year of independence (1964). This obliged Zambia to rely heavily on white officers of the former Federal forces (usually those of Zambian residence) and British loan service personnel. Neither proved satisfactory — the former Federal officers often had Rhodesian sympathies, several having to be replaced. The arrangements with Britain proved politically unpopular, from the military point of view the British government forbade their use in combat, making them much less valuable to Zambia. Pressures for rapid Africanisation built up; the British training team was withdrawn in 1968—9 and in 1970 the Army Commander (a former Federal officer) and almost all the remaining contract white officers were dismissed. Officer cadets were sent to Britain until the early 1970s, others were sent to India, Canada and Eire. Some Indian and Tanzanian officers have assisted the army's training in Zambia; recent reports suggest the arrival of large Soviet, GDR and Czechoslovak training teams.

The overall standard of military training, however, remains very poor. The para-military forces appear better trained.

EQUIPMENT AND ARMS INDUSTRY

Zambia's armoured regiment includes four elderly T-34 tanks and some thirty assorted T-54/55 and Type 59s. Other armour includes a number, perhaps as high as 150, BRDM-1 and 2 vehicles, twelve BTR-60 armoured personnel carriers and the survivors of some twenty-five old Ferret scout cars. The artillery includes thirty 130mm and eighteen 105 M-56 pieces, twenty five 122mm howitzers, a number as yet unconfirmed, of BM-21 artillery rocket launchers and some 76mm guns. Anti-aircraft defence includes fifty 20mm, forty 37mm, fifty 57mm and sixteen 85mm guns, together with SAM-7 equipments. One report suggests that Zambia also possesses a few SAM-3 missiles and launchers. Reports of an order for Tigercat missiles need to be treated with reserve. Rapier missiles ordered in the 1970s appear to have been wasted through poor maintenance. Infantry weapons include Carl Gustav 84mm rocket launchers and RPG-7s.

The Air Force possesses two fighter squadrons, one of twelve MIG-19s and one of sixteen MIG-21s. There are also two light air to ground strike aircraft squadrons, one of six Yugoslav Jastreb Soko and one with fifteen Aermacchi MB-326, and two transport squadrons which together possess some thirty-five medium transport aircraft drawn from the USA, Canada, the USSR, West Germany and the UK. A light communication squadron is equipped with twenty SAAB Supporter machines known locally as Safari; these can quickly be adapted for light bombing duties. Some twenty training machines exist in theory, not all may be operational; they include two MIG 21s, eight Siai-Marchetti SF 260 Warriors, two Soko Galebs and twelve Chinese Shenyang BT-6s. The one helicopter squadron possesses six Agusta-Bell 205 variants, one Agusta-Bell 212, eleven MI-8s and two Bell light Sioux machines. Shortages of pilots and of fuel greatly reduce the efficiency of the force.

RANK, DRESS AND DISTINCTIONS

Ranks follow the British system; dress is similar to that of the former King's African Rifles, dark green being the distinguishing colour.

CURRENT DEVELOPMENTS

Zambia's problems are those of national cohesion, worsened by those of the economy and, until 1980, the Rhodesian situation. These are reflected in its military policy.

The ending of the Rhodesian conflict has not entirely eased this problem, as a number of 'freedom fighters', particularly those associated with the Nkomo faction, have preferred to remain in Zambia rather than return to Zimbabwe; they constitute a nuisance, sometimes a violent one, in Zambia. Both from unrest in Zaïre and from present and future overspills of fighting in Angola and Namibia, threats are developing which preclude any great improvement in Zambia's military situation. However the country's economic position fails to improve, and she may find it difficult to effect the necessary military precautions.

Lloyd Mathews

ZIMBABWE

The Republic of Zimbabwe emerged from the former British white settler-controlled colony of Southern Rhodesia on April 18th, 1980, after fourteen years of mounting civil war, conducted in the latter stages with great ferocity and bloodshed.

The government at independence reflected the result of the March 1980 general election held under Commonwealth monitoring arrangements, including a small military force drawn from several Commonwealth countries. The overall winner was the Zimbabwe African National Union (ZANU) party of Mr Robert Mugabe, who became Prime Minister. As a junior partner in the post election coalition, and resenting his status as such, was the veteran nationalist leader Mr J. Nkomo, leader of the Zimbabwe African Peoples Union (ZAPU) party. The two parties were linked before the election in a Patriotic Front (PF) coalition; they fought the election separately, but in the resulting coalition both parties retained the words 'Patriotic Front' linked to their names.

The government also represents the domination of the Shona group of peoples over the minority Ndebele supported by one Shona people the Kalanga, a reversal of the historic pre-colonial situation in which the Ndebele were the conquerors and the Shona the vanquished. Nkomo is himself a Kalanga, his home is Bulawayo, the heart of Ndebele country.

During the civil war the two parties had each operated an insurgency force, that of ZANU was known as ZANLA (the Zimbabwe National Liberation Army) that of ZAPU was known as ZIPRA (the Zimbabwe Peoples Revolutionary Army). These two forces operated in rivalry, occasionally fighting against each other, and more frequently, betraying each other to the authorities.

ZANLA was largely based in Mozambique, it recruited mainly from the Shona group of peoples, it attached a great importance to mass political indoctrination in its operations.

ZIPRA was largely based in Zambia, it recruited mainly but far from exclusively, from the Ndebele and fought a more conventional operationally-styled insurgency campaign.

The Zimbabwe government, on British advice and with British help has embarked on an amalgamation of the two guerrilla forces with those elements of the former Rhodesian Army that were politically acceptable, in practice the black battalions (of the 'Rhodesian African Rifles') raised in the late 1970s, the logistic and service units and one or two other special forces. Their personnel include substantial percentages from the Kalanga group of the Shona, and from the Ndebele. These units had, and many of their individual members still in service retain, a high level of professional skill. These units also had another significance, of much importance in a neo-revolutionary situation. They were recruited very often from members of a large middle class of Africans that had been growing steadily since the middle 1960s; these soldiers were nationalist but not revolutionary.

Shortly after the election, an amalgamation committee was created in March 1980, which blossomed forth into a Joint Military High Command four days before independence. This body included the ZANLA leader, Rex Nhongo, the ZIPRA leader, Lookout Masuku, the (white) commander of the former Army, Lieutenant-General Sandy Maclean, and of the former Air Force, Air Marshal Frank Mussel, and the (at that time white) Permanent Secretary for Defence. The command was directly responsible to the Prime Minister, who appointed one of his most trusted Ministers, E. Munangawa, to be its Chairman, and soon retired the last Rhodesian Defence Forces Commander, General P. Walls. It maintained its own staff, appointed functional sub-committees on which all three groupings were represented and issued orders and directives to all the forces of the new Zimbabwe National Army and Air Force; orders to the former guerrilla units were, however, sent through the respective insurgent force chain of command until integration. Both in its 'image' as a symbol of reconciliation and cohesion, and in its operation, the Command proved a considerable success; by August 1981 it was considered to have fulfilled its purpose and was dissolved.

Another remarkable success story, beginning in the days of the Commonwealth Monitoring Group's British military team, has been the work of BMATT, the British Military Advisory and Training Team. Early on (and despite the consideration that some blame might perhaps be thought to attach to Britain for Rhodesia's colonial structure and the consequential insurgent campaign), officers and men of the team appear to have successfully tapped and fostered a vein of unity and loyalty to a new national non-political army. The magnitude of the task, scores of thousands of guerrillas assembling with their weapons in concentrations of various sizes but including some frighteningly large, the men suspicious, resentful and at times revengeful, cannot be exaggerated and this successful integration may be seen as a repayment to Zimbabwe by Britain for errors, more of omission than commission, of the past. Whether this newly-aroused sentiment is a short-lived independence euphoria, to decline into ethnic violence as the realities of post-independence life become more clear and severe, or whether it is a true new national pride and cohesion remains to be seen.

Indications, encouraging and discouraging, abound. In early 1981 violent clashes involving some mutinous former ZIPRA personnel occurred near Bulawayo, over three hundred people being killed. Three battalions of the Army that were in origin former Rhodesian African Rifles units and the air force had to be committed. Arms caches, of weaponry and ammunition, property of former insurgent groups — and of the old Rhodesian Army — are still hidden around the country. The discovery of a number of these, and their unexpectedly large size, led to the dismissal of Nkomo by Mugabe early in 1982; the official rhetoric took and has continued to develop the theme that the rift is not an ethnic or mass political divide, and that opportunities and preferment will still be given to ex-ZAPU and ZIPRA men providing they abandon their maverick and self-seeking leader Nkomo. This theme appears to be meeting with some success — in only five out of the forty-five army major units that existed at the time was there any trouble, and this was easily contained; and this success was achieved despite the subsequent arrest of General Lookout Masuku and several other senior ZIPRA officers serving in the new Zimbabwe National Army hierarchy, arrests made despite the support given to the government by Masuku at the time of the early 1981 violence. The appeal produced, obviously, a particular response from the non-Ndebele members of ZAPU/ZIPRA. The stresses, however, remain; two events that occurred in 1981 only too clearly witness to residual bitterness, a bomb attack in June on the house of Mugabe and the sabotage of Zimbabwe Air Force aircraft at Gwelo. This latter event was blamed (for reasons that represent an unpleasant mixture of continuing white versus black racial hatred and political expediency) on the senior white officers of the Air Force, alleged to be in the service of South Africa. Several were arrested, tortured – and then released but not reinstated. Occasional grenade attacks, police and military searches for ZIPRA caches, and also former ZIPRA soldiers who have deserted from the new Army, continue in a number of areas of western Zimbabwe.

STRENGTH AND BUDGET

Population: 7,500,000.

Strength: Army 60,000 (in the process of being reduced); Air Force 3000 (establishment). The Police in Zimbabwe has always been organised on gendarmerie lines; it totals 10,000 with a permanent barrack unit of 1500 for riot or other internal security duties. A Peoples Militia is to be organised.

GNP: no figure available.

Defence Expenditure: $555,000,000 (1981); a higher figure for 1982 may be anticipated.

COMMAND AND CONSTITUTIONAL STATUS

The non-executive President of the Republic of Zimbabwe, the Rev Canaan Banana, is Commander-in-Chief of the Armed Forces; the Zimbabwe Cabinet is headed by the Prime Minister, Mr Robert Mugabe, who is also Minister for Defence. A Minister of State in the Prime Minister's office, Mr S. Sekeramayi is believed to hold day-to-day control of defence. The titular commander of the defence forces is the last of the senior Rhodesian regime officers, Lieut-General Sandy Maclean, but the appointment is little more than honorary and Maclean is due to retire shortly. The Army Commander is in theory Lieutenant-General R. Nhongo (ZANLA), away on a course in Pakistan. The acting army commander, Major General J. Tungamirai, his quartermaster-general and four out of the five brigade commanders are all former ZANLA men. A few ex-ZIPRA officers are still to be found in senior appointments but these appear to be from among the less militant supporters of Nkomo, not prepared to go out into the wilderness, whether this reluctance is for overall patriotic or for personal status reasons is not clear.

There is some reason to speculate that one brigade of the Zimbabwe National Army, the 5th Brigade, trained by North Korea may have been, and perhaps still is, intended to serve additionally as a small private political force. Its membership is entirely ZANLA. One battalion of this brigade was sent to Mozambique in July 1982 and its personnel figured again in the seizure of the aircraft intended to transport Princess Anne, and the roughing-up of the RAF crew, in October, 1982.

Interestingly, however, one or two former Rhodesian army units have been left virtually as they were – the reason being the regime's need to have available units on whose professionalism, reliability and impartiality there could be no question. One of these is the paratroop battalion, the key personnel of which are former (white) Rhodesian Light Infantry. A second is the horsed mounted infantry patrol force known as Grey's Scouts (which was unusual in pre-independence days in that it was completely mixed racially); others include the armoured-car unit, the three former RAR battalions to which only very limited numbers of former insurgents have been admitted, and the commando unit which still includes a number of former Selous Scouts personnel. These units at present retain ex-Rhodesian Army commanding

officers and other officers as well, their value and importance was evident in the 1981 troubles.

ROLE, COMMITMENT, DEPLOYMENT AND RECENT OPERATIONS

The Past

The three component parts of the new Zimbabwe National Army have of course three differing recent operational experiences. These may perhaps be briefly set out before noting the present circumstances.

Former Rhodesian African Rifles, and other Rhodesian Army personnel serving in the new Army will have had experience, at a low level only as few were officers and none higher than captain, of a counter-insurgency campaign fought with very considerable skill despite severe difficulties of *matériel* caused by sanctions. They may have first-hand knowledge of, and perhaps skills in, the efficient organising of intelligence, ambushes, patrolling in small detachments, tracking from the air, the speedy despatch by lorry, aircraft or helicopter of patrols to areas in which insurgents are reported, of bomb, napalm, rocket and air-to-ground strikes, and of pursuit and the use of pseudo-gangs. They will have seen, and perhaps participated in, heli-borne troop or helicopter gunship strikes. They will have had experience of the defensive side of counter-insurgency work, minefields, radar-surveillance trip-wires, electronic devices, floodlights, barbed-wire, the improvisation of armoured troop carriers and convoy procedures in destabilised areas. They will also have seen, from the government authority's perspective, the effects of the use of terror and of mass political indoctrination, by insurgents. Their weaponry experience will be that of the equipment of the old Rhodesian Army.

The remaining senior officers of the old Rhodesian Army will have had considerable middle-level combat command experience in the 1970s.

The former insurgents will have had experience of the reverse side of the coin; in the early stages of the insurgency campaign fieldcraft, tactics and weapon-handling was often poor but in the latter stages attacks were mounted with much greater skill and proficiency. Their weapon training was of course based upon Soviet made or Soviet patterned issues.

The New Role

The post-independence role of the Zimbabwe National Army, as perceived at Harare, appears to be three-fold. The first is obviously the regime's favourite, to figure conspicuously on the southern African stage, perhaps to play a leading role in the overthrow of the South African government and at least to secure Zimbabwe against any overspill from the southern African racial confrontation. The second role is to offer assistance, if so requested, to friendly (ideologically compatible) regimes in southern Africa under pressure; a not-entirely fortunate example of this was the commitment of a battalion of the Zimbabwe Army to operations in Mozambique in July 1982. The third role, viewed perhaps as a regrettable necessity, is internal security operations, when necessary, in Zimbabwe itself.

The Present

Units of Zimbabwe's army have in fact been committed to duties linked to all three of these roles.

A few clashes have occurred with South African forces on the Limpopo river border, the most notable in August 1982 when three South African soldiers who had crossed the river were killed. More seriously, the regime fears that South Africa will seek to undermine the regime's political, economic and military life by subversion and sabotage, for which purpose it will seek to use the remaining local whites. There was almost certainly South African direction of the sabotage of the Zimbabwe Air Force in August 1982. Not surprisingly, the fear of South Africa is in danger of becoming paranoiac and is one reason why the government plans to form a People's Militia, which together with 'youth brigades' also to be raised, will be used for surveillance and security work. Obvious dangers of oppression will present themselves.

Units of the Army have continued to be deployed in Matabeleland in support of the police in internal security duties, especially following the kidnapping of whites. The clashes of early 1981 involved a move of three ZIPRA columns, at least one of which was motorised, moving out from two camps in the Bulawayo area; they were confronted by three loyal army battalions, former Rhodesian African Rifles, and the Air Force. After skirmishes the ZIPRA columns surrendered, which served firstly to break the mystique of an especial ZIPRA invincibility and secondly to enable the government to secure firm control of certain ZIPRA held equipment, including Soviet BTR 152 armoured personnel carriers.

In July 1982 one battalion of the North Korean trained 5 Brigade was sent into Mozambique to assist the Mosambique army to suppress insurgent MNR activity in the border area. It does not appear to have been involved in any major operations.

ORGANISATION

The Zimbabwe Army is to be built around five infantry brigades each of three battalions, together with two extra brigade type district headquarters for Harare and Bulawayo; there will also be an armoured regiment, an artillery regiment, a parachute battalion, a commando unit, and a number of engineer, signals and logistic units. The number of units to be attached to the two city commands is unclear.

At present the number of infantry battalions is very much larger, in the neighbourhood of 45; this reflects the transitional post-war stage of the Army's reconstruction. Of these 45 about 40 are integrated units.

5 Brigade has been described by Prime Minister Mugabe as having as a *gukurahundi* (anti-dissident) role.

RECRUITMENT, TRAINING AND RESERVES

The Zimbabwe National Army is at present an all-volunteer force, though it is possible some form of national service with military service as one of several options may be introduced in due course.

Before independence, the Kalanga ethnic group, one of the Shona peoples but with a measure of Ndebele acculturation, traditionally supplied African soldiers for Rhodesia's army. In the second half of the last decade, when a vast expansion took place, Ndebele recruits accounted for a great proportion of the recruits (some 35—40% according to some sources), than percentage of Ndebele within the total population. Recruitment is now said to be without favour. Some 200 to 250 local whites continue to serve, a few in key command and administrative appointments, others in training and technical services.

Pre-independence, Rhodesian African Rifles soldiers were given a three month basic training, followed by three months' continuation training, some selected cadres were then given courses at the School of Infantry at Gwelo. These courses included an officer cadet course, a junior leaders course, a

company commanders' course and a joint air/army counter-insurgency course. NCO training took place in Bulawayo.

The first Africans selected by the Rhodesian regime for officer cadet training began their six months' course in 1976; some 100 appear to have been trained by 1979.

The insurgents received training in Tanzania, Mozambique and Zambia in Africa, and a variety of revolutionary-minded countries including the Soviet Union, China, Yugoslavia, Romania and North Korea outside Africa. The training varied very greatly in quality, ZIPRA personnel being in general the more capable reflecting ZIPRA's greater military commitment. Their subsequent British training has included the separation of leaders from the rank and file so that they become adjusted to the status and responsibilities of officers and NCOs, drill, signals, mechanical transport, map-reading and weapon training, unit administration and last but by no means least, sports. From the Commonwealth Monitoring Group time onwards a carefully prepared 'reconciliation' programme was evolved, beginning with exchange visits and sports fixtures, and ending with two months integration training — and the all important inclusion on the pay-roll.

Since independence Britain has figured much in training, a sizeable British training mission being posted to Zimbabwe (at the time of writing, October 1982, approximately 100 officers and NCOs). The team is headed by Major-General C. Shortis. A small number of cadets are sent to Sandhurst and other specialist British training establishments; a few others are sent to equivalent foundations in Nigeria. The British Army Staff College at Camberley ran a special 'crash' course for Zimbabwe officers in 1980; a few continue to attend.

A North Korean team of over 100 trained one brigade, 5 Brigade, almost certainly with a view to its role as a politicised elite force; its soldiers are entirely Shona. The North Koreans were not popular for social reasons, their training was regarded as very poor and in the summer of 1982, almost all the North Koreans departed. The British training team was then asked to advise on the training of the brigade.

Zimbabwe's major training weakness lies in the technical arms (and of course the Air Force). Many of the skilled white technical officers and NCOs have left the country. Training their successors to a satisfactory standard is a long and costly undertaking, in some fields only barely begun.

A cadet academy and a staff college course have both been instituted.

Although training has achieved a surprising measure of success, the violence of the last years has left its mark. Reports of soldiers molesting civilians appear with disturbing frequency.

An additional complication is that of the continuing return to the country of 'insurgents'; some of these have only now completed their training, others for political or personal reasons delayed an earlier return. Some of these have to be absorbed into the army. Others, it is hoped, might join agricultural development projects. Women ex-insurgents pose an especial problem.

EQUIPMENT AND ARMS INDUSTRY

Zimbabwe has industrial capacity for a limited range of weapon manufacture. During the civil war, pistols and a 9mm carbine were produced, also napalm. Some somewhat improvised armoured fighting vehicles also appeared, adaptions from civilian chassis. The new army is not to resort to such improvisations.

The army's equipment reflects the army's very mixed parentage. The armoured unit includes ten Soviet-built T-34 and eighteen T-54 tanks, twenty-eight Panhard AML 90 Eland armoured cars of South African manufacture, and fifteen elderly British Ferret and a small number of Soviet BRDM-2 armoured reconnaissance vehicles. Armoured troop carriers include a number of West German Henschel UR-146 and survivors from the Rhodesian-produced civil war improvisations such as the Leopard and the Rhino, and a few Soviet BTR-152s.

Artillery is again of mixed origin, eighteen British 25 pounders, a few 1971 105mm guns, a battery of M-56 105mm pack howitzers, eight Soviet 122mm pieces, and eight British 5.5 gun-howitzers. Infantry weapons include 81mm mortars, SAM-7 surface-to-air missiles, RPG-7, type 69s and 106mm recoilless guns. Anti-aircraft weaponry includes 20mm and 23mm guns. Most of the larger items of Soviet equipment, the tanks, BRDMs and artillery were provided by North Korea for the 5th Brigade.

The Air Force possesses a bomber squadron of seven Canberra bombers, two fighter squadrons one of nine Hawker Hunter and one of five Gloster Vampire aircraft, both capable of air-to-ground strike attacks; a counter-insurgency squadron of ten Cessna 337 and nine Aermacchi Trojan light piston-engined aircraft, a reconnaissance, liaison and training squadron of about ten Siai-Marchetti SF-260 Warriors, a transport squadron of eighteen medium and small transports, and two helicopter squadrons in total equipped with twenty seven Alouette and eleven Agusta-Bell 205 helicopters.

The Air Force has on order eight British Aerospace Hawk counter-insurgency and training machines. Of an initial delivery, four were destroyed, with some nine other aircraft, by saboteurs at Gwelo in August 1982; replacements are understood to have been ordered.

Air Force stations are at New Sarum (near Harare), Thornhill (near Gwelo), Bulawayo, Chiredzi and Umtali. The strike aircraft are normally stationed at Thornhill. The Air Force's actual strength is some way below its establishment, and serious shortages of pilots and technical ground staff mean that only a limited number of its machines can be flown.

RANK, DRESS AND DISTINCTIONS

The process of achieving sartorial uniformity has been as difficult as that of overall cohesion. Full uniform (for those in possession of it) follows the old Rhodesian Army adaptation of British style. The normal working dress is a dark green pullover with light beige trousers. Sometimes light canvas shoes are preferred to brown ones.

Rank badges are modifications of the British system, the crown being replaced by a local symbol. For some time some officers, particularly of ZANLA origin, were averse to wearing rank insignia epaulettes, but this aversion seems now to have been overcome.

The Rhodesian regime inaugurated a local honours system of decorations and medals for bravery, long service, etc. This system has been discontinued by the new regime.

CURRENT DEVELOPMENTS

Zimbabwe's major problems are the containing of its own political and ethnic tensions, and the adjustment of an economy structured to suit a high earn/high spend white settler elite to the new African majority rule political order at a time of world recesssion, increasing population and land hunger among blacks. The problems occasioned by the former have already been outlined; the Mugabe regime appears to be moving in the direction of an executive President and one party state system as the longer term political solution, despite the fact that ZANU enjoys total power at present, other parties being reduced to tokens. This could involve the politicisation of the army, probably to its disadvantage. The second major problem is in the longer term the more serious, that of the continued and efficient economic operation of the sophisticated institutions, and much sophisticated technology of the old order by the often inadequately trained personnel of the new; not all members of the new government even grasp the difficulties of this, or the consequences of failure. Racial outbursts against South Africa, which would be quite content to leave Zimbabwe alone providing Zimbabwe does not sponsor ANC insurgents, merely obscure these issues.

The Army will be in danger of becoming one of the arenas in which tensions may be fought out if the remarkable spirit of reconciliation and national unity evaporates. The British prescription for this situation, a high standard of professionalism, is certainly the best and probably the only hope. And if the army succeeds in preserving cohesion it may prove a decisive example for the nation.

ADDENDUM

Unrest, and the deployment of troops to contain banditry continue in the Bulawayo area. A major military operation, 'Operation Octopus' was in progress at the time of writing, the operation was being commanded by the (white) commanding officer of the 1st Paratroop Battalion (formerly the old Rhodesian Light Infantry) which still includes a number of whites. Other units committed are from the North Korean trained 5th Brigade. Some reports suggest that up to 2–3000 men, mostly former ZIPRA personnel, are engaged in full or part-time banditry, their activities have extended to railway sabotage.

In view of the worsening internal security situation in Mozambique, a ZNA battalion has once again had to be loaned: the battalion appears to have been one of the 5th Brigade units and its role is protection of the Sofala-Mutare pipeline.

North Korean training staff has returned to Zimbabwe; a mission of some 60 has re-appeared to train a new 6th Brigade, likely to be the garrison force for one — or both — of the city commands noted above.

Lloyd Mathews

APPENDIX 1

The Armies of Africa

Information at present available on these armies remains limited; the difficulties of obtaining up-to-date information are particularly severe and enquiries unwelcome, particularly when these originate from a former colonial power. It is hoped that the publication of this work, however, may arouse sufficient interest to promote a more free exchange of information in the future.

Almost all African nations have armies: even Lesotho and Gambia, which at independence decided not to have an army, maintain a small barrack police gendarmerie, and Botswana, Seychelles and Swaziland have all recently decided to raise a small army. The need for an army was generally perceived at independence to be part of the assumption of nationhood, essential both for self-respect and international status. African armies are, in consequence, a projection of the new nation as an institution; in some cases they share the State's divisions or essential unreality. While in a number of new nations the valour of fighting men in pre-colonial politics may be recalled with pride by the military, in no nation are the armies based on any traditional groupings, ethnic, social or regional. Further, some of the border 'disputes' to which new armies may find themselves posted are also a projection of nation-building. Sometimes deliberately, sometimes not so, these disputes disseminate a concept of nationhood.

Whether many of the armed forces of black Africa can fully and properly be termed 'armies' is an open question. Few of black Africa's armies have the logistic back-up to mount a campaign in a neighbouring territory — many would even find defence of their own borders beyond them. The chief of staff of one of Africa's larger and better armies recently remarked that over half of his Army's vehicles purchased in the last five years were already damaged beyond repair. Some teeth-arm units can participate in a multi-nation or United Nations force if the logistic arrangements are provided for from other sources. Post-independence Africa's relative peace (among black nations) has however been one of military incapacity; but in the 1980s the sanctity of coloni-ally drawn frontiers is being seriously undermined, each year, by the increasing number of border disputes. A few States, e.g. Uganda and Nigeria, have the equipment to mount a very brief attack, but all the problems of reserves, supplies, repair facilities and ammunition preclude any long campaign — unless backed by an outside power. For most African nations then, armies have three roles: prestige and ceremonial; internal security; and in varying dimensions a very important and valuable part in the process of modernisation and nation-building. In the internal security commitment the army may not be the only force; Kenya, for example, maintains a strong barrack police gendarmerie and Tanzania a workers' militia; a counter-balancing role is clearly envisaged for both these forces. Most Francophone African States have a pattern of army, gendarmerie and republican guards to eye each other. The prestige and ceremonial role is important in the dissemina-tion of the concept of 'nation' to the general population; the modernisation role may be limited, in more conservative armies, to simple education for pre-literate soldiers and their families, or may in other armies extend to rural development work or political propaganda duties. Many armies have impres-sive-appearing ranges of weapons in their armouries, but it must be remembered that for some of these ammunition may be exceedingly difficult to obtain — in some cases the weapon

representing an alliance with a particular great power now out of favour, in other cases through the age and obsolescence of the weapon. Many artillery weapons, proudly paraded on various independence days, could only fire a handful of rounds, in some cases none at all.

France and Britain left their African possessions with a military model — in Britain's case reinforced by successful earlier developments of the model in the old and Asian Commonwealth countries; only Tanzania and Guinea have specifically and totally rejected the model as entirely unsuit-able and potentially dangerous socially. The British model gained added prestige from being 'non-political' and based on a volunteer force; both models transferred concepts of effici-ency, honesty, frugality, hierarchy and order, and a perceived repository of true disinterested patriotism; the two latter con-cepts often produced officers whose nationalism was conserva-tive and non-radical. The British model was further transferred smoothly and easily by virtue of the British organisation of colonial African battalions by territory; handover was there-fore a devolutionary change involving Africanisation of the officer corps, conversion of lightly armed battalions into a conventional but unsophisticated field army and provision of logistic and support units, including artillery and armoured cars. These armies in turn are now frequently having to enter the more sophisticated world of tanks, missiles, radar and air-to-ground strike aircraft, and despite the impoverished state of many of the countries concerned, expenditure often seems no object. Africa is becoming the continent of the armoured car.

From the early colonial period, France saw her African territories as a source of reserve military manpower; the *Troupes Coloniales* formally created in 1900 was to be a reserve army loyal only to France and formed therefore of units with no particular territorial affiliations. A large military establishment with centralised training and promotion arrange-ments, was thereby created — in the inter-war period, for example, there were over 40 battalions with even greater numbers in war-time. Conscription measures of varying severity were applied both in war-time and in peace. African units saw service on various fronts in World War I, in the post-1918 garrisoning of Germany, again on various fronts in World War II and in both the long Indo-China operation and the short Suez operation after 1945.

This structure lasted until the very end of the 1950s, and even with the 1960 grant of independence to all the French African colonies and Malagasy (with the exception of Guinea, which had opted for independence in 1958, and the Afar and Issa Coast), French thinking altered surprisingly little for several years. Arrangements were made for the handing over of certain units and their officers to new nations, the splitting-up of logistic services and training facilities, and French military aid. These arrangements formed part of the 'treaties of co-operation', to which enormous importance was attached by France; indeed, independence without such a treaty was seen as secession. The treaties were a package; it was not possible for a territory to opt out of the military commit-ments while retaining general aid; further, the treaties provid-ed for staging rights and, in some territories, bases for French troops, and also asserted a monopoly position in respect of military co-operation. France's perceptions of these arrange-ments was that their own world military position, and the new nations' frontiers, would be secured by French units, referred to as (French) 'community troops'; the new nations' own armies were to be useful internal security adjuncts. The whole process was made possible by the personal charisma of de Gaulle, and except in the case of Mali and to some extent the Congo, the arrangements lasted during his presidency. Since that time in almost all Francophone territories popular demands for the revision of the 'treaties of co-operation' have led to a number of changes, and there is now a growing tendency to diversify the sources of weapon purchase.

No British parallels to the complex French treaties were arranged, and Britain maintains no garrison in sub-Saharan Africa. In colonial days the military establishment in Africa was very small; it was also very often a source of income to certain areas of some colonies and only rarely resented. Britain has made less formal arrangements which have included the provision of British army (and other services') training teams and missions, single instructors for special subjects, and the large-scale provision of places in a very wide variety of British Armed Forces' training schools and establishments. The training so provided does, of course, tend to reinforce the organisational legacy, the British organisational mould of military units: their approximate size; regimental organisation and the different responsibilities of officers and non-commissioned officers; regulations and disciplinary procedures; training methods; roles of the various arms of a service (e.g. the difference between army engineers, electrical and mechanical engineers, signals and pioneers — all of which are separate corps in the British army and have generally been reproduced as small separate corps in new African nations); and perhaps most important of all, command and staff procedures. A number of countries have judged that officers trained outside the British system have found it difficult to adjust on their return; this difficulty led several African countries to seek Canadian, Indian or Pakistani help, since these nations followed the overall British pattern. The service of the various colonial battalions — as units from their individual territories — in World Wars I and II gave each new army a sense of continuity and proud tradition; in the case of the Ghanaian and Nigerian units, strengthened by service in the UN Congo Force.

There were political difficulties, particularly in East Africa, and also legal problems in each territory, but transition began in West Africa in 1951. A few general, if unrelated, features of the transition merit mention. In the transition years it was possible to note three types of officer — the very few (Gold Coast only) commissioned in World War II, promoted warrant officers and sergeants, and young school leavers trained (usually) at the Royal Military Academy, Sandhurst. Sandhurst's courses have never been very testing academically and the colonial school systems were, after a slow start, able to produce men well able to deal with them. Particular problems arose with technical and administrative units which had sometimes been centralised by region, e.g. east Africa, where each service had to be split and then rebuilt; on the other hand regional groupings enabled certain services, e.g. initial officer training and some technical training, to be undertaken regionally. In these difficult and complex situations many political and military leaders inevitably turned to the British, who at least knew the background and had some realistic idea of what was possible; after independence it was normally only Britain who posted a Defence Adviser (Attaché) to its mission in the newly independent capital. These officers were often very influential in the early years.

West Africa was particularly fortunate in the foresight of the British West African Command General, Sir L. Whistler, appointed in 1951. He urged an immediate increase in African NCOs and a programme of Africanisation of officers to produce captains in 5—10 years, and majors in 10—15 years. Places were reserved at Sandhurst — which at first could not all be filled — and preliminary training courses for potential officers began at Teshie, near Accra, for both Nigeria (to 1960) and the Gold Coast. The first Nigerians arrived at Sandhurst and at other British officer cadet schools in 1952, the first Gold Coast cadets a few months later. Because of settler prejudices in Kenya and the Mau Mau campaign, east Africa was much slower, the first warrant officers being given commissioned status under the title of *effendi* in 1957 after a course run for all three territories in Kenya. Northern Rhodesia and Nyasaland were dominated by Southern Rhodesian prejudices, and their first officers were not commissioned until 1964, immediately prior to independence as Zambia and Malawi. Southern Rhodesia's first African officers were only commissioned in 1977.

The colonial units had always had a small role as a vehicle of modernisation; this tradition, and the exhortations of new political leaders to soldiers to see themselves as agents of nation-building, reinforced a British-transmitted attitude of armies being custodians of true patriotism at a soldier's level. The British vocational view of an officer's calling has led some commentators to observe that military officers formed a very important part of an alleged post-colonial elitist structure in Africa. Certainly the first generally very conservative generation of African officers were often less nationalist (when nationalism was meant to equate with radicalism) than their political leaders; many saw their professional links with Britain as strengthening their own position *vis-à-vis* political leaders who had hoped their armies would turn into armed political support groups. These political leaders then began to pressure their armies, either by starvation of funds, the creation of rival units, or a total theoretical reappraisal of the role of the army — all policies which led to tension. Sometimes difficulties would be created by unauthorised actions of individual ministers — notably in Kenya, where one minister made his own unauthorised training arrangements. Elsewhere bribery played an unattractive role in the arrangement of military assistance to replace the departing colonial power. One or two minor oddities in the British system (inconsequential in Britain) occasionally became serious on transplantation to Africa, e.g. excesses of regimental loyalty, suspicions of short-service or promoted NCO officers towards Sandhurst officers, friction between young inexperienced Sandhurst subalterns and older experienced sergeants, and the traditional British military slowness to adjust to changing political situations. It is perhaps only barely necessary to add that in the period of handover, no British colonial officials, in London or in any territory, foresaw military intervention in politics; the training of African officers was seen of no more political importance than weights and measures inspectors.

Both the French and the British systems had admirers — because they had clearly been successful. Africa is now being offered a new, immediately successful and dazzling model, the Soviet—Cuban pattern. This new pattern gains admirers; in Africa success is infectious. The Soviets too have always prodigious quantities of only slightly obsolescent military hardware to give to their friends.

In conclusion the reader should perhaps first be cautioned in respect of the great weight of theoretical material, some briefly mentioned above, that is now appearing on the various themes of army—State relationships in Africa, the causes of coups, personal, military and political ambitions, military professionalism, 'corporatism', 'praetorian' armies, armies as 'sections of the *élite* armed with guns', etc. The sum total of the factors that lead armies to behave in a particular way are generally different in their composition in each particular

State: no generalisations apply to all African armies and only very few to a majority. A glance at the entries for, for example, Benin or Uganda will indicate the difficulties of proposing paradigms. One theme, however, that does merit especial mention is the dangers arising from linkages between the urban poor (unemployed, under-employed or under-paid) in African countries with the junior leader grades, officer and N.C.O. in the armed forces. Such linkages caused the recent upheavals in Ghana and Liberia and the time of writing, appear to have been a major cause of the August 1982 events in Kenya.

Finally it is hoped that no reader will underestimate the qualities of African soldiers when properly trained and led.

The current poor performances of many African armies are products of the transitional nature of their States and societies, training and logistic shortcomings, and poor command. An historical note cannot do better than conclude firstly with General Smuts's assessment, in the World War I German East African Campaign, that of all the British, South African, Indian and colonial troops under his command, the best were those from West Africa, and secondly with a reminder of the sturdy performance put up by divisions from both East and West Africa in the arduous Burma campaign.

Lloyd Mathews

APPENDIX 2

The Armies of India, Pakistan, Burma, Sri Lanka and Bangladesh

These armies all descend, directly or indirectly, from that of the British Indian Empire, which was garrisoned by units of the British army and by a single Indian Army.

Until 1937, military force in Burma was provided by a regiment of the Indian Army, the 20th Burma Rifles, and by battalions of Burma Military Police officered from India. Subsequently the Burma Rifles and the Military Police came under the control of the Government of Burma. Until 1947 the Indian and Pakistan armies were one — the Indian Army. It was then partitioned, each new State receiving a number of regiments of infantry and cavalry proportionate to its population. So strong were regimental loyalties in the Indian Army, however, that its separated officers made no attempt to remodel the manpower each army received. India and Pakistan continue to preserve the titles and numbering of the old regiments to this day, so that the army of one is half the jigsaw to which the other can supply the missing pieces. The army of Bangladesh was a creation of the State of Pakistan, since East Pakistan (Bangladesh) was not a recruiting area before independence, and provided no local regiments. Pakistan raised on the old British-India pattern two regiments, the East Bengal Regiment (of several battalions) and the East Bengal Rifles (a paramilitary force akin to India's Assam Rifles). These formed the basis of the Bangladesh army after independence was secured in 1971. The Sri Lanka army is not directly descended from the British-Indian, but Ceylon was garrisoned from British India and its volunteer forces (until 1947 all that existed) were modelled on the lines of the Auxiliary Force of India (*q.v.*). It was from these volunteer forces that the Sri Lanka army grew. Finally, the Nepalese army, though always a sovereign force, has, through the service of so many Nepalese in the Gurkha regiments of the Indian army, been much influenced by it, and may be said to belong within its military tradition.

John Keegan